Collins Cobuild

Compact
ENGLISH LEARNER'S
DICTIONARY

P9-CSV-388

THE UNIVERSITY
OF BIRMINGHAM

COLLINS
COBUILD

HarperCollins*Publishers*

first edition 2004

© HarperCollins Publishers 2004

HarperCollins Publishers
Westerhill Road, Bishopbriggs, Glasgow G64 2QT
Great Britain

www.cobuild.collins.co.uk

Collins®, COBUILD® and Bank of English® are registered
trademarks of HarperCollins Publishers Limited

ISBN 0-00-717523-X

Andrew Betsis ELT
31 Pyrgou, 18542 Pireas
Greece

ISBN 0-00-770584-0

Disal S.A.
Av. Marquês de São Vicente 182
Barra Funda
01139-000 São Paulo
Brazil

ISBN 0-00-770712-6

A catalogue record for this book is available from the
British Library

Typeset by Morton Word Processing, Scarborough

Printed and bound in Great Britain by Clays Ltd, St Ives plc

CONTENTS

Corpus Acknowledgements

We would like to acknowledge the assistance of the many hundreds of individuals and companies who have kindly given permission for copyright material to be used in the Bank of English. The written sources include many national and regional newspapers in Britain and overseas; magazines and periodical publishers; and book publishers in Britain, the United States and Australia. Extensive spoken data has been provided by radio and television broadcasting companies; research workers at many universities and other institutions; and numerous individual contributors. We are grateful to them all.

Founding Editor-in-Chief
John Sinclair

Publishing Director
Lorna Sinclair Knight

Editorial Director
Michela Clari

Managing Editor
Maree Airlie

We would also like to thank all the people involved in
the *Cobuild New Student's Dictionary*, whose original work
provided impetus for this book:

| **Publishing Director** | **Editorial Manager** |
| Gwyneth Fox | Stephen Bullon |

Senior Editors

| Rosalind Combley | Michael Murphy |
| Christina Rammell | Laura Wedgeworth |

Editors

| Isabel Griffiths | Ceri Hewitt |
| Sean Lynch | Carole Murphy |

Usage notes
John Williams

INTRODUCTION

A dictionary is probably the single most important reference book that a student of English can buy. This dictionary is especially important, because for many of its users it may be the first dictionary entirely in English that they use.

Like all COBUILD dictionaries, the **Compact English Learner's Dictionary** is based on the analysis of real language in use. Over the last few years, we have built up a huge collection of text, both written and spoken, called *The Bank of English*®, which now stands at over 524 million words. Because it is all held on computer, *The Bank of English*® provides very fast and accurate access to all sorts of information about the language. One very significant area is word frequency. This information is absolutely vital in helping to prepare dictionary entries as it provides a sensible list of words that need to be included and defined.

The words explained in this dictionary account for over 90% of the language that is written and spoken. That is because there is a relatively small number of words which are used over and over again, while there is a large number of words which are not used very frequently. This dictionary concentrates on the words that occur over and over again, and the entries represent the language that students really do need to know and to use.

The information about the words in this dictionary has been carefully chosen and presented in order to enable the student to write better English as well as understand English better. The entries provide a detailed account of the main uses and meanings of each word. Each of the forms is listed at the start of each entry, along with information about variant spellings where they exist. Explanations are written in full sentences, and reflect typical grammatical behaviour as well as providing a clear description of meaning. And of course, the thousands of examples are taken directly from *The Bank of English*®, showing typical patterns of use and grammatical structure.

As always we welcome any comments that readers may have about our books, so please contact us if you have any observations, criticisms or questions. You can contact us on our website at:

http://www.cobuild.collins.co.uk

or by email directly to: cobuild@ref.collins.co.uk

or you can write to us at the following address:

Collins COBUILD
Westerhill Road
Bishopbriggs
Glasgow G64 2QT

GRAMMAR

Introduction

Nearly all the words that are explained in this dictionary have grammar information given about them. For each word or meaning, its word class is shown in capital letters, just before the definition. Examples of word classes are N-C, VERB, PRON and ADV. The sections below contain further information about each word class.

Verbs

VERB

A **verb** is a word which is used to say what someone or something does or what happens to them, or to give information about them.

eat: *We ate chips every night.*
lose: *My husband lost his job.*
sleep: *She slept till noon.*

PHR-VERB

A **phrasal verb** is a combination of a verb and an adverb (for example *catch up*) or a verb and a preposition (for example *call for*), which together have a particular meaning. Some phrasal verbs have both an adverb and a preposition (for example *add up to*).

catch up: *I stopped and waited for her to catch up.*
call for: *I shall be calling for you at seven o'clock.*
cut off: *He threatened to cut my hair off.*
add up to: *Profits can add up to millions of dollars.*

PASSIVE-VERB

A **passive verb** is a verb that is formed using a form of 'be' followed by the past participle of the main verb. Passive verbs focus on the person or thing that is affected by the action.

glue: *She was glued to the television.*
born: *My mother was 40 when I was born.*

LINK-VERB

A **link verb** is a verb such as 'be', 'become', 'feel', or 'seem'. These verbs connect the subject of a sentence to a complement. Most link verbs do not occur in the passive.

be: *He was the tallest in the room.*
feel: *We felt very happy.*
seem: *He seemed to like me.*

MODAL

A **modal verb** is a verb such as 'may', 'must', or 'would'.

can: *Can I help you?*
must: *I must leave fairly soon.*
shall: *I shall do what you suggest.*

Nouns

N-C

Count nouns refer to things which can be counted, and they have both singular and plural forms. When a count noun is used in the singular, it must normally have a word such as 'a', 'an', 'the', or 'my' in front of it.

head: *She turned her head away from him.*
room: *Does the hotel have large rooms?*

N-U

Uncount nouns refer to things that are not normally counted or not considered to be individual items. Uncount nouns do not have a plural form, and are used with a singular verb.

help: *I need help with my homework.*
electricity: *Electricity is dangerous.*
bread: *Please buy some bread when you go to town.*

N-VAR

Variable nouns are uncount when they refer to something in general, and count nouns when they refer to a particular instance of something.

conversation: *I found her in* ***conversation*** *with Mrs Williams.*
I struck up a ***conversation*** *with him.*

Other variable nouns refer to substances. They are uncount when they refer to a mass of the substance, and count nouns when they refer to types or brands.

shampoo: *... a bottle of* ***shampoo***.
... bubble baths, soaps, and ***shampoos***.

N-SING

A **singular noun** is always singular and must have a word such as 'a', 'an', 'the', or 'my' in front of it.

sun: *The* ***sun*** *was shining.*
wash: *His grey socks were in the* ***wash***.

N-PL

A **plural noun** is always plural and is used with plural verbs.

clothes: *His* ***clothes*** *looked terribly dirty.*
expenses: *They have agreed to pay for travel and* ***expenses***.

N-TITLE

A **title noun** is a noun that is used to refer to someone who has a particular role or position. Titles come before the name of the person and begin with a capital letter.

President: *He believes there probably was a conspiracy to kill* ***President*** *Kennedy in 1963.*
Sir: *...* ***Sir*** *Christopher Wren.*

N-VOC

A **vocative noun** is a noun that is used when speaking directly to someone or writing to them.

darling: *Thank you,* ***darling***.
dad: *How do you feel,* ***Dad***?

N-PROPER

A **proper noun** refers to one person, place, thing, or institution, and begins with a capital letter.

God: *He believes in* ***God***.
Senate: *All of the president's cabinet appointments must be confirmed by the* ***Senate***.

Adjectives

ADJ

An **adjective** is a word which is used to tell you more about a person or thing, such as their appearance, colour, size, or other qualities.

white: *She bought a loaf of* ***white*** *bread.*
angry: *I felt* ***angry***.
blank: *He tore a* ***blank*** *page from his notebook.*

ADJ BEFORE N

This is used to mean an adjective that is normally used only in front of a noun. For example, you can talk about an *'indoor swimming pool'*, but you do not say 'The swimming pool was indoor'.

maximum: *We want the* ***maximum*** *number of people to attend.*
northern: *Matilda was born in* ***northern*** *Italy.*

ADJ AFTER LINK-V

This is used to mean an adjective that is normally used only after a link verb. For example, you can say *'She was glad'*, but you do not talk about 'a glad woman'.

alone: *I want to be* ***alone***.
sure: *I'm not quite* ***sure***.

Adverbs

ADV

An **adverb** is a word that gives more information about when, how, where, or in what circumstances something happens.

tomorrow: *I'll see you* ***tomorrow***, *all right?*
quickly: *He dressed* ***quickly***.
home: *She wanted to go* ***home***.

Other word classes

PHRASE

A **phrase** is a group of words which have a particular meaning when they are used together. This meaning is not always understandable from the separate parts.

in the bag: *It's **in the bag**. Unofficially, the job's yours.*
sit tight: ***Sit tight**, I'll be right back.*

PREP

A **preposition** is a word such as 'by', 'with', or 'from' which is always followed by a noun group or the '-ing' form of a verb.

near: *He stood **near** the door.*
of: *He had little chance **of** winning.*

PRON

A **pronoun** is used to refer to someone or something that has already been mentioned or whose identity is already known.

he: *My father is fat. **He** weighs over fifteen stone.*
them: *Did you give it to **them**?*
this: ***This** is what I wanted to say: it wasn't my idea.*
someone: *He has a reputation of being **someone** who is independent.*

CONJ

A **conjunction** is a word such as 'and', 'but', 'although', or 'nor', which is used to link two words or two clauses in a sentence.

since: *So much has changed in the sport **since** I was a teenager.*
before: *He phoned on Tuesday, just **before** you came.*

DET

A **determiner** is a word such as 'a', 'the', 'my', or 'every' which is used at the beginning of a noun group.

an: *We went to **an** art exhibition.*

the: *The man began to run towards **the** boy.*
every: *She spoke to **every** person at that party.*

CONVENTION

This is used to mean a word or fixed phrase which is used in conversation, for example when greeting someone, apologizing, or replying. Examples of conventions are 'hello', 'sorry', and 'I'm afraid'.

QUANT

A **quantifier** is a word or phrase like 'plenty' or 'a lot' which allows you to say in a general way how many there are of something, or how much there is of something. Quantifiers are often followed by 'of'.

all: *He was talking to **all** of us.*
enough: *They had **enough** cash for a one-way ticket.*
little: ***Little** is known about his childhood.*
whole: *We spent the **whole** summer in Italy.*

NUM

This is used to mean **number**.

eighteen: *He was employed by them for **eighteen** years.*
billion: *... 3 **billion** dollars.*

ORD

An **ordinal** is a number that is used like an adjective or an adverb.

hundredth: *The bank celebrates its **hundredth** anniversary in December.*
first: *There's no time for boyfriends, my career comes **first**.*

PREDET

A **predeterminer** is a word such as 'all' or 'half' which can come before a determiner.

all: *She's worked **all** her life.*
half: ***Half** the letter was in Swedish.*

EXCLAM

An **exclamation** is a word or phrase which is spoken suddenly, loudly, or with emphasis in order to express a strong emotion.

oh: *'Oh!'* Kenny blinked. *'Has everyone gone?'*
gee: *Gee, it's hot.*

Some words and meanings have two word classes, and the definition and example sentences show how the word is used in those two word classes.

For example:

control 2: VERB & N-U If you **control** a person or machine, or if you have **control** of them, you are able to make them do what you want them to do.

*I can't **control** what the judge says or what people think... He lost **control** of his car.*

behind 1: PREP & ADV

*I put one of the cushions **behind** his head... She led the way upstairs, with Terry following **behind**.*

PRONUNCIATION

IPA Symbols

VOWEL SOUNDS		CONSONANT SOUNDS	
ɑː	calm, ah	b	bed, rub
æ	act, mass	d	done, red
aɪ	dive, cry	f	fit, if
aɪə	fire, tyre	g	good, dog
aʊ	out, down	h	hat, horse
aʊə	flour, sour	j	yellow, you
e	met, lend, pen	k	king, lick
eɪ	say, weight	l	lip, bill
eə	fair, care	m	mat, ram
ɪ	fit, win	n	not, tin
iː	seem, me	p	pay, lip
ɪə	near, beard	r	run, read
ɒ	lot, spot	s	soon, bus
əʊ	note, coat	t	talk, bet
ɔː	claw, faun	v	van, love
ɔɪ	boy, joint	w	win, wool
ʊ	could, stood	x	loch
uː	you, choose	z	zoo, buzz
ʊə	lure, pure	ʃ	ship, wish
ɜː	turn, third	ʒ	measure, leisure
ʌ	fund, must	ŋ	sing, working
ə	*the first vowel in* about	tʃ	cheap, witch
i	*the second vowel in* very	θ	thin, myth
		ð	then, bathe
		dʒ	joy, bridge

Notes

In this dictionary the International Phonetic Alphabet (IPA) is used to show how the words are pronounced. The symbols used in the International Phonetic Alphabet are shown in the table above. Primary and secondary stress are shown by marks above and below the line, in front of the stressed syllable. For example, in the word 'abbreviation', represented /əˌbriːviˈeɪʃən/, the second syllable has secondary stress and the fourth syllable has primary stress.

Compound words, that is words which are made up of more than one word with either a space or a hyphen between them, are not usually given pronunciations. Pronunciations for the individual words that make up the compounds can be found at their entries at other parts of the dictionary. However, compound words are given stress markers.

Where appropriate, American pronunciations are given immediately after the British English pronunciations and are preceded by the abbreviation AM.

/ɑː/ or /æ/

A number of words are shown in the dictionary with alternative pronunciations with /ɑː/ and /æ/, such as 'path' /pɑːθ, pæθ/. In this case, /pɑːθ/ is the standard British pronunciation. However, in many other accents of English, including standard American English, the pronunciation is /pæθ/.

A a

a /ə, STRONG eɪ/ or **an** /ən, STRONG æn/. The form **an** is used in front of words that begin with vowel sounds. **1** DET You use **a** or **an** when you are referring to someone or something for the first time, or when you do not want to be specific. *Today you've got a new teacher... A waiter entered with a tray... He refused to work with an orchestra ever again.* **2** DET You can use **a** or **an** in front of nouns when the noun is followed by other words that describe it more fully. *...a happiness she had never believed possible.* **3** DET You can use **a** or **an** instead of the number 'one' in front of some numbers and measurements. *...a hundred miles.* **4** DET You use **a** or **an** in expressions such as **eight hours a day** to express a rate or ratio. *Prices start at £13.95 a metre.*

aback /ə'bæk/. PHRASE If you are **taken aback**, you are very surprised or shocked by something. *His resignation may have taken most people aback.*

abandon /ə'bændən/ **abandons, abandoning, abandoned.** **1** VERB If you **abandon** a thing, place, or person, you leave them permanently or for a long time. *His parents had abandoned him.* ♦**abandoned** ADJ *...an abandoned village.* ♦**abandonment** N-U *...her father's complete abandonment of her.* **2** VERB If you **abandon** an activity or idea, you stop doing it or thinking about it before it is finished. *He abandoned his studies after two years.* ♦**abandonment** N-U *Rain forced the abandonment of the next day's competitions.* **3** N-U If you do something with **abandon**, you do it in a carefree way. *...smoking and drinking with abandon.*

abate /ə'beɪt/ **abates, abating, abated.** VERB When something **abates**, it becomes much less strong or widespread; FORMAL. *...a crime wave that shows no sign of abating.*

abbey /'æbi/ **abbeys.** N-C An **abbey** is a church with buildings attached to it in which monks or nuns live or used to live.

abbreviate /ə'bri:vieɪt/ **abbreviates, abbreviating, abbreviated.** VERB If a word or a phrase, **is abbreviated**, it is made shorter. *'Compact disc' is often abbreviated to 'CD'... He persuaded his son to abbreviate his first name to Alec.* ♦**abbreviated** ADJ *...a very abbreviated description of the project.*

abbreviation /ə,bri:vi'eɪʃən/ **abbreviations.** N-C An **abbreviation** is a short form of a word or phrase. *The postal abbreviation for Kansas is KS.*

abdicate /'æbdɪkeɪt/ **abdicates, abdicating, abdicated.** **1** VERB If a king or queen **abdicates**, he or she resigns. *...when King Constantine was forced to abdicate the Greek throne.* ♦**abdication** N-U *...the abdication of Edward VIII.* **2** VERB If you **abdicate** responsibility for something, you refuse to accept the responsibility for it any longer. *Their parents have abdicated their responsibilities.* ♦**abdication** N-U *...an outrageous abdication of*

their duties.

abdomen /'æbdəmən/ **abdomens.** N-C Your **abdomen** is the part of your body below your chest where your stomach is. ♦**abdominal** /æb'dɒmɪnəl/ ADJ BEFORE N *...the abdominal muscles.*

abduct /æb'dʌkt/ **abducts, abducting, abducted.** VERB If someone **is abducted**, he or she is taken away illegally. *He was charged with abducting a taxi driver.* ♦**abduction, abductions** N-VAR *...the abduction of four black youths.*

aberration /,æbə'reɪʃən/ **aberrations.** N-VAR An **aberration** is an incident or way of behaving that is not normal; FORMAL. *...whether today's coup attempt is a minor aberration on the road to democracy.*

abide /ə'baɪd/ **abides, abiding, abided.** PHRASE If you say that you **can't abide** someone or something, you are emphasizing that you dislike them intensely. *I can't abide people who can't make up their minds.*
▸ **abide by.** PHR-VERB If you **abide by** a law, agreement, or decision, you do what it says.

abiding /ə'baɪdɪŋ/. ADJ BEFORE N An **abiding** feeling or memory is one that you have for a very long time. *He also acquired an abiding interest in history.* ● See also **law-abiding.**

ability /ə'bɪlɪti/ **abilities.** N-VAR Your **ability** is the quality or skill that you have which makes it possible for you to do something. *Her drama teacher spotted her ability. ...his leadership abilities. ...the human ability to recognise complex sound patterns.*

abject /'æbdʒekt/. ADJ You use **abject** to emphasize that a situation or quality is shameful or depressing. *...abject poverty... This scheme was an abject failure.*

ablaze /ə'bleɪz/. ADJ AFTER LINK-V Something that is **ablaze** is burning fiercely. *Within seconds, curtains and woodwork were ablaze... Two houses were set ablaze.*

able /'eɪbəl/ **abler, ablest.** **1** PHRASE If someone or something **is able** to do something, they have the skills, freedom, or other means which make it possible for them to do it. *I was never able to play any sports.* **2** ADJ An **able** person is clever or good at doing something. ♦**ably** /'eɪbli/ ADV *He was ably assisted by Robert James... She campaigns so ably for one-parent families.*

abnormal /æb'nɔ:məl/. ADJ Someone or something that is **abnormal** is unusual or exceptional in a way that is worrying. *...an abnormal fear of strangers.* ♦**abnormally** ADV *...abnormally high levels of stress.*

abnormality /,æbnɔ:'mælɪti/ **abnormalities.** N-VAR An **abnormality** is an unusual part or feature of something that is worrying or dangerous. *...a genetic abnormality.*

aboard /ə'bɔ:d/. PREP & ADV If you are **aboard** a ship or plane, you are on or in it. *No-one else was aboard the plane... It had taken two hours to load all the people aboard.*

abolish /əˈbɒlɪʃ/ **abolishes, abolishing, abolished.** VERB If someone in authority **abolishes** a practice or organization, they put an end to it. *Parliament voted to abolish the death penalty.* ♦**abolition** /ˌæbəˈlɪʃən/ N-U *...the total abolition of slavery.*

abominable /əˈbɒmɪnəbəl/. ADJ Something that is **abominable** is very unpleasant or very bad. *Their treatment of him was abominable. ...this abominable war.*

aboriginal /ˌæbəˈrɪdʒɪnəl/ **Aboriginals.** N-C An **Aboriginal** is a member of one of the tribes which were living in Australia when Europeans arrived. *...health and housing for aboriginals. ...Aboriginal art.*

Aborigine /ˌæbəˈrɪdʒɪni/ **Aborigines.** N-C **Aborigine** means the same as **Aboriginal.** Some people consider **Aborigine** to be a racist word.

abort /əˈbɔːt/ **aborts, aborting, aborted.** ① VERB If an unborn baby **is aborted,** the pregnancy is ended deliberately and the baby is not born alive. *...the lover who walked out on her after she had aborted their child.* ② VERB If you **abort** a process, plan, or activity, you stop it before it is finished. *The take-off was aborted.*

abortion /əˈbɔːʃən/ **abortions.** N-VAR An **abortion** is a medical operation in which a pregnancy is deliberately ended and the baby is not born alive. *...the Vatican's teaching on abortion.*

abortive /əˈbɔːtɪv/. ADJ An **abortive** attempt or action is unsuccessful. *...the abortive rebellion.*

abound /əˈbaʊnd/ **abounds, abounding, abounded.** VERB If things **abound,** or if a place **abounds** with things, there are very large numbers of them; FORMAL. *Stories abound about when he was in charge... San Francisco abounds with lawyers.*

about /əˈbaʊt/. ① PREP You use **about** to introduce who or what something relates to or concerns. *Helen's told me about you. ...advice about exercise... He felt helpless to do anything about it.* ② PREP When you say that there is a particular quality **about** someone or something, you mean that they have this quality. *There is something special about her.* ③ ADV **About** in front of a number means approximately. *The child is about eight years old.* ④ ADV & PREP If someone or something moves **about,** they keep moving in different directions. *The kids ran about in the garden... From 1879 to 1888 he wandered about Germany.* ⑤ ADJ AFTER LINK-V If someone or something is **about,** they are present or available. *There's lots of money about.* ⑥ PHRASE If you **are about to** do something, you are going to do it soon. *The film was about to start.* ⑦ See note at **around.** ● **how about:** see **how.** ● **what about:** see **what.** ● **just about:** see **just.**

above /əˈbʌv/. ① PREP & ADV If one thing is **above** another one, it is directly over it or higher than it. *He lifted his hands above his head. ...the flat above mine... A long scream sounded from somewhere above.* ② ADV & N-SING & ADJ BEFORE N You use **above** in writing to refer to something that has already been mentioned. *...the results described above... For additional information, contact any of the above... I may be reached at the above address.* ③ PREP & ADV If

an amount or measurement is **above** a particular level, it is greater than that level. *The temperature crept up to just above 40 degrees. ...above average levels of rainfall. ...people of 18 years and above.* ④ PREP & ADV If someone is **above** you, they are in a position of authority over you. *...the people above you in the positions of power... I had orders from above.* ⑤ PREP If someone thinks that they are **above** something, they think that they are too good or too important for it; used showing disapproval. *He would consider himself above such petty personal comments.* ⑥ PREP If someone is **above** criticism or suspicion, they cannot be criticized or suspected because of their good qualities or their position. *He was a respected academic and above suspicion.* ⑦ **over and above:** see **over.**

abrasive /əˈbreɪsɪv/. ① ADJ If you describe someone's manner as **abrasive,** you think they are rude and unkind. *The abrasive style that prompted one member of Congress to describe him as a pit bull.* ② ADJ An **abrasive** substance is rough and can be used to clean hard surfaces.

abreast /əˈbrest/. ① ADV If people or things walk or move **abreast,** they are side by side. *...they walked three abreast.* ② PREP If you keep **abreast** of a subject, you know all the most recent facts about it. *He will be keeping abreast of the news.*

abroad /əˈbrɔːd/. ADV If you go **abroad,** you go to a foreign country. *I would love to go abroad this year.*

abrupt /əˈbrʌpt/. ① ADJ An **abrupt** action is very sudden and often unpleasant. *Rosie's idyllic world came to an abrupt end when her parents' marriage broke up.* ♦**abruptly** ADV *He stopped abruptly.* ② ADJ Someone who is **abrupt** is rather rude and unfriendly. ♦**abruptly** ADV *'Good night, then,' she said abruptly.*

absence /ˈæbsəns/ **absences.** ① N-VAR Someone's **absence** from a place is the fact that they are not there. *...letters which had arrived for me in my absence. ...her husband's frequent absences.* ② N-SING The **absence** of something is the fact that it is not there. *In the absence of a will, the courts decide who the guardian is.*

absent /ˈæbsənt/. ① ADJ If someone or something is **absent** from a place or situation, they are not there. *He was absent from work for over 35 days.* ② ADJ If someone appears **absent,** they are not paying attention. ♦**absently** ADV *He nodded absently.*

absentee /ˌæbsənˈtiː/ **absentees.** N-C An **absentee** is a person who should be in a particular place but who is not there. *...absentees from work. ...absentee landlords.*

absent-minded. ADJ An **absent-minded** person is very forgetful or does not pay attention to what they are doing. ♦**absent-mindedly** ADV *He did it automatically, almost absentmindedly.*

absolute /ˈæbsəluːt/ **absolutes.** ① ADJ BEFORE N **Absolute** means total and complete. *...absolute beginners. ...the absolute proof that we needed... It's absolute nonsense.* ② N-C & ADJ BEFORE N **Absolutes** or **absolute** rules or principles are believed to be true or right for all situations.

absolutely /ˌæbsə'luːtli/. **1** ADV **Absolutely** means totally and completely. *Jill is absolutely right... It's an absolutely brilliant book... I absolutely refuse to get married.* **2** ADV **Absolutely** is an emphatic way of saying yes or agreeing with someone. **Absolutely not** is an emphatic way of saying no or disagreeing with someone. *'Was it worth it?'—'Absolutely.'... 'Did they approach you?'—'No, absolutely not.'*

absorb /əb'zɔːb/ **absorbs, absorbing, absorbed.** **1** VERB To **absorb** a substance means to soak it up or take it in. *Plants absorb carbon dioxide from the air... Refined sugars are absorbed into the bloodstream very quickly.* ◆**absorption** /əb'zɔːpʃən/ N-U *...the absorption of iron from food.* **2** VERB If a group **is absorbed** into a larger group, it becomes part of the larger group. *The Colonial Office was absorbed into the Foreign Office. ...the ability of a bigger bank to absorb a smaller one.* ◆**absorption** N-U *...East Germany's absorption into the Federal Republic.* **3** VERB If you **absorb** information, you understand and remember it. *Too often he only absorbs half the information. ...to give employees time to absorb the bad news.* **4** VERB If something **absorbs** you, it interests you and gets all your attention. **5** VERB If something **absorbs** a force, it reduces its effect. *...shoes that are not designed to absorb the impact of running.*

absorbed /əb'zɔːbd/. ADJ AFTER LINK-V If you are **absorbed** in a person, activity, or subject, they get all your attention. *She was totally absorbed in her partner.*

absorbing /əb'zɔːbɪŋ/. ADJ An **absorbing** activity interests you a great deal and takes up all your attention. *...an absorbing hobby.*

absorption. See **absorb.**

abstain /æb'steɪn/ **abstains, abstaining, abstained.** **1** VERB If you **abstain** from something you like doing, you deliberately do not do it. *Overeaters can't totally abstain from eating.* ◆**abstention** /æb'stenʃən/ N-U *...abstention from alcohol.* **2** VERB If you **abstain** during a vote, you do not vote. ◆**abstention, abstentions** N-VAR *The voting was twenty in favour, six against, and sixteen abstentions.*

abstinence /'æbstɪnəns/. N-U **Abstinence** is the practice of not having something you enjoy, often for health or religious reasons. *...lifelong abstinence from alcohol.*

abstract /'æbstrækt/ **abstracts.** **1** ADJ & PHRASE An **abstract** idea or way of thinking is based on general ideas rather than on particular things. You can also talk or think about something **in the abstract.** *Money was a commodity she never thought about except in the abstract.* **2** ADJ BEFORE N & N-C **Abstract** art makes use of shapes and patterns rather than showing people or things as they actually are. An **abstract** is an abstract work of art. **3** N-C An **abstract** of an article or speech is a short piece of writing that summarizes the main points.

abstraction /æb'strækʃən/ **abstractions.** N-C An **abstraction** is a general idea rather than one relating to a specific thing. *Is it worth*

fighting a big war, in the name of an abstraction like sovereignty?

absurd /æb'sɜːd/. ADJ & N-SING If you say that something is **absurd**, you think that it is ridiculous or does not make sense. **The absurd** is something that is absurd. *The thought of being a movie star was absurd to her. ...a highly developed sense of the absurd.* ◆**absurdly** ADV *Prices were still absurdly low.* ◆**absurdity** /æb'sɜːdɪti/ **absurdities** N-VAR *...the absurdity of all wars.*

abundance /ə'bʌndəns/. N-SING & PHRASE If there is an **abundance** of something, or if something is in **abundance**, there is a large quantity of it. *...an abundance of safe beaches... Food was in abundance.*

abundant /ə'bʌndənt/. ADJ Something that is **abundant** is present in large quantities. *...an abundant supply of cheap labour.*

abuse, abuses, abusing, abused; noun /ə'bjuːs/, verb /ə'bjuːz/. **1** VERB & N-VAR If someone **is abused**, or if they are victims of **abuse**, they are treated cruelly and violently. *...parents who feel they cannot cope or might abuse their children. ...human rights abuses.* **2** VERB & N-U You can say that someone **is abused** if rude and insulting things are said to them. **Abuse** is rude and insulting things that people say when they are angry. *He was verbally abused by other soldiers... I was left shouting abuse as the car sped off.* **3** VERB & N-U If you **abuse** something, you use it in a wrong way or for a bad purpose. **Abuse** of something is the use of it in this way. *...how the rich and powerful can abuse their position. ...an abuse of power. ...alcohol abuse.*

abusive /ə'bjuːsɪv/. **1** ADJ Someone who is **abusive** says rude and insulting things. *...abusive language.* **2** ADJ Someone who is **abusive** is cruel and violent towards someone else. *...her cruel and abusive husband.*

abysmal /ə'bɪzməl/. ADJ **Abysmal** means very bad or poor in quality. *My ignorance on the subject of drugs was abysmal.* ◆**abysmally** ADV *Standards of hygiene are abysmally low.*

abyss /æ'bɪs/ **abysses.** **1** N-C An **abyss** is a hole in the ground which is so deep that it is impossible to measure. *He crawled to over the edge of the abyss.* **2** N-C You can refer to a frightening situation which could have terrible consequences as an **abyss**; WRITTEN. *...taking his country to the abyss of war.*

academic /ˌækə'demɪk/ **academics.** **1** ADJ BE-FORE N **Academic** means relating to work done in schools, colleges, and universities, especially work which involves studying and reasoning rather than practical or technical skills. *...the academic year... Their academic standards are high.* ◆**academically** ADV *He is academically gifted.* **2** ADJ Someone who is **academic** is good at studying. **3** N-C An **academic** is a member of a university or college who teaches or does research. **4** ADJ If you say that something is **academic**, you mean that it has no real relevance or effect. *If Andy had been fit it might have been a different story. But it's all academic now.*

academy /ə'kædəmi/ **academies.** N-C A school or college specializing in a particular subject is sometimes called an **academy**. ...*the Royal Academy of Music.*

accelerate /æk'seləreɪt/ **accelerates, accelerating, accelerated.** VERB When the rate or speed of something **accelerates**, it increases. *Growth will accelerate to 2.9 per cent next year... We need to accelerate the pace of change... The car accelerated.* ♦**acceleration** N-U ...*acceleration to 60 mph.*

accelerator /æk'seləreɪtə/ **accelerators.** N-C In a vehicle, the **accelerator** is the pedal you press to go faster.

accent /'æksənt/ **accents.** [1] N-C Someone who speaks with a particular **accent** pronounces the words of a language in a way that indicates their country, region, or social class. ...*a slight American accent.* [2] N-C An **accent** is a mark written above or below certain letters in some languages to show how they are pronounced. [3] N-SING If you put the **accent** on a particular feature of something, you give it special importance or emphasis.

accentuate /æk'sentʃueɪt/ **accentuates, accentuating, accentuated.** VERB To **accentuate** something means to emphasize it or make it more noticeable. *His shaven head accentuates his large round face.*

accept /æk'sept/ **accepts, accepting, accepted.** [1] VERB If you **accept** something that you have been offered, you say yes to it or agree to take it. *I accepted his offer of permanent employment... All those invited to next week's peace conference have accepted.* ♦**acceptance** /æk'septəns/ N-U ...*acceptance of the invitation to Moscow.* [2] VERB If you **accept** a fact, you believe that it is true or valid. *Her parents accepted her decision.* ♦**acceptance** N-U ...*a theory that is steadily gaining acceptance.* [3] VERB To **accept** a difficult or unpleasant situation means to recognize that it cannot be changed. *Urban dwellers often accept noise as part of city life... We also accept that some marriages die.* ♦**acceptance** N-U ...*his calm acceptance of whatever comes his way.* [4] VERB If you **accept** the blame or responsibility for something, you admit that you are responsible for it. [5] VERB When an organization or group **accepts** someone, they give them a job or allow them to join their group. *They refused to accept women as bus drivers... Stephen was accepted into the family.* ♦**acceptance** N-U *Would he be popular enough to gain acceptance?* [6] See also **accepted.**

acceptable /æk'septəbəl/. [1] ADJ If a situation or action is **acceptable**, people generally approve of it or allow it to happen. *It is becoming more acceptable for women to drink... The air pollution exceeds acceptable levels.* ♦**acceptability** N-U ...*increasing the social acceptability of divorce.* ♦**acceptably** ADV *Teach children to behave acceptably.* [2] ADJ If something is **acceptable**, it is good enough or fairly good. *We've made an acceptable start.*

accepted /æk'septɪd/. ADJ **Accepted** ideas are agreed by most people to be correct or reasonable. *It was generally accepted that men disliked shopping.*

access /'ækses/ **accesses, accessing, accessed.** [1] N-U If you have **access** to a building or other place, you are able or allowed to go into it; FORMAL. ...*unlimited access to the swimming pool.* [2] N-U Your **access** to someone is the opportunity or right you have to see them. *His ex-partner denies him access to his children.* [3] VERB & N-U If you **access** information, or if you have **access** to it, you are able to see or get it. ...*to give patients right of access to their medical records.*

accessible /æk'sesɪbəl/. [1] ADJ If a place is **accessible**, you are able to reach it or get into it. ...*a low cupboard that's easily accessible.* ♦**accessibility** /æk,sesɪ'bɪlɪti/ N-U ...*accessibility to the city centre.* [2] ADJ If something is **accessible** to people, they can easily use it or obtain it. ...*making computers truly accessible to people.* ♦**accessibility** N-U ...*the cost, quality and accessibility of health care.*

accessory /æk'sesəri/ **accessories.** [1] N-C **Accessories** are extra parts added to something to make it more efficient, useful, or decorative. ...*bathroom accessories.* [2] N-C An **accessory** to a crime is someone who willingly helps the person who commits it, but does not take part in the crime itself; TECHNICAL. *She was charged with being an accessory.*

accident /'æksɪdənt/ **accidents.** [1] N-VAR An **accident** is an event which happens completely by chance. You can also say that something happens by **accident**. *Is it destiny that brings people together, or is it accident?... She discovered the problem by accident.* [2] N-C An **accident** is something unpleasant that happens and that often causes injury or death. ...*a serious car accident.*

accidental /ˌæksɪ'dentəl/. ADJ An **accidental** event happens by chance or as the result of an accident. *The fire was accidental.* ♦**accidentally** ADV *Names were accidentally erased from computer disks.*

acclaim /ə'kleɪm/ **acclaims, acclaiming, acclaimed.** VERB & N-U If someone or something is **acclaimed**, or wins **acclaim**, they are praised publicly and enthusiastically; FORMAL. *She has been acclaimed for the TV dramas 'Prime Suspect' and 'Civvies'... He was acclaimed as England's greatest modern painter... Angela Bassett has won critical acclaim for her excellent performance.* ♦**acclaimed** ADJ ...*six highly acclaimed novels.*

acclimatize (BR also **acclimatise**) /ə'klaɪmətaɪz/ **acclimatizes, acclimatizing, acclimatized.** VERB When you **acclimatize** or **are acclimatized** to a new situation, place, or climate, you become used to it. *The athletes are acclimatising to the heat... He has left for St Louis early to acclimatise himself... It would take her two years to get acclimatized.*

accolade /'ækəleɪd/ **accolades.** N-C An **accolade** is something that is done or said about someone which shows how much people admire them; FORMAL. ...*the ultimate international accolade, the Nobel Peace Prize.*

accommodate /ə'kɒmədeɪt/ **accommodates, accommodating, accommodated.** [1] VERB If a building or space can **accommodate** someone or something, it has enough room for them. *The school in Poldown was not* *big enough to accommodate all the children.* 2 VERB To **accommodate** someone means to provide them with a place to stay. *...a hotel built to accommodate guests for the wedding.* 3 VERB To **accommodate** someone means to help them. *...the full-service beauty salon which accommodates both men and women.* ♦**accommodating** ADJ *Lindi seemed a nice, accommodating girl.*

accommodation /əˌkɒmə'deɪʃən/. N-U **Accommodation** is used to refer to rooms or buildings where people live, stay, or work. *Travel and overnight accommodation are included.*

accompaniment /ə'kʌmpnɪmənt/ **accompaniments.** 1 N-U The **accompaniment** to a singer or instrument is the music that is played at the same time, forming a background to it. *...a lively musical accompaniment.* 2 N-VAR An **accompaniment** to something is another thing that happens or exists at the same time, usually something that complements the first thing. *Eclairs make an ideal accompaniment to morning coffee... The procession wends its way through the streets to the accompaniment of wildly excited shouting.*

accompany /ə'kʌmpəni/ **accompanies, accompanying, accompanied.** 1 VERB If you **accompany** someone, you go somewhere with them; FORMAL. *Children must be accompanied by an adult.* 2 VERB If one thing **accompanies** another, the two things happen or exist at the same time. *...sauces that accompany chicken dishes.* 3 VERB When you **accompany** a singer or a musician, you play one part of a piece of music while they sing or play the main tune.

accomplice /ə'kʌmplɪs, AM ə'kɒm-/ **accomplices.** N-C An **accomplice** is a person who helps to commit a crime.

accomplish /ə'kʌmplɪʃ, AM ə'kɒm-/ **accomplishes, accomplishing, accomplished.** VERB If you **accomplish** something, you succeed in doing it. *If we'd all work together, I think we could accomplish our goal.* ♦**accomplishment** N-U *...the accomplishment of his highly important mission.*

accomplished /ə'kʌmplɪʃt, AM ə'kɒm-/. ADJ If someone is **accomplished**, they are very good at something. *...an accomplished linguist.*

accomplishment /ə'kʌmplɪʃmənt, AM ə'kɒm-/ **accomplishments.** 1 N-C Your **accomplishments** are the things you have achieved or the things that you do well; FORMAL. *The list of her accomplishments is staggering.* 2 See also **accompany.**

accord /ə'kɔːd/ **accords, according, accorded.** 1 VERB If you **are accorded** a particular kind of treatment, people treat you in that way; FORMAL. *...the military honours accorded to all visiting heads of state.* 2 N-C An **accord** between countries or groups of people is a formal agreement, for example to end a war. *...the 1991 peace accords.*
PHRASES • If one person, action, or fact is **in accord with** another, there is no conflict between them. You can also say that two people or things are **in accord**. • When you do something **of** your **own accord**, you do it freely and because you want to. If something happens **of** its **own accord**, it seems to happen

automatically, without anybody making it happen. *He had left her of his own accord.*

accordance /ə'kɔːdəns/. PHRASE If something is done **in accordance with** a rule or system, it is done in the way that the rule or system says it should be done. *Act in accordance with the law.*

accordingly /ə'kɔːdɪŋli/. ADV You use **accordingly** to say that one thing happens as a result of another thing. *It is a difficult job and they should be paid accordingly.*

ac'cording to. 1 PREP If something is true **according to** a particular person or book, that person or book claims that it is true. *Philip stayed at the hotel, according to Mr Hemming.* 2 PREP If something is done **according to** a particular principle or plan, this principle or plan is used as the basis for the way it is done. *Things really did work out according to plan.*

account /ə'kaʊnt/ **accounts, accounting, accounted.** 1 N-C If you have an **account** with a bank, you leave money with the bank and withdraw it when you need it. *...a savings account.* 2 N-C In business, a regular customer of a company can be referred to as an **account**. *The marketing agency, has won two Edinburgh accounts.* 3 N-C **Accounts** are detailed records of all the money that a person or business receives and spends. *He kept detailed accounts.* 4 N-C An **account** is a written or spoken report of something that has happened. *He gave a detailed account of what happened... He is, by all accounts, a superb teacher.*
PHRASES • If someone **is called, held,** or **brought to account** for something they have done wrong, they are made to explain why they did it, and are often criticized or punished for it. • If you **take** something **into account**, you consider it when you are thinking about a situation. • If you tell someone not to do something **on** your **account**, you mean that they should do it only if they want to, and not because they think it will please you. *Don't leave on my account.* • If you say that something should **on no account** be done, you are emphasizing that it should not be done under any circumstances. *When asked for your views about your current job, on no account must you be negative.*

▶ **account for.** 1 PHR-VERB If you can **account for** something, you explain it or give the necessary information about it. *How do you account for the company's alarmingly high staff turnover?* 2 PHR-VERB If something **accounts for** a particular proportion of a whole thing, it is what that proportion consists of. *Computers account for 5% of the country's commercial electricity consumption.*

accountable /ə'kaʊntəbəl/. ADJ If you are **accountable** for something that you do, you are responsible for it. *Public officials can finally be held accountable for their actions.* ♦**accountability** N-U *...the system of local accountability for the police.*

accountancy /ə'kaʊntənsi/. N-U **Accountancy** is the work of keeping financial accounts.

accountant /ə'kaʊntənt/ **accountants.** N-C An **accountant** is a person whose job is to keep financial accounts.

accumulate /əˈkjuːmjʊleɪt/ **accumulates, accumulating, accumulated.** VERB When you **accumulate** things or when they **accumulate**, they collect or are gathered over a period of time. *Chemicals can accumulate in processed foods.* ♦**accumulation, accumulations** N-C *...accumulation of wealth. ...accumulations of dirt.*

accurate /ˈækjʊrət/. **1** ADJ Something that is **accurate** is correct to a detailed level. *This is the most accurate description of the killer to date... Quartz watches are very accurate.* ♦**accuracy** N-U *...the accuracy of the story.* ♦**accurately** ADV *The questions have been accurately recorded.* **2** ADJ A person, device, or machine that is **accurate** is able to perform a task without making a mistake. *The rifle was extremely accurate.* ♦**accuracy** N-U *Every bank pays close attention to the speed and accuracy of its staff.* ♦**accurately** ADV *...shooting back accurately, aiming to kill.*

accusation /ˌækjʊˈzeɪʃən/ **accusations.** N-C If you make an **accusation** against someone, you express the belief that they have done something wrong.

accuse /əˈkjuːz/ **accuses, accusing, accused.** VERB If you **accuse** someone of something, you say that you believe they did something wrong or dishonest. *He was accusing her of having an affair... Prosecutors had accused him of stealing about $26 million.*

accused /əˈkjuːzd/. **Accused** is the singular and plural. N-C The **accused** refers to the person or people charged with a crime or on trial for it. *The accused is alleged to be a member of a right-wing gang... The accused are out on bail.*

accustom /əˈkʌstəm/ **accustoms, accustoming, accustomed.** VERB If you **accustom** yourself to something, you experience it or learn about it, so that it becomes familiar or natural. *Shakespeare has accustomed us to a mixture of humor and tragedy in the same play.* ♦**accustomed** ADJ AFTER LINK-V *He was accustomed to hard work.*

ace /eɪs/ **aces.** **1** N-C An **ace** is a playing card with a single symbol on it. *...the ace of hearts.* **2** N-C In tennis, an **ace** is a serve which is so good that the other player cannot return the ball.

ache /eɪk/ **aches, aching, ached.** **1** VERB & N-C If part of your body **aches**, or if you have an **ache**, you feel a steady, fairly strong pain. *He really was aching, tired, and hungry. ...an effective remedy for aches and pains.* **2** VERB If you **ache** for something or **ache** to do something, you want it very much. *She still ached for the lost intimacy and sexual contact of marriage. ...a country aching to get away from its past.*

achieve /əˈtʃiːv/ **achieves, achieving, achieved.** VERB If you **achieve** a particular aim or effect, you succeed in doing it or causing it to happen, usually after a lot of effort. *Achieving our goals makes us feel good.*

achievement /əˈtʃiːvmənt/ **achievements.** **1** N-C An **achievement** is something which someone has succeeded in doing, especially after a lot of effort. **2** N-U **Achievement** is the process of achieving something. *It is only the*

achievement of these goals that will finally bring lasting peace.

achiever /əˈtʃiːvə/ **achievers.** N-C A high **achiever** is someone who is successful in their studies or their work, usually as a result of their efforts. A low achiever is someone who is unsuccessful.

acid /ˈæsɪd/ **acids.** **1** N-VAR An **acid** is a liquid or substance with a pH value of less than 7. Strong acids can damage your skin and clothes. *...citric acid... Acids in the stomach destroy the virus.* **2** ADJ An **acid** substance contains acid. *These shrubs must have an acid, lime-free soil.* **3** ADJ An **acid** fruit or drink has a sour or sharp taste. *These wines may taste rather hard and somewhat acid.* **4** ADJ An **acid** remark is unkind or critical.

acidic /əˈsɪdɪk/. ADJ Something that is **acidic** contains acid or has a pH value of less than 7.

acidity /æˈsɪdɪti/. N-U **Acidity** is the quality of having a pH value lower than 7.

acknowledge /ækˈnɒlɪdʒ/ **acknowledges, acknowledging, acknowledged.** **1** VERB If you **acknowledge** a fact, you accept that it is true; FORMAL. *Naylor acknowledged, in a letter to the judge, that he was a drug addict... This is now acknowledged as an urgent national problem.* **2** VERB If you **acknowledge** someone, you show that you have seen and recognized them. *She never even acknowledged the man who opened the door.* **3** VERB If you **acknowledge** a message or letter, you tell the person who sent it that you have received it. *The army sent me a postcard acknowledging my request.*

acknowledgement (or **acknowledgment**) /ækˈnɒlɪdʒmənt/ **acknowledgements.** **1** N-SING An **acknowledgement** of something is a statement or action that recognizes that it is true. *The President's resignation appears to be an acknowledgment that he has lost all hope.* **2** N-VAR If you receive an **acknowledgement** of something you have sent to someone, you are told officially that it has arrived. **3** N-PL The **acknowledgements** in a book are the parts in which the author thanks the people who have helped.

acne /ˈækni/. N-U **Acne** is a skin disease which causes spots on the face and neck.

acorn /ˈeɪkɔːn/ **acorns.** N-C An **acorn** is a pale oval nut that is the fruit of an oak tree.

acoustic /əˈkuːstɪk/ **acoustics.** **1** ADJ BEFORE N An **acoustic** guitar is not made louder by an electrical amplifier. **2** N-PL The **acoustics** of a room are the structural features which determine how well you can hear sound in it. *The acoustics of the theatre are still superb.* **3** ADJ **Acoustic** means relating to sound or hearing. *...acoustic signals.*

acquaint /əˈkweɪnt/ **acquaints, acquainting, acquainted.** VERB If you **acquaint** someone with something, you tell them about it, so that they know it or become familiar with it; FORMAL. *I want to acquaint myself with your abilities.*

acquaintance /əˈkweɪntəns/ **acquaintances.** **1** N-C An **acquaintance** is someone who you have met but do not know particularly well. *Rose and Jim Gordon were old acquaintances.* **2** N-VAR If you have an **acquaintance** with someone, you have met them and you know them. *I struck up an acquaintance with a shop-keeper.* **3** N-SING Your **acquaintance** with a subject is your knowledge or experience of it. *They had little or no acquaintance with Chinese history.*

acquainted /ə'kweɪntɪd/. **1** ADJ AFTER LINK-V If you are **acquainted** with something, you know about it because you have learned it or experienced it; FORMAL *He was well acquainted with the literature of France.* **2** ADJ AFTER LINK-V If you are **acquainted** with someone, you know them but they are not a close friend. You can also say that two people are **acquainted**.

acquire /ə'kwaɪə/ **acquires, acquiring, acquired.** **1** VERB If you **acquire** something, you obtain it. *General Motors acquired a 50% stake in Saab.* **2** VERB If you **acquire** a skill or habit, you learn it or develop it. *He had acquired the habit of observing people... Salt is an acquired taste.*

acquisition /ˌækwɪ'zɪʃən/ **acquisitions.** **1** N-C An **acquisition** is something that you have obtained. *His latest acquisition is a 1928 Lancia.* **2** N-U The **acquisition** of something is the process of getting it or being given it. *...the acquisition of land by force.* **3** N-U The **acquisition** of a skill or habit is the process of learning it or developing it. *...language acquisition.*

acquit /ə'kwɪt/ **acquits, acquitting, acquitted.** **1** VERB If someone **is acquitted** of a crime, it is formally declared in court that they did not commit it. *Mr Ling was acquitted of disorderly behaviour... All the accused were acquitted.* **2** VERB If you **acquit** yourself in a particular way, other people feel that you behave in that way; FORMAL *Most officers and men acquitted themselves well.*

acquittal /ə'kwɪtəl/ **acquittals.** N-VAR The **acquittal** of someone who has been accused of a crime is a formal declaration that they are innocent. *The judge ordered their acquittal.*

acre /'eɪkə/ **acres.** N-C An **acre** is a unit of area equal to 4,840 square yards or approximately 4,047 square metres.

acrimonious /ˌækrɪ'məʊniəs/. ADJ **Acrimonious** words or quarrels are bitter and angry; FORMAL.

acronym /'ækrənɪm/ **acronyms.** N-C An **acronym** is a word made of the initial letters of the words in a phrase, especially when this is the name of something. An example of an acronym is NATO.

across /ə'krɒs, AM ə'krɔːs/. **1** PREP & ADV If you go or look **across** somewhere, you go or look from one side of it to the other. *He watched Karl run across the street... He glanced across at his sleeping wife.* **2** PREP & ADV Something that is situated **across** a street, river, or area is on the other side of it, or stretches from one side to the other. *I saw you across the room... They parked across from the Castro Theatre... The floating bridge across Lake Washington.* **3** ADV **Across** is used to indicate the width of something. *This hand-decorated plate measures 30cm across.* **4** PREP When something happens **across** a place or organization, it happens equally everywhere within it. *The film opens across America on December 11.* ● **across the board:** see **board**.

acrylic /æ'krɪlɪk/. ADJ **Acrylic** material is man-made, manufactured by a chemical process. *...new acrylic wigs.*

act /ækt/ **acts, acting, acted.** **1** VERB When you **act**, you do something for a particular purpose. *...when police acted to stop widespread looting... We have acted properly and responsibly in this case.* **2** N-C An **act** is a single action or thing that someone does. *...the act of reading... My insurance excludes acts of sabotage.* **3** VERB If someone **acts** in a particular way, they behave in that way. *...a gang of youths who were acting suspiciously... He acted as if he hadn't heard.* **4** VERB If someone or something **acts** as a particular thing, they have that role or function. *He acted both as the ship's surgeon and as chaplain for the men.* **5** N-SING If you say that someone's behaviour is an **act**, you mean that it does not express their real feelings. **6** VERB If you **act** in a play or film, you have a part in it. *Every time I see her act I am filled with admiration.* **7** N-C An **act** in a play, opera, or ballet is one of the main parts into which it is divided. **8** N-C An **act** in a show is one of the short performances in the show. *...the best new comedy acts.* **9** N-C An **Act** is a law passed by the government. *...the Tax Reform Act of 1986.*

acting /'æktɪŋ/. **1** N-U **Acting** is the activity or profession of performing in plays or films. *The acting was superb. ...her acting career.* **2** ADJ BEFORE N You use **acting** before the title of a job to indicate that someone is doing that job temporarily. *...the new acting President.*

action /'ækʃən/ **actions.** **1** N-U **Action** is doing something for a particular purpose. *She was anxious to avoid any action which might harm him.* **2** N-C An **action** is something that you do on a particular occasion. *Peter had a reason for his action.* **3** N-SING The **action** refers to all the important and exciting things that are happening in a situation. *Hollywood is where the action is now.* **4** N-U **Action** is fighting in a war. *He'd been listed as missing in action.* PHRASES ● If you **put** an idea or policy **into action**, you begin to use it. ● If someone is **out of action**, they are injured and cannot work. You can also say that something is **out of action**. *...the lifts went out of action.*

activate /'æktɪveɪt/ **activates, activating, activated.** VERB If a device or process **is activated**, something causes it to start working. *Video cameras can be activated by movement.*

active /'æktɪv/. **1** ADJ An **active** person is energetic and always busy. *Having an active youngster about the house can be quite wearing.* **2** ADJ If someone is **active** in an organization or cause, they are involved in it and work hard for it. *...an active member of the Conservative Party... He is active on Tyler's behalf.* ♦ **actively** ADV *They actively campaigned for the vote.* **3** ADJ BEFORE N **Active** is used to emphasize that someone is taking action in order to achieve something, rather than just waiting for it to happen. *They are taking active steps to reduce stress.* ♦ **actively** ADV *They have never been* *actively encouraged to take such risks.* **4** ADJ An **active** volcano has erupted recently.

activist /'æktɪvɪst/ **activists.** N-C An **activist** is a person who works to bring about political or social changes. *...animal rights activists.*

activity /æk'tɪvɪti/ **activities.** **1** N-U **Activity** is a situation in which a lot of things are happening. *Other boats came and went in a flurry of activity.* **2** N-C An **activity** is something that you spend time doing. *...outdoor activities.* **3** N-PL The **activities** of a group are the things they do to achieve their aims. *...terrorist activities.*

actor /'æktə/ **actors.** N-C An **actor** is someone whose job is acting in plays or films.

actress /'æktrəs/ **actresses.** N-C An **actress** is a woman whose job is acting in plays or films.

actual /'æktʃʊəl/ **1** ADJ BEFORE N **Actual** is used to emphasize that you are referring to something real or genuine. *The actual number of AIDS victims is much higher than statistics reflect.* **2** ADJ BEFORE N You use **actual** to contrast the important aspect of something with a less important aspect. *The exercises in this chapter can guide you, but it will be up to you to do the actual work.* ● **in actual fact:** see **fact.**

actually /'æktʃʊəli/ **1** ADV You use **actually** to indicate that a situation exists or that it is true. *I grew bored and actually fell asleep for a few minutes... Interest is only payable on the amount actually borrowed.* **2** ADV You use **actually** as a way of being more polite, especially when you are correcting or contradicting someone, advising them, or when you are introducing a new topic of conversation. *No, I'm not a student. I'm a doctor, actually... Well actually, John, I rang you for some advice.*

> **Actual** and **actually** are not used to refer to something which is happening now, at the present time. For this meaning, you need to use adjectives such as **current** or **present**, or adverbs such as **currently** or **now**. **Actual** and **actually** are used to emphasize what is true or genuine in a situation, often when this is surprising, or a contrast with what has just been said.

acumen /'ækjʊmen, AM ə'kju:mən/ N-U **Acumen** is the ability to make good judgments and quick decisions. *...business acumen.*

acupuncture /'ækjʊpʌŋktʃə/ N-U **Acupuncture** is the treatment of a person's illness or pain by sticking small needles into their body.

acute /ə'kju:t/ **1** ADJ An **acute** situation or feeling is very intense or unpleasant. *...a very acute infection.* ◆**acutely** ADV *It was an acutely uncomfortable journey.* **2** ADJ If a person's or animal's senses are **acute**, they are sensitive and powerful. *Cats have very acute hearing.* ◆**acutely** ADV *He was acutely aware of the odour of cooking oil.* **3** ADJ In geometry, an **acute** angle is less than 90°.

ad /æd/ **ads.** N-C An **ad** is an advertisement; IN-FORMAL.

AD /ˌeɪ 'di:/. You use **AD** in dates to indicate a number of years or centuries since the year in which Jesus Christ is believed to have been born. *...the Great Fire of 1136 AD.*

adamant /'ædəmənt/. ADJ If you are **adamant** about something, you are determined not to change your mind. *The prime minister is adamant that he will not resign.* ◆**adamantly** ADV *She adamantly refused to put the book back.*

adapt /ə'dæpt/ **adapts, adapting, adapted.** **1** VERB If you **adapt** to a new situation, you change your ideas or behaviour in order to deal with it. *MPs have quickly adapted themselves to the cameras.* **2** VERB If you **adapt** something, you change it to make it suitable for a new purpose or situation. *Shelves were built to adapt the library for use as an office.* **3** VERB If you **adapt** a book or play, you change it so that it can be made into a film or a television programme. *The scriptwriter helped him to adapt his novel for the screen.* **4** See also **adapted.**

adaptable /ə'dæptəbəl/. ADJ Someone or something that is **adaptable** is able to change or be changed in order to suit new situations. *Humans are infinitely adaptable... an adaptable piece of summer clothing.* ◆**adaptability** N-U *...this adaptability which many animals do indeed show.*

adaptation /ˌædæp'teɪʃən/ **adaptations.** **1** N-C An **adaptation** of a story is a play or film based on it. *...his screen adaptation of Shakespeare's Henry the Fifth.* **2** N-U **Adaptation** is the act of changing something to make it suitable for a new purpose or situation. *Most living creatures are capable of adaptation.*

adapted /ə'dæptɪd/. ADJ AFTER LINK-V If something is **adapted** to a particular situation or purpose, it is especially suitable for it. *Plants are adapted to being short of water in summer.*

add /æd/ **adds, adding, added.** **1** VERB If you **add** one thing to another, you put it with the other thing, to complete or improve it. *Add the grated cheese to the sauce... He wants to add a huge sports complex to Binfield Manor.* **2** VERB & PHR-VERB If you **add** numbers or amounts, or **add** them **up**, you calculate their total. *Banks add all the interest and other charges together.* **3** VERB If one thing **adds** to another, it makes the other thing greater in degree or amount, or it gives it a particular quality. *Cheerful faces added to the general gaiety.* ◆**added** ADJ BEFORE N *For added protection choose moisturising lipsticks with a sun screen.* **4** VERB If you **add** something when you are speaking, you say something more. *Hunt added his congratulations.*

▸ **add in.** PHR-VERB If you **add in** something, you include it as a part of something else. *Once the vegetables start to cook add in a couple of tablespoons of water.*

▸ **add on.** **1** PHR-VERB If something **is added on**, it is attached to or made part of something else. *The colour is either drab or garish and is obviously added on.* **2** PHR-VERB If you **add on** an extra item or amount to a list or total, you include it in the list or total. *Many loan application forms automatically add on insurance.*

▸ **add up.** **1** See **add 2.** **2** PHR-VERB If facts or events do not **add up**, they make you confused about the true nature of the situation. *This* *charge of burglary just doesn't add up.* **3** PHR-VERB If small amounts of something **add up**, they gradually increase. *It's the little minor problems that add up.*

▶ **add up to.** PHR-VERB If amounts **add up to** a particular total, they result in that total when they are put together. *Profits can add up to millions of dollars.*

addict /ˈædɪkt/ **addicts. 1** N-C An **addict** is someone who cannot stop taking harmful drugs. *...a drug addict.* **2** N-C You can say that someone is an **addict**, when they like a particular activity very much. *Caroline is a TV addict.*

addicted /əˈdɪktɪd/. **1** ADJ Someone who is **addicted** to a drug cannot stop taking it. *Many of the women are addicted to heroin.* **2** ADJ If you are **addicted** to something, you like it very much. *She had become addicted to golf.*

addiction /əˈdɪkʃən/ **addictions. 1** N-VAR **Addiction** is the condition of being addicted to drugs. *...drug addiction.* **2** N-VAR An **addiction** to something is a very strong desire or need for it. *...his addiction to gambling.*

addictive /əˈdɪktɪv/. **1** ADJ If a drug is **addictive**, people who start taking it find that they cannot stop. *Cigarettes are highly addictive.* **2** ADJ Something that is **addictive** is so enjoyable that it makes you want to do it or have it a lot. *Video movie-making can quickly become addictive.*

addition /əˈdɪʃən/ **additions. 1** PHRASE You use **in addition** or **with the addition of** to mention another item connected with the subject you are discussing. *There's a postage and packing fee in addition to the repair charge.* **2** N-C An **addition** to something is a thing which is added to it. *...recent additions to the range of 4x4 cars.* ◆ **additional** ADJ *The US is sending additional troops to the region.* **3** N-U **Addition** is the process of calculating the total of two or more numbers.

additionally /əˈdɪʃənəli/. **1** ADV You use **additionally** to introduce an extra fact; FORMAL. *All teachers are qualified to teach their native language. Additionally, we select our teachers for their engaging personalities.* **2** ADV **Additionally** is used to say that something happens to a greater extent than before. *The birds are additionally protected in the reserves at Birsay.*

additive /ˈædɪtɪv/ **additives.** N-C An **additive** is a substance which is added to food by the manufacturer for a particular purpose, such as colouring it. *Strict safety tests are carried out on food additives. ...additive-free baby foods.*

address /əˈdres, AM ˈædres/ **addresses, addressing, addressed. 1** N-C Your **address** is the number of the house, the name of the street, and the town where you live or work. *The address is 2025 Main Street, Northwest, Washington, DC, 20036.* **2** VERB If a letter is **addressed** to you, your name and address has been written on it. *Applications should be addressed to the business affairs editor.* **3** VERB & N-C If you **address** a group of people or if you give an **address**, you give a speech to them. *He turned to address the multitude. ...an address to the American people.* **4** VERB If you **address**

someone or **address** a remark to someone, you say something to them. *The two foreign ministers did not address each other directly.* **5** VERB If you **address** someone by a name or a title such as 'sir', you call them that name or title. *I heard him address her as darling.* **6** VERB If you **address** a problem or if you **address** yourself to it, you try to understand it or deal with it. *Mr King sought to address those fears when he spoke at the meeting... Throughout the book we have addressed ourselves to the problem of ethics.*

adept /əˈdept/. ADJ Someone who is **adept** at something does it skilfully. *He's usually very adept at keeping his private life out of the media... He is an adept guitar player.*

adequate /ˈædɪkwət/. ADJ If something is **adequate**, there is enough of it or it is good enough for a particular purpose. *...an amount adequate to purchase another house.* ◆ **adequacy** N-U *...the adequacy of the diet.* ◆ **adequately** ADV *I speak the language adequately.*

adhere /ædˈhɪə/ **adheres, adhering, adhered. 1** VERB If you **adhere** to a rule, you act in the way that it says you should. *All members of the association adhere to a strict code of practice.* ◆ **adherence** /ædˈhɪərəns/ N-U *...strict adherence to the constitution.* **2** VERB If you **adhere** to an opinion or belief, you support or hold it. *...those who adhered to more traditional views.* **3** VERB If a substance **adheres** to a surface or object, it sticks to it; FORMAL. *Small particles adhere to the seed.*

adhesive /ædˈhiːsɪv/ **adhesives.** N-VAR & ADJ An **adhesive** or an **adhesive** substance is used to make things stick together. *...adhesive tape.*

ad hoc /ˌæd ˈhɒk/. ADJ An **ad hoc** activity or organization is done or formed only when it becomes necessary, rather than being planned in advance. *I would accept opportunities in TV on an ad hoc basis. ...ad hoc committees.*

adjacent /əˈdʒeɪsənt/. ADJ If two things are **adjacent**, they are next to each other. *He sat in an adjacent room. ...offices adjacent to the museum.*

adjective /ˈædʒɪktɪv/ **adjectives.** N-C In grammar, an **adjective** is a word such as 'big', 'dead', or 'financial' that describes a person or thing, or gives extra information about them. Adjectives usually come before nouns or after link verbs.

adjoin /əˈdʒɔɪn/ **adjoins, adjoining, adjoined.** VERB If one room, place, or object **adjoins** another, they are next to each other; FORMAL. *We waited in an adjoining office.*

adjourn /əˈdʒɜːn/ **adjourns, adjourning, adjourned.** VERB If a meeting or trial is **adjourned** or if it **adjourns**, it is stopped for a short time. *The proceedings have now been adjourned until next week.* ◆ **adjournment** /əˈdʒɜːnmənt/ **adjournments.** N-C *The court ordered a four month adjournment.*

adjust /əˈdʒʌst/ **adjusts, adjusting, adjusted. 1** VERB When you **adjust** to a new situation, you get used to it by changing your behaviour or your ideas. *It has been hard to adjust.* ◆ **adjustment** /əˈdʒʌstmənt/ **adjustments.** N-C *He will have to make major adjustments to* his thinking. [2] VERB If you **adjust** something, you change it so that it is more effective or appropriate. *Panama has adjusted its tax and labour laws.* ♦**adjustment** N-C *Investment is up by 5.7% after adjustment for inflation.* [3] VERB If you **adjust** something, you correct or alter its position or setting. *You can manually adjust the camera.* ♦**adjustment** N-C *...a large workshop for repairs and adjustments.*

adjustable /ə'dʒʌstəbəl/. ADJ If something is **adjustable**, it can be changed to different positions or sizes. *The bags have adjustable shoulder straps... The seats are fully adjustable.*

administer /æd'mɪnɪstə/ **administers, administering, administered.** [1] VERB If someone **administers** something such as a country, the law, or a test, they take responsibility for organizing and supervising it. *The plan calls for the UN to administer the country until elections can be held.* [2] VERB If a doctor or a nurse **administers** a drug, they give it to a patient; FORMAL.

administration /æd,mɪnɪ'streɪʃən/. [1] N-U **Administration** is the range of activities connected with organizing and supervising the way that an organization functions. *Too much time is spent on administration. ...business administration.* [2] N-SING The **administration** of a company or institution is the group of people who organize and supervise it. *They would like the college administration to exert more control.* [3] See note at **government**.

administrative /æd'mɪnɪstrətɪv, AM -streɪt-/. ADJ **Administrative** work involves organizing and supervising an organization. *...administrative costs.*

administrator /æd'mɪnɪstreɪtə/ **administrators.** N-C An **administrator** is a person whose job involves helping to organize and supervise the way that an organization functions.

admirable /'ædmɪrəbəl/. ADJ An **admirable** quality or action deserves to be praised and admired. *He was, in many ways, a very admirable person.* ♦**admirably** ADV *Peter had dealt admirably with the sudden questions.*

admiral /'ædmərəl/ **admirals.** N-C & N-TITLE An **admiral** is a naval officer of the highest rank.

admiration /,ædmɪ'reɪʃən/. N-U **Admiration** is a feeling of great liking and respect. *I have always had the greatest admiration for him.*

admire /əd'maɪə/ **admires, admiring, admired.** [1] VERB If you **admire** someone or something, you like and respect them. *All those who knew him will admire him for his work.* ♦**admirer, admirers** N-C *He was an admirer of her grandfather's paintings.* [2] VERB If you **admire** someone or something, you look at them with pleasure. *We took time to stop and admire the view.*

admission /æd'mɪʃən/ **admissions.** [1] N-VAR If you gain **admission** to a place or organisation, you are allowed to enter it or join it. *Students apply for admission to a particular college. ...increases in hospital admissions.* [2] N-U **Admission** or an **admission fee** is the amount of money you pay to enter a place such as a park or museum. [3] N-VAR An **admission** is a statement that something bad or embarrassing is

true. *She wanted some admission of guilt from her father.*

admit /æd'mɪt/ **admits, admitting, admitted.** [1] VERB If you **admit** that something bad or embarrassing is true, you agree, often reluctantly, that it is true. *Up to two thirds of 14 to 16 year olds admit to buying drink illegally... None of these people will admit responsibility.* [2] VERB If someone **is admitted** to hospital, they are taken into hospital for treatment. [3] VERB If someone **is admitted** to a place or organization, they are allowed to enter it or join it. *He was admitted to university after the war... Journalists are rarely admitted to the region.*

admittedly /æd'mɪtɪdli/. ADV You use **admittedly** when you are saying something which weakens the force of your statement. *It's only a theory, admittedly, but the pieces fit together.*

adolescent /,ædə'lesənt/ **adolescents.** ADJ & N-C **Adolescent** is used to describe young people who are no longer children but who have not yet become adults. An **adolescent** is a young person. *An adolescent boy.* ♦**adolescence** /,ædə'lesəns/ N-U *...children who have reached adolescence.*

adopt /ə'dɒpt/ **adopts, adopting, adopted.** [1] VERB If you **adopt** someone else's child, you take it into your own family and make it legally your own. *...an adopted child.* ♦**adoption, adoptions** N-VAR *They gave their babies up for adoption.* [2] VERB If you **adopt** a new attitude or plan, you begin to have it. *Pupils should be helped to adopt a positive approach to the environment.* ♦**adoption** N-U *...the adoption of Japanese management practices.*

adorable /ə'dɔːrəbəl/. ADJ If you say that someone or something is **adorable**, you are emphasizing that they are very attractive and you feel great affection for them. *We had three adorable children.*

adore /ə'dɔː/ **adores, adoring, adored.** [1] VERB If you **adore** someone, you love and admire them. ♦**adoration** N-U *He had been used to female adoration.* [2] VERB If you **adore** something, you like it very much; INFORMAL. *My mother adores bananas.*

adoring /ə'dɔːrɪŋ/. ADJ An **adoring** person loves and admires someone else very much. ♦**adoringly** ADV *She gazes adoringly at her husband.*

adorn /ə'dɔːn/ **adorns, adorning, adorned.** VERB If something **adorns** a place or an object, it makes it look more beautiful. *Several magnificent oil paintings adorn the walls.* ♦**adornment** /ə'dɔːnmənt/ **adornments** N-VAR *...a building without any adornment or decoration.*

adrenalin (or **adrenaline**) /ə'drenəlɪn/. N-U **Adrenalin** is a substance produced by your body which makes your heart beat faster and gives you more energy.

adrift /ə'drɪft/. [1] ADJ AFTER LINK-V If a boat is **adrift**, it is floating on the water without being controlled. *They were spotted after three hours adrift in a dinghy.* [2] ADJ AFTER LINK-V If something or someone has gone **adrift**, they no longer seem to have any purpose or direction. *...a policy that has gone adrift.*

adult /'ædʌlt, AM ə'dʌlt/ **adults.** N-C & ADJ BEFORE
N An **adult** is a mature, fully developed person
or animal. **Adult** means relating to the time
when you are an adult, or typical of adults. ...*a
pair of adult birds... I've lived most of my adult
life in London.*

adultery /ə'dʌltəri/. N-C If a married person
commits **adultery**, they have sex with someone that they are not married to.

adulthood /'ædʌlthʊd, AM -'dʌlt-/. N-U **Adulthood** is the state of being an adult. ...*children
coming into adulthood.*

advance /æd'vɑːns, -'væns/ **advances, advancing, advanced.** 1 VERB & N-VAR To **advance** or to make an **advance** means to move
forward, often in order to attack someone. *Rebel forces are advancing on the capital... The
defences are intended to obstruct any advance
by tanks.* 2 VERB & N-VAR If you **advance** or
make an **advance** in something you are doing,
you make progress in it. *Japan has advanced
from a rural, feudal society to an urban, industrial power. ...the dramatic advances of the
1970s.* 3 VERB & N-C If you **advance** someone a
sum of money, or if you give them an **advance**,
you give them money earlier than arranged.
*The bank advanced $1.2 billion... She was paid
a £100,000 advance for her next two novels.*
4 VERB To **advance** an event, or its time or
date, means to bring it forward to an earlier
time or date. *Too much protein in the diet may
advance the ageing process.* 5 ADJ BEFORE N **Advance** booking or warning is done or given before an event happens. *The event received little
advance publicity.* 6 PHRASE If you do something **in advance**, you do it before a particular
date or event. If one thing happens or is done
in advance of another, it happens or is done
before the other thing. *I had asked everyone to
submit questions in advance of the meeting.*

advanced /æd'vɑːnst, -'vænst/. 1 ADJ An **advanced** system, method, or design is modern
and has been developed from an earlier version of the same thing. ...*the most advanced
optical telescope in the world.* 2 ADJ A country
that is **advanced** has reached a high level of industrial or technological development. ...*the
educational levels reached in other advanced
countries.* 3 ADJ An **advanced** student is doing
more difficult work.

advancement /æd'vɑːnsmənt, -'væns-/. 1 N-U
Advancement is promotion in your job, or to a
higher social class. *He cared little for social advancement.* 2 N-U The **advancement** of something is the process of helping it to progress.
...*the advancement of education.*

advantage /æd'vɑːntɪdʒ, -'væn-/ **advantages.**
1 N-VAR An **advantage** is something that puts
you in a better position than other people. **Advantage** is the state of being in a better position than others who are competing against
you. *A good crowd will be a definite advantage
to me and the rest of the team... Men have created a social and physical position of advantage for themselves.* 2 N-C An **advantage** is a
way in which one thing is better than another.
*The great advantage of home-grown oranges is
their magnificent flavour.* 3 PHRASE If you **take
advantage of** something, you make good use
of it while you can. *I intend to take full advantage of this trip to buy the things we need.*
4 PHRASE If someone **takes advantage of** you,
they treat you unfairly for their own benefit.
5 PHRASE If you **use** something **to** your **advantage** or **turn** something **to** your **advantage**,
you exploit it in order to benefit from it.

advantageous /ˌædvən'teɪdʒəs/. ADJ Something that is **advantageous** to you is likely to
benefit you. ...*very advantageous prices.*

advent /'ædvent/. N-U The **advent** of something
is the fact of it starting or coming into existence; FORMAL. ...*the advent of the computer.*

adventure /æd'ventʃə/ **adventures.** N-VAR An
adventure is a series of events that you become involved in that are unusual, exciting,
and perhaps dangerous. *I set off for a new adventure in the United States. ...a feeling of adventure.* ◆**adventurer, adventurers.** N-C ...*a
true adventurer's paradise.*

adventurous /æd'ventʃərəs/. ADJ An **adventurous** person is willing to take risks and eager to
have new experiences. Something that is **adventurous** involves new things or ideas. *The
menu seemed more adventurous before.*

adverb /'ædvɜːb/ **adverbs.** N-C In grammar, an
adverb is a word such as 'slowly' or 'very'
which adds information about time, place, or
manner.

adversary /'ædvəsəri, AM -seri/ **adversaries.**
N-C Your **adversary** is someone you are competing with or fighting against. ...*political adversaries.*

adverse /'ædvɜːs, AM æd'vɜːrs/. ADJ **Adverse** effects or conditions are unfavourable to you.
*Stress can have an adverse effect on their
health.* ◆**adversely** ADV ...*countries adversely
affected by the increase in the price of oil.*

adversity /æd'vɜːsɪti/. N-U **Adversity** is a very
difficult situation. ...*ways in which people
manage to enjoy life despite adversity.*

advert /'ædvɜːt/ **adverts.** N-C An **advert** is the
same as an advertisement; INFORMAL.

advertise /'ædvətaɪz/ **advertises, advertising, advertised.** 1 VERB If you **advertise**
something such as a product, event, or job,
you tell people about it in newspapers, on television, or on posters. *Religious groups are currently not allowed to advertise on television.*
◆**advertiser, advertisers** N-C ...*campaigns by
the advertiser in support of the film.* 2 VERB If
you **advertise** for someone to do something
for you, you place an advertisement for it in a
newspaper, on television, or on a poster, saying that you need someone to do it. *We advertised for staff in a local newspaper.*

advertisement /æd'vɜːtɪsmənt, AM ˌædvə'taɪz-/
advertisements. N-C An **advertisement** is an
announcement in a newspaper, on television,
or on a poster that tells people about a product, event, or job vacancy. ...*job advertisements.*

advertising /'ædvətaɪzɪŋ/. N-U **Advertising** is
the business activity of encouraging people to
buy products, go to events, or apply for jobs.
...*a ban on tobacco advertising.*

advice /ædˈvaɪs/. N-U If you give someone **advice**, you tell them what you think they should do. *Take my advice and stay away from him!*

advisable /ædˈvaɪzəbəl/. ADJ AFTER LINK-V If you tell someone that it is **advisable** to do something, you are suggesting that they should do it, because it is sensible and likely to achieve the result they want. *It's always advisable to book for dinner at leading restaurants.*

advise /ædˈvaɪz/ **advises, advising, advised.** [1] VERB If you **advise** someone to do something, you tell them what you think they should do. *Could you advise me how to use a telescope with a camera?* [2] VERB If you **advise** people on a particular subject, you give them help and information on it. *...a new booklet advising on financial problems.* [3] VERB If you **advise** someone of a fact or situation, you tell them the fact or explain what the situation is; FORMAL. *A counselor will advise you of your rights.*

adviser (or **advisor**) /ædˈvaɪzə/ **advisers.** N-C An **adviser** is an expert whose job is to advise people on a particular subject. *...a university careers adviser.*

advisory /ædˈvaɪzəri/. ADJ An **advisory** committee gives people help and information on a particular subject. *...the advisory committee on the safety of nuclear installations.*

advocacy /ˈædvəkəsi/. [1] N-SING Someone's **advocacy** of a particular action or plan is their act of recommending it publicly; FORMAL. *...the president's advocacy of higher taxes.* [2] N-U **Advocacy** is the way in which lawyers deal with cases in court; FORMAL.

advocate, advocates, advocating, advocated; verb /ˈædvəkeɪt/, noun /ˈædvəkət/. [1] VERB & N-C If you **advocate** a particular action or plan, or if you are an **advocate** of it, you support it publicly; FORMAL. *Mr Williams is a conservative who advocates fewer government controls on business.* [2] N-C An **advocate** is a lawyer who speaks in favour of someone or defends them in a court of law; TECHNICAL.

aerial /ˈeəriəl/ **aerials.** [1] ADJ BEFORE N You use **aerial** to talk about things which happen in the air or are done from the air, particularly from an aeroplane. *...aerial photographs.* [2] N-C In British English, an **aerial** is a piece of metal equipment that receives television or radio signals. The American word is **antenna**.

aeroplane /ˈeərəpleɪn/ **aeroplanes.** N-C An **aeroplane** is a vehicle with wings and engines that enable it to fly through the air; the usual American word is **airplane**.

aerosol /ˈeərəsɒl, AM -sɔːl/ **aerosols.** N-C An **aerosol** is a small container in which a liquid such as paint is kept under pressure. When you press a button, the liquid is forced out as a fine spray or foam.

aesthetic (or **esthetic**) /iːsˈθetɪk, AM esˈ-/. ADJ **Aesthetic** is used to talk about beauty or art, and people's appreciation of beautiful things. *...products chosen for their aesthetic appeal.* ◆**aesthetically** ADV *...aesthetically pleasing furniture and carpets.*

affable /ˈæfəbəl/. ADJ **Affable** people are pleasant and friendly. *...his gentle, affable nature.*

affair /əˈfeə/ **affairs.** [1] N-C You refer to an event as an **affair** when you are talking about it in a general way. *The government has mishandled the whole affair.* [2] N-PL In politics and journalism, **affairs** is used to refer to a particular type of activity or to the activities in a particular place. *...our foreign affairs correspondent.* ● See also **current affairs, state of affairs.** [3] N-PL Your **affairs** are your personal concerns. *The unexpectedness of my father's death meant that his affairs were not entirely in order.* [4] N-SING If you say that a decision or situation is someone's **affair**, you mean that other people should not interfere. *If you wish to make a fool of yourself, that is your affair.* [5] N-C If two people who are not married to each other have an **affair**, they have a sexual relationship.

affect /əˈfekt/ **affects, affecting, affected.** [1] VERB When something **affects** someone or something, it influences them or causes them to change. *...decisions that would affect me for the rest of my life... More than seven million people have been affected by drought.* [2] VERB If a disease **affects** you, it makes you ill. *AIDS seems to affect men and women in equal numbers.*

affection /əˈfekʃən/ **affections.** [1] N-U If you regard someone or something with **affection**, you are fond of them. [2] N-PL Your **affections** are your feelings of love or fondness for someone. *She had focused her affections on her father.*

affectionate /əˈfekʃənət/. ADJ If you are **affectionate**, you show your fondness for another person in your behaviour. *They were more affectionate towards the younger child.* ◆**affectionately** ADV *He looked affectionately at his niece.*

affidavit /ˌæfɪˈdeɪvɪt/ **affidavits.** N-C An **affidavit** is a written statement which you swear is true and which may be used as evidence in a court of law.

affiliate, affiliates, affiliating, affiliated. [1] N-C /əˈfɪliət/ An **affiliate** is an organization which is officially connected with another, larger organization or is a member of it. [2] VERB /əˈfɪlieɪt/ If an organization **affiliates to** or **with** another larger organization, it forms a close connection with it or becomes a member of it. *...the United Nations and its affiliated organisations.* ◆**affiliation, affiliations** N-C *The group has no affiliation to any political party.*

affinity /əˈfɪnɪti/ **affinities.** [1] N-SING If you have an **affinity** with someone or something, you feel that you belong with them and understand them. *...fishermen who have a natural affinity for the water.* [2] N-C If people or things have an **affinity** with each other, they are similar in some ways. *The festival has affinities with the Roman festival of Cybele.*

affirm /əˈfɜːm/ **affirms, affirming, affirmed.** [1] VERB If you **affirm** that something is true, you state firmly and publicly that it is true; FORMAL. *...a speech in which he affirmed a commitment to lower taxes.* ◆**affirmation** /ˌæfəˈmeɪʃən/ **affirmations** N-VAR *...affirmation that Mr Green was a man of courage.* [2] VERB If an event **affirms** something, it shows that it is true or exists; FORMAL. ♦**affirmation** N-U ...*the youngsters' expression of violence, which he saw as the affirmation of their rebellion.*

affirmative /ə'fɜːmətɪv/. ADJ An **affirmative** word or gesture indicates that you agree with someone or that the answer to a question is 'yes'; FORMAL. ...*an affirmative nod.*

afflict /ə'flɪkt/ **afflicts, afflicting, afflicted.** VERB If you **are afflicted** with something, it affects you badly. *Both people who died were afflicted with a rare genetic disease... Italy has been afflicted by political corruption for decades.*

affliction /ə'flɪkʃən/ **afflictions.** N-VAR An **affliction** is something which causes suffering; FORMAL. *Baldness is an affliction that can ruin a young man's life.*

affluent /'æfluənt/. ADJ **Affluent** people have a lot of money. ...*Philadelphia's affluent suburbs.* ♦**affluence** N-U *The postwar era was one of new affluence for the working class.*

afford /ə'fɔːd/ **affords, affording, afforded.** [1] VERB If you cannot **afford** something, you do not have enough money to pay for it. *We can't afford to pay private fees.* [2] VERB If you cannot **afford** to do something or allow it to happen, you must not do it or you must prevent it from happening because it would be harmful or embarrassing to you. *The country could not afford the luxury of an election.*

affordable /ə'fɔːdəbl/. ADJ If something is **affordable**, people have enough money to buy it. ...*affordable housing.* ♦**affordability** N-U ...*advertisements that emphasized affordability.*

affront /ə'frʌnt/ **affronts, affronting, affronted.** VERB & N-C If something **affronts** you, or if it is an **affront** to you, it makes you feel insulted. ...*results which would affront the good sense of right-thinking persons... She has taken my enquiry as a personal affront.*

afield /ə'fiːld/. [1] PHRASE **Further afield** or **farther afield** mean in places other than the nearest or most obvious one. *Lucerne is a good base for travelling further afield.* [2] PHRASE If people come from **far afield**, they come from a long way away.

afloat /ə'fləʊt/. [1] ADV When someone or something is **afloat**, they remain partly above the surface of water and do not sink. [2] ADV If a person or business manages to stay **afloat**, they have just enough money to pay their debts. *He and his family kept afloat by doing odd jobs.*

afoot /ə'fʊt/. ADJ AFTER LINK-V If something such as a plan is **afoot**, it is already happening or being planned, often secretly. *US workers claim plans are afoot to move work to Germany.*

aforementioned /ə'fɔːmenʃənd/. ADJ BEFORE N When you refer to the **aforementioned** person or subject, you mean the person or subject that has already been mentioned; FORMAL.

afraid /ə'freɪd/. [1] ADJ AFTER LINK-V If you are **afraid** of someone or **afraid** to do something, you are frightened because you think that something horrible is going to happen. *I was afraid of the other boys.* [2] ADJ AFTER LINK-V If

you are **afraid** that something unpleasant will happen, you are worried that it may happen. *The Government is afraid of losing the election.* [3] ADJ AFTER LINK-V If you are **afraid** for someone else, you are worried that they are in danger. *She's afraid for her family in Somalia.* [4] CONVENTION When you want disagree with someone or apologize to them in a polite way, you can say **I'm afraid**. *I'm afraid I can't agree with you on that John.*

afresh /ə'freʃ/. ADV If you do something **afresh**, you do it again in a different way.

African /'æfrɪkən/ **Africans.** [1] ADJ **African** means belonging or relating to the continent of Africa. ...*African art.* [2] N-C An **African** is someone who comes from Africa.

aft /ɑːft, æft/. ADV & ADJ BEFORE N If you go **aft** in a boat or plane, you go to the back of it. The **aft** end of a boat or plane is towards the back. *Clark shook hands with the pilot and walked aft. ...the aft cabin.*

after /'ɑːftə, 'æftə/ In addition to the uses below, **after** is used in phrasal verbs such as 'ask after' or 'look after'. [1] PREP & CONJ If something happens or is done **after** a particular event or date, it happens or is done during the period of time that follows it. *I went for a walk after lunch... After completing and signing it, please return the form to us... She's leaving the day after tomorrow.* [2] PREP In American English, **after** is used when telling the time. [3] PREP If you are **after** someone, you follow or chase them. *He would be smart enough to know the police were after him.* [4] PREP If you shout or stare **after** someone, you shout or stare at them as they move away from you. [5] PREP If you are **after** something, you are trying to get it. *I'm not after Rick's job.* [6] PREP To be named **after** someone or something means to be given the same name as them. *Phillimore Island is named after Sir Robert Phillimore.* [7] PREP You use **after** in order to give the most important aspect of something when comparing it with something else. *After Germany, America is Britain's second-biggest customer.* [8] CONVENTION If you say **'after you'** to someone, you are being polite and allowing them to go in front of you. [9] **after all:** see **all**.

aftermath /'ɑːftəmɑːθ, 'æftəmæθ/. N-SING The **aftermath** of an important or serious event is the situation that results from it. *In the aftermath of the coup, the troops opened fire on the demonstrators.*

afternoon /,ɑːftə'nuːn, ,æf-/ **afternoons.** N-C The **afternoon** is the part of each day which begins at 12 o' clock lunchtime and ends at about six o'clock.

afterwards /'ɑːftəwədz, 'æf-/. The form **afterward** is also used, mainly in American English. ADV If something is done or happens **afterwards**, it is done or happens later than a particular event or time that has already been described. *Shortly afterwards, police arrested four suspects... James was taken to hospital but died soon afterwards.*

again /ə'gen, ə'geɪn/. [1] ADV You use **again** to indicate that something happens a second time, or after it has already happened before. *He kissed her again... I don't ever want to go* *through anything like that again.* [2] PHRASE You can use **again and again** or **time and again** to emphasize that something happens many times. *Time and again political parties have failed to tackle this issue.* [3] ADV You use **again** to indicate that something has returned to the particular state or place that it used to be in. *She opened the door and closed it again.* [4] **every now and again:** see **now**.

against /ə'genst, ə'geɪnst/. [1] PREP If something is leaning or pressing **against** something else, it is touching it. *She leaned against him. ...the rain beating against the window panes.* [2] PREP & ADV If you are **against** an idea, policy, or system, you think it is wrong or stupid. *...a march to protest against job losses. ...12 votes in favour, 2 votes against.* [3] PREP If you take action **against** someone or something, you try to harm them. *...the crime of violence against women.* [4] PREP If you do something **against** someone's wishes, advice, or orders, you do it although they tell you not to. *He discharged himself from hospital against the advice of doctors.* [5] PREP If you compete **against** someone in a game, you try to beat them. *The tour will include games against the Australians.* [6] PREP If you do something to protect yourself **against** something unpleasant, you do something which will make its effects on you less serious. *This cream protects against damage from sunlight.* [7] PREP Something that is **against** the law is forbidden by law. [8] PREP & ADV The odds **against** something happening are the odds that it will not happen.

age /eɪdʒ/ **ages, ageing** (or **aging**), **aged.** [1] N-VAR Your **age** is the number of years that you have lived. *She has a nephew who is just ten years of age... At the age of sixteen he qualified for a place at the University.* [2] N-U **Age** is the state of being old. *This cologne, like wine, improves with age... At 67, he is showing signs of age.* [3] VERB When someone **ages**, they become or seem much older. *He seemed to have aged in the last few months... Worry had aged him.* ◆**ageing** N-U *Inadequate fluid intake and poor diet all contribute to ageing.* [4] N-C An **age** is a period in history. *We're living in the age of television. ...the Bronze Age.* [5] See also **aged, middle age.**

PHRASES ● Someone who is **under age** is not legally old enough to do something. *Many of the drinkers in the town's pubs are under age. ...under age smoking.* ● When someone **comes of age**, they legally become an adult.

aged. [1] ADJ /eɪdʒd/ You use **aged** followed by a number to say how old someone is. *They have a son aged five.* [2] ADJ BEFORE N & N-PL /'eɪdʒɪd/ An **aged** person is very old. You can refer to people who are very old as **the aged.** *...his aged parents. ...a home for the aged.* [3] See also **middle-aged.**

agency /'eɪdʒənsi/ **agencies.** [1] N-C An **agency** is a business which provides services for a person or another business. *...a dating agency. ...an advertising agency.* [2] N-C An **agency** is an administrative organization run by a government. *...the Central Intelligence Agency.*

agenda /ə'dʒendə/ **agendas.** [1] N-C An **agenda** is a list of items to be discussed at a meeting.

This is sure to be an item on the agenda next week. [2] N-C You can refer to the political issues which are important at a particular time as an **agenda.** *His speech today will set the agenda for Labour's general election campaign.*

agent /'eɪdʒənt/ **agents.** [1] N-C An **agent** is someone who arranges work or business for someone else, especially actors or musicians. *You are buying direct, rather than through an agent.* ● See also **estate agent, travel agent.** [2] N-C An **agent** is someone who works for a country's secret service.

age of con'sent. N-SING The **age of consent** is the age at which a person can legally marry or agree to have a sexual relationship.

age-old. ADJ BEFORE N An **age-old** story, tradition, or problem has existed for a very long time.

aggravate /'ægrəveɪt/ **aggravates, aggravating, aggravated.** [1] VERB If someone or something **aggravates** a situation, they make it worse. *Tipping the head may aggravate any neck injury.* [2] VERB If someone or something **aggravates** you, they make you annoyed; INFORMAL. *It's been aggravating me for months.* ◆**aggravating** ADJ *It's very aggravating to be so low on merchandise.* ◆**aggravation, aggravations** N-VAR *The sounds were a constant aggravation.*

aggregate /'ægrɪgət/ **aggregates.** [1] N-C & ADJ BEFORE N An **aggregate** or **aggregate** amount is an amount made up of several smaller amounts. *An aggregate of twelve hundred acres spread over four separate parks. ...an aggregate loss of £353 million.* [2] PHRASE If one team beats another team **on aggregate**, it wins by getting the higher total over a series of games; BRITISH. *Raith Rovers lost 1-0 away to the Icelandic side, Akranes, but went through 3-2 on aggregate.*

aggression /ə'greʃən/. N-U **Aggression** is angry or violent behaviour towards someone. *...an act of aggression.*

aggressive /ə'gresɪv/. [1] ADJ An **aggressive** person behaves angrily or violently towards other people. *Some children are much more aggressive than others. ...aggressive behaviour.* ◆**aggressively** ADV *...rumours she always aggressively denies.* [2] ADJ If you are **aggressive** in your work or other activities, you behave in a forceful way because you are eager to succeed. *...a very aggressive and competitive executive.*

aggressor /ə'gresə/ **aggressors.** N-C The **aggressor** is the person or country that starts a fight.

aggrieved /ə'griːvd/. ADJ If you feel **aggrieved**, you feel upset and angry because of the way you have been treated.

aghast /ə'gɑːst, ə'gæst/. ADJ If you are **aghast**, you are filled with horror and surprise; FORMAL.

agile /'ædʒaɪl, AM -dʒəl/. [1] ADJ Someone who is **agile** can move with surprising ease and speed. *He is very agile for a big man.* ◆**agility** /ə'dʒɪlɪti/ N-U *He lacks Bruce's natural agility.* [2] ADJ If you have an **agile** mind, you think quickly and intelligently. ◆**agility** N-U *...exercises in mental agility.*

agitate /'ædʒɪteɪt/ **agitates, agitating, agitated.** VERB If people **agitate** for something, they protest or take part in political activity in order to get it. *The women who worked in these mills had begun to agitate for better conditions.* ♦**agitation** N-U *...continuing agitation against the decision.*

agitated /'ædʒɪteɪtɪd/. ADJ If someone is **agitated**, they are very worried or upset, and show this in their behaviour or voice. *Susan seemed agitated about something.*

agitation /,ædʒɪ'teɪʃən/. N-U **Agitation** is worry. *Sheila lit a cigarette, trying to mask her agitation.* ● See also **agitate**.

ago /ə'gəʊ/. ADV You use **ago** to refer to past time. For example, if something happened one year **ago**, it is one year since it happened. *She died long ago.*

agonize (BR also **agonise**) /'ægənaɪz/ **agonizes, agonizing, agonized.** VERB If you **agonize** over something, you feel anxious and spend a long time thinking about it. *I agonize over what to give my wife for Christmas.*

agonizing (or **agonising**) /'ægənaɪzɪŋ/. ADJ Something that is **agonizing** causes you to feel great physical or mental pain. *The wait was agonizing... It was an agonizing decision.*

agony /'ægəni/ **agonies.** N-VAR **Agony** is great physical or mental pain. *She called out in agony. ...the agonies of parenthood.*

agree /ə'griː/ **agrees, agreeing, agreed.** 1 VERB If you **agree** with someone, you have the same opinion about something. *I agree with you entirely... We agreed that she was not to be told.* 2 VERB If you **agree** to do something, you say that you will do it. *He agreed to meet me at my hotel.* 3 VERB If people **agree** on something or **agree** something, they all decide to have or do something. *We never agreed a date.* 4 VERB If you **agree** with an action or a suggestion, you approve of it. *The Cabinet agreed with his plan.* 5 VERB If two stories or totals **agree**, they are the same as each other. *His second statement agrees with facts as stated by the other witnesses.*

agreeable /ə'griːəbəl/. 1 ADJ If something or someone is **agreeable**, they are pleasant and people like them. *...an agreeable surprise... He had been a very agreeable guest.* 2 ADJ AFTER LINK-V If you are **agreeable** to something or if it is **agreeable** to you, you are willing to do it or to allow it; FORMAL *...a solution that would be agreeable to all.*

agreement /ə'griːmənt/ **agreements.** 1 N-C An **agreement** is a decision that two or more people, groups, or countries have made together. *...a ceasefire agreement.* 2 N-U & PHRASE **Agreement** with someone means having the same opinion they have. You can also say that you are **in agreement** with someone. *The unions had reached broad agreement on the resolution... James nodded his head in agreement.*

agriculture /'ægrɪkʌltʃə/. N-U **Agriculture** is farming and the methods used to look after crops and animals. ♦**agricultural** /,ægrɪ'kʌltʃərəl/ ADJ *...agricultural research.*

aground /ə'graʊnd/. ADV If a ship or boat runs

aground, it gets stuck on the ground in a shallow area of water.

ahead /ə'hed/. 1 ADV Something that is **ahead** is in front of you. If you look **ahead**, you look directly in front of you. *The road ahead is now blocked solid... Ahead, he saw the side railings of First Bridge... Brett looked straight ahead.* 2 ADV If you are **ahead** in your work or achievements, you have made more progress than you expected. *Children in small classes were 1.5 months ahead in reading.* 3 ADV If a person or a team is **ahead** in a competition, they are winning. *A goal would have put Dublin 6-1 ahead... Clinton was ahead in the polls.* 4 ADV If you go on **ahead**, you leave for a place before other people. *I'd have to send Tina on ahead with Rachael.* 5 ADV **Ahead** means in the future. *A much bigger battle is ahead for the president... Book ahead as the restaurant is very popular. ...the days ahead.*

a'head of. 1 PREP If someone or something is **ahead of** you, they are in front of you. *I saw a man in a blue jacket thirty metres ahead of me... She walked ahead of Helene up the steps.* 2 PREP If an event or period of time lies **ahead of** you, it is going to happen or come soon or in the future. *We have a very busy day ahead of us.* 3 PREP If something happens **ahead of** an event, it happens before that event. If something happens **ahead of** time, it happens earlier than was planned. *The Prime Minister was speaking ahead of today's meeting... The election was held six months ahead of schedule.* 4 PREP If one person is **ahead of** another, they have made more progress and are more advanced in what they are doing. *Henry generally stayed ahead of the others in the academic subjects.* 5 **ahead of one's time:** see **time.**

aid /eɪd/ **aids, aiding, aided.** 1 VERB & N-U To **aid** a person, country, or organization, or to give them **aid**, means to help them by giving them money, equipment, or services. *...American efforts to aid the refugees... They have already pledged billions of dollars in aid.* ♦**-aided** *...state-aided schools.* 2 VERB & N-U To **aid** someone or give them **aid**, means to help or assist them. *...a software system to aid managers in advanced decision-making... He was forced to turn for aid to his former enemy.* 3 VERB & N-C If something **aids** a process, it makes it easier or more likely to happen. An **aid** is something that makes things easier to do. *The export sector will continue to aid the economic recovery. ...slimming aids.* 4 See also **first aid.**

PHRASES ● If an activity or event is **in aid of** a particular cause, it raises money for that cause. *...a charity performance in aid of Great Ormond Street Children's Hospital.* ● If you **come** or **go to** someone's **aid**, you try to help them when they are in danger or difficulty. *Horrified neighbours rushed to his aid as he fell.*

aide /eɪd/ **aides.** N-C An **aide** is an assistant to a person with an important job. *...a presidential aide.*

AIDS /eɪdz/. N-U **AIDS** is an illness which destroys the natural system of protection that the body has against disease. **AIDS** is an abbreviation for **acquired immune deficiency syndrome**.

ailing /'eɪlɪŋ/. ① ADJ If someone is **ailing**, they are ill and not getting better. ② ADJ An **ailing** business is in difficulty and is becoming weaker.

ailment /'eɪlmənt/ **ailments**. N-C An **ailment** is an illness, especially one that is not very serious.

aim /eɪm/ **aims, aiming, aimed**. ① VERB If you **aim** for something or **aim** to do it, you plan or hope to achieve it. *He said he would aim for the 100 metres world record. ...an appeal which aims to raise funds for children with special needs.* ② N-C The **aim** of something that you do is the purpose for which you do it or the result that it is intended to achieve. *The aim of the festival is to increase awareness of Hindu culture.* ③ PASSIVE-VERB If an action or plan **is aimed** at achieving something, it is intended to achieve it. *The new measures are aimed at tightening existing sanctions.* ④ VERB If your action **is aimed** at a particular person, you intend it to affect and influence them. *Much of cigarette advertising is aimed at women.* ⑤ VERB & N-SING If you **aim** a weapon **at** someone or something, you point it towards them before firing. Your **aim** is the act of pointing a weapon at a target or your ability to hit the target. *He was aiming the rifle at Wade.* ⑥ PHRASE If you **take aim** at someone or something, you point a loaded weapon at them.

aimless /'eɪmləs/. ADJ A person or activity that is **aimless** has no clear purpose or plan. *...several hours of aimless searching.* ♦ **aimlessly** ADV *I wandered around aimlessly.*

ain't /eɪnt/. **Ain't** is used in some dialects of English instead of 'am not', 'aren't', or 'isn't'; SPOKEN.

air /eə/ **airs, airing, aired**. ① N-U **Air** is the mixture of gases which forms the earth's atmosphere and which we breathe. *Keith opened the window and leaned out into the cold air.* ② N-SING The **air** is the space around things or above the ground. *...firing their guns in the air.* ③ N-U **Air** is used to refer to travel in aircraft. *Amy had never travelled by air before. ...help towards the air fare.* ④ N-SING If someone or something has a particular **air**, they give this general impression. *...regarding him with an air of faint amusement... The meal gave the occasion an almost festive air.* ⑤ VERB If you **air** your opinions, you make them known to people. *Both sides agreed they had aired all their differences.* ♦ **airing** N-SING *Their views would at long last get an airing.* ⑥ VERB If you **air** a room, you let fresh air circulate around it. When you **air** clothes, you put them in a place where warm air can circulate around them, helping to dry them.

PHRASES ● If you do something to **clear the air**, you do it in order to get rid of any misunderstandings that there might be. *...an inquiry just to clear the air and settle the facts of the case.* ● If a person or programme is **on the air**, they are broadcasting or being broadcast on radio or television. *I was on the air for two hours... The show first went on the air in 1964.*

'air base (or **airbase**) **air bases**. N-C An **air base** is a military airport.

airborne /'eəbɔːn/. ADJ **Airborne** means flying in the air or coming from the air. *The aircraft was soon airborne again. ...airborne troops.*

,air-con'ditioned. ADJ If a room is **air-conditioned**, the air in it is kept cool and dry by means of a special machine.

,air-con'ditioning (or **air conditioning**). N-U **Air-conditioning** is a method of providing buildings and vehicles with cool dry air.

aircraft /'eəkrɑːft, -kræft/; **aircraft** is both the singular and the plural form. N-C An **aircraft** is a vehicle which can fly, for example an aeroplane or a helicopter.

airfield /'eəfiːld/ **airfields**. N-C An **airfield** is a place where aircraft take off and land, usually small planes or military aircraft.

'air force (or **airforce**) **air forces**. N-C An **air force** is the part of a country's military organization that is concerned with fighting in the air.

airlift /'eəlɪft/ **airlifts, airlifting, airlifted**. VERB & N-C If people or goods **are airlifted** somewhere, they are carried by air, especially in a war or when land routes are closed. An **airlift** is an operation to do this. *The injured were airlifted to hospital in Prestwick. ...an airlift of food, medicines and blankets.*

airline /'eəlaɪn/ **airlines**. N-C An **airline** is a company which provides regular services carrying people or goods in aeroplanes.

airliner /'eəlaɪnə/ **airliners**. N-C An **airliner** is a large aeroplane used for carrying passengers.

airman /'eəmæn/ **airmen**. N-C An **airman** is a man who serves in his country's air force.

airplane /'eəpleɪn/ **airplanes**. N-C An **airplane** is the same as an **aeroplane**; AMERICAN.

airport /'eəpɔːt/ **airports**. N-C An **airport** is a place where aircraft land and take off, usually with a lot of buildings and facilities.

'air raid, air raids. N-C An **air raid** is an attack in which military aircraft drop bombs on people or places.

airspace /'eəspeɪs/. N-U A country's **airspace** is the part of the sky that is over that country and is considered to belong to that country.

airtight /'eətaɪt/. ADJ If a container is **airtight**, its lid fits so tightly that no air can get in or out.

airwaves /'eəweɪvz/. N-PL If someone says something over the **airwaves** or on the **airwaves**, they say it on the radio or television; JOURNALISM.

airy /'eəri/. ADJ If a building or room is **airy**, it is large and has plenty of fresh air inside. *The bathroom has a light and airy feel.*

aisle /aɪl/ **aisles**. N-C An **aisle** is a long narrow gap that people can walk along between rows of seats in a church or an aeroplane, or between rows of shelves in a supermarket.

aka. **aka** is an abbreviation for 'also known as'; it is used especially when referring to a nickname or stage name. *...Anna Mae Bullock, aka Tina Turner.*

akin /ə'kɪn/. ADJ AFTER LINK-V If one thing is **akin** to another, it is similar to it in some way; FOR-

MAL. *The journey will be more akin to air travel than to a conventional train.*

alarm /əˈlɑːm/ **alarms, alarming, alarmed.** ① VERB & N-U If something **alarms** you, it makes you afraid or anxious that something unpleasant might happen. This feeling is called **alarm**. *We could not see what had alarmed him... She sat up in alarm.* ♦**alarmed** ADJ *They should not be too alarmed by the press reports.* ♦**alarming** ADJ *The statistics were even more alarming.* ♦**alarmingly** ADV *...the alarmingly high rate of heart disease.* ② N-C An **alarm** is an automatic device that warns you of something, for example by ringing a bell. *He heard the alarm go off.*

a'larm clock, alarm clocks. N-C An **alarm clock** is a clock that you can set to make a noise so that it wakes you up at a particular time.

alas /əˈlæs/. ADV **Alas** is used to express sadness or regret about something that has happened; FORMAL. *Many wonderful people who are, alas, no longer here.*

albeit /ɔːlˈbiːɪt/. ADV You use **albeit** to introduce a fact or comment which reduces the force or significance of what you have just said; FORMAL. *He has a majority, albeit a small one.*

album /ˈælbəm/ **albums.** ① N-C An **album** is a CD, record, or cassette with music op it, usually several different tracks. *This new single is taken from their latest album.* ② N-C An **album** is a book in which you put things such as photographs or stamps that you have collected.

alcohol /ˈælkəhɒl, AM -hɔːl/. ① N-U Drinks that can make people drunk, such as beer, wine, and whisky, can be referred to as **alcohol**. ② N-U **Alcohol** is a colourless liquid which is found in drinks such as beer, wine, and whisky. It is also used in products such as perfumes and cleaning fluids.

alcoholic /ˌælkəˈhɒlɪk, AM -ˈhɔːl-/ **alcoholics.** ① N-C An **alcoholic** is someone who is addicted to alcohol. ♦**alcoholism** /ˈælkəhɒlɪzəm/ N-U *His sister died two years ago as a result of alcoholism.* ② ADJ **Alcoholic** drinks contain alcohol.

ale /eɪl/ **ales.** N-VAR **Ale** is the same as beer.

alert /əˈlɜːt/ **alerts, alerting, alerted.** ① ADJ If you are **alert**, you are paying full attention to things around you and are ready to deal with anything that might happen. *We all have to stay alert... He had been spotted by an alert neighbour.* ♦**alertness** N-U *A doctor's alertness saved her son.* ② ADJ AFTER LINK-V & VERB If you are **alert** to a problem, you are fully aware of it. You can also **alert** someone to a dangerous or unpleasant situation. *The bank is alert to the danger... He wanted to alert people to the activities of the group.* ③ N-C An **alert** is a situation in which people prepare themselves for something dangerous that may happen soon. *...a security alert.* ④ PHRASE When soldiers, police, or other authorities are **on alert**, they are ready to deal with anything that may happen.

'A level, A levels. N-VAR **A levels** are British educational qualifications which schoolchildren take when they are about eighteen years old.

algae /ˈældʒiː, ˈælgaɪ/. N-U **Algae** is a type of plant with no stems or leaves that grows in water or on damp surfaces.

algebra /ˈældʒɪbrə/. N-U **Algebra** is a type of mathematics in which letters are used to represent quantities.

alias /ˈeɪliəs/ **aliases.** N-C & PREP An **alias** is a false name, especially one used by a criminal or actor. *He was travelling under an alias. ...Richard Thorp, alias Alan Turner.*

alibi /ˈælɪbaɪ/ **alibis.** N-C If you have an **alibi**, you can prove that you were somewhere else when a crime was committed.

alien /ˈeɪliən/ **aliens.** ① ADJ **Alien** is used to describe someone or something that belongs to a different country, race, group, or culture. This use is considered offensive by some people. *...alone in an alien culture.* ② N-C An **alien** is someone who is not a legal citizen of the country in which they live; TECHNICAL. ③ ADJ AFTER LINK-V If something **is alien** to you, it is not the way you would normally feel or behave. *Such an attitude is alien to most businessmen.* ④ N-C In science fiction, an **alien** is a creature from outer space.

alienate /ˈeɪliəneɪt/ **alienates, alienating, alienated.** ① VERB If you **alienate** someone such as a friend, you cause them to lose their friendly relationship with you. *The government cannot afford to alienate either group.* ② VERB If you **are alienated from** something, you are emotionally or intellectually separated from it. *Gambling was alienating me from anyone who'd ever loved me.* ♦**alienated** ADJ *Most of these students also feel alienated from their parents.* ♦**alienation** N-U *...her sense of alienation from the world.*

alight /əˈlaɪt/ **alights, alighting, alighted.** ① ADJ AFTER LINK-V If something is **alight**, it is burning. *Several buildings were set alight.* ② ADJ AFTER LINK-V If you describe someone's face or expression as **alight**, you mean it shows that they are feeling a strong emotion such as excitement or happiness. *Her eyes were alight with a girlish enjoyment of life.* ③ VERB When you **alight** from a train or bus, you get out of it after a journey; FORMAL.

align /əˈlaɪn/ **aligns, aligning, aligned.** ① VERB If you **align** yourself with a particular group, you support their political aims. ♦**alignment, alignments** N-VAR *He refused to compromise the church by a particular political alignment.* ② VERB If objects **are aligned** with each other, they are placed in a precise position in relation to each other. *Align the two sections of wood so that the grain flows from one to the other.* ♦**alignment** N-U *...the alignment of the planets.*

alike /əˈlaɪk/. ① ADJ AFTER LINK-V & ADV If two or more people or things are **alike**, they are similar. *We looked very alike. ...their assumption that all men and women think alike.* ② ADV You use **alike** after mentioning two or more people, groups, or things in order to emphasize that you are referring to both or all of them. *The techniques are being applied by big and small firms alike.*

alive /əˈlaɪv/. ① ADJ AFTER LINK-V If people or animals are **alive**, they are living. *They kept her alive on a life support machine.* ② ADJ AFTER

LINK-V If an activity, organization, or situation is **alive**, it continues to exist or to function. *The big factories are trying to stay alive by cutting costs.* ③ ADJ If you say that someone seems **alive**, you mean that they seem to be lively and to enjoy everything that they do. *I never expected to feel so alive in my life again.* ④ ADJ & PHRASE If a place is **alive** with something, a lot of people or things are there and it seems busy or exciting. You can say people, places, or events **come alive** when they start to be active or lively. *The forest had been alive with the sounds of squawking birds.*

all /ɔːl/ ① QUANT You use **all** to indicate that you are referring to the whole of a group or thing or to everyone or everything of a particular kind. *He was talking to all of us... I'd spent all I had, every last penny... We all admire professionalism and dedication.* ● See note at **whole**. ② DET & PREDET You use **all** to refer to the whole of a period of time. *George had to cut grass all afternoon... She's worked all her life.* ③ PRON You use **all** to refer to a situation or to life in general. *All is silent on the island now.* ④ ADV You use **all** to emphasize the extent to which something happens or is true. *I got scared and I ran and left her all alone. ...universities all round the world.* ⑤ ADV **All** is used in expressions such as **all the more** or **all the better** to mean even more or even better than before. *The living room is decorated in pale colours that make it all the more airy.* ⑥ ADV You use **all** when you are talking about an equal score in a game. For example, if the score is three **all**, both players or teams have three points.

PHRASES ● You say **above all** to emphasize that the thing you are mentioning is the most important point. ● You use **after all** when introducing a statement which supports or helps explain something you have just said. *They know only too well that the stakes are high. After all, health care is a $900 billion industry.* ● You use **after all** when you are saying that something that you thought might not be true is in fact true. *There wasn't much wrong after all.* ● You use **all in all** to introduce a summary or generalization. *All in all, it appeared that a pretty depressing summer awaited Jones.* ● You use **at all** to emphasize a negative or a question. *Robin never really liked him at all.* ● You use **for all** to say that a particular fact does not affect or contradict what you are saying, although it may seem to do so. *For all his shortcomings, he was kind and considerate.* ● **In all** means in total. *In all some 15 million people live in the selected areas.* ● You use **of all** to emphasize the words 'first' or 'last', or a superlative adjective or adverb. *First of all, answer these questions... Now she faces her toughest task of all.*

Allah /ˈælə, ˈælɑː/. N-PROPER **Allah** is the name of God in Islam.

,all-A'merican. ADJ BEFORE N If you describe someone as an **all-American** boy or girl, you mean that they seem to have all the typical qualities that are valued by ordinary Americans, such as patriotism and healthy good looks.

allay /əˈleɪ/ **allays, allaying, allayed.** VERB If you **allay** someone's fears or doubts, you stop them feeling afraid or doubtful; FORMAL. *He did what he could to allay his wife's fears.*

allegation /ˌælɪˈɡeɪʃən/ **allegations.** N-C An **allegation** is a statement saying that someone has done something wrong. *...allegations of brutality and theft.*

allege /əˈledʒ/ **alleges, alleging, alleged.** VERB If you **allege** that someone has done something wrong, you say it but do not prove it; FORMAL. *The accused is alleged to have killed a man... It is alleged that the restaurant discriminated against black customers. ...protests at the alleged beatings.* ◆ **allegedly** ADV *His van allegedly struck them as they were crossing a street.*

allegiance /əˈliːdʒəns/ **allegiances.** N-VAR Your **allegiance** is your support for and loyalty to a group, person, or belief. *My allegiance to Kendall and his company ran deep.*

allergic /əˈlɜːdʒɪk/. ADJ If you are **allergic** to something, or have an **allergic** reaction to it, you become ill or get a rash when you eat it, smell it, or touch it.

allergy /ˈælədʒi/ **allergies.** N-VAR If you have a particular **allergy**, you become ill or get a rash when you eat, smell, or touch something that does not normally make people ill. *Allergy to cats is one of the commonest causes of asthma. ...food allergies.*

alleviate /əˈliːvieɪt/ **alleviates, alleviating, alleviated.** VERB If you **alleviate** pain, suffering, or an unpleasant condition, you make it less intense or severe. *...the problem of alleviating mass poverty.* ◆ **alleviation** N-U *...the alleviation of the refugees' misery.*

alley /ˈæli/ **alleys.** N-C An **alley** or **alleyway** is a narrow passage or street with buildings or walls on both sides.

alliance /əˈlaɪəns/ **alliances.** N-VAR An **alliance** is a relationship in which different countries, political parties, or organizations work together for some purpose. You can also refer to the group that is formed in this way as an **alliance**. *...a movement of professionals in alliance with progressive businessmen and politicians.*

allied /ˈælaɪd, AM əˈlaɪd/. ① ADJ BEFORE N **Allied** countries, political parties, or groups are united by a formal agreement. *...forces from three allied nations.* ② ADJ If one thing or group is **allied** to another, the two things are related because they have particular qualities or characteristics in common. *...lectures on subjects allied to health, beauty and fitness. ...doctors, and allied medical professionals.* ③ See also **ally**.

alligator /ˈælɪɡeɪtə/ **alligators.** N-C An **alligator** is a large reptile with short legs, a long tail and very powerful jaws.

allocate /ˈæləkeɪt/ **allocates, allocating, allocated.** VERB If one item or share of something **is allocated** to a particular person or for a particular purpose, it is given to that person or used for that purpose. *The budget allocated $7.3 billion for development programmes... Our plan is to allocate one member of staff to handle appointments.* ◆ **allocation** N-U *...the allocation of land for new homes.*

allot /ə'lɒt/ **allots, allotting, allotted.** VERB If something **is allotted** to someone, it is given to them as their share. *The seats are allotted to the candidates who have won the most seats... We were allotted half an hour to address the committee.* ♦**allotment, allotments.** N-C *...their full allotment of $300 million.*

allotment /ə'lɒtmənt/ **allotments.** N-C In Britain, an **allotment** is a small area of land which a person rents to grow vegetables on.

,all-'out. ADJ BEFORE N & ADV You use **all-out** to talk about actions that are carried out in a very energetic and determined way, using all the resources available. *...an all-out effort to bring the fire under control... We will be going all out to ensure it doesn't happen again.*

allow /ə'laʊ/ 1 VERB If someone **is allowed** to do something, it is all right for them to do it. *The children are not allowed to watch violent TV programmes.* 2 VERB If you **are allowed** something, you are given permission to have it or are given it. *Gifts like chocolates or flowers are allowed... He should be allowed the occasional treat.* 3 VERB If you **allow** something to happen, you do not prevent it. *If the soil is allowed to dry out the tree could die.* 4 VERB If something **allows** a particular thing to happen, it makes it possible. *The money it saved allowed them to distribute aid more widely to others.* 5 VERB If you **allow** a length of time or an amount of something for a particular purpose, you include it in your planning. *Please allow 28 days for delivery.*

▸ **allow for.** PHR-VERB If you **allow for** certain problems or expenses, you include some extra time or money in your planning so that you can deal with them if they occur. *You should allow for the possibility that taxes will be 15 to 20 per cent higher.*

allowance /ə'laʊəns/ **allowances.** 1 N-C An **allowance** is money that is given regularly to someone. 2 PHRASE If you **make allowances** for certain circumstances in a situation, you take them into consideration when making your plans. *The raw exam results make no allowance for social background.* 3 PHRASE If you **make allowances** for someone who is behaving badly, you deal with them less severely than you would normally, usually because of a problem that they have. *You make allowances for your children when they are feeling ill.*

,all 'right (or alright). 1 ADJ AFTER LINK-V If you say that someone or something is **all right**, you mean that you find them satisfactory but not especially good. *Most of the teachers are all right... The red wine sauce was all right.* 2 ADJ AFTER LINK-V If someone is **all right**, they are well or safe. *I'm all right now... Are you feeling all right?* 3 CONVENTION You say **'all right'** when you are agreeing to something. *'I think you should go now.'—'All right.'*

'all-time. ADJ **All-time** is used when you are comparing all the things of a particular type that there have ever been. *...her all-time favourite film.*

allude /ə'luːd/ **alludes, alluding, alluded.** VERB If you **allude** to something, you mention

it in an indirect way; FORMAL. *She alluded to his absence in vague terms.*

allure /ə'ljʊə, AM ə'lʊr/. N-U The **allure** of something is a pleasing or exciting quality that it has. *Novels without stories have lost their allure for the young author.*

allusion /ə'luːʒən/ **allusions.** N-VAR An **allusion** to something is an indirect or vague reference to it. *She made an allusion to the events in Los Angeles... His poetry is dense with many literary allusions.*

ally, allies, allying, allied. 1 N-C/'æli/ An **ally** is a country, organization, or person that helps and supports another. *...the Western allies.* 2 VERB /ə'laɪ/ If you **ally** yourself with someone, you support them. *Ten years later he allied himself with the British.* ● See also **allied.**

almighty /ɔːl'maɪti/. 1 N-PROPER The **Almighty** is another name for God. *...a hymn to the Almighty.* 2 ADJ BEFORE N An **almighty** row, problem, or mistake is a very serious one. *Apparently they kicked up an almighty fuss.*

almond /'ɑːmənd/ **almonds.** N-C An **almond** is a kind of pale oval nut.

almost /'ɔːlməʊst/. ADV **Almost** means very nearly, but not completely. *The camps are now almost full... I stood up and almost fell.*

aloft /ə'lɒft, AM ə'lɔːft/. ADV Something that is **aloft** is in the air or off the ground. LITERARY. *After the result was announced, Mr Peres was raised aloft by his supporters.*

alone /ə'ləʊn/. 1 ADJ AFTER LINK-V When you are **alone**, you are not with any other people. *She wanted to be alone.* 2 ADJ AFTER LINK-V A person who is **alone** is also someone who has no family or friends. *Never in her life had she felt so alone, so abandoned.* 3 ADJ AFTER LINK-V If one person is **alone** with another, they are together, with nobody else present. *I couldn't imagine why he would want to be alone with me... We'll be alone together, quite like old times.* 4 ADV If you do something **alone**, you do it without help from other people. *He was working alone and did not have an accomplice.* 5 ADV You say that one person or thing **alone** does something when you are emphasizing that only one person or thing is involved. *The cost of the damage in Florida alone would amount to billions of dollars.* 6 to **leave** someone **alone**: see **leave.**

along /ə'lɒŋ, AM ə'lɔːŋ/. 1 PREP If you move or look **along** something, you move or look towards one end of it. *Newman walked along the street... The young man led Mark along a corridor... I looked along the length of the building.* 2 PREP & ADV If something is situated **along** a road, river, or corridor, it is situated in it or beside it. *Half the houses along the road were for sale... Two thirds of the way along, turn right and take the path across the park.* 3 ADV If something is going **along** in a particular way, it is progressing in that way. *Everything was coming along fine after all.* 4 ADV If you take someone **along** when you go somewhere, you take them with you. If someone comes **along**, they come to a particular place. *Some of the men would take their wives along... Bring along your friends and colleagues.*

PHRASES ● You use **all along** to say that something has existed or been the case throughout a period of time. *She had been planning all along to leave Hungary.* • If you do something **along with** someone else, you both do it. • If you take one thing **along with** another, you take both things. *The baby's mother escaped along with two other children.*

alongside /ə,lɒŋ'saɪd, AM -,lɔ:ŋ-/. ① PREP & ADV If something is **alongside** something else, it is next to it. *He crossed the street and walked alongside Central Park... I rode the bicycle and he ran alongside.* ② PREP If people or systems work or exist **alongside** each other, they work or exist in the same place or in the same situation. *Volunteers work alongside local staff.*

aloof /ə'lu:f/. ① ADJ If you say that someone is **aloof**, you think they are not very friendly and that they try to keep away from other people. ② ADJ AFTER LINK-V If you stay **aloof** from something, you do not become involved with it. *The Government is keeping aloof from the controversy.*

aloud /ə'laʊd/. ADV When you speak or read **aloud**, you speak so that other people can hear you. *When we were children, our father read aloud to us, usually after supper.*

alphabet /'ælfəbet/ **alphabets**. N-C The **alphabet** is the set of letters in a fixed order which is used for writing the words of a language.

alphabetical /,ælfə'betɪkəl/. ADJ BEFORE N **Alphabetical** means arranged according to the normal order of the letters in the alphabet. *...arranged in strict alphabetical order.*

alpine /'ælpaɪn/. ADJ **Alpine** means existing in or relating to mountains. *...alpine plants.*

already /ɔːl'redi/. ① ADV If something has **already** happened, it has happened before the present time. Speakers of British English usually use **already** with a verb in a perfect tense, putting it after 'have', 'has', or 'had', or at the end of a clause. Some speakers of American English use **already** with the simple past tense of the verb instead of a perfect tense. *I have already started making baby clothes... They've spent nearly a billion dollars on it already... She says she already told the neighbors not to come over for a couple of days.* • See note at **yet**. ② ADV You use **already** to say that a situation exists at this present moment or that it exists at an earlier time than expected. You use **already** after the verb 'be' or an auxiliary verb, or before a verb if there is no auxiliary. *He was already late for his appointment with the Prime Minister... Is it five o'clock already?... Various insurance schemes already exist for this purpose.*

alright /ɔːl'raɪt/. See **all right**.

also /'ɔːlsəʊ/. ① ADV You use **also** when you are giving more information about a person or thing. *Furniture designer Linley, who also owns a nearby restaurant, employs up to 20 craftsmen... We've got a big table and also some stools and benches.* ② ADV You can use **also** to say that the same fact applies to someone or something else. *The UN says six other civilians were also injured.*

altar /'ɔːltə/ **altars**. N-C An **altar** is a holy table in a church or temple.

alter /'ɔːltə/ **alters, altering, altered.** VERB If something **alters**, or if you **alter** it, it changes. *Little had altered in the village... The government has altered the rules.* ◆**alteration, alterations** N-VAR *There were a few minor alterations to the cast.*

alternate, alternates, alternating, alternated. ① VERB /'ɔːltəneɪt/ When you **alternate** between two things, you regularly do or use one thing and then the other. *I alternated between feeling freezing cold and boiling hot.* ② VERB When one thing **alternates** with another, the two things occur regularly, one after the other. *Her aggressive moods alternated with gentle or more co-operative states.* ③ ADJ BEFORE N /ɔːl'tɜːnət/ **Alternate** actions, events, or processes regularly occur after each other. *They were streaked with alternate bands of colour.* ◆**alternately** ADV *He lived alternately in Florence and Naples.* ④ ADJ BEFORE N If something happens on **alternate** days, it happens on one day, then happens on every second day after that. In the same way, something can happen in **alternate** weeks or years. *Some government offices open on alternate Saturdays.* ⑤ ADJ BEFORE N In American English, **alternate** is used to describe something that can exist or you can do instead of something else. The British word is **alternative**. *He also sent Congress an alternate version of the bill.* ◆**alternately** ADV *Alternately, the coconut can be toasted under the broiler.*

alternative /ɔːl'tɜːnətɪv/ **alternatives**. ① N-C & ADJ BEFORE N In British English, an **alternative** is something that can exist or you can do instead of something else. The American adjective is **alternate**. *How about natural gas? Is that an alternative?... There were alternative methods of travel available.* ② ADJ BEFORE N **Alternative** is used to describe things which are different from traditional or established things of their kind. *...alternative medicine.*

alternatively /ɔːl'tɜːnətɪvli/. ADV You use **alternatively** to introduce a suggestion or to mention something different from what has just been stated. *Allow about eight hours for the drive from Calais. Alternatively, you can fly to Brive.*

although /ɔːl'ðəʊ/. ① CONJ You use **although** to introduce a statement which contrasts with something else that you are saying. *Although I was only six, I can remember seeing it on TV... Their system worked after a fashion, although no one was sure how.* ② CONJ **Although** is used to introduce clauses that modify what is being said or that add further information. *Something about the man was familiar, although Hillsden could not immediately place him.*

altitude /'æltɪtjuːd, AM -tuːd/ **altitudes**. N-VAR If something is at a particular **altitude**, it is at that height above sea level. *As we lost altitude, the wind became stronger.*

alto /'æltəʊ/ **altos**. N-C An **alto** is a woman with a low singing voice, or a man with a high singing voice.

altogether /,ɔːltə'geðə/. ① ADV You use **altogether** to emphasize that something has stopped, been done, or finished completely. *His tour may have to be cancelled altogether.*

2 ADV You use **altogether** in front of an adjective or adverb to emphasize that adjective or adverb. *This wine has an altogether stronger, more pronounced flavour... The choice of language is altogether different.* **3** ADV You use **altogether** to indicate that the amount you are mentioning is a total. *There were 11 of us altogether.*

altruism /'æltruːɪzəm/. N-U **Altruism** is unselfish concern for other people's happiness and welfare. ♦**altruistic** ADJ *The company was not being entirely altruistic.*

aluminium /ˌæluː'mɪniəm/ (AM **aluminum** /ə'luːmɪnəm/). N-U **Aluminium** is a lightweight metal used for making things such as cooking equipment and aircraft parts.

always /'ɔːlweɪz/. **1** ADV If you **always** do something, you do it regularly, whenever a particular situation arises. *Always lock your garage... David always collects Alistair from school.* **2** ADV If you **always** do a particular thing, you do it all the time, continuously. *He has always been the family solicitor... He was always cheerful.* **3** ADV You use **always** in expressions such as **can always** or **could always** when you are making suggestions or giving advice. *I guess I can always ring Jean.*

am /əm, STRONG æm/. **Am** is the first person singular of the present tense of **be**.

a.m. /ˌeɪ 'em/. **a.m.** after a number indicates that the number refers to a particular time between midnight and noon. *Visitor Centre and shop open 9 a.m. – 5 p.m.*

amalgamate /ə'mælgəmeɪt/ **amalgamates, amalgamating, amalgamated.** VERB When two or more organizations **amalgamate**, or when they are **amalgamated**, they become one large organization. *The firm has amalgamated with an American company.* ♦**amalgamation** N-U *...an amalgamation of the two parties.*

amass /ə'mæs/ **amasses, amassing, amassed.** VERB If you **amass** something such as money, you gradually get a lot of it. *She has amassed a personal fortune of £8 million.*

amateur /'æmətə, AM -tʃɜːr/ **amateurs.** N-C An **amateur** is someone who does a particular activity as a hobby, not as a job. *He was encouraged to continue racing for another year as an amateur. ...amateur dramatic productions.*

amaze /ə'meɪz/ **amazes, amazing, amazed.** VERB If something **amazes** you, it surprises you very much. *He amazed us by his knowledge of Welsh history.* ♦**amazed** ADJ *I was amazed to learn she was still writing her stories.*

amazement /ə'meɪzmənt/. N-U **Amazement** is what you feel if you are very surprised by something. *Both men stared at her in amazement... To my amazement, Peterson disagreed.*

amazing /ə'meɪzɪŋ/. ADJ If something is **amazing**, it is very surprising and makes you feel pleasure or admiration. *It's the most amazing thing to watch... It's amazing how people collect so much stuff.* ♦**amazingly** ADV *She was an amazingly good cook.*

ambassador /æm'bæsədə/ **ambassadors.** N-C An **ambassador** is an important official living in a foreign country who represents the government of his or her own country.

amber /'æmbə/. ADJ Something that is **amber** in colour is orange or yellowish-brown.

ambience (or **ambiance**) /'æmbiəns/. N-SING The **ambience** of a place is its character and atmosphere; LITERARY. *The overall ambience of the room is cosy.*

ambiguity /ˌæmbɪ'gjuːɪti/ **ambiguities.** N-VAR You say that there is **ambiguity** when something can be understood in more than one way.

ambiguous /æm'bɪgjuəs/. ADJ Something that is **ambiguous** can be understood in more than one way. *There had been a few ambiguous remarks.* ♦**ambiguously** ADV *...an ambiguously worded document.*

ambition /æm'bɪʃən/ **ambitions.** **1** N-C If you have an **ambition** to achieve something, you want very much to achieve it. *His ambition is to sail round the world.* **2** N-U **Ambition** is the desire to be successful, rich, or powerful. *He is full of ambition and resolve.*

ambitious /æm'bɪʃəs/. **1** ADJ Someone who is **ambitious** wants to be successful, rich, or powerful. **2** ADJ An **ambitious** idea or plan is on a large scale and needs a lot of work in order to be successful.

ambivalent /æm'bɪvələnt/. ADJ If you are **ambivalent** about something, you are not sure exactly what you think about it. *She remained ambivalent about her marriage.*

amble /'æmbəl/ **ambles, ambling, ambled.** VERB When you **amble** somewhere, you walk there slowly and in a relaxed manner. *Slowly they ambled back to the car.*

ambulance /'æmbjʊləns/ **ambulances.** N-C An **ambulance** is a vehicle for taking people to and from hospital.

ambush /'æmbʊʃ/ **ambushes, ambushing, ambushed.** VERB & N-C If people **ambush** their enemies, they attack them after hiding and waiting for them. The attack is called an **ambush**. *The Guatemalan army says rebels ambushed and killed 10 patrolmen.*

amen /ˌɑː'men, ˌeɪ-/. CONVENTION **Amen** is said or sung by Christians at the end of a prayer.

amend /ə'mend/ **amends, amending, amended.** **1** VERB If you **amend** something that has been written or said, you change it. *They voted unanimously to amend the constitution.* **2** PHRASE If you **make amends** when you have harmed someone, you show you are sorry by doing something to please them. *He wanted to make amends for causing their marriage to fail.*

amendment /ə'mendmənt/ **amendments.** N-C An **amendment** is a section that is added to a law or rule in order to change it.

amenity /ə'miːnɪti, AM -'men-/ **amenities.** N-C **Amenities** are things such as shopping centres or sports facilities that are for people's convenience or enjoyment. *The hotel amenities include health clubs, and conference facilities.*

American /ə'merɪkən/ **Americans.** ADJ & N-C **American** means belonging or relating to the United States of America. An **American** is someone who comes from the United States of America. *...the American economy.*

A,merican 'football. See **football**.

amiable /'eɪmiəbəl/. ADJ Someone who is **amiable** is friendly and pleasant. *...an educated, amiable and decent man.* ♦**amiably** ADV We chatted amiably about old friends.

amicable /'æmɪkəbəl/. ADJ When people have an **amicable** relationship, they are pleasant to each other and solve their problems without quarrelling. *Our discussions were amicable and productive. ...an amicable agreement.* ♦**amicably** ADV Mr Black divorced amicably from his wife.

amid /ə'mɪd/. 1 PREP If something happens **amid** other things, it happens while the other things are happening; LITERARY. *Amid the tumult, she jumped into her car.* 2 PREP If something is **amid** other things, it is surrounded by them; LITERARY. *...a tiny bungalow amid clusters of trees.*

amidst /ə'mɪdst/. **Amidst** means the same as **amid**.

amiss /ə'mɪs/. ADJ AFTER LINK-V If you say that something is **amiss**, you mean there is something wrong.

ammonia /ə'məʊniə/. N-U **Ammonia** is a colourless liquid or gas with a strong sharp smell.

ammunition /ˌæmjʊ'nɪʃən/. 1 N-U **Ammunition** consists of bullets and rockets that are made to be fired from guns. 2 N-U If you use information as **ammunition**, you use it against someone. *It helps to have details as ammunition.*

amnesty /'æmnɪsti/ **amnesties.** 1 N-C If a prisoner is granted an **amnesty**, they are officially pardoned. *...a general amnesty for political prisoners.* 2 N-C An **amnesty** is a period of time during which people can confess to a crime or give up weapons without being punished.

among /ə'mʌŋ/. 1 PREP A person or thing that is **among** a group of people or things is surrounded by them or is with them. *They walked among the crowds. ...houses set among well-tended gardens... I was brought up among people who read and wrote a lot.* 2 PREP If someone or something is **among** a group, they are a member of that group. *A British man was among the people killed... Among his purchases were several books.* 3 PREP If an opinion or situation exists **among** a group of people, they have it or experience it. If something happens **among** a group of people, they do it. *...concern among book and magazine retailers. ...when we discuss it among ourselves.* 4 PREP If something is divided **among** three or more people, they all get a part of it.

amongst /ə'mʌŋst/. PREP **Amongst** means the same as **among**.

amount /ə'maʊnt/ **amounts, amounting, amounted.** 1 N-C An **amount** of something is how much of it you have, need, or get. *He needs that amount of money to survive... I still do a certain amount of work.* 2 VERB If something **amounts** to a particular total, all the parts of it add up to that total. *The total rain and snowfall amounted to 50mm.* 3 PHRASE If you say that there are **any amount of** things or

people, you mean that there are a lot of them. *There are any amount of clubs you could join.*

▶ **amount to.** PHR-VERB If you say that one thing **amounts** to something else, you mean the first thing is the same as the second. *The banks have what amounts to a monopoly.*

amp /æmp/ **amps.** N-C An **amp** is a unit which is used for measuring electric current. *...a 3 amp fuse.*

ample /'æmpəl/. ADJ If there is an **ample** amount of something, there is enough of it and some extra. *There'll be ample opportunity to relax. ...ample space for a good-sized kitchen.* ♦**amply** ADV Its 160 pages are amply illustrated.

amplifier /'æmplɪfaɪə/ **amplifiers.** N-C An **amplifier** is an electronic device in a radio or stereo system, which causes sounds or signals to become louder.

amplify /'æmplɪfaɪ/ **amplifies, amplifying, amplified.** 1 VERB To **amplify** a sound means to make it louder. *This landscape seemed to trap and amplify sounds.* ♦**amplification** /ˌæmplɪfɪ'keɪʃən/ N-U *...an electronic amplification system.* 2 VERB To **amplify** an idea, feeling, or statement means to increase its strength or intensity. *Her anxiety about the world was amplifying her personal fears.*

amputate /'æmpjʊteɪt/ **amputates, amputating, amputated.** VERB If a surgeon **amputates** someone's arm or leg, he or she cuts it off in an operation. *He had to have one leg amputated.* ♦**amputation, amputations** N-VAR *...the amputation of limbs.*

amuse /ə'mjuːz/ **amuses, amusing, amused.** 1 VERB If something **amuses** you, it makes you want to laugh or smile. *The thought seemed to amuse him.* 2 VERB If you **amuse** yourself, you do something in order to pass the time and not become bored. *I always invented stories to amuse myself... Archie kept us amused.*

amused /ə'mjuːzd/. ADJ If you are **amused** by something, it makes you want to laugh or smile. *He was amused to learn that he and O'Brien had similar ideas.*

amusement /ə'mjuːzmənt/ **amusements.** 1 N-U **Amusement** is the feeling that you have when you think that something is funny. *He stopped and watched with amusement.* 2 N-U **Amusement** is the pleasure that you get from being entertained or from doing something interesting. *He wrote for the amusement of his friends.* 3 N-C **Amusements** are ways of passing the time pleasantly. *People had very few amusements to choose from.*

amusing /ə'mjuːzɪŋ/. ADJ An **amusing** person or thing makes you laugh or smile. *...a capable and amusing companion.* ♦**amusingly** ADV It must be amusingly written.

an /ən, STRONG æn/. DET **An** is used instead of 'a' in front of words that begin with vowel sounds.

anaemia (or **anemia**) /ə'niːmiə/. N-U **Anaemia** is a medical condition in which there are too few red cells in your blood, so that you feel tired and look pale. ♦**anaemic** ADJ Losing a lot of blood makes you tired and anaemic.

anaesthetic (or **anesthetic**) /ˌænɪs'θetɪk/ **anaesthetics.** N-VAR **Anaesthetic** is a substance used to stop you feeling pain during an operation. ...*while they are under the anaesthetic.*

anaesthetist (or **anesthetist**) /əˈniːsθətɪst/ **anaesthetists.** N-C An **anaesthetist** is a doctor or nurse who gives anaesthetics to patients.

anal /ˈeɪnəl/. ADJ **Anal** means relating to the anus.

analogy /əˈnælədʒi/ **analogies.** N-C If you draw an **analogy** between two things, you show that they are similar. ...*the analogy of looking for a needle in a haystack.* ◆**analogous** /əˈnæləgəs/ ADJ *Swimming has no event that is analogous to the 100 metres in athletics.*

analyse. See **analyze.**

analysis /əˈnælɪsɪs/ **analyses** /əˈnælɪsiːz/. ① N-VAR **Analysis** is the process of considering something or examining it in order to understand it or to find out what it consists of. ...*a careful analysis of the situation... They collect blood samples for analysis.* ② PHRASE You say **in the final analysis** or **in the last analysis** to indicate that the statement you are making is about the basic facts of a situation. *Violence in the last analysis produces more violence.*

analyst /ˈænəlɪst/ **analysts.** ① N-C An **analyst** is a person whose job is to analyse a subject and give opinions about it. ...*a political analyst.* ② N-C An **analyst** is someone who is trained to examine and treat people who have emotional problems. *My analyst has helped me not to feel guilty.*

analytic /ˌænəˈlɪtɪk/. ADJ **Analytic** means the same as **analytical**.

analytical /ˌænəˈlɪtɪkəl/. ADJ **Analytical** skills or methods involve the use of logical reasoning. ...*your analytical and leadership skills.*

analyze (BR also **analyse**) /ˈænəlaɪz/ **analyzes, analyzing, analyzed.** VERB If you **analyze** something, you consider it or examine it in order to understand it or to find out what it consists of. *Analyse what is causing the stress in your life... They had their tablets analysed.*

anarchist /ˈænəkɪst/ **anarchists.** N-C An **anarchist** is someone who believes the laws and power of governments should be replaced by people working together freely. ◆**anarchism** N-U *...fervent political anarchism.*

anarchy /ˈænəki/. N-U **Anarchy** is a situation where nobody obeys rules or laws. ...*an attempt to stop the country slipping into anarchy.* ◆**anarchic** /æˈnɑːkɪk/ ADJ ...*the near anarchic level of violence.*

anatomy /əˈnætəmi/ **anatomies.** N-VAR **Anatomy** is the study of the bodies of people or animals. The **anatomy** of a person or animal is the structure of their body. ...*a professor of anatomy.* ...*the female anatomy.* ◆**anatomical** /ˌænəˈtɒmɪkəl/ ADJ ...*the minute anatomical differences between insects.*

ancestor /ˈænsestə/ **ancestors.** N-C Your **ancestors** are the people from whom you are descended. ...*our daily lives, so different from those of our ancestors.* ◆**ancestral** /ænˈsestrəl/ ADJ ...*the family's ancestral home.*

ancestry /ˈænsestri/ **ancestries.** N-C Your **ancestry** consists of the people from whom you are descended. ...*a family who could trace their ancestry back to the sixteenth century.*

anchor /ˈæŋkə/ **anchors, anchoring, anchored.** ① N-C An **anchor** is a heavy hooked object at the end of a chain that is dropped from a boat into the water to make the boat stay in one place. ② VERB When a boat **anchors**, or when you **anchor** it, its anchor is dropped into the water to make it stay in one place. *We could anchor off the pier.* ③ VERB If you **anchor** an object, you fix it to something so that it will not move. *The roots anchor the plant in the earth.*

ancient /ˈeɪnʃənt/. ADJ **Ancient** means very old, or having existed for a long time. ...*ancient Greece and Rome. ...ancient Jewish traditions.*

and /ənd, STRONG ænd/. ① CONJ You use **and** to link two or more words, groups, or clauses. *She and Simon had already gone... I'm 53 and I'm very happy.* ② CONJ You use **and** to link two identical words or phrases to emphasize their degree or to suggest that something continues or increases over a period of time. *We talked for hours and hours... Learning becomes more and more difficult.* ③ CONJ **And** links two statements about events which follow each other. *I waved goodbye and went down the stone harbour steps... I looked up and found her staring at me.* ④ CONJ You use **and** to link two statements when the second statement continues the point that has been made in the first statement. *You could only really tell the effects of the disease in the long term, and five years wasn't long enough... 'He used to be so handsome.'—'And now?'.* ⑤ CONJ **And** indicates that two numbers are to be added together. *What does two and two make?*

anecdote /ˈænɪkdəʊt/ **anecdotes.** N-C An **anecdote** is a short entertaining account of something that has happened. *Pete was telling them an anecdote about their mother.* ◆**anecdotal** /ˌænɪkˈdəʊtəl/ ADJ ...*anecdotal accounts of journeys and encounters.*

anemia /əˈniːmiə/. See **anaemia.**

anemic /əˈniːmɪk/. See **anaemia.**

anesthetic /ˌænɪsˈθetɪk/. See **anaesthetic.**

anesthetist /əˈniːsθətɪst/. See **anaesthetist.**

anew /əˈnjuː, AM əˈnuː/. ADV If you do something **anew**, you do it again, often in a different way; LITERARY. *She's ready to start anew.*

angel /ˈeɪndʒəl/ **angels.** ① N-C **Angels** are spiritual beings that some people believe are God's messengers and servants in heaven. ② N-C If you refer to someone as an **angel**, you mean that they are good, kind, and gentle. *Thank you a thousand times. You're an angel.*

angelic /ænˈdʒelɪk/. ADJ You can describe someone as **angelic** when they are very good, kind, and gentle. ...*an angelic face.*

anger /ˈæŋgə/ **angers, angering, angered.** ① N-U **Anger** is the strong emotion that you feel when you think someone has behaved in an unfair, cruel, or unacceptable way. *He cried with anger and frustration.* ② VERB If someone or something **angers** you, they make you angry. *His coldness angered her.*

angle /ˈæŋgəl/ **angles, angling, angled.** ① N-C If something is **at an angle**, it is leaning in a particular direction so that it is not straight, horizontal, or vertical. *The boat is now leaning at a 30 degree angle. ...brackets to ad-*

just the steering wheel's angle. **2** N-C An **angle** is the direction from which you look at something. *Thanks to the angle at which he stood, he could just see the sunset.* **3** N-C You can refer to a way of presenting something or thinking about it as a particular **angle**. *He was considering the idea from all angles.* **4** VERB If you are **angling for** something, you are trying to make someone offer it to you without asking for it directly. *It sounds very much as if he's just angling for sympathy.* **5** See also **right angle**.

angler /ˈæŋglə/ **anglers.** N-C An **angler** is someone who fishes with a fishing rod as a hobby.

angling /ˈæŋglɪŋ/. N-U **Angling** is the activity of fishing with a fishing rod.

Anglo-. **Anglo-** is added to adjectives indicating nationality to form adjectives describing something which involves relations between Britain and another country. *...his contribution to Anglo-American relations.*

angry /ˈæŋgri/ **angrier, angriest.** ADJ When you are **angry**, you feel strong emotion about something that you consider unfair, cruel, or insulting. *She was angry at her husband. ...an angry mob.* ♦**angrily** ADV *France and Italy reacted angrily to the decision.*

Angry is normally used to talk about someone's mood or feelings on a particular occasion. If someone is often angry, you can describe them as **bad-tempered.** *She's a bad-tempered young lady.* If someone is very angry, you can describe them as **furious.** *Senior police officers are furious at the blunder.* If they are less angry, you can describe them as **annoyed** or **irritated.** *The Premier looked annoyed but calm. ... a man irritated by the barking of his neighbour's dog.* Typically, someone is **irritated** by something because it happens constantly or continually.

---

angst /æŋst/. N-U **Angst** is a feeling of anxiety and worry. *Many kids suffer from acne and angst.*

anguish /ˈæŋgwɪʃ/. N-U **Anguish** is great mental or physical suffering. *For a few brief minutes we forgot the anxiety and anguish.*

anguished /ˈæŋgwɪʃt/. ADJ **Anguished** means feeling or showing great mental or physical suffering; WRITTEN. *She let out an anguished cry.*

angular /ˈæŋgjʊlə/. ADJ **Angular** things have shapes that contain a lot of straight lines and sharp points. *She has a very angular face.*

animal /ˈænɪməl/ **animals.** **1** N-C Any living creature other than a human being can be referred to as an **animal**. *He was attacked by wild animals.* **2** N-C An **animal** is any living thing that is not a plant, including people. *...members of the animal kingdom.* **3** ADJ **Animal** qualities or feelings relate to your physical nature and instincts rather than your mind. *...an animal panic to run and hide.* **4** N-C If you say that someone is an **animal**, you find their behaviour disgusting or very unpleasant. *This man is an animal, a beast.*

animate /ˈænɪmət/. ADJ Something that is **animate** has life, in contrast to things like stones and machines which do not. *...all aspects of the material world, animate and inanimate.*

animated /ˈænɪmeɪtɪd/. **1** ADJ Someone or something that is **animated** is lively and interesting. *She was seen in animated conversation with the singer.* **2** ADJ BEFORE N An **animated** film is one in which puppets or drawings appear to move. *...Disney's animated film 'Lady and the Tramp.'*

animation /ˌænɪˈmeɪʃən/. **1** N-U **Animation** is the quality of being lively and interesting. *They both spoke with great animation.* **2** N-U **Animation** is the use of puppets or drawings that appear to move in films. *...traditional cartoon animation.*

animosity /ˌænɪˈmɒsɪti/ **animosities.** N-VAR **Animosity** is a feeling of strong dislike and anger. *The animosity between the two men grew.*

ankle /ˈæŋkəl/ **ankles.** N-C Your **ankle** is the joint where your foot joins your leg.

annex (or **annexe**) **annexes, annexing, annexed.** **1** N-C/ˈæneks/ An **annex** is a building which is joined to or is next to a larger main building. **2** VERB /æˈneks/ If a country **annexes** another country or an area of land, it seizes it and takes control of it. *...the plan to invade and annex Kuwait.* ♦**annexation** N-U *...Indonesia's annexation of East Timor.*

annihilate /əˈnaɪəleɪt/ **annihilates, annihilating, annihilated.** VERB If something **is annihilated**, it is destroyed completely. *The lava annihilates everything in its path.* ♦**annihilation** N-U *Leaders fear the annihilation of their people.*

anniversary /ˌænɪˈvɜːsəri/ **anniversaries.** N-C An **anniversary** is a date which is remembered or celebrated because a special event happened on that date in a previous year. *...their third wedding anniversary.*

announce /əˈnaʊns/ **announces, announcing, announced.** **1** VERB If you **announce** something, you tell people about it publicly or officially. *She was planning to announce her engagement... He will announce tonight that he is resigning.* **2** VERB If you **announce** something, you say it in a deliberate and rather aggressive way. *He announced that he was leaving... 'I'm having a bath and going to bed,' she announced.*

announcement /əˈnaʊnsmənt/ **announcements.** **1** N-C An **announcement** is a public statement which gives information about something that has happened or that will happen. *...an announcement of a cut in the bank loan rate.* **2** N-SING The **announcement** of something is the act of telling people about it. *...the announcement of Jeanne's engagement.*

announcer /əˈnaʊnsə/ **announcers.** N-C An **announcer** is someone who introduces programmes on radio or television.

annoy /əˈnɔɪ/ **annoys, annoying, annoyed.** VERB If someone **annoys** you, they make you fairly angry and impatient. *Try making a note of the things which annoy you... It annoyed me that I didn't have time to do more ironing.*

annoyance /əˈnɔɪəns/. N-U **Annoyance** is the feeling that you get when someone annoys you. *To her annoyance the stranger did not go away.*

annoyed /ə'nɔɪd/. ADJ If you are **annoyed**, you are fairly angry about something. *Eleanor was annoyed at having had to wait so long.* ● See note at **angry**.

annoying /ə'nɔɪɪŋ/. ADJ An **annoying** person or action makes you feel fairly angry and impatient. *It's very annoying when this happens.*

annual /'ænjʊəl/. [1] ADJ BEFORE N **Annual** means happening or done once every year. *...our annual holiday.* ◆**annually** ADV *Interest will be paid annually.* [2] ADJ BEFORE N **Annual** quantities or rates relate to a period of one year. *...annual sales of about $80 million.* ◆**annually** ADV *El Salvador produces nearly 100,000 tons of refined copper annually.*

annum /'ænəm/. See **per annum**.

anomaly /ə'nɒməli/ **anomalies.** N-C If something is an **anomaly**, it is different from what is normal or usual; FORMAL.

anonymous /ə'nɒnɪməs/. [1] ADJ If you remain **anonymous** when you do something, you do not let people know that you were the person who did it. Something that is **anonymous** does not reveal who you are. *You can remain anonymous if you wish. ...anonymous phone calls.* ◆**anonymously** ADV *Reports can be made anonymously.* ◆**anonymity** /,ænə'nɪmɪti/ N-U *The official requested anonymity.* [2] ADJ Something that is **anonymous** has no interesting features. *...an anonymous holiday villa.*

anorak /'ænəræk/ **anoraks.** N-C An **anorak** is a warm waterproof jacket, usually with a hood.

anorexia /,ænə'reksiə/. N-U **Anorexia** or **anorexia nervosa** is an illness in which a person refuses to eat enough because they have an overwhelming fear of becoming fat.

another /ə'nʌðə/. [1] DET & PRON **Another** thing or person means one more in addition to those that already exist or are known about. *We're going to have another baby... Drink up, there's time for another.* [2] DET & PRON **Another** can be used to mean a different thing or person from the one just mentioned. *Her doctor referred her to another therapist... He said one thing and has done quite another.* [3] PHRASE You use **one another** to indicate that each member of a group does something to or for the other members. *...women learning to help themselves and one another.* [4] PHRASE If you talk about **one** thing **after** another, you are referring to a series of repeated or continuous events. *They kept going, destroying one store after another.*

answer /'ɑːnsə, 'æn-/ **answers, answering, answered.** [1] VERB When you **answer** someone who has asked you something, you say something back to them. *Just answer the question... 'When?' asked Alba, calmly. 'Tonight', answered Hunter.* [2] VERB If you **answer** a letter or advertisement, you write to the person who wrote it. *She answered an advert for a job.* [3] N-C An **answer** is something that you say or write when you answer someone. *I wrote to him but I never had an answer back.* [4] VERB & N-C When you **answer** the telephone, you pick it up when it rings. When you **answer** the door, you open it when you hear a knock or the bell.

If no-one picks up the phone or opens the door, you can say there is no **answer**. *She answered her phone on the first ring.* [5] N-C An **answer** to a problem is a possible solution to it. *Legislation is only part of the answer.* [6] VERB & N-C When you **answer** a question in a test, or give an **answer** to it, you write or say something in an attempt to give the facts that are asked for. *She answered 81 questions... Simply marking an answer wrong will not help the pupil.*

▶ **answer back.** PHR-VERB If someone, especially a child, **answers** you **back**, or if they **answer back**, they speak rudely to you when you speak to them. *She was beaten by teachers for answering back.*

▶ **answer for.** PHR-VERB If you have to **answer for** something bad or wrong you have done, you are punished for it. *He must be made to answer for his terrible crimes.*

'answering machine, answering machines. N-C An **answering machine** is a device which records telephone messages while you are out.

ant /ænt/ **ants.** N-C **Ants** are small crawling insects that live in large groups.

antagonism /æn'tægənɪzəm/. N-U **Antagonism** is hatred or hostility. *...a history of antagonism between the two sides.*

antagonist /æn'tægənɪst/ **antagonists.** N-C Your **antagonist** is your opponent or enemy.

antagonize (BR also **antagonise**) /æn'tægənaɪz/ **antagonizes, antagonizing, antagonized.** VERB If you **antagonize** someone, you make them feel hostile towards you. *Jordan does not wish to antagonise Saudi Arabia.*

antenna /æn'tenə/ **antennae** /æn'teniː/ or **antennas.** For meaning 2 the plural is usually **antennas.** [1] N-C The **antennae** of an insect are the two long thin parts attached to its head that it uses to feel things with. [2] N-C An **antenna** is a device that sends and receives television or radio signals.

anthem /'ænθəm/ **anthems.** N-C An **anthem** is a song or hymn written for a special occasion. *...the Olympic anthem.* ● See also **national anthem**.

anthology /æn'θɒlədʒi/ **anthologies.** N-C An **anthology** is a collection of writings by different writers published together in one book.

anthropology /,ænθrə'pɒlədʒi/. N-U **Anthropology** is the study of people, society, and culture. ◆**anthropologist, anthropologists** N-C *...an anthropologist who had been in China.*

antibiotic /,æntibaɪ'ɒtɪk/ **antibiotics.** N-C **Antibiotics** are drugs that are used in medicine to kill bacteria and to cure infections.

anticipate /æn'tɪsɪpeɪt/ **anticipates, anticipating, anticipated.** [1] VERB If you **anticipate** an event, you realize in advance that it may happen and you are prepared for it. *We couldn't have anticipated the result of our campaigning.* ◆**anticipation** N-U *They hoard food in anticipation of future shortages.* [2] VERB If you **anticipate** a question, request, or need, you do what is necessary or required before the question, request, or need occurs. *Do you expect your partner to anticipate your needs?*

3 VERB If you **anticipate** something pleasant or exciting that is going to happen, you look forward to it with pleasure. ◆**anticipation** N-U *His eyes gleamed in anticipation.*

anti-clockwise /ˌænti'klɒkwaɪz/. ADV & ADJ In British English, if something is moving **anti-clockwise**, it is moving in a circle in the opposite direction to the hands of a clock. The usual American word is **counterclockwise**.

antics /'æntɪks/. N-PL **Antics** are funny, silly, or unusual ways of behaving.

antidote /'æntidəʊt/ **antidotes.** N-C An **antidote** is a chemical substance that controls the effect of a poison.

antiquated /'æntɪkweɪtɪd/. ADJ **Antiquated** things seem very old or old-fashioned. *Many factories are so antiquated they are not worth saving.*

antique /æn'tiːk/ **antiques.** N-C An **antique** is an old object which is valuable because of its beauty or rarity. *...antique silver jewellery.*

antiquity /æn'tɪkwɪti/ **antiquities.** **1** N-U **Antiquity** is the distant past, especially the time of the ancient Egyptians, Greeks, and Romans. *...famous monuments of classical antiquity.* **2** N-C **Antiquities** are interesting old things, such as buildings and statues, that you can visit.

antiseptic /ˌænti'septɪk/ **antiseptics.** N-VAR **Antiseptic** is a substance that kills bacteria.

anti-'social. **1** ADJ **Anti-social** people are unwilling to meet and be friendly with other people. *...an anti-social loner.* **2** ADJ **Anti-social** behaviour is annoying or upsetting to others.

anus /'eɪnəs/ **anuses.** N-C A person's **anus** is the hole between their buttocks, from which faeces leave their body.

anxiety /æŋ'zaɪɪti/ **anxieties.** N-VAR **Anxiety** is a feeling of nervousness or worry. *Her voice was full of anxiety. ...anxieties about money.*

anxious /'æŋkʃəs/. **1** ADJ AFTER LINK-V If you are **anxious** to do something or **anxious** that something should happen, you very much want to do it or want it to happen. *I was anxious to get him here... He is anxious that there should be no delay.* **2** ADJ If you are feeling **anxious**, you are worried about something. You can also use **anxious** to describe a time when someone feels anxious. *She had become very anxious and alarmed... They had to wait 10 anxious days.* ◆**anxiously** ADV *They waited anxiously for news.*

any /'eni/. **1** QUANT You use **any** in negative statements to mean none of a particular thing. *I never make any big decisions... You don't know any of my friends... The children needed new school clothes and Kim couldn't afford any.* **2** ADV You can use **any** to emphasize a comparative adjective or adverb in a negative statement. *I can't see things getting any easier.* **3** QUANT You use **any** in questions and conditional clauses to ask if there is some of a particular thing or to suggest that there might be. *Do you speak any foreign languages?... Do you use any of the following?... I'll be happy to answer any questions if there are any.* **4** QUANT You use **any** in positive statements when you are referring to something or someone without

saying exactly what, who, or which kind you mean. *I'm prepared to take any advice. ...the biggest mistake any of them could remember... Clean the mussels and discard any that do not close.* **5** PHRASE If something does not happen or is not true **any more** or **any longer**, it has stopped happening or is no longer true. *I don't want to see her any more... I couldn't keep the tears hidden any longer.*

anybody /'enibɒdi/. See **anyone**.

anyhow /'enihaʊ/. See **anyway**.

anymore /ˌeni'mɔː/ or **any more.** ADV If something does not happen or is not true **anymore**, it has stopped happening or is no longer true. Some people think this spelling is incorrect and prefer to use **any more**. *People are not interested in movies anymore.*

anyone /'eniwʌn/ or **anybody** /'enibɒdi/. **1** PRON You use **anyone** in negative statements to indicate that nobody is present or involved in an action. *You needn't talk to anyone if you don't want to... He was far too scared to tell anybody.* **2** PRON You use **anyone** in questions and conditional clauses to ask or talk about someone who might be involved in a particular situation or action. *Did you tell anyone?... If anybody wants me, I'll be at the police station.* **3** PRON You use **anyone** before words which indicate the kind of person you are talking about. *It's not a job for anyone who is slow with numbers.* **4** PRON You use **anyone** to say that a particular thing would be true of any person out of a very large number of people. *Al Smith could make anybody laugh.*

> Do not confuse **anyone** with **any one**. **Anyone** always refers to people. In the phrase **any one**, 'one' is a pronoun or a determiner that can refer to either a person or a thing, depending on the context. It is often followed by the word **of**. *Parting from any one of you for even a short time is hard... None of us stay in any one place for a very long time.* In these examples, **any one** is a more emphatic way of saying **any**.

anyplace /'enipleɪs/. **Anyplace** means the same as **anywhere**; AMERICAN.

anything /'eniθɪŋ/. **1** PRON You use **anything** in negative statements to say that nothing is present or an action or event does not happen. *She couldn't see or hear anything... I couldn't manage anything.* **2** PRON You use **anything** in questions and conditional clauses to ask or talk about whether something is present or happening. *Did you find anything? ...if there's anything I could do for him.* **3** PRON You use **anything** to emphasize that a particular thing could be true about any one of a very large number of things. *Anything could happen... He can have anything. ...anything from 25 to 40 litres of milk.* **4** PRON You use **anything** before words which indicate the kind of thing you are talking about. *She collects anything that has charm.* **5** PRON You use **anything** in expressions such as **anything near**, **anything close to**, and **anything like** to emphasize a statement that you are making. ...*the only way he can live anything near a normal life.*

anytime /'enɪ,taɪm/. ADV You use **anytime** to mean at an unspecified point in time. *The college admits students anytime during the year... He can leave anytime he wants.*

anyway /'enɪweɪ/ or **anyhow** /'enɪhaʊ/. [1] ADV You use **anyway** to indicate that a statement explains or supports a previous point. *I'm certain David's told you his business troubles. Anyway, it's no secret that he owes money.* [2] ADV You use **anyway** to suggest that a statement is true or relevant in spite of other things that have been said. *I wasn't qualified to apply for the job really but I got it anyhow.* [3] ADV You use **anyway** to correct or modify a statement. *Ann doesn't want to have children. Not right now, anyway.* [4] ADV You use **anyway** to change the topic or return to a previous topic. *'I've got a terrible cold.'—'Have you? Oh dear. Anyway, so you're not going to go away this weekend?'.*

anyways /'enɪweɪz/. ADV Some people use **anyways** instead of **anyway**; AMERICAN.

anywhere /'enɪweə/. [1] ADV You use **anywhere** in negative statements, questions, and conditional clauses to refer to a place without saying exactly where you mean. *Did you try to get help from anywhere?... I haven't got anywhere to live.* [2] ADV You use **anywhere** in positive statements to emphasize an expression that refers to a place or area. *...jokes that are so funny they always work anywhere... He'll meet you anywhere you want.* [3] ADV When you do not want to be exact, you use **anywhere** to refer to a particular range of things. *His shoes cost anywhere from $200 up.*

apart /ə'pɑːt/. [1] ADV When someone or something is positioned **apart** from a person or thing, they are some distance from them. *He was standing a bit apart from the rest of us... He was standing, feet apart... He tried in vain to keep the two dogs apart.* [2] ADV If two people are **apart**, they are no longer living together or spending time together. *Mum and Dad live apart.* [3] ADV If something comes **apart**, its parts separate from each other. *The handles of two of Ivanisevic's new rackets came apart.* [4] PREP You use **apart from** when you are giving an exception to a general statement. *The room was empty apart from one man seated beside the fire.* [5] PREP You use **apart from** to indicate that you are aware of one aspect of a situation, but that you are going to focus on another aspect. *The Queen remains above criticism, apart from the issue of her tax liability.*

apartment /ə'pɑːtmənt/ **apartments.** N-C An **apartment** is a set of rooms for living in, usually on one floor of a large building. This word can be used in British and American English, although **flat** is the more commonly used word in Britain. *...concrete apartment blocks.*

apathy /'æpəθi/. N-U **Apathy** is a state of mind in which you are not interested in or enthusiastic about anything. *...the political apathy of young Americans.* ♦**apathetic** /,æpə'θetɪk/ ADJ *The voters seem so apathetic about European issues.*

ape /eɪp/ **apes, aping, aped.** [1] N-C **Apes** are animals such as chimpanzees or gorillas. [2] VERB If you **ape** someone's behaviour, you imitate it. *...French films which merely aped Hollywood.*

aperture /'æpətʃə/ **apertures.** N-C An **aperture** is a narrow hole or gap, for example the opening in a camera through which light passes into it; FORMAL. *Through the aperture he could clearly see daylight.*

apex /'eɪpeks/ **apexes.** [1] N-SING The **apex** of an organization or system is the highest and most important position in it. *At the apex of the party was its central committee.* [2] N-C The **apex** of something such as a pyramid is its pointed top.

apiece /ə'piːs/. ADV If people have a particular number of things **apiece**, they have that number each. *He and I had two fish apiece.*

apologetic /ə,pɒlə'dʒetɪk/. ADJ If you are **apologetic**, you show or say that you are sorry that you have hurt someone or caused trouble for them. *He sounded very apologetic about his activities.* ♦**apologetically** ADV *Mary Ann smiled at her apologetically.*

apologize (BR also **apologise**) /ə'pɒlədʒaɪz/ **apologizes, apologizing, apologized.** VERB When you **apologize** to someone, you say that you are sorry that you have hurt them or caused trouble for them. You can say **'I apologize'** as a formal way of saying sorry. *I apologize for being late.*

apology /ə'pɒlədʒi/ **apologies.** N-VAR An **apology** is something that you say or write in order to tell someone that you are sorry that you have hurt them or caused trouble for them. *I make no apologies for the way we played. ...a letter of apology.*

apostrophe /ə'pɒstrəfi/ **apostrophes.** N-C An **apostrophe** is the mark ', written to indicate that one or more letters have been omitted from a word, as in 'isn't'. It is also added to nouns to form possessives, as in 'Mike's car'.

appal (AM **appall**) /ə'pɔːl/ **appals, appalling, appalled.** VERB If something **appals** you, it shocks you because it is so bad. *My wife now looks like her mother, which appals me.* ♦**appalled** ADJ *I am absolutely appalled at what this man has done.*

appalling /ə'pɔːlɪŋ/. ADJ Something that is **appalling** is so bad that it shocks you. *They have been living under the most appalling conditions.* ♦**appallingly** ADV *...an appallingly bad speech.*

apparatus /,æpə'reɪtəs, -'ræt-/ **apparatuses.** [1] N-VAR The **apparatus** of an organization or system is its structure and method of operation. *...the technical apparatus of management.* [2] N-U **Apparatus** is the equipment which is used to do a particular job or activity. *...firemen wearing breathing apparatus.*

apparent /ə'pærənt/. [1] ADJ BEFORE N An **apparent** situation seems to be the case, although you cannot be certain that it is. *The apparent failure of the mission is a serious blow.* [2] ADJ AFTER LINK-V If something is **apparent**, it is clear and obvious. *It was apparent that he had got very confused.*

apparently /ə'pærəntli/. ADV You use **apparently** to refer to something that seems to be the case although it may not be. *The news apparently came as a complete surprise.*

appeal /ə'piːl/ **appeals, appealing, appealed.** ⓵ VERB & N-C If you **appeal** for something that you need, or make an **appeal** for it, you make a serious and urgent request for it. *The UN has appealed for help from the international community. ...a last-minute appeal to him to call off his trip.* ⓶ VERB & N-C If you **appeal** to someone in authority against a decision, or if you make an **appeal**, you formally ask them to change it. *The government has appealed against the court's decision... Maguire has appealed to the Supreme Court.* ⓷ VERB & N-U If something **appeals** to you, or if it has **appeal**, you find it attractive or interesting. *The idea appealed to him. ...tiny dolls with great appeal to young girls.*

appealing /ə'piːlɪŋ/. ADJ Someone or something that is **appealing** is pleasing and attractive. *...a sense of humour that I found very appealing.*

appear /ə'pɪə/ **appears, appearing, appeared.** ⓵ LINK-VERB If you say that something **appears** to be the case or **appears** to have a certain quality, you mean that you have the impression that it is the case or that it has that quality. *He appeared to be depressed... The aircraft appears to have crashed... There appears to be no problem with your baby's breathing... He is anxious to appear a gentleman.* ⓶ VERB When something or someone **appears**, it becomes possible to see them or obtain them. *A woman appeared at the far end of the street. ...white flowers which appear in early summer... New diet books appear at a rate of nearly one a week.* ⓷ VERB When someone **appears** in a play, a show, or a television programme, they take part in it. ⓸ VERB When someone **appears** before a court of law, they go there to answer charges or to give information.

appearance /ə'pɪərəns/ **appearances.** ⓵ N-C When someone makes an **appearance** at a public event or in a broadcast, they take part in it. *...the president's second public appearance. ...a brief appearance on television.* ⓶ N-SING The **appearance** of someone or something in a place is the fact of their arriving or becoming visible there. *...the welcome appearance of Cousin Fred... Flowering plants were making their first appearance.* ⓷ N-SING Your **appearance** is what you look like or how you present yourself. *She used to be so fussy about her appearance... It adds nothing to the value or appearance of the house.*

appease /ə'piːz/ **appeases, appeasing, appeased.** VERB If you try to **appease** someone, you try to maintain a peaceful situation by giving them what they want; often used showing disapproval. *The government tried to appease discontented workers.* ♦ **appeasement** N-U *Appeasement didn't work with Hitler.*

appendix /ə'pendɪks/ **appendices** /ə'pendɪsiːz/. ⓵ N-C Your **appendix** is a small tube inside your body at the end of your digestive system. ⓶ N-C An **appendix** to a book is extra information that is placed at the end of it.

appetite /'æpɪtaɪt/ **appetites.** ⓵ N-VAR Your **appetite** is your desire to eat. *He has a healthy appetite. ...loss of appetite.* ⓶ N-C If you have an **appetite** for something, you have a strong desire for it. *...his appetite for success.*

appetizing (BR also **appetising**) /'æpɪtaɪzɪŋ/. ADJ **Appetizing** food looks and smells nice, so that you want to eat it.

applaud /ə'plɔːd/ **applauds, applauding, applauded.** ⓵ VERB When a group of people **applaud**, they clap their hands to show that they have enjoyed a performance. *I didn't applaud him because it was a very bad speech.* ⓶ VERB When a person or their behaviour **is applauded**, people praise it. *He should be applauded for his courage... We applaud her determination.*

applause /ə'plɔːz/. N-U **Applause** is the noise made by a group of people clapping their hands to show approval. *They greeted him with thunderous applause.*

apple /'æpəl/ **apples.** N-VAR An **apple** is a round fruit with a smooth skin and firm white flesh.

appliance /ə'plaɪəns/ **appliances.** N-C An **appliance** is a device such as a vacuum cleaner that does a particular job in your home. *...electrical appliances.*

applicable /'æplɪkəbəl, ə'plɪkə-/. ADJ Something that is **applicable** to a particular situation is relevant to it. *...standards applicable to all police officers... One knows their name and also, where applicable, their professional post.*

applicant /'æplɪkənt/ **applicants.** N-C An **applicant** for a job or position is someone who applies for it.

application /ˌæplɪ'keɪʃən/ **applications.** ⓵ N-VAR An **application** for something such as a job or a place at a college is a formal written request to be given it. *Tickets are available on application.* ⓶ N-VAR The **application** of a rule or piece of knowledge is the use of it in a particular situation. *...the practical application of the theory. ...artificial intelligence and its application to robotics.*

applied /ə'plaɪd/. ADJ An **applied** subject of study is practical rather than theoretical. *...applied research.*

apply /ə'plaɪ/ **applies, applying, applied.** ⓵ VERB If you **apply** for something or to do something, you write asking formally to be allowed to have it or do it. *I am continuing to apply for jobs... They may apply to join the organization.* ⓶ VERB If you **apply** yourself to something, you concentrate hard on it. *They would have to apply their minds to many questions.* ⓷ VERB If something **applies** to a person or a situation, it is relevant to them. *The convention does not apply to us.* ⓸ VERB If you **apply** a rule or piece of knowledge, you use it in a situation or activity. *...applying the technology to practical business problems.* ⓹ VERB If you **apply** something to a surface, you put it onto the surface or rub it into it; FORMAL. *Apply direct pressure to the wound... Applying the dye can be messy.*

appoint /ə'pɔɪnt/ **appoints, appointing, appointed.** VERB If you **appoint** someone to a job or post, you formally choose them for it. *The Prime Minister has appointed a civilian as* *defence minister.* ♦**appointment** N-U *...his appointment as foreign minister.*

appointed /əˈpɔɪntɪd/. ADJ BEFORE N If something happens at the **appointed** time, it happens at the time that was decided in advance; FORMAL.

appointment /əˈpɔɪntmənt/ **appointments**. [1] N-C An **appointment** is a job or position of responsibility. *Mr Fay is to take up an appointment as a researcher.* [2] N-VAR If you have an **appointment** with someone, you have arranged to see them at a particular time. If something can be done **by appointment**, you can make an appointment to do it.

appraisal /əˈpreɪzəl/ **appraisals**. N-VAR If you make an **appraisal** of something, you consider it carefully and form an opinion about it. *...a calm appraisal of the situation.*

appraise /əˈpreɪz/ **appraises, appraising, appraised**. VERB If you **appraise** something or someone, you consider them carefully and form an opinion about them. *I carefully appraised the situation.*

appreciate /əˈpriːʃieɪt/ **appreciates, appreciating, appreciated**. [1] VERB If you **appreciate** something, you like it because you recognize its good qualities. *Anyone can appreciate our music.* ♦**appreciation** N-U *...children's understanding and appreciation of art.* [2] VERB If you **appreciate** a situation or problem, you understand it and know what it involves. *We appreciate how tough it is in business... You'll appreciate the reason for secrecy.* ♦**appreciation** N-U *They lacked appreciation of social and political issues.* [3] VERB If you say that you **appreciate** something someone has done for you, you mean that you are grateful for it. *I'd appreciate it if you wouldn't mention it.* ♦**appreciation** N-U *...gifts presented to them in appreciation of their work.* [4] VERB If something **appreciates** over a period of time, its value increases. *Houses will always appreciate in value.* ♦**appreciation** N-U *...long-term price appreciation.*

appreciative /əˈpriːʃətɪv/. ADJ If you are **appreciative**, you are grateful. *We have been very appreciative of their support.* ♦**appreciatively** ADV *Michael smiled appreciatively.*

apprehension /ˌæprɪˈhenʃən/ **apprehensions**. N-VAR **Apprehension** is a feeling of fear that something bad may happen; FORMAL. *...her apprehensions about the big risks she was taking.*

apprehensive /ˌæprɪˈhensɪv/. ADJ Someone who is **apprehensive** is afraid that something bad may happen.

apprentice /əˈprentɪs/ **apprentices**. N-C An **apprentice** is a young person who works with someone in order to learn their skill.

apprenticeship /əˈprentɪsʃɪp/ **apprenticeships**. N-VAR Someone who has an **apprenticeship** works for a fixed period of time for someone who teaches them a particular skill. **Apprenticeship** is the system of learning a skill like this. *He served an apprenticeship as an engineer.*

approach /əˈprəʊtʃ/ **approaches, approaching, approached**. [1] VERB & N-C When someone **approaches**, they come nearer to you. You

can also talk about their **approach**. *He didn't approach the front door at once. ...the approaching car... At their approach the little boy ran away.* [2] N-C The **approach** to a place is the road or path that leads to it. *The path serves as an approach to the boat house.* [3] VERB & N-C If you **approach** someone about something or if you make an **approach** to them, you speak to them because you want them to do something for you. *Chappel approached me about the job... Anna approached several builders.* [4] VERB & N-C When you **approach** a situation in a particular way, you think about it or deal with it in that way. You can call this your **approach** to it. *The Bank has approached the issue in a practical way. ...different approaches to gathering information.* [5] VERB & N-SING As a future time or event **approaches**, or as you **approach** it, it gradually comes nearer. You can also talk about the **approach** of a future time or event. *...the approaching crisis. ...the approach of crucial elections.* [6] VERB If something **approaches** a particular level or state, it almost reaches that level or state. *...speeds approaching 200mph.*

appropriate, appropriates, appropriating, appropriated. [1] ADJ /əˈprəʊprɪət/ Something that is **appropriate** is suitable or acceptable for a particular situation. *...an outfit appropriate to the job... The teacher can then take appropriate action... It is appropriate that the exhibition should be sponsored by BMW.* ♦**appropriately** ADV *Dress appropriately.* [2] VERB /əˈprəʊprieɪt/ If you **appropriate** something which does not belong to you, you take it for yourself; FORMAL. *Several other newspapers have appropriated the idea.* ♦**appropriation** N-U *...illegal appropriation of land.*

approval /əˈpruːvəl/. [1] N-U If a plan or request gets someone's **approval**, they agree to it. *He gave his personal approval to the security arrangements. ...the royal seal of approval.* [2] N-U If someone has your **approval**, you like and admire them.

approve /əˈpruːv/ **approves, approving, approved**. [1] VERB If you **approve** of something or someone, you like them or think they are good. *Not everyone approves of the festival... You don't approve, do you?* [2] VERB If someone in authority **approves** a plan or idea, they formally agree to it.

approved /əˈpruːvd/. ADJ An **approved** method or person is generally or officially recommended or acceptable for a particular job. *...tuition from an approved driving instructor.*

approving /əˈpruːvɪŋ/. ADJ An **approving** reaction shows support for something, or satisfaction with it. ♦**approvingly** ADV *He nodded approvingly.*

approximate, approximates, approximating, approximated. [1] ADJ /əˈprɒksɪmət/ **Approximate** quantities are close to the correct quantity, but are not exact. *The times are approximate only... Could you tell me its approximate age?* ♦**approximately** ADV *The conservatory measures approximately 13ft x 16ft.* [2] VERB /əˈprɒksɪmeɪt/ If something **approximates** to something else, it is similar to it but not exactly the same. *Something approximating to a just outcome will be ensured.*

approximation /ə‚prɒksɪˈmeɪʃən/ **approximations.** N-C An **approximation** is a fact, description, or calculation that is not exact. *This story is probably a good approximation to the truth.*

apricot /ˈeɪprɪkɒt/ **apricots.** N-C An **apricot** is a small, soft, round fruit with yellow-orange flesh and a stone inside.

April /ˈeɪprɪl/. N-U **April** is the fourth month of the year.

apron /ˈeɪprən/ **aprons.** N-C An **apron** is a piece of clothing that you put on over the front of your clothes to prevent them from getting dirty.

apt /æpt/. [1] ADJ If someone **is apt to** behave in a particular way, they often behave in that way. *She was apt to raise her voice.* [2] ADJ **Apt** means suitable. ◆**aptly** ADV *...the beach in the aptly named town of Oceanside.*

aptitude /ˈæptɪtjuːd, AM -tuːd/ **aptitudes.** N-VAR If you have an **aptitude** for something, you are able to learn it quickly and do it well. *Alan has no aptitude for music.*

aquatic /əˈkwætɪk/. ADJ **Aquatic** means existing or happening in water. *...aquatic plants.*

arable /ˈærəbəl/. ADJ **Arable** farming involves growing crops rather than keeping animals. **Arable** land is land that is used for arable farming.

arbitrary /ˈɑːbɪtri, AM -treri/. ADJ An **arbitrary** decision or action is not based on any principle or plan, and therefore may seem unfair. *...arbitrary arrests and detention without trial.* ◆**arbitrarily** ADV *Prisoners-of-war are being arbitrarily killed.*

arbitrate /ˈɑːbɪtreɪt/ **arbitrates, arbitrating, arbitrated.** VERB When someone **arbitrates** between two people who are in dispute, they consider all the facts and decide who is right. *The tribunal had been set up to arbitrate in the dispute.* ◆**arbitration** N-U *Both sides hope to settle through arbitration.*

arc /ɑːk/ **arcs.** N-C An **arc** is a smoothly curving line or movement.

arcade /ɑːˈkeɪd/ **arcades.** N-C An **arcade** is a covered passageway where there are shops. *...a shopping arcade.*

arch /ɑːtʃ/ **arches, arching, arched.** [1] N-C An **arch** is a structure which is made when two columns join at the top in a curve. *...railway arches.* [2] VERB If something **arches** or if you **arch** it, it forms a curved shape or line. *Don't arch your back.*

archaeology (or **archeology**) /‚ɑːkiˈɒlədʒi/. N-U **Archaeology** is the study of the past by examining the remains of things such as buildings and tools. ◆**archaeological** /‚ɑːkiəˈlɒdʒɪkəl/ ADJ BEFORE N *...archaeological sites.* ◆**archaeologist** **archaeologists** N-C *...archaeologists uncovering Mayan treasures.*

archaic /ɑːˈkeɪɪk/. ADJ **Archaic** means very old or very old-fashioned. *The existing law is archaic.*

archbishop /‚ɑːtʃˈbɪʃəp/ **archbishops.** N-C In the Roman Catholic church, and in some other churches, an **archbishop** is a bishop of the highest rank.

arched /ɑːtʃt/. See **arch**.

archeology. See **archaeology**.

archetype /ˈɑːkɪtaɪp/ **archetypes.** N-C The **archetype** of a particular kind of person or thing is a perfect or typical example of it. ◆**archetypal** ADJ *Cricket is the archetypal English game.*

architect /ˈɑːkɪtekt/ **architects.** [1] N-C An **architect** is a person who designs buildings. [2] N-C The **architect** of an idea or event is the person who invented it or made it happen. *...the architect of Russia's economic reforms.*

architecture /ˈɑːkɪtektʃə/. [1] N-U **Architecture** is the art of designing and constructing buildings. ◆**architectural** /‚ɑːkɪˈtektʃərəl/ ADJ *...architectural drawings.* ◆**architecturally** ADV *...sites which are architecturally interesting.* [2] N-U The **architecture** of a building is the style in which it is constructed. *...a fine example of Moroccan architecture.*

archive /ˈɑːkaɪv/ **archives.** N-C **Archives** are collections of documents that contain information about the history of an organization or group of people. *...Soviet military archives.*

ardent /ˈɑːdənt/. ADJ Someone who is **ardent** about something is very enthusiastic or passionate about it. *...ardent fans.* ◆**ardently** ADV *Its electorate ardently supports abortion rights.*

arduous /ˈɑːdʒuəs/. ADJ Something that is **arduous** is difficult and involves a lot of physical effort. *...a long, arduous journey.*

are /ə, STRONG ɑː/. **Are** is the plural and the second person singular of the present tense of **be**. **Are** is often abbreviated to '**re** after pronouns.

area /ˈeəriə/ **areas.** [1] N-C An **area** is a particular part of a city, a country, or the world. *Half the French population still lived in rural areas.* [2] N-C A particular **area** of a room or other place is a part that is used for a particular activity. *...Gatwick airport's luggage area.* [3] N-C The **area** of a shape or piece of land is the amount that it covers, expressed as a measurement. *The islands cover a total area of 625.6 square kilometers.* [4] N-C You can use **area** to refer to a particular subject or to a particular part of a general situation or activity. *...awards to the best writers in every area of the arts.*

arena /əˈriːnə/ **arenas.** [1] N-C An **arena** is a place where public events such as concerts take place. *...a spectacular sports arena.* [2] N-C You can refer to a particular field of activity, especially one where there is a lot of conflict, as an **arena.** *He entered the political arena in 1987.*

aren't /ɑːnt, AM ˈɑːrənt/. [1] **Aren't** is the usual spoken form of 'are not'. [2] **Aren't** is used instead of 'am not' in negative questions.

arguably /ˈɑːgjuəbli/. ADV You can use **arguably** when you are stating your opinion or belief, as a way of giving more authority to it. *We now have arguably the best bookshops in the world.*

argue /ˈɑːgjuː/ **argues, arguing, argued.** [1] VERB If you **argue** with someone, you disagree with them about something, often angrily. *...arguing with patients about smoking...*

They argued about the cost of a taxi. [2] VERB If you **argue** that something is true, you give the reasons why you think it is true. If you **argue for** or **against** an idea or policy, you state the reasons why you support or oppose it. *His lawyers are arguing that he is unfit to stand trial... The report argues against tax increases.*

argument /'ɑːgjʊmənt/ **arguments.** [1] N-C If people have an **argument**, they disagree with each other, often angrily. *She got into an argument with one of the marchers.* [2] N-VAR An **argument** is a set of statements that you use to try to convince people that your opinion is correct. *There's a strong argument for lowering the price.*

arid /'ærɪd/. ADJ **Arid** land is so dry that very few plants can grow on it.

arise /ə'raɪz/ **arises, arising, arose** /ə'rəʊz/ **arisen.** /ə'rɪzən/. [1] VERB If a situation or problem **arises**, it begins to exist or people start to become aware of it. *Language problems arose when their families moved from England.* [2] VERB If something **arises from** a particular situation, or **arises out of it**, it is created or caused by the situation. *...claim for damages arising from the Piper Alpha disaster... The charges arise out of a fraud enquiry.*

aristocracy /ˌærɪ'stɒkrəsi/ **aristocracies.** N-C The **aristocracy** is a class of people in some countries who have a high social rank and special titles.

aristocrat /'ærɪstəkræt, ə'rɪst-/ **aristocrats.** N-C An **aristocrat** is someone whose family has a high social rank, especially someone with a title. ♦**aristocratic** ADJ *...aristocratic values.*

arithmetic /ə'rɪθmɪtɪk/. N-U **Arithmetic** is the part of mathematics that deals with adding, subtracting, multiplying, and dividing numbers.

arm /ɑːm/ **arms.** [1] N-C Your **arms** are the parts of your body between your hands and your shoulders. [2] N-C The **arm** of a piece of clothing is the part of it that covers your arm. [3] N-C The **arm** of a chair is the part on which you rest your arm. [4] N-PL **Arms** are weapons, especially bombs and guns. *...nuclear arms reductions.* [5] VERB To **arm** someone with a weapon means to provide them with it. *Governments have been reluctant to arm all police officers.* [6] PHRASE If something gives you **a shot in the arm**, it gives you help and encouragement when you need it very much.

armaments /'ɑːməmənts/. N-PL A particular country's **armaments** are its weapons and military equipment.

armchair /'ɑːmtʃeə/ **armchairs.** N-C An **armchair** is a comfortable chair with a support on each side for your arms.

armed /ɑːmd/. ADJ Someone who is **armed** is carrying a weapon. You can also use **armed** to describe crimes or conflicts involving weapons. *He may be armed. ...armed robbery.*

armed 'forces. N-PL The **armed forces** or the **armed services** of a country are its army, navy, and air force.

armour (AM **armor**) /'ɑːmə/. [1] N-U **Armour** is a metal covering that protects a military vehicle against attack. *...a warhead that can penetrate the armour of most tanks.* [2] N-U In former times, **armour** was the protective metal clothing worn by soldiers.

armoured (AM **armored**) /'ɑːməd/. ADJ An **armoured** vehicle has a metal covering that protects it from gunfire and other missiles.

armoury (AM **armory**) /'ɑːməri/ **armouries.** [1] N-C An **armoury** is a place where weapons, bombs, and other military equipment are stored. You can also refer to all a country's weapons and military equipment as its **armoury**. [2] N-C You can refer to a large number of things which someone can use to achieve a particular goal as their **armoury**. *...a large armoury of drugs for the treatment of mental illness.*

armpit /'ɑːmpɪt/ **armpits.** N-C Your **armpits** are the areas of your body under your arms where your arms join your shoulders.

army /'ɑːmi/ **armies.** [1] N-C An **army** is a large organized group of people who are armed and trained to fight. [2] N-C An **army** of people, animals, or things is a large number of them together. *...an army of volunteers.*

aroma /ə'rəʊmə/ **aromas.** N-C An **aroma** is a strong pleasant smell. *...the wonderful aroma of freshly baked bread.*

aromatic /ˌærə'mætɪk/. ADJ **Aromatic** plants, food, or oil has a strong pleasant smell.

arose /ə'rəʊz/. **Arose** is the past tense of **arise**.

around /ə'raʊnd/. [1] **Around** means the same as the preposition and adverb uses of **round**. [2] ADV & PREP If someone or something is **around**, they are near, present, or available. *The idea has been around for ages without catching on... Most people around here no longer care.* [3] ADV **Around** means approximately. *My salary was around £19,000... He expects the elections to be held around November.*

> **Around** and **round** are used in various ways as prepositions and adverbs, often as part of phrasal verbs. In most cases, you can use either word without any difference of meaning. In American English, **around** is much more common than **round**.
> When you are talking about casual or random movement in no particular direction, you can use **about** as well as **around** and **round**. *It's so romantic up there, flying around in a small plane... I spent a couple of hours driving round Richmond... Police constables walk about with guns on their hips.*
> When you are talking about something being generally present or available, you can use **around** or **about**, but not **round**, as adverbs. *There is a lot of talent around at the moment... There's not that many jobs about.*
> **Round** has a lot of other meanings, as a noun, verb, and adjective. You cannot use **around** in these cases.

arousal /ə'raʊzəl/. N-U If you are in a state of **arousal**, you are excited or alert.

arouse /ə'raʊz/ **arouses, arousing, aroused.** [1] VERB If something **arouses** a particular reaction or feeling in you, it causes you to have that reaction or feeling. *She had a knack of arousing strong emotions.* [2] ADJ To **arouse** someone means to make them feel sexually excited.

arrange /əˈreɪndʒ/ arranges, arranging, arranged. [1] VERB If you **arrange** something such as an event or meeting, you make the plans and preparations that are necessary for it to happen. *We arranged a social event once a year... I've arranged to see him on Friday morning... I will arrange for someone to take you.* [2] VERB If you **arrange** objects, you place them in a particular position. *She enjoys arranging dried flowers.*

arrangement /əˈreɪndʒmənt/ arrangements. [1] N-PL **Arrangements** are plans and preparations which you make so that something can happen. *I must make all the arrangements for the burial.* [2] N-C An **arrangement** of things is a group of them displayed in a particular way. *...imaginative flower arrangements.*

array /əˈreɪ/. N-C An **array** of different things is a large number of them. *She experienced a bewildering array of emotions.*

arrears /əˈrɪəz/. N-PL **Arrears** are amounts of money that someone owes. If someone is **in arrears** with regular payments, they have not paid them. *The arrears have been mounting in recent months.*

arrest /əˈrest/ arrests, arresting, arrested. VERB & N-VAR When the police **arrest** someone or make an **arrest**, they take them to a police station in order to decide whether they should be charged with an offence. *Police arrested five young men in connection with the attacks... Detectives placed him under arrest.*

arrival /əˈraɪvl/ arrivals. [1] N-VAR Your **arrival** at a place is the act of arriving there. [2] N-SING If you talk about the **arrival** of something new, you are referring to the fact that it has begun to exist or become available. *...the arrival of modern technologies.* [3] N-C An **arrival** is someone who has just arrived at a place. *Each day there are new arrivals in the camp.*

arrive /əˈraɪv/ arrives, arriving, arrived. [1] VERB When you **arrive** at a place, you reach it at the end of a journey. *Fresh groups of guests arrived... I've just arrived from England.* [2] VERB When something **arrives**, it is brought to you or it becomes available to you. *Your letter arrived yesterday.* [3] VERB When you **arrive** at an idea, decision, or conclusion, you reach it or decide on it. *The jury cannot arrive at a unanimous decision.*

arrogant /ˈærəgənt/. ADJ If you say that someone is **arrogant**, you disapprove of them because they behave as if they are better than other people. ♦**arrogance** N-U *The arrogance of those in power is quite blatant.* ♦**arrogantly** ADV *The doctor arrogantly dismissed their cry for help.*

arrow /ˈærəʊ/ arrows. [1] N-C An **arrow** is a long, thin weapon with a sharp point at one end which is shot from a bow. [2] N-C An **arrow** is a written sign which points in a particular direction to indicate where something is.

arsenal /ˈɑːsənəl/ arsenals. N-C An **arsenal** is a large collection of weapons and military equipment. *...reductions in Britain's nuclear arsenal.*

arson /ˈɑːsən/. N-U **Arson** is the crime of deliberately setting fire to a building or vehicle.

art /ɑːt/ arts. [1] N-U **Art** is paintings, drawings, and sculpture which are beautiful or which express an artist's ideas. **Art** is also the activity of creating these things. *...contemporary American art. ...an art class for children.* [2] N-VAR The **arts** are activities such as music, painting, literature, cinema, and dance. *...people working in the arts. ...the art of cinema.* [3] N-PL At a university or college, **arts** are subjects such as history or languages in contrast to scientific subjects. *...arts and social science graduates.* [4] N-C If you describe an activity as an **art**, you mean that it requires a lot of skill. *...the art of acting.* [5] See also **fine art**, **martial art**, **state-of-the-art**, **work of art**.

artefact (AM **artifact**) /ˈɑːtɪfækt/ artefacts. N-C An **artefact** is an ornament, tool, or other object made by a human being, especially one that has archaeological or cultural interest.

artery /ˈɑːtəri/ arteries. N-C Your **arteries** are the tubes that carry blood from your heart to the rest of your body.

arthritis /ɑːˈθraɪtɪs/. N-U **Arthritis** is a condition in which the joints in someone's body are swollen and painful. ♦**arthritic** /ɑːˈθrɪtɪk/ ADJ *...arthritic hands.*

artichoke /ˈɑːtɪtʃəʊk/ artichokes. [1] N-VAR An **artichoke** or a **globe artichoke** is a round vegetable with thick green leaves arranged like the petals of a flower. [2] N-VAR An **artichoke** or a **Jerusalem artichoke** is a small, yellow-white vegetable similar to a potato.

article /ˈɑːtɪkl/ articles. [1] N-C An **article** is a piece of writing in a newspaper or magazine. [2] N-C You can refer to objects as **articles** of some kind; FORMAL. *...articles of clothing.* [3] N-C An **article** of a formal document is a section dealing with a particular point. *...Article 50 of the UN charter.* [4] See also **definite article**, **indefinite article**.

articulate, articulates, articulating, articulated. [1] ADJ /ɑːˈtɪkjʊlət/ If you are **articulate**, you are able to express yourself well. *...an articulate description.* [2] VERB /ɑːˈtɪkjʊleɪt/ When you **articulate** your ideas or feelings, you express them clearly in words; FORMAL. *Encourage her to articulate her views.*

articulated /ɑːˈtɪkjʊleɪtɪd/. ADJ An **articulated** vehicle, especially a lorry, is made in two sections with a moving joint between them; BRITISH.

artifact. See **artefact**.

artificial /ˌɑːtɪˈfɪʃəl/. [1] ADJ **Artificial** objects, materials, or situations do not occur naturally and are created by people. *...artificial limbs. ...the artificial environment of an office.* ♦**artificially** ADV *...artificially sweetened lemonade. ...artificially high prices.* [2] ADJ If you describe someone's behaviour as **artificial**, you disapprove of them because they are pretending to have attitudes and feelings which they do not really have. *...a fixed, artificial smile.*

artificial intelligence. N-U **Artificial intelligence** is a type of computer technology concerned with making machines work in a similar way to the human mind.

artillery /ɑːˈtɪləri/. N-U & N-SING **Artillery** consists of large, powerful guns which are transported on wheels. The **artillery** is the section of the army which uses these guns.

artist /ˈɑːtɪst/ **artists**. 1 N-C An **artist** is someone who draws, paints, or produces other works of art. 2 N-C You can refer to a musician, actor, dancer, or other performer as an **artist**. ...a popular artist who has sold millions of records.

artistic /ɑːˈtɪstɪk/. 1 ADJ Someone who is **artistic** is good at drawing or painting, or arranging things in a beautiful way. They encourage boys to be sensitive and artistic. 2 ADJ **Artistic** also means relating to art or artists. ...the campaign for artistic freedom. ◆**artistically** ADV ...artistically gifted children.

artistry /ˈɑːtɪstri/. N-U **Artistry** is great skill. ...his artistry as a cellist.

as /əz, STRONG æz/. 1 CONJ If something happens **as** something else happens, it happens at the same time. We shut the door behind us as we entered. 2 PREP You use **as** when you are referring to the appearance or function of something. I only told them that as a joke... He has worked as a diplomat. 3 CONJ You use **as** when you are saying how something is done. I'll behave toward them as I would like to be treated. 4 PREP You use the structure **as...as** when you are comparing things, or emphasizing how large or small something is. This was not as easy as we imagined. ...as many as eight thousand letters. 5 CONJ You can use **as** to mean 'because'. This is important as it sets the mood for the rest of the day. 6 PREP You use **as** in expressions like **as a result** and **as a consequence** to indicate how two situations or events are related to each other. Large shoals of fish are dying as a result of pollution in the oceans. 7 CONJ You use **as if** and **as though** when you are comparing one situation to another. He burst into a high-pitched laugh, as though he'd said something funny. 8 PREP You use **as for** and **as to** to introduce a slightly different subject. I feel that there's a lot of pressure put on policemen. And as for putting guns in their hands, I don't think that's a very good idea at all. 9 PREP You use **as to** to indicate what something refers to. They should make decisions as to whether the student needs more help. 10 PREP If you say that something will happen **as of** or **as from** a particular date or time, you mean that it will happen from that time onwards. She is to retire as from 1 October.

asbestos /æsˈbestɒs/. N-U **Asbestos** is a grey material which does not burn.

ascend /əˈsend/ **ascends, ascending, ascended**. 1 VERB If you **ascend** a hill or a staircase, you go up it; WRITTEN. Mrs Clayton had to hold Lizzie's hand as they ascended the steps... Then we ascend steeply through forests of rhododendron. 2 VERB If something **ascends**, it leads or goes upward; WRITTEN. They ascended 55,900 feet in their balloon... A number of staircases ascend from the cobbled streets.

ascending /əˈsendɪŋ/. ADJ BEFORE N If a group of things is arranged in **ascending** order, each thing is greater in size, amount, or importance than the thing before it. The batteries were lettered in ascending order of size.

ascent /əˈsent/ **ascents**. N-C An **ascent** is a steep upward slope, or a journey up a steep slope. ...the first ascent of the world's highest peak.

ascertain /ˌæsəˈteɪn/ **ascertains, ascertaining, ascertained**. VERB If you **ascertain** the truth about something, you find out what it is; FORMAL. They had ascertained that he was not a spy... They were unable to ascertain the extent of the damage.

ascribe /əˈskraɪb/ **ascribes, ascribing, ascribed**. VERB If you **ascribe** something to a person, thing, or event, you believe that they cause it or have it; FORMAL. They ascribe every setback to some kind of conspiracy. ...mystical characteristics which are sometimes ascribed to cats.

ash /æʃ/ **ashes**. 1 N-U & N-PL **Ash** or **ashes** is the grey powder-like substance that is left after something is burnt. ...volcanic ash... He ordered their villages burned to ashes. 2 N-VAR An **ash** is a kind of tree. **Ash** is the wood of this tree.

ashamed /əˈʃeɪmd/. ADJ AFTER LINK-V If someone is **ashamed** of something or someone, they feel embarrassed about it or guilty because of it. I felt incredibly ashamed of myself for getting so angry... She was ashamed that she looked so shabby... Women are often ashamed to admit they are being abused.

ashore /əˈʃɔː/. ADV Something that comes **ashore** comes from the sea onto the shore. Oil from the tanker has come ashore at two beaches in Devon.

ashtray /ˈæʃtreɪ/ **ashtrays**. N-C An **ashtray** is a small dish in which people put the ash from their cigarettes and cigars.

Asian /ˈeɪʃən, ˈeɪʒən/ **Asians**. 1 ADJ **Asian** means belonging or relating to Asia. ...Asian music. 2 N-C An **Asian** is a person who comes from India, Pakistan, or some other part of Asia. Many of the shops were run by Asians.

aside /əˈsaɪd/. 1 ADV If you move something **aside**, you move it to one side of you. If you move **aside**, you move to one side. Sarah closed the book and laid it aside... She stood aside and allowed Hillsden to enter. 2 ADV If you take someone **aside**, you take them away from a group of people in order to talk to them in private. An officer took us aside and told us everyone was okay. 3 PREP **Aside from** means the same as **apart from**; AMERICAN. Does he look O.K., aside from his clothes?

ask /ɑːsk, æsk/ **asks, asking, asked**. 1 VERB If you **ask** someone something, you say something in the form of a question because you want some information. 'How is Frank?' he asked... I asked him his name... I wasn't the only one asking questions... She asked me if I'd enjoyed my dinner. 2 VERB If you **ask** someone to do something, you tell them that you want them to do it. If you **ask** to do something, you tell someone that you want to do it. We had to ask him to leave... I asked to see the Director.

3 VERB If you **ask for** something, you say that you would like it. If you **ask for** someone, you say that you want to see them or speak to them. *I decided to go to the next house and ask for food... There's a man at the gate asking for you.* **4** VERB If you **ask** someone's permission or forgiveness, you try to obtain it. *He asked permission to leave.* **5** VERB If you **ask** someone somewhere, you invite them there. *Couldn't you ask Jon to the party?* **6** PHRASE You can say **'if you ask me'** to emphasize that you are stating your personal opinion. *He was too sarcastic for his own good, if you ask me.*

asleep /ə'sli:p/. ADJ AFTER LINK-V Someone who is **asleep** is sleeping. *He was asleep on Mum's bed.*
PHRASES ● When you **fall asleep**, you start sleeping. *I was so tired I fell asleep.* ● Someone who is **fast asleep** or **sound asleep** is sleeping deeply.

asparagus /ə'spærəgəs/. N-U **Asparagus** is a vegetable with green shoots that you cook and eat.

aspect /'æspekt/ **aspects**. **1** N-C An **aspect** of something is one of the parts of its character or nature. *Climate and weather affect every aspect of our lives.* **2** N-C A room or a window with a particular **aspect** faces in that direction; FORMAL. *The house had a south-west aspect.*

aspiration /ˌæspɪ'reɪʃən/ **aspirations**. N-VAR Someone's **aspirations** are their ambitions to achieve something. *The girl had aspirations to a movie career.*

aspire /ə'spaɪə/ **aspires, aspiring, aspired.** VERB If you **aspire** to something such as an important job, you have a strong desire to have it. *He aspired to a career in diplomacy.*

aspirin /'æspɪrɪn/ **aspirins**. N-VAR **Aspirin** is a mild drug which reduces pain and fever.

aspiring /ə'spaɪərɪŋ/. ADJ BEFORE N **Aspiring** describes someone who is trying to become successful in a particular career. *...aspiring young artists.*

ass /æs/ **asses**. **1** N-C An **ass** is the same as a donkey; DATED. **2** N-C If you call someone an **ass**, you mean that they are behaving in a silly way; INFORMAL.

assailant /ə'seɪlənt/ **assailants**. N-C Someone's **assailant** is a person who has physically attacked them; FORMAL.

assassin /ə'sæsɪn/ **assassins**. N-C An **assassin** is a person who assassinates someone.

assassinate /ə'sæsɪneɪt/ **assassinates, assassinating, assassinated.** VERB If someone important **is assassinated**, they are murdered as a political act. *Robert Kennedy was assassinated in 1968.* ◆**assassination, assassinations** N-VAR *...an assassination plot.* ● See note at **kill**.

assault /ə'sɔ:lt/ **assaults, assaulting, assaulted.** **1** VERB & N-VAR To **assault** someone means to attack them physically. An **assault** on a person is a physical attack on them. *The gang assaulted him with iron bars. ...sexual assaults.* **2** N-C An **assault** on someone is a strong criticism of them. *...a fierce personal assault on Tony Blair.* **3** N-C An **assault** by an army is a strong attack made against an enemy.

assemble /ə'sembəl/ **assembles, assembling, assembled.** **1** VERB When people **assemble**, or when someone **assembles** them, they come together in a group. *...a convenient place for students to assemble between classes.* **2** VERB To **assemble** something means to fit the different parts of it together. *Workers were assembling planes.*

assembly /ə'sembli/ **assemblies**. **1** N-C An **assembly** is a group of people gathered together for a particular purpose. *...an assembly of party members from the Russian republic.* **2** N-VAR The **assembly** of a machine or device is the process of fitting its parts together.

as'sembly line, assembly lines. N-C An **assembly line** is an arrangement of workers and machines in a factory where the product passes from one worker to another until it is finished.

assent /ə'sent/ **assents, assenting, assented.** **1** N-U If someone gives their **assent** to something, they formally agree to it. *He gave his assent to the proposed legislation.* **2** VERB To **assent** to something means to agree to it; FORMAL. *They reluctantly assented to having their picture taken.*

assert /ə'sɜ:t/ **asserts, asserting, asserted.** **1** VERB If you **assert** a fact or belief, you state it firmly; FORMAL. *The company asserts that it won't be held responsible... He asserted his innocence.* ◆**assertion, assertions** N-VAR *Police accepted his assertion that the men had threatened him.* **2** VERB If you **assert** yourself or **assert** your authority, you speak and act in a firm, forceful way. *He's speaking up and asserting himself.*

assertive /ə'sɜ:tɪv/. ADJ Someone who is **assertive** speaks and acts in a firm, forceful way. *Assertive behaviour gets positive results.* ◆**assertiveness** N-U *...assertiveness training.*

assess /ə'ses/ **assesses, assessing, assessed.** VERB If you **assess** something or someone, you consider them carefully and make a judgement about their quality or value. *I looked around and assessed the situation; I was safe... You can ask the court to assess whether the bill is fair.* ◆**assessment, assessments** N-VAR *...the assessment of future senior managers.*

asset /'æset/ **assets**. **1** N-C If something that you have is an **asset**, it is useful to you. *He's been a great asset to the company.* **2** N-PL The **assets** of a company or a person are the things that they own.

assign /ə'saɪn/ **assigns, assigning, assigned.** **1** VERB If you **assign** a task or function to someone, you give it to them. *She'll assign them research papers. ...when teachers assign homework.* **2** VERB If you **are assigned** to a place or group, you are sent to work in the place or with the group. *Did you choose Russia or were you simply assigned there?*

assignment /ə'saɪnmənt/ **assignments**. N-VAR An **assignment** is a piece of work that you are given to do, as part of your job or studies. *...written assignments and practical tests. ...a photographer on assignment for Life magazine.*

assimilate /ə'sɪmɪleɪt/ **assimilates, assimilating, assimilated.** **1** VERB When immigrants **are assimilated** into a community, or when that community **assimilates** them, they become an accepted part of it. *His family tried to assimilate into the white and Hispanic communities... The Vietnamese are trying to assimilate themselves.* ◆**assimilation** N-U ...*assimilation of minority ethnic groups.* [2] VERB If you **assimilate** new ideas, customs, or methods, you learn them and make use of them. ...*someone who assimilates facts well.* ◆**assimilation** N-U ...*assimilation of knowledge.*

assist /ə'sɪst/ **assists, assisting, assisted.** VERB If someone or something **assists** you, they help you; FORMAL. *The family decided to assist me with my chores. ...information to assist you in making the best selection.*

assistance /ə'sɪstəns/. N-U If you give someone **assistance**, you help them. Someone or something that is **of assistance** is helpful or useful; FORMAL. *I would be grateful for any assistance.*

assistant /ə'sɪstənt/ **assistants.** [1] ADJ BEFORE N **Assistant** is used in front of titles or jobs to indicate a slightly lower rank. ...*the assistant secretary of defense.* [2] N-C Someone's **assistant** is a person who helps them in their work. ...*a research assistant.* [3] N-C An **assistant** is a person who sells things in a shop. ...*a sales assistant.*

associate, associates, associating, associated. [1] VERB /ə'səʊsieɪt/ If you **associate** one thing with another, the two are connected or you think of them as connected. *I associate her with feelings of well-being... Poverty is associated with old age.* [2] VERB If you **are associated** with an organization, cause, or point of view, you support it publicly. *I have no wish to associate myself with stupidity.* [3] VERB If you **associate** with a person or group of people, you spend a lot of time with them. *I began associating with different crowds of people.* [4] N-U /ə'səʊsiət/ Your **associates** are your business colleagues.

association /ə,səʊsi'eɪʃən/ **associations.** [1] N-C An **association** is an official group of people who have the same occupation, aim, or interest. ...*the British Astronomical Association.* [2] N-U Your **association** with a person, group, or organization is the connection that you have with them. If someone does something in **association** with someone else, they do it together. ...*his recently published biography written in association with Tony Cosier.* [3] N-C If something has particular **associations** for you, it is connected in your mind with a particular memory or feeling. ...*a flood of unhappy associations.*

assorted /ə'sɔːtɪd/. ADJ A group of **assorted** things of a particular kind have different sizes, colours, or qualities. ...*paper in assorted sizes.*

assortment /ə'sɔːtmənt/ **assortments.** N-C An **assortment** is a group of similar things that have different sizes, colours, or qualities.

assume /ə'sjuːm, AM -'suːm/ **assumes, assuming, assumed.** [1] VERB If you **assume** that something is true, you suppose that it is true, sometimes wrongly. *I can safely assume the eggs will be fresh... Mistakes were assumed to be the fault of the commander.* [2] VERB If someone **assumes** power or responsibility,

they take power or responsibility. *It is usually the woman who assumes overall care of the baby.* [3] VERB If you **assume** a particular expression, quality, or way of behaving, you start to look or behave in this way. *His face assumed a weary expression.*

assuming /ə'sjuːmɪŋ, AM -'suːm-/. CONJ You use **assuming** or **assuming that** when you are supposing that something is true, so that you can think about what the consequences would be. *Assuming he's still alive, what is he doing now?*

assumption /ə'sʌmpʃən/ **assumptions.** N-C If you make an **assumption**, you suppose that something is true, sometimes wrongly. ...*their assumption that all men and women think alike.*

assurance /ə'ʃʊərəns/ **assurances.** [1] N-VAR If you give someone an **assurance** about something, you say that it is the case, in order to make them less worried. *He gave written assurance that he would start work at once.* [2] N-U If you do something with **assurance**, you do it with confidence and certainty. *Masur led the orchestra with assurance.*

assure /ə'ʃʊə/ **assures, assuring, assured.** [1] VERB If you **assure** someone that something is true or will happen, you tell them that it is the case, to make them less worried. *I can assure you that the animals are well cared for.* [2] VERB To **assure** someone of something means to make certain that they will get it. *The series is assured of success.*

assured /ə'ʃʊəd/. ADJ Someone who is **assured** is very confident and relaxed. *It was an assured performance.*

asterisk /'æstərɪsk/ **asterisks.** N-C An **asterisk** is the symbol *.

asthma /'æsmə, AM 'æz-/. N-U **Asthma** is an illness which affects the chest and makes breathing difficult.

asthmatic /æs'mætɪk, AM æz-/. N-C & ADJ An **asthmatic** or someone who is **asthmatic** suffers from asthma.

astonish /ə'stɒnɪʃ/ **astonishes, astonishing, astonished.** VERB If someone or something **astonishes** you, they surprise you very much. ◆**astonished** ADJ *I was shocked and astonished by his stupidity.*

astonishing /ə'stɒnɪʃɪŋ/. ADJ Something that is **astonishing** is very surprising. ◆**astonishingly** ADV ...*an astonishingly beautiful young woman.*

astonishment /ə'stɒnɪʃmənt/. N-U **Astonishment** is a feeling of great surprise. *She looked at her husband in astonishment.*

astound /ə'staʊnd/ **astounds, astounding, astounded.** VERB If something **astounds** you, you are amazed by it. ◆**astounding** ADJ ...*an astounding discovery.*

astray /ə'streɪ/ [PHRASES] ● If you **are led astray** by someone or something, they make you behave badly or foolishly. *He was led astray by this older woman.* ● If something **goes astray**, it gets lost. *Many items of mail being sent to her have gone astray.*

astride /ə'straɪd/. PREP If you sit or stand **astride** something, you sit or stand with one leg on each side of it. ...*three youths who stood astride their bicycles.*

astrology /ə'strɒlədʒi/. N-U **Astrology** is the study of the movements of the planets, sun, moon, and stars in the belief that they can influence people's lives. ◆**astrologer, astrologers** N-C *He consulted an astrologer.*

astronaut /'æstrənɔːt/ **astronauts**. N-C An **astronaut** is a person who travels in a spacecraft.

astronomical /ˌæstrə'nɒmɪkəl/. ADJ If you describe an amount as **astronomical**, you are emphasizing that it is very large. *The cost will be astronomical.*

astronomy /ə'strɒnəmi/. N-U **Astronomy** is the scientific study of the stars, planets, and other natural objects in space. ◆**astronomer, astronomers** N-C *...an amateur astronomer.*

astute /ə'stjuːt, AM ə'stuːt/. ADJ Someone who is **astute** is clever and skilful at understanding behaviour and situations. *She was politically astute. ...astute business decisions.*

asylum /ə'saɪləm/ **asylums**. ① N-C An **asylum** is a mental hospital. ② N-U **Asylum** is protection given to foreigners who have left their own country for political reasons. *He applied for asylum in 1987.*

at /ət, STRONG æt/. ① PREP You use **at** to say where something happens or is situated. *We had dinner at a restaurant. ...muscles at the back of the thigh... Graham was already at the door... I majored in psychology at Hunter College.* ② PREP If you look at something or someone, you look towards them. If you direct something **at** someone, you direct it towards them. *He looked at Michael and laughed... They threw petrol bombs at the police.* ③ PREP You use **at** to say when something happens. *We closed our offices at 2:00 p.m... He only sees her at Christmas.* ④ PREP You use **at** to express a rate, frequency, level, or price. *I drove back down the highway at normal speed... Oil prices were closing at $19.76 a barrel.* ⑤ PREP If you are working **at** something, you are dealing with it. If you are aiming **at** something, you are trying to achieve it. *She has worked hard at her marriage. ...a $1.04m grant aimed at improving student performance.* ⑥ PREP If something is done at someone's command or invitation, it is done as a result of it. *I visited Japan in 1987 at the invitation of the Foreign Minister.* ⑦ PREP You use **at** to say that someone or something is in a particular state or condition. *Their countries had been at war for nearly six weeks.* ⑧ PREP You use **at** to say how something is done. *...shots fired at random from a minibus... Mr Martin was taken out of his car at gunpoint.* ⑨ PREP If you are good at something, you do it well. If you are bad at something, you do it badly. ⑩ PREP If you are delighted, pleased, or appalled **at** something, that is the effect it has on you.

ate /et, eɪt/. **Ate** is the past tense of **eat**.

atheism /'eɪθiɪzəm/. N-U **Atheism** is the belief that there is no God. ◆**atheist** /'eɪθiɪst/ **atheists** N-C *...a confirmed atheist.*

athlete /'æθliːt/ **athletes**. N-C An **athlete** is a person who takes part in athletics competitions.

athletic /æθ'letɪk/. ① ADJ BEFORE N **Athletic**

means relating to athletes and athletics. ② ADJ An **athletic** person is fit, healthy, and active.

athletics /æθ'letɪks/. N-U **Athletics** consists of sports such as running, the high jump, and the javelin.

atlas /'ætləs/ **atlases**. N-C An **atlas** is a book of maps.

atmosphere /'ætməsfɪə/ **atmospheres**. ① N-C A planet's **atmosphere** is the layer of air or other gas around it. ◆**atmospheric** /ˌætməs'ferɪk/ ADJ *...atmospheric pressure.* ② N-C The **atmosphere** of a place is the air that you breathe there. *...the smoky atmosphere of the gaming room.* ③ N-SING The **atmosphere** of a place is the general impression that you get of it. *We try and provide a very homely atmosphere.*

atom /'ætəm/ **atoms**. N-C An **atom** is the smallest possible amount of a chemical element.

atomic /ə'tɒmɪk/. ADJ BEFORE N **Atomic** means relating to atoms or to the power produced by splitting atoms. *...atomic particles. ...an atomic bomb.*

atrocious /ə'trəʊʃəs/. ADJ If you describe something as **atrocious**, you mean it is extremely bad and unpleasant. *The food here is atrocious. ...atrocious weather conditions.*

atrocity /ə'trɒsɪti/ **atrocities**. N-VAR An **atrocity** is a very cruel, shocking action. *Rebel forces have committed atrocities against civilians.*

attach /ə'tætʃ/ **attaches, attaching, attached**. ① VERB If you **attach** something to an object, you join it or fasten it to the object. *We attach labels to things before we file them away... Don't forget to attach the completed entry form.* ② VERB If you **attach** a quality to something or someone, you consider that they have that quality. *We attach great importance to the food at all our hotels.*

attached /ə'tætʃt/. ADJ AFTER LINK-V If you are **attached to** someone or something, you are very fond of them. *She is very attached to her family.*

attachment /ə'tætʃmənt/ **attachments**. ① N-VAR An **attachment** to someone or something is a fondness for them. *Mother and child form a close attachment.* ② N-C An **attachment** is a device that can be fixed onto a machine in order to enable it to do different jobs. *...a close-up lens attachment for your camera.*

attack /ə'tæk/ **attacks, attacking, attacked**. ① VERB & N-VAR To **attack** a person or place, or to launch an **attack** on them, means to try to hurt or damage them using physical violence. *I thought he was going to attack me... He commanded his troops to attack. ...a vicious attack by a gang of youths... The police came under attack.* ◆**attacker, attackers** N-C *She struggled with her attacker.* ② N-C An **attack** of an illness is a short period in which you suffer badly from it. *...an attack of asthma.* ③ VERB & N-VAR If you **attack** a person, belief, or idea, or if you launch an **attack** on them, you criticize them strongly. *The union has attacked the plan... He attacked greedy bosses for awarding themselves big rises. ...his response to attacks on his work.* ④ VERB If you **attack** a job or a problem, you start to deal with it in an energetic way. *Parents shouldn't attack the problem on their own.*

5 VERB In a game such as football, when players **attack**, they try to score. **6** See also **counter-attack, heart attack**.

attain /əˈteɪn/ **attains, attaining, attained.**
VERB If you **attain** something, you gain it, often after a lot of effort; FORMAL. *Jim is halfway to attaining his pilot's licence.* ♦ **attainment** N-U *...the attainment of independence.*

attempt /əˈtempt/ **attempts, attempting, attempted.** **1** VERB & N-C If you **attempt** to do something or **attempt** it, or if you make an **attempt** to do it, you try to do it. *They are accused of attempting to murder British soldiers... He attempted a brave smile. ...a deliberate attempt to mislead people.* ♦ **attempted** ADJ BEFORE N *...a case of attempted murder.* **2** N-C If someone makes an **attempt on** a person's life, they try to kill that person. *There were several attempts on her life.*

attend /əˈtend/ **attends, attending, attended.** **1** VERB If you **attend** a meeting or other event, you are present at it; FORMAL. *Thousands of people attended the funeral... They had been invited but were not expected to attend.* ♦ **attendance** N-U *...his lack of attendance at classes.* **2** VERB If you **attend** an institution such as a school or church, you go to it regularly; FORMAL. *They attended college together.* **3** VERB If you **attend to** something, you deal with it. *The staff will helpfully attend to your needs.*

attendance /əˈtendəns/ **attendances.** N-VAR The **attendance** at an event is the number of people who are present there. *...falling church attendances.*

attendant /əˈtendənt/ **attendants.** **1** N-C An **attendant** is someone whose job is to serve people, for example in a petrol station or a cloakroom. **2** ADJ You use **attendant** to describe something that results from or is connected to a thing already mentioned. *Mr Brady's victory, and all the attendant publicity.*

attention /əˈtenʃən/ **1** N-U If something has your **attention** or if you are **paying attention** to it, you have noticed it and are interested in it. *A gleam of light had attracted his attention... They have sought to draw world attention to human rights abuses... He never paid much attention to his audience.* **2** N-U If something needs **attention**, it needs care or action. *If you are badly burnt, seek medical attention.*

attentive /əˈtentɪv/ **1** ADJ If you are **attentive**, you watch or listen carefully. *...an attentive audience.* ♦ **attentively** ADV *He listened attentively.* **2** ADJ Someone who is **attentive** is helpful and polite. *He is attentive to his wife.*

attest /əˈtest/ **attests, attesting, attested.** VERB To **attest** something or to **attest** to it means to show that it is true; FORMAL. *Police records attest to his long history of violence... I can attest that this approach is effective.*

attic /ˈætɪk/ **attics.** N-C An **attic** is a room at the top of a house, just below the roof.

attitude /ˈætɪtjuːd, AM -tuːd/ **attitudes.** N-VAR Your **attitude** to something is the way you think and feel about it. *...the general change in attitude towards handicapped people. ...negative attitudes to work.*

attorney /əˈtɜːni/ **attorneys.** N-C In American English, an **attorney** is a lawyer.

attract /əˈtrækt/ **attracts, attracting, attracted.** **1** VERB If someone or something **attracts** you, they have qualities which make it easy for you to like or admire them. *The theory attracted him by its logic... What first attracted me to her was her incredible experience of life.* ♦ **attracted** ADJ *I wasn't deeply attracted to him.* **2** VERB If something **attracts** attention, publicity, or support, it gets it. *His country would also like to attract investment from private companies.* **3** VERB If something **attracts** people or animals, it has features that make them want to go to it. *The Cardiff Bay project is attracting many visitors.* **4** VERB If something magnetic **attracts** an object, it causes the object to move towards it.

attraction /əˈtrækʃən/ **attractions.** **1** N-C An **attraction** is a feature which makes something interesting or desirable. *...America's top tourist attraction, Disney World... What's the attraction of trains and train books?* **2** N-U **Attraction** is a feeling of liking someone. *...our level of attraction to the opposite sex.*

attractive /əˈtræktɪv/ **1** ADJ An **attractive** person or thing is pleasant to look at. *He was immensely attractive to women... The flat was small but attractive.* ♦ **attractiveness** N-U *...the attractiveness of the region.* ● See note at **beautiful.** **2** ADJ You say that something is **attractive** when it seems desirable. *Making easy money has always been an attractive proposition.*

attribute, attributes, attributing, attributed. **1** VERB /əˈtrɪbjuːt/ If you **attribute** something to a person, thing, or event, you believe that they cause it or have it; FORMAL. *Women tend to attribute their success to luck... People were beginning to attribute superhuman qualities to him.* **2** VERB If a piece of writing or a remark **is attributed to** someone, people say that that person created it or said it. *...a play attributed to William Shakespeare.* **3** N-C /ˈætrɪbjuːt/ An **attribute** is a quality or feature. *Cruelty is a normal attribute of human behaviour.*

aubergine /ˈəʊbəʒiːn/ **aubergines.** N-VAR An **aubergine** is a vegetable with a smooth purple skin.

auburn /ˈɔːbən/. ADJ **Auburn** hair is reddish brown.

auction /ˈɔːkʃən/ **auctions, auctioning, auctioned.** **1** N-VAR An **auction** is a sale where goods are sold to the person who offers the highest price. *Lord Salisbury bought the picture at auction.* **2** VERB If something **is auctioned**, it is sold in an auction. *We'll auction them for charity.*
▶ **auction off.** PHR-VERB If you **auction off** a number of things, you get rid of them all by selling them at an auction. *They're coming to auction off my farm.*

auctioneer /ˌɔːkʃəˈnɪə/ **auctioneers.** N-C An **auctioneer** is a person in charge of an auction.

audacious /ɔːˈdeɪʃəs/. ADJ Something or someone that is **audacious** is very daring and takes a lot of risks. *...an audacious plan to win the presidency.* ♦ **audacity** /ɔːˈdæsɪti/ N-U *He had* the audacity to make a 200-1 bet on himself to win.

audible /'ɔːdɪbəl/. ADJ An **audible** sound can be heard. ♦**audibly** ADV *Hugh sighed audibly.*

audience /'ɔːdɪəns/ **audiences**. [1] N-C The **audience** is all the people who are watching or listening to a play, concert, film, or programme. *The entire audience broke into loud applause.* [2] N-C You can use **audience** to refer to the people who read someone's books or hear about their ideas. *...books that are accessible to a general audience.*

audio /'ɔːdiəʊ/. ADJ BEFORE N **Audio** equipment is used for recording and reproducing sound. *...audio tapes.*

audit /'ɔːdɪt/ **audits, auditing, audited.** VERB & N-C When an accountant **audits** an organization's accounts or conducts an **audit** on them, he or she examines them to make sure that they are correct. ♦**auditor, auditors** N-C *...the group's internal auditors.*

audition /ɔː'dɪʃən/ **auditions, auditioning, auditioned.** N-C & VERB If someone does an **audition**, or if they **audition**, they give a short performance so that a director or conductor can decide if they are good enough to be in a play, film, or orchestra. You can also say that a director or conductor **auditions** someone. *He made a mess of his audition... She wrote to Paramount Studios and asked if they would audition her.*

auditorium /ˌɔːdɪ'tɔːriəm/ **auditoriums** (or **auditoria** /ˌɔːdɪ'tɔːriə/). N-C In a theatre or concert hall, the **auditorium** is the part of the building where the audience sits.

augment /ɔːg'ment/ **augments, augmenting, augmented.** VERB To **augment** something means to make it larger by adding something to it; FORMAL. *...searching for a way to augment the family income.*

August /'ɔːgəst/. N-U **August** is the eighth month of the year.

aunt /ɑːnt, ænt/ **aunts.** N-C Your **aunt** is the sister of your mother or father, or the wife of your uncle. *...Aunt Vera.*

auntie (or **aunty**) /'ɑːnti, 'ænti/ **aunties.** N-C **Auntie** means the same as **aunt**; INFORMAL.

au pair /əʊ 'peə, AM ˌɔː -/ **au pairs.** N-C An **au pair** is a young person who lives with a family in a foreign country in order to learn their language and help around the house.

aura /'ɔːrə/ **auras.** N-C An **aura** is a quality or feeling that appears to surround a person or place. *She had an aura of authority.*

aural /'ɔːrəl, 'aʊrəl/. ADJ **Aural** means related to the sense of hearing. *...astonishing visual and aural effects.*

auspices /'ɔːspɪsɪz/. PHRASE If something is done **under the auspices of** a person or organization, it is done with their support; FORMAL. *...a conference held in 1961 under British auspices.*

austere /ɔː'stɪə/. [1] ADJ Something that is **austere** is plain and not decorated. ♦**austerity** /ɔː'sterɪti/ N-U *...the austerity of the priest's coat.* [2] ADJ An **austere** person is strict and serious. *...a rather austere, distant, somewhat cold person.* [3] ADJ An **austere** way of life is rather

harsh, with no luxuries. *The life of the troops was still comparatively austere.* ♦**austerity** N-U *...the years of austerity which followed the war.*

authentic /ɔː'θentɪk/. ADJ If something is **authentic**, it is genuine or accurate. *...authentic Italian food.* ♦**authenticity** /ˌɔːθen'tɪsɪti/ N-U *...factors that have cast doubt on the statue's authenticity.*

author /'ɔːθə/ **authors.** [1] N-C The **author** of a piece of writing is the person who wrote it. *...Rick Rogers, the author of the report.* [2] N-C An **author** is a person whose occupation is writing books. *Tolstoy's my favourite author.*

authorise /'ɔːθəraɪz/. See **authorize**.

authoritarian /ɔːˌθɒrɪ'teəriən, AM -'tɔːr-/ **authoritarians.** N-C & ADJ An **authoritarian** or an **authoritarian** person wants to control other people rather than letting them decide things themselves; used showing disapproval. *...authoritarian governments.*

authoritative /ɔː'θɒrɪtətɪv, AM ə'θɔːrɪtetɪv/. [1] ADJ An **authoritative** statement or piece of writing is based on a complete knowledge of the subject. *...the first authoritative study of polio.* ♦**authoritatively** ADV *I can't speak authoritatively on that.* [2] ADJ An **authoritative** person seems powerful and in control; used showing approval. *...a calm and authoritative voice.*

authority /ɔː'θɒrɪti, AM -'tɔːr-/ **authorities.** [1] N-C An **authority** is an official organization that has the power to make decisions. You can refer generally to these organizations, especially government ones, as **the authorities**. *...the Health Education Authority. ...a pretext for the authorities to cancel the elections.* [2] N-U If you have **authority** to do something, you have been given the power or permission to do it. *The judge had no authority to order a second trial... The bank changed my current account to a business account without my authority.* [3] N-C Someone who is an **authority on** a subject knows a lot about it. *...a world authority on heart-diseases.*

authorize (BR also **authorise**) /'ɔːθəraɪz/ **authorizes, authorizing, authorized.** VERB If someone **authorizes** something, they give their official permission for it to happen. *Only the President could authorize the use of the atomic bomb... The police have been authorized to break up any large gatherings.* ♦**authorization, authorizations** N-VAR *We didn't have authorization to go.*

autobiography /ˌɔːtəbaɪ'ɒgrəfi/ **autobiographies.** N-C Your **autobiography** is an account of your life, which you write yourself. ♦**autobiographical** /ˌɔːtəbaɪə'græfɪkəl/ ADJ *...a highly autobiographical novel.*

autograph /'ɔːtəgrɑːf, -græf/ **autographs, autographing, autographed.** N-C & VERB If a famous person puts their **autograph** on something, or if they **autograph** it, they write their signature on it for you. *They asked for his autograph. ...an autographed photo.*

automated /'ɔːtəmeɪtɪd/. ADJ An **automated** factory, office, or process uses machines to do the work instead of people.

automatic /ˌɔːtə'mætɪk/ **automatics.** [1] ADJ & N-C An **automatic** machine can keep running without someone operating its controls. You can refer to an automatic gun, car, or washing machine as an **automatic**. *Modern trains have automatic doors... The weapons were automatics.* ♦**automatically** ADV *...equipment to automatically bottle the wine.* [2] ADJ An **automatic** action is one that you do without thinking about it. *His response was automatic.* ♦**automatically** ADV *He switched automatically into interview mode.* [3] ADJ If something such as an action or a punishment is **automatic**, it happens as the normal result of something else. *Israel offers automatic citizenship to all Jews who want it.* ♦**automatically** ADV *Many loan application forms automatically add on insurance.*

automobile /ˈɔːtəməbiːl, AM -məʊˈbiːl/ **automobiles.** N-C In American English, cars are sometimes called **automobiles**.

autonomy /ɔːˈtɒnəmi/ N-U If a country, person, or group has **autonomy**, they control themselves rather than being controlled by others. *Activists stepped up their demands for local autonomy.* ♦**autonomous** ADJ *...the autonomous regional government of Andalucia.*

autopsy /ˈɔːtɒpsi/ **autopsies.** N-C An **autopsy** is an examination of a dead body by a doctor in order to discover the cause of death.

autumn /ˈɔːtəm/ **autumns.** N-VAR In British English, **autumn** is the season between summer and winter. The American word is **fall**. *The best time to visit is in autumn... She died last autumn.*

auxiliary /ɔːgˈzɪljəri, AM -ləri/ **auxiliaries.** [1] N-C & ADJ BEFORE N An **auxiliary**, or an **auxiliary** staff member, is a person who is employed to assist other people, often in the health service or the armed forces. *...nursing auxiliaries.* [2] ADJ BEFORE N **Auxiliary** equipment is extra equipment that is available for use when necessary. *...auxiliary fuel tanks.* [3] N-C In grammar, the **auxiliary verbs** are 'be', 'have', and 'do'. They are used with a main verb to form tenses, negatives and questions.

avail /əˈveɪl/ PHRASE If an action is **to no avail**, it does not achieve what you want. *His efforts were to no avail... Matt fought back but to little avail.*

available /əˈveɪləbəl/ [1] ADJ If something is **available**, you can use it or obtain it. *Breakfast is available to fishermen from 6 a.m... There are three small boats available for hire. ...the best available information.* ♦**availability** N-U *...the easy availability of guns.* [2] ADJ AFTER LINK-V Someone who is **available** is free to talk to you or spend time with you. *Mr Leach is on holiday and was not available for comment.*

avalanche /ˈævəlɑːntʃ, -læntʃ/ **avalanches.** [1] N-C An **avalanche** is a large mass of snow or rock that falls down the side of a mountain. [2] N-SING You can refer to a large quantity of things that arrive or happen at the same time as an **avalanche** of them. *The newcomer was greeted with an avalanche of publicity.*

avant-garde /ˌævɒ̃ ˈgɑːd/ ADJ **Avant-garde** theatre or writing is modern and experimental. *...avant-garde concert music.*

avenge /əˈvendʒ/ **avenges, avenging, avenged.** VERB If you **avenge** a wrong or harmful act, you hurt or punish the person who did it; FORMAL. *He was trying to avenge the death of his friend.*

avenue /ˈævɪnjuː, AM -nuː/ **avenues.** [1] N-C An **avenue** is a wide road, with shops or houses on each side. *...the most expensive stores on Park Avenue.* [2] N-C An **avenue** is a way of getting something done. *...potential avenues of investigation.*

average /ˈævərɪdʒ/ **averages, averaging, averaged.** [1] N-C & ADJ BEFORE N An **average**, or an **average** amount, is the result you get when you add several amounts together and divide the total by the number of amounts. *The boats remain at sea for an average of ten days... The average age was 63.* [2] PHRASE You say **on average** to indicate that a number is the average of several numbers. *Women are, on average, paid 25 per cent less than men.* [3] VERB To **average** a particular amount means to be that amount as an average over a period of time. *We averaged 42 miles per hour.* [4] ADJ & N-SING Something that is **average** or **the average** is normal in quality or amount for a particular group of things or people. *His first novel is much, much better than the average novel. ...what is found in an average British dustbin.*

aversion /əˈvɜːʃən, AM -ʒən/ **aversions.** N-VAR If you have an **aversion** to someone or something, you dislike them very much; FORMAL. *I've always had an aversion to being part of a group.*

avert /əˈvɜːt/ **averts, averting, averted.** [1] VERB If you **avert** something unpleasant, you prevent it from happening. *Talks with the teachers' union have averted a strike.* [2] VERB If you **avert** your eyes, you look away from something.

aviation /ˌeɪviˈeɪʃən/ N-U **Aviation** is the operation and production of aircraft.

avid /ˈævɪd/ ADJ You use **avid** to describe someone who is very enthusiastic about something. *He's an avid reader.* ♦**avidly** ADV *...a most entertaining magazine, which I read avidly each month.*

avocado /ˌævəˈkɑːdəʊ/ **avocados.** N-VAR An **avocado** is a fruit in the shape of a pear with a dark green skin and a large stone inside it.

avoid /əˈvɔɪd/ **avoids, avoiding, avoided.** [1] VERB If you **avoid** something unpleasant that might happen, you take action in order to prevent it from happening. *...emergency action to avoid a disaster... Drink lots of water to avoid becoming dehydrated.* [2] VERB If you **avoid** doing something, you make a deliberate effort not to do it. *I avoid working in places which are too public... He fled to Costa Rica to avoid military service.* ♦**avoidance** N-U *...tips regarding health maintenance and stress avoidance.*

> When you try not to do something, you say that you **avoid doing it**, not that you 'avoid to do it'. *This leaflet tells you how to avoid getting ill.*
> If you want to suggest that you cannot stop yourself from doing something, you

should use the expression **can't help**.
*I'm sorry, I can't help being suspicious...
Nobody liked her to cough, but she
couldn't help it.*

3 VERB If you **avoid** someone or something,
you try not to have contact with them. *She
thought he was trying to avoid her.* **4** VERB If a
person or vehicle **avoids** someone or something, they change the direction they are moving in, so that they do not hit them. *She
dashed across the road to avoid an oncoming
car.*

await /ə'weɪt/ **awaits, awaiting, awaited.**
1 VERB If you **await** someone or something,
you wait for them; FORMAL. *We awaited the arrival of the chairman.* **2** VERB Something that
awaits you is going to happen to you in the future; FORMAL. *A nasty surprise awaited them.*

awake /ə'weɪk/ **awakes, awaking, awoke,
awoken.** **1** ADJ AFTER LINK-V If you are **awake**,
you are not sleeping. If you are **wide awake**,
you are fully awake. **2** VERB When you **awake**,
or when something **awakes** you, you wake up;
LITERARY. *The sound of many voices awoke her.*

awaken /ə'weɪkən/ **awakens, awakening,
awakened.** **1** VERB To **awaken** a feeling in a
person means to cause them to have this feeling; FORMAL. *...struggling to awaken people's interest in local issues.* ♦**awakening,
awakenings** N-C *...the awakening of national
consciousness in people.* **2** VERB When you
awaken, or when something **awakens** you, you
wake up; LITERARY.

award /ə'wɔːd/ **awards, awarding, awarded.**
1 N-C An **award** is a prize or certificate you get
for doing something well. *...the Booker Prize,
Britain's top award for fiction.* **2** VERB If you
are awarded something, you get a prize or certificate for doing something well. *The Mayor
awarded him a medal of merit.* **3** VERB If a
judge or referee **awards** someone something,
they decide that a sum of money should be
given to the person. *A High Court judge had
awarded him £6 million damages.* **4** N-C An
award is a sum of money that a judge or referee decides should be given to someone.
...workmen's compensation awards.

aware /ə'weə/ **1** ADJ AFTER LINK-V If you are
aware of a fact or situation, you know about it.
*Smokers are well aware of the dangers to their
own health... We are aware that we might lose
our jobs.* ♦**awareness** N-U *...general awareness
about bullying.* **2** ADJ AFTER LINK-V If you are
aware of something, you realize that it is present or is happening because you hear it, see it,
smell it, or feel it. *She was acutely aware of the
noise of the city.* **3** ADJ AFTER LINK-V Someone
who is **aware** notices events that are happening around them. *They are politically very
aware.*

awash /ə'wɒʃ/ ADJ AFTER LINK-V If an area or a
floor is **awash**, there is a lot of water on it.
Slum areas are awash with mud and sewage.

away /ə'weɪ/ **1** ADV If you move **away** from a
place, you move so that you are no longer
there. If you are **away**, you are not in the usual
place. *He walked away from his car... The waitress whipped the plate away... Jason was away*
on a business trip. **2** ADV If you put something
away, you put it in a safe place. *All her letters
were carefully filed away... I have $100m hid-
den away.* **3** PREP & ADV If something is **away**
from a person or place, it is at a distance from
that person or place. *The two women were sitting as far away from each other as possible...
The nearest river was four miles away.* • See
note at **far**. **4** ADJ BEFORE N & ADV When a sports
team plays an **away** game, or when it plays
away, it plays at its opponents' ground. **5** ADV
You can use **away** to say that something slowly
disappears, or changes so that it is no longer
the same. *So much snow has already melted
away... The Liberal Democrats' support fell
away.* **6** ADV You use **away** to talk about future
events. For example, if an event is a week
away, it will happen in a week. **7** ADV **Away** is
used to emphasize that an action is continuous or repeated. *He would often be working
away on his word processor.* **8** **right away**: see
right. • **far and away**: see **far**.

awe /ɔː/ **awes, awed.** N-U & VERB **Awe** is the respect and amazement that you feel when you
are faced with something wonderful and rather frightening. When you have this feeling
you are **in awe of it** or **are awed** by it. *She
gazed in awe at the great stones... I am still
awed by David's courage.*

awesome /'ɔːsəm/ ADJ Something that is **awesome** is very impressive and often frightening.
The responsibility is awesome.

awful /'ɔːfʊl/ **1** ADJ If you say that something
is **awful**, you mean that it is very bad. *...the
same awful jokes... Her injuries were massive.
It was awful... I hardly slept at all and felt pretty awful.* **2** ADJ BEFORE N You can use **awful** to
emphasize how large an amount or how long a
time is; INFORMAL. *I've got an awful lot of work
to do.*

awfully /'ɔːfʊli/ ADV You use **awfully** to emphasize how much of a quality someone or something has; INFORMAL. *The caramel looks awfully
good... I'm awfully sorry.*

awhile /ə'waɪl/ ADV **Awhile** means for a short
time; AMERICAN. *He worked awhile as a pharmacist in Cincinnati.*

awkward /'ɔːkwəd/ **1** ADJ An **awkward** situation is embarrassing and difficult to deal with.
If you feel **awkward**, you feel embarrassed and
shy. *It was a bit awkward for me. ...awkward
questions.* ♦**awkwardly** ADV *Awkwardly, we
took our places.* **2** ADJ Something that is **awkward** to use or carry is difficult to use or carry
because of its design. An **awkward** job is difficult to do. *It was small but heavy enough to
make it awkward to carry.* ♦**awkwardly** ADV
...an awkwardly shaped room. **3** ADJ An **awkward** movement or position is uncomfortable
or clumsy. *Amy made an awkward gesture with
her hands.* ♦**awkwardly** ADV *He fell awkwardly.*
4 ADJ Someone who is **awkward** deliberately
causes problems for other people. *Don't be
awkward.*

awoke /ə'wəʊk/. **Awoke** is the past tense of
awake.

awoken /ə'wəʊkən/. **Awoken** is the past participle of **awake**.

axe (AM **ax**) /æks/ **axes, axing, axed.** [1] N-C An **axe** is a tool used for chopping wood. It consists of a blade attached to the end of a long handle. [2] VERB If someone's job or something such as a service or programme **is axed**, it is ended suddenly.

axis /'æksɪs/ **axes,** /'æksiːz/. [1] N-C An **axis** is an imaginary line through the middle of something. ...*the daily rotation of the earth upon its axis.* [2] N-C An **axis** of a graph is one of the two lines on which the scales of measurement are marked.

B b

babble /'bæbəl/ **babbles, babbling, babbled.** VERB & N-SING If someone **babbles**, they talk in a confused or excited way. You can refer to people's voices as a **babble** of sound when they babble. *Momma babbled on and on. ...the high babble of voices.*

babe /beɪb/ **babes.** [1] N-VOC Some people use **babe** as an affectionate way of addressing someone; INFORMAL. *I'm sorry, babe.* [2] N-C A **babe** is the same as a baby; DATED.

baby /'beɪbi/ **babies.** [1] N-C A **baby** is a very young child that cannot yet walk or talk. [2] N-VOC & N-C Some people use **baby** as an affectionate way of addressing someone; INFORMAL. *He was confused, poor baby.*

babysit (or **baby-sit**) /'beɪbɪsɪt/ **babysits, babysitting, babysat.** VERB If you **babysit** for someone, you look after their children while they are out. *You can take it in turns to babysit.* ◆**babysitter, babysitters** N-C *It's difficult to find a good babysitter.*

bachelor /'bætʃələ/ **bachelors.** N-C A **bachelor** is a man who has never married. *Benfield, a bachelor, enjoyed the respect of his colleagues.*

back 1 adverb uses

back /bæk/. [1] ADV If someone moves **back**, they move in the opposite direction to the one in which they are facing. *She stepped back from the door.* [2] ADV You use **back** to say that someone or something returns to a particular place or state. *I went back to bed... I'll be back as soon as I can... Denise hopes to be back at work soon.* [3] ADV If you give or put something **back**, you return it to the person who had it or to the place where it was before you took it. If you get or take something **back**, you then have it again after not having it for a while. *She handed the knife back... Put it back in the freezer... You'll get your money back.* [4] ADV You use **back** to indicate that you are talking or thinking about something that happened in the past. *The story starts back in 1950. ...that terrorist attack a few years back.* [5] ADV If you do something **back**, you do to someone what they have done to you. *If the phone rings say you'll call back... Lee looked at Theodora. She stared back.* [6] ADV If someone or something is kept or situated **back** from a place, they are at a distance from it. *Keep back from the edge of the platform.* [7] PHRASE If someone moves **back and forth**, they repeatedly move in one direction and then in the opposite direction. *He paced back and forth.*

back 2 opposite of front; noun and adjective uses

back /bæk/ **backs.** [1] N-C Your **back** is the part of your body from your neck to your waist that is on the opposite side to your chest. [2] N-C & ADJ BEFORE N The **back** or the **back** part of something is the part of it that is towards the rear or farthest from the front. ...*the back of her neck. ...the index at the back of the book. ...the back door.* [3] N-C The **back** of a chair is the part that you lean against.

PHRASES • If you do something **behind** someone's **back**, you do it without them knowing about it. • If you **turn** your **back on** someone or something, you ignore them or refuse to help them. • If you are wearing something **back to front**, you are wearing it with the back of it on the front of your body.

back 3 verb uses

back /bæk/ **backs, backing, backed.** [1] VERB If a building **backs** onto something, the back of it faces in the direction of that thing or touches the edge of that thing. ...*a ground floor flat which backs on to a busy street.* [2] VERB When you **back** a vehicle somewhere, or when it **backs** somewhere, it moves backwards. *He got into his car and backed out of the drive.* [3] VERB If you **back** a person or a course of action, you support them. ...*a new witness to back his claim that he is a victim of mistaken identity.* [4] VERB If you **back** someone in a competition, you bet money that they will win. [5] See also **backing**.

▶ **back away.** PHR-VERB If you **back away**, you move away because you are nervous or frightened. *Jupe backed away from the door.*

▶ **back down.** PHR-VERB If you **back down**, you withdraw a claim or demand that you made earlier.

▶ **back off.** PHR-VERB If you **back off**, you move away in order to avoid problems or a fight.

▶ **back out.** PHR-VERB If you **back out**, you decide not to do something that you previously agreed to do. *The Hungarians backed out of the project in 1989.*

▶ **back up.** [1] PHR-VERB If someone or something **backs up** a statement, they supply evidence to show it is true. [2] PHR-VERB If you **back** someone **up**, you help and support them. [3] See also **back-up**.

backbone /'bækbəʊn/ **backbones.** N-C A **backbone** is the column of small linked bones along the middle of your back.

backer /'bækə/ **backers.** N-C A **backer** is someone who gives support or financial help to a person or project.

backfire /ˌbæk'faɪə, AM -'faɪr/ **backfires, backfiring, backfired.** [1] VERB If a plan **backfires**, it has the opposite result to the one that was intended. [2] VERB When a motor vehicle or its engine **backfires**, it produces an explosion in the exhaust pipe.

background /'bækgraʊnd/ **backgrounds.** [1] N-C Your **background** is the kind of family you come from and the kind of education you have had. *She came from a working-class York-shire background.* [2] N-C The **background** to an event or situation consists of the facts that explain what caused it. *...a background of continuing political violence.* [3] N-SING The **background** refers to things, shapes, colours, or sounds that are not the main ones and are often partly hidden by other things. *...the sound of applause in the background... It had a pattern of white flowers on a green background. ...background music.*

backing /'bækɪŋ/ **backings.** [1] N-U **Backing** is money, resources, or support given to a person or organization. *Mr Bach set up his own consulting business with the backing of his old boss.* [2] N-VAR A **backing** is a layer of strong material that is put onto the back of something in order to protect or strengthen it.

backlash /'bæklæʃ/. N-SING A **backlash** against a tendency or recent development in society or politics is a sudden strong reaction against it. *...the backlash against working women.*

backlog /'bæklɒg, AM -lɔːg/ **backlogs.** N-C A **backlog** is a number of things which have not yet been done, but which need to be done. *...a backlog of repairs and maintenance in schools.*

backside /'bæk'saɪd/ **backsides.** N-C Your **backside** is the part of your body that you sit on; INFORMAL.

backstage /'bæk'steɪdʒ/. ADV In a theatre, **backstage** refers to the areas behind the stage. *He went backstage and asked for her autograph.*

'back-up (or **backup**) **back-ups.** [1] N-VAR **Back-up** consists of extra equipment, resources, or people that you can get help or support from if necessary. *Does the company have a 24-hour backup service?* [2] N-VAR If you have something such as a second set of plans as **back-up**, you have arranged for them to be available for use in case the first one does not work. *Computer users should make regular back-up copies.*

backward /'bækwəd/ **backwards.** In American English and in formal British English, **backward** is often used as an adverb instead of **backwards**. [1] ADV & ADJ BEFORE N If you move or look **backwards**, you move or look in the direction that your back is facing. A **backward** movement or look is in the direction that your back is facing. *The diver flipped over backwards into the water... He took two steps backward. ...a backward glance.* [2] ADV If you do something **backwards**, you do it in the opposite way to the usual way. *He works backwards, building a house from the top downwards.* [3] ADJ A **backward** country or society does not have modern industries and machines; used showing disapproval. [4] PHRASE If someone or something moves **backwards and forwards**, they move repeatedly first in one direction and then in the opposite direction. *...people travelling backwards and forwards.*

backwater /'bækwɔːtə/ **backwaters.** N-C A **backwater** is a place or an institution that is isolated from modern ideas or influences; used showing disapproval. *The city was a provincial backwater for more than seven centuries.*

backyard /'bæk'jɑːd/ **backyards.** N-C A **backyard** is an area of land at the back of a house.

bacon /'beɪkən/. N-U **Bacon** is salted or smoked meat taken from the back or sides of a pig.

bacteria /bæk'tɪəriə/. N-PL **Bacteria** are very small organisms which can cause disease. ♦**bacterial** ADJ BEFORE N *Cholera is a bacterial infection.*

bad /bæd/ **worse, worst.** [1] ADJ Something that is **bad** is unpleasant, harmful, or of poor quality. *...a bad day at work... The floods are described as the worst in nearly fifty years.* [2] ADJ You can say that something is **not bad** to mean that it is quite good or acceptable. *The wine wasn't bad.* [3] ADJ Someone who is **bad** at doing something is not very skilful at it. *Dad was really bad at getting to places on time... He was a bad driver.* [4] ADJ If you feel **bad** about something, you feel sorry or guilty about it. *I feel bad that he's doing most of the work.* [5] ADJ If you have a **bad** back, heart, leg, or eye, there is something wrong with it. [6] ADJ **Bad** language is language that contains rude or offensive words. [7] ADJ If you are in a **bad** mood, you are cross and behave unpleasantly to people. [8] PHRASE If you say **'too bad'**, you are indicating in a rather harsh way that nothing can be done to change the situation. *Too bad if you missed the bus.*

bade /bæd, beɪd/. **Bade** is the past tense of some senses of **bid**.

badge /bædʒ/ **badges.** N-C A **badge** is a small piece of metal or cloth which you attach to your clothes for decoration.

badger /'bædʒə/ **badgers, badgering, badgered.** [1] N-C A **badger** is a wild animal with a white head with two wide black stripes on it. [2] VERB If you **badger** someone, you repeatedly tell them to do something or repeatedly ask them questions.

badly /'bædli/ **worse, worst.** [1] ADV If something is done **badly**, it is done with very little success or effect. *The project was badly managed.* [2] ADV **Badly** is used to say that something bad happens to a great degree. *...fires which badly damaged the prison's chapel... In all twelve people were badly injured... Low exam results will reflect badly on them.* [3] ADV If you need or want something **badly**, you need or want it very much. [4] See also **worse, worst.**

badly 'off, worse off, worst off. ADJ If you are **badly off**, you are in a bad situation or condition, especially financially. *Surely you can't be that badly off... There are people much worse off than me, crippled, or in pain.*

badminton /'bædmɪntən/. N-U **Badminton** is a game played on a rectangular court by two or four players. They hit a feathered object called a shuttlecock across a high net.

bad-'tempered. ADJ Someone who is **badtempered** is not very cheerful and gets angry easily. *I became bad tempered and tearful with my boyfriend.* ● See note at **angry**.

baffle /'bæfəl/ **baffles, baffling, baffled.** VERB If something **baffles** you, you cannot understand it or explain it. *Scientists are baffled by the find.* ◆**baffling** ADJ *...a baffling array of wires.*

bag /bæg/ **bags.** [1] N-C A **bag** is a container made of paper, plastic, or leather which is used to carry things. *...a clear polythene bag. ...a bag of sweets.* [2] N-PL If you have **bags** under your eyes, you have folds of skin there, usually because you have not had enough sleep. [3] PHRASE If you say that something is **in the bag,** you mean that you are certain to get it or achieve it; INFORMAL.

baggage /'bægɪdʒ/. [1] N-U Your **baggage** consists of the suitcases and bags that you take with you when you travel. [2] N-U You can use **baggage** to refer to someone's problems or prejudices. *He's carrying a lot of old emotional baggage.*

baggy /'bægi/. ADJ **Baggy** clothes hang loosely on your body.

bail /beɪl/ **bails, bailing, bailed**; also spelled **bale** for meaning 2, and for meaning 1 of the phrasal verb. [1] VERB & N-U In Britain, if someone who is awaiting trial **is bailed**, or if they are released on **bail**, they are set free until they are due to appear in court, provided someone agrees to pay a sum of money if they fail to appear. *He has been granted bail until the hearing resumes in late September.* [2] VERB If you **bail** water from a boat, you remove it using a container. *We kept her afloat for a couple of hours by bailing frantically.*

▶ **bail out.** [1] PHR-VERB If you **bail** someone **out,** you help them out of a difficult situation, often by giving them money. [2] PHR-VERB If you **bail** someone **out,** you pay bail on their behalf.

bailiff /'beɪlɪf/ **bailiffs.** N-C A **bailiff** is a law officer who makes sure that the decisions of a court are obeyed; BRITISH.

bait /beɪt/ **baits, baiting, baited.** [1] N-U & VERB **Bait** is food which you put on a hook or in a trap in order to catch fish or animals. When you **bait** a hook or trap, you put bait on it. [2] N-U If someone or something is being used as **bait,** they are being used to tempt someone to do something. *He lured the youngsters by using his own children as bait.* [3] VERB If someone **baits** you, they deliberately try to make you angry by teasing you. *The defense lawyers may be able to bait him and get him to act aggressively.*

bake /beɪk/ **bakes, baking, baked.** [1] VERB When you **bake** food, or when it **bakes,** you cook it in the oven without any extra liquid or fat. *Bake the cake for 50 minutes. ...baked potatoes.* [2] VERB When you **bake,** you prepare and mix together ingredients to make cakes, biscuits, or bread. You then put them in the oven to cook. *Mary Rathbun loves to bake... How did you learn to bake cakes?* ◆**baking** N-U *Christine describes her main activities as 'cooking, cleaning, ironing and baking'.* [3] See note at **cook**. ● See also **baking**.

baker /'beɪkə/ **bakers.** N-C A **baker** is a person whose job is to bake and sell bread and cakes.

You also refer to the shop where bread and cakes are sold as a **baker** or a **baker's**.

bakery /'beɪkəri/ **bakeries.** N-C A **bakery** is a building where bread and cakes are baked, or the shop where they are sold.

baking /'beɪkɪŋ/. ADJ & ADV You can use **baking** to describe weather or a place that is very hot indeed. *...a baking July day. ...the baking hot summer of 1969.*

balance /'bæləns/ **balances, balancing, balanced.** [1] VERB If something or someone **balances** somewhere, or if you **balance** them there, they remain steady and do not fall over. *I balanced on the ledge... She had balanced a glass on her chest.* [2] N-U **Balance** is the stability that someone or something has when they are balanced on something. *He lost his balance as his foot slipped on the ice.* [3] N-SING A **balance** is a situation or combination of things in which all the different parts are equal or correct in strength or importance. *...the ecological balance of the forest.* [4] VERB If you **balance** one thing with something different, or if one thing **balances** with another, each of the things has the same strength or importance. *...trying to balance his demanding career with the demands of his wife.* [5] VERB To **balance** a budget or **balance** the books means to make sure that the amount of money that is spent is not greater than the amount that is received. [6] N-C The **balance** in your bank account is the amount of money in it. [7] N-SING The **balance** to be paid on something is the total amount of money which remains to be paid for it. *They were due to pay the balance on delivery.*

PHRASES ● If something is **in the balance,** its future is uncertain. ● You can say **on balance** to indicate that you are stating an opinion only after considering all the relevant facts or arguments. *On balance he agreed with Christine.*

balanced /'bælənst/. [1] ADJ A **balanced** account or report is fair and reasonable. [2] ADJ Something that is **balanced** is pleasing or beneficial because its different parts are in the correct proportions. *...a balanced diet.*

balcony /'bælkəni/ **balconies.** [1] N-C A **balcony** is a platform on the outside of a building with a wall or railing around it. [2] N-C The **balcony** in a theatre or cinema is an upstairs seating area.

bald /bɔːld/ **balder, baldest.** [1] ADJ Someone who is **bald** has little or no hair on the top of their head. ◆**baldness** N-U *He wears a cap to cover a spot of baldness.* [2] ADJ A **bald** tyre has become worn down and it is no longer safe or legal to use. [3] ADJ BEFORE N A **bald** statement has no unnecessary words in it. ◆**baldly** ADV *Phrased so baldly, the point seems obvious.*

balding /'bɔːldɪŋ/. ADJ A **balding** person is beginning to lose the hair on the top of their head.

bale /beɪl/ **bales, baling, baled.** [1] N-C A **bale** of something such as hay or paper is a large quantity tied into a tight bundle. [2] VERB When hay or paper **is baled,** it is tied together in a tight bundle. See also **bail**.

balk (or **baulk**) /bɔːlk, AM bɔːk/, **balks, balking, balked.** VERB If you **balk** at something, you are very reluctant to do it. *Even biology* *undergraduates may balk at animal experiments.*

ball /bɔːl/ **balls.** [1] N-C A **ball** is a round object used in games such as football. [2] N-C A **ball** is something that has a round shape. *Thomas screwed the letter up into a ball.* [3] N-C The **ball** of your foot or on the **ball** of your thumb is the rounded part where your toes join your foot or where your thumb joins your hand. [4] N-C A **ball** is a large formal dance.

PHRASES • If you **are having a ball**, you are having a wonderful time; INFORMAL. • If you start **the ball rolling**, you start something happening.

ballad /'bæləd/ **ballads.** [1] N-C A **ballad** is a slow, romantic, popular song. [2] N-C A **ballad** is a long song or poem which tells a story using simple language.

ballet /'bæleɪ, AM bæ'leɪ/ **ballets.** [1] N-U **Ballet** is a type of artistic dancing with carefully planned movements. [2] N-C A **ballet** is an artistic work performed by ballet dancers.

balloon /bə'luːn/ **balloons, ballooning, ballooned.** [1] N-C A **balloon** is a small, thin, rubber bag that becomes larger when you blow air into it. [2] N-C A **balloon** is a large strong bag filled with gas or hot air, which can carry passengers in a compartment underneath it. [3] VERB When something **balloons**, it quickly becomes bigger. *Her weight ballooned from 8 stone to 11 stone.*

ballot /'bælət/ **ballots, balloting, balloted.** [1] N-C A **ballot** is a secret vote in which people select a candidate in an election, or express their opinion about something. [2] VERB If you **ballot** a group of people, you find out what they think about something by organizing a secret vote. *The union said they will ballot members on whether to strike.*

balm /bɑːm/ **balms.** N-VAR **Balm** is a sweet-smelling oil that is obtained from some tropical trees and is used to make ointments that heal wounds or lessen pain.

bamboo /bæm'buː/ **bamboos.** N-VAR **Bamboo** is a tall tropical plant with hard hollow stems.

ban /bæn/ **bans, banning, banned.** [1] VERB & N-C To **ban** something or place a **ban** on it means to state officially that it must not be done, shown, or used. *Canada will ban smoking in all offices later this year... The General also lifted a ban on political parties.* [2] VERB If you **are banned** from doing something, you are officially prevented from doing it. *He was banned from driving for three years.*

banal /bə'nɑːl, -'næl/. ADJ If you describe something as **banal**, you mean that it is so ordinary that it is not at all effective or interesting. *...a banal conversation.* ◆**banality** /bə'nælɪti/ N-U *...the sheer banality of colonial life.*

banana /bə'nɑːnə, -'næn-/ **bananas.** N-VAR A **banana** is a long curved fruit with a yellow skin.

band /bænd/ **bands, banding, banded.** [1] N-C A **band** is a group of musicians who play jazz, rock, or pop music, or who play brass instruments together. [2] N-C A **band** of people is a group of people who have joined together because they share an interest or belief. *...a band of rebels.* [3] N-C A **band** is a flat narrow strip of

cloth which you wear round your head or wrists, or round a piece of clothing. *...a black arm-band.* [4] N-C A **band** is a strip or loop of metal or other strong material which strengthens something, or which holds several things together. [5] N-C A **band** is a range of numbers or values within a system of measurement. *...a new tax band of 20p in the pound.*

▶ **band together.** PHR-VERB If people **band together**, they act as a group in order to try and achieve something.

bandage /'bændɪdʒ/ **bandages, bandaging, bandaged.** [1] N-C A **bandage** is a long strip of cloth that is tied around a wounded part of someone's body in order to protect or support it. [2] VERB If you **bandage** a wound or part of someone's body, you tie a bandage round it. *...a man with a bandaged head.*

B&'B, B&Bs. See bed and breakfast.

bandit /'bændɪt/ **bandits.** N-C A **bandit** is an armed robber.

bandwagon /'bændwægən/ **bandwagons.** N-C If you say that someone has jumped on the **bandwagon**, you mean that they have become involved in an activity only because it has become fashionable. *Many conservative politicians have jumped on the anti-immigrant bandwagon.*

bang /bæŋ/ **bangs, banging, banged.** [1] N-C A **bang** is a sudden loud noise such as an explosion. [2] VERB If you **bang** something such as a door, or if it **bangs**, it closes suddenly with a loud noise. *The door banged shut behind them.* [3] VERB If you **bang** on something, or if you **bang** it, you hit it so that it makes a loud noise. *I banged on the wall... There is no point in shouting or banging the table... Daryl banged his fist on the desk.* [4] VERB & N-C If you **bang** part of your body against something, you accidentally knock into it and hurt yourself. A **bang** is a knock or blow. *He hurried into the hall, banging his shin against a chair. ...a nasty bang on the head.*

bank /bæŋk/ **banks, banking, banked.** [1] N-C A **bank** is a place where you can keep your money in an account. [2] N-C You use **bank** to refer to a large amount of something, stored for use. For example, a blood **bank** is a store of blood. [3] N-C The **banks** of a river, canal, or lake are the raised areas of ground along its edge. [4] N-C A **bank** of ground is a raised area of it with a flat top and one or two sloping sides. *...a grassy bank.* [5] N-C A **bank** of something is a long high row or mass of it. *...a bank of fog.*

▶ **bank on.** PHR-VERB If you **bank on** something happening, you rely on it happening. *You might be able to get it altered – but don't bank on it.*

banker /'bæŋkə/ **bankers.** N-C A **banker** is someone involved in banking at a senior level.

bank 'holiday, bank holidays. N-C A **bank holiday** is a public holiday; BRITISH.

banking /'bæŋkɪŋ/. N-U **Banking** is the business activity of banks and similar institutions.

banknote (or **bank note**) /'bæŋknəʊt/ **banknotes.** N-C A **banknote** is a piece of paper money. *...coins and banknotes.*

bankrupt /'bæŋkrʌpt/ **bankrupts, bankrupting, bankrupted.** [1] ADJ People or organizations that go **bankrupt** do not have enough money to pay their debts. *He was declared bankrupt after failing to pay a £114m loan guarantee.* [2] VERB To **bankrupt** a person or organization means to make them go bankrupt. *The cost of the court case bankrupted him.* [3] ADJ You use **bankrupt** to say that someone or something is completely without a particular quality. *He thinks that European civilisation is morally bankrupt.*

bankruptcy /'bæŋkrʌptsi/ **bankruptcies.** [1] N-U **Bankruptcy** is the state of being bankrupt. *Many established firms were facing bankruptcy.* [2] N-C A **bankruptcy** is an instance of an organization or person going bankrupt.

banner /'bænə/ **banners.** N-C A **banner** is a long strip of cloth with a message or slogan on it.

banquet /'bæŋkwɪt/ **banquets.** N-C A **banquet** is a grand formal dinner.

banter /'bæntə/. N-U **Banter** is friendly teasing or joking talk.

baptism /'bæptɪzəm/ **baptisms.** N-VAR A **baptism** is a ceremony in which a person is baptized. *...adult baptism.*

baptize (BR also **baptise**) /bæp'taɪz/ **baptizes, baptizing, baptized.** VERB When someone **is baptized,** water is sprinkled on them or they are immersed in water as a sign that they have become a member of the Christian Church.

bar /bɑː/ **bars, barring, barred.** [1] N-C A **bar** is a place where you can buy and drink alcoholic drinks. [2] N-C A **bar** is a counter on which alcoholic drinks are served. *He leaned forward across the bar.* [3] N-C A **bar** is a long, straight, rigid piece of metal. *...an iron bar.* [4] N-C A **bar** of something is a roughly rectangular piece of it. *...a bar of soap.* [5] VERB If you **bar** someone from going somewhere or doing something, you prevent them from going there or doing it. *She stood in the doorway, barring his way out... Many jobs were barred to them.* [6] PREP You can use **bar** to mean 'except'. For example, all the work **bar** the washing means all the work except the washing. FORMAL. [7] N-PROPER The **Bar** is used to refer to the profession of a barrister in England, or of any kind of lawyer in the United States. *Robert was planning to read for the Bar.* [8] N-C In music, a **bar** is one of the several short parts of the same length into which a piece of music is divided. [9] See also **barring.**

PHRASES • If someone is **behind bars,** they are in prison. • You say that there are **no holds barred** when people are competing forcefully, without following any rules in their efforts to win.

barbaric /bɑː'bærɪk/. ADJ **Barbaric** behaviour is extremely cruel. *...the most barbaric form of execution still in existence today.* ◆**barbarism** /'bɑːbərɪzəm/ N-U *...an act of barbarism.* ◆**barbarity** /bɑː'bærɪti/ **barbarities** N-VAR *...the barbarities of the Nazi regime.*

barbecue /'bɑːbɪkjuː/ **barbecues, barbecuing, barbecued.** [1] N-C A **barbecue** is a grill used to cook food outdoors. [2] N-C A **barbecue** is an outdoor party at which people eat food

cooked on a barbecue. [3] VERB If you **barbecue** food, you cook it on a barbecue. *Tuna can be grilled, fried or barbecued. ...barbecued chicken.*

barbed 'wire. N-U **Barbed wire** is strong wire with sharp points sticking out of it, which is used to make fences.

barber /'bɑːbə/ **barbers.** [1] N-C A **barber** is a man whose job is cutting men's hair. [2] N-SING The shop where a barber works is called the **barber's.**

bard /bɑːd/ **bards.** N-C A **bard** is a poet; LITERARY.

bare /beə/ **barer, barest; bares, baring, bared.** [1] ADJ If a part of your body is **bare,** it is not covered by any clothing. *Her feet were bare.* [2] ADJ A **bare** surface is not covered or decorated with anything. *...bare wooden floors.* [3] ADJ If a room, cupboard, or shelf is **bare,** it is empty. *His fridge was bare apart from three very withered tomatoes.* [4] ADJ You use **bare** to talk about the least amount of something or its most basic elements. *...a ship at sea with the bare minimum of crew... She's obviously given them the barest details of her illness.* [5] If you **bare** something, you uncover it and show it; WRITTEN. *She bared her teeth like a dog.*

PHRASES • If someone does something **with** their **bare hands,** they do it without using any weapons or tools. *...using their bare hands to reach the trapped miners.*

barefoot /'beəfut/. ADJ If you are **barefoot** or **barefooted,** you are wearing nothing on your feet.

barely /'beəli/. ADV You use **barely** to say that something is only just true or possible. *Anastasia could barely remember the ride to the hospital... The water had barely come to a simmer when she cracked four eggs into it.*

bargain /'bɑːgɪn/ **bargains, bargaining, bargained.** [1] VERB When people **bargain** with each other, they discuss what each of them will do, pay, or receive. *Shop in small local markets and don't be afraid to bargain.* ◆**bargaining** N-U *The government has called for sensible pay bargaining.* [2] N-C A **bargain** is a formal agreement on what two people will do, pay, or receive. *The treaty was based on a bargain between the French and German governments.* [3] N-C A **bargain** is something which is good value for money, usually because it has been sold at a lower price than normal. *At this price the wine is a bargain.* [4] PHRASE You use **into the bargain** when mentioning an additional quantity, feature, fact, or action, to emphasize that it is also involved. *...designed to save you time and effort, and keep your work surfaces neat and tidy into the bargain.*

▶ **bargain for.** PHR-VERB If someone gets something they had not **bargained for,** or if they get more than they **bargained for,** something happens that they did not expect or something happens to a much greater degree than they had expected.

barge /bɑːdʒ/ **barges, barging, barged.** [1] N-C A **barge** is a narrow boat with a flat bottom, used for carrying heavy loads. [2] VERB If you **barge** into a place or person, you rush into it or push past them in a rude or rough way; INFORMAL. *He barged past her and sprang at*

Gillian... Students tried to barge into the buildings.

baritone /'bærɪtəʊn/ **baritones.** N-C A **baritone** is a man with a fairly deep singing voice.

bark /baːk/ **barks, barking, barked.** [1] VERB & N-C When a dog **barks** or gives a **bark**, it makes a short loud noise. *A small dog barked at a seagull.* [2] N-U **Bark** is the tough material that covers the outside of a tree.

barley /'baːli/. N-U **Barley** is a crop which has seeds that are used in the production of food, beer, and whisky.

barmaid /'baːmeɪd/ **barmaids.** N-C In British English, a **barmaid** is a woman who serves drinks in a bar or pub. The American word is **bartender**.

barman /'baːmən/ **barmen.** N-C In British English, a **barman** is a man who serves drinks in a bar or pub. The American word is **bartender**.

barn /baːn/ **barns.** N-C A **barn** is a building on a farm in which crops or animal food are kept.

barometer /bə'rɒmɪtə/ **barometers.** N-C A **barometer** is an instrument that measures air pressure and shows when the weather is changing. *The barometer was falling.*

baron /'bærən/ **barons.** [1] N-C & N-TITLE A **baron** is a man who is a member of the nobility. [2] N-C You use **baron** to refer to someone who controls a large amount of an industry and who is therefore extremely powerful. ...*drug barons.*

baroness /'bærənes/ **baronesses.** N-C & N-TITLE A **baroness** is a woman who has the same rank as a baron, or who is the wife of a baron.

barracks /'bærəks/. N-C A **barracks** is a building or group of buildings where members of the armed forces live.

barrage /'bærɑːʒ, AM bə'rɑːʒ/ **barrages.** [1] N-C If you get a lot of questions or complaints about something, you can say that you are getting a **barrage** of them. *He was faced with a barrage of angry questions.* [2] N-C A **barrage** is continuous firing on an area with a large number of artillery weapons such as heavy guns and tanks. ...*a barrage of anti-aircraft fire.*

barrel /'bærəl/ **barrels.** [1] N-C A **barrel** is a large round container for liquids or food. Barrels are usually wider in the middle than at the top or bottom. ...*oak barrels.* [2] N-C The **barrel** of a gun is the long metal tube through which the bullet moves when the gun is fired.

barren /'bærən/. ADJ **Barren** land has soil of such bad quality that plants cannot grow on it. ...*a bleak, barren desert.*

barricade /'bærɪkeɪd/ **barricades, barricading, barricaded.** [1] N-C A **barricade** is a line of vehicles or other objects placed across a road or passage to stop people getting past. [2] VERB If people **barricade** a road or passage, they put something across it to stop other people reaching it. *The rioters barricaded streets with piles of blazing tyres.* [3] VERB If you **barricade** yourself inside a room or building, you put something heavy against the door so that other people cannot get in. *The students have barricaded themselves into their dormitory building.*

barrier /'bæriə/ **barriers.** [1] N-C A **barrier** is a fence or wall that prevents people or things from moving from one area to another. [2] N-C A **barrier** is something such as a law or policy that makes it difficult or impossible for something to happen. *Duties and taxes are the most obvious barrier to free trade.*

barring /'baːrɪŋ/. PREP You use **barring** to indicate that the person, thing, or event that you are mentioning is an exception to the point that you are making. *Barring accidents, I believe they will succeed.*

barrister /'bærɪstə/ **barristers.** N-C A **barrister** is a lawyer who represents people in the higher courts of law; BRITISH.

bartender /'baːtendə/ **bartenders.** N-C In American English, a **bartender** is a person who serves drinks in a bar. The British word is **barman** or **barmaid**.

barter /'baːtə/ **barters, bartering, bartered.** VERB & N-U If you **barter** goods, you exchange them for other goods, rather than selling them. **Barter** is the act of exchanging goods in this way. *They have been bartering wheat for cotton and timber. ...the old barter system.*

base /beɪs/ **bases, basing, based.** [1] N-C The **base** of something is its lowest edge or part, or the part at which it is attached to something else. ...*a cake tin with a removable base. ...the base of the cliffs.* [2] N-C A position or thing that is a **base** for something is one from which that thing can be developed or achieved. *The family base was crucial to my development.* [3] VERB If you **base** one thing on another thing, or if one thing **is based** on another, the first thing is developed from the second one. *He based his conclusions on the evidence... Three of the new products are based on traditional herbal medicines.* [4] N-C & ADJ Your **base** is the main place where you work, stay, or live. If you **are based** in a particular place, that is the place where you live or do most of your work. *Her base was her home in Scotland... Both firms are based in Kent.* [5] N-VAR A military **base** is a place which part of an army, navy, or air force works from. ...*a British army base near Hanover.*

baseball /'beɪsbɔːl/. N-U **Baseball** is a game played by two teams of nine players. Each player from one team hits a ball with a bat and then tries to run round all four bases before the other team can get the ball back.

basement /'beɪsmənt/ **basements.** N-C The **basement** of a building is a room or rooms partly or completely below ground level, with a room or rooms in it. ...*a damp basement flat.*

bases. [1] /'beɪsɪz/ **Bases** is the plural and the third person singular of **base**. [2] /'beɪsiːz/ **Bases** is the plural of **basis**.

bash /bæʃ/ **bashes, bashing, bashed.** [1] N-C A **bash** is a party or celebration; INFORMAL. ...*one of the biggest showbiz bashes of the year.* [2] VERB If you **bash** someone or something, you hit them hard in a rough way. *I bashed him on the head... Too many golfers try to bash the ball out of sand.*

basic /'beɪsɪk/ **basics.** [1] ADJ & N-PL You use **basic** or the **basics** to describe the most important or the simplest aspects of something. ...*access to justice is a basic right... Let's get* down to basics. ...*teaching the basics of reading, writing and arithmetic.* [2] ADJ **Basic** goods and services are very simple ones which every human being needs. ...*shortages of even the most basic foodstuffs.* ...*the basic needs of food and water.* [3] ADJ AFTER LINK-V An activity, situation, or plan that is **basic** to the achievement or success of something else is necessary for it. *There are certain ethical principles that are basic to all the great religions.* [4] ADJ You describe something as **basic** when it has only the most important features and no luxuries. ...*basic cooking and camping equipment.*

basically /'beɪsɪkli/. ADV You use **basically** to indicate that the most important feature of something is, or to give a general description of something complicated. *He is basically healthy... There are basically three types of club... This gun is designed for one purpose — it's basically to kill people.*

basin /'beɪsən/ **basins.** [1] N-C A **basin** is a deep bowl that you use for holding liquids, or for mixing food in. [2] N-C A **basin** is the same as a **washbasin**. [3] N-C The **basin** of a large river is the area of land around it from which water and streams run down into it. ...*the Amazon basin.*

basis /'beɪsɪs/ **bases** /'beɪsiːz/. [1] N-C The **basis** of something is the central and most important part of it, from which it can be developed. *Technical skill is a fundamental basis for most, if not all, great art.* [2] N-C The **basis** for something is the thing that provides a reason for it. *The idea has its basis in fact.* [3] PHRASE If something happens or is done **on a** particular **basis**, it happens or is done in that way. *We're going to be meeting there on a regular basis... Most members work on a voluntary basis.*

bask /bɑːsk, bæsk/ **basks, basking, basked.** [1] VERB If you **bask** in the sunshine, you lie in it and enjoy its warmth. [2] VERB If you **bask** in someone's approval, favour, or admiration, you thoroughly enjoy it. *For now, though, the company can bask in its success.*

basket /'bɑːskɪt, 'bæs-/ **baskets.** N-C A **basket** is a container made of thin strips of cane woven together.

basketball /'bɑːskɪtbɔːl, 'bæs-/. N-U **Basketball** is a game in which two teams of five players each try to score points by throwing a large ball through a circular net fixed to a metal ring at each end of the court.

bass /beɪs/ **basses.** [1] N-C A **bass** is a man with a deep singing voice. [2] ADJ BEFORE N A **bass** instrument has a range of notes of low pitch. ...*a bass guitar.*

bastion /'bæstiən, AM -tʃən/ **bastions.** N-C If you describe a system or organization as a **bastion** of a particular way of life, you mean that it is important and effective in defending that way of life; LITERARY. ...*a town which had been a bastion of white prejudice.*

bat /bæt/ **bats, batting, batted.** [1] N-C A **bat** is a specially shaped piece of wood that is used for hitting the ball in cricket, baseball, or table tennis. ...*a baseball bat.* [2] VERB When you **bat**, you have a turn at hitting the ball with a bat in cricket or baseball. *Penney also batted well to make 57.* [3] N-C A **bat** is a small flying animal

that looks like a mouse with wings. Bats fly at night.

batch /bætʃ/ **batches.** N-C A **batch** of things or people is a group of them, especially one that is dealt with at the same time. *Bread is baked in batches throughout the day.* ...*the current batch of trainee priests.*

bath /bɑːθ, bæθ/ **baths, bathing, bathed.** [1] N-C In British English, a **bath** is a container which you fill with water and sit in while you wash your body. The American word is **bathtub**. [2] N-C When you have a **bath** or take a **bath**, you wash your body while sitting in a bath filled with water. *I took a long hot bath.* [3] VERB & N-C If you **bath** a child or other person, or if you give them a **bath**, you wash them in a bath. *Don't feel you have to bath your child every day.*

bathe /beɪð/ **bathes, bathing, bathed.** [1] VERB When you **bathe** in a sea, river, or lake, you swim or play there; FORMAL BRITISH. *The water's 45 degrees centigrade, it's so nice to bathe in.* ◆**bathing** N-U ...*bathing beaches.* [2] VERB When you **bathe**, you have a bath; AMERICAN. *At least 60% of us now bathe or shower once a week.* [3] VERB When you **bathe** a wound, you wash it gently. *Bathe the infected area in a salt solution.* [4] VERB If a place is **bathed** in light, it is very bright. *I was led to a small room bathed in soft red light.*

bathroom /'bɑːθruːm, 'bæθ-/ **bathrooms.** [1] N-C A **bathroom** is a room in a house that contains a bath or shower, a washbasin, and sometimes a toilet. [2] N-SING In American English, a **bathroom** is a room in a house or public building that contains a toilet. The usual British word is **toilet**.

bathtub /'bɑːθtʌb, 'bæθ-/ **bathtubs.** N-C In American English, a **bathtub** is a container which you fill with water and sit in while you wash your body. The British word is **bath**.

baton /'bætɒn, AM bə'tɑːn/ **batons.** [1] N-C A **baton** is a stick, for example one which is used by the conductor of an orchestra, or by athletes in a relay race. [2] N-C A **baton** is a short heavy stick which is sometimes used as a weapon by the police.

batsman /'bætsmən/ **batsmen.** N-C In a game of cricket, the **batsman** is the person who is batting.

battalion /bə'tæliən/ **battalions.** N-C A **battalion** is a large group of soldiers consisting of three or more companies.

batter /'bætə/ **batters, battering, battered.** [1] VERB To **batter** someone or something means to hit them many times. ...*who witness fathers battering their mothers.* ...*battered wives... Batter the steaks flat.* [2] N-U **Batter** is a mixture of flour, eggs, and milk used to make pancakes.

battered /'bætəd/. ADJ Something that is **battered** is old, worn, and damaged. ...*a battered leather suitcase.*

battering /'bætərɪŋ/ **batterings.** N-C If something takes a **battering**, it suffers very badly as a result of a particular event or action. *We took an awful battering during the war.*

battery /'bætəri/ **batteries.** [1] N-C **Batteries** are the devices that you put in electrical items to provide the power that makes these devices work. [2] N-C A **battery** of things, people, or events is a large number of them. ...*a battery of journalists and television cameras.*

battle /ˈbætəl/ **battles, battling, battled.**
[1] N-VAR In a war, a **battle** is a fight between armies or between groups of ships or planes. ...*a gun battle*... ...*men who die in battle.* [2] N-C & VERB A **battle** is a conflict in which different people or groups compete for power or try to achieve opposite things. Opposing groups can also **battle** with one another. ...*a major legal battle*... *2,000 fans battled with riot police... The sides must battle again for a quarter-final place.* [3] VERB To **battle** means to try hard to be successful in spite of very difficult circumstances. *Doctors battled throughout the night to save her life... He is battling with a leg injury.* [4] PHRASE If one person or group **does battle** with another, they take part in a battle or contest against them.

battlefield /ˈbætəlfiːld/ **battlefields.** N-C A **battlefield** is a place where a battle is fought.

battleground /ˈbætəlgraʊnd/ **battlegrounds.**
[1] N-C A **battleground** is the same as a **battlefield.** [2] N-C You can refer to a subject over which people disagree or compete as a **battleground.** ...*the battleground of education.*

battleship /ˈbætəlʃɪp/ **battleships.** N-C A **battleship** is a very large, heavily armoured warship.

baulk /bɔːlk, AM bɔːk/. See **balk**.

bawl /bɔːl/ **bawls, bawling, bawled.** [1] VERB If you **bawl,** you shout or sing something loudly and harshly. *Laura and Peter were shouting and bawling at each other.* [2] VERB If a child is **bawling,** it is crying loudly. ...*a bawling baby.*

bay /beɪ/ **bays, baying, bayed.** [1] N-C A **bay** is a part of a coastline where the land curves inwards. ...*San Francisco Bay.* [2] N-C A **bay** is a partly enclosed area used for a particular purpose. *The car reversed into the loading bay.* [3] PHRASE If you **keep** something or someone **at bay,** or **hold** them **at bay,** you prevent them from reaching or affecting you. *Eating oranges keeps colds at bay.* [4] VERB If you say that a number of people **are baying** for something, you mean that they are shouting or calling for it angrily. *The referee ignored voices baying for a penalty.*

bayonet /ˈbeɪənət/ **bayonets.** N-C A **bayonet** is a long sharp blade that can be fixed to the end of a rifle and used as a weapon.

bazaar /bəˈzɑː/ **bazaars.** [1] N-C A **bazaar** is an area with many small shops and stalls, especially in the Middle East and India. [2] N-C A **bazaar** is a sale to raise money for charity.

BC /ˌbiː ˈsiː/. You use **BC** in dates to indicate a number of years or centuries before the year in which Jesus Christ is believed to have been born. ...*the fourth century BC.*

be /bɪ, STRONG biː/ **am, are, is, being, was, were, been.** [1] LINK-VERB You use **be** to introduce more information about the subject, such as its identity, nature, qualities, or position. *She's my mother... Cheney was in Madrid... He's still alive isn't he?* [2] LINK-VERB You use **be,** with 'it' as the subject, in clauses where you are describing something or giving your

judgement of a situation. *Sometimes it is necessary to say no... It's nice having friends to chat to... It's a good idea to avoid refined food.* [3] LINK-VERB You use **be** as a link between a subject and a clause and in certain other clause structures, as exemplified below. *It was me she didn't like... Our greatest problem is convincing me.* [4] LINK-VERB You use **be** in 'there' expressions like **there is** and **there are** to say that something exists or happens. *Clearly there is a problem here... There are very few cars on this street.*

beach /biːtʃ/ **beaches.** N-C A **beach** is an area of sand or pebbles by the sea. ...*a beautiful sandy beach.*

beacon /ˈbiːkən/ **beacons.** N-C A **beacon** is a light or a fire on a hill or tower, which acts as a signal or a warning.

bead /biːd/ **beads.** [1] N-C **Beads** are small pieces of coloured glass, wood, or plastic with a hole through the middle which are used for jewellery or decoration. [2] N-C A **bead** of liquid or moisture is a small drop of it. ...*the beads of sweat on his forehead.*

beak /biːk/ **beaks.** N-C A bird's **beak** is the hard curved or pointed part of its mouth. ...*a black bird with a yellow beak.*

beaker /ˈbiːkə/ **beakers.** [1] N-C A **beaker** is a plastic cup. [2] N-C A **beaker** is a glass or plastic jar which is used in chemistry.

beam /biːm/ **beams, beaming, beamed.** [1] VERB If someone **is beaming,** they are smiling because they are happy; WRITTEN. *The bartender was beaming at him.* [2] VERB If something such as radio signals or television pictures **are beamed** somewhere, or if they **beam** somewhere, they are sent there by means of electronic equipment. *Soon, CMTV will be beaming into British homes. ...beaming radio broadcasts to China.* [3] N-C A **beam** of light is a line of light that shines from an object such as a torch or the sun. [4] VERB If something such as the sun or a lamp **beams** down, it sends light to a place and shines on it. *A sharp white spot-light beamed down on a small stage.* [5] N-C A **beam** is a long thick bar of wood, metal, or concrete, especially one which is used to support the roof of a building. ...*oak beams.*

bean /biːn/ **beans.** [1] N-C **Beans** are the pods of a climbing plant, or the seeds that the pods contain, which are eaten as a vegetable. [2] N-C Beans such as coffee **beans** or cocoa **beans** are the seeds of a plant that is used in the production of coffee and chocolate.

bear /beə/ **bears, bearing, bore, borne.** [1] N-C A **bear** is a large strong wild animal with thick fur and sharp claws. [2] VERB If you **bear** something somewhere, you carry it there; LITERARY. *They bore the oblong hardwood box into the kitchen.* [3] VERB If something **bears** the weight of something else, it supports the weight of that thing. *The ice was not thick enough to bear their weight.* [4] VERB If you **bear** something difficult, you accept it and are able to deal with it. *They will have to bear the misery of living in constant fear... He can't bear to talk about it.* [5] VERB If you **bear** someone a feeling such as love or hate, you feel that emotion towards them; FORMAL. *She bore no ill will. If people didn't like her, too bad.* [6] PHRASE If you **bring** pressure or influence **to bear on** someone, you use it to try and persuade them to do something. *His companions brought pressure to bear on him, urging him to stop wasting money.* [7] **bear the brunt of:** see **brunt**. ● **bear in mind:** see **mind**.

▶ **bear out.** PHR-VERB If someone **bears** someone **out** or **bears out** what they are saying, it supports what they are saying. *Unhappily the facts do not wholly bear out the theory.*

▶ **bear with.** PHR-VERB If you ask someone to **bear with** you, you are asking them to be patient. *Bear with me, Frank, just let me try to explain.*

bearable /'beərəbəl/. ADJ If something is **bearable,** you can accept it, although it is rather unpleasant. *...the small luxuries that made life bearable.*

beard /biəd/ **beards.** N-C A man's **beard** is the hair that grows on his chin and cheeks.

bearded /'biədid/. ADJ A **bearded** man has a beard.

bearer /'beərə/ **bearers.** [1] N-C The **bearer** of something such as a document or a piece of news is the person who has it in their possession, or the person who brings it to you. *Spanish identity documents state the bearer's profession... I hate to be the bearer of bad news.* [2] N-C A **bearer** is a person who carries a stretcher or coffin.

bearing /'beəriŋ/ **bearings.** [1] PHRASE If something **has a bearing on** a situation or event, it is relevant to it. *Diet has an important bearing on your general health.* [2] PHRASE If you **get** your **bearings** or **find** your **bearings,** you find out where you are or what you should do next. If you **lose** your **bearings,** you do not know where you are or what you should do next.

beast /biːst/ **beasts.** N-C A **beast** is an animal, especially a large one; LITERARY.

beat /biːt/ **beats, beating, beat, beaten.** [1] VERB To **beat** someone or something means to hit them very hard. *They were beaten to death with baseball bats... The rain was beating on the windowpanes.* ◆ **beating, beatings.** N-C *...the beating of the rain.* [2] VERB & N-C When your heart or pulse **beats,** it continually makes regular rhythmic movements. The **beat** of your heart or pulse is a single movement of it. *I felt my heart beating faster. ...more than 70 beats per minute.* ◆ **beating** N-SING *...the beating of my heart.* [3] N-C The **beat** of a piece of music is the main rhythm that it has. *...the thumping beat of rock music.* [4] VERB If you **beat** eggs, cream, or butter, you mix them thoroughly using a fork or whisk. [5] VERB To **beat** someone in a competition means to do better than them. *She was easily beaten into third place.* ◆ **beating** N-SING *The candidates the government liked took a beating.*

▶ **beat down.** [1] PHR-VERB When the sun **beats down,** it is very hot and bright. [2] PHR-VERB When the rain **beats down,** it rains very hard. [3] PHR-VERB If you **beat down** a person who is selling you something, you force them to accept a lower price for it.

▶ **beat up.** PHR-VERB If someone **beats** a person **up,** they hit or kick the person many times.

beautiful /'bjuːtiful/. [1] ADJ **Beautiful** means attractive to look at. *...the most beautiful child on earth... New England is beautiful.* ◆ **beautifully** ADV *...a beautifully clear, sunny day.*

> When you are describing someone's appearance, you can only use **beautiful** and **pretty** to describe women, girls, and babies. **Beautiful** is a much stronger word than **pretty**. The equivalent word for a man is **handsome**. **Good-looking** and **attractive** can be used to describe people of either sex.

[2] ADJ You can describe something that someone does as **beautiful** when they do it very skilfully. *...the finest and most beautiful display of bowling.* ◆ **beautifully** ADV *He writes beautifully.*

beauty /'bjuːti/ **beauties.** [1] N-U **Beauty** is the state or quality of being beautiful. *...an area of outstanding natural beauty. ...the idea of feminine beauty.* [2] N-C A beautiful woman is sometimes described as a **beauty.** [3] N-C The **beauties** of something are its attractive qualities or features; LITERARY. *...the beauties of the countryside.* [4] N-C If you say that a particular feature is the **beauty** of something, you mean that this feature is what makes the thing so good. *That's the beauty of it. Any fool can make this.*

beaver /'biːvə/ **beavers, beavering, beavered.** N-C A **beaver** is a furry animal like a large rat with a big flat tail.

▶ **beaver away.** PHR-VERB If you **are beavering away** at something, you are working very hard at it.

became /bɪ'keɪm/. **Became** is the past tense of **become.**

because /bɪ'kʌz, bɪ'kɒz/. [1] CONJ You use **because** when stating the reason or explanation for something. *He is called Mitch, because that's his name is Mitchell... Maybe they just didn't want to ask too many questions, because they rented us a room without even asking to see our papers.* [2] PREP If an event or situation occurs **because of** something, that thing is the reason or cause. *Many families break up because of a lack of money.*

beckon /'bekən/ **beckons, beckoning, beckoned.** [1] VERB If you **beckon** to someone, you signal to them to come to you. *He beckoned to the waiter... I beckoned her over.* [2] VERB If something **beckons,** it is so attractive that you want to become involved in it. *...the warm bars and restaurants which now beckoned.*

become /bɪ'kʌm/ **becomes, becoming, became become.** [1] LINK-VERB If someone or something **becomes** a particular thing, they start being that thing. *He became a professional footballer... The wind became stronger.* [2] PHRASE If you wonder **what has become of** someone, you wonder where they are and what has happened to them.

bed /bed/ beds. **1** N-VAR A **bed** is a piece of furniture that you lie on when you sleep. *We finally went to bed at about 4am... Sam and Robina put the children to bed.* **2** PHRASE To **go to bed with** someone means to have sex with them. **3** N-C A flower **bed** is an area of earth in which you grow plants. **4** N-C The sea **bed** or a river **bed** is the ground at the bottom of the sea or of a river.

,bed and 'breakfast. N-U **Bed and breakfast** is a system of accommodation in a hotel or guest house in which you pay for a room for the night and for breakfast the following morning. The abbreviation **B&B** is also used.

bedclothes /'bedkləʊðz/. N-PL **Bedclothes** are the sheets and covers which you put over you when you get into bed.

bedding /'bedɪŋ/. N-U **Bedding** consists of sheets, blankets, and other covers used on beds.

bedrock /'bedrɒk/. N-U The **bedrock** of something refers to all the principles, ideas, or facts on which it is based. *Trust is the bedrock of a relationship.*

bedroom /'bedru:m/ bedrooms. N-C A **bedroom** is a room which is used for sleeping in.

bedside /'bedsaɪd/. **1** N-SING Your **bedside** is the area beside your bed. *He drew a chair up to the bedside and sat down.* **2** N-SING If you talk about being at someone's **bedside**, you are talking about seeing near them when they are ill in bed. *She was called to her brother's bedside.*

bee /bi:/ bees. N-C A **bee** is an insect with a yellow-and-black striped body that makes a buzzing noise as it flies.

beef /bi:f/. beefs, beefing, beefed. N-U Beef is the meat of a cow, bull, or ox.

▶ **beef up.** PHR-VERB If you **beef** something **up**, you increase, strengthen, or improve it. *...a campaign to beef up security.*

been /bɪn, bi:n/. **1** **Been** is the past participle of **be**. **2** VERB If you have **been** to a place, you have gone to it or visited it. *Mr Li has already been to Egypt.*

beer /bɪə/ beers. N-VAR **Beer** is a bitter alcoholic drink made from grain. A **beer** is a glass of beer. *Would you like a beer?*

beet /bi:t/ beets. **1** N-U **Beet** is a root vegetable that is used as food for animals. **2** N-VAR In American English, **beets** are **beetroot**.

beetle /'bi:tal/ beetles. N-C A **beetle** is an insect with a hard covering to its body.

beetroot /'bi:tru:t/ beetroots. N-VAR In British English, **beetroot** is a dark red root vegetable which can be cooked or pickled. The American word is **beets**.

befall /bɪ'fɔ:l/ befalls, befalling, befell, /bɪ'fel/ befallen. VERB If something bad or unlucky **befalls** you, it happens to you; LITERARY. *...the disaster that befell the island of Flores.*

befit /bɪ'fɪt/ befits, befitting, befitted. VERB If something **befits** a person or thing, it is suitable or appropriate for them. *He writes beautifully, as befits a poet.*

before /bɪ'fɔ:/. **1** PREP & CONJ & ADV If something happens **before** a time or event, it happens earlier than that time or event. *My husband rarely comes to bed before 2 or 3am. ...Greenwich, where Mary lived before moving to Newtown... He phoned on Tuesday, just before you came... The war had ended only a month or so before.* **2** ADJ If something happened the day **before**, it happened during the previous day. *I'd been to a housewarming party the night before.* **3** ADV If someone has done something **before**, they have done it on a previous occasion. 'Have you been to York before?' ...conversation with people she has never met before.* **4** PREP If someone is **before** something, they are in front of it; FORMAL. *They stopped before a large white villa.* **5** PREP When you have a task or difficult situation **before** you, you have to deal with it. *...the duty which lay before him.*

beforehand /bɪ'fɔ:hænd/. ADV If you do something **beforehand**, you do it earlier than a particular event. *Make a list of your questions beforehand.*

befriend /bɪ'frend/ befriends, befriending, befriended. VERB If you **befriend** someone, you make friends with them.

beg /beg/ begs, begging, begged. **1** VERB If you **beg** someone to do something, you ask them anxiously or eagerly to do it. *I begged to be allowed to leave... We are not going to beg for help. ...weeping and begging forgiveness... 'Please leave,' I begged.* **2** VERB If someone **is begging**, they are asking people to give them food or money. *I was surrounded by people begging for food... She was living alone, begging food from neighbors.* **3** PHRASE If you say that something **begs** a particular **question**, you mean that it makes people want to ask this question. Some people think this use is incorrect. *Hopewell's success begs the question: why aren't more companies doing the same?* **4** I **beg your pardon:** see pardon.

began /bɪ'gæn/. **Began** is the past tense of **begin**.

beggar /'begə/ beggars. N-C A **beggar** is someone who lives by asking people for money or food.

begin /bɪ'gɪn/ begins, beginning, began /bɪ'gæn/, begun /bɪ'gʌn/. **1** VERB When someone or something **begins** to do something, they start doing it. *He stood up and began to move around the room... Snow began falling again... 'Professor Theron,' he began, 'I'm very pleased to see you.'* **2** VERB When something **begins** or when you begin it, it takes place from a particular time onwards. *The concert begins at 5 p.m... He had begun his career as a painter.* **3** PHRASE You use the phrase **to begin with** when you are talking about the first stage of a situation, event, or process, or to introduce the first of several things that you want to say. *To begin with, jobs in journalism were scarce... 'What do scientists you've spoken with think about that?'—'Well, to begin with, they doubt it's going to work.'*

beginner /bɪ'gɪnə/ beginners. N-C A **beginner** is someone who has just started learning to do something and cannot do it well yet.

beginning /bɪ'gɪnɪŋ/ beginnings. N-C The **beginning** of something is the first part of it. *This was the beginning of her recording career... She* *contacted me at the beginning of August... I had the beginnings of a headache.*

begun /bɪˈgʌn/. **Begun** is the past participle of **begin**.

behalf /bɪˈhɑːf, -ˈhæf/. PHRASE If you do something **on** someone's **behalf**, you do it as their representative. *She made an emotional public appeal on her son's behalf.*

behave /bɪˈheɪv/ **behaves, behaving, behaved**. [1] VERB The way that you **behave** is the way that you do and say things, and the things that you do and say. *He'd behaved badly.* [2] VERB If you **behave** yourself, you act in the way that people think is correct and proper. *You're going to behave and do what you're told.*

behaviour (AM **behavior**) /bɪˈheɪvjə/ **behaviours**. N-VAR A person's **behaviour** is the way they behave. *...anti-social behaviour... Being over-expressive is a behaviour typical of people with no authority.*

behavioural (AM **behavioral**) /bɪˈheɪvjərəl/. ADJ BEFORE N **Behavioural** means relating to the behaviour of a person or animal, or to the study of their behaviour. *...infant behavioural patterns.*

behind /bɪˈhaɪnd/ **behinds**. In addition to the uses shown below, **behind** is also used in phrasal verbs such as 'fall behind' and 'lie behind'. [1] PREP & ADV If someone or something is **behind** another person or thing, they are facing the back of that person or thing. *I put one of the cushions behind his head... They were parked behind the truck... She led the way upstairs, with Terry following behind.* [2] ADV If you stay **behind**, you remain in a place after other people have gone. [3] ADV If you leave something or someone **behind**, you do not take them with you when you go. [4] PREP When someone or something is **behind**, they are delayed or are making less progress than they should. *The train was seven minutes behind schedule.* [5] PREP The people or events **behind** a situation are the causes of it or the things that are responsible for it. *It is still not clear who was behind the killing.* [6] PREP If something or someone is **behind** you, they support and help you. *His family are completely behind him, whatever he decides.* [7] N-C Your **behind** is the part of your body that you sit on; INFORMAL. [8] to **do something behind someone's back**: see **back**. ● **behind bars**: see **bar**. ● **behind the scenes**: see **scene**.

being /ˈbiːɪŋ/ **beings**. [1] **Being** is the present participle of **be**. [2] N-U **Being** is existence. Something that comes **into being** begins to exist. *The committee came into being in 1993.* [3] N-C You can refer to any real or imaginary creature as a **being**. *...beings from outer space.*

belated /bɪˈleɪtɪd/. ADJ A **belated** action happens later than it should have done. *...John Hall's belated return to the international side.* ◆ **belatedly** ADV *People have belatedly become aware of how fragile the planet is.*

belch /beltʃ/ **belches, belching, belched**. [1] VERB & N-C If someone **belches**, they make a sudden noise, called a **belch**, in their throat because air has risen up from their stomach. [2] VERB If an engine or factory **belches** smoke,

or if smoke **belches** from it, large amounts of smoke come from it. *Clouds of steam started to belch from the engine.*

beleaguered /bɪˈliːgəd/. ADJ **Beleaguered** people or places are being attacked or criticized; FORMAL. *...the beleaguered city of Vukovar.*

belie /bɪˈlaɪ/ **belies, belying, belied**. VERB If one thing **belies** another, it creates a false idea or image of someone or something. *...a man with energy that belies his years.*

belief /bɪˈliːf/ **beliefs**. N-VAR **Belief** is a feeling of certainty that something exists, is true, or is good. *...a belief in reincarnation.*

believable /bɪˈliːvəbl/. ADJ Something that is **believable** makes you think that it could be true or real. *This book is full of believable characters.*

believe /bɪˈliːv/ **believes, believing, believed**. [1] VERB If you **believe** that something is true, you think that it is true. *Experts believe that the drought will be extensive.* ● See note at **think**. [2] VERB If you **believe** someone, you accept that they are telling the truth. *He did not sound as if he believed her... Don't believe what you read in the papers.* [3] VERB If you **believe** in things such as God, fairies, or miracles, you are sure that they exist or happen. [4] VERB If you **believe** in a way of life or an idea, you think it is good or right. *He believed in marital fidelity.*

believer /bɪˈliːvə/ **believers**. [1] N-C If you are a **believer** in something, you think that it is good or right. *Mum was a great believer in herbal medicines.* [2] N-C A **believer** is someone who is sure that God exists or that the teachings of their religion are true.

bell /bel/ **bells**. [1] N-C A **bell** is a device that makes a ringing sound which attracts people's attention. *I've been ringing the door bell.* [2] N-C A **bell** is a hollow metal object with a loose piece hanging inside it that hits the sides and makes a sound. *...church bells.*

belligerent /bɪˈlɪdʒərənt/ **belligerents**. ADJ A **belligerent** person is hostile and aggressive. ◆ **belligerence** N-U *He could be accused of passion, but never belligerence.*

bellow /ˈbeləʊ/ **bellows, bellowing, bellowed**. [1] VERB & N-C If someone **bellows**, they shout angrily in a loud deep voice. You call a sound like this a **bellow**. *'I didn't ask to be born!' she bellowed... The owner bellowed orders at the teenager... Alfred let out a bellow.* [2] N-C A **bellows** is a device used for blowing air into a fire in order to make it burn more fiercely. The plural is also 'bellows'.

belly /ˈbeli/ **bellies**. N-C A person's or animal's **belly** is their stomach or abdomen.

belong /bɪˈlɒŋ, AM -ˈlɔːŋ/ **belongs, belonging, belonged**. [1] VERB If something **belongs to** you, you own it. *At one time the jeep had belonged to the army... The handwriting belongs to a male.* [2] VERB If someone or something **belongs to** a particular group, they are a member of it. *I used to belong to a youth club.* [3] VERB If a person or thing **belongs** in a particular category, group, or place, they are of that category or group, or are usually found in that place. *The judges could not decide which category it belonged in.*

belongings /bɪˈlɒŋɪŋz, AM -ˈlɔːŋ-/. N-PL Your **belongings** are the things that you own.

beloved /bɪˈlʌvɪd/; also pronounced /bɪˈlʌvd/ when used after a noun or after the verb 'be'. ADJ A **beloved** person, thing, or place is one that you feel great love or affection for. *He lost his beloved wife last year.*

below /bɪˈləʊ/. [1] PREP & ADV If something is **below** something else, it is in a lower position. *To the west, the sun dipped below the horizon... The path runs below a long brick wall... Please write to me at the address below.* [2] PREP & ADV If something is **below** a particular amount or level, it is less than that it. *Rainfall has been below average. ...temperatures at zero or below.* [3] **below par:** see **par**.

belt /belt/ **belts, belting, belted.** [1] N-C A **belt** is a strip of leather or cloth that you fasten round your waist. [2] N-C A **belt** is a circular strip of rubber used in machines to drive moving parts or to move objects along. [3] N-C A **belt** of land or sea is a long, narrow area of it that has some special feature. *...Zambia's northern copper belt.* [4] VERB & N-C If someone **belts** you or gives you a belt, they hit you very hard; INFORMAL. [5] See also **safety belt**, **conveyor belt**.
PHRASES • If you have to **tighten** your **belt**, you must manage without things because you have less money than you used to have. • If you have something **under** your **belt**, you have already achieved it or done it. *Colvin already has two albums under her belt.*

bemused /bɪˈmjuːzd/. ADJ If you are **bemused**, you look slightly puzzled or confused. *Mary looked at her with a bemused expression.*

bench /bentʃ/ **benches.** [1] N-C A **bench** is a long seat of wood or metal. [2] N-C A **bench** is a long narrow table in a factory, laboratory, or workshop. [3] N-COLL-SING In a court of law, the **bench** consists of the judge or magistrates. *Allgood served on the bench for more than 50 years.*

bend /bend/ **bends, bending, bent** /bent/. [1] VERB When you **bend**, you move the top part of your body downwards and forwards. *I bent over and kissed her cheek... She was bent over the sink.* [2] VERB When you **bend** a part of your body such as your arm or leg, or when it **bends**, you change its position so that it is no longer straight. *Stand up straight, then slightly bend one leg... As you walk faster, you will find the arms bend naturally.* ◆**bent** ADJ *Keep your knees slightly bent.* [3] VERB When you **bend** something that is flat or straight, you use force to make it curved or angular. *Bend the bar into a horseshoe.* ◆**bent** ADJ *...a length of bent wire.* [4] VERB When a road or river **bends**, it changes direction to form a curve or angle. *The road bent sharply to the left.* [5] N-C A **bend** in a road, river, or pipe is a curved part in it. [6] VERB If someone **bends** the rules, they do something which is not allowed, either to gain an advantage or to help someone else. [7] See also **bent**. • **to bend double:** see **double**.

beneath /bɪˈniːθ/. PREP & ADV Something that is **beneath** another thing is under it. *She could see the muscles of his shoulders beneath his T-shirt... Beneath the surface gaiety were traces of sadness... On a shelf beneath he spotted a photo album.*

benefactor /ˈbenɪfæktə/ **benefactors.** N-C Your **benefactor** is a person who helps you by giving you money.

beneficial /ˌbenɪˈfɪʃəl/. ADJ Something that is **beneficial** helps people or improves their lives. *Wine in moderation is beneficial to health.*

beneficiary /ˌbenɪˈfɪʃəri, AM -ʃieri/ **beneficiaries.** N-C Someone who is a **beneficiary** of something is helped by it. *The main beneficiaries of pension equality so far have been men.*

benefit /ˈbenɪfɪt/ **benefits, benefiting, benefited,** or **benefitting, benefitted.** [1] VERB & N-VAR If you **benefit** from something or if you have **the benefit of** it, it helps you or improves your life. *He hopes to benefit from the tax cuts. ...government programs benefiting children... Steve didn't have the benefit of a formal college education... I hope what I have written will be of benefit to someone else.* [2] N-U **Benefit** is money given by the government to people who are poor, ill, or unemployed. *...unemployment benefit.* [3] PHRASE If you give someone **the benefit of the doubt**, you accept what they say as true, because you cannot prove that it is not true.

benevolent /bɪˈnevələnt/. ADJ A **benevolent** person is kind, helpful, and tolerant. ◆**benevolence** N-U *He chuckles often and radiates benevolence.*

benign /bɪˈnaɪn/. [1] ADJ You use **benign** to describe someone who is kind, gentle, and harmless. *...a good-looking man with a benign expression.* ◆**benignly** ADV *I just smiled benignly.* [2] ADJ A **benign** disease or substance will not cause death or serious harm; TECHNICAL.

bent /bent/. [1] **Bent** is the past tense and past participle of **bend**. [2] ADJ AFTER LINK-V When someone is **bent** on doing something, they are determined to do it. *They seem bent on destroying the city.* [3] N-SING If you have a **bent** for something, you have a natural ability to do it or a natural interest in it. *...his bent for history.*

bequeath /bɪˈkwiːð/ **bequeaths, bequeathing, bequeathed.** VERB If you **bequeath** something to someone, you formally state that they should have it when you die, usually in your will. *Fields's will bequeathed them the sum of twenty thousand dollars... He bequeathed all his silver to his children.*

bereaved /bɪˈriːvd/. ADJ & N-PL A **bereaved** person has a relative or close friend who has recently died. Bereaved people are sometimes called **the bereaved**; FORMAL. *Mr Dinkins visited the bereaved family to offer comfort... He wanted to show his sympathy for the bereaved.* ◆**bereavement** /bɪˈriːvmənt/ **bereavements** N-VAR *...those who have suffered a bereavement.*

bereft /bɪˈreft/. ADJ If a person or thing is **bereft** of something, they no longer have it; FORMAL. *The place seemed to be utterly bereft of human life... They were bereft of ideas.*

berry /ˈberi/ **berries.** N-C **Berries** are small round fruit that grow on a bush or a tree.

berth /bɜːθ/ **berths, berthing, berthed.** [1] N-C A **berth** is a space in a harbour where a ship stays for a period of time. [2] VERB When a ship **berths**, it sails into harbour and stops at the quay. *As soon as they berthed, the boxes of fish would be unloaded. ...the port where the ferry is berthed.* [3] N-C A **berth** is a bed on a boat or train, or in a caravan.

beset /bɪˈset/ **besets, besetting, beset.** VERB If someone or something **is beset** by problems or fears, they have many problems or fears which affect them severely. *...the problems now besetting the country.*

beside /bɪˈsaɪd/ [1] PREP Something that is **beside** something else is at the side of it or next to it. *Beside his plate was a pile of books... I moved from behind my desk to sit beside her.* [2] PHRASE If you are **beside yourself** with anger or excitement, you are extremely angry or excited. [3] **beside the point**: see **point.**

besides /bɪˈsaɪdz/ [1] PREP & ADV **Besides** or **beside** something means in addition to it. *I think she has many good qualities besides being very beautiful. ...the shortage of training, ill health and much else besides.* [2] ADV You use **besides** to make an additional point or give an additional reason. *'I don't need any help. Besides, I'm nearly finished.'*

besiege /bɪˈsiːdʒ/ **besieges, besieging, besieged.** [1] VERB If you **are besieged** by people, many people want something from you and continually bother you. *She was constantly besieged by the press.* [2] VERB If soldiers **besiege** a place, they surround it and wait for the people in it to surrender.

best /best/. [1] **Best** is the superlative of **good.** [2] **Best** is the superlative of **well.** [3] N-SING Your **best** is the greatest effort or the highest achievement that you are capable of. *Miss Blockey was at her best when she played the piano.* [4] N-SING The **best** is used to refer to things of the highest quality or standard. *He'll have the best of care.* [5] ADV If you like something **best** or like it the **best,** you prefer it. *What music do you like best?... What was the role you loved the best?* [6] PHRASE You use **at best** to indicate that even if you describe something as favourably as possible, it is still not very good. *At best Nella would be an invalid; at worst she would die.* [7] PHRASE If you **make the best of** an unsatisfactory situation, you accept it and try to be cheerful about it. *He was determined to be cheerful and make the best of a bad job.* [8] **the best part of** something: see **part.** • **the best of both worlds**: see **world.**

bestow /bɪˈstəʊ/ **bestows, bestowing, bestowed.** VERB To **bestow** something on someone means to give it to them; FORMAL. *The Mayor bestowed medals on the police.*

best-'seller (or **bestseller**), **best-sellers.** N-C A **best-seller** is a book of which a very large number of copies have been sold.

best-'selling (or **bestselling**). [1] ADJ BEFORE N A **best-selling** product is very popular and a large quantity of it has been sold. [2] ADJ BEFORE N A **best-selling** author is an author who has sold a very large number of copies of his or her book.

bet /bet/ **bets, betting, bet.** [1] VERB & N-C If you **bet** on the result of a horse race, football match, or other event, or you put a **bet** on it, you give someone a sum of money which they give you back with extra money if the result is what you predicted, or which they keep if it is not. *I bet £10 on a horse called Premonition... He bet him 500 pounds they would lose... He had already placed a bet on one of the horses.* ♦**betting** N-U *...off-course betting shops.* [2] PHRASE You say **'You bet'** or **'you bet your life'** as an emphatic way of saying 'yes' or of emphasizing a statement; INFORMAL. *'It's settled, then?'—'You bet.'* [3] PHRASE If you use a phrase such as **'I bet', 'I'll bet',** or **'you can bet',** you mean that you are sure something is true. *I bet you were good at games when you were at school.*

betray /bɪˈtreɪ/ **betrays, betraying, betrayed.** [1] VERB If you **betray** someone who trusts you, you do something which hurts and disappoints them. *When I tell someone I will not betray his confidence I keep my word.* [2] VERB If someone **betrays** their country or their comrades, they give information to an enemy, putting their country's security or their comrades' safety at risk. *They betrayed the plan to the enemy.* [3] VERB If you **betray** your feelings or thoughts, you show them without intending to. *Jeremy's voice betrayed little emotion.*

betrayal /bɪˈtreɪəl/ **betrayals.** N-VAR A **betrayal** is an action that betrays someone or something. *She felt that what she had done was a betrayal of Patrick.*

better /ˈbetə/. [1] ADJ **Better** is the comparative of **good.** [2] ADV **Better** is the comparative of **well.** [3] ADV If you like one thing **better** than another, you like it more. *I always liked you better than Sandra... They liked it better when it rained.* [4] ADJ AFTER LINK-V If you are **better** after an illness or injury, you are less ill. If you feel **better,** you no longer feel so ill. • See note at **recover.** [5] ADV You can tell someone that they **are better** doing one thing than another, or **it is better** doing one thing than another when you are advising them about what they should do. *You are better eating just a small snack than hurrying a main meal.* [6] PHRASE If you say that someone **had better** do something, you mean that they ought to do it. *I think we had better go home.* [7] PHRASE If someone **is better off,** they are in a more pleasant situation than before. *A baby or child is better off in its country of birth.* [8] PHRASE If something changes **for the better,** it improves. [9] PHRASE If something **gets the better of** you, you are unable to resist it. [10] **the better part of**: see **part.**

between /bɪˈtwiːn/. [1] PREP & ADV If something is **between** two things or is **in between** them, it has one of the things on one side of it and the other thing on the other side. *There was a cigarette stuck between his lips. ...raised flower beds that have brick paths in between.* [2] PREP If people or things travel **between** two places, they travel regularly from one place to the other and back again. *I often travel between Britain, France and Germany.* [3] PREP A relationship, discussion, or difference **between** two people, groups, or things is one that involves them both or relates to them both. *...the relationship between patients and doctors.* [4] PREP If something stands **between** you and what you want, it prevents you from having it. [5] PREP If something is **between** or **in between** two amounts or ages, it is greater or older than the first one and smaller or younger than the second one. *A third of its population is aged between 18 and 30.* [6] PREP & ADV If something happens **between** or **in between** two times or events, it happens after the first time or event and before the second one. *The canal was built between 1793 and 1797. ...pain lasting a few minutes, with periods of calm in between.* [7] PREP If you must choose **between** two things, you must choose one thing or the other one. [8] PREP If people have a particular amount of something **between** them, this is the total amount that they have. *The three sites employ 12,500 people between them.* [9] PREP When something is divided or shared **between** people, they each have a share of it. *All the tasks are shared between us.*

beverage /ˈbevərɪdʒ/ **beverages.** N-C A **beverage** is a drink; FORMAL. *...alcoholic beverages.*

beware /bɪˈweə/. VERB If you tell someone to **beware** of a person or thing, you are warning them that the person or thing may harm them. **Beware** is only used as an imperative or infinitive. It does not have any other forms. *Beware of being too impatient with others... Motorists were warned to beware of slippery conditions.*

bewildered /bɪˈwɪldəd/. ADJ If you are **bewildered**, you are very confused and cannot understand something or decide what you should do. *Some shoppers looked bewildered by the sheer variety.* ◆**bewildering** ADJ *The choice of excursions was bewildering.*

bewilderment /bɪˈwɪldəmənt/. N-U **Bewilderment** is the feeling of being bewildered. *He shook his head in bewilderment.*

bewitch /bɪˈwɪtʃ/ **bewitches, bewitching, bewitched.** VERB If someone or something **bewitches** you, you find them so attractive that you cannot think about anything else. *The doctor is bewitched by Maya's beauty.* ◆**bewitching** ADJ *...bewitching brown eyes.*

beyond /bɪˈjɒnd/. [1] PREP & ADV If something is **beyond** a place or barrier, it is on the other side of it. *They heard footsteps in the main room, beyond a door. ...a fabulous view out to the Strait of Georgia and the Rockies beyond.* [2] PREP & ADV If something extends **beyond** a particular thing, it affects or includes other things. If something happens **beyond** a particular time or date, it continues after that time or date has passed. *His interests extended beyond the fine arts to international politics and philosophy. ...through the 1990s and beyond.* [3] PREP If something is, for example, **beyond** understanding or **beyond** belief, it is so extreme in some way that it cannot be understood or believed. *By the year 2000, business computing will have changed beyond recognition.* [4] PREP If you say that something is **beyond** someone, you mean that they are incapable of dealing with it. *Any practical help would almost certainly be beyond him.*

bias /ˈbaɪəs/ **biases.** [1] N-VAR **Bias** is prejudice against one group and favouritism towards another, which may badly affect someone's judgment. *...the bias in favour of new road schemes. ...allegations of bias against women.* [2] N-VAR **Bias** is a concern with or interest in one thing more than others. *The Department has a strong bias towards neuroscience.*

biased /ˈbaɪəst/. [1] ADJ AFTER LINK-V Someone or something that is **biased** towards one thing is more concerned with it than with other things. *University funding was tremendously biased towards scientists.* [2] ADJ If someone or something is **biased**, they show prejudice against one group and favouritism towards another, or are influenced so much by something that any judgment they make is likely to be unfair. *She claimed that judges were biased against women victims.*

bible /ˈbaɪbəl/ **bibles.** [1] N-PROPER The **Bible** is the sacred book of the Christian religion. ◆**biblical** /ˈbɪblɪkəl/ ADJ *...the biblical story of creation.* [2] N-C A **bible** is a copy of the Bible.

bibliography /ˌbɪbliˈɒɡrəfi/ **bibliographies.** [1] N-C A **bibliography** is a list of books on a particular subject. [2] N-C A **bibliography** is a list of the books and articles referred to in a particular book.

bicker /ˈbɪkə/ **bickers, bickering, bickered.** VERB When people **bicker**, they quarrel about unimportant things. *They bickered endlessly over procedure.* ◆**bickering** N-U *...months of political bickering.*

bicycle /ˈbaɪsɪkəl/ **bicycles.** N-C A **bicycle** is a vehicle with two wheels which you ride by sitting on it and pushing two pedals with your feet.

bid /bɪd/ **bids, bidding, bid.** [1] N-C A **bid** for something or a **bid** to do something is an attempt to obtain it or do it. *...his successful bid for the US presidency... He may have changed his appearance in a bid to evade capture.* [2] N-C & VERB If you make a **bid** for something or if you **bid** for it, you offer to pay a particular amount of money to buy it. *Hanson made an agreed takeover bid of £351 million... He certainly wasn't going to bid $18 billion for this company.* ◆**bidder, bidders** N-C *The sale will be made to the highest bidder.*

big /bɪɡ/ **bigger, biggest.** [1] ADJ Something that is **big** is large in size or great in degree, extent, or importance. *Australia's a big country... Her husband was a big man. ...the big backlog of applications. ...one of Britain's biggest companies... Her problem was just too big for her to tackle on her own.* [2] ADJ BEFORE N Children often refer to their older brother or sister as their **big** brother or sister; INFORMAL. *I asked my big brother Peter what it meant.*

Big, large, and great are all used to talk about size. In general, large is more formal than big, and great is more formal than large.
Big and large are normally used to describe objects. If you use great to describe an object, you are suggesting that it is impressive because of its size. *The great bird of prey was a dark smudge*

against the sun.
You can use **large** or **great**, but not **big**, to describe amounts. *He noticed a large amount of blood on the laundry floor... The coming of tourists in great numbers changes things.*
Great is often used with nouns referring to things such as feelings or ideas. It is the only one of the three words that can be used in front of an uncount noun. *It gives me very great pleasure to welcome you to Kings Norton... This must be a great disappointment for Roger.*
Remember that **great** has several other meanings, when it does not refer to size, but to something that is remarkable, very good, or enjoyable.

,big 'business. N-U Something that is **big business** has become an important commercial activity. *Sport has become big business.*

,big 'deal. ⒈ N-SING If you say that something is a **big deal**, you mean that it is important or significant. *Winning was such a big deal for the whole family.* ⒉ CONVENTION If you say **'big deal'** to someone, you mean that you are not impressed by something or someone that they consider important or impressive; INFORMAL. *'You'll miss The Brady Bunch.' 'Big deal'.*

bigot /'bɪgət/ **bigots.** N-C If you describe someone as a **bigot**, you disapprove of them because they have strong unreasonable prejudices or opinions. *...a narrow-minded bigot.*

bigotry /'bɪgətri/. N-U **Bigotry** is the fact of having or expressing strong unreasonable prejudices or opinions. *He deplored religious bigotry.*

bike /baɪk/ **bikes.** N-C A **bike** is a bicycle or a motorcycle; INFORMAL. *I used to ride a bike years ago. ...to encourage motorists to go by bike.*

bikini /bɪ'kiːni/ **bikinis.** N-C A **bikini** is a two-piece swimming costume worn by women.

bilingual /baɪ'lɪŋgwəl/. ADJ **Bilingual** means involving or using two languages. *...bilingual education. ...the Collins bilingual dictionaries... He is bilingual in an Asian language and English.*

bill /bɪl/ **bills, billing, billed.** ⒈ N-C In British English, a **bill** is a written statement of money that you owe for goods or services. The American word is **check**. *He paid his bill for the newspapers. ...phone bills.* ⒉ N-C In British English, **the bill** in a restaurant is a piece of paper on which the price of the meal you have just eaten is written and which you are given before you pay. The American word is **check**. ⒊ VERB If you **are billed** for something, you are given or sent a bill for it. *Are you going to bill me for this?* ⒋ N-C In American English, a **bill** is a piece of paper money. The usual British word is **note**. ⒌ N-C In parliament, a **bill** is a formal statement of a proposed new law that is discussed and then voted on. *...the toughest crime bill that Congress has passed in a decade.*

billboard /'bɪlbɔːd/ **billboards.** N-C A **billboard** is a very large board on which posters are displayed.

billion /'bɪljən/ **billions.** ⒈ NUM A **billion** is a thousand million. *...3 billion dollars.* ⒉ QUANT You can use **billions** and **billion** to mean an extremely large amount. *They've sold billions of them... It must be worth billions.*

billionaire /,bɪljə'neə/ **billionaires.** N-C A **billionaire** is an extremely rich person who has money or property worth at least a thousand million pounds or dollars.

billow /'bɪləʊ/ **billows, billowing, billowed.** VERB When something **billows**, it swells out and moves slowly in the wind. *Her pink dress billowed out around her... Dense smoke swirled and billowed.*

bin /bɪn/ **bins.** N-C A **bin** is a container that you put rubbish in.

bind /baɪnd/ **binds, binding, bound.** ⒈ VERB If something **binds** people together, it makes them feel as if they are all part of the same group. *...the social and political ties that bind the USA to Britain.* ⒉ VERB If you **are bound** by something such as a rule or agreement, you are forced or required to act in a certain way. *The authorities will be legally bound to arrest any suspects... The treaty binds them to respect their neighbour's independence.* ⒊ VERB If you **bind** something, you tie string or rope tightly round it. *Bind the ends of the cord together with thread.* ⒋ VERB When a book **is bound**, the pages are joined together and the cover is put on. ⒌ See also **bound**.

binding /'baɪndɪŋ/ **bindings.** ⒈ ADJ A **binding** agreement or decision must be obeyed or carried out. *...a legally binding commitment... The panel's decisions are secret and not binding on the government.* ⒉ N-VAR The **binding** of a book is its cover. *Its books are noted for the quality of their paper and bindings.*

binge /bɪndʒ/ **binges, binging, binged.** N-C & VERB If you go on a **binge**, or if you **binge**, you do too much of something, such as drinking alcohol or eating; INFORMAL. *I binged on pizzas.*

bingo /'bɪŋgəʊ/. N-U **Bingo** is a game in which players aim to match the numbers that someone calls out with the numbers on a card that they have been given. *Do you play bingo?.*

binoculars /bɪ'nɒkjʊləz/. N-PL **Binoculars** consist of two small telescopes joined together side by side, which you look through in order to see things that are a long way away. You can also say **a pair of binoculars.**

biochemical /,baɪəʊ'kemɪkəl/. ADJ BEFORE N **Biochemical** processes are the chemical processes that happen in living things.

biochemistry /,baɪəʊ'kemɪstri/. N-U **Biochemistry** is the study of the chemical processes that happen in living things. ♦**biochemist, biochemists** N-C *...a team of biochemists from Cambridge University.*

biographer /baɪ'ɒgrəfə/ **biographers.** N-C Someone's **biographer** is a person who writes an account of their life.

biography /baɪ'ɒgrəfi/ **biographies.** N-C A **biography** of a person is an account of their life, written by someone else. ♦**biographical** /,baɪə'græfɪkəl/ ADJ *...a 14-minute biographical film.*

biological /ˌbaɪəˈlɒdʒɪkəl/. **1** ADJ **Biological** is used to describe processes and states that occur in the bodies and cells of living things. ...a natural biological response. ◆**biologically** ADV Much of our behaviour is biologically determined. **2** ADJ BEFORE N **Biological** studies are connected with research in biology. ...biological sciences. **3** ADJ **Biological** weapons and **biological** warfare involve the use of organisms which damage living things. ...biological pest control.

biology /baɪˈɒlədʒi/. N-U **Biology** is the science concerned with the study of living things. ◆**biologist, biologists** N-C ...biologists studying the fruit fly.

biotechnology /ˌbaɪəʊtekˈnɒlədʒi/. N-U **Biotechnology** is the use of living parts such as cells or bacteria in industry and medicine; TECHNICAL.

birch /bɜːtʃ/ **birches.** N-VAR A **birch** is a tall tree with thin branches. **Birch** is the wood of this tree.

bird /bɜːd/ **birds.** N-C A **bird** is a creature with feathers and wings.

Biro /ˈbaɪərəʊ/ **Biros.** N-C A **Biro** is a pen with a small metal ball at its tip. **Biro** is a trademark.

birth /bɜːθ/ **births.** **1** N-VAR When a baby is born, you refer to this event as its **birth.** When a woman **gives birth,** she produces a baby from her body. The twins were separated at birth. **2** N-U You can refer to the beginning or origin of something as its **birth.** ...the birth of popular democracy.

'birth control. N-U **Birth control** means planning whether to have children and using contraception to prevent unwanted pregnancy.

birthday /ˈbɜːθdeɪ, -di/ **birthdays.** N-C Your **birthday** is the anniversary of the date on which you were born. ...his 24th birthday... I'm getting a bike for my birthday... Happy Birthday!

birthplace /ˈbɜːθpleɪs/ **birthplaces.** **1** N-C Your **birthplace** is the place where you were born; WRITTEN. **2** N-C The **birthplace** of something is the place where it began or originated. ...Athens, the birthplace of the ancient Olympics.

'birth rate, birth rates. N-C The **birth rate** is the number of babies born for every 1000 people during a particular period.

biscuit /ˈbɪskɪt/ **biscuits.** N-C In British English, a **biscuit** is a small flat cake that is crisp and usually sweet. The usual American word is **cookie.**

bisexual /ˌbaɪˈsekʃʊəl/ **bisexuals.** ADJ & N-C A **bisexual** person or a **bisexual** is sexually attracted to both men and women.

bishop /ˈbɪʃəp/ **bishops.** N-C A **bishop** is a clergyman of high rank.

bistro /ˈbiːstrəʊ/ **bistros.** N-C A **bistro** is a small restaurant or bar.

bit /bɪt/ **bits.** **1** QUANT A **bit** of something is a small amount of it, or a small piece or part of it; INFORMAL. ...a little bit of money. ...crumpled bits of paper... Now comes the really important bit. **2** PHRASE **A bit** means to a small extent or degree; INFORMAL. This girl was a bit strange... I

have a bit more to offer. **3** PHRASE You can use **a bit of** to make a statement less extreme. It's all a bit of a mess. **4** N-C In computing, a **bit** is the smallest unit of information that is held in a computer's memory. **5** **Bit** is the past tense of **bite.**

PHRASES ● You can say that someone's behaviour is **a bit much** when you are annoyed about it; INFORMAL. It seems to be a bit much to say, 'well we don't trust you to drink'. ● You say that one thing is **every bit as** good or interesting as another to emphasize that they are just as good or interesting as each other. My dinner jacket is every bit as good as his. ● If you do something **for a bit,** you do it for a short period of time; INFORMAL. That should keep you busy for a bit. ● **Quite a bit** means a lot; INFORMAL. He's quite a bit older than me.

bitch /bɪtʃ/ **bitches.** N-C A **bitch** is a female dog.

bite /baɪt/ **bites, biting, bit, bitten.** **1** VERB & N-C When a person or animal **bites** something, they use their teeth to cut into it or through it. A **bite** is an act of biting something. He bit into his sandwich... Llamas won't bite or kick... You cannot eat a bun in one bite. **2** VERB & N-C If an insect or a snake **bites** you, it makes a mark or hole in your skin, called a **bite.** A poisonous snake bit his ankle... Try not to scratch insect bites.

> Note that animals, snakes, mosquitoes, and ants **bite** you, but wasps and bees **sting** you.

3 VERB When an action or policy begins to **bite,** it begins to have a serious or harmful effect. The recession started biting deeply into British industry. **4** PHRASE If you **bite your lip,** or if you **bite your tongue,** you stop yourself from saying something that you want to say, because it would be wrong in the circumstances.

biting /ˈbaɪtɪŋ/. **1** ADJ A **biting** wind is extremely cold. **2** ADJ **Biting** criticism or wit is very harsh or unkind. This was the most biting criticism made against her.

bitten /ˈbɪtən/. **Bitten** is the past participle of **bite.**

bitter /ˈbɪtə/ **bitterest; bitters.** **1** ADJ In a **bitter** argument or conflict, people argue very angrily or fight very fiercely. ...a bitter attack on the Government. **2** ADJ If someone is **bitter,** they feel angry and resentful. She is said to be very bitter about the way she was sacked. ◆**bitterly** ADV ...bureaucrats who bitterly resented their loss of power. ◆**bitterness** N-U She still feels bitterness towards him. **3** ADJ You can use **bitter** to emphasize feelings of disappointment. ◆**bitterly** ADV I was bitterly disappointed to have lost. **4** ADJ A **bitter** wind or **bitter** weather is extremely cold. ◆**bitterly** ADV It's bitterly cold here in Moscow. **5** ADJ A **bitter** taste is sharp, not sweet, and often slightly unpleasant. **6** N-VAR **Bitter** is a kind of British beer. ...a pint of bitter.

bizarre /bɪˈzɑː/. ADJ Something that is **bizarre** is very odd and strange. What a bizarre story! ◆**bizarrely** ADV She dressed bizarrely.

black /blæk/ **blacker, blackest; blacks, blacking, blacked.** [1] ADJ & N-VAR Something that is **black** is of the darkest colour that there is. ...*a flowing black gown*... *He was dressed all in black.* ♦**blackness** N-U ...*the blackness of night.* [2] ADJ & N-C A **black** person belongs to a race of people with dark skins, especially a race from Africa. You can refer to black people as **blacks**, but some people find this use offensive. ...*black musicians*... *I'm black and I'm proud to be black.* [3] ADJ **Black** coffee or tea has no milk or cream added to it. *I drink coffee black.* [4] ADJ If you describe a situation as **black**, you are emphasizing that it is very bad indeed. ...*one of the blackest days of his political career.* [5] ADJ **Black** humour involves jokes about things that are sad or unpleasant. ...*a black comedy.* [6] VERB When a group **blacks** particular goods or people, it refuses to handle the goods or to have dealings with the people. *The Union had blacked incoming goods at the London Docks.*
▶ **black out.** PHR-VERB If you **black out**, you lose consciousness for a short time. ● See also **blackout.**

,black and 'white. [1] ADJ & N-U In a **black and white** photograph or film, everything is shown in black, white, and grey. *The pictures were in black and white.* [2] PHRASE You say that something is **in black and white** when it has been written or printed, and not just spoken. *He'd seen the proof in black and white.*

blackberry /'blækbəri, AM -beri/ **blackberries.** N-C A **blackberry** is a small dark purple fruit.

blackboard /'blækbɔːd/ **blackboards.** N-C A **blackboard** is a dark-coloured board which teachers write on with chalk.

blackcurrant /,blæk'kʌrənt, AM -'kɜːrənt/ **blackcurrants.** N-C Blackcurrants are very small, dark purple fruits that grow in bunches.

blacken /'blækən/ **blackens, blackening, blackened.** VERB To **blacken** something means to make it black or very dark in colour. *Smoke from the wood fire had blackened the kitchen walls.* ...*his blackened teeth.*

,black 'eye, black eyes. N-C A **black eye** is a dark-coloured bruise around the eye. *Smith gave him a black eye.*

blackmail /'blækmeɪl/ **blackmails, blackmailing, blackmailed.** N-U & VERB **Blackmail** is the action of threatening to do something unpleasant to someone unless they do what you want them to do. If one person **blackmails** another person, they use blackmail against them. *She was a prime target for blackmail*... *He was trying to blackmail me into saying whatever he wanted.* ♦**blackmailer, blackmailers** N-C ...*a blackmailer who threatened to poison supermarket food.*

,black 'market, black markets. N-C If something is bought or sold on the **black market**, it is bought or sold illegally. *There is a plentiful supply of guns on the black market.*

blackout /'blækaʊt/ **blackouts.** [1] N-C A **blackout** is a period of time during a war in which the buildings in an area are made dark for safety reasons. *The last show had to be over before the blackout began.* [2] N-C If you have a **blackout**, you temporarily lose consciousness.

blacksmith /'blæksmɪθ/ **blacksmiths.** N-C A **blacksmith** is someone whose job is making things out of metal, for example horseshoes.

bladder /'blædə/ **bladders.** N-C Your **bladder** is the part of your body where urine is held until it leaves your body.

blade /bleɪd/ **blades.** [1] N-C The **blade** of a knife, axe, or saw is the sharp edge of it that is used for cutting. [2] N-C The **blades** of a propeller are the parts that turn round.

blame /bleɪm/ **blames, blaming, blamed.** [1] VERB & PHRASE If you **blame** a person or thing for something bad, or if you think or say they are **to blame**, you think or say that they are responsible for it. *The police blamed the explosion on terrorists.* ...*who is to blame?.* [2] N-U The **blame** for something bad that has happened is the responsibility for causing it or letting it happen. *I'm not going to take the blame for that.* [3] VERB If you say that you do not **blame** someone for doing something, you mean that it was a reasonable thing to do in the circumstances. *He slammed the door and stormed off. I could hardly blame him.*

blanch /blɑːntʃ, blæntʃ/ **blanches, blanching, blanched.** VERB If you **blanch**, you suddenly become very pale. *She felt herself blanch at the unpleasant memories.*

bland /blænd/ **blander, blandest.** [1] ADJ If you describe someone or something as **bland**, you mean that they are dull and very ordinary. ...*a bland beige or tan carpet.* [2] ADJ **Bland** food has very little flavour. ...*bland kidney beans.*

blank /blæŋk/ **blanker, blankest.** [1] ADJ Something that is **blank** has nothing on it. ...*a blank page.* ...*blank cassettes.* [2] ADJ If you look **blank**, your face shows no feeling or understanding. *He gave her a blank look.* ♦**blankly** ADV *She stared at him blankly.* [3] ADJ & N-SING If your mind or memory **goes blank** or if it is a **blank**, you cannot think of anything or remember anything. [4] See also **point-blank.**

blanket /'blæŋkɪt/ **blankets, blanketing, blanketed.** [1] N-C A **blanket** is a large piece of thick cloth, especially one which you put on a bed to keep you warm. [2] N-SING & VERB If there is a **blanket** of something such as snow, or if snow **blankets** an area, it covers it. *Heavy cloud and rain blanketed the valley.* [3] ADJ You use **blanket** to describe something which affects or refers to every person or thing in a group. *There's already a blanket ban on foreign unskilled labour.*

blare /bleə/ **blares, blaring, blared.** VERB & N-SING When something such as a siren or radio **blares** or **blares out**, it makes a loud, unpleasant noise called a **blare**. *Music blared from the flat behind me.* ...*the blare of a radio through a thin wall.*

blasphemy /'blæsfəmi/ **blasphemies.** N-VAR You can describe something that shows disrespect for God or a religion as **blasphemy**. ♦**blasphemous** /'blæsfəməs/ ADJ *The book was blasphemous, and offended Muslims worldwide.*

blast /blɑːst, blæst/ **blasts, blasting, blasted.** [1] N-C A **blast** is a big explosion. *250 people were killed in the blast.* [2] VERB If people or things **blast** something, they destroy or damage it with a bomb or an explosion. *They're using dynamite to blast away rocks.* ③ N-C A **blast** of air or wind, or of a sound, is a sudden strong rush of it. *Blasts of cold air swept down from the mountains. ...the loud blast of a horn.* ④ VERB To **blast** someone means to shoot them with a gun; JOURNALISM. *Suddenly all the men pull out pistols and begin blasting away.*

▶ **blast off.** PHR-VERB When a space rocket **blasts off**, it leaves the ground at the start of its journey.

blatant /'bleɪtənt/. ADJ If you describe something you think is bad as **blatant**, you mean that rather than hide it, those responsible actually seem to be making it obvious. *...the most blatant discrimination. ...a blatant attempt to blackmail me.* ◆**blatantly** ADV *...a blatantly sexist question... Blatantly false assertions have gone unchallenged.*

blaze /bleɪz/ **blazes, blazing, blazed.** ① VERB When a fire **blazes**, it burns strongly and brightly. *...a blazing fire.* ② N-C A **blaze** is a large fire in which things are damaged. *...a blaze which swept through a tower block.* ③ VERB Something that **blazes** with light or colour is extremely bright. ④ N-C A **blaze** of light or colour is a large amount of it. ⑤ N-SING A **blaze** of publicity or attention is a great amount of it. *He wanted his presidency to end in a blaze of glory.* ⑥ PHRASE If someone **blazes a trail**, they discover or explore something new. *These surgeons have blazed the trail in the treatment of bomb victims.*

blazer /'bleɪzə/ **blazers.** N-C A **blazer** is a kind of jacket.

blazing /'bleɪzɪŋ/. ① ADJ BEFORE N You use **blazing** or **blazing hot** to describe the weather when it is very hot and sunny. *...blazing hot summers.* ② ADJ BEFORE N When people have a **blazing** row, they quarrel in a very noisy and excited way.

bleach /bliːtʃ/ **bleaches, bleaching, bleached.** ① VERB To **bleach** material means to use a chemical to make it white or pale. The sun can also **bleach** things, especially someone's hair. *She bleached her hair blonde... They put cloth out to bleach in the sun.* ② N-U **Bleach** is a chemical that is used to make cloth white, or to clean things thoroughly. *...a solution of household bleach.*

bleak /bliːk/ **bleaker, bleakest.** ① ADJ If a situation is **bleak**, it is bad, and seems unlikely to improve. *The immediate outlook remains bleak.* ◆**bleakness** N-U *...the continued bleakness of the American job market.* ② ADJ If you describe something as **bleak**, you mean it looks cold or unpleasant. *...bleak inner-city streets... The weather can be quite bleak on the coast.* ③ ADJ If someone looks or sounds **bleak**, they seem depressed or unfriendly. *Julian's face took on a bleak look.* ◆**bleakly** ADV *'There is nothing left,' she says bleakly.*

bleed /bliːd/ **bleeds, bleeding, bled.** VERB When you **bleed**, you lose blood from your body as a result of injury or illness. *She's going to bleed to death... His head had struck the sink and was bleeding.* ◆**bleeding** N-U *...internal bleeding.*

blemish /'blemɪʃ/ **blemishes, blemishing, blemished.** ① N-C A **blemish** is a mark that spoils the appearance of something. *If there is the slightest blemish it is rejected.* ② VERB If something **blemishes** your reputation, or if it is a **blemish** on it, it spoils it. *He wasn't about to blemish that pristine record... These are minor blemishes on a remarkably smooth operation.*

blend /blend/ **blends, blending, blended.** ① VERB & N-C When you **blend** substances together, you mix them together so that they become one substance. A **blend** of substances is a mix of them. *Blend the butter with the sugar. ...a blend of spices.* ② VERB When colours or sounds **blend**, they combine in a pleasing way. *Paint the walls and ceilings the same colour so they blend together.*

▶ **blend into,** or **blend in.** PHR-VERB If something **blends into** the background or **blends in**, it is so similar to the background in appearance or sound that it is difficult to see or hear it separately. *The toad had changed its colour to blend in with its new environment.*

bless /bles/ **blesses, blessing, blessed.** ① VERB When a priest **blesses** people or things, he or she asks for God's favour and protection for them. ② PASSIVE-VERB If someone **is blessed** with a good quality or skill, they have it. *Both are blessed with uncommon ability to fix things.*

PHRASES When people say **God bless** or **bless you** to someone, they are expressing their affection or thanks. *Bless you, you're so kind.*

blessed /'blesɪd/. ADJ BEFORE N You use **blessed** to describe something that you are thankful for or relieved about. *Rainy weather brings blessed relief to hay fever victims.* ◆**blessedly** ADV *Most British election campaigns are blessedly brief.*

blessing /'blesɪŋ/ **blessings.** ① N-C A **blessing** is something good that you are thankful for. *...the blessings of prosperity.* ② N-C If something is done with your **blessing**, you approve of it. ③ PHRASE If you say that a situation is a **mixed blessing**, you mean that it has disadvantages as well as advantages. *...the mixed blessing of modern technology.*

blew /bluː/. **Blew** is the past tense of **blow**.

blight /blaɪt/ **blights, blighting, blighted.** ① N-C You can refer to something as a **blight** when it causes great difficulties or damage to something. *This discriminatory policy has really been a blight on America.* ② VERB If something **blights** something else, it damages it. *An embarrassing blunder nearly blighted his career.*

blind /blaɪnd/ **blinds, blinding, blinded.** ① ADJ & N-PL Someone who is **blind** cannot see because their eyes are damaged. You can refer to people who are **blind** as the **blind**. *...a blind person... He went blind.* ◆**blindness** N-U *Early diagnosis and treatment can usually prevent blindness.* ② VERB If something **blinds** you, you become unable to see, either for a short time or permanently. *The strong sunlight blinded him.* ③ ADJ AFTER LINK-V & VERB If you are **blind** to a fact or situation or if something **blinds** you to it, you take no notice of it or are unaware of it. *All the time I was blind to your suffering.* [4] ADJ If you describe someone's beliefs or actions as **blind**, you think that they do not question or think about what they are doing. *...her blind faith in the wisdom of the Church.* [5] PHRASE If you say that someone **is turning a blind eye** to something bad or illegal, you mean that they are pretending not to notice that it is happening so that they will not have to do anything about it. *I can't turn a blind eye when someone is being robbed.* [6] ADJ BEFORE N A **blind** corner is one that you cannot see round. [7] N-C A **blind** is a roll of material which you pull down over a window to keep out the light.

blindfold /'blaɪndfəʊld/ **blindfolds, blind-folding, blindfolded.** [1] N-C A **blindfold** is a strip of cloth that is tied over someone's eyes so that cannot see. [2] VERB If you **blindfold** someone, you tie a blindfold over their eyes. *He had been blindfolded and his hands were tied.*

blinding /'blaɪndɪŋ/. ADJ A **blinding** light is extremely bright.

blindly /'blaɪndli/. [1] ADV If you do something **blindly**, you do it when you cannot see properly. *Lettie groped blindly for the glass.* [2] ADV You use **blindly** to say that someone does something without having enough information, or without thinking about it. *Don't just blindly follow what the banker says.*

blink /blɪŋk/ **blinks, blinking, blinked.** [1] VERB & N-C When you **blink** or when you give a **blink**, you shut your eyes and very quickly open them again. *She was blinking her eyes rapidly... He kept giving quick blinks.* [2] VERB When a light **blinks**, it flashes on and off. *A warning light blinked on.*

bliss /blɪs/. N-U **Bliss** is a state of complete happiness. *It was a scene of such domestic bliss.*

blissful /'blɪsfʊl/. ADJ A **blissful** time or state is a very happy one. *We spent a blissful week together.* ♦ **blissfully** ADV *We're blissfully happy.*

blister /'blɪstə/ **blisters, blistering, blistered.** [1] N-C A **blister** is a painful swelling containing clear liquid on the surface of your skin. [2] VERB When your skin **blisters**, blisters appear on it as a result of burning or rubbing. *The affected skin turns red and may blister... The sap of this plant blisters the skin.*

blistering /'blɪstərɪŋ/. [1] ADJ **Blistering** heat is very great heat. *...a blistering summer day.* [2] ADJ A **blistering** remark expresses great anger or sarcasm. *...a blistering attack on his critics.*

blithe /blaɪð/. ADJ You use **blithe** to indicate that something is done casually, without serious thought. *...blithe disregard for best scientific practice.* ♦ **blithely** ADV *Your editorial blithely ignores the hard facts.*

blitz /blɪts/ **blitzes, blitzing, blitzed.** [1] VERB & N-C If a city or building **is blitzed** during a war, bombs are dropped on it by enemy aircraft. You can refer to an attack like this as a **blitz**. [2] N-C If you have a **blitz** on something, you make a big effort to deal with it or to improve it; INFORMAL. *There is to be a blitz on incorrect grammar.*

blizzard /'blɪzəd/ **blizzards.** N-C A **blizzard** is a storm in which snow falls heavily and there are strong winds.

bloated /'bləʊtɪd/. ADJ Something that is **bloated** is much larger than normal, usually because it has a lot of liquid or gas inside it. *...the bloated body of a dead bullock.*

blob /blɒb/ **blobs.** N-C A **blob** of thick or sticky liquid is a small amount of it. *...a blob of cream.*

bloc /blɒk/ **blocs.** N-C A **bloc** is a group of countries who act together because they have similar political aims and interests. *...the former Soviet bloc.*

block /blɒk/ **blocks, blocking, blocked.** [1] N-C A **block** of flats or offices is a large building containing them. *...a white-painted apartment block.* [2] N-C In a town, a **block** is a group of buildings with streets on all four sides. *She walked four blocks down High Street.* [3] N-C A **block** of a substance is a large rectangular piece of it. [4] VERB To **block** a road or channel means to put something across or in it so that nothing can go through it or along it. *Police blocked the entrance to Westminster Bridge. ...a blocked drain.* [5] VERB If something **blocks** your view, it prevents you from seeing something by being between you and that thing. *...a row of trees that blocked his view.* [6] VERB When people **block** something, they do not allow it to happen. *The country has tried to block imports of various cheap foreign products.*

▶ **block out.** PHR-VERB If you **block out** a thought, you try not to think about it. *She accuses me of having blocked out the past.*

▶ **block up.** PHR-VERB If you **block** something **up** or if it **blocks up**, it becomes completely blocked so that nothing can get through it. *'Any holes in the kitchen where the mice are getting through?'—'I've blocked them up.'.*

blockade /blɒ'keɪd/ **blockades, blockading, blockaded.** N-C & VERB A **blockade** is an action that is taken to prevent goods from entering or leaving a place. You can also say that people **blockade** a place. *...a blockade of the harbour... Warships are blockading the port.*

blockage /'blɒkɪdʒ/ **blockages.** N-C A **blockage** in a pipe or tunnel is something that is blocking it. *...a fatal blockage in the lung.*

blockbuster /'blɒkbʌstə/ **blockbusters.** N-C A **blockbuster** is a very popular and successful film or book; INFORMAL.

bloke /bləʊk/ **blokes.** N-C A **bloke** is a man; INFORMAL, BRITISH.

blonde (or **blond**) /blɒnd/ **blondes.** ADJ & N-C A **blonde** person or a **blonde** has pale yellow-coloured hair. The form **blonde** is used to refer to women, and **blond** to refer to men. *Do blondes really have more fun?... The baby had blond curls.*

blood /blʌd/. [1] N-U **Blood** is the red liquid that flows inside your body. [2] N-U You can use **blood** to refer to the race or social class of someone's parents or ancestors. *There was Greek blood in his veins.*

PHRASES • If something violent and cruel is done **in cold blood**, it is done deliberately and in an unemotional way. • New people who are introduced into an organization and whose fresh ideas are likely to improve it are referred to as **new blood**, **fresh blood**, or **young blood**. *There's been a major reshuffle of the cabinet to bring in new blood.* ● **own flesh and blood**: see **flesh**.

'blood pressure. N-U Your **blood pressure** is a measure of the force with which blood is pumped around your body. *Your doctor will monitor your blood pressure.*

bloodshed /'blʌdʃed/. N-U **Bloodshed** is violence in which people are killed or wounded. *...rioting and bloodshed.*

bloodstream /'blʌdstriːm/ **bloodstreams.** N-C Your **bloodstream** is your blood as it flows around your body. *The disease releases toxins into the bloodstream.*

'blood test, blood tests. N-C A **blood test** is a medical examination of a sample of your blood.

'blood vessel, blood vessels. N-C **Blood vessels** are the narrow tubes through which your blood flows.

bloody /'blʌdi/ **bloodier, bloodiest.** 1 **Bloody** is a swear word. Some people use 'bloody' to emphasize what they are saying, especially when they are angry about something someone has said or done. BRITISH. 2 ADJ A situation or event that is **bloody** is one in which there is a lot of violence and people are killed. *...the bloody riots of 1981.*

bloom /bluːm/ **blooms, blooming, bloomed.** 1 N-C A **bloom** is the flower on a plant. 2 PHRASE A plant or tree that is **in bloom** has flowers on it. 3 VERB When a plant or tree **blooms**, it produces flowers. When a flower **blooms**, the flower bud opens.

blossom /'blɒsəm/ **blossoms, blossoming, blossomed.** 1 N-VAR **Blossom** is the flowers that appear on a tree before the fruit. *...cherry blossom.* 2 VERB When a tree **blossoms**, it produces blossom. 3 VERB If someone or something **blossoms**, they develop good, attractive, or successful qualities. *What began as a local festival has blossomed into an international event.*

blot /blɒt/ **blots, blotting, blotted.** N-C A **blot** is a drop of liquid that has been spilled on a surface and has dried. *...an ink blot.*
▶ **blot out.** 1 PHR-VERB If one thing **blots out** another thing, it is in front of the other thing and prevents it from being seen. *Clouds blotted out the sun.* 2 PHR-VERB If you try to **blot out** a memory, you try to forget it. *She's trying to blot out all memory of the incident.*

blotch /blɒtʃ/ **blotches.** N-C A **blotch** is a small area of colour, for example on someone's skin. *His face was covered in red blotches.*

blouse /blaʊz, AM blaʊs/ **blouses.** N-C A **blouse** is a kind of shirt worn by girls or women.

blow /bloʊ/ **blows, blowing, blew, blown.** 1 VERB When a wind or breeze **blows**, the air moves. *A chill wind blew at the top of the hill.* 2 VERB If the wind **blows** something somewhere, or if something **blows** there, it is moved there by the wind. *The wind blew her hair back from her forehead... Sand blew in our eyes.* 3 VERB If you **blow**, you send out a stream of air from your mouth. *Danny blew on his fin-*

gers to warm them. 4 VERB When a whistle or horn **blows**, or when someone **blows** it, they make a sound by blowing into it. 5 VERB When you **blow** your nose, you force air out of it through your nostrils in order to clear it. 6 VERB To **blow** something out, off, or away means to violently remove or destroy it with an explosion. *The can exploded, wrecking the kitchen and bathroom and blowing out windows... Rival gunmen blew the city to bits.* 7 N-C If someone receives a **blow**, they are hit by someone or something. *He went off to hospital after a blow to the face.* 8 N-C A **blow** is something that happens which makes you very disappointed or unhappy. *It was a terrible blow when he was made redundant.* 9 VERB If you **blow** a chance or attempt to do something, you make a mistake which wastes the chance or causes the attempt to fail; INFORMAL. *I had probably blown my chances for this job... Oh you fool! You've blown it!* 10 VERB If you **blow** a large amount of money, you spend it quickly on luxuries; INFORMAL.
▶ **blow out.** PHR-VERB If you **blow out** a flame or a candle, you blow at it so that it stops burning.
▶ **blow over.** PHR-VERB If something such as trouble or an argument **blows over**, it comes to an end. *Wait, and it'll all blow over.*
▶ **blow up.** 1 PHR-VERB If someone **blows** something **up**, or if it **blows up**, it is destroyed by an explosion. *Their boat blew up.* 2 PHR-VERB If you **blow up** something such as a balloon or a tyre, you fill it with air.

blown /bloʊn/. **Blown** is the past participle of **blow**.

bludgeon /'blʌdʒən/ **bludgeons, bludgeoning, bludgeoned.** VERB If someone **bludgeons** you into doing something, they make you do it by bullying or threatening you. *Their approach simply bludgeons you into submission.*

blue /bluː/ **bluer, bluest; blues.** 1 ADJ & N-VAR Something that is **blue** is the colour of the sky on a sunny day. 2 PHRASE Something that happens **out of the blue** happens suddenly and unexpectedly. *Turner's resignation came out of the blue.* 3 N-U The **blues** is a type of music which is similar to jazz, with a slow tempo and a strong rhythm.

,blue-'collar. ADJ **Blue-collar** workers work in industry, doing physical work, rather than in offices.

blueprint /'bluːprɪnt/ **blueprints.** N-C A **blueprint** for something is an original plan or description of how it is expected to work. *...his blueprint for the country's future.*

bluff /blʌf/ **bluffs, bluffing, bluffed.** 1 N-VAR A **bluff** is an attempt to make someone believe that you will do something when you do not really intend to do it. *The letter was a bluff. ...a game of bluff.* 2 PHRASE If you **call** someone's **bluff**, you tell them to do what they have been threatening to do, because you are sure that they will not really do it. 3 VERB If you **bluff**, you try to make someone believe that you will do something although you do not really intend to do it, or that you know something when you really do not know it. *Either side, or* *both, could be bluffing... He tried to bluff his way through another test.*

blunder /'blʌndə/ **blunders, blundering, blundered.** [1] N-C & VERB If you make a **blunder**, or if you **blunder**, you make a stupid mistake. *It had been a monumental blunder to give him the assignment... The company admitted it had blundered.* [2] VERB If you **blunder** somewhere, you move there in a clumsy way. *He had blundered into the table.*

blunt /blʌnt/ **blunter, bluntest; blunts, blunting, blunted.** [1] ADJ If you are **blunt**, you say exactly what you think without trying to be polite. *His blunt response surprised them.* ◆**bluntly** ADV *'I don't believe you!' Jeanne said bluntly.* ◆**bluntness** N-U *His bluntness got him into trouble.* [2] ADJ BEFORE N A **blunt** object has a rounded or flat end rather than a sharp one. *He had been battered to death with a blunt instrument.* [3] ADJ A **blunt** knife is no longer sharp and does not cut well. [4] VERB If something **blunts** an emotion or feeling, it weakens it. *Our appetite was blunted by the beer.*

blur /blɜː/ **blurs, blurring, blurred.** [1] N-C A **blur** is a shape or area which you cannot see clearly because it has no distinct outline or because it is moving very fast. *Her face is a blur.* [2] VERB If an image **blurs**, or if it is **blurred**, it becomes a blur. *A dizziness overcame him, blurring his vision.* ◆**blurred** ADJ *...slightly blurred images.* [3] VERB If something **blurs** a distinction between things, the differences between them are no longer clear. *Television is blurring the distinction between sport and show business.* ◆**blurred** ADJ *Fiction and reality were increasingly blurred.*

blurt /blɜːt/ **blurts, blurting, blurted.**
▶ **blurt out.** PHR-VERB If you **blurt** something **out**, you say it suddenly, after trying hard to keep quiet or to keep it secret. *'You're mad,' the driver blurted out... Richard blurted out what was on his mind.*

blush /blʌʃ/ **blushes, blushing, blushed.** VERB & N-C When you **blush**, or when a **blush** spreads over your face, your face becomes redder than usual because you are ashamed or embarrassed. *I felt myself blush... Ann accepted it with a blush.*

bluster /'blʌstə/ **blusters, blustering, blustered.** VERB & N-U If you say that someone is **blustering** or that what they say is **bluster**, you mean that they are speaking aggressively or proudly but without authority. *'That's lunacy,' he blustered... At the heart of Tom's bluster was a great shyness.*

boar /bɔː/; the plural is **boar** or **boars.** [1] N-C A **boar** or a **wild boar** is a wild pig. [2] N-C A **boar** is a male pig.

board /bɔːd/ **boards, boarding, boarded.** [1] N-C A **board** is a flat piece of wood, plastic, or cardboard which is used for a particular purpose. *...a chopping board. ...a chess board... They put down wooden boards, and laid new carpets on top.* [2] N-C You can refer to a blackboard or a noticeboard as a **board**. *He wrote a few more notes on the board.* [3] N-C The **board** of a company or organization is the group of people who control it. *...the board of directors. ...board meetings.* [4] VERB & PHRASE When you

board a train, ship, or aircraft, or when you go **on board**, you get on it. *Are you ready to board?... There were four people on board the aircraft.* [5] N-U **Board** is the food which is provided when you stay somewhere, for example in a hotel. *Free room and board are provided for all hotel staff.* [PHRASES] ● If a policy or a situation applies **across the board**, it affects everything or everyone in a particular group. *...to increase salaries across the board.* ● If you **take on board** an idea or suggestion, you begin to accept it or take it into consideration. *I shall be hoping that the council will take that message on board.*

▶ **board up.** PHR-VERB If you **board up** a door or window, you fix pieces of wood over it so that it is covered up. *Half the shops are boarded up.*

'boarding school, boarding schools. N-VAR A **boarding school** is a school where the pupils live during the term. *Now she is away at boarding school.*

boardroom /'bɔːdruːm/ **boardrooms.** N-C The **boardroom** is a room where the board of a company meets.

boast /bəʊst/ **boasts, boasting, boasted.** VERB & N-C If someone **boasts** about something that they have done or that they own, they talk about it proudly in a way that other people may find irritating or offensive. A **boast** is what someone says when they boast. *Carol boasted about her costume... Furci boasted that he took part in killing them. ...her boast of being a great lover.*

boat /bəʊt/ **boats.** [1] N-C A **boat** is something in which people can travel across water. *...a small fishing boat... The island may be reached by boat.* [2] N-C You can refer to a passenger ship as a **boat**. *My father met me off the boat... It would be just his luck to miss the last boat.* [PHRASES] ● If you say that someone is **rocking the boat**, you mean that they are upsetting a calm situation and causing trouble. ● If two or more people are **in the same boat**, they are in the same unpleasant situation. *She's in the same boat as me. She's unemployed herself.*

boating /'bəʊtɪŋ/. N-U **Boating** is travelling on a lake or river in a small boat for pleasure. *...a boating accident... I wanted to go boating.*

bob /bɒb/ **bobs, bobbing, bobbed.** VERB If something **bobs**, it moves up and down, like something does when it is floating on water. *The raft bobbed along... Huge balloons bobbed about in the sky above.*

bode /bəʊd/ **bodes, boding, boded.** VERB If something **bodes** ill, it makes you think that something bad will happen in the future. If something **bodes** well, it makes you think that something good will happen. LITERARY. *The way the bill was passed bodes ill for democracy.*

bodily /'bɒdɪli/. [1] ADJ BEFORE N Your **bodily** needs and functions are the needs and functions of your body. [2] ADV You use **bodily** to indicate that an action involves the whole of someone's body. *I was hurled bodily to the deck.*

body /'bɒdi/ **bodies.** [1] N-C Your **body** is all your physical parts, including your head, arms, and legs. *My whole body hurt.* [2] N-C You can refer to the main part of your body, excluding your arms, head, and legs, as your **body**. *Gently pull your leg toward your body.* [3] N-C A **body** is a dead person's body. *Police later found a body.* [4] N-C A **body** is an organized group of people who deal with something officially. *...public bodies such as local authorities.* [5] N-C The **body** of a car or plane is its main part, excluding its engine, wheels, and wings.

bodyguard /ˈbɒdigɑːd/ **bodyguards.** N-C Someone's **bodyguard** is the person or group of people employed to protect them.

body language. N-U Your **body language** is the way you show your feelings or thoughts by means of the movements of your body.

bog /bɒg/ **bogs.** N-C A **bog** is wet muddy area of land.

bogged down. ADJ If you are **bogged down** in something, it prevents you from making progress or getting something done; INFORMAL. *Why get bogged down in legal details?*

boggle /ˈbɒgəl/ **boggles, boggling, boggled.** VERB If you say that the mind **boggles** at something, you mean that it is so strange or amazing that it is difficult to imagine or understand; INFORMAL. *The mind boggles at how much work they have to do... The implications of this boggle the mind.*

bogus /ˈbəʊgəs/. ADJ If you describe something as **bogus**, you mean that it is not genuine. *...their bogus insurance claim.*

bohemian /bəʊˈhiːmiən/ **bohemians.** ADJ & N-C You can describe someone as **bohemian**, or as a **bohemian**, if they are artistic and live in an unconventional way.

boil /bɔɪl/ **boils, boiling, boiled.** [1] VERB When a hot liquid **boils**, or when you **boil** it, bubbles appear in it and it starts to change into steam or vapour. *Boil the water in the saucepan. ...a large pan of boiling water.* [2] PHRASE When you **bring** a liquid **to the boil**, you heat it until it boils. [3] VERB When you **boil** a kettle, or when you put it on to **boil**, you heat the water inside it until it boils. *Marianne put the kettle on to boil.* [4] VERB When you **boil** food, or when you put it on to **boil**, you cook it in boiling water. *Boil the potatoes for 10 minutes.* ● See note at **cook.** [5] N-C A **boil** is a red painful swelling on your skin.

▶ **boil down to.** PHR-VERB If you say that a situation or problem **boils down to** a particular thing, you mean that this is the most important aspect of it. *It all boils down to money again.*

▶ **boil over.** PHR-VERB When a liquid that is being heated **boils over**, it rises and flows over the edge of the container.

boiler /ˈbɔɪlə/ **boilers.** N-C A **boiler** is a device which burns fuel to provide hot water.

boiling /ˈbɔɪlɪŋ/. ADJ Something that is **boiling** or **boiling hot** is very hot. *It's boiling in here. ...boiling hot plates.* ● See note at **hot.**

boisterous /ˈbɔɪstərəs/. ADJ Someone who is **boisterous** is noisy, lively, and full of energy. *...a boisterous but good-natured crowd.*

bold /bəʊld/ **bolder, boldest.** [1] ADJ Someone who is **bold** is brave or confident. *I don't feel I'm being bold. ...bold economic reforms.*
♦ **boldly** ADV *You can and must act boldly...*

'You should do it,' the girl said, boldly.
♦ **boldness** N-U *...the boldness of his economic programme.* [2] ADJ **Bold** colours or designs are painted or drawn in a clear strong way. *...bold handwriting.*

bolster /ˈbəʊlstə/ **bolsters, bolstering, bolstered.** VERB If you **bolster** someone's confidence or courage, you make them more confident or more courageous. *...measures intended to bolster morale.*

bolt /bəʊlt/ **bolts, bolting, bolted.** [1] N-C A **bolt** is a long metal object which screws into a nut and is used to fasten things together. *...nuts and bolts that haven't been tightened up.* [2] VERB If you **bolt** one thing to another, you fasten them firmly together, using a bolt. *Bolt the components together. ...a wooden bench which was bolted to the floor.* [3] N-C A **bolt** on a door or window is a metal bar that you slide across in order to fasten the door or window. *...the sound of a bolt being slowly and reluctantly slid open.* [4] VERB If you **bolt** a door or window, you slide the bolt across to fasten it. *Lock and bolt the kitchen door.* [5] VERB If a person or animal **bolts**, they suddenly start to run very fast, often because something has frightened them. *I made some excuse and bolted for the exit.*

bomb /bɒm/ **bombs, bombing, bombed.** [1] N-C A **bomb** is a device which explodes, damaging a large area or killing people. [2] VERB When a place **is bombed**, it is attacked with bombs. *Airforce jets bombed the airport.*
♦ **bombing, bombings** N-VAR *...the bombing of Dresden.*

bombard /bɒmˈbɑːd/ **bombards, bombarding, bombarded.** [1] VERB If someone **bombards** you with something, they make you face a great deal of it. *We have been bombarded with requests for information... He began bombarding her with love letters.* [2] VERB When soldiers **bombard** a place, they attack it with continuous heavy gunfire or bombs.
♦ **bombardment** N-U *...the sound of heavy aerial bombardment.*

bomber /ˈbɒmə/ **bombers.** [1] N-C A **bomber** is an aeroplane that drops bombs. [2] N-C **Bombers** are people who plant bombs in public places.

bombshell /ˈbɒmʃel/ **bombshells.** N-C A **bombshell** is a sudden piece of bad or unexpected news. *His resignation after thirteen years is a political bombshell.*

bonanza /bəˈnænzə/ **bonanzas.** N-C You can refer to a time or situation when people suddenly become much richer as a **bonanza**. *...a sales bonanza for computer makers.*

bond /bɒnd/ **bonds, bonding, bonded.** [1] N-C A **bond** between people is a close link between them, for example feelings of love, or a special agreement. *...the bond between mothers and babies... The republic is successfully breaking its bonds with Moscow.* [2] VERB When people **bond** with each other, they form a relationship based on love or shared experiences. *Belinda was having trouble bonding with the baby... We were bonded by years of mutual history.* [3] N-PL **Bonds** are feelings, duties, or customs that force you to behave in a particular way. *...the* *bonds of tradition.* [4] VERB When things **bond** together, they stick to each other or become joined in some way. *In graphite sheets, carbon atoms bond together in rings.* [5] N-C A **bond** is a certificate issued by a government or company which shows that you have lent them money and that they will pay you interest.

bondage /'bɒndɪdʒ/. N-U **Bondage** is the condition of being a slave; LITERARY. *Masters sometimes allowed slaves to buy their way out of bondage.*

bone /bəʊn/ **bones, boning, boned.** [1] N-VAR Your **bones** are the hard parts inside your body which together form your skeleton. *Stephen fractured a thigh bone... The body is made up primarily of bone, muscle, and fat.* [2] VERB If you **bone** a piece of meat or fish, you remove the bones from it before cooking it.

bonfire /'bɒnfaɪə/ **bonfires.** N-C A **bonfire** is a fire built outdoors, usually to burn rubbish.

bonnet /'bɒnɪt/ **bonnets.** [1] N-C In British English, the **bonnet** of a car is the metal cover over the engine at the front. The American word is **hood**. [2] N-C A **bonnet** is a hat worn by babies which has ribbons that are tied under the chin.

bonus /'bəʊnəs/ **bonuses.** [1] N-C A **bonus** is an amount of money that is added to someone's pay, usually because they have worked very hard. [2] N-C A **bonus** is something good that you get in addition to something else, usually something which is unexpected. *When we qualified for both the finals it was an extra bonus.*

bony /'bəʊni/. ADJ If someone has, for example, a **bony** face or **bony** hands, their face or hands are too thin.

boo /buː/ **boos, booing, booed.** VERB & N-C If you **boo** a speaker or performer, you shout 'boo' or make other loud sounds to indicate that you do not like them. The sounds you make are called **boos**. *He was booed off the stage... She was greeted with boos and hisses.* ♦**booing** N-U *The stadium became a riot of booing and ill feeling.*

book /bʊk/ **books, booking, booked.** [1] N-C A **book** consists of pieces of paper, usually with words printed on them, which are fastened together and fixed inside a cover of strong paper or cardboard. [2] N-C A **book** of something such as stamps is a small number of them fastened together between thin cardboard or plastic covers. [3] N-PL An organization's **books** are written records of money that has been spent and earned, or of the names of people who belong to it. *An accountant has gone over the books... Many of the people on our books are in the computing industry.* [4] VERB When you **book** something such as a hotel room or a ticket, you arrange to have it or use it at a particular time; BRITISH. *I have booked a table in the nearby restaurant.* [5] PHRASE If a hotel, restaurant, or theatre is **fully booked**, **booked solid**, or **booked up**, it has no rooms, tables, or tickets left.

▸ **book into** or **book in.** PHR-VERB In British English, when you **book into** a hotel or when you **book in**, you officially state that you have arrived to stay there, usually by signing your name in a register. The American term is **check in**.

bookcase /'bʊkkeɪs/ **bookcases.** N-C A **bookcase** is a piece of furniture with shelves for books.

bookie /'bʊki/ **bookies.** N-C A **bookie** is the same as a **bookmaker**; INFORMAL.

booklet /'bʊklət/ **booklets.** N-C A **booklet** is a small paperback book, containing information on a particular subject.

bookmaker /'bʊkmeɪkə/ **bookmakers.** N-C A **bookmaker** is a person whose job is to take your money when you bet and to pay you money if you win.

boom /buːm/ **booms, booming, boomed.** [1] N-C & VERB If there is a **boom** in something such as the economy, or if it is **booming**, it increases or develops very quickly. *...the 1980s property boom... Sales are booming.* [2] VERB & N-C When something such as a cannon or someone's voice **booms** out, it makes a loud, deep, echoing sound called a **boom**. *'Ladies,' boomed Helena, 'we all know why we're here tonight'... The stillness of the night was broken by the boom of a cannon.*

boon /buːn/ **boons.** N-C You say that something is a **boon** to people or for people when it makes their life better or easier. *Fans that follow the games will provide a boon to local hotels.*

boost /buːst/ **boosts, boosting, boosted.** [1] VERB & N-C If one thing **boosts** another, or if it gives it a **boost**, it causes the second thing to increase or be more successful. *The campaign had boosted sales... That would provide a tremendous boost to education.* [2] VERB & N-C If something **boosts** your confidence or morale, or if it gives it a **boost**, it improves it. *It did give me a boost to win such a big event.*

boot /buːt/ **boots, booting, booted.** [1] N-C **Boots** are strong heavy shoes that cover your whole foot and the lower part of your legs. [2] VERB If you **boot** something such as a ball, you kick it hard; INFORMAL. [3] N-C In British English, the **boot** of a car is a covered space at the back or front that is used for luggage. The usual American word is **trunk**.

PHRASES ● If you **get the boot**, you are forced to leave your job; INFORMAL. ● You can say **to boot** after the last item in a list of things in order to emphasize that particular thing. *He was a liar, a cheat and a bad businessman to boot.*

booth /buːð/ **booths.** [1] N-C A **booth** is a small area separated from a larger public area by screens or thin walls where, for example, you can make a telephone call. [2] N-C A **booth** is a small tent or stall, usually at a fair, in which you can buy goods or watch some entertainment.

booze /buːz/ **boozes, boozing, boozed.** [1] N-U **Booze** is alcoholic drink; INFORMAL. [2] VERB When people **booze**, they drink a lot of alcohol; INFORMAL. *...a load of drunken businessmen who had been boozing all afternoon.*

border /'bɔːdə/ **borders, bordering, bordered.** [1] N-C The **border** between two countries is the dividing line between them. *They fled across the border.* [2] VERB If one thing **bor-**

ders another, it is next to it. ...*the countries bordering Iran.* ...*mile of white sand beach bordered by palm trees.* [3] N-C A **border** is a strip or band around the edge of something. ...*a wall of plain tiles with a bright border.* [4] VERB When you say that something **borders** on a particular state, you mean that it has almost reached that state. *He admitted last night that his feelings bordered on despair.*

bore /bɔː/ **bores, boring, bored.** [1] VERB If someone or something **bores** you, you find them dull and uninteresting. *Dick bored him all the way through the meal.* [2] N-C You describe someone as a **bore** when you think that they talk in a very uninteresting way. [3] N-SING You can describe a situation as **a bore** when you find it annoying or a nuisance. *It's a bore to be sick.* [4] VERB If you **bore** a hole in something, you make a deep round hole in it using a drilling tool. [5] **Bore** is the past tense of **bear**.

boredom /'bɔːdəm/. N-U **Boredom** is the state of being bored. *He had given up attending lectures out of sheer boredom.*

boring /'bɔːrɪŋ/. ADJ If you say that someone or something is **boring**, you think that they are very dull and uninteresting. ...*a boring job.*

born /bɔːn/. [1] PASSIVE-VERB When a baby **is born**, it comes out of its mother's body. You can refer to a baby's parents by saying that he or she **is born** of or **born** to those people. *My mother was 40 when I was born... He was born of German parents and lived most of his life abroad.* [2] ADJ BEFORE N You use **born** to describe someone who has a natural ability to do a particular activity or job. For example, a **born** cook has a natural ability to cook well.

-born. **-born** is added to the name of a place or nationality to indicate where a person was born. ...*the German-born photographer.*

borne /bɔːn/. **Borne** is the past participle of **bear**.

borough /'bʌrə, AM 'bɜːrəʊ/ **boroughs.** N-C A **borough** is a town or district, which has its own council. ...*the New York City borough of Queens.*

borrow /'bɒrəʊ/ **borrows, borrowing, borrowed.** VERB If you **borrow** something that belongs to someone else, you take it, usually with their permission, intending to return it. *Can I borrow a pen please?... He borrowed $200 from his wife.* ◆**borrowing** N-U *Government borrowing is set to surge.*

borrower /'bɒrəʊə/ **borrowers.** N-C A **borrower** is a person or organization that borrows money. *Most borrowers repay a fixed amount each month.*

bosom /'bʊzəm/ **bosoms.** [1] N-C A woman's breasts are sometimes referred to as her **bosom** or her **bosoms**; DATED. [2] N-SING If you are in the **bosom** of your family or of a community, you are among people who love and protect you; LITERARY. ...*after five long months away from the bosom of his family.* [3] ADJ BEFORE N A **bosom** friend is a very close friend. ...*his bosom buddy.*

boss /bɒs/ **bosses, bossing, bossed.** [1] N-C Your **boss** is the person in charge of the organization or department where you work. *He cannot stand his boss.* [2] PHRASE If you **are your**

own boss, you work for yourself or do not have to ask other people for permission to do something. *I'm very much my own boss and no one interferes with what I do.* [3] VERB & PHR-VERB If someone **bosses** you, or if they **boss** you **around**, they keep telling you what to do. *We cannot boss them into doing more.*

bossy /'bɒsi/. ADJ A **bossy** person enjoys telling other people what to do; used showing disapproval. ...*a rather bossy little girl.*

botany /'bɒtəni/. N-U **Botany** is the scientific study of plants. ◆**botanical** ADJ BEFORE N *The area is of great botanical interest.* ◆**botanist** /'bɒtənɪst/ **botanists** N-C *He trained as a botanist.*

botch /bɒtʃ/ **botches, botching, botched.** VERB & PHR-VERB If you **botch** a piece of work, or if you **botch** it **up**, you do it badly or clumsily; INFORMAL. *What if I botched it?... I hate having builders botch up repairs on my house.*

both /bəʊθ/. [1] QUANT You use **both** when you are referring to two people or things and saying that something is true about each of them. *Put both vegetables into a bowl... Both of us had tears in our eyes... Well, I'll leave you both then.* [2] CONJ You use the structure **both...and** when you are giving two facts or alternatives and emphasizing that each of them is true or possible. *Now, many women work both before and after having their children.*

> Notice that all these sentences mean the same thing: '**Both boys have been ill**', '**Both the boys have been ill**', '**Both of the boys have been ill**', '**The boys have both been ill**'. However, you cannot say 'Both of boys have been ill'.

bother /'bɒðə/ **bothers, bothering, bothered.** [1] VERB If you do not **bother** to do something or if you do not **bother** with it, you do not do it, consider it, or use it because you think it is unnecessary or because you are too lazy. *Lots of people don't bother to go through a marriage ceremony... The papers didn't even bother reporting it... He does not bother with a helmet.* [2] PHRASE If you say that you **can't be bothered** to do something, you mean that you are not going to do it because you think it is unnecessary or because you are too lazy. *I just can't be bothered to look after the house.* [3] N-U **Bother** is trouble, fuss, or difficulty. *I usually buy sliced bread – it's less bother... Going to the police is a bother.* [4] VERB If something **bothers** you, it worries, annoys, or upsets you. *It bothered me that boys weren't interested in me... Never bother about people's opinions.* ◆**bothered** ADJ AFTER LINK-V *I was bothered about the blister on my hand.* [5] VERB If you **bother** someone, you talk to them or interrupt them when they are busy. *I just don't know why he bothers me with this kind of rubbish.*

bottle /'bɒtəl/ **bottles, bottling, bottled.** [1] N-C A **bottle** is a glass or plastic container for keeping liquids in. ...*two empty beer bottles... He had drunk half a bottle of whisky.* [2] VERB To **bottle** liquid means to put it into bottles after it has been made. ...*equipment to auto-*

matically bottle the wine. ◆**bottled** ADJ *...bottled water.*

▶ **bottle up.** PHRASE-VERB If you **bottle up** feelings, you do not express them or show them. *Tension in the home increases if you bottle things up... Be assertive rather than bottle up anger.*

bottom /'bɒtəm/ **bottoms, bottoming, bottomed.** [1] N-C The **bottom** of something is the lowest part of it. *He sat at the bottom of the stairs. ...the bottom of page 8.* [2] ADJ BEFORE N The **bottom** thing in a series of things is the lowest one. *...the bottom drawer. ...the bottom shelf.* [3] N-SING If someone is **bottom** or at the **bottom** in a survey, test, or league, their performance is worse than that of all the other people involved. *He was always bottom of the class.* [4] N-C Your **bottom** is the part of your body that you sit on. [5] PHRASE If you **get to the bottom** of something, you discover the real cause of it. *I have to get to the bottom of this mess.*

▶ **bottom out.** PHRASE-VERB If a trend such as a fall in prices **bottoms out,** it stops getting worse or decreasing. *He expects the recession to bottom out.*

,**bottom 'line, bottom lines.** N-SING The **bottom line** in a decision or situation is the most important factor that you have to consider. *The bottom line is that it's not profitable.*

bought /bɔːt/. **Bought** is the past tense and past participle of **buy.**

boulder /'bəʊldə/ **boulders.** N-C A **boulder** is a large rounded rock.

boulevard /'buːləvɑːd, AM 'bʊl-/ **boulevards.** N-C A **boulevard** is a wide street in a city, usually with trees along each side. *...Lenton Boulevard.*

bounce /baʊns/ **bounces, bouncing, bounced.** [1] VERB & N-C When something such as a ball **bounces,** or when you **bounce** it, it moves upwards or away immediately after hitting a surface. This movement is called a **bounce.** *...a falling pebble, bouncing down the eroded cliff... I bounced a ball against the house. ...two bounces of the ball.* [2] VERB If you **bounce** on something, you jump up and down on it repeatedly. *She lets us do anything, even bounce on our beds.* [3] VERB If something **bounces** or if something **bounces** it, it swings or moves up and down. *Her long black hair bounced as she walked... The wind was bouncing the branches of the big oak trees.* [4] VERB If a cheque **bounces** or if a bank **bounces** it, the bank refuses to accept it and pay out the money.

bouncer /'baʊnsə/ **bouncers.** N-C A **bouncer** is a man who is employed to prevent unwanted people from entering a nightclub or causing trouble in it.

bouncy /'baʊnsi/. ADJ Someone or something that is **bouncy** is very lively and enthusiastic. *...good, bouncy pop songs... She was bouncy and full of energy.*

bound /baʊnd/ **bounds, bounding, bounded.** [1] **Bound** is the past tense and past participle of **bind.** [2] PHRASE If one thing is **bound up with** another, it is closely connected with it. *My fate was bound up with hers.* [3] PHRASE If something **is bound to** happen or be true, it is

certain to happen or be true. *There are bound to be price increases next year... He's bound to know.* [4] ADJ AFTER LINK-V If a vehicle is **bound for** a particular place, it is travelling towards it. *The ship was bound for Italy.* [5] N-PL **Bounds** are limits which restrict what can be done. *Visitors are kept firmly within bounds—no noise, no photographs.* [6] PHRASE If a place is **out of bounds,** people are not allowed to go there. [7] VERB When animals or people **bound,** they move quickly with large leaps. *He bounded up the steps.*

boundary /'baʊndəri/ **boundaries.** N-C The **boundary** of an area of land is an imaginary line that separates it from other areas. *...that disputed boundary between the two countries.*

bounty /'baʊnti/ **bounties.** N-VAR You can refer to something that is provided in large amounts as **bounty;** LITERARY. *...autumn's bounty of fruits, seeds and berries.*

bouquet /bəʊ'keɪ, buː-/ **bouquets.** N-C A **bouquet** is a bunch of flowers arranged in an attractive way. *...a bouquet of dried violets.*

bourgeois /'bʊəʒwɑː/. ADJ **Bourgeois** means typical of fairly rich middle-class people; used showing disapproval. *...his privileged bourgeois family.*

bout /baʊt/ **bouts.** [1] N-C If you have a **bout** of something such as an illness, you have it for a short period. *...a severe bout of flu.* [2] N-C A **bout** of activity is a short time during which it happens a great deal or in which you do it a great deal. *...the latest bout of violence.*

boutique /buː'tiːk/ **boutiques.** N-C A **boutique** is a small shop that sells fashionable clothes, shoes, or jewellery.

bow 1 bending or submitting

bow /baʊ/ **bows, bowing, bowed.** [1] VERB & N-C When you **bow** to someone, or if you give them a **bow,** you briefly bend your body towards them as a formal way of greeting them or showing respect. *They bowed low to Louis and hastened out of his way... I gave a theatrical bow.* [2] VERB If you **bow** your head, you bend it downwards so that you are looking towards the ground. *He bowed his head, ashamed.* [3] VERB If you **bow to** pressure or to someone's wishes, you agree to do what they want you to do. *Some shops are bowing to consumer pressure and stocking organically grown vegetables.*

▶ **bow out.** PHRASE-VERB If you **bow out** of something, you stop taking part in it. *He would bow out of politics after the next election... He had bowed out gracefully.*

bow 2 objects

bow /bəʊ/ **bows.** [1] N-C A **bow** is a knot with two loops and two loose ends that is used in tying shoelaces and ribbons. *...a length of ribbon tied in a bow.* [2] N-C A **bow** is a weapon for shooting arrows, consisting of a long curved piece of wood with a string attached to both its ends. [3] N-C The **bow** of a violin or other stringed instrument is a long thin piece of wood with horse hair stretched along it, which you move across the strings of the instrument in order to play it.

bowed. [1] ADJ /bəud/ Something that is **bowed** is curved. ...*an old lady with bowed legs.* [2] ADJ /baud/ If a person's body is **bowed**, it is bent forward. *Head bowed, she was listening or praying.*

bowel /'bauəl/ **bowels.** N-C Your **bowels** are the tubes in your body through which digested food passes from your stomach to your anus.

bowl /bəul/ **bowls, bowling, bowled.** [1] N-C A **bowl** is a circular container with a wide uncovered top that is used for mixing and serving food. ...*decorative wooden bowls.* ...*a bowl of soup.* [2] N-C You can refer to the hollow rounded part of an object as its **bowl**. ...*the toilet bowl.* [3] VERB In cricket, when a bowler **bowls**, they throw the ball down the pitch towards the batsman. [4] N-U **Bowls** is a game in which the players try to roll large wooden balls as near as possible to a small ball.

▶ **bowl over.** [1] PHR-VERB To **bowl** someone **over** means to push into them and make them fall to the ground. [2] PHR-VERB If you **are bowled over** by something, you are very impressed or surprised by it. *I was bowled over by the beauty of Cornwall.*

bowler /'bəulə/ **bowlers.** [1] N-C In cricket, the **bowler** is the person who is bowling. [2] N-C A **bowler** or a **bowler hat** is a round stiff hat with a narrow curved brim.

box /bɒks/ **boxes, boxing, boxed.** [1] N-C A **box** is a square or rectangular container with stiff sides and sometimes with a lid. ...*a small wooden box.* ...*a box of chocolates.* [2] N-C A **box** on a form is a square or rectangular space in which you have to write something. [3] N-C In a theatre or at a sports ground, a **box** is a small enclosed area where a small number of people can sit to watch the performance or game. [4] VERB To **box** means to fight someone according to the rules of the sport of boxing. *At school I boxed and played rugby.* ◆ **boxer, boxers.** N-C ...*a professional boxer.*

▶ **box in.** PHR-VERB If you **are boxed in**, you are unable to move because you are surrounded by other people or cars. *The black cabs cut in front of them, trying to box them in.*

boxing /'bɒksɪŋ/. N-U **Boxing** is a sport in which two people wearing padded gloves fight, using only their hands.

'box office, box offices. [1] N-C The **box office** in a theatre or cinema is the place where the tickets are sold. [2] N-SING People talk about the **box office** when they are referring to the success of a film or play in terms of the number of people who go to see it. *The movie looks set to be the biggest box office success of all time.*

boy /bɔɪ/ **boys.** [1] N-C A **boy** is a male child. [2] N-C You can refer to a young man as a **boy**, especially when talking about relationships between young men and women. ...*the age when girls get interested in boys.*

boycott /'bɔɪkɒt/ **boycotts, boycotting, boycotted.** VERB & N-C When people **boycott** a product they disapprove of, or organize a **boycott** against it, they refuse to buy it. People also **boycott** events and organizations by refusing to have anything to do with them. *The main opposition parties are boycotting the elec-*

tions. ...*the lifting of the economic boycott against Israel.*

boyfriend /'bɔɪfrend/ **boyfriends.** N-C Someone's **boyfriend** is the man with whom they are having a romantic or sexual relationship.

boyhood /'bɔɪhud/. N-U **Boyhood** is the period of a man's life during which he is a boy. *He has been a Derby County supporter since boyhood.*

boyish /'bɔɪʃ/. ADJ If you describe a man as **boyish**, you mean that his appearance or behaviour is like that of a boy, and you find this attractive. ...*a boyish grin.* ...*a boyish enthusiasm for life.* ◆ **boyishly** ADV *John grinned boyishly.*

Br. Br. is a written abbreviation for **British**.

bra /brɑː/ **bras.** N-C A **bra** is a piece of underwear that a woman wears to support her breasts.

brace /breɪs/ **braces, bracing, braced.** [1] VERB If you **brace** yourself for something unpleasant or difficult, you prepare yourself for it. *He braced himself for the icy plunge into the black water.* [2] VERB If you **brace** yourself against something, you press against it in order to steady yourself or to avoid falling. *He braced his back against one wall.* [3] N-C A **brace** is a device attached to a person's leg to strengthen or support it. [4] N-C A **brace** is a metal device fastened to a child's teeth to help them grow straight. [5] N-PL In British English, **braces** are a pair of straps that you wear over your shoulders to prevent your trousers from falling down. The American word is **suspenders**.

bracelet /'breɪslɪt/ **bracelets.** N-C A **bracelet** is a piece of jewellery that you wear round your wrist.

bracing /'breɪsɪŋ/. ADJ If you describe a place, climate, or activity as **bracing**, you mean that it makes you feel fit and full of energy.

bracket /'brækɪt/ **brackets.** [1] N-C If you say that someone or something is in a particular **bracket**, you mean that they are within a particular range. ...*a low income bracket.* [2] N-C **Brackets** are pieces of metal, wood, or plastic that are fastened to a wall in order to support something such as a shelf. [3] N-C **Brackets** are a pair of written marks such as ( ) that you place round a word or sentence in order to indicate that you are giving extra information.

brag /bræg/ **brags, bragging, bragged.** VERB If someone **brags**, they talk very proudly about what they have done or what they own; used showing disapproval. *He's always bragging about his ability as a cricketer... The chairman never tires of bragging that he and Mr. Bush are old friends.*

braid /breɪd/ **braids, braiding, braided.** [1] N-U **Braid** is a narrow piece of decorated cloth or twisted threads, used to decorate clothes or curtains. [2] VERB In American English, if you **braid** hair, you twist three or more lengths of it over and under each other to make one thick length. The usual British word is **plait**. [3] N-C In American English, a **braid** is a length of hair which has been plaited and tied. The usual British word is **plait**.

brain /breɪn/ **brains.** **1** N-C Your **brain** is the organ inside your head that controls your body's activities and enables you to think and to feel things. **2** N-C Your **brain** is your mind and the way that you think. *Once you stop using your brain you soon go stale.* **3** N-C If you say that someone has a good **brain**, you mean that they are intelligent and have the ability to make good decisions. *You've got brains, you've got ideas, get on with it.* **4** N-C The person who plans the activities of an organization can be referred to as the **brains** behind it; INFORMAL. *Some investigators regarded her as the brains of the gang.*

brainchild /ˈbreɪntʃaɪld/. N-SING The **brainchild** of a person is an idea or invention that they have thought up or created.

brake /breɪk/ **brakes, braking, braked.** **1** N-C A vehicle's **brakes** are devices that make it go slower or stop. **2** VERB When the driver of a vehicle **brakes**, or when the vehicle **brakes**, the driver presses the vehicle's brake, to make it slow down or stop. *She braked sharply to avoid another car.*

bran /bræn/. N-U **Bran** consists of small brown flakes that are left when wheat grains have been used to make white flour.

branch /brɑːntʃ, bræntʃ/ **branches, branching, branched.** **1** N-C The **branches** of a tree are the parts that grow out from its trunk. **2** N-C A **branch** of a business or other organization is one of the offices, shops, or local groups which belong to it. *The local branch of Bank of America is handling the accounts.* **3** N-C A **branch** of a subject is a part or type of it. *...a new branch of mathematics known as complexity theory.*

▸ **branch off.** PHR-VERB A road or path that **branches off** from another one starts from it and goes in a slightly different direction. If you **branch off** somewhere, you change the direction in which you are going. *After a few miles, a small road branched off to the right.*

▸ **branch out.** PHR-VERB If you **branch out**, you do something different from your normal activities or work. *...as telephone companies branch out into new information services.*

brand /brænd/ **brands, branding, branded.** **1** N-C A **brand** of a product is the version made by one particular manufacturer. *...a brand of cigarette. ...a supermarket's own brand.* **2** VERB If someone **is branded** as something bad, many people decide that they are that thing. *The company has been branded racist by some of its own staff... They recently branded him a war criminal.* **3** VERB When someone **brands** an animal, they burn a permanent mark onto its skin in order to show who it belongs to.

brandish /ˈbrændɪʃ/ **brandishes, brandishing, brandished.** VERB If you **brandish** something, especially a weapon, you hold it in a threatening way. *He appeared in the lounge brandishing a knife.*

'brand name, brand names. N-C A product's **brand name** is the name the manufacturer gives it and under which it is sold.

,brand-'new. ADJ Something that is **brand-new** is completely new.

brandy /ˈbrændi/ **brandies.** N-VAR **Brandy** is a strong alcoholic drink.

brash /bræʃ/ **brasher, brashest.** ADJ If you describe someone as **brash**, you disapprove of them because you think that they are aggressive and too confident. ♦**brashly** ADV *...the young man who had brashly challenged his leadership.* ♦**brashness** N-U *...a brashness bordering on arrogance.*

brass /brɑːs, bræs/. **1** N-U **Brass** is a yellow metal made from copper and zinc. *...shining brass buttons.* **2** N-PL The **brass** section of an orchestra is the part which consists of brass wind instruments such as trumpets and horns.

brat /bræt/ **brats.** N-C If you call a child a **brat**, you disapprove of their bad or annoying behaviour.

bravado /brəˈvɑːdəʊ/. N-U **Bravado** is an appearance of courage that someone shows in order to impress other people.

brave /breɪv/ **braver, bravest; braves, braving, braved.** **1** ADJ Someone who is **brave** is willing to do dangerous things, and does not show fear in difficult or dangerous situations. *...your mother's brave fight with the dread disease... He was not brave enough to report the loss of the documents.* ♦**bravely** ADV *The enemy fought bravely.* **2** VERB If you **brave** a difficult or dangerous situation, you deliberately experience it, in order to achieve something. *Thousands have braved icy rain to demonstrate their support.* **3** PHRASE If you say that someone is **putting a brave face on** a difficult situation, you mean that they are pretending that they are happy or coping with a problem when they are not.

bravery /ˈbreɪvəri/. N-U **Bravery** is brave behaviour or the quality of being brave.

brawl /brɔːl/ **brawls, brawling, brawled.** VERB & N-C If you **brawl** with each other, or become involved in a **brawl**, you fight in a rough disorganized way. *He was suspended for a year from University after brawling with police.*

brazen /ˈbreɪzən/. ADJ If you describe someone as **brazen**, you mean that they are very bold and do not care if other people think that they are behaving wrongly. *They have been more brazen about taking the law into their own hands.* ♦**brazenly** ADV *Every taboo was brazenly violated in a spirit of reckless adventure.*

breach /briːtʃ/ **breaches, breaching, breached.** **1** N-VAR & VERB If there is a **breach** of an agreement or a law, or if you **breach** an agreement or a law, you break it. *His employer sued him for breach of contract.* **2** N-C A **breach** in a relationship is a serious disagreement which often results in the relationship ending. *...a serious breach in relations between the two countries.* **3** VERB If someone or something **breaches** a barrier, they make an opening in it, usually leaving it weakened or destroyed. *The blast is thought to have breached a fire wall.* **4** N-C A **breach** in a barrier is a wide gap in it. **5** VERB & N-C If someone **breaches** security or defences, or if there is a **breach** in security or defences, they manage to get through and attack an area that is heavily guarded and protected.

bread /bred/. N-U Bread is a food made from flour, water, and often yeast. The mixture is made into a soft dough and baked in an oven. ...*a loaf of bread.*

breadth /bretθ, AM bredθ/. [1] N-U The **breadth** of something is the distance between its two sides. *The breadth of the whole camp was 400 paces.* [2] N-U **Breadth** is the quality of consisting of or involving many different things. *Older people have a tremendous breadth of experience.*

breadwinner /ˈbredwɪnə/ **breadwinners.** N-C In a family, the **breadwinner** is the person who earns the money that the family needs.

break /breɪk/ **breaks, breaking, broke, broken.** [1] VERB When an object **breaks** or when you **break** it, it suddenly separates into two or more pieces, often because it has been hit or dropped. *The plane broke into three pieces... He fell through the window, breaking the glass... Break the cauliflower into florets.* [2] VERB When a tool or piece of machinery **breaks** or when you **break** it, it is damaged and no longer works. *He accused her of breaking the stereo. ...broken washing machines.* [3] VERB If you **break** a rule or agreement, you do something that the rule or agreement indicates you should not do. *We didn't know we were breaking the law. ...broken promises.* [4] VERB If you **break free** or **break loose**, you free yourself from something or escape from it. *She broke free by thrusting her elbow into his chest.* [5] VERB To **break** a difficult or unpleasant situation that has existed for some time means to end it suddenly. *...to break the vicious circle between disadvantage and crime.* [6] VERB To **break** someone means to destroy their determination, their success, or their career. *He never let his jailers break him.* [7] N-C & VERB If you have a **break** or if you **break**, you stop what you are doing and do something else or have a rest. *Do you want to have a little break?... They broke for lunch.* [8] VERB To **break** the force of something such as a blow or fall means to weaken its effect. *Here the trees might have broken his fall.* [9] VERB If you **break** a piece of bad news to someone, you tell it to them. *Then Louise broke the news that she was leaving me.* [10] N-C A **break** is a lucky opportunity; INFORMAL. *Her big break came when she appeared on network TV.* [11] VERB If you **break** a record, you beat the previous record for a particular achievement. [12] VERB When day or dawn **breaks**, it starts to grow light after the night has ended. [13] VERB When a wave **breaks**, it passes its highest point and turns downwards. [14] VERB If you **break** a secret code, you work out how to understand it. [15] VERB When a boy's voice **breaks**, it becomes permanently deeper. [16] See also **broke, broken.** [17] To **break even**: see **even**.

▶ **break down.** [1] PHR-VERB If a machine or a vehicle **breaks down**, it stops working. [2] PHR-VERB When a discussion, relationship, or system **breaks down**, it fails because of a problem or disagreement. *Talks with business leaders broke down last night.* [3] PHR-VERB If someone **breaks down**, they start crying. [4] PHR-VERB When a substance **breaks down** or

when something **breaks** it **down**, it changes into a different form because of a chemical process. *The oil is attacked by naturally occurring microbes which break it down.* [5] PHR-VERB If you **break down** a door or barrier, you hit it so hard that it falls down. *His father failed to break the door down.* [6] See also **breakdown.**

▶ **break in.** [1] PHR-VERB If someone **breaks in**, they get into a building by force. *Masked robbers broke in and made off with $8,000.* ● See also **break-in.** [2] PHR-VERB If you **break in** on someone's conversation, you interrupt them. *'She told you to stay here,' Mike broke in.*

▶ **break into.** [1] PHR-VERB If someone **breaks into** a building, they get into it by force. [2] PHR-VERB You can use **break into** to indicate that someone suddenly starts doing something. *I feel as if I should break into song.* [3] PHR-VERB If you **break into** a new area of activity, you become involved in it. *She finally broke into films after an acclaimed stage career.*

▶ **break off.** [1] PHR-VERB When part of something **breaks off** or when you **break** it **off**, it is snapped off or torn away. *Lee broke off a small piece of orange.* [2] PHR-VERB If you **break off** when you are doing or saying something, you suddenly stop doing it or saying it. *Northern Ireland broke off the talks.* [3] PHR-VERB If you **break off** a relationship, you end it. *...the courage to break it off with her.*

▶ **break out.** [1] PHR-VERB If something such as a fight or disease **breaks out**, it begins suddenly. *He was 29 when war broke out.* [2] PHR-VERB If you **break out** in a rash or a sweat or if it **breaks out**, it appears on your skin.

▶ **break through.** [1] PHR-VERB If you **break through** a barrier, you succeed in forcing your way through. *About fifteen inmates broke through onto the roof.* [2] See also **breakthrough.**

▶ **break up.** [1] PHR-VERB When something **breaks up** or when you **break** it **up**, it separates or is divided into several smaller parts. *Break up the chocolate and melt it... He broke the bread up into chunks.* [2] PHR-VERB If you **break up** with your partner, you end your relationship with them; INFORMAL. *My girlfriend had broken up with me... The marriage broke up.* [3] PHR-VERB If an activity **breaks up** or if you **break** it **up**, it is brought to an end. *Police used tear gas to break up a demonstration.* [4] PHR-VERB When schools or their pupils **break up**, the term ends and the pupils start their holidays; BRITISH. *...the last week before they break up.* [5] See also **break-up.**

breakaway /ˈbreɪkəweɪ/. ADJ BEFORE N A **breakaway** group is a group of people who have separated from a larger group. *...the breakaway republic of Croatia.*

breakdown /ˈbreɪkdaʊn/ **breakdowns.** [1] N-C The **breakdown** of a system, plan, or discussion is its failure or ending. *...the breakdown of trade talks between the US and EU officials.* [2] N-C If you suffer a **breakdown**, you become so depressed that you cannot cope with life. *They often seem depressed and close to emotional breakdown.* ● See also **nervous breakdown.** [3] N-C A **breakdown** of a car or piece of machinery is when it stops working. [4] N-C A

breakdown of something is a list of its separate parts. *The organisers were given a breakdown of the costs.*

breakfast /'brekfəst/ **breakfasts.** N-VAR **Breakfast** is the first meal of the day, which is usually eaten early in the morning. *He likes two eggs for breakfast... I have breakfast at 9am.* ● See note at **meal**.

'**break-in, break-ins.** N-C When there is a **break-in,** someone gets into a building by force.

'**breaking point.** N-U If something or someone has reached **breaking point,** they have so many problems that they may soon be unable to continue. *My nerves are almost at breaking point.*

breakneck /'breiknek/. ADJ BEFORE N Something that happens or travels at **breakneck** speed happens or travels very fast. *The company has expanded at a breakneck pace.*

breakout (or **break-out**) /'breikaʊt/ **breakouts.** N-C If there has been a **break-out,** someone has escaped from prison. *High Point prison had the highest number of breakouts of any jail.*

breakthrough /'breikθruː/ **breakthroughs.** N-C A **breakthrough** is an important development or achievement. *The company looks poised to make a significant breakthrough in China.*

'**break-up, break-ups.** N-C The **break-up** of a group, relationship, or system is its end. *...since the break-up of his marriage.*

breast /brest/ **breasts.** [1] N-C A woman's **breasts** are the two soft round pieces of flesh on her chest that can produce milk to feed a baby. [2] N-C A person's chest can be referred to as his or her **breast**; LITERARY. *He struck his breast.* [3] N-C A bird's **breast** is the front part of its body. [4] N-VAR A piece of **breast** is a piece of meat that is cut from the front of a bird or lamb. *...grilled chicken breast.*

breath /breθ/ **breaths.** [1] N-VAR Your **breath** is the air which you take into and let out of your lungs when you breathe. *I could smell the whisky on his breath.* [2] N-VAR When you take a **breath,** you breathe in once. *He took a deep breath... He spoke for one and a half hours and barely paused for breath.*

PHRASES ● If you are **out of breath**, you are breathing very quickly and with difficulty because you have been doing something energetic. ● If you **hold** your **breath**, you make yourself stop breathing for a few moments. ● If you say something **under** your **breath**, you say it in a very quiet voice. ● If you describe something new or different as **a breath of fresh air**, you mean that you approve of it as it makes a situation or subject more interesting or exciting. *Her brisk treatment of an almost taboo subject was a breath of fresh air.* ● If you say that something **takes** your **breath away**, you mean that it is extremely beautiful or amazing. *I heard this song on the radio and it just took my breath away.*

breathalyze (or **breathalyse**) /'breθəlaɪz/ **breathalyzes, breathalyzing, breathalyzed.** VERB If the driver of a car **is breathalyzed** by the police, they ask him or her to breathe into a special device in order to test whether he or she has drunk too much alcohol.

breathe /briːð/ **breathes, breathing, breathed.** [1] VERB When people or animals **breathe,** they take air into their lungs and let it out again. *No American should have to drive out of town to breathe clean air... A thirteen year old girl is being treated after breathing in smoke.* ◆**breathing** N-U *Her breathing became slow and heavy.* [2] VERB If someone says something very quietly, you can say that they **breathe** it; LITERARY. *'You don't understand,' he breathed.* [3] VERB If someone **breathes** life, confidence, or excitement **into** something, they improve it by adding this quality; WRITTEN.

▶ **breathe in.** PHR-VERB When you **breathe in,** you take some air into your lungs.

▶ **breathe out.** PHR-VERB When you **breathe out,** you send air out of your lungs through your nose or mouth.

breather /'briːðə/ **breathers.** N-C If you take a **breather,** you stop what you are doing for a short time and have a rest; INFORMAL.

'**breathing space.** N-U A **breathing space** is a short period of time in which you can recover from one activity and prepare for a second one. *We hope that it will give us some breathing space.*

breathless /'breθləs/. ADJ If you are **breathless,** you have difficulty in breathing properly, for example because you have been running. ◆**breathlessly** ADV *'I'll go in,' he said breathlessly.* ◆**breathlessness** N-U *Asthma causes wheezing and breathlessness.*

breathtaking (or **breath-taking**) /'breθteɪkɪŋ/. ADJ If you say that something is **breathtaking,** you mean that it is extremely beautiful or amazing. *The house has breathtaking views from every room.* ◆**breathtakingly** ADV *...a breathtakingly simple gadget.*

breed /briːd/ **breeds, breeding, bred** /bred/. [1] N-C A **breed** of animal is a particular type of it. For example, terriers are a breed of dog. [2] VERB If you **breed** animals or plants, you keep them for the purpose of producing more animals or plants. *He used to breed dogs for the police... New varieties of rose are bred each year.* ◆**breeder, breeders.** N-C *...horse breeders.* ◆**breeding** N-U *...selective breeding for better yields.* [3] VERB When animals **breed,** they mate and produce offspring. ◆**breeding** N-U *...the breeding season.* [4] VERB If something **breeds** a situation or feeling, it causes it to develop. *If they are unemployed it's bound to breed resentment.* [5] PHRASE Someone who was **born and bred** in a particular place was born there and spent their childhood there. *...a Londoner born and bred.* [6] N-C A particular **breed** of person is a type of person, with special qualities or skills. *...one of the new breed of British women squash players.*

breeze /briːz/ **breezes, breezing, breezed.** [1] N-C A **breeze** is a gentle wind. *I imagined a breeze blowing against my face. ...a cool salty sea breeze.* [2] VERB When you **breeze** into a place, you enter it in a casual and carefree way. *He was late, but eventually he breezed in.*

breezy /'bri:zi/. [1] ADJ Someone who is **breezy** behaves in a brisk, casual, cheerful, and confident way. *...his bright and breezy personality.* [2] ADJ When the weather is **breezy**, there is a fairly strong but pleasant wind blowing. *The day was breezy and warm.*

brethren /'breðrɪn/. See **brother**.

brew /bru:/ **brews, brewing, brewed.** [1] VERB When you **brew** tea or coffee, you make it by pouring hot water over tea leaves or ground coffee. [2] N-C A **brew** is a pot of tea or coffee. *...a mild herbal brew.* [3] VERB If someone **brews** beer, they make it. [4] VERB If an unpleasant situation **is brewing**, it is starting to develop. *A crisis was brewing.*

brewer /'bru:ə/ **brewers.** N-C A **brewer** is a person or company that makes beer.

brewery /'bru:əri/ **breweries.** N-C A **brewery** is a place where beer is made.

bribe /braɪb/ **bribes, bribing, bribed.** N-C & VERB If you are offered a **bribe** or if you **are bribed**, you are offered a sum of money or something valuable in order to persuade you to do something. *He was being investigated for receiving bribes... He bribed the workers to silence.*

bribery /'braɪbəri/. N-U **Bribery** is the action of giving someone a bribe. *He was jailed on charges of bribery.*

brick /brɪk/ **bricks.** N-VAR **Bricks** are rectangular blocks of baked clay used for building walls. *...a huge brick building.*

bride /braɪd/ **brides.** N-C A **bride** is a woman who is getting married or who has just got married. *The guests had crowded around the bride and groom.* ♦**bridal** ADJ BEFORE N *...a bridal shop.*

bridegroom /'braɪdgru:m/ **bridegrooms.** N-C A **bridegroom** is a man who is getting married.

bridesmaid /'braɪdzmeɪd/ **bridesmaids.** N-C A **bridesmaid** is a woman or a girl who accompanies a bride on her wedding day.

bridge /brɪdʒ/ **bridges.** [1] N-C A **bridge** is a structure built over a river, road, or railway so that people or vehicles can cross from one side to the other. *I walked across the bridge.* [2] VERB & N-C If something **bridges** the gap between two people or things, or if it acts as a **bridge** between them, it makes it easier for the differences or disagreements between them to be reduced or overcome. *It is unlikely that the two sides will be able to bridge their differences.* [3] N-U **Bridge** is a card game for four players.

bridle /'braɪdəl/ **bridles, bridling, bridled.** N-C & VERB A **bridle** is a set of straps that is put around a horse's head and mouth so that the person riding or driving the horse can control it. When you **bridle** a horse, you put a bridle on it.

brief /bri:f/ **briefer, briefest; briefs, briefing, briefed.** [1] ADJ Something that is **brief** lasts for only a short time. *She once made a brief appearance on television. ...a brief statement.* [2] ADJ AFTER LINK-V If you are **brief**, you say what you want to say in as few words as possible. *I hope to be brief and to the point.* [3] N-PL Men's or women's underpants can be referred to as

briefs. [4] VERB If someone **briefs** you, they give you information or instructions that you need. *The Prime Minister has been briefed by her parliamentary aides.*

briefcase /'bri:fkeɪs/ **briefcases.** N-C A **briefcase** is a case for carrying documents.

briefing /'bri:fɪŋ/ **briefings.** N-VAR A **briefing** is a meeting at which information or instructions are given to people. *They're holding a press briefing tomorrow.*

briefly /'bri:fli/. [1] ADV Something that happens **briefly** happens for a very short period of time. *He smiled briefly... The couple chatted briefly on the doorstep.* [2] ADV If you say something **briefly**, you use very few words or give very few details. *She told them briefly what had happened... Briefly, these are some of my main findings.*

brigade /brɪ'geɪd/ **brigades.** N-C A **brigade** is one of the groups which an army is divided into. ● See also **fire brigade**.

brigadier /ˌbrɪgə'dɪə/ **brigadiers.** N-C & N-TITLE A **brigadier** is an army officer of high rank.

bright /braɪt/ **brighter, brightest.** [1] ADJ A **bright** colour is strong and noticeable, and not dark. *...a bright red dress.* ♦**brightly** ADV *...brightly coloured wallpaper.* [2] ADJ A **bright** light, object, or place is shining strongly or is full of light. *...a bright October day.* ♦**brightly** ADV *...a warm, brightly lit room... The sun shone brightly.* ♦**brightness** N-U *...the brightness of each star.* [3] ADJ **Bright** people or ideas are clever and original. *Were you always fairly bright at school?* [4] ADJ If someone looks or sounds **bright**, they look or sound cheerful. *'May I help you?' said a bright American voice.* ♦**brightly** ADV *He smiled brightly.* [5] ADJ If the future is **bright**, it is likely to be pleasant and successful. *Both had successful careers and the future looked bright.*

brighten /'braɪtən/ **brightens, brightening, brightened.** [1] VERB If you **brighten**, or if you **brighten up**, you suddenly look happier. *They brightened up at the mention of departure.* [2] VERB If someone or something **brightens** a situation, or if the situation **brightens**, it becomes more pleasant or favourable. *Prospects for the industry may be brightening.* [3] VERB & PHR-VERB If something **brightens** a place, or if it **brightens** it **up**, the place becomes brighter or lighter. *It could do with a lick of paint to brighten up its premises.*

brilliant /'brɪliənt/. [1] ADJ If you describe people or ideas as **brilliant**, you mean that they are extremely clever. *He was a brilliant musician... She had a brilliant mind.* ♦**brilliantly** ADV *...a very high quality production, brilliantly written and acted.* ♦**brilliance** N-U *...his brilliance as a director.* [2] ADJ You can say something is **brilliant** when it is very successful. *...his brilliant career... She knew she could have a brilliant future.* [3] ADJ BEFORE N A **brilliant** light or colour is extremely bright. *The woman had brilliant green eyes.* ♦**brilliantly** ADV *...brilliantly coloured flowers.*

brim /brɪm/ **brims, brimming, brimmed.** [1] N-C The **brim** of a hat is the wide part that sticks outwards at the bottom. [2] VERB If something **is brimming** with things of a particular kind, it is full of them. *Her eyes were brimming with tears now.*

bring /brɪŋ/ **brings, bringing, brought.**
[1] VERB If you **bring** someone or something with you when you come to a place, they come with you or you have them with you. *Remember to bring an apron... Someone went upstairs and brought down a huge kettle... Come to my party and bring a girl with you.* [2] VERB If you **bring** something somewhere, you move it there. *Reaching into her pocket, she brought out a cigarette... Her mother brought her hands up to her face... He poured a brandy for Dena and brought it to her.* [3] VERB To **bring** something or someone to a place means to cause them to come to that place. *I told you about what brought me here.* [4] VERB To **bring** something or someone into a particular state or condition means to cause them to be in it. You can also say something **brings** a particular feeling, situation, or quality. *He brought the car to a stop... They have brought down income taxes... Her three children brought her joy.* [5] VERB If you cannot **bring** yourself to do something, you cannot make yourself do it. *I just cannot bring myself to talk about it.*

Bring and **take** are both used to talk about carrying something or accompanying someone somewhere, but **bring** is used to suggest movement towards the speaker and **take** is used to suggest movement away from the speaker. *Martin had brought the book into hospital with him... Anna took the book to bed with her.* In the first sentence, *brought* suggests that Martin is coming to the same place as the speaker, that is, the speaker is in the hospital too. In the second sentence, *took* suggests that Anna moved away from the speaker when she went to bed, or alternatively that the speaker is merely reporting something that he or she was not involved in.
The difference between **bring** and **take** is equivalent to that between **come** and **go**. **Bring** and **come** suggest movement towards the speaker, while **take** and **go** suggest movement away.

▶ **bring about.** PHR-VERB To **bring** something **about** means to cause it to happen. *...the only way to bring about political change... That's what's brought it all about.*

▶ **bring along.** PHR-VERB If you **bring** someone or something **along**, you bring them with you when you come to a place. *Dad brought a notebook along... Bring along your friends.*

▶ **bring back.** [1] PHR-VERB If something **brings back** a memory, it makes you start thinking about it. *Your article brought back sad memories for me.* [2] PHR-VERB When people **bring back** a fashion or practice that existed at an earlier time, they introduce it again. *...whether to bring back the death penalty.*

▶ **bring down.** PHR-VERB To **bring down** a government or ruler means to cause them to lose power. *They were threatening to bring down the government.*

▶ **bring forward.** [1] PHR-VERB To **bring forward** an event means to arrange for it to take place at an earlier time than had been planned. *He had to bring forward an 11 o'clock meeting... We decided to bring the wedding forward.* [2] PHR-VERB If you **bring forward** an argument or proposal, you state it so that people can consider it. *The Government will bring forward proposals for legislation.*

▶ **bring in.** [1] PHR-VERB When an organization **brings in** a new law or system, they introduce it. *The government brought in a controversial law.* [2] PHR-VERB To **bring in** money means to earn it; INFORMAL. *I have three part-time jobs, which bring in about £6,000 a year.*

▶ **bring off.** PHR-VERB If you **bring off** something difficult, you succeed in doing it; INFORMAL. *They were about to bring off an even bigger coup... He thought his book would change society. But he didn't bring it off.*

▶ **bring out.** [1] PHR-VERB When a person or company **brings out** a new product, they produce it and sell it. *He's now brought out a book.* [2] PHR-VERB Something that **brings out** a particular kind of behaviour in you causes you to behave in that way. *A challenge brought out the best in him.*

▶ **bring up.** [1] PHR-VERB To **bring up** a child means to look after it until it is grown up. *She brought up four children... I bring my children up to be trusting, honest and helpful.* [2] PHR-VERB If you **bring up** a particular subject, you introduce it into a discussion or conversation. *Why are you bringing it up now?* [3] PHR-VERB If you **bring up** food, you vomit; INFORMAL. *If I taste anything, I bring it up again directly.*

brink /brɪŋk/. N-SING If you are on the **brink** of something important, terrible, or exciting, you are just about to do it or experience it. *I was on the brink of poverty... He was driven to the brink of madness.*

brisk /brɪsk/ **brisker, briskest.** [1] ADJ A **brisk** action is done quickly and in an energetic way. *...a brisk walk.* ◆**briskly** ADV *Eve walked briskly down the corridor.* [2] ADJ If someone's behaviour is **brisk**, they behave in a busy confident way which shows that they want to get things done quickly. *Her voice was brisk and professional.* ◆**briskly** ADV *'Anyhow,' she added briskly, 'it's none of my business'.* [3] ADJ If the weather is **brisk**, it is cold and refreshing. *...a brisk winter's day.*

bristle /ˈbrɪsəl/ **bristles, bristling, bristled.** [1] N-C **Bristles** are short thick hairs that feel hard and rough. [2] N-C The **bristles** of a brush are the thick hairs attached to the handle. [3] VERB If the hair on your body **bristles**, it rises away from your skin because you are cold, frightened, or angry. *It makes the hairs at the nape of the neck bristle.* [4] VERB If you **bristle** at something, you react to it angrily. *He still bristles at the suggestion that he is arrogant.*

▶ **bristle with.** PHR-VERB If a place **bristles with** objects or people, there are a lot of them there. *The island was bristling with soldiers.*

British /ˈbrɪtɪʃ/. [1] ADJ **British** means belonging or relating to Great Britain. *...the British gov-*

ernment. [2] N-PL The **British** are the people who come from Great Britain.

Briton /'brɪtən/ **Britons.** N-C A **Briton** is a person who comes from Great Britain. *...seventeen-year-old Briton Jane March.*

brittle /'brɪtəl/. ADJ A **brittle** object or substance is hard but easily broken. *...the dry, brittle ends of the hair.*

broach /brəʊtʃ/ **broaches, broaching, broached.** VERB When you **broach** a subject, you mention it in order to start a discussion on it. *I broached the subject of her early life.*

broad /brɔːd/ **broader, broadest.** [1] ADJ Something that is **broad** is wide. *His shoulders were broad. ...the broad river.* [2] ADJ You use **broad** to describe something that involves many different things or people. *A broad range of issues was discussed.* [3] ADJ A **broad** description is general rather than detailed. *...a broad outline of the Society's development.* [4] ADJ BEFORE N A **broad** hint is a very obvious one. *They've been giving broad hints about what to expect.* [5] ADJ A **broad** accent is strong and noticeable. *He has a broad Yorkshire accent.*

broadcast /'brɔːdkɑːst, -kæst/ **broadcasts, broadcasting, broadcasted** or **broadcast.** [1] N-C A **broadcast** is something that you hear on the radio or see on television. *A broadcast of the speech was heard in San Francisco.* [2] VERB To **broadcast** a programme means to send it out by radio waves, so that it can be heard on the radio or seen on television. *The concert will be broadcast live on television.* ◆**broadcasting** N-U *...the BBC Weather Service celebrated 70 years of broadcasting.*

broadcaster /'brɔːdkɑːstə, -kæst-/ **broadcasters.** N-C A **broadcaster** is someone who gives talks or takes part in discussions on radio or television.

broaden /'brɔːdən/ **broadens, broadening, broadened.** [1] VERB When something **broadens**, it becomes wider. *The smile broadened to a grin... As we drove towards Chamdo, the river broadened.* [2] VERB If you **broaden** something, or if it **broadens**, you make it involve or affect more things or people. *We must broaden our appeal... The political spectrum has broadened.*

broadly /'brɔːdli/. [1] ADV You use **broadly** to indicate that something is generally true. *The idea that software is capable of any task is broadly true.* [2] ADV You use **broadly** to say that something is true to a large extent. *The new law has been broadly welcomed.* [3] ADV If someone smiles **broadly**, their mouth is stretched very wide.

broad-'minded. ADJ Someone who is **broad-minded** does not disapprove of actions or attitudes that many other people disapprove of; used showing approval. *...a shrewd, broad-minded man of high intelligence.*

broccoli /'brɒkəli/. N-U **Broccoli** is a vegetable with green stalks and green or purple flower buds.

brochure /'brəʊʃə, AM brəʊ'fʊr/ **brochures.** N-C A **brochure** is a booklet with pictures that gives you information about a product or service. *...holiday brochures.*

broil /brɔɪl/ **broils, broiling, broiled.** VERB In American English, if you **broil** food, you cook

it using strong heat directly above or below it. The British word is **grill**. ● See note at **cook**.

broke /brəʊk/. [1] **Broke** is the past tense of **break.** [2] ADJ If you are **broke**, you have no money; INFORMAL. *He was broke when I married him.* [3] PHRASE If a company or person **goes broke**, they lose money and are unable to continue in business or to pay their debts.

broken /'brəʊkən/. [1] **Broken** is the past participle of **break.** [2] ADJ BEFORE N A **broken** line is not continuous but has gaps in it. [3] ADJ BEFORE N You use **broken** to describe a marriage that has ended in divorce, or a home in which the parents of the family are divorced, when you think this is a sad thing. *...children from broken homes.* [4] ADJ BEFORE N If someone talks in **broken** English or in **broken** French, for example, they speak slowly and make a lot of mistakes because they do not know the language very well.

broker /'brəʊkə/ **brokers, brokering, brokered.** [1] N-C A **broker** is a person whose job is to buy and sell shares, foreign money, or goods for other people. [2] VERB If a country or government **brokers** an agreement, they try to negotiate or arrange it. *The United Nations brokered a peace in Mogadishu.*

bronze /brɒnz/ **bronzes.** [1] N-U **Bronze** is a yellowish-brown metal made from copper and tin. [2] N-C A **bronze** is a sculpture made of bronze. *...a bronze of Napoleon on horseback.* [3] ADJ Something that is **bronze** is yellowish-brown in colour. *Her hair shone bronze and gold.*

,bronze 'medal, bronze medals. N-C If you win a **bronze medal**, you come third in a competition, especially a sports contest, and are often given a medal made of bronze as a prize.

brooch /brəʊtʃ/ **brooches.** N-C A **brooch** is a small piece of jewellery which can be pinned on a dress, blouse, or coat.

brood /bruːd/ **broods, brooding, brooded.** [1] N-C A **brood** is a group of baby birds belonging to the same mother. [2] VERB If someone **broods** over something, they think about it a lot, seriously and often unhappily. *She constantly broods about her family.*

brooding /'bruːdɪŋ/. [1] ADJ **Brooding** is used to describe an atmosphere or feeling that causes you to feel disturbed or slightly afraid; LITERARY. *...a heavy, brooding silence.* [2] ADJ If you describe someone's expression as **brooding**, you mean that they look as if they are thinking deeply about something. *...his dark, brooding eyes.*

brook /brʊk/ **brooks.** N-C A **brook** is a small stream.

broom /bruːm/ **brooms.** N-C A **broom** is a long-handled brush which is used to sweep the floor.

broth /brɒθ, AM brɔːθ/. N-U **Broth** is a kind of soup. It usually has vegetables or rice in it.

brothel /'brɒθəl/ **brothels.** N-C A **brothel** is a building where men pay to have sex with prostitutes.

brother /'brʌðə/ **brothers.** The old-fashioned form **brethren** is also used as the plural for meaning 2. [1] N-C Your **brother** is a boy or a man who has the same parents as you. ...*my younger brother.* ● See also **half-brother.**

> Note that there is no common English word that can refer to both a brother and a sister. You simply have to use both words. *She has 13 brothers and sisters.* The word **sibling** exists, but it is rare and very formal.

2 N-C Some people describe a man as their **brother** when he belongs to the same group as them. *Sri Lankans share a common ancestry with their Indian brethren.* **3** N-TITLE **Brother** is a title given to a man who belongs to a religious institution such as a monastery. ...*Brother Otto.*

brotherhood /'brʌðəhʊd/ **brotherhoods.** **1** N-U **Brotherhood** is the affection and loyalty that you feel for people who you have something in common with. *He believed in socialism and the brotherhood of man.* **2** N-C A **brotherhood** is an organization whose members all have the same political aims and beliefs or the same job or profession.

'brother-in-law, **brothers-in-law.** N-C Someone's **brother-in-law** is the brother of their husband or wife, or the man who is married to their sister.

brought /brɔːt/. **Brought** is the past tense and past participle of **bring.**

brow /braʊ/ **brows.** **1** N-C Your **brow** is your forehead. *He wiped his brow with the back of his hand.* **2** N-C Your **brows** are your eyebrows. **3** N-C The **brow** of a hill is the top part of it.

brown /braʊn/ **browner, brownest; browns, browning, browned.** **1** ADJ & N-VAR Something that is **brown** is the colour of earth or wood. ...*her deep brown eyes.* **2** ADJ You can describe a white-skinned person as **brown** when they have been sitting in the sun until their skin is darker than usual. *I don't want to be really brown, just have a nice light golden colour.* **3** VERB If someone **browns** in the sun or if the sun **browns** them, they become brown in colour. When food **browns** or when you **brown** food, you cook it, usually for a short time on a high flame. ...*gorgeous females busy browning themselves... Cook for ten minutes until the sugar browns.*

browse /braʊz/ **browses, browsing, browsed.** **1** VERB & N-C If you **browse** or have a **browse** in a shop, you look at things in a casual way, without intending to buy anything. *I stopped in several bookstores to browse... I'm just browsing around. ...a browse around the shops.* **2** VERB If you **browse** through a book or magazine, you look through it in a casual way. ...*browsing through brochures.*

bruise /bruːz/ **bruises, bruising, bruised.** **1** N-C A **bruise** is an injury which appears as a purple mark on your body. **2** VERB If you **bruise** a part of your body, a bruise appears on it, for example because something hits you. *I had only bruised my knee.* ◆**bruised** ADJ ...*a badly bruised leg.*

brunt /brʌnt/. PHRASE If someone or something **bears the brunt** or **takes the brunt** of something unpleasant, they suffer the main part or force of it. *Young people are bearing the brunt of unemployment.*

brush /brʌʃ/ **brushes, brushing, brushed.** **1** N-C A **brush** is an object with a large number of bristles fixed to it. You use brushes for painting, for cleaning things, and for tidying your hair. ...*a hair brush.* **2** VERB & N-SING When you **brush** something or when you give it a **brush**, you clean it or tidy it using a brush. ...*he brushed away the fine sawdust.* **3** VERB If you **brush** something somewhere, you remove it with quick light movements of your hands. *He brushed the snow off the windshield.* **4** VERB If one thing **brushes** against another or if you **brush** one thing against another, the first thing touches the second thing lightly while passing it. *She brushed her lips softly across Michael's cheek.*

▶ **brush aside** or **brush away.** PHR-VERB If you **brush aside** or **brush away** an idea, remark, or feeling, you refuse to consider it because you think it is not important or useful, even though it may be. *Perhaps you shouldn't brush the idea aside too hastily.*

▶ **brush up.** PHR-VERB If you **brush up** something or if you **brush up on** it, you practise it or improve your knowledge of it. *Eleanor spent much of the summer brushing up on her driving.*

brusque /bruːsk/. ADJ If you describe a person as **brusque**, you mean that they deal with people quickly and abruptly, without showing much consideration for their feelings. *The doctors are brusque and busy.* ◆**brusquely** ADV *'It's only a sprain,' Paula said brusquely.*

,brussels 'sprout (or **Brussels sprout**) **brussels sprouts.** N-C **Brussels sprouts** or **sprouts** are vegetables that look like tiny cabbages.

brutal /'bruːtəl/. **1** ADJ A **brutal** act or person is cruel and violent. ...*the brutal suppression of anti-government protests.* ◆**brutally** ADV *Her real parents had been brutally murdered.* **2** ADJ If someone expresses something unpleasant with **brutal** honesty or frankness, they express it in a clear and accurate way, without attempting to disguise or reduce its unpleasant effect. *She spoke with a brutal honesty.* ◆**brutally** ADV *The talks had been brutally frank.*

brutality /bruː'tælɪti/ **brutalities.** N-VAR **Brutality** is cruel and violent treatment or behaviour. A **brutality** is an instance of cruel and violent treatment or behaviour. ...*police brutality.* ...*the brutalities of civil war.*

brute /bruːt/ **brutes.** **1** N-C If you call a man a **brute**, you mean that he is rough and insensitive. ...*a drunken brute.* **2** ADJ BEFORE N When you refer to **brute** strength or force, you are contrasting it with gentler methods or qualities. *He used brute force to take control.*

BSE /,biː es 'iː/. N-U **BSE** is a fatal disease which affects the nervous system of cattle. It is an abbreviation for 'bovine spongiform encephalopathy'.

bubble /'bʌbəl/ **bubbles, bubbling, bubbled.** **1** N-C **Bubbles** are small balls of air or gas in a liquid. ...*a bubble of gas.* **2** N-C A **bub-**

ble is a hollow delicate ball of soapy liquid floating in the air or standing on a surface. *...soap bubbles.* **3** VERB When a liquid **bubbles**, bubbles move in it, for example because it is boiling or moving quickly. *The water bubbled to the surface.* **4** VERB If you are **bubbling** with a good feeling, you are full of it. *She came to the phone bubbling with excitement.*

bubbly /'bʌbli/ **bubblier, bubbliest.** **1** ADJ If something is **bubbly**, it has a lot of bubbles in it. *...warm, bubbly water.* **2** N-U Champagne is sometimes called **bubbly**; INFORMAL. **3** ADJ Someone who is **bubbly** is very lively and cheerful. *...a bubbly girl who loves to laugh.*

buck /bʌk/ **bucks, bucking, bucked.** **1** N-C A **buck** is a US or Australian dollar; INFORMAL. *That would probably cost you about fifty bucks.* **2** PHRASE When someone makes **a fast buck** or makes **a quick buck**, they earn a lot of money quickly and easily, often by doing something which is considered to be dishonest; INFORMAL. **3** N-C A **buck** is the male of various animals, including the deer and rabbit. **4** VERB If a horse **bucks**, it jumps into the air wildly with all four feet off the ground. **5** PHRASE If you **pass the buck**, you refuse to accept responsibility for something. *David says the responsibility is Mr Smith's and it's no good trying to pass the buck.*

▶ **buck up.** **1** PHR-VERB If you **buck** someone **up** or if you **buck up** their spirits, you say or do something to make them more cheerful; INFORMAL. **2** PHR-VERB If you tell someone to **buck up** or to **buck up** their ideas, you are telling them to start behaving in a more positive manner; INFORMAL. *If we don't buck up we'll be in trouble.*

bucket /'bʌkɪt/ **buckets.** N-C A **bucket** is a deep round metal or plastic container with a handle. *...a blue bucket. ...a bucket of water.*

buckle /'bʌkəl/ **buckles, buckling, buckled.** **1** N-C & VERB A **buckle** is a piece of metal or plastic attached to one end of a belt or strap and used to fasten it. When you **buckle** a belt or strap, you fasten it with a buckle. *...a big silver belt buckle... He always buckles his seat belt.* **2** VERB If an object **buckles** or if something **buckles** in, it becomes bent as a result of severe heat or force. *A freak wave had buckled the deck.* **3** VERB If your legs **buckle**, they bend because they have become very weak. *His knees buckled and he fell backwards.*

▶ **buckle down.** PHR-VERB If you **buckle down** to something, you start working seriously at it. *I just buckled down and got on with playing.*

bud /bʌd/ **buds, budding, budded.** **1** N-C A **bud** is a small pointed lump that appears on a tree or plant and develops into a leaf or flower. **2** VERB When a tree or plant **is budding**, buds are appearing on it or are beginning to open. **3** PHRASE To **nip** something **in the bud** means to stop it before it can develop very far; INFORMAL. *It is important to recognize jealousy and to nip it in the bud before it gets out of hand.*

Buddhist /'bʊdɪst/ **Buddhists.** N-C & ADJ **Buddhists** believe in a religion which teaches that the way to end suffering is by overcoming your desires. **Buddhist** means relating to this religion. *She has been a Buddhist since 1976. ...a*

Buddhist temple. ♦**Buddhism.** N-U *...the doctrine of Buddhism.*

budding /'bʌdɪŋ/. ADJ BEFORE N You use **budding** to describe someone who is just beginning to succeed or become interested in a certain activity. You also use **budding** to describe a situation that is just beginning. *...a budding actress. ...our budding romance.*

buddy /'bʌdi/ **buddies.** **1** N-C A **buddy** is a close friend, usually a male friend of a man; INFORMAL. *We became great buddies.* **2** N-VOC Men sometimes address other men as **buddy**; AMERICAN, INFORMAL.

budge /bʌdʒ/ **budges, budging, budged.** **1** VERB If someone will not **budge** on a matter, or if nothing **budges** them, they refuse to change their mind or to compromise. *Both sides say they will not budge... No amount of prodding will budge him.* **2** VERB If someone or something will not **budge**, or if you cannot **budge** them, they will not move. *Her mother refused to budge from London... I got a grip on the boat and pulled but I couldn't budge it.*

budget /'bʌdʒɪt/ **budgets, budgeting, budgeted.** **1** N-C A **budget** is a plan showing how much money a person or organization has available and how it will be spent. The **budget** for something is the amount of money that a person, organization, or country has available to spend on it. *I do try and buy within my budget. ...this year's budget for AIDS prevention.* **2** VERB If you **budget** certain amounts of money for particular things, you decide that you can afford to spend those amounts on those things. *The movie is only budgeted at $10 million... I'm learning how to budget.* ♦**budgeting** N-U *...our budgeting for the current year.* **3** ADJ BEFORE N **Budget** is used to suggest that something is being sold cheaply. *...a budget-priced CD.*

buff /bʌf/ **buffs, buffing, buffed.** **1** N-C You use **buff** to talk about people who know a lot about a particular subject; INFORMAL. *...an avid film buff.* **2** VERB If you **buff** the surface of something, you rub it with a piece of soft material in order to make it shine.

buffalo /'bʌfələʊ/; the plural is **buffalo** or **buffaloes**. N-C A **buffalo** is a wild animal like a large cow with long curved horns.

buffer /'bʌfə/ **buffers.** **1** N-C A **buffer** is something that prevents something else from being harmed. *Keep savings as a buffer against unexpected cash needs.* **2** N-C The **buffers** on a train or at the end of a railway line are two metal discs on springs that reduce the shock when they are hit.

buffet, buffets, buffeting, buffeted. **1** N-C /'bʌfeɪ, AM bʊ'feɪ/ A **buffet** is a café in a station. **2** N-C A **buffet** is a meal of cold food at a special occasion. Guests may help themselves to the food. **3** N-C On a train, the **buffet** or the **buffet car** is the carriage where meals and snacks are sold; BRITISH. **4** VERB /'bʌfɪt/ If something is **buffeted** by rough winds or seas, it is repeatedly struck or blown around by them. *Their plane had been severely buffeted by storms.*

bug /bʌg/ **bugs, bugging, bugged.** **1** N-C A **bug** is a tiny insect, especially one that causes damage; INFORMAL. [2] N-C A **bug** is a minor illness such as a cold. *...a stomach bug... There was a bug going around.* [3] N-C If there is a **bug** in a computer program, there is an error in it. [4] VERB If a place **is bugged,** tiny microphones are hidden there to secretly record what people are saying. [5] VERB If something or someone **bugs** you, they worry or annoy you; INFORMAL. *I only did it to bug my parents. ...this little short guy who really bugged me.*

build /bɪld/ **builds, building, built** /bɪlt/. [1] VERB If you **build** a structure, you make it by joining things together. *Developers are now proposing to build a hotel on the site... Workers at the plant build the F-16 jet fighter.* [2] VERB If you **build** something into a wall or object, you make it in such a way that it is in the wall or object, or is part of it. *The TV was built into the ceiling.* [3] VERB If people **build** an organization or a society, they gradually form it. *Their purpose is to build a fair society and a strong economy.* [4] VERB If you **build** an organization, system, or product on something, you base it on it. *...a firmer foundation of fact on which to build theories... Build on the qualities you are satisfied with.* [5] VERB If you **build** something into a policy, system, or product, you make it a part of it. *We have to build computers into the school curriculum.* [6] N-C Your **build** is the shape that your bones and muscles give to your body. *He is of medium build.* • See also **built.**

▶ **build up** [1] PHR-VERB If an amount of something **builds up,** or if you **build** it **up,** it gradually gets bigger as a result of more being added to it. *Slowly a thick layer of fat builds up on the pan's surface.* [2] PHR-VERB If you **build** someone **up,** you help them to feel stronger or more confident. [3] See also **build-up, built-up.**

builder /ˈbɪldə/ **builders.** N-C A **builder** is a person whose job is to build or repair buildings.

building /ˈbɪldɪŋ/ **buildings.** N-C A **building** is a structure with a roof and walls.

'**building society, building societies.** N-C In Britain, a **building society** is a business in which people can invest their money, and which lends people money to buy houses.

'**build-up,** (also **buildup** or **build up**) **build-ups.** [1] N-C A **build-up** is a gradual increase in something. *There has been a build-up of troops on both sides of the border.* [2] N-C The **build-up** to an event is the way that people talk about it a lot in the period immediately before it. *...the build-up to Christmas.*

built /bɪlt/. [1] **Built** is the past tense and past participle of **build.** [2] ADJ If you say that someone is **built** in a particular way, you are describing the kind of body they have. *He is heavily built.*

,**built-'in.** ADJ BEFORE N **Built-in** features are included in something as an essential part of it. *...built-in cupboards in the bedrooms.*

'**built-up.** ADJ A **built-up** area is one where there are many buildings.

bulb /bʌlb/ **bulbs.** [1] N-C A **bulb** is the glass part of an electric lamp which gives out light when electricity passes through it. [2] N-C A **bulb** is an onion-shaped root that grows into a plant.

bulge /bʌldʒ/ **bulges, bulging, bulged.** [1] VERB If something **bulges,** it sticks out. *His eyes were bulging.* [2] VERB If something **is bulging** with things, it is very full of them. *...a bulging briefcase.* [3] N-C A **bulge** is a lump on an otherwise flat surface. *...those bulges on your hips and thighs.*

bulimia /buːˈlɪmiə/. N-U **Bulimia** or **bulimia nervosa** is a mental illness in which a person eats very large amounts and then makes themselves vomit. ♦ **bulimic** /buːˈlɪmɪk/ ADJ *Nobody knew I was bulimic.*

bulk /bʌlk/ **bulks.** [1] N-SING You can refer to the **bulk** of a person or thing when you want to indicate that they are very large and heavy. *Despite his bulk he moved lightly on his feet.* [2] QUANT The **bulk** of something is most of it. *...the bulk of the world's great poetry... They come from all over the world, though the bulk is from the Indian subcontinent.* [3] N-U If you buy or sell something in **bulk,** you buy or sell it in large quantities. *I've got a big freezer and buy everything in bulk.*

bulky /ˈbʌlki/ **bulkier, bulkiest.** ADJ Something that is **bulky** is large and heavy. *...a bulky grey sweater.*

bull /bʊl/ **bulls.** [1] N-C A **bull** is a male animal of the cow family. [2] N-C Male elephants and whales are called **bulls.**

bulldog /ˈbʊldɒg, AM -dɔːg/ **bulldogs.** N-C A **bulldog** is a type of dog with a large square head and powerful jaws.

bulldoze /ˈbʊldəʊz/ **bulldozes, bulldozing, bulldozed.** VERB To **bulldoze** something means to knock it down with a bulldozer.

bulldozer /ˈbʊldəʊzə/ **bulldozers.** N-C A **bulldozer** is a large tractor with a broad metal blade at the front, used for moving earth or knocking down buildings.

bullet /ˈbʊlɪt/ **bullets.** N-C A **bullet** is a small piece of metal which is fired from a gun.

bulletin /ˈbʊlɪtɪn/ **bulletins.** [1] N-C A **bulletin** is a short news report on radio or television. *...NBC's evening news bulletin.* [2] N-C A **bulletin** is a regular newspaper or leaflet produced by a group or organization.

'**bullet-proof** (or **bulletproof**). ADJ Something that is **bullet-proof** is made of a strong material that bullets cannot pass through. *...bullet-proof glass.*

bullion /ˈbʊliən/. N-U **Bullion** is gold or silver in the form of bars.

bullock /ˈbʊlək/ **bullocks.** N-C A **bullock** is a young bull that has been castrated.

bully /ˈbʊli/ **bullies, bullying, bullied.** [1] VERB & N-C If someone **bullies** you, or if someone is a **bully,** they use their strength or power to hurt or frighten you. ♦ **bullying** N-U *...schoolchildren who were victims of bullying.* [2] VERB If someone **bullies** you into something, they make you do it by using force or threats. *She should never have bullied us into going.*

bum /bʌm/ **bums.** [1] N-C A **bum** is a person who has no permanent home or job and who gets money by doing occasional work or by begging; INFORMAL AMERICAN. [2] N-C Your **bum** is the part of your body which you sit on; INFORMAL.

bump /bʌmp/ bumps, bumping, bumped. **1** VERB & N-C If you **bump** into something, you accidentally hit it while you are moving. You can also talk about a **bump**. *The boat bumped against something... He bumped his head... Small children often cry after a minor bump.* **2** N-C A **bump** is a minor swelling that you get on your body if you hit something or if something hits you. *He had a huge bump on his head.* **3** VERB If a vehicle **bumps** over a surface, it travels in a rough, bouncing way because the surface is very uneven. *We left the road, and again bumped over the mountainside.* **4** N-C A **bump** on a road is a raised, uneven part.
▸ **bump into.** PHR-VERB If you **bump into** someone you know, you meet them by chance; INFORMAL. *I bumped into a friend of yours today.*

bumper /ˈbʌmpə/ bumpers. **1** N-C **Bumpers** are bars at the front and back of a vehicle which protect it if it bumps into something. **2** ADJ BEFORE N A **bumper** crop or harvest is larger than usual.

bumpy /ˈbʌmpi/ bumpier, bumpiest. **1** ADJ A **bumpy** road or path has a lot of bumps on it. **2** ADJ A **bumpy** journey is uncomfortable and rough. *...a hot and bumpy ride across the desert.*

bun /bʌn/ buns. **1** N-C A **bun** is a small round cake. **2** N-C If a woman has her hair in a **bun**, it is fastened into a round shape at the back of her head.

bunch /bʌntʃ/ bunches, bunching, bunched. **1** N-C A **bunch** of people or things is a group of them. *The players were a great bunch... We did a bunch of songs together.* **2** N-C A **bunch** of flowers or fruit is a group of them held or tied together, or growing on the same stem.
▸ **bunch up** or **bunch together.** PHR-VERB If people or things **bunch up** or **bunch together**, they move close to each other so that they form a small tight group. *A cluster of Iraqi prisoners appeared, bunched together on a truck.*

bundle /ˈbʌndəl/ bundles, bundling, bundled. **1** N-C A **bundle** is a number of things tied together or wrapped in a cloth so that they can be carried or stored. *...a bundle of five pound notes. ...bundles of clothing.* **2** N-SING If you describe someone as, for example, a **bundle** of fun, you are emphasizing that they are full of fun. *Stan was a bundle of nerves.* **3** VERB If you **bundle** someone somewhere, you push them there in a rough and hurried way. *He was bundled into a car.*

bungalow /ˈbʌŋɡələʊ/ bungalows. N-C A **bungalow** is a house with only one storey.

bungle /ˈbʌŋɡəl/ bungles, bungling, bungled. VERB If you **bungle** something, you fail to do it properly, because you make mistakes or are clumsy. *Two prisoners bungled an escape bid. ...a bungled kidnap attempt.*

bunk /bʌŋk/ bunks. N-C A **bunk** is a bed fixed to a wall, especially in a ship or caravan.

bunker /ˈbʌŋkə/ bunkers. **1** N-C A **bunker** is an underground shelter, built with strong walls to protect it against heavy gunfire and bombing. **2** N-C A **bunker** is a container for coal or other fuel. **3** N-C On a golf course, a **bunker** is a large hollow filled with sand that golfers must try and avoid.

bunny /ˈbʌni/ bunnies. N-C Small children call a rabbit a **bunny** or a **bunny rabbit**.

buoy /bɔɪ, AM ˈbuːi/ buoys, buoying, buoyed. N-C A **buoy** is a floating object that shows ships and boats where they can go and warns them of danger.
▸ **buoy up.** PHR-VERB If someone in a difficult situation is **buoyed up** by something, it makes them feel more cheerful and optimistic. *They are buoyed up by a sense of hope.*

buoyant /ˈbɔɪənt/. **1** ADJ If you are **buoyant**, you feel lively and cheerful. *He sounded buoyant once again.* ♦**buoyancy** /ˈbɔɪənsi/ N-U *...a mood of buoyancy and optimism.* **2** ADJ Something that is **buoyant** floats on a liquid or in the air. ♦**buoyancy** N-U *Air can be pumped into the diving suit to increase buoyancy.*

burden /ˈbɜːdən/ burdens, burdening, burdened. **1** N-C Something that is a **burden** causes you a lot of worry or hard work. *Her death will be an impossible burden on Paul.* **2** VERB If someone **burdens** you with something that is likely to worry you, they tell you about it. *We decided not to burden him with the news.* **3** N-C A **burden** is a heavy load that is difficult to carry; FORMAL.

burdened /ˈbɜːdənd/. ADJ If you are **burdened** with something, it causes you a lot of worry or hard work. *Developing countries are already burdened with debt.*

bureau /ˈbjʊərəʊ/ bureaux or bureaus. **1** N-C A **bureau** is an office, organization, or government department that collects and distributes information. *...the Australian Bureau of Statistics.* **2** N-C A **bureau** is a desk with drawers and a lid that opens to form a writing surface; BRITISH.

bureaucracy /bjʊˈrɒkrəsi/ bureaucracies. **1** N-C A **bureaucracy** is an administrative system operated by a large number of officials following rules and procedures. *State bureaucracies can tend to stifle enterprise.* **2** N-U **Bureaucracy** is all the rules and procedures followed by government departments and similar organizations; often used showing disapproval. *People usually complain about too much bureaucracy.*

bureaucrat /ˈbjʊərəkræt/ bureaucrats. N-C A **bureaucrat** is an official who works in a bureaucracy, especially one who seems to follow rules and procedures too strictly.

bureaucratic /ˌbjʊərəˈkrætɪk/. ADJ **Bureaucratic** rules and procedures are complicated and can cause long delays. *The department has become a bureaucratic nightmare.*

bureaux /ˈbjʊərəʊz/. **Bureaux** is a plural of **bureau**.

burgeon /ˈbɜːdʒən/ burgeons, burgeoning, burgeoned. VERB If something **burgeons**, it grows or develops rapidly; LITERARY. *...Japan's burgeoning satellite-TV industry.*

burger /ˈbɜːɡə/ burgers. N-C A **burger** is a flat round mass of minced meat or vegetables, which is grilled or fried.

burglar /ˈbɜːglə/ **burglars.** N-C A **burglar** is a thief who breaks into houses and steals things.

burglary /ˈbɜːgləri/ **burglaries.** N-VAR If someone commits **burglary,** they enter a building by force and steal things. *He's been arrested for burglary... Basement flats are very vulnerable to burglaries.*

burgle /ˈbɜːgəl/ **burgles, burgling, burgled.** VERB If a house **is burgled,** someone breaks in and steals things. *He admitted that he was trying to burgle the surgery.*

burial /ˈberiəl/ **burials.** N-VAR A **burial** is the ceremony that takes place when a dead body is put into a grave. *The priest prepared the body for burial.*

burly /ˈbɜːli/. ADJ A **burly** man has a broad body and strong muscles. *...a burly security guard.*

burn /bɜːn/ **burns, burning, burned** or **burnt.** [1] VERB If there is a fire or a flame somewhere, you say that there is a fire or flame **burning** there. *Fires were burning out of control.* [2] VERB If something **is burning,** it is on fire. *When I arrived one of the vehicles was still burning.* ♦**burning** N-U *...a terrible smell of burning.* ♦**burnt** ADJ *...the smell of burnt toast.* [3] VERB If you **burn** something, you destroy it with fire. *Protesters set cars on fire and burned a building.* [4] VERB & N-C If you **burn** yourself, or if you suffer **burns,** you are injured by fire or by something very hot. *...the amount of time you can stay in the sun without burning... She suffered appalling burns to her back.* [5] VERB If you **are burning** with an emotion, you feel it very strongly. *Shannon was burning with impatience.*

▸ **burn down.** PHR-VERB If a building **burns down** or if someone **burns** it **down,** it is completely destroyed by fire. *Anarchists burnt down a restaurant.*

burner /ˈbɜːnə/ **burners.** N-C A **burner** is a device which produces heat or a flame.

burning /ˈbɜːnɪŋ/. ADJ If something is extremely hot, you can say that it is **burning** or **burning hot.** *...the burning desert of Central Asia.*

burnt /bɜːnt/. **Burnt** is a past tense and past participle of **burn.**

burnt-out /bɜːnt-ˈaʊt/; also spelled **burned-out.** ADJ **Burnt-out** vehicles or buildings are very badly damaged by fire.

burrow /ˈbʌrəʊ, AM ˈbɜː-/ **burrows, burrowing, burrowed.** VERB & N-C When an animal **burrows,** or digs a **burrow,** it digs a tunnel or hole in the ground.

burst /bɜːst/ **bursts, bursting, burst.** [1] VERB When something **bursts** or when you **burst** it, it suddenly splits open, and air or some other substance comes out. *A tyre burst... It is not a good idea to burst a blister.* [2] VERB If you **burst** into or through something, you suddenly go into it or through it with a lot of energy. *Gunmen burst into his home and opened fire.* [3] N-C A **burst** of something is a sudden short period of it. *...a burst of gunfire.*

▸ **burst into.** PHR-VERB If you **burst into** tears or laughter, you suddenly begin to cry or laugh.
● to **burst into flames:** see **flame.**

▸ **burst out.** PHR-VERB If you **burst out** laughing or crying, you suddenly begin laughing or crying loudly.

bursting /ˈbɜːstɪŋ/. [1] ADJ AFTER LINK-V If a place is **bursting** with people or things, it is full of them. *The wardrobes were bursting with clothes.* [2] ADJ AFTER LINK-V If you are **bursting** with a feeling, you are full of it. *I was bursting with curiosity.* [3] ADJ If you are **bursting** to do something, you are very eager to do it. *She was bursting to tell everyone.*

bury /ˈberi/ **buries, burying, buried.** [1] VERB To **bury** something means to put it into a hole in the ground and cover it up, often in order to hide it. *...squirrels who bury nuts and seeds.* [2] VERB When a dead person **is buried,** their body is put into a grave and covered with earth. [3] VERB If you **are buried** under something that falls on top of you, you are completely covered and may not be able to get out. *...people buried under the collapsed buildings.* [4] VERB If you **bury** yourself in your work, you concentrate hard on it.

bus /bʌs/ **buses.** N-C A **bus** is a large motor vehicle which carries passengers.

bush /bʊʃ/ **bushes.** [1] N-C A **bush** is a plant which is like a very small tree. [2] N-SING The wild parts of some hot countries are referred to as the **bush.** *...the dense Mozambican bush.*

bushy /ˈbʊʃi/ **bushier, bushiest.** ADJ **Bushy** hair or fur grows very thickly. *...bushy eyebrows.*

busily /ˈbɪzɪli/. ADV If you do something **busily,** you do it in a very active way. *Her father was busily taking notes.*

business /ˈbɪznɪs/ **businesses.** [1] N-U **Business** is work relating to the production, buying, and selling of goods or services. *...young people seeking a career in business. ...Harvard Business School.* [2] N-C A **business** is an organization which produces and sells goods or provides a service. *...small businesses.* [3] N-U **Business** is used when talking about how many products or services a company is able to sell. *...German companies would lose business... Business is booming.* [4] PHRASE If a shop or company goes **out of business,** it has to stop trading because it is not making enough money. [5] N-U You can use **business** to refer to any activity, situation, or series of events. *I've got some unfinished business to attend to.* [6] N-SING If you say that something is your **business,** you mean that it concerns you personally and that other people should not get involved in it. *If she doesn't want the police involved, that's her business... My marriage is none of your business, David.* [7] See also **big business.**

PHRASES ● If you say that someone **has no business** to do something, you mean that they have no right to do it. *I had no business to be there at all.* ● If someone **means business,** they are serious and determined about what they are doing; INFORMAL.

businesslike /ˈbɪznɪslaɪk/. ADJ Someone who is **businesslike** deals with things in an efficient way.

businessman /ˈbɪznɪsmæn/ **businessmen.** N-C A **businessman** is a man who works in business.

businesswoman /ˈbɪznɪswʊmən/ **business-**

women. N-C A **businesswoman** is a woman who works in business.

busk /bʌsk/ busks, busking, busked. VERB People who **busk** play music or sing for money in public places; BRITISH. ♦**busking** N-U Restrictions on busking may be eased. ♦**busker, buskers** N-C He earned a living as a busker.

bust /bʌst/ busts, busting, busted. [1] VERB When you **bust** something, you break it or damage it so badly that it cannot be used; INFORMAL. They will have to bust the door to get him out. [2] PHRASE If a company **goes bust**, it loses so much money that it is forced to close down; INFORMAL. [3] N-C A **bust** is a statue of someone's head and shoulders. ...a bronze bust of the Queen. [4] N-C You can refer to a woman's breasts as her **bust**. Good posture also helps your bust look bigger.

bustle /'bʌsəl/ bustles, bustling, bustled. [1] VERB If someone **bustles** somewhere, they move there in a hurried and determined way. My mother bustled around the kitchen. [2] VERB A place that **is bustling** with people or activity is full of people who are very busy or lively. The harbour bustled with activity. ...the bustling market. [3] N-U **Bustle** is busy noisy activity. There was a good deal of cheerful bustle.

'**bust-up, bust-ups.** N-C If you have a **bust-up** with someone, you have a serious quarrel, often resulting in the end of a relationship; INFORMAL.

busy /'bɪzi/ busier, busiest; busies, busying, busied. [1] ADJ If you are **busy**, you are working hard at something, so that you are not free to do anything else. They are busy preparing for a hectic day's activity... She would be too busy to come. [2] VERB If you **busy** yourself with something, you occupy yourself by dealing with it. She busied herself getting towels ready. [3] ADJ A **busy** street or place is full of traffic and people moving about.

but /bət, STRONG bʌt/. [1] CONJ You use **but** to introduce something which contrasts with what you have just said. 'You said you'd stay till tomorrow.'—'I know, Bel, but I think I would rather go back.'. [2] CONJ You use **but** when you are adding something or changing the subject. I still can't figure out why he did what he did – but anyway, he succeeded. [3] CONJ You use **but** to link an excuse or apology with what you are about to say. I'm sorry, but it's nothing to do with you. [4] ADV **But** can mean 'only'; FORMAL. This is but one of the methods used. [5] PREP **But** means 'except'. He didn't speak anything but Greek. [6] PHRASE You use **but for** to introduce the only factor that causes a particular thing not to happen or not to be completely true. ...the small square below, empty but for a delivery van.

butcher /'bʊtʃə/ butchers, butchering, butchered. [1] N-C A **butcher** is a shopkeeper who sells meat. You can refer to a shop where meat is sold as a **butcher** or a **butcher's**. [2] VERB You say that someone **has butchered** people when they have killed a lot of them in a very cruel way, and you want to express your horror and disgust. Guards butchered 1,350 prisoners.

butler /'bʌtlə/ butlers. N-C A **butler** is the chief male servant in the house of a wealthy family.

butt /bʌt/ butts, butting, butted. [1] N-C The **butt** of a weapon is the thick end of its handle. [2] N-C The **butt** of a cigarette or cigar is the small part that is left when you have finished smoking it. [3] N-C A **butt** is a large barrel used for collecting or storing liquid. ...a water butt. [4] N-SING If you are **the butt** of teasing or criticism, people keep teasing you or criticizing you. He is the butt of countless jokes. [5] VERB If a person or animal **butts** you, they hit you with the top of their head. [6] N-C Someone's **butt** is their bottom; AMERICAN, INFORMAL.

▶ **butt in.** PHR-VERB If you **butt in**, you rudely join in a private conversation without being asked to. 'I should think not,' Sarah butted in.

butter /'bʌtə/ butters, buttering, buttered. [1] N-U **Butter** is a yellowish substance made from cream which you spread on bread or use in cooking. [2] VERB When you **butter** bread, you spread butter on it.

butterfly /'bʌtəflaɪ/ butterflies. N-C A **butterfly** is an insect with large colourful wings and a thin body.

buttock /'bʌtək/ buttocks. N-C Your **buttocks** are the two rounded fleshy parts of your body you sit on.

button /'bʌtən/ buttons, buttoning, buttoned. [1] N-C **Buttons** are small hard objects sewn on to pieces of clothing, which you use to fasten the clothing. [2] VERB & PHR-VERB If you **button** or **button up** a shirt, coat, or other piece of clothing, you fasten it by pushing its buttons through the buttonholes. I buttoned up my mink coat. [3] N-C A **button** is a small object that you press in order to operate something. He reached for the remote control and pressed the 'play' button. [4] N-C In American English, a **button** is a small piece of metal or plastic which you pin onto your clothes to show your support for someone or something. The British word is **badge**. ...campaign buttons bearing pictures of Bill Clinton.

▶ **button up.** See button 2.

buttonhole /'bʌtənhəʊl/ buttonholes, buttonholing, buttonholed. [1] N-C A **buttonhole** is a hole that you push a button through in order to fasten a piece of clothing. [2] N-C A **buttonhole** is a flower that you wear on your lapel; BRITISH. [3] VERB If you **buttonhole** someone, you stop them and make them listen to you.

buttress /'bʌtrəs/ buttresses, buttressing, buttressed. [1] N-C **Buttresses** are supports, usually made of stone or brick, that support a wall. [2] VERB To **buttress** an argument or system means to give it support and strength. As always, his argument is buttressed by facts and quotations.

buy /baɪ/ buys, buying, bought. [1] VERB If you **buy** something, you obtain it by paying money for it. He could not afford to buy a house... Lizzie bought herself a mountain bike... I'd like to buy him lunch. ♦**buyer, buyers** N-C Car buyers are more interested in safety. [2] N-C If something is a good **buy**, it is of good quality and not very expensive. Good buys this week include broccoli, avocados, and tomatoes.

3 VERB If you **buy** something such as time or freedom, you obtain it but only by offering or giving up something in return. *It was a risky operation, but might buy more time.*

▶ **buy out.** PHR-VERB If you **buy** someone **out**, you buy their share of something that you previously owned together. *The bank had to pay to buy out most of the 200 former partners.*

▶ **buy up.** PHR-VERB If you **buy up** land, property, or a commodity, you buy large amounts of it, or all that is available. *His officials were yesterday buying up vast stocks of corn.*

▶ **buy into.** PHR-VERB If someone **buys into** a company or an organization, they buy part of it, often in order to gain some control of it.

buyout (or **buy-out**) /ˈbaɪaʊt/ **buyouts.** N-C A **buyout** is the buying of a company, especially by its managers or employees. *...a management buyout.*

buzz /bʌz/ **buzzes, buzzing, buzzed.** **1** N-SING A **buzz** is a continuous sound, like the sound of a bee when it is flying. *...the incessant buzz of insects. ...the buzz of a chainsaw. ...the excited buzz of conversation.* **2** VERB If something **buzzes**, it makes a long continuous sound, like a bee. *A fly buzzed on the windowpane... Helicopter gunships buzzed overhead.* **3** VERB If a place **is buzzing** with activity or conversation, there is a lot of activity or conversation there, especially because something important or exciting is about to happen. *...Hong Kong's buzzing, pulsating atmosphere.*

buzzer /ˈbʌzə/ **buzzers.** N-C A **buzzer** is a device that makes a buzzing sound, for example in an alarm clock.

buzzword (or **buzz word**) /ˈbʌzwɜːd/ **buzzwords.** N-C A **buzzword** is a word or expression that has become fashionable in a particular field. *Specialisation is the new buzzword.*

by /baɪ/ **1** PREP If something is done **by** a person or thing, that person or thing does it. *The boys had to be rescued by firemen... He was so fascinated by her beauty.* **2** PREP **By** is used to say how something is done. *...if you're travelling by car. ...dinners by candlelight... Make the sauce by boiling the cream... I'd like to pay by cheque.* **3** PREP If you say that a book, a piece of music, or a painting is **by** someone, you mean that they wrote it or created it. *...detective stories by American writers.* **4** PREP If you hold someone or something **by** a particular part of them, you hold that part. *He caught her by the shoulder.* **5** PREP & ADV Someone or

something that is **by** something else is beside it and close to it. *...a rocking-chair by the window... Large numbers of security police stood by.* **6** PREP & ADV If a person or vehicle goes **by** you, it moves past without stopping. *A few cars passed close by me... A police patrol went by.* **7** PREP If something happens **by** a particular time, it happens at or before that time. *By eight o'clock he had arrived.* **8** PREP Things that are made or sold **by** the million or **by** the dozen are made or sold in those quantities. *Parcels arrived by the dozen from America.* **9** PREP If something increases or decreases **by** a particular amount, that amount is gained or lost. *Violent crime has increased by 10 percent.* **10** PREP You use **by** in expressions such as 'day by day' to say that something happens gradually. **11** PREP If you are **by** yourself, you are alone. If you do something **by** yourself, you do it without any help.

bye /baɪ/. CONVENTION **'Bye'** and **'bye-bye'** are informal ways of saying goodbye.

'by-election, by-elections. N-C A **by-election** is an election that is held to choose a new member of parliament when a member has resigned or died.

bygone /ˈbaɪɡɒn, AM -ɡɔːn/. ADJ BEFORE N **Bygone** means happening or existing a very long time ago. *...a bygone era. ...bygone generations.*

bypass /ˈbaɪpɑːs, -pæs/ **bypasses, bypassing, bypassed.** **1** VERB If you **bypass** someone in authority, you avoid asking their permission to do something. **2** N-C A **bypass** is a main road which takes traffic round the edge of a town rather than through its centre. **3** VERB If you **bypass** a place, you go round it rather than through it. **4** N-C A **bypass** is an operation in which the flow of blood is redirected so that it does not flow through a part of the heart which is diseased or blocked. *...heart bypass surgery.*

'by-product, by-products. N-C A **by-product** is something which is made during the manufacture or processing of another product. *Glycerine is a by-product of soap-making.*

bystander /ˈbaɪstændə/ **bystanders.** N-C A **bystander** is a person who sees something happen but does not take part in it. *...an innocent bystander.*

byte /baɪt/ **bytes.** N-C In computing, a **byte** is a unit of storage approximately equivalent to one printed character.

C c

cab /kæb/ **cabs.** **1** N-C A **cab** is a taxi. *She called a cab.* **2** N-C The **cab** of a lorry is the part in which the driver sits.

cabaret /ˈkæbəreɪ, AM -ˈreɪ/ **cabarets.** N-VAR **Cabaret** is live entertainment consisting of dancing, singing, or comedy acts that are performed in the evening in restaurants or nightclubs. *He began singing in bars and cabarets. ...a cabaret act.*

cabbage /ˈkæbɪdʒ/ **cabbages.** N-VAR A **cabbage** is a round vegetable with green leaves.

cabin /ˈkæbɪn/ **cabins.** **1** N-C A **cabin** is a small room in a ship or boat, or one of the areas inside a plane. *...the First Class cabin.* **2** N-C A **cabin** is a small wooden house.

cabinet /ˈkæbɪnɪt/ **cabinets.** **1** N-C A **cabinet** is a cupboard used for storing things such as medicines or alcoholic drinks or for displaying decorative things in. *...a medicine cabinet.*

2 N-C The **Cabinet** is a group of the most senior ministers in a government. • See note at **government**.

cable /ˈkeɪbəl/ **cables, cabled, cabling.** **1** N-U **Cable** is used to refer to television systems in which the signals are sent along underground wires rather than by radio waves. *They ran commercials on cable systems across the country.* **2** VERB If an area or building **is cabled**, cables and other equipment are put in place so that the people there can receive cable television. **3** N-VAR A **cable** is a thick wire, or a bundle of wires inside a rubber or plastic covering, which is used to carry electricity or electronic signals. ...*overhead power cables.*

cache /kæʃ/ **caches.** N-C A **cache** is a quantity of things such as weapons that have been hidden.

cactus /ˈkæktəs/ **cactuses** (or **cacti** /ˈkæktaɪ/). N-C A **cactus** is a desert plant with a thick stem, often with spikes.

cadet /kəˈdet/ **cadets.** N-C A **cadet** is a young person who is being trained in the armed forces or police.

café /ˈkæfeɪ, AM kæˈfeɪ/ **cafés.** N-C A **café** is a place where you can buy and have simple meals, snacks, and drinks.

> In Britain, a **café** serves tea, coffee, soft drinks, and light meals, but not usually alcoholic drinks. If you want an alcoholic drink, you can go to a **pub**. Many pubs serve food, especially at lunchtime, but for a larger or more special meal, you might want to go to a **restaurant**.

cafeteria /ˌkæfɪˈtɪəriə/ **cafeterias.** N-C A **cafeteria** is a self-service restaurant in a large shop or workplace.

caffeine /ˈkæfiːn, AM kæˈfiːn/. N-U **Caffeine** is a chemical substance found in coffee, tea, and cocoa, which makes your brain and body more active.

cage /keɪdʒ/ **cages.** N-C A **cage** is a structure of wire or metal bars in which birds or animals are kept.

caged /keɪdʒd/. ADJ A **caged** bird or animal is inside a cage.

cajole /kəˈdʒəʊl/ **cajoles, cajoling, cajoled.** VERB If you **cajole** someone, you get them to do something after persuading them for some time. *It was he who had cajoled Garland into doing the film.*

cake /keɪk/ **cakes.** **1** N-VAR A **cake** is a sweet food made by baking a mixture of flour, eggs, sugar, and fat. ...*a piece of chocolate cake.* **2** N-C Food that is formed into flat round shapes before it is cooked can be referred to as **cakes**. ...*fish cakes.*

calamity /kəˈlæmɪti/ **calamities.** N-C A **calamity** is an event that causes a great deal of damage or distress; FORMAL. ...*the calamity of war.*

calcium /ˈkælsiəm/. N-U **Calcium** is a soft white element found in bones and teeth, and also in limestone, chalk, and marble.

calculate /ˈkælkjʊleɪt/ **calculates, calculating, calculated.** **1** VERB If you **calculate** a number or amount, you work it out by doing some arithmetic. *We calculate that the average size farm in Lancaster County is 65 acres.* ◆**calculation** /ˌkælkjʊˈleɪʃən/ **calculations** N-VAR *The machine does the calculations.* **2** VERB If you **calculate** the effects of something, you consider what they will be. *I believe I am capable of calculating the political consequences accurately.* ◆**calculation** N-VAR ...*political calculation.*

calculated /ˈkælkjʊleɪtɪd/. ADJ If something is **calculated**, it is deliberately planned to have a particular effect. *Everything she said seemed deliberately calculated to make him feel guilty.* ...*a calculated attempt to cover up her crime.*

calculating /ˈkælkjʊleɪtɪŋ/. ADJ If you describe someone as **calculating**, you disapprove of the fact that they deliberately plan to get what they want, often by harming other people. ...*a cool, calculating and clever criminal.* ◆**calculation** /ˌkælkjʊˈleɪʃən/ N-U *cold, unspeakably cruel calculation.*

calculation. See **calculate, calculating.**

calculator /ˈkælkjʊleɪtə/ **calculators.** N-C A **calculator** is a small electronic device used for doing mathematical calculations.

calendar /ˈkælɪndə/ **calendars.** **1** N-C A **calendar** is a chart or device which displays the date and the day of the week, and often the whole of a particular year. **2** N-C A **calendar** month is one of the twelve periods of time that a year is divided into. **3** N-C A **calendar** is a list of dates within a year that are important for a particular organization or activity. ...*one of the most popular fixtures in the racing calendar.*

calf /kɑːf, AM kæf/ **calves.** **1** N-C A **calf** is a young cow. **2** N-C The young of some animals, such as elephants, giraffes, and whales, are called **calves**. **3** N-C Your **calves** are the backs of your legs between your ankles and knees.

calibre (AM **caliber**) /ˈkælɪbə/ **calibres.** **1** N-U The **calibre** of someone or something is their qualities, abilities, or high standards. *The calibre of the teaching was very high.* **2** N-C The **calibre** of a gun is the width of the inside of its barrel; TECHNICAL.

call /kɔːl/ **calls, calling, called.** **1** VERB If you **call** someone or something by a particular name or title, you give them that name or title. *Everybody called each other by their surnames... There are two Labour politicians called Jim Callaghan.* **2** VERB If you **call** a person or situation something, that is how you describe them. *They called him a traitor... She calls me lazy.* **3** VERB & PHR-VERB If you **call** something, or if you **call** it **out**, you say it in a loud voice. *I heard someone calling my name... The train stopped and a porter called out, 'Middlesbrough!'.* **4** VERB & N-C If you **call** someone, or make a telephone **call**, you telephone them. *He called me at my office... I think we should call the doctor... I made a phone call to the United States.* **5** PHRASE If someone is **on call**, they are ready to go to work at any time if they are needed. ...*a doctor on call.* **6** VERB If you **call** a meeting, you arrange for it to take place. **7** VERB & N-C If you **call** somewhere, or pay a **call** there, you make a short visit there. *A market researcher called at the house... He decided to pay a call on Tommy.* **8** N-C If there is a **call**

for something, someone demands that it should happen. *...a call for all businessmen to work together.* **9** to **call it a day**: see **day**.

▶ **call back.** PHR-VERB If you **call** someone **back**, you telephone them again or in return for a telephone call that they have made to you.

▶ **call for.** **1** PHR-VERB If you **call for** someone or something, you go to collect them. *I shall be calling for you at seven o'clock.* **2** PHR-VERB If you **call for** an action, you demand that it should happen. *They angrily called for Robinson's resignation.* **3** PHR-VERB If something **calls for** a particular action or quality, it needs it. *Does the situation call for military intervention?*

▶ **call in.** **1** PHR-VERB If you **call** someone **in**, you ask them to come and help you or do something for you. *Call in an architect or surveyor to oversee the work.* **2** PHR-VERB If you **call in** somewhere, you make a short visit there. *He just calls in occasionally.*

▶ **call off.** PHR-VERB If you **call off** an event that has been planned, you cancel it. *The deal was called off.*

▶ **call on** or
▶ **call upon.** **1** PHR-VERB If you **call on** someone to do something, you say publicly that you want them to do it. *One of Kenya's leading churchmen has called on the government to resign.* **2** PHR-VERB If you **call on** someone, you pay them a short visit.

▶ **call out.** **1** PHR-VERB If you **call** someone **out**, you order them to come to help, especially in an emergency. *Colombia has called out the army.* **2** See also **call** 3.

▶ **call up.** **1** PHR-VERB If you **call** someone **up**, you telephone them. *When I'm in Pittsburgh, I call him up.* **2** PHR-VERB If someone **is called up**, they are ordered to join the armed forces.

▶ **call upon.** See **call on**.

caller /'kɔːlə/ **callers.** **1** N-C A **caller** is a person who is making a telephone call. **2** N-C A **caller** is a person who comes to see you for a short visit.

callous /'kæləs/. ADJ A **callous** person or action is cruel and shows no concern for other people. *...his callous disregard for human life.* ◆**callously** ADV *...callously ill-treating his wife.* ◆**callousness** N-U *...the callousness of Raymond's murder.*

calm /kɑːm/ **calmer, calmest; calms, calming, calmed.** **1** ADJ & N-U A **calm** person does not show or feel any worry, anger, or excitement. You can refer to someone's feeling of **calm**. *...a calm and diplomatic woman... Try to keep calm... He felt a sudden sense of calm.* ◆**calmly** ADV *She speaks slowly and calmly.* **2** N-U **Calm** is a state of being quiet and peaceful. *...the rural calm of Grand Rapids, Michigan.* **3** ADJ If the weather is **calm**, there is little or no wind. If the sea is **calm**, the water is not moving very much. **4** VERB If you **calm** someone, you do something to make them less upset or excited. *Isabella had helped calm her fears.* ◆**calming** ADJ *...a very calming effect on the mind.*

▶ **calm down.** PHR-VERB If you **calm down** or if someone **calms** you **down**, you become less

upset or excited. *I'll try a herbal remedy to calm him down.*

calorie /'kæləri/ **calories.** N-C A **calorie** is a unit of measurement for the energy value of food.

calves /kɑːvz, AM kævz/. **Calves** is the plural of **calf**.

camcorder /'kæmkɔːdə/ **camcorders.** N-C A **camcorder** is a portable video camera.

came /keɪm/. **Came** is the past tense of **come**.

camel /'kæməl/ **camels.** N-C A **camel** is a desert animal with one or two humps on its back.

cameo /'kæmiəʊ/ **cameos.** **1** N-C A **cameo** is a short descriptive piece of acting or writing. *...memorable cameos of Scottish history.* **2** N-C A **cameo** is a brooch with a raised design on a flat stone of another colour.

camera /'kæmrə/ **cameras.** **1** N-C A **camera** is a piece of equipment for taking photographs or for making a film. *...a video camera.* **2** PHRASE If someone or something is **on camera**, they are being filmed.

cameraman /'kæmrəmən/ **cameramen.** N-C A **cameraman** is a person who operates a television or film camera.

camouflage /'kæməflɑːʒ/. **1** N-U **Camouflage** consists of things such as leaves, branches, or paint, used to make military forces difficult to see. *...a camouflage jacket.* **2** VERB When military forces **camouflage** themselves or their weapons, they use camouflage to make themselves or their weapons difficult to see. ◆**camouflaged** ADJ *You won't see them from the air. They'd be very well camouflaged.* **3** N-U **Camouflage** is the way in which some animals are coloured and shaped to look as though they are part of their natural surroundings.

camp /kæmp/ **camps, camping, camped.** **1** N-VAR A **camp** is a place where people live or stay in tents or caravans. **2** VERB If you **camp** somewhere, you stay there in a tent or caravan. *We camped near the beach... For six months they camped out in a caravan in a meadow.* ◆**camping** N-U *We recently went on a camping trip to Africa.* **3** N-C A **camp** is a collection of buildings for people such as soldiers, refugees, or prisoners. *...refugee camps.* **4** N-C You can use **camp** to refer to a group of people with a particular idea or belief. *The press release provoked furious protests from the Clinton camp.*

campaign /ˌkæm'peɪn/ **campaigns, campaigning, campaigned.** N-C & VERB A **campaign** is a planned set of actions aimed at achieving a particular result. To **campaign** means to carry out a campaign. *...an advertising campaign to attract more people. ...a bombing campaign... They have been campaigning to improve the legal status of women.* ◆**campaigner, campaigners** N-C *...peace campaigners.*

camper /'kæmpə/ **campers.** **1** N-C A **camper** is a person who goes camping. **2** N-C A **camper** is a van equipped with beds and cooking equipment.

campsite /'kæmpsaɪt/ **campsites.** N-C A **campsite** or a **camping site** is a place where people who are on holiday can stay in tents.

campus /'kæmpəs/ **campuses**. N-C A **campus** is the area of land containing the main buildings of a college or university.

can 1 modal uses

can /kən, STRONG kæn/ **1** MODAL If you **can** do something, you have the ability or opportunity to do it. *I can take care of myself... See if you can find Karlov... You can't be with your baby all the time.* **2** MODAL If you **can** do something, you are allowed to do it. *You must buy the credit life insurance before you can buy the disability insurance... I can't tell you what he said.* **3** MODAL You use **can** to indicate that something is true sometimes or is true in some circumstances. *...long-term therapy that can last five years or more... Exercising alone can be boring.* **4** MODAL You use **cannot** or **can't** to state that you are certain that something is not true or will not happen. *She feels sure the person can't have been Douglas.* **5** MODAL You use **can** in order to make suggestions or requests, or to offer to do something. *You can always try the beer... Can I have a look at that?... Can I help you?*

can 2 container

can /kæn/ **cans, canning, canned**. **1** N-C A **can** is a sealed metal container for food, drink, or paint. *...empty beer cans.* **2** VERB When food or drink is **canned**, it is put into a metal container and sealed.

canal /kə'næl/ **canals**. N-C A **canal** is a long, narrow, man-made stretch of water.

cancel /'kænsəl/ **cancels, cancelling, cancelled** (AM **canceling, canceled**). **1** VERB If you **cancel** something that has been arranged, you stop it from happening. If you **cancel** an order for goods or services, you tell the person or organization supplying them that you no longer wish to receive them. *Many trains have been cancelled and a limited service is operating... There is normally no refund should a client choose to cancel.* ◆**cancellation, cancellations** N-VAR *The cancellation of his visit has disappointed many people.* **2** VERB If someone in authority **cancels** a document or a debt, they officially declare that it is no longer valid or no longer legally exists. *...a government order cancelling his passport.* ◆**cancellation** N-U *...cancellation of Third World debt.*

▸ **cancel out.** PHR-VERB If one thing **cancels out** another thing, the two things have opposite effects which combine to produce no real effect. *Gary Bannister's goal was cancelled out by Chris Waddle's. ...cooling and heating effects seem to cancel each other out.*

cancer /'kænsə/ **cancers**. N-VAR **Cancer** is a serious illness in which abnormal body cells increase, producing growths. *Ninety per cent of lung cancers are caused by smoking.* ◆**cancerous** ADJ *Nine out of ten lumps are not cancerous.*

candid /'kændɪd/. ADJ If you are **candid** with someone or about something, you speak honestly. *I haven't been completely candid with him. ...a candid interview.* ◆**candidly** ADV *He has stopped taking heroin now, but admits candidly that he will always be a drug addict.*

candidacy /'kændɪdəsi/. N-U Someone's **candidacy** is their position of being a candidate in an election. *Today he is formally announcing his candidacy for President.*

candidate /'kændɪdeɪt/ **candidates**. **1** N-C A **candidate** is someone who is being considered for a position, for example in an election or for a job. *...the Democratic candidate... He is a candidate for the office of Governor.* **2** N-C A **candidate** is someone taking an examination. **3** N-C A **candidate** is a person or thing regarded as suitable for a particular purpose, or as likely to be or do a particular thing. *The director looked like a candidate for a heart attack.*

candle /'kændəl/ **candles**. N-C A **candle** is a stick of hard wax with a piece of string (called a wick through the middle. You light the wick so the candle produces light.

candour (AM **candor**) /'kændə/. N-U **Candour** is the quality of speaking honestly and openly about things. *He covered a wide range of topics with unusual candour.*

candy /'kændi/ **candies**. N-VAR In American English, sweet foods such as toffees, chocolates, and mints are referred to as **candy**. The British word is **sweets**. *...a piece of candy.*

cane /keɪn/ **canes, caning, caned**. **1** N-U **Cane** is the long hollow stems of a plant such as bamboo. *...cane baskets and furniture.* **2** N-C A **cane** is a long narrow stick. *He wore a grey suit and leaned heavily on his cane.* **3** VERB & N-SING When schoolchildren **were caned** or were given the **cane**, they were hit with a cane as a punishment. *...if you misbehaved you would get the cane.*

canine /'keɪnaɪn/. ADJ **Canine** means relating to or resembling a dog.

canister /'kænɪstə/ **canisters**. N-C A **canister** is a metal container.

cannabis /'kænəbɪs/. N-U **Cannabis** is a drug which some people smoke. It is illegal in many countries.

cannibal /'kænɪbəl/ **cannibals**. N-C A **cannibal** is a person who eats human flesh. ◆**cannibalism** /'kænɪbəlɪzəm/ N-U *...tales of cannibalism among the starving explorers.*

cannon /'kænən/ the plural is **cannon** or **cannons**. **1** N-C A **cannon** is a large gun on wheels, formerly used in battles. **2** N-C A **cannon** is a heavy automatic gun, especially one fired from an aircraft.

cannot /'kænɒt, kə'nɒt/. **Cannot** is the negative form of **can**.

canoe /kə'nuː/ **canoes**. N-C A **canoe** is a small narrow boat that you row using a paddle.

canon /'kænən/ **canons**. N-C A **canon** is one of the clergy on the staff of a cathedral.

canopy /'kænəpi/ **canopies**. N-C A **canopy** is a decorated cover which hangs above something such as a bed or throne.

can't /kɑːnt, AM kænt/. **Can't** is the usual spoken form of 'cannot'.

canteen /kæn'tiːn/ **canteens**. N-C A **canteen** is a place in a factory, office, or shop where the workers can have meals.

canter /'kæntə/ **canters, cantering, cantered**. VERB & N-SING When a horse **canters** or when it moves at a **canter**, it moves at a speed between a gallop and a trot.

canvas /'kænvəs/ **canvases.** [1] N-U **Canvas** is strong heavy cloth used for making tents, sails, and bags. [2] N-VAR A **canvas** is a piece of canvas on which an oil painting is done, or the painting itself. *...canvases by masters like Carpaccio, Canaletto and Guardi.*

canvass /'kænvəs/ **canvasses, canvassing, canvassed.** [1] VERB If you **canvass** for a person or political party, you try to persuade people to vote for them. *I have gone around my community canvassing for the Labor Party.* [2] VERB If you **canvass** public opinion, you find out how people feel about something. *The poll canvassed the views of almost eighty economists.*

canyon /'kænjən/ **canyons.** N-C A **canyon** is a long narrow valley with very steep sides.

cap /kæp/ **caps, capping, capped.** [1] N-C A **cap** is a soft flat hat usually worn by men or boys. [2] N-C The **cap** of a bottle is its lid. [3] VERB You can say that the last event in a series of events **caps** the others. *The unrest capped a weekend of right-wing attacks on foreigners.*

capable /'keɪpəbəl/. [1] ADJ AFTER LINK-V If you are **capable** of doing something, you are able to do it. *He had been hardly capable of standing up... I realised he was capable of murder.* ◆**capability** /ˌkeɪpə'bɪlɪti/ **capabilities** N-VAR *The standards set four years ago will be far below the athletes' capabilities now.* [2] ADJ Someone who is **capable** has the ability to do something well. *She's a very capable speaker.* ◆**capably** ADV *It was all dealt with very capably.*

capacity /kə'pæsɪti/ **capacities.** [1] N-U & ADJ BEFORE N The **capacity** of something is the maximum amount that it can hold or produce. A **capacity** crowd completely fills a theatre or stadium. *Each stadium had a seating capacity of about 50,000... The restaurant was packed to capacity. ...a feature which gave the vehicles a much greater fuel capacity.* [2] N-C Your **capacity** to do something is your ability to do it. *Our capacity for giving care, love and attention.* [3] N-C If someone does something in a particular **capacity**, they do it as part of their duties. *He was visiting the territory in his capacity as an official.*

cape /keɪp/ **capes.** [1] N-C A **cape** is a large piece of land that sticks out into the sea. [2] N-C A **cape** is a short cloak.

capital /'kæpɪtəl/ **capitals.** [1] N-U **Capital** is a sum of money used to start or expand a business or invested to make more money. [2] N-C The **capital** of a country is the city where its government meets. *...Kathmandu, the capital of Nepal.* [3] N-C & ADJ BEFORE N A **capital** or a **capital** letter is the large form of a letter used at the beginning of sentences and names.

> Note that you must always use a capital letter with days of the week, months of the year, and festivals. *...on Monday the 13th of January. ...at Christmas.* Names of seasons, however, usually be-

gin with a small letter. *...in spring.* Capitals must also be used with the names of countries and other places, as well with the adjectives and nouns derived from them, such as those which refer to their inhabitants or languages. *...in Portugal. ...the Swiss police... Thousands of Germans filled the streets of Berlin... He spoke fluent Arabic.*

[4] ADJ BEFORE N A **capital** offence is one that is punished by death.

capitalise /'kæpɪtəlaɪz/. See **capitalize.**

capitalism /'kæpɪtəlɪzəm/. N-U **Capitalism** is an economic and political system in which property, business, and industry are owned by private individuals and not by the state. ◆**capitalist, capitalists.** N-C *...the industrialized capitalist countries. ...industrial capitalists.*

capitalize (BR also **capitalise**) /'kæpɪtəlaɪz/ **capitalizes, capitalizing, capitalized.** VERB If you **capitalize** on a situation, you use it to gain some advantage. *The rebels seem to be trying to capitalize on the public's discontent with the government.*

ˌcapital 'punishment. N-U Capital **punishment** is the legal killing of a person who has committed a serious crime.

capitulate /kə'pɪtʃʊleɪt/ **capitulates, capitulating, capitulated.** VERB If you **capitulate**, you stop resisting and do what someone else wants you to do. *Cohen capitulated to virtually every demand.* ◆**capitulation** N-U *Acceptance of the plan would mean capitulation.*

capsize /kæp'saɪz, AM 'kæpsaɪz/ **capsizes, capsizing, capsized.** VERB If you **capsize** a boat or if it **capsizes**, it turns upside down in the water.

capsule /'kæpsjuːl, AM 'kæpsəl/ **capsules.** [1] N-C A **capsule** is a small container with powdered or liquid medicine inside which you swallow. [2] N-C The **capsule** of a spacecraft is the part in which the astronauts travel.

captain /'kæptɪn/ **captains, captaining, captained.** [1] N-C & N-TITLE A **captain** is a military officer of middle rank. [2] N-C The **captain** of an aeroplane or ship is the officer in charge of it. [3] N-C The **captain** of a sports team is its leader. [4] VERB If you **captain** a ship or team, you are the captain of it. *The team was captained by Keegan.*

captaincy /'kæptɪnsi/. N-U The **captaincy** of a team is the position of being captain. *Under his captaincy, Leeds lost twice to Rangers.*

caption /'kæpʃən/ **captions.** N-C The **caption** of a picture consists of the words which are printed underneath.

captivate /'kæptɪveɪt/ **captivates, captivating, captivated.** VERB If you **are captivated** by someone or something, you find them fascinating and attractive. *For 40 years she has captivated the world with her radiant looks.* ◆**captivating** ADJ *...her captivating smile.*

captive /'kæptɪv/ **captives.** [1] ADJ BEFORE N A **captive** animal or person is being kept in a particular place and is not allowed to escape. *...captive rats, mice, and monkeys.* [2] PHRASE If someone **takes** or **holds** you **captive**, they take or keep you as a prisoner. [3] N-C A **captive** is a prisoner; LITERARY.

captivity /kæpˈtɪvɪti/. N-U **Captivity** is the state of being kept as a captive. *The great majority of barn owls are reared in captivity.*

capture /ˈkæptʃə/ **captures, capturing, captured.** [1] VERB & N-U If you **capture** someone or something, you catch them or take possession of them, especially in a war, or after a chase. You can also talk about the **capture** of someone or something. *The guerrillas shot down one aeroplane and captured the pilot. ...the final battles which led to the army's capture of the town.* [2] VERB To **capture** something means to gain control of it. *In 1987, McDonald's captured 19 percent of all fast-food sales.* [3] VERB If someone **captures** the atmosphere or quality of something, they represent it successfully in pictures, music, or words. *...a portrait photographer poised to capture the moment.*

car /kɑː/ **cars.** [1] N-C A **car** is a motor vehicle with room for a small number of passengers. *They arrived by car.* [2] N-C In American English, a **car** is one of the separate sections of a train that carries passengers. The usual British word is **carriage.** [3] N-C In Britain, railway carriages are called **cars** when they are used for a particular purpose. *...the dining car.*

caramel /ˈkærəmel/ **caramels.** [1] N-C A **caramel** is a kind of toffee. [2] N-U **Caramel** is burnt sugar used for colouring and flavouring food.

carat /ˈkærət/ **carats.** [1] N-C A **carat** is a unit equal to 0.2 grams used for measuring the weight of diamonds and other precious stones. *...a huge eight-carat diamond.* [2] N-C A **carat** is a unit for measuring the purity of gold. The purest gold is 24-carat gold. *...a 14-carat gold fountain pen.*

caravan /ˈkærəvæn/ **caravans.** [1] N-C A **caravan** is a vehicle in which people live or spend their holidays. It is usually pulled by a car. *...a caravan holiday in France.* [2] N-C A **caravan** is a group of people and animals that travel together in deserts and other similar places. *...a caravan of horses.*

carbohydrate /ˌkɑːbəʊˈhaɪdreɪt/ **carbohydrates.** N-VAR **Carbohydrates** are energy-giving substances found in foods such as sugar and bread.

carbon /ˈkɑːbən/. N-U **Carbon** is a chemical element that diamonds and coal are made of.

carbon di'oxide. N-U **Carbon dioxide** is a gas that animals and people breathe out.

carbon mon'oxide /ˌkɑːbən məˈnɒksaɪd/. N-U **Carbon monoxide** is a poisonous gas produced for example by cars.

carcass (or **carcase**) /ˈkɑːkəs/ **carcasses.** N-C A **carcass** is the body of a dead animal.

card /kɑːd/ **cards.** [1] N-C A **card** is a piece of stiff paper or thin cardboard on which something is written or printed. [2] N-U **Card** is strong stiff paper or thin cardboard. [3] N-C A **card** is a piece of stiff paper with a picture and a message which you send to someone on a special occasion. *She sends me a card on my birthday.* [4] N-C **Cards** are thin pieces of cardboard decorated with numbers or pictures used to play various games. *...a pack of cards... I taught Rachel how to play cards.* [5] N-C You

can use **card** to refer to something that gives you an advantage in a particular situation. *This permitted Western manufacturers to play their strong cards: capital and technology.*

cardboard /ˈkɑːdbɔːd/. N-U **Cardboard** is thick stiff paper used to make boxes and other containers. *...a thin cardboard folder.*

cardiac /ˈkɑːdiæk/. ADJ BEFORE N **Cardiac** means relating to the heart; TECHNICAL. *...a top cardiac surgeon.*

cardigan /ˈkɑːdɪɡən/ **cardigans.** N-C A **cardigan** is a knitted woollen garment that fastens at the front.

cardinal /ˈkɑːdnəl/ **cardinals.** [1] N-C A **cardinal** is a priest of high rank in the Catholic church. [2] ADJ BEFORE N **Cardinal** means extremely important; FORMAL. *One of the cardinal rules of movie reviewing is not to give away too much.*

care /keə/ **cares, caring, cared.** [1] VERB If you **care** about something, you are concerned about it or interested in it. *...a company that cares about the environment... I really didn't care whether he came or not.* [2] VERB If you **care** for someone, you feel a lot of affection for them. *He still cared for me. ...people who are your friends, who care about you.* [3] VERB To **care** to do something or **care** for it means to want or choose to do it; FORMAL. *He said he was off to the beach and would we care to join him... Would you care for some orange juice?* [4] VERB & N-U If you **care** for someone or something, or if you take **care** of them, you look after them and keep them in a good state or condition. *They hired a nurse to care for her... There was no one else to take care of their children. ...sensitive teeth which need special care.* [5] N-U Children who are in **care** are looked after by the state. *She was taken into care as a baby.* [6] N-U If you do something with **care**, you do it with great attention to avoid mistakes or damage. *We'd taken enormous care in choosing the location.* [7] CONVENTION You can say **'Take care'** when saying goodbye to someone; INFORMAL. [8] N-C Your **cares** are your worries, anxieties, or fears. [9] See also **caring.**

career /kəˈrɪə/ **careers, careering, careered.** [1] N-C A **career** is a job or profession. *...a career in journalism. ...a political career.* [2] N-C Your **career** is the part of your life that you spend working. *During his career, he wrote more than fifty plays.* [3] VERB If a person or vehicle **careers** somewhere, they move fast and in an uncontrolled way. *His car careered into a river.*

carefree /ˈkeəfriː/. ADJ A **carefree** person or period of time does not have any problems or responsibilities. *...carefree summers at the beach.*

careful /ˈkeəfʊl/. [1] ADJ If you are **careful**, you give serious attention to what you are doing in order to avoid damage or mistakes. *Be very careful with this stuff, it can be dangerous... We had to be very careful not to be seen.* ◆**carefully** ADV *Drive carefully... He had chosen his words carefully.* [2] ADJ **Careful** work, thought, or examination is thorough and shows a concern for details. *The trip needs careful planning. ...keeping careful records.* ◆**carefully** ADV *All her letters were carefully filed away.*

careless /'keələs/. ADJ If you are **careless**, you do not pay enough attention to what you are doing, and so you make mistakes. *The company denied that it was careless about safety.*
◆ **carelessly** ADV *She was fined £100 for driving carelessly.* ◆ **carelessness** N-U *The fire had resulted from extreme carelessness.*

caress /kə'res/ **caresses, caressing, caressed.** VERB & N-C If you **caress** someone, you stroke them gently and affectionately. A **caress** is an act of caressing someone. *He was gently caressing her golden hair... She smoothed his forehead with a caress.*

caretaker /'keəteɪkə/ **caretakers.** N-C A **caretaker** is a person who looks after a large building such as a school or a block of flats.

cargo /'kɑːgəʊ/ **cargoes.** N-VAR The **cargo** of a ship or plane is the goods that it is carrying. *...a cargo of bananas... cargo planes.*

caricature /'kærɪkətʃʊə, AM -tʃər/ **caricatures, caricaturing, caricatured.** [1] N-VAR A **caricature** is a drawing or description of someone that exaggerates their appearance or behaviour. *...a caricature of Hitler with a devil's horns.* [2] VERB If you **caricature** someone, you draw or describe them in an exaggerated way in order to make people laugh. *...being caricatured as the proverbial American tourist.*

caring /'keərɪŋ/. ADJ A **caring** person is affectionate, helpful, and sympathetic. *...a loving, caring husband.*

carnage /'kɑːnɪdʒ/. N-U **Carnage** is the violent killing of a lot of people; LITERARY. *...his strategy for stopping the carnage in Bosnia.*

carnation /kɑː'neɪʃən/ **carnations.** N-C A **carnation** is a plant with white, pink, or red flowers.

carnival /'kɑːnɪvəl/ **carnivals.** N-C A **carnival** is a public festival with music, processions, and dancing.

carol /'kærəl/ **carols.** N-C **Carols** are Christian religious songs that are sung at Christmas.

'car park, car parks. N-C In British English, a **car park** is an area or building where people can leave their cars. The American word is **parking lot.**

carpenter /'kɑːpɪntə/ **carpenters.** N-C A **carpenter** is a person whose job is making and repairing wooden things.

carpet /'kɑːpɪt/ **carpets.** [1] N-C A **carpet** is a thick covering for a floor or staircase, made of wool or a similar material. [2] N-C A **carpet** of something is a layer of it covering the ground. *...the carpet of leaves in my yard.*

carpeted /'kɑːpɪtɪd/. [1] ADJ If a floor or room is **carpeted**, it has a carpet on the floor. *...the gray-carpeted dining room.* [2] ADJ If the ground is **carpeted** with something, there is a layer of it covering the ground. *The ground was thickly carpeted with pine needles.*

carriage /'kærɪdʒ/ **carriages.** [1] N-C In British English, a **carriage** is one of the separate sections of a train that carries passengers. The usual American word is **car.** [2] N-C A **carriage** is an old-fashioned vehicle pulled by horses.

carriageway /'kærɪdʒweɪ/ **carriageways.** N-C A **carriageway** is one of the two sides of a motorway or major road; BRITISH.

carrier /'kæriə/ **carriers.** [1] N-C A **carrier** is a vehicle that is used for carrying people, especially soldiers, or things. *...armoured personnel carriers and tanks.* [2] N-C A **carrier** is a passenger airline. *...Switzerland's national carrier, Swissair.* [3] N-C A **carrier** or a **carrier bag** is a paper or plastic bag with handles; BRITISH.

carrot /'kærət/ **carrots.** [1] N-VAR **Carrots** are long, thin, orange-coloured vegetables that grow under the ground. [2] N-C Something that is offered to people in order to persuade them to do something can be referred to as a **carrot**. *They will be set targets, with a carrot of extra cash and pay if they achieve them.*

carry /'kæri/ **carries, carrying, carried.** [1] VERB If you **carry** something, you take it with you, holding it so that it does not touch the ground. *He was carrying a briefcase... She carried her son to the car.* [2] VERB To **carry** something means to have it with you wherever you go. *He always carried a gun.* [3] VERB To **carry** someone or something means to take them somewhere. *...carrying a message of thanks to President Mubarak... The ship could carry seventy passengers.* [4] VERB If someone is **carrying** a disease, they are infected with it and can pass it on to other people. *...people carrying the AIDS virus.* [5] VERB If an action or situation **carries** a particular quality or consequence, it has it. *Exposure to the sun carries the risk of developing skin cancer. ...an offence which can carry the death penalty.* [6] VERB If you **carry** an idea or a method further, you use or develop it or apply it in new circumstances. *It's not such a new idea, but I carried it to extremes.* [7] VERB If a newspaper **carries** a picture or an article, it contains it. [8] VERB If a proposal or motion **is carried** in a debate, a majority of people vote in favour of it. [9] VERB If a sound **carries**, it can be heard a long way away. *He doubted if the sound would carry far.* [10] PHRASE If you **get carried away**, you are so eager or excited about something that you do something hasty or foolish.

▶ **carry on.** [1] PHR-VERB If you **carry on** doing something, you continue to do it. *The assistant carried on talking.* [2] PHR-VERB If you **carry on** an activity, you take part in it. *They carried on a conversation through most of the morning.*

▶ **carry out.** PHR-VERB If you **carry out** a threat, task, or instruction, you do it or act according to it. *The security forces carried out the arrests.*

▶ **carry through.** PHR-VERB If you **carry** something **through**, you do it, often in spite of difficulties. *It would carry through its military operation to the very end.*

cart /kɑːt/ **carts, carting, carted.** [1] N-C A **cart** is an old-fashioned wooden vehicle, usually pulled by an animal. [2] VERB If you **cart** things somewhere, you carry or transport them there, often with difficulty; INFORMAL. *He carted off the entire contents of the house.*

cartel /kɑː'tel/ **cartels.** N-C A **cartel** is an association of companies or countries involved in the same industry who act together to control competition and prices.

cartilage /'kɑːtɪlɪdʒ/. N-U **Cartilage** is a strong flexible substance which surrounds the joints in your body.

carton /'kɑːtən/ **cartons.** [1] N-C A **carton** is a plastic or cardboard container in which food or drink is sold. ...*a two-pint carton of milk.* [2] N-C A **carton** is a large strong cardboard box; AMERICAN.

cartoon /kɑː'tuːn/ **cartoons.** [1] N-C A **cartoon** is a humorous drawing in a newspaper or magazine. [2] N-C A **cartoon** is a film in which all the characters and scenes are drawn rather than being real people or objects.

cartoonist /kɑː'tuːnɪst/ **cartoonists.** N-C A **cartoonist** is a person whose job is to draw cartoons for newspapers and magazines.

cartridge /'kɑːtrɪdʒ/ **cartridges.** [1] N-C In a gun, a **cartridge** is a tube containing a bullet and an explosive substance. [2] N-C A **cartridge** is a part of a machine that can be easily removed and replaced when it is worn out or empty.

carve /kɑːv/ **carves, carving, carved.** [1] VERB If you **carve** an object, you cut it out of stone or wood. You **carve** wood or stone in order to make the object. *One of the prisoners has carved a beautiful wooden chess set.* [2] VERB If you **carve** writing or a design on an object, you cut it into the surface. *He carved his name on his desk.* [3] VERB If you **carve** meat, you cut slices from it. [4] VERB & PHR-VERB If you **carve** a career or a niche for yourself, or if you **carve out** a career or niche, you succeed in getting the career or the position that you want by your own efforts. *She has carved a niche for herself as a comic actor.*

► **carve up.** PHR-VERB If someone **carves** something **up**, they divide it into smaller areas or pieces; used showing disapproval. *They have begun carving the country up like a pie.*

carving /'kɑːvɪŋ/ **carvings.** [1] N-C A **carving** is an object or design that has been cut out of stone or wood. [2] N-U **Carving** is the act of carving objects or designs.

cascade /kæs'keɪd/ **cascades, cascading, cascaded.** [1] N-C A **cascade** of something is a large amount of it; LITERARY. ...*a cascade of laughter.* [2] VERB When water **cascades**, it pours downwards very fast and in large quantities. *The freezing, rushing water cascaded past her.*

case /keɪs/ **cases.** [1] N-C A **case** is a particular situation or instance, especially one that you are using as an example of something more general. *Suffering can have beneficial results and certainly I know that was true in my case... In extreme cases, insurance companies can prosecute.* [2] N-C A **case** is a person that a professional such as a doctor is dealing with. *Child protection workers were meeting to discuss her case.* [3] N-C A crime, or a trial that takes place after a crime, can be called a **case**. ...*her connection with the kidnapping case. ...trying to determine the outcome of court cases.* [4] N-C In an argument, the **case** for or against something consists of the facts and reasons used to support or oppose it. *He sat there while I made the case for his dismissal.* [5] N-C A **case** is a container that is designed to hold or protect something. ...*a black case for his spectacles... The room was filled with cases of liquor.* [6] N-C A **case** is the same as a **suit-case**.

PHRASES ● You say **in any case** when you are adding another reason for something you have said or done. *The concert was booked out, and in any case, most of the people gathered in the square could not afford the price of a ticket.* ● You say **in case** to indicate that you have something or are doing something because a particular thing might happen or might have happened. *All exits must be kept clear in case of fire... I'm waiting for Mary, in case you're wondering... She carried her pills in her purse, just in case.* ● You say **in that case** or **in which case** to indicate that you are assuming that a previous statement is correct or true. *You may, of course, disagree, in which case, don't hesitate to let me know.* ● When you say that a job or task **is a case of** doing a particular thing, you mean that the job or task consists of doing that thing. *Every team has a weakness; it's just a case of finding it.*

'case study, case studies. N-C A **case study** is a written account that gives detailed information about a person, group, or thing and their development over a period of time. ...*a large case study of malaria in West African children.*

cash /kæʃ/ **cashes, cashing, cashed.** [1] N-U **Cash** is money, especially money in the form of notes and coins. *We were desperately short of cash. ...two thousand pounds in cash.* [2] VERB If you **cash** a cheque, you exchange it at a bank for the amount of money that it is worth.

► **cash in** PHR-VERB If someone **cashes in** on a situation, they use it to gain an advantage for themselves. *Local Conservatives have been accused of cashing in on racial tension in the area.*

cashier /kæ'ʃɪə/ **cashiers.** N-C A **cashier** is the person that customers pay money to or get money from in a shop or bank.

cashmere /ˌkæʃ'mɪə, AM 'kæʒmɪr/. N-U **Cashmere** is a kind of very fine soft wool.

casino /kə'siːnəʊ/ **casinos.** N-C A **casino** is a place where people play gambling games.

casserole /'kæsərəʊl/ **casseroles.** [1] N-VAR A **casserole** is a meal made by cooking food in liquid in an oven. ...*lamb casserole.* [2] N-C A **casserole** or **casserole dish** is a large heavy container with a lid used for cooking casseroles.

cassette /kə'set/ **cassettes.** N-C A **cassette** is a small, flat, rectangular, plastic container with magnetic tape inside which is used for recording and playing back sounds.

cast /kɑːst, kæst/ **casts, casting, cast.** [1] N-C The **cast** of a play or film is all the people who act in it. In the singular **cast** may be followed by a singular or plural verb. *Most of the cast was amazed by the play's success.* [2] VERB To **cast** an actor means to choose them to act a particular role. *He was cast as a college professor.* [3] VERB If you **cast** something somewhere, you throw it there; LITERARY. *He cast the stone away.* [4] VERB If you **cast** your eyes or **cast** a look somewhere, you look there; WRITTEN. *He cast a stern glance at the two men.* [5] VERB If you **cast** doubt or suspicion on something, you make other people unsure about it. *New tests have cast doubt on the cause of the blast.* [6] VERB When you **cast** your vote in an election, you vote. [7] VERB To **cast** an object means to make it by pouring hot liquid metal into a container and leaving it until it becomes hard.

▸ **cast about** or **cast around**. PHR-VERB If you **cast about** or **cast around** for something, you try to find it. *She had been casting around for a good excuse.*

▸ **cast aside**. PHR-VERB If you **cast** someone or something **aside**, you get rid of them. *In America we seem to cast aside our elderly people.*

▸ **cast off**. PHR-VERB If you **cast** something **off**, you get rid of it or no longer use it; WRITTEN. *...having cast off a grossly inefficient economic system.*

caste /kɑːst, kæst/ **castes**. N-VAR A **caste** is one of the social classes into which people in a Hindu society are divided. *India divides in many ways: by caste, religion, language, region.*

castigate /ˈkæstɪgeɪt/ **castigates, castigating, castigated**. VERB If you **castigate** someone, you scold or criticize them severely; FORMAL.

'cast-iron. [1] ADJ **Cast-iron** objects are made of a special type of iron containing carbon. *...a cast-iron bath.* [2] ADJ A **cast-iron** excuse, guarantee, or solution is absolutely certain to be effective.

castle /ˈkɑːsəl, ˈkæsəl/ **castles**. N-C A **castle** is a large building with thick high walls, built by important people, such as kings, in former times, for protection during wars and battles.

castrate /kæˈstreɪt, AM ˈkæstreɪt/ **castrates, castrating, castrated**. VERB To **castrate** a male animal means to remove its testicles. ◆**castration, castrations** N-VAR *...the castration of male farm animals.*

casual /ˈkæʒuəl/. [1] ADJ If you are **casual**, you are relaxed and not very concerned about what is happening. ◆**casually** ADV *'No need to hurry,' Ben said casually.* [2] ADJ BEFORE N Something that is **casual** happens by chance or without planning. *...a casual remark.* [3] ADJ BEFORE N **Casual** clothes are ones that you normally wear at home or on holiday, and not for formal occasions. ◆**casually** ADV *They were smartly but casually dressed.* [4] ADJ BEFORE N **Casual** work is done for short periods and is not permanent. *...establishments which employ people on a casual basis.*

casualty /ˈkæʒuəlti/ **casualties**. [1] N-C A **casualty** is a person who is injured or killed in a war or in an accident. *The casualties on our side were frightful.* [2] N-C A **casualty** of an event or situation is a person or a thing that has suffered badly as a result of it. *Small companies were early casualties of the recession.* [3] N-U **Casualty** is the department of a hospital where people are taken for emergency treatment; BRITISH.

cat /kæt/ **cats**. [1] N-C A **cat** is a small furry animal with a tail, whiskers, and sharp claws. Cats are often kept as pets. [2] N-C **Cats** are a group of animals which includes lions, tigers, and domestic cats. [3] PHRASE In a fight or contest, if the stronger person or group plays **cat and mouse** with the other, they choose to defeat their opponent slowly, using skill and deceit, rather than force or violence.

catalogue (AM **catalog**) /ˈkætəlɒg/ **catalogues, cataloguing, catalogued**. [1] N-C A **catalogue** is a list of things, such as the goods you can buy from a company, the objects in a museum, or the books in a library. [2] VERB To **catalogue** things means to make a list of them. [3] N-C A **catalogue of** similar things, especially bad things, is a number of them happening one after another. *Mr Wills struggled to explain the catalogue of errors.*

catalyst /ˈkætəlɪst/ **catalysts**. [1] N-C You can describe a person or thing as a **catalyst** when they cause a change or event to happen. *I think the report will serve as a catalyst to bring all of the parties together.* [2] N-C In chemistry, a **catalyst** is a substance that causes a reaction to take place more quickly.

catapult /ˈkætəpʌlt/ **catapults, catapulting, catapulted**. [1] N-C A **catapult** is a device for shooting small stones. It consists of a Y-shaped stick with a piece of elastic tied between the two top parts. [2] VERB If someone or something **catapults** through the air, they move or are thrown very suddenly and violently through it. *His car catapulted off the kerb... Georgina was catapulted through the windscreen.*

cataract /ˈkætərækt/ **cataracts**. N-C A **cataract** is a layer that has grown over a person's eye that prevents them from seeing properly.

catastrophe /kəˈtæstrəfi/ **catastrophes**. N-C A **catastrophe** is an unexpected event that causes great suffering or damage. *From all points of view, war would be a catastrophe.*

catastrophic /ˌkætəˈstrɒfɪk/. ADJ **Catastrophic** means extremely bad or serious, often causing great suffering or damage. *Even a small oil spill would be catastrophic. ...a catastrophic mistake.*

catch /kætʃ/ **catches, catching, caught**. [1] VERB If you **catch** a person or animal, you capture them. *Police say they are confident of catching the gunman. ...an animal caught in a trap.* [2] VERB If you **catch** an object which is moving through the air, you seize it with your hands. *I jumped up to catch the ball.* [3] VERB If something which is moving **catches** something else, it hits it. *He caught her on the side of her head with his other hand.* [4] VERB If something **catches** on or in an object, or if it **is caught** on or in it, it becomes trapped by it. *Her heel caught on a rusty bedspring.* [5] VERB If you **catch** a bus, train, or plane, you get on it to travel somewhere. [6] VERB If you **catch** someone doing something wrong, you discover them doing it. *He caught a youth breaking into a car... They caught him with $30,000 cash in a briefcase.* [7] PASSIVE-VERB If you **are caught** in a storm or other unpleasant situation, it happens when you cannot avoid its effects. *Visitors to the area were caught between police and the rioters.* [8] VERB If something **catches** your attention or your eye, you notice it or become interested in it. [9] VERB If you cannot **catch** what someone says, you cannot manage to hear it. *I do not believe I caught your name.*

10 VERB If you **catch** a cold or a disease, you become ill with it. **11** VERB If something **catches** the light, or if the light **catches** it, it reflects the light and looks bright or shiny. **12** N-C A **catch** on a window or door is a device that fastens it. **13** N-SING A **catch** is a hidden problem or difficulty in a plan or course of action. *'It's your money. You deserve it.'—'What's the catch?'*

▶ **catch on.** **1** PHR-VERB If you **catch on** to something, you understand it, or realize that it is happening. *I was slow to catch on to what she was trying to tell me.* **2** PHR-VERB If something **catches on**, it becomes popular. *Photography began to catch on as a respectable activity.*

▶ **catch out.** PHR-VERB To **catch** someone **out** means to cause them to make a mistake that reveals that they are lying about something. *His clumsy attempts to catch her out had failed.*

▶ **catch up.** **1** PHR-VERB If you **catch up** with someone, you reach them by walking faster than them. *I stopped and waited for her to catch up.* **2** PHR-VERB To **catch up** with someone means to reach the same standard or level that they have reached. *The school is used by kids who want to catch up on English.* **3** PHR-VERB If you **catch up** on an activity that you have not had much time to do, you spend time doing it. *I was catching up on a bit of reading.* **4** PHR-VERB If you **are caught up** in something, you are involved in it, usually unwillingly. *...innocent people caught up in the fighting.*

▶ **catch up with.** **1** PHR-VERB When people **catch up with** someone who has done something wrong, they succeed in finding them. **2** PHR-VERB If something **catches up with** you, you find yourself in an unpleasant situation which you have been able to avoid but which you are now forced to deal with. *His criminal past caught up with him.*

catchy /'kætʃi/ **catchier, catchiest.** ADJ A **catchy** tune, name, or phrase is attractive and easy to remember.

categorical /ˌkætɪˈgɒrɪkəl, AM -ˈgɔːr-/. ADJ If you are **categorical** about something, you state your views with certainty and firmness. *...his categorical denial of the charges.* ◆ **categorically** ADV *I categorically refused to leave.*

categorize (BR also **categorise**) /'kætɪgəraɪz/ **categorizes, categorizing, categorized.** VERB If you **categorize** people or things, you say which set they belong to. *They categorized me as a rock 'n' roll player.* ◆ **categorization, categorizations.** N-VAR *...the labeling and categorization of people in news reports.*

category /'kætɪgri, AM -gɔːri/ **categories.** N-C If people or things are divided into **categories**, they are divided into groups according to their qualities and characteristics. *The law covers four categories of experiments.*

cater /'keɪtə/ **caters, catering, catered.** VERB In British English, to **cater for** people means to provide them with the things they need. In American English, you **cater to** people. *...shops that cater for the needs of men.*

caterer /'keɪtərə/ **caterers.** N-C A **caterer** is a person or a company that provides food in a particular place or on a special occasion.

catering /'keɪtərərɪŋ/. N-U **Catering** is the activity or business of providing food for people. *...a catering company.*

caterpillar /'kætəpɪlə/ **caterpillars.** N-C A **caterpillar** is a small worm-like animal that eventually develops into a butterfly or moth.

cathedral /kəˈθiːdrəl/ **cathedrals.** N-C A **cathedral** is a large important church which has a bishop in charge of it.

Catholic /'kæθlɪk/ **Catholics.** ADJ & N-C The **Catholic** Church is the branch of the Christian Church that accepts the Pope as its leader. A **Catholic** is a member of the Catholic Church. *...Catholic priests. ...a very devout Catholic.* ◆ **Catholicism** /kəˈθɒlɪsɪzəm/ N-U *...her conversion to Catholicism.*

cattle /'kætəl/. N-PL **Cattle** are cows and bulls.

catwalk /'kætwɔːk/ **catwalks.** N-C At a fashion show, the **catwalk** is the narrow platform that models walk along to display clothes.

caucus /'kɔːkəs/ **caucuses.** N-C A **caucus** is an influential group of people within an organization who share similar aims and interests; FORMAL. *...the black caucus in the US Congress.*

caught /kɔːt/. **Caught** is the past tense and past participle of **catch**.

cauldron /'kɔːldrən/ **cauldrons.** N-C A **cauldron** is a very large round metal pot used for cooking over a fire; LITERARY.

cauliflower /'kɒlɪflaʊə, AM 'kɔː-/ **cauliflowers.** N-VAR A **cauliflower** is a large, round, white vegetable surrounded by green leaves.

cause /kɔːz/ **causes, causing, caused.** **1** N-C & VERB The **cause** of an event or the thing that **causes** it is the thing that makes it happen. *Oil pollution is the commonest cause of death for seabirds. ...the factors that caused prices to rise... They never really caused us problems.* **2** N-U If you **have cause** for a particular feeling or action, you have good reason for it. *It seems that you have cause for celebration. ...if you've ever had cause to be angry at a computer.* **3** N-C A **cause** is an aim which a group of people supports or is fighting for. *...present-day champions of the cause.*

caution /'kɔːʃən/ **cautions, cautioning, cautioned.** **1** N-U **Caution** is great care taken in order to avoid danger. *Extreme caution should be exercised when buying part-worn tyres.* **2** VERB & N-U If someone **cautions** you, or if they give you a **caution**, they warn you. *Tony cautioned against misrepresenting the situation... They caution that the process is long and difficult... One word of caution. It is not wise to become totally dependent on others.*

cautionary /'kɔːʃənri, AM -neri/. ADJ A **cautionary** story is intended to give a warning. *...her cautionary tales of men.*

cautious /'kɔːʃəs/. ADJ A **cautious** person acts very carefully in order to avoid danger. *Employers may become overly cautious about taking on new staff.* ◆ **cautiously** ADV *David moved cautiously forward.*

cavalier /ˌkævəˈlɪə/. ADJ If you describe a person as **cavalier**, you disapprove of them because you think that they do not consider other people's feelings or take account of the seriousness of a situation. *The Editor takes a cavalier attitude to the concept of fact checking.*

cavalry /'kævəlri/. N-SING **The cavalry** used to be the soldiers who rode horses in an army. Nowadays, it is usually the soldiers who use armoured vehicles in an army.

cave /keɪv/ **caves, caving, caved.** N-C A **cave** is a large hole in the side of a cliff or hill, or under the ground.

▶ **cave in.** [1] PHR-VERB When a roof or wall **caves in**, it collapses inwards. [2] PHR-VERB If you **cave in**, you suddenly stop arguing or resisting. *The Government has caved in to pressure from property developers.*

cavern /'kævən/ **caverns.** N-C A **cavern** is a large deep cave.

cavernous /'kævənəs/. ADJ A **cavernous** room or building is very large inside.

caviar (or **caviare**) /'kæviɑː/ **caviars.** N-VAR **Caviar** is a food that consists of the salted eggs of a fish called the sturgeon.

cavity /'kævɪti/ **cavities.** N-C A **cavity** is a small space or hole in something solid. *...the decay that causes cavities in your teeth.*

cc. cc. is an abbreviation for 'cubic centimetres', used when referring to the volume or capacity of something. *...1,500 cc sports cars.*

CD /ˌsiː'diː/ **CDs.** N-C A **CD** is a small shiny disc on which music or information is stored. **CD** is an abbreviation for 'Compact Disc'.

'**CD player, CD players.** N-C A **CD player** is a machine on which you can play CDs.

CD ROM /ˌsiː diː 'rɒm/ **CD ROMs.** N-C A **CD ROM** is a disc which can be read by a computer, and on which a very large amount of data is stored.

cease /siːs/ **ceases, ceasing, ceased.** [1] VERB If something **ceases**, it stops happening; FORMAL. *At one o'clock the rain had ceased.* [2] VERB To **cease** to do something means to stop doing it; FORMAL. *A small number of firms have ceased trading.*

ceasefire /'siːsfaɪə/ **ceasefires.** N-C A **ceasefire** is an arrangement in which countries at war agree to stop fighting for a time.

cedar /'siːdə/ **cedars.** N-VAR A **cedar** is a kind of evergreen tree. **Cedar** is the wood of this tree.

cede /siːd/ **cedes, ceding, ceded.** VERB If someone in a position of authority **cedes** land or power to someone else, they let them have it; FORMAL. *The General had promised to cede power by January.*

ceiling /'siːlɪŋ/ **ceilings.** [1] N-C A **ceiling** is the top inside surface of a room. *...a small air vent in the ceiling.* [2] N-C A **ceiling** is an official upper limit on prices or wages. *...an informal agreement to put a ceiling on salaries.*

celebrate /'selɪbreɪt/ **celebrates, celebrating, celebrated.** [1] VERB If you **celebrate** something, you do something enjoyable because of a special occasion. *The England football team have been celebrating their victory... I was in a mood to celebrate.* ◆ **celebration, celebrations.** N-VAR *Only a few people can find any cause for celebration. ...his eightieth birthday celebrations.* [2] VERB When priests **celebrate**

Holy Communion or Mass, they officially perform the actions and ceremonies that are involved.

celebrated /'selɪbreɪtɪd/. ADJ A **celebrated** person or thing is famous and much admired. *...his most celebrated film.*

celebrity /sɪ'lebrɪti/ **celebrities.** N-C A **celebrity** is someone who is famous. *At the age of 30, Hersey suddenly became a celebrity.*

celery /'seləri/. N-U **Celery** is a vegetable with long pale green stalks.

celestial /sɪ'lestiəl/. ADJ **Celestial** is used to describe things connected with heaven or the sky; LITERARY.

celibate /'selɪbət/. ADJ Someone who is **celibate** does not marry or have sex; FORMAL. ◆ **celibacy** N-U *...a monk who took the vow of celibacy.*

cell /sel/ **cells.** [1] N-C A **cell** is the smallest part of an animal or plant. All animals and plants are made up of millions of cells. [2] N-C A **cell** is a small room in which a prisoner is locked. *...police cells.*

cellar /'selə/ **cellars.** N-C A **cellar** is a room underneath a building.

cello /'tʃeləʊ/ **cellos.** N-VAR A **cello** is a musical instrument that looks like a large violin. You hold it upright and play it sitting down. ◆ **cellist, cellists.** N-C *...the world's greatest cellist.*

cellular /'seljʊlə/. ADJ **Cellular** means relating to the cells of animals or plants. *...molecular and cellular mechanisms.*

cellulite /'seljʊlaɪt/. N-U **Cellulite** is lumpy fat which people may get under their skin, especially on their thighs.

Celsius /'selsiəs/. ADJ **Celsius** is a scale for measuring temperature, in which water freezes at 0° and boils at 100°. Another word for this is 'centigrade'. *Night temperatures can drop below 15 degrees Celsius.* ● See note at **temperature.**

cement /sɪ'ment/ **cements, cementing, cemented.** [1] N-U **Cement** is a grey powder which is mixed with sand and water in order to make concrete. [2] VERB If things **are cemented** together, they are stuck or fastened together. *The lice eggs are cemented to the hairs on the scalp.* [3] VERB Something that **cements** a relationship or agreement makes it stronger. *Nothing cements a friendship between countries so much as trade.*

cemetery /'semɪtri/ **cemeteries.** N-C A **cemetery** is a place where dead people are buried.

censor /'sensə/ **censors, censoring, censored.** [1] VERB If someone **censors** a letter or the media, they officially examine it and cut out any parts that they consider unacceptable. *Television companies tend to censor bad language.* [2] N-C A **censor** is a person who has been officially appointed to censor things.

censorship /'sensəʃɪp/. N-U When there is **censorship**, letters or the media are censored. *I am totally against censorship.*

censure /'senʃə/ **censures, censuring, censured.** VERB & N-U If someone **is censured** or if they attract **censure**, they are criticized strongly; FORMAL. *I would not presume to censure*

Osborne for hating his mother. ...a controversial policy which has attracted international censure.

census /ˈsensəs/ **censuses.** N-C A **census** is an official survey of the population of a country.

cent /sent/ **cents.** N-C A **cent** is a small unit of money in many countries, for example in the United States and Australia. ● See also **per cent**.

centenary /senˈtiːnəri, AM -ˈten-/ **centenaries.** N-C A **centenary** is the one hundredth anniversary of an event; BRITISH. *...the centenary of the death of Lord Tennyson.*

center /ˈsentə/. See **centre**.

Centigrade /ˈsentɪgreɪd/. ADJ **Centigrade** means the same as **Celsius**. *...daytime temperatures of up to forty degrees centigrade.* ● See note at **temperature**.

centimetre (AM **centimeter**) /ˈsentimiːtə/ **centimetres.** N-C A **centimetre** is a unit of length equal to ten millimetres or one-hundredth of a metre.

central /ˈsentrəl/. [1] ADJ BEFORE N A **central** group or organization makes all the important decisions for a larger organization or country. *...the central committee of the Cuban communist party.* ◆**centrally** ADV *...a centrally planned economy.* [2] ADJ Something that is **central** is in the middle of a place or area. *...central London.* ◆**centrally** ADV *...a full-sized double bed centrally placed.* [3] ADJ The **central** person or thing in a particular situation is the most important one. *...a central part of their culture.*

central heating. N-U **Central heating** is a heating system in which water or air is heated and passed round a building through pipes and radiators.

centralise /ˈsentrəlaɪz/. See **centralize**.

centralize (BR also **centralise**) /ˈsentrəlaɪz/ **centralizes, centralizing, centralized.** VERB To **centralize** a country or organization means to create a system in which one central authority gives instructions to regional groups. *Multinational firms tended to centralize their operations.* ◆**centralized** ADJ *...a centralized economy.* ◆**centralization** N-U *The centralization of political power.*

centre (AM **center**) /ˈsentə/ **centres, centring, centred.** [1] N-C The **centre** of something is the middle of it. *...the centre of the room.* [2] N-C A **centre** is a place where people have meetings, get help of some kind, or take part in a particular activity. *...the medical centre. ...the National Exhibition Centre.* [3] N-C If an area or town is a **centre** for an industry or activity, that industry or activity is very important there. *London is also the major international insurance centre.* [4] N-C If something is the **centre** of attention or interest, people are giving it a lot of attention. *The centre of attraction was Pierre Auguste Renoir's oil painting.* [5] PASSIVE-VERB Someone or something that is **centred** in a particular place is based there. *...the silk industry, which was centered in Valencia.* [6] VERB If something **centres** or **is centred** on a particular thing or person, that thing or person is the main subject of attention. *...talks which centred on the Cambodia problem... All his concerns were centred around*

himself rather than Rachel. ◆**-centred** *...a child-centred approach to teaching.*

century /ˈsentʃəri/ **centuries.** [1] N-C A **century** is a period of a hundred years that is used when stating a date. For example, the 19th century was the period from 1801 to 1900. [2] N-C A **century** is any period of a hundred years.

ceramic /sɪˈræmɪk/ **ceramics.** [1] N-VAR **Ceramic** is clay that has been heated to a very high temperature so that it becomes hard. [2] N-C **Ceramics** are ceramic ornaments or objects. [3] N-U **Ceramics** is the art of making ceramic objects.

cereal /ˈsɪəriəl/ **cereals.** [1] N-VAR **Cereal** is a food made from grain, usually mixed with milk and eaten for breakfast. [2] N-C **Cereals** are plants such as wheat or rice that produce grain. *...4 million hectares of cereal crops.*

cerebral /ˈserɪbrəl/. [1] ADJ **Cerebral** means relating to thought or reasoning rather than to emotions; FORMAL. *Some think him too cerebral to win the support of voters.* [2] ADJ BEFORE N **Cerebral** means relating to the brain; TECHNICAL. *...a cerebral haemorrhage.*

ceremonial /ˌserɪˈməʊniəl/ **ceremonials.** ADJ BEFORE N Something that is **ceremonial** is used in a ceremony or relates to a ceremony. *He represented the nation on ceremonial occasions.*

ceremony /ˈserɪməni, AM -məʊni/ **ceremonies.** [1] N-C A **ceremony** is a formal event such as a wedding or a coronation. [2] N-U **Ceremony** consists of the special things that are said and done on very formal occasions. *...the pomp and ceremony of the Pope's visit.*

certain /ˈsɜːtən/. [1] ADJ If you are **certain** about something or if it is **certain**, you firmly believe it is true and have no doubt about it. *She's absolutely certain she's going to make it... It wasn't a balloon – I'm certain of that... The scheme is certain to meet opposition.* [2] ADJ You use **certain** to indicate that you are referring to one particular thing or person, although you are not saying exactly which it is. *There will be certain people who'll say 'I told you so!'... You owe a certain person a sum of money.*

PHRASES ● If you know something **for certain**, you have no doubt about it. *She couldn't know what time he'd go, or even for certain that he'd go at all.* ● When you **make certain** that something happens, you take action to ensure that it happens. *He had made certain he hadn't shown his face.*

certainly /ˈsɜːtənli/. [1] ADV You can use **certainly** to emphasize what you are saying. *The public is certainly getting tired of hearing about it... Certainly, pets can help children develop friendship skills.* [2] ADV You use **certainly** when you are agreeing or disagreeing strongly with what someone has said. *'You keep out of their way don't you?'—'I certainly do.'... 'Perhaps it would be better if I withdrew altogether.'—'Certainly not!'*

certainty /ˈsɜːtənti/ **certainties.** [1] N-U **Certainty** is the state of having no doubts at all. *I have told them with absolute certainty there'll be no change of policy.* [2] N-C **Certainties** are things that nobody has any doubts about. *In politics there are never any certainties.*

certificate /sə'tɪfɪkət/ **certificates.** N-C A certificate is an official document which states that particular facts are true, or which you receive when you have successfully completed a course of study or training. *...birth certificates. ...the Post-Graduate Certificate of Education.*

certify /'sɜːtɪfaɪ/ **certifies, certifying, certified.** [1] VERB If someone in an official position **certifies** something, they officially state that it is true or genuine. *The president certified that the project would receive at least $650m... The National Election Council is supposed to certify the results.* ◆ **certification** /sə,tɪfɪ'keɪʃən/ **certifications** N-VAR *...written certification that the relative is really ill.* [2] VERB If someone **is certified** as a particular kind of worker, they are given a certificate stating that they have successfully completed a course of training in their profession. *They wanted to get certified as divers.* ◆ **certification** N-U *...training leading to the certification of their skill in a particular field.*

cervix /'sɜːvɪks/. The plural is **cervixes** or **cervices.** N-C The **cervix** is the entrance to the womb; TECHNICAL. ◆ **cervical** /'sɜːvɪkəl, sə'vaɪkəl/ ADJ BEFORE N *...cervical cancer.*

CFC /ˌsiː ef 'siː/ **CFCs.** N-C CFCs are chemicals that are used in aerosols, refrigerators, and cooling systems, and in the manufacture of various plastics. **CFC** is an abbreviation for 'chlorofluorocarbon'.

chain /tʃeɪn/ **chains, chaining, chained.** [1] N-C A **chain** consists of metal rings connected together in a line. *His open shirt revealed a fat gold chain.* [2] VERB If a person or thing **is chained** to something, they are fastened to it with a chain. *The dog was chained to the leg of the garden seat... She chained her bike to the railings.* [3] N-C A **chain** of things is a group of them arranged in a line. *...a chain of islands.* [4] N-C A **chain** of shops or hotels is a number of them owned by the same company. *...a large supermarket chain.* [5] N-C A **chain** of events is a series of them happening one after another.

chair /tʃeə/ **chairs, chairing, chaired.** [1] N-C A **chair** is a piece of furniture for one person to sit on, with a back and four legs. [2] N-C At British universities, a **chair** is the post of professor. [3] VERB If you **chair** a meeting, you are the person in charge of it. *...a committee chaired by Dr Robert Song.* [4] N-C The **chair** of a meeting is the chairperson.

chairman /'tʃeəmən/ **chairmen.** N-C The **chairman** of a meeting or organization is the person in charge of it.

chairperson /'tʃeəpɜːsən/ **chairpersons.** N-C The **chairperson** of a meeting or organization is the person in charge of it.

chairwoman /'tʃeəwʊmən/ **chairwomen.** N-C The **chairwoman** of a meeting or organization is the woman in charge of it.

chalet /'ʃæleɪ, AM ʃæ'leɪ/ **chalets.** N-C A **chalet** is a small wooden house, especially in a mountain area or holiday camp.

chalk /tʃɔːk/ **chalks, chalking, chalked.** [1] N-U **Chalk** is soft white rock. *...the highest*

chalk cliffs in Britain. [2] N-C **Chalk** refers to small pieces of chalk used for writing or drawing. *...coloured chalks.*

▶ **chalk up.** PHR-VERB If you **chalk up** a success, you achieve it. *The team chalked up another victory.*

challenge /'tʃælɪndʒ/ **challenges, challenging, challenged.** [1] N-VAR A **challenge** is something new and difficult which requires great effort and determination. *The new government's first challenge is the economy.* [2] PHRASE If someone **rises to the challenge**, they successfully act in response to a difficult situation. *They rose to the challenge of entertaining 80 schoolchildren.* [3] VERB & N-C If you **challenge** someone or if you present them with a **challenge**, you invite them to fight or compete with you. *He left a note at the scene of the crime, challenging detectives to catch him... A third presidential candidate emerged to mount a serious challenge.* [4] VERB & N-VAR To **challenge** ideas or people means to question their truth, value, or authority. A **challenge** is an act of challenging someone or something. *Rose challenged him to come on stage and explain his opinions... The details are open to challenge. ...a direct challenge to the authority of the government.* [5] ADJ If you say that someone is **challenged** in a particular way, you mean that they have a disability in that area. **Challenged** is often used for humorous effect. **Challenged** is only used after an adverb for this meaning. *She ran off with an intellectually challenged ski instructor.*

challenger /'tʃælɪndʒə/ **challengers.** N-C A **challenger** is someone who competes for a position or title. *...the sixth challenger for the 1995 Americas Cup.*

challenging /'tʃælɪndʒɪŋ/. [1] ADJ A **challenging** job or activity requires great effort and determination. *I'm ready to do all those things which are more challenging.* [2] ADJ **Challenging** behaviour seems to be inviting people to argue or compete. *Mona gave him a challenging look.*

chamber /'tʃeɪmbə/ **chambers.** [1] N-C A **chamber** is a large room that is used for formal meetings, or that is designed and equipped for a particular purpose. *...the Council chamber. ...a burial chamber.* [2] N-C You can refer to a country's parliament or to one section of it as a **chamber.**

,**chamber of 'commerce, chambers of commerce.** N-C A **chamber of commerce** is a group of business people who work together to improve business and industry in their area.

champ /tʃæmp/ **champs.** N-C A **champ** is the same as a **champion;** INFORMAL.

champagne /ʃæm'peɪn/. N-U **Champagne** is an expensive French sparkling white wine. It is often drunk to celebrate something.

champion /'tʃæmpiən/ **champions, championing, championed.** [1] N-C A **champion** is someone who has won the first prize in a competition. *...a former Olympic champion. ...champion boxer Lennox Lewis.* [2] N-C & VERB If you are a **champion** of a person, a cause or a principle or if you **champion** them, you support or defend them. *He was once known as a* *champion of social reform... He passionately championed the poor.*

championship /'tʃæmpiənʃip/ **championships.** [1] N-C A **championship** is a competition to find the best player or team in a particular sport. ...*the world chess championship.* [2] N-SING **The championship** refers to the title or status of being a sports champion. *He went on to take the championship.*

chance /tʃɑːns, tʃæns/ **chances, chancing, chanced.** [1] N-VAR If there is a **chance** of something happening, it is possible that it will happen. *His chances of winning are slim... There seems little chance of the situation improving.* [2] N-SING If you have a **chance** to do something, you have the opportunity to do it. *All eligible people would get a chance to vote... I felt I had to give him a chance.* [3] N-U & ADJ BEFORE N Something that happens by **chance** was not planned. *He was found by chance on Tuesday by a relative. ...a chance meeting.*

| PHRASES | • If you say that someone **stands a chance** of achieving something, you mean that they are likely to achieve it. If you say that they do not **stand a chance**, you mean that they cannot possibly achieve it. • When you **take a chance**, you try to do something although there is a large risk of danger or failure. *You take a chance on the weather if you holiday in the UK.* |

chancellor /'tʃɑːnslə, 'tʃæns-/ **chancellors.** [1] N-TITLE In several European countries, the **Chancellor** is the head of government. ...*Chancellor Kohl.* [2] N-C The heads of British universities and some American universities are called **Chancellors**.

chandelier /ˌʃændə'liə/ **chandeliers.** N-C A **chandelier** is an ornamental frame hanging from a ceiling, which holds a number of light bulbs or candles.

change /tʃeɪndʒ/ **changes, changing, changed.** [1] N-VAR If there is a **change** in something, it becomes different. *What is needed is a change of attitude on the part of architects... Political change is on its way.* [2] VERB When something **changes** or when you **change** it, it becomes different. *She has now changed into a happy, self-confident woman... They should change the law to make it illegal to own replica weapons.* [3] N-SING If you say that something is a **change** or makes a **change**, you mean that it is enjoyable because it is different from what you are used to. *A dinner party on a Spanish theme would certainly make a delicious change.* [4] PHRASE If you say that something is happening **for a change**, you mean that you are glad that it is happening because usually it does not. *Now let me ask you a question, for a change.* [5] VERB & N-C To **change** something means to replace it with something new or different. A **change** of something is an act of replacing something. *All they did was change a fuse... A change of leadership alone will not be enough.* [6] VERB When you **change** your clothes, you take them off and put on different ones. *They had allowed her to shower and change... I changed into a tracksuit... I've got to get changed first.* • See note at **wear**. [7] VERB When you **change** a baby or **change** its

nappy, you take off its dirty nappy and put on a clean one. [8] VERB When you **change** buses or trains, you get off one and get on to another to continue your journey. [9] VERB When you **change** a bed or **change** the sheets, you take off the dirty sheets and put on clean ones. [10] N-U Your **change** is the money that you receive when you pay for something with more money than it costs. [11] N-U **Change** is coins, rather than notes.

▸ **change over** PHR-VERB If you **change over** from one thing to another, you stop doing one thing and start doing the other. *We are gradually changing over to a completely metric system.*

channel /'tʃænəl/ **channels, channelling, channelled** (AM **channeling, channeled**). [1] N-C A **channel** is a wavelength on which television programmes are broadcast. ...*movie channels.* [2] N-C If something has been done through particular **channels**, a particular group of people have arranged for it to be done. *The President will contact other leaders either directly or through diplomatic channels.* [3] VERB If you **channel** money into something, you arrange for it to be used for that purpose. ...*a system set up to channel funds to the poor countries.* [4] N-C A **channel** is a passage along which water flows. ...*a drainage channel.* [5] N-PROPER The **Channel** or the **English Channel** is the narrow area of water between England and France.

chant /tʃɑːnt, tʃænt/ **chants, chanting, chanted.** [1] N-C A **chant** is a word or group of words that is repeated over and over again. ...*chants of 'four more years'.* [2] N-C A **chant** is a religious song or prayer that is sung on only a few notes. ...*a Gregorian chant.* [3] VERB If you **chant** something, you repeat the same words over and over again. *Demonstrators chanted slogans.* ♦ **chanting** N-U *A lot of the chanting was in support of the deputy Prime Minister.*

chaos /'keɪɒs/. N-U **Chaos** is a state of complete disorder and confusion. *Their gigs often ended in chaos.*

chaotic /keɪ'ɒtɪk/. ADJ If a situation is **chaotic**, it is in a state of disorder and confusion.

chap /tʃæp/ **chaps.** N-C A **chap** is a man or boy; BRITISH, INFORMAL.

chapel /'tʃæpəl/ **chapels.** [1] N-C A **chapel** is a part of a church which has its own altar and which is used for private prayer. [2] N-C A **chapel** is a small church in a school, hospital, or prison.

chaplain /'tʃæplɪn/ **chaplains.** N-C A **chaplain** is a member of the Christian clergy who does religious work in places such as hospitals, schools, or prisons.

chapped /tʃæpt/. ADJ If your skin is **chapped**, it is dry, cracked, and sore.

chapter /'tʃæptə/ **chapters.** [1] N-C A **chapter** is one of the parts that a book is divided into. *Turn to Chapter 1.* [2] N-C You can refer to a part of your life or a period in history as a **chapter**; WRITTEN. *This had been a particularly difficult chapter in Lebanon's recent history.* [3] N-C A **chapter** is a branch of a society, club, or union.

character /'kæriktə/ **characters.** [1] N-C The **character** of a person or place consists of all the qualities they have that make them distinct. *There is a negative side to his character... The character of this country has been formed by immigration.* [2] PHRASE If someone behaves **in character**, they behave in the way you expect them to. If they behave **out of character**, they do not behave as you expect. [3] N-VAR Someone's **character** is their reputation. *...her opponent's attack on her character. ...his previous good character.* [4] N-C The **characters** in a film, book, or play are the people in it. [5] N-C You can refer to a person as a **character**, especially when describing their qualities. *He's a very strange character.* [6] N-C A **character** is a letter, number, or other symbol that is written or printed.

characteristic /ˌkærəktə'rɪstɪk/ **characteristics.** [1] N-C A **characteristic** is a quality or feature that is typical of someone or something. *Genes determine the characteristics of every living thing.* [2] ADJ If something is **characteristic** of a person, thing, or place, it is typical of them. *Refusal to admit defeat was characteristic of Davis.* ♦**characteristically** ADV *He replied in characteristically robust style.*

characterize (BR also **characterise**) /'kæriktəraiz/ **characterizes, characterizing, characterized.** [1] VERB If something **is characterized** by a particular feature or quality, that feature or quality is very evident in it; FORMAL. *...the greed that characterized the 1980s.* [2] VERB If you **characterize** someone or something **as** a particular thing, you describe them as that thing; FORMAL. *Both companies have characterized the relationship as friendly.* ♦**characterization, characterizations.** N-VAR *...his characterisation of other designers as 'thieves'.*

charade /ʃə'rɑːd, AM -'reɪd/ **charades.** N-C A **charade** is a pretence which is so obvious that nobody is deceived.

charcoal /'tʃɑːkəʊl/. N-U **Charcoal** is a black substance used as a fuel and for drawing, obtained by burning wood without much air.

charge /tʃɑːdʒ/ **charges, charging, charged.** [1] VERB If you **charge** someone an amount of money, you ask them to pay that amount for something. *Local nurseries charge £100 a week. ...the architect who charged us a fee of seven hundred pounds.* [2] N-C A **charge** is an amount of money that you have to pay for a service. *We can arrange this for a small charge.* [3] PHRASE If something is **free of charge**, it does not cost anything. [4] N-C A **charge** is a formal accusation that someone has committed a crime. *He may still face criminal charges.* [5] VERB When the police **charge** someone, they formally accuse them of having done something illegal. *Police have charged Mr Smith with murder.* [6] N-U If you have **charge of** or are **in charge** of something or someone, you have responsibility for them. *A few years ago Bacryl took charge of the company. ...the Swiss governess in charge of the smaller children.* [7] VERB If you **charge** towards someone or something, you move quickly and aggressively towards them. *He charged through the door to*

my mother's office. [8] VERB To **charge** a battery means to pass an electrical current through it to make it more powerful or to make it last longer.

charisma /kə'rɪzmə/. N-U If someone has **charisma**, they can attract, influence, and inspire people by their personal qualities. ♦**charismatic** /ˌkærɪz'mætɪk/ ADJ *...a charismatic politician.*

charitable /'tʃærɪtəbəl/. [1] ADJ Someone who is **charitable** is kind and tolerant. [2] ADJ BEFORE N A **charitable** organization or activity helps and supports people who are ill, handicapped, or poor.

charity /'tʃærɪti/ **charities.** [1] N-C A **charity** is an organization which raises money to help people who are ill, handicapped, or poor. [2] N-U People who live on **charity** live on money or goods which are given to them because they are poor. *She wouldn't accept charity.* [3] N-U **Charity** is kindness and tolerance towards other people. *...acts of charity.*

charm /tʃɑːm/ **charms, charming, charmed.** [1] N-VAR **Charm** is the quality of being attractive and pleasant. *The 1937 Disney classic has lost none of its original charm.* [2] VERB If you **charm** someone, you please them by using your charm. *He charmed all of us.* [3] N-C A **charm** is an action, saying, or object that is believed to have magic powers. *...a good luck charm.*

charming /'tʃɑːmɪŋ/. ADJ If someone or something is **charming**, they are very pleasant and attractive. *What a charming man! ...a charming little village.* ♦**charmingly** ADV *Moira smiled charmingly.*

charred /tʃɑːd/. ADJ Something that is **charred** is black as a result of being badly burnt. *...charred wreckage.*

chart /tʃɑːt/ **charts, charting, charted.** [1] N-C A **chart** is a diagram or graph which displays information. *Consult the chart on page 44 for the correct cooking times.* [2] N-C A **chart** is a map of the sea or stars. [3] VERB If you **chart** the development or progress of something, you observe and record it carefully. *The book charts the history of four generations of the family.* [4] N-PL The **charts** are the official lists that show which pop records have sold the most copies each week.

charter /'tʃɑːtə/ **charters, chartering, chartered.** [1] N-C A **charter** is a formal document describing the rights, aims, or principles of an organization. *...the United Nations Charter.* [2] ADJ BEFORE N A **charter** plane or boat is hired for use by a particular person or group. *...charter flights to Spain.* [3] VERB If someone **charters** a plane or boat, they hire it for their own use. *He chartered a jet to fly her home.*

chase /tʃeɪs/ **chases, chasing, chased.** [1] VERB & N-C If you **chase** someone, you run after or follow them in order to catch them or force them to leave a place. A **chase** is an act of chasing someone. *She chased the thief for 100 yards... Many farmers will then chase you off their land... He was reluctant to give up the chase.* [2] VERB If you **are chasing** something you want, such as work or money, you are trying hard to get it. *14 people are chasing every job. ...booksellers chasing after profits.*

chasm /ˈkæzəm/ **chasms.** ① N-C A **chasm** is a very deep crack in rock or ice. ② N-C If there is a **chasm** between two things or between two groups, there is a very large difference between them. *...the chasm that divides the worlds of university and industry.*

chat /tʃæt/ **chats, chatting, chatted.** VERB & N-C When people **chat**, or when they have a **chat**, they talk in an informal and friendly way. *I was chatting to him the other day... We chatted about old times... I had a chat with John.*

▶ **chat up.** PHR-VERB If you **chat** someone **up**, you talk to them in a friendly way because you are sexually attracted to them; BRITISH, INFORMAL. *He'd spent most of that evening chatting up one of my friends.*

château /ˈʃætəʊ/ (or **chateau**) **châteaux** /ˈʃætəʊz/. N-C A **château** is a large country house in France.

'chat show, chat shows. N-C In British English, a **chat show** is a television or radio show in which an interviewer and his or her guests talk in a friendly informal way about different topics. The usual American expression is **talk show**.

chatter /ˈtʃætə/ **chatters, chattering, chattered.** ① VERB & N-C If you **chatter**, you talk quickly and continuously about unimportant things. **Chatter** is this kind of talk. *...chattering away in different languages... Erica was friendly and chattered about Andrew's children. ...idle chatter.* ② VERB If your teeth **chatter**, they rattle together because you are cold.

chauffeur /ˈʃəʊfə, ʃəʊˈfɜː/ **chauffeurs, chauffeuring, chauffeured.** ① N-C A **chauffeur** is a person whose job is to drive and look after another person's car. ② VERB If you **chauffeur** someone somewhere, you drive them there in a car, usually as part of your job. *It was certainly useful to have her there to chauffeur him around.*

chauvinism /ˈʃəʊvɪnɪzəm/. ① N-U If you accuse a man of **chauvinism**, you are criticizing him because he believes that men are naturally better and more important than women. ♦ **chauvinist, chauvinists.** N-C *...the male chauvinist pig who wants women in the home.* ② N-U **Chauvinism** is a strong and unreasonable belief that your own country is better and more important than other people's. ♦ **chauvinist** N-C *...the emergence of extreme nationalist and chauvinist forces.*

cheap /tʃiːp/ **cheaper, cheapest.** ① ADJ **Cheap** goods or services cost less money than usual or than you expected. *Tickets are still unbelievably cheap.* ♦ **cheaply** ADV *...to help you to plan your holiday more cheaply.* ② ADJ BEFORE N **Cheap** goods cost less money than similar products but their quality is poor. *...some cheap material. ...cheap clothes shops.* ③ ADJ BEFORE N **Cheap** remarks are unkind and unnecessary. *...accusing him of making cheap remarks.*

cheat /tʃiːt/ **cheats, cheating, cheated.** ① VERB & N-C If someone **cheats**, or if they are a **cheat**, they do not obey a set of rules which they should be obeying, for example in a game

or exam. *Students may be tempted to cheat... His wife knew him to be a cheat and a liar.* ♦ **cheating** N-U *He was accused of cheating.* ② VERB If someone **cheats** you out of something, they get it from you by behaving dishonestly. *...a deliberate effort to cheat them out of their pensions.* ③ PHRASE If you **feel cheated**, you feel that you have been let down or treated unfairly. *They may feel cheated when the actual holiday doesn't match their fantasies.*

▶ **cheat on.** PHR-VERB If someone **cheats on** their husband, wife, or partner, they have a sexual relationship with another person; INFORMAL.

check /tʃek/ **checks, checking, checked.** ① VERB & N-C If you **check** something, or if you make a **check** on it, you make sure that it is satisfactory, safe, or correct. *I think there is an age limit, but I'd have to check... She hadn't checked whether she had a clean ironed shirt... Stephen checked on her several times during the night. ...regular checks on his blood pressure.* ② VERB To **check** something, usually something bad, means to stop it from continuing or spreading. *Sex education is also expected to help check the spread of AIDS.* ③ PHRASE If something **is held** or **kept in check**, they are prevented from becoming too great or powerful. *Life on Earth will become unsustainable unless population growth is held in check.* ④ N-C In American English, **the check** in a restaurant is a piece of paper on which the price of the meal you have just eaten is written and which you are given before you pay. The British word is **bill.** ⑤ N-C A pattern of squares, usually of two colours, can be referred to as **checks** or a **check.** *...check trousers.* ⑥ See also **cheque.**

▶ **check in** or

▶ **check into.** ① PHR-VERB When you **check into** a hotel or clinic, or when you **check in**, you arrive and go through the necessary procedures before staying there. *I'll tell them we'll check in tomorrow... He has checked into an alcohol treatment centre.* ② PHR-VERB When you **check in** at an airport, you arrive and show your ticket before going on a flight. ♦ **check-in, check-ins.** N-C *Ask at the check-in if families can board early.*

▶ **check out.** ① PHR-VERB When you **check out** of a hotel, you pay the bill and leave. ② PHR-VERB If you **check** someone or something **out**, you find out about them. *The police had to check out the call.* ③ See also **checkout.**

▶ **check up.** PHR-VERB If you **check up** on someone or something, you find out information about them.

checkout /ˈtʃekaʊt/ **checkouts.** N-C In a supermarket, a **checkout** is a counter where you pay for your goods.

checkpoint /ˈtʃekpɔɪnt/ **checkpoints.** N-C A **checkpoint** is a place where traffic has to stop and be checked.

'check-up, check-ups. N-C A **check-up** is a routine examination by a doctor or dentist.

cheek /tʃiːk/ **cheeks.** ① N-C Your **cheeks** are the sides of your face below your eyes. ② N-SING You say that someone has a **cheek** when you are annoyed at something unacceptable they have done; INFORMAL. *I'm amazed they had the cheek to ask.*

cheekbone /'tʃiːkbəʊn/ **cheekbones.** N-C Your **cheekbones** are the two bones in your face just below your eyes.

cheeky /'tʃiːki/ **cheekier, cheekiest.** ADJ Someone who is **cheeky** is rude to someone they ought to respect, but often in a charming or amusing way. *The boy was cheeky and casual. ...a cheeky grin.*

cheer /tʃɪə/ **cheers, cheering, cheered.** 1 VERB & N-C When people **cheer**, they shout loudly to show approval or encouragement. A **cheer** is the sound made when people do this. *Swiss fans cheered Jakob Hlasek during yesterday's match. ...a resounding cheer.* 2 VERB If you **are cheered** by something, it makes you feel happier. *He has been cheered by the hundreds of letters of support.* 3 CONVENTION People say **'Cheers'** just before they drink an alcoholic drink.

▸ **cheer on.** PHR-VERB If you **cheer** someone **on**, you shout loudly in order to encourage them. *500,000 spectators lined the course to cheer on the runners.*

▸ **cheer up.** PHR-VERB When you **cheer up**, you stop feeling depressed and become more cheerful. *I wrote that song just to cheer myself up... Cheer up, better times may be ahead.*

cheerful /'tʃɪəfʊl/ 1 ADJ A **cheerful** person is happy. *They are both very cheerful in spite of their colds.* ♦**cheerfully** ADV *'We've come with good news,' Pat said cheerfully.* ♦**cheerfulness** N-U *...his unfailing cheerfulness.* 2 ADJ **Cheerful** things are pleasant and make you feel happy. *The nursery is bright and cheerful.*

cheery /'tʃɪəri/ ADJ **Cheery** means cheerful and happy. ♦**cheerily** ADV *'Come on in,' she said cheerily.*

cheese /tʃiːz/ **cheeses.** N-VAR **Cheese** is a solid food made from milk.

chef /ʃef/ **chefs.** N-C A **chef** is a cook in a restaurant or hotel.

chemical /'kemɪkəl/ **chemicals.** 1 ADJ BEFORE N **Chemical** means involving or resulting from a reaction between two or more substances, or relating to the substances that something consists of. *...chemical reactions. ...the chemical composition of the ocean.* ♦**chemically** ADV *...chemically treated foods.* 2 N-C **Chemicals** are substances that are used in or made by a chemical process.

chemist /'kemɪst/ **chemists.** 1 N-C In Britain, a **chemist** or a **chemist's** is a shop where medicines are sold or given out. You can also refer to the specially qualified person who prepares and sells the medicines in this shop as a **chemist**. ● See note at **pharmacy.** 2 N-C A **chemist** is a person who studies chemistry.

chemistry /'kemɪstri/ N-U **Chemistry** is the scientific study of the characteristics and composition of substances.

cheque (AM **check**) /tʃek/ **cheques.** N-C A **cheque** is a printed form on which you write an amount of money and say who it is to be paid to. Your bank then pays the money to that person from your account. *He wrote them a cheque for £10,000... I'd like to pay by cheque.*

cherish /'tʃerɪʃ/ **cherishes, cherishing, cherished.** 1 VERB If you **cherish** something such as a hope or a pleasant memory, you keep it in your mind for a long period of time. *The president will cherish the memory of this visit to Ohio.* ♦**cherished** ADJ *...the cherished dream of a world without wars.* 2 VERB If you **cherish** someone or something, you take good care of them because you love them. ♦**cherished** ADJ BEFORE N *...his most cherished possession.* 3 VERB If you **cherish** a right or a privilege, you regard it as important and try hard to keep it. *They cherish their independence.* ♦**cherished** ADJ BEFORE N *...some deeply cherished beliefs.*

cherry /'tʃeri/ **cherries.** 1 N-C **Cherries** are small, round fruit with red or black skins. 2 N-C A **cherry** or a **cherry tree** is a tree that cherries grow on.

chess /tʃes/ N-U **Chess** is a game for two people played on a board with 64 black and white squares. Each player has 16 pieces including a King. The aim is to trap your opponent's King.

chest /tʃest/ **chests.** 1 N-C Your **chest** is the top part of the front of your body. *He was shot in the chest. ...mild chest pain.* 2 N-C A **chest** is a large heavy box, used for storing things.

chestnut /'tʃesnʌt/ **chestnuts.** 1 N-C A **chestnut** or **chestnut tree** is a tall tree with broad leaves. 2 N-C The nuts that grow on chestnut trees are called **chestnuts.** 3 ADJ & N-VAR Something that is **chestnut** is dark reddish-brown. *...a woman with chestnut hair.*

chew /tʃuː/ **chews, chewing, chewed.** VERB When you **chew** food, you break it up with your teeth and make it easier to swallow. *He chewed on his toast... Polly took a bite of the apple, chewed and swallowed.*

chic /ʃiːk/ ADJ Something or someone that is **chic** is fashionable and sophisticated. *...very chic bars and restaurants.*

chick /tʃɪk/ **chicks.** N-C A **chick** is a baby bird.

chicken /'tʃɪkɪn/ **chickens, chickening, chickened.** 1 ADJ BEFORE N **Chickens** are birds which are kept on a farm for their eggs and their meat. 2 N-U **Chicken** is the meat of a chicken eaten for food.

▸ **chicken out.** PHR-VERB If someone **chickens out** of something, they do not do it because they are afraid; INFORMAL. *I chickened out of producing the album myself.*

chide /tʃaɪd/ **chides, chiding, chided.** VERB If you **chide** someone, you scold them; DATED. *Cross chided himself for worrying.*

chief /tʃiːf/ **chiefs.** 1 N-C The **chief** of an organization or department is its leader or the person in charge of it. *...the chief test pilot. ...the police chief.* 2 ADJ BEFORE N The **chief** cause, part, or member of something is the most important one. *The job went to one of his chief rivals.*

chiefly /'tʃiːfli/ ADV You use **chiefly** to indicate that a particular reason, emotion, or feature is the main or most important one. *The museum is hoped to be self-financing, chiefly through education... He painted chiefly portraits.*

chiffon /'ʃɪfɒn, AM ʃɪ'fɑːn/ N-U **Chiffon** is a kind of very thin silk or nylon cloth.

child /tʃaɪld/ **children.** **1** N-C A **child** is a human being who is not yet an adult. ...*when I was a child... It was only suitable for children.* **2** N-PL Someone's **children** are their sons and daughters. *His children have left home.*

childbirth /ˈtʃaɪldbɜːθ/. N-U **Childbirth** is the act of giving birth to a child. *She died in childbirth.*

childhood /ˈtʃaɪldhʊd/ **childhoods.** N-VAR A person's **childhood** is the time when they are a child. *She had a happy childhood. ...a story heard in childhood.*

childish /ˈtʃaɪldɪʃ/. **1** ADJ **Childish** means relating to or typical of a child. ...*childish enthusiasm.* **2** ADJ If you describe someone, especially an adult, as **childish**, you mean their behaviour is silly and more like that of a child than an adult. ...*very childish behaviour.* ♦**childishly** ADV *Such remarks were childishly simplistic.*

childless /ˈtʃaɪldləs/. ADJ Someone who is **childless** has no children.

childlike /ˈtʃaɪldlaɪk/. ADJ You describe someone as **childlike** when they seem like a child in their appearance or behaviour.

children /ˈtʃɪldrən/. **Children** is the plural of **child**.

chili /ˈtʃɪli/. See **chilli**.

chill /tʃɪl/ **chills, chilling, chilled.** **1** VERB To **chill** something means to make it cold. *Chill the cheesecake for two hours before serving... The wind chilled our wet bodies to the bone. ...a glass of chilled champagne.* **2** VERB & N-C If something that you see, hear, or feel **chills** you, it frightens you. If something sends a **chill** through you, it gives you a sudden feeling of fear or anxiety. WRITTEN. *Some films chill you to the marrow of your bones. ...a chill of fear.* ♦**chilling** ADJ ...*a chilling reminder of the destruction.* **3** N-C A **chill** is a mild illness which can give you a slight fever.
▶ **chill out.** PHR-VERB If you **chill out**, you relax after doing something tiring or stressful; INFORMAL. ...*music to chill out to.*

chilli (or **chili**) /ˈtʃɪli/ **chillies.** N-C **Chillies** are small red or green seed pods with a hot, spicy taste.

chilly /ˈtʃɪli/. **1** ADJ **Chilly** means uncomfortably cold. *It was a chilly afternoon... The house itself felt chilly.* **2** ADJ You say that relations between people are **chilly** or that a person's response is **chilly** when they are not at all friendly or enthusiastic. *The students received a very chilly welcome.*

chime /tʃaɪm/ **chimes, chiming, chimed.** **1** VERB When a bell or clock **chimes**, it makes ringing sounds. *The clock chimed three o'clock.* **2** N-C A **chime** is a ringing sound made by a bell, especially when it is part of a clock. *The chimes of midnight struck.*
▶ **chime in.** PHR-VERB If someone **chimes in**, they say something just after someone else has spoken. *'Why?' Pete asked impatiently.—'Yes, why?' Bob chimed in.*

chimney /ˈtʃɪmni/ **chimneys.** N-C A **chimney** is a pipe above a fireplace or furnace through which smoke can go up into the air.

chimpanzee /ˌtʃɪmpænˈziː/ **chimpanzees.** N-C A **chimpanzee** is a kind of small African ape.

chin /tʃɪn/ **chins.** N-C Your **chin** is the part of your face below your mouth and above your neck.

china /ˈtʃaɪnə/. **1** N-U **China** or **china clay** is a very thin clay used to make cups, plates, and ornaments. **2** N-U Cups, plates, and ornaments made of china are referred to as **china**. *Judy collects blue and white china.*

chink /tʃɪŋk/ **chinks, chinking, chinked.** **1** N-C A **chink** is a very narrow opening. ...*a chink in the curtains.* **2** VERB When objects **chink**, they touch each other, making a light ringing sound. ...*cutlery chinking in the silence.*

chip /tʃɪp/ **chips, chipping, chipped.** **1** N-C In British English, **chips** are long thin pieces of fried potato eaten hot. The American expression is **French fries.** **2** N-C In American English, **chips** or **potato chips** are very thin slices of potato that have been fried until they are hard and crunchy and that are eaten cold as a snack. The British word is **crisps.** **3** N-C A silicon **chip** is a very small piece of silicon with electronic circuits on it. **4** VERB If you **chip** something, a small piece is broken off it. *A singer chipped a tooth on his microphone... Steel baths are lighter but chip easily.* ♦**chipped** ADJ ...*a chipped tooth.* **5** N-C A **chip** is a small piece of something, especially a piece which has been broken off something. ...*chocolate chips. ...wood chips.* **6** PHRASE If you say that someone has a **chip on** their **shoulder**, you mean they behave aggressively, because they believe they have been treated unfairly; INFORMAL.
▶ **chip in.** PHR-VERB When a number of people **chip in**, each person gives some money so that they can pay for something together; INFORMAL. *The brothers chip in a certain amount of money each month.*

chisel /ˈtʃɪzəl/ **chisels, chiselling, chiselled.** (AM **chiseling, chiseled**). **1** N-C A **chisel** is a tool that has a long metal blade with a sharp edge at the end. It is used for cutting and shaping wood and stone. **2** VERB If you **chisel** wood or stone, you cut and shape it using a chisel. *They chisel the stone to size.*

chlorine /ˈklɔːriːn/. N-U **Chlorine** is a gas that is used to disinfect water and to make cleaning products.

chocolate /ˈtʃɒklɪt, AM ˈtʃɔːk-/ **chocolates.** **1** N-VAR **Chocolate** is a sweet food made from cocoa beans. **2** N-C **Chocolates** are small sweets or nuts covered with a layer of chocolate. **3** N-U **Chocolate** is a hot drink made from a powder containing chocolate.

choice /tʃɔɪs/ **choices; choicer; choicest.** **1** N-C If there is a **choice** of things, there are several of them and you can choose the one you want. *It's available in a choice of colours... At lunchtime, there's a choice between the buffet or the set menu.* **2** N-C Your **choice** is the thing or things that you choose. *His choice of words made Rodney angry. ...tickets to see the football team of your choice.* **3** PHRASE If you **have no choice** but to do something, or **have little choice** but to do it, you cannot avoid doing it. **4** ADJ BEFORE N **Choice** means of very high quality; FORMAL. ...*his choicest cuts of meat.*

choir /kwaɪə/ **choirs.** N-C A **choir** is a group of people who sing together.

choke /tʃəʊk/ **chokes, choking, choked.** [1] VERB If you **choke** on something, it prevents you from breathing properly. *The girl choked to death after breathing in smoke... The parachute tangled round his body, almost choking him.* [2] VERB To **choke** someone means to squeeze their neck until they are dead. [3] VERB If a place **is choked** with things or people, it is full of them and they prevent movement in it. *The village's roads are choked with traffic... The gutters were choked by fallen leaves.* [4] N-C A vehicle's **choke** is a device that reduces the amount of air going into the engine and makes it easier to start.

cholera /ˈkɒlərə/. N-U **Cholera** is a serious disease that affects your digestive organs.

cholesterol /kəˈlestərɒl, AM -rɔːl/. N-U **Cholesterol** is a substance that exists in the fat, tissues, and blood of all animals. Too much cholesterol in a person's blood can cause heart disease.

choose /tʃuːz/ **chooses, choosing, chose, chosen.** [1] VERB If you **choose** someone or something from all the people or things that are available, you decide to have that person or thing. *They will be able to choose their own leaders... She chose a chair slightly behind her husband's.* [2] VERB If you **choose** to do something, you do it because you want to or because you feel that it is right. *The NRDC chose to inform the public about the risks.*

chop /tʃɒp/ **chops, chopping, chopped.** [1] VERB If you **chop** something, you cut it into pieces with a knife or axe. *Finely chop the onion.* [2] N-C A **chop** is a small piece of meat cut from the ribs of a sheep or pig. *...lamb chops.*
► **chop down.** PHR-VERB If you **chop down** a tree, you cut through its trunk with an axe so that it falls to the ground.
► **chop off.** PHR-VERB To **chop off** something such as a part of someone's body means to cut it off. *They both chopped off their hair.*
► **chop up.** PHR-VERB If you **chop** something **up**, you chop it into small pieces. *Chop up three firm tomatoes.*

chopper /ˈtʃɒpə/ **choppers.** N-C A **chopper** is a helicopter; INFORMAL.

choral /ˈkɔːrəl/. ADJ **Choral** music is sung by a choir.

chord /kɔːd/ **chords.** N-C A **chord** is a number of musical notes played or sung together with a pleasing effect. *...the opening chords of 'Stairway to Heaven'.*

chore /tʃɔː/ **chores.** N-C A **chore** is an unpleasant task. *Making pasta by hand with a rolling pin can be a real chore. ...household chores.*

choreograph /ˈkɒriəgrɑːf, AM ˈkɔːriəgræf/ **choreographs, choreographing, choreographed.** VERB When someone **choreographs** a ballet or other dance, they invent the steps and movements and tell the dancers how to perform them. *...one of the first dance pieces to be choreographed by Morris.* ♦ **choreographer** /ˌkɒriˈɒgrəfə, AM ˌkɔː-/ **choreographers** N-C *...dancer and choreographer Rudolph Nureyev.*

choreography /ˌkɒriˈɒgrəfi, AM ˌkɔː-/. N-U **Choreography** is the inventing of steps and move-

ments for ballets and other dances. ♦ **choreographic** /ˌkɒriəˈgræfɪk, AM ˌkɔː-/ ADJ *...his choreographic work for The Birmingham Royal Ballet.*

chorus /ˈkɔːrəs/ **choruses, chorusing, chorused.** [1] N-C A **chorus** is a large group of people who sing together. [2] N-C The **chorus** of a song is the part which is repeated after each verse. [3] N-SING When there is a **chorus** of criticism, disapproval, or praise, that attitude is expressed by a lot of people at the same time. *...the growing chorus of complaint.* [4] VERB When people **chorus** something, they say or sing it together. *'Hi,' they chorused.*

chose /tʃəʊz/. **Chose** is the past tense of **choose.**

chosen /ˈtʃəʊzən/. **Chosen** is the past participle of **choose.**

christen /ˈkrɪsən/ **christens, christening, christened.** [1] VERB When a baby **is christened**, he or she is given Christian names during a christening. *She was christened Susan.* [2] VERB You say that you **christen** a person, place, or object if you choose a name for them and start calling them by that name. *...his car, which he had christened Lola.*

christening /ˈkrɪsənɪŋ/ **christenings.** N-C A **christening** is a ceremony in which a baby is made a member of the Christian church and is given his or her Christian names.

Christian /ˈkrɪstʃən/ **Christians.** N-C & ADJ A **Christian** or **Christian** person follows the teachings of Jesus Christ. *...the Christian Church.*

Christianity /ˌkrɪstiˈænɪti/. N-U **Christianity** is a religion based on the teachings of Jesus Christ.

'Christian name, Christian names. N-C A person's **Christian name** is the name given to them when they were born or christened.

Christmas /ˈkrɪsməs/ **Christmases.** N-VAR **Christmas** is the period around the 25th of December when Christians celebrate the birth of Jesus Christ. *Merry Christmas. ...Christmases past.*

,**Christmas 'Day.** N-U **Christmas Day** is the 25th of December.

,**Christmas 'Eve.** N-U **Christmas Eve** is the 24th of December.

'**Christmas tree, Christmas trees.** N-C A **Christmas tree** is a real or artificial fir tree, which people put in their houses at Christmas and decorate with lights and balls.

chrome /krəʊm/. N-U **Chrome** is a hard silver-coloured metal, used to coat other metals.

chromium /ˈkrəʊmiəm/. N-U **Chromium** is the same as chrome.

chromosome /ˈkrəʊməsəʊm/ **chromosomes.** N-C A **chromosome** is a part of a cell in an animal or plant. It contains genes which determine what characteristics the animal or plant will have.

chronic /ˈkrɒnɪk/. [1] ADJ A **chronic** illness lasts for a very long time. *...chronic depression.* ♦ **chronically** ADV *Most of them were chronically ill.* [2] ADJ A **chronic** situation is very severe and unpleasant. *...chronic housing shortages.* ♦ **chronically** ADV *Counselling services are chronically underfunded.*

chronicle /ˈkrɒnɪkəl/ **chronicles, chronicling, chronicled.** [1] VERB If you **chronicle** a series of events, you describe them in the order in which they happened. *The book chronicles baseball's disgraceful incidents.* [2] N-C A **chronicle** is an account or record of a series of events. *...this vast chronicle of Napoleonic times.*

chronological /ˌkrɒnəˈlɒdʒɪkəl/. ADJ If things are described or shown in **chronological** order, they are described or shown in the order in which they happened. *...chronological tables of China's history.* ♦**chronologically** ADV *The exhibition is organised chronologically.*

chubby /ˈtʃʌbi/. ADJ A **chubby** person is rather fat. ● See note at **fat**.

chuck /tʃʌk/ **chucks, chucking, chucked.** VERB When you **chuck** something somewhere, you throw it there in a casual way; INFORMAL. *He screwed the paper up and chucked it in the bin.*

▸ **chuck away** or **chuck out.** PHR-VERB If you **chuck** something **away** or **chuck** it **out**, you throw it away; INFORMAL.

chuckle /ˈtʃʌkəl/ **chuckles, chuckling, chuckled.** VERB & N-C When you **chuckle**, you laugh quietly. A quiet laugh is called a **chuckle**. *He gave a little chuckle.*

chug /tʃʌɡ/ **chugs, chugging, chugged.** VERB When a vehicle **chugs** somewhere, it goes there slowly with its engine making short thudding sounds. *The train chugs down the track.*

chum /tʃʌm/ **chums.** N-C In British English, your **chums** are your friends; INFORMAL. *...his old chum Anthony.*

chunk /tʃʌŋk/ **chunks.** [1] N-C A **chunk** of something is a thick solid piece of it. *...chunks of ice.* [2] N-C A **chunk** of something is a large amount or part of it; INFORMAL. *...a chunk of farmland near Gatwick Airport.*

chunky /ˈtʃʌŋki/. ADJ A **chunky** person or thing is large and heavy. *...a chunky girl from California. ...a chunky sweater.*

church /tʃɜːtʃ/ **churches.** [1] N-VAR A **church** is a building in which Christians worship. *I didn't see you in church on Sunday.* [2] N-C A **Church** is one of the groups of people within the Christian religion that have their own beliefs, clergy, and forms of worship. *...the Catholic Church.*

churn /tʃɜːn/ **churns, churning, churned.** [1] N-C A **churn** is a container used for making butter. [2] VERB & PHR-VERB If something **churns** mud, water, or dust, or **churns** it **up**, it moves it about violently. *Ferries churn the waters of Howe Sound. ...dust churned up by the passing trucks.* [3] VERB If you say that your stomach **is churning**, you mean that you feel sick. You can also say that something **churns** your stomach. *My stomach churned as I stood up.*

▸ **churn out.** PHR-VERB To **churn** something **out** means to produce large quantities of it very quickly; INFORMAL. *...those fantasy novels he churned out in the 1960s.*

▸ **churn up.** See **churn** 2.

chute /ʃuːt/ **chutes.** [1] N-C A **chute** is a steep narrow slope down which people or things can slide. *...a laundry chute.* [2] N-C A **chute** is a parachute; INFORMAL. *The chute failed to open.*

chutney /ˈtʃʌtni/ **chutneys.** N-VAR **Chutney** is a strong-tasting mixture of fruit, vinegar, sugar, and spices.

cider /ˈsaɪdə/ **ciders.** N-VAR **Cider** is an alcoholic drink made from apples.

cigar /sɪˈɡɑː/ **cigars.** N-C **Cigars** are rolls of dried tobacco leaves which people smoke.

cigarette /ˌsɪɡəˈret/ **cigarettes.** N-C **Cigarettes** are small tubes of paper containing tobacco which people smoke.

cinder /ˈsɪndə/ **cinders.** N-C **Cinders** are the pieces of blackened material that are left after wood or coal has burned.

cinema /ˈsɪnɪmɑː/ **cinemas.** [1] N-C In British English, a **cinema** is a place where people go to watch films. The American term is **movie theater** or **movie house.** [2] N-C **Cinema** is the business and art of making films. *...the greatest director in the history of cinema.* ♦**cinematic** /ˌsɪnɪˈmætɪk/ ADJ *...the cinematic industry.*

cinnamon /ˈsɪnəmən/. N-U **Cinnamon** is a spice used for flavouring sweet food.

circa /ˈsɜːkə/. PREP If you write **circa** in front of a year, you mean that the date is approximate. *...circa 1850.*

circle /ˈsɜːkəl/ **circles, circling, circled.** [1] N-C A **circle** is a round shape. Every part of its edge is the same distance from the centre. *The flag was red, with a large white circle in the center... Cut out 4 circles of pastry.* [2] VERB To **circle** someone or something, or to **circle** around them, means to move around them in a circle. *I circled my living room half a dozen times... A police helicopter circled overhead.* [3] N-C You can refer to a group of people as a **circle.** *He has a small circle of friends... It was common knowledge in financial circles.* [4] N-SING The **circle** in a theatre is an area of seats on the upper floor. [5] See also **vicious circle.**

circuit /ˈsɜːkɪt/ **circuits.** [1] N-C An electrical **circuit** is a complete route which an electric current can flow around. ● See also **closed-circuit.** [2] N-C A **circuit** is a series of places that are visited regularly by a person or group. *...the Australian comedy circuit.* [3] N-C A racing **circuit** is a track on which cars, motorbikes, or cycles race; BRITISH. [4] N-C A **circuit** of a place or area is a journey all the way round it; FORMAL. *She made a slow circuit of the room.*

circular /ˈsɜːkjʊlə/ **circulars.** [1] ADJ Something that is **circular** is shaped like a circle. *...a circular hole twelve feet wide. ...a circular motion. ...a long, circular route.* [2] N-C A **circular** is a letter or advertisement which is sent to a large number of people at the same time.

circulate /ˈsɜːkjʊleɪt/ **circulates, circulating, circulated.** [1] VERB When something **circulates** or **is circulated**, it is passed round or spread among a group of people. *He has circulated a discussion document, asking for comments... Rumours began to circulate about his health.* ♦**circulation** N-U *...the circulation of leaflets aimed at discrediting both men.* [2] VERB When something **circulates**, it moves easily and freely within a closed place or system. *...a*

virus which circulates via the bloodstream.
♦ **circulation** N-U *...free circulation of goods.*

circulation /ˌsɜːkjʊˈleɪʃən/ **circulations.** [1] N-C The **circulation** of a newspaper or magazine is the number of copies sold each time it is produced. *The Daily News once had the highest circulation of any daily in the country.* [2] N-SING Your **circulation** is the movement of blood around your body. *...cold spots in the fingers caused by poor circulation.* [3] PHRASE If something such as money is **in circulation**, it is being used by the public. *...America, with perhaps 180 million guns in circulation.*

circumcise /ˈsɜːkəmsaɪz/ **circumcises, circumcising, circumcised.** VERB If a boy or man is **circumcised**, the loose skin at the end of his penis is cut off. ♦ **circumcision** /ˌsɜːkəmˈsɪʒən/ N-U *Jews and Moslems practise circumcision for religious reasons.*

circumference /səˈkʌmfrəns/ **circumferences.** N-C The **circumference** of a circle, place, or round object is the distance around its edge. *The island is 3.5 km in circumference.*

circumstance /ˈsɜːkəmstæns/ **circumstances.** [1] N-C **Circumstances** are the conditions which affect what happens in a particular situation. *60 percent favor abortion under certain circumstances... I wish we could have met under happier circumstances... Everton last night insisted they would not increase their offer under any circumstances.* [2] PHRASE You can use **in the circumstances** or **under the circumstances** before or after a statement to indicate that you have considered the conditions affecting the situation before making the statement. *In the circumstances, Paisley's plans looked highly appropriate.* [3] N-PL Your **circumstances** are the conditions of your life, especially the amount of money that you have. *...help and support for the single mother, whatever her circumstances.*

circus /ˈsɜːkəs/ **circuses.** N-C A **circus** is a travelling show performed in a large tent, with performers such as clowns and trained animals.

citation /saɪˈteɪʃən/ **citations.** [1] N-C A **citation** is an official document or speech which praises a person for something brave or special that they have done. [2] N-C A **citation** from a book or piece of writing is a quotation from it.

cite /saɪt/ **cites, citing, cited.** VERB If you **cite** something, you quote it or mention it, especially as an example or proof of what you are saying; FORMAL. *She cites a favourite poem by George Herbert... I am merely citing his reaction as typical of British industry.*

citizen /ˈsɪtɪzən/ **citizens.** [1] N-C If someone is a **citizen** of a country, they are legally accepted as belonging to that country. *...American citizens living in Canada.* [2] N-C The **citizens** of a town are the people who live there. *...the citizens of Buenos Aires.* [3] See also **senior citizen**.

citizenship /ˈsɪtɪzənʃɪp/ N-U If you have **citizenship** of a country, you are legally accepted as belonging to it.

citrus /ˈsɪtrəs/ ADJ BEFORE N A **citrus** fruit is a sharp-tasting fruit such as an orange, lemon, or grapefruit.

city /ˈsɪti/ **cities.** [1] N-C A **city** is a large town. *...a busy city centre.* [2] N-PROPER The **City** is the part of London where many financial institutions have their main offices. *The City fears that profits could fall.*

civic /ˈsɪvɪk/ ADJ BEFORE N Civic means having an official status in a town. *...the businessmen and civic leaders of Manchester.*

civil /ˈsɪvəl/ [1] ADJ You use **civil** to describe things that relate to the people of a country, and their activities, often in contrast with the armed forces. *...civil unrest. ...the US civil aviation industry. ...civil and political rights.* [2] ADJ A **civil** person is polite in a formal way, but not particularly friendly; FORMAL. ♦ **civility** /sɪˈvɪlɪti/ **civilities** N-VAR *She treats the press with civility.*

civilian /sɪˈvɪliən/ **civilians.** N-C A **civilian** is anyone who is not a member of the armed forces. *...the country's civilian population.*

civilization (BR also **civilisation**) /ˌsɪvɪlaɪˈzeɪʃən/ **civilizations.** [1] N-VAR A **civilization** is a human society with its own social organization and culture. *...the ancient civilizations of Central and Latin America.* [2] N-U **Civilization** is the state of having an advanced level of social organization and a comfortable way of life. *...our advanced state of civilisation.*

civilize (BR also **civilise**) /ˈsɪvɪlaɪz/ **civilizes, civilizing, civilized.** VERB To **civilize** a person or society means to educate them and improve their way of life. *What does this play do to civilize the audience?*

civilized (BR also **civilised**) /ˈsɪvɪlaɪzd/. [1] ADJ A **civilized** society has an advanced level of social organization. *I believed that in civilized countries, torture had ended long ago.* [2] ADJ If you describe a person or their behaviour as **civilized**, you mean that they are polite and reasonable.

civil 'servant, civil servants. N-C A **civil servant** is a person who works in the Civil Service.

Civil 'Service. N-SING The **Civil Service** of a country consists of the government departments and the people who work in them.

civil 'war, civil wars. N-C A **civil war** is a war which is fought between different groups of people living in the same country.

clad /klæd/. ADJ AFTER LINK-V If you are **clad** in particular clothes, you are wearing them; LITERARY. *...the figure of a woman, clad in black.*

claim /kleɪm/ **claims, claiming, claimed.** [1] VERB & N-C If someone **claims** that something is true, or if they make a **claim** that it is true, they say that it is true but they have not proved it and it may be false. *...a man claiming to be a journalist... He claims a 70 to 80 per cent success rate... He repeated his claim that the people of Trinidad and Tobago backed his action.* [2] VERB If someone **claims** responsibility, or **claims** the credit for something, they say that they are responsible for it. *He was too modest to claim the credit.* [3] VERB & N-C If you **claim** something such as money, property, or land, or if you make a **claim** for it, you ask for it because you have a right to it. *Now they are returning to claim what was theirs. ...the office which has been dealing with their claim for* *benefit.* [4] VERB If a fight or disaster **claims** someone's life, they are killed in it; WRITTEN. *Heart disease is the biggest killer, claiming 180,000 lives a year.* [5] N-C If you have a **claim** on someone or their attention, you have a right to demand things from them or to demand their attention. *He was surrounded by people, all with claims on his attention.*

PHRASES ● Someone's **claim to fame** is something quite important or interesting that they have done or that is connected with them. *His claim to fame is that he climbed Mount Everest.* ● If you **lay claim to** something, you say that it is yours; FORMAL. ● If you **stake your claim**, you show or say that you have a right to be something or to have something. *Jane is determined to stake her claim as an actress.*

claimant /ˈkleɪmənt/ **claimants.** N-C A **claimant** is someone who has applied for something such as compensation, an insurance payment, or unemployment benefit which they think they are entitled to.

clam /klæm/ **clams.** N-C A **clam** is a kind of shellfish.

clamber /ˈklæmbə/ **clambers, clambering, clambered.** VERB If you **clamber** somewhere, you climb there with difficulty. *They clambered up the stone walls.*

clamour (AM **clamor**) /ˈklæmə/ **clamours, clamouring, clamoured.** [1] VERB & N-U If people **are clamouring** for something, or if there is a **clamour** for it, people are demanding it noisily or angrily; JOURNALISM. *...competing parties clamouring for the attention of the voter. ...the clamour for his resignation.* [2] N-SING **Clamour** is used to describe the loud noise of a large group of people talking or shouting together. *She could hear a clamour in the road outside.*

clamp /klæmp/ **clamps, clamping, clamped.** [1] N-C A **clamp** is a device that holds two things firmly together. [2] VERB When you **clamp** one thing to another, you fasten them together with a clamp. *Clamp the microphones to the pole.* [3] VERB To **clamp** something in a particular place means to put it there firmly and tightly. *He clamped his lips together.*

▶ **clamp down.** PHR-VERB To **clamp down** on something means to stop it or control it; JOURNALISM. *The authorities are now determined to clamp down on the media.*

clan /klæn/ **clans.** N-C A **clan** is a group of families related to each other.

clandestine /klænˈdestɪn/. ADJ Something that is **clandestine** is hidden or secret, and often illegal; FORMAL. *...their clandestine meetings.*

clap /klæp/ **claps, clapping, clapped.** [1] VERB & N-SING When you **clap**, you hit your hands together to express appreciation or attract attention. This action is called a **clap**. *Midge clapped her hands, calling them back to order... As long as the crowd give them a clap, they're quite happy.* [2] VERB If you **clap** an object or your hand onto something, you put it there quickly and firmly. *I clapped a hand over her mouth.* [3] N-C A **clap** of thunder is a sudden and loud noise of thunder.

claret /ˈklærət/ **clarets.** N-VAR **Claret** is a type of red French wine.

clarify /ˈklærɪfaɪ/ **clarifies, clarifying, clarified.** VERB To **clarify** something means to make it easier to understand. *A bank spokesman was unable to clarify the situation.* ◆**clarification** /ˌklærɪfɪˈkeɪʃən/ N-U *The union has written to Zurich asking for clarification of the situation.*

clarinet /ˌklærɪˈnet/ **clarinets.** N-C A **clarinet** is a wind instrument with a single reed in its mouthpiece.

clarity /ˈklærɪti/. N-U **Clarity** is the quality of being clear and easy to understand. *...a fascinating book, written with clarity.*

clash /klæʃ/ **clashes, clashing, clashed.** [1] VERB & N-C When people **clash**, or when they are involved in a **clash**, they disagree, argue, or fight with each other. *...the two countries clashed over human rights. ...clashes between police in riot gear and demonstrators.* [2] VERB & N-C Beliefs, ideas, or qualities that **clash** are very different from each other and are therefore opposed. You can also talk about a **clash** of these things. *...policy decisions which clash with official company thinking. ...a clash of views.* [3] VERB If one event **clashes** with another, they happen at the same time and so you cannot go to both of them. *His wedding clashed with a golf fixture... We'll go to both of them if the times don't clash.*

clasp /klɑːsp, klæsp/ **clasps, clasping, clasped.** [1] VERB & N-C If you **clasp** someone or something you hold them tightly. A **clasp** is an act of clasping someone or something. *She clasped the children to her... With one last clasp of his hand, she left him.* [2] N-C A **clasp** is a small metal fastening.

class /klɑːs, klæs/ **classes, classing, classed.** [1] N-C A **class** is a group of pupils or students who are taught together. [2] N-C A **class** is a course of teaching in a particular subject. *He acquired a law degree by taking classes at night.* [3] N-U If you do something **in class**, you do it during a lesson in school. *There is lots of reading in class.* [4] N-VAR **Class** is used to refer to the division of people in a society according to their social status. *...the British class structure. ...the relationship between social classes.* [5] N-C A **class** of things is a group of them with similar characteristics. *The largest class of racing sailboats in the world.* [6] N-U If you say that someone has **class**, you mean that they are elegant and sophisticated. [7] VERB If someone or something **is classed as** a particular thing, they are considered as belonging to that group of things. *I would like to know why this film is classed as political.* [8] PHRASE If you say that someone is **in a class of** their **own**, you mean that they have more of a particular skill or quality than anyone else. [9] See also **middle class, upper class, working class.**

classic /ˈklæsɪk/ **classics.** [1] ADJ A **classic** example of something has all the features which you expect that kind of thing to have. *His first two goals were classic cases of being in the right place at the right time.* ◆**classically** ADV *He's not classically handsome.* [2] ADJ BEFORE N & N-C A **classic** piece of writing or film, or a **classic**, is a piece of writing or film of high quality that has become a standard against which similar things are judged. ...*a classic study of the American penal system.* ...*a film classic.* [3] N-U **Classics** is the study of ancient Greek and Roman civilizations, especially their languages, literature, and philosophy.

classical /'klæsɪkəl/ [1] ADJ You use **classical** to describe something that is traditional in form, style, or content. ...*classical, rock and jazz music.* ♦ **classically** ADV ...*classically trained dancers.* [2] ADJ **Classical** is used to describe things relating to ancient Greek or Roman civilization. ...*ancient Egypt and classical Greece.*

classified /'klæsɪfaɪd/. ADJ **Classified** information is officially secret. *The document was highly classified.*

classify /'klæsɪfaɪ/ **classifies, classifying, classified.** VERB To **classify** things means to divide them into groups or types so that things with similar characteristics are in the same group. *The coroner immediately classified his death as a suicide.* ♦ **classification** /,klæsɪfɪ'keɪʃən/ **classifications** N-VAR ...*the classification of people into racial subtypes.*

classless /'klɑːsləs, 'klæs-/. ADJ If politicians refer to a **classless** society, they mean a society in which people are not affected by differences in social status; used showing approval.

classmate /'klɑːsmeɪt, 'klæs-/ **classmates.** N-C Your **classmates** are students in the same class as you at school or college.

classroom /'klɑːsruːm, 'klæs-/ **classrooms.** N-C A **classroom** is a room in a school where lessons take place.

classy /'klɑːsi, 'klæsi/ **classier, classiest.** ADJ If you describe someone or something as **classy**, you mean they are stylish and sophisticated; INFORMAL. *They need classier brand names to sell upmarket cars.*

clatter /'klætə/ **clatters, clattering, clattered.** [1] VERB If you say that people or things **clatter** somewhere, you mean that they move there noisily. *He turned and clattered down the stairs.* [2] VERB & N-SING When something hard **clatters**, or when it makes a **clatter**, it makes repeated short noises as it hits against another hard thing; LITERARY. *She set her cup down, and it clattered against the saucer.* ...*the clatter of a typewriter.*

clause /klɔːz/ **clauses.** [1] N-C A **clause** is a section of a legal document. [2] N-C In grammar, a **clause** is a group of words containing a verb.

claw /klɔː/ **claws, clawing, clawed.** [1] N-C The **claws** of a bird or animal are the thin curved nails on its feet. [2] VERB When people or animals **claw** something, or when they **claw** at it, they damage it or try to get hold of it with their nails or claws. *His fingers clawed at Blake's wrist.*

clay /kleɪ/. N-U **Clay** is a type of earth that is soft when it is wet and hard when it is baked dry.

clean /kliːn/ **cleaner, cleanest; cleans, cleaning, cleaned.** [1] ADJ Something that is **clean** is free from dirt or unwanted marks. ...*the cleanest beach in Europe.* *Tiled kitchen floors are easy to keep clean.* [2] VERB & N-SING If you **clean** something, or if you give it a **clean**, you make it free from dirt and unwanted marks. *It took half an hour to clean the orange powder off the bath...* *Give the cooker a good*

clean. ♦ **cleaning** N-U *I do the cleaning myself.* [3] ADJ If something such as a book, joke, or lifestyle is **clean**, it is not sexually immoral or offensive; used showing approval. ...*clean, wholesome, decent movies.* [4] ADJ If someone's reputation or record is **clean**, they have never done anything illegal or wrong. ...*a clean driving licence.* [5] ADJ BEFORE N If you make a **clean** break or start, you end a situation completely and start again in a different way. *Voters have chosen to make a clean break with the communist past.* [6] PHRASE If you **come clean** about something that you have been keeping secret, you admit it; INFORMAL.

▸ **clean out.** PHR-VERB If you **clean out** a cupboard or room, you clean and tidy it thoroughly.

▸ **clean up.** PHR-VERB If you **clean up** something, you clean it thoroughly. *Many regional governments cleaned up their beaches.*

cleaner /'kliːnə/ **cleaners.** [1] N-C A **cleaner** is someone who is employed to clean the rooms and furniture inside a building or someone whose job is to clean a particular type of thing. *He was a window cleaner.* [2] N-VAR A **cleaner** is a substance or device for cleaning things. ...*oven cleaner.* ...*an air cleaner.* [3] N-C A **cleaner** or a **cleaner's** is a shop where things such as clothes are dry-cleaned. [4] See also **vacuum cleaner.**

cleanliness /'klenlɪnəs/. N-U **Cleanliness** is the degree to which people keep themselves and their surroundings clean. *Many of Britain's beaches fail to meet minimum standards of cleanliness.*

cleanse /klenz/ **cleanses, cleansing, cleansed.** [1] VERB To **cleanse** a person, place, or organization of something dirty, unpleasant, or evil means to make them free of it. ...*the safest way to cleanse your body of poisons.* [2] VERB If you **cleanse** your skin or a wound, you clean it.

cleanser /'klenzə/ **cleansers.** N-VAR A **cleanser** is a liquid or cream that you use for cleaning something, especially your skin.

clear /klɪə/ **clearer, clearest; clears, clearing, cleared.** [1] ADJ Something that is **clear** is easy to understand, see, or hear. ...*a pretty clear account of the sequence of events.* ...*television which transmits far clearer pictures.* ♦ **clearly** ADV *It was important for children to learn to express themselves clearly.* [2] ADJ Something that is **clear** is obvious. *It was a clear case of homicide... It became clear that I hadn't been able to convince Mike.* ♦ **clearly** ADV *Clearly, the police cannot break the law.* [3] ADJ If you are **clear** about something, you understand it completely. *She paused, trying to be clear about her feelings.* [4] ADJ If you have a **clear** mind or way of thinking, you are able to think sensibly and logically. *She needed a clear head to carry out their instructions.* ♦ **clearly** ADV *I can think clearly when I'm alone.* [5] ADJ If a substance is **clear**, it has no colour and you can see through it. ...*a clear glass panel.* ...*a clear gel.* [6] ADJ **Clear** skin or eyes look healthy. [7] ADJ If it is a **clear** day, there is no mist, rain, or cloud. [8] VERB When fog or mist **clears**, it gradually disappears. [9] ADJ If a sur-

face or place is **clear**, it is free from obstructions or unwanted objects. *The runway is clear – go ahead and land.* [10] VERB When you **clear** a place, you remove unwanted things from it. *Firemen were still clearing rubble from apartments.* [11] ADJ If your conscience is **clear**, you do not feel guilty about anything. *I can look back on things with a clear conscience.* [12] ADJ AFTER LINK-V If one thing is **clear** of another, the two things are not touching. *He lifted him clear of the deck.* [13] VERB If an animal or person **clears** a fence, wall, or hedge, they jump over it without touching it. [14] VERB If a course of action **is cleared**, people in authority give permission for it to happen. *The helicopter was cleared for take-off.* [15] VERB If someone **is cleared** of a crime or mistake, they are proved to be not guilty of it. [16] See also **clearing**.
[PHRASES] ● If you **stay clear** or **steer clear** of a person or place, you do not go near them. ● If someone is **in the clear**, they are free from blame, suspicion, or danger; INFORMAL. *The Audit Commission said that the ministry was in the clear.* ● to **clear** your throat: see **throat**.

▸ **clear away.** PHR-VERB When you **clear things away**, or when you **clear away**, you put away things that you have been using. *The waitress had cleared away the plates... Tania cooked, served, and cleared away.*

▸ **clear off.** PHR-VERB If you tell someone to **clear off**, you are telling them in a rude way to go away; INFORMAL.

▸ **clear out.** [1] PHR-VERB If you tell someone to **clear out** of a place or to **clear out**, you are telling them rather rudely to leave the place; INFORMAL. *'Clear out!' he bawled. 'Private property!'* [2] PHR-VERB If you **clear out** a cupboard or room, you tidy it and throw away unwanted things.

▸ **clear up.** [1] PHR-VERB When you **clear up**, or when you **clear** a place **up**, you tidy a place and put things away. *I cleared up my room.* [2] PHR-VERB To **clear up** a problem, misunderstanding, or mystery means to settle it or find a satisfactory explanation for it. [3] PHR-VERB When bad weather **clears up**, it stops raining or being cloudy.

clearance /'klɪərəns/ **clearances.** [1] N-VAR **Clearance** is the removal of old or unwanted buildings, trees, or other things from an area. *The UN pledged to help supervise the clearance of mines.* [2] N-VAR If you get **clearance** to do or have something, you get official approval or permission to do or have it. *The plane had been given clearance to land.*

,clear-'cut. ADJ Something that is **clear-cut** is easy to understand and definite or distinct. *This was a clear-cut case of the original land owner being in the right.*

clearing /'klɪərɪŋ/ **clearings.** N-C A **clearing** is a small area in a forest where there are no trees.

clench /klentʃ/ **clenches, clenching, clenched.** [1] VERB When you **clench** your fist, you curl your fingers up tightly, usually because you are very angry. *...angry protestors with clenched fists.* [2] VERB When you **clench** your teeth, you squeeze them together firmly, usually because you are angry or upset. *Slowly, he released his breath through clenched teeth.*

clergy /'klɜːdʒi/. N-PL The **clergy** are the religious leaders of a particular group of believers. *...Catholic clergy.*

clergyman /'klɜːdʒimən/ **clergymen.** N-C A **clergyman** is a male member of the clergy.

cleric /'klerɪk/ **clerics.** N-C A **cleric** is a member of the clergy.

clerical /'klerɪkəl/. [1] ADJ BEFORE N **Clerical** jobs, skills, and workers are concerned with work that is done in an office. *...a clerical error.* [2] ADJ BEFORE N **Clerical** means relating to the clergy. *...Iran's clerical leadership.*

clerk /klɑːk, AM klɜːrk/ **clerks.** N-C A **clerk** is a person who works in an office, bank, or law court and whose job is to look after records or accounts. *...an accounts clerk with a travel firm.*

clever /'klevə/ **cleverer, cleverest.** [1] ADJ A **clever** person is intelligent and able to understand things easily or to plan things well. *My sister was always a lot cleverer than I was.* ◆ **cleverly** ADV *He did this much more cleverly than I could have done.* ◆ **cleverness** N-U *He sat back, smiling complacently at his own cleverness.* [2] ADJ A **clever** idea, book, or invention is extremely effective and shows the skill of the people involved. *It is a clever and gripping novel. ...this clever new gadget.* ◆ **cleverly** ADV *...a cleverly designed swimsuit.*

cliché (or **cliche**) /'kliːʃeɪ, AM kliː'ʃeɪ/ **clichés.** N-C A **cliché** is an idea or phrase which has been used so much that it is no longer interesting or effective; used showing disapproval. *It has become a cliche to describe Asia-Pacific as the world's most dynamic economic area.*

click /klɪk/ **clicks, clicking, clicked.** [1] VERB & N-C If something **clicks**, or if you **click** it, it makes a short sharp sound, called a **click**. *He clicked off the radio... Blake clicked his fingers at a passing waiter. ...a click of a button.* [2] VERB When you suddenly understand something, you can say that it **has clicked**; INFORMAL. *It suddenly clicked that this was fantastic fun.*

client /'klaɪənt/ **clients.** N-C A **client** is someone for whom a professional person or organization is providing a service or doing some work. *The company required clients to pay substantial fees.* ● See note at **customer**.

clientele /ˌkliːɒn'tel, ˌklaɪən-/. N-SING The **clientele** of a place or business are its customers or clients. *This pub had a mixed clientele.*

cliff /klɪf/ **cliffs.** N-C A **cliff** is a high area of land with a very steep side, especially one next to the sea.

climate /'klaɪmət/ **climates.** [1] N-VAR The **climate** of a place is the general weather conditions that are typical of it. *...the hot and humid climate of Cyprus.* [2] N-C You can use **climate** to refer to the atmosphere or situation somewhere. *...the existing climate of violence and intimidation.*

climax /'klaɪmæks/ **climaxes, climaxing, climaxed.** N-C & VERB The **climax** of something is the most exciting or important moment in it, usually near the end. You can say something **climaxes** with a particular event. *Reaching an Olympics was the climax of her career... The poem climaxes with an outbreak of his jealousy.*

climb /klaɪm/ **climbs, climbing, climbed.**
1 VERB & N-C If you **climb** something such as a tree, mountain, or ladder, or if you **climb up** it, you move towards the top of it. Climbing something is called a **climb**. *Climb up the steps on to the bridge... Children love to climb. ...an hour's leisurely climb through olive groves.* **2** VERB If you **climb** somewhere, you move there carefully and often awkwardly, for example because you are moving into a small space. *The girls climbed into the car.* **3** VERB When something like an aeroplane **climbs**, it moves upwards. *The plane climbed to 370 feet.* **4** VERB When something **climbs**, it increases in value or amount. *Prices have climbed by 21%.*
▶ **climb down.** **1** PHR-VERB If you **climb down** something such as a tree, mountain, or ladder, you move towards the bottom of it. **2** PHR-VERB If you **climb down** in an argument or dispute, you admit that you are wrong, or change your intentions or demands.

climber /ˈklaɪmə/ **climbers.** N-C A **climber** is someone who climbs rocks or mountains as a sport.

climbing /ˈklaɪmɪŋ/. N-U **Climbing** is the activity of climbing rocks or mountains.

clinch /klɪntʃ/ **clinches, clinching, clinched.** VERB To **clinch** an agreement or argument means to settle it; INFORMAL. *He is about to clinch a deal with an American engine manufacturer.*

cling /klɪŋ/ **clings, clinging, clung.** **1** VERB If you **cling** to something or someone, you hold onto them tightly. *She had to cling onto the door handle... They hugged each other, clinging together.* **2** VERB Clothes that **cling** stay pressed against your body when you move. *Her sweat-stained clothing clung to her body.* **3** VERB If you **cling to** an idea or way of behaving, you continue to believe in its value or importance, even though it may no longer be valid or useful. *She clings to a romantic fantasy of wedded bliss.*

clinic /ˈklɪnɪk/ **clinics.** N-C A **clinic** is a building where people receive medical advice or treatment.

clinical /ˈklɪnɪkəl/. **1** ADJ BEFORE N **Clinical** means involving or relating to the medical treatment or testing of patients. *...a clinical psychologist.* ◆**clinically** ADV *She was diagnosed as being clinically depressed.* **2** ADJ **Clinical** thought or behaviour is very logical and does not involve any emotion; used showing disapproval. *All this questioning is so analytical and clinical.*

clink /klɪŋk/ **clinks, clinking, clinked.** VERB & N-C When glass or metal objects **clink**, or when you **clink** them, they touch each other and make a short light sound, called a **clink**. *She clinked her glass against his. ...the clink of a spoon in a cup.*

clip /klɪp/ **clips, clipping, clipped.** **1** N-C A **clip** is a small metal or plastic device that is used for holding things together. *She took the clip out of her hair.* **2** VERB If you **clip** one thing to another, you fasten it there with a clip. You can also say that one thing **clips** to another. *He clipped his cufflinks neatly in place. ...an electronic pen which clips to the casing.* **3** N-C

A **clip** from a film or a radio or television programme is a short piece of it that is broadcast separately. *...an historical film clip of Lenin speaking.* **4** VERB If you **clip** something, you cut small pieces from it. *I saw an old man out clipping his hedge.*

clipped /klɪpt/. **1** ADJ **Clipped** means neatly trimmed. *...a quiet street of clipped hedges.* **2** ADJ If you have a **clipped** way of speaking, you speak with quick short sounds. *'Come in', a clipped voice said.*

clipping /ˈklɪpɪŋ/ **clippings.** N-C A **clipping** is an article, picture, or advertisement that has been cut from a newspaper or magazine. *...newspaper clippings.*

clique /kliːk/ **cliques.** N-C If you describe a group of people as a **clique**, you mean that they spend a lot of time together and seem unfriendly towards people who are not in the group; used showing disapproval. *...a clique of privileged students.*

cloak /kləʊk/ **cloaks, cloaking, cloaked.** **1** N-C A **cloak** is a wide loose coat that fastens at the neck and does not have sleeves. **2** VERB & N-SING To **cloak** something, or to put a **cloak** around it, means to hide the truth about it or cover it up. *The subject remains cloaked in mythology and mystery... Preparations for the wedding were made under a cloak of secrecy.*

cloakroom /ˈkləʊkruːm/ **cloakrooms.** N-C A **cloakroom** is a small room in a public building where people can leave their coats.

clobber /ˈklɒbə/ **clobbers, clobbering, clobbered.** VERB If you **clobber** someone, you hit them; BRITISH, INFORMAL.

clock /klɒk/ **clocks, clocking, clocked.** N-C A **clock** is an instrument, for example in a room or on the outside of a building, that shows you what the time is. ● See also **o'clock**.
PHRASES ● If you work **round the clock**, you work all day and all night without stopping. *She will no longer be guarded round the clock. ...an around-the-clock service.* ● If you want to **turn the clock back** or **put the clock back**, you want to return to a situation that used to exist, for example because you would like to have avoided certain things that have happened.
▶ **clock up.** PHR-VERB To **clock up** a large total means to reach that total; BRITISH. *Rude taxi drivers clocked up a total of 239 offences in 1990.*

clockwise /ˈklɒkwaɪz/. ADV & ADJ BEFORE N When something is moving **clockwise** or when it is moving in a **clockwise** direction, it is moving in a circle, in the same direction as the hands on a clock.

clockwork /ˈklɒkwɜːk/. **1** ADJ BEFORE N A **clockwork** toy or device has machinery inside it which makes it move or operate when it is wound up with a key. **2** PHRASE If something happens **like clockwork**, it happens without problems or delays. *The Queen's holiday is arranged to go like clockwork.*

clog /klɒg/ **clogs, clogging, clogged.** **1** VERB & PHR-VERB When something **clogs** a hole or place, or when it **clogs up** a hole or place, it blocks it so that nothing can pass through. *The traffic clogged the Thames*

bridges... The lungs clog up with a thick mucus.
♦**clogged** ADJ *The streets were clogged with people.* [2] N-C **Clogs** are heavy leather or wooden shoes with thick wooden soles.

clone /kləʊn/ **clones.** N-C If you say that someone is a **clone** of someone else, you disapprove of them because they try to look and behave exactly like that person. *They believe we all want to be supermodel clones.*

close 1 verb uses

close /kləʊz/ **closes, closing, closed.** [1] VERB When you **close** a door, window, or lid, or when it **closes**, it moves so that a hole, gap, or opening is covered. *If you are cold, close the window... Zacharias heard the door close.* [2] VERB When a place **closes**, or when it **is closed**, people cannot use it, or all work stops there. *Shops close only on Christmas Day. ...if they do close the local college.* [3] VERB To **close** a matter or event means to bring it to an end. *He needs another $30,000 to close the deal. ...the closing ceremony of the National Political Conference.* [4] N-SING The **close** of a period of time or an activity is the end of it. To **bring something to a close** or to **draw something to a close** means to end it. *Applications would still be received until the close of business tomorrow.* [5] VERB If you **are closing** on someone or something that you are following, you are getting nearer and nearer to them. *I was within 15 seconds of the guy in second place and closing in on him.*

▶ **close down.** PHR-VERB If a factory or a business **closes down**, or if it **is closed down**, all work or activity stops there, usually for ever. *The Government has already closed down two newspapers.*

▶ **close in.** PHR-VERB If people **close in** on a person or place, they come nearer and gradually surround them. *Forces were closing in on Berlin.*

close 2 adjective uses

close /kləʊs/ **closer, closest.** [1] ADJ AFTER LINK-V Something that is **close** to something else is near to it. *The man moved closer... The tables were pushed close together.* ♦**closely** ADV *They were closely followed by security men.* [2] ADJ People who are **close** know each other well and like each other a lot. *She and Linda became very close. ...a close friend from school.* ♦**closeness** N-U *...her closeness to her mother.* [3] ADJ BEFORE N Your **close** relatives are the members of your family most directly related to you, for example your parents, brothers, or sisters. [4] ADJ BEFORE N **Close** contact or co-operation involves seeing or communicating with someone often. *He lived alone, keeping close contact with his three grown-up sons.* ♦**closely** ADV *We work closely with the careers officers.* [5] ADJ If there is a **close** connection or resemblance between two things, they are strongly connected or are very similar. *There is a close connection between pain and tension. ...Clare's close resemblance to his elder sister.* ♦**closely** ADV *...a pattern closely resembling a cross.* [6] ADJ When a competition or election is **close**, it is only won or lost by a small amount. *It is still a close contest between two leading opposition parties.* [7] ADJ BEFORE N **Close** inspec-

tion or observation of something is careful and thorough. *Let's have a closer look.* ♦**closely** ADV *...if you look closely at many of the problems in society.* [8] ADJ AFTER LINK-V If you are **close** to something, or if it is **close**, it is likely to happen or come soon. *She sounded close to tears... A senior White House official said the agreement is close... He's close to signing a contract.* [9] ADJ If the atmosphere in a place is **close**, it is uncomfortably warm and does not have enough fresh air. [10] See also **closing.**

PHRASES ● Something that is **close by** or **close at hand** is near to you. ● If you describe an event as **a close shave** or **a close call**, you mean that an accident nearly happened. ● If something is **close to** or **close on** a particular amount or distance, it is slightly less than that amount or distance. *Sisulu spent close to 30 years in prison.* ● If you look at something **close up** or **close to**, you look at it when you are very near to it. *They always look smaller close up.* ● See also **close-up.**

closed /kləʊzd/. ADJ A **closed** group of people does not welcome new people or ideas from outside. *It is a closed society in the sense that they've not been exposed to many things.*

,closed-'circuit. ADJ **Closed-circuit** television is a television system used to film people, for example in shops so thieves can be identified. *...closed-circuit cameras.*

closet /'klɒzɪt/ **closets.** [1] N-C In American English, a **closet** is a piece of furniture with doors at the front and shelves inside, which is used for storing things. The usual British word is **cupboard.** [2] ADJ BEFORE N **Closet** is used to describe a person who has beliefs, habits, or feelings which they keep secret. *He is a closet Fascist.*

close-up /'kləʊs ʌp/ **close-ups.** N-C A **close-up** is a photograph or a picture in a film that shows a lot of detail because it is taken very near to the subject.

closing /'kləʊzɪŋ/. ADJ BEFORE N The **closing** part of an activity or period of time is its final part. *...in the closing stages of the war.* ● See also **close.**

closure /'kləʊʒə/ **closures.** [1] N-VAR The **closure** of a business or factory is the permanent shutting of it. *Almost three in four clinics say they face closure.* [2] N-C The **closure** of a road or border is the blocking of it to prevent people from using it.

clot /klɒt/ **clots, clotting, clotted.** [1] N-C A blood **clot** is a thick lump of blood inside the body. *...surgery to remove a blood clot from his brain.* [2] VERB When blood **clots** it thickens and forms a clot.

cloth /klɒθ, AM klɔːθ/ **cloths.** [1] N-VAR **Cloth** is fabric which is made by weaving or knitting a substance such as cotton or wool. [2] N-C A **cloth** is a piece of cloth used for a particular purpose, such as cleaning. *Clean it with a damp cloth.*

clothed /kləʊðd/. ADJ AFTER LINK-V If you are **clothed** in a certain way, you are dressed in that way. *He lay down on the bed fully clothed... She was clothed in a flowered dress.*

clothes /kləʊðz/. N-PL **Clothes** are the things

that people wear, such as shirts, coats, trousers, and dresses. See note on page 111.

> There is no singular form of **clothes**. You cannot talk about 'a clothe'. In formal English, you can talk about a **garment**, a **piece of clothing**, an **article of clothing**, or an **item of clothing**, but in ordinary conversation, you usually name the piece of clothing you are talking about.
> For the different verbs associated with clothes, see the note at **wear**.

clothing /'kləʊðɪŋ/. N-U **Clothing** is the clothes people wear. *...protective clothing.* • See note at **clothes**.

cloud /klaʊd/ **clouds, clouding, clouded.** [1] N-VAR A **cloud** is a mass of water vapour that is seen as a white or grey mass in the sky. *The sky was almost entirely obscured by cloud.* [2] N-C A **cloud** of smoke or dust is a mass of it floating in the air. [3] VERB If you say that something **clouds** your view of a situation, you mean that it makes you unable to understand the situation or judge it properly. *Religious mania clouded his mind.* [4] VERB If something **clouds** an event or situation, it makes it less pleasant. *Poor job prospects have clouded the outlook for the economy.*
▸ **cloud over.** PHR-VERB If your face or eyes **cloud over**, you suddenly look sad or angry.

cloudy /'klaʊdi/. [1] ADJ If it is **cloudy**, there are a lot of clouds in the sky. [2] ADJ A **cloudy** liquid is less clear than it should be.

clout /klaʊt/ **clouts, clouting, clouted.** [1] VERB & N-C If you **clout** someone, or if you give them a **clout**, you hit them; INFORMAL. *The officer clouted her on the head... I was half tempted to give one of them a clout.* [2] N-U A person or institution that has **clout** has influence and power. *The two firms wield enormous clout in financial markets.*

clove /kləʊv/ **cloves.** [1] N-VAR **Cloves** are small dried flower buds used as a spice. [2] N-C A **clove** of garlic is one of the small sections of a garlic bulb.

clown /klaʊn/ **clowns, clowning, clowned.** [1] N-C A **clown** is a performer who wears funny clothes and bright make-up, and does silly things to make people laugh. [2] VERB If you **clown**, you do silly things to make people laugh.

club /klʌb/ **clubs, clubbing, clubbed.** [1] N-C A **club** is an organization of people who are all interested in a particular activity. *...a chess club.* [2] N-C A **club** is a team which competes in professional or amateur sporting competitions. *...the Italian football club, AC Milan.* [3] N-C A **club** is a place where the members of a particular club or organization meet. [4] N-C A **club** is the same as a **nightclub**. *...an occasional night of dancing at a club.* [5] N-C A **club** is a thick heavy stick that can be used as a weapon. [6] VERB To **club** a person or animal means to hit them hard with a thick heavy stick or a similar weapon. *Riot police clubbed a student to death.* [7] N-C A golf **club** is a long thin metal stick with a piece of wood or metal at one end.

[8] N-VAR **Clubs** is one of the four suits in a pack of playing cards. Each card in the suit is called a **club** and is marked with one or more black symbols: ♣.

clubhouse (or **club house**) /'klʌbhaʊs/ **clubhouses.** N-C A **clubhouse** is the place where the members of a sports club meet.

clue /kluː/ **clues.** [1] N-C A **clue** to a problem, mystery, or puzzle is something that helps you find the answer. *...a crossword puzzle clue. ...clues to the girls' killer.* [2] PHRASE If you **haven't a clue** about something, you know nothing about it. *I haven't a clue what I'll give Carl for his birthday.*

clump /klʌmp/ **clumps, clumping, clumped.** N-C A **clump** of things is a small group of them growing together or collected together in one place. *...a clump of trees... Her hair fell out in clumps.*

clumsy /'klʌmzi/ **clumsier, clumsiest.** [1] ADJ A **clumsy** person moves or handles things in an awkward way. ◆**clumsily** /'klʌmzɪli/ ADV *She rose clumsily.* ◆**clumsiness** N-U *Her clumsiness embarrassed him.* [2] ADJ A **clumsy** action or statement is not skilful or is without tact and likely to upset people. *...the German bank's clumsy handling of German monetary policy.* ◆**clumsily** ADV *...the exciting but clumsily written account of a captured crew of an RAF Tornado.* ◆**clumsiness** N-U *...clumsiness of expression.* [3] ADJ A **clumsy** object is ugly and awkward to use. *The keyboard is a large and clumsy instrument.*

clung /klʌŋ/. **Clung** is the past tense and past participle of **cling**.

cluster /'klʌstə/ **clusters, clustering, clustered.** [1] N-C A **cluster** of people or things is a small group of them close together. [2] VERB If people or things **cluster** together, they gather together or are found together in small groups. *The children clustered around me. ...small cottages that are clustered together.*

clutch /klʌtʃ/ **clutches, clutching, clutched.** [1] VERB If you **clutch** something, you hold it very tightly. *Michelle clutched my arm.* [2] N-PL If you are in another person's **clutches**, that person has control over you. [3] N-C In a car, the **clutch** is the pedal that you press before you change gear, and the mechanism that it operates.

clutter /'klʌtə/ **clutters, cluttering, cluttered.** [1] N-U **Clutter** is a lot of unnecessary or useless things in an untidy state. *Caroline prefers her worktops to be clear of clutter.* [2] VERB If things **clutter** a place, they fill it untidily. *The roads were cluttered with cars.* ◆**cluttered** ADJ *...a cluttered desk.*

cm. cm. is the written abbreviation for **centimetre**. *His height had increased by 2.5 cm.*

co- /kəʊ-/. **Co-** is used to form words that refer to people sharing things or doing things together. *He co-produced the album with Bowie... His co-workers hated him.*

coach /kəʊtʃ/ **coaches, coaching, coached.** [1] N-C A **coach** is a large comfortable bus that carries passengers on long journeys. *I hate travelling by coach.* [2] N-C A **coach** is one of the separate sections of a train that carries passengers; BRITISH. [3] N-C A **coach** is an enclosed four-wheeled vehicle pulled by horses, in which people used to travel. **4** VERB If you **coach** someone, you help them to become better at a particular sport or subject. *He coached the North Carolina State University basketball team.* **5** N-C A **coach** is someone who coaches a person or sports team. *...a drama coach. ...a football coach.*

coal /kəʊl/ **coals.** **1** N-U **Coal** is a hard black substance taken from underground and burned as fuel. **2** N-PL **Coals** are burning pieces of coal.

coalition /ˌkəʊəˈlɪʃən/ **coalitions.** **1** N-C A **coalition** is a government consisting of people from two or more political parties. *...a coalition government.* **2** N-C A **coalition** is a group consisting of people from different political or social groups. *...a coalition of consumer and environmental groups.*

coarse /kɔːs/ **coarser, coarsest.** **1** ADJ **Coarse** things have a rough texture. *...a beach of coarse sand.* ♦**coarsely** ADV *...coarsely ground black pepper.* **2** ADJ A **coarse** person talks and behaves in a rude and offensive way. ♦**coarsely** ADV *The women laughed coarsely at some vulgar joke.*

coast /kəʊst/ **coasts, coasting, coasted.** **1** N-C The **coast** is an area of land next to the sea. ♦**coastal** /ˈkəʊstəl/ ADJ BEFORE N *...coastal areas.* **2** VERB If a person or a team **is coasting**, they are doing something easily and without effort. *Charles was coasting at school... Ivan Lendl coasted to a 6-3, 6-2, 6-3 victory.*

coastguard /ˈkəʊstɡɑːd/ **coastguards.** N-C A **coastguard** is an official who watches the sea near a coast, in order to get help when it is needed and to prevent smuggling.

coastline /ˈkəʊstlaɪn/ **coastlines.** N-VAR A country's **coastline** is the edge of its coast. *...two patrol boats to watch five miles of coastline.*

coat /kəʊt/ **coats, coating, coated.** **1** N-C A **coat** is a piece of clothing with long sleeves worn over your other clothes when you go outside. **2** N-C An animal's **coat** is its fur or hair. **3** VERB If you **coat** something with a substance, you cover it with a thin layer of the substance. *...a dying bird coated with oil.* ♦**-coated** *...chocolate-coated sweets.* **4** N-C A **coat** of paint or varnish is a thin layer of it.

coating /ˈkəʊtɪŋ/ **coatings.** N-C A **coating** of a substance is a thin layer of it. *...a coating of breadcrumbs.*

coax /kəʊks/ **coaxes, coaxing, coaxed.** VERB If you **coax** someone to do something, you gently try to persuade them to do it. *I had to coax him to tell me what was wrong.*

cobble /ˈkɒbəl/ **cobbles, cobbling, cobbled.**
▸ **cobble together** PHR-VERB If you say that someone has **cobbled** something **together**, you mean that they have made or produced it roughly or quickly. *The group had cobbled together a few decent songs.*

cobra /ˈkəʊbrə/ **cobras.** N-C A **cobra** is a kind of poisonous snake.

cobweb /ˈkɒbweb/ **cobwebs.** N-C A **cobweb** is the fine net that a spider makes in order to catch insects.

cocaine /kəʊˈkeɪn/. N-U **Cocaine** is an addictive drug which people take for pleasure.

cock /kɒk/ **cocks, cocking, cocked.** **1** N-C A **cock** is an adult male chicken. **2** VERB If you **cock** a part of your body towards a particular direction, you lift it or point it in that direction. *He paused and cocked his head.*

cockpit /ˈkɒkpɪt/ **cockpits.** N-C The **cockpit** in a small plane or racing car is the part where the pilot or driver sits.

cockroach /ˈkɒkrəʊtʃ/ **cockroaches.** N-C A **cockroach** is a large brown insect that is often found in dirty or damp places.

cocktail /ˈkɒkteɪl/ **cocktails.** **1** N-C A **cocktail** is an alcoholic drink containing several ingredients. *...a champagne cocktail.* **2** N-C A mixture of a number of different things can be called a **cocktail**. *...a fruit cocktail... Children and guns are a potentially lethal cocktail.*

cocky /ˈkɒki/. ADJ A **cocky** person is very self-confident and pleased with themselves; INFORMAL. *He had a confident, even cocky, air.*

cocoa /ˈkəʊkəʊ/. **1** N-U **Cocoa** is a brown powder used in making chocolate. **2** N-U **Cocoa** is a hot drink made with cocoa powder and milk.

coconut /ˈkəʊkənʌt/ **coconuts.** N-VAR A **coconut** is a very large nut with a hairy shell, white flesh, and milky juice inside. **Coconut** is the white flesh of a coconut.

cocoon /kəˈkuːn/ **cocoons.** **1** N-C A **cocoon** is a covering of silky threads made by the larvae of moths and other insects before they grow into adults. **2** N-C You can use **cocoon** to describe a safe and protective environment. *She is looking for a cocoon to retreat to or bring up children.*

cod /kɒd/. N-VAR A **cod** is a large sea fish with white flesh. **Cod** is the flesh of this fish eaten as food.

code /kəʊd/ **codes, coding, coded.** **1** N-C A **code** is a set of rules about how people should behave. *...a strict code of practice. ...the strict Islamic dress code.* **2** N-C A **code** is a system of replacing the words in a message with other words or symbols, so that people who do not know the system cannot understand it. *If you can't remember your number, write it in code in a diary.* **3** N-C A **code** is a group of numbers or letters used to identify something such as a postal address. *Callers dialing the wrong area code will not get through.* **4** N-C A **code** is any system of signs or symbols that has a meaning. *...digital code.*

coded /ˈkəʊdɪd/. ADJ **Coded** messages have words or symbols which represent other words, so that the message is secret unless you know the system behind the code. *...coded instructions to waiting terrorists.*

coding /ˈkəʊdɪŋ/. N-U **Coding** is a method of making it easy to see the difference between several things, for example by marking them in different colours.

coerce /kəʊˈɜːs/ **coerces, coercing, coerced.** VERB If you **coerce** someone into doing something, you make them do it against their will; FORMAL. *Clark had somehow been able to coerce Jenny into doing whatever he told her to* do. ◆**coercion** /kəʊˈɜːʃən/ N-U *The growth in its membership was due to official coercion.*

coffee /ˈkɒfi, AM ˈkɔːfi/ **coffees.** [1] N-VAR **Coffee** is the roasted beans of the coffee plant. [2] N-VAR **Coffee** is a drink made from boiling water and ground roasted coffee beans. *Would you like to come back for coffee?.*

'**coffee shop, coffee shops.** N-C A **coffee shop** is a restaurant that sells coffee, tea, cakes, and sometimes sandwiches and snacks.

coffers /ˈkɒfəz/ N-PL The **coffers** of an organization consist of the money that it has to spend.

coffin /ˈkɒfɪn, AM ˈkɔːfɪn/ **coffins.** N-C A **coffin** is a box in which a dead body is buried or cremated.

cognac /ˈkɒnjæk, AM ˈkəʊn-/ **cognacs.** N-VAR **Cognac** is a kind of brandy.

cognitive /ˈkɒgnɪtɪv/ ADJ BEFORE N **Cognitive** means relating to the mental process involved in knowing, learning, and understanding things; TECHNICAL. *...physical, emotional and cognitive growth.*

coherent /kəʊˈhɪərənt/ [1] ADJ If something is **coherent**, it is well planned, so that it is clear and sensible. *...a coherent campaign to change the laws.* ◆**coherence** /kəʊˈhɪərəns/ N-U *...political coherence.* [2] ADJ If someone is **coherent**, they express their thoughts in a clear and calm way. *He appeared hardly capable of conducting a coherent conversation.* ◆**coherently** ADV *Many young people are unable to express themselves coherently.*

cohesion /kəʊˈhiːʒən/ N-U If there is **cohesion** within a society, organization, or group, the different members fit together well and form a united whole. *The cohesion of the armed forces was rapidly breaking down.*

cohesive /kəʊˈhiːsɪv/ ADJ Something that is **cohesive** consists of parts that fit together well and form a united whole. *...a reasonably cohesive and supportive family.*

coil /kɔɪl/ **coils, coiling, coiled.** [1] N-C A **coil** of rope or wire is a length of it that has been wound into a series of loops. *He slung the coil of rope over his shoulder.* [2] VERB & PHR-VERB If something **coils**, or if you **coil** it **up**, it curves into a series of loops or into the shape of a ring. *A huge rattlesnake lay coiled on the blanket... Once we have the wire, we can coil it up.*

coin /kɔɪn/ **coins, coining, coined.** [1] N-C A **coin** is a small piece of metal used as money. [2] VERB If you **coin** a word or a phrase, you are the first person to say it. *Jaron Lanier coined the term 'virtual reality'.*

coinage /ˈkɔɪnɪdʒ/ [1] N-U **Coinage** consists of the coins used in a country. [2] N-U **Coinage** is the system of money used in a country.

coincide /ˌkəʊɪnˈsaɪd/ **coincides, coinciding, coincided.** [1] VERB If one event **coincides** with another, they happen at the same time. *The shop's opening coincided with the Christmas rush.* [2] VERB If the opinions or ideas of two or more people **coincide**, they are the same. *The beliefs of the patient and the doctor ideally should coincide. ...people whose interests coincided with his own.*

coincidence /kəʊˈɪnsɪdəns/ **coincidences.** N-VAR A **coincidence** happens when two or more things occur at the same time by chance. *It's been pure coincidence that he's followed my career. ...a string of amazing coincidences.*

coincidentally /ˌkəʊɪnsɪˈdentli/ ADV You say **coincidentally** when you want to draw attention to a coincidence. *Coincidentally, I had once found myself in a similar situation.*

coke /kəʊk/ **cokes.** [1] N-VAR **Coke** is sweet, brown, non-alcoholic fizzy drink. **Coke** is a trademark. [2] N-U **Coke** is **cocaine**; INFORMAL.

cola /ˈkəʊlə/ N-U **Cola** is a sweet, brown, non-alcoholic fizzy drink.

cold /kəʊld/ **colder, coldest, colds.** [1] ADJ & N-U If something or someone is **cold**, they have a very low temperature. **The cold** is cold weather or a low temperature. *...cold running water... This is the coldest winter I can remember... It was windy and Jake felt cold... He must have come inside to get out of the cold.* ◆**coldness** N-U *...the coldness of the night.*

If you want to emphasize how cold the weather is, you can say that it is **freezing**, especially in winter when there is ice or frost. In summer, if the temperature is below average, you can say that it is **cool**. In general, **cold** suggests a lower temperature than **cool**, and **cool** things may be pleasant or refreshing. *A cool breeze swept off the sea; it was pleasant out there.*
See also the note at **hot**.

---

[2] ADJ **Cold** food, such as salad or meat that has been cooked and cooled, is not intended to be eaten hot. [3] ADJ A **cold** person does not show much emotion or affection and therefore seems unfriendly. *What a cold, unfeeling woman she was.* ◆**coldly** ADV *I'll see you in the morning,' Hugh said coldly.* ◆**coldness** N-U *His coldness angered her.* [4] N-C & PHRASE If you have a **cold**, you have a mild, very common illness which makes you sneeze a lot and gives you a sore throat or a cough. If you **catch cold**, or if you **catch a cold**, you become ill with a cold. [5] **in cold blood**: see **blood**.

collaborate /kəˈlæbəreɪt/ **collaborates, collaborating, collaborated.** [1] VERB When people **collaborate**, they work together on a particular project. *Students collaborate in group exercises and projects... He collaborated with his son Michael on the English translation.* ◆**collaboration, collaborations** N-VAR *Drummond was working on a book in collaboration with the band.* ◆**collaborator,** /kəˈlæbəreɪtə/ **collaborators** N-C *He completed the book in two years, with Hugh Lynn his collaborator.* [2] VERB If someone **collaborates** with an enemy which has occupied their country, he or she helps them; used showing disapproval. ◆**collaboration** N-U *...rumors of his collaboration with the occupying forces.* ◆**collaborator** N-C *...a secret collaborator with the Communists' security police.*

collaborative /kəˈlæbərətɪv, AM -reɪt-/ ADJ BEFORE N A **collaborative** piece of work is done by

two or more people working together; FORMAL.
...*a collaborative research project.*

collage /'kɒlɑːʒ, AM kə'lɑːʒ/ **collages.** N-VAR A
collage is a picture made by sticking pieces of
paper or cloth onto paper. **Collage** is the
method of making these pictures.

collapse /kə'læps/ **collapses, collapsing,
collapsed.** [1] VERB & N-U If something **collapses**, or if there is a **collapse** of it, it suddenly
falls down or falls inwards. *The roof support
structure had collapsed. ...an inquiry into the
freeway's collapse.* [2] VERB & N-U If you **collapse**,
or if you have a **collapse**, you suddenly fall
down because you are ill or tired. *Jimmy collapsed on the floor... A few days after his collapse he was sitting up in bed.* [3] VERB & N-U If a
system or institution **collapses**, or if there is a
collapse, it fails completely and suddenly. *His
business empire collapsed under a massive burden of debt... The medical system is facing collapse.*

collar /'kɒlə/ **collars, collaring, collared.**
[1] N-C The **collar** of a shirt or coat is the part
which fits round the neck and is usually folded
over. [2] N-C A **collar** is a leather band which is
put round the neck of a dog or cat. [3] VERB If
you **collar** someone who has done something
wrong or who is running away, you catch them
and hold them so that they cannot escape; IN-
FORMAL. *As Kerr fled towards the exit, Boycott
collared him at the ticket barrier.*

collate /kə'leɪt/ **collates, collating, collated.**
VERB When you **collate** pieces of information,
you gather them all together and examine
them. *The 1992 figures have not yet been collated.*

collateral /kə'lætərəl/. N-U **Collateral** is money
or property which is used as a guarantee that
someone will repay a loan; FORMAL. *Many people use personal assets as collateral for small
business loans.*

colleague /'kɒliːg/ **colleagues.** N-C Your **colleagues** are the people you work with, especially in a professional job. *...a business colleague.*

collect /kə'lekt/ **collects, collecting, collected.** [1] VERB If you **collect** a number of things,
you bring them together from several places.
*Two young girls were collecting firewood... 1.5
million signatures have been collected.* [2] VERB
If you **collect** things as a hobby, you get a large
number of them over a period of time because
you are interested in them. *He collected antique furniture.* ♦**collecting** N-U *...stamp collecting.* ♦**collector, collectors.** N-C *...a respected
collector of Indian art.* [3] VERB When you **collect** someone or something, you go and get
them from a place where they are waiting for
you or have been left for you. *David always
collects Alistair from school... After collecting
the cash, the kidnapper made his escape.*
♦**collection** N-U *...services such as rubbish collection.* [4] VERB If a substance **collects** somewhere, or something **collects** it, it keeps arriving over a period of time and is held in that
place or thing. *Methane gas does collect in the
mines. ...water tanks which collect rainwater.*
[5] VERB If you **collect** for a charity or for a present, you ask people to give you money for it.

*They collected donations for a fund to help
military families.* ♦**collection, collections.** N-C
There was a collection for a wreath. [6] VERB If
you **collect** yourself or **collect** your thoughts,
you make an effort to calm or prepare yourself. *...a chance to relax and collect his
thoughts.*

collection /kə'lekʃən/ **collections.** [1] N-C A
collection of things is a group of similar or related things. *...the world's largest collection of
sculptures by Henry Moore. ...a collection of essays from foreign affairs experts. ...Guy
Laroche's autumn collection of day and evening
wear.* [2] See also **collect**.

collective /kə'lektɪv/. [1] ADJ BEFORE N **Collective** means shared by or involving every member of a group of people. *It was a collective decision... Scientists breathed a collective sigh of
relief, about the finding.* ♦**collectively** ADV *The
Cabinet is collectively responsible for policy.*
[2] N-C A **collective** is a business or farm whose
employees share the decision-making and the
profits.

collector /kə'lektə/ **collectors.** [1] N-C A **collector** is someone whose job is to take something
such as money or tickets from people. *...rent
collectors. ...Council rubbish collectors.* [2] See
also **collect**.

college /'kɒlɪdʒ/ **colleges.** [1] N-VAR A **college** is
an institution where students study after they
have left school. *Joanna is doing business studies at a local college... I'm going to college in
September.* [2] N-C A **college** in a university is
one of the institutions which some British universities are divided into. *...Balliol College, Oxford.* [3] N-C A **college** of a particular kind is an
organized group of people who have special
duties and powers; FORMAL. *...the Royal College
of Nursing.*

collide /kə'laɪd/ **collides, colliding, collided.**
VERB If people or vehicles **collide**, they bump
into each other. *Two trains collided head-on...
Racing up the stairs, he almost collided with
Daisy.*

colliery /'kɒljəri/ **collieries.** N-C A **colliery** is a
coal mine; BRITISH.

collision /kə'lɪʒən/ **collisions.** N-VAR A **collision** occurs when a moving object hits something. *Their van was involved in a collision
with a car. ...a head-on collision between two
aeroplanes.*

collude /kə'luːd/ **colludes, colluding, col-
luded.** VERB If one person **colludes** with another, they co-operate secretly or illegally. *Several local officials are in jail on charges of colluding with the Mafia.* ♦**collusion** /kə'luːʒən/
N-U *Critics have accused banks of being in collusion over the plans.*

colon /'kəʊlən/ **colons.** N-C A **colon** is the
punctuation mark (:).

colonel /'kɜːnəl/ **colonels.** N-C & N-TITLE A **colonel** is a senior military officer.

colonial /kə'ləʊniəl/. ADJ BEFORE N **Colonial**
means relating to countries that are colonies,
or to colonialism. *...independence from British
colonial rule. ...the colonial civil service.*

colonialism /kə'ləʊniəlɪzəm/. N-U **Colonialism**
is the practice by which a powerful country di-

rectly controls less powerful countries. *...the residual effects of colonialism.*

colonist /'kɒlənɪst/ **colonists.** N-C **Colonists** are people who start a colony. *...the early American colonists.*

colonize (BR also **colonise**) /'kɒlənaɪz/ **colonizes, colonizing, colonized.** VERB When large numbers of people or animals **colonize** a place, they go to live there and make it their home. *The first British attempt to colonize Ireland was in the twelfth century... Toads are colonising the whole place.* ◆**colonization** N-U *...the European colonization of America.*

colony /'kɒləni/ **colonies.** 1 N-C A **colony** is a country which is controlled by a more powerful country. 2 N-C A **colony** is a group of people or animals of a particular sort living together. *...an artists' colony. ...a seal colony.*

color /'kʌlə/. See **colour**.

colorless /'kʌlələs/. See **colourless**.

colossal /kə'lɒsəl/. ADJ Something that is **colossal** is very large. *...a colossal waste of money.*

colour (AM **color**) /'kʌlə/ **colours, colouring, coloured.** 1 N-C The **colour** of something is the appearance that it has as a result of reflecting light. Red, blue, and green are colours. *'What colour is the car?' – 'Red.'... Her silk dress was sky-blue, the colour of her eyes.* 2 N-C Someone's **colour** is the colour of their skin. People often use **colour** in this way to refer to a person's race. *The ANC has always welcomed South Africans of all colours.* 3 ADJ A **colour** television, film, or photograph shows things in all their colours, and not just in black and white. *...colour illustrations.* 4 N-U **Colour** is a quality that makes something interesting or exciting. *Check shirts add colour to a sober work suit.* 5 VERB If something **colours** your opinion, it affects your opinion.
▶ **colour in.** PHR-VERB If you **colour in** a drawing, you give it different colours using crayons or paints.

coloured (AM **colored**) /'kʌləd/. 1 ADJ **Coloured** means having a particular colour or combination of colours. *...a cheap gold-coloured bracelet. ...brightly coloured silks.* 2 ADJ A **coloured** person belongs to a race of people with dark skins; an offensive use.

colourful (AM **colorful**) /'kʌləfʊl/. 1 ADJ Something that is **colourful** has bright colours. *...colourful flowers.* 2 ADJ **Colourful** means interesting and exciting. *...boxing's colourful history. ...the island's colourful past.*

colouring (AM **coloring**) /'kʌlərɪŋ/ **colourings.** 1 N-U Someone's **colouring** is the colour of their hair, skin, and eyes. 2 N-U **Colouring** is a substance that is used to give colour to food.

colourless (AM **colorless**) /'kʌlələs/. 1 ADJ A **colourless** substance is clear or invisible. *...a colourless, almost odourless liquid.* 2 ADJ **Colourless** people or places are dull and uninteresting. *We hurried through the colourless little town.*

colt /kəʊlt/ **colts.** N-C A **colt** is a young male horse.

column /'kɒləm/ **columns.** 1 N-C A **column** is a tall solid cylinder, especially one supporting part of a building. 2 N-C A **column** is something that has a tall narrow shape. *...a column of smoke.* 3 N-C A **column** of people, animals, or vehicles is a group of them moving in a line. *...a column of tanks.* 4 N-C In a newspaper or magazine, a **column** is a vertical section of writing, or a regular section written by the same person. *He writes a column for The Wall Street Journal.*

columnist /'kɒləmɪst/ **columnists.** N-C A **columnist** is a journalist who writes a regular article in a newspaper or magazine.

coma /'kəʊmə/ **comas.** N-C If someone is in a **coma**, they are deeply unconscious.

comb /kəʊm/ **combs, combing, combed.** 1 N-C A **comb** is a flat piece of plastic or metal with long thin pointed parts, which you use to tidy your hair. 2 VERB When you **comb** your hair, you tidy it using a comb. 3 VERB If you **comb** a place for something, you search thoroughly for it. *Officers combed the woods for the murder weapon.*

combat, combats, combating, combated. 1 N-VAR /'kɒmbæt/ **Combat** is fighting that takes place in a war. *Over 16 million men had died in combat.* 2 VERB /kəm'bæt/ If people in authority **combat** something, they try to stop it happening. *...new government measures to combat crime.*

combatant /'kɒmbətənt, AM kəm'bæt-/ **combatants.** N-C A **combatant** is someone who takes part in a fight or a war.

combative /'kɒmbətɪv, AM kəm'bætɪv/. ADJ A **combative** person is aggressive and eager to fight or argue.

combination /ˌkɒmbɪ'neɪʃən/ **combinations.** 1 N-C A **combination** is a mixture of things. *...a fantastic combination of colours.* 2 N-C The **combination** of a lock is the series of letters or numbers used to open it. *He's the only one who knows the combination to the safe.*

combine, combines, combining, combined. 1 VERB /kəm'baɪn/ If you **combine** two or more things, or if they **combine**, they exist or join together. *Combine the flour with 3 tablespoons water... Disease and starvation combine to kill thousands.* ◆**combined** ADJ BEFORE N *Their combined assets total £20 billion.* 2 VERB If someone or something **combines** two qualities or features, they have both of them. *Their system seems to combine the two ideals... He combines legal expertise with social concern.* 3 VERB If someone **combines** two activities, they do them both at the same time. *It is possible to combine a career with being a mother... He will combine the two jobs.* 4 N-C /'kɒmbaɪn/ A **combine** is a group of people or organizations that are working together.

combustion /kəm'bʌstʃən/. N-U **Combustion** is the act of burning something or the process of burning; TECHNICAL.

come /kʌm/ **comes, coming, came, come.** 1 VERB You use **come** to say that someone or something arrives somewhere, or moves towards you. *Two police officers came into the hall... He came to a door... Beryl came round this morning to apologize.* 2 VERB If something **comes** to a particular point, it reaches it. *I wore a large shirt of Jamie's which came down over my hips.* 3 VERB You use **come** in expressions which state what happens to someone or something. *The door knobs came off... The Communists came to power in 1944... Their worst fears may be coming true.* **4** VERB If someone **comes** to do something, they gradually start to do it. *She said it so many times that she came to believe it.* **5** VERB When a particular time or event **comes**, it arrives or happens. *The announcement came after a meeting at the Home Office... The time has come for us to move on.* **6** VERB If a thought or idea **comes** to you, you suddenly realize it. **7** VERB If something such as a sum **comes to** a particular amount, it adds up to it. *Lunch came to $80.* **8** VERB If someone or something that **comes from** a particular place or thing, that place or thing is their origin or source. *Nearly half the students come from abroad... Chocolate comes from the cacao tree.* **9** VERB Something that **comes from** something else or **comes of** it is the result of it. *...a feeling of power that comes from driving fast.* **10** VERB If someone or something **comes** first, next, or last, they are first, next, or last in a series, list, or competition. **11** VERB If a type of thing **comes** in a range of colours, styles, or sizes, it can have any of those colours, styles, or sizes. *The wallpaper comes in black and white only.* **12** See note at **bring.** ● See also **coming.**

▸ **come about.** PHR-VERB When you say how or when something **came about,** you say how or when it happened. *This situation came about when I encouraged him to give up his job.*

▸ **come across.** **1** PHR-VERB If you **come across** someone or something, or **come upon** them, you meet or find them by chance. *This is the worst place I've come across.* **2** PHR-VERB The way that someone **comes across** is the impression they make on other people. *He can come across as an extremely pleasant young man.*

▸ **come along.** **1** PHR-VERB If you ask someone to **come along** to a place or event where you are going to be, you are inviting them to come with you or go there. **2** PHR-VERB When something **comes along,** it arrives or happens, perhaps by chance. *It was lucky you came along.* **3** PHR-VERB If something **is coming along,** it is developing or making progress. *How's your husband's research coming along?*

▸ **come around** or **come round.** **1** PHR-VERB If you **come around** to an idea, you eventually change your mind and accept it. *It looks like they're coming around to our way of thinking.* **2** PHR-VERB When something **comes around,** it happens as a regular or predictable event. *...when the World Cup comes around next year.* **3** PHR-VERB When someone who is unconscious **comes round,** or **comes to** they recover consciousness.

▸ **come at.** PHR-VERB If a person or animal **comes at** you, they move towards you in a threatening way and try to attack you.

▸ **come back.** **1** PHR-VERB If something that you had forgotten **comes back** to you, you remember it. *I'll think of his name in a moment when it comes back to me.* **2** PHR-VERB When something **comes back,** it becomes fashionable again. *I'm glad hats are coming back.*

♦**comeback, comebacks.** N-C *Tight fitting T-shirts are making a comeback.*

▸ **come by.** PHR-VERB To **come by** something means to find or obtain it.

▸ **come down.** **1** PHR-VERB If the cost, level, or amount of something **comes down,** it becomes less than it was before. *The price of petrol is coming down.* **2** PHR-VERB If something **comes down,** it falls to the ground.

▸ **come down on.** **1** PHR-VERB If you **come down on** one side of an argument, you declare that you support that side. **2** PHR-VERB To **come down on** someone means to criticize them or treat them harshly.

▸ **come down to.** PHR-VERB If a problem or decision **comes down to** a particular thing, that thing is the most important factor involved. *The problem comes down to money.*

▸ **come down with.** PHR-VERB If you **come down with** an illness, you get it.

▸ **come for.** PHR-VERB If people such as soldiers **come for** you, they come to find you.

▸ **come forward.** PHR-VERB If someone **comes forward,** they offer to do something in response to a request for help. *A vital witness came forward to say that she saw Tanner wearing the boots.*

▸ **come in.** **1** PHR-VERB If information or a report **comes in,** you receive it. *Reports are now coming in of trouble at yet another jail.* **2** PHR-VERB If you have money **coming in,** you receive it regularly as your income. **3** PHR-VERB If someone or something **comes in,** or **comes into** a situation, they are involved in it. *Finally, he could do no more, which is where Jacques came in.* **4** PHR-VERB When a new idea, fashion, or product **comes in,** it becomes popular or available.

▸ **come in for.** PHR-VERB If someone or something **comes in for** criticism or blame, they receive it.

▸ **come into.** **1** PHR-VERB If someone **comes into** money or property, they inherit it. **2** See also **come in** 3.

▸ **come off.** PHR-VERB If something **comes off,** it is successful or effective. *It was a good try but it didn't quite come off.*

▸ **come on.** **1** PHR-VERB You say '**Come on**' to someone to encourage them to do something. *Come on Doreen, let's dance.* **2** PHR-VERB When a machine **comes on,** it starts working. **3** PHR-VERB If you have an illness or a headache **coming on,** you can feel it starting. **4** PHR-VERB If something **is coming on,** it is developing or making progress. *The knee's coming on fine, I'm walking comfortably already.*

▸ **come on to.** PHR-VERB When you **come on to** a particular topic, you start discussing it. *We're now looking at a smaller system but I'll come on to that later.*

▸ **come out.** **1** PHR-VERB When a new product **comes out,** it becomes available to the public. *Christian Slater has a new movie coming out.* **2** PHR-VERB If a fact **comes out,** it becomes known to people. *The truth is beginning to come out about what happened.* **3** PHR-VERB If you **come out** for or against something, you declare that you support it or that you do not support it. **4** PHR-VERB If a photograph does not **come out,** it is blank or unclear when it is developed and printed. **[5]** PHR-VERB When the sun, moon, or stars **come out**, they appear in the sky.

▶ **come over.** PHR-VERB If a feeling **comes over** you, it affects you. *An eerie feeling came over me.*

▶ **come round.** See **come around**.

▶ **come through.** **[1]** PHR-VERB To **come through** a dangerous or difficult situation means to survive it. *The city had faced racial crisis and come through it.* **[2]** PHR-VERB If something **comes through**, you receive it. *The news came through at about five o'clock.* **[3]** PHR-VERB If a quality or impression **comes through**, it is clearly shown in what is said or done. *I hope my love for the material came through.*

▶ **come to.** See **come round** 3.

▶ **come under.** **[1]** PHR-VERB If you **come under** attack or pressure, for example, people attack you or put pressure on you. **[2]** PHR-VERB If something **comes under** your authority, you control how it is managed.

▶ **come up.** **[1]** PHR-VERB If someone **comes up** to you, they walk over to you. **[2]** PHR-VERB If an event **is coming up**, it is about to take place. *We do have elections coming up.* **[3]** PHR-VERB If something **comes up**, it happens unexpectedly. *I was delayed – something came up at home.* **[4]** PHR-VERB If a topic **comes up** in a conversation, it is mentioned. **[5]** PHR-VERB If a job **comes up** or if something **comes up** for sale, it becomes available. **[6]** PHR-VERB When the sun or moon **comes up**, it rises. *It will be so great watching the sun come up.*

▶ **come up against.** PHR-VERB If you **come up against** a problem or difficulty, you have to deal with it. *We came up against a great deal of resistance in dealing with the case.*

▶ **come upon.** See **come across** 1.

comeback /'kʌmbæk/ **comebacks.** See **come back** 2.

comedian /kə'miːdiən/ **comedians.** N-C A **comedian** is an entertainer whose job is to make people laugh by telling jokes.

comedy /'kɒmədi/ **comedies.** **[1]** N-U **Comedy** consists of types of entertainment that are intended to make people laugh. *...his career in comedy.* *...a TV comedy series.* **[2]** N-C A **comedy** is a play, film, or television programme that is intended to make people laugh.

comet /'kɒmɪt/ **comets.** N-C A **comet** is an object that travels around the sun leaving a bright trail behind it.

comfort /'kʌmfət/ **comforts, comforting, comforted.** **[1]** N-U **Comfort** is the state of being physically or mentally relaxed. *The shoe has padding around the collar, heel and tongue for added comfort.* **[2]** N-U If you are living in **comfort**, you have enough money to have everything you need. **[3]** N-C **Comforts** are things that make your life easier and more pleasant. *She enjoys the material comforts married life has brought her.* **[4]** VERB & N-U If you **comfort** someone, or if you offer them **comfort**, you make them feel less worried or unhappy. *Ned put his arm around her, trying to comfort her... We have offered comfort to some new residents who felt lost and lonely.*

comfortable /'kʌmfətəbl/. **[1]** ADJ You describe things such as furniture as **comfortable** when they make you feel physically relaxed. When you are physically comfortable you can also say that you are **comfortable**. *...a comfortable fireside chair... Lie down on your bed and make yourself comfortable.* ♦ **comfortably** ADV *Are you sitting comfortably?* **[2]** ADJ If someone is **comfortable**, they have enough money to be able to live without financial problems. ♦ **comfortably** ADV *Cayton describes himself as comfortably well-off.* **[3]** ADJ AFTER LINK-V If you feel **comfortable** with a particular situation or person, you feel confident and relaxed with them. *I'll talk to them, but I won't feel comfortable about it.*

comforting /'kʌmfətɪŋ/. ADJ If something is **comforting**, it makes you feel less worried or unhappy. *It may be comforting to know that some things never change.*

comic /'kɒmɪk/ **comics.** **[1]** ADJ Something that is **comic** makes you want to laugh. *The novel is comic and tragic. ...a fine comic actor.* **[2]** N-C A **comic** is an entertainer who tells jokes in order to make people laugh. **[3]** N-C In British English, a **comic** is a magazine that contains stories told in pictures. The usual American term is **comic book**.

comical /'kɒmɪkəl/. ADJ If something is **comical**, it makes you want to laugh because it seems funny or silly. *Her expression is almost comical.*

'comic book, comic books. N-C A **comic book** is the same as a **comic**; AMERICAN.

coming /'kʌmɪŋ/. ADJ BEFORE N A **coming** event or time will happen soon. *...the weather in the coming months.*

comma /'kɒmə/ **commas.** N-C A **comma** is the punctuation mark (,).

command /kə'mɑːnd, -'mænd/ **commands, commanding, commanded.** **[1]** VERB & N-C If you **command** someone to do something, or if you give them a **command** to do it, you order them to do it. *'Get in your car and follow me,' he commanded... The tanker failed to respond to a command to stop.* **[2]** VERB If you **command** something such as obedience or attention, you obtain it as a result of being popular or important. *...an excellent physician who commanded the respect of all his colleagues.* **[3]** VERB & N-U An officer who **commands** part of an army, navy, or air force or has **command** of it, is in charge of it. *Who would command the troops in the event of war?... In 1942 he took command of 108 Squadron.* **[4]** N-U Your **command** of something is your knowledge of it and ability to use it. *...his excellent command of English.*

commandant /'kɒməndænt/ **commandants.** N-C A **commandant** is an army officer in charge of a particular place or group of people.

commander /kə'mɑːndə/ **commanders.** **[1]** N-C & N-TITLE A **commander** is an officer in charge of a military operation. **[2]** N-C & N-TITLE A **commander** is an officer in the navy.

commanding /kə'mɑːndɪŋ/. **[1]** ADJ If you are in a **commanding** position, you are in a strong or powerful position. *The French vessel has a commanding lead.* **[2]** ADJ If you have a **com-**

manding voice or manner, you seem powerful and confident. ...*his commanding presence.*

commando /kəˈmɑːndəʊ/ **commandos** (or **commandoes**). N-C **Commandos** are soldiers specially trained to carry out raids.

commemorate /kəˈmeməreɪt/ **commemorates, commemorating, commemorated.** VERB If you **commemorate** a person or event, you remember them by means of a special action or ceremony, or a specially created object. ...*a plaque commemorating the 169 Australians who died.* ◆**commemoration, commemorations** N-VAR ...*a service of commemoration.*

commemorative /kəˈmemərətɪv/. ADJ BEFORE N A **commemorative** object or event is intended to make people remember an event or person. ...*a commemorative plaque.*

commence /kəˈmens/ **commences, commencing, commenced.** VERB When something **commences**, or when you **commence** it, it begins; FORMAL. *He commenced laughing.* ◆**commencement** N-U ...*the subsequent commencement of oil and gas production.*

commend /kəˈmend/ **commends, commending, commended.** VERB If you **commend** someone or something, you praise them formally to other people. *I commended her for that action.* ◆**commendation, commendations** N-VAR ...*a letter of commendation.*

commendable /kəˈmendəbəl/. ADJ If you describe someone's behaviour as **commendable**, you approve of it; FORMAL. *Mr Sparrow has acted with commendable speed.* ◆**commendably** ADV *Her manner was commendably restrained.*

comment /ˈkɒment/ **comments, commenting, commented.** VERB & N-VAR If you **comment** on something, or if you make a **comment** on it, you give your opinion about it or make a statement about it. *Stuart commented that this was very true... He made his comments at a news conference.*

commentary /ˈkɒməntri, AM -teri/ **commentaries.** [1] N-VAR A **commentary** is a spoken description of an event that is broadcast on radio or television while it is taking place. *He turned on his car radio to listen to the commentary.* [2] N-C A **commentary** is a book or article which explains or discusses something. ...*a lengthy commentary on the situation in India.*

commentate /ˈkɒməntteɪt/ **commentates, commentating, commentated.** VERB To **commentate** means to give a radio or television commentary on an event. *They are in Sweden to commentate on the European Championships.*

commentator /ˈkɒməntteɪtə/ **commentators.** [1] N-C A **commentator** is a broadcaster who gives a commentary on an event. [2] N-C A **commentator** is someone who often writes or broadcasts about a particular subject. ...*Hugo Young, the political commentator of the Guardian.*

commerce /ˈkɒmɜːs/. N-U **Commerce** is the activity of buying and selling things on a large scale. *They have made their fortunes from industry and commerce.*

commercial /kəˈmɜːʃəl/ **commercials.** [1] ADJ **Commercial** means relating to the buying and selling of goods. ...*English commercial law.*

[2] ADJ **Commercial** activities, organizations, and products are concerned with making a profit. ...*the commercial exploitation of the forests.* ◆**commercially** ADV *About five more species are grown commercially.* [3] ADJ **Commercial** television and radio are paid for by advertising. [4] N-C A **commercial** is an advertisement broadcast on television or radio.

commission /kəˈmɪʃən/ **commissions, commissioning, commissioned.** [1] VERB & N-C If you **commission** a piece of work, or if you give someone a **commission** to do it, you formally arrange to pay for someone to do it to you. *A Japanese publishing house commissioned a book from me.* [2] N-VAR **Commission** is a sum of money paid to a salesperson for every sale that they make. *The adviser gets commission on every new policy sold.* [3] N-C A **commission** is a group of people appointed to find out about something or to control something. **Commission** can take the singular or plural form of the verb. ...*the Press Complaints Commission.* [4] VERB & N-C If a member of the armed forces is **commissioned**, or if they receive a **commission**, they are made an officer.

commissioner /kəˈmɪʃənə/ **commissioners.** N-C A **commissioner** is an important official in a government department or other organization. ...*the European Commissioner for External Affairs.*

commit /kəˈmɪt/ **commits, committing, committed.** [1] VERB If someone **commits** a crime or a sin, they do something illegal or bad. *They believe they know who committed the murder.* [2] VERB To **commit** money or resources to something means to use them for a particular purpose. ...*one of the first nations to commit forces to the Gulf.* [3] VERB If you **commit** yourself to a way of life or course of action, you accept it fully or definitely decide to do it. *Mary had committed herself to becoming a teacher.* ◆**commitment, commitments** N-VAR ...*commitment to the ideals of Bolshevism... They made a commitment to peace.* [4] VERB If someone **is committed** to a hospital or prison, they are officially sent there.

commitment /kəˈmɪtmənt/ **commitments.** N-C A **commitment** is a regular task which takes up some of your time. *I've got a lot of work commitments.*

committee /kəˈmɪti/ **committees.** N-C A **committee** is a group of people who represent a larger group or organization and make decisions for them. **Committee** can take the singular or plural form of the verb. ...*the Committee for Safety in Medicine.*

commodity /kəˈmɒdɪti/ **commodities.** N-C A **commodity** is something that is sold for money; TECHNICAL. ...*basic commodities like bread and meat.*

common /ˈkɒmən/ **commoner, commonest; commons.** [1] ADJ If something is **common**, it is found in large numbers or it happens often. ...*Hansen, a common name in Norway.* ...*a common mistake.* ◆**commonly** ADV *Parsley is probably the most commonly used of all herbs.* [2] ADJ If something is **common** to two or more people or groups, it is possessed, done, or used by them all. *Moldavians and Romanians share* *a common language.* **3** PHRASE If two or more people or things have the same interests, experiences, characteristics or features. **4** ADJ BEFORE N **Common** is used to indicate that something is ordinary and not special. *The scientific name for common salt is sodium chloride.* **5** ADJ If you describe someone as **common**, you mean they behave in a way that shows lack of taste, education, and good manners. **6** N-C A **common** is an area of grassy land where the public is allowed to go.

common 'law. **1** N-U **Common law** is the system of law which is based on judges' decisions and on custom rather than on written laws. **2** ADJ BEFORE N A **common law** relationship is regarded as a marriage because it has lasted a long time, although no official marriage contract has been signed. *...his common law wife.*

commonplace /ˈkɒmənpleɪs/. ADJ & N-C If something is **commonplace** or a **commonplace**, it happens often or is often found. *...a commonplace event. ...the sort of comment that has become a commonplace among conservatives.*

common 'sense (or **commonsense**). N-U **Common sense** is the natural ability to make good judgments and behave sensibly.

Commonwealth /ˈkɒmənwelθ/. N-PROPER The **Commonwealth** is an association of countries that used to belong to the British Empire.

commotion /kəˈməʊʃən/ **commotions.** N-VAR A **commotion** is a lot of noise and confusion. *I heard yelling and a lot of commotion.*

communal /ˈkɒmjʊnəl, AM kəˈmjuːnəl/. **1** ADJ BEFORE N **Communal** means relating to particular groups in a country or society. *...the communal violence in Sri Lanka.* **2** ADJ Something that is **communal** is shared by a group of people. *...communal ownership.*

commune /ˈkɒmjuːn/ **communes.** N-C A **commune** is a group of people who live together and share everything.

communicate /kəˈmjuːnɪkeɪt/ **communicates, communicating, communicated.** **1** VERB If you **communicate** with someone, you give them information, for example by speaking, writing, or sending radio signals. *They communicated in sign language.* ♦**communication** N-U *She has no means of communication.* **2** VERB If you **communicate** an idea or a feeling to someone, you make them aware of it. *I was having trouble communicating my feelings to others.* **3** VERB If you say that people are able to **communicate**, you mean they talk to each other openly, which allows them to understand each other's feelings or attitudes. *...the inability of husbands and wives to communicate.*

communication /kəˌmjuːnɪˈkeɪʃən/ **communications.** **1** N-PL **Communications** are the systems and processes that are used to communicate or broadcast information. *...a communications satellite.* **2** N-C A **communication** is a message that is sent to someone by, for example, sending a letter; FORMAL.

communion /kəˈmjuːnjən/. **1** N-U **Communion** is the Christian ceremony in which people

eat bread and drink wine as a symbol of Christ's death and resurrection. **2** N-U **Communion** with nature or some other power or spirit, or **communion** with a person is the feeling that you are sharing thoughts or feelings with them.

communiqué /kəˈmjuːnɪkeɪ, AM -ˈkeɪ/ **communiqués.** N-C A **communiqué** is an official statement. *...the joint communique, issued by China and Saudi Arabia.*

communist /ˈkɒmjʊnɪst/ **communists.** N-C & ADJ A **communist** is someone who supports a political system in which the state controls the means of production, and everyone is supposed to be equal. *...communist rebels.* ♦**communism** N-U *...the collapse of communism in Eastern Europe.*

community /kəˈmjuːnɪti/ **communities.** **1** N-SING & N-C A **community** is a group of people who live in a particular area or are alike in some way. *The event was well supported by the local community. ...the business community.* **2** N-U **Community** is friendship between different people or groups, and a sense of having something in common. **Community** can take the singular or plural form of the verb. *...a neighbourhood which has no sense of community.*

com'munity centre, community centres. N-C A **community centre** is a place where the people, groups, and organizations in a particular area can go and meet one another and do things.

com,munity 'service. N-U **Community service** is unpaid work that criminals sometimes do as a punishment instead of being sent to prison. *He was sentenced to 140 hours community service.*

commute /kəˈmjuːt/ **commutes, commuting, commuted.** **1** VERB If you **commute**, you travel a long distance to work every day. ♦**commuter, commuters** N-C *The number of commuters to London has dropped by 100,000.* **2** VERB If a prisoner's sentence **is commuted**, it is changed to a less serious sentence.

compact /kəmˈpækt/ **compacts, compacting, compacted.** **1** ADJ Something that is **compact** is small or takes up very little space. *...a compact camera.* **2** VERB To **compact** something means to press it so that it becomes more dense; FORMAL. *The boy was compacting the trash. ...a pile of compacted earth.*

compact disc /ˌkɒmpækt ˈdɪsk/ **compact discs.** N-C **Compact discs** are small discs on which sound, especially music, is recorded. The abbreviation 'CD' is also used.

companion /kəmˈpænjən/ **companions.** N-C A **companion** is someone who you spend time with or travel with. *He has been her constant companion for the last four months.*

companionship /kəmˈpænjənʃɪp/. N-U **Companionship** is having someone you know and like with you, rather than being on your own. *I was glad of her companionship.*

company /ˈkʌmpəni/ **companies.** **1** N-C A **company** is a business organization that makes money by selling goods or services. *...an insurance company.* **2** N-C A **company** is a group of opera singers, dancers, actors, or other performers who work together. **3** N-U **Company** is the state of having companionship. *'I won't stay long.'—'No, please. I need the company'.* **4** PHRASE If you **keep** someone **company**, you spend time with them and stop them feeling lonely or bored. *Why don't you stay here and keep Emma company?*

comparable /ˈkɒmpərəbəl/. **1** ADJ Something that is **comparable** to something is roughly similar, for example in amount or importance. *Farmers were meant to get an income comparable to that of townspeople.* ♦**comparably** ADV *...comparably qualified students.* **2** ADJ If two or more things are **comparable**, they are similar and so can be reasonably compared. *In other comparable countries real wages increased much more rapidly.* ♦**comparability** N-U *...comparability between the accounts of similar companies.*

comparative /kəmˈpærətɪv/ **comparatives.** **1** ADJ You use **comparative** to show that your description of something is accurate only when it is compared to something else, or to what is usual. *He met the higher demands with comparative ease.* ♦**comparatively** ADV *...a comparatively small nation.* **2** ADJ BEFORE N A **comparative** study involves the comparison of two or more things of the same kind. *...the comparative study of English and Latin authors.* **3** N-C & ADJ BEFORE N In grammar, the **comparative** or the **comparative** form of an adjective or adverb is used to indicate that something has more of a quality than it used to have or than something else has. For example, 'bigger' is the comparative form of 'big'. ● Compare **superlative**.

compare /kəmˈpeə/ **compares, comparing, compared.** **1** VERB If you **compare** things, you consider them and discover the differences or similarities between them. *Compare the two illustrations in Fig 60.* **2** VERB If you **compare** one person or thing to another, you say that they are like the other person or thing. *Some commentators compared his work to that of James Joyce.*

compared /kəmˈpeəd/. PREP You can use **compared with** and **compared to** when you want to contrast two things or situations. For example, if you say that one thing is large compared with another or compared to another, you mean that it is larger than the other thing.

comparison /kəmˈpærɪsən/ **comparisons.** **1** N-VAR When you make a **comparison** between two or more things, you consider them and discover the differences between them. *...a comparison of the British and German economies.* **2** N-VAR When you make a **comparison**, you say that one thing is like another in some way. *...the comparison of her life to a sea voyage.*

compartment /kəmˈpɑːtmənt/ **compartments.** **1** N-C A **compartment** is one of the separate sections of a railway carriage. **2** N-C A **compartment** is one of the separate parts of an object that is used for keeping things in. *I put a bottle of champagne in the freezer compartment.*

compass /ˈkʌmpəs/ **compasses.** **1** N-C A **compass** is an instrument that you use for

finding directions. It has a dial and a magnetic needle that always points to the north. **2** N-PL **Compasses** are a hinged V-shaped instrument that you use for drawing circles accurately. *...a pair of compasses.*

compassion /kəmˈpæʃən/. N-U **Compassion** is a feeling of pity, sympathy, and understanding for people who are suffering. *...his compassion and concern for a helpless woman.*

compassionate /kəmˈpæʃənət/. ADJ A **compassionate** person feels pity, sympathy, and understanding for people who are suffering. *...a deeply compassionate man.* ♦**compassionately** ADV *He smiled compassionately at her.*

compatible /kəmˈpætɪbəl/. **1** ADJ If things, systems, or ideas are **compatible**, they work well together or can exist together successfully. *His evidence is fully compatible with other data.* ♦**compatibility** N-U *...compatibility with VHS video recorders.* **2** ADJ If you are **compatible** with someone, you have a good relationship with them because you have similar opinions and interests. ♦**compatibility** N-U *The basis of friendship is compatibility.*

compatriot /kəmˈpætriət, AM -ˈpeɪt-/ **compatriots.** N-C Your **compatriots** are people from your own country.

compel /kəmˈpel/ **compels, compelling, compelled.** VERB If a situation, a rule, or a person **compels** you to do something, they force you to do it. *...legislation to compel cyclists to wear a helmet.*

compelling /kəmˈpelɪŋ/. ADJ A **compelling** argument or reason for something convinces you that something is true or that something should be done. *...a compelling reason to spend money.*

compensate /ˈkɒmpənseɪt/ **compensates, compensating, compensated.** **1** VERB If someone **is compensated** for something unpleasant which has happened to them, they receive compensation for it. *The allied nations want Iraq to compensate victims of the war.* **2** VERB To **compensate** for something, especially something harmful or unwanted, means to do something which balances it or makes it ineffective. *The built-in safety device compensates for a fall in water pressure.*

compensation /ˌkɒmpənˈseɪʃən/ **compensations.** **1** N-U **Compensation** is money that someone who has undergone loss or suffering claims from the person or organization responsible. *He received one year's salary as compensation.* **2** N-VAR If something is a **compensation**, it reduces the effects of something bad that has happened. *Helen gained some compensation for her earlier defeat by winning the final open class.*

compete /kəmˈpiːt/ **competes, competing, competed.** **1** VERB If one person or organization **competes** with another for something, they try to get that thing for themselves and stop the other getting it. *Local residents fear competing with foreigners for jobs.* **2** VERB If you **compete** in a contest or a game, you take part in it. *Eight entrants competed for prizes totalling $1000.*

competent /'kɒmpɪtənt/. ADJ Someone who is **competent** is efficient and effective. *He was a very competent civil servant.* ♦**competently** ADV *The government performed competently.* ♦**competence** N-U *They have a high level of competence.*

competition /ˌkɒmpɪ'tɪʃən/ **competitions.** [1] N-U **Competition** is a situation in which two or more people or groups are trying to get something which not everyone can have. *There's been some fierce competition for the title.* [2] N-VAR A **competition** is an event in which people take part in order to find out who is best at a particular activity. *...a surfing competition.*

competitive /kəm'petɪtɪv/. [1] ADJ **Competitive** situations or activities are ones in which people compete with each other. *We are working in a very competitive market.* ♦**competitively** ADV *...skiing competitively.* [2] ADJ A **competitive** person is eager to be more successful than other people. *...ambitious and fiercely competitive.* ♦**competitively** ADV *They worked hard together, competitively and under pressure.* ♦**competitiveness** N-U *I can't stand the pace, I suppose, and the competitiveness.* [3] ADJ You can say goods or services are at a **competitive** price or rate when they are less expensive than other goods of the same kind. ♦**competitively** ADV *...competitively priced vehicles.*

competitor /kəm'petɪtə/ **competitors.** [1] N-C A company's **competitors** are other companies that sell similar kinds of goods or services. *The bank isn't performing as well as some of its competitors.* [2] N-C A **competitor** is a person who takes part in a competition.

compilation /ˌkɒmpɪ'leɪʃən/ **compilations.** N-C A **compilation** is a record containing music from many different artists or music from different periods of one artist's career. *...a compilation of his jazz works over the past decade.*

compile /kəm'paɪl/ **compiles, compiling, compiled.** VERB To **compile** something such as a book, report, or TV programme, you produce it by putting together pieces of information. *Councils were required to compile a register of all adults living in their areas.* ♦**compilation** /ˌkɒmpɪ'leɪʃən/ N-U *...the compilation of data.*

complacent /kəm'pleɪsənt/. ADJ If someone is **complacent** about something like a threat or danger, they behave as if there is nothing to worry about. *We cannot afford to be complacent about our health.* ♦**complacency** /kəm'pleɪsənsi/ N-U *...complacency about the risks of infection from AIDS.* ♦**complacently** ADV *...smiling complacently at his own cleverness.*

complain /kəm'pleɪn/ **complains, complaining, complained.** [1] VERB If you **complain** about something, you say you are not satisfied with it. *People always complain that the big banks are unfriendly and unhelpful... They are liable to face more mistreatment if they complain to the police.* [2] VERB If you **complain** of a pain or illness, you say you have it.

complaint /kəm'pleɪnt/ **complaints.** [1] N-VAR A **complaint** is a statement of dissatisfaction about a situation or a reason for it. *...com-plaints about the standard of service on Britain's railways.* [2] N-C A **complaint** is an illness. *Eczema is a common skin complaint.*

complement, complements, complementing, complemented. [1] VERB /'kɒmplɪment/ If people or things **complement** each other, they have different qualities which go well together. *Choose a superb wine to complement your meal. ...a written examination to complement the practical test.* [2] N-C /'kɒmplɪmənt/ Something that is a **complement** to something else complements it. *The green wallpaper is the perfect complement to the old pine.* [3] N-C In grammar, the **complement** of a link verb is an adjective group or noun group which comes after the verb and describes or identifies the subject. For example, in the sentence 'They felt very tired', 'very tired' is the complement.

complementary /ˌkɒmplɪ'mentri/. ADJ If two different things are **complementary**, they form a complete unit when they are brought together, or they combine well with each other. *The two groups had complementary skills.*

complete /kəm'pliːt/ **completes, completing, completed.** [1] ADJ If something is **complete**, it contains all the parts that it should contain. *No garden is complete without a bed of rose bushes. ...a complete set of keys to the shop.* [2] ADJ You use **complete** to emphasize that something is as great in degree or amount as it possibly can be. *The resignation came as a complete surprise.* ♦**completely** ADV *Dozens of flats had been completely destroyed.* [3] VERB If you **complete** something, you finish doing or producing it. *Peter Mayle has just completed his first novel.* ♦**completion** N-U *The project is nearing completion.* [4] ADJ AFTER V-LINK If a task is **complete**, it is finished. *The work of restoring the farmhouse is complete.* [5] VERB To **complete** a set or group means to provide the last item that is needed to make it a full set or group. *Put a word in each space to complete the sentence.* [6] VERB To **complete** a form means to write the necessary information on it. [7] PHRASE If one thing comes **complete with** another, it has that thing as an extra or additional part. *The diary comes complete with a gold-coloured ballpoint pen.*

complex /'kɒmpleks/ **complexes.** [1] ADJ **Complex** things have many different parts and are hard to understand. *...a complex system of voting. ...her complex personality. ...complex machines.* [2] N-C A **complex** is a group of buildings used for a particular purpose. *...a new stadium and leisure complex.* [3] N-C If someone has a **complex** about something, they have a mental or emotional problem relating to it, often because of an unpleasant experience in the past. *I have never had a complex about my height.*

complexion /kəm'plekʃən/ **complexions.** N-C Your **complexion** is the natural colour or condition of the skin on your face. *He had a pale complexion.*

complexity /kəm'pleksɪti/ **complexities.** N-VAR **Complexity** is the state of having many different parts connected or related to each other in a complicated way. *...the increasing* *complexity of modern weapon systems. ...legal complexities.*

compliance /kəmˈplaɪəns/. N-U **Compliance** with something, for example a law or agreement, means doing what you are required or expected to do; FORMAL. *The company says it is in full compliance with US labor laws.*

complicate /ˈkɒmplɪkeɪt/ **complicates, complicating, complicated.** VERB To **complicate** something means to make it more difficult to deal with or understand. *You have enough worries without me complicating matters.*

complicated /ˈkɒmplɪkeɪtɪd/. ADJ Something that is **complicated** has many parts and is therefore difficult to understand. *...the complicated voting system.*

complication /ˌkɒmplɪˈkeɪʃən/ **complications.** N-C A **complication** is a problem or difficulty. *The age difference was a complication to the relationship.*

complicity /kəmˈplɪsɪti/. N-U **Complicity** is involvement with other people in an illegal activity; FORMAL. *Recently a number of policemen were sentenced to death for their complicity in the murder.*

compliment, compliments, complimenting, complimented; verb /ˈkɒmplɪmənt/, noun /ˈkɒmplɪmənt/. [1] VERB & N-C If you **compliment** someone, or if you pay them a **compliment**, you say something nice about them. *They complimented me on the way I looked.* [2] N-PL **Compliments** is used in expressing good wishes or respect; FORMAL. *My compliments to the chef.*

complimentary /ˌkɒmplɪˈmentəri/. [1] ADJ If you are **complimentary** about something, you express admiration for it. *We often get complimentary remarks regarding the cleanliness of our patio.* [2] ADJ A **complimentary** seat, ticket, or book is given to you free.

comply /kəmˈplaɪ/ **complies, complying, complied.** VERB If you **comply** with a demand or rule, you do what you are required to do; FORMAL. *There are calls for his resignation, but there is no sign yet that he will comply.*

component /kəmˈpəʊnənt/ **components.** N-C The **components** of something are its parts. *The management plan has four main components.*

compose /kəmˈpəʊz/ **composing, composed.** [1] VERB The things that something **is composed of** are its parts or members. The separate things that **compose** something are the parts or members that form it. *The force would be composed of troops from NATO countries... Protein molecules compose all the complex working parts of living cells.* [2] VERB When someone **composes** music, a speech, or a letter, they write it. [3] VERB If you **compose** yourself, you become calm after being angry or excited. ♦**composed** ADJ *Laura was standing beside him, very calm and composed.*

composer /kəmˈpəʊzə/ **composers.** N-C A **composer** is a person who writes music.

composition /ˌkɒmpəˈzɪʃən/ **compositions.** [1] N-U The **composition** of something is the things that it consists of and the way that they are arranged. *Forests vary greatly in composi-*

tion. [2] N-C A **composition** is a piece of written work, especially one that children write at school. [3] N-C A composer's **compositions** are the pieces of music he or she has written.

compost /ˈkɒmpɒst, AM -pəʊst/. N-U **Compost** is a mixture of decaying plants and manure which is used to improve soil. *...a small compost heap.*

composure /kəmˈpəʊʒə/. N-U Someone's **composure** is their appearance or feeling of calm and their control of their feelings, often in a difficult situation; FORMAL.

compound, compounds, compounding, compounded; noun and adjective /ˈkɒmpaʊnd/, verb /kəmˈpaʊnd/. [1] N-C A **compound** is an enclosed area of land used for a particular purpose. *...a military compound.* [2] N-C In chemistry, a **compound** is a substance consisting of two or more elements. [3] ADJ BEFORE N In grammar, a **compound** noun, adjective, or verb is made up of two or more words, for example 'fire engine'. [4] VERB To **compound** a problem means to make it worse by increasing it in some way; FORMAL. *Additional bloodshed and loss of life will only compound the tragedy.*

comprehend /ˌkɒmprɪˈhend/ **comprehends, comprehending, comprehended.** VERB If you cannot **comprehend** something, you cannot understand it; FORMAL. *Whenever she failed to comprehend she invariably laughed.*

comprehension /ˌkɒmprɪˈhenʃən/ **comprehensions.** [1] N-U **Comprehension** is the ability to understand something or the process of understanding something. *This was utterly beyond her comprehension... They turned to one another with the same expression of dawning comprehension.* [2] N-VAR A **comprehension** is an exercise to find out how well you understand a piece of text.

comprehensive /ˌkɒmprɪˈhensɪv/ **comprehensives.** [1] ADJ Something that is **comprehensive** includes everything necessary or relevant. *...a comprehensive guide to the region.* ♦**comprehensively** ADV *The book is comprehensively illustrated.* [2] ADJ BEFORE N & N-C In Britain, a **comprehensive** school or a **comprehensive** is where children of all abilities are taught together.

compress /kəmˈpres/ **compresses, compressing, compressed.** VERB If you **compress** something, or if it **compresses**, it is pressed or squeezed so that it takes up less space. *Compressing a gas heats it up... As air in the lungs compresses, the flexible ribs contract.* ♦**compression** /kəmˈpreʃən/ N-U *The compression of the wood is easily achieved.*

comprise /kəmˈpraɪz/ **comprises, comprising, comprised.** VERB If something **comprises** or **is comprised of** a number of things or people, it has them as its parts or members; FORMAL. *The exhibition comprises 50 oils and watercolours.*

compromise /ˈkɒmprəmaɪz/ **compromises, compromising, compromised.** N-VAR & VERB If you reach a **compromise** with someone or if you **compromise** with them, you reach an agreement whereby you both give up something that you originally wanted. *...the govern-*

ment's policy of compromise... He would be prepared to compromise on his original demands... Make an effort to compromise with colleagues. [2] VERB If someone **compromises** themselves or their beliefs, they do something which causes people to doubt their honesty, loyalty, or moral principles. He would rather shoot himself than compromise his principles.

compromising /'kɒmprəmaɪzɪŋ/. ADJ If you describe information or a situation as **compromising**, you mean that it reveals an embarrassing or guilty secret about someone. ...compromising photographs.

compulsion /kəm'pʌlʃən/ **compulsions**. [1] N-C A **compulsion** is a strong desire to do something. He felt a sudden compulsion to drop the bucket and run. [2] N-U If someone uses **compulsion** to make you do something, they force you to do it. They were in classes out of choice rather than compulsion.

compulsive /kəm'pʌlsɪv/. [1] ADJ BEFORE N You use **compulsive** to describe people who cannot stop doing something. ...a compulsive liar. ◆**compulsively** ADV John is compulsively neat and clean. [2] ADJ If you say a book is **compulsive** reading or a film is **compulsive** viewing, you find it so interesting that you do not want to stop reading the book or watching the film; BRITISH.

compulsory /kəm'pʌlsəri/. ADJ If something is **compulsory**, you must do it because a law or someone in authority says you must. In East Germany learning Russian was compulsory.

computer /kəm'pjuːtə/ **computers**. N-C A **computer** is an electronic machine which makes quick calculations and deals with large amounts of information.

computerize (BR also **computerise**) /kəm'pjuːtəraɪz/ **computerizes, computerizing, computerized.** VERB To **computerize** a system or type of work means to introduce computers into it. ◆**computerized** ADJ Organizations can access computerized data banks to search for information.

computing /kəm'pjuːtɪŋ/. N-U **Computing** is the activity of using a computer and writing programs for it.

comrade /'kɒmreɪd, AM -ræd/ **comrades**. N-C Someone's **comrades** are their friends or companions; LITERARY.

con /kɒn/ **cons, conning, conned.** VERB & N-C If someone **cons** you, or if what they do is a **con**, they trick you into doing or believing something by saying things that are not true; INFORMAL. The businessman had conned him of £10,000... It was all a con. ● **pros and cons**: see **pro.**

conceal /kən'siːl/ **conceals, concealing, concealed.** VERB To **conceal** something means to hide it or keep it secret. The hat concealed her hair... She knew at once that he was concealing something from her. ◆**concealment** N-U ...the concealment of weapons.

concede /kən'siːd/ **concedes, conceding, conceded.** VERB If you **concede** something, you admit it or accept that it is true, often unwillingly. Bess finally conceded that Nancy was right... 'Well,' he conceded, 'I do sometimes mumble a bit'.

conceivable /kən'siːvəbəl/. ADJ If something is **conceivable**, you can imagine it or believe it. It is just conceivable that a single survivor might be found. ◆**conceivably** ADV The mission could conceivably be accomplished within a week.

conceive /kən'siːv/ **conceives, conceiving, conceived.** [1] VERB If you cannot **conceive** of something, you cannot imagine it or believe it. He couldn't conceive of anyone arguing with his results. [2] VERB If you **conceive** a plan or idea, you think of it and work out how it can be done. He conceived the idea of making a photographic study of German society. ◆**conception** /kən'sepʃən/ N-U The symphony is admirable in conception. [3] VERB When a woman **conceives**, she becomes pregnant. ◆**conception, conceptions.** N-VAR Six weeks after conception your baby is the size of your little fingernail. [4] See also **conception.**

concentrate /'kɒnsəntreɪt/ **concentrates, concentrating, concentrated.** [1] VERB If you **concentrate** on something, you give it all your attention. He sat back and concentrated on his driving... At work you need to be able to concentrate. [2] VERB When something **is concentrated** in one place, it is all there rather than being spread around. The high-status jobs were increasingly concentrated in the big cities.

concentrated /'kɒnsəntreɪtɪd/. [1] ADJ A **concentrated** liquid has been increased in strength by having water removed from it. [2] ADJ A **concentrated** activity is done with great intensity in one place. ...a more concentrated effort to reach out to troubled kids.

concentration /ˌkɒnsən'treɪʃən/ **concentrations.** [1] N-U **Concentration** on something involves giving all your attention to it. We lacked concentration and it cost us the goal. [2] N-VAR A **concentration** of something is a large amount of it or large numbers of it in a small area. ...one of the world's greatest concentrations of wildlife.

concen'tration camp, concentration camps. N-C A **concentration camp** is a prison where non-military prisoners are kept in very bad conditions, usually in wartime.

concept /'kɒnsept/ **concepts.** N-C A **concept** is an idea or abstract principle. ...the concept of arranged marriages. ◆**conceptual** /kən'septʃuəl/ ADJ BEFORE N ...the conceptual framework for this evaluation.

conception /kən'sepʃən/ **conceptions.** [1] N-VAR A **conception** is an idea that you have in your mind. ...someone with not the slightest conception of teamwork. [2] See also **conceive.**

concern /kən'sɜːn/ **concerns, concerning, concerned.** [1] N-U **Concern** is worry about a situation. There is no cause for concern. [2] VERB If something **concerns** you, it worries you. It concerns me that we're not being told about this. ◆**concerned** ADJ I've been concerned about you lately. [3] N-C A **concern** is a fact or situation that worries you. Unemployment was the electorate's main concern. [4] VERB If you **concern** yourself with something, you give attention to it because you think that it is important. I didn't concern myself with politics. [5] N-U Your **concern** for someone is a feeling that you want them to be happy, safe, and well. He had only gone along out of concern for his two grandsons. **6** VERB If a book, speech, or piece of information **concerns** a particular subject, it is about that subject. *Chapter 2 concerns itself with the methodological difficulties.* ◆**concerned** ADJ AFTER LINK-V *Randolph's work was exclusively concerned with the effects of pollution.* **7** VERB If a situation, event, or activity **concerns** you, it affects you or involves you. *'That doesn't concern you,' Zlotin retorted sharply.* ◆**concerned** ADJ *It's a very stressful situation for everyone concerned.* **8** N-SING If a situation or problem is your **concern**, it is your duty or responsibility. *The technical aspects were the concern of the Army.* **9** N-C A **concern** is a company or business. *The Minos Beach Hotel is a family concern.*

PHRASES ● You say **as far as** something **is concerned** to indicate the subject that you are talking about. *As far as my career was concerned, the affair did me more good than harm.* ● You say **as far as I'm concerned** to indicate that you are giving your own opinion. *The only problem, as far as I'm concerned, is Iris.*

concerning /kən'sɜːnɪŋ/. PREP You use **concerning** to indicate what a question or piece of information is about. *...various questions concerning pollution and the environment.*

concert /'kɒnsət/ **concerts.** N-C A **concert** is a performance of music. *...live rock concerts.*

concerted /kən'sɜːtɪd/. **1** ADJ A **concerted** action is done by several people or groups working together. *...a concerted attack on poverty.* **2** ADJ If you make a **concerted** effort to do something, you try very hard to do it. *I'm going to make a concerted effort to write more letters.*

concerto /kən'tʃeətəʊ/ **concertos.** N-C A **concerto** is a piece of music for a solo instrument and an orchestra.

concession /kən'seʃən/ **concessions.** N-C If you make a **concession** to someone, you agree to let them do or have something, especially in order to end an argument or conflict. *He has refused to make any concessions to the kidnappers.*

conciliation /kən,sɪli'eɪʃən/. N-U **Conciliation** is trying to end a disagreement. *...a mood of conciliation.*

conciliatory /kən'sɪliətri, AM -tɔːri/. ADJ If you are **conciliatory** in your actions or behaviour, you show you are willing to end a disagreement with someone. *...a conciliatory gesture.*

concise /kən'saɪs/. ADJ Something that is **concise** gives all the necessary information in a very brief form. *Burton's text is concise and informative.* ◆**concisely** ADV *He'd delivered his report clearly and concisely.*

conclude /kən'kluːd/ **concludes, concluding, concluded.** **1** VERB If you **conclude** that something is true, you decide that it is true using the facts you know. *He concluded that Oswald was somewhat abnormal... What can we conclude from this debate?* **2** VERB When you **conclude** something, or when it **concludes**, it finishes; FORMAL. *I would like to conclude by saying that I do enjoy your magazine... The evening concluded with dinner and speeches.* **3** VERB If people or groups **conclude**

a treaty or business deal, they arrange it or agree it; FORMAL.

conclusion /kən'kluːʒən/ **conclusions.** **1** N-C When you come to a **conclusion**, you decide that something is true after you have thought about it carefully. *I've come to the conclusion that she's a very great musician... Other people will no doubt draw their own conclusions.* **2** N-SING The **conclusion** of something is its ending. **3** PHRASE You can describe something that seems certain to happen as a **foregone conclusion**. **4** PHRASE You say **'in conclusion'** to introduce the last thing that you want to say. *In conclusion, walking is a cheap, safe, enjoyable and readily available form of exercise.*

conclusive /kən'kluːsɪv/. ADJ **Conclusive** evidence shows that something is definitely true. *There is no conclusive proof that this is harmful.* ◆**conclusively** ADV *A new study proved conclusively that smokers die younger than non-smokers.*

concoct /kən'kɒkt/ **concocts, concocting, concocted.** **1** VERB If you **concoct** an excuse, you invent one. *The prisoner concocted the story to get a lighter sentence.* **2** VERB If you **concoct** something, especially something unusual, you make it by mixing several things together. *Eugene was concocting Rossini Cocktails.*

concoction /kən'kɒkʃən/ **concoctions.** N-C A **concoction** is something that has been made out of several things mixed together. *...a concoction of honey, yogurt, oats, and apples.*

concrete /'kɒŋkriːt/. **1** N-U **Concrete** is a substance used for building. It is made from cement, sand, small stones, and water. **2** ADJ Something that is **concrete** is definite and specific. *He had no concrete evidence.*

concur /kən'kɜː/ **concurs, concurring, concurred.** VERB If two or more people **concur**, they agree; FORMAL. *Local feeling does not necessarily concur with the press.*

concurrent /kən'kʌrənt, AM -'kɜːr-/. ADJ If two things are **concurrent**, they happen at the same time. *He will actually be serving three concurrent five-year sentences.* ◆**concurrently** ADV *There were three races running concurrently.*

concussion /kən'kʌʃən/. N-U If you suffer **concussion** after a blow to your head, you lose consciousness or feel sick or confused.

condemn /kən'dem/ **condemns, condemning, condemned.** **1** VERB If you **condemn** something, you say that it is bad and unacceptable. *Mr Davies condemned the fee increase.* ◆**condemnation** /,kɒndem'neɪʃən/ **condemnations** N-VAR *There was widespread condemnation of Saturday's killings.* **2** VERB If someone **is condemned** to a punishment, they are given it. *He was condemned to life imprisonment.* **3** VERB If authorities **condemn** a building, they officially decide that it is not safe and must be pulled down.

condemned /kən'demd/. ADJ A **condemned** prisoner is going to be executed. *...a condemned man's last request.*

condense /kən'dens/ **condenses, condensing, condensed.** **1** VERB If you **condense** a piece of writing or speech, you make it shorter. *...how to condense serious messages into short,* *self-contained sentences.* [2] VERB When a gas or vapour **condenses**, or when you **condense** it, it changes into a liquid.

condescend /ˌkɒndɪ'send/ **condescends, condescending, condescended.** [1] VERB If you say that someone **condescends** to do something, you disapprove of them because they agree to do it in a way which shows that they think they are superior to other people and should not have to do it. *He wouldn't condescend to talk to the nurse.* [2] VERB If you say that someone **condescends** to other people, you disapprove of them because they behave in a way which shows that they think they are superior to other people. *Don't condescend to me.* ◆**condescending** ADJ ...*his condescending attitude.* ◆**condescension** /ˌkɒndɪ'senʃən/ N-U ...*a smile of condescension.*

condition /kən'dɪʃən/ **conditions, conditioning, conditioned.** [1] N-SING The **condition** of someone or something is the state they are in. *He remains in a critical condition in a California hospital... The boat is in good condition.* [2] N-PL The **conditions** in which people live or do things are the factors that affect their comfort, safety, or success. *People are living in appalling conditions. ...the adverse weather conditions.* [3] N-C A **condition** is something which must happen in order for something else to be possible. *One of the conditions of our release was that we had to leave the country immediately.* [4] PHRASE When you agree to do something **on condition that** something else happens, you mean that you will only do it if this other thing happens or is agreed to first. *He spoke to reporters on condition that he was not identified.* [5] N-C You can refer to an illness or medical problem as a particular **condition**. ...*a heart condition.* [6] VERB If someone **is conditioned** to think or do something in a particular way, they do it as a result of their upbringing or training. *You have been conditioned to believe that it is weak to be scared.* ◆**conditioning** N-U ...*social conditioning.*

conditional /kən'dɪʃənl/. ADJ If a situation or agreement is **conditional** on something, it will only happen if this thing happens. *Their support is conditional on his proposals meeting their approval. ...a conditional offer.*

condolence /kən'dəʊləns/ **condolences.** N-PL & N-U When you offer your **condolences**, or when you send a message of **condolence**, you express sympathy for someone whose friend or relative has died recently.

condom /'kɒndəm/ **condoms.** N-C A **condom** is a rubber covering which a man wears on his penis as a contraceptive.

condone /kən'dəʊn/ **condones, condoning, condoned.** VERB If someone **condones** behaviour that is wrong, they accept it and allow it to happen. *I cannot condone violence.*

conducive /kən'dju:sɪv, AM -'du:sɪv/. ADJ If one thing is **conducive** to another, it makes the other thing likely to happen. *Make your bedroom as conducive to sleep as possible.*

conduct **conducts, conducting, conducted;** verb /kən'dʌkt/, noun /'kɒndʌkt/. [1] VERB & N-SING When you **conduct** an activity or task, you organize it and do it. You can also talk

about the **conduct** of an activity or task. *I decided to conduct an experiment. ...the conduct of free and fair elections.* [2] N-U & VERB Your **conduct**, or the way you **conduct** yourself, is the way you behave. ...*basic principles of civilised conduct... The way he conducts himself reflects on the party.* [3] VERB When someone **conducts** an orchestra or choir, they stand in front of it and direct its performance. *Solti will continue to conduct here and abroad.* ◆**conductor, conductors** N-C ...*several hundred musicians and their conductor.* [4] VERB If something **conducts** heat or electricity, it allows heat or electricity to pass through it.

cone /kəʊn/ **cones.** [1] N-C A **cone** is a shape with a circular base and smooth curved sides ending in a point at the top. [2] N-C A **cone** is the fruit of a pine or fir tree. It consists of a cluster of scales containing seeds.

confederation /kənˌfedə'reɪʃən/ **confederations.** N-C A **confederation** is an organization of groups or states, especially one that exists for political or business purposes. ...*a confederation of independent republics.*

confer /kən'fɜ:/ **confers, conferring, conferred.** [1] VERB When you **confer** with someone, you discuss something with them in order to make a decision. *He conferred with Hill... His doctors conferred by telephone.* [2] VERB If someone or something **confers** power or honour on you, they give it to you. *Never imagine that rank confers genuine authority.*

conference /'kɒnfrəns/ **conferences.** N-C A **conference** is a meeting, often lasting a few days, which is organized on a particular subject. ...*a conference on education. ...the Conservative Party conference.*

confess /kən'fes/ **confesses, confessing, confessed.** VERB If you **confess** to doing something wrong or something that you are ashamed of, you admit that you did it. *He had confessed to seventeen murders... Ed later confessed that he was worried the whole time.*

confession /kən'feʃən/ **confessions.** [1] N-C A **confession** is a signed statement by someone in which they admit that they have committed a particular crime. *They forced him to sign a confession.* [2] N-VAR **Confession** is the act of admitting that you have done something that you are ashamed of or embarrassed about. *I have a confession to make.*

confide /kən'faɪd/ **confides, confiding, confided.** VERB If you **confide** in someone, you tell them a secret. *She had confided in me a year earlier... He confided to me that he felt like he was being punished.*

confidence /'kɒnfɪdəns/ **confidences.** [1] N-U If you have **confidence** in someone, you feel you can trust them. *I have every confidence in you.* [2] N-U If you have **confidence**, you feel sure about your abilities, qualities, or ideas. *The team was full of confidence.* [3] N-U If you tell someone something in **confidence**, you tell them a secret. *We told you all these things in confidence.* [4] N-C A **confidence** is a secret that you tell someone.

confident /'kɒnfɪdənt/. [1] ADJ If you are **confident** about something, you are certain that it will happen in the way you want it to. *I'm con-*

fident that we will succeed. ♦ **confidently** ADV *I can confidently promise that this year is going to be very different.* [2] ADJ People who are **confident** feel sure of their own abilities, qualities, or ideas. *In time he became more confident and relaxed.* ♦ **confidently** ADV *She walked confidently across the hall.*

confidential /ˌkɒnfɪˈdenʃəl/. ADJ Information that is **confidential** is meant to be kept secret. *...confidential information about her private life.* ♦ **confidentially** ADV *Any information they give will be treated confidentially.* ♦ **confidentiality** N-U *...the confidentiality of the client-solicitor relationship.*

configuration /kənˌfɪgʊˈreɪʃən, AM -ˌfɪgjə-/ **configurations.** N-C A **configuration** is an arrangement of a group of things; FORMAL. *...an ancient configuration of giant stones.*

confine, confines, confining, confined. [1] VERB /kənˈfaɪn/ To **confine** something or someone to a particular place or group means to prevent them from spreading beyond it or from leaving it. *The US will soon be taking steps to confine the conflict... The army and police had been confined to barracks.* ♦ **confinement** N-U *...his confinement to a wheelchair.* [2] VERB If you **confine** yourself to something, you do only that thing. *Yoko had largely confined her activities to the world of big business.* [3] N-PL /ˈkɒnfaɪnz/ The **confines** of a building or area are its boundaries; FORMAL. *The movie is set entirely within the confines of the abandoned factory.*

confined /kənˈfaɪnd/. [1] ADJ AFTER LINK-V If something is **confined to** a particular place or group, it exists only there. *The problem is not confined to Germany.* [2] ADJ A **confined** space or area is small and enclosed by walls.

confirm /kənˈfɜːm/ **confirms, confirming, confirmed.** [1] VERB If something **confirms** what you believe, it shows that it is definitely true. *X-rays have confirmed that he has not broken any bones... These new statistics confirm our worst fears.* ♦ **confirmation** /ˌkɒnfəˈmeɪʃən/ N-U *Rejections are simply confirmation of what they thought all along.* [2] VERB If you **confirm** something that has been stated or suggested, you say that it is definitely true. *The spokesman confirmed that the area was now in rebel hands.* ♦ **confirmation** N-U *She glanced over at James for confirmation.* [3] VERB If you **confirm** an arrangement or appointment, you make it definite. *You make the reservation, and I'll confirm it in writing.* ♦ **confirmation** N-U *Travel arrangements are subject to confirmation.*

confiscate /ˈkɒnfɪskeɪt/ **confiscates, confiscating, confiscated.** VERB If you **confiscate** something from someone, you take it away from them, often as a punishment. *The court confiscated his passport.*

conflict, conflicts, conflicting, conflicted. [1] N-U /ˈkɒnflɪkt/ **Conflict** is serious disagreement and argument. If two people or groups are in **conflict**, they have had a serious disagreement and have not yet reached agreement. *Try to keep any conflict between you and your ex-partner to a minimum.* [2] N-VAR **Conflict** is fighting between countries or groups of people. *...a military conflict.* [3] VERB /kənˈflɪkt/

If ideas, beliefs, or accounts **conflict**, they are very different from each other and it seems impossible for them to exist together. *...opinions which usually conflicted with my own.* ♦ **conflicting** ADJ *...conflicting reports about the identity of the hostage.*

conform /kənˈfɔːm/ **conforms, conforming, conformed.** [1] VERB If something **conforms** to a law or to someone's wishes, it is what is required or wanted. *These activities do not conform with diplomatic rules.* [2] VERB If you **conform**, you behave in the way that you are expected to behave. *People feel a failure if they don't conform.*

conformity /kənˈfɔːmɪti/. N-U **Conformity** is behaviour, thought, or appearance that is the same as that of most other people.

confound /kənˈfaʊnd/ **confounds, confounding, confounded.** VERB If someone or something **confounds** you, they make you confused or surprised. *The choice of Governor may confound us all.*

confront /kənˈfrʌnt/ **confronts, confronting, confronted.** [1] VERB If you **are confronted** with a problem or task, you have to deal with it. *...the magnitude of the task confronting them.* [2] VERB If you **confront** someone, you stand or sit in front of them, especially when you are going to fight or argue with them. *The candidates confronted each other during a televised debate.* [3] VERB If you **confront** someone with facts or evidence, you present it to them in order to accuse them of something. *How do managers react when we confront them with this fact?*

confrontation /ˌkɒnfrʌnˈteɪʃən/ **confrontations.** N-VAR A **confrontation** is a dispute, fight, or battle. *...confrontation with the enemy.* ♦ **confrontational** /ˌkɒnfrʌnˈteɪʃənəl/ ADJ *...the committee's confrontational style of campaigning.*

confuse /kənˈfjuːz/ **confuses, confusing, confused.** [1] VERB If you **confuse** two things, you get them mixed up, so that you think one is the other. *I can't see how anyone could confuse you with another!* ♦ **confusion** N-U *Use different colours of felt pen on your sketch to avoid confusion.* ● See also **confusion.** [2] VERB To **confuse** someone means to make it difficult for them to know what is happening or what to do. *German politics surprised and confused him.* [3] VERB To **confuse** a situation means to make it complicated or difficult to understand. *In attempting to present two sides, you managed only to confuse the issue.*

confused /kənˈfjuːzd/. [1] ADJ If you are **confused**, you do not know what to do or you do not understand what is happening. *People are confused about what they should eat to stay healthy.* [2] ADJ Something that is **confused** does not have any order or pattern and is difficult to understand. *...a modern society in which values have become increasingly confused.*

confusing /kənˈfjuːzɪŋ/. ADJ Something that is **confusing** makes it difficult for people to know what to do or what is happening. *This situation must be confusing for you.*

confusion /kənˈfjuːʒən/ **confusions.** [1] N-VAR
If there is **confusion** about something, it is not
clear what the true situation is. *There's still
confusion about the number of casualties.*
[2] N-U **Confusion** is a situation in which everything is in disorder, especially because there
are lots of things happening at the same time.
There was confusion when a man fired shots.
[3] N-U If your mind is in a state of **confusion**,
you do not know what to believe or what you
should do. [4] See also **confuse**.

congenial /kənˈdʒiːniəl/ ADJ A **congenial** person, place, or environment is pleasant; FORMAL.

congested /kənˈdʒestɪd/ ADJ A **congested** road
or area is extremely crowded and blocked with
traffic or people.

congestion /kənˈdʒestʃən/ N-U If there is **congestion** in a place, the place is extremely congested. *...the problems of traffic congestion.*

conglomerate /kənˈglɒmərət/ **conglomer-
ates.** N-C A **conglomerate** is a large business
consisting of several different companies. *Fiat
is Italy's largest industrial conglomerate.*

congratulate /kənˈɡrætʃʊleɪt/ **congratulates,
congratulating, congratulated.** VERB If you
congratulate someone, you express pleasure
for something good that has happened to
them, or you praise them for something they
have achieved. *She congratulated him on the
birth of his son.* ♦**congratulation** N-U *...letters
of congratulation.*

congratulations /kən.ɡrætʃʊˈleɪʃənz/. CONVEN-
TION You say **'congratulations'** to someone in
order to congratulate them. *Congratulations,
you have a healthy baby boy.*

congregate /ˈkɒŋɡrɪɡeɪt/ **congregates, con-
gregating, congregated.** VERB When people
congregate, they gather together. *Youngsters
love to congregate here in the evenings.*

congregation /ˌkɒŋɡrɪˈɡeɪʃən/ **congrega-
tions.** N-C The people who attend a church
service are the **congregation**. **Congregation**
can take the singular or plural form of the
verb.

congress /ˈkɒŋɡres/ **congresses.** N-C A **congress** is a large meeting held to discuss ideas
and policies. **Congress** can take the singular or
plural form of the verb.

Congress /ˈkɒŋɡres/. N-PROPER **Congress** is the
elected group of politicians that is responsible
for making the law in the USA.
♦**congressional** /kənˈɡreʃənəl/ ADJ BEFORE N *...a
congressional report.* ● See note at **government**.

congressman /ˈkɒŋɡrɪsmən/ **congressmen.**
N-C & N-TITLE A **congressman** is a male member
of the US Congress. ● See note at **government**.

congresswoman /ˈkɒŋɡrɪswʊmən/
congresswomen. N-C & N-TITLE A **congresswoman** is a female member of the US Congress. ● See note at **government**.

conjecture /kənˈdʒektʃə/ **conjectures.** N-VAR
Conjecture is a guess based on incomplete or
doubtful information; FORMAL. *The attitudes of
others were matters of conjecture.*

conjunction /kənˈdʒʌŋkʃən/ **conjunctions.**
[1] PHRASE If one thing is done or used **in conjunction with** another, the two things are done

or used together; FORMAL. *The army should
have operated in conjunction with the fleet.*
[2] N-C In grammar, a **conjunction** is a word
that joins together words, groups, or clauses.
For example, 'and' and 'or' are conjunctions.

conjure /ˈkʌndʒə, AM ˈkɑːn-/ **conjures, con-
juring, conjured.** VERB & PHR-VERB If you **conjure** something out of nothing, or if you **conjure up** something, you produce it as if by
magic. *Every day a different chef will be conjur-
ing up delicious dishes.*

▶ **conjure up.** PHR-VERB To **conjure up** a memory, picture, or idea means to create it in your
mind. *He could conjure up in exact colour almost every event of his life.*

connect /kəˈnekt/ **connects, connecting,
connected.** [1] VERB To **connect** one thing to
another means to join them together. *Connect
the wires... The trailer was connected to the car.
...the long hallway that connects the rooms.*
[2] VERB If a piece of equipment or a place **is
connected** to a source of power or water, it is
joined to that source. *Ischia was now connected to the mainland water supply.* [3] VERB If a
telephone operator **connects** you, he or she
enables you to speak to another person by
telephone. [4] VERB If one train or plane **connects** with another, it arrives at a time which
allows passengers to change to the other one
in order to continue their journey. *...a train
connecting with a ferry to Ireland.* [5] VERB If
you **connect** a person or thing with something,
you realize that there is a link between them. *I
wouldn't have connected the two things.*

connected /kəˈnektɪd/. ADJ If one thing is connected with another, there is a link between
them. *The dispute is not directly connected to
the negotiations.*

connection /kəˈnekʃən/ **connections.** [1] N-C
A **connection** is a relationship between two
people, groups, or things. *He had no connection with the security forces.* [2] N-C A **connection** is the joint where two wires or pipes are
joined together. [3] N-C If you get a **connection**
at a station or airport, you continue your journey by catching another train, bus, or plane.
My flight was late and I missed the connection.
[4] PHRASE If you talk to someone **in connection with** something, you talk to them about
that thing. *I am writing in connection with
Michael Shower's letter.*

connoisseur /ˌkɒnəˈsɜː/ **connoisseurs.** N-C A
connoisseur is someone who knows a lot
about the arts, food, or drink. *...connoisseurs of
good food.*

connotation /ˌkɒnəˈteɪʃən/ **connotations.** N-C
The **connotations** of a word are the ideas or
qualities that it makes you think of. *...the title's
sexual connotations.*

conquer /ˈkɒŋkə/ **conquers, conquering,
conquered.** [1] VERB If one country or group
of people **conquers** another, they take complete control of their land. *During 1940,
Mussolini conquered Abyssinia.* ♦**conqueror,
conquerors.** N-C *...the attitudes of European
conquerors.* [2] VERB If you **conquer** something
such as a problem, you succeed in ending it or
dealing with it. *He has never conquered his addiction.*

conquest /'kɒŋkwest/. N-U **Conquest** is the act of conquering a country or group of people. *He had led the conquest of southern Poland.*

conscience /'kɒnʃəns/ **consciences.** [1] N-C Your **conscience** is the part of your mind that tells you if what you are doing is wrong. If you have a **guilty conscience**, or if you have something **on** your **conscience**, you feel guilty because you know you have done something wrong. *I have battled with my conscience over whether I should actually send this letter.* [2] N-U **Conscience** is doing what you believe is right even though it might be unpopular or difficult. *He refused for reasons of conscience to sign a new law legalising abortion.*

conscientious /,kɒnʃi'enʃəs/. ADJ Someone who is **conscientious** is very careful to do their work properly. *...a conscientious and dedicated mother.* ♦**conscientiously** ADV *He studied conscientiously.*

conscious /'kɒnʃəs/. [1] ADJ AFTER LINK-V If you are **conscious** of something, you notice it or are aware of it. *He was conscious of the faint, musky aroma of aftershave.* [2] ADJ **Conscious** is used in expressions such as 'politically conscious' to describe someone who believes that a particular aspect of life is important. *She was very health-conscious.* [3] ADJ BEFORE N A **conscious** decision or effort is one that you are aware of making. *I don't think we ever made a conscious decision to have a big family.* ♦**consciously** ADV *Sophie was not consciously seeking a replacement after her father died.* [4] ADJ Someone who is **conscious** is awake rather than asleep or unconscious. *She was fully conscious.*

consciousness /'kɒnʃəsnəs/. [1] N-U Your **consciousness** consists of your mind, thoughts, beliefs and attitudes. *She let her consciousness drift. ...a necessary change in the European consciousness.* [2] N-U If you lose **consciousness**, you become unconscious. When you regain **consciousness**, you become conscious again.

conscript, conscripts, conscripting, conscripted. [1] VERB /kən'skrɪpt/ If someone **is conscripted**, they are officially made to join the armed forces of a country. *He was conscripted into the army.* ♦**conscription** N-U *All adult males will be liable for conscription.* [2] N-C /'kɒnskrɪpt/ A **conscript** is a person who has been made to join the armed forces of a country.

consecrate /'kɒnsɪkreɪt/ **consecrates, consecrating, consecrated.** VERB When a building, place, or object **is consecrated**, it is officially declared to be holy. ♦**consecration** N-U *...the consecration of the new Coventry Cathedral.*

consecutive /kən'sekjʊtɪv/. ADJ **Consecutive** events or periods of time happen one after the other without interruption. *...his second consecutive win.*

consensus /kən'sensəs/. N-SING A **consensus** is general agreement amongst a group of people. *There is a growing consensus in Europe that more vigorous action is needed.*

consent /kən'sent/ **consents, consenting, consented.** [1] N-U **Consent** is permission given to someone to do something. *Can my child be medically examined without my consent?* [2] N-U **Consent** is agreement about something between people. *By common consent it was the best game of these Championships.* [3] VERB If you **consent** to something, you agree to do it or agree to it being done.

consequence /'kɒnsɪkwens/ **consequences.** [1] N-C The **consequences** of something are the results or effects of it. *One consequence of the reforms was a sharp tax increase.* [2] PHRASE If one thing happens and then another thing happens **in consequence**, the second thing happens as a result of the first. *His death was totally unexpected and, in consequence, no plans had been made for his replacement.* [3] N-U Someone or something that is **of consequence** is important or valuable. Someone or something that is **of no consequence** is not important or valuable.

consequent /'kɒnsɪkwənt/. ADJ **Consequent** means happening as a direct result of something; FORMAL. *...the warming of the Earth and the consequent climatic changes.* ♦**consequently** ADV *Ellen's father teased her about her weight. Consequently, she sees herself as much heavier than she really is.*

conservation /,kɒnsə'veɪʃən/. N-U **Conservation** is the preservation and protection of the environment. *...wildlife conservation.* ● See also **conserve**.

conservationist /,kɒnsə'veɪʃənɪst/ **conservationists.** N-C A **conservationist** is someone who works and campaigns for the conservation of the environment.

conservative /kən'sɜːvətɪv/ **conservatives.** [1] N-C & ADJ A **Conservative** or a **Conservative** politician or voter is a member of or votes for the Conservative Party. *...Conservative MPs.* ♦**conservatism** N-U *...one of the hallmarks of Conservatism under John Major.* [2] ADJ & N-C Someone who is **conservative** or who is a **conservative** has right-wing views. [3] ADJ Someone who is **conservative** is unwilling to accept changes and new ideas. *Older people tend to be more conservative than younger ones.* ♦**conservatism** N-U *Designers blame UK manufacturers' conservatism.* [4] ADJ A **conservative** estimate is very cautious. *Conservative estimates put her wealth at £5 million.* ♦**conservatively** ADV *...a player conservatively valued at £500,000.*

conservatory /kən'sɜːvətri, AM -tɔːri/ **conservatories.** N-C A **conservatory** is a glass room built onto a house.

conserve /kən'sɜːv/ **conserves, conserving, conserved.** [1] VERB If you **conserve** a supply of something, you use it carefully so that it lasts longer than it normally would. *Rationing has been introduced to conserve stocks.* ♦**conservation** N-U *...energy conservation.* [2] VERB To **conserve** something means to protect it from harm, loss, or change. *...aid to help developing countries conserve their forests.*

consider /kən'sɪdə/ **considers, considering, considered.** [1] VERB If you **consider** a person or thing to be something, this is your opinion of them. *I consider him a coward... Others consider the move premature... He considers that* *this is the worst recession this century.* • See note at **think**. **2** VERB If you **consider** something, you think about it carefully. *You do have to consider the feelings of those around you.* ♦**consideration** N-U *He said the draft treaty needed further consideration.* **3** See also **considering**.

considerable /kən'sɪdərəbəl/. ADJ **Considerable** means great in amount or degree. *...his considerable wealth... Vets' fees can be considerable.* ♦**considerably** ADV *Children vary considerably in the rate at which they learn.*

considerate /kən'sɪdərət/. ADJ A **considerate** person pays attention to the needs, wishes, or feelings of other people.

consideration /kən,sɪdə'reɪʃən/ **considerations.** **1** N-U Someone who shows **consideration** pays attention to the needs, wishes, or feelings of other people. *Show consideration for other rail travellers.* **2** N-C A **consideration** is something that should be thought about when you are planning or deciding something. *A further important consideration is the weather.* **3** See also **consider**.

PHRASES • If you **take** something **into consideration**, you think about it because it is relevant to what you are doing. *In sentencing, he took into consideration the defendants' ages.* • If something is **under consideration**, it is being discussed. *Several proposals are under consideration.*

considering /kən'sɪdərɪŋ/. CONJ & PREP You use **considering** to indicate that you are taking a particular fact into account when giving an opinion. *Considering that you are no longer involved with this man, your response is a little extreme... The former hostage is in remarkably good shape considering his ordeal.*

consign /kən'saɪn/ **consigns, consigning, consigned.** VERB If you **consign** someone or something **to** a particular place or situation, you put or place them there. *For decades, many of Malevich's works were consigned to the basements of Soviet museums.*

consignment /kən'saɪnmənt/ **consignments.** N-C A **consignment** of goods is a load that is being delivered to a place or person.

consist /kən'sɪst/ **consists, consisting, consisted.** VERB Something that **consists** of particular things is formed from them. *His diet consisted of bread, cheese and lager.*

consistency /kən'sɪstənsi/. N-U The **consistency** of a substance is the extent to which it is thick or smooth. *Dilute the paint with water until it is the consistency of milk.*

consistent /kən'sɪstənt/. **1** ADJ A **consistent** person always behaves or responds in the same way. *Becker has never been the most consistent of players.* ♦**consistency** N-U *He has shown remarkable consistency throughout.* ♦**consistently** ADV *...something I have consistently denied.* **2** ADJ If facts or ideas are **consistent**, there is no contradiction between or within them. *This result is consistent with the findings.*

consolation /,kɒnsə'leɪʃən/ **consolations.** N-VAR If something is a **consolation**, it makes you feel more cheerful when you are unhappy.

He knew then he was right, but it was no consolation.

console, consoles, consoling, consoled. **1** VERB /kən'səʊl/ If you **console** someone who is unhappy, you try to make them more cheerful. *I could say nothing to console him.* **2** N-C /'kɒnsəʊl/ A **console** is a panel with switches or knobs that is used to operate a machine.

consolidate /kən'sɒlɪdeɪt/ **consolidates, consolidating, consolidated.** VERB If you **consolidate** something such as your power or success, you strengthen it so that it becomes more effective or secure. *This album should further consolidate their success.* ♦**consolidation** N-U *The report is expected to recommend some consolidation of police powers.*

consonant /'kɒnsənənt/ **consonants.** N-C A **consonant** is a sound such as 'p' or 'f' which you pronounce by stopping the air flowing freely through your mouth.

consortium /kən'sɔːtiəm/ **consortiums** or **consortia** /kən'sɔːtiə/. N-C A **consortium** is a group of people or firms who have agreed to work together. **Consortium** can take the singular or plural form of the verb.

conspicuous /kən'spɪkjʊəs/. ADJ If someone or something is **conspicuous**, people can see or notice them very easily. *I felt very conspicuous.* ♦**conspicuously** ADV *Johnston's name was conspicuously absent from the list.*

conspiracy /kən'spɪrəsi/ **conspiracies.** N-VAR **Conspiracy** is the secret planning by a group of people to do something wrong or illegal. *...a conspiracy to undermine public education.*

conspirator /kən'spɪrətə/ **conspirators.** N-C A **conspirator** is a person who joins a conspiracy.

conspire /kən'spaɪə/ **conspires, conspiring, conspired.** **1** VERB If two or more people **conspire** to do something illegal or harmful, they make a secret agreement to do it. *...a defendant convicted of conspiring with his brother to commit robberies.* **2** VERB If events **conspire** to produce a particular result, they seem to cause this result. *The weather and the recession conspired to hit wine production and sales.*

constable /'kʌnstəbəl, 'kɒn-/ **constables.** N-C & N-TITLE In Britain, a **constable** is a police officer of the lowest rank.

constant /'kɒnstənt/. **1** ADJ Something that is **constant** happens all the time or is always there. *...constant interruptions. ...constant noise.* ♦**constantly** ADV *The direction of the wind is constantly changing.* **2** ADJ An amount or level that is **constant** stays the same over a particular period of time. *The temperature remains more or less constant.*

constellation /,kɒnstə'leɪʃən/ **constellations.** N-C A **constellation** is a group of stars which form a fixed pattern.

consternation /,kɒnstə'neɪʃən/. N-U **Consternation** is a feeling of anxiety or fear; FORMAL. *The announcement has caused consternation.*

constipation /,kɒnstɪ'peɪʃən/. N-U **Constipation** is a medical condition which causes people to have difficulty getting rid of waste matter from their bowels.

constituency /kən'stɪtʃʊənsi/ **constituencies.** N-C A **constituency** is an area for which someone is elected as the representative in parliament.

constituent /kən'stɪtʃʊənt/ **constituents.** [1] N-C A **constituent** is someone who lives in a particular constituency. [2] N-C & ADJ BEFORE N A **constituent** or a **constituent** part of something is one of the things that it is made from. ...caffeine, one of the major constituents of coffee.

constitute /'kɒnstɪtjuːt, AM -tuː-/ **constitutes, constituting, constituted.** [1] LINK-VERB If something **constitutes** a particular thing, it can be regarded as being that thing. ...the question of what constitutes normal behaviour. [2] LINK-VERB If a number of things or people **constitute** something, they are the parts or members that form it. Hindus constitute 83% of India's population.

constitution /,kɒnstɪ'tjuːʃən, AM -'tuː-/ **constitutions.** [1] N-C The **constitution** of a country or organization is the system of laws which formally states people's rights and duties. ...the French constitution. ◆**constitutional** /,kɒnstɪ'tjuːʃənəl, AM -'tuː-/ ADJ ...Italy's constitutional reforms. [2] N-C Your **constitution** is your health. He must have an extremely strong constitution.

constrain /kən'streɪn/ **constrains, constraining, constrained.** VERB To **constrain** someone or something means to limit their development or activities; FORMAL. Women are too often constrained by family commitments. ◆**constrained** ADJ ...constrained budgets.

constraint /kən'streɪnt/ **constraints.** [1] N-C A **constraint** is something that limits or controls what you can do. ...new legal constraints. [2] N-U **Constraint** is control over the way you behave which prevents you from doing what you want to do. The Republics wanted democracy after years of constraint.

constrict /kən'strɪkt/ **constricts, constricting, constricted.** [1] VERB If a part of your body, especially your throat, **is constricted**, something causes it to become narrower. ...a drug which constricts the blood vessels... His throat began to feel swollen and constricted. ◆**constriction** N-U ...constriction of the blood vessels. [2] VERB If something **constricts** you, it limits your actions so that you cannot do what you want to do. Men and women alike have been constricted by traditional sexual roles. ◆**constriction, constrictions** N-C ...the constrictions placed upon me as a child.

construct /kən'strʌkt/ **constructs, constructing, constructed.** [1] VERB /kən'strʌkt/ If you **construct** something, you build, make, or create it. ...the campaign to construct a temple on the site... Construct a spending plan. [2] N-C /'kɒnstrʌkt/ A **construct** is a complex idea; FORMAL.

construction /kən'strʌkʃən/ **constructions.** [1] N-U **Construction** is the building or creating of something. ...a new community centre is under construction... This is the finest wood for boat construction. [2] N-C A **construction** is an object that has been made or built. ...an impressive steel and glass construction.

constructive /kən'strʌktɪv/. ADJ A **constructive** discussion, comment, or approach is useful and helpful. ...constructive criticism. ◆**constructively** ADV Use the time constructively.

construe /kən'struː/ **construes, construing, construed.** VERB If something **is construed** in a particular way, its nature or meaning is interpreted in that way; FORMAL. She construed my concern as nosiness.

consul /'kɒnsəl/ **consuls.** N-C A **consul** is a government official who lives in a foreign city and looks after all the people there who are from his or her own country. ◆**consular** /'kɒnsjʊlə, AM -sə-/ ADJ BEFORE N ...British Consular officials.

consulate /'kɒnsjʊlət, AM -sə-/ **consulates.** N-C A **consulate** is the place where a consul works. ...the British consulate in Lyons.

consult /kən'sʌlt/ **consults, consulting, consulted.** [1] VERB If you **consult** someone or something, you refer to them for advice or information. Consult your doctor about how much exercise you should attempt... He needed to consult with an attorney... Consult the chart on page 44 for the correct cooking times. ◆**consultation, consultations** N-VAR ...a consultation with a nutritionist. [2] See also **consultation**.

consultancy /kən'sʌltənsi/ **consultancies.** [1] N-C A **consultancy** is a company that gives expert advice on a particular subject. ...a management consultancy. [2] N-U **Consultancy** is expert advice which a person or group is paid to provide. The project provides both consultancy and training.

consultant /kən'sʌltənt/ **consultants.** [1] N-C A **consultant** is an experienced doctor specializing in one area of medicine; BRITISH. ...a consultant heart surgeon. [2] N-C A **consultant** is a person who gives expert advice on a particular subject. He was a consultant to the Swedish government.

consultation /,kɒnsəl'teɪʃən/ **consultations.** [1] N-VAR **Consultations** are meetings which are held to discuss something. **Consultation** is discussion about something. ...consultations with President Mitterrand. [2] See also **consult**.

consultative /kən'sʌltətɪv/. ADJ A **consultative** committee or document is one which gives advice or makes proposals about a particular problem or subject.

consume /kən'sjuːm, AM -'suːm/ **consumes, consuming, consumed.** [1] VERB If you **consume** something, you eat or drink it; FORMAL. Martha would consume nearly a pound of cheese per day. [2] VERB To **consume** an amount of fuel, energy, or time means to use it up. A computer circuit consumes a tiny amount of electricity. ◆**-consuming** ...oil-consuming countries. ...a time-consuming job.

consumed /kən'sjuːmd, AM -'suːmd/. ADJ AFTER LINK-V If you are **consumed** with a feeling or idea, it affects you very strongly. He's consumed with ambition.

consumer /kən'sjuːmə, AM -'suː-/ **consumers.** N-C A **consumer** is a person who buys things or uses services. ...consumer rights.

consuming /kən'sju:mɪŋ, AM -'su:-/. ADJ A **consuming** passion or interest is more important to you than anything else. *He has developed a consuming passion for chess.*

consummate, consummates, consummating, consummated. [1] ADJ /'kɒnsjəmət/ You use **consummate** to describe someone who is extremely skilful; FORMAL. *...a consummate politician... He acted the part with consummate skill.* [2] VERB /'kɒnsəmeɪt/ If two people **consummate** a marriage or relationship, they make it complete by having sex. ◆**consummation** N-U *...the consummation of their marriage.* [3] VERB To **consummate** an agreement means to complete it; FORMAL. *No one has been able to consummate a deal.*

consumption /kən'sʌmpʃən/. [1] N-U The **consumption** of fuel or energy is the amount of it that is used, or the act of using it. *...a reduction in fuel consumption.* [2] N-U The **consumption** of food or drink is the act of eating or drinking something; FORMAL. *The wine was unfit for human consumption.* [3] N-U **Consumption** is the act of buying and using things; TECHNICAL. *...the production and consumption of goods and services.*

contact /'kɒntækt/ **contacts, contacting, contacted.** [1] N-VAR **Contact** involves meeting or communicating with someone. *I had very little contact with teenagers... I shall be in contact with my family by telephone... He started writing poetry, and making contact with other poets.* [2] VERB If you **contact** someone, you telephone them or write to them. *Could he be contacted?* [3] N-U If you come into **contact** with something, you have some experience of it in the course of your work or other activities. *The college has brought me into contact with western ideas.* [4] N-C A **contact** is someone you know in an organization who helps you or gives you information. *Their contact in the United States Embassy was called Phil.* [5] N-U If people or things are in **contact**, they are touching each other. *...where the foot and shoe are in contact... There was no physical contact.*

'contact lens, contact lenses. N-C **Contact lenses** are small lenses that you put on your eyes to help you to see better.

contagious /kən'teɪdʒəs/. [1] ADJ A **contagious** disease can be caught by touching people or things that are infected with it. [2] ADJ A **contagious** feeling or attitude spreads quickly among a group of people. *Laughing is contagious.*

contain /kən'teɪn/ **contains, containing, contained.** [1] VERB If something such as a box or a room **contains** things, those things are in it. *The bag contained a Christmas card... The 77,000-acre estate contains five of the highest peaks in Scotland.* [2] VERB If something **contains** a particular substance, that substance is part of it. *Alcohol contains sugar.* [3] VERB To **contain** something such as a feeling, problem, or activity means to control it and prevent it from increasing. *Evans could barely contain his delight... Firemen are still trying to contain the fire.*

container /kən'teɪnə/ **containers.** [1] N-C A **container** is something such as a box or bottle that is used to hold things. [2] N-C A **container** is a very large metal or wooden box used for transporting goods so that they can be loaded easily onto ships and lorries. *...the country's busiest container port.*

contaminate /kən'tæmɪneɪt/ **contaminates, contaminating, contaminated.** VERB If something **is contaminated** by dirt, chemicals, or radiation, it becomes impure or harmful. *...waste water contaminated by hazardous chemicals... He received a contaminated blood transfusion.* ◆**contamination** N-U *...the contamination of the sea.*

contemplate /'kɒntəmpleɪt/ **contemplates, contemplating, contemplated.** [1] VERB If you **contemplate** something, you consider it as a possibility. *He contemplated a career as an army medical doctor... He will not contemplate discussion on the issue.* [2] VERB If you **contemplate** an idea or subject, you think about it for a long time. *He cried as he contemplated his future.* ◆**contemplation** N-U *It is a place of quiet contemplation.* [3] VERB To **contemplate** something or someone means to look at them for a long time. *He contemplated his hands.*

contemporary /kən'tempərəri, AM -pəreri/ **contemporaries.** [1] ADJ **Contemporary** means existing now or at the time you are talking about. *...contemporary music. ...the reports of contemporary witnesses.* [2] N-C Someone's **contemporaries** are people who are or were alive at the same time as them. *...Shakespeare and his contemporaries.*

contempt /kən'tempt/. N-U If you have **contempt** for someone or something, you have no respect for them. *They were regarded with contempt.*

contemptuous /kən'temptʃʊəs/. ADJ If you are **contemptuous** of someone or something, you have no respect for them. *He's openly contemptuous of all the major political parties.* ◆**contemptuously** ADV *'A deal!' she said contemptuously, 'I hate all deals.'*

contend /kən'tend/ **contends, contending, contended.** [1] VERB If you have to **contend** with a problem or difficulty, you have to deal with it or overcome it. *They had a severely disturbed child to contend with.* [2] VERB If you **contend** with someone for something, you compete with them to try to get it. *...the two main groups contending for power.* ◆**contender** /kən'tendə/ N-C *...a strong contender for an Olympic gold medal.* [3] VERB If you **contend** that something is true, you state or argue that it is true; FORMAL. *Lawyers contend that smokers use the tobacco products voluntarily.*

content 1 noun uses

content /'kɒntent/ **contents.** [1] N-PL The **contents** of a container such as a bottle, box, or room are the things inside it. *Empty the contents of the pan into the sieve. ...Sandon Hall and its contents.* [2] N-VAR The **content** of a piece of writing, speech, or television programme is its subject and the ideas expressed in it. *Stricter controls were placed on the content of video films. ...the letter's contents.* [3] N-PL The **contents** of a book are its different chapters and sections. *There is no initial list of* *contents.* **4** N-SING You can use **content** to refer to the amount or proportion of something that a substance contains. **Content** is always used after a noun for this meaning. *Sunflower margarine has the same fat content as butter.*

content 2 adjective and verb uses

content /kən'tent/ **contents, contenting, contented.** **1** ADJ AFTER LINK-V If you are **content** to do something or **content with** something, you are willing to accept it, rather than wanting something more or better. *I am content to admire the mountains from below... Not content with rescuing one theatre, Sally Green has taken on another.* **2** VERB If you **content** yourself **with** something, you accept it and do not try to do or have other things. *He wisely contented himself with his family.* **3** ADJ AFTER LINK-V If you are **content**, you are happy and satisfied with your way of life. **4** See also **contentment.**

contented /kən'tentɪd/. ADJ If you are **contented**, you are satisfied with your life or the situation you are in. ♦**contentedly** ADV *The landlady sighed contentedly.*

contention /kən'tenʃən/ **contentions.** **1** N-C Someone's **contention** is the opinion that they are expressing. *My contention is not that men don't talk. We do.* **2** N-U **Contention** is disagreement or argument about something. *The major area of contention among the Democrats is abortion.* **3** PHRASE If you are **in contention** in a contest, you have a chance of winning it. *Four others are in contention for the prize.*

contentious /kən'tenʃəs/. ADJ A **contentious** issue causes disagreement and arguments. *The strategy was highly contentious.*

contentment /kən'tentmənt/. N-U **Contentment** is the feeling of being content.

contest, contests, contesting, contested. **1** N-C /'kɒntest/ A **contest** is a competition or game. *...a writing contest.* **2** N-C A **contest** is a struggle to win power or control. *...next year's presidential contest.* **3** VERB /kən'test/ If someone **contests** an election or competition, they take part in it in order to win. **4** VERB If you **contest** a statement or decision, you disagree with it formally. *He has to reply within 14 days in order to contest the case.*

contestant /kən'testənt/ **contestants.** N-C A **contestant** in a competition or quiz is a person who takes part in it.

context /'kɒntekst/ **contexts.** **1** N-VAR The **context** of an idea or event is the general situation in which it occurs. *It is important that we put Jesus into the context of history... The drugs problem has to be seen in context.* **2** N-VAR The **context** of a word or sentence consists of the words or sentences before it and after it. *He said his remarks had been taken out of context.*

continent /'kɒntɪnənt/ **continents.** **1** N-C A **continent** is a very large area of land, such as Africa or Asia, that consists of several countries. **2** N-PROPER In Britain, the mainland of Europe is sometimes referred to as the **Continent.** ♦**continental** ADJ BEFORE N *...the continental street-side cafe.*

contingency /kən'tɪndʒənsi/ **contingencies.** N-C A **contingency** is something that might happen in the future. *I need to examine all possible contingencies. ...military contingency plans.*

contingent /kən'tɪndʒənt/ **contingents.** **1** N-C A **contingent** is a group of people representing a country or organization. *A contingent of Belgian paratroops is also said to have arrived. ...European scientists, including a British contingent.* **2** ADJ If an event is **contingent on** something, it can only happen if that thing happens or exists; FORMAL. *...the premise that people's rights are contingent on their abilities.*

continual /kən'tɪnjʊəl/. ADJ BEFORE N **Continual** means happening without stopping, or happening again and again. *...continual pain... She suffered continual police harassment.* ♦**continually** ADV *Malcolm was continually changing his mind.*

continuation /kən,tɪnjʊ'eɪʃən/. **1** N-U The **continuation** of something is the fact that it continues to happen or exist. *...the continuation of the war.* **2** N-SING Something that is a **continuation** of something else is closely connected with it and develops it in some way. *This chapter is a continuation of Chapter 8.*

continue /kən'tɪnjuː/ **continues, continuing, continued.** **1** VERB If something **continues**, it does not stop. If you **continue** to do something, you do not stop doing it. *The conflict would continue until conditions were met for a ceasefire... Interest rates continue to fall... Diana and Roy are determined to continue working.* **2** VERB If something **continues**, or if you **continue** it, it starts again after stopping for a period of time. *The trial continues today... I went up to my room to continue with my packing.* **3** VERB To **continue** means to begin speaking again after a pause or interruption. *'Anyway, that was what gave us the idea,' she continued after a pause.* **4** VERB If you **continue** in a particular direction, you keep going in that direction. *He continued rapidly up the path.*

continuity /,kɒntɪ'njuːɪti, AM -'nuː-/ **continuities.** N-VAR The **continuity** of something is the fact that it happens, exists, or develops without stopping or changing suddenly. *...political stability and continuity.*

continuous /kən'tɪnjʊəs/. **1** ADJ A **continuous** process or event continues for a period of time without stopping. *...a continuous stream of phone calls.* ♦**continuously** ADV *The machinery should go on working continuously for twelve hours.* **2** ADJ A **continuous** line or surface has no gaps in it. **3** ADJ In English grammar, **continuous** tenses are formed using the auxiliary 'be' and the present participle of a verb, as in 'I'm feeling a bit tired'. Compare **simple.**

contort /kən'tɔːt/ **contorts, contorting, contorted.** VERB When something **contorts**, it changes into an unnatural and unattractive shape. *His face contorted with pain.* ♦**contortion, contortions** N-VAR *...the contortions of the gymnasts.*

contour /'kɒntʊə/ **contours.** **1** N-C The **contours** of something are its shape or outline. *...the contours of the body.* **2** N-C On a map, a **contour** is a line joining points of equal height.

contraception /ˌkɒntrə'sepʃən/. N-U Methods of preventing pregnancy are called **contraception**.

contraceptive /ˌkɒntrə'septɪv/ **contraceptives**. N-C A **contraceptive** is a device or pill used to prevent pregnancy.

contract, contracts, contracting, contracted. [1] N-C /'kɒntrækt/ A **contract** is a legal agreement, usually between two companies or between an employer and employee, which involves doing work for a stated sum of money. *...a prestigious contract for work on Europe's tallest building*. [2] VERB /kən'trækt/ If you **contract** with someone to do something, you legally agree to do it for them or for them to do it for you; FORMAL. [3] VERB When something **contracts**, it becomes smaller or shorter. *When you are anxious, your muscles contract*. ◆**contraction, contractions**. N-VAR *...the contraction and expansion of blood vessels*. [4] VERB If you **contract** a serious illness, you become ill with it; FORMAL.

contractor /'kɒntræktə, kən'træk-/ **contractors**. N-C A **contractor** is a person or company that works for other people or companies.

contractual /kən'træktʃʊəl/. ADJ A **contractual** arrangement or relationship involves a legal agreement between people; FORMAL. ◆**contractually** ADV *Rank was contractually obliged to hand him a cheque for $30 million*.

contradict /ˌkɒntrə'dɪkt/ **contradicts, contradicting, contradicted**. [1] VERB If you **contradict** someone, you say or suggest that what they have just said is wrong. *She dared not contradict her*. [2] VERB If one statement or action **contradicts** another, the first one makes the second appear to be wrong. *Her version contradicted the Government's claim*.

contradiction /ˌkɒntrə'dɪkʃən/ **contradictions**. [1] N-VAR A **contradiction** is an aspect of a situation which appears to conflict with other aspects, so that they cannot all exist or be successful. *...the contradictions between her private life and the public persona*. [2] PHRASE If you say that something is a **contradiction in terms**, you mean that it is described as having a quality that it cannot have. *A public service run for profit – a contradiction in terms if there ever was one*.

contradictory /ˌkɒntrə'dɪktəri, AM -tɔːri/. ADJ If two or more facts, ideas, or statements are **contradictory**, they state or imply that opposite things are true. *...advice that sometimes is contradictory and confusing*.

contrary /'kɒntrəri, AM -treri/. [1] ADJ **Contrary** ideas or opinions are completely different from each other. *Clearly there's room for a contrary view to mine... Contrary to popular belief, moderate exercise actually decreases your appetite*. [2] PHRASE You use **on the contrary** when you are contradicting what has just been said. *'People just don't do things like that.'—'On the contrary, they do them all the time.'*

> Do not confuse **on the contrary** with **on the other hand**. **On the contrary** is used to contradict someone, to say that they are wrong. **On the other hand** is used to state a different, often contrast-

ing aspect of the situation you are considering. *Prices of other foods and consumer goods fell. Wages on the other hand increased.*

[3] PHRASE Evidence or statements **to the contrary** contradict what you are saying or what someone else has said. *Despite the report's conclusions to the contrary, the city had an excellent emergency plan.*

contrast, contrasts, contrasting, contrasted. [1] N-VAR /'kɒntrɑːst, -træst/ A **contrast** is a great difference between two or more things. *...the contrast between town and country... His public statements have always been in marked contrast to those of his son*. [2] PHRASE You use **contrast** in expressions such as **by contrast** or **in contrast**, to show that you are mentioning a very different situation from the one you have just mentioned. *After the ecstatic hugs and kisses of the team-members, the award ceremony was, in contrast, cold and flat*. [3] VERB /kən'trɑːst, -'træst/ If one thing **contrasts** with another, it is very different from it. *Paint the wall in a contrasting colour*. [4] VERB If you **contrast** one thing with another, you show the differences between them. *In this section we contrast four possible broad approaches*.

contravene /ˌkɒntrə'viːn/ **contravenes, contravening, contravened**. VERB To **contravene** a law or rule means to do something that is forbidden by it; FORMAL. ◆**contravention** /ˌkɒntrə'venʃən/ **contraventions** N-VAR *Child labour is exploited in contravention of labour laws.*

contribute /kən'trɪbjuːt/ **contributes, contributing, contributed**. [1] VERB If you **contribute** to something, you say or do something to help make it successful. *Each of the girls is expected to contribute to community work*. [2] VERB If a person, organization, or country **contributes** money or resources to something, they help to pay for it or achieve it. *The US is contributing $4 billion in loans, credits and grants*. ◆**contributor** /kən'trɪbjʊtə/ **contributors** N-C *...contributors to EU funds*. [3] VERB If something **contributes** to a situation, it is one of its causes. *Stress, both human and mechanical, may also be a contributing factor*. ◆**contributor** N-C *Old buses are major contributors to pollution*. [4] VERB If you **contribute** to a magazine or book, you write things that are published in it. *She contributes regularly to Vogue magazine*. ◆**contributor** N-C *...a regular contributor to this magazine*.

contribution /ˌkɒntrɪ'bjuːʃən/ **contributions**. [1] N-C If you make a **contribution** to something, you do something to help make it successful or to produce it. *He was awarded a prize for his contribution to world peace*. [2] N-C A **contribution** is a sum of money that you give in order to help pay for something. *...companies that make charitable contributions*.

contrive /kən'traɪv/ **contrives, contriving, contrived**. [1] VERB If you **contrive** to do something difficult, you manage to do it; FORMAL. *He contrived to see her most days and nights*. [2] VERB If you **contrive** an event or situation, you succeed in making it happen;

FORMAL. *The oil companies were accused of contriving a shortage of gasoline.*

contrived /kən'traɪvd/. ADJ If you say that something is **contrived**, you think it is false or unconvincing; used showing disapproval. *The plotting is contrived, the dialogue inane and the romance implausible.*

control /kən'trəʊl/ **controls, controlling, controlled.** [1] VERB & N-U If someone **controls** an organization, place, or system, or if they have **control** of it, they have the power to take all the important decisions about the way it is run. You can also say they are **in control** of it or it is **under** their **control**. *The restructuring involves Mr Ronson giving up control of the company... People feel more in control of their own lives. ...its controlling interest in both firms.* ◆**-controlled** *AGA Gas is Swedish-controlled.* ◆**controller, controllers** N-C *...the job of controller of BBC 1.* [2] VERB & N-U If you **control** a person or machine, or if you have **control** of them, you are able to make them do what you want them to do. *I can't control what the judge says or what people think... He lost control of his car... Some teachers have more control over pupils than their parents have.* [3] VERB & N-U If you **control** yourself or your feelings, or show **control**, you make yourself behave calmly even though you are feeling angry, excited, or upset. *I couldn't control my temper... Sometimes he would completely lose control.* ◆**controlled** ADJ *Her manner was quiet and very controlled.* [4] VERB & N-U To **control** prices, wages, or undesirable activities means to restrict them to an acceptable level. **Control** is the act of controlling something in this way. If something is **out of control**, it cannot be restricted by anyone. If it is **under control**, it is being dealt with successfully. *The priorities are to control prices. ...the need to control environmental pollution... Control of inflation remains the government's absolute priority... The fire is burning out of control.* [5] N-PL **Controls** are the methods an organization uses to restrict something. *The price controls announced yesterday will lower electricity bills.* [6] N-U A **control** is a device such as a switch or lever which you use in order to operate a machine or other piece of equipment. *He was at the controls of the plane when it crashed.*

> You do not use **control** as a verb to talk about inspecting documents. The word you use is **check**. *Police were searching cars and checking identity documents.* However, at an airport or port, the place where passports are checked is called **passport control**.

controversial /ˌkɒntrə'vɜːʃəl/. ADJ Someone or something that is **controversial** causes intense public argument, disagreement, or disapproval. *...the controversial new book.*

controversy /'kɒntrəvɜːsi, kən'trɒvəsi/ **controversies.** N-VAR **Controversy** is a lot of discussion and disagreement about something, often involving strong anger or disapproval. *...a fierce political controversy over human rights.*

convalesce /ˌkɒnvə'les/ **convalesces, convalescing, convalesced.** VERB If you **are convalescing**, you are resting and regaining your health after an illness or operation. *...those convalescing from illness or surgery.* ◆**convalescent** ADJ *...his convalescent wife.* ◆**convalescence** /ˌkɒnvə'lesəns/ ADJ *I visited him during his convalescence.*

convene /kən'viːn/ **convenes, convening, convened.** VERB If you **convene** a meeting, you arrange for it to take place. You can also say that people **convene** at a meeting. *Senior officials convened in October.*

convenience /kən'viːniəns/ **conveniences.** [1] N-U If something is done for your **convenience**, it is done in a way that is useful or suitable for you. *He was happy to make a detour for her convenience.* [2] N-C If you describe something as a **convenience** you mean it is useful. *Mail order is a convenience for buyers who are too busy to shop.* [3] N-C **Conveniences** are pieces of equipment designed to make your life easier. *...an apartment with all the modern conveniences.*

convenient /kən'viːniənt/. [1] ADJ Something that is **convenient** is easy, useful, or suitable for a particular purpose. *...a flexible and convenient way of paying... It was more convenient to eat in the kitchen.* ◆**conveniently** ADV *The body spray slips conveniently into your sports bag.* ◆**convenience** /kən'viːniəns/ N-U *...the convenience of a fast non-stop flight.* [2] ADJ A place that is **convenient** is near to where you are, or near to another place where you want to go. *Martin drove along until he found a convenient parking place.* ◆**conveniently** ADV *The resort is conveniently close to Phoenix International Airport.* [3] ADJ A **convenient** time to do something is a time when you are free to do it or would like to do it. *Would this evening be convenient for you?*

convent /'kɒnvənt/ **convents.** N-C A **convent** is a building in which a community of nuns live.

convention /kən'venʃən/ **conventions.** [1] N-VAR A **convention** is an accepted way of behaving or of doing something. *It's just a social convention that men don't wear skirts.* [2] N-C A **convention** is an official agreement between countries or organizations. *...the UN convention on climate change.* [3] N-C A **convention** is a large meeting of an organization or group. *...the annual convention of the World Boxing Council.*

conventional /kən'venʃənəl/. [1] ADJ **Conventional** people behave in a way that is accepted as normal in their society. *...a respectable married woman with conventional opinions.* ◆**conventionally** ADV *People still wore their hair short and dressed conventionally.* [2] ADJ A **conventional** method or product is the one that is usually used. *...a conventional computer floppy disk.* ◆**conventionally** ADV *...conventionally grown crops.* [3] ADJ **Conventional** wars and weapons do not involve nuclear explosives.

converge /kən'vɜːdʒ/ **converges, converging, converged.** [1] VERB When roads or lines **converge**, they meet or join. *As they flow south, the five rivers converge.* [2] VERB When people or vehicles **converge** on a place, they move towards it from different directions. *Hundreds of coaches will converge on the capital.* **3** VERB If different ideas or societies **converge**, they gradually become similar to each other. *The views of the richest householders converged with those of the poorest.* ♦**convergence** /kənˈvɜːdʒəns/ **convergences.** N-U *...economic convergence between the European economies.*

conversation /ˌkɒnvəˈseɪʃən/ **conversations.** **1** N-VAR If you have a **conversation** with someone, you talk to them, usually in an informal situation. *I struck up a conversation with him.* ♦**conversational** ADJ *...the author's easy, conversational style.* ♦**conversationally** ADV *Lyrics are written almost conversationally, yet sung with passion.* **2** PHRASE When you **make conversation**, you talk to someone in order to be polite rather than because you want to.

converse, converses, conversing, conversed. **1** VERB /kənˈvɜːs/ If you **converse** with someone, you talk to each other; FORMAL. *They were conversing in German.* **2** N-SING /ˈkɒnvɜːs/ The **converse** of a statement or fact is its opposite or reverse. *If great events produce great men, the converse is also true.* ♦**conversely** /ˈkɒnvɜːsli, kənˈvɜːsli/ ADV *Some people mistake politeness for weakness, and conversely, they think that rudeness is a sign of strength.*

convert, converts, converting, converted. **1** VERB /kənˈvɜːt/ To **convert** one thing into another means to change it into a different shape or form. *The signal will be converted into digital code. ...a table that converts into an ironing board. ...a converted farmhouse.* ♦**conversion** /kənˈvɜːʃən/ **conversions.** N-VAR *...the conversion of military industries to civilian use.* **2** VERB If someone **converts** you, they persuade you to change your religious or political beliefs. *He converted to Catholicism in 1917.* ♦**conversion** N-VAR *...his conversion to Christianity.* **3** N-C /ˈkɒnvɜːt/ A **convert** is someone who has changed their religious or political beliefs. *...new converts to democracy.*

convertible /kənˈvɜːtɪbəl/ **convertibles.** **1** N-C A **convertible** is a car with a soft roof that can be folded down or removed. **2** ADJ **Convertible** money can be easily exchanged for other forms of money; TECHNICAL.

convey /kənˈveɪ/ **conveys, conveying, conveyed.** **1** VERB To **convey** facts or feelings means to cause them to be known or understood. *I tried to convey the wonder of this machine to my husband... Officials convey a sense of alarm.* **2** VERB To **convey** someone or something to a place means to transport them there; FORMAL. *The minibus picked us up and conveyed us to the station.*

conveyor belt /kənˈveɪə belt/ **conveyor belts.** N-C A **conveyor belt** or a **conveyor** is a continuously moving strip which is used in factories for moving objects along.

convict, convicts, convicting, convicted. **1** VERB /kənˈvɪkt/ If someone **is convicted** of a crime, they are found guilty of it in a law court. *He was convicted of murder... There was insufficient evidence to convict him.* **2** N-C /ˈkɒnvɪkt/

A **convict** is someone who is in prison, convicted of committing a crime.

conviction /kənˈvɪkʃən/ **convictions.** **1** N-C A **conviction** is a strong belief or opinion. *...the conviction that Europe may be losing its competitive edge... We had an absolute conviction that we were on the side of good.* **2** N-C If someone has a **conviction**, they have been found guilty of a crime. *He will appeal against his conviction.*

convince /kənˈvɪns/ **convinces, convincing, convinced.** **1** VERB If someone or something **convinces** you of something, they make you believe that it is true or that it exists. *I soon convinced him of my innocence... The waste disposal industry is finding it difficult to convince the public that its operations are safe.* ♦**convinced** ADJ *He became convinced that the marriage could soon end.* **2** VERB If someone or something **convinces** you to do something, they persuade you to do it. *He convinced her to go ahead and marry Bud.*

convincing /kənˈvɪnsɪŋ/ ADJ If someone or something is **convincing**, you believe them. *He sounded very convincing.* ♦**convincingly** ADV *He argued forcefully and convincingly.*

convoy /ˈkɒnvɔɪ/ **convoys.** N-C A **convoy** is a group of vehicles or ships travelling together. *They travel in convoy.*

convulsion /kənˈvʌlʃən/ **convulsions.** N-C If someone has **convulsions**, they suffer uncontrollable movements of their muscles.

cook /kʊk/ **cooks, cooking, cooked.** **1** VERB When you **cook** a meal, you prepare and heat food so it can be eaten. *Let the vegetables cook gently for about 10 minutes... Chefs at the St James Court restaurant have cooked for the Queen... We'll cook them a nice Italian meal.* ♦**cooking** N-U *You do a lot of cooking don't you?*

> You often use a more specific verb instead of **cook** when you are talking about preparing food using heat. For example, you **roast** meat in an oven, but you **bake** bread and cakes, or you **boil** vegetables in hot water, or you can **steam** them over a pan of boiling water. You can **fry** meat and vegetables in oil or fat. You can also **grill** them directly under or over a flame. In American English, **broil** is used instead of **grill**. You do not normally talk about **grilling** bread. Instead, you **toast** it.

2 N-C A **cook** is a person whose job is to prepare and cook food. **3** See also **cooking**.
▶ **cook up.** PHR-VERB If someone **cooks up** a dishonest scheme, they plan it; INFORMAL. *He must have cooked up his scheme on the spur of the moment.*

cookbook /ˈkʊkbʊk/ **cookbooks.** N-C A **cookbook** is a book that contains recipes for preparing food.

cooker /ˈkʊkə/ **cookers.** N-C A **cooker** is a large metal device used for cooking food using gas or electricity.

cookery /ˈkʊkəri/. N-U **Cookery** is the activity of preparing and cooking food.

cookie /'kʊki/ **cookies.** N-C In American English, a **cookie** is a small, sweet, flat cake. The usual British word is **biscuit.**

cooking /'kʊkɪŋ/. [1] N-U **Cooking** is cooked food. *I like your cooking.* [2] See also **cook.**

cool /kuːl/ **cooler, coolest, cools, cooling, cooled.** [1] ADJ Something that is **cool** has a low temperature but is not cold. *There was a cool breeze... The vaccines were kept cool in refrigerators.* ♦**coolness** N-U *...the coolness of the tiled floor.* ● See note at **cold.** [2] VERB When something **cools** or when you **cool** it, it becomes lower in temperature. You can also say it **cools** down or you **cool** it **down.** *As the droplets evaporated they cooled the air... Avoid putting your car away until the engine has cooled down.* [3] ADJ If you stay **cool** in a difficult situation, you remain calm. ♦**coolly** ADV *Everyone must think this situation through calmly and coolly.* ♦**coolness** N-U *Detectives praised him for his coolness.* [4] ADJ If you say that a person or their behaviour is **cool,** you mean that they are unfriendly or lack enthusiasm. ♦**coolly** ADV *'It's your choice, Nina,' David said coolly.* ♦**coolness** N-U *...the sudden coolness of her friend's manner.* [5] ADJ If you say that someone is **cool,** you mean that they are fashionable and attractive; INFORMAL.
▶ **cool down.** [1] See **cool** 2. [2] PHR-VERB If someone **cools down** or if you **cool** them **down,** they become less angry. *He has had time to cool down.*
▶ **cool off.** PHR-VERB If someone or something **cools off** or if you **cool** them **off,** they become cooler after being hot. *Cool off in the pool.*

co-operate /kəʊ-'ɒpəreɪt/ **co-operates, co-operating, co-operated.** [1] VERB If you **co-operate** with someone, you work with them or help them. *The UN had been co-operating with the State Department... The couple spoke about how they would co-operate in the raising of their child.* ♦**co-operation** /kəʊ-ˌɒpə'reɪʃən/ N-U *...economic co-operation with East Asia.* [2] VERB If you **co-operate,** you do what someone asks you to do. *He agreed to co-operate with the police investigation.* ♦**co-operation** N-U *...the importance of the public's co-operation in the hunt for the bombers.*

co-operative /kəʊ-'ɒpərətɪv/ **co-operatives.** [1] N-C A **co-operative** is a business or organization run by the people who work for it, who share its benefits and profits. [2] ADJ A **co-operative** activity is done by people working together. *...a smooth co-operative effort between Egyptian and US authorities.* ♦**co-operatively** ADV *They agreed to work co-operatively.* [3] ADJ Someone who is **co-operative** does what you ask them to do. *I made every effort to be co-operative.*

co-ordinate (or **coordinate**) **co-ordinates, co-ordinating, co-ordinated.** [1] VERB /kəʊ-'ɔːdɪneɪt/ If you **co-ordinate** an activity, you organize it. *...an advisory committee to co-ordinate police work. ...a rapid and well co-ordinated international rescue operation.* ♦**co-ordination** N-U *...more effective co-ordination of disaster relief.* ♦**co-ordinator, co-ordinators.** N-C *...the party's campaign co-ordinator.* [2] VERB If you **co-ordinate** the parts

of your body, you make them work together efficiently. ♦**co-ordination** N-U *...clumsiness and lack of co-ordination.* [3] N-C /kəʊ-'ɔːdɪnət/ The **co-ordinates** of a point on a map or graph are the two sets of numbers or letters that you need in order to find that point.

cop /kɒp/ **cops.** N-C A **cop** is a policeman or policewoman; INFORMAL.

cope /kəʊp/ **copes, coping, coped.** VERB If you **cope** with a problem, task, or difficult situation, you deal with it successfully. *She has had to cope with losing all her money... Don't worry, Clarrie. I'll cope.*

copious /'kəʊpiəs/. ADJ A **copious** amount is a large amount. *...copious amounts of red wine.* ♦**copiously** ADV *He bled copiously.*

copper /'kɒpə/ **coppers.** [1] N-U **Copper** is a soft reddish-brown metal. [2] N-C A **copper** is a policeman or policewoman; BRITISH, INFORMAL. [3] N-C **Coppers** are brown metal coins of low value; BRITISH. *I gave him a few coppers.*

copy /'kɒpi/ **copies, copying, copied.** [1] N-C If you make a **copy** of something, you produce something that looks like the original thing. *...a copy of Steve's resignation letter.* [2] VERB & PHR-VERB If you **copy** something which has been written or **copy** it **out,** you write it again exactly. *He copied the data into a notebook... We're copying from textbooks... Concentrating hard, the pupils copied out the text.* [3] VERB If you **copy** a person or their ideas, you behave like them. *Children can be seen to copy the behaviour of others whom they admire.* [4] N-C A **copy** of a book, newspaper, or record is one of many identical ones that have been printed or produced. *...a copy of 'USA Today'.*
▶ **copy down.** PHR-VERB If you **copy down** what someone says or writes, you write it down yourself. *I copied it down the way my lawyer read it.*
▶ **copy out.** See **copy** 2.

copyright /'kɒpiraɪt/ **copyrights.** N-VAR If someone has the **copyright** on a piece of writing or music, it is illegal to reproduce or perform it without their permission.

coral /'kɒrəl, AM 'kɔːr-/ **corals.** N-U **Coral** is a hard substance formed from the skeletons of very small sea animals.

cord /kɔːd/ **cords.** [1] N-VAR **Cord** is strong thick string. *...a length of nylon cord.* [2] N-VAR **Cord** is electrical wire covered in rubber or plastic. *...electrical cord.*

cordial /'kɔːdiəl, AM -dʒəl/ **cordials.** ADJ **Cordial** means warm and friendly. *They struck up a cordial relationship.* ♦**cordiality** /ˌkɔːdi'æltɪ, AM -'dʒæl-/ N-U *...an atmosphere of cordiality.* ♦**cordially** ADV *They all greeted me very cordially.*

cordon /'kɔːdən/ **cordons, cordoning, cordoned.** N-C A **cordon** is a line of police, soldiers, or vehicles preventing people from entering or leaving an area.
▶ **cordon off.** PHR-VERB If police or soldiers **cordon off** an area, they prevent people from entering or leaving it.

core /kɔː/ **cores.** [1] N-C The **core** of a fruit is the central part containing seeds or pips. *...an apple core.* [2] N-C The **core** of something is the central or most important part. ...*the core of the city... Get straight to the core of a problem*.

cork /kɔːk/ **corks.** [1] N-U **Cork** is a soft light substance which forms the bark of a Mediterranean tree. [2] N-C A **cork** is a piece of cork or plastic that is pushed into the opening of a bottle to close it.

corkscrew /'kɔːkskruː/ **corkscrews.** N-C A **corkscrew** is a device for pulling corks out of bottles.

corn /kɔːn/ **corns.** [1] N-U **Corn** refers to crops such as wheat and barley, or their seeds; BRITISH. ...*fields of corn*. [2] N-U **Corn** is the same as **maize**; AMERICAN. ...*fresh-baked corn bread*.

corner /'kɔːnə/ **corners, cornering, cornered.** [1] N-C A **corner** is a place where two sides or edges of something meet, or where a road meets another road. ...*a card table in the corner of the living room... He waited until the man had turned a corner*. [2] VERB If you **corner** a person or animal, you force them into a place they cannot escape from. *The gang was cornered by armed police. ...like a cornered animal.* [3] VERB If a company or place **corners** an area of trade, they gain control over it so that no one else can have any success in it. *This restaurant has cornered the Madrid market for specialist paellas.* [4] PHRASE If you say that something is **round the corner**, you mean that it will happen very soon. ...*economic recovery is just around the corner*.

cornerstone /'kɔːnəstəʊn/ **cornerstones.** N-C The **cornerstone** of something is the basis of its existence or success; FORMAL. *Research is the cornerstone of the profession.*

corny /'kɔːni/. ADJ If you describe something as **corny**, you mean that it is obvious or sentimental and not at all original. *I know it sounds corny, but I'm really not motivated by money.*

coronary /'kɒrənri, AM 'kɔːrəneri/ **coronaries.** [1] ADJ BEFORE N **Coronary** means relating to the heart; TECHNICAL. ...*the coronary arteries*. [2] N-C If someone has a **coronary**, blood cannot reach their heart because of a blood clot.

coronation /ˌkɒrə'neɪʃən, AM ˌkɔːr-/ **coronations.** N-C A **coronation** is the ceremony at which a king or queen is crowned.

coroner /'kɒrənə, AM 'kɔːr-/ **coroners.** N-C A **coroner** is an official who is responsible for investigating sudden or unusual deaths.

corporal /'kɔːprəl/ **corporals.** N-C & N-TITLE A **corporal** is a non-commissioned officer in the army.

corporal punishment. N-U **Corporal punishment** is the punishment of people by hitting them.

corporate /'kɔːprət/. ADJ BEFORE N **Corporate** means relating to business corporations. ...*a corporate lawyer*.

corporation /ˌkɔːpə'reɪʃən/ **corporations.** N-C A **corporation** is a large business or company.

corps /kɔː/. **Corps** is both the singular and the plural form. [1] N-C A **corps** is a part of the army which has special duties. ...*the Army Medical Corps.* [2] N-C A **corps** is a small group of people who do a special job. ...*the diplomatic corps.*

corpse /kɔːps/ **corpses.** N-C A **corpse** is a dead body.

correct /kə'rekt/ **corrects, correcting, corrected.** [1] ADJ Something that is **correct** is accurate and has no mistakes. *Check the label is correct.* ◆**correctly** ADV *Did I pronounce your name correctly?* [2] ADJ AFTER LINK-V If you are **correct**, what you have said or thought is true. *If Casey is correct, the total cost of the cleanup would come to $110 billion.* [3] ADJ BEFORE N The **correct** thing or method is the one that is most suitable in a particular situation. ...*the correct way to produce a crop of tomato plants.* ◆**correctly** ADV *The exercises, correctly performed, will stretch and tone muscles.* [4] VERB If you **correct** a mistake, problem, or fault, you put it right. *Most companies willingly correct what went wrong.* [5] VERB When someone **corrects** a piece of writing, they mark the mistakes in it. [6] VERB If you **correct** someone, you say something which is more accurate or appropriate than what they have just said. *I must correct him on a minor point.* [7] ADJ **Correct** behaviour is considered socially acceptable. ◆**correctly** ADV *The High Court of Parliament began very correctly.* ◆**correctness** N-U ...*political correctness.*

correction /kə'rekʃən/ **corrections.** [1] N-VAR A **correction** is something which puts right something that is wrong. *We will then make the necessary corrections.* [2] N-C **Corrections** are marks or comments made on a piece of written work which indicate where there are mistakes and what are the right answers.

corrective /kə'rektɪv/ **correctives.** ADJ **Corrective** measures are intended to put right something that is wrong. ...*corrective surgery.*

correlate /'kɒrəleɪt, AM 'kɔːr-/ **correlates, correlating, correlated.** VERB If one thing **correlates** with another, there is a close similarity or connection between them. *Obesity correlates with increased risk for hypertension and stroke... Earnings and performance aren't always correlated.*

correlation /ˌkɒrə'leɪʃən, AM ˌkɔːr-/ **correlations.** N-C A **correlation** between things is a link between them; FORMAL. ...*the correlation between smoking and disease.*

correspond /ˌkɒrɪ'spɒnd, AM ˌkɔːr-/ **corresponds, corresponding, corresponded.** [1] VERB If one thing **corresponds** to another, there is a close similarity or connection between them. *The two maps of London correspond closely.* ◆**corresponding** ADJ BEFORE N *March and April sales this year were up 8% on the corresponding period in 2002.* ◆**correspondingly** ADV *Local loans are easier to monitor and are correspondingly less risky.* [2] VERB If you **correspond** with someone, you write letters to them. *We corresponded regularly.*

correspondence /ˌkɒrɪ'spɒndəns, AM ˌkɔːr-/ **correspondences.** [1] N-U **Correspondence** is the act of writing letters to someone. ...*a long correspondence with a close college friend.* [2] N-U Someone's **correspondence** is the letters that they receive or send. [3] N-C If there is a **correspondence** between two things, there is a similarity between them. *...correspondences between Eastern religions and Christianity.*

correspondent /ˌkɒrɪ'spɒndənt, ᴀᴍ ˌkɔːr-/ **correspondents.** N-C A **correspondent** is a television or newspaper reporter.

corridor /'kɒrɪdɔː, ᴀᴍ 'kɔːrɪdər/ **corridors.** N-C A **corridor** is a long passage in a building or train, with rooms on one or both sides.

corroborate /kə'rɒbəreɪt/ **corroborates, corroborating, corroborated.** VERB To **corroborate** something that has been said means to provide evidence that supports it; FORMAL. *...a wide range of documents which corroborated the story.* ◆**corroboration** N-U *...independent corroboration.*

corrode /kə'rəʊd/ **corrodes, corroding, corroded.** VERB When metal or stone **corrodes**, it is gradually destroyed by rust or by a chemical. *The structure had been corroded by moisture.* ◆**corroded** ADJ *The underground pipes were badly corroded.* ◆**corrosion** N-U *Zinc is used to protect other metals from corrosion.*

corrugated /'kɒrəgeɪtɪd, ᴀᴍ 'kɔːr-/. ADJ **Corrugated** metal or cardboard has been folded into a series of small parallel folds to make it stronger.

corrupt /kə'rʌpt/ **corrupts, corrupting, corrupted.** [1] ADJ A **corrupt** person behaves in a way that is morally wrong, especially by doing illegal things for money. [2] VERB If someone **is corrupted** by something, it causes them to become dishonest and unable to be trusted. *...a man so corrupted by the desire for money.*

corruption /kə'rʌpʃən/. N-U **Corruption** is dishonesty and illegal behaviour by people in positions of power. *The President faces 54 charges of corruption and tax evasion.*

cosmetic /kɒz'metɪk/ **cosmetics.** [1] N-C **Cosmetics** are substances such as lipstick or face powder. [2] ADJ **Cosmetic** measures or changes improve the appearance of something without changing its basic character or without solving a basic problem. *They believe the changes in South Africa are still largely cosmetic.*

cosmic /'kɒzmɪk/. ADJ **Cosmic** means occurring in, or coming from, the part of space that lies outside Earth and its atmosphere. *...cosmic radiation.*

cosmopolitan /ˌkɒzmə'pɒlɪtən/. ADJ **Cosmopolitan** means influenced by many different countries and cultures. *London has always been a cosmopolitan city.*

cosmos /'kɒzmɒs, ᴀᴍ -məs/. N-SING The **cosmos** is the universe; TECHNICAL.

cost /kɒst, ᴀᴍ kɔːst/ **costs, costing, cost.** [1] N-C The **cost** of something is the amount of money needed to buy, do, or make it. *Badges are also available at a cost of £2.50.* [2] VERB If something **costs** a particular amount of money, you can buy, do, or make it for that amount. *It's going to cost me over $100,000 to buy new trucks.* [3] N-SING The **cost** of achieving something is the loss, damage or injury involved in achieving it. *Factories in the West Country are to be closed at a cost of 150 jobs.* [4] VERB If an event or mistake **costs** you something, you lose that thing because of it. *...an operation that cost him his sight.* [5] PHRASE If you say that something must be avoided **at all**

costs, you are emphasizing that it must not be allowed to happen under any circumstances.

'co-star, co-stars. [1] N-C An actor or actress who is a **co-star** of a film has one of the most important parts in it. [2] VERB If an actor or actress **co-stars** with another actor or actress, the two of them have the main parts in a film. *They co-starred in the movie State Of Grace.*

'cost-ef'fective. ADJ Something that is **cost-effective** saves or makes more money than it costs to make or maintain.

costly /'kɒstli, ᴀᴍ 'kɔːst-/ **costlier, costliest.** [1] ADJ Something that is **costly** is very expensive. [2] ADJ If you describe someone's action or mistake as **costly**, you mean that it results in a serious disadvantage for them. *This sort of scandal in international banking has been politically costly*

,cost of 'living. N-SING The **cost of living** is the average amount of money that people need to spend on food, housing, and clothing.

costume /'kɒstjuːm, ᴀᴍ -tuːm/ **costumes.** N-U A **costume** is a set or style of clothes worn by people at a particular time in history, or in a particular country.

cosy (ᴀᴍ **cozy**) /'kəʊzi/ **cosier, cosiest.** [1] ADJ A **cosy** house or room is comfortable and warm. [2] ADJ You use **cosy** to describe activities that are pleasant and friendly. *...a cosy chat between friends.*

cot /kɒt/ **cots.** N-C In British English, a **cot** is a bed for a baby, with bars or panels round it so that the baby cannot fall out. The American word is **crib.**

cottage /'kɒtɪdʒ/ **cottages.** N-C A **cottage** is a small house, usually in the country.

cotton /'kɒtən/ **cottons, cottoning, cottoned.** [1] N-VAR **Cotton** is cloth made from the soft fibres from the cotton plant. *Summer sheets are generally made of cotton. ...a cotton shirt.* [2] N-U **Cotton** is a plant which produces the soft fibres used in making cotton cloth. [3] N-VAR **Cotton** is sewing thread; BRITISH. *...a needle and cotton.*

▸ **cotton on.** PHR-VERB If you **cotton on** to something, you understand it or realize it; INFORMAL. *I knew exactly what I was arguing about but she didn't cotton on.*

,cotton 'wool. N-U **Cotton wool** is soft fluffy cotton, often used for applying creams to your skin.

couch /kaʊtʃ/ **couches, couching, couched.** [1] N-C A **couch** is a long soft piece of furniture for sitting or lying on. [2] VERB If a statement **is couched** in a particular style of language, it is expressed in that style of language; WRITTEN. *The statement was couched in polite terms.*

cough /kɒf, ᴀᴍ kɔːf/ **coughs, coughing, coughed.** [1] VERB & N-C When you **cough**, you force air out of your throat with a sudden harsh noise. A **cough** is an act of coughing. *Graham began to cough violently... She heard a muffled cough behind her.* ◆**coughing** N-U *...a terrible fit of coughing.* [2] N-C A **cough** is an illness in which you cough a lot. *Contact your doctor if the cough persists.* [3] VERB If you **cough** blood, it comes up out of your throat or mouth when you cough.

▶ **cough up.** PHR-VERB If you **cough up** money, you give someone money, usually when you would prefer not to; INFORMAL. *I'll have to cough up $10,000 a year for tuition.*

could /kəd, STRONG kʊd/ [1] MODAL If you **could** do something, you were able to do it. *I could see that something was terribly wrong... He could not resist telling her the truth... I couldn't read or write.* [2] MODAL You use **could** after 'if' when you are imagining what would happen if something was the case. *If I could afford it I'd have four television sets.* [3] MODAL You use **could** to indicate that something sometimes happened. *He could be very pleasant when he wanted to.* [4] MODAL You use **could have** to indicate that something was a possibility in the past, although it did not actually happen. *He could have made a fortune as a lawyer.* [5] MODAL You use **could** to indicate that something is possibly true, or that it may possibly happen. *The disease could have been caused by years of working in smokey clubs.* [6] MODAL You use **could** when making offers and suggestions. *I could call the local doctor... Couldn't you go for walks with your friends?* [7] MODAL You use **could** in questions to make polite requests. *Could I stay tonight?... He asked if he could have a cup of coffee.*

couldn't /ˈkʊdənt/. **Couldn't** is the usual spoken form of 'could not'.

could've /ˈkʊdəv/. **Could've** is the usual spoken form of 'could have', when 'have' is an auxiliary verb.

council /ˈkaʊnsəl/ **councils.** [1] N-C A **council** is a group of people elected to govern a town or other area. *...Cheshire County Council.* [2] ADJ BEFORE N **Council** houses or flats are owned by the local council and people pay rent to live in them; BRITISH.

councillor (AM **councilor**) /ˈkaʊnsələ/ **councillors.** N-C A **councillor** is a member of a local council.

counsel /ˈkaʊnsəl/ **counsels, counselling, counselled** (or AM **counseling, counseled**). [1] N-U **Counsel** is careful advice; FORMAL. *It is wise to seek help and counsel.* [2] VERB If you **counsel** someone to do something, you advise them to do it; FORMAL. *My advisers counselled me to do nothing.* [3] VERB If you **counsel** people, you give them advice about their problems. *...a psychologist who counsels people with eating disorders.* ◆**counselling** N-U *...marriage counseling.* ◆**counsellor, counsellors** N-C *Take your problems to a trained counsellor.* [4] N-C Someone's **counsel** is the lawyer who gives advice on a legal case and speaks for them in court.

count /kaʊnt/ **counts, counting, counted.** [1] VERB When you **count**, you say all the numbers in order up to a particular number. *He was counting slowly under his breath... Brian counted to twenty.* [2] VERB & PHR-VERB If you **count** all the things in a group, or if you **count** them **up**, you add them up to see how many there are. *I counted the money... They counted up all the hours the villagers work.* [3] N-C A **count** is the action of counting, or the number that you get after counting. *Bill's mother had been five times divorced at the last count.* [4] VERB If something or someone **counts for** something, or if they **count**, they are important or valuable. *Experience counts for a lot in poker... It's as if your opinions, your likes and dislikes just don't count.* [5] VERB If something **counts** as a particular thing, it is regarded as being that thing. *A conservatory counts as an extension... It can be counted a success.* [6] N-C & N-TITLE A **Count** is a male member of the nobility. [7] PHRASE If you **keep count** of a number of things, you keep a record of how many have occurred. If you **lose count** of a number of things, you cannot remember how many have occurred. *She'd lost count of the interviews she'd been called for.*

▶ **count against.** PHR-VERB If something **counts against** you, it may cause you to be punished or rejected. *...his youth might count against him.*

▶ **count on** or **count upon.** PHR-VERB If you **count on** someone or something, you rely on them to support you. *I can always count on you to cheer me up.*

▶ **count out.** PHR-VERB If you **count out** a sum of money, you count it as you put the notes or coins in a pile.

▶ **count up.** See **count** 2.

▶ **count upon.** See **count on.**

countable noun /ˌkaʊntəbəl ˈnaʊn/ **countable nouns.** N-C A **countable noun** is the same as a **count noun.**

countdown /ˈkaʊntdaʊn/ **countdowns.** N-C A **countdown** is the counting aloud of numbers in reverse order before something happens.

countenance /ˈkaʊntɪnəns/ **countenances, countenancing, countenanced.** [1] VERB If someone will not countenance something, they do not agree with it and will not allow it to happen; FORMAL. *Jake would not countenance Janis's marrying.* [2] N-C Someone's **countenance** is their face; LITERARY.

counter /ˈkaʊntə/ **counters, countering, countered.** [1] N-C In a shop, a **counter** is a long flat surface at which customers are served. *...the cosmetics counter.* [2] VERB & N-C If you **counter** something that is being done, or do something as **a counter to** it, you take action to make it less effective. *...those in the community who are working to counter the drug and gang problem. ...a danger that Muslim terrorism will emerge as a counter to Hindu violence.* [3] VERB If you **counter** something that has been said, you say something in reaction to it or in opposition to it. *Both of them had to counter fierce criticism.* [4] PHRASE If one thing **runs counter to** another, or if one thing **is counter to** another, the first thing is the opposite of the second thing or conflicts with it. *Much of the plan runs counter to European Union policy.* [5] N-C A **counter** is a small, flat, round object used in a board game.

counteract /ˌkaʊntərˈækt/ **counteracts, counteracting, counteracted.** VERB To **counteract** something means to reduce its effect by doing something that has the opposite effect. *...pills to counteract high blood pressure.*

'counter-attack, counter-attacks, counter-attacking, counter-attacked.

VERB & N-VAR When an army **counter-attacks**, or when it makes a **counter-attack**, it attacks an enemy that has just attacked it.

counterclockwise /ˌkaʊntəˈklɒkwaɪz/. ADV & ADJ **Counterclockwise** means the same as **anti-clockwise**; AMERICAN.

counterfeit /ˈkaʊntəfɪt/ **counterfeits, counterfeiting, counterfeited.** [1] N-C & ADJ **Counterfeits**, or **counterfeit** banknotes, goods, or documents are not genuine, but have been made to look exactly like genuine ones in order to deceive people. *Counterfeits of the company's jeans are flooding Europe. ...counterfeit currency.* [2] VERB To **counterfeit** something means to make a counterfeit version of it. ◆**counterfeiting** N-U *...the business of counterfeiting.*

counterpart /ˈkaʊntəpɑːt/ **counterparts.** N-C Someone's or something's **counterpart** is another person or thing that has a similar function in a different place. *The Foreign Secretary telephoned his German and Italian counterparts.*

ˌcounter-proˈductive (or **counterproductive**). ADJ Something that is **counterproductive** has the opposite effect from what you intend. *Exercising alone can be boring and often counter-productive.*

countess /ˈkaʊntɪs/ **countesses.** N-C & N-TITLE A **Countess** is a female member of the nobility.

countless /ˈkaʊntləs/. ADJ BEFORE N **Countless** means very many. *She brought joy to countless people.*

ˈcount noun, count nouns. N-C A **count noun** is a noun such as 'bird', 'chair', or 'year' which has a singular and a plural form and is always used after a determiner in the singular.

country /ˈkʌntri/ **countries.** [1] N-C A **country** is one of the political areas which the world is divided into, covering a particular area of land. You can refer to the people who live in a particular country as **the country**. *Indonesia is the fifth most populous country in the world... The country was going through the final throes of civil war.*

> **Country** is the most usual word to use when you are talking about the major political units that the world is divided into. **State** is used when you are talking about politics or government institutions. *...the new German state created by the unification process. ...Italy's state-controlled telecommunications company.* **State** can also refer to a political unit within a particular country. *...the American state of California.* **Nation** is often used when you are talking about a country's inhabitants, and their cultural or ethnic background. *Wales is a proud nation with its own traditions... Zambia's President Kaunda is due to address the nation later tonight.* **Land** is a less precise and more literary word, which you can use, for example, to talk about the feelings you have for a particular country. *They was fascinated to learn about this strange land at the edge of Europe.*

[2] N-SING **The country** is land away from towns and cities. *...a healthy life in the country.* [3] N-U **Country** is used to refer to an area with particular characteristics or connections. *...mountainous country east of Genoa.* [4] N-U **Country** music is a style of popular music from the USA.

countryman /ˈkʌntrimən/ **countrymen.** N-C Your **countrymen** are people from your own country.

countryside /ˈkʌntrisaɪd/. N-U The **countryside** is land away from towns and cities. ● See note at **landscape**.

county /ˈkaʊnti/ **counties.** N-C A **county** is a region of Britain, Ireland, or the USA with its own local government.

coup /kuː/ **coups.** [1] N-C A **coup** is the same as a **coup d'état.** [2] N-C A **coup** is an achievement thought to be especially brilliant because of its difficulty. *The sale is a big coup for the auction house.*

coup d'état /ˌkuː deɪˈtɑː/ **coups d'état.** The plural is pronounced the same as the singular. N-C When there is a **coup d'état**, a group of people seize power in a country.

couple /ˈkʌpəl/ **couples, coupling, coupled.** [1] QUANT If you refer to a **couple** of people or things, you mean two or approximately two of them. *I think the trouble will clear up in a couple of days.* [2] N-C A **couple** is two people who are married, or having a sexual or romantic relationship. *The couple have no children.* [3] N-C A **couple** is two people that you see together on a particular occasion or that are associated in some way. *The four couples began the opening dance.* [4] VERB If one thing produces a particular effect when it **is coupled with** another, the two things combine to produce that effect. *Over-use of those drugs, coupled with poor diet, leads to physical degeneration.*

coupon /ˈkuːpɒn/ **coupons.** [1] N-C A **coupon** is a piece of printed paper which is issued by the maker or supplier of a product and which allows you to pay less than usual for something. [2] N-C A **coupon** is a small form which you fill in and send off to ask for information, or to enter a competition.

courage /ˈkʌrɪdʒ, AM ˈkɜːr-/. N-U **Courage** is the quality shown by someone who does something difficult or dangerous, even though they may be afraid. *One of the girls plucked up the courage to tell police he was a drugs dealer.*

courageous /kəˈreɪdʒəs/. ADJ Someone who is **courageous** shows courage. *...his courageous defiance of the government.* ◆**courageously** ADV *Smith fought courageously.*

courgette /kʊəˈʒet/ **courgettes.** N-VAR In British English, **courgettes** are long thin green vegetables; the American word is **zucchini**.

courier /ˈkʊriə/ **couriers.** [1] N-C A **courier** is a person who is paid to take letters and parcels direct from one place to another. [2] N-C A **courier** is a person employed by a travel company to look after people who are on holiday.

course /kɔːs/ **courses, coursing, coursed.** [1] See **of course.** [2] N-U The **course** of a vehicle is the route along which it is travelling. *The captain altered course a few degrees to the right.* [3] N-C A **course** of action is an action or a

series of actions that you can do in a particular situation. *Vietnam is trying to decide on its course for the future.* [4] N-SING You can refer to the way that events develop as the **course** of history, nature, or events. [5] N-C A **course** is a series of lessons or lectures on a particular subject. *...a course in business administration.* [6] N-C A **course** of medical treatment is a series of treatments that a doctor gives someone. *...a course of antibiotics.* [7] N-C A **course** is one part of a meal. *...a three-course dinner.* [8] VERB If a liquid **courses** somewhere, it flows there quickly; LITERARY. *The tears coursed down his cheeks.* [9] N-C In sport, a **course** is an area of land where races are held or golf is played.
PHRASES ● If you are **on course for** something, you are likely to achieve it. ● If something **runs its course** or **takes its course**, it develops naturally and comes to a natural end. *20,000 cows would die before the epidemic had run its course.* ● **in due course:** see **due**.

court /kɔːt/ **courts, courting, courted.** [1] N-C A **court** is a place where legal matters are decided by a judge and jury or by a magistrate. You can also refer to a judge, jury, or magistrates as a **court**. *Would she be willing to testify in court?... The court awarded the man one and a half million pounds.* [2] N-C A **court** is an area for playing a game such as tennis or squash. [3] N-C The **court** of a king or queen is the place where he or she lives and works. [4] PHRASE You can say someone **holds court** when they are surrounded by a lot of people who are paying them a lot of attention because they are interesting or famous; used showing disapproval. [5] VERB If you say that someone **is courting** disaster, you think they are acting in a way that makes it likely to happen. [6] VERB If you **court** something such as publicity or popularity, you try to obtain it for yourself.

courteous /ˈkɜːtɪəs/. ADJ Someone who is **courteous** is polite, respectful, and considerate. *He is so courteous and so helpful.* ◆**courteously** ADV *He nodded courteously to me.*

courtesy /ˈkɜːtɪsi/ **courtesies.** [1] N-U **Courtesy** is polite, respectful, and considerate behaviour. [2] N-C **Courtesies** are polite and respectful things that you say or do; FORMAL. *Hugh and John were exchanging courtesies.* [3] ADJ BEFORE N **Courtesy** is used to describe services that are provided free of charge by an organization to its customers. *A courtesy shuttle bus operates between the hotel and the town.*

courthouse /ˈkɔːthaʊs/ **courthouses.** N-C In American English, a **courthouse** is a building in which a law court meets. The usual British word is **court**.

courtier /ˈkɔːtɪə/ **courtiers.** N-C **Courtiers** were members of the nobility at the court of a king or queen.

court-'martial, court-martials, court-martialling, court-martialled. [1] N-VAR A **court-martial** is a military court of a member of the armed forces. [2] VERB If a member of the armed forces **is court-martialled**, he or she is tried in a military court.

courtroom /ˈkɔːtruːm/ **courtrooms.** N-C A

courtroom is a room in which a law court meets.

courtship /ˈkɔːtʃɪp/. N-U **Courtship** is the activity in which a man and a woman spend a lot of time together, because they are intending to get married; FORMAL.

courtyard /ˈkɔːtjɑːd/ **courtyards.** N-C A **courtyard** is a flat open area of ground surrounded by buildings or walls.

cousin /ˈkʌzən/ **cousins.** N-C Your **cousin** is the child of your uncle or aunt.

cove /kəʊv/ **coves.** N-C A **cove** is a small bay on the coast.

covenant /ˈkʌvənənt/ **covenants.** [1] N-C A **covenant** is a formal written agreement between two or more people which is recognized in law. [2] N-C A **covenant** is a formal written promise to pay a sum of money each year for a fixed period, especially to a charity.

cover /ˈkʌvə/ **covers, covering, covered.** [1] VERB & PHR-VERB If you **cover** one thing with another, or if you **cover** it **up**, you place the second thing over the first in order to protect it, hide it, or close it. *...the black patch which covered his left eye.* [2] N-C A **cover** is something which is put over an object, usually in order to protect it. The **cover** of a book or a magazine is the protective outside part of it. [3] N-PL Bed **covers** are sheets, blankets, and quilts. [4] VERB If one thing **is covered** in or another, the second forms a layer over its surface. *The desk was covered with papers... Black clouds covered the sky.* [5] VERB If you **cover** a particular distance, you travel that distance. [6] VERB & N-U When an insurance policy **covers** a person or thing, or provides **cover**, it guarantees that money will be paid in relation to that person or thing. *...travel insurance covering you and your family against theft. ...unlimited cover for Freezer Contents.* [7] VERB If you **cover** a particular topic, you discuss it in a lecture, course, or book. *Other subjects covered included nerves and how to overcome them.* [8] VERB If a journalist **covers** an event, he or she reports on it. [9] VERB If a sum of money **covers** something, it is enough to pay for it. *...£1.50 to cover postage and administration.* [10] N-U & PHRASE You can refer to trees, rocks, or other places where you shelter from the weather or hide from some one as **cover**. If you **take cover**, you shelter from the weather or from an attack. *They ran for cover.*

▶ **cover up.** [1] PHR-VERB If you **cover up** something that you do not want people to know about, you conceal the truth about it. *How do we know you're not just covering up for your friend?* [2] See also **cover** 1. ● See also **cover-up.**

coverage /ˈkʌvərɪdʒ/. N-U The **coverage** of something in the news is the reporting of it. *...TV coverage of college football.*

covering /ˈkʌvərɪŋ/ **coverings.** N-VAR A **covering** is a layer of something over something else. *Sawdust was used as a hygienic floor covering.*

covert /ˈkʌvət, ˈkəʊvɜːt/. ADJ **Covert** activities or situations are secret or hidden; FORMAL. *They have been supplying covert military aid to* *the rebels.* ◆**covertly** ADV *Joanna studied him covertly through her lashes.*

'**cover-up, cover-ups.** N-C A **cover-up** is an attempt to hide a crime or mistake.

covet /ˈkʌvɪt/ **covets, coveting, coveted.** VERB If you **covet** something belonging to someone else, you want very much to have it for yourself; FORMAL. *She coveted his job so openly that conversations between them were tense.*

coveted /ˈkʌvɪtɪd/. ADJ You use **coveted** to describe something that very many people would like to have. *...one of sport's most coveted trophies.*

cow /kaʊ/ **cows, cowing, cowed.** ① N-C A **cow** is a large female animal kept on farms for its milk. ② N-C Some female animals, including elephants and whales, are called **cows**. ③ VERB If someone **is cowed**, they are frightened into behaving in a particular way; FORMAL. *The government, far from being cowed by these threats, has vowed to continue its policy.* ◆**cowed** ADJ *She was so cowed by the beatings that she meekly obeyed.*

coward /ˈkaʊəd/ **cowards.** N-C A **coward** is someone who is easily frightened and avoids dangerous or difficult situations.

cowardice /ˈkaʊədɪs/. N-U **Cowardice** is cowardly behaviour.

cowardly /ˈkaʊədli/. ADJ Someone who is **cowardly** is easily frightened and so avoids doing dangerous or difficult things. *I know it would be cowardly not to respond to the invitation.*

cowboy /ˈkaʊbɔɪ/ **cowboys.** ① N-C A **cowboy** is a man employed to look after cattle in the United States of America. ② N-C You can refer to someone, especially a builder, as a **cowboy** if you think they are dishonest or do bad work.

coy /kɔɪ/. ① ADJ If you describe someone as **coy**, you disapprove of them pretending to be shy and modest. *Carol charmed all the men by turning coy.* ◆**coyly** ADV *She smiled coyly at Algie as he took her hand.* ◆**coyness** N-U *...her coyness and flirting.* ② ADJ If someone is being **coy**, they are unwilling to talk about something that they feel guilty or embarrassed about. *The hotel are understandably coy about the incident.*

cozy /ˈkaʊzi/. See **cosy**.

crab /kræb/ **crabs.** N-C A **crab** is a sea creature with a flat round body covered by a shell, and five pairs of legs with claws on the front pair. Crabs walk sideways.

crack 1 verb uses

crack /kræk/ **cracks, cracking, cracked.** ① VERB If something **cracks**, or if you **crack** it, it becomes slightly damaged, with lines appearing on its surface. *One of the stones cracked the glass panel in the front door. ...a cracked mirror.* ② VERB If you **crack** something, you hit it and it breaks or is damaged. *Crack the eggs into a bowl... He cracked his head on the pavement.* ③ VERB If you **crack** a problem or a code, you solve it, especially after a lot of thought. *He has finally cracked the system.* ④ VERB If someone **cracks**, they lose control of their emotions or actions because they are under a lot of pressure. *She's calm and*

strong, and she is just not going to crack. ⑤ VERB If you **crack** a joke, you tell it.

▶ **crack down.** PHR-VERB If people in authority **crack down** on a group of people, they become stricter in making them obey rules or laws. *We are cracking down now. Anyone who gets caught is fired.* ● See also **crackdown**.

▶ **crack up.** PHR-VERB If someone **cracks up**, they are under such emotional strain that they become mentally ill; INFORMAL.

crack 2 noun and adjective uses

crack /kræk/ **cracks.** ① N-C A **crack** is a very narrow gap between two things. *Kathryn had seen him through a crack in the curtains.* ② N-C A **crack** is a line that appears on the surface of something when it is slightly damaged. *The plate had a crack in it.* ③ N-C A **crack** is a sharp sound, like the sound of a piece of wood breaking. *There was a loud crack and glass flew into the car.* ④ N-SING If you have a **crack at** something, you make an attempt to do or achieve something; INFORMAL. *I should love to have a crack at the Olympia title.* ⑤ N-C A **crack** is a slightly rude or cruel joke. ⑥ ADJ BEFORE N A **crack** soldier or sportsman is highly trained and very skilful. *...a crack undercover police officer.*

crackdown /ˈkrækdaʊn/ **crackdowns.** N-C A **crackdown** is strong official action taken to punish people who break laws.

cracker /ˈkrækə/ **crackers.** N-C A **cracker** is a hollow cardboard tube covered with coloured paper. Crackers make a bang when they are pulled apart and usually contain a small toy, joke, and a paper hat.

crackle /ˈkrækəl/ **crackles, crackling, crackled.** VERB & N-C If something **crackles**, it makes a series of short harsh noises called **crackles**. *The radio crackled again. ...the crackle of gunfire.*

cradle /ˈkreɪdəl/ **cradles, cradling, cradled.** ① N-C A **cradle** is a baby's bed with high sides. ② N-SING A place that is referred to as the **cradle of** something is the place where it began. *...New York, the cradle of capitalism.* ③ VERB If you **cradle** someone or something in your arms, you hold them carefully. *I stood cradling the phone.*

craft /krɑːft, kræft/ **crafts, crafting, crafted.** ① N-C You can refer to a boat, a spacecraft, or an aircraft as a **craft**. **Craft** is both the singular and plural form. *Hundreds of small craft sounded their foghorns.* ② N-C A **craft** is an activity that involves doing something skilfully, especially an activity such as weaving, carving, or pottery that involves making things skilfully with your hands. *...the craft of writing. ...traditional arts and crafts.* ③ VERB If something **is crafted**, it is made skilfully. *Many delegates were willing to craft a compromise.*

craftsman /ˈkrɑːftsmən, ˈkræft-/ **craftsmen.** N-C A **craftsman** is a man who makes things skilfully with his hands.

craftsmanship /ˈkrɑːftsmənʃɪp, ˈkræft-/. ① N-U **Craftsmanship** is the skill that someone uses when they make beautiful things with their hands. *...the craftsmanship of Armani.* ② N-U **Craftsmanship** is the quality that something has when it is beautiful and has been carefully made. *His canoes are known for their style, fine detail and craftsmanship.*

crafty /ˈkrɑːfti, ˈkræfti/ **craftier, craftiest.** ADJ If you describe someone as **crafty**, you mean that they get what they want in a clever way, often by deceiving people. *...a crafty, lying character.*

cram /kræm/ **crams, cramming, crammed.** VERB If you **cram** things or people into a place, or if they **cram** it, there are so many of them in it at one time that it is completely full. *I crammed my bag full of swimsuits and T-shirts... Friends and admirers crammed the chapel.*

crammed /kræmd/. ADJ If a place is **crammed** with things or people, it is very full of them. *The house is crammed with priceless furniture.*

cramp /kræmp/ **cramps, cramping, cramped.** N-U & N-PL **Cramp** is a sudden strong pain caused by a muscle suddenly contracting. *...stomach cramps.*

cramped /kræmpt/. ADJ A **cramped** room or building is not big enough for the people or things in it. *...a rather cramped little flat.*

crane /kreɪn/ **cranes, craning, craned.** [1] N-C A **crane** is a large machine that moves heavy things by lifting them in the air. [2] N-C A **crane** is a kind of large bird with a long neck and long legs. [3] VERB If you **crane** your neck, you stretch your neck in a particular direction in order to see or hear something better. *She craned forward to look at me.*

crank /kræŋk/ **cranks, cranking, cranked.** [1] N-C If you call someone a **crank**, you think they have peculiar ideas or behaviour; INFORMAL. [2] VERB If you **crank** a device or machine, you make it move by turning a handle. *The chauffeur got out to crank the motor.*

crash /kræʃ/ **crashes, crashing, crashed.** [1] VERB & N-C If a moving vehicle **crashes**, or if it has a **crash**, it hits something and is damaged or destroyed. *His car crashed into the rear of a van... His mother crashed her car into a tree. ...a car crash.* [2] VERB & N-C To **crash** means to move or fall violently, making a sudden loud noise, called a **crash**. *The walls above us crashed down... Two people in the flat recalled hearing a loud crash about 1.30 a.m.* [3] VERB & N-C If a business or financial system **crashes**, it fails suddenly, often with serious effects. Its sudden failure is called a **crash**. *When the market crashed, they assumed the deal would be cancelled. ...a stock market crash.* [4] VERB If a computer or a computer program **crashes**, it fails suddenly.

crass /kræs/. ADJ **Crass** behaviour is stupid and insensitive.

crate /kreɪt/ **crates.** N-C A **crate** is a large box used for transporting or storing things.

crater /ˈkreɪtə/ **craters.** N-C A **crater** is a large hole in the ground, which has been caused by something hitting it or by an explosion.

crave /kreɪv/ **craves, craving, craved.** VERB If you **crave** something, you want to have it very much. *...a vulnerable, unhappy girl who craved affection... You may be craving for some fresh air.* ◆**craving, cravings.** N-C *...a craving for sugar.*

crawl /krɔːl/ **crawls, crawling, crawled.** [1] VERB When you **crawl**, you move forward on your hands and knees. *I began to crawl towards the door.* [2] VERB & N-SING If someone or something **crawls** somewhere, or if they move there at a **crawl**, they move there slowly or with great difficulty. *I watched the moth crawl up the outside of the lampshade... The traffic on the approach road slowed to a crawl.* [3] VERB If you say that a place **is crawling** with people or things, you mean that it is full of them; INFORMAL. *This place is crawling with police.*

crayon /ˈkreɪɒn/ **crayons.** N-C A **crayon** is a rod of coloured wax used for drawing.

craze /kreɪz/ **crazes.** N-C If there is a **craze** for something, it is very popular for a short time. *Walking is the latest fitness craze.*

crazed /kreɪzd/. ADJ **Crazed** people are wild and uncontrolled, and perhaps insane. *A crazed gunman slaughtered five people last night.*

crazy /ˈkreɪzi/ **crazier, craziest.** [1] ADJ If you describe someone or something as **crazy**, you think they are very foolish or strange; INFORMAL. *People thought they were all crazy to try to make money from manufacturing.* ◆**crazily** ADV *Our policies are crazily extravagant.* [2] ADJ AFTER LINK-V If you are **crazy about** something, you are very enthusiastic about it. If you are **crazy about** someone, you are deeply in love with them. *He was crazy about gardening... We're crazy about each other.* [3] ADJ AFTER LINK-V If something makes or drives you **crazy**, it makes you extremely annoyed or upset. *This sitting around is driving me crazy.*

creak /kriːk/ **creaks, creaking, creaked.** VERB & N-C If something **creaks**, it makes a short high-pitched sound, called a **creak**, when it moves. *The steps creaked beneath his feet... The door was pulled open with a creak.*

cream /kriːm/ **creams, creaming, creamed.** [1] N-U **Cream** is a thick liquid that is produced from milk. You can use it in cooking or put it on fruit or puddings. *...strawberries and cream.* [2] N-VAR A **cream** is a substance that you rub into your skin, for example to keep it soft or to heal or protect it. *...sun protection creams.* [3] ADJ Something that is **cream** in colour is yellowish-white. [4] N-SING **The cream** is used to refer to the best people or things of a particular kind. *...the cream of society.*
▶ **cream off.** PHR-VERB If you **cream off** part of a group of people, you separate them and treat them differently, because you think they are better than the rest. *The private schools cream off many of the best pupils.*

creamy /ˈkriːmi/. ADJ **Creamy** food or drink contains a lot of cream or milk or has a soft smooth texture like cream. *...rich, creamy coffee. ...creamy mashed potato.*

crease /kriːs/ **creases, creasing, creased.** [1] VERB & N-C If cloth or paper **creases**, or if you **crease** it, lines called **creases** form in it because it has been crushed or folded. *If you iron the collar last, you will crease the rest of the shirt... Papa flattened the creases of the map.* ◆**creased** ADJ *His clothes were creased, as if he had slept in them.* [2] VERB & N-C If your face **creases**, lines called **creases** appear on it because you are frowning or smiling. *His face* *creased into an unwilling smile. ...the tiny creases at the corners of his eyes.* ◆**creased** ADJ *...Jock's creased drunken face.*

create /kri'eɪt/ **creates, creating, created.** VERB To **create** something means to cause it to happen or exist. *It is really great for a radio producer to create a show like this... She could create a fight out of anything.* ◆**creator, creators** N-C *...Ian Fleming, the creator of James Bond.*

creation /kri'eɪʃən/ **creations.** [1] N-U The **creation** of something is the act of bringing it into existence. *These businesses stimulate the creation of local jobs.* [2] N-U In many religions, **creation** is the making of the universe, earth, and creatures by God. *...the biblical story of creation.* [3] N-C You can refer to something that someone has made as a **creation**. *The bathroom is entirely my own creation.*

creative /kri'eɪtɪv/ [1] ADJ A **creative** person has the ability to invent and develop original ideas, especially in art. **Creative** activities involve inventing and developing original ideas. *...creative writing.* ◆**creativity** /ˌkriːeɪ'tɪvɪti/ N-U *American art reached a peak of creativity in the '50s and 60s.* [2] ADJ If you use something in a **creative** way, you use it in a new way that produces interesting and unusual results. *...his creative use of words.*

creature /'kriːtʃə/ **creatures.** N-C You can refer to any living thing that is not a plant as a **creature**. *Like all living creatures, birds need a regular supply of water.*

crèche /kreʃ/ **crèches.** N-C A **crèche** is a place where small children are left and looked after while their parents are doing something else.

credence /'kriːdəns/. N-U If something gives or lends **credence** to a theory or story, it makes it easier to believe.

credentials /krɪ'denʃəlz/. [1] N-PL Your **credentials** are your previous achievements, training, and general background, which indicate that you are qualified to do something. *I can testify to the credentials of the clientele.* [2] N-PL Someone's **credentials** are a letter or certificate that proves their identity or qualifications. *Egypt's new ambassador to Syria has presented his credentials to President Assad.*

credible /'kredɪbəl/. [1] ADJ **Credible** means able to be trusted or believed. *We have two very credible witnesses.* ◆**credibility** N-U *The police have lost their credibility.* [2] ADJ A **credible** candidate, policy, or system is one that appears to have a chance of being successful. *...a more credible opponent.*

credit /'kredɪt/ **credits, crediting, credited.** [1] N-U **Credit** is a system where you pay for goods or services several weeks or months after you have received them. *Pay cash or buy on credit.* [2] N-U If a person or their bank account is **in credit**, the bank account has money in it. *I made sure the account stayed in credit. ...the interest earned on a credit balance.* [3] N-U If you get the **credit** for something good, people praise you because you are thought to be responsible for it. *Some of the credit for her relaxed manner must go to Andy.* [4] VERB If people **credit** someone **with** an achievement, people say or believe that they were responsible

for it. *The staff are crediting him with having saved Hythe's life.* [5] N-C The **credits** refers the list of people who helped to make a film, a record, or a television programme.

PHRASES ● If you say that, **to** someone's **credit**, they did something, you mean that they deserve praise for it. *To his credit, Mr Molyneaux always opposed the use of violence.* ● If you have one or more achievements **to** your **credit**, you have achieved them. *I have countless magazine stories to my credit.*

creditable /'kredɪtəbəl/. ADJ A **creditable** performance or achievement is of a reasonably high standard.

'credit card, credit cards. N-C A **credit card** is a plastic card that you use to buy goods on credit.

creditor /'kredɪtə/ **creditors.** N-C Your **creditors** are the people who you owe money to.

creed /kriːd/ **creeds.** [1] N-C A **creed** is a set of beliefs or principles that influence the way people live or work. *...their devotion to their creed of self-help.* [2] N-C A **creed** is a religion; FORMAL. *...young South Africans of every race and creed.*

creek /kriːk/ **creeks.** [1] N-C A **creek** is a narrow inlet where the sea comes a long way into the land; BRITISH. [2] N-C A **creek** is a small stream or river; AMERICAN.

creep /kriːp/ **creeps, creeping, crept.** [1] VERB To **creep** somewhere means to move there quietly and slowly. *He crept up the stairs... Mist had crept in again from the sea.* [2] VERB **Creep** can be used to indicate that something gradually reaches a particular level or that it is gradually introduced into a particular situation. *The inflation rate has been creeping up to 9.5 per cent. ...if you suspect a fault is creeping into your game.* [3] N-C If you describe someone as a **creep**, you mean that you dislike them, because they flatter people but are not sincere; INFORMAL.

creepy /'kriːpi/. ADJ If you say that something or someone is **creepy**, you mean they make you feel very uneasy; INFORMAL. *...places that were really creepy at night.*

cremate /krɪ'meɪt, AM 'kriːmeɪt/ **cremates, cremating, cremated.** VERB When someone **is cremated**, their dead body is burned, usually as part of a funeral service. ◆**cremation, cremations.** N-VAR *We finalized the arrangements for her cremation.*

crept /krept/. **Crept** is the past tense and past participle of **creep**.

crescendo /krɪ'ʃendəʊ/. N-C A **crescendo** is a noise that gets louder and louder. Some people use **crescendo** to refer to the point when a noise is at its loudest. *The applause quickly rose to a crescendo.*

crescent /'kresənt, 'krez-/ **crescents.** N-C A **crescent** is a curved shape like the shape of the moon during its first and last quarters.

crest /krest/ **crests.** [1] N-C The **crest** of a hill or a wave is the highest part of it. [2] N-C A **crest** is a design that is the symbol of a noble family, a town, or an organization.

crevice /'krevɪs/ **crevices.** N-C A **crevice** is a narrow crack in a rock.

crew /kruː/ **crews.** [1] N-C The **crew** of a ship, an aircraft, or a spacecraft consists of the people who work on it and operate it. **Crew** can take the singular or plural form of the verb. [2] N-C A **crew** is a group of people with special technical skills who work together on a task or project. **Crew** can take the singular or plural form of the verb. ...*a two-man film crew.*

crib /krɪb/ **cribs.** N-C In American English, a **crib** is a bed for a baby, with bars or panels round it so that the baby cannot fall out. The British word is **cot**.

cricket /ˈkrɪkɪt/ **crickets.** [1] N-U **Cricket** is an outdoor game played by two teams who try to score points, called runs, by hitting a ball with a wooden bat. ...*the scene of the crime.* [2] N-C A **cricket** is a small jumping insect that produces sharp sounds by rubbing its wings together.

cricketer /ˈkrɪkɪtə/ **cricketers.** N-C A **cricketer** is a person who plays cricket.

crime /kraɪm/ **crimes.** N-VAR A **crime** is an illegal action or activity for which a person can be punished by law. ...*the alarming rise in crime... It's not a crime to be stupid.*

criminal /ˈkrɪmɪnəl/ **criminals.** [1] N-C A **criminal** is a person who has committed a crime. [2] ADJ **Criminal** means connected with crime. *He had a criminal record for petty theft. ...criminal assault.* ◆**criminally** ADV ...*a hospital for the criminally insane.*

crimson /ˈkrɪmzən/. ADJ Something that is **crimson** is deep red in colour.

cringe /krɪndʒ/ **cringes, cringing, cringed.** VERB If you **cringe** at something, you feel embarrassed or disgusted, and perhaps show this in your expression or by making a slight movement. *Chris had cringed at the thought of using her own family for publicity.*

cripple /ˈkrɪpəl/ **cripples, crippling, crippled.** [1] N-C A person with a physical disability or a serious permanent injury is sometimes referred to as a **cripple**. Some people find this use offensive. [2] VERB If someone **is crippled** by an injury, they are so seriously affected by it that they can never move their body properly again. [3] VERB To **cripple** a machine, organization, or system means to damage it severely or prevent it from working properly. *A total cut-off of supplies would cripple Jordan's economy.*

crippling /ˈkrɪplɪŋ/. [1] ADJ BEFORE N A **crippling** illness or disability severely damages your health or body. ...*crippling diseases such as arthritis.* [2] ADJ If you say that an action, policy, or situation has a **crippling** effect on something, you mean it has a very harmful effect.

crisis /ˈkraɪsɪs/ **crises** /ˈkraɪsiːz/. N-VAR A **crisis** is a situation in which something or someone is affected by one or more very serious problems. ...*the continent's economic crisis. ...someone to turn to in moments of crisis.*

crisp /krɪsp/ **crisper, crispest; crisps.** [1] ADJ **Crisp** food is pleasantly hard and crunchy. *Grill under a medium grill until the bacon is crisp. ...crisp lettuce.* [2] N-C In British English, **crisps** are very thin slices of potato that have been fried until they are hard and crunchy and that are eaten cold as a snack. The American word is **chips** or **potato chips.** [3] ADJ **Crisp** air

is pleasantly fresh, cold, and dry. [4] ADJ A **crisp** remark or response is brief and perhaps unfriendly. *'Very well,' I said, adopting a crisp authoritative tone.*

criss-cross /ˈkrɪs krɒs, AM - krɔːs/ **criss-crosses, criss-crossing, criss-crossed.** [1] VERB If a person or thing **criss-crosses** an area, they travel from one side to the other and back again many times. If a number of things **criss-cross** an area, they cross it, and cross over each other. *They criss-crossed the country by bus.* [2] ADJ BEFORE N A **criss-cross** pattern or design consists of lines crossing each other.

criterion /kraɪˈtɪəriən/ **criteria** /kraɪˈtɪəriə/. N-C A **criterion** is a factor on which you judge or decide something. *The bank is reassessing its criteria for lending money.*

critic /ˈkrɪtɪk/ **critics.** [1] N-C A **critic** is a person who writes reviews and expresses opinions about books, films, music, and art. *Mather was film critic on the Daily Telegraph.* [2] N-C Someone who is a **critic** of a person or system disapproves of them and criticizes them publicly. *Her critics accused her of caring only about success.*

critical /ˈkrɪtɪkəl/. [1] ADJ A **critical** time or situation is extremely important. *The incident happened at a critical point in the campaign... How you finance a business is critical to the success of your venture.* ◆**critically** ADV *Economic prosperity depends critically on an open world trading system.* [2] ADJ A **critical** situation is very serious and dangerous. *The German authorities are considering an airlift if the situation becomes critical.* ◆**critically** ADV *Moscow is running critically low on food supplies.* [3] ADJ If you are **critical** of someone or something, you criticize them. *He has apologised for critical remarks he made about the referee.* ◆**critically** ADV *She spoke critically of Laura.* [4] ADJ BEFORE N A **critical** approach to something involves examining and judging it carefully. ...*the critical analysis of political ideas.* ◆**critically** ADV *Wyman watched them critically.*

criticism /ˈkrɪtɪsɪzəm/ **criticisms.** [1] N-VAR **Criticism** is the action of expressing disapproval of something or someone. A **criticism** is a statement that expresses disapproval. ...*the criticism that the English do not truly care about their children.* [2] N-U **Criticism** is a serious examination and judgement of something such as a book or play. ...*literary criticism.*

criticize (BR also **criticise**) /ˈkrɪtɪsaɪz/ **criticizes, criticizing, criticized.** VERB If you **criticize** someone or something, you express your disapproval of them by saying what you think is wrong with them. *The regime has been harshly criticized for serious human rights violations.*

critique /krɪˈtiːk/ **critiques.** N-C A **critique** is a written examination and judgement of a situation or of a person's work or ideas; FORMAL. ...*a feminist critique of Victorian high novelists.*

croak /krəʊk/ **croaks, croaking, croaked.** [1] VERB When a frog or bird **croaks**, it makes a harsh low sound. [2] VERB When someone **croaks** something, they say it in a hoarse rough voice. *Tiller moaned and managed to croak, 'Help me'.*

crockery /'krɒkəri/. N-U **Crockery** consists of plates, cups, and saucers.

crocodile /'krɒkədaɪl/ **crocodiles.** N-C A **crocodile** is a large reptile with a long body. Crocodiles live in rivers.

croissant /'kwæsɒn, AM kwɑː'sɑːn/ **croissants.** N-VAR **Croissants** are small crescent-shaped pieces of sweetened bread that are eaten for breakfast.

crony /'krəʊni/ **cronies.** N-C Your **cronies** are the friends who you spend a lot of time with; INFORMAL. *...the governor and his cronies.*

crook /krʊk/ **crooks.** [1] N-C A **crook** is a criminal or a dishonest person; INFORMAL. *The man is a crook and a liar.* [2] N-C The **crook** of your arm or leg is the soft inside part where you bend your elbow or knee.

crooked /'krʊkɪd/. [1] ADJ Something that is **crooked** is bent or twisted. *She has a crooked nose.* [2] ADJ If you describe a person or an activity as **crooked**, you mean that they are dishonest or criminal. *...crooked business deals.*

croon /kruːn/ **croons, crooning, crooned.** VERB If you **croon**, you sing or say something quietly and gently. *Lewis began to croon another Springsteen song.*

crop /krɒp/ **crops, cropping, cropped.** [1] N-C **Crops** are plants such as wheat and potatoes that are grown in large quantities for food. *Farmers here still plant and harvest their crops by hand.* [2] N-C The plants or fruits that are collected at harvest time are referred to as a **crop**. *...this year's corn crop.* [3] N-SING You can refer to a group of people or things that have appeared together as a **crop of** them. *...the current crop of young British designers.* [4] VERB To **crop** someone's hair means to cut it short.

▶ **crop up.** PHR-VERB If something **crops up**, it happens or appears unexpectedly. *Problems will crop up and hit you before you are ready.*

croquet /'krəʊkeɪ, AM krəʊ'keɪ/. N-U **Croquet** is a game in which the players use long-handled wooden mallets to hit balls through metal arches stuck in a lawn.

cross 1 verb and noun uses

cross /krɒs, AM krɔːs/ **crosses, crossing, crossed.** [1] VERB If you **cross** a room, road, or area of land, you move to the other side of it. If you **cross** to a place, you move over a room, road, or area in order to reach that place. *Nine Albanians have crossed the border into Greece... Egan crossed to the drinks cabinet and poured a Scotch.* [2] VERB A road, railway, or bridge that **crosses** an area of land or water passes over it. *The Defford to Eckington road crosses the river.* [3] VERB When lines or roads **cross**, they meet and go across each other. [4] VERB If you **cross** your arms, legs, or fingers, you put one of them on top of the other. *Pop crossed his arms over his chest.* [5] VERB If an expression **crosses** someone's face, it appears briefly on their face; LITERARY. [6] VERB When a thought **crosses** your mind, you think of or remember something. ♦ N-C A **cross** is a shape that consists of a vertical line with a shorter horizontal line across it. *...a cross on a silver chain.* [8] N-C A **cross** is a written mark in the shape of an X.

[9] N-C Something that is **a cross between** two things is neither one thing nor the other, but a mixture of both. *The snowmobile is a cross between a sledge and a motorcycle.*

▶ **cross out.** PHR-VERB If you **cross out** words, you draw a line through them.

cross 2 adjective use

cross /krɒs, AM krɔːs/ **crosser, crossest.** ADJ Someone who is **cross** is angry or irritated. *I'm terribly cross with him.* ♦ **crossly** ADV *'No, no, no,' Morris said crossly.*

cross-'country. [1] N-U **Cross-country** is the sport of running, riding, or skiing across open countryside. [2] ADJ BEFORE N & ADV A **cross-country** journey involves less important roads or railway lines, or takes you from one side of a country to the other. *...cross-country rail services... I drove cross-country in his van.*

cross-ex'amine, cross-examines, cross-examining, cross-examined. VERB When a lawyer **cross-examines** someone during a trial or hearing, he or she questions them about the evidence that they have given. ♦ **cross-examination, cross-examinations** N-VAR *...the cross-examination of a witness.*

crossing /'krɒsɪŋ, AM 'krɔːs-/ **crossings.** [1] N-C A **crossing** is a boat journey to the other side of a sea. [2] N-C A **crossing** is a place where you can cross something such as a road or a border.

crossover /'krɒsəʊvə, AM 'krɔːs-/ **crossovers.** [1] N-VAR A **crossover** of one style and another is a combination of the two different styles. *...the contemporary crossover of pop, jazz and funk.* [2] N-SING A **crossover** is a change from one type of activity to another. *...the crossover from actress to singer.*

crossroads /'krɒsrəʊdz, AM 'krɔːs-/. N-C A **crossroads** is a place where two roads meet and cross. **Crossroads** is the singular and plural.

'**cross-section, cross-sections.** [1] N-C A **cross-section** of something such as a group of people is a typical or representative sample. *I was surprised at the cross-section of people there.* [2] N-C A **cross-section** of an object is what you would see if you cut straight through the middle of it. *...a cross-section of an airplane.*

crossword /'krɒswɜːd, AM 'krɔːs-/ **crosswords.** N-C A **crossword** or **crossword puzzle** is a word game in which you work out answers to clues, and write the answers in the white squares of a pattern of black and white squares. *...doing the crossword puzzle in the daily paper.*

crotch /krɒtʃ/ **crotches.** [1] N-C Your **crotch** is the part of your body between the tops of your legs. [2] N-C The **crotch** of a pair of trousers is the part that covers the area between the tops of your legs.

crouch /kraʊtʃ/ **crouches, crouching, crouched.** [1] VERB & N-SING If you **are crouching**, or if you **crouch down**, your legs are bent under you so that you are close to the ground and leaning forward slightly. If you are in a **crouch**, your body is in this position. *We were crouching in the bushes... He crouched down beside him... They walked in a crouch.* [2] VERB

If you **crouch over** something, you bend over it so that you are very near to it. *He crouched over the steering wheel.*

crow /krəʊ/ **crows, crowing, crowed.** [1] N-C A **crow** is a large black bird which makes a loud harsh noise. [2] VERB When a cock **crows**, it utters a loud sound, early in the morning. [3] VERB If you say that someone **is crowing** about something they have achieved, they keep talking about it proudly in a way that annoys you; INFORMAL. *They outraged journalists by crowing about America's superiority to England.*

crowd /kraʊd/ **crowds, crowding, crowded.** [1] N-C A **crowd** is a large group of people who have gathered together. *A huge crowd had gathered.* [2] N-C A particular **crowd** is a group of friends, or people with the same interests or occupation; INFORMAL. *All the old crowd have come out.* [3] VERB When people **crowd** around someone or something, they gather closely together around them. *The children crowded around him.* [4] VERB If people **crowd** into a place or **are crowded into** it, large numbers of them enter it so that it becomes very full. *One group of journalists were crowded into a mini-bus.*

crowded /ˈkraʊdɪd/ ADJ A **crowded** place is full of people or things. *The old town square was crowded with people. ...a crowded city.*

crown /kraʊn/ **crowns, crowning, crowned.** [1] N-C A **crown** is a circular ornament, usually made of gold and jewels, which a king or queen wears on their head at official ceremonies. [2] VERB When a king or queen is **crowned**, a crown is placed on their head as part of a ceremony in which they are officially made king or queen. [3] VERB If one thing **crowns** another, it is on top of it; LITERARY. *Another rugged castle crowns the cliffs.* [4] N-C Your **crown** is the top part of your head, at the back.

crucial /ˈkruːʃəl/ ADJ Something that is **crucial** is extremely important. *An animal's sense of smell is still crucial to its survival. ...crucial decisions.* ◆ **crucially** ADV *Education is crucially important.*

crucify /ˈkruːsɪfaɪ/ **crucifies, crucifying, crucified.** VERB In former times, if someone **was crucified**, they were killed by being tied or nailed to a cross and left to die. ◆ **crucifixion** /ˌkruːsɪˈfɪkʃən/ **crucifixions** N-VAR *...the crucifixion of Christians in Rome.*

crude /kruːd/ **cruder, crudest.** [1] ADJ Something that is **crude** is simple and not sophisticated. *...an important but crude way of assessing the risk of heart disease. ...crude wooden boxes.* ◆ **crudely** ADV *...a crudely carved wooden form.* [2] ADJ If you describe someone as **crude**, you disapprove of them because they speak or behave in a rude or offensive way. *Must you be quite so crude?* ◆ **crudely** ADV *He hated it when she spoke so crudely.*

crude 'oil. N-U **Crude oil** is oil in its natural state before it has been processed.

cruel /ˈkruːəl/ **crueller, cruellest.** ADJ Someone who is **cruel** deliberately causes pain or distress. *Children can be so cruel. ...her cruel and abusive husband.* ◆ **cruelly** ADV *...the cruelly treated, faithful wife.* ◆ **cruelty** /ˈkruːəltɪ/

cruelties N-VAR *Britain has laws against cruelty to animals.*

cruise /kruːz/ **cruises, cruising, cruised.** [1] N-C A **cruise** is a holiday spent on a ship or boat which visits a number of places. *He and his wife were planning to go on a world cruise.* [2] VERB If you **cruise** a sea, river, or canal, you travel around it or along it on a cruise. *You could cruise to Australia.* [3] VERB If a car or a ship **cruises**, it moves at a constant moderate speed. *A black and white police car cruised past.*

cruiser /ˈkruːzə/ **cruisers.** [1] N-C A **cruiser** is a motor boat with a cabin for people to sleep in. [2] N-C A **cruiser** is a large fast warship.

crumb /krʌm/ **crumbs.** N-C **Crumbs** are tiny pieces that fall from bread, biscuits, or cake when you cut or eat them.

crumble /ˈkrʌmbəl/ **crumbles, crumbling, crumbled.** [1] VERB When something soft or brittle **crumbles**, or when you **crumble** it, it breaks into a lot of small pieces. *The flint crumbled into fragments.* [2] VERB If an old building or piece of land **is crumbling**, or if it **is crumbling away**, parts of it keep breaking off. *...a big gray mountain crumbling into the sea.* [3] VERB If something such as a system, relationship, or hope **crumbles**, it comes to an end. *The traditional marriage is crumbling fast.*

crumbly /ˈkrʌmblɪ/. ADJ Something that is **crumbly** is easily broken into a lot of little pieces. *...crumbly cheese.*

crumple /ˈkrʌmpəl/ **crumples, crumpling, crumpled.** [1] VERB & PHR-VERB If you **crumple** something such as paper or cloth, or if you **crumple** it **up**, you squash it and it becomes full of creases and folds. *She crumpled the paper in her hand... Nancy looked at the note angrily, then crumpled it up.* ◆ **crumpled** ADJ *His uniform was crumpled.* [2] VERB If someone's face **crumples**, they suddenly look very disappointed or as if they want to cry.

► **crumple up.** See **crumple** 1.

crunch /krʌntʃ/ **crunches, crunching, crunched.** [1] VERB If you **crunch** something hard, you crush it noisily between your teeth. *Richard crunched into the apple.* [2] VERB & N-C If something **crunches**, it makes a breaking or crushing noise, called a **crunch**. *...wheels crunching over a stony surface. ...the crunch of tires on the gravel driveway.*

crunchy /ˈkrʌntʃɪ/. ADJ **Crunchy** food is pleasantly hard or crisp, and makes a noise when you eat it.

crusade /kruːˈseɪd/ **crusades.** N-C A **crusade** is a long and determined attempt to achieve something. *He made it his crusade to teach children to love books.* ◆ **crusader, crusaders** N-C *...a crusader for the rights of women.*

crush /krʌʃ/ **crushes, crushing, crushed.** [1] VERB To **crush** something means to press it very hard so that its shape is destroyed or so that it breaks into pieces. *Andrew crushed his empty can. ...crushed ice.* [2] VERB If you **are crushed** against someone or something, you are pushed or pressed against them. *We were at the front, crushed against the stage.* [3] N-C A **crush** is a dense crowd of people. *He somehow*

crust 142

got separated in the crush. [4] VERB To **crush** a protest, army, or political organization means to defeat it completely. ♦**crushing** N-U *...the violent crushing of anti-government demonstrations.* [5] N-C If you have a **crush on** someone, you feel you are in love with them but you do not have a relationship with them; INFORMAL.

crust /krʌst/ **crusts.** [1] N-U The **crust** on a loaf of bread is the outside part. [2] N-C The earth's **crust** is its outer layer.

crusty /ˈkrʌsti/. ADJ Something that is **crusty** has a hard, crisp, outer layer. *...crusty French loaves.*

crutch /krʌtʃ/ **crutches.** N-C A **crutch** is a stick which someone with an injured foot or leg uses to support them when walking.

crux /krʌks/. N-SING The **crux** of an argument is the most important or difficult part, which affects everything else. *The crux of their disagreement came down to two things: money and power.*

cry /kraɪ/ **cries, crying, cried.** [1] VERB & N-SING When you **cry**, or when you have a **cry**, tears come from your eyes, usually because you are unhappy or hurt. *I hung up the phone and started to cry... He cried with anger and frustration... I like a good cry.* ♦**crying** N-U *...her 13-week-old son's crying.* [2] VERB & PHR-VERB To **cry** something, or to **cry** something **out**, means to shout or say something loudly. *'Nancy Drew,' she cried, 'you're under arrest!'... 'You're wrong, quite wrong!' Henry cried out.* [3] N-C A **cry** is a loud high sound that you make when you feel a strong emotion such as fear, pain, or pleasure. *A cry of horror broke from me.* [4] PHRASE If you say that something is **a far cry** from something else, you mean it is very different from it. *Their lives are a far cry from his own poor childhood.*

▶ **cry out.** [1] PHR-VERB If you **cry out**, you call out loudly because you are frightened, unhappy or in pain. *He was crying out in pain when the ambulance arrived.* [2] See **cry** 2.

▶ **cry out for.** PHR-VERB If you say that something **cries out for** a particular thing, you mean that it needs that thing very much. *His body was crying out for some exercise.*

cryptic /ˈkrɪptɪk/. ADJ A **cryptic** remark or message contains a hidden meaning. *My father's notes are more cryptic here.* ♦**cryptically** ADV *'Not necessarily,' she says cryptically.*

crystal /ˈkrɪstəl/ **crystals.** [1] N-C A **crystal** is a piece of a mineral that has formed naturally into a regular symmetrical shape. *...salt crystals.* [2] N-U **Crystal** is a transparent rock used in jewellery and ornaments. [3] N-U **Crystal** is very high quality glass, usually with its surface cut into patterns. *...crystal glasses.*

crystal 'clear. ADJ An explanation that is **crystal clear** is very easy to understand. *The message is crystal clear – if you lose weight, you will have a happier, healthier, better life.*

crystallize (BR also **crystallise**) /ˈkrɪstəlaɪz/ **crystallizes, crystallizing, crystallized.** [1] VERB If you **crystallize** an opinion or idea, or if it **crystallizes**, it becomes fixed and definite in your mind. *I hope the above points have helped to crystallize your thoughts.* [2] VERB

When a substance **crystallizes**, it turns into crystals. *Don't stir or the sugar will crystallise.*

cub /kʌb/ **cubs.** N-C A **cub** is a young wild animal such as a lion, wolf, or bear. *...three five-week-old lion cubs.*

cube /kjuːb/ **cubes.** N-C A **cube** is a solid shape with six square surfaces which are all the same size.

cubic /ˈkjuːbɪk/. ADJ BEFORE N **Cubic** is used to express units of volume. *...3 billion cubic metres of soil.*

cubicle /ˈkjuːbɪkəl/ **cubicles.** N-C A **cubicle** is a small enclosed area, for example one where you can have a shower or change your clothes.

cuckoo /ˈkʊkuː/ **cuckoos.** N-C A **cuckoo** is a grey bird which makes an easily recognizable sound consisting of two quick notes.

cucumber /ˈkjuːkʌmbə/ **cucumbers.** N-VAR A **cucumber** is a long dark green vegetable.

cuddle /ˈkʌdəl/ **cuddles, cuddling, cuddled.** VERB & N-C If you **cuddle** someone, or if you give them a **cuddle**, you put your arms round them and hold them close. *They used to kiss and cuddle in front of everyone... It would have been nice to give him a cuddle.*

cuddly /ˈkʌdəli/ **cuddlier, cuddliest.** ADJ If you describe people or animals as **cuddly**, you find them attractive because they are plump or soft and look nice to cuddle.

cue /kjuː/ **cues.** [1] N-C A **cue** is something said or done by a performer that is a signal for another performer to begin speaking or to begin doing something. *I had never known him miss a cue.* [2] PHRASE If you **take** your **cue** from someone, you use their behaviour as an indication of what you should do. *Taking his cue from his companion, he apologized.* [3] PHRASE If you say that something happened **on cue**, you mean that it happened just when it was expected to happen, or just at the right time. *Kevin arrived right on cue.*

cuff /kʌf/ **cuffs, cuffing, cuffed.** [1] N-C The **cuffs** of a piece of clothing are the end parts of the sleeves. [2] PHRASE An **off-the-cuff** remark is made without being prepared or thought about in advance. *Mr Baker was speaking off the cuff when he made those suggestions.*

cuisine /kwɪˈziːn/ **cuisines.** N-VAR The **cuisine** of a region is its characteristic style of cooking. *...traditional French cuisine.*

culinary /ˈkʌlɪnəri, AM ˈkjuːləneri/. ADJ BEFORE N **Culinary** means related to cooking. *...culinary delights.*

cull /kʌl/ **culls, culling, culled.** [1] VERB If items or ideas **are culled from** a particular source or number of sources, they are taken and gathered together. *All this, needless to say, had been culled second-hand from radio reports.* [2] VERB & N-C To **cull** animals means to kill some of them in order to reduce their numbers. You can also talk about a **cull**. *...a proposal to cull the Forest deer. ...the annual seal cull off the Namibian coast.* ♦**culling** N-U *The culling of seal cubs has led to an outcry.*

culminate /ˈkʌlmɪneɪt/ **culminates, culminating, culminated.** VERB If you say that an activity, process, or series of events **culminates in** or **with** a particular event, you mean that event happens at the end of it. *They had an argument, which culminated in Tom getting drunk.* ♦**culmination** N-SING *The protests were the culmination of a week of demonstrations.*

culprit /'kʌlprɪt/ **culprits.** [1] N-C The person who committed a crime or did something wrong can be referred to as the **culprit.** *The real culprits in the fight have not been identified.* [2] N-C The cause of a problem or bad situation can be referred to as the **culprit.** *...carbon dioxide – the main culprit in the greenhouse effect.*

cult /kʌlt/ **cults.** [1] N-C A **cult** is a fairly small religious group, especially one which is considered strange. *The teenager may have been abducted by a religious cult.* [2] N-SING & ADJ When a person, object, or activity becomes a **cult,** they become very popular or fashionable. *The film is destined to become a cult classic.*

cultivate /'kʌltɪveɪt/ **cultivates, cultivating, cultivated.** [1] VERB If you **cultivate** land, you prepare it and grow crops on it. *She also cultivated a small garden of her own. ...cultivated land.* ♦**cultivation** N-U *...the cultivation of fruit and vegetables.* [2] VERB If you **cultivate** an attitude, image, or skill, you develop it and make it stronger. *He has cultivated the image of an elder statesman.* ♦**cultivation** N-U *...the cultivation of a positive approach to life.*

cultivated /'kʌltɪveɪtɪd/ [1] ADJ If you describe someone as **cultivated,** you mean that they are well-educated and have good manners. *...an elegant, cultivated woman.* [2] ADJ BEFORE N **Cultivated** plants have been developed for growing on farms or in gardens. *...a mixture of wild and cultivated varieties.*

cultural /'kʌltʃərəl/ ADJ **Cultural** means relating to the arts generally, or to the arts and customs of a particular society. *...sports and cultural events. ...cultural and educational exchanges between Britain and India.* ♦**culturally** ADV *Culturally, they have much in common with their neighbours just across the border.*

culture /'kʌltʃə/ **cultures.** [1] N-U **Culture** consists of activities such as the arts and philosophy, which are considered to be important for the development of civilization and of people's minds. *...France's Minister of Culture and Education.* [2] N-C A **culture** is a particular society or civilization, especially considered in relation to its beliefs, way of life, or art. *...people from different cultures.* [3] N-C In science, a **culture** is a group of bacteria or cells grown in a laboratory as part of an experiment.

cultured /'kʌltʃəd/ ADJ If you describe someone as **cultured,** you mean that they are well educated and know a lot about the arts. *He is a cultured man with a wide circle of friends.*

-cum- /-kʌm-/. You put **-cum-** between two words to form a compound noun referring to something or someone that is partly one thing and partly another. *...a dining-room-cum-study.*

cumbersome /'kʌmbəsəm/ [1] ADJ Something that is **cumbersome** is large and heavy and difficult to carry, wear, or handle. *Although the machine looks cumbersome, it is actually easy to use.* [2] ADJ A **cumbersome** system or process is complicated and inefficient. *The proposed regulations are ill-defined and cumbersome.*

cumulative /'kjuːmjʊlətɪv/. ADJ If a series of events have a **cumulative** effect, each event makes the effect greater. *The benefits from eating fish are cumulative.*

cunning /'kʌnɪŋ/ [1] ADJ A **cunning** person is clever and deceitful. ♦**cunningly** ADV *They were cunningly disguised in golf clothes.* [2] N-U **Cunning** is the ability to plan things cleverly, often by deceiving people. *...one more example of the cunning of today's art thieves.*

cup /kʌp/ **cups, cupping, cupped.** [1] N-C A **cup** is a small round container with a handle, which you drink from. [2] N-C A **cup** is something which is small, round, and hollow, like a cup. *...the brass cups of the small chandelier.* [3] N-C A **cup** is a large metal cup on a stem given as a prize to the winner of a game or competition. [4] VERB If you **cup** your hands, you make them into a curved dish-like shape. *He cupped his hands around his mouth and called out for Diane.* [5] VERB If you **cup** something in your hands, you make your hands into a curved dish-like shape and support it or hold it gently. *He cupped her chin in the palm of his hand.*

cupboard /'kʌbəd/ **cupboards.** N-C A **cupboard** is a piece of furniture with doors at the front and usually shelves inside.

curable /'kjʊərəbəl/. ADJ A **curable** disease or illness can be treated.

curate /'kjʊərət/ **curates.** N-C A **curate** is a clergyman who helps a vicar or priest.

curator /kjʊ'reɪtə/ **curators.** N-C The **curator** of a museum or art gallery is the person in charge of the exhibits or works of art.

curb /kɜːb/ **curbs, curbing, curbed.** [1] VERB & N-C If you **curb** something, you control it and keep it within limits. You can also talk about a **curb** on something. *...advertisements aimed at curbing the spread of Aids... He called for much stricter curbs on immigration.* [2] See also **kerb.**

cure /kjʊə/ **cures, curing, cured.** [1] VERB If a doctor or a medical treatment **cures** someone, or **cures** their illness, they make the person well again. *Now doctors believe they have cured him of the disease.* [2] N-C A **cure** for an illness is a medicine or other treatment that cures the illness. [3] VERB If someone or something **cures** a problem, they bring it to an end. *We need to cure our environmental problems.* [4] N-C A **cure** to a problem is something which brings it to an end. *The magic cure for inflation does not exist.* [5] VERB When food, tobacco, or animal skin **is cured,** it is dried, smoked, or salted so that it will last for a long time. *...sliced cured ham.*

curfew /'kɜːfjuː/ **curfews.** N-C A **curfew** is a law stating that people must stay inside their houses after a particular time at night. *The village was placed under curfew.*

curiosity /ˌkjʊəri'ɒsɪti/ **curiosities.** [1] N-U **Curiosity** is a desire to know about things. *To satisfy our own curiosity we traveled to Baltimore.* [2] N-C A **curiosity** is something which is interesting and fairly rare. *...castles, curiosities, and museums.*

curious /ˈkjʊəriəs/. **1** ADJ If you are **curious** about something, you are interested in it and want to learn more about it. *Steve was intensely curious about the world I came from. ...a group of curious villagers.* ♦**curiously** ADV *The woman in the shop had looked at them curiously.* **2** ADJ Something that is **curious** is unusual or difficult to understand. *There is a curious thing about her writings.* ♦**curiously** ADV *Harry was curiously silent through all this.*

curl /kɜːl/ **curls, curling, curled.** **1** N-C **Curls** are lengths of hair shaped in curves and circles. *...the little girl with blonde curls.* **2** VERB If your hair **curls**, or if you **curl** it, it is full of curls. *Maria had curled her hair for the event.* **3** N-C A **curl** of something is a piece or quantity of it that is curved or spiral in shape. *...curls of lemon peel.* **4** VERB If something **curls** somewhere, it moves there in circles or spirals. *Smoke was curling up the chimney... He curled the ball into the net.*

▸ **curl up.** **1** PHR-VERB When someone who is lying down **curls up**, they bring their arms, legs, and head in towards their stomach. *In colder weather, your cat will curl up into a tight, heat-conserving ball.* **2** PHR-VERB When something such as a leaf or a piece of paper **curls up**, its edges bend up or towards its centre. *The corners of the lino were curling up.*

curly /ˈkɜːli/ **curlier, curliest.** **1** ADJ **Curly** hair is full of curls. **2** ADJ **Curly** objects are curved or spiral-shaped. *...cauliflowers with extra long curly leaves.*

currency /ˈkʌrənsi, AM ˈkɜːr-/ **currencies.** **1** N-VAR The money used in a country is referred to as its **currency**. *...a single European currency. ...foreign currency.* **2** N-U If ideas, expressions, or customs have **currency**, they are generally used and accepted by people at that time; FORMAL. *'Loop' is one of those computer words that has gained currency.*

current /ˈkʌrənt, AM ˈkɜːr-/ **currents.** **1** N-C A **current** is a steady, continuous, flowing movement of water or air. *The couple were swept away by the strong current.* **2** N-C An electric **current** is electricity flowing through a wire or circuit. **3** ADJ Something that is **current** is happening, being done, or being used at the present time. *The current situation is very different... He plans to repeal a number of current policies.* ♦**currently** ADV *Twelve potential AIDS vaccines are currently being tested.*

current acˈcount, current accounts. N-C A **current account** is a bank account which you can take money out of at any time; BRITISH.

current afˈfairs. N-PL **Current affairs** are political events and problems which are discussed in the media. *...the BBC's current affairs programme 'Panorama'.*

curriculum /kəˈrɪkjʊləm/ **curriculums** or **curricula** /kəˈrɪkjʊlə/. **1** N-C A **curriculum** consists of all the different courses of study that are taught in a school, college, or university. *Not having Shakespeare in the school curriculum is madness.* **2** N-C A particular course of study can be referred to as a **curriculum**. *...the history curriculum.*

curry /ˈkʌri, AM ˈkɜːri/ **curries.** N-VAR **Curry** is an

Asian dish made with hot spices. *I went for a curry last night.*

curse /kɜːs/ **curses, cursing, cursed.** **1** VERB & N-C If you **curse**, or if you utter a **curse**, you swear or say rude words because you are angry about something; WRITTEN. *I cursed and hobbled to my feet... Groans and curses filled the air.* **2** VERB If you **curse** someone or something, you say insulting things to them or complain strongly about them because you are angry with them. *We set off again, cursing the delay... He cursed himself for not making a note of it.* **3** N-C If you say that there is a **curse** on someone, you mean that a supernatural power is causing unpleasant things to happen to them. **4** N-C You can refer to something that causes a lot of trouble as a **curse**. *...the curse of high unemployment.*

cursor /ˈkɜːsə/ **cursors.** N-C On a computer screen, the **cursor** is a small, movable shape which indicates where anything typed by the user will appear.

curt /kɜːt/. ADJ If someone is **curt**, they speak in a brief and rather rude way. *'The matter is closed,' was the curt reply.* ♦**curtly** ADV *'I'm leaving,' she said curtly.*

curtail /kɜːˈteɪl/ **curtails, curtailing, curtailed.** VERB If you **curtail** something, you reduce or restrict it. *Public spending is far too high, and must be curtailed.* ♦**curtailment** N-U *...the curtailment of presidential power.*

curtain /ˈkɜːtən/ **curtains.** **1** N-C **Curtains** are hanging pieces of material which you can pull across a window to keep light out or prevent people from looking in. *Her bedroom curtains were drawn.* **2** N-SING In a theatre, the **curtain** is a large piece of material that hangs in front of the stage until a performance begins.

curve /kɜːv/ **curves, curving, curved.** **1** N-C A **curve** is a smooth, gradually bending line, for example part of the edge of a circle. *...a curve in the road.* **2** VERB If something **curves**, it is shaped like a curve, or moves in a curve. *A stone wall curves away to the left... The ball curved strangely in the air.* ♦**curved** ADJ *...a curved blade.* **3** N-C You can refer to a change in something as a particular **curve**, especially when it is represented on a graph. *...the rising curve of youth unemployment.*

cushion /ˈkʊʃən/ **cushions, cushioning, cushioned.** **1** N-C A **cushion** is a fabric case filled with soft material, which you put on a seat to make it more comfortable. **2** VERB To **cushion** an impact means to reduce its effect. *...steps to cushion the impact of the economic slump.*

custard /ˈkʌstəd/. N-U **Custard** is a sweet yellow sauce made from milk and eggs or from milk and a powder. It is eaten with puddings.

custodial /kʌˈstəʊdiəl/. ADJ BEFORE N **Custodial** means relating to keeping people in prison; FORMAL. *He will be given a custodial sentence.*

custodian /kʌˈstəʊdiən/ **custodians.** N-C The **custodian** of an official building, a company's assets, or other valuable thing is the person in charge of it. *The Prime Minister is the ultimate custodian of the national interest.*

custody /ˈkʌstədi/. **1** N-U **Custody** is the legal right to look after a child, especially the right given to a child's father or mother when they get divorced. *I'm going to go to court to get custody of the children.* [2] PHRASE Someone who is **in custody** has been arrested and is being kept in prison until they can be tried.

custom /'kʌstəm/ **customs.** [1] N-VAR A **custom** is an activity, a way of behaving, or an event which is usual or traditional in a particular society or in particular circumstances. *...an ancient Japanese custom... It was the custom to give presents at such occasions.* [2] See also **customs.**

customary /'kʌstəmri, AM -meri/. ADJ **Customary** means usual. *It is customary to offer a drink or a snack to guests... Yvonne took her customary seat.*

customer /'kʌstəmə/ **customers.** N-C A **customer** is someone who buys goods or services, especially from a shop. *The shop was full of customers.*

> When you buy goods from a particular shop or company, you are one of its **customers**. If you use the professional services of someone such as a lawyer or an accountant, you are one of their **clients**. Doctors and hospitals have **patients**, while hotels have **guests**. People who travel on public transport are referred to as **passengers**, or sometimes **customers**.

customize /'kʌstəmaɪz/ (BR also **customise**) **customizes, customizing, customized.** VERB If you **customize** something, you change its appearance or features to suit your tastes or needs. *Kids customised their bikes.*

customs /'kʌstəmz/. [1] N-PROPER **Customs** is the official organization responsible for collecting taxes on goods coming into a country and preventing illegal goods from being brought in. *Spanish customs seized 400lb of marijuana. ...customs officers.* [2] N-U **Customs** is the place where people arriving from a foreign country have to declare goods that they bring with them. *He walked through customs.*

cut /kʌt/ **cuts, cutting, cut.** [1] VERB & N-C If you **cut** something, or if you make a **cut** in it, you push a knife or similar tool into it in order to remove a piece of it, or to mark or damage it. *Cut the tomatoes in half... The thieves cut a hole in the fence... You've had your hair cut, it looks great... The operation involves making several cuts in the cornea.* [2] VERB If you **cut** yourself, you accidentally injure yourself on a sharp object and you bleed. *Johnson cut himself shaving. ...blood from his cut lip.* [3] N-C A **cut** is an injury caused by touching or being touched by something sharp. *...a cut on his left eyebrow.* [4] VERB If you **cut across** or **through** an area, you go through it because it is a short route to another place. *He decided to cut across the Heath.* [5] VERB & N-C To **cut** something, or to make a **cut** in it, means to reduce it. *The first priority is to cut costs. ...a deal to cut 50 billion dollars from the federal deficit. ...an immediate 2 per cent cut in interest rates.* [6] VERB & N-C When a part of a piece of writing or performance **is cut**, or when **cuts** have been made to

it, parts of it are not printed, broadcast, or performed. *We've cut some scenes... It has been found necessary to make some cuts in the text.* [7] VERB & N-C To **cut** a supply of something means to stop providing it or stop it being provided. A **cut** in the supply of something is the action of stopping it. *...cutting food and water supplies. ...cuts in electricity supplies.* [8] PHRASE If something is **a cut above** other things of the same kind, it is better than them. [9] See also **cutting.**

▶ **cut across.** PHR-VERB If an issue or problem **cuts across** the division between two or more groups of people, it affects or matters to people in all the groups. *This health-care issue cuts across all the generations.*

▶ **cut back.** PHR-VERB If you **cut back** some money that you are spending, or if you **cut back** on it, you reduce it. *They will be concerned to cut back expenditure... The Government has cut back on defence spending.* ● See also **cutback.**

▶ **cut down.** [1] PHR-VERB If you **cut down** on something, you use or do less of it. *He cut down on coffee... Car owners were asked to cut down travel.* [2] PHR-VERB If you **cut down** a tree, you cut through its trunk so that it falls to the ground. [3] PHR-VERB If you **cut down** something, you reduce it. *We'd like politicians to get together and agree ways to cut down atmospheric pollution.*

▶ **cut in.** PHR-VERB If you **cut in** on someone, you interrupt them when they are speaking. *Daniel cut in on Joanne's attempts at reassurance.*

▶ **cut off.** [1] PHR-VERB If you **cut** something **off**, you remove it with a knife or a similar tool. *Mrs Kreutz cut off a generous piece of the meat... He threatened to cut my hair off.* [2] PHR-VERB To **cut off** a place or a person means to separate them from things they are normally connected with. *The storm has cut us off... Without a car we still felt very cut off.* [3] PHR-VERB To **cut off** a supply of something means to stop providing it or stop it being provided. *The rebels have cut off electricity from the capital.* [4] PHR-VERB If you get **cut off** when you are talking on the telephone, the line is suddenly disconnected.

▶ **cut out.** [1] PHR-VERB If you **cut** something **out**, you remove it from what surrounds it using scissors or a knife. *Cut out the coupon and send those cheques off today.* [2] PHR-VERB If you **cut out** a part of a text, you do not print, publish, or broadcast that part, in order to shorten the text or make it more acceptable. *They'd cut out all the interesting stuff.* [3] PHR-VERB To **cut out** something unnecessary means to remove it completely from a situation. *It would be wiser to cut out all alcohol during pregnancy.* [4] PHR-VERB If an object **cuts out** the light, it prevents light from reaching a place. *The curtains were half drawn to cut out the sunlight.* [5] PHR-VERB If an engine **cuts out**, it suddenly stops working.

▶ **cut up.** PHR-VERB If you **cut** something **up**, you cut it into several pieces. *Halve the tomatoes, then cut them up.*

cutback /'kʌtbæk/ (or **cut-back**) **cutbacks.** N-C A **cutback** is a reduction in something. *...cutbacks in defence spending.*

cute /kjuːt/ **cuter, cutest.** ADJ **Cute** means pretty or attractive. *Oh, look at that dog! He's so cute. ...a cute little house.*

cutlery /'kʌtləri/ N-U The knives, forks, and spoons that you eat with are referred to as **cutlery.**

cutter /'kʌtə/ **cutters.** N-VAR A **cutter** is a tool that you use for cutting something. *...a pastry cutter. ...a pair of wire cutters.*

cutting /'kʌtɪŋ/ **cuttings.** [1] N-C A **cutting** is a piece of writing cut from a newspaper or magazine; BRITISH. *...old newspaper cuttings.* [2] N-C A **cutting** is a piece of stalk that you cut from a plant and use to grow a new plant. [3] ADJ A **cutting** remark is unkind and hurts people's feelings.

cutting 'edge. N-SING If you are at the **cutting edge** of a field of activity, you are involved in its most important or exciting developments. *This shipyard is at the cutting edge of world shipbuilding technology.*

CV /ˌsiː 'viː/ **CV's.** N-C In British English, your **CV** is a brief written account of your personal details, your education, and jobs you have had, which you send when you are applying for a job. The American word is **resumé.**

cyanide /'saɪənaɪd/ N-U **Cyanide** is a highly poisonous substance.

cycle /'saɪkəl/ **cycles, cycling, cycled.** [1] VERB If you **cycle**, you ride a bicycle. *I cycle to work at least twice a week.* ◆**cycling** N-U *Quiet country roads are ideal for cycling.* [2] N-C A **cycle** is a bicycle. [3] N-C A **cycle** is a series of events or processes that is continually repeated, always in the same order. *...the cycles of nature... They must break out of the cycle of violence.*

cyclical /'sɪklɪkəl, 'saɪk-/ or **cyclic** /'sɪklɪk, 'saɪk-/. ADJ A **cyclical** process happens again and again in cycles. *...the cyclical downturns that the stockmarket was bound to suffer.*

cyclist /'saɪklɪst/ **cyclists.** N-C A **cyclist** is someone who rides a bicycle.

cyclone /'saɪkləʊn/ **cyclones.** N-C A **cyclone** is a violent tropical storm.

cylinder /'sɪlɪndə/ **cylinders.** N-C A **cylinder** is a shape or container with flat circular ends and long straight sides. *...a cylinder of foam. ...a gas cylinder.*

cynic /'sɪnɪk/ **cynics.** N-C A **cynic** is someone who always thinks the worst of people or things.

cynical /'sɪnɪkəl/. ADJ If you describe someone as **cynical**, you think that they always think the worst of people or things. *...his cynical view of the world... It has also made me more cynical about relationships.* ◆**cynically** ADV *He laughed cynically, but without bitterness.* ◆**cynicism** /'sɪnɪsɪzəm/ N-U *...growing public cynicism about politicians.*

cyst /sɪst/ **cysts.** N-C A **cyst** is a growth containing liquid that appears inside your body or under your skin.

D d

dab /dæb/ **dabs, dabbing, dabbed.** [1] VERB If you **dab** something, you touch it several times using quick light movements. *She dabbed iodine on the cuts... He dabbed at his lips with the napkin.* [2] N-C A **dab** of something is a small amount of it that is put onto a surface; INFORMAL. *...a dab of glue.*

dabble /'dæbəl/ **dabbles, dabbling, dabbled.** VERB If you **dabble** in something, you take part in it but not very seriously. *He dabbled in politics.*

dad /dæd/ **dads.** N-C & N-VOC Your **dad** is your father; INFORMAL. *Help me Dad!... He's living with his mum and dad.*

daddy /'dædi/ **daddies.** N-C & N-VOC Children often call their father **daddy;** INFORMAL. *Little children like to watch their daddies shave... Look at me, Daddy!*

daffodil /'dæfədɪl/ **daffodils.** N-C A **daffodil** is a yellow flower that blooms in the spring.

daft /dɑːft, dæft/ **dafter, daftest.** ADJ **Daft** means stupid and not sensible; BRITISH, INFORMAL. *That's a daft question.*

dagger /'dægə/ **daggers.** N-C A **dagger** is a weapon like a knife with two sharp edges.

daily /'deɪli/ **dailies.** [1] ADV & ADJ BEFORE N If something happens **daily**, it happens every day. *The exhibition is open daily from 11am... I set out for my daily walk.* [2] ADJ BEFORE N **Daily** means relating to a single day or to one day at a time. *...the recommended daily intake of vitamins.* [3] N-C & ADJ BEFORE N A **daily** or a **daily** newspaper is a newspaper that is published every day except Sunday.

dainty /'deɪnti/. ADJ A **dainty** movement, person, or object is small, delicate, or pretty. *...dainty feet.* ◆**daintily** ADV *He noticed how daintily they all ate.*

dairy /'deəri/ **dairies.** [1] N-C A **dairy** is a shop or company that sells milk, butter, and cheese. [2] N-C A **dairy** on a farm is a building where milk is kept or where cream, butter, and cheese are made. [3] ADJ BEFORE N **Dairy** is used to refer to foods such as butter and cheese that are made from milk. *...dairy products.*

daisy /'deɪzi/ **daisies.** N-C A **daisy** is a small wild flower with a yellow centre and white petals.

dam /dæm/ **dams, damming, dammed.** [1] N-C A **dam** is a wall built across a river to stop the flow of the water and make a lake. [2] VERB To **dam** a river means to build a dam across it.

damage /'dæmɪdʒ/ **damages, damaging, damaged.** [1] VERB To **damage** something means to injure or harm it. *Halliday damaged his knee during training. ...the attempt to damage his reputation.* ◆**damaging** ADJ *...damaging allegations about his relationship with an actress.* [2] N-U **Damage** is injury or harm that is caused to something. *The bomb caused extensive damage to the restaurant. ...the damage done to our international image by the recent* *violence.* **3** N-PL When a court of law awards **damages** to someone, it orders money to be paid to them by a person who has harmed them.

dame /deɪm/ **dames.** N-TITLE In Britain, **Dame** is a title given to a woman as a special honour. *...Dame Joan Sutherland.*

damn /dæm/. **1** EXCLAM & ADJ BEFORE N & ADV **Damn** is a swear word which people use to express anger or frustration or for emphasis. *Damn! she muttered... The damn thing's burst... As it turned out, I was damn right.* **2** PHRASE If you say that someone **does not give a damn** about something, you mean that they do not care about it at all; INFORMAL.

damned /dæmd/. A swear word which people use to express anger or frustration or for emphasis. *...a damned nuisance... We are making a damned good profit.*

damning /ˈdæmɪŋ/. ADJ Something that is **damning** suggests strongly that someone is guilty of a crime or error. *...damning evidence.*

damp /dæmp/ **damper, dampest; damps, damping, damped.** **1** ADJ **Damp** means slightly wet. *...a damp towel.* ♦**dampness** N-U *...the dampness of the wall.* **2** N-U **Damp** is slight moisture in the air or on the walls of a house.

▸ **damp down.** PHR-VERB To **damp down** a difficult situation means to make it calmer or less intense. *Mr Blair tried to damp down the row yesterday.*

dampen /ˈdæmpən/ **dampens, dampening, dampened.** **1** VERB To **dampen** something means to make it less lively or intense. *It did nothing to dampen his enthusiasm for motor sport.* **2** VERB If you **dampen** something, you make it slightly wet. *...dampen a sponge.*

dance /dɑːns, dæns/ **dances, dancing, danced.** **1** VERB When you **dance**, you move around in time to music. *...a couple dancing together... We all danced the Charleston.* ♦**dancing** N-U *Let's go dancing tonight.* **2** N-C A **dance** is a series of steps and rhythmic movements which you do to music. It is also a piece of music which people can dance to. *She describes the tango as a very sexy dance.* **3** N-C A **dance** is a social event where people dance with each other. **4** N-U **Dance** is the activity of performing dances as a public entertainment or art form. *...an evening of dance.*

'dance floor (or **dancefloor**) **dance floors.** N-C In a restaurant or night club, the **dance floor** is the area where people can dance.

dancer /ˈdɑːnsə, ˈdæns-/ **dancers.** N-C A **dancer** is a person who earns money by dancing, or a person who is dancing.

dandelion /ˈdændɪlaɪən/ **dandelions.** N-C A **dandelion** is a wild plant which has yellow flowers first, then fluffy balls of seeds.

danger /ˈdeɪndʒə/ **dangers.** **1** N-U **Danger** is the possibility that someone may be harmed or killed. *My friends endured tremendous danger in order to help me... Your life is in danger.* **2** N-C A **danger** is something or someone that can hurt or harm you. *...the dangers of smoking.* **3** N-SING If there is a **danger** of something unpleasant happening, it is possible that it will

happen. *There is a danger of infection developing.*

dangerous /ˈdeɪndʒərəs/. ADJ If something is **dangerous**, it may hurt or harm you. *...dangerous drugs.* ♦**dangerously** ADV *He rushed downstairs dangerously fast.*

dangle /ˈdæŋɡəl/ **dangles, dangling, dangled.** VERB If something **dangles** from somewhere, it hangs or swings loosely. *A gold bracelet dangled from his left wrist.*

dare /deə/ **dares, daring, dared.** **1** VERB & MODAL If you **dare** to do something, you have enough courage to do it. *He has also dared to take unpopular, but principled stands at times... I didn't dare look at Ellen... They daren't leave him.* **2** VERB & N-C If you **dare** someone to do something, or challenge them to do it for a **dare**, you challenge them to prove that they are not frightened of doing it. *He glared at the German, daring him to disagree. ...two students accused of murdering a stranger for a dare.*

PHRASES ● You say **'how dare you'** when you are very shocked and angry about something that someone has done. *How dare you insult my singing!* ● You say **I dare say** or **I daresay** to show that you think something is probably true; SPOKEN. *I dare say they're right.*

daren't /deənt/. 'Dare not' is usually written or said as **daren't**; INFORMAL.

daring /ˈdeərɪŋ/. **1** ADJ A **daring** person does things which might be dangerous or shocking. *...a daring escape by helicopter.* **2** N-U **Daring** is the courage to do things which might be dangerous or shocking. *His daring may have cost him his life.*

dark /dɑːk/ **darker, darkest.** **1** ADJ When it is **dark**, there is not enough light to see properly. *People usually draw the curtains once it gets dark. ...a dark corridor... After dark, park in a well-lit, busy place.* ♦**darkness** N-U *The whole city was plunged into darkness.* **2** N-SING **The dark** is the lack of light in a place. *I've always been afraid of the dark.* **3** ADJ Something that is **dark** or a **dark** colour is black or a shade close to black. *...a dark suit. ...a dark blue dress.* **4** ADJ Someone who is **dark** has brown or black hair, and often brown skin. **5** ADJ **Dark** looks or remarks suggest that something horrible is going to happen. *...dark rumours abound.* ♦**darkly** ADV *They shake their heads and mutter darkly.* **6** PHRASE If you are **in the dark** about something, you do not know anything about it.

darken /ˈdɑːkən/ **darkens, darkening, darkened.** **1** VERB If something **darkens**, it becomes darker; WRITTEN. *The sky darkened abruptly... He may have darkened his hair.* **2** VERB If someone's face **darkens**, they suddenly look angry; WRITTEN.

darkroom /ˈdɑːkruːm/ **darkrooms.** N-C A **darkroom** is a room which is lit only by red light, so that photographs can be developed there.

darling /ˈdɑːlɪŋ/ **darlings.** **1** N-VOC You call someone **darling** if you love them or like them very much. *Thank you, darling.* **2** ADJ BEFORE N & N-C You can describe someone as **darling** or say that they are a **darling** when you love or like them very much. ...*our darling child... She is a darling.*

darn /dɑːn/ **darns, darning, darned.** [1] VERB When you **darn** something made of cloth, you mend a hole in it by sewing stitches across the hole and then weaving stitches in and out of them. [2] ADJ BEFORE N & ADV People sometimes use **darn** or **darned** to express anger or frustration or for emphasis. ...*darned kids... You're darn right.*

dart /dɑːt/ **darts, darting, darted.** [1] VERB If a person or animal **darts** somewhere, they move there suddenly and quickly; WRITTEN. *Ingrid darted across the deserted street.* [2] VERB If you **dart** a glance at someone or something, or if your eyes **dart** to them, you look at them very quickly; WRITTEN. *Her eyes darted from one face to another.* [3] N-C A **dart** is a small, narrow object with a sharp point which you can throw or shoot. [4] N-U **Darts** is a game in which you throw darts at a round board with numbers on it.

dash /dæʃ/ **dashes, dashing, dashed.** [1] VERB & N-SING If you **dash** somewhere, or if you make a **dash** there, you go there quickly and suddenly. *He dashed upstairs... Frank considered making a dash for the front door.* [2] N-C A **dash** of something is a small quantity or amount of it. *Add a dash of lemon juice.* [3] VERB If an event or person **dashes** someone's hopes, it destroys them by making it impossible that the thing that is hoped for will ever happen. ...*the injury which dashed his hopes of Olympic gold.* [4] N-C A **dash** is a short horizontal line (—) used in writing.

▶ **dash off.** [1] PHR-VERB If you **dash off** to a place, you go there very quickly. [2] PHR-VERB If you **dash off** something such as a letter, you write it quickly without thinking much about it. *He dashed off a couple of novels.*

dashboard /'dæʃbɔːd/ **dashboards.** N-C The **dashboard** in a car is the panel facing the driver's seat where most of the instruments and switches are.

dashing /'dæʃɪŋ/. ADJ A **dashing** person or thing is very stylish and attractive; DATED. ...*a dashing young officer.*

data /'deɪtə/. N-U & N-PL **Data** is information, usually in the form of facts or statistics, that you can analyse. *The study was based on data from 2,100 women.*

database or **data base** /'deɪtəbeɪs/ **databases.** N-C A **database** is a collection of data stored in a computer in a way that makes it easy to obtain. ...*a database of hotels that cater for businesswomen.*

date /deɪt/ **dates, dating, dated.** [1] N-C A **date** is a particular day or year, for example 7th June 1990, or 1066. *What's the date today?... You will need to give the dates you wish to stay.* [2] VERB When you **date** something, you give the date when it began or was made. *Archaeologists have dated the fort to the reign of Emperor Antoninus Pius.* [3] VERB When you **date** a letter or a cheque, you write a particular day's date on it. [4] PHRASE **To date** means up until the present time. *'Dottie' is by far his best novel to date.* [5] VERB If something **dates**, it goes out of fashion. ◆ **dated** ADJ ...*people in dated*

dinner-jackets. [6] N-C A **date** is an appointment to meet someone or go out with them, especially someone of the opposite sex. You can also refer to the person you go out with as your **date**. *I have a date with Bob... His date was one of the girls in the show.* [7] VERB If you **are dating** someone of the opposite sex, you go out regularly with them. *For a year I dated a woman who was a research assistant... They've been dating for three months.* [8] N-C A **date** is a small, sticky, dark brown fruit with a stone inside. [9] See also **out of date, up-to-date.**

▶ **date back** or **date from.** PHR-VERB If something **dates back** to a particular time, or **dates from** that time, it started or was made at that time. *The treasure dates back to the sixth century BC.*

daub /dɔːb/ **daubs, daubing, daubed.** VERB When you **daub** a substance such as mud or paint on something, you spread it on that thing roughly or carelessly. *They daubed his home with slogans.*

daughter /'dɔːtə/ **daughters.** N-C Your **daughter** is your female child. *I have two daughters.*

'daughter-in-law, daughters-in-law. N-C Your **daughter-in-law** is the wife of your son.

daunt /dɔːnt/ **daunts, daunting, daunted.** VERB If something **daunts** you, it makes you feel afraid or worried about dealing with it. ...*a gruelling journey that would have daunted a woman half her age.* ◆ **daunted** ADJ AFTER LINK-V *I was quite daunted by the prospect of coping with teenagers.* ◆ **daunting** ADJ ...*the daunting task of restoring the gardens to their former splendour.*

dawn /dɔːn/ **dawns, dawning, dawned.** [1] N-VAR **Dawn** is the time of day when light first appears in the sky, before the sun rises. *Nancy woke at dawn.* [2] VERB When you say that a particular day **dawned**, you mean it began; WRITTEN. *The next day dawned sombre and gloomy.* [3] N-SING The **dawn** of a period of time or a situation is the beginning of it; LITERARY. ...*the dawn of the radio age.* [4] VERB If something **is dawning**, it is beginning to develop or come into existence; LITERARY. *A new railway age has dawned.* ◆ **dawning** N-C ...*the dawning of the space age.*

▶ **dawn on** or **dawn upon.** PHR-VERB If a fact or idea **dawns on** you, or if it **dawns upon** you, you realize it. *It gradually dawned on me that I still had talent.*

day /deɪ/ **days.** [1] N-C A **day** is one of the seven twenty-four hour periods of time in a week. [2] N-VAR **Day** is the part of a day when it is light or the time when you are awake and doing things. *He arranged for me to go down to London one day a week... The snack bar is open during the day.* [3] N-C You can refer to a period in history as a particular **day** or as particular **days**. *He began to talk about the Ukraine of his uncle's day... She is doing just fine these days.*

PHRASES ● If you **call it a day**, you stop what you are doing and leave it to be finished later. *I want Alan Whicker's job when he calls it a day.* ● **One day**, **some day**, or **one of these days** means at some future time. *Maybe one day*

you'll find true love. • **day and night**: see
night. • **night and day**: see **night.**

'day care. N-U **Day care** is care that is provided
during the day for people who cannot look after themselves, such as small children, old
people, or people who are ill.

daydream /'deɪdriːm/ **daydreams, day-
dreaming, daydreamed.** VERB & NOUN When
you **daydream**, or when you have a **daydream**,
you think about pleasant things that you
would like to happen. *He daydreams of being a
famous journalist... Janis emerged from her
daydream.*

daylight /'deɪlaɪt/. N-U **Daylight** is the light that
there is during the day, or the time of day
when it is light. *It was still daylight... Quinn returned shortly after daylight.*

daytime /'deɪtaɪm/. N-U **Daytime** is the part of a
day when it is light. *In the daytime he stayed
up in his room.*

,day-to-'day. ADJ BEFORE N **Day-to-day** things
or activities exist or happen every day as part
of ordinary life. *...the day-to-day lives of students.*

dazed /deɪzd/. ADJ If someone is **dazed**, they are
confused and unable to think clearly, often because of shock or a blow to the head.

dazzle /'dæzəl/ **dazzles, dazzling, dazzled.**
[1] VERB If someone or something **dazzles** you,
you are extremely impressed by their skill or
beauty. *George dazzled her with his knowledge
of the world.* [2] N-U The **dazzle** of a light is its
brightness, which makes it impossible for you
to see properly for a short time. [3] VERB If a
bright light **dazzles** you, you cannot see properly for a short time.

dazzling /'dæzlɪŋ/. [1] ADJ Something that is
dazzling is very impressive or beautiful. *...a
dazzling smile.* ♦**dazzlingly** ADV *The view was
dazzlingly beautiful.* [2] ADJ A **dazzling** light is
very bright and makes you unable to see properly for a short time. ♦**dazzlingly** ADV *The bay
seemed dazzlingly bright.*

dead /ded/. [1] ADJ & N-PL **Dead** people or the
dead are no longer living. *My husband's been
dead a year now.*

> Do not confuse **dead** with **died**. **Died** is
> the past tense and past participle of the
> verb **die**, and thus indicates the action of
> dying. *She died in 1934... Two men have
> died since the rioting broke out.* You do
> not use **died** as an adjective. You use
> **dead** instead. *More than 2,200 dead
> birds have been found.*

[2] ADJ A telephone or piece of electrical equipment that is **dead** is not functioning. *Duke answered the phone and the line went dead.*
[3] ADJ BEFORE N **Dead** is used to mean complete or absolute, especially with the words
'silence', 'centre', and 'stop'. *He adjusted each
chesspiece so that it stood dead centre in its
square.* [4] ADV **Dead** means precisely or exactly. *Mars was visible, dead in the centre of the
telescope... A fishing boat came out of nowhere,
dead ahead.* [5] ADV **Dead** is sometimes used to
mean very; INFORMAL. *His poems sound dead
boring, actually.* [6] PHRASE To **stop dead**

means to suddenly stop moving or doing
something. *We all stopped dead and looked at
it.*

,dead 'end, dead ends. [1] N-C If a street is a
dead end, there is no way out at one end of it.
[2] N-C A job or course of action that is a **dead
end** does not lead to further developments or
progression. *Waitressing was a dead-end job.*

deadline /'dedlaɪn/ **deadlines.** N-C A **deadline**
is a time or date before which a particular task
must be finished or a particular thing must be
done. *The deadline for submissions to the competition will be Easter 2004.*

deadlock /'dedlɒk/. N-U If a dispute or series of
negotiations reaches **deadlock**, neither side is
willing to give in, and so no agreement can be
reached. *Peace talks between the two sides ended in deadlock.*

deadly /'dedli/ **deadlier, deadliest.** [1] ADJ If
something is **deadly**, it is likely or able to cause
death. *...a deadly disease... Some have turned
to more deadly weapons.* [2] ADJ If you describe
a person or their behaviour as **deadly**, you
mean they are unpleasant or dangerous. A
deadly situation has unpleasant or dangerous
consequences. *My aim was deadly accurate.
...the deadliest blizzard to hit the United States
since January 1966.*

deaf /def/ **deafer, deafest.** [1] ADJ & N-PL **Deaf**
people or the **deaf** are unable to hear anything
or unable to hear very well. *She is now profoundly deaf... Many regular TV programs are
captioned for the deaf.* ♦**deafness** N-U *...perma-
nent deafness.* [2] ADJ AFTER LINK-V If you say that
someone is **deaf** to people's pleas or criticisms,
you disapprove of them because they refuse to
pay attention to them. *She kept her eyes down,
deaf to what was happening around her.*

deafen /'defən/ **deafens, deafening, deafened.** VERB If you **are deafened** by a noise, it is
so loud that you cannot hear anything else.
The noise of the typewriters deafened her.

deafening /'defənɪŋ/. ADJ A **deafening** noise is
a very loud noise.

deal /diːl/ **deals, dealing, dealt** /delt/.
[1] QUANT **A good deal** or **a great deal** of something is a lot of it. *Lawrence Durrell wrote a
great deal of poetry... She had certainly known
a good deal more than she'd admitted.* [2] N-C A
deal is an agreement or arrangement, especially in business. *Japan will have to do a deal
with America on rice imports.* [3] VERB If a person, company, or shop **deals in** a particular
type of goods, their business involves buying
or selling those goods. *They deal in antiques.*
♦**dealer, dealers.** N-C *...an antique dealer.*
[4] VERB & PHR-VERB When you **deal** cards, or
when you **deal** them **out**, you give them out to
the players in a game of cards. *The croupier
dealt each player a card... Dalton dealt out five
cards to each player.*

▸ **deal out.** PHR-VERB If someone **deals out** a
punishment or harmful action, they punish or
harm someone. *It also deals out sharp criticism
to the Department.* • See also **deal** 5.

▸ **deal with.** [1] PHR-VERB When you **deal with** a
situation or problem, you do what is necessary
to achieve the result you want. *...the way that
building societies deal with complaints.*

2 PHR-VERB If a book, speech, or film **deals with** a subject, it is concerned with it. *...the parts of his book which deal with contemporary Paris.* **3** PHR-VERB If you **deal with** a particular person or organization, you have business relations with them. *When I worked in Florida I dealt with British people all the time.*

dealings /'di:lɪŋz/. N-PL Someone's **dealings** with a person or organization are the relations that they have with them or the business that they do with them. *He has learnt little in his dealings with the international community.*

dean /di:n/ **deans.** **1** N-C A **dean** is an important administrator at a university or college. **2** N-C A **dean** is a priest who is the main administrator of a cathedral.

dear /dɪə/ **dearer, dearest; dears.** **1** ADJ BEFORE N You use **dear** to describe someone or something that feel affection for. *Mrs Cavendish is a dear friend of mine.* **2** ADJ AFTER LINK-V If something is **dear to** you or **dear to** your heart, you care deeply about it. *His family life was very dear to him.* **3** N-VOC You can call someone **dear** as a sign of affection. *You're a lot like me, dear.* **4** ADJ BEFORE N **Dear** is written at the beginning of a letter, followed by the name or title of the person you are writing to. *'Dear sir,' she began.* **5** ADJ Something that is **dear** costs a lot of money. *They're too dear.*

dearest /'dɪərɪst/. **1** N-VOC You can call someone **dearest** when you are very fond of them; DATED. *What's wrong, my dearest? You look tired.* **2** ADJ When you are writing to someone you are very fond of, you can use **dearest** at the beginning of the letter before the person's name. *Dearest Maria, Sorry I haven't written for so long.*

dearly /'dɪəli/. **1** ADV If you love someone **dearly**, you love them very much. **2** ADV If you would **dearly** like to do or have something, you would very much like to do it or have it. *I would dearly love to marry.* **3** PHRASE If you **pay dearly** for doing something or if it **costs** you **dearly**, you suffer a lot as a result; FORMAL. *He drank too much and is paying dearly for his pleasure.*

death /deθ/ **deaths.** N-VAR **Death** is the end of the life of a person or animal. *1.5 million people are in immediate danger of death from starvation. ...the thirtieth anniversary of her death.*
PHRASES ● If you say that something is a matter of **life and death**, you are emphasizing that it is extremely important, often because someone may die if people do not act immediately. *We're dealing with a life-and-death situation here.* ● If someone **is put to death**, they are executed. ● You use **to death** to indicate that a particular action or process results in someone's death. *He was stabbed to death.* ● You use **to death** after an adjective or a verb to emphasize the action, state, or feeling mentioned. *He scares teams to death with his pace and power... I went out last night, but not for very long. I was bored to death.*

'death penalty. N-SING The **death penalty** is the punishment of death, used in some countries for people who have committed very serious crimes. *Both youngsters could face the death penalty.*

death row /,deθ 'rəʊ/. N-U If someone is on **death row**, they are in the part of a prison which contains the cells for criminals who have been sentenced to death.

'death toll (or **death-toll**) **death tolls.** N-C The **death toll** of an accident, disaster, or war is the number of people who die in it.

debacle (or **débâcle**) /deɪ'bɑːkəl, AM dɪ'bɑː-/ **de-bacles.** N-C A **debacle** is an event or attempt that is a complete failure. *It will be hard for the republic to recover from this debacle.*

debatable /dɪ'beɪtəbəl/. ADJ Something that is **debatable** is not definitely true or not certain. *Whether the Bank of England would do any better is highly debatable.*

debate /dɪ'beɪt/ **debates, debating, debated.** **1** N-VAR A **debate** is a discussion about a subject on which people have different views. *There has been a lot of debate among scholars about this.* **2** VERB When people **debate** a topic, they discuss it fairly formally, putting forward different views. You can also say that one person **debates** a topic with another person. *The United Nations Security Council will debate the issue today.* **3** N-C A **debate** is a formal discussion, for example in a parliament, in which people express different opinions about a subject and then vote on it. *...a debate on defence spending.* **4** VERB If you **debate** what to do, you think about possible courses of action before deciding what to do. *At the moment we are debating what furniture to buy for the house... I debated going back inside.*

debit /'debɪt/ **debits, debiting, debited.** **1** VERB When your bank **debits** your account, money is taken from it and paid to someone else. **2** N-C A **debit** is a record of the money taken from your bank account.

debris /'deɪbri, AM deɪ'briː/. N-U **Debris** consists of pieces of things that have been destroyed, or rubbish that is lying around. *A number of people were killed by flying debris.*

debt /det/ **debts.** **1** N-VAR A **debt** is a sum of money that you owe someone. *He is still paying off his debts.* **2** N-U **Debt** is the state of owing money. *He was already deeply in debt through gambling losses.*

debtor /'detə/ **debtors.** N-C A **debtor** is a country, organization, or person who owes money.

debut /'deɪbjuː, AM deɪ'bjuː/ **debuts.** N-C The **debut** of a performer or sports player is his or her first public performance or recording. *...her debut album 'Sugar Time'.*

decade /'dekeɪd/ **decades.** N-C A **decade** is a period of ten years, especially one that begins with a year ending in 0, for example 1980 to 1989. *...the last decade of the nineteenth century.*

decadent /'dekədənt/. ADJ If you say that a person or society is **decadent**, you mean that they have low standards, especially low moral standards. *...their decadent rock 'n' roll lifestyles.* ◆**decadence** N-U *The empire had for years been falling into decadence.*

decay /dɪ'keɪ/ **decays, decaying, decayed.** **1** VERB & N-U When something **decays**, it becomes rotten. This process is called **decay**. *The bodies buried in the fine ash slowly decayed. ...decaying leaves.* ◆**decayed** ADJ *...de-*

cayed teeth. [2] VERB & N-U If a society, system, or institution **decays**, it gradually becomes weaker or its condition gets worse. This process is called **decay**. ...*decaying urban and rural areas.* ...*a film about inner city decay.*

deceased /dɪ'siːst/; **deceased** is both the singular and the plural form. [1] N-C **The deceased** is used to refer to a person or a group of people who have recently died; FORMAL. *Do you know the last address of the deceased?* [2] ADJ A **deceased** person is one who has recently died; FORMAL. ...*his recently deceased mother.*

deceit /dɪ'siːt/ **deceits**. N-VAR **Deceit** is behaviour that is intended to make people believe something which is not true. ...*the deceit and lies of the past.*

deceitful /dɪ'siːtfʊl/ ADJ If you say that someone is **deceitful**, you mean that they behave in a dishonest way by making other people believe something that is not true. *The ambassador called the report deceitful and misleading.*

deceive /dɪ'siːv/ **deceives, deceiving, deceived.** VERB If you **deceive** someone, you make them believe something that is not true. *I was really hurt that he had deceived me... The alleged offences include deceiving the council into giving her son a house.*

December /dɪ'sembə/. N-U **December** is the twelfth and last month of the year in the Western calendar.

decency /'diːsənsi/. N-U **Decency** is behaviour which follows accepted moral standards. *His sense of decency forced him to resign... No-one had the decency to tell me to my face.*

decent /'diːsənt/. [1] ADJ **Decent** means acceptable in standard or quality. *The lack of a decent education did not defeat Rey.* ♦**decently** ADV *The allies say they will treat their prisoners decently.* [2] ADJ **Decent** is used to describe behaviour which is morally correct or acceptable. *After a decent interval, trade relations began to return to normal.* ♦**decently** ADV *I don't want to go back to the regiment in Egypt, if I can decently avoid it.*

decentralized (BR also **decentralised**) /,diː'sentrəlaɪzd/. ADJ In a **decentralized** political system, decisions are made by departments in local areas. *This decentralized structure made it difficult to control developments within the various party branches.* ♦**decentralization** /,diː,sentrəlaɪ'zeɪʃən/ N-U *He seems set against the idea of increased decentralisation.*

deception /dɪ'sepʃən/ **deceptions.** N-VAR **Deception** is the act of deceiving someone. *He admitted conspiring to obtain property by deception.*

deceptive /dɪ'septɪv/. ADJ If something is **deceptive**, it encourages you to believe something which is not true. *First impressions proved deceptive.* ♦**deceptively** ADV *The storyline is deceptively simple.*

decibel /'desɪbel/ **decibels.** N-C A **decibel** is a unit of measurement which is used to indicate how loud a sound is.

decide /dɪ'saɪd/ **decides, deciding, decided.** [1] VERB If you **decide** to do something, you choose to do it. *She decided to do a secretarial course... He decided that he would drive back to town at once.* [2] VERB If a person or group of people **decides** something, they choose what something should be like or how a particular problem should be solved. *She was still young, he said, and that would be taken into account when deciding her sentence.* [3] VERB If you **decide** that something is the case, you form that opinion after considering the facts. *He decided Franklin must be suffering from a bad cold... For a long time I couldn't decide whether the original settlers were insane or just stupid.* [4] VERB If an event or fact **decides** something, it makes a particular result definite or unavoidable. *The results will decide if he will win a place at a good university... Luck is certainly not the only deciding factor.*

▸ **decide on.** PHR-VERB If you **decide on** something or **decide upon** something, you choose it from two or more possibilities. *Therese decided on a career in publishing.*

decided /dɪ'saɪdɪd/. ADJ BEFORE N **Decided** means clear and definite. *He's a man of very decided opinions.*

decidedly /dɪ'saɪdɪdli/. ADV **Decidedly** means to a great extent and in a way that is obvious. *He admits there will be moments when he's decidedly uncomfortable at what he sees.*

deciduous /dɪ'sɪdʒuəs/. ADJ A **deciduous** tree loses its leaves in autumn every year.

decimal /'desɪməl/ **decimals.** [1] ADJ A **decimal** system involves counting in units of ten. ...*the decimal system of metric weights and measures.* [2] N-C A **decimal** is a fraction written in the form of a dot followed by one or more numbers representing tenths, hundredths, and so on, for example .5, .51, .517.

,**decimal 'point, decimal points.** N-C A **decimal point** is the dot in front of a decimal fraction.

decimate /'desɪmeɪt/ **decimates, decimating, decimated.** VERB To **decimate** a group of people or animals means to destroy a very large number of them. *The pollution could decimate the river's thriving population of kingfishers.*

decipher /dɪ'saɪfə/ **deciphers, deciphering, deciphered.** VERB If you **decipher** a piece of writing or a message, you work out what it says, even though it is difficult to read or understand.

decision /dɪ'sɪʒən/ **decisions.** [1] N-C When you make a **decision**, you choose what should be done or which is the best of various alternatives. *I think I made the right decision... The decision to discipline Marshall was taken by the party chairman.* [2] N-U **Decision** is the act of deciding something. *The moment of decision can't be too long delayed.*

de'cision-making. N-U **Decision-making** is the process of reaching decisions, especially in a large organization or in government. *She wants to see more women involved in decision making.*

decisive /dɪ'saɪsɪv/. [1] ADJ If a fact, action, or event is **decisive**, it makes it certain that there will be a particular result. *The election campaign has now entered its final, decisive phase.* ♦**decisively** ADV *The plan was decisively reject-*

ed. [2] ADJ If someone is **decisive**, they have the ability to make quick decisions. *He should give way to a younger, more decisive leader.* ◆**decisively** ADV *'I'll call for you at half ten,' she said decisively.* ◆**decisiveness** N-U *His supporters admire his decisiveness.*

deck /dek/ **decks, decking, decked.** [1] N-C A **deck** on a bus or ship is a downstairs or upstairs area. *...the top deck of the number 13 bus.* [2] N-SING The **deck** of a ship is a floor in the open air which you can walk on. [3] N-C A tape **deck** or a record **deck** is a piece of equipment on which you play tapes or records. [4] N-C In American English, a **deck** of cards is a complete set of playing cards. The usual British word is **pack**.

▸ **deck out.** PHR-VERB If someone or something **is decked out** with or in something, they are decorated with it or wearing it. *She had decked him out from head to foot in expensive clothes.*

declaration /ˌdeklə'reɪʃən/ **declarations.** [1] N-C A **declaration** is an official announcement or statement. *...Somaliland's declaration of independence.* [2] N-C A **declaration** is a firm statement which shows that you have no doubts about what you are saying. *...a declaration of undying love.*

declare /dɪ'kleə/ **declares, declaring, declared.** [1] VERB If you **declare** that something is the case, you say that it is true in a firm deliberate way. *He declared his intention to become the best golfer in the world.* [2] VERB If you **declare** something, you state it officially and formally. *A petition was filed in court to have him declared insane... Representatives addressed the rally and declared their support for Lithuania.* [3] VERB If you **declare** goods that you have bought abroad or money that you have earned, you say how much you have bought or earned so that you can pay tax on it.

decline /dɪ'klaɪn/ **declines, declining, declined.** [1] VERB & N-VAR If something **declines**, or if there is a **decline** in something, it becomes smaller, weaker, or worse. *The number of staff has declined from 217,000 to 114,000. ...declining standards of literacy. ...the rate of decline in tobacco consumption.* [2] PHRASE If something is **in decline**, falling **into decline**, or **on the decline**, it is gradually growing smaller, weaker, or worse. *U.S. oil production is in decline... Thankfully the smoking of cigarettes is on the decline.* [3] VERB If you **decline** something or **decline** to do something, you politely refuse to accept it or do it; FORMAL. *I declined his offer of coffee and dessert... Her band declined to comment on the story.*

decompose /ˌdiːkəm'pəʊz/ **decomposes, decomposing, decomposed.** VERB When dead plants, humans, or animals **decompose**, they change chemically and begin to rot. *The debris slowly decomposes into compost... Her decomposed body was found in a remote wood.* ◆**decomposition** /ˌdiːˌkɒmpə'zɪʃən/ N-U *...the four mutilated bodies were all in advanced stages of decomposition.*

decor /'deɪkɔː/ N-U The **decor** of a house or of a room is the style in which it is furnished and decorated.

decorate /'dekəreɪt/ **decorates, decorating, decorated.** [1] VERB If you **decorate** something, you make it more attractive by adding things to it. *He decorated his room with pictures.* [2] VERB If you **decorate** a building, room, you paint it or wallpaper it. ◆**decorating** N-U *I did a lot of the decorating myself.* ◆**decorator, decorators** N-C *...a firm of painters and decorators.* [3] VERB If someone **is decorated**, they are given a medal or other honour as an official reward for something that they have done.

decoration /ˌdekə'reɪʃən/ **decorations.** [1] N-VAR **Decorations** are features added to something to make it more attractive. *...Christmas decorations... Whole currants look very pretty as decoration for cakes.* [2] N-U The **decoration** of a room or building is the furniture, wallpaper, and ornaments there. *Everybody has their own ideas of decoration – especially with pine.* [3] N-C A **decoration** is a medal or a title given to someone as an official honour.

decorative /'dekərətɪv/ ADJ Something that is **decorative** is intended to look attractive. *...decorative accessories, designed to give your kitchen that personal touch.*

decoy /'diːkɔɪ/ **decoys.** N-C A **decoy** is a person or object that you use to lead someone away from where they intended to go, especially so that you can catch them.

decrease, decreases, decreasing, decreased. [1] VERB /dɪ'kriːs/ When something **decreases**, or when you **decrease** it, it becomes less in quantity, size, or intensity. *Population growth is decreasing by 1.4% each year... Some groups have decreased their cigarette consumption. ...decreasing interest rates.* [2] N-C /'diːkriːs/ A **decrease** is a reduction in the quantity or size of something. *...a decrease in the number of young people out of work.*

decree /dɪ'kriː/ **decrees, decreeing, decreed.** [1] VERB If someone in authority **decrees** that something must happen, they order this officially. *The government decreed that all who wanted to live and work in Kenya must hold Kenyan passports.* [2] N-C A **decree** is an official order made by the ruler of a country. *...reform by presidential decree.*

dedicate /'dedɪkeɪt/ **dedicates, dedicating, dedicated.** [1] VERB If you say that someone **has dedicated** themselves to something, you approve of the fact that they have given a lot of time and effort to it because they think that it is important. *Bessie has dedicated her life to caring for others.* ◆**dedicated** ADJ *...a dedicated doctor.* ◆**dedication** N-U *...his obvious dedication to the job.* [2] VERB If you **dedicate** something such as a book or a piece of music **to** someone, you say that the work is written for them, as a sign of affection or respect. ◆**dedication, dedications** N-C *Normally such dedications are reserved for special concert guests.*

deduce /dɪ'djuːs, AM -'duːs/ **deduces, deducing, deduced.** VERB If you **deduce** that something is true, you reach that conclusion because of what you know to be true. *Galileo deduced that the planets were closer to Earth than* *the stars were... The date of the document can be deduced from references to the Civil War.*

deduct /dɪ'dʌkt/ **deducts, deducting, deducted.** VERB When you **deduct** an amount from a total, you subtract it from the total. *He could deduct the fees he paid to the accountant.*

deduction /dɪ'dʌkʃən/ **deductions.** [1] N-VAR A **deduction** is a conclusion that you reach because of what you know to be true. *...her own shrewd deductions about what was going on.* [2] N-VAR A **deduction** is an amount subtracted from a total. *...tax deductions.*

deed /diːd/ **deeds.** [1] N-C A **deed** is something that is done, especially something very good or very bad; LITERARY. *...the warm feeling one gets from doing a good deed.* [2] N-C A **deed** is a legal document containing the terms of an agreement, especially an agreement concerning the ownership of land or a building.

deem /diːm/ **deems, deeming, deemed.** VERB If something **is deemed** to have a quality or to do something, it is considered to have that quality or do that thing; FORMAL. *Many people have ideas that their society deems to be outrageous... She leads polls, but lacks the political machine deemed necessary to win.*

deep /diːp/ **deeper, deepest.** [1] ADJ & ADV If something is **deep**, it extends a long way down from the surface. *The water is very deep. ...the deep cut on his left hand... Gingerly, she put her hand in deeper.* [2] ADJ You use **deep** to talk or ask about how much something measures from the surface to the bottom, or from front to back. *I found myself in water only three feet deep.* [3] ADV **Deep** in an area means a long way inside it. *Oil and gas were trapped deep inside the earth when it was formed. ...invasion armies advancing deep into Europe.* [4] ADJ You use **deep** to emphasize the seriousness, strength, importance, or degree of something. *...his deep love of Israel.* ♦**deeply** ADV *Our conversations left me deeply depressed... She slept deeply but woke early.* [5] ADJ A **deep** breath uses the whole of your lungs. ♦**deeply** ADV *She sighed deeply.* [6] ADJ A **deep** colour is strong and fairly dark. [7] ADJ A **deep** sound is a low one. *His voice was deep and mellow.* [8] ADJ You can describe someone as **deep** when you think that they have qualities such as intelligence or determination. [9] PHRASE If you say that something **goes deep** or **runs deep**, you mean that it is very serious or strong and is hard to change. *His anger and anguish clearly went deep.*

deepen /'diːpən/ **deepens, deepening, deepened.** [1] VERB If a situation or emotion **deepens**, or if something **deepens** it, it becomes more intense. *As her feelings for Jay deepened, so did her desire for a permanent relationship.* [2] VERB When a sound **deepens** or **is deepened**, it becomes lower in tone. *Her voice has deepened and coarsened with the years.* [3] VERB To **deepen** something means to make it deeper. *The authority wants to widen and deepen the River Soar.* [4] VERB Where a river or a sea **deepens**, the water gets deeper.

deep-'seated. ADJ A **deep-seated** problem, feeling, or belief is difficult to change because its causes have been there for a long time. *...deep-seated economic problems.*

deer /dɪə/ **Deer** is both the singular and the plural form. N-C A **deer** is a large wild animal. Male deer usually have large, branching horns.

deface /dɪ'feɪs/ **defaces, defacing, defaced.** VERB If someone **defaces** something such as a wall, they spoil it by writing or drawing things on it.

default /dɪ'fɔːlt/ **defaults, defaulting, defaulted.** [1] VERB & N-U If someone **defaults** on something that they have legally agreed to do, or if they are in **default** on it, they fail to do it. *More borrowers are defaulting on loans.* [2] PHRASE If something happens **by default**, it happens only because something else has not happened.

defeat /dɪ'fiːt/ **defeats, defeating, defeated.** [1] VERB If you **defeat** someone, you win a victory over them in a battle or contest. *His forces were defeated by Syrian-Lebanese troops in October.* [2] VERB To **defeat** an action, plan, or proposal means to cause it to fail. *The socialist motion was defeated by 88 votes to 489.* [3] VERB If a task or a problem **defeats** you, it is so difficult that you cannot do it or solve it. *The structural challenges of constructing such a huge novel almost defeated her.* [4] N-VAR **Defeat** is the state of being beaten in a battle, game, or contest, or of failing to achieve what you wanted to. *The most important thing is not to admit defeat... The vote is seen as something of a defeat for the anti-abortion lobby.*

defect, defects, defecting, defected. [1] N-C /'diːfekt/ A **defect** is a fault or imperfection in a person or thing. *He was born with a hearing defect.* [2] VERB /dɪ'fekt/ If someone **defects**, they leave their own country, political party, or other group, and join an opposing one. *He tried to defect to the West last year.* ♦**defection, defections** N-VAR *There have been no reports yet of any defections from the elite Republican Guard.* ♦**defector, defectors** N-C *The government has attracted defectors from other parties.*

defective /dɪ'fektɪv/. ADJ If something is **defective**, there is something wrong with it. *...defective brakes.*

defence (AM **defense**) /dɪ'fens/ **defences.** [1] N-U **Defence** is action taken to protect someone or something from attack. *The land was flat, giving no scope for defence. ...chanting slogans in defence of Baltic freedom.* [2] N-U **Defence** is the organization of a country's armies and weapons to protect the country or its interests. *Twenty eight percent of the federal budget is spent on defense.* [3] N-PL The **defences** of a country or region are its armed forces and weapons. [4] N-C A **defence** is something that people or animals can use or do to protect themselves. *The immune system is our main defence against disease.* [5] N-C A **defence** is something that you say or write in support of ideas or actions that have been criticized. *Chomsky's defence of his approach goes further.* [6] N-C In a court of law, an accused person's **defence** is the process of presenting evidence in their favour. *He has insisted on conducting his own defence.* [7] N-SING The **defence** is the case presented by a lawyer in a trial for the person who has been accused of a crime. *You* can also refer the lawyers for this person as the **defence**. [8] N-C In a sports team, the **defence** is the group of players who try to stop the opposing team scoring. For this meaning, **defence** can take the singular or plural form of the verb.

defenceless (AM **defenseless**) /dɪˈfensləs/. ADJ If someone is **defenceless**, they are weak and cannot defend themselves. *...a savage attack on a defenceless young girl.*

defend /dɪˈfend/ **defends, defending, defended.** [1] VERB If you **defend** someone or something, you take action to protect them. *In 1991 he and his friends defended themselves against some racist thugs.* [2] VERB If you **defend** someone or something when they have been criticized, you argue in support of them. *Clarence's move was unpopular, but Matt had to defend it... He is defending himself against a charge of sexual harassment.* [3] VERB When a lawyer **defends** a person who has been accused of something, the lawyer argues on their behalf in a court of law that the charges are not true. [4] VERB If a sports champion **defends** his or her title, he or she is in a contest against someone who will become the new champion if they win.

defendant /dɪˈfendənt/ **defendants.** N-C The **defendant** in a trial is the person accused of a crime.

defender /dɪˈfendə/ **defenders.** [1] ADJ If you are a **defender** of a particular thing or person that has been criticized or attacked, you support that thing or person in public. *...a strong defender of human rights or religious freedom.* [2] N-C A **defender** in a game such as football is a player whose main task is to try and stop the other side scoring.

defense /dɪˈfens/. See **defence**.

defensive /dɪˈfensɪv/. [1] ADJ You use **defensive** to describe things that are intended to protect someone or something. *The union leaders were pushed into a more defensive position.* [2] ADJ & PHRASE If someone is **defensive**, or if they are **on the defensive**, they are behaving in a way that shows that they feel unsure or threatened. *She heard the blustering, defensive note in his voice.* ♦**defensively** *'It's nothing to be ashamed of', she replied somewhat defensively.*

defer /dɪˈfɜː/ **defers, deferring, deferred.** [1] VERB If you **defer** an event or action, you arrange that it will take place at a later date than was planned. *Customers often defer payment for as long as possible.* [2] VERB If you **defer to** someone, you accept their opinion or do what they want because you respect them. *She defers to her husband on everything.*

deference /ˈdefrəns/. N-U **Deference** is polite and respectful behaviour to someone in a superior social position.

defiance /dɪˈfaɪəns/. N-U **Defiance** is behaviour or an attitude which shows that you are not willing to obey someone. *...his courageous defiance of the government... People have taken to the streets in defiance of the curfew.*

defiant /dɪˈfaɪənt/. ADJ If you are **defiant**, you refuse to obey someone or you ignore their disapproval of you. *The newspaper remained defiant over its latest confrontation with the*

royals. ♦**defiantly** ADV *They defiantly rejected any talk of a compromise.*

deficiency /dɪˈfɪʃənsi/ **deficiencies.** [1] N-VAR **Deficiency** in something, especially something that your body needs, is a lack of it; FORMAL. *...iron deficiency.* [2] N-VAR A **deficiency** is a weakness or imperfection in someone or something; FORMAL. *...the deficiencies of the British transport system.*

deficient /dɪˈfɪʃənt/. [1] ADJ If someone or something is **deficient** in a particular thing, they do not have as much of it as they need; FORMAL. *...a diet deficient in vitamin B.* [2] ADJ Something that is **deficient** is not good enough; FORMAL. *...deficient landing systems.*

deficit /ˈdefəsɪt/ **deficits.** N-C A **deficit** is the amount by which the money received by a country or organization is less than the money it has spent. *...Britain's trade deficit.*

define /dɪˈfaɪn/ **defines, defining, defined.** VERB If you **define** something, you say exactly what it is or exactly what it means. *...a speech defining America's role in modern Europe... My dictionary defines morning as 'the first part of the day, ending at or about noon'.*

definite /ˈdefɪnɪt/. [1] ADJ If something is **definite**, it is firm and clear, and unlikely to be changed. *It's too soon to give a definite answer.* [2] ADJ **Definite** means true rather than being someone's opinion or guess. *The police had nothing definite against her.*

definite 'article, definite articles. N-C In grammar, the word 'the' is sometimes called the **definite article**.

definitely /ˈdefɪnɪtli/. ADV You use **definitely** to emphasize that something is the case and will not change. *I definitely agree with you... They've definitely decided on the name Fiona.*

definition /ˌdefɪˈnɪʃən/ **definitions.** [1] N-C A **definition** of a word or term is a statement giving its meaning, especially in a dictionary. [2] PHRASE If you say that something has a particular quality **by definition**, you mean that it has this quality simply because of what it is. *Fashion is by definition fickle.* [3] N-U **Definition** is the quality of being clear and distinct. *Their foreign policy lacks definition.*

definitive /dɪˈfɪnɪtɪv/. [1] ADJ Something that is **definitive** provides a firm, unquestionable conclusion. *No one has come up with a definitive answer as to why this should be so.* ♦**definitively** ADV *The Constitution did not definitively rule out divorce.* [2] ADJ A **definitive** book or performance is thought to be the best of its kind ever.

deflate /dɪˈfleɪt/ **deflates, deflating, deflated.** [1] VERB If you **deflate** a person, you cause them to lose confidence. ♦**deflated** ADJ *When she refused I felt deflated.* [2] VERB When a tyre or balloon **deflates**, all the air comes out of it.

deflect /dɪˈflekt/ **deflects, deflecting, deflected.** [1] VERB If you **deflect** something such as someone's attention, you cause them to turn their attention to something else or to do something different. *We won't let it deflect us from what we are doing.* [2] VERB If you **deflect** something that is moving, you make it go in a slightly different direction, for example by hitting it or pushing it. *He stuck out his boot and* *deflected the shot over the bar.* ♦**deflection, deflections.** N-VAR *...the gravitational deflection of light-rays by the Sun.*

deforestation /ˌdiːˈfɒrɪsˈteɪʃən, AM -ˈfɔːr-/. N-U **Deforestation** is the cutting down of trees over a large area. *...the deforestation of the Amazon.*

deform /dɪˈfɔːm/ **deforms, deforming, deformed.** VERB If something **deforms** something such as a person's body, it causes it to have an unnatural shape. *...people hideously deformed by acne.* ♦**deformed** ADJ *He was born with a deformed right leg.*

deformity /dɪˈfɔːmɪti/ **deformities.** [1] N-C A **deformity** is a part of someone's body which is not the normal shape because of injury or illness, or because they were born like this way. [2] N-U **Deformity** is the condition of having a deformity. *The bones begin to grind against each other, leading to pain and deformity.*

defraud /dɪˈfrɔːd/ **defrauds, defrauding, defrauded.** VERB If someone **defrauds** you, they use tricks or lies to take something away from you or stop you from getting something that belongs to you. *He was convicted of defrauding investors out of millions of dollars.*

deft /deft/. ADJ A **deft** action is skilful and often quick; WRITTEN. ♦**deftly** ADV *One of the waiting servants deftly caught him as he fell.*

defunct /dɪˈfʌŋkt/. ADJ If something is **defunct**, it no longer exists or it is no longer functioning. *...the now defunct Social Democratic Party.*

defuse /ˌdiːˈfjuːz/ **defuses, defusing, defused.** [1] VERB If you **defuse** a dangerous or tense situation, you calm it. *...a series of measures to try to defuse the crisis in Yugoslavia.* [2] VERB If someone **defuses** a bomb, they remove the fuse from it so that it cannot explode.

defy /dɪˈfaɪ/ **defies, defying, defied.** [1] VERB If you **defy** people or laws, you refuse to obey them. *Nearly eleven-thousand people have been arrested for defying the ban on street trading.* [2] VERB If you **defy** someone to do something which you think is impossible, you challenge them to do it. *I defy you not to want to know what happens next.* [3] VERB If something **defies** description or understanding, it is so strange or surprising that it is almost impossible to describe it or understand it. *...a devastating and barbaric act that defies all comprehension.*

degenerate, degenerates, degenerating, degenerated. [1] VERB /dɪˈdʒenəreɪt/ To **degenerate** means to become worse. *...fear that the present unrest could degenerate into violence.* ♦**degeneration** N-U *...the degeneration of our political system.* [2] ADJ & N-C /dɪˈdʒenərət/ If you say that someone is **degenerate**, or if you say they are a **degenerate**, you think they show very low standards of morality.

degrade /dɪˈgreɪd/ **degrades, degrading, degraded.** [1] VERB Something that **degrades** someone humiliates them and makes them feel they are not respected. *...the notion that pornography degrades women.* ♦**degrading** ADJ *...degrading treatment.* ♦**degradation** /ˌdegrəˈdeɪʃən/ **degradations.** N-VAR *She described the degradations she had been forced to suffer.* [2] VERB To **degrade** something means to

damage it so that it becomes worse or weaker; FORMAL. *The very success of tourism has degraded the natural environment.* ♦**degradation** N-U *...the degradation of democracy.*

degree /dɪˈgriː/ **degrees.** [1] N-C You use **degree** to indicate the extent to which something happens or is the case. *These barriers will ensure a very high degree of protection.* [2] N-C A **degree** is a unit of measurement for temperatures, angles, and longitude and latitude; often written as '°', for example 23°. [3] N-C A **degree** is a university qualification gained after completing a course of study there. *She has a degree in English.*

dehydrate /ˌdiːhaɪˈdreɪt, -ˈhaɪdreɪt/ **dehydrates, dehydrating, dehydrated.** [1] VERB When food is **dehydrated**, all the water is removed from it. *...dehydrated soup.* [2] VERB If you **are dehydrated**, you feel ill because you have lost too much water from your body. ♦**dehydration** N-U *I needed to drink three litres a day to prevent dehydration.*

deity /ˈdeɪti, AM ˈdiː-/ **deities.** N-C A **deity** is a god or goddess; FORMAL.

delay /dɪˈleɪ/ **delays, delaying, delayed.** [1] VERB If you **delay** doing something, you do not do it until a later time. *This morning's decision to delay the launch seems like unfavorable weather conditions.* [2] VERB To **delay** someone or something means to make them late or slow them down. *Various set-backs and problems delayed production.* [3] N-VAR If there is a **delay**, something does not happen until later than planned or expected. *...a seven-hour stoppage that caused delays on most flights.*

delegate, delegates, delegating, delegated. [1] N-C /ˈdelɪgət/ A **delegate** is a person chosen to vote or make decisions on behalf of a group of people, especially at a conference or meeting. [2] VERB /ˈdelɪgeɪt/ If you **delegate** duties, responsibilities, or power to someone, you give them those duties or responsibilities or that power, so that they can act on your behalf.

delegation /ˌdelɪˈgeɪʃən/ **delegations.** N-C A **delegation** is a group of people chosen to represent a larger group of people.

delete /dɪˈliːt/ **deletes, deleting, deleted.** VERB If you **delete** something that has been written down or stored in a computer, you cross it out or remove it.

deliberate, deliberates, deliberating, deliberated. [1] ADJ /dɪˈlɪbərət/ If something that you do is **deliberate**, you intended to do it. *...a deliberate act of sabotage.* ♦**deliberately** ADV *It looks as if the blaze was started deliberately.* [2] ADJ A **deliberate** action or movement is slow and careful. ♦**deliberately** ADV *He spoke slowly and deliberately.* [3] VERB /dɪˈlɪbəreɪt/ If you **deliberate**, you think about something carefully before making a decision. *The jury deliberated for five days before reaching a verdict.*

deliberation /dɪˌlɪbəˈreɪʃən/ **deliberations.** [1] N-U **Deliberation** is careful consideration of a subject. *After much deliberation, the winners have been chosen.* [2] N-PL **Deliberations** are formal discussions.

delicacy /'delɪkəsi/ **delicacies.** N-C A **delicacy** is a rare or expensive food that is considered especially nice to eat. ...delicacies such as sturgeon.

delicate /'delɪkət/. **1** ADJ Something that is **delicate** is narrow and graceful or attractive. ...her long, delicate nose. ♦**delicately** ADV ...a small and delicately formed chin. ♦**delicacy** N-U ...the sculpted, nearly Asiatic delicacy of his face. **2** ADJ A **delicate** colour, taste, or smell is pleasant and not intense. Smoked trout has a delicate flavour. ♦**delicately** ADV ...a soup delicately flavoured with nutmeg. **3** ADJ A **delicate** object is fragile and needs to be handled carefully. **4** ADJ Someone who is **delicate** is not healthy and strong, and becomes ill easily. He was a delicate child. **5** ADJ A **delicate** situation or problem needs very careful and tactful treatment. ...the delicate issue of adoption. ♦**delicately** ADV ...his delicately worded assessment of the course. ♦**delicacy** N-U ...a matter of some delicacy.

delicatessen /ˌdelɪkə'tesən/ **delicatessens.** N-C A **delicatessen** is a shop that sells unusual or foreign foods.

delicious /dɪ'lɪʃəs/. ADJ **Delicious** food or drink has an extremely pleasant taste. ♦**deliciously** ADV This new yoghurt has a deliciously creamy flavour.

delight /dɪ'laɪt/ **delights, delighting, delighted.** **1** N-U **Delight** is a feeling of very great pleasure. Andrew roared with delight... To my great delight, it worked. **2** N-C You can refer to someone or something that gives you great pleasure as a **delight**. The aircraft was a delight to fly. **3** VERB If something **delights** you, it gives you a lot of pleasure. ...a style of music that has delighted audiences all over the world. **4** VERB & PHRASE If you **delight in** something, especially doing something, or if you **take delight in** it, you get a lot of pleasure from it. Ford delighted in showing visitors around... Haig took obvious delight in proving his critics wrong.

delighted /dɪ'laɪtɪd/. ADJ If you are **delighted**, you are extremely pleased and excited about something. He said that he was delighted with the public response. ♦**delightedly** ADV She smiled delightedly up at him.

delightful /dɪ'laɪtful/. ADJ Someone or something that is **delightful** is very pleasant. ...a most delightful woman. ♦**delightfully** ADV ...a delightfully mellow flavour.

delinquent /dɪ'lɪŋkwənt/ **delinquents.** N-C & ADJ A **delinquent** is a young person who repeatedly commits minor crimes. You can also describe their behaviour as **delinquent**. ♦**delinquency** N-U He had no history of delinquency.

delirious /dɪ'lɪəriəs/. **1** ADJ Someone who is **delirious** is unable to think or speak in a rational way, usually because they have a fever. **2** ADJ Someone who is **delirious** is extremely excited and happy. I was delirious with joy. ♦**deliriously** ADV Chelsea fans went home deliriously happy.

deliver /dɪ'lɪvə/ **delivers, delivering, delivered.** **1** VERB If you **deliver** something somewhere, you take it there. The Canadians plan

to deliver more food to southern Somalia... We were told the pizza would be delivered in 20 minutes. **2** VERB If you **deliver** a lecture or speech, you give it. **3** VERB When someone **delivers** a baby, they help the woman who is giving birth. **4** VERB If someone **delivers** a blow to someone else, they hit them. Those blows to the head could have been delivered by a woman.

delivery /dɪ'lɪvəri/ **deliveries.** **1** N-U **Delivery** is the act of bringing letters, parcels, or goods to someone's house or office. Please allow 28 days for delivery. **2** N-C A **delivery** of letters or goods is an occasion when they are delivered. I got a delivery of fresh eggs this morning. **3** N-U Someone's **delivery** of a speech is the way in which they give it. His speeches were magnificently written but his delivery was hopeless. **4** N-VAR **Delivery** is the process of giving birth to a baby. In the end, it was an easy delivery: a fine baby boy.

delta /'deltə/ **deltas.** N-C A **delta** is a triangle shaped area of flat land, where a river spreads out into several smaller rivers before entering the sea.

delude /dɪ'luːd/ **deludes, deluding, deluded.** VERB If you **delude** someone, you make them believe something that is not true. We delude ourselves that we are in control.

deluge /'deljuːdʒ/ **deluges, deluging, deluged.** **1** VERB & N-C If you **are deluged** with things, or if you receive a **deluge** of things, a very large number of them arrive or happen at the same time. Papen's office was deluged with complaints... A deluge of manuscripts began to arrive in the post. **2** N-C & VERB A **deluge** is a sudden heavy fall of rain. You can say that rain **deluges** a place when it falls very heavily there.

delusion /dɪ'luːʒən/ **delusions.** N-VAR A **delusion** is a false belief. I was under the delusion that he intended to marry me.

deluxe or **de luxe** /dɪ'lʌks/. ADJ BEFORE N **Deluxe** goods or services are better and more expensive than ordinary ones. ...a five-star deluxe hotel.

delve /delv/ **delves, delving, delved.** **1** VERB If you **delve** into a subject, you try to discover more about it. Jenny delved into her mother's past. **2** VERB If you **delve** inside something such as a bag, you search inside it. She delved into her rucksack and pulled out a folder.

demand /dɪ'mɑːnd, -'mænd/ **demands, demanding, demanded.** **1** VERB & N-C If you **demand** something, or if you make a **demand** for something, you ask for it forcefully. The Labour Party has demanded an explanation from the government... They demanded that a police officer arrest the pair... They consistently rejected the demand to remove US troops. **2** PHRASE If something is available **on demand**, you can have it whenever you ask for it. **3** VERB If one thing **demands** another, the first needs the second in order to happen or be dealt with successfully. The task of rebuilding would demand much patience. **4** N-U & PHRASE If there is **demand** for something, a lot of people want it. You can also say that something or someone is **in demand**. Demand for coal is down... He was much in demand as a lecturer. **5** N-C You talk about the **demands** of something or someone, or their **demands** on you when you mean the things they require or want from you, which will take a lot of effort on your part. ...*the demands and challenges of a new job*... *I had no right to make demands on his time.*

demanding /dɪˈmɑːndɪŋ, -ˈmænd-/. [1] ADJ A **demanding** job requires a lot of time, energy, or attention. [2] ADJ Someone who is **demanding** always wants something and is not easily satisfied. ...*a very demanding child.*

demean /dɪˈmiːn/ **demeans, demeaning, demeaned.** VERB To **demean** someone or something means to make people have less respect for them. *Pornography demeans women.* ♦**demeaning** ADJ *Addressing women as 'girls' is demeaning.*

demeanour (AM **demeanor**) /dɪˈmiːnə/. N-U Your **demeanour** is the way you behave, which gives people an impression of your character and feelings; FORMAL. ...*a cheerful demeanour.*

demented /dɪˈmentɪd/. [1] ADJ Someone who is **demented** is mentally ill. [2] ADJ If you describe someone as **demented**, you think that their actions are strange, foolish, or uncontrolled.

dementia /dɪˈmenʃə/ **dementias.** N-VAR **Dementia** is a disease of the brain which leads to a progressive loss of intellectual power and memory; TECHNICAL. ...*senile dementia.*

demilitarize (BR also **demilitarise**) /ˌdiːˈmɪlɪtəraɪz/ **demilitarizes, demilitarizing, demilitarized.** VERB To **demilitarize** an area means to remove all military forces from it.

demise /dɪˈmaɪz/. N-SING The **demise** of something or someone is their end or death; FORMAL. ...*the demise of communism in Eastern Europe.*

demo /ˈdemoʊ/ **demos.** N-C A **demo** is a demonstration by a group of people to show their opposition to something or their support for something; BRITISH. ...*an anti-racist demo.*

demobilize (BR also **demobilise**) /ˌdiːˈmoʊbɪlaɪz/ **demobilizes, demobilizing, demobilized.** VERB If a country **demobilizes** its troops, or if its troops **demobilize**, they are released from service and go home. ♦**demobilization** N-U ...*the demobilisation of its 100,000 strong army.*

democracy /dɪˈmɒkrəsi/ **democracies.** [1] N-U **Democracy** is a political system in which people choose their government by voting for them in elections. [2] N-C A **democracy** is a country in which the people choose their government by voting for it.

democrat /ˈdeməkræt/ **democrats.** N-C A **democrat** is a person who believes in the ideals of democracy, personal freedom, and equality.

democratic /ˌdeməˈkrætɪk/. [1] ADJ A **democratic** country, organization, or system is governed by representatives who are elected by the people. ♦**democratically** ADV ...*Russia's first democratically elected President.* [2] ADJ Something that is **democratic** is based on the idea that everyone should have equal rights and should be involved in making important decisions. *We work in a very democratic way.* ♦**democratically** ADV *This committee will enable decisions to be made democratically.*

demolish /dɪˈmɒlɪʃ/ **demolishes, demolishing, demolished.** [1] VERB When a building **is demolished**, it is knocked down, often because it is old or dangerous. *A storm moved directly over the island, demolishing buildings.* ♦**demolition** /ˌdeməˈlɪʃən/ **demolitions** N-VAR *The project required the total demolition of the old bridge.* [2] VERB If you **demolish** someone's idea, argument, or belief, you prove that it is completely wrong.

demon /ˈdiːmən/ **demons.** N-C A **demon** is an evil spirit. ♦**demonic** /dɪˈmɒnɪk/ ADJ ...*a form of demonic possession.*

demonstrate /ˈdemənstreɪt/ **demonstrates, demonstrating, demonstrated.** [1] VERB To **demonstrate** a fact or theory means to make it clear to people. *Women's groups said the case demonstrated the law's bias against women... They are anxious to demonstrate to the voters that they have practical policies.* ♦**demonstration, demonstrations** N-C *We want a demonstration of commitment.* [2] VERB If you **demonstrate** a skill, quality, or feeling, you show that you have it. *He demonstrated his courage in the Korean war.* [3] VERB If you **demonstrate** something to someone, you show them how to do it or how it works. *The BBC has just successfully demonstrated a new digital radio transmission system.* ♦**demonstration** N-C ...*a cookery demonstration.* [4] VERB When people **demonstrate**, they take part in a march or a meeting to show that they oppose or support something. *In Rostock, more than 10,000 people demonstrated against racism yesterday.* ♦**demonstration** N-C *Riot police used tear gas and truncheons this afternoon to break up a demonstration.* ♦**demonstrator, demonstrators** N-C ...*a crowd of demonstrators.*

demoralize (BR also **demoralise**) /dɪˈmɒrəlaɪz, AM -ˈmɔːr-/ **demoralizes, demoralizing, demoralized.** VERB If something **demoralizes** you, it makes you lose confidence and feel depressed. ♦**demoralized** ADJ ...*a demoralized police force.* ♦**demoralizing** ADJ *It can be very demoralizing to struggle with a painting which offers little possibility of success.* ♦**demoralization** N-U ...*the lingering demoralization that followed defeat.*

demote /dɪˈmoʊt/ **demotes, demoting, demoted.** VERB If someone in authority **demotes** you, they lower your rank, often as a punishment. ♦**demotion, demotions** N-VAR *He faces demotion or even the sack.*

den /den/ **dens.** [1] N-C A **den** is the home of certain types of wild animals such as foxes. [2] N-C A **den** is a secret place where people meet, usually for a dishonest purpose. ...*illegal drinking dens.*

denial /dɪˈnaɪəl/ **denials.** [1] N-VAR A **denial** of something such as an accusation is a statement that it is not true, does not exist, or did not happen. ...*denial of the Russian Mafia's existence.* [2] N-U If there is **denial** of something to someone, they are not allowed to have it. ...*the denial of visas to international relief workers.*

denigrate /ˈdenɪgreɪt/ **denigrates, denigrating, denigrated.** VERB If you **denigrate** someone or something, you criticize or insult them,

denim 158

damaging their reputation; FORMAL. *...an article denigrated Aboriginal ceremonies.* ◆**denigration** N-U *...men's denigration of women.*

denim /'denɪm/. N-U **Denim** is a thick cotton cloth used to make clothes.

denomination /dɪ,nɒmɪ'neɪʃən/ **denominations.** [1] N-C A **denomination** is a religious group which has slightly different beliefs from other groups within the same faith. [2] N-C The **denomination** of a banknote or coin is its official value. *...a pile of bank notes, mostly in small denominations.*

denote /dɪ'nəʊt/ **denotes, denoting, denoted.** VERB If one thing **denotes** another, it is a sign or indication of it; FORMAL. *Red eyes denote strain and fatigue.*

denounce /dɪ'naʊns/ **denounces, denouncing, denounced.** VERB If you **denounce** someone or something, you criticize them severely and publicly. *Some 25,000 demonstrators denounced him as a traitor.* ● See also **denunciation**

dense /dens/ **denser, densest.** [1] ADJ Something that is **dense** contains a lot of things or people in relation to its size. *...a dense forest.* ◆**densely** ADV *...a densely populated island.* [2] ADJ **Dense** fog or smoke is thick and difficult to see through.

density /'densɪti/ **densities.** [1] N-VAR The **density** of something is the extent to which it fills a place. *...the law which restricts the density of housing.* [2] N-VAR The **density** of a substance or object is the relation of its mass or weight to its volume.

dent /dent/ **dents, denting, dented.** [1] VERB If something **dents** your ideas or your pride, it makes you believe that you or your ideas are not as good as you thought. [2] VERB & N-C If you **dent** something, you damage it by hitting or pressing it, causing a hollow dip to form in it. The hollow is called a **dent**. *There was a dent in the bonnet.*

dental /'dentəl/. ADJ BEFORE N **Dental** is used to describe things relating to teeth. *...free dental treatment.*

dentist /'dentɪst/ **dentists.** N-C A **dentist** is a person qualified to treat people's teeth.

dentures /'dentʃəz/; the form **denture** is used as a modifier. N-PL **Dentures** are artificial teeth.

denunciation /dɪ,nʌnsɪ'eɪʃən/ **denunciations.** N-VAR A **denunciation** of someone or something is a severe public criticism of them.

deny /dɪ'naɪ/ **denies, denying, denied.** [1] VERB If you **deny** something, you say that it is not true. *She denied both accusations... They all denied ever having seen her.* [2] VERB If you **deny** someone something, you do not let them have it. *His ex-partner denies him access to his children.*

deodorant /di'əʊdərənt/ **deodorants.** N-VAR **Deodorant** is a substance that you put on your body to reduce or hide the smell of perspiration.

depart /dɪ'pɑːt/ **departs, departing, departed.** VERB To **depart** from a place means to leave it and start a journey to another place;

FORMAL. *Our tour departs from Heathrow Airport.*

department /dɪ'pɑːtmənt/ **departments.** N-C A **department** is one of the sections of a large shop or organization such as a university. *...Bloomingdale's cosmetics department. ...the geography department of Moscow University.* ◆**departmental** /,diːpɑːt'mentəl/ ADJ BEFORE N *...a bigger departmental budget.*

de'partment store, department stores. N-C A **department store** is a large shop which sells many different kinds of goods.

departure /dɪ'pɑːtʃə/ **departures.** [1] N-VAR **Departure** is the act of leaving a place or a job. *...the President's departure for Helsinki. ...his departure from the post of Prime Minister.* [2] N-C If an action is a **departure** from what was planned or what is usually done, it is different from it. *That decision is a major departure from previous American policy.*

depend /dɪ'pend/ **depends, depending, depended.** [1] VERB If you say that one thing **depends** on another, you mean that the first thing will be affected or decided by the second. *The cooking time needed depends on the size of the potato.* [2] VERB & PHRASE You use **depends** in expressions such as **it depends** or **depending on** to indicate that you cannot give a clear answer to a question because other factors will affect the answer. *'But how long can you stay in the house?'—'I don't know. It depends.'* [3] VERB If you **depend** on someone or something, you need them in order to be able to survive. *Their survival depends on him.* [4] VERB If you can **depend** on someone or something, you know that they will help you or support you when you need them. *You can depend on me.*

dependable /dɪ'pendəbəl/. ADJ If someone or something is **dependable**, you know that they will always do what you need or expect them to do. *...a faithful and dependable companion.*

dependant (or **dependent**) /dɪ'pendənt/ **dependants.** N-C Your **dependants** are the people who you support financially, such as your children. *...a single man with no dependants.*

dependent /dɪ'pendənt/. ADJ AFTER LINK-V To be **dependent** on someone or something means to need them in order to succeed or be able to survive. *Britain became increasingly dependent upon American technology.* ◆**dependence** N-U *...the effects of alcoholism and drug dependence.* ◆**dependency** N-U *Ukraine is handicapped by its near-total dependency on Russian oil.*

depict /dɪ'pɪkt/ **depicts, depicting, depicted.** VERB To **depict** someone or something means to represent them in drawing, painting, or writing. *...pictures depicting Nelson's most famous battles.* ◆**depiction, depictions** N-VAR *...their depiction in the book as thieves.*

deplete /dɪ'pliːt/ **depletes, depleting, depleted.** VERB To **deplete** a stock or amount of something means to reduce it, usually to a very low level. *...substances that deplete the ozone layer.* ◆**depleted** ADJ *...Robert E. Lee's worn and depleted army.* ◆**depletion** N-U *...the depletion of underground water supplies.*

deplorable /dɪˈplɔːrəbəl/. ADJ If you say that something is **deplorable**, you mean that it is extremely bad or unpleasant; FORMAL. ...*deplorable working and living conditions.*

deplore /dɪˈplɔː/ **deplores, deploring, deplored.** VERB If you **deplore** something, you think it is very wrong or immoral; FORMAL. *He deplores violence.*

deploy /dɪˈplɔɪ/ **deploys, deploying, deployed.** VERB To **deploy** troops or resources means to organize or position them so that they are ready to be used. ♦**deployment** N-U ...*the deployment of extra forces in the gulf.*

deport /dɪˈpɔːt/ **deports, deporting, deported.** VERB If a government **deports** someone, it sends them out of the country. *More than 240 England football fans are being deported from Italy.* ♦**deportation, deportations** N-VAR ...*migrants facing deportation.*

depose /dɪˈpəʊz/ **deposes, deposing, deposed.** VERB If a ruler or political leader **is deposed**, they are forced to give up their position. ♦**deposition** /ˌdepəˈzɪʃən/ N-U ...*the deposition of the king.*

deposit /dɪˈpɒzɪt/ **deposits, depositing, deposited.** [1] N-C A **deposit** is a sum of money given as part payment for something, or as security when you rent something. *A £50 deposit is required when ordering.* ...*the equivalent of a month's rent as a deposit.* [2] VERB & N-C If you **deposit** a sum of money into your bank account, or if you put a **deposit** in your account, you pay a sum of money into a bank account or other savings account. *The customer has to deposit a minimum of £100 monthly.* [3] N-C & VERB A **deposit** is an amount of a substance that has been left somewhere as a result of a chemical or geological process. You say the substance has been **deposited** there. ...*underground deposits of gold and diamonds.*

depot /ˈdepəʊ, AM ˈdiː-/ **depots.** [1] N-C A **depot** is a place where large amounts of raw materials, equipment, or other supplies are kept. ...*a government arms depot.* [2] N-C A **depot** is a large building or yard where buses or railway engines are kept when they are not being used. [3] N-C A **depot** is a bus station or a railway station.

depreciate /dɪˈpriːʃieɪt/ **depreciates, depreciating, depreciated.** VERB If something such as currency **depreciates**, or if something **depreciates**, it loses some of its original value. *The pound depreciated by a quarter.* ♦**depreciation, depreciations** N-VAR ...*machinery depreciation and wages.*

depress /dɪˈpres/ **depresses, depressing, depressed.** [1] VERB If someone or something **depresses** you, they make you feel sad and disappointed. *The state of the country depresses me.* [2] VERB If something **depresses** prices, wages, or figures, it causes them to become less. *The stronger U.S. dollar depressed sales.*

depressed /dɪˈprest/. [1] ADJ If you are **depressed**, you are sad and feel you cannot enjoy anything, because your situation is difficult and unpleasant. *He seemed somewhat depressed.* [2] ADJ A **depressed** place or industry does not have enough business or employ-

ment to be prosperous. *The construction industry is no longer as depressed as it was.*

depressing /dɪˈpresɪŋ/. ADJ Something that is **depressing** makes you feel sad and disappointed. *The hospital was a very depressing place to be.* ♦**depressingly** ADV *It all sounded depressingly familiar.*

depression /dɪˈpreʃən/ **depressions.** [1] N-VAR **Depression** is a mental state in which someone feels unhappy and has no energy or enthusiasm. ...*suffering from depression... I slid into a depression.* [2] N-C A **depression** is a time when there is very little economic activity, which results in a lot of unemployment and poverty. [3] N-C A **depression** in a surface is an area which is lower than the parts surrounding it.

deprive /dɪˈpraɪv/ **deprives, depriving, deprived.** VERB If you **deprive** someone of something that they want or need, you take it away from them or prevent them from having it. *She was deprived of her passport.* ♦**deprived** ADJ ...*a deprived inner city area.* ♦**deprivation** /ˌdeprɪˈveɪʃən/ **deprivations** N-VAR *Crime flourishes in conditions of deprivation.*

dept. Dept is a written abbreviation for 'department'.

depth /depθ/ **depths.** [1] N-VAR The **depth** of something such as a hole is the distance between its top and bottom surfaces. *The water was some 12 to 18 inches in depth.* [2] N-VAR The **depth** of a solid structure is the distance between its front surface and its back. [3] N-U If an emotion is very strongly felt, you can talk about its **depth**. *I am well aware of the depth of feeling that exists in Londonderry.* [4] N-PL **The depths of** an area are the parts of it which are very remote. ...*somewhere in the depths of the pine forest.* [5] N-PL The **depths** of something difficult or unpleasant are the middle and most severe or intense part of it. ...*the depths of a recession.* ...*the depths of winter... I was in the depths of despair.* [6] PHRASE If you deal with a subject **in depth**, you consider all the aspects of it thoroughly. ...*an in-depth investigation.* [7] PHRASE If you say that someone is **out of** their **depth**, you mean that they are in a situation that is much too difficult for them to be able to cope with it.

deputy /ˈdepjʊti/ **deputies.** N-C A **deputy** is the second most important person in an organization or department. Someone's deputy often acts on their behalf when they are absent. ...*the academy's deputy director.*

derail /ˌdiːˈreɪl/ **derails, derailing, derailed.** [1] VERB If someone or something **derails** a plan or a series of negotiations, they prevent it from continuing as planned. ...*people trying to derail peace talks.* [2] VERB If a train **is derailed**, or if it **derails**, it comes off the track on which it is running. ♦**derailment** /ˌdiːˈreɪlmənt/ **derailments** N-VAR *Rail services have been suspended because of a derailment.*

deranged /dɪˈreɪndʒd/. ADJ Someone who is **deranged** behaves in a wild or strange way, often as a result of mental illness. *A deranged man shot and killed 14 people.*

derelict /ˈderɪlɪkt/. ADJ A **derelict** place is empty and in a bad condition because it has not been used or lived in for a long time. ...*a derelict warehouse.*

deride /dɪˈraɪd/ **derides, deriding, derided.**
VERB If you **deride** someone or something, you say that they are stupid or have no value; FORMAL. *Other countries are derided for selling arms to the enemy.* ♦**derision** /dɪˈrɪʒən/ N-U *He was greeted with shouts of derision.*

derivative /dɪˈrɪvətɪv/ **derivatives.** [1] N-C A **derivative** is something which has been developed or obtained from something else. ...*a poppy-seed derivative similar to heroin.* [2] ADJ If you say that something is **derivative**, you are criticizing it because it is not new or original but has been developed from something else. ...*their dull, derivative debut album.*

derive /dɪˈraɪv/ **derives, deriving, derived.** [1] VERB If you **derive** something such as pleasure or benefit **from** someone or something, you get it from them. ...*one of those happy people who derive pleasure from helping others.* [2] VERB If something **derives** or **is derived from** something, it comes from that thing. *The name Anastasia is derived from a Greek word meaning 'of the resurrection'.*

descend /dɪˈsend/ **descends, descending, descended.** [1] VERB If you **descend**, or if you **descend** something, you move downwards; FORMAL. ...*as we descend to the cellar.* [2] VERB If a mood **descends** somewhere, it starts to affect the people there. *An uneasy calm descended on the area.* [3] VERB If people **descend** on a place, a lot of them arrive there suddenly. *Reporters from around the globe are descending upon the peaceful villages.* [4] VERB If you say that someone **descends** to something which you consider unacceptable or unworthy of them, you are expressing your disapproval of the fact that they do it. *We're never going to descend to such methods.*

descendant /dɪˈsendənt/ **descendants.** N-C Someone's **descendants** are the people in later generations who are related to them.

descended /dɪˈsendɪd/ ADJ AFTER LINK-V A person who is **descended from** someone who lived a long time ago is directly related to them. *She was descended from some Scottish Lord.*

descent /dɪˈsent/ **descents.** [1] N-VAR A **descent** is a movement from a higher to a lower level. *The airliner began its descent towards the airfield.* [2] N-C A **descent** is a surface that slopes downwards, for example the side of a steep hill. [3] N-U You use **descent** to talk about a person's family background, for example their nationality or social status. *All the contributors were of African descent.*

describe /dɪˈskraɪb/ **describes, describing, described.** [1] VERB If you **describe** someone or something, you say what they are like. *We asked her to describe what kind of things she did in her spare time. ...a poem by Carver which describes their life together.* [2] VERB If you **describe** someone or something **as** a particular thing, you say that they are like that thing. *They described themselves as liberals.*

When you use **describe** with an indirect object, you must put **to** in front of the in-

direct object. *He later described to me what he had found... Could you describe the man to the police?* You do not say, for example, 'He described me what he had found'.

description /dɪˈskrɪpʃən/ **descriptions.** [1] N-VAR A **description** of someone or something is an account which explains what they are or what they look like. *Police have issued a description of the man.* [2] N-SING If something is **of** a particular **description** is belongs to the general class of items that are mentioned. *Events of this description occurred daily.*

descriptive /dɪˈskrɪptɪv/ ADJ **Descriptive** language indicates what something is like. *The poem is very descriptive.*

desecrate /ˈdesɪkreɪt/ **desecrates, desecrating, desecrated.** VERB If someone **desecrates** something considered sacred or special, they deliberately damage or insult it. ♦**desecration** N-U ...*the desecration of the cemetery.*

desert, deserts, deserting, deserted. [1] N-VAR /ˈdezət/ A **desert** is a large area of land, usually in a hot region, which has almost no water, rain, trees, or plants. [2] VERB /dɪˈzɜːt/ If people **desert** a place, they leave it and it becomes empty. *Medical staff have deserted the city's main hospital.* ♦**deserted** ADJ ...*a deserted side street.* [3] VERB If someone **deserts** you, they leave you and no longer help or support you. *Mrs Roding's husband deserted her years ago.* ♦**desertion, desertions.** N-VAR ...*alone and vulnerable after her father's desertion.* [4] VERB If someone **deserts** from the armed forces, they leave without permission. ♦**desertion** N-VAR *Two soldiers face charges of desertion.* ♦**deserter, deserters** N-C ...*a young army deserter.*

deserve /dɪˈzɜːv/ **deserves, deserving, deserved.** VERB If you say that someone **deserves** something, you mean that they should have it or do it because of their qualities or actions. *It's your money. You deserve it... 'He deserved to die,' said Penelope viciously... Every patient deserves better than that.*

deserving /dɪˈzɜːvɪŋ/ ADJ If you describe a person or organization as **deserving**, you think they should be helped; FORMAL. *The money saved could be used for more deserving causes.*

design /dɪˈzaɪn/ **designs, designing, designed.** [1] VERB & N-U When you **design** something new, or when you are responsible for its **design**, you plan what it should be like. *He approached me to create and design the restaurant... The plan is designed to reduce some of the company's mountainous debt. ...a born mechanic with a flair for design.* [2] N-U The **design** of something is the way in which it has been planned and made. ...*a new design of clock.* [3] N-C A **design** is a drawing which someone produces to show how they would like something to be built or made. ...*his design for a new office tower.* [4] N-C A **design** is a decorative pattern of lines, flowers, or shapes. ...*swirling leaf designs.*

designate, designates, designating, designated. [1] VERB /ˈdezɪgneɪt/ When you **desig-**

nate something or someone as a particular thing, you formally give them a description or name. *1991 has been designated the Year of Sport... Designate someone as the spokesperson.* ♦**designation, designations.** N-VAR *...the designation of Madrid as European City of Culture.* [2] VERB If something **is designated** for a particular purpose, it is set aside for that purpose. *Smoking is allowed in designated areas.* [3] ADJ /'dezɪgnət/ You use **designate** after a job title to refer to someone who has been formally chosen to do that job, but has not yet started doing it. *...Japan's Prime Minister-designate.*

designer /dɪ'zaɪnə/ **designers.** [1] N-C A **designer** is a person whose job involves planning the form of a new object. *...a fashion designer.* [2] ADJ BEFORE N **Designer** clothes are expensive fashionable clothes created by a famous designer.

desirable /dɪ'zaɪərəbəl/. [1] ADJ Something that is **desirable** is worth having or doing. *Prolonged negotiation was not desirable.* ♦**desirability** N-U *...the debate on the desirability of banning the ivory trade.* [2] ADJ Someone who is **desirable** is sexually attractive.

desire /dɪ'zaɪə/ **desires, desiring, desired.** [1] VERB & N-C If you **desire** something, or if you have a **desire** for it, you want it; FORMAL. *Fred was bored and desired to go home... I had a strong desire to help and care for people.* ♦**desired** *His warnings have provoked the desired response.* [2] VERB & N-U If you **desire** someone, or if you feel **desire** for them, you want to have sex with them.

desk /desk/ **desks.** N-C A **desk** is a table which you sit at in order to write or work.

desolate /'desələt/. [1] ADJ A **desolate** place is empty and lacking in comfort. [2] ADJ If someone is **desolate**, they feel very lonely and depressed.

desolation /,desə'leɪʃən/. [1] N-U The **desolation** of a place is its depressing emptiness. *...a scene of desolation and ruin.* [2] ADJ **Desolation** is a feeling of great unhappiness. *...an overwhelming sense of loneliness and desolation.*

despair /dɪ'speə/ **despairs, despairing, despaired.** [1] VERB & N-U If you **despair**, or if you feel **despair**, you feel that everything is wrong and that nothing will improve. *I despair at the attitude with which their work is received... I looked at my wife in despair.* [2] VERB If you **despair** of something, you feel that there is no hope that it will happen or improve. *They despaired of ever having a family of their own.*

despatch /dɪ'spætʃ/. See **dispatch**.

desperate /'despərət/. [1] ADJ If you are **desperate**, you are in such a bad situation that you will try anything to change it. *...a desperate attempt to hijack a plane... Many refugees were in a desperate state.* ♦**desperately** ADV *I tried desperately to bandage him.* [2] ADJ AFTER LINK-V If you are **desperate** for something or **desperate** to do something, you want to have it or do it very much. *People are desperate for him to do something.* ♦**desperately** ADV *...a boy who desperately needed affection.*

desperation /,despə'reɪʃən/. N-U **Desperation** is the feeling that you have when you are in such

a bad situation that you will try anything to change it. *...acts of sheer desperation.*

despicable /dɪ'spɪkəbəl, AM 'despɪk-/. ADJ If you say that a person or action is **despicable**, you are emphasizing that they are extremely nasty or cruel. *It was a despicable crime.*

despise /dɪ'spaɪz/ **despises, despising, despised.** VERB If you **despise** someone or something, you hate them very much. *How I despised myself for my cowardice!*

despite /dɪ'spaɪt/. PREP You use **despite** to introduce a fact which makes the other part of the sentence surprising. *Despite a thorough investigation, no trace of Dr Southwell has been found.*

dessert /dɪ'zɜːt/ **desserts.** N-VAR **Dessert** is something sweet, such as fruit or a pudding, that you eat at the end of a meal. *She had homemade ice cream for dessert.*

destabilize (BR also **destabilise**) /diː'steɪbəlaɪz/ **destabilizes, destabilizing, destabilized.** VERB To **destabilize** something such as a country or government means to create a situation which reduces its power or influence. *Their sole aim is to destabilize the Indian government.*

destination /,destɪ'neɪʃən/ **destinations.** N-C Your **destination** is the place you are going to. *...his preferred holiday destination, Hawaii.*

destined /'destɪnd/. ADJ AFTER LINK-V If something is **destined** to happen, or if someone is **destined** to do something, that thing will definitely happen. *Muriel was destined for great things.*

destiny /'destɪni/ **destinies.** [1] N-C A person's **destiny** is everything that happens to them during their life, including what will happen in the future. [2] N-U **Destiny** is the force which some people believe controls the things that happen to you. *Is it destiny that brings people together?*

destitute /'destɪtjuːt, AM -tuːt/. ADJ Someone who is **destitute** has no money or possessions; FORMAL. *...destitute people living on the streets.*

destroy /dɪ'strɔɪ/ **destroys, destroying, destroyed.** VERB To **destroy** something means to cause so much damage to it that it is completely ruined or does not exist any more. *He destroyed my confidence... The building was completely destroyed.* ♦**destruction** /dɪ'strʌkʃən/ N-U *...the destruction of the ozone layer.*

destructive /dɪ'strʌktɪv/. ADJ Something that is **destructive** causes or is capable of causing great damage, harm, or injury. *...the awesome destructive power of nuclear weapons... Guilt can be very destructive.*

detach /dɪ'tætʃ/ **detaches, detaching, detached.** VERB If you **detach** one thing from another that it is fixed to, you remove it. If one thing **detaches** from another, it becomes separated from it. *Detach the white part of the application form.*

detached /dɪ'tætʃt/. [1] ADJ Someone who is **detached** is not emotionally or personally involved in something. *He tries to remain emotionally detached from the prisoners.* [2] ADJ A

detached house is not joined to any other house.

detachment /dɪˈtætʃmənt/. N-U **Detachment** is a feeling of not being emotionally or personally involved in something. ...*a well-developed sense of professional detachment.*

detail /ˈdiːteɪl/ **details, detailing, detailed.** ① N-VAR The **details** of something are its small, individual features or elements. If you examine or discuss something **in detail**, you examine all these features. ...*the details of a peace agreement... I recall every detail of the party. ...his scrupulous attention to detail.* ② N-PL **Details** about something are items of information about it. *See the bottom of this page for details of how to apply.* ③ VERB If you **detail** things, you list them or give full information about them; FORMAL. *The report detailed the human rights abuses committed during the war.*

detailed /ˈdiːteɪld, AM dɪˈteɪld/. ADJ A **detailed** report or plan contains a lot of details. ...*a detailed account of the decisions.*

detain /dɪˈteɪn/ **detains, detaining, detained.** ① VERB When people such as the police **detain** someone, they keep them in a place under their control. *The act allows police to detain a suspect for up to 48 hours.* ② VERB To **detain** someone means to delay them, for example by talking to them; FORMAL. *Thank you. We won't detain you any further.*

detainee /ˌdiːteɪˈniː/ **detainees.** N-C A **detainee** is someone who is being held prisoner by a government or being held by the police.

detect /dɪˈtekt/ **detects, detecting, detected.** VERB If you **detect** something, you find it or notice it. ...*equipment used to detect radiation... Arnold could detect a certain sadness in the old man's face.* ◆**detection** N-U ...*the early detection of breast cancer.*

detective /dɪˈtektɪv/ **detectives.** N-C A **detective** is someone, for example a police officer, whose job is to discover the facts about a crime or other situation.

detector /dɪˈtektə/ **detectors.** N-C A **detector** is an instrument which is used to find or measure something. ...*smoke detectors.*

detente (or **détente**) /deɪˈtɒnt/. N-U **Detente** is a state of friendly relations between two countries when previously there had been problems between them; FORMAL. ...*a policy of detente.*

detention /dɪˈtenʃən/ **detentions.** N-VAR **Detention** is the arrest or imprisonment of someone, especially for political reasons. ...*the detention without trial of government critics.*

deter /dɪˈtɜː/ **deters, deterring, deterred.** VERB To **deter** someone from doing something means to make them not want to do it. *Tougher sentences would do nothing to deter crime.*

detergent /dɪˈtɜːdʒənt/ **detergents.** N-VAR **Detergent** is a chemical substance used for washing things such as clothes or dishes.

deteriorate /dɪˈtɪəriəreɪt/ **deteriorates, deteriorating, deteriorated.** VERB If something **deteriorates**, it becomes worse. *Grant's health steadily deteriorated.* ◆**deterioration** N-U ...*a sharp deterioration in Anglo-Irish relations.*

determination /dɪˌtɜːmɪˈneɪʃən/. N-U **Determination** is the quality that you show when you have decided to do something and you will not let anything stop you. ...*the government's determination to beat inflation.*

determine /dɪˈtɜːmɪn/ **determines, determining, determined.** ① VERB If something **determines** what will happen, it controls it. *The size of the chicken pieces will determine the cooking time.* ◆**determination** N-U *We must take into our own hands the determination of our future. ...the gene which is responsible for male sex determination.* ② VERB To **determine** something means to discover it or discover the facts about it. *The investigation will determine what really happened... My aim was first of all to determine what to do next.* ◆**determination** N-U ...*procedures for the determination of refugee status.*

determined /dɪˈtɜːmɪnd/. ADJ If you are **determined** to do something, you have made a firm decision to do it and will not let anything stop you. *England made several determined efforts to score.* ◆**determinedly** ADV *She shook her head, determinedly.*

determiner /dɪˈtɜːmɪnə/ **determiners.** N-C In grammar, a **determiner** is a word such as 'the' or 'my' that is used before a noun to indicate which particular thing or person you are referring to.

deterrent /dɪˈterənt, AM -ˈtɜːr-/ **deterrents.** N-C & ADJ BEFORE N A **deterrent**, or something that has a **deterrent** effect, is something that prevents people from doing something by making them afraid of what will happen to them if they do. *They seriously believe that capital punishment is a deterrent.* ◆**deterrence** N-U ...*nuclear deterrence.*

detest /dɪˈtest/ **detests, detesting, detested.** VERB If you **detest** someone or something, you dislike them very much. *Jean detested being photographed.*

detonate /ˈdetəneɪt/ **detonates, detonating, detonated.** VERB If someone **detonates** a bomb, or if it **detonates**, it explodes. ◆**detonation, detonations** N-VAR ...*accidental detonation of nuclear weapons.*

detour /ˈdiːtʊə/ **detours.** N-C If you make a **detour** on a journey, you go by a route which is not the shortest way.

detract /dɪˈtrækt/ **detracts, detracting, detracted.** VERB If one thing **detracts** from another, it makes it seem less good or less impressive. *Even Sarah's sour comments could not detract from the excitement Meg felt.*

detriment /ˈdetrɪmənt/. PHRASE If something happens **to the detriment of** something or someone, it causes them harm or damage. *These tests will give too much importance to written exams to the detriment of other skills.*

detrimental /ˌdetrɪˈmentəl/. ADJ Something that is **detrimental** to something else has a harmful or damaging effect on it. *The experts emphasized the detrimental effects of these drugs.*

devalue /ˌdiːˈvæljuː/ **devalues, devaluing, devalued.** ① VERB To **devalue** something means to cause it to be thought less important or less worthy of respect. *They spread tales about her in an attempt to devalue her work.* ② VERB To **devalue** the currency of a country means to reduce its value in relation to other currencies. ◆**devaluation, devaluations** N-VAR ...*the devaluation of the dollar.*

devastate /'devəsteɪt/ **devastates, devastating, devastated.** VERB If something **devastates** a place, it damages it very badly or destroys it. *A fire had devastated large parts of Windsor Castle.* ◆**devastation** N-U *A huge bomb blast brought chaos and devastation.*

devastated /'devəsteɪtɪd/. ADJ AFTER LINK-V If you are **devastated** by something, you are very shocked and upset by it.

devastating /'devəsteɪtɪŋ/. ADJ You describe something as **devastating** when it is very damaging or upsetting. *Affairs do have a devastating effect on marriages... The diagnosis was devastating. She had cancer.*

develop /dɪ'veləp/ **develops, developing, developed.** ① VERB When someone or something **develops**, or when someone **develops** something, the person or thing grows or changes over a period of time and usually becomes more advanced or complete. *As children develop, some of the most important things they learn have to do with their sense of self... Most of these settlements developed from agricultural centres... These clashes could develop into open warfare... We must develop closer ties with Germany.* ◆**development** N-U ...*the development of the embryo.* ② VERB If someone **develops** something such as a habit or illness, they begin to have it. *She later developed a taste for expensive nightclubs... Smokers are most prone to develop lung cancer.* ③ VERB If someone **develops** a new product, they design it and produce it. *He claims that several countries have developed nuclear weapons secretly.* ◆**developer, developers** N-C ...*a software developer.* ◆**development** N-VAR ...*investment in product development.* ④ VERB When a country **develops**, it changes from being a poor agricultural country to a rich industrial country. ◆**developed** ADJ ...*the developed nations.* ⑤ VERB To **develop** an area of land means to build houses or factories on it to make it more useful or profitable. ...*the cost of acquiring or developing property.* ◆**developer.** N-C ...*property developers.* ◆**development** N-U ...*the fostering of development in the rural areas.* ⑥ VERB When a photographic film **is developed**, prints or negatives are made from it.

developing /dɪ'veləpɪŋ/. ADJ BEFORE N If you talk about **developing** countries or the **developing** world, you mean the countries or the parts of the world that are poor and have little industry.

development /dɪ'veləpmənt/ **developments.** ① N-C A **development** is an event which is likely to have an effect on a situation. ...*the latest developments in Moscow.* ② N-C A **development** is an area of houses or buildings which have been built by property developers.

deviant /'diːviənt/ **deviants.** N-C & ADJ A **deviant** or someone who shows **deviant** behaviour behaves in a way that is different from what is normally considered to be acceptable. *Not all alcoholics and drug abusers produce deviant offspring.* ◆**deviance** N-U ...*social deviance.*

deviate /'diːvieɪt/ **deviates, deviating, deviated.** VERB To **deviate** from a plan or from a usual way of behaving means not to behave in the planned or usual way. *He planned his schedule far in advance, and he didn't deviate from it. A deviation from the norm is not tolerated.* ◆**deviation, deviations** N-VAR

device /dɪ'vaɪs/ **devices.** ① N-C A **device** is an object that has been made for a particular purpose. ...*a timer device for a bomb.* ② N-C A **device** is a method of achieving something. ...*a device to pressurise Mr Neill into negotiating.* ③ PHRASE If you **leave** someone **to their own devices,** you leave them alone to do as they wish.

devil /'devəl/ **devils.** ① N-PROPER In Christianity, Judaism, and Islam, **the Devil** is the most powerful evil spirit. ② N-C A **devil** is an evil spirit. ③ N-C You can use **devil** when showing how you feel about someone. For example, you can call someone a poor devil to show that you feel sorry for them; INFORMAL.

devious /'diːviəs/. ADJ A **devious** person does dishonest things in a clever complicated way. *You have a very devious mind.*

devise /dɪ'vaɪz/ **devises, devising, devised.** VERB If you **devise** something, you have the idea for it and design it. *We devised a plan.*

devoid /dɪ'vɔɪd/. ADJ AFTER LINK-V If you say that someone or something is **devoid of** a quality or thing, you are emphasizing that they have none of it. ...*a face that was so devoid of feeling.*

devolve /dɪ'vɒlv/ **devolves, devolving, devolved.** VERB If you **devolve** power, authority, or responsibility to a less important or powerful person or group, or if it **devolves** upon them, it is transferred to them. *Companies have been learning to devolve authority to workers.* ◆**devolution** /,diːvə'luːʃən, ,dev-/ N-U ...*the devolution of power to the regions.*

devote /dɪ'vəʊt/ **devotes, devoting, devoted.** VERB If you **devote** yourself, your time, or your energy to something, you spend all or most of your time or energy on it. *He abandoned his political life and devoted himself to business.*

devoted /dɪ'vəʊtɪd/. ADJ If you are **devoted** to someone or something, you care about them or love them very much. ...*a loving and devoted husband... Horace is so devoted to his garden.*

devotee /,devə'tiː/ **devotees.** N-C A **devotee** of a subject or activity is someone who is very enthusiastic about it.

devotion /dɪ'vəʊʃən/. N-U Your **devotion** to someone or something is your great love of them and commitment to them. *At first she was flattered by his devotion. ...his devotion to his job.*

devour /dɪ'vaʊə/ **devours, devouring, devoured.** VERB If a person or animal **devours** something, they eat it quickly and eagerly. *She devoured two bars of chocolate.*

devout /dɪ'vaʊt/. ① ADJ A **devout** person has deep religious beliefs. *They were devout, serious girls.* ② ADJ BEFORE N A **devout** believer in something supports it very strongly and enthusiastically. ...*devout Marxists.*

diabetes /,daɪə'biːtiːz, AM -tɪs/. N-U **Diabetes** is a condition in which someone's body is unable to control the level of sugar in their blood.

diabetic /ˌdaɪə'betɪk/ **diabetics.** N-C & ADJ A **diabetic** or a person who is **diabetic** suffers from diabetes.

diagnose /ˈdaɪəgnəʊz, AM -nəʊs/ **diagnoses, diagnosing, diagnosed.** VERB If someone or something **is diagnosed** as having a particular illness or problem, their illness or problem is identified. *The soldiers were diagnosed as having flu... He could diagnose an engine problem simply by listening.*

diagnosis /ˌdaɪəg'nəʊsɪs/ **diagnoses.** N-VAR **Diagnosis** is identifying what is wrong with someone who is ill or with something that is not working properly. *...a doctor making a diagnosis.*

diagnostic /ˌdaɪəg'nɒstɪk/. ADJ BEFORE N **Diagnostic** devices or methods are used for discovering what is wrong with someone or something. *...X-rays and other diagnostic tools.*

diagonal /daɪ'ægənəl/. ADJ A **diagonal** line or movement goes in a slanting direction. ♦ **diagonally** ADV *He ran diagonally across the pitch.*

diagram /ˈdaɪəgræm/ **diagrams.** N-C A **diagram** is a drawing which is used to explain something.

dial /daɪəl/ **dials, dialling, dialled.** (AM **dialing, dialed**). **1** N-C The **dial** on a clock or meter is the part where the time or a measurement is indicated. **2** N-C The **dial** on a radio is the control which you move in order to change the frequency. **3** N-C The **dial** on a telephone is a circular disc that you rotate according to the number that you want to call. **4** VERB If you **dial**, or if you **dial** a number, you turn the dial or press the buttons on a telephone.

dialect /ˈdaɪəlekt/ **dialects.** N-C A **dialect** is a form of a language spoken in a particular area. *They began to speak rapidly in dialect.*

dialogue (AM **dialog**) /ˈdaɪəlɒg, AM -lɔːg/ **dialogues.** **1** N-VAR **Dialogue** is communication or discussion between people or groups. *...a direct dialogue between the two nations.* **2** N-VAR The **dialogue** in a book, film, or play consists of the things the characters in it say to each other. *He writes great dialogue.*

diameter /daɪ'æmɪtə/ **diameters.** N-C The **diameter** of a circle or sphere is the length of a straight line through the middle of it. *...thin pancakes 6 inches in diameter.*

diamond /ˈdaɪəmənd/ **diamonds.** **1** N-C A **diamond** is a hard bright precious stone. *...diamond earrings.* **2** N-C A **diamond** is a shape with four straight sides of equal length which are not at right angles to each other. **3** N-U **Diamonds** is one of the four suits in a pack of playing cards. Each card in the suit is called a **diamond** and is marked with one or more bold symbols: ♦.

diaper /ˈdaɪəpə/ **diapers.** N-C In American English, a **diaper** is something which you put round a baby's bottom in order to soak up its urine and faeces. The British word is **nappy**.

diaphragm /ˈdaɪəfræm/ **diaphragms.** N-C Your **diaphragm** is a muscle between your lungs and your stomach.

diarrhoea (AM **diarrhea**) /ˌdaɪə'riːə/. N-U When someone has **diarrhoea**, a lot of liquid faeces comes out of their body because they are ill.

diary /ˈdaɪəri/ **diaries.** N-C A **diary** is a notebook with a separate space for each day of the year.

dice /daɪs/ **dices, dicing, diced.** **Dice** is the singular and plural of the noun. **1** N-C A **dice** is a small cube with one to six spots on each face, used in games. *Roll the dice.* **2** VERB When you **dice** food, you cut it into small cubes.

dictate, dictates, dictating, dictated. **1** VERB /dɪk'teɪt, AM 'dɪkteɪt/ If you **dictate** something, you say it aloud for someone else to write down. *Mr Phillips dictated a memo to his secretary.* **2** VERB If you **dictate** to someone, you tell them what they must do. *What right has one country to dictate the environmental standards of another?* **3** N-C /ˈdɪkteɪt/ A **dictate** is an order which you have to obey; FORMAL. *...the dictates of the Party.*

dictator /dɪk'teɪtə, AM 'dɪkteɪt-/ **dictators.** N-C A **dictator** is a ruler who has complete power in a country; used showing disapproval.

dictatorial /ˌdɪktə'tɔːriəl/. ADJ If you describe someone's behaviour as **dictatorial**, you mean that they tell people what to do in a forceful and unfair way; used showing disapproval. *...his dictatorial management style.*

dictatorship /dɪk'teɪtəʃɪp/ **dictatorships.** **1** N-VAR **Dictatorship** is system in which a country is governed by a dictator. **2** N-C A **dictatorship** is a country ruled by a dictator.

dictionary /ˈdɪkʃənri, AM -neri/ **dictionaries.** N-C A **dictionary** is a book in which the words and phrases of a language are listed, usually in alphabetical order, together with their meanings or corresponding words of another language.

did /dɪd/. **Did** is the past tense of **do**.

didn't /ˈdɪdnt/. **Didn't** is the usual spoken form of 'did not'.

die /daɪ/ **dies, dying, died.** **1** VERB When people, animals, or plants **die**, they stop living. *My mother died of cancer. ...friends who died young.* ● See note at **dead.** **2** VERB When something **dies**, or when it **dies away** or **dies down**, it becomes less intense, until it disappears. *My love for you will never die. ...the echoes of the thunder dying away across the peaks... The wind had died down.* **3** See also **dying.**

PHRASES If you say that old habits or attitudes **die hard**, you mean that they take a very long time to change, and may never disappear completely.

▶ **die out.** PHR-VERB If something **dies out**, it becomes less and less common and eventually disappears. *How did the dinosaurs die out?*

diesel /ˈdiːzəl/ **diesels.** **1** ADJ **Diesel** describes a type of engine in which oil is burnt by very hot air. It also describes a vehicle with this type of engine, or the heavy oil used as fuel in it. *Many people think diesel cars are smelly and dirty.* **2** N-VAR A **diesel** is a vehicle which has a diesel engine, or the heavy oil used as fuel in it.

diet /daɪət/ **diets, dieting, dieted.** **1** N-VAR Your **diet** is the type and range of food that you regularly eat. *...a healthy diet.* **2** N-C & VERB

If you are on a **diet**, or if you **are dieting**, you eat only certain foods because you are trying to lose weight. ◆**dieter, dieters** N-C *Most dieters are miserable.*

dietary /'daɪətri, AM -teri/. ADJ Dietary means relating to the kind of food you eat. *...dietary changes.*

differ /'dɪfə/ **differs, differing, differed.** 1 VERB If two or more things **differ**, they are not like each other. *Their attitudes to promotion also differ from ours.* 2 VERB If people **differ**, they disagree with each other about something. *They differ on lots of issues.*

difference /'dɪfrəns/ **differences.** 1 N-VAR The **difference** between things is the way in which they are different from each other. *...the vast difference in size... The difference is that I expect so much of her, but not of him.* 2 N-SING The **difference** between two amounts is the amount by which one is less than the other. 3 N-C If people have their **differences**, they disagree about things. 4 PHRASE If you say that something **makes a difference**, you mean that it changes a situation. *We had terrible rows over his homework, but it made no difference.*

different /'dɪfrənt/. 1 ADJ If one thing is **different** from another, it is not like the other thing. *We have totally different views.* ◆**differently** ADV *Every individual learns differently.* 2 ADJ BEFORE N When you refer to two or more **different** things of a particular kind, you mean two or more separate things of that kind. *...different brands of drinks.* 3 ADJ AFTER LINK-V You can describe something as **different** when it is unusual and not like other things of the same kind. *The result is interesting and different.*

> In British English, people sometimes say that one thing is **different to** another. *You're so different to what I imagined.* Some people consider this use to be incorrect, and insist that you should say **different from**. *We human beings are vastly different from all other species.* In American English, you can say that one thing is **different than** another. This use is often considered incorrect in British English, but it is sometimes the simplest possibility when the comparison implies a clause. *I am no different than I was 50 years ago.*

differential /,dɪfə'renʃəl/ **differentials.** N-C A **differential** is a difference between two values in a scale, for example a difference between rates of pay within a company; TECHNICAL. *...the differential between their two currencies. ...wage differentials.*

differentiate /,dɪfə'renʃieɪt/ **differentiates, differentiating, differentiated.** VERB To **differentiate** between things means to show or recognize the difference between them. *At this age your baby cannot differentiate one person from another. ...policies that differentiate them from the other parties.* ◆**differentiation** N-U *...the differentiation between the sexes.*

difficult /'dɪfɪkəlt/. 1 ADJ Something that is **difficult** is not easy to do, understand, or cope with. *I find it difficult to speak up for myself.*

2 ADJ If you say that someone is **difficult**, you think they are behaving in an unreasonable and unhelpful way. *I could be difficult about it, but why bother?*

difficulty /'dɪfɪkəlti/ **difficulties.** 1 N-VAR A **difficulty** is a problem. If you are in **difficulty** or in **difficulties**, you are having a lot of problems. *...economic difficulties.* 2 N-U If you have **difficulty** doing something, you are not able to do it easily. *Do you have difficulty getting up?*

diffident /'dɪfɪdənt/. ADJ Someone who is **diffident** is shy and lacks confidence. ◆**diffidence** /'dɪfɪdəns/ N-U *...her diffidence towards the opposite sex.*

diffuse, diffuses, diffusing, diffused. 1 VERB /dɪ'fjuːz/ If something such as knowledge or information **is diffused**, or if it **diffuses**, it is made available over a wide area or to a lot of people; FORMAL. *Interest in books is more widely diffused than ever.* ◆**diffusion** /dɪ'fjuːʒən/ N-U *...the diffusion of political power.* 2 ADJ /dɪ'fjuːs/ Something that is **diffuse** is spread over a large area rather than concentrated in one place; FORMAL. *...a cold, diffuse light.*

dig /dɪg/ **digs, digging, dug** /dʌg/. 1 VERB When people or animals **dig**, they make a hole in the ground or in a pile of stones or debris. *He dug a hole in the lawn... Rescue workers are digging through the rubble.* 2 VERB If you **dig** one thing **into** another, or if one thing **digs into** another, the first thing is pushed hard into the second, or presses hard into it. *He could feel the beads digging into his palm.* 3 N-C A **dig** is a critical remark. *They have used the occasion to have a dig at the Press.*
▸ **dig out** or **dig up**. PHR-VERB If you **dig** something **out** or **dig** it **up**, you discover it after it has been stored, hidden, or forgotten for a long time.

digest /daɪ'dʒest/ **digests, digesting, digested.** 1 VERB When you **digest** food, it passes through your body to your stomach, your stomach removes the substances that you need, and your body gets rid of the rest. *Fats are hard to digest.* ◆**digestion** N-U *...a fruit which aids digestion.* 2 VERB If you **digest** information, you think about it carefully so that you understand it or are capable of dealing with it. *She read everything, digesting every fragment of news.*

digestive /daɪ'dʒestɪv/. ADJ BEFORE N Digestive refers to the digestion of food. *...digestive disorders.*

digit /'dɪdʒɪt/ **digits.** 1 N-C A **digit** is a written symbol for any of the ten numbers from 0 to 9. 2 N-C A **digit** is a finger, thumb, or toe.

digital /'dɪdʒɪtəl/. 1 ADJ Digital systems record or transmit information in the form of thousands of very small signals. *...digital audio broadcasting.* 2 ADJ BEFORE N Digital watches or clocks show the time by displaying numbers.

dignified /'dɪgnɪfaɪd/. ADJ If you say that someone or something is **dignified**, you mean they are calmly impressive and worthy of respect.

dignitary /'dɪgnɪtri, AM -teri/ **dignitaries.** N-C A **dignitary** is someone who has a high rank in government or in the Church.

dignity /'dɪgnɪti/. **1** N-U If someone behaves with **dignity**, they are serious, calm, and controlled. **2** N-U **Dignity** is the quality of being worthy of respect. ...*respect for human dignity.*

dike /daɪk/. See **dyke**.

dilapidated /dɪ'læpɪdeɪtɪd/. ADJ A **dilapidated** building is old and in bad condition.

dilate /daɪ'leɪt/ **dilates, dilating, dilated.** VERB When things such as blood vessels or the pupils of your eyes **dilate**, or when something **dilates** them, they become wider or bigger. *Exercise dilates blood vessels.* ◆**dilated** ADJ *His eyes seemed slightly dilated.*

dilemma /daɪ'lemə, AM dɪl-/ **dilemmas.** N-C A **dilemma** is a difficult situation in which you have to choose between two or more alternatives. ...*the dilemma of whether or not to return to his country.*

diligent /'dɪlɪdʒənt/. ADJ **Diligent** people work hard and carefully. ...*a diligent student.* ◆**diligence** N-U *The police are pursuing their inquiries with great diligence.* ◆**diligently** ADV *We worked diligently on our school assignments.*

dilute /daɪ'luːt/ **dilutes, diluting, diluted.** VERB If a liquid is **diluted**, or if it **dilutes**, it is added to or mixes with water or another liquid, and becomes weaker. *Dilute it well with cooled, boiled water.*

dim /dɪm/ **dimmer, dimmest; dims, dimming, dimmed.** **1** ADJ **Dim** light is not bright. You can also say that something is **dim** when the light is not bright enough to see very well. *Below decks, the lights were dim... He saw a dim outline of a small boat.* ◆**dimly** ADV ...*a dimly lit kitchen...* *The shoreline could be dimly seen.* **2** VERB If you **dim** a light, or if it **dims**, it becomes less bright.

dime /daɪm/ **dimes.** N-C A **dime** is an American coin worth ten cents.

dimension /daɪ'menʃən, dɪm-/ **dimensions.** **1** N-C A particular **dimension** of something is a particular aspect of it. *Works of art have a spiritual dimension.* **2** N-PL You can refer to the measurements of something as its **dimensions**. ...*the dimensions of the new oilfield.*

diminish /dɪ'mɪnɪʃ/ **diminishes, diminishing, diminished.** VERB When something **diminishes**, or when it **is diminished**, its importance, size, or intensity is reduced. *The threat of nuclear war has diminished.*

diminutive /dɪ'mɪnjʊtɪv/. ADJ A **diminutive** person or object is very small; FORMAL. ...*the diminutive figure of Mr. Nerette.*

din /dɪn/. N-SING A **din** is a very loud and unpleasant noise that lasts for some time. ...*the din of the crowd.*

dine /daɪn/ **dines, dining, dined.** VERB When you **dine**, you have dinner; FORMAL. *The two men dined at Wilson's club.*

diner /'daɪnə/ **diners.** **1** N-C In the United States, a **diner** is a small cheap restaurant that is open all day. **2** N-C The **diners** in a restaurant are the people who are eating there.

dinghy /'dɪŋgi/ **dinghies.** N-C A **dinghy** is a small boat that you sail or row.

dingy /'dɪndʒi/. ADJ A **dingy** place is dark and depressing. ...*his rather dingy office.*

'dining room, dining rooms. N-C The **dining room** is the room in a house or hotel where people have their meals.

dinner /'dɪnə/ **dinners.** **1** N-VAR **Dinner** is the main meal of the day, eaten in the evening. *She invited us to her house for dinner.* **2** N-VAR Some people use **dinner** to refer to the meal you eat in the middle of the day; BRITISH. **3** N-C A **dinner** is a formal social event in the evening at which a meal is served. *The Foundation is holding a dinner.* **4** See note at **meal**.

'dinner table, dinner tables. N-C You refer to a table as the **dinner table** when it is being used for dinner; BRITISH. *Sam was left at the dinner table with Peg.*

dinosaur /'daɪnəsɔː/ **dinosaurs.** N-C **Dinosaurs** were large reptiles which lived in prehistoric times.

dioxide /daɪ'ɒksaɪd/. See **carbon dioxide**.

dip /dɪp/ **dips, dipping, dipped.** **1** VERB If you **dip** something into a liquid, you put it in and then quickly take it out again. *They dip the food into the sauce.* **2** VERB If something **dips**, it makes a downward movement. *The sun dipped below the horizon.* **3** N-C A **dip** in a surface is a place that is lower than the rest of the surface. *The pitch has a slight dip in the middle.*

diploma /dɪ'pləʊmə/ **diplomas.** N-C A **diploma** is a university or college qualification.

diplomacy /dɪ'pləʊməsi/. **1** N-U **Diplomacy** is the activity of managing relations between the governments of different countries. *Force will have to be used if diplomacy fails.* **2** N-U **Diplomacy** is the skill of saying or doing things without offending people. *Mr Smith sometimes lacked diplomacy.*

diplomat /'dɪpləmæt/ **diplomats.** N-C A **diplomat** is a senior official, usually based at an embassy, who negotiates with another country on behalf of his or her own country.

diplomatic /dɪplə'mætɪk/. **1** ADJ **Diplomatic** means relating to diplomacy and diplomats. *Iran and Iraq have agreed to resume diplomatic relations.* ◆**diplomatically** ADV *The conflict can be resolved diplomatically.* **2** ADJ Someone who is **diplomatic** is able to say or do things without offending people. ◆**diplomatically** ADV *She could have put it more diplomatically.*

dire /daɪə/. ADJ **Dire** is used to emphasize how serious or terrible a situation or event is. *He was in dire need of hospital treatment.*

direct /daɪ'rekt, dɪ-/ **directs, directing, directed.** **1** ADJ & ADV **Direct** means going or aimed straight towards a place or object. ...*a direct train service from Calais to Strasbourg... You can fly direct to Amsterdam from most British airports.* ◆**directly** ADV *Roads and railways went directly to seaports.* ◆ See also **directly**. **2** ADJ & ADV You use **direct** to describe something such as contact or a relationship between two things or people which only involves the things or people that are mentioned, with nothing or nobody in between. *He seemed to be in direct contact with the Boss... 100 million have died this century as a direct result of war... Ensure that babies are kept out of direct sunlight... I can deal direct with your Inspector.* ◆**directly** ADV *People lost* *money directly because of some kind of criminal action.* [3] ADJ If you describe a person or their behaviour as **direct**, you mean that they are honest and say exactly what they mean. *He avoided giving a direct answer.* ◆**directness** N-U *I like the openness and directness of northerners.* [4] VERB Something that **is directed** at a particular person or thing is aimed at them or is intended to affect them. *The demonstrators directed their rage at symbols of wealth.* [5] VERB If you **direct** someone somewhere, you tell them how to get there. *Could you direct them to Dr Lamont's office, please?* [6] VERB If someone **directs** a project or a group of people, they organize it and are in charge of it. ◆**director, directors.** N-C *...the director of the intensive care unit.* [7] VERB If someone **directs** a film, play, or television programme, they decide how it should be made and performed. *Andrew acts and directs.* ◆**director** N-C *...the film director Franco Zeffirelli.* ● See also **director**.

direction /daɪˈrekʃən, dɪr-/ **directions.** [1] N-VAR A **direction** is the general line that someone or something is moving or pointing in. *St Andrews was ten miles in the opposite direction... Civilians were fleeing in all directions.* [2] N-VAR **Directions** are instructions that tell you what to do or how to get to a place. *He proceeded to give Dan directions to the computer room... The house was built under the direction of John's partner.*

directive /daɪˈrektɪv, dɪr-/ **directives.** N-C A **directive** is an official instruction that is given by someone in authority. *...a new EU directive.*

directly /daɪˈrektli, dɪr-/. [1] ADV If something is, for example, **directly** above something or in front of something, it is exactly that position. *There, directly below me, was a guy.* [2] ADV If you do one action **directly** after another, you do the second action as soon as the first one is finished. *Directly after lunch we were packed and ready to go.* [3] See also **direct**.

di,rect 'object, direct objects. N-C The **direct object** of a transitive verb is the noun group which is used to refer to someone or something directly affected by or involved in the action performed by the subject. For example, in 'I saw him yesterday', 'him' is the direct object. Compare **indirect object**.

director /daɪˈrektə, dɪr-/ **directors**. N-C The **directors** of a company are its most senior managers. *...the board of directors.* ● See also **direct**.

directorate /daɪˈrektərət, dɪr-/ **directorates.** [1] N-C A **directorate** is a board of directors in a company. [2] N-C A **directorate** is a part of a government department which is responsible for one particular thing. *...the Health and Safety Directorate of the EU.*

di,rector 'general, directors general. N-C The **director general** of a large organization is the person who is in charge of it.

directory /daɪˈrektəri, dɪr-/ **directories.** N-C A **directory** is a book which gives lists of information such as people's names, addresses, and telephone numbers. *...a telephone directory.*

dirt /dɜːt/. [1] N-U If there is **dirt** on something,

there is dust, mud, or a stain on it. [2] N-U You can refer to the earth on the ground as **dirt**.

dirty /ˈdɜːti/ **dirtier, dirtiest; dirties, dirtying, dirtied.** [1] ADJ & VERB If you get something **dirty**, or if you **dirty** it, it becomes marked or covered with stains, spots, or mud. *The kids have got their clothes dirty... The dog's hairs might dirty the seats.* [2] ADJ **Dirty** jokes, books, or language refer to sex in a way that many people find obscene or offensive.

disability /ˌdɪsəˈbɪlɪti/ **disabilities.** N-C A **disability** is a physical or mental condition that restricts the way someone can live their life. *...facilities for people with disabilities.*

disable /dɪˈseɪbəl/ **disables, disabling, disabled.** [1] VERB If an injury or illness **disables** someone, it restricts the way they can live their life. [2] VERB To **disable** a system or mechanism means to stop it working. *...if you need to disable a car alarm.*

disabled /dɪˈseɪbəld/. ADJ & N-PL **Disabled** people or **the disabled** have an illness, injury, or condition that restricts the way they can live their lives.

disadvantage /ˌdɪsədˈvɑːntɪdʒ, -ˈvæn-/ **disadvantages.** [1] N-C A **disadvantage** is a part of a situation which causes problems. *...the advantages and disadvantages of allowing their soldiers to marry.* [2] PHRASE If you are **at a disadvantage**, you have a problem that other people do not have. *The children from poor families were at a distinct disadvantage.*

disadvantaged /ˌdɪsədˈvɑːntɪdʒd, -ˈvæn-/. ADJ & N-C **Disadvantaged** people or **the disadvantaged** live in bad economic or social conditions.

disaffected /ˌdɪsəˈfektɪd/. ADJ **Disaffected** people no longer fully support something which they previously supported. *...people disaffected with the government.*

disagree /ˌdɪsəˈɡriː/ **disagrees, disagreeing, disagreed.** [1] VERB If you **disagree** with someone, you have a different opinion to them about something. *They can communicate even when they strongly disagree... Well, I disagree.* [2] VERB If you **disagree** with an action or suggestion, you disapprove of it. *I disagree with drug laws in general.*

disagreement /ˌdɪsəˈɡriːmənt/ **disagreements.** [1] N-U **Disagreement** means objecting to something. *Britain and France have expressed some disagreement with the proposal.* [2] N-VAR When there is a **disagreement** about something, people disagree or argue about what should be done. *My driving instructor and I had a brief disagreement.*

disallow /ˌdɪsəˈlaʊ/ **disallows, disallowing, disallowed.** VERB If something **is disallowed**, it is not allowed or accepted officially, because it has not been done correctly. *Antony Cole was standing for President, but the election was disallowed.*

disappear /ˌdɪsəˈpɪə/ **disappears, disappearing, disappeared.** [1] VERB If someone or something **disappears**, they go where they cannot be seen or found. *The airliner disappeared off their radar. ...a Japanese woman who disappeared thirteen years ago.* ◆**disappearance, disappearances.** N-VAR *Her disappearance has baffled police.* [2] VERB To

disappear means to stop existing or happening. *Year by year great swathes of this small nation's countryside disappear.* ♦**disappearance** N-C *...the virtual disappearance of common dolphins.*

disappoint /ˌdɪsə'pɔɪnt/ **disappoints, disappointing, disappointed.** VERB If things or people **disappoint** you, they are not as good as you had hoped, or do not do what you hoped they would have done. *I'm sorry if this reply will disappoint you.* ♦**disappointing** ADJ *The meat was overdone and the vegetables disappointing.* ♦**disappointingly** ADV *Progress is disappointingly slow.*

disappointed /ˌdɪsə'pɔɪntɪd/. ADJ If you are **disappointed**, you are sad because something has not happened or because something is not as good as you hoped it would be. *I was disappointed that Kluge was not there... I'm surprised and disappointed in you.*

disappointment /ˌdɪsə'pɔɪntmənt/ **disappointments.** 1 N-U **Disappointment** is the state of feeling disappointed. *Book early to avoid disappointment.* 2 N-C Someone or something that is a **disappointment** is not as good as you hoped. *He was such a disappointment to his family.*

disapproval /ˌdɪsə'pruːvəl/. N-U If you express **disapproval** of something, you indicate that you do not like it or that you think it is wrong. *His action had been greeted with almost universal disapproval.*

disapprove /ˌdɪsə'pruːv/ **disapproves, disapproving, disapproved.** VERB If you **disapprove** of something, you do not like it or you think it is wrong. *Her mother disapproved of her working in a pub... No matter how much I disapprove, I still love her.* ♦**disapproving** ADJ *Janet gave him a disapproving look.* ♦**disapprovingly** ADV *Antonio looked at him disapprovingly.*

disarm /dɪs'ɑːm/ **disarms, disarming, disarmed.** 1 VERB To **disarm** a person or group means to take away their weapons. *We will agree to disarming troops.* 2 VERB If a country or group **disarms**, it gives up the use of its weapons. *We're not ready to disarm ourselves.* 3 VERB If a person or their behaviour **disarms** you, they cause you to feel less angry, hostile, or critical towards them. *She did her best to disarm her critics.* ♦**disarming** ADJ *...a disarming smile.* ♦**disarmingly** ADV *He is, as ever, business-like, and disarmingly honest.*

disarmament /dɪs'ɑːməmənt/. N-U **Disarmament** is the act of reducing the number of weapons that a country has.

disarray /ˌdɪsə'reɪ/. N-U If people or things are in **disarray** they have become very confused and disorganized. *The nation is in disarray following rioting.*

disaster /dɪ'zɑːstə, -'zæs-/ **disasters.** 1 N-C A **disaster** is a very bad accident such as an earthquake or a plane crash. *It was the second air disaster in the region.* 2 N-C If you refer to something as a **disaster**, you are emphasizing that you think it is extremely bad. *It would be a disaster for them not to reach the semi-finals.* 3 N-U **Disaster** is something which has very bad consequences for you. *The best way of*

coping with disaster is not to confront it directly.

disastrous /dɪ'zɑːstrəs, -'zæs-/. ADJ Something that is **disastrous** has extremely bad consequences and effects or is very unsuccessful. *...the recent, disastrous earthquake... England's cricketers have had another disastrous day.* ♦**disastrously** ADV *Their scheme went disastrously wrong.*

disband /dɪs'bænd/ **disbands, disbanding, disbanded.** VERB When someone **disbands** a group of people, it stops operating as a single unit. *All the armed groups will be disbanded... The rebels were to have fully disbanded by June.*

disbelief /ˌdɪsbɪ'liːf/. N-U **Disbelief** is not believing that something is true or real. *She looked at him in complete disbelief.*

disc (AM **disk**) /dɪsk/ **discs.** 1 N-C A **disc** is a flat, circular shape or object. 2 N-C A **disc** is a piece of cartilage between the bones in your spine. 3 N-C A **disc** is a gramophone record or a compact disc. 4 See also **disk**.

discard /dɪs'kɑːd/ **discards, discarding, discarded.** VERB If you **discard** something, you get rid of it because it is not wanted. *Read the manufacturer's guidelines before discarding the box. ...discarded cigarette butts.*

discern /dɪ'sɜːn/ **discerns, discerning, discerned.** 1 VERB If you can **discern** something, you are aware of it and know what it is; FORMAL. *It was hard to discern why this was happening.* 2 VERB If you can **discern** something, you can just see it, but not clearly; FORMAL. *We could just discern a narrow, weedy ditch.*

discernible /dɪ'sɜːnəbəl/. ADJ If something is **discernible**, you can see it or recognize that it exists. *Far away the outline of the island is just discernible.*

discerning /dɪ'sɜːnɪŋ/. ADJ A **discerning** person is good at judging the quality of something. *...holidays to suit the more discerning traveller.*

discharge, discharges, discharging, discharged. verb /dɪs'tʃɑːdʒ/, noun /'dɪstʃɑːdʒ/. 1 VERB & N-U When someone is **discharged** from hospital, prison, or the armed forces, or when they are given a **discharge**, they are allowed to leave, or told that they must leave. *He has a broken nose but may be discharged today... He was given a conditional discharge.* 2 VERB If someone **discharges** their duties or responsibilities, they carry them out; FORMAL. *...the quiet competence with which he discharged his many college duties.* 3 VERB If something is **discharged** from inside a place, it comes out; FORMAL. *The resulting salty water will be discharged at sea.* 4 N-C When there is a **discharge** of a substance, the substance comes out from inside somewhere. *...a watery discharge from their eyes.*

disciple /dɪ'saɪpl/ **disciples.** N-C If you are someone's **disciple**, you are influenced by their teachings and try to follow their example. *...a major intellectual figure with disciples throughout Europe.*

disciplinary /'dɪsɪplɪnəri, AM -neri/. ADJ BEFORE N **Disciplinary** matters are concerned with rules, making sure that people obey them, and punishing people who do not.

discipline /'dɪsɪplɪn/ **disciplines, disciplining, disciplined.** [1] N-U **Discipline** is the practice of making people obey rules or standards of behaviour, and punishing them when they do not. ...*discipline problems in the classroom.* [2] VERB If someone **is disciplined** for something that they have done wrong, they are punished for it. *The workman was disciplined by his company but not dismissed.* [3] N-U **Discipline** is the quality of being able to behave or work in a controlled way. ...*calm, control and discipline.* [4] N-C A **discipline** is an area of study, especially a subject of study in a college or university; FORMAL. ...*people from a wide range of disciplines.*

'disc jockey, disc jockeys. N-C A **disc jockey** is the same as a **DJ.**

disclose /dɪs'kləʊz/ **discloses, disclosing, disclosed.** VERB If you **disclose** new or secret information, you tell it to someone. *He will not disclose the names of his patients... The company disclosed that its chairman will step down in May.*

disclosure /dɪs'kləʊʒə/ **disclosures.** N-VAR **Disclosure** is the act of revealing new or secret information. ...*a series of unauthorised newspaper disclosures.*

disco /'dɪskəʊ/ **discos.** N-C A **disco** is a place or event where people dance to pop music.

discomfort /dɪs'kʌmfət/ **discomforts.** [1] N-U **Discomfort** is an unpleasant or painful feeling in a part of your body. *Steve had some discomfort, but no real pain.* [2] N-U **Discomfort** is a feeling of worry or embarrassment. *He sniffed, fidgeting in discomfort.* [3] N-C **Discomforts** are conditions which cause you to feel physically uncomfortable. ...*the discomforts of camping.*

disconcerting /ˌdɪskən'sɜːtɪŋ/. ADJ If you say that something is **disconcerting,** you mean that it makes you feel uneasy, confused, or embarrassed. *He had a disconcerting habit of looking down at the ground as he spoke.* ♦**disconcertingly** ADV *She could be almost disconcertingly absent-minded.*

disconnect /ˌdɪskə'nekt/ **disconnects, disconnecting, disconnected.** VERB To **disconnect** a piece of equipment means to detach it from its source of power.

disconnected /ˌdɪskə'nektɪd/. ADJ **Disconnected** things are not linked in any way. ...*sequences of utterly disconnected events.*

discontent /ˌdɪskən'tent/. N-U **Discontent** is the feeling of not being satisfied with your situation.

discontinue /ˌdɪskən'tɪnjuː/ **discontinues, discontinuing, discontinued.** [1] VERB If you **discontinue** something that you have been doing regularly, you stop doing it; FORMAL. *Do not discontinue the treatment without consulting your doctor.* [2] VERB If a product **is discontinued,** the manufacturer stops making it.

discord /'dɪskɔːd/ **discords.** N-U **Discord** is disagreement; LITERARY. ...*arranging schedules so as to prevent discord.*

discount, discounts, discounting, discounted. [1] N-C /'dɪskaʊnt/ A **discount** is a reduction in the price of something. *All full-time staff get a 20% discount.* [2] VERB /dɪs'kaʊnt/ If

you **discount** something, you reject or ignore it. *Traders tended to discount the rumor.*

discourage /dɪs'kʌrɪdʒ, AM -'kɜːr-/ **discourages, discouraging, discouraged.** [1] VERB If someone or something **discourages** you, they cause you to lose your enthusiasm about doing something. *It may be difficult to do at first. Don't let this discourage you.* ♦**discouraged** ADJ *She was determined not to be too discouraged.* ♦**discouraging** ADJ *Today's report is more discouraging for the economy.* [2] VERB To **discourage** an action, or to **discourage** someone from doing it, means to try and persuade them not to do it. ...*a campaign to discourage children from smoking.* ♦**discouragement** N-U ...*active discouragement from teachers.*

discourse /'dɪskɔːs/ **discourses.** N-C **Discourse** is spoken or written communication between people. ...*a long tradition of political discourse.*

discover /dɪs'kʌvə/ **discovers, discovering, discovered.** [1] VERB If you **discover** something that you did not know about before, you become aware of it or learn of it. *She discovered that they'd escaped... It was difficult for the inspectors to discover which documents were important.* [2] VERB If someone or something **is discovered,** someone finds them. *A few days later his badly beaten body was discovered.* [3] VERB When someone **discovers** something new, they are the first person to find it or become aware of it. ...*the first European to discover America... People discovered how to cultivate cereals thousands of years ago.*

discovery /dɪs'kʌvəri/ **discoveries.** [1] N-VAR If someone makes a **discovery,** they become aware of something or learn of something that they did not know about before. *I felt I'd made an incredible discovery.* [2] N-C If someone makes a **discovery,** they are the first person to find or become aware of something that no one knew about before. ...*the discovery of the ozone hole over the South Pole.* [3] N-VAR When the **discovery** of people or objects happens, someone finds them.

discredit /dɪs'kredɪt/ **discredits, discrediting, discredited.** [1] VERB To **discredit** someone or something means to cause other people to stop trusting or respecting them. ...*trying to discredit government foreign-aid policies.* ♦**discredited** ADJ ...*discredited police evidence.* [2] VERB To **discredit** evidence or an idea means to make it appear false or doubtful.

discreet /dɪs'kriːt/. ADJ If you are **discreet,** you are careful to avoid attracting attention or revealing private information. *He followed at a discreet distance. ...discreet jewellery. ...discreet inquiries.* ♦**discreetly** ADV *He glanced discreetly around the room.*

discrepancy /dɪs'krepənsi/ **discrepancies.** N-C If there is a **discrepancy** between two things that ought to be the same, there is a difference between them. ...*discrepancies in their accounting systems.*

discretion /dɪs'kreʃən/. [1] N-U **Discretion** is the quality of behaving in a quiet and controlled way without attracting attention or giving away private information. *Larsson sometimes* *joined in the fun, but with more discretion.* [2] N-U If someone in a position of authority has the **discretion** to do something in a situation, they have the freedom and authority to decide what to do; FORMAL. *School governors have the discretion to allow parents to withdraw pupils... The rules are often bent at the organiser's discretion.*

discretionary /dɪsˈkreʃənri, AM -neri/. ADJ **Discretionary** matters are not fixed by rules but are decided by the people in authority. *You are entitled to a discretionary grant for your course.*

discriminate /dɪsˈkrɪmɪneɪt/ **discriminates, discriminating, discriminated.** [1] VERB If you can **discriminate** between two things, you can recognize the difference between them. *He is incapable of discriminating between a good idea and a terrible one.* [2] VERB To **discriminate** against a group of people or in favour of a group of people means to unfairly treat them worse or better than other groups. *They believe the law discriminates against women.*

discrimination /dɪsˌkrɪmɪˈneɪʃən/. [1] N-U **Discrimination** is the practice of treating one person or group of people less fairly or less well than other people or groups. *...sex discrimination laws. ...discrimination against immigrants.* [2] N-U **Discrimination** is awareness of what is good or of high quality. *They cooked without skill and ate without discrimination.*

discriminatory /dɪsˈkrɪmɪnətri, AM -tɔːri/. ADJ **Discriminatory** laws or practices are unfair because they treat one group of people worse than other groups. *...racially discriminatory laws.*

discuss /dɪsˈkʌs/ **discusses, discussing, discussed.** VERB If people **discuss** something, they talk about it, often in order to reach a decision. *I will be discussing the situation with colleagues tomorrow... The groups are also to discuss how to bring peace and unity to the country.*

Note that **discuss** is never used as an intransitive verb. You cannot say, for example, 'They discussed', 'I discussed with him', or 'They discussed about politics'. Instead, you can say that you **have a discussion** with someone about something. *I had a long discussion about all this with Stephen.* If the discussion is less formal, you can simply use the verb *talk. They come here and sit for hours talking about politics... We talked all night long.*

---

discussion /dɪsˈkʌʃən/ **discussions.** N-VAR If there is **discussion** about something, people talk about it, often in order to reach a decision. *Council members are due to have informal discussions later on today... The proposals are still under discussion.*

disdain /dɪsˈdeɪn/ **disdains, disdaining, disdained.** N-U If you feel **disdain** for someone or something, you dislike them because you think they are inferior or unimportant. *Janet looked at him with disdain.*

disease /dɪˈziːz/ **diseases.** N-VAR A **disease** is an illness which affects people, animals, or

plants. *...the rapid spread of disease in the area. ...heart disease.*

diseased /dɪˈziːzd/. [1] ADJ Something that is **diseased** is affected by a disease. *Clear away dead or diseased plants.* [2] ADJ If you say that someone's mind is **diseased**, you are emphasizing that you think it is not normal or balanced. *Gardner describes the book as 'the product of a diseased and evil mind'.*

disenchanted /ˌdɪsɪnˈtʃɑːntɪd, -ˈtʃænt-/. ADJ If you are **disenchanted** with something, you no longer think that it is good. *I'm disenchanted with the state of British theatre.* ♦**disenchantment** /ˌdɪsɪnˈtʃɑːntmənt, -ˈtʃænt-/ N-U *There's growing disenchantment with the Government.*

disengage /ˌdɪsɪnˈɡeɪdʒ/ **disengages, disengaging, disengaged.** [1] VERB If you **disengage** something, you separate it from the thing which it has become attached to. *John gently disengaged himself from his sister's tearful embrace... His front brake cable disengaged.* [2] VERB If an army **disengages** from a conflict or an area, it withdraws from the fight or the area. ♦**disengagement** N-U *...this policy of disengagement from the European war.*

disengaged /ˌdɪsɪnˈɡeɪdʒd/. ADJ If someone is **disengaged** from something, they are not as involved with it as you would expect. *Both of the parents are emotionally disengaged from the patient.*

disfigure /dɪsˈfɪɡə, AM -ɡjər/ **disfigures, disfiguring, disfigured.** [1] VERB If someone **is disfigured**, their appearance is spoiled. *Many of the wounded had been badly disfigured.* ♦**disfigured** ADJ *...the scarred, disfigured face.* [2] VERB To **disfigure** an object or a place means to spoil its appearance. *Wind turbines are noisy and they disfigure the landscape.*

disgrace /dɪsˈɡreɪs/ **disgraces, disgracing, disgraced.** [1] N-U & N-SING If you say that someone is in **disgrace**, you are emphasizing that other people disapprove of them and do not respect them because of something they have done. *His vice president also had to resign in disgrace... What went on was a scandal. It was a disgrace to Britain.* [2] N-SING If you say that something is a **disgrace**, you are emphasizing that it is very bad or wrong. *To withold any information is an absolute disgrace.* [3] VERB If you say that someone **disgraces** someone else, you are emphasizing that their behaviour causes the other person to feel ashamed. *I have disgraced my family's name.*

disgraced /dɪsˈɡreɪst/. ADJ You use **disgraced** to describe someone whose bad behaviour has caused them to lose the approval and respect of the public or of people in authority. *...the disgraced leader of the coup.*

disgraceful /dɪsˈɡreɪsfʊl/. ADJ If you say that something is **disgraceful**, you disapprove of it strongly. *...his most disgraceful behaviour.* ♦**disgracefully** ADV *His brother had behaved disgracefully.*

disgruntled /dɪsˈɡrʌntəld/. ADJ If you are **disgruntled**, you are cross and dissatisfied about something. *Disgruntled employees recently called for his resignation.*

disguise /dɪsˈgaɪz/ **disguises, disguising, disguised.** [1] VERB & N-VAR If you **disguise** yourself, or if you are **in disguise**, you alter your appearance so that people will not recognize you. *She disguised herself as a man... He was wearing that ridiculous disguise.* ◆**disguised** ADJ *The extremists entered the building disguised as medical workers.* [2] VERB To **disguise** something means to hide it or change its appearance, so that people do not know about it or will not recognize it. *He made no attempt to disguise his agitation.* ◆**disguised** ADJ *...a thinly disguised warning.*

disgust /dɪsˈgʌst/ **disgusts, disgusting, disgusted.** [1] N-U **Disgust** is a strong feeling of dislike or disapproval. *He spoke of his disgust at the incident.* [2] VERB To **disgust** someone means to make them feel a strong sense of dislike and disapproval. *He disgusted many with his boorish behaviour.*

disgusted /dɪsˈgʌstɪd/. ADJ If you are **disgusted**, you have a strong feeling of dislike or disapproval. *I'm disgusted with the way that he was treated.* ◆**disgustedly** ADV *'It's a little late for that,' Ritter said disgustedly.*

disgusting /dɪsˈgʌstɪŋ/. ADJ If you say that something is **disgusting**, you think it is extremely unpleasant or unacceptable. *...one of the most disgusting sights I had ever seen... I think it's disgusting that women of 60 are having babies.*

dish /dɪʃ/ **dishes, dishing, dished.** [1] N-C A **dish** is a shallow container used for cooking or serving food. *...a dish of spaghetti.* [2] N-C Food that is prepared in a particular style or combination can be referred to as a **dish**. *There are plenty of vegetarian dishes to choose from.* [3] N-C You can use the word **dish** to refer to anything that is round and hollow in shape with a wide uncovered top. *...a satellite dish.*

▸ **dish out** [1] PHR-VERB If you **dish out** something, you distribute it among a number of people; INFORMAL. *Doctors, not pharmacists, are responsible for dishing out drugs.* [2] PHR-VERB If someone **dishes out** criticism or punishment, they give it to someone. [3] PHR-VERB If you **dish out** food, you serve it to people. *She dished him out a plate of stew.*

▸ **dish up.** PHR-VERB If you **dish up** food, you serve it to people. *They dished up a superb meal... I'll dish up.*

dishonest /dɪsˈɒnɪst/. ADJ If you say someone is **dishonest**, you mean that they are not honest and you cannot trust them. *It would be dishonest to mislead people.* ◆**dishonestly** ADV *They acted dishonestly.*

dishonesty /dɪsˈɒnɪsti/. N-U **Dishonesty** is dishonest behaviour.

disillusion /ˌdɪsɪˈluːʒən/ **disillusions, disillusioning, disillusioned.** [1] VERB If someone or something **disillusions** you, they make you realize that something is not as good as you thought. *He said he had been bitterly disillusioned by his country's failure to change.* ◆**disillusioned** ADJ *I've become very disillusioned with local politics.* [2] N-U **Disillusion** is the same as **disillusionment**.

disillusionment /ˌdɪsɪˈluːʒənmənt/. N-U **Disillusionment** is the disappointment that you

feel when you discover that someone or something is not as good as you had expected or thought. *...a general sense of disillusionment with the government.*

disinfect /ˌdɪsɪnˈfekt/ **disinfects, disinfecting, disinfected.** VERB If you **disinfect** something, you clean it using a substance that kills germs. *Your contact lenses should be disinfected daily.*

disinfectant /ˌdɪsɪnˈfektənt/ **disinfectants.** N-VAR **Disinfectant** is a substance that kills germs.

disintegrate /dɪsˈɪntɪgreɪt/ **disintegrates, disintegrating, disintegrated.** [1] VERB If something **disintegrates**, it becomes seriously weakened and is divided or destroyed. *During October 1918 the Austro-Hungarian Empire began to disintegrate.* ◆**disintegration** N-U *...the disintegration of an ordinary marriage.* [2] VERB If an object **disintegrates**, it breaks into many small pieces and is destroyed. *At 420 mph the windscreen disintegrated.*

disinterested /dɪsˈɪntrəstɪd/. [1] ADJ Someone who is **disinterested** is not involved in a situation or not likely to benefit from it and is therefore able to act in a fair and unselfish way. *Scientists, of course, can be expected to be impartial and disinterested.* [2] ADJ If you are **disinterested** in something, you are not interested in it. *Doran was disinterested in food.*

disk /dɪsk/. N-C In a computer, the **disk** is the part where information is stored. *The program takes up 2.5 megabytes of disk space.*

dislike /ˌdɪsˈlaɪk/ **dislikes, disliking, disliked.** [1] VERB & N-U If you **dislike** someone or something, or if you have a feeling of **dislike** towards them, you think they are unpleasant and you do not like them. *David began to dislike all his television heroes who smoked... She looked at him with dislike.* [2] N-PL Your **dislikes** are the things that you do not like. *Consider what your likes and dislikes are about your job.*

dislocate /ˈdɪsləkeɪt/ **dislocates, dislocating, dislocated.** VERB If you **dislocate** a bone or a joint in your body, it moves out of its proper position. *Harrison dislocated a finger. ...a dislocated shoulder.*

dislodge /ˌdɪsˈlɒdʒ/ **dislodges, dislodging, dislodged.** VERB To **dislodge** someone or something from a place or position means to make them move from that place or position. *Rainfall from a tropical storm dislodged the debris from the slopes of the volcano.*

dismal /ˈdɪzməl/. [1] ADJ Something that is **dismal** is depressingly bad. *My prospects of returning to a suitable job are dismal.* [2] ADJ Something that is **dismal** is bleak, sad, and depressing. *The main hospital is pretty dismal. ...a dark dismal day.*

dismantle /ˌdɪsˈmæntəl/ **dismantles, dismantling, dismantled.** VERB If you **dismantle** a machine or structure, you take it apart carefully.

dismay /ˌdɪsˈmeɪ/ **dismays, dismaying, dismayed.** N-U & VERB If you have a feeling of **dismay**, or if something **dismays** you, it makes you feel afraid, worried, or disappointed; FORMAL. *Mr Reynolds expressed dismay at this idea... McKee suddenly realized she was crying* *and the thought dismayed him.* ♦**dismayed** ADJ *He was dismayed to find that his hands were shaking.*

dismember /,dɪs'membə/ **dismembers, dismembering, dismembered.** VERB To **dismember** the body of a dead person means to cut or pull it to pieces. ♦**dismemberment** N-U *...many bodies in various states of decay and dismemberment.*

dismiss /dɪs'mɪs/ **dismisses, dismissing, dismissed.** [1] VERB If you **dismiss** something, you decide that it is not important enough for you to think about. *Mr Wakeham dismissed the reports as speculation.* [2] VERB When an employer **dismisses** an employee, they order the employee to leave his or her job. *He was dismissed for incompetence.* [3] VERB If you **are dismissed** by someone in authority, they tell you that you can go away from them. *Two more witnesses were called, heard and dismissed.*

dismissal /dɪs'mɪsəl/ **dismissals.** [1] N-VAR When an employee is dismissed from their job, you can refer to their **dismissal.** *...Mr Low's dismissal from his post at the head of the commission.* [2] N-U **Dismissal** of something means deciding or saying that it is not important. *...high-handed dismissal of public opinion.*

dismissive /dɪs'mɪsɪv/. ADJ If you are **dismissive** of someone or something, you say or show that you think they are not important or have no value. *...the dismissive attitude scientists often take.* ♦**dismissively** ADV *He describes Sally dismissively as 'that woman'.*

disobedience /,dɪsə'biːdiəns/. N-U **Disobedience** is deliberately refusing to do what someone in authority tells you to do, or to follow rules. *The penalty for disobedience was death.*

disobey /,dɪsə'beɪ/ **disobeys, disobeying, disobeyed.** VERB When someone **disobeys** a person or an order, they deliberately do not do what they have been told to do. *...a naughty boy who often disobeyed his mother and father.*

disorder /dɪs'ɔːdə/ **disorders.** [1] N-VAR A **disorder** is a problem or illness which affects a person's mind or body. *...a rare nerve disorder that can cause paralysis of the arms.* [2] N-U **Disorder** is a state of being untidy, badly prepared, or badly organized. *The emergency room was in disorder.* [3] N-U **Disorder** is violence or rioting in public. *...forms of civil disorder – most notably, football hooliganism.*

disorderly /,dɪs'ɔːdəli/. ADJ If you describe something as **disorderly**, you mean that it is untidy, irregular, or disorganized; FORMAL. *...the large and disorderly room.*

disorganized (BR also **disorganised**) /,dɪs'ɔːgənaɪzd/. ADJ **Disorganized** means badly organized, planned, or managed, often leading to a state of confusion. *The lectures are very disorganized... I'm completely disorganized.*

disorientated /,dɪs'ɔːrienteɪtɪd/. ADJ **Disorientated** means the same as **disoriented.**

disoriented (BR also **disorientated**) /,dɪs'ɔːrientɪd/. ADJ If you feel **disoriented**, you lose your sense of direction, or you feel generally lost and uncertain. *He is completely disoriented by what is going on.*

disown /dɪs'əʊn/ **disowns, disowning, disowned.** VERB If you **disown** someone or some-thing, you no longer have any connection with them. *His wealthy parents had disowned him.*

disparage /,dɪs'pærɪdʒ/ **disparages, disparaging, disparaged.** VERB If you **disparage** someone or something, you speak about them in a way which shows that you do not have a good opinion of them. *...Larkin's tendency to disparage literature.* ♦**disparagement** N-U *...their disparagement of this book.* ♦**disparaging** ADJ *A lot of very disparaging things have been said about Seattle.*

disparate /'dɪspərət/. ADJ **Disparate** things are clearly different from each other in quality or type; FORMAL. *Scientists are trying to pull together disparate ideas in astronomy.*

disparity /dɪs'pærɪti/ **disparities.** N-VAR A **disparity** between two or more things is a noticeable difference between them; FORMAL. *...disparities between poor and wealthy school districts.*

dispatch (BR also **despatch**) /dɪs'pætʃ/ **dispatches, dispatching, dispatched.** [1] VERB & N-U If you **dispatch** someone or something to a place, you send them there. You can also talk about the **dispatch** of people or things to a place. *The Italian government was preparing to dispatch 4,000 soldiers to search the island.* [2] N-C A **dispatch** is an official report sent to a person or organization by their representative in another place.

dispel /dɪs'pel/ **dispels, dispelling, dispelled.** VERB To **dispel** an idea or feeling means to stop people believing in it or feeling it. *The President is attempting to dispel the notion that he has neglected the economy.*

dispense /dɪs'pens/ **dispenses, dispensing, dispensed.** [1] VERB To **dispense** something means to give it to people; FORMAL. *...High Court circuit judges dispensing justice.* [2] VERB When a chemist **dispenses** medicine, he or she prepares it and gives it to the patient.

▶ **dispense with.** PHR-VERB If you **dispense with** something, you stop using it or get rid of it altogether. *The princess dispensed with her official bodyguards at the beginning of the year.*

dispenser /dɪs'pensə/ **dispensers.** N-C A **dispenser** is a machine or container from which you can get things. *...cash dispensers.*

disperse /dɪs'pɜːs/ **disperses, dispersing, dispersed.** [1] VERB When a group of people **disperses**, the group splits up and the people leave in different directions. *The crowd dispersed peacefully... Police eventually dispersed them with tear gas.* [2] VERB When things **disperse**, or when you **disperse** them, they spread over a wide area. *The leaflets were dispersed throughout the country.*

displace /dɪs'pleɪs/ **displaces, displacing, displaced.** [1] VERB If one thing **displaces** another, it forces the other thing out and occupies its position. *It might even displace the war news from the front page.* [2] VERB If someone **is displaced**, they are forced to move away from the area where they live. *...resettling refugees and displaced persons.* ♦**displacement** N-U *...the gradual displacement of the American Indian.*

display /dɪs'pleɪ/ **displays, displaying, displayed.** [1] VERB & N-U If you **display** something, or if you put it on **display**, you put it in a place where people can see it. *...war veterans proudly displaying their medals. ...the other artists whose work is on display.* [2] VERB & N-VAR If you **display** a quality or emotion, you behave in a way which shows that you have it. You can also talk about a **display** of particular quality or emotion. *It was unlike Gordon to display his feelings. ...his determined display of courage.* [3] N-C A **display** is something which is intended to attract people's attention, for example an event or attractive arrangement of different things. *...a permanent display of 300 of the artist's paintings. ...the firework display.*

displeasure /dɪsˈpleʒə/. N-U Someone's **displeasure** with someone or something is a feeling of annoyance towards that person or about that thing. *He has been very vocal in his displeasure over the results.*

disposable /dɪsˈpəʊzəbəl/. ADJ **Disposable** things are designed to be thrown away after use. *...disposable nappies.*

disposal /dɪsˈpəʊzəl/. [1] PHRASE If you have something **at** your **disposal**, you are able to use it whenever you want. If you are at someone's **disposal**, you are willing to help them in any way you can. *Do you have this information at your disposal?* [2] N-U The **disposal** of something is the act of getting rid of it. *...the permanent disposal of radioactive wastes.*

dispose /dɪsˈpəʊz/ **disposes, disposing, disposed.**
▸ **dispose of.** PHR-VERB If you **dispose of** something, you get rid of it, usually because you no longer want or need it. *Matthew told police he disposed of the murder weapon for Charles.*

disposed /dɪsˈpəʊzd/. [1] ADJ AFTER LINK-V If you are **disposed** to do something, you are willing to do it; FORMAL. *We passed one or two dwellings, but were not disposed to stop.* [2] ADJ You can use **disposed** when you are talking about someone's general attitude or opinion. *Every government is ill-disposed to the press.*

disposition /ˌdɪspəˈzɪʃən/ **dispositions.** N-C Your **disposition** is the way that you tend to behave or feel. *...people of a nervous disposition.*

disprove /dɪsˈpruːv/ **disproves, disproving, disproved.** VERB If you **disprove** an idea or belief, you show that it is not true.

dispute /dɪsˈpjuːt/ **disputes, disputing, disputed.** [1] N-VAR A **dispute** is a disagreement or quarrel between people. *...pay disputes with the government.* [2] VERB & PHRASE If you **dispute** a fact or opinion, you say that it is incorrect or untrue. If an issue is **in dispute**, people cannot agree about whether it is correct or true. *Nobody disputed that Davey was clever.* [3] VERB When people **dispute** something, they fight for control of it. *Fishermen from Bristol disputed fishing rights with the Danes.*

disqualify /dɪsˈkwɒlɪfaɪ/ **disqualifies, disqualifying, disqualified.** VERB When someone **is disqualified** from an event or an activity, they are officially stopped from taking part in it. *He was disqualified from driving for three years.* ♦**disqualification** /ˌdɪsˌkwɒlɪfɪˈkeɪʃən/ **disqualifications** N-VAR *...a four-year disqualification from athletics.*

disquiet /dɪsˈkwaɪət/. N-U **Disquiet** is a feeling of worry or anxiety; FORMAL. *There is growing disquiet about the cost of such policing.*

disregard /ˌdɪsrɪˈɡɑːd/ **disregards, disregarding, disregarded.** VERB & N-U If you **disregard** something, or if you show **disregard** for it, you ignore it or do not take account of it. *He disregarded the advice of his executives. ...a total disregard for the safety of the public.*

disrepute /ˌdɪsrɪˈpjuːt/. PHRASE If something is brought **into disrepute** or falls **into disrepute**, it loses its good reputation, because it is connected with activities that people do not approve of.

disrupt /dɪsˈrʌpt/ **disrupts, disrupting, disrupted.** VERB If someone or something **disrupts** an event or process, they cause problems that prevent it from continuing normally. *Anti-war protesters disrupted the debate.* ♦**disruption, disruptions** N-VAR *The strike is expected to cause delays and disruption to flights.*

disruptive /dɪsˈrʌptɪv/. ADJ If you say that someone is **disruptive**, you think they are preventing an activity or system from continuing normally. *He was a disruptive influence.*

dissatisfaction /ˌdɪˌsætɪsˈfækʃən/. N-U If you feel **dissatisfaction** with something, you are not satisfied with it. *Low pay is the main cause of job dissatisfaction among teachers.*

dissatisfied /ˌdɪˈsætɪsfaɪd/. ADJ If you are **dissatisfied** with something, you are not contented or pleased with it. *82% of voters are dissatisfied with the way their country is being governed.*

dissect /daɪˈsekt, dɪ-/ **dissects, dissecting, dissected.** VERB To **dissect** a dead body means to cut it up in order to examine it. ♦**dissection, dissections** N-VAR *Researchers need a growing supply of corpses for dissection.*

disseminate /dɪˈsemɪneɪt/ **disseminates, disseminating, disseminated.** VERB To **disseminate** information means to distribute it, so that it reaches many people; FORMAL. *It took years to disseminate information about Aids.* ♦**dissemination** N-U *...the dissemination of scientific ideas.*

dissent /dɪˈsent/ **dissents, dissenting, dissented.** VERB & N-U If you **dissent**, or if you express **dissent**, you express disagreement with a decision or established opinion; FORMAL. *One member Martha Seger dissented from the final vote. ...voices of dissent.* ♦**dissenting** ADJ *He suppressed dissenting views among his colleagues.* ♦**dissenter, dissenters** N-C *The Party does not tolerate dissenters in its ranks.*

dissertation /ˌdɪsəˈteɪʃən/ **dissertations.** N-C A **dissertation** is a long formal piece of writing, especially for a university degree.

dissident /ˈdɪsɪdənt/ **dissidents.** N-C **Dissidents** are people who criticize their repressive government. *...arrests of political dissidents.*

dissipate /ˈdɪsɪpeɪt/ **dissipates, dissipating, dissipated.** [1] VERB When something **dissipates**, or when you **dissipate** it, there is less of it or it becomes less strong, until it goes away completely. *The tension in the room had dissipated.* ♦**dissipation** N-U *...the dissipation of my child-rearing energies.* [2] VERB If someone **dis-**

sipates money, time, or effort, they waste it. *A wayward son dissipated the fortune.* ♦**dissipation** N-U *...the dissipation of remaining pensions assets.*

dissociate /dɪˈsəʊʃieɪt/ **dissociates, dissociating, dissociated.** VERB If you **dissociate** yourself **from** someone or something, you say that you are not connected with them. *It seems harder and harder for the president to dissociate himself from the scandals.*

dissolve /dɪˈzɒlv/ **dissolves, dissolving, dissolved.** [1] VERB If a substance **dissolves** in liquid, or if you **dissolve** a substance, it mixes with the liquid, becoming weaker until it finally disappears. *Heat gently until the sugar dissolves.* [2] VERB When something **is dissolved,** it is officially ended; FORMAL. *The marriage was dissolved in 1976.* ♦**dissolution** /ˌdɪsəˈluːʃən/ N-U *...the dissolution of parliament.*

dissuade /dɪˈsweɪd/ **dissuades, dissuading, dissuaded.** VERB If you **dissuade** someone from doing something, you persuade them not to do it; FORMAL. *He considered emigrating, but his family managed to dissuade him.*

distance /ˈdɪstəns/ **distances, distancing, distanced.** [1] N-VAR The **distance** between two places is the amount of space between them. *...the distance between the island and the nearby shore. ...within walking distance.* [2] PHRASE If you are **at a distance** from something, or if you remember it **from a distance,** you are thinking about something which happened a long time ago. *...now that I can look back on the whole tragedy from a distance of nearly forty years.* [3] N-U **Distance** is detachment and remoteness in the way that someone behaves, so that they do not seem friendly. *There were periods of sulking, and of pronounced distance.* [4] VERB If you **distance** yourself **from** someone or something, you become less involved with them. *The United States has distanced itself from the British plan.* ♦**distanced** ADJ AFTER LINK-V *He'd become too distanced from his fans.*

distant /ˈdɪstənt/ [1] ADJ **Distant** means far away; WRITTEN. *The mountains rolled away to a distant horizon.* ♦**distantly** ADV *Rose heard a buzzer sound distantly.* [2] ADJ An event or time that is **distant** is far away in the past or future. *Things will improve in the not too distant future.* [3] ADJ A **distant** relative is one that you are not closely related to. ♦**distantly** ADV *His father's distantly related to the Royal family.* [4] ADJ AFTER LINK-V If you describe someone as **distant,** you find them emotionally detached and unfriendly. [5] ADJ If you describe someone as **distant,** you mean that they are not paying attention because they are thinking about something else. *There was a distant look in her eyes.* ♦**distantly** ADV *'He's in the interview room,' she said distantly.*

distaste /ˌdɪsˈteɪst/. N-U If you feel **distaste** for someone or something, you dislike or disapprove of them. *Roger looked at her with distaste.*

distasteful /ˌdɪsˈteɪstfʊl/. ADJ If something is **distasteful** to you, you dislike or disapprove of it. *I find her gossip distasteful.*

distil (AM **distill**) /dɪsˈtɪl/ **distils, distilling, distilled.** VERB If a liquid such as whisky **is distilled,** it is heated until it evaporates and then cooled until it becomes liquid again. *...a gallon of distilled water.* ♦**distillation** N-U *The water is warm because of the distillation process.*

distinct /dɪˈstɪŋkt/. [1] ADJ If one thing is **distinct** from another, there is an important difference between them. *Engineering and technology are disciplines distinct from one another. ...oily fish, as distinct from fatty meat.* ♦**distinctly** ADV *...a banking industry with two distinctly different sectors.* [2] ADJ If something is **distinct,** you hear or see it clearly. *...a distinct smell of burning coal.* ♦**distinctly** ADV *I distinctly heard the loudspeaker.* [3] ADJ If an idea, thought, or intention is **distinct,** it is clear and definite. *There was a distinct change in her attitude.* ♦**distinctly** ADV *I distinctly remember wishing I had not got involved.*

distinction /dɪˈstɪŋkʃən/ **distinctions.** [1] N-C A **distinction** is a difference between similar things. If you **draw** or **make** a **distinction** between two things, you say that they are different. *...obvious distinctions between the two wine-making areas... He draws a distinction between art and culture.* [2] N-U **Distinction** is the quality of being excellent. *...furniture of distinction.*

distinctive /dɪˈstɪŋktɪv/. ADJ Something that is **distinctive** has special qualities that make it easily recognizable. *His voice was very distinctive.* ♦**distinctively** ADV *...the distinctively fragrant taste of elderflowers.*

distinguish /dɪˈstɪŋgwɪʃ/ **distinguishes, distinguishing, distinguished.** [1] VERB If you can **distinguish** one thing from another, you can see or understand the difference between them. *Could he distinguish right from wrong? ...distinguishing between areas of light and dark.* [2] VERB A feature or quality that **distinguishes** one thing from another causes the two things to be regarded as different. *There is something about music that distinguishes it from all other art forms.* [3] VERB If you can **distinguish** something, you can see, hear, or taste it although it is very difficult to detect; FORMAL. *He could distinguish voices.* [4] VERB If you **distinguish** yourself, you do something that makes you famous or important. *He distinguished himself as a long distance runner.*

distinguished /dɪˈstɪŋgwɪʃt/. ADJ A **distinguished** person is very successful, famous, or important. *...a distinguished academic family.*

distinguishing /dɪˈstɪŋgwɪʃɪŋ/. ADJ The **distinguishing** features of something are the features which make it different from other things of the same type. *One of the most distinguishing characteristics of the Algerians was religion.*

distort /dɪˈstɔːt/ **distorts, distorting, distorted.** [1] VERB If you **distort** a statement, fact, or idea, you report or represent it in an untrue way. *The media distorts reality.* ♦**distorted** ADJ *These figures give a distorted view.* ♦**distortion, distortions.** N-VAR *He later accused reporters of wilful distortion and bias.* [2] VERB If something you can see or hear **is distorted,** its appearance or sound is changed so that it seems strange. *A painter may exaggerate* *or distort shapes.* ♦**distorted** ADJ *...the slightly distorted image caused by the projector.* ♦**distortion** N-VAR *Audio signals could be transmitted along cables without distortion.*

distract /dɪ'strækt/ **distracts, distracting, distracted.** VERB If something **distracts** you, or if it **distracts** your attention, it stops you concentrating. *Playing video games sometimes distracts him from his homework.* ♦**distracting** ADJ *The yapping of the little dog was very distracting.*

distracted /dɪ'stræktɪd/. ADJ If you are **distracted**, you are very worried or are not concentrating. ♦**distractedly** ADV *He looked up distractedly. 'Be with you in a second'.*

distraction /dɪ'strækʃən/ **distractions.** [1] N-VAR A **distraction** is something that takes your attention away from what you are doing. *This is getting to be a distraction from what I really want to do.* [2] N-C A **distraction** is an activity that is intended to entertain people. *Their national distraction is going to the disco.*

distraught /dɪ'strɔːt/. ADJ If someone is **distraught**, they are extremely upset or worried. *Mr Barker's distraught parents were last night being comforted by relatives.*

distress /dɪ'stres/ **distresses, distressing, distressed.** [1] N-U **Distress** is extreme sorrow, suffering, or pain. *Jealousy causes distress and painful emotions.* [2] N-U **Distress** is the state of being in extreme danger and needing urgent help. *The ship might be in distress.* [3] VERB If someone or something **distresses** you, they cause you to be upset or worried. *The idea of Toni being in danger distresses him enormously.* ♦**distressed** ADJ *She was too exhausted and distressed to talk.* ♦**distressing** ADJ *...distressing news.* ♦**distressingly** ADV *Her face had grown distressingly old.*

distribute /dɪ'strɪbjuːt/ **distributes, distributing, distributed.** [1] VERB If you **distribute** things, you hand them or deliver them to a number of people. *Soldiers are working to distribute food and blankets.* ♦**distribution** N-U *...the distribution of leaflets and posters.* [2] VERB When a company **distributes** goods, it supplies them to the shops or businesses that sell them. ♦**distribution** N-U *...the production and distribution of goods and services.* ♦**distributor, distributors.** N-C *...Spain's largest distributor of petroleum products.* [3] VERB If you **distribute** things among the members of a group, you share them among those members. *Distribute chores evenly among all family members.*

distribution /ˌdɪstrɪ'bjuːʃən/ **distributions.** N-VAR The **distribution** of something is how much of it there is in each place or at each time. *...a more equitable distribution of wealth.*

district /'dɪstrɪkt/ **districts.** [1] N-C A **district** is an area of a town or country. *I drove around the business district.* [2] N-C A **district** is an area of a town or country which has been given official boundaries for the purpose of administration. *...Glasgow District Council.*

,district at'torney, district attorneys. N-C In the United States, a **District Attorney** is a lawyer who works as the State prosecutor in a district. The abbreviation **D.A.** is also used.

distrust /dɪs'trʌst/ **distrusts, distrusting, distrusted.** VERB & N-U If you **distrust** someone or something, or if you feel **distrust** for them, you think that they are not honest, reliable, or safe. *I don't have any particular reason to distrust them. ...a profound distrust of all political authority.*

disturb /dɪ'stɜːb/ **disturbs, disturbing, disturbed.** [1] VERB If you **disturb** someone, you interrupt what they are doing and cause them inconvenience. *She slept in a separate room in order not to disturb him.* [2] VERB If something **disturbs** you, it makes you feel upset or worried. *...dreams so vivid that they disturb me for days.* [3] VERB If something **is disturbed**, its position or shape is changed. *He'd placed his notes in the brown envelope. They hadn't been disturbed.*

disturbance /dɪ'stɜːbəns/ **disturbances.** [1] N-C A **disturbance** is an incident in which people behave violently in public. *During the disturbance which followed, three Englishmen were hurt.* [2] N-U **Disturbance** means upsetting or disrupting something which was previously in a calm and orderly state. *The old people's home would cause less disturbance to local residents than a school.*

disturbed /dɪ'stɜːbd/. ADJ Someone who is **disturbed** is extremely worried, unhappy, or mentally ill. *...severely emotionally disturbed children.*

disturbing /dɪ'stɜːbɪŋ/. ADJ Something that is **disturbing** makes you feel upset or worried. *There was something about him she found disturbing.* ♦**disturbingly** ADV *...the disturbingly high frequency of racial attacks.*

disused /ˌdɪs'juːzd/. ADJ A **disused** place or building is no longer used. *...a disused airfield.*

ditch /dɪtʃ/ **ditches, ditching, ditched.** [1] N-C A **ditch** is a long narrow channel cut into the ground at the side of a road or field. [2] VERB If you **ditch** something, you get rid of it; INFORMAL. *I decided to ditch the sofa bed.*

dither /'dɪðə/ **dithers, dithering, dithered.** VERB If someone **dithers**, they hesitate because they are unable to make a quick decision about something. *We're still dithering over whether to marry.*

dive /daɪv/ **dives, diving, dived** (AM also **dove**). [1] VERB & N-C If you **dive**, or if you do a **dive**, you jump head-first into water with your arms straight above your head. *She was standing by a pool, about to dive in. ...a dive of 80 feet from the Chasm Bridge.* [2] VERB & N-C If you **dive**, or if you do a **dive**, you go under the surface of the sea or a lake, using special breathing equipment. ♦**diver, divers** N-C *Police divers have recovered the body of a sixteen year old boy.* ♦**diving** N-U *...the most popular spots to go diving.* [3] VERB When birds and animals **dive**, they go quickly downwards, head-first, through the air or water. *The shark dived down and swam under the boat.* [4] VERB & N-C If you **dive**, or if you make a **dive**, in a particular direction, you jump or rush in that direction. *They dived into a taxi... He made a sudden dive for Uncle Jim's legs.*

diverge /daɪ'vɜːdʒ, AM dɪ-/ **diverges, diverging, diverged.** [1] VERB When things **diverge**, they are different, or become different. *His interests increasingly diverged from those of his colleagues.* [2] VERB When roads or paths **diverge**, they begin leading in different directions. *At Orte, the railway lines for Florence and Ancona diverge.*

divergent /daɪˈvɜːdʒənt, AM dɪ-/. ADJ Things that are **divergent** are different from each other. *Similar customs were known in widely divergent cultures.* ♦**divergence, divergences.** N-VAR *There's a substantial divergence of opinion within the party.*

diverse /daɪˈvɜːs, AM dɪ-/. ADJ If a group or range is **diverse**, it is made up of a wide variety of things. *...shops selling a diverse range of gifts.*

diversify /daɪˈvɜːsɪfaɪ, AM dɪ-/ **diversifies, diversifying, diversified.** VERB When an organization or person **diversifies** into other things, or when they **diversify** their activities, they increase the variety of things that they do or make. *Manufacturers have been encouraged to diversify.* ♦**diversification** /daɪˌvɜːsɪfɪˈkeɪʃən, AM dɪ-/ **diversifications** N-VAR *...diversification of agriculture.*

diversion /daɪˈvɜːʃən, AM dɪˈvɜːrʒən/ **diversions.** [1] N-C A **diversion** is an action or event that attracts your attention away from what you are doing. *...armed robbers who escaped after throwing smoke bombs to create a diversion.* ♦**diversionary** ADJ *...a diversionary tactic, taking attention away from what the case is all about.* [2] N-C A **diversion** is a special route arranged for traffic when the normal route cannot be used; BRITISH. ● See also **divert**.

diversity /daɪˈvɜːsɪti, AM dɪ-/ **diversities.** [1] N-VAR The **diversity** of something is the fact that it contains many very different elements. *...to introduce more choice and diversity into the education system.* [2] N-SING A **diversity of** things is a range of things which are very different from each other. *...how to grow a diversity of vegetables .*

divert /daɪˈvɜːt, AM dɪ-/ **diverts, diverting, diverted.** [1] VERB To **divert** people or vehicles means to change their course. *Police are diverting traffic away from the Square.* [2] VERB To **divert** money or resources means to cause them to be used for a different purpose. *The government is trying to divert more public funds from west to east.* ♦**diversion** N-U *...the illegal diversion of profits from secret arms sales.* [3] VERB If someone **diverts** your attention from something important or serious, they stop you thinking about it by making you think about something else. *They want to divert the attention of the people from the real issues.*

divide /dɪˈvaɪd/ **divides, dividing, divided.** [1] VERB & PHR-VERB To **divide** something or to **divide** it **up**, means to split it up and separate it into two or more parts. *Divide the pastry in half... The idea is to divide up the country into four sectors... Paul divides most of his spare time between the study and his bedroom.* [2] VERB If you **divide** a larger number by a smaller number, you calculate how many times the smaller number can go exactly into the larger number. *Measure the floor area of the greenhouse and divide it by six.* [3] VERB If a border or line **divides** two areas, it keeps them

separate from each other. *...the long frontier dividing Mexico from the United States.* [4] VERB If something **divides** people, it causes strong disagreement between them. *...the enormous differences that still divide the two sides.* ♦**divided** ADJ *The democrats are divided over whether to admit him into their group.* [5] N-C A **divide** is a significant difference between two groups. *...a Hindu-Muslim divide in India.*
▶ **divide up.** See **divide** 1.

dividend /ˈdɪvɪdend/ **dividends.** [1] N-C A **dividend** is the part of a company's profits which is paid to people who have shares in the company. [2] PHRASE If something **pays dividends**, it brings advantages at a later date. *Steps taken now to maximise your health will pay dividends later on.*

divine /dɪˈvaɪn/. ADJ You use **divine** to describe something that is provided by or relates to a god or goddess. *...a divine punishment.* ♦**divinely** ADV *The law was divinely ordained.* ♦**divinity** /dɪˈvɪnɪti/ N-U *...the divinity of Christ's word.*

diving /ˈdaɪvɪŋ/. See **dive**.

division /dɪˈvɪʒən/ **divisions.** [1] N-U The **division** of something is the act of separating it into two or more different parts. *...the unification of Germany, after its division into two states. ...the current division of labor between workers and management.* [2] N-C A **division** is a significant distinction or difference of opinion between two groups. *...the division between the prosperous west and the impoverished east.* [3] N-U **Division** is the mathematical process of dividing one number by another. [4] N-C A **division** is a department in a large organization. *...the bank's Latin American division.* ♦**divisional** ADJ BEFORE N *...the divisional headquarters.*

divisive /dɪˈvaɪsɪv/. ADJ Something that is **divisive** causes hostility between people; FORMAL. *Abortion has always been a divisive issue.*

divorce /dɪˈvɔːs/ **divorces, divorcing, divorced.** [1] VERB & N-VAR When someone **divorces** their husband or wife, or obtains a **divorce** from them, their marriage is legally ended. *He and Lillian had got divorced... Numerous marriages now end in divorce.* ♦**divorced** ADJ *Princess Margaret is divorced from Lord Snowdon.* [2] VERB If one thing **is divorced from** another, they become separate from each other; FORMAL. *You can't divorce finance from manufacturing.*

divulge /daɪˈvʌldʒ, AM dɪ-/ **divulges, divulging, divulged.** VERB If you **divulge** a piece of information, you tell someone about it; FORMAL. *I do not want to divulge where the village is.*

DIY /ˌdiː aɪ ˈwaɪ/. N-U **DIY** is the activity of making or repairing things in your home. **DIY** is an abbreviation for 'do-it-yourself'.

dizzy /ˈdɪzi/. ADJ If you feel **dizzy**, you feel that you are losing your balance and are about to fall. *He kept getting dizzy spells.* ♦**dizziness** N-U *A wave of dizziness swept over her.*

DJ (or **d j**) /ˈdiː ˌdʒeɪ/ **DJs.** N-C A **DJ** is someone who plays and introduces pop records on the radio or at a disco.

DNA /ˌdiː en ˈeɪ/. N-U **DNA** is an acid that is contained in the cells of living things. It determines the particular structure and functions of every cell. **DNA** is an abbreviation for 'deoxyribonucleic acid'.

do /də, STRONG duː/ **does, doing, did, done.**
Two of the major uses of **do** is in forming negatives and questions. [1] VERB You use **do** to say that someone performs an action, activity, or task. *I was trying to do some work.* [2] VERB To **do** something about a problem means to try to solve it. *Though he didn't like it there wasn't much he could do about it.* [3] VERB You use **do** to say that something has a particular result or effect. *A few bombs can do a lot of damage... The publicity did her career no harm.* [4] VERB If you ask someone what they **do**, you are asking what their job is. [5] VERB If someone **does** well or badly, they are successful or unsuccessful. *Connie did well at school.* [6] VERB If you **do** a subject, you study it at school or college. *I'd like to do maths at university.* [7] VERB You use **do** when referring to the speed that something achieves or can achieve. *They were doing 70 miles an hour.* [8] VERB If you say that something will **do**, you mean that it is satisfactory. *Give them a prize. Anything will do.* [9] N-C A **do** is a party, dinner party, or other social event; BRITISH, INFORMAL. *A friend of his is having a do in Stoke... They always have all-night dos there.* [10] See also **done.**

PHRASES • If you say that you **could do with** something, you mean that you need it or would benefit from it. *I could do with a cup of tea.* • If you ask **what** someone **is doing** in a particular place, you are expressing surprise that they are there. *What was he doing in Hyde Park at that time of the morning?* • What something **has to do with** or **is to do with** is what it is connected or concerned with. *They were shouting at each other. It was something to do with money.*

▶ **do away with.** PHR-VERB To **do away with** something means to get rid of it. *The long-range goal must be to do away with nuclear weapons.*

▶ **do out of.** PHR-VERB If you **do** someone **out of** something, you unfairly cause them not to have it; INFORMAL. *The others have done him out of his share.*

▶ **do up.** [1] PHR-VERB If you **do** something **up**, you fasten it. *Mari did up the buttons... Do your coat up.* [2] PHR-VERB To **do up** an old building means to repair and decorate it; FORMAL. *Nicholas has bought a barn in Provence and is spending August doing it up.*

▶ **do without.** PHR-VERB If you **do without** something, you manage or survive in spite of not having it. *We can't do without the help of your organisation.*

dock /dɒk/ **docks, docking, docked.** [1] N-C A **dock** is an enclosed area of water where ships are loaded, unloaded, or repaired. [2] VERB When a ship **docks** or is **docked**, it is brought into a dock. *The vessel docked at Liverpool.* [3] VERB When one spacecraft **docks** or is **docked** with another, they join together in space. [4] N-SING In a law court, the **dock** is the place where the person accused of a crime sits; BRITISH. [5] VERB If you **dock** something such as someone's salary, you take some of it away as

a punishment. *Soccer's governing body has recommended docking two points from the league champions.*

doctor /'dɒktə/ **doctors, doctoring, doctored.** [1] N-C & N-TITLE & N-VOC A **doctor** is someone qualified in medicine who treats people who are ill. *Don't hesitate to call the doctor if you are at all uneasy... Doctor Paige will be here right after lunch.* [2] N-SING **The doctor's** is used to refer to the surgery or clinic where a doctor works. *I have an appointment at the doctor's.* [3] N-C & N-TITLE **Doctor** is the title given to someone who has been awarded the highest academic degree by a university. *...a doctor of philosophy.* [4] VERB To **doctor** something means to deliberately change it in order to deceive people. *They doctored the prints, deepening the lines to make her look as awful as possible.*

doctorate /'dɒktərət/ **doctorates.** N-C A **doctorate** is the highest degree awarded by a university.

doctrine /'dɒktrɪn/ **doctrines.** N-VAR A **doctrine** is a set of principles or beliefs. *...orthodox Christian doctrine.* ♦**doctrinal** /dɒk'traɪnəl, AM 'dɑːktrɪnəl/ ADJ *...the pursuit of doctrinal goals.*

document, documents, documenting, documented. [1] N-C /'dɒkjəmənt/ A **document** is an official piece of paper with writing on it. *...travel documents.* [2] VERB /'dɒkjəment/ If you **document** something, you make a detailed record of it on film, tape, or paper. *...a book documenting his prison experiences.*

documentary /,dɒkjə'mentri/ **documentaries.** [1] N-C A **documentary** is a radio or television programme, or a film which provides factual information about a particular subject. *...a TV documentary on homelessness.* [2] ADJ BEFORE N **Documentary** evidence consists of things that are written down.

documentation /,dɒkjəmən'teɪʃən/ N-U **Documentation** consists of documents which provide a record of something. *I had full documentation of our additional expenses.*

dodge /dɒdʒ/ **dodges, dodging, dodged.** [1] VERB If you **dodge** somewhere, you move there suddenly to avoid being hit, caught, or seen. *We dodged behind a pillar out of sight of the tourists.* [2] VERB If you **dodge** a moving object, you avoid it by quickly moving aside. *He desperately dodged a speeding car trying to run him down.* [3] VERB If you **dodge** something such as a problem, you avoid thinking about it or dealing with it. *...dodging military service by feigning illness.*

dodgy /'dɒdʒi/ **dodgier, dodgiest.** [1] ADJ If you describe someone or something as **dodgy**, you disapprove of them because they seem rather dishonest and unreliable. [2] ADJ If you say that something is **dodgy**, you mean that it seems rather risky or unreliable. *...some pretty dodgy airport food.*

does /dəz, STRONG dʌz/. **Does** is the third person singular of the present tense of **do**.

doesn't /'dʌzənt/. **Doesn't** is the usual spoken form of 'does not'.

dog 178

dog /dɒg, AM dɔːg/ **dogs, dogging, dogged.**
[1] N-C A **dog** is an animal that is often kept as a pet or used to guard or hunt things. [2] VERB If problems or injuries **dog** you, they keep affecting you. *His retirement was dogged by illnesses.*

dogged /'dɒgɪd, AM 'dɔːg-/. ADJ BEFORE N If you describe someone's actions as **dogged**, you mean that they are determined to continue with something, however difficult it becomes. *...one man's dogged determination to do something everyone else considered eccentric.*
♦**doggedness** N-U *Most of my accomplishments came as the result of sheer doggedness.*
♦**doggedly** ADV *She would fight doggedly for her rights.*

dogma /'dɒgmə, AM 'dɔːg-/ **dogmas.** N-VAR If you refer to a belief or a system of beliefs as a **dogma**, you are criticizing it for expecting people to accept that it is true without questioning it. *The unions accuse the government of political dogma.*

dogmatic /dɒg'mætɪk, AM dɔːg-/. ADJ If you say that someone is **dogmatic**, you are criticizing them for following rules or principles rigidly without paying any attention to other factors. *...a dogmatic approach to solving political issues.* ♦**dogmatically** ADV *He would not dogmatically oppose government intervention.*
♦**dogmatism** /'dɒgmətɪzəm, AM 'dɔːg-/ N-U *We cannot allow dogmatism to stand in the way of progress.*

do-it-your'self. N-U Do-it-yourself is the activity of making or repairing things in your home yourself, rather than employing other people.

doldrums /'dɒldrəmz/. PHRASE If an area of activity is **in the doldrums**, nothing new or exciting is happening.

doll /dɒl/ **dolls.** N-C A **doll** is a child's toy which looks like a small person or baby.

dollar /'dɒlə/ **dollars.** N-C The **dollar** is a unit of money in the USA, Canada, and some other countries. It is represented by the symbol $.

dolphin /'dɒlfɪn/ **dolphins.** N-C A **dolphin** is a mammal with fins and a pointed nose which lives in the sea.

domain /dəʊ'meɪn/ **domains.** [1] N-C A **domain** is a particular area of activity or interest; FORMAL. *...the great experimenters in the domain of art.* [2] N-C Someone's **domain** is the area where they have control or influence; FORMAL. *The kitchen is by no means his wife's domain.*

dome /dəʊm/ **domes.** N-C A **dome** is a round roof. *...the dome of St Paul's cathedral.*

domestic /də'mestɪk/. [1] ADJ **Domestic** political activities and situations happen or exist within one particular country. *...a mixture of domestic and foreign news. ...over 100 domestic flights a day to 15 UK destinations.* [2] ADJ BEFORE N **Domestic** means relating to or concerned with the home and family. *...domestic violence between husband and wife. ...domestic appliances.* [3] ADJ BEFORE N **Domestic** animals are not wild, and are kept as pets or on farms.

dominant /'dɒmɪnənt/. ADJ Someone or something that is **dominant** is more powerful or noticeable than other people or things. *She was a dominant figure in the French film industry.*
♦**dominance** N-U *...the dominance of the scientific method in the modern world.*

dominate /'dɒmɪneɪt/ **dominates, dominating, dominated.** [1] VERB To **dominate** a situation means to be the most powerful or important person or thing in it. *The book is expected to dominate the best-seller lists. ...countries where life is dominated by war.*
♦**domination** N-U *...the domination of the market by a small number of organizations.* [2] VERB If one person **dominates** another, they have power over them. *Women are no longer dominated by the men in their relationships.*
♦**dominating** ADJ *He had a very dominating personality.* ♦**domination** N-U *...five centuries of domination by the Romans.*

domino /'dɒmɪnəʊ/ **dominoes.** N-VAR **Dominoes** is a game played using small rectangular blocks, called **dominoes**, which are marked with two groups of spots on one side.

donate /dəʊ'neɪt/ **donates, donating, donated.** [1] VERB If you **donate** something to a charity or other organization, you give it to them. *Others donated second-hand clothes.*
♦**donation, donations** N-U *...the donation of his collection to the art gallery.* [2] VERB If you **donate** your blood or a part of your body, you allow doctors to use it to help somebody who is ill. ♦**donation** N-U *...kidney donation.*

done /dʌn/. [1] **Done** is the past participle of **do**. [2] ADJ AFTER LINK-V A task that is **done** has been completed. *The damage was done by the time Giggs came... As soon as the cake is done, remove it from the oven.*

donkey /'dɒŋki/ **donkeys.** N-C A **donkey** is an animal like a small horse with long ears.

donor /'dəʊnə/ **donors.** [1] N-C A **donor** is someone who gives a part of their body or some of their blood to be used by doctors to help a person who is ill. [2] N-C A **donor** is someone who gives something such as money to a charity or other organization.

don't /dəʊnt/. **Don't** is the usual spoken form of **do not**.

donut /'dəʊnʌt/ **donuts.** See **doughnut**.

doom /duːm/. N-U **Doom** is a terrible state or event in the future which you cannot prevent. *I awoke with a terrible sense of doom and fear.*

doomed /duːmd/. [1] ADJ Someone or something that is **doomed** is certain to fail. *...a doomed attempt to rescue the children.* [2] ADJ If someone is **doomed** to an unpleasant fate, they are certain to suffer it. *If he lived, he would be doomed to spend the rest of his life in misery.*

door /dɔː/ **doors.** [1] N-C A **door** is a swinging or sliding piece of wood, glass, or metal, which is used to open and close the entrance to a building, room, cupboard, or vehicle. *I was knocking at the front door; there was no answer.* [2] N-C A **door** is the space in a wall when a door is open. *She looked through the door.*

PHRASES ● When you **answer the door**, you go and open the door because a visitor has knocked on it or rung the bell. ● If someone goes **from door to door** or goes **door to door**, they go along a street calling at each house in turn, for example selling something. ● When you are **out of doors**, you are not inside a building, but in the open air. *The weather was fine enough for working out of doors.* • See also **next door.**

doorstep /ˈdɔːstep/ **doorsteps.** [1] N-C A **doorstep** is a step on the outside of a building, in front of a door. [2] PHRASE If a place is **on your doorstep**, it is very near to where you live. *...a giant oil refinery right on their doorstep.*

doorway /ˈdɔːweɪ/ **doorways.** N-C A **doorway** is the space in a wall where a door opens and closes. *He stood in the doorway, smiling.*

dope /dəʊp/ **dopes, doping, doped.** [1] N-U **Dope** is an illegal drug, especially cannabis; INFORMAL. [2] VERB If someone **dopes** a person or animal, they force them or trick them into taking drugs.

dormant /ˈdɔːmənt/. ADJ Something that is **dormant** has not been active or used for a long time, but is capable of becoming active. *...the long dormant volcano... The buds will remain dormant until spring.*

dormitory /ˈdɔːmɪtri, AM -tɔːri/ **dormitories.** N-C A **dormitory** is a large bedroom where several people sleep, for example in a boarding school.

dosage /ˈdəʊsɪdʒ/ **dosages.** N-C The **dosage** of a medicine or drug is the amount that should be taken. *...in order to inject the correct dosage of insulin.*

dose /dəʊs/ **doses, dosing, dosed.** [1] N-C A **dose** of a medicine or drug is a measured amount of it. *One dose of penicillin can wipe out the infection.* [2] VERB To **dose** someone means to give them a medicine or drug. *...the machine that was dosing her with painkillers.*

dossier /ˈdɒsieɪ, -ɪə/ **dossiers.** N-C A **dossier** is a collection of papers containing information on a particular subject. *The government kept dossiers on thousands of its citizens.*

dot /dɒt/ **dots.** N-C A **dot** is a very small round mark. *...a black dot in the middle of the circle.*

dote /dəʊt/ **dotes, doting, doted.** VERB If you **dote** on someone, you love them very much and ignore their faults. *He dotes on his nine-year-old son.* ♦ **doting** ADJ *...his doting parents.*

dotted /ˈdɒtɪd/. [1] ADJ **Dotted** lines are made of a row of dots. *Cut along the dotted line.* [2] ADJ AFTER LINK-V If an area **is dotted with** things, it has many of those things scattered over its surface. *The maps were dotted with the names of small towns... Many pieces of sculpture are dotted around the house.*

double /ˈdʌbl/ **doubles, doubling, doubled.** [1] ADJ BEFORE N You use **double** to describe a pair of similar things. *...a pair of double doors... Ring four two, double two, double two if you'd like to speak to our financial adviser. ...an extremely nasty double murder.* [2] ADJ You use **double** to describe something which is twice the normal size or twice the normal capacity. *...a large double garage... Allow the loaves to rise until just about double in size.* [3] ADJ & N-C A **double** room, or a **double**, is a room that is intended to be used by two people. *The Great Western Hotel is ideal, costing around £40 a night for a double.* [4] VERB If something **doubles**, or if you **double** it, it becomes twice as large. *The program will double the amount of money available.* [5] VERB If a

person or thing **doubles as** someone or something else, they have a second job or purpose as well as their main one. *...drug dealers who double as police informers.* [6] N-U **Doubles** is a game of tennis or badminton in which two people play against two other people. [7] PHRASE If you **bend double**, you bend right over. If you **are bent double**, you are bending right over. [8] **in double figures:** see **figure.**

▶ **double up** or **double over.** PHR-VERB If you **double up**, or if you **double over**, you bend your body quickly or violently. *She doubled up with laughter... I was doubled over in agony.*

double bass /ˌdʌbl ˈbeɪs/ **double basses.** N-VAR A **double bass** is the largest instrument in the violin family. You play it standing up.

double-glaze, double-glazes, double-glazing, double-glazed. VERB If someone **double-glazes** a house or its windows, they fit the windows with a second layer of glass which keeps the inside of the house warmer and quieter. ♦ **double-glazing** N-U *Doreen had double glazing put into their bungalow.*

doubly /ˈdʌbli/. [1] ADV You use **doubly** to say that a situation has two aspects or features. *She now felt doubly guilty; she had embarrassed Franklin and she had cost her partner money.* [2] ADV You use **doubly** to say that something happens or is true to a greater degree than usual. *Secretly he was afraid; doubly so.*

doubt /daʊt/ **doubts, doubting, doubted.** [1] N-VAR If you feel **doubt** or **doubts** about something, you feel uncertain about it. *This raises doubts about the point of advertising... There can be little doubt that you can try too hard.* [2] VERB If you **doubt** something, or if you **doubt** whether something is true or possible, you believe that it is probably not true, genuine, or possible. *No one doubted his ability... He doubted if he would learn anything new.* [3] VERB If you **doubt** someone, or if you **doubt** their word, you think they might not be telling the truth. *Don't think I'm doubting you.*

PHRASES • If you are **in doubt** about something, or if it is **in doubt**, you are uncertain about it. *He is in no doubt as to what is needed... The outcome was still in doubt.* • If something is **beyond doubt**, or if it is **beyond reasonable doubt**, you are certain that it is true. *She knew no one beyond doubt that her husband loved her.* • You use **no doubt** to emphasize that something seems very likely to you. *No doubt we will meet again.* • You use **without doubt** or **without a doubt** to emphasize that something is true. *He is, without doubt, the best player in the world.* • to **give** someone **the benefit of the doubt:** see **benefit.**

doubtful /ˈdaʊtful/. [1] ADJ Something that is **doubtful** seems unlikely or uncertain. *It is doubtful whether he will appear again.* [2] ADJ If you are **doubtful** about something, you are uncertain about it. *I was still very doubtful about the chances for success.* ♦ **doubtfully** ADV *Keeton shook his head doubtfully.*

doubtless /ˈdaʊtləs/. ADV If you say that something is **doubtless** the case, you mean that you think it is probably or almost certainly the case. *They will doubtless get their land back.*

dough /dəʊ/. N-U **Dough** is a mixture of flour and water, and sometimes also sugar and fat, which is cooked to make bread, pastry, and biscuits.

doughnut (or **donut**) /ˈdəʊnʌt/ **doughnuts**. N-C A **doughnut** is a lump or ring of sweet dough cooked in hot fat.

dour /dʊə, daʊə/. ADJ Someone who is **dour** has a severe and unfriendly manner.

douse (or **dowse**) /daʊs/ **douses, dousing, doused.** ① VERB If you **douse** a fire, you stop it burning by pouring a lot of water over it. ② VERB If you **douse** someone or something with a liquid, you throw a lot of that liquid over them. *Douse the pasta in olive oil.*

dove, doves. ① N-C /dʌv/ A **dove** is a bird that looks like a pigeon. ② /dəʊv/ **Dove** is a past tense of **dive**; AMERICAN.

down 1 preposition and adverb uses

down /daʊn/. ① PREP & ADV **Down** means towards the ground or a lower level, or in a lower place. *A man came down the stairs. ...a ledge 40ft down the rock face... She was still looking down at her papers.* ② ADV If you put something **down**, you put it onto a surface. *Danny put down his glass.* ③ PREP If you go **down** a road or river, you go along it. *...a few miles down the road at Burnham.* ④ ADV **Down** is often used to mean in the south or towards the south. *I went down to L.A. all the way from Seattle.* ⑤ ADV If the amount or level of something goes **down**, it decreases. *My weight went down to seventy pounds.* ⑥ PREP If someone or something is **down for** something, it has been arranged that they will do it or it will happen to them. *Mark had told me that he was down for an interview.* ⑦ **up and down**: see **up**. ● **ups and downs**: see **up**.

down 2 adjective uses

down /daʊn/. ① ADJ AFTER LINK-V If you are feeling **down**, you are feeling unhappy or depressed; INFORMAL. ② ADJ AFTER LINK-V If something is **down** on paper, it has been written on the paper. *That date wasn't down on our news sheet.* ③ ADJ AFTER LINK-V If a piece of equipment, especially a computer system, is **down**, it is temporarily not working because of a fault.

down 3 noun use

down /daʊn/. N-U **Down** consists of the small soft feathers on young birds.

downfall /ˈdaʊnfɔːl/. ① N-U The **downfall** of a successful or powerful person or institution is their failure. *His lack of experience had led to his downfall.* ② N-U Something that is someone's **downfall** is the thing that causes them to fail. *His honesty had been his downfall.*

downgrade /ˌdaʊnˈgrɪd/ **downgrades, downgrading, downgraded.** VERB If someone or something is **downgraded**, their situation is changed to a lower level of importance or value. *The boy's condition has been downgraded from critical to serious... I was downgraded to a clerical job.*

downhill /ˌdaʊnˈhɪl/. ① ADV & ADJ BEFORE N If someone or something is moving **downhill**, they are moving down a slope. *He headed*

downhill *towards the river. ...downhill ski runs.* ② ADV You can say that something is going **downhill** when it is becoming worse.

'down payment, down payments. N-C If you make a **down payment** on something, you pay a percentage of the total cost when you buy it. You pay the remaining amount later.

downpour /ˈdaʊnpɔː/ **downpours.** N-C A **downpour** is a heavy fall of rain.

downright /ˈdaʊnraɪt/. ADV & ADJ BEFORE N You use **downright** to emphasize unpleasant or bad qualities or behaviour. *...ideas that would have been downright dangerous. ...suspicion and downright hostility.*

downside /ˈdaʊnsaɪd/. N-SING The **downside** of a situation is the aspect of it which is less positive, pleasant, or useful than its other aspects. *The downside of this approach is a lack of clear leadership.*

downstairs /ˌdaʊnˈsteəz/. ① ADV If you go **downstairs** in a building, you go down a staircase towards the ground floor. ② ADV & ADJ BEFORE N If something or someone is **downstairs**, they are on the ground floor or on a lower floor than you. *...the flat downstairs. ...the downstairs rooms.*

downstream /ˌdaʊnˈstriːm/. ADV & ADJ BEFORE N **Downstream** means towards the mouth of a river. *We had drifted downstream. ...Baghdad and other downstream cities.*

down-to-'earth. ADJ Someone who is **down-to-earth** is concerned with practical things, rather than with theories; used showing approval.

downtown /ˈdaʊntaʊn/. ADV & ADJ BEFORE N **Downtown** means in or towards the centre of a city. *By day he worked downtown. ...downtown Chicago.*

downturn /ˈdaʊntɜːn/ **downturns.** N-C If there is a **downturn** in the economy, it becomes worse or less successful.

downwards /ˈdaʊnwədz/. In usual British English, **downwards** is an adverb and **downward** is an adjective. In formal British English and in American English, **downward** is both an adjective and an adverb. ① ADV & ADJ If you move or look **downwards**, you move or look towards the ground or a lower level. *Benedict pointed downwards. ...a firm downward movement of the hands.* ② ADV & ADJ If an amount or rate moves **downwards**, it decreases. *...the downward trend in home ownership.*

dowse /daʊs/. See **douse**.

doze /dəʊz/ **dozes, dozing, dozed.** VERB & N-SING When you **doze**, or when you have **a doze**, you sleep lightly or for a short period. ▶ **doze off.** PHR-VERB If you **doze off**, you fall into a light sleep. *Salter dozed off for a few moments.*

dozen /ˈdʌzən/ **dozens.** ① NUM A **dozen** means twelve. *...two dozen eggs.* ② QUANT If you refer to **dozens of** things or people, you are emphasizing that there are many of them. *...dozens of homes.*

Dr, Drs. **Dr** is a written abbreviation for **Doctor**.

drab /dræb/. ADJ Something that is **drab** is dull and not attractive or exciting. ◆ **drabness** N-U *...the dusty drabness of nearby villages.*

draconian /drə'kəʊniən/. ADJ **Draconian** laws or measures are extremely harsh; FORMAL.

draft /drɑːft, dræft/ **drafts, drafting, drafted.**
[1] VERB & N-C When you **draft** a piece of writing, you write the first version of it, called a **draft.** *He drafted a standard letter to the editors.* [2] VERB If you **are drafted,** you are ordered to serve in the armed forces. [3] VERB If people **are drafted** into a place, they are moved there to do a particular job. *Extra police officers had to be drafted in.* [4] See also **draught.**

drag /dræg/ **drags, dragging, dragged.**
[1] VERB If you **drag** something or someone somewhere, you pull them there with difficulty. *He got up and dragged his chair towards the table... He drags his leg, and he can hardly lift his arm.* [2] VERB If you **drag** someone somewhere, you make them go there, although they may be unwilling. *...when you can drag him away from his work... I find it really hard to drag myself out and exercise regularly.* [3] VERB If a period of time or an event **drags,** it is very boring and seems to last a long time. *The minutes dragged past.* [4] VERB If the police **drag** a river or lake, they pull nets or hooks across the bottom of it in order to look for something. [PHRASES] ● If you **drag your feet,** or if you **drag your heels,** you delay doing something or do it very slowly because you do not want to do it. ● If a man is **in drag,** he is wearing women's clothes.

▶ **drag out.** [1] PHR-VERB If you **drag** something **out,** you make it last for longer than is necessary. *...a company that was willing to drag out the proceedings for years.* [2] PHR-VERB If you **drag** something **out** of someone, you persuade them to tell you something that they do not want to tell you.

dragon /'drægən/ **dragons.** N-C In stories and legends, a **dragon** is an animal like a big lizard. It has wings and claws, and breathes out fire.

dragonfly /'drægənflaɪ/ **dragonflies.** N-C A **dragonfly** is a brightly coloured insect with a long thin body and two sets of wings.

drain /dreɪn/ **drains, draining, drained.**
[1] VERB If you **drain** a liquid from a place or object, you remove the liquid by causing it to flow somewhere else. If a liquid **drains** somewhere, it flows there. *Miners built the tunnel to drain water out of the mines. ...springs and rivers that drain into lakes.* [2] N-C A **drain** is a pipe that carries water or sewage away from a place, or an opening in a surface that leads to the pipe. [3] VERB If you **drain** a place or object, you remove the liquid that has been in it or surrounding it. *Drain the pasta well... The soil drains freely.* [4] VERB If something **drains** you, it exhausts you physically and emotionally. ◆**drained** ADJ *She sighed and collapsed, completely drained.* ◆**draining** ADJ *I've been through a very draining, demanding time.* [5] N-SING If something or someone is a **drain** on resources, they use them up. *Citizens who are a drain on public resources.* [6] PHRASE If you say that something is going **down the drain,** you mean that it is being destroyed or wasted; INFORMAL.

drainage /'dreɪnɪdʒ/. N-U **Drainage** is the sys-

tem or process by which water or other liquids are drained from a place.

drama /'drɑːmə/ **dramas.** [1] N-C A **drama** is a serious play for the theatre, television, or radio. [2] N-U You refer to plays in general as **drama.** *He knew nothing of Greek drama.* [3] N-VAR You can refer to exciting or dangerous aspects of a real situation as its **drama.** *The meeting had all the ingredients of high political drama.*

dramatic /drə'mætɪk/ **dramatics.** [1] ADJ A **dramatic** change is sudden and noticeable. *Air safety has not improved since the dramatic advances of the 1970s.* ◆**dramatically** ADV *The cost of living has increased dramatically.* [2] ADJ A **dramatic** action, event, or situation is exciting and impressive. *...a dramatic display of fireworks.*

dramatics /drə'mætɪks/. The form **dramatic** is used as a modifier. N-U You use **dramatics** to refer to activities connected with the theatre and drama. *...an amateur dramatics class. ...a dramatic arts major in college.*

dramatist /'dræmətɪst/ **dramatists.** N-C A **dramatist** is someone who writes plays.

dramatize (BR also **dramatise**) /'dræmətaɪz/ **dramatizes, dramatizing, dramatized.** [1] VERB If a book or story **is dramatized,** it is written or presented as a play, a film, or a television drama. ◆**dramatization, dramatizations** N-C *...a dramatisation of D H Lawrence's novel, 'Lady Chatterley's Lover'.* [2] VERB If someone **dramatizes** an event or situation, they try to make it seem more serious or exciting than it really is; used showing disapproval. *They have tried very hard to dramatize their own experience as victims.*

drank /dræŋk/. **Drank** is the past tense of **drink.**

drape /dreɪp/ **drapes, draping, draped.**
[1] VERB If you **drape** a piece of cloth somewhere, you place it there so that it hangs down. *Natasha took the coat and draped it over her shoulders... He draped himself in the Canadian flag.* [2] N-PL In American English, **drapes** are pieces of heavy fabric you hang across a window and close to keep the light out or stop people looking in. The British word is **curtains.**

drastic /'dræstɪk/. [1] ADJ A **drastic** course of action is extreme and is usually taken urgently. *He's not going to do anything drastic about economic policy.* [2] ADJ A **drastic** change is a very great change. ◆**drastically** ADV *Services have been drastically reduced.*

draught (AM **draft**) /drɑːft, dræft/ **draughts.** N-C A **draught** is an unwelcome current of air coming into a room or vehicle. *You need fresh air but obviously don't want to be in a draught.*

draw /drɔː/ **draws, drawing, drew, drawn.**
[1] VERB When you **draw,** or when you **draw** something, you use a pencil, pen, or crayon to produce a picture, pattern, or diagram. *He starts a painting by quickly drawing simplified shapes.* ◆**drawing** N-U *I like dancing, singing and drawing.* [2] VERB You can use **draw** to indicate that someone or something moves somewhere or is moved there. *Claire had seen the taxi drawing away... I drew her close to him... He drew his chair nearer the fire.* [3] VERB If you **draw** a curtain or blind, you pull it

across a window to cover or uncover the window. [4] VERB If someone **draws** a gun, knife, or other weapon, they pull it out of its holder so that it is ready to use. [5] VERB If you **draw** a deep breath, you breathe in deeply once. [6] VERB If you **draw** something into or out of a particular place, you cause it to go into or come out of that place. *Villagers still have to draw their water from wells.* [7] VERB If you **draw** money out of a bank or building society, you take it out so that you can use it. [8] VERB If you **draw** a comparison, conclusion, or distinction, you decide that it exists or is true. *He draws a comparison between what's going on in the country now and what happened in Germany.* [9] VERB If you **draw** someone's attention to something, you make them aware of it. *He was waving his arms to draw their attention.* [10] VERB If someone or something **draws** a particular reaction, people react to it in that way. *Such a policy would inevitably draw fierce resistance from farmers.* [11] PHRASE When an event or period of time **draws to an end**, or when it **draws to a close**, it finishes. *The conflict was drawing to a close.* [12] See also **drawing**, **drawn**.

▶ **draw in** or **draw into**. PHR-VERB If you **draw** someone **in**, or if you **draw** them **into** something you are involved with, you cause them to become involved with it. *She is said to be the perfect hostess, drawing everyone into the conversation.*

▶ **draw on** or **draw upon**. [1] PHR-VERB If you **draw on** or **draw upon** something such as your skills or experience, you use them. *He drew on his experience as a yachtsman to make a documentary programme.* [2] PHR-VERB As a period of time **draws on**, it passes and the end of it gets closer. *...as the afternoon drew on.*

▶ **draw up**. [1] PHR-VERB When you **draw up** a document, list, or plan, you prepare it and write it out. *...a working party to draw up a formal agreement.* [2] PHR-VERB If you **draw up** a chair, you move it nearer to a person or place.

▶ **draw on**. See **draw on** 1.

drawback /ˈdrɔːbæk/ **drawbacks.** N-C A **drawback** is an aspect of something that makes it less acceptable. *The apartment's only drawback was that it was too small.*

drawer /ˈdrɔːə/ **drawers.** N-C A **drawer** is a part of a desk or other piece of furniture that is shaped like a rectangular box. You pull it towards you to open it.

drawing /ˈdrɔːɪŋ/ **drawings.** N-C A **drawing** is a picture made with a pencil, pen, or crayon. *She did a drawing of me.* ● See also **draw**.

'**drawing room**, **drawing rooms.** N-C A **drawing room** is a room, especially a large room in a large house, where people sit and relax; DATED.

drawl /drɔːl/ **drawls**, **drawling**, **drawled.** VERB & N-C If someone **drawls**, or if they speak in a **drawl**, they speak slowly, with long vowel sounds. *'You guys don't mind if I smoke?' he drawled. ...Jack's southern drawl.*

drawn /drɔːn/ [1] **Drawn** is the past participle of **draw**. [2] ADJ If someone looks **drawn**, they look very tired or ill.

,**drawn-'out.** ADJ You describe something as **drawn-out** when it lasts longer than you think it should. *...a long drawn-out war.*

dread /dred/ **dreads**, **dreading**, **dreaded.** [1] VERB If you **dread** something unpleasant which may happen, you feel anxious about it. *I dreaded coming back... I'd been dreading that the birth would take a long time.* [2] N-U **Dread** is a feeling of great anxiety and fear about something that may happen.

dreaded /ˈdredɪd/. ADJ BEFORE N **Dreaded** means terrible and greatly feared. *...how to treat this dreaded disease.*

dreadful /ˈdredfʊl/. ADJ If you say that something is **dreadful**, you mean that it is very unpleasant or very poor in quality. *They told us the dreadful news... My financial situation is dreadful.* ◆ **dreadfully** ADV *I've behaved absolutely dreadfully.*

dream /driːm/ **dreams**, **dreaming**, **dreamed** or **dreamt** /dremt/. [1] VERB & N-C When you **dream**, or when you **have** a **dream**, you experience imaginary events in your mind while you are asleep. *Ivor dreamed that he was on a bus... He had a dream about Claire.* [2] VERB If you often think about something that you would very much like to happen or have, you can say that you **dream** of it. *I dream that my son will attend college.* [3] N-C You can describe something that you would very much like to happen or have as your **dream**. *...his dream of becoming a full pilot.* [4] VERB If you say you would not **dream** of doing something, you are emphasizing that you would not do it. *I wouldn't dream of making fun of you.*

▶ **dream up**. PHR-VERB If you **dream up** a plan or idea, you work it out or create it in your mind. *I dreamed up a plan to solve both problems.*

dreamer /ˈdriːmə/ **dreamers.** N-C Someone who is a **dreamer** looks forward to pleasant things that may never happen, rather than being realistic and practical.

dreamy /ˈdriːmi/ **dreamier**, **dreamiest.** ADJ If someone has a **dreamy** expression, they are not paying attention to things around them and look as if they are thinking about something pleasant. *He smiled, an odd, dreamy smile.*

dreary /ˈdrɪəri/ **drearier**, **dreariest.** ADJ If something is **dreary**, it is so dull that it makes you feel bored or depressed. *...a dreary little town.*

dredge /dredʒ/ **dredges**, **dredging**, **dredged.** VERB To **dredge** a river means to clear a channel by removing mud from the bottom.

▶ **dredge up**. PHR-VERB If someone **dredges up** a piece of information they learnt a long time ago, or if they **dredge up** a distant memory, they manage to remember it. *...an American trying to dredge up some French or German learned in high school.*

drench /drentʃ/ **drenches**, **drenching**, **drenched.** VERB To **drench** something or someone means to make them completely wet. *...getting drenched by icy water.* ◆ **drenched** ADJ *We were completely drenched and cold.*

dress /dres/ **dresses, dressing, dressed.**
[1] N-C A **dress** is a piece of clothing worn by a woman or girl which covers her body and extends down over her legs. [2] N-U You can refer to clothes worn by men or women as **dress**. *He's usually smart in his dress. ...evening dress.* [3] VERB When you **dress**, or when you **dress** yourself, you put clothes on yourself. *He told Sarah to wait while he dressed.* ● See note at **wear**.
▸ **dress up.** PHR-VERB If you **dress up**, you put on different clothes, in order to look smarter or to disguise yourself. *You do not need to dress up for dinner... He was dressed up as Father Christmas.*
▸ **dress down.** PHR-VERB If you **dress down**, you wear clothes that are less smart than usual.

dressed /drest/. [1] ADJ AFTER LINK-V If you are **dressed**, you are wearing clothes rather than being naked. *He was fully dressed, including shoes.* ● See note at **wear**. [2] ADJ AFTER LINK-V If you are **dressed** in a particular way, you are wearing clothes of a particular kind or colour. *He was dressed in a black suit.*

dresser /'dresə/ **dressers.** [1] N-C A **dresser** is a piece of furniture which is usually used for storing china; BRITISH. [2] N-C A **dresser** is a chest of drawers, usually with a mirror on the top; AMERICAN. [3] N-C You use **dresser** to refer to the kind of clothes that a person wears. *...smart dressers.*

dressing /'dresɪŋ/ **dressings.** [1] N-C A **dressing** is a protective covering that is put on a wound. [2] N-VAR A salad **dressing** is a mixture of oil, vinegar, and herbs, which you pour over a salad.

'dressing gown, dressing gowns. N-C A **dressing gown** is a loose-fitting coat worn over pyjamas or other night clothes.

'dressing room, dressing rooms. N-C A **dressing room** is a room in a theatre or sports stadium where performers or players can change their clothes.

'dressing table, dressing tables. N-C A **dressing table** is a small table in a bedroom with drawers and a mirror.

drew /druː/. **Drew** is the past tense of **draw**.

dribble /'drɪbəl/ **dribbles, dribbling, dribbled.** [1] VERB If a liquid **dribbles** somewhere, or if you **dribble** it, it drips down slowly or flows in a thin stream. *Sweat dribbled down Hart's face.* [2] VERB When a person **dribbles**, saliva trickles from their mouth. [3] VERB When players **dribble** the ball in a game such as football, they give it several quick kicks or taps in order to keep it moving.

dried /draɪd/. **Dried** is the past tense and past participle of **dry**.

drier /draɪə/. See **dry, dryer**.

drift /drɪft/ **drifts, drifting, drifted.** [1] VERB When something **drifts** somewhere, it is carried there by the wind or by water. *Mist drifted silently across the water.* [2] VERB & N-C To **drift** somewhere, or to move there in a **drift**, means to move there slowly or gradually. *Half the crowd drifted outside before the end. ...the drift towards the cities.* [3] VERB To **drift** into a situation means to get into it in a way that is not planned or controlled. *...young people drifting*

into crime. [4] N-C A **drift** of snow is a deep pile formed by the wind.
▸ **drift off.** PHR-VERB If you **drift off** to sleep, you gradually fall asleep.

drill /drɪl/ **drills, drilling, drilled.** [1] N-C A **drill** is a tool for making holes. *...pneumatic drills.* [2] VERB When you **drill** into something or **drill** a hole in it, you make a hole using a drill. [3] N-VAR A **drill** is a procedure which a group of people, especially soldiers, practice so that they can do something quickly and efficiently. *...the military drill used by soldiers to load and fire the big guns.*

drink /drɪŋk/ **drinks, drinking, drank, drunk.** [1] VERB When you **drink** a liquid, you take it into your mouth and swallow it. *He drank some tea.* ♦**drinker, drinkers** N-C *...if you're a heavy coffee drinker.* [2] N-C A **drink** is an amount of a liquid which you drink. *I'll get you a drink of water.* [3] VERB To **drink** means to drink alcohol. *He was smoking and drinking too much.* ♦**drinking** N-U *She had left him because of his drinking.* ♦**drinker** N-C *He was a heavy drinker.* [4] N-VAR **Drink** is alcohol, such as beer, wine, or whisky. A **drink** is an alcoholic drink. *Too much drink is bad for your health.* [5] See also **drunk**.
▸ **drink to.** PHR-VERB If you **drink to** someone or something, you raise your glass before drinking, and say that you hope they will be happy or successful. *We drank to our success.*

drip /drɪp/ **drips, dripping, dripped.** [1] VERB When liquid **drips** somewhere, it falls in small drops. *Rain dripped from the brim of his baseball cap.* [2] VERB When something **drips**, drops of liquid fall from it. *A tap in the kitchen was dripping.* [3] N-C A **drip** is a small individual drop of a liquid. *...drips of water.* [4] N-C A **drip** is a piece of medical equipment by which a liquid is slowly passed through a tube into a patient's bloodstream. *I had to be put on a drip.*

drive /draɪv/ **drives, driving, drove, driven** /'drɪvən/. [1] VERB To **drive** a vehicle means to control it so that it goes where you want it to go. *She never learned to drive... His daughter Carly drove him to the train station.* ♦**driving** N-U *...dangerous driving.* ♦**driver, drivers** N-C *The driver got out of his van.* [2] N-C A **drive** is a journey in a vehicle such as a car. *I thought we might go for a drive.* [3] N-C A **drive** is a private road leading from a public road to a house. [4] VERB If something **drives** a machine, it supplies the power that makes it work. *...electric motors that drive the wheels.* [5] N-C You use **drive** to refer to the mechanical part of a computer which reads the data on disks and tapes, or writes data onto them. [6] VERB If you **drive** one thing into another, you push it in or hammer it in using a lot of effort. *Drive the pegs into the side of the path.* [7] VERB If you **drive** people or animals somewhere, you make them go to or from that place. *The last offensive drove thousands of people into Thailand.* [8] VERB The desire or feeling that **drives** someone to do something, especially something extreme, is what causes them to do it. *Jealousy drives people to murder.* [9] N-U **Drive** is energy and determination. *John will be best remem-*

bered for his drive and enthusiasm. [10] N-SING A **drive** is a special effort by a group of people to achieve something. ...*a demonic drive to succeed.* [11] See also **driving, drove**.

▶ **drive away.** PHR-VERB To **drive** people **away** means to make them want to go away or stay away. *Increased crime is driving away customers.*

driveway /'draɪvweɪ/ **driveways.** N-C A **driveway** is a private road that leads from a public road to a house or garage.

driving /'draɪvɪŋ/. ADJ BEFORE N The **driving** force behind something is the person, group, or thing mainly responsible for it. *Consumer spending was the driving force behind the economic growth.*

'driving licence, driving licences. N-C In British English, a **driving licence** is a card showing that you are qualified to drive. The usual American term is **driver's license**.

drizzle /'drɪzl/ **drizzles, drizzling, drizzled.** [1] VERB If it is **drizzling**, light rain is falling in fine drops. [2] N-U **Drizzle** is light rain falling in fine drops.

drone /drəʊn/ **drones, droning, droned.** VERB & N-SING If something **drones**, it makes a low continuous humming noise called a **drone**. *The occasional plane droned overhead.* ...*the constant drone of the motorways.*

▶ **drone on.** PHR-VERB If someone **drones on** about something, they keep talking about it in a boring way.

drool /druːl/ **drools, drooling, drooled.** [1] VERB If someone **drools**, saliva falls from their mouth. [2] VERB If you **drool** over someone or something, you look at them with great pleasure; used showing disapproval. *He is drooled over by women.*

droop /druːp/ **droops, drooping, drooped.** VERB If something **droops**, it hangs or leans downwards with no strength or firmness. *Pale wilting roses drooped from a blue vase.*

drop /drɒp/ **drops, dropping, dropped.** [1] VERB & N-C If a level or amount **drops**, or if there is a **drop** in it, it quickly becomes less. *Temperatures can drop to freezing at night... He had dropped the price of his London home by £1.25m... He was prepared to take a drop in wages.* [2] VERB If you **drop** something, or if it **drops**, it falls straight down. *I dropped my glasses and broke them... He dropped his plate into the sink.* ♦ **dropping** N-U ...*the dropping of the first atomic bomb.* [3] N-C You use **drop** to talk about vertical distances. *It's only a four-foot drop.* [4] VERB If a person or a part of their body **drops** to a lower position, or if they **drop** a part of their body to a lower position, they move to that position, often in a tired way. *Nancy dropped into a nearby chair... She let her head drop.* [5] VERB If your voice **drops**, or if you **drop** your voice, you speak more quietly. *He dropped his voice and glanced round at the door.* [6] VERB & PHR-VERB If the driver of a vehicle **drops** you somewhere, or if they **drop** you **off**, they stop the vehicle and you get out. *He dropped me outside the hotel... Just drop me off at the airport.* [7] VERB If you **drop** an idea, course of action, or habit, you decide not to continue with it. *He was told to drop the idea.*

[8] PHRASE If you **drop a hint**, you give someone a hint in a casual way. [9] N-C A **drop** of a liquid is a very small amount of it shaped like a little ball.

▶ **drop by** or **drop in.** PHR-VERB If you **drop by**, or if you **drop in**, you visit someone informally. *He tried to drop by the office... Why not drop in for a chat?*

▶ **drop off.** [1] See **drop** 6 [2] PHR-VERB If you **drop off** to sleep, you go to sleep.

▶ **drop out.** PHR-VERB If someone **drops out** of college or a race, for example, they leave it without finishing what they started.

droplet /'drɒplət/ **droplets.** N-C A **droplet** is a very small drop of liquid. ...*tiny droplets of water.*

drought /draʊt/ **droughts.** N-VAR A **drought** is a long period of time during which no rain falls. ...*drought and famines have killed up to two million people.*

drove /drəʊv/ **droves.** [1] **Drove** is the past tense of **drive**. [2] N-C **Droves** of people are very large numbers of them. *They are leaving in droves.*

drown /draʊn/ **drowns, drowning, drowned.** [1] VERB When someone **drowns**, or when they **are drowned**, they die because they have gone under water and cannot breathe. *Forty-eight people have drowned after their boat capsized... She fell into the water and was drowned.* [2] VERB & PHR-VERB If something **drowns** a sound, or if it **drowns** it **out**, it is louder than the sound and makes it impossible to hear it. *His speech was drowned by loud cries... Her voice was drowned out by a loud crash.*

drowsy /'draʊzi/ **drowsier, drowsiest.** ADJ If you are **drowsy**, you feel sleepy and cannot think clearly. *He felt pleasantly drowsy.* ♦ **drowsiness** N-U *Big meals during the day cause drowsiness.*

drug /drʌg/ **drugs, drugging, drugged.** [1] N-C A **drug** is a chemical substance given to people to treat or prevent an illness or disease. [2] N-C **Drugs** are substances that some people smoke or inject into their blood because of their stimulating effects. *She was sure Leo was taking drugs.* [3] VERB If you **drug** a person or animal, you give them a chemical substance in order to make them sleepy or unconscious. *They drugged the guard dog.*

drugstore /'drʌgstɔː/ **drugstores.** N-C In America, a **drugstore** is a shop where medicines, cosmetics, and some other goods are sold. • See note at **pharmacy**.

drum /drʌm/ **drums, drumming, drummed.** [1] N-C A **drum** is a musical instrument consisting of a skin stretched tightly over a round frame. ♦ **drummer, drummers** N-C ...*a pop-group drummer.* [2] N-C A **drum** is a large container in the shape of a cylinder which is used for storing fuel or other substances. ...*an oil drum.* [3] VERB If something **drums** on a surface, or if you **drum** something on a surface, it hits it regularly, making a continuous beating sound. *He drummed his fingers on the leather top of his desk.*

▶ **drum into.** PHR-VERB If you **drum** something **into** someone, you keep saying it to make them understand or remember it. *We had it* drummed into us that you need a degree to get a job.

▶ **drum up.** PHR-VERB If you **drum up** support or business, you try to get it. *The organisers failed to drum up much public support.*

drunk /drʌŋk/ **drunks.** [1] ADJ If someone is **drunk**, they have consumed too much alcohol. *I got drunk.* [2] N-C A **drunk** is someone who is drunk or who often gets drunk. [3] **Drunk** is the past participle of **drink**.

drunken /ˈdrʌŋkən/. ADJ BEFORE N A **drunken** person is drunk or is frequently drunk; used showing disapproval. *...groups of drunken hooligans.* ◆**drunkenly** ADV *Bob stormed drunkenly into her house.* ◆**drunkenness** N-U *He was arrested for drunkenness.*

dry /draɪ/ **drier** (or **dryer**), **driest; dries, drying, dried.** [1] ADJ If something is **dry**, it has no water or other liquid on it or in it. *...a soft dry cloth... Pat it dry with a soft towel.* ◆**dryness** N-U *...the parched dryness of the air.* [2] VERB When you **dry** something, or when it **dries**, it becomes dry. *Wash and dry the lettuce... Leave your hair to dry naturally.* [3] ADJ When the weather or a place is **dry**, there is no rain or much less rain than average. [4] ADJ If you say that your skin or hair is **dry**, you mean that it is less oily or soft than normal. *Dry hair is damaged by washing it too frequently.* ◆**dryness** N-U *...dryness of the skin.* [5] ADJ **Dry** humour is amusing, mocking people in a subtle way. ◆**dryly** ADV *'I've never done anything like this,' she replied dryly. – 'That's a comfort,' she replied dryly.* [6] ADJ If you describe something such as a book, play, or activity as **dry**, you mean that it is dull and uninteresting. *...the dry, academic phrases.* [7] ADJ **Dry** sherry or wine does not taste sweet. [8] See also **dried, dryer.**

▶ **dry off.** PHR-VERB If something **dries off**, or if you **dry it off**, the moisture on its surface disappears or is removed. *I got out, dried myself off, and dressed.*

▶ **dry out.** PHR-VERB If something **dries out**, it becomes completely dry. *If the soil is allowed to dry out the tree could die.*

▶ **dry up.** [1] PHR-VERB If something **dries up**, it loses all its water or moisture. *As the day goes on, the pollen dries up and becomes hard.* [2] PHR-VERB If a supply of something **dries up**, it stops. *Tourism is expected to dry up completely this summer.* [3] PHR-VERB If you **dry up** or **dry up** the dishes, you wipe the water off them with a cloth after they have been washed.

dry-'clean, dry-cleans, dry-cleaning, dry-cleaned. VERB When clothes **are dry-cleaned**, they are cleaned with a liquid chemical rather than with water.

dryer (or **drier**) /ˈdraɪə/ **dryers.** N-C A **dryer** is a machine for drying things, for example clothes or people's hair. *...hair dryers.* ● See also **dry.**

dual /ˈdjuːəl/. AM ˈduː-/. ADJ BEFORE N **Dual** means having two parts, functions, or aspects. *...his dual role as head of the party and head of state. ...dual nationality.*

dub /dʌb/ **dubs, dubbing, dubbed.** [1] VERB If someone or something **is dubbed** a particular thing, it is given that description or name.

Orson Welles dubbed her 'the most exciting woman in the world'. [2] VERB If a film **is dubbed**, a different soundtrack is added with actors speaking in a different language. *It was dubbed into Spanish for Mexican audiences.*

dubious /ˈdjuːbiəs, AM ˈduː-/. [1] ADJ You describe something as **dubious** when you think it is not completely honest, safe, or reliable. *This claim seems to us to be rather dubious.* ◆**dubiously** ADV *He was dubiously convicted of shooting three white men.* [2] ADJ AFTER LINK-V If you are **dubious** about something, you are unsure about it. *My parents were a bit dubious about it all at first.* ◆**dubiously** ADV *He eyed Coyne dubiously.*

duchess /ˈdʌtʃɪs/ **duchesses.** N-C A **duchess** is a woman who has the same rank as a duke, or is a duke's wife or widow.

duck /dʌk/ **ducks, ducking, ducked.** [1] N-C A **duck** is a common water bird with short legs and a large flat beak. [2] N-U **Duck** is the meat of a duck eaten as food. [3] VERB If you **duck**, you move your head or body quickly downwards to avoid being seen or hit. *He ducked in time to save his head from a blow... I wanted to duck down and slip past but they saw me... Hans deftly ducked their blows.* [4] VERB You say that someone **ducks** a duty or responsibility when you disapprove of the fact that they avoid it. *He is an indecisive leader who ducks crucial decisions.*

▶ **duck out.** PHR-VERB If you **duck out** of something that you are supposed to do, you avoid doing it. *George ducked out of his forced marriage to a cousin.*

duct /dʌkt/ **ducts.** N-C A **duct** is a pipe or channel which carries a liquid or gas. *...a big air duct in the ceiling.*

dud /dʌd/ **duds.** ADJ & N-C You say that something is **dud** or a **dud** when it does not work properly; INFORMAL. *He replaced a dud valve.*

dude /djuːd, AM duːd/ **dudes.** N-C A **dude** is a man; INFORMAL. *My doctor is a real cool dude.*

due /djuː, AM duː/ **dues.** [1] PREP If an event or situation is **due** to something else, it happens or exists as a result of it. *A lot of this will be due to Mr Green's efforts.* [2] ADJ AFTER LINK-V If something is **due** at a particular time, it is expected to happen or to arrive at that time. *The results are due at the end of the month... Mr Carter is due in London on Monday.* [3] PHRASE If you say that something will happen **in due course**, you mean that it will happen eventually, when the time is right. *The arrangements will be published in due course.* [4] ADJ AFTER LINK-V If something is **due** to you, you have a right to it. *I've got some leave due to me... No further pension was due.* [5] ADJ AFTER LINK-V If someone is **due for** something, that thing is planned to happen or be given to them now, or very soon. *Miss Smith, you know you are due for a move?* [6] ADJ BEFORE N If you give something **due** consideration, you give it the consideration it deserves. *After due consideration it was decided to send him away.* [7] N-PL **Dues** are sums of money that you pay regularly to an organization that you belong to. [8] PHRASE You can say **'with due respect'** when you are about to disagree politely with someone. *With all due respect I sub-*

mit to you that you're asking the wrong question.

duel /'djuːəl, AM 'duː-/ **duels.** [1] N-C A **duel** is a fight between two people in which they use guns or swords in order to settle a quarrel. [2] N-C You can refer to a conflict between two people or groups as a **duel**.

duet /djuːˈet, AM duːˈet/ **duets.** N-C A **duet** is a piece of music sung or played by two people.

dug /dʌɡ/. **Dug** is the past tense and past participle of **dig**.

duke /djuːk, AM duːk/ **dukes.** N-C A **duke** is a noble of high rank.

dull /dʌl/ **duller, dullest; dulls, dulling, dulled.** [1] ADJ If you describe someone or something as **dull**, you mean that they are not interesting or exciting. They are both nice people but can be rather dull. ◆**dullness** N-U ...the dullness of their routine life. [2] ADJ A **dull** colour or light is not bright. The stamp was a dark, dull blue colour. ◆**dully** ADV The street lamps gleamed dully. [3] ADJ A **dull** sound or feeling is weak and not intense. ...the dull boom of the explosion. ...a dull ache. ◆**dully** ADV His arm throbbed dully. [4] VERB If something **dulls**, or if it **is dulled**, it becomes less intense, bright, or lively. He can dull your senses with facts.

duly /'djuːli, AM 'duː-/. ADV **Duly** is used to say that something is done at the correct time or in the correct way; FORMAL. He is a duly elected president of the country.

dumb /dʌm/ **dumber, dumbest.** [1] ADJ Someone who is **dumb** is completely unable to speak. ...a young deaf and dumb man. [2] ADJ AFTER LINK-V If someone is **dumb** on a particular occasion, they cannot speak because they are angry or shocked. We were all struck dumb for a minute. [3] ADJ If you call a person **dumb**, you mean that they are stupid or foolish. I've met a lot of dumb people. [4] ADJ If you say that something is **dumb**, you think that it is silly and annoying; AMERICAN, INFORMAL. I came up with this dumb idea.

dummy /'dʌmi/ **dummies.** [1] N-C A **dummy** is a model of a person, often used to display clothes. ...a shop-window dummy. [2] N-C In British English, a **dummy** is a rubber or plastic object that you give to a baby to suck so that it feels comforted. The American word is **pacifier**. [3] ADJ You use **dummy** to describe objects that are not real, but have been made to look as if they are real. ...dummy weapons.

dump /dʌmp/ **dumps, dumping, dumped.** [1] VERB If something **is dumped** somewhere, it is put there because it is no longer wanted or needed. The getaway car was dumped near a motorway tunnel. ◆**dumping** N-U ...the dumping of hazardous waste. [2] VERB If you **dump** something somewhere, you put it there quickly and carelessly; INFORMAL. We dumped our bags at the nearby Grand Hotel and hurried towards the market. [3] N-C A **dump** is a site provided for people to leave their rubbish. [4] N-C If you refer to a place as a **dump**, you mean it is unattractive and unpleasant to live in or visit; INFORMAL.

dune /djuːn, AM duːn/ **dunes.** N-C A **dune** is a hill of sand near the sea or in a desert.

dung /dʌŋ/. N-U **Dung** is faeces from large animals. ...little piles of cow dung.

dungeon /'dʌndʒən/ **dungeons.** N-C A **dungeon** is a dark underground prison in a castle.

dunno /də'nəʊ/. **Dunno** is sometimes used to represent a way of saying 'don't know'; WRITTEN, INFORMAL. 'How did she get it?'—'I dunno.'

duo /'djuːəʊ, AM duː-/ **duos.** N-C A **duo** consists of two people who do something together, especially perform together. ...a famous dancing and singing duo.

dupe /djuːp, AM duːp/ **dupes, duping, duped.** VERB If someone **dupes** you, they trick you. ...a plot to dupe stamp collectors into buying fake rarities.

duplicate, duplicates, duplicating, duplicated; verb /'djuːplɪkeɪt, AM 'duː-/, noun /'djuːplɪkət, AM 'duː-/. [1] VERB & N-C If you **duplicate** something that has already been done, or if you perform a **duplicate** of it, you repeat or copy it. His task will be to duplicate his success overseas here at home... It was an exact duplicate of what happened in Vegas. ◆**duplication** N-U ...unnecessary duplication of work. [2] VERB If you **duplicate** something which has been written, drawn, or recorded onto tape, you make exact copies of it. ...a business which duplicates video and cinema tapes. [3] N-C A **duplicate** is an object which is a copy of something. I've lost my card. I've got to get a duplicate. ...a duplicate key.

durable /'djʊərəbəl, AM 'dʊr-/. ADJ **Durable** materials or products are strong and last a long time. ...hard, durable plastic. ◆**durability** N-U Airlines recommend hard-sided cases for durability.

duration /djʊ'reɪʃən, AM dʊr-/. N-U The **duration** of an event or state is the time that it lasts for. Courses are of two years' duration.

during /'djʊərɪŋ, AM 'dʊrɪŋ/. [1] PREP If something happens **during** a period of time or **during** an event, it happens continuously, or happens several times between the beginning and end of that period or event. Sandstorms are common during the Saudi Arabian winter. [2] PREP An event that happens **during** a period of time happens at some point or moment in that period. During the night a gust of wind had blown the pot over.

> You do not use **during** to say how long something lasts. You use **for**. You do not say, for example, 'I went to Wales during two weeks'. You say 'I went to Wales for two weeks'.

dusk /dʌsk/. N-U **Dusk** is the time just before night when it is not yet completely dark.

dust /dʌst/ **dusts, dusting, dusted.** [1] N-U **Dust** consists of very small dry particles of earth, sand, or dirt. I could see a thick layer of dust on the stairs. [2] VERB When you **dust** furniture or other objects, you remove dust from them using a dry cloth. [3] PHRASE If you say that **the dust has settled**, you mean that a situation has become calmer after a series of confusing or chaotic events.

dustbin /'dʌstbɪn/ **dustbins.** N-C In British English, a **dustbin** is a large container for rubbish. The usual American term is **garbage can.**

dusty /'dʌsti/ **dustier, dustiest.** ADJ Something that is **dusty** is covered with dust.

dutiful /'djuːtɪfʊl, AM 'duː-/. ADJ If you are **dutiful**, you do everything that you are expected to do. ...the dutiful wife, who sacrifices her career for her husband. ♦ **dutifully** ADV The inspector dutifully recorded the date.

duty /'djuːti, AM 'duːti/ **duties.** 1 N-VAR **Duty** is the work that you have to do as your job. Staff must report for duty at their normal place of work... I carried out my duties conscientiously. 2 PHRASE If someone such as a policeman or a nurse is **off duty**, they are not working. If they are **on duty**, they are working. Extra staff had been put on duty. 3 N-SING If you say that something is your **duty**, you believe that you ought to do it because it is your responsibility. I consider it my duty to write to you and thank you. 4 N-VAR **Duties** are taxes which you pay to the government on goods that you buy. ...import duties.

,duty-'free. ADJ **Duty-free** goods are sold at airports or on planes or ships at a cheaper price than usual because they are not taxed.

duvet /'duːveɪ, AM duː'veɪ/ **duvets.** N-C A **duvet** is a large cover filled with feathers or similar material, which you use to cover yourself in bed instead of a sheet and blankets; BRITISH.

dwarf /dwɔːf/ **dwarfs, dwarfing, dwarfed.** VERB If one person or thing **is dwarfed** by another, the second is so much bigger than the first that it makes them look very small. The US air travel market dwarfs that of Britain.

dwell /dwel/ **dwells, dwelling, dwelled** or **dwelt.** 1 VERB If you **dwell on** something, especially something unpleasant, you think, speak, or write about it a lot or for quite a long time. I'd rather not dwell on the past. 2 VERB If you **dwell** somewhere, you live there; FORMAL. ...the fate of the forest and the Indians who dwell in it.

dweller /'dwelə/ **dwellers.** N-C A city **dweller** or slum **dweller**, for example, is a person who lives in the kind of place or house indicated. ...to encourage town dwellers to grow vegetables.

dwelling /'dwelɪŋ/ **dwellings.** N-C A **dwelling** is a house or other place where someone lives; FORMAL. Some 3500 new dwellings are planned for the area.

dwelt /dwelt/. **Dwelt** is the past tense and past participle of **dwell**.

dwindle /'dwɪndəl/ **dwindles, dwindling, dwindled.** VERB If something **dwindles**, it becomes smaller, weaker, or less in number. The factory's workforce has dwindled from over 4,000 to a few hundred. ...his dwindling authority.

dye /daɪ/ **dyes, dyeing, dyed.** 1 VERB If you **dye** something, you change its colour by soaking it in a special liquid. The women prepared, spun and dyed the wool. 2 N-VAR **Dye** is a substance which is used to dye something.

dying /'daɪɪŋ/. 1 **Dying** is the present participle of **die**. 2 ADJ BEFORE N & N-PL **Dying** people or **the dying** are people who are very ill and likely to die soon. ...a dying man... The dead and the dying were everywhere. 3 ADJ BEFORE N A **dying** tradition or industry is becoming less important and is likely to end altogether. 4 ADJ AFTER LINK-V You say that you **are dying** for something or **are dying** to do something to emphasize that you very much want to have it or do it; INFORMAL. I was dying for a cigarette... She was dying to talk to Frank.

dyke (or **dike**) /daɪk/ **dykes.** N-C A **dyke** is a thick wall that prevents river or sea water flooding onto land.

dynamic /daɪ'næmɪk/ **dynamics.** 1 ADJ A **dynamic** person is full of energy; used showing approval. ...a dynamic and energetic leader. ♦ **dynamically** ADV ...one of the most dynamically imaginative jazz pianists. ♦ **dynamism** /'daɪnəmɪzəm/ N-U ...a situation that calls for dynamism and new thinking. 2 N-PL The **dynamics** of a situation or group of people are the opposing forces within it that cause it to change. ...an understanding of family dynamics.

dynamite /'daɪnəmaɪt/. N-U **Dynamite** is a type of explosive.

dynamo /'daɪnəməʊ/ **dynamos.** N-C A **dynamo** is a device that uses the movement of a machine to produce electricity.

dynasty /'dɪnəsti, AM 'daɪn-/ **dynasties.** N-C A **dynasty** is a series of rulers of a country who all belong to the same family.

E e

each /iːtʃ/. 1 QUANT If you refer to **each** thing or person in a group, or if you refer to **each one** of the members of a group, you are referring to every member, considered as individuals. Each book is beautifully illustrated. ...two bedrooms, each with three beds. ...tickets at six pounds each... He handed each of them a page of photos... He picked up forty of these publications and read each one of them. 2 PRON You use **each other** when you are saying that each member of a group does something to the others. We stared at each other.

eager /'iːgə/. ADJ If you are **eager** to do or have something, you very much want to do it or have it. They're very eager to get money. ...the crowd of eager faces around him. ♦ **eagerly** ADV Scientists throughout Europe are eagerly awaiting the results. ♦ **eagerness** N-U ...an eagerness to learn.

eagle /'iːgəl/ **eagles.** N-C An **eagle** is a large bird that hunts and kills small animals for food.

ear /ɪə/ **ears.** 1 N-C Your **ears** are the two parts of your body with which you hear sounds. 2 N-SING If you have an **ear** for music or language, you are able to hear its sounds accurately and to interpret them or reproduce them well. 3 N-C The **ears** of a cereal plant such as wheat are the top parts containing the seeds.

earlier /'ɜːliə/. **1** **Earlier** is the comparative of **early**. **2** ADJ & ADV **Earlier** means occurring at a point in time before the present or before the one you are talking about. ...*earlier reports of gunshots.* ...*political reforms announced earlier this year.*

earliest /'ɜːliɪst/. **1** **Earliest** is the superlative of **early**. **2** PHRASE **At the earliest** means not before the date or time mentioned. *The tests won't be completed until next April at the earliest.*

earlobe /'ɪələʊb/ **earlobes**. N-C Your **earlobes** are the soft parts at the bottom of your ears.

early /'ɜːli/ **earlier, earliest.** **1** ADJ & ADV BEFORE N **Early** means before the usual time that something happens or before the time that was arranged or expected. *Why do we have to go to bed so early?.* ...*early retirement.* **2** ADV & ADJ BEFORE N **Early** means near the beginning of an activity, process, or period of time. ...*the early stages of pregnancy... It's too early to declare his efforts a success.* ...*an incident which occurred much earlier in the game.* ...*the early 1980s.*

earmark /'ɪəmɑːk/ **earmarks, earmarking, earmarked.** VERB If something is **earmarked** for a particular purpose, it is reserved for that purpose. *China has earmarked more than $20bn for oil exploration.*

earn /ɜːn/ **earns, earning, earned.** **1** VERB If you **earn** money, you receive it in return for work that you do. *She earns £17,000 a year.* **2** VERB If something **earns** money, it produces money as profit. ...*a current account which earns little or no interest.* ...*the money earned from oil imports.* **3** VERB If you **earn** something such as praise, you get it because you deserve it. *Companies must earn a reputation for honesty... I think that's earned him very high admiration.*

earner /'ɜːnə/ **earners.** N-C An **earner** is someone or something that earns money or produces profit. ...*a typical wage earner... Sugar is Fiji's second biggest export earner.*

earnest /'ɜːnɪst/. **1** PHRASE If something is done **in earnest**, it is done to a much greater extent and more seriously than before. *Campaigning will begin in earnest tomorrow.* **2** ADJ **Earnest** people are very serious and sincere. ♦**earnestly** ADV *I earnestly hope Mrs Smith will find it in her heart to forgive me.*

earnings /'ɜːnɪŋz/. N-PL Your **earnings** are the money that you earn by working. *Average weekly earnings rose by 1.5% in July.*

earring /'ɪərɪŋ/ **earrings.** N-C **Earrings** are pieces of jewellery which you attach to your ears.

earth /ɜːθ/ **earths.** **1** N-PROPER The **Earth** is the planet on which we live. **2** N-SING The **earth** is the surface of the Earth. *The earth shook.* **3** N-U **Earth** is the substance on the land surface of the earth in which plants grow. ...*a huge mound of earth.* **4** N-SING The **earth** in an electric plug or appliance is a wire through which electricity can pass into the ground, to make the equipment safe even if something goes wrong with it.

PHRASES ● You use **on earth** for emphasis in questions which begin with words such as 'how', 'why', 'what', or 'where'. *Why on earth would he want to go to such a place?* ● If you come **down to earth**, you have to face the reality of everyday life after a period of great excitement. *I was shocked, brought down to earth by this revelation.* ● See also **down-to-earth.**

earthly /'ɜːθli/. **1** ADJ BEFORE N **Earthly** means happening in the material world of our life on earth and not in any spiritual life or life after death. *The priest emphasized the need to confront evil during the earthly life.* **2** PHRASE If you say that there is no **earthly reason** for something, you are emphasizing that there is no possible reason for it. *What earthly reason would they have for lying?*

earthquake /'ɜːθkweɪk/ **earthquakes.** N-C An **earthquake** is a shaking of the ground caused by movement of the earth's crust.

earthy /'ɜːθi/ **earthier, earthiest.** **1** ADJ If you describe someone as **earthy**, you mean they are open and direct about subjects which other people avoid or feel ashamed about. ...*his extremely earthy humour.* **2** ADJ Something that is **earthy** looks, smells, or feels like earth. ...*a strong, earthy smell.*

earwig /'ɪəwɪg/ **earwigs.** N-C An **earwig** is a small, thin brown insect that has a pair of pincers at the back end of its body.

ease /iːz/ **eases, easing, eased.** **1** PHRASE If you do something **with ease**, you do it without difficulty or effort. *Anne was intelligent and capable of passing her exams with ease.* **2** N-U If you talk about the **ease of** a particular activity, you mean that it is easy to do or has been made easier to do. *For ease of reference, only the relevant extracts are included.* ...*the camera's ease of use.* **3** PHRASE If you are **at ease**, you feel confident and comfortable. If you are **ill at ease**, you feel anxious or awkward. **4** VERB If something **eases**, or if it **eases** off, it is reduced in degree, speed, or intensity. *I gave him some brandy to ease the pain... These days, the pressure has eased off... The rain had eased up.* ♦**easing** N-U ...*the easing of sanctions.* **5** VERB If you **ease** your way somewhere or **ease** somewhere, you move there slowly, carefully, and gently. If you **ease** something somewhere, you move it there slowly, carefully, and gently. *She eased back into the chair... He eased his foot off the accelerator.*

▶ **ease up.** PHR-VERB If you **ease up**, you start to make less effort. *He told supporters not to ease up even though he's leading in the presidential race.*

easel /'iːzəl/ **easels.** N-C An **easel** is a wooden frame that supports a picture which an artist is painting.

easily /'iːzɪli/. **1** ADV You use **easily** to emphasize that something is very likely to happen, or is certainly true. *The cost could easily be three times that amount.* ...*an ancient barn that is easily the length of two tennis courts.* **2** ADV You use **easily** to say that something happens more quickly than normal. *He had always cried very easily.* **3** See also **easy.**

east /iːst/. **1** N-SING The **east** is the direction in which you look to see the sun rise. **2** N-SING &

ADJ The **east** of a place, or the **east** part of a place, is the part which is towards the east. ...*a village in the east of the country.* ...*the east coast.* ③ ADV **East** means towards the east, or positioned to the east of a place or thing. *Go east on Route 9.* ...*just east of the center of town.* ④ ADJ An **east** wind blows from the east. ⑤ N-SING The **East** is used to refer either to the countries in the southern and eastern part of Asia, including China, India, and Japan, or to the former USSR and other countries in eastern Europe. ● See also **Far East**, **Middle East**.

Easter /ˈiːstə/. N-U **Easter** is a Christian festival and holiday, when the resurrection of Jesus Christ is celebrated.

easterly /ˈiːstəli/. ① ADJ An **easterly** point, area, or direction is to the east or towards the east. ...*a more easterly direction.* ② ADJ An **easterly** wind blows from the east.

eastern /ˈiːstən/. ① ADJ **Eastern** means in or from the east of a region or country. ② ADJ **Eastern** means coming either from the people or countries of the East, such as India, China, and Japan, or from the countries in the East of Europe and the former USSR.

easterner /ˈiːstənə/ **easterners**. N-C An **easterner** is a person who was born in or who lives in the eastern part of a place or country.

eastward /ˈiːstwəd/ (or **eastwards**). ADV & ADJ **Eastward** or **eastwards** means towards the east. *A powerful snowstorm is moving eastwards.* ...*travel in an eastward direction.*

easy /ˈiːzi/ **easier**, **easiest**. ① ADJ If a job or action is **easy**, you can do it without difficulty. *That kind of calculation is fairly easy to do.* ...*making easy conversation with people she has never met before.* ◆**easily** ADV *These journeys are most easily made by plane.* ② ADJ An **easy** life or time is comfortable and without any problems. *It ought to make life much easier.* ③ PHRASE If someone tells you to **take it easy**, they mean that you should relax and not do very much; INFORMAL.

easy-'going. ADJ If you describe someone as **easy-going**, you mean that they are not easily worried or upset; used showing approval.

eat /iːt/ **eats**, **eating**, **ate**, **eaten**. VERB When you **eat** something, you put it into your mouth, chew it, and swallow it. *I ate my chicken quickly.*

▶ **eat away**. PHR-VERB If one thing **eats away** another or **eats away** at another, it gradually destroys or uses it up. *The sea eats away at coastlines.*

▶ **eat into**. PHR-VERB If something **eats into** your time or resources, it uses them, when they should be used for other things. *Responsibilities at home and work eat into his time.*

eater /ˈiːtə/ **eaters**. N-C You use **eater** to refer to someone who eats in a particular way or eats particular kinds of food. ...*a fussy eater.* ...*meat eaters.*

eavesdrop /ˈiːvzdrɒp/ **eavesdrops**, **eavesdropping**, **eavesdropped**. VERB If you **eavesdrop** on someone, you listen secretly to what they are saying. ◆**eavesdropper**, **eavesdroppers**. N-C ...*a telephone call recorded by an eavesdropper.*

ebb /eb/ **ebbs**, **ebbing**, **ebbed**. ① VERB When the tide or the sea **ebbs**, its level falls. ② N-C The **ebb** or the **ebb tide** is one of the regular periods when the sea gradually falls to a lower level. ③ VERB If a feeling or a person's strength **ebbs**, it weakens and gradually disappears; FORMAL. *Popular sympathy for the government could ebb.*

PHRASES ● If someone or something is at a **low ebb**, they are not being very successful or profitable. *The club's fortunes were at a low ebb.* ● You can use **ebb and flow** to describe the way that something repeatedly increases and decreases. ...*the ebb and flow of the fighting.*

ebullient /ɪˈbʌliənt, -ˈbʊl-/. ADJ An **ebullient** person is lively and full of enthusiasm or excitement about something; FORMAL. ◆**ebullience** N-U ...*his characteristic ebullience.*

eccentric /ɪkˈsentrɪk/ **eccentrics**. ADJ & N-C An **eccentric** person or an **eccentric** has habits or opinions that other people think strange. ◆**eccentricity** /ˌeksenˈtrɪsɪti/ **eccentricities** N-VAR ...*a performer noted for his eccentricity... We all have our eccentricities.*

ecclesiastical /ɪˌkliːziˈæstɪkəl/. ADJ **Ecclesiastical** means belonging to or connected with the Christian Church.

echelon /ˈeʃəlɒn/ **echelons**. N-C An **echelon** in an organization or society is a level or rank in it; FORMAL. ...*the lower echelons of society.*

echo /ˈekəʊ/ **echoes**, **echoing**, **echoed**. ① N-C An **echo** is a sound caused by a noise being reflected off a surface such as a wall. *He heard the echo of his footsteps along the hallway.* ② VERB If sounds **echo**, or a place **echoes** with sounds, the sounds are reflected off a surface there and can be heard again. *The corridor echoed with the barking of a dozen dogs.* ...*the echoing hall.* ③ VERB If you **echo** someone's words, you repeat them or express the same thing. *Other US military personnel echoed the sentiments of Captain Ryan.* ④ N-C An **echo** is an expression of an attitude, opinion, or statement which has already been expressed. *Political attacks work only if they find an echo with voters.*

eclectic /ɪˈklektɪk/. ADJ If you describe a collection of objects, ideas, or beliefs as **eclectic**, you mean that they are wide ranging and come from many different sources; FORMAL. ...*the most eclectic mix of styles imaginable.*

eclipse /ɪˈklɪps/ **eclipses**, **eclipsing**, **eclipsed**. ① N-C When there is an **eclipse** of the sun or a **solar eclipse**, the moon is between the earth and the sun, so that part or all of the sun is hidden. When there is an **eclipse** of the moon or a **lunar eclipse**, the earth is between the sun and the moon, so that part or all of the moon is hidden. ② VERB If one thing **eclipses** another, the first thing becomes more important so that the second thing is no longer noticed. *Nothing is going to eclipse winning the Olympic title.*

ecology /ɪˈkɒlədʒi/. ① N-U When you talk about the **ecology** of a place, you are referring to the relationships between living things and their environment. *The region has a unique ecology.* ◆**ecological** /ˌiːkəˈlɒdʒɪkəl/ ADJ BEFORE N

...Siberia's delicate ecological balance.
♦**ecologically** ADV China is very ecologically conscious. [2] N-U **Ecology** is the study of the relationship between living things and their environment. ♦**ecologist, ecologists.** N-C ...an ecologist who visited Sri Lanka to study endangered animals.

economic /,i:kə'nɒmɪk, ,ek-/. [1] ADJ **Economic** means concerned with the organization of the money, industry, and trade of a country, region, or society. ...China's economic reforms. ♦**economically** ADV ...an economically depressed area. [2] ADJ If something is **economic**, it produces a profit. The new system may be more economic.

economical /,i:kə'nɒmɪkəl, ,ek-/. [1] ADJ Something that is **economical** does not require a lot of money to operate. ...economical cars. ♦**economically** ADV Services could be operated more efficiently and economically. [2] ADJ If someone is **economical**, they spend money carefully and sensibly. ♦**economically** ADV We must all live as economically as possible.

economics /,i:kə'nɒmɪks, ,ek-/. [1] N-U **Economics** is the study of the way in which money, industry, and trade are organized in a society. [2] N-U The **economics** of a society or industry is the system of organizing money and trade in it. ...the economics of the newspaper business.

economist /ɪ'kɒnəmɪst/ **economists.** N-C An **economist** is a person who studies, teaches, or writes about economics.

economy /ɪ'kɒnəmi/ **economies.** [1] N-C The **economy** of a country or region is the system by which money, industry, and trade are organized. ...changes in the Indian economy. [2] N-U **Economy** is careful spending or the careful use of things to save money or avoid waste. ...improvements in the fuel economy of cars.

economy class. ADJ On an aeroplane, an **economy class** ticket or seat is the cheapest available. The price includes two economy class airfares from Brisbane to Los Angeles.

ecosystem /'i:kəʊsɪstəm, AM 'ekə-/ **ecosystems.** N-C An **ecosystem** is all the plants and animals that live in a particular area together with the relationship that exists between them and their environment; TECHNICAL. ...Antarctica's ecosystem.

ecstasy /'ekstəsi/ **ecstasies.** [1] N-VAR **Ecstasy** is a feeling of great happiness. ...a state of almost religious ecstasy... The dancing roused the audience to ecstasies. [2] N-U **Ecstasy** is an illegal drug which acts as a stimulant and can cause hallucinations.

ecstatic /ek'stætɪk/. ADJ If you are **ecstatic**, you feel very enthusiastic and happy. The audience reception was ecstatic... The Russian President was given an ecstatic welcome. ♦**ecstatically** ADV ...ecstatically happy.

eczema /'eksmə, AM ɪg'zi:mə/. N-U **Eczema** is a skin condition which makes your skin itch and become sore and broken.

edge /edʒ/ **edges, edging, edged.** [1] N-C The **edge** of something is the place or line where it stops, or the part of it that is furthest from the

middle. We were on a hill, right on the edge of town... She was standing at the water's edge. [2] N-C The **edge** of something sharp such as a knife is its sharp or narrow side. ...the sharp edge of the sword. [3] VERB If you **edge** somewhere, you move there very slowly. He edged closer to the telephone. [4] N-SING If you have an **edge** over someone, you have an advantage over them. The three days France have to prepare could give them the edge over England... Manufacturers will do almost anything to gain a competitive edge. [5] PHRASE If you are **on edge**, you are nervous and unable to relax.
▸ **edge out.** PHR-VERB If someone **edges out** someone else, they just manage to beat them or get in front of them in a contest. McGregor's effort was enough to edge Johnson out of top spot.

edgy /'edʒi/. ADJ If you feel **edgy**, you are nervous and anxious; INFORMAL.

edible /'edɪbəl/. ADJ If something is **edible**, it is safe to eat. ...edible mushrooms.

edict /'i:dɪkt/ **edicts.** N-C An **edict** is a command given by someone in authority; FORMAL.

edifice /'edɪfɪs/ **edifices.** [1] N-C An **edifice** is a large impressive building; FORMAL. ...a large sandstone edifice built in the early part of the century. [2] N-C You can describe a system of beliefs or a traditional institution as an **edifice**. ...the ancient edifice of monarchy.

edit /'edɪt/ **edits, editing, edited.** [1] VERB If you **edit** a text, you correct it so that it is suitable for publication. She had helped him by editing his manuscript. [2] VERB If you **edit** a book, you collect pieces of writing by different authors and prepare them for publication. ...a collection of essays, edited by Toni Morrison. [3] VERB If you **edit** a film or a television or radio programme, you choose some of what has been filmed or recorded and arrange it in a particular order. He taught me how to edit and splice film... He is editing together excerpts of some of his films. [4] VERB Someone who **edits** a newspaper or magazine is in charge of it and makes decisions concerning the contents.
▸ **edit out.** PHR-VERB If you **edit** something **out** of a book or film, you remove it. His voice will be edited out of the final film.

edition /ɪ'dɪʃən/ **editions.** [1] N-C An **edition** is a particular version of a book, magazine, or newspaper that is printed at one time. This is the second edition of a popular book. ...a paperback edition. [2] N-C An **edition** is a single television or radio programme that is one of a series. ...the Monday edition of 'Eastenders'.

editor /'edɪtə/ **editors.** [1] N-C An **editor** is a person in charge of a newspaper or magazine, or a section of a newspaper or magazine, who makes decisions concerning the contents. [2] N-C An **editor** is a person who checks and corrects texts before they are published. [3] N-C An **editor** is a person who is collecting pieces of writing by different authors and preparing them for publication. Michael Rosen is the editor of the anthology. [4] N-C An **editor** is a person who selects recorded material for a film or for a radio or television programme.

editorial /ˌedɪ'tɔːrɪəl/ **editorials.** [1] ADJ BEFORE N **Editorial** means involved in preparing a newspaper, magazine, or book for publication. *...the editorial staff of 'Private Eye'.* [2] ADJ BEFORE N **Editorial** means involving the attitudes, opinions, and contents of a newspaper, magazine, or television programme. *We are not about to change our editorial policy.* [3] N-C An **editorial** is an article in a newspaper which gives the opinion of the editor or publisher on a particular topic.

educate /'edʒukeɪt/ **educates, educating, educated.** [1] VERB When someone **is educated**, they are taught at a school or college. *He was educated at Haslingden Grammar School.* [2] VERB To **educate** people means to improve their understanding of a particular problem or issue. *...a game designed to help educate teenagers about AIDS.*

> Note that you do not use **educate** or **education** to talk about the way parents look after their children and gradually teach them about good behaviour and life in general. Instead, you should use the verb **bring up** or the noun **upbringing**. *His parents brought him up to be polite and courteous. ...the effect that this religious upbringing has had on me.*

educated /'edʒukeɪtɪd/. ADJ **Educated** people have reached a high standard of learning.

education /ˌedʒu'keɪʃən/ **educations.** N-VAR **Education** means learning and teaching. *They're cutting funds for education... Parents are the most important factor in a child's education.* ◆**educational** ADJ *...declining educational standards.*

Edwardian /ed'wɔːdiən/ **Edwardians.** [1] ADJ **Edwardian** means connected with or typical of Britain in the first decade of the 20th century, when Edward VII was King. *...the Edwardian era.* [2] N-C People associated with the Edwardian period are sometimes called **Edwardians**.

eel /iːl/ **eels.** N-C An **eel** is a fish with a long, thin body.

eerie /'ɪəri/. ADJ Something that is **eerie** is strange and frightening. *...an eerie silence.* ◆**eerily** ADV *The streets were eerily deserted.*

effect /ɪ'fekt/ **effects, effecting, effected.** [1] N-VAR An **effect** is a change, reaction, or impression that is caused by something or is the result of something. *...the effect of divorce on children... Head injuries can cause long-lasting psychological effects... She paused, obviously for effect.* [2] VERB If you **effect** something, you succeed in causing it to happen; FORMAL. *...prospects for effecting real political change.* [3] See also **side-effect**.

PHRASES ● You add **in effect** to a statement which you feel is a reasonable description or summary of something. *That deal would create, in effect, the world's biggest airline.* ● You use **to this effect, to that effect**, or **to the effect that** when you are summarizing what someone has said, rather than repeating their actual words. *...statements to the effect that they're not prepared to negotiate with this regime.* ● When something **takes effect, comes into effect**, or **is**

put into effect, it begins to apply or starts to have results. ● You use **effect** in expressions such as **to good effect** and **to no effect** in order to indicate how successful or impressive an action is. *Mr Charles complained, to no effect.*

effective /ɪ'fektɪv/. [1] ADJ Something that is **effective** produces the intended results. *...the most effective way of teaching writing... The vaccine is effective against most allergies.* ◆**effectively** ADV *I learned to exert my authority more effectively.* ◆**effectiveness** N-U *...the effectiveness of computers as an educational tool.* [2] ADJ **Effective** means having a particular role or result in practice, though not officially. *The rebels have been in effective control of the island since March.* [3] ADJ AFTER LINK-V When a law or an agreement becomes **effective**, it begins officially to apply.

effectively /ɪ'fektɪvli/. ADV You use **effectively** with a statement which you feel is a reasonable description or summary of a particular situation. *President Elchibey has effectively lost power.*

efficacy /'efɪkəsi/. N-U The **efficacy** of something is its effectiveness in producing the intended results. *The World Health Organisation is to analyse the drug to test its safety and efficacy.*

efficient /ɪ'fɪʃənt/. ADJ Something or someone that is **efficient** does a job successfully, without wasting time or energy. *Cycling is the most efficient form of transport. ...energy-efficient lighting.* ◆**efficiently** ADV *...a campaign to encourage consumers to use energy more efficiently.* ◆**efficiency** /ɪ'fɪʃənsi/ N-U *They marvelled at her efficiency.*

effort /'efət/ **efforts.** [1] N-VAR If you make an **effort** to do something, you try hard to do it. *He made no effort to hide his disappointment... He died despite the frantic efforts of lifeguards.* [2] N-VAR If you do something with **effort**, or if it is an **effort**, you can do it but you find it physically or mentally demanding. *She took a deep breath and sat up slowly and with great effort... With an effort he rose to his feet... Even carrying the camcorder while hiking in the forest was an effort.*

effortless /'efətləs/. ADJ If an action is **effortless**, it is achieved easily. *...the sense of seemingly effortless movement.* ◆**effortlessly** ADV *Peter adapted effortlessly to his new surroundings.*

EFL /ˌiː ef 'el/. N-U **EFL** is used to describe things connected with the teaching of English to people whose first language is not English. **EFL** is an abbreviation for 'English as a Foreign Language'. *...an EFL teacher.*

e.g. /ˌiː 'dʒiː/. **e.g.** is an abbreviation that means 'for example'. It is used before a noun, or to introduce another sentence. *...products made from cream, e.g., cheese, butter, etc.*

egg /eg/ **eggs, egging, egged.** [1] N-C An **egg** is the rounded object produced by a female bird from which a baby bird later emerges. Reptiles, fish, and insects also produce eggs. *...a baby bird hatching from its egg.* [2] N-VAR An **egg** is a hen's egg considered as food. *Break the eggs into a shallow bowl. ...bacon and egg.*

3 N-C An **egg** is a cell in a female person or animal which can develop into a baby.

▶ **egg on.** PHR-VERB If you **egg** someone **on**, you encourage them to do something that is daring or foolish.

ego /ˈiːgəʊ, ˈegəʊ/. **egos.** N-VAR Someone's **ego** is their sense of their own self and their worth. *It's a great blow to your ego... She's got a lot of ego invested in her career.*

eight /eɪt/ **eights.** NUM **Eight** is the number 8.

eighteen /ˌeɪˈtiːn/. NUM **Eighteen** is the number 18.

eighteenth /ˌeɪˈtiːnθ/. ORD The **eighteenth** item in a series is the one that you count as number eighteen.

eighth /eɪtθ/ **eighths.** **1** ORD The **eighth** item in a series is the one that you count as number eight. *...the eighth century.* **2** N-C An **eighth** is one of eight equal parts of something. *...an eighth of an inch thick.*

eightieth /ˈeɪtiəθ/. ORD The **eightieth** item in a series is the one that you count as number eighty.

eighty /ˈeɪti/ **eighties.** **1** NUM **Eighty** is the number 80. **2** N-PL When you talk about the **eighties**, you are talking about numbers between 80 and 89. For example, if you are **in your eighties**, you are aged between 80 and 89. If the temperature is **in the eighties**, the temperature is between 80 and 89 degrees. If something happened **in the eighties**, it happened between 1980 and 1989.

either /ˈaɪðə, ˈiːðə/. **1** CONJ You use **either** in front of the first of two or more alternatives, when you are stating the only possibilities or choices that there are. The other alternatives are introduced by 'or'. *Sightseeing is best done either by tour bus or by bicycles... He should be either put on trial or set free... Either she goes or I go.* **2** PRON & DET You can use **either** to refer to one of two things, people, or situations, when you want to say that they are both possible and it does not matter which one is chosen or considered. *There were glasses of iced champagne and cigars. Unfortunately not many of either were consumed. ...the authority to pursue suspects into either country... Do either of you smoke cigarettes?* **3** PRON & DET & CONJ You can use **either** in a negative statement to refer to each of two things, people, or situations to indicate that the negative statement includes both of them. *She warned me that I'd never marry or have children.—'I don't want either.'... He sometimes couldn't remember either man's name. ...music that fails to be either funny or funky.* **4** DET You use **either** to introduce a noun that refers to each of two things when you are talking about both of them. *The basketball nets hung down from the ceiling at either end of the gymnasium.* **5** ADV You use **either** by itself in negative statements to indicate that there is a similarity or connection with a person or thing that you have just mentioned. *He did not even say anything to her, and she did not speak to him either.*

eject /ɪˈdʒekt/ **ejects, ejecting, ejected.** **1** VERB If someone **ejects** you from a place, they force you to leave. *Officials used guard dogs to eject the protesters.* ♦**ejection, ejec-**

tions N-VAR *...the ejection and manhandling of hecklers at the meeting.* **2** VERB To **eject** something means to remove it or push it out forcefully. *...the volcanic dust that is sometimes ejected into the stratosphere.*

elaborate, elaborates, elaborating, elaborated. **1** ADJ /ɪˈlæbərət/ You use **elaborate** to describe something that consists of many different parts, making it very detailed or complex. *...an elaborate ceremony that lasts for eight days.* ♦**elaborately** ADV *...elaborately costumed dolls.* **2** VERB /ɪˈlæbəreɪt/ If you **elaborate on** a plan or a theory, or if you **elaborate** a plan or theory, you give more details about it. *Lieutenant Cerezzi refused to elaborate on possible motives for the killing.* ♦**elaboration** N-U *...the elaboration of specific policies.*

elapse /ɪˈlæps/ **elapses, elapsing, elapsed.** VERB When time **elapses**, it passes; FORMAL. *Forty-eight hours have elapsed since his arrest.*

elastic /ɪˈlæstɪk/. **1** N-U **Elastic** is a rubber material that stretches when you pull it and returns to its original size when you let it go. *...bouncing around on a piece of elastic.* **2** ADJ Something that is **elastic** stretches easily. *Like all arteries, it is elastic and muscular.*

elasticity /ˌiːlæˈstɪsɪti, ˌlæst-/. N-U The **elasticity** of a material or substance is its ability to return to its original shape, size, and condition after it has been stretched. *Daily facial exercises help her to retain the skin's elasticity.*

elated /ɪˈleɪtɪd/. ADJ If you are **elated**, you are extremely happy and excited because of something that has happened. *'That was one of the best races of my life,' said an elated Mansell.* ♦**elation** /ɪˈleɪʃən/ N-U *His supporters have reacted to the news with elation.*

elbow /ˈelbəʊ/. **elbows, elbowing, elbowed.** **1** N-C Your **elbow** is the joint where your arm bends in the middle. **2** VERB If you **elbow** someone away, you push them aside with your elbow. If you **elbow** your way somewhere, you move there by pushing other people out of the way, using your elbows. *The security team elbowed aside a steward... Her burly boyfriend elbowed him into the gutter.* **3** VERB If someone **elbows** you, they intentionally hurt you by hitting you with their elbow. *He blatantly elbowed Harding right in the eye.*

elder /ˈeldə/ **elders.** **1** ADJ The **elder** of two people is the one who was born first. *...his elder brother.*

> In British English, the adjective **elder** is usually only used to describe brothers and sisters. *...her elder sister.* **Elder** cannot be followed by **than** but **older** can be followed by **than**. *I've got a sister who is older than me.*

2 N-C A person's **elder** is someone who is older than them. **3** N-C In some societies, an **elder** is one of the respected older people who have influence and authority.

elderly /ˈeldəli/. ADJ & N-PL You use **elderly** as a polite way of saying that someone is old. **The elderly** are people who are old. *...an elderly couple. ...programs that provide health care to the elderly.*

eldest /'eldɪst/. ADJ The **eldest** person in a group is the one who was born before all the others. ...*her eldest daughter, Lisa.*

elect /ɪ'lekt/ **elects, electing, elected.** [1] VERB When people **elect** someone, they choose that person to represent them, by voting. *Manchester College elected him Principal in 1956. ...electing a woman as its new president. ...the country's democratically elected president.* [2] VERB If you **elect** to do something, you choose to do it; FORMAL. *Those electing to smoke will be seated at the rear.*

election /ɪ'lekʃən/ **elections.** [1] N-VAR An **election** is a process in which people vote to choose a person or group of people to hold an official position. ...*Poland's first fully free elections for more than fifty years. ...his election campaign.* [2] N-U The **election** of a person or a political party is their success in winning an election. ...*the election of the Labour government in 1964. ...Vaclav Havel's election as president.* [3] See also **by-election, general election.**

elector /ɪ'lektə/ **electors.** N-C An **elector** is a person who has the right to vote in an election.

electoral /ɪ'lektərəl/. ADJ BEFORE N **Electoral** means connected with an election. ...*Italy's electoral system.* ♦**electorally** ADV *A period of recession was electorally damaging.*

electorate /ɪ'lektərət/ **electorates.** N-C The **electorate** of a country is the people there who have the right to vote in an election. **Electorate** can take the singular or plural form of the verb. *He has the backing of almost a quarter of the electorate.*

electric /ɪ'lektrɪk/. [1] ADJ BEFORE N An **electric** device works by means of electricity. [2] ADJ BEFORE N An **electric** current, voltage, or charge is one that is produced by electricity. **Electric** plugs, sockets, or power lines are designed to carry electricity. [3] ADJ If you describe the atmosphere of a place or event as **electric**, you mean that people are in a state of great excitement.

electrical /ɪ'lektrɪkəl/. [1] ADJ BEFORE N **Electrical** devices work by means of electricity. ...*electrical equipment.* ♦**electrically** ADV ...*electrically-powered vehicles.* [2] ADJ BEFORE N **Electrical** engineers and industries are involved in the production or maintenance of electricity or electrical goods.

electrician /ɪlek'trɪʃən, ˌiːlek-/ **electricians.** N-C An **electrician** is a person whose job is to install and repair electrical equipment.

electricity /ɪlek'trɪsɪti, ˌiːlek-/. N-U **Electricity** is a form of energy used for heating and lighting, and to provide power for machines.

e,lectric 'shock, electric shocks. See shock meaning 7.

electrify /ɪ'lektrɪfaɪ/ **electrifies, electrifying, electrified.** [1] VERB If something **electrifies** you, it excites and surprises you a lot. *The world was electrified by his courage and resistance.* ♦**electrifying** ADJ ...*an electrifying performance.* [2] VERB When a railway system is **electrified**, it is connected by overhead wires or by a special rail to a supply of electricity. ♦**electrification** /ɪˌlektrɪfɪ'keɪʃən/ N-U ...*the electrification of the Oxted to Uckfield line.*

electrocute /ɪ'lektrəkjuːt/ **electrocutes, electrocuting, electrocuted.** VERB If someone **is electrocuted**, they are accidentally killed or injured when they touch something connected to a source of electricity. *He accidentally electrocuted himself.* ♦**electrocution** N-U ...*safety switches designed to switch off in a second to prevent electrocution.*

electron /ɪ'lektrɒn/. N-C An **electron** is a tiny particle of matter that is smaller than an atom and has a negative electrical charge.

electronic /ɪlek'trɒnɪk, ˌiː-/. [1] ADJ BEFORE N An **electronic** device has transistors, silicon chips, or valves which control and change the electric current passing through it. [2] ADJ An **electronic** process involves the use of electronic devices. ...*electronic surveillance.* ♦**electronically** ADV ...*electronically operated gates.*

electronics /ɪlek'trɒnɪks/. [1] N-U **Electronics** is the technology of using transistors and silicon chips, especially in devices such as radios, televisions, and computers. ...*Europe's three main electronics companies.* [2] N-PL You can refer to electronic devices, or the part of a piece of equipment that consists of electronic devices, as the **electronics**. *It is hoped that all the electronics could be contained in a microchip.*

elegant /'elɪgənt/. [1] ADJ If you describe a person or thing as **elegant**, you think they are pleasing and graceful. ...*an elegant restaurant.* ♦**elegance** N-U ...*Princess Grace's understated elegance.* ♦**elegantly** ADV *a tall, elegantly dressed man.* [2] ADJ If you describe a piece of writing, an idea, or a plan as **elegant**, you mean that it is simple, clear, and clever. ♦**elegance** N-U *The delight comes from the simple elegance of the writing.* ♦**elegantly** ADV ...*her funny and elegantly written memoirs.*

element /'elɪmənt/ **elements.** [1] N-C An **element** of something is one of the parts which make up the whole thing. ...*one of the key elements of the UN's peace plan... Fitness has now become an important element in our lives.* [2] N-C When you talk about the particular **elements** within a society or organization, you are referring to groups of people who have similar aims, beliefs, or habits. ...*criminal elements.* [3] N-C If something has an **element** of a particular quality, it has a certain amount of it. *These reports clearly contain elements of propaganda.* [4] N-C The **element** in an electrical appliance is the metal part which changes the electric current into heat. [5] N-PL You can refer to the weather, especially wind and rain, as the **elements**. *Our open boat is exposed to the elements.* [6] PHRASE If someone is **in** their **element**, they are doing something that they enjoy and do well. *My stepmother was in her element, organizing everything.*

elemental /ˌelɪ'mentəl/. ADJ **Elemental** feelings and behaviour are simple and forceful; LITERARY. *Jamie resorted to a more elemental tactic.*

elementary /ˌelɪ'mentri/. ADJ **Elementary** things are very simple, straightforward, and basic. ...*elementary computer skills.*

elephant /'elɪfənt/ **elephants.** N-C An **elephant** is a very large animal with a long trunk.

elevate /'elɪveɪt/ **elevates, elevating, elevated.** [1] VERB When someone or something **is elevated** to a more important rank or status, they achieve it; FORMAL. *He was elevated to the post of prime minister.* ◆**elevation** N-U *...his elevation to the papacy.* [2] VERB To **elevate** something means to increase it in amount or intensity; FORMAL. *Emotional stress can elevate blood pressure.* [3] VERB If you **elevate** something, you raise it above a horizontal level; FORMAL.

elevation /ˌelɪ'veɪʃən/ **elevations.** N-C The **elevation** of a place is its height above sea level.

elevator /'elɪveɪtə/ **elevators.** N-C In American English, an **elevator** is a device that carries people up and down inside buildings. The usual British word is **lift**.

eleven /ɪ'levən/. NUM **Eleven** is the number 11.

eleventh /ɪ'levənθ/. ORD The **eleventh** item in a series is the one that you count as number eleven.

elicit /ɪ'lɪsɪt/ **elicits, eliciting, elicited.** [1] VERB If you **elicit** a response or a reaction, you do or say something which makes other people respond or react. *He was hopeful that his request would elicit a positive response.* [2] VERB If you **elicit** a piece of information, you get it by asking the right questions. *Several phone calls elicited no further information.*

eligible /'elɪdʒɪbəl/. ADJ Someone who is **eligible** for something is entitled or able to have it. *Almost half the population are eligible to vote.* ◆**eligibility** N-U *...the rules covering eligibility for benefits.*

eliminate /ɪ'lɪmɪneɪt/ **eliminates, eliminating, eliminated.** [1] VERB To **eliminate** something means to remove it completely; FORMAL. *If you think you may be allergic to a food or drink, eliminate it from your diet.* ◆**elimination** N-U *...the complete elimination of nuclear weapons.* [2] VERB When a person or team **is eliminated** from a competition, they are defeated and so take no further part in it.

elite /ɪ'liːt, eɪ-/ **elites.** N-C & ADJ BEFORE N You can refer to the most powerful, rich, or talented people within a particular group or society as the **elite**. You can also talk about an **elite** group of people. *...China's intellectual elite. ...elite troops.*

elitist /ɪ'liːtɪst, eɪ-/ **elitists.** [1] ADJ If you describe an activity, a profession, or a system as **elitist**, you mean that it is practised only by a small group of powerful, rich, or talented people, or that it favours only this group of people; used showing disapproval. *The legal profession is starting to be less elitist.* ◆**elitism** N-U *...the arrogance and elitism of gallery owners. ...a conference against elitism.* [2] N-C An **elitist** is someone who believes that they are part of an elite; used showing disapproval.

elm /elm/ **elms.** N-VAR An **elm** is a tree with broad leaves which it loses in winter.

eloquent /'eləkwənt/. ADJ A person who is **eloquent** is good at speaking and able to persuade people; used showing approval. *...one particularly eloquent German critic. ...a very eloquent speech.* ◆**eloquence** N-U *...his eloquence and persuasiveness.* ◆**eloquently** ADV *Jan speaks eloquently about her art.*

else /els/. [1] ADV You use **else** after words such as 'anywhere', 'someone', 'what', 'everyone' and 'everything' to refer vaguely to another place, person, or thing, or to refer to all the other people, places, or things except the one you are talking about. *What else have you had for your birthday?... I never wanted to live anywhere else... Cigarettes are in short supply, like everything else here... London seems so much dirtier than everywhere else here.* [2] CONJ You use **or else** after stating a logical conclusion, to indicate that what you are about to say is evidence for that conclusion. *Evidently no lessons have been learnt or else the government would not have handled the problem so sloppily.* [3] CONJ You use **or else** to introduce a possibility or alternative. *Make sure you are strapped in very well, or else you will fall out... You are either a total genius or else you must be absolutely raving mad.* [4] PHRASE You can say **'if nothing else'** to indicate that what you are mentioning is, in your opinion, the only good thing in a particular situation. *If nothing else, you'll really enjoy meeting them.*

elsewhere /ˌels'weə/. ADV **Elsewhere** means in other places or to another place. *Almost 80 percent of the state's residents were born elsewhere... But if you are not satisfied then go elsewhere.*

ELT /ˌiː el 'tiː/. N-U **ELT** is the teaching of English to people whose first language is a language other than English. **ELT** is an abbreviation for 'English Language Teaching'.

elude /ɪ'luːd/ **eludes, eluding, eluded.** [1] VERB If something that you want **eludes** you, you fail to obtain it. *Sleep eluded her... The appropriate word eluded him.* [2] VERB If you **elude** someone or something, you avoid them or escape from them. *He eluded the police for 13 years.*

elusive /ɪ'luːsɪv/. ADJ Something or someone that is **elusive** is difficult to find, achieve, describe, or remember. *In London late-night taxis are always elusive.*

e-mail (or **E-mail**) /'iːmeɪl/. N-U **E-mail** is a system of sending written messages electronically from one computer to another. **E-mail** is an abbreviation for 'electronic mail'.

emanate /'eməneɪt/ **emanates, emanating, emanated.** [1] VERB If a quality, idea, or feeling **emanates** from you, or if you **emanate** a quality or feeling, you give people a strong sense that you have that quality or feeling; FORMAL. *He emanates sympathy.* [2] VERB If something **emanates** from somewhere, it comes from there; FORMAL. *...reports emanating from America.*

emancipate /ɪ'mænsɪpeɪt/ **emancipates, emancipating, emancipated.** VERB If people **are emancipated**, they are freed from unpleasant or degrading social, political, or legal restrictions; FORMAL. *That war preserved the Union and emancipated the slaves.* ◆**emancipation** N-U *...women's emancipation.*

embankment /ɪm'bæŋkmənt/ **embankments.** N-C An **embankment** is a thick wall built of earth, often supporting a railway line or road.

embargo /ɪmˈbɑːgəʊ/ **embargoes.** N-C An embargo is an order made by a government to
stop trade with another country.

embark /ɪmˈbɑːk/ **embarks, embarking, em-
barked.** [1] VERB If you **embark** on something
new, you start doing it. *He's embarking on a
new career as a writer.* [2] VERB When you embark on a ship, you go on board before the
start of a journey.

embarrass /ɪmˈbærəs/ **embarrasses, embarrassing, embarrassed.** [1] VERB If something
or someone **embarrasses** you, it makes you
feel shy or ashamed. *It embarrassed him that
he had no idea of what was going on.*
♦**embarrassing** ADJ *That was an embarrassing
situation for me.* ♦**embarrassingly** ADV
*Stephens had beaten him embarrassingly easi-
ly.* [2] VERB If something **embarrasses** a politician, it causes political problems for them. *The
Government has been embarrassed by the affair.* ♦**embarrassing** ADJ *He has put the Bonn
government in an embarrassing position.*

embarrassed /ɪmˈbærəst/. ADJ A person who is
embarrassed feels shy, ashamed, or guilty
about something.

embarrassment /ɪmˈbærəsmənt/ **embarrass-
ments.** [1] N-U **Embarrassment** is a feeling of
shyness, shame, or guilt. *We apologise for any
embarrassment this may have caused.* [2] N-C If
you refer to a person as **an embarrassment**,
you mean that you disapprove of them but
cannot avoid your connection with them. *His
wife's family were something of an embarrassment to him.*

embassy /ˈembəsi/ **embassies.** N-C An embassy is a group of officials, headed by an ambassador, who represent their government in a
foreign country. The building in which they
work is also called an **embassy**.

embedded /ɪmˈbedɪd/. [1] ADJ If an object is
embedded in something, it is fixed there firmly
and deeply. *There is glass embedded in the cut.*
[2] ADJ If an attitude or feeling is **embedded** in a
society or in someone's personality, it has become a permanent feature of it. *...the racism
still so strongly embedded in our society.*

embellish /ɪmˈbelɪʃ/ **embellishes, embel-
lishing, embellished.** [1] VERB If something
is **embellished** with decorative features, they
are added to make it more attractive. *Ivy leaves
embellish the front of the dresser.*
♦**embellishment** /ɪmˈbelɪʃmənt/ **embellish-
ments.** N-VAR *...buildings with little bits of decoration and embellishment.* [2] VERB If you embellish a story, you make it more interesting by
adding details which may be untrue.

embezzle /ɪmˈbezəl/ **embezzles, embez-
zling, embezzled.** VERB If someone **embezzles** money that their organization or company
has placed in their care, they take it and use it
illegally for their own purposes.
♦**embezzlement** N-U *...charges of forgery and
embezzlement.*

emblem /ˈembləm/ **emblems.** [1] N-C An emblem is a design representing a country or organization. [2] N-C An **emblem** is something
symbolizing a quality or idea. *The eagle was an
emblem of strength and courage.*

embodiment /ɪmˈbɒdɪmənt/. N-SING If you describe someone or something as the **embodiment** of a quality or idea, you mean that it is
their most noticeable characteristic or the basis of all they do; FORMAL. *A baby is the embodiment of vulnerability.*

embody /ɪmˈbɒdi/ **embodies, embodying,
embodied.** [1] VERB If someone or something
embodies an idea or quality, they are a symbol
or expression of that idea or quality. *Jack Kennedy embodied all the hopes of the 1960s.*
[2] VERB If something **is embodied** in a particular thing, the second thing contains or consists
of the first. *This strategy was embodied in two
early pieces of legislation.*

embrace /ɪmˈbreɪs/ **embraces, embracing,
embraced.** [1] VERB & N-C When you **embrace**
someone, you put your arms around them in
order to show your affection for them. This action is called an **embrace**. *The couple in the
corridor were embracing each other. ...a young
couple locked in an embrace.* [2] VERB If you
embrace a change, political system, or idea,
you start supporting it or believing in it wholeheartedly; FORMAL. *The new rules have been
embraced by government watchdog organizations.* [3] VERB If something **embraces** a group
of people, things, or ideas, it includes them;
FORMAL. *...a theory that would embrace the
whole field of human endeavour.*

embroider /ɪmˈbrɔɪdə/ **embroiders, embroidering, embroidered.** VERB If cloth is embroidered with a design, the design is stitched
into it. *Matilda was embroidering an altar
cloth.*

embroidery /ɪmˈbrɔɪdəri/ **embroideries.**
[1] N-VAR **Embroidery** consists of designs sewn
onto cloth. [2] N-U **Embroidery** is the activity of
sewing designs onto cloth.

embroiled /ɪmˈbrɔɪld/. ADJ If you become embroiled in an argument or with a person, you
become deeply involved in that argument or in
a relationship with that person, often causing
problems for yourself.

embryo /ˈembriəʊ/ **embryos.** N-C An embryo is
an animal or human in the very early stages of
development in the womb.

embryonic /ˌembriˈɒnɪk/. ADJ **Embryonic**
means in a very early stage of development;
FORMAL. *...Romania's embryonic democracy.*

emerald /ˈemərəld/ **emeralds.** N-C An emerald
is a bright green precious stone.

emerge /ɪˈmɜːdʒ/ **emerges, emerging,
emerged.** [1] VERB When you **emerge**, you
come out from a place where you could not be
seen. *The postman emerged from his van
soaked.* [2] VERB If you **emerge** from a difficult
or bad experience, you come to the end of it.
*The nation is emerging from the recession slow-
ly.* [3] VERB When something **emerges** as a political
movement **emerges**, it comes into existence;
JOURNALISM. ♦**emergence** N-U *...the emergence
of new democracies in East and Central Europe.*

emergency /ɪˈmɜːdʒənsi/ **emergencies.**
[1] N-C An **emergency** is an unexpected and serious situation such as an accident, which
must be dealt with quickly. *The hospital will
cater only for emergencies.* [2] ADJ BEFORE N An
emergency action is one that is done or ar-

ranged quickly, in response to an emergency. *...an emergency meeting of parliament.* [3] ADJ BEFORE N **Emergency** equipment or supplies are those intended for use in an emergency. *...an emergency exit.*

emigrate /ˈemɪɡreɪt/ **emigrates, emigrating, emigrated.** VERB If you **emigrate**, you leave your own country to live in another. *He emigrated to Belgium.* ◆**emigration** N-U *...the huge emigration of workers to the West.*

eminent /ˈemɪnənt/. ADJ An **eminent** person is well-known and respected. *...an eminent scientist.* ◆**eminence** /ˈemɪnəns/ N-U *Beveridge was a man of great eminence.*

eminently /ˈemɪnəntli/. ADV You use **eminently** in front of an adjective describing a positive quality in order to emphasize the quality expressed by that adjective. *His family was eminently respectable.*

emission /ɪˈmɪʃən/ **emissions.** N-VAR An **emission** of light, heat, radiation, or a harmful gas is the release of it into the atmosphere; FORMAL.

emit /ɪˈmɪt/ **emits, emitting, emitted.** VERB To **emit** a sound, smell, or substance means to produce it or send it out; FORMAL. *Polly blinked and emitted a long, low whistle.*

emotion /ɪˈməʊʃən/ **emotions.** N-VAR Emotion is strong feeling such as joy or love. An **emotion** is one of these feelings. *Her voice trembled with emotion... Jealousy is a destructive emotion, and one I avoid.*

emotional /ɪˈməʊʃənəl/. [1] ADJ **Emotional** means relating to emotions and feelings. ◆**emotionally** ADV *He'd learned never to become emotionally involved.* [2] ADJ When someone is **emotional**, they show their feelings openly, especially because they are upset.

emotive /ɪˈməʊtɪv/. ADJ An **emotive** situation or issue is likely to make people feel strong emotions. *Embryo research is an emotive issue.*

empathy /ˈempəθi/. N-U **Empathy** is the ability to share another person's feelings as if they were your own feelings. *He had a natural empathy with children.*

emperor /ˈempərə/ **emperors.** N-C An **emperor** is a man who rules an empire.

emphasis /ˈemfəsɪs/ **emphases** /ˈemfəsiːz/. [1] N-VAR **Emphasis** is special importance that is given to one part or aspect of something. *A family-run hotel and restaurant, with the emphasis firmly on comfort.* [2] N-VAR **Emphasis** is extra force that you put on a syllable, word, or phrase when you are speaking. *The emphasis is on the first syllable of the last word.*

emphasize (BR also **emphasise**) /ˈemfəsaɪz/ **emphasizes, emphasizing, emphasized.** VERB To **emphasize** something means to indicate that it is particularly important or true, or to draw special attention to it. *Your letter should emphasize how your skills will benefit the employer.*

emphatic /ɪmˈfætɪk/. [1] ADJ An **emphatic** statement is made forcefully. ◆**emphatically** ADV *The president emphatically denied that suggestion.* [2] ADJ An **emphatic** victory is one where the winner wins easily.

empire /ˈempaɪə/ **empires.** [1] N-C An **empire** is a group of countries controlled by one power-

ful country. [2] N-C A business **empire** is a group of companies controlled by one powerful person. *...the big Mondadori publishing empire.*

empirical /ɪmˈpɪrɪkəl/. ADJ **Empirical** knowledge or evidence is based on observation, experiment, and experience rather than theories. ◆**empirically** ADV *To some extent it can be demonstrated empirically.*

employ /ɪmˈplɔɪ/ **employs, employing, employed.** [1] VERB If a person or company **employs** you, they pay you to work for them. *3,000 local workers are employed in the tourism industry.* [2] VERB If you **employ** methods, materials, or expressions, you make use of them; FORMAL. *...the clever advertising employed by U.S. cigarette companies.*

employee /ɪmˈplɔɪiː/ **employees.** N-C An **employee** is a person who is paid to work for a company or organization. *He is an employee of Fuji Bank.*

employer /ɪmˈplɔɪə/ **employers.** N-C Your **employer** is the organization or person that you work for.

employment /ɪmˈplɔɪmənt/. N-U If you are in **employment**, you have a paid job. *She was unable to find employment.*

empower /ɪmˈpaʊə/ **empowers, empowering, empowered.** VERB If someone or something **empowers** you, they give you the means to achieve something, for example to become more successful. *...to empower people, to give them ways to help them get well.* ◆**empowerment** N-U *...the empowerment of women.*

empress /ˈemprɪs/ **empresses.** N-C An **empress** is a woman who rules an empire, or the wife of an emperor.

empty /ˈempti/ **emptier, emptiest; empties, emptying, emptied.** [1] ADJ An **empty** place, vehicle, or container has no people or things in it. *The room was bare and empty... The roads were nearly empty of traffic.* ◆**emptiness** N-U *...the emptiness of the desert.* [2] VERB If you **empty** a container, or if you **empty** something out of it, you remove its contents. *Empty the noodles and liquid into a serving bowl... He emptied the contents out into the palm of his hand.* [3] VERB If someone **empties** a room or place, or if it **empties**, everyone in that place leaves. *The stadium emptied at the end of the first day of athletics.* [4] ADJ If you describe something as **empty**, you mean that it has no real value or meaning. *Sometimes I even make empty threats that I have no intention of carrying out.* ◆**emptiness** N-U *In my private life there was emptiness.*

empty-'handed. ADJ If you come back from somewhere **empty-handed**, you have failed to get what you intended to get.

emulate /ˈemjʊleɪt/ **emulates, emulating, emulated.** VERB If you **emulate** someone or something, you imitate them because you admire them; FORMAL. *Sons are traditionally expected to emulate their fathers.*

enable /ɪnˈeɪbəl/ **enables, enabling, enabled.** VERB If someone or something **enables** you to do something, they make it possible for you to do it. *The new test should enable doctors to detect the disease early.*

enact /ɪn'ækt/ **enacts, enacting, enacted.** [1] VERB When a government **enacts** a proposal, they make it into a law; TECHNICAL. ◆**enactment, enactments** N-VAR ...*the enactment of a Bill of Rights.* [2] VERB If people **enact** a story or play, they act it; FORMAL.

enamel /ɪ'næməl/ **enamels.** N-U **Enamel** is a substance which can be heated and put onto metal in order to decorate or protect it.

encapsulate /ɪn'kæpsjʊleɪt/ **encapsulates, encapsulating, encapsulated.** VERB If something **encapsulates** facts or ideas, it contains or represents them in a very small space or in a single object or event. *The editorial encapsulated the views of many conservatives.*

encase /ɪn'keɪs/ **encases, encasing, encased.** VERB If something **is encased** in a container or material, it is completely enclosed within it or covered by it. *The procedure involves encasing the concrete columns with steel.*

enchant /ɪn'tʃɑːnt, -'tʃænt/ **enchants, enchanting, enchanted.** [1] VERB If you are **enchanted** by someone or something, you think they are very pleasing. ◆**enchanting** ADJ *She's an absolutely enchanting child.* [2] VERB In fairy stories and legends, to **enchant** someone means to put a magic spell on them.

encircle /ɪn'sɜːkəl/ **encircles, encircling, encircled.** VERB To **encircle** something or someone means to surround them completely. *A forty-foot-high concrete wall encircles the jail.*

enclave /'eŋkleɪv/ **enclaves.** N-C An **enclave** is a place that is different from the areas surrounding it, for example because the people there are from a different culture.

enclose /ɪn'kləʊz/ **encloses, enclosing, enclosed.** [1] VERB If a place or object is **enclosed** by something, the place or object is completely surrounded by that thing or is inside it. *The garden was enclosed by a privet hedge... Enclose the pot in a clear polythene bag.* [2] VERB If you **enclose** something with a letter, you put it in the same envelope. *Please remember to enclose a stamped addressed envelope when writing.*

enclosure /ɪn'kləʊʒə/ **enclosures.** N-C An **enclosure** is an area of land surrounded by a wall or fence and used for a special purpose. ...*seats in the VIP enclosure.*

encode /ɪ'kəʊd/ **encodes, encoding, encoded.** VERB When information **is encoded**, it is put into a code. *Throughout the 20th century spies have used random noise to encode their messages.*

encompass /ɪn'kʌmpəs/ **encompasses, encompassing, encompassed.** VERB If something **encompasses** certain things, it includes all of them. *The map shows the rest of the western region, encompassing nine states.*

encore /'ɒŋkɔː, -'kɔː/ **encores.** N-C & CONVEN-TION An **encore** is a short extra performance at the end of a longer one, which an entertainer gives because the audience asks for it, often by shouting 'encore'.

encounter /ɪn'kaʊntə/ **encounters, encountering, encountered.** [1] VERB If you encoun-ter problems or difficulties, you experience them. ...*the practical problems encountered by disabled people.* [2] VERB & N-C If you **encounter** someone, or if you have an **encounter** with them, you meet them; FORMAL. ...*that first encounter with Daniel.*

encourage /ɪn'kʌrɪdʒ, AM -'kɜːr-/ **encourages, encouraging, encouraged.** [1] VERB If you **encourage** someone, you give them confidence, for example by letting them know that what they are doing is good. *When things aren't going well, he encourages me, telling me not to give up.* [2] VERB If someone is **encouraged by** something, it gives them hope or confidence. *She has been encouraged by the unwavering support of her family.* ◆**encouraged** ADJ *He was encouraged that there seemed to be some progress.* [3] VERB If you **encourage** someone to do something, you try to persuade them to do it, for example by trying to make it easier for them to do it. *We want to encourage people to go fishing... Their task is to help encourage private investment.* [4] VERB If something **encourages** a particular activity or state, it causes it to happen or increase. ...*a natural substance that encourages cell growth.*

encouragement /ɪn'kʌrɪdʒmənt, AM -'kɜːr-/ **encouragements.** N-VAR **Encouragement** is the activity of encouraging someone, or something that is said or done in order to encourage them. *Thanks for your advice and encouragement.*

encouraging /ɪn'kʌrɪdʒɪŋ, AM -'kɜːr-/. ADJ Something that is **encouraging** gives you hope or confidence. *It was encouraging that he recognised the dangers.* ◆**encouragingly** ADV ...*encouragingly large audiences.*

encroach /ɪn'krəʊtʃ/ **encroaches, encroaching, encroached.** [1] VERB If one thing **encroaches** on another, it spreads or becomes stronger, and slowly begins to restrict the power, range, or effectiveness of the second thing; used showing disapproval. *The Church is resisting government attempts to encroach upon its authority.* ◆**encroachment, encroachments** N-VAR ...*the encroachment of commercialism in medicine.* [2] VERB If something **encroaches** on a place, it spreads and takes over more and more of that place; FOR-MAL. *Sand dunes began encroaching on agricultural land.*

encyclopedia (BR also **encyclopaedia**) /ɪn,saɪklə'piːdiə/ **encyclopedias.** N-C An **encyclopedia** is a book or set of books in which many facts are arranged for reference, usually in alphabetical order.

end /end/ **ends, ending, ended.** [1] N-SING The **end** of something such as a period of time or an activity is the last part of it or the final point in it. ...*at the end of the 18th century... You will have the chance to ask questions at the end.* [2] VERB & PHRASE When a situation, process, or activity **ends**, or when something or someone **ends** it, it reaches its final point and stops. You can also say that something has **come to an end** or is **at an end**. *The Vietnam War was just about to end... She began to weep. That ended our discussion... The cold war came to an end.* ◆**ending** N-SING ...*the ending of a marriage.*

3 VERB A journey, road, or river that **ends** at a particular place stops there. *The road ended at a T-junction.* **4** The **end** of a long narrow object is the tip or smallest edge of it. *...the end of her cigarette.* **5** N-C An **end** is the purpose for doing something. *The police force is being manipulated for political ends.* **6** See also **ending, dead end.**

PHRASES • If you find it difficult to **make ends meet**, you do not have enough money. • When something happens for days or weeks **on end**, it happens continuously during that time.

▶ **end up.** PHR-VERB If you **end up** in a particular place or situation, you are in that place or situation after a series of events. *The painting ended up at the Tate Gallery... You might end up getting something you don't want.*

endanger /ɪnˈdeɪndʒə/ **endangers, endangering, endangered.** VERB To **endanger** something or someone means to put them in a situation where they might be harmed or destroyed. *Toxic waste could endanger lives. ...endangered species.*

endear /ɪnˈdɪə/ **endears, endearing, endeared.** VERB If something **endears** you to someone, or if you **endear** yourself to them, you become well liked by them. *He has endeared himself to the American public.* ♦**endearing** ADJ *...an endearing personality.*

endeavour (AM endeavor) /ɪnˈdevə/ **endeavours, endeavouring, endeavoured.** **1** VERB If you **endeavour** to do something, you try to do it; FORMAL. *I will endeavour to arrange it.* **2** N-VAR An **endeavour** is an attempt to do something, especially if it is new or original. *...scientific endeavour.*

endemic /enˈdemɪk/. ADJ If a disease or illness is **endemic** in a place, it is frequently found among the people who live there; FORMAL. *Polio was then endemic among children my age.*

ending /ˈendɪŋ/ **endings.** N-C The **ending** of a book, play, or film is the last part of it. *The film has a Hollywood happy ending.* • See also **end.**

endless /ˈendləs/. **1** ADJ If you describe something as **endless**, you mean that it lasts so long that it seems as if it will never end. *...endless meetings and tedious functions.* ♦**endlessly** ADV *They talk about it endlessly.* **2** ADJ **Endless** means very large or long, with no variation. ♦**endlessly** ADV *Rolling green pastures stretch endlessly to the horizon.*

endorse /ɪnˈdɔːs/ **endorses, endorsing, endorsed.** **1** VERB If you **endorse** someone or something, you say publicly that you support or approve of them. *I can endorse their opinion wholeheartedly.* ♦**endorsement, endorsements** N-C *...the committee's endorsement of the idea.* **2** VERB If you **endorse** a product or company, you appear in advertisements for it. *The twins endorsed a line of household cleaning products.* ♦**endorsement** N-C *Her income from endorsements is around $7 million a year.*

endow /ɪnˈdaʊ/ **endows, endowing, endowed.** **1** VERB If someone or something is **endowed** with a quality, they have it or are given it; FORMAL. *Herbs endow a whole range of food with subtle flavours.* **2** VERB If someone **endows** an institution, they provide them with

a large amount of money which is invested to produce an annual income.

endowment /ɪnˈdaʊmənt/ **endowments.** **1** N-C An **endowment** is a gift of money that is made to an institution such as a school. **2** N-C Someone's **endowments** are their natural qualities and abilities; FORMAL. *...their natural mental endowments.*

,end reˈsult, end results. N-C You can describe the result of a lengthy process or activity as its **end result.** *Carbon dioxide is the end result of carbon oxidation.*

endurance /ɪnˈdjʊərəns, AM -ˈdʊr-/. N-U **Endurance** is the ability to continue with a difficult experience or activity over a long period of time. *...his powers of endurance.*

endure /ɪnˈdjʊə, AM -ˈdʊr/ **endures, enduring, endured.** **1** VERB If you **endure** a painful or difficult situation, you bear it calmly and patiently, usually because you have no other choice. *The company endured heavy financial losses. ...unbearable pain, which they had to endure in solitude.* **2** VERB If something **endures**, it continues to exist. *Somehow the language endures.* ♦**enduring** ADJ *...the start of an enduring friendship.*

enemy /ˈenəmi/ **enemies.** **1** N-C Your **enemy** is someone who intends to harm you. **2** N-SING In a war, the **enemy** is the army or country that you are fighting. **Enemy** can take the singular or plural form of the verb for this meaning. *The enemy is approaching the city from all sides... The enemy are all around us.*

energetic /ˌenəˈdʒetɪk/. ADJ An **energetic** person has a lot of energy. **Energetic** activities require a lot of energy. *As young people we were very energetic. ...an energetic display onstage which involves a lot of jumping about.* ♦**energetically** ADV *...dancing energetically around the fire.*

energy /ˈenədʒi/ **energies.** **1** N-U **Energy** is the ability and strength to do active physical things. *He was saving his energy for next week's race.* **2** N-VAR If you put all your **energy** or **energies** into something, you put all your time and effort into it. *He began to put more of his energies into bringing up his son.* **3** N-U **Energy** is power obtained from electricity, coal, or water, that makes machines work or provides heat. *...nuclear energy.*

enforce /ɪnˈfɔːs/ **enforces, enforcing, enforced.** **1** VERB If people in a position of authority **enforce** a law or rule, they make sure that it is obeyed. *The Croatian government was going to enforce a ban on any new refugees.* ♦**enforcement** N-U *The doctors want stricter enforcement of existing laws.* **2** VERB If you **enforce** a particular condition, you force it to be done or to happen. *...the enforced intimacy of life on a small, overcrowded island.*

engage /ɪnˈgeɪdʒ/ **engages, engaging, engaged.** **1** VERB If you **are engaged in** an activity, you are doing it; FORMAL. *You were never engaged in the drug trade.* **2** VERB If something **engages** you, it keeps you interested in it and thinking about it; FORMAL. *The subject has been engaging the attention of many researchers.* **3** VERB If you **engage** someone **in** conversation, you have a conversation with them; FOR-

MAL. *We want to engage recognized leaders in discussion.* [4] VERB If you **engage** someone to do a particular job, you hire them to do it; FORMAL.

engaged /ɪn'geɪdʒd/. [1] ADJ If two people are **engaged**, they have agreed to marry each other. [2] ADJ AFTER LINK-V Someone who is **engaged in** or **on** a particular activity is doing it or involved with it. *The police said they found the three engaged in target practice.* [3] ADJ AFTER LINK-V When a telephone line is **engaged**, it is already being used, so that you are unable to speak to the person you are phoning.

engagement /ɪn'geɪdʒmənt/ **engagements.** [1] N-C An **engagement** is an arrangement that you have made to do something at a particular time; FORMAL. *He had an engagement at a restaurant in Greek Street at eight.* [2] N-C An **engagement** is an agreement that two people have made to get married. You can also refer to the period of time during which they have this agreement as their **engagement**. [3] N-C A military **engagement** is a battle.

engaging /ɪn'geɪdʒɪŋ/. ADJ An **engaging** person or thing is pleasant, interesting, or entertaining.

engender /ɪn'dʒendə/ **engenders, engendering, engendered.** VERB If someone or something **engenders** a particular feeling or situation, they cause it; FORMAL. *He has what it takes to engender loyalty.*

engine /'endʒɪn/ **engines.** [1] N-C A vehicle's **engine** is the part that produces the power to make it move. [2] N-C An **engine** is the large vehicle that pulls a railway train.

engineer /ˌendʒɪ'nɪə/ **engineers, engineering, engineered.** [1] N-C An **engineer** is a skilled person who uses scientific knowledge to design, construct, and maintain engines and machines or structures such as roads and bridges. [2] VERB When a vehicle, bridge, or building **is engineered**, it is planned and constructed using scientific methods. [3] N-C An **engineer** is a person who repairs mechanical or electrical devices. *...a service engineer.* [4] VERB If you **engineer** an event or situation, you cause it to happen, in a clever or indirect way. *The officers engineered a second coup on 19th June.*

engineering /ˌendʒɪ'nɪərɪŋ/. N-U **Engineering** is the work involved in designing and constructing machinery, electrical devices, or roads and bridges.

English /'ɪŋglɪʃ/. [1] ADJ **English** means belonging or relating to England. *...the English way of life.* [2] N-PL The **English** are the people who come from England. [3] N-U **English** is the language spoken by people who live in Great Britain and Ireland, the United States, Canada, Australia, and many other countries.

engraved /ɪn'greɪvd/. ADJ If an object is **engraved**, a design or some writing has been cut into its surface. *...a headstone engraved with the Star of David. ...exquisite engraved glass.*

engrossed /ɪn'grəʊst/. ADJ If you are **engrossed** in something, it holds your attention completely. *Tony didn't notice because he was too engrossed in his work.*

engulf /ɪn'gʌlf/ **engulfs, engulfing, engulfed.** [1] VERB If one thing **engulfs** another, it spreads quickly through it or over it, covering it completely; LITERARY. *A landslide engulfed a block of flats.* [2] VERB If something such as a conflict or hatred **engulfs** a place or a group of people, it spreads uncontrollably through that place or group, effecting everybody strongly; LITERARY. *A revolutionary wave now threatens to engulf the country.*

enhance /ɪn'hɑːns, -'hæns/ **enhances, enhancing, enhanced.** VERB To **enhance** something means to improve its value, quality, or attractiveness. *They'll be keen to enhance their reputation abroad.* ♦**enhancement, enhancements** N-VAR *He was concerned with the enhancement of the human condition.*

enigma /ɪ'nɪgmə/ **enigmas.** N-C If you describe something or someone as an **enigma**, you mean they are mysterious or difficult to understand.

enigmatic /ˌenɪg'mætɪk/. ADJ **Enigmatic** means mysterious and difficult to understand. *...one of Orson Welles's most enigmatic films.* ♦**enigmatically** ADV *His words hung enigmatically in the air.*

enjoy /ɪn'dʒɔɪ/ **enjoys, enjoying, enjoyed.** [1] VERB If you **enjoy** something, it gives you pleasure and satisfaction. *I enjoyed playing cricket.* [2] VERB If you **enjoy yourself**, you do something you like doing. *Eleanor went to Baltimore with Franklin, but did not enjoy herself.* [3] VERB If you **enjoy** something such as a privilege, you have it. *The average German will enjoy 40 days' paid holiday this year.*

enjoyable /ɪn'dʒɔɪəbəl/. ADJ Something that is **enjoyable** gives you pleasure. *Shopping for clothes should be an enjoyable experience.*

enjoyment /ɪn'dʒɔɪmənt/. N-U Your **enjoyment** of something is the pleasure you get from having or experiencing it. *I apologise if your enjoyment of the movie was spoiled.*

enlarge /ɪn'lɑːdʒ/ **enlarges, enlarging, enlarged.** [1] VERB If you **enlarge** something, or if it **enlarges**, it becomes bigger. *...the plan to enlarge Ewood Park into a 30,000 all-seater stadium... The glands in the neck may enlarge. ...an enlarged peacekeeping force.* ♦**enlargement** N-U *...the enlargement of the European Union.* [2] VERB If you **enlarge on** or **upon** something that has been mentioned, you give more details about it.

enlighten /ɪn'laɪtən/ **enlightens, enlightening, enlightened.** VERB To **enlighten** someone means to give them more knowledge and greater understanding about something; FORMAL. *This book will entertain and enlighten the reader.* ♦**enlightening** ADJ *...an enlightening talk on the work done at the zoo.*

enlightened /ɪn'laɪtənd/. ADJ If you describe someone as **enlightened**, you admire them for having sensible modern attitudes. You can also talk about an **enlightened** place or period of history. *We now lived in more enlightened times.*

enlist /ɪn'lɪst/ **enlists, enlisting, enlisted.** [1] VERB If someone **enlists**, he or she joins the army, navy, or air force. *He enlisted as a private in the Mexican War... Many students* sought to avoid being drafted and sent to Vietnam as enlisted men. [2] VERB If you **enlist** someone's help, you persuade them to help you or support you.

enliven /ɪnˈlaɪvən/ **enlivens, enlivening, enlivened.** VERB If something **enlivens** an event or situation, it makes it more lively or cheerful. *Flirtation can enliven even the most mundane situation.*

en masse /ˌɒn ˈmæs/. ADV If a group of people do something **en masse**, they all do it together. *They were threatening to resign en masse.*

enormous /ɪˈnɔːməs/. ADJ **Enormous** means extremely large in size, amount, or degree. *The main bedroom is enormous... It was an enormous disappointment.* ♦**enormously** ADV *I admired him enormously.*

enough /ɪˈnʌf/. [1] QUANT **Enough** means as much as you need or as much as is necessary. *They had enough cash for a one-way ticket... I was old enough to work and earn money... Although the UK says efforts are being made, they are not doing enough.* [2] QUANT If you say that something is **enough**, you mean that you do not want it to continue. *I think I have said enough... Ann heard enough of this... Would you shut up, please! I'm having enough trouble with these children!* [3] ADV You use **enough** to say that something is the case to a moderate or fairly large degree. *Winter is a common enough German surname... The rest of the evening passed pleasantly enough.* [4] ADV You use **enough** in expressions such as **strangely enough** and **interestingly enough** to indicate that you think a fact is strange or interesting. *...an Italian who, interestingly enough, doesn't speak a word of his native language.* • **sure enough:** see **sure**.

enquire /ɪnˈkwaɪə/. See **inquire**.

enquiry /ɪnˈkwaɪəri/. See **inquiry**.

enrage /ɪnˈreɪdʒ/ **enrages, enraging, enraged.** VERB If you **are enraged** by something, it makes you extremely angry. *He enraged the government by renouncing the agreement.* ♦**enraged** ADJ *I began getting more and more enraged at my father.*

enrich /ɪnˈrɪtʃ/ **enriches, enriching, enriched.** VERB To **enrich** something means to improve its quality by adding something to it. *It is important to enrich the soil prior to planting.* ♦**enrichment** N-U *...spiritual enrichment.*

enrol (AM **enroll**) /ɪnˈrəʊl/ **enrols, enrolling, enrolled.** VERB If you **enrol** for a course, or if you **are enrolled** in a college or university, you officially join it and pay a fee. *Cherny was enrolled at the University in 1945... I thought I'd enrol you with an art group at the school.* ♦**enrolment** N-U *A fee is payable at enrolment.*

en route /ˌɒn ˈruːt/. ADV If you are **en route** to a place, you are travelling there.

enshrined /ɪnˈʃraɪnd/. ADJ If something such as an idea or a right is **enshrined** in a society, constitution, or a law, it is protected by it. *Freedom of speech is enshrined in the US constitution.*

ensue /ɪnˈsjuː, AM -ˈsuː/ **ensues, ensuing, ensued.** VERB If something **ensues**, it happens immediately after something else, usually as a result of it. *A brief but rather embarrassing silence ensued.*

ensuing /ɪnˈsjuːɪŋ/. ADJ BEFORE N **Ensuing** events happen immediately after other events. *The ensuing argument had been bitter.*

ensure /ɪnˈʃʊə/ **ensures, ensuring, ensured.** VERB To **ensure** that something happens means to make certain that it happens; FORMAL. *Ensure that your name and address is correct.*

entail /ɪnˈteɪl/ **entails, entailing, entailed.** VERB If one thing **entails** another, it involves it or causes it. *The job entails dealing with members of the public.*

entangle /ɪnˈtæŋɡəl/ **entangles, entangling, entangled.** [1] VERB If something **is entangled** in something such as a rope or net, it is caught in it very firmly. *Drift nets entangle hundreds of thousands of animals annually.* [2] VERB If something **entangles** you in problems or difficulties, it involves you in problems or difficulties from which you find it hard to escape. *Military involvement could eventually entangle Britain in a war.* ♦**entangled** ADJ *He became entangled in further controversy.* ♦**entanglement, entanglements.** N-VAR *...the US becoming involved in foreign entanglements.*

enter /ˈentə/ **enters, entering, entered.** [1] VERB When you **enter** a place, you come or go into it; FORMAL. *He entered the room briskly and stood near the door... As soon as I entered, they stopped.* [2] VERB If you **enter** an organization or institution, you start to work there or become a member of it. *She entered Parliament in 1959.* [3] VERB When something **enters** a new period in its development or history, it begins this period. *...as the war enters its second month.* [4] VERB If you **enter** a competition, race, or examination, you officially take part in it. *His wife Marie secretly entered him for the Championship.* [5] VERB When you **enter** something in a book or computer, you write or type it in. *Prue entered the passage in her notebook.*

▶ **enter into.** [1] PHR-VERB If you **enter into** something such as an agreement, discussion, or relationship with someone, you become involved in it; FORMAL. *She is prepared to enter into talks with the strike leaders.* [2] PHR-VERB Something that **enters into** something else is a factor in it. *Self-interest didn't enter into it.*

enterprise /ˈentəpraɪz/ **enterprises.** [1] N-C An **enterprise** is a company or business. *...state-owned enterprises.* [2] N-C An **enterprise** is something new that you try to do, especially something difficult or involving a degree of risk. *Horse breeding is indeed a risky enterprise.* [3] N-U If you say that someone shows **enterprise**, you approve of their willingness to try out new ways of doing something. *Sadly, his enterprise was not rewarded.* ♦**enterprising** ADJ *...an enterprising young man.*

entertain /ˌentəˈteɪn/ **entertains, entertaining, entertained.** [1] VERB If you **entertain** people, you do something that amuses or interests them. *Children's television not only entertains but also teaches.* ♦**entertaining** ADJ *...a highly entertaining movie.* [2] VERB If you **entertain** guests, you give them food and hospitality. ...*an enthusiastic cook who loves to entertain.* ♦**entertaining** N-U *The magnificent hall is often used for entertaining.* [3] VERB If you **entertain** an idea or suggestion, you consider it; FORMAL. *They flatly refuse to entertain any idea of reform.*

entertainer /ˌentəˈteɪnə/ **entertainers.** N-C An **entertainer** is a person whose job is to entertain audiences, for example by telling jokes, singing, or dancing.

entertainment /ˌentəˈteɪnmənt/ **entertainments.** N-VAR **Entertainment** consists of performances or activities that give people pleasure. *We have to present athletics as entertainment. ...discos and other entertainments.*

enthral (AM **enthrall**) /ɪnˈθrɔːl/ **enthrals, enthralling, enthralled.** VERB To **enthral** someone means to hold their attention and interest completely. *He enthralled audiences in Paris.* ♦**enthralling** ADJ *...an enthralling book.*

enthuse /ɪnˈθjuːz/, AM -ˈθuːz/ **enthuses, enthusing, enthused.** [1] VERB If you **enthuse** about something, you talk about it in a way that shows how excited you are about it. *'I've found the most wonderful house to buy!' she enthused.* [2] VERB If you are **enthused** by something, it makes you feel enthusiastic. *Holst was enthused by William Morris's ideas on art.*

enthusiasm /ɪnˈθjuːziæzəm, AM -ˈθuː-/ **enthusiasms.** [1] N-U **Enthusiasm** is great eagerness to do something or to be involved in something. *If her son showed enough enthusiasm, maybe Warren would take him into the business.* [2] N-C An **enthusiasm** is an activity or subject that interests you a lot. *Racing was one of Pat Meaney's many enthusiasms.*

enthusiast /ɪnˈθjuːziæst, AM -ˈθuː-/ **enthusiasts.** N-C An **enthusiast** is a person who is very interested in a particular activity or subject. *...keep-fit enthusiasts.*

enthusiastic /ɪnˌθjuːziˈæstɪk, AM -ˌθuː-/. ADJ If you are **enthusiastic** about something, you show how much you like or enjoy it by the way that you behave and talk. *They are very enthusiastic about the proposal.* ♦**enthusiastically** ADV *The announcement was greeted enthusiastically.*

entice /ɪnˈtaɪs/ **entices, enticing, enticed.** VERB To **entice** someone means to try to persuade them to go somewhere or to do something. *She resisted attempts to entice her into politics.* ♦**enticement, enticements.** N-VAR *There is a range of enticements to open an account.*

enticing /ɪnˈtaɪsɪŋ/. ADJ Something that is **enticing** is extremely attractive. *It was an enticing proposition.*

entire /ɪnˈtaɪə/. ADJ You use **entire** when you want to emphasize that you are referring to the whole of something. *He had spent his entire life in China as a doctor... The entire family was staring at him.*

entirely /ɪnˈtaɪəli/. ADV **Entirely** means completely. *...an entirely new approach... Paul was not entirely happy with this suggestion... I agree with you entirely.*

entirety /ɪnˈtaɪərɪti/. PHRASE If you refer to something **in its entirety**, you mean all of it. *...plans to publish the journal in its entirety.*

entitle /ɪnˈtaɪtl/ **entitles, entitling, entitled.** [1] VERB If you are **entitled** to something, you have the right to have it or do it. *They are also entitled to free school meals.* ♦**entitlement, entitlements.** N-VAR *They lose their entitlement to benefit when they start work.* [2] ADJ You say that a book, film, or painting is **entitled** a particular thing when you are mentioning its title. *...a book entitled Decorative Designs.*

entity /ˈentɪti/ **entities.** N-C An **entity** is something that exists separately from other things and has a clear identity; FORMAL. *The domestic and international tourism markets are separate entities.*

entourage /ˌɒntʊˈrɑːʒ/ **entourages.** N-C The **entourage** of someone famous or important is the group of assistants or other people who travel with them. *Her entourage included her personal assistant, hairdresser, and bodyguard.*

entrance, entrances, entrancing, entranced. [1] N-C /ˈentrəns/ An **entrance** is a way into a place, for example a door or gate. *Beside the entrance to the church, turn right.* [2] N-C Someone's **entrance** is their arrival in a room. *If she had noticed her father's entrance, she gave no indication.* [3] N-U If you gain **entrance** to a place, profession, or institution, you are able to go into it or are accepted as a member of it. *Entrance to universities and senior secondary schools was restricted.* [4] VERB /ɪnˈtrɑːns, -ˈtræns/ If something **entrances** you, it makes you feel delight and wonder. *She entranced the audience with classical Indian singing.* ♦**entranced** ADJ *For the next three hours we sat entranced.*

entrant /ˈentrənt/ **entrants.** N-C An **entrant** is a person who officially enters a competition or institution. *...competition entrants. ...a young school entrant.*

entrench /ɪnˈtrentʃ/ **entrenches, entrenching, entrenched.** VERB If something such as power, a custom, or an idea is **entrenched**, it is firmly established and difficult to change. ♦**entrenched** ADJ *Religious disputes are deeply entrenched and will not be easily overcome.*

entrepreneur /ˌɒntrəprəˈnɜː/ **entrepreneurs.** N-C An **entrepreneur** is a person who sets up businesses and business deals. ♦**entrepreneurial** ADJ *...his entrepreneurial skills.*

entrust /ɪnˈtrʌst/ **entrusts, entrusting, entrusted.** VERB If you **entrust** something important to someone, or if you **entrust** them with it, you make them responsible for it. *Miss Conway was entrusted with the children's education.*

entry /ˈentri/ **entries.** [1] N-C An **entry** is something that you complete in order to take part in a competition, for example the answers to a set of questions. *The closing date for entries is 31st December.* [2] N-C An **entry** in a diary, computer file, or reference book is a single short item in it. *The event is recorded in Waite's diary, in the entry for 23 March 1936.* [3] N-C A person's **entry** is their arrival in a room. *...hardly noticing Sue's triumphant entry into the room.* [4] N-U If you gain **entry** to a particular place, you are able to go in. *He was refused entry to France... No entry after 11pm.* [5] N-U Someone's

entry into a society or group is their joining of it. *His entry into the navy had to be delayed.* [6] N-C The **entry** to a place is the way into it, for example a door or gate.

envelop /ɪn'veləp/ **envelops, enveloping, enveloped.** VERB If one thing **envelops** another, it covers or surrounds it completely. *...a thick fog enveloped the airport.*

envelope /'envələʊp, 'ɒn-/ **envelopes.** N-C An **envelope** is the rectangular paper cover in which you send a letter through the post.

enviable /'enviəbəl/. ADJ An **enviable** quality is one that someone else has and that you wish you had too. *They have enviable reputations as athletes.*

envious /'enviəs/. ADJ If you are **envious** of someone else, you envy them. ♦**enviously** ADV *Ferguson could only look on enviously.*

environment /ɪn'vaɪərənmənt/ **environments.** [1] N-VAR Someone's **environment** is their surroundings, especially the conditions in which they grow up, live, or work. *The twins were separated at birth and brought up in entirely different environments.* [2] N-SING The **environment** is the natural world of land, sea, air, plants, and animals. *...persuading people to respect the environment.* ♦**environmental** /ɪn,vaɪərən'mentəl/ ADJ BEFORE N *Ireland's strict environmental protection laws ensure that these industries operate safely and cleanly.*

environmentalist /ɪn,vaɪərən'mentəlɪst/ **environmentalists.** N-C An **environmentalist** is a person who wants to protect and preserve the natural environment.

envisage /ɪn'vɪzɪdʒ/ **envisages, envisaging, envisaged.** VERB If you **envisage** a situation or event, you imagine it, or think that it is likely to happen. *He had never envisaged spending the whole of his working life in that particular job.*

envision /ɪn'vɪʒən/ **envisions, envisioning, envisioned.** VERB If you **envision** something, you envisage it; AMERICAN.

envoy /'envɔɪ/ **envoys.** N-C An **envoy** is a diplomat sent to a foreign country.

envy /'envi/ **envies, envying, envied.** VERB & N-U If you **envy** someone, you wish that you had the same things or qualities that they have. This feeling is called **envy**. *I envied her relationship with our mother... Her sisters watched with envy.*

enzyme /'enzaɪm/ **enzymes.** N-C An **enzyme** is a chemical substance that is found in living creatures which produces changes in other substances without being changed itself; TECHNICAL.

epic /'epɪk/ **epics.** [1] N-C An **epic** is a long book, poem, or film whose story extends over a long period of time or tells of great events. *...Mel Gibson's historical epic, Braveheart.* [2] ADJ Something that is described as **epic** is considered very impressive or ambitious. *...Columbus's epic voyage of discovery.*

epidemic /,epɪ'demɪk/ **epidemics.** N-C If there is an **epidemic** of a particular disease somewhere, it spreads quickly to a very large number of people there. *...a flu epidemic.*

epilepsy /'epɪlepsi/. N-U **Epilepsy** is a brain condition which causes a person to suddenly lose consciousness and sometimes to have fits.

epileptic /,epɪ'leptɪk/ **epileptics.** [1] N-C An **epileptic** is a person who suffers from epilepsy. [2] ADJ **Epileptic** means suffering from or relating to epilepsy. *...an epileptic fit.*

episode /'epɪsəʊd/ **episodes.** [1] N-C You can refer to an event or a short period of time as an **episode** if you want to suggest that it is important or unusual, or has some particular quality. *...an unhappy episode in our long (and previously friendly) relationship.* [2] N-C An **episode** is one of the programmes in a serial on television or radio.

epitome /ɪ'pɪtəmi/. N-SING If you say that someone or something is **the epitome** of a particular thing, you mean that they are a perfect example of it. *Maureen was the epitome of sophistication.*

epitomize (BR also **epitomise**) /ɪ'pɪtəmaɪz/ **epitomizes, epitomizing, epitomized.** VERB If you say that someone or something **epitomizes** a particular thing, you mean that they are a perfect example of it. *...the American heiress who is said to have epitomised Parisian chic in her day.*

epoch /'iːpɒk, AM 'epək/ **epochs.** N-C If you refer to a long period of time as an **epoch**, you mean that important events or great changes took place during it. *The birth of Christ was the beginning of a major epoch of world history.*

equal /'iːkwəl/ **equals, equalling, equalled;** (AM **equaling, equaled**). [1] ADJ If two things are **equal**, or if one thing is **equal** to another, they are the same in size, number, or value. *...equal numbers of men and women... Research and teaching are of equal importance. ...an amount equal to their monthly wages.* ♦**equally** ADV *All these techniques are equally effective... The prize was divided equally between the six of us.* [2] ADJ If people are **equal**, they all have the same rights and are treated in the same way. *...the commitment to equal opportunities... They have agreed to meet on reasonably equal terms.* ♦**equally** ADV *...a court system that is supposed to treat everyone equally.* [3] N-C If someone is your **equal** they have the same ability or status that you have. *You should have married somebody more your equal.* [4] VERB To **equal** something or someone means to be as good or as great as them. *The victory equalled Southend's best in history.* [5] ADJ AFTER LINK-V If someone is **equal to** a job or situation, they have the necessary abilities, strength, or courage to deal successfully with it. *He was confident that the two people would be equal to the task ahead of them.*

equality /ɪ'kwɒlɪti/. N-U **Equality** is a situation or state where all the members of a society or group have the same status, rights, and opportunities. *...equality of the sexes.*

equalize (BR also **equalise**) /'iːkwəlaɪz/ **equalizes, equalizing, equalized.** VERB To **equalize** a situation means to give everyone the same rights or opportunities. *...modern divorce laws that equalize the rights of husbands and wives.* ♦**equalization** N-U *...the equaliza-*

tion of parenting responsibilities between men and women.

equally /'iːkwəli/. ADV **Equally** is used to introduce a comment which balances or contrasts with another comment that has just been made. *In that situation, he would lie. Equally, in my situation, I would want to believe he was lying.* ● See also **equal**.

equate /ɪ'kweɪt/ **equates, equating, equated.** VERB If you **equate** one thing with another, or if one thing **equates** with another, you believe that they are strongly connected. *I'm always wary of men wearing suits, as I equate this with power and authority... The author doesn't equate liberalism and conservatism.*

equation /ɪ'kweɪʒən/ **equations.** N-C An **equation** is a mathematical statement saying that two amounts or values are the same, for example $6 \times 4 = 12 \times 2$.

equator /ɪ'kweɪtə/. N-SING The **equator** is an imaginary line round the middle of the earth, halfway between the North and South poles.

equestrian /ɪ'kwestriən/. ADJ **Equestrian** means connected with the activity of riding horses. *...equestrian skills.*

equilibrium /ˌiːkwɪ'lɪbriəm/. N-VAR **Equilibrium** is a state of balance or stability in a situation or in someone's mind. *For the economy to be in equilibrium, income must equal expenditure... He had recovered his equilibrium and even his good humour.*

equip /ɪ'kwɪp/ **equips, equipping, equipped.** [1] VERB If you **equip** a person or thing with something such as a tool or a machine, you provide them with it. *The country did not possess the modern guns to equip the reserve army properly. ...well-equipped research buildings.* [2] VERB If something **equips** you for a particular task or experience, it gives you the knowledge, skills, and personal qualities you need for it. *A basic two-hour first aid course would equip you to deal with any of these incidents.*

equipment /ɪ'kwɪpmənt/. N-U **Equipment** consists of the things such as tools or machines which are used for a particular purpose.

equitable /'ekwɪtəbəl/. ADJ Something that is **equitable** is fair and reasonable in a way that gives equal treatment to everyone. *...a fair and equitable settlement.*

equivalent /ɪ'kwɪvələnt/ **equivalents.** [1] N-SING & ADJ If one amount or value is the **equivalent** of another, or if one is **equivalent** to the other, they are the same. *It is common to ask for the equivalent of one month's rent as a deposit... A unit is equivalent to a glass of wine.* [2] N-C & ADJ The **equivalent** of someone or something is a person or thing that has the same function in a different place, time, or system. *...the civil administrator of the West Bank and his equivalent in Gaza. ...a decrease of 10% in property investment compared with the equivalent period in 1991.*

era /'ɪərə/ **eras.** N-C An **era** is a period of time that is considered as a single unit because it has a particular feature.

eradicate /ɪ'rædɪkeɪt/ **eradicates, eradicating, eradicated.** VERB To **eradicate** something means to get rid of it completely; FORMAL.

They are already battling to eradicate illnesses such as malaria and tetanus. ◆**eradication** N-U *...the eradication of their country's Communist past.*

erase /ɪ'reɪz, AM ɪ'reɪs/ **erases, erasing, erased.** [1] VERB If you **erase** a thought or feeling, you destroy it completely so that you can no longer remember it or feel it. *They are desperate to erase the memory of that last defeat.* [2] VERB If you **erase** sound which has been recorded on a tape or information which has been stored in a computer, you completely remove or destroy it. *The names were accidentally erased from computer disks.* [3] VERB If you **erase** something such as writing or a mark, you remove it.

erect /ɪ'rekt/ **erects, erecting, erected.** [1] VERB If people **erect** something such as a building or bridge, they build it; FORMAL. *The Eiffel Tower was erected for the World Exhibition in 1889.* ◆**erection** N-U *...the erection of temporary fencing.* [2] ADJ People or things that are **erect** are straight and upright. *Her head was erect and her back was straight.*

erection /ɪ'rekʃən/ **erections.** N-C If a man has an **erection** his penis is stiff and sticking up because he is sexually aroused.

erode /ɪ'rəʊd/ **erodes, eroding, eroded.** [1] VERB If rock or soil **erodes**, or if it **is eroded** by the weather or sea, it cracks and breaks so that it is gradually destroyed. *Soil is quickly eroded by wind and rain.* ◆**erosion** /ɪ'rəʊʒən/ N-U *...erosion of the river valleys.* [2] VERB If something strong or something with a high value **erodes** or **is eroded**, it gradually weakens or decreases; FORMAL. *His fumbling of the issue of reform has eroded his authority.* ◆**erosion** N-U *...the erosion of moral standards.*

erotic /ɪ'rɒtɪk/. ADJ If you describe something as **erotic**, you mean that it involves or arouses sexual desire. *It wasn't an erotic experience at all.*

err /ɜː/ **errs, erring, erred.** [1] VERB If you **err**, you do something wrong; FORMAL. *If you make a threat be sure to carry it out if he errs again.* [2] PHRASE If you **err on the side of** a way of behaving, you tend to behave in that way. *They may be wise to err on the side of caution.*

errand /'erənd/ **errands.** N-C If you go on an **errand** for someone, you go a short distance in order to do something for them, for example to buy something from a shop.

erratic /ɪ'rætɪk/. ADJ Something that is **erratic** happens at unexpected times or moves in an irregular way. *...Argentina's erratic inflation rate.* ◆**erratically** ADV *Police stopped him for driving erratically.*

erroneous /ɪ'rəʊniəs/. ADJ **Erroneous** beliefs or opinions are incorrect. *...the erroneous notion that one can contract AIDS by giving blood.* ◆**erroneously** ADV *It had been widely and erroneously reported that Armstrong had refused.*

error /'erə/ **errors.** [1] N-VAR An **error** is a mistake. *NASA discovered a mathematical error in its calculations... The plane was shot down in error.* [2] **trial and error**: see **trial**.

erupt /ɪ'rʌpt/ **erupts, erupting, erupted.** [1] VERB When a volcano **erupts**, it throws out a lot of hot lava, ash, and steam. ◆**eruption,**

eruptions. N-VAR ...*the volcanic eruption of Tambora in 1815.* [2] VERB **Erupt** is used to indicate that something suddenly begins or intensifies. *Heavy fighting erupted there today... The neighborhood known as Watts erupted into riots... Without warning she erupts into laughter.* ◆**eruption** N-C ...*this sudden eruption of violence.*

escalate /ˈeskəleɪt/ **escalates, escalating, escalated.** VERB If an unpleasant situation **escalates**, or if someone or something **escalates** it, it becomes worse; JOURNALISM. *Protests escalated into five days of rioting.* ◆**escalation** N-SING ...*a sudden escalation of violence.*

escalator /ˈeskəleɪtə/ **escalators.** N-C An **escalator** is a moving staircase.

escape /ɪˈskeɪp/ **escapes, escaping, escaped.** [1] VERB & N-C If you **escape** from a place, or if you make your **escape** from a place, you succeed in getting away from it. *A prisoner has escaped from a jail in northern England.* [2] VERB & N-C You can say that you **escape** when you survive something such as an accident. You can also talk about a particular kind of **escape**. *The two officers were extremely lucky to escape serious injury... The man's girlfriend managed to escape unhurt... I hear you had a very narrow escape.* [3] N-C If something is an **escape**, it makes people think about pleasant things instead of the tedious unpleasant aspects of their life. *For me television is an escape.* [4] VERB If something **escapes** you, or if it **escapes** your attention, you forget it or are unaware of it. ...*an actor whose name escapes me for the moment.*

escapism /ɪˈskeɪpɪzəm/. N-U If you describe an activity or type of entertainment as **escapism**, you mean that it makes people think about pleasant things instead of the tedious or unpleasant aspects of their life. ◆**escapist** ADJ ...*escapist movies.*

escort, escorts, escorting, escorted. [1] N-C & PHRASE /ˈeskɔːt/ An **escort** is a person or group of people travelling with someone in order to protect or guard them. If someone is taken somewhere **under escort**, they are accompanied by guards, either because they have been arrested or because they need to be protected. *He arrived with a police escort.* [2] N-C An **escort** is a person who accompanies someone of the opposite sex to a social event; FORMAL. [3] VERB /ɪˈskɔːt/ If you **escort** someone somewhere, you go there with them to make sure that they go somewhere. *I escorted him to the door.*

esoteric /ˌiːsəʊˈterɪk, AM ˌesə-/. ADJ Something that is **esoteric** is understood by only a small number of people with special knowledge; FORMAL. *Where did you obtain this esoteric piece of information?*

especially /ɪˈspeʃəli/. [1] ADV You use **especially** to emphasize that what you are saying applies more to one person or thing than to any others. *Re-apply sunscreen every two hours, especially if you have been swimming... He liked the American country singers, especially George Jones.* [2] ADV You use **especially** to emphasize a characteristic or quality. *She was especially fond of a little girl named Betsy.*

espionage /ˈespiənɑːʒ/. N-U **Espionage** is the activity of finding out the political, military, or industrial secrets of your enemies or rivals by using spies.

espouse /ɪˈspaʊz/ **espouses, espousing, espoused.** VERB If you **espouse** a policy or plan, you support it; FORMAL.

essay /ˈeseɪ/ **essays.** N-C An **essay** is a piece of writing on a particular subject. ...*Thomas Malthus's essay on population.*

essence /ˈesəns/. N-U The **essence** of something is its basic and most important characteristic. *The essence of good managing is caring.*
| PHRASES | ● You use **in essence** to indicate that you are talking about the basic and most important characteristic of something; FORMAL. *Local taxes are in essence simple.* ● If you say that something **is of the essence**, you mean that it is absolutely necessary in a particular situation. *Time is of the essence – a matter of life or death.*

essential /ɪˈsenʃəl/ **essentials.** [1] ADJ Something that is **essential** is absolutely necessary. *It is essential that you take specialist legal advice... Play is an essential part of a child's development.* [2] N-C The **essentials** are things that are absolutely necessary in a situation. *The flat contained the basic essentials.*

essentially /ɪˈsenʃəli/. [1] ADV You use **essentially** to emphasize that you are talking about the most basic and important aspects of someone or something. *He was essentially a simple man.* [2] ADV You use **essentially** to indicate that what you are saying is basically or generally true, although it may not cover all the minor details. *He develops his opinions essentially by reading the newspapers.*

establish /ɪˈstæblɪʃ/ **establishes, establishing, established.** [1] VERB If someone **establishes** an organization or a system, they create it. ...*the right to establish independent trade unions.* ◆**establishment** N-SING ...*the establishment of the regional government in 1980.* [2] VERB If you **establish** contact with a group of people, you start to have discussions with them; FORMAL. ◆**establishment** N-SING ...*discussions to explore the establishment of diplomatic relations.* [3] VERB If you **establish** that something is true, you discover facts that show that it is definitely true; FORMAL. *Medical tests established that she was not their own child... An autopsy had been done to establish the cause of death. ...an established medical fact.*

established /ɪˈstæblɪʃt/. ADJ An **established** person or organization has a good reputation or a secure position, usually because they have existed for a long time. ...*the established names of Paris fashion.*

establishment /ɪˈstæblɪʃmənt/ **establishments.** [1] N-C An **establishment** is a shop, restaurant, or other business premises; FORMAL. ...*a scientific research establishment. ...commercial establishments.* [2] N-SING You refer to the people who have power and influence in the running of a country or organization as **the establishment**. ...*the literary establishment.*

estate /ɪˈsteɪt/ **estates.** [1] N-C An **estate** is a large area of land in the country owned by one person or organization. [2] N-C In Britain, people sometimes use **estate** to refer to a housing estate. **3** N-C Someone's **estate** is the money and property they leave when they die. *His estate was valued at $150,000.* **4** See also **housing estate**, **real estate**.

es'tate agent, estate agents. N-C In British English, an **estate agent** is someone who works for a company selling houses and land. The American word is **realtor**.

esteem /ɪˈstiːm/. N-U **Esteem** is admiration and respect; FORMAL. *He is held in very high esteem by colleagues.*

esthetic /iːsˈθetɪk, AM esˈθ-/. See **aesthetic**.

estimate, estimates, estimating, estimated. verb /ˈestɪmeɪt/, noun /ˈestɪmət/. **1** VERB & N-C If you **estimate** a quantity or value, or if you make an **estimate**, you make an approximate judgement or calculation of it. *It's difficult to estimate how much money is involved. ...the official estimate of the election result.* ◆**estimated** *There are an estimated 90,000 gangsters in the country.* **2** N-C An **estimate** is a judgement about a person or situation which you make based on the available evidence. *...my estimate of his grandson's capabilities.*

estranged /ɪˈstreɪndʒd/. ADJ You refer to someone as **estranged** from their family or friends when they are living separately from them and not communicating with them because they have quarrelled; FORMAL. *...his estranged wife... She spent most of her twenties virtually estranged from her father.* ◆**estrangement** N-U *They are anxious to end the estrangement between them.*

estuary /ˈestʃʊri, AM ˈestʃʊeri/ **estuaries.** N-C An **estuary** is the wide part of a river where it joins the sea.

etc. etc is used at the end of a list to indicate that there are other items which you could mention if you had enough time or space. **Etc** is a written abbreviation for 'etcetera'. *She knew all about my schoolwork, my hospital work, etc.*

etcetera (or **et cetera**) /etˈsetrə/. See **etc**

etch /etʃ/ **etchs, etching, etched.** **1** VERB If a line or pattern **is etched** into a surface, it is cut into the surface using acid or a sharp tool. *Crosses were etched into the walls.* **2** VERB If something **is etched** on your memory, you remember it very clearly because it made a strong impression on you; LITERARY. *The ugly scene in the study was still etched in her mind.*

etching /ˈetʃɪŋ/ **etchings.** N-C An **etching** is a picture printed from a metal plate that has had a design cut into it.

eternal /ɪˈtɜːnəl/. **1** ADJ Something that is **eternal** lasts for ever. *...eternal life. ...the quest for eternal youth.* ◆**eternally** ADV *She is eternally grateful to her family for their support.* **2** ADJ BEFORE N **Eternal** truths and values never change and are thought to be true in all situations. *...the eternal and immutable principles of right and wrong.*

eternity /ɪˈtɜːnɪti/ **eternities.** **1** N-U **Eternity** is time without an end, or a state of existence outside time, especially the state which some people believe they will pass into after they have died. *I have always found the thought of eternity terrifying.* **2** N-SING You can refer to a

period of time as **an eternity** when it seems very long; INFORMAL. *The war continued for an eternity.*

ethereal /ɪˈθɪəriəl/. ADJ If you describe someone or something as **ethereal**, you mean that they have a delicate beauty that seems almost supernatural; FORMAL.

ethic /ˈeθɪk/ **ethics.** **1** N-PL **Ethics** are moral beliefs and rules about right and wrong. *Its members are bound by a rigid code of ethics.* **2** N-SING An **ethic** of a particular kind is moral belief that influences the behaviour and attitudes of a group of people. *The work ethic is very strong in their household.*

ethical /ˈeθɪkəl/. **1** ADJ **Ethical** means influenced by a system of moral beliefs about right and wrong. *...the ethical aspects of animal experimentation.* ◆**ethically** ADV *We can defend ethically and morally everything we stand for.* **2** ADJ If you describe something you do as **ethical**, you mean that it is morally right or acceptable. *My involvement has not been altogether, shall we say, ethical.* ◆**ethically** ADV *Mayors want local companies to behave ethically.*

ethnic /ˈeθnɪk/. ADJ **Ethnic** means relating to different racial or cultural groups of people. *...Britain's ethnic minorities.* ◆**ethnically** /ˈeθnɪkli/ ADV *...a predominantly young, ethnically mixed audience.*

ethos /ˈiːθɒs/. N-SING The **ethos** of a group of people is the set of ideas and attitudes associated with it. *The whole ethos of the hotel is effortless service.*

etiquette /ˈetɪket/. N-U **Etiquette** is a set of customs and rules for polite behaviour. *...the rules of diplomatic etiquette.*

euphemism /ˈjuːfəmɪzəm/ **euphemisms.** N-U A **euphemism** is a polite word or expression that people use to talk about something unpleasant or embarrassing, such as death or sex.

euphemistic /ˌjuːfəˈmɪstɪk/. ADJ **Euphemistic** language consists of polite words or expressions for unpleasant or embarrassing things. ◆**euphemistically** ADV *...political prisons, called euphemistically 're-education camps'.*

euphoria /juːˈfɔːriə/. N-U **Euphoria** is a feeling of great happiness. ◆**euphoric** /juːˈfɒrɪk/ ADJ *It had received euphoric support from the public.*

European /ˌjʊərəˈpiːən/ **Europeans.** **1** ADJ **European** means coming from or relating to Europe. *...European countries.* **2** N-C A **European** is a person who comes from Europe.

euthanasia /ˌjuːθəˈneɪziə, AM -ʒə/. N-U **Euthanasia** is the practice of painlessly killing a dying person in order to stop their suffering.

evacuate /ɪˈvækjueɪt/ **evacuates, evacuating, evacuated.** VERB If people **are evacuated** from a place, or if they **evacuate** a place, they move out of it because it has become dangerous. *18,000 people have been evacuated from the area... Officials ordered the residents to evacuate.* ◆**evacuation, evacuations** N-VAR *...the mass evacuation of the Bosnian town of Srebrenica.*

evacuee /ɪˌvækjuˈiː/ **evacuees.** N-C An **evacuee** is someone who has been sent away from a dangerous place to somewhere safe.

evade /ɪ'veɪd/ **evades, evading, evaded.**
VERB If you **evade** something unpleasant or difficult, you avoid dealing with it. *By his own admission, he evaded taxes... He managed to evade capture.*

evaluate /ɪ'væljʊeɪt/ **evaluates, evaluating, evaluated.** VERB If you **evaluate** something or someone, you consider them in order to make a judgement about them, for example about how good or bad they are. *Evaluate what you are doing and work to get better.* ◆**evaluation,** **evaluations** N-VAR *...the opinions and evaluations of college supervisors.*

evaporate /ɪ'væpəreɪt/ **evaporates, evaporating, evaporated.** VERB When a liquid **evaporates**, it changes into a gas, because its temperature has increased. ◆**evaporation** N-U *...the evaporation of the sweat on the skin.*

evasion /ɪ'veɪʒən/ **evasions.** N-VAR If you accuse someone of **evasion,** you mean that they are deliberately avoiding dealing with something that is unpleasant or difficult. *...an evasion of responsibility.*

evasive /ɪ'veɪsɪv/. ADJ If you describe someone as **evasive,** you mean that they deliberately avoid answering questions. ◆**evasively** ADV *'I can't come to any conclusion about that,' Millson said evasively.*

eve /iːv/ **eves.** N-C The **eve** of an event is the day before it, or the period of time just before it; JOURNALISM. *...on the eve of his 27th birthday.*

even 1 discourse uses

even /'iːvən/. [1] ADV You use **even** to suggest that what comes just after or just before it in the sentence is surprising. *He kept calling me for years, even after he got married... Even dark-skinned women should use sunscreens.* [2] PHRASE You use **even so** to introduce a surprising fact that relates to what you have just said. *The bus was only half full. Even so, a young man asked Nina if the seat next to her was taken.* [3] ADV You use **even** with comparative adjectives and adverbs to emphasize a quality that someone or something has. *It was on television that he made an even stronger impact as an interviewer... Stan was speaking even more slowly than usual.* [4] CONJ You use **even if** or **even though** to indicate that a particular fact does not make the rest of your statement untrue. *Even if you are on a fairly strict diet you can still go out for a good meal.*

even 2 adjective uses

even /'iːvən/. [1] ADJ An **even** measurement or rate stays at about the same level. *How important is it to have an even temperature?* ◆**evenly** ADV *He looked at Ellen, breathing evenly in her sleep.* [2] ADJ An **even** surface is smooth and flat. *The tables are fitted with a glass top to provide an even surface.* [3] ADJ If there is an **even** division of something, each person, group, or area involved has an equal amount. *Divide the dough into 12 even pieces.* ◆**evenly** ADV *The money will be evenly distributed.* [4] ADJ If a contest or competition is **even,** the people taking part are all equally skilful. ◆**evenly** ADV *...two evenly matched candidates.* [5] ADJ AFTER LINK-V If you are **even** with someone, you do not owe them anything, such as money or a favour. [6] PHRASE When a company or a person

running a business **breaks even,** they make neither a profit nor a loss. [7] PHRASE If you say you will **get even** with someone, you mean that you intend to harm them because they have harmed you; INFORMAL. [8] ADJ An **even** number can be divided exactly by the number two.

even 3 phrasal verb uses

even /'iːvən/ **evens, evening, evened.**
▶ **even out.** PHR-VERB When an amount of something **evens out,** or when you **even** it **out,** it becomes more evenly distributed or steadier. *Rates of house price inflation have evened out.*

evening /'iːvnɪŋ/ **evenings.** N-VAR The **evening** is the part of each day between the end of the afternoon and the time when you go to bed. *All he did that evening was sit around. ...6.00 in the evening. ...a proper evening meal.*

event /ɪ'vent/ **events.** [1] N-C An **event** is something that happens. *...recent events in Europe... The event was an undoubted success.* [2] N-C An **event** is an organized occasion. *...major sporting events.* [3] PHRASE You use **in the event of, in the event that,** and **in that event** when you are talking about a possible future situation, especially when you are planning what to do if it occurs. *...in the unlikely event of an error being made.*

eventual /ɪ'ventʃʊəl/. ADJ BEFORE N The **eventual** result of something is what happens at the end of it. *...events leading to his imprisonment and his eventual death.*

eventuality /ɪ,ventʃʊ'ælɪti/ **eventualities.** N-C An **eventuality** is a possible future event or result; FORMAL. *Every eventuality is covered, from running out of petrol to needing water.*

eventually /ɪ'ventʃʊəli/. [1] ADV **Eventually** means in the end, especially after a lot of delays, problems, or arguments. *The flight eventually got away six hours late.* [2] ADV **Eventually** means at the end of a situation or process or as the final result of it. *She eventually plans to run her own chain of country inns.*

ever /'evə-/. [1] ADV **Ever** means at any time. It is used in questions and negative statements. *Neither of us had ever skied... Have you ever experienced failure?... You won't hear from Gaston ever again.* [2] ADV You use **ever** after comparatives and superlatives to emphasize the degree to which something is true. *She's got a great voice and is singing better than ever... This is the most awful evening I can ever remember.*
PHRASES ● You say **as ever** in order to indicate that something is not unusual. *He was by himself, alone as ever.* ● You use **ever since** to emphasize that something has been true since the time mentioned, and is still true now. *He's been there ever since you left!* ● You use **ever so** and **ever such** to emphasize that someone or something has a lot of a particular quality; BRITISH, INFORMAL. *He was very lively and ever such a good dancer... I like him ever so much.*

ever- /'evə-/. You use **ever-** in adjectives such as **ever-increasing** and **ever-present,** to show that something exists or continues all the time. *...an ever-changing world.*

evergreen /'evəgriːn/ **evergreens.** N-C An

evergreen is a tree or bush which has green leaves all the year round.

every /'evri/. [1] DET & ADJ You use **every** to indicate that you are referring to all the members of a group or all the parts of something. ...*recipes for every occasion. ...parents who would fulfil his every need.* [2] DET You use **every** to say how often something happens or to indicate that something happens at regular intervals. *We were made to attend meetings every day... A burglary occurs every three minutes in London.* [3] DET You use **every** before some nouns in order to emphasize what you are saying. *There is every chance that you will succeed... I made every effort to be co-operative... He has every intention of staying.* | PHRASES | ● You use the expressions **every now and then**, **every now and again**, **every once in a while**, and **every so often** to indicate that something happens occasionally. ● If something happens **every other** day or week, for example, or **every second** day or week, it happens on one day or week in each period of two days or weeks. *Their local committees are usually held every other month.*

everybody /'evribɒdi/. See **everyone**.

everyday /'evridei/. ADJ You use **everyday** to describe something which happens or is used every day, or forms a regular and basic part of your life. ...*your everyday routine. ...the joys and sorrows of everyday living.*

everyone /'evriwʌn/ (or **everybody**). PRON **Everyone** or **everybody** means all the people in a group or all people in general. *Everyone in the street was shocked... Everyone else goes home around 7 p.m... Everyone needs some free time for rest and relaxation.*

> Do not confuse **everyone** with **every one**. **Everyone** always refers to people. In the phrase **every one**, 'one' is a pronoun that can refer to any person or thing, depending on the context. It is often followed by the word **of**. *We've saved seeds from every one of our plants... Every one of them phoned me.* In these examples, **every one** is a more emphatic way of saying **all**.

everything /'evriθɪŋ/. [1] PRON You use **everything** to refer to all the objects, activities, or facts in a situation. *Everything else in his life had changed. ...everything that they will need for the day's hike.* [2] PRON You use **everything** to refer to a whole situation or to life in general. *Is everything all right?*

everywhere /'evriweə/. [1] ADV You use **everywhere** to refer to a whole area or to all the places in a particular area. *Working people everywhere object to paying taxes... We went everywhere together.* [2] ADV You use **everywhere** to refer to all the places that someone goes to. *Everywhere he went he was introduced as the current United States Open Champion.* [3] PRON If you say that someone or something is **everywhere**, you mean that they are present in a place in very large numbers. *There were cartons of cigarettes everywhere.*

evict /ɪ'vɪkt/ **evicts, evicting, evicted.** VERB When people **are evicted**, they are officially forced to leave the house where they are living. *The city police evicted ten families.* ◆**eviction, evictions** N-VAR *He was facing eviction, along with his wife and family.*

evidence /'evidəns/. N-U **Evidence** is anything that makes you believe that something is true or exists. ...*evidence that stress is partly responsible for disease... There is no evidence to support this theory.* | PHRASES | ● If you **give evidence** in a court of law, you give a statement saying what you know about something. ● If someone or something is **in evidence**, they are present and can be clearly seen. *Few soldiers were in evidence.*

evident /'evidənt/. ADJ If something is **evident**, you notice it easily and clearly. *His footprints were clearly evident in the heavy dust... It was evident that she had once been a beauty.*

evidently /'evidəntli/. ADV You use **evidently** to say that something is true, because you have seen evidence of it yourself or because someone has told you it is true. *The two Russians evidently knew each other.*

evil /'iːvəl/ **evils.** [1] N-U **Evil** is used to refer to all the wicked and bad things that happen in the world. ...*a conflict between good and evil.* [2] N-C An **evil** is a very unpleasant or harmful situation or activity. ...*the evils of alcohol.* [3] ADJ If you describe someone or something as **evil**, you mean that they are wicked and cause harm to people. ...*the country's most evil terrorists. ...condemning slavery as evil.*

evocative /ɪ'vɒkətɪv/. ADJ If something like a description is **evocative**, it strongly reminds you of something or gives you a powerful impression of what it is like. *Her story is sharply evocative of Italian provincial life.*

evoke /ɪ'vəʊk/ **evokes, evoking, evoked.** VERB To **evoke** a particular memory, idea, emotion, or response means to cause it to happen or exist. ...*the scene evoking memories of those old movies.*

evolution /,iːvə'luːʃən, ,ev-/. [1] N-U **Evolution** is a process of gradual change during which animals and plants change some of their characteristics and sometimes develop into new species. [2] N-U You can use **evolution** to refer to any gradual process of change and development. ...*the evolution of modern physics.*

evolutionary /,iːvə'luːʃənri, AM -neri/. ADJ **Evolutionary** means relating to a process of gradual change and development. ...*a period of evolutionary change.*

evolve /ɪ'vɒlv/ **evolves, evolving, evolved.** [1] VERB When animals and plants **evolve**, they gradually change and develop into different forms. *Maize evolved from a wild grass. ...when amphibians evolved into reptiles.* [2] VERB If something **evolves**, or if you **evolve** it, it gradually develops into something different and usually more advanced. ...*a tiny airline which eventually evolved into Pakistan International Airlines.*

ewe /juː/ **ewes.** N-C A **ewe** is an adult female sheep.

exacerbate /ɪg'zæsəbeɪt/ **exacerbates, exacerbating, exacerbated.** VERB If something

exacerbates a bad situation, it makes it worse; FORMAL. ♦**exacerbation** N-U ...*the exacerbation of global problems.*

exact /ɪgˈzækt/ **exacts, exacting, exacted.** [1] ADJ Something that is **exact** is correct, accurate, and complete in every way. *I don't remember the exact words... The exact number of protest calls has not been revealed... A small number – five, to be exact – have been bad.* ♦**exactly** ADV *Try to locate exactly where the smells are entering the room.* [2] ADJ BEFORE N You use **exact** before a noun to emphasize that you are referring to that particular thing and no other. *Do you really think I could get the exact thing I want?* [3] VERB When someone **exacts** something, they demand and obtain it from someone else; FORMAL. *Already he has exacted a written apology from the chairman of the commission.* [4] See also **exactly.**

exacting /ɪgˈzæktɪŋ/. ADJ An **exacting** person or task requires you to work very hard. *They seem to have the same exacting standards.*

exactly /ɪgˈzæktli/. [1] ADV **Exactly** means precisely, and not just approximately. *Agnew's car pulled into the driveway at exactly five o'clock. ...exactly in the middle of the picture.* [2] ADV If you say **'Exactly'**, you are agreeing with someone or emphasizing the truth of what they say. If you say **'Not exactly'**, you are telling them politely that not everything they are saying is true or accurate. *'We don't know the answer to that.'—'Exactly, so shut up... 'And you refused?'—'Well, not exactly. I couldn't say yes.'* [3] ADV You use **not exactly** to indicate that a meaning or situation is slightly different from what people think or expect. *He's not exactly homeless, he just hangs out in this park.*

exaggerate /ɪgˈzædʒəreɪt/ **exaggerates, exaggerating, exaggerated.** [1] VERB If you **exaggerate**, you make the thing that you are talking about seem bigger or more important than it actually is. *She did sometimes exaggerate the demands of her job.* ♦**exaggeration, exaggerations** N-VAR *It would be an exaggeration to call the danger urgent.* [2] VERB If something **exaggerates** a situation, quality, or feature, it makes it appear greater, more obvious, or more important than it really is. *The dress exaggerates her slim waist.*

exaggerated /ɪgˈzædʒəreɪtɪd/. ADJ Something that is **exaggerated** is or seems larger, better, worse, or more important than it needs to be. *...exaggerated claims for what such courses can achieve.*

exalted /ɪgˈzɔːltɪd/. ADJ An **exalted** person is very important; LITERARY. *...the more exalted members of the British government.*

exam /ɪgˈzæm/ **exams.** N-C An **exam** is a formal test taken to show your knowledge of a subject. *Did you pass any exams?... I was due to sit exams at university.*

> Note that to **pass** an exam always means to succeed in it. If you do not pass an exam, you **fail** it. If you simply do an exam or take part in it, you can say that you **take** the exam, or, more formally, that you **sit** the exam.

examination /ɪgˌzæmɪˈneɪʃən/ **examinations.** N-C An **examination** is an exam; FORMAL.

examine /ɪgˈzæmɪn/ **examines, examining, examined.** [1] VERB If you **examine** something, you look at it or consider it carefully. *He examined her passport... The plans will be examined by EU environment ministers.* ♦**examination, examinations** N-VAR *Further examination is needed to exclude the chance of disease.* [2] VERB If you **are being examined**, you are being given a formal test in order to show your knowledge of a subject

examiner /ɪgˈzæmɪnə/ **examiners.** N-C An **examiner** is a person who sets or marks an exam.

example /ɪgˈzɑːmpəl, -ˈzæmp-/ **examples.** [1] N-C An **example** is something which represents or is typical of a particular group of things. *...an outstanding example of a small business that grew into a big one... Let me give another example.* [2] PHRASE You use **for example** to show that you are giving an example of a particular kind of thing. *...intelligent money management, for example paying big bills monthly.* [3] N-C In a dictionary entry, an **example** is a phrase which shows how a word is used. [4] N-C If you refer to a person as an **example** to other people, you mean that he or she behaves in a good way that other people should copy. *He had always been held up as an example to the younger ones.*

> PHRASES If you **follow** someone's **example**, you copy their behaviour, especially because you admire them. If you **set an example**, you encourage people by your behaviour to behave in a similar way.

exasperate /ɪgˈzɑːspəreɪt, -ˈzæs-/ **exasperates, exasperating, exasperated.** VERB If someone or something **exasperates** you, they annoy you, making you feel frustrated. *The sheer futility of it all exasperates her.* ♦**exasperated** ADJ *Bertha was exasperated at the delay.* ♦**exasperation** N-U *Mahoney clenched his fist in exasperation.*

excavate /ˈekskəveɪt/ **excavates, excavating, excavated.** VERB To **excavate** a piece of land means to remove earth carefully from it and look for the remains of pots or buildings, in order to find out about the past. ♦**excavation, excavations** N-VAR *...the excavation of a bronze-age boat.*

exceed /ɪkˈsiːd/ **exceeds, exceeding, exceeded.** [1] VERB If something **exceeds** a particular amount, it is greater than that amount. *Its research budget exceeds $700 million a year.* [2] VERB If you **exceed** a limit, you go beyond it. *I would be exceeding my powers if I ordered the march to be halted.*

exceedingly /ɪkˈsiːdɪŋli/. ADV **Exceedingly** means very much indeed; DATED. *...an exceedingly good lunch.*

excel /ɪkˈsel/ **excels, excelling, excelled.** VERB If someone **excels** in something, they are very good at it. *He began to excel.*

Excellency /ˈeksələnsi/ **Excellencies.** N-VOC People use expressions such as **Your Excellency** or **His Excellency** when they are addressing or referring to officials of very high rank, for example ambassadors or governors. *...His excellency the President.*

excellent /'eksələnt/. ADJ Something that is **excellent** is very good indeed. *Sue is very efficient and does an excellent job as Fred's personal assistant.* ♦**excellence** N-U *...the top US award for excellence in journalism.* ♦**excellently** ADV *They're both playing excellently.*

except /ɪk'sept/. PREP & CONJ You use **except** or **except for** to introduce the only thing or person that a statement does not apply to, or a fact that prevents a statement from being completely true. *I don't take any drugs whatsoever, except aspirin... Everyone was late, except for Richard... The log cabin stayed empty, except when we came.*

exception /ɪk'sepʃən/ **exceptions.** N-VAR An **exception** is a situation, thing, or person that is not included in a general statement. *Normally she wore little make-up, but this evening was clearly an exception. ...a day off for everybody, with the exception of Lawrence.*

PHRASES • If you **make an exception** you consider or allow something that you would normally not consider or allow. *It is not a good idea to eat in hotels, but I made an exception for the Chinese restaurant in the Mandarin Hotel.* • If you **take exception** to something, you feel offended or annoyed by it. *The striker took exception when he was dropped from the team.*

exceptional /ɪk'sepʃənəl/. ① ADJ You use **exceptional** to describe someone or something that has a particular quality to an unusually high degree. *...children with exceptional ability.* ♦**exceptionally** ADV *...an exceptionally talented dancer.* ② ADJ **Exceptional** situations are very unusual or rare. *The courts hold that this case is exceptional.*

excerpt /'eksɜːpt/ **excerpts.** N-C An **excerpt** is a short piece of writing or music taken from a larger piece. *...an excerpt from Tchaikovsky's Nutcracker.*

excess, excesses; noun /ɪk'ses/, adjective /'ekses/. ① N-VAR & ADJ BEFORE N An **excess** of something or an **excess** amount of it is a larger amount than is needed or usual. *...the problems created by an excess of wealth... The major reason for excess weight is excess eating.* ② PHRASE **In excess of** means more than a particular amount. *Avoid deposits in excess of £20,000 in any one account.* ③ N-VAR **Excess** is behaviour that is unacceptable because it is too extreme or immoral. *...the bloody excesses of warfare.* ④ PHRASE If you do something **to excess**, you do it too much. *Red meat, eaten to excess, is very high in fat.*

excessive /ɪk'sesɪv/. ADJ If something is **excessive**, it is too great in amount or degree. *...use of excessive force by police.* ♦**excessively** ADV *...excessively high salaries.*

exchange /ɪks'tʃeɪndʒ/ **exchanges, exchanging, exchanged.** ① VERB & N-C If two or more people **exchange** things, or if there is an **exchange** of them, they give them to each other at the same time. *We exchanged addresses... He exchanged a quick smile with her. ...the exchange of prisoners of war.* ② VERB If you **exchange** something, or if you **exchange** it for something else, you replace it with something. *We will gladly exchange your goods, or refund your money.* ③ PHRASE If you give someone one thing **in exchange** for another, you give it to them because they are giving the other thing to you. If you do something for someone **in exchange** for another, you do it for someone because they did something for you. *He paid her a huge salary. In exchange, he was assured of her vote.* ④ N-C An **exchange** is a brief conversation; FORMAL. *...angry exchanges between opposition and government delegates.*

ex'change rate, exchange rates. N-C The **exchange rate** of a country's unit of currency is the amount of another country's currency that you get in exchange for it.

excise /'eksaɪz/. N-U **Excise** is a tax that the government of a country puts on goods produced for sale in that country.

excitable /ɪk'saɪtəbl/. ADJ An **excitable** person becomes excited very easily.

excite /ɪk'saɪt/ **excites, exciting, excited.** ① VERB If something **excites** you, it makes you feel very happy or enthusiastic. *I only take on work that excites me.* ② VERB If something **excites** a reaction or feeling, it causes it. *These comings and goings excited some curiosity.*

excited /ɪk'saɪtɪd/. ADJ If you are **excited**, you are looking forward to something eagerly. *I'm very excited about the possibility of playing for England's first team.* ♦**excitedly** ADV *A little boy came running up and tugged at his coat sleeve excitedly.*

excitement /ɪk'saɪtmənt/ **excitements.** N-VAR You use **excitement** to refer to the state of being excited, or to something that excites you. *...in a state of great excitement... This game had its challenges, excitements and rewards.*

exciting /ɪk'saɪtɪŋ/. ADJ Something that is **exciting** makes you feel very happy or enthusiastic. *...the most exciting adventure of their lives.*

exclaim /ɪks'kleɪm/ **exclaims, exclaiming, exclaimed.** VERB Writers sometimes use **exclaim** to show that someone is speaking suddenly, loudly, or emphatically. *'There!' Jackson exclaimed delightedly... She exclaimed that she could not possibly do something like that.*

excla'mation mark, exclamation marks. N-C In British English, an **exclamation mark** is the punctuation mark (!). The American expression is **exclamation point**.

exclude /ɪks'kluːd/ **excludes, excluding, excluded.** ① VERB If you **exclude** someone from a place or activity, you prevent them from entering it or taking part in it. *The Academy excluded women from its classes... Many of the youngsters feel excluded.* ♦**exclusion** /ɪks'kluːʒən/ **exclusions.** N-VAR *...his continued exclusion from the England team.* ② VERB If you **exclude** something that has some connection with what you are doing, you deliberately do not use it or consider it. *Christmas carols are being modified to exclude any reference to Christ.* ♦**exclusion** N-VAR *...the exclusion of all commercial lending institutions from the college loan program.* ③ VERB To **exclude** a possibility means to decide or prove that it is wrong and not worth considering.

excluding /ɪks'kluːdɪŋ/. PREP You use **excluding** before mentioning a person or thing to show that you are not including them in your statement. *Excluding water, half of the body's weight is protein.*

exclusive /ɪkˈskluːsɪv/. **1** ADJ Something that is **exclusive** is available only to people who are rich. *...Britain's most exclusive club.* **2** ADJ **Exclusive** means used or owned by only one person or group. *Our group will have exclusive use of a 60-foot boat.* **3** ADJ If two things are mutually **exclusive**, they cannot exist together. *Ambition and successful fatherhood can be mutually exclusive.*

exclusively /ɪkˈskluːsɪvli/. ADV **Exclusively** is used to refer to situations or activities that involve only the thing or things mentioned, and nothing else. *...an exclusively male domain.*

excrete /ɪkˈskriːt/ **excretes, excreting, excreted.** VERB When you **excrete** waste matter from your body, you get rid of it, usually through your bowels; FORMAL.

excruciating /ɪkˈskruːʃieɪtɪŋ/. ADJ **Excruciating** pain is extremely painful.

excursion /ɪkˈskɜːʃən, AM -ʒən/ **excursions.** N-C An **excursion** is a short journey or visit. *...a coach excursion to Trondheim.*

excuse, excuses, excusing, excused. **1** N-C /ɪkˈskjuːs/ An **excuse** is a reason which you give in order to explain why something has been done or has not been done, or to avoid doing something. *I made some excuse and bolted for the exit... Once I had had a baby I had the perfect excuse to stay at home.* **2** VERB /ɪkˈskjuːz/ To **excuse** someone or to **excuse** their behaviour means to provide reasons for their actions, especially when other people disapprove of these actions. *That doesn't excuse my mother's behaviour.* **3** VERB If you **excuse** someone for something wrong that they have done, you forgive them. *Many people might have excused them for avoiding some of their responsibilities.* **4** VERB If someone **is excused** from a duty or responsibility, they are told that they do not have to carry it out. *...a medical certificate excusing him from court.* **5** VERB If you **excuse** yourself, you use a phrase such as **'Excuse me'** as a polite way of saying that you are about to leave. *He excused himself and went up to his room.*

PHRASES ● You say **'Excuse me'** when you want to politely get someone's attention. *Excuse me, but are you Mr Honig?* ● You use **'excuse me'** to apologize for interrupting someone. *Excuse me interrupting, but there's a thing I feel I've got to say.*

execute /ˈeksɪkjuːt/ **executes, executing, executed.** **1** VERB To **execute** someone means to kill them as a punishment. *This boy's father had been executed for conspiring against the throne.* ◆**execution, executions.** N-VAR *...execution by lethal injection.* ◆**executioner, executioners.** N-C *...the executioner's axe.* **2** VERB If you **execute** a plan, you carry it out; FORMAL. ◆**execution** N-U *...the making and execution of monetary policy.* **3** VERB If you **execute** a difficult action or movement, you perform it. *The landing was skilfully executed.*

executive /ɪgˈzekjʊtɪv/ **executives.** **1** N-C An **executive** is someone employed by a company at a senior level. **2** N-SING The **executive** of an organization is a committee which makes im-

portant decisions. *Some executive members have called for his resignation.*

exemplary /ɪgˈzempləri/. ADJ If you describe someone or something as **exemplary**, you consider them to be extremely good. *He showed outstanding and exemplary courage.*

exemplify /ɪgˈzemplɪfaɪ/ **exemplifies, exemplifying, exemplified.** VERB If something or someone **exemplifies** something, they are a typical example of it. *The room's style exemplifies Conran's ideal of 'beauty and practicality'.*

exempt /ɪgˈzempt/ **exempts, exempting, exempted.** **1** ADJ If you are **exempt** from a rule or duty, you do not have to obey it or perform it. *Men in college were exempt from military service.* **2** VERB To **exempt** a person from a rule or duty means to state officially that they do not have to obey it or perform it. ◆**exemption, exemptions** N-VAR *...new exemptions for students and the low-paid.*

exercise /ˈeksəsaɪz/ **exercises, exercising, exercised.** **1** VERB & N-SING If you **exercise** your authority, your rights, or a good quality such as mercy, you put it into use. The **exercise** of these things is the act of using them; FORMAL. *They are merely exercising their right to free speech. ...the exercise of political and economic power.* **2** VERB & N-U When you **exercise**, you move your body energetically in order to get fit and remain healthy. The activity is referred to as **exercise**. *Exercising the body does a great deal to improve one's health... Lack of exercise can lead to feelings of depression. ...stomach exercises.* **3** N-C **Exercises** are a series of movements you do in order to get fit and remain healthy. **4** N-C **Exercises** are activities which you do in order to maintain a skill or to train for a particular skill. *...creative writing exercises. ...military exercises.*

exert /ɪgˈzɜːt/ **exerts, exerting, exerted.** **1** VERB If someone or something **exerts** influence or pressure on someone, they use their influence or put pressure on that person to do something. *...exerting political influence on newspaper editors.* **2** VERB If you **exert yourself**, you make a physical or mental effort to do something. *Do not exert yourself unnecessarily.* ◆**exertion, exertions.** N-VAR *He clearly found the physical exertion exhilarating.*

exhale /eksˈheɪl/ **exhales, exhaling, exhaled.** VERB When you **exhale**, you breathe out; FORMAL.

exhaust /ɪgˈzɔːst/ **exhausts, exhausting, exhausted.** **1** VERB If something **exhausts** you, it makes you very tired. *Walking in deep snow had totally exhausted him.* ◆**exhausted** ADJ *She was too exhausted and distressed to talk.* ◆**exhausting** ADJ *It's a pretty exhausting job.* ◆**exhaustion** N-U *He is suffering from exhaustion.* **2** VERB If a supply of something such as money or food is **exhausted**, it has all been spent or eaten. *People are now living longer and exhausting natural resources.* **3** VERB If you **have exhausted** a subject, you have talked about it so much that there is nothing more to say about it. **4** N-C The **exhaust** on a motor vehicle is the series of pipes which carry waste gases from the engine. **5** N-U **Exhaust** is the waste gases produced by the engine of a motor vehicle.

exhaustive /ɪgˈzɔːstɪv/. ADJ An **exhaustive** study or search is thorough and complete. ...*exhaustive inquiries.* ◆**exhaustively** ADV *You covered everything pretty exhaustively.*

exhibit /ɪgˈzɪbɪt/ **exhibits, exhibiting, exhibited.** [1] VERB To **exhibit** a particular quality, feeling, or type of behaviour means to show it; FORMAL. *He has exhibited symptoms of anxiety.* [2] VERB When an object of interest **is exhibited**, it is put in a public place for people to come and look at it. ...*a massive elephant exhibited by London Zoo.* ◆**exhibition** N-U *Pieces of the wall are currently on exhibition.* [3] N-C An **exhibit** is an object of interest that is displayed in a museum or art gallery. [4] VERB When artists **exhibit**, they show their work in public. *By 1936 she was exhibiting at the Royal Academy.* [5] N-C An **exhibit** is an object that is shown in court as evidence in a legal case.

exhibition /ˌeksɪˈbɪʃən/ **exhibitions.** [1] N-C An **exhibition** is an event at which objects of interest are displayed in a public place. ...*an exhibition of expressionist art.* [2] N-SING If a player or team plays particularly well in a game, you can say that they give an **exhibition** of their skills. ...*treating the fans to an exhibition of power and speed.* [3] See also **exhibit**.

exhibitor /ɪgˈzɪbɪtə/ **exhibitors.** N-C An **exhibitor** is a person whose work is being shown in an exhibition.

exhilarating /ɪgˈzɪləreɪtɪŋ/. ADJ If you describe an experience or feeling as **exhilarating**, you mean that it makes you feel very happy and excited. *It was one of the most exhilarating journeys I have ever made!*

exhort /ɪgˈzɔːt/ **exhorts, exhorting, exhorted.** VERB If you **exhort** someone to do something, you try hard to persuade them to do it; FORMAL. *Kennedy exhorted his listeners to turn away from violence.* ◆**exhortation, exhortations.** N-VAR ...*exhortations to reform.*

exile /ˈeksaɪl, ˈegz-/ **exiles, exiling, exiled.** [1] VERB & N-U If someone **is exiled**, or if they are living in **exile**, they are living in a foreign country because they cannot live in their own country, usually for political reasons. *He was exiled from the Soviet Union.* ...*six years of exile.* [2] N-C An **exile** is someone who lives in exile.

exist /ɪgˈzɪst/ **exists, existing, existed.** [1] VERB If something **exists**, it is present in the world as a real thing. *He thought that if he couldn't see something, it didn't exist.* ...*if you hide away something and pretend that they don't exist.* [2] See also **existing**.

existence /ɪgˈzɪstəns/ **existences.** [1] N-U The **existence** of something is the fact that it is present in the world as a real thing. ...*the existence of other galaxies.* [2] N-C You can refer to someone's way of life as a particular **existence**. *Portia is a gentle person who has led a fairly comfortable existence.*

existing /ɪgˈzɪstɪŋ/. ADJ BEFORE N **Existing** is used to describe something which is now present or is now available. ...*the need to improve existing products.*

exit /ˈegzɪt, ˈeksɪt/ **exits.** [1] N-C An **exit** is a doorway through which you can leave a public building. *He picked up the case and walked towards the exit.* [2] N-C An **exit** on a motorway is a place where traffic can leave it. *Take the A422 exit at Old Stratford.* [3] N-C If you refer to someone's **exit**, you are referring to the fact that they left it. *I made a hasty exit.* [4] VERB If you **exit** a room or building, you leave it; FORMAL.

exodus /ˈeksədəs/. N-SING When there is an **exodus** of people from a place, a lot of people leave it at the same time. ...*the exodus of refugees from a war zone.*

exotic /ɪgˈzɒtɪk/. ADJ Something that is **exotic** is unusual and interesting, usually because it comes from a distant tropical country. ...*brilliantly coloured, exotic flowers.* ◆**exotically** ADV ...*an exotically plumed bird.*

expand /ɪkˈspænd/ **expands, expanding, expanded.** VERB If something **expands**, it becomes larger. *The money supply expanded by 14.6%... I owned a bookshop and desired to expand the business.* ◆**expansion** /ɪkˈspænʃən/ **expansions.** N-VAR *The company has abandoned plans for further expansion.*

• **expand on** or **expand upon.** PHR-VERB If you **expand on** something, you give more information about it. *The president used today's speech to expand on remarks he made last month.*

expanse /ɪkˈspæns/ **expanses.** N-C An **expanse** of sea, sky, or land is a very large area of it.

expansion. See **expand**.

expansive /ɪkˈspænsɪv/. [1] ADJ BEFORE N **Expansive** means covering or including a large area or many things. ...*an expansive grassy play area.* [2] ADJ If you are **expansive**, you talk a lot, or are friendly or generous, because you are happy and relaxed. *Fritz was a large and expansive man who loved to entertain.*

expatriate /eksˈpætriət, -ˈpeɪt-/ **expatriates.** N-C An **expatriate** is someone who is living in a country other than the one where they were born.

expect /ɪkˈspekt/ **expects, expecting, expected.** [1] VERB If you **expect** something to happen, you believe that it will happen. *He expects to lose his job in the next few weeks... They no longer expect profits to improve.* [2] VERB If you **are expecting** something or someone, you believe that they will be delivered or arrive soon. *I am expecting several important letters... We were expecting him home.* [3] VERB If you **expect** something, or if you **expect** someone to do something, you believe that it is your right to have that thing, or it is that person's duty to do it for you. *I do expect to have some time to myself... I wasn't expecting you to help.* [4] VERB If a woman **is expecting** a baby, she is pregnant. *I hear Dawn's expecting again.*

expectant /ɪkˈspektənt/. [1] ADJ If you are **expectant**, you are excited because you think something interesting is about to happen. ◆**expectantly** ADV *The others waited, looking at him expectantly.* ◆**expectancy** N-U ...*a tremendous air of expectancy.* • See also **life expectancy**. [2] ADJ BEFORE N An **expectant** mother or father is someone whose baby is going to be born soon.

expectation /ˌekspek'teɪʃən/ **expectations.**
[1] N-VAR Your **expectations** are your beliefs that a particular thing will happen. *One broker said, 'My expectation is that the stock will go as high as $2.50'... Even the dark night air was tense with expectation.* [2] N-C A person's **expectations** are beliefs which they have about the way someone should behave or something should happen. *...living up to other people's expectations.*

expedient /ɪk'spiːdiənt/ **expedients.** N-C & ADJ An **expedient** is an action that achieves a particular purpose, but may not be morally right. You can also say that it is **expedient** to do something. *I cut my purchases dramatically by the simple expedient of destroying my credit card... It was expedient to be nice to him if you wanted to get on.* ◆**expediency** N-U *Their enthusiasm was partly motivated by political expediency.*

expedition /ˌekspɪ'dɪʃən/ **expeditions.** N-C An **expedition** is a journey made for a particular purpose such as exploration. *...Byrd's 1928 expedition to Antarctica.*

expel /ɪk'spel/ **expels, expelling, expelled.**
[1] VERB If someone is **expelled** from a school or organization, they are officially told to leave because they have behaved badly. *...a 14-year-old boy expelled from school for refusing to take a shower.* ◆**expulsion** /ɪk'spʌlʃən/ N-U *...her expulsion from high school.* [2] VERB If people **are expelled** from a place, they are made to leave it, usually by force. *...numerous examples of patients being expelled from hospital.* ◆**expulsion** N-U *...the expulsion of illegal immigrants.* [3] VERB To **expel** something such as a gas means to force it out. *He groaned, expelling the air from his lungs.*

expend /ɪk'spend/ **expends, expending, expended.** VERB To **expend** energy, time, or money means to spend it or use it.

expenditure /ɪk'spendɪtʃə/ **expenditures.**
[1] N-VAR **Expenditure** is the spending of money on something, or the money that is spent on something. *...reduced public expenditure... They should cut their expenditure on defence.* [2] N-U **Expenditure** of energy or time is using it for a particular purpose.

expense /ɪk'spens/ **expenses.** [1] N-VAR **Expense** is the money that something costs you or that you need to spend in order to do something. *The tunnel is an unnecessary expense. ...household expenses.* [2] N-PL Your **expenses** are the money you spend while doing something in the course of your work, which will be paid back to you afterwards. *...travelling expenses.*

PHRASES ● If you do something **at your own expense**, you pay for it. *She traveled at her own expense to the Soviet Union.* ● If someone makes a joke **at** your **expense**, they do it to make you seem foolish.

expensive /ɪk'spensɪv/. ADJ If something is **expensive**, it costs a lot of money. *Wine's so expensive in this country. ...a lot of expensive equipment.* ◆**expensively** ADV *She was expensively dressed.*

experience /ɪk'spɪəriəns/ **experiences, experiencing, experienced.** [1] N-U **Experience**
is knowledge or skill in a particular job or activity, which you have gained from doing that job or activity. *He has also had managerial experience on every level.* ◆**experienced** ADJ *...very experienced nurses.* [2] N-U **Experience** is used to refer to the past events, knowledge, and feelings that make up someone's life or character. *Experience has taught me caution.* [3] N-C An **experience** is something that happens to you or something that you do. *Unfair dismissal can be a traumatic experience for an employee.* [4] VERB If you **experience** a situation or feeling, it happens to you or you are affected by it. *Widows seem to experience more distress than do widowers.*

experiment /ɪk'sperɪmənt/ **experiments, experimenting, experimented.** [1] N-VAR An **experiment** is a scientific test which is done to discover what happens to something in particular conditions. *...conducting experiments on behalf of NASA and the Japanese scientific community.* [2] VERB If you **experiment with** something, or if you **experiment on** it, you do scientific tests to discover what happens to that thing in particular conditions. *...a professor who had been experimenting on rabbits.* ◆**experimentation** N-U *...animal experimentation.* [3] N-VAR An **experiment** is the trying out of a new idea or method in order to see what it is like and what effects it has. *...the country's five year experiment in democracy.* [4] VERB To **experiment** means to try out a new idea or method, in order to see what it is like and what kind of effects it has. *Students should be encouraged to experiment with bold ideas.* ◆**experimentation** N-U *...his sexual experimentation.*

experimental /ɪk,sperɪ'mentəl/. [1] ADJ Something that is **experimental** is new or uses new ideas or methods. *...highly experimental pieces of music.* [2] ADJ BEFORE N **Experimental** means relating to scientific experiments. *Scientists know that all experimental results are variable.* ◆**experimentally** ADV *A species can be studied experimentally.*

expert /'eksp3ːt/ **experts.** [1] ADJ & N-C If someone is **expert** at doing something, or if they are an **expert**, he or she is very skilled at doing something or knows a lot about a particular subject. *...an expert gardener. ...experts on terrorism.* ◆**expertly** ADV *Shopkeepers expertly rolled spices up in bay leaves.* [2] ADJ BEFORE N **Expert** advice or help is given by someone who has studied a subject thoroughly or who is very skilled at a particular job. *We'll need an expert opinion.*

expertise /ˌeksp3ː'tiːz/. N-U **Expertise** is special skill or knowledge. *...legal expertise.*

expire /ɪk'spaɪə/ **expires, expiring, expired.**
[1] VERB When something such as a contract or a visa **expires**, it comes to an end or is no longer valid. *My passport has expired.* [2] VERB When someone **expires**, they die; LITERARY.

explain /ɪk'spleɪn/ **explains, explaining, explained.** [1] VERB If you **explain** something, you give details about it or describe it so that it can be understood. *Don't sign anything until your solicitor has explained the contract to you... 'He and Mrs Stein have a plan,' she ex-*

plained. [2] VERB If you **explain** something that has happened, you give reasons for it. *The receptionist apologized for the delay, explaining that it had been a hectic day... Explain yourself to me.*

▶ **explain away** PHR-VERB If someone **explains away** a mistake or a bad situation that they are responsible for, they try to indicate that it is unimportant or that it is not really their fault. *I had noticed blood on my husband's clothing but he explained it away.*

explanation /ˌeksplə'neɪʃən/ explanations. N-VAR If you give an **explanation**, you give reasons why something happened, or describe something in detail. *The authorities have given no explanation for his arrest. ...an in-depth explanation of the gas furnace and how it works.*

explanatory /ɪk'splænətəri, AM -tɔːri/. ADJ Something that is **explanatory** explains something by giving details about it; FORMAL. *...explanatory notes.*

explicit /ɪk'splɪsɪt/. [1] ADJ Something that is **explicit** is shown or expressed clearly and openly, without hiding anything. *...sexually explicit scenes in films.* ◆ **explicitly** ADV *...explicitly political activities.* [2] ADJ AFTER LINK-V If you are **explicit** about something, you express yourself clearly and openly. *He has been so vocal and so explicit about his annoyance.* ◆ **explicitly** ADV *She has been talking very explicitly about AIDS.*

explode /ɪk'spləʊd/ explodes, exploding, exploded. [1] VERB If something such as a bomb **explodes**, it bursts with great force. *The grenade exploded, killing both men. ...gunfire which exploded the fuel tank.* [2] VERB You can say that a person **explodes** when they express strong feelings suddenly and violently. *Simon exploded with anger.*

exploit, exploits, exploiting, exploited. [1] VERB/ɪk'splɔɪt/ If someone **exploits** you, they unfairly use your work or ideas and give you little in return. *Critics claim he exploited black musicians.* ◆ **exploitation** N-U *...to protect the interests of the staff and prevent exploitation.* [2] VERB To **exploit** something means to use it to gain an advantage for yourself. *...a talent for seeing, creating and exploiting opportunities.* ◆ **exploitation** N-U *...her exploitation of the social security system.* [3] VERB To **exploit** resources or raw materials means to develop them and use them for industry or commercial activities. ◆ **exploitation** N-U *...the planned exploitation of its potential oil and natural gas reserves.* [4] N-C /'eksplɔɪt/ Someone's **exploits** are the brave or interesting things they have done. *...his wartime exploits.*

exploratory /ɪk'splɒrətri, AM -'plɔːrətɔːri/. ADJ **Exploratory** actions are done to discover or learn something. *...exploratory surgery.*

explore /ɪk'splɔː/ explores, exploring, explored. [1] VERB If you **explore** a place, you travel around it to find out what it is like. *The best way to explore the area is in a boat.* ◆ **exploration** /ˌeksplə'reɪʃən/ explorations N-VAR *...space exploration.* ◆ **explorer, explorers** N-C *...Arctic explorers.* [2] VERB If you **explore** an idea, you think about it carefully to decide whether it is a good one. *The city is exploring the idea of converting the building into*

a youth hostel. [3] VERB If people **explore for** a substance such as oil or minerals, they study an area and do tests on the land to see whether they can find it. ◆ **exploration** N-U *...oil exploration.*

explosion /ɪk'spləʊʒən/ explosions. [1] N-C An **explosion** is a sudden violent burst of energy, for example one caused by a bomb. *Six soldiers were injured in the explosion.* [2] N-C An **explosion** of something is a large and rapid increase of it. *...the population explosion in North Africa.*

explosive /ɪk'spləʊsɪv/ explosives. [1] N-VAR & ADJ An **explosive**, or an **explosive** substance or device, is a substance or device that can cause an explosion. [2] ADJ An **explosive** situation is likely to have serious or dangerous effects.

exponent /ɪk'spəʊnənt/ exponents. [1] N-C An **exponent** of an idea, theory, or plan is someone who speaks or writes in support of it; FORMAL. *...an exponent of free speech.* [2] N-C An **exponent** of a particular skill or activity is a person who is good at it. *...the great exponent of expressionist dance, Kurt Jooss.*

export, exports, exporting, exported; verb /ɪk'spɔːt/, noun /'ekspɔːt/. [1] VERB & N-U To **export** goods means to sell them to another country. Selling goods to another country is called **export**. *The lumber is exported worldwide. ...200,000 cars a year, mostly for export.* ◆ **exporter, exporters** N-C *...arms exporters.* [2] N-C **Exports** are goods which are sold to another country and sent there. *Ghana's main export is cocoa.*

expose /ɪk'spəʊz/ exposes, exposing, exposed. [1] VERB To **expose** something means to uncover it and make it visible. *For an instant his whole back was exposed.* [2] VERB If you **are exposed** to something dangerous, you are put in a situation in which it might harm you. *...workers exposed to chemicals that damage their health.* [3] VERB To **expose** a person or situation means to reveal the truth about them. *...church officials exposed him as a fake.* [4] ADJ An **exposed** place has no natural protection against bad weather or enemies. *...an exposed hillside.*

exposition /ˌekspə'zɪʃən/ expositions. N-C An **exposition** of an idea or theory is a detailed explanation of it; FORMAL.

exposure /ɪk'spəʊʒə/ exposures. [1] N-U **Exposure** to something dangerous means being in a situation where it might affect you. *Exposure to lead is known to damage the brains of young children.* [2] N-U **Exposure** is the harmful effect on your body caused by very cold weather. *At least two people died of exposure.* [3] N-U **Exposure** is publicity. *His aim is to get the artists more exposure.* [4] N-U The **exposure** of a well-known person is the revealing of the fact that they are bad or immoral in some way. *...the exposure of Anthony Blunt as a former Soviet spy.* [5] N-C In photography, an **exposure** is a single photograph.

expound /ɪk'spaʊnd/ expounds, expounding, expounded. VERB If you **expound** an idea or opinion, you give a clear and detailed explanation of it; FORMAL. *Schmidt continued to expound his views on economics.*

express /ik'spres/ expresses, expressing, expressed. [1] VERB When you **express** an idea or feeling, you show what you think or feel. *He expressed grave concern... I didn't know how to express myself properly.* [2] VERB If an idea or feeling **expresses** itself in some way, it can be clearly seen in someone's actions. *The anxiety of the separation often expresses itself as anger.* [3] VERB If you **express** a quantity in a particular form, you write it down in that form; TECHNICAL. *It is expressed as a percentage.* [4] ADJ BEFORE N An **express** command or order is stated clearly; FORMAL. *The visit to the nightclub was against the express wishes of the coach.* ♦**expressly** ADV *Suicide is expressly forbidden in Buddhism.* [5] ADJ BEFORE N An **express** intention or purpose is deliberate or specific. *I had obtained my first camera for the express purpose of taking railway photographs.* ♦**expressly** ADV *...projects expressly designed to support cattle farmers.* [6] ADJ BEFORE N An **express** service is one in which things are done faster than usual. *...an express delivery service.* [7] N-C An **express** is a fast train or coach which stops at very few places.

expression /ik'spreʃən/ expressions. [1] N-C An **expression** is a word or phrase. *...an Irish expression for fun.* [2] N-VAR The **expression** of ideas or feelings is the showing of them through words, actions, or art. *The announcement led to some expressions of concern from ministers. ...freedom of artistic expression.* [3] N-VAR Your **expression** is the way that your face shows what you are thinking or feeling.

expressive /ik'spresiv/. ADJ Something that is **expressive** indicates clearly a person's feelings or intentions. *...her wonderfully expressive face. ...love poems, expressive of love for someone.* ♦**expressively** ADV *He moved his hands very expressively.*

expulsion. See **expel**.

exquisite /ik'skwizit, 'ekskwizit/. ADJ **Exquisite** means extremely beautiful. *His voice is exquisite. ...her exquisite manners.* ♦**exquisitely** ADV *...exquisitely crafted dolls' houses.*

extend /ik'stend/ extends, extending, extended. [1] VERB If something **extends** for a particular distance or time, it continues for that distance or time. *...a playing career in first-class cricket that extended from 1894 to 1920.* [2] VERB If an object **extends** from a surface, it sticks out from it. *...a brightly coloured awning extended from the wall.* [3] VERB If something **extends** to a group of people, things, or activities, it includes or affects them. *The service also extends to wrapping and delivering gifts... His influence extends beyond the TV viewing audience.* [4] VERB If you **extend** something, you make it bigger, or make it last longer or include more. *We thought about extending the house... They have extended the deadline by twenty-four hours.* [5] VERB If you **extend** a part of your body, you straighten it or stretch it out. *Marshall extended his hand to Kelly.* [6] VERB To **extend** an offer or invitation to someone means to make it; FORMAL.

extension /ik'stenʃən/ extensions. [1] N-C An **extension** is a new room or building which is added to an existing building. *...the new exten-*sion to London's National Gallery.* [2] N-C An **extension** is an extra period of time for which something continues to exist or be valid. *...an extension to their visas.* [3] N-C Something that is an **extension** of something else is a development of it that includes or affects more people, things, or activities. *...the difficulties of an extension of unemployment benefits.* [4] N-C An **extension** is a telephone line that is connected to the switchboard of a company or institution, and that has its own number. *...extension 308.*

extensive /ik'stensiv/. [1] ADJ Something that is **extensive** covers a large area. *The hospital stands in extensive grounds.* ♦**extensively** ADV *She has travelled extensively.* [2] ADJ If something is **extensive**, it is very great. *The blast caused extensive damage.* ♦**extensively** ADV *This edition has been extensively revised.* [3] ADJ **Extensive** means covering many details, ideas, or items. *The summit is given extensive coverage in today's newspapers.* ♦**extensively** ADV *All these issues have been extensively researched.*

extent /ik'stent/. [1] N-SING The **extent** of something is its length, area, or size. *Climatic alterations reduced the extent of the rain forest.* [2] N-SING The **extent** of a situation is how great, important, or serious it is. *There's no word on the extent of his injuries.* [3] N-U You use **extent** to say how true something is. *It was and, to a large extent, still is a good show... I was getting more nervous to the extent that I was almost physically sick.*

exterior /ik'stiəriə/ exteriors. [1] N-C The **exterior** of something is its outside surface. *...the stone exterior of the building.* [2] N-C You can refer to someone's outward appearance and behaviour as their **exterior**. *Pat's tough exterior hides a shy and sensitive soul.* [3] ADJ BEFORE N You use **exterior** to refer to the outside parts of something, or to things that are outside something. *...exterior walls.*

exterminate /ik'stɜːmineit/ exterminates, exterminating, exterminated. VERB To **exterminate** a group of people or animals means to kill all of them. *A huge effort was made to exterminate the rats.* ♦**extermination** N-U *...the extermination of wild dogs.*

external /ik'stɜːnəl/ externals. [1] ADJ BEFORE N **External** means happening, coming from, or existing outside a place, person, or area of activity. *...external walls. ...the commissioner for external affairs.* ♦**externally** ADV *Vitamins can be applied externally to the skin.* [2] ADJ BEFORE N **External** is used to describe people who come into an organization from outside to do a job there. *...external examiners.*

extinct /ik'stiŋkt/. [1] ADJ If a species of animals is **extinct**, it no longer has any living members. *It is 250 years since the wolf became extinct in Britain.* [2] ADJ An **extinct** volcano does not erupt or is unlikely to erupt.

extinction /ik'stiŋkʃən/. N-U The **extinction** of a species of animal is the death of all its remaining members. *Tigers could face extinction within 10 years.*

extinguish /ik'stiŋgwiʃ/ extinguishes, extinguishing, extinguished. VERB If you **extinguish** a fire or a light, you stop it burning or shining. *It took about 50 minutes to extinguish the fire.*

extol /ɪkˈstəʊl/ **extols, extolling, extolled.** VERB If you **extol** something, you praise it enthusiastically. *...you hear people extolling the virtues of higher education.*

extra /ˈekstrə/ **extras.** [1] ADJ BEFORE N & ADV An **extra** thing, person, or amount is another one that is added to others of the same kind. *...extra blankets. ...extra staff... They should get up to £13,500 extra a year to spend on staff.* [2] N-C **Extras** are things that are not necessary but make something more comfortable, useful, or enjoyable. *Extras include an introduction to scuba diving.* [3] N-C **Extras** are additional amounts of money added to the basic price of something. *There are no hidden extras.* [4] N-C An **extra** is a person who plays an unimportant part in a film. [5] ADV You can use **extra** in front of adjectives and adverbs to emphasize the quality that they are describing; INFORMAL. *I'd have to be extra careful.*

extract, extracts, extracting, extracted; verb /ɪkˈstrækt/, noun /ˈekstrækt/. [1] VERB & N-VAR To **extract** a substance means to obtain it from something else, for example by using industrial or chemical processes. An **extract** is a substance that has been obtained in this way. *Citric acid can be extracted from the juice of oranges. ...a plant extract which acts as a natural tonic.* ♦**extraction** N-U *...the extraction of oil.* [2] VERB If you **extract** something from a place, you take it out or pull it out; LITERARY. *She reached into the wardrobe and extracted another tracksuit.* [3] VERB If you **extract** information or a response **from** someone, you get it from them with difficulty. *He was unable to extract any information from the three men.* [4] VERB When a dentist **extracts** a tooth, he or she removes it from the patient's mouth. ♦**extraction, extractions** N-VAR *Extractions were carried out without anaesthetic.* [5] N-C An **extract** from a book or piece of writing is a small part of it that is printed or published separately.

extradite /ˈekstrədaɪt/ **extradites, extraditing, extradited.** VERB If someone is **extradited**, they are officially sent back to their own country to stand trial for a crime; FORMAL. ♦**extradition** /ˌekstrəˈdɪʃən/ **extraditions** N-VAR *...the British government's request for his extradition.*

extraordinary /ɪkˈstrɔːdənri/, AM -neri/. [1] ADJ An **extraordinary** person or thing has some extremely good or special quality. *...an extraordinary musician... We've made extraordinary progress.* ♦**extraordinarily** /ɪkˈstrɔːdənrɪli, AM -nerɪli/ ADV *She's extraordinarily disciplined.* [2] ADJ If you describe something as **extraordinary**, you mean that it is very unusual or surprising. *What an extraordinary thing to happen!* ♦**extraordinarily** ADV *Rainfall was extraordinarily high.*

extravagance /ɪkˈstrævəgəns/ **extravagances.** N-C An **extravagance** is something that you spend money on but cannot really afford. *Her only extravagance was horses.*

extravagant /ɪkˈstrævəgənt/. [1] ADJ Someone who is **extravagant** spends more money than

they can afford or uses more of something than is reasonable. *We are not extravagant; restaurant meals are a luxury.* ♦**extravagantly** ADV *Jeff had shopped extravagantly for presents.* ♦**extravagance** N-U *...gross mismanagement and financial extravagance.* [2] ADJ Something that is **extravagant** costs more money than you can afford or uses more of something than is reasonable. *Her Aunt Sallie gave her an uncharacteristically extravagant gift.* ♦**extravagantly** ADV *...an extravagant expensive piece of equipment.* [3] ADJ **Extravagant** behaviour is extreme behaviour that is often done for a particular effect. *...extravagant shows of generosity.* ♦**extravagantly** ADV *She had on occasions praised him extravagantly.* [4] ADJ **Extravagant** claims or ideas are unrealistic or impractical; used showing disapproval. *...extravagant claims for success.*

extravaganza /ɪkˌstrævəˈɡænzə/ **extravaganzas.** N-C An **extravaganza** is a very elaborate and expensive show or performance. *...a magnificent firework extravaganza.*

extreme /ɪkˈstriːm/ **extremes.** [1] ADJ **Extreme** means very great in degree or intensity. *...people living in extreme poverty. ...Japan, with its extreme housing shortage.* ♦**extremely** ADV *My mobile phone is extremely useful.* [2] ADJ You use **extreme** to describe situations and behaviour which are much more severe or unusual than you would expect. *'I would rather die than do anything so extreme,' she said.* [3] ADJ The **extreme** point or edge of something is its farthest point or edge. *...winds from the extreme north.* [4] N-C You can use **extremes** to refer to situations or types of behaviour that have completely opposite qualities to each other. *...the extremes of success and failure.* [5] PHRASE You use **in the extreme** after an adjective to emphasize how bad or undesirable something is. *He had been foolish in the extreme.*

extremist /ɪkˈstriːmɪst/ **extremists.** N-C If you describe someone as an **extremist**, you disapprove of them because they try to bring about political change by using violent or extreme methods. *...a previously unknown extremist group.* ♦**extremism** N-U *...right-wing extremism.*

extrovert /ˈekstrəvɜːt/ **extroverts.** N-C & ADJ An extrovert, or someone who is **extrovert**, is very active, lively, and sociable. *His footballing skills and extrovert personality won the hearts of the public.*

exuberant /ɪɡˈzjuːbərənt, AM -ˈzuːb-/. [1] ADJ Someone who is **exuberant** is full of energy, excitement, and cheerfulness. *She was a bubbly, exuberant personality.* ♦**exuberance** N-U *...her burst of exuberance.* ♦**exuberantly** ADV *They both laughed exuberantly.* [2] ADJ If you describe something as **exuberant**, you like it because it is lively, exciting, and full of energy and life. *His clothes had a kind of exuberant style.* ♦**exuberance** N-U *...the sheer exuberance of the sculpture.* ♦**exuberantly** ADV *...exuberantly decorated.*

exude /ɪɡˈzjuːd, AM -ˈzuːd/ **exudes, exuding, exuded.** [1] VERB If someone **exudes** a quality or feeling, or if it **exudes**, they show that they have it to a great extent; FORMAL. *Men dressed like this exude an air of quiet confidence.* [2] VERB If something **exudes** a liquid or smell, or if a liquid or smell **exudes** from it, the liquid or smell comes out of it; FORMAL. *...a factory which exuded a pungent smell.*

eye /aɪ/ **eyes, eyeing** (or **eying**), **eyed.** [1] N-C Your **eyes** are the parts of your body with which you see. ♦-**eyed** *...a blonde-haired, blue-eyed little girl... She watched open-eyed.* [2] N-C You use **eye** when you are talking about a person's ability to judge things or about the way in which they are considering or dealing with things. *...a man of discernment, with an eye for quality... He turned his critical eye on the United States... The practice of religion in America sometimes seems strange to European eyes.* [3] VERB If you **eye** someone or something in a particular way, you look at them carefully in that way. *Sally eyed Claire with interest... Martin eyed the bottle.*

> PHRASES • If you say that something happens **before** your **eyes**, **in front of** your **eyes**, or **under** your **eyes**, you are emphasizing that it happens where you can see it clearly or while you are watching it. *The man was bleeding to death before his eyes.* • If something **catches** your **eye**, you suddenly notice it. *A quick movement across the aisle caught his eye.* • If you **catch** someone's **eye**, you do something to attract their attention, so that you can speak to them. *He tried to catch her eye, but she was sunk in deep thought.* • To **clap eyes on** someone or something, or **set** or **lay eyes on** them, means to see them; INFORMAL. *It was the most cruel, evil human face I ever set eyes on.* • If you **have** your **eye on** something, you want to have it; INFORMAL. *...a new outfit you've had your eye on.* • If you **keep an eye on** something or someone, you watch them carefully, for example to make sure that they are safe, or are not

causing trouble. *He had been sent here to keep an eye on Benedict.* • If you **keep** your **eyes open** or **keep an eye out** for someone or something, you watch for them carefully; IN-FORMAL. *As we walked along, we kept our eyes open for mushrooms... You and your friends keep an eye out.* • If you **look** someone **in the eye** or **meet** their **eyes**, you look directly at them in a bold open way, for example in order to make them realize that you are not afraid of them or that you are telling the truth. *She felt so foolish she could barely look Robert in the eye... She met my eyes steadily, but offered no explanations.* • If someone sees something **through** your **eyes**, they see it from your point of view.

eyeball /ˈaɪbɔːl/ **eyeballs.** N-C Your **eyeballs** are the parts of your eyes that are like white balls.

eyebrow /ˈaɪbraʊ/ **eyebrows.** [1] N-C Your **eyebrows** are the lines of hair which grow above your eyes. [2] PHRASE If something causes you to **raise an eyebrow** or to **raise** your **eyebrows**, it causes you to feel surprised or disapproving. *He raised his eyebrows over some of the suggestions.*

'**eye-catching.** ADJ Something that is **eye-catching** is very noticeable. *...an eye-catching headline on the front page of the Sunday Times.*

eyelash /ˈaɪlæʃ/ **eyelashes.** N-C Your **eyelashes** are the hairs which grow on the edges of your eyelids.

eyelid /ˈaɪlɪd/ **eyelids.** N-C Your **eyelids** are the two flaps of skin which cover your eyes when they are closed.

eyesight /ˈaɪsaɪt/. N-U Your **eyesight** is your ability to see. *He suffered from poor eyesight.*

eyewitness, eyewitnesses. N-C An **eyewitness** is a person who has seen an event and can therefore describe it, for example in a law court.

F f

fable /ˈfeɪbəl/ **fables.** N-VAR A **fable** is a traditional story which teaches a moral lesson.

fabric /ˈfæbrɪk/ **fabrics.** [1] N-VAR **Fabric** is cloth. *...red cotton fabric. ...silk and other delicate fabrics.* [2] N-SING The **fabric** of a society is its structure and customs; FORMAL. *Years of civil war have wrecked the country's social fabric.* [3] N-SING The **fabric** of a building is its walls, roof, and other parts; FORMAL.

fabricate /ˈfæbrɪkeɪt/ **fabricates, fabricating, fabricated.** VERB If someone **fabricates** information, they invent it in order to deceive people; FORMAL. *Officers fabricated evidence against them.* ♦**fabrication, fabrications** N-VAR *China calls the report pure fabrication.*

fabulous /ˈfæbjʊləs/. ADJ You use **fabulous** to emphasize how wonderful or impressive you think something is. ♦**fabulously** ADV *...their fabulously rich parents.*

facade or **façade** /fəˈsɑːd/ **facades.** [1] N-C The **facade** of a large building is the outside of its front wall. *...the refurbishing of the cathedral's facade.* [2] N-SING You say that something is a

facade when its outward appearance deliberately gives a wrong impression. *They hid the troubles plaguing their marriage behind a facade of family togetherness.*

face 1 noun uses

face /feɪs/ **faces.** [1] N-C Your **face** is the front of your head from your chin to your forehead. *She had a beautiful face... His face was covered with wrinkles.* [2] N-C The **face** of a cliff, mountain, or building is a vertical surface or side of it. [3] N-C The **face** of a clock is the surface which shows the time. [4] N-SING If you refer to a particular **face** of something, you mean one particular aspect of it. *...the unacceptable face of capitalism.* [5] N-U If you lose **face**, something that you do or something that happens makes people lose respect for you. If you are able to save **face**, you do something which restores your reputation. *To cancel the airport project would mean a loss of face for the governor.* [6] See also **face value**.

> PHRASES • If you take a particular action or attitude **in the face of** a problem or difficulty,

you respond to that problem or difficulty in that way. *He persevered in the face of active discouragement from those around him.* ● If an action or belief **flies in the face of** accepted ideas or rules, it seems to completely contradict them. *...scientific principles that seem to fly in the face of common sense.* ● If you **make** or **pull a face**, you show your dislike for something by, for example, sticking out your tongue. ● If you manage to keep **a straight face**, you manage to look serious, although you want to laugh.

face 2 verb uses

face /feɪs/ **faces, facing, faced.** [1] VERB To **face** a particular direction means to look in that direction from a position directly opposite it. *They stood facing each other... The garden faces south.* [2] VERB If you **are faced** with something difficult or unpleasant, you have to deal with it. *We are faced with a serious problem.* [3] VERB If you cannot **face** something, you do not feel able to deal with it because it seems so difficult or unpleasant. *My children want me with them for Christmas Day, but I can't face it... I couldn't face seeing anyone.*

▶ **face up to.** PHR-VERB If you **face up to** something difficult or unpleasant, you accept it and try to deal with it. *You can help an alcoholic parent by facing up to the problem.*

faceless /feɪsləs/. ADJ If you describe someone or something as **faceless**, you dislike them because they have no character or individuality. *...faceless bureaucrats.*

facet /fæsɪt, -set/ **facets.** N-C A **facet** of something is a single part or aspect of it. *The government is involved in every facet of people's lives.*

face 'value. [1] N-SING The **face value** of things such as banknotes or tickets is the price stated on it. *Tickets were selling at twice their face value.* [2] PHRASE If you take something at **face value**, you accept it without thinking about it very much.

facial /feɪʃəl/. ADJ BEFORE N **Facial** is used to describe things that relate to your face. *...his facial expression.*

facilitate /fəˈsɪlɪteɪt/ **facilitates, facilitating, facilitated.** VERB To **facilitate** a process means to make it easier; FORMAL. *...facilitating the release of hostages.*

facility /fəˈsɪlɪti/ **facilities.** [1] N-C **Facilities** are buildings, equipment, or services that are provided for a particular purpose. *...nursery facilities.* [2] N-C A **facility** is a useful service or feature provided by an organization or machine. *...an overdraft facility... This system has an electronic mail facility.*

fact /fækt/ **facts.** [1] N-C **Facts** are pieces of information which can be proved to be true. *...the facts about the murder.* [2] N-U When you refer to something as **fact**, you mean that it is true or correct. *...a statement of verifiable historical fact.*

[PHRASES] ● You use **the fact that** after some verbs and prepositions, for example in expressions such as **despite the fact that** and **apart from the fact that**, to link the verb or preposition with a clause. *Despite the fact that the disease is so prevalent, treatment is still far from*

satisfactory... *My family now accepts the fact that I don't eat sugar or bread.* ● You use **in fact, in actual fact, as a matter of fact,** or **in point of fact** to indicate that you are giving more detailed information about what you have just said. *We've had a pretty bad time while you were away. In fact, we very nearly split up.*

faction /fækʃən/ **factions.** N-C A **faction** is an organized group of people within a larger group who oppose some of the ideas of the larger group. *...the leaders of the country's warring factions.* ◆**factional** ADJ *The factional fighting has killed more than 4,000 people.*

factor /fæktə/ **factors.** N-C A **factor** is one of the things that affects an event or situation. *...environmental factors, such as air pollution.*

factory /fæktri/ **factories.** N-C A **factory** is a large building where machines are used to make goods in large quantities.

factual /fæktʃuəl/. ADJ Something that is **factual** contains or refers to facts rather than theories or opinions. *The editorial contained several factual errors.*

faculty /fækəlti/ **faculties.** [1] N-C Your **faculties** are your physical and mental abilities. *...losing our faculties of memory and reason.* [2] N-C In some universities, a **faculty** is a group of related departments. *...the Faculty of Social and Political Sciences.*

fad /fæd/ **fads.** N-C You can refer to an activity or topic of interest that is very popular for a short time as a **fad**.

fade /feɪd/ **fades, fading, faded.** [1] VERB When something fades, or when something **fades** it, it slowly becomes less intense in brightness, colour, or sound. *They observed the comet for 70 days before it faded from sight... Ultraviolet light will fade the colours in organic materials... His voice faded away.* ◆**faded** ADJ *...faded blue jeans.* [2] VERB If memories, feelings, or possibilities **fade**, they slowly become less strong. *Prospects for peace had already started to fade.*

▶ **fade away** or **fade out.** PHR-VERB When something fades **away** or **fades out**, it slowly becomes less noticeable or less important until it ends completely. *With time, they said, criticism will fade away.*

faeces (AM **feces**) /ˈfiːsiːz/. N-U **Faeces** is the solid waste substance that people and animals get rid of from their body through the anus; FORMAL.

Fahrenheit /færənhaɪt/. ADJ & N-U **Fahrenheit** is a scale for measuring temperature, in which water freezes at 32 degrees and boils at 212 degrees. It is represented by the symbol °F. ● See note at **temperature.**

fail /feɪl/ **fails, failing, failed.** [1] VERB If you **fail** to do something that you were trying to do, you do not succeed in doing it. *He failed to win sufficient votes... We tried to develop plans for them to get along, which all failed miserably.* [2] VERB If someone or something **fails** to do something that they should have done, they do not do it. *He failed to file tax returns for 1982... The bomb failed to explode.* [3] VERB If someone **fails** you, they do not do what you expected or trusted them to do. ...*communities who feel that the political system has failed them.* [4] VERB If someone **fails** an examination, they do not reach the standard that is required. ● See note at **exam**. [5] VERB If something **fails**, it stops working properly. *The lights mysteriously failed.*

failing /'feɪlɪŋ/ **failings.** [1] N-C The **failings** of someone or something are their faults or unsatisfactory features. *The new law's failings could send many companies bankrupt.* [2] PHRASE You say **failing that** to introduce an alternative, in case what you have just said is not possible. *Talk things through, or failing that, write down your thoughts.*

failure /'feɪljə/ **failures.** [1] N-VAR **Failure** is a lack of success in doing or achieving something. *This policy is doomed to failure... The marriage was a failure.* [2] N-U Your **failure** to do something you were expected to do is the fact that you do not do it. ...*their disgraceful failure to support British citizens.* [3] N-VAR When there is a **failure** of something, it stops working properly. ...*engine failures... Anthony was being treated for kidney failure.*

faint /feɪnt/ **fainter, faintest; faints, fainted.** [1] ADJ Something that is **faint** is not strong or intense. ...*the soft, faint sounds of water dripping... Their voices grew fainter.* ◆**faintly** ADV *She smiled faintly.* [2] VERB & N-C If you **faint**, or if you fall into a **faint**, you lose consciousness for a short time. [3] ADJ AFTER LINK-V Someone who feels **faint** feels dizzy and unsteady.

fair /feə/ **fairer, fairest; fairs.** [1] ADJ & PHRASE Something or someone that is **fair** is reasonable, right, and just. *It didn't seem fair to leave out her father. ...a very fair and broadminded man... He has been critical of me but, to be fair, he's very encouraging and wants me to perform at my best.* ◆**fairly** ADV ...*solving their problems quickly and fairly.* ◆**fairness** N-U *...concern about the fairness of the election campaign.* [2] ADJ BEFORE N A **fair** amount, degree, size, or distance is quite large. *I spent a fair bit of time finding directions.* [3] ADJ **Fair** hair or skin is light or pale in colour. [4] ADJ When the weather is **fair**, it is not cloudy or rainy; FORMAL. [5] N-C A **fair** is an event held in a field at which people pay to ride on machines for amusement or try to win prizes in games; BRITISH. [6] N-C A **fair** is an event at which people display or sell goods. ...*an antiques fair.* [7] See also **fairly**.

[PHRASES] ● You use **fair enough** when you want to say that a statement, decision, or action seems reasonable to a certain extent, but that perhaps someone has gone beyond what is reasonable. *If you don't like it, fair enough, but that's hardly a justification to attack the whole thing.* ● You say **fair enough** to acknowledge what someone has just said and to indicate that you think it is reasonable. *'The message was addressed to me and I don't see why I should write it to you.'*—*'Fair enough.'*

fairground /'feəɡraʊnd/ **fairgrounds.** N-C A **fairground** is a part of a park or field where people pay to ride on various machines for amusement or try to win prizes in games.

fairly /'feəli/. ADV **Fairly** means to quite a large degree. *We did fairly well... Were you always fairly bright at school?* ● See note at **rather**. See also **fair**.

fairy /'feəri/ **fairies.** N-C A **fairy** is an imaginary creature with magical powers.

'fairy tale, fairy tales. N-C A **fairy tale** is a story for children involving magical events and imaginary creatures.

faith /feɪθ/ **faiths.** [1] N-U If you have **faith** in someone or something, you feel confident about their ability or goodness. *She had placed a great deal of faith in Mr Penleigh... People have lost faith in the British Parliament.* [2] N-C A **faith** is a particular religion, such as Christianity or Buddhism. *The College welcomes students of all races, faiths, and nationalities.* [3] N-U **Faith** is strong religious belief. *I don't think his faith should be ridiculed.* [4] PHRASE If you do something **in good faith**, you sincerely believe that it is the right thing to do in the circumstances.

faithful /'feɪθfʊl/. [1] ADJ & N-PL If you are **faithful** to a person, organization, or idea, you remain firm in your support for them. People like this can be referred to as **the faithful**. *The government remained faithful to its peace initiative. ...gatherings of the Party faithful.* ◆**faithfully** ADV *She had served the police force faithfully for so many years.* [2] ADJ Someone who is **faithful** to their husband, wife, or lover does not have a sexual relationship with anyone else. *I'm very faithful when I love someone.* [3] ADJ A **faithful** account, version, or copy of something represents or reproduces the original accurately. *Colin Welland's screenplay is faithful to the novel.* ◆**faithfully** ADV *I translate from one meaning to another as faithfully as I can.*

faithfully /'feɪθfʊli/. CONVENTION In British English, when you start a formal or business letter with 'Dear Sir' or 'Dear Madam', you write **Yours faithfully** before your signature at the end. The usual American expression is **Sincerely yours.**

fake /feɪk/ **fakes, faking, faked.** [1] ADJ & N-C **Fake** things or **fakes** have been made to look valuable or genuine, although they are not. *The bank manager is said to have issued fake certificates... It is filled with famous works of art, and every one of them is a fake.* [2] VERB If someone **fakes** something, they try to make it look genuine, although it is not. *He faked his own death... I leant against the glass partition and faked a yawn.*

fall /fɔːl/ **falls, falling, fell, fallen.** [1] VERB If someone or something **falls**, they move quickly downwards. *Her father fell into the sea... He held the bag so that everything fell out... Bombs fell in the town.* [2] VERB & N-C If a person or structure **falls**, **falls down**, or **falls over**, they move from an upright position, so that they are lying on the ground. You can also say that a person has a **fall**. *The woman gripped the shoulders of her man to stop herself from falling... We watched buildings fall on top of people... I hit him so hard he fell down... Roads have been blocked by fallen trees.* [3] VERB & N-C When rain or snow **falls**, or when there is a **fall**

of it, it comes down from the sky. [4] VERB & N-C
If something **falls**, or if there is a **fall** in it, decreases in amount, value, or strength. *Her
weight fell to under seven stones... Oil product
prices fell 0.2 per cent. ...a sharp fall in the
value of the pound.* [5] VERB & N-SING If a powerful or successful person **falls**, they suddenly
lose their power or position. You can also talk
about that person's **fall**. *Mrs Thatcher fell from
power. ...the fall of the military dictator.*
[6] VERB You can use **fall** to show that someone
or something passes into another state. For example, if someone **falls** ill, they become ill.
These women fall victim to exploitation.
[7] VERB If you say that something or someone
falls into a particular category, you mean that
they belong in that category. *Both women fall
into the highest-risk group.* [8] VERB If silence or
a feeling of sadness or tiredness **falls** on a
group of people, they become silent, sad, or
tired; WRITTEN. *Silence fell on the passengers as
the police checked identity cards.* [9] VERB When
light or shadow **falls** on something, it covers it.
*...the shadow that suddenly fell across the door-
way.* [10] VERB When night or darkness **falls**,
night begins and it becomes dark. [11] N-PL You
can refer to a waterfall as the **falls**. *...Niagara
Falls.* [12] N-VAR In American English, **fall** is the
season between summer and winter. The Brit-
ish word is **autumn**. *The Supreme Court will not hear the case until next
fall.* [13] to **fall flat**: see **flat**.

▶ **fall apart.** [1] PHR-VERB If something **falls
apart**, it breaks into pieces because it is old or
badly made. *Bit by bit the building fell apart.*
[2] PHR-VERB If an organization or system **falls
apart**, it becomes disorganized and inefficient.
*Europe's monetary system is falling apart... I've
tried everything to stop our marriage falling
apart.*

▶ **fall back on.** PHR-VERB If you **fall back on**
something, you do it or use it after other things
have failed. *Unable to defeat him by logical discussion, she fell back on her old habit of criticizing his speech.*

▶ **fall behind.** PHR-VERB If you **fall behind**, you
do not make progress or move forward as fast
as other people. *He missed school and fell behind... Boris is falling behind all the top players.*

▶ **fall for.** [1] PHR-VERB If you **fall for** someone,
you are strongly attracted to them and start
loving them. *I just fell for him right away.*
[2] PHR-VERB If you **fall for** a lie or trick, you believe it or are deceived by it; INFORMAL. *It was
just a line to get you out here, and you fell for it!*

▶ **fall off.** PHR-VERB If something **falls off**, it separates from the thing to which it was attached.
*When your exhaust falls off, you have to replace
it.*

▶ **fall out.** [1] PHR-VERB If a person's hair or a
tooth **falls out**, it becomes loose and separates
from their body. [2] PHR-VERB If you **fall out**
with someone, you have an argument with
them and stop being friendly. *Mum and I used
to fall out a lot.* ● See also **fallout**.

▶ **fall through.** PHR-VERB If an arrangement **falls
through**, it fails to happen. *My house sale is
just on the verge of falling through.*

▶ **fall to.** PHR-VERB If a responsibility or duty **falls
to** someone, it becomes their responsibility or
duty. *It fell to me to get rid of them.*

fallacy /'fæləsi/ **fallacies.** N-C A **fallacy** is an
idea which many people believe to be true, but
which is false. *It is a fallacy that mass tourism
has spoiled Mallorca.*

fallen /'fɔːlən/. **Fallen** is the past participle of
fall.

fallout /'fɔːlaʊt/. N-U **Fallout** is the radiation
that affects an area after a nuclear explosion.

false /fɔːls/. [1] ADJ If something is **false**, it is incorrect, untrue, or mistaken. *The President was
being given false information... He had deliberately given the hospital a false name.* ♦ **falsely**
ADV *...a man who is falsely accused of a crime.*
[2] ADJ You use **false** to describe objects which
are artificial but which are intended to look
like the real thing or to be used instead of the
real thing. *...the false bottom of her suitcase.
...a set of false teeth.* [3] ADJ If you describe a
person or their behaviour as **false**, you are
criticizing them for not being sincere or for
hiding their real feelings. *She bowed her head
and smiled in false modesty.* ♦ **falsely** ADV *He
was falsely jovial.*

false a'larm, false alarms. N-C When you
think something dangerous is about to happen, but then discover that you were mistaken,
you can say that it was a **false alarm**. *...a
bomb threat that turned out to be a false
alarm.*

false 'start, false starts. N-C A **false start** is
an attempt to start something, such as a
speech, project, or plan, which fails because
you were not properly prepared or ready to begin.

falsify /'fɔːlsɪfaɪ/ **falsifies, falsifying, falsified.** VERB If someone **falsifies** a written record, they change it in a misleading way or add
untrue details to it in order to deceive people.
Wise allegedly falsified bank records.

falter /'fɔːltə/ **falters, faltering, faltered.**
[1] VERB If something **falters**, it weakens and
seems likely to collapse or to stop. *The economy is faltering. ...the faltering peace process.*
[2] VERB If you **falter**, you hesitate and become
unsure or unsteady. *Her voice faltered and she
had to stop a moment to control it.*

fame /feɪm/. N-U If you achieve **fame**, you become very well-known. *The film earned him
international fame.*

famed /feɪmd/. ADJ If you are **famed** for something, you are very well-known because of it.
The city is famed for its outdoor restaurants.

familiar /fə'mɪliə/. [1] ADJ If someone or something is **familiar** to you, you recognize them or
know them well. *They are already familiar
faces on our TV screens.* ♦ **familiarity**
/fəmɪliˈærɪti/ N-U *...the uncanny familiarity of
her face.* [2] ADJ AFTER LINK-V If you are **familiar
with** something, you know it or understand it
well. *He was not very familiar with the area.*
♦ **familiarity** N-U *The enemy would always have
the advantage of familiarity with the rugged
terrain.* [3] ADJ If you behave in a **familiar** way
towards someone, you treat them very informally, so that you may offend them if you are
not close friends. *John's 'crime' was being too*

familiar with the manager. ♦**familiarly** ADV
'Gerald, isn't it?' I began familiarly.
♦**familiarity** N-U ...the easy familiarity with
which her host greeted the head waiter.

family /ˈfæmɪli/ **families. Family** can take the
singular or plural form of the verb. **1** N-C A
family is a group of people who are related to
each other, especially parents and their children. ...a family of five... His family are completely behind him... They decided to start a
family. **2** N-C When people talk about their
family, they sometimes mean their ancestors.
Her family came to Los Angeles at the turn of
the century.

family 'planning. N-U **Family planning** is the
practice of using contraception to control the
number of children you have.

famine /ˈfæmɪn/ **famines.** N-VAR A **famine** is a
serious shortage of food in a country, which
may cause many deaths.

famous /ˈfeɪməs/. ADJ Someone or something
that is **famous** is very well known. ...England's
most famous landscape artist... New Orleans is
famous for its cuisine.

> A **famous** person or thing is known to
> more people than a **well-known** one. A
> **notorious** person or thing is famous be-
> cause they are connected with some-
> thing bad or undesirable. **Infamous** is
> not the opposite of famous. It has a simi-
> lar meaning to notorious, but is a strong-
> er word. Someone or something that is
> **notable** is important or remarkable.

famously /ˈfeɪməsli/. ADV You use **famously** to
refer to a fact that is well known, usually because it is remarkable. Authors are famously ignorant about the realities of publishing.

fan /fæn/ **fans, fanning, fanned.** **1** N-C If you
are a **fan** of someone or something, you admire them and are very interested in them. If
you're a Billy Crystal fan, you'll love this movie.
2 N-C A **fan** is a device that keeps a room or
machine cool. **3** VERB If you **fan** yourself, you
wave a fan or other flat object in order to make
yourself cooler. **4** VERB If you **fan** a fire, you
wave something flat next to it in order to make
it burn more strongly.

▶ **fan out.** PHR-VERB If a group of people or
things **fan out**, they move forwards away from
a particular point in different directions. The
main body of British, American, and French
troops had fanned out to the west.

fanatic /fəˈnætɪk/ **fanatics.** **1** N-C If you describe someone as a **fanatic**, you disapprove of
them because you consider their behaviour or
opinions to be very extreme. I am not a religious fanatic but I am a Christian. ♦**fanatical**
ADJ ...a fanatical group of fundamentalists.
2 N-C If you say that someone is a **fanatic**, you
mean that they are very enthusiastic about a
particular activity, sport, or way of life; INFOR-
MAL. Both Rod and Phil are football fanatics.

fanciful /ˈfænsɪfʊl/. ADJ If you describe an idea
as **fanciful**, you disapprove of it because you
think it comes from someone's imagination,
and is therefore unrealistic or unlikely to be
true. ...fanciful ideas about Martian life.

fancy 1 wanting, liking, or thinking

fancy /ˈfænsi/ **fancies, fancying, fancied.**
1 VERB If you **fancy** something, you want to
have it or do it; BRITISH, INFORMAL. Do you fancy
going to see a movie sometime?... I just fancied
a drink. **2** VERB If you **fancy** someone, you feel
attracted to them, especially in a sexual way;
INFORMAL. I didn't really fancy him anyway.
3 N-VAR A **fancy** is an idea that is unlikely, untrue, or imaginary; LITERARY. ...a childhood fancy. **4** EXCLAM You say 'fancy' or 'fancy that'
when you want to express surprise or disapproval. Fancy coming to a funeral in brown
boots!.

PHRASE If something **takes your fancy** when
you see or hear it, you like it; INFORMAL. ...copy-
ing any fashion which takes her fancy.

fancy 2 elaborate or expensive

fancy /ˈfænsi/ **fancier, fanciest.** **1** ADJ If you
describe something as **fancy**, you mean that it
is special, unusual, or elaborate. ...fancy jewellery. **2** ADJ If you describe something as **fancy**,
you mean that it is very expensive or of very
high quality, and you often dislike it because
of this. They sent me to a fancy private school.

fanfare /ˈfænfeə/ **fanfares.** N-C A **fanfare** is a
short loud tune played on trumpets to an-
nounce a special event.

fang /fæŋ/ **fangs.** N-C **Fangs** are the two long,
sharp, upper teeth that some animals have.

fantasize (BR also **fantasise**) /ˈfæntəsaɪz/ **fan-
tasizes, fantasizing, fantasized.** VERB If
you **fantasize** about something that you would
like to happen, you think imaginatively about
it. She fantasised that he was still alive.

fantastic /fænˈtæstɪk/. **1** ADJ If you say that
something is **fantastic**, you are emphasizing
that you think it is very good; INFORMAL. I have
a fantastic social life. **2** ADJ BEFORE N You use
fantastic to emphasize the size, amount, or
degree of something; INFORMAL. ...fantastic
amounts of money. ♦**fantastically** ADV ...a fantastically expensive restaurant. **3** ADJ You describe something as **fantastic** when it seems
strange and wonderful or unlikely. Unlikely
and fantastic legends grew up around a great
many figures.

fantasy /ˈfæntəzi/ **fantasies.** **1** N-C A **fantasy**
is a situation or event that you think about and
that you want to happen, especially one that is
unlikely to happen. ...fantasies of romance and
true love. **2** N-VAR You can refer to a story or
situation that someone creates from their imagination and that is not based on reality as
fantasy. ...the words from a Disney fantasy.

far /fɑː/ **farther** or (**further**) **farthest** or (**furthest**) Far has two comparatives, **farther** and
further, and two superlatives, **farthest** and
furthest. **Farther** and **farthest** are used mainly
in sense 1, and are dealt with here. **Further**
and **furthest** are dealt with in separate entries.
1 ADV If one place, thing, or person is **far** away
from another, there is a great distance between them. ...a nice little Italian restaurant
not far from here... Both of my sisters moved
even farther away from home... He had wandered to the far end of the room. **2** ADV You use
far in questions and statements about distances. How far is it to Malcy?... How far can

you throw?... She followed the tracks as far as the road.

Far is used in negative sentences and questions about distance, but not usually in affirmative sentences. If you want to state the distance of a particular place from where you are, you can say that it is that distance **away**. *...Durban, which is over 300 kilometres away.* If a place is very distant, you can say that it is a **long way away**, or that it is a **long way from** another place.

---

3 ADJ BEFORE N You use **far** to refer to the part of an area or object that is the greatest distance from the centre in a particular direction. *...at the far left of the blackboard.* **4** ADV A time or event that is **far** away in the future or the past is a long time from the present. *...conflicts whose roots lie far back in time... I can't see any farther than the next six months... The first day of term seemed so far away.* **5** ADV You use **far** to indicate the extent to which something happens. *How far did the film tell the truth about Barnes Wallis?* **6** ADV You can use **far** when talking about the progress that someone or something makes. *Discussions never progressed very far.* **7** ADV You can use **far** when talking about the degree to which someone's behaviour or actions are extreme. *This time he's gone too far.* **8** ADV You can use **far** to mean 'very much' when you are comparing two things and emphasizing the difference between them. *Women who eat plenty of fresh vegetables are far less likely to suffer anxiety... These trials are simply taking far too long.*

PHRASES • You can use **by far** or **far and away** in comparisons to emphasize that something is better or greater than anything else. *By far the most important issue for them is unemployment... Rangers are far and away the best team.* • If you say that something is **far from** a particular thing or **far from** being the case, you are emphasizing that it is not that particular thing or not at all the case. *Much of what they recorded was far from the truth.* • If an answer or idea is **not far wrong**, **not far out**, or **not far off**, it is almost correct. *I hadn't been far wrong in my estimate.* • **So far** means up until the present point in time or in a situation. *So far, they have met with no success.* • If people come from **far and wide**, they come from a large number of places, some of them far away. If things spread **far and wide**, they spread over a very large area or distance. • **as far as** I am **concerned**: see concern. • **a far cry from**: see cry.

faraway /ˌfɑːrəˈweɪ/ **1** ADJ BEFORE N **Faraway** means a long distance from you or from a particular place. *...photographs of a faraway country.* **2** ADJ BEFORE N If you describe someone or their thoughts as **faraway**, you mean that they are thinking about something that is very different from the situation around them. *She smiled with a faraway look in her eyes.*

farce /fɑːs/ **farces. 1** N-C A **farce** is a humorous play in which the characters become involved in unlikely and complicated situations.

2 N-C If you describe a situation or event as a **farce**, you mean that it is so disorganized or ridiculous that you cannot take it seriously. *The increasing traffic on our roads is going to make cycling a complete farce.* ♦ **farcical** ADJ *The whole scheme is farcical.*

fare /feə/ **fares, faring, fared. 1** N-C The **fare** is the money that you pay for a journey by bus, taxi, train, boat, or aeroplane. *He could barely afford the railway fare.* **2** VERB If you say that someone or something **fares** well or badly, you are referring to the degree of success they achieve in a particular situation or activity. *It is unlikely that the marine industry will fare any better in September.*

,Far 'East. N-PROPER The **Far East** consists of all the countries of Eastern Asia, including China and Japan.

farewell /ˌfeəˈwel/ **farewells.** CONVENTION & N-C **Farewell** means goodbye; LITERARY. *'Farewell', my friend... They said their farewells.*

,far-'fetched. ADJ If you describe a story or idea as **far-fetched**, you are criticizing it because you think it is unlikely to be true or practical. *The storyline was too far-fetched.*

farm /fɑːm/ **farms, farming, farmed. 1** N-C A **farm** is an area of land consisting of fields and buildings, where crops are grown or animals are raised. *Both boys liked to work on the farm.* **2** VERB If you **farm** an area of land, you grow crops or raise animals on it. *He has lived and farmed in the area for 46 years.*

farmer /ˈfɑːmə/ **farmers.** N-C A **farmer** is a person who owns or manages a farm.

farmhouse /ˈfɑːmhaʊs/ **farmhouses.** N-C A **farmhouse** is the main house on a farm, usually where the farmer lives.

farmland /ˈfɑːmlænd/ **farmlands.** N-VAR **Farmland** is land which is farmed or which is suitable for farming.

farmyard /ˈfɑːmjɑːd/ **farmyards.** N-C On a farm, the **farmyard** is an area near the farmhouse which is enclosed by walls or buildings.

,far 'off, further off, furthest off. 1 ADJ A **far off** time is a long time away in the future or past. *The day this would happen was not far off.* **2** ADJ & ADV A **far off** place is a long distance away. *...stars in far-off galaxies... The children who lived far off didn't go home.*

,far-'reaching. ADJ **Far-reaching** actions, events, or changes have a very great influence and affect a great number of things. *...technology with far-reaching effects on human society.*

farther /ˈfɑːðə/. **Farther** is a comparative of **far**.

farthest /ˈfɑːðɪst/. **Farthest** is a superlative of **far**.

fascinate /ˈfæsɪneɪt/ **fascinates, fascinating, fascinated.** VERB If something or someone **fascinates** you, you find them extremely interesting. *Politics fascinated Franklin's father.*

fascinated /ˈfæsɪneɪtɪd/. ADJ If you are **fascinated**, you are extremely interested by something. *I sat on the stairs and watched, fascinated.*

fascinating /ˈfæsɪneɪtɪŋ/. ADJ If you find something **fascinating**, you find it extremely interesting. *Madagascar is the most fascinating place I have ever been to.*

fascination /ˌfæsɪˈneɪʃən/. N-U **Fascination** is the state of being extremely interested in something. *I've had a lifelong fascination with the sea.*

fascist /ˈfæʃɪst/ **fascists.** [1] N-C & ADJ A **fascist** or a person with **fascist** views has a set of right-wing political beliefs that includes strong control by the state and a powerful role for the armed forces. ♦**fascism** N-U *...the menace of fascism.* [2] N-C If you refer to someone as a **fascist**, you disapprove of the fact that they have extreme views on something, and do not tolerate alternative views.

fashion /ˈfæʃən/ **fashions, fashioning, fashioned.** [1] N-U **Fashion** is the area of activity that involves styles of clothing and appearance. [2] N-C & PHRASE A **fashion** is a style of clothing or a way of behaving that is popular at a particular time. If something is **in fashion**, it is a fashion at a particular time, and if it is **out of fashion** it is not. [3] N-SING If you do something in a particular **fashion**, you do it in that way; FORMAL. *There is another drug called DHE that works in a similar fashion.* [4] VERB If you **fashion** something, you make it; FORMAL. [5] See also **old-fashioned**.

fashionable /ˈfæʃənəbəl/. ADJ Something that is **fashionable** is popular or approved of at a particular time. *It became fashionable to eat certain kinds of fish.* ♦**fashionably** ADV *...women who are perfectly made up and fashionably dressed.*

fast /fɑːst, fæst/ **faster, fastest; fasts, fasting, fasted.** [1] ADJ & ADV **Fast** means moving, acting, or happening with great speed. *...fast cars. ...a faster pace of political reform... They work terrifically fast.* [2] ADV You use **fast** in questions or statements about speed. *How fast were you driving?... The only question is how fast the process will be.* [3] ADV & ADJ **Fast** means happening without any delay. *We'd appreciate your leaving as fast as possible. ...an astonishingly fast action on the part of the Congress.* [4] ADJ AFTER V-LINK If a watch or clock is **fast**, it is showing a time that is later than the real time. [5] ADV If something is held or fixed **fast**, it is held or fixed very firmly. *The tanker is stuck fast on the rocks.* [6] ADV If you hold **fast** to a principle or idea, or if you stand **fast**, you do not change your mind about it. [7] VERB & N-C If you **fast**, or if you go on a **fast**, you eat no food for a period of time, usually for religious reasons. *They fasted for three days... The fast is broken at sunset.* • **fast asleep**: see **asleep**.

fasten /ˈfɑːsən, ˈfæs-/ **fastens, fastening, fastened.** [1] VERB When you **fasten** something, or when it **fastens**, you do it up or close it by means of buttons or a strap, buckle, or other device. *Fasten your seat belt. ...the dress, which fastens with a long back zip.* [2] VERB If you **fasten** one thing to another, you attach the first thing to the second.

fastening /ˈfɑːsənɪŋ, ˈfæs-/ **fastenings.** N-C A **fastening** is something such as a clasp, cord, or latch that you use to fasten something.

fast food. N-U **Fast food** is hot food such as hamburgers which is served quickly after you order it.

fastidious /fæˈstɪdiəs/. ADJ If you say that someone is **fastidious**, you mean that they pay great attention to detail because they like everything to be accurate and very orderly. *He was fastidious about his appearance.* ♦**fastidiously** ADV *He fastidiously copied every word of his notes.*

fat /fæt/ **fatter, fattest; fats.** [1] ADJ A **fat** person has a lot of flesh on their body and weighs too much. *I could eat what I liked without getting fat.* ♦**fatness** N-U *...a child's tendency towards fatness.*

> If you describe someone as **fat**, you are speaking in a very direct way, and this may be considered rude. If you want to say more politely that someone is rather fat, it is better to describe them as **plump**, or more informally, as **chubby**, but in general you should avoid using any of these words in the presence of the person you are describing. The same is true of **overweight** and **obese**, which are used to describe someone who may have health problems because of their size or weight. **Obese** is a medical term used to describe someone who is extremely fat or overweight.

[2] N-U **Fat** is the extra flesh that animals and humans have under their skin, which is used to store energy and to help keep them warm. [3] N-VAR **Fat** is a substance contained in many foods which your body uses to produce energy. *...low-fat yogurts.* [4] N-VAR **Fat** is a substance used in cooking which is obtained from vegetables or the flesh of animals. *Avoid dishes cooked in fat.* [5] ADJ A **fat** object, especially a book, is very thick or wide. *He took out his fat wallet.*

fatal /ˈfeɪtəl/. [1] ADJ A **fatal** action has undesirable results. *He made the fatal mistake of lending her some money.* ♦**fatally** ADV *Failure now could fatally damage his chances.* [2] ADJ A **fatal** accident or illness causes someone's death. *...the fatal stabbing of a police sergeant.* ♦**fatally** ADV *He was shot and fatally injured.*

fatality /fəˈtælɪti/ **fatalities.** N-C A **fatality** is a person's death, caused by an accident or violence; FORMAL.

fate /feɪt/ **fates.** [1] N-U **Fate** is a power that some people believe controls everything that happens. *Could these facts be attributed to fate?* [2] N-C Someone's **fate** is what happens to them. *His fate is now in the hands of his bankers.*

fateful /ˈfeɪtfʊl/. ADJ If you describe an action or event as **fateful**, you mean that it had important, and often bad, effects on later events. *It was a fateful decision, one which was to break the Government.*

father /ˈfɑːðə/ **fathers, fathering, fathered.** [1] N-C Your **father** is your male parent. [2] VERB When a man **fathers** a child, he makes a woman pregnant and their child is born. [3] N-C The **father of** something is the man who invented or started it. *...Max Dupain, regarded as the father of modern photography.* [4] N-VOC & N-TITLE

In some Christian churches, priests are addressed or referred to as **Father**.

fatherhood /ˈfɑːðəhʊd/. N-U **Fatherhood** is the state of being a father. ...*the joys of fatherhood*.

father-in-law, fathers-in-law. N-C Your **father-in-law** is the father of your husband or wife.

fathom /ˈfæðəm/ **fathoms, fathoming, fathomed.** [1] N-C A **fathom** is a unit of length used for describing the depth of the sea. One fathom is equal to 6 feet or approximately 1.8 metres. [2] VERB & PHR-VERB If you cannot **fathom** something, or you cannot **fathom** it **out**, you cannot understand it, although you think carefully about it. *I really couldn't fathom what Steiner was talking about.*

fatigue /fəˈtiːg/. N-U **Fatigue** is a feeling of extreme physical or mental tiredness.

fatigues /fəˈtiːgz/. N-PL **Fatigues** are clothes that soldiers wear when they are on the battlefield or when they are doing routine jobs.

fattening /ˈfætənɪŋ/. ADJ **Fattening** food is thought to make people fat.

fatty /ˈfæti/. [1] ADJ **Fatty** food contains a lot of fat. ...*fatty meat such as sausages*. [2] ADJ BEFORE N **Fatty** acids or **fatty** tissue contain or consist of fat.

fault /fɔːlt/ **faults, faulting, faulted.** [1] N-SING & PHRASE If a bad situation is your **fault**, or if you are **at fault**, you caused it or are responsible for it. *It was all his fault... Individuals had suffered hardship through no fault of their own... He could never accept that he had been at fault.* [2] N-C A **fault** is a weakness or imperfection in a person or a piece of equipment. *His biggest fault was his desire to do too much... There is a fault in the computer programme.* [3] VERB If you say that you cannot **fault** someone, you approve of the hard work they put into doing something or the efficient way that they do it. *It is hard to fault the way he runs his own operation.* [4] N-C A **fault** is a large crack in the earth's surface. ...*the San Andreas Fault.* [5] PHRASE If you **find fault** with something, you complain about it.

faultless /ˈfɔːltləs/. ADJ Something that is **faultless** contains no mistakes. *Hans's English was faultless.*

faulty /ˈfɔːlti/. ADJ A **faulty** machine or piece of equipment is not working properly. *His car has faulty brakes.*

fauna /ˈfɔːnə/. N-PL Animals, especially those in a particular area, can be referred to as **fauna**; TECHNICAL. ...*the Lake's remarkable flora and fauna.*

favour (AM **favor**) /ˈfeɪvə/ **favours, favouring, favoured.** [1] N-U If you regard something or someone with **favour**, you like or support them. *The changes found favour with most competitors.* [2] N-C If you ask someone to do a **favour** for you, you ask them to do something which will help you. *Can you do me a favor?* [3] VERB If you **favour** something, you prefer it to the other choices available. *They favour a transition to democracy.* [4] VERB If you **favour** someone, you treat them better than you treat other people. *My brother felt that my mum favoured me.*

PHRASES ● If you are **in favour of** something,

you think that it is a good thing. *I wouldn't be in favour of income tax cuts.* ● If one thing is rejected **in favour of** another, the second thing is done or chosen instead of the first. ...*when ordinary machine tools are scrapped in favour of new computerized ones.* ● If someone makes a judgement **in** your **favour**, they say that you are right. *A federal judge ruled in their favour.* ● If something is **in** your **favour**, it helps you or gives you an advantage. ...*the allegation that the media were biased in favour of Mr Clinton.* ● If someone or something is **in favour**, people like or support them. If they are **out of favour**, people no longer like or support them.

favourable (AM **favorable**) /ˈfeɪvərəbl/. [1] ADJ If you are **favourable** to something, you agree with it or approve of it. *We've already had a lot of favourable comment from customers.* ◆**favourably** ADV *He listened intently, and responded favourably to both my suggestions.* [2] ADJ If something makes a **favourable** impression on you, or if it is **favourable to** you, you like it and approve of it. *He was desperate to make a favourable impression on General MacArthur... These terms were favourable to India.* [3] ADJ If you make a **favourable** comparison between two things, you say that the first is better than or as good as the second. ◆**favourably** ADV *These figures compare favourably with more established methods.* [4] ADJ **Favourable** conditions make something more likely to succeed. ...*attempts to influence the government to choose policies favourable to industry.* ...*favourable weather conditions.* ◆**favourably** ADV *Japan is thus favourably placed to maintain its economic lead.*

favourite (AM **favorite**) /ˈfeɪvərɪt/ **favourites.** [1] N-C & ADJ BEFORE N Your **favourite**, or your **favourite** thing or person, is the one that you like most. *I love all sports but soccer is my favourite... Her favourite writer is Hans Christian Andersen.* [2] N-C The **favourite** in a race or contest is the person or animal expected to win. *The Belgian Cup has been won by the favourites F.C. Liege.*

fawn /fɔːn/ **fawns, fawning, fawned.** [1] ADJ & N-U Something that is **fawn** is pale yellowish-brown. [2] N-C A **fawn** is a very young deer. [3] VERB If you say that someone **fawns** over a powerful or rich person, you disapprove of them because they flatter that person in order to get something for themselves. *People fawn over you when you're famous.* ...*200 pages of fawning praise.*

fax /fæks/ **faxes, faxing, faxed.** [1] N-C A **fax** or a **fax machine** is a piece of equipment used to send and receive documents electronically along a telephone line. [2] VERB & N-C If you **fax** a document, you send a document from one fax machine to another. *Did you fax him a reply?... Pop it in the post, or get your secretary to fax it.* [3] N-C You can refer to a copy of a document that is transmitted by a fax machine as a **fax**. *I sent him a fax... Did she get my fax yesterday?*

fear /fɪə/ **fears, fearing, feared.** [1] N-VAR **Fear** is the unpleasant feeling of worry that you get when you think that you are in danger or that something horrible is going to happen. *I stood there crying and shaking with fear.* ...*his fears* *about the forthcoming operation.* [2] PHRASE If you do not do something **for fear of** another thing happening, you do not do it because you do not wish that other thing to happen. *He did not dare move his feet for fear of disturbing anything.* [3] VERB If you **fear** something unpleasant, you are worried that it might happen, or might have happened. *She had feared she was going down with pneumonia... More than two million refugees have fled the area, fearing attack.* [4] VERB & N-VAR If you **fear for** someone or something, or if you have **fears for** them, you are worried that they might be in danger. *Carla fears for her son... There are fears for the safety of a 15-year-old girl.*

fearful /ˈfɪəfʊl/. [1] ADJ If you are **fearful** of something, you are afraid of it. *Bankers were fearful of a world banking crisis.* ♦**fearfully** ADV *'What are you going to do to me?' Alex asked fearfully.* [2] ADJ BEFORE N You use **fearful** to emphasize how serious or bad something is. *The region is in a fearful recession.* ♦**fearfully** ADV *It's fearfully expensive!*

fearless /ˈfɪələs/. ADJ If you describe someone as **fearless**, you admire their courage. *They were young and strong and fearless.* ♦**fearlessly** ADV *...a fearlessly outspoken politician.*

fearsome /ˈfɪəsəm/. ADJ If you describe something as **fearsome**, you are emphasizing the fact that it is terrible or frightening. *...a fearsome array of weapons.*

feasible /ˈfiːzəbəl/. ADJ If something is **feasible**, it can be done, made, or achieved. *Are these experiments technically feasible?* ♦**feasibility** N-U *Two companies are studying the feasibility of building a mill in the region.*

feast /fiːst/ **feasts, feasting, feasted.** [1] N-C A **feast** is a large and special meal. *...wedding feasts.* [2] VERB If you **feast**, you take part in a feast; LITERARY. ♦**feasting** N-U *The marriage is celebrated with much dancing and feasting.* [3] VERB If you **feast on** a particular food, you eat a large amount of it with great enjoyment. *We feasted on nuts and candies and cake.* [4] N-SING You can refer to a large number of good, interesting, or enjoyable things as a **feast** of them. *...a feast of special effects.*

feat /fiːt/ **feats.** N-C A **feat** is an impressive and difficult act or achievement. *A racing car is an extraordinary feat of engineering.*

feather /ˈfeðə/ **feathers.** N-C A bird's **feathers** are the light soft things covering its body.

feathered /ˈfeðəd/. ADJ **Feathered** is used to describe something covered in feathers or made from feathers. *...extravagant feathered hats.*

feature /ˈfiːtʃə/ **features, featuring, featured.** [1] N-C A particular **feature** of something is an interesting or important part or characteristic of it. *The spacious gardens are a special feature of this property... The making of pilgrimages is an essential feature of Hindu life.* [2] N-PL Your **features** are your eyes, nose, mouth, and other parts of your face. [3] VERB When a film or exhibition **features** someone or something, they are an important part of it. *The series featured top stars from snooker, cricket and rugby.* [4] VERB If someone or some-

thing **features in** something such as an exhibition or magazine, they are an important part of it. *Most projects featured in the book are small scale.* [5] N-C A **feature** is a special article in a newspaper or magazine, or a special programme on radio or television. *...our special feature on breast cancer.* [6] N-C A **feature** or a **feature film** is a full-length film about a fictional subject.

February /ˈfebjʊəri, AM -jʊəri/. N-U **February** is the second month of the year.

feces /ˈfiːsiːz/. See **faeces.**

fed /fed/. **Fed** is the past tense and past participle of **feed.** See also **fed up.**

federal /ˈfedərəl/. [1] ADJ BEFORE N In a **federal** country or system, a group of states is controlled by a central government. [2] ADJ BEFORE N **Federal** means belonging or relating to the national government of a federal country rather than to one of the states within it. *...a federal judge.* ♦**federally** ADV *...federally subsidized apartments.*

federation /ˌfedəˈreɪʃən/ **federations.** N-C A **federation** is a group of organizations or states that have joined together for a common purpose. *...the British Athletic Federation.*

fed 'up. ADJ AFTER LINK-V Someone who is **fed up** is bored or annoyed; INFORMAL. *I am fed up with reading how women should dress to please men.*

fee /fiː/ **fees.** [1] N-C A **fee** is a sum of money that you pay to be allowed to do something. *...his television licence fee.* [2] N-C A **fee** is the money that someone is paid for a particular job or service. *...solicitors' fees.*

feeble /ˈfiːbəl/ **feebler, feeblest.** [1] ADJ If you describe someone or something as **feeble**, you mean that they are physically weak. *He was old and feeble.* ♦**feebly** ADV *His left hand moved feebly at his side.* [2] ADJ If you say that someone or something is **feeble**, you mean that they are not very good, convincing, or effective. *This is a particularly feeble argument.* ♦**feebly** ADV *I said 'Sorry', very feebly, feeling rather embarrassed.*

feed /fiːd/ **feeds, feeding, fed.** [1] VERB If you **feed** a person or animal, you give them food. *She fed him a cookie... He spooned the ice cream into a cup and fed it to her.* ♦**feeding, feedings** N-VAR *...the feeding of dairy cows.* [2] VERB To **feed** a family or a community means to supply food for them. *Feeding a hungry family can be expensive.* [3] VERB When an animal **feeds**, it eats something. *...insects that feed on wood.* [4] VERB & N-C When a baby **feeds**, or when it has a **feed**, it drinks breast milk or milk from its bottle. [5] VERB If you **feed** something somewhere, you put it in there at a steady rate. *She was feeding documents into a paper shredder. ...blood vessels that feed blood to the brain.*

feedback /ˈfiːdbæk/. N-U When you get **feedback** on your work or progress, someone tells you how well or badly you are doing. *I was getting great feedback from my boss.*

feel /fiːl/ **feels, feeling, felt.** [1] LINK-VERB If you **feel** an emotion or a physical sensation, you experience it. *I am feeling very depressed... I felt a sharp pain in my shoulder.* [2] LINK-VERB If you talk about how an experience or event **feels**, you are describing the emotions and sensations connected with it. *It feels good to have finished a piece of work... It felt like I'd had two babies instead of one.* [3] N-SING & LINK-VERB The **feel** of an object, or the way it **feels**, is the physical quality that you notice when you touch it. *He remembered the feel of her skin... The metal felt smooth and cold.* [4] VERB If you **feel** an object, you touch it so that you can learn what it is like. *The doctor felt his head... Feel how soft the skin is.* [5] VERB If you **feel** something, you are aware that it is touching or happening to your body. *He felt her leg against his... I felt myself blush.* [6] VERB If you **feel** something, you become aware of it, even though you cannot see or hear it. *I could feel that a man was watching me.* [7] VERB If you **feel** that something is the case, you have a strong idea in your mind that it is the case. *I feel certain that it will all turn out well... She felt him to be responsible.* [8] VERB If you **feel** that you should do something, you think that you should do it. *You need not feel obliged to contribute.* [9] VERB If you talk about how you **feel** about something, you talk about your opinion, attitude, or reaction to it. *She feels guilty about spending less time lately with her two kids.* [10] VERB If you **feel like** doing or having something, you want to do or have it. *Neither of them felt like going back to sleep.* [11] N-SING The **feel** of something is the general impression that it gives you. *The room has a warm, cosy feel.* [12] See also **feeling**, **felt**.

▶ **feel for.** [1] PHR-VERB If you **feel for** something, you try to find it using your hands rather than your eyes. *I felt for my wallet.* [2] PHR-VERB If you **feel for** someone, you have sympathy for them.

feeling /ˈfiːlɪŋ/ **feelings.** [1] N-VAR A **feeling** is an emotion. *It gave me a feeling of satisfaction.* [2] PHRASE **Bad feeling** or **ill feeling** is resentment or anger which exists between people, for example after an argument. *There's been some bad feeling between the two families.* [3] N-SING If you have a **feeling** that something is the case, you think that it is probably the case. *I have a feeling that everything will come right for us.* [4] N-SING If you have a **feeling** of being in a particular situation, you feel that you are in that situation. *I had the terrible feeling of being left behind.* [5] N-PL Your **feelings** about something are the things that you think and feel about it, or your attitude towards it. *I had mixed feelings about meeting him.* [6] N-PL When you refer to someone's **feelings**, you are talking about the things that might embarrass or upset them. If you hurt someone's **feelings**, you say or do something that upsets them. [7] N-U **Feeling** for someone is affection or sympathy for them. *It's incredible that Peter can behave with such stupid lack of feeling.* [8] N-C A **feeling** is a physical sensation. *I also had a strange feeling in my neck.* [9] N-U **Feeling** in part of your body is the ability to experience the sense of touch in this part of your body. *After the accident he had no feeling in his legs.*

feet /fiːt/. **Feet** is the plural of **foot**.

feign /feɪn/ **feigns, feigning, feigned.** VERB If someone **feigns** a feeling or attitude, they pretend to have it; FORMAL. *I didn't want to go to school, and decided to feign illness.*

fell /fel/ **fells, felling, felled.** [1] **Fell** is the past tense of **fall**. [2] VERB If trees are **felled**, they are cut down.

fella (or **feller**) /ˈfelə/ **fellas.** N-C You can refer to a man as a **fella**; informal. *He's an intelligent man and a nice fella.*

fellow /ˈfeləʊ/ **fellows.** [1] ADJ BEFORE N You use **fellow** to describe people who are in the same situation as you, or people you feel you have something in common with. *He knew his fellow teachers in Cincinnati shared his frustrations.* [2] N-C A **fellow** is a man or boy; DATED, INFORMAL. *...the fellow who came to collect our drinks.* [3] N-C A **fellow** of a society or academic institution is a member of it.

fellowship /ˈfeləʊʃɪp/ **fellowships.** [1] N-C A **fellowship** is a group of people that join together for a common purpose. *...the Fellowship of World Christians.* [2] N-U **Fellowship** is a feeling of friendship that people have when they are talking or doing something together. *...a sense of community and fellowship.* [3] N-C A **fellowship** at a university is a post which involves research work.

felony /ˈfeləni/ **felonies.** N-C A **felony** is a very serious crime such as armed robbery; TECHNICAL.

felt /felt/. [1] **Felt** is the past tense and past participle of **feel**. [2] N-U **Felt** is a type of thick cloth made from wool or other fibres packed tightly together.

female /ˈfiːmeɪl/ **females.** [1] ADJ Someone who is **female** is a woman or a girl. *...a female singer.* [2] N-C Women and girls are sometimes referred to as **females** when they are being considered as a type. *Hay fever affects males more than females.* [3] ADJ BEFORE N **Female** is used to describe things that relate to or affect women rather than men. *...female infertility.* [4] N-C & ADJ You can refer to any creature that can lay eggs or produce babies from its body as a **female**, or as a **female** creature. *Each female will lay just one egg. ...the female blue whale.*

feminine /ˈfemɪnɪn/. ADJ **Feminine** means relating to women or considered typical of or suitable for them. *...traditional feminine roles.* ◆**femininity** /ˌfemɪˈnɪnɪti/ N-U *...the ideology of motherhood and femininity.*

feminism /ˈfemɪnɪzəm/. N-U **Feminism** is the belief that women should have the same rights and opportunities as men. ◆**feminist, feminists** N-C *...the feminist movement.*

fence /fens/ **fences, fencing, fenced.** [1] N-C A **fence** is a barrier made of wood or wire supported by posts. [2] VERB & PHR-VERB If you **fence** an area of land, or if you **fence** it **off**, or if you **fence** it **in**, you surround it with a fence. *We could fence off the cliff top... He plans to fence in about 100 acres of his ranch.* [3] PHRASE You say that someone **is sitting on the fence** to express your disapproval of them because they refuse to state a definite opinion or to say who they support in a conflict. *The Republicans criticised the president for sitting on the fence.*

fencing /ˈfensɪŋ/. **1** N-U **Fencing** is a sport in which two competitors fight using very thin swords. **2** N-U **Fencing** consists of materials that are used to make fences.

fend /fend/ **fends, fending, fended.** VERB If you have to **fend for** yourself, you have to look after yourself without relying on other people.
▶ **fend off.** PHR-VERB If you **fend off** someone or something, you defend yourself against them, using either words or physical strength. *Earlier, Marianne had fended off questions about her marriage... I fended him off with my elbow.*

ferment, ferments, fermenting, fermented.
1 N-U /ˈfɜːment/ **Ferment** is excitement and trouble caused by change or uncertainty. *The whole country has been in a state of political ferment.* **2** VERB /fəˈment/ If a food or drink **ferments**, or if it **is fermented**, a chemical change takes place in it so that alcohol is produced. ♦ **fermentation** N-U *...the fermentation that produces alcohol.*

fern /fɜːn/ **ferns.** N-C A **fern** is a plant with long stems, thin leaves, and no flowers.

ferocious /fəˈrəʊʃəs/. ADJ A **ferocious** animal, person, or action is fierce and violent. *...a pack of ferocious dogs.* ♦ **ferociously** ADV *She kicked out ferociously.*

ferocity /fəˈrɒsɪti/. N-U When something is done with **ferocity**, it is done in a fierce and violent way.

ferry /ˈferi/ **ferries, ferrying, ferried.** **1** N-C A **ferry** is a boat that carries passengers or vehicles across a river or a narrow stretch of sea. **2** VERB To **ferry** people or goods means to transport them, usually by means of regular journeys between the same two places. *A plane arrives to ferry guests to and from Bird Island Lodge.*

fertile /ˈfɜːtaɪl, AM -təl/. **1** ADJ Land or soil that is **fertile** is able to support a large number of strong healthy plants. ♦ **fertility** /fɜːˈtɪlɪti/ N-U *...the fertility of the soil.* **2** ADJ BEFORE N You describe a place or situation as **fertile** ground when you think that something is likely to succeed or develop there. *...a fertile breeding ground for this kind of violent racism.* **3** ADJ Someone who is **fertile** is able to reproduce and have babies. ♦ **fertility** N-U *Pregnancy is the only sure test for fertility.*

fertilize (BR also **fertilise**) /ˈfɜːtɪlaɪz/ **fertilizes, fertilizing, fertilized.** **1** VERB When an egg or plant **is fertilized**, the process of reproduction begins by sperm joining with the egg, or by pollen coming into contact with the reproductive part of a plant. ♦ **fertilization** N-U *...the average length of time from fertilization until birth.* **2** VERB To **fertilize** land means to spread manure or chemicals on it to make plants grow well.

fertilizer (BR also **fertiliser**) /ˈfɜːtɪlaɪzə/ **fertilizers.** N-VAR **Fertilizer** is a substance that you spread on the ground to make plants grow more successfully.

fervent /ˈfɜːvənt/. ADJ Someone who is **fervent** about something has strong and enthusiastic feelings about it. *...a fervent admirer of Morisot's work.* ♦ **fervently** ADV *Their claims will be fervently denied.*

fervour (AM **fervor**) /ˈfɜːvə/. N-U **Fervour** is a very great enthusiasm for something or belief in something; FORMAL. *...religious fervour.*

fester /ˈfestə/ **festers, festering, festered.** **1** VERB If a situation or problem **is festering**, it is growing worse, because it is not being properly recognized or dealt with. *Resentments are starting to fester.* **2** VERB If a wound **festers**, it becomes infected; LITERARY.

festival /ˈfestɪvəl/ **festivals.** **1** N-C A **festival** is an organized series of events and performances. *...summer festivals of music, theatre, and dance.* **2** N-C A **festival** is a day or period when people have a holiday and celebrate some special event, often a religious one.

festive /ˈfestɪv/. **1** ADJ Something that is **festive** is special, colourful, or exciting, especially because of a holiday or celebration. *The town has a festive holiday atmosphere.* **2** ADJ BEFORE N **Festive** means relating to a holiday or celebration, especially Christmas. *...the festive period.*

festivity /feˈstɪvɪti/ **festivities.** **1** N-U **Festivity** is the celebration of something in a happy way. *There was a general air of festivity and abandon.* **2** N-PL **Festivities** are events organized to celebrate something.

fetch /fetʃ/ **fetches, fetching, fetched.** **1** VERB If you **fetch** something or someone, you go and get them from where they are. *Sylvia fetched a towel from the bathroom... Fetch me a glass of water.* **2** VERB If something **fetches** a particular sum of money, it is sold for that amount. *The house is expected to fetch around £400,000.* **3** See also **far-fetched.**

fete /feɪt/ **fetes, feting, feted.** **1** N-C A **fete** is an event held out of doors that includes competitions and the selling of home-made goods. **2** VERB If someone **is feted**, they are celebrated, welcomed, or admired by the public.

fetus /ˈfiːtəs/. See **foetus.**

feud /fjuːd/ **feuds, feuding, feuded.** **1** N-C A **feud** is a long-lasting and bitter dispute between two people or groups. **2** N-C If two people or groups **feud**, there is a feud between them. *He feuded with his ex-wife.*

feudal /ˈfjuːdəl/. ADJ BEFORE N **Feudal** means relating to the system in which people were given land and protection by people of higher rank, and worked and fought for them in return.

fever /ˈfiːvə/ **fevers.** **1** N-VAR If you have a **fever**, your temperature is higher than usual because you are ill. • See also **hay fever.** **2** N-C A **fever** is extreme excitement or agitation. *Angie waited in a fever of excitement.*

feverish /ˈfiːvərɪʃ/. **1** ADJ **Feverish** emotion or activity shows great excitement or agitation. *...feverish last minute negotiations.* ♦ **feverishly** ADV *Volunteers are working feverishly to remove the heavy snow.* **2** ADJ If you are **feverish**, you are suffering from a fever.

few /fjuː/ **fewer, fewest.** **1** QUANT **Few** is used to indicate a small number of things or people. *I gave a dinner party for a few close friends... A strict diet is appropriate for only a few. ...a little tea-party I'm giving for a few of the teachers.* **2** QUANT **Few** is used to indicate that a number of things or people is smaller than is desirable or than was expected. *She had few friends... The trouble is that few want to buy... Few of the beach houses still had lights on.*

Few and **a few** are both used in front of the plural of count nouns, but they do not have the same meaning. For example, if you say '**I have a few friends**', this is a positive statement and you are saying that you have some friends. However, if you say '**I have few friends**', this is a kind of negative statement and you are saying that you have almost no friends or that you do not have enough friends.

PHRASES ● You use **a good few** when you are referring to quite a lot of things or people. *He was a good few years older than me.* ● You use **as few as** before a number to suggest that it is surprisingly small. *The factory may make as few as 1,500 cars this year.* ● Things that are **few and far between** are very rare or uncommon. *Successful women politicians are few and far between.* ● You use **no fewer than** to suggest that a number is surprisingly large. *He had invited no fewer than 4,000 young people.*

fiancé /fiˈɒnseɪ, AM ˌfiːɑːˈnseɪ/ **fiancés.** N-C A woman's **fiancé** is the man to whom she is engaged to be married.

fiancée /fiˈɒnseɪ, AM ˌfiːɑːˈnseɪ/ **fiancées.** N-C A man's **fiancée** is the woman to whom he is engaged to be married.

fiasco /fiˈæskəʊ/ **fiascos.** N-C When something fails completely, you can describe it as a **fiasco**, especially if it seems ridiculous or disorganized. *The race had been a complete fiasco.*

fibre (AM **fiber**) /ˈfaɪbə/ **fibres.** 1 N-C A **fibre** is a thin thread of a natural or artificial substance, especially one used to make cloth or rope. 2 N-C A **fibre** is a thin piece of flesh like a thread which connects nerve cells in your body or which muscles are made of. *...the nerve fibres.* 3 N-U **Fibre** consists of the parts of plants or seeds that your body cannot digest, but which help food pass quickly through your digestive system.

fickle /ˈfɪkəl/ 1 ADJ A **fickle** person keeps changing their mind about what they like or want; used showing disapproval. *...a handsome but fickle young actor.* 2 ADJ If you say that something is **fickle**, you mean that it often changes and is unreliable. *Orta's weather can be fickle.*

fiction /ˈfɪkʃən/ **fictions.** 1 N-U **Fiction** is stories about imaginary people and events. ◆**fictional** ADJ *Ulverton is a fictional village on the Wessex Downs.* 2 N-VAR A statement or report that is **fiction** is not true. *The truth or fiction of this story has never been truly determined.*

fictitious /fɪkˈtɪʃəs/ ADJ Something that is **fictitious** is false or does not exist. *We're interested in the source of these fictitious rumours.*

fiddle /ˈfɪdəl/ **fiddles, fiddling, fiddled.** 1 VERB If you **fiddle** with an object, you keep moving it or touching it with your fingers. *She fiddled nervously with the buttons of her cardigan.* 2 VERB If someone **fiddles** financial documents, they alter them dishonestly to get money for themselves; INFORMAL. ◆**fiddling** N-U *...evidence of fiddling in the firm's Treasury-bond department.* 3 N-C A **fiddle** is a dishonest action or scheme to get money; BRITISH, INFORMAL. *...a £1 million car insurance fiddle.* 4 N-C Some people call violins **fiddles.**

fiddly /ˈfɪdli/ ADJ Something that is **fiddly** is difficult to do or use, because it involves small or complicated objects; INFORMAL. *Fish can be fiddly to cook.*

fidelity /fɪˈdelɪti/ 1 N-U **Fidelity** is loyalty to a person, organization, or set of beliefs; FORMAL. *I had to promise fidelity to the Queen.* 2 N-U The **fidelity** of something such as a report or translation is its degree of accuracy; FORMAL.

fidget /ˈfɪdʒɪt/ **fidgets, fidgeting, fidgeted.** VERB If you **fidget**, you keep moving your hands or feet or changing position slightly, because you are nervous or bored. *Brenda fidgeted in her seat... He fidgeted with his tie.*

field /fiːld/ **fields, fielding, fielded.** 1 N-C A **field** is an enclosed area of land where crops are grown or animals are kept. *...a field of wheat.* 2 N-C A sports **field** is a grassy area where sports are played. 3 N-C A **field** is an area of land or sea bed under which large amounts of a mineral have been found. *...an extensive natural gas field.* ● See also **minefield, playing field.** 4 PHRASE Your **field of vision** is the area that you can see without turning your head. *...a big red rubber ball that bounced suddenly across his field of vision.* 5 N-C A particular **field** is a subject or area of interest. *Each of the authors of the tapes is an expert in his field.* 6 ADJ **Field** work involves research that is done in a real, natural environment rather than in a theoretical way or in controlled conditions. *...field trips to observe plants and animals.* 7 VERB The team that **is fielding** in a game of cricket or baseball is the team trying to catch the ball. ◆**fielder, fielders** N-C *The right fielder threw the ball back.* ◆**fielding** N-U *Their bowling performance was very good, their fielding very sharp.* 8 PHRASE If someone **is having a field day**, they are very busy doing something that they enjoy, even though it may hurt other people. *In our absence the office gossips are probably having a field day.*

fierce /fɪəs/ **fiercer, fiercest.** 1 ADJ A **fierce** animal or person is very aggressive or angry. ◆**fiercely** ADV *'I don't know,' she said fiercely.* 2 ADJ **Fierce** feelings, actions, or conditions are very intense and strong. *...a fierce storm which went on for five days.* ◆**fiercely** ADV *He has always been ambitious and fiercely competitive.*

fiery /ˈfaɪəri/ 1 ADJ Something that is **fiery** is burning strongly or contains fire; LITERARY. *A helicopter crashed in a fiery explosion in Vallejo.* 2 ADJ You can use **fiery** for emphasis when you are referring to bright colours such as red or orange; LITERARY. *Overhead the sky is a fiery red.* 3 ADJ If you describe someone as **fiery**, you mean that they express very strong emotions, especially anger. *She had a fiery temper.*

fifteen /ˌfɪfˈtiːn/ NUM **Fifteen** is the number 15.

fifteenth 228

fifteenth /ˌfɪfˈtiːnθ/. ORD The **fifteenth** item in a series is the one that you count as number fifteen.

fifth /fɪfθ/ **fifths.** ① ORD The **fifth** item in a series is the one that you count as number five. ② N-C A **fifth** is one of five equal parts of something.

fiftieth /ˈfɪftiəθ/. ORD The **fiftieth** item in a series is the one that you count as number fifty.

fifty /ˈfɪfti/ **fifties.** NUM **Fifty** is the number 50. For examples of how numbers such as **fifty** and **eighty** are used see **eighty**.

fig /fɪɡ/ **figs.** N-C A **fig** is a soft sweet fruit full of tiny seeds. Figs grow on trees in hot countries.

fight /faɪt/ **fights, fighting, fought** /fɔːt/. ① VERB & N-C If you **fight** something, you try in a determined way to prevent it or stop it happening. A **fight** against something is an attempt to stop it. *More units to fight forest fires are planned... I've spent a lifetime fighting against racism. ...the fight against drug addiction.* ② VERB & N-C If you **fight for** something, you try in a determined way to get it or achieve it. A **fight for** something is an attempt to get it. *We had fought to hold on to the company. ...the fight for justice.* ③ VERB If a person or army **fights**, they oppose each other with weapons. *I would sooner go to prison than fight for this country... The rival militias have been fighting for more than two years.* ♦ **fighting** N-U *More than nine hundred people have died in the fighting.* ④ VERB & N-C If one person **fights** with another, or if they have a **fight**, they hit or kick each other because they want to hurt each other. *I did fight him, I punched him but it was like hitting a wall... He had had a fight with Smith.* ⑤ VERB & N-C When people **fight** about something, or when they have a **fight**, they quarrel. *Mostly, they fight about paying bills... He had a big fight with his dad.* ⑥ VERB When politicians **fight** an election, they try to win it. ⑦ VERB If you **fight** your way to a place, you move towards it with great difficulty, usually because there are a lot of people in your way. *Female fans fought their way past bodyguards and tore at his clothes.* ⑧ VERB When you **fight** an emotion or desire, you try very hard not to feel it, show it, or act on it. *He fought with the urge to smoke.*
▶ **fight back.** ① PHR-VERB If you **fight back** against someone who has attacked you or made difficulties for you, you defend yourself by taking action against them. *The teenage attackers fled when the two men fought back.* ② PHR-VERB When you **fight back** an emotion, you try very hard not to feel it, show it, or act on it. *She fought back the tears.*
▶ **fight off.** ① PHR-VERB If you **fight off** something such as an illness, a desire, or an unpleasant feeling, you succeed in getting rid of it. *All day she had fought off the impulse to telephone Harry.* ② PHR-VERB If you **fight off** someone who has attacked you, you succeed in driving them away by fighting them. *The woman fought off the attacker.*

fighter /ˈfaɪtə/ **fighters.** ① N-C A **fighter** or a **fighter plane** is a fast military aircraft used for destroying other aircraft. ② N-C A **fighter** is

someone who physically fights another person, especially a boxer.

figurative /ˈfɪɡərətɪv, AM -ɡjər-/. ADJ If you use a word or expression in a **figurative** sense, you use it with a more abstract or imaginative meaning than its ordinary literal one. ♦ **figuratively** ADV *A lot more children are abandoned today both literally and figuratively.*

figure /ˈfɪɡə, AM -ɡjər/ **figures, figuring, figured.** ① N-C A **figure** is a particular amount expressed as a number, especially a statistic. *Government figures predict that one in two marriages will end in divorce.* ② N-C A **figure** is any of the ten written symbols from 0 to 9 that are used to represent a number. ③ N-PL An amount or number that is in single **figures** is between nought and nine. An amount or number that is in double **figures** is between ten and ninety-nine. ④ N-C A **figure** is the shape of a person you cannot see clearly. *A figure in a blue dress appeared in the doorway.* ⑤ N-C In art, a **figure** is a person in a drawing or a painting, or a statue of a person. ⑥ N-C Your **figure** is the shape of your body. *Janet was a natural blonde with a good figure.* ⑦ N-C Someone who is referred to as a particular type of **figure** is well-known and important in some way. *...key figures in the three main political parties.* ⑧ N-C If you say that someone is, for example, a mother **figure** or a hero **figure**, you mean that they have the qualities typical of mothers or heroes. *...authority figures such as parents and teachers.* ⑨ VERB If you **figure that** something is the case, you think or guess that it is the case; INFORMAL. *I figured that's what she wanted.* ⑩ VERB A thing or person that **figures** in something appears in it or is included in it. *Human rights violations figured prominently in the report.*
▶ **figure out.** PHR-VERB If you **figure out** a solution to a problem or the reason for something, you succeed in solving it or understanding it; INFORMAL. *It took them about one month to figure out how to start the equipment.*

figurehead /ˈfɪɡəhed, AM -ɡjər-/ **figureheads.** N-C If you refer to someone as the **figurehead** of an organization or political movement, you mean that they are recognized as its leader, although they have no real power.

file /faɪl/ **files, filing, filed.** ① N-C A **file** is a box or folder in which documents are kept. ② N-C & PHRASE To keep a **file** on someone or something means to collect information about them. Information that is **on file** is recorded as part of a collection of information. *We already have files on people's tax details... We'll keep your details on file.* ③ VERB & PHR-VERB If you **file** a document, or if you **file** it **away**, you put it in the correct file. *I'd completed all the case notes and filed them away.* ④ VERB When you **file** an accusation, complaint, or request, you make it officially. *I filed for divorce on the grounds of adultery.* ⑤ VERB & PHRASE When a group of people **files** somewhere, or when they walk somewhere **in single file**, they walk one behind the other in a line. *The children filed out of the house.* ⑥ N-C A **file** is a tool with rough surfaces, used for smoothing and shaping hard materials. [7] VERB If you **file** an object, you smooth or shape it with a file.

fill /fɪl/ **fills, filling, filled.** [1] VERB & PHR-VERB If you **fill** a container, or if you **fill** it **up**, you keep putting or pouring something into it until it is full. You can also say a container or something shaped like a container **fills** with something. *Fill a saucepan with water... The victims' lungs fill quickly with fluid... Pass me your cup, Amy, and I'll fill it up for you.* [2] VERB & PHR-VERB If something **fills** a space, or if it **fills up** a space, it is so large, or there are such large quantities of it, that there is very little room left. *The text fills 231 pages. ...the complicated machines that fill up today's laboratories.* ♦**filled** ADJ *...four museum buildings filled with historical objects. ...a flower-filled garden.* [3] VERB & PHR-VERB If you **fill** a crack or hole, or if you **fill** it **in**, you put a substance into it in order to make the surface smooth again. [4] VERB If something **fills** you with an emotion, you experience this emotion strongly. *He was filled with pride at his creation.* [5] VERB & PHR-VERB If you **fill** a period of time with a particular activity, or if you **fill** it **up** with that activity, you spend the time in this way. *She went to her yoga class, glad to have something to fill up the evening.* [6] VERB If something **fills** a need or gap, it means that the need or gap no longer exists. *...a sense of fun, of gaiety that filled a gap in his life.* [7] VERB If something **fills** a role or position, that is their role or position. *I was asked to fill the role of escort.* [8] PHRASE If you **have had your fill** of something, you do not want to experience it or do it any more.

▸ **fill in.** [1] PHR-VERB When you **fill in** a form, you write information in the spaces on it. [2] PHR-VERB If you **fill** someone **in**, you give them detailed information about something; INFORMAL. *He filled her in on Wilbur Kantor's visit.* [3] PHR-VERB If you **fill in** for someone else, you do their job for them in their absence. [4] See also **fill** 3.

▸ **fill out.** PHR-VERB To **fill out** a form means the same as to **fill in** a form. *Fill out the application carefully, and keep copies of it.*

▸ **fill up.** [1] PHR-VERB A type of food that **fills** you **up** makes you feel that you have eaten a lot, even though you have only eaten a small amount. [2] See also **fill** 1, 2, 5.

fillet /'fɪlɪt, AM fɪ'leɪ/ **fillets, filleting, filleted.** [1] N-VAR A **fillet** of fish or meat is a piece that has no bones in it. *...chicken fillets.* [2] VERB When you **fillet** fish or meat, you prepare it by taking the bones out.

filling /'fɪlɪŋ/ **fillings.** [1] N-C A **filling** is a small amount of metal or plastic that a dentist puts in a tooth. [2] N-VAR The **filling** in a pie, chocolate, sandwich or cake is the mixture inside it. [3] ADJ Food that is **filling** makes you feel full when you have eaten it. *...a filling meal.*

film /fɪlm/ **films, filming, filmed.** [1] N-VAR A **film** is a motion picture or a series of moving pictures recorded so that they can be shown in a cinema or on television. *In the evening we saw a film starring William Holden... The programme showed film of the four children laughing.* [2] VERB If you **film** someone or

something, you use a camera to take moving pictures which can be shown in a cinema or on television. *...a camera crew filming her for French television.* ♦**filming** N-U *Filming begins early next year.* [3] N-VAR A **film** is the roll of thin plastic that you use in a camera to take photographs. *...a roll of film.* [4] N-C A **film** of powder, liquid, or grease is a very thin layer of it. *A film of dust covered every surface.*

filter /'fɪltə/ **filters, filtering, filtered.** [1] VERB To **filter** a substance, or to **filter** particles out of a substance, means to pass it through a device which removes the particles from it. *The best prevention for cholera is to boil or filter water.* [2] N-C A **filter** is a device through which a substance is passed when it is being filtered. *...an oil filter.* [3] VERB When light or sound **filters** into a place, it comes in faintly. [4] N-C A **filter** is a device through which sound or light is passed and which blocks or reduces particular frequencies. *...a pale blue filter gives the correct colour balance.* [5] VERB When news or information **filters** through to people, it gradually reaches them. *Reports filtered out of deep disagreements within the leadership.*

filth /fɪlθ/. [1] N-U **Filth** is a disgusting amount of dirt. *The floor and furniture are covered in filth.* [2] N-U People refer to words or pictures as **filth** when they think that they describe or represent something such as sex or nudity in a disgusting way.

filthy /'fɪlθi/ **filthier, filthiest.** [1] ADJ Something that is **filthy** is very dirty indeed. *...a pair of filthy jeans.* [2] ADJ People describe things as **filthy** when they think that they are disgusting. *...a filthy habit.*

fin /fɪn/ **fins.** [1] N-C A fish's **fins** are the flat objects which stick out of its body and help it to swim. [2] N-C A **fin** on something such as an aeroplane is a flat part which sticks out and helps to control its movement.

final /'faɪnəl/ **finals.** [1] ADJ BEFORE N In a series of events, things, or people, the **final** one is the last one, or the one that happens at the end. *This is my final offer... The final effect was eerily realistic.* [2] ADJ If a decision is **final**, it cannot be changed or questioned. *I'm not going, and that's final.* [3] N-C A **final** is the last game or contest in a series, which decides the overall winner. *...the Scottish Cup Final.* ● See also **quarter-final, semi-final.** [4] N-PL **Finals** are the last and most important examinations in a university course. *Anna sat her finals in the summer.*

finale /fɪ'nɑːli, -'næli/ **finales.** [1] N-C The **finale** is the last section of a show or a piece of music. *... the finale of Shostakovich's Fifth Symphony.* [2] N-C If you say that an event provides a particular kind of **finale** to something, you mean that it provides it with that kind of ending. *...a sad finale to an otherwise spectacular career.*

finalist /'faɪnəlɪst/ **finalists.** N-C A **finalist** is a person or team that takes part in the final of a competition. *...World Cup finalists.*

finalize (BR also **finalise**) /'faɪnəlaɪz/ **finalizes, finalizing, finalized.** VERB If you **finalize** something that you are arranging, you complete the arrangements for it. *They have until today to finalise their orders.*

finally /'faɪnəli/ **1** ADV If something **finally** happens, it happens after a long delay. *Finally, he answered the phone himself.* **2** ADV You use **finally** to indicate that something is the last in a series. *She moves from Germany to Russia and finally America.* **3** ADV You use **finally** to introduce a final point or topic. *And finally, a word about the winner.*

finance /'faɪnæns, fɪ'næns/ **finances, financing, financed.** **1** VERB & N-U To **finance** a project or purchase, or to provide **finance** for it, means to provide money to pay for it. *These funds are then used to finance the purchase of equipment. ...an American whom he hoped would provide finance for the magazine.* **2** N-U **Finance** is the management of money, especially on a national level. *...the world of high finance. ...Canada's Minister of Finance.* **3** N-PL Your **finances** are the amount of money that you have. *...tips on how to work out your finances.*

financial /faɪ'nænʃəl, fɪ-/. ADJ **Financial** means relating to or involving money. *...financial difficulties.* ♦**financially** ADV *She would like to be more financially independent.*

fi,nancial 'year, financial years. N-C A **financial year** is a twelve month period beginning and ending in April, which governments and businesses use to plan their finances; BRITISH.

financier /faɪ'nænsɪə, fɪ-/ **financiers.** N-C A **financier** is a person who provides money for projects or enterprises.

finch /fɪntʃ/ **finches.** N-C A **finch** is a small bird with a short strong beak.

find /faɪnd/ **finds, finding, found.** **1** VERB If you **find** someone or something, you see them or learn where they are. *The police also found a pistol... I can't find the boys' shampoo.* **2** VERB If you **find** something that you need or want, you succeed in getting it. *We have to find him a job... My sister helped me find the money for a private operation.* **3** PASSIVE-VERB If you say that something **is found** in a particular place, you mean that it is in that place. *Fibre is found in cereal foods, beans, fruit and vegetables.* **4** VERB If you **find** yourself doing something, you are doing it without intending to. *It's not the first time that you've found yourself in this situation.* **5** VERB If you **find** that something is the case, you become aware of it or realize it. *At my age I would find it hard to get another job... I've never found my diet a problem... She returned to her east London home to find her back door forced open.* **6** VERB When a court or jury **finds** a person guilty or not guilty, they decide if that person is guilty or innocent. *She was found guilty of manslaughter.* **7** VERB You can use **find** to express your reaction to someone or something. *We're sure you'll find it exciting!... But you'd find him a good worker if you showed him what to do.* **8** N-C If you describe something that has been discovered as a **find**, you mean that it is good or useful. *...the botanical find of the century.* **9** PHRASE If you **find** your **way** somewhere, you get there by choosing the right way to go. *He was an expert at finding his way, even in strange surround-*

ings. **10** See also **finding, found.** ● **to find fault with:** see **fault.**

▶ **find out.** **1** PHR-VERB If you **find** something **out,** you learn it, often by making a deliberate effort. *...their campaign to find out the truth.* **2** PHR-VERB If you **find** someone **out,** you discover they have been doing something dishonest.

finding /'faɪndɪŋ/ **findings.** N-C Someone's **findings** are the information they get as the result of an investigation. *The committee has just reported its findings.*

fine 1 adjective uses

fine /faɪn/ **finer, finest.** **1** ADJ You use **fine** to describe someone or something that is very good. *...an excellent journalist and a very fine man. ...London's finest art deco cinema.* ♦**finely** ADV *They are finely engineered boats.* **2** ADJ AFTER LINK-V If you say that you are **fine,** you mean that you are feeling well and reasonably happy. **3** ADJ & ADV If you say that something is **fine,** you mean that it is satisfactory or acceptable. *All the instruments are working fine.* **4** ADJ When the weather is **fine,** it is sunny and not raining. **5** ADJ Something that is **fine** is very delicate, narrow, or small. *...the fine hairs on her arms.* ♦**finely** ADV *Chop the ingredients finely.* **6** ADJ A **fine** adjustment, detail, or distinction is very delicate, small, or exact.

fine 2 punishment

fine /faɪn/ **fines, fining, fined.** N-C & VERB If you get a **fine,** or if you **are fined,** you are punished by being ordered to pay a sum of money. *They fined him $10,000.*

,fine 'art, fine arts. N-VAR Painting and sculpture can be referred to as **fine art** or as **the fine arts.** *He deals in antiques and fine art.*

finesse /fɪ'nes/. N-U If you do something with **finesse,** you do it with great skill and elegance. *His boxing style is crude and lacks finesse.*

,fine-'tune, fine-tunes, fine-tuning, fine-tuned. VERB If you **fine-tune** something, you make very small and precise changes to it in order to make it work better. *Computers allow the plans to be fine-tuned and to be altered quickly.*

finger /'fɪŋgə/ **fingers, fingering, fingered.** **1** N-C Your **fingers** are the four long moveable parts at the end of your hands. *There was a ring on each of his fingers.* **2** VERB If you **finger** something, you touch or feel it with your fingers. *He fingered the few coins in his pocket.*

PHRASES ● If you **cross your fingers,** you put one finger on top of another and hope for good luck. If someone **is keeping their fingers crossed,** they are hoping for good luck. ● If you **point the finger** at someone, you blame them or accuse them of something. *He said he wasn't pointing an accusing finger at anyone in the government.* ● If you **put your finger on** something such as a problem or an idea, you see and identify exactly what it is. *He could never quite put his finger on who or what was responsible for all this.*

fingernail /'fɪŋgəneɪl/ **fingernails.** N-C Your **fingernails** are the hard areas on the ends of your fingers.

fingerprint /ˈfɪŋɡəprɪnt/ **fingerprints.** N-C & PHRASE Your **fingerprints** are the unique marks made by the tip of your fingers when you touch something. If the police **take** someone's **fingerprints**, they make a record of that person's fingerprints.

fingertip /ˈfɪŋɡətɪp/ **fingertips.** [1] N-C Your **fingertips** are the ends of your fingers. [2] PHRASE If something is **at** your **fingertips**, you can reach or get it easily. *I had the information at my fingertips.*

finish /ˈfɪnɪʃ/ **finishes, finishing, finished.** [1] VERB & PHR-VERB When you **finish** doing something, or when you **finish** it **off**, you do the last part of it, so that there is no more for you to do. In American English, you can also say **finish up**. *I've practically finished the ironing... The consultants had been working to finish a report... She is busy finishing off a biography.* [2] PHRASE If you put **the finishing touches** to something, you do the last things that are necessary to complete it. [3] VERB When something **finishes**, it ends. *The teaching day finishes at around 4pm.* [4] N-SING The **finish** of something is the last part of it. *I intend to continue it and see the job through to the finish.* [5] N-C An object's **finish** is the appearance or texture of its surface. *...the finish and workmanship of the woodwork.* [6] See also **finished**.

▶ **finish off.** PHR-VERB When you **finish off** something that you have been eating or drinking, you eat or drink the last part of it. ● See also **finish** 2.

▶ **finish up.** PHR-VERB If you **finish up** in a particular place or situation, you are in that place or situation after doing something. *He's probably going to finish up in jail.* ● See also **finish** 2.

▶ **finish with.** PHR-VERB When you **finish with** someone or something, you stop being involved with them. *My boyfriend was threatening to finish with me.*

finished /ˈfɪnɪʃt/. [1] ADJ AFTER LINK-V If you are **finished with** something, you are no longer doing it or interested in it. *One suspects he will be finished with boxing.* [2] ADJ AFTER LINK-V Someone or something that is **finished** is no longer important or effective. *Her power over me is finished... I thought I was finished.*

finite /ˈfaɪnaɪt/. ADJ Something that is **finite** has a limited size or extent; FORMAL. *Coal and oil are finite resources.*

fir /fɜː/ **firs.** N-C A **fir** or a **fir tree** is a tall pointed evergreen tree.

fire 1 burning, heat

fire /faɪə/ **fires, firing, fired.** [1] N-U **Fire** consists of the flames produced by things that are burning. *...a great orange ball of fire.* [2] N-VAR A **fire** is an occurrence of uncontrolled burning which destroys things. *Much of historic Rennes was destroyed by fire. ...a forest fire.* [3] N-C A **fire** is a burning pile of coal, wood, or other fuel that you make. *I started to clear the grate to light a fire.* [4] N-C A **fire** is a device that uses electricity or gas to heat a room.
PHRASES ● If something **catches fire**, it starts burning. ● If something is **on fire**, it is burning

fiercely. ● If you **set fire to** something, or if you **set it on fire**, you start it burning.

fire 2 shooting or attacking

fire /faɪə/ **fires, firing, fired.** [1] VERB & N-U If someone **fires** a gun or a bullet, a bullet is sent from a gun that they are using. You can refer to the shots fired as **fire**. *...an exchange of fire during a police raid.* ◆**firing** N-U *The firing continued.* [2] VERB If you **fire** questions **at** someone, you ask them a lot of questions very quickly, one after another.

fire 3 dismiss

fire /faɪə/ **fires, firing, fired.** VERB If your employer **fires** you, he or she dismisses you from your job. *You're fired!*

firearm /ˈfaɪərɑːm/ **firearms.** N-C **Firearms** are guns. *...illegal possession of firearms.*

'fire brigade, fire brigades. N-C The **fire brigade** is an organization which has the job of putting out fires.

'fire engine, fire engines. N-C A **fire engine** is a large vehicle that carries firemen and equipment for putting out fires.

fireman /ˈfaɪəmən/ **firemen.** N-C A **fireman** is a person whose job is to put out fires.

fireplace /ˈfaɪəpleɪs/ **fireplaces.** N-C In a room, the **fireplace** is the place where a fire can be lit.

firepower /ˈfaɪəpaʊə/. N-U The **firepower** of an army or military vehicle is the amount of ammunition it can fire.

firewood /ˈfaɪəwʊd/. N-U **Firewood** is wood that has been cut up for burning on a fire.

firework /ˈfaɪəwɜːk/ **fireworks.** N-C **Fireworks** are small objects that are lit to entertain people on special occasions. They burn in a bright, attractive, and often noisy way.

firm /fɜːm/ **firms; firmer, firmest.** [1] N-C A **firm** is a business selling or producing something. *...a firm of heating engineers.* [2] ADJ Something that is **firm** is fairly hard and does not change much in shape when it is pressed. *Choose a soft, medium or firm mattress.* ◆**firmness** N-U *Vegetables should retain some firmness.* [3] ADJ A **firm** grasp or push is one which is strong and controlled. *The quick handshake was firm and cool.* ◆**firmly** ADV *She held me firmly by the elbow.* [4] ADJ A **firm** person behaves in a fairly strict way, and will not change their mind. *She had to be firm with him. 'I don't want to see you again'.* ◆**firmly** ADV *'A good night's sleep is what you want,' he said firmly.* ◆**firmness** N-U *...a manner that combines friendliness with compassion and firmness.* [5] PHRASE If someone **stands firm**, they refuse to surrender or change their mind about something. *The council is standing firm against the barrage of protest.* [6] ADJ A **firm** decision or piece of information is definite and unlikely to change. *We have no firm evidence.* ◆**firmly** ADV *He is firmly convinced that it is vital to do this.*

first /fɜːst/. [1] ORD & PRON & ADV The **first** thing or person is the one that happens or comes before all the others of the same kind. *...the first month of her diet... Johnson came first in the one hundred metres... The second paragraph startled me even more than the first. ...two years* *after they had first started going out.* [2] ADV If you do something **first**, you do it before anyone else does, or before you do anything else. *I do not remember who spoke first... First, tell me what you think of my products.* [3] N-SING An event that is described as **a first** has never happened before. *The meeting between financial analysts was a first for the company.* [4] PRON **The first** you hear of something or **the first** you know about it is the time when you first become aware of it. *That was the first we heard of it.* [5] ADV & ORD You use **first** when you are talking about what happens in the early part of an event or experience, in contrast to what happens later. *At first, he seemed surprised by my questions... Her first reaction was disgust.* [6] ADV & PHRASE You use **first** or **first of all** to introduce the first of a number of things that you want to say. *First of all, we can encourage people to buy their homes.* [7] ADJ **First** refers to the best or most important thing or person of a particular kind. *The first duty of any government must be to protect the interests of the taxpayers.* [8] PHRASE If you **put** someone or something **first**, you treat them as more important than anything else.

first 'aid. N-U **First aid** is medical treatment given as soon as possible to a sick or injured person. *Onlookers thought she was giving first aid.*

first 'class. [1] ADJ Something or someone that is **first class**, is of the highest quality or standard. *The food was first class.* [2] N-U & ADJ & ADV **First class**, or **first class** accommodation, is the best and most expensive accommodation on an aeroplane, ship, or train. *...a cabin in first class. ...two first-class tickets to Dublin... She had never flown first class before.*

first-'hand (or **firsthand**). ADJ **First-hand** information or experience is gained directly, rather than from other people. *She has little first-hand knowledge of Quebec... We've been through Germany and seen first-hand what's happening there.*

firstly /ˈfɜːstli/. ADV You use **firstly** when you are about to mention the first in a series of items. *Noise affects us in two ways. Firstly, it can damage hearing.*

first 'name, first names. N-C Your **first name** is the first of the names that you were given when you were born, as opposed to your surname. *Her first name is Mary.*

first 'rate. ADJ If someone or something is **first rate**, they are of the highest quality. *...a first-rate scientist.*

fiscal /ˈfɪskəl/. ADJ BEFORE N **Fiscal** means related to government money or public money, especially taxes. *...fiscal policy.*

fish /fɪʃ/ **fishes, fishing, fished.** [1] N-VAR A **fish** is a creature with a tail and fins that lives in water. The plural is **fish** or **fishes**. **Fish** is the flesh of a fish eaten as food. [2] VERB If you **fish**, you try to catch fish. [3] VERB If you **fish** a particular area of water, you try to catch fish there. *On Saturday we fished the River Arno.*

▶ **fish out.** PHR-VERB If you **fish** something **out** from somewhere, you take or pull it out. *He fished out three files from the cabinet.*

fisherman /ˈfɪʃəmən/ **fishermen.** N-C A **fisherman** is a person who catches fish as a job or for sport.

fishing /ˈfɪʃɪŋ/. N-U **Fishing** is the sport or business of catching fish.

fist /fɪst/ **fists.** N-C You refer to someone's hand as their **fist** when they have bent their fingers towards their palm. *He swore and shook his fist at me.*

fit 1 being right or going in the right place

fit /fɪt/ **fits, fitting, fitted** (AM **fit**). [1] VERB & N-SING If something **fits**, or if it is a good **fit**, it is the right size and shape to go onto a person's body or into a particular position. *The sash, kimono, and other garments were made to fit a child. ...a pocket computer which is small enough to fit into your pocket... The sills and doors were a reasonably good fit.* [2] VERB If you **fit** something into a particular space or place, you put it there. *...she fitted her key in the lock.* [3] VERB If you **fit** something somewhere, you attach it there securely. *Fit hinge bolts to give extra support to the door lock... Peter had built the overhead ladders, and the next day he fitted them to the wall.* [4] ADJ If someone or something is **fit** for a particular purpose, they are suitable or appropriate for it. *You're not fit to be a mother!... The meat is fit to eat.* ◆**fitness** N-U *You should consult your doctor about your fitness to travel.* [5] PHRASE If someone **sees fit** to do something, they decide that it is the right thing to do; used showing disapproval. *He's not a friend, you say, yet you saw fit to lend him money.*

▶ **fit in.** [1] PHR-VERB If you manage to **fit** a person or task **in**, you manage to find time to deal with them. *I find that I just can't fit in regular domestic work.* [2] PHR-VERB If you **fit into** a group, or if you **fit in**, you seem to belong in the group because you are similar to other people in it. *It's hard to see how he would fit into the team.*

▶ **fit out** or **fit up.** PHR-VERB If you **fit** someone or something **out**, or if you **fit** them **up**, you provide them with equipment and other things that they need. *We helped to fit him out for a trip to the Baltic.*

fit 2 healthy

fit /fɪt/ **fitter, fittest.** ADJ Someone who is **fit** is healthy and physically strong. ◆**fitness** N-U *...women who regularly engage in sports and fitness activities.*

fit 3 uncontrollable movements or emotions

fit /fɪt/ **fits.** [1] N-C If someone has a **fit**, they suddenly lose consciousness and their body makes uncontrollable movements. *...epileptic fits.* [2] N-C A **fit** of coughing, laughter, anger, or panic is a sudden uncontrolled outburst of it. *Pattie shot Tom in a fit of jealous rage.*

fitted /ˈfɪtɪd/. [1] ADJ **Fitted** clothes or furnishings are designed to be exactly the right size for their purpose. *...a fitted jacket. ...a fitted carpet.* [2] ADJ **Fitted** furniture is designed to fill a particular space and is fixed in place. *...fitted wardrobes.* [3] ADJ If a room is **fitted with** objects, those objects are in the room and are normally fixed in place. *...an exercise room fitted with an electronic bicycle.*

fitting /ˈfɪtɪŋ/ **fittings.** ① ADJ If something is **fitting**, it is right or suitable. ...*a fitting end to a bitter campaign.* ♦**fittingly** ADV *Fittingly, the hearing is being conducted by a former Supreme Court judge.* ② N-C A **fitting** is a small part on the outside of a piece of equipment or furniture, such as a handle or a tap. ...*brass light fittings.* ③ N-PL **Fittings** are things such as cookers or electric fires that are fixed inside a building but can be removed if necessary.

five /faɪv/ **fives.** NUM **Five** is the number 5.

fiver /ˈfaɪvə/ **fivers.** N-C A **fiver** is a British five pound note; INFORMAL.

fix /fɪks/ **fixes, fixing, fixed.** ① VERB If something **is fixed** somewhere, it is attached there securely. *It is fixed on the wall... He fixed a bayonet to the end of his rifle.* ② VERB If you **fix** something, for example a date, price, or policy, you decide what it will be or you arrange it. *He's going to fix a time when I can see him... He vanished after you fixed him with a job.* ③ VERB To **fix** something means to repair it or to make it satisfactory. *If something is broken, we get it fixed... It's not too late to fix the problem.* ④ VERB If you **fix** your eyes or attention on something, you look at it or think about it with concentration. *Her soft brown eyes fixed on Kelly... Fix your attention on the practicalities of financing your schemes.* ⑤ VERB & N-C If someone **fixes** a race, election, contest, or other event, they make unfair or illegal arrangements to affect the result. A **fix** is a situation where this happens. *They offered opposing players bribes to fix a decisive league match... It's all a fix, a deal they've made.* ⑥ N-C An injection of an addictive drug such as heroin can be referred to as a **fix**; INFORMAL. ⑦ See also **fixed**.

▸ **fix up.** ① PHR-VERB If you **fix** someone **up** with something they need, you provide it. *He was fixed up with a job.* ② PHR-VERB If you **fix** something **up**, you arrange it. *I fixed up an appointment to see her.*

fixed /fɪkst/. ADJ You use **fixed** to describe something which stays the same and does not vary. ...*fixed interest rates.* ...*people who have fixed ideas about things.* ...*a fixed grin.*

fixture /ˈfɪkstʃə/ **fixtures.** ① N-C **Fixtures** are pieces of furniture or equipment, for example baths, which are permanently fixed inside a building. ② N-C If something or someone is a **fixture** in a particular place, they are always there. *She was a fixture in New York's nightclubs.* ③ N-C In sport, a **fixture** is a competition arranged for a particular date; BRITISH. *City won this fixture 3-0.*

fizz /fɪz/ **fizzes, fizzing, fizzed.** VERB & N-U If a drink **fizzes**, or if it has **fizz**, it produces lots of little bubbles of gas and makes a hissing sound. ...*what it is that makes cola fizz... The champagne began to lose its fizz.*

fizzy /ˈfɪzi/. ADJ **Fizzy** drinks are full of little bubbles of gas.

flag /flæg/ **flags, flagging, flagged.** ① N-C A **flag** is a piece of coloured cloth used as a sign for something or as a signal. ...*the American flag.* ② PHRASE If you **fly the flag**, you show that you are proud of your country, or that you support a particular cause. *Don't expect him to be flying the flag for his home country.* ③ VERB If you **flag**, or if your spirits **flag**, you begin to lose enthusiasm or energy. *By 4,000m he was beginning to flag.*

flagrant /ˈfleɪgrənt/. ADJ BEFORE N. You can use **flagrant** to describe an action or situation that is bad or shocking in an obvious or deliberate way. ...*a flagrant violation of international law.*

flagship /ˈflægʃɪp/ **flagships.** ① N-C A **flagship** is the most important ship in a fleet. ② N-C The **flagship** of a group of things that are owned or produced by a particular organization is the most important one. *The hospital has been the government's flagship.*

flail /fleɪl/ **flails, flailing, flailed.** VERB If your arms or legs **flail**, **flail around**, or **flail about**, they wave about in an energetic but uncontrolled way. *His arms were flailing in all directions.*

flair /fleə/. ① N-SING If you have a **flair for** a particular thing, you have a natural ability to do it well. ...*a dentist with a flair for invention.* ② N-U If you have **flair**, you do things in an interesting, and stylish way. *Their work has all the usual punch, panache and flair you'd expect.*

flak /flæk/. N-U If you get a lot of **flak** from someone, they criticize you severely. If you take the **flak**, you get the blame for something; INFORMAL.

flake /fleɪk/ **flakes, flaking, flaked.** ① N-C A **flake** is a small thin piece of something that has broken off a larger piece. *A flake of plaster from the ceiling fell into his eye.* ② VERB If paint **flakes**, or if it **flakes off**, small pieces of it come off.

flamboyant /flæmˈbɔɪənt/. ADJ If you say that someone or something is **flamboyant**, you mean that they are very noticeable and stylish. *Freddie Mercury was a flamboyant star.* ♦**flamboyance** N-U ...*his usual mixture of flamboyance and flair.* ♦**flamboyantly** ADV *She dressed flamboyantly.*

flame /fleɪm/ **flames.** N-VAR A **flame** is a hot bright stream of burning gas that comes from something that is burning. *The heat from the flames was so intense that roads melted.*

PHRASES • If something is **in flames**, it is on fire. • If something **bursts into flames**, it suddenly starts burning fiercely.

flaming /ˈfleɪmɪŋ/. ① ADJ **Flaming** is used to describe something that is burning and producing a lot of flames. ...*the crash, which sent flaming debris hurtling through the city centre.* ② ADJ BEFORE N Something that is **flaming** red or **flaming** orange is bright red or orange in colour.

flank /flæŋk/ **flanks, flanking, flanked.** ① N-C An animal's **flanks** are the sides of its body. ② N-C A **flank** of an army or naval force is one side of it when it is organized for battle. ③ VERB If something is **flanked** by things, it has them at its side. *Bookcases flank the bed.*

flannel /ˈflænəl/ **flannels.** N-U **Flannel** is a lightweight cloth used for making clothes. ...*a faded red flannel shirt.*

flap /flæp/ **flaps, flapping, flapped.** ① VERB If something that is attached at one end **flaps**, or if you **flap** it, it moves quickly up and down or from side to side. *The bird flapped its wings furiously.* [2] N-C A **flap** of cloth or skin is a flat piece of it that moves freely because it is attached by only one edge. *He drew back the tent flap.*

flare /fleə/ **flares, flaring, flared.** [1] N-C A **flare** is a small device that produces a bright flame. Flares are used as signals, for example on ships. [2] VERB If a fire **flares**, or if it **flares up**, the flames suddenly become larger. *Don't spill too much fat on the barbecue as it could flare up.* [3] VERB If something such as violence or anger **flares**, or if it **flares up**, it becomes worse. *Trouble flared in several American cities... Dozens of people were injured as fighting flared up.*

'flare-up, flare-ups. N-C If there is a **flare-up** of violence or of an illness, it suddenly starts or gets worse. *...a flare-up in her arthritis.*

flash /flæʃ/ **flashes, flashing, flashed.** [1] N-C A **flash** of light is a sudden, short burst of it. *A sudden flash of lightning lit everything up.* [2] VERB If a light **flashes**, or if you **flash** a light, it shines brightly and suddenly. *Lightning flashed among the distant dark clouds... A driver flashed her headlights.* [3] VERB Something that **flashes** past moves or happens very quickly. *Cars flashed by every few minutes... A ludicrous thought flashed through Harry's mind.* [4] PHRASE If you say that something happens **in a flash**, you mean that it happens very quickly. *The answer had come to him in a flash.*

flashback /'flæʃbæk/ **flashbacks.** [1] N-C In a film, novel, or play, a **flashback** to the past is a scene that returns to events in the past. [2] N-C If you have a **flashback** to a past experience, you have a sudden and vivid memory of it. *He has recurring flashbacks to the night his friends died.*

flashlight /'flæʃlaɪt/ **flashlights.** N-C A **flashlight** is a small portable electric light which gets its power from batteries.

flashy /'flæʃi/ **flashier, flashiest.** ADJ If you describe a person or thing as **flashy**, you mean they are smart and noticeable, but in a rather vulgar way; INFORMAL. *...a flashy sports car.*

flask /flɑːsk, flæsk/ **flasks.** N-C A **flask** is a bottle used for carrying alcoholic or hot drinks around with you. *...a flask of coffee.*

flat /flæt/ **flats; flatter, flattest.** [1] N-C In British English, a **flat** is a set of rooms for living in, that is part of a larger building. The usual American word is **apartment**. *...a block of flats.* [2] ADJ Something that is **flat** is level and smooth, rather than sloping, curved, or bumpy. *His right hand moved across the cloth, smoothing it flat... The sea was calm, perfectly flat.* [3] ADJ A **flat** object is not very tall or wide in relation to its length and width. *...a square flat box.* [4] ADJ A **flat** tyre or ball does not have enough air in it. [5] ADJ A **flat** battery has lost some or all of its electrical power. [6] ADJ BEFORE N A **flat** refusal or rejection is definite and firm. *The Foreign Ministry has issued a flat denial of any involvement.* ♦ **flatly** ADV *He flatly refused to discuss it.* [7] ADV If something is done in a particular amount of time **flat**, it is done in exactly that amount of time. *I had it all explained*

to me in two minutes flat. [8] ADJ You use **flat** to describe someone's voice when they are saying something without expressing any emotion. *'Whatever you say,' he said in a deadly flat voice.* ♦ **flatly** ADV *I know you,' he said flatly.* [9] ADJ BEFORE N A **flat** rate, price, or percentage is one that is fixed and which applies in every situation. *Sometimes there's a flat fee for carrying out a particular task.* [10] ADJ **Flat** is used after a letter representing a musical note to show that the note should be played or sung half a tone lower than the note which otherwise corresponds to that letter. **Flat** is often represented by the symbol ♭ after the letter. [11] ADV & ADJ If a musical note is played or sung **flat**, it is slightly lower in pitch than it should be.

PHRASES ● If an event or attempt to do something **falls flat**, it fails. *Liz meant it as a joke but it fell flat.* ● If you do something **flat out**, you do it as fast or as hard as you can; BRITISH. *He is working flat out to trap those responsible.*

flatten /'flætən/ **flattens, flattening, flattened.** [1] VERB & PHR-VERB If you **flatten** something, or if you **flatten** it **out**, you make it flat or flatter. You can also say that something **flattens** or **flattens out**. *Flatten the dough out and cut it into pieces.* [2] VERB If you **flatten** yourself against something, you press yourself flat against it. *He flattened himself against a brick wall as I passed.*

flatter /'flætə/ **flatters, flattering, flattered.** [1] VERB If someone **flatters** you, they praise you in an exaggerated way that is not sincere. *I knew she was just flattering me.* [2] VERB If you **flatter** yourself that something is the case, you believe, perhaps wrongly, something good about yourself. *He flatters himself that his work will be found useful.*

flattered /'flætəd/. ADJ AFTER LINK-V If you are **flattered** by something that has happened, you are pleased about it because it makes you feel important. *I am flattered that they should be so supportive.*

flattering /'flætərɪŋ/. [1] ADJ If something is **flattering**, it makes you appear more attractive. *Her hair has been cut in a shorter, more flattering style.* [2] ADJ If someone's remarks or behaviour are **flattering**, they are pleasing because they show that the person has a high opinion of you. *It is always flattering to be asked to judge.*

flaunt /flɔːnt/ **flaunts, flaunting, flaunted.** VERB If you say that someone **flaunts** their possessions or qualities, you mean that they display them in a very obvious way in. *They drove around in Rolls-Royces, openly flaunting their wealth.*

flavour (AM **flavor**) /'fleɪvə/ **flavours, flavouring, flavoured.** [1] N-VAR The **flavour** of a food or drink is its taste. *This cheese has a crumbly texture with a strong flavour.* ♦ **-flavoured** *...fruit-flavoured sparkling water.* [2] VERB If you **flavour** food or drink, you add something to give it a particular taste. *Flavour your favourite dishes with exotic herbs and spices.* [3] N-U The **flavour** of something is its distinctive characteristic or quality. *Claude's landscapes have a strong Italian flavour.*

flavouring (AM **flavoring**) /ˈfleɪvərɪŋ/ **flavourings.** N-VAR **Flavourings** are substances that are added to food or drink to give it a particular taste.

flaw /flɔː/ **flaws.** [1] N-C A **flaw** in something such as a theory is a mistake in it. *Almost all of these studies have serious flaws.* [2] N-C A **flaw** in someone's character is an undesirable quality which they have. *The only flaw in his character seems to be a short temper.*

flawed /flɔːd/. ADJ Something that is **flawed** has a mark or fault in it. *The research was seriously flawed. ...a flawed genius.*

flawless /ˈflɔːləs/. ADJ If you say that something or someone is **flawless**, you mean that they have no faults or imperfections. *...her flawless complexion.* ◆**flawlessly** ADV *I wanted to do my job flawlessly.*

flea /fliː/ **fleas.** N-C A **flea** is a small jumping insect that sucks human or animal blood.

fleck /flek/ **flecks.** N-C **Flecks** are small marks on a surface, or objects that look like small marks. *Flecks of dark blue paint.*

fled /fled/. **Fled** is the past tense and past participle of **flee**.

fledgling /ˈfledʒlɪŋ/ **fledglings.** [1] N-C A **fledgling** is a young bird. [2] ADJ BEFORE N You use **fledgling** to describe an inexperienced person or a new organization. *...fledgling writers.*

flee /fliː/ **flees, fleeing, fled.** VERB If you **flee** from something or someone, or if you **flee** them, you escape from them by running away. *In 1984 he fled to Costa Rica to avoid military service. ...refugees fleeing persecution.*

fleece /fliːs/ **fleeces, fleecing, fleeced.** [1] N-C A sheep's **fleece** is its coat of wool. [2] N-C A **fleece** is the wool, in a single piece, that is cut off one sheep during shearing. [3] VERB If someone **fleeces** you, they get a lot of money from you by tricking you; INFORMAL. *He fleeced her out of thousands of pounds.*

fleet /fliːt/ **fleets.** [1] N-C A **fleet** is an organized group of ships. *...local fishing fleets.* [2] N-C You can refer to a group of vehicles as a **fleet**, especially when they all belong to a particular organization or when they are all going somewhere together. *With its own fleet of trucks, the company delivers most orders overnight.*

fleeting /ˈfliːtɪŋ/. ADJ **Fleeting** is used to describe something which lasts only for a very short time. *The girls caught only a fleeting glimpse of the driver.* ◆**fleetingly** ADV *He smiled fleetingly.*

flesh /fleʃ/ **fleshes, fleshing, fleshed.** [1] N-U **Flesh** is the soft part of a person's or animal's body between the bones and the skin. *...the pale pink flesh of trout.* [2] N-U You can use **flesh** to refer to human skin and the human body, especially when you are considering it in a sexual way. *...the sins of the flesh.* [3] N-U The **flesh** of a fruit or vegetable is the soft inner part. [4] PHRASE If you meet or see someone **in the flesh**, you meet or see them in person. [5] PHRASE If you say that someone is your **own flesh and blood**, you are emphasizing that they are a member of your family.

▸ **flesh out.** PHR-VERB If you **flesh out** something such as a story, you add more details to it. *He talked with him for an hour and a half, fleshing out the details of his original five-minute account.*

flew /fluː/. **Flew** is the past tense of **fly**.

flex /fleks/ **flexes, flexing, flexed.** [1] N-VAR A **flex** is an electric cable containing wires that is connected to an electrical appliance. [2] VERB If you **flex** your muscles or parts of your body, you bend, move, or stretch them to exercise them.

flexible /ˈfleksɪbəl/. [1] ADJ A **flexible** object or material can be bent easily without breaking. *...brushes with long, flexible bristles.* ◆**flexibility** N-U *The plastic's flexibility makes it possible to create a much larger range of shapes.* [2] ADJ Something or someone that is **flexible** is able to change and adapt easily to new conditions and circumstances. *Look for software that's flexible enough for a range of abilities.* ◆**flexibility** N-U *Manville has the financial flexibility to buy other companies at the best moment.*

flick /flɪk/ **flicks, flicking, flicked.** [1] VERB & N-C If something **flicks** in a particular direction, or if someone **flicks** it, it moves with a short, sudden movement. This action is called a **flick**. *His tongue flicked across his lips... She sighed and flicked a dishcloth at the counter. ...a flick of the whip.* [2] VERB If you **flick** a switch, you press it quickly. *He flicked a light-switch... Pearle flicked off the TV.* [3] VERB If you **flick** through a book or magazine, you turn the pages quickly.

flicker /ˈflɪkə/ **flickers, flickering, flickered.** [1] VERB & N-C If a light or flame **flickers**, it shines unsteadily. You can also talk about a **flicker** of light. *A television flickered in the corner... I saw the flicker of flames.* [2] N-C A **flicker** of feeling is one that is experienced or visible only faintly and briefly. *He felt a flicker of regret.* [3] VERB If an expression **flickers** across your face, it appears briefly. *A smile flickered across Vincent's grey features.*

flight /flaɪt/ **flights.** [1] N-C A **flight** is a journey made by flying, usually in an aeroplane. *The flight will take four hours.* [2] N-C You can refer to an aeroplane carrying passengers on a particular journey as a particular **flight**. *I'll try to get on the flight down to Karachi tonight... BA flight 286 was two hours late.* [3] N-U **Flight** is the action of flying, or the ability to fly. *...supersonic flight... These hawks are magnificent in flight.* [4] N-U **Flight** is the act of running away from something. *Frank was in full flight when he reached them. ...others who came to this country in desperate flight from wars or famines.* [5] PHRASE If someone **takes flight**, they run away. [6] N-C A **flight** of steps or stairs is a row of them leading from one level to another.

flimsy /ˈflɪmzi/ **flimsier, flimsiest.** [1] ADJ Something that is **flimsy** is easily damaged because it is badly made or made of a weak material. *...a flimsy wooden door.* [2] ADJ **Flimsy** cloth or clothing is thin and does not give much protection. [3] ADJ If you describe something such as evidence or an excuse as **flimsy**, you mean that it is not very convincing.

flinch /flɪntʃ/ **flinches, flinching, flinched.** [1] VERB If you **flinch**, you make a small, sudden movement without meaning to, usually because you are startled or frightened. *She flinched as though he'd slapped her.* [2] VERB If you do not **flinch** from something unpleasant, you do not attempt to avoid it. *The world community should not flinch in the face of this challenge.*

fling /flɪŋ/ **flings, flinging, flung** /flʌŋ/. [1] VERB If you **fling** something or someone somewhere, you throw it there suddenly, using a lot of force. *Peter flung his shoes into the corner... He flung himself to the floor.* [2] N-C If two people have a **fling**, they have a brief sexual relationship; INFORMAL. [3] N-SING You can refer to a short period of enjoyment as a **fling**, especially when it might be the last one that you will have. *...that last fling before you finally give up and take up a job.*

flip /flɪp/ **flips, flipping, flipped.** [1] VERB If you **flip** through a book, you turn the pages quickly. [2] VERB If something **flips** over, or if you **flip** it over, it suddenly turns over. *The plane then flipped over and burst into flames... He flipped it neatly on to the plate.*

flirt /flɜːt/ **flirts, flirting, flirted.** [1] VERB If you **flirt** with someone, you behave as if you are sexually attracted to them, in a playful or not very serious way. *He flirts outrageously.* ◆**flirtation, flirtations** N-VAR *...a professor who has a flirtation with a student.* [2] N-C A **flirt** is someone who flirts a lot. [3] VERB If you **flirt** with an idea or belief, you consider it or adopt it briefly, but do not become completely committed to it. *My mother used to flirt with Socialism.*

float /fləʊt/ **floats, floating, floated.** [1] VERB If something is **floating** in or on a liquid, it is lying or moving slowly on or just below the surface. *A tree branch was floating down the river.* [2] VERB Something that **floats** in the air hangs in it or moves slowly through it. *The white cloud of smoke floated away.* [3] N-C A **float** is a light object that is used to help someone or something float in water. [4] VERB To **float** a new company means to make shares in it available for the public to buy. To **float** new shares means to make them available for the public to buy.

flock /flɒk/ **flocks, flocking, flocked.** [1] N-C A **flock** of birds, sheep, or goats is a group of them. **Flock** can take the singular or plural form of the verb. [2] N-C You can refer to a group of people or things as a **flock of** them to emphasize that there are a lot of them. *These cases all attracted flocks of famous writers.* [3] VERB If people **flock** to a place or event, a lot of them go there. *The criticisms will not stop people flocking to see the film.*

flog /flɒg/ **flogs, flogging, flogged.** [1] VERB If someone tries to **flog** something, they try to sell it; BRITISH, INFORMAL. [2] VERB If someone is **flogged**, they are hit very hard with a whip or stick as a punishment. ◆**flogging, floggings** N-VAR *He urged the restoration of hanging and flogging.*

flood /flʌd/ **floods, flooding, flooded.** [1] N-VAR If there is a **flood**, a large amount of water, for example from an overflowing river, covers an area which is usually dry. *More than 70 people were killed in the floods.* [2] VERB If

something such as a river or a burst pipe **floods** an area that is usually dry, or if the area **floods**, it becomes covered with water. *The Chicago River flooded the city's underground tunnel system... That February the river flooded.* ◆**flooding** N-U *The flooding is thought to be the worst this century.* [3] VERB & N-C If you say that people or things **flood** into a place, or that there is a **flood** of them arriving somewhere, you are emphasizing that they arrive there in large numbers. *...the refugees flooding out of Bosnia... He received a flood of letters.*

floodlight /ˈflʌdlaɪt/ **floodlights, floodlighting, floodlit.** [1] N-C **Floodlights** are powerful lamps which are used to light sports grounds and the outsides of public buildings. [2] VERB If a building or place **is floodlit**, it is lit by floodlights. *A police helicopter hovered above, floodlighting the area. ...a floodlit forecourt.*

floor /flɔː/ **floors, flooring, floored.** [1] N-C The **floor** of a room is the part that you walk on. *Jack's sitting on the floor watching TV.* [2] N-C A **floor** of a building is all the rooms on a particular level. *It is on the fifth floor of the hospital.*

> In British English, the **ground floor** of a building is the floor which is level with the ground. The floor on the next level is called the **first floor**. In American English, the **first floor** is the floor which is level with the ground and the next floor up is the **second floor**.

[3] N-C The ocean **floor** is the ground at the bottom of an ocean. The valley **floor** is the ground at the bottom of a valley. [4] VERB If you **are floored** by something, you are unable to respond to it because you are so surprised by it. *He was floored by the announcement.* [5] VERB If someone **is floored**, they are knocked to the ground. *Police Sergeant John Shepherd floored him with a rugby tackle.* [6] See also **shop floor**.

floorboard /ˈflɔːbɔːd/ **floorboards.** N-C **Floorboards** are the long pieces of wood that some floors are made of.

flop /flɒp/ **flops, flopping, flopped.** [1] VERB If someone or something **flops** somewhere, they fall there heavily or untidily. *His hair flopped over his left eye.* [2] VERB & N-C If something **flops**, or if it is a **flop**, it is a total failure. *The film flopped badly at the box office... The policy is destined to be another embarrassing flop.*

floppy /ˈflɒpi/. ADJ **Floppy** things are loose and tend to hang downwards. *...a floppy hat.*

floppy 'disk (BR also **floppy disc**), **floppy disks.** N-C A **floppy disk** is a small magnetic disk that is used for storing computer data and programs.

flora /ˈflɔːrə/. N-U You can refer to plants as **flora**, especially the plants growing in a particular area; FORMAL. **Flora** can take the singular or plural form of the verb. *The soil is rich in lime and affects the flora.*

floral /ˈflɔːrəl/. [1] ADJ A **floral** fabric or design has a pattern of flowers on it. [2] ADJ BEFORE N You use **floral** to describe something that contains flowers or is made of flowers. ...*eye-catching floral arrangements.*

florist /ˈflɒrɪst, AM ˈflɔːr-/ **florists.** [1] N-C A **florist** is a shopkeeper who sells flowers and indoor plants. [2] N-C A **florist** or a **florist's** is a shop where flowers and indoor plants are sold.

flounder /ˈflaʊndə/ **flounders, floundering, floundered.** [1] VERB If something **is floundering**, it has many problems and may soon fail completely. *What a pity that his career was left to flounder.* [2] VERB If someone **is floundering**, they do not know what to do or say. *I was floundering. I worked in a number of jobs. I had no direction in my life.*

flour /ˈflaʊə/ **flours.** N-VAR **Flour** is a white or brown powder that is made by grinding grain. It is used to make bread, cakes, and pastry.

flourish /ˈflʌrɪʃ, AM ˈflɜːr-/ **flourishes, flourishing, flourished.** [1] VERB If something **flourishes**, it is successful or widespread, and developing quickly and strongly. *Business flourished and within six months they were earning 18,000 roubles a day.* ◆**flourishing** ADJ *London quickly became a flourishing port.* [2] VERB If a plant or animal **flourishes**, it grows well or is healthy. ◆**flourishing** ADJ *...the largest and most flourishing fox population in Europe.* [3] N-C If you do something with a **flourish**, you do it with a bold sweeping movement, intended to make people notice it. *She tended to finish dancing with a flourish.*

flout /flaʊt/ **flouts, flouting, flouted.** VERB If you **flout** a law, order, or rule of behaviour, you deliberately and openly disobey it.

flow /fləʊ/ **flows, flowing, flowed.** [1] VERB & N-VAR If a liquid, gas, or electrical current **flows** somewhere, it moves there steadily and continuously. This movement is called a **flow**. *A stream flowed gently down into the valley. ...increases in blood flow.* [2] VERB & N-C If a number of people or things **flow** from one place to another, they move there steadily in large groups. This movement is called a **flow**. *Refugees continue to flow from the region. ...the frantic flow of cars and buses along the street.* [3] VERB & N-C If information or money **flows** somewhere, it moves freely between people or organizations. This movement is called a **flow**. *A lot of this information flowed through other police departments. ...the opportunity to control the flow of information.* [4] VERB If someone's hair or clothing **flows**, it hangs freely and loosely; LITERARY.

flower /ˈflaʊə/ **flowers, flowering, flowered.** [1] N-C A **flower** is the brightly coloured part of a plant which grows at the end of a stem. *...a bunch of flowers.* [2] VERB & PHRASE When a plant **flowers**, or when it is **in flower**, its flowers have appeared and opened. [3] VERB When something **flowers**, it gets stronger and more successful. *Their relationship flowered.* ◆**flowering** N-U *...the flowering of new thinking.*

'flower ˌbed, flower beds. N-C A **flower bed** is an area of earth in which you grow plants.

flown /fləʊn/. **Flown** is the past participle of **fly**.

flu /fluː/. N-U **Flu** is an illness caused by a virus. The symptoms are like those of a bad cold but more serious. *He had come down with the flu.*

fluctuate /ˈflʌktjʊeɪt/ **fluctuates, fluctuating, fluctuated.** VERB If something **fluctuates**, it changes a lot in an irregular way. *Body temperature can fluctuate if you are ill.* ◆**fluctuation, fluctuations** N-VAR *Don't worry about tiny fluctuations in your weight.*

fluent /ˈfluːənt/. [1] ADJ Someone who is **fluent** in a particular language can speak it easily and correctly. You can also say that someone speaks **fluent** French, Chinese, or other language. ◆**fluently** ADV *He spoke three languages fluently.* ◆**fluency** N-U *To work as a translator, you need fluency in at least one foreign language.* [2] ADJ If your speech, reading, or writing is **fluent**, you speak, read, or write easily, with no hesitation or mistakes. ◆**fluently** ADV *Alex didn't read fluently till he was nearly seven.*

fluff /flʌf/ **fluffs, fluffing, fluffed.** [1] N-U **Fluff** is the small masses of soft light thread that you find on clothes or in dusty corners of a room. *...some bits of fluff on the sleeve of his sweater.* [2] VERB & PHR-VERB If you **fluff** something, or if you **fluff** it **up**, you get a lot of air into it, for example by shaking or brushing it, in order to make it seem larger and lighter. *I resent you fluffing the pillows.*

fluffy /ˈflʌfi/. ADJ Something such as a towel or a toy animal that is **fluffy** is very soft and woolly.

fluid /ˈfluːɪd/ **fluids.** [1] N-VAR A **fluid** is a liquid; FORMAL. *Make sure that you drink plenty of fluids.* [2] ADJ **Fluid** movements, lines, or designs are smooth and graceful. ◆**fluidity** /fluːˈɪdɪti/ N-U *...an exquisite fluidity of movement.* [3] ADJ A situation that is **fluid** is likely to change often.

fluke /fluːk/ **flukes.** N-C If you say that something good is a **fluke**, you mean that it happened accidentally rather than by being planned or arranged; INFORMAL. *The discovery was something of a fluke.*

flung /flʌŋ/. **Flung** is the past tense and past participle of **fling**.

fluorescent /flʊəˈresənt/. [1] ADJ A **fluorescent** surface or colour has a very bright appearance when light is directed onto it. *...a piece of fluorescent tape.* [2] ADJ A **fluorescent** light shines with a very hard bright light and is usually in the form of a long strip.

flurry /ˈflʌri, AM ˈflɜːri/ **flurries.** [1] N-C A **flurry** of activity or speech is a short, energetic amount of it. *...a flurry of diplomatic activity aimed at ending the war.* [2] N-C A **flurry** of snow or wind is a small amount of it that moves suddenly.

flush /flʌʃ/ **flushes, flushing, flushed.** [1] VERB & N-C If you **flush**, or if there is a **flush** on your cheeks, your face goes red because you are embarrassed or hot. *There was a slight flush on his cheeks.* ◆**flushed** ADJ *Her face was flushed with anger.* [2] VERB & N-C When you **flush** a toilet, or when it **flushes**, you press a handle and water flows into the toilet bowl, cleaning it. This action is called a **flush**. [3] VERB If you **flush** people or animals out of a place, you force them to come out. *...operations to flush out anti-government rebels.* [4] ADJ AFTER LINK-V If something is **flush** with a surface, it is level with it and does not stick up.

fluster 238

Make sure the tile is flush with the surrounding tiles.

fluster /ˈflʌstə/ **flusters, flustering, flustered.** VERB If you **fluster** someone, you make them feel nervous and confused by rushing or interrupting them. *She was a very calm person. Nothing could fluster her.* ♦ **flustered** ADJ *She was so flustered that she forgot her reply.*

flute /fluːt/ **flutes.** N-C A **flute** is a musical wind instrument consisting of a long tube with holes in it. You play it by blowing over a hole at one end while holding it sideways.

flutter /ˈflʌtə/ **flutters, fluttering, fluttered.** **1** VERB If something light **flutters,** or if you **flutter** it, it moves through the air with small quick movements. *Her chiffon skirt was fluttering in the night breeze.* **2** VERB If your heart or stomach **flutters,** you experience a strong feeling of excitement or anxiety.

flux /flʌks/. N-U If something is in a state of **flux,** it is changing constantly. *...a period of economic flux.*

fly /flaɪ/ **flies, flying, flew, flown.** **1** N-C A **fly** is a small insect with two wings. **2** VERB When something such as a bird, insect, or aircraft **flies,** it moves through the air. *The planes flew through the clouds... The bird flew away.* ♦ **flying** ADJ BEFORE N *...species of flying insects.* **3** VERB If you **fly** somewhere, you travel there in an aircraft. If you **fly** something or someone somewhere, you send them there in an aircraft. *It may be possible to fly the women and children out on Thursday.* **4** VERB When a pilot **flies** an aircraft, he or she controls its movement. *He flew a small plane to Cuba. ...his inspiration to fly.* ♦ **flyer, flyers** N-C *...a highly experienced flyer.* **5** VERB If something **flies** or is **flying,** it moves about freely and loosely. *His long, uncovered hair flew back in the wind... A red and black flag was flying from the balcony.* **6** VERB If you say that someone or something **flies** in a particular direction, you are emphasizing that they move there with a lot of speed or force. *She flew to their bedsides when they were ill... The blow sent the young man flying.* **7** N-C The front opening on a pair of trousers is referred to as the **fly** or the **flies.** **8** PHRASE If you get **off to a flying start,** you start something very well, for example a race or a new job.

▶ **fly into.** PHR-VERB If you **fly into** a rage or a panic, you suddenly become very angry or anxious and show this in your behaviour. *Losing a game would cause him to fly into a rage.*

flyer /ˈflaɪə/ **flyers.** N-C A **flyer** is a small printed notice which is used to advertise a particular company or event.

foal /fəʊl/ **foals.** N-C A **foal** is a very young horse.

foam /fəʊm/ **foams, foaming, foamed.** **1** N-U **Foam** consists of a mass of small bubbles that are formed when air and a liquid are mixed together. *The water curved round the rocks in great bursts of foam.* **2** VERB If a liquid **foams,** it is full of small bubbles and keeps moving slightly. **3** N-U **Foam** or **foam rubber** is soft rubber full of small holes which is used, for example, to make mattresses and cushions.

focal point /ˈfəʊkəl pɔɪnt/ **focal points.** N-C The **focal point** of something is the thing that people concentrate on or pay most attention to.

focus /ˈfəʊkəs/ **focuses, focusing, focused** (or **focusses, focussing, focussed**). **1** VERB If you **focus** on a particular topic, or if your attention **is focused** on it, you concentrate on it and deal with it. *Today he was able to focus his message exclusively on the economy.* **2** The **focus** of something is the main topic or main thing that it is concerned with. *The new system is the focus of controversy.* **3** N-C Your **focus** on something is the special attention that you pay it. *IBM has also shifted its focus from mainframes to personal computers.* **4** VERB If you **focus** your eyes, or if your eyes **focus,** you adjust so that you can clearly see the thing that you want to look at. If you **focus** a camera, telescope, or other instrument, you adjust it so that you can see clearly through it. *His eyes slowly began to focus on what looked like a small dark ball.* **5** PHRASE If an image or a camera, telescope, or other instrument is **in focus,** the edges of what you see are clear and sharp. If it is **out of focus,** the edges of what you see are blurred. **6** VERB If you **focus** rays of light on a particular point, you pass them through a lens or reflect them from a mirror so that they meet at that point.

fodder /ˈfɒdə/. N-U **Fodder** is food that is given to animals such as cows or horses.

foe /fəʊ/ **foes.** N-C Someone's **foe** is their enemy; LITERARY.

foetus (or **fetus**) /ˈfiːtəs/ **foetuses.** N-C A **foetus** is an unborn animal or human being in its later stages of development.

fog /fɒg/ **fogs.** N-VAR When there is **fog,** there are tiny drops of water in the air which form a thick cloud and make it difficult to see things. *The crash happened in thick fog... Halfway down the river we ran into a bank of fog.*

foggy /ˈfɒgi/ **foggier, foggiest.** ADJ When it is **foggy,** there is fog.

foil /fɔɪl/ **foils, foiling, foiled.** **1** N-U **Foil** is metal that is as thin as paper. It is used to wrap food in. **2** VERB If you **foil** someone's plan or attempt at something, you prevent it from being successful; JOURNALISM. *He foiled an armed robbery.* **3** N-C If you say that one thing or person is a **foil** for another, you think that they contrast with each other and go well together. *A cold beer is the perfect foil for a curry.*

fold /fəʊld/ **folds, folding, folded.** **1** VERB & PHR-VERB If you **fold** a piece of paper or cloth, or if you **fold** it **up,** you bend it so that one part covers another part. *He folded the paper carefully... Fold the omelette in half.* **2** N-C A **fold** in a piece of paper or cloth is a bend that you make in it when you put one part of it over another part and press the edge. **3** N-C The **folds** in a piece of cloth are the curved shapes which are formed when it is not hanging or lying flat. **4** VERB & PHR-VERB If a piece of furniture or equipment **folds,** or if you **fold** it **up,** you make it smaller or flatter by bending or closing parts of it. *This portable seat folds flat for easy storage... Fold the ironing board up so that it is flat. ...a folding beach chair.* **5** VERB If you **fold**

your arms or hands, you bring them together and cross them or link them. [6] VERB If a business or organization **folds**, it is unsuccessful and has to close.

folder /ˈfəʊldə/ **folders.** N-C A **folder** is a thin piece of cardboard in which you can keep loose papers.

foliage /ˈfəʊliɪdʒ/. N-U The **foliage** of a plant consists of its leaves.

folk /fəʊk/ **folks.** [1] N-PL & N-VOC You can refer to people as **folk** or **folks**. ...*country folk*... *It's a question of money, folks.* [2] N-PL You can refer to your close family, especially your mother and father, as your **folks**; INFORMAL. *I've been avoiding my folks lately.* [3] ADJ BEFORE N **Folk** art and customs are traditional or typical of a particular community or nation. ...*Irish folk music.*

folklore /ˈfəʊklɔː/. N-U **Folklore** consists of the traditional stories, customs, and habits of a particular community or nation. *In Chinese folklore the bat is an emblem of good fortune.*

follow /ˈfɒləʊ/ **follows, following, followed.** [1] VERB If you **follow** someone who is going somewhere, you move along behind them. *We followed him up the steps... They took him into a small room and I followed.* [2] VERB If you **follow** someone to a place, you go to join them there at a later time. *He followed Janice to New York.* [3] VERB To **follow** an event, activity, or period of time means to happen or come after it, at a later time. ...*the days following Daddy's death... He was arrested in the confusion which followed.* [4] VERB & PHR-VERB If you **follow** one thing **with** another, or if you **follow** it **up with** another, you do or say the second thing after you have done or said the first thing. *Warm up first, then follow this with a series of simple stretching exercises.* [5] PHRASE You use **followed by** to say what comes after something else in a list or ordered set of things. *Potatoes are still the most popular food, followed by white bread.* [6] VERB If it **follows** that a particular thing is the case, that thing is a logical result of something else being true or being the case. *Just because a bird does not breed one year, it does not follow that it will fail the next.* [7] PHRASE You use **as follows** to introduce something such as a list, description, or explanation. *The winners are as follows: E. Walker; R. Foster; R. Gates.* [8] VERB If you **follow** a path or route, you go somewhere using the path or route to direct you. [9] VERB If you **follow** advice or instructions, you act or do something in the way that it indicates. [10] VERB If you **follow** something, you understand it. *Do you follow the plot so far?* [11] VERB If you **follow** something, you take an interest in it. *Do you follow the football at all?*
▸ **follow through** PHR-VERB If you **follow through** an action or plan, you continue doing or thinking about it until it is completed.

follower /ˈfɒləʊə/ **followers.** N-C The **followers** of a person or belief are the people who support the person or accept the belief.

following /ˈfɒləʊɪŋ/. [1] PREP **Following** a particular event means after that event. ...*the centuries following Christ's death.* [2] ADJ The fol-

lowing day, week, or year is the day, week, or year after the one you have just mentioned. *We went to dinner the following Monday evening.* [3] ADJ & PRON You use **the following** to refer to something that you are about to mention. *The method of helping such patients is explained in the following chapters... Add small pinches of any of the following: paprika, nutmeg, dried herbs.* [4] N-SING If you have a **following**, a group of people support or admire your beliefs or actions. *Australian rugby league enjoys a huge following in New Zealand.*

follow-up, follow-ups. N-VAR A **follow-up** is something that is done as a continuation or second part of something done previously. *Patients are asked to return for a one-day follow-up workshop.*

folly /ˈfɒli/ **follies.** N-VAR If you say that an action or way of behaving is **folly** or is a **folly**, you mean that it is foolish. ...*the follies of war.*

fond /fɒnd/ **fonder, fondest.** [1] ADJ AFTER LINK-V If you are **fond of** someone or something, you like that person or thing. *I am very fond of Michael.* ◆ **fondness** N-U *I've always had a fondness for jewels.* [2] ADJ BEFORE N You use **fond** to describe people or their behaviour when they show affection. *He gave him a fond smile.* ◆ **fondly** ADV *Their eyes meet fondly across the table.* [3] ADJ BEFORE N If you have **fond** memories of someone or something, you remember them with pleasure. ◆ **fondly** ADV *I remembered it fondly.*

food /fuːd/ **foods.** [1] N-VAR **Food** is what people and animals eat. *Enjoy your food.* ...*frozen foods.* [2] PHRASE If you give someone **food for thought**, you make them think carefully about something. *Lord Fraser's speech offers much food for thought.*

foodstuff /ˈfuːdstʌf/ **foodstuffs.** N-C **Foodstuffs** are substances which people eat. ...*basic foodstuffs such as sugar, cooking oil and cheese.*

fool /fuːl/ **fools, fooling, fooled.** [1] N-C If you call someone a **fool**, you are indicating that you think they are not sensible and show a lack of good judgement. *'You fool!' she shouted... He'd been a fool to get involved with her!* [2] PHRASE If you **make a fool of** someone, you make people think they are silly. *He was drinking and making a fool of himself.* [3] VERB If someone **fools** you, they deceive or trick you. *They tried to fool you into coming after us.*
▸ **fool about** or **fool around.** PHR-VERB If you **fool about**, or if you **fool around**, you behave in a playful and silly way.

foolish /ˈfuːlɪʃ/. ADJ If you say that someone's behaviour is **foolish**, you mean that it is not sensible and shows a lack of good judgement. *It would be foolish to raise hopes unnecessarily.* ◆ **foolishly** ADV *He admitted that he had acted foolishly.* ◆ **foolishness** N-U *They don't accept any foolishness.*

foot /fʊt/ **feet.** [1] N-C & PHRASE Your **feet** are the parts of your body that are at the ends of your legs and that you stand on. If you are **on your feet**, you are standing up. If you rise **to your feet**, you stand up. *Everyone was on their feet applauding.* [2] N-SING The **foot** of something is the part that is farthest from its top. *David*

called to the children from the foot of the stairs.
3 N-C A **foot** is a unit of length, equal to 12 inches or approximately 30.48 centimetres. The plural can be either 'foot' or 'feet'. *...a cell 10 foot long, 6 foot wide and 10 foot high.*

PHRASES ● If you say that someone or something is **on** their **feet** again after a difficult period, you mean that they have recovered and are back to normal. ● If you go somewhere **on foot**, you walk, rather than use any form of transport. ● If someone **puts** their **foot down**, they use their authority in order to stop something happening. *He had planned to go skiing on his own in March but his wife had decided to put her foot down.* ● If you **put** your **feet up**, you relax or have a rest, especially by sitting or lying with your feet supported off the ground. ● To **set foot** in a place means to go there. *I left that place and never set foot in Texas again.* ● If someone has to **stand on** their **own two feet**, they have to manage without help from other people.

footage /ˈfʊtɪdʒ/. N-U **Footage** of a particular event is a film, or the part of a film, showing this event. *...exclusive footage from this summer's festivals.*

football /ˈfʊtbɔːl/ **footballs**. **1** N-U In British English, **football** is a game played by two teams of eleven players who try to score by kicking or heading a ball into their opponent's goal. The American word is **soccer**. *Several boys were still playing football.* **2** N-U In American English, **football** is a game played by two teams of eleven players who try to score by taking the ball into their opponent's end. The British term is **American football**. **3** N-C A **football** is a ball that is used for playing football.

footballer /ˈfʊtbɔːlə/ **footballers**. N-C In British English, a **footballer** is a person who plays football. The American term is 'soccer player'.

foothills /ˈfʊthɪlz/. N-PL The **foothills** of a mountain or a range of mountains are the lower hills or mountains around its base. *Pasadena lies in the foothills of the San Gabriel mountains.*

foothold /ˈfʊthəʊld/ **footholds**. **1** N-C A **foothold** is a strong position from which further advances or progress may be made. *Companies must establish a firm foothold in Europe.* **2** N-C A **foothold** is a ledge or hollow where you can safely put your foot when climbing.

footing /ˈfʊtɪŋ/. **1** N-U You use **footing** to describe the basis on which something is done or exists. *...research that is aimed at placing training on a more scientific footing.* **2** N-U You use **footing** to refer to your position and how securely your feet are placed on the ground. *He lost his footing and slid into the water.*

footnote /ˈfʊtnəʊt/ **footnotes**. N-C A **footnote** is a note at the bottom of a page which gives more information about something on the page.

footpath /ˈfʊtpɑːθ, -pæθ/ **footpaths**. N-C A **footpath** is a path for people to walk on.

footprint /ˈfʊtprɪnt/ **footprints**. N-C A **footprint** is the mark of a person's or animal's foot left on a surface.

footstep /ˈfʊtstep/ **footsteps**. **1** N-C A **footstep** is the sound made by someone's feet touching the ground when they are walking or running. *They heard footsteps in the main room.* **2** PHRASE If you **follow in** someone's **footsteps**, you do the same things as they did earlier. *He followed in the footsteps of his father, a former professional boxer.*

footwear /ˈfʊtweə/. N-U **Footwear** refers to things that people wear on their feet, for example shoes, boots, and sandals.

for /fə, STRONG fɔː/. **1** PREP If something is **for** someone, they are intended to have it or benefit from it. *I have some free advice for you. ...a table for two.* **2** PREP If you work **for** someone, you are employed by them. *...a buyer for one of the largest chain stores.* **3** PREP & ADV If you are **for** something, you are in favour of it. *Are you for or against public transport?.* **4** PHRASE If you are **all for** something, you are very much in favour of it. *I was all for it, but Wolfe said no.* **5** PREP If you are **for** something, or if something is **for** you, you like it or intend to do it or have it. *Right, who's for a toasted sandwich then?... I'm afraid German beer isn't for me.* **6** PREP You use **for** after words such as 'time', 'space', 'money', or 'energy' when you say how much there is or whether there is enough of it in order to be able to do or use a particular thing. *Many new trains have space for wheelchair users... It would take three to six hours for a round trip.* **7** PREP You use **for** when you are describing the purpose of something, the reason for something, or the cause of something. *...a room for rent. ...a comfortable chair, suitable for use in the living room. ...a speech in parliament explaining his reasons for going.* **8** PREP A word or term **for** something is a way of referring to it. *The technical term for sunburn is erythema.* **9** PREP You use **for** to say how long something lasts or continues. *For a few minutes she sat on her bed... They talked for a bit.* **10** PHRASE You use an expression such as **for the first time** when you are talking about how often something has happened. *Mr Lukman is visiting the United States for the second time this year.* **11** PREP You use **for** to say how far something extends. *We drove on for a few miles.* **12** PREP You use **for** with 'every' when you state the second part of a ratio. *There had been one divorce for every 100 marriages before the war.* **13** PREP You use **for** when you are talking about the cost of something. *The Martins sold their house for about 1.4 million pounds.* **14** PREP You use **for** when you are mentioning a person or thing that you have feelings about. *He began to feel sympathy for this slightly mysterious man.* **15** PREP You use **for** when you are saying how something affects someone. *It would be excellent experience for him to travel a little.* **16** PREP You use **for** when you say that an aspect of something or someone is surprising in relation to other aspects of them. *He was tall for an eight-year-old.* **17** PREP If something is planned **for** a particular time or occasion, it is planned to happen then. *The party was scheduled for 7:00... I'll be home for Christmas.* **18** PREP If you leave **for** a place, or if you take a train, plane, or boat **for** a place, you are going there. [19] **as for**: see **as**. ● **but for**: see **but**. ● **for all**: see **all**.

forage /'fɒrɪdʒ, AM 'fɔːr-/ **forages, foraging, foraged**. [1] VERB To **forage** for something such as food means to search for it. *We disturbed a wild boar that had been foraging by the roadside.* [2] N-U **Forage** is crops that are grown as food for cattle and horses.

foray /'fɒreɪ, AM 'fɔːreɪ/ **forays**. [1] N-C If you make a **foray** into a new or unfamiliar type of activity, you start to become involved in it. *...her first forays into politics.* [2] N-C If a group of soldiers make a **foray** into an area, they make a quick attack there, usually in order to steal supplies.

forbid /fə'bɪd/ **forbids, forbidding, forbade** /fə'bæd, -'beɪd/, **forbidden**. [1] VERB If you **forbid** someone to do something, or if you **forbid** an activity, you order that it must not be done. *They'll forbid you to marry... Brazil's constitution forbids the military use of nuclear energy.* [2] VERB If something **forbids** an event or course of action, it makes it impossible. *His own pride forbids him to ask Arthur's help.*

forbidden /fə'bɪdən/. ADJ If something is **forbidden**, you are not allowed to do it or have it. *Smoking was forbidden... It is forbidden to drive faster than 20mph.*

force /fɔːs/ **forces, forcing, forced**. [1] VERB If something or someone **forces** you to do something, they make you do it, even though you do not want to. *A back injury forced her to withdraw from the competition... I cannot force you in this. You must decide... He tried to force her into a car... To force this agreement on the nation is wrong.* [2] VERB If you **force** something, you use a lot of strength to move it. *He forced the key clumsily into the ignition... Police forced the door of the flat and arrested Mr Roberts.* [3] N-U **Force** is power or strength. *...the guerrillas' efforts to seize power by force... the force of the explosion shattered the windows.* [4] N-C Someone or something that is a **force** in a situation has a strong influence on it. *The FLN is still a big political force in the country.* [5] VERB If you **force** a smile or a laugh, you manage to smile or laugh even though you do not want to. ◆**forced** ADJ *He pushed her away with a forced smile.* [6] N-C A **force** in physics is the pulling or pushing effect that one thing has on another. *...the earth's gravitational force.* [7] N-C **Forces** are groups of soldiers or military vehicles that are organized for a particular purpose. *...the deployment of American forces in the region.*

PHRASES ● A law or system that is **in force** exists or is being used. *Martial law is in force.* ● If you **join forces** with someone, you work together to achieve a common aim or purpose. *African nations joined forces to combat cholera.* ● to **force someone's hand**: see **hand**.

forceful /'fɔːsful/. [1] ADJ Someone who is **forceful** expresses their opinions in a strong and confident way. *She was a forceful intellectual, unafraid to speak her mind.* ◆**forcefully** ADV *He argued forcefully and convincingly.* [2] ADJ Something that is **forceful** causes you to think or feel something very strongly. *The re-*

cent bomb attack is a forceful reminder that we must continue to strive for peace.

forcible /'fɔːsɪbəl/. ADJ **Forcible** actions involve physical force or violence. *...the forcible resettlement of villagers.* ◆**forcibly** ADV *Student leaders were forcibly removed from the university.*

fore /fɔː/. [1] PHRASE When something or someone comes **to the fore**, they suddenly become important or popular. *A number of low-budget independent films brought new directors and actors to the fore.* [2] ADJ BEFORE N & ADV **Fore** is used to refer to parts at the front of a ship or aircraft. *Our yacht was well equipped with two double cabins fore and aft.*

forearm /'fɔːrɑːm/ **forearms**. N-C Your **forearms** are the parts of your arms between your elbows and your wrists.

forecast /'fɔːkɑːst, -kæst/ **forecasts, forecasting, forecasted** or **forecast**. VERB & N-C If you **forecast** future events, you say what you think is going to happen. A **forecast** is a prediction of future events. *He forecasts that average salary increases will remain around 4 per cent... The forecast is for changeable weather.* ◆**forecaster, forecasters** N-C *...our senior weather forecaster.*

forefinger /'fɔːfɪŋgə/ **forefingers**. N-C Your **forefinger** is the finger next to your thumb.

forefront /'fɔːfrʌnt/. N-SING If you are at the **forefront** of a campaign or other activity, you have a leading and influential position in it. *They have been at the forefront of the campaign for political change.*

forego (or **forgo**) /fɔː'gəu/ **foregoes, foregoing, forewent, foregone**. VERB If you **forego** something, you decide not to have it or do it, although you would like to; FORMAL. *Keen skiers are happy to forego a summer holiday to go skiing.*

foreground /'fɔːgraund/. [1] N-SING The **foreground** of a picture is the part that seems nearest to you. *...the bowler-hatted figure in the foreground.* [2] N-SING If something or someone is in the **foreground**, they receive a lot of attention. *...issues that were placed in the foreground.*

forehead /'fɒrɪd, 'fɔːhed/ **foreheads**. N-C Your **forehead** is the flat area at the front of your head above your eyebrows and below where your hair grows.

foreign /'fɒrɪn, AM 'fɔːr-/. [1] ADJ Something that is **foreign** comes from or relates to a country that is not your own. *She was on her first foreign holiday without her parents. ...a foreign language.* [2] ADJ BEFORE N In politics and journalism, **foreign** is used to describe people and activities relating to countries that are not the country of the person or government concerned. *...the German foreign minister. ...the effects of US foreign policy.* [3] ADJ A **foreign** body is an object that has got into something, usually by accident, and should not be there; FORMAL. *...a foreign body in the eye.* [4] ADJ Something that is **foreign** to a particular person or thing is not typical of them or is unknown to them. *The whole concept of being gentle with anyone is foreign to most men.*

foreigner /'fɒrɪnə, AM 'fɔːr-/ **foreigners.** N-C A **foreigner** is someone who belongs to a country that is not your own. • See note at **stranger**.

foreman /'fɔːmən/ **foremen.** N-C A **foreman** is a person who is in charge of a group of workers.

foremost /'fɔːməʊst/ [1] ADJ The **foremost** thing or person in a group is the most important or best. ...one of the world's foremost scholars of ancient Indian culture. [2] PHRASE You use **first and foremost** to emphasize the most important quality of something or someone. This book aims first and foremost to improve your painting skills.

forename /'fɔːneɪm/ **forenames.** N-C Your **forenames** are your first names, as opposed to your surname; FORMAL.

forensic /fə'rensɪk/ [1] ADJ BEFORE N When a **forensic** analysis is done, objects are examined scientifically in order to discover information about a crime. Forensic experts searched the area for clues. [2] ADJ BEFORE N **Forensic** means relating to the legal profession. ...a senior forensic psychiatrist.

forerunner /'fɔːrʌnə/ **forerunners.** N-C The **forerunner** of something is a similar thing that existed before it and influenced its development. ...a machine which, in some respects, was the forerunner of the modern helicopter.

foresee /fɔː'siː/ **foresees, foreseeing, foresaw, foreseen.** VERB If you **foresee** something, you expect and believe that it will happen. He did not foresee any problems. ...a dangerous situation which could have been foreseen.

foreseeable /fɔː'siːəbəl/ PHRASE When you talk about **the foreseeable future**, you are referring to the period of time in the future during which it is possible to say what will happen. She will not be seeking a divorce in the foreseeable future.

foresight /'fɔːsaɪt/ N-U **Foresight** is the ability to see what might happen in the future and to take appropriate action; used showing approval. Thankfully they had the foresight to invest in new technology.

forest /'fɒrɪst, AM 'fɔːr-/ N-VAR A **forest** is a large area where trees grow close together. ...25 million hectares of forest.

forestall /fɔː'stɔːl/ **forestalls, forestalling, forestalled.** VERB If you **forestall** someone, you realize what they are likely to do and prevent them from doing it. O'Leary made to open the door, but Bunbury forestalled him.

forestry /'fɒrɪstri, AM 'fɔːr-/ N-U **Forestry** is the science or skill of growing trees in forests.

forever /fə'revə/; also spelled **for ever** for meanings 1 and 2. [1] ADV Something that will happen or continue **forever** will always happen or continue. It was great fun but we knew it wouldn't go on for ever... I am forever grateful to the friend who helped us. [2] ADV If something has gone or changed **forever**, it has gone and will never reappear. The old social order was gone forever. [3] ADV If you say that someone is **forever** doing something, you are emphasizing that they do it very often. He was forever attempting to arrange deals.

forewent. Forewent is the past tense of **forego**.

forfeit /'fɔːfɪt/ **forfeits, forfeiting, forfeited.** [1] VERB If you **forfeit** a right, privilege, or possession, you have to give it up because you have done something wrong. He argues that murderers forfeit their own right to life. [2] N-C A **forfeit** is something that you have to give up because you have done something wrong. That is the forfeit he must pay.

forgave /fə'geɪv/. **Forgave** is the past tense of **forgive**.

forge /fɔːdʒ/ **forges, forging, forged.** [1] VERB If someone **forges** banknotes, documents, or paintings, they make false copies of them in order to deceive people. Taylor had forged her signature. ◆**forger, forgers** N-C ...the most prolific art forger in the country. [2] VERB If you **forge** an alliance or relationship, you succeed in creating it. The programme aims to forge links between higher education and small businesses. [3] N-C A **forge** is a place where a blacksmith makes metal things such as horseshoes.

▶ **forge ahead.** PHR-VERB If you **forge ahead** with something, you make a lot of progress with it. George began to forge ahead with his studies.

forgery /'fɔːdʒəri/ **forgeries.** [1] N-U **Forgery** is the crime of forging banknotes, documents, or paintings. [2] N-C You can refer to a forged banknote, document, or painting as a **forgery**.

forget /fə'get/ **forgets, forgetting, forgot, forgotten.** [1] VERB If you **forget** something, or if you **forget** how to do something, you cannot think of it or think of how to do it, although you knew it in the past. I forgot how to speak English, I could only speak Spanish... She forgot where she left the car. [2] VERB If you **forget** to do something, you do not remember to do it. She forgot to lock her door one day and two men got in... Don't forget that all dogs need a supply of fresh water. [3] VERB If you **forget** something that you had intended to bring with you, you do not remember to bring it. Once when we were going to Paris, I forgot my passport. [4] VERB If you **forget** something or someone, you deliberately do not think about them any more. I can't forget what happened... I found it very easy to forget about Sam. [5] VERB If someone **forgets** himself or **herself**, he or she behaves in an uncontrolled or unacceptable way.

forgetful /fə'getfʊl/. ADJ Someone who is **forgetful** often forgets things. ◆**forgetfulness** N-U Her forgetfulness is due to advancing age.

forgive /fə'gɪv/ **forgives, forgiving, forgave, forgiven.** VERB If you **forgive** someone who has done something wrong, you stop being angry with them. She'd find a way to forgive him for the theft of the money. ◆**forgiving** ADJ I don't think people are in a very forgiving mood. ◆**forgiveness** N-U He would fall to his knees sobbing and begging for forgiveness.

forgo /fɔː'gəʊ/. See **forego**.

forgot /fə'gɒt/. **Forgot** is the past tense of **forget**.

forgotten /fə'gɒtən/. **Forgotten** is the past participle of **forget**.

fork /fɔːk/ **forks, forking, forked.** [1] N-C A **fork** is an implement that you use when you are eating food. It consists of three or four long thin points on the end of a handle. **2** N-C A garden **fork** is a tool that you use to dig your garden. It consists of three or four long thin points attached to a long handle. **3** N-C & VERB If there is a **fork** in something such as a road or a river, or if it **forks**, it divides into two parts in the shape of a 'Y'. *You should take the right fork... The path dipped down to a sort of cove, and then it forked in two directions.*

▶ **fork out.** PHR-VERB If you **fork out** for something, you pay for it; INFORMAL. *Britons fork out more than a billion pounds a year on toys.*

forlorn /fɔːˈlɔːn/. **1** ADJ If you are **forlorn**, you are lonely and unhappy. ◆ **forlornly** ADV *...waiting forlornly in the rain.* **2** ADJ A **forlorn** hope or attempt has no chance of success. *...the forlorn hope of finding a better life in cities.*

form 1 type and shape

form /fɔːm/ **forms**. **1** N-C A **form** of something is a type or kind of it. *He contracted a rare form of cancer... I am against hunting in any form.* **2** PHRASE If someone's behaviour is **true to form**, it is typical of them. *True to form, she kept her guests waiting for more than 90 minutes.* **3** N-C The **form** of something is its shape. *...the form of the body.* **4** N-C You can refer to something that you can see as a **form**, especially if you cannot see it clearly. *She thought she'd never been so glad to see his bulky form.*

form 2 making things

form /fɔːm/ **forms, forming, formed**. **1** VERB When a particular shape **forms** or **is formed**, people or things move or are arranged so that this shape is made. *They formed a circle and sang... The General gave orders for the cadets to form into lines.* **2** VERB If something is arranged so that it has a particular shape or function, you can say that it **forms** something with that shape or function. *All the buildings have names and form a half circle.* **3** VERB If something consists of particular things or people, you can say that they **form** that thing. *Cereals form the staple diet.* **4** VERB If you **form** an organization, group, or company, you start it. ◆ **formation** N-U *...the formation of a new government.* **5** VERB When something **forms**, it begins to exist. *Huge ice sheets were formed.*

form 3 document

form /fɔːm/ **forms**. N-C A **form** is a piece of paper with questions on it. You write the answers on the same piece of paper. *You will be asked to fill in a form.*

form 4 someone's physical condition

form. N-U & PHRASE In sport, an athlete's **form** refers to their ability or success over a period of time. If they are **off form**, they are performing badly; if they are **on form**, they are performing well. *His form this season has been brilliant.*

formal /ˈfɔːməl/. **1** ADJ **Formal** speech or behaviour is correct and serious, rather than relaxed and friendly, and is used especially in official situations. *...a formal letter of apology.* ◆ **formally** ADV *'Good afternoon, Mr Benjamin,' Schumacher said formally.* ◆ **formality** /fɔːˈmælɪti/ N-U *...the stifled formality of the office.* **2** ADJ BEFORE N A **formal** statement, action, or event is an official one. *No formal an-*

nouncement had been made. *...a formal dinner.* ◆ **formally** ADV *They are now formally separated.* **3** ADJ BEFORE N **Formal** education or training is given in a school or college. *Although his formal education stopped after primary school, he was an avid reader.*

formality /fɔːˈmælɪti/ **formalities**. **1** N-C **Formalities** are formal actions that are carried out on particular occasions. *...immigration and customs formalities.* **2** See also **formal**.

formalize (BR also **formalise**) /ˈfɔːməlaɪz/ **formalizes, formalizing, formalized**. VERB If you **formalize** a plan or arrangement, you make it official. *The arrangement, he added, need not be formalized in court.*

format /ˈfɔːmæt/ **formats, formatting, formatted**. **1** N-C The **format** of something is the way it is arranged and presented. *I had met with him to explain the format of the programme.* **2** VERB To **format** a computer disk means to run a program so that the disk can be written on.

formation /fɔːˈmeɪʃən/ **formations**. **1** N-U The **formation** of something is its start or creation. *The name was changed two years after the club's formation. ...the formation of an interim government.* **2** N-C A rock or cloud **formation** is rock or clouds of a particular shape. **3** N-U If things are in **formation**, they are arranged in a particular pattern. *He was flying in formation with seven other jets.*

formative /ˈfɔːmətɪv/. ADJ A **formative** period in your life or experience is one that has an important influence on your character and attitudes. *She spent her formative years growing up in east London.*

former /ˈfɔːmə/. **1** ADJ BEFORE N **Former** is used to indicate what someone or something used to be, but no longer is. *...former President Richard Nixon. ...the former home of Sir Christopher Wren.* **2** ADJ BEFORE N **Former** is used to describe a situation or period of time which came before the present one. *He would want you to remember him as he was in former years.* **3** PRON From two people, things, or groups that have just been mentioned, you can refer to the first of them as **the former**. *If the family home and joint pension rights are of equal value, the wife may choose the former and the husband the latter.*

formerly /ˈfɔːməli/. ADV If something happened or was **formerly** true, it happened or was true in the past. *He had formerly been in the Navy.*

formidable /ˈfɔːmɪdəbəl, fəˈmɪd-/. ADJ If you describe something or someone as **formidable**, you mean that you feel frightened by them because they are very impressive or considerable. *We have a formidable task ahead of us.*

formula /ˈfɔːmjʊlə/ **formulas** or **formulae** /ˈfɔːmjʊliː/. **1** N-C A **formula** is a plan that is made as a way of dealing with a problem. *...this simple formula for a long and happy life.* **2** N-C A **formula** is a group of letters, numbers, or other symbols which represents a scientific or mathematical rule. *...a mathematical formula.* **3** N-C In science, the **formula** for a substance tells you what amounts of other substances are needed in order to make that substance. [4] N-U **Formula** is a powder which you mix with water to make artificial milk for babies.

formulate /ˈfɔːmjʊleɪt/ **formulates, formulating, formulated.** [1] VERB If you **formulate** a plan or proposal, you develop it, thinking about the details carefully. ◆ **formulation** N-U ...the process of policy formulation. [2] VERB If you **formulate** a thought or opinion, you express it in words.

forsake /fəˈseɪk/ **forsakes, forsaking, forsook** /fəˈsʊk/, **forsaken.** [1] VERB If someone **forsakes** you, they leave you when they should have stayed, or stop helping you or looking after you. ...children who've been forsaken by individual teachers. [2] VERB If you **forsake** something, you stop doing or having it; LITERARY. She forsook her notebook for new technology.

fort /fɔːt/ **forts.** N-C A **fort** is a strong building that is used as a military base.

forth /fɔːθ/ [1] ADV To go **forth** from a place means to leave it; LITERARY. Go forth into the desert. [2] ADV To bring something **forth** means to produce it or make it visible; LITERARY. ...ways to bring forth new ideas. [3] **and so forth:** see **so**. ● **back and forth:** see **back**.

forthcoming /ˌfɔːθˈkʌmɪŋ/ [1] ADJ BEFORE N A **forthcoming** event is going to happen soon. ...the forthcoming election. [2] ADJ AFTER LINK-V When something such as help or information is **forthcoming**, it is provided or made available. They promised that the money would be forthcoming. [3] ADJ If someone is **forthcoming**, they willingly give you information when you ask.

forthright /ˈfɔːθraɪt/ ADJ If you describe someone as **forthright**, you admire them because they say clearly and forcefully what they think and feel. ...forthright language.

fortieth /ˈfɔːtiəθ/ ORD The **fortieth** item in a series is the one that you count as number forty.

fortify /ˈfɔːtɪfaɪ/ **fortifies, fortifying, fortified.** [1] VERB To **fortify** a place means to make it stronger and less easy to attack, often by building a wall or ditch round it. ...British soldiers working to fortify an airbase. [2] VERB If food or drink **is fortified**, another substance is added to it to make it healthier or stronger. ...wine fortified with brandy.

fortnight /ˈfɔːtnaɪt/ **fortnights.** N-C A **fortnight** is a period of two weeks. I hope to be back in a fortnight.

fortress /ˈfɔːtrɪs/ **fortresses.** N-C A **fortress** is a castle or other strong, well protected building, which is difficult for enemies to enter.

fortunate /ˈfɔːtʃʊnɪt/ ADJ If someone or something is **fortunate**, they are lucky. He was extremely fortunate to survive. ◆ **fortunately** ADV Fortunately, the weather that winter was reasonably mild.

fortune /ˈfɔːtʃuːn/ **fortunes.** [1] N-U **Fortune** or good **fortune** is good luck. Ill **fortune** is bad luck. [2] N-PL The **fortunes** of someone or something are the extent to which they are doing well or being successful. The film follows the fortunes of two women. [3] N-C A **fortune** is a very large amount of money.

forty /ˈfɔːti/ **forties.** NUM **Forty** is the number 40. For examples of how numbers such as forty and eighty are used see **eighty**.

forum /ˈfɔːrəm/ **forums.** N-C A **forum** is a place, situation, or event in which people exchange ideas and discuss issues that are important to them. The organisation would provide a forum where problems could be discussed.

forward /ˈfɔːwəd/ **forwards, forwarding, forwarded. Forwards** is often used as an adverb instead of **forward** in senses 1 and 4. [1] ADV If you move or look **forward** or **forwards**, you move or look in a direction that is in front of you. She fell forwards on to her face... He continued to walk, didn't look at the car, kept his face forward. [2] ADV & ADJ BEFORE N **Forward** means in a position near the front of something such as a building or vehicle. The best seats are in the aisle and as far forward as possible. ...to allow more troops to move to forward positions. [3] ADV If something or someone is put **forward**, they are suggested or offered as suitable for a particular purpose. If someone comes **forward**, they present themselves as suitable for a particular purpose. Next month the Commission is to bring forward its first proposals... No witnesses have come forward. [4] ADV **Forward** and **forwards** are used to indicate that someone is making progress. They just couldn't see any way forward. [5] VERB If a letter or message is **forwarded**, it is sent to the place where they are, after having been sent to a different place earlier. [6] ADJ If you describe someone as **forward**, you mean they speak very confidently and openly, sometimes offending people or not showing them enough respect. ◆ **forwardness** N-U He shocked me with his forwardness. [7] **backwards and forwards:** see **backwards**.

fossil /ˈfɒsəl/ **fossils.** N-C A **fossil** is the hardened remains or impression of a prehistoric animal or plant inside a rock.

fossil 'fuel, fossil fuels. N-VAR **Fossil fuels** are fuels such as coal, oil, and natural gas.

foster /ˈfɒstə, AM ˈfɔːst-/ **fosters, fostering, fostered.** [1] ADJ BEFORE N **Foster** parents are people who officially take a child into their family for a period of time, without becoming the child's legal parents. The child is referred to as their **foster** child. [2] VERB If you **foster** a child, you take him or her into your family as a foster child. [3] VERB If you **foster** a feeling, activity, or idea, you help it to develop. ...a responsibility to foster global economic growth.

fought /fɔːt/ **Fought** is the past tense and past participle of **fight**.

foul /faʊl/ **fouler, foulest; fouls, fouling, fouled.** [1] ADJ If you describe something as **foul**, you mean it is dirty and smells or tastes unpleasant. [2] VERB If a place **is fouled** by someone or something, they make it dirty. Two oil-related accidents near Los Angeles have fouled the ocean. [3] ADJ **Foul** language is offensive and contains swear words or rude words. [4] ADJ If someone is in a **foul** temper or mood, they are very angry. [5] PHRASE If you **fall foul of** someone, you do something which gets you into trouble with them. [6] N-C In sports such as football, a **foul** is an action that is against the rules.

found /faʊnd/ founds, founding, founded. [1] **Found** is the past tense and past participle of **find**. [2] VERB When an organization, company, or city **is founded** by someone, they start it or create it. *He founded the Centre for Journalism Studies at University College Cardiff.* ◆ **foundation** N-SING *...the foundation of Kew Gardens.* ◆ **founder,** founders N-C *He was one of the founders of the university's medical faculty.*

foundation /faʊnˈdeɪʃən/ foundations. [1] N-C The **foundation** of something such as a belief or way of life is the idea or experience on which it is based. *This laid the foundations for later modern economic growth.* [2] N-PL The **foundations** of a building or other structure are the layer of bricks or concrete below the ground that it is built on. [3] N-C A **foundation** is an organization which provides money for a special purpose. *...the National Foundation for Educational Research.* [4] N-U If a story, idea, or argument has no **foundation,** there are no facts to prove that it is true. *The allegations were without foundation.*

founded /ˈfaʊndɪd/. ADJ AFTER LINK-V If something is **founded on** a particular thing, it is based on it. *The criticisms are founded on facts.*

founder /ˈfaʊndə/ founders, foundering, foundered. [1] VERB If something such as a plan or a project **founders,** it fails. [2] VERB If a ship **founders,** it fills with water and sinks.

founding /ˈfaʊndɪŋ/. N-SING & ADJ The **founding** of an organization, tradition, or club is the creation of it. You can also use **founding** to describe a person or thing relating to the founding of something. *I have been a member of The Wine Club since its founding in 1973. ...a founding member of the Communist Party.*

foundry /ˈfaʊndri/ foundries. N-C A **foundry** is a place where metal or glass is melted and made into particular objects.

fountain /ˈfaʊntɪn/ fountains. [1] N-C A **fountain** is an ornamental feature in a pool which consists of a jet of water that is forced up into the air by a pump. [2] N-C A **fountain** of a liquid is an amount of it which is sent up into the air and falls back.

four /fɔː/ fours. [1] NUM **Four** is the number 4. [2] PHRASE If you are **on all fours,** your knees, feet, and hands are on the ground. *She crawled on all fours over to the window.*

foursome /ˈfɔːsəm/ foursomes. N-C A **foursome** is a group of four people or things.

fourteen /ˌfɔːˈtiːn/. NUM **Fourteen** is the number 14.

fourteenth /ˌfɔːˈtiːnθ/. ORD The **fourteenth** item in a series is the one that you count as number fourteen.

fourth /fɔːθ/ fourths. [1] ORD The **fourth** item in a series is the one that you count as number four. [2] N-C In American English, a **fourth** is one of four equal parts of something. The British word is **quarter.**

fowl /faʊl/. N-C A **fowl** is a bird, especially a duck, goose, or chicken. The plural is **fowl** or **fowls.**

fox /fɒks/ foxes, foxing, foxed. [1] N-C A **fox** is a wild animal which looks like a dog and has reddish-brown fur and a thick tail. [2] VERB If you **are foxed** by something, you cannot understand it or solve it; BRITISH. *...a question which foxed one of these formidable experts.*

foyer /ˈfɔɪə, ˈfwaɪeɪ/ foyers. N-C The **foyer** is the large area where people meet or wait just inside the doors of a theatre, cinema, or hotel.

fraction /ˈfrækʃən/ fractions. [1] N-C A **fraction** is a tiny amount or proportion of something. *I opened my eyes just a fraction.* [2] N-C In arithmetic, a **fraction** is a part of a whole number. For example, $\frac{1}{2}$ and $\frac{1}{3}$ are fractions of 1.

fracture /ˈfræktʃə/ fractures, fracturing, fractured. [1] VERB If something such as a bone **fractures,** or if it **is fractured,** it cracks or breaks. *He suffered a fractured skull.* [2] N-C A **fracture** is a crack or break in something. *...a hip fracture.*

fragile /ˈfrædʒaɪl, AM -dʒəl/. [1] ADJ If you describe a situation as **fragile,** you mean that it is weak or uncertain, and unlikely to be able to resist strong pressure or attack. *...the fragile peace agreed this month.* ◆ **fragility** /frəˈdʒɪlɪti/ N-U *...the fragility of the environment.* [2] ADJ Something that is **fragile** is easily broken or damaged. *He leaned back in his fragile chair.* ◆ **fragility** N-U *...the fragility of their bones.* [3] ADJ Something that is **fragile** is very delicate in appearance. *...her fragile beauty.*

fragment, fragments, fragmenting, fragmented. [1] N-C A **fragment** of something is a small piece or part of it. *...glass fragments... She read everything, digesting every fragment of news.* [2] VERB /frægˈment/ If something **fragments,** or if another thing **fragments** it, it breaks or separates into small pieces. *By the first century BC, Buddhism was in danger of fragmenting into small sects.* ◆ **fragmentation** N-U *...the fragmentation of the Soviet Union.* ◆ **fragmented** ADJ *Europe had become infinitely more unstable and fragmented.*

fragrance /ˈfreɪɡrəns/ fragrances. N-VAR A **fragrance** is a pleasant or sweet smell.

fragrant /ˈfreɪɡrənt/. ADJ Something that is **fragrant** has a sweet or pleasant smell. *The air was fragrant with the smell of orange blossoms.*

frail /freɪl/ frailer, frailest. [1] ADJ Someone who is **frail** is not very strong or healthy. [2] ADJ Something that is **frail** is easily broken or damaged.

frame /freɪm/ frames, framing, framed. [1] N-C The **frame** of a picture or mirror is the part around its edges. *...a photograph of her mother in a silver frame.* [2] VERB If a picture or photograph **is framed,** it is put in a frame. [3] N-C A **frame** is a structure, for example of bars or posts, which gives an object its shape and strength. *We painted our table to match the window frame.* [4] N-C A **frame** of cinema film is one of the many separate photographs that it consists of. [5] N-C You can refer to someone's body as their **frame,** especially when you are describing its general shape. *...their bony frames.* [6] VERB If you **frame** something in a particular kind of language, you express it in that way. *Let me frame the* *question a little differently.* **7** VERB If someone **frames** an innocent person, they make other people think that person is guilty of a crime, by lying or inventing evidence; INFORMAL. *He had been framed by the police.*

,frame of 'mind. N-SING Your **frame of mind** is your mood or attitude at a particular time. *Clearly, Lewis was not in the right frame of mind to continue.*

framework /ˈfreɪmwɜːk/ **frameworks.** **1** N-C A **framework** is a set of rules, ideas, or beliefs which you use in order to decide what to do. *...topical issues within a Christian framework.* **2** N-C A **framework** is a structure that forms a support or frame for something. *...wooden shelves on a steel framework.*

franchise /ˈfræntʃaɪz/ **franchises.** **1** N-C If a large company or organization grants a **franchise** to a smaller company, the smaller company is allowed to sell the products of the larger company or participate in an activity controlled by the larger company. *...the franchise to build and operate the tunnel.* **2** N-SING In politics, **the franchise** is the right to vote in an election, especially one to elect a parliament.

frank /fræŋk/ **franker, frankest.** ADJ If someone is **frank**, they state things openly and honestly. *...a frank discussion.* ◆**frankly** ADV *You can talk frankly to me.* ◆**frankness** N-U *The reaction to his frankness was hostile.*

frankly /ˈfræŋkli/. ADV You use **frankly** when you are expressing an opinion or feeling to emphasize that you mean what you are saying. *Frankly, Thomas, this question of your loan is beginning to worry me.*

frantic /ˈfræntɪk/. ADJ If someone is **frantic**, they are behaving in a desperate, wild, and disorganized way, because they are frightened, worried, or in a hurry. *A bird had been locked in and was by now quite frantic.* ◆**frantically** ADV *We have been frantically trying to save her life.*

fraternity /frəˈtɜːnɪti/ **fraternities.** **1** N-U **Fraternity** is friendship between people who feel they are closely linked to each other. *Bob needs the fraternity of others who share his mission.* **2** N-C You can refer to a group of people with the same profession or interests as a particular **fraternity**. *...the sailing fraternity.* **3** N-C In the United States, a **fraternity** is a society of male students at a university or college.

fraud /frɔːd/ **frauds.** **1** N-VAR **Fraud** is the crime of gaining money by deceit. *He was jailed for two years for fraud. ...tax frauds.* **2** N-C If you call someone or something a **fraud**, you are criticizing them because you think they are not genuine, or are less good than they claim or appear to be. *You're a fraud and a spy, Simons.*

fraudulent /ˈfrɔːdjʊlənt/. ADJ **fraudulent** activity is deceitful or dishonest. *...fraudulent claims about being a nurse.* ◆**fraudulently** ADV *All 5,000 of the homes were fraudulently obtained.*

fraught /frɔːt/. **1** ADJ AFTER LINK-V If a situation or action is **fraught with** problems or difficulties, it is full of them. *Operations employing this technique were fraught with dangers.* **2** ADJ If you say that a situation or action is

fraught, you mean that it is worrying or stressful. *...a somewhat fraught day.*

fray /freɪ/ **frays, fraying, frayed.** **1** VERB If something such as cloth or rope **frays**, its threads or fibres become worn and it is likely to tear or break. *The stitching had begun to fray at the edges.* **2** N-SING If you say that someone joins **the fray**, you mean that they become involved in an exciting or challenging activity or situation. *...a second round of voting when new candidates can enter the fray.*

freak /friːk/ **freaks.** **1** ADJ BEFORE N A **freak** event or action is very unusual or extreme. *...a freak accident.* **2** N-C People are sometimes referred to as **freaks** when their behaviour or appearance is very different from that of most people; used showing disapproval. *...a place where minorities are treated like freaks.*

freckle /ˈfrekəl/ **freckles.** N-C If someone has **freckles**, they have small light brown spots on their skin.

free /friː/ **freer, freest; frees, freeing, freed.** **1** ADJ If something is **free**, you can have it or use it without paying. *...a free brochure... The company won the contract by essentially saying it would do the job for free.* ● **free of charge:** see **charge**. **2** ADJ Someone or something that is **free** is not controlled or limited by rules or custom or by other people. *Women should be free to dress and act as they please. ...organising free and fair elections.* **3** PHRASE You say **'feel free'** to someone who has asked you if they can do something as a way of giving them permission. *Go right ahead. Feel free... If you have any questions at all, please feel free to ask me.* **4** VERB If you **free** someone of something unpleasant or restricting, you remove it from them. *It will free us of a whole lot of debt.* **5** ADJ A person or thing that is **free** of something unpleasant does not have it or is not affected by it. *...a future far more free of fear... The carnival got off to a virtually trouble-free start.* **6** ADJ Someone who is **free** is no longer a prisoner or a slave. *He walked from the court house a free man... More than ninety prisoners have been set free.* **7** VERB To **free** a prisoner or slave means to release them. **8** VERB If you **free** someone or something, you make them available for a task or purpose. *His deal with Disney will run out shortly, freeing him to pursue his own project.* **9** ADJ If you have a **free** period of time, or if you are **free** at a particular time, you are not working or occupied then. *She spent her free time shopping.* **10** ADJ If something such as a table or seat is **free**, it is not being used or occupied, or is not reserved for someone to use. *They took the only free table.* **11** ADJ AFTER LINK-V If something gets **free**, it is no longer trapped by something or attached to something. *He pulled his arm free.* **12** VERB If you **free** someone or something, you remove or loosen them from the place where they have been trapped or become fixed. *Firemen tried to free the injured and put out the blaze.*

freedom /ˈfriːdəm/ **freedoms.** **1** N-VAR **Freedom** is the state of being allowed to do what you want. *...freedom of speech. ...the need for individual freedoms and human rights.* **2** N-U

When prisoners or slaves gain their **freedom**, they are set free or they escape. *...what he wanted, which was release from prison and freedom.* **3** N-U **Freedom from** something you do not want means not being affected by it. *...all the freedom from pain that medicine could provide.*

,free 'enterprise. N-U **Free enterprise** is an economic system in which businesses compete for profit without much government control.

freelance /'fri:lɑ:ns, -læns/. ADJ & ADV Someone who does **freelance** work or who is, for example, a **freelance** journalist or photographer, organizes their own work, income, and taxes, rather than being employed by someone who pays them regularly. *She decided to go freelance.*

freely /'fri:li/. **1** ADV You use **freely** to indicate that something happens or is done many times or in large quantities, often without restraint. *We have referred freely to his ideas... Consumer goods are freely available.* **2** ADV If you can talk **freely**, you do not need to be careful about what you say. **3** ADV If someone gives or does something **freely**, they give or do it without being forced to do it. *Danny shared his knowledge freely.* **4** ADV If something or someone moves **freely**, they move easily and smoothly, without any obstacles or resistance. *...to ensure that traffic flows freely throughout the country.*

freer /'fri:ə/. **Freer** is the comparative of **free**.

freest /'fri:ɪst/. **Freest** is the superlative of **free**.

freeway /'fri:weɪ/ **freeways.** N-C In American English, a **freeway** is a major road that has been specially built for fast travel over long distances. The usual British word is **motorway**.

,free 'will. PHRASE If you do something **of your own free will**, you do it because you want to and not because you are forced to. *If he does not leave of his own free will then we will have to force him out.*

freeze /fri:z/ **freezes, freezing, froze frozen.** **1** VERB If a liquid **freezes**, or if something **freezes** it, it becomes solid because of low temperatures. *If the temperature drops below 0°C, water freezes.* **2** VERB If you **freeze** something such as food, you preserve it by storing it at a temperature below 0° Celsius. You can also talk about how well food **freezes**. **3** VERB If you **freeze**, you feel very cold. *Your hands will freeze doing this.* **4** VERB If someone who is moving **freezes**, they suddenly stop and become completely still. *She froze when the beam of the flashlight struck her.* **5** VERB & N-C If the government or a company **freeze** an activity, prices, or wages, or if it puts a **freeze** on them, it states officially that it will not allow them to increase for a fixed period of time. *OPEC has agreed to freeze its global oil production. ...a wage freeze.* **6** VERB If someone in authority **freezes** your bank accounts or other financial concerns, they obtain a legal order which stops you having access to them or using them. **7** See also **freezing**, **frozen**.

▸ **freeze out.** PHR-VERB If you **freeze** someone **out** of an activity or situation, you prevent them from being involved in it by creating difficulties or by being unfriendly.

freezer /'fri:zə/ **freezers.** N-C A **freezer** is a fridge in which the temperature is kept below freezing point so that you can store food inside it for long periods.

freezing /'fri:zɪŋ/. ADJ If you say that something or someone is **freezing** or **freezing cold**, you are emphasizing that they are very cold. *...a freezing January afternoon... You must be freezing.* ● See note at **cold.**

freight /freɪt/. **1** N-U **Freight** is the movement of goods by lorries, trains, ships, or aeroplanes. *The whole thing will have to go by air freight.* **2** N-U **Freight** consists of the goods that are transported by lorries, trains, ships, or aeroplanes. *...26 tons of freight.*

freighter /'freɪtə/ **freighters.** N-C A **freighter** is a ship or aeroplane designed to carry goods.

frenetic /frɪ'netɪk/. ADJ **Frenetic** activity is fast and energetic, but rather uncontrolled. *...the frenetic pace of life in New York.*

frenzied /'frenzid/. ADJ **Frenzied** actions are carried out by someone who has lost control of their mind, senses, or feelings and is acting in a wild and violent way. *...a frenzied attack.*

frenzy /'frenzi/ **frenzies.** N-VAR **Frenzy** is great excitement or wild behaviour that often results from losing control of your feelings. *'Get out!' she ordered in a frenzy.*

frequency /'fri:kwənsi/ **frequencies.** **1** N-U The **frequency** of an event is the number of times it happens. *The frequency of Kara's phone calls increased.* **2** N-VAR The **frequency** of a sound wave or radio wave is the rate at which it vibrates; TECHNICAL.

frequent, frequents, frequenting, frequented. **1** ADJ /'fri:kwənt/ If something is **frequent**, it happens often. *She gives frequent performances of her work... He is a frequent visitor to the house.* ◆ **frequently** ADV *He was frequently depressed.* **2** VERB /frɪ'kwent/ If someone **frequents** a particular place, they regularly go there; FORMAL. *I hear he frequents Kenny's, the Cajun restaurant.*

fresco /'freskəʊ/ **frescoes.** N-C A **fresco** is a picture that is painted on a plastered wall when the plaster is still wet.

fresh /freʃ/ **fresher, freshest.** **1** ADJ BEFORE N A **fresh** thing or amount replaces or is added to a previous one. *Make fresh inquiries... I need a new challenge and a fresh start.* **2** ADJ Something that is **fresh** has been done, made, or experienced recently. *There were no fresh car tracks. ...with the memory of the bombing fresh in her mind.* **3** ADJ **Fresh** food has been produced or picked recently, and has not been preserved. *...locally caught fresh fish.* ◆ **freshly** ADV *...freshly baked bread.* ◆ **freshness** N-U Pay attention to the freshness of your food. **4** ADJ If you describe something as **fresh**, you mean you like it because it is new and exciting. *These designers are full of fresh ideas.* ◆ **freshness** N-U *There was a freshness and enthusiasm about the new students.* **5** ADJ If something smells, tastes, or feels **fresh**, it is clean, cool, or refreshing. *The air was fresh.* **6** ADJ **Fresh** water is water that is not salty, for example the water

in streams and lakes. • See also **freshwater**.
[7] ADJ AFTER LINK-V If you **are fresh from** or **are fresh out of** a particular place or experience, you have just come from that place or you have just had that experience. *I returned to the office, fresh from Heathrow.*

,fresh 'air. N-U You can describe the air outside as **fresh air**, especially when you mean that it is good for you. *Take exercise, preferably in the fresh air.*

freshman /'freʃmən/ **freshmen.** N-C Freshmen are students who are in their first year at an American university or college.

freshwater /'freʃwɔːtə/. ADJ BEFORE N A **freshwater** lake or pool contains water that is not salty.

fret /fret/ **frets, fretting, fretted.** VERB If you **fret** about something, you worry about it. *Vera is fretting about her sick children.*

friction /'frikʃən/ **frictions.** [1] N-VAR **Friction** between people is disagreement and quarrels between them. *The friction between us was becoming evident.* [2] N-U **Friction** is the force that makes it difficult for things to move freely when they are touching each other. [3] N-U **Friction** is the rubbing of one thing against another. *...the friction of his leg against hers.*

Friday /'fraɪdeɪ, -di/ **Fridays.** N-VAR **Friday** is the day after Thursday and before Saturday.

fridge /frɪdʒ/ **fridges.** N-C In British English, a **fridge** is a large metal container for storing food at low temperatures to keep it fresh. The usual American word is **refrigerator**.

friend /frend/ **friends.** [1] N-C A **friend** is someone who you know well and like, but who is not related to you. *Joanie's my best friend.* [2] N-PL If you are **friends** with someone, you are their friend and they are yours. *Sarah and Ella have been friends for seven years.* [3] PHRASE If you **make friends** with someone, you begin a friendship with them. *I've never found it hard to make friends.* [4] N-PL The **friends** of an organization, a country, or a cause are the people and organizations who help and support them. *...The Friends of Birmingham Royal Ballet.*

friendly /'frendli/ **friendlier, friendliest; friendlies.** [1] ADJ A **friendly** person is kind and pleasant. *...a man with a pleasant, friendly face.* ♦**friendliness** N-U *She also loves the friendliness of the people.* [2] ADJ AFTER LINK-V If you are **friendly with** someone, you like each other and enjoy spending time together. *I'm friendly with his mother.* [3] N-C In sport, a **friendly** is a game which is not part of a competition, and is played for entertainment or practice.

-friendly /-'frendli/. **-friendly** combines with nouns to form adjectives which describe things that do not harm or that help the thing or person mentioned. *Palm oil is environment-friendly. ...ozone-friendly fridges. ...customer-friendly banking facilities.*

friendship /'frendʃɪp/ **friendships.** N-VAR A **friendship** is a relationship or state of friendliness between two people who like each other. *...the quickest way to end a good friendship... The two countries signed treaties of friendship and co-operation.*

frigate /'frɪgət/ **frigates.** N-C A **frigate** is a small naval ship that can move at fast speeds.

fright /fraɪt/ **frights.** [1] N-U **Fright** is a sudden feeling of fear. *Franklin uttered a shriek and jumped with fright.* [2] N-C A **fright** is an experience which makes you suddenly afraid. *The last time you had a real fright, you nearly crashed the car.* [3] PHRASE If someone **takes fright**, they experience a sudden feeling of fear.

frighten /'fraɪtən/ **frightens, frightening, frightened.** VERB If something or someone **frightens** you, they cause you to suddenly feel afraid or anxious. *He knew that Soli was trying to frighten him.*

▸ **frighten away** or **frighten off.** [1] PHR-VERB If you **frighten away** a person or animal, or if you **frighten** them **off**, you make them afraid so that they run away or stay some distance away from you. *The fishermen said the company's seismic survey was frightening away fish.* [2] PHR-VERB To **frighten** someone **away** or **frighten** them **off** means to make them nervous so that they decide not to do something. *Let's not frighten visitors off by making them feel they're not welcome.*

▸ **frighten into.** PHR-VERB If you **frighten** someone **into** doing something, you force them to do it by making them afraid.

▸ **frighten off.** See **frighten away**.

frightened /'fraɪtənd/. ADJ If you are **frightened**, you feel anxious or afraid. *She was frightened of flying.*

frightening /'fraɪtənɪŋ/. ADJ If something is **frightening**, it makes you feel afraid or anxious. *It was a very frightening experience.* ♦**frighteningly** ADV *She was frighteningly ill.*

frightful /'fraɪtfʊl/. [1] ADJ Something that is **frightful** is very bad or unpleasant; DATED. *My father was unable to talk about the war, it was so frightful.* [2] ADJ BEFORE N **Frightful** is used to emphasize the extent or degree of something; DATED. *He got himself into a frightful muddle.* ♦**frightfully** ADV *I'm most frightfully sorry.*

frill /frɪl/ **frills.** [1] N-C A **frill** is a long, narrow, folded strip of cloth which is attached to something as a decoration. [2] N-PL If something has no **frills**, it is simple and has no unnecessary or additional features. *...Volkswagen's no-frills cars.*

fringe /frɪndʒ/ **fringes.** [1] N-C A **fringe** is hair which is cut so that it hangs over your forehead. [2] N-C A **fringe** is a decoration attached to clothes and other objects, consisting of a row of hanging threads. *...curtains of white silk with a fringe edging.* [3] N-C To be on the **fringe** or on the **fringes** of a place means to be on the outside edge of it. *...black townships located on the fringes of the city.* [4] N-C The **fringes** of an activity or organization are its least typical or most extreme parts. *...fringe theatre style.* [5] N-C **Fringe benefits** are extra things that some people get from their job in addition to their salary, for example a car.

fringed /frɪndʒd/. [1] ADJ BEFORE N **Fringed** clothes, curtains, or furnishings are decorated with fringes. [2] ADJ AFTER LINK-V If a place or object **is fringed with** things, they are situated along its edges. ...*tiny islands fringed with golden sand.*

frivolous /ˈfrɪvələs/. **1** ADJ If you describe someone as **frivolous**, you mean they behave in a silly or light-hearted way, rather than being serious and sensible. *Isabelle was a frivolous little fool.* **2** ADJ If you describe an activity as **frivolous**, you disapprove of it because it is not useful and wastes time or money. ...*a business as fickle and frivolous as fashion.*

fro /frəʊ/. **to and fro**: see **to**.

frock /frɒk/ **frocks.** N-C A **frock** is a woman's or girl's dress; DATED.

frog /frɒg, AM frɔːg/ **frogs.** N-C A **frog** is a small creature with smooth skin, big eyes, and long back legs which it uses for jumping.

frolic /ˈfrɒlɪk/ **frolics, frolicking, frolicked.** VERB & N-SING When people or animals **frolic**, they run around and play in a lively way. *Frolic* is this behaviour. *Tourists sunbathe and frolic in the ocean.* ...*fun and frolic.*

from /frəm, STRONG frɒm, AM frʌm/. **1** PREP You use **from** to say what the source, origin, or starting point of something is. ...*an anniversary present from his wife... The results were taken from six surveys.* ...*wines from France.* **2** PREP If someone or something moves or is taken **from** a place, they leave it or are removed from it. *The guests watched as she fled from the room... Remove the bowl from the ice.* **3** PREP If you take something **from** an amount, you reduce the amount by that much. *The £103 is deducted from Mrs Adams' salary every month.* **4** PREP If you are away **from** a place, you are not there. *Her husband worked away from home a lot.* **5** PREP If you return **from** a place or activity, you return after being there or doing it. *My son Colin has just returned from Amsterdam.* **6** PREP If you see or hear something **from** a particular place, you are in that place when you see it or hear it. *They see the painting from behind a plate glass window.* **7** PREP Something that sticks out or hangs **from** an object is attached to it or touches it. *Hanging from his right wrist is a heavy gold bracelet.* ...*large fans hanging from ceilings.* **8** PREP You can use **from** when giving distances. For example, if one place is fifty miles **from** another, the distance between them is fifty miles. *How far is it from here?* **9** PREP If a road goes **from** one place to another, you can travel along it between the two places. ...*the road from St Petersburg to Tallinn.* **10** PREP **From** is used, especially in the expression **made from**, to say what substance has been used to make something. ...*bread made from white flour.* **11** PREP If something happens **from** a particular time, it begins to happen then. *She studied painting from 1926.* **12** PREP You say **from** one thing to another when you are stating the range of things that are possible. *There are 94 countries represented in Barcelona, from Algeria to Zimbabwe.* **13** PREP If something changes **from** one thing to another, it stops being the first thing and becomes the second thing. *The expression on his face changed from sympathy to surprise.* **14** PREP You use **from** when mentioning the

cause of something. *The problem simply resulted from a difference of opinion... He is suffering from eye ulcers.* **15** PREP You use **from** to give the reason for an opinion. *I guessed from his name that Jose must have been Spanish.*

front /frʌnt/ **fronts.** **1** N-C & ADJ BEFORE N The **front** of something, or the **front** part of it, is the part of it that faces you or faces forward. *Stand at the front of the line... Her cotton dress had ripped down the front... She was only six and still missing her front teeth.* **2** N-C In a war, the **front** is the place where two armies are fighting. *Her husband is fighting at the front.* **3** N-C If something happens on a particular **front**, it happens with regard to a particular situation or activity. ...*research across a wide academic front.* **4** N-SING If someone puts on a **front**, they pretend to have feelings which they do not have. *Michael kept up a brave front.* **5** N-C An organization or activity that is a **front** for another one that is illegal or secret is used to hide it. ...*a firm later identified by the police as a front for crime syndicates in the city.*

PHRASES • If a person or thing is **in front**, they are ahead of others in a moving group. ...*motorists who speed or drive too close to the car in front.* • If you are **in front** in a competition or contest, you are winning. • If someone or something is **in front of** a particular thing, they are facing it, almost in front of it, or close to the front part of it. *She sat down in front of her dressing-table mirror... Something darted out in front of my car.* • If you do something **in front of** someone, you do it in their presence. *They never argued in front of their children.*

frontal /ˈfrʌntəl/. **1** ADJ A **frontal** attack or challenge criticizes or threatens something in a very strong direct way. ...*a frontal attack on conventional marriage.* **2** ADJ **Frontal** means relating to or involving the front of something. ...*the frontal region of the brain.*

frontier /ˈfrʌntɪə, -ˈtɪə/ **frontiers.** **1** N-C A **frontier** is a border between two countries. **2** N-C The **frontiers** of a subject are the limits to which it can be known or done. ...*pushing back the frontiers of science.*

front 'line, front lines. N-C The **front line** is the place where two armies are fighting each other.

front-'page. ADJ A **front-page** article or picture appears on the front page of a newspaper because it is very important or interesting.

front-'runner, front-runners. N-C In a competition or contest, the **front-runner** is the person who seems most likely to win it.

frost /frɒst, AM frɔːst/ **frosts.** N-VAR When there is a **frost**, the outside temperature drops below freezing and the ground is covered with ice crystals.

frosty /ˈfrɒsti, AM ˈfrɔːsti/. **1** ADJ If the weather is **frosty**, the temperature is below freezing. ...*sharp, frosty nights.* **2** ADJ You describe the ground or an object as **frosty** when it is covered with frost. ...*the frosty stones.* **3** ADJ If you describe someone's behaviour as **frosty**, you think it is unfriendly. ...*Ros's frosty glance.*

froth /frɒθ, AM frɔːθ/ **froths, frothing, frothed.** **1** VERB If a liquid **froths**, small bubbles appear on the surface. *The sea froths over* *my feet.* [2] N-U **Froth** is a mass of small bubbles on the surface of a liquid. *...the froth of bubbles on the top of a glass of beer.*

frown /fraʊn/ **frowns, frowning, frowned.** VERB & N-C If you **frown**, or if you have a **frown** on your face, you move your eyebrows close together because you are annoyed, worried, or thinking hard. *He frowned at her anxiously... There was a deep frown on the boy's face.*

▶ **frown on** or **frown upon.** PHR-VERB If something **is frowned on,** or if it **is frowned upon,** people disapprove of it. *This practice is frowned upon as being wasteful.*

froze /frəʊz/. **Froze** is the past tense of **freeze.**

frozen /ˈfrəʊzən/. [1] **Frozen** is the past participle of **freeze.** [2] ADJ If the ground is **frozen,** it has become very hard because the weather is very cold. *It was bitterly cold now and the ground was frozen hard.* [3] ADJ **Frozen** food has been preserved by being kept at a very low temperature. *Frozen fish is a very healthy convenience food.* [4] ADJ If you say that you are **frozen,** you mean that you are very cold. *He put one hand up to his frozen face.*

frugal /ˈfruːgəl/. [1] ADJ Someone who is **frugal** spends very little money on themselves. *She lives a frugal life.* ◆ **frugality** /fruːˈgælɪti/ N-U *We must practise the strictest frugality and economy.* [2] ADJ A **frugal** meal is small and inexpensive. *The diet was frugal.*

fruit /fruːt/ The plural is **fruit** or **fruits.** [1] N-VAR **Fruit** is something which grows on a tree or bush and which contains seeds or a stone covered with edible flesh. Apples, oranges, and bananas are all fruit. *Fresh fruit and vegetables provide fibre and vitamins.* [2] N-C The **fruits** of someone's work or activity are the good things that result from it. *The findings are the fruit of more than three years research.* [3] PHRASE If an action **bears fruit,** it produces good results.

fruitful /ˈfruːtfʊl/. ADJ Something that is **fruitful** produces good and useful results. *...a long, happy, fruitful relationship.*

fruition /fruːˈɪʃən/. N-U When something comes to **fruition,** it starts to produce the intended results. *These plans take time to come to fruition.*

fruitless /ˈfruːtləs/. ADJ **Fruitless** actions, events, or efforts do not achieve anything at all. *It was a fruitless search... Talks have so far have been fruitless.*

fruity /ˈfruːti/ **fruitier, fruitiest.** [1] ADJ Something that is **fruity** smells or tastes of fruit. *This shampoo smells fruity. ...a lovely rich fruity wine.* [2] ADJ A **fruity** laugh or voice is rich and deep.

frustrate /frʌˈstreɪt, AM ˈfrʌstreɪt/ **frustrates, frustrating, frustrated.** [1] VERB If something **frustrates** you, it upsets or angers you because you are unable to do anything about the problems it creates. *These questions frustrated me... Do you get very frustrated by slow-moving traffic?* ◆ **frustrated** ADJ *Roberta felt frustrated and angry.* ◆ **frustrating** ADJ *I found it very frustrating to teach Ted.* ◆ **frustration, frustrations** N-VAR *...frustration among hospital doctors.* [2] VERB To **frustrate** something such as a plan means to prevent it. *The government has delib-erately frustrated his efforts to gain work permits.*

fry /fraɪ/ **fries, frying, fried.** [1] VERB When you **fry** food, you cook it in a pan containing hot fat. *Fry the breadcrumbs until golden brown.* ◆ **fried** ADJ *...fried fish.* ● See note at **cook.** [2] N-PL **Fry** are very small young fish. [3] N-PL **Fries** are the same as **chips.**

'frying pan, frying pans. N-C A **frying pan** is a flat metal pan with a long handle, in which you fry food.

ft. N-C **ft** is a written abbreviation for **foot** or **feet.** *...flying at 1,000 ft.*

fudge /fʌdʒ/ **fudges, fudging, fudged.** [1] N-U **Fudge** is a soft brown sweet made from butter, milk, and sugar. [2] VERB If you **fudge** something, you avoid making clear or definite decisions about it. *Both have fudged their calculations.*

fuel /ˈfjuːəl/ **fuels, fuelling, fuelled** (AM **fueling, fueled**). [1] N-VAR **Fuel** is a substance such as coal, oil, or petrol that is burned to provide heat or power. *...the fuel necessary to heat their homes.* ● See also **fossil fuel.** [2] VERB A machine or vehicle that **is fuelled** by a particular substance works by burning that substance. *...power stations fuelled by oil.*

fugitive /ˈfjuːdʒɪtɪv/ **fugitives.** N-C A **fugitive** is someone who is running away or hiding, usually in order to avoid being caught by the police.

fulfil (or **fulfill**) /fʊlˈfɪl/, **fulfils, fulfilling, fulfilled.** [1] VERB If you **fulfil** a promise, dream, or ambition, you do what you said or hoped you would do. *...to fulfil her ambitions and become an actress.* [2] VERB To **fulfil** a task, role, or function means to do what is required by it. [3] VERB If something **fulfils** you, you feel happy and satisfied with what you are doing. *...a hobby that fulfilled her.* ◆ **fulfilling** ADJ *...a fulfilling career.* ◆ **fulfilled** ADJ *I feel more fulfilled doing this than I've ever done.* ◆ **fulfilment** N-U *...a great sense of fulfilment.*

full /fʊl/ **fuller, fullest.** [1] ADJ Something that is **full** contains as much of a substance or as many objects as it can. *...a full tank of petrol... The main car park was full.* [2] ADJ AFTER LINK-V If a place is **full** of things or people, it contains a large number of them. *His mouth was full of peas. ...a useful recipe leaflet full of ideas.* [3] ADJ AFTER LINK-V If someone or something is **full** of a feeling or quality, they have a lot of it. *I feel full of confidence.* [4] ADJ AFTER LINK-V If you feel **full,** you have eaten so much that you do not want anything else. ◆ **fullness** N-U *High fibre diets give the feeling of fullness.* [5] ADJ BEFORE N & ADV You can use **full** to indicate the greatest possible amount of something. *...the sound of Mahler, playing at full volume. ...in full daylight. ...a two-seater Lotus, parked with its headlamps full on.* [6] ADJ BEFORE N You can use **full** to indicate that you are referring to the whole of something, or to emphasize the amount of a quality that it has. *Full details will be sent to you... May I have your full name?... The farm was in full view of the house.* [7] ADJ If someone has a **full** life, they are always busy. [8] ADJ When there is a **full** moon, the moon appears as a bright, complete circle. [9] ADJ A

full flavour is strong and rich. *...a dry, grapey wine with a full flavour.*

PHRASES ● Something that has been done **in full** has been done or finished completely. *The medical experts have yet to report in full.* ● Something that is done or experienced **to the full** is done to as great an extent as is possible. *...a good mind which should be used to the full.*

,**full-'blown.** ADJ BEFORE N **Full-blown** means having all the characteristics of a particular type of thing or person. *Before becoming a full-blown director, he worked as the film editor.*

,**full-'length.** [1] ADJ BEFORE N A **full-length** book, record, or film is the normal length, rather than being shorter than normal. [2] ADJ BEFORE N A **full-length** coat or skirt is long enough to reach the lower part of a person's leg. [3] ADJ BEFORE N A **full-length** mirror or portrait shows the whole of a person. [4] ADV Someone who is lying **full-length** is lying down flat and stretched out. *She stretched herself out full-length.*

,**full-'scale.** [1] ADJ BEFORE N **Full-scale** means as complete, intense, or great in extent as possible. *...a full-scale nuclear war.* [2] ADJ BEFORE N A **full-scale** drawing or model is the same size as the thing that it represents.

,**full-'size** or **full-sized.** ADJ BEFORE N A **full-size** or **full-sized** model or picture is the same size as the thing or person that it represents.

,**full 'stop, full stops.** N-C In British English, a **full stop** is the punctuation mark (.) which you use at the end of a sentence when it is not a question or exclamation. The American word is **period.**

,**full-'time** or **full time.** ADJ & ADV **Full-time** work or study takes up the whole of each normal working week. *...a full-time job... Deirdre works full-time.*

fully /'fʊli/. [1] ADV **Fully** means to the greatest degree or extent possible. *She was fully aware of my thoughts... I don't fully agree.* [2] ADV If you describe, answer, or deal with something **fully**, you leave out nothing that should be mentioned or dealt with. *These debates are discussed more fully later in this book.*

fumble /'fʌmbəl/ **fumbles, fumbling, fumbled.** VERB If you **fumble** for something, or if you **fumble** with it, you clumsily try and reach for it or hold it. *She crept from the bed and fumbled for her dressing gown.*

fume /fjuːm/ **fumes, fuming, fumed.** [1] N-PL **Fumes** are unpleasantly strong or harmful gases or smells. *...car exhaust fumes.* [2] VERB If you **are fuming** over something, you are very angry about it. *'It's monstrous!' Jackie fumed... Mrs. Vine was still fuming.*

fun /fʌn/. [1] N-U **Fun** is pleasant, enjoyable, and light-hearted activity or amusement. *We had so much fun doing it... You still have time to join in the fun.* [2] ADJ If someone is **fun**, you enjoy their company. If something is **fun**, you enjoy doing it. *Liz was wonderful fun to be with...* It was a fun evening.

PHRASES ● If you do something **in fun**, you do it as a joke or for amusement, without intending to cause any harm. *Don't say such things, even in fun.* ● If you **make fun of** someone or something, or if you **poke fun at** them, you tease someone or make jokes about them. *They all made fun of my plan.*

function /'fʌŋkʃən/ **functions, functioning, functioned.** [1] N-C The **function** of something or someone is the useful thing that they do or are intended to do. *The main function of the merchant banks is to raise capital for industry.* [2] VERB If a machine or system is **functioning**, it is working or operating. *Conservation programs cannot function without local support.* [3] VERB If someone or something **functions as** a particular thing, they do the work or fulfil the purpose of that thing. *One third of the room functions as workspace.* [4] N-C A **function** is a large formal dinner or party.

functional /'fʌŋkʃənəl/. [1] ADJ **Functional** things are useful rather than decorative. *...modern, functional furniture.* [2] ADJ **Functional** equipment works or operates in the way that it is supposed to. *We have fully functional smoke alarms.* [3] ADJ BEFORE N **Functional** means relating to the way something works or operates. *...decreased functional ability in the knees.*

fund /fʌnd/ **funds, funding, funded.** [1] N-PL **Funds** are amounts of money that are available to be spent. *The concert will raise funds for research into Aids. ...government funds.* [2] N-C A **fund** is an amount of money that is collected for a particular purpose. *...a scholarship fund for undergraduate engineering students.* [3] VERB To **fund** something means to provide money for it. *They will use the grant to fund the appointment of a Welfare Visitor. ...government-funded institutions.* ♦**funding** N-U *They hope for government funding for the scheme.* [4] N-C If you have a **fund** of something, you have a lot of it. *...an extraordinary fund of energy.*

fundamental /ˌfʌndə'mentəl/. ADJ If something is **fundamental**, it is very important or basic. *Technical skill is a fundamental basis for most, if not all, great art... Better relations with others are fundamental to the well-being of the area.* ♦**fundamentally** ADV *He can be very charming but he is fundamentally a bully.*

fundamentalism /ˌfʌndə'mentəlɪzəm/. N-U **Fundamentalism** is belief in the original form of a religion or theory, without accepting any later ideas. ♦**fundamentalist** /ˌfʌndə'mentəlɪst/ **fundamentalists** N-C *...fundamentalist Christians.*

fundamentals /ˌfʌndə'mentəlz/. N-PL The **fundamentals** of something are its simplest, most important elements, ideas, or principles. *...the fundamentals of road safety.*

fundraiser /'fʌndreɪzə/ **fundraisers.** [1] N-C A **fundraiser** is an event which is intended to raise money for a particular purpose. *Organize a fundraiser for your church.* [2] N-C A **fundraiser** is someone who works to raise money for a particular purpose.

'**fund-raising.** N-U **Fund-raising** is the activity of collecting money for a particular purpose.

funeral /'fjuːnərəl/ **funerals.** N-C A **funeral** is a ceremony for the burial or cremation of someone who has died. *His funeral will be on Thursday at Blackburn Cathedral.*

fungus /'fʌŋgəs/ **fungi** /'fʌŋgiː, 'fʌndʒaɪ/. N-VAR A **fungus** is a plant that has no flowers, leaves, or green colouring, such as a mushroom or mould. ♦**fungal** /'fʌŋgəl/ ADJ ...*fungal growth.*

funnel /'fʌnəl/ **funnels, funnelling, funnelled** (AM **funneling, funneled**). [1] N-C A **funnel** is an object with a wide top and a tube at the bottom, which is used to pour substances into a container. [2] N-C A **funnel** is a chimney on a ship. [3] VERB If something **funnels** somewhere, or if it **is funnelled** there, it is directed through a narrow space. *The winds came from the north, across the plains, funnelling down the valley.* [4] VERB If you **funnel** money or resources somewhere, you send them there from several sources. ...*a plan to funnel environmental aid through the World Bank.*

funny /'fʌni/ **funnier, funniest.** [1] ADJ **Funny** things are amusing and make you smile or laugh. ...*a funny story... What's so funny?* [2] ADJ You say that something is **funny** when it is strange, surprising, or puzzling. *It's funny how fast things change.* [3] ADJ If you feel **funny**, you feel slightly ill; INFORMAL.

fur /fɜː/ **furs.** [1] N-U **Fur** is the thick hair that grows on the bodies of many animals, and is sometimes used to make clothes or rugs. You can also refer to an artificial material that resembles this hair as **fur**. ...*a black coat with a fur collar.* [2] N-C A **fur** is a coat made from fur. ...*women in furs.*

furious /'fjʊəriəs/. [1] ADJ If someone is **furious**, they are extremely angry. *He is furious at the way his wife has been treated.* ♦**furiously** ADV *'You clumsy idiot,' he said furiously.* • See note at **angry.** [2] ADJ You can use **furious** to indicate that something involves great energy, speed, or violence. ...*months of furious debate.* ♦**furiously** ADV *I started writing furiously.*

furlong /'fɜːlɒŋ, AM -lɔːŋ/ **furlongs.** N-C A **furlong** is an imperial unit of length that is equal to 220 yards or 201.2 metres.

furnace /'fɜːnɪs/ **furnaces.** N-C A **furnace** is a container or enclosed space in which a very hot fire is made, for example to melt metal, burn rubbish, or produce steam.

furnish /'fɜːnɪʃ/ **furnishes, furnishing, furnished.** [1] VERB When you **furnish** a room, you put furniture in it. ♦**furnished** ADJ ...*a furnished flat... The room was tastefully furnished.* [2] VERB To **furnish** something means to provide it or supply it; FORMAL. *They'll be able to furnish you with all the rest of the details.*

furnishings /'fɜːnɪʃɪŋz/. N-PL The **furnishings** of a room or house are the furniture, curtains, carpets, and decorations such as pictures.

furniture /'fɜːnɪtʃə/. N-U **Furniture** consists of large movable objects such as tables, chairs, or beds that are used in a room for sitting on or for putting things on or in. ...*bedroom furniture.*

> Note that **furniture** is only ever used as an uncount noun. You cannot say 'a furniture' or 'furnitures'. If you want to refer in general terms to something such such as a table, a chair, or a bed, you can say a **piece of furniture** or an **item of furniture.**

furore (AM **furor**) /fjʊ'rɔːri, 'fjʊərɔː/. N-SING A **furore** is a very angry or excited reaction by people to something. ...*the furore over his remarks about Northern Ireland.*

furrow /'fʌrəʊ, AM 'fɜːr-/ **furrows, furrowing, furrowed.** [1] N-C A **furrow** is a long line in the earth made for planting seeds. [2] N-C **Furrows** in someone's skin are deep folds or lines. ...*the deep furrows that marked the corners of his mouth.* [3] VERB If someone **furrows** their brow or forehead, deep folds appear in it because they are frowning; WRITTEN. *Her father furrowed his forehead... Occasionally her brow furrowed.*

furry /'fɜːri/ **furrier, furriest.** [1] ADJ A **furry** animal is covered with thick soft hair. ...*a long furry tail.* [2] ADJ Something that is **furry** resembles fur. ...*a furry hat.*

further /'fɜːðə/ **furthers, furthering, furthered.** [1] ADV **Further** means to a greater degree or extent. *Inflation is below 5% and set to fall further.* [2] ADV If someone or something goes **further** or takes something **further**, they progress to a more advanced or detailed stage. *He did not develop that idea any further.* [3] ADJ BEFORE N A **further** thing or amount is an additional one. *Doctors are carrying out further tests.* [4] ADV **Further** means a greater distance than before or than something else. *Now we live further away from the city centre.* ...*a crossroads fifty yards further on.* [5] ADV **Further** is used in expressions such as **'further back'** and **'further ahead'** to refer to a point in time that is earlier or later than the time you are talking about. *Ministers have been looking further ahead, beyond the current conflicts in the region.* [6] VERB If you **further** something, you help it to progress or to be successful. *Education isn't only about furthering your career.*

further edu'cation. N-U In Britain, **further education** is education after leaving school, at a college rather than a university. The usual American term is **continuing education.**

furthermore /,fɜːðə'mɔː/. ADV **Furthermore** is used to introduce a statement adding to or supporting the previous one. *It is nearly dark, and furthermore it's going to rain.*

furthest /'fɜːðɪst/. [1] ADV **Furthest** means to a greater extent or degree than ever before or than anything or anyone else. ...*the south of England, where prices have fallen furthest.* [2] ADJ & ADV The **furthest** one of a number of things is the one that is the greatest distance away. ...*the furthest point from earth.* ...*areas furthest from the coast.*

furtive /'fɜːtɪv/. ADJ If you describe someone's behaviour as **furtive**, you disapprove of them behaving as if they want to keep something secret or hidden. ...*furtive meetings.* ♦**furtively** ADV *He glanced around furtively.*

fury /'fjʊəri/. N-U **Fury** is very strong anger. *His face was contorted with fury.*

fuse /fjuːz/ **fuses, fusing, fused.** [1] N-C In an electrical appliance, a **fuse** is a wire safety device which melts and stops the electric current if there is a fault. [2] VERB When an electric device **fuses**, or when you **fuse** it, it stops working because of a fault. *The light fused.* [3] N-C A **fuse** is part of a bomb or firework which delays the explosion and gives people time to move away. [4] VERB When one thing **fuses** with another, they join together, usually to become one thing. *Manufactured glass is made by fusing various types of sand.* [5] VERB To **fuse** ideas, qualities, or things means to combine them. *...Latin American music fused with jazz.*

fuselage /ˈfjuːzɪlɑːʒ/ **fuselages**. N-C The **fuselage** of an aeroplane or rocket is its main part.

fusion /ˈfjuːʒən/ **fusions**. [1] N-VAR When two ideas, qualities, or things are combined, you can say that there is a **fusion** of them. *...a fusion of Eastern and Western cooking.* [2] N-U **Fusion** is the process in which atomic particles combine and produce a large amount of nuclear energy; TECHNICAL. *...research into nuclear fusion.*

fuss /fʌs/ **fusses, fussing, fussed.** [1] N-SING & N-U **Fuss** is unnecessarily anxious or excited behaviour. *I don't know what all the fuss is about.* [2] VERB When people **fuss**, they behave in an unnecessarily anxious or excited way. *My mother is fussing about the journey.* [3] VERB If you **fuss over** someone or something, you pay them too much attention or worry about them too much. *All the Sisters fussed over her.* [4] PHRASE If you **make a fuss of** someone, you pay a lot of attention to them.

fussy /ˈfʌsi/ **fussier, fussiest.** [1] ADJ Someone who is **fussy** is very concerned with unimportant details and is difficult to please. *He was very fussy about cleanliness.* [2] ADJ If you describe things as **fussy**, you are criticizing them because they are too elaborate or detailed. *...fussy curtains.*

futile /ˈfjuːtaɪl, AM -təl/. ADJ If you say that something is **futile**, you mean there is no point in doing it, usually because it has no chance of succeeding. *...their futile attempts to avoid publicity.* ◆ **futility** /fjuːˈtɪlɪti/ N-U *...the futility of arguing with him.*

future /ˈfjuːtʃə/ **futures.** [1] N-SING The **future** is the period of time after the present. *No decision on the proposal was likely in the immediate future.* [2] ADJ BEFORE N **Future** things will happen or exist after the present time. *...the UK's future role in Europe.* [3] N-C The **future** of someone or something is what will happen to them after the present time. *...his future as prime minister.* [4] N-C Something that has a **future** is likely to be successful or to survive. *There's no future in this relationship.* [PHRASES] ● You use **in future** when you are telling someone what you want or expect to happen from now on. *Be more careful in future.* ● If you say something will happen **in the near future**, you mean it will happen quite soon.

future 'tense. N-SING In grammar, the **future tense** is used to refer to things that will come after the present.

futuristic /ˌfjuːtʃəˈrɪstɪk/. ADJ Something that is **futuristic** looks like something from the future. *...a futuristic building.*

fuzzy /ˈfʌzi/ **fuzzier, fuzziest.** [1] ADJ **Fuzzy** hair sticks up in a soft curly mass. [2] ADJ A **fuzzy** picture or image is blurred and unclear. *...fuzzy photographs.* [3] ADJ BEFORE N **Fuzzy** logic is a type of computer logic that is supposed to imitate the way that humans think.

G g

gadget /ˈgædʒɪt/ **gadgets.** N-C A **gadget** is a small machine or device which does a useful task. *...consumer gadgets such as CD players.*

gag /gæg/ **gags, gagging, gagged.** [1] N-C A **gag** is a piece of cloth that is tied round or put inside someone's mouth to stop them from speaking. [2] VERB If someone **gags** you, they tie a piece of cloth around your mouth in order to stop you speaking. *The raiders bound and gagged her.* [3] VERB If a person **is gagged** by someone in authority, they are prevented from expressing their opinion or from publishing certain information; used showing disapproval. [4] N-C A **gag** is a joke; INFORMAL.

gain /geɪn/ **gains, gaining, gained.** [1] VERB If you **gain** something, you acquire it gradually. *Students can gain valuable experience by working on the campus radio... The helicopter gained speed as it headed toward the mainland.* [2] VERB If you **gain** from something, you get some advantage from it. *Many areas of the world would actually gain from global warming.* [3] N-C A **gain** is an improvement or increase. *News on new home sales is brighter, showing a gain of nearly 8% in June.* [4] PHRASE If you do something **for gain**, you do it in order to get some profit for yourself; FORMAL. *...buying art solely for financial gain.* [5] VERB If you **gain** something, you obtain it, usually after a lot of effort. *Passing exams is no longer enough to gain a place at university.*

gait /geɪt/ **gaits.** N-C Someone's **gait** is their particular way of walking; WRITTEN. *...a rolling gait.*

gala /ˈgɑːlə, AM ˈgeɪlə/ **galas.** N-C A **gala** is a special public celebration, performance, or festival. *...a gala evening at the Royal Opera House.*

galaxy /ˈgæləksi/ **galaxies.** N-C A **galaxy** is a huge group of stars and planets extending over millions of miles.

gale /geɪl/ **gales.** N-C A **gale** is a very strong wind. *...fierce winter gales.*

gall /gɔːl/ **galls, galling, galled.** [1] N-SING If someone has the **gall** to do something dangerous or dishonest, they have the daring to do it; used showing disapproval. *She had the gall to suggest that I might supply her with information.* [2] VERB If someone's action **galls** you, it makes you angry because you cannot do anything about it. *What really galled Dana was that Caroline knew where she would be staying.*

gallant /ˈgælənt/; also pronounced /gəˈlænt/ for meaning 2. [1] ADJ A **gallant** person behaves

very bravely and honourably in a dangerous or difficult situation. *...gallant soldiers.*
♦ **gallantly** ADV *The town responded gallantly to the War.* [2] ADJ If you say that a man is **gallant**, you think he is polite and considerate towards other people, especially women; DATED.

gallery /ˈgæləri/ **galleries.** [1] N-C A **gallery** is a place that has permanent exhibitions of works of art in it. *...an art gallery.* [2] N-C The **gallery** in a theatre or concert hall is a raised area at the back like a large balcony.

galley /ˈgæli/ **galleys.** N-C On a ship or aircraft, the **galley** is the kitchen.

gallon /ˈgælən/ **gallons.** N-C A **gallon** is a unit of measurement for liquids that is equal to eight pints. In Britain, it is equal to 4.564 litres. In America, it is equal to 3.785 litres.

gallop /ˈgæləp/ **gallops, galloping, galloped.** [1] VERB & N-SING When a horse **gallops**, or when it runs at a **gallop**, it runs very fast, so that during each stride all four legs are off the ground at the same time. *The horses galloped away... He whipped his horse into a gallop.* [2] VERB & N-SING If you **gallop**, you ride a horse that is galloping. A **gallop** is a ride on a galloping horse. *Major Winston galloped into the distance. ...early morning gallops at his Lambourne stables.*

galore /gəˈlɔː/ ADJ You use **galore** to emphasize that something that you like exists in very large quantities. *There were bargains galore.*

galvanize (BR also **galvanise**) /ˈgælvənaɪz/ **galvanizes, galvanizing, galvanized.** VERB If you **are galvanized** into doing something, you are motivated by excitement, fear, or anger into doing it straight away. *These murders may galvanise the country into throwing the weight of the state against racial violence.*

gamble /ˈgæmbəl/ **gambles, gambling, gambled.** [1] VERB & N-SING If you **gamble** on something, or if you take a **gamble**, you take a risky action or decision in the hope of gaining money, success, or an advantage. *Few firms will be willing to gamble on new products... They are not prepared to gamble their careers on this matter. ...the French president's risky gamble in calling a referendum.* [2] VERB If you **gamble**, you bet money on the result of a game, a race, or competition. *John gambled heavily on the horses... He gambled away his family estates.*
♦ **gambler, gamblers** N-C *I used to be a very heavy gambler.* ♦ **gambling** N-U *The laws regulating gambling are tough.*

game /geɪm/ **games.** [1] N-C A **game** is an activity or sport usually involving skill, knowledge, or chance, in which you follow fixed rules and try to win against an opponent or to solve a puzzle. *...the wonderful game of football.* [2] N-C In sport, a **game** is a match, or part of a match. *We won three games against Australia. ...the last three points of the second game.* [3] N-PL **Games** are organized events involving several different sports. *...the 1996 Olympic Games.* [4] N-C You can describe a way of behaving as a **game** when it is used to try to gain advantage. *The Americans have been playing a very delicate political game.* [5] N-U **Game** is wild animals or birds that are hunted for sport or food. [6] ADJ AFTER LINK-V If you say that someone is

game or **game for** something, you mean that they are willing to do something new, unusual, or risky. *He still had new ideas and was game to try them... He said he's game for a similar challenge next year.*

PHRASES ● If someone or something **gives the game away**, they reveal a secret or reveal their feelings. *The faces of the two conspirators gave the game away!* ● If you beat someone **at their own game**, you use the same methods that they have used, but more successfully, so that you gain an advantage over them. ● If you say that something is **the name of the game**, you mean that it is the most important aspect of the activity you are talking about. *In the current economic climate, survival is the name of the game.*

gaming /ˈgeɪmɪŋ/. N-U **Gaming** means the same as **gambling**, especially at cards, roulette, and other games of chance.

gang /gæŋ/ **gangs, ganging, ganged.** [1] N-C A **gang** is a group of people who join together for some purpose, often criminal. *...members of a rival gang. ...a gang of masked robbers.* [2] N-C A **gang** is a group of manual workers who work together. *...a gang of labourers.*

▸ **gang up.** PHR-VERB If people **gang up** on someone, they unite against them; INFORMAL. *All the girls in my class seemed to gang up against me.*

gangster /ˈgæŋstə/ **gangsters.** N-C A **gangster** is a member of a group of violent criminals.

gaol /dʒeɪl/. See **jail**.

gap /gæp/ **gaps.** [1] N-C A **gap** is a space between two things or a hole in something solid. *...the wind tearing through gaps in the window frames.* [2] N-C A **gap** is a period of time when you are not doing what you normally do. *There followed a gap of four years, during which William joined the Army.* [3] N-C If there is something missing from a situation which prevents it from being complete, you can also say that there is a **gap**. *Tony recognised a gap in the market for a true specialist in cheese.* [4] N-C A **gap** is a great difference between two things, people, or ideas. *...the gap between rich and poor... America's trade gap widened.*

gape /geɪp/ **gapes, gaping, gaped.** [1] VERB If you **gape**, you look at someone or something in surprise, with your mouth open. *His secretary stopped taking notes to gape at me.* [2] VERB If you say that something such as a hole or a wound **gapes**, you are emphasizing that it is deep or wide. *A hole gaped in the roof.*
♦ **gaping** ADJ *...a gaping wound in her chest.*

garage /ˈgærɑːʒ, -rɪdʒ, AM gəˈrɑːʒ/ **garages.** [1] N-C A **garage** is a building in which you keep a car. [2] N-C A **garage** is a place where you can get your car repaired, buy a car, or buy petrol.

garbage /ˈgɑːbɪdʒ/. N-U In American English, **garbage** is rubbish, especially waste from a kitchen. The usual British word is **rubbish**. *...garbage collection.* ● See note at **rubbish**.

garden /ˈgɑːdən/ **gardens, gardening, gardened.** [1] N-C In British English, a **garden** is an area of land next to a house, with plants, trees, and grass. The usual American word is **yard**. [2] VERB If you **are gardening**, you are doing work in your garden such as weeding or planting. ◆**gardener, gardeners.** N-C ...*a keen gardener.* ◆**gardening** N-U *I have taken up gardening again.* [3] N-U **Gardens** are a park with plants, trees, and grass. ...*the botanical gardens.*

garish /'geərɪʃ/. ADJ If you describe something as **garish**, you dislike it because it is very bright in an unattractive showy way. ...*garish, illuminated signs.*

garland /'gɑːlənd/ **garlands.** N-C A **garland** is a circular decoration made from flowers and leaves, worn round the neck or head.

garlic /'gɑːlɪk/. N-U **Garlic** is the small, white, round bulb of a plant related to the onion plant, which is used as a flavouring. ...*a clove of garlic.*

garment /'gɑːmənt/ **garments.** N-C A **garment** is a piece of clothing; FORMAL. ● See note at **clothes**.

garner /'gɑːnə/ **garners, garnering, garnered.** VERB If you say that someone has **garnered** something useful or valuable, you mean that they have collected or gained it; FORMAL.

garnish /'gɑːnɪʃ/ **garnishes, garnishing, garnished.** [1] N-VAR A **garnish** is a small amount of herbs, salad, or other food that is used to decorate prepared food. [2] VERB To **garnish** food means to decorate it with a garnish.

garrison /'gærɪsən/ **garrisons.** N-C A **garrison** is a group of soldiers whose job is to guard the town or building where they live. You can also refer to the buildings which the soldiers live in as a **garrison**.

gas /gæs/ **gases, gasses, gassing, gassed.** The form **gases** is the plural of the noun. The form **gasses** is the third person singular of the verb. [1] N-VAR A **gas** is any substance that is neither liquid nor solid, such as oxygen or hydrogen. Some gases burn easily and are used as a fuel for heating and cooking. ...*gas and dust from the volcanic eruption.* ● See also **tear gas.** [2] N-VAR **Gas** is a poisonous gas that can be used as a weapon. ...*mustard gas.* [3] VERB To **gas** a person or animal means to kill them by making them breathe poisonous gas. [4] N-U In American English, **gas** is the liquid used as a fuel for motor vehicles. The British word is **petrol.**

gash /gæʃ/ **gashes, gashing, gashed.** [1] N-C A **gash** is a long deep cut. [2] VERB If you **gash** something, you accidentally make a long deep cut in it. *He gashed his leg while felling trees.*

'gas mask, gas masks. N-C A **gas mask** is a device worn over someone's face in order to protect them from poisonous gases.

gasoline /'gæsəliːn/. N-U In American English, **gasoline** is the liquid used as a fuel for motor vehicles. The British word is **petrol.**

gasp /gɑːsp, gæsp/ **gasps, gasping, gasped.** VERB & N-C If you **gasp**, or if you give a **gasp**, you take a short, quick breath through your mouth, especially when you are surprised or in pain. *She gasped for air... An audible gasp went round the court.*

gastric /'gæstrɪk/. ADJ BEFORE N **Gastric** is used to describe things which occur in the stomach; TECHNICAL. ...*gastric ulcers.*

gate /geɪt/ **gates.** [1] N-C A **gate** is a structure like a door which is used at the entrance to a field, a garden, or the grounds of a building. [2] N-C In an airport, a **gate** is an exit through which passengers reach their aeroplane. ...*the departure gate.*

gateway /'geɪtweɪ/ **gateways.** [1] N-C A **gateway** is an entrance where there is a gate. *The ruined castle has an attractive gateway.* [2] N-C A **gateway to** something is a way of reaching, achieving, or discovering it. *New York is the great gateway to America.*

gather /'gæðə/ **gathers, gathering, gathered.** [1] VERB When people **gather** somewhere, or if someone **gathers** them there, they come together in a group. *We gathered around the fireplace... The man signalled for me to gather the children together.* [2] VERB & PHR-VERB If you **gather** things, or if you **gather** them **up**, you collect them together. *I suggest we gather enough firewood to last the night. ...a private detective using a hidden tape recorder to gather information... I needed a few minutes to gather my thoughts... When Sutcliffe had gathered up his papers, he went out.* [3] VERB If something **gathers** speed, momentum, or force, it gradually becomes faster or more powerful. *Demands for his dismissal have gathered momentum in recent weeks.* [4] VERB You use **gather** in expressions such as '**I gather**' and '**as far as I can gather**' when you are introducing information that you have found out, especially when you have found it out in an indirect way. *I gather his report is highly critical of the trial judge... 'He speaks English,' she said to Graham.— 'I gathered that.'*

▸ **gather up.** See **gather** 2.

gathering /'gæðərɪŋ/ **gatherings.** N-C A **gathering** is a group of people meeting together. ...*polite social gatherings.*

gaudy /'gɔːdi/. ADJ If you describe something as **gaudy**, you mean it is very bright-coloured and obvious, and often you are suggesting that it is vulgar. ...*gaudy fake jewellery.*

gauge /geɪdʒ/ **gauges, gauging, gauged.** [1] VERB If you **gauge** something, you measure it or judge it. *He gauged the wind at over thirty knots... To gauge consumer reaction, we canvassed shoppers in London's West End.* [2] N-C A **gauge** is a device that measures the amount or quantity of something and shows the amount measured. ...*temperature gauges.* [3] N-SING A **gauge** of a situation is a fact or event that can be used to judge it. *They run businesses and see money as a gauge of efficiency.*

gaunt /gɔːnt/. ADJ If someone looks **gaunt**, they look very thin, usually because of illness.

gauntlet /'gɔːntlɪt/ **gauntlets.** N-C **Gauntlets** are long, thick, protective gloves.

PHRASES ● If you **run the gauntlet**, you are attacked or criticized by a lot of hostile people, especially because you are obliged to pass through a group of them. *She was forced to run a gauntlet of some 300 jeering demonstrators.* ● If you **throw down the gauntlet** to someone, you say or do something that challenges them to argue or compete with you. If someone **takes up the gauntlet**, they accept a challenge that has been offered.

gave /geɪv/. Gave is the past tense of **give**.

gay /geɪ/ gays; gayer, gayest. [1] ADJ & N-PL Gay people or **gays** are homosexuals. [2] ADJ **Gay** means lively and cheerful; DATED. *I felt almost gay as I waited for Hank.*

gaze /geɪz/ gazes, gazing, gazed. [1] VERB If you **gaze** at someone or something, you look steadily at them for a long time. *He gazed reflectively at the fire... The girls stood still, gazing around the building.* [2] N-C You can talk about someone's **gaze** as a way of describing how they are looking at something, especially when they are looking steadily at it. *She felt increasingly uncomfortable under the woman's steady gaze.*

The verbs **gaze** and **stare** are both used to talk about looking at something for a long time. If you **gaze at** something, it is often because you think it is marvellous or impressive. *A fresh-faced little girl gazes in wonder at the bright fairground lights.* If you **stare at** something or someone, it is often because you think they are strange or shocking. *Various families came out and stared at us.*

---

gazette /gə'zet/ gazettes. N-C A **gazette** is a newspaper or journal. *...the Arkansas Gazette.*

GCE /ˌdʒiː siː 'iː/. A **GCE** is an examination taken by British school students at Advanced level, during their last year at school. GCE is an abbreviation for 'General Certificate of Education'. ● See also **A level**.

GCSE /ˌdʒiː siː es 'iː/ GCSEs. A **GCSE** is an examination taken by British school students when they are fifteen or sixteen years old. GCSE is an abbreviation for 'General Certificate of Secondary Education'.

gear /gɪə/ gears, gearing, geared. [1] N-C A **gear** is a piece of machinery, for example in a car or on a bicycle, which controls the rate at which energy is converted into motion. When a vehicle's engine is operating at a particular rate, you can say it is in a particular **gear**. *The car was in fourth gear... He put the truck in gear and drove on.* [2] N-U The **gear** for a particular activity is the equipment and special clothes that you use. *...fishing gear.* [3] ADJ If someone or something is **geared to** or **geared towards** a particular purpose, they are organized or designed in order to achieve that purpose. *My training was geared towards winning gold in Munich.*

▸ **gear up.** PHR-VERB If someone **is gearing up** for a particular activity, they are preparing to do it. If they **are geared up** for it, they are prepared and able to do it. *All the parties will be gearing up for a general election... The factory was geared up to make 1,100 cars a day.*

gearbox /'gɪəbɒks/ gearboxes. N-C A **gearbox** is the system of gears in an engine or vehicle.

gee /dʒiː/. EXCLAM People sometimes say **gee** in order to express a strong reaction to something or to introduce a remark or response; AMERICAN, INFORMAL. *Gee, it's hot.*

geese /giːs/. Geese is the plural of **goose**.

gel (or **jell**) /dʒel/ gels, gelling, gelled. [1] VERB If people, things, or ideas **gel**, they or

their different parts begin to work well together to form a successful whole. *They have gelled very well with the rest of the team. ...episodes that never quite manage to gel into a plot.* [2] N-VAR **Gel** is a smooth, soft, jelly-like substance, especially one used to keep your hair in a particular style.

gem /dʒem/ gems. [1] N-C A **gem** is a jewel. *...precious gems.* [2] N-C If you describe something or someone as a **gem**, you mean that they are especially good or helpful. *...a gem of a hotel.*

gender /'dʒendə/ genders. [1] N-VAR A person's **gender** is the fact that they are male or female. *Women are sometimes denied opportunities solely because of their gender.* [2] N-C You can refer to all male people or all female people as a particular **gender**. *...the different abilities and skills of the two genders.*

gene /dʒiːn/ genes. N-C A **gene** is the part of a cell in a living thing which controls its physical characteristics, growth, and development.

genealogy /ˌdʒiːni'ælədʒi/ genealogies. [1] N-U **Genealogy** is the study of the history of families. ◆ **genealogical** /ˌdʒiːniə'lɒdʒɪkəl/ ADJ BEFORE N *...genealogical research on his family.* [2] N-C A **genealogy** is the history of a family over several generations.

genera /'dʒenərə/. Genera is the plural of **genus**.

general /'dʒenrəl/ generals. [1] N-C & N-TITLE A **general** is an officer of a high-rank in the armed forces. [2] ADJ BEFORE N If you talk about the **general** situation somewhere or talk about something in **general** terms, you are describing the situation as a whole rather than considering its details or exceptions. *The figures represent a general decline in employment... She recounted in very general terms some of the events of recent months.* [3] ADJ BEFORE N You use **general** to describe something that involves or affects most people, or most people in a group. *...general awareness about bullying.* [4] ADJ BEFORE N **General** is used to describe something that is not restricted to any one thing or area. *...a general store. ...a general ache radiating from the back of the neck. ...a general sense of well-being.* [5] ADJ BEFORE N **General** is used to describe a person who has an average amount of knowledge or interest in a particular subject. *This book is intended for the general reader.* [6] ADJ BEFORE N **General** is used to describe someone's job, to indicate that they have responsibility for the whole of an organization. *He is the general manager of the museum.* [7] See also **generally**.

PHRASES ● You say **in general** when you are talking about the whole of a situation without going into details, or when you are referring to most people or things in a group. *We need to improve our educational system in general... People in general will support us.* ● **In general** is used to indicate that a statement is true in most cases. *In general, it was the better-educated voters who voted Yes.*

general election, general elections. N-C A **general election** is an election for a new government, in which all the citizens of a country may vote.

generalize (BR also **generalise**) /'dʒenrəlaɪz/ **generalizes, generalizing, generalized.** VERB If you **generalize**, you say something that is true in most cases. *It is virtually impossible to generalize about the state of the country's health.* ◆**generalization, generalizations.** N-VAR *You cannot make sweeping generalizations out of the isolated cases.*

generalized (BR also **generalised**) /'dʒenrəlaɪzd/. ADJ **Generalized** means involving many different things, rather than one or two specific things. *The symptoms may have become more generalized and less easily detected.*

generally /'dʒenrəli/. [1] ADV You use **generally** to summarize a situation, activity, or idea without referring to the particular details of it. *University teachers generally have admitted a lack of enthusiasm.* [2] ADV You use **generally** to say that something happens or is used on most occasions but not on every occasion. *As women we generally say and feel too much.*

general prac'titioner, general practitioners. N-C A **general practitioner** is a doctor who treats all types of illnesses instead of specializing in one area of medicine. The abbreviation **GP** is also used.

general 'public. N-SING The **general public** is all the people in a society. *You get to know what the general public is really thinking.*

generate /'dʒenəreɪt/ **generates, generating, generated.** [1] VERB To **generate** something means to cause it to begin and develop. *The reforms would generate new jobs.* [2] VERB To **generate** electricity or other forms of energy means to produce it. *...solar panels for generating power.* ◆**generation** N-U *...the fuels used for electricity generation.*

generation /,dʒenə'reɪʃən/ **generations.** [1] N-C A **generation** consists of all the people in a group or country who are of a similar age. *He's of a younger generation. ...the leading American playwright of his generation.* [2] N-C A **generation** is the period of time that it takes for children to grow up and become adults and have children of their own. *Its centuries-old culture will be wiped out within a few generations.* [3] N C You can use **generation** to refer to a stage of development in the design and manufacture of machines or equipment. *...the next generation of computers.*

generator /'dʒenəreɪtə/ **generators.** N-C A **generator** is a machine which produces electricity.

generic /dʒɪ'nerɪk/. [1] ADJ BEFORE N **Generic** means applying to a whole group of similar things; FORMAL. *Parmesan is a generic term used to describe a family of hard Italian cheeses.* [2] N-C & ADJ A **generic** or a **generic** drug is a drug that does not have a trademark and is known by a general name; TECHNICAL.

generous /'dʒenərəs/. [1] ADJ A **generous** person gives more of something, especially money, than is usual or expected. *German banks are more generous in their lending. The gift is generous by any standards.* ◆**generosity** /,dʒenə'rɒsɪti/ N-U *She is well known for her generosity.* ◆**generously** ADV *...the judges who gave so generously of their time.* [2] ADJ **Generous**

means friendly, helpful, and willing to see the good qualities in people or things. *That's a very generous interpretation of what he said.* ◆**generously** ADV *He said, very generously, that the campaign had been a huge success.* [3] ADJ Something that is **generous** is much larger than is usual or necessary. *...a generous portion of spaghetti.* ◆**generously** ADV *Sprinkle generously with sugar.*

genetics /dʒɪ'netɪks/. The form **genetic** is used as a modifier. [1] N-U **Genetics** is the study of how characteristics are passed from one generation to another by means of genes. [2] ADJ **Genetic** means concerned with genetics or genes. *...genetic scientists.* ◆**genetically** ADV *...genetically altered tomatoes.*

genial /'dʒiːniəl/. ADJ A **genial** person is kind and friendly. ◆**genially** ADV *Liz laughed genially.* ◆**geniality** N-U *...his habitual geniality.*

genital /'dʒenɪtəl/ **genitals.** N-PL Your **genitals** are your external sexual organs.

genius /'dʒiːniəs/ **geniuses.** [1] N-U **Genius** is very great ability or skill in something. *...his genius for chess.* [2] N-C A **genius** is a highly intelligent, creative, or talented person.

genocide /'dʒenəsaɪd/. N-U **Genocide** is the murder of a whole community or race; FORMAL.

genre /'ʒɒnrə/ **genres.** N-C A **genre** is a particular style of literature, art, or music; FORMAL. *...novels in the horror genre.*

gent /dʒent/ **gents.** [1] N-C A **gent** is a gentleman; DATED. [2] N-SING People sometimes refer to a men's public toilet as **the gents**; BRITISH, INFORMAL.

genteel /dʒen'tiːl/. ADJ A **genteel** person is polite, respectable, and refined. *...a genteel middle-class family.*

gentle /'dʒentəl/ **gentler, gentlest.** [1] ADJ A **gentle** person is kind, mild, and calm. *...a quiet and gentle man. ...her gentle nature.* ◆**gently** ADV *She smiled gently.* ◆**gentleness** N-U *...his gentleness towards the children.* [2] ADJ If an action is **gentle**, it has little force. *...light, gentle strokes. ...a gentle breeze.* ◆**gently** ADV *Patrick took her gently by the arm.* [3] ADJ A **gentle** slope or curve is not steep or severe. *...gentle, rolling meadows.* ◆**gently** ADV *...a gently sloping hill.* [4] ADJ A **gentle** heat is a fairly low heat.

gentleman /'dʒentəlmən/ **gentlemen.** [1] N C A **gentleman** is a man from a family of high social standing. *...the traditional country gentleman.* [2] N-C A **gentleman** is a man who is polite and well-educated. *He was always such a gentleman.* [3] N-C You can refer politely to men as **gentlemen**. *This way, please, gentlemen.*

gentry /'dʒentri/. N-PL The **gentry** are people of high social status; BRITISH, DATED.

genuine /'dʒenjʊɪn/. [1] ADJ Something that is **genuine** is real and exactly what it appears to be. *...genuine leather... They're convinced the picture is genuine.* ◆**genuinely** ADV *I was genuinely surprised.* [2] ADJ Someone who is **genuine** is honest and sincere. *She was a very genuine woman.*

genus /'dʒenəs, AM 'dʒiː-/ **genera.** N-C A **genus** is a class or group of similar animals or plants; TECHNICAL.

geographical /ˌdʒiːəˈɡræfɪkəl/ or **geographic** /ˌdʒiːəˈɡræfɪk/. ADJ **Geographical** means relating to geography. *...a vast geographical area.* ◆**geographically** ADV *Geographically, it's the highest point in London.*

geography /dʒiˈɒɡrəfi/. ① N-U **Geography** is the study of the countries of the world and of such things as land formations, seas, and climate. ② N-U The **geography** of a place is the way that features such as rivers, mountains, and towns are arranged. *...policemen who knew the local geography.*

geology /dʒiˈɒlədʒi/. ① N-U **Geology** is the study of the earth's structure, surface, and origins. ◆**geological** /ˌdʒiːəˈlɒdʒɪkəl/ ADJ *...a lengthy geological survey.* ◆**geologist, geologists** N-C *...the latest discovery by geologists in Australia.* ② N-U The **geology** of an area is the structure of its land.

geometric /ˌdʒiːəˈmetrɪk/. ① ADJ **Geometric** means relating to geometry. *...geometric laws.* ② ADJ **Geometric** patterns or shapes consist of regular shapes or lines. *...geometric designs.*

geometry /dʒiˈɒmɪtri/. ① N-U **Geometry** is a mathematical science concerned with the measurement of lines, angles, curves, and shapes. ② N-U The **geometry** of an object is its shape or the relationship of its parts to each other; FORMAL. *...the geometry of the car's nose.*

geriatric /ˌdʒeriˈætrɪk/. ADJ BEFORE N **Geriatric** is used to describe things relating to the illnesses and medical care of old people; TECHNICAL. *...the future of geriatric care.*

germ /dʒɜːm/ **germs**. ① N-C A **germ** is a very small organism that causes disease. *...cholera germs.* ② N-C The **germ** of something such as an idea is the beginning of it.

germinate /ˈdʒɜːmɪneɪt/ **germinates, germinating, germinated**. VERB If a seed **germinates** or is **germinated**, it starts to grow; TECHNICAL. *Heat will encourage seeds to germinate.* ◆**germination** N-U *To speed up germination, it is worth soaking the seed in water.*

gesture /ˈdʒestʃə/ **gestures, gesturing, gestured**. ① VERB & N-C If you **gesture**, you use movements of your hands or head called **gestures** to convey a message or feeling. *She gestured towards the front door... With a gesture of the head, she beckoned him back.* ② N-C A **gesture** is something that you say or do in order to express your attitude or intentions. *Iraq said it made the offer as a gesture of goodwill.*

get 1 changing, causing, moving, or reaching

get /ɡet/ **gets, getting, got** (AM also **gotten**). In most of its uses **get** is a fairly informal word. ① LINK-VERB **Get** often has the same meaning as 'become'. For example, if something **gets** cold, it becomes cold. *The boys were getting bored... From here on, it can only get better... It's getting late.* ② **Get** is often used in place of 'be' as an auxiliary verb to form the passive. *Does she ever get asked for her autograph?... A pane of glass got broken.* ③ VERB If someone or something **gets** into a particular state or situation, or if someone or something **gets** them into it, they start being in that state or situation. *Perhaps I shouldn't say that – I might get into trouble... How did we get into this recession... I*

don't know if I can get it clean... Brian will get them out of trouble.* ④ VERB To **get** somewhere means to move or arrive there. *I got off the bed and opened the door... Generally I get to work at 9.30am... It was dark by the time she got home.* ⑤ VERB If you **get** something or someone into a particular place or position, you move them there by means of a particular action or effort. *Mack got his wallet out... Go and get your coat on... The UN was supposed to be getting aid to where it was most needed.* ⑥ VERB If you **get** someone to do something, they do it because you asked, persuaded, or told them to do it. *Tom's on the phone. Can I get him to call you back?* ⑦ VERB If you **get** something done, you arrange for it to be done. *I have to get my car repaired.* ⑧ VERB If you **get** to do something, you manage to do it or have the opportunity to do it. *Do you get to see him often?... They get to stay in nice hotels.* ⑨ VERB You can use **get** in expressions like **get moving, get going**, and **get working** when you want to tell people to begin moving, going, or working quickly. ⑩ VERB If you **get** to a particular stage in an activity, you reach that stage. *Patrick had got as far as finding some clients.* ⑪ VERB If something **gets** you, it annoys you; INFORMAL. *What gets me is the attitude of so many of these people.*

get 2 obtaining, receiving, or catching

get /ɡet/ **gets, getting, got** (or AM **gotten**). ① VERB If you **get** something that you want or need, you obtain it or receive it. *The problem was how to get enough food to sustain life... I asked him to get me some information... They get a salary of $11,000 a year... Whenever I get the chance I go to Maxim's for dinner.* ② VERB If you **get** someone or something, you go and bring them to a particular place. *Go and get your daddy for me... Get me a large brandy.* ③ VERB You can use **you get** instead of 'there is' or 'there are' to say that something exists, happens, or can be experienced; SPOKEN. *You get a lot of youngsters hanging around the Common.* ④ VERB If you **get** an illness or disease, you become ill with it. *When I was five I got measles.* ⑤ VERB If you **get** an idea, impression, or feeling, you have it or experience it. *Charles got a shock when he saw him... I get the feeling that you're an honest man.* ⑥ VERB If you **get** a joke or **get** the point of something, you understand it. ⑦ VERB When you **get** a train, bus, plane, or boat, you travel by that means of transport. ⑧ See also **got**. ● **to give as good as you get**: see **give**.

get 3 phrasal verbs

get /ɡet/ **gets, getting, got** (or AM **gotten**). ▶ **get about.** PHR-VERB If you **get about**, you move or travel from place to place. *Rail travel through France is the perfect way to get about.* ② See **get around**.

▶ **get across.** PHR-VERB If you **get** an idea or argument **across**, you succeed in making people understand it. *Officers felt their point of view was not getting across to ministers... Wally got his message across very well.*

▶ **get along.** PHR-VERB If you **get along** with someone, you have a friendly relationship with them. *It's impossible to get along with him.*

▶ **get around.** [1] PHR-VERB If you **get around**, you go to a lot of different places as part of your way of life. [2] PHR-VERB If news **gets around**, **gets about**, or **gets round**, it is told to lots of people. *Word got around that he was taking drugs.* [3] PHR-VERB If you **get around** or **get round** a difficulty or restriction, you manage to avoid it or deal with it. *Although tobacco ads are prohibited, companies get around the ban by sponsoring music shows.*

▶ **get around to** or **get round to.** PHR-VERB When you **get around to** doing something that you have delayed or have been too busy to do, you finally do it. *I haven't got round to talking to him yet.*

▶ **get at.** [1] PHR-VERB To **get at** something means to succeed in reaching it. *A goat was standing up against a tree on its hind legs, trying to get at the leaves.* [2] PHR-VERB If you **get at** someone, you keep criticizing or teasing them in an unkind way; INFORMAL. *I'm just tired of you getting at me all the time.* [3] PHR-VERB If you ask someone what they are **getting at**, you ask them to explain what they mean. *What are you getting at now?*

▶ **get away.** [1] PHR-VERB If you **get away**, you succeed in leaving a place or situation that you do not want to be in. *Dr Dunn was apparently trying to get away when he was shot.* [2] PHR-VERB If you **get away**, you go away for a period of time in order to have a holiday.

▶ **get away with.** PHR-VERB If you **get away with** doing something wrong or risky, you do not suffer any punishment or other bad consequences because of it. *The criminals know how to play the system and get away with it.*

▶ **get back.** PHR-VERB If you get something **back** after you have lost it or after it has been taken from you, you have it again. *You can cancel the contract and get your money back.*

▶ **get back to.** [1] PHR-VERB If you **get back to** a previous activity or subject, you start doing the activity or talking about the subject again. *I couldn't get back to sleep... We got back to the subject of Tom Halliday.* [2] PHR-VERB To **get back to** a previous state or level means to return to it. *Life started to get back to normal.*

▶ **get by.** PHR-VERB If you can **get by** with the few resources you have, you can manage to live or do things satisfactorily. *Melville managed to get by on a small amount of money.*

▶ **get down to.** PHR-VERB When you **get down to** something, you start doing it. *With the election out of the way, the government can get down to business.*

▶ **get in.** [1] PHR-VERB When a train, bus, or plane **gets in**, it arrives. *Her train gets in at about ten to two.* [2] PHR-VERB When a political party or a politician **gets in**, they are elected. [3] PHR-VERB If you **get** something you want to say **in**, you eventually manage to say it, usually in a situation where other people are talking a lot. *It was hard to get a word in.*

▶ **get in on.** PHR-VERB If you **get in on** an activity, you start taking part in it, perhaps without being invited; INFORMAL. *Now baseball is trying to get in on the European market.*

▶ **get into.** [1] PHR-VERB If you **get into** an activity, you start doing it or being involved in it. *He was eager to get into politics.* [2] PHR-VERB If you

get into a school, college, or university, you are accepted there as a student. [3] PHR-VERB If you ask what has **got into** someone, you mean that they are behaving in an unexpected way; INFORMAL. *He didn't know what could have got into him, to steal a watch.*

▶ **get off.** [1] PHR-VERB If someone who has broken a law or rule **gets off**, they are not punished, or only slightly punished. *He is likely to get off with a small fine.* [2] PHR-VERB You can tell someone to **get off** when they are touching you and you do not want them to. *I kept telling him to get off... 'Get off me!' I screamed.*

▶ **get off with.** PHR-VERB If you **get off with** someone, you have a romantic or sexual encounter with them; INFORMAL.

▶ **get on.** [1] PHR-VERB If you **get on** with someone, you have a friendly relationship with them. *I get on very well with his wife.* [2] PHR-VERB If you **get on** with an activity, you continue doing it or start doing it. *Jane got on with her work.* [3] PHR-VERB If someone **is getting on** well or badly, they are making good or bad progress. *Livy's getting on very well in Russian.* [4] PHR-VERB If you try to **get on**, you try to be successful in your career. *She's keen. She's ambitious. She wants to get on.* [5] PHR-VERB If someone **is getting on**, they are getting old; INFORMAL.

▶ **get on to.** [1] PHR-VERB If you **get on to** a particular topic, you start talking about it. *We got on to the subject of relationships.* [2] PHR-VERB If you **get on to** someone, you contact them. *I got on to him and explained some of the things.*

▶ **get out.** [1] PHR-VERB If you **get out** of a place or situation, you leave it. *I told him to leave and get out... Getting out of the contract would be no problem.* [2] PHR-VERB If you **get out**, you go to places and meet people. *Get out and enjoy yourself, make new friends.* [3] PHR-VERB If news or information **gets out**, it becomes known. *If word got out now, a scandal could be disastrous.*

▶ **get out of.** PHR-VERB If you **get out of** doing something that you do not want to do, you avoid doing it. *It's amazing what people will do to get out of paying taxes.*

▶ **get over.** [1] PHR-VERB If you **get over** an unpleasant experience or an illness, you recover from it. *It took me a very long time to get over the shock of her death.* [2] PHR-VERB If you **get over** a problem, you manage to deal with it.

▶ **get over with.** PHR-VERB If you **get** something unpleasant **over with**, you do it or experience it quickly, since you cannot avoid it. *The sooner we start, the sooner we'll get it over with.*

▶ **get round.** [1] See **get around**. [2] PHR-VERB If you **get round** someone, you persuade them to like you or do what you want, by pleasing or flattering them. *Max could always get round her.*

▶ **get round to.** See **get around to**.

▶ **get through.** [1] PHR-VERB If you **get through** a task, you complete it. *I think you can get through the first two chapters.* [2] PHR-VERB If you **get through** an unpleasant experience or time, you manage to live through it. *It is hard to see how people will get through the winter.* [3] PHR-VERB If you **get through** a large amount of something, you use it up. *You'll get through at least ten nappies a day.* [4] PHR-VERB If you **get through** to someone, you succeed in making them understand what you are trying to say. *An old friend might well be able to get through to her and help her.* [5] PHR-VERB If you **get through** to someone, you succeed in contacting them on the telephone. *I've been trying to ring up all day and I couldn't get through.*

▸ **get together.** [1] PHR-VERB When people **get together**, they meet in order to discuss something or to spend time together. [2] PHR-VERB If you collect or assemble things or people for a particular purpose, you can say that you **get them together.** *We'll give you three days to get the money together.*

▸ **get up.** [1] PHR-VERB If you are sitting or lying and then **get up**, you rise to a standing position. [2] PHR-VERB When you **get up**, you get out of bed. *They have to get up early in the morning.*

▸ **get up to.** PHR-VERB If you say that someone **gets up to** something, you mean that they do it and you do not approve of it; BRITISH. *They get up to all sorts behind your back.*

getaway /ˈɡetəweɪ/ **getaways.** N-C When someone makes a **getaway**, they leave a place in a hurry, especially after committing a crime. *They made their getaway on a stolen motorcycle.*

ghastly /ˈɡɑːstli, ˈɡæstli/ ADJ If you describe someone or something as **ghastly**, you mean that they are very unpleasant. *...a mother accompanied by her ghastly unruly child.*

ghetto /ˈɡetəʊ/ **ghettos** or **ghettoes.** N-C A **ghetto** is a part of a town in which many poor people or many people of a particular race, religion, or nationality live. *...the black ghettos of New York.*

ghost /ɡəʊst/ **ghosts.** N-C A **ghost** is the spirit of a dead person that someone thinks they can see or feel. *...the ghost of the drowned girl.*

ghostly /ˈɡəʊstli/ ADJ Something that is **ghostly** seems unreal or supernatural and may be frightening because of this. *The moon shone, shedding a ghostly light on the fields.*

GI /ˌdʒiː ˈaɪ/ **GIs.** N-C A **GI** is a soldier in the United States army.

giant /ˈdʒaɪənt/ **giants.** [1] ADJ BEFORE N You use **giant** to describe something that is much larger or more important than most other things of its kind. *...Italy's giant car maker, Fiat. ...a giant oak table.* [2] N-C A large successful organization or country can be referred to as a **giant**; JOURNALISM. *...Japanese electronics giant Sony.* [3] N-C In children's stories, a **giant** is a person who is very big and strong.

gibe /dʒaɪb/ See **jibe.**

giddy /ˈɡɪdi/ ADJ If you feel **giddy**, you feel that you are about to fall over, usually because you are not well.

gift /ɡɪft/ **gifts.** [1] N-C A **gift** is something that you give someone as a present. *...suggestions for Christmas gifts.* [2] N-C If someone has a **gift** for doing something, they have a natural ability for doing it. *He discovered a gift for teaching.*

gifted /ˈɡɪftɪd/ ADJ A **gifted** person has a natural

ability for doing most things or for doing a particular activity. *...a school for gifted children.*

gig /ɡɪɡ/ **gigs.** N-C A **gig** is a live performance by a pop or jazz musician, comedian, or disc jockey; INFORMAL. *The Stones only do outdoor gigs.*

gigantic /dʒaɪˈɡæntɪk/ ADJ If you describe something as **gigantic**, you are emphasizing that it is extremely large in size, amount, or degree. *...a gigantic oak tree... It's come as a gigantic surprise.*

giggle /ˈɡɪɡəl/ **giggles, giggling, giggled.** VERB & N-C If you **giggle**, or if you let out a **giggle**, you laugh in a childlike helpless way. *'I beg your pardon?' she giggled... She gave a little giggle.*

gilded /ˈɡɪldɪd/ ADJ If something is **gilded**, it has been covered with a thin layer of gold or gold paint. *...gilded statues.*

gilt /ɡɪlt/ ADJ A **gilt** object is covered with a thin layer of gold or gold paint.

gimmick /ˈɡɪmɪk/ **gimmicks.** N-C A **gimmick** is an unusual and unnecessary feature or action whose purpose is to attract attention or publicity; used showing disapproval. *It is just a public relations gimmick.*

gin /dʒɪn/ **gins.** N-VAR **Gin** is a colourless alcoholic drink.

ginger /ˈdʒɪndʒə/ [1] N-U **Ginger** is the root of a plant that is used to flavour food. It has a sweet spicy flavour. [2] ADJ & N-U **Ginger** is used to describe something, usually a person's hair, that is orange-brown.

gingerly /ˈdʒɪndʒəli/ ADV If you do something **gingerly**, you do it in a careful hesitant manner; WRITTEN. *I drove gingerly past the security check points.*

gipsy /ˈdʒɪpsi/ **gipsies.** See **gypsy.**

giraffe /dʒɪˈrɑːf, -ˈræf/ **giraffes.** N-C A **giraffe** is a large African animal with a very long neck, long legs, and dark patches on its body.

girl /ɡɜːl/ **girls.** [1] N-C A **girl** is a female child. [2] N-C Young women are often referred to as **girls**. Some people find this use offensive. *...a pretty twelve-year old girl.*

girlfriend /ˈɡɜːlfrend/ **girlfriends.** [1] N-C Someone's **girlfriend** is a girl or woman with whom they are having a romantic or sexual relationship. *He had been going out with his girlfriend for seven months.* [2] N-C A **girlfriend** is a female friend. *I met a girlfriend for lunch.*

girth /ɡɜːθ/ **girths.** N-VAR The **girth** of an object is its width or thickness; FORMAL. *...a 43 inch long fish with a 9 inch girth.*

gist /dʒɪst/ N-SING The **gist** of a speech, conversation, or piece of writing is its general meaning. *I could not get the gist of their conversation.*

give 1 used with nouns describing actions

give /ɡɪv/ **gives, giving, gave, given.** [1] VERB You can use **give** with nouns that refer to physical actions. The whole expression refers to the performing of the action. For example, **'She gave a smile'** means almost the same as 'She smiled'. *George gave a tremendous yawn... She gave my hand a quick squeeze.* [2] VERB You use **give** to say that a person does a particular thing for someone else. For example, if you **give** someone a lift, you take them somewhere in your car. *She began to give piano lessons to some of the local children... He was given mouth-to-mouth resuscitation.* [3] VERB You use **give** with nouns that refer to information, opinions, or greetings to indicate that something is communicated. For example, if you **give** someone some news, you tell it to them. *He gave no details... He asked me to give his regards to all of you.* [4] VERB If someone or something **gives** you a particular idea, impression, or feeling, they cause you to have it. *They gave me the impression that they were doing exactly what they wanted... It will give great pleasure to many thousands of children.* [5] VERB If you **give** something thought or attention, you think about it or deal with it. *I've been giving it some thought... Priority will be given to those who apply early.* [6] VERB If you **give** a speech or a performance, you speak or perform in public. *...Mrs Butler who gave us such an interesting talk last year.* [7] VERB If you **give** a party or other social event, you organize it.

give 2 transferring

give /gɪv/ **gives, giving, gave, given.** [1] VERB If you **give** someone something that you own or have bought, you provide them with it, so that they have it or can use it. *Many leading industrialists gave money to the Conservative Party... She gave me a doll for my birthday.* [2] VERB If you **give** someone something that you are holding or that is near you, you pass it to them, so that they are then holding it. *He pulled a handkerchief from his pocket and gave it to him.* [3] VERB To **give** someone or something a particular right or power means to allow them to have it. *...a citizen's charter giving rights to gays.*

give 3 other uses, phrases, and phrasal verbs

give /gɪv/ **gives, giving, gave, given.** [1] VERB If something **gives**, it collapses or breaks under pressure. *My knees gave under me.* [2] VERB You use **give** in phrases such as **I'd give anything**, **I'd give my right arm**, and **what wouldn't I give** to emphasize that you are very keen to do or have something. *I'd give anything to be like you.*

PHRASES ● If someone **gives as good as** they **get**, they fight or argue as well or intensely as the person they are fighting or arguing with. ● If you say something requires **give and take**, you mean that people must compromise for it to be successful. ● **Give or take** is used to indicate that an amount is approximate. *They grow to a height of 12 inches – give or take a couple of inches.* ● to **give way**: see **way**.

▶ **give away.** [1] PHR-VERB If you **give away** something that you own, you give it to someone because you no longer want it. *He was giving his collection away for nothing.* [2] PHR-VERB If you **give away** information that should be kept secret, you reveal it to other people. *Her voice gave nothing away.*

▶ **give back.** PHR-VERB If you **give** something **back**, you return it to the person who gave it to you. *I gave the textbook back to him.*

▶ **give in.** [1] PHR-VERB If you **give in**, you admit that you are defeated or that you cannot do something. *All right. I give in. What did you do with the ship?* [2] PHR-VERB If you **give in**, you

agree to do something that you do not want to do. *They won't give in to the workers' demands.*

▶ **give off** or **give out.** PHR-VERB If something **gives off** or **gives out** a gas, heat, or a smell, it produces it and sends it out into the air. *...natural gas, which gives off less carbon dioxide than coal.*

▶ **give out.** PHR-VERB If you **give out** a number of things, you distribute them among a group of people. *They were giving out leaflets.* ● See also **give off.**

▶ **give over to.** PHR-VERB If something **is given over to** or **given up to** a particular use, it is used entirely for that purpose. *Much of the garden was given over to vegetables.*

▶ **give up.** [1] PHR-VERB If you **give up** something, you stop doing it or having it. *I was trying to give up drugs... The doctors gave up hope as her condition worsened.* [2] PHR-VERB If you **give up**, you decide that you cannot do something and stop trying to do it. *After a fruitless morning sitting at his desk he had given up.* [3] PHR-VERB If you **give up** your job, you resign from it.

▶ **give up to.** See **give over to.**

given /'gɪvən/. [1] **Given** is the past participle of **give.** [2] ADJ AFTER LINK-V If you are **given to** doing something, you often do it; FORMAL. *I am not very given to emotional displays.* [3] ADJ If something happens in a **given** situation, it happens in that particular situation. If something happens at a **given** time, it happens at that particular time. *Do you regularly work for more than 10 hours on any given day?* [4] PREP **Given** is used when indicating a possible situation in which someone has the opportunity or ability to do something. For example, **given the chance** means 'if I had the chance'. *Given patience, successful breeding of this species can be achieved.* [5] CONJ If you say **given that** something is the case, you mean taking that fact into account. *This may seem an odd view to take, given that I am strongly in favour of the Maastricht treaty.* [6] PREP If you say **given** a particular thing, you mean taking that thing into account. *Given the uncertainty over Leigh's future I was left with little other choice.*

glacial /'gleɪʃəl/. ADJ **Glacial** means relating to or produced by glaciers or ice; TECHNICAL. *...a true glacial landscape with U-shaped valleys.*

glacier /'glæsɪə, AM 'gleɪʃə/ **glaciers.** N-C A **glacier** is a huge mass of ice which moves very slowly, often down a mountain.

glad /glæd/. [1] ADJ AFTER LINK-V If you are **glad** about something, you are happy and pleased about it. *I'm glad I relented in the end... The people seem genuinely glad to see you... I ought to be glad about what happened.* ♦ **gladly** ADV *If this offer is genuine I will gladly accept it.* [2] ADJ If you say that you will be **glad** to do something, you mean that you are willing and eager to do it. *I'll be glad to show you everything.* ♦ **gladly** ADV *If you'd prefer something else I'll gladly have it changed for you.*

glamorous /'glæmərəs/. ADJ If you describe someone or something as **glamorous**, you mean that they are more attractive, exciting, or interesting than ordinary people or things.

...the glamorous lifestyle of the rich and famous.

glamour (AM **glamor**) /'glæmə/. N-U **Glamour** is the quality of being more attractive, exciting, or interesting than ordinary people or things. *He loved the glamour of show business.*

glance /glɑːns, glæns/ **glances, glancing, glanced.** ⑴ VERB & N-C If you **glance** at someone or something, or if you give them a **glance**, you look at them very quickly and then look away. *He glanced at his watch... The boys exchanged glances.* ⑵ VERB If you **glance through** or **at** a newspaper or book, you spend a short time looking at it without reading it carefully. *She glanced at her diary.* ⑶ PHRASE If you say that something appears to be true **at first glance**, you mean that it seems to be true when you first see it, but that your first impression may be wrong. *At first glance, everything appeared normal.*

gland /glænd/ **glands.** N-C **Glands** are organs in your body that produce chemical substances which your body needs in order to function. *...sweat glands.*

glare /gleə/ **glares, glaring, glared.** ⑴ VERB & N-C If you **glare** at someone, or if you give them a **glare**, you look at them angrily. *Joe glared at his brother... The waiter lowered his eyes to avoid Harold's furious glare.* ⑵ VERB & N-SING If the sun or a light **glares**, it shines with a very bright light which is difficult to look at, called a **glare**. *The sun glared down on the station platform. ...the glare of the headlights.* ⑶ N-SING If you are in the **glare** of publicity or public attention, you are constantly being watched and talked about by the public.

glaring /'gleərɪŋ/. ADJ If you describe something bad as **glaring**, you mean that it is very obvious. *...glaring errors.* ♦**glaringly** ADV *It was glaringly obvious.*

glass /glɑːs, glæs/ **glasses.** ⑴ N-U **Glass** is the hard transparent substance that windows and bottles are made from. *...a pane of glass. ...a sliding glass door.* ⑵ N-C A **glass** is a container made of glass which you can drink from. *Jack held his glass out and Carl poured it full... I drank a glass of water.* ⑶ N-U Objects made of glass can be referred to as **glass**. *...a glittering array of glass.* ⑷ N-PL **Glasses** are two lenses in a frame that some people wear in front of their eyes in order to see better. *He took off his glasses.*

glaze /gleɪz/ **glazes.** N-C A **glaze** is a thin layer of a hard shiny substance on a piece of pottery.

glazed /gleɪzd/. ⑴ ADJ If someone's eyes are **glazed**, their expression is dull or dreamy, because they are tired or are having difficulty concentrating. *There was a glazed look in her eyes.* ⑵ ADJ **Glazed** pottery is covered with a thin layer of a hard shiny substance. ⑶ ADJ A **glazed** window or door has glass in it.

gleam /gliːm/ **gleams, gleaming, gleamed.** ⑴ VERB & N-SING If an object or the surface of something **gleams**, it shines because it is reflecting light. The light reflecting off something is called a **gleam**. *The cutlery gleamed... I could see the gleam of brass.* ⑵ N-C A **gleam** of light is a faint light; WRITTEN. *...the first gleam of*

dawn. ⑶ VERB & N-SING If your eyes **gleam**, or if there is a **gleam** in your eyes, your eyes look bright and show that you are excited or happy; WRITTEN.

glean /gliːn/ **gleans, gleaning, gleaned.** VERB If you **glean** information, you obtain it slowly and with difficulty. *At present we're gleaning information from all sources.*

glee /gliː/. N-U **Glee** is a feeling of happiness and excitement, often caused by someone else's misfortune. *Investors have reacted with glee.*

gleeful /'gliːfəl/. ADJ Someone who is **gleeful** is happy or excited, often because of someone else's misfortune. ♦**gleefully** ADV *The media gleefully reports the bitterness between the two groups.*

glib /glɪb/. ADJ If you describe what someone says as **glib**, you disapprove of it because it suggests that something is simple or easy, when this is not the case. ♦**glibly** ADV *We talk glibly of equality of opportunity.*

glide /glaɪd/ **glides, gliding, glided.** ⑴ VERB If you **glide** somewhere, you move there smoothly and silently. *Waiters glide between tightly packed tables bearing trays.* ⑵ VERB When birds or aeroplanes **glide**, they float on air currents. *Pelicans glide over the waves.*

glider /'glaɪdə/ **gliders.** N-C A **glider** is an aircraft without an engine which flies by floating on air currents.

glimmer /'glɪmə/ **glimmers, glimmering, glimmered.** ⑴ VERB & N-C If something **glimmers**, it produces a faint, often unsteady light called a **glimmer**. *...a few stars still glimmered. ...the glimmer of daylight.* ⑵ N-C A **glimmer of** something is a faint sign of it. *...the first glimmer of hope.*

glimpse /glɪmps/ **glimpses, glimpsing, glimpsed.** ⑴ VERB & N-C If you **glimpse** someone or something, or if you get a **glimpse** of them, you see them very briefly and not very well. *...a window through which you could glimpse a few of the soldiers inside... I had a glimpse of a swimming pool through the trees.* ⑵ N-C A **glimpse** of something is a brief experience of it or an idea about it that helps you understand it better. *The trip will give them a glimpse of a world they have barely encountered.*

glint /glɪnt/ **glints, glinting, glinted.** ⑴ VERB & N-C If something **glints**, or if there is a **glint** of light from it, it produces or reflects a quick flash of light; WRITTEN. *The sea glinted in the sun. ...the glint of gold.* ⑵ VERB & N-SING If someone's eyes **glint**, they shine and express a particular emotion. You can talk about a **glint** in someone's eyes; WRITTEN. *...her eyes glinting with pride... Was there a glint of mockery in his eyes?*

glisten /'glɪsən/ **glistens, glistening, glistened.** VERB If something **glistens**, because it is smooth, wet, or oily. *Her eyes glistened with tears. ... a man with glistening black hair.*

glitter /'glɪtə/ **glitters, glittering, glittered.** ⑴ VERB If something **glitters**, it shines and sparkles. *The sunlight made the water glitter.* ⑵ N-U You can use **glitter** to refer to the superficial attractiveness or excitement connected with something. ...*the glitter of the pop world.*

gloat /gləʊt/ **gloats, gloating, gloated.** VERB When someone **gloats**, they show great pleasure at their own success or at other people's failure. *No doubt you're gloating over the result.*

global /ˈgləʊbəl/. ADJ **Global** means concerning or including the whole world. ...*a global ban on nuclear testing.* ◆ **globally** ADV ...*products sold globally.*

,global 'warming. N-U The problem of the gradual rise in the earth's temperature is referred to as **global warming**.

globe /gləʊb/ **globes.** [1] N-SING You can refer to the Earth as the **globe**. ...*performers from around the globe.* [2] N-C A **globe** is a ball-shaped object with a map of the world on it.

gloom /gluːm/. [1] N-SING **Gloom** is a state of partial darkness. *My eyes were becoming accustomed to the gloom.* [2] N-U **Gloom** is a feeling of unhappiness or despair. ...*the deepening gloom over the economy.*

gloomy /ˈgluːmi/ **gloomier, gloomiest.** [1] ADJ Something that is **gloomy** is dark and rather depressing. ...*the gloomy days of winter.* [2] ADJ If someone is **gloomy**, they are unhappy and have no hope. *They are gloomy about their chances of success.* ◆ **gloomily** ADV *Mark shook his head gloomily.* [3] ADJ If a situation is **gloomy**, it does not give you much hope of success or happiness. *The economic outlook remains gloomy.*

glorify /ˈglɔːrɪfaɪ/ **glorifies, glorifying, glorified.** VERB If you say that someone **glorifies** something, you mean that they praise it or make it seem good or special, usually when it is not. ...*music which glorifies drugs.* ◆ **glorification** /ˌglɔːrɪfɪˈkeɪʃən/ N-U ...*the increasing glorification of violence.*

glorious /ˈglɔːriəs/. [1] ADJ If you describe something as **glorious**, you are emphasizing that it is very beautiful or wonderful. ...*a glorious rainbow.* ◆ **gloriously** ADV ...*a gloriously sunny morning.* [2] ADJ A **glorious** career, victory, or occasion involves great fame or success.

glory /ˈglɔːri/ **glories, glorying, gloried.** [1] N-U **Glory** is fame and admiration that you get for an achievement. *It was her moment of glory.* [2] N-U The **glory** of something is its great beauty or quality of being impressive. *Spring arrived in all its glory.*
▸ **glory in.** PHR-VERB If you **glory in** a situation or activity, you enjoy it very much. *The workers were glorying in their new-found freedom.*

gloss /glɒs, AM glɔːs/ **glosses, glossing, glossed.** [1] N-SING A **gloss** is a bright shine on a surface. *It gives hair a rich gloss.* [2] N-VAR **Gloss** or **gloss paint** is paint that forms a shiny surface when it dries.
▸ **gloss over.** PHR-VERB If you **gloss over** a problem or mistake, you try to make it seem unimportant by ignoring it or by dealing with it very quickly.

glossy /ˈglɒsi, AM ˈglɔːsi/. [1] ADJ Something that is **glossy** is smooth and shiny. ...*glossy black hair.* [2] ADJ BEFORE N **Glossy** magazines, brochures, or photographs are produced on expensive shiny paper.

glove /glʌv/ **gloves.** N-C **Gloves** are pieces of clothing which cover your hand and wrist and have individual sections for each finger.

glow /gləʊ/ **glows, glowing, glowed.** [1] VERB & N-C If something **glows**, it produces a dull, steady light called a **glow**. *He blew on the charcoal until it glowed orange.* ...*the glow of the fire.* [2] VERB If something **glows**, it looks bright because it is reflecting light. *The ship's sails glowed in the morning sun.* [3] VERB & N-SING If someone's skin **glows**, or if there is a **glow** to their skin, it looks healthy and pink, for example because they are excited or have been exercising. *Alison's skin seem to glow with health.* [4] VERB & N-SING If someone **glows** with an emotion such as pride or pleasure, the expression in their face shows they feel it. A **glow** of something like pride or pleasure is a strong feeling of it. *I felt a glow of achievement.*

glowing /ˈgləʊɪŋ/. ADJ A **glowing** description of someone or something praises them highly. ...*glowing school reports.*

glucose /ˈgluːkəʊz, -əʊs/. N-U **Glucose** is a type of sugar.

glue /gluː/ **glues, glueing** (or **gluing**), **glued.** [1] N-VAR **Glue** is a sticky substance used for joining things together. [2] VERB If you **glue** one object to another, you stick them together, using glue. *Glue the two halves together.* [3] PASSIVE-VERB If you say that someone **is glued to** something, you mean that they are giving it all their attention. *She was glued to the television.*

glum /glʌm/ **glummer, glummest.** ADJ Someone who is **glum** is sad and quiet, because they are disappointed or unhappy. ◆ **glumly** ADV *Charles was sitting glumly in the front seat.*

glut /glʌt/ **gluts.** N-C If there is a **glut** of something such as goods or raw materials, there is so much of it that it cannot all be sold or used. ...*a glut of summer fruit.*

gm. gm is a written abbreviation for **gram**.

GMT /ˌdʒiː em ˈtiː/. **GMT** is an abbreviation for 'Greenwich Mean Time', the standard time in Great Britain which is used to calculate the time in the rest of the world.

gnaw /nɔː/ **gnaws, gnawing, gnawed.** [1] VERB If animals or people **gnaw** something, they bite it repeatedly. *Woodlice attack living plants and gnaw at the stems.* [2] VERB If a feeling or thought **gnaws** at you, it causes you to keep worrying; LITERARY. ...*a question gnawed at him.* ...*gnawing doubts about the value of the whole affair.*

gnome /nəʊm/ **gnomes.** N-C In children's stories, a **gnome** is a tiny old man with a beard and a pointed hat.

go 1 moving or leaving

go /gəʊ/ **goes, going, went, gone.** In most cases the past participle of **go** is **gone**, but occasionally you use 'been': see **been**. [1] VERB When you **go** somewhere, you move or travel there. *We went to Rome... I went home at the weekend... It took us an hour to go three miles.* [2] VERB You use **go** to say that someone leaves the place where they are and does an activity, often a leisure activity. *We went swimming very early... He went for a walk.* [3] VERB When someone **goes** to do something, they move somewhere in order to do it, and they do it. In British English, someone can also **go and** do something. In American English, someone can also **go do** something, but you say that someone **went and** did something. *Paddy had gone to live in Canada... I must go and see this film.* [4] VERB When you **go**, you leave the place where you are. *Let's go.* [5] VERB If you **go to** school, work, or church, you attend it regularly as part of your normal life. *His son went to a top university.* [6] VERB When you say where a road or path **goes**, you are saying where it begins or ends, or what places it is in. *...a mountain road that goes from Blairstown to Millbrook Village.* [7] VERB If you say where money **goes**, you are saying what it is spent on. *Most of my money goes on bills.* [8] VERB If you say that something **goes to** someone, you mean that it is given to them. *A lot of credit must go to the chairman... The job went to Yuri Skokov.* [9] VERB When something **goes**, someone gets rid of it. *100,000 jobs will go.* [10] VERB If something **goes** into something else, it fits into it or it is put into it. *He was trying to push it through the hole and it wouldn't go... This knob goes here...* *The shoes go on the shoe shelf.* [11] VERB If something such as a piece of machinery **is going**, it is no longer working properly and may soon stop working altogether. You can also talk, for example, about someone's hearing or mental powers **going**. *The battery was going... His eyes are going.* [12] See note at **bring**.

go 2 link verb uses

go /gəʊ/ **goes, going, went, gone.** [1] LINK-VERB You can use **go** to say that someone or something changes to another state or condition. For example, if someone **goes crazy**, they become crazy. *50,000 companies have gone out of business.* [2] LINK-VERB You can use **go** when indicating whether or not someone wears or has something. For example, if someone **goes barefoot**, they do not wear any shoes.

go 3 other verb uses, noun uses, and phrases

go /gəʊ/ **goes, going, went, gone.** [1] VERB You use **go** to talk about how successful an event or situation is. For example, if you say that an event **went well**, you mean that it was successful, and if you ask how something **is going**, you are asking how much success people are having with it. *Some colours go together and some don't.* [3] N-C A **go** is an attempt at doing something. *I always wanted to have a go at football.* [4] N-C If it is your **go** in a game, it is your turn to do something. [5] See also **going**, **gone**.

PHRASES • If you **go all out** to do something or **go all out** for something, you make the greatest possible effort to do it or get it; INFORMAL. • If someone **has a go at** you, they criticize you, often unfairly; INFORMAL. • If someone is **making a go of** something such as a business or relationship, they are beginning to make it successful. • If you **have** something **on the go**, you have started it and are busy doing it. *Do you like to have many projects on the go at any one time?* • If someone is always **on the go**, they are busy and active; INFORMAL. • If you say that there is a certain amount of time **to go**, you mean that there is that amount of time left before something happens or ends. *There is a week to go until the first German elections.* • to **go without saying**: see **say**. • **there you go**: see **there**.

go 4 phrasal verbs

go /gəʊ/ **goes, going, went, gone.**
▶ **go about.** [1] PHR-VERB The way you **go about** a task or problem is the way you deal with it. [2] PHR-VERB When you **are going about** your normal activities, you are doing them. [3] PHR-VERB If you **go about** in a particular way, you behave or dress in that way. *He went about looking ill and unhappy.*
▶ **go after.** PHR-VERB If you **go after** something, you try to get it, catch it, or hit it. *We're not going after civilian targets.*
▶ **go against.** PHR-VERB If someone **goes against** your wishes, beliefs, or expectations, their behaviour is the opposite of what you want, believe in, or expect.
▶ **go ahead.** [1] PHR-VERB If someone **goes ahead** with something, they begin to do it or make it. [2] PHR-VERB If a process or an organized event **goes ahead**, it takes place or is carried out.
▶ **go along with.** [1] PHR-VERB If you **go along with** someone or something such as a rule or an idea, you agree with that person or accept that idea. [2] PHR-VERB If you **go along with** a person or an idea, you agree with them.
▶ **go around** or **go round.** [1] PHR-VERB If you **go around** or **go round** to someone's house, you visit them at their house; INFORMAL. [2] PHR-VERB If there is enough of something to **go around** or **go round**, there is enough of it for people's needs.
▶ **go around with** or **go round with.** PHR-VERB If you **go around with** or **go round with** a person or group of people, you are friends with them and go to places together; BRITISH.
▶ **go back on.** PHR-VERB If you **go back on** a promise or agreement, you do not do what you promised or agreed to do.
▶ **go back to.** PHR-VERB If you **go back to** a task or activity, you start doing it again after you have stopped for a period of time.
▶ **go before.** PHR-VERB When people or their case **goes before** a judge, they appear in court as part of a legal process.
▶ **go down.** [1] PHR-VERB If a price, level, or amount **goes down**, it becomes lower than it was. *Crime has gone down 70%.* [2] PHR-VERB If you **go down** on your knees or on all fours, you lower your body until it is supported by your knees, or by your hands and knees. [3] PHR-VERB When the sun **goes down**, it drops below the horizon. [4] PHR-VERB If a ship **goes down**, it sinks. If a plane **goes down**, it crashes. [5] PHR-VERB If you say that a remark, idea, or type of behaviour **goes down** in a particular way, you mean that it gets that reaction. *Solicitors advised their clients that a tidy look went down well with the magistrates.*

▶ **go down with.** PHR-VERB If you **go down with** an illness or a disease, you catch it.

▶ **go for.** [1] PHR-VERB If you **go for** a particular thing or way of doing something, you choose it. *People tried to persuade him to go for a more gradual reform programme.* [2] PHR-VERB If you **go for** someone or something, you like them very much; INFORMAL. *I tend to go for large dark men.* [3] PHR-VERB If someone **goes for** you, they attack you. *Pantieri went for him, gripping him by the throat.*

▶ **go in.** PHR-VERB If the sun **goes in**, it is behind a cloud.

▶ **go in for.** PHR-VERB If you **go in for** a particular activity, you start doing it.

▶ **go into.** [1] PHR-VERB If you **go into** something, you describe it in detail. *I don't want to go into details about what was said.* [2] PHR-VERB If you **go into** a particular occupation, you start doing that job. *Mr Pok has now gone into the tourism business.*

▶ **go off.** [1] PHR-VERB If you **go off** something or someone, you stop liking them; INFORMAL. [2] PHR-VERB If an explosive device or a gun **goes off**, it explodes or fires. [3] PHR-VERB If an alarm bell **goes off**, it makes a sudden loud noise. [4] PHR-VERB If an electrical device **goes off**, it stops operating. *All the lights went off.* [5] PHR-VERB Food or drink that has **gone off** is unfit to eat or drink; BRITISH.

▶ **go on.** [1] PHR-VERB If you **go on** doing something, or **go on with** an activity, you continue to do it. *I'm all right here. Go on with your work.* [2] PHR-VERB If a process or institution **goes on**, it continues to happen or exist. *The population failed to understand the necessity for the war to go on.* [3] PHR-VERB If something **is going on**, it is happening. *While this conversation was going on, I was listening.* [4] PHR-VERB If you **go on**, you continue saying something or talking about something. *Meer cleared his throat several times before he went on.* [5] PHR-VERB The information you have to **go on** is the information you have available to base an opinion or judgement on. [6] PHR-VERB If an electrical device **goes on**, it begins operating.

▶ **go out.** [1] PHR-VERB When you **go out**, you do something enjoyable away from your home , for example go to a bar or the cinema. [2] PHR-VERB If you **go out** with someone, you have a romantic or sexual relationship with them. [3] PHR-VERB If a light **goes out**, it stops shining. [4] PHR-VERB If flames **go out**, they stop burning. [5] PHR-VERB When the tide **goes out**, the level of sea in a particular place gets lower.

▶ **go over.** PHR-VERB If you **go over** a document, incident, or problem, you examine it very carefully and systematically. *An accountant has gone over the books.*

▶ **go over to.** [1] PHR-VERB If someone or something **goes over** to a different way of doing things, they change to it. [2] PHR-VERB If you **go over** to a group or political party, you join them after previously belonging to an opposing group or party. *Only a small number of tanks and paratroops have gone over to his side.*

▶ **go round.** PHR-VERB **Go round** means the same as **go around**.

▶ **go through.** [1] PHR-VERB If you **go through** a difficult experience or period of time, you experience it. [2] PHR-VERB If you **go through** a lot of things such as papers or clothes, you look at them, usually in order to search for a particular item. *Someone had gone through my possessions.* [3] PHR-VERB When someone **goes through** a particular routine, they perform a task in a particular way. [4] PHR-VERB If a law, agreement, or official decision **goes through**, it is approved by a parliament or committee.

▶ **go through with.** PHR-VERB If you **go through with** an action you have decided on, you do it, even though it may be very difficult for you.

▶ **go towards.** PHR-VERB If an amount of money **goes towards** something, it is used to pay part of the cost of it.

▶ **go under.** [1] PHR-VERB If a business **goes under**, it becomes bankrupt. [2] PHR-VERB If a boat or a person **goes under**, they sink below the surface of some water.

▶ **go up.** [1] PHR-VERB If a price, amount, or level **goes up**, it becomes higher or greater than it was. [2] PHR-VERB If something **goes up**, it explodes or suddenly starts to burn. *The hotel went up in flames.*

▶ **go with.** [1] PHR-VERB If one thing **goes with** another thing, the two things officially belong together, so that if you get one, you also get the other. *...the lucrative £150,000 salary that goes with the job.* [2] PHR-VERB If one thing **goes with** another thing, they are usually found or experienced together. *...the shame that goes with being on the dole.*

▶ **go without.** PHR-VERB If you **go without** something that you need, you do not get it. *I have known what it is like to go without food for days.*

goad /gəʊd/ **goads, goading, goaded.** VERB If you **goad** someone, you deliberately make them angry in order to get them to react in some way. *The psychiatrist was trying to goad him into some unguarded response.*

'go-ahead. [1] N-SING If you give someone **the go-ahead**, you give them permission to do something. *The Greek government today gave the go-ahead for five major road schemes.* [2] ADJ BEFORE N A **go-ahead** person or organization tries hard to succeed, often by using new methods.

goal /gəʊl/ **goals.** [1] N-C In games such as football or hockey, the **goal** is the space into which the players try to get the ball in order to score. [2] N-C In games such as football or hockey, if a player scores a **goal**, they get the ball into the goal. [3] N-C Your **goal** is something that you hope to achieve. *The goal is to raise as much money as possible.*

goalkeeper /'gəʊlkiːpə/ **goalkeepers.** N-C A **goalkeeper** is the player in a sports team whose job is to guard the goal.

goat /gəʊt/ **goats.** N-C A **goat** is an animal which is a bit bigger than a sheep and has horns.

gobble /'gɒbəl/ **gobbles, gobbling, gobbled.** VERB If you **gobble** food, you eat it quickly and greedily.

'go-between, go-betweens. N-C If someone acts as a **go-between**, they take messages between people who are unable or unwilling to meet each other.

god /gɒd/ **gods.** [1] N-PROPER The name **God** is given to the spirit or being who is worshipped as the creator and ruler of the world, especially by Christians, Jews, and Muslims. [2] CONVENTION People sometimes use **God** in exclamations for emphasis, or to express surprise, fear, or excitement. Some people find this use offensive. *Oh my God he's shot somebody.* [3] N-C A **god** is one of the spirits or beings believed in many religions to have power over an aspect of the world. *...Pan, the God of nature.*

goddess /ˈgɒdes/ **goddesses.** N-C In many religions, a **goddess** is a female spirit or being that is believed to have power over a particular aspect of the world. *...Diana, the goddess of war.*

goggles /ˈgɒgəlz/. N-PL **Goggles** are large glasses that fit closely to your face around your eyes to protect them.

going /ˈgəʊɪŋ/. [1] VERB If you say that something **is going** to happen, you mean that it will happen in the future. *I think it's going to be successful... You're going to enjoy this... He's going to resign.* [2] N-U The **going** is the conditions that affect your ability to do something. *He has her support to fall back on when the going gets tough.* [3] ADJ BEFORE N The **going** rate for something is the usual amount of money that you expect to pay or receive for it. [4] See also **go**.

PHRASES • When you **get going**, you start doing something or start a journey, especially after a delay. • If you **keep going**, you continue doing something difficult or tiring. • If someone or something **has** a lot **going for** them, they have a lot of advantages.

,goings-'on. N-PL **Goings-on** are strange, amusing, or improper activities.

gold /gəʊld/ **golds.** [1] N-U **Gold** is a valuable yellow-coloured metal used for making jewellery, and as an international currency. *The price of gold was going up. ...gold coins.* [2] N-U **Gold** is jewellery and other things that are made of gold. *We handed over all our gold and money.* [3] ADJ & N-C Something that is **gold** in colour is bright yellow. *...Michel's black and gold shirt.*

golden /ˈgəʊldən/. [1] ADJ Something that is **golden** is bright yellow. *...an endless golden beach.* [2] ADJ **Golden** things are made of gold. [3] ADJ BEFORE N If you describe something as **golden**, you mean it is wonderful because it is likely to be successful, or because it is the best of its kind. *There's a golden opportunity for peace.*

goldfish /ˈgəʊldfɪʃ/. N-C A **goldfish** is a small orange-coloured fish which is often kept as a pet in a bowl or a garden pond. **Goldfish** is both the singular and the plural form.

,gold 'medal, gold medals. N-C A **gold medal** is a medal made of gold which is awarded as first prize in a contest or competition.

golf /gɒlf/. N-U **Golf** is a game in which you use long sticks called clubs to hit a ball into holes that are spread out over a large area of grassy land. ♦**golfer, golfers.** N-C *About 150 golfers* had arrived for a match. ♦**golfing** N-U *...a golfing holiday in Spain.*

'golf club, golf clubs. [1] N-C A **golf club** is a long, thin, metal stick with a piece of wood or metal at one end that you use to hit the ball in golf. [2] N-C A **golf club** is a social organization which provides a golf course and a clubhouse for its members.

'golf course, golf courses. N-C A **golf course** is an area of land where people play golf.

gone /gɒn, AM gɑːn/. [1] **Gone** is the past participle of **go**. [2] ADJ AFTER LINK-V Someone or something that is **gone** is no longer present or no longer exists. *While he was gone she had tea with the Colonel... By morning the smoke will be all gone.* [3] PREP If it is **gone** a particular time, it is later than that time; BRITISH, INFORMAL. *It was just gone 7 o'clock this evening when I finished.*

gong /gɒŋ, AM gɔːŋ/ **gongs.** N-C A **gong** is a flat, circular piece of metal that you hit with a hammer to make a loud sound.

gonna /ˈgɒnə, AM ˈgɔːnə/. **Gonna** is used in written English to represent the words 'going to' when they are pronounced informally. *What am I gonna do?*

good /gʊd/ **better, best.** [1] ADJ **Good** means pleasant or enjoyable. *We had a really good time together... There's nothing better than a cup of hot coffee... It's so good to hear your voice after all this time.* [2] ADJ **Good** means of a high quality, standard, or level. *Exercise is just as important to health as good food... He was very good at his work.* [3] ADJ A **good** idea, reason, method, or decision is a sensible or valid one. *It was a good idea to make some different kinds of community service... Could you give me some advice on the best way to do this?* [4] ADJ Someone who is in a **good** mood is cheerful and pleasant to be with. [5] ADJ A **good** person is kind and thoughtful. *You are good to me.* [6] ADJ A child or animal that is **good** is well-behaved. [7] N-U **Good** is what is considered to be right according to moral standards or religious beliefs. *...good and evil.* [8] N-SING If something is done for the **good** of a person or organization, it is done in order to benefit them. *I'm only telling you this for your own good!* [9] N-U If you say that doing something is **no good** or does **not** do **any good**, you mean that doing it is not of any use or will not bring any success. *It's no good worrying about it now... We gave them water and kept them warm, but it didn't do any good.* [10] ADJ BEFORE N You use **good** to emphasize the great extent or degree of something. *We waited a good fifteen minutes.*

PHRASES • **'As good as'** can be used to mean 'almost.' *His career is as good as over.* • If something changes or disappears **for good**, it never changes back or reappears as it was before. *This drug cleared up the disease for good.* • If someone **is good for** something, you can rely on them to provide that thing. *He was good for a few laughs.* • If you **make good** some damage or a loss, you repair the damage or replace what has been lost. • If someone **makes good**, they become successful. *Both men are poor boys made good.* • See also **better, best, goods.**

,good after'noon. CONVENTION You say 'Good afternoon' when you are greeting someone in the afternoon; FORMAL.

goodbye (or **good-bye**) /,gʊd'baɪ/ **good-byes.** ① CONVENTION You say 'Goodbye' to someone when you or they are leaving, or at the end of a telephone conversation. ② N-VAR When you say **goodbye** to someone or say your **goodbyes**, you say something such as 'goodbye' or 'bye' when you leave. *They came to the front door to wave goodbye.*

,good 'evening. CONVENTION You say 'Good evening' when you are greeting someone in the evening; FORMAL.

goodie /'gʊdi/. See **goody**.

,good-'looking,   better-looking,   best-looking. ADJ A **good-looking** person has an attractive face. ● See note at **beautiful**.

,good 'morning. CONVENTION You say 'Good morning' when you are greeting someone in the morning; FORMAL.

,good-'natured. ADJ A **good-natured** person or animal is naturally friendly and does not get angry easily.

goodness /'gʊdnəs/. ① CONVENTION People say 'goodness' or 'my goodness' to express surprise or for emphasis. *Goodness, I wonder if he knows... My goodness, he's earned millions in his career.* ● **thank goodness**: see **thank**. ② N-U **Goodness** is the quality of being kind and honest. *He retains a faith in human goodness.*

goodnight (or **good night**) /,gʊd'naɪt/. CONVENTION You say 'Goodnight' to someone late in the evening, before one of you goes home or goes to sleep.

goods /gʊdz/. N-PL **Goods** are things that are made to be sold. *...consumer goods.*

goodwill /,gʊd'wɪl/. N-U **Goodwill** is a friendly or helpful attitude towards other people, countries, or organizations. *...a gesture of goodwill.*

goody (or **goodie**) /'gʊdi/ **goodies.** ① N-C You can refer to pleasant, exciting, or attractive things as **goodies**; INFORMAL. *...a little bag of goodies.* ② N-C You can refer to the heroes and the morally good characters in a story or situation as the **goodies**; INFORMAL. *There are few goodies and baddies in this industrial dispute.*

goose /guːs/ **geese.** N-VAR A **goose** is a large bird similar to a duck, with a long neck. The meat of this bird is also referred to as **goose**.

gorge /gɔːdʒ/ **gorges, gorging, gorged.** ① N-C A **gorge** is a narrow steep-sided valley, usually where a river passes through mountains or an area of hard rock. ② VERB If you **gorge** on something, you eat lots of it in a very greedy way. *We gorged ourselves on delicious bread.*

gorgeous /'gɔːdʒəs/. ADJ Someone or something that is **gorgeous** is extremely pleasant or attractive; INFORMAL. *It's a gorgeous day... All the girls in my house are mad about Ryan, they think he's gorgeous.*

gorilla /gə'rɪlə/ **gorillas.** N-C A **gorilla** is a very large ape.

gosh /gɒʃ/. CONVENTION Some people say 'Gosh' to indicate surprise or shock; INFORMAL. *Gosh, that was a heavy bag!*

gospel /'gɒspəl/ **gospels.** ① N-C The **Gospels** are the four books of the Bible describing the life and teachings of Jesus Christ. ② N-C You can use **gospel** to refer humorously to a particular way of thinking that a person or group urges others to accept. *...the gospel according to my mom.* ③ ADJ If you take something as **gospel**, or as the **gospel truth**, you believe that it is completely true. ④ N-U **Gospel** or **gospel music** is a style of religious music that uses strong rhythms and vocal harmony.

gossip /'gɒsɪp/ **gossips, gossiping, gossiped.** ① N-U **Gossip** is informal conversation, often about other people's private affairs. *There has been much gossip about the possible reasons for his absence.* ② VERB If you **gossip** with someone, you talk informally with them, especially about other people or local events. *We spoke, debated, gossiped into the night.* ③ N-C If you describe someone as a **gossip**, you disapprove of them because they often talk about other people's private affairs. *He was a vicious gossip.*

got /gɒt/. ① **Got** is the past tense and past participle of **get**. ② VERB You use **have got** in spoken English when you are saying that someone owns, possesses, or is holding a particular thing, or when you are mentioning a quality or characteristic that someone or something has. In American English, the 'have' is sometimes omitted. *I've got a coat just like this... Have you got any ideas?... After a pause he asked, 'You got any identification?'* ③ VERB You use **have got to** in spoken English when you are saying that something is necessary or must happen in the way stated. In American English, the 'have' is sometimes omitted. *I'm not happy with the situation, but I've just got to accept it... See, you got to work very hard.* ④ VERB People sometimes use **have got to** in spoken English in order to emphasize that they are certain that something is true. In American English, the 'have' is sometimes omitted. *He's got to be very happy with these results.*

Gothic /'gɒθɪk/. ① ADJ **Gothic** is used to describe a style of architecture or church art, dating from the Middle Ages, that is distinguished by tall pillars, high curved ceilings, and pointed arches. ② ADJ **Gothic** is used to describe stories in which strange, mysterious adventures happen in dark and lonely places such as the ruins of a castle.

gotta /'gɒtə/. Gotta is used to represent the words 'got to' when they are pronounced informally, as a way of saying 'have to' or 'must'; WRITTEN. *Prices are high and our kid's gotta eat.*

gotten /'gɒtən/. **Gotten** is the past participle of **get** in American English.

gouge /gaʊdʒ/ **gouges, gouging, gouged.** VERB If you **gouge** something, you make a hole or a long cut in it, usually with a sharp object. *...quarries which have gouged great holes in the hills.*

▶ **gouge out.** PHR-VERB To **gouge out** a piece or part of something means to cut, dig, or force it from the surrounding surface. ...*threatening to gouge his eyes out.*

gourmet /'guəmeɪ/ **gourmets.** [1] ADJ BEFORE N **Gourmet** food is more unusual or sophisticated than ordinary food. [2] N-C A **gourmet** is someone who enjoys good food, and who knows a lot about food and wine.

govern /'gʌvən/ **governs, governing, governed.** [1] VERB To **govern** a country means to officially control and organize its economic, social, and legal systems. [2] VERB If a situation or activity **is governed** by a particular factor or rule, it is controlled by or depends on that factor or rule. *Marine insurance is governed by a strict series of rules and regulations.*

government /'gʌvənmənt/ **governments.** [1] N-C The **government** of a country is the group of people who are responsible for governing it. When it is singular **government** can take the singular or plural form of the verb. *The Government are to carry out a review of the Shops Act. ...fighting between government forces and left-wing rebels.* [2] N-U **Government** consists of the activities, methods, and principles involved in governing a country or other political unit. ...*our system of government.* ◆**governmental** /ˌgʌvən'mentəl/ ADJ BEFORE N ...*participation in the governmental process.*

> In Britain, the head of the government is the **Prime Minister**. The Prime Minister appoints the other **ministers**, who are responsible for particular areas of policy. The Prime Minister and other senior ministers together form the **Cabinet**. The policies of the government are debated and approved by **Parliament**, which consists of the **House of Commons** and the **House of Lords**. There are about 650 elected **Members of Parliament** (or **MPs**) in the House of Commons.
> In the United States, the head of the government is the **President**, who appoints the members of his **administration**. Policies are debated and approved by **Congress**, which consists of the **House of Representatives** and the **Senate**. Members of the House of Representatives are known as **congressmen** and **congresswomen**, and members of the **Senate** are called **senators**.

governor /'gʌvənə/ **governors.** N-C A **governor** is a person who is responsible for the political administration of a region, or for the administration of an institution. *Governor Deukmejian called for an inquiry. ...the BBC board of governors. ...the prison governor.*

gown /gaʊn/ **gowns.** [1] N-C A **gown** is a long dress which women wear on formal occasions. [2] N-C A **gown** is a loose black cloak worn on formal occasions by lawyers and academics.

GP /ˌdʒiː 'piː/ **GPs.** N-C A **GP** is a doctor who treats all types of illness, instead of specializing in one area of medicine. **GP** is an abbreviation for 'general practitioner'.

grab /græb/ **grabs, grabbing, grabbed.** [1] VERB If you **grab** something, you take it or pick it up roughly. *I grabbed him by the neck.*

[2] VERB & N-C If you **grab at** something, or if you make a **grab** for it, you try to get hold of it. *I made a grab for the knife.* [3] VERB If you **grab** an opportunity, you take advantage of it eagerly. *She grabbed the chance of a job interview.* [4] PHRASE If something is **up for grabs**, it is available to anyone who is interested.

grace /greɪs/ **graces, gracing, graced.** [1] N-U If someone moves with **grace**, they move smoothly and elegantly. [2] N-U If someone behaves with **grace**, they behave in a polite and dignified way, even when they are upset. *He accepted defeat with grace.* [3] VERB If you say that something or someone **graces** a place, you mean that they make the place more pleasant or attractive; FORMAL. *The Tartar cities were graced with many gates and temples... Her face has graced the cover of more than 500 magazines.* [4] N-U A period of **grace** is an extra period of time that you have been given to do something. *Businesses were given a year's grace and payments began from March 1, 1996.* [5] PHRASE If you refer to someone's **fall from grace**, you are talking about the fact that they are suddenly no longer approved of or popular, often because they have done something unacceptable. You can also say that someone **has fallen from grace**.

graceful /'greɪsfʊl/. [1] ADJ Someone or something that is **graceful** moves in a smooth and elegant way that is attractive to watch. ◆**gracefully** ADV *She stepped gracefully onto the stage.* [2] ADJ Something that is **graceful** is attractive because it has a pleasing shape or style. ...*a graceful medieval cathedral.* [3] ADJ **Graceful** behaviour is polite and pleasant. ◆**gracefully** ADV *We managed to decline gracefully.*

gracious /'greɪʃəs/. [1] ADJ If someone is **gracious**, they are considerate and pleasant. ...*a gracious speech of thanks.* ◆**graciously** ADV *Hospitality at the Presidential guest house was graciously declined.* [2] ADJ You use **gracious** to describe the comfortable way of life of wealthy people. ...*gracious suburbs with swimming pools and tennis courts.*

grade /greɪd/ **grades, grading, graded.** [1] VERB If something **is graded**, its quality is judged or classified. *The oil is tasted and graded according to quality... South Point College does not grade the students' work.* [2] N-C The **grade** of a product is its quality. ...*a good grade of plywood.* [3] N-C Your **grade** in an examination is the mark that you get. ...*GCSE O level, grade B.* [4] N-C Your **grade** in a company or organization is your level of importance or your rank. ...*senior management grades.* [5] N-C In schools in the United States, a **grade** is a group of classes in which all the children are of a similar age. [6] PHRASE If someone **makes the grade**, they succeed, especially by reaching the required standard; INFORMAL.

gradient /'greɪdiənt/ **gradients.** N-C A **gradient** is a slope or the degree to which the ground slopes.

gradual /'grædʒʊəl/. ADJ A **gradual** change or process happens in small stages over a long period of time, rather than suddenly. *You can expect her progress at school to be gradual ra-*

ther than brilliant. ◆**gradually** ADV *Gradually we learned to cope.*

graduate, graduates, graduating, graduated. verb /ˈgrædʒʊeɪt/, noun /ˈgrædʒʊət/. [1] VERB & N-C In Britain, when a student **graduates** from university, they have successfully completed a first degree course. A **graduate** is someone who has graduated from university. *She graduated in English and Drama from Manchester University. ...graduates in engineering.* [2] VERB In the United States, when a student **graduates**, they have successfully completed their studies at university, college, or school studies. [3] N-C In the United States, a **graduate** is a student who has successfully completed high school. [4] VERB If you **graduate** from one thing to another, you go from a less important job or position to a more important one. *From commercials she quickly graduated to television shows.*

graduation /ˌgrædʒʊˈeɪʃən/. [1] N-U **Graduation** is the successful completion of a course of study at a university, college, or school, for which you receive a degree or diploma. *Upon graduation he joined a small law firm.* [2] N-C A **graduation** is a special ceremony at which degrees or diplomas are given to students who have successfully completed their studies.

graffiti /grəˈfiːti/. N-U **Graffiti** are words or pictures that are scribbled or drawn in public places, for example on walls or trains.

graft /grɑːft, græft/ **grafts, grafting, grafted.** [1] VERB If a piece of healthy skin or bone **is grafted** on to a damaged part of your body, it is attached to that part of your body by a medical operation. [2] N-C A **graft** is skin or bone which is grafted onto your body. *I am having a skin graft on my arm soon.* [3] VERB If a part of one plant **is grafted** onto another plant, they are joined together so that they will become one plant. [4] N-U **Graft** means hard work; BRITISH. *His career has been one of hard graft.* [5] N-U **Graft** refers to the activity of using power to obtain money dishonestly; AMERICAN. *Her wealth was obtained by graft and corruption.*

Grail /greɪl/. [1] N-PROPER The **Grail** or the **Holy Grail** is the cup that was used by Jesus Christ at the Last Supper. [2] N-SING If you describe something as a **grail** or a **holy grail**, you mean that someone is trying very hard to obtain or achieve it.

grain /greɪn/ **grains.** [1] N-C A **grain** of wheat, rice, or other cereal crop is a seed from it. [2] N-VAR **Grain** is a cereal crop, especially wheat or corn, that has been harvested for food. *...a bag of grain.* [3] N-C A **grain** of something such as sand or salt is a tiny piece of it. [4] N-SING A **grain** of a quality is a very small amount of it. *There's more than a grain of truth in that.* [5] N-C The **grain** of a piece of wood is the direction of its fibres. You can also refer to the pattern of lines on the surface of the wood as **the grain.** *Brush the paint generously over the wood in the direction of the grain.* [6] PHRASE If you say that an idea or action **goes against the grain**, you mean it is very difficult to accept it or do it, because it conflicts with your beliefs.

gram (or **gramme**) /græm/ **grams.** N-C A **gram** is a unit of weight equal to one thousandth of a kilogram.

grammar /ˈgræmə/ **grammars.** [1] N-U **Grammar** is the ways that words can be put together in order to make sentences. *He studied hard at his Latin grammar.* [2] N-U Someone's **grammar** is the way in which they obey or do not obey the rules of a language. *...a deterioration in spelling and grammar among teenagers.* [3] N-C A **grammar** is a book that describes the rules of a language.

grammar school, grammar schools. N-C A **grammar school** is a school in Britain for children aged between eleven and eighteen with a high academic ability.

grammatical /grəˈmætɪkəl/. ADJ BEFORE N **Grammatical** is used to describe something relating to grammar.

gramme /græm/. See **gram.**

gran /græn/ **grans.** N-C & N-VOC Your **gran** is your grandmother; INFORMAL.

grand /grænd/ **grander, grandest.** [1] ADJ If you describe a building or landscape as **grand**, you mean that it is splendid or impressive. *...their rather grand house.* [2] ADJ **Grand** plans or actions are ambitious and intended to achieve important results. *The grand design of Europe's monetary union is already agreed.* [3] ADJ If you describe people as **grand**, you mean they seem or act important or socially superior. [4] ADJ If you describe an activity or experience as **grand**, you think that it is pleasant and enjoyable. *He was having a grand time meeting new sorts of people.* [5] ADJ BEFORE N A **grand** total is a total obtained by adding a series of things together. [6] N-SING A **grand** is a thousand pounds or a thousand dollars; INFORMAL.

grandad (or **granddad**) /ˈgrændæd/ **grandads.** N-C & N-VOC Your **grandad** is your grandfather; INFORMAL.

grandchild, /ˈgræntʃaɪld/ **grandchildren.** N-C Someone's **grandchild** is the child of their son or daughter.

granddaughter /ˈgrændɔːtə/ **granddaughters.** N-C Someone's **granddaughter** is the daughter of their son or daughter.

grandeur /ˈgrændʒə/. [1] N-U **Grandeur** is the quality in something which makes it seem impressive and elegant. *...the grandeur of the country mansion.* [2] N-U Someone's **grandeur** is the great importance and social status that they have, or think that they have. *...mansions built by nineteenth-century men with delusions of grandeur.*

grandfather /ˈgrændfɑːðə/ **grandfathers.** N-C & N-VOC Your **grandfather** is the father of your father or mother.

grandiose /ˈgrændiəʊs/. ADJ If you describe something as **grandiose**, you mean it is bigger or more elaborate than necessary; used showing disapproval. *Not one of Kim's grandiose plans has even begun.*

grand jury, grand juries. N-C A **grand jury** is a jury, usually in the United States, which considers a criminal case in order to decide if someone should be tried in a court of law.

grandma /'grænmɑː/ **grandmas.** N-C & N-VOC
Your **grandma** is your grandmother; INFORMAL.

grandmother /'grænmʌðə/ **grandmothers.**
N-C & N-VOC Your **grandmother** is the mother of
your father or mother.

grandpa /'grænpɑː/ **grandpas.** N-C & N-VOC Your
grandpa is your grandfather; INFORMAL.

grandparent /'grænpeərənt/ **grandparents.**
N-C Your **grandparents** are the parents of your
father or mother.

grandson /'grænsʌn/ **grandsons.** N-C
Someone's **grandson** is the son of their son or
daughter.

grandstand /'grændstænd/ **grandstands.** N-C
A **grandstand** is a covered stand for spectators
at sporting events.

granite /'grænɪt/. N-U **Granite** is a very hard rock
used in building.

granny (or **grannie**) /'græni/ **grannies.** N-C &
N-VOC Your **granny** is your grandmother; INFOR-
MAL.

grant /grɑːnt, grænt/ **grants, granting, granted.** ① N-C A **grant** is an amount of money that
the government or other institution gives to a
person or an organization for a particular purpose. *They'd got a special grant to encourage
research.* ② VERB If someone in authority
grants you something, they give it to you. *Permission was granted a few weeks ago.* ③ VERB If
you **grant** that something is true, you admit
that it is true; FORMAL. *The magistrates granted
that the RSPCA was justified in bringing the action.*
PHRASES ● If you say that someone **takes** you
for granted, you are complaining that they
benefit from your help, efforts, or presence
without showing that they are grateful. ● If you
take it for granted that something is the case,
or if you **take** something **for granted**, you believe that it is true or you accept it as normal
without thinking about it. *He seemed to take it
for granted that he should speak as a representative... All the things I took for granted up
north just didn't happen in London.*

ˌgrant-mainˈtained school. ADJ A **grant-maintained
school** is one which receives money directly
from the national government rather than
from a local authority; BRITISH.

grape /greɪp/ **grapes.** ① N-C **Grapes** are small
green or purple fruit that can be eaten raw or
used for making wine. ② PHRASE If you describe someone's attitude as **sour grapes**, you
mean that they say something is worthless or
undesirable because they want it but cannot
have it themselves.

grapefruit /'greɪpfruːt/; the plural is **grapefruit**
or **grapefruits.** N-VAR A **grapefruit** is a large,
round, yellow fruit that has a sharp taste.

grapevine /'greɪpvaɪn/ **grapevines.** ① PHRASE
If you hear something **on the grapevine**, you
hear it in casual conversation with other people. ② N-C A **grapevine** is a climbing plant on
which grapes grow.

graph /grɑːf, græf/ **graphs.** N-C A **graph** is a
mathematical diagram which shows the relationship between two or more sets of numbers
or measurements.

graphic /'græfɪk/ **graphics.** ① ADJ A **graphic**
description or account of something unpleasant is very clear and detailed. *...graphic scenes
of drug taking.* ◆ **graphically** ADV *Here, graphically displayed, was confirmation of the entire
story.* ② N-U **Graphics** is the activity of drawing
or making pictures, especially in publishing,
industry, or computing. ③ N-U **Graphics** are
drawings and pictures that are made using
simple lines. *The Agriculture Department today
released a new graphic to replace the old symbol.*

graphite /'græfaɪt/. N-U **Graphite** is a hard black
substance that is a form of carbon.

grapple /'græpəl/ **grapples, grappling, grappled.** ① VERB If you **grapple** with someone,
you take hold of them and struggle with them.
*They grappled desperately for control of the
weapon.* ② VERB If you **grapple** with a problem, you try hard to solve it.

grasp /grɑːsp, græsp/ **grasps, grasping,
grasped.** ① VERB & N-SING If you **grasp** something, you hold it firmly. A **grasp** is a firm hold
or grip. *She was trying to grasp at something...
His hand was taken in a warm, firm grasp.*
② N-SING If something is in your **grasp**, you
possess or control it. If something slips from
your **grasp**, you lose it or lose control of it. *She
allowed victory to slip from her grasp.* ③ VERB &
N-SING If you **grasp** something that is complicated or difficult to understand, you understand it. A **grasp** of something is an understanding of it. *He instantly grasped that
Stephen was talking about his wife... They have
a good grasp of foreign languages.* ④ N-SING If
you say that something is within someone's
grasp, you mean that it is very likely that they
will achieve it.

grass /grɑːs, græs/ **grasses.** N-VAR **Grass** is a
very common green plant with narrow leaves
that forms a layer covering an area of ground.

grasshopper /'grɑːshɒpə, 'græs-/ **grass-
hoppers.** N-C A **grasshopper** is an insect with
long back legs that jumps high into the air and
makes a high, vibrating sound.

grassland /'grɑːslænd, 'græs-/ **grasslands.**
N-VAR **Grassland** is land covered with wild
grass.

ˌgrass ˈroots (also **grass-roots** or
grassroots). N-PL The **grass roots** of an organization are the ordinary people in it, rather
than its leaders. *You have to join the party at
grass-roots level.*

grassy /'grɑːsi, 'græs-/. ADJ A **grassy** area of
land is covered in grass.

grate /greɪt/ **grates, grating, grated.** ① N-C A
grate is a framework of bars in a fireplace,
which holds the coal or wood. ② VERB When
you **grate** food, you shred it into very small
pieces using a tool called a grater. ③ VERB
When something **grates**, it rubs against something else, making a harsh unpleasant sound.
The gun barrel grated against the floor. ④ VERB
If something such as someone's behaviour
grates on you, it irritates you. *...a loud, grating
Brooklyn accent.*

grateful /'greɪtfʊl/. ADJ If you are **grateful** for
something that someone has given you or
done for you, you are pleased and wish to

thank them. *I am grateful to you for your help.*
♦ **gratefully** ADV *I gratefully accepted the offer.*

gratify /'grætɪfaɪ/ **gratifies, gratifying, gratified.** [1] VERB If you **are gratified** by something, it gives you pleasure or satisfaction; FORMAL. *Sarah was gratified by the figures.* ♦ **gratifying** ADJ *It is very gratifying to watch our business grow.* ♦ **gratification** /ˌgrætɪfɪˈkeɪʃən/ N-U *Israelis reacted with gratification.* [2] VERB If you **gratify** a desire, you satisfy it; FORMAL. *We gratified our friend's curiosity.* ♦ **gratification** N-U *...sexual gratification.*

gratitude /'grætɪtjuːd, AM -tuːd/. N-U **Gratitude** is the state of feeling grateful. *I wish to express my gratitude to Kathy Davis for her help.*

gratuitous /grə'tjuːɪtəs, AM -'tuː-/. ADJ If you describe something as **gratuitous**, you mean that it is unnecessary, and often harmful or upsetting. *...gratuitous violence.*
♦ **gratuitously** ADV *...something less gratuitously offensive.*

grave /greɪv/ **graves; graver, gravest.** [1] N-C A **grave** is a place where a dead person is buried. [2] ADJ A **grave** situation is very serious. *...the grave crisis facing the country.* ♦ **gravely** ADV *...his gravely ill wife.* [3] ADJ A **grave** person is quiet and serious. *Mrs Williams was looking very grave.* ♦ **gravely** ADV *'I think you should see this', she said gravely.*

gravel /'grævəl/. N-U **Gravel** consists of very small stones. *...a gravel path.*

graveyard /'greɪvjɑːd/ **graveyards.** N-C A **graveyard** is an area of land where dead people are buried.

gravitational /ˌgrævɪˈteɪʃənəl/. ADJ BEFORE N **Gravitational** means relating to the force of gravity. *...the earth's gravitational pull.*

gravity /'grævɪti/. [1] N-U **Gravity** is the force which makes things fall when you drop them. [2] N-U The **gravity** of a situation is its importance and seriousness. *No one questioned the gravity of the crime itself.*

gravy /'greɪvi/. N-U **Gravy** is a sauce made from the juices that come from meat when it cooks.

gray /greɪ/. See **grey**.

graze /greɪz/ **grazes, grazing, grazed.** [1] VERB When animals **graze**, or when they **are grazed**, they eat the grass or other plants that are growing in a particular place. *He used to graze some sheep up on the high slopes.* [2] VERB If you **graze** a part of your body, you injure the skin by scraping against something. [3] N-C A **graze** is a small wound caused by scraping against something. *...minor cuts and grazes.* [4] VERB If one thing **grazes** another thing, it touches that thing lightly as it passes by. *A bullet grazed my cheek.*

grease /griːs/ **greases, greasing, greased.** [1] N-U **Grease** is a thick substance used to oil the moving parts of machines. [2] N-U **Grease** is an oily substance produced by your skin. [3] N-U **Grease** is animal fat produced by cooking meat. *...bacon grease.* [4] VERB If you **grease** something, you put grease or fat on it. *Lightly grease a baking tray.*

greasy /'griːsi, -zi/ **greasier, greasiest.** ADJ Something that is **greasy** is covered with grease or contains a lot of grease. *...greasy hair.*

great /greɪt/ **greats; greater, greatest.** [1] ADJ BEFORE N You use **great** to describe something that is very large. *...great columns of ice.* [2] ADJ **Great** is used to emphasize the large amount or degree of something. *She had great difficulty in keeping her eyes open.* ♦ **greatly** ADV *He will be greatly missed.* [3] ADJ You use **great** to describe someone or something that is important, famous, or exciting. *...the great novels of the 19th century. ...the greatest scientist since Einstein.* ♦ **greatness** N-U *...her conviction of her husband's greatness.* [4] ADJ If something is **great**, it is very good; INFORMAL. *I thought it was a great idea... It would make a great film... Oh great! That'll be good for Fergus.* [5] See note at **big**.

greed /griːd/. N-U **Greed** is a desire for more of something than is necessary or fair.

greedy /'griːdi/. **greedier, greediest.** ADJ Someone who is **greedy** wants more of something than is necessary or fair. *...greedy bosses who award themselves huge pay rises.*
♦ **greedily** ADV *Livy ate the pasties greedily.*

green /griːn/ **greener, greenest; greens.** [1] ADJ & N-VAR Something that is **green** is the colour of grass or leaves. *...green olives. ...a paler and softer shade of green.* [2] ADJ A place that is **green** is covered with grass, plants, and trees. ♦ **greenness** N-U *...the lush greenness of the river valleys.* [3] ADJ BEFORE N **Green** issues relate to the protection of the environment. *...the power of the Green movement in Germany.* [4] N-C A **green** is a smooth, flat area of grass, for example the area around a hole on a golf course.

greenery /'griːnəri/. N-U Plants that make a place look attractive are referred to as **greenery**.

greenhouse /'griːnhaʊs/ **greenhouses.** N-C A **greenhouse** is a glass building in which you grow plants that need to be protected from bad weather.

greenhouse effect. N-SING The **greenhouse effect** is the rise in the earth's temperature caused by a build-up of gases around the earth.

greet /griːt/ **greets, greeting, greeted.** [1] VERB When you **greet** someone, you say something friendly such as 'hello' when you meet them. [2] VERB If something **is greeted** in a particular way, people react to it in that way. *The move was greeted with dismay by union leaders.* [3] VERB If you **are greeted** by something, it is the first thing you notice in a place; LITERARY. *Customers are greeted by a wonderful waft of smells from the kitchen.*

greeting /'griːtɪŋ/ **greetings.** N-VAR A **greeting** is something friendly that you say or do when you meet someone. *He raised a hand in greeting.*

grenade /grɪ'neɪd/ **grenades.** N-C A **grenade** is a small bomb that can be thrown by hand.

grew /gruː/. **Grew** is the past tense of **grow**.

grey (AM **gray**) /greɪ/ **greyer, greyest; greys.** ADJ & N-VAR **Grey** is the colour of ashes or of clouds on a rainy day. *...grey trousers... His hair is a dark shade of grey.*

greyhound /'greɪhaʊnd/ **greyhounds.** N-C

A **greyhound** is a thin dog that can run very fast.

grid /grɪd/ **grids.** [1] N-C A **grid** is a pattern of straight lines that cross over each other to form squares. *...a grid of narrow streets.* [2] N-C A **grid** is a network of wires and cables by which sources of power, such as electricity, are distributed throughout an area. *...the national electricity grid.*

gridlock /'grɪdlɒk/. [1] N-U **Gridlock** is the situation that exists when all the roads in a particular place are so full of vehicles that none of them can move. [2] N-U You can use **gridlock** to refer to a situation in an argument or dispute when neither side is prepared to give in, so no agreement can be reached. *...political gridlock.*

grief /griːf/. [1] N-U **Grief** is extreme sadness. *...her grief at her husband's suicide.* [2] PHRASE If someone or something **comes to grief**, they fail or are harmed. *So many marriages have come to grief over lack of money.*

grievance /'griːvəns/ **grievances.** N-VAR A **grievance** is a reason for complaining. *...an opportunity for them to air their grievances.*

grieve /griːv/ **grieves, grieving, grieved.** [1] VERB If you **grieve** over something, especially someone's death, you feel very sad about it. *He still grieves for his wife, who died of cancer three years ago.* [2] VERB If something **grieves** you, it makes you feel unhappy or upset. *It grieved Elaine to be separated from her son.*

grievous /'griːvəs/. ADJ Something that is **grievous** is extremely serious or worrying in its effects. *...a very grievous mistake.* ♦**grievously** ADV *Michael was grievously injured.*

grill /grɪl/ **grills, grilling, grilled.** [1] VERB In British English, if you **grill** food, you cook it using strong heat directly above or below it. The American word is **broil**. *...grilled chicken.* • See note at **cook**. [2] N-C A **grill** is a part of a cooker where food is grilled. [3] VERB If you **grill** someone, you ask them a lot of questions for a long period of time; INFORMAL. *The police grilled him for hours.* ♦**grilling, grillings.** N-C *Bank chiefs face a grilling over the plan.*

grille /grɪl/ **grilles.** N-C A **grille** is a protective framework of bars or wire placed in front of a window or a piece of machinery.

grim /grɪm/ **grimmer, grimmest.** [1] ADJ A situation or news that is **grim** is unpleasant. *There was further grim economic news yesterday.* [2] ADJ A **grim** place is unattractive and depressing. [3] ADJ If someone is **grim**, they are very serious or stern; LITERARY. *Her face was grim.* ♦**grimly** ADV *'That was no accident,' Frank said grimly.*

grimace /grɪ'meɪs, 'grɪməs/ **grimaces, grimacing, grimaced.** VERB & N-C If you **grimace**, or if you make a **grimace**, you twist your face in an ugly way because you are unhappy, disgusted, or in pain. *He grimaced at his reflection. ...a little grimace of pain.*

grin /grɪn/ **grins, grinning, grinned.** VERB & N-C If you **grin**, or if you give a **grin**, you smile broadly. *Nancy grinned at him.*

grind /graɪnd/ **grinds, grinding, ground.** [1] VERB When something such as corn or coffee **is ground**, it is crushed until it becomes a fine powder. *...freshly ground coffee.* [2] VERB If you **grind** something into a surface, you press it hard into the surface. *He ground his cigar stub into the ashtray.* [3] PHRASE If something **grinds to a halt**, it gradually slows down until it stops completely. *The industry would grind to a halt.* [4] N-SING You can refer to tiring, boring, and routine work as the **grind**; INFORMAL. *...the daily grind of shaving.* [5] See also **ground**.

▶ **grind down.** PHR-VERB If you **grind** someone **down**, you treat them very harshly, so that they do not have the will to resist you.

grinder /'graɪndə/ **grinders.** N-C A **grinder** is a machine or device which crushes something into small pieces. *...coffee grinders.*

grip /grɪp/ **grips, gripping, gripped.** [1] VERB & N-SING If you **grip** something, or if you take a **grip** on it, you hold it firmly. *She gripped the rope... His strong hand eased the bag from her grip.* [2] N-U If things such as shoes or car tyres have **grip**, they do not slip. [3] N-SING Someone's **grip** on a person or situation is the control they have over them. If you **get a grip on** something, you make an effort to control it. *The president maintains an iron grip on his country... He wondered if he was getting old and losing his grip.* [4] VERB If something **grips** you, it affects you strongly and your attention is concentrated on it. *The entire community has been gripped by fear.* ♦**gripping** ADJ *The film turned out to be a gripping thriller.*

PHRASES If you **get to grips with** a problem, or if you **come to grips with** it, you consider it seriously, and start taking action to deal with it. *The government's first task is to get to grips with the economy.*

gripe /graɪp/ **gripes, griping, griped.** VERB & N-C If you say that someone is **griping** about something, you mean they are complaining about something in an annoying way. A **gripe** is a complaint; INFORMAL. *I am sick of hearing motorists griping about the state of the roads.* ♦**griping** N-U *Still, the griping went on.*

grisly /'grɪzli/. ADJ Something that is **grisly** is horrible and shocking. *...grisly murders.*

grit /grɪt/ **grits, gritting, gritted.** [1] N-U **Grit** consists of tiny pieces of stone, often put on roads in winter to make them less slippery. [2] N-U If you say that someone has **grit**, you mean that they have determination and courage. *...the inner grit to hang on when things go wrong.* [3] VERB If you **grit** your teeth, you decide to say nothing or to carry on, even though you are very angry or the situation is very difficult. *Ms Warner said she coped with such abuse 'through gritted teeth'.*

gritty /'grɪti/. [1] ADJ Something that is **gritty** is covered with grit or has a texture like grit. *...coarse, gritty ash.* [2] ADJ Someone who is **gritty** is determined and courageous. *...gritty determination.*

groan /grəʊn/ **groans, groaning, groaned.** VERB & N-C If you **groan**, you make a long low sound of pain, unhappiness, or disapproval, called a **groan**. *He began to groan with pain... A groan of disappointment went up from the crew.*

grocer /'grəʊsə/ **grocers.** N-C A **grocer** is a shopkeeper who sells foods such as flour, sugar, and tinned foods. You can refer to a shop where these goods are sold as a **grocer** or a **grocer's**.

grocery /ˈgrəʊsəri/ **groceries.** [1] N-C A **grocery** or a **grocery store** is a grocer's shop; AMERICAN. [2] N-PL **Groceries** are foods you buy at a grocer's or at a supermarket. ...*two bags of groceries.*

groin /grɔɪn/ **groins.** N-C Your **groin** is the part of your body where your legs meet your abdomen.

groom /gruːm/ **grooms, grooming, groomed.** [1] N-C A **groom** is the same as a **bridegroom.** [2] N-C A **groom** is someone whose job is to look after horses in a stable. [3] VERB If you **groom** an animal, you brush its fur. [4] VERB If you **are groomed** for a special job, someone prepares you for it. *Marshall was groomed to run the family companies.*

groomed /gruːmd/. ADJ You use **groomed** in expressions such as **well groomed** and **badly groomed** to say how neat, clean, and smart a person is. ...*a well-groomed appearance.*

grooming /ˈgruːmɪŋ/. N-U **Grooming** refers to the things that people do to keep themselves clean and make their face, hair, and skin look nice. ...*a growing concern for personal grooming.*

groove /gruːv/ **grooves.** N-C A **groove** is a deep line cut into a surface.

grope /grəʊp/ **gropes, groping, groped.** [1] VERB If you **grope** for something that you cannot see, you search for it with your hands. *Bunbury groped in his breast pocket for his wallet... I didn't turn on the light, but groped my way across the room.* [2] VERB If you **grope** for something such as the solution to a problem, you try to think of it, when you have no real idea what it could be. *She groped for a simple word to express a simple idea.*

gross /grəʊs/ **grosser, grossest.** [1] ADJ BEFORE N You use **gross** to emphasize the degree to which something is unacceptable or unpleasant. *He was dismissed from his job for gross misconduct.* ◆**grossly** ADV ...*grossly overpaid corporate lawyers.* [2] ADJ If you describe something or someone as **gross**, you think that they are very ugly, tasteless, or repulsive; INFORMAL. *He wears really gross holiday outfits... Don't be so gross!* [3] ADJ BEFORE N & ADV A **gross** amount is the total amount after all the relevant amounts have been added together, and before any deductions are made. *Gross sales in June totalled £709 million.* ...*a father earning £20,000 gross a year.* [4] ADJ BEFORE N The **gross** weight of something is its total weight, including its container or wrapping.

grotesque /grəʊˈtesk/. [1] ADJ You say that something is **grotesque** when it is so unnatural, unpleasant, or exaggerated that it upsets or shocks you. ...*a country where grotesque abuses are taking place.* ◆**grotesquely** ADV *He says the law is grotesquely unfair.* [2] ADJ If something is **grotesque**, it is very ugly. ...*a grotesque face with its gaping mouth.* ◆**grotesquely** ADV ...*grotesquely deformed beggars.*

ground /graʊnd/ **grounds, grounding, grounded.** [1] N-SING The **ground** is the surface of the earth or the floor of a room. *We slid down the roof and dropped to the ground. ...the marshy ground of the river delta... They sat on the ground.* [2] N-SING If you say that something takes place on the **ground**, you mean it takes place on the surface of the earth and not in the air. ...*American naval, air and ground forces.* [3] N-U A **ground** is an area which is used for a particular purpose. ...*Indian hunting grounds. ...the city's football ground.* [4] N-PL The **grounds** of a large or important building are the garden or area of land which surrounds it. ...*the palace grounds. ...the grounds of the University.* [5] VERB If aircraft or pilots **are grounded**, they are not allowed to fly. [6] N-VAR You can use **ground** to refer to a place or situation in which particular methods or ideas can develop and be successful. *The company has maintained its reputation as the developing ground for new techniques.* [7] N-U **Ground** is used in expressions such as **gain ground** and **lose ground** in order to talk about the progress which someone or something makes in a situation or in a particular field; JOURNALISM. *The IJI's election campaign gained ground during the last week... These novels are breaking new ground.* [8] N-VAR The **ground** or **grounds** for a particular feeling or course of action is the reason or justification for it. *Owen was against it, on the grounds of expense.* [9] VERB If an argument or opinion **is grounded** in or on something, it is based on that thing. *Her argument was grounded in fact.* [10] **Ground** is the past tense and past participle of **grind**.

PHRASES ● If something such as a project **gets off the ground**, it begins or starts functioning. *We help small companies to get off the ground.* ● If you **stand** your **ground** or **hold** your **ground**, you do not run away from a danger or threat, but face it bravely. ● If people or things of a particular kind are **thin on the ground**, there are very few of them; BRITISH. *Good managers are thin on the ground.*

grounding /ˈgraʊndɪŋ/. N-SING If you have a **grounding** in a subject, you know the basic facts or principles of that subject. *The degree provides a grounding in law.*

'ground rule, ground rules. N-C The **Ground rules** for something are the basic principles on which future action will be based. *Rudy set ground rules for our meeting.*

groundwork /ˈgraʊndwɜːk/. N-SING The **groundwork** for something is the early work on it which forms the basis for the rest. *Yesterday's meeting was to lay the groundwork for the task ahead.*

group /gruːp/ **groups, grouping, grouped.** [1] N-C A **group** of people or things is a number of them together in one place at one time. **Group** can take the singular or plural form of the verb. *The trouble involved a small group of football supporters... The students work in groups.* [2] N-C A **group** is a set of people who have the same interests or objectives, and who organize themselves to work or act together. ...*the Minority Rights Group. ...members of an environmental group.* [3] N-C A **group** is a set of people or things which have something in common. ...*the most promising players in her age group.* ● See also **pressure group.** [4] N-C A

group is a number of musicians who perform pop music together. [5] VERB If a number of things or people are **grouped together**, they are together in one place or within one organization or system. *The fact sheets are grouped into seven sections. ...the Arab Maghreb Union, which groups together the five North African states.*

grouping /ˈgruːpɪŋ/ **groupings.** N-C A **grouping** is a set of people or things that have something in common. *There were two main political groupings.*

grouse /graʊs/ **grouses, grousing, groused.** [1] N-C **Grouse** are small sized birds which are often shot for sport and can be eaten. **Grouse** is the singular and plural form. [2] VERB & N-C If you **grouse**, you complain. A **grouse** is a complaint. *They groused about the parking regulations.*

grove /graʊv/ **groves.** N-C A **grove** is a group of trees that are close together. *...an olive grove.*

grovel /ˈgrɒvəl/ **grovels, grovelling, grovelled** (AM **groveling, groveled**). [1] VERB If someone **grovels**, they behave very humbly towards another person, for example because they are frightened or because they want something; used showing disapproval. *I don't grovel to anybody.* ♦**grovelling** ADJ *The Senator has been accused of grovelling.* [2] VERB If you **grovel**, you crawl on the ground, for example in order to find something. *We grovelled around the club on our knees.*

grow /graʊ/ **grows, growing, grew, grown.** [1] VERB When something or someone **grows**, they develop and increase in size or intensity. *All children grow at different rates... The economy continues to grow... This political row threatens to grow into a full blown crisis.* [2] VERB If a plant or tree **grows** in a particular place, it is alive there. *Trees and bushes grew down to the water's edge.* [3] VERB When you **grow** something, you cause it to develop or increase in size or length. *I always grow a few red onions... I'm growing my hair.* ♦**grower, growers** N-C *...England's apple growers.* [4] LINK-VERB You use **grow** to say that someone or something gradually changes until they have a new quality, feeling, or attitude. *I grew a little afraid of the guy next door... He's growing old... He grew to love his work.* [5] See also **grown**.

▶ **grow apart.** PHR-VERB If people who have a close relationship **grow apart**, they gradually start to have different interests and opinions, and their relationship starts to fail. *It sounds as if you have grown apart from Tom.*

▶ **grow into.** PHR-VERB When a child **grows into** a piece of clothing that is too big for them, they get bigger so that it fits them properly.

▶ **grow on.** PHR-VERB If someone or something **grows on** you, you start to like them more and more. *The place began to grow on me.*

▶ **grow out of.** [1] PHR-VERB If you **grow out of** a type of behaviour, you stop behaving in that way as you develop or change. *Most children who stammer grow out of it.* [2] PHR-VERB When a child **grows out of** a piece of clothing, they become so big that it no longer fits them.

▶ **grow up.** [1] PHR-VERB When someone **grows up**, they gradually change from being a child

into being an adult. [2] PHR-VERB If something **grows up**, it starts to exist and becomes larger or more important. *A variety of heavy industries grew up alongside the port.* [3] See also **grown-up**.

growl /graʊl/ **growls, growling, growled.** [1] VERB & N-C When an animal **growls**, it makes a low rumbling noise, called a **growl**, usually because it is angry. *The dog growled at him.* [2] VERB & N-C If someone **growls** something, they say it in a low rough voice, called a **growl**; WRITTEN. *'I should have killed him,' Sharpe growled.*

grown /graʊn/. [1] **Grown** is the past participle of **grow**. [2] ADJ A **grown** man or woman is one who is fully developed and mature. *Dad, I'm a grown woman. I know what I'm doing.*

grown-'up, grown-ups. [1] N-C Children, or people talking to children, often refer to adults as **grown-ups**. *Tell children to tell a grown-up if they're being bullied.* [2] ADJ Someone who is **grown-up** is mature and no longer dependent on their parents or another adult. *She was a widow with grown-up children.*

growth /graʊθ/ **growths.** [1] N-U The **growth** of something such as an industry, organization, or idea is its development in size, wealth, or importance. *...the growth of nationalism. ...Japan's enormous economic growth.* [2] N-U **Growth** in a person, animal, or plant is the process of increasing in size and development. *...hormones which control fertility and body growth.* [3] N-C A **growth** is an abnormal lump that grows inside or on a person, animal, or plant.

grub /grʌb/ **grubs, grubbing, grubbed.** [1] N-C A **grub** is an insect which has just hatched from its egg. [2] N-U **Grub** is food; INFORMAL.

grubby /ˈgrʌbi/ **grubbier, grubbiest.** ADJ **Grubby** people or things are rather dirty; INFORMAL. *...kids with grubby faces.*

grudge /grʌdʒ/ **grudges, grudging, grudged.** N-C If you have a **grudge** against someone, you have unfriendly feelings towards them because they have harmed you in the past.

grudging /ˈgrʌdʒɪŋ/. ADJ A **grudging** feeling or action is one that you feel or do unwillingly. *He even earned his opponents' grudging respect.* ♦**grudgingly** ADV *The studio grudgingly agreed to allow him to continue working.*

gruelling (AM **grueling**) /ˈgruːəlɪŋ/. ADJ A **gruelling** activity is extremely difficult and tiring.

gruesome /ˈgruːsəm/. ADJ Something that is **gruesome** is horrible and shocking. *...gruesome murders.*

grumble /ˈgrʌmbəl/ **grumbles, grumbling, grumbled.** VERB & N-C If you **grumble** about something, you complain about it. You can refer to complaints like this as **grumbles**. *A tourist grumbled that the waiter spoke too much Spanish... 'This is inconvenient,' he grumbled... Its high price has brought grumbles from some customers.*

grumpy /ˈgrʌmpi/. ADJ If you say that someone is **grumpy**, you think that they are bad-tempered and miserable; INFORMAL. ♦**grumpily** ADV *I rolled grumpily out of bed.*

grunt /grʌnt/ **grunts, grunting, grunted.**
[1] VERB & N-C If someone **grunts**, they make a low rough noise called a **grunt**, often because they do not want to talk. *'Rubbish,' I grunted... He grunted his thanks. ...grunts of acknowledgement.* [2] VERB When an animal, usually a pig, **grunts**, it makes a low rough noise.

guarantee /ˌgærənˈtiː/ **guarantees, guaranteeing, guaranteed.** [1] VERB & N-C If one thing **guarantees** another, or if one thing is a **guarantee** of another, the first is certain to cause the second thing to happen. *...a man whose fame guarantees that his calls will nearly always be returned... Reports of this kind are guaranteed to cause anxiety... A famous old name on a firm is not necessarily a guarantee of quality.* [2] VERB & N-C If you **guarantee** something, you promise that it is definitely true, or that you will do or provide it for someone. You refer to a promise like this as your **guarantee**. *We guarantee to refund your money if you are not delighted. ...a guaranteed income... The Editor can give no guarantee that they will fulfil their obligations.* [3] VERB & N-C If a company **guarantees** its product or work it has carried out, it provides a written promise called a **guarantee** which states that if the product or work has any faults within a specified time, it will be repaired or replaced free of charge.

guard /gɑːd/ **guards, guarding, guarded.**
[1] VERB If you **guard** a place, person, or object, you watch them carefully, either to protect them or to stop them from escaping. *A few men were left outside to guard her. ...the heavily guarded border.* [2] N-C & PHRASE A **guard** is someone such as a soldier or prison officer who is guarding a particular place or person. When a soldier or prison officer is guarding someone or something, you say that they are **on guard** or **standing guard**. [3] N-SING A **guard** is a specially organized group of people, such as soldiers or policemen, who protect or watch someone or something. *We have a security guard around the whole area.* [4] N-C A **guard** is a person whose job is to check tickets on a train and ensure that the train travels safely and punctually. [5] VERB If you **guard** something important or secret, you protect or hide it. *He closely guarded her identity.* ◆**guarded** ADJ *He was hoping to keep the visit a closely guarded secret.* [6] N-C A **guard** is a protective device which covers a part of someone's body or a dangerous part of a piece of equipment. *...safety guards.*

PHRASES ● If someone **catches** you **off guard**, they surprise you by doing something when you are not expecting it. ● If you are **on your guard**, or if you are **on guard**, you are being very careful because you think a situation might become difficult or dangerous. *He is constantly on guard against any threat of humiliation.*

▶ **guard against.** PHR-VERB If you **guard against** something, you are careful to prevent it from happening, or you take action to avoid being affected by it. *We always have to guard against complacency.*

guardian /ˈgɑːdiən/ **guardians.** [1] N-C A **guardian** is someone who has been legally ap-

pointed to look after another person's affairs, for example those of a child or someone who is mentally ill. [2] N-C If you consider someone a defender or protector of something, you can call them its **guardian**. *...guardians of public morality.*

guerrilla (or **guerilla**) /gəˈrɪlə/ **guerrillas.** N-C A **guerrilla** is a person who fights as part of an unofficial army, usually an army which is fighting against the existing government of a country.

guess /ges/ **guesses, guessing, guessed.**
[1] VERB & N-C If you **guess** something, or if you make a **guess** about something, you form an idea or opinion about it, knowing that it may not be true or accurate because you do not have all the relevant facts. *Wood guessed that he was a very successful publisher or a banker... You can only guess at what mental suffering they endure... My guess is that the answer will be negative.* [2] VERB If you **guess** that something is the case, you correctly form the opinion that it is the case, although you do not have definite knowledge about it. *He should have guessed what would happen... Someone might have guessed our secret.* [3] PHRASE You say **I guess** to indicate slight uncertainty or reluctance about what you are saying. *I guess he's right.*

guest /gest/ **guests, guesting, guested.**
[1] N-C A **guest** is someone who has been invited to stay in your home, attend an event, or appear on a radio or television show. *She was a guest at the wedding. ...a frequent chat show guest.* [2] VERB If someone **guests** on something such as a television show, they appear or perform on it as a guest. *Last month she guested with New York City Ballet.* [3] N-C A **guest** is someone who is staying in a hotel.

guidance /ˈgaɪdəns/. N-U **Guidance** is help and advice. *...the reports which were produced under his guidance.*

guide /gaɪd/ **guides, guiding, guided.** [1] N-C A **guide** is a person who shows tourists round places such as museums or cities, or shows people the way through difficult country. [2] VERB If you **guide** someone somewhere, you go there with them in order to show them the way, and perhaps to explain points of interest to them. *He took the bewildered Elliott by the arm and guided him out. ...a guided tour of the eight-bedroom mansion.* [3] N-C A **guide** or **guide book** is a book which gives information about a town, area, or country, or information to help you understand something. *...the Pocket Guide to Butterflies.* [4] N-C A **guide** is something that can be used to help you plan your actions or to form an opinion about something. *As a rough guide, a horse needs 2.5 per cent of his body weight in food every day.* [5] VERB If you **guide** someone, you influence their actions or decisions. *He should have let his instinct guide him.*

guideline /ˈgaɪdlaɪn/ **guidelines.** N-C A **guideline** is a rule or piece of advice about how to do something. *Are there strict guidelines for animal experimentation?*

guild /gɪld/ **guilds.** N-C A **guild** is an organization of people who do the same job or who share an interest. ...*the Guild of Food Writers.*

guilt /gɪlt/. [1] N-U **Guilt** is an unhappy feeling that you have because you have done something bad. ...*his feeling of guilt towards his son.* [2] N-U **Guilt** is the fact that you have done something bad or illegal. ...*the determination of guilt according to criminal law.*

guilty /'gɪlti/ **guiltier, guiltiest.** [1] ADJ If you feel **guilty**, you feel unhappy because you have done something bad or have failed to do something which you should have done. ♦**guiltily** ADV *He glanced guiltily over his shoulder.* [2] ADJ BEFORE N You use **guilty** to describe an action or fact that you feel guilty about. ...*a guilty secret.* [3] ADJ If someone is **guilty** of doing something bad or committing a crime, they have done a bad thing or committed a crime. *Mr Brooke had been guilty of a 'gross error of judgment'... He has agreed to plead guilty to six felonies.*

'guinea pig, guinea pigs. [1] N-C If someone is used as a **guinea pig** in an experiment, a drug or other treatment is tested for the first time on them. *The Doctor used himself as a human guinea pig to perfect a treatment.* [2] N-C A **guinea pig** is a small furry animal without a tail.

guise /gaɪz/ **guises.** N-C If something is done or appears under the **guise** of something else, the first thing looks like the second thing or is made to look like it, in order to hide its true appearance or nature. ...*the men who committed this murder under the guise of a political act... The new leaders are merely the old guard in a different guise.*

guitar /gɪ'tɑː/ **guitars.** N-C A **guitar** is a wooden musical instrument with six strings which are plucked or strummed. ♦**guitarist** /gɪ'tɑːrɪst/ **guitarists.** N-C ...*the world's best jazz guitarists.*

gulf /gʌlf/ **gulfs.** [1] N-C A **gulf** is an important or significant difference between two people, things, or groups. *There is a growing gulf between rich and poor.* [2] N-C A **gulf** is a large area of sea which extends a long way inland. ...*the Gulf of Mexico.*

gullible /'gʌlɪbəl/. ADJ If you say that someone is **gullible**, you think they are easily tricked. ♦**gullibility** N-U ...*the unending gullibility of his poor customers.*

gully /'gʌli/ **gullies.** N-C A **gully** is a long narrow valley with steep sides.

gulp /gʌlp/ **gulps, gulping, gulped.** [1] VERB & N-C If you **gulp** food or drink down, or if you take **gulps** of food or drink, you swallow large quantities of it. *She quickly gulped her tea... He'd gulped it down in one bite... He took the burger carefully from my fingers and swallowed it in two gulps.* [2] VERB & N-C If you **gulp**, you swallow air, making a noise in your throat called a **gulp** as you do so, usually because you are nervous. *I gulped, and then proceeded to tell her the whole story... He slumped back, gulping for air.*

gum /gʌm/ **gums.** [1] N-U **Gum** is a substance, often mint-flavoured, which you chew for a long time but do not swallow. [2] N-U **Gum** is a type of glue that you use to stick paper together. [3] N-C Your **gums** are the areas of firm pink

flesh inside your mouth, which your teeth grow out of.

gun /gʌn/ **guns, gunning, gunned.** [1] N-C A **gun** is a weapon from which bullets or pellets are fired. [2] PHRASE If you **stick to your guns**, you continue to have your own opinion about something, even though other people disagree or try to make you change your mind; INFORMAL.
▸ **gun down.** PHR-VERB If someone **is gunned down**, they are shot and severely injured or killed.

gunfire /'gʌnfaɪə/. N-U **Gunfire** is the repeated shooting of guns. *He died during an exchange of gunfire.*

gunman /'gʌnmən/ **gunmen.** N-C A **gunman** is someone who uses a gun to commit a crime.

gunpoint /'gʌnpɔɪnt/. PHRASE If someone holds you **at gunpoint**, they threaten to shoot you if you do not obey them.

gunshot /'gʌnʃɒt/ **gunshots.** [1] N-C A **gunshot** is the firing of a gun or the sound of a gun being fired. *He heard gunshots.* [2] N-U **Gunshot** is used to refer to bullets that are fired from a gun. *A policeman suffered gunshot wounds.*

gurgle /'gɜːgəl/ **gurgles, gurgling, gurgled.** [1] VERB When water **gurgles**, it makes a bubbling sound. ...*the sound of hot water gurgling through the van's engine.* [2] VERB When a baby **gurgles**, it makes bubbling sounds in its throat, usually because it is happy.

guru /'gʊruː/ **gurus.** [1] N-C A **guru** is a spiritual leader and teacher, especially in Hinduism. [2] N-C A **guru** is someone whom many people regard as an expert or leader. ...*fashion gurus.*

gush /gʌʃ/ **gushes, gushing, gushed.** [1] VERB & N-SING When liquid **gushes** out of something, or if there is a **gush** of liquid from something, a large quantity of liquid flows out very quickly. *Piping-hot water gushed out... A supertanker continues to gush oil off the coast of Spain... I heard a gush of water.* [2] VERB If you say that someone **gushes** about something, you mean that they express their admiration or pleasure in a way that seems exaggerated and false. *He gushes about his new-found happiness with a girl almost half his age.* ♦**gushing** ADJ *She was very gushing and very effusive.*

gust /gʌst/ **gusts, gusting, gusted.** [1] N-C A **gust** is a short, strong, sudden rush of wind. [2] VERB When the wind **gusts**, it blows with short, strong, sudden rushes. *The wind gusted up to 164 miles an hour.*

gut /gʌt/ **guts, gutting, gutted.** [1] N-PL A person's or animal's **guts** are all their internal organs. [2] VERB If someone **guts** a fish or a dead animal, they remove its internal organs. [3] N-SING The **gut** is the tube inside your body through which food passes while it is being digested. [4] N-U **Guts** is courage; INFORMAL. *The new Chancellor has the guts to push through unpopular tax increases.* [5] ADJ A **gut** feeling or response is based on instinct or emotion rather than on reason. *My gut reaction was very positive.* [6] VERB If a building **is gutted**, the inside is destroyed, leaving only the outside walls. *A firebomb gutted a building where 60 people lived.*

gutter /'gʌtə/ **gutters.** **1** N-C The **gutter** is the edge of a road next to the pavement, where rain collects and flows away. **2** N-C A **gutter** is a channel fixed to the edge of a roof, which rain water drains into. **3** N-SING You can use **the gutter** to refer to a condition of life in which someone is poor and has no self-respect. *Instead of ending up in jail or in the gutter he was remarkably successful.*

guy /gaɪ/ **guys.** **1** N-C A **guy** is a man; INFORMAL. *I was working with a guy from Manchester.* **2** N-VOC & N-PL Americans sometimes address a group of people, whether they are male or female, as **guys** or **you guys**.

gym /dʒɪm/ **gyms.** **1** N-C A **gym** is the same as a **gymnasium.** **2** N-U **Gym** means **gymnastics.**

gymnasium /dʒɪm'neɪziəm/ **gymnasiums.** N-C A **gymnasium** is a club or room, usually containing special equipment, where people can exercise.

gymnastic /dʒɪm'næstɪk/ **gymnastics.** N-PL **Gymnastics** consists of physical exercises that develop your strength, co-ordination, and agility. The form **gymnastic** is used as a modifier. *...gymnastic exercises.*

gynaecology (AM **gynecology**) /ˌgaɪnɪ'kɒlədʒi/. N-U **Gynaecology** is the branch of medical science which deals with women's diseases and medical conditions.

gypsy (or **gipsy**) /'dʒɪpsi/ **gypsies.** N-C A **gypsy** is a member of a race of people who travel from place to place in caravans, rather than living in one place.

H h

habit /'hæbɪt/ **habits.** **1** N-VAR A **habit** is something that you do often or regularly. *He had the endearing habit of smiling at everyone he saw... After twenty years as a chain smoker Mr Nathe has given up the habit. ...a survey on eating habits in the UK.* **2** PHRASE If you **are in the habit of** doing something or **make a habit of** doing it, you do it regularly or often. If you **get into the habit of** doing something, you begin to do it regularly or often. *You can phone me at work as you you don't make a habit of it.* **3** N-C A drug **habit** is an addiction to a drug such as heroin.

habitat /'hæbɪtæt/ **habitats.** N-C The **habitat** of an animal or plant is its natural environment in which it normally lives or grows.

habitual /hə'bɪtʃuəl/. ADJ A **habitual** state or way of behaving is one that someone usually has or does, especially one that is considered to be typical or characteristic of them. *He soon recovered his habitual geniality.* ♦**habitually** ADV *They habitually used foul language.*

hack /hæk/ **hacks, hacking, hacked.** **1** VERB If you **hack** something, or if you **hack away** at it, you cut it with strong, rough strokes using a sharp tool such as an axe or knife. *Some were hacked to death with machetes... He started to hack away at the tree bark.* **2** N-C If you refer to a professional writer such as a journalist as a **hack**, you disapprove of them because they write for money without worrying very much about the quality of their writing. **3** VERB When someone **hacks** into a computer system, they break into the system, especially in order to get secret information that is stored there. ♦**hacker** /'hækə/ **hackers** N-C *Once inside their systems, the hackers could steal information.* ♦**hacking** N-U *...the common and often illegal art of computer hacking.*
▶ **hack away.** See hack 1.
▶ **hack off.** PHR-VERB If you **hack** something **off**, you cut it off with strong, rough strokes using a sharp tool such as an axe or knife. *Kim even hacked off her long hair.*

had /hæd/. **Had** is the past tense and past participle of **have.**

haddock /'hædək/. N-VAR A **haddock** is a type of sea fish. The form 'haddock' is also used as the plural. **Haddock** is the flesh of this fish eaten as food.

hadn't /'hædənt/. **Hadn't** is the usual spoken form of 'had not'.

haemorrhage (AM **hemorrhage**) /'hemərɪdʒ/ **haemorrhages, haemorrhaging, haemorrhaged.** VERB & N-VAR If someone **is haemorrhaging**, or if they have a **haemorrhage**, they are bleeding heavily because of broken blood vessels inside their body. *If this is left untreated, one can actually haemorrhage to death.* ♦**haemorrhaging** N-U *A post mortem showed he died from shock and haemorrhaging.*

haggle /'hægəl/ **haggles, haggling, haggled.** VERB If you **haggle**, you argue about something before reaching an agreement, especially about the cost of something. *Of course he'll still haggle over the price.* ♦**haggling** N-U *After months of haggling, they recovered only three-quarters of what they had lent.*

hail /heɪl/ **hails, hailing, hailed.** **1** VERB If a person or event **is hailed** as important or successful, they are praised publicly. *US magazines hailed her as the greatest rock'n'roll singer in the world.* **2** N-SING **Hail** consists of tiny balls of ice that fall like rain from the sky. **3** N-SING A **hail** of things, usually small objects, is a large number of them that hit you at the same time and with great force. *The riot police were met with a hail of stones.* **4** VERB If someone or something **hails from** a particular place or background, they come from it. *I hail from Brighton.* **5** VERB If you **hail** a taxi, you wave at it in order to stop it and ask the driver to take you somewhere.

hair /heə/ **hairs.** **1** N-VAR Your **hair** is the mass of fine thread-like strands that grow on your head. **2** N-VAR **Hair** is all the short, fine, thread-like material that grows on different parts of your body. *The majority of men have hair on their chest.* **3** N-VAR **Hair** is the rough, thread-like material that covers the body of an animal such as a dog, or makes up a horse's mane and tail. **4** N-C **Hairs** are very fine thread-like strands that grow on some insects and plants.

haircut /'heəkʌt/ **haircuts.** [1] N-C If you have a **haircut**, someone cuts your hair for you. [2] N-C A **haircut** is the style in which your hair has been cut. *Who's that guy with the funny haircut?*

hairdresser /'heədresə/ **hairdressers.** N-C A **hairdresser** is a person who cuts, washes, and styles people's hair. You can also refer to the shop where a hairdresser works as a **hairdresser** or a **hairdresser's**. ◆**hairdressing** N-U ...*personal services such as hairdressing.*

hairstyle /'heəstaɪl/ **hairstyles.** N-C Your **hairstyle** is the style in which your hair has been cut or arranged. *I think her new short hairstyle looks simply great.*

hairy /'heəri/ **hairier, hairiest.** [1] ADJ Someone or something that is **hairy** is covered with a lot of hair. [2] ADJ If you describe a situation as **hairy**, you mean that it is exciting but rather frightening; INFORMAL. *His driving was a bit hairy.*

half /hɑːf, AM hæf/ **halves.** [1] N-C & PREDET & ADJ **Half** of an amount or object is one of two equal parts that together make up the whole amount or object. *Cut the tomatoes in half vertically... The bridge was re-built in two halves... She's half his age. ...the first half hour.* [2] N-C In games such as football and rugby, matches are divided into two equal periods of time which are called **halves**. *...early in the second half.* [3] ADV You use **half** to say that something is only partly the case or happens to only a limited extent. *His refrigerator frequently looked half empty... She'd half expected him to withdraw from the course.* [4] ADV You can use **half** to say that someone has parents of two different nationalities. For example, if you are **half** German, one of your parents is German. [5] PREP You use **half past** to refer to a time that is thirty minutes after a particular hour. *...half past twelve.* [6] PHRASE If you increase something **by half**, half of the original amount is added to it. If you decrease it **by half**, half of the original amount is taken away from it. *The number of 7 year olds who read poorly has increased by half over the past 5 years.*

'half-brother, half-brothers. N-C Someone's **half-brother** is a boy or man who has either the same mother or the same father as they have. *Peter, my half-brother, considers himself Candian.*

half-'hearted. ADJ If someone does something in a **half-hearted** way, they do it without any real interest or effort. *...a half-hearted apology... Her application was a bit half-hearted.* ◆**half-heartedly** ADV *I can't do anything half-heartedly. I have to do everything 100 per cent.*

'half-sister, half-sisters. N-C Someone's **half-sister** is a girl or woman who has either the same mother or the same father as they have.

half-'time. N-U In sport, **half-time** is the short rest period between the two parts of a game.

halfway (or **half-way**). /,hɑːfˈweɪ, AM ,hæf-/. [1] ADV **Halfway** means in the middle of a place or in between two points, at an equal distance from each of them. *He was halfway up the ladder.* [2] ADV & ADJ BEFORE N **Halfway** means at the middle of a period of time or an event. *We were more than halfway through our tour. ...the halfway point of the tournament.*

hall /hɔːl/ **halls.** [1] N-C In a house or other building, the **hall** is the area just inside the front door. [2] N-C A **hall** is a large room or building which is used for public events such as concerts, exhibitions, and meetings. *...a dance in the village hall. ...the Royal Albert Hall.*

hallmark /'hɔːlmɑːk/ **hallmarks.** [1] N-C The **hallmark** of something or someone is their most typical quality or feature. *It's a technique that has become the hallmark of Amber Films.* [2] N-C A **hallmark** is an official mark that is put on objects made of gold, silver, or platinum that indicates the quality of the metal.

hallo /hæˈləʊ/. See **hello.**

hallowed /'hæləʊd/. [1] ADJ **Hallowed** is used to describe something that is respected and admired, usually because it is old or important. *...the hallowed turf of Lord's Cricket Ground.* [2] ADJ **Hallowed** is used to describe something that is considered to be holy. *...hallowed ground.*

Halloween /,hæləʊˈiːn/ (also **Hallowe'en**). N-U **Halloween** is the night of the 31st of October and it is traditionally said to be the time when ghosts and witches can be seen.

hallucination /hə,luːsɪˈneɪʃən/ **hallucinations.** N-C A **hallucination** is something that is not real that someone sees because they are ill or have taken a drug. *The drug induces hallucinations at high doses.*

hallway /'hɔːlweɪ/ **hallways.** N-C A **hallway** is the entrance hall of a house or other building.

halo /'heɪləʊ/ **haloes** (or **halos**). N-C A **halo** is a circle of light that is drawn in pictures round the head of a holy figure such as a saint.

halt /hɔːlt/ **halts, halting, halted.** [1] VERB & PHRASE When a vehicle or person **halts** or when something **halts** them, they stop moving along and stand still. You can also say that they come **to a halt**. *She held her hand out flat, to halt him... The elevator creaked to a halt.* [2] VERB & PHRASE When something such as development or activity **halts**, or when you **halt** it, it stops completely. You can also say that these things come **to a halt**. *He criticised the government for failing to halt economic decline... In the ensuing chaos, agricultural production was brought to a halt.*

halve /hɑːv, AM hæv/ **halves, halving, halved.** [1] VERB When you **halve** something, or when it **halves**, it is reduced to half its previous size or amount. *Sales of vinyl records halved in 1992 to just 6.7m.* [2] VERB If you **halve** something, you divide it into two equal parts. *Halve the pineapple and scoop out the inside.* [3] **Halves** is the plural of **half**.

ham /hæm/ **hams.** N-VAR **Ham** is meat from the top of the back leg of a pig, usually eaten cold. *...a huge baked ham. ...ham sandwiches.*

hamburger /'hæmbɜːgə/ **hamburgers.** N-C A **hamburger** is a flat round mass of minced beef, fried and eaten in a bread roll.

hamlet /'hæmlɪt/ **hamlets.** N-C A **hamlet** is a small village.

hammer /'hæmə/ **hammers, hammering, hammered.** [1] N-C A **hammer** is a tool used for hitting things. It consists of a heavy piece of metal at the end of a handle. [2] VERB & PHR-VERB If you **hammer** something such as a nail, you hit it with a hammer. If you **hammer** it **in**, you hit it into a surface, using a hammer. *Hammer a wooden peg into the hole.* [3] VERB If you **hammer** a surface or **hammer** on it, you hit it several times. *He hammered his two clenched fists on the table.* [4] VERB If a person or organization **is being hammered**, they are being severely attacked, defeated, or harmed; BRITISH, INFORMAL. *The company has been hammered by the downturn in the construction and motor industries.*

▸ **hammer in.** See **hammer** 2.

▸ **hammer out.** PHR-VERB If you **hammer out** something such as a plan, you reach an agreement about it after a long or difficult discussion. *Diplomats met to hammer out a draft resolution.*

hamper /'hæmpə/ **hampers, hampering, hampered.** [1] VERB If someone or something **hampers** you, they make it difficult for you to do what you are trying to do. *I was hampered by a lack of information.* [2] N-C A picnic **hamper** is a large basket with a lid, used for carrying food.

hamstring /'hæmstrɪŋ/ **hamstrings, hamstringing, hamstrung.** [1] N-C A **hamstring** is a tendon behind your knee joining the muscles of your thigh to the bones of your lower leg. [2] VERB If you **are hamstrung** by something, it makes it very difficult for you to take any action; JOURNALISM. *These countries are often hamstrung by lack of money and facilities.*

hand 1 noun and phrase uses

hand /hænd/ **hands.** [1] N-C Your **hands** are the parts of your body at the ends of your arms, below the wrist. [2] N-C The **hands** of a clock or watch are the thin pieces of metal or plastic that indicate what time it is. [3] N-SING If you ask someone for a **hand** with something, you are asking them to help you. *Come and give me a hand in the garden... I'd be glad to lend a hand.* [4] N-C In a game of cards, your **hand** is the cards which are dealt to you.

PHRASES ● If something is **at hand**, **near at hand**, or **close at hand**, it is very near in place or time. *His retirement was near at hand.* ● If you do something **by hand**, you do it using your hands rather than a machine. *...quilts stitched entirely by hand.* ● When something **changes hands**, its ownership changes, usually because it is sold to someone else. ● If you **force** someone's **hand**, you force them to do something before they are ready to do it, or to do something they do not want to do. ● If someone gives you **a free hand**, they allow you to do what you want in a particular situation. ● If two things go **hand in hand**, they are closely connected and cannot be considered separately from each other. *Yvette's rise to fame went hand in hand with the growth of the club.* ● If you **have a hand in** something, you are one of the people involved in doing it or

creating it. ● If a situation is **in hand**, it is under control. *The Olympic organisers say that matters are well in hand.* ● If someone lives from **hand to mouth**, they have hardly enough food or money to live on. ● If someone or something is **on hand**, they are near and able to be used if they are needed. *The Bridal Department will have experts on hand to give you all the help and advice you need.* ● You use **on the other hand** to introduce the second of two contrasting points, facts, or ways of looking at something. You can use **on the one hand** in an earlier sentence to introduce the first part of the contrast. *On the one hand, if the body doesn't have enough cholesterol, we would not be able to survive. On the other hand, if the body has too much cholesterol, the excess begins to line the arteries.* ● See note at **contrary.** ● If you reject an idea **out of hand**, you reject it without hesitating and without discussing it or considering it first. *The Russian Federation leader did not dismiss the proposals out of hand.* ● If you have something **to hand** or **near to hand**, you have it with you or near you, ready to use when needed. *You may want to keep this brochure safe, so you have it to hand whenever you may need it.* ● If you **try** your **hand** at an activity, you attempt to do it, usually for the first time. ● If you **wash** your **hands of** someone or something, you refuse to be involved with them any more or to take responsibility for them.

hand 2 verb uses

hand /hænd/ **hands, handing, handed.** VERB If you **hand** something to someone, you pass it to them. *He handed me a little rectangle of white paper.*

▸ **hand down** or **hand on.** PHR-VERB If you **hand** something such as your knowledge or possessions **down**, or **hand** it **on**, you pass it on to other people, often people of a younger generation. *...a Ukrainian folk heritage handed down from their parents.*

▸ **hand in.** PHR-VERB If you **hand** something **in**, you give it to someone in authority, so that they can deal with it. *My advice to anyone who finds anything on a bus is to hand it in to the police... All eighty opposition members of parliament have handed in their resignation.*

▸ **hand on.** See **hand down.**

▸ **hand out.** [1] PHR-VERB If you **hand** something **out**, you give it to people. *One of my jobs was to hand out the prizes.* [2] See also **hand-out.**

▸ **hand over.** PHR-VERB If you **hand** something **over** to someone, you give it to them. *He handed over a letter of apology from the Minister.*

▸ **hand over to.** PHR-VERB If you **hand over to** someone, you give them the responsibility for dealing with a particular situation which was previously your responsibility. *The present leaders have to decide whether to stand down and hand over to a younger generation.*

handbag /'hændbæg/ **handbags.** N-C In British English, a **handbag** is a small bag used by women to carry things such as money and keys. The usual American word is **purse.**

handbook /'hændbʊk/ **handbooks.** N-C A **handbook** is a book giving advice or instructions on how to do a practical task.

handcuff /'hændkʌf/ **handcuffs, handcuffing, handcuffed.** [1] N-PL **Handcuffs** are two metal rings linked by a short chain which are locked round a prisoner's wrists. *He was led away to jail in handcuffs.* [2] VERB If the police **handcuff** someone, they put handcuffs around their wrists. *She was handcuffed to a woman police officer during the court hearing.*

handful /'hændfʊl/ **handfuls.** [1] N-SING If there is only **a handful** of people or things, there are not very many of them. *...the handful of customers at the bar.* [2] N-C A **handful** of something is the amount of it that you can hold in your hand. *She scooped up a handful of sand.* [3] N-C If you describe someone, especially a child, as a **handful**, you mean that he or she is difficult to control; INFORMAL. *Zara can be a handful sometimes.*

handicap /'hændikæp/ **handicaps, handicapping, handicapped.** [1] N-C A **handicap** is a physical or mental disability. *He lost his leg when he was ten, but learnt to overcome his handicap.* [2] VERB & N-C If an event or a situation **handicaps** someone or something, or if it is a **handicap** to them, it places them at a disadvantage. *Greater levels of stress may seriously handicap some students... The tax issue was undoubtedly a handicap to Labour.*

handicapped /'hændikæpt/. ADJ & N-PL A **handicapped** person has a physical or mental disability. You can refer to people who are handicapped as **the handicapped**. *Alex was mentally handicapped.*

handkerchief /'hæŋkətʃɪf/ **handkerchiefs.** N-C A **handkerchief** is a small square of fabric which you use for blowing your nose.

handle /'hændl/ **handles, handling, handled.** [1] N-C A **handle** is the part of an object such as a tool, bag, or cup that you hold in order to be able to pick up and use the object. [2] N-C A **handle** is a small round object or a lever that is attached to a door and is used for opening and closing it. *I turned the handle and went in.* [3] VERB When you **handle** something such as a weapon or car, you use or control it effectively. You can also say that a vehicle **handles** well or badly, depending on how easy it is to steer. *I wanted someone who could handle a gun, just in case... His ship had handled like a dream!* [4] VERB If you **handle** a problem or a particular area of work, you deal with it. *You must learn how to handle your feelings... She handled travel arrangements for the press.* ◆ **handling** N-U *The family has criticized the military's handling of Robert's death.* [5] VERB When you **handle** an object or a person, you hold them or touch them with your hands. *When it sunk in that I might be handling a new born baby my heart skipped a beat.*

handler /'hændlə/ **handlers.** N-C A **handler** is someone whose job is to be in charge of a particular type of thing. *...baggage handlers at Gatwick airport. ...dog handlers.*

handmade /ˌhænd'meɪd/. ADJ If something is **handmade**, it is made without using machines. *...a pair of handmade shoes.*

handout /'hændaʊt/ **handouts.** [1] N-C A **handout** is money, clothing, or food which is given to people who are badly in need of it. *Soldiers oversee the food handouts.* [2] N-C A **handout** is a document which gives information about something.

handshake /'hændʃeɪk/ **handshakes.** N-C If you give someone a **handshake**, you grasp their right hand with your right hand and move it up and down as a greeting, or to show that you have agreed about something.

handsome /'hænsəm/. [1] ADJ A **handsome** man has an attractive face. [2] ADJ A **handsome** woman has an attractive appearance with large regular features rather than small delicate ones. [3] ADJ BEFORE N A **handsome** sum of money is a large or generous amount of it; FORMAL. *They will make a handsome profit.* [4] See note at **beautiful**.

hands-'on. ADJ **Hands-on** experience or work involves actually doing a particular thing, rather than just talking about it or getting someone else to do it. *...hands-on experience of computers.*

handwriting /'hændraɪtɪŋ/. N-U Your **handwriting** is your style of writing with a pen or pencil.

handwritten /ˌhænd'rɪtən/. ADJ A **handwritten** piece of writing was written with a pen or pencil, rather than being typed.

handy /'hændi/ **handier, handiest.** [1] ADJ Something that is **handy** is useful. *...handy hints on looking after indoor plants.* [2] ADJ A thing or place that is **handy** is nearby and convenient; INFORMAL. *Keep a pen and pad handy by the phone.* [3] ADJ AFTER LINK-V Someone who is **handy** with a particular tool or weapon is skilful at using it; INFORMAL.

hang /hæŋ/ **hangs, hanging, hung.** The form **Hanged** is used as the past tense and past participle in meaning 3. [1] VERB & PHR-VERB If something **hangs** in a high place or position, or if you **hang** it there, it is attached there so it does not touch the ground. **Hang up** means the same as **hang**. *A young woman came out of the house to hang clothes on a line... Some of the prisoners climbed onto the roof and hung up a banner... The walls are hung with old cinema posters.* [2] VERB If a piece of clothing or fabric **hangs** in a particular way or position, that is how it is worn or arranged. *...the shawl hanging loose from her shoulders.* [3] VERB If someone **is hanged**, they are killed by having a rope tied around their neck and the support taken away from under their feet. *He was hanged last month after being found guilty of spying.* [4] VERB If a future event or a possibility **hangs over** you, it worries you. *Threat of unemployment hangs over thousands of university researchers.* [5] PHRASE If you **get the hang of** something, you begin to understand how to do it; INFORMAL.

▶ **hang about** or **hang around** or **hang round.** PHR-VERB If you **hang about**, **hang around**, or **hang round** somewhere, you stay or wait there; INFORMAL. *He got sick of hanging around waiting for me.*

▶ **hang back.** PHR-VERB If you **hang back**, you move or stay slightly behind a person or group, usually because you are nervous about something. *He hung back shyly.*

▶ **hang on.** [1] PHR-VERB If you ask someone to **hang on**, you mean you want them to wait for a moment; INFORMAL. *Hang on a second. I'll come with you.* [2] PHR-VERB If you **hang on**, you manage to survive until a situation improves. *Manchester United hung on to take the Cup.* [3] PHR-VERB If you **hang on** to or **hang onto** something that gives you an advantage, you succeed in keeping it for yourself. *The President has been trying hard to hang onto power.* [4] PHR-VERB If you **hang on** to or **hang onto** something, you hold it very tightly. [5] PHR-VERB If one thing **hangs on** another, it depends on it. *The survival of the sport hangs on this race.*

▶ **hang out.** [1] PHR-VERB When you **hang out** washing, you hang it on a clothes line to dry. [2] PHR-VERB If you **hang out** in a particular place or area, you go and stay there for no particular reason, or spend a lot of time there; INFORMAL. *We can just hang out and have a good time.*

▶ **hang round.** See **hang around**.

▶ **hang up.** [1] See **hang 1**. [2] PHR-VERB If you **hang up** when you are on the phone, or if you **hang up on** someone, you end the phone call suddenly and unexpectedly by putting back the receiver. *Don't hang up!... He said he'd call again, and hung up on me.*

hangar /'hæŋə/ **hangars.** N-C A **hangar** is a large building in which aircraft are kept.

hanger /'hæŋə/ **hangers.** N-C A **hanger** is a curved piece of metal or wood used for hanging clothes on.

hangover /'hæŋəʊvə/ **hangovers.** [1] N-C A **hangover** is a headache and feeling of sickness that you have after drinking too much alcohol. [2] N-C Something that is a **hangover** from the past is an idea or way of behaving which people used to have in the past but which people no longer generally have. *...the official trade union, a hangover from the Soviet past.*

haphazard /hæp'hæzəd/. ADJ If you describe something as **haphazard**, you are critical of it because it is not at all organized or is not arranged according to a plan. *Students find the transition from school to college haphazard and confusing.* ◆ **haphazardly** ADV *...books jammed haphazardly in the shelves.*

hapless /'hæpləs/. ADJ BEFORE N A **hapless** person is unlucky; FORMAL. *...his hapless victim.*

happen /'hæpən/ **happens, happening, happened.** [1] VERB When something **happens**, it occurs or is done without being planned. *Tell me what happened... The accident was similar to one that happened in 1973.* [2] VERB When something **happens to** you, it takes place and affects you. *It's the best thing that ever happened to me.* [3] VERB If you **happen** to do something, you do it by chance. If it **happens** that something is the case, it occurs by chance. *I looked in the nearest paper, which happened to be the Daily Mail.* [4] PHRASE You use **as it happens** in order to introduce a statement, especially one that is rather surprising. *As it hap-*

pened, the demonstration was smaller than expected.

happening /'hæpənɪŋ/ **happenings.** N-C **Happenings** are things that happen, often in a way that is unexpected or hard to explain. *They plan to hire freelance reporters to cover the latest happenings in the towns.*

happy /'hæpi/ **happier, happiest.** [1] ADJ Someone who is **happy** has feelings of joy or contentment. *Marina was a confident, happy child.* ◆ **happily** ADV *Joe and Irene were still happily married.* ◆ **happiness** N-U *Money can't buy happiness.* [2] ADJ A time or place that is **happy** is full of pleasant feelings, or has an atmosphere in which people feel happy. *She had had a particularly happy childhood.* [3] ADJ AFTER LINK-V If you are **happy** with a situation or arrangement, you are satisfied with it. *I wasn't too happy with what I'd written so far.* [4] ADJ AFTER LINK-V If you are **happy** to do something, you are willing to do it. *That's a risk I'm happy to take.* [5] ADJ BEFORE N You use **happy** in greetings to say that you hope someone will enjoy a special occasion. *Happy Birthday!* ● **many happy returns**: see **return**. [6] ADJ You use **happy** to describe something that is fortunate or lucky. *By happy coincidence, Robert met Richard and Julia.* ◆ **happily** ADV *Happily, his neck injuries were not serious.*

harass /'hærəs, hə'ræs/ **harasses, harassing, harassed.** VERB If you **harass** someone, you continually trouble them. *We are almost routinely harassed by the police.* ◆ **harassment** N-U *...sexual harassment.*

harassed /'hærəst, hə'ræst/. ADJ If you are **harassed**, you are anxious and tense because you have too much to do or too many problems to cope with. *I grew more and more harassed over lack of funds and too much to do.*

harbour (AM **harbor**) /'hɑːbə/ **harbours, harbouring, harboured.** [1] N-C A **harbour** is an area of deep water which is protected from the sea by land or walls, so that boats can be left there safely. [2] VERB If you **harbour** an emotion, you have it for a long period of time. *He had always harboured political ambitions.* [3] VERB If a person or country **harbours** someone who is wanted by the police, they let them stay in their house or country and offer them protection.

hard /hɑːd/ **harder, hardest.** [1] ADJ Something that is **hard** is very firm to touch and is not easily bent, cut, or broken. *...the hard wooden floor.* ◆ **hardness** N-U *...the hardness of the iron railing.* [2] ADJ Something that is **hard** is very difficult. *At my age I would find it hard to get another job... I have had a hard life... It was a very hard problem.* [3] ADV & ADJ If you try or work **hard**, you make a great effort to achieve something. *Am I trying too hard?... I admired him as a true scientist and hard worker... Their work is hard and unglamorous.* [4] ADV & ADJ **Hard** means with a lot of force. *I kicked a dustbin very hard... He gave her a hard push.* [5] ADJ & ADV Someone who is **hard** shows no kindness or pity. *His father was a hard man... Don't be so hard on him... The security forces would continue to crack down hard on the protesters.* [6] ADJ A **hard** winter or a **hard**

frost is very cold. **7** ADJ BEFORE N **Hard** evidence or facts are definitely true. *Yeltsin had no hard information that any American POWs are still alive.* **8** ADJ **Hard** drugs are strong illegal drugs such as heroin.

PHRASES • If you say that something is **hard going**, you mean it is difficult and requires a lot of effort. *The talks had been hard going at the start.* • If someone is **hard put** or **hard pushed** to do something, they have difficulty doing it. *I'd be hard pushed to teach him anything.*

hardback /'hɑːdbæk/ **hardbacks.** N-VAR A **hardback** is a book which has a stiff cover. *'The Secret History' was published in hardback.*

'hard core. You can refer to the members of a group who are most involved with its activities as the **hard core**. *...a hard-core group of right-wing senators.*

,hard 'currency, hard currencies. N-VAR A **hard currency** is one which is unlikely to lose its value and so is considered to be a good one to have or to invest in.

harden /'hɑːdən/ **hardens, hardening, hardened.** **1** VERB When something **hardens**, it becomes stiff or firm. *Give the cardboard two or three coats of varnish to harden it.* **2** VERB When you **harden** your ideas or attitudes, they become fixed and you become determined that you will not change them. ♦ **hardening** N-U *...a hardening of the government's attitude.* **3** VERB When people **harden**, or when events **harden** them, they become less sympathetic and gentle. *Witnessing the horrors of the Bosnian war hardened her.*

hardline (or **hard-line**) /,hɑːd'laɪn/. ADJ If you describe someone's policy or attitude as **hardline**, you mean that it is strict or extreme, and they refuse to change it. *He will continue with the same hardline policies towards drugs.*

hardly /'hɑːdli/. **1** ADV If you use **hardly** to say that something is only just true. *I hardly know you... Hardly anyone slept that night.* **2** ADV If you say **hardly** had one thing happened when something else happened, you mean that the first event was followed immediately by the second. *He had hardly collected the papers on his desk when the door burst open.* **3** ADV You use **hardly** to mean 'not' when you want to suggest that you are expecting your listener or reader to agree with your comment. *It's hardly surprising his ideas didn't catch on.*

,hard-'pressed. **1** ADJ If someone is **hard-pressed**, they are under a lot of strain and worry. *...hard-pressed, poorly paid professionals.* **2** ADJ If you will be **hard-pressed** to do something, you will have great difficulty doing it. *The airline will be hard-pressed to make a profit.*

hardship /'hɑːdʃɪp/ **hardships.** N-VAR **Hardship** is a situation in which your life is difficult or unpleasant. *Many people are suffering economic hardship.*

hardware /'hɑːdweə/. **1** N-U Computer **hardware** is computer equipment as opposed to the programs that are written for it. **2** N-U Military **hardware** is the equipment that is used by the armed forces, such as tanks and missiles. **3** N-U **Hardware** is equipment such as hammers and screws for use in the home and garden.

hardy /'hɑːdi/ **hardier, hardiest.** ADJ People, animals, and plants that are **hardy** are strong and able to endure difficult conditions. *...the ten hardy football supporters who had made the trek to Dublin.*

hare /heə/ **hares.** N-C A **hare** is an animal like a large rabbit, but with longer ears and legs.

hark /hɑːk/ **harks, harking, harked.**
▶ **hark back to.** **1** PHR-VERB If you say that one thing **harks back** to another thing in the past, you mean that it is similar to it or takes it as a model. *...pitched roofs, which hark back to the Victorian era.* **2** PHR-VERB When people **hark back** to something in the past, they remember it or tell someone about it. *...whether Puttnam should be harking back to a conflict that happened nearly fifty years ago.*

harm /hɑːm/ **harms, harming, harmed.** **1** VERB & N-U To **harm** someone or something, or to cause them **harm**, means to injure or damage them. *The hijackers seemed anxious not to harm anyone... To cut taxes would probably do the economy more harm than good.* **2** PHRASE If you say that **there is no harm in** doing something, you mean that it might be worth doing, and you will not be blamed for doing it. *They are not always willing to take on untrained workers, but there's no harm in asking.*

harmful /'hɑːmfʊl/. ADJ Something that is **harmful** has a bad effect on someone or something else. *...the harmful effects of smoking.*

harmless /'hɑːmləs/. **1** ADJ Something that is **harmless** does not have any bad effects. *This experiment was harmless to the animals.* **2** ADJ If you describe someone or something as **harmless**, you mean that they are not important and therefore unlikely to annoy other people or cause trouble. *He seemed harmless enough.*

harmonic /hɑː'mɒnɪk/. ADJ **Harmonic** means composed, played, or sung using two or more notes which sound right and pleasing together. *...harmonic and rhythmic structures.*

harmonious /hɑː'məʊniəs/. **1** ADJ A **harmonious** relationship, agreement, or discussion is friendly and peaceful. ♦ **harmoniously** ADV *It is unfortunate when neighbours cannot live harmoniously.* **2** ADJ Something that is **harmonious** has parts which go well together. *...a harmonious balance of mind, body, and spirit.*

harmonize (BR also **harmonise**) /'hɑːmənaɪz/ **harmonizes, harmonizing, harmonized.** VERB If two or more things **harmonize** with each other, they fit in well with each other. *...slabs of pink and beige stone that harmonize with the carpet... Their tastes don't harmonize.*

harmony /'hɑːməni/ **harmonies.** **1** N-U If people are living in **harmony** with each other, they are in a state of peaceful agreement and co-operation. *...racial harmony.* **2** N-VAR **Harmony** is the pleasant combination of different notes of music played at the same time. *...complex vocal harmonies. ...singing in harmony.* **3** N-U The **harmony** of something is the way in which its parts are combined into a pleasant arrangement. ...*the ordered harmony of the universe.*

harness /'hɑːnɪs/ **harnesses, harnessing, harnessed.** 1 VERB To **harness** something means to control it and use it. ...*the movement's ability to harness the anger of all Ukrainians... Turkey plans to harness the waters of the Tigris and Euphrates rivers.* 2 N-C A **harness** is a set of straps which fits around a person or animal, for example to attach a piece of equipment to them. 3 VERB If a horse or other animal **is harnessed**, a harness is put on it. *The horses were harnessed to a heavy wagon.*

harp /hɑːp/ **harps, harping, harped.** N-C A **harp** is a large musical instrument consisting of a triangular frame with vertical strings which you pluck with your fingers.

▸ **harp on.** PHR-VERB If someone **harps on** about something, they keep talking about it; used showing disapproval. *She concentrated on the good parts of her trip instead of harping on about the bad.*

harrowing /'hærəʊɪŋ/. ADJ A **harrowing** sight or experience is very upsetting or disturbing. ...*harrowing pictures of the children who had been murdered.*

harsh /hɑːʃ/ **harsher, harshest.** 1 ADJ **Harsh** climates or living conditions are very difficult for people, animals, and plants to exist in. *The weather grew harsh, chilly and unpredictable.* ♦**harshness** N-U ...*the harshness of their living conditions.* 2 ADJ **Harsh** actions or remarks are unkind and show no understanding or sympathy. ...*the cold, harsh cruelty of her husband.* ♦**harshly** ADV *Her husband is being harshly treated in prison.* ♦**harshness** N-U *She apologizes for the harshness of her words.* 3 ADJ Something that is **harsh** is so hard, bright, or rough that it seems unpleasant or harmful. ...*harsher detergents that can leave hair dirtier.*

harvest /'hɑːvɪst/ **harvests, harvesting, harvested.** 1 VERB & N-SING When farmers **harvest** a crop, they gather it in. You can refer to this activity as **the harvest.** ...*there was about 300 million tons of grain in the fields at the start of the harvest.* 2 N-C A crop is called a **harvest** when it has been gathered. ...*a bumper potato harvest.*

has The auxiliary verb is pronounced /həz/, STRONG hæz/. The main verb is usually pronounced /hæz/. **Has** is the third person singular of the present tense of **have.**

hash /hæʃ/. PHRASE If you **make a hash of** a job, you do it very badly; INFORMAL. *Watson had made a thorough hash of it.*

hasn't /'hæzənt/. **Hasn't** is the usual spoken form of 'has not'.

hassle /'hæsəl/ **hassles, hassling, hassled.** 1 N-VAR A **hassle** is a situation that is difficult and involves problems, effort, or arguments with people. ...*all the usual hassles at airport check-in.* 2 VERB If someone **hassles** you, they irritate you by repeatedly telling you or asking you to do something that you do not want to do; INFORMAL. ...*if you are tired of being hassled by unreasonable parents.*

haste /heɪst/. N-U **Haste** is the quality of doing something quickly, so that you are careless and make mistakes. *The translations bear the signs of inaccuracy and haste... Loneliness can lead to people remarrying in haste.*

hasten /'heɪsən/ **hastens, hastening, hastened.** 1 VERB If you **hasten** an event or process, you make it happen faster or sooner; WRITTEN. *He may hasten the collapse of his own country.* 2 VERB If you **hasten** to do something, you are quick to do it. *'There's no threat in this, Freddie,' Arnold hastened to say.*

hasty /'heɪsti/. 1 ADJ **Hasty** means done or arranged in a hurry, without planning or preparation. *The signs of the Serbs hasty departure could be seen everywhere.* ♦**hastily** ADV *'No, I'm sure it's not,' said Virginia hastily.* 2 ADJ If you describe what someone does or says as **hasty**, you mean that they are acting too quickly, without thinking carefully; used showing disapproval. *The Government should not be pressured into making hasty decisions.*

hat /hæt/ **hats.** N-C A **hat** is a covering that you wear on your head.

hatch /hætʃ/ **hatches, hatching, hatched.** 1 VERB When an egg **hatches**, or when it **is hatched**, a baby bird or animal comes out by breaking the shell. *The young disappeared soon after they were hatched.* 2 VERB If someone **hatches** a plot or a scheme, they think of it and work it out; used showing disapproval. *He was accused opposition parties of hatching a plot to assassinate the Pope.* 3 N-C A **hatch** is a small covered opening in a floor, wall, or ceiling.

hatchet /'hætʃɪt/ **hatchets.** N-C A **hatchet** is a small axe.

hate /heɪt/ **hates, hating, hated.** 1 VERB & N-U If you **hate** someone or something, or if you have feelings of **hate** towards them, you have an extremely strong dislike for them. *Most people hate him, but they don't dare to say so. ...a violent bully, destructive and full of hate.* 2 VERB You can use **hate** in expressions such as **I hate to say it** and **I hate to tell you** when you want to express regret about what you are about to say. *I hate to tell you this, but tomorrow's your last day.*

hatred /'heɪtrɪd/. N-U **Hatred** is an extremely strong feeling of dislike for someone or something. *Her hatred of authority led to her expulsion from high school.*

'hat-trick, hat-tricks. N-C A **hat-trick** is a series of three achievements, for example three goals scored by the same person in a football match.

haul /hɔːl/ **hauls, hauling, hauled.** 1 VERB If you **haul** a heavy object somewhere, you pull it there with a great effort. *A crane had to be used to haul the car out of the stream.* 2 PHRASE If you say that a task or a journey is a **long haul**, you mean that it takes a long time and a lot of effort. *Revitalising the Romanian economy will be a long haul.*

haunt /hɔːnt/ **haunts, haunting, haunted.** 1 VERB If something unpleasant **haunts** you, you keep thinking or worrying about it over a long period of time. *The decision to leave her children now haunts her.* 2 N-C A place that is the **haunt** of a particular person is one which they often visit because they enjoy going there. *Morris came up to New York to revisit his old haunts.* 3 VERB If people say that a ghost or spirit **haunts** a place or a person, they mean that a ghost or spirit regularly appears in that place or is seen by that person. *His ghost is said to haunt some of the rooms.*

haunted /ˈhɔːntɪd/. **1** ADJ A **haunted** building or other place is one where a ghost regularly appears. **2** ADJ Someone who has a **haunted** expression looks very worried or troubled. *She looked so haunted, I almost didn't recognize her.*

haunting /ˈhɔːntɪŋ/. ADJ **Haunting** sounds, images, or words remain in your thoughts because they are very beautiful or sad. *...the haunting calls of wild birds.* ♦**hauntingly** ADV *Each one of these ancient towns is hauntingly beautiful.*

have /həv, STRONG hæv/ **has, having, had.** **1** MODAL You use **have to** when you are saying that something is necessary, obligatory, or must happen. If you do not **have to** do something, it is not necessary or obligatory for you to do it. *He had to go to Germany... We'll have to find a taxi... They didn't have to pay tax.* **2** VERB You **have** when you are saying that someone or something owns, possesses, or holds a particular thing, or when you are mentioning one of their qualities or characteristics. *Oscar had a new bicycle... You have beautiful eyes... Do you have any brothers and sisters?... I have no doubt at all in my own mind about this... I have my microphone with me.* **3** VERB If a woman **has** a baby, she gives birth to it. If she **is having** a baby, she is pregnant. **4** VERB If you **have** something to do, you are responsible for doing it or must do it. *He had plenty of work to do... I have some important calls to make.* **5** VERB If you **have** something such a part of your body in a particular position or state, it is in that position or state. *Mary had her eyes closed... They had the curtains open.* **6** VERB If someone **has** you by a part of your body, they are holding you there and they are trying to hurt you or force you to go somewhere. *Larry had him by the ear and was beating his head against the pavement.* **7** VERB If you **have** something done, someone does it for you or you arrange for it to be done. *I had your rooms cleaned and aired... You've had your hair cut.* **8** VERB If someone or something **has** something happen to them, usually something unpleasant, it happens to them. *We had our money stolen.* **9** PHRASE You can use **has it** in expressions like '**rumour has it that**' and '**as legend has it**' when you are quoting something that you have heard, but you do not necessarily think it is true. *Rumour has it that tickets were being sold for £300.*

haven /ˈheɪvən/ **havens.** N-C A **haven** is a place where people or animals are safe from trouble or danger. *...Lake Baringo, a freshwater haven for a mixed variety of birds.*

haven't /ˈhævənt/. **Haven't** is the usual spoken form of 'have not'.

havoc /ˈhævək/. **1** N-U **Havoc** is a state of chaos, confusion, and disorder. *Rioters caused havoc in the centre of the town.* **2** PHRASE If one thing **plays havoc with** another or **wreaks havoc on** it, it prevents it from continuing or

functioning as normal, or damages it. *The weather played havoc with airline schedules.*

hawk /hɔːk/ **hawks, hawking, hawked.** N-C A **hawk** is a large bird that hunts other animals.

hay /heɪ/. N-U **Hay** is grass which has been cut and dried so that it can be used to feed animals. *...bales of hay.*

'hay fever. N-U If someone suffers from **hay fever**, they have an allergy to pollen which makes their nose, throat, and eyes become red and swollen.

hazard /ˈhæzəd/ **hazards, hazarding, hazarded.** **1** N-C A **hazard** is something which could be dangerous to you. *The deer are a hazard to motorists.* **2** VERB If you **hazard** a guess that something is the case, you make a guess about it which you know might be wrong. *'Five miles?' Sharpe hazarded.*

hazardous /ˈhæzədəs/. ADJ **Hazardous** things are dangerous, especially to people's health or safety. *Lead is especially hazardous to unborn babies.*

haze /heɪz/ **hazes.** **1** N-VAR **Haze** is a light mist caused by heat or dust in the air. *...the shimmering heat haze.* **2** N-SING If there is a **haze** of something such as smoke or steam, you cannot see clearly through it; LITERARY. *...a haze of cigarette smoke.*

hazel /ˈheɪzəl/ **hazels.** **1** N-VAR A **hazel** is a small tree which produces edible nuts. **2** ADJ **Hazel** eyes are greenish-brown.

hazy /ˈheɪzi/ **hazier, haziest.** **1** ADJ When the sky or a view is **hazy**, you cannot see it clearly because there is a haze. *...a warm, hazy summer afternoon.* **2** ADJ If you are **hazy** about things, or if your thoughts are **hazy**, you are confused. *I have only a hazy memory of what he was really like.*

he /hi, STRONG hiː/. PRON You use **he** to refer to a man, boy, or male animal. **He** is used as the subject of a verb. *He lives in Rapid City... I cried when he died.*

head 1 noun uses

head /hed/ **heads.** **1** N-C Your **head** is the part of your body which has your eyes, mouth, nose, and brain in it. *She turned her head away from him.* **2** N-C You can use **head** to refer to your mind and your mental abilities. *I can't get that song out of my head. ...an exceptional analyst who could do complex maths in his head.* **3** N-C The **head** of an organization, school, or department is the person in charge of it. *...heads of government from more than 100 countries... She became head of a girls' school.* **4** N-SING The **head** of something is the top, start, or most important end. *...the head of the stairs... A different name was placed at the head of the chart.*

head 2 verb uses

head /hed/ **heads, heading, headed.** **1** VERB If someone or something **heads** a line or procession, they are at the front of it. **2** VERB If something **heads** a list or group, it is at the top of it. *Running a business heads the list of ambitions.* **3** VERB If a piece of writing **is headed** a particular title, it has that title written at the beginning of it. *One chapter is headed, 'Beating the Test'.* **4** VERB If you **are heading** for a particular place or in a particular direction, you are going towards that place or in that direction. You can also say that you **are headed** for a particular place. *It is not clear how many of them will be heading back to Saudi Arabia. ...a truck headed west.* [5] VERB If something or someone **is heading for** a particular result, the situation they are in is developing in a way that makes that result very likely. You can also say that something or someone **is headed** towards a particular result. *The centuries-old ritual seems headed for extinction.* [6] VERB When you **head** a ball, you hit it with your head. *He headed the ball across the face of the goal.* [7] See also **heading**.

head 3 phrases

head /hed/ **heads.**

PHRASES ● The cost or amount **per head** or **a head** is the cost or amount for one person. *This simple chicken dish costs less than £1 a head.* ● If a problem or disagreement **comes to a head** or if you **bring** it **to a head**, it reaches a state where you have to do something about it urgently. *These problems came to a head in September when five of the station's journalists were sacked.* ● If you **get** something **into your head**, you suddenly decide that it is true and you will not change your mind about it. ● If you say that something such as praise or success **goes to** someone's **head**, you mean that they become arrogant as a result of it. ● If you **keep** your **head**, you remain calm in a difficult situation. If you **lose** your **head**, you panic or do not remain calm.

headache /'hedeɪk/ **headaches.** [1] N-C If you have a **headache**, you have a pain in your head. [2] N-C If you say that something is a **headache**, you mean that it causes you difficulty or worry. *The biggest headache for mothers hoping to return to study is childcare.*

heading /'hedɪŋ/ **headings.** N-C A **heading** is the title of a piece of writing, written or printed at the top of the page. *...chapter headings.*

headlight /'hedlaɪt/ **headlights.** N-C A vehicle's **headlights** are the large bright lights at the front.

headline /'hedlaɪn/ **headlines.** [1] N-C A **headline** is the title of a newspaper story, printed in large letters at the top of it. *The headline says 'Pentagon plans major cuts'.* [2] N-PL The **headlines** are the main points of a radio or television news broadcast. *Here are the headlines.* [3] PHRASE Someone or something that **hits the headlines** gets a lot of publicity from the media.

headlined /'hedlaɪnd/. ADJ AFTER LINK-V If a newspaper story is **headlined** something, that is its title. *...an article headlined 'Don't Panic'.*

headlong /'hedlɒŋ, AM -lɔːŋ/. [1] ADV If you move **headlong** in a particular direction, you move there very quickly. *He ran headlong for the open door.* [2] ADV & ADJ BEFORE N If you rush **headlong** into something, you do it quickly, without thinking carefully about it. *Do not leap headlong into decisions. ...the headlong rush to independence will cause further problems.*

headmaster /ˌhed'mɑːstə, -'mæst-/ **headmasters.** N-C A **headmaster** is a man who is the head teacher of a school; BRITISH.

headmistress /ˌhed'mɪstrɪs/ **headmistresses.** N-C A **headmistress** is a woman who is the head teacher of a school; BRITISH.

,**head of 'state, heads of state.** N-C A **head of state** is the leader of a country, for example a president or queen.

,**head-'on.** [1] ADV & ADJ BEFORE N If two vehicles hit each other **head-on**, they hit each other with their front parts pointing towards each other. *The car collided head-on with a van. ...a head-on collision.* [2] ADJ BEFORE N & ADV A **head-on** disagreement is firm and direct and has no compromises. *...a head-on clash between the president and the assembly... I chose to confront the issue head-on.*

headphones /'hedfəʊnz/. N-PL **Headphones** are small speakers which you wear over your ears in order to listen to music or other sounds without other people hearing.

headquarters /'hedkwɔːtəz/. N-C The **headquarters** of an organization are its main offices. **Headquarters** can take the singular or plural form of the verb. *...the army's headquarters in Buenos Aires.*

,**head 'start.** N-SING If you have a **head start** on other people, you have an advantage over them in a competition or race. *A good education gives your child a head start in life.*

,**head 'teacher** (or **headteacher**), **head teachers.** N-C A **head teacher** is a teacher who is in charge of a school; BRITISH.

headway /'hedweɪ/. PHRASE If you **make headway**, you make progress towards achieving something. *Police were making little headway in the investigation.*

heady /'hedi/ **headier, headiest.** ADJ A **heady** atmosphere or experience strongly affects your senses, for example by making you feel drunk or excited. *...the heady days just after their marriage.*

heal /hiːl/ **heals, healing, healed.** [1] VERB When an injury such as a broken bone heals, it becomes healthy and normal again. *It will take three to four weeks before the fracture fully heals.* [2] VERB If you **heal** something such as a disagreement between people, you restore the situation to its former state. *...the man most likely to heal the wounds in the party.*

healer /'hiːlə/ **healers.** N-C A **healer** is a person who treats sick people, especially one who believes that they are able to heal people through prayer or a supernatural power.

health /helθ/. [1] N-U Your **health** is the condition of your body. *Smoking is bad for your health.* [2] N-U **Health** is a state in which you are fit and well. *They nursed me back to health.* [3] N-U The **health** of an organization or system is the success that it has and the fact that it is working well. *...the longer-term improvement in the health of the economy.*

healthy /'helθi/ **healthier, healthiest.** [1] ADJ Someone who is **healthy** is well and is not suffering from any illness. Something that is **healthy** shows that a person is well. *She was a very healthy child. ...the glow of healthy skin.* ◆**healthily** ADV *What I really want is to live healthily for as long as possible.* [2] ADJ Something that is **healthy** is good for you. *...a healthy diet.* [3] ADJ A **healthy** organization or system is successful. ...*recent collapses of apparently healthy companies.* [4] ADJ A **healthy** amount of something is a large amount that shows success. ...*healthy profits.*

heap /hiːp/ **heaps, heaping, heaped.** [1] N-C A **heap** of things is an untidy pile of them. ...*a heap of clothes.* ● See note at **pile.** [2] VERB & PHR-VERB If you **heap** things, or if you **heap** them **up**, you arrange them in a pile. *Mrs. Madrigal heaped more carrots onto Michael's plate... The militia was heaping up wood for a bonfire.* [3] VERB If you **heap** praise or criticism on someone or something, you give them a lot of praise or criticism. [4] QUANT **Heaps of** something or a **heap of** it is a large quantity of it; IN-FORMAL. *You have heaps of time... Mansell managed to get himself in a whole heap of trouble.*

hear /hɪə/ **hears, hearing, heard** /hɜːd/. [1] VERB When you **hear** sounds, you are aware of them because they reach your ears. *I heard the sound of gunfire.*

Do not confuse **hear** and **listen.** You use **hear** to talk about sounds that you are aware of because they reach your ears. You often use **can** with **hear.** *I can hear him yelling and swearing.* If you want to say that someone is paying attention to something they can hear, you say that they **are listening to** it. *He turned on the radio and listened to the news.* Note that **listen** is not followed directly by an object. You must always say that you listen **to** something. However, **listen** can also be used on its own without an object. *I was laughing too much to listen.*

---

[2] VERB When a judge or a court **hears** a case or **hears** evidence, they listen to it officially in order to make a decision about it; FORMAL. *The case will be heard next week.* [3] VERB If you **hear from** someone, you receive a letter or a telephone call from them. *The police are anxious to hear from anyone who may know her.* [4] VERB If you **hear** some news or information, you learn it because someone tells it to you or it is mentioned on the radio or television. *My mother heard of this school through Leslie... I heard that he was forced to resign... You mean you still haven't heard anything of Ian?*

PHRASES ● If you **have** never **heard of** someone or something, you know nothing about them. ● If you **won't hear of** someone doing something, you refuse to let them do it.

hearing /ˈhɪərɪŋ/ **hearings.** [1] N-U **Hearing** is the sense which makes it possible for you to be aware of sounds. *My hearing has grown sharper.* [2] N-C A **hearing** is an official meeting held to collect facts about an incident or problem. [3] N-C If someone gives you a **hearing** or a **fair hearing**, they listen to you when you give your opinion about something.

heart /hɑːt/ **hearts.** [1] N-C Your **heart** is the organ in your chest that pumps the blood around your body. ...*the beating of his heart.* [2] N-C You can refer to someone's **heart** when you are talking about their deep feelings and

beliefs; LITERARY. *Alik's words filled her heart with pride.* [3] N-VAR You use the word **heart** when you are talking about someone's character and attitude towards other people. *She's got a good heart.* [4] N-SING If you refer to things of **the heart**, you mean love and romance. [5] N-SING The **heart** of something is the most important part of it. *The heart of the problem is supply and demand.* [6] N-SING The **heart** of a place is its centre. ...*the heart of London's West End.* [7] N-C A **heart** is a shape that is sometimes used as a symbol of love. [8] N-VAR **Hearts** is one of the four suits in a pack of playing cards. Each card in the suit is called a **heart** and is marked with one or more symbols: ♥.

PHRASES ● If you feel or believe something **with all** your **heart**, you feel or believe it very strongly. *My own family I loved with all my heart.* ● If someone is a particular kind of person **at heart**, this is what they are really like. ● If someone or something **breaks** your **heart**, or if they give you a **broken heart**, they make you very unhappy. ● If you know something such as a poem **by heart**, you have learnt all the words and can remember them. ● If you have a **change of heart**, your feelings about something change. ● If something is **close to** your **heart**, or if it is **dear to** your **heart**, you care deeply about it. ● If you say something **from the heart**, you sincerely mean what you say. *I don't want to go away without thanking you from the bottom of my heart.* ● If your **heart sinks**, you suddenly feel very disappointed or unhappy. *Our hearts sank when we saw this awful hotel.* ● If you **take heart** from something, you are made to feel encouraged and optimistic by it. ● If you **take** something **to heart**, you are deeply affected and upset by it.

heartache /ˈhɑːteɪk/ **heartaches.** N-VAR **Heartache** is very great sadness and emotional suffering; JOURNALISM. ...*the heartache of her divorce.*

heart attack, heart attacks. N-C If someone has a **heart attack**, their heart begins to beat irregularly or stops completely.

heartbeat /ˈhɑːtbiːt/ **heartbeats.** [1] N-SING Your **heartbeat** is the regular movement of your heart as it pumps blood around your body. *Your baby's heartbeat will be monitored continuously.* [2] N-C A **heartbeat** is one of the movements of your heart. *Smoking could lead to irregular heartbeats.*

heartbreak /ˈhɑːtbreɪk/ **heartbreaks.** N-VAR **Heartbreak** is very great sadness or unhappiness. ...*suffering and heartbreak for those close to the victims.*

heartbreaking /ˈhɑːtbreɪkɪŋ/. ADJ Something that is **heartbreaking** makes you feel extremely sad and upset. *They have taken the heartbreaking decision to have no more children.*

heartbroken /ˈhɑːtbrəʊkən/. ADJ Someone who is **heartbroken** is extremely sad and upset.

hearten /ˈhɑːtən/ **heartens, heartening, heartened.** VERB If you **are heartened** by something, it encourages you and makes you cheerful. *The news heartened everybody.* ◆ **heartened** ADJ AFTER LINK-V *I feel heartened by her progress.* ◆ **heartening** ADJ *It has been very heartening to see new writing emerging.*

'heart failure. N-U Heart failure is a serious medical condition in which someone's heart stops working properly or stops completely.

heartfelt /'hɑːtfelt/. ADJ Heartfelt is used to describe a deep or sincere feeling or wish. *My heartfelt sympathy goes out to all the relatives.*

hearth /hɑːθ/ **hearths.** N-C The hearth is the floor of a fireplace, which sometimes extends into the room.

heartland /'hɑːtlænd/ **heartlands.** N-C Heartland or heartlands is used to refer to the area or region where a particular set of activities or beliefs is most significant. *...the industrial heartland of America.*

hearty /'hɑːti/ **heartier, heartiest.** [1] ADJ Hearty people or actions are loud, cheerful, and energetic. ♦**heartily** ADV *He laughed heartily.* [2] ADJ Hearty feelings or opinions are strongly felt. *Arnold was in hearty agreement.* ♦**heartily** ADV *I heartily agree with her favourable comments.* [3] ADJ A hearty meal is large and very satisfying. *The boys ate a hearty breakfast.*

heat /hiːt/ **heats, heating, heated.** [1] VERB & PHR-VERB When you heat something, or when you heat it up, you raise its temperature. *Heat the tomatoes and oil in a pan... Freda heated up a pie for me.* [2] N-U Heat is warmth or the quality of being hot. *...the fierce heat of the sun.* [3] N-U The heat of something is its temperature. *Adjust the heat of the barbecue.* [4] N-SING The heat of a particular activity is the point when there is the greatest activity or excitement. *...in the heat of the election campaign.* [5] N-C A heat is one of a series of races or competitions. The winners of a heat take part in another race or competition, against the winners of other heats.

▸ **heat up.** PHR-VERB When something heats up, it gradually becomes hotter. *...when her mobile home heats up like an oven.* [2] See also heat 1.

heated /'hiːtɪd/. ADJ If someone is heated about something, they get angry and excited about it. A heated discussion or quarrel is one where the people involved are angry and excited. ♦**heatedly** ADV *The crowd continued to argue heatedly about the best way to tackle the problem.*

heater /'hiːtə/ **heaters.** N-C A heater is a piece of equipment which is used to warm a place or to heat water.

heather /'heðə/. N-U Heather is a low spreading plant with small purple, pink, or white flowers that grows wild on hills or moorland.

heating /'hiːtɪŋ/. N-U Heating is the process or equipment involved in keeping a building warm. *...cottages for £150 a week, including heating.* ● See also central heating.

heave /hiːv/ **heaves, heaving, heaved.** [1] VERB & N-C If you heave an object that is heavy or difficult to move, or if you move it with a heave, you push, pull, or lift it using a lot of effort. *It took five strong men to heave it up a ramp... It took only one heave to hurl him into the river.* [2] VERB If something heaves, it moves up and down with large regular movements. *His chest heaved, and he took a deep breath.*

heaven /'hevən/ **heavens.** [1] N-PROPER In some religions, heaven is said to be the place where God lives and where good people go when they die. [2] N-PL The heavens are the sky; DATED. *The stars glittered in the heavens.*
[PHRASES] ● You say 'good Heavens' to express surprise. *Good Heavens! That explains a lot!* ● You can say 'Heaven knows' to emphasize that you do not know something, or that you find something very surprising; BRITISH, INFORMAL. *Heaven knows what they put in it.* ● You can say 'Heaven knows' to emphasize something that you feel or believe very strongly; BRITISH, INFORMAL. *Heaven knows they have enough money.* ● thank heavens: see thank.

heavenly /'hevənli/. [1] ADJ Heavenly describes things relating to heaven. *...heavenly beings whose function it is to serve God.* [2] ADJ If you describe something as heavenly, you mean that it is very pleasant and enjoyable; INFORMAL. *The idea of spending two weeks with him may seem heavenly.*

heavily /'hevɪli/. ADV You can use heavily to indicate that something is great in amount, degree, or intensity. *...heavily armed soldiers... The agency was heavily criticised.*

heavy /'hevi/ **heavier, heaviest.** [1] ADJ Something that is heavy weighs a lot. *He opened the heavy Bible.* ♦**heaviness** N-U *...a sensation of warmth and heaviness in the muscles.* [2] ADJ You use heavy to ask or talk about how much someone or something weighs. *How heavy are you?... Protons are nearly 2000 times as heavy as electrons.* [3] ADJ Someone or something that is heavy is solid in appearance or structure. *...heavy old brown furniture... He was short and heavy.* ♦**heavily** ADV *...a big man of about forty, wide-shouldered and heavily built.* [4] ADJ Heavy means great in amount, degree, or intensity. *Heavy fighting has been going on. ...the heavy responsibility that parents take on.* ♦**heaviness** N-U *...the heaviness of the blood loss.* [5] ADJ If a person's breathing is heavy, it is very loud and deep. ♦**heavily** ADV *She sank back on the pillow and closed her eyes, breathing heavily.* [6] ADJ BEFORE N A heavy movement or action is done with a lot of force or pressure. *You sustained a heavy blow on the back of the skull.* ♦**heavily** ADV *I sat down heavily on the ground.* [7] ADJ If you describe a period of time or a schedule as heavy, you mean it involves a lot of work. *It's been a heavy day and I'm tired.* [8] ADJ Heavy work requires a lot of physical strength. [9] ADJ Heavy air or weather is unpleasantly still, hot, and damp. [10] ADJ A situation that is heavy is difficult or unpleasant to cope with; INFORMAL. *...when you can't handle your best friends' heavy conversation.*

heavy-'duty. ADJ A heavy-duty machine is strong and can be used a lot. *...a heavy-duty polythene bag.*

heavy-'handed. ADJ If you say that someone is heavy-handed, you mean that they are unnecessarily forceful and thoughtless. *...heavy-handed police tactics.*

heavyweight /'heviweit/ **heavyweights.** [1] N-C A heavyweight is a boxer or wrestler in the heaviest class. [2] N-C If you refer to a person or organization as a heavyweight, you

Hebrew /'hiːbruː/. N-U **Hebrew** is a language spoken by Jews.

heck /hek/. [1] EXCLAM You say **'heck!'** to express slight irritation or surprise; INFORMAL. *Oh, heck. What can I write about?... What the heck's that?* [2] PHRASE People use **a heck of** to emphasize how big something is or how much of it there is; INFORMAL. *They're spending a heck of a lot of money.*

heckle /'hekəl/ **heckles, heckling, heckled.** VERB & N-C If people in an audience **heckle** public speakers, they interrupt them by making rude remarks, called **heckles.** *A small group of youths stayed behind to heckle. ...a heckle from an audience member.* ◆**heckling** N-U *...the heckling and jeers of his audience.* ◆**heckler, hecklers.** N-C *He was interrupted by hecklers.*

hectare /'hekteə/ **hectares.** N-C A **hectare** is a unit of area equal to 10,000 square metres.

hectic /'hektɪk/. ADJ A **hectic** situation involves a lot of rushed activity. *...his hectic work schedule.*

he'd /hɪd, hiːd/. **He'd** is the usual spoken form of 'he had', especially when 'had' is an auxiliary verb. **He'd** is also a spoken form of 'he would'.

hedge /hedʒ/ **hedges, hedging, hedged.** [1] N-C A **hedge** is a row of bushes along the edge of a garden, field, or road. [2] VERB If you **hedge,** you avoid answering a question or committing yourself to a particular action. *'I can't give you an answer now,' he hedged.* [3] PHRASE If you **hedge your bets,** you reduce the risk of losing a lot by supporting more than one person or thing.

hedgehog /'hedʒhɒg, AM -hɔːg/ **hedgehogs.** N-C A **hedgehog** is a small brown animal with sharp spikes covering its back.

hedgerow /'hedʒrəʊ/ **hedgerows.** N-C A **hedgerow** is a row of bushes, trees, and plants, usually growing along a country lane or between fields.

hedonist /'hiːdənɪst/ **hedonists.** N-C A **hedonist** is someone who believes that having pleasure is the most important thing in life; FORMAL. ◆**hedonistic** ADJ *...the hedonistic pleasures of partying.* ◆**hedonism** N-U *...a life of hedonism and glamour.*

heed /hiːd/ **heeds, heeding, heeded.** [1] VERB If you **heed** someone's advice or warning, you pay attention to it and do what they suggest; FORMAL. *Few at the conference in London last week heeded his warning.* [2] PHRASE If you **take heed** of what someone says, or if you **pay heed to** them, you pay attention to them and consider carefully what they say.

heel /hiːl/ **heels.** [1] N-C Your **heel** is the back part of your foot, just below your ankle. [2] N-C The **heel** of a shoe is the raised part on the bottom at the back.

hefty /'hefti/ **heftier, heftiest.** ADJ **Hefty** means very large in size, weight, or amount; INFORMAL. *He faces a hefty fine.*

height /haɪt/ **heights.** [1] N-VAR The **height** of a person or thing is their measurement from bottom to top. *Her weight is about normal for her height.* [2] N-U **Height** is the quality of being tall. *Her height is intimidating for some men.* [3] N-VAR A particular **height** is the distance that something is above the ground. *...a 6.3 kilogram weight was dropped on it from a height of 1 metre.* [4] N-C A **height** is a high position or place above the ground. *From a height, it looks like a desert.* [5] N-SING When an activity, situation, or organization is at its **height,** it is at its most successful, powerful, or intense. *Emigration from Britain to Brittany was at its height.* [6] N-SING If you say that something is **the height of** a quality, you are emphasizing that it has that quality to the greatest degree possible. *I think it's the height of bad manners to be dressed badly.*

heighten /'haɪtən/ **heightens, heightening, heightened.** VERB If something **heightens** a feeling, the feeling increases in degree or intensity. *The move has heightened tension in the state... Cross's interest heightened.*

heir /eə/ **heirs.** N-C Someone's **heir** is the person who will inherit their money, property, or title when they die. *Her son was the sole heir to his grandparents' fortune.*

heiress /'eərɪs/ **heiresses.** N-C An **heiress** is a woman who will inherit property, money, or a title.

held /held/. **Held** is the past tense and past participle of **hold.**

helicopter /'helikɒptə/ **helicopters.** N-C A **helicopter** is an aircraft with no wings. It hovers or moves vertically and horizontally by means of large overhead blades which rotate.

hell /hel/ **hells.** [1] N-PROPER According to some religions, **Hell** is the place where the Devil lives, and where wicked people are sent to be punished when they die. [2] N-VAR If you say that a particular situation or place is **hell,** you are emphasizing that it is extremely unpleasant; INFORMAL. *June says her life has been hell since her marriage ended nine months ago.* [3] PHRASE You can use **from hell** after a noun when you are emphasizing that something or someone is extremely unpleasant or evil. *...the holiday from hell.*

he'll /hɪl, hiːl/. **He'll** is the usual spoken form of 'he will'.

hello (also **hallo** or **hullo**) /he'ləʊ/ **hellos.** CONVENTION & N-C You say **'Hello'** when you are greeting someone or starting a telephone conversation. *Hello, Trish. I won't shake hands, because I'm filthy... The salesperson greeted me with a warm hello.*

helmet /'helmɪt/ **helmets.** N-C A **helmet** is a hard hat which you wear to protect your head.

help /help/ **helps, helping, helped.** [1] VERB If you **help** someone, you make something easier for them to do for example by doing part of their work or by giving them advice or money. *He has helped to raise a lot of money... America's priority is to help nations defend themselves... You can of course help by giving them a donation directly... He began to help with the chores.* [2] VERB & N-SING If something **helps,** or if someone or something is a **help,** they make something easier to do or get, or they improve a situation. *The right style of swimsuit can help to hide a lot... It will do very little indeed to help our environment... The books were not much help.* [3] VERB If you **help** yourself to something, you serve yourself or you take it for yourself. *'Help yourself to a Pepsi.'... There's bread on the table. Help yourself.* [4] N-U & EXCLAM **Help** is the assistance that someone gives when they go to rescue a person who is in danger. You shout **'help!'** when you are in danger in order to attract someone's attention so that they can come and rescue you. *He was screaming for help.*

| PHRASES | ● If you **can't help** the way you feel or behave, you cannot control it or stop it happening. You can also say that you **can't help** yourself. *'Please don't cry.'—'I can't help it.'* ● See note at **avoid**. ● If something or someone **is of help**, they make things easier or better. *Can I be of help to you?*

▶ **help out.** PHR-VERB If you **help** someone **out**, you help them by doing some work for them or by lending them some money.

helper /'helpə/ **helpers.** N-C A **helper** is a person who helps another person or group with a job they are doing, usually an organized activity.

helpful /'helpfʊl/ [1] ADJ If someone is **helpful**, they help you by doing work for you or by giving you advice or information. *The staff in the London office are helpful.* ♦**helpfully** ADV *They had helpfully provided us with instructions.* [2] ADJ Something that is **helpful** makes a situation more pleasant or easier to tolerate. *Having the right equipment at hand will be enormously helpful.*

helpless /'helpləs/ ADJ If you are **helpless**, you do not have the strength or power to do anything useful or to protect yourself. *...seeing your child develop from a helpless baby to an independent toddler.* ♦**helplessly** ADV *Their son watched helplessly as they vanished beneath the waves.* ♦**helplessness** N-U *...his overwhelming sense of helplessness.*

hem /hem/ **hems, hemming, hemmed.** [1] N-C The **hem** of a piece of cloth is an edge which is folded over and sewn. *The hem of a skirt or dress is the hem along its lower edge.* [2] VERB If you **hem** a piece of cloth, you fold the edge over and sew it to make it neat.

▶ **hem in.** PHR-VERB If you **are hemmed in** by something, you are completely surrounded by it so that you cannot move. You can also say that a place is **hemmed in** when it is surrounded by something tall such as mountains or tall buildings. *You feel hemmed in. Find open spaces, get in touch with nature. ...a small valley hemmed in by rocks.*

hemisphere /'hemɪsfɪə/ **hemispheres.** N-C A **hemisphere** is one half of the earth. *...the northern hemisphere.*

hemorrhage /'hemərɪdʒ/. See **haemorrhage**.

hen /hen/ **hens.** [1] N-C A **hen** is a female chicken. [2] N-C The female of any bird can be referred to as a **hen**. *...ostrich hens.*

hence /hens/. [1] ADV **Hence** means for the reason just mentioned. *The Socialist Party was profoundly divided and hence very weak.* [2] ADV If something will happen a particular length of

time **hence**, it will happen that length of time from now. *The election two years hence may seem a long way off.*

henceforth /ˌhens'fɔːθ/. ADV **Henceforth** means from this time onwards; FORMAL. *Henceforth, all churches and religious societies will be legally recognised.*

hepatitis /ˌhepə'taɪtɪs/. N-U **Hepatitis** is a serious disease which affects the liver.

her /hə, STRONG hɜː/. [1] PRON & DET You use **her** to refer to a woman, girl, or female animal. *I really thought I'd lost her... Liz travelled round the world for a year with her boyfriend James.* [2] PRON & DET **Her** is sometimes used to refer to a country or nation. *...Britain's apparently deep-rooted distrust of her EU partner.* [3] PRON & DET People sometimes use **her** to refer informally to a car, ship, or machine. *Kemp got out of his car. 'Just fill her up, thanks.'*

herald /'herəld/ **heralds, heralding, heralded.** [1] VERB & N-C Something that **heralds** a future event or situation, or is a **herald** of it, is a sign that it is going to happen or appear. *Their discovery could herald a cure for some forms of impotence.* [2] VERB If an important event or action **is heralded** by people, announcements are made about it so that it is publicly known and expected. *Tonight's clash between Real Madrid and Arsenal is being heralded as the match of the season.*

herb /hɜːb, AM ɜːb/ **herbs.** N-C A **herb** is a plant whose leaves are used in cookery to add flavour to food, or as a medicine. ♦**herbal** /'hɜːbəl, AM 'ɜːb-/ ADJ *...herbal remedies for colds.*

herd /hɜːd/ **herds, herding, herded.** [1] N-C A **herd** is a large group of animals of one kind that live together. *...dairy herds.* [2] VERB If you **herd** people or animals somewhere, you make them move there in a group. *The group was herded into a bus.*

here /hɪə/. [1] ADV You use **here** when you are referring to the place where you are. *I'm here all by myself... I can't stand here chatting all day... Sheila was in here a minute ago.* [2] ADV You use **here** when you are pointing towards a place that is near you, in order to draw someone else's attention to it. *...if you will just sign here... Come and sit here, Lauren.* [3] ADV You use **here** at the beginning of a sentence in order to draw attention to something or someone who has just arrived in the place where you are, or to draw attention to the place you have just arrived at. *'Here's the taxi,' she said politely... Here comes your husband.* [4] ADV You use **here** to refer to a particular point or stage of a situation or subject that you have come to or that you are dealing with. *The book goes into recent work in greater detail than I have attempted here.* [5] ADV You use **here** when you are offering or giving something to someone. *Here's my mother's number... Here's some letters I want you to sign.*

hereditary /hɪ'redɪtri/. [1] ADJ A **hereditary** characteristic or illness is passed on to a child from its parents before it is born. *Cystic fibrosis is the commonest fatal hereditary disease.* [2] ADJ A **hereditary** title or position in society is passed on as a right from parent to child.

heresy /ˈherɪsi/ **heresies**. N-VAR **Heresy** is a belief or way of behaving that disagrees with generally accepted beliefs, especially religious ones. *Galileo's heresy lay in declaring the Sun to be the fixed point and not the Earth.*

heritage /ˈherɪtɪdʒ/. N-SING A country's **heritage** consists of all the qualities and traditions that have continued over many years, especially when they are considered to be of historical importance. *Bullfighting is part of Spain's heritage.*

hermit /ˈhɜːmɪt/ **hermits**. N-C A **hermit** is a person who deliberately lives alone, away from people and society.

hernia /ˈhɜːniə/ **hernias**. N-C A **hernia** is a medical condition in which one of your internal organs sticks through a weak point in the surrounding tissue.

hero /ˈhɪərəʊ/ **heroes**. [1] N-C The **hero** of a book, play, or film is the main male character, who usually has good qualities. [2] N-C A **hero** is someone who has done something brave or good and is admired by a lot of people. *He called Mr Mandela a hero who had inspired millions.*

heroic /hɪˈrəʊɪk/ **heroics**. [1] ADJ **Heroic** people or actions are brave and determined. *A heroic six-year-old saved his playmate from being burned to death. ...his heroic effort to negotiate the release of hostages.* ◆**heroically** ADV *He had acted heroically.* [2] N-PL You can describe actions involving bravery or determination as **heroics**. *...his wartime heroics as a fighter pilot.* [3] N-PL If you describe someone's actions as **heroics**, you mean that they are foolish or dangerous because they are too difficult for the situation in which they occur; SPOKEN. *His advice was: 'No heroics, stay within the law'.*

heroin /ˈherəʊɪn/. N-U **Heroin** is a powerful addictive drug used to prevent pain. Some people take it for pleasure.

heroine /ˈherəʊɪn/ **heroines**. [1] N-C The **heroine** of a book, play, or film is its main female character, who usually has good qualities. [2] N-C A **heroine** is a woman who has done something brave or good and is admired by a lot of people. *...our national heroines.*

heroism /ˈherəʊɪzəm/. N-U **Heroism** is great courage and bravery. *...acts of heroism.*

herpes /ˈhɜːpiːz/. N-U **Herpes** is the name used for several viruses which cause painful red spots to appear on the skin; TECHNICAL.

herring /ˈherɪŋ/; the plural is **herring** or **herrings**. N-VAR A **herring** is a long silver-coloured fish. **Herring** is the flesh of this fish eaten as food.

hers /hɜːz/. PRON You use **hers** to indicate that something belongs or relates to a woman, girl, or female animal that has already been mentioned, or whose identity is known. *His hand as it shook hers was warm and firm. ...a great friend of hers.*

herself /həˈself/. [1] PRON You use **herself** to refer to the same woman, girl, or female animal that is mentioned as the subject of the clause, or as a previous object in the clause. *She let herself out of the room... Robin didn't feel good about herself.* [2] PRON You use **herself** to emphasize the female subject or object of a clause, and to make it clear who you are referring to. *Has anyone thought of consulting Bethan herself?* [3] PRON If a girl or woman does something **herself**, she does it without any help or interference from anyone else. *The jam was marvellous. She had made it herself.*

he's /hɪz, hiːz/. **He's** is the usual spoken form of 'he is' or 'he has', especially when 'has' is an auxiliary verb.

hesitant /ˈhezɪtənt/. ADJ If you are **hesitant** about doing something, you do not do it quickly or immediately, usually because you are uncertain, embarrassed, or worried. *At first he was hesitant to accept the role.* ◆**hesitancy** /ˈhezɪtənsi/ N-U *...Ukraine's hesitancy over abandoning the weapons.* ◆**hesitantly** ADV *'Would you do me a favour?' she asked hesitantly.*

hesitate /ˈhezɪteɪt/ **hesitates, hesitating, hesitated**. [1] VERB If you **hesitate**, you pause slightly while you are doing something or just before you do it, usually because you are uncertain, embarrassed, or worried. *She hesitated before replying.* ◆**hesitation, hesitations** N-VAR *After a moment's hesitation, the others followed him.* [2] VERB If you **hesitate** to do something, you are unwilling to do it because you are not certain whether it is the right thing to do. *Many women hesitate to discuss money... Don't hesitate to say no if you'd rather not.* ◆**hesitation** N-VAR *He promised there would be no more hesitations in pursuing reforms.*

heterosexual /ˌhetərəʊˈsekʃuəl/ **heterosexuals**. ADJ & N-C Someone who is **heterosexual** or a **heterosexual**, is sexually attracted to people of the opposite sex. ◆**heterosexuality** N-U *...the assumption that heterosexuality was 'normal'.*

hey /heɪ/. CONVENTION You say or shout **'hey'** to attract someone's attention or show surprise, interest, or annoyance; INFORMAL. *Hey! You!*

heyday /ˈheɪdeɪ/. N-SING The **heyday** of someone or something is the time when they are most powerful, successful, or popular. *...the heyday of the railways.*

hi /haɪ/. CONVENTION You say **'hi'** when you are greeting someone; INFORMAL. *'Hi, Darren.'*

hiccup (or **hiccough**) /ˈhɪkʌp/, **hiccups, hiccuping, hiccuped** (or **hiccupping, hiccupped**). [1] VERB & N-U When you **hiccup**, or when you have **hiccups**, you make repeated sharp sounds in your throat, often because you have been eating or drinking too quickly. [2] N-C You can refer to a minor problem as a **hiccup**. *Preparations have been hit by only one slight hiccup.*

hid /hɪd/. **Hid** is the past tense of **hide**.

hidden /ˈhɪdən/. [1] **Hidden** is the past participle of **hide**. [2] ADJ Something that is **hidden** is not easily noticed. *...hidden dangers.* [3] ADJ A place that is **hidden** is difficult to find. *...a hidden valley.*

hide /haɪd/ **hides, hiding, hid, hidden**. [1] VERB To **hide** something means to cover it or put it somewhere so that it cannot be seen. *She hid her face in her hands. ...a bomb hidden in a briefcase.* [2] VERB If you **hide**, or if you **hide** yourself, you go somewhere where you cannot easily be seen or found. *They hid themselves behind a tree.* [3] VERB If you **hide** what you feel or know, you keep it a secret. *Lee tried to hide his excitement.* [4] N-C A **hide** is a place which is built to look like its surroundings, so that people can watch or photograph animals and birds without being seen by them; BRITISH. [5] N-VAR A **hide** is the skin of a large animal, used for making leather. ...*cow hides.*

hideous /'hɪdiəs/. ADJ If you say that someone or something is **hideous**, you mean that they are extremely unpleasant or ugly. ...*a hideous crime.* ...*his hideous face.* ◆**hideously** ADV He has been left hideously disfigured.

hiding /'haɪdɪŋ/ **hidings.** N-U If someone is in **hiding**, they have secretly gone somewhere where they cannot be found. *He went into hiding 18 months ago.*

hierarchy /'haɪərɑːki/ **hierarchies.** [1] N-VAR A **hierarchy** is a system in which people have different ranks or positions depending on how important they are. ...*a society which is ordered by hierarchy.* ◆**hierarchical** /haɪə'rɑːkɪkəl/ ADJ ...*a hierarchical society.* [2] N-C The **hierarchy** of an organization such as the Church is the group of people who manage and control it.

hi-fi /'haɪ faɪ/ **hi-fis.** N-C A **hi-fi** is a set of stereo equipment which you use to play records, tapes, and compact discs.

high /haɪ/ **higher, highest; highs.** [1] ADJ & ADV A **high** structure or mountain measures a great amount from the bottom to the top. ...*a house, with a high wall all around it.* ...*the highest mountain in the Adirondacks.* ...*high-heeled shoes.* ...*a sofa piled high with cushions.*

> You do not use **high** to describe people. The word you should use is **tall**. *She was rather tall for a woman.* **Tall** is also used to describe buildings such as skyscrapers, and other things whose height is much greater than their width. ...*tall pine trees.* ...*a tall glass vase.*

[2] ADJ You use **high** to talk or ask about how much something upright measures from the bottom to the top. ...*an elegant bronze horse only nine inches high... How high is the door?* [3] ADJ & ADV If something is **high**, it is a long way above the ground, above sea level, or above a person or thing. *I looked down from the high window... The sun was high in the sky. ...being able to run faster or jump higher than other people.* [4] ADJ & ADV **High** means great in amount, degree, or intensity. *Official reports said casualties were high... High winds have knocked down trees and power lines... He expects the unemployment figures to rise even higher.* [5] ADJ If a number or level is in the **high** eighties, it is more than eighty-five, but not as much as ninety. [6] ADJ AFTER LINK-V If a food or other substance is **high in** a particular ingredient, it contains a large amount of that ingredient. ...*a superb compost, high in calcium.* [7] N-C If something reaches a **high** of a particular amount or degree, that is the greatest it has ever been. *Sales of Russian vodka have reached an all-time high.* [8] ADJ If you say that something is a **high** priority or is **high** on your list, you mean that you consider it to be one of the most important things you have to

do. [9] ADJ **High** means advanced or complex. ...*the rise of Japan's high technology industries.* [10] ADJ Someone who is **high** in a particular profession or society, or has a **high** position, has an important position and has great authority and influence. [11] ADJ If people have a **high** opinion of you, they respect you very much. [12] ADJ If the quality or standard of something is **high**, it is very good indeed. [13] ADJ If someone has **high** principles or standards, they are morally good. [14] ADJ If your spirits are **high**, you feel happy and excited. [15] to **be high time**: see **time**.

,high-'class. ADJ **High-class** is used to describe people and things which are the very best of their type. ...*a high-class hotel.* ...*a high-class international jockey.*

higher /haɪə/. **Higher** is the comparative form of **high**.

,higher edu'cation. N-U **Higher education** is education at universities and colleges.

,high-'flying. ADJ A **high-flying** person is very ambitious and is likely to be successful in their career. ...*a high-flying executive.*

highlands /'haɪləndz/. N-PL **Highlands** are mountainous areas. ...*the highlands of Scotland.*

highlight /'haɪlaɪt/ **highlights, highlighting, highlighted.** [1] VERB If you **highlight** a point or problem, you draw attention to it. *The report highlights the need to set aside areas for the development of airports.* [2] N-C The **highlights** of an event, activity, or period of time are the most interesting or exciting parts of it.

highly /'haɪli/. [1] ADV You use **highly** to emphasize that a particular quality exists to a great degree. ...*highly confidential information.* ...*highly skilled craftsmen.* [2] ADV You use **highly** to indicate that someone has an important position in an organization or set of people. ...*a highly placed government source.* [3] ADV If you think **highly** of something or someone, you think they are very good indeed.

Highness /'haɪnɪs/ **Highnesses.** N-VOC You use expressions such as **Your Highness** and **His Highness** to address a member of a royal family.

,high-'pitched. ADJ A **high-pitched** sound is high and shrill. ...*a high-pitched scream.*

,high-'powered. ADJ **High-powered** professional people are in a job which carries a lot of responsibility or status. ...*a high-powered businessman.*

,high-'profile. ADJ A **high-profile** person or event attracts a lot of attention or publicity. ...*high-profile court cases.*

'high-rise. N-C & ADJ BEFORE N A **high-rise**, or a **high-rise** building, is a very tall modern building. ...*high-rise flats.*

'high school, high schools. [1] N-VAR In Britain, a **high school** is a school for children aged between eleven and eighteen. [2] N-VAR In the United States, a **high school** is a school for children aged between fourteen and eighteen.

'high street, high streets. N-C The **high street** of a town is the main street where most of the shops and banks are; BRITISH.

,high 'tech (or **hi tech**). ADJ **High tech** activities or equipment involve or result from the use of high technology. ...*such high-tech industries as computers.*

,high tech'nology. N-U **High technology** is the development and use of advanced electronics and computers.

highway /'haɪweɪ/ **highways.** N-C A **highway** is a main road, especially one that connects towns or cities; AMERICAN.

hijack /'haɪdʒæk/ **hijacks, hijacking, hijacked.** VERB & N-C If someone **hijacks** a plane or other vehicle, they illegally take control of it by force while it is travelling from one place to another. An illegal action like this is called a **hijack.** ♦**hijacker, hijackers** N-C *There was a scuffle between the hijackers and the pilots.* ♦**hijacking, hijackings** N-C ...*attempted hijackings in the Soviet Union.*

hike /haɪk/ **hikes, hiking, hiked.** ① VERB & N-C If you **hike,** or if you go on a **hike,** you go for a long walk in the country. *You could hike through the Fish River Canyon.* ♦**hiker, hikers** N-C ...*hikers with rucksacks and maps.* ♦**hiking** N-U ...*strenuous hiking on cliff pathways.* ② VERB & PHR-VERB To **hike** prices, rates, or taxes, or to **hike** them **up,** means to increase them suddenly or by a large amount; JOURNALISM. *The federal government hiked the tax on hard liquor.*

hilarious /hɪ'leəriəs/. ADJ If something is **hilarious,** it is extremely funny. ♦**hilariously** ADV *She found it hilariously funny.*

hill /hɪl/ **hills.** N-C A **hill** is an area of land that is higher than the land that surrounds it, but not as high as a mountain.

hilly /'hɪli/ **hillier, hilliest.** ADJ A **hilly** area has a lot of hills.

him /hɪm/. ① PRON You use **him** to refer to a man, boy, or male animal. *Elaine met him at the bus station.* ② PRON **Him** can be used to refer to someone whose sex is not known or stated; WRITTEN.

himself /hɪm'self/. ① PRON You use **himself** to refer to the same man, boy, or male animal that is mentioned as the subject of the clause. *A driver blew up his car and himself... He poured himself a whisky... William went away muttering to himself.* ② PRON You use **himself** to emphasize the male subject or object of a clause, and to make it clear who you are referring to. ...*the judgment pronounced by Pope John Paul II himself.* ③ PRON If a man or boy does something **himself,** he does it without any help. *Goldrims had written it himself.*

hind /haɪnd/. ① ADJ BEFORE N An animal's **hind** legs are at the back of its body. ② N-C A **hind** is a female deer.

hinder /'hɪndə/ **hinders, hindering, hindered.** VERB If something **hinders** you, it makes it more difficult for you to do something. *A thigh injury increasingly hindered her mobility.*

hindrance /'hɪndrəns/ **hindrances.** ① N-C A **hindrance** is someone or something that hinders you. ② N-U **Hindrance** is the act of hindering someone or something. *They boarded their flight to Paris without hindrance.*

hindsight /'haɪndsaɪt/. N-U **Hindsight** is the ability to understand something about an event after it has happened, although you did not understand or realize it at the time. *With hindsight, we'd all do things differently.*

Hindu /'hɪnduː, hɪn'duː/ **Hindus.** ① N-C A **Hindu** is a person who believes in Hinduism. ② ADJ **Hindu** is used to describe things that belong or relate to Hinduism. ...*a Hindu temple.*

Hinduism /'hɪnduːɪzəm, hɪn'duː/. N-U **Hinduism** is an Indian religion, which has many gods and teaches that people have another life after they die.

hinge /hɪndʒ/ **hinges, hinging, hinged.** ① N-C A **hinge** is a moveable joint made of metal, wood, or plastic that joins two things so that one of them can swing freely. ② ADJ Something that is **hinged** is joined to another thing by means of a hinge. *The hinged seat lifts up to reveal a useful storage space.*

▶ **hinge on.** PHR-VERB Something that **hinges on** one thing or event depends entirely on it. *The plan hinges on a deal being struck.*

hint /hɪnt/ **hints, hinting, hinted.** ① VERB & N-C If you **hint** at something, or if you drop a **hint** about it, you suggest it in an indirect way. *The President hinted he might make some changes.* ② N-C A **hint** is a helpful piece of advice. *The book gives handy hints on looking after indoor plants.* ③ N-SING A **hint** of something is a very small amount of it. *She added only a hint of vermouth to the gin.*

hip /hɪp/ **hips.** ① N-C Your **hips** are the two areas or bones at the sides of your body between the tops of your legs and your waist. ② ADJ If you say that someone is **hip,** you mean that they are fashionable; INFORMAL. ...*a hip young character with tight-cropped blond hair.*

hippie (or **hippy**) /'hɪpi/ **hippies.** N-C In the 1960s and 1970s, **hippies** were people who rejected conventional society and tried to live a life based on peace and love.

hire /haɪə/ **hires, hiring, hired.** ① VERB & N-U If you **hire** something, or if you have it on hire, you pay money to use it for a period of time; BRITISH. *Hire of skis, boots and clothing, are all available.* ② PHRASE If something is **for hire,** it is available for you to hire; BRITISH. ③ VERB If you **hire** someone, you pay them to work for you. *He will be in charge of all hiring and firing at PHA.*

▶ **hire out.** PHR-VERB If you **hire out** something such as a car or a person's services, you allow them to be used in return for payment. *His agency hires out security guards and bodyguards.*

his /hɪz/. ① DET & PRON You use **his** to indicate that something belongs or relates to a man, boy, or male animal. *He spent a large part of his career in Hollywood... My dinner jacket is every bit as good as his.* ② DET **His** can be used to refer to someone whose sex is not known or stated. ...*the relations between a teacher and his pupils.*

Hispanic /hɪ'spænɪk/ **Hispanics.** ADJ & N-C If you describe someone from the United States as **Hispanic,** or if you refer to them as a **His-**

panic, you mean that they or their family originally came from Latin America.

hiss /hɪs/ **hisses, hissing, hissed.** [1] VERB & N-C To **hiss** means to make a sound like a long 's', called a **hiss**. *The tires of Lenny's bike hissed over the wet pavement.* ◆**hissing** N-U *...a silence broken only by a steady hissing from above my head.* [2] VERB If you **hiss** something, you say it in a strong angry whisper. *'Now, quiet,' my mother hissed.*

historian /hɪˈstɔːriən/ **historians.** N-C A **historian** is a person who specializes in the study of history and who writes about it.

historic /hɪˈstɒrɪk, AM -ˈtɔːr-/. ADJ A **historic** event is important in history, or likely to be considered important at some time in the future. *...the historic changes in the Soviet Union.*

historical /hɪˈstɒrɪkəl, AM -ˈtɔːr-/. [1] ADJ BEFORE N **Historical** people, situations, or things existed in the past and are considered to be a part of history. ◆**historically** ADV *Historically, royal marriages have been cold, calculating affairs.* [2] ADJ BEFORE N **Historical** books, works of art, or studies are concerned with people, situations, or things that existed in the past.

history /ˈhɪstəri/ **histories.** [1] N-U You can refer to the events of the past as **history**. You can also refer to the past events which concern a particular topic or place as its **history**. *He later studied history and folklore at Indiana University. ...great moments in baseball history.* [2] N-C A **history** is an account of events that have happened in the past in a particular subject. *...his magnificent history of broadcasting.* [3] N-C Someone's **history** is the set of facts that are know about their past. *...the boy's medical history.* [4] N-C If someone has a **history** of something bad, they keep doing that thing or it keeps happening to them. *He had a long history of drink problems.*

hit /hɪt/ **hits, hitting, hit.** [1] VERB If you **hit** someone or something, you deliberately strike or touch them forcefully, with your hand or with an object held in your hand. *Both men had been hit in the stomach with baseball bats.* [2] VERB & N-C When a moving object **hits** another object, it strikes or touches it with a lot of force. This impact is called a **hit**. *The car had apparently hit a traffic sign... A house took a direct hit and then the rocket exploded.* [3] VERB If something **hits** a person, place, or thing, it affects them badly. *...the earthquake which hit northern Peru.* [4] VERB When a feeling or an idea **hits** you, it suddenly comes into your mind. *Then the answer hit me.* [5] N-C If a record, play, or film is a **hit**, it is very popular and successful. [6] PHRASE If two people **hit it off**, they become friendly as soon as they meet.

▸ **hit on** or **hit upon**. PHR-VERB If you **hit on** an idea or a solution to a problem, or if you **hit upon** it, you think of it.

hit-and-'run. ADJ BEFORE N In a **hit-and-run** accident, the driver of a vehicle hits someone and then drives away without stopping. *...a hit-and-run driver in a stolen car.*

hitch /hɪtʃ/ **hitches, hitching, hitched.** [1] N-C A **hitch** is a slight problem. [2] VERB If you **hitch**, or if you **hitch** a lift, you hitch-hike. *Philippe had hitched all over Europe.* [3] VERB

If you **hitch** one thing onto something else, you fasten it there. *We hitched the horse to the cart.*

hitchhike (or **hitch-hike**) /ˈhɪtʃhaɪk/ **hitchhikes, hitchhiking, hitchhiked.** VERB If you **hitchhike**, you travel by getting free lifts from passing vehicles. *Neff hitchhiked to New York.* ◆**hitchhiker, hitchhikers** N-C *On my way to Vancouver I picked up a hitchhiker.*

,hi 'tech. See **high tech**.

hitherto /ˌhɪðəˈtuː/. ADV You use **hitherto** to indicate that something was true up until the time you are talking about, although it may no longer be the case; FORMAL *Hitherto, the main emphasis has been on the need to resist aggression.*

'**hit list, hit lists.** N-C A terrorist's or gangster's **hit list** are the people they intend to kill.

HIV /ˌeɪtʃ aɪ ˈviː/. [1] N-U **HIV** is a virus which reduces people's resistance to illness and can cause AIDS. [2] PHRASE If someone is **HIV positive**, they are infected with the HIV virus, and may develop AIDS.

hive /haɪv/ **hives, hiving, hived.** [1] N-C A **hive** is a structure in which bees are kept. [2] N-C If you describe a place as a **hive of** activity, you approve of the fact that there is a lot of activity there or that people are busy working there.

hoard /hɔːd/ **hoards, hoarding, hoarded.** [1] VERB If you **hoard** things such as food or money, you save or store them, often in secret, because they are valuable or important to you. *They've begun to hoard food and gasoline and save their money.* [2] N-SING A **hoard** is a store of things you have hoarded or secretly hidden.

hoarding /ˈhɔːdɪŋ/ **hoardings.** N-C In British English, a **hoarding** is a large board used for advertising which stands at the side of a road. The usual American word is **billboard**.

hoarse /hɔːs/ **hoarser, hoarsest.** ADJ If you are **hoarse**, your voice sounds rough and unclear, for example because your throat is sore. ◆**hoarsely** ADV *'Thank you,' Maria said hoarsely.*

hoax /həʊks/ **hoaxes.** N-C A **hoax** is a trick in which someone tells people something that is not true, for example that there is a bomb somewhere.

hob /hɒb/ **hobs.** N-C A **hob** is a surface on top of a cooker which can be heated in order to cook things.

hobble /ˈhɒbəl/ **hobbles, hobbling, hobbled.** [1] VERB If you **hobble**, you walk with difficulty because you are in pain. *He got up slowly and hobbled over to the coffee table.* [2] VERB To **hobble** something or someone means to make it more difficult for them to be successful or to achieve what they want. *...the poor transport system that has hobbled the area.*

hobby /ˈhɒbi/ **hobbies.** N-C A **hobby** is something that you enjoy doing in your spare time.

hockey /ˈhɒki/. [1] N-U **Hockey** is a sport played between two teams of 11 players who use long curved sticks to hit a small ball and try to score goals. [2] See also **ice hockey**.

hog /hɒg, AM hɔːg/ **hogs, hogging, hogged.** [1] N-C A **hog** is a pig. [2] VERB If you **hog** something, you take all of it in a selfish or rude way;

hoist

INFORMAL. *Have you done hogging the bath-room?*

hoist /hɔɪst/ **hoists, hoisting, hoisted.**
[1] VERB If you **hoist** a heavy object somewhere, you lift it or pull it up there, often using equipment or machinery of some kind. *Hoisting my suitcase on to my shoulder, I turned and headed toward my hotel... A twenty-foot steel pyramid is to be hoisted into position.* [2] N-C A **hoist** is a machine for lifting heavy things. [3] VERB If you **hoist** a flag or a sail, you pull it up to its correct position using ropes.

hold 1 *physically touching, supporting, or containing*

hold /həʊld/ **holds, holding, held.** [1] VERB & N-C When you **hold** something, you carry or support it, using your hands or your arms. Your **hold** on something is the fact that you are holding it. *Hold the knife at an angle... Hold the baby while I load the car... He released his hold on the camera.* [2] N-U **Hold** is used in expressions such as **grab hold of**, **catch hold of**, and **get hold of**, to indicate that you close your hand tightly around something. *Mother took hold of the barking dogs by their collars.* [3] VERB If you **hold** your body or part of your body in a particular position, you keep it in that position. *Hold your hands in front of your face.* [4] VERB If one thing **holds** another in a particular position, it keeps it in that position. *...the wooden wedge which held the heavy door open.* [5] VERB If one thing is used to **hold** another, it is used to store it. *Two knife racks held her favourite knives.* [6] VERB If something **holds** a particular amount of something, it can contain that amount. *The small bottles don't seem to hold much.* [7] N-C The **hold** of a ship or aeroplane is the place where cargo is stored. [8] See also **holding**.

hold 2 *having or doing*

hold /həʊld/ **holds, holding, held.** [1] VERB If you **hold** a particular opinion or belief, that is your opinion or belief. *He held firm opinions which usually conflicted with my own.* [2] VERB You can use **hold** to say that something has a particular quality or characteristic. *Death doesn't hold any fear for me.* [3] VERB **Hold** is used with nouns such as 'office', 'power', and 'responsibility' to indicate that someone has a particular position of power or authority. *She has never held ministerial office.* [4] VERB **Hold** is used with nouns such as 'permit', 'degree', or 'ticket' to indicate that someone has a particular document that allows them to do something. *He did not hold a firearm certificate.* ♦**holder, holders.** N-C *...season-ticket holders.* [5] VERB If you **hold** an event, you organize it and it takes place. *The German sports federation said it would hold an investigation.* [6] VERB If you **hold** a conversation with someone, you talk with them. *The Prime Minister is holding consultations with his colleagues.* [7] VERB If you **hold** someone's interest or attention, you keep them interested. *It's done in a way that will hold children's attention.* [8] See also **holding**.

hold 3 *controlling or remaining*

hold /həʊld/ **holds, holding, held.** [1] VERB If someone **holds** you in a place, they keep you

there as a prisoner. *Somebody is holding your wife hostage.* [2] N-SING If you have a **hold** over someone, you have power or control over them. *Because he once loved her, she still has a hold on him.* [3] VERB You ask someone to **hold** when you are answering a telephone if you are asking them to wait for a short time. *Could you hold the line and I'll just get my pen.* [4] VERB If something **holds**, it remains the same. *Cattle prices held at yesterday's sales... Would the weather hold?* [5] CONVENTION If you say '**Hold it**', you are telling someone to stop what they are doing and to wait. [6] CONVENTION If you say '**Hold on**', you are telling someone to wait a short time. [7] See also **holding**.

hold 4 *phrases*

hold /həʊld/ **holds, holding, held.**
PHRASES • If you **get hold of** something or someone, you manage to get them or find them. *It is hard to get hold of guns in this country.* • If you put something **on hold**, you decide not to do it now, but to leave it till later. *He put his retirement on hold to work 16 hours a day.* • If you **hold** your own, you are not defeated by someone. *She can hold her own against almost any player.* • If something **takes hold**, it finally gains complete control or influence over something or someone. *She felt a strange excitement taking hold of her.*

hold 5 *phrasal verbs*

hold /həʊld/ **holds, holding, held.**
► **hold against.** PHR-VERB If you **hold** something **against** someone, you resent or dislike them because of something which they did in the past.
► **hold back.** [1] PHR-VERB If you **hold back**, you hesitate before doing something. *My fear of failure always held me back.* [2] PHR-VERB If you **hold** someone or something **back**, you prevent them from advancing or increasing. *Stagnation in home sales is holding back economic recovery.* [3] PHR-VERB If you **hold** something **back**, you do not tell someone the full details about it. *You seem to be holding something back.*
► **hold down.** PHR-VERB If you **hold down** a job, you manage to keep it.
► **hold off.** PHR-VERB If you **hold off** doing something, you delay doing it or delay making a decision about it. *They have threatened military action but held off until now.*
► **hold on** or **hold onto.** [1] PHR-VERB If you **hold on** or **hold onto** something, you keep your hand firmly round something. [2] PHR-VERB If you **hold onto** something that gives you an advantage, you succeed in keeping it for yourself, and prevent other people getting it. *...a politician who knew how to hold onto power.* [3] PHR-VERB If you **hold onto** something, you keep it for a longer time than would normally be expected. *People hold onto letters for years and years.*
► **hold out.** [1] PHR-VERB If you **hold out** your hand or something that is in your hand, you move it towards someone. *'I'm Nancy Drew,' she said, holding out her hand.* [2] PHR-VERB If you **hold out** for something, you refuse to accept something inferior or you refuse to surrender. *He can only hold out a few more weeks.*

▶ **hold up.** [1] PHR-VERB If someone or something **holds** you **up**, they delay you. [2] PHR-VERB If someone **holds up** a place such as a bank, they rob it using a weapon. • See also **hold-up**.

▶ **hold with.** PHR-VERB If you do not **hold with** something, you do not approve of it.

holder /ˈhəʊldə/ **holders.** N-C A **holder** is a device for storing a particular thing. ...*a Victorian cigar holder.* ...*a toothbrush holder.*

holding /ˈhəʊldɪŋ/ **holdings.** [1] N-C If you have a **holding** in a company, you own shares in it. ...*holdings in commercial and merchant banks.* [2] N-C A **holding** is an area of farm land rented or owned by the person who cultivates it. [3] N-PL The **holdings** of a place such as a library or art gallery consists of the collection of items which are kept there.

hold-up, hold-ups. [1] N-C A **hold-up** is a situation in which someone is threatened with a weapon in order to make them hand over money or valuables. [2] N-C A **hold-up** is something which causes a delay, for example traffic delays.

hole /həʊl/ **holes, holing, holed.** N-C A **hole** is an opening or hollow space in something. *The builders had cut holes into the soft stone.*

▶ **hole up.** PHR-VERB If you **hole up** somewhere, you hide or shut yourself away there; INFORMAL. *She spent her free time holed up in her apartment with a book.*

holiday /ˈhɒlɪdeɪ/ **holidays, holidaying, holidayed.** [1] N-C & PHRASE In British English, a **holiday** is a period of time when you are not working and are away from home for relaxation. You can also say that you are **on holiday** during this time. The American word is **vacation**. *We're going to Scotland for our holidays... I went on holiday with friends to Ibiza.* [2] VERB If you **are holidaying** in a place, you are on holiday there; BRITISH. [3] N-C A **holiday** is a day when people do not go to work or school because of a religious or national festival. ...*dozens of flight cancellations over the holiday weekend.* • See also **bank holiday**. [4] N-PL In British English, the **holidays** are the time when children do not have to go to school. The American word is **vacation**. ...*the first day of the school holidays.*

holidaymaker (or **holiday-maker**) /ˈhɒlɪdeɪmeɪkə/ **holidaymakers.** N-C A **holidaymaker** is a person who is away from home on holiday; BRITISH.

holiness /ˈhəʊlɪnəs/. [1] N-U **Holiness** is the state or quality of being holy. [2] N-VOC People say **Your Holiness** or **His Holiness** when they address or refer respectfully to the Pope or to leaders of some other religions.

holistic /həʊˈlɪstɪk/. ADJ A **holistic** approach to something treats it as a whole, rather than as a number of different parts; FORMAL.

holler /ˈhɒlə/ **hollers, hollering, hollered.** VERB If you **holler**, you shout loudly; AMERICAN, INFORMAL. *He'll be hollering at me for coming in late.*

hollow /ˈhɒləʊ/ **hollows, hollowing, hollowed.** [1] ADJ Something that is **hollow** has a hole or space inside it. ...*a hollow tree.* [2] ADJ A surface that is **hollow** curves inwards. ...*sharp-featured, with hollow cheeks.* [3] N-C A **hollow** is an area that is lower than the surrounding surface. *Water gathers in a hollow and forms a pond.* [4] ADJ If you describe a statement, situation, or person as **hollow**, you mean they have no real value, worth, or effectiveness. ◆**hollowness** N-U ...*the hollowness of these promises.* [5] ADJ BEFORE N A **hollow** sound is dull and echoing. ...*the hollow sound of a gunshot.*

▶ **hollow out.** PHR-VERB If you **hollow** something **out**, you remove the inside part of it. *Someone had hollowed out a large block of stone.*

holly /ˈhɒli/ **hollies.** N-VAR **Hollies** are a group of evergreen trees and shrubs which have hard, shiny, prickly leaves, and also have bright red berries in winter.

holocaust /ˈhɒləkɔːst/ **holocausts.** [1] N-VAR A **holocaust** is an event in which there is large-scale destruction and loss of life, especially in war. ...*nuclear holocaust.* [2] N-SING The **holocaust** was the killing by the Nazis of millions of Jews during the Second World War.

holy /ˈhəʊli/ **holier, holiest.** [1] ADJ Something that is **holy** is considered to be special because it relates to God or to a particular religion. *This is a holy place.* [2] ADJ Someone who is **holy** leads a pure and good life which is dedicated to God or to a particular religion.

homage /ˈhɒmɪdʒ/. N-U **Homage** is respect shown towards someone or something you admire, or to someone who is in authority. ...*films that pay homage to our literary heritage.*

home /həʊm/ **homes, homing, homed.** [1] N-C & ADV Someone's **home** is the house or flat where they live. *They stayed at home and watched TV... She wanted to go home... Hi, Mom, I'm home!* [2] N-C Your **home** is the place or country where you live or feel that you belong. *Ms Highsmith has made Switzerland her home.* [3] N-C A **home** is a building where people who cannot care for themselves are looked after. ...*a home for handicapped children.* [4] N-SING The **home** of something is the place where it began or where it is most typically found. *This south-west region of France is the home of claret.* [5] ADV If you press, drive, or hammer a message or an opinion **home**, you emphasize it strongly. *It is now up to all of us to debate this issue and press home the argument.* [6] N-U & ADJ BEFORE N When a team plays at **home**, or when they play a **home** game, they play a game on their own ground, rather than on the opposing team's ground. [7] PHRASE If you feel **at home**, you feel comfortable and at ease in the place or situation that you are in.

homecoming /ˈhəʊmkʌmɪŋ/ **homecomings.** N-C Your **homecoming** is your return to your home or country after you have been away for a long time.

home-grown. [1] ADJ **Home-grown** fruit and vegetables have been grown in your garden, rather than bought in a shop. [2] ADJ If you describe something as **home-grown**, you mean that it develops in your own country or area rather than another country or area.

homeland /ˈhəʊmlænd/ **homelands.** N-C Your **homeland** is your native country.

homeless /'həʊmləs/. ADJ & N-PL You describe people who have nowhere to live as **homeless**. You can also refer to them as **the homeless**. ♦**homelessness** N-U ...*the only way to solve homelessness.*

homely /'həʊmli/. ADJ If you describe a room or house as **homely**, you like it because it makes you feel comfortable and at ease. ...*a very homely atmosphere.*

home-'made (also **homemade**). ADJ Home-made things are made in someone's home, rather than in a shop or factory. ...*a home-made bomb.*

homeopathy (BR also **homoeopathy**) /,həʊmi'ɒpəθi/. N-U **Homeopathy** is a way of treating illness in which the patient is given very small amounts of a drug which would produce symptoms of the illness if taken in large quantities. ♦**homeopathic** /,həʊmiəʊ'pæθɪk/ADJ ...*homeopathic medicine.*

homesick /'həʊmsɪk/. ADJ If you are **homesick**, you feel unhappy because you are away from home and are missing your family and friends. ♦**homesickness** N-U *There were inevitable bouts of homesickness.*

homestead /'həʊmsted/ **homesteads.** N-C A **homestead** is a farmhouse, together with the land around it.

home 'town (also **hometown**) **home towns.** N-C Someone's **home town** is the town where they live or the town that they come from.

homework /'həʊmwɜːk/. [1] N-U **Homework** is school work given to pupils to do at home. *Have you done your homework?* [2] N-U If you do your **homework**, you find out what you need to know in preparation for something. *Serious bargain hunters will do their homework before taking a tour.*

homicidal /,hɒmɪ'saɪdəl/. ADJ **Homicidal** is used to describe someone who is dangerous because they are likely to kill someone.

homicide /'hɒmɪsaɪd/ **homicides.** N-VAR **Homicide** is the deliberate and unlawful killing of a person.

homogeneous (also **homogenous**) /'hɒmə,dʒiːniəs, 'həʊ-/. ADJ **Homogeneous** is used to describe a group or thing which has members or parts that are all the same. *The unemployed are not a homogeneous group.*

homophobia /,hɒmə'fəʊbiə/. N-U **Homophobia** is a strong and unreasonable dislike of homosexual people. ♦**homophobic** ADJ ...*homophobic violence.*

homosexual /'hɒməʊ,sekʃʊəl, 'həʊ-/ **homosexuals.** ADJ & N-C Someone who is **homosexual**, or who is a **homosexual**, is sexually attracted to people of the same sex. ...*a homosexual relationship.* ♦**homosexuality** N-U ...*a place where gays could openly discuss homosexuality.*

hone /həʊn/ **hones, honing, honed.** VERB If you **hone** something, for example a skill or idea, you carefully develop it for a special purpose. *His body is honed and kept in trim with constant exercise.*
► **hone in.** PHR-VERB If you **hone in** on one particular aspect of something, you concentrate

all your attention on it. *You must hone in on what is important to your topic.*

honest /'ɒnɪst/. [1] ADJ If you describe someone as **honest**, you mean that they always tell the truth, and do not try to deceive people or break the law. *He is a very honest, decent man.* ♦**honestly** ADV *She fought honestly for a just cause and for freedom.* [2] ADJ If you are **honest** in a particular situation, you are telling the complete truth or giving your sincere opinion, even if this is not very pleasant. *What do you think of the school, in your honest opinion?* ♦**honestly** ADV *It came as a shock to hear an old friend speak so honestly about Ted.* [3] ADV You say '**honest**' before or after a statement to emphasize that you are telling the truth; INFORMAL. *I'm not sure, honest.* ♦**honestly** ADV *Honestly, I don't know anything about it.*

honestly /'ɒnɪstli/. ADV You use **honestly** to emphasize that you are annoyed or impatient; SPOKEN. *Oh, honestly, I don't know what they will think of next.*

honesty /'ɒnɪsti/. N-U **Honesty** is the quality of being honest. *I can answer you with complete honesty.*

honey /'hʌni/. N-U **Honey** is a sweet, sticky, edible substance made by bees.

honeymoon /'hʌnimuːn/ **honeymoons, honeymooning, honeymooned.** [1] N-C A **honeymoon** is a holiday taken by a couple who have just married. [2] VERB When a couple who have just married **honeymoon** somewhere, they go there on their honeymoon. *They honeymooned in Venice.* [3] N-C You can use **honeymoon** to refer to a period of time when someone has just started in a new job or role and everyone is pleased with them and does not criticize them. *The new Prime Minister will enjoy a honeymoon period.*

honor /'ɒnə/. See **honour**.

honorable /'ɒnərəbəl/. See **honourable**.

honorary /'ɒnərəri, AM -reri/. [1] ADJ BEFORE N An **honorary** title or membership is given as a mark of respect to someone who does not qualify for it in the normal way. ...*an honorary member of the Golf Club.* [2] ADJ BEFORE N An **Honorary** is used to describe an official job that is done without payment. ...*the honorary secretary of the Cheshire Beekeepers' Association.*

honour (AM **honor**) /'ɒnə/ **honours, honouring, honoured.** [1] N-U **Honour** means doing what you believe to be right and being confident that you have done what is right. *I do not believe I can any longer serve with honour as a member of your government.* [2] N-C An **honour** is a special award or job that is given to someone for something they have done. *He was showered with honours – among them an Oscar.* [3] VERB If someone is **honoured**, they are given public praise or an award for something they have done. *Two American surgeons were last week honoured with the 1990 Nobel Prize for Medicine and Physiology.* [4] PHRASE If something is arranged **in honour of** a particular event, it is arranged in order to celebrate that event. [5] N-SING If you describe something that has happened to you as **an honour**, you mean that you are pleased and proud about it. *It's an honour to finally work with her.* [6] VERB

If you say that you would **be honoured** to do something, you are saying very politely and formally that you would be pleased to do it. *It's a very flattering offer, and I'm honoured by your confidence in me.* [7] VERB If you **honour** an arrangement or promise, you keep to it. *The two sides agreed to honour a new ceasefire.* [8] N-VOC Judges are sometimes called **Your Honour** or referred to as **His Honour** or **Her Honour.**

honourable (AM **honorable**) /'ɒnrəbəl/. ADJ If you describe people or actions as **honourable**, you mean that they are worthy of being respected or admired. ♦**honourably** ADV *She had not behaved honorably in the leadership election.*

hood /hʊd/ **hoods.** [1] N-C A **hood** is a part of some coats which covers your head. [2] N-C A **hood** is a bag made of cloth, which is put over someone's head and face so that they cannot be recognized or so that they cannot see. [3] N-C In American English the **hood** of a car is the cover over the engine at the front. The British word is **bonnet.**

hooded /'hʊdɪd/. [1] ADJ A **hooded** piece of clothing has a hood. *...a hooded sweatshirt.* [2] ADJ A **hooded** person is wearing a hood or a piece of clothing pulled down over their face, so they are difficult to recognize. *...a hooded gunman.*

hoof /huːf/ **hoofs** or **hooves.** N-C The **hooves** of an animal such as a horse are the hard parts of its feet.

hook /hʊk/ **hooks, hooking, hooked.** [1] N-C A **hook** is a bent piece of metal or plastic that is used for catching or holding things, or for hanging things up. *He felt a fish pull at his hook. ...curtain hooks.* [2] VERB If you **hook** one thing onto another, you attach it there using a hook. If something **hooks** somewhere, it can be hooked there. *...one of those can openers that hooked onto the wall.* [3] N-C A **hook** is a short sharp punch that you make with your elbow bent.

PHRASES ● If someone gets **off the hook**, they manage to get out of the awkward or unpleasant situation that they are in. *Government officials accused of bribery and corruption often get off the hook.* ● If you take a phone **off the hook**, you take the receiver off the part that it normally rests on, so that the phone will not ring.

▸ **hook up.** PHR-VERB When someone **hooks up** a computer or other electronic machine, they connect it to other similar machines or to a central power supply. *...technicians who hook up computer systems and networks.*

hooked /hʊkt/. [1] ADJ **Hooked** objects are shaped like a hook. *...hooked claws.* [2] ADJ AFTER LINK-V If you are **hooked** on something, you enjoy it so much that it takes up a lot of your interest and attention. *Open this book and read a few pages and you will be hooked.* [3] ADJ AFTER LINK-V If someone is **hooked** on a drug, they are addicted to it.

hooker /'hʊkə/ **hookers.** N-C A **hooker** is a prostitute; INFORMAL.

hooligan /'huːlɪɡən/ **hooligans.** N-C If you describe young people as **hooligans**, you are critical of them because they behave in a noisy and violent way in a public place.

hooliganism /'huːlɪɡənɪzəm/. N-U **Hooliganism** is the behaviour and action of hooligans. *...football hooliganism.*

hoop /huːp/ **hoops.** N-C A **hoop** is a large ring made of wood, metal, or plastic.

hoot /huːt/ **hoots, hooting, hooted.** [1] VERB & N-C If you **hoot** the horn on a vehicle, it makes a loud noise called a **hoot.** *I never hoot my horn when I pick a girl up for a date.* [2] VERB & N-C If you **hoot**, you make a loud high-pitched noise, called a **hoot**, when you are laughing. *Bev hooted with laughter.* ♦*...derisive hoots.* [3] VERB & N-C When an owl **hoots**, it makes a sound like a long 'oo'. The sound is called a **hoot.**

hoover /'huːvə/ **hoovers, hoovering, hoovered.** [1] N-C A **hoover** is an electrical machine which sucks up dust and dirt from carpets. **Hoover** is a trademark. BRITISH. [2] VERB If you **hoover** a carpet, you clean it using a vacuum cleaner; BRITISH. ♦**hoovering** N-U *I finished off the hoovering.*

hooves /huːvz/. **Hooves** is a plural of **hoof.**

hop /hɒp/ **hops, hopping, hopped.** [1] VERB & N-C When you **hop**, you move along by jumping on one foot. A movement like this is called a **hop.** [2] VERB & N-C When birds and some small animals **hop**, they move in small jumps, called **hops**, with two feet together. *...toads hopping across the road.* [3] VERB If you **hop** somewhere, you move there quickly or suddenly; INFORMAL. *I hopped out of bed quickly.* [4] N-C A **hop** is a short quick journey, usually by plane. *...a 20-minute hop in a private helicopter.*

hope /həʊp/ **hopes, hoping, hoped.** [1] VERB If you **hope** that something is true, or if you **hope** for something, you want it to be true or to happen, and you usually believe that it is possible or likely. *I hope to get a job within the next two weeks... 'Will it happen again?'—'I hope not, but you never know.'* [2] N-VAR **Hope** is a feeling of desire and expectation that things will go well in the future. *Kevin hasn't given up hope of being fit.* [3] N-C If someone wants something to happen, and considers it likely or possible, you can refer to their **hopes** of doing that thing, or to their **hope** that it will happen. *My hope is that, in the future, I will go over there and marry her.*

PHRASES ● If you **hope for the best**, you hope that everything will happen in the way you want, although you know that it may not. *Some companies are cutting costs and hoping for the best.* ● If you do one thing **in the hope** of another thing happening, you do it because you think it might cause or help the other thing to happen, which is what you want. *He was studying in the hope of being admitted to an engineering college.*

hopeful /'həʊpfʊl/ **hopefuls.** [1] ADJ If you are **hopeful**, you are fairly confident that something that you want to happen will happen. *Surgeons were hopeful of saving the sight in Sara's left eye.* [2] ADJ If something such as a sign or event is **hopeful**, it makes you feel that what you want to happen will happen. *The* *leadership election has not been a hopeful sign for Labour's future.* **3** N-C If you refer to someone as a **hopeful**, you mean that they have a particular ambition and it is possible that they will achieve it. *...his job as football coach to young hopefuls.*

hopefully /'həʊpfʊli/. ADV **Hopefully** is often used when mentioning something that you hope are and fairly confident will happen. *Hopefully, you won't have any problems after reading this.*

hopeless /'həʊpləs/. **1** ADJ If you feel **hopeless**, you feel desperate because there seems to be no possibility of success. *Even able pupils feel hopeless about job prospects.* ◆**hopelessly** ADV *...a young woman hopelessly in love with a handsome hero.* ◆**hopelessness** N-U *She had a feeling of hopelessness about the future.* **2** ADJ Someone or something that is **hopeless** is certain to be unsuccessful. *I don't believe your situation is as hopeless as you think.* **3** ADJ You use **hopeless** to emphasize how bad an event or situation is. ◆**hopelessly** ADV *He was hopelessly in debt.*

horde /hɔːd/ **hordes.** N-C If you describe a large crowd of people as a **horde**, you mean that they are excited and, often, rather frightening or unpleasant. *...a horde of people was screaming for tickets.*

horizon /hə'raɪzən/ **horizons.** **1** N-SING The **horizon** is the distant line where the sky seems to touch the land or the sea. **2** N-C Your **horizons** are the limits of what you want to do or of what you are interested or involved in. *As your horizons expand, these new ideas can give a whole new meaning to life.* **3** PHRASE If something is **on the horizon**, it is going to happen or be done quite soon.

horizontal /hɒrɪ'zɒntəl, AM 'hɔːr-/ **horizontals.** **1** ADJ Something that is **horizontal** is flat and parallel with the ground. *The board consists of vertical and horizontal lines.* ◆**horizontally** ADV *...a horizontally striped tie.* **2** N-C The **horizontal** is a line or structure that is horizontal. *Do not raise your left arm above the horizontal.*

hormone /'hɔːməʊn/ **hormones.** N-C A **hormone** is a chemical, usually occurring naturally in your body, that stimulates certain organs of your body. ◆**hormonal** /hɔː'məʊnəl/ ADJ *...our individual hormonal balance.*

horn /hɔːn/ **horns.** **1** N-C On a vehicle such as a car, the **horn** is the device that makes a loud noise as a signal or warning. **2** N-C The **horns** of an animal such as a cow or deer are the hard pointed things that grow from its head. **3** N-U **Horn** is the hard substance that the horns of animals are made of. **4** N-C A **horn** is a brass musical instrument, consisting of a pipe that is narrow at one end and wide at the other.

horoscope /'hɒrəskəʊp, AM 'hɔːr-/ **horoscopes.** N-C Your **horoscope** is a forecast of events which some people believe will happen to you in the future, based on the position of the stars when you were born.

horrendous /hə'rendəs, AM hɔːr'r-/. ADJ Something that is **horrendous** is very bad or unpleasant. *The violence used was horrendous.*

◆**horrendously** ADV *The restaurant is horrendously expensive.*

horrible /'hɒrɪbəl, AM 'hɔːr-/. ADJ If you say that something is **horrible**, you mean that it is very unpleasant. *...a horrible small boy... Unless you respect other people's religions, horrible mistakes and conflict will occur.* ◆**horribly** /'hɒrɪbli, AM 'hɔːr-/ ADV *Everything's gone horribly wrong.*

horrid /'hɒrɪd, AM 'hɔːr-/. ADJ If you describe someone or something as **horrid**, you mean they are very unpleasant; INFORMAL. *What a horrid smell!... I love both my parents, but they're horrid to each other.*

horrific /hə'rɪfɪk, AM hɔːr'r-/. ADJ If you describe something as **horrific**, you mean that it is so bad that people are horrified and shocked by it. *I have never seen such horrific injuries.* ◆**horrifically** ADV *He had been horrifically assaulted.*

horrify /'hɒrɪfaɪ, AM 'hɔːr-/ **horrifies, horrifying, horrified.** VERB If someone is **horrified**, they feel shocked, disappointed, or disgusted. *...a crime trend that will horrify all parents.* ◆**horrifying** ADJ *These were such horrifying experiences.*

horror /'hɒrə, AM 'hɔːr-/ **horrors.** **1** N-U **Horror** is a strong feeling of alarm caused by something extremely unpleasant. *I felt numb with horror.* **2** N-SING If you have a **horror** of something, you are afraid of it or dislike it strongly. *...his horror of death.* **3** N-C You can refer to extremely unpleasant or frightening experiences as **horrors**. *...the horrors of war.* **4** ADJ A **horror** film or story is intended to be very frightening.

horse /hɔːs/ **horses.** N-C A **horse** is a large animal which people can ride.

horseback /'hɔːsbæk/. **1** N-U If you do something on **horseback**, you do it while riding a horse. **2** ADJ BEFORE N & ADV **Horseback** riding is the activity of riding a horse. *Many people in this area ride horseback.*

horseman /'hɔːsmən/ **horsemen.** N-C A **horseman** is a man who is riding a horse, or who rides horses well.

horseshoe /'hɔːsʃuː/ **horseshoes.** N-C A **horseshoe** is a piece of metal shaped like a U which is fixed to a horse's hoof.

horticulture /'hɔːtɪkʌltʃə/. N-U **Horticulture** is the study and practice of growing plants. ◆**horticultural** /ˌhɔːtɪ'kʌltʃərəl/ ADJ *...the horticultural show.*

hose /həʊz/ **hoses, hosing, hosed.** **1** N-C A **hose** is a long, flexible pipe through which water is carried in order to do things such as put out fires or water gardens. **2** VERB & PHR-VERB If you **hose** something, or if you **hose** it **down**, you wash it using a hose. *The beaches were hosed with hot water... Crewmen hosed down the decks.*

hospice /'hɒspɪs/ **hospices.** N-C A **hospice** is a hospital for people who are dying.

hospitable /hɒ'spɪtəbəl, 'hɒspɪt-/. ADJ A **hospitable** person is friendly, generous, and welcoming to guests or strangers. *He was very hospitable to me when I came to New York.*

hospital /ˈhɒspɪtəl/ **hospitals.** N-VAR A **hospital** is a place where people who are ill are looked after by doctors and nurses. *My mother went into hospital.*

hospitality /ˌhɒspɪˈtælɪti/. N-U **Hospitality** is friendly, welcoming behaviour towards guests or strangers.

hospitalize (BR also **hospitalise**) /ˈhɒspɪtəlaɪz/ **hospitalizes, hospitalizing, hospitalized.** VERB If someone is **hospitalized**, they are sent or admitted to hospital. ♦**hospitalization** N-U *Occasionally hospitalization is required.*

host /həʊst/ **hosts, hosting, hosted.** ① N-C & VERB The **host** at a party is the person who has invited the guests and who provides the food, drink, or entertainment. You can say they **host** the party. *He attended a private lunch hosted by the Prime Minister.* ② N-C & VERB A country, city, or organization that is the **host** of an event provides the facilities for that event to take place. You can say they **host** the event. *In March Luxembourg hosted a meeting of justice-ministry officials.* ③ N-C & VERB The **host** of a radio or television show is the person who introduces it and talks to the people taking part. You can say they **host** the show. ④ QUANT A **host** of things is a lot of them. *...a whole host of gadgets powered by electricity.*

hostage /ˈhɒstɪdʒ/ **hostages.** N-C & PHRASE A **hostage** is a person who is illegally held prisoner and threatened with injury or death unless certain demands are met by other people. If someone **is taken hostage** or **is held hostage**, they are captured and kept in this way.

hostel /ˈhɒstəl/ **hostels.** N-C A **hostel** is a large house where people can stay cheaply for a short time.

hostess /ˈhəʊstɪs/ **hostesses.** N-C The **hostess** at a party is the woman who has invited the guests and provides the food, drink, or entertainment.

hostile /ˈhɒstaɪl, AM -təl/. ① ADJ If someone is **hostile** to another person or to an idea or suggestion, they show their dislike for them in an aggressive way. *The Governor faced hostile crowds.* ♦**hostility** /hɒˈstɪlɪti/ N-U *...hostility to Black and ethnic groups.* ② ADJ A **hostile** environment is one in which humans and animals find it difficult to live. *...some of the most hostile climatic conditions in the world.*

hostilities /hɒˈstɪlɪtiz/. N-PL You can refer to fighting between two countries or groups who are at war as **hostilities**.

hot /hɒt/ **hotter, hottest, hots, hotting, hotted.** ① ADJ If something is **hot**, it has a high temperature. *...hot water. ...a hot meal.*

In informal English, if you want to emphasize how hot the weather is, you can say that it is **boiling**. In winter, if the temperature is above average, you can say that it is **mild**. In general, **hot** suggests a higher temperature than **warm**, and **warm** things are usually pleasant. *I would imagine that I was back home in England, sitting in the garden on a warm evening.* See also the note at **cold**.

② ADJ If you are **hot**, you feel uncomfortable because of the high temperature of your body or your surroundings. ③ ADJ You can say food is **hot** when it has a burning taste caused by spices. *...hot curries.* ④ ADJ You can use **hot** to describe an issue or event that is very important, exciting, or popular at the present time; INFORMAL. *...the hottest movie of the summer... Labour is now hot favourite to win the election.*
▶ **hot up.** PHR-VERB When something **hots up**, it becomes more active or exciting; BRITISH. *Poland's presidential campaign is hotting up.*

ˈhot air ˌballoon. See **balloon**.

ˈhot dog, hot dogs. N-C A **hot dog** is a long bread roll with a sausage in it.

hotel /ˌhəʊˈtel/ **hotels.** N-C A **hotel** is a building where people stay, paying for their rooms and meals.

hotelier /ˌhəʊˈteliə, AM ˌəʊteˈljeɪ/ **hoteliers.** N-C A **hotelier** is a person who owns or manages a hotel or several hotels.

hotline /ˈhɒtlaɪn/ **hotlines.** ① N-C A **hotline** is a telephone line that the public can use to contact an organization about a particular subject. ② N-C A **hotline** is a direct telephone line between heads of government for use in an emergency.

hotly /ˈhɒtli/. ① ADV If you say something **hotly**, you say it angrily. *'That's not true,' Robyn said hotly... The bank hotly denies any wrongdoing.* ② ADV If something is being **hotly** pursued or **hotly** contested, the people involved are very determined to catch it or to win it. *This year's final will be as hotly contested as ever.*

hound /haʊnd/ **hounds, hounding, hounded.** ① N-C A **hound** is a type of dog, often used for hunting or racing. *...a pack of hounds.* ② VERB If someone **hounds** you, they constantly disturb you or pester you. *I was constantly hounded by classmates.*

hour /aʊə/ **hours.** ① N-C An **hour** is a period of sixty minutes. *The journey took three hours... They returned half an hour later.* ② N-PL You can refer to the period of time during which something happens or operates each day as the **hours** during which it happens or operates. *...the hours of darkness... Phone us during office hours... Peter came home in the early hours of the morning.* ③ N-SING The **hour** is used in expressions like **on the hour** to refer to times when it is exactly one o'clock, two o'clock, and so on. *Trains will leave Reading at 36 minutes past the hour.* ④ See also **rush hour**.

hourly /ˈaʊəli/. ① ADJ BEFORE N & ADV An **hourly** event happens once every hour. *...hourly news bulletins... The hospital issued press releases hourly.* ② ADJ BEFORE N Your **hourly** earnings are the amount of money that you earn each hour. *...the decision to cut their hourly pay.*

house, houses /ˈhaʊzɪz/, **housing, housed.** ① N-C A **house** is a building in which people live. You can also refer to all the people who live together in a house as the **house**. *It would wake the whole house.* ② PHRASE If someone **puts** their **house in order**, they arrange their affairs and solve their problems. ③ N-C **House** is used in the names of some types of companies and establishments. *...a steak house. ...a publishing house.* **4** N-C You can refer to the two main bodies of Britain's and the United States of America's parliament as **the House** or a **House**. *Some members of the House and Senate worked all day yesterday.* **5** N-C In a theatre or cinema, the **house** is the part where the audience sits. *The show played to packed houses.* **6** VERB /haʊz/ To **house** someone means to provide a house or flat for them to live in. **7** VERB If a building **houses** something, that thing is kept or located in the building. *The gallery will house the university's art collection.*

‚house ar'rest. N-U If someone is under **house arrest**, they are officially ordered not to leave their home, because they are suspected of being involved in an illegal activity.

household /'haʊshəʊld/ **households.** **1** N-C A **household** is all the people in a family or group who live together in a house. *...women-only households.* **2** N-SING The **household** is your home and everything connected with looking after it. *My husband gave me cash to manage the household. ...household chores.* **3** ADJ BEFORE N Someone or something that is a **household** name is very well known.

householder /'haʊshəʊldə/ **householders.** N-C A **householder** is the owner or tenant of a house.

housekeeper /'haʊskiːpə/ **housekeepers.** N-C A **housekeeper** is a person employed to do the cleaning and cooking in a house.

housekeeping /'haʊskiːpɪŋ/. N-U Housekeeping is the work, organization, and financial planning involved in running a home.

housewife /'haʊswaɪf/ **housewives.** N-C A **housewife** is a married woman who does not have a paid job, but instead looks after her home and children.

housework /'haʊswɜːk/. N-U Housework is the work such as cleaning and cooking that you do in your home.

housing /'haʊzɪŋ/. N-C **Housing** is the buildings that people live in. *...affordable housing.*

'housing estate, housing estates. N-C A **housing estate** is a large number of houses or flats built close together; BRITISH.

hover /'hɒvə, AM 'hʌv-/ **hovers, hovering, hovered.** **1** VERB To **hover** means to stay in the same position in the air without moving forwards or backwards. *Butterflies hovered above the wild flowers... A police helicopter hovered overhead.* **2** VERB If someone **is hovering**, they are hesitating because they cannot decide what to do. *Judith was hovering in the doorway.*

how /haʊ/. **How** is mainly used in questions. **1** ADV & CONJ You use **how** to ask about the way in which something happens or is done. *I don't want to know how he died... How do you manage to keep the place so tidy?* **2** ADV & CONJ You use **how** when you are asking for news about someone's health or life, or whether something was successful or enjoyable. *Hi! How are you doing?... How's the job?... How was your trip down to Orlando?... She asked how he had been feeling.* **3** ADV You use **how** in expressions such as **'how about...'** or **'how would you

like...'** when you are making an offer or a suggestion. *How about a cup of coffee?* **4** ADV You use **how** to emphasize the degree to which something is true. *I didn't realize how heavy that shopping was going to be.* **5** ADV You use **how** to ask questions about the quantity or degree of something. *How long will you be staying?... How old is your son now?* **6** CONVENTION You can say **'How about you?'** when you are asking someone their opinion. *Well, I enjoyed that. How about you two?*

> You do not use **how** to ask questions about the appearance or character of someone or something. You use an expression with **what** and **like**. For example, if you ask **'How is Susan?'**, you are asking about her health. If you want to know about her appearance, you ask **'What does Susan look like?'** If you want to know about her personality, you ask **'What is Susan like?'**

---

however /haʊ'evə/. **1** ADV You use **however** when you are adding a comment which contrasts with what has just been said. *Some of the food crops failed. However, the cotton did quite well.* **2** CONJ & ADV You use **however** to say that it makes no difference how something is done or to what degree or extent something is done. *Wear your hair however you want... However hard she tried, nothing seemed to work.* **3** ADV & CONJ You can use **however** in questions to express surprise at something. *However did you find this place?*

howl /haʊl/ **howls, howling, howled.** **1** VERB & N-C If a wolf or a dog **howls** or lets out a **howl**, it utters a long, loud, crying sound. **2** VERB & N-C If a person **howls** or lets out a **howl**, they make a long, loud cry expressing pain, anger, or unhappiness. *Vincent let out a howl of anguish.* **3** VERB & N-C If people **are howling** with laughter, or if there are **howls** of laughter, people are laughing very loudly. **4** VERB When the wind **howls**, it blows hard, making a loud noise.

HQ /,eɪtʃ 'kjuː/ **HQs.** N-VAR **HQ** is an abbreviation for 'headquarters'.

hr, hrs. hr is a written abbreviation for 'hour'. *...1 hr 15 mins.*

hub /hʌb/ **hubs.** **1** N-C The **hub** of a wheel is the part at the centre. **2** N-C If you describe a place as a **hub** of an activity, you mean that it is a very important centre for that activity. *The area around Red Square was the hub of Moscow's business life.*

huddle /'hʌdəl/ **huddles, huddling, huddled.** **1** VERB If you **huddle** somewhere, you sit, stand, or lie there holding your arms and legs close to your body, usually because you are cold or frightened. *She huddled inside the porch.* **2** VERB If people **huddle** together or **huddle** round something, they stand, sit, or lie close to each other, usually because they all feel cold or frightened. *We huddled round a small coal fire.* **3** N-C A **huddle** of people or things is a small group standing or sitting close together. *...a huddle of stone buildings.*

hue /hju:/ **hues.** N-C A **hue** is a colour; LITERARY. *...an intricately woven cloth of many hues.*

huff /hʌf/ **huffs, huffing, huffed.** [1] VERB If you **huff**, you indicate that you are annoyed or offended about something, usually by the way that you say something. *'I don't like ultimatums,' Michelle huffed.* [2] PHRASE If someone is **in a huff**, they are behaving in a bad-tempered way because they are annoyed or offended.

hug /hʌg/ **hugs, hugging, hugged.** [1] VERB & N-C If you **hug** someone, or if you give them a **hug**, you put your arms around them and hold them tightly, as a sign of affection. *Lynn and I hugged each other... There were lots of hugs and kisses.* [2] VERB If you **hug** something, you hold it close to your body with your arms tightly round it. *She hugged her legs tight to her chest.* [3] VERB Something that **hugs** the ground or a stretch of land or water stays very close to it; WRITTEN. *The road hugs the coast for hundreds of miles.*

huge /hju:dʒ/. ADJ Something that is **huge** is extremely large in size, amount, or degree. *...a huge window... They have made huge profits.* ♦ **hugely** ADV *...a hugely successful career.*

hull /hʌl/ **hulls.** N-C The **hull** of a boat is the main part of its body.

hullo /hʌ'ləʊ/. See **hello.**

hum /hʌm/ **hums, humming, hummed.** [1] VERB & N-SING If something **hums**, or if it makes a **hum**, it makes a low continuous noise. *The air conditioner hummed. ...the hum of traffic.* [2] VERB When you **hum** a tune, you sing it with your lips closed. *She was humming to herself.*

human /'hju:mən/ **humans.** [1] ADJ BEFORE N **Human** means relating to or concerning people. *...the human body. ...human history... The crash was the result of human error.* [2] N-C You can refer to people as **humans** when you are comparing them with animals or machines. *In humans, the same process takes about three months.*

,**human 'being, human beings.** N-C A **human being** is a man, woman, or child.

humane /,hju:'meɪn/. ADJ Someone who is **humane** is kind and compassionate. *...the desire for a more humane society.* ♦ **humanely** ADV *All detainees are being humanely treated.*

humanism /'hju:mənɪzəm/. N-U **Humanism** is the belief that people can achieve happiness and fulfilment without the need for religion. ♦ **humanist, humanists.** N-C *...the country's leading humanists.*

humanitarian /hju:,mænɪ'teəriən/ **humanitarians.** N-C & ADJ If someone is a **humanitarian**, or if they hold **humanitarian** views, they try to avoid making people suffer or to help people who are suffering. *He says he acted on humanitarian grounds.*

humanity /hju:'mænɪti/ **humanities.** [1] N-U All the people in the world can be referred to as **humanity.** *He has rendered a great service to humanity.* [2] N-U A person's **humanity** is their state of being a human being, rather than an animal or an object; FORMAL. *He was under discussion and it made him feel deprived of his humanity.* [3] N-U **Humanity** is the quality of being kind, thoughtful, and sympathetic. *Her speech showed great maturity and humanity.* [4] N-PL The **humanities** are subjects such as literature, philosophy, and history which are concerned with human ideas and behaviour.

,**human 'nature.** N-U **Human nature** is the natural qualities and behaviour that most people show. *It seems to be human nature to worry.*

,**human 'race.** N-SING You can refer to all the people in the world as the **human race.**

humble /'hʌmbəl/ **humbler, humblest; humbles, humbling, humbled.** [1] ADJ A **humble** person is not proud and does not believe that they are better than other people. ♦ **humbly** ADV *'I'm a lucky man, undeservedly lucky,' he said humbly.* [2] ADJ People and things that are considered very ordinary and unimportant can be described as **humble**. *...a humble fisherman. ...the humble potato.* [3] VERB If something or someone **humbles** you, they make you realize that you are not as important or clever as you thought you were. *I felt humbled by the power of the sea.* ♦ **humbling** ADJ *...a very humbling experience.*

humid /'hju:mɪd/. ADJ You use **humid** to describe an atmosphere or climate that is very damp, and usually very hot. *Visitors can expect hot and humid conditions.*

humidity /hju:'mɪdɪti/. N-U **Humidity** is dampness in the air. *The humidity is relatively low.*

humiliate /hju:'mɪlieɪt/ **humiliates, humiliating, humiliated.** VERB To **humiliate** someone means to say or do something which makes them feel ashamed or stupid. *He enjoyed humiliating me.* ♦ **humiliated** ADJ *I have never felt so humiliated in my life.* ♦ **humiliating** ADJ *...a humiliating defeat.*

humiliation /hju:,mɪli'eɪʃən/ **humiliations.** N-VAR **Humiliation** is the embarrassment and shame you feel when someone makes you appear stupid, or when you make a mistake in public. A **humiliation** is an occasion or situation in which you feel this. *The result is a humiliation for the prime minister.*

humility /hju:'mɪlɪti/. N-U Someone who has **humility** is not proud and does not believe that they are better than other people. *He should learn a little humility.*

humor /'hju:mə/. See **humour.**

humorous /'hju:mərəs/. ADJ If someone or something is **humorous**, they are amusing and witty. *...humorous stories.* ♦ **humorously** ADV *He regarded the whole thing humorously.*

humour (AM **humor**) /'hju:mə/ **humours, humouring, humoured.** [1] N-U You can refer to the amusing things that people say as their **humour.** *She is a fan of his outrageous humour.* [2] N-U If something has **humour**, it is funny and makes you want to laugh. *He tries to find the humour in most situations.* [3] N-U If you are in good **humour**, you feel happy; WRITTEN. [4] VERB If you **humour** someone, you try to please them, so that they will not become upset. *I nodded, partly to humour him.*

hump /hʌmp/ **humps, humping, humped.** [1] N-C A **hump** is a small hill or raised piece of ground. *The path goes over a large hump.* [2] N-C A camel's **hump** is the large lump on its back. [3] VERB If you **hump** a heavy object somewhere, you carry it there with difficulty; BRITISH, INFORMAL. *Charlie humped his rucksack up the stairs.*

hunch /hʌntʃ/ **hunches, hunching, hunched.** **1** N-C If you have a **hunch** that something is true, you think that it is likely to be true; INFORMAL. *I had a hunch it was lead poisoning.* **2** VERB If you **hunch** your shoulders or **hunch** forward, you raise your shoulders, lower your head, and lean forward. *Pupils sat hunched over their books.*

hundred /ˈhʌndrəd/ **hundreds.** **1** NUM A **hundred** or one **hundred** is the number 100. **2** N-PL & PRON You can use **hundreds** to mean an extremely large number. *He received hundreds of letters... Hundreds died in the fighting.* **3** PHRASE You can use **a hundred per cent** or **one hundred per cent** to emphasize that something is definitely the case; INFORMAL. *I'm a hundred per cent certain that's what I saw.*

hundredth /ˈhʌndrədθ/ **hundredths.** **1** ORD The **hundredth** item in a series is the one that you count as number one hundred. *...the hundredth anniversary of his birth.* **2** N-C A **hundredth** is one of a hundred equal parts of something. *...one hundredth of a second.*

hung /hʌŋ/ **1** Hung is the past tense and past participle of most senses of **hang.** **2** ADJ A **hung** parliament, council, or jury consists of different groups of people who have different opinions, but no group forms a majority.

hunger /ˈhʌŋgə/ **hungers, hungering, hungered.** **1** N-U **Hunger** is the feeling of weakness or discomfort that you get when you need something to eat. *...pangs of hunger.* **2** N-U **Hunger** is a serious lack of food which causes suffering or death. *...thousands could easily die of hunger.* **3** VERB & N-SING If you **hunger** for something, or if you have a **hunger** for it, you want it very much; FORMAL. *Jules hungered for adventure.*

'hunger strike, hunger strikes. N-VAR If someone goes on **hunger strike,** they refuse to eat as a way of protesting about something. *The refugees began a hunger strike.*

hungry /ˈhʌŋgri/ **hungrier, hungriest.** **1** ADJ When you are **hungry,** you want food. ♦**hungrily** ADV *James ate hungrily.* **2** PHRASE If people **go hungry,** they suffer from hunger, either for a long period because they are poor or for a short period because they miss a meal. **3** ADJ If you are **hungry** for something, you want it very much; LITERARY. *...an ambitious club who are hungry to win things.*

hunk /hʌŋk/ **hunks.** N-C A **hunk** of something is a large piece of it. *...a hunk of cheese.*

hunt /hʌnt/ **hunts, hunting, hunted.** **1** VERB & N-C When people or animals **hunt,** or they go on a **hunt,** they chase and kill wild animals for food or as a sport. *He liked to hunt rabbits. ...a bear hunt.* ♦**hunting** N-U *...a ban on fox hunting.* **2** VERB & N-C If you **hunt** for someone or something, or if you have a **hunt** for them, you search for them. *He hunted for an apartment... More than 70 police officers are involved in the hunt for her killer.* ♦**hunting** N-U *...job hunting.*

▶ **hunt down.** PHR-VERB If you **hunt** someone or something **down,** you succeed in finding them

after searching for them. *It took her four months to hunt him down.*

hunter /ˈhʌntə/ **hunters.** **1** N-C A **hunter** is a person who hunts wild animals for food or as a sport. *...deer hunters.* **2** N-C People who are searching for things of a particular kind can be referred to as **hunters.** *...bargain hunters.*

hurdle /ˈhɜːdəl/ **hurdles.** **1** N-C A **hurdle** is a difficulty that you must overcome in order to achieve something. *...preparing a CV, the first hurdle in a job search.* **2** N-C **Hurdles** is a race in which people run and jump over a number of hurdles.

hurdler /ˈhɜːdlə/ **hurdlers.** N-C A **hurdler** is an athlete whose special event is the hurdles.

hurl /hɜːl/ **hurls, hurling, hurled.** **1** VERB If you **hurl** an object, you throw it with a lot of force. *Groups of angry youths hurled stones at police.* **2** VERB If you **hurl** abuse or insults at someone, you shout at them aggressively.

hurricane /ˈhʌrɪkən, AM ˈhɜːrɪkeɪn/ **hurricanes.** N-C A **hurricane** is a very violent storm with strong winds.

hurried /ˈhʌrid, AM ˈhɜːr-/. ADJ A **hurried** action is done quickly. *...a hurried breakfast.* ♦**hurriedly** ADV *She blushed and hurriedly left the room.*

hurry /ˈhʌri, AM ˈhɜːri/ **hurries, hurrying, hurried.** **1** VERB If you **hurry** somewhere, you go there quickly. *Claire hurried along the road... She had to hurry home and look after her son.* **2** VERB If you **hurry** to do something, you start doing it as soon as you can, or you try to get it done quickly. *Traders hurried to buy up supplies before the long weekend.* **3** VERB & PHR-VERB If you **hurry** someone or something, **hurry** them **up,** or **hurry** them **along,** you try to make something happen more quickly. *Sorry to hurry you, John... Can you advise me how I can hurry up the process?... Petter saw no reason to hurry the divorce along.* **4** PHRASE If you are **in a hurry** to do something, you need or want to do something quickly. If you do something **in a hurry,** you do it quickly. *My colleague was in a hurry to get back to work.*

▶ **hurry up.** **1** PHR-VERB If you tell someone to **hurry up,** you are telling them to do something more quickly. *Hurry up with that coffee, will you.* **2** See **hurry 3.**

hurt /hɜːt/ **hurts, hurting, hurt.** **1** VERB & ADJ If you **hurt** yourself, or if you are **hurt,** you are injured. *He fell and hurt his back... His comrades asked him if he was hurt.* **2** VERB If you **hurt** someone, you cause them to feel pain. *I didn't mean to hurt her... Ouch. That hurt.* **3** VERB If a part of your body **hurts,** you feel pain there. *His collar bone only hurt when he lifted his arm.* **4** VERB & ADJ If someone **hurts** you, or if you are **hurt,** you are upset because someone has said or done something rude or inconsiderate. *He is afraid of hurting Bessy's feelings... He gave me a slightly hurt look.* **5** VERB You can say that something **hurts** someone or something when it damages them. *They may fear hurting their husbands' careers.*

hurtle /ˈhɜːtəl/ **hurtles, hurtling, hurtled.** VERB If someone or something **hurtles** somewhere, they move there very quickly, often in a rough or violent way. *I hurtled down the stairs.*

husband /'hʌzbənd/ **husbands.** N-C A woman's **husband** is the man she is married to.

hush /hʌʃ/ **hushes, hushing, hushed.**
[1] CONVENTION You say **'Hush!'** to someone when you are asking or telling them to be quiet. [2] N-SING You say that there is a **hush** in a place when it is quiet and peaceful, or when it suddenly becomes quiet. *A hush fell over the crowd.*

▸ **hush up.** PHR-VERB If someone in authority **hushes up** something bad or wrong, they prevent other people from finding out about it. *They had to hush it up.*

hushed /hʌʃt/. ADJ **Hushed** means quiet and calm. *...a hushed and dignified atmosphere.*

hustle /'hʌsəl/ **hustles, hustling, hustled.**
[1] VERB If you **hustle** someone, you make them move quickly, usually by pulling or pushing them. *The guards hustled Harry out of the car.* [2] VERB If you **hustle**, you go somewhere or do something hurriedly. *He hustled straight up the aircraft steps.*

hut /hʌt/ **huts.** N-C A **hut** is a small, simple building, often made of wood, mud, or grass.

hybrid /'haɪbrɪd/ **hybrids.** [1] N-C A **hybrid** is an animal or plant that has been bred from two different types of animal or plant; TECHNICAL. [2] N-C You can use **hybrid** to refer to something that is a mixture of other things. *...a hybrid of solid and liquid fuel.*

hydraulic /haɪ'drɒlɪk, AM -'drɔːl-/. ADJ BEFORE N **Hydraulic** means involving a fluid that is under pressure, such as water or oil. *...hydraulic pumps.*

hydrogen /'haɪdrədʒən/. N-U **Hydrogen** is a colourless gas that is the lightest and most common element in the universe.

hygiene /'haɪdʒiːn/. N-U **Hygiene** is the practice of keeping yourself and your surroundings clean, especially in order to prevent the spread of disease. ♦**hygienic** /haɪ'dʒiːnɪk, AM ˌhaɪ'dʒiɛnɪk/ ADJ *...extremely hygienic conditions.*

hymn /hɪm/ **hymns.** N-C A **hymn** is a song sung by Christians to praise God.

hype /haɪp/. N-U If you describe the publicity for something such as a new film as **hype**, you disapprove of it because it is very intensive and exaggerated. *My products aren't based on advertising hype, they sell by word of mouth.*

hyphen /'haɪfən/ **hyphens.** N-C A **hyphen** is the punctuation sign (-) used to join words together to make a compound.

hypnosis /hɪp'nəʊsɪs/. [1] N-U **Hypnosis** is a state of unconsciousness produced when someone has been hypnotized. [2] N-U **Hypnosis** is the art or practice of hypnotizing someone.

hypnotic /hɪp'nɒtɪk/. [1] ADJ Something that is **hypnotic** makes you feel as if you have been hypnotized. *...the TV screen's hypnotic power.* [2] ADJ If someone is in a **hypnotic** state, they have been hypnotized.

hypnotize (BR also **hypnotise**) /'hɪpnətaɪz/ **hypnotizes, hypnotizing, hypnotized.**
[1] VERB If someone **hypnotizes** you, they put you into a state of unconsciousness in which you seem to be asleep but can respond to certain things you see or hear. ♦**hypnotism** /'hɪpnətɪzəm/ N-U *...the use of acupuncture and hypnotism.* ♦**hypnotist, hypnotists.** N-C *...regular visits to a hypnotist.* [2] VERB If you **are hypnotized** by someone or something, you are so fascinated by them that you cannot think of anything else. *He's hypnotized by that black hair and that white face.*

hypocrisy /hɪ'pɒkrɪsi/ **hypocrisies.** N-VAR If you accuse someone of **hypocrisy**, you disapprove of them because they act in a way which goes against the beliefs or qualities they say they have. *He accused newspapers of hypocrisy in their treatment of the story.*

hypocrite /'hɪpəkrɪt/ **hypocrites.** N-C If you accuse someone of being a **hypocrite**, you disapprove of them because they act in a way which goes against the beliefs or qualities they say they have.

hypocritical /ˌhɪpə'krɪtɪkəl/. ADJ If you accuse someone of being **hypocritical**, you disapprove of them because they act in a way which goes against the beliefs or qualities they say they have. *If someone is being hypocritical then it is fair to expose that.*

hypothesis /haɪ'pɒθɪsɪs/ **hypotheses.** N-C A **hypothesis** is an explanation or theory which has not yet been proved to be correct; FORMAL.

hypothetical /ˌhaɪpə'θetɪkəl/. ADJ If something is **hypothetical**, it is based on possible situations, not actual ones. *...a purely hypothetical question.* ♦**hypothetically** /ˌhaɪpə'θetɪkli/ ADV *We're talking hypothetically.*

hysterectomy /ˌhɪstə'rektəmi/ **hysterectomies.** N-C A **hysterectomy** is a surgical operation to remove a woman's womb.

hysteria /hɪ'stɪəriə, AM -'ster-/. [1] N-U **Hysteria** among a group of people is a state of uncontrolled excitement or panic. *No one could help getting carried away by the hysteria.* [2] N-U A person who is suffering from **hysteria** is mentally disturbed, often as a result of shock; TECHNICAL.

hysterical /hɪ'sterɪkəl/. [1] ADJ Someone who is **hysterical** is in a state of uncontrolled excitement or panic. *Calm down. Don't get hysterical.* ♦**hysterically** ADV *Everyone was laughing hysterically.* [2] ADJ If you describe someone or something as **hysterical**, you mean that you think they are very funny; INFORMAL. ♦**hysterically** ADV *It wasn't supposed to be a comedy but I found it hysterically funny.* [3] ADJ A **hysterical** illness is caused by mental disturbance that is often the result of shock; TECHNICAL. *Her hysterical symptoms included paralysis.*

hysterics /hɪ'sterɪks/. [1] N-PL If someone is in **hysterics** or is having **hysterics**, they are in a state of uncontrolled excitement or panic. [2] N-PL You can say that someone is in **hysterics** or is having **hysterics** when they are laughing uncontrollably; INFORMAL. *She collapsed in hysterics when I told her about the horse.*

I i

I /aɪ/. PRON **I** is used as the subject of a verb. A speaker or writer uses **I** to refer to himself or herself. *She liked me, I think... Jim and I are getting married.*

ice /aɪs/, **ices, icing, iced**. [1] N-U **Ice** is frozen water. *Hans ground his skate blade against the ice. ...a bitter lemon with ice.* [2] VERB To **ice** cakes means to cover them with icing. *We were all given little iced cakes.* [3] N-C An **ice** is an ice cream.

PHRASES ● If you **break the ice** at a party or meeting, or in a new situation, you do something to make people feel relaxed. *Break the ice with tea or coffee and get to know your client a little better.* ● If you say that something **cuts no ice** with you, you mean that you are not impressed or influenced by it. *That sort of romantic attitude cuts no ice with money-men.* ● If someone puts a plan or project **on ice**, they delay doing it. ● See also **iced, icing**.

iceberg /'aɪsbɜːg/ **icebergs**. N-C An **iceberg** is a large, tall mass of ice floating in the sea. ● **tip of the iceberg**: see **tip**.

ice 'cream, ice creams. [1] N-U **Ice cream** is a very cold sweet food made from frozen milk, fats, and sugar. [2] N-C An **ice cream** is a portion of ice cream.

iced /aɪst/. ADJ BEFORE N An **iced** drink has been made very cold, often by putting ice in it. *...iced tea.* ● See also **ice**.

ice hockey. N-U **Ice hockey** is a game like hockey played on ice.

'ice-skate, ice-skates. N-C **Ice-skates** are boots with a thin metal bar underneath that people wear to move quickly on ice.

'ice-skating. N-U **Ice-skating** is a sport or leisure activity which involves people moving about on ice wearing ice-skates.

icicle /'aɪsɪkəl/ **icicles**. N-C An **icicle** is a long pointed piece of ice hanging from a surface.

icing /'aɪsɪŋ/. N-U **Icing** is a sweet substance made from powdered sugar that is used to cover and decorate cakes.

icon (or **ikon**) /'aɪkɒn/ **icons**. [1] N-C If you describe something or someone as an **icon**, you mean that they are important as a symbol of something. *...Britain's favourite fashion icon, the Princess of Wales. ...Picasso and the other icons of modernism.* [2] N-C An **icon** is a picture of Christ or a saint painted on a wooden panel. Icons are regarded as holy by some Christians. [3] N-C An **icon** is a picture on a computer screen representing a particular computer function. If you want to use it, you move the cursor onto the icon using a mouse.

icy /'aɪsi/ **icier, iciest**. [1] ADJ **Icy** air or water is extremely cold. *...an icy wind... His shoes and clothing were wet through and icy cold.* [2] ADJ An **icy** road has ice on it.

ID /ˌaɪ 'diː/ **IDs**. N-VAR If you have **ID**, you are carrying a document such as an identity card or driving licence which proves that you are a particular person. *I had no ID on me so the po-*

lice couldn't establish I was the owner of the car.

I'd /aɪd/. **I'd** is the usual spoken form of 'I had', especially when 'had' is an auxiliary verb. **I'd** is also a spoken form of 'I would'. *I'd seen her before... There are some questions I'd like to ask.*

idea /aɪ'diːə/ **ideas**. [1] N-C An **idea** is a plan or possible course of action. *It's a good idea to avoid refined food... I really like the idea of helping people... She told me she'd had a brilliant idea.* [2] N-C Your **idea** of something is your belief about what it is like or what it should be like. *My idea of physical perfection is to be very slender... Everyone has their own ideas about how to bring up children. ...a theory which supports the idea that there are many other solar systems.* [3] N-SING If you have an **idea** of something, you have some general understanding or knowledge of it, although you may not know many details about it. *Could you give us an idea of the range of complaints you've been receiving?... I had an idea that he joined the army later, after university... We haven't the faintest idea where he is.* [4] N-SING The **idea** of an action or activity is its aim or purpose. *The idea is to give children the freedom to explore.* [5] PHRASE If someone **gets the idea**, they understand how to do something or understand what you are telling them. *It isn't too difficult once you get the idea.*

ideal /aɪ'diːəl/ **ideals**. [1] N-C An **ideal** is a principle, idea, or standard that you believe is right and worth trying to achieve. *...pursuing his ideals of democracy, justice and human rights.* [2] N-SING Your **ideal** of something is the person or thing that seems to you to be the best possible example of it. *Throughout his career she remained his feminine ideal.* [3] ADJ The **ideal** person or thing for a particular purpose is the best one for it. *I was the ideal person to take over the job... The conditions were ideal for racing.* ◆**ideally** ADV *The hotel is ideally situated for country walks.* [4] ADJ BEFORE N An **ideal** society or world is the best possible one that you can imagine. ● See also **ideally**.

idealise /aɪ'diːəlaɪz/. See **idealize**.

idealism /aɪ'diːəlɪzəm/. N-U **Idealism** is the behaviour and beliefs of someone who has ideals and tries to follow them, even though this may be impractical or naive. ◆**idealist, idealists** N-C *He is not such an idealist that he cannot see the problems.*

idealistic /ˌaɪdiə'lɪstɪk/. ADJ **Idealistic** people base their behaviour on ideals, even though this may be impractical or naive.

idealize (BR also **idealise**) /aɪ'diːəlaɪz/ **idealizes, idealizing, idealized**. VERB If you **idealize** someone or something, you think of them as perfect or much better than they really are. *People idealize the past.*

ideally /aɪ'diːəli/. ADV If you say that **ideally** something should happen, you mean that you would like it to happen, although it may not be possible. *Ideally, she would love to become pregnant again.* ● See also **ideal**.

identical /aɪˈdentɪkəl/. ADJ Things that are **identical** are exactly the same. *Nearly all the houses were identical.* ◆**identically** ADV *...nine identically dressed female dancers.*

identifiable /aɪˌdentɪˈfaɪəbəl/. ADJ Something or someone that is **identifiable** can be recognized. *It is instantly identifiable as a Catholic church.*

identification /aɪˌdentɪfɪˈkeɪʃən/. N-U When someone asks you for **identification**, they are asking to see something such as a driving licence which proves who you are.

identify /aɪˈdentɪfaɪ/ **identifies, identifying, identified.** [1] VERB If you can **identify** someone or something, you can recognize them and say who or what they are. *Police have already identified around 10 murder suspects... Having identified the problem, the question arises of how to overcome it.* ◆**identification** /aɪˌdentɪfɪˈkeɪʃən/ **identifications** N-VAR *He's made a formal identification of the body.* [2] VERB If something **identifies** you, it makes it possible for people to recognize you. *She wore a little nurse's hat on her head to identify her.* [3] VERB If you **identify with** someone or something, you feel that you understand them. *She would only play a role if she could identify with the character.* ◆**identification** N-VAR *Marilyn had an intense identification with animals.* [4] VERB If you **identify** one thing **with** another, you consider them to be closely associated. *Candidates want to identify themselves with reform.* ◆**identification** N-VAR *...the identification of Spain with Catholicism.*

identity /aɪˈdentɪti/ **identities.** [1] N-C Your **identity** is who you are. *The police soon established his true identity.* [2] N-VAR The **identity** of a person or place is the characteristics that they have that distinguish them from others. *Palestinians see Jerusalem as a symbol of national identity.*

i'dentity card, identity cards. N-C An **identity card** is a card with a person's name, photograph, date of birth, and other information about them on it.

ideology /ˌaɪdiˈɒlədʒi/ **ideologies.** N-VAR An **ideology** is a set of beliefs, especially the political beliefs on which people, parties, or countries base their actions. *...capitalist ideology.* ◆**ideological** /ˌaɪdiəˈlɒdʒɪkəl/ ADJ *...the ideological divisions between the parties.* ◆**ideologically** ADV *The army was ideologically opposed to the kind of economic solution proposed.*

idiom /ˈɪdiəm/ **idioms.** [1] N-C A particular **idiom** is a particular style of something such as music or architecture; FORMAL. *McCartney was also keen to write in a classical idiom, rather than a pop one.* [2] N-C An **idiom** is a group of words which have a different meaning when used together from the one they would have if you took the meaning of each word individually. For example, 'to give someone the cold shoulder' is an idiom meaning to ignore someone.

idiot /ˈɪdiət/ **idiots.** N-C If you call someone an **idiot**, you mean that they are very stupid. *I knew I'd been an idiot to stay there.*

idle /ˈaɪdəl/ **idles, idling, idled.** [1] ADJ If you describe someone as **idle**, you disapprove of them not doing anything when they should be doing something. *...idle bureaucrats who spent the day reading newspapers.* ◆**idly** ADV *We were not idly sitting around.* [2] ADJ AFTER LINK-V Workers who are **idle** have no jobs or work. Machines or factories that are **idle** are not being used. *The machine is lying idle.* [3] ADJ BEFORE N **Idle** is used to describe something that is done for no particular reason, or does not achieve anything useful. *...idle chatter.* ◆**idly** ADV *We talked idly about magazines.*

idol /ˈaɪdəl/ **idols.** N-C An **idol** is someone such as a film star or pop star, who is greatly admired or loved by their fans. *...a teen idol.*

idolize (or **idolise**) /ˈaɪdəlaɪz/ **idolizes, idolizing, idolized.** VERB If you **idolize** someone, you admire them very much. *Naomi idolised her father.*

idyllic /ɪˈdɪlɪk, AM aɪd-/. ADJ Something that is **idyllic** is extremely pleasant and peaceful without any difficulties. *...an idyllic setting for a summer romance... Married life was not as idyllic as he had imagined.*

i.e. /ˌaɪ ˈiː/. **i.e.** is used to introduce a word or sentence expressing what you have just said in a different and clearer way. *The Uzbeks speak a Turkic language (i.e. one related to Turkish).*

if /ɪf/. [1] CONJ You use **if** in conditional sentences to introduce the circumstances in which an event or situation might happen or might have happened. *She gets very upset if I exclude her from anything... Are you a student with a knack for coming up with great ideas? If so, we would love to hear from you.* [2] CONJ You use **if** in indirect questions when the answer is either 'yes' or 'no'. *I wonder if you'd be kind enough to give us some information, please?.* [3] CONJ You use **if** to suggest that something might be slightly different from what you are stating in the main part of the sentence, for example that there might be slightly more or less of a particular quality. *That standard is quite difficult, if not impossible, to achieve... What one quality, if any, do you like the most about your partner?*

PHRASES ● You use **'if anything'** when you are saying something which confirms a negative statement that you have just made. *There has yet to be an improvement. If anything, the situation has deteriorated.* ● You use **as if** to describe something or someone by comparing them with another thing or person. *He points two fingers at his head, as if he were holding a gun.* ● You use **if only** when you are mentioning a reason for doing something. *She always writes me once a month, if only to scold me because I haven't answered her last letter yet.* ● You use **if only** to express a wish or desire, especially one that cannot be fulfilled. *If only you had told me that some time ago... If only it were that simple!*

ignite /ɪgˈnaɪt/ **ignites, igniting, ignited.** VERB When you **ignite** something, or when it **ignites**, it starts burning. *The bombs ignited a fire which destroyed some 60 houses.*

I

ignition 306

ignition /ɪgˈnɪʃən/. N-SING In a car, the **ignition** is the mechanism which ignites the fuel and starts the engine, usually operated by turning a key. *Uncle Jim put the key in the ignition.*

ignorant /ˈɪgnərənt/. **1** ADJ If you refer to someone as **ignorant**, you mean that they are not very knowledgeable or well educated. If someone is **ignorant** of a fact, they do not know it. *People don't like to ask questions for fear of appearing ignorant... Many people are worryingly ignorant of the facts about global warming.* ♦**ignorance** N-U *I am embarrassed by my complete ignorance of non-European history.* **2** ADJ People are sometimes described as **ignorant** when they behave in a rude or inconsiderate way. Some people think this use is not correct.

ignore /ɪgˈnɔː/. **ignores, ignoring, ignored.** VERB If you **ignore** someone or something, you deliberately take no notice of them. *Her husband ignored her... She ignored legal advice to drop the case.*

ikon /ˈaɪkɒn/. See **icon**.

ill /ɪl/ **ills. 1** ADJ & N-PL Someone who is **ill** is suffering from a disease or health problem. People who are ill in some way can be referred to as, for example, the mentally **ill**. *I was feeling ill.*

The words **ill** and **sick** are very similar in meaning but are used in slightly different ways. **Ill** is never used before a noun, and can be used in verbal expressions such as **fall ill** and **be taken ill**. *He fell ill shortly before Christmas... The trial was delayed after one of the jury members was taken ill.* **Sick** is often used before a noun. *...sick children.*
In British English, **ill** is a slightly more polite, less direct word than **sick**. **Sick** often suggests the actual physical feeling of being ill, for example nausea or vomiting. *I spent the next 24 hours in bed, groaning and being sick.*
In American English, **sick** is often used where British people would say **ill**. *Some people get hurt in accidents or get sick.*

---

2 N-PL Difficulties or problems can be referred to as **ills**; FORMAL. *His critics maintain that he's responsible for many of Algeria's ills.* **3** ADJ BEFORE N **Ill** can be used in front of some nouns to mean 'bad'; FORMAL. *She had brought ill luck into their family.* **4** N-U **Ill** is evil or harm; LITERARY. *They say they mean you no ill.* **5** **ill at ease**: see **ease**.

I'll /aɪl/. **I'll** is the usual spoken form of 'I will' or 'I shall'. *I'll drive you back to your hotel later, if you like.*

illegal /ɪˈliːgəl/. ADJ If something is **illegal**, the law says that it is not allowed. *It is illegal to intercept radio messages. ...illegal drugs.* ♦**illegally** ADV *The previous government had acted illegally... Illegally parked cars will be towed away.*

illegitimate /ˌɪlɪˈdʒɪtɪmət/. **1** ADJ A person who is **illegitimate** was born of parents who were not legally married to each other. **2** ADJ Something that is **illegitimate** is not right, according to the law or to accepted standards. *The election would have been dismissed as illegitimate by the international community.*

ill-'fated. ADJ If you describe something as **ill-fated**, you mean that it ended or will end in an unsuccessful or unfortunate way. *...Scott's ill-fated expedition to the South Pole.*

ill 'health. N-U Someone who suffers from **ill health** has an illness or is often ill.

illicit /ɪˈlɪsɪt/. ADJ An **illicit** activity or substance is not allowed according to the law or to social customs. *...the use of illicit drugs.*

illiterate /ɪˈlɪtərət/. ADJ Someone who is **illiterate** cannot read or write.

illness /ˈɪlnəs/ **illnesses. 1** N-U **Illness** is the fact or experience of being ill. *Mental illness is still a taboo subject... He has not taken a day off work due to illness in 25 years.* **2** N-C An **illness** is a particular disease such as a cold, measles, or pneumonia.

illogical /ɪˈlɒdʒɪkəl/. ADJ An **illogical** feeling or action is not rational and does not result from ordered thinking. *It is illogical to have two houses of parliament with the same powers. ...his completely illogical arguments.*

illuminate /ɪˈluːmɪneɪt/ **illuminates, illuminating, illuminated. 1** VERB To **illuminate** something means to shine light on it and make it brighter; WRITTEN. *The sandstone walls were illuminated by moonlight.* ♦**illumination** N-U *...the days before illumination by electricity.* **2** VERB If you **illuminate** something that is difficult to understand, you make it clearer by explaining it or giving examples; FORMAL. *The instructors use games and drawings to illuminate their subject.* ♦**illuminating** ADJ *This is a most illuminating book.* ♦**illumination** N-U *...a growing sense of illumination.*

illusion /ɪˈluːʒən/ **illusions. 1** N-VAR An **illusion** is a false idea or belief. *No one really has any illusions about winning the war.* **2** N-C An **illusion** is something that appears to exist or to be a particular thing but in reality does not exist or is something else. *Her upswept hair gave the illusion of above average height.*

illustrate /ˈɪləstreɪt/ **illustrates, illustrating, illustrated. 1** VERB If something **illustrates** a situation, it shows that the situation exists. *The incident illustrates how tricky it is to design a safe system... The case also illustrates that some women are now trying to fight back.* ♦**illustration, illustrations.** N-VAR *An illustration of China's dynamism is that a new company is formed in Shanghai every 11 seconds.* **2** VERB If you use an example, story, or diagram to **illustrate** a point, you use it to show that what you are saying is true or to make your meaning clearer. *Throughout, she illustrates her analysis with excerpts from discussions.* ♦**illustration** N-VAR *Here, by way of illustration, are some extracts from our new catalogue.* **3** VERB To **illustrate** a book means to put pictures or diagrams into it. ♦**illustration** N-VAR *The text is embellished with medical illustrations.*

illustrious /ɪˈlʌstriəs/. ADJ An **illustrious** person is famous and distinguished.

I'm /aɪm/. **I'm** is the usual spoken form of 'I am'. *I'm having a bath and going to bed.*

image /'ɪmɪdʒ/ **images.** [1] N-C If you have an **image** of someone or something, you have a picture or idea of them in your mind. *The words 'Cote d'Azur' conjure up images of sunny days in Mediterranean cafes.* [2] N-C The **image** of a person or organization is the way that they appear to other people. *He has cultivated the image of an elder statesman... The tobacco industry has been trying to improve its image.* [3] N-C An **image** is a picture or reflection of someone or something. *...glamorous images of women on record sleeves.* [4] N-C An **image** is a description or symbolic representation of something in a poem or other work of art. *...the image of 'star-laden seas' in the first stanza.*

imagery /'ɪmɪdʒri/. N-U You can talk about, for example, a poem's or film's **imagery** when you are referring to the symbols or descriptions in it which create a strong picture in your mind. *...the nature imagery of the ballad.*

imaginable /ɪ'mædʒɪnəbəl/. ADJ You use **imaginable** in expressions like 'the worst thing imaginable' or 'every imaginable thing' to emphasize that it is the most extreme example of something, or all the possible examples of something. *...their imprisonment under some of the most horrible circumstances imaginable... He had had the worst imaginable day.*

imaginary /ɪ'mædʒɪnəri, AM -neri/. ADJ An **imaginary** person, place, or thing exists only in your mind or in a story, and not in real life. *Lots of children have imaginary friends.*

imagination /ɪˌmædʒɪ'neɪʃən/ **imaginations.** N-VAR Your **imagination** is your ability to form pictures or ideas in your mind of new, exciting, or imaginary things. *Antonia is a woman with a vivid imagination... Long before I ever went there, Africa was alive in my imagination... The Government approach displays a lack of imagination.*

imaginative /ɪ'mædʒɪnətɪv/. ADJ Someone who is **imaginative** or has **imaginative** ideas is easily able to think of or create new or exciting things. *...hundreds of cooking ideas and imaginative recipes.* ◆**imaginatively** ADV The hotel is decorated imaginatively and attractively.

imagine /ɪ'mædʒɪn/ **imagines, imagining, imagined.** [1] VERB If you **imagine** a situation, your mind forms a picture or idea of it. *He could not imagine a more peaceful scene... Can you imagine how she must have felt?... Imagine you're lying on a beach.* [2] VERB If you **imagine** that something is true, you think that it is true. *We tend to imagine that the Victorians were very prim and proper... 'Was he meeting someone?'—'I imagine so.'* [3] VERB If you **imagine** something, you think that you have seen, heard, or experienced something, although actually you have not. *I realised that I must have imagined the whole thing.*

imbalance /ɪm'bæləns/ **imbalances.** N-VAR If there is an **imbalance** in a situation, the things involved are not the same size, or are not the right size in proportion to each other. *...the imbalance between the two sides in this war.*

imbue /ɪm'bjuː/ **imbues, imbuing, imbued.** VERB If you **imbue** something **with** a quality, you fill it with the quality; FORMAL. *His presence imbued her with a feeling of security.*

imitate /'ɪmɪteɪt/ **imitates, imitating, imitated.** [1] VERB If you **imitate** someone, you copy what they do or produce. *...a genuine German musical which does not try to imitate the American model.* ◆**imitator, imitators** N-C *...that slickness which sets Bruce Willis's movies apart from their imitators.* [2] VERB If you **imitate** someone or something, you copy the way they speak or behave, often as a joke.

imitation /ˌɪmɪ'teɪʃən/ **imitations.** [1] N-C An **imitation** of something is a copy of it. *...the most accurate imitation of Chinese architecture in Europe.* [2] N-U **Imitation** means copying someone else's actions. *Molly learned her golf by imitation.* [3] ADJ BEFORE N **Imitation** things are not genuine but are made to look as if they are. *...imitation leather.* [4] N-C If someone does an **imitation** of another person, they copy the way they speak or behave, often as a joke.

immaculate /ɪ'mækjʊlət/. [1] ADJ If something is **immaculate**, it is extremely clean, tidy, or neat. *Her front room was kept immaculate.* ◆**immaculately** ADV As always he was immaculately dressed. [2] ADJ If something is **immaculate**, it is perfect, without any mistakes or flaws at all. *Moreno produced an immaculate performance.*

immaterial /ˌɪmə'tɪəriəl/. ADJ AFTER LINK-V If something is **immaterial**, it is not important or not relevant. *Whether we like him or not is immaterial.*

immature /ˌɪmə'tjʊə, AM -'tʊr/. [1] ADJ Something that is **immature** is not yet fully developed. *...babies with particularly immature respiratory systems.* [2] ADJ If you describe someone as **immature**, you mean that they do not behave in a sensible and adult way. *...grossly immature drivers who flout the rules of the road... She's just being childish and immature.*

immediate /ɪ'miːdiət/. [1] ADJ An **immediate** result, action, or reaction happens or is done without any delay. *These tragic incidents have had an immediate effect... My immediate reaction was just disgust.* ◆**immediately** ADV He immediately flung himself to the floor... Ingrid answered Peter's letter immediately. [2] ADJ **Immediate** needs and concerns must be dealt with quickly. *The immediate problem is not a lack of food, but transportation.* [3] ADJ BEFORE N **Immediate** means very close to something or someone else in time or space, or in a sequence. *...the immediate aftermath of the riots. ...his immediate superior, General Geichenko.* ◆**immediately** ADV She always sits immediately behind the driver. [4] ADJ BEFORE N Your **immediate** family are your parents, brothers, and sisters.

immediately /ɪ'miːdiətli/. [1] If something is **immediately** apparent, it can be seen or understood without any delay. *The reasons for this may not be immediately obvious.* [2] CONJ If one thing happens **immediately** something else happens, it happens after that event, without any delay. *Immediately he had said it,*

Leonidas cursed himself. **3** See also **immediate**.

immense /ɪ'mens/. ADJ **Immense** means extremely large or great. *With immense relief I stopped running... The job ahead is immense and will take time.*

immensely /ɪ'mensli/. ADV **Immensely** means to a very great extent or degree. *Chess is immensely popular in Russia... I enjoyed this movie immensely.*

immerse /ɪ'mɜːs/ **immerses, immersing, immersed.** **1** VERB If you **immerse** yourself **in** something that you are doing, you become completely involved in it. *I had to immerse myself in the new job.* ◆**immersed** ADJ AFTER LINK-V *He's really becoming immersed in his work.* **2** VERB If you **immerse** something **in** a liquid, you put it into the liquid so that it is completely covered.

immigrant /'ɪmɪgrənt/ **immigrants.** N-C An **immigrant** is a person who has come to live in a country from another country.

immigration /ˌɪmɪ'greɪʃən/. **1** N-U **Immigration** is the fact or process of people coming into a country in order to live and work there. *The government has decided to tighten its immigration policy.* **2** N-U **Immigration** or **immigration control** is the place at a port, airport, or international border where officials check the passports of people who wish to come into the country.

imminent /'ɪmɪnənt/. ADJ Something that is **imminent** will happen very soon. *There appeared no imminent danger.*

immoral /ɪ'mɒrəl, AM -'mɔːr-/. ADJ If you describe someone or their behaviour as **immoral**, you mean that their behaviour is morally wrong. *...those who think that birth control and abortion are immoral.*

immortal /ɪ'mɔːtəl/ **immortals.** **1** ADJ & N-C Someone or something that is **immortal** or an **immortal** is famous and likely to be remembered for a long time. *...Wuthering Heights, Emily Bronte's immortal love story... He called Moore 'one of the immortals of soccer'.* ◆**immortality** /ˌɪmɔː'tælɪti/ N-U *Some people want to achieve immortality through their works.* **2** ADJ & N-C In stories, someone who is **immortal** or an **immortal** lives for ever. ◆**immortality** N-U *The Greeks accepted belief in the immortality of the soul.*

immortalize (BR also **immortalise**) /ɪ'mɔːtəlaɪz/ **immortalizes, immortalizing, immortalized.** VERB If someone or something is **immortalized** in something such as a film or a book, they are made famous and will be remembered for a very long time because of it.

immune /ɪ'mjuːn/. **1** ADJ AFTER LINK-V If you are **immune** to a disease, you cannot be affected by it. *Most adults are immune to Rubella.* ◆**immunity** /ɪ'mjuːnɪti/ N-U *Birds in outside cages develop immunity to airborne bacteria.* **2** ADJ AFTER LINK-V If you are **immune** to something that happens or is done, you are not affected by it. *He did not become immune to the sight of death.* **3** ADJ AFTER LINK-V Someone or something that is **immune** from a particular process or situation is able to escape it. *No one is immune from scandal.* ◆**immunity** N-U *The*

police are offering immunity to witnesses who help identify the murderers.

im'mune system, immune systems. N-C Your **immune system** consists of all the cells and processes in your body which protect you from illness and infection.

immunize (BR also **immunise**) /'ɪmjʊnaɪz/ **immunizes, immunizing, immunized.** VERB If you **are immunized** against a disease, you are given with a drug which prevents you from being affected by it. *Every student is immunized against hepatitis B... He proposed a national program to immunize children.* ◆**immunization, immunizations** N-VAR *...universal immunization against childhood diseases.*

impact, impacts, impacting, impacted; noun /'ɪmpækt/, verb /ɪm'pækt/. **1** N-C & VERB If something makes an **impact** on a situation or person, or if something **impacts** on a situation or person, it has a strong effect on them. *They expect the meeting to have a marked impact on the future of the country... Such schemes mean little unless they impact on people.* **2** N-U The **impact** of one object on another is the force with which it hits it. *A running track should be capable of absorbing the impact of a runner's foot landing on it.*

impair /ɪm'peə/ **impairs, impairing, impaired.** VERB To **impair** something such as an ability or the way that something functions means to damage it, preventing it from working properly; FORMAL. *Consumption of alcohol impairs your ability to drive a car.* ◆**impaired** ADJ *...permanently impaired hearing.*

impairment /ɪm'peəmənt/ **impairments.** N-C If someone has an **impairment**, they have a medical condition which prevents their eyes, ears, or brain from working properly.

impart /ɪm'pɑːt/ **imparts, imparting, imparted.** **1** VERB If you **impart** information to someone, you tell it to them; FORMAL. **2** VERB If something **imparts** a particular quality to something, it gives it that quality; FORMAL. *His production of Harold Pinter's play fails to impart a sense of excitement or danger.*

impartial /ɪm'pɑːʃəl/. ADJ Someone who is **impartial** is able to act fairly because they are not personally involved in a situation. *...impartial advice on investments.* ◆**impartially** ADV *He has vowed to oversee the elections impartially.* ◆**impartiality** /ˌɪmpɑːʃi'ælɪti/ N-U *...a justice system lacking impartiality.*

impasse /'æmpæs, 'ɪm-/. N-SING An **impasse** is a situation in which it is impossible to make any progress. *The company says it has reached an impasse in negotiations with the union.*

impassioned /ɪm'pæʃənd/. ADJ If someone makes an **impassioned** speech or plea, they express strong personal feelings about an issue in a forceful way; WRITTEN.

impassive /ɪm'pæsɪv/. ADJ An **impassive** person does not show any emotion. ◆**impassively** ADV *Mr Miyazawa sat impassively through a barrage of insults from the opposition.*

impatient /ɪm'peɪʃənt/. **1** ADJ If you are **impatient**, you are annoyed because you have had to wait too long for something. *Some countries are growing impatient with the slow pace of re-*

form. ◆**impatiently** ADV *Frank hit the elevator button and waited impatiently for the elevator to arrive.* ◆**impatience** /ɪm'peɪʃəns/ N-U *There is considerable impatience with the slow pace of political change.* [2] ADJ AFTER LINK-V If you are **impatient** to do something or **impatient for** something to happen, you are eager to do it or eager for it to happen and do not want to wait. *He was impatient to get home.*

impeccable /ɪm'pekəbəl/. ADJ If you describe something such as someone's behaviour or appearance as **impeccable**, you are emphasizing that it is excellent and has no faults. *She had impeccable taste in clothes.* ◆**impeccably** ADV ...*the impeccably manicured garden.*

impede /ɪm'piːd/ **impedes, impeding, impeded.** VERB To **impede** someone or something means to make their movement, development, or progress difficult; FORMAL. *Fallen rock are impeding the progress of the rescue workers.*

impediment /ɪm'pedɪmənt/ **impediments.** [1] N-C An **impediment** to something prevents it from happening, or from progressing or developing easily; FORMAL. *The current level of rates was not an impediment to economic recovery.* [2] N-C A speech **impediment** is a disability such as a stammer which makes speaking difficult.

impending /ɪm'pendɪŋ/. ADJ BEFORE N An **impending** event is one that is going to happen very soon; FORMAL. ...*a feeling of impending disaster.*

impenetrable /ɪm'penɪtrəbəl/. [1] ADJ An **impenetrable** wall or barrier is impossible to get through. [2] ADJ If you describe something such as a book as **impenetrable**, you are emphasizing that it is impossible to understand.

imperative /ɪm'perətɪv/ **imperatives.** [1] ADJ & N-C You can say that it is **imperative** that something is done, or that there is an **imperative** to do it when you want to emphasize that it must be done. *The killings made it all the more imperative that the cycle of violence be ended... Many see it as a moral imperative to reduce animal experiments.* [2] N-SING In grammar, a clause that is in **the imperative** contains the base form of a verb and usually has no subject. Imperative clauses are used to tell someone to do something. Examples are 'Go away' and 'Please be careful'.

imperfect /ɪm'pɜːfɪkt/. [1] ADJ Something that is **imperfect** has faults. ...*an imperfect world.* [2] N-SING In grammar, **the imperfect** or the **imperfect** tense of a verb is used in describing continuous situations or repeated actions in the past.

imperfection /ˌɪmpə'fekʃən/ **imperfections.** N-VAR An **imperfection** is a fault or weakness.

imperial /ɪm'pɪəriəl/. [1] ADJ BEFORE N **Imperial** means belonging or relating to an empire, emperor, or empress. ...*the Imperial Palace in Tokyo.* [2] ADJ BEFORE N The **imperial** system of measurement uses miles, yards, feet, and inches to measure length, ounces and pounds to measure weight, and pints and gallons to measure volume.

imperialism /ɪm'pɪəriəlɪzəm/. N-U **Imperialism** is a system in which a rich and powerful country controls other countries. ◆**imperialist** N-C ...*an imperialist power that insists on meddling in the affairs of weaker countries.*

impersonal /ɪm'pɜːsənəl/. [1] ADJ If you describe a place, organization, or activity as **impersonal**, you think that the people there are acting in an unfriendly way towards you, making you feel unimportant or unwanted. ...*impersonal cold rooms in large, cheap, white hotels.* [2] ADJ **Impersonal** means not concerned with any particular person. *Redundancy selection will probably be carried out on a fairly impersonal basis.*

impersonate /ɪm'pɜːsəneɪt/ **impersonates, impersonating, impersonated.** VERB If you **impersonate** someone, you pretend to be that person, either to deceive people or to entertain them. *He was once jailed for impersonating a doctor.* ◆**impersonation, impersonations** N-C *He was doing an impersonation of an Elvis.*

impetus /'ɪmpɪtəs/. N-U Something that gives a process **impetus** or gives it an **impetus** makes it happen or progress more quickly. *The article gave new impetus to the debate over mercy killing.*

implacable /ɪm'plækəbəl/. ADJ If you describe someone as **implacable**, you mean that their attitude or feelings about something are firm and will not be changed by other people's opinion. ...*a ruthless and implacable enemy.* ◆**implacably** ADV *His union was implacably opposed to the privatization of the company.*

implant, implants, implanting, implanted. [1] VERB /ɪm'plɑːnt, -'plænt/ If something such as a heart **is implanted** into a person's body, it is put there by means of a medical operation. *For diabetes the capsule is implanted under the skin.* [2] N-C /'ɪmplɑːnt, -'plænt/ An **implant** is something implanted into a person's body. ...*silicone breast implants.*

implement, implements, implementing, implemented. [1] VERB /'ɪmplɪmənt/ If you **implement** a plan, system, or law, you carry it out. ◆**implementation** N-U ...*the implementation of the peace agreement.* [2] N-C /'ɪmplɪmənt/ An **implement** is a tool or other piece of equipment.

implicate /'ɪmplɪkeɪt/ **implicates, implicating, implicated.** VERB If you **implicate** someone in a crime or something bad, you show that they were involved in it. *Allegations had appeared in the press implicating the army and police in some of the killings.*

implication /ˌɪmplɪ'keɪʃən/ **implications.** N-C The **implications** of something are the things that are likely to happen as a result of it. ...*the political implications of his decision.*

implicit /ɪm'plɪsɪt/. [1] ADJ Something that is **implicit** is expressed in an indirect way. ◆**implicitly** ADV *Mr Jones's role was implicitly criticised in the report.* [2] ADJ If you have an **implicit** belief or faith in something, you believe it completely and have no doubts about it. *He had implicit faith in the noble intentions of the Emperor.* ◆**implicitly** ADV *I trust him implicitly.*

implore /ɪm'plɔː/ **implores, imploring, implored.** VERB If you **implore** someone to do something, you beg them to do it; FORMAL. *Michael, I implore you. Don't say anything.*

imply /ɪmˈplaɪ/ implies, implying, implied. VERB To **imply** that something is the case means to say or do something to make it appear that it is the case. *The tone of the report implied that his death was inevitable... The meeting in no way implies a resumption of contacts with the terrorists.*

import, imports, importing, imported. [1] VERB /ɪmˈpɔːt/ When a country or organization **imports** a product, they buy it from another country for use in their own country. *To import from Russia, a Ukrainian firm needs Russian roubles. ...the price of imported oil.* ◆**importation** N-U *...restrictions concerning the importation of birds.* ◆**importer, importers** N-C *...oil importers.* [2] N-C /ˈɪmpɔːt/ **Imports** are products or raw materials bought from another country for use in your own country.

important /ɪmˈpɔːtənt/. [1] ADJ Something that is **important** is very significant, valuable, or necessary. *Her sons are the most important thing in her life.* ◆**importantly** ADV *I was hungry, and, more importantly, my children were hungry.* ◆**importance** N-U *Safety is of paramount importance.* [2] ADJ An **important** person has influence or power. *...a very important criminal lawyer.* ◆**importance** N-U *Penn photographed just about everyone of importance in the arts.*

> You do not use **important** to say that an amount or quantity is very large. You do not talk, for example, about 'an important sum of money'. Instead, you use words such as **large**, **considerable**, or **substantial**. *...a large sum of money. ...a man with considerable influence... Britain's armed forces face substantial cuts.*

impose /ɪmˈpəʊz/ imposes, imposing, imposed. [1] VERB If you **impose** something on people, you force them to accept it. *Parents should beware of imposing their own tastes on their children.* ◆**imposition** /ˌɪmpəˈzɪʃən/ N-U *...the imposition of a day-time ban on cycling in the city centre.* [2] VERB If someone **imposes on** you, they expect you to do something for them which you do not want to do. *I was afraid you'd simply feel we were imposing on you... I didn't want to impose myself on my married friends.* ◆**imposition, impositions** N-C *I know this is an imposition. But please hear me out.*

imposing /ɪmˈpəʊzɪŋ/. ADJ If you describe someone or something as **imposing**, you think their appearance or manner is very impressive. *...the imposing gates at the entrance to the estate.*

impossible /ɪmˈpɒsɪbəl/. [1] ADJ Something that is **impossible** cannot be done or cannot happen. *The tax is impossible to administer.* ◆**impossibly** ADV *Mathematical physics is an almost impossibly difficult subject.* ◆**impossibility, impossibilities** N-VAR *...the impossibility of knowing absolute truth.* [2] ADJ You can say that a situation or person is im-

possible when they are very difficult to deal with. *The Government was now in an almost impossible position... You are an impossible man!*

impotent /ˈɪmpətənt/. [1] ADJ If someone feels **impotent**, they feel that they have no power to influence people or events. *The aggression of a bully leaves people feeling hurt, angry and impotent.* ◆**impotence** N-U *...a sense of impotence in the face of deplorable events.* [2] ADJ If a man is **impotent**, he is unable to have sex normally. ◆**impotence** N-U *...the many men who suffer from impotence.*

impound /ɪmˈpaʊnd/ impounds, impounding, impounded. VERB If policemen or other officials **impound** something that you own, they legally confiscate it; FORMAL. *The police moved in, arrested him and impounded the cocaine.*

impoverish /ɪmˈpɒvərɪʃ/ impoverishes, impoverishing, impoverished. VERB To **impoverish** someone or something means to make them poor. *We need to reduce the burden of taxes that impoverish the economy.* ◆**impoverished** ADJ *...one of the most impoverished and crime-infested suburbs of Rio de Janeiro.*

impractical /ɪmˈpræktɪkəl/. ADJ If an idea or course of action is **impractical**, it is not sensible or practical. *Narrow fields several kilometres in length are highly impractical for farmers.*

impress /ɪmˈpres/ impresses, impressing, impressed. [1] VERB If someone or something **impresses** you, you feel great admiration for them. *...a group of students who were trying to impress their girlfriends.* ◆**impressed** ADJ AFTER LINK-V *I'm very impressed with the new airport.* [2] VERB If you **impress** something on someone, you make them understand its importance. *I had always impressed upon the children that if they worked hard they would succeed.*

impression /ɪmˈpreʃən/ impressions. [1] N-C Your **impression** of someone or something is what you think they are like. Your **impression** of a situation is what you think is going on. *What were your first impressions of college?... My impression is that they are totally out of control.* [2] N-SING If someone or something gives a particular **impression**, they cause you to believe that something is the case, often when it is not actually the case. *They certainly gave the impression of a carefree couple who delighted in each other's company.* [3] N-C If you do an **impression** of someone, you imitate their voice or manner in an amusing way. [4] N-C An **impression** of an object is the mark that it has left after being pressed hard onto a surface.
PHRASES ● If you are **under the impression** that something is the case, you believe it to be the case. *His family was under the impression that he died while en route to the hospital.* ● If someone or something **makes an impression**, they have a strong effect on people or a situation. *He has told me his plans and he's made a good impression on me.*

impressive /ɪm'presɪv/. ADJ **Impressive** is used to describe people or things which impress you. *The film's special effects are particularly impressive.* ♦ ...*an impressively bright and energetic American woman.*

imprint, imprints, imprinting, imprinted; noun /'ɪmprɪnt/ verb /ɪm'prɪnt/. **1** N-C & VERB If something leaves an **imprint** on your mind, or if it **is imprinted** on your mind, you cannot forget it because it has had a strong effect on you. *The problem of unemployment left a deep imprint on his attitude towards such social issues... He could not dislodge the images imprinted on his brain.* **2** N-C An **imprint** is a mark made by the pressure of an object on a surface. **3** VERB If a surface **is imprinted** with a mark or design, that mark or design is printed on the surface or pressed into it.

imprison /ɪm'prɪzən/ **imprisons, imprisoning, imprisoned.** VERB If someone **is imprisoned**, they are locked up or kept somewhere. ♦ **imprisonment** N-U *She was sentenced to seven years' imprisonment.*

improbable /ɪm'prɒbəbəl/. **1** ADJ Something that is **improbable** is unlikely to be true or to happen. *It is improbable that the Prime Minister will be forced to resign.* ♦ **improbability, improbabilities.** N-VAR ...*the improbability of such an outcome.* **2** ADJ If you describe something as **improbable**, you mean it is strange or ridiculous. *Their marriage seems an improbable alliance.* ♦ **improbably** ADV ...*an improbably glamorous female cop.*

impromptu /ɪm'prɒmptjuː, AM -tuː/. ADJ An **impromptu** action is one that you do without planning it in advance. *The children put on an impromptu concert for the visitors.*

improper /ˌɪm'prɒpə/. **1** ADJ **Improper** activities are illegal or dishonest; FORMAL. *Mr Matthews maintained that he had done nothing improper.* ♦ **improperly** ADV *I acted neither fraudulently nor improperly.* **2** ADJ BEFORE N **Improper** conditions or methods of treatment are not suitable or adequate for a particular purpose. *The improper use of medicine could lead to severe adverse reactions.* ♦ **improperly** ADV *Doctors were improperly trained.* **3** ADJ If you describe someone's behaviour as **improper**, you mean that it is rude or shocking; DATED. *It would be improper to speculate on Dr Holt's suicide.* ♦ **improperly** ADV ...*improperly dressed.*

improve /ɪm'pruːv/ **improves, improving, improved.** **1** VERB If something **improves**, or if you **improve** it, it gets better. *The weather is beginning to improve... He improved their house.* ♦ **improvement** /ɪm'pruːvmənt/ **improvements** N-VAR *There is considerable room for improvement in state facilities for treating the mentally handicapped.* **2** VERB If you **improve on** a previous achievement, you achieve a better standard or result. ...*whether annual profits can improve on last year's £65.8 million.* ♦ **improvement** N-C *The system we introduced in 1980 has been a great improvement.*

improvise /'ɪmprəvaɪz/ **improvises, improvising, improvised.** **1** VERB If you **improvise**, you make or do something using whatever you have or without having planned it in advance. ...*tents improvised from sheets of heavy plastic... His improvised bomb must have started a fire.* **2** VERB When actors or musicians **improvise**, they make up the words or music while they are performing. *He'd had to improvise a dramatic suicide scene.*

impulse /'ɪmpʌls/ **impulses.** **1** N-C An **impulse** is a sudden desire to do something. *All day she had fought off the impulse to telephone Harry.* **2** PHRASE If you do something **on impulse**, you suddenly decide to do it, without planning it. *After lunch she decided on impulse to take a bath.* **3** N-C An **impulse** is a short electrical signal sent along a wire or nerve, or through the air.

impulsive /ɪm'pʌlsɪv/. ADJ Someone who is **impulsive** does things suddenly without thinking about them carefully first. *Avoid making an impulsive decision.* ♦ **impulsively** ADV *Impulsively she patted him on the arm.*

impure /ɪm'pjʊə/. ADJ An **impure** substance is not of good quality because it has other substances mixed with it.

impurity /ɪm'pjʊərɪti/ **impurities.** N-C **Impurities** are substances that are present in small quantities in another substance and make it dirty or of an unacceptable quality.

in 1 position or movement

in /ɪn/. **1** PREP Something that is **in** something else is enclosed by it or surrounded by it. *He was in his car... Put the knives in the kitchen drawer... Mix the sugar and the water in a cup.* **2** PREP If something happens **in** a place, it happens there. *Those rockets landed in the desert.* **3** ADV If you **are in**, you are present at your home or place of work. *My flatmate was in at the time.* **4** ADV When someone comes **in**, they enter a room or building. *They shook hands and went in.* **5** ADV If a train, boat, or plane is **in** or has come **in**, it has arrived. *Look. The train's in.* **6** ADV When the sea or tide comes **in**, the sea moves towards the shore rather than away from it. **7** PREP Something that is **in** a window, especially a shop window, is just behind the window so that you can see it from outside. *There was a camera for sale in the window.* **8** PREP When you see something **in** a mirror, you see its reflection. **9** PREP If you are dressed **in** a piece of clothing, you are wearing it. *They are still in their pyjamas. ...three women in black.*

in 2 inclusion or movement

in /ɪn/. **1** PREP If something is **in** a book, film, play, or picture, you can read it or see it there. ...*one of the funniest scenes in the film.* **2** PREP If you are **in** something such as a play or a race, you are one of the people taking part. *Alf offered her a part in the play he was directing.* **3** PREP Something that is **in** a group or collection is a member of it or part of it. *There were about 12 students in my class.* **4** PREP You use **in** to specify a general subject or field of activity. ...*future developments in medicine and surgery.*

in 3 time and numbers

in /ɪn/. **1** PREP If something happens **in** a particular year, month, or other period of time, it happens during that time. *In the evening, the people assemble in the mosques... He believes* food prices will go up in the future. [2] PREP If you do something **in** a particular period of time, that is how long it takes you to do it. *He completed the book in two years.* [3] PREP If something will happen **in** a particular length of time, it will happen after that length of time. *They'll be back in a few months.* [4] PREP You use **in** to indicate roughly how old someone is. For example, if someone is **in** their fifties, they are between 50 and 59 years old. [5] PREP You use **in** to indicate roughly how many people or things do something. *The jugs were produced in their millions.* [6] PREP You use **in** to express a ratio, proportion, or probability. *He had a one in 500 chance of survival.*

in 4 states and qualities

in /ɪn/. [1] PREP If something or someone is **in** a particular state or situation, that is their present state or situation. *Their equipment was in poor condition... Dave was in a hurry.* [2] PREP You use **in** to indicate the feeling or desire which someone has when they do something, or which causes them to do it. *Simpson looked at them in surprise... Carl pushed ahead in his eagerness to reach the wall.* [3] PREP You use **in** to indicate how someone is expressing something. *'Good evening,' Frank said in Russian... All requests must be made in writing.* [4] PREP You use **in** to describe the arrangement or shape of something. *He was curled up in a ball.* [5] PREP You use **in** to specify which feature or aspect of something you are talking about. *The movie is nearly two hours in length. ...a real increase in the standard of living.*

in 5 other uses and phrases

in /ɪn/. ADJ Something that is **in** is fashionable or popular; INFORMAL. *A few years ago jogging was the in thing.*
PHRASES • If you say that someone **is in for** a shock or a surprise, you mean they are going to experience it. • If someone **has it in for** you, they dislike you and try to cause problems for you; INFORMAL. • If you are **in on** something, you are involved in it or know about it. *I'm going to let you in on a little secret.* • You use **in that** to explain a statement you have just made. *I'm lucky in that I've got four sisters.*

in. In. is a written abbreviation for 'inch'. The plural can be 'in.' or 'ins'.

inability /ˌɪnəˈbɪlti/. N-U Someone's **inability** to do something is the fact that they are unable to do it. *...her inability to concentrate.*

inaccessible /ˌɪnækˈsesɪbəl/. [1] ADJ An **inaccessible** place is impossible or very difficult to reach. *It is far away in a wild, inaccessible part of the island.* [2] ADJ Someone or something that is **inaccessible** is difficult or impossible to understand or appreciate. *...language that is inaccessible to working people.*

inaccurate /ɪnˈækjʊrət/. ADJ If a statement or measurement is **inaccurate**, it is not accurate or correct. ◆**inaccuracy, inaccuracies** N-VAR *There are many inaccuracies in her article.*

inaction /ɪnˈækʃən/. N-U If you refer to someone's **inaction**, you disapprove of the fact that they are doing nothing. *He is bitter about the inaction of the other political parties.*

inactive /ɪnˈæktɪv/. ADJ Someone or something that is **inactive** is not doing anything or is not

working. *Most volcanoes are inactive most of the time.* ◆**inactivity** /ˌɪnækˈtɪvɪti/ N-U *After years of inactivity I started running.*

inadequate /ɪnˈædɪkwət/. [1] ADJ If something is **inadequate**, there is not enough of it or it is not good enough. *The problem lies with inadequate staffing.* ◆**inadequacy, inadequacies** N-VAR *...the inadequacy of the water supply.* ◆**inadequately** ADV *The projects were inadequately funded.* [2] ADJ If someone feels **inadequate**, they feel that they do not have the qualities necessary to do something or to cope with life. ◆**inadequacy** N-U *...her chronic sense of inadequacy.*

inadvertent /ˌɪnədˈvɜːtənt/. ADJ An **inadvertent** action is one that you do without realizing what you are doing. *She giggled at the inadvertent pun.* ◆**inadvertently** ADV *You may have inadvertently pressed the wrong button.*

inappropriate /ˌɪnəˈprəʊpriət/. ADJ Something that is **inappropriate** is not suitable for a particular situation or purpose. *His behavior was inappropriate and insensitive.*

inasmuch as (or **in as much as**) /ˌɪnəzˈmʌtʃ æz/. CONJ You use **inasmuch as** to introduce a statement which explains something you have just said, and adds to it; FORMAL. *I am extremely lucky in as much as I have a very strong and loving wife.*

inaugural /ɪnˈɔːgjʊrəl/. ADJ BEFORE N An **inaugural** meeting or speech is the first one of a new organization or leader.

inaugurate /ɪnˈɔːgjʊreɪt/ **inaugurates, inaugurating, inaugurated.** [1] VERB When a new leader **is inaugurated**, they are formally given their new position at an official ceremony. ◆**inauguration, inaugurations** N-VAR *...the inauguration of the new Governor.* [2] VERB If you **inaugurate** a new system or organization, you start it; FORMAL.

incapable /ɪnˈkeɪpəbəl/. ADJ Someone who is **incapable** of doing something is unable to do it. *He was a man incapable of violence.*

incarcerate /ɪnˈkɑːsəreɪt/ **incarcerates, incarcerating, incarcerated.** VERB If someone **is incarcerated**, they are imprisoned; FORMAL. ◆**incarceration** N-U *...her mother's incarceration in a psychiatric hospital.*

incarnation /ˌɪnkɑːˈneɪʃən/ **incarnations.** [1] N-C If you say that someone is the **incarnation of** a particular quality, you mean that they represent that quality or are typical of it in an extreme form. *She is the incarnation of courage.* [2] N-C An **incarnation** is one of the lives that a person has, according to some religions.

incendiary /ɪnˈsendiəri, AM -eri/. ADJ BEFORE N **Incendiary** attacks or weapons are ones which cause large fires. *More than 10,000 incendiary bombs were dropped.*

incense, incenses, incensing, incensed. [1] N-U /ˈɪnsens/ **Incense** is a substance that is burned for its sweet smell, often during a religious ceremony. [2] VERB /ɪnˈsens/ Something that **incenses** you makes you extremely angry. ◆**incensed** ADJ *Mum was incensed at his lack of compassion.*

incentive /ɪnˈsentɪv/ **incentives.** N-VAR An **incentive** is something that encourages you to do something. *...tax incentives for companies that create jobs.*

incessant /ɪn'sesənt/. ADJ An **incessant** process or activity never stops. *...incessant rain.* ♦**incessantly** ADV *Dee talked incessantly.*

incest /'ɪnsest/. N-U **Incest** is the crime of two members of the same family having sexual intercourse.

inch /ɪntʃ/ **inches, inching, inched.** 1 N-C An **inch** is a unit of length, equal to approximately 2.54 centimetres. 2 VERB To **inch** somewhere means to move there very slowly and carefully. To **inch** something somewhere means to move it there in this way. *...a climber inching up a vertical wall of rock... He inched the van forward.*

incidence /'ɪnsɪdəns/ **incidences.** N-VAR The **incidence** of something bad is the frequency with which it occurs, or the occasions when it occurs. *...the high incidence of child mortality.*

incident /'ɪnsɪdənt/ **incidents.** N-C An **incident** is an event, especially one involving something unpleasant; FORMAL. *Police were still investigating the incident yesterday.*

incidental /ˌɪnsɪ'dentəl/. ADJ If one thing is **incidental** to another, it is less important than the other thing or is not a major part of it. *At the bottom of the bill, you will notice various incidental expenses.*

incidentally /ˌɪnsɪ'dentli/. ADV You use **incidentally** to introduce a point which is not directly relevant to what you are saying. *The tower, incidentally, dates from the twelfth century.*

incinerate /ɪn'sɪnəreɪt/ **incinerates, incinerating, incinerated.** VERB When authorities **incinerate** rubbish or waste material, they burn it in a furnace. ♦**incineration** N-U *...an incineration plant.*

incinerator /ɪn'sɪnəreɪtə/ **incinerators.** N-C An **incinerator** is a furnace for burning rubbish.

incisive /ɪn'saɪsɪv/. ADJ **Incisive** speech or writing is clear and forceful.

incite /ɪn'saɪt/ **incites, inciting, incited.** VERB If someone **incites** people to behave in a violent or unlawful way, they encourage them to behave in that way. *The party agreed not to incite its supporters to violence. ...material likely to incite racial hatred.* ♦**incitement, incitements.** N-VAR *British law forbids incitement to murder.*

inclination /ˌɪnklɪ'neɪʃən/. N-VAR An **inclination** is a feeling that makes you want to act in a particular way. *She showed no inclination to go. ...his artistic inclinations.*

incline, inclines, inclining, inclined. 1 VERB /ɪn'klaɪn/ If you **incline** to a particular view or action, you want to take that view or perform that action, or often take or perform it; FORMAL. *I incline to the view that he is right.* ♦**inclined** ADJ AFTER LINK-V *Nobody felt inclined to argue with Smith.* 2 N-C /'ɪnklaɪn/ An **incline** is a slope; FORMAL.

inclined /ɪn'klaɪnd/. 1 ADJ AFTER LINK-V If you say that you are **inclined** to have a particular opinion, you mean that you hold this opinion but you are not expressing it strongly. *I am inclined to agree with Alan.* 2 ADJ Someone who is, for example, mathematically or artistically

inclined has a natural talent for mathematics or art.

include /ɪn'kluːd/ **includes, including, included.** VERB If something **includes** something else, it has it as one of its parts. If you **include** one thing in another, you make it part of it. *The program includes swimming, fishing and canoeing... Food is included in the price... Most people, myself included, aren't very happy about it.*

including /ɪn'kluːdɪŋ/. PREP You use **including** to introduce examples of people or things that are part of the group of people or things that you are talking about. *Twelve people, including six police officers, were taken to hospital.*

inclusion /ɪn'kluːʒən/ **inclusions.** N-VAR The **inclusion** of one thing in another is the act of making it a part of the second thing. *...his inclusion in the team.*

inclusive /ɪn'kluːsɪv/. 1 ADJ & ADV If a price is **inclusive**, it includes all the charges connected with the goods or services offered. *The price of the trip was £824 (inclusive of flights). ...a special introductory offer of £5,995 fully inclusive.* 2 ADJ You use **inclusive** to indicate that the first and last things mentioned are included in a series. *Only children aged 6 to 15 inclusive are eligible.*

incoherent /ˌɪnkəʊ'hɪərənt/. ADJ If someone is **incoherent**, they are talking in a confused and unclear way. *The man was almost incoherent with fear.*

income /'ɪnkʌm/ **incomes.** N-C The **income** of a person or organization is the money that they earn or receive. *...families on low incomes.* ● See note at **pay.**

incoming /'ɪnkʌmɪŋ/. 1 ADJ BEFORE N An **incoming** message or phone call is one that you receive. *We keep a tape of incoming calls.* 2 ADJ BEFORE N An **incoming** plane or passenger is one that is arriving at a place. *...a passenger off the incoming flight.*

incompatible /ˌɪnkəm'pætɪbəl/. ADJ If one thing or person is **incompatible** with another, they are very different from each other and therefore cannot exist or work together. *Their interests were mutually incompatible.* ♦**incompatibility** N-U *He sees no incompatibility between poetry and science.*

incompetent /ɪn'kɒmpɪtənt/. ADJ If you describe someone as **incompetent**, you are criticizing them because they cannot do their job or a task properly. *...lazy and incompetent colleagues.* ♦**incompetence** N-U *Our manager was sacked for incompetence.*

incomplete /ˌɪnkəm'pliːt/. ADJ Something that is **incomplete** is not yet finished, or does not have all the parts or details that it needs. *The clearing of rubbish and drains is still incomplete.*

incomprehensible /ˌɪnkɒmprɪ'hensɪbəl/. ADJ Something that is **incomprehensible** is impossible to understand.

inconceivable /ˌɪnkən'siːvəbəl/. ADJ If something is **inconceivable**, it is very unlikely to happen or be true. *It was inconceivable that he was a criminal.*

inconclusive /ˌɪnkənˈkluːsɪv/. ADJ If something is **inconclusive**, it does not provide any clear answer or result. *Our research has so far proved inconclusive.*

incongruous /ɪnˈkɒŋɡruːəs/. ADJ Something that is **incongruous** seems strange because it does not fit in with the rest of a situation; FORMAL. *She was small and fragile and looked incongruous in an army uniform.* ♦**incongruously** ADV *...Western-style buildings perched incongruously in a high green valley.*

inconsiderate /ˌɪnkənˈsɪdərət/. ADJ If you describe someone as **inconsiderate**, you are criticizing them for not taking enough care over how their behaviour affects other people.

inconsistent /ˌɪnkənˈsɪstənt/. [1] ADJ If you describe someone as **inconsistent**, you are criticizing them for not behaving in the same way every time a similar situation occurs. *...the leadership's hesitant and inconsistent behaviour.* ♦**inconsistency, inconsistencies.** N-VAR *His worst fault was his inconsistency.* [2] ADJ AFTER LINK-V Something that is **inconsistent** with a particular set of ideas or values is not in accordance with them. *His theory is inconsistent with modern observations.*

incontinent /ɪnˈkɒntɪnənt/. ADJ Someone who is **incontinent** is unable to control their bladder or bowels. ♦**incontinence** N-U *Incontinence is not just a condition of old age.*

inconvenience /ˌɪnkənˈviːnɪəns/ **inconveniences, inconveniencing, inconvenienced.** [1] N-VAR If someone or something causes **inconvenience**, they cause problems or difficulties. *We apologize for any inconvenience caused during the repairs.* [2] VERB If someone **inconveniences** you, they cause problems or difficulties for you. *He promised to be very quick so as not to inconvenience them any further.*

inconvenient /ˌɪnkənˈviːnɪənt/. ADJ Something that is **inconvenient** causes problems or difficulties for someone. *She arrived at an extremely inconvenient moment.*

incorporate /ɪnˈkɔːpəreɪt/ **incorporates, incorporating, incorporated.** VERB If something such as a group or device **incorporates** a particular thing, the group or device has that thing in it as one of its parts; FORMAL. *The new cars will incorporate a number of major improvements.*

incorrect /ˌɪnkəˈrekt/. ADJ Something that is **incorrect** is wrong or untrue. *The findings were based on incorrect data.* ♦**incorrectly** ADV *The doors had been fitted incorrectly.*

increase, increases, increasing, increased; verb /ɪnˈkriːs/, noun /ˈɪnkriːs/. [1] VERB & N-C If something **increases**, or if there is an **increase** in it, it becomes larger in number, level, or amount. *Japan's industrial output increased by 2%... We are experiencing an increasing number of problems. ...a sharp increase in productivity.* [2] PHRASE If something is **on the increase**, it is becoming more frequent. *Divorce rates and births outside marriage are on the increase.*

increasingly /ɪnˈkriːsɪŋli/. ADV You use **increasingly** to indicate that a situation or quality is becoming greater in intensity or more common. *He was finding it increasingly difficult to make decisions... Increasingly, their goals have become more radical.*

incredible /ɪnˈkredɪbəl/. [1] ADJ If you describe someone or something as **incredible**, you like them very much or are impressed by them, because they are extremely or unusually good. *The wildflowers will be incredible after this rain.* [2] ADJ Something that is **incredible** is amazing or very difficult to believe. *...the incredible stories that children may tell us.* ♦**incredibly** ADV *Incredibly, some people don't like the name.* [3] ADJ You use **incredible** to emphasize the amount or intensity of something. *We import an incredible amount of cheese from the Continent.* ♦**incredibly** ADV *It was incredibly hard work.*

incredulous /ɪnˈkredʒʊləs/. ADJ If someone is **incredulous**, they cannot believe something because it is very surprising or shocking. *There was a brief, incredulous silence.* ♦**incredulously** ADV *'You told Pete?' Rachel said incredulously.*

incriminate /ɪnˈkrɪmɪneɪt/ **incriminates, incriminating, incriminated.** VERB If something **incriminates** you, it suggests that you are the person responsible for something bad, especially a crime. *They are afraid of incriminating themselves and say no more than is necessary.* ♦**incriminating** ADJ *...incriminating evidence.*

incumbent /ɪnˈkʌmbənt/ **incumbents.** N-C An **incumbent** is the person who is holding an official post at a particular time; FORMAL. *...measures to secure the re-election of incumbent congressmen next month.*

incur /ɪnˈkɜː/ **incurs, incurring, incurred.** VERB If you **incur** something unpleasant, it happens to you because of something you have done; FORMAL. *The government had also incurred huge debts.*

incurable /ɪnˈkjʊərəbəl/. [1] ADJ An **incurable** disease cannot be cured. ♦**incurably** ADV *...youngsters who are disabled, or incurably ill.* [2] ADJ You can use **incurable** to indicate that someone has a particular quality or attitude and will not change. *Poor old William is an incurable romantic.* ♦**incurably** ADV *I know you think I'm incurably nosey.*

indebted /ɪnˈdetɪd/. ADJ AFTER LINK-V If you say that you are **indebted** to someone, you mean that you are very grateful to them for something. *I am deeply indebted to him for his help.*

indecent /ɪnˈdiːsənt/. ADJ Something that is **indecent** is shocking, usually because it relates to sex or nakedness. *He accused Mrs Moore of making an indecent suggestion.* ♦**indecency** N-U *...the indecency of their language.* ♦**indecently** ADV *...an indecently short skirt.*

indecision /ˌɪndɪˈsɪʒən/. N-U **Indecision** is uncertainty about what you should do. *After months of indecision, the government finally gave the plan the go-ahead.*

indecisive /ˌɪndɪˈsaɪsɪv/. ADJ If someone is **indecisive**, they find it difficult to make decisions.

indeed /ɪnˈdiːd/. [1] ADV You use **indeed** to confirm or agree in an emphatic way with something that has just been said. *The payments* had indeed been made... 'Did you know him?'—'I did indeed.'... 'Know what I mean?'—'Indeed I do.' [2] ADV You use **indeed** to introduce a further comment or statement which strengthens the point you have already made. *We have nothing against diversity; indeed, we want more of it.* [3] ADV You use **indeed** at the end of a clause to give extra force to the word 'very', or to emphasize a particular word. *The wine was very good indeed... It's rare indeed for an Irish Prime Minister to visit Belfast.*

indefinite /ɪnˈdefɪnɪt/. [1] ADJ If something is **indefinite**, people have not decided when it will end. *The trial was adjourned for an indefinite period.* ◆**indefinitely** ADV *The visit has now been postponed indefinitely.* [2] ADJ If something such as a plan is **indefinite**, it is not exact or clear. *...at some indefinite time in the future.*

in,definite 'article, indefinite articles. N-C In grammar, the words 'a' and 'an' are sometimes called **indefinite articles.**

in,definite 'pronoun, indefinite pronouns. N-C An **indefinite pronoun** is a pronoun such as 'someone', 'anything', or 'nobody', which you use to refer in a general way to a person or thing without saying who or what they are, or what kind of person or thing you mean.

independent /ˌɪndɪˈpendənt/. [1] ADJ If one thing or person is **independent** of another, they are separate and not connected, so the first one is not affected or influenced by the second. *Your questions should be independent of each other.* ◆**independently** ADV *...several people working independently in different areas of the world.* [2] ADJ Someone who is **independent** does not rely on other people. *She would like to be financially independent.* ◆**independently** ADV *...helping disabled students to live and study as independently as possible. ...the independently-minded females of the Nineties.* ◆**independence** N-U *He was afraid of losing his independence.* [3] ADJ **Independent** countries and states are not ruled by other countries but have their own government. ◆**independence** N-U *In 1816, Argentina declared its independence from Spain.*

index /ˈɪndeks/ **indices, indexes, indexing, indexed. Indexes** is the usual plural, but the form **indices** can be used for meaning 1. [1] N-C An **index** is a system by which changes in the value of something can be compared or measured. *...the UK retail price index.* [2] VERB If a quantity or value is **indexed** to another, a system is arranged so that it increases or decreases whenever the other one increases or decreases. *Minimum pensions and wages are to be indexed to inflation.* [3] N-C An **index** is an alphabetical list at the back of a book saying where particular things are referred to in the book. [4] VERB If a book or collection of books **has been indexed**, someone has made an alphabetical list of the items in it. *A quarter of this vast archive has been indexed.*

indicate /ˈɪndɪkeɪt/ **indicates, indicating, indicated.** [1] VERB If one thing **indicates** another, the first thing shows that the second is true or exists. *A survey of retired people has indicated that most are independent and enjoying life.* [2] VERB If you **indicate** an opinion, an intention, or a fact, you mention it in a rather indirect way. *Mr Rivers has indicated that he may resign.* [3] VERB If you **indicate** something to someone, you point to it. *He indicated a chair.* [4] VERB When the driver of a car **indicates**, they operate flashing lights on one side of their vehicle which show the direction they are going to turn.

indication /ˌɪndɪˈkeɪʃən/ **indications.** N-VAR An **indication** is a sign which gives you an idea of what someone feels, what is happening, or what is likely to happen. *I cannot come to a decision about it now or given any indication of my own views... He gave no indication that he was ready to compromise.*

indicative /ɪnˈdɪkətɪv/. [1] ADJ If something is **indicative of** the existence or nature of something, it is a sign of it. *Often physical appearance is indicative of how a person feels.* [2] N-SING In grammar, a clause that is in **the indicative**, or in **the indicative mood**, has a subject followed by a verb group. Examples are 'I'm hungry' and 'She was followed'.

indicator /ˈɪndɪkeɪtə/ **indicators.** [1] N-C An **indicator** is a measurement or value which gives you an idea of what something is like. *...vital economic indicators, such as inflation, growth and the trade gap.* [2] N-C A car's **indicators** are the flashing lights that tell you that it is going to turn left or right.

indices /ˈɪndɪsiːz/. **Indices** is one of the plurals of **index**.

indict /ɪnˈdaɪt/ **indicts, indicting, indicted.** VERB When someone **is indicted** for a crime, they are officially charged with it. *Jones was later indicted on criminal charges.* ◆**indictment, indictments.** N-VAR *He is currently under indictment in Switzerland.*

indictment /ɪnˈdaɪtmənt/ **indictments.** N-C If you say that a fact or situation is an **indictment** of something, you mean that it shows how bad that thing is. *It's a sad indictment of society that policeman are regarded as easy targets by thugs.*

indifferent /ɪnˈdɪfərənt/. [1] ADJ If you are **indifferent** to something, you have no interest in it. *People have become indifferent to the suffering of others.* ◆**indifferently** ADV *'Not that it matters,' said Tench indifferently.* ◆**indifference** N-U *...the prejudice and indifference which surround the Aids epidemic.* [2] ADJ If you describe something or someone as **indifferent**, you mean that it is of a rather low standard. *She had starred in several very indifferent movies.*

indigenous /ɪnˈdɪdʒɪnəs/. ADJ **Indigenous** people or things belong to the country in which they are found, rather than coming there or being brought there from another country. *The Chumash were a tribe indigenous to California.*

indigestion /ˌɪndɪˈdʒestʃən/. N-U If you have **indigestion**, you have pains in your stomach that are caused by difficulties in digesting food.

indignant /ɪnˈdɪgnənt/. ADJ If you are **indignant**, you are shocked and angry, because you think that something is unjust or unfair. ◆**indignantly** ADV *'That is not true,' Erica said indignantly.*

indignation /ˌɪndɪgˈneɪʃən/. N-U **Indignation** is a feeling of shock and anger which you have when you think that something is unjust or unfair. *He could hardly contain his indignation.*

indignity /ɪnˈdɪɡnɪti/ **indignities.** N-VAR If you talk about the **indignity** of doing something, you mean that doing it is humiliating or embarrassing. *He suffered the indignity of having to flee angry protesters.*

indirect /ˌɪndaɪˈrɛkt, -dɪr-/. **1** ADJ An **indirect** result or effect is not caused immediately and obviously by a thing or person, but happens because of something else that they have done. *Millions could die of hunger as an indirect result of the war.* ♦**indirectly** ADV *Drugs are directly or indirectly responsible for much of the violence.* **2** ADJ An **indirect** route or journey does not use the shortest way between two places. **3** ADJ An **indirect** answer or reference does not directly mention the thing that is actually being talked about.

indirect 'object, indirect objects. N-C An **indirect object** is an object which is used with a transitive verb to indicate who benefits from an action or gets something as a result. For example, in 'She gave him her address', 'him' is the indirect object. Compare **direct object**.

indirect 'speech. Indirect speech is the same as **reported speech**.

indiscriminate /ˌɪndɪˈskrɪmɪnət/. ADJ If you describe an action as **indiscriminate**, you are critical of it because it does not involve any careful thought or choice. *...the indiscriminate killing of refugees.* ♦**indiscriminately** ADV *It is worth being patient rather than buying indiscriminately.*

indispensable /ˌɪndɪˈspɛnsəbəl/. ADJ If someone or something is **indispensable**, they are absolutely essential and other people or things cannot function without them. *She was becoming indispensable to him.*

indisputable /ˌɪndɪˈspjuːtəbəl/. ADJ If a fact is **indisputable**, it is obviously and definitely true. *It is indisputable that birds in the UK are harbouring this illness.* ♦**indisputably** ADV *She has an indisputably lovely voice.*

indistinguishable /ˌɪndɪˈstɪŋɡwɪʃəbəl/. ADJ If one thing is **indistinguishable** from another, the two things are so similar that it is difficult to know which is which. *In most cases the copies were indistinguishable from the originals.*

individual /ˌɪndɪˈvɪdʒuəl/ **individuals.** **1** ADJ BEFORE N **Individual** means relating to one person or thing, rather than to a large group. *Homeopathic treatment is always geared towards each individual person.* ♦**individually** ADV *...cheeses which come in individually wrapped segments.* **2** N-C An **individual** is a person.

individuality /ˌɪndɪvɪdʒuˈælɪti/. N-U The **individuality** of a person or thing consists of the qualities that make them different from other people or things. *People should be free to express their individuality.*

indoor /ˈɪndɔː/. ADJ BEFORE N **Indoor** activities or things are ones that happen or are used inside a building, rather than outside. *...a weekly indoor market.*

indoors /ˌɪnˈdɔːz/. ADV If something happens **indoors**, it happens inside a building. *Perhaps we should go indoors.*

induce /ɪnˈdjuːs, AM -ˈduːs/ **induces, inducing, induced.** **1** VERB To **induce** a particular state or condition means to cause it. *Surgery could induce a heart attack.* **2** VERB If you **induce** someone to do something, you persuade or influence them to do it. *I would do anything to induce them to stay.*

inducement /ɪnˈdjuːsmənt, AM -ˈduːs-/ **inducements.** N-C An **inducement** is something which might persuade someone to do a particular thing. *My friends were offered financial inducements to give the press information.*

induction /ɪnˈdʌkʃən/ **inductions.** N-VAR **Induction** is a procedure or ceremony for introducing someone to a new job or way of life. *...the induction of the girls into the sport. ...Elvis' induction into the army.*

indulge /ɪnˈdʌldʒ/ **indulges, indulging, indulged.** **1** VERB If you **indulge** in something, you allow yourself to have or do something that you know you will enjoy. *You can indulge yourself without spending a fortune.* **2** VERB If you **indulge** someone, you let them have or do whatever they want. *He did not really agree with indulging children.*

indulgent /ɪnˈdʌldʒənt/. ADJ If you are **indulgent**, you treat a person with special kindness. *His indulgent mother was willing to let him do anything he wanted.* ♦**indulgently** ADV *Ned smiled at him indulgently.* ♦**indulgence, indulgences** N-VAR *...the king's indulgence towards his sons.*

industrial /ɪnˈdʌstriəl/. **1** ADJ **Industrial** means relating to industry. *...industrial machinery and equipment.* **2** ADJ An **industrial** city or country is one in which industry is important or highly developed.

in,dustrial 'action. N-U If a group of workers take **industrial action**, they stop working or take other action to protest about their pay or working conditions.

in'dustrial estate, industrial estates. N-C An **industrial estate** is an area which has been specially planned for a lot of factories; BRITISH.

industrialist /ɪnˈdʌstriəlɪst/ **industrialists.** N-C An **industrialist** is a person who owns or controls large industrial companies or factories.

industrialize (BR also **industrialise**) /ɪnˈdʌstriəlaɪz/ **industrializes, industrializing, industrialized.** VERB When a country **industrializes**, or when it **is industrialized**, it develops a lot of industries. *Energy consumption rises as countries industrialise... Stalin's methods had industrialized the Russian economy.* ♦**industrialization** N-U *Industrialization began early in Spain.*

in,dustrial re'lations. N-PL Industrial relations refers to the relationship between employers and workers.

industry /ˈɪndəstri/ **industries.** **1** N-U **Industry** is the work and processes involved in making things in factories. **2** N-C A particular **industry** consists of all the people and activities involved in making a particular product or providing a particular service. *...the motor vehicle and textile industries.*

inedible /ɪnˈedɪbəl/. ADJ Something that is **inedible** is poisonous or tastes too bad to eat.

ineffective /ˌɪnɪˈfektɪv/. ADJ If you say that something is **ineffective**, you mean that it has no effect on a process or situation. ...*an ineffective method of controlling your dog.*

ineffectual /ˌɪnɪˈfektʃʊəl/. ADJ If someone or something is **ineffectual**, they fail to do what they are expected to do or are trying to do. *The government appears to be both ineffectual and indecisive.* ♦ **ineffectually** ADV *I tried, ineffectually, to comfort her.*

inefficient /ˌɪnɪˈfɪʃənt/. ADJ A person, organization, system, or machine that is **inefficient** does not work in the most economical way. ...*the closure of outdated and inefficient factories.* ♦ **inefficiency** N-U ...*the inefficiency of the distribution system.* ♦ **inefficiently** ADV *We still use power very inefficiently.*

inept /ɪnˈept/. ADJ Someone who is **inept** does something with a complete lack of skill. *You are completely inept at writing.* ...*his inept effort at finding a girlfriend.*

inequality /ˌɪnɪˈkwɒlɪti/ **inequalities.** N-VAR **Inequality** is a difference in social status, wealth, or opportunity between people or groups. *People are concerned about corruption and social inequality.*

inert /ɪnˈɜːt/. ADJ Someone or something that is **inert** does not move at all and appears to be lifeless. *The body was cold and inert.*

inertia /ɪnˈɜːʃə/. N-U If you have a feeling of **inertia**, you feel very lazy and unwilling to do anything. *He resented her inertia, her lack of energy.*

inescapable /ˌɪnɪˈskeɪpəbəl/. ADJ If something is **inescapable**, it is impossible not to notice it or be affected by it. *That is the inescapable conclusion of the reports.*

inevitable /ɪnˈevɪtəbəl/. ADJ & N-SING If something is **inevitable**, it is certain to happen and cannot be prevented or avoided. You can refer to something inevitable as **the inevitable**. *If the case succeeds, it is inevitable that other trials will follow... There's no point in putting off the inevitable.* ♦ **inevitability** N-U *We are all bound by the inevitability of death.* ♦ **inevitably** /ɪnˈevɪtəbli/ ADV *Technological changes will inevitably lead to unemployment.*

inexorable /ɪnˈeksərəbəl/. ADJ Something that is **inexorable** cannot be prevented from continuing; FORMAL. ...*the seemingly inexorable rise in unemployment.* ♦ **inexorably** ADV *The crisis is moving inexorably towards war.*

inexpensive /ˌɪnɪkˈspensɪv/. ADJ Something that is **inexpensive** does not cost much. ...*a large variety of good inexpensive restaurants.*

inexperience /ˌɪnɪkˈspɪəriəns/. N-U If you refer to someone's **inexperience**, you mean that they have little knowledge or experience of a particular situation or activity. *Critics attacked the youth and inexperience of his staff.*

inexperienced /ˌɪnɪkˈspɪəriənst/. ADJ If you are **inexperienced**, you have little or no experience of a particular activity. *They are inexperienced when it comes to decorating.*

inexplicable /ˌɪnɪkˈsplɪkəbəl/. ADJ If something is **inexplicable**, you cannot explain it.

♦ **inexplicably** ADV *She suddenly and inexplicably announced her retirement.*

inextricably /ˌɪnekˈstrɪkəbəli/. ADV If two or more things are **inextricably** linked, they cannot be separated. *Our survival is inextricably linked to the survival of the rainforest.*

infamous /ˈɪnfəməs/. ADJ **Infamous** people or things are well-known because of something bad. ...*the infamous massacre of Indians at Wounded Knee.* ● See note at **famous**.

infancy /ˈɪnfənsi/. [1] N-U **Infancy** is the period in your life when you are a very young child. *Fewer children die at birth or in infancy than ever before.* [2] N-U If something is in its infancy, it is new and has not developed very much. *Computing science was still in its infancy.*

infant /ˈɪnfənt/ **infants.** N-C An **infant** is a very young child or baby; FORMAL.

infantry /ˈɪnfəntri/. N-U The **infantry** are the soldiers in an army who fight on foot.

infect /ɪnˈfekt/ **infects, infecting, infected.** VERB To **infect** people, animals, plants, or food means to cause them to suffer from germs or to carry germs. ...*people infected with HIV... Europeans infected Indians with smallpox.* ♦ **infection** N-U ...*plants that are resistant to infection.*

infection /ɪnˈfekʃən/ **infections.** N-C An **infection** is a disease caused by germs. *I had an ear infection.*

infectious /ɪnˈfekʃəs/. [1] ADJ If you have an **infectious** disease, people near you can catch it from you. [2] ADJ If a feeling is **infectious**, it spreads to other people. ...*the infectious enthusiasm of the workforce.*

infer /ɪnˈfɜː/ **infers, inferring, inferred.** VERB If you **infer** that something is true, you decide that it is true on the basis of information you have. ...*information from which he can infer the future course of events.*

inference /ˈɪnfərəns/ **inferences.** N-C An **inference** is a conclusion that you draw about something. *There were two inferences to be drawn from her letter.*

inferior /ɪnˈfɪəriə/ **inferiors.** [1] ADJ Something that is **inferior** is not as good as something else. *The cassettes were of inferior quality... Comprehensive schools were perceived as inferior to grammar schools.* [2] ADJ & N-C If one person is regarded as **inferior** to another or as that person's **inferior**, they are considered to have less ability, status, or importance. *Most career women make me feel inferior... It was a gentleman's duty always to be civil, even to his inferiors.* ♦ **inferiority** /ɪnfɪəriˈɒrɪti, AM -ˈɔːr-/ N-U ...*feelings of inferiority that come from childhood.*

infertile /ɪnˈfɜːtaɪl, AM -təl/. [1] ADJ Someone who is **infertile** is unable to produce babies. ♦ **infertility** /ˌɪnfɜːˈtɪlɪti/ N-U *Male infertility is becoming commonplace.* [2] ADJ **Infertile** land has poor quality soil, so plants cannot grow well there.

infested /ɪnˈfestd/. ADJ If a place is **infested** with something undesirable such as insects or other pests, there are lots of them in it. *The prison is infested with rats.* ...*shark-infested waters.*

infidelity

infidelity /ˌɪnfɪˈdelɪti/ **infidelities.** N-VAR Infidelity occurs when a person who is married or in a steady relationship has sex with another person. *Andrews learned of his wife's infidelity.*

infiltrate /ˈɪnfɪltreɪt/ **infiltrates, infiltrating, infiltrated.** VERB If people **infiltrate** an organization, they join it secretly in order to spy on it or influence it. *The movement has been infiltrated by anarchists.* ◆**infiltration, infiltrations** N-VAR ...*the problem of alleged infiltration of the armed forces.*

infinite /ˈɪnfɪnɪt/. ADJ Something that is **infinite** is extremely large in amount or degree, or has no limit. *No company has infinite resources.* ◆**infinitely** ADV *His design was infinitely better than anything I could have done.*

infinitive /ɪnˈfɪnɪtɪv/ **infinitives.** N-C The **infinitive** of a verb is its base form or simplest form, such as 'do', 'take', and 'eat'. The infinitive is often used with 'to' in front of it.

infinity /ɪnˈfɪnɪti/. [1] N-U **Infinity** is a number that is larger than any other number and so can never be given an exact value. [2] N-U **Infinity** is a point that is further away than any other point and so can never be reached. ...*the darkness of a starless night stretching to infinity.*

infirmary /ɪnˈfɜːməri/ **infirmaries.** N-C Some hospitals are called **infirmaries.** ...*the Radcliffe Infirmary in Oxford.*

inflame /ɪnˈfleɪm/ **inflames, inflaming, inflamed.** VERB If something **inflames** a situation, or if it **inflames** people's feelings, it makes people more angry or feel more strongly; JOURNALISM. *Political passions have been inflamed by the scandal.*

inflamed /ɪnˈfleɪmd/. ADJ If part of your body is **inflamed**, it is red or swollen because of an infection or injury; FORMAL.

inflammation /ˌɪnfləˈmeɪʃən/ **inflammations.** N-VAR An **inflammation** is a swelling in your body that results from an infection or injury; FORMAL. ...*inflammation of the liver.*

inflammatory /ɪnˈflæmətəri, AM -tɔːri/. ADJ An **inflammatory** action or remark is likely to make people react very angrily. *Someone made an inflammatory racist remark.*

inflatable /ɪnˈfleɪtəbəl/ **inflatables.** ADJ An **inflatable** object is one that you fill with air when you want to use it. ...*an inflatable boat.*

inflate /ɪnˈfleɪt/ **inflates, inflating, inflated.** VERB If you **inflate** something such as a balloon or tyre, or if it **inflates**, it becomes bigger as it is filled with air or another gas. *Don's lifejacket had failed to inflate.*

inflated /ɪnˈfleɪtɪd/. [1] ADJ If you say that someone has an **inflated** opinion of themselves, you mean that they think that they are better or more important than they really are. [2] ADJ If you describe a price or salary as **inflated**, you mean that it is higher than is reasonable.

inflation /ɪnˈfleɪʃən/. N-U **Inflation** is a general increase in the prices of goods and services in a country. ...*an inflation rate of only 2.2%.*

inflationary /ɪnˈfleɪʃənri, AM -neri/. ADJ **Inflationary** means connected with inflation or causing inflation. ...*inflationary wage claims.*

inflect /ɪnˈflekt/ **inflects, inflecting, inflected.** VERB If a word **inflects**, its ending or form changes in order to show its grammatical function or number. If a language **inflects**, it has words in it that inflect. ◆**inflection, inflections** N-VAR ...*the rules of inflection.*

inflexible /ɪnˈfleksɪbəl/. ADJ Something or someone that is **inflexible** cannot or will not change or be altered, even if the situation changes. *Workers insisted the new system was too inflexible.* ◆**inflexibility** N-U *Joyce was irritated by the inflexibility of her colleagues.*

inflict /ɪnˈflɪkt/ **inflicts, inflicting, inflicted.** VERB To **inflict** something unpleasant on someone or something means to make them suffer it. ...*sports that inflicted cruelty on animals.*

influence /ˈɪnfluəns/ **influences, influencing, influenced.** [1] N-U **Influence** is the power to make other people agree with your opinions or make them do what you want. *Did Eva Braun have any influence on Hitler?... The government should continue to use its influence for the release of all hostages.* [2] VERB If you **influence** someone, you use your power to make them agree with you or do what you want. *My dad influenced me to do electronics.* [3] N-C & VERB If someone or something has an **influence** on people or events, or if they **influence** people or events, they affect the way people think or act, or what happens. *The Shropshire landscape was an influence on Owen. ...driving under the influence of alcohol... What you eat may influence your risk of getting cancer.* [4] N-C Someone or something that is a good or bad **influence** has a good or bad effect on someone. *TV is a bad influence on people.*

influential /ˌɪnfluˈenʃəl/. ADJ Someone who is **influential** has a lot of influence over people or events. *It helps to have influential friends... He had been influential in shaping economic policy.*

influx /ˈɪnflʌks/. N-SING An **influx** of people or things into a place is their steady arrival there in large numbers. ...*an influx of refugees.*

info /ˈɪnfəʊ/. N-U **Info** is information; INFORMAL. *For more info phone 414-3935.*

inform /ɪnˈfɔːm/ **informs, informing, informed.** VERB If you **inform** someone of something, you tell them about it. ...*efforts to inform people about the dangers of AIDS... My daughter informed me that she was pregnant.* ● See also **informed.**

informal /ɪnˈfɔːməl/. ADJ You use **informal** to describe behaviour, speech, or situations that are relaxed and casual rather than correct and serious. *She is refreshingly informal.* ◆**informally** ADV *They frequently chat informally over coffee.*

informant /ɪnˈfɔːmənt/ **informants.** N-C An **informant** is someone who gives another person information, especially someone who gives information to the police.

information /ˌɪnfəˈmeɪʃən/. N-U If you have **information** about a particular thing, you know something about it. *We will be looking at every piece of information we receive... For further information contact the number below.*

Note that **information** is only ever used as an uncount noun. You cannot say 'an information' or 'informations'. However, you can say a **piece of information** or an **item of information** when you are referring to a particular fact that someone has informed you of.

infor,mation tech'nology. N-U **Information technology** is the theory and practice of using computers to store and analyse information.

informative /ɪn'fɔːmətɪv/. ADJ Something that is **informative** gives you useful information. *It is an informative and readable book.*

informed /ɪn'fɔːmd/. ADJ Someone who is **informed** knows about a subject. An **informed** guess or decision is based on knowledge about a subject. *Consumers can now make a more informed choice about what they buy.*

informer /ɪn'fɔːmə/ **informers.** N-C An **informer** is someone who tells the police that another person has done something wrong.

infra-red /ˌɪnfrə 'red/. ADJ BEFORE N **Infra-red** radiation is similar to light but has a longer wavelength, so we cannot see it without special equipment, referred to as **infra-red** equipment.

infrastructure /'ɪnfrəstrʌktʃə/ **infrastructures.** N-VAR The **infrastructure** of a country or society consists of the basic facilities such as transport, communications, power supplies, and buildings, which enable the country or society to function properly.

infringe /ɪn'frɪndʒ/ **infringes, infringing, infringed.** [1] VERB If someone **infringes** a law or an agreement, they break it. *The film exploited his image and infringed his copyright.* ♦**infringement** /ɪn'frɪndʒmənt/ **infringements** N-VAR *Infringement of the regulation is punishable by a fine.* [2] VERB If something **infringes** people's rights or freedoms, or if it **infringes on** them, it prevents them from having the rights or freedoms they are entitled to. ♦**infringement** N-VAR *The wide-ranging police powers are an infringement of civil liberties.*

infuriate /ɪn'fjʊərɪeɪt/ **infuriates, infuriating, infuriated.** VERB If something or someone **infuriates** you, they make you extremely angry. *...a teenage craze guaranteed to infuriate your parents.* ♦**infuriating** ADV *Lizzie is messy to an infuriating degree.*

infuse /ɪn'fjuːz/ **infuses, infusing, infused.** VERB To **infuse** a quality into someone or something, or to **infuse** them with a quality, means to fill them with it; FORMAL. *The girls seemed to be infused with excitement on seeing the snow.*

ingenious /ɪn'dʒiːniəs/. ADJ Something that is **ingenious** is very clever and involves new ideas or equipment. *...a truly ingenious invention.*

ingenuity /ˌɪndʒə'njuːɪti, AM -'nuː-/. N-U **Ingenuity** is skill at inventing things or at working out how to achieve things.

ingrained /ˌɪn'greɪnd/. ADJ **Ingrained** habits and beliefs are difficult to change or remove. *...deeply ingrained family loyalty.*

ingredient /ɪn'griːdiənt/ **ingredients.** [1] N-C **Ingredients** are the things that are used to make something, especially all the different foods you use when you are cooking a particular dish. [2] N-C An **ingredient** of a situation is one of the essential parts of it.

inhabit /ɪn'hæbɪt/ **inhabits, inhabiting, inhabited.** VERB If a place or region is **inhabited** by a group of people or a species of animal, those people or animals live there. *...the people who inhabit these beautiful islands.*

inhabitant /ɪn'hæbɪtənt/ **inhabitants.** N-C The **inhabitants** of a place are the people who live there.

inhale /ɪn'heɪl/ **inhales, inhaling, inhaled.** VERB When you **inhale**, you breathe in. When you **inhale** something such as smoke, you take it into your lungs when you breathe in. *He was treated for the effects of inhaling smoke.*

inherent /ɪn'herənt, -'hɪər-/. ADJ The **inherent** qualities of something are the necessary and natural parts of it. *...the dangers inherent in an outbreak of war.* ♦**inherently** ADV *Aeroplanes are not inherently dangerous.*

inherit /ɪn'herɪt/ **inherits, inheriting, inherited.** [1] VERB If you **inherit** money or property, you receive it from someone who has died. *...paintings that he inherited from his father.* [2] VERB If you **inherit** something such as a situation or attitude, you take it over from people who came before you. *A future Labour government would inherit a difficult economic situation.* [3] VERB If you **inherit** a characteristic, you are born with it, because your parents or ancestors had it. *Her children have inherited her love of sport.*

inheritance /ɪn'herɪtəns/ **inheritances.** [1] N-VAR An **inheritance** is money or property which you receive from someone who is dead. *...families fighting over their inheritance.* [2] N-C If you get something such as a problem or attitude from someone who used to have it, you can refer to this as an **inheritance**. *...starvation and disease over much of Europe and Asia, which was Truman's inheritance as President.*

inhibit /ɪn'hɪbɪt/ **inhibits, inhibiting, inhibited.** VERB If something **inhibits** an event or process, it prevents it or slows it down. *Wine or sugary drinks inhibit digestion.*

inhibited /ɪn'hɪbɪtɪd/. ADJ If you say that someone is **inhibited**, you mean they find it difficult to behave naturally and show their feelings, and that you think this is a bad thing. *The English are very inhibited.*

inhibition /ˌɪnɪ'bɪʃən/ **inhibitions.** N-VAR **Inhibitions** are feelings of fear or embarrassment that make it difficult for you to behave naturally. *They behave with a total lack of inhibition.*

inhuman /ˌɪn'hjuːmən/. [1] ADJ If you describe something as **inhuman**, you mean that it is extremely cruel. *The barbaric slaughter of whales is unnecessary and inhuman.* [2] ADJ Something that is **inhuman** is not human or does not seem human, and is strange or frightening. *...inhuman shrieks.*

initial /ɪ'nɪʃəl/ **initials, initialling, initialled** (AM **initialing, initialed**). [1] ADJ BEFORE N You use **initial** to describe something that happens at the beginning of a process. *The ini-*

tial reaction has been excellent. **2** N-C **Initials** are the capital letters which begin each word of a name. **3** VERB When you **initial** a document, you write your initials on it to show that you have seen it or have officially approved it.

initially /ɪˈnɪʃəli/. ADV **Initially** means in the early stages of a process or situation. *Initially, they were wary of Simon.*

initiate /ɪˈnɪʃieɪt/ **initiates, initiating, initiated. 1** VERB If you **initiate** something, you start it or cause it to happen. *They wanted to initiate a discussion on economics.* ◆**initiation** N-U *There was a year between initiation and completion.* **2** VERB If someone **is initiated** into a particular group or society, they become a member of it by taking part in ceremonies at which they learn its special knowledge or customs. *She was initiated into the London Temple of the Alpha and Omega in 1919.* ◆**initiation, initiations** N-VAR *...initiation rites.*

initiative /ɪˈnɪʃətɪv/ **initiatives. 1** N-C An **initiative** is an important act intended to solve a problem. *There's talk of a new peace initiative.* **2** N-SING In a fight or contest, if you have **the initiative**, you are in a stronger position than your opponents. **3** N-U If you have **initiative**, you are able to take action without needing other people to tell you what to do. *She was disappointed by his lack of initiative.* **4** PHRASE If you **take the initiative** in a situation, you are the first person to act, and are therefore able to control the situation.

inject /ɪnˈdʒekt/ **injects, injecting, injected. 1** VERB To **inject** someone with a substance such as a medicine, or to **inject** it into them, means to use a needle and a syringe to put it into their body. *He needs to inject himself once a month.* **2** VERB If you **inject** a new, exciting, or interesting quality into a situation, you add it. *She kept trying to inject a little fun into their relationship.* **3** VERB If you **inject** money or resources into a business or organization, you provide more money or resources for it.

injection /ɪnˈdʒekʃən/ **injections. 1** N-C If you have an **injection**, a doctor or nurse puts a medicine into your body using a needle and a syringe. *It has to be given by injection, usually twice daily.* **2** N-C An **injection** of money or resources into a business or organization is the act of providing more money or resources for it.

injunction /ɪnˈdʒʌŋkʃən/ **injunctions.** N-C An **injunction** is a court order, usually one telling someone not to do something; LEGAL. *...an injunction banning her from his home.*

injure /ˈɪndʒə/ **injures, injuring, injured.** VERB If you **injure** a person or animal, you damage some part of their body. *...motorists who kill, maim, and injure.* ● See note at **wound.**

injured /ˈɪndʒəd/. **1** ADJ & N-PL An **injured** person has physical damage to part of their body, usually as a result of an accident or fighting. **The injured** are people who are injured. *Many of them will have died because they were so badly injured.* ● See note at **wound.** **2** ADJ If you feel **injured**, or if your feelings are **injured**, you feel upset because you believe something unfair has been done to you. *...a look of injured pride.*

injury /ˈɪndʒəri/ **injuries.** N-VAR An **injury** is damage done to a person's body. *The two other passengers escaped serious injury.* ● See note at **wound.**

injustice /ɪnˈdʒʌstɪs/ **injustices.** N-VAR **Injustice** is a lack of fairness in a situation. *...the injustice and futility of terrorism.*

ink /ɪŋk/ **inks, inking, inked. 1** N-VAR **Ink** is the coloured liquid used for writing or printing. *The letter was handwritten in black ink.* **2** VERB If you **ink** something, you put ink on it.

inland. 1 ADV /ɪnˈlænd/ If something is situated **inland**, it is away from the coast, towards or near the middle of a country. *The vast majority live further inland.* **2** ADJ BEFORE N /ˈɪnlænd/ **Inland** lakes and places are not on the coast, but in or near the middle of a country.

in-laws. N-PL Your **in-laws** are the parents and close relatives of your husband or wife.

inlet /ˈɪnlet/ **inlets.** N-C An **inlet** is a narrow strip of water which goes from a sea or lake into the land.

inmate /ˈɪnmeɪt/ **inmates.** N-C The **inmates** of a prison or a psychiatric hospital are the prisoners or patients who are living there.

inn /ɪn/ **inns.** N-C An **inn** is a small hotel or a pub, usually an old one; DATED.

innate /ɪˈneɪt/. ADJ An **innate** quality or ability is one which a person is born with. *Americans have an innate sense of fairness.* ◆**innately** ADV *...her innately feminine qualities.*

inner /ˈɪnə/. **1** ADJ BEFORE N The **inner** parts of something are the parts which are contained or are enclosed inside the other parts, and which are closest to the centre. *She got up and went into an inner office.* **2** ADJ BEFORE N Your **inner** feelings are feelings which you have but do not show to other people.

,inner 'circle, inner circles. N-C An **inner circle** is a group of people who have a lot of power or control in a group or organization, and who work together in secretive ways. *...the inner circle of scientists who produced the atomic bomb.*

,inner 'city, inner cities. N-C You use **inner city** to refer to areas near the centre of a city where people live and where there are often social and economic problems. *...the fear of living in the inner city. ...inner-city areas.*

innings /ˈɪnɪŋz/. **Innings** is both the singular and the plural form. N-C An **innings** is a period in a game of cricket during which a particular player or team is batting.

innocence /ˈɪnəsəns/. **1** ADJ **Innocence** is the quality of having no experience or knowledge of the more complex or unpleasant aspects of life. *...childhood innocence.* **2** N-U If someone proves their **innocence**, they prove that they are not guilty of a crime.

innocent /ˈɪnəsənt/ **innocents. 1** ADJ If someone is **innocent**, they did not commit a crime which they have been accused of. *He was sure that the man was innocent of any crime.* **2** ADJ & N-C If someone is **innocent** or is an **innocent**, they have no experience or knowledge of the more complex or unpleasant aspects of life. *They seemed so young and innocent. ...a hopeless innocent where women were concerned.*

♦**innocently** ADV *The baby gurgled innocently on the bed.* [3] ADJ **Innocent** people are those who are not involved in a crime, conflict, or other situation, but who nevertheless get injured or killed. *All those wounded were innocent victims.* [4] ADJ An **innocent** remark or action is not meant to offend people, although it may do so. *It was probably an innocent question.*

innocuous /ɪˈnɒkjuəs/. ADJ Something that is **innocuous** is not at all harmful; FORMAL. *Both mushrooms look innocuous but are in fact deadly.*

innovation /ˌɪnəˈveɪʃən/ **innovations.** [1] N-C An **innovation** is a new thing or new method of doing something. [2] N-U **Innovation** is the introduction of new things or new methods. *We must promote originality, inspire creativity and encourage innovation.*

innovative /ˈɪnəveɪtɪv/. [1] ADJ Something that is **innovative** is new and original. [2] ADJ An **innovative** person introduces changes and new ideas.

innovator /ˈɪnəveɪtə/ **innovators.** N-C An **innovator** is someone who introduces changes and new ideas.

innuendo /ˌɪnjuˈendəʊ/ **innuendoes** or **innuendos.** N-VAR **Innuendo** is indirect reference to something rude or unpleasant. *...magazines which are full of sexual innuendo.*

innumerable /ɪˈnjuːmərəbəl, AM -ˈnuː-/. ADJ **Innumerable** means very many, or too many to be counted. *He has invented innumerable excuses, told endless lies.*

inordinate /ɪnˈɔːdɪnɪt/. ADJ If you describe something as **inordinate**, you are emphasizing that it is unusually or excessively great in amount or degree; FORMAL. *...their inordinate number of pets.* ♦**inordinately** ADV *He is inordinately proud of his wife.*

input /ˈɪnpʊt/ **inputs, inputting, input.** [1] N-VAR **Input** consists of information or resources that a group or project receives. *...inputs and advice on how to improve the management of their farms.* [2] VERB If you **input** information into a computer, you feed it in, for example by typing it on a keyboard. [3] N-U **Input** is information fed into a computer.

inquest /ˈɪnkwest/ **inquests.** N-C An **inquest** is an official inquiry into the cause of someone's death.

inquire (or **enquire**) /ɪnˈkwaɪə/ **inquires, inquiring, inquired.** [1] VERB If you **inquire** about something, you ask for information about it; FORMAL. *'Is something wrong?' he enquired... He asked for his key and inquired whether there had been any messages for him.* [2] VERB If you **inquire** into something, you investigate it carefully. *Inspectors were appointed to inquire into the affairs of the company.*

▸ **inquire after.** PHR-VERB If you **inquire after** someone, you ask how they are or what they are doing. *Elsie called to inquire after my health.*

inquiring (or **enquiring**) /ɪnˈkwaɪərɪn/. [1] ADJ BEFORE N If you have an **inquiring** mind, you have a great interest in learning new things. *...an inquiring attitude to learning.* [2] ADJ BEFORE N If someone has an **inquiring** expression

on their face, they are showing that they want to know something; WRITTEN.

inquiry (or **enquiry**) /ɪnˈkwaɪəri/ **inquiries.** [1] N-C An **inquiry** is a question which you ask in order to get information. *He made some inquiries and discovered she had gone to the Continent.* [2] N-C An **inquiry** is an official investigation. [3] N-U **Inquiry** is the process of investigating something to get information about it. *...a new line of inquiry.*

inquisitive /ɪnˈkwɪzɪtɪv/. ADJ An **inquisitive** person likes finding out about things, especially secret things. *Barrow had an inquisitive nature.*

inroads /ˈɪnrəʊdz/. PHRASE If one thing **makes inroads** into another, the first thing starts affecting or destroying the second. *...television has made deep inroads into cinema.*

insane /ɪnˈseɪn/. [1] ADJ & N-PL Someone who is **insane** has a mind that does not work in a normal way, with the result that their behaviour is very strange. **The insane** are people who are insane. *His first wife went insane.* ♦**insanity** /ɪnˈsænɪti/ N-U *...a woman's descent into insanity.* [2] ADJ If you describe a decision or action as **insane**, you think it is very foolish or excessive. ♦**insanely** ADV *I would be insanely jealous if Bill left me for another woman.* ♦**insanity** N-U *...the final financial insanity of the 1980s.*

insatiable /ɪnˈseɪʃəbəl/. ADJ If someone has an **insatiable** desire for something, they want as much of it as they can possibly get. *He had an insatiable appetite for publicity.*

inscribe /ɪnˈskraɪb/ **inscribes, inscribing, inscribed.** VERB If you **inscribe** words on an object, you write or carve them on it. *...stone slabs inscribed with Buddhist texts.*

inscription /ɪnˈskrɪpʃən/ **inscriptions.** N-C An **inscription** is a piece of writing carved into a surface, or written on a book or photograph.

insect /ˈɪnsekt/ **insects.** N-C An **insect** is a small creature with six legs. Most insects have wings.

insecticide /ɪnˈsektɪsaɪd/ **insecticides.** N-VAR **Insecticide** is a chemical used to kill insects.

insecure /ˌɪnsɪˈkjʊə/. [1] ADJ If you feel **insecure**, you feel that you are not good enough or are not loved. *Most mothers are insecure about their performance as mothers.* ♦**insecurity** /ˌɪnsɪˈkjʊərɪti/ **insecurities** N-VAR *It was his shyness and insecurity which let him down.* [2] ADJ Something that is **insecure** is not safe or protected. *...low-paid, insecure jobs.* ♦**insecurity** N-U *...the insecurity of agricultural life.*

insensitive /ɪnˈsensɪtɪv/. ADJ If you describe someone as **insensitive**, you mean that they are not aware of or sympathetic to other people's feelings or problems. *My husband is very insensitive about my problem.* ♦**insensitivity** /ɪnˌsensɪˈtɪvɪti/ N-U *...my clumsiness and insensitivity towards her.*

inseparable /ɪnˈsepərəbəl/. [1] ADJ If two things are **inseparable**, they cannot be considered separately. *Liberty is inseparable from social justice.* [2] ADJ Friends who are **inseparable** are always together.

insert /ɪnˈsɜːt/ **inserts, inserting, inserted.** [1] VERB If you **insert** an object into something, you put the object inside it. *He took a small key from his pocket and slowly inserted it into the lock.* ◆**insertion, insertions.** N-VAR *...the insertion of needles at precise points on the body.* [2] VERB If you **insert** a comment or detail in a piece of writing or a speech, you include it.

inside /ɪnˈsaɪd/ **insides.** [1] PREP & ADV Something or someone that is **inside** a place, container, or object is in it or surrounded by it. *Inside the box were a dozen or so papers... There is a telephone inside the entrance hall... He ripped open the envelope and read what was inside.* [2] N-C The **inside** of something is the part or area that its sides surround or contain. *I painted the inside of the house. ...an inside lavatory.* [3] ADJ BEFORE N On a wide road, the **inside** lanes are the ones closest to the edge of the road. [4] N-PL Your **insides** are your internal organs, especially your stomach; INFORMAL. [5] ADJ BEFORE N **Inside** knowledge is obtained from someone who is involved in a situation and therefore knows a lot about it. *The attackers had inside information about the targets.* [6] PHRASE If something such as a piece of clothing is **inside out**, the inside part has been turned so that it faces outwards.

insider /ɪnˈsaɪdə/ **insiders.** N-C An **insider** is someone who is involved in a situation and who knows more about it than other people. *Insiders say there are simply too many chiefs. ...insider knowledge.*

insidious /ɪnˈsɪdiəs/. ADJ Something that is **insidious** is unpleasant and develops gradually without being noticed. *The changes are insidious, and will not produce a noticeable effect for 15 to 20 years.*

insight /ˈɪnsaɪt/ **insights.** N-VAR If you gain **insight** into a complex situation or problem, you learn something useful or valuable about it. *...an insight into the practical problems encountered by disabled people.*

insignificant /ˌɪnsɪɡˈnɪfɪkənt/. ADJ Something that is **insignificant** is unimportant, especially because it is very small. *In 1949 Bonn was a small, insignificant city.* ◆**insignificance** N-U *...the sense of insignificance that everybody has felt.*

insist /ɪnˈsɪst/ **insists, insisting, insisted.** [1] VERB If you **insist** that something should be done, you say very firmly that it must be done. *She insisted on being present... I didn't want to join in, but Kenneth insisted.* ◆**insistence** N-U *She had attended an interview at her boyfriend's insistence.* [2] VERB If you **insist** that something is true, you say it very firmly and refuse to change your mind. *The president insisted that he was acting out of compassion.*

insistent /ɪnˈsɪstənt/. [1] ADJ Someone who is **insistent** keeps insisting that a particular thing should be done or is the case. *Abramov had been insistent that the matter be resolved quickly.* ◆**insistently** ADV *'What is it?' his wife asked again, gently but insistently.* [2] ADJ An **insistent** noise or rhythm continues for a long time and holds your attention.

insofar as /ˌɪnsəˈfɑːr æz/. CONJ You use **insofar as** to introduce a statement which explains and adds to something you have just said; FOR-MAL. *She was not ashamed of her addiction, except insofar as it troubled her husband.*

insomnia /ɪnˈsɒmniə/. N-U Someone who suffers from **insomnia** finds it difficult to sleep.

inspect /ɪnˈspekt/ **inspects, inspecting, inspected.** VERB If you **inspect** something, you examine it or check it carefully. *His wife tilted his head to the side and inspected the wound.* ◆**inspection, inspections.** N-VAR *Officials will have to make an inspection of the dam.*

inspector /ɪnˈspektə/ **inspectors.** [1] N-C An **inspector** is someone whose job is to inspect things. *The mill was finally shut down by state safety inspectors.* [2] N-C & N-TITLE In Britain, an **inspector** is a police officer who is higher in rank than a sergeant and lower in rank than a superintendent. *...Inspector Joplin.*

inspiration /ˌɪnspəˈreɪʃən/ **inspirations.** [1] N-U **Inspiration** is a feeling of excitement and enthusiasm gained from new ideas. *Daphne played extremely well and it will give a lot of inspiration to other women.* [2] N-SING The **inspiration** for something such as a piece of work or a theory is the person or thing that provides the basic idea or example for it. *My inspiration comes from poets like Baudelaire.*

inspire /ɪnˈspaɪə/ **inspires, inspiring, inspired.** [1] VERB If a work of art or an action is **inspired** by something, that thing is the source of the idea or the motivation for it. *The book was inspired by a real person... What inspired you to change your name?* ◆**-inspired** *...Mediterranean-inspired ceramics.* [2] VERB If someone or something **inspires** you, they give you new ideas and a strong feeling of enthusiasm. *...the personal charisma to inspire people.* ◆**inspiring** ADJ *...a brilliant and inspiring young teacher.* [3] VERB Someone or something that **inspires** a particular emotion or reaction in people makes them feel it. *He inspires fierce loyalty in his friends.*

instability /ˌɪnstəˈbɪlɪti/ **instabilities.** N-VAR **Instability** is a lack of stability in a place, situation, or person. *...political instability.*

install /ɪnˈstɔːl/ **installs, installing, installed.** [1] VERB If you **install** a piece of equipment, you fit it or put it somewhere so that it is ready to be used. *They had installed a new phone line.* ◆**installation** /ˌɪnstəˈleɪʃən/ N-U *...the installation of alarms.* [2] VERB If someone **is installed** in a new job or important position, they are officially given the job or position. *The army has promised to install a new government within a week.*

instalment (AM **installment**) /ɪnˈstɔːlmənt/ **instalments.** [1] N-C If you pay for something in **instalments**, you pay small sums of money at regular intervals over a period of time. *...his next instalment on the mortgage.* [2] N-C An **instalment** of a story is one of its separate parts that are published or broadcast one after the other. *...the latest instalment in Douglas Adams's 'Hitchhiker' trilogy.*

instance /ˈɪnstəns/ **instances.** [1] PHRASE You use **for instance** when you are mentioning something or someone that is an example of what you are talking about. *They will be concerned to do the right thing – to dress properly, for instance.* [2] N-C An **instance** is a particular example or occurrence of something. ...*another instance of robbery.* [3] PHRASE You say **in the first instance** to mention the first of a series of actions or possibilities; FORMAL. *Try to resolve the problem with the Tax Office in the first instance.*

instant /ˈɪnstənt/ **instants.** [1] N-C An **instant** is an extremely short period of time or a point in time. *The pain disappeared in an instant... At that instant the museum was plunged into total darkness.* [2] CONJ If you say that someone does something the **instant** something else happens, you are emphasizing that they do the first thing immediately after the second thing happens. *She would know the instant he walked in whether it was true.* [3] ADJ You use **instant** to describe something that happens immediately. *He had taken an instant dislike to Mortlake.* ♦**instantly** ADV *The man was killed instantly.* [4] ADJ BEFORE N **Instant** food can be prepared very quickly, for example by just adding water. ...*instant coffee.*

instantaneous /ˌɪnstənˈteɪniəs/. ADJ Something that is **instantaneous** happens immediately and very quickly. *The coroner said that death was instantaneous.* ♦**instantaneously** ADV *Airbags inflate instantaneously on impact.*

instead /ɪnˈsted/. PREP & ADV If you do one thing **instead** of another, you do the first thing and not the second thing, especially as the result of a choice or a change of behaviour. *She had to spend nearly four months away from him that summer, instead of the usual two... When we feel anger, we bury the emotion and feel guilty instead.*

instigate /ˈɪnstɪɡeɪt/ **instigates, instigating, instigated.** VERB To **instigate** an event or situation means to cause it to happen. ...*those who are instigating violence.* ♦**instigation** N-U *The talks are taking place at the instigation of Germany.* ♦**instigator** N-C *He was accused of being the main instigator of the coup.*

instil (AM **instill**) /ɪnˈstɪl/ **instils, instilling, instilled.** VERB If you **instil** an idea or feeling into someone, you make them think it or feel it. *Their work will instil a sense of responsibility in children.*

instinct /ˈɪnstɪŋkt/ **instincts.** [1] N-VAR An **instinct** is the natural tendency that a person has to behave or react in a particular way. *I didn't have a strong maternal instinct.* ...*the dog's natural instinct to hunt.* [2] N-C An **instinct** is a feeling that you have about a particular situation, rather than an opinion based on facts. *I should've gone with my first instinct, which was not to do the interview.*

instinctive /ɪnˈstɪŋktɪv/. ADJ An **instinctive** feeling, idea, or action is one that you have or do without thinking. *It's an absolutely instinctive reaction – if a child falls down, you pick it up.* ♦**instinctively** ADV *He knew instinctively that here was more bad news.*

institute /ˈɪnstɪtjuːt, AM -tuːt/ **institutes, instituting, instituted.** [1] N-C An **institute** is an organization or building where a particular type of work is done, especially research or teaching. ...*the National Cancer Institute.* [2] VERB If you **institute** a system, rule, or plan,

you start it; FORMAL. *We will institute a number of measures to better safeguard the public.*

institution /ˌɪnstɪˈtjuːʃən, AM -ˈtuː-/ **institutions.** [1] N-C An **institution** is an official organization which is important in society. Parliament, the Church, and large banks are all institutions. ♦**institutional** ADJ BEFORE N ...*the power of the institutional church.* [2] N-C An **institution** is a place such as a mental hospital, children's home, or prison, where people are kept and looked after. *Larry has been in an institution since he was four.* [3] N-C An **institution** is a custom that is considered an important or typical feature of society, because it has existed for a long time. ...*the institution of marriage.*

institutionalized (BR also **institutionalised**) /ˌɪnstɪˈtjuːʃənəlaɪzd, AM -ˈtuː-/. [1] ADJ If you say that something bad has become **institutionalized**, you are critical of the fact that it has become part of a culture, social system, or organization. ...*a form of institutionalized racism.* [2] ADJ If a person becomes **institutionalized**, they have lived for so long in an institution that they are no longer able to live an independent life.

instruct /ɪnˈstrʌkt/ **instructs, instructing, instructed.** [1] VERB If you **instruct** someone to do something, you formally tell them to do it. *The family has instructed solicitors to sue the company.* [2] VERB Someone who **instructs** people in a subject or skill teaches it to them. *He instructed family members in nursing techniques.*

instruction /ɪnˈstrʌkʃən/ **instructions.** [1] N-PL **Instructions** are clear and detailed information on how to do something. ...*some basic instructions on how to cook a turkey.* [2] N-C An **instruction** is something that someone tells you to do. *He had instructions to keep this guest satisfied.* [3] N-U **Instruction** in a subject or skill is teaching that someone gives you about it. ...*religious instruction.*

instructive /ɪnˈstrʌktɪv/. ADJ Something that is **instructive** gives useful information. ...*an entertaining and instructive documentary.*

instructor /ɪnˈstrʌktə/ **instructors.** N-C An **instructor** is a teacher, especially of driving, skiing, or swimming. ...*his karate instructor.*

instrument /ˈɪnstrəmənt/ **instruments.** [1] N-C An **instrument** is a tool or device that is used to do a particular task. ...*navigation instruments.* ...*instruments for cleaning and polishing teeth.* [2] N-C A musical **instrument** is an object such as a piano, guitar, or flute which you play in order to produce music. [3] N-C Something that is an **instrument** for achieving a particular aim is used by people to achieve that aim. ...*the use of the law as an instrument of political repression.*

instrumental /ˌɪnstrəˈmentəl/. [1] ADJ Someone or something that is **instrumental** in a process or event helps to make it happen. *He was instrumental in getting the legislation passed.* [2] ADJ & N-C **Instrumental** music is performed using musical instruments and not voices. An **instrumental** is a piece of instrumental music.

insufficient /ˌɪnsəˈfɪʃənt/. ADJ Something that is **insufficient** is not enough for a particular purpose; FORMAL. *There are insufficient funds to pay the debt.* ♦**insufficiently** ADV *The general workforce is insufficiently educated.*

insular /'ɪnsjʊlə, AM -sə-/. ADJ **Insular** people are unwilling to meet new people or to consider new ideas. ♦**insularity** /ˌɪnsjʊ'lærɪti, AM -sə-/ N-U ...*the growing insularity of Russian politics.*

insulate /'ɪnsjʊleɪt, AM -sə-/ **insulates, insulating, insulated.** [1] VERB To **insulate** something means to cover it or surround it in a thick layer, in order to prevent heat or sound from passing through it. *Is there any way we can insulate our home from the noise?* [2] VERB If you or a group is **insulated** from harmful things, they are protected from them. *The country was insulated from the worst effects of the recession.* [3] VERB If a piece of equipment is **insulated**, it is covered with rubber or plastic to prevent electricity passing through it and giving the person using it an electric shock.

insulation /ˌɪnsjʊ'leɪʃən, AM -sə-/. N-U **Insulation** is a thick layer of material used to insulate something.

insulin /'ɪnsjʊlɪn, AM -sə-/. N-U **Insulin** is a substance that most people produce naturally in their body and which controls the level of sugar in their blood.

insult, insults, insulting, insulted. [1] VERB /ɪn'sʌlt/ If you **insult** someone, you offend them by being rude to them. *I did not mean to insult you.* ♦**insulted** ADJ *I was deeply insulted.* ♦**insulting** ADJ ...*an insulting remark.* [2] N-C /'ɪnsʌlt/ An **insult** is a rude remark or action which offends someone. *They shouted insults at each other.* [3] PHRASE If an action or event **adds insult to injury**, it makes an unfair or unacceptable situation even worse.

insurance /ɪn'ʃʊərəns/. [1] N-U **Insurance** is an arrangement in which you pay money regularly to a company, and they pay money to you if something unpleasant happens to you, for example if your property is stolen. ...*health insurance.* [2] N-SING If you do something as an **insurance** against something unpleasant, you do it in order to protect yourself in case the unpleasant thing happens. *Farmers grow a mixture of crops as an insurance against crop failure.*

insure /ɪn'ʃʊə/ **insures, insuring, insured.** VERB If you **insure** yourself or your property, you pay money to an insurance company so that if you become ill or if your property is stolen, the company will pay you a sum of money. *Women can now insure themselves against contracting breast cancer.* ● See also **ensure.**

insurer /ɪn'ʃʊərər/ **insurers.** N-C An **insurer** is a company that sells insurance.

insurgency /ɪn'sɜːdʒənsi/ **insurgencies.** N-VAR An **insurgency** is an attempt by a group of people to remove the government of their country by force.

insurrection /ˌɪnsə'rekʃən/ **insurrections.** N-VAR An **insurrection** is violent action taken by a group of people against the rulers of their country. ...*an armed insurrection.*

intact /ɪn'tækt/. ADJ Something that is **intact** is complete and has not been damaged or spoilt. *The roof was still intact... His reputation remained intact.*

intake /'ɪnteɪk/ **intakes.** [1] N-C Your **intake** of food, drink, or air is the amount that you eat, drink, or breathe in, or the process of taking it into your body. *Cut down your alcohol intake.* [2] N-C The people who are accepted into an institution or organization at a particular time are referred to as a particular **intake.** ...*one of this year's intake of students.*

intangible /ɪn'tændʒɪbəl/. ADJ & N-PL A quality or idea that is **intangible** is hard to define or explain. You can refer to qualities or ideas like this as **intangibles.** *The culture is shaped by many factors, some of them intangible.*

integral /'ɪntɪgrəl/. ADJ If something is an **integral** part of another thing, it is an essential part of it. *The nude scenes are integral to the story.*

integrate /'ɪntɪgreɪt/ **integrates, integrating, integrated.** [1] VERB If people **integrate** into a social group, or if they **are integrated** into it, they join it and become a part of it. ...*attempts to integrate immigrants more firmly into French society.* ♦**integrated** ADJ ...*integrated schooling.* ♦**integration** N-U ...*the integration of disabled people into mainstream society.* [2] VERB If you **integrate** things, you combine them so that they are closely linked or so that they form one thing. *The two airlines will integrate their services.* ♦**integrated** ADJ ...*integrated computer systems.*

integrity /ɪn'tegrɪti/. N-U **Integrity** is the quality of being honest and firm in your moral principles. ...*a man of integrity.*

intellect /'ɪntɪlekt/ **intellects.** [1] N-VAR **Intellect** is the ability to think and to understand ideas and information. ...*good health and a lively intellect.* [2] N-VAR **Intellect** is the quality of being very intelligent or clever. *I was intrigued by him, stirred by his intellect.*

intellectual /ˌɪntɪ'lektʃʊəl/ **intellectuals.** [1] ADJ BEFORE N **Intellectual** means involving a person's ability to think and to understand ideas and information. ...*the intellectual development of children.* ♦**intellectually** ADV ...*intellectually demanding work.* [2] N-C & ADJ An **intellectual** is someone who spends a lot of time studying and thinking about complicated ideas. You can say that someone like this is **intellectual.** *They were very intellectual and she found it difficult, I think, to fit in.*

intelligence /ɪn'telɪdʒəns/. [1] N-U Someone's **intelligence** is their ability to understand and learn things. ...*a woman of exceptional intelligence.* [2] N-U **Intelligence** is the ability to think and understand instead of doing things by instinct. *Whales have intelligence and are capable of exercising choice.* [3] N-U **Intelligence** is information gathered by the government about their country's enemies. ...*the intelligence services.*

intelligent /ɪn'telɪdʒənt/. [1] ADJ An **intelligent** person has the ability to think, understand, and learn things quickly and well. ...*the most intelligent man I have ever met.* ♦**intelligently** ADV *They are incapable of thinking intelligently about politics.* [2] ADJ Something that is **intelligent** has the ability to think and understand instead of doing things by instinct. ...*the biggest-ever search for intelligent life elsewhere in the universe.*

intend /ɪnˈtend/ intends, intending, intended. [1] VERB If you intend to do something, you have decided or planned to do it. *I intend to go to university. ...the hotel in which they intended staying.* [2] VERB Something that is intended for a particular person or purpose, or intended to have a particular effect, has been planned for that person or purpose, or planned to have that effect. *The money is intended for food and medical supplies... Today's announcement was intended as a warning.*

intense /ɪnˈtens/ [1] ADJ Something that is intense is very great in strength or degree. *The pain was intense. ...intense heat.* ◆intensely ADV *She is intensely irritating.* ◆intensity /ɪnˈtensɪti/ N-U ...*the intensity of the work.* [2] ADJ An intense person is very serious. *...an intense young man.*

intensify /ɪnˈtensɪfaɪ/ intensifies, intensifying, intensified. VERB If you intensify something, or if it intensifies, it becomes greater in strength or degree. *His lawyers have intensified their efforts to halt his execution.*

intensive /ɪnˈtensɪv/ [1] ADJ An intensive activity involves the concentration of energy or people on one particular task. *...four weeks of intensive study.* ◆intensively ADV *Wilson has worked intensively on his speed and strength.* [2] ADJ Intensive farming involves producing as many crops or animals as possible from your land, usually with the aid of chemicals.

in,tensive 'care. N-U If someone is in intensive care, they are in hospital being cared for very thoroughly and watched very closely because they are seriously ill.

intent /ɪnˈtent/ intents. [1] N-U A person's intent is their intention to do something; FORMAL. *...his intent to appeal against the decision. ...this strong statement of intent on arms control.* [2] ADJ If someone is intent, they appear to be concentrating very seriously on what they are doing or feeling; WRITTEN. *Amy watched the child's intent face.* ◆intently ADV *She stared intently at the TV screen.* [3] ADJ AFTER LINK-V If you are intent on doing something, you are determined to do it. *He is intent on repeating his victory.* [4] PHRASE You say to all intents and purposes to suggest that a situation is not exactly as you describe it but the effect is the same as if it were. *To all intents and purposes he was my father.*

intention /ɪnˈtenʃən/ intentions. N-VAR An intention is an idea or plan of what you are going to do. *...his intention to return to Berlin... I have no intention of resigning.*

intentional /ɪnˈtenʃənəl/ ADJ Something that is intentional is deliberate. *The kick was intentional.* ◆intentionally ADV *I've never intentionally hurt anyone.*

interact /ˌɪntərˈækt/ interacts, interacting, interacted. VERB The way that two people or things interact is the way that they communicate or work in relation to each other. *Addictive substances interact with the chemicals in the brain.* ◆interaction, interactions N-VAR ...*studies on parent-child interaction.*

interactive /ˌɪntərˈæktɪv/ ADJ An interactive computer program or television system is one which allows direct communication between the user and the machine.

intercept /ˌɪntəˈsept/ intercepts, intercepting, intercepted. VERB If you intercept someone or something that is travelling from one place to another, you stop them. *He asked why the bombers had not been intercepted by Army patrols.* ◆interception, interceptions. N-VAR ...*the interception of a ship off the west coast of Scotland.*

interchange, interchanges; verb /ˌɪntəˈtʃeɪndʒ/, noun /ˈɪntətʃeɪndʒ/. VERB & N-VAR If you interchange things, or if there is an interchange of things, you exchange one thing for the other. *Your task is to interchange words so that the sentence makes sense.*

interchangeable /ˌɪntəˈtʃeɪndʒəbəl/ ADJ Things that are interchangeable can be exchanged with each other without making any difference. ◆interchangeably ADV *...two different words used interchangeably to describe one action.*

interconnect /ˌɪntəkəˈnekt/ interconnects, interconnecting, interconnected. VERB Things that interconnect or that are interconnected are connected to or with each other. *Virtually all urban problems are really interconnected with each other. ...interconnecting rooms.* ◆interconnection, interconnections. N-VAR ...*the variety of interconnections between music and other arts.*

intercontinental /ˌɪntəkɒntɪˈnentəl/ ADJ BEFORE N Intercontinental is used to describe something that exists or happens between continents. *...intercontinental flights.*

intercourse /ˈɪntəkɔːs/ N-U If people have intercourse, they have sex; FORMAL.

interdependent /ˌɪntədɪˈpendənt/ ADJ People or things that are interdependent all depend on each other. *Most economies today are highly interdependent with one another.* ◆interdependence N-U ...*the interdependence of the world's economies.*

interest /ˈɪntrəst, -tərest/ interests, interesting, interested. [1] N-SING & N-U If you have an interest in something, you like it and want to learn or hear more about it. *He showed a great interest in animals... She'd liked him at first, but soon lost interest.* [2] N-C Your interests are the things that you enjoy doing. *His interests include cooking and photography.* [3] VERB If something interests you, you want to learn more about it or to continue doing it. *These are the stories that interest me.* [4] N-C If you have an interest in something being done, you want it to be done because you will benefit from it. *The US clearly has an interest in promoting free trade.* [5] N-C A person or organization that has interests in a company owns shares in this company. *Her other business interests include a theme park in Scandinavia.* [6] N-U Interest is extra money that you receive if you have invested a sum of money, or extra money that you pay if you have borrowed money. *Does your current account pay interest?* [7] See also self-interest, vested interest.

PHRASES Something that is in the interests of a person or group will benefit them in some way. *...a compromise that would be in the in-*

terests of the British fishing industry. If you do something **in the interests of** a particular result or situation, you do it in order to achieve that result or maintain that situation. ...*a call for all businessmen to work together in the interests of national stability.*

interested /ˈɪntrɪstɪd/. [1] ADJ AFTER LINK-V If you are **interested** in something, you think it is important and you are keen to learn more about it or spend time doing it. *I wasn't particularly interested in physics... I'd be interested to know what people's views were.* [2] ADJ BEFORE N An **interested** party or group of people is affected by or involved in a particular event or situation.

interesting /ˈɪntrɪstɪŋ/. ADJ If you find something **interesting**, it attracts you or holds your attention. *It was interesting to be in a different environment. ...a very interesting book.* ◆**interestingly** ADV *Interestingly enough, a few weeks later, Benjamin remarried.*

interfere /ˌɪntəˈfɪə/ **interferes, interfering, interfered.** [1] VERB If someone **interferes** in a situation, they get involved in it although it does not concern them and their involvement is not wanted. *I wish everyone would stop interfering. ...interfering neighbours.* [2] VERB If something **interferes with** a situation, process, or activity, it has a damaging effect on it. *Drug problems frequently interfered with his work.*

interference /ˌɪntəˈfɪərəns/. [1] N-U **Interference** is the act of interfering in something. *...interference in the republic's internal affairs.* [2] N-U When there is **interference**, a radio signal is affected by other radio waves so that it cannot be received properly.

interim /ˈɪntərɪm/. [1] ADJ BEFORE N **Interim** describes things that are intended to be used until something permanent is arranged or established. *...an interim government. ...an interim report.* [2] PHRASE **In the interim** means until a particular thing happens.

interior /ɪnˈtɪəriə/ **interiors.** [1] N-C The **interior** of something is the inside or central part of it. *...the boat's interior. ...the interior walls.* [2] N-SING The **interior** of a country or continent is the central area of it. *...a 5-day hike into the interior.*

interlude /ˈɪntəluːd/ **interludes.** N-C An **interlude** is a short period of time during which an activity or event stops. *...a happy interlude in the Kents' life.*

intermediary /ˌɪntəˈmiːdiəri/ **intermediaries.** N-C An **intermediary** is a person who passes messages between two people or groups.

intermediate /ˌɪntəˈmiːdiət/. [1] ADJ An **intermediate** stage or level is one that occurs between two other stages or levels. [2] ADJ **Intermediate** students are no longer beginners, but are not yet advanced.

interminable /ɪnˈtɜːmɪnəbəl/. ADJ If you describe something as **interminable**, you think it lasts too long and wish it would stop. *...an interminable wait of six hours.* ◆**interminably** ADV *The programme droned interminably on.*

intermittent /ˌɪntəˈmɪtənt/. ADJ Something that is **intermittent** happens occasionally rather than continuously. *...three hours of intermittent rain.* ◆**intermittently** ADV *The talks went on intermittently for years.*

intern /ɪnˈtɜːn/ **interns, interning, interned.** VERB If someone **is interned**, they are put in prison for political reasons. *He was interned as an enemy alien.*

internal /ɪnˈtɜːnəl/. [1] ADJ BEFORE N You use **internal** to describe things that exist or happen inside a place or organization. *The country stepped up internal security. ...the internal mail box.* [2] ADJ BEFORE N **Internal** is used to describe things that exist or happen inside a particular person, object, or place. *The internal bleeding had been massive.* ◆**internally** ADV *The herb has gentle calming effect when taken internally.*

international /ˌɪntəˈnæʃənəl/. ADJ **International** means between or involving different countries. *...an international embargo on arms supplies to Iraq.* ◆**internationally** ADV *...internationally recognised certificates.*

Internet /ˈɪntənet/. N-PROPER **The Internet** is the worldwide network of computer links which allows computer users to connect with computers all over the world.

interpersonal /ˌɪntəˈpɜːsənəl/. ADJ BEFORE N **Interpersonal** means relating to relationships between people. *...interpersonal relationships.*

interpret /ɪnˈtɜːprɪt/ **interprets, interpreting, interpreted.** [1] VERB If you **interpret** something in a particular way, you decide that this is its meaning or significance. *The judge has to interpret the law as it's been passed.* [2] VERB If you **interpret** what someone is saying, you translate it immediately into another language. *The chambermaid spoke little English, so her husband came with her to interpret.* ◆**interpreter, interpreters** N-C *Interpreters and translators are employed by local authorities.*

interpretation /ɪnˌtɜːprɪˈteɪʃən/ **interpretations.** [1] N-VAR An **interpretation** of something is an opinion of what it means. *The Labour Party put a different interpretation on the figures.* [2] N-VAR A performer's **interpretation** of a piece of music or a dance is the particular way in which they choose to perform it.

interrogate /ɪnˈtɜːrəgeɪt/ **interrogates, interrogating, interrogated.** VERB If someone, especially a police officer, **interrogates** someone, they question him or her for a long time, in order to get information from them. ◆**interrogation, interrogations** N-VAR *Two men have died under interrogation.*

interrogative /ˌɪntəˈrɒgətɪv/ **interrogatives.** N-SING A clause that is in the **interrogative** is in the form of a question.

interrupt /ˌɪntəˈrʌpt/ **interrupts, interrupting, interrupted.** [1] VERB If you **interrupt** someone who is speaking, you say or do something that causes them to stop. *They interrupted me every time I said tried to say something... Turkin tapped him on the shoulder. 'Sorry to interrupt, Colonel.'* ◆**interruption, interruptions** N-VAR *The sudden interruption stopped Beryl in mid-flow. ...the constant interruptions of delivery men.* [2] VERB If someone or something **interrupts** a process or activity, they stop it for a period of time. *He has rightly interrupted his holiday in Spain.* ◆**interruption** N-VAR *...interruptions in the supply of food.*

intersection /ˌɪntəˈsekʃən/ **intersections.** N-C An **intersection** is a place where roads cross each other. ...*a busy highway intersection.*

interspersed /ˌɪntəˈspɜːst/. ADJ If one group of things are **interspersed with** or **among** another, the second things occur between or among the first things. ...*a series of bursts of gunfire, interspersed with single shots.*

interstate /ˈɪntəsteɪt/. [1] ADJ BEFORE N **Interstate** means between states, especially the states of the United States. *The action prohibits interstate movement of certain fruits.* [2] N-C In the US, an **interstate** is a major road linking states.

interval /ˈɪntəvəl/ **intervals.** [1] N-C The **interval** between two events or dates is the period of time between them. *There was a long interval of silence.* [2] N-C An **interval** during a play, concert, or game is a short break between two of the parts.

PHRASES ● If something happens **at intervals**, it happens several times with gaps or pauses in between. ● If things are placed **at** particular **intervals**, there are spaces of a particular size between them. *Several barriers marked the road at intervals of about a mile.*

intervene /ˌɪntəˈviːn/ **intervenes, intervening, intervened.** VERB If you **intervene** in a situation, you become involved in it and try to change it. *The situation calmed down when police intervened.* ◆**intervention** /ˌɪntəˈvenʃən/ **interventions** N-VAR ...*its intervention in the internal affairs of many countries.*

intervening /ˌɪntəˈviːnɪŋ/. [1] ADJ BEFORE N An **intervening** period of time is one which separates two events or points in time. *I had spent the intervening time in London.* [2] ADJ BEFORE N An **intervening** object or area comes between two other objects or areas.

interview /ˈɪntəvjuː/ **interviews, interviewing, interviewed.** [1] VERB & N-C When an employer **interviews** you, or when you go for an **interview**, he or she asks you questions in order to find out whether you are suitable for a job. *He was interviewed for a management job.* ...*an interview for a job as a TV researcher.* [2] VERB & N-C When a journalist **interviews** someone such as a famous person, they ask them a series of questions. This type of discussion is also called an **interview**. ...*an interview with American Vogue fashion editor Carlyn Cerf.* ◆**interviewer, interviewers** N-C ...*a wealthy figure much sought after by TV interviewers.*

interviewee /ˌɪntəvjuːˈiː/ **interviewees.** N-C An **interviewee** is a person who is being interviewed.

intestine /ɪnˈtestɪn/ **intestines.** N-C Your **intestines** are the tubes in your body through which food from your stomach passes. ◆**intestinal** /ɪnˈtestɪnəl/ ADJ BEFORE N ...*the intestinal wall.*

intimacy /ˈɪntɪməsi/. N-U When there is **intimacy** between people, they have a close relationship. ...*a few precious moments of intimacy with a lover.*

intimate, intimates, intimating, intimated; adjective and noun /ˈɪntɪmət/, verb /ˈɪntɪmeɪt/. [1] ADJ If two people have an **intimate** friendship, they are very good friends. ◆**intimately**

ADV *He did not feel he had got to know them intimately.* [2] ADJ You use **intimate** to describe an occasion or the atmosphere of a place that you like because it is quiet and pleasant, and seems suitable for close conversations between friends. ...*an intimate candlelit dinner for two.* [3] ADJ To be **intimate** with someone means to have a sexual relationship with them. ...*their intimate moments with their boyfriends.* ◆**intimately** ADV *Get to know yourself and your partner intimately.* [4] ADJ If you have an **intimate** knowledge of something, you know it in great detail. ...*their intimate knowledge of the motor industry.* ◆**intimately** ADV ...*musicians whose work she knew intimately.* [5] VERB If you **intimate** that something is the case, you say it in an indirect way; FORMAL. *He went on to intimate that he was indeed contemplating a shake-up of the company.*

intimidate /ɪnˈtɪmɪdeɪt/ **intimidates, intimidating, intimidated.** VERB To **intimidate** someone means to frighten them, sometimes as a deliberate way of making them do something. ...*attempts to intimidate people into voting for the governing party.* ◆**intimidated** ADJ *Women can come in here and not feel intimidated.* ◆**intimidating** ADJ ...*the intimidating atmosphere that greeted them as they took to the pitch.* ◆**intimidation** N-U ...*an aggressive campaign of intimidation against supporters of the prime minister.*

into /ɪntuː/. In addition to the uses shown below, **into** is used with verbs of movement, such as 'walk into', and in phrasal verbs such as 'enter into'. [1] PREP To go **into** a place or object means to go inside it. *I have no idea how he got into Iraq... He got into bed... Put them into a dish... All olives were packed into jars by hand.* [2] PREP If you bump or crash **into** something, you hit it accidentally. *The Belgian hit the kerb and smashed into the barriers.* [3] PREP If you get **into** a piece of clothing, you put it on. *She could change into a different outfit.* [4] PREP To get **into** a particular state means to start being in that state. *That caused him to get into trouble... I slid into a depression.* [5] PREP If something changes **into** something else, it then has a new form, shape, or nature. ...*to turn a nasty episode into a little bit of a joke.* [6] PREP An investigation **into** a subject or event is concerned with that subject or event. ...*research into Aids.* [7] PREP You use **into** with many verbs to do with persuading someone to do something. *Gerome tried to talk her into taking an apartment in Paris.* [8] PREP If something is cut or split **into** a number of pieces or sections, it is divided so that it becomes several smaller pieces or sections. *Sixteen teams are taking part, divided into four groups.*

intolerable /ɪnˈtɒlərəbəl/. ADJ If something is **intolerable**, it is so bad that no one can accept it. *This would put intolerable pressure on them.* ◆**intolerably** ADV ...*intolerably cramped conditions for the actors.*

intolerant /ɪnˈtɒlərənt/. ADJ If you describe someone as **intolerant**, you mean that they do not accept behaviour and opinions that are different from their own; used showing disapproval. *He was intolerant of both suggestions* *and criticisms.* ◆**intolerance** N-U ...*his intolerance of any opinion other than his own.*

intractable /ɪnˈtræktəbəl/. **1** ADJ **Intractable** people are very difficult to influence or control; FORMAL. *He protested, but Wright was intractable.* **2** ADJ **Intractable** problems are very difficult to deal with; FORMAL. *A final settlement of the intractable Afghan conflict is still far off.*

intransigent /ɪnˈtrænsɪdʒənt/. ADJ If you describe someone as **intransigent**, you mean that they refuse to change their behaviour or opinions; used showing disapproval. FORMAL. *They put pressure on the Government to change its intransigent stance.* ◆**intransigence** N-U *He often appeared angry and frustrated by the intransigence of both sides.*

intransitive /ɪnˈtrænsɪtɪv/. ADJ An **intransitive** verb does not have an object.

intravenous /ˌɪntrəˈviːnəs/. ADJ **Intravenous** foods or drugs are given to sick people through their veins, rather than their mouths. ...*an intravenous drip.* ◆**intravenously** ADV *Premature babies have to be fed intravenously.*

intrepid /ɪnˈtrepɪd/. ADJ An **intrepid** person acts bravely, ignoring difficulties and danger. ...*an intrepid space traveller.*

intricate /ˈɪntrɪkət/. ADJ Something that is **intricate** has many small parts or details. ...*intricate patterns and motifs.* ◆**intricately** ADV ...*intricately carved sculptures.* ◆**intricacy** N-U ...*the rich intricacy of traditional Japanese porcelain.*

intrigue, **intrigues**, **intriguing**, **intrigued**. **1** N-VAR /ˈɪntriːɡ/ **Intrigue** is the making of secret plans that are intended to harm or deceive other people. ...*the plots and intrigues in the novel.* **2** VERB /ɪnˈtriːɡ/ If something **intrigues** you, you are fascinated by it and curious about it. *She had hesitated, even though the job intrigued her.* ◆**intrigued** ADJ *I would be intrigued to hear others' views.*

intriguing /ɪnˈtriːɡɪŋ/. ADJ If you describe someone or something as **intriguing**, you mean that they interest you and you are curious about them. *This intriguing book is both thoughtful and informative.* ◆**intriguingly** ADV *The results are intriguingly different each time.*

intrinsic /ɪnˈtrɪnsɪk/. ADJ If something has **intrinsic** value or **intrinsic** interest, it is valuable or interesting because of its basic nature or character, and not because of its connection with other things; FORMAL. *Diamonds have little intrinsic value.* ◆**intrinsically** ADV *Sometimes I wonder if people are intrinsically evil.*

introduce /ˌɪntrəˈdjuːs, AM -ˈduːs/ **introduces**, **introducing**, **introduced**. **1** VERB To **introduce** something means to cause it to enter a place or exist in a system for the first time. *The word 'Pagoda' was introduced to Europe by the 17th century Portuguese.* **2** VERB If you **introduce** someone to something, you cause them to learn about it or to have their first experience of it. *He introduced her to both literature and drugs.* **3** VERB If you **introduce** one person to another, or if you **introduce** two people, you tell them each other's names, so that they can get to know each other. *Let me introduce myself.* **4** VERB The person who **introduces** a television or radio programme speaks at the beginning of it, and often between the different

items in it, in order to explain what the programme or the items are about. *'Health Matters' is introduced by Dick Oliver.*

introduction /ˌɪntrəˈdʌkʃən/ **introductions**. **1** N-U The **introduction** of something into a place or system is the occasion when it enters the place or exists in the system for the first time. ...*the introduction of student loans.* **2** N-SING Someone's **introduction** to something is the occasion when they experience it for the first time. *His introduction to public life came as an office-holder in a trade union.* **3** N-VAR When you make an **introduction**, you tell two people each other's names so that they can get to know each other. **4** N-C The **introduction** to a book or talk comes at the beginning and tells you what the rest of the book or talk is about. **5** N-C If you refer to a book as an **introduction** to a particular subject, you mean that it explains the basic facts about it.

introductory /ˌɪntrəˈdʌktəri/. **1** ADJ An **introductory** remark, book, or course is intended to give you a general idea of a particular subject, often before more detailed information is given. **2** ADJ An **introductory** offer or price on a new product is something such as a free gift or a low price that is meant to attract new customers.

intrude /ɪnˈtruːd/ **intrudes**, **intruding**, **intruded**. VERB If you say that someone or something **is intruding** into a particular place or situation, you mean that they are not wanted or welcome there. *I hope I'm not intruding... Personal feelings cannot be allowed to intrude.*

intruder /ɪnˈtruːdə/ **intruders**. N-C An **intruder** is a person who enters a place without permission.

intrusion /ɪnˈtruːʒən/ **intrusions**. N-VAR If you describe something as an **intrusion**, you mean that it disturbs you when you are in a private place or in a private situation. *I hope you don't mind this intrusion.* ...*intrusion into private grief.*

intrusive /ɪnˈtruːsɪv/. ADJ Something that is **intrusive** disturbs your mood or your life in an unwelcome way. *Staff are courteous but never intrusive.*

intuition /ˌɪntjuˈɪʃən, AM -tuː-/ **intuitions**. N-VAR Your **intuitions** are feelings you have that something is true even when you have no evidence or proof of it. *Her intuition was telling her that something was wrong.*

intuitive /ɪnˈtjuːɪtɪv, AM -ˈtuː-/. ADJ If you have an **intuitive** idea or feeling about something, you feel that it is true although you have no evidence or proof of it. ◆**intuitively** ADV *He seemed to know intuitively that I must be missing my mother.*

inundate /ˈɪnʌndeɪt/ **inundates**, **inundating**, **inundated**. VERB If you **are inundated** with letters or demands, you receive so many that you cannot deal with them all. *They have inundated me with fan letters.*

invade /ɪnˈveɪd/ **invades**, **invading**, **invaded**. **1** VERB To **invade** a country means to enter it by force with an army. ◆**invader**, **invaders**. N-C ...*action against a foreign invader.* **2** VERB If you say that people or animals **invade** a place, you mean that they enter it in large numbers, often in a way that is unpleasant or difficult to deal with. *Every so often the kitchen would be invaded by ants.*

invalid, invalids. [1] N-C /'ɪnvəlɪd/ An **invalid** is someone who is very ill or disabled and needs to be cared for by someone else. [2] ADJ /ɪn'vælɪd/ If an action, procedure, or document is **invalid**, it cannot be accepted, because it breaks the law or some official rule. *The trial was stopped and the results declared invalid.* [3] ADJ An **invalid** argument or conclusion is wrong because it is based on a mistake.

invaluable /ɪn'væljəbəl/. ADJ If you describe something as **invaluable**, you mean that it is extremely useful. *I was able to gain invaluable experience over that year.*

invariably /ɪn'veəriəbli/. ADV If something **invariably** happens or is **invariably** true, it always happens or is always true. *They almost invariably get it wrong.*

invasion /ɪn'veɪʒən/ **invasions.** [1] N-VAR If there is an **invasion** of a country, a foreign army enters it by force. *...the Roman invasion of Britain.* [2] N-U If you refer to the arrival of a large number of people or things as an **invasion**, you are emphasizing that they are unpleasant or difficult to deal with. *...this year's annual invasion of flies.* [3] N-VAR If you describe an action as an **invasion**, you disapprove of it because it affects someone or something in a way that is not desirable. *Is reading a child's diary always a gross invasion of privacy?*

invasive /ɪn'veɪsɪv/. ADJ You use **invasive** to describe something undesirable which spreads very quickly and which is very difficult to stop from spreading. *They found invasive cancer during a routine examination.*

invent /ɪn'vent/ **invents, inventing, invented.** [1] VERB If you **invent** something, you are the first person to think of it or make it. *He invented the first electric clock.* ◆**inventor, inventors.** N-C *Alexander Graham Bell, the inventor of the telephone.* [2] VERB If you **invent** a story or excuse, you try to persuade people that it is true when it is not. *I must invent something I can tell my mother.*

invention /ɪn'venʃən/ **inventions.** [1] N-C An **invention** is a machine or system that has been invented by someone. *The spinning wheel was a Chinese invention.* [2] N-VAR If you refer to someone's account of something as an **invention**, you mean that it is not true and that they have made it up. *The story was certainly a favourite one, but it was undoubtedly pure invention.* [3] N-U **Invention** is the act of inventing something that has never been made or used before. *...the invention of the wheel.*

inventive /ɪn'ventɪv/. ADJ An **inventive** person is good at inventing things or has clever and original ideas. *She inspired me to be more inventive with my own cooking.* ◆**inventiveness** N-U *He has surprised us before with his inventiveness.*

inventory /'ɪnvəntri, AM -tɔːri/ **inventories.** [1] N-C An **inventory** is a written list of all the objects in a place. [2] N-C An **inventory** is a supply or stock of something; AMERICAN.

invert /ɪn'vɜːt/ **inverts, inverting, inverted.** [1] VERB If you **invert** something, you turn it upside down or back to front; FORMAL. *Invert the cake onto a cooling rack. ...a black inverted triangle.* [2] VERB If you **invert** something, you change it to its opposite; FORMAL. *...inverted moral values.*

in,verted 'commas. N-PL In British English, **inverted commas** are the punctuation marks (' ') or (" ") which are used in writing to show where speech or a quotation begins and ends. The usual American term is **quotation marks**.

invest /ɪn'vest/ **invests, investing, invested.** [1] VERB If you **invest** in something, or if you **invest** a sum of money, you use your money in a way that you hope will increase its value, for example by buying shares or property. *He wants advice on how to invest the money.* ◆**investor, investors.** N-C *It is likely that investors will face losses.* [2] VERB If you **invest** in something useful, you buy it because it will help you to do something more efficiently or more cheaply. *The company has invested a six-figure sum in an electronic order-control system.* [3] VERB If you **invest** time or energy in something, you spend a lot of time or energy on something that you consider to be useful or likely to be successful. *I would rather invest time in Rebecca than in the kitchen.* [4] VERB To **invest** someone with rights or responsibilities means to give them those rights or responsibilities legally or officially; FORMAL. *The constitution had invested him with certain powers.*

investigate /ɪn'vestɪgeɪt/ **investigates, investigating, investigated.** VERB If someone, especially an official, **investigates** an event or allegation, they try to find out what happened or what is the truth. *Police are still investigating how the accident happened.* ◆**investigation, investigations.** N-VAR *He is currently under investigation for corruption.*

investigative /ɪn'vestɪgətɪv, AM -geɪt-/. ADJ **Investigative** work, especially journalism, involves investigating things. *...an investigative reporter.*

investigator /ɪn'vestɪgeɪtə/ **investigators.** N-C An **investigator** is someone who investigates things, especially as part of their job.

investment /ɪn'vesmənt/ **investments.** [1] N-U **Investment** is the activity of investing money. *The government must introduce tax incentives to encourage investment.* [2] N-C An **investment** is an amount of money that you invest, or the thing that you invest in. *...an average rate of return of 8% on your investments. ...people's desire to buy a house as an investment.* [3] N-C If you describe something you buy as an **investment**, you mean that it will be useful, especially because it will help you to do a task more cheaply or efficiently. *A small-screen portable TV can be a good investment.*

invigorating /ɪn'vɪgəreɪtɪŋ/. ADJ Something that is **invigorating** makes you feel refreshed and more energetic. *...the invigorating northern air.*

invincible /ɪn'vɪnsɪbəl/. ADJ If you describe an army or a sports team as **invincible**, you believe that they cannot be defeated. *He knocked out the seemingly invincible Mike Tyson.*

invisible /ɪnˈvɪzɪbəl/. **1** ADJ If something is **invisible**, you cannot see it, because it is hidden or because it is very small or faint. *The belt is invisible even under the thinnest garments.* ♦ **invisibly** ADV *A thin coil of smoke rose almost invisibly.* **2** ADJ If you say that a particular problem or situation is **invisible**, you are complaining that it is being ignored. *The problems of the poor are largely invisible.* ♦ **invisibility** N-U *...the invisibility of women and women's concerns in society.*

invitation /ˌɪnvɪˈteɪʃən/ **invitations**. **1** N-C An **invitation** is a written or spoken request to come to an event such as a party or a meeting. *The Syrians have not yet accepted an invitation to attend.* **2** N-C An **invitation** is the card or paper on which an invitation is written or printed. **3** N-SING If you believe that someone's action is likely to have a particular result, especially a bad one, you can refer to the action as an **invitation** to that result. *Don't leave your shopping on the back seat of your car – it's an open invitation to a thief.*

invite, **invites**, **inviting**, **invited**. **1** VERB /ɪnˈvaɪt/ If you **invite** someone to something such as a party or a meal, you ask them to come to it. *I invited her in for a coffee... Barron invited her to accompany him to the races.* **2** VERB If you **are invited** to do something, you are formally asked to do it. *Managers will be invited to apply for a management buy-out.* **3** VERB If something you say or do **invites** trouble or criticism, it makes trouble or criticism more likely. *Their refusal to compromise will inevitably invite more criticism from the UN.* **4** N-C /ˈɪnvaɪt/ An **invite** is an invitation to something such as a party or a meal; INFORMAL.

inviting /ɪnˈvaɪtɪŋ/. ADJ If you say that something is **inviting**, you mean it has qualities that attract you. *The February air was soft, cool, and inviting.* ♦ **invitingly** ADV *The waters of the tropics are invitingly clear.*

invoice /ˈɪnvɔɪs/ **invoices**. **1** N-C An **invoice** is an official document that lists goods or services that you have received and says how much money you owe for them. **2** VERB If you **invoice** someone, you send them an invoice.

invoke /ɪnˈvəʊk/ **invokes**, **invoking**, **invoked**. **1** VERB If you **invoke** a law, you state that you are taking a particular action because that law allows or obliges you to. *The judge invoked an international law that protects refugees.* **2** VERB If you **invoke** something such as a saying or a famous person, you refer to them in order to support what you are saying. *Adam Smith's name is frequently invoked by the promoters of such policies.*

involuntary /ɪnˈvɒləntri/. ADJ If you make an **involuntary** movement or sound, you make it suddenly and without intending to. *Another surge of pain in my ankle caused me to give an involuntary shudder.* ♦ **involuntarily** /ˈɪnvɒləntrəli/. ADV *His left eyelid twitched involuntarily.*

involve /ɪnˈvɒlv/ **involves**, **involving**, **involved**. **1** VERB If an activity **involves** something, that thing is a necessary part of it. *Nicky's job as a public relations director involves spending quite a lot of time with other people.* **2** VERB If a situation or activity **involves** someone, they are taking part in it. *...a riot involving a hundred inmates.* **3** VERB If you **involve** someone in something, you get them to take part in it. *Before too long he started involving me in the more confidential aspects of the job.*

involved /ɪnˈvɒlvd/. **1** ADJ AFTER LINK-V If you are **involved** in a situation or activity, you are taking part in it or have a strong connection with it. *...an organisation for people involved in agriculture.* **2** ADJ AFTER LINK-V The things **involved** in something such as a job or system are the necessary parts of it. *Let's take a look at some of the figures involved.* **3** ADJ If a situation or activity is **involved**, it is very complicated. **4** ADJ AFTER LINK-V If one person is **involved** with another, especially someone they are not married to, they are having a close relationship. *He became romantically involved with a married woman.*

involvement /ɪnˈvɒlvmənt/. **1** N-U Your **involvement** in something is the fact that you are taking part in it. *She disliked his involvement with the group.* **2** N-U **Involvement** is the enthusiasm that you feel when you care deeply about something. *Ben has always felt a deep involvement with animals.*

inward /ˈɪnwəd/ **inwards**. **1** ADJ BEFORE N Your **inward** thoughts or feelings are the ones that you do not express or show to other people. *I sighed with inward relief.* ♦ **inwardly** ADV *He pretended to be mildly affronted, but inwardly he was pleased.* **2** ADJ BEFORE N An **inward** movement is one towards the inside or centre of something. *...a sharp, inward breath like a gasp.*

inwards /ˈɪnwədz/. The form **inward** is also used. In American English, **inward** is more usual. ADV If something moves or faces **inwards**, it moves or faces towards the inside or centre of something. *She pressed back against the door until it swung inwards.*

iodine /ˈaɪədiːn, AM -daɪn/. N-U **Iodine** is a dark-coloured substance often used in medicine and photography.

IQ /ˌaɪ ˈkjuː/ **IQs**. N-VAR Your **IQ** is your level of intelligence, as indicated by a special test. *His IQ is above average.*

irate /aɪˈreɪt/. ADJ If someone is **irate**, they are very angry about something. *Bob was very irate, shouting and swearing about the flight delay.*

iris /ˈaɪərɪs/ **irises**. **1** N-C The **iris** is the round coloured part of a person's eye. **2** N-C An **iris** is a tall plant with long leaves and large purple, yellow, or white flowers.

iron /ˈaɪən/ **irons**, **ironing**, **ironed**. **1** N-U **Iron** is an element which usually takes the form of a hard, dark-grey metal. *...the huge, iron gate.* **2** ADJ BEFORE N You can use **iron** to describe the character or behaviour of someone who is very firm in their decisions and actions, or who can control their feelings well. *...a man of icy nerve and iron will.* **3** N-C An **iron** is an electrical device with a flat metal base. You heat it until the base is hot, then rub it over clothes to remove creases. **4** VERB If you **iron** clothes, you remove the creases from them using an iron. ...*a freshly ironed shirt.* ♦**ironing** N-U *I managed to get all the ironing done.* **5** See also **cast-iron.**

▶ **iron out.** PHR-VERB If you **iron out** difficulties, you resolve them and bring them to an end.

ironic /aɪˈrɒnɪk/. **1** ADJ When you make an **ironic** remark, you say something that you do not mean, as a joke. *People used to call me Mr Popularity at high school, but they were being ironic.* ♦**ironically** ADV *'A very good year for women!' she said ironically.* **2** ADJ An **ironic** situation is strange or amusing because it is the opposite of what you expect. *It seems ironic that it takes a recession to improve choice.* ♦**ironically** ADV *Ironically, for a man who hated war, he would have made a superb war cameraman.*

irony /ˈaɪrəni/ **ironies.** **1** N-U **Irony** is a form of humour which involves saying things that you do not mean. *There seemed to be no hint of irony in his voice.* **2** N-VAR The **irony** of a situation is an aspect of it which is strange or amusing, because it is just the opposite of what you expect. *The irony is this document may become more available in the US than in Britain where it was commissioned.*

irrational /ɪˈræʃənəl/. ADJ **Irrational** feelings or behaviour are not based on logical reasons or thinking. *...an irrational fear of science.* ♦**irrationally** ADV *He is in a disturbed state of mind and could act irrationally.* ♦**irrationality** N-U *His cruelty increased, as did his irrationality.*

irreconcilable /ˌɪrekəˈnsaɪləbəl/. **1** ADJ If two things such as opinions or proposals are **irreconcilable**, they are so different from each other that it is not possible to have them both; FORMAL. *These old concepts are irreconcilable with modern life.* **2** ADJ An **irreconcilable** disagreement is so serious that it cannot be settled; FORMAL. *...an irreconcilable clash of personalities.*

irregular /ɪˈreɡjʊlə/. **1** ADJ If events or actions occur at **irregular** intervals, the periods of time between them are of different lengths. *She was taken to hospital suffering from an irregular heartbeat... He worked irregular hours.* ♦**irregularly** ADV *Epileptic fits occur irregularly and without warning.* ♦**irregularity** /ɪˌreɡjʊˈlærɪti/ **irregularities** N-VAR *...a dangerous irregularity in her heartbeat.* **2** ADJ Something that is **irregular** is not smooth or straight, or does not form a regular pattern. *The paint was drying in irregular patches.* ♦**irregularly** ADV *...the irregularly shaped lake.* **3** ADJ **Irregular** behaviour is dishonest or not in accordance with the normal rules. *...the minister accused of irregular business practices.* ♦**irregularity** N-VAR *...alleged financial irregularities.*

irrelevant /ɪˈreləvənt/. ADJ If you say that something is **irrelevant**, you mean that it is not important to or not connected with the present situation or discussion. *He either ignored questions or gave irrelevant answers... He said politics has become increasingly irrelevant to most Americans.* ♦**irrelevance** N-SING *Whether the book shocks or not is an irrelevance.*

irresistible /ˌɪrɪˈzɪstɪbəl/. **1** ADJ If your wish to do something is **irresistible**, it is so powerful that you cannot prevent yourself doing it. *He experienced an irresistible urge to yawn.* ♦**irresistibly** ADV *He found himself being irresistibly drawn to Gail's home.* **2** ADJ If you describe something or someone as **irresistible**, you mean that they are so good or attractive that you cannot stop yourself from liking them or wanting them. *What is it about Tim that you find so irresistible?* ♦**irresistibly** ADV *She had a charm which men found irresistibly attractive.*

irrespective /ˌɪrɪˈspektɪv/. PREP If something is true or happens **irrespective** of other things, those things do not affect it; FORMAL. *This service should be available to everybody, irrespective of whether they can afford it.*

irresponsible /ˌɪrɪˈspɒnsɪbəl/. ADJ If you describe someone as **irresponsible**, you are criticizing them because they do things without properly considering their possible consequences. *Many people have an irresponsible attitude towards marriage.* ♦**irresponsibly** ADV *They have behaved irresponsibly.* ♦**irresponsibility** N-U *She was greatly embarrassed by her son's irresponsibility.*

irreverent /ɪˈrevərənt/. ADJ If you describe someone as **irreverent**, you mean that they do not show respect for people or things that are generally respected. ♦**irreverence** N-U *...his irreverence for authority.*

irreversible /ˌɪrɪˈvɜːsɪbəl/. ADJ If a change is **irreversible**, things cannot be changed back to the way they were before. *She could suffer irreversible brain damage.*

irrevocable /ɪˈrevəkəbəl/. ADJ Actions or decisions that are **irrevocable** cannot be stopped or changed; FORMAL. *His mother's death was an irrevocable loss.* ♦**irrevocably** ADV *My relationships with friends have been irrevocably altered.*

irrigate /ˈɪrɪɡeɪt/ **irrigates, irrigating, irrigated.** VERB To **irrigate** land means to supply it with water in order to help crops to grow. *None of the water from Lake Powell is used to irrigate the area.* ♦**irrigation** N-U *...a sophisticated irrigation system.*

irritable /ˈɪrɪtəbəl/. ADJ If you are **irritable**, you are easily annoyed. *He had missed his dinner, and grew irritable.* ♦**irritably** ADV *'Why are you whispering?' he asked irritably.* ♦**irritability** N-U *She showed no sign of irritability.*

irritant /ˈɪrɪtənt/ **irritants.** **1** N-C If you describe something as an **irritant**, you mean that it keeps annoying you; FORMAL. *He said the issue was not a major irritant.* **2** N-C An **irritant** is a substance which causes a part of your body to become tender, sore, or itchy; FORMAL.

irritate /ˈɪrɪteɪt/ **irritates, irritating, irritated.** **1** VERB If something **irritates** you, it keeps annoying you. *Her high voice really irritated Maria.* ♦**irritated** ADJ *Her teacher is getting irritated with her.* ● See note at **angry.** ♦**irritating** ADJ *...the irritating habit of interrupting.* ♦**irritatingly** ADV *They can be irritatingly indecisive at times.* **2** VERB If something **irritates** a part of your body, it causes it to itch or be sore. *Skin is easily irritated.*

irritation 332

irritation /ˌɪrɪˈteɪʃən/ **irritations.** [1] N-U **Irritation** is a feeling of annoyance. *He tried not to let his irritation show.* [2] N-C An **irritation** is something that keeps annoying you. *He describes the tourists as an irritation.* [3] N-U **Irritation** in your skin or eyes is a feeling of soreness or itching there.

is /ɪz/. **Is** is the third person singular of the present tense of **be**.

Islam /ˈɪzlɑːm, AM ɪsˈlɑːm/. N-U **Islam** is the religion of the Muslims, which teaches that there is only one God and that Mohammed is His prophet. ♦ **Islamic** /ɪzˈlæmɪk/ ADJ *...Islamic law.*

island /ˈaɪlənd/ **islands.** N-C An **island** is a piece of land that is completely surrounded by water. *...the picturesque island of Gozo... We spent a day on Caldey Island.*

islander /ˈaɪləndə/ **islanders.** N-C **Islanders** are people who live on an island.

isle /aɪl/ **isles.** N-C **Isle** is used in the names of some islands. *...the Isle of Man.*

isn't /ˈɪzənt/. In informal English, **is not** is usually said or written as **isn't**.

isolate /ˈaɪsəleɪt/ **isolates, isolating, isolated.** VERB To **isolate** someone or something means to make them become separate from other people or things of the same kind, either physically or socially. *We can use genetic engineering techniques to isolate the gene.* ♦ **isolated** ADJ *They are finding themselves increasingly isolated within the teaching profession.* ♦ **isolation** N-U *...the public isolation of the Prime Minister.*

isolated /ˈaɪsəleɪtɪd/. [1] ADJ An **isolated** place is a long way away from large towns and is difficult to reach. *Aubrey's family's farm is very isolated.* [2] ADJ BEFORE N An **isolated** example is an example of something that is not very common. *...an isolated case of cheating.*

isolation /ˌaɪsəˈleɪʃən/. [1] PHRASE If someone does something **in isolation**, they do it without other people being present or without their help. [2] See also **isolate**.

issue /ˈɪsjuː, ˈɪʃuː/ **issues, issuing, issued.** [1] N-C An **issue** is an important subject that people are arguing about or discussing. *...the issue of human rights... Is it right for the Church to express a view on political issues?* [2] N-SING If something is **the issue**, it is the thing you consider to be the most important part of a situation or discussion. *I was earning a lot of money, but that was not the issue... She avoided the issue.* [3] N-C An **issue** of a magazine or newspaper is a particular edition of it. *...the latest issue of the Lancet.* [4] VERB If someone **issues** a statement, they make it formally or publicly. *His kidnappers issued a second threat to kill him.* [5] VERB If you **are issued with** something, it is officially given to you. *Staff will be issued with new grey-and-yellow designer uniforms.* [6] VERB When something such as a liquid, sound, or smell **issues from** something, it comes out of that thing; FORMAL. [7] PHRASE The question or point **at issue** is the question or point that is being argued about or discussed. *The point at issue is who controls the company.*

it /ɪt/ **It** is used as the subject of a verb or as the object of a verb or preposition. [1] PRON You use **it** to refer to an object, animal, or other thing that has already been mentioned, or to a situation that you have just described. *He saw the grey Land-Rover down the by-pass. It was more than a hundred yards from him... Antonia will not be jealous, or if she is, she will not show it.* [2] PRON You use **it** before certain nouns, adjectives, and verbs to introduce your feelings or point of view about a situation. *It was nice to see Steve again... It's a pity you never got married, Sarah.* [3] PRON You use **it** in passive clauses which report a situation or event. *It has been said that stress causes cancer.* [4] PRON You use **it** to say what the time, day, or date is. *It's three o'clock in the morning... It was a Monday, so she was at home.* [5] PRON You use **it** to describe the weather, the light, or the temperature. *It was very wet and windy... It's getting dark. Let's go inside.* [6] PRON You use **it** when you are telling someone who you are, or asking them who they are. 'Who is it?' he called... Hello Freddy, it's only me, Maxine.* [7] PREP When you are emphasizing or drawing attention to something, you can put that thing immediately after **it** and a form of the verb 'be'. *It's my father they're accusing.*

italic /ɪˈtælɪk/ **italics.** N-PL & ADJ **Italics** or **italic** letters are letters which slope to the right. They can be used to emphasize particular words. The examples in this dictionary are printed in italics.

itch /ɪtʃ/ **itches, itching, itched.** [1] VERB & N-C If you **itch**, or if a part of your body **itches**, you have an unpleasant feeling on your skin, called an **itch**, that makes you want to scratch. *His body regularly itched from head to toe... Scratch my back – I've got an itch.* ♦ **itching** N-U *The itching is caused by contact with irritant material.* ♦ **itchy** ADJ *...itchy, sore eyes.* [2] VERB & N-SING If you **are itching** to do something, or if you have an **itch** to do something, you are very eager or impatient to do it; INFORMAL. *I was itching to get involved. ...an itch to be rich.*

it'd /ˈɪtəd/. **It'd** is a spoken form of 'it had', especially when 'had' is an auxiliary. **It'd** is also a spoken form of 'it would'. *It'd just started... It'd be fun.*

item /ˈaɪtəm/ **items.** [1] N-C An **item** is one of a collection or list of objects. *The most valuable item on show will be a Picasso drawing.* [2] N-C An **item** is one of a list of things for someone to do, deal with, or talk about. *The other item on the agenda is the tour.*

itinerary /aɪˈtɪnərəri, AM -eri/ **itineraries.** N-C An **itinerary** is a plan of a journey, including the route and the places that will be visited. *The next place on our itinerary was Silistra.*

it'll /ˈɪtəl/. **It'll** is a spoken form of 'it will'.

its /ɪts/. DET You use **its** to indicate that something belongs or relates to a thing, place, or animal that has just been mentioned or whose identity is known. *The British Labor Party concludes its annual conference today.*

Do not confuse **its** and **it's**. **It's** is short for 'it is' or 'it has'. *The horse raised its head... It's hot in here... It's stopped raining.*

it's /ɪts/. **It's** is a spoken form of 'it is' or 'it has', especially when 'has' is an auxiliary verb. ● See note at **its**.

itself /ɪt'sɛlf/. [1] PRON **Itself** is used as the object of a verb or preposition when it refers to something that is the same thing as the subject of the verb. *The body rebuilds itself while we sleep... The back part of the chair bends double and folds into itself.* [2] PRON You use **itself** to emphasize the thing you are referring to. *I think life itself is a learning process.* [3] PRON If you say that someone is, for example, politeness **itself** or kindness **itself**, you are emphasizing they are extremely polite or extremely kind. *I was never really happy there, although the people were kindness itself.*

I've /aɪv/. **I've** is the usual spoken form of 'I have', especially when 'have' is an auxiliary. *I think I've got a stomach ulcer.*

ivory /'aɪvəri/. N-U **Ivory** is a valuable type of bone, which forms the tusks of an elephant. *...intricate ivory carvings. ...the international ban on the sale of ivory.*

ivy /'aɪvi/. N-U **Ivy** is an evergreen plant that grows up walls or along the ground.

J j

jab /dʒæb/ **jabs, jabbing, jabbed.** [1] VERB If you **jab** something, you push it with a quick sudden movement. *A needle was jabbed into the baby's arm... He jabbed at me with his forefinger.* [2] N-C A **jab** is an injection to prevent illness; INFORMAL, BRITISH.

jack /dʒæk/ **jacks, jacking, jacked.** [1] N-C A **jack** is a device for lifting a heavy object such as a car off the ground. [2] N-C A **jack** is a playing card whose value is between a ten and a queen.

▸ **jack up.** PHR-VERB If you say that someone or something **jacks up** a price or amount, you mean the price or amount rises to an unreasonable level; INFORMAL. *Inflation has jacked up the rate of unemployment.*

jacket /'dʒækɪt/ **jackets.** [1] N-C A **jacket** is a short coat. ● See also **lifejacket**. [2] N-C The **jacket** of a book is the paper cover that protects it. [3] N-C In American English, the **jacket** of a record is the cover in which it is kept. The usual British word is **sleeve**.

jackpot /'dʒækpɒt/ **jackpots.** N-C A **jackpot** is a large sum of money which is the most valuable prize in a game or lottery.

Jacuzzi /dʒə'ku:zi/ **Jacuzzis.** N-C A **Jacuzzi** is a large round bath which is fitted with a special device that makes the water bubble. **Jacuzzi** is a trademark.

jade /dʒeɪd/. N-U **Jade** is a hard green type of stone used for making jewellery and ornaments.

jaded /'dʒeɪdɪd/. ADJ If you are **jaded**, you have no enthusiasm because you are tired and bored.

jagged /'dʒægɪd/. ADJ Something that is **jagged** has a rough uneven shape or edge with lots of sharp points. *...a piece of iron with jagged edges.*

jail /dʒeɪl/ **jails, jailing, jailed.** [1] N-VAR A **jail** is a place where criminals are kept in order to punish them. *He served six months in jail for theft.* [2] VERB If someone **is jailed**, they are put in jail.

jam /dʒæm/ **jams, jamming, jammed.** [1] N-VAR **Jam** is a food that you spread on bread, made by cooking fruit with a large amount of sugar. The usual American word is **jelly**. [2] VERB If you **jam** something somewhere, you push it there roughly. *Pete jammed his hands into his pockets.* [3] VERB If something

jams, or if you **jam** it, it becomes fixed in one position and cannot move freely or work properly. *The second time he fired, his gun jammed... A rope jammed the boat's propeller.* [4] VERB To **jam** a radio or electronic signal means to interfere with it and prevent it from being received or heard clearly. ♦ **jamming** N-U *The plane is used for electronic jamming and radar detection.* [5] VERB If a lot of people **jam** a place, or if they **jam** into it, they are packed tightly together and can hardly move. *Thousands of people jammed the streets.* ♦ **jammed** ADJ *The stadium was jammed.* [6] N-C If there is a **jam** on a road, there are so many vehicles there that they cannot move. [7] N-SING If you are **in a jam**, you are in a very difficult situation; INFORMAL.

jangle /'dʒæŋgəl/ **jangles, jangling, jangled.** VERB & N-C If metal objects **jangle**, or if they **are jangled**, they strike against each other and make an unpleasant ringing noise, called a **jangle**. *...her jangling bracelets.*

janitor /'dʒænɪtə/ **janitors.** N-C A **janitor** is a person whose job is to look after a building; AMERICAN.

January /'dʒænjəri, AM -jʊeri/. N-U **January** is the first month of the year in the Western calendar.

jar /dʒɑ:/ **jars, jarring, jarred.** [1] N-C A **jar** is a glass container with a lid, used for storing food. *...two jars of filter coffee.* [2] VERB If something **jars** on you, you find it unpleasant or shocking. *...televised congressional hearings that jarred the nation's faith in the presidency.* ♦ **jarring** ADJ *Dore's comments strike a jarring note.* [3] VERB If an object **jars**, or if something **jars** it, the object moves with a fairly hard shaking movement. *The impact jarred his arm.*

jargon /'dʒɑ:gən/. N-U **Jargon** consists of words and expressions that are used in special or technical ways by particular groups of people, often making the language difficult to understand. *...600,000 C2 males (marketing jargon for skilled manual workers).*

jaunty /'dʒɔ:nti/ **jauntier, jauntiest.** ADJ If you describe someone or something as **jaunty**, you mean that they are full of confidence and energy. *Tremain's novel is altogether jauntier.* ♦ **jauntily** ADV *He walked jauntily into the cafe.*

javelin /'dʒævlɪn/ **javelins.** ① N-C A **javelin** is a long spear that is thrown in sports competitions. ② N-SING You can refer to the competition in which the javelin is thrown as **the javelin**.

jaw /dʒɔː/ **jaws.** ① N-C Your **jaw** is the part of your face below your mouth. ② N-C A person's or animal's **jaws** or **jawbones** are the two bones in their head which their teeth are attached to.

jazz /dʒæz/. N-U **Jazz** is a style of music invented by black American musicians in the early part of the twentieth century. It has very strong rhythms and the musicians often improvise.

jealous /'dʒeləs/. ① ADJ If someone is **jealous**, they feel angry or bitter because they think that another person is trying to take a lover, friend, or possession away from them. *She got insanely jealous and there was a terrible fight.* ◆**jealously** ADV *The formula is jealously guarded.* ② ADJ If you are **jealous** of another person's possessions or qualities, you feel angry or bitter because you do not have them. *You're jealous because the record company rejected your idea.* ◆**jealously** ADV *Gloria eyed them jealously.*

jealousy /'dʒeləsi/ **jealousies.** N-VAR **Jealousy** is the feeling of anger or bitterness which someone has when they think that another person is trying to take a lover, friend, or possession away from them, or when they wish that they could have the qualities or possessions that another person has. *We all know the sharp stab of jealousy as an old girlfriend comes back into view... Her beauty causes envy and jealousy.*

jeans /dʒiːnz/. N-PL **Jeans** are casual trousers that are usually made of strong blue denim. You can also say **a pair of jeans**.

Jeep /dʒiːp/ **Jeeps.** N-C A **Jeep** is a small four-wheeled vehicle that can travel over rough ground. **Jeep** is a trademark.

jeer /dʒɪə/ **jeers, jeering, jeered.** ① VERB If people **jeer** at someone, they show that they do not respect them by saying rude and insulting things to them. *His motorcade was jeered by angry residents.* ◆**jeering** N-U *There was constant jeering and interruption from the floor.* ② N-C **Jeers** are the rude and insulting things which people shout in order to show that they do not respect someone.

jell /dʒel/. See **gel**.

jelly /'dʒeli/ **jellies.** ① N-VAR **Jelly** is a transparent food made from gelatine, fruit juice, and sugar, which is eaten as a dessert; BRITISH. ② N-VAR **Jelly** is a food that you spread on bread, made by cooking fruit with a large amount of sugar. The British word is **jam**.

jeopardize (BR also **jeopardise**) /'dʒepədaɪz/ **jeopardizes, jeopardizing, jeopardized.** VERB If someone or something **jeopardizes** a situation or activity, they do something that may destroy it or cause it to fail. *The talks may still be jeopardized by disputes.*

jeopardy /'dʒepədi/. PHRASE If someone or something is **in jeopardy**, they are in a dangerous situation. *A series of setbacks have put the whole project in jeopardy.*

jerk /dʒɜːk/ **jerks, jerking, jerked.** VERB & N-C If you **jerk** something or someone, or if they **jerk** in a particular direction, they move a short distance very suddenly and quickly. A **jerk** is a short sudden movement. *...jerking his head in my direction... The car jerked to a halt... He indicated the bedroom with a jerk of his head.*

jerky /'dʒɜːki/ **jerkier, jerkiest.** ADJ **Jerky** movements are very sudden and abrupt and do not flow smoothly. *Mr Griffin made a jerky gesture.* ◆**jerkily** ADV *... he moved jerkily towards the car.*

jersey /'dʒɜːzi/ **jerseys.** ① N-C A **jersey** is a knitted piece of clothing that covers the upper part of your body and your arms; DATED. ② N-U **Jersey** is a knitted fabric used especially to make women's clothing. *... a black jersey top.*

jet /dʒet/ **jets, jetting, jetted.** ① N-C A **jet** is an aeroplane that is powered by jet engines. ② VERB If you **jet** somewhere, you travel there in a fast aeroplane. *...jetting off on a two-week holiday.* ③ N-C A **jet** of liquid or gas is a strong, fast, thin stream of it. *A jet of water.*

jet 'engine, jet engines. N-C A **jet engine** works by pushing hot air and gases out at the back.

'jet lag (also **jetlag**). N-U If you are suffering from **jetlag**, you feel tired and slightly confused after a long journey by aeroplane.

jettison /'dʒetɪsən/ **jettisons, jettisoning, jettisoned.** VERB If someone **jettisons** something that is not needed, they throw it away or get rid of it. *The crew jettisoned excess fuel... The Government seems to have jettisoned the plan.*

jetty /'dʒeti/ **jetties.** N-C A **jetty** is a wide stone wall or wooden platform where boats stop to let people get on and off, or to load or unload goods.

Jew /dʒuː/ **Jews.** N-C A **Jew** is a person who believes in and practises the religion of Judaism.

jewel /'dʒuːəl/ **jewels.** N-C A **jewel** is a precious stone used to decorate valuable things such as rings or necklaces. *...precious jewels.*

jeweller (AM **jeweler**) /'dʒuːələ/ **jewellers.** ① N-C A **jeweller** is a person who makes, sells, and repairs jewellery and watches. ② N-C A **jeweller** or a **jeweller's** is a shop where jewellery and watches are made, sold, and repaired.

jewellery (AM **jewelry**) /'dʒuːəlri/. N-U **Jewellery** consists of ornaments that people wear such as rings and bracelets.

Jewish /'dʒuːɪʃ/. ADJ **Jewish** means belonging or relating to the religion of Judaism or to Jews. *...the Jewish festival of the Passover.*

jibe (also **gibe**) /dʒaɪb/ **jibes, jibing, jibed.** VERB & N-C If someone **jibes**, they say something rude and insulting, called a **jibe**, which is intended to make another person look foolish; WRITTEN. *'No doubt he'll give me the chance to fight him again,' he jibed. ...a cheap jibe about his loss of hair.*

jig /dʒɪg/ **jigs, jigging, jigged.** ① N-C A **jig** is a lively folk dance. ② VERB To **jig** means to dance or move energetically, especially bouncing up and down. *You didn't just jig about by yourself, I mean you danced properly.*

jigsaw /'dʒɪgsɔː/ **jigsaws.** N-C A **jigsaw** or **jig-saw puzzle** is a picture on cardboard or wood that has been cut up into odd shapes and which has to be put back together again.

jingle /'dʒɪŋgəl/ **jingles, jingling, jingled.** [1] VERB When something **jingles**, or when you **jingle** it, it makes a gentle ringing noise, like small bells. *Brian put his hands in his pockets and jingled some change.* [2] N-C A **jingle** is a short and simple tune, often with words, used to advertise a product on radio or television.

jitters /'dʒɪtəz/. N-PL If someone has the **jitters**, they are very nervous or uncertain about something; INFORMAL. *He cut interest rates in December to calm the jitters of investors.*

jittery /'dʒɪtəri/. ADJ If someone is **jittery**, they are very nervous or uncertain about something; INFORMAL. *International investors have become jittery about the country's economy.*

job /dʒɒb/ **jobs.** [1] N-C A **job** is the work that someone does to earn money. *Once I'm in America I can get a job... Thousands have lost their jobs.* [2] N-C A **job** is a particular task. *He was given the job of tending the fire... Save major painting jobs for the spring or summer.* [3] N-C The **job** of a particular person or thing is their duty or function. *Their main job is to preserve health rather than treat illness.* [4] N-SING If you say, for example, that someone has done a good **job** or an excellent **job** of something, you mean that they have done it well. *He didn't do a very good job of explaining the sequence of events... You could make a better job of running a restaurant.*

jobless /'dʒɒbləs/. ADJ Someone who is **jobless** does not have a job, but would like one. *...the number of jobless people.*

jockey /'dʒɒki/ **jockeys.** N-C A **jockey** is someone who rides a horse in a race.

jog /dʒɒg/ **jogs, jogging, jogged.** [1] VERB & N-C If you **jog**, or if you go for a **jog**, you run slowly, often as a form of exercise. *I got up early the next morning to jog.* ♦**jogger, joggers** N-C *The park was full of joggers.* ♦**jogging** N-U *Many students are keeping fit through jogging.* [2] VERB If you **jog** something, you push or bump it slightly so that it moves. *Avoid jogging the camera.*

join /dʒɔɪn/ **joins, joining, joined.** [1] VERB If one person or vehicle **joins** another, they move or go to the same place. *His wife and children moved to join him in their new home.* [2] VERB If you **join** an organization, you become a member of it. *He joined the Army five years ago.* [3] VERB & PHR-VERB If you **join** an activity, or if you **join in** an activity, you become involved in it. *The Egyptian Prime Minister has now joined the debate... Tens of thousands of people are expected to join in the celebrations.* [4] VERB If you **join** a queue, you go and stand at the end of it. [5] VERB If two roads or rivers **join**, or if one **joins** the other, they meet or come together at a particular point. *Do you know the highway to Tulsa? The airport road joins it.* [6] VERB & N-C To **join** two things means to fasten, fix, or connect them together. A **join** is a place where two things are fastened or fixed together. *'And' is frequently used to join two sentences. ...the conjunctiva, the skin* which joins the eye to the lid... *The car parks are joined by a footpath... Don't worry – you can't see the join.* [7] to **join forces**: see **force**. • to **join the ranks**: see **rank**.

▸ **join in.** See **join** 3.
▸ **join up.** [1] PHR-VERB If someone **joins up**, they become a member of the armed forces; BRITISH. [2] PHR-VERB If a person or thing **joins up** with another, or if the two of them **join up**, they move or go to the same place. *Hawkins joined up with Mick in Malaga, and the two went touring.*

joint /dʒɔɪnt/ **joints.** [1] ADJ BEFORE N **Joint** means shared by or belonging to two or more people. *...a joint bank account.* ♦**jointly** ADV *The Port Authority is an agency jointly run by New York and New Jersey.* [2] N-C A **joint** is a part of your body such as your elbow or knee where two bones meet and are able to move together. *Her joints ache if she exercises.* [3] N-C A **joint** is a place where two things meet or are fixed together. *...weeds that grow in joints between paving blocks.*

joke /dʒəʊk/ **jokes, joking, joked.** [1] VERB & N-C If you **joke**, or if you make a **joke**, you say something amusing or tell a funny story to make people laugh. *She would joke about her appearance... Don't get defensive, Charlie. I was only joking... He made a joke about poisoning his wife.* ♦**joker, jokers** N-C *He is, by nature, a joker.* [2] N-SING If you say that someone or something is a **joke**, you mean that they are ridiculous and not worthy of respect; INFORMAL. *The decision was a joke.*

PHRASES • You say **you're joking** or **you must be joking** to someone when they have just told you something very surprising or difficult to believe; SPOKEN. *One hundred and forty quid for a pair of headphones, you've got to be joking!* • If you describe a situation as **no joke**, you are emphasizing that it is very difficult or unpleasant; INFORMAL. *Two hours on a bus is no joke.*

joker /'dʒəʊkə/ **jokers.** N-C The **joker** in a pack of cards is the card which does not belong to any of the four suits.

jolly /'dʒɒli/ **jollier, jolliest.** [1] ADJ A **jolly** person is happy and cheerful. [2] ADJ A **jolly** event is lively and enjoyable. *I was looking forward to a jolly party.* [3] ADV You can use **jolly** to emphasize something; BRITISH, DATED. *It was jolly hard work.*

jolt /dʒəʊlt/ **jolts, jolting, jolted.** [1] VERB & N-C If something **jolts**, or if something else **jolts** it, it moves suddenly and violently. A **jolt** is a sudden violent movement. *The train lolted into motion... Three people fell overboard when their raft was jolted... One tiny jolt could worsen her injuries.* [2] VERB & N-C If you **are jolted** by something, it gives you an unpleasant surprise or shock. A **jolt** is a surprise or shock like this. *...scandals that have jolted the Catholic church... An uproar from the hallway jolted her awake... The campaign came at a time when America needed such a jolt.*

jostle /'dʒɒsəl/ **jostles, jostling, jostled.** [1] VERB If people **jostle** you, they bump against you or push you in a crowd. *I was jostled by a group of fans... Journalists and photographers* *jostled for space... Chee jostled his way through the crowd.* [2] VERB If people or things **are jostling for** something such as attention or a reward, they are competing with each other for it. *...the contenders who have been jostling for the top job.*

jot /dʒɒt/ **jots, jotting, jotted.**
▶ **jot down.** PHR-VERB If you **jot** something **down**, you write it down in the form of a short informal note. *Keep a pad handy to jot down queries.*

journal /ˈdʒɜːnəl/ **journals.** [1] N-C A **journal** is a magazine or newspaper, especially one that deals with a specialized subject. *...scientific journals.* [2] N-C A **journal** is an account which you write of your daily activities. *On the plane he wrote in his journal.*

journalist /ˈdʒɜːnəlɪst/ **journalists.** N-C A **journalist** is a person whose job is to collect news, and write about it in newspapers or magazines or talk about it on television or radio. *...a journalist with the Financial Times.* ♦ **journalism** N-U *He began a career in journalism.*

journey /ˈdʒɜːni/ **journeys, journeying, journeyed.** VERB & N-C If you **journey** somewhere, or if you make a **journey** there, you travel there. *Naomi journeyed to the United States for the first time... During the journey to the airport he was pursued by photographers.*

joy /dʒɔɪ/ **joys.** [1] N-U **Joy** is a feeling of great happiness. *Salter shouted with joy. ...tears of joy.* [2] N-C Something that is a **joy** makes you feel happy or gives you great pleasure. *That is one of the joys of being a chef.*

joyful /ˈdʒɔɪfʊl/ [1] ADJ Something that is **joyful** causes happiness and pleasure. *A wedding is a joyful celebration of love.* [2] ADJ A **joyful** person is extremely happy. *...crowds of joyful students.* ♦ **joyfully** ADV *They greeted him joyfully.*

joyous /ˈdʒɔɪəs/ ADJ **Joyous** means extremely happy; LITERARY. *...a joyous celebration of life.* ♦ **joyously** ADV *Sarah accepted joyously.*

joyrider /ˈdʒɔɪraɪdə/ **joyriders.** N-C A **joyrider** is someone who steals a car and drives it around at high speed for fun.

jubilant /ˈdʒuːbɪlənt/ ADJ If you are **jubilant**, you feel extremely happy because of a success. *I was jubilant at how things had gone.*

jubilee /ˈdʒuːbɪliː/ **jubilees.** N-C A **jubilee** is a special anniversary of an event, especially the 25th or 50th anniversary. *...Queen Victoria's jubilee.*

Judaism /ˈdʒuːdeɪɪzəm/ N-U **Judaism** is the religion of the Jewish people, which is based on the Old Testament of the Bible and the laws written in the Talmud.

judge /dʒʌdʒ/ **judges, judging, judged.** [1] N-C A **judge** is the person in a court of law who decides how the law should be applied, for example how criminals should be punished. *Tomorrow they will be brought before a judge... Judge Mr Justice Schiemann jailed him for life.* [2] VERB If you **judge** someone or something, you form an opinion about them based on the evidence or information that you have. *It will take a few more years to judge the impact of these ideas... He judged that this was the moment to say what had to be said... Judging by the opinion polls, he seems to be succeeding.*

[3] N-C If someone is a good **judge** of something, they can understand it and make decisions about it. *I think I am a reasonable judge of character.* [4] N-C A **judge** is a person who chooses the winner of a competition. *A panel of judges is now selecting the finalists.* [5] VERB If you **judge** a competition, you decide who the winner is. *Entrants will be judged in two age categories.*

judgment (BR also **judgement**) /ˈdʒʌdʒmənt/ **judgments.** [1] N-C A **judgment** is an opinion that you have or express after thinking carefully about something. *In your judgment, what has changed over the past few years?... I don't really want to make any judgments on the decisions they made.* [2] N-U **Judgment** is the ability to make sensible guesses about a situation or sensible decisions about what to do. *I think you have made a bad error of judgement... I have never had anyone question my judgement.* [3] N-VAR A **judgment** is a decision made by a judge or by a court of law. *The industry was awaiting a judgment from the European Court... The Appeal Court reserved judgment on Mrs Thornton's second appeal.*

judicial /dʒuːˈdɪʃl/ ADJ BEFORE N **Judicial** means relating to the legal system and to judgements made in a court of law. *...an independent judicial inquiry.*

judiciary /dʒuːˈdɪʃəri, AM -ʃieri/ N-SING The **judiciary** is the branch of authority in a country which is concerned with justice and the legal system; FORMAL.

judicious /dʒuːˈdɪʃəs/ ADJ An action or decision that is **judicious** shows very good judgment and sense; FORMAL. *The President authorizes the judicious use of military force to protect our citizens.* ♦ **judiciously** ADV *Fertilisers should be used judiciously.*

judo /ˈdʒuːdəʊ/ N-U **Judo** is a sport or martial art in which two people wrestle and try to throw each other to the ground.

jug /dʒʌɡ/ **jugs.** N-C A **jug** is a container which is used for holding and pouring liquids.

juggle /ˈdʒʌɡl/ **juggles, juggling, juggled.** [1] VERB If you have to **juggle** lots of different things, you have difficulty fitting them all in so that you have enough time for all of them. *Mike juggled the demands of a family of 11 with a career as a TV reporter.* [2] VERB If you **juggle**, you entertain people by throwing things into the air, catching each one and throwing it up again so that there are several of them in the air at the same time. *Soon she was juggling five eggs.* ♦ **juggling** N-U *...mime and juggling.* ♦ **juggler, jugglers** N-C *...a professional juggler.*

juice /dʒuːs/ **juices.** [1] N-VAR **Juice** is the liquid that can be obtained from a fruit. *...a glass of fresh orange juice.* [2] N-PL The **juices** of a joint of meat are the liquid that comes out of it when you cook it. [3] N-PL The **juices** in your stomach are the fluids that help you to digest food.

juicy /ˈdʒuːsi/ **juicier, juiciest.** [1] ADJ If food is **juicy**, it has a lot of juice in it and is very enjoyable to eat. *...a thick, juicy steak.* [2] ADJ You can describe information as **juicy** if it is exciting or scandalous; INFORMAL.

July /dʒʊˈlaɪ/. N-U **July** is the seventh month of the year.

jumble /ˈdʒʌmbəl/ **jumbles, jumbling, jumbled**. [1] N-C A **jumble** of things is a lot of different things that are all mixed together in a disorganized or confused way. ...*a jumble of huge boulders. ...a meaningless jumble of words.* [2] VERB & PHR-VERB If you **jumble** things, or if they **jumble**, they become mixed together so that things are untidy or not in the correct order. To **jumble up** means the same as to **jumble**. *They jumble together shampoos, toys, chocolate, clothes, electronic goods and hair slides. ...wires jumbled up, tied together, all painted black.* [3] N-U **Jumble** is old or unwanted things that people give away to charity; BRITISH.

jumbo /ˈdʒʌmbəʊ/ **jumbos**. [1] ADJ BEFORE N **Jumbo** is used to describe things which are very large. ...*a jumbo box of tissues.* [2] N-C A **jumbo** or a **jumbo jet** is a very large jet aeroplane.

jump /dʒʌmp/ **jumps, jumping, jumped**. [1] VERB & N-C When you **jump**, you bend your knees, push against the ground with your feet, and move quickly upwards into the air. This action is called a **jump**. *He jumped 25 feet from his third floor flat to avoid the man. ...the longest jumps by a man.* [2] VERB If you **jump** something such as a fence, you move quickly up and through the air over or across it. [3] VERB If you **jump** somewhere, you move there quickly and suddenly. *She jumped to her feet and ran downstairs.* [4] VERB If something makes you **jump**, it makes you make a sudden movement because you are frightened or surprised. [5] VERB & N-C If an amount or level **jumps**, or if there is a **jump** in an amount or level, it suddenly increases by a large amount in a short time. *Sales jumped from $94 million to over $101 million. ...a big jump in energy conservation.* [6] VERB If you **jump at** an offer or opportunity, you accept it quickly and eagerly. *Members of the public would jump at the chance to become part owners.*

jumper /ˈdʒʌmpə/ **jumpers**. N-C In British English, a **jumper** is a knitted piece of clothing which covers the upper part of your body and your arms. The American word is **sweater**.

junction /ˈdʒʌŋkʃən/ **junctions**. N-C A **junction** is a place where roads or railway lines join. The usual American word is **intersection**. *Follow the road to a junction and turn left.*

June /dʒuːn/. N-U **June** is the sixth month of the year.

jungle /ˈdʒʌŋgəl/ **jungles**. [1] N-VAR A **jungle** is a forest in a tropical country where tall trees and other plants grow very closely together. [2] N-SING If you describe a situation as a **jungle**, you dislike it because it is complicated and difficult to get what you want from it. ...*a jungle of complex rules.*

junior /ˈdʒuːniə/ **juniors**. [1] N-C & ADJ A **junior**, or a **junior** official or employee, holds a lower-ranking position in an organization or profession. ...*a junior minister attached to the prime minister's office.* [2] N-SING If you are

someone's **junior**, you are younger than they are. ...*a woman 12 years his junior.*

junk /dʒʌŋk/. [1] N-U **Junk** is an amount of old or useless things; INFORMAL. *What are you going to do with all that junk, Larry?* [2] N-U You can use **junk** to refer to old and second-hand goods that people buy and collect.

junkie /ˈdʒʌŋki/ **junkies**. N-C A **junkie** is a drug addict; INFORMAL.

junta /ˈdʒʌntə, ˈhʊntə/ **juntas**. N-C If you refer to a government as a **junta**, you mean that it is a military dictatorship that has taken power by force.

jurisdiction /ˌdʒʊərɪsˈdɪkʃən/. N-U **Jurisdiction** is the power that a court of law or an official has to carry out legal judgements or enforce laws. *The British police have no jurisdiction over foreign bank accounts.*

juror /ˈdʒʊərə/ **jurors**. N-C A **juror** is a member of a jury.

jury /ˈdʒʊəri/ **juries**. When it is in the singular, **jury** can take the singular or plural form of the verb. [1] N-C In a court of law, the **jury** is the group of people who have been chosen from the general public to listen to the facts about a crime and to decide whether the person accused is guilty or not. *The jury found him guilty of murder.* [2] N-C A **jury** is a group of people who choose the winner of a competition.

just 1 adverb uses and phrases

just /dʒʌst/. [1] ADV If you say that something has **just** happened, you mean that it happened a very short time ago. *I've just bought a new house.* [2] ADV If you say that you are **just** doing something, you mean that you will finish doing it very soon. If you say that you are **just** going to do something, you mean that you will do it very soon. *I'm just making the sauce for the cauliflower... I'm just going to walk down the lane now and post some letters.* [3] ADV You use **just** to indicate that something is no more important, interesting, or difficult, for example, than you say it is. *It's just a suggestion... I am sure you can tell just by looking at me that I am all right.* [4] ADV You use **just** to indicate that what you are saying is the case, but only by a very small degree or amount. *Her hand was just visible.* [5] ADV You use **just** to emphasize the word or phrase following it, in order to express feelings such as annoyance, admiration, or certainty. *She just won't relax... I don't see the point in it really. It's just stupid.* [6] ADV You use **just** with instructions, polite requests, or statements of intention, to make your request or statement seem less difficult than someone might think. *I'm just going to ask you a bit more about your father's business.* [7] ADV You use **just** to mean exactly, when you are specifying something precisely or asking for precise information. *There are no statistics about just how many people won't vote... My arm hurts too, just here.*

PHRASES ● You use **just about** to indicate that what you are talking about is so close to being the case that it can be regarded as being the case. *What does she read? Just about everything.* ● You use **it's just that** when you are making a complaint, suggestion, or excuse, so that the person you are talking to will not get annoyed with you. *Your hair is all right; it's just that you need a haircut.* ● **just now**: see **now**. ● **only just**: see **only**.

just 2 adjective use

just /dʒʌst/. ADJ If you describe a situation, action, or idea as **just**, you mean that it is right or acceptable according to particular moral principles; FORMAL. *...a just cause.* ◆**justly** ADV *They were not treated justly in the past.*

justice /'dʒʌstɪs/ **justices.** [1] N-U **Justice** is fairness in the way that people are treated. *He only wants freedom, justice and equality.* [2] N-U The **justice** of a claim, argument, or cause is its quality of being reasonable and right. *We must win people round to the justice of our cause.* [3] N-U **Justice** is the system that a country uses in order to deal with people who break the law. *A lawyer is part of the machinery of justice.* [4] N-C In American English, a **justice** is a judge. [5] N-TITLE **Justice** is used before the names of judges. *...Mr Justice Hutchison.*

PHRASES ● If a criminal **is brought to justice**, he or she is tried in a court of law and punished. *They demanded that those responsible be brought to justice.* ● If you **do justice** to someone or something, you deal with them properly and completely. *No one article can ever do justice to the topic of fraud.*

justifiable /ˌdʒʌstɪ'faɪəbəl/. ADJ An opinion, action, or fact that is **justifiable** is acceptable or correct because there is a good reason for it. *When, if ever, is it morally justifiable to allow a patient to die?* ◆**justifiably** ADV *He was justifiably proud of his achievements.*

justification /ˌdʒʌstɪfɪ'keɪʃən/ **justifications.** N-VAR A **justification** for something is an acceptable reason or explanation for it. *To me the only justification for a zoo is educational.*

justified /'dʒʌstɪfaɪd/. ADJ AFTER LINK-V An action that is **justified** is reasonable and acceptable. *In my opinion, the decision was wholly justified... He's absolutely justified in resigning.*

justify /'dʒʌstɪfaɪ/ **justifies, justifying, justified.** VERB If someone or something **justifies** a particular decision, action, or idea, they show or prove that it is reasonable or necessary. *No argument can justify a war.*

jut /dʒʌt/ **juts, jutting, jutted.** VERB If something **juts** out, it sticks out above or beyond a surface. *The northern end of the island juts out like a long, thin finger into the sea.*

juvenile /'dʒuːvənaɪl/ **juveniles.** [1] N-C A **juvenile** is a child or young person who is not yet old enough to be regarded as an adult; FORMAL. [2] ADJ If you describe someone's behaviour as **juvenile**, you are critical of it because you think that it is silly or immature.

juxtapose /ˌdʒʌkstə'pəʊz/ **juxtaposes, juxtaposing, juxtaposed.** VERB If you **juxtapose** two contrasting objects, images, or ideas, you put them together, so that the differences between them are strongly emphasized; FORMAL. *Interviews with politicians were juxtaposed with news items of quite astonishing triviality.* ◆**juxtaposition** /ˌdʒʌkstəpə'zɪʃən/ **juxtapositions** N-VAR *...the juxtaposition of sound and picture.*

K k

k /keɪ/. **K** or **k** is used to represent the number 1000, especially when referring to sums of money. For example, £10k means £10,000.

kangaroo /ˌkæŋgə'ruː/ **kangaroos.** N-C A **kangaroo** is a large Australian animal. Female kangaroos carry their babies in a pouch on their stomachs.

karate /kə'rɑːti/. N-U **Karate** is a martial art in which people fight using their hands, elbows, feet, and legs.

keel /kiːl/ **keels, keeling, keeled.** PHRASE If something is **on an even keel**, it is working or progressing smoothly and steadily, without any sudden changes. *There is enough income to keep the family on an even keel.*
▸ **keel over.** PHR-VERB If something or someone **keels over**, they fall over sideways. *She must have had a heart attack and keeled over.*

keen /kiːn/ **keener, keenest.** [1] ADJ AFTER LINK-V If you are **keen** on doing something, you very much want to do it. If you are **keen** that something should happen, you very much want it to happen. *He's keen on a return match... She's still keen to keep in touch.* ◆**keenness** N-U *...the country's keenness for better economic ties with China.* [2] ADJ AFTER LINK-V If you are **keen on** something or someone, you like them a lot. ◆**keenness** N-U *...his keenness for the arts.* [3] ADJ If someone is

keen, they have a lot of enthusiasm for a particular activity or for things in general. *I've interviewed him and he seems very keen... She was a keen amateur photographer.* ◆**keenness** N-U *...the keenness of the students.* [4] ADJ A **keen** sense or emotion is very strong and intense. *...his keen sense of loyalty.* ◆**keenly** ADV *Charles listened keenly... The 1994 contest should be very keenly fought.*

keep /kiːp/ **keeps, keeping, kept.** [1] LINK-VERB If someone **is kept** in a particular state, they remain in it. *The noise kept him awake... To keep warm they burnt wood... Their main aim is to help keep youngsters out of trouble.* [2] VERB If you **keep** in a particular position or place, or if someone **keeps** you in it, you remain in it. *Keep away from the doors while the train is moving... He kept his head down... Doctors will keep her in hospital for at least another week.* [3] VERB & PHR-VERB If you **keep** doing something, or if you **keep on** doing it, you do it repeatedly or continue to do it. You can also say that someone or something **keeps** you doing something. *I keep forgetting it's December... Did he give up or keep on trying?* [4] VERB **Keep** is used with some nouns to indicate that someone does something for a period of time or continues to do it. For example, if you **keep a grip** on something, you continue to hold or control it. *One of them would keep a look-out on the road.* [5] VERB If you **keep** something that you possess, you continue to have it. If you **keep** it somewhere, you store it there. *The city of Leningrad was deciding whether to keep its name... I thought it easier to contact us, keep this card handy... She kept her money under the mattress.* [6] VERB When you **keep** something such as a promise or an appointment, you do what you said you would do. [7] VERB If you **keep** a record of a series of events, you make a written record of it. *Eleanor began to keep a diary.* [8] VERB If someone or something **keeps** you from doing something, they prevent you from doing it. *What can you do to keep it from happening again?* [9] VERB If someone or something **keeps** you, they delay you and make you arrive somewhere later than expected. *'What kept you?'—'I went in the wrong direction'.* [10] VERB If you **keep** something from someone, you do not tell them about it. *He had to keep the truth from his children.* [11] N-SING Your **keep** is the cost of food and other things that you need every day. *Ray will earn his keep on local farms while studying.*

PHRASES ● If you **keep yourself to yourself**, or if you **keep to yourself**, you stay on your own most of the time and do not mix with other people. ● If something is **in keeping** with something else, it is appropriate or suitable according to that thing. *In keeping with tradition, the Emperor and Empress did not attend the ceremony.* ● To **keep your head**: see **head**.

▶ **keep down.** PHR-VERB If you **keep** the amount of something **down**, you do not let it increase. *Administration costs were kept down to just £460.*

▶ **keep on.** [1] See **keep** 3. [2] PHR-VERB If you **keep** someone **on**, you continue to employ them, for example after other employees have lost their jobs. *A skeleton staff of 20 is being kept on.*

▶ **keep to.** [1] PHR-VERB If you **keep** to a rule, plan, or agreement, you do exactly what you are expected or supposed to do. *You've got to keep to the speed limit.* [2] PHR-VERB If you **keep** something **to** a particular number or quantity, you limit it to that number or quantity. *Keep costs to a minimum.*

▶ **keep up.** [1] PHR-VERB If someone or something **keeps up** with another person or thing, the first one moves or progresses as fast as the second. *She shook her head and started to walk on. He kept up with her... Things are changing so fast, it's hard to keep up.* [2] PHR-VERB If you **keep** something **up**, you continue to do it or provide it. *They can no longer keep up the repayments.*

kennel /'kenəl/ **kennels.** [1] N-C A **kennel** is a small hut made for a dog to sleep in. [2] N-C **Kennels** or a **kennels** or a **kennel** is a place where dogs are bred and trained, or looked after when their owners are away.

kept /kept/. **Kept** is the past tense and past participle of **keep**.

kerb (AM **curb**) /kɜːb/ **kerbs.** N-C The **kerb** is the raised edge of a pavement which separates it from the road.

kerosene /'kerəsiːn/. N-U In American English, **kerosene** is a strong-smelling liquid which is used as a fuel in heaters, lamps, and engines. The usual British word is **paraffin**.

kettle /'ketəl/ **kettles.** N-C A **kettle** is a covered container that you use for boiling water.

key /kiː/ **keys.** [1] N-C A **key** is a specially shaped piece of metal which fits in a lock and is turned in order to open it. [2] N-C The **keys** of a typewriter or computer keyboard are the buttons that you press in order to operate it. [3] N-C The **keys** of a piano or organ are the black and white bars that you press in order to play it. [4] N-C In music, a **key** is a scale of musical notes that starts at one particular note. *...the key of A minor.* [5] ADJ BEFORE N The **key** person or thing in a group is the most important one. *Education is likely to be a key issue in the next election.* [6] N-C The **key** to a desirable situation or result is the way in which it can be achieved. *Diet and relaxation are two important keys to good health.*

keyboard /'kiːbɔːd/ **keyboards.** [1] N-C The **keyboard** of a typewriter or computer is the set of keys that you press in order to operate it. [2] N-C The **keyboard** of a piano or organ is the set of black and white keys that you press in order to play it.

kg. kg is an abbreviation for 'kilogram'.

khaki /'kɑːki, AM 'kæki/. ADJ Something that is **khaki** is greenish brown.

kick /kık/ **kicks, kicking, kicked.** [1] VERB & N-C If you **kick** someone or something, or if you give them a **kick**, you hit them with your foot. *She kicked him in the leg... He escaped by kicking open the window... He suffered a kick to the knee.* [2] VERB If you **kick**, you move your legs with very quick, small, and forceful movements, once or repeatedly. *They were struggling and kicking... The baby beamed and kicked her legs.* [3] PHRASE If someone **gets a kick** from something, they get pleasure or excitement from it; INFORMAL. [4] VERB If you **kick** a bad habit, you stop having that habit; INFORMAL. *I've kicked cigarettes.*

▶ **kick off.** PHR-VERB If an event, game, series, or discussion **kicks off**, or if someone **kicks** it **off**, it begins; INFORMAL. *The Mayor kicked off the party.*

▶ **kick out.** PHR-VERB To **kick** someone **out** of a place means to force them to leave it; INFORMAL. *Her family kicked her out.*

'kick-off, kick-offs. N-VAR In football, **kick-off** is the time at which a particular match starts.

'kick-start, kick-starts, kick-starting, kick-started. VERB To **kick-start** a process that has stopped working or progressing is to take a course of action that will quickly start it going again. *The President has chosen to kick-start the economy by slashing interest rates.*

kid /kıd/ **kids, kidding, kidded.** [1] N-C You can refer to a child as a **kid**; INFORMAL. *They've got three kids.* [2] N-C Young people who are no longer children are sometimes referred to as **kids**; INFORMAL. *...gangs of kids on motorbikes.* [3] VERB If you **are kidding**, you are saying something that is not really true, as a joke; INFORMAL. *Oh come on, I was just kidding... I'm not kidding, Frank. There's a cow out there.*

4 VERB If people **kid** themselves, they allow themselves to believe something that is not true; INFORMAL. *Anyone who thinks he'll resign is kidding himself.* **5** N-C A **kid** is a young goat.

kidnap /ˈkɪdnæp/ **kidnaps, kidnapping, kidnapped.** **1** VERB To **kidnap** someone is to take them away illegally and by force, and usually to hold them prisoner in order to demand something from their family, employer, or government. *Police in Brazil uncovered a plot to kidnap him.* ♦**kidnapper, kidnappers** N-C *He has been set free by his kidnappers.* ♦**kidnapping, kidnappings.** N-VAR *He was shot during the kidnapping.* **2** N-VAR **Kidnap** or a **kidnap** is the crime of kidnapping someone. *He was charged with the kidnap of a 25 year-old woman.*

kidney /ˈkɪdni/ **kidneys.** N-C Your **kidneys** are the two organs in your body that filter waste matter from your blood and send it out of your body in your urine. *...kidney disease.*

kill /kɪl/ **kills, killing, killed.** **1** VERB If a person, animal, or other living thing **is killed**, something or someone causes them to die. *Six people have been killed in a road crash... The earthquake killed 62 people... Heroin can kill.* ♦**killing, killings** N-VAR *...a brutal killing.*

There are several words which mean similar things to **kill**. To **murder** someone means to kill them deliberately. **Assassinate** is used to talk about the murder of an important person, often for political reasons. If a large number of people are murdered, the words **slaughter** or **massacre** are sometimes used. **Slaughter** can also be used to talk about killing animals for their meat.

---

2 VERB & PHR-VERB If something **kills** an activity, process, or feeling or **kills** it **off**, it prevents it from continuing. *His objective was to kill the space station project altogether... An election like that kills off your interest in politics for ever.* **3** VERB If you **are killing** time, you are doing something because you have some time available, not because you really want to do it. *To kill the hours while she waited, Anna worked in the garden.*

▸ **kill off. 1** See kill 2. **2** PHR-VERB If you **kill** things **off**, you destroy or kill all of them. *Their natural predators have all been killed off... All blood products are now heat treated to kill off any infection.*

killer /ˈkɪlə/ **killers.** **1** N-C A **killer** is a person who has killed someone. *The police are searching for his killers.* **2** N-C You can refer to anything that causes death as a **killer**. *Heart disease is the biggest killer of men in most developed countries.*

kilo /ˈkiːləʊ/ **kilos.** N-C A **kilo** is the same as a **kilogram**.

kilogram (or **kilogramme**) /ˈkɪləɡræm/ **kilograms.** N-C A **kilogram** is a metric unit of weight. One kilogram is a thousand grams, and is equal to 2.2 pounds.

kilometre (AM **kilometer**) /ˈkɪləmiːtə, kɪˈlɒmɪtə/ **kilometres.** N-C A **kilometre** is a metric unit of distance or length. One kilo-

metre is a thousand metres, and is equal to 0.62 miles.

kin /kɪn/. N-U Your **kin** are your relatives; DATED.

kind /kaɪnd/ **kinds; kinder, kindest.** **1** N-VAR If you talk about a particular **kind** of thing, you are talking about one of the classes or sorts of that thing. *Had Jamie ever been in any kind of trouble?... I'm not the kind of person to get married... This book prize is the biggest of its kind in the world... Donations came from all kinds of people.* **2** ADJ Someone who is **kind** behaves in a gentle, caring, and helpful way towards other people. *She is warm-hearted and kind to everyone... It was very kind of you to come.* ♦**kindly** ADV *He had very kindly asked me to the cocktail party.* ♦**kindness** N-U *We have been treated with such kindness by everybody.* **3** ADJ AFTER LINK-V You can use **kind** in expressions such as **please be so kind as to** in order to ask someone to do something in a firm but polite way. *I wonder if you'd be kind enough to call him.*

PHRASES ● You use **kind of** when you want to say that something or someone can be roughly described in a particular way; SPOKEN. *She wasn't beautiful. But she was kind of cute... It kind of gives us an idea of what's happening.* ● Payment **in kind** is payment in the form of goods or services, rather than money. *...the child's dream of working in a chocolate factory and being paid in kind.* ● See also **kindly**.

kindergarten /ˈkɪndəɡɑːtən/ **kindergartens.** N-VAR A **kindergarten** is a school for young children who are not old enough to go to a primary school. *She's in kindergarten now.*

kindly /ˈkaɪndli/. **1** ADJ A **kindly** person is kind, caring, and sympathetic. **2** ADV If someone asks you to **kindly** do something, they are asking you in a way which shows that they have authority over you, or that they are angry with you. *Will you kindly obey the instructions?* **3** PHRASE If someone **does not take kindly to** something, they do not like it. *She did not take kindly to being offered advice.* ● See also **kind**.

king /kɪŋ/ **kings.** **1** N-C A **king** is a man who is a member of the royal family of a country, and who is the head of state of that country. *...the king and queen of Spain.* **2** N-C In chess, the **king** is the piece which each player must try to capture. **3** N-C A **king** is a playing card with a picture of a king on it.

kingdom /ˈkɪŋdəm/ **kingdoms.** **1** N-C A **kingdom** is a country or region that is ruled by a king or queen. **2** N-SING All the animals, birds, and insects in the world can be referred to together as the animal **kingdom**. All the plants can be referred to as the plant **kingdom**.

kiosk /ˈkiːɒsk/ **kiosks.** N-C A **kiosk** is a small shop in a public place such as a street or station. It sells things such as snacks or newspapers which you buy through a window.

kiss /kɪs/ **kisses, kissing, kissed.** VERB & N-C If you **kiss** someone, or if you give them a **kiss**, you touch them with your lips to show affection or to greet them. *She leaned up and kissed him on the cheek... They kissed for almost half-a-minute.*

kit /kɪt/ **kits, kitting, kitted.** **1** N-C A **kit** is a group of items that are kept together because they are used for similar purposes. *...a first aid kit.* **2** N-U Your **kit** is the special clothing you use for a particular activity or sport; BRITISH. *I forgot my gym kit.* **3** N-C A **kit** is a set of parts that can be put together in order to make something. *...model aeroplane kits.*

▶ **kit out.** PHR-VERB If someone or something **is kitted out**, they have all the clothing or equipment they need at a particular time; BRITISH, INFORMAL. *Kit yourself out in crash helmet and goggles.*

kitchen /'kɪtʃɪn/ **kitchens.** N-C A **kitchen** is a room used for cooking and related jobs such as washing dishes.

kite /kaɪt/ **kites.** N-C A **kite** is an object consisting of a light frame covered with paper or cloth, which you fly in the air at the end of a long string.

kitsch /kɪtʃ/. N-U & ADJ You can refer to a work of art or an object as **kitsch** if it is showy and in bad taste, for example because it is designed to appeal to people's sentimentality. *...collectors of Fifties kitsch... Green eye shadow has long been considered kitsch.*

kitten /'kɪtən/ **kittens.** N-C A **kitten** is a very young cat.

kitty /'kɪti/ **kitties.** N-C A **kitty** is an amount of money collected from several people, which is used to buy things that they will share or use together. *You haven't put any money in the kitty.*

'kiwi fruit, kiwi fruits; kiwi fruit can also be used as the plural form. N-VAR A **kiwi fruit** is a fruit with a brown hairy skin and green flesh.

km. km is a written abbreviation for **kilometre**.

knack /næk/. N-SING If you have the **knack** of doing something difficult or skilful, you are able to do it easily. *He's got the knack of getting people to listen.*

knead /ni:d/ **kneads, kneading, kneaded.** VERB When you **knead** dough, you press and squeeze it with your hands to make it smooth.

knee /ni:/ **knees.** **1** N-C Your **knee** is the place where your leg bends. *The snow was up to his knees. ...a knee injury.* **2** N-C If something or someone is on your **knee**, they are resting or sitting on the upper part of your legs when you are sitting down. *I sat in the back of the taxi with my son on my knee.* **3** N-PL If you are on your **knees**, you are kneeling. *She fell to the ground on her knees and prayed.* **4** PHRASE If a country or organization **is brought to its knees**, it is almost completely destroyed by someone or something.

kneel /ni:l/ **kneels, kneeling, knelt** /nelt/ (or **kneeled**). VERB & PHR-VERB When you **kneel** or **kneel down**, you move your body into a position with your knees on the ground and your lower legs stretched out behind them. If you **are kneeling**, you are in this position. *She kneeled down beside him... She was kneeling in prayer.*

knew /nju:, AM nu:/. **Knew** is the past tense of **know**.

knickers /'nɪkəz/. N-PL **Knickers** are a piece of underwear worn by women and girls which have holes for the legs and elastic around the

top; BRITISH. *...six pairs of knickers.*

knife /naɪf/ **knives, knifes, knifing, knifed; knives** is the plural form of the noun and **knifes** is the third person singular of the present tense of the verb. **1** N-C A **knife** is a tool consisting of a sharp flat piece of metal attached to a handle, used to cut things or as a weapon. *...a knife and fork. ...a surgeon's knife.* **2** VERB To **knife** someone means to attack and injure them with a knife. *She was knifed in the back.*

knight /naɪt/ **knights, knighting, knighted.** **1** N-C In medieval times, a **knight** was a man of noble birth, who served his king or lord in battle. **2** VERB If someone **is knighted**, they are given a knighthood. **3** N-C In chess, a **knight** is a piece shaped like a horse's head.

knighthood /'naɪthʊd/ **knighthoods.** N-C A **knighthood** is a title given to a man in Britain for outstanding achievements or for service to his country. A man with a knighthood puts 'Sir' in front of his name.

knit /nɪt/ **knits, knitting, knitted.** VERB When someone **knits** something, they make it from wool or a similar thread using knitting needles or a machine. *She knitted him 10 pairs of socks. ...her grey knitted cardigan.* ♦ **knitting** N-U *...a relaxing hobby, such as knitting.*

knitting /'nɪtɪŋ/. N-U **Knitting** is something, such as a piece of clothing, that is being knitted. *Miss Marple sits in the corner with her knitting.*

knives /naɪvz/. **Knives** is the plural of **knife**.

knob /nɒb/ **knobs.** **1** N-C A **knob** is a round handle or switch. *She reached for the door knob... He twiddled a knob on the dashboard.* **2** N-C A **knob of** butter is a small amount of it; BRITISH.

knock /nɒk/ **knocks, knocking, knocked.** **1** VERB & N-C If you **knock** on something such as a door or window, you hit it, usually several times, to attract someone's attention. A **knock** is the action or sound of knocking. *She went directly to Simon's apartment and knocked on the door... They heard a knock.* ♦ **knocking** N-SING *...a loud knocking at the door.* **2** VERB & N-C If you **knock** something, or if you give it a **knock**, you touch it or hit it roughly and it moves or falls over. *She accidentally knocked the tea tin off the shelf. ...materials to protect against knocks.* **3** VERB To **knock** someone into a particular place or condition means to hit them very hard so that they fall over or become unconscious. *Someone had knocked him unconscious.* **4** VERB If something **knocks**, it makes a repeated banging noise. *The walls squeaked and the pipes knocked.* **5** VERB If you **knock** something or someone, you criticize them; INFORMAL.

▶ **knock about** or **knock around.** **1** PHR-VERB If someone **knocks** you **around** or **knocks** you **about**, they hit or kick you several times; BRITISH. *He started knocking her about.* **2** PHR-VERB If someone **knocks around** or **knocks about** somewhere, they spend time there; BRITISH. *Do you have a big group of friends that you knock around with?*

▶ **knock down.** **1** PHR-VERB If someone **is knocked down**, they are hit by a vehicle and are injured or killed. [2] PHR-VERB To **knock down** a building means to demolish it.

▶ **knock off.** PHR-VERB To **knock off** an amount from a price, time, or level means to reduce it by that amount. *He has knocked 10 seconds off the world record.*

▶ **knock out.** [1] PHR-VERB To **knock** someone **out** means to cause them to become unconscious. *I nearly knocked him out.* [2] PHR-VERB If a person or team **is knocked out** of a competition, they are defeated in a game, so that they take no more part in the competition. ● See also **knockout**.

'**knock-on.** ADJ BEFORE N If something has a **knock-on** effect, it causes a series of events to happen, one after another; BRITISH. *Their problems could have a knock-on effect on the banking sector.*

knockout (or **knock-out**) /'nɒkaʊt/ **knockouts.** [1] N-C If a boxer wins a fight by a **knockout**, his opponent falls to the ground and is unable to stand up before the referee has counted to ten. [2] ADJ BEFORE N A **knockout** blow is an action or event that completely destroys an opponent. [3] ADJ BEFORE N In a **knockout** competition, the loser of each game leaves the competition, until one competitor is left as the winner; BRITISH.

knot /nɒt/ **knots, knotting, knotted.** [1] VERB & N-C If you **knot** something such as a piece of string, or if you tie a **knot** in it, you pass one end of it through a loop and pull it tight. [2] PHRASE If you say that two people **tie the knot**, you mean that they get married; INFORMAL. [3] N-SING A **knot** of people is a group of them standing very close together. *...a little knot of children.* [4] VERB & N-C If your stomach **knots**, or if there is a **knot** in your stomach, it feels tight because you are afraid or excited. *I felt my stomach knot with apprehension.* [5] N-C A **knot** is a unit used for measuring the speed of ships and aircraft, equal to approximately 1.85 kilometres per hour. *...speeds of up to 30 knots.*

know /nəʊ/ **knows, knowing, knew, known.** [1] VERB If you **know** something, you have it correctly in your mind. *Everyone knows his name... You know what happened there... 'How did he meet your mother?'—'I don't know.'* [2] VERB If you **know** about something or **know** how to do something, you understand part or all of it, or have the necessary skills and understanding to do it. *She didn't know anything about music... Do you know any English?... The health authorities now know how to deal with the disease.* [3] VERB If **know** of something, you have heard about it but you do not necessarily have a lot of information about it. *We know of the incident but have no further details.* [4] VERB If you **know** a person, place, or thing, you are familiar with them. *I'd known him for nine years... I don't know whether you know Birmingham well.* [5] VERB If someone or something **is known** as a particular name, they are

called by that name. *The disease is more commonly known as Mad Cow Disease... Everyone knew him as Dizzy.* [6] See also **known**.

PHRASES ● If you **get to know** someone, you find out what they are like by spending time with them. ● You say '**I know**' to indicate that you agree with what has just been said, or to indicate that you realize something is true. *'This country is so awful.'—'I know, I know.'* ● Someone who is **in the know** has information about something that only a few people have any knowledge of. ● You say '**you know**' to emphasize something or to make your statement clearer. *The conditions in there are awful, you know.* ● You say '**You never know**' or '**One never knows**' to indicate that something is possible, although it is unlikely. *There might be an even bigger one – I doubt it, but you never know.*

knowingly /'nəʊɪŋli/. [1] ADV If you **knowingly** do something wrong, you are aware that it is wrong when you do it. *He had never knowingly taken illegal drugs.* [2] ADV If you look or gesture **knowingly**, you show that you understand something, even though it has not been mentioned directly. *The officers nodded knowingly to each other.*

knowledge /'nɒlɪdʒ/. N-U **Knowledge** is information and understanding of a subject, which someone has in their mind. *He denies any knowledge of the payments. ...the latest advances in scientific knowledge.*

PHRASES ● If you say that something is true **to the best of** your **knowledge**, you mean that you think that it is true, although you are not completely sure. ● If you do something **safe in the knowledge** that something else is the case, you do the first thing confidently because you are sure of the second thing; WRITTEN. *I arrived late, safe in the knowledge that no demonstration leaves on time.*

knowledgeable /'nɒlɪdʒəbəl/. ADJ A **knowledgeable** person knows a lot about many different things or a lot about a particular subject. *Youngsters seem very knowledgeable about drugs.*

known /nəʊn/. [1] **Known** is the past participle of **know**. [2] ADJ You use **known** to describe someone or something that is clearly recognized by or familiar to all people, or to a particular group of people. *...a known criminal.* [3] PHRASE If you **let it be known** that something is the case, you make sure that people know it, without telling them directly. *The Prime Minister has let it be known that he is against it.* [4] See also **well-known**.

knuckle /'nʌkəl/ **knuckles.** N-C Your **knuckles** are the rounded pieces of bone where your fingers join your hands, and where your fingers bend.

Koran /kɔː'rɑːn/. N-PROPER The **Koran** is the sacred book on which the religion of Islam is based.

L l

l, l is a written abbreviation for 'litre'.

lab /læb/ **labs.** N-C A **lab** is the same as a **laboratory;** INFORMAL.

label /'leɪbəl/ **labels, labelling, labelled,** (AM **labeling, labeled**). [1] N-C A **label** is a piece of paper or plastic that is attached to an object, giving information about it. [2] VERB If something **is labelled**, a label is attached to it, giving information about it or what it is. *All the products are labelled with comprehensive instructions.* [3] N-C If you say that someone gets a particular **label**, you mean that people describe them with a particular critical word or phrase. *Her treatment of her husband earned her the label of the most hated woman in America.* [4] VERB If you say that someone or something **is labelled** as a particular thing, you mean that people generally describe them that way and you think that this is unfair. *They are afraid to contact the social services in case they are labelled a problem family.*

labor /'leɪbə/. See **labour.**

laboratory /lə'bɒrətri, AM 'læbrətɔːri/ **laboratories.** N-C A **laboratory** is a building or room where scientific experiments and research are carried out.

laborer. See **labourer.**

laborious /lə'bɔːriəs/. ADJ A **laborious** task or process takes a lot of effort. ♦**laboriously** ADV *He sat behind a desk laboriously writing.*

labour (AM **labor**) /'leɪbə/ **labours, labouring, laboured.** [1] ADJ A **labour** politician or voter is a member of the Labour Party or votes for the Labour Party. *...the labour of seeding, planting and harvesting... The chef at the barbecue looked up from his labours.* [3] VERB If you **labour** to do something, you do it with difficulty. *For 25 years now he has laboured to build a religious community.* [4] N-U **Labour** is used to refer to the people who work in a country or industry. *...skilled labour.* [5] VERB If you **labour under** an illusion that something is the case, you continue to believe it to be true when it is not. *Both authors labour under the strange delusion that the world is run by feminists.* [6] VERB If you **labour** a point or an argument, you keep making the same point or saying the same thing, although it is unnecessary. [7] N-U **Labour** is the last stage of pregnancy, in which a woman gives birth to a baby. *She was in labour.*

labourer /'leɪbərə/ **labourers.** N-C A **labourer** is a person who does a job which involves a lot of hard physical work. *...a farm labourer.*

labyrinth /'læbɪrɪnθ/ **labyrinths.** [1] N-C A **labyrinth** is a complicated series of paths or passages, through which it is difficult to find your way. [2] N-C If you describe a situation, process, or area of knowledge as a **labyrinth**, you mean that it is very complicated. *...the labyrinth of human nature.*

lace /leɪs/ **laces, lacing, laced.** [1] N-U **Lace** is very delicate cloth which is made by twisting together fine threads, leaving holes in between. [2] N-C **Laces** are thin pieces of material that are used to fasten some types of clothing, especially shoes. *He'd put on his shoes and tied the laces.* [3] VERB & PHR-VERB If you **lace** something such as a pair of shoes, or if you **lace** them **up**, you tighten them by pulling the laces through the holes, and tying them together. [4] VERB To **lace** food or drink with a substance such as alcohol or a drug means to put a small amount of the substance into the food or drink. *She laced his food with sleeping pills.*

lack /læk/ **lacks, lacking, lacked.** [1] N-U If there is a **lack** of something, there is not enough of it, or there is none at all. *Despite his lack of experience, he got the job... The charges were dropped for lack of evidence.* [2] VERB If you say that someone or something **lacks** something, or that something **is lacking** in them, you mean they do not have any or enough of that thing. *It lacked the power of the Italian cars... Certain vital information is lacking in the report.* ♦**lacking** ADJ AFTER LINK-V *She felt nervous, increasingly lacking in confidence.*

lacklustre (AM **lackluster**) /'læklʌstə/. ADJ If you describe something or someone as **lacklustre**, you mean that they are not very impressive or lively. *...his party's lacklustre performance during the election campaign.*

lacquer /'lækə/ **lacquers.** N-VAR **Lacquer** is a special type of liquid which is put on wood or metal to protect it and make it shiny.

lacy /'leɪsi/. ADJ **Lacy** things are made from lace or have pieces of lace attached to them. *...lacy nightgowns.*

lad /læd/ **lads.** N-C A **lad** is a boy or young man; BRITISH, INFORMAL. *He's always been a big lad for his age.*

ladder /'lædə/ **ladders.** N-C A **ladder** is a piece of equipment used for climbing up something such as a wall. It consists of two long pieces of wood or metal with steps fixed between them.

laden /'leɪdən/. [1] ADJ If someone or something is **laden** with a lot of heavy things, they are holding or carrying them; LITERARY. *...buffet tables laden with exotic fruit. ...a car heavily laden with skis.* [2] VERB If you describe a person or thing as **laden with** something, particularly something bad, you mean that they have a lot of it or are full of it. *We're so laden with guilt.*

lady /'leɪdi/ **ladies.** [1] N-C & N-VOC You can use the word **lady** when you are referring to a woman, especially when you are showing politeness or respect. *Your table is ready, ladies.* [2] N-TITLE **Lady** is a title used in front of the names of some women from the upper classes. *...Lady Diana Spencer.* [3] N-SING People sometimes refer to a public toilet for women as **the ladies.**

lag /læg/ **lags, lagging, lagged.** [1] VERB To **lag behind** someone or something means to make slower progress than them. *He now lags 10 points behind the champion.* [2] N-C A time **lag** is a period of time between two related events.

There's a time lag between infection with HIV and developing AIDS.

lager /ˈlɑːgə/ **lagers**. N-VAR **Lager** is a kind of light beer.

lagoon /ləˈguːn/ **lagoons**. N-C A **lagoon** is an area of calm sea water that is separated from the ocean by sand or rock.

laid /leɪd/. **Laid** is the past tense and past participle of **lay**.

,laid-'back. ADJ If you describe someone as **laid-back**, you mean that they behave in a calm relaxed way as if nothing ever worries them.

lain /leɪn/. **Lain** is the past participle of some meanings of **lie**.

lake /leɪk/ **lakes**. N-C A **lake** is a large area of fresh water, surrounded by land.

lamb /læm/ **lambs**. ① N-C A **lamb** is a young sheep. ② N-U **Lamb** is the flesh of a lamb eaten as food. *...leg of lamb.*

lame /leɪm/. ① ADJ A **lame** person cannot walk properly because an injury or illness has damaged one or both of their legs. *She was lame in one leg... His horse went lame.* ② ADJ If you describe an excuse or effort as **lame**, you mean that it is weak. *He mumbled some lame excuse about having gone to sleep.* ♦ **lamely** ADV *'Lovely house,' I said lamely.*

lament /ləˈment/ **laments, lamenting, lamented**. ① VERB If you **lament** something, you express your regret about it; LITERARY. *He laments that people in Villa El Salvador are suspicious of the police... 'Prices are down 40 per cent since Christmas,' he lamented.* ② N-C Someone's **lament** is something that they say that expresses their regret or disappointment about something. *...the professional woman's lament that a woman's judgment is questioned more than a man's.*

lamp /læmp/ **lamps**. N-C A **lamp** is a light that works by using electricity or by burning oil or gas. *She switched on the bedside lamp.*

land /lænd/ **lands, landing, landed**. ① N-U **Land** is an area of ground. *...agricultural land... It isn't clear whether the plane went down over land or sea.* ② N-C A particular **land** is a particular country; LITERARY. *...2,000 miles away in a strange land.* ● See note at **country**. ③ VERB When someone or something **lands**, they come down to the ground after moving through the air or falling. *He was sent flying into the air and landed 20ft away.* ④ VERB When a plane or spacecraft **lands**, or when someone **lands** it, it arrives somewhere after a journey. *The jet landed after a flight of just under three hours.* ♦ **landing, landings**. N-C *I had to make a controlled landing into the sea.* ⑤ VERB To **land** goods somewhere means to successfully unload them there at the end of a journey, especially by ship. *The vessels will have to land their catch at designated ports.* ⑥ VERB If something **lands** you **in** an unpleasant situation, or it if **lands** you **with** it, it causes you to have to deal with it; BRITISH, INFORMAL. *This is not the first time his exploits have landed him in trouble... The other options simply complicate the situation and could land him with more expense.*

landing /ˈlændɪŋ/ **landings**. N-C In a building, a **landing** is a flat area at the top of a staircase.

landlady /ˈlændleɪdi/ **landladies**. N-C Someone's **landlady** is the woman who allows them to live or work in a building which she owns, in return for rent.

landlord /ˈlændlɔːd/ **landlords**. N-C Someone's **landlord** is the man who allows them to live or work in a building which he owns, in return for rent.

landmark /ˈlændmɑːk/ **landmarks**. ① N-C A **landmark** is a building or feature which is easily noticed and can be used to judge your position or the position of other buildings or features. *The Ambassador Hotel is a Los Angeles landmark.* ② N-C You can refer to an important stage in the development of something as a **landmark**. *The baby was one of the big landmarks in our relationship.*

landscape /ˈlændskeɪp/ **landscapes, landscaping, landscaped**. ① N-VAR The **landscape** is everything that you can see when you look across an area of land, including hills, rivers, buildings, and trees. *...Arizona's harsh desert landscape.*

> Do not confuse **landscape**, **scenery**, **countryside**, and **nature**. With **landscape**, the emphasis is on the physical features of the land, while **scenery** includes everything you can see when you look out over an area of land in the country. *...perfect Alpine scenery.* **Countryside** is land which is away from towns and cities. *...3,500 acres of mostly flat countryside.* **Nature** includes the landscape, the weather, animals, and plants, which are not created by man. *These creatures roamed the Earth as the finest and rarest wonders of nature.*

② N-C A **landscape** is a painting of the countryside. ③ VERB If an area of land **is landscaped**, it is altered to create a pleasing artistic effect. ♦ **landscaping** N-U *The landowner insisted on a high standard of landscaping.*

landslide /ˈlændslaɪd/ **landslides**. ① N-C If an election is won by a **landslide**, it is won by a large number of votes. ② N-C A **landslide** is a large amount of earth and rocks falling down a cliff or the side of a mountain.

lane /leɪn/ **lanes**. ① N-C A **lane** is a type of road, especially in the country. ② N-C Roads, race courses, and swimming pools are sometimes divided into parallel strips called **lanes**. *...the slow lane.* ③ N-C A **lane** is a route that is frequently used by aircraft or ships. *...the busiest shipping lanes in the world.*

language /ˈlæŋgwɪdʒ/ **languages**. ① N-C A **language** is a system of sounds and written symbols used by the people of a particular country, area, or tribe to communicate with each other. *...the English language... Students are expected to master a second language.* ② N-U **Language** is the ability to use words in order to communicate. *...how children acquire language.* ③ N-U You can refer to the words used in connection with a particular subject as the **language** of that subject. *...the language of* business. [4] N-U The **language** of a piece of writing or a speech is the style in which it is written or spoken. ...*a booklet summarising it in plain language.*

languid /ˈlæŋɡwɪd/. ADJ If someone is **languid**, they show little energy or interest and are very slow and casual in their movements; LITERARY.
♦ **languidly** ADV *We sat about languidly.*

languish /ˈlæŋɡwɪʃ/ **languishes, languishing, languished.** VERB If someone **languishes** somewhere, they are forced to remain and suffer in an unpleasant situation. *Pollard continues to languish in prison.*

lantern /ˈlæntən/ **lanterns.** N-C A **lantern** is a lamp in a metal frame with glass sides.

lap /læp/ **laps, lapping, lapped.** [1] N-C Your **lap** is the flat area formed by your thighs when you are sitting down. *She waited quietly with her hands in her lap.* [2] N-C In a race, you say that a competitor has completed a **lap** when he or she has gone round the course once. [3] VERB If you **lap** another competitor in a race, you pass them while they are still on the previous lap. [4] VERB When water **laps** against something such as the shore or the side of a boat, it touches it gently and makes a soft sound; WRITTEN. *Water lapped the walls.*
♦ **lapping** N-U *The only sound was the lapping of the waves.* [5] VERB & PHR-VERB When an animal **laps** a drink, or when it **laps** it **up**, it uses its tongue to flick the liquid into its mouth.
▸ **lap up.** PHR-VERB If someone **laps up** information or attention, they accept it eagerly. *They just haven't been to school before. They're so eager to learn, they lap it up.* See **lap** 5.

lapel /ləˈpel/ **lapels.** N-C The **lapels** of a jacket or coat are the two flaps at the front that are folded back on each side.

lapse /læps/ **lapses, lapsing, lapsed.** [1] N-C A **lapse** of something such as concentration or judgement is a temporary lack of it, which can cause you to make a mistake. [2] VERB & N-C If you **lapse** into a particular kind of behaviour, or have a **lapse** into that behaviour, you start behaving that way. *He lapsed into long silences... Her lapse into German didn't seem peculiar.* [3] N-SING A **lapse** of time is a period that is long enough for a situation to change. *Traditional management is being restored after a lapse of nearly 50 years.* [4] VERB If a period of time **lapses**, it passes. ...*in the days that had lapsed since Grace's death.* [5] VERB If a situation, relationship, or legal contract **lapses**, it is allowed to end or to become invalid.

large /lɑːdʒ/ **larger, largest.** [1] ADJ A **large** thing or person is greater in size than usual or average. *The pike lives mainly in large rivers and lakes... He was a large man with a thick square head.* [2] ADJ A **large** amount or number of people or things is more than the average amount or number. *There are a large number of centres where you can take full-time courses.* [3] ADJ **Large** is used to indicate that a problem or issue which is being discussed is very important or serious. ...*the already large problem of under-age drinking.* [4] See note at **big**.

PHRASES • You use **at large** to indicate that you are talking about most of the people mentioned. ...*the chances of getting reforms accept-*

ed by the community at large. • You use **by and large** to indicate that a statement is mostly but not completely true. *By and large, he does not watch many movies.*

largely /ˈlɑːdʒli/. [1] ADV You use **largely** to say that a statement is mostly but not completely true. *The early studies were done on men, largely by male researchers.* [2] ADV You use **largely** to introduce the main reason for an event or situation. *Today, largely because of their diets, over 50 percent of Americans are at risk for heart disease.*

large-'scale (or large scale). [1] ADJ BEFORE N A **large-scale** action or event happens over a wide area or involves a lot of people or things. ...*a large scale military operation.* [2] ADJ BEFORE N A **large-scale** map or diagram represents a small area of land or a building or machine in a way that shows small details of it.

lark /lɑːk/ **larks.** N-C A **lark** is a small brown bird that has a pleasant song.

larva /ˈlɑːvə/ **larvae** /ˈlɑːviː/. N-C A **larva** is an insect at the stage before it becomes an adult.

laser /ˈleɪzə/ **lasers.** [1] N-C A **laser** is a narrow beam of concentrated light produced by a special machine. [2] N-C A **laser** is a machine that produces a laser beam.

lash /læʃ/ **lashes, lashing, lashed.** [1] N-C Your **lashes** are the hairs that grow on the edge of your eyelids. [2] VERB If you **lash** something somewhere, you tie it firmly to something. *Secure the anchor by lashing it to the rail... All the equipment is very securely lashed down.* [3] VERB If wind, rain, or water **lashes** someone or something, it hits them violently; WRITTEN. *Suddenly rain lashed against the windows.* [4] VERB & N-C If someone **lashes** another person, they hit that person with a whip. This action is called a **lash**. *The villagers sentenced one man to five lashes.*
▸ **lash out.** [1] PHR-VERB If you **lash out**, you try to hit someone with your hands or feet or with a weapon. [2] PHR-VERB If you **lash out at** someone or something, you speak to them very angrily or cruelly, criticizing or scolding them.

lass /læs/ **lasses.** N-C A **lass** is a young woman or girl; INFORMAL, BRITISH.

last /lɑːst, læst/ **lasts, lasting, lasted.** [1] ADJ & PRON You use **last** to describe the most recent period of time, event, or thing. *I got married last July... Much has changed since my last visit... The next tide would be even higher than the last.* [2] ORD & PRON The **last** thing, person, event, or period of time is the one that happens or comes after all the others of the same kind. ...*the last three pages of the chapter... The trickiest bits are the last on the list.* [3] DET & N-SING **Last** is used to refer to the only thing, person, or part of something that remains. ...*the last piece of pizza... He finished off the last of the wine.* [4] DET & PRON You can use **last** to emphasize that you do not want to do something or that something is unlikely to happen. *The last thing I wanted to do was teach... I would be the last to say that science has explained everything.* [5] ADV If something **last** happened on a particular occasion, it has not happened since then. *When were you there last?... The house is a little more dilapidated* *than when I last saw it.* [6] ADV If something happens **last**, it happens after everything else. *I was always picked last for the football team.* [7] PRON If you are the **last** to do or know something, everyone else does or knows it before you. [8] VERB If something **lasts**, it continues to exist or happen. *The games lasted only half the normal time... Enjoy it because it won't last.* [9] VERB If something **lasts** for a particular length of time, it continues to be able to be used for that time, for example because there is some of it left. *This battery lasts twice as long as batteries made by other battery makers.* [10] See also **lasting**.

[PHRASES] ● If something has happened **at last** or **at long last**, it has happened after you have been hoping for it for a long time. *I'm so glad that we've found you at last!* ● You use expressions such as **the night before last**, **the election before last**, and **the leader before last**, to refer to the period of time, event, or person that happened or came immediately before the most recent one in a series. ● You can use expressions such as **the last I heard** and **the last she heard** to introduce a piece of information that is the most recent that you have on a particular subject. *The last I heard, Joe and Irene were still happily married.* ● You use expressions such as **to the last detail** and **to the last man** to indicate that a plan, situation, or activity includes every single person, thing, or part involved. ● to **have the last laugh**: see **laugh**. ● **the last straw**: see **straw**.

last-'ditch ADJ BEFORE N A **last-ditch** action is done only because there are no other ways left to try to achieve something or to prevent something happening. *...a last-ditch attempt to prevent civil war.*

lasting /ˈlɑːstɪŋ, ˈlæst-/. ADJ Something that is **lasting** continues to exist or to be effective for a very long time. *She left a lasting impression on him.*

lastly /ˈlɑːstli, ˈlæst-/. [1] ADV You use **lastly** when you want to make a final point that is connected with the ones you have already mentioned. *Lastly, I would like to ask about your future plans.* [2] ADV You use **lastly** when you are saying what happens after everything else in a series of actions or events. *Spot all the differences between the two pictures opposite, then circle them in red. Lastly, complete the tie-breaker.*

last-'minute. See **minute**.

latch /lætʃ/ **latches, latching, latched**. [1] N-C A **latch** is a fastening on a door or gate. It consists of a metal bar which you lower to lock the door and raise to open it. [2] N-C A **latch** is a lock on a door which locks automatically when you shut the door. *...a key clicked in the latch of the front door.*

▶ **latch onto** or **latch on**. [1] PHR-VERB If someone **latches onto** a person or an idea, or if someone **latches on**, they become very interested in the person or idea, often because they find them useful. *Other trades have been quick to latch on.* [2] PHR-VERB If one thing **latches onto** another, or if it **latches on**, it attaches itself to it. *...antibodies in their blood that latch onto the virus and kill it.*

late /leɪt/ **later, latest**. [1] ADV & ADJ BEFORE N **Late** means near the end of a period of time. *It was late in the afternoon. ...the late 1960's.* [2] ADV & ADJ **Late** means after the time that was arranged or expected. *Steve arrived late... His campaign got off to a late start.* [3] ADJ AFTER LINK-V If it is **late**, it is near the end of the day or it is past the time that you feel something should have been done. *We've got to go now. It's getting late.* ♦**lateness** N-U *A large crowd had gathered despite the lateness of the hour.* [4] ADV & ADJ BEFORE N **Late** means after the usual time that a particular event or activity happens. *We went to bed very late... They had a late lunch.* ♦**lateness** N-U *He apologised for his lateness.* [5] ADJ BEFORE N You use **late** when you are talking about someone who is dead. *...the late Mr Parkin.* [6] See also **later, latest**.

[PHRASES] ● If you say that someone is doing something **late in the day**, you mean that it may fail because they have waited too long before doing it. *I'd left it all too late in the day to get anywhere with these strategies.* ● You use **of late** to refer to an event or state of affairs that happened or began to exist a short time ago; FORMAL. *Neither player has been performing well of late.*

lately /ˈleɪtli/ ADV **Lately** means recently. *Dad's health hasn't been too good lately.*

latent /ˈleɪtənt/. ADJ **Latent** is used to describe something which is hidden and not obvious at the moment, but which may develop further in the future. *It may also appeal to the latent chauvinism of many ordinary people.*

later /ˈleɪtə/. [1] **Later** is the comparative of **late**. [2] ADV & ADJ You use **later** or **later on** to refer to a time or situation that is after the one that you have been talking about or after the present one. *Later on I'll be speaking to Patty Davis... The competition should have been rescheduled for a later date.* [3] ADJ You use **later** to refer to the last part of someone's life or career or of a period in history. *He found happiness in later life.*

lateral /ˈlætərəl/. ADJ **Lateral** means relating to the sides of something, or moving in a sideways direction. *...the lateral movement of the bridge.*

latest /ˈleɪtɪst/. [1] **Latest** is the superlative of **late**. [2] ADJ You use **latest** to describe something that is the most recent thing of its kind. *...her latest book.* [3] ADJ You can use **latest** to describe something that is extremely modern and up-to-date, and is therefore better than the other things of its type. *Computers have always represented the latest in technology.* [4] PHRASE You use **at the latest** to emphasize that something must happen at or before a particular time. *She should be back by ten o'clock at the latest.*

lathe /leɪð/ **lathes**. N-C A **lathe** is a machine for shaping wood or metal.

latitude /ˈlætɪtjuːd, AM -tuːd/ **latitudes**. [1] N-VAR The **latitude** of a place is its distance from the Equator. Compare **longitude**. *The army must cease military operations above 36 degrees latitude north.* [2] N-U **Latitude** is the freedom to choose how to do something; FOR-

MAL. *He would be given every latitude in forming a new government.*

latter /'lætə/ [1] PRON & ADJ BEFORE N When two people, things, or groups have just been mentioned, you can refer to the second one as the **latter** or describe them as the **latter** person, thing, or group. *He tracked down his cousin and uncle. The latter was sick.* [2] ADJ BEFORE N You use **latter** to describe the later part of a period of time or an event. *The latter part of the debate concentrated on abortion.*

'latter-day. ADJ BEFORE N **Latter-day** is used to describe a person or thing that is a modern equivalent of someone or something in the past. *He holds the sincere belief that he is a latter-day prophet.*

lattice /'lætɪs/ **lattices.** N-C A **lattice** is a pattern or structure made of strips which cross over each other diagonally leaving holes in between. *...the narrow steel lattice of the bridge.*

laugh /lɑːf, læf/ **laughs, laughing, laughed.** [1] VERB & N-C When you **laugh**, or when you give a **laugh**, you make a sound with your throat while smiling. *The British don't laugh at the same jokes as the French... He gave a deep rumbling laugh.* [2] VERB If people **laugh** at someone or something, they mock them or make jokes about them. *I thought they were laughing at me because I was ugly.* [3] PHRASE If you say that you **have the last laugh**, you mean that you make your critics or opponents look foolish or wrong, by being successful when you were not expected to be.

▶ **laugh off.** PHR-VERB If you **laugh off** a difficult or serious situation, you try to suggest that it is amusing and unimportant. *Whilst I used to laugh it off, I'm now getting irritated by it.*

laughter /'lɑːftə, 'læf-/. N-U **Laughter** consists of people laughing. *Everybody in the room roared with laughter.*

launch /lɔːntʃ/ **launches, launching, launched.** [1] VERB & N-C To **launch** a ship or a lifeboat means to put it into water, often for the first time. The occasion when this happens is called its **launch**. *Coastguards launched three lifeboats... The launch of a ship was a big occasion.* [2] VERB & N-VAR To **launch** a rocket, missile, or satellite means to send it into the air or into space. You can refer to its **launch**. *A Delta II rocket was launched from Cape Canaveral... This morning's launch of the space shuttle Columbia has been delayed.* [3] VERB & N-C To **launch** a large and important activity, for example a military attack, means to start it. The start of something like this is its **launch**. *Mr Gorbachev was on holiday when the coup was launched. ...the launch of a campaign to restore law and order.* [4] VERB & N-C If a company **launches** a new product, it starts to make it available to the public. You say this is the **launch** of the product. *Crabtree & Evelyn has just launched a new jam... British Airways has broken new ground with the launch of a new service to Taipei.*

▶ **launch into.** PHR-VERB If you **launch into** something such as a speech, task, or fight, you start it enthusiastically. *Geoff has launched himself into fatherhood with great enthusiasm.*

launder /'lɔːndə/ **launders, laundering, laundered.** [1] VERB When you **launder** clothes, bed linen, or towels, you wash and iron them. *...a freshly laundered and starched white shirt.* [2] VERB To **launder** money that has been obtained illegally means to process it through a legitimate business or to send it abroad to a foreign bank, so that nobody knows that it was illegally obtained. *...banks that launder drug money.* ◆**launderer, launderers.** N-C *...a businessman and self-described money launderer and arms dealer.*

laundry /'lɔːndri/ **laundries.** [1] N-U **Laundry** is used to refer to clothes, sheets, and towels that are about to be washed, are being washed, or have just been washed. *I'll do your laundry. ...dirty laundry.* [2] N-C A **laundry** is a place where clothes, sheets, and towels are washed and dried.

laurel /'lɒrəl, AM 'lɔːr-/ **laurels.** N-VAR A **laurel** or a **laurel tree** is a small evergreen tree with shiny leaves.

lava /'lɑːvə/. N-U **Lava** is the very hot liquid rock that comes out of a volcano.

lavatory /'lævətri, AM -tɔːri/ **lavatories.** N-C A **lavatory** is a toilet; BRITISH.

lavender /'lævɪndə/. N-U **Lavender** is a garden plant with sweet-smelling purple flowers.

lavish /'lævɪʃ/ **lavishes, lavishing, lavished.** [1] ADJ If you describe something as **lavish**, you mean that a lot of time, effort, or money is being spent on it to make it as impressive as possible. *...a lavish party.* ◆**lavishly** ADV *IBM spent lavishly on their workers' education.* [2] ADJ If you say that something is **lavish**, you mean it is extravagant and wasteful. *...stealing antique jewellery and paintings to finance a lavish lifestyle.* [3] VERB If you **lavish** something such as money, affection, or time on someone or something, you spend a lot of money on them or give them a lot of affection or attention. *The emperor promoted the general and lavished him with gifts.*

law /lɔː/ **laws.** [1] N-SING **The law** is a system of rules that a society or government develops in order to deal with crime, business agreements, and social relationships. *Obscene and threatening phone calls are against the law.* [2] N-PL The **laws** of an organization or activity are its rules, which are used to organize and control it. [3] N-C A **law** is a rule or set of rules for good behaviour which is considered right and important by the majority of people for moral, religious, or emotional reasons. *...inflexible moral laws.* [4] N-C A **law** is a natural process in which a particular event or thing always leads to a particular result, or a scientific rule that someone has invented to explain such a process. *...the law of gravity.* [5] N-U **Law** or **the law** is all the professions which deal with advising people about the law, representing people in court, or giving decisions and punishments. **Law** is also the study of systems of law and how laws work. *...a career in law. ...a law degree.* [6] PHRASE If someone **takes the law into their own hands**, they punish someone according to their own ideas of justice, often when this involves breaking the law.

'law-abiding. ADJ A **law-abiding** person always obeys the law. *Gun ownership by law-abiding people was not a problem.*

,law and 'order. N-U When there is **law and order** in a country, the laws are generally accepted and obeyed there. *If there were a breakdown of law and order, the army might be tempted to intervene.*

lawful /ˈlɔːfʊl/. ADJ If an activity, organization, or product is **lawful**, it is allowed by law; FORMAL. ♦**lawfully** ADV ...*whether the police acted lawfully in shooting him.*

lawless /ˈlɔːləs/. ADJ **Lawless** actions break the law, especially in a wild and violent way. ...*the lawless gangs who have been terrorizing the city.* ♦**lawlessness** N-U ...*acts of lawlessness.*

lawn /lɔːn/ **lawns.** N-VAR A **lawn** is an area of grass that is kept cut short and is usually part of a garden or park.

lawsuit /ˈlɔːsuːt/ **lawsuits.** N-C A **lawsuit** is a case in a court of law which concerns a dispute between two people or organizations; FORMAL.

lawyer /ˈlɔɪə/ **lawyers.** N-C A **lawyer** is a person who is qualified to advise people about the law and represent them in court.

lax /læks/. ADJ If you say that a person's behaviour or a system is **lax**, you mean they are not careful or strict in making or obeying rules or maintaining high standards. *One of the problem areas is lax security.* ♦**laxity** N-U *The laxity of export control authorities has made a significant contribution to the problem.*

laxative /ˈlæksətɪv/ **laxatives.** N-VAR & ADJ A **laxative**, or a **laxative** substance, is something which you eat or drink which helps you to pass faeces through your body.

lay 1 placing and putting

lay /leɪ/ **lays, laying, laid.** [1] **Lay** is the past tense of some meanings of **lie**. [2] VERB If you **lay** something somewhere, you put it there in a careful or neat way. *Mothers routinely lay babies on their backs to sleep.* [3] VERB If you **lay** something such as carpets, cables, or foundations, you put them into their permanent position. *Public utilities dig up roads to lay pipes.* [4] VERB When someone **lays** a trap, they prepare it to catch someone or something. *They were laying a trap for the kidnapper.* [5] VERB When a female bird **lays** an egg, an egg comes out of its body. [6] VERB **Lay** is used with some nouns to talk about making preparations for something. For example, if you **lay the basis** for something or **lay plans** for it, you prepare it carefully so that you can continue with it, develop it, or benefit from it later. *His work laid the foundations of modern psychology.* [7] VERB **Lay** is used with some nouns in expressions about accusing or blaming someone. For example, if you **lay the blame** for a mistake on someone, you say it is their fault. *Police have decided not to lay charges.* [8] See note at **lie**.

▶ **lay aside.** PHR-VERB If you **lay aside** a feeling or belief, you reject it or give it up in order to progress with something. *To make a success of any future talks, both sides will have to lay aside their long-term differences.*

▶ **lay down.** PHR-VERB If rules or people in authority **lay down** what people must do, they tell people what they must do. *The Companies Act lays down a set of minimum requirements.*

▶ **lay into.** PHR-VERB If you **lay into** someone, you start attacking them physically or criticizing them severely; INFORMAL. *A mob of women laid into him with handbags.*

▶ **lay off.** [1] PHR-VERB If workers **are laid off** by their employers, they are told to leave their jobs, usually because there is no more work for them to do. *They did not sell a single car for a month and had to lay off workers.* [2] PHR-VERB If you tell someone to **lay off**, you mean that they should leave you or someone else alone; INFORMAL.

▶ **lay on.** PHR-VERB If you **lay on** food, entertainment, or a service, you provide it or supply it, especially in a generous or grand way. *They laid on a superb evening.*

▶ **lay out.** [1] PHR-VERB To **lay out** ideas or plans means to explain or present them clearly, for example in a document or a meeting. *Maxwell listened closely as Johnson laid out his plan.* [2] PHR-VERB To **lay out** an area of land or a building means to plan and design how its different parts should be arranged. [3] See also **layout.**

lay 2 non-professional

lay /leɪ/. [1] ADJ BEFORE N You use **lay** to describe people who are involved with a Christian church but are not monks, nuns, or members of the clergy. ...*a Methodist lay preacher.* [2] ADJ BEFORE N You use **lay** to describe someone who is not an expert or professional in a particular subject or activity. *It is difficult for a lay person to gain access to medical libraries.*

layer /ˈleɪə/ **layers, layering, layered.** [1] N-C A **layer** of a material or substance is a quantity or flat piece of it that covers a surface or that is between two other things. *A fresh layer of snow covered the street... Dress warmly, in layers.* [2] N-C If something such as a system or an idea has many **layers**, it has many different levels or parts. *He is not concerned with deeper layers of meaning.* [3] VERB If you **layer** something, you arrange it in layers. *Continue layering the pastry sheets. ...a layered white dress.*

layman /ˈleɪmən/ **laymen.** N-C A **layman** is a person who is not an expert or a professional in a particular subject or activity. ...*explaining scientific breakthroughs in layman's terms.*

layout /ˈleɪaʊt/ **layouts.** N-C The **layout** of a garden, building, or piece of writing is the way in which the parts of it are arranged.

lazy /ˈleɪzi/ **lazier, laziest.** [1] ADJ If someone is **lazy**, they do not want to work or make an effort. *I was too lazy to learn how to read music.* ♦**laziness** N-U *I dislike laziness.* [2] ADJ BEFORE N **Lazy** actions or activities are done in a slow and relaxed way, without making much effort. *We would have a lazy lunch and then lie on the beach.* ♦**lazily** ADV *She smiled lazily.*

lb; the plural is **lbs** or **lb.** **lb** is a written abbreviation for **pound**, when 'pound' refers to weight.

lead 1 being ahead or taking someone somewhere

lead /liːd/ **leads, leading, led.** [1] VERB If you **lead** a group of moving people, you walk or ride in front of them. *They threatened to lead a* *mass walk-out... Tom was leading, a rifle slung over his back.* ② VERB If you **lead** someone to a particular place or thing, you take them there. *The nurse led me to a large room.* ③ VERB If something such as a road or door **leads** to a place, you can get to that place by following the road or going through the door. *...a main highway leading north.* ④ VERB If you **are leading** in a race or competition, you are winning. *So far Fischer leads by five wins to two.* ⑤ N-SING If you have the **lead** or are in the **lead** in a race or competition, you are winning. The amount by which someone is winning can also be referred to as their **lead**. *England took the lead after 31 minutes... Sainz now has a lead of 28 points.* ⑥ VERB If you **lead** a group or organization or an activity, you are in charge of it. *He led the country between 1949 and 1984.* ⑦ N-C If you give a **lead**, you do something which is considered a good example to follow. *...the need for the president to give a moral lead... Many others followed his lead.* ⑧ VERB You can use **lead** when you are saying what kind of life someone has. For example, if you **lead** a busy life, your life is busy. ⑨ VERB If something **leads** to a situation or event, it causes that situation or event to happen. *Ethnic tensions among the republics could lead to civil war... What led you to do this work?* ⑩ VERB If someone or something **leads** you to think or expect something, they cause you to think or expect it, although it is not true or does not happen. *It was not as straightforward as we were led to believe.* ⑪ VERB To **lead** a discussion or person onto a particular subject means to cause the discussion to develop in such a way that the subject is introduced. *After a while I led the conversation around to her job.* ⑫ N-C A **lead** is a piece of information or an idea which may help people to discover the facts in a situation. *Police say they have no leads so far on the murder.* ⑬ N-SING The **lead** in a play, film, or show is the most important role in it. The person who plays this part can also be called the **lead**. *She has recently played the lead in Bertolucci's Stealing Beauty.* ⑭ N-C A dog's **lead** is a long chain or piece of leather attached to the dog's collar so that you can control the dog. ⑮ N-C A **lead** in a piece of electrical equipment is a piece of wire which supplies electricity to the equipment. ⑯ See also **leading**. ● to **lead** someone **astray**: see **astray**.

▶ **lead on to.** PHR-VERB If one event or action **leads on to** another, it causes it or makes it possible; BRITISH. *This discovery led on to studies of the immune system.*

▶ **lead up to.** ① PHR-VERB Events that **lead up to** a situation happen one after the other until that situation is reached. *...the events that led up to the deaths.* ② PHR-VERB The period of time **leading up to** an event is the period of time immediately before it happens. *...the weeks leading up to Christmas.*

lead 2 substances

lead /led/ **leads.** ① N-U **Lead** is a soft, grey, heavy metal. ② N-C The **lead** in a pencil is the centre part of it which makes a mark on paper.

leader /'li:də/ **leaders.** ① N-C The **leader** of an organization or a group of people is the person who is in charge of it. *...the Liberal Party leader.* ② N-C The **leader** in a race or competition is the person who is winning at a particular time.

leadership /'li:dəʃɪp/ **leaderships.** ① N-SING You can refer to the people who are in charge of a group or organization as the **leadership**. *...the Labour leadership of Haringey council.* ② N-U Someone's **leadership** is their position or state of being in control of a group of people. *The agency quadrupled in size under her leadership.* ③ N-U **Leadership** refers to the qualities or methods that make someone a good leader. *There will be times when firm leadership is required.*

leading /'li:dɪŋ/ ① ADJ BEFORE N The **leading** people or things in a group are the most important or successful. *...a leading industrial nation.* ② ADJ BEFORE N The **leading** role in a play or film is the main one. A **leading** lady or man is an actor who plays this role.

leaf /li:f/ **leaves; leafs, leafing, leafed.** N-C A **leaf** is one of the parts of a tree or plant that is flat, thin, and usually green. The plural is **leaves**.

▶ **leaf through.** PHR-VERB If you **leaf through** a book or magazine, you turn the pages quickly without looking at them carefully. The third person singular, present tense, is **leafs through**.

leaflet /'li:flət/ **leaflets.** N-C A **leaflet** is a little book or a piece of paper containing information about a particular subject. *...a leaflet called 'Sexual Harassment at Work'.*

leafy /'li:fi/. ① ADJ **Leafy** trees and plants have a lot of leaves. *...green leafy vegetables.* ② ADJ You say that a place is **leafy** when there are a lot of trees and plants there. *...London's leafy suburbs.*

league /li:g/ **leagues.** ① N-C A **league** is a group of people, clubs, or countries that have joined together for a particular purpose or because they share a common interest. *...the League of Nations.* ② N-C You use the word **league** to make comparisons between different people or things, especially in terms of their quality. *Their record sales would put them in the same league as The Rolling Stones.* ③ PHRASE If you say that someone is **in league** with someone else to do something bad, they are working together to do that thing. *Secretly, he was in league with the nation's top mobsters.*

leak /li:k/ **leaks, leaking, leaked.** ① VERB & N-C If a container or other object **leaks**, or if it has a **leak**, there is a hole or crack in it which lets liquid or gas escape. You can also say the liquid or gas **leaks** from its container. *The roof leaked... The tanker is still leaking oil. ...a gas leak.* ② VERB & N-C If a secret document or piece of information **is leaked** or if there is a **leak** involving it, someone lets the public know about it. *A civil servant was imprisoned for leaking a document to the press. ...serious leaks, possibly involving national security.*

leakage /'li:kɪdʒ/ **leakages.** N-VAR **Leakage** is

the escape of liquid or gas from a container through a crack or hole.

lean /liːn/ **leans, leaning, leaned** (BR also **leant** /lent/); **leaner leanest.** [1] VERB When you **lean** in a particular direction, you bend your body in that direction. *They stopped to lean over a gate.* [2] VERB If you **lean** on something, you rest against it so that it partly supports you. If you **lean** an object somewhere, you place the object so that its weight is partly supported. *A man was leaning on the railing... Lean the plants against a wall.* [3] VERB If you **lean** towards an idea or a way of behaving, you tend to think or act in that way. *Voters have been leaning in the direction of the Democrats.* [4] ADJ A **lean** person is thin but looks strong and fit. [5] ADJ **Lean** meat has very little fat. [6] ADJ A **lean** period of time is one in which people have little money or success. *It is a lean time for the oil business.*

▶ **lean on.** PHR-VERB If you **lean on** someone, you depend on them for support and help. *You can lean on me.*

leap /liːp/ **leaps, leaping, leaped** (or **leapt** /lept/). [1] VERB & N-C If you **leap**, or if you take a **leap**, you jump high in the air or jump a long distance. *He had leapt from a window in the building and escaped.* [2] VERB To **leap** somewhere means to move there suddenly and quickly. *The two men leaped into the jeep... The car leapt forward.* [3] VERB & N-C You can say that things **leap** or take a **leap** when they suddenly advance or increase by a large amount. *Their share will leap to about 15 per cent. ...a giant leap in productivity.* [4] VERB If you **leap** at a chance or opportunity, you accept it quickly and eagerly.

learn /lɜːn/ **learns, learning, learned, learnt** /lɜːnt/. In British English, the forms **learned** and **learnt** can both be used for the past tense and past participle. [1] VERB When you **learn**, you obtain knowledge or a skill through studying or training. *Their children were going to learn English... He is learning to play the piano... You need to learn how to use the office computer.* ◆**learner, learners** N-C *...a new aid for younger children or slow learners.* ◆**learning** N-U *...a bilingual approach to the learning of English.* [2] VERB If you **learn** something such as a poem or the script of a play, you study or repeat the words so that you can remember them. [3] VERB If people **learn** to behave or react in a particular way, their attitudes gradually change and they start behaving that way. *He learned to conceal his views... We are learning how to confront death.* [4] VERB If you **learn from** an experience, you change the way you behave so that it does not happen again, or so that you can deal with it if it happens again. *He has learned from his mistakes.* [5] VERB If you **learn** of something, you find out about it. *She learned of his affair with Betty... She wasn't surprised to learn that he was involved.*

lease /liːs/ **leases, leasing, leased.** [1] N-C A **lease** is a legal agreement under which someone pays money to another person in exchange for the use of a building or piece of land for a specified period of time. *He took up*

a 10 year lease on the house. [2] VERB If you **lease** property or something such as a car, or if someone **leases** it to you, they allow you to use it in return for regular payments of money. *He leased an apartment... She hopes to lease the building to students.* [3] PHRASE If you say that someone or something has been given **a new lease of life**, you are emphasizing that they are much more lively or successful than they have been in the past.

least /liːst/. **Least** is often considered to be the superlative form of **little**. [1] ADJ & ADV & PRON You use **the least** to mean a smaller amount or extent than anyone or anything else, or the smallest amount or extent possible. *If you like cheese, go for the ones with the least fat... I'm the least experienced guy... We might get caught when we least expect it. ...the gap between those earning the most and those earning the least.* [2] ADJ You use **least** in structures where you are emphasizing that a particular situation or event is much less important or serious than other possible or actual ones. *Feeling sick is the least of her worries.*

PHRASES ● You use **at least** to say that a number, amount, or action is the minimum possible or likely, and that more may be possible. The forms **at the least** and **at the very least** are also used. *...a dinner menu featuring at least 15 different sorts of fish... She could take a nice holiday at least.* ● You use **at least** when you are mentioning an advantage that still exists in a bad situation. *At least we know he is still alive.* ● You can use **in the least** and **the least bit** to emphasize a negative. *I'm not like that at all. Not in the least... Alice wasn't the least bit frightened.* ● You can use **not least** to emphasize an important example or reason. *Dieting itself can be bad for you, not least because it is a cause of chronic stress.* ● You can use **to say the least** to suggest that a situation is actually much more extreme or serious than you say it is. *Accommodation was basic to say the least.*

leather /'leðə/ **leathers.** [1] N-VAR **Leather** is treated animal skin which is used for making shoes, clothes, bags, and furniture. *...a leather jacket.* [2] N-PL **Leathers** are leather clothes, especially those worn by motorcyclists.

leave /liːv/ **leaves, leaving, left** /left/. [1] VERB If you **leave** a place or person, you go away from that place or person. *I simply couldn't bear to leave my little girl... My flight leaves in less than an hour... The last of the older children had left for school.* [2] VERB If you **leave** an institution, group, or job, you stop attending that institution, being a member of that group, or doing that job. *He left school with no qualifications. ...a leaving present.* [3] VERB If someone **leaves** their husband, wife, or partner, they end the relationship and stop living with him or her. *Bill left me for another woman.* [4] VERB If you **leave** something somewhere, you put it there and it remains there when you go away. *I left my bags in the car... Leave your key with a neighbour... He left me a nice little welcoming note.* [5] VERB If someone or something **leaves** an amount of something, that amount remains available after the rest has been used or has gone. *He always left a little food for the next day... It doesn't leave me much time.* [6] VERB If something **leaves** a mark, effect, or sign, it causes that mark, effect, or sign to remain as a result. *A muscle tear will leave a scar after healing... She left a lasting impression on him.* [7] VERB If an event **leaves** people or things in a particular state, they are in that state when the event has finished. *...violent disturbances which have left at least ten people dead.* [8] VERB If you **leave** someone to do something, you go away from them so that they do it on their own, or you give them the responsibility for dealing with it. *I'd better leave you to get on with it... Left to myself, I don't go to church much.* [9] PHRASE If you **leave** someone or something **alone**, you do not bother them or try to do anything with them. *He just would not leave me alone, he followed me everywhere... Cigarettes and alcohol are best left alone.* [10] VERB If you **leave** something until a particular time, you delay dealing with it. *Don't leave it all until the last minute.* [11] VERB If you **leave** property or money to someone, you arrange for it to be given to them after you have died. [12] VERB If you say that someone **leaves** a wife, husband, or a particular number of children, you mean that the wife, husband, or children remain alive after that person has died. [13] N-U & PHRASE **Leave** is a period of time when you are not working at your job. If you are **on leave**, you are not at your job. *Why don't you take a few days' leave?*

▸ **leave behind.** [1] PHR-VERB If you **leave** someone or something **behind**, you go away from them permanently from them. *When he fled Liberia, he left behind a wife and two young children.* [2] PHR-VERB If someone or something **leaves behind** an object or a situation, that object or situation remains after they have gone. *The tenant has already left, leaving behind a mess of broken furniture.* [3] PHR-VERB If a person, country, or organization **is left behind**, they do not achieve as much as others or they do not progress as quickly, so they are at a disadvantage.

▸ **leave off.** PHR-VERB If someone or something **is left off** a list, they are not included in that list.

▸ **leave out.** PHR-VERB If you **leave** someone or something **out** of something such as an activity or a collection, you do not include them in it. *I never left him out of my team.*

leaves /liːvz/. **Leaves** is the plural form of **leaf**.

lecture /ˈlektʃə/ **lectures, lecturing, lectured.** [1] N-C A **lecture** is a talk that someone gives in order to teach people about a particular subject, usually at a university. [2] VERB If you **lecture** on a particular subject, you give a lecture or a series of lectures about it. *She then invited him to Atlanta to lecture on the history of art.* [3] VERB & N-C If someone **lectures** you about something, or if they give you a **lecture**, they criticize you or tell you how they think you should behave. *Chuck would lecture me, telling me to get a haircut... Our captain gave us a stern lecture on safety.*

lecturer /ˈlektʃərə/ **lecturers.** N-C A **lecturer** is a teacher at university or college.

led /led/. **Led** is the past tense and past participle of **lead**.

ledge /ledʒ/ **ledges.** [1] N-C A **ledge** is a narrow shelf along the bottom edge of a window. [2] N-C A **ledge** is a piece of rock shaped like a narrow shelf on the side of a cliff or mountain.

ledger /ˈledʒə/ **ledgers.** N-C A **ledger** is a book in which a company or other organization writes down the amounts of money it spends and receives.

leek /liːk/ **leeks.** N-VAR **Leeks** are long green and white vegetables which smell similar to onions.

leer /lɪə/ **leers, leering, leered.** VERB & N-C If someone **leers** at you, or if they look at you with a **leer**, they smile unpleasantly, usually in a sexually suggestive way; used showing disapproval. *The soldier leered at Thomasina... When I asked the clerk for my room key, he gave it to me with a leer.*

left /left/. [1] **Left** is the past tense and past participle of **leave**. [2] ADJ & PHRASE If there is a certain amount of something **left**, or if you have a certain amount of it **left over**, it remains when the rest has gone or been used. *Is there any gin left?... They still have six games left to play.* [3] N-SING & ADV & ADJ BEFORE N The **left** is one of two opposite directions, sides, or positions. In the word 'to', the 't' is to the left of the 'o'. If you are facing north and you turn **left**, you will be facing west. **Left** is used to describe the one of two things that someone has, for example their arm or leg, that is on the left. *In Britain cars drive on the left... To my left, I noticed a light... Go left at the traffic lights... Drummond had the baton in his left hand.* [4] N-SING You can refer to political ideas which are closer to socialism than to capitalism or conservatism, or to people who support these ideas, as **the left**. *The change has been bitterly opposed by the left.*

'left-hand. ADJ BEFORE N **Left-hand** describes the position of something when it is on the left side. *...the back left-hand corner of the drawer.*

,left-'handed. ADJ Someone who is **left-handed** finds it easier to use their left hand rather than their right hand for activities such as writing and throwing a ball.

leftist /ˈleftɪst/ **leftists.** N-C & ADJ BEFORE N Socialists and communists are sometimes referred to as **leftists**. *...an alliance of seven leftist parties.*

leftover /ˈleftəʊvə/ **leftovers.** ADJ BEFORE N & N-PL **Leftover** things or **leftovers** are things which remain after the other similar things have been used, especially food which remains after a meal.

,left-'wing (or **left wing**). [1] ADJ **Left-wing** people have political ideas that are based on socialism. *They would not be voting for him because he was too left-wing.* [2] N-SING The **left wing** of a political group consists of the members of it whose beliefs are closer to socialism than are those of its other members.

leg /leg/ **legs.** [1] N-C A person or animal's **legs** are the long parts of their body that they use to stand on and walk with. [2] N-C The **legs** of a pair of trousers are the parts that cover your legs. [3] N-C A **leg** of lamb or pork is a piece of meat from the thigh of a sheep, lamb, or pig.

4 N-C The **legs** of a table, chair, or other piece of furniture are the parts that rest on the floor, supporting the furniture's weight. **5** N-C A **leg** of a long journey is one part of it. *The first leg of the journey was by boat to Lake Naivasha.*

legacy /ˈlegəsi/ **legacies.** **1** N-C A **legacy** is money or property which someone leaves to you in their will when they die. **2** N-C The **legacy** of an event or period of history is something which is a direct result of it and which continues to exist after it is over. *...the legacy of inequality and injustice created by Apartheid.*

legal /ˈliːgəl/. **1** ADJ BEFORE N **Legal** is used to describe things that relate to the law. *He vowed to take legal action. ...the British legal system.* ◆**legally** ADV *It could be a bit problematic, legally speaking.* **2** ADJ An action or situation that is **legal** is allowed by law. *...drivers who have more than the legal limit of alcohol.* ◆**legally** ADV *...a legally binding contract.* ◆**legality** /liˈgælɪti/. N-U *The auditor questioned the legality of the deal.*

legalize (BR also **legalise**) /ˈliːgəlaɪz/ **legalizes, legalizing, legalized.** VERB If something is **legalized**, the law is changed so that it is allowed. *...a 1973 ruling which legalized abortion.*

legend /ˈledʒənd/ **legends.** **1** N-VAR A **legend** is a very old and popular story that may be based on real events. *...the legends of ancient Greece.* **2** N-C If you refer to someone as a **legend**, you mean that they are very famous and admired. *...Hollywood legend Audrey Hepburn.*

legendary /ˈledʒəndri, AM -deri/. **1** ADJ If you describe someone or something as **legendary**, you mean that they are very famous and that many stories are told about them. *...the legendary Jazz singer Adelaide Hall.* **2** ADJ A **legendary** person, place, or event is described in a legend.

leggings /ˈlegɪŋz/. N-PL **Leggings** are tight trousers that are made out of a fabric which stretches easily.

legion /ˈliːdʒən/ **legions.** **1** N-C A **legion** is a large group of soldiers who form one section of an army. **2** N-C A **legion** of people or things is a large number of them. *...a legion of stories about noisy neighbours.*

legislate /ˈledʒɪsleɪt/ **legislates, legislating, legislated.** VERB When a government **legislates**, it passes a new law. *You can't legislate against prejudice.*

legislation /ˌledʒɪˈsleɪʃən/. N-U **Legislation** consists of a law or laws passed by a government. *...legislation to protect women's rights.*

legislative /ˈledʒɪslətɪv, AM -leɪ-/. ADJ BEFORE N **Legislative** means involving or relating to the process of making and passing laws.

legislator /ˈledʒɪsleɪtə/ **legislators.** N-C A **legislator** is someone involved in making or passing laws.

legislature /ˈledʒɪslətʃə, AM -leɪ-/ **legislatures.** N-C The **legislature** of a state or country is the group of people within it who have the power to make and pass laws; FORMAL.

legitimate /lɪˈdʒɪtɪmət/. **1** ADJ Something that is **legitimate** is acceptable according to the

law. *...the restoration of the legitimate government.* ◆**legitimacy** /lɪˈdʒɪtɪmsi/ N-U *...the legitimacy of the board's activities.* ◆**legitimately** ADV *He still claims to be the legitimately elected president.* **2** ADJ If you say that something such as a feeling or opinion is **legitimate**, you think that it is reasonable and acceptable. *That's a perfectly legitimate fear.* ◆**legitimacy** N-U *The comment is not without legitimacy.* ◆**legitimately** ADV *You can legitimately claim to feel angry and disappointed.*

leisure /ˈleʒə, AM ˈliːʒ-/. **1** N-U **Leisure** is the time when you do not have to work and can do things that you enjoy. *...a relaxing way to fill my leisure time.* **2** PHRASE If someone does something **at leisure** or **at their leisure**, they do it when they want to, without hurrying. *Stroll at leisure through the gardens.*

leisurely /ˈleʒəli, AM ˈliːʒ-/. ADJ & ADV A **leisurely** action is done in a relaxed and unhurried way. *Tweed walked at a leisurely pace.*

lemon /ˈlemən/ **lemons.** N-VAR A **lemon** is a sour yellow citrus fruit. *...a slice of lemon.*

lemonade /ˌleməˈneɪd/. N-VAR **Lemonade** is a clear, sweet, fizzy drink, or a drink that is made from lemons, sugar, and water.

lend /lend/ **lends, lending, lent.** **1** VERB When people or organizations such as banks **lend** you money, they give it to you and you agree to pay it back at a future date, often with an extra amount as interest. *I had to lend him ten pounds to take his children to the pictures... The White House said that America would lend another $1.5 billion.* ◆**lender, lenders** N-C *...the six leading mortgage lenders.* ◆**lending** N-U *...a slump in bank lending.* **2** VERB If you **lend** something that you own, you allow someone to have or to use it for a period of time. *Will you lend me your jacket?* **3** VERB To **lend** something such as a particular quality to something means to give it that quality. *Enthusiastic applause lent a sense of occasion to the proceedings... He lent his support to the abolition of existing divorce laws.* **4** VERB If something **lends** itself to a particular activity, it is very suitable for it. *The room lends itself well to summer eating.*

length /leŋθ/ **lengths.** **1** N-VAR The **length** of something is the amount that it measures from one end to the other. *It is about a metre in length. ...the length of the fish.* **2** N-U The **length** of something is its quality of being long. *I noticed, too, the length of her fingers.* **3** N-VAR The **length** of something such as a piece of writing is the amount of writing that is contained in it. **4** N-VAR The **length** of an event, activity, or situation is the time it lasts. *...his film, over two hours in length.* **5** N-C A **length** of wood, string, cloth, or other material is a piece of it. *Hang lengths of fabric behind the glass.* **6** N-C If you swim a **length** in a swimming pool, you swim from one end to the other. **7** N-SING If something happens or exists along **the length of** something, it happens or exists for the whole way along it. *I looked along the length of the building.*

PHRASES ● If someone does something **at length**, they do it for a long time and in great detail. *They spoke at length.* ● If someone **goes**

to great lengths to achieve something, they try very hard and may do extreme things in order to achieve it. *Garbo went to great lengths to hide from reporters.*

lengthen /ˈleŋθən/ **lengthens, lengthening, lengthened.** VERB When something **lengthens**, or when you **lengthen** it, it becomes longer. *Vacations have lengthened.*

lengthy /ˈleŋθi/. [1] ADJ Something that is **lengthy** lasts for a long time. ...*the lengthy process of filling out passport application forms.* [2] ADJ A **lengthy** report, book, or document contains a lot of speech or writing.

lenient /ˈliːniənt/. ADJ When someone in authority is **lenient**, they are not as strict or as severe as expected. *He received an unexpectedly lenient sentence.* ◆**leniently** ADV *Reckless drivers are treated too leniently.*

lens /lenz/ **lenses.** N-C A **lens** is a thin, curved piece of glass or plastic in something such as a camera or pair of glasses which makes things appear larger or clearer.

lent /lent/. **Lent** is the past tense and past participle of **lend**.

lentil /ˈlentɪl/ **lentils.** N-C **Lentils** are a type of dried seed used in cooking.

leopard /ˈlepəd/ **leopards.** N-C A **leopard** is a type of large wild cat from Africa or Asia. Leopards have yellow fur and black spots.

lesbian /ˈlezbiən/ **lesbians.** N-C & ADJ A **lesbian** or a **lesbian** woman is a woman who is sexually attracted to women.

less /les/. [1] QUANT & ADV You use **less** to indicate that there is a smaller number of things or a smaller amount of something than before or than average, or than something else. *People should eat less fat... Over here, things have been a bit less dramatic... He still eats cheese, but far less often. ...spending less and saving more... Last year less of the money went into high-technology companies.* [2] PREP You use **less** than before a number or amount to say that the actual number or amount is smaller than this. *Motorways actually cover less than 0.1 percent of the countryside.* [3] PREP When you are referring to amounts, you use **less** in front of a number or quantity to indicate that it is to be subtracted from another number or quantity already mentioned. ...*Fees: £750, less £400.*

PHRASES ● You use **less and less** to say that something is becoming smaller all the time in degree or amount. *The couple seem to spend less and less time together.* ● You can use **no less** as an emphatic way of expressing surprise or admiration at the amount or importance of someone or something. *He had returned to England in an aircraft carrier no less.* ● You use **no less than** before an amount to indicate that you think the amount is larger than you expected. *He is lined up for no less than four US television interviews.* ● You use **less than** to say that something does not have a particular quality. For example, something that is **less than** perfect is not perfect. ● **more or less:** see **more.**

lessen /ˈlesən/ **lessens, lessening, lessened.** VERB If something **lessens**, or if you **lessen** it, it becomes smaller in amount, degree, or importance. ...*changes to their diet that would lessen the risk of premature death.* ◆**lessening** N-U ...*a lessening of tension.*

lesser /ˈlesə/. ADJ & ADV You use **lesser** in order to indicate that something is smaller in extent or amount than another thing that has been mentioned. *The responsibility lies with Harris and, to a lesser extent, Clarke. ...lesser known works by famous artists.*

lesson /ˈlesən/ **lessons.** [1] N-C A **lesson** is a fixed period of time during which people are taught something. *Johanna took piano lessons.* [2] N-C If an experience teaches you a **lesson**, it makes you realize that one thing or realize what should be done. *There's still one lesson to be learned from the crisis.* [3] PHRASE If you say that you are going to **teach** someone **a lesson**, you mean that you are going to punish them for something that they have done so that they do not do it again.

lest /lest/. CONJ If you do something **lest** something unpleasant should happen, you do it to try to prevent the unpleasant thing from happening; FORMAL. *I was afraid to open the door lest he should follow me.*

let /let/ **lets, letting, let.** [1] VERB If you **let** something happen, you allow it to happen. *Thorne let him talk... I love sweets but Mum doesn't let me have them... I can't let myself be distracted.* [2] VERB If you **let** someone into, out of, or through a place, you allow them to enter, leave, or go through it. *I let myself into the flat... I'd better go and let the dog out.* [3] VERB You use **let me** when you are introducing something you want to do, or something you are offering to do. *Let me explain... Let me get you something to drink.* [4] VERB You use **let's** or **let us** when you are making a suggestion. *I'm bored. Let's go home... 'Shall we go in and have some supper?'—'Yes, let's.'* [5] VERB & PHR-VERB If you **let** your house or land to someone, or if you **let** it **out**, you allow them to use it in exchange for regular payments.

PHRASES ● **Let alone** is used after a statement, usually a negative one, to indicate that the statement is even more true of the person or situation that you are going to mention next. *It is incredible that the 12-year-old managed to even reach the pedals, let alone drive the car.* ● If you **let go** of someone or something, you stop holding them. *She let go of Mona's hand.* ● If you **let** someone **know** something, you make sure that they know about it. *If you do want to go, please let me know.*

▶ **let down.** [1] PHR-VERB If you **let** someone **down**, you disappoint them, usually by not doing something that you said you would. *Don't worry, Xiao, I won't let you down.* [2] PHR-VERB If you **let down** something filled with air, such as a tyre, you allow air to escape from it.

▶ **let in.** PHR-VERB If an object **lets in** something such as air or water, it allows air or water to get into it or pass through it. *There is no glass in the front door to let in light.*

▶ **let in on.** PHR-VERB If you **let** someone **in on** something that is a secret from most people, you allow them to know about it.

▶ **let off** [1] PHR-VERB If someone in authority **lets** you **off** a task or duty, they give you permission not to do it; BRITISH. *Having a new baby lets you off going to boring dinner-parties.* [2] PHR-VERB If you **let** someone **off**, you give them a lighter punishment than they expect or no punishment at all. [3] PHR-VERB If you **let off** an explosive or a gun, you explode or fire it. *His neighbourhood had let off fireworks to celebrate the Revolution.*

▶ **let on** PHR-VERB If you do not **let on** that something is true, you do not tell anyone that it is true; BRITISH. *I'd be in trouble if I let on.*

▶ **let out** [1] PHR-VERB If something or someone **lets** water, air, or breath **out**, they allow it to flow out or escape. *It lets sunlight in but doesn't let heat out.* [2] See also **let** 5.

▶ **let up** PHR-VERB If an unpleasant, continuous process **lets up**, it stops or reduces. *The rain had let up.*

lethal /ˈliːθəl/. ADJ Something that is **lethal** can kill you. ...*a lethal dose of sleeping pills.*

lethargic /lɪˈθɑːdʒɪk/. ADJ If you are **lethargic**, you have no energy or enthusiasm. *He felt too miserable and lethargic to get dressed.*

lethargy /ˈleθədʒi/. N-U **Lethargy** is a condition in which you have no energy or enthusiasm.

let's /lets/. **Let's** is the usual spoken and written form of **let us**.

letter /ˈletə/ **letters**. [1] N-C When you write a **letter**, you write a message on paper and send it to someone. *I had received a letter from a very close friend. ...a letter of resignation.* [2] N-C **Letters** are written symbols which represent the sounds of a language. ...*the letter E.*

letterbox (or **letter box**) /ˈletəbɒks/ **letterboxes**. N-C A **letterbox** is a rectangular hole in a door through which letters are delivered.

lettering /ˈletərɪŋ/. N-U You can use the word **lettering** to refer to writing, especially when you are describing the type of letters used. ...*a small blue sign with white lettering.*

lettuce /ˈletɪs/ **lettuces**. N-VAR A **lettuce** is a plant with large green leaves that you eat in salads.

leukaemia (AM **leukemia**) /luˈkiːmiə/. N-U **Leukaemia** is a serious disease of the blood.

level /ˈlevəl/ **levels**, **levelling**, **levelled** (AM **leveling**, **leveled**). [1] N-C A **level** is a point on a scale, for example a scale of amount, importance, or difficulty. ...*the lowest level of inflation for some years... Michael's roommate had been pleasant on a superficial level.* [2] N-SING The **level** of something is its height or the height of its surface. *He had the gun held at waist level... The water level of the Mississippi River is already 6.5 feet below normal.* [3] ADJ AFTER LINK-V If one thing is **level** with another thing, it is at the same height. *Amy knelt down so that their eyes were level.* [4] ADJ Something that is **level** is completely flat. ...*a plateau of fairly level ground.* [5] VERB If someone or something such as a violent storm **levels** a building or area of land, they flatten or demolish it completely. *Further tremors could level more buildings.* [6] ADV & ADJ AFTER LINK-V If you draw **level** with someone or something, you get closer to them until you are by their side.

He waited until they were level with the door. [7] VERB If an accusation or criticism **is levelled** at someone, they are criticized for something they have done or are accused of doing something wrong. *He leveled bitter criticism against the US.* ● a **level playing field**: see **playing field**.

▶ **level off** or **level out**. PHR-VERB If an amount or something that is changing **levels off** or **levels out**, it stops changing so quickly. *Inflation is finally levelling out at around 11% a month.*

lever /ˈliːvə, AM ˈlev-/ **levers**. [1] N-C A **lever** is a handle or bar that you pull or push to operate a piece of machinery. *Pull the gear lever.* [2] N-C A **lever** is a long bar, one end of which is placed under a heavy object so that when you press down on the other end you can move the object. [3] N-C A **lever** is an idea or action that you can use to make people do what you want them to do. ...*using the hostages as a lever to gain concessions.*

leverage /ˈliːvərɪdʒ, AM ˈlev-/. [1] N-U **Leverage** is the ability to influence and control situations or people. *His function as a Mayor affords him the leverage to get things done.* [2] N-U **Leverage** is the force that is applied to an object when something such as a lever is used.

levy /ˈlevi/ **levies**, **levying**, **levied**. [1] N-C A **levy** is a sum of money that you have to pay, for example as a tax to the government. [2] VERB If a government or organization **levies** a tax or other sum of money, it demands it.

liability /ˌlaɪəˈbɪlɪti/ **liabilities**. [1] N-C If you say that someone or something is a **liability**, you mean that they cause a lot of problems or embarrassment. *She had become a liability to her party.* [2] N-C An organization's **liabilities** are the sums of money which it owes.

liable /ˈlaɪəbəl/. [1] ADJ AFTER LINK-V If people or things are **liable** to do something or **liable** to something, they have a tendency to do it or to experience it; FORMAL. ...*equipment that is liable to break. ...a woman particularly liable to depression.* [2] ADJ AFTER LINK-V If you are **liable** for something, you are legally responsible for it. *The airline's insurer is liable for damages.* ◆ **liability** /ˌlaɪəˈbɪlɪti/ N-U *The Government will not admit liability for his injuries.*

liaise /liˈeɪz/ **liaises**, **liaising**, **liaised**. VERB When organizations or people **liaise**, or when one organization **liaises** with another, they co-operate and inform each other about their work; BRITISH. *Social services and health workers liaise closely.*

liaison /liˈeɪzɒn, AM ˈliːeɪz-/ **liaisons**. [1] N-U **Liaison** is co-operation and the exchange of information between different organizations or people. *We work in close liaison with the Doping Control Unit.* [2] N-C You can refer to a romantic relationship between two people as a **liaison**.

liar /ˈlaɪə/ **liars**. N-C A **liar** is someone who tells lies.

libel /ˈlaɪbəl/ **libels**, **libelling**, **libelled**. [1] N-VAR **Libel** is something in writing which wrongly accuses someone of something, and which is therefore against the law; LEGAL. *Warren sued him for libel over the remarks.*

2 VERB If someone **libels** you, they write something in a newspaper or book which wrongly damages your reputation and is therefore against the law.

liberal /ˈlɪbərəl/ **liberals.** **1** ADJ & N-C If someone has **liberal** views, or if they are a **liberal**, they are tolerant and believe in people's right to behave differently or hold their own opinions. *She is known to have liberal views on divorce.* **2** ADJ BEFORE N & N-C A **liberal** politician or voter or a **liberal** is a member of a Liberal Party or votes for a Liberal Party. **3** ADJ **Liberal** means giving, using, or taking a lot of something. *...the country's liberal use of the death penalty.* ◆**liberally** ADV *...coffee liberally laced with whiskey.*

liberalize (BR also **liberalise**) /ˈlɪbrəlaɪz/ **liberalizes, liberalizing, liberalized.** VERB When a country or government **liberalizes**, or **liberalizes** its laws or its attitudes, it allows people more freedom in their actions. *...the decision to liberalize travel restrictions.* ◆**liberalization** N-U *...the liberalization of divorce laws.*

liberate /ˈlɪbəreɪt/ **liberates, liberating, liberated.** **1** VERB To **liberate** a place or the people in it means to free them from the political or military control of another country, area, or group of people. *They planned to march on and liberate the city.* ◆**liberation** N-U *...a mass liberation movement.* **2** VERB To **liberate** someone from something means to help them escape from it or overcome it, and lead a better way of life. *He asked how committed the leadership was to liberating its people from poverty.* ◆**liberating** ADJ *It can be a very liberating experience.* ◆**liberation** N-U *...the women's liberation movement.*

liberated /ˈlɪbəreɪtɪd/. ADJ If you describe someone as **liberated**, you mean that they do not accept their society's traditional values or restrictive way of behaving.

liberty /ˈlɪbəti/ **liberties.** **1** N-VAR **Liberty** is the freedom to live your life in the way that you want and go where you want to go. *...the rights and liberties of the English people.* **2** PHRASE If someone is **at liberty** to do something, they have been given permission to do it. *We are not at liberty to disclose that information.*

librarian /laɪˈbreəriən/ **librarians.** N-C A **librarian** is a person who works in, or is in charge of a library.

library /ˈlaɪbrəri, AM -breri/ **libraries.** N-C A public **library** is a building where things such as books, newspapers, videos, and music are kept for people to read, use, or borrow.

lice /laɪs/. **Lice** is the plural of **louse**.

licence (AM **license**) /ˈlaɪsəns/ **licences.** **1** N-C A **licence** is an official document which gives you permission to do, use, or own something. *...his pilot's licence.* **2** PHRASE If someone does something **under licence**, they do it by special permission from a government or some other authority.

license /ˈlaɪsəns/ **licenses, licensing, licensed.** VERB If a government or other authority **licenses** a person, organization, or activity, they officially give permission for the person or organization to do something, or for

the activity to take place. *The council can license a U.S. company to produce the drug.*

licensed /ˈlaɪsənst/. **1** ADJ If you are **licensed** to do something, you are given the official authority to do it. *...the club, which was licensed to hold parties.* **2** ADJ If something that you own or use is **licensed**, you have official permission to own it or use it. *...a licensed rifle.*

'license plate, license plates. N-C In American English, a **license plate** is a sign on the front and back of a vehicle that shows its registration number. The British expression is **number plate.**

lick /lɪk/ **licks, licking, licked.** VERB & N-C When you **lick** something, or when you give it a **lick**, you move your tongue across its surface. *She folded up her letter, licking the envelope flap. ...taking tiny licks at a pistachio ice-cream.*

lid /lɪd/ **lids.** **1** N-C A **lid** of a container is the top which you open to reach inside. **2** N-C Your **lids** are the pieces of skin which cover your eyes when you close them.

lie 1 position or situation

lie /laɪ/ **lies, lying, lay, lain.** **1** VERB If you **are lying** somewhere, you are in a horizontal position and are not standing or sitting. *There was a child lying on the ground... He lay awake watching her.* **2** VERB If an object **lies** in a particular place, it is in a flat position in that place. *Broken glass lay scattered on the carpet.* **3** VERB If a place **lies** in a particular position, it is situated there. *The islands lie at the southern end of the Kurile chain.* **4** LINK-VERB You can use **lie** to say that something is or remains in a particular state or condition. *His country's economy lies in ruins.* **5** VERB You can use **lie** to say what position someone is in during a competition; BRITISH. *Blyth Tait is lying in second place.* **6** VERB You can talk about where something such as a problem, solution, or fault **lies** to say what you think it involves or is caused by. *The problem lay in the large amounts spent on defence.* **7** VERB If something **lies** ahead, it is going to happen in the future.

> Do not confuse the verb **lie** with the verb **lay**. The past tense of **lie** is **lay** and the past participle is **lain**. It is an intransitive verb. *I lay on the floor with my legs in the air... He had lain in great pain in a darkened room.* However, **lay**, whose past tense and past participle are **laid**, is usually a transitive verb. *They laid him on the floor.* Because **lay** is used to talk about putting something in a particular place or position, it is related to the verb **lie**. If someone **lays** something somewhere, it **lies** there. Because of their related meanings, people sometimes confuse the two verbs, and produce sentences like 'He likes to lay on the beach and get a tan.' However, sentences of this kind are not considered correct by most speakers of English.

▶ **lie around.** PHR-VERB If things are left **lying around** or **lying about**, they are not tidied away. *My dad had a couple of Bob Dylan and Beatles song-books lying around the house.*

▶ **lie behind.** PHR-VERB If you refer to what **lies behind** a situation or event, you are referring to the reason the situation exists or the event happened. *What lay behind the clashes was disagreement over the list of candidates.*

lie 2 things that are not true

lie /laɪ/ **lies, lying, lied.** [1] VERB & N-C If someone **is lying**, or if they are telling a **lie**, they are saying something that they know is untrue. *He lies about his age... She lied to her husband so she could meet her lover... All the boys told lies about their adventures.* ◆**lying** N-U *Lying is something that I will not tolerate.* [2] PHRASE If you say that someone **is living a lie**, you mean that in every part of their life they are hiding the truth about themselves from other people.

lieutenant, /lef'tenənt, AM luː-/ **lieutenants.** A **lieutenant** is a junior officer in the army, navy, or air force.

life /laɪf/ **lives.** [1] N-U **Life** is the quality which people, animals, and plants have when they are not dead. *...a baby's first minutes of life.* [2] N-U You can use **life** to refer to things or groups of things which are alive. *...some useful facts about animal and plant life.* [3] N-C Someone's **life** is their state of being alive, or the period of time during which they are alive. *Your life is in danger... He spent the last fourteen years of his life in retirement.* [4] N-U **Life** is the events and experiences that happen to people. *...the sort of life we can only fantasise about living.* [5] N-C You can use **life** to refer to particular activities which people regularly do during their lives. *My personal life has had to take second place to my career.* [6] N-U A person or place that is full of **life** is full of activity and excitement. *The town itself was full of life and character.* [7] N-SING The **life** of something such as a machine or organization is the period of time that it lasts for. *The repairs did not increase the value or the life of the equipment.* [8] N-U If someone is sentenced to **life**, they are sent to prison for the rest of their life, or for a very long time. [9] PHRASE If someone **is fighting for** their **life**, they are very seriously ill or injured and may die; JOURNALISM. ● **a new lease of life**: see **lease**.

lifeboat /'laɪfbəʊt/ **lifeboats.** N-C A **lifeboat** is a boat used to rescue people who are in danger at sea.

'life-cycle, life-cycles. N-C The **life-cycle** of an animal or plant is the series of changes it passes through from the beginning of its life until its death.

,life ex'pectancy, life expectancies. N-VAR The **life expectancy** of a person, animal, or plant is the length of time that they are normally likely to live. *Smoking reduces life expectancy.*

lifeguard /'laɪfɡɑːd/ **lifeguards.** N-C A **lifeguard** is a person who works at a beach or swimming pool and rescues people when they are in danger of drowning.

lifejacket (or **life jacket**) /'laɪfdʒækɪt/ **lifejackets.** N-C A **life jacket** is a sleeveless jacket which keeps you afloat in water; BRITISH.

lifeless /'laɪfləs/. [1] ADJ A person or animal that is **lifeless** is dead, or so still that they appear to be dead. [2] ADJ A **lifeless** place or area does not

have anything living or growing there at all. *...the Antarctic, mile for mile one of the planet's most lifeless areas.* [3] ADJ If you describe a person, or something such as an artistic performance or a town as **lifeless**, you mean they lack any lively or exciting qualities. *With one exception his novels are shallow and lifeless things.*

lifeline /'laɪflaɪn/ **lifelines.** N-C A **lifeline** is something that enables an organization or group to survive or to continue with an activity. *The orders will throw a lifeline to Britain's shipyards.*

lifelong /'laɪflɒŋ, AM -lɔːŋ/. ADJ BEFORE N **Lifelong** means existing or happening for the whole of a person's life. *...her lifelong friendship with Naomi.*

lifespan /'laɪfspæn/ **lifespans.** N-C The **lifespan** of a person, animal, or plant is the period of time for which they live or are normally expected to live. *A 15-year lifespan is not uncommon for a dog.*

lifestyle (or **life-style**) /'laɪfstaɪl/ **lifestyles.** N-C Your **lifestyle** is the way you live, for example the things you normally do. *They enjoyed an income and lifestyle that many people would envy.*

'life-threatening. ADJ A **life-threatening** situation or illness is one in which there is a strong possibility that someone will die.

lifetime /'laɪftaɪm/ **lifetimes.** [1] N-C A **lifetime** is the length of time that someone is alive. *During my lifetime I haven't got around to much travelling.* [2] N-SING The **lifetime** of something is the period of time that it lasts. *...the lifetime of a parliament.* [3] PHRASE If you describe something, for example an opportunity, as the opportunity **of a lifetime**, you are emphasizing that it is the most memorable or important opportunity that you are ever likely to have.

lift /lɪft/ **lifts, lifting, lifted.** [1] VERB & PHR-VERB If you **lift** something, or if you **lift** it **up**, you move it to a higher position. *She lifted the last of her drink to her lips... Amy lifted her arm to wave... She put her arms around him and lifted him up.* [2] VERB If fog, cloud, or mist **lifts**, it reduces, making the weather brighter or less misty. [3] N-C In British English, a **lift** is a device that carries people or goods up and down inside tall buildings. The American word is **elevator.** [4] N-C If you give someone a **lift**, you drive them from one place to another. [5] VERB If people in authority **lift** a law or rule, they end it. *Mr Bush said he'd never been enthusiastic about sanctions in the first place and would lift them.* [6] VERB To **lift** something means to increase it. *The bank lifted its basic home loans rate to 10.99% from 10.75%.*

ligament /'lɪɡəmənt/ **ligaments.** N-C A **ligament** is a band of strong tissue in your body, which connects bones.

light 1 brightness or illumination

light /laɪt/ **lights, lighting, lit, lighted; lighter, lightest.** The form **lit** is the usual past tense and past participle, but the form **lighted** is also used. [1] N-U **Light** is the brightness that lets you see things. Light comes from the sun, moon, lamps, and fire. *It was difficult to see in* the dim light. ...ultraviolet light. **2** N-C A **light** is anything that produces light, especially an electric bulb. *The janitor comes round to turn the lights out. ...street lights.* **3** VERB A place or object that **is lit** by something has light shining in it or on it. *The room was lit by only the one light.* **4** ADJ If it is **light**, there is enough natural daylight to see by. *It was still light when we arrived.* **5** ADJ If a building or room is **light**, it has a lot of natural light in it. **6** VERB If you **light** something, you make it start burning. *She lit the fire as soon as I arrived.* **7** N-SING If someone asks you for a **light**, they want a match or a cigarette lighter so they can start smoking; INFORMAL. **8** N-C If something is presented in a particular **light**, it is presented so that you think about it in a particular way or so that it appears to be of a particular nature. *He has worked hard in recent months to portray New York in a better light.* PHRASES ● If you **set light to** something, you make it start burning. ● If someone or something **sheds light on**, **throws light on**, or **casts light on** something, they add to the information people have about it, helping them to understand it more. *A new approach offers an answer, and may shed light on an even bigger question.* ● If something **comes to light** or is **brought to light**, it becomes known. *The truth is unlikely to be brought to light by the promised enquiry.* ● If something is possible **in the light of** particular information or knowledge, it becomes possible because you have this information or knowledge. *In the light of this information it is now possible to identify a number of key issues.* ● See also **lighter, lighting.**

▶ **light up.** **1** PHR-VERB If you **light** something **up**, or if it **lights up**, it becomes bright. *...a keypad that lights up when you pick up the handset.* **2** PHR-VERB If your face or eyes **light up**, you suddenly look very surprised or happy.

light 2 not great in weight, amount, or intensity

light /laɪt/ **lighter, lightest. 1** ADJ Something that is **light** does not weigh very much. *Try to wear light, loose clothes.* ♦ **lightness** N-U *It is fashioned completely of steel for lightness and strength.* **2** ADJ Something that is **light** is not very great in amount, degree, or intensity. *...the usual light traffic in the city... There was a light knock at the door.* ♦ **lightly** ADV *Put the onions in the pan and cook until lightly browned... He kissed her lightly on the mouth.* **3** ADJ Something that is **light** is very pale in colour. *He is light haired with gray eyes... We know he has a light green van.* **4** ADJ **Light** work does not involve much physical effort.

light 3 unimportant or not serious

light /laɪt/ **lighter, lightest. 1** ADJ You can describe things such as books or music as **light** when they are entertaining without making you think very deeply. **2** ADJ If you say something in a **light** way, you sound as if you think it is not important or serious. *Talk to him in a friendly, light way about the relationship. ...to finish on a lighter note.* ♦ **lightly** ADV *'Once a detective, always a detective,' he said lightly.*

'light bulb, light bulbs. N-C A **light bulb** is the round glass part of an electric light or lamp which light shines from.

lighten /ˈlaɪtən/ **lightens, lightening, lightened. 1** VERB When something **lightens**, or when you lighten it, it becomes less dark. *She was asked to lighten her hair for a TV series.* **2** VERB If your attitude or mood **lightens**, you feel more cheerful, happy, and relaxed. *The sun was streaming in through the window, yet it did nothing to lighten his mood.* **3** VERB If you **lighten** something, you make it less heavy.

lighter /ˈlaɪtə/ **lighters.** N-C A **lighter** is a small device that produces a flame that you can use to light cigarettes.

,light·ˈhearted. 1 ADJ **Light-hearted** things are intended to be entertaining or amusing, and not at all serious. *The opera is viewed as light-hearted fantasy.* **2** ADJ Someone who is **light-hearted** is cheerful and happy. *They were light-hearted and prepared to enjoy life.*

lighthouse /ˈlaɪthaʊs/ **lighthouses.** N-C A **lighthouse** is a tower near the sea which contains a powerful flashing lamp to guide ships or to warn them of danger.

lighting /ˈlaɪtɪŋ/ N-U The **lighting** in a place is the way that it is lit, or the quality of the light in it. *The whole room is bathed in soft lighting. ...street lighting.*

lightning /ˈlaɪtnɪŋ/ **1** N-U **Lightning** is the bright flashes of light in the sky that you see during a thunderstorm. **2** ADJ BEFORE N **Lightning** describes things that happen very quickly or last for only a short time. *Driving today demands lightning reflexes.*

lightweight /ˈlaɪtweɪt/ **1** ADJ Something that is **lightweight** weighs less than most other things of the same type. *The company manufactures a range of lightweight cycles.* **2** N-C A **lightweight** is a boxer or wrestler in one of the lightest classes. **3** ADJ & N-C If you describe someone as **lightweight**, or as a **lightweight**, you are criticizing them for not being important or skilful in a particular area of activity. *Some of the discussion in the book is lightweight and unconvincing.*

'light-year, light-years. 1 N-C A **light-year** is the distance that light travels in a year. **2** N-C You can say that two things are **light years** apart to emphasize a very great difference or a very long distance or period of time between them; INFORMAL. *She says the French education system is light years ahead of the English one.*

likable /ˈlaɪkəbəl/. See **likeable.**

like 1 expressing similarity

like /laɪk/ **likes. 1** PREP If one person or thing is **like** another, they have similar characteristics or behave in similar ways. *Kathy is a great mate, we are like sisters... It's a bit like going to the dentist; it's never as bad as you fear.* ♦ **-like** *...flu-like illnesses.* **2** PREP If you ask or talk about what someone or something is **like**, you are asking or talking about their qualities, features, or characteristics. *What was Bulgaria like?* **3** PREP You use **like** to introduce an example of the thing that you have just mentioned. *The neglect that large cities like New York have received over the past 12 years is tremendous.* **4** PREP If you say that someone is behaving **like** something or someone else, you mean that they are behaving in a way that is typical of that kind of thing or person. *Greenfield was behaving like an irresponsible idiot.* **5** PREP **Like** is sometimes used in order to say that something appears to be the case when it is not. Some people consider this use to be incorrect and prefer to use 'as if'. *I felt like I was going on an adventure.* **6** PREP You can use **like** in expressions such as **nothing like** to make an emphatic negative statement. *Three hundred million dollars will be nothing like enough.*

PHRASES ● You say **'and the like'** to indicate that there are other similar things or people that can be included in what you are saying. *...keeping fit through jogging, aerobics, weight training, and the like.* ● You say **'like this'**, **'like that'**, or **'like so'** when you are showing someone how something is done. *It opens and closes, like this.* ● You use the expression **something like** with an amount, number, or description to indicate that it is approximately accurate. *They can get something like £3,000 a year.*

like 2 expressing preferences and wishes

like /laɪk/ **likes, liking, liked.** **1** VERB If you **like** something or someone, you think they are interesting, enjoyable, or attractive. *I can't think why Grace doesn't like me... Do you like to go swimming?... That's one of the things I like about you.* **2** N-PL Someone's **likes** are the things that they enjoy or find pleasant. *I knew everything about Jemma: her likes and dislikes.* **3** VERB If you **like** something such as a particular course of action or way of behaving, you approve of it. *Opal, his wife, didn't really like him drinking so much.* **4** VERB If you say that you would **like** something or would **like** to do something, you are expressing a wish or desire. *I'd like a huge bubble bath... Would you like to come back for coffee?* **5** PHRASE You say **if you like** when you are expressing something in a different way, or in a way that you think some people might disagree with or find strange. *This is more like a down payment, or a deposit, if you like.* **6** See also **liking**.

likeable (or **likable**) /ˈlaɪkəbəl/. ADJ Someone or something that is **likeable** is pleasant and easy to like. *He was an immensely likeable chap.*

likelihood /ˈlaɪklihʊd/. N-U The **likelihood** of something happening is how likely it is to happen. *The likelihood of infection is minimal... There is every likelihood that sanctions will work.*

likely /ˈlaɪkli/ **likelier, likeliest.** **1** ADJ If something is **likely** to happen, it probably will happen. *Once people have seen that something actually works, they are much more likely to accept change.* **2** ADJ If something is **likely**, it is probably true. *It appeared most likely that a new engine would be required.* **3** ADJ BEFORE N A **likely** person, place, or thing is one that will probably be suitable for a particular purpose. *He had always seemed a likely candidate to become Prime Minister.*

'like-minded. ADJ **Like-minded** people have similar opinions, ideas, or interests.

liken /ˈlaɪkən/ **likens, likening, likened.** VERB If you **liken** one thing or person **to** another, you say that they are similar. *She likens marriage to slavery.*

likeness /ˈlaɪknəs/ **likenesses.** **1** N-SING If one thing has a **likeness** to another, it is similar to it in appearance. *There might be a likeness between their features, but their eyes were totally dissimilar.* **2** N-C If a picture is a good **likeness** of someone, it looks very much like them.

likewise /ˈlaɪkwaɪz/. **1** ADV You use **likewise** when you are comparing two things and saying that they are similar. *The V2 was not an ordinary weapon: it could only be used against cities. Likewise the atom bomb.* **2** ADV If you do one thing, and someone else does **likewise**, they do the same thing. *He lent money, made donations and encouraged others to do likewise.*

liking /ˈlaɪkɪŋ/. N-SING If you have a **liking** for something or someone, you like them. *She had a liking for good clothes.*

PHRASES ● If something is, for example, too fast **for** your **liking**, you would prefer it to be slower. *He had become too powerful for their liking.* ● If something is **to** your **liking**, it suits your interests, tastes, or wishes. *London was more to his liking than Rome.*

lilac /ˈlaɪlək/ **lilacs.** The plural is **lilac** or **lilacs**. **1** N-VAR A **lilac** is a small tree with pleasant-smelling purple, pink, or white flowers. **2** ADJ & N-C Something that is **lilac** is pale pinkish-purple in colour.

lily /ˈlɪli/ **lilies.** N-C A **lily** is a plant with large flowers that are often white.

limb /lɪm/ **limbs.** N-C Your **limbs** are your arms and legs. *She would be able to stretch out her cramped limbs.*

PHRASES ● If someone has gone **out on a limb**, they have done or said something that is risky or extreme.

limbo /ˈlɪmbəʊ/. N-U If you are in **limbo**, you are in a situation where you seem to be caught between two stages and it is unclear what will happen next. *I've made no firm decisions yet— I'm in limbo.*

lime /laɪm/ **limes.** **1** N-C A **lime** is a small, round citrus fruit with green skin. **2** N-U **Lime** is a drink that tastes of limes. **3** N-C A **lime** is a large tree with pale green leaves. **4** N-U **Lime** is a substance containing calcium. It is found in soil and water.

limelight /ˈlaɪmlaɪt/. N-U If someone is in the **limelight**, they are getting a lot of attention, because they are famous or because they have done something very unusual or exciting.

limestone /ˈlaɪmstəʊn/ **limestones.** N-VAR **Limestone** is a white rock which is used for building and making cement.

limit /ˈlɪmɪt/ **limits, limiting, limited.** **1** N-C A **limit** is the greatest amount, extent, or degree of something that is possible. *Her love for him was being tested to its limits... There is no limit to how much fresh fruit you can eat in a day.* **2** N-C A **limit** is the largest or smallest amount of something such as time or money that is allowed because of a rule, law, or decision. *The three month time limit will be up in mid-June.* **3** VERB If you **limit** something, you prevent it from becoming greater than a particular amount or degree. *This would limit unemployment to around 2.5 million.* ◆**limitation** N-U *...the limitation of nuclear weapons.* [4] VERB If you **limit** yourself to something, or if someone or something **limits** you, the number of things that you have or do is reduced. *Men should limit themselves to 20 units of alcohol a week.* ◆**limiting** ADJ *The conditions laid down to me were not too limiting.* [5] VERB If something **is limited** to a particular place or group of people, it exists only in that place, or is had or done only by that group. *Entry to this prize draw is limited to UK residents only.*

PHRASES ● If a place is **off limits**, you are not allowed to go there. *These establishments are off limits to ordinary citizens.* ● If someone **is over the limit**, they have drunk more alcohol than they are legally allowed to when driving a vehicle; BRITISH.

limitation /ˌlɪmɪˈteɪʃən/ **limitations.** [1] N-VAR A **limitation** on something is a rule or decision which prevents that thing from growing or extending beyond certain limits. *...a limitation on the tax deductions for top earners.* [2] N-PL The **limitations** of someone or something are the things that they cannot do, or the things that they do badly. *Parents are too likely to blame schools for the educational limitations of their children.* [3] N-VAR A **limitation** is a fact or situation that allows only some actions and makes others impossible. *...an acute disc collapse in the spine, causing limitation of movement.* [4] See also **limit**.

limited /ˈlɪmɪtɪd/. [1] ADJ Something that is **limited** is not very great in amount, range, or degree. *They may only have a limited amount of time.* [2] ADJ BEFORE N A **limited** company is one in which the shareholders are legally responsible for only a part of any money that it may owe if it goes bankrupt; BRITISH.

limited e'dition, limited editions. N-C A **limited edition** is something such as a book or a set of coins which has been produced in very small numbers, so that each one will be valuable in the future.

limitless /ˈlɪmɪtləs/. ADJ If you describe something as **limitless**, you mean that there is or appears to be so much of it that it will never be used up. *...a limitless supply of energy.*

limousine /ˌlɪməˈziːn/ **limousines.** N-C A **limousine** is a large and very comfortable car. Limousines are usually driven by a chauffeur and are used by very rich or important people.

limp /lɪmp/ **limps, limping, limped.** [1] VERB & N-C If you **limp**, or if you walk with a **limp**, you walk in an uneven way because one of your legs or feet is hurt. *He had to limp off with a leg injury... A stiff knee following surgery forced her to walk with a limp.* [2] ADJ If something is **limp**, it is soft or weak when it should be firm or strong. *...adding volume and lift to limp hair.* ◆**limply** ADV *He let the newspaper hang limply from his fingers.*

line 1 noun uses

line /laɪn/ **lines.** [1] N-C A **line** is a long thin mark on a surface. *Draw a line down that page's center.* [2] N-C The **lines** on someone's face are the wrinkles that appear there as they grow older.

[3] N-C A **line** of people or things is a number of them that are arranged in a row. *...a line of women queueing for bread.* [4] N-C You can refer to a long piece of string or wire as a **line** when it is being used for a particular purpose. *She put her washing on the line. ...a piece of fishing-line.* [5] N-C **Line** is used to refer to a route along which people or things move or are sent. *The telephone lines went dead... They've got to ride all the way to the end of the line.* [6] N-C You can use **line** to refer to the edge, outline, or shape of something. [7] N-C **Line** refers to the boundary between certain areas, things, or types of people. *...just over the California state line in Nevada... Thirteen per cent of the population live below the poverty line.* [8] N-C An actor's **lines** are the words they speak in a play or film. [9] N-C The **line** that someone takes on a problem or topic is their attitude or policy towards it. *The government has taken a hard line against the continuing influx of Albanian boat people.* [10] N-C Your **line** of work is the kind of work that you do. [11] N-C A **line** is a type of product that a company makes or sells. *His best selling line is the cheapest lager.* [12] See also **lining, bottom line, front line, production line**.

line 2 verb uses

line /laɪn/ **lines, lining, lined.** [1] VERB If people or things **line** a place such as a road, large numbers of them are present along its edges or sides. *Thousands of cheering Albanians lined the streets. ...a long tree-lined drive.* [2] VERB If you **line** something such as a container, you put a layer of something on the inside surface of it. *Bears tend to line their dens with leaves or grass.* [3] VERB If something **lines** a container or area, it forms a layer on the inside surface. *...the muscles that line the intestines.*

▶ **line up.** [1] PHR-VERB If people or things **are lined up**, they move so that they stand in a row or form a queue. *I would line up my toys on this windowsill and play... The senior leaders lined up behind him in orderly rows.* [2] PHR-VERB If you **line up** an event or activity, you arrange for it to happen. If you **line** someone **up** for an event or activity, you arrange for them to be available for that event or activity. *Bob Dylan was lining up a two-week UK tour.*

line 3 phrases

line /laɪn/ **lines.**

PHRASES ● If something happens somewhere **along the line** or somewhere **down the line**, it happens during the course of a situation or activity. *Somewhere along the line he picked up an engineering degree.* ● If you **draw the line** at a particular activity, you refuse to do it, usually because you disapprove of it. *They would draw the line at hitting an old lady.* ● If you are **in line for** something, you are likely to get it. *He must be in line for a place in the Guinness Book of Records.* ● If one thing is **in line** with another, or is brought **into line** with it, the first thing is, or becomes, similar to the second, especially in a way that has been agreed, planned, or expected. *The structure of our schools is now broadly in line with the major countries of the world.* ● If you do something **on line**, you do it using a computer or a computer network. ● If something such as your job, career, or reputation is **on the line**, you may lose or harm it as a result of the situation you are in. *He wouldn't put his career on the line to help a friend.* ● If someone steps **out of line**, they disobey someone or behave in an unacceptable way. ● If you **read between the lines**, you understand what someone really means, or what is really happening in a situation, even though it is not said openly. ● to **toe the line**: see **toe**.

linear /'lɪniə/. **1** ADJ A **linear** process is one in which something progresses straight from one stage to another. *...life as a series of events, progressing in a linear way from beginning to end.* **2** ADJ A **linear** shape consists of straight lines.

linen /'lɪnɪn/. N-U **Linen** is a kind of cloth that is made from a plant called flax.

liner /'laɪnə/ **liners**. N-C A **liner** is a large passenger ship.

linesman /'laɪnzmən/ **linesmen**. N-C A **linesman** is an official in games such as football and tennis who indicates when the ball goes outside the boundary lines.

'**line-up, line-ups**. N-C A **line-up** is a group of people or a series of things that are assembled to take part in a particular activity or event. *...a new series with a great line-up of musicians.*

linger /'lɪŋgə/ **lingers, lingering, lingered**. **1** VERB If something **lingers**, it continues to exist for a long time. *The scent of her perfume lingered on in the room. ...the lingering effects of radiation.* **2** VERB If you **linger** somewhere, you stay there for a longer time than is necessary. *Customers are welcome to linger over coffee until around midnight.*

lingerie /'lænʒəri, AM -'reɪ/. N-U You can refer to women's underwear and night clothes as **lingerie**.

linguist /'lɪŋgwɪst/ **linguists**. **1** N-C A **linguist** is someone who is good at speaking or learning foreign languages. **2** N-C A **linguist** is someone who studies or teaches linguistics.

linguistics /lɪŋ'gwɪstɪks/ The form **linguistic** is used as a modifier. **1** N-U **Linguistics** is the study of the way in which language works. **2** ADJ **Linguistic** abilities or ideas relate to language or linguistics. *...linguistic theory.*

lining /'laɪnɪŋ/ **linings**. **1** N-C The **lining** of a piece of clothing or a curtain is a material attached to the inside of it in order to make it thicker or warmer, or to make it hang better. *...a padded satin jacket with quilted lining.* **2** N-C The **lining** of your stomach or other organ is a layer of tissue on the inside of it. *...the uterine lining.*

link /lɪŋk/ **links, linking, linked**. **1** VERB & N-C If something **links** two things, or if there is a **link** between them, there is a logical relationship between them. *Liver cancer is linked to the hepatitis B virus. ...the link between alcohol and violence.* **2** VERB & N-C If something **links** two places or objects, or if there is a link between them, there is a physical connection between them. *...the Rama Road, which links the capital, Managua, with the Caribbean coast. ...the high-speed rail link between London and the Channel Tunnel.* **3** VERB If you **link** one person or thing to another, you claim that there is a relationship or connection between

them. *Jones has linked the crime to social circumstances.* **4** VERB If you **link** one thing with another, you join them by putting one thing through the other. *She linked her arm through his.* **5** N-C A **link** of a chain is one of the rings in it.

▶ **link up**. **1** PHR-VERB If you **link up** with someone, you join them for a particular purpose. *The Russian and American armies linked up for the first time.* **2** PHR-VERB If one thing **is linked up** to another, the two things are connected to each other. *CD-ROM discs, which can be linked up to a hi-fi and personal computer.*

'**link-up, link-ups**. N-C A **link-up** is a relationship or partnership between two organizations. *The US airline has just announced a formal link-up with British Airways.*

lion /laɪən/ **lions**. N-C A **lion** is a large wild member of the cat family that is found in Africa. Lions have yellowish fur, and male lions have long hair on their head and neck.

'**lion's share**. N-SING If a person, group, or project gets the **lion's share** of something, they get the largest part of it. *The lion's share of the work will go to American companies.*

lip /lɪp/ **lips**. **1** N-C Your **lips** are the two outer parts of the edge of your mouth. **2** PHRASE If you say that someone keeps a **stiff upper lip**, you mean that they do not show any emotion even though it is difficult for them not to. **3** **bite your lip**: see **bite**.

'**lip-service**. N-U If you say that someone pays **lip-service** to an idea, you are criticizing them because they say they are in favour of it, but do nothing to support it. *He had done no more than pay lip service to their views.*

lipstick /'lɪpstɪk/ **lipsticks**. N-VAR **Lipstick** is a coloured substance which women put on their lips.

liqueur /lɪ'kjʊə, AM -'kɜːr/ **liqueurs**. N-VAR A **liqueur** is a strong sweet alcoholic drink.

liquid /'lɪkwɪd/ **liquids**. N-VAR A **liquid** is a substance such as water which is not solid and which can be poured. *Solids turn to liquids at certain temperatures. ...liquid nitrogen.*

liquidate /'lɪkwɪdeɪt/ **liquidates, liquidating, liquidated**. VERB To **liquidate** a company means to close it down and sell all its assets, usually because it is in debt. ♦ **liquidation, liquidations**. N-VAR *The company went into liquidation.* ♦ **liquidator, liquidators** N-C *The firm has been passed into the hands of liquidators.*

liquor /'lɪkə/ **liquors**. N-U In American English, alcoholic drink such as whisky and vodka is sometimes referred to as **liquor**. The British word is **spirits**.

list /lɪst/ **lists, listing, listed**. **1** N-C A **list** is a set of things which all belong to a particular category, written down one below the other. *...the hotel's exhaustive wine list.* **2** VERB To **list** a set of things means to write them or say them one after another, usually in a particular order. *Ingredients are listed in order of the amount used.*

listen /'lɪsən/ **listens, listening, listened**. **1** VERB If you **listen** to someone who is talking or to a sound, you give your attention to them. *Sonia was not listening... He spent his time listening to the radio.* **2** VERB If you **listen** for a sound, you keep alert, ready to hear it if it occurs. *They spend the flight listening for any little noise that may seem odd.* ③ VERB If you **listen** to someone, you do what they advise you to do, or you believe them. *When I asked him to stop, he would not listen.* ④ CONVENTION You say **listen** when you want someone to pay attention to you because you are going to say something. *Listen, I finish at one.* ⑤ See note at **hear**.

▸ **listen in.** PHR-VERB If you **listen in** to a private conversation, you secretly listen to it. *He assigned federal agents to listen in on Martin Luther King's phone calls.*

listener /ˈlɪsnə/ **listeners.** N-C People who listen to the radio are often referred to as **listeners.** *I'm a regular listener to her show.*

listless /ˈlɪstləs/. ADJ Someone who is **listless**, has no energy or enthusiasm. ◆**listlessly** ADV *Usually, you would just sit listlessly, too hot to do anything.*

lit /lɪt/. **Lit** is a past tense and past participle of **light**.

liter /ˈliːtə/. See **litre**.

literacy /ˈlɪtərəsi/. N-U **Literacy** is the ability to read and write. *Many adults have some problems with literacy and numeracy.*

literal /ˈlɪtərəl/. ① ADJ The **literal** meaning of a word is its most basic meaning. *People there are fighting, in a literal sense, for their homes.* ② ADJ A **literal** translation is one in which you translate each word separately, rather than expressing the meaning in a more natural way. *A literal translation of the name Tapies is 'walls'.* ◆**literally** ADV *The word 'volk' translates literally as 'folk'.*

literally /ˈlɪtərəli/. ADV You can use **literally** to emphasize a word or expression which is being used in a creative way to exaggerate a situation. Some careful speakers of English think that this use is incorrect. *The views are literally breath-taking.*

literary /ˈlɪtərəri, AM -reri/. ① ADJ **Literary** means connected with literature. *...a literary masterpiece.* ② ADJ **Literary** words are often unusual in some way and are used to create a special effect in a poem, speech, or novel.

literate /ˈlɪtərət/. ① ADJ Someone who is **literate** is able to read and write. *Over one-quarter of the adult population are not fully literate.* ② ADJ If you describe someone as **literate**, you mean that they are intelligent and well-educated, especially about literature and the arts. *Scientists should be literate and articulate as well as able to handle figures.*

literature /ˈlɪtrətʃə, AM -tərətʃʊr/ **literatures.** ① N-U Novels, plays, and poetry are referred to as **literature**. *...teaching literature to large groups of young people.* ② N-U **Literature** is printed information about something. *...the literature on immigration policy.*

litigation /ˌlɪtɪˈɡeɪʃən/. N-U **Litigation** is the process of taking legal action; TECHNICAL. *The settlement ends more than four years of litigation on behalf of the residents.*

litre (AM **liter**) /ˈliːtə/ **litres.** N-C A **litre** is a metric unit of volume. It is equal to approximately 1.76 British pints or 2.11 American pints. *...15 litres of water.*

litter /ˈlɪtə/ **litters, littering, littered.** ① N-U **Litter** is rubbish which is left lying around outside. ② VERB If a number of things **litter** a place, they are scattered around in it. *Glass from broken bottles litters the pavement.* ◆**littered** ADJ *Debris was littered over the race track.* ③ ADJ AFTER LINK-V If you say that something such as history or someone's speech is **littered with** something, you mean that there are many examples of the second thing in the first. *Charles's speech is littered with lots of marketing buzzwords like 'package' and 'product'.*

little /ˈlɪtəl/. ① QUANT You use **little** to emphasize that there is only a small amount of something. *I need very little sleep these days... Little is known about his childhood.* ② QUANT A **little** of something is a small amount of it. *A little food would do us all some good... Pour a little of the sauce over the chicken.* ③ ADV **Little** means not very often or to only a small extent. *On their way back to Marseille they spoke very little.* ④ ADJ **Little** things are small in size. **Little** is slightly more informal than **small**. *We sat around a little table. ...the little group of art students.* ⑤ ADJ BEFORE N A **little** distance, period of time, or event is short in length. *Just go down the road a little way.* ⑥ ADJ BEFORE N You use **little** to indicate that something is not serious or important. *Harry found himself getting angry over little things.* ⑦ See note at **small**.

Little and **a little** are both used as determiners in front of uncount nouns, but they do not have the same meaning. For example, if you say '**I have a little money**', this is a positive statement and you are saying that you have some money. However, if you say '**I have little money**', this is a kind of negative statement and you are saying that you have almost no money or that you do not have enough money.
Note that when **little** is used with count nouns, it is an adjective, meaning **small**. *...a little house. ...little children.*
See also the note at **small.**

PHRASES ● A **little** or a **little bit** means to a small extent or degree or for a short period. *He was a little bit afraid of his father's reaction... He walked a little by himself.* ● If something happens **little by little**, it happens very gradually. *Little by little he was becoming weaker.*

live 1 verb uses

live /lɪv/ **lives, living, lived.** ① VERB If someone **lives** in a particular place, their home is there. *She has lived here for 10 years... We used to live in the same road... He still lives with his parents.*

When you are talking about someone's home, the verb **live** has a different meaning in the continuous tenses than it does in the simple tenses. For example, if you say '**I'm living in London**', this suggests that the situation is temporary and you may soon move to a different place. If you say '**I live in London**', this

live 362

suggests that London is your permanent home.

The verb **work** behaves in a similar way. You use the continuous tenses, with the '-ing' form, to talk about a temporary job, but the simple tenses to talk about a permanent job.

2 VERB The way someone **lives** is the kind of life they have or the circumstances they are in. *We lived quite grandly... We can start living a normal life again now.* **3** VERB To **live** means to be alive. *He's got a terrible disease and will not live long... He lived to see his first grandson... Ian was her only living relative.* **4** VERB If people **live by** doing a particular activity, they get the money, food, or clothing they need by doing that activity. *...the last indigenous people to live by hunting.* **5** VERB If you say that someone **lives for** a particular thing, you are emphasizing that it is the most important thing in their life. *Laura lived for those kids.* **6** **hand to mouth**: see **hand**. ● to **live a lie**: see **lie**.

▶ **live down.** PHR-VERB If you are unable to **live down** a mistake, failure, or bad reputation, you are unable to make people forget about it. *I thought I'd never live it down.*

▶ **live off.** **1** PHR-VERB If you **live off** another person, you rely on them to provide you with money. *...a man who all his life had lived off his father.* **2** See **live on** 1.

▶ **live on.** **1** PHR-VERB If you **live on** a particular amount of money, or if you **live off** it, you have that amount of money to buy things. *Most students are unable to live on £3000 per year.* **2** PHR-VERB If someone **lives on** a particular kind of food, it is, or seems to be, the only thing that they eat. *The children live on chips.* **3** PHR-VERB If a person or occasion **lives on** in someone's mind or in history, they are remembered because they are significant or important.

▶ **live up to.** PHR-VERB If someone or something **lives up to** what they were expected to be or do, they achieve what they expected.

live 2 adjective and adverb uses

live /laɪv/. **1** ADJ BEFORE N **Live** animals or plants are alive, rather than being dead or artificial. **2** ADJ & ADV A **live** television or radio programme is one in which an event is broadcast at the time that it happens. *...live pictures of the current weather... It was broadcast live in 50 countries.* **3** ADJ & ADV A **live** performance is given in front of an audience, rather than being recorded. *She's much happier performing live.* **4** ADJ A **live** wire or piece of electrical equipment is directly connected to a source of electricity.

livelihood /ˈlaɪvlihʊd/ **livelihoods.** N-VAR Your **livelihood** is your job or the source of your income. *...fishermen who depend on the seas for their livelihood.*

lively /ˈlaɪvli/ **livelier, liveliest.** **1** ADJ You can describe someone as **lively** when they behave in an enthusiastic and cheerful way. ♦ **liveliness** N-U *Amy could sense his liveliness.* **2** ADJ A **lively** event or a **lively** discussion, for example, has lots of interesting and exciting things happening in it or being said in it. *...a lively debate.* **3** ADJ BEFORE N You use **lively** to describe a feeling which is strong and enthusiastic. *He had a lively interest in Buddhism.*

liven /ˈlaɪvən/ **livens, livening, livened.**

▶ **liven up.** **1** PHR-VERB If a place or event **livens up**, or if you **liven it up**, it becomes more interesting and exciting. *How could we decorate the room to liven it up?* **2** PHR-VERB If people **liven up**, or if something **livens** them **up**, they become more cheerful and energetic. *Talking about her daughters livens her up.*

liver /ˈlɪvə/ **livers.** **1** N-C Your **liver** is a large organ in your body which cleans your blood. **2** N-U **Liver** is the liver of some animals, which is cooked and eaten.

lives. **1** /laɪvz/ **Lives** is the plural of **life**. **2** /lɪvz/ **Lives** is the third person singular form of **live**.

livestock /ˈlaɪvstɒk/. N-U Animals such as cattle and sheep which are kept on a farm are referred to as **livestock**.

livid /ˈlɪvɪd/. ADJ Someone who is **livid** is extremely angry; INFORMAL *I am absolutely livid about it.*

living /ˈlɪvɪŋ/. **1** N-SING The work that you do for a **living** is the work that you do to earn the money that you need. *He earns his living doing all kinds of things.* **2** N-U You use **living** when talking about the quality of people's daily lives. *...the stresses of urban living.* **3** N-PL **The living** are people who are alive, rather than people who have died.

'living-room, living-rooms. N-C The **living-room** in a house is the room where people sit and relax.

lizard /ˈlɪzəd/ **lizards.** N-C A **lizard** is a reptile with short legs and a long tail.

load /ləʊd/ **loads, loading, loaded.** **1** VERB & PHR-VERB If you **load** a vehicle or container, or if you **load** it **up**, you put a large quantity of things or heavy things into it. *The three men seemed to have finished loading the truck... Mr. Dambar had loaded his plate with lasagne.* **2** N-C A **load** is something large or heavy which is being carried. *...a big load of hay.* **3** VERB To **load** a gun, camera, or other piece of equipment means to put something such as a bullet or film in it so that it is ready to use. *He carried a loaded gun.* **4** QUANT A **load of** something or **loads of** it is a large amount of it. A **load of** people or things or **loads of** them is a large number of them. *I've got loads of money.*

loaded /ˈləʊdɪd/. **1** ADJ A **loaded** remark or question has more meaning or purpose than it appears to have, because the person who uses it hopes it will cause people to respond in a particular way. **2** ADJ If something is **loaded** with things, it has a large number of them in it or on it. *...a fully loaded jet airliner.* **3** ADJ If you say that something is **loaded in favour of** someone or something, you mean that it works unfairly to their advantage. If you say it is **loaded against** them, you mean that it works unfairly to their disadvantage.

loaf /ləʊf/ **loaves** /ləʊvz/. N-C A **loaf** of bread is bread in a shape that can be cut into slices.

loan /ləʊn/ **loans, loaning, loaned.** [1] N-C A **loan** is a sum of money that you borrow. [2] VERB & N-SING If someone **loans** something to you, or if they give you a **loan** of it, they lend it to you. [3] PHRASE If something or someone is **on loan** to a person or organization, that person or organization is borrowing them.

loath or **loth** /ləʊθ/. ADJ AFTER LINK-V If you are **loath** to do something, you do not want to do it.

loathe /ləʊð/ **loathes, loathing, loathed.** VERB If you **loathe** something or someone, you dislike them very much. ...a play universally loathed by the critics. ◆**loathing** N-U She looked at him with loathing.

loaves /ləʊvz/. **Loaves** is the plural of **loaf**.

lob /lɒb/ **lobs, lobbing, lobbed.** VERB & N-C If you **lob** something such as a ball, you throw or hit it high in the air. A **lob** is a throw or hit like this. Thugs lobbed a grenade into the crowd.

lobby /'lɒbi/ **lobbies, lobbying, lobbied.** [1] N-C The **lobby** of a building is the main entrance area with corridors and staircases leading off it. [2] VERB To **lobby** a member of a government means to try to persuade them that a particular thing should be done. Gun control advocates are lobbying hard for new laws. [3] N-C A **lobby** is a group of people who represent a particular organization or campaign, and who try to persuade the government to do something. ...a fierce anti-nuclear lobby.

lobe /ləʊb/ **lobes.** N-C The **lobe** of your ear is the soft part at the bottom.

lobster /'lɒbstə/ **lobsters.** N-C A **lobster** is a sea creature with a hard shell, two large claws, and eight legs.

local /'ləʊkəl/ **locals.** [1] ADJ **Local** means existing in or belonging to the area where you live, or to the area that you are talking about. ...the local newspaper... Some local residents joined the students' protest. ◆**locally** ADV Her clothes were bought locally. [2] N-C You can refer to the people who live in a particular district as the **locals**; INFORMAL.

locality /ləʊ'kælɪti/ **localities.** N-C A **locality** is a small area of a country or city. ...details of the drinking water quality in your locality.

locate /ləʊ'keɪt, AM 'ləʊkeɪt/ **locates, locating, located.** [1] VERB If you **locate** something or someone, you find them; FORMAL. [2] VERB If you **locate** something in a particular place, you put, build, or set it there; FORMAL. ◆**located** ADJ The restaurant is located near the cathedral.

location /ləʊ'keɪʃən/ **locations.** [1] N-C A **location** is a place, especially the place where something happens or is situated. Macau's newest small luxury hotel has a beautiful location. [2] PHRASE If a film is made **on location**, it is made away from a studio.

loch /lɒx, lɒk/ **lochs.** N-C A **loch** is a large Scottish lake.

lock /lɒk/ **locks, locking, locked.** [1] VERB When you **lock** something, you fasten it by means of a key. ...the locked door. [2] N-C The **lock** on something such as a door is the device which fastens it when you turn a key in it. He heard a key turning in the lock. [3] VERB If you **lock** something or someone in a place, room,

or container, you put them there and fasten the lock. They beat them up and locked them in a cell. [4] VERB When you **lock** something in a particular position or place, or when it **locks** there, it is held or fitted firmly in that position or place. He locked his fingers behind his head... The undercarriage locked into position. [5] N-C A **lock** is a place on a canal or river which can be closed at each end by gates, so boats can move to a higher or lower section by changing the water level inside the gates. [6] N-C A **lock** of hair is a small bunch of hairs on your head that grow together in the same direction.

▶ **lock away.** [1] PHR-VERB If you **lock** something **away** in a place or container, you put or hide it there and fasten the lock. He had even locked away all the videos. [2] PHR-VERB To **lock** someone **away** or to **lock** them **up** means to put them in prison or in a secure psychiatric hospital. Locking them away is not sufficient, you have to give them treatment.

▶ **lock up.** [1] PHR-VERB When you **lock up** a building or car, or when you **lock up**, you make sure that all the doors and windows are locked so that nobody can get in. [2] See **lock away** 2.

locker /'lɒkə/ **lockers.** N-C A **locker** is a small cupboard for someone's personal belongings, for example in a changing room.

locomotive /'ləʊkəməʊtɪv/ **locomotives.** N-C A **locomotive** is a railway engine; FORMAL.

locust /'ləʊkəst/ **locusts.** N-C **Locusts** are insects that live in hot countries. They fly in large groups and eat crops.

lodge /lɒdʒ/ **lodges, lodging, lodged.** [1] N-C A **lodge** is a house or hut in the country or the mountains where people stay on holiday. ...a Victorian hunting lodge. [2] VERB If you **lodge** in someone else's house, you live there paying rent. ◆**lodger, lodgers** N-C Jennie took in a lodger to help with the mortgage. [3] VERB If something **lodges** somewhere, it becomes stuck there. The bullet lodged in the sergeant's leg... His car has a bullet lodged in the passenger door. [4] VERB If you **lodge** a complaint, you formally make it.

lodging /'lɒdʒɪŋ/ **lodgings.** N-VAR You can refer to a room that is rented in someone's house as a person's **lodging** or **lodgings**. He was given free lodging.

loft /lɒft, AM lɔːft/ **lofts.** N-C A **loft** is the space inside the sloping roof of a building.

lofty /'lɒfti, AM 'lɔːf-/. [1] ADJ A **lofty** idea or aim is noble, important, and admirable. ...the gap between lofty ideals and grubby reality. [2] ADJ A **lofty** building or room is very high; FORMAL. ...a light, lofty apartment. [3] ADJ If you say that someone behaves in a **lofty** way, you are criticizing them for behaving in a proud way, as if they think they are very important. ...the lofty disdain he often expresses for his profession.

log /lɒg, AM lɔːg/ **logs, logging, logged.** [1] N-C A **log** is a thick piece of wood cut from a branch or trunk of a tree. [2] N-C A **log** is an official written account of what happens each day, for example on a ship. He wrote about what he had seen in his ship's log. [3] VERB If you **log** an event or fact, you record it officially in writing.

Details of the crime are then logged in the computer.

▶ **log in** or **log on.** PHR-VERB When someone **logs in** or **logs on**, or when they **log into** a computer system, they gain access to the system, usually by typing their name and a password.

▶ **log out** or **log off.** PHR-VERB When someone who is using a computer system **logs out** or **logs off**, they finish using the system by typing a particular command.

logic /'lɒdʒɪk/. N-U **Logic** is a way of reasoning that involves a series of statements, each of which must be true if the statement before it is true.

logical /'lɒdʒɪkəl/. [1] ADJ In a **logical** argument or analysis, each step or point must be true if the step before it is true. *...when each logical step has been checked by other mathematicians.* ◆**logically** ADV *My professional training has taught me to look at things logically.* [2] ADJ A **logical** conclusion or result is the only reasonable one. *If the climate gets drier, then the logical conclusion is that even more drought will occur.* ◆**logically** ADV *Logically, the Universe cannot be younger than any of the stars it contains.* [3] ADJ A **logical** course of action seems reasonable or sensible in the circumstances. *It is logical to take precautions.*

logistics /lə'dʒɪstɪks/. The form **logistic** is used as a modifier. [1] N-PL If you refer to the **logistics** of doing a complicated task, you are referring to the skilful organization of people and equipment, so that it can be done. *...the logistics of getting such a big show on the road.* [2] ADJ **Logistic** or **logistical** means relating to the organization of something complicated. *Producing a musical so far from home posed a variety of logistical problems.*

logo /'ləʊgəʊ/. **logos.** N-C The **logo** of an organization is the special design that it puts on all its products.

loiter /'lɔɪtə/. **loiters, loitering, loitered.** VERB If you **loiter** somewhere, you stay there or walk about there without any real purpose. *Men loiter at the entrance of the factory.*

lone /ləʊn/. ADJ BEFORE N A **lone** person or thing is alone or is the only one in a particular place. *He was shot by a lone gunman.*

lonely /'ləʊnli/. **lonelier, loneliest.** [1] ADJ A **lonely** person is unhappy because they are alone, or because they do not have any friends. You can also use **lonely** to describe a situation or period of time in which someone feels lonely. *...those long, lonely nights.* ◆**loneliness** N-U *He felt a sudden inexpressible loneliness.* [2] ADJ A **lonely** place is one where very few people come. *...dark, lonely streets.*

loner /'ləʊnə/. **loners.** N-C A **loner** is a person who likes being alone.

long /lɒŋ, AM lɔːŋ/. **longer, longest.** [1] ADV & ADJ **Long** means a great amount of time or for a great amount of time. *Repairs to the cable did not take too long... I learned long ago to avoid these invitations... The railway had obviously been built long after the house... I went for a long walk around Odessa.* [2] ADV & ADJ You use **long** to ask or talk about amounts of time. *How*

long can you stay?... The average commuter journey there is five hours long.

PHRASES • If you say that something is true **as long as** or **so long as** something else is true, you mean that it is true only if the second thing is true. *Tiles can be fixed to any surface as long as it's flat.* • The expression **for long** is used to mean 'for a great amount of time'. *'Did you live there?'—'Not for long'.* • Something that is **no longer** true, or that is not true **any longer**, used to be true but is not true now. *Food shortages are no longer a problem... He wasn't sitting by the door any longer.* • If you say that someone **won't be long**, you think that they will arrive or return soon.

long /lɒŋ, AM lɔːŋ/. **longer, longest.** [1] ADJ Something that is **long** measures a great distance from one end to the other. *...a long table. ...places quite a long way from here.* [2] ADJ You use **long** to talk about or ask about the distance something measures from one end to the other. *An eight-week-old embryo is only an inch long... How long is the tunnel? ...centipedes as long as a pencil.* [3] ADJ A **long** book or other piece of writing contains a lot of words.

long /lɒŋ, AM lɔːŋ/. **longs, longing, longed.** VERB If you **long** for something, you want it very much. *He longed for the winter to be over... I'm longing to meet her.* ◆**longing, longings** N-VAR *...her longing to return home.*

long-'distance. ADJ BEFORE N & ADV **Long-distance** travel or communication involves places that are far apart. *...long-distance journeys... I phoned Nicola long-distance.*

longevity /lɒn'dʒevɪti/. N-U **Longevity** is living for a long time or lasting for a long time; FORMAL. *He attributed his longevity to a happy family life.*

longitude /'lɒndʒɪtjuːd, AM -tuːd/. **longitudes.** N-VAR The **longitude** of a place is its distance to the west or east of a line passing through Greenwich in England. Compare **latitude**.

long-'lost. ADJ BEFORE N You use **long-lost** to describe someone or something that you have not seen for a long time. *...the arrival of their long-lost cousins.*

long-'range. ADJ A **long-range** plan or prediction relates to a period extending a long time into the future. *...a long-range strategy for improving US education.*

long-'standing. ADJ A **long-standing** situation has existed for a long time. *...their long-standing dispute over money.*

long-'suffering. ADJ Someone who is **long-suffering** patiently bears continual trouble or bad treatment. *...his loyal, long-suffering wife.*

long 'term. [1] ADJ Something that is **long term** has continued for a long time or will continue for a long time in the future. *...the long-term unemployed. ...a long-term solution to credit card fraud.* [2] N-SING When you talk about what happens in **the long term**, you are talking about what happens over a long period of time. *In the long term the company hopes to open a shop in Moscow.*

'long-time. ADJ You use **long-time** to describe something that has existed or been a particular thing for a long time. *...her long-time boyfriend.*

loo /luː/ **loos.** N-C A **loo** is a toilet; BRITISH, INFORMAL.

look 1 using your eyes or your mind

look /lʊk/ **looks, looking, looked.** [1] VERB & N-SING If you **look**, or if you have a **look**, in a particular direction, you direct your eyes there in order to see what is there. *I looked down the hallway... Ducks! Look, right there!... Lucille took a last look in the mirror... Assisi has a couple of churches that are worth a look.* • See note at **see.** [2] N-C A **look** is an expression on someone's face, showing what they are feeling or thinking. *He gave her a blank look, as if he had no idea who she was... A look of disgust came over his face.* [3] VERB & N-C If you **look** for something or someone, or if you have a **look** for them, you try to find them. *I'm looking for my friend... Have you looked at the piano?... Go and have another look.* [4] VERB & N-C To **look** at a subject or situation, or to have a look at it, means to examine it, consider it, or judge it. *Can you look at my back? I think something's wrong... Next term we'll be looking at the Second World War period. ...a quick look at the morning newspapers... Brian had learned to look at her with new respect.* [5] VERB You can use **look** to draw attention to something or someone, for example because you find them very significant or annoying. *Look what a mess you've made of your life.* [6] CONVENTION You say **look** when you want someone to pay attention to what you are going to say. *Look, I'm sorry. I didn't mean it.* [7] VERB If a building or part of a building **looks** out onto something, it has a view of it. *Each front door looks across a narrow alley.* [8] to **look** someone **in the eye:** see **eye.**

▶ **look around.** See **look round.**

▶ **look after.** [1] PHR-VERB If you **look after** someone or something, you keep them healthy, safe, or in good condition. *I love looking after the children.* [2] PHR-VERB If you **look after** something, it is your responsibility to deal with it. *We'll help you look after your finances.*

▶ **look back.** PHR-VERB If you **look back**, you think about things that happened in the past. *Looking back, I see that I did the best I could.*

▶ **look down on.** PHR-VERB If you say that someone **looks down on** someone or something, you mean that they consider that person or thing to be inferior, usually when this is not the case. *I wasn't successful, so they looked down on me.*

▶ **look forward to.** PHR-VERB If you **are looking forward** to something, you want it to happen because you think you will enjoy it. *I'm really looking forward to meeting him.*

▶ **look into.** PHR-VERB If you **look into** something, you find out about it. *He had once looked into buying his own island.*

▶ **look on.** [1] PHR-VERB If you **look on** while something happens, you watch it happening without taking part yourself. *Local people looked on in silence as the two coffins were tak-* *en into the church.* [2] PHR-VERB If you **look on** someone or something in a particular way, you think of them in that way. *Employers look favourably on applicants who have work experience.*

▶ **look out.** PHR-VERB You say **'look out'** to warn someone of danger. • See also **lookout.**

▶ **look out for.** PHR-VERB If you **look out for** something, you stay alert so that you will notice it if or when it happens. *Look out for special deals.*

▶ **look round.** PHR-VERB If you **look round** a place, or if you **look around** it, you walk round it and look at the different parts of it. *We went to look round the show homes... I'm going to look around and see what I can find.*

▶ **look through.** PHR-VERB If you **look through** a book, a magazine, or a group of things, you get an idea of what is in it by examining a lot of the items in it. *Peter starts looking through the mail as soon as the door shuts.*

▶ **look to.** PHR-VERB If you **look to** someone or something for a particular thing, you expect or hope that they will provide it. *The nation looks to them for guidance.*

▶ **look up.** [1] PHR-VERB If you **look up** a piece of information, you find it out by looking in a book or list. *I looked up your address in the personnel file.* [2] PHR-VERB If you **look** someone **up**, you visit them after you have not seen them for a long time. [3] PHR-VERB If a situation **is looking up**, it is improving; INFORMAL.

▶ **look up to.** PHR-VERB If you **look up to** someone, you respect and admire them.

look 2 appearance

look /lʊk/ **looks, looking, looked.** [1] LINK-VERB & N-SING You use **look** when describing the appearance of a person or thing or the impression that they give. *I shall use the money to make my home look lovely... They look like stars to the naked eye... He looked as if he was going to smile... She had the look of someone deserted and betrayed.* [2] N-PL When you refer to someone's **looks**, you are referring to how physically attractive they are. *...a young woman with wholesome good looks.* [3] LINK-VERB You use **look** when indicating what you think will happen in the future or how a situation seems to you. *He had lots of time to think about the future, and it didn't look good... It looks like Warner Brothers' gamble is paying off.*

PHRASES • You use expressions such as **by the look of him** and **by the looks of it** when you want to give an opinion based on the appearance of someone or something. *He was not a well man by the look of him.* • If you **don't like the look** of something or someone, their appearance suggests that they might be the cause of something unpleasant. *I don't like the look of those clouds... I didn't like the look of him one bit.*

lookout /'lʊkaʊt/ **lookouts.** [1] N-C A **lookout** is a place from which you can see clearly in all directions. *Troops tried to set up a lookout post.* [2] N-C A **lookout** is someone who is watching for danger. [3] PHRASE If you are **on the lookout** for something, you are watching out for it. *He was always on the lookout for good new music.*

loom /lu:m/ **looms, looming, loomed.**
1 VERB If something **looms** over you, or if it **looms up**, it appears as a large or unclear shape, often in a frightening way. ...*the bleak mountains that loomed out of the blackness.*
2 VERB If a worrying or threatening event or situation **is looming**, it seems likely to happen soon. *The threat of renewed civil war looms ahead.* **3** PHRASE If a problem or event **looms large**, it occupies a lot of your thoughts and seems to be a frightening prospect that you cannot avoid. ...*the terrible problem of armed crime now looming large in our society.* **4** N-C A **loom** is a device that is used for weaving thread into cloth.

loony /'lu:ni/ **loonies.** ADJ & N-C If you describe someone's behaviour as loony, or if you refer to someone as a **loony**, you mean that they behave in a way that seems mad or strange; IN-FORMAL. ...*loony feminist nonsense... They all thought I was a loony.*

loop /lu:p/ **loops, looping, looped.** **1** N-C A **loop** is a curved or circular shape in something long, such as a piece of string. **2** VERB If you **loop** something such as a piece of rope around an object, you tie a length of it in a loop around the object. *He looped the rope over the wood.* **3** VERB If something **loops** somewhere, it goes there in a circular direction. ...*the road which looped through the hills.*

loophole /'lu:phəʊl/ **loopholes.** N-C A **loophole** in the law is a small mistake or omission which some people use to avoid doing something that the law intends them to do. ...*exploiting some loophole in the law to avoid prosecution.*

loose /lu:s/ **looser, loosest.** **1** ADJ Something that is **loose** is not firmly held or fixed in place. *Two wooden beams had come loose from the ceiling.* ...*a loose thread.* ◆**loosely** ADV ...*a shirt tied loosely at the waist.* **2** ADJ If people or animals break **loose** or are set **loose**, they are freed after they have been restrained. *She broke loose from his embrace.* **3** PHRASE If a person or animal is **on the loose**, they are free because they have escaped from a person or place. **4** ADJ **Loose** clothes do not fit closely. ◆**loosely** ADV *His shirt hung loosely over his thin shoulders.* **5** ADJ A **loose** grouping or arrangement is flexible rather than strictly controlled or organized. ...*a loose coalition of leftwing forces.* ◆**loosely** ADV ...*a loosely organised studio band.*

loose 'end, loose ends. N-C A **loose end** is part of a story or situation that has not yet been explained. *There are some annoying loose ends in the plot.*

loosen /'lu:sən/ **loosens, loosening, loosened.** **1** VERB If someone in authority **loosens** restrictions or laws, they make them less severe. ◆**loosening** N-SING ...*a loosening of state control over economic matters.* **2** VERB If you **loosen** something that is tied or fastened, you move it or undo it slightly so that it is less tight or less firmly held in place.
▶ **loosen up.** **1** PHR-VERB If a person or situation **loosens up**, they become more relaxed. **2** PHR-VERB If you **loosen up**, you do simple exercises to get your muscles ready for a physical activity.

loot /lu:t/ **loots, looting, looted.** **1** VERB If people **loot** a building, or if they **loot** things from it, they steal things from it during a battle or a riot. ...*thugs who have looted food supplies.* ◆**looting** N-U *There has been rioting and looting.* ◆**looter, looters** N-C *He saw looters carrying off items from evacuated apartments.* **2** N-U **Loot** is stolen money and goods; INFORMAL.

lopsided (or **lop-sided**) /,lɒp'saɪdɪd/. ADJ Something that is **lopsided** is uneven because one side is, for example, higher or much greater than the other. ...*a friendly, lopsided grin.* ...*lopsided economic relations.*

lord /lɔ:d/ **lords.** **1** N-C In Britain, a **lord** is a man who has a high rank in the nobility. *She married a lord.* **2** N-TITLE **Lord** is a title used in front of the names of some male members of the nobility, and of judges, bishops, and some high ranking officials. BRITISH. *He was Lord Chancellor from 1970 until 1974.* **3** N-PROPER In the Christian church, people refer to God and to Jesus Christ as **the Lord**.

lore /lɔ:/. N-U The **lore** of a particular country or culture is its traditional stories and history. ...*ancient Catalan lore.* ● See also **folklore**.

lorry /'lɒri, AM 'lɔ:ri/ **lorries.** N-C In British English, a **lorry** is a large vehicle used to transport goods by road. The American word is **truck**.

lose /lu:z/ **loses, losing, lost.** **1** VERB If you **lose** a fight or an argument, someone else defeats you. *A C Milan lost the Italian Cup Final... No one likes to be on the losing side.* **2** VERB If you **lose** something, you cannot find it, or you no longer have it because it has been taken away from you. *I lost my keys... He lost his place in the team.* **3** VERB If someone **loses** a quality or belief, they no longer have it. *He lost all sense of reason.* **4** VERB You say you **lose** something when you have less of it. *She lost a lot of blood... The best way to lose weight is to exercise... The company was losing money.* **5** VERB If you **lose** a relative or friend, they die. **6** VERB If you **lose** an opportunity or **lose** time, you waste it. *They did not lose the opportunity to say what they thought of events.* **7** **Lose** is used in a large number of expressions which are explained under other words in this dictionary. For example, the expression **lose** your **balance** is explained at **balance**. ● See also **lost**.
▶ **lose out.** PHR-VERB If you **lose out**, you suffer a loss or disadvantage. *Women have lost out in this new pay flexibility.*

loser /'lu:zə/ **losers.** N-C The **losers** of a contest or struggle are the people who are defeated. If you say someone is a **good loser** you mean that they accept that they have lost a contest without complaining. If you say that someone is a **bad loser**, you mean that they hate losing and complain a lot about it.

loss /lɒs, AM lɔ:s/ **losses.** **1** N-U **Loss** is the fact of no longer having something or of having less of it than before. ...*loss of sight... The loss of income for the government is about $250 million a month.* **2** N-C A **loss** is the disadvantage you suffer when a valuable and useful person or thing leaves or is taken away. *His death* *was a great loss to herself. ...a terrible loss of human life... Military sources put the army's losses at about twenty.* ⓷ N-U *Loss* is the feeling of sadness you experience when someone you like is taken away from you. *...your feelings of loss and grief.* ⓸ N-VAR If a business makes a **loss**, it earns less than it spends.

PHRASES ● If you are **at a loss**, you do not know what to do in a particular situation. ● If you **cut** your **losses**, you stop what you are doing because it is making a bad situation become worse.

lost /lɒst, AM lɔːst/ ⓵ *Lost* is the past tense and past participle of *lose*. ⓶ ADJ If you are **lost**, you do not know where you are or you are unable to find your way. *I realised I was lost.* ⓷ ADJ If something gets **lost**, you cannot find it. ⓸ ADJ If you feel **lost**, you feel uncomfortable or vulnerable because you are in an unfamiliar situation. ⓹ PHRASE If advice or a comment **is lost on someone**, they do not understand it, or they pay no attention to it.

lot /lɒt/ **lots.** ⓵ QUANT A *lot* of something or *lots* of it is a large amount of it. *A lot of our land is used to grow crops... He drank lots of milk... I learned a lot from him.* ⓶ ADV A *lot* means to a great extent or degree. *They went out a lot.* ⓷ N-C You can use **lot** to refer to a set or group of things or people. *We've just sacked one lot of builders.* ⓸ N-SING You can refer to a specific group of people as a particular **lot**; INFORMAL. *They're a boring lot.* ⓹ N-C A **lot** in an auction is one of the objects or groups of objects that is being sold. *Lot 432 is described as a Baroque Pearl and Diamond Pin.* ⓺ PHRASE If people **draw lots** to decide who will do something, they each take a piece of paper from a container. One or more pieces of paper is marked, and the people who take marked pieces are chosen. ⓻ See also **parking lot**.

loth /ləʊθ/. See **loath**.

lotion /'ləʊʃən/ **lotions.** N-VAR A *lotion* is a liquid that you use to clean, improve, or protect your skin or hair. *...suntan lotion.*

lottery /'lɒtəri/ **lotteries.** ⓵ N-C A *lottery* is a type of gambling in which people bet on a number or a series of numbers being chosen as the winner. Lotteries usually offer large cash prizes and are often organized so that a percentage of the profits is donated to good causes. ⓶ N-SING If you describe something as a **lottery**, you mean that what happens depends entirely on luck or chance. *Which judges are assigned to a case is always a bit of a lottery.*

loud /laʊd/ **louder, loudest.** ⓵ ADJ & ADV If a noise is **loud**, the level of sound is very high and it can easily be heard. Someone or something that is **loud** produces a lot of noise. *There was a loud bang... He turns the television up very loud.* ◆**loudly** ADV *His footsteps echoed loudly in the tiled hall.* ⓶ PHRASE If you say something **out loud**, you say it so that it can be heard, rather than just thinking it. *I laughed out loud.* ⓷ ADJ If someone is **loud** in their support or condemnation of something, they express their opinion very often and in a very strong way. ◆**loudly** ADV *Mac talked loudly in favour of the good works done by the Church.* ⓸ ADJ If you describe a piece of clothing as

loud, you dislike it because it is too bright and tasteless.

loudspeaker /ˌlaʊd'spiːkə/ **loudspeakers.** N-C A *loudspeaker* is a piece of equipment, for example part of a radio, through which sound comes out.

lounge /laʊndʒ/ **lounges, lounging, lounged.** ⓵ N-C A *lounge* is a room in a house, or in a hotel, where people sit and relax. ⓶ N-C At an airport, the departure **lounge** is a large room where passengers go before boarding their plane. ⓷ VERB If you **lounge** somewhere, you lean against something or lie somewhere in a relaxed way. *They ate and drank and lounged in the shade.*
▶ **lounge about** or **lounge around.** PHR-VERB If you **lounge about** or **lounge around**, you spend your time in a relaxed and lazy way. *He remembered mowing the lawn, lounging around the swimming pool.*

louse /laʊs/ **lice.** N-C *Lice* are small insects that live on the bodies of people or animals.

lousy /'laʊzi/. ⓵ ADJ If you describe something as **lousy**, you mean that it is of bad quality; INFORMAL. *The food was lousy.* ⓶ ADJ If you feel **lousy**, you feel very ill; INFORMAL. *I felt lousy.*

lout /laʊt/ **louts.** N-C If you describe a young man as a **lout**, you are critical of him because he behaves in a rude or aggressive way. *...a drunken lout.*

lovable /'lʌvəbəl/. ADJ If you describe someone as **lovable**, you mean they have attractive qualities and are easy to like.

love /lʌv/ **loves, loving, loved.** ⓵ VERB & N-U If you **love** someone, or if you have **love** for them, you feel romantically or sexually attracted to them, and they are very important to you. *Oh, Amy, I love you... Our love for each other has been increased by what we've been through together.* ⓶ VERB & N-U If you **love** someone, or if you have **love** for them, you care for them very much. *You'll never know anyone the way you love your baby... My love for all my children is unconditional.* ⓷ VERB & N-U If you **love** something, or if you have a **love** of it, you like it very much. *I love taking photographs. ...one of these people that loves to be in the outdoors. ...a love of literature.* ⓸ VERB You can say that you **love** something when you consider that it is important and want to protect or support it. *I love my country as you love yours.* ⓹ VERB If you would **love** to have or do something, you very much want to have or do it. *I would love a hot bath and clean clothes... His wife would love him to give up his job.* ⓺ CONVENTION You can write **love** or **love from**, followed by your name, when you end an informal letter. *...with love from Grandma.* ⓻ N-VOC Some people use **love** as an affectionate way of addressing someone; INFORMAL. *Well, I'll take your word for it then, love.* ⓼ NUM In tennis, **love** is a score of zero.

PHRASES ● If you fall **in love** with someone, you start to feel romantically or sexually attracted to them, and they are very important to you. *We fell madly in love.* ● When two people **make love**, they have sex. ● See also **loving**.

'love affair, love affairs. N-C A **love affair** is a romantic and usually sexual relationship between two people.

'love life, love lives. N-C Someone's **love life** is the part of their life that consists of their romantic and sexual relationships.

lovely /'lʌvli/ **lovelier, loveliest.** ADJ If you describe someone or something as **lovely**, you mean that they are very beautiful or that you like them very much. *You look lovely, Marcia... He had a lovely voice.* ◆**loveliness** N-U *You are a vision of loveliness.*

'love-making. N-U **Love-making** refers to sexual activities that take place between two people who love each other.

lover /'lʌvə/ **lovers.** [1] N-C Someone's **lover** is someone who they are having a sexual relationship with but are not married to. [2] N-C If you are a **lover** of something such as animals or the arts, you enjoy them very much and take great pleasure in them. *She is a great lover of horses. ...art lovers.*

loving /'lʌvɪŋ/. [1] ADJ Someone who is **loving** feels or shows love to other people. *...a most loving husband.* ◆**lovingly** ADV *Brian gazed lovingly at Mary Ann.* [2] ADJ **Loving** actions are done with great enjoyment and care. *The house has been restored with loving care.* ◆**lovingly** ADV *...lovingly prepared food.*

low /ləʊ/ **lower, lowest; lows.** [1] ADJ Something that is **low** measures a short distance from the bottom to the top. *She put it down on the low table. ...low, rolling hills.* [2] ADJ If something is **low**, it is close to the ground, to sea level, or to the bottom of something. *He bumped his head on the low beams... It was late afternoon and the sun was low in the sky.* [3] ADJ **Low** means small in amount or degree, or at the bottom of a particular scale or system. *...low incomes. ...temperatures in the low 80s... World stocks of wheat were getting very low. ...the low rank of 'legal adviser'.* [4] N-C A **low** is a level or amount that is less than it was before. *The shares plunged to a new low.* [5] ADJ If the quality or standard of something is **low**, it is poor. *...work of very low quality.* [6] ADJ If someone is **low**, or if their spirits are **low**, they are feeling depressed. *We are all very tired and morale is low.* [7] ADJ If you have a **low** opinion of someone, you disapprove of them or dislike them. [8] ADJ A **low** sound is deep and quiet. *Father whistled a few low notes... 'The police are here,' she said in a low voice.* [9] ADJ If something such as a radio or a light is **low**, it is only producing a small amount of sound, heat, or light. *I've got the heater on low.* [10] PHRASE If you **are lying low**, you are avoiding being seen or drawing attention to yourself; INFORMAL. *It would be safer to lie low till the men were gone.* ● **at a low ebb:** see **ebb.** ● **a low profile:** see **profile.**

lower /'ləʊə/ **lowers, lowering, lowered.** [1] **Lower** is the comparative of **low.** [2] ADJ You can use **lower** to refer to the bottom one of a pair of things. *She bit her lower lip.* [3] VERB If you **lower** something, you move it slowly downwards. *Gracefully she lowered herself into a chair.* [4] VERB To **lower** an amount, value, or quality means to make it less. *The Central*

Bank has lowered interest rates. ◆**lowering** N-SING *...the lowering of the voting age to 18.*

lower 'class (also **lower-class**), **lower classes.** N-C & ADJ Some people use **the lower class** or **the lower classes** to refer to the division of society that they consider to have the lowest social status. **The lower class** can take the singular or plural form of the verb. *Most of the victims come from the lower classes. ...students from lower-class families.*

low-'key. ADJ Something that is **low-key** is restrained rather than noticeable or intense. *The wedding will be a very low-key affair.*

lowly /'ləʊli/ **lowlier, lowliest.** ADJ Something that is **lowly** is low in position or status. *...the team's lowly position in the First Division.*

loyal /'lɔɪəl/. ADJ If you describe someone as **loyal**, you mean they remain firm in their friendship or support for someone or something. *They had remained loyal to the president.* ◆**loyally** ADV *They have loyally supported their party.*

loyalty /'lɔɪəlti/ **loyalties.** [1] N-U **Loyalty** is behaviour in which you stay firm in your friendship or support for someone or something. *I have sworn an oath of loyalty to the monarchy.* [2] N-C **Loyalties** are feelings of friendship, support, or duty. *Mr Armstrong has divided loyalties when England play Scotland at rugby.*

LP /ˌel 'piː/ **LPs.** N-C An **LP** is a record which usually has about 25 minutes of music or speech on each side.

Ltd. In Britain, **Ltd** is a written abbreviation for **limited**, used after the name of a company.

lubricate /'luːbrɪkeɪt/ **lubricates, lubricating, lubricated.** VERB If you **lubricate** something such as a part of a machine, you put oil onto it to make it move smoothly. *Lubricate the hinges and springs.* ◆**lubrication** N-U *Use a touch of linseed oil for lubrication.*

lucid /'luːsɪd/. [1] ADJ **Lucid** writing or speech is clear and easy to understand. *...his lucid explanation of the work.* ◆**lucidly** ADV *...the ability to present matters lucidly.* ◆**lucidity** /luː'sɪdɪti/ N-U *...the force and lucidity of his arguments.* [2] ADJ When someone is **lucid**, they are able to think clearly again after a period of illness or confusion. ◆**lucidity** N-U *Gordie had occasional months of lucidity.*

luck /lʌk/. N-U **Luck** is success or good things that happen to you, which do not come from your own abilities or efforts. *He does deserve some good luck... We have had no luck finding accommodation.*

PHRASES ● You can say **'Bad luck'**, **'Hard luck'**, or **'Tough luck'** to someone when you want to express your sympathy to them. ● You say **'Good luck'** or **'Best of luck'** to someone when you are wishing them success in something they are trying to do. ● When someone **tries** their **luck** at something, they try to succeed at it. *She went back to Japan last June to try her luck as a model.* ● You can add **with luck** or **with any luck** to a statement to indicate that you hope that a particular thing will happen. *With any luck, she thought, the money would turn up somewhere.*

luckily /'lʌkɪli/. ADV You add **luckily** to your statement to indicate that you are glad that something happened or is the case. *Luckily, we both love football.*

lucky /'lʌki/ **luckier, luckiest.** [1] ADJ If someone is **lucky**, they are in a very desirable situation. *I am luckier than most. I have a job.* [2] ADJ A **lucky** person always has good luck. *He had always been lucky at cards.* [3] ADJ If an event or situation is **lucky**, it has good effects or consequences, which happen by chance. *Five of the kids were taken to hospital, it's just lucky that no lives were lost.* [4] ADJ A **lucky** object is something that someone believes helps them to be successful. *Seven is my lucky number.* [5] PHRASE If you say that someone **will be lucky** to do or get something, you mean that they are very unlikely to do or get it. *You'll be lucky if you get any breakfast.*

lucrative /'lu:krətɪv/. ADJ A **lucrative** business or activity earns you a lot of money.

ludicrous /'lu:dɪkrəs/. ADJ If you describe something as **ludicrous**, you mean that it is very foolish or unreasonable. *It was ludicrous to suggest that the visit could be kept secret.* ♦**ludicrously** ADV *The prices are ludicrously low.*

lug /lʌg/ **lugs, lugging, lugged.** VERB If you **lug** a heavy object somewhere, you carry it there with difficulty; INFORMAL. *Nobody wants to lug around huge suitcases.*

luggage /'lʌgɪdʒ/. N-U **Luggage** consists of the suitcases and bags that take when you travel.

> **Luggage** is an uncount noun. You can have **a piece of luggage** or **some luggage** but you cannot have 'a luggage' or 'some luggages'.

lukewarm /,lu:k'wɔ:m/. [1] ADJ **Lukewarm** water is only slightly warm. [2] ADJ If you describe a person or their attitude as **lukewarm** towards someone or something, you mean they do not show much enthusiasm or interest towards them. *The new design received the same lukewarm response as his first proposal.*

lull /lʌl/ **lulls, lulling, lulled.** [1] N-C A **lull** is a period of quiet or of little activity. *...a lull in the conversation.* [2] VERB If you **are lulled into** feeling safe, someone or something causes you to feel safe at a time when you are not safe. *It is easy to be lulled into a false sense of security.*

lumber /'lʌmbə/ **lumbers, lumbering, lumbered.** [1] N-U In American English, **lumber** consists of wood that has been roughly cut up; the British word is **timber.** [2] VERB If someone **lumbers** around, they move slowly and clumsily. *He turned and lumbered back to his chair.*

▶ **lumber with.** PHR-VERB If you **are lumbered with** someone or something, you have to take responsibility for them, although you do not want to; BRITISH, INFORMAL. *I was lumbered with the job of taking charge of all the money.*

luminous /'lu:mɪnəs/. ADJ Something that is **luminous** shines or glows in the dark. *...the luminous dial on the clock.*

lump /lʌmp/ **lumps, lumping, lumped.** [1] N-C A **lump** is a solid piece of something. *...a lump of clay.* [2] N-C A **lump** on someone's body is a small, hard piece of flesh caused by an injury or an illness.

▶ **lump together.** PHR-VERB If a number of different people or things **are lumped together**, they are considered as a group rather than separately; INFORMAL. *People tend to lump them all together.*

'lump sum, lump sums. N-C A **lump sum** is a large amount of money that is given or received all at once. *...a tax-free lump sum of £50,000.*

lumpy /'lʌmpi/ **lumpier, lumpiest.** ADJ Something that is **lumpy** contains lumps or is covered in lumps. *She stretched out on the lumpy mattress.*

lunar /'lu:nə/. ADJ BEFORE N **Lunar** means relating to the moon. *...man's first lunar landing.*

lunatic /'lu:nətɪk/ **lunatics.** N-C & ADJ If you describe someone as a **lunatic**, or if you say that their behaviour is **lunatic**, you mean they behave in a stupid and possibly dangerous way.

lunch /lʌntʃ/ **lunches, lunching, lunched.** [1] N-VAR **Lunch** is a meal that you have in the middle of the day. *We all went out for lunch.* ● See note at **meal.** [2] VERB When you **lunch** somewhere, you eat lunch there; FORMAL.

luncheon /'lʌntʃən/ **luncheons.** N-VAR **Luncheon** is a formal meal in the middle of the day.

lung /lʌŋ/ **lungs.** N-C Your **lungs** are the two organs inside your chest which you use for breathing.

lunge /lʌndʒ/ **lunges, lunging, lunged.** VERB & N-C If you **lunge**, or if you make a **lunge**, in a particular direction, you move there suddenly and clumsily. *He lunged at me, grabbing me violently.*

lurch /lɜ:tʃ/ **lurches, lurching, lurched.** VERB & N-C To **lurch**, or to give a **lurch** means to make a sudden, jerky movement, especially forwards. *Henry looked, stared, and lurched to his feet... The car took a lurch forward.*

lure /ljʊə, AM lʊr/ **lures, luring, lured.** [1] VERB To **lure** someone means to trick them into a particular place or to trick them into doing something that they should not do. *They were being lured into a trap.* [2] N-C A **lure** is an attractive quality that something has. *The lure of rural life is proving as strong as ever.*

lurid /'ljʊərɪd, AM 'lʊrɪd/. [1] ADJ If you say that something is **lurid**, you disapprove of it because it involves a lot of violence, sex, or shocking detail. *...lurid accounts of Claire's sexual exploits.* [2] ADJ If you describe something as **lurid**, you do not like it because it is very brightly coloured. *...a lurid red.*

lurk /lɜ:k/ **lurks, lurking, lurked.** [1] VERB If someone **lurks** somewhere, they hide there, usually because they intend to do something bad. *...the trees where Harper lurked with his seven-barrelled gun.* [2] VERB If something such as a memory, suspicion, or danger **lurks**, it exists, but you are only slightly aware of it. *Around every corner lurked doubt and uncertainty.*

luscious /'lʌʃəs/. ADJ **Luscious** food is juicy and delicious.

lush /lʌʃ/ **lusher, lushest.** ADJ **Lush** fields or gardens have a lot of very healthy grass or plants.

lust 370

lust /lʌst/ **lusts, lusting, lusted.** [1] VERB & N-U
If you **lust** after someone or **lust** for them, you
feel a very strong sexual desire for them. **Lust**
is this feeling. *He is obsessed by his lust for her.*
[2] VERB & N-U If you **lust** for something or **lust**
after it, you have a very strong and eager desire
to have it. A **lust** for something is this desire.
Sheard lusted after the Directorship.

luxurious /lʌgˈʒʊəriəs/. [1] ADJ Something that
is **luxurious** is very comfortable and expensive. *...Roberto's luxurious life-style.*
♦ **luxuriously** ADV *The dining-room is luxuriously furnished.* [2] ADJ **Luxurious** actions express great pleasure and comfort.
♦ **luxuriously** ADV *Liz laughed, stretching luxuriously.*

luxury /ˈlʌkʃəri/ **luxuries.** [1] N-U **Luxury** is very
great comfort, especially among beautiful and
expensive surroundings. *He leads a life of considerable luxury.* [2] N-C & ADJ BEFORE N A **luxury**

is something expensive which you do not really need but which you enjoy. *I do like the luxuries of life – good wine, clothes, holidays.
...luxury food.* [3] N-SING A **luxury** is a pleasure
which you do not often experience. *Hot baths
are my favourite luxury.*

lying /ˈlaɪɪŋ/. **Lying** is the present participle of
lie.

lynch /lɪntʃ/ **lynchs, lynching, lynched.** VERB
If an angry crowd of people **lynch** someone
they believe is guilty of committing a crime,
they kill that person by hanging them, without
letting them have a trial.

lyric /ˈlɪrɪk/ **lyrics.** [1] ADJ BEFORE N **Lyric**
poetry is written in a simple and direct style. [2] N-PL
The **lyrics** of a song are its words.

lyrical /ˈlɪrɪkəl/. ADJ Something that is **lyrical** is
poetic and romantic. *His paintings became
more lyrical.*

M m

m. m is a written abbreviation for 'metres' or
'metre'. *...a ditch 1m wide.*

ma'am /mæm, mɑːm/. N-VOC People sometimes
say **ma'am** as a formal and polite way of addressing a woman whose name they do not
know, or a woman of superior rank.

macabre /məˈkɑːbrə/. ADJ You describe something such as an event or story as **macabre**
when it is strange and horrible, usually because it involves death or injury.

machete /məˈʃeti/ **machetes.** N-C A **machete** is
a large knife with a broad blade.

machine /məˈʃiːn/ **machines.** [1] N-C A **machine** is a piece of equipment which uses electricity or an engine in order to do a particular
kind of work. *...a machine to pump water out
of mines.* [2] N-C You use **machine** to refer to a
large, well-controlled organization. *...the former Soviet military machine.*

ma'chine gun, machine guns. N-C A **machine gun** is a gun which fires a lot of bullets
very quickly one after the other. *...a burst of
machine-gun fire.*

machinery /məˈʃiːnəri/. [1] N-U **Machinery** is
machines in general, or machines that are
used in a factory. [2] N-U The **machinery** of a
government or organization is the system that
it uses to deal with things. *...strengthening the
machinery of the United Nations.*

machinist /məˈʃiːnɪst/ **machinists.** N-C A **machinist** is a person whose job is to operate a
machine, especially in a factory.

macho /ˈmætʃəʊ, AM ˈmɑː-/. ADJ You use **macho**
to describe men who behave in an aggressively
masculine way; INFORMAL. *He likes to project a
macho image.*

mackerel /ˈmækərəl/. N-VAR A **mackerel** is a
greenish-blue edible sea fish. **Mackerel** is the
flesh of this fish eaten as food. **Mackerel** is
both the singular and plural.

mad /mæd/ **madder, maddest.** [1] ADJ Someone who is **mad** has a mental illness which
makes them behave in strange ways. *She was
afraid of going mad.* ♦ **madness** N-U *...the clas-*

sic symptoms of madness. [2] ADJ You describe
someone as **mad** when they do or say things
that you think are very foolish. *He'd be mad to
refuse.* ♦ **madness** N-U *It would be madness to
lose the jury system.* [3] ADJ You use **mad** to describe wild uncontrolled behaviour. *There
would be a mad rush for our bicycles... The
audience went mad.* [4] ADJ You can say that
someone is **mad** when they are very angry; IN-
FORMAL. *They both got mad at me for interfering.* [5] ADJ AFTER LINK-V If you are **mad** about
something or someone, you like them very
much indeed; INFORMAL. *He was mad about
golf.*

PHRASES ● If you say that someone or something **drives** you **mad**, you mean that you find
them extremely annoying; INFORMAL. *This itching is driving me mad.* ● If you do something
like mad, you do it very energetically or enthusiastically; INFORMAL. *We trained like mad.*

madam /ˈmædəm/. N-VOC **Madam** is a formal
and polite way of addressing a woman. *This
way, madam.*

madden /ˈmædən/ **maddens, maddening,
maddened.** VERB If something **maddens** you,
it makes you feel very angry or annoyed.
♦ **maddening** ADJ *...her maddening vagueness.*
♦ **maddeningly** ADV *The service is maddeningly
slow.*

made /meɪd/. [1] **Made** is the past tense and
past participle of **make.** [2] ADJ AFTER LINK-V If
something is **made of** or **made out of** a particular substance or material, that substance or
material was used to build or construct it. *...a
cross made of silver.*

madly /ˈmædli/. [1] ADV If you do something
madly, you do it in a fast, excited, or eager
way. *...waving madly to catch the attention of
those on board.* [2] ADV If you are **madly** in love
with someone, you love them very much.

mag /mæg/ **mags.** N-C A **mag** is the same as a
magazine; INFORMAL. *...sports mags.*

magazine /ˌmægəˈziːn, AM -ziːn/ **magazines.**
N-C A **magazine** is a weekly or monthly publi-

cation which contains articles, stories, photographs and advertisements. ...*a women's magazine*.

maggot /'mægət/ **maggots.** N-C **Maggots** are tiny creatures that look like very small worms and turn into flies.

magic /'mædʒɪk/. [1] N-U & ADJ **Magic** is a special power that occurs in stories and that some people believe in, that can make apparently impossible things happen. ...*a magic charm*. [2] N-U **Magic** is the art of performing tricks to entertain people, for example by seeming to make things appear and disappear. [3] N-U & ADJ The **magic** of something is a special quality that makes it seem wonderful and exciting. ...*part of the magic of Christmas*. ...*those magic moments*.

magical /'mædʒɪkəl/. [1] ADJ Something that is **magical** seems to use magic or to be able to produce magic. ...*a little boy who has magical powers*. ◆**magically** ADV ...*rub gently with a pencil and the picture will magically appear*. [2] ADJ You can say that something is **magical** when it has a special mysterious quality that makes it seem wonderful and exciting. *Paris is a magical city*.

magician /mə'dʒɪʃən/ **magicians.** [1] N-C A **magician** is a person who entertains people by doing magic tricks. [2] N-C In fairy stories, a **magician** is a man who has magic powers.

magistrate /'mædʒɪstreɪt/ **magistrates.** N-C A **magistrate** is a person who is appointed to act as a judge in law courts which deal with minor crimes or disputes.

magnate /'mægneɪt/ **magnates.** N-C A **magnate** is someone who has earned a lot of money from a particular business or industry. ...*a shipping magnate*.

magnet /'mægnɪt/ **magnets.** N-C A **magnet** is a piece of iron which attracts iron or steel towards it.

magnetic /mæg'netɪk/. [1] ADJ If something is **magnetic**, it has the power of a magnet or functions like a magnet. ...*magnetic particles*. [2] ADJ **Magnetic** tapes or objects are coated in a magnetic substance which contains coded information that can be read or written on by computers. ...*a magnetic strip*. [3] ADJ If you describe something or someone as **magnetic**, you mean that they have qualities which people find very attractive. ...*her magnetic personality*.

magnetism /'mægnɪtɪzəm/. [1] N-U **Magnetism** is a power that attracts some substances towards others. [2] N-U Someone with **magnetism** has unusual and exciting qualities which people find very attractive. ...*his animal magnetism*.

magnificent /mæg'nɪfɪsənt/. ADJ Something or someone that is **magnificent** is extremely good, beautiful, or impressive. ...*a magnificent achievement*. ◆**magnificence** N-U ...*the magnificence of the sunset*. ◆**magnificently** ADV *The team played magnificently*.

magnify /'mægnɪfaɪ/ **magnifies, magnifying, magnified.** [1] VERB To **magnify** an object means to make it appear larger than it really is, by means of a special lens or mirror. ...*classifying lenses by how much they magnify the im-*

age. ◆**magnification** /,mægnɪfɪ'keɪʃən/ N-U *Pores are visible without magnification*. [2] VERB To **magnify** something means to increase its effect, size, or intensity. *Advances in shipping have magnified the problem*.

magnitude /'mægnɪtjuːd, AM -tuːd/. N-U The **magnitude** of something is its great size or importance. *They underestimated the magnitude of the task*.

magpie /'mægpaɪ/ **magpies.** N-C A **magpie** is a black and white bird with a long tail.

mahogany /mə'hɒgəni/. N-U **Mahogany** is a dark reddish-brown wood that is used to make furniture.

maid /meɪd/ **maids.** N-C A **maid** is a female servant.

maiden /'meɪdən/ **maidens.** [1] N-C A **maiden** is a young girl or woman; LITERARY. [2] ADJ BEFORE N **Maiden** is used to describe some activities and events when they are the first of that kind that a particular person or thing has done. ...*the ship's maiden voyage*.

mail /meɪl/ **mails, mailing, mailed.** [1] N-U **Mail** is the letters and parcels that are delivered to you. *Nora looked through the mail*. [2] N-SING The **mail** is the system used for collecting and delivering letters and parcels. *It's illegal to use the mail for those purposes... Ford will contact owners by mail*. [3] VERB If you **mail** something, you post it. *I just mailed a letter to you yesterday... Mail me the current issue immediately*. [4] See also **e-mail**.

mailbox /'meɪlbɒks/ **mailboxes.** [1] N-C In the United States, a **mailbox** is a box outside your house where letters are delivered. [2] N-C In American English, a **mailbox** is a metal box with a hole in it where you put letters that you want to send. The British word is **post box**.

,mail 'order. N-U If you buy things by **mail order**, you chose them from a catalogue and they are sent to you by post.

maim /meɪm/ **maims, maiming, maimed.** VERB To **maim** someone means to injure them so badly that part of their body is permanently damaged. *She saw children horrifically maimed by landmines*.

main /meɪn/ **mains.** [1] ADJ The **main** thing is the most important one. ...*one of the main tourist areas of Amsterdam... My main concern now is to protect the children*. [2] PHRASE If something is true **in the main**, it is generally true, although there may be exceptions. *In the main, her old friends are happy for her*. [3] N-C The **mains** are the pipes which supply gas or water to buildings, or which take sewage away from them. ...*a new gas main*. [4] N-PL The **mains** are the wires which supply electricity to buildings, or the place where the wires end inside the building; BRITISH. ...*amplifiers which plug into the mains*.

,main 'clause, main clauses. N-C In grammar, a **main clause** is a clause that can stand alone as a complete sentence.

mainframe /'meɪnfreɪm/ **mainframes.** N-C A **mainframe** or a **mainframe computer** is a large computer which can be used by many people at the same time.

mainland /'meɪnlænd/. N-SING The **mainland** is the large main part of a country, in contrast to the islands around it. ...*the coast of mainland Britain.*

mainly /'meɪnli/. ADV You use **mainly** to say that a statement is true in most cases or to a large extent. *The staff were mainly Russian.*

,main 'road, main roads. N-C A **main road** is an important road that leads from one town or city to another.

mainstay /'meɪnsteɪ/ **mainstays.** N-C The **mainstay** of something is the most important part of it. *Fish and rice were the mainstays of the country's diet.*

mainstream /'meɪnstriːm/. N-SING People or ideas that are part of the **mainstream** are regarded as normal and conventional. ...*those outside the mainstream of society.* ...*mainstream opinion.*

maintain /meɪn'teɪn/ **maintains, maintaining, maintained.** **1** VERB If you **maintain** something, you continue to have it, and do not let it stop or grow weaker. *I've tried to maintain contact with the children.* **2** VERB If you **maintain** something at a particular rate or level, you keep it at that rate or level. *The government was right to maintain interest rates at a high level.* **3** VERB To **maintain** someone means to provide them with money and the things that they need. *the basic costs of maintaining a child.* **4** VERB If you **maintain** a building, vehicle, road, or machine, you keep it in good condition. **5** VERB If you **maintain** that something is true, you state your opinion very strongly. *He had always maintained his innocence.*

maintenance /'meɪntɪnəns/. **1** N-U The **maintenance** of a building, road, vehicle, or machine is the process of keeping it in good condition. **2** N-U **Maintenance** is money that someone gives regularly to another person to pay for the things that they need.

maize /meɪz/. N-U **Maize** is a tall plant which produces sweetcorn.

majestic /mə'dʒestɪk/. ADJ If you describe something or someone as **majestic**, you think they are very beautiful, dignified, and impressive. ...*a majestic country home.* ♦**majestically** ADV *She rose majestically to her feet.*

majesty /'mædʒɪsti/ **majesties.** **1** N-VOC & N-C **Your Majesty, His Majesty, Her Majesty,** or **Their Majesties** are used to address or refer to Kings or Queens. **2** N-U The **majesty** of a place or thing is its quality of being beautiful, dignified, and impressive. ...*the breathtaking majesty of the view.*

major /'meɪdʒə/ **majors.** **1** ADJ BEFORE N You use **major** to describe something that is more important, serious, or significant than other things. *Drug abuse has long been a major problem.* **2** N-C & N-TITLE A **major** is an army officer of medium rank.

majority /mə'dʒɒrɪti, AM -'dʒɔːr-/ **majorities.** **1** N-SING & PHRASE The **majority** of people or things in a group is more than half of them. When there is more of one group than another, you can say they are **in a majority** or **in the majority.** *The vast majority of our cheeses are made with pasteurised milk.* ...*those*

parts of India where Hindus were in a majority. **2** N-C In an election or vote, a **majority** is the difference between the number of votes gained by the winner and the number gained by the person or party that comes second. *The decision was passed by a majority of eight to two.*

make /meɪk/ **makes, making, made.** **Make** is used with many nouns to talk about performing actions, and creating, constructing, or preparing something. **1** VERB If someone or something **makes** you do something, they cause or force you to do it. *Mama made him clean up the plate... Grit from the highway made him cough... I was made to feel guilty.* **2** VERB You use **make** to talk about causing someone or something to be a particular thing or to have a particular quality. ...*James Bond, the role that made him a star... She made life very difficult for me.* **3** VERB If you **make** yourself understood, heard, or known, you succeed in getting people to understand you, hear you, or know that you are there. *He almost had to shout to make himself heard above the music.* **4** VERB If you **make** something **into** something else, you change it in some way so that it becomes that other thing. *The middle valley was made into public gardens for recreation.* **5** VERB If you **make** money, you get it by working, by selling something, or by winning it. *What interested Dyer was making money.* **6** VERB If you **make** friends or enemies, someone becomes your friend or enemy, often because of a particular thing you have done. **7** VERB If something **makes** something else, it is responsible for the success of that thing. *What really makes the book are the beautiful designs.* **8** VERB You can use **make** to say that someone or something has the right qualities for a particular task or role. *She'll make a good actress, if she gets the right training.* **9** VERB If someone **makes** a particular team or **makes** a particular high position, they do so well that they are put in that team or get that position. *The athletes are just happy to make the British team.* **10** VERB You can use **make** to say that two numbers add up to. *Four twos make eight.* **11** N-C The **make** of a product such as a car or radio is the name of the company that made it. ...*a certain make of wristwatch.*

PHRASES ● If you **make do** with something, you use or have it instead of something else that you do not have, although it is not as good. *Why make do with a copy if you can afford the genuine article?* ● If you **make it** somewhere, you succeed in getting there, especially in time to do something. *So you did make it to America, after all.* ● If you **make it,** you are successful in achieving something difficult, or in surviving through a very difficult period. *You're brave and courageous. You can make it.*

▶ **make for.** PHR-VERB If you **make for** a place, you move towards it. *He rose from his seat and made for the door.*

▶ **make of.** PHR-VERB If you ask someone what they **make of** something, you want to know what their impression or opinion of it is. *Nancy wasn't sure what to make of Mick's apology.*

▶ **make off.** PHR-VERB If you **make off**, you leave somewhere as quickly as possible. *They broke free and made off in a stolen car.*

▶ **make out.** [1] PHR-VERB If you can **make** something **out**, you can see, hear, or understand it. *I could just make out a tall, pale, shadowy figure... For a moment he couldn't make out what she was saying.* [2] PHR-VERB If you **make out** that something is the case, you try to get people to believe it. *They were trying to make out that I'd actually done it.* [3] PHR-VERB When you **make out** a cheque or receipt, you write all the necessary information on it.

▶ **make up.** [1] PHR-VERB The people or things that **make up** something are the members or parts that form that thing. *Women officers make up 13 per cent of the police force.* [2] PHR-VERB If you **make up** a story or excuse, you invent it. [3] PHR-VERB If two people **make up** after a quarrel or disagreement, or if they **make it up**, they become friends again. [4] PHR-VERB To **make up** for something that is lost or missing means to replace it or compensate for it. *...an extra compensation payment to make up for the stress you have been caused.* [5] PHR-VERB If you **make it up to** someone for disappointing them, you do something for them to show how sorry you are. *I must make it up to him for the awful intrusion of last night.*

maker /'meɪkə/ **makers.** N-C The **maker** of something is the person or company that makes it. *...Japan's two largest car makers.*

makeshift /'meɪkʃɪft/. ADJ **Makeshift** things are temporary and of poor quality, and are used because there is nothing better available. *20,000 Liberians were living in makeshift shelters.*

'make-up. [1] N-U **Make-up** consists of things such as lipstick or eye shadow which you can put on your face to make yourself look more attractive, or creating it. [2] N-U The **make-up** of something is the different parts that it consists of, and the way these parts are arranged. *...the chemical make-up of the oceans and atmosphere.*

making /'meɪkɪŋ/ **makings.** N-U The **making** of something is the act of producing, constructing, or creating it. *...the making of this movie.*

PHRASES ● If you describe a person or thing as something **in the making**, you mean that they are going to become known or recognized as that thing. *Her drama teacher is confident Julie is a star in the making.* ● If something **is the making of** a person or thing, it is the reason that they become successful or become very much better than they used to be. ● If someone or something has **the makings of** something, it seems possible or likely that they will become that thing, as they have the necessary qualities. *Godfrey had the makings of a successful journalist.* ● If something such as a problem you have is **of** your **own making**, you have caused or created it yourself. *The university's financial troubles are of its own making.*

malaria /mə'leəriə/. N-U **Malaria** is a serious disease caught from mosquitoes.

male /meɪl/ **males.** [1] N-C & ADJ A **male** is a person or animal that belongs to the sex that cannot have babies or lay eggs. *...a deep male voice.* [2] ADJ A **male** flower or plant fertilizes the part that will become the fruit.

malfunction /,mæl'fʌŋkʃən/ **malfunctions, malfunctioning, malfunctioned.** VERB & N-C If a machine or computer **malfunctions**, it fails to work properly. If this happens, you say there is a **malfunction**. *...a malfunctioning satellite. ...a technical malfunction.*

malice /'mælɪs/. N-U **Malice** is a deliberate desire to harm people. *There was no malice on his part.*

malicious /mə'lɪʃəs/. ADJ **Malicious** talk or behaviour is intended to harm people or their reputation, or to embarrass or upset them. *...malicious gossip.* ♦**maliciously** ADV *Sue grinned maliciously in the darkness.*

malignant /mə'lɪgnənt/. ADJ A **malignant** tumour or disease is serious, spreads rapidly to other parts of the body, and may cause death.

maligned /mə'laɪnd/. ADJ If you describe someone or something as **maligned**, you mean that people often criticize them and say unpleasant things about them, and that this is unfair. *Potatoes are a much-maligned vegetable.*

mall /mɔːl, mæl/ **malls.** N-C A **mall** is a large enclosed shopping area.

mallet /'mælɪt/ **mallets.** N-C A **mallet** is a wooden hammer with a square head.

malnutrition /,mælnju:'trɪʃən, AM -nu:t-/. N-U If someone is suffering from **malnutrition**, they are physically weak and extremely thin because they have not eaten enough food.

malpractice /,mæl'præktɪs/ **malpractices.** N-VAR If you accuse someone of **malpractice**, you are accusing them of breaking the law or the rules of their profession in order to gain some advantage for themselves; FORMAL.

malt /mɔːlt/. N-U **Malt** is a substance made from grain that is used to make some alcoholic drinks.

mammal /'mæməl/ **mammals.** N-C **Mammals** are animals that give birth to babies rather than laying eggs, and feed their young with milk.

mammoth /'mæməθ/ **mammoths.** [1] ADJ You can use **mammoth** to emphasize that a task is very great and needs a lot of effort to achieve. *...the mammoth task of relocating the library.* [2] N-C A **mammoth** was a prehistoric animal like a large elephant with long curling tusks.

man /mæn/ **men; mans, manning, manned.** [1] N-C A **man** is an adult male human. [2] N-VAR **Man** and **men** are sometimes used to refer to all humans. Some people dislike this use. *Anxiety is modern man's natural state.* [3] N-PL In the armed forces, the **men** are the ordinary soldiers, sailors, or airmen, but not the officers. [4] VERB. If you **man** something such as a place, vehicle or machine, you operate it or are in charge of it. *The station is seldom manned in the evening.* [5] **the man in the street**: see **street.**

manage /'mænɪdʒ/ **manages, managing, managed.** [1] VERB If someone **manages** an organization, business, or system, they are responsible for controlling it. *Within two years he was managing the store.* [2] VERB If you **manage** time, money, or other resources, you deal with them carefully and do not waste them. *In a busy world, managing your time is increasingly important.* [3] VERB If you **manage** to do something, especially something difficult, you succeed in doing it. *I managed to pull myself up onto a wet, sloping path.* [4] VERB If you **manage**, you succeed in coping with a difficult situation. *How did your mother manage when your father left?*

manageable /ˈmænɪdʒəbəl/. ADJ Something that is **manageable** is of a size, quantity, or level of difficulty that people are able to deal with. *Cut down the task to a manageable size.*

management /ˈmænɪdʒmənt/ **managements**. [1] N-U **Management** is the control and organizing of something. *The zoo needed better management. ...time management.* [2] N-VAR You can refer to the people who control and organize a business or other organization as the **management**. **Management** can take the singular or plural form of the verb. *The management is doing its best.*

manager /ˈmænɪdʒə/ **managers**. N-C A **manager** is the person responsible for running part of or the whole of a business organization.

manageress /ˌmænɪdʒəˈres/ **manageresses**. N-C The **manageress** of a shop, restaurant, or other small business is the woman who is responsible for running it.

managerial /ˌmænɪˈdʒɪəriəl/. ADJ **Managerial** means relating to the work of a manager. *...managerial skills.*

managing diˈrector, managing directors. N-C The **managing director** of a company is the most important working director, and is in charge of the way the company is managed.

mandate /ˈmændeɪt/ **mandates, mandating, mandated**. [1] N-C A government's **mandate** is the authority it has to carry out particular policies or tasks as a result of winning an election or vote. *...a mandate for continued economic reform.* [2] VERB & N-C When someone is **mandated** to do something, or when they are given a **mandate** to do it, they are given the authority to do it, or are instructed to do it. *He'd now been mandated by the West African Economic Community to go in and to enforce a ceasefire.*

mandatory /ˈmændətri, AM -tɔːri/. ADJ If an action or procedure is **mandatory**, people have to do it, because it is a rule or it is fixed by law; FORMAL. *...the mandatory life sentence for murder.*

mane /meɪn/ **manes**. N-C The **mane** on a horse or lion is the long thick hair that grows from its neck.

maneuver /məˈnuːvə/. See manoeuvre.

mangle /ˈmæŋɡəl/ **mangles, mangling, mangled**. VERB If something **is mangled**, it is very forcefully crushed and twisted out of shape. *...the mangled wreckage.*

mango /ˈmæŋɡəʊ/ **mangoes** or **mangos**. N-C A **mango** is a large, sweet yellowish fruit which grows in hot countries.

manhood /ˈmænhʊd/. N-U **Manhood** is the state of being a man rather than a boy, or the period of a man's adult life. *They were failing to help their sons grow from boyhood to manhood.*

mania /ˈmeɪniə/ **manias**. N-C If you say that a person or group has a **mania** for something, you mean that they enjoy it very much or devote a lot of time to it. *The media have a mania about rugby.*

maniac /ˈmeɪniæk/ **maniacs**. N-C A **maniac** is a mad person who is violent and dangerous.

manic /ˈmænɪk/. ADJ If you describe someone as **manic**, you mean that they do things extremely quickly or energetically, often because they are very excited or anxious. ◆**manically** ADV *We cleaned the house manically.*

manicure /ˈmænɪkjʊə/ **manicures, manicuring, manicured**. VERB & N-C If you **manicure** your hands or nails, or if you have a **manicure**, you care for them by softening your skin and cutting and painting your nails.

manifest /ˈmænɪfest/ **manifests, manifesting, manifested**. [1] ADJ If you say that something is **manifest**, you mean it is clearly true and that nobody would disagree with it if they saw it or considered it; FORMAL. *...the manifest failure of the policies.* ◆**manifestly** ADV *She manifestly failed to last the mile and a half of the race.* [2] VERB & ADJ If you **manifest** a particular quality, feeling, or illness, or if it becomes **manifest**, it becomes visible or obvious; FORMAL. *The virus needs two weeks to manifest itself... The same alarm is manifest everywhere.*

manifestation /ˌmænɪfeˈsteɪʃən/ **manifestations**. N-C A **manifestation** of something is one of the different ways in which it can appear; FORMAL. *... different manifestations of the disease.*

manifesto /ˌmænɪˈfestəʊ/ **manifestos** or **manifestoes**. N-C A **manifesto** is a statement published by a person or group of people, especially a political party, in which they say what their aims and policies are. *...the Labour Party's election manifesto.*

manipulate /məˈnɪpjʊleɪt/ **manipulates, manipulating, manipulated**. [1] VERB If you say that someone **manipulates** people or events, you disapprove of them because they control or influence them to produce a particular result. *They felt he had been cowardly in manipulating the system.* ◆**manipulation**, **manipulations** N-VAR *...accusations of political manipulation.* [2] VERB If you **manipulate** something that requires skill, such as a complicated piece of equipment or a difficult idea, you operate it or process it. *The technology uses a pen to manipulate a computer.* ◆**manipulation** N-VAR *Making circuits requires controlled manipulation.*

manipulative /məˈnɪpjʊlətɪv/. ADJ If you describe someone as **manipulative**, you disapprove of them because they manipulate people. *...aggressive and manipulative behaviour.*

mankind /ˌmænˈkaɪnd/. N-U You can refer to all human beings as **mankind** when you are considering them as a group. *...the evolution of mankind.*

manly /ˈmænli/. ADJ If you describe a man's behaviour as **manly**, you approve of it because it shows qualities that are considered ideal in a man. ◆**manliness** N-U *He has no doubts about his manliness.*

,man-'made ADJ Man-made things are created or caused by people, rather than occurring naturally. ...*man-made lakes.*

manned /mænd/. See **man**.

manner /'mænə/ **manners.** [1] N-SING The **manner** in which you do something is the way that you do it. *She smiled again in a friendly manner.* [2] N-SING Someone's **manner** is the way in which they behave and talk when they are with other people. *His manner was self-assured.* ♦**-mannered** *He was a quiet, mild-mannered man.* [3] N-PL If someone has **good manners**, they are polite and observe social customs. If someone has **bad manners**, they are not polite and do not observe these customs. [4] PHRASE If you refer to **all manner of** objects or people, you are talking about objects or people of many different kinds. ...*all manner of wildlife.*

manoeuvre (AM **maneuver**) /mə'nu:və/ **manoeuvres, manoeuvring, manoeuvred.** [1] VERB & N-VAR If you **manoeuvre** something into or out of an awkward position, you skilfully move it there. A **manoeuvre** is a movement like this. *I manoeuvred my way among the tables. ...a ship capable of high speed and rapid manoeuvre.* [2] N-C A **manoeuvre** is something clever which you do to change a situation to your advantage. ...*manoeuvres to block the electoral process.* [3] PHRASE If you have **room for manoeuvre**, you have the opportunity to change your plans if it becomes necessary or desirable. *With an election looming, he has little room for manoeuvre.* [4] N-PL Military **manoeuvres** are training exercises which involve the movement of soldiers and equipment over a large area.

manor /'mænə/ **manors.** N-C A **manor** is a large country house with land.

manpower /'mænpaʊə/. N-U Workers are sometimes referred to as **manpower** when they are being considered as a part of the process of producing goods or providing services.

mansion /'mænʃən/ **mansions.** N-C A **mansion** is a very large house.

manslaughter /'mænslɔ:tə/. N-U **Manslaughter** is the unlawful killing of a person by someone who did not intend to kill them; TECHNICAL. ...*she was guilty of manslaughter, not murder.*

mantelpiece (also **mantlepiece**) /'mæntəlpi:s/ **mantelpieces.** N-C A **mantelpiece** is a shelf over a fireplace.

mantra /'mæntrə/ **mantras.** N-C A **mantra** is a chant used by Buddhists and Hindus when they meditate.

manual /'mænjʊəl/ **manuals.** [1] ADJ **Manual** work is unskilled work using your hands or your physical strength. ...*skilled manual workers.* [2] ADJ BEFORE N **Manual** equipment is operated by hand, rather than by electricity or by a motor. ♦**manually** ADV *The device is manually operated.* [3] N-C A **manual** is a book which tells you how to do something or how a piece of machinery works. ...*the instruction manual.*

manufacture /,mænjʊ'fæktʃə/ **manufactures, manufacturing, manufactured.** [1] VERB & N-U To **manufacture** things means to make them in a factory. The **manufacture** of things is the process of making them in a factory. *They manufacture the class of plastics known as thermoplastic materials.* ♦**manufacturing** N-U ...*management headquarters for manufacturing in China.* [2] VERB If you say that someone **manufactures** information, you are criticizing them because the information is not true. *The officers manufactured an elaborate story.*

manufacturer /,mænjʊ'fæktʃərə/ **manufacturers.** N-C A **manufacturer** is a business that makes goods in large quantities.

manure /mə'njʊə, AM -'nʊr/. N-U **Manure** is animal faeces that is spread on the ground in order to improve the growth of plants.

manuscript /'mænjʊskrɪpt/ **manuscripts.** [1] N-C A **manuscript** is a handwritten or typed document, especially a writer's first version of a book before it is published. [2] N-C A **manuscript** is an old document that was written by hand before printing was invented. ...*early printed books and rare manuscripts.*

many /'meni/. [1] QUANT **Many** is used to indicate a large number of people or things. *I don't think many people would argue with that... In many of these neighborhoods a lot of people don't have telephones.* [2] QUANT **Many** is used to talk and ask questions about numbers or quantities. *No-one knows how many people have been killed... How many do you smoke a day?*

PHRASES ● You use **as many as** before a number to suggest that it is surprisingly large. ...*as many as four and a half million people watched today's parade.* ● You use **a good many** or **a great many** to emphasize that you are referring to a large number of things or people. *We've both had a good many beers.* ● **in so many words**: see **word**.

map /mæp/ **maps, mapping, mapped.** N-C A **map** is a drawing of a particular area, showing its main features as they would appear if you looked at them from above. *Have you got a map of the city centre?*

▸ **map out** PHR-VERB If you **map out** a plan or task, you work out how you will do it. *We had mapped out our future.*

maple /'meɪpəl/ **maples.** N-VAR A **maple** is a tree with large leaves with five points. **Maple** is the wood of this tree.

mar /mɑ:/ **mars, marring, marred.** VERB To **mar** something means to spoil or damage it; WRITTEN. *That election was marred by massive cheating.*

marathon /'mærəθən, AM -θɒn/ **marathons.** [1] N-C A **marathon** is a race in which people run a distance of 26 miles (about 42 km). [2] ADJ BEFORE N A **marathon** task takes a long time to do and is very tiring. ...*a marathon session of talks.*

marble /'mɑ:bəl/ **marbles.** [1] N-U **Marble** is a very hard rock used, for example, to make statues and fireplaces. ...*classical marble busts of Caesar.* [2] N-VAR **Marbles** are small coloured glass balls used by children to play a game called **marbles**.

march /mɑ:tʃ/ **marches, marching, marched.** [1] VERB & N-C When soldiers **march** somewhere, or when a commanding officer **marches** them somewhere, they walk there with very regular steps, as a group. You can also say they go on a **march**. *We marched fifteen miles to Yadkin River.* ◆[2] VERB & N-C When a large group of people march, or when they hold a **march**, they walk somewhere together in order to protest about something. *The demonstrators then marched through the capital. ...a march for peace.* ◆**marcher, marchers** N-C *Police stopped the marchers.* ◆[3] VERB If you **march** somewhere, you walk there quickly, for example because you are angry. *He marched into the kitchen without knocking.* ◆[4] VERB If you **march** someone somewhere, you force them to walk there with you by holding their arm. *I marched him across the room and out on to the doorstep.* ◆[5] N-SING The **march** of something is its steady progress. *...the relentless march of technology.* ◆[6] PHRASE If you give someone their **marching orders**, you tell them that you no longer want or need them. *Seven board members either resigned or were given their marching orders.*

March /mɑːtʃ/. N-U **March** is the third month of the year.

mare /meə/ **mares**. N-C A **mare** is an adult female horse.

margarine /ˌmɑːdʒəˈriːn, AM -rɪn/. N-U **Margarine** is a substance similar to butter, made from vegetable oil and sometimes animal fats.

margin /ˈmɑːdʒɪn/ **margins**. [1] N-C A **margin** is the difference between two amounts, especially the difference in the number of votes or points between the winner and the loser in a contest. *They could end up with a 50-point winning margin.* ◆[2] N-C If there is a **margin** for something in a situation, there is some freedom to choose what to do or decide how to do it. *He knew he had to be very fast; there was no margin for error.* ◆[3] N-C The **margins** on a page are the blank spaces at each side.

marginal /ˈmɑːdʒɪnəl/. ADJ Something that is **marginal** is small and not very important. *...a marginal improvement in output.* ◆**marginally** ADV *Sales last year were marginally higher than in 1991.*

marijuana /ˌmærɪˈwɑːnə/. N-U **Marijuana** is an illegal drug which is usually smoked.

marina /məˈriːnə/ **marinas**. N-C A **marina** is a small harbour for pleasure boats.

marinade /ˌmærɪˈneɪd/ **marinades, marinading, marinaded**. [1] N-C A **marinade** is a sauce of oil, vinegar, and spices, which you soak meat or fish in before cooking it, in order to flavour it. ◆[2] VERB To **marinade** means the same as to **marinate**.

marinate /ˈmærɪneɪt/ **marinates, marinating, marinated**. VERB If you **marinate** meat or fish or if it **marinates**, you soak it in vinegar, oil, and spices before cooking it, in order to flavour it.

marine /məˈriːn/ **marines**. [1] N-C A **marine** is a soldier who is trained for duties at sea and on land. ◆[2] ADJ BEFORE N **Marine** is used to describe things relating to the sea. *...marine life. ...a solicitor specialising in marine law.*

marital /ˈmærɪtəl/. ADJ BEFORE N **Marital** means relating to marriage. *...their marital problems.*

maritime /ˈmærɪtaɪm/. ADJ BEFORE N **Maritime**

means relating to the sea and to ships. *...the National Maritime Museum.*

mark /mɑːk/ **marks, marking, marked**. [1] VERB & N-C If something **marks** a surface, or if it makes a **mark** on it, a small area of the surface is stained or damaged. *Wood marks easily... The dogs are always rubbing against the wall and making dirty marks.* ◆[2] VERB & N-C If you **mark** something with a particular word or symbol, you write that word or symbol on it. *This word or symbol is called a **mark**. The bank marks the check 'certified'... He made marks with a pencil.* ◆[3] VERB & N-C When a teacher **marks** a student's work, he or she decides how good it is and writes comments or a score on it. *This score is called a **mark**. He was marking essays in his small study... He did well to get such a good mark.* ◆[4] N-C When something reaches a particular **mark**, it reaches that particular number, point, or stage. *Unemployment is rapidly approaching the one million mark.* ◆[5] N-C The **mark** of a particular thing, feeling, or quality is something which enables you to recognize it or which shows that it exists. *The mark of a civilized society is that it looks after its weakest members.* ◆[6] VERB If something **marks** a place or position, it shows where a particular thing is or was. *...the river which marks the border with Thailand.* ◆**marker, markers** N-C *...a boundary marker.* ◆[7] VERB An event that **marks** a particular stage or point is a sign that something different is about to happen. *The announcement marks the end of an extraordinary period in European history.* ◆[8] See also **marked, marking**.

PHRASES ● If something or someone **leaves** their **mark** or **leaves a mark**, they have a lasting effect. *His experiences in Spain have left their mark on him.* ● If you **make** your **mark** or **make a mark**, you become noticed or famous by doing something impressive or unusual. *She made her mark in the film industry in the 1960s.* ● If something is **off the mark** or **wide of the mark**, it is inaccurate or incorrect. If it is **on the mark**, it is accurate or correct. *That comparison isn't as wide of the mark as it seems.*

▸ **mark down**. [1] PHR-VERB If you **mark** something **down**, you write it down. *I had the date marked down in my diary.* ◆[2] PHR-VERB To **mark** an item **down** or **mark** its price **down** means to reduce its price. *Clothes are the best bargain, with many items marked down.*

▸ **mark off**. PHR-VERB If you **mark off** an item on a list, you put a mark on it, for example to indicate that it has been dealt with. *Read the text through and mark off the sections you find particularly applicable.*

marked /mɑːkt/. ADJ Something that is **marked** is very obvious and easily noticed. *...a marked increase in crimes against property.* ◆**markedly** /ˈmɑːkɪdli/ ADV *The film is markedly different from the play.*

market /ˈmɑːkɪt/ **markets, marketing, marketed**. [1] N-C A **market** is a place where goods are bought and sold, usually in the open air. *He sold boots on a market stall.* ◆[2] N-C The **market** for a commodity or product is the total number of people who want to buy it. *The* *housing market was in a state of serious decline.* ③ VERB To **market** a product means to organize its sale, by deciding on its price, where it should be sold, and how it should be advertised. *Touch-tone telephones have been marketed in America since 1963.* ♦**marketing** N-U *...Renault's marketing department.* ④ PHRASE If something is **on the market** or comes **onto the market**, it is available for people to buy.

marketplace (or **market place**) /'mɑːkɪtpleɪs/, **marketplaces**. ① N-C In business, **the marketplace** refers to the activity of buying and selling products. *Alternative fuels can't compete in the marketplace alongside gasoline.* ② N-C A **marketplace** is a small area in a town where goods are bought and sold, often in the open air.

marking /'mɑːkɪŋ/ **markings**. N-C **Markings** are lines or patterns on an animal or object which help to identify it. *...the distinctive markings on their tails.*

marmalade /'mɑːməleɪd/ **marmalades**. N-VAR **Marmalade** is a food like jam made from oranges or lemons.

maroon /mə'ruːn/ **maroons, marooning, marooned**. ① ADJ & N-U Something that is **maroon** is a dark reddish-purple. *...maroon velvet curtains.* ② VERB If someone **is marooned** somewhere, they are left in a place that is difficult for them to escape from. *He spent twenty-four hours marooned in the cab of his vehicle.*

marquis (or **marquess**) /'mɑːkwɪs/ **marquises**. N-C A **marquis** is a male member of the nobility.

marriage /'mærɪdʒ/ **marriages**. ① N-VAR A **marriage** is the relationship between a husband and wife, or the state of being married. *...a good marriage. ...six years of marriage.* ② N-VAR A **marriage** is the act of marrying someone, or the ceremony at which this is done. *I opposed her marriage to Darryl.*

married /'mærɪd/. ① ADJ If you are **married**, you have a husband or wife. *She is married to an Englishman. ...a married man.* ② ADJ BEFORE N **Married** means relating to marriage. *...the first ten years of our married life.*

marry /'mæri/ **marries, marrying, married**. ① VERB When two people **get married** or **marry**, they become each other's husband and wife during a special ceremony. *Laura just got married to Jake... They married a month after they met... He wants to marry her.* ② VERB When a clergyman or registrar **marries** two people, he or she is in charge of their marriage ceremony.

marsh /mɑːʃ/ **marshes**. N-VAR A **marsh** is a wet muddy area of land.

marshal /'mɑːʃəl/ **marshals, marshalling, marshalled** (AM **marshaling marshaled**). ① VERB If you **marshal** people or things, you gather them together and organize them. *Richard was marshalling the doctors and nurses.* ② N-C A **marshal** is an official who helps to organize a public event. *The grand prix is controlled by well-trained marshals.* ③ N-C In the United States and some other countries, a **marshal** is a police officer, often one who is responsible for a particular area.

martial /'mɑːʃəl/. ADJ **Martial** is used to describe things that relate to soldiers or war; FORMAL. *He declared martial law and immediately started arresting political opponents.* ● See also **court-martial**.

,**martial 'art, martial arts**. N-C A **martial art** is one of the techniques of self-defence that come from the Far East, for example karate and judo.

martyr /'mɑːtə/ **martyrs, martyred**. ① N-C A **martyr** is someone who is killed or made to suffer greatly because of their religious or political beliefs. *...a Christian martyr.* ② VERB If someone **is martyred**, they are killed or made to suffer greatly because of their religious or political beliefs.

marvel /'mɑːvəl/ **marvels, marvelling, marvelled** (AM **marveling, marveled**). ① VERB If you **marvel** at something, you express your great surprise or admiration. *Her fellow members marveled at her seemingly infinite energy.* ② N-C A **marvel** is something that makes you feel great surprise or admiration. *...the marvels of creation.*

marvellous (AM **marvelous**) /'mɑːvələs/. ADJ If you describe someone or something as **marvellous**, you are emphasizing that they are very good indeed. *...a marvellous actor... He looked marvellous.* ♦**marvellously** ADV *He always painted marvellously.*

mascara /mæ'skɑːrə, AM -'kær-/. N-U **Mascara** is a substance used to colour eyelashes.

mascot /'mæskɒt/ **mascots**. N-C A **mascot** is an animal, toy, or symbol which is associated with a particular organization or event, and which is thought to bring good luck. *...the official mascot of the Barcelona Games.*

masculine /'mæskjʊlɪn/. ADJ **Masculine** characteristics or things relate to or are considered typical of men, rather than women. *...masculine characteristics like a husky voice and facial hair.* ♦**masculinity** /,mæskjʊ'lɪnɪti/ N-U *Why do men seem to need to prove their masculinity?*

mash /mæʃ/ **mashes, mashing, mashed**. VERB If you **mash** food that is solid but soft, you crush it so that it forms a soft mass. *Mash the bananas with a fork.*

mask /mɑːsk, mæsk/ **masks, masking, masked**. ① N-C A **mask** is something which you wear over your face for protection or to disguise yourself. *...actors wearing masks.* ② VERB & N-C If you **mask** your feelings, you deliberately do not show them. This type of behaviour can be referred to as a **mask**. *His mask of detachment cracked.* ③ VERB If one thing **masks** another, the first thing prevents people from noticing or recognizing the second thing. *A thick grey cloud masked the sun.*

masked /mɑːskt/. ADJ Someone who is **masked** is wearing a mask.

masochism /'mæsəkɪzəm/. N-U **Masochism** is behaviour in which someone gets sexual pleasure from their own pain or their own suffering. ♦**masochist, masochists** N-C *...sexual masochists.* ♦**masochistic** /,mæsə'kɪstɪk/ ADJ *...masochistic tendencies.*

mason /'meɪsən/ **masons**. N-C A **mason** is a person who makes things out of stone.

masonry /ˈmeɪsənri/. N-U **Masonry** consists of the parts of a building which are built from brick or stone.

masquerade /ˌmæskəˈreɪd/ **masquerades, masquerading, masqueraded.** VERB To **masquerade as** someone or something means to pretend to be that person or thing. *He masqueraded as a doctor and fooled everyone.*

mass /mæs/ **masses, massing, massed.**
[1] N-SING A **mass** of something is a large amount of it. *She had a mass of auburn hair.*
[2] QUANT **Masses** of something means a large amount of it; INFORMAL. *There's masses of work for her to do.* [3] ADJ BEFORE N **Mass** is used to describe something which involves or affects a very large number of people. *...weapons of mass destruction.* [4] N-PL **The masses** are the ordinary people in society. *His music is commercial. It is aimed at the masses.* [5] VERB When people or things **mass** somewhere, large numbers of them gather there. *The General was massing his troops for a counterattack.* ♦ **massed** ADJ BEFORE N *...the massed ranks of newsmen.* [6] N-VAR The **mass** of an object is the amount of physical matter that it has; TECHNICAL. [7] N-VAR **Mass** is a Christian church ceremony during which people eat bread and drink wine in order to remember the last meal of Jesus Christ.

massacre /ˈmæsəkə/ **massacres, massacring, massacred.** [1] N-VAR A **massacre** is the killing of many people in a violent and cruel way. [2] VERB If people **are massacred**, a large number of them are killed in a violent and cruel way. *300 civilians are believed to have been massacred by the rebels.* [3] See note at **kill**.

massage /ˈmæsɑːʒ, AM məˈsɑːʒ/ **massages, massaging, massaged.** VERB & N-VAR If you **massage** someone, or if you give them a **massage**, you rub their body to make them relax or to stop their muscles from hurting. *She continued massaging her right foot... Massage isn't a long-term cure for stress.*

masse. See **en masse**.

massive /ˈmæsɪv/. ADJ Something that is **massive** is very large in size. *There was evidence of massive fraud.* ♦ **massively** ADV *Interest rates will rise massively.*

mass 'media. N-SING The **mass media** are television, radio, and newspapers.

mass-pro'duce, mass-produces, mass-producing, mass-produced. VERB To **mass-produce** something means to manufacture it in large quantities, using machinery. *...machinery to mass-produce footwear.* ♦ **mass-produced** ADJ BEFORE N *...the first mass-produced mountain bike.*

mast /mɑːst, mæst/ **masts.** [1] N-C The **masts** of a boat are the tall upright poles that support its sails. [2] N-C A radio or television **mast** is a very tall pole that is used as an aerial.

master /ˈmɑːstə/ **masters, mastering, mastered.** [1] N-C A servant's **master** is the man that he or she works for; DATED. [2] ADJ BEFORE N You use **master** to describe someone's job when they are very skilled at it. *...a master craftsman.* [3] N-U If you are **master** of a situation, you have control over it. *Jackson re-*

mained calm and always master of his passions. [4] VERB If you **master** something, you manage to learn how to do it properly or understand it completely. *Students are expected to master a second language.* [5] N-C A **master** is a male schoolteacher. ● See also head-**master**.

mastermind /ˈmɑːstəmaɪnd, ˈmæs-/ **masterminds, masterminding, masterminded.** [1] VERB If you **mastermind** a complicated activity, you plan and organize it. *The finance minister will continue to mastermind Poland's economic reform.* [2] N-C The **mastermind** behind a complicated plan, often a criminal one, is the person who plans and organizes it.

masterpiece /ˈmɑːstəpiːs, ˈmæs-/ **masterpieces.** N-C A **masterpiece** is an extremely good painting, novel, film, or other work of art.

mastery /ˈmɑːstəri, ˈmæs-/. [1] N-U If you show **mastery** of a particular skill or language, you show you have learnt or understood it completely and have no difficulty using it. *He doesn't have mastery of the basic rules of grammar.* [2] N-U **Mastery** is power or control over something. *...his mastery over early, painful emotions.*

mat /mæt/ **mats.** [1] N-C A **mat** is a small piece of material which you put on a table to protect it from a hot plate or cup. [2] N-C A **mat** is a small piece of carpet or other thick material that you put on the floor. [3] See also **matt**.

match /mætʃ/ **matches, matching, matched.** [1] N-C A **match** is an organized game of football, cricket, or other sport. [2] N-C A **match** is a small wooden stick with a substance on one end that produces a flame when you strike it against a rough surface. [3] VERB If one thing **matches** another, or if the two things **match**, they look good together, usually because they have similar colours or designs. *You don't have to match your lipstick exactly to your outfit.* ♦ **matching** ADJ BEFORE N *...a matching handbag.* [4] VERB If something such as an amount or a quality **matches** with another, or if the two things **match**, they are both the same or equal. *Our value system does not match with their value system... Their strengths in memory and spatial skills matched.* [5] VERB To **match** something means to be equal to it in speed, size, or quality. *They played some fine attacking football, but I think we matched them in every department.* [6] PHRASE If one person or thing **is no match for** another, they are unable to compete successfully with the other person or thing. *Hand-held guns proved no match for heavy armor.*

matched /mætʃt/. [1] ADJ If two people are well **matched**, they are suited to one another and are likely to have a successful relationship. *My parents were not very well matched.* [2] ADJ In competitive situations, if opponents are well **matched**, they are both of the same standard in strength or ability.

mate /meɪt/ **mates, mating, mated.** [1] N-C You can refer to someone's friends as their **mates**; BRITISH, INFORMAL. [2] N-C An animal's **mate** is its sexual partner. [3] VERB When animals **mate**, they have sex in order to produce young. *They want the males to mate with wild females.*

material /məˈtɪəriəl/ **materials.** [1] N-VAR A **material** is a solid substance. *...a conducting material such as a metal.* [2] N-VAR **Material** is cloth. *...the thick material of her skirt.* [3] N-PL **Materials** are the things that you need for a particular activity. *...sewing materials.* [4] ADJ **Material** things are possessions or money, rather than abstract things. *She enjoys the material comforts married life has brought her.* ◆**materially** ADV *He has tried to help this child materially and spiritually.*

materialism /məˈtɪəriəlɪzəm/. N-U **Materialism** is the attitude of someone who attaches a lot of importance to money and possessions.

materialize (BR also **materialise**) /məˈtɪəriəlaɪz/ **materializes, materializing, materialized.** VERB If an event does not **materialize**, it does not happen. *A rebellion by radicals failed to materialize.*

maternal /məˈtɜːnəl/. ADJ **Maternal** feelings or actions are typical of those of a mother towards her child. *She had little maternal instinct.*

maternity /məˈtɜːnɪti/. ADJ BEFORE N **Maternity** is used to describe things relating to pregnancy and birth. *...the city's maternity hospital.*

math /mæθ/. See **maths**.

mathematical /ˌmæθəˈmætɪkəl/. ADJ BEFORE N Something that is **mathematical** involves numbers and calculations. ◆**mathematically** ADV *...a mathematically complicated formula.*

mathematician /ˌmæθəməˈtɪʃən/ **mathematicians.** N-C A **mathematician** is a person who is trained in the study of numbers and in the study of calculations.

mathematics /ˌmæθəˈmætɪks/. N-U **Mathematics** is the study of numbers, quantities, or shapes.

maths /mæθs/. N-U In British English, mathematics is usually referred to as **maths**. The American word is **math**.

matinee (or **matinée**) /ˈmætɪneɪ, AM -ˈneɪ/ **matinees.** N-C A **matinee** is a performance of a play or a showing of a film in the afternoon.

matrix /ˈmeɪtrɪks/ **matrices** /ˈmeɪtrɪsiːz/. N-C A **matrix** is the environment in which something such as a society develops and grows; FORMAL. *...the matrix of their culture.*

matt /mæt/. ADJ A **matt** colour, paint, or surface is dull rather than shiny.

matter /ˈmætə/ **matters, mattering, mattered.** [1] N-C A **matter** is a task, situation, or event which you have to deal with or think about. *...business matters.* [2] N-PL You use **matters** to refer to the situation you are talking about. *It is hard to see how this would improve matters.* [3] N-U You can refer to books, newspapers, and other texts as printed **matter** or reading **matter**. [4] N-U **Matter** is the physical part of the universe consisting of solids, liquids, and gases. [5] N-SING You use **matter** in expressions such as 'What's the matter?' or 'Is anything the matter?' when you think that someone has a problem and you want to know what it is. [6] N-SING You can use **matter** in expressions such as 'a matter of weeks' when

you are emphasizing that it is a short period of time. [7] VERB If something **matters**, it is important because it has an effect on a situation. *It does not matter how long their hair is.*

PHRASES ● If you say that something is **another matter** or **a different matter**, you mean that it is very different from the situation that you have just discussed or is an exception to a rule or general statement that you have just made. *Being responsible for one's own health is one thing, but being responsible for another person's health is quite a different matter.* ● You say '**it doesn't matter**' to tell someone who is apologizing to you that you are not angry or upset, and that they should not worry. ● You use **no matter** in expressions such as **no matter how** and **no matter what** to indicate that something is true or happens in all circumstances. *Any dog bite, no matter how small, needs immediate medical attention.* ● If you are going to do something **as a matter of** urgency or priority, you are going to do it as soon as possible, because it is important. ● If you say that something is just **a matter of time**, you mean that it is certain to happen at some time in the future. *It would be only a matter of time before he went through with it.* ● **as a matter of fact**: see **fact**.

,**matter-of-'fact.** ADJ If you say someone is being **matter-of-fact**, you mean that they are being unemotional in a tense or difficult situation. *John was doing his best to give Francis the news in a matter-of-fact way.* ◆**matter-of-factly** ADV *'She thinks you're a spy,' Scott said matter-of-factly.*

mattress /ˈmætrəs/ **mattresses.** N-C A **mattress** is a large flat pad which is put on a bed to make it comfortable to sleep on.

mature /məˈtjʊə/ **matures, maturing, matured.** [1] VERB When a child or young animal **matures**, it becomes an adult. [2] ADJ A **mature** person or animal is fully grown. ◆**maturity** /məˈtjʊərɪti/ N-U *We stop growing at maturity.* [3] ADJ If you describe someone as **mature**, you think that their behaviour is responsible and sensible. ◆**maturity** N-U *Her speech showed great maturity.* [4] VERB When something **matures**, it reaches a state of complete development. *When the trees matured they were cut.*

maul /mɔːl/ **mauls, mauling, mauled.** VERB If someone **is mauled** by an animal, they are attacked and badly injured by it. *The dog went berserk and mauled one of the girls.*

maverick /ˈmævrɪk/ **mavericks.** N-C If you describe someone as a **maverick**, you mean that they do not think or behave in the same way as other people.

maxim /ˈmæksɪm/ **maxims.** N-C A **maxim** is a rule for good or sensible behaviour, especially one in the form of a saying. *I believe in the maxim 'if it ain't broke, don't fix it'.*

maximize (BR also **maximise**) /ˈmæksɪmaɪz/ **maximizes, maximizing, maximized.** VERB To **maximize** something means to make it as large or important as you can. *In order to maximize profit the firm would obviously seek to maximize output.*

maximum /ˈmæksɪməm/. [1] ADJ BEFORE N & N-SING The **maximum** amount or the **maxi-**

mum is the amount which is the largest that is possible, allowed, or required. ...*the maximum height for a fence or hedge is 2 metres.* ...*a maximum of two years in prison.* [2] ADJ BEFORE N You use **maximum** to emphasize how great an amount is. ...*the maximum amount of information... It was achieved with minimum fuss and maximum efficiency.* [3] ADV If you say that something is a particular amount **maximum**, you mean that this is the greatest amount it should be or could possibly be, although a smaller amount is acceptable or very possible. *We need an extra 6g a day maximum.*

may /meɪ/. [1] MODAL If you say that something **may** happen or be true, you mean that it is possible. *We may have some rain today... I don't know if they'll publish it or not. They may... Cancer may not show up for many years.* [2] MODAL If someone **may** do something, they are allowed to do it. *May we come in?... You may leave... Adolescents under the age of 18 may not work in jobs that require them to drive.* [3] MODAL You use **may** in statements where you are accepting the truth of a situation, but contrasting it with something that is more important. *I may be almost 50, but there's not a lot of things I've forgotten.*

May /meɪ/ N-U/N-C May is the fifth month of the year.

maybe /ˈmeɪbi/. [1] ADV You use **maybe** to express uncertainty, for example when you do not know that something is definitely true. *Maybe she is in love... I do think about having children, maybe when I'm 40... 'Is she coming back?'—'Maybe'.* [2] ADV You use **maybe** when you are making a rough guess at a number, quantity, or value, rather than stating it exactly. *The men were maybe a hundred feet away.*

mayhem /ˈmeɪhem/. N-U **Mayhem** is a situation that is not controlled or ordered, when people are behaving in a disorganized, confused, and often violent way. *Their arrival caused mayhem as crowds of refugees rushed towards them.*

mayonnaise /ˌmeɪəˈneɪz/. N-U **Mayonnaise** is a sauce made from egg yolks, oil, and vinegar, eaten cold.

mayor /meə, ˈmeɪə/ **mayors**. N-C The **mayor** of a town or city is the person who has been elected to represent it for a fixed period of time.

maze /meɪz/ **mazes**. N-C A **maze** is a complex system of passages or paths separated by walls or hedges. *The palace has extensive gardens, a maze, and tennis courts.*

me /mi, STRONG miː/. PRON A speaker or writer uses **me** to refer to himself or herself. **Me** is used as the object of a verb or a preposition. ...*decisions that would affect me for the rest of my life... She looked up at me.*

meadow /ˈmedəʊ/ **meadows**. N-C A **meadow** is a field with grass and flowers growing in it.

meagre (AM **meager**) /ˈmiːgə/. ADJ Something that is **meagre** is very small in amount. ...*a meagre 3.1% pay rise... Their food supply is meager and they are frequently without water.*

meal /miːl/ **meals**. N-C A **meal** is an occasion when people eat. You can refer to the food that

they eat at that time as a **meal**. *The waiter offered him red wine or white wine with his meal.*

> The first meal of the day is called **breakfast**. The most common word for the midday meal is **lunch**, but in some parts of Britain, and in some contexts, **dinner** is used as well. ...*school dinners.* ...*Christmas dinner.* However, **dinner** is used mainly to refer to a meal in the evening. In American English, this is the normal term, but in British English it may suggest a formal or special meal. If you want to avoid this suggestion, you can refer simply to your **evening meal**. **Supper** and **tea** are sometimes also used to refer to this meal, but there is some disagreement over usage. For some people, **supper** can only be a snack in the late evening and **tea** is a light meal in the afternoon, at which tea is drunk.

mean 1 signify

mean /miːn/ **means, meant**. [1] VERB If you want to know what something or someone **means**, you want to know what they are referring to, or what message they are conveying. *What does 'evidence' mean?... What do you think he means by that?... In modern Welsh, 'glas' means 'blue'... The red signal means you can shoot.* [2] VERB If something **means** a lot to you, it is important to you. *It would mean a lot to them to win.* [3] VERB If one thing **means** another, it shows that the second thing is true or makes it certain to happen. *Becoming a millionaire didn't mean an end to money worries.* [4] VERB If you **mean** what you say, you are serious and not joking, exaggerating, or just being polite. *He could see if I meant what I said... Does he really mean it when he says he is sorry?* [5] VERB If you **mean** to do something, you intend to do it. *I have been meaning to write this letter for some time now... I didn't mean to hurt you.*

PHRASES ● You say **'I mean'** when you are explaining, justifying, or correcting what you have just said. *It was his idea. Gordon's, I mean... I'm sure he wouldn't mind. I mean, I was the one who asked him... It was law or classics – I mean English or classics.* ● to **mean business**: see **business**.

mean 2 unkind

mean /miːn/ **meaner, meanest**. [1] ADJ If you say that someone is **mean**, you disapprove of them because they are unwilling to spend much money or to use very much of a particular thing. *He's basically mean with money. ...a rather mean portion of apple tart.* ♦**meanness** N-U ...*the meanness of some employers.* [2] ADJ If you are **mean** to someone, you are unkind to them. ♦**meanness** N-U *You provoked him out of meanness.* [3] PHRASE You use **no mean** to emphasize that someone or something is good or remarkable. *She was no mean performer.*

mean 3 average

mean /miːn/. N-SING The **mean** is a number that

is the average of a set of numbers. *...the mean score for 26-year-olds.* • See also **means**.

meander /mi'ændə/ **meanders, meandering, meandered.** 1 VERB If a river or road **meanders**, it has a lot of bends in it. *A rural single railway track meanders through the valley.* 2 VERB If you **meander** through a place, you move slowly through it for pleasure. *It's so restful to meander along Irish country roads.*

meaning /'mi:nɪŋ/ **meanings.** 1 N-VAR The **meaning** of something such as a word, symbol, or gesture is the thing that it refers to or the message that it conveys. *...two words with similar meanings... I have been trying hard to interpret the meaning of this dream.* 2 N-U If an activity or action has **meaning**, it has a purpose and is worthwhile. *...a challenge that gives meaning to life.*

meaningful /'mi:nɪŋful/. 1 ADJ If you describe something as **meaningful**, you mean that it is serious, important, or useful in some way. *...satisfying, meaningful work.* ♦**meaningfully** ADV *By joining voluntary organisations they can participate actively and meaningfully.* 2 ADJ BEFORE N A **meaningful** look, gesture, or remark is intended to express something which is not obvious, but which is understood. ♦**meaningfully** ADV *She rolled her eyes meaningfully.*

meaningless /'mi:nɪŋləs/. ADJ Something that is **meaningless** has no meaning or purpose. *The sentence 'kicked the ball the man' is meaningless. ...the conviction that life is meaningless.*

means /mi:nz/. 1 N-C A **means** of doing something is a method or instrument which can be used to do it. **Means** is both the singular and the plural form. *They didn't provide me with any means of transport... The move is a means to fight crime.* 2 N-PL You can refer to the money that someone has as their **means**; FORMAL. *...a health service that's available to all, regardless of means... As a student you're always living beyond your means.*

PHRASES • You can say **'by all means'** to tell someone that you are willing to allow them to do something. *'Can I come and have a look at your house?'—'Yes, by all means'.* • If you do something **by means of** a particular method or instrument, you do it using that method or instrument. *This is a two year course taught by means of lectures and seminars.* • You use expressions such as **'by no means'** and **'not by any means'** to emphasize that something is not true. *This is by no means out of the ordinary.*

meant /ment/. 1 **Meant** is the past tense and past participle of **mean**. 2 ADJ AFTER LINK-V If something or someone is **meant** to do a particular thing or is **meant** for a particular purpose, that is what was intended or planned. *The tales were never meant for publication... I'm meant to be on holiday.* 3 ADJ AFTER LINK-V If you say that something is **meant** to have a particular quality or characteristic, you mean it has a reputation for being like that. *Spurs are meant to be one of the top teams in the world.*

meantime /'mi:ntaɪm/. N-U In the **meantime** means in the period of time between two events, or while an event is happening. *Reduce*

the heat and simmer for 30 minutes. *In the meantime, fry the spicy sausage.*

meanwhile /'mi:nwaɪl/. ADV **Meanwhile** means in the period of time between two events, or while an event is happening. *I'll be ready to greet them. Meanwhile I'm off to discuss the Fowler's party with Felix.*

measles /'mi:zəlz/. N-U **Measles** is an infectious illness that gives you a high temperature and red spots.

measurable /'meʒərəbəl/. ADJ If something is **measurable**, it is large enough to be noticed or to be significant; FORMAL. *Both leaders seemed to expect measurable progress.*

measure /'meʒə/ **measures, measuring, measured.** 1 VERB If you **measure** the quality, quantity, or value of something, you decide how great it is, by using particular procedures or instruments. *I continued to measure his progress against the charts in the doctor's office... The swelling is measured with a ruler.* 2 VERB If something **measures** a particular length, width, or amount, that is its size or intensity, expressed in numbers. *This hand-decorated plate measures 30cm across.* 3 N-SING A **measure** of a particular quality, feeling, or activity is a fairly large amount of it; FORMAL. *Each attained a measure of success.* 4 N-SING If something is a **measure** of a particular situation, it shows that the situation is very serious or has developed to a very great extent. *That is a measure of how bad things have become.* 5 N-C When someone takes **measures** to do something, they carry out particular actions in order to achieve a particular result. *...new government measures to combat crime.* 6 PHRASE If something is done **for good measure**, it is done in addition to a number of other things. *I repeated my question for good measure.*

▸ **measure up.** PHR-VERB If you do not **measure up** to a standard or to someone's expectations, you are not good enough to achieve the standard or fulfil the person's expectations. *She's always comparing me to other people, and somehow I never measure up.*

measurement /'meʒəmənt/ **measurements.** 1 N-C A **measurement** is a result that you obtain by measuring something. *We took lots of measurements.* 2 N-VAR **Measurement** of something is the process or activity of measuring it. 3 N-PL Your **measurements** are the size of your chest, waist, hips, and other parts of your body.

meat /mi:t/ **meats.** N-VAR **Meat** is the flesh of a dead animal that people cook and eat. *...cold meats and salads.*

mechanic /mɪ'kænɪk/ **mechanics.** 1 N-C A **mechanic** is someone whose job is to repair and maintain machines and engines, especially car engines. 2 N-PL The **mechanics** of a system or activity are the way in which it works or the way in which it is done. *What are the mechanics of this new process?*

mechanical /mɪ'kænɪkəl/. 1 ADJ A **mechanical** device has moving parts and uses power in order to do a particular task. ♦**mechanically** ADV *The locks are mechanically operated.* 2 ADJ A **mechanical** action is done automatically, without thinking about it. ♦**mechanically** ADV

He nodded mechanically, his eyes fixed on the girl.

mechanism /'mekənɪzm/ **mechanisms.**
[1] N-C A **mechanism** is a part of a machine that does a particular task. *...the locking mechanism.* [2] N-C A **mechanism** is a way of getting something done within a particular system. *...a mechanism for protecting minority rights.*

mechanize (BR also **mechanise**) /'mekənaɪz/ **mechanizes, mechanizing, mechanized.** VERB If a type of work **is mechanized**, it is done by machines. ♦**mechanization** N-U *...the mechanisation of agriculture.*

medal /'medəl/ **medals.** N-C A **medal** is a small metal disc, given as an award for bravery or as a prize in a sporting event.

medallist /'medəlɪst/ **medallists.** N-C A **medallist** is a person who has won a medal in sport.

meddle /'medəl/ **meddles, meddling, meddled.** VERB If you say that someone **meddles** in something, you are criticizing the fact that they try to influence or change it without being asked. *She told me not to meddle in things that don't concern me.*

media /'miːdiə/. [1] N-SING You can refer to television, radio, and newspapers as the **media**. **Media** can take the singular or plural form of the verb. *The media has brought more unwelcome attention to the Royal Family.* [2] **Media** is a plural of **medium**.

mediaeval. See **medieval**.

mediate /'miːdieɪt/ **mediates, mediating, mediated.** VERB If someone **mediates** between two groups, or **mediates** an agreement between them, they try to settle a dispute between them. *The Vatican successfully mediated in a territorial dispute between Argentina and Chile.* ♦**mediation** N-U *...United Nations mediation between the two sides.* ♦**mediator, mediators** N-C *An archbishop has been acting as mediator between the rebels and the authorities.*

medical /'medɪkəl/ **medicals.** [1] ADJ BEFORE N **Medical** means relating to illness and injuries and to their treatment or prevention. *Four of our men needed medical treatment.* ♦**medically** ADV *I am not medically qualified.* [2] N-C A **medical** is a thorough examination of your body by a doctor.

medication /,medɪ'keɪʃən/ **medications.** N-VAR **Medication** is medicine that is used to cure an illness. *She is not on any medication.*

medicinal /me'dɪsənəl/. ADJ **Medicinal** substances are used to treat and cure illness. *...medicinal plants.*

medicine /'medsən, AM 'medɪsɪn/ **medicines.** [1] N-U **Medicine** is the treatment of illness and injuries by doctors and nurses. *He pursued a career in medicine.* [2] N-VAR A **medicine** is a substance that you swallow in order to cure an illness.

medieval (or **mediaeval**) /,medi'iːvəl, AM ,miːd-/. ADJ **Medieval** things relate to or date from the period in European history between about 500 AD and about 1500 AD. *...a medieval castle.*

mediocre /,miːdi'əʊkə/. ADJ If you describe someone or something as **mediocre**, you

mean that it is of rather poor quality. *His school record was mediocre.* ♦**mediocrity** /,miːdi'ɒkrɪti, ,med-/ N-U *...the mediocrity of most contemporary literature.*

meditate /'medɪteɪt/ **meditates, meditating, meditated.** [1] VERB If you **meditate** on something, you think about it carefully and deeply for a long time. [2] VERB If you **meditate**, you remain in a calm, silent state for a period of time, often as part of a religious training. ♦**meditation** N-U *Many busy executives have begun to practice meditation.*

medium /'miːdiəm/; the plural of the noun is **mediums** or **media**. [1] ADJ You use **medium** to describe something which is average in size, degree or amount, or approximately half way along a scale between two extremes. *He was of medium height... Only a low or medium heat is necessary. ...medium brown hair.* [2] N-C A **medium** is the means that you use to communicate or express something. *In Sierra Leone, English is used as the medium of instruction.*
● See also **media**.

meek /miːk/. ADJ & N-PL A **meek** person is quiet and timid and does what other people say. **The meek** are people who are **meek**. ♦**meekly** ADV *'Thank you, Peter', Amy said meekly.*

meet /miːt/ **meets, meeting, met.** [1] VERB If you **meet** someone, or if you **meet up** with them, you happen to be in the same place as them and have a conversation with them. *He's the kindest and sincerest person I've ever met... Hey, Terry, come and meet my Dad... We met by chance... When he was parking my automobile, he met up with a buddy he had at Oxford.* [2] VERB If two or more people **meet**, or if they **meet up**, they go to the same place, which they have earlier arranged to do, so that they can talk or do something together. *Meet me down at the beach tomorrow... Mr Levy will meet with President Bush on Thursday... We tend to meet up for lunch once a week... The committee met twice last week to discuss the company's problems.* [3] VERB If you **meet** someone who is travelling, or if you **meet** their train, plane, or bus, you go to the station, airport, or bus stop in order to be there when they arrive. *Lili and my father met me off the boat.* [4] VERB If something **meets** a need, requirement, or condition, it is satisfactory or sufficiently large to fulfil it. *Employees must meet certain eligibility requirements.* [5] VERB If you **meet** something such as a problem or challenge, you deal satisfactorily with it. *They had worked heroically to meet the deadline.* [6] VERB If you **meet** the cost of something, you provide the money for it. *The government said it will help meet some of the cost of the damage.* [7] VERB If someone or something **meets** an attitude or reaction, or if they **meet with** it, they experience that attitude or get that reaction from people. *Never had she met such spite and pettiness... The idea met with a cool response.* [8] VERB The place where two areas or lines **meet** is the place where they aren't next to one another or join. *The track widened as it met the road.* [9] to **make ends meet**: see **end**. ● to **meet** someone's **eyes**: see **eye**.

▶ **meet up.** See **meet** 1, 2.

meeting /ˈmiːtɪŋ/ **meetings.** ⓵ N-C A **meeting** is an event at which a group of people come together to discuss things or make decisions. You can also refer to the people at a meeting as **the meeting**. *He still travels to London regularly for business meetings... The meeting decided that further efforts were needed.* ⓶ N-C A **meeting** is an occasion when you meet someone. *...a chance meeting.*

megabyte /ˈmeɡəbaɪt/ **megabytes.** N-C In computing, a **megabyte** is one million bytes of data.

melancholy /ˈmelənkɒli/. ADJ & N-U Someone who is **melancholy** or has **melancholy** feelings has an intense feeling of sadness. This feeling can be called **melancholy**; LITERARY.

mellow /ˈmeləʊ/ **mellower, mellowest; mellows, mellowing, mellowed.** ⓵ ADJ **Mellow** is used to describe things that have a pleasant, soft, rich colour, usually red, yellow, or brown. *...the softer, mellower light of evening.* ⓶ ADJ A **mellow** flavour or sound is pleasant, smooth, and rich. ⓷ VERB & ADJ If someone **mellows**, or if they become more **mellow**, they become kinder or less extreme in their behaviour. *Marriage had not mellowed him... Is she more mellow and tolerant?*

melodrama /ˈmelədrɑːmə/ **melodramas.** N-VAR A **melodrama** is a story or play in which there are a lot of exciting or sad events and in which people's emotions are very exaggerated.

melodramatic /ˌmelədrəˈmætɪk/. ADJ If you are being **melodramatic**, you treat a situation as much more serious than it really is.

melody /ˈmelədi/ **melodies.** N-C A **melody** is a tune; LITERARY.

melon /ˈmelən/ **melons.** N-VAR A **melon** is a large, sweet, juicy fruit with a thick green or yellow skin.

melt /melt/ **melts, melting, melted.** ⓵ VERB When a solid substance **melts**, or when it **is melted**, it changes to a liquid because of being heated. *The snow had melted... Break up the chocolate and melt it.* ⓶ VERB & PHR-VERB If something **melts**, or if it **melts away**, it gradually disappears. *The youths dispersed and melted into the darkness... His anger melted away.*
▸ **melt down.** PHR-VERB If an object **is melted down**, it is heated until it melts. *Their equipment would be melted down as scrap metal.*

member /ˈmembə/ **members.** N-C A **member** of a group or organization is one of the people, animals, or things belonging to it. *Their lack of training could put members of the public at risk. ...a sunflower or a similar member of the daisy family... Britain is a full member of NATO.*

Member of Parliament, Members of Parliament. N-C A **Member of Parliament** is a person who has been elected to represent people in a country's parliament. It is usually abbreviated to 'MP'. ● See note at **government**.

membership /ˈmembəʃɪp/ **memberships.** ⓵ N-U **Membership** is the fact or state of being a member of an organization. *...his membership of the Communist Party.* ⓶ N-VAR The **membership** of an organization is the people

who belong to it. *The party membership reached 97,000.*

membrane /ˈmembreɪn/ **membranes.** N-C A **membrane** is a thin skin which connects or covers parts of a person's or animal's body.

memo /ˈmeməʊ/ **memos.** N-C A **memo** is an official note from one person to another within the same organization.

memoirs /ˈmemwɑːz/. N-PL If someone writes their **memoirs**, they write a book about their life.

memorabilia /ˌmemərəˈbɪliə/. N-PL **Memorabilia** consists of things that you collect because they are connected with a person or an organization in which you are interested. *...rock and pop memorabilia.*

memorable /ˈmemərəbəl/. ADJ Something that is **memorable** is likely to be remembered, because it is special or unique. *It had been a memorable day.*

memorandum /ˌmeməˈrændəm/; the plural is **memoranda** or **memorandums.** N-C A **memorandum** is a memo; FORMAL.

memorial /mɪˈmɔːriəl/ **memorials.** ⓵ N-C A **memorial** is a structure built in order to remind people of a famous person or event. *...a memorial to Columbus... Every village had its war memorial.* ⓶ ADJ BEFORE N A **memorial** event or prize is in honour of someone who has died, so that they will be remembered. *A memorial service is being held for her at St Paul's Church.*

memorize (BR also **memorise**) /ˈmeməraɪz/ **memorizes, memorizing, memorized.** VERB If you **memorize** something, you learn it so that you can remember it exactly.

memory /ˈmeməri/ **memories.** ⓵ N-C Your **memory** is your ability to remember things. *All the details of the meeting are fresh in my memory... He had a good memory for faces... He claims to have lost his memory.* ⓶ N-C A **memory** is something that you remember about the past. *He had happy memories of his father.* ⓷ N-SING If you talk about the **memory** of someone who has died, especially someone who was loved or respected, you are referring to the ways in which they are remembered. *The congress opened with a minute's silence in memory of those who died in the struggle.* ⓸ N-C A computer's **memory** is the capacity of the computer to store information. ⓹ PHRASE If you do something **from memory**, you do it without looking at anything written or printed. *Many members of the church sang from memory.*

men /men/. **Men** is the plural of **man**.

menace /ˈmenɪs/ **menaces, menacing, menaced.** ⓵ N-C Something or someone that is a **menace** is likely to cause serious harm. *In my view you are a menace to the public. ...the menace of fascism.* ⓶ N-U **Menace** is a quality or atmosphere of danger or threat. *...a vague feeling of menace.* ⓷ VERB If someone or something **menaces** you, they threaten to harm you or are likely to do so. *...a Franco-Spanish fleet which menaced the English coast.* ◆ **menacing** ADJ *Mary Ann gave her a menacing look.* ◆ **menacingly** ADV *James moved menacingly towards him.*

mend /mend/ **mends, mending, mended.**
1 VERB If you **mend** something that is damaged or broken, you do something to it so that it works properly or can be used. *My father always mended shoes... I should have had the catch mended.* **2** PHRASE If you are **on the mend**, you are recovering after an illness or injury.

meningitis /ˌmenɪnˈdʒaɪtɪs/. N-U **Meningitis** is a serious infectious illness which affects your brain and spinal cord.

menopause /ˈmenəpɔːz/. N-SING The **menopause** is the time during which a woman stops menstruating, usually when she is about fifty. ♦ **menopausal** ADJ *...a menopausal woman.*

menstrual /ˈmenstruəl/. ADJ BEFORE N **Menstrual** means relating to menstruation. *...the menstrual cycle.*

menstruate /ˈmenstrueɪt/ **menstruates, menstruating, menstruated.** VERB When a woman **menstruates**, a flow of blood comes from her womb; FORMAL. ♦ **menstruation** N-U *...the cycles of menstruation and fertility.*

menswear /ˈmenzweə/. N-U **Menswear** is clothing for men.

mental /ˈmentl/. **1** ADJ BEFORE N **Mental** means relating to the mind and the process of thinking. *...the mental development of children.* ♦ **mentally** ADV *He became mentally ill.* **2** ADJ BEFORE N A **mental** act is one that involves only thinking and not physical action. *...mental arithmetic.* ♦ **mentally** ADV *I mentally rehearsed what I would do.*

mentality /menˈtælɪti/ **mentalities.** N-C Your **mentality** is your attitudes or ways of thinking. *...the criminal mentality.*

mention /ˈmenʃən/ **mentions, mentioning, mentioned.** **1** VERB & N-VAR If you **mention** something, or if you give a **mention** to it, you say something about it, usually briefly. *I may not have mentioned it before... She had mentioned that it was her husband's birthday... There was no mention of elections.* **2** PHRASE You use **not to mention** when you want to add extra information which emphasizes the point that you are making. *The audience, not to mention the bewildered cast, were not amused.*

mentor /ˈmentɔː/ **mentors.** N-C Someone's **mentor** is a person who teaches them and gives them a lot of advice over a period of time; FORMAL. *...his political mentor.*

menu /ˈmenjuː/ **menus.** **1** N-C In a restaurant or café, the **menu** is a list of the available meals and drinks. *They ordered everything on the menu.* **2** N-C On a computer, a **menu** is a list of choices of things that you can do using the computer.

MEP /ˌem iː ˈpiː/ **MEPs.** N-C An **MEP** is a person who has been elected to the European Parliament. **MEP** is an abbreviation for 'Member of the European Parliament'.

mercenary /ˈmɜːsənri, AM -neri/ **mercenaries.** **1** N-C A **mercenary** is a soldier who is paid to fight by a country or group that he or she does not belong to. **2** ADJ If you describe someone as **mercenary**, you mean that they are only interested in the money that they can get from a particular person or situation.

merchandise /ˈmɜːtʃəndaɪz, -daɪs/. N-U **Merchandise** is goods that are bought or sold; FORMAL. *The merchandise is reasonably priced.*

merchandising /ˈmɜːtʃəndaɪzɪŋ/. N-U **Merchandising** is used to refer to the way shops and businesses organize the sale of their products, for example the way they are displayed and the prices that are chosen.

merchant /ˈmɜːtʃənt/ **merchants.** **1** N-C A **merchant** is a person whose business is buying or selling goods in large quantities. *...a wine merchant.* **2** ADJ BEFORE N **Merchant** seamen or ships are involved in carrying goods for trade.

mercifully /ˈmɜːsɪfʊli/. ADV You can use **mercifully** to show that you are glad about something, because it avoids a dangerous or unpleasant situation. *Mercifully, a friend came to the rescue... Crime is mercifully rare here.*

merciless /ˈmɜːsɪləs/. ADJ If you describe someone as **merciless**, you mean that they are very cruel or determined and do not show any concern for the effect that their actions have on other people. ♦ **mercilessly** ADV *We teased him mercilessly.*

mercury /ˈmɜːkjʊri/. N-U **Mercury** is a silver-coloured liquid metal, used in thermometers.

mercy /ˈmɜːsi/. **1** N-U If someone in authority shows **mercy**, they choose not to harm or punish someone they have power over. *They cried for mercy.* **2** PHRASE If you are **at the mercy of** something or someone, you cannot prevent yourself being affected or harmed by them. *Ordinary people are at the mercy of faceless bureaucrats.*

mere /mɪə/ **merest.** ADJ BEFORE N You use **mere** to emphasize how unimportant, insufficient, or small something is. **Mere** does not have a comparative form. The superlative form **merest** is used for emphasis, rather than in comparisons. *Tickets are a mere £7.50... She'd never received the merest hint of any communication from him.* ♦ **merely** ADV *The brain accounts for merely three per cent of body weight.*

merely /ˈmɪəli/. **1** ADV You use **merely** to emphasize that something is only what you say and not better, more important, or more exciting. *Michael is now merely a good friend.* **2** ADV You use **not merely** before the less important of two statements, as a way of emphasizing the more important statement. *His were not merely crimes of theft but of violence.*

merge /mɜːdʒ/ **merges, merging, merged.** VERB If one thing **merges with** another, or if one thing **is merged with** another, they combine or come together to make one whole thing. *The two countries merged into one. ...how to merge the graphic with text on the same screen.*

merger /ˈmɜːdʒə/ **mergers.** N-C A **merger** is the joining together of two separate companies or organizations so that they become one. *...the proposed merger of two Japanese banks.*

merit /ˈmerɪt/ **merits, meriting, merited.** **1** N-VAR If you refer to the **merit** or **merits** of something, you mean that it has good or useful qualities. *Box-office success mattered more than artistic merit... Whatever its merits, their work would never be used.* **2** VERB If someone or something **merits** a particular action or treatment, they are good, important, or serious enough for someone to treat them in this way; FORMAL *Such ideas merit careful consideration.* ③ PHRASE If you judge something or someone **on merit** or on **their merits**, your judgement is based on their actual qualities, rather than on particular rules, traditions, or prejudices. *Everybody is selected on merit... Each case is judged on its merits.*

mermaid /ˈmɜːmeɪd/ **mermaids.** N-C In fairy stories and legends, a **mermaid** is a woman with a fish's tail instead of legs, who lives in the sea.

merry /ˈmeri/. ADJ **Merry** means happy and cheerful. *...a merry little tune... We wished them a Merry Christmas.* ♦ **merrily** ADV *Chris threw back his head and laughed merrily.*

mesh /meʃ/ **meshes, meshing, meshed.** ① N-VAR **Mesh** is material like a net made from wire, thread, or plastic. *...wire mesh.* ② VERB If two things or ideas **mesh**, or if they **are meshed**, they go together well. *This story never quite meshed with the facts.*

mesmerize (BR also **mesmerise**) /ˈmezməraɪz/ **mesmerizes, mesmerizing, mesmerized.** VERB If you **are mesmerized** by something, you are so fascinated by it that you cannot think about anything else. *Jack walked around the hotel and was mesmerized by its sheer size.*

mess /mes/ **messes, messing, messed.** ① N-SING If something is a **mess** or in a **mess**, it is dirty or untidy. *I'll clear up the mess later... The wrong shampoo can leave curly hair in a tangled mess.* ② N-C If you say that a situation is a **mess**, you mean that it is full of trouble or problems. You can also say that something is in a **mess**. *I've made such a mess of my life. ...the many reasons why the economy is in such a mess.*

▶ **mess around** (BR also **mess about**) ① PHR-VERB If you **mess around**, you spend time doing silly or casual things without any particular purpose or result. *Boys and girls will enjoy messing about with any kind of machine.* ② PHR-VERB If you say that someone **is messing around with** something, you mean that they are interfering with it in a harmful way. *I'd like to know who's been messing about with the pram.*

▶ **mess up.** ① PHR-VERB If someone **messes** something **up**, or if they **mess up**, they cause something to fail or be spoiled; INFORMAL *He had messed up one career... If I messed up, I would probably be fired.* ② PHR-VERB If you **mess up** a place or a thing, you make it untidy or dirty. *I hope they haven't messed up your video tapes.*

message /ˈmesɪdʒ/ **messages.** ① N-C A **message** is a piece of information or a request that you send to someone or leave for them when you cannot speak to them directly. *I got a message you were trying to reach me.* ② N-C The **message** that someone is trying to communicate is the idea, argument, or opinion that they are trying to communicate. *I think they got the message that this is wrong.*

messenger /ˈmesɪndʒə/ **messengers.** N-C A **messenger** takes a message to someone, or takes messages regularly as their job. *...instruction for the document to be sent by messenger.*

Messiah /mɪˈsaɪə/. N-PROPER For Jews, the **Messiah** is a king or leader who will be sent to them by God. For Christians, the **Messiah** is Jesus Christ.

Messrs /ˈmesəz/. **Messrs** is used as the plural of **Mr** in front of the names of two or more men; FORMAL *...Messrs Clegg & Sons of Balham.*

messy /ˈmesi/. ① ADJ A **messy** person or activity makes things dirty or untidy. *She was a good, if messy, cook... The work tends to be a bit messy.* ② ADJ Something that is **messy** is dirty or untidy. *This first coat of paint looks messy.* ③ ADJ If you describe a situation as **messy**, you dislike it because it is confused or complicated. *Negotiations would be messy and time-consuming.*

met /met/. **Met** is the past tense and past participle of **meet**.

metabolic /ˌmetəˈbɒlɪk/. ADJ BEFORE N **Metabolic** means relating to a person's or animal's metabolism; TECHNICAL *People who have inherited a low metabolic rate will gain weight.*

metabolism /mɪˈtæbəlɪzəm/ **metabolisms.** N-VAR Your **metabolism** is the way that chemical processes in your body cause food to be used in an efficient way, for example to give you energy; TECHNICAL

metal /ˈmetəl/ **metals.** N-VAR **Metal** is a hard substance such as iron, steel, copper, or lead. *...furniture in wood, metal and glass. ...a metal bar.*

metallic /məˈtælɪk/. ADJ **Metallic** things consist of metal or sound or look like they consist of metal. *...a nonstick metallic dish... It gave a metallic clang, like a cracked bell.*

metamorphosis /ˌmetəˈmɔːfəsɪs/ **metamorphoses.** N-VAR When a **metamorphosis** occurs, a person or thing develops and changes into something completely different; FORMAL *...his metamorphosis from Communist to nationalist.*

metaphor /ˈmetəfɔːr/ **metaphors.** N-VAR A **metaphor** is an imaginative way of describing something by referring to something else which has the qualities that you want to express. *...using a dinner party as a metaphor for life.*

metaphorical /ˌmetəˈfɒrɪkəl, AM -ˈfɔːr-/. ADJ You use the word **metaphorical** to indicate that you are not using words with their ordinary meaning, but are describing something by means of an image or symbol. *The ride is the literal and metaphorical high point of the park.* ♦ **metaphorically** ADV *You're speaking metaphorically, I hope.*

mete /miːt/ **metes, meting, meted.**
▶ **mete out.** PHR-VERB To **mete out** a punishment means to punish someone; FORMAL *...the two year sentence meted out to a convicted child molester.*

meteor /ˈmiːtiə/ **meteors.** N-C A **meteor** is a piece of rock flying through space, especially one that is shining or burning brightly.

meteorite /ˈmiːtiəraɪt/ **meteorites.** N-C A **meteorite** is a large piece of rock or metal from space that has landed on the earth.

meteorological /ˌmiːtiərəˈlɒdʒɪkəl/ ADJ BEFORE N **Meteorological** means relating to the weather or to weather forecasting; TECHNICAL. ...*adverse meteorological conditions.*

meter /ˈmiːtə/ **meters.** [1] N-C A **meter** is a device that measures and records something such as the amount of gas or electricity that you have used. ...*the electricity meter.* [2] See also **metre**.

methane /ˈmiːθeɪn, AM ˈmeθ-/. N-U **Methane** is a colourless gas that has no smell.

method /ˈmeθəd/ **methods.** N-VAR A **method** is a particular way of doing something. *The pill is the most efficient method of birth control.* ...*new teaching methods.*

methodical /məˈθɒdɪkəl/. ADJ If you describe someone as **methodical**, you mean that they do things carefully, thoroughly, and in order. *Da Vinci was methodical in his research.* ◆**methodically** ADV *She methodically put the things into her suitcase.*

methodology /ˌmeθəˈdɒlədʒi/ **methodologies.** N-VAR A **methodology** is a system of methods and principles for doing something; FORMAL. *Teaching methodologies vary according to the topic.* ◆**methodological** ADJ ...*methodological issues raised by the study of literary texts.*

meticulous /məˈtɪkjʊləs/. ADJ If someone is **meticulous**, they do things very carefully and with great attention to detail. ◆**meticulously** ADV *The flat had been meticulously cleaned.*

metre (AM **meter**) /ˈmiːtə/ **metres.** N-C A **metre** is a unit of length equal to 100 centimetres. *The scarves are 2.3 metres long.*

metric /ˈmetrɪk/. ADJ The **metric** system of measurement uses metres, grammes, and litres.

metro /ˈmetrəʊ/ **metros.** N-C The **metro** is the underground railway system in some cities, for example in Paris.

metropolis /məˈtrɒpəlɪs/ **metropolises.** N-C You can refer to a large, important, busy city as a **metropolis**. *Ho Chi Minh City will be a thriving metropolis in the future.*

metropolitan /ˌmetrəˈpɒlɪtən/. ADJ BEFORE N **Metropolitan** means belonging to or typical of a large busy city. ...*major metropolitan hospitals.*

mg. mg is a written abbreviation for 'milligram' or 'milligrams'. ...*300 mg of calcium.*

mice /maɪs/. **Mice** is the plural of **mouse**.

microbe /ˈmaɪkrəʊb/ **microbes.** N-C A **microbe** is a very small living thing, which you can only see with a microscope.

microchip /ˈmaɪkrəʊtʃɪp/ **microchips.** N-C A **microchip** is a small piece of silicon inside a computer, on which electronic circuits are printed.

microcosm /ˈmaɪkrəʊkɒzəm/ **microcosms.** N-C A place or event that is a **microcosm** of a larger one has all the main features of the larger one and seems like a smaller version of it; FORMAL. *In many ways, Pennsylvania is a microcosm of the United States.*

micro-'organism, micro-organisms. N-C A **micro-organism** is a very small living thing which you can only see with a powerful microscope; TECHNICAL.

microphone /ˈmaɪkrəfəʊn/ **microphones.** N-C A **microphone** is a device used to record sounds or make them louder.

microprocessor /ˌmaɪkrəʊˈprəʊsesə/ **microprocessors.** N-C A **microprocessor** is a microchip which can be programmed to do a large number of tasks or calculations.

microscope /ˈmaɪkrəskəʊp/ **microscopes.** N-C A **microscope** is an instrument which magnifies very small objects so that you can study them.

microscopic /ˌmaɪkrəˈskɒpɪk/. ADJ **Microscopic** objects are extremely small, and usually can be seen only through a microscope. ...*microscopic particles.*

microwave /ˈmaɪkrəʊweɪv/ **microwaves, microwaving, microwaved.** [1] N-C A **microwave** or a **microwave oven** is an oven which cooks food very quickly by a kind of radiation rather than by heat. [2] VERB To **microwave** food or drink means to cook or heat it in a microwave oven.

mid-'air (or **midair**). N-U If something happens in **mid-air**, it happens in the air rather than on the ground. *The aircraft exploded in mid-air.* ...*a mid-air collision.*

midday /ˌmɪdˈdeɪ/. N-U **Midday** is twelve o'clock in the middle of the day.

middle /ˈmɪdəl/ **middles.** [1] N-C The **middle** of something is the part that is farthest from its edges, ends, or outside surface. *Howard stood in the middle of the room... Father told her to make sure the roast potatoes weren't raw in the middle.* [2] ADJ BEFORE N The **middle** thing or person in a row or series is the one with an equal number of things or people on each side, or before it and after it. *The middle drawer contained stockings.* ...*the middle child in a family of seven children.* [3] N-SING & ADJ BEFORE N The **middle** of an event or period of time, or the **middle** part of it, is the part that comes after the first part and before the last part. *I woke up in the middle of the night.* ...*the middle month of each quarter.* [4] ADJ BEFORE N The **middle** course or way is a moderate course of action that lies between two opposite and extreme courses. ...*an attempt to find a middle way between doing nothing and doing everything.*

PHRASES ● If you are in the middle of doing something, you are busy doing it. *I'm in the middle of writing a book.* ● the middle of nowhere: see nowhere.

middle 'age. N-U **Middle age** is the period in your life when you are between about 40 and 60 years old.

middle-'aged. ADJ **Middle-aged** people are between the ages of about 40 and 60.

middle 'class, middle classes. N-C & ADJ The **middle class** or **middle classes** are the people in a society who are not working class or upper class, for example managers, doctors, and lawyers. You can say people like this are **middle class.** ...*middle-class voters.*

,**Middle 'East.** N-PROPER The **Middle East** is the area around the eastern Mediterranean that includes Iran and all the countries in Asia that are to the west and south-west of Iran. ...*the two great rivers of the Middle East.*

middleman /'mɪdəlmæn/ **middlemen.** 1 N-C A **middleman** is a person or company that buys things from the people who produce them and sells them to other people at a profit. 2 N-C A **middleman** is a person who helps in negotiations between people who are unwilling to meet each other directly. *The two sides would only meet indirectly, through middlemen.*

midnight /'mɪdnaɪt/. N-U **Midnight** is twelve o'clock in the middle of the night.

midst /mɪdst/.
PHRASES ● If you are **in the midst of** doing something, you are doing it at present. *Susan's students are in the midst of their first research project.* ● If something happens **in the midst of** a situation or an event, it happens during that situation or event. *Eleanor arrived in the midst of a blizzard.* ● If someone or something is **in the midst of** a group of people or things, they are among them or surrounded by them. ...*a house in the midst of huge trees.*

midway /,mɪd'weɪ/. 1 ADV & ADJ BEFORE N If something is **midway** between two places, it is between them and the same distance from each of them. ...*a cottage midway between London and Oxford.* ...*the midway point between Gloucester, Hereford and Worcester.* 2 ADV & ADJ BEFORE N If something happens **midway** through a period of time, it happens during the middle part of it. *He returned midway through the afternoon.* ...*the midway point in the season.*

midweek /,mɪd'wiːk/. ADJ BEFORE N & ADV **Midweek** describes something that happens in the middle of the week. ...*midweek flights from Gatwick...* *They'll be able to go up to London midweek.*

midwife /'mɪdwaɪf/ **midwives.** N-C A **midwife** is a nurse who advises pregnant women and helps them to give birth.

might /maɪt/. 1 MODAL You use **might** to indicate that something will possibly happen or be true in the future. *Smoking might be banned totally in most buildings... I might well regret it later... He might not be back until tonight.* 2 MODAL You use **might** to indicate that there is a possibility that something is true. *You might be right... He might not be interested in her any more... I heard what might have been an explosion.* 3 MODAL You use **might** to make a suggestion or to give advice in a very polite way. *You might try the gas station down the street... I thought we might go for a drive on Sunday.* 4 MODAL You use **might** as a polite way of interrupting someone, asking a question, making a request, or introducing what you are going to say next; FORMAL, SPOKEN. *Might I make a suggestion?... Might I trouble you for a drop more tea?* 5 N-U **Might** is power or strength; FORMAL. ...*the great might of the Soviet Union.*

mightily /'maɪtɪli/. ADV **Mightily** means to a great extent or to a great degree; DATED. *I was mightily impressed.*

mightn't /'maɪtənt/. **Mightn't** is a spoken form of 'might not'.

might've /'maɪtəv/. **Might've** is the usual spoken form of 'might have', especially when 'have' is an auxiliary verb.

mighty /'maɪti/ **mightier, mightiest.** 1 ADJ **Mighty** means very large or powerful; LITERARY. ...*a mighty explosion.* ...*one of the mightiest armies in history.* 2 ADV **Mighty** means very; AMERICAN, INFORMAL. *You look mighty pretty tonight.*

migraine /'miːɡreɪn, AM 'maɪ-/ **migraines.** N-VAR A **migraine** is a very severe headache.

migrant /'maɪɡrənt/ **migrants.** N-C A **migrant** is a person who moves from one place to another, especially in order to find work. ...*migrant workers.*

migrate /maɪ'ɡreɪt, AM 'maɪɡreɪt/ **migrates, migrating, migrated.** 1 VERB If people **migrate**, they move from one place to another, especially in order to find work. *Lacking opportunities in the countryside, peasants have migrated to the cities.* ◆**migration, migrations.** N-VAR ...*the migration of Soviet Jews to Israel.* 2 VERB When birds, fish, or animals **migrate**, they go and live in a different area for part of the year, in order to breed or to find food. ◆**migration** N-VAR ...*the migration of swallows.*

mike /maɪk/ **mikes.** N-C A **mike** is a microphone; INFORMAL.

mild /maɪld/ **milder, mildest.** 1 ADJ Something that is **mild** is not very strong or severe. ...*a mild onion flavour.* ...*a mild headache.* ◆**mildly** ADV ...*mildly spiced rice... I felt mildly alarmed.* 2 ADJ **Mild** weather is less cold than usual. ● See note at **hot.**

mile /maɪl/ **miles.** 1 N-C A **mile** is a unit of distance equal to approximately 1.6 kilometres. *The hurricane is moving to the west at about 18 miles per hour.* 2 N-PL **Miles** is used to refer to a long distance. *The nearest doctor is miles away... 'Shall I come to see you?'—'Are you kidding? It's miles.'*

mileage /'maɪlɪdʒ/ **mileages.** 1 N-VAR **Mileage** refers to a distance that is travelled, measured in miles. *They had to keep track of their mileage.* 2 N-U The **mileage** in a particular course of action is its usefulness in getting you what you want. *It's obviously important to get as much mileage out of the convention as possible.*

milestone /'maɪlstəʊn/ **milestones.** N-C A **milestone** is an important event in the history or development of something. *The decision is being seen as a milestone in relations between the two countries.*

milieu /'miːljɜː, AM mɪ'ljuː/ **milieux** or **milieus.** N-C The **milieu** in which you live or work is the group of people that you live or work among; FORMAL. ...*a very different cultural milieu.*

militant /'mɪlɪtənt/ **militants.** ADJ & N-C Someone who is **militant**, or who is a **militant**, is active in trying to bring about political change. ...*one of the most militant unions.* ...*an attack by militants.* ◆**militancy** N-U ...*the growing militancy of French university students.*

military /'mɪlɪtri, AM -teri/. **1** ADJ **Military** means relating to a country's armed forces. *Military action may become necessary.* ♦**militarily** /ˌmɪlɪ'teərɪli/ ADV *...suggestions that the United States should intervene militarily.* **2** N-SING **The military** are the armed forces of a country, especially the officers of high rank. **Military** can take the singular or plural form of the verb. *Did you serve in the military?*

militia /mɪ'lɪʃə/ **militias.** N-C A **militia** is an organization that operates like an army but whose members are not professional soldiers.

milk /mɪlk/ **milks, milking, milked.** **1** N-U **Milk** is the white liquid produced by cows and goats, which people drink and make into butter, cheese, and yoghurt. **2** VERB When someone **milks** a cow or goat, they get milk from it from an organ called the udder, which hangs beneath its body. ♦**milking** N-U *...helping to bring in the cows for milking.* **3** N-U **Milk** is the white liquid produced by women to feed their babies. **4** VERB If you say that someone **milks** something, you mean that they get as much benefit or profit as they can from it, without caring about other people; used showing disapproval. *The callous couple milked money from a hospital charity to fund a lavish lifestyle.*

milky /'mɪlki/. **1** ADJ Something that is **milky** in colour is pale white. *A milky mist filled the valley.* **2** ADJ **Milky** food or drink contains a lot of milk. *...milky coffee.*

mill /mɪl/ **mills, milling, milled.** **1** N-C A **mill** is a building where grain is crushed to make flour. **2** N-C A **mill** is a small device used for grinding something such as coffee or pepper. *...a pepper mill.* **3** N-C A **mill** is a factory used for making and processing materials such as steel, wool, or cotton.

▶ **mill around** (BR also **mill about**). PHR-VERB When a crowd of people **are milling around**, they are moving around in a disorganized way.

millennium /mɪ'leniəm/ **millennia** or **millenniums.** N-C A **millennium** is a thousand years.

milligram (or **milligramme**) /'mɪlɪɡræm/ **milligrams.** N-C A **milligram** is a metric unit of weight equal to one thousandth of a gram. *...0.5 milligrams of mercury.*

millilitre (AM **milliliter**) /'mɪlɪliːtə/ **millilitres.** N-C A **millilitre** is a metric unit of volume for liquids and gases that is equal to a thousandth of a litre. *...100 millilitres of blood.*

millimetre (AM **millimeter**) /'mɪlɪmiːtə/ **millimetres.** N-C A **millimetre** is a metric unit of length equal to one tenth of a centimetre. *The dots can be as small as a quarter of a millimetre across.*

million /'mɪljən/ **millions.** **1** NUM A **million** or one **million** is the number 1,000,000. **2** QUANT People say that there are **millions of** people or things when they are emphasizing that there is a very large number of them. *The programme was viewed on television in millions of homes... This long and wretched war has brought misery to millions.*

millionaire /ˌmɪljə'neə/ **millionaires.** N-C A **millionaire** is someone who has money or property worth at least a million pounds or dollars.

millionth /'mɪljənθ/. ORD The **millionth** item in a series is the one you count as number one million.

mime /maɪm/ **mimes, miming, mimed.** **1** N-VAR **Mime** is the use of movements and gestures to express something or tell a story without using speech. *...a mime artist.* **2** VERB If you **mime** something, you describe or express it using mime rather than speech. *I remember asking her to mime getting up in the morning.*

mimic /'mɪmɪk/ **mimics, mimicking, mimicked.** **1** VERB If you **mimic** someone's actions or voice, you imitate them in an amusing or entertaining way. *He could mimic anybody.* **2** N-C A **mimic** is a person who is able to mimic people.

min. Min. is a written abbreviation for **minimum**, or for **minutes** or **minute**.

mince /mɪns/ **minces, mincing, minced.** **1** N-U In British English, **mince** is meat cut into very small pieces. The usual American word is **hamburger meat**. **2** VERB If you **mince** food such as meat, you cut it into very small pieces. **3** PHRASE If you say someone does not **mince** their **words** or does not **mince words**, you mean they speak in a forceful direct way, especially when saying something unpleasant to someone.

mind 1 thinking

mind /maɪnd/ **minds.** N-C Your **mind** is your ability to think and reason. You also talk about someone having a particular type of **mind** when it is part of their character, or a result of their education or professional training. *She moved to London, meeting some of the best minds of her time... Andrew, you have a very suspicious mind.*

PHRASES ● If you say that an idea or possibility never **crossed** your **mind**, you mean that you did not think of it. ● If you see something **in** your **mind's eye**, you are able to imagine it clearly in your mind. *In his mind's eye, he could see the headlines in the newspapers.* ● If you tell someone to **bear** something **in mind** or to **keep** something **in mind**, you are reminding or warning them about something important which they should think about and remember. ● If you **make up** your **mind** or **make** your **mind up**, you decide which of a number of possible things you will have or do. ● If something is **on** your **mind**, you are worried or concerned about it and think about it a lot. *This game has been on my mind all week.* ● If your **mind is on** something or you **have** your **mind on** something, you are thinking about that thing rather than something else. *He tried the first page but his mind was on other things.* ● If you have or keep **an open mind**, you avoid forming an opinion or making a decision until you know all the facts. *Police said they were keeping an open mind about the mystery death.* ● If you say that someone is **out of their mind**, you mean that they are mad or very foolish. ● Your **state of mind** is your mental state at a particular time. *Over time the patient's state of mind gradually improved.* ● If something **takes** your **mind off** a problem or unpleasant situation, it helps you to forget about it for a while.

mind 2 expressing opinion

mind /maɪnd/ **minds, minding, minded.**
[1] VERB If you do not **mind** something, you are not annoyed or bothered by it. *Do you mind being alone?... I hope you don't mind me calling in like this, without an appointment... It involved a little extra work, but nobody seemed to mind.* [2] VERB If someone does not **mind** what happens or what something is like, they do not have a strong preference for any particular thing. *I don't mind what we play, really.*

PHRASES ● If you **change** your **mind**, or if someone or something **changes** your **mind**, you change a decision you have made or an opinion that you had. ● You use **never mind** to tell someone that you do not think that they need to do something or to worry about something. *'I'll go up in one second, I promise.'—'Never mind,' I said with a sigh. 'I'll do it.'... 'Was his name David?'—'No I don't think it was, but never mind, go on.'* ● You use **to my mind** to indicate that the statement you are making is your own opinion. *There are scenes in this play which to my mind are incredibly violent.* ● If you say that you **wouldn't mind** something, you mean that you would quite like it. *I wouldn't mind a coffee... Anne said she wouldn't mind going to Italy to live.*

mind 3 care

mind /maɪnd/ **minds, minding, minded.**
[1] VERB If you tell someone to **mind** something or to **mind that** they do something, you are warning them to be careful so that they do not hurt themselves or other people, or damage something. *Mind that bike!... Mind you don't burn those sausages.* [2] VERB If you **mind** a child or something such as a shop or luggage, you look after it, usually while the person who owns it or is usually responsible for it is elsewhere. *Jim Coulters will mind the store while I'm away.*

minder /'maɪndə/ **minders.** N-C A **minder** is a person whose job is to protect someone such as a celebrity or businessman.

mindful /'maɪndfʊl/. ADJ AFTER LINK-V If you are **mindful** of something, you think about it and consider it when taking action; FORMAL. *Always be mindful of safety.*

mindless /'maɪndləs/. [1] ADJ If you describe a destructive action as **mindless**, you mean that it is not at all sensible and is done for no good reason. *...mindless violence.* [2] ADJ If you describe an activity as **mindless**, you mean that it is so dull that people do it without thinking. *...the mindless repetitiveness of some tasks.* ◆**mindlessly** ADV *...mindlessly banging a tennis ball against the wall.*

mine /maɪn/ **mines, mining, mined.** [1] PRON **Mine** is the first person singular possessive pronoun. A speaker or writer uses **mine** to indicate that something belongs or relates to himself or herself. *Her right hand is inches from mine... That wasn't his fault, it was mine.* [2] N-C A **mine** is a place where deep holes or tunnels are dug under the ground in order to extract minerals. *...a coal mine.* [3] VERB When a mineral **is mined**, it is obtained from the

ground by digging deep holes and tunnels. *The pit no longer has enough coal that can be mined economically.* ◆**miner, miners.** N-C *My father was a miner.* ◆**mining** N-U *...traditional industries such as coal mining.* [4] N-C A **mine** is a bomb hidden in the ground or in water which explodes when something touches it.

minefield /'maɪnfiːld/ **minefields.** N-C A **minefield** is an area of land or water where explosive mines have been hidden.

mineral /'mɪnərəl/ **minerals.** N-C A **mineral** is a substance such as tin, salt, or coal that is formed naturally in rocks and in the earth.

'mineral water, mineral waters. N-VAR **Mineral water** is water that comes out of the ground naturally and is considered healthy to drink.

mingle /'mɪŋgəl/ **mingles, mingling, mingled.** [1] VERB If things such as sounds, smells, or feelings **mingle**, they become mixed together but are usually still recognizable. *Foreboding mingled with his excitement. ...the mingled scents of flowers, cigar smoke and Chanel.* [2] VERB If you **mingle**, you move among a group of people, chatting to different people. *Guests ate and mingled. ...reporters who mingled freely with the crowd.*

miniature /'mɪnɪtʃə, AM 'mɪnɪətʃʊr/ **miniatures.** [1] ADJ BEFORE N **Miniature** things are much smaller than other things of the same kind. *...miniature roses.* [2] PHRASE If you describe one thing as another thing **in miniature**, you mean that it is much smaller than the other thing, but is otherwise exactly the same. *Ecuador provides a perfect introduction to South America; it's a continent in miniature.* [3] N-C A **miniature** is a very small detailed painting, often of a person.

minibus /'mɪnɪbʌs/ **minibuses.** N-C A **minibus** is a large van which has seats in the back and windows along its sides. *He was then taken by minibus to the military base.*

minimal /'mɪnɪml/. ADJ Something that is **minimal** is very small in quantity or degree. *The co-operation between the two is minimal.* ◆**minimally** ADV *He was paid, but only minimally.*

minimalist /'mɪnɪməlɪst/ **minimalists.** ADJ & N-C **Minimalist** ideas, artists, or designers are influenced by a style in which a small number of very simple things are used to create a particular effect. Artists and designers like this are called **minimalists.** *The two designers settled upon a minimalist approach.* ◆**minimalism** N-U *...austere minimalism.*

minimize (BR also **minimise**) /'mɪnɪmaɪz/ **minimizes, minimizing, minimized.** [1] VERB If you **minimize** a risk or problem, you reduce it to the lowest possible level. *Concerned people want to minimize the risk of developing cancer.* [2] VERB If you **minimize** something, you make it seem smaller or less important than it really is. *At his trial, he had tried to minimize his behavior.*

minimum /'mɪnɪməm/. [1] ADJ BEFORE N & N-SING A **minimum** amount of something, or a **minimum**, is the smallest amount that is possible, allowed, or required. *...five feet nine, the minimum height for a policeman... This will take a*

minimum of one hour. **2** ADJ BEFORE N & N-SING
You use **minimum**, or a **minimum**, to state
how small an amount is. *He goes about his job
with a minimum of fuss.*

mining /ˈmaɪnɪŋ/. See **mine**.

minister /ˈmɪnɪstə/ **ministers, ministering,
ministered.** **1** N-C A **minister** is a person who
is in charge of a government department. *...the
new Defence Minister.* ● See note at **government.** **2** N-C A **minister** is a member of the
clergy, especially in a Protestant church.
3 VERB If you **minister to** people or **to** their
needs, you serve them or help them, for example by making sure that they have everything
they need or want. *For 44 years he had ministered to the poor.*

ministerial /ˌmɪnɪˈstɪəriəl/. ADJ BEFORE N **Ministerial** means relating to government ministers.
A ministerial meeting was being held.

ministry /ˈmɪnɪstri/ **ministries.** **1** N-C A **ministry** is a government department. *...the Ministry
of Justice.* **2** N-C The **ministry** of a religious
person is the work that they do that is inspired
by their religious beliefs. *His ministry is among
the poor.* **3** N-SING Members of the clergy belonging to some branches of the Christian
church are referred to as the **ministry**. *So
what prompted him to enter the ministry?*

mink /mɪŋk/; the plural is **mink** or **minks**.
1 N-C A **mink** is a small furry animal with
highly valued fur. **2** N-U **Mink** is the fur of a
mink. **3** N-C A **mink** is a coat or other garment
made from the fur of a mink.

minor /ˈmaɪnə/ **minors.** **1** ADJ You use **minor**
to describe something that is less important,
serious, or significant than other things in a
group or situation. *...a number of minor roles
in films...* *The problem is minor, and should be
quickly overcome.* **2** N-C A **minor** is a person
who is still legally a child. In Britain, people
are minors until they reach the age of eighteen.

minority /maɪˈnɒrɪti, AM -ˈnɔːr-/ **minorities.**
1 N-SING If you talk about a **minority** of people
or things in a larger group, you are referring to
a number of them that forms less than half of
the larger group. *In a tiny minority of cases
mistakes have been made. ...minority shareholders.* **2** PHRASE If people are **in a minority**
or **in the minority**, they belong to a group of
people or things that form less than half of a
larger group. **3** N-C A **minority** is a group of
people of the same race, culture, or religion
who live in a place where most of the people
around them are of a different race, culture, or
religion. *...the region's ethnic minorities.*

mint /mɪnt/ **mints, minting, minted.** **1** N-U
Mint is a fresh-tasting herb. **2** N-C A **mint** is a
sweet with a peppermint flavour. **3** N-SING The
mint is the place where the official coins of a
country are made. **4** VERB To **mint** coins or
medals means to make them in a mint.
♦**minting** N-U *...the minting of new gold coins.*

minus /ˈmaɪnəs/ **minuses.** **1** CONJ You use **minus** to show that one number or quantity is
being subtracted from another. *One minus one
is zero. ...their full July salary minus the hardship payment.* **2** ADJ **Minus** before a number
or quantity means that the number or quantity

is less than zero. *...temperatures of minus 65
degrees.* **3** PREP If someone or something is
minus something, they do not have that thing.
*The film company collapsed, leaving Chris job-
less and minus his life savings.* **4** N-C A **minus**
is a disadvantage. *The minuses far outweigh
that possible gain.*

minuscule /ˈmɪnɪskjuːl/. ADJ If you describe
something as **minuscule**, you mean it is very
small.

minute, minutes. **1** N-C /ˈmɪnɪt/ A **minute** is
one of the sixty equal parts of an hour. People
often say **'a minute'** or **'minutes'** when they
mean a short length of time. *The pizza will
then take about twenty minutes to cook... See
you in a minute.* **2** CONVENTION People often
use expressions such as **wait a minute** or **just
a minute** when they want to stop you doing or
saying something. *Wait a minute, folks, something is wrong here.* **3** N-PL The **minutes** of a
meeting are the written records of the things
that are discussed or decided at it. **4** ADJ
/maɪˈnjuːt, AM -ˈnuːt/. If you say that something
is **minute**, you mean that it is very small. *Only
a minute amount is needed.* ♦**minutely** ADV
*The benefit of an x-ray far outweighs the mi-
nutely increased risk of cancer.*

PHRASES ● If you say that something will or
may happen **at any minute** or **any minute
now**, you are emphasizing that it is likely to
happen very soon. ● A **last-minute** action is
done at the latest time possible. *He will probably wait until the last minute.* ● You use the
expression **the next minute** or expressions
such as **'one minute** he was there, **the next** he
was gone' to emphasize that something happens suddenly. *The next minute my father
came in.* ● If you say that something happens
the minute something else happens, you are
emphasizing that it happens immediately after
the other thing. *The minute you do this, you'll
lose control.* ● If you say that something must
be done **this minute**, you mean that it must be
done immediately. *Sit down this minute.*

miracle /ˈmɪrəkəl/ **miracles.** **1** N-C If you say
that an event or invention is a **miracle**, you
mean that it is very surprising and fortunate. *It
is a miracle no one was killed.* **2** N-C A **miracle**
is a wonderful and surprising event that is believed to be caused by God. *... Jesus's ability to
perform miracles.*

miraculous /mɪˈrækjʊləs/. **1** ADJ If you describe something as **miraculous**, you mean
that it is very surprising and fortunate. *The
horse made a miraculous recovery.*
♦**miraculously** ADV *Miraculously, the guards
escaped death.* **2** ADJ If someone describes a
wonderful event as **miraculous**, they believe
the event has been caused by God.
♦**miraculously** ADV *He was miraculously
healed of a severe fever.*

mirror /ˈmɪrə/ **mirrors, mirroring, mirrored.**
1 N-C A **mirror** is an object made of glass in
which you can see your reflection. **2** VERB If
you see something reflected in water, you can
say that the water **mirrors** it; LITERARY. **3** VERB
If something **mirrors** something else, it has
similar features to it, and therefore seems like

a copy or representation of it. *The book inevitably mirrors my own interests and experiences.*

miscalculate /ˌmɪsˈkælkjʊleɪt/ **miscalculates, miscalculating, miscalculated.** VERB If you **miscalculate**, you make a mistake in judging a situation or in making a calculation. *He has badly miscalculated the mood of the people.* ◆**miscalculation, miscalculations.** N-VAR *The coup failed because of miscalculations by the plotters.*

miscarriage /ˌmɪsˈkærɪdʒ/ **miscarriages.** N-C If a woman has a **miscarriage**, she gives birth to a foetus before it is properly formed and it dies.

miscellaneous /ˌmɪsəˈleɪniəs/. ADJ BEFORE N A **miscellaneous** group consists of many different kinds of things or people that are difficult to put into a particular category. *...a hoard of miscellaneous junk.*

mischief /ˈmɪstʃɪf/. **1** N-U **Mischief** is eagerness to have fun, especially by embarrassing people or by playing harmless tricks. *He was always up to mischief.* **2** N-U **Mischief** is trouble or harm that is caused by something. *...the mischief that young people get up to when they're not employed. ...old attitudes and prejudices which have done so much mischief.*

mischievous /ˈmɪstʃɪvəs/. **1** ADJ A **mischievous** person is eager to have fun by embarrassing people or by playing harmless tricks. ◆**mischievously** ADV *Kathryn winked mischievously.* **2** ADJ A **mischievous** act or suggestion is intended to cause trouble. *The Foreign Office dismissed the story as mischievous and false.*

misconception /ˌmɪskənˈsepʃən/ **misconceptions.** N-C A **misconception** is an idea that is not correct or which has been misunderstood. *There are many fears and misconceptions about cancer.*

misconduct /ˌmɪsˈkɒndʌkt/. N-U **Misconduct** is bad or unacceptable behaviour, especially by a professional person or someone who is normally respected by people. *She was found guilty of professional misconduct.*

misdemeanour (AM **misdemeanor**) /ˌmɪsdɪˈmiːnə/ **misdemeanours.** N-C A **misdemeanour** is an act that some people consider to be wrong or unacceptable; FORMAL. *Emily knew nothing about her husband's misdemeanours.*

miserable /ˈmɪzərəbəl/. **1** ADJ If you are **miserable**, you are very unhappy. ◆**miserably** ADV *He looked miserably down at his plate.* **2** ADJ A **miserable** place or **miserable** weather makes you feel depressed, for example because it is very dull. *...a grey, wet, miserable day.*

misery /ˈmɪzəri/ **miseries.** **1** N-VAR **Misery** is great unhappiness. *All that money brought nothing but sadness and misery.* **2** N-U **Misery** is the way of life and unpleasant living conditions of people who are very poor. *A tiny, educated elite profited from the misery of their two million fellow countrymen.*

misfit /ˈmɪsfɪt/ **misfits.** N-C A **misfit** is a person who is not easily accepted by other people, often because their behaviour is very different from that of everyone else.

misfortune /ˌmɪsˈfɔːtʃuːn/ **misfortunes.** N-VAR A **misfortune** is something unpleasant or un-

lucky that happens to someone. *She seemed to enjoy the misfortunes of others.*

misgiving /ˌmɪsˈɡɪvɪŋ/ **misgivings.** N-VAR If you have **misgivings** about something that is being proposed or done, you feel that it is not quite right, and are worried that it may have undesirable consequences. *I have misgivings about going anywhere away from home.*

misguided /ˌmɪsˈɡaɪdɪd/. ADJ If you describe an opinion or plan as **misguided**, you are critical of it because you think it is based on a mistake or misunderstanding. *He is misguided in expecting honesty from her.*

mishap /ˈmɪshæp/ **mishaps.** N-VAR A **mishap** is an unfortunate but not very serious event that happens to you. *After a number of mishaps she did manage to get back to Germany.*

misinterpret /ˌmɪsɪnˈtɜːprɪt/ **misinterprets, misinterpreting, misinterpreted.** VERB If you **misinterpret** something, you understand it wrongly. *He was totally amazed that he'd misinterpreted the situation so completely.* ◆**misinterpretation** N-U *The message left no room for misinterpretation.*

misjudge /ˌmɪsˈdʒʌdʒ/ **misjudges, misjudging, misjudged.** VERB If you say that someone **has misjudged** a person or situation, you mean that they have formed an incorrect idea or opinion about them, and often that they have made a wrong decision as a result of this. *Perhaps I had misjudged him, and he was not so predictable after all.*

mislead /ˌmɪsˈliːd/ **misleads, misleading, misled.** VERB If you say that someone **has misled** you, you mean that they have made you believe something which is not true, either by telling you a lie or by giving you a wrong idea or impression.

misleading /ˌmɪsˈliːdɪŋ/. ADJ If you describe something as **misleading**, you mean that it gives you a wrong idea or impression. *It would be misleading to say that we were friends.* ◆**misleadingly** ADV *The data had unfortunately been presented misleadingly.*

misled /ˌmɪsˈled/. **Misled** is the past tense and past participle of **mislead**.

mismanage /ˌmɪsˈmænɪdʒ/ **mismanages, mismanaging, mismanaged.** VERB To **mismanage** something means to manage it badly. *75% of voters think the President has mismanaged the economy.* ◆**mismanagement** N-U *His gross mismanagement left the company desperately in need of restructuring.*

misplaced /ˌmɪsˈpleɪst/. ADJ If you describe a feeling or action as **misplaced**, you are critical of it because you think it is inappropriate, or directed towards the wrong thing or person. *Your concern is misplaced. Ackroyd is no threat to anyone.*

misread, misreads, misreading, misread; present tense /ˌmɪsˈriːd/, past tense and past participle /ˌmɪsˈred/. **1** VERB If you **misread** a situation or someone's behaviour, you do not understand it properly. *The government largely misread the mood of the electorate.* ◆**misreading, misreadings.** N-C *...a misreading of opinion in France.* **2** VERB If you **misread** something that has been written or printed, you look at it and think that it says something that it does not say. *I misread the map.*

misrepresent /ˌmɪsreprɪˈzent/ **misrepresents, misrepresenting, misrepresented.** VERB If someone **misrepresents** a person or situation, they give a wrong or inaccurate account of what the person or situation is like. *The press had misrepresented him as arrogant and bullying.* ♦**misrepresentation** N-U *The programme's researchers are most certainly guilty of bias and misrepresentation.*

miss /mɪs/ **misses, missing, missed.** **1** N-TITLE You use **Miss** in front of the name of a girl or unmarried woman. *The club was run by Miss Ivy Streeter.* **2** VERB & N-C If you **miss** when you are trying to hit something, you fail to hit it. A **miss** is an occasion when you miss something. *She hurled the ashtray across the room, narrowly missing my head... Striker Alan Smith was guilty of two glaring misses.* **3** VERB If you **miss** something, you fail to notice it. *It's the first thing you see as you come round the corner. You can't miss it.* **4** VERB If you **miss** the point or **miss** the joke, you fail to understand or appreciate it. **5** VERB If you **miss** someone or something, you feel sad because the person is no longer with you, or because you no longer have the thing. *Your mama and I are gonna miss you at Christmas... He missed having good friends.* **6** VERB If you **miss** something such as a plane or train, you arrive too late to catch it. *He missed the last bus home.* **7** VERB If you **miss** an event or activity, you do not go to it or take part in it, because you are unable to or have forgotten to. *Makku and I had to miss our lesson... 'Are you coming to the show?'—'I wouldn't miss it for the world.'* **8** See also **missing.**

▶ **miss out.** **1** PHR-VERB If you **miss out** on something that would be beneficial or interesting to you, you are not involved in it or do not take part in it. *We're missing out on a tremendous opportunity.* **2** PHR-VERB If you **miss out** something or someone, you do not include them; BRITISH. *What about Sally? You've missed her out.*

missile /ˈmɪsaɪl, AM -səl/ **missiles.** **1** N-C A **missile** is a tube-shaped weapon that moves long distances through the air and explodes when it reaches its target. **2** N-C Anything that is thrown as a weapon can be called a **missile**; FORMAL. *Supporters hurled missiles at rival fans.*

missing /ˈmɪsɪŋ/ **1** ADJ If someone or something is **missing** or has **gone missing**, they are not where you expect them to be, and you cannot find them. *His wallet was missing... She reported him to the police as a missing person.* **2** ADJ If a part of something is **missing**, it has been removed or has come off and has not been replaced. *Three buttons were missing from his shirt.*

mission /ˈmɪʃən/ **missions.** **1** N-C A **mission** is an important task that you are given to do, especially one that involves travelling to another country. *In 1987, he disappeared on a mission to Beirut.* **2** N-C A **mission** is a group of people who have been sent to a foreign country to carry out an official task. *...the head of South*

Africa's trade mission to Zimbabwe. **3** N-C A **mission** is a special journey made by a military aeroplane or space rocket. *The plane was on a bombing mission.* **4** N-C If you have a **mission**, there is something that you believe it is your duty to try to achieve. *Her mission in life is to show that being disabled doesn't mean being helpless.*

missionary /ˈmɪʃənri, -neri/ **missionaries.** N-C A **missionary** is a Christian who has been sent to a foreign country to teach people about Christianity.

mist /mɪst/ **mists, misting, misted.** N-VAR Mist consists of many tiny drops of water in the air, which make it difficult to see very far. *I couldn't see anything through the mist.*

▶ **mist over** or **mist up.** PHR-VERB When a piece of glass **mists over** or **mists up**, it becomes covered with tiny drops of water, so that you cannot see through it easily. *The windscreen was misting up.*

mistake /mɪˈsteɪk/ **mistakes, mistaking, mistook, mistaken.** **1** N-C & PHRASE If you make a **mistake**, or if you do something **by mistake**, you do something wrong, for example because you do not know what is right or because you are not thinking clearly. *...spelling mistakes... The official who ignored the warning might have made a mistake... Someone must have sold it by mistake.* **2** VERB If you **mistake** one person or thing for another, you wrongly think that they are the other person or thing. *I mistook you for Carlos.* **3** PHRASE You can say **there is no mistaking** something when you are emphasizing that you cannot fail to recognize or understand it. *There's no mistaking his voice.*

mistaken /mɪˈsteɪkən/ ADJ If you are **mistaken**, or if you have a **mistaken** belief, you are wrong about something. *You couldn't be more mistaken, Alex. ...a victim of mistaken identity.* ♦**mistakenly** ADV *Some of the crew mistakenly believed the ship was under attack.*

mister /ˈmɪstə/ See **Mr.**

mistook /mɪˈstʊk/ **Mistook** is the past tense and past participle of **mistake**.

mistress /ˈmɪstrəs/ **mistresses.** **1** N-C A married man's **mistress** is a woman he is having a sexual relationship with, but who is not his wife. **2** N-C A **mistress** is a female teacher; DATED. *...Miss Moore, the geography mistress.*

mistrust /ˌmɪsˈtrʌst/ **mistrusts, mistrusting, mistrusted.** VERB & N-U If you **mistrust** someone or something, you do not trust them. **Mistrust** is the feeling that you have towards someone who you do not trust. *There was mutual mistrust between the two men.*

misty /ˈmɪsti/ ADJ If it is **misty**, there is a lot of mist in the air.

misunderstand /ˌmɪsʌndəˈstænd/ **misunderstands, misunderstanding, misunderstood.** VERB If you **misunderstand** someone or something, you do not understand them properly. *He had misunderstood the rules.*

misunderstanding /ˌmɪsʌndəˈstændɪŋ/ **misunderstandings.** **1** N-VAR A **misunderstanding** is a failure to understand something such as a situation or a person's remarks. *It is a simple misunderstanding.* **2** N-C You can refer to a disagreement or slight quarrel as a **misunderstanding**. *We had a misunderstanding.*

misunderstood /ˌmɪsʌndəˈstʊd/. [1] **Misunderstood** is the past tense and past participle of **misunderstand**. [2] ADJ If you describe someone as **misunderstood**, you mean that people have wrong ideas about them, and do not recognize their qualities or achievements. ...*a misunderstood genius.*

misuse, misuses, misusing, misused. [1] VERB /ˌmɪsˈjuːz/ If you **misuse** something, you use it incorrectly, carelessly, or dishonestly. *Mr Chung was accused of misusing company funds.* [2] N-VAR /ˌmɪsˈjuːs/ The **misuse** of something is incorrect, careless, or dishonest use of it. ...*the misuse of language.*

mite /maɪt/ **mites.** [1] PHRASE A **mite** means to a small extent or degree. *I can't help feeling just a mite uneasy about it.* [2] N-C **Mites** are very tiny creatures that live, for example, on plants or in animals' fur.

mitigate /ˈmɪtɪgeɪt/ **mitigates, mitigating, mitigated.** VERB To **mitigate** something means to make it less unpleasant, less serious, or less painful; FORMAL. ...*ways of mitigating the effects of an explosion.*

mitigating /ˈmɪtɪgeɪtɪŋ/. ADJ BEFORE N **Mitigating** circumstances are facts which make a crime less serious or more justifiable; FORMAL.

mix /mɪks/ **mixes, mixing, mixed.** [1] VERB If two substances **mix**, or if you **mix** one substance with another, they combine to form a single substance. *Oil and water don't mix... Mix the ingredients together slowly.* [2] VERB If you **mix** something, you prepare it by mixing two or more things together. *He mixed himself a drink.* [3] N-VAR A **mix** is a powder containing all the substances that you need in order to make something, to which you add liquid. ...*cake mix.* [4] N-C A **mix** is two or more things combined together. *The story is a magical mix of fantasy and reality.* [5] VERB If you **mix** with other people, you meet them and talk to them. ...*giving both younger and older students the opportunity to mix.* [6] See also **mixed up**.

▸ **mix up.** PHR-VERB If you **mix up** two things or people, you confuse them, so that you think that one of them is the other one. *I had mixed her up with someone else.*

mixed /mɪkst/. [1] ADJ You use **mixed** to describe something which consists of different people or things of the same general kind. *His clubs attract a mixed crowd... I had mixed feelings about this news.* [2] ADJ **Mixed** means involving people from two or more different races. ...*a woman of mixed race.* ...*mixed marriages.* [3] ADJ **Mixed** education or accommodation is intended for both males and females. ...*a mixed secondary school.*

mixed 'up. [1] ADJ If you are **mixed up**, you are confused. *I get mixed up about times and places... Elena is a very mixed up child.* [2] ADJ AFTER LINK-V If you say that someone is **mixed up** with a person or in an activity that you disapprove of, you mean they are involved with that person or activity. *She got herself mixed up in terrorism.*

mixer /ˈmɪksə/ **mixers.** N-C A **mixer** is a ma-

chine used for mixing things together. ...*a food mixer.*

mixture /ˈmɪkstʃə/ **mixtures.** [1] N-SING A **mixture** of things consists of several different things together. ...*trembling in a mixture of fear and excitement.* [2] N-C A **mixture** is a substance that consists of other substances which have been stirred or shaken together. ...*a sticky mixture of flour and water.*

ml, ml is a written abbreviation for 'millilitre' or 'millilitres'. ...*300 ml water.*

mm, mm is a written abbreviation for 'millimetre' or 'millimetres'. *45 mm of rain fell.*

moan /məʊn/ **moans, moaning, moaned.** [1] VERB & N-C If you **moan**, you make a low, miserable cry called a **moan**, because you are unhappy or in pain. *Lauren moaned in her sleep... She let out a faint moan.* [2] VERB To **moan** means to speak in a way which shows that you are very unhappy. *'Look what he did,' she moaned... Carol is always moaning about how she detests her bottom.*

mob /mɒb/ **mobs, mobbing, mobbed.** [1] N-C A **mob** is a large disorganized crowd of people. *The mob then set fire to the police station.* [2] VERB If someone is **mobbed**, a disorderly crowd of people gathers very closely around them. *They are mobbed by fans wherever they go.*

mobile /ˈməʊbaɪl, AM -bəl/. [1] ADJ Something or someone that is **mobile** is able to move or be moved easily. *He is now mobile thanks to a powered wheelchair.* ...*a mobile library.* ♦ **mobility** /məʊˈbɪlɪti/ N-U *It's intended to give patients greater mobility.* [2] ADJ If you are socially **mobile**, you are able to move to a different social class. ♦ **mobility** N-U ...*class barriers which prevented social mobility.* [3] N-C A **mobile** is the same as a **mobile phone**.

,mobile 'phone, mobile phones. N-C A **mobile phone** is a telephone that you can carry with you and use to make or receive calls wherever you are.

mobilize (BR also **mobilise**) /ˈməʊbɪlaɪz/ **mobilizes, mobilizing, mobilized.** [1] VERB If you **mobilize** a group of people, or if you **mobilize** support, you get people to support something in an active way. *The king had wanted to mobilise popular support.* ♦ **mobilization** N-U ...*the rapid mobilization of international opinion in support of the revolution.* [2] VERB If a country **mobilizes** its armed forces, or if it **mobilizes**, it prepares for war; FORMAL. *The French mobilized 160,000 troops.* ♦ **mobilization** N-U ...*a demand for full-scale mobilisation to defend the republic.*

mock /mɒk/ **mocks, mocking, mocked.** [1] VERB If you **mock** someone, you laugh at them, tease them, or try to make them look foolish. ♦ **mocking** ADJ ...*a mocking mocking tone.* [2] ADJ BEFORE N You use **mock** to describe something which is not genuine, but which is intended to be very similar to the real thing. *Tex's voice was raised in mock horror.* ...*mock exams.*

mockery /ˈmɒkəri/. [1] N-U **Mockery** is words, behaviour, or opinions that are unkind and scornful. *There was a hint of mockery in his voice.* [2] N-SING If something makes a **mockery**

of something, it makes it appear worthless and foolish. *Allowing her to avoid prison would make a mockery of the law.*

modal /'məʊdəl/ **modals.** N-C In grammar, a **modal** or a **modal verb** is a word such as 'can' or 'would' which is used in a verbal group and which expresses ideas such as possibility, intention, and necessity.

mode /məʊd/ **modes.** N-C A **mode** of something is one of the different forms it can take; FORMAL. *...road, rail and other modes of transport.*

model /'mɒdəl/ **models, modelling, modelled** (AM **modeling, modeled**). 1 N-C A **model** of an object is a smaller copy of it that shows what it looks like or how it works. *...an architect's model of a wooden house. ...a model aeroplane.* 2 N-C A **model** is a system that is being used and that people might want to copy in order to achieve similar results. *...the Chinese model of economic reform.* 3 N-C If you say that someone or something is a **model of** a particular quality, you approve of them because they have that quality to a large degree. *His marriage is a model of propriety.* 4 ADJ BEFORE N A **model** wife or a **model** teacher, for example, is an excellent wife or an excellent teacher. *She had been a model pupil.* 5 VERB If one thing **is modelled** on another, the first thing is made so that it is like the second thing in some way. *She asked the author if she had modelled her hero on anybody in particular.* 6 N-C A particular **model** of a machine is a version of it. *To keep the cost down, opt for a basic model.* 7 N-C An artist's **model** is a person who is painted, drawn, or sculpted by them. 8 N-C A fashion **model** is a person whose job is to display clothes by wearing them. 9 VERB If someone **models** clothes, they display them by wearing them. ◆ **modelling** N-U *She was being offered a modelling contract.*

moderate, moderates, moderating, moderated. 1 ADJ & N-C /'mɒdərət/ **Moderate** political opinions or policies are not extreme. A person who has these opinions can be referred to as a **moderate.** *...an easy-going man of very moderate views.* 2 ADJ A **moderate** amount is neither large nor small. *...moderate exercise.* ◆ **moderately** ADV *...a reasonably attractive woman.* 3 VERB /'mɒdəreɪt/ If you **moderate** something, or if it **moderates,** it becomes less extreme or violent. *The immediate sense of crisis has moderated somewhat.*

moderation /ˌmɒdə'reɪʃən/. 1 N-U If someone's behaviour shows **moderation,** they act in a way that is reasonable and not extreme. *He urged the African National Congress to show moderation.* 2 PHRASE If you do something **in moderation,** you do not do it too much. *Many adults are able to drink in moderation.*

modern /'mɒdən/. 1 ADJ BEFORE N **Modern** means relating to the present time. *...the risks facing every modern marriage.* 2 ADJ Something that is **modern** is new and involves the latest ideas or equipment. *...modern technology.*

modernize (BR also **modernise**) /'mɒdənaɪz/ **modernizes, modernizing, modernized.** VERB To **modernize** a system means to replace old equipment or methods with new ones.

...plans to modernize the refinery. ◆ **modernization** N-U *...a five-year modernization programme.*

modest /'mɒdɪst/. 1 ADJ A **modest** house or other building is not large or expensive. *She lives in a modest apartment in Santa Monica.* 2 ADJ Something that is **modest** is quite small in amount. *...a modest improvement.* ◆ **modestly** ADV *Sales are expected to drop only modestly this year.* 3 ADJ If you say that someone is **modest,** you approve of them because they do not talk much about their abilities, achievements, or possessions. ◆ **modestly** ADV *Hubbard modestly described himself as an average runner.*

modesty /'mɒdɪsti/. N-U Someone who shows **modesty** does not talk much about their abilities, achievements, or possessions; used showing approval.

modifier /'mɒdɪfaɪə/ **modifiers.** N-C A **modifier** is a word which comes in front of a noun in a noun group.

modify /'mɒdɪfaɪ/ **modifies, modifying, modified.** VERB If you **modify** something, you change it slightly in order to improve it. *He planned to modify existing legislation.* ◆ **modification** /ˌmɒdɪfɪ'keɪʃən/ **modifications.** N-C *Relatively minor modifications were required.*

module /'mɒdʒuːl/ **modules.** 1 N-C A **module** is one of the units that some university or college courses are divided into; BRITISH. 2 N-C A **module** is part of a spacecraft which can operate independently of the main part, often at a distance from it.

moist /mɔɪst/ **moister, moistest.** ADJ Something that is **moist** is slightly wet.

moisture /'mɔɪstʃə/. N-U **Moisture** is tiny drops of water in the air or on a surface.

mold /məʊld/. See **mould.**

mole /məʊl/ **moles.** 1 N-C A **mole** is a natural dark spot on someone's skin. 2 N-C A **mole** is a small animal with black fur that lives underground. 3 N-C A **mole** is a member of a government or organization who secretly reveals confidential information to the press or to a rival organization.

molecular /mə'lekjʊlə/. ADJ BEFORE N **Molecular** means relating to molecules. *...recent advances in molecular genetics.*

molecule /'mɒlɪkjuːl/ **molecules.** N-C A **molecule** is the smallest amount of a chemical substance which can exist. *...water molecules.*

molest /mə'lest/ **molests, molesting, molested.** VERB A person who **molests** a woman or child interferes with them sexually against their will.

molten /'məʊltən/. ADJ **Molten** rock, metal, or glass has been heated to a very high temperature and has become a hot thick liquid.

mom /mɒm/ **moms.** N-C & N-VOC Your **mom** is your mother; AMERICAN, INFORMAL.

moment /'məʊmənt/ **moments.** 1 N-C A **moment** is a very short period of time. *She stared at him a moment, then turned away... In moments, I was asleep.* 2 N-C A particular **moment** is the point in time at which something happens. *Many people still remember the mo-*

ment when they heard that President Kennedy _had been_ assassinated.

PHRASES ● You use **at the moment** to indicate that a particular situation exists at the time when you are speaking. _At the moment, no one is talking to me._ ● If someone does something at **the last moment**, they do it at the latest possible time. _They changed their minds at the last moment and refused to go._ ● You use **for the moment** to indicate that something is true now, even if it will not be true later or in the future. _For the moment, however, the government is happy to live with it._ ● If you say that something happens **the moment** something else happens, you are emphasizing that it happens immediately after the other thing. _The moment I closed my eyes, I fell asleep._

momentary /ˈməʊməntəri, AM -teri/. ADJ Something that is **momentary** lasts for only a very short time. ◆**momentarily** /ˌməʊmənˈteərɪli/ ADV _She paused momentarily._

momentous /məʊˈmentəs/. ADJ A **momentous** event is very important.

momentum /məʊˈmentəm/. ① N-U If a process or movement gains **momentum**, it develops or progresses increasingly quickly, and becomes increasingly less likely to stop. _The campaign against him was gathering momentum._ ② N-U **Momentum** is the force that causes an object to continue moving, because of its mass and speed; TECHNICAL.

monarch /ˈmɒnək/ **monarchs.** N-C A **monarch** is a king or queen.

monarchist /ˈmɒnəkɪst/ **monarchists.** ADJ & N-C If someone has **monarchist** opinions or if they are a **monarchist**, they believe that their country should have a monarch.

monarchy /ˈmɒnəki/ **monarchies.** N-C A **monarchy** is a system in which a monarch rules over a country. _...a serious debate on the future of the monarchy._

monastery /ˈmɒnəstri, AM -teri/ **monasteries.** N-C A **monastery** is a building in which monks live.

Monday /ˈmʌndeɪ, -di/ **Mondays.** N-VAR **Monday** is the day after Sunday and before Tuesday.

monetary /ˈmʌnɪtri, AM ˈmɑːnɪteri/. ADJ BEFORE N **Monetary** means relating to money, or to the money supply; FORMAL. _...monetary policy._

money /ˈmʌni/. ① N-U **Money** consists of the coins or banknotes that you can spend, or a sum that can be represented by these. _They spent all their money on that building... I needed to earn some money._ ② PHRASE If you **get** your **money's worth**, you are satisfied with it because you think it is worth the amount of money you have spent on it. _The fans get their money's worth._

monitor /ˈmɒnɪtə/ **monitors, monitoring, monitored.** ① VERB If you **monitor** something, you regularly check its development or progress. _Officials had not been allowed to monitor the voting._ ② N-C A **monitor** is a machine used to check or record things. _...a heart monitor._ ③ N-C A **monitor** is a screen which is used to display information, for example in airports or television studios.

monk /mʌŋk/ **monks.** N-C A **monk** is a member of a male religious community.

monkey /ˈmʌŋki/ **monkeys.** N-C A **monkey** is an animal that lives in hot countries that has a long tail and climbs trees.

monogamy /məˈnɒgəmi/. N-U **Monogamy** is the state or custom of having a sexual relationship with only one partner or of being married to only one person. ◆**monogamous** ADJ _...a monogamous relationship._

monolithic /ˌmɒnəˈlɪθɪk/. ADJ If you describe an organization or system as **monolithic**, you are critical of it because it is very large and very slow to change. _...a monolithic bureaucracy._

monologue /ˈmɒnəlɒg, AM -lɔːg/ **monologues.** N-C If you refer to a long speech by one person during a conversation as a **monologue**, you mean it prevents other people from talking or expressing their opinions. _Morris ignored the question and continued his monologue._

monopolize (BR also **monopolise**) /məˈnɒpəlaɪz/ **monopolizes, monopolizing, monopolized.** VERB If someone **monopolizes** something, they have a very large share of it and prevent other people from having a share. _Johnson, as usual, monopolized the conversation._

monopoly /məˈnɒpəli/ **monopolies.** ① N-VAR If a company, person, or state has a **monopoly** on something such as an industry, they have complete control over it. _...a state monopoly on land ownership._ ② N-C A **monopoly** is a company which is the only one that makes a particular product or offers a particular service and which therefore completely controls an industry.

monotonous /məˈnɒtənəs/. ADJ Something that is **monotonous** is very boring because it has a regular repeated pattern which never changes. _It's monotonous work, like most factory jobs._

monsoon /mɒnˈsuːn/ **monsoons.** N-C The **monsoon** is the season of very heavy rain in Southern Asia.

monster /ˈmɒnstə/ **monsters.** ① N-C A **monster** is a large imaginary creature that is very frightening. ② ADJ BEFORE N **Monster** means extremely large. _The film will be a monster hit._

monstrous /ˈmɒnstrəs/. ① ADJ If you describe a situation or someone's actions as **monstrous**, you mean that it is very shocking or unfair. ◆**monstrously** ADV _Your husband's family has behaved monstrously._ ② ADJ If you describe something, especially an unpleasant thing, as **monstrous**, you mean that it is extremely large. _...monstrous waves and severe winds._

month /mʌnθ/ **months.** N-C A **month** is one of the twelve periods of time that a year is divided into, for example January or February. _I sent him fifteen dollars a month._

monthly /ˈmʌnθli/. ADJ BEFORE N & ADV A **monthly** publication or event appears or happens every month. _...a monthly newsletter... I get paid monthly._

monument /ˈmɒnjʊmənt/ **monuments.** N-C A **monument** is a large structure, usually made of stone, which is built to remind people of an event in history or of a famous person.

monumental /ˌmɒnjʊˈmentəl/. ADJ You can use **monumental** to emphasize the size or extent of something. *It had been a monumental blunder. ...his monumental work on Chinese astronomy.*

mood /muːd/ **moods.** ① N-C Your **mood** is the way you are feeling at a particular time. *Lily was in one of her aggressive moods.* ② N-SING The **mood** of a group of people is the way that they think and feel about an idea, event, or question at a particular time. *They largely misread the mood of the electorate.* ③ N-C If someone is in a **mood**, their behaviour shows that they are feeling angry and impatient.

moody /ˈmuːdi/. ADJ A **moody** person often becomes depressed or angry without any warning. ♦**moodily** ADV *He sat and stared moodily out of the window.* ♦**moodiness** N-U *His moodiness may have been caused by his poor health.*

moon /muːn/ **moons.** ① N-SING The **moon** is the object in the sky that goes round the Earth once every four weeks and that you can often see at night as a circle or part of a circle. *...the light of a full moon.* ② N-C A **moon** is an object like a small planet that travels around a planet. *...Neptune's large moon.* ③ PHRASE If you say that you are **over the moon**, you mean that you are very pleased about something; INFORMAL.

moonlight /ˈmuːnlaɪt/ **moonlights, moonlighting, moonlighted.** ① N-U **Moonlight** is the light that comes from the moon at night. *They walked along the road in the moonlight.* ② VERB If someone **moonlights**, they have a second job in addition to their main job, often without informing their main employers or the tax office. *...an engineer who was moonlighting as a taxi driver.*

moor /mʊə/ **moors, mooring, moored.** ① N-VAR A **moor** is an area of high open ground covered mainly with rough grass and heather; BRITISH. ② VERB If you **moor** a boat, you attach it to the land with a rope or cable so that it cannot drift away. *I decided to moor near some tourist boats.*

mooring /ˈmʊərɪŋ/ **moorings.** N-C A **mooring** is a place or object on land to which a boat is tied so that it cannot drift away.

moorland /ˈmʊələnd/ **moorlands.** N-VAR **Moorland** is land which consists of moors.

moose /muːs/. N-C A **moose** is a large North American deer. **Moose** is both the singular and plural form.

mop /mɒp/ **mops, mopping, mopped.** ① N-C A **mop** consists of a sponge or many pieces of string attached to a long handle and is used for washing floors. ② VERB If you **mop** a floor, you clean it with a mop. ③ VERB If you **mop** sweat from your forehead, you wipe the sweat away with a handkerchief. *The Inspector took out a handkerchief and mopped his brow.*
▸ **mop up.** PHR-VERB If you **mop up** a liquid, you clean it with a cloth so that the liquid is absorbed. *A waiter mopped up the mess.*

mope /məʊp/ **mopes, moping, moped.** VERB If you **mope**, or if you **mope around** or **mope**

about, you feel miserable and are not interested in anything. *Get on with life and don't sit back and mope... He moped around the office for a while, feeling bored.*

moped /ˈməʊped/ **mopeds.** N-C A **moped** is a small motorcycle which you start by pedalling like a bicycle.

moral /ˈmɒrəl, AM ˈmɔːr-/ **morals.** ① N-PL **Morals** are principles and beliefs concerning right and wrong behaviour. *They have no morals.* ② ADJ BEFORE N **Moral** means relating to beliefs about what is right or wrong. ♦**morally** ADV *When, if ever, is it morally justifiable to allow a patient to die?* ③ ADJ A **moral** person behaves in a way that is believed by most people to be good and right. ♦**morally** ADV *Art is not there to improve you morally.* ④ ADJ BEFORE N If you give someone **moral** support, you encourage them in what they are doing by expressing approval. ⑤ N-SING The **moral** of a story or event is what you learn from it about how you should or should not behave.

morale /məˈrɑːl, -ˈræl/. N-U **Morale** is the amount of confidence and optimism that people have. *Many pilots are suffering from low morale.*

morality /məˈrælɪti/ **moralities.** ① N-U **Morality** is the belief that some behaviour is right and acceptable and that other behaviour is wrong. *...standards of morality and justice.* ② N-U The **morality** of something is how right or acceptable it is. *...debates over the morality of the death penalty.*

moratorium /ˌmɒrəˈtɔːriəm, AM ˌmɔːr-/ **moratoriums** or **moratoria.** N-C If there is a **moratorium** on a particular activity, it is officially stopped for a period of time; FORMAL. *Spain imposed a moratorium on the building of nuclear power stations.*

morbid /ˈmɔːbɪd/. ADJ If someone has a **morbid** interest in a particular subject, especially a strange or unpleasant subject, they are fascinated by it. *...a morbid fear of cancer.* ♦**morbidly** ADV *I slid into a depression and became morbidly fascinated with death.*

more /mɔː/. **More** is often considered to be the comparative form of **much** and **many**. ① QUANT You use **more** to indicate that there is a greater number of things or a greater amount of something than before or than average, or than something else. *...teaching more children foreign languages... Prison conditions have become more brutal... We can satisfy our basic wants more easily than in the past... He had four hundred dollars in his pocket. Billy had more... As the afternoon drew on we were joined by more of the regulars.* ② PREP You use **more than** before a number or amount to say that the actual number or amount is even greater. *...a survey of more than 1,500 schools.* ③ ADV You can use **more** or **some more** to indicate that something continues to happen for a further period of time. *We can talk more about Leo on Thursday... Would you mind if I just stayed in my room and read some more?* ④ ADV You use **more** to indicate that something is repeated. *Aubrey sighed once more... The breathing exercises should be repeated several times more.* ⑤ DET & PRON You use **more** to refer to an additional thing or amount. *Are you sure you wouldn't like some more wine?... They should do more to help themselves.*

PHRASES ● You can use **more and more** to indicate that something is becoming greater in amount, extent, or degree all the time. *Bob became more and more furious... More and more women are wearing men's fragrances.* ● You use **more than** to say that something is true to a greater degree than is necessary or than average. *Lithuania produces more than enough food to feed itself.* ● You use **no more than** or **not more than** when you want to emphasize how small a number or amount is. *Each box requires no more than a few hours of labor to build.* ● If something is **more or less** true, it is true in a general way, but is not completely true. *The Conference is more or less over.* ● You can use **what is more** or **what's more** to introduce an extra piece of information which supports or emphasizes the point you are making. *You should remember it, and what's more, you should get it right.* ● **all the more**: see **all**. ● **any more**: see **any**.

moreover /mɔːˈrəʊvə/. ADV You use **moreover** to introduce a piece of information that adds to or supports the previous statement; FORMAL. *There was indeed a man immediately behind her. Moreover, he was observing her strangely.*

morgue /mɔːg/ **morgues.** N-C A **morgue** is a building or room where dead bodies are kept before being cremated or buried.

morning /ˈmɔːnɪŋ/ **mornings.** 1 N-VAR The **morning** is the part of a day between the time that people wake up and noon. *On Sunday morning Bill was woken by the telephone.* 2 N-C If you refer to a particular time in the **morning**, you mean a time during the part of a day between midnight and noon. *I often stayed up until two or three in the morning.* 3 PHRASE If you say that something will happen **in the morning**, you mean that it will happen during the morning of the following day. *I'll fly to London in the morning.*

morose /məˈrəʊs/. ADJ Someone who is **morose** is miserable, bad-tempered, and not willing to talk very much to other people.. ♦**morosely** ADV *One elderly man sat morosely at the bar.*

morphine /ˈmɔːfiːn/. N-U **Morphine** is a drug used to relieve pain.

morsel /ˈmɔːsəl/ **morsels.** N-C A **morsel** is a very small amount of something, especially a very small piece of food. *...a delicious little morsel of meat.*

mortal /ˈmɔːtəl/ **mortals.** 1 ADJ If you refer to the fact that people are **mortal**, you mean that they have to die and cannot live forever. ♦**mortality** N-U *She has suddenly come face to face with her own mortality.* 2 N-C You can describe someone as a **mortal** when you want to say that they are an ordinary person, rather than someone who has power or has achieved something. *Musicians, like the rest of us, are mere mortals.* 3 ADJ BEFORE N You can use **mortal** to show that something is very serious or may cause death. *Our citizens' lives were in mortal danger.* ♦**mortally** ADV *...a mortally wounded soldier.*

mortality /mɔːˈtælɪti/. N-U The **mortality** in a

particular place or situation is the number of people who die. *...the infant mortality rate in Britain is higher.*

mortar /ˈmɔːtə/ **mortars.** 1 N-C A **mortar** is a short cannon which fires shells high into the air for a short distance. 2 N-U **Mortar** is a mixture of sand, water, and cement, which is put between bricks to make them stay firmly together.

mortgage /ˈmɔːgɪdʒ/ **mortgages, mortgaging, mortgaged.** 1 N-C A **mortgage** is a loan of money which you get from a bank or building society in order to buy a house. 2 VERB If you **mortgage** your house or land, you use it as a guarantee to a company in order to borrow money from them.

mortician /mɔːˈtɪʃən/ **morticians.** N-C In American English, a **mortician** is a person whose job is to deal with the bodies of people who have died and to arrange funerals. The British word is **undertaker**.

mortuary /ˈmɔːtʃʊəri, AM -eri/ **mortuaries.** N-C A **mortuary** is building or a room in a hospital where dead bodies are kept before they are buried or cremated.

mosaic /məʊˈzeɪɪk/ **mosaics.** N-VAR A **mosaic** is a design made of small pieces of coloured stone or glass set in concrete or plaster.

Moslem /ˈmʊzlɪm/. See **Muslim**.

mosque /mɒsk/ **mosques.** N-C A **mosque** is a building where Muslims go to worship.

mosquito /mɒˈskiːtəʊ/ **mosquitoes** (or **mosquitos**). N-C **Mosquitoes** are small flying insects which bite people in order to suck their blood.

moss /mɒs, AM mɔːs/ **mosses.** N-VAR **Moss** is a very small soft green plant which grows on damp soil, or on wood or stone.

most /məʊst/. **Most** is often considered to be the superlative form of **much** and **many**. 1 QUANT You use **most** to refer to the majority of a group of people or things or the largest part of something. *Most people think the Queen has done a good job... Most of the book is completely true... All of the rooms have private baths, and most have radios and TV.* 2 ADJ & PRON You use **the most** to mean a larger amount than anyone or anything else, or the largest amount possible. *The President himself won the most votes... The most they earn in a day is ten roubles.* 3 ADV & PHRASE You use **most** or **most of all** to indicate that something is true or happens to a greater degree or extent than anything else. *What she feared most was becoming like her mother. ...Professor Morris, the person he most hated... She said she wanted most of all to be fair.* 4 ADV You use **most** to indicate that someone or something has a greater amount of a particular quality than other things of its kind. *He was one of the most influential performers of modern jazz.* 5 ADV If you do something **the most**, you do it to the greatest extent possible or with the greatest frequency. *What question are you asked the most?* 6 ADV You use **most** to emphasize an adjective or adverb; FORMAL. *I believe he is most painfully anxious about Diana.*

PHRASES ● You use **at most** or **at the most** to say that a number or amount is the maximum that is possible or likely. *I was probably only about twelve or thirteen years old at most.* • If you **make the most of** something, you get the maximum use or advantage from it. *Make the most of every opportunity.*

mostly /ˈməʊstli/. ADV You use **mostly** to indicate that a statement is true about the majority of a group of things or people, true most of the time, or true in most respects. *I am working with mostly highly motivated people... Cars are mostly metal.*

motel /məʊˈtel/ **motels.** N-C A **motel** is a hotel intended for people who are travelling by car.

moth /mɒθ, AM mɔːθ/ **moths.** N-C A **moth** is an insect like a butterfly, which usually flies about at night.

mother /ˈmʌðə/ **mothers, mothering, mothered.** ① N-C & N-VOC Your **mother** is the woman who gave birth to you. *She's an English teacher and a mother of two children.* ② VERB If you **mother** someone, you treat them with great care and affection, as if they were a small child.

motherhood /ˈmʌðəhʊd/. N-U **Motherhood** is the state of being a mother.

'mother-in-law, mothers-in-law. N-C Someone's **mother-in-law** is the mother of their husband or wife.

motherland /ˈmʌðəlænd/. N-SING The **motherland** is the country in which you were born and to which you still feel emotionally linked.

motherly /ˈmʌðəli/. ADJ **Motherly** feelings or actions are like those of a mother. *It was an incredible display of motherly love and forgiveness.*

motif /məʊˈtiːf/ **motifs.** N-C A **motif** is a design used as a decoration or as part of an artistic pattern. *...a rose motif.*

motion /ˈməʊʃən/ **motions, motioning, motioned.** ① N-U **Motion** is continual movement. *The wind from the car's motion whipped her hair around her head.* ② N-C A **motion** is an action, gesture, or movement. *He made a neat chopping motion with his hand.* ③ VERB If you **motion** to someone, you move your hand or head as a way of telling them to do something or where to go. *She motioned for the locked front doors to be opened... I motioned him to join us.* ④ N-C A **motion** in a meeting or debate is a proposal which is discussed and voted on. ⑤ See also **slow motion**.

PHRASES • If you say that someone **is going through the motions**, you think they are only saying or doing something because it is expected of them and not because they are interested in it, enthusiastic about it, or sympathetic to it. • If a process or event is **set in motion**, something causes it to happen or begin to happen. *Our desires in food are largely set in motion by our sense of smell.*

motionless /ˈməʊʃənləs/. ADJ Someone or something that is **motionless** is not moving at all. *He remained quite motionless behind his desk.*

'motion picture, motion pictures. N-C A **motion picture** is a film made for cinema; AMERICAN.

motivate /ˈməʊtɪveɪt/ **motivates, motivating, motivated.** ① VERB If you **are motivated** by something, especially an emotion, it causes you to behave in a particular way. *The crime was not politically motivated... What motivates athletes to takes drugs?* ② VERB If someone **motivates** you to do something, they make you feel determined to do it. *Better schools are able to motivate students to do their best.* ♦ **motivated** ADJ *...highly motivated employees.*

motivation /ˌməʊtɪˈveɪʃən/ **motivations.** ① N-C Your **motivation** for doing something is what causes you to want to do it. *The prime motivation is usually money.* ② N-U If you have the **motivation** to do something, you feel determined to do it. *The players were tired and they lacked motivation.*

motive /ˈməʊtɪv/ **motives.** N-C Your **motive** for doing something is your reason for doing it. *Police have ruled out robbery as a motive for the killing.*

motor /ˈməʊtə/ **motors, motoring, motored.** ① N-C A **motor** in a machine, vehicle, or boat is the part that uses electricity or fuel to produce movement, so that the machine, vehicle, or boat can work. ② ADJ BEFORE N **Motor** vehicles and boats have a petrol or diesel engine. ③ ADJ BEFORE N **Motor** is used to describe activities relating to motor vehicles. *...the future of the British motor industry.* ④ See also **motoring**.

motorbike /ˈməʊtəbaɪk/ **motorbikes.** N-C A **motorbike** is the same as a **motorcycle**.

'motor car, motor cars. N-C A **motor car** is the same as a **car**; DATED.

motorcycle /ˈməʊtəsaɪkəl/ **motorcycles.** N-C A **motorcycle** is a two-wheeled vehicle with an engine.

motorcyclist /ˈməʊtəsaɪklɪst/ **motorcyclists.** N-C A **motorcyclist** is someone who rides a motorcycle.

motoring /ˈməʊtərɪŋ/. ADJ BEFORE N **Motoring** means relating to cars and to driving. *...one of Britain's largest motoring organisations.*

motorist /ˈməʊtərɪst/ **motorists.** N-C A **motorist** is someone who drives a car.

motorized (BR also **motorised**) /ˈməʊtəraɪzd/. ADJ A **motorized** vehicle has an engine. *...the first time motorized vehicles were used in a war.*

motorway /ˈməʊtəweɪ/ **motorways.** N-VAR In British English, a **motorway** is a wide road specially built for fast travel over long distances. The usual American word is **freeway**.

motto /ˈmɒtəʊ/ **mottoes** (or **mottos**). N-C A **motto** is a short sentence or phrase that expresses the attitude to life of a particular person or group. *The motto of the club is: THINK QUICK!*

mould (AM **mold**) /məʊld/ **moulds, moulding, moulded.** ① N-C A **mould** is a container used to make something into a particular shape. ② VERB If you **mould** plastic or clay, you make it into a particular shape. *Mould the cheese mixture into small balls.* ③ VERB To **mould** someone or something means to change or influence them over a period of time so that they develop in a particular way. *We try to mold our children into something they do* not wish to be. [4] N-VAR **Mould** is a soft grey, green, or blue substance that sometimes forms on old food or on damp walls or clothes.

mound /maʊnd/ **mounds.** N-C A **mound** of things is a large heap or pile of them. *The bulldozers piled up huge mounds of dirt.*

mount /maʊnt/ **mounts, mounting, mounted.** [1] VERB To **mount** a campaign or event means to organize it and make it take place. *The ANC announced it was mounting a major campaign of mass political protests.* [2] VERB If something **mounts**, or if it **mounts up**, it increases. *For several hours, tension mounted... Her medical bills mounted up.* [3] VERB If you **mount** the stairs or a platform, you go up the stairs or go up onto the platform; FORMAL. *The vehicle mounted the pavement.* [4] VERB If you **mount** a horse or cycle, you climb on to it so that you can ride it. *They all mounted and rode off.* [5] VERB If you **mount** an object on something, you fix it there firmly. *Her husband mounts the work on velour paper.* ♦-**mounted** *...a wall-mounted electric fan.* [6] **Mount** is used as part of the name of a mountain. *...Mount Everest.* [7] See also **mounted**.

mountain /ˈmaʊntɪn, AM -tən/ **mountains.** [1] N-C A **mountain** is a very high area of land with steep sides. *...the north side of the mountain. ...a lovely little mountain village.* [2] N-C A **mountain** of something is a very large amount of it; INFORMAL. *They have mountains of coffee to sell.*

'**mountain bike, mountain bikes.** N-C A **mountain bike** is a type of bicycle with a strong frame and thick tyres.

mountaineer, /ˌmaʊntɪˈnɪə/ **mountaineers.** N-C A **mountaineer** is someone who climbs mountains as a hobby or sport.

mountainous /ˈmaʊntɪnəs/. ADJ A **mountainous** place has a lot of mountains. *...the mountainous region of Campania.*

mountainside /ˈmaʊntɪnsaɪd/ **mountainsides.** N-C A **mountainside** is one of the steep sides of a mountain.

mounted /ˈmaʊntɪd/. ADJ BEFORE N **Mounted** police or soldiers ride horses when they are on duty. ● See also **mount**.

mourn /mɔːn/ **mourns, mourning, mourned.** [1] VERB If you **mourn** someone who has died, you are very sad that they have died and show your sorrow in the way that you behave. *The whole nation had mourned the death of their great leader.* [2] VERB If you **mourn** something, you regret that you no longer have it and show your regret in the way that you behave. *We mourned the loss of our cities.*

mourner /ˈmɔːnə/ **mourners.** N-C You can refer to the people at a funeral as the **mourners**.

mournful /ˈmɔːnfʊl/. ADJ If you are **mournful**, you are very sad. *He looked mournful, even near to tears.* ♦**mournfully** ADV *He stood mournfully at the gate waving bye bye.*

mouse /maʊs/ **mice** /maɪs/. [1] N-C A **mouse** is a small furry animal with a long tail. [2] N-C A **mouse** is a device that you use with a computer system. By moving it across a surface and pressing its buttons, you can perform operations without using the keyboard.

mousse /muːs/ **mousses.** N-VAR **Mousse** is a sweet light food made from eggs and cream.

moustache (AM **mustache**) /məˈstɑːʃ, AM ˈmʌstæʃ/ **moustaches.** N-C A man's **moustache** is the hair that grows on his upper lip.

mouth, mouths, mouthing, mouthed; noun /maʊθ/ in the singular, /maʊðz/ in the plural. [1] N-C Your **mouth** is your lips, or the space behind your lips where your teeth and tongue are. *She clamped her hand against her mouth... His mouth was full of peas.* ♦-**mouthed** *...a tough, wide-mouthed, gray-haired policeman.* [2] N-C The **mouth** of a cave, hole, or bottle is its entrance or opening. [3] N-C The **mouth** of a river is the place where it flows into the sea. [4] VERB /maʊð/ If you **mouth** something, you form words with your lips without making any sound. *I mouthed a goodbye and hurried in... 'It's for you,' he mouthed.* [5] **from hand to mouth:** see **hand**.

mouthful /ˈmaʊθfʊl/ **mouthfuls.** N-C A **mouthful** of food or drink is an amount that you put or have in your mouth. *Chew each mouthful fully before the next bite.*

mouthpiece /ˈmaʊθpiːs/ **mouthpieces.** [1] N-C The **mouthpiece** of a telephone is the part that you speak into. [2] N-C The **mouthpiece** of a musical instrument is the part that you blow into. [3] N-C The **mouthpiece** of an official person or organization is someone who informs other people of the opinions and policies of that organization or person. *Their mouthpiece is the vice-president.*

movable (or **moveable**) /ˈmuːvəbl/. ADJ Something that is **movable** can be moved from one place or position to another. *It's a vinyl doll with movable arms and legs.*

move /muːv/ **moves, moving, moved.** [1] VERB When you **move** something, or when it **moves**, its position changes. *She moved the sheaf of papers into position... The train began to move.* [2] VERB & N-C When you **move**, or when you make a **move**, you change your position or go to a different place. *She moved away from the window... Daniel's eyes followed her every move.* [3] VERB & N-C If a person or company **moves**, they leave the building where they have been living or working, and go to live or work in a different place. A **move** is an act of moving. *She had often considered moving to London... The move to Prague was a daunting prospect.* [4] VERB & N-C If you **move** from one job or interest to another, you change to it. A **move** is an act of moving. *Christina moved jobs to get experience. ...his move to the chairmanship.* [5] VERB & N-C If you **move** towards a particular state, activity, or opinion, you start to be in that state, do that activity, or have that opinion. A **move** is an act of moving in this way. *...the need to move towards greater economic convergence. ...fifteen Japanese banks made a move to pull out.* [6] VERB If a situation is moving, it is developing or progressing. *...events are moving fast.* [7] VERB If something **moves** you to do something, it causes you to do it. *It was punk that first moved him to join a band.* [8] VERB If something **moves** you, it causes you to feel a deep emotion, usually sadness or sympathy.

His prayer moved me to tears. ◆**moved** ADJ AFTER LINK-V *Walesa himself appeared to be deeply moved.* [9] N-C A **move** is an action that you take in order to achieve something. *It may also be a good move to suggest she talks things over.* [10] PHRASE If you are **on the move**, you are going from one place to another. [11] See also **moving**.

▶ **move about** or **move around.** PHR-VERB If you **move about** or **move around**, you keep changing your job or keep changing the place where you live. *He moved around the country working in orange groves.*

▶ **move in.** [1] PHR-VERB If you **move in** somewhere, or if you **move into** a new house or place, you begin to live in a different house or place. *Her husband had moved in with a younger woman... I want you to move into my apartment.* [2] PHR-VERB If soldiers or police **move in**, they go towards a place or person in order to attack them or deal with them. *Forces were moving in on the town of Knin.*

▶ **move off.** PHR-VERB When vehicles or people **move off**, they start moving away from a place. *Gil waved his hand and the car moved off.*

▶ **move on.** PHR-VERB When you **move on** somewhere, you leave the place where you have been staying or waiting and go or travel somewhere else. *What's wrong with his wanting to sell his land and move on?... Mr Li moves on to Jordan later today.*

▶ **move out.** PHR-VERB If you **move out**, you leave the house or place where you have been living, and go and live somewhere else.

▶ **move up.** PHR-VERB If you **move up**, you change your position, especially in order to be nearer someone or to make room for someone else. *Move up, John, and let the lady sit down.*

moveable /'mu:vəbəl/. See **movable.**

movement /'mu:vmənt/ **movements.** [1] N-VAR **Movement** involves changing position or going from one place to another. *They actually monitor the movement of the fish going up river... Her hand movements are becoming more animated.* [2] N-VAR **Movement** is a gradual development or change of an attitude, opinion, or policy. *...the movement towards democracy in Latin America.* [3] N-PL Your **movements** are everything which you do or plan to do during a period of time. *I want a full account of your movements the night Mr Gower was killed.* [4] N-C A **movement** is a group of people who share the same beliefs, ideas, or aims. *...the women's movement.*

movie /'mu:vi/ **movies.** [1] N-C In American English, a **movie** is a motion picture. The British word is **film**. *...a horror movie.* [2] N-PL In American English, when people go to **the movies**, they see a movie in a movie theater. The British term is **the cinema**.

moving /'mu:vɪŋ/. [1] ADJ If something is **moving**, it makes you feel a strong emotion such as pity. *It was a moving moment.* ◆**movingly** ADV *You write very movingly of your sister Diana's suicide.* [2] ADJ BEFORE N A **moving** model or part of a machine moves or is able to move. [3] See also **move.**

mow /məʊ/ **mows, mowing, mowed, mown** (or **mowed**). VERB If you **mow** an area of grass, you cut it using a mower.

▶ **mow down.** PHR-VERB If a large number of people **are mown down**, they are killed violently by a vehicle or gunfire.

mower /'məʊə/ **mowers.** N-C A **mower** is a machine for cutting grass, corn, or wheat.

MP /,em 'pi:/ **MPs.** N-C In Britain, an **MP** is a person who has been elected to represent the people from a particular area in the House of Commons. **MP** is an abbreviation for 'Member of Parliament'.

mph. mph is written after a number to indicate the speed of something such as a vehicle. It is an abbreviation for 'miles per hour'.

Mr /'mɪstə/. N-TITLE **Mr** is used before a man's name when you are speaking or referring to him. *Hello, Mr Simpson. ...Mr Bob Price.*

Mrs /'mɪsɪz/. N-TITLE **Mrs** is used before the name of a married woman when you are speaking or referring to her. *Hello, Mrs Miles. ...Mrs Anne Pritchard.*

Ms /məz, mɪz/. N-TITLE **Ms** is used before a woman's name when you are speaking to her or referring to her. If you use **Ms**, you are not specifying if the woman is married or not. *...Ms Elizabeth Harman.*

much /mʌtʃ/. [1] ADV You use **much** to indicate the great intensity, extent, or degree of something such as an action, feeling, or change. **Much** is usually used with 'so', 'too', and 'very', and in negative clauses for this meaning. *She laughs too much... Thank you very much... My hairstyle hasn't changed much since I was five.* [2] ADV You use **much** in order to emphasize that there is a large amount of a particular quality. *The skin is much too delicate... You'd be so much happier if you could see yourself the way I see you.* [3] ADV If one thing is **much** the same as another thing, it is very similar to it. *Sheep's milk is produced in much the same way as goat's milk... It looks pretty much like Michael's signature.* [4] QUANT You use **much** to indicate that you are referring to a large amount of something. *Grapes are grown on the hillsides in full sun, without much water... There was so much to talk about... She does much of her work abroad.* [5] QUANT You use **much** to ask questions or make statements about the amount or degree of something. *How much do you earn?... She knows how much this upsets me.* [6] ADV If something does not happen **much**, it does not happen very often. *His father never talked much about the war.*

PHRASES ● If you describe something as **not much of** a particular type of thing, you mean that it is small or of poor quality. *It hasn't been much of a holiday.* ● If something is **not so much** one thing as another, it is more like the second thing than the first. *I don't really think of her as a daughter so much as a very good friend.* ● You say **nothing much** to refer to something that is not very interesting or important. *'What was stolen?'—'Oh, nothing much.'* ● You use **much less** after a statement to indicate that the statement is even more true of the person, thing, or situation that you are going to mention next. *They are always short of water to drink, much less to bathe in.* ● If you say **so much for** a particular thing, you mean that it has not been successful or helpful; INFORMAL. *So much for all his damn theories!* ● If a situation or action is **too much** for you, you cannot cope with it. *His inability to stay at one job for long had finally proved too much for her.* ● **a bit much**: see **bit**.

muck /mʌk/ **mucks, mucking, mucked.** N-U **Muck** is dirt or some other unpleasant substance; INFORMAL.

▶ **muck about.** PHR-VERB If you **muck about** or **muck around**, you behave in a stupid way and waste time; BRITISH, INFORMAL. *He'd spent his boyhood summers mucking about in boats.*

mucus /'mju:kəs/. N-U **Mucus** is a liquid that is produced in some parts of your body, for example the inside of your nose; FORMAL.

mud /mʌd/. N-U **Mud** is a sticky mixture of earth and water.

muddle /'mʌdəl/ **muddles, muddling, muddled.** [1] N-VAR A **muddle** is a confused state or situation. *My thoughts are all in a muddle.* [2] VERB & PHR-VERB If you **muddle** things or people, or if you **muddle** them **up**, you get them mixed up, so that you do not know which is which. *One or two critics have begun to muddle the two names... He sometimes muddles me up with other patients.* ◆ **muddled up** ADJ *I am getting my words muddled up.*

▶ **muddle through.** PHR-VERB If you **muddle through**, you manage to do something even though you do not really know how to do it properly.

▶ **muddle up.** See **muddle** 2.

muddled /'mʌdəld/. ADJ If someone is **muddled**, they are confused about something.

muddy /'mʌdi/ **muddier, muddiest; muddies, muddying, muddied.** [1] ADJ Something that is **muddy** contains or is covered in mud. *...his muddy boots.* [2] ADJ BEFORE N A **muddy** colour is dull and brownish. *...a muddy green-brown.* [3] VERB If you **muddy** something, you cause it to be muddy. *They muddied their shoes.* [4] VERB If someone or something **muddies** a situation or issue, they cause it to seem less clear and less easy to understand. *Their relationship has sometimes been muddied by politics and personal rivalry.*

muffle /'mʌfəl/ **muffles, muffling, muffled.** VERB If something **muffles** a sound, it makes it quieter and more difficult to hear. *Blake held his handkerchief over the mouthpiece to muffle his voice.*

mug /mʌg/ **mugs, mugging, mugged.** [1] N-C A **mug** is a large deep cup with straight sides. *She sipped from her coffee mug. ...a mug of sweet tea.* [2] VERB If someone **mugs** you, they attack you in order to steal your money. ◆ **mugging, muggings** N-VAR *...a victim of mugging.* ◆ **mugger, muggers** N-C *If you come face to face with a mugger, what do you do?*

mule /mju:l/ **mules.** N-C A **mule** is an animal whose parents are a horse and a donkey.

mull /mʌl/ **mulls, mulling, mulled.**

▶ **mull over.** PHR-VERB If you **mull** something **over**, you think about it for a long time before deciding what to do.

multilateral /ˌmʌlti'lætərəl/. ADJ **Multilateral** means involving at least three different groups of people or nations. *...multilateral trade talks in Geneva.*

multimedia /ˌmʌlti'mi:diə/. [1] N-U In computing, you use **multimedia** to refer to programs and products which involve the use of sound, pictures, and film, as well as ordinary text. [2] N-U In education, **multimedia** is the use of television and other different media in a lesson, instead of only textbooks.

multinational (or **multi-national**) /ˌmʌlti'næʃənəl/ **multinationals.** [1] ADJ & N-C A **multinational** company or a **multinational** has branches in many different countries. *...multinationals such as Ford and IBM.* [2] ADJ **Multinational** is used to describe something that involves several different countries. *The US troops would be part of a multinational force.*

multiple /'mʌltɪpəl/ **multiples.** [1] ADJ You use **multiple** to describe things that consist of many parts, involve many people, or have many uses. *He died of multiple injuries... The most common multiple births are twins.* [2] N-C If one number is a **multiple** of a smaller number, it can be exactly divided by that smaller number. *We count the seconds, minutes and hours in multiples of six and ten.*

multiple sclerosis /ˌmʌltɪpəl sklə'rəusɪs/. N-U **Multiple sclerosis** is a serious disease of the nervous system. The abbreviation 'MS' is also used.

multiplicity /ˌmʌltɪ'plɪsɪti/. QUANT A **multiplicity** of things is a large number or large variety of them; FORMAL. *...a writer who uses a multiplicity of styles.*

multiply /'mʌltɪplaɪ/ **multiplies, multiplying, multiplied.** [1] VERB When something **multiplies**, or when you **multiply** it, it increases greatly in number or amount. *Her husband multiplied his demands on her time.* ◆ **multiplication** /ˌmʌltɪplɪ'keɪʃən/ N-U *...the multiplication of bacteria.* [2] VERB If you **multiply** one number by another, you calculate the total which you get when you add the number to itself as many times as is indicated by the second number. *Twenty-five multiplied by one point one two is twenty eight. ...the remarkable ability to multiply huge numbers.* ◆ **multiplication** N-U *...subtraction, multiplication and division.*

multitude /'mʌltɪtjuːd, AM -tuːd/ **multitudes.** QUANT A **multitude** of things or people is a very large number of them. *There are a multitude of small quiet roads to cycle along.*

mum /mʌm/ **mums.** N-C & N-VOC Your **mum** is your mother; BRITISH, INFORMAL. *He misses his mum.*

mumble /'mʌmbəl/ **mumbles, mumbling, mumbled.** VERB & N-C If you **mumble** something, or if you speak in a **mumble**, you speak very quietly and not clearly so that the words are difficult to understand. *He mumbled a few words.*

mummy /'mʌmi/ **mummies.** [1] N-C & N-VOC Some people, especially children, call their mother **mummy**; BRITISH, INFORMAL. [2] N-C A **mummy** is a dead body which was preserved long ago by being rubbed with oils and wrapped in cloth.

munch /mʌntʃ/ **munches, munching, munched.** VERB To **munch** food means to chew it steadily and thoroughly. *Sheep were munching their way through a yellow carpet of leaves.*

mundane /ˌmʌn'deɪn/. ADJ Something that is **mundane** is ordinary and not interesting. ...*the mundane realities of life.*

municipal /mjuː'nɪsɪpəl/. ADJ BEFORE N **Municipal** means associated with the local government of a city or town.

municipality /mjuːˌnɪsɪ'pælɪti/ **municipalities.** N-C A **municipality** is a city or town with its own local council and officials. You can also refer to that city or town's local government as the **municipality**. ...*public woodlands, belonging to the municipality.*

munitions /mjuː'nɪʃənz/. N-PL **Munitions** are bombs, guns, and other military supplies.

mural /'mjʊərəl/ **murals.** N-C A **mural** is a picture which is painted on a wall.

murder /'mɜːdə/ **murders, murdering, murdered.** [1] N-VAR **Murder** is the crime of deliberately killing a person. *He was jailed for life after being found guilty of murder... She was convicted of three murders.* [2] VERB To **murder** someone means to commit the crime of killing them deliberately. ◆**murderer, murderers** N-C ...*a notorious murderer.* [3] See note at **kill**.

murderous /'mɜːdərəs/. ADJ If you describe a person or their actions as **murderous**, you mean that they intend to kill someone or are likely to kill someone. *This murderous lunatic could kill them both.*

murky /'mɜːki/ **murkier, murkiest.** [1] ADJ A **murky** place or time of day is dark and rather unpleasant. ...*one murky November afternoon.* [2] ADJ **Murky** water is dark and dirty. [3] ADJ If you describe an activity or situation as **murky**, you suspect that it is dishonest; BRITISH. ...*a murky conspiracy to keep them out of power.* [4] ADJ If you describe something as **murky**, you mean that it is difficult to understand. *The law here is a little bit murky.*

murmur /'mɜːmə/ **murmurs, murmuring, murmured.** [1] VERB & N-C If you **murmur** something, or if you speak in a **murmur**, you speak very quietly, so that not many people can hear what you are saying. *He turned and murmured something to the professor... They spoke in low murmurs.* [2] N-SING A **murmur** is a continuous low sound, like the noise of a river or of distant voices. *I could hear the murmur of the sea.*

muscle /'mʌsəl/ **muscles, muscling, muscled.** [1] N-VAR Your **muscles** are the internal pieces of body tissue which connect your bones together, and which you expand and contract when you make a movement. *Exercise will tone up your stomach muscles.* [2] N-U If you say that someone has **muscle**, you mean that they have power and influence. *Eisenhower used his muscle to persuade Congress to change the law.* [3] PHRASE If a group, organization, or

country **flexes** its **muscles**, it behaves in a way designed to show people that it has power and is considering using it.

▶ **muscle in.** PHR-VERB If someone **muscles in** on something, they force their way into a situation where they have no right to be and where they are not welcome; used showing disapproval. *They are hoping to tie up the deal before any other rivals muscle in.*

muscular /'mʌskjʊlə/. [1] ADJ BEFORE N **Muscular** means involving or affecting your muscles. ...*muscular effort.* [2] ADJ A **muscular** person has strong, firm muscles. ...*his tanned muscular legs.*

muse /mjuːz/ **muses, musing, mused.** VERB If you **muse** on something, you think about it, usually saying or writing what you are thinking at the same time; WRITTEN. *General George Patton once mused that Americans love a winner.* ◆**musing, musings** N-C *His musings were interrupted by Montagu.*

museum /mjuː'ziːəm/ **museums.** N-C A **museum** is a public building where interesting and valuable objects are kept and displayed.

mushroom /'mʌʃruːm/ **mushrooms, mushrooming, mushroomed.** [1] N-VAR **Mushrooms** are fungi with short stems and round tops. You can eat some kinds of mushrooms. ...*mushroom omelette.* [2] VERB If something **mushrooms**, it grows or appears very quickly. *A sleepy capital of a few hundred thousand people has mushroomed to a crowded city of 2 million.*

music /'mjuːzɪk/. [1] N-U **Music** is the pattern of sounds produced by people singing or playing instruments. ...*classical music.* [2] N-U **Music** is the symbols written on paper that represent musical sounds. *He's never been able to read music.*

musical /'mjuːzɪkəl/ **musicals.** [1] ADJ BEFORE N **Musical** describes things that are concerned with playing or studying music. ...*Stan Getz's musical career.* ◆**musically** ADV *Musically there is a lot to enjoy.* [2] N-C A **musical** is a play or film that uses singing and dancing in the story. [3] ADJ Someone who is **musical** has a natural ability in music. *My father was very musical.*

musical 'instrument, musical instruments. N-C A **musical instrument** is an object such as a piano, guitar, or violin which you play in order to produce music.

musician /mjuː'zɪʃən/ **musicians.** N-C A **musician** is a person who plays a musical instrument as their job or hobby.

Muslim (or **Moslem**) /'mʊzlɪm/ **Muslims.** N-C & ADJ A **Muslim** or a person who is **Muslim** is someone who believes in Islam and lives according to its rules.

muslin /'mʌzlɪn/. N-U **Muslin** is a very thin cotton cloth.

mussel /'mʌsəl/ **mussels.** N-C A **mussel** is a kind of shellfish.

must /məst, STRONG mʌst/. [1] MODAL You use **must** to indicate that you think it is very important or necessary for something to happen. *What you wear should be stylish and clean, and must definitely fit well... The doctor must not* allow the patient to be put at risk. [2] MODAL You use **must** to express your firm intention to do something. *I must be getting back.* [3] MODAL You use **must** to make forceful suggestions or invitations. *You must see a doctor, Frederick... You must see the painting Paul has given me.* [4] MODAL You use **must** in questions to express your anger or irritation about something that someone has done. *Why must you do everything as if you have to win?* [5] PHRASE You say **'if you must'** when you know that you cannot stop someone doing something that you think is wrong, stupid, or annoying. *'Could I have a word?'—'Oh dear, if you must.'* [6] N-C If something is a **must**, it is absolutely necessary; INFORMAL. *A trip to this important religious monument is a must for all visitors.* [7] MODAL You use **must** to indicate that you are fairly sure that something is the case, often because of the available evidence. *At 29 Russell may be one of the youngest ever Wembley referees... He must have brought them home in order to continue his work.*

mustache /məˈstɑːʃ, AM ˈmʌstæʃ/. See **moustache**.

mustard /ˈmʌstəd/. N-U **Mustard** is a yellow or brown paste made from seeds which tastes spicy.

muster /ˈmʌstə/ **musters, mustering, mustered.** [1] VERB If you **muster** support, strength, or energy, you gather as much as you can in order to do something. *He travelled around West Africa trying to muster support for his movement.* [2] VERB When soldiers **muster** or **are mustered**, they gather in one place in order to take part in military action.

mustn't /ˈmʌsənt/. **Mustn't** is the usual spoken form of 'must not'.

must've /ˈmʌstəv/. **Must've** is a spoken form of 'must have', especially when 'have' is an auxiliary verb.

mutant /ˈmjuːtənt/ **mutants.** N-C A **mutant** is an animal or plant that is physically different from others of the same species as the result of a change in its genetic structure.

mutate /mjuːˈteɪt, AM ˈmjuːteɪt/ **mutates, mutating, mutated.** VERB If an animal or plant **mutates**, or if something **mutates** it, it develops different characteristics as a result of a change in its genes. *HIV may have mutated into a new, as yet undetected virus.* ◆**mutation, mutations** N-VAR *...accidental mutations of the genes.*

mute /mjuːt/ **mutes, muting, muted.** [1] ADJ Someone who is **mute** does not speak. *He was mute, distant, and indifferent.* [2] VERB If you **mute** a noise or sound, you make it quieter. ◆**muted** ADJ *'Yes,' he muttered, his voice so muted I hardly heard his reply.* [3] VERB If someone **mutes** something such as their feelings or their activities, they reduce the strength or intensity of them. *It accuses the Bush administration of muting its criticism of repression.* ◆**muted** ADJ *Reaction to the news was muted.*

mutilate /ˈmjuːtɪleɪt/ **mutilates, mutilating, mutilated.** VERB If a person or animal **is mutilated**, their body is damaged very severely, usually by someone who physically attacks

them. ◆**mutilation, mutilations** N-VAR *...cases of torture and mutilation.*

mutiny /ˈmjuːtɪni/ **mutinies.** N-VAR A **mutiny** is a rebellion by a group of people, usually soldiers or sailors, against a person in authority.

mutter /ˈmʌtə/ **mutters, muttering, muttered.** VERB & N-C If you **mutter**, or if you speak in a **mutter**, you speak very quietly so that you cannot easily be heard, often because you are complaining about something. *She can hear the old woman muttering about consideration. ...a mutter of protest.* ◆**muttering, mutterings** N-VAR *He heard muttering from the front of the crowd.*

mutton /ˈmʌtən/. N-U **Mutton** is meat from an adult sheep.

mutual /ˈmjuːtʃuəl/. ADJ You use **mutual** to describe a situation, feeling, or action that is experienced, felt, or done by both of two people mentioned. *The East and the West can work together for their mutual benefit... It's plain that he adores his daughter, and the feeling is mutual.* ◆**mutually** ADV *...a mutually convenient time.*

muzzle /ˈmʌzəl/ **muzzles, muzzling, muzzled.** [1] N-C The **muzzle** of a gun is the end where the bullets come out when it is fired. [2] N-C A **muzzle** is a device that is put over a dog's nose and mouth so that it cannot bite people or bark. [3] VERB If you **muzzle** a dog, you put a muzzle over its nose and mouth.

my /maɪ/. DET A speaker or writer uses **my** to indicate that something belongs or relates to himself or herself. *I invited him back to my flat... John's my best friend.*

myriad /ˈmɪriəd/ **myriads.** QUANT You can use **myriad** to refer to a very large number or great variety of people or things. *They face a myriad of problems bringing up children... The myriad other tasks we are trying to perform in the world. ...these myriads of fish.*

myself /maɪˈself/. [1] PRON A speaker or writer uses **myself** to refer to himself or herself. **Myself** is used as the object of a verb or preposition when the subject refers to the same person. *I asked myself what I would have done... I looked at myself in the mirror.* [2] PRON You use **myself** to emphasize a first person singular subject. Some speakers use **myself** instead of 'me' as the object of a verb or preposition. *I myself enjoy cinema. ...a complete beginner like myself.* [3] PRON If you say something such as 'I did it **myself**', you are emphasizing that you did it, rather than anyone else.

mysterious /mɪˈstɪəriəs/. [1] ADJ Someone or something that is **mysterious** is strange, not known about, or not understood. *He died in mysterious circumstances. ...a mysterious illness.* ◆**mysteriously** ADV *A couple of messages had mysteriously disappeared.* [2] ADJ AFTER LINK-V If someone is **mysterious** about something, they deliberately do not talk about it, often because they want people to be curious about it. *As for his job—well, he was very mysterious about it.* ◆**mysteriously** ADV *Asked what she meant, she said mysteriously: 'Work it out for yourself'.*

mystery /ˈmɪstəri/ **mysteries.** [1] N-C A **mystery** is something that is not understood or known about. *The source of the gunshots still remains a mystery.* [2] N-U If you talk about the **mystery** of someone or something, you are talking about how difficult they are to understand or to know about. *She's a lady of mystery... It is an elaborate ceremony, shrouded in mystery.* [3] ADJ BEFORE N A **mystery** person or thing is one whose identity or nature is not known. *A mystery buyer purchased 1.5 million MGN shares.* [4] N-C A **mystery** is a story in which strange things happen that are not explained until the end.

mystic /'mɪstɪk/ **mystics.** [1] N-C A **mystic** is a person who believes in religious practices in which people search for truth, knowledge, and unity with God through meditation and prayer. ♦ **mysticism** /'mɪstɪsɪzəm/ N-U ...*a mixture of mysticism and Roman Catholicism.* [2] ADJ BEFORE N **Mystic** means the same as **mystical**. ...*mystic union with God.*

mystical /'mɪstɪkəl/. ADJ Something that is **mystical** involves spiritual powers and influences that most people do not understand. *That was clearly a deep mystical experience.*

mystify /'mɪstɪfaɪ/ **mystifies, mystifying, mystified.** VERB If you **are mystified** by something, you find it impossible to explain or understand. *There was something strange in her attitude which mystified me.* ♦ **mystifying** ADJ *I find your attitude a little mystifying.*

mystique /mɪ'stiːk/. N-U **Mystique** is an atmosphere of mystery and secrecy which is associated with a particular person or thing. ...*the mystique that surrounds fine art.*

myth /mɪθ/ **myths.** [1] N-VAR A **myth** is a well-known story which was made up in the past to explain natural events or to justify religious beliefs or social customs. ...*a famous Greek myth.* ♦ **mythical** ADJ ...*the Hydra, the mythical beast that had seven or more heads.* [2] N-VAR If you describe a belief or explanation as a **myth**, you mean that many people believe it but it is actually untrue. *Contrary to the popular myth, women are not reckless spendthrifts.*

mythical /'mɪθɪkəl/. ADJ If you describe something as **mythical**, you think it is untrue or does not exist. ...*the mythical, romanticized West of cowboys.*

mythology /mɪ'θɒlədʒi/. N-U **Mythology** is a group of myths, especially those from a particular country, religion, or culture. ...*Greek mythology.* ♦ **mythological** ADJ ...*the mythological beast that was part lion and part goat.*

N n

nag /næg/ **nags, nagging, nagged.** [1] VERB If you say that someone **is nagging** you, you are annoyed with them because they are continuously asking you to do something. *My girlfriend nagged me to cut my hair.* ♦ **nagging** N-U *Her endless nagging drove him away from home.* [2] VERB If something such as a doubt or worry **nags** at you, or **nags** you, it keeps worrying you. ...*the anxiety that had nagged Amy all through lunch.*

nail /neɪl/ **nails, nailing, nailed.** [1] N-C A **nail** is a thin piece of metal with one pointed end and one flat end. You hit the flat end with a hammer in order to push the nail into something such as a wall. [2] VERB If you **nail** something somewhere, you fix it there using one or more nails. *The windows were all nailed shut.* [3] N-C Your **nails** are the thin hard parts that grow at the ends of your fingers and toes.
► **nail down.** [1] PHR-VERB If you **nail down** something unknown or uncertain, you find out exactly what it is. *It would be useful if you could nail down the source of this tension.* [2] PHR-VERB If you **nail down** an agreement, you manage to reach a firm agreement with a definite result.

naive (also **naïve**) /naɪ'iːv, AM nɑː-/. ADJ If you describe someone as **naive**, you think they lack experience, causing them to expect things to be uncomplicated or easy, or people to be honest or kind when they are not. *I must have been naive to think we would get my parents' blessing.* ♦ **naively** ADV ...*naively applying Western solutions to Eastern problems.* ♦ **naivety** /naɪ'iːvɪti/ N-U *I was alarmed by his naivety and ignorance of international affairs.*

naked /'neɪkɪd/. [1] ADJ Someone who is **naked** is not wearing any clothes. *Her naked body was found wrapped in a sheet.* ♦ **nakedness** N-U *He had pulled the blanket over his body to hide his nakedness.* [2] ADJ You can describe an object as **naked** when it does not have its normal covering. ...*a naked light bulb.* [3] ADJ BEFORE N **Naked** emotions are easily recognized because they are very strongly felt; WRITTEN. ...*the naked hatred in the woman's face.* ♦ **nakedly** ADV ...*showing her fear so nakedly.* [4] PHRASE If you say that something cannot be seen by **the naked eye**, you mean that it cannot be seen without the help of equipment such as a telescope or microscope.

name /neɪm/ **names, naming, named.** [1] N-C The **name** of a person, thing, or place is the word or words that you use to identify them. *His name is Michael... They changed the name of the street.* [2] VERB When you **name** someone or something, you give them a name. If you **name** someone or something after a person or thing, you give them the same name as that person or thing. *My mother insisted on naming me Horace... Why have you not named any of your sons after yourself?* [3] VERB If you **name** someone, you identify them by stating their name. *One of the victims of the weekend's snowstorm has been named as twenty-year-old John Barr.* [4] N-C You can refer to the reputation of a person or thing as their **name**. *He had a name for good judgement... She's never had any drug problems or done anything to give jazz a bad name.* [5] See also **brand name, Christian name.**
PHRASES ● You can use **by name**, or **by the name of,** when you are saying what someone

is called. *This guy, Jack Smith, does he go by the name of Jackal?* ● If someone **calls** you **names**, they insult you by saying unpleasant things to you or about you. *They had called her rude names.* ● If something is **in** your **name**, it officially belongs to you or has been reserved for you. *A double room had been reserved for him in the name of Muller.* ● If you do something **in the name of** an ideal or a person, you do it because you believe in or represent that ideal or person. *...the things people did in the name of business.* ● If you **make a name for** yourself or **make** your **name** as something, you become well-known for that thing. *He made his name with several collections of short stories.* ● If you say that something is **the name of the game**, you mean that it is the most important aspect of a situation; INFORMAL. *Family values are suddenly the name of the game.*

namely /'neɪmli/. ADV You use **namely** to introduce more detailed information about what you have just said. *One group of people seems to be forgotten, namely pensioners.*

nanny /'næni/ **nannies.** N-C A **nanny** is a woman who is paid by the parents to look after their children in some families.

nap /næp/ **naps, napping, napped.** VERB & N-C If you **nap**, or if you have a **nap**, you sleep for a short period of time, usually during the day.

napkin /'næpkɪn/ **napkins.** N-C A **napkin** is a small piece of cloth or paper used to protect your clothes when you are eating.

nappy /'næpi/ **nappies.** N-C In British English, a **nappy** is a piece of thick cloth or paper which is fastened round a baby's bottom in order to soak up its urine and faeces. The usual American word is **diaper.**

narcotic /nɑːˈkɒtɪk/ **narcotics.** N-C & ADJ **Narcotics,** or **narcotic** drugs, are drugs such as opium or heroin which make you sleepy and stop you feeling pain, but are also addictive.

narrate /nəˈreɪt, AM ˈnæreɪt/ **narrates, narrating, narrated.** VERB If you **narrate** a story, you tell it; FORMAL. *The book is narrated by Richard Papen.* ◆**narration** N-U *...its story-within-a-story method of narration.* ◆**narrator, narrators** N-C *The story's narrator is an actress in her late thirties.*

narrative /'nærətɪv/ **narratives.** N-C A **narrative** is a story or an account of events.

narrow /'næraʊ/ **narrower, narrowest; narrows, narrowing, narrowed.** [1] ADJ Something that is **narrow** measures a very small distance from one side to the other, especially compared to its length or height. *...the town's narrow streets... She had long, narrow feet.* [2] VERB If something **narrows,** it becomes less wide. *The wide track narrows before crossing another stream.* [3] ADJ If you describe someone's ideas, attitudes, or beliefs as **narrow,** you disapprove of them because they are not imaginative but are old-fashioned or very strict, and often ignore the more important aspects of a situation. *...a narrow and outdated view of family life.* ◆**narrowness** N-U *...the narrowness of their mental and spiritual outlook.* [4] VERB If something **narrows,** or if you **narrow** it, its extent, range, or scope becomes smaller.

The European Community and America had narrowed their differences over farm subsidies. ◆**narrowing** N-U *...a narrowing of the gap between rich members and poor.* [5] ADJ If you have a **narrow** victory, you succeed in winning but only by a small amount. *Delegates have voted by a narrow majority in favour of considering electoral reform.* ◆**narrowly** ADV *She narrowly failed to win enough votes.* [6] ADJ BEFORE N If you have a **narrow** escape, something unpleasant nearly happens to you. ◆**narrowly** ADV *Five firemen narrowly escaped death.*

▸ **narrow down.** PHR-VERB If you **narrow down** a range of things, you reduce the number of things included in it. *I've managed to narrow the list down to twenty-three.*

nasal /'neɪzəl/. [1] ADJ If someone's voice is **nasal,** it sounds as if air is passing through their nose as well as their mouth when they are speaking. *She talked in a deep nasal monotone.* [2] ADJ BEFORE N **Nasal** is used to describe things relating to the nose. *...inflamed nasal passages.*

nasty /'nɑːsti, ˈnæsti/ **nastier, nastiest.** [1] ADJ Something that is **nasty** is very unpleasant or unattractive. *This divorce could turn nasty. ...Emily's nasty little house.* ◆**nastiness** N-U *...the nastiness of war.* [2] ADJ A **nasty** problem or question is a difficult one. *This firm action had defused a very nasty situation.* [3] ADJ If you describe a disease or injury as **nasty,** you mean that it is serious or looks very unpleasant. *Lili had a nasty chest infection.* [4] ADJ If you describe a person or their behaviour as **nasty,** you mean that they behave in an unkind and unpleasant way. *The guards looked really nasty... She is so nasty to me.* ◆**nastily** ADV *She took the money and eyed me nastily.*

nation /'neɪʃən/ **nations.** N-C A **nation** is an individual country, especially when it is considered from the point of view of its cultural or ethnic identity. *...the Arab nations of the Gulf.* ● See note at **country.**

national /'næʃənəl/ **nationals.** [1] ADJ **National** means relating to the whole of a country, rather than to part of it or to other nations. *...national and local elections. ...major national and international issues.* ◆**nationally** ADV *...a nationally televised speech.* [2] ADJ BEFORE N **National** means typical of the people or customs of a particular country or nation. *Baseball is the national pastime.* [3] N-C A **national** of a country is a citizen of that country who is staying in a different country. *...a Sri Lankan-born British national.*

national 'anthem, national anthems. N-C A **national anthem** is a nation's official song.

nationalise /'næʃənəlaɪz/. See **nationalize.**

nationalist /'næʃənəlɪst/ **nationalists.** [1] ADJ BEFORE N & N-C **Nationalist** ideas or movements are connected with attempts to obtain political independence for a particular group of people. A **nationalist** is a person with nationalist beliefs. *The crisis has set off a wave of nationalist feelings in Quebec.* ◆**nationalism** N-U *...the rising tide of Slovak nationalism.* [2] ADJ BEFORE N & N-C **Nationalist** is used when describing people's great love for their nation, or their belief that their nation is better than others. A **nationalist** is someone with nationalist views.

Political life has been infected by growing na-tionalist sentiment. ♦**nationalistic** ADJ *There is still a lot of nationalistic pride in being the best in the country.* ♦**nationalism** N-U *...this kind of fierce nationalism.*

nationality /ˌnæʃəˈnælɪti/ **nationalities.** N-VAR If you have the **nationality** of a particular country, you have the legal right to be a citizen of it. *Asked his nationality, he said British.*

nationalize (BR also **nationalise**) /ˈnæʃənəlaɪz/ **nationalizes, nationalizing, nationalized.** VERB If a government **national-izes** a private industry, that industry becomes owned by the state and controlled by the gov-ernment. *The coffee industry was nationalised at the time of independence.* ♦**nationalization, nationalizations** N-VAR *...the nationalization of the coal mines.*

,national 'park, national parks. N-C A na-**tional park** is a large area of natural land pro-tected by the government because of its natu-ral beauty, plants, or animals.

nationwide /ˌneɪʃənˈwaɪd/. ADJ & ADV **Nation-wide** activities or situations happen or exist in all parts of a country. You can say they happen or exist **nationwide**. *The rising number of car crimes is a nationwide problem. ...available from department stores nationwide.*

native /ˈneɪtɪv/ **natives.** [1] ADJ BEFORE N Your **native** country or area is the country or area where you were born and brought up. *Mother Teresa visited her native Albania.* [2] N-C & ADJ A **native** of a particular country or region, or a person who is **native** to that country or region, is a person who was born there. *Dr Aubin is a native of St Blaise. ...men and women native to countries such as Japan.* [3] ADJ BEFORE N Your **native** language or tongue is the first language that you learned to speak when you were a child. [4] N-C & ADJ Animals or plants that are **natives** of a region, or are **native** to it, grow there naturally and have not been brought there. *The coconut palm is a native of Malay-sia. ...a 50 acre forest of native Caledonian pines.*

natural /ˈnætʃərəl/ **naturals.** [1] ADJ If you say that it is **natural** for someone to act in a par-ticular way, you mean that it is reasonable in the circumstances. *It is only natural for young-sters to crave excitement... Grief is a perfectly natural response.* [2] ADJ If someone's behav-iour is **natural**, they are relaxed and do not ap-pear to be hiding anything or pretending to be something they are not. ♦**naturally** ADV *You can talk quite naturally to her.* ♦**naturalness** N-U *...the naturalness of the acting.* [3] ADJ **Natural** behaviour or ability is instinctive and has not been learned. *...the insect's natural in-stinct to feed... Martin was a natural commu-nicator.* ♦**naturally** ADV *Some children are naturally more timid than others.* [4] N-C If you describe someone as a **natural**, you mean that they do something very well and very easily. *He's a natural with any kind of engine.* [5] ADJ BEFORE N **Natural** things exist in nature and were not created by people. *...a natural disas-ter like an earthquake. ...the gigantic natural harbour of Poole.* ♦**naturally** ADV *Nitrates are chemicals that occur naturally in water.*

naturalist /ˈnætʃərəlɪst/ **naturalists.** N-C A **naturalist** is a person who studies plants, ani-mals, and other living things.

naturally /ˈnætʃərəli/. [1] ADV You use **naturally** to indicate that something is obvious and not surprising. *He will never play again. Naturally he is devastated.* [2] ADV If one thing develops **naturally** from another, it develops as a nor-mal result of it. *A study of yoga leads naturally to meditation.* [3] PHRASE If a skill or quality **comes naturally** to you, you have it instinc-tively, without having to work very hard to get it. *Ambition and self-confidence came naturally to Sergei.*

,natural re'sources. N-PL The **natural re-sources** of a place are all its land, forests, ener-gy sources, and minerals which exist naturally there and can be used by people. *...a country rich in natural resources.*

nature /ˈneɪtʃə/ **natures.** [1] N-U **Nature** refers to all the animals, plants, and other things in the world that are not made by people, and all the events and processes that are not caused by people. *...grasses that grow wild in nature. ...the ecological balance of nature.* ● See note at **landscape.** [2] N-U The **nature** of something is its basic quality or character. *...the ambitious nature of the programme... The protests had been non-political by nature.* [3] N-C Someone's **nature** is their character, which they show by their behaviour. *Her ambitious nature made her unsuitable for an arranged marriage... He was by nature affectionate.*

PHRASES ● If you say that something has a particular characteristic **by** its **nature** or **by** its **very nature**, you mean that things of that type always have that characteristic. *Youth is by its very nature rebellious.* ● A way of behaving is **second nature** to you, you do it almost with-out thinking because it is easy or obvious to you. *Secrecy is second nature to these people.*

naughty /ˈnɔːti/. [1] ADJ You say that small chil-dren are **naughty** when they behave badly. *Girls, you're being very naughty.* [2] ADJ **Naugh-ty** books, pictures, or words are slightly rude or relate to sex. *...naughty magazines.*

nausea /ˈnɔːziə/. N-U **Nausea** is a feeling of sick-ness and dizziness. *I was overcome with a feel-ing of nausea.*

nautical /ˈnɔːtɪkəl/. ADJ **Nautical** things and people are involved with ships. *...a nautical chart of the region.*

naval /ˈneɪvəl/. ADJ BEFORE N **Naval** people and things belong to a country's navy. *...the US na-val base at Guantanamo Bay.*

navel /ˈneɪvəl/ **navels.** N-C Your **navel** is the small hollow just below your waist at the front of your body.

navigate /ˈnævɪgeɪt/ **navigates, navigating, navigated.** [1] VERB When someone **navigates** an area, or when they **navigate**, they steer a ship or plane through the area towards a par-ticular destination. *Every year they navigate the Greek and Turkish islands in a sailing boat.* ♦**navigation** N-U *The expedition was wrecked by bad planning and poor navigation.* ♦**navigator, navigators** N-C *He became an RAF navigator during the war.* [2] VERB If a passen-ger in a car **navigates**, he or she tells the driver, often using a road map, what roads the car should be driven along in order to get somewhere. *You drive. I'll navigate.* **3** VERB If you **navigate** your way somewhere, you go there with difficulty, because the route is complicated or there are obstacles. *He attempted to navigate his way through the crowds.*

navy /'neɪvi/ **navies.** **1** N-C A country's **navy** is the part of its armed forces that fights at sea. *Her own son was also in the Navy.* **2** ADJ & N-U **Navy** or **navy blue** is very dark blue.

NB /ˌen 'biː/. You write **NB** to draw someone's attention to what you are going to write next. *NB: A small charge will be made.*

near /nɪə/ **nearer, nearest; nears, nearing, neared.** **1** PREP & ADV & ADJ If something is **near** a place or thing or **near** to it, it is a short distance from it. *...a farmhouse near the cottage... He crouched as near to the door as he could... He collapsed into the nearest chair.* **2** ADV & PREP & ADJ If you are **near to** a particular state or **near** it, you have almost reached it. *The repairs to the Hafner machine were near to completion... He was near tears... She was believed to have died in near poverty.* **3** ADV & PREP If two things are similar, you can say that they are **near** to each other or **near** each other. *...a sickening sensation that was near to nausea... The legal profession is the nearest thing to a recession-proof industry... Her feelings were nearer hatred than love.* **4** PREP & ADV If something happens **near** a particular time or **near to** it, it happens just before or just after that time. *I'll tell you nearer the day... The announcement, so near to Christmas, had come as a shock.* **5** ADV If a time or event is **near**, it will happen very soon. *The time for my departure from Japan was drawing nearer.* **6** VERB If someone or something **is nearing** a particular place, stage, or point in time, they will soon reach it. *As he neared the stable, he slowed the horse... His age was hard to guess – he must have been nearing fifty.* **7** PREP & ADJ You use **near** to say that something is a little more or less than an amount or number stated. *...the pound, which ended last year near its annual low. ...the near 5 per cent fall in the exchange rate.*

PHRASES • If something is **near enough** a quantity or **near enough** true, it is almost that quantity or almost true. *I've been working at it now for near enough an hour.* • You use **nowhere near** and **not anywhere near** to emphasize that something is not the case. *They are nowhere near good enough.* • **in the near future:** see **future.**

nearby /ˌnɪə'baɪ/. ADV & ADJ If something is **nearby**, it is only a short distance away. *...someone who lived nearby. ...a nearby table.*

nearly /'nɪəli/. **1** ADV If something is **nearly** a quantity, it is very close to that quantity but slightly less than it. If something is **nearly** a certain state, it is very close to that state but has not quite reached it. *Goldsworth stared at me in silence for nearly twenty seconds... It was already nearly eight o'clock... I've nearly finished.* **2** PHRASE You use **not nearly** to emphasize that something is not the case. For example, if something is **not nearly** big enough, it is

much too small. *Father's flat in Paris wasn't nearly as grand as this.*

neat /niːt/ **neater, neatest.** **1** ADJ A **neat** place, thing, or person is tidy, smart, and orderly. *She undressed and put her wet clothes in a neat pile.* ◆ **neatly** ADV *He folded his paper neatly.* ◆ **neatness** N-U *...the crisp neatness of her appearance.* **2** ADJ A **neat** explanation or method is clever and convenient. *It had been such a neat, clever plan.* ◆ **neatly** ADV *Real people do not fit neatly into these categories.* ◆ **neatness** N-U *...the extreme neatness of his conclusions.* **3** ADJ If you drink an alcoholic drink **neat**, you drink it without anything added. *...neat whisky.*

necessarily /ˌnesɪ'serɪli, -srɪli/. **1** ADV If you say that something is **not necessarily** true, you mean that it may not be true or is not always true. *Women do not necessarily have to imitate men to be successful... 'He was lying, of course.'—'Not necessarily.'* **2** ADV If you say that something **necessarily** happens, you mean that it has to happen and cannot be any different. *Business relationships are necessarily a bit more formal.*

necessary /'nesɪsəri/. **1** ADJ Something that is **necessary** is needed to get a particular result or effect. *It might be necessary to leave fast... We will do whatever is necessary... The army needs men who are willing to fight, when necessary.* **2** ADJ BEFORE N A **necessary** consequence or connection must happen or exist, because of the nature of the things or events involved. *Wastage was no doubt a necessary consequence of war.*

necessitate /nɪ'sesɪteɪt/ **necessitates, necessitating, necessitated.** VERB If something **necessitates** a particular course of action, it makes it necessary; FORMAL. *...a letter to the Pope, which necessitates careful phrasing.*

necessity /nɪ'sesɪti/ **necessities.** **1** N-U **Necessity** is the need to do something. *He'd learned the necessity of hiding his feelings... Most women, like men, work from economic necessity.* **2** PHRASE If something is **of necessity** true, it is true because nothing else is possible or imaginable in the circumstances. **3** N-C **Necessities** are things that you must have to live. *Water is a basic necessity of life.*

neck /nek/ **necks.** **1** N-C Your **neck** is the part of your body which joins your head to the rest of your body. *She threw her arms round his neck and hugged him.* **2** N-C The **neck** of a dress or shirt is the part which is round your neck or just below it. **3** N-C The **neck** of something such as a bottle or a guitar is the long narrow part at one end of it. **4** PHRASE If two or more competitors are **neck and neck**, they are level with each other and have an equal chance of winning. **5** **a pain in the neck:** see **pain.**

necklace /'nekləs/ **necklaces.** N-C A **necklace** is a piece of jewellery such as a chain or string of beads, which someone wears round their neck.

nectarine /'nektəriːn, -rɪn/ **nectarines.** N-C A **nectarine** is a kind of peach with a smooth skin.

née /neɪ/. **née** is used before a name to indicate

that it was a woman's surname before she got married; FORMAL. ...*Nicola Lewis (née May).*

need /niːd/ **needs, needing, needed.** [1] VERB If you **need** something, or **need** to do something, you cannot successfully achieve what you want or live properly without it. *He desperately needed money... I need to make a phone call... I need you to do something for me... I need you here, Wally.* [2] N-C If you have a **need** to do or have something, you cannot successfully achieve what you want without it. *Charles has never felt the need to compete. ...his need for attention.* [3] VERB If an object or place **needs** something doing to it, that action must or should be done to improve the object or place, or to improve a situation. If a task **needs** doing, it must or should be done to improve a situation. *The building needs quite a few repairs... The flavour sometimes needs to be disguised.* [4] N-SING If there is a **need** for something, that thing would improve a situation. *There is a need for other similar schools.* [5] MODAL & VERB If you say that someone **needn't** do something, or that they **don't need** to do it, you are telling them not to do it, or advising or suggesting that they should not do it. *Look, you needn't shout... She need not know I'm here... Come along, Mother, we don't need to take up any more of Mr Kemp's time.* [6] MODAL & VERB If someone **needn't** have done something, or if they **didn't need** to do it, it was not necessary or useful for them to do it, although they did it. *I was a little nervous when I announced my engagement to Grace, but I needn't have worried... You didn't need to give me any more money you know.*

[PHRASES] ● If you say that you will do something, especially an extreme action, **if need be**, or **if needs be**, you mean that you will do it if is necessary. *We can survive down here for three months, if need be.* ● People **in need** do not have enough of essential things such as money, food, or good health. *When both of you were in need, I was the one who loaned you money.* ● If someone or something is **in need of** something, they need it or ought to have it. *I was all right but in need of rest.*

needle /ˈniːdəl/ **needles, needling, needled.** [1] N-C A **needle** is a small very thin piece of metal with a hole at one end and a sharp point at the other, which is used for sewing. [2] N-C Knitting **needles** are thin metal or plastic sticks that are used for knitting. [3] N-C The **needle** on a record player is the small pointed instrument that touches the record and picks up the sound signals. [4] N-C A **needle** is a thin hollow metal rod with a sharp point, which forms part of a syringe. It is used to give injections. [5] N-C On an instrument measuring speed, weight, or electricity, the **needle** is the thin piece of metal or plastic which moves backwards and forwards and shows the measurement. [6] N-C The **needles** of a fir or pine tree are its thin pointed leaves. [7] VERB If someone **needles** you, they annoy you by criticizing you repeatedly. *He had needled Jerrold, which might be unwise.*

needless /ˈniːdləs/. [1] ADJ Something that is **needless** is completely unnecessary. *His death*

was so needless. ◆**needlessly** ADV *A lot of women suffer needlessly.* [2] PHRASE You say **needless to say** to emphasize that what you are saying is obvious. *Needless to say, I am thrilled.*

needn't /ˈniːdənt/. **Needn't** is the usual spoken form of 'need not'.

needy /ˈniːdi/ **needier, neediest.** ADJ & N-PL **Needy** people do not have enough food, medicine, or clothing or an adequate house to live in. **The needy** are people who are needy. *...housing for needy families. ...raising funds for the needy.*

negate /nɪˈɡeɪt/ **negates, negating, negated.** VERB If one thing **negates** another, it causes that other thing to lose the effect or value that it had; FORMAL. *An incorrect diet may negate the effects of training.*

negative /ˈneɡətɪv/ **negatives.** [1] ADJ A fact, situation, or experience that is **negative** is unpleasant, depressing, or harmful. *The news is not all negative. ...the negative effect of persistent job insecurity.* [2] ADJ A **negative** reply or decision indicates the answer 'no'. *The question invites a negative response.* ◆**negatively** ADV *60 percent of the sample answered negatively.* [3] ADJ If someone is **negative**, they consider only the bad aspects of a situation, rather than the good ones. *...the public's overall negative view of the Government's economic policies.* ◆**negatively** ADV *Why do so many people think negatively?* ◆**negativity** N-U *She has been accused of negativity.* [4] N-C A **negative** is a word, expression, or gesture that means 'no' or 'not'. *He uses five negatives in fifty-three words.* [5] ADJ If a medical test or scientific test is **negative**, it shows that something has not happened or is not present. *The results were negative.* [6] N-C A **negative** is the image that is first produced when you take a photograph. [7] ADJ A **negative** number is less than zero. *...a negative score.*

neglect /nɪˈɡlekt/ **neglects, neglecting, neglected.** [1] VERB & N-U If you **neglect** someone or something, you do not look after them properly. **Neglect** is failure to look after someone or something properly. *Don't neglect your health... The house had suffered years of neglect.* ◆**neglected** ADJ *...neglected children.* [2] VERB If you **neglect** to do something, you fail to do it. *He had neglected to give her his telephone number... They never neglect their duties.*

negligent /ˈneɡlɪdʒənt/. ADJ When someone is **negligent**, they fail to do something that they should do. *The doctors have denied they were negligent.* ◆**negligently** ADV *...a claim that they have acted negligently.* ◆**negligence** N-U *They accuse the airline of negligence.*

negligible /ˈneɡlɪdʒɪbəl/. ADJ Something that is **negligible** is so small or unimportant that it is not worth considering. *The risks are negligible.*

negotiable /nɪˈɡəʊʃəbəl/. ADJ Something that is **negotiable** can be changed or agreed by means of discussion. *The fee is negotiable.*

negotiate /nɪˈɡəʊʃieɪt/ **negotiates, negotiating, negotiated.** [1] VERB If one person or group **negotiates** with another, they talk about a problem or a situation such as a business arrangement in order to solve the problem or complete the arrangement. You can also say that two people or groups **negotiate**. *The local government and the army negotiated a truce... His publishing house had just begun negotiating for her next books.* ♦ **negotiator, negotiators** N-C *...Japanese trade negotiators.* ② VERB If you **negotiate** a place or an obstacle, you successfully travel across it or around it. *I negotiated my way out of the airport.*

ne'gotiating table. N-SING If you say that people are at **the negotiating table**, you mean that they are having discussions in order to settle a dispute or reach an agreement.

negotiation /nɪ,gəʊʃi'eɪʃən/ **negotiations.** N-VAR **Negotiations** are discussions that take place between people with different interests, in which they try to reach an agreement. *Four years of negotiation ended fruitlessly.*

Negro /'niːgrəʊ/ **Negroes.** N-C A **Negro** is someone with dark skin who comes from Africa or whose ancestors came from Africa. Many people find this word offensive.

neighbour (AM **neighbor**) /'neɪbə/ **neighbours.** ① N-C Your **neighbours** are the people who live near you, especially the people who live in the house or flat which is next to yours. ② N-C Your **neighbour** is the person who is standing or sitting next to you. *The woman prodded her neighbour.* ③ N-C You can refer to something which is near or next to something else of the same kind as its **neighbour**. *Consider the shape and colour of each plant in relation to its neighbours.*

neighbourhood (AM **neighborhood**) /'neɪbəhʊd/ **neighbourhoods.** N-C A **neighbourhood** is one of the parts of a town where people live. *Margaret no longer takes evening strolls around her neighbourhood.*

neighbouring (AM **neighboring**) /'neɪbərɪŋ/. ADJ BEFORE N **Neighbouring** describes the places and things that are near to the place or thing that you are talking about. *...Thailand and its neighbouring countries.*

neither /'naɪðə, 'niːðə/. ① CONJ You use **neither** in front of the first of two or more words or expressions when you are linking two or more things which are not true or do not happen. The other thing, or the last of the other things, is introduced by 'nor'. *Professor Hisamatsu spoke neither English nor German... The play is neither as funny nor as disturbing as Tabori thinks it is.* ② DET & PRON You use **neither** to refer to each of two things or people, when you are making a negative statement that includes both of them. *At first, neither man could speak... Neither of us felt like going out... Neither seemed likely to be aware of my absence for long.* ③ CONJ If you say that one person or thing does not do something and **neither** does another, what you say is true of all the people or things that you are mentioning. *I never learned to swim and neither did they.*

neon /'niːɒn/. ① N-U **Neon** is a gas which exists in very small amounts in the atmosphere. ② ADJ **Neon** lights or signs are made from glass tubes filled with neon gas which produce a bright electric light.

nephew /'nefjuː, 'nev-/ **nephews.** N-C Your **nephew** is the son of your sister or brother.

nerve /nɜːv/ **nerves.** ① N-C **Nerves** are long thin fibres that transmit messages between your brain and other parts of your body. ② N-PL If you talk about someone's **nerves**, you mean their ability to remain calm and not become worried in a stressful situation. *Jill's nerves are stretched to breaking point.* ③ N-PL You can refer to someone's feelings of anxiety or tension as **nerves**. *I don't suffer from nerves.* ④ N-U **Nerve** is the courage you need to do something difficult or dangerous. *He never got up enough nerve to meet me.*

PHRASES ● If someone or something **gets on** your **nerves**, they annoy or irritate you; INFORMAL. ● If you say that someone **had a nerve** or **had the nerve** to do something, you mean that they made you angry by doing something rude or lacking in respect; INFORMAL. *He had the nerve to ask me to prove who I was.*

nervous /'nɜːvəs/. ① ADJ If you are **nervous**, you are worried and frightened, and show this in your behaviour. *It has made me very nervous about going out.* ♦ **nervously** ADV *Joe giggled nervously.* ♦ **nervousness** N-U *I smiled warmly so he wouldn't see my nervousness.* ② ADJ A **nervous** person is very tense and easily upset. ③ ADJ BEFORE N A **nervous** illness or condition is one that affects your mental state.

nervous 'breakdown, nervous breakdowns. N-C If someone has a **nervous breakdown**, they become extremely depressed and anxious, and have to be treated by a psychiatrist. This illness is caused by mental stress.

'nervous system, nervous systems. N-C Your **nervous system** is all the nerves in your body together with your brain and spinal cord, which control your movements and feelings.

nest /nest/ **nests, nesting, nested.** ① N-C A **nest** is a place that birds, insects and other animals make to lay eggs in or give birth to their young in. *...a wasps' nest.* ② VERB When a bird **nests** somewhere, it builds a nest and settles there to lay its eggs. *Owls nested in the trees.*

nestle /'nesəl/ **nestles, nestling, nestled.** ① VERB If you **nestle** somewhere, you move into a comfortable position, often by pressing against someone or something soft. *The two little girls nestled against their mother.* ② VERB If a building, place, or thing **nestles** somewhere, it is in that place or position and seems safe or sheltered. *The house nestles in 40 acres of parkland.*

net /net/ **nets, netting, netted;** also spelled **nett** in British English for meanings 5 and 6. ① N-U **Net** is a kind of material made of threads, strings, or wires woven together so that there are small equal spaces between them. *...net curtains.* ② N-C A **net** is a piece of net which you use, for example, to protect something or to catch fish. *...a fisherman who sat mending his nets.* ③ N-C The **net** is the piece of netting used to divide the two halves of a tennis court, or to form the back of a goal in football. *Both girls were eager to come to the* *net to volley.* [4] VERB If you **net** something, you manage to get it, often by using skill. *He stands to net a fortune.* [5] ADJ BEFORE N & ADV A **net** amount or result is the final amount or result, when everything necessary has been considered or included. *...a rise in sales and net profit. ...a net gain of nearly 50 seats... The London Share Account now pays 7.75% gross 5.81% net.* [6] ADJ BEFORE N The **net** weight of something is its weight without its container or wrapping.

netball /ˈnetbɔːl/. N-U **Netball** is a game played by two teams of seven players, usually women. Each team tries to score goals by throwing a ball through a net at the top of a pole at each end of the court.

nett. See **net**.

nettle /ˈnetəl/ **nettles.** N-C A **nettle** is a wild plant with leaves that sting when you touch them.

network /ˈnetwɜːk/ **networks.** [1] N-C A **network** of lines, roads, veins, or other long thin things is a large number of them which cross each other or meet at many points. *...the network of streets surrounding the park... Butterfly wings are covered with a network of veins.* [2] N-C A **network** of people or organizations is a large number of them that have a connection with each other and work together as a system. *...their widespread network of offices.* [3] N-C A radio or television **network** is a company or group of companies that broadcasts the same radio or television programmes throughout an area.

networking /ˈnetwɜːkɪŋ/. N-U **Networking** is the process of establishing business contacts, often through social activities. *Quite a bit of networking goes on.*

neurosis /njʊəˈrəʊsɪs, AM nʊr-/ **neuroses.** N-VAR **Neurosis** is a mental condition which causes people to have unreasonable fears and worries. *She got a neurosis about chemicals.*

neurotic /njʊəˈrɒtɪk, AM nʊr-/ **neurotics.** ADJ & N-C If someone is **neurotic**, or if they are a **neurotic**, they continually show a lot of unreasonable fears and worry. *They were neurotic about their health.*

neutral /ˈnjuːtrəl, AM nuːt-/. [1] ADJ A **neutral** person or country does not support anyone in a disagreement, war, or contest. *It is morally impossible to remain neutral in this conflict.* ◆**neutrality** /njuːˈtrælɪti, AM ˈnuːt-/ N-U *...a reputation for political neutrality.* [2] ADJ If someone's facial expression or language is **neutral**, they do not show what they are thinking or feeling. *After a pause I said in my most neutral voice: 'Really'.* [3] N-U **Neutral** is the position between the gears of a vehicle, in which the gears are not connected to the engine. *Graham put the van in neutral and jumped out.* [4] ADJ In an electrical device or system, the **neutral** wire is one of the three wires needed to complete the circuit so that the current can flow.

neutralize (BR also **neutralise**) /ˈnjuːtrəlaɪz, AM ˈnuːt-/ **neutralizes, neutralizing, neutralized.** VERB To **neutralize** something means to prevent it from having any effect or from working properly. *Does alcohol neutralise the effects of contraceptive measures?*

never /ˈnevə/. [1] ADV **Never** means at no time in the past or future. *I have never lost the weight I put on in my teens... Never say that... This is never to happen again.* [2] ADV **Never** means not in any circumstances. *Divorce is never easy for children.* [3] PHRASE **Never ever** is an emphatic expression for 'never'; SPOKEN. *He's vowed never ever to talk about it.* [4] ADV **Never** is used to refer to the past and to say that something did not happen. *He never achieved anything... I was to meet Nick in London, but he never appeared.* [5] **never mind:** see **mind**.

never-'ending. ADJ If you describe something bad or unpleasant as **never-ending**, you are emphasizing that it seems to last a very long time. *...a never-ending series of scandals.*

nevertheless /ˌnevəðəˈles/. ADV You use **nevertheless** when saying something that contrasts with what has just been said; FORMAL. *All of this is perfectly true, but the episode is incredible nevertheless.*

new /njuː, AM nuː/ **newer, newest.** [1] ADJ Something that is **new** has been recently created or invented. *They've just opened a new hotel... Their epic fight is the subject of a new film... These ideas are nothing new in America.* [2] ADJ Something that is **new** has not been used or owned by anyone. *There are many boats, new and used, for sale.* [3] ADJ You use **new** to describe something which has replaced another thing because someone no longer has it, or because it is no longer useful. *I had to find somewhere new to live... They told me I needed a new battery.* [4] ADJ **New** is used to describe something that has only recently been discovered or noticed. *The new planet is about ten times the size of the earth.* [5] ADJ BEFORE N **New** is used to describe someone or something that has recently acquired a particular status. *...the usual exhaustion of a new mother.* [6] ADJ AFTER LINK-V If you are **new** to a situation or place, or if the situation or place is **new** to you, you have not previously seen it or had any experience of it. *She wasn't new to the company... His name was new to me then... I'm new here.*

newborn (or **new-born**) /ˈnjuːbɔːn, AM ˈnuː-/ **newborns.** ADJ & N-C A **newborn** baby or animal or a **newborn** is a baby or animal that has just been born. *...a cradle for his newborn child.*

newcomer /ˈnjuːkʌmə, AM ˈnuː-/ **newcomers.** N-C A **newcomer** is a person who has recently started a new activity, arrived in a place, or joined an organization. *The candidates are both relative newcomers to politics.*

new-'found (or **newfound**). ADJ BEFORE N A **new-found** quality or ability is one that you have discovered recently. *...his new-found sense of confidence.*

newly /ˈnjuːli, AM ˈnuːli/. ADV **Newly** is used before past participles or adjectives to indicate that an action or a situation is very recent. *...a newly married man. ...the newly independent countries of Africa and Asia.*

news /njuːz, AM nuːz/. [1] N-U **News** is information about a recently changed situation or a recent event. *We waited and waited for news of him... I wish I had better news for you... Mr*

Forsberg welcomed the news. [2] N-U **News** is information that is published in newspapers and broadcast on radio and television. *...some of the top stories in the news.* [3] N-SING **The news** is a television or radio broadcast which consists of information about recent events. *...the six o'clock news.*

> Note that, although **news** looks like a plural, it is in fact an uncount noun in meanings 1 and 2. *Good news is always worth waiting for.* You cannot say 'a news', but you can say a **piece of news** when you are referring to a particular fact or message. *One of my Dutch colleagues told me a very exciting piece of news.* When you are talking about television and radio news, or newspapers, you can refer to an individual story or report as a **news item**.

'**news agency, news agencies.** N-C A **news agency** is an organization which collects news stories from all over the world and sells them to journalists.

newsagent /'njuːzeɪdʒənt, AM 'nuːz-/ **newsagents.** N-C In Britain, a **newsagent** or a **newsagent's** is a shop where newspapers, sweets, cigarettes, and stationery are sold. You can also refer to the shopkeeper as a **newsagent**.

newscaster /'njuːzkɑːstər, AM 'nuːzkæst/ **newscasters.** N-C A **newscaster** is a person who reads the news on television or radio.

'**news conference, news conferences.** N-C A **news conference** is a meeting held by a famous or important person in which they answer journalists' questions.

newsletter /'njuːzletə, AM 'nuːz-/ **newsletters.** N-C A **newsletter** is one or more printed sheets of paper containing information about an organization that is sent regularly to its members.

newspaper /'njuːspeɪpə, AM 'nuːz-/ **newspapers.** [1] N-VAR A **newspaper** is a publication consisting of a number of large sheets of folded paper, on which news is printed. *They read their daughter's allegations in the newspaper. ...two pots, each wrapped in newspaper.* [2] N-C A **newspaper** is an organization that produces a newspaper. *He worked for a small newspaper in Queensland.*

newsprint /'njuːzprɪnt, AM 'nuːz-/. N-U **Newsprint** is the cheap paper on which newspapers are printed.

,**new 'wave, new waves.** N-C In the arts or in politics, a **new wave** is a group or movement that deliberately introduces new or unconventional ideas. *...the new wave of satirical comedy.*

,**New 'Year.** [1] N-U **New Year** or **the New Year** is the time when people celebrate the start of a year. *Happy New Year, everyone... The restaurant was closed over the New Year.* [2] N-SING **The New Year** is the first few weeks of a year. *Isabel was expecting their baby in the New Year.*

next /nekst/. [1] ORD The **next** period of time, event, person, or thing is the one that comes immediately after the present one or after the previous one. *I got up early the next morning. ...the next available flight... Who will be the next prime minister?... I don't want to be the next to die.* [2] DET & PRON You use **next** in expressions such as **next Friday** and **next year** to refer, for example, to the Friday or year which follows immediately after the present one or after the previous one. *Let's plan a big night next week... John would be coming the weekend after next.* [3] ADJ The **next** place or person is the one nearest to you or the first one that you come to. *Trish could hear it in the next room... Stop at the next corner.* [4] ADV The thing that happens **next** is the thing that happens immediately after something else. *Allow the sauce to cool. Next, add the parsley... The news is next.* [5] ADV When you **next** do something, you do it for the first time since you last did it. *I next saw him at his house.* [6] ADV You use **next** to say that something has more of a quality than all other things except one. *He didn't have a son. I think he felt that a grandson is the next best thing.* [7] PHRASE You can say **the next thing I knew** to suggest that a new situation which you are describing was surprising because it happened very suddenly; INFORMAL SPOKEN. *The next thing I knew, the bungalow was on fire.* [8] PREP If one thing is **next to** another, it is at the side of it. *She sat down next to him on the sofa.* [9] PHRASE You use **next to** before a negative, or a word that suggests something negative, to mean almost. *Most pre-prepared weight loss products are next to useless.*

,**next 'door.** [1] ADV & ADJ BEFORE N If a room or building is **next door**, it is the next one to the right or left. *He lived in the house next door to me. ...the old lady who lived next door... Juan came out of the next-door room.* [2] ADV & ADJ The people **next door** are the people who live in the house to the right or left of yours. *...our next door neighbour.*

nibble /'nɪbl/ **nibbles, nibbling, nibbled.** [1] VERB & N-C If you **nibble** food, or if you eat in **nibbles**, you eat it by biting very small pieces off it. *She nibbled at the corner of a piece of dry toast.* [2] VERB When animals **nibble** at something, or when they **nibble away** at it, they take small bites of it quickly and repeatedly.

nice /naɪs/ **nicer, nicest.** [1] ADJ If you say that something is **nice**, you mean that it is pleasant, enjoyable, or attractive. *It's nice to be here together again... We had a nice meal.* ◆**nicely** ADV *He's just written a book, nicely illustrated and not too technical.* [2] ADJ If you say that it is **nice of** someone to say or do something, you are saying that they are being kind and thoughtful. This is often used as a way of thanking someone. *'How are your boys?' — 'How nice of you to ask.'.* [3] ADJ If someone is **nice**, they are friendly and pleasant. *He was a nice fellow, very quiet and courteous... They were extremely nice to me.* ◆**nicely** ADV *He treated you very nicely.*

nicely /'naɪsli/. ADV Something that is happening or working **nicely** is happening or working in a satisfactory way. *She has a bit of private money, so they manage quite nicely.*

niche /niːʃ, AM nɪtʃ/ **niches.** [1] N-C A **niche** is a hollow in a wall or a natural hollow part in a cliff. *...a niche in the rock where the path ended.* [2] N-C Your **niche** is the job or activity which is exactly suitable for you. *Simon Lane quickly found his niche as a busy freelance model maker.*

nick /nɪk/ **nicks, nicking, nicked.** [1] VERB If someone **nicks** something, they steal or take it; INFORMAL, BRITISH. *He's nicked all your ideas... Michelle had her purse nicked.* [2] VERB If you **nick** something, you accidentally make a small cut or scratch into the surface of it. *He'd also nicked himself on the chin with his razor.* [3] N-C A **nick** is a small cut or scratch in the surface of something. *There was a bad nick at the nape of his neck.* [4] PHRASE If something is achieved **in the nick of time**, it is achieved successfully, at the last possible moment; INFORMAL. *Seems we got here just in the nick of time.*

nickel /ˈnɪkəl/ **nickels.** [1] N-U **Nickel** is a silver-coloured metal that is used in making steel. [2] N-C In the United States and Canada, a **nickel** is a coin worth five cents.

nickname /ˈnɪkneɪm/ **nicknames, nicknaming, nicknamed.** [1] N-C A **nickname** is an informal name for someone or something. *Red got his nickname for his red hair.* [2] VERB If someone or something is **nicknamed** a particular name, they are given that name as a nickname. *Which newspaper was once nicknamed The Thunderer?*

nicotine /ˈnɪkətiːn/. N-U **Nicotine** is an addictive substance in tobacco.

niece /niːs/ **nieces.** N-C Your **niece** is the daughter of your sister or brother. *... his niece from America.*

niggle /ˈnɪɡəl/ **niggles, niggling, niggled.** VERB & N-C If something **niggles** you, it makes you worry slightly over a long time. You can call a worry like this a **niggle**. *The truth might niggle him for ever... Why is there a little niggle at the back of my mind?*

night /naɪt/ **nights.** [1] N-VAR The **night** is the part of each period of twenty-four hours when it is dark outside, especially the time when most people are sleeping. *He didn't leave the house all night... Finally night fell.* [2] N-C The **night** is the period of time between the end of the afternoon and the time that you go to bed. *So whose party was it last night?... I really enjoy going out on Friday night.* [3] N-U If you refer to a particular time at **night**, you mean a time during the part of a day after it gets dark and before midnight. *We got back about eleven o'clock at night.*
PHRASES ● If something happens **day and night** or **night and day**, it happens all the time without stopping. *His team is working day and night to finish.* ● If you have **an early night**, you go to bed early. If you have **a late night**, you go to bed late. *All I want is an early night.*

nightclub /ˈnaɪtklʌb/ **nightclubs.** N-C A **nightclub** is a place where people go late in the evening to drink and dance.

nightlife /ˈnaɪtlaɪf/. N-U The **nightlife** in a place is the entertainment and social activities that are available at night, such as nightclubs and bars. *It's a university town, with lots of nightlife.*

nightly /ˈnaɪtli/. ADJ BEFORE N & ADV A **nightly** event happens every night. *Air raids were a nightly occurrence... Dinner is served nightly.*

nightmare /ˈnaɪtmeə/ **nightmares.** [1] N-C A **nightmare** is a very frightening dream. *All the victims still suffered nightmares.* [2] N-C If you say that an experience is a **nightmare**, you mean that it is very unpleasant; INFORMAL. *The bus journey up there was a nightmare.*

'night time. N-U **Night time** is the period of time between when it gets dark and when the sun rises. *He likes to have his bath at night time.*

nil /nɪl/. [1] NUM **Nil** means the same as zero. It is often used in scores of sports games. *They lost two nil to Italy.* [2] N-U If you say that something is **nil**, you mean that it does not exist at all. *Their legal rights are virtually nil.*

nimble /ˈnɪmbəl/ **nimbler, nimblest.** [1] ADJ Someone who is **nimble** is able to move their fingers, hands, or legs quickly and easily. *...jobs which demand nimble fingers.* [2] ADJ Someone who has a **nimble** mind is clever and can think quickly.

nine /naɪn/ **nines.** NUM **Nine** is the number 9.

nineteen /ˌnaɪnˈtiːn/ **nineteens.** NUM **Nineteen** is the number 19.

nineteenth /ˌnaɪnˈtiːnθ/. ORD The **nineteenth** item in a series is the one that you count as number nineteen.

ninetieth /ˈnaɪntiəθ/. ORD The **ninetieth** item in a series is the one that you count as number ninety.

ninety /ˈnaɪnti/ **nineties.** NUM **Ninety** is the number 90. For examples of how numbers such as ninety and eighty are used see **eighty**.

ninth /naɪnθ/. ORD The **ninth** item in a series is the one that you count as number nine.

nip /nɪp/ **nips, nipping, nipped.** [1] VERB If you **nip** somewhere, usually somewhere nearby, you go there quickly or for a short time; INFORMAL, BRITISH. *Should I nip out and get some groceries?* [2] VERB If a person or an animal **nips** you, they pinch or bite you lightly. *He was nipped by a rat.* ● to **nip** something **in the bud**: see **bud**.

nipple /ˈnɪpəl/ **nipples.** N-C The **nipples** on someone's body are the two small pieces of slightly hard flesh on their chest. Babies suck milk through their mothers' nipples. *Sore nipples can inhibit milk supply.*

nitrate /ˈnaɪtreɪt/ **nitrates.** N-VAR A **nitrate** is a chemical compound that includes nitrogen and oxygen. Nitrates are used as fertilizers.

nitrogen /ˈnaɪtrədʒən/. N-U **Nitrogen** is a colourless element that has no smell and is usually found as a gas.

no /nəʊ/; the plural of the noun can be **noes** or **no's**. [1] CONVENTION You use **no** to give a negative answer to a question, to say that something is not true, to refuse an offer, or to refuse permission. *'Any problems?'—'No, I'm O.K.'... 'You're getting worse than me.'—'No I'm not.'... 'Here, have mine.'—'No, this is fine.'... No. I forbid it.* [2] CONVENTION You use **no** to say that you agree with or understand a negative statement that someone else has made. *'I don't know him, do I?'—'No, you don't.'* ③ CONVENTION You use **no** to express shock or disappointment at something. *Oh no, not another day of this.* ④ CONVENTION You use **no** as a way of introducing a correction to what you have just said. *It means the whole group, no, more than that, it means the entire species.* ⑤ DET You use **no** to mean not any or not one person or thing. *He had no intention of paying the cash... No letters survive from this early period.* ⑥ DET You use **no** to emphasize that someone or something is not a particular thing or does not have a particular quality. *He is no singer... Today's elections in Peking are of no great importance.* ⑦ ADV You use **no** when emphasizing that something does not exceed a particular amount or number, or does not have more of a particular quality than something else. *...no later than the end of 1994... No fewer than thirty climbers reached the summit... He will be no more effective than his predecessors.* ⑧ DET **No** is used in notices or instructions to say that a particular thing is forbidden. *...'no smoking' signs... No talking after lights out.* ⑨ N-C A **no** is the answer 'no' or a vote against something. *Is that a yes or a no?* ⑩ PHRASE If you say **there is no** doing a particular thing, you mean that it is impossible to do that thing. *There is no going back to the life she had.*

No., Nos. No. is a written abbreviation for 'number'. *...No. 10 Downing Street.*

nobility /nəʊˈbɪlɪti/. ① N-U **Nobility** is the quality of being noble; FORMAL. *...instincts of nobility and generosity.* ② N-SING The **nobility** of a society are all the people who have titles and high social rank. *They married into the nobility.*

noble /ˈnəʊbəl/ **nobler, noblest; nobles.** ① ADJ If you say that someone is a **noble** or their behaviour is **noble**, you admire and respect them because they are honest, brave, and not selfish. *He was an upright and noble man who was always willing to help.* ♦ **nobly** ADV *They have supported us nobly in this war.* ② ADJ Something that is **noble** is very impressive in quality or appearance. *...the great parks with their noble trees.* ③ ADJ & N-C If someone is **noble** or a **noble**, they belong to a high social class and have a title. *...rich and noble families.*

nobody /ˈnəʊbɒdi/ **nobodies.** ① PRON **Nobody** means not a single person. *Nobody realizes how bad things are... For a long time, nobody spoke.* ② N-C If someone says that a person is a **nobody**, they are saying in an unkind way that the person is not at all important. *A man in my position has nothing to fear from a nobody like you.*

> You do not use **nobody** or **no one** in front of **of** to talk about a particular group of people. The word you need is **none**. *None of the men have been injured... Virtually none of them know English.*

nocturnal /nɒkˈtɜːnəl/. ① ADJ **Nocturnal** means occurring at night. *...teenagers' nocturnal activities.* ② ADJ **Nocturnal** creatures are active mostly at night.

nod /nɒd/ **nods, nodding, nodded.** ① VERB & N-C If you **nod**, or if you give a **nod**, you move your head down and up to show that you are answering 'yes' to a question, or to show agreement, understanding, or approval. *'Are you okay?' I asked. She nodded... Todd agreed with a nod of his head.* ② VERB & N-C If you **nod** in a particular direction, or if you give a **nod** in a particular direction, you bend your head once in a that direction in order to indicate something. *'Does it work?' he asked, nodding at the piano... 'It was on the news earlier,' said Leo, with a nod towards the television.* ③ VERB & N-C If you **nod**, or if you give a **nod**, you bend your head once, as a way of saying hello or goodbye. *All the girls nodded and said 'Hi'... He gave Sabrina a quick nod of acknowledgement.*

▸ **nod off.** PHR-VERB If you **nod off**, you fall asleep, especially when you had not intended to; INFORMAL. *I almost nodded off listening to it.*

noise /nɔɪz/ **noises.** ① N-U **Noise** is a loud or unpleasant sound. *There was too much noise in the room.* ② N-C A **noise** is a sound that someone or something makes. *...animal noises... He heard a noise somewhere under his window.*

noisy /ˈnɔɪzi/ **noisier, noisiest.** ① ADJ Someone or something that is **noisy** makes a lot of loud or unpleasant noise. *...my noisy old typewriter.* ♦ **noisily** ADV *He slammed the car door noisily.* ② ADJ A place that is **noisy** is full of loud or unpleasant noise. *...the crowded and noisy terrace of the cafe.*

nomadic /nəʊˈmædɪk/. ADJ **Nomadic** people travel from place to place rather than living in one place all the time. *...gypsies who have given up their nomadic way of life.*

'no-man's land. N-U **No-man's land** is an area of land that is not owned or controlled by anyone, for example the area of land between two opposing armies. *...the no-man's land between the Jordanian and Iraqi frontier posts.*

nominal /ˈnɒmɪnəl/. ① ADJ You use **nominal** to indicate that someone or something is supposed to have a particular identity or status, but in reality does not have it. *As he was still not allowed to run a company, his wife became its nominal head.* ♦ **nominally** ADV *...South Africa's nominally independent homeland of Transkei.* ② ADJ A **nominal** price or sum of money is very small in comparison with the real cost or value of the thing that is being bought or sold. *All the ferries carry bicycles free or for a nominal charge.*

nominate /ˈnɒmɪneɪt/ **nominates, nominating, nominated.** VERB If someone is **nominated** for a job, position, or prize, their name is formally suggested as a candidate for it. *The UN Secretary General has nominated Mrs Ogata as its next High Commissioner for Refugees.*

nomination /ˌnɒmɪˈneɪʃən/ **nominations.** N-C A **nomination** is an official suggestion of someone for a job, position, or prize. *...a list of nominations for senior lectureships.*

nominee /ˌnɒmɪˈniː/ **nominees.** N-C A **nominee** is someone who is nominated for something. *...nominees for the 1992 Nobel Peace Prize.*

nonchalant /ˈnɒnʃələnt, AM -ˈlɑːnt/. ADJ Someone who is **nonchalant** seems very calm and appears not to worry or care about things. *Denis tried to look nonchalant and uninterested.* ♦**nonchalance** /ˈnɒnʃələns, AM -ˈlɑːns/ N-U *Despite everyone's apparent nonchalance the air crackled with nervous energy.* ♦**nonchalantly** ADV *'Does Will intend to return with us?' Joanna asked as nonchalantly as she could.*

none /nʌn/. QUANT **None of** something means not even a small amount of it. *None of* a group of people or things means not even one of them. *She did none of the maintenance on the vehicle... None of us knew how to treat her... They asked me for fresh ideas, but I had none.*

PHRASES • You use **none the** to say that someone or something does not have any more of a particular quality than they did before. *He became convinced that his illness was purely imaginary: that made it none the better.* • You use **none too** in front of an adjective or adverb in order to emphasize that the quality mentioned is not present. *He was none too thrilled to hear from me at that hour.*

nonetheless /ˌnʌnðəˈles/. ADV You use **nonetheless** when saying something that contrasts with what has just been said; FORMAL. *His face is serious but nonetheless very friendly.*

non-ex'istent. ADJ If you say that something is **non-existent**, you mean that it does not exist when you feel that it should. *Hygiene was non-existent: no running water, no bathroom.*

no-'nonsense. ADJ If you describe someone as a **no-nonsense** person or something as a **no-nonsense** thing, you approve of the fact that they are efficient and concentrate on important matters rather than trivial things. *The decor is straightforward and no- nonsense.*

nonsense /ˈnɒnsəns/. [1] N-U If you say that something spoken or written is **nonsense**, you mean that you consider it to be untrue or silly. *...all that poetic nonsense about love... 'I'm putting on weight.'—'Nonsense my dear.'* [2] N-U You can use **nonsense** to refer to something that you think is foolish or that you disapprove of. *I think there is a limit to how much of this nonsense people are going to put up with.* [3] PHRASE To **make a nonsense** of something or to **make nonsense of** it means to make it seem ridiculous or pointless. *The fighting made a nonsense of peace pledges made in London last week.*

non-'smoker, non-smokers. N-C A **non-smoker** is someone who does not smoke.

non-'stick. ADJ **Non-stick** cooking equipment such as pans or baking tins has a special coating, which prevents food from sticking to it.

non-'stop (or **nonstop**). ADJ Something that is **non-stop** continues without any pauses or breaks. *...80 minutes of non-stop music.*

non-'violent. [1] ADJ **Non-violent** methods of bringing about change do not involve hurting people or causing damage. ♦**non-violence** N-U *...a firm public commitment to non-violence.* [2] ADJ You can refer to someone or to something such as a crime as **non-violent** when that person or thing does not hurt or injure people. *...non-violent offenders.*

noodles /ˈnuːdəlz/. N-C **Noodles** are long, thin pieces of pasta.

noon /nuːn/. N-U **Noon** is twelve o'clock in the middle of the day. *The long day of meetings started at noon.*

'no one (or **no-one**). PRON **No-one** means not a single person, or not a single member of a particular group or set. *No one can open mail except the person to whom it has been addressed.* • See note at **nobody**.

noose /nuːs/ **nooses**. N-C A **noose** is a loop at the end of a piece of rope or wire that is used to trap animals or hang people.

nope /nəʊp/. CONVENTION **Nope** is sometimes used instead of 'no' as a response; INFORMAL SPOKEN. *'Has the prisoner next door talked to you'—'Nope,' the man answered.*

nor /nɔː/. [1] CONJ You use **nor** after 'neither' to introduce the second thing that a negative statement applies to. *Neither Mr Rose nor Mr Woodhead was available for comment... I can give you neither an opinion nor any advice.* [2] CONJ You use **nor** after a negative statement in order to indicate that the negative statement also applies to you or to someone or something else. *'If my husband has no future,' she said, 'then nor do my children.'.*

norm /nɔːm/ **norms**. [1] N-C **Norms** are ways of behaving that are considered normal in a particular society. *...the commonly accepted norms of democracy. ...a social norm that says drunkenness is inappropriate behaviour.* [2] N-SING If you say that a situation is **the norm**, you mean that it is usual and expected. *Families of six or seven are the norm in Borough Park.*

normal /ˈnɔːməl/. ADJ Something that is **normal** is usual and ordinary, and in accordance with what people expect. *There's no reason why you can't have a perfectly normal child... The two countries resumed normal diplomatic relations.*

normality /nɔːˈmælɪti/. N-U **Normality** is a situation in which everything is normal. *A semblance of normality has returned.*

normalize (BR also **normalise**) /ˈnɔːmǝlaɪz/ **normalizes, normalizing, normalized.** VERB When you **normalize** a situation, or when it **normalizes**, it becomes normal or returns to normal. *Vietnam has been pressing for some time to normalise ties. ...some deep-seated emotional reason which has to be dealt with before your eating habits normalize.* ♦**normalization** N-U *...the normalisation of diplomatic relations between them.*

normally /ˈnɔːməli/. [1] ADV If you say that something **normally** happens or that you **normally** do a particular thing, you mean that it is what usually happens or what you usually do. *All airports in the country are working normally today... Normally, the transportation system in Paris carries 950,000 passengers a day.* [2] ADV If you do something **normally**, you do it in the usual or conventional way. *She would apparently eat normally and then make herself sick.*

north /nɔːθ/. **1** N-SING The **north** is the direction on your left when you are looking towards the direction where the sun rises. *Birds usually migrate from north to south.* **2** N-SING & ADJ The **north** of a place or the **north** part of it is the part which is towards the north. *...people in the North and Midlands. ...the north coast of Crete.* **3** ADV **North** means towards the north, or positioned to the north of a place. *Anita drove north up Pacific Highway. ...a little village a few miles north of Portsmouth.* **4** ADJ A **north** wind blows from the north.

north-'east. **1** N-SING The **north-east** is the direction halfway between north and east. *The land to the north-east fell away into meadows.* **2** N-SING & ADJ The **north-east** of a place or the north-east part of it is the part which is towards the north-east. *...in the north-east of England. ...the north-east outskirts of London.* **3** ADV **North-east** means towards the north-east, or positioned to the north-east of a place or thing. *...army convoys moving north-east. ...Careysburg, twenty miles north-east of the capital, Monrovia.* **4** ADJ A **north-east** wind blows from the north-east.

north-'eastern (or **north eastern**). ADJ **North-eastern** means in or from the north-east of a region or country. *...the north-eastern coast of the United States.*

northerly /ˈnɔːðəli/. **1** ADJ **Northerly** means towards the north. *...the most northerly island in the British Isles... I wanted to go a more northerly route across Montana.* **2** ADJ A **northerly** wind blows from the north.

northern /ˈnɔːðən/. ADJ **Northern** means in or from the north of a region or country. *...Northern Ireland... Prices at three-star hotels fell furthest in several northern cities.*

northward /ˈnɔːθwəd/ (or **northwards**) /ˈnɔːθwədz/. ADV & ADJ **Northward** or **northwards** means towards the north. *...the flow of immigrants northward... The northward journey from Jalalabad was no more than 120 miles.*

north-'west. **1** N-SING The **north-west** is the direction halfway between north and west. *...Ushant, five miles out to the north-west.* **2** N-SING & ADJ The **north-west** of a place or the north-west part of it is the part which is towards the north-west. *...the extreme north-west of South America. ...the North-West Regional Health Authority.* **3** ADV **North-west** means towards the north-west, or positioned to the north-west of a place or thing. *Take the narrow lane going north-west parallel with the railway line.* **4** ADJ A **north-west** wind blows from the north-west.

north-'western. ADJ **North-western** means in or from the north-west of a region or country. *He was from north-western Russia.*

nose /nəʊz/ **noses, nosing, nosed.** **1** N-C Your **nose** is the part of your face which sticks out above your mouth. You use it for smelling and breathing. *She wiped her nose with a tissue.* **2** N-C The **nose** of a car or plane is its front part. **3** PHRASE If you do something **under** someone's **nose**, you do it in front of them, so that they could easily see you doing it. *She stole items from right under the noses of other shoppers.*

nostalgia /nɒˈstældʒə/. N-U **Nostalgia** is an affectionate feeling for things you have experienced in the past. *...nostalgia for his happy youth.*

nostalgic /nɒsˈtældʒɪk/. ADJ If you feel **nostalgic**, you think affectionately about experiences you have had in the past. *Many people were nostalgic for the good old days.* ♦ **nostalgically** ADV *People look back nostalgically on the period.*

nostril /ˈnɒstrɪl/ **nostrils.** N-C Your **nostrils** are the two openings at the end of your nose.

not /nɒt/. **1** You use **not**, usually in the form **n't**, to form questions to which you expect the answer 'yes'. *Haven't they got enough problems there already?* **2** You use **not**, usually in the form **n't**, in questions which imply that someone should have done something or should do something, or to express surprise that something is not the case. *Why didn't you do it months ago?... Hasn't anyone ever kissed you before?* **3** You use **not**, usually in the form **n't**, in question tags after a positive statement. *You will take me tomorrow, won't you?* **4** You use **not**, usually in the form **n't**, in polite suggestions. *Why don't you fill out our application?* **5** You use **not** to represent the negative of a word, group, or clause that has just been used. *'Have you found Paula?'—'I'm afraid not.'... I really didn't care whether he came or not.* **6** You use **not** before 'all', 'every', or 'always' to say that there are exceptions to something that is generally true. You also use **not** before words like 'only' and 'just' to say that something is true, but it is not the whole truth. *Not every applicant had a degree... Brendel is not only a great pianist, but a great musician.* **7** You can use **not** or **not even** in front of 'a' or 'one' to emphasize that there is none at all of what is being mentioned. *I sent report after report. But not one word was published.* **8** You use **not** when you are contrasting something that is true with something that people might wrongly believe to be true. *Training is an investment not a cost.* **9** CONJ You use **not that** to introduce a negative clause that contradicts or modifies what the previous statement implies. *His death took me a year to get over; not that you're ever really over it.* **10** CONVENTION **Not at all** is an emphatic way of saying 'No' or of agreeing that the answer to a question is 'No'. *'Sorry. I sound like Abby, don't I?'—'No. Not at all.'* **11** **not least:** see **least**. • **not to mention:** see **mention**. • **nothing if not:** see **nothing**. • **more often than not:** see **often**.

notable /ˈnəʊtəbəl/. ADJ Something or someone that is **notable** is important or interesting. *...a sleepy fishing town notable for its church.* • See note at **famous**.

notably /ˈnəʊtəbli/. ADV You use **notably** before mentioning the most important example of the thing you are talking about. *...more important problems, notably the fate of the children.*

notch /nɒtʃ/ **notches, notching, notched.** **1** N-C A **notch** is a small V-shaped or circular cut in the surface or edge of something. **2** N-C You can refer to a step on a scale of measurement or achievement as a **notch**; JOURNALISM. *Average earnings in the economy moved up another notch in August.*

▸ **notch up.** PHR-VERB If you **notch up** something such as a score or total, you achieve it; JOURNALISM. *Selfridges notched up sales worth £1 million before lunch.*

note /nəʊt/ **notes, noting, noted.** ① N-C A **note** is a short letter. *I'll have to leave a note for Karen. Remember to write a note to say where you are.* ② N-C A **note** is something that you write down to remind you about something. *Take notes during the consultation.* ③ VERB & PHR-VERB When you **note** something, or when you **note** it **down**, you write it down so that you have a record of it. You can also say that a piece of writing **notes** something when it is recorded there. *She was, she noted in her diary, 'very indignant with him.'... He noted down the address... The report notes that a dramatic drop in military violence took place.* ④ VERB If you **note** a fact, you become aware of it. *Those who met her noted the facial resemblance to the famous actress... Please note that there are a limited number of tickets.* ⑤ N-C In a book or article, a **note** is a short piece of additional information. *See Note 16 on page p. 223.* ⑥ N-C In music, a **note** is a sound of a particular pitch, or a written symbol representing this sound. ⑦ N-C In British English, a **note** is a piece of paper money. The usual American word is **bill**. *...a five pound note.* ⑧ N-SING You can use **note** to refer to a quality or feeling that something has, or the impression that it gives you. You can say that someone or something strikes or sounds a particular **note**. *He could discern the note of urgency in their voices... The film ends on a positive note... He welcomed the campaign but sounded a note of caution.*

PHRASES ● If you **compare notes** with someone or the two of you **compare notes**, you talk to them and find out whether they have the same opinion, information, or experiences as yourself. *...the chance to compare notes with other suffering mothers.* ● Someone or something that is **of note** is important, worth mentioning, or well-known. *He has published nothing of note in the last ten years.* ● If you **take note** of something, you pay attention to it because you think that it is important. *He advises you to take note of where the exits are.* ● See also **noted**.

▸ **note down** See **note** ③.

notebook /ˈnəʊtbʊk/ **notebooks.** N-C A **notebook** is a small book for writing notes in.

noted /ˈnəʊtɪd/. ADJ Someone who is **noted** for something they do or have is well-known and admired for it. *...a television programme noted for its attacks on organised crime.*

nothing /ˈnʌθɪŋ/. ① PRON **Nothing** means not a single thing, or not a single part of something. *He said nothing to reporters... There is nothing wrong with the car.* ② PRON You use **nothing** to indicate that something or someone is not important or significant. *Because he had always had money it meant nothing to him... She kept bursting into tears over nothing.*

PHRASES ● **Nothing but** a particular thing means only that thing. *All that money brought*

nothing but sadness... She did nothing but complain about him.* ● You use **nothing if not** to indicate that someone or something clearly has a lot of a particular quality. *Professor Fish has been nothing if not professional.* ● You can use **nothing less than** to emphasize your next words, often indicating that something seems very surprising or important. *You're nothing less than a murderer!* ● You say **nothing of the sort** to emphasize a refusal or a negative statement. *It was supposed to have been a triumph. It was nothing of the sort.* ● to **say nothing of**: see **say**. ● to **think nothing of**: see **think**.

notice /ˈnəʊtɪs/ **notices, noticing, noticed.** ① VERB If you **notice** something, you become aware of it. *You didn't notice anything special about him?... Mrs Shedden noticed a bird sitting on the garage... He noticed he was acting strangely.* ② PHRASE If something **comes to** your **notice** or **is brought to** your **notice**, you become aware of it. If it **escapes** your **notice**, you are not aware of it. *He was later thanked for bringing the matter to their notice.* ③ PHRASE If you **take notice** of something, you pay attention to it. *Noel was someone people took notice of... I always knew something was wrong, but no one would take any notice.* ④ N-C A **notice** is a written announcement in a place where everyone can read it. *A few guest houses had 'No Vacancies' notices in their windows.* ⑤ N-U **Notice** is advanced warning about something. *I was given four days' notice to prepare for the wedding... She was transferred without notice... Thank you all for coming along at such short notice.*

PHRASES ● If a situation will exist **until further notice**, it will continue until someone changes it. ● If your employer **gives** you **notice**, he or she tells you that you must leave within a set period of time. If you **give notice** or **hand in** your **notice**, you tell your employer that you intend to leave within a set period of time.

noticeable /ˈnəʊtɪsəbəl/. ADJ Something that is **noticeable** is very obvious, so that it is easy to see or recognize. *It was noticeable that his face and arms were red.* ◆**noticeably** ADV *The baby became noticeably more agitated.*

notify /ˈnəʊtɪfaɪ/ **notifies, notifying, notified.** VERB If you **notify** someone of something, you officially inform them of it. *We have notified the police.* ◆**notification** /ˌnəʊtɪfɪˈkeɪʃən/ **notifications** N-VAR *All clubs should have received notification by now.*

notion /ˈnəʊʃən/ **notions.** N-C A **notion** is a belief or idea. *...the notion that pornography degrades women.*

notoriety /ˌnəʊtəˈraɪɪti/. N-U If someone or something achieves **notoriety**, they become well-known for something bad.

notorious /nəʊˈtɔːriəs/. ADJ Someone or something that is **notorious** is well known for something bad. *The area is notorious for drug dealing.* ◆**notoriously** ADV *Doctors notoriously neglect their own health.* ● See note at **famous.**

notwithstanding /ˌnɒtwɪðˈstændɪŋ/. PREP & ADV If something is true **notwithstanding** something else, it is true in spite of that other thing; FORMAL. *He despised William Pitt, not-*

withstanding the similar views they both held... Such realism notwithstanding, the film was a disaster.

nought /nɔːt/ **noughts. Nought** is the number 0.

noun /naʊn/ **nouns.** N-C A **noun** is a word such as 'woman', 'guilt', or 'John' which is used to refer to a person or thing.

nourish /ˈnʌrɪʃ, AM ˈnɜːrɪʃ/ **nourishes, nourishing, nourished.** VERB To **nourish** a person, animal, or plant means to provide them with the food that is necessary for growth and health. *...microbes in the soil which nourish the plant.* ♦ **nourishing** ADJ *...sensible, nourishing food.* ♦ **nourishment** N-U *Breast milk is your baby's best source of nourishment.*

novel /ˈnɒvəl/ **novels.** [1] N-C A **novel** is a book containing a long story about imaginary people and events. [2] ADJ **Novel** things are unlike anything that has been done, experienced, or created before. *...taking scraps of past music and making them into something novel.*

novelist /ˈnɒvəlɪst/ **novelists.** N-C A **novelist** is a person who writes novels. *...a romantic novelist*

novelty /ˈnɒvəlti/ **novelties.** [1] N-U **Novelty** is the quality of being different, new, and unusual. *The novelty of the situation intrigued him.* [2] N-C A **novelty** is something that is new and therefore interesting. *...the days when a motor car was a novelty.* [3] N-C **Novelties** are cheap unusual objects sold as gifts or souvenirs.

November /nəʊˈvembə/. N-U **November** is the eleventh month of the year.

novice /ˈnɒvɪs/ **novices.** N-C A **novice** is someone who has been doing a job or other activity for only a short time and so is not experienced at it. *Most of us are novices on the computer. ...a novice writer.*

now /naʊ/. [1] ADV & PRON You use **now** to refer to the present time, often in contrast to the past or the future. *Beef now costs well over 30 roubles a pound... I must go now... She should know that by now... Now is your chance to talk to him.* [2] CONJ You use **now** or **now that** to indicate that an event has occurred and as a result something else may or will happen. *Now you're settled, why don't you take up some serious study?* [3] ADV You use **now** in statements which specify the length of time up to the present that something has lasted. *They've been married now for 30 years.* [4] ADV You can say **'Now'** to introduce new information into a story or account. *Now, I hadn't told him these details, so he must have done some research on his own.*
[PHRASES] ● If you say that something will happen **any day now**, **any moment now**, or **any time now**, you mean that it will happen very soon. *We were expecting him home again any day now.* ● **Just now** means a very short time ago. *You looked pretty upset just now.* ● If you say that something happens **now and then** or **every now and again**, you mean that it happens sometimes but not very often or regularly. *Now and then they heard the roar of a heavy truck.*

nowadays /ˈnaʊədeɪz/. ADV **Nowadays** means at the present time, in contrast with the past. *I don't see much of Tony nowadays.*

nowhere /ˈnəʊweə/. [1] ADV You use **nowhere** to emphasize that a place has more of a particular quality than any other places, or that it is the only place where something happens or exists. *Nowhere is language a more serious issue than in Hawaii... This kind of forest exists nowhere else in the world.* [2] ADV You use **nowhere** when making negative statements to say that a suitable place of the specified kind does not exist. *There was nowhere to hide and nowhere to run... I have nowhere else to go.*
[PHRASES] ● If you say that something or someone appears **from nowhere** or **out of nowhere**, you mean that they appear suddenly and unexpectedly. *A car came from nowhere, and I had to jump back.* ● If you say that you **are getting nowhere** or that something **is getting** you **nowhere**, you mean that you are not achieving anything or having any success. *Oh, stop it! This is getting us nowhere.* ● If you say that a place is **in the middle of nowhere**, you mean it is a long way from other places. ● **nowhere near:** see **near**.

nuance /ˈnjuːɑːns, AM ˈnuː-/ **nuances.** N-VAR A **nuance** is a small and subtle difference in sound, feeling, appearance, or meaning. *...every subtle nuance of emotion.*

nuclear /ˈnjuːkliə, AM ˈnuːk-/. ADJ BEFORE N **Nuclear** means relating to the nuclei of atoms, or to the energy produced when these nuclei are split or combined. *...a nuclear power station. ...nuclear weapons.*

nuclear reˈactor, nuclear reactors. N-C A **nuclear reactor** is a machine which produces nuclear energy.

nucleus /ˈnjuːkliəs, AM ˈnuː-/ **nuclei.** [1] N-C The **nucleus** of an atom or cell is the central part of it. [2] N-C The **nucleus** of a group of people is the small number of members which form the most important part of the group. *...the nucleus of people who started Private Eye magazine.*

nude /njuːd, AM nuːd/ **nudes.** [1] ADJ & PHRASE Someone who is **nude** or who is **in the nude** is not wearing any clothes. ♦ **nudity** /ˈnjuːdɪti, AM ˈnuː-/ N-U *...nudity and bad language on TV.* [2] N-C A **nude** is a picture or statue of a nude person.

nudge /nʌdʒ/ **nudges, nudging, nudged.** VERB & N-C If you **nudge** someone, or if you give them a **nudge**, you push them gently with your elbow. *I nudged Alexander and pointed again.*

nuisance /ˈnjuːsəns, AM ˈnuː-/ **nuisances.** N-C If you say that someone or something is a **nuisance**, you mean that they annoy you or cause you problems. If you say that someone **makes a nuisance** of themselves, you mean that they are a nuisance. *He could be a bit of a nuisance when he was drunk.*

numb /nʌm/ **numbs, numbing, numbed.** [1] ADJ If a part of your body is **numb**, you cannot feel anything there. *He could feel his fingers growing numb.* ♦ **numbness** N-U *Nerve injury can cause numbness in the thigh.* [2] VERB If a blow or cold weather **numbs** a part of your

number 418

body, you can no longer feel anything in it. *The cold numbed my fingers.* **3** ADJ If you are **numb** with shock or fear, you are so shocked or frightened that you cannot think clearly or feel any emotion. **4** VERB If an event or experience **numbs** you, you can no longer think clearly or feel any emotion. ◆**numbed** ADJ *I'm so numbed with shock that I can hardly think.*

number /ˈnʌmbə/ **numbers, numbering, numbered.** **1** N-C A **number** is a word such as 'two', 'nine', or 'twelve', or a symbol such as 1, 3, or 47, which is used in counting something. *I don't know the room number. ...number 3, Argyll Street.* **2** N-C Someone's **number** is the series of digits that you dial when you telephone them. *Sarah sat down and dialled a number... 'You must have a wrong number,' she said. 'There's no one of that name here.'* **3** VERB If you **number** something, you give it a number in a series and write the number on it. *He cut his paper up into tiny squares, and he numbered each one.* **4** N-C You use **number** with words such as 'large' or 'small' to say approximately how many things or people there are. *I have had an enormous number of letters.* **5** N-SING If there are **a number of** things or people, there are several of them. If there are **any number of** things or people, there is a large quantity of them. *Sam told a number of lies... There must be any number of people in my position.* **6** VERB If a group of people or things **numbers** a particular total, that is how many there are. *a paramilitary force which numbered 100,000 men.*

,**number 'one.** ADJ **Number one** means better, more important, or more popular than anything else of its kind. *The economy is the number one issue by far.*

'**number plate, number plates.** N-C In British English, a **number plate** is a sign on the front and back of a vehicle that shows its registration number. The American expression is **license plate.**

numerical /njuːˈmerɪkəl, AM ˈnuː-/. ADJ **Numerical** means expressed in numbers or relating to numbers. *Put them in numerical order.* ◆**numerically** ADV *...a numerically small nation.*

numerous /ˈnjuːmərəs, AM ˈnuːm-/. ADJ If people or things are **numerous**, they exist or are present in large numbers. *Sex crimes were just as numerous as they are today.*

nun /nʌn/ **nuns.** N-C A **nun** is a member of a female religious community.

nurse /nɜːs/ **nurses, nursing, nursed.** **1** N-C

A **nurse** is a person whose job is to care for people who are ill. **2** VERB If you **nurse** someone, you care for them while they are ill. *In hospital they nursed me back to health.* ◆**nursing** N-U *I wanted to go into something like nursing or dentistry.*

nursery /ˈnɜːsəri/ **nurseries.** **1** N-C A **nursery** is a place where children who are not old enough to go to school are looked after. *Her company ran its own workplace nursery.* **2** N-C A **nursery** is a place where plants are grown in order to be sold to the public.

'**nursery rhyme, nursery rhymes.** N-C A **nursery rhyme** is a traditional poem or song for young children.

'**nursing home, nursing homes.** N-C A **nursing home** is a private hospital for old people.

nurture /ˈnɜːtʃə/ **nurtures, nurturing, nurtured.** **1** VERB If you **nurture** a young child or a young plant, you care for it while it is growing and developing; FORMAL. *Parents want to know the best way to nurture and raise their child.* **2** VERB If you **nurture** plans, ideas, or people, you encourage their development and success; FORMAL. *She has always interrupted her own work to nurture the talent of others.*

nut /nʌt/ **nuts.** **1** N-C The firm shelled fruit of some trees and bushes are called **nuts.** **2** N-C A **nut** is a small piece of metal with a hole through which you put a bolt. Nuts and bolts are used to hold things together such as pieces of machinery.

nutrient /ˈnjuːtriənt, AM ˈnuː-/ **nutrients.** N-C **Nutrients** are chemical substances that people and animals need from food and plants need from soil. *...minerals and other essential nutrients.*

nutrition /njuːˈtrɪʃən, AM ˈnuː-/. N-U **Nutrition** is the process of taking and absorbing nutrients from food. *There are alternative sources of nutrition to animal meat.*

nutritional /njuːˈtrɪʃənəl, AM ˈnuː-/. ADJ The **nutritional** content of food is all the proteins, vitamins, and minerals that are in it which help you to remain healthy. ◆**nutritionally** ADV *...a nutritionally balanced diet.*

nutritious /njuːˈtrɪʃəs, AM nuː-/. ADJ **Nutritious** food contains the proteins, vitamins, and minerals which help your body to be healthy. *...a hot, nutritious meal.*

nylon /ˈnaɪlɒn/. N-U **Nylon** is a strong, flexible, artificial material. *Green nylon nets were piled up.*

oak /əʊk/ **oaks.** N-VAR An **oak** or an **oak tree** is a type of large tree. **Oak** is the wood of this tree. *...a stout oak door.*

oar /ɔː/ **oars.** N-C **Oars** are long poles with flat ends which are used for rowing a boat.

oasis /əʊˈeɪsɪs/ **oases** /əʊˈeɪsiːz/. **1** N-C An **oasis** is a small area in a desert where water and plants are found. **2** N-C You can refer to any pleasant place or situation as an **oasis**

when it is surrounded by unpleasant ones. *The gardens are an oasis in the midst of Cairo's urban sprawl.*

oath /əʊθ/ **oaths.** **1** N-C An **oath** is a formal promise. *He took an oath of loyalty to the government.* **2** N-SING In a court of law, if someone takes **the oath**, they formally promise to tell the truth . You can say that someone is on

oath or **under oath** when they have made this promise.

oats /əʊts/. N-C **Oats** are a cereal crop or its grains, used for making porridge or for feeding animals.

obedient /əʊˈbiːdiənt/. ADJ An **obedient** person or animal does what they are told to do. *He was always very obedient to his parents.* ♦**obedience** N-U *...unquestioning obedience to the law.* ♦**obediently** ADV *He was looking obediently at Keith.*

obese /əʊˈbiːs/. ADJ Someone who is **obese** is extremely fat. *Three-fifths of English women are overweight or obese.* ♦**obesity** N-U *There is a link between diet, obesity, and disease.* ● See note at **fat**.

obey /əʊˈbeɪ/. **obeys, obeying, obeyed.** VERB If you **obey** a rule, instruction, or person, you do what you are told to do. *Most people obey the law... It was Baker's duty to obey.*

obituary /əʊˈbɪtjʊəri, AM -tʃʊeri/. **obituaries.** N-C Someone's **obituary** is an account of their character and achievements which is published shortly after they have died. *I read your brother's obituary in the Times.*

object, objects, objecting, objected. ① N-C /ˈɒbdʒɪkt/ An **object** is anything that has a fixed shape or form and that is not alive. *...an object the shape of a coconut. ...everyday objects such as wooden spoons.* ② N-C The **object** of what someone is doing is their aim or purpose. *The object of the exercise is to raise money.* ③ N-C The **object of** a particular feeling or reaction is the person or thing it is directed towards, or the person or thing that causes it. *The object of her hatred was 24-year-old Ros French.* ④ N-C In grammar, the **object** of a clause is a noun group which refers to a person or thing that is affected by the action of the verb. In the sentence 'She married a young engineer', 'a young engineer' is the object. ● See also **direct object, indirect object**. ⑤ PHRASE If you say, for example, that **money is no object**, you are emphasizing that you are willing or able to spend as much money as necessary. *For him price is no object.* ⑥ VERB /əbˈdʒekt/ If you **object** to something, you express your dislike or disapproval of it. *Working people everywhere object to paying taxes... The Labour Party objects that the government's scheme is elitist.*

objection /əbˈdʒekʃən/. **objections.** N-VAR If you make an **objection** to something, you say that you do not like it or agree with it. *Two main objections to the proposal have been raised... I have no objection to banks making money.*

objective /əbˈdʒektɪv/. **objectives.** ① N-C Your **objective** is what you are trying to achieve. *His objective was to win.* ② ADJ BEFORE N **Objective** means based on facts and not influenced by personal feelings. *He had no objective evidence that anything extraordinary was happening... A journalist should be completely objective.* ♦**objectively** ADV *We simply want to inform people objectively about events.* ♦**objectivity** /ˌɒbdʒekˈtɪvɪti/ N-U *...the objectivity of science.*

obligation /ˌɒblɪˈgeɪʃən/. **obligations.** N-VAR If you have an **obligation** to do something, it is your duty to do it. If you have an **obligation** to a person, it is your duty to look after them. *He had not felt an obligation to help save his friend... We have an obligation to the children.*

obligatory /əˈblɪgətri, AM -tɔːri/. ① ADJ If something is **obligatory**, you must do it, because there is a rule or law about it. *Sixteenth-century dress was obligatory for guests. ...an obligatory AIDS test.* ② ADJ BEFORE N If you describe something as **obligatory**, you mean that it is done from habit or custom rather than out of enthusiasm. *His lips curved up in the obligatory smile.*

oblige /əˈblaɪdʒ/ **obliges, obliging, obliged.** ① VERB If you **oblige** someone, you help them by doing what they have asked you to do. *If you ever need help with the babysitting, I'd be glad to oblige... They obliged with very straightforward answers.* ② VERB If a situation or law **obliges** you to do something, it makes it necessary for you to do it; FORMAL. *This decree obliges unions to delay strikes.*

obliged /əˈblaɪdʒd/. ADJ If you feel **obliged** to do something, you feel that you should do it, or a rule insists that you do it.

obliging /əˈblaɪdʒɪŋ/. ADJ If you describe someone as **obliging**, you think that they are willing and eager to be helpful. *...an extremely pleasant and obliging man.* ♦**obligingly** ADV *Benedict obligingly held the door open.*

oblique /əʊˈbliːk/. ADJ An **oblique** statement is not expressed directly or openly, making it difficult to understand. *Mr Golding delivered an oblique warning.* ♦**obliquely** ADV *He obliquely referred to the US.*

obliterate /əˈblɪtəreɪt/ **obliterates, obliterating, obliterated.** ① VERB If something **obliterates** an object or place, it destroys it completely. *Whole villages were obliterated by fire.* ♦**obliteration** N-U *...the obliteration of three rainforests.* ② VERB If you **obliterate** something such as a memory or emotion, you remove it completely from your mind; LITERARY. *There was time enough to obliterate memories of how things once were.*

oblivion /əˈblɪviən/. ① N-U **Oblivion** is the state of not being aware of what is happening around you, for example because you are asleep or unconscious. *He had slipped once again into deep and dreamless oblivion.* ② N-U **Oblivion** is the state of having been forgotten. *His football career seemed to be heading for oblivion.*

oblivious /əˈblɪviəs/. ADJ If you are **oblivious** to something, you are not aware of it. *She lay motionless where she was, oblivious to pain.*

obnoxious /ɒbˈnɒkʃəs/. ADJ If you describe someone as **obnoxious**, you think that they are very unpleasant. *He was a most obnoxious character. No-one liked him.*

obscene /ɒbˈsiːn/. ADJ If you describe something as **obscene**, you mean it offends you because it relates to sex or violence in an unpleasant and shocking way. *I think all these photographs are obscene.*

obscenity /ɒbˈsenɪti/. **obscenities.** ① N-U **Obscenity** is behaviour that offends people because it relates to sex in an unpleasant or indecent way. *The photographs were not art but ob-*

scenity. [2] N-C An **obscenity** is a very rude word or expression. *They shouted obscenities at us.*

obscure /əbˈskjʊə/ **obscurer, obscurest; obscures, obscuring, obscured.** [1] ADJ If something or someone is **obscure**, they are unknown, or are known by only a few people. *The origin of the custom is obscure. ...an obscure Greek composer.* ♦**obscurity** N-U *The latter half of his life was spent in obscurity.* [2] VERB If one thing **obscures** another, it prevents it from being seen or heard properly. *Trees obscured his vision; he couldn't see much of the square.* [3] ADJ If you describe something as **obscure**, you find it is difficult to understand or deal with, usually because it involves so many parts or details. *The contracts are written in obscure language.* ♦**obscurity** N-U *Hunt was irritated by the obscurity of Henry's reply.*

observation /ˌɒbzəˈveɪʃən/ **observations.** [1] N-U **Observation** is the action or process of carefully watching someone or something. *...careful observation of the movement of the planets... In hospital she'll be under observation all the time.* ♦**observational** ADJ *...observational studies of the early emotional relationships of young children.* [2] N-C An **observation** is something that you have learned by seeing or watching something and thinking about it. *This book contains observations about the causes of addictions.* [3] N-C If a person makes an **observation**, they make a comment about something or someone, usually as a result of watching how they behave. *He makes the observation that writing can be a kind of salvation for certain people.* [4] N-U **Observation** is the ability to notice things that are not usually noticed. *My powers of observation and memory had improved.*

observatory /əbˈzɜːvətri, AM -tɔːri/ **observatories.** N-C An **observatory** is a building with a large telescope from which scientists study the stars and planets.

observe /əbˈzɜːv/ **observes, observing, observed.** [1] VERB If you **observe** someone or something, you watch them carefully. *Professor Stern studies and observes the behaviour of babies.* [2] VERB If you **observe** someone or something, you see or notice them; FORMAL. *Hooke observed a reddish spot on the surface of the planet.* [3] VERB If you **observe** something such as a law or custom, you obey it or follow it. *...forcing motorists to observe speed restrictions.* ♦**observance** N-U *...the observance of religious rituals.*

observer /əbˈzɜːvə/ **observers.** [1] N-C An **observer** is someone who sees or notices something. *Observers say the woman pulled a knife out and stabbed him.* [2] N-C An **observer** is someone who studies current events and situations. *...an independent political observer.*

obsess /əbˈses/ **obsesses, obsessing, obsessed.** VERB If something **obsesses** you, you keep thinking about it and find it difficult to think about anything else. *The idea of hunting big game had obsessed me since I was about six... She stopped drinking but began obsessing about her weight.* ♦**obsessed** ADJ *He was obsessed with American gangster movies.*

obsession /əbˈseʃən/ **obsessions.** N-VAR If you say that someone has an **obsession** with someone or something, you feel they are spending too much of their time thinking about that person or thing. *She would try to forget her obsession with Christopher.*

obsessive /əbˈsesɪv/. ADJ If someone's behaviour is **obsessive**, they cannot stop doing something or thinking about something. *Williams is obsessive about motor racing.* ♦**obsessively** ADV *He couldn't help worrying obsessively about what would happen.*

obsolete /ˌɒbsəˈliːt/. ADJ Something that is **obsolete** is no longer needed because a better thing now exists. *So much equipment becomes obsolete almost as soon as it's made.*

obstacle /ˈɒbstəkəl/ **obstacles.** N-C An **obstacle** is something which makes it difficult for you to go forward or do something. *A rabbit can jump obstacles up to three feet high... Overcrowding remains a large obstacle to improving housing conditions.*

obstetrician /ˌɒbstəˈtrɪʃən/ **obstetricians.** N-C An **obstetrician** is a doctor who is trained to deal with childbirth and the care of pregnant women.

obstinate /ˈɒbstɪnət/. ADJ If you describe someone as **obstinate**, you are critical of them because they are very determined to do what they want, and refuse to be persuaded to do something else. *He is obstinate and determined and will not give up.* ♦**obstinately** ADV *Smith obstinately refused to carry out the order.* ♦**obstinacy** N-U *She was capable of great obstinacy.*

obstruct /əbˈstrʌkt/ **obstructs, obstructing, obstructed.** [1] VERB To **obstruct** someone or something means to block their path, making it difficult for them to move forward. *Lorries have completely obstructed the road.* [2] VERB To **obstruct** something such as justice or progress means to prevent it from happening properly or from developing. *The authorities are obstructing a United Nations investigation.*

obstruction /əbˈstrʌkʃən/ **obstructions.** [1] N-VAR An **obstruction** is something that blocks a road or path. *...drivers parking near his house and causing an obstruction.* [2] N-U **Obstruction** is the act of deliberately preventing something from happening. *Obstruction of justice is a federal offence.*

obtain /əbˈteɪn/ **obtains, obtaining, obtained.** VERB To **obtain** something means to get it or achieve it; FORMAL. *Evans was trying to obtain a false passport.*

obvious /ˈɒbviəs/. ADJ If something is **obvious**, it is easy to see or understand. *It's obvious he's worried about us. ...her obvious creative talents.*

obviously /ˈɒbviəsli/. [1] ADV You use **obviously** when you are stating something that you expect your listener to know already. *Obviously I'd be disappointed if we don't make it, but it wouldn't be the end of the world.* [2] ADV You use **obviously** to indicate that something is easily noticed, seen, or recognized. *They obviously appreciate you very much.*

occasion /əˈkeɪʒən/ **occasions.** [1] N-C An **occasion** is a time when something happens. *On one occasion, his father threw a radio at his* mother. [2] N-C An **occasion** is an important event, ceremony, or celebration. *The launch of a ship was a big occasion.* [3] N-C An **occasion for** doing something is an opportunity for doing it; FORMAL. *It is an occasion for all the family to celebrate.* [4] PHRASE If something happens **on occasion** or **on occasions**, it happens sometimes, but not very often. *Some of the players may, on occasion, break the rules.*

occasional /əˈkeɪʒənəl/. ADJ **Occasional** means happening sometimes, but not regularly or often. *I've had occasional mild headaches.* ◆**occasionally** ADV *He still misbehaves occasionally.*

occult /ɒˈkʌlt, ˈɒkʌlt/. N-SING The **occult** is the knowledge and study of supernatural or magical forces.

occupancy /ˈɒkjʊpənsi/. N-U **Occupancy** is the act of using a room, building, or area of land for a fixed period of time. *Hotel occupancy has been as low as 40%.*

occupant /ˈɒkjʊpənt/ **occupants**. N-C The **occupants** of a building or room are the people who live or work there. *Most of the occupants had left before the fire broke out.*

occupation /ˌɒkjʊˈpeɪʃən/ **occupations**. [1] N-C Your **occupation** is your job or your profession. ◆**occupational** ADJ *...the occupational hazards of mining.* [2] N-C An **occupation** is something that you do for pleasure or as part of your daily life. *Parachuting is a dangerous occupation.* [3] N-U The **occupation** of a country is its invasion and control by a foreign army. *The communist regime was established in Romania during the Soviet occupation.*

occupy /ˈɒkjʊpaɪ/ **occupies, occupying, occupied**. [1] VERB The people who **occupy** a building or place are the people who live or work there. *Land is, in most instances, purchased by those who occupy it.* ◆**occupier, occupiers** N-C *...junk mail addressed to 'the occupier'.* [2] PASSIVE-VERB If something such as a seat **is occupied**, someone is using it, so that it is not available for anyone else. *I saw three camp beds, two of which were occupied.* [3] VERB If something **occupies** you, or if you **occupy** yourself with it, you are busy doing it or thinking about it. *Her parliamentary career has occupied all of her time... He occupied himself with packing the car.* ◆**occupied** ADJ *I had been so occupied with other things.* [4] VERB If soldiers **occupy** a place or country, they move into it, using force in order to gain control of it. *U.S. forces now occupy a part of the country.* [5] VERB If someone or something **occupies** a particular place in a system, process, or plan, they have that place. *Many men still occupy more positions of power than women.*

occur /əˈkɜː/ **occurs, occurring, occurred**. [1] VERB When an event **occurs**, it happens. *The crash occurred on a sharp bend... Events of this description occurred daily.* [2] VERB When something **occurs** in a particular place, it exists or is present there. *Nitrates are chemicals that occur naturally in water.* [3] VERB If a thought or idea **occurs** to you, you suddenly think of it or realize it. *It did not occur to me to check my insurance policy... It occurred to me that I could have the book sent to me.*

occurrence /əˈkʌrəns, AM -ˈkɜːr-/ **occurrences**. N-C An **occurrence** is something that happens; FORMAL. *Complaints seemed to be an everyday occurrence.*

ocean /ˈəʊʃən/ **oceans**. N-C The **ocean** is the sea. *There were few sights as beautiful as the calm ocean. ...the Indian Ocean.*

o'clock /əˈklɒk/. ADV You use **o'clock** after numbers from one to twelve to say what time it is. *It's almost eight o'clock. ...ten o'clock last night.*

October /ɒkˈtəʊbə/. N-U **October** is the tenth month of the year.

octopus /ˈɒktəpəs/ **octopuses**. N-VAR An **octopus** is a sea creature with eight tentacles.

odd /ɒd/ **odder, oddest**. [1] ADJ If you say that someone or something is **odd**, you mean that they are strange or unusual. *He'd seem odd... What an odd coincidence.* ◆**oddly** ADV *...an oddly shaped hill... He was behaving extremely oddly.* [2] ADJ You use **odd** before a noun to indicate that the type or size of something is not important. *...moving from place to place where she could find the odd bit of work... He likes the odd drink.* [3] ADJ You say that two things are **odd** when they do not belong to the same set or pair. *...odd socks.* [4] ADJ **Odd** numbers cannot be divided exactly by the number two. [5] ADV You use **odd** after a number to indicate that it is approximate; INFORMAL. *I've lived here for forty odd years.*

PHRASE ● In a group of people or things, the **odd one out** is the one that is different from all the others.

oddity /ˈɒdɪti/ **oddities**. [1] N-C An **oddity** is someone or something that is strange or unusual. *Tourists are still something of an oddity.* [2] N-C The **oddity** of something is the fact that it is strange. *...one of the oddities of human intelligence.*

odds /ɒdz/. N-PL You refer to the probability of something happening as the **odds** that it will happen. *What are the odds of winning a prize?*

PHRASES ● If something happens **against** all **odds**, it happens or succeeds although it seemed impossible or very unlikely. *Some women do manage to achieve business success against all odds.* ● If you are **at odds** with someone, you are disagreeing or quarrelling with them.

odour (AM **odor**) /ˈəʊdə/ **odours**. N-C An **odour** is a smell. *...the odour of tobacco.*

odyssey /ˈɒdɪsi/ **odysseys**. N-C An **odyssey** is a long exciting journey on which a lot of things happen; LITERARY.

of /əv, STRONG ɒv, AM ʌv/. [1] PREP You use **of** to say who or what someone or something belongs to, or is connected with. *...the immaculately maintained homes of the rich. ...the new mayor of Los Angeles. ...the superb temples of India.* [2] PREP You use **of** to say what something relates to or concerns. *...feelings of jealousy. ...cancer of the breast.* [3] PREP You use **of** to say who or what a feeling or quality relates to. *I have grown very fond of Alec... She would be guilty of betraying her mother.* [4] PREP You use **of** to talk about someone or something else who is also involved in an action. *He'd been dreaming of her... The Americans cannot accuse him of ignoring the problem.* [5] PREP You use **of** to show that someone or something is part of a larger group. *Gita Saghal is the youngest child of three. ...a blade of grass.* [6] PREP You use **of** to talk about amounts. *...a rise of 13.8%. ...a glass of beer. ...eight years of war.* [7] PREP You use **of** to say how old someone or something is. *She is a young woman of twenty-six... I feel like a girl of 18.* [8] PREP You use **of** to say the date when talking about what day of the month it is. *...the 4th of July.* [9] PREP You use **of** to say when something happened. *Some of the economic errors of the past are at last being put right... Rene announced his retirement at the end of the month.* [10] PREP You use **of** to say what substance or materials something is formed from. *...a mixture of paint-thinner and petrol... The traditional thermometer is made of brass.* [11] PREP You use **of** to say what caused or is causing a person's or animal's death. *One of her ex-husbands is dying of cancer.* [12] PREP You use **of** to talk about someone's qualities or characteristics. *Andrew is a man of honour... She's a woman of few words, but the few words are potent.* [13] PREP You use **of** to describe someone's behaviour. *That's very kind of you.*

of 'course. [1] ADV You say **of course** to say that something is not surprising because it is normal, obvious, or well-known. *Of course there were lots of other interesting things at the exhibition.* [2] ADV You use **of course** in order to emphasize a statement that you are making. *Of course I'm not afraid!* [3] CONVENTION You say **of course** as a polite way of giving permission; SPOKEN. *'Could I see these documents?'—'Of course.'* [4] CONVENTION **Of course not** is an emphatic way of saying no; SPOKEN. *'You won't tell him, will you?'—'Of course not.'*

off /ɒf, AM ɔːf/. [1] PREP & ADV When something is taken **off** something else or moves **off** it, it is no longer touching that thing. *He took his feet off the desk... Hugh wiped the blood off his face... Lee broke off a small piece of orange.* [2] PREP & ADV When you get **off** a bus, train, or plane, you get out of it. *As he stepped off the aeroplane, he was shot dead... At the next stop the man got off too and introduced himself.* [3] ADV When you go **off**, you leave the place where you were. *He was just about to drive off.* [4] PREP & ADV If you keep **off** a street or piece of land, you do not go onto it. *The police had warned visitors to keep off the beach. ...a sign saying 'Keep Off'.* [5] PREP & ADV If something is situated **off** a place such as a room or road, it is near to it, but not exactly in it. *The boat was anchored off the northern coast. ...a penthouse just off Park Avenue.* [6] ADV If you fight something **off** or keep it **off**, you make it go away or prevent it. *...the body's effort to fight off the common cold.* [7] ADV & PREP If you have time **off**, you do not go to work for a period of time. *The rest of the men had the day off... He could not get time off work.* [8] ADJ & ADV If something such as a machine or an electric light is **off**, it is not in use. *He saw her bedroom light was off... The microphones had been switched off.*

[9] ADJ If an agreement or an arranged event is **off**, it has been cancelled. *The deal's off... Greenpeace refused to call off the event.* [10] ADJ AFTER LINK-V If food has gone **off**, it tastes and smells unpleasant because it is going bad. [11] PREP If you are **off** something, you have stopped using it or liking it; INFORMAL. *I'm off coffee at the moment... The psychiatrist took her off drug therapy.* [12] ADV If something is a long time **off**, it will not happen for a long time. *The required technology is probably still two years off.* [13] PHRASE If something happens **on and off** or **off and on**, it happens occasionally, or only for part of a period of time, not in a regular or continuous way. *I was still working on and off as a waitress.*

offal /ˈɒfəl, AM ˈɔːfəl/. N-U **Offal** is the liver, kidneys, and other internal organs of an animal, when they are used for food.

off-'balance (or **off balance**). ADJ AFTER LINK-V If someone or something is **off-balance**, they can easily fall or be knocked over because they are not standing firmly. *She was thrown off-balance.*

off 'duty (or **off-duty**). ADJ When someone such as a soldier or policeman is **off duty**, they are not working. *...an off-duty policeman.*

offence (AM **offense**) /əˈfens/ **offences.** [1] N-C An **offence** is a crime; FORMAL. *He has committed hundreds of offences.* [2] N-U If you give **offence**, you upset or embarrass someone. *We did not mean to cause any offence.* [3] PHRASE If you **take offence**, you are upset by something that someone says or does. *She never takes offence at anything.*

offend /əˈfend/ **offends, offending, offended.** [1] VERB If you **offend** someone, you upset or embarrass them. ♦**offended** ADJ *She is terribly offended and hurt by this.* [2] VERB To **offend** against a law, rule, or principle means to break it. *His vulgarity offended the code of his circle.* [3] VERB If someone **offends**, they commit a crime. *Girls are far less likely to offend than boys.* ♦**offender, offenders** N-C *...a prison for young offenders.*

offense /əˈfens, AM ˈɒfens/. See **offence**.

offensive /əˈfensɪv/ **offensives.** [1] ADJ Something that is **offensive** upsets or embarrasses people because it is rude or insulting. *...an offensive remark.* [2] N-C An **offensive** is a strong attack. *...a military offensive on the guerrilla base.* [3] PHRASE If you **go on the offensive**, **go over to the offensive**, or **take the offensive**, you begin to take strong action against people who have been attacking you.

offer /ˈɒfə, AM ˈɔːfər/ **offers, offering, offered.** [1] VERB If you **offer** something to someone, you ask them if they would like to have it or to use it. *I was brought up to offer my seat to a lady on the tube... She offered him a cup of tea. ...a new magazine offering advice on finance.* [2] VERB If you **offer** to do something, you say that you are willing to do it. *Greg offered to teach him to ski... 'Can I get you a drink,' she offered.* [3] VERB If you **offer** a particular amount of money for something, you say that you will pay that much for it. *The UN has offered $25,000 reward for information leading to his arrest.* [4] N-C An **offer** is something that someone says they will give you or do for you. *He was made a film offer he could not refuse... Ingrid would not accept Steele's offer to drive her to her car.* **5** N-C An **offer** in a shop is a specially low price for a product, or something extra that you get by buying the product. *...special offers on alcohol.* **6** PHRASE If something is **on offer**, it is available to be used or bought. *...some of the excellent books on offer.*

office /'ɒfɪs, AM 'ɔːf-/ **offices. 1** N-C An **office** is a room or a part of a building where people work sitting at desks. *I arrived at the office early.* **2** N-C An **office** is a department of an organization, especially the government, where people deal with a particular kind of administrative work. *Contact your local tax office.* **3** N-C An **office** is a small building or room where people can go for information, tickets, or a service of some kind. *...the tourist office.* **4** N-U Someone who holds **office** has an important job or a position of authority in an organization. *...events to mark the President's first ten years in office.*

officer /'ɒfɪsə, AM 'ɔːf-/ **officers. 1** N-C In the armed forces, an **officer** is a person in a position of authority. *...army officers.* **2** N-C An **officer** is a person who has a responsible position in an organization, especially a government organization. *...a local authority education officer.* **3** N-C & N-VOC Members of the police force can be referred to as **officers**. *...senior police officers... Thank you, Officer.*

official /ə'fɪʃəl/ **officials. 1** ADJ Something that is **official** is approved by the government or by someone else in authority. *...the official unemployment figures.* ♦ **officially** ADV *The election results have still not been officially announced.* **2** ADJ BEFORE N **Official** is used to describe things which are done or used by people in authority as part of their job or position. *Mr Ridley is currently on an official visit to Hungary. ...the Irish President's official residence.* **3** N-C An **official** is a person who holds a position of authority in an organization. *...a senior UN official.*

'**off-licence, off-licences.** N-C In Britain, an **off-licence** is a shop which sells alcoholic drinks. The usual American expression is **liquor store**.

,**off-'peak.** ADJ BEFORE N & ADV **Off-peak** things are available at a time when there is little demand for them, so that they are cheaper than usual. *...off-peak electricity... Calls cost 39p a minute off-peak.*

offset /,ɒf'set, AM ,ɔːf-/ **offsets, offsetting, offset.** VERB If one thing **is offset** by another, the effect of the first thing is reduced by the second, so that any advantage or disadvantage is cancelled out. *The slump in sales was offset by a surge in exports.*

offshoot /'ɒfʃuːt, AM 'ɔːf-/ **offshoots.** N-C If one thing is an **offshoot** of another thing, it has developed from the other thing. *The technology we use is an offshoot of the motor industry.*

offshore (or **off-shore**) /,ɒf'ʃɔː, AM ,ɔːf-/. ADJ & ADV **Offshore** means situated or happening in the sea, near to the coast. *...an offshore island... One day a larger ship anchored offshore.*

offside (or **off-side**) /,ɒf'saɪd, AM ,ɔːf-/. **1** ADJ & ADV If a player in a game of football or hockey is **offside**, they have broken the rules by moving too far forward. *Rush was clearly offside... Wise was standing at least ten yards offside.* **2** N-SING The **offside** of a vehicle is the side farthest from the pavement when you are driving; BRITISH.

offspring /'ɒfsprɪŋ, AM 'ɔːf-/; **offspring** is both the singular and plural form. N-C You can refer to a person's children or to an animal's young as their **offspring**; FORMAL.

often /'ɒfən, AM 'ɔːf-/. **1** ADV If something happens **often**, it happens many times or much of the time. *They often spent Christmas at Prescott Hill... They used these words freely, often in front of their parents too... That doesn't happen very often.* **2** ADV You use **often** after 'how' to ask questions about frequency. You also use **often** in statements to give information about the frequency of something. *How often do you brush your teeth?... They jog twice as often as the general population.*

> You do not use **often** to talk about something that happens several times within a short period of time. You do not say, for example, 'I often phoned her yesterday'. You say 'I phoned her several times yesterday' or 'I kept phoning her yesterday'.

PHRASES ● If something happens **every so often**, it happens regularly, but with fairly long intervals between each occasion. *Every so often he would turn round and look at her.* ● If you say that something happens **more often than not** or **as often as not**, you mean that it happens fairly frequently, and that this can be considered as typical of the kind of situation you are talking about. *Behind many successful men there is, more often than not, a woman who makes this success possible.*

oh /əʊ/. **1** CONVENTION You use **oh** to introduce a response or a comment on something that has just been said; SPOKEN. *'Would you like me to phone and explain the situation?'—'Oh, would you?'.* **2** EXCLAM You use **oh** to express a feeling such as surprise, pain, annoyance, or joy; SPOKEN. *'Oh!' Kenny blinked. 'Has everyone gone?'... 'Oh, my God,' Korontzis moaned.* **3** CONVENTION You use **oh** when you are hesitating while speaking, for example because you are trying to estimate something, or because you are searching for the right word. *I've been here, oh, since the end of June.*

oil /ɔɪl/ **oils, oiling, oiled. 1** N-VAR **Oil** is a smooth thick liquid used as a fuel and for lubricating machines. Oil is found underground. *The company buys and sells about 600,000 barrels of oil a day. ...a small oil-lamp.* **2** VERB If you **oil** something, you put oil onto it or into it in order to make it work smoothly or to protect it. *A crew of assistants oiled and adjusted the release mechanism.* **3** N-VAR **Oil** is a smooth thick liquid made from plants or fish and used in cookery. *...olive oil.*

'**oil paint, oil paints.** N-VAR **Oil paint** is a thick paint used by artists.

'oil painting, oil paintings. N-C An **oil painting** is a picture which has been painted using oil paints.

'oil slick, oil slicks. N-C An **oil slick** is a layer of oil that floats on the sea or on a lake. It is formed when oil accidentally spills out of a ship or container.

oily /'ɔɪli/. ADJ Something that is **oily** is covered with oil, contains oil, or looks, feels, or tastes like oil. ...*an oily rag*... *Paul found the tomato sauce too oily.* ...*a skin tonic for oily, blemished complexions.*

ointment /'ɔɪntmənt/ **ointments.** N-VAR An **ointment** is a smooth thick substance that is put on sore skin or a wound to help it heal. *A range of ointments and creams is available for the treatment of eczema.*

okay (or **OK**) /,əʊ'keɪ/. [1] ADJ & ADV If you say that something is **okay**, you mean that it is acceptable; INFORMAL. *Is it okay if I come by myself?... We seemed to manage okay for the first year.* [2] ADJ AFTER LINK-V If you say that someone is **okay**, you mean that they are safe and well. *Check that the baby's okay.* [3] CONVENTION You can say **okay** to show that you agree to something. *'Shall I give you a ring on Friday?'—'Yeah okay.'* [4] CONVENTION You can say **'Okay?'** to check whether the person you are talking to understands what you have said and accepts it. *We'll get together next week, OK?*

old /əʊld/ **older, oldest.** [1] ADJ & N-PL Someone who is **old** has lived for many years and is no longer young. You can refer to old people as **the old.** ...*a white-haired old man.* [2] ADJ Something that is **old** has existed for a long time. *These books must be very old.* ...*an old Arab proverb.* [3] ADJ Something that is **old** is no longer in good condition because of its age or because it has been used a lot. ...*an old toothbrush.* [4] ADJ You use **old** to talk or ask about the age of someone or something. See usage note at **elder.** *The paintings in the chapel were perhaps a thousand years old... How old are you now?* [5] ADJ BEFORE N You use **old** to refer to something that is no longer used, that no longer exists, or that has been replaced by something else. *The old road had disappeared under grass.* [6] ADJ BEFORE N You use **old** to refer to something that used to belong to you, or to a person or thing that used to have a particular role in your life. *I'll make up the bed in your old room.* ...*when Jane returned to her old boyfriend.* [7] ADJ BEFORE N An **old** friend or enemy is someone who has been your friend or enemy for a long time.

PHRASES ● You use **any old** to emphasize that the quality or type of something is not important. If you say that a particular thing is not **any old** thing, you are emphasizing how special or famous it is. *Any old paper will do... This is not just any old front room.*

,old 'age. [1] N-U Your **old age** is the period of years towards the end of your life. *They worry about how they will support themselves in their old age.* [2] N-U **Old age** is the quality or state of being old and near the end of one's life. *We tend to consider old age as a social problem.*

,old-'fashioned. ADJ Something that is **old-fashioned** is no longer used, done, or believed by most people, because it has been replaced by something that is more modern. *The house was dull, old-fashioned and in bad condition... They still make cheese the old-fashioned way.*

olive /'ɒlɪv/ **olives.** [1] N-VAR **Olives** are small green or black fruit with a bitter taste. The tree on which olives grow is called an **olive tree** or an **olive.** [2] ADJ & N-VAR Something that is **olive** is yellowish-green in colour.

'olive oil. N-U **Olive oil** is edible oil obtained by pressing olives.

Olympic /ə'lɪmpɪk/ **Olympics.** [1] ADJ BEFORE N **Olympic** means relating to the Olympic Games. ... *the reigning Olympic champion.* [2] N-PROPER **The Olympics** are the Olympic Games.

O,lympic 'Games. N-PROPER The **Olympic Games** are a set of international sports competitions which take place every four years, each time in a different country. **Olympic Games** can take the singular or plural form of the verb.

omelette (AM **omelet**) /'ɒmlət/ **omelettes.** N-C An **omelette** is a food made by beating eggs and cooking them in a flat pan.

omen /'əʊmən/ **omens.** N-C If you say that something is an **omen**, you think it indicates what is likely to happen in the future and whether it will be good or bad. *Her appearance at this moment is an omen of disaster.*

ominous /'ɒmɪnəs/. ADJ If you describe something as **ominous**, you mean that it worries you because it makes you think that something unpleasant is going to happen. *The rolls of distant thunder were growing more ominous.* ◆**ominously** ADV *The bar seemed ominously quiet.*

omission /əʊ'mɪʃən/ **omissions.** N-VAR An **omission** is the act of not including something or not doing something. *We overcame the prosecution's seemingly malicious omission of recorded evidence.*

omit /əʊ'mɪt/ **omits, omitting, omitted.** [1] VERB If you **omit** something, you do not include it in an activity or piece of work. *Omit the salt in this recipe... Our apologies to David Pannick for omitting his name from last week's article.* [2] VERB If you **omit** to do something, you do not do it; FORMAL. *His new girlfriend had omitted to tell him she was married.*

on /ɒn/. [1] PREP If someone or something is **on** a surface or object, the surface or object is underneath them and is supporting their weight. *He is sitting beside her on the sofa... On top of the cupboards are vast straw baskets.* ...*the Chinese rug on the floor.* [2] PREP If something is **on** a surface or object, it is stuck to it or attached to it. ...*the peeling paint on the ceiling... There was a smear of gravy on his chin.* [3] PREP If you get **on** a bus, train, or plane, you go in it in order to travel somewhere. You say you are **on** the bus, train, or plane when you are travelling in it. *I never go on the bus into the town.* [4] PREP If there is something **on** a piece of paper, it has been written or printed there. ...*the writing on the back of the card.* ...*the numbers she put on the chart.* [5] ADV When you put a piece of clothing **on**, you place it over a part of your body in order to wear it. If you have it **on**, you are wearing it. *He put his coat on... I had a hat on.* **6** PREP You can say that you have something **on** if you are carrying it in your pocket or in a bag. *I didn't have any money on me.* **7** PREP If something happens **on** a particular day or date, that is when it happens. *This year's event will take place on June 19th... She travels to Korea on Monday.* **8** PREP You use **on** when mentioning an event that was followed by another one. *She waited in her hotel to welcome her children on their arrival from London... On reaching Dubai the evacuees were taken straight to Dubai international airport.* **9** PREP If something is done **on** an instrument, machine, or system, it is done using that instrument, machine, or system. *I could do all my work on the computer.* **10** ADV If something such as a machine or an electric light is **on**, it is functioning or in use. *The light was on and the door was open... I've turned the central heating on again.* **11** PREP Books, discussions, or ideas **on** a particular subject are concerned with that subject. *...any book on baby care. ...a free counselling service which can offer help and advice on legal matters.* **12** PREP If something affects you, you can say that it has an effect **on** you. **13** PREP When you buy something or pay for something, you spend money **on** it. *I resolved not to waste money on a hotel.* **14** PREP When you spend time or energy **on** a particular activity, you spend time or energy doing it. *Children spend so much time on computer games.* **15** ADV You use **on** to say that someone is continuing to do something. *They walked on in silence... Read on for further hints.* **16** PREP If you are **on** a council or committee, you are a member of it. *Claire and Beryl were on the organizing committee.* **17** PREP If someone is **on** a medicine or drug they are taking it regularly. If someone lives **on** a particular kind of food, they eat it. *She was on antibiotics for an eye infection... The caterpillars feed on a wide range of trees, shrubs and plants.* **18** PREP If you are **on** a particular kind of income, that is the kind of income you have. *...young people who are unemployed or on low wages.* **19** ADV When an activity is taking place, you can say that it is **on**. *It tells you what here what's on at the cinema.* **20** PREP If something is being broadcast, you can say that it is **on** the radio or television. *...every sporting event on television and satellite.* **21** ADV If you say that someone goes **on** at you, you mean that they continually criticize you, complain to you, or ask you to do something. *She's been on at me for weeks to show her round the stables... He used to keep on at me about the need to win.* **22** PHRASE If you **have a lot on**, you are very busy. If you **do not have much on**, you are not busy; SPOKEN. **23** **and so on**: see **so**.

once /wʌns, wɒns/. **1** ADV If something happens **once**, it happens one time only, or one time within a particular period of time. *I met Wilma once, briefly... Since then I haven't once slept through the night... Mary had only been to Manchester once before.* **2** ADV If something was **once** true, it was true at some time in the past, but is no longer true. *The house where she lives was once the village post office.* **3** CONJ If something happens **once** another thing has happened, it happens immediately afterwards. *Once customers come to rely on these systems they almost never take their business elsewhere.*

PHRASES ● If something happens **once and for all**, it happens completely or finally. *We have to resolve this matter once and for all.* ● If you do something **at once**, you do it immediately. *I have to go, I really must, at once.* ● If several things happen **at once** or **all at once**, they all happen at the same time. *You can't be doing two things at once.* ● **For once** is used to emphasize that something happens on this particular occasion, especially if it has never happened before, and may never happen again. *For once, dad is not complaining.* ● **once upon a time**: see **time**. ● **once in a while**: see **while**.

one /wʌn, wɒn/ **ones**. **1** NUM One is the number 1. *They had three sons and one daughter. ...one thousand years ago. ...one of the children killed in the crash.* **2** DET & PRON You can use **one** to refer to the first of two or more things that you are comparing. *Prices vary from one shop to another... The twins were dressed differently and one was thinner than the other.* **3** PRON You can use **one** or **ones** when it is clear what type of thing or person you are referring to and you are describing them or giving more information about them. *They are selling their house to move to a smaller one.* **4** DET You can use **one** when referring to a time in the past or in the future. For example, if you say that you did something **one day**, you mean that you did it on a day in the past. *How would you like to have dinner one night?* **5** PRON Speakers and writers sometimes use **one** to make statements about people in general which also apply to themselves. **One** can be used as the subject or object of a sentence. FORMAL. *Where does one go from there?... Shares and bonds can bring one quite a considerable additional income.*

PHRASES ● If you say that someone is **at one with** the world, their feelings, or other people, you mean that they feel happy and relaxed in the situation they are in. *Take a stroll through the countryside and be at one with nature.* ● You use **one or other** to refer to one or more things or people in a group, when it does not matter which one is thought of or chosen. *...discrimination against one or other of the sexes.* ● **One or two** means a few. *We may make one or two changes.* ● **one another**: see **another**.

onerous /ˈəʊnərəs, AM ˈɑːn-/. ADJ If you describe a task as **onerous**, you dislike having to do it because you find it difficult or unpleasant; FORMAL. *...the onerous task of bringing up a very difficult child.*

one's /wʌnz/. **1** DET Speakers and writers use **one's** to indicate that something belongs to or relates to people in general, or to themselves in particular; FORMAL. *It is natural to care for one's family and one's children.* **2** **One's** can be used as a spoken form of 'one is' or 'one has', especially when 'has' is an auxiliary verb. *No one's going to hurt you... 'No-one's got respect for him any more.'*

oneself /wʌn'self/. **1** PRON A speaker or writer uses **oneself** to refer to themselves or to any person in general. *...a way of making oneself feel sophisticated... To work one must have time to oneself.* **2** PRON To do something **oneself** means to do it without any help or interference from anyone else; FORMAL. *Some things one must do oneself.* **3** PRON You use **oneself** to emphasize that something happens to you rather than to people in general. *It is better to die oneself than to kill.*

one-'sided. **1** ADJ In a **one-sided** activity or relationship, one of the people or groups involved does much more than the other or is much stronger than the other. *The negotiating was completely one-sided. ...a very one-sided match.* **2** ADJ If you describe someone as **one-sided**, you are critical of them because they have considered only one side of an issue or event. *Historians should be less one-sided, pay more attention to the contributions of women.*

'one-time (also **onetime**). ADJ BEFORE N **One-time** can be used to describe something such as a job or role which someone used to have, or something which happened or existed in the past. *...a one-time body builder.*

one-to-'one. ADJ BEFORE N & ADV In a **one-to-one** relationship, you deal with only one other person. *...one-to-one counselling is the answer... She would like to talk to people one to one.*

one-'way. **1** ADJ In **one-way** streets or traffic systems, vehicles can only travel in one direction. **2** ADJ A **one-way** ticket enables you to travel to a place, but not to come back again. *The fare is £85 one-way.*

ongoing /ˈɒnɡəʊɪŋ/. ADJ An **ongoing** situation is continuing to happen. *There is an ongoing debate on the issue.*

onion /ˈʌnjən/ **onions.** N-VAR An **onion** is a small round vegetable. It is white with a brown skin, and has a strong smell and taste.

onlooker /ˈɒnlʊkə/ **onlookers.** N-C An **onlooker** is someone who is watching an event. *A small crowd of onlookers were there to watch Mrs Thatcher.*

only /ˈəʊnli/. **1** ADV You use **only** to indicate the one thing that is true, appropriate, or necessary in a particular situation. *Only the President could authorize the use of the atomic bomb... A business can only be built on a sound financial base.* **2** ADV You use **only** to introduce the thing which must happen before the thing mentioned in the main part of the sentence can happen. *The lawyer is paid only if he wins.* **3** ADJ BEFORE N If you talk about the **only** person or thing involved in a particular situation, you mean there are no others involved in it. *She was the only woman in the legal department.* **4** ADJ BEFORE N An **only** child is a child who has no brothers or sisters. **5** ADV You use **only** to emphasize that something is unimportant or small. *I was only joking... Child car seats only cost about £10 a week to hire... Teenagers typically earn only half the adult wage.* **6** ADV You use **only** to emphasize a wish or hope. *We can only hope that she can recover.* **7** CONJ **Only** can be used to add a comment

which slightly changes or corrects what you have just said; INFORMAL. *It's a bit like my house, only nicer... It's just as dramatic as a film, only it's real.* **8** CONJ **Only** can be used after a clause with 'would' to indicate why something is not done; SPOKEN. *I'd invite you to come with me, only it's such a long way.* **9** ADV You can use **only** before an infinitive to introduce an event which happens immediately after one you have just mentioned, and which is rather surprising or unfortunate. *I tried ringing them dozens of times only to find the number engaged.* **10** ADV You can use **only** to emphasize how appropriate a certain course of action or type of behaviour is. *It's only fair to let her know that you intend to apply... She appeared to have changed considerably, which was only to be expected.*

▭ PHRASES ▭ ● You can say that something has **only just** happened when you want to emphasize that it happened a very short time ago. *I've only just arrived.* ● You use **only just** to emphasize that something is true, but by such a small degree that it is almost not true at all. *For centuries farmers there have only just managed to survive.* ● **if only:** see **if.**

When **only** is used as an adverb, its position in the sentence depends on the word or phrase it applies to. If **only** applies to the subject of a clause, you put it in front of the subject. *Only strong characters can make such decisions.* Otherwise, you normally put it in front of the verb, or after the first auxiliary, or after the verb **be**. *I only want my son back, that is all... He had only agreed to see me because we had met before... I was only able to visit him once.*

However, some people think it is more correct to put **only** directly in front of the word or phrase it applies to. This is the best position if you want to be quite clear or emphatic. *It applies only to passengers carrying British passports... She'd done it only because it was necessary.*

For extra emphasis, you can put **only** after the word or phrase it applies to. *The event will be for women only... I'll say this once and once only.*

on-'screen (also **onscreen**). **1** ADJ BEFORE N **On-screen** means appearing on the screen of a television, cinema, or computer. *...a clear and easy-to-follow menu-driven on-screen display.* **2** ADJ BEFORE N & ADV **On-screen** means relating to the roles being played by film or television actors. *...her on-screen romance with Pierce Lawton... He was immensely attractive to women, onscreen and offscreen.*

onset /ˈɒnset/. N-SING The **onset** of something unpleasant is the beginning of it. *...the onset of the disease.*

onslaught /ˈɒnslɔːt/ **onslaughts.** **1** N-C An **onslaught** on someone or something is a very violent attack against them. *The attackers launched another vicious onslaught on their victim.* **2** N-C If you refer to an **onslaught** of something, you mean that there is a large amount of it, often so that it is very difficult to deal with. *The onslaught of orders should keep aircraft manufacturers busy.*

onto (or **on to**) /'ɒntuː/. [1] PREP If someone or something moves **onto** an object, or if they are put onto it, they are then on that object or surface. *I lowered myself onto the bed and switched on the TV... Smear cream on to your baby's skin.* [2] PREP When you get **onto** a bus, train, or plane, you enter it. [3] PREP **Onto** is used after verbs such as 'hold', 'hang', and 'cling' to indicate what someone is holding firmly or where something is being held firmly. *She had to cling onto the door-handle until the pain passed.* [4] PREP If people who are talking get **onto** a different subject, they begin talking about it. *Let's get on to more important matters.* [5] PREP If someone **is onto** something, they are about to make a discovery; INFORMAL. *Archaeologists knew they were onto something big when they started digging.* [6] PREP If someone **is onto** you, they have discovered that you are doing something illegal or wrong; INFORMAL. *I had told people what he had been doing, so now the police were onto him.*

onus /'əʊnəs/. N-SING If you say that the **onus** is on someone to do something, you mean it is their duty or responsibility to do it. *The onus is on the shopkeeper to provide quality goods.*

onward /'ɒnwəd/ or **onwards**. [1] ADJ & ADV **Onward** means moving forward or continuing a journey. *British Airways have two flights a day to Bangkok, and there are onward flights to Phnom Penh... He led us onwards through the forest... The bus continued onward.* [2] ADJ & ADV **Onward** means developing, progressing, or becoming more important over a period of time. *...the onward march of progress in the British aircraft industry... The White House feels no compulsion to rush onwards to a new agreement.* [3] ADV If something happens from a particular time **onwards** or **onward**, it begins to happen at that time and continues to happen afterwards. *...from the turn of the century onward.*

ooze /uːz/ **oozes, oozing, oozed.** [1] VERB When a thick or sticky liquid **oozes** from something, the liquid flows slowly and in small quantities. *The wounds were still oozing blood... He could see the cut now, still oozing slightly.* [2] VERB If you say that someone or something **oozes** a quality or characteristic, you mean that they show it very strongly. *The Elizabethan house oozes charm.*

opaque /əʊ'peɪk/. [1] ADJ If an object or substance is **opaque**, you cannot see through it. *...opaque glass windows.* [2] ADJ If you say that something is **opaque**, you mean that it is difficult to understand. *...the opaque language of the inspector's reports.*

open 1 uncovering

open /'əʊpən/ **opens, opening, opened.** [1] VERB When you **open** something such as a door or the lid of a box, or when it **opens**, you move it so that it no longer covers a hole or gap. *He opened the window... The church doors would open and the crowd would surge out.* [2] VERB If you **open** something such as a container or a letter, you remove, or cut

part of it so that you can take out what is inside. *The Inspector opened the packet of cigarettes.* [3] VERB If you **open** something such as a book, an umbrella, or your hand, or if it **opens**, the different parts of it move away from each other so that the inside of it can be seen. *He opened the heavy Bible... The officer's mouth opened.* [4] VERB When you **open** your eyes, or when they **open**, you move your eyelids upwards so that you can see. [5] VERB If people **open** something such as a blocked road or a border, or if it **opens**, people can then pass along it or through it. *The rebels have opened the road from Monrovia to the Ivory Coast.* [6] ADJ You use **open** to describe something which has been opened. *...an open window... I tore the letter open... Her eyes were open.* [7] ADJ If an item of clothing is **open**, it is not fastened. *His open shirt revealed a fat gold chain.* [8] VERB When flowers **open**, their petals spread out.

> You do not use **open** as a verb or adjective to talk about electrical devices. If someone causes an electrical device to work by pressing a switch or turning a knob, you say that they **put it on**, **switch it on**, or **turn it on**. If the device is already working, you say that it is **on**. *The answering machine is on... He cannot sleep with the light on.*

open 2 buildings, places, and events

open /'əʊpən/ **opens, opening, opened.** [1] VERB When a shop, office, or public building **opens**, or when it **is opened**, its doors are unlocked and the people in it start working. *Banks closed on Friday afternoon and did not open again until Monday morning.* [2] ADJ AFTER LINK-V When a shop, office, or public building is **open**, its doors are unlocked and the people in it are working. *His shop is open Monday through Friday.* [3] VERB When a public building, factory, or company **opens** or when someone **opens** it, it starts operating for the first time. *The original station opened in 1754.* ◆**opening, openings** N-C *He was there for the official opening.* [4] VERB When an event such as a conference or a play **opens**, it begins to take place or to be performed. *...an emergency session of Parliament due to open later this morning.* ◆**opening** N-SING *...the opening of the talks.* [5] VERB If a place **opens** into another, larger place, you can move from one directly into the other. *The corridor opened into a low smoky room.* [6] ADJ An **open** area is a large area that does not have many structures or obstructions in it. *Officers will continue their search of nearby open ground.* [7] ADJ BEFORE N An **open** structure or object is not covered or enclosed. *...a room with an open fire.*

open 3 other meanings

open /'əʊpən/ **opens, opening, opened.** [1] ADJ If you describe a person or their character as **open**, you mean they are honest and do not want or try to hide anything or to deceive anyone. *He had always been open with her.* ◆**openness** N-U *I was impressed by his openness.* [2] ADJ AFTER LINK-V If you are **open to** suggestions or ideas, you are ready and willing to consider or accept them. *They are open to suggestions on how working conditions might be improved.* **3** ADJ AFTER LINK-V If you say that a system, person, or idea is **open to** something such as abuse or criticism, you mean they might receive it because of the qualities they possess or the effects they have had. *They left themselves wide open to accusations of double standards.* **4** VERB If you **open** an account with a bank or a commercial organization, you begin to use their services. **5** See also **opening**, **openly**.

<hr>

open 4 phrases

open /ˈəʊpən/ **opens, opening, opened.**
PHRASES ● If you do something **in the open**, you do it out of doors. ● If a situation is brought out **into the open**, people are told about it and it is no longer a secret.

▶ **open up. 1** PHR-VERB If something **opens up** opportunities or possibilities, or if opportunities or possibilities **open up**, they are able to arise or develop. *New opportunities are opening up for investors.* **2** PHR-VERB If a place, economy, or area of interest **opens up**, or if someone **opens it up**, it becomes accessible to more people. *As the market opens up, I think people are going to be able to spend more money on consumer goods.* **3** PHR-VERB When you **open up** a building, you unlock and open the door so that people can get in. *The postmaster and his wife arrived to open up the shop.*

open-'air (or **open air**). **1** ADJ An **open-air** place or event is outside rather than in a building. *...the Open Air Theatre in Regents Park.* **2** N-SING If you are in the **open air**, you are outside rather than in a building.

open-'ended. ADJ When people begin an **open-ended** discussion or activity, they do not start with any intention of achieving a particular decision or result. *...open-ended questions about what passengers expect of an airline.*

opener /ˈəʊpənə/ **openers.** N-C An **opener** is a tool which is used to open containers.

opening /ˈəʊpənɪŋ/ **openings. 1** ADJ BEFORE N The **opening** event, item, day, or week in a series is the first one. *...the season's opening game.* **2** N-SING The **opening** of something such as a book or concert is the first part of it. *...the opening of the film.* **3** N-C An **opening** is a hole or empty space through which things can pass. *...a narrow opening in the fence.* **4** N-C An **opening** is a good opportunity to do something. *All she needed was an opening to show her capabilities.* **5** N-C An **opening** is a job that is available. *We don't have any openings now.* **6** See also **open**.

openly /ˈəʊpənli/. ADV If you do something **openly**, you do it without trying to hide anything. *We can now talk openly about AIDS... They were openly gay.*

open-'minded. ADJ If you describe someone as **open-minded**, you approve of them because they are willing to listen to and consider other people's ideas. ◆**open-mindedness** N-U *...honesty, open-mindedness and willingness to learn.*

opera /ˈɒprə/ **operas.** N-VAR An **opera** is a musical entertainment. It is like a play, but most

of the words are sung. ◆**operatic** /ˌɒpəˈrætɪk/ ADJ *...the local amateur operatic society.*

operate /ˈɒpəreɪt/ **operates, operating, operated. 1** VERB If you **operate** a business or organization, you work to keep it running properly. If a business or organization **operates**, it carries out its work. *Greenwood owned and operated an enormous pear orchard. ...allowing commercial banks to operate in the country.* ◆**operation** N-U *...funds for the everyday operation of the business.* **2** VERB The way that something **operates** is the way that it works or has an effect. *Ceiling and wall lights can operate independently.* ◆**operation** N-U The operation of the new tax is being studied.* **3** VERB When you **operate** a machine or device, you make it work. ◆**operation** N-U *...the operation of the aeroplane.* **4** VERB When surgeons **operate** on a patient, they cut open the patient's body in order to remove, replace, or repair a diseased or damaged part.

'operating theatre, operating theatres. N-C An **operating theatre** is a room in a hospital where surgeons carry out operations.

operation /ˌɒpəˈreɪʃən/ **operations. 1** N-C An **operation** is a highly organized activity that involves many people doing different things. *The rescue operation began on Friday afternoon. ...a military operation.* **2** N-C A business or company can be referred to as an **operation**. *...Thorn's electronic's operation.* **3** N-C If a patient has an **operation**, a surgeon cuts open their body in order to remove, replace, or repair a diseased or damaged part. **4** N-U If a system is in **operation**, it is being used. *Until the rail links are in operation, passengers can only travel through the tunnel by coach.* **5** N-U If a machine or device is in **operation**, it is working. *There are three ski lifts in operation.* **6** See also **operate**.

operational /ˌɒpəˈreɪʃənəl/. **1** ADJ A machine or piece of equipment that is **operational** is in use or is ready to be used. *The whole system will be fully operational by December 2005.* **2** ADJ **Operational** factors or problems relate to the working of a system, device, or plan. *Every operational aspect had been fully researched.* ◆**operationally** ADV *An all-female political section would have been operationally ineffective.*

operative /ˈɒpərətɪv/ **operatives. 1** ADJ Something that is **operative** is working or having an effect. *The Youth Training Scheme was operative by the end of 1983.* **2** N-C An **operative** is a worker, especially one with a manual skill; FORMAL. **3** N-C An **operative** is someone who works for a government agency such as the intelligence service; AMERICAN.

operator /ˈɒpəreɪtə/ **operators. 1** N-C An **operator** is a person who works at a telephone exchange or on the switchboard of an office or hotel. *He dialled the operator.* **2** N-C An **operator** is someone who is employed to operate or control a machine. **3** N-C An **operator** is a person or a company that runs a business. *...the nation's largest cable TV operator.*

opinion /əˈpɪnjən/ **opinions. 1** N-C Your **opinion** about something is what you think or believe about it. *I wasn't asking for your opinion.*

2 N-SING Your **opinion** of someone is your judgment of their character or ability. *That improved Mrs Goole's already favourable opinion of him.* **3** N-U You can refer to the beliefs or views that people have as **opinion**. *Scientific opinion is divided over the health risks.*

o'pinion poll, opinion polls. N-C An **opinion poll** involves asking people for their opinion on a particular subject, especially one concerning politics.

opium /'əupiəm/. N-U **Opium** is a powerful drug made from the seeds of a type of poppy.

opponent /ə'pəunənt/ **opponents.** **1** N-C A politician's **opponents** are other politicians who belong to a different party or have different aims or policies. **2** N-C In a sporting contest, your **opponent** is the person who is playing against you. **3** N-C The **opponents** of an idea or policy do not agree with it. *...opponents of the spread of nuclear weapons.*

opportunist /ˌɒpə'tjuːnɪst, AM -'tuːn-/ **opportunists.** **1** ADJ & N-C If you describe someone as **opportunist**, or if you call them an **opportunist**, you are critical of them because they take advantage of any situation in order to gain money or power. *...corrupt and opportunist politicians.* ♦**opportunism** N-U *...political opportunism.* **2** ADJ **Opportunist** actions are not planned, but take advantage of the immediate situation. *...a brilliant opportunist goal.*

opportunistic /ˌɒpətjuː'nɪstɪk, AM -tuː-/. ADJ If you describe someone's behaviour as **opportunistic**, you are critical of them because they take advantage of situations in order to gain money or power. *Many of the party's members joined only for opportunistic reasons.*

opportunity /ˌɒpə'tjuːnɪti, AM -'tuːn-/ **opportunities.** N-VAR An **opportunity** is a situation in which it is possible for you to do something that you want to do. *I had an opportunity to go to New York... The best reason for a trip to London is the super opportunity for shopping.*

oppose /ə'pəuz/ **opposes, opposing, opposed.** VERB If you **oppose** someone or their plans or ideas, you disagree with what they want to do and try to prevent them from doing it. *...protesters opposed planned nuclear tests by France.*

opposed /ə'pəuzd/. **1** ADJ AFTER LINK-V If you **are opposed** to something, you disagree with it or disapprove of it. *I am utterly opposed to any form of terrorism.* **2** ADJ You say that two ideas or systems are **opposed** when they are opposite to each other or very different from each other. *...two opposed ideologies.* **3** PHRASE You use **as opposed to** when you want to make it clear that you are talking about a particular thing and not something else. *We ate in the restaurant, as opposed to the bistro.*

opposing /ə'pəuzɪŋ/. **1** ADJ BEFORE N **Opposing** ideas or tendencies are totally different from each other. *I have a friend who has the opposing view and felt that the war was immoral.* **2** ADJ BEFORE N **Opposing** groups of people disagree about something or are in competition with one another.

opposite /'ɒpəzɪt/ **opposites.** **1** PREP & ADV If one thing is **opposite** another, it is facing it.

Two young people sat opposite me... I glanced up at the building opposite. **2** ADJ BEFORE N The **opposite** side or part of something is the one that is farthest away from you. *...the opposite corner of the room.* **3** ADJ **Opposite** is used to describe things of the same kind which are as different as possible in a particular way. *...a word with the opposite meaning. ...a car going in the opposite direction.* **4** N-C The **opposite** of someone or something is the person or thing that is most different from them. *He was the complete opposite of Raymond.*

'opposite 'sex. N-SING If you are talking about men and refer to **the opposite sex**, you mean women. If you are talking about women and refer to **the opposite sex**, you mean men.

opposition /ˌɒpə'zɪʃən/. **1** N-U **Opposition** is strong, angry, or violent disagreement and disapproval. *The government is facing a new wave of opposition.* **2** N-C The **opposition** refers to the politicians or political parties that form part of a country's parliament but are not in the government.

oppress /ə'pres/ **oppresses, oppressing, oppressed.** **1** VERB To **oppress** someone means to treat them cruelly or unfairly. *These people often are oppressed by their governments.* ♦**oppressed** ADJ *...oppressed minorities.* ♦**oppression** /ə'preʃən/ N-U *...the oppression of black people throughout history.* ♦**oppressor, oppressors** N-C *They sought to drive out their oppressors.* **2** VERB If something **oppresses** you, it makes you feel depressed and uncomfortable; LITERARY. *It was not just the weather which oppressed her.*

oppressive /ə'presɪv/. **1** ADJ **Oppressive** laws, societies, and customs treat people cruelly and unfairly. *The new laws will be just as oppressive as those they replace.* **2** ADJ You say that the weather is **oppressive** when it is hot and humid. *...the oppressive afternoon heat.* **3** ADJ An **oppressive** situation makes you feel depressed or uncomfortable. *...the oppressive sadness that weighed upon him.*

opt /ɒpt/ **opts, opting, opted.** VERB If you **opt** for something, you choose it or decide to do it in preference to anything else. *She opted to spend Christmas with her younger brother.*
▶ **opt out.** PHR-VERB If you **opt out** of something, you choose not to be involved in it. *Under the agreement the Vietnamese can opt out at any time.*

optic /'ɒptɪk/. ADJ BEFORE N **Optic** means relating to the eyes or to sight. *...the optic nerve.*

optical /'ɒptɪkəl/. **1** ADJ **Optical** instruments, devices, or processes involve or relate to vision or light. *...optical telescopes.* **2** ADJ BEFORE N **Optical** means relating to the way that things appear to people. *...an optical illusion.*

optician /ɒp'tɪʃən/ **opticians.** N-C An **optician** is someone whose job involves testing people's eyesight and making and selling glasses and contact lenses.

optimism /'ɒptɪmɪzəm/. N-U **Optimism** is the feeling of being hopeful about the future or about the success of something. *The president expressed optimism about reaching a peaceful settlement.* ♦**optimist, optimists** N-C *Susan remains an optimist.*

optimistic /ˌɒptɪˈmɪstɪk/. ADJ Someone who is **optimistic** is hopeful about the future or about the success of something. *She is optimistic that an agreement can be worked out soon.* ◆**optimistically** ADV *He talked optimistically about the future.*

optimum /ˈɒptɪməm/. ADJ The **optimum** level or state of something is the best level or state that it could achieve; FORMAL. *...the basic requirements for optimum health.*

option /ˈɒpʃən/ **options.** [1] N-C An **option** is a choice between one or more things. *...frustrated artists who became lawyers at an early age because it seemed a safe option... What other options do you have?* [2] N-SING If you have the **option** to do something, you can choose whether to do it or not. *Women should be given the option of having the treatment.* [3] PHRASE If you **keep** your **options open** or **leave** your **options open**, you avoid making an immediate decision about something.

optional /ˈɒpʃənəl/. ADJ If something is **optional**, you can choose whether or not you do it or have it. *Optional extras include cooking tuition.*

opulent /ˈɒpjʊlənt/. ADJ **Opulent** things look grand and expensive; FORMAL. *...his opulent new office.* ◆**opulence** N-U *...the opulence of Napoleon III's court.*

opus /ˈəʊpəs, ˈɒpəs/ **opuses** or **opera.** N-C An **opus** is a musical composition. The abbreviation 'op.' is also used.

or /ə, STRONG ɔː/. [1] CONJ You use **or** to link alternatives. *Would you like tea or coffee?... He said he would try to write or call... Everyone thought she was either lying or mad... I don't know whether people will buy it or not.* [2] CONJ **Or** is used between two numbers to indicate that you are giving an approximate amount. *Drink two or three glasses of water after exercising.* [3] CONJ You use **or** to introduce a comment which corrects or modifies what you have just said. *The man was a fool, or at least incompetent... There was nothing more he wanted, or so he thought.* [4] CONJ You can use **or** to introduce an explanation or justification for what you have just said. *She had to have the operation, or she would die... He must have thought Jane was worth it or he wouldn't have wasted time on her.* [5] **or else**: see **else**. ● **or so**: see **so**.

oral /ˈɔːrəl/ **orals.** [1] ADJ **Oral** is used to describe things that involve speaking rather than writing. *...an oral exam in the form of an interview.* ◆**orally** ADV *...the tradition that is passed down orally.* [2] N-C An **oral** is an examination, especially in a foreign language, that is spoken rather than written. [3] ADJ BEFORE N **Oral** medicines are ones that you swallow. *...an oral typhoid vaccine.* ◆**orally** ADV *...tablets taken orally.*

orange /ˈɒrɪndʒ, AM ˈɔːr-/ **oranges.** [1] ADJ & N-VAR Something that is **orange** is of a colour between red and yellow. [2] N-C An **orange** is a round orange fruit that is juicy and sweet. [3] N-U **Orange** is a drink that is made from or tastes of oranges.

oratory /ˈɒrətəri, AM ˈɔːrətɔːri/. N-U **Oratory** is the art of making formal speeches; FORMAL. *...American political oratory.*

orbit /ˈɔːbɪt/ **orbits, orbiting, orbited.** [1] N-VAR An **orbit** is the curved path followed by an object going round a planet, a moon, or the sun. *Mars and Earth have orbits which change with time.* [2] VERB If something such as a satellite **orbits** a planet, a moon, or the sun, it goes round and round it.

orbital /ˈɔːbɪtəl/. [1] ADJ BEFORE N An **orbital** road goes all the way round a large city. [2] ADJ BEFORE N **Orbital** describes things relating to the orbit of an object in space. *...the Earth's orbital velocity.*

orchard /ˈɔːtʃəd/ **orchards.** N-C An **orchard** is an area of land on which fruit trees are grown.

orchestra /ˈɔːkɪstrə/ **orchestras.** N-C An **orchestra** is a large group of musicians who play a variety of different instruments together. ◆**orchestral** /ɔːˈkestrəl/ ADJ BEFORE N *...orchestral music.*

orchestrate /ˈɔːkɪstreɪt/ **orchestrates, orchestrating, orchestrated.** [1] VERB If you **orchestrate** something, you organize it very carefully in order to produce a particular result or situation. *The colonel was able to orchestrate a rebellion from inside an army jail.* ◆**orchestration** N-U *...the orchestration of criminal justice policy.* [2] VERB When someone **orchestrates** a piece of music, they rewrite it so that it can be played by an orchestra. ◆**orchestration** N-U *...Ravel's orchestration of Mussorgsky's piano work.*

orchid /ˈɔːkɪd/ **orchids.** N-C An **orchid** is a plant which has brightly coloured, unusually shaped flowers.

ordain /ɔːˈdeɪn/ **ordains, ordaining, ordained.** VERB When someone is **ordained**, they are made a member of the clergy in a religious ceremony.

ordeal /ɔːˈdiːl/ **ordeals.** N-C An **ordeal** is an extremely unpleasant and difficult experience. *She described her agonising ordeal.*

order 1 conjunction uses

order /ˈɔːdə/. [1] CONJ If you do something **in order to** achieve a particular thing, you do it because you want to achieve that thing. *Schools are extremely unwilling to cut down on staff in order to cut costs... No agenda was drawn up, in order that all matters could be raised.* [2] CONJ If something must happen **in order for** something else to happen, the second thing cannot happen if the first thing does not happen. *In order for him to win, he has to get at least nine Democratic votes.*

order 2 commands and requests

order /ˈɔːdə/ **orders, ordering, ordered.** [1] VERB & N-C If someone in authority **orders** something, **orders** you to do something, or gives you an **order**, they tell you to do something. *The President has ordered a full investigation... He ordered his men to cease firing... She was fined £1,200 for disobeying orders.* [2] N-C An **order** is something that you ask to be brought or sent to you, and that you are going to pay for. *The waiter returned with their order.* [3] VERB When you **order** something that you are going to pay for, you ask for it to be brought or sent to you. *Iris ordered coffees for herself and Tania.* [4] PHRASE If you are **under**

orders to do something, you have been told to do it by someone in authority. *I am under orders not to discuss my mission.* [5] See also **mail order**. • **a tall order**: see **tall**.

▶ **order around** or **order about**. PHR-VERB If someone **is ordering** you **around**, they are telling you what to do as if they have authority over you.

order 3 arrangements, situations, and groupings

order /'ɔ:də/ **orders**. [1] N-U If a set of things are arranged or done in a particular **order**, one thing is put first or done first, another thing second, another thing third, and so on. *Arrange the entries in numerical order.* [2] N-U **Order** is the situation that exists when everything is in the correct place or is done at the correct time. *She ached for some order in her life.* [3] N-U **Order** is the situation that exists when people live together peacefully rather than fighting or causing trouble. *Troops were sent to the islands to restore order.* [4] N-SING When people talk about a particular **order**, they mean the way society is organized at a particular time. *...questioning the existing social order.* [5] N-C A religious **order** is a group of monks or nuns who live according to certain rules. [6] N-C If you refer to something of a particular **order**, you mean something of a particular quality, amount, or degree; FORMAL. *...a poet of the highest order.* [7] PREP You use **in the order of** or **of the order of** when giving an approximate figure. *They borrowed something in the order of £10 million.* [8] See also **law and order**.
PHRASES • A machine or device that is **in working order** is functioning properly and is not broken. *...a ten-year-old car that is in perfect working order.* • A machine or device that is **out of order** is broken and does not work.

orderly /'ɔ:dəli/ **orderlies**. [1] ADJ Something that is **orderly** is well organized or well arranged. *...a beautiful, clean and orderly city.* ♦ **orderliness** N-U *...parents' concerns with neatness and orderliness.* [2] N-C An **orderly** is an untrained hospital attendant.

ordinal /'ɔ:dɪnəl/ **ordinals**. N-C An **ordinal** or an **ordinal number** is a number such as 'first', 'third', or 'tenth', which tells you what position something has in an ordered group of things.

ordinance /'ɔ:dɪnəns/ **ordinances**. N-C An **ordinance** is an official rule or order; FORMAL.

ordinarily /'ɔ:dɪnərəli, AM 'ɔ:rdɪli/. ADV If something is **ordinarily** the case, it is usually the case. *The streets would ordinarily have been full of people.*

ordinary /'ɔ:dɪnri, AM -neri/. [1] ADJ **Ordinary** people or things are not special or different in any way. *Most ordinary people would agree with me... It was just an ordinary weekend.* [2] PHRASE Something that is **out of the ordinary** is unusual or different. *The boy's knowledge was out of the ordinary.*

ordination /,ɔ:dɪ'neɪʃən/ **ordinations**. N-VAR When someone's **ordination** takes place, they are made a member of the Christian clergy in a special ceremony.

ore /ɔ:/ **ores**. N-VAR **Ore** is rock or earth from which metal can be obtained.

organ /'ɔ:gən/ **organs**. [1] N-C An **organ** is a part of your body that has a particular purpose or function, for example your heart or your lungs. *...the liver and other organs.* [2] N-C An **organ** is a large musical instrument with pipes of different lengths through which air is forced. It has keys and pedals rather like a piano. ♦ **organist, organists** N-C *...the acclaimed organist Christopher Wrench.*

organic /ɔ:'gænɪk/. [1] ADJ **Organic** gardening or farming uses only natural animal and plant products and does not use artificial fertilizers or pesticides. ♦ **organically** ADV *...organically grown vegetables.* [2] ADJ Something that is **organic** is produced by or found in living things. *...decaying organic matter.*

organisation /,ɔ:gənaɪ'zeɪʃən/. See **organization**.

organisational /,ɔ:gənaɪ'zeɪʃənəl/. See **organizational**.

organise /'ɔ:gənaɪz/. See **organize**.

organism /'ɔ:gənɪzəm/ **organisms**. N-C An **organism** is an animal or plant, especially one that is so small that you cannot see it without using a microscope.

organization (BR also **organisation**) /,ɔ:gənaɪ'zeɪʃən/ **organizations**. [1] N-C An **organization** is an official group of people, for example a political party, a business, a charity, or a club. *...charitable organizations. ...the International Labour Organisation.* ♦ **organizational** ADJ BEFORE N *This problem needs to be dealt with at an organizational level.* [2] N-U The **organization** of something is the way in which its different parts are arranged or relate to each other. *...the proposed changes in the organization of the Health Service.* ♦ **organizational** ADJ BEFORE N *Big organizational changes are needed.* [3] N-U The **organization** of an activity or public event involves making all the arrangements for it. *He was involved in the organization of conferences and seminars.* ♦ **organizational** ADJ BEFORE N *...Evelyn's excellent organisational skills.*

organize (BR also **organise**) /'ɔ:gənaɪz/ **organizes, organizing, organized**. [1] VERB If you **organize** an activity or event, you make all the arrangements for it. *Maggie was the one that organized the trip to the railway museum.* ♦ **organizer, organizers** N-C *...the complete lack of planning by festival organizers.* [2] VERB If you **organize** something that someone wants or needs, you make sure that it is provided. *He asked her to organize coffee and sandwiches.* [3] VERB If you **organize** things, you put them into order. *He began to organize his materials.*

organized (BR also **organised**) /'ɔ:gənaɪzd/. [1] ADJ BEFORE N An **organized** activity or group involves a number of people doing something together in a structured way, rather than doing it by themselves. *...organised groups of art thieves. ...organised religion.* [2] ADJ People who are **organized** work in an efficient and effective way.

orgasm /'ɔ:gæzəm/ **orgasms**. N-C An **orgasm** is the moment of greatest pleasure and excitement during sexual activity.

orgy /'ɔ:dʒi/ **orgies**. [1] N-C An **orgy** is a party in which people behave in a very uncontrolled

way, especially one involving sexual activity.
[2] N-C You can refer to an activity as an **orgy** to emphasize that it is done to an excessive extent. ...*an orgy of destruction.*

oriental /ˌɔːriˈentəl/. ADJ **Oriental** means coming from or associated with eastern Asia, especially China and Japan. ...*oriental carpets.*

orientated /ˈɔːrienteitid/. ADJ **Orientated** means the same as **oriented**. ...*a lesbian and gay orientated radio programme.*

orientation /ˌɔːriənˈteiʃən/. [1] N-U You can refer to the aims and interests of an organization as its **orientation**. ...*a marketing orientation.* [2] N-U Someone's **orientation** is their basic beliefs or preferences. ...*sexual orientation.*

oriented /ˈɔːrientid/. ADJ AFTER LINK-V You use **oriented** to indicate what someone or something is interested in or concerned with. For example, if someone is politically **oriented**, they are interested in politics. *Most students here are oriented to computers.*

origin /ˈɒrɪdʒɪn, AM ˈɔːr-/ **origins.** [1] N-VAR You can refer to the beginning, cause, or source of something as its **origin** or its **origins.** ...*theories about the origin of life.* ...*many drugs which have their origins in herbs.* [2] N-VAR Your **origin** or **origins** is the country, race, or social class of your parents or ancestors. ...*people of Asian origin.* ...*their country of origin.*

original /əˈrɪdʒɪnəl/ **originals.** [1] ADJ You use **original** to refer to something that existed at the beginning of a process or activity, or the characteristics that something had when it first existed. ...*Strathclyde police, which carried out the original investigation.* ♦**originally** ADV *France originally refused to sign the treaty.* [2] N-C If something such as a document or work of art is an **original**, it is not a copy or a later version. *Copy the questionnaire and send the original to your employer.* [3] ADJ An **original** piece of writing or music was written recently and has not been published or performed before. ...*its policy of commissioning original work.* [4] ADJ If you describe someone or their work as **original**, you mean that they are very imaginative and have new ideas. ...*a wholly original form of humour.* ♦**originality** /əˌrɪdʒɪˈnæliti/ N-U *He was capable of writing things of startling originality.*

originate /əˈrɪdʒɪneit/ **originates, originating, originated.** VERB If something **originated** at a particular time or in a particular place, it began to happen or exist at that time or in that place. *All carbohydrates originate from plants.*

ornament /ˈɔːnəmənt/ **ornaments.** [1] N-C An **ornament** is an attractive object that you display in your home or garden. [2] N-U **Ornament** refers to decorations and patterns on a building or piece of furniture.

ornamental /ˌɔːnəˈmentəl/. ADJ Something that is **ornamental** is intended to be attractive rather than useful. ...*an ornamental pond.*

ornate /ɔːˈneit/. ADJ Something that is **ornate** has a lot of decoration on it. ...*an ornate iron staircase.*

orphan /ˈɔːfən/ **orphans, orphaned.** [1] N-C An **orphan** is a child whose parents are dead. [2] PASSIVE-VERB If a child **is orphaned**, his or

her parents die. *Jones was orphaned at the age of ten.*

orphanage /ˈɔːfənidʒ/ **orphanages.** N-C An **orphanage** is a place where orphans are looked after.

orthodox /ˈɔːθədɒks/. [1] ADJ **Orthodox** beliefs, methods, or systems are the ones that are accepted or used by most people. ...*orthodox medicine.* [2] ADJ If you describe someone as **orthodox**, you mean that they hold the older and more traditional ideas of their religion or party. ...*Orthodox Jews.*

orthodoxy /ˈɔːθədɒksi/ **orthodoxies.** [1] N-C An **orthodoxy** is an accepted view about something. *These ideas rapidly became the new orthodoxy in linguistics.* [2] N-VAR The old traditional beliefs of a religion, political party, or philosophy can be referred to as **orthodoxy**. ...*a return to Marxist orthodoxy.*

ostensibly /ɒˈstensibli/. ADV If something is **ostensibly** true, it seems or is officially stated to be true, but you or other people have doubts about whether it is. ...*ostensibly independent organisations.*

ostentatious /ˌɒstenˈteiʃəs/. [1] ADJ If you describe something or someone as **ostentatious**, you disapprove of them because their content, appearance, or behaviour is intended to impress people with its wealth and importance. ...*an ostentatious wedding reception.* ♦**ostentatiously** ADV *They lived comfortably, but not ostentatiously.* [2] ADJ An **ostentatious** action is done in an exaggerated way in order to attract people's attention. ♦**ostentatiously** ADV *He yawned ostentatiously.*

ostrich /ˈɒstritʃ, AM ˈɔːst-/ **ostriches.** N-C An **ostrich** is a very large African bird that cannot fly.

other /ˈʌðə/ **others.** When **other** follows the determiner 'an', it is written as one word: see **another.** [1] ADJ BEFORE N & PRON You use **other** to refer to an additional thing or person of the same type as one that has been mentioned or is known about. *They were just like any other young couple... Four crewmen were killed, one other was injured.* [2] ADJ BEFORE N & PRON You use **other** to indicate that something is not the thing already mentioned, but something else. *Calls cost 36p per minute cheap rate and 48p per minute at all other times... Some of these methods will work. Others will not.* [3] ADJ BEFORE N & PRON You use **other** to refer to the second of two things or people when the identity of the first is already known or understood, or has already been mentioned. *The Captain was at the other end of the room. ...a cigarette in one hand and a martini in the other.* [4] ADJ BEFORE N & PRON You use **other** to refer the rest of the people or things in a group, or to people or things like the ones just mentioned. *When the other pupils were taken to an exhibition, he was left behind. ...the new physics and astronomy of Copernicus, Galileo, and others.* [5] ADJ BEFORE N & PRON **Other** people are people in general, excluding yourself and the particular person you have mentioned. *She likes to be with other people. ...a brave man who died helping others.* [6] ADJ BEFORE N You use **other** in expressions of time such as **the other day** or **the**

other week to refer to a day or week in the recent past; INFORMAL. *The other evening we had a party.*

PHRASES ● You use **none other than** and **no other than** to emphasize the name of a person or thing when something about that person or thing is surprising. *The manager was none other than his son.* ● You use **other than** after a negative in order to introduce an exception to what you have said. *Geoffrey was left no choice other than to resign.* ● **each other**: see **each**. ● **every other**: see **every**. ● **one or other**: see **one**. ● **in other words**: see **word**.

otherwise /'ʌðəwaɪz/. [1] ADV You use **otherwise** after stating a situation or fact, to say what the result or consequence would be if this situation or fact was not the case. *I'm lucky that I'm interested in school work, otherwise I'd go mad.* [2] ADV You use **otherwise** when stating the general condition or quality of something, when you are also mentioning an exception to this. *He woke at about 7 am, very hungry but otherwise happy.* [3] ADV You use **otherwise** to refer to actions or ways of doing something that are different from the one mentioned in your main statement. *Take approximately 60mg up to four times a day, unless advised otherwise by a doctor.*

ought /ɔːt/. [1] MODAL If you say that someone **ought to** do something, you mean that it is the right or sensible thing to do. If you say that someone **ought to have** done something, you mean that it would have been the right or sensible thing to do, but they did not do it. *You've got a good wife. You ought to take care of her... You ought to ask a lawyer's advice... Perhaps I ought not to interfere... I realize I ought to have told you about it.* [2] MODAL If you say that something **ought to** be true, you mean that you expect it to be true. If you say that something **ought to have** happened, you mean that you expect it to have happened. *'This ought to be fun,' he told Alex, eyes gleaming... He ought to have reached the house some time ago.*

oughtn't /'ɔːtənt/. **Oughtn't** is a spoken form of 'ought not'.

ounce /aʊns/ **ounces.** [1] N-C An **ounce** is a unit of weight used in Britain and the USA. There are sixteen ounces in a pound and one ounce is equal to 28.35 grams. *... four ounces of sugar.* [2] N-SING You can refer to a very small amount of something, such as a quality or characteristic, as an **ounce**. *I spent every ounce of energy trying to hide.*

our /aʊə/. [1] DET A speaker or writer uses **our** to indicate that something belongs or relates both to himself or herself and to one or more other people. *We're expecting our first baby... I locked myself out of our apartment.* [2] DET A speaker or writer sometimes uses **our** to indicate that something belongs or relates to people in general. *The quality of our life depends on keeping well.*

ours /aʊəz/. PRON A speaker or writer uses **ours** to refer to something that belongs or relates to a group of people which includes himself or herself. *There are few strangers in a town like ours.*

ourselves /aʊə'selvz/. [1] PRON A speaker or writer uses **ourselves** to refer to himself or herself and one or more other people as a group. *We sat round the fire to keep ourselves warm... We admitted to ourselves that we were tired.* [2] PRON A speaker or writer sometimes uses **ourselves** to refer to people in general. *When we exert ourselves our heart rate increases.* [3] PRON You use **ourselves** to emphasize the first person plural subject, or to emphasize that you are referring to a particular group of people and nobody else. *Others are feeling just the way we ourselves would feel in the same situation... We did it ourselves.*

oust /aʊst/ **ousts, ousting, ousted.** VERB If someone **is ousted** from a position of power or from a job or place, they are forced to leave it. *They tried to oust him in a parliamentary vote of no confidence.* ◆**ousting** N-U *...the ousting of Mr Perez.*

out /aʊt/. [1] ADV When you go **out** of a place or get **out** of something such as a vehicle, you leave it, so that you are no longer inside it. If you keep **out** of a place, you do not go into it. *The waitress came out of the kitchen... She got out of bed and put on her robe... Nurses and doctors rushed out... Electric fences are erected to keep out animals.* [2] ADV If you are **out**, you are not at home or not at your usual place of work. *She almost certainly left the house while you were out... I went out looking for the kids.* [3] ADV If you take something **out** of a place or container, you remove it from there. *Carefully pull out the centre pages... He took out his notebook... I always took my key out of my bag and put it in my pocket.* [4] ADV If you look or shout **out** of a window, you look or shout through it at someone or something that is outside. *He went to the window and stared out at the dark sky... Her mother waved at her out of the train window.* [5] PREP If you get **out of** a situation or **out of** something such as the rain or wind, you are no longer in it. *Children may lie to get out of trouble... Stay out of politics... Keep your child out of the sun.* [6] ADJ AFTER LINK-V & ADV If a light or fire is **out**, it is no longer shining or burning. If it goes **out**, it stops burning or shining. *The candle went out.* [7] ADJ AFTER LINK-V & ADV If flowers are **out**, their petals have opened. If they come **out**, their petals open. [8] ADJ AFTER LINK-V & ADV If something such as a book or record is **out** or comes **out**, it is available for people to buy. *Our new spring catalogue is out now.* [9] ADJ AFTER LINK-V In a game or sport, if someone is **out**, they can no longer take part either because the rules say so or because they are unable to. [10] ADJ AFTER LINK-V If you say that a proposal or suggestion is **out**, you mean that it is unacceptable or impossible. [11] ADJ AFTER LINK-V If you say that a calculation or measurement is **out**, you mean that it is incorrect. *They were only a few inches out.* [12] ADJ AFTER LINK-V If you say that someone is **out** to do something, usually something that you disapprove of, you mean they intend to do it; INFORMAL. *Most companies these days are just out to make a quick profit.* [13] PREP You use **out of** to say what causes someone to do something. For example, if you do something **out of** pity, you do it because you pity someone. *He took up office out of a sense of duty.* **14** PREP If you get something such as pleasure, an advantage, or information **out of** something or someone, they give it to you or cause you to have it. *To get the most out of your money, you have to invest... Employers are looking to get more work out of fewer people.* **15** PREP If you are **out of** something, you no longer have any of it. *We're out of milk.* **16** PREP If something is made **out of** a particular material, it is formed or constructed using it. **17** PREP You use **out of** to indicate what proportion of a group of things something is true of. For example, if something is true of one **out of** five things, it is true of one fifth of all things of that kind. *One out of every two households owns a microwave.*

outback /ˈaʊtbæk/. N-SING The parts of Australia where very few people live are referred to as the **outback**.

outbreak /ˈaʊtbreɪk/ **outbreaks.** N-C An **outbreak** of something unpleasant is a sudden occurrence of it. *...the outbreak of war.*

outburst /ˈaʊtbɜːst/ **outbursts.** **1** N-C An **outburst** of an emotion, especially anger, is a sudden strong expression of that emotion. *...a spontaneous outburst of cheers and applause.* **2** N-C An **outburst** of violent activity is a sudden period of this activity. *Five people were reported killed today in a fresh outburst of violence.*

outcast /ˈaʊtkɑːst, -kæst/ **outcasts.** N-C An **outcast** is someone who is rejected by a group of people. *All of us felt like social outcasts.*

outcome /ˈaʊtkʌm/ **outcomes.** N-C The **outcome** of an action or process is the result of it. *It's too early to know the outcome of her illness.*

outcry /ˈaʊtkraɪ/ **outcries.** N-C An **outcry** is a reaction of strong disapproval and anger shown by the public or media about a recent event. *The killing caused an international outcry.*

outdated /ˌaʊtˈdeɪtɪd/. ADJ Something that is **outdated** is old-fashioned and no longer useful. *...outdated and inefficient factories.*

outdo /ˌaʊtˈduː/ **outdoes, outdoing, outdid, outdone.** VERB If you **outdo** someone, you are more successful than they are at a particular activity. *...each man trying to outdo the other in boasts of his wartime exploits.*

outdoor /ˌaʊtˈdɔː/. ADJ BEFORE N **Outdoor** activities or things take place or are used outside, rather than in a building. *She excelled at outdoor sports. ...outdoor furniture.*

outdoors /ˌaʊtˈdɔːz/. ADV & N-SING If something happens **outdoors**, or if it happens in **the outdoors**, it happens outside in the fresh air rather than in a building. *It was warm enough to be outdoors all afternoon.*

outer /ˈaʊtə/. ADJ BEFORE N The **outer** parts of something are the parts which enclose the other parts, and which are farthest from the centre. *...burns that damage only the outer layer of skin. ...the outer suburbs of the city.*

,outer ˈspace. N-U **Outer space** refers to the area outside the Earth's atmosphere where planets and stars are.

outfit /ˈaʊtfɪt/ **outfits, outfitting, outfitted.** **1** N-C An **outfit** is a set of clothes. *...smart new outfits for work. ...a maid's outfit.* **2** N-C You can refer to a group of people or an organization as an **outfit**; INFORMAL. *We are a professional outfit.* **3** VERB To **outfit** someone or something means to provide them with equipment for a particular purpose; AMERICAN. *I outfitted an attic bedroom as a studio.*

outflow /ˈaʊtfləʊ/ **outflows.** N-C When there is an **outflow** of money or people, a large amount of money or people move from one place to another.

outgoing /ˌaʊtˈɡəʊɪŋ/. **1** ADJ BEFORE N An **outgoing** president, chairman, or minister is one who is going to leave. **2** ADJ An **outgoing** person is very friendly and likes meeting people. **3** ADJ BEFORE N **Outgoing** things such as planes, mail, and passengers are leaving somewhere or being sent somewhere.

outgoings /ˈaʊtɡəʊɪŋz/. N-PL Your **outgoings** are the regular amounts of money which you have to spend every week or every month, for example in order to pay your rent or bills; BRITISH.

outgrow /ˌaʊtˈɡrəʊ/ **outgrows, outgrowing, outgrew, outgrown.** VERB If you **outgrow** a piece of clothing, you get bigger and can no longer wear it.

outing /ˈaʊtɪŋ/ **outings.** N-C An **outing** is a short enjoyable trip, usually with a group of people, away from your home, school, or place of work. *...a family outing to London.*

outlaw /ˈaʊtlɔː/ **outlaws, outlawing, outlawed.** **1** VERB When something is **outlawed**, it is made illegal. *In 1975, gambling was outlawed.* **2** N-C An **outlaw** is a criminal who is hiding from the authorities; DATED.

outlay /ˈaʊtleɪ/ **outlays.** N-C An **outlay** is an amount of money that is invested in a piece of equipment, project, or business; FORMAL.

outlet /ˈaʊtlet/ **outlets.** **1** N-C If someone has an **outlet** for their feelings or ideas, they have a means of expressing and releasing them. *Boxing now became one of the main outlets for his incredible energy.* **2** N-C An **outlet** is a shop or organization which sells the goods made by a particular manufacturer. *...the largest retail outlet in the city.* **3** N-C An **outlet** is a hole or pipe through which water or air can flow away. *...the sewage outlet.* **4** N-C In American English, an **outlet** is a device in a wall where you can connect electrical equipment to the electricity supply. The British word is **socket**.

outline /ˈaʊtlaɪn/ **outlines, outlining, outlined.** **1** VERB & N-C If you **outline** an idea or plan, or if you present an **outline** of it, you explain it in a general way. *The mayor outlined his plan to clean up the town's image. ...an outline of the survey findings.* **2** N-C The **outline** of an object is the general shape of it that you can see, for example when there is a light behind it. *...the hazy outline of the goalposts.* **3** VERB When an object **is outlined**, you can see its general shape because there is a light behind it. *The hotel was outlined against the lights.*

outlive /ˌaʊtˈlɪv/ **outlives, outliving, outlived.** VERB If one person **outlives** another, they are still alive after the other person has died. If one thing **outlives** another thing, the first thing continues to exist after the second has disappeared or been replaced. *I'm sure Rose will outlive many of us... The UN is an organisation which has long since outlived its usefulness.*

outlook /ˈaʊtlʊk/. [1] N-C Your **outlook** is your general attitude towards life. *The experience improved my outlook on life.* [2] N-SING The **outlook** for something is whether or not it is going to be prosperous, successful, or safe. *He said the inflation outlook remained good.*

outlying /ˈaʊtlaɪɪŋ/. ADJ BEFORE N **Outlying** places are far away from the main cities of a country. *Tourists can visit outlying areas like the Napa Valley.*

outnumber /ˌaʊtˈnʌmbə/ **outnumbers, outnumbering, outnumbered.** VERB If one group of people or things **outnumbers** another, the first group has more people or things in it than the second group. *...a town where men outnumber women four to one.*

out of 'date. ADJ Something that is **out of date** is old-fashioned and no longer useful. *Think how rapidly medical knowledge has gone out of date. ...out-of-date computers.*

out of 'work. ADJ Someone who is **out of work** does not have a job.

outpost /ˈaʊtpəʊst/ **outposts.** N-C An **outpost** is a small settlement in a foreign country or in a distant area. *...a remote mountain outpost.*

output /ˈaʊtpʊt/ **outputs.** [1] N-VAR You use **output** to refer to the amount of something that a person or thing produces. *...the largest drop in industrial output for ten years.* [2] N-VAR The **output** from a computer is the information that it displays on a screen or prints on paper as a result of a particular program.

outrage, outrages, outraging, outraged; verb /aʊtˈreɪdʒ/, noun /ˈaʊtreɪdʒ/. [1] VERB If something **outrages** you, it makes you extremely shocked and angry. *The Civil Liberties Union is outraged by the court's decision.* ♦**outraged** ADJ *Outraged readers said the story was extremely offensive.* [2] N-U **Outrage** is a feeling of shock and anger about something. *The decision provoked outrage from women.* [3] N-C You can refer to an act or event which you find very shocking as an **outrage**. *It is an outrage that women are denied the same financial assistance as men.*

outrageous /aʊtˈreɪdʒəs/. ADJ If you describe something as **outrageous**, you are emphasizing that it is unacceptable or very shocking. *...his outrageous drunken behaviour.* ♦**outrageously** ADV *...outrageously expensive clothes.*

outright; adjective /ˈaʊtraɪt/, adverb /aʊtˈraɪt/. [1] ADJ BEFORE N & ADV You use **outright** to describe actions and behaviour that are open and direct, rather than indirect. *...an outright lie... Why don't you tell me outright?* [2] ADJ BEFORE N & ADV **Outright** means complete and total. *She had failed to win an outright victory... The peace plan wasn't rejected outright.* [3] PHRASE If someone **is killed outright**, they die immediately, for example in an accident.

outset /ˈaʊtset/. PHRASE If something happens **at the outset** of an event, process, or period of time, it happens at the beginning of it. If something happens **from the outset** it happens from the beginning and continues to happen. *Decide at the outset what kind of learning programme you want... It's clear from the outset that their love is doomed.*

outside /ˌaʊtˈsaɪd/ **outsides.** [1] N-C & ADJ BEFORE N The **outside** of something such as a building or a container is the part which surrounds or encloses the rest of it. *The moth was on the outside of the glass. ...the outside wall.* [2] ADV & PREP & ADJ BEFORE N If you are **outside** a building, place, or country, you are not in it. *They heard voices coming from outside... The victim was outside a shop when he was attacked. ...an outside lavatory.* [3] ADJ BEFORE N When you talk about the **outside** world, you are referring to things that exist or happen in places other than your own home or community. *...a side of her character she hid carefully from the outside world.* [4] ADJ BEFORE N On a road with two or more lanes, the **outside** lane is the one for overtaking or for travelling at high speed. [5] ADJ BEFORE N & PREP **Outside** people or organizations are not part of a particular organization or group. *...outside consultants... He is hoping to recruit a chairman from outside the company.* [6] PREP You use **outside** to refer to a particular thing or range of things which are not part of something or not included within it. *She is a beautiful boat, but way, way outside my price range.* [7] PREP Something that happens **outside** a particular period of time does not happen during that time. *They are open outside normal daily banking hours.*

outsider /ˌaʊtˈsaɪdə/ **outsiders.** [1] N-C An **outsider** is someone who does not belong to a particular group or organization, or is not accepted by them. *Malone, a cop, felt as much an outsider as any of them.* [2] N-C In a competition, an **outsider** is a competitor who is unlikely to win.

outskirts /ˈaʊtskɜːts/. N-PL The **outskirts** of a city or town are the parts that are farthest from its centre. *...the outskirts of New York.*

outspoken /ˌaʊtˈspəʊkən/. ADJ If you are **outspoken**, you give your opinions about things openly, even if they shock people. *...his outspoken criticism of the prime minister.* ♦**outspokenness** N-U *Her outspokenness had alienated many voters.*

outstanding /aʊtˈstændɪŋ/. [1] ADJ If you describe a person or their work as **outstanding**, you think that they are remarkable and impressive. *...an outstanding athlete.* ♦**outstandingly** ADV *...outstandingly successful schools.* [2] ADJ **Outstanding** means very obvious or important. *...an outstanding example of a small business that grew into a big one.* [3] ADJ Money that is **outstanding** has not yet been paid and is still owed to someone. *The total debt outstanding is $70 billion.* [4] ADJ **Outstanding** issues or problems have not yet been resolved.

outstretched /aʊtˈstretʃt/. ADJ If your arms, fingers, legs, or feet are **outstretched**, they are stretched as far as they can go. *He was* *wrapped in a blanket and held his arms out-stretched.*

outstrip /ˌaʊtˈstrɪp/ **outstrips, outstripping, outstripped.** VERB If one thing **outstrips** another, the first thing becomes larger in amount, or more successful or important, than the second thing. *...wage rises that far out-stripped productivity.*

outward /ˈaʊtwəd/ **1** ADJ BEFORE N An **outward** journey is a journey that you make away from a place that you are intending to return to later. *Tickets must be bought in advance, with outward and return dates specified.* **2** ADJ BE-FORE N The **outward** feelings, qualities, or attitudes of someone or something are the ones they appear to have rather than the ones they actually have. *What the military rulers have done is to restore the outward appearance of order.* ♦ **outwardly** ADV *People were outwardly hostile.* **3** ADJ BEFORE N The **outward** features of something are the ones that you can see from the outside. *Mark was lying unconscious but with no outward sign of injury.*

outwards /ˈaʊtwədz/; the form **outward** is also used. In American English, **outward** is more usual. ADV If something moves or faces **outwards**, it moves or faces away from the place you are in or the place you are talking about. *The top door opened outwards.*

outweigh /ˌaʊtˈweɪ/ **outweighs, outweighing, outweighed.** VERB If, for example, the benefits of something **outweigh** the disadvantages, it has some disadvantages but is more beneficial than harmful; FORMAL. *The medical benefits of x-rays far outweigh the risk of having them.*

outwit /ˌaʊtˈwɪt/ **outwits, outwitting, outwitted.** VERB If you **outwit** someone, you use your intelligence or a clever trick to defeat them or to gain an advantage over them. *To win the presidency he had first to outwit his rivals.*

oval /ˈəʊvəl/ **ovals.** N-C & ADJ An **oval** or an **oval** shape is a round shape which is similar to a circle, but is wider in one direction than the other. *...a pale oval face.*

ovary /ˈəʊvəri/ **ovaries.** N-C A woman's **ovaries** are the two organs in her body that produce eggs.

ovation /əʊˈveɪʃən/ **ovations.** N-C An **ovation** is a long burst of applause from an audience for a particular performer.

oven /ˈʌvən/ **ovens.** N-C An **oven** is a cooker or part of a cooker that is like a box with a door. You cook food inside an oven.

over 1 position and movement

over /ˈəʊvə/. **1** PREP & ADV If one thing is **over** another thing or is moving **over** it, the first thing is directly above the other, either resting on it, or with a space between them. *He looked at himself in the mirror over the table. ...the small iron bridge over the stream. ...planes flying over every 10 or 15 minutes.* **2** PREP & ADV If one thing is **over** another thing, it covers part or all of it. *He was wearing a light-grey suit over a shirt... The workers decided it would be too difficult to recover it so they covered it over.* **3** PREP & ADV If you lean **over** an object, you bend your body so that the top part of it is above the object. *She bent over the*

table, frowning... Sam leant over to open the door of the car. **4** PREP If you look **over** or talk **over** an object, you look or talk across the top of it. *I went and stood beside him, looking over his shoulder.* **5** PREP If a window has a view **over** an area of land or water, you can see the land or water through the window. **6** PREP & ADV If someone or something goes **over** a barrier or boundary, they get to the other side of it by going across it, or across the top of it. *Policemen jumped over the wall in pursuit... I climbed over into the back seat.* **7** PREP If something is on the opposite side of a road or river, you can say that it is **over** the road or **over** the river. *...Richard Garrick, who lived in the house over the road.* **8** ADV You use **over** to indicate a particular position or place away from you. *He noticed Rolfe standing silently over by the window.* **9** PHRASE **Over here** means near you, or in the country you are in. **Over there** means in a place a short distance away from you, or in another country. *Why don't you come over here tomorrow evening... She'd married some American and settled down over there.* **10** ADV If something rolls **over** or is turned **over**, its position changes so that the part that was facing upwards is now facing downwards. *His car rolled over after a tyre punctured.*

over 2 amounts and time

over /ˈəʊvə/. **1** PREP & ADV If something is **over** a particular amount, measurement, or age, it is more than that amount, measurement, or age. *Cigarettes kill over a hundred thousand Britains every year. ...people aged 65 and over.* **2** PHRASE **Over and above** an amount, especially a normal amount, means more than that amount or in addition to it. *Expenditure on education has gone up by seven point eight per cent over and above inflation.* **3** ADJ AFTER LINK-V If an activity is **over** or all **over**, it is completely finished. *The bad times were over... I am glad it's all over.* **4** PREP If something happens **over** a period of time, it happens during that time. *Many strikes over the last few years have not ended successfully.* **5** PREP If you are **over** an illness or an experience, it has finished and you have recovered from its effects. *I'm glad that you're over the flu.*

over 3 cause and influence

over /ˈəʊvə/. **1** PREP You use **over** to indicate what a disagreement or feeling relates to or is caused by. *...concern over recent events in Burma.* **2** PREP If you have control or influence **over** someone or something, you are able to control them or influence them. *The oil companies have lost their power over oil prices.*

overall, overalls; adjective and adverb /ˌəʊvərˈɔːl/, noun /ˈəʊvərɔːl/. **1** ADJ BEFORE N & ADV You use **overall** to indicate that you are talking about a situation in general or about the whole of something. *Cut down your overall amount of physical activity. ...the quality of education overall.* **2** N-PL **Overalls** are a piece of clothing that combine trousers and a shirt which you wear over your clothes to protect them while you are working. **3** N-C An **overall**

is a type of coat that you wear over your clothes to protect them while you are working.

overboard /ˈəʊvəbɔːd/. ADV If you fall **overboard**, you fall over the side of a ship into the water.

overcame /ˌəʊvəˈkeɪm/. **Overcame** is the past tense of **overcome**.

overcharge /ˌəʊvəˈtʃɑːdʒ/ **overcharges, overcharging, overcharged.** VERB If someone **overcharges** you, they charge you too much for their goods or services.

overcoat /ˈəʊvəkəʊt/ **overcoats.** N-C An **overcoat** is a thick warm coat.

overcome /ˌəʊvəˈkʌm/ **overcomes, overcoming, overcame, overcome.** [1] VERB If you **overcome** a problem or a feeling, you successfully deal with it and control it. *Molly had fought and overcome her fear of flying.* [2] VERB If you **are overcome** by a feeling, you feel it very strongly. *The night before the test I was overcome by fear and despair.* [3] VERB If you **are overcome** by smoke or a poisonous gas, you become very ill or die from breathing it in.

overcrowded /ˌəʊvəˈkraʊdɪd/. ADJ An **overcrowded** place has too many things or people in it. *...one of the most overcrowded prisons in the country.*

overcrowding /ˌəʊvəˈkraʊdɪŋ/. N-U If there is **overcrowding** in a place, there are more people living there than it was designed for. *...overcrowding and lack of facilities for patients.*

overdo /ˌəʊvəˈduː/ **overdoes, overdoing, overdid, overdone.** [1] VERB If someone **overdoes** something, they behave in an exaggerated or extreme way. *He thought Dan was overdoing the charity bit.* [2] VERB If you **overdo** an activity, you try to do more than you can physically manage. *Satisfy your urge to take exercise but don't overdo it.*

overdose /ˈəʊvədəʊs/ **overdoses, overdosing, overdosed.** N-C & VERB If someone takes an **overdose** of a drug, or if they **overdose** on it, they take more of it than is safe. *Guitarist Jimi Hendrix died of a drug overdose... He'd overdosed on heroin.*

overdraft /ˈəʊvədrɑːft, -dræft/ **overdrafts.** N-C If you have an **overdraft**, you have spent more money than you have in your bank account, and so you are in debt to the bank.

overdue /ˌəʊvəˈdjuː, -ˈduː/. [1] ADJ If you say that a change or an event is **overdue**, you mean that it should have happened before now. *This debate is long overdue.* [2] ADJ **Overdue** sums of money have not been paid, even though it is later than the date on which they should have been paid.

overeat /ˌəʊvəˈiːt/ **overeats, overeating, overate, overeaten.** VERB If you **overeat**, you eat more than you should.

overestimate /ˌəʊvərˈestɪmeɪt/ **overestimates, overestimating, overestimated.** VERB If you **overestimate** someone or something, you think that they are better, bigger, or more important than they really are. *I think you overestimate me, Fred.*

overflow, overflows, overflowing, overflowed. [1] VERB /ˌəʊvəˈfləʊ/ If a liquid or a river er **overflows**, it flows over the edges of the container or the place it is in. *The sewers were overflowing and the river was bursting its banks.* [2] VERB If a place or container is **overflowing** with people or things, there are too many of them in it. *The great hall was overflowing with people.* [3] VERB If someone **is overflowing** with a feeling, or if the feeling **overflows**, the person is experiencing it very strongly and shows this in their behaviour. *Kenneth overflowed with friendliness and hospitality.* [4] N-C /ˈəʊvəfləʊ/ An **overflow** is a hole or pipe through which liquid can flow out of a container when it gets too full.

overgrown /ˌəʊvəˈɡrəʊn/. ADJ If a place is **overgrown**, it is thickly covered with plants because it has not been looked after. *...a courtyard overgrown with weeds.*

overhang /ˌəʊvəˈhæŋ/ **overhangs, overhanging, overhung.** VERB If one thing **overhangs** another, it sticks out over and above it. *Part of the rock wall overhung the path.*

overhaul, overhauls, overhauling, overhauled; verb /ˌəʊvəˈhɔːl/, noun /ˈəʊvəhɔːl/. [1] VERB & N-C If a piece of equipment **is overhauled**, or if you give it an **overhaul**, it is cleaned, checked thoroughly, and repaired if necessary. *He had had his little Fiat car overhauled three times.* [2] VERB & N-C If you **overhaul** a system or method, or if you give it an **overhaul**, you examine it carefully and change it in order to improve it. *...a complete overhaul of air traffic control systems.*

overhead; adjective /ˈəʊvəhed/, adverb /ˌəʊvəˈhed/. ADJ BEFORE N & ADV You use **overhead** to indicate that something is above you or above the place you are talking about. *...the overhead light... Helicopters have been flying overhead.*

overheads /ˈəʊvəhedz/. N-PL The **overheads** of a business are its regular and essential expenses.

overhear /ˌəʊvəˈhɪə/ **overhears, overhearing, overheard.** VERB If you **overhear** someone, you hear what they are saying when they are not talking to you and do not know that you are listening. *I overheard two doctors discussing my case.*

overheat /ˌəʊvəˈhiːt/ **overheats, overheating, overheated.** VERB If a machine **overheats**, or if you **overheat** it, it becomes hotter than is necessary or desirable. *The engine was overheating and the car was not handling well.* ♦**overheated** ADJ *...that stuffy, overheated apartment.*

overhung /ˌəʊvəˈhʌŋ/. **Overhung** is the past tense and past participle of **overhang**.

overjoyed /ˌəʊvəˈdʒɔɪd/. ADJ If you are **overjoyed**, you are extremely pleased about something. *Shelley was overjoyed to see me.*

overland /ˈəʊvəlænd/. ADJ BEFORE N & ADV An **overland** journey is made across land rather than by ship or aeroplane. *...the overland route... They're travelling to Baghdad overland.*

overlap, overlaps, overlapping, overlapped; verb /ˌəʊvəˈlæp/, noun /ˈəʊvəlæp/. [1] VERB If one thing **overlaps** another, one part of the first thing covers a part of the other. You can also say that two things **overlap**. *Overlap* the slices carefully so there are no gaps... The edges must overlap each other. [2] VERB & N-C If one idea or activity **overlaps** another, they involve some of the same subjects, people, or periods of time. You can also say that two ideas or activities **overlap**, or that there is an **overlap** between them. ...the overlap between civil and military technology.

overleaf /ˌəʊvəˈliːf/. ADV **Overleaf** is used in books and magazines to say that something is on the other side of the page you are reading. Answer the questionnaire overleaf.

overload /ˌəʊvəˈləʊd/ **overloads, overloading, overloaded.** [1] VERB If you **overload** a vehicle, you put more things or people in it than it was designed to carry. Don't overload the boat or it will sink. ♦**overloaded** ADJ Some trains were so overloaded that their suspension collapsed. [2] VERB & N-C To **overload** someone **with** work or problems means to give them more work or problems than they can manage. This can also be called an **overload**. ...an effective method that will not overload staff with yet more paperwork... 57 per cent complained of work overload. ♦**overloaded** ADJ The bar waiter was already overloaded with orders.

overlook /ˌəʊvəˈlʊk/ **overlooks, overlooking, overlooked.** [1] VERB If a building or window **overlooks** a place, you can see the place from the building or window. Pretty and comfortable rooms overlook a flower-filled garden. [2] VERB If you **overlook** a fact or problem, you do not notice it, or do not realize how important it is. We overlook all sorts of warning signals about our own health. [3] VERB If you **overlook** someone's faults or bad behaviour, you forgive them and take no action. ...satisfying relationships that enable them to overlook each other's faults.

overly /ˈəʊvəli/. ADV **Overly** means more than is normal, necessary, or reasonable. Employers may become overly cautious about taking on new staff.

overnight /ˌəʊvəˈnaɪt/. [1] ADV & ADJ BEFORE N **Overnight** means throughout the night or at some point during the night. The weather remained calm overnight. ...overnight accommodation. [2] ADV & ADJ BEFORE N You can say that something happens **overnight** when it happens quickly and unexpectedly. The rules are not going to change overnight... He became an overnight success.

overpower /ˌəʊvəˈpaʊə/ **overpowers, overpowering, overpowered.** [1] VERB If you **overpower** someone, you seize them despite their struggles because you are stronger than they are. It took ten guardsmen to overpower him. [2] VERB If a feeling **overpowers** you, it suddenly affects you very strongly. A sudden dizziness overpowered him. ♦**overpowering** ADJ The desire for revenge can be overpowering.

overpowering /ˌəʊvəˈpaʊərɪŋ/. ADJ An **overpowering** person makes other people feel uncomfortable because they have such a strong personality.

overran (or **over-ran**) /ˌəʊvəˈræn/. **Overran** is the past tense of **overrun**.

overrate (or **over-rate**) /ˌəʊvəˈreɪt/ **overrates, overrating, overrated.** VERB If you say that

something or someone **is overrated**, you mean that people have a higher opinion of them than they deserve. More men are finding out that the joys of work have been overrated. ♦**overrated** ADJ Life in the wild is vastly overrated.

override (or **over-ride**) /ˌəʊvəˈraɪd/ **overrides, overriding, overrode, overridden.** [1] VERB If one thing in a situation **overrides** other things, it is more important than them. The welfare of a child should always override the wishes of its parents. ♦**overriding** ADJ ...the overriding need to cut the budget. [2] VERB If someone in authority **overrides** a person or their decisions, they cancel their decisions. ...the authority to override him.

overrule (or **over-rule**) /ˌəʊvəˈruːl/ **overrules, overruling, overruled.** VERB If someone in authority **overrules** a person or their decision, they officially decide that the decision is incorrect or not valid. In 1991, the Court of Appeal overruled this decision.

overrun (or **over-run**) /ˌəʊvəˈrʌn/ **overruns, overrunning, overran.** [1] VERB If an army **overruns** a country, it succeeds in occupying it quickly. [2] VERB If you say that a place is **overrun** with things that you consider undesirable, you mean that there are a large number of them there. The flower beds were overrun with grasses. [3] VERB If an event or meeting **overruns**, it continues for a longer time than it should have. Tuesday's lunch overran by three-quarters of an hour.

overseas /ˌəʊvəˈsiːz/. [1] ADJ BEFORE N & ADV You use **overseas** to describe things that happen or exist abroad. ...his long overseas trip. ...if you're staying for more than three months or working overseas. [2] ADJ BEFORE N An **overseas** student or visitor comes from abroad.

oversee /ˌəʊvəˈsiː/ **oversees, overseeing, oversaw, overseen.** VERB If someone in authority **oversees** a job or an activity, they make sure that it is done properly. ...an architect or surveyor to oversee the work.

overshadow /ˌəʊvəˈʃædəʊ/ **overshadows, overshadowing, overshadowed.** [1] VERB If an unpleasant event or feeling **overshadows** something, it makes it less happy or enjoyable. Fears for the President's safety could overshadow his peace-making mission. [2] VERB If someone or something **is overshadowed** by another person or thing, they are less successful, important, or impressive than the other person or thing. Hester is overshadowed by her younger and more attractive sister.

oversight /ˈəʊvəsaɪt/ **oversights.** N-C If there has been an **oversight**, someone has forgotten to do something which they should have done. By an unfortunate oversight, full instructions do not come with the product.

oversized /ˈəʊvəsaɪzd/. ADJ **Oversized** things are bigger than usual. ...an oversized bed.

overstate /ˌəʊvəˈsteɪt/ **overstates, overstating, overstated.** VERB If you say that someone is **overstating** something, you mean they are describing it in a way that makes it seem more important or serious than it really is. Many scientists think this method overstates the dangers.

overt /ˌəʊˈvɜːt/. ADJ An **overt** action or attitude is done or shown in an open and obvious way. *Although there is no overt hostility, black and white students do not mix much.* ◆**overtly** ADV *...overtly political issues.*

overtake /ˌəʊvəˈteɪk/ **overtakes, overtaking, overtook, overtaken.** [1] VERB If you **overtake** a moving vehicle or person, you pass them because you are moving faster than they are. [2] VERB If an event **overtakes** you, it happens unexpectedly or suddenly. *Something like panic overtook me in a flood.*

overthrow, overthrows, overthrowing, overthrew, overthrown; verb /ˌəʊvəˈθrəʊ/, noun /ˈəʊvəθrəʊ/. VERB & N-SING When a government or a leader is **overthrown**, they are removed from power by force. You can also talk about the **overthrow** of a government or leader. *That government was overthrown in a military coup. ...the overthrow of the state.*

overtime /ˈəʊvətaɪm/. N-U **Overtime** is time that you spend doing your job in addition to your normal working hours. *He would work overtime, without pay, to finish a job.*

overtone /ˈəʊvətəʊn/ **overtones.** N-C If something has **overtones** of a particular thing or quality, it has a small amount of that thing or quality but does not openly express it. *...a speech that had overtones of a sermon.*

overtook /ˌəʊvəˈtʊk/. **Overtook** is the past tense of **overtake.**

overture /ˈəʊvətʃʊə/ **overtures.** N-C An **overture** is a piece of music, often one that is used as the introduction to an opera or play.

overturn /ˌəʊvəˈtɜːn/ **overturns, overturning, overturned.** [1] VERB If something **overturns**, or if you **overturn** it, it turns upside down or on its side. *Alex jumped up so violently that he overturned his glass of sherry.* [2] VERB If someone in authority **overturns** a legal decision, they officially decide that that decision is incorrect or not valid. [3] VERB To **overturn** a government or system means to remove it or destroy it.

overview /ˈəʊvəvjuː/ **overviews.** N-C An **overview** of a situation is a general understanding or description of it as a whole. *...a historical overview of drug use.*

overweight /ˌəʊvəˈweɪt/. ADJ Someone who is **overweight** weighs more than is considered healthy or attractive. ● See note at **fat.**

overwhelm /ˌəʊvəˈwelm/ **overwhelms, overwhelming, overwhelmed.** [1] VERB If you are **overwhelmed** by a feeling or event, it affects you very strongly and you do not know how to deal with it. *Her brightness overwhelmed me.* ◆**overwhelmed** ADJ *...overwhelmed by the crowds and noise.* [2] VERB If a group of people **overwhelm** a place or another group, they gain control over them. *One massive Allied offensive would overwhelm the weakened enemy.*

overwhelming /ˌəʊvəˈwelmɪŋ/. [1] ADJ If something is **overwhelming**, it affects you very strongly, and you do not know how to deal with it. *...an overwhelming desire to have another child.* ◆**overwhelmingly** ADV *Women found him overwhelmingly attractive.* [2] ADJ You can use **overwhelming** to emphasize that an amount or quantity is much greater than other amounts or quantities. *The overwhelming majority of small businesses go broke within the first twenty-four months.* ◆**overwhelmingly** ADJ *The House of Commons has overwhelmingly rejected calls to bring back the death penalty.*

overwork /ˌəʊvəˈwɜːk/ **overworks, overworking, overworked.** VERB & N-U If you **overwork**, or if you suffer from **overwork**, you work too hard, and are likely to become very tired or ill. *He overworks and underpays the poor clerk whom he employs. ...a heart attack brought on by overwork.* ◆**overworked** ADJ *...an overworked doctor.*

ovulate /ˈɒvjʊleɪt/ **ovulates, ovulating, ovulated.** VERB When a woman **ovulates**, she produces eggs from her ovary. ◆**ovulation** N-U *The woman can tell when ovulation is about to occur.*

owe /əʊ/ **owes, owing, owed.** [1] VERB If you **owe** money to someone, they have lent it to you and you have not yet paid it back. *The company owes money to more than 60 banks... Blake already owed him nearly £50.* [2] VERB If someone or something **owes** a particular quality, their success, or their existence to a person or thing, they only have it because of that person or thing. *I owe him my life.* [3] VERB If you say that you **owe** someone gratitude, respect, or loyalty, you mean that they deserve it from you; FORMAL. *I owe you an apology... I owe a big debt of gratitude to her.* [4] VERB If you say that you **owe it to** someone to do something, you mean that you should do that thing because they deserve it. *I can't go. I owe it to him to stay.* [5] PREP You use **owing to** to introduce the reason for something. *He was out of work owing to a physical injury.*

owl /aʊl/ **owls.** N-C An **owl** is a bird with large eyes which hunts small animals at night.

own /əʊn/ **owns, owning, owned.** [1] ADJ & PRON You use **own** to indicate that something belongs to or is typical of a particular person or thing. *My wife decided I should have my own shop... I let her tell me about it in her own way. ...a sense of style that is very much her own.* [2] ADJ & PRON You use **own** to emphasize that someone does something without any help from other people. *He'll have to make his own arrangements... There's no career structure, you have to create your own.* [3] VERB If you **own** something, it is your property. *His father owns a local pub.*

PHRASES ● When you are **on** your **own**, you are alone. ● If you do something **on your own**, you do it without any help from other people. *I work best on my own.* ● If someone or something **comes into** their **own**, they become very successful or start to perform very well because the circumstances are right. *The goalkeeper came into his own with a series of brilliant saves.*

▸ **own up.** PHR-VERB If you **own up** to something wrong that you have done, you admit that you did it. *Last year my husband owned up to an affair with his secretary.*

owner /ˈəʊnə/ **owners.** N-C The **owner** of something is the person to whom it belongs. *...the* *owner of the store... Every pet owner knows their animal has its own personality.*

ownership /'əʊnəʃɪp/. N-U **Ownership** of something is the state of owning it. *...the growth of home ownership in Britain.*

ox /ɒks/ **oxen.** N-C An **ox** is a castrated bull.

oxygen /'ɒksɪdʒən/. N-U **Oxygen** is a colourless gas in the air which is needed by all plants and animals.

oyster /'ɔɪstə/ **oysters.** N-C An **oyster** is a large flat shellfish.

oz. **oz** is a written abbreviation for 'ounce'.

ozone /'əʊzəʊn/. N-U **Ozone** is a form of oxygen. There is a layer of ozone high above the earth's surface.

'ozone layer. N-SING The **ozone layer** is the part of the Earth's atmosphere that has the highest number of ozone molecules.

P p

p /piː/. **p** is an abbreviation for 'pence' or 'page'. *They cost 5p each... See Note 16 on p. 223.*

pace /peɪs/ **paces, pacing, paced.** [1] N-U The **pace** of something is the speed at which it happens or is done. *Many people were not satisfied with the pace of change.* [2] N-SING Your **pace** is the speed at which you walk. *He moved at a brisk pace.* [3] N-C A **pace** is the distance you move when you take one step. *I took a pace backwards.* [4] VERB If you **pace** a small area, you keep walking up and down it, because you are anxious or impatient. *Kravis paced the room nervously... He found John pacing around the flat.*

PHRASES • To **keep pace** with something that is changing means to change quickly in response to it. *...a world changing far too fast for her to keep pace.* • If you do something at your **own pace**, you do it at a speed that is comfortable for you.

pacifier /'pæsɪfaɪə/ **pacifiers.** N-C In American English, a **pacifier** is a rubber or plastic object that you give to a baby to suck so that it feels comforted. The British word is **dummy**.

pacifist /'pæsɪfɪst/ **pacifists.** N-C & ADJ A **pacifist** or someone with **pacifist** views believes that war and violence are always wrong. ♦**pacifism** N-U *He didn't hide his pacifism.*

pack /pæk/ **packs, packing, packed.** [1] VERB & PHR-VERB When you **pack**, or when you **pack up**, you put your belongings into a bag, because you are leaving. *I packed my bags and left home... He began packing his things.* ♦**packing** N-U *She left Frances to finish her packing.* [2] VERB To **pack** things, for example in a factory, means to put them into containers or parcels so that they can be transported and sold. *Machines now exist to pack olives in jars.* [3] VERB If people or things **pack into** a place, or if they **pack** a place, there are so many of them that the place is full. *A thousand supporters packed into the stadium... Thousands of people packed the square.* ♦**packed** ADJ *The stores were packed with shoppers.* [4] N-C A **pack** of things is a collection of them in one packet. *...a free information pack. ...a pack of cigarettes.* [5] N-C A **pack** is a bag containing your belongings that you carry on your back when you are travelling. *I hid the money in my pack.* [6] N-C A **pack** of wolves or dogs is a group of them hunting together. [7] N-C In British English, a **pack** of cards is a complete set of playing cards. The usual American word is **deck**.

▸ **pack off.** PHR-VERB If you **pack** someone **off** somewhere, you send them there; INFORMAL. *At the age of nine she was packed off to boarding school in England.*

package /'pækɪdʒ/ **packages, packaging, packaged.** [1] N-C A **package** is a small parcel. *The package was addressed to Yusuf.* [2] N-C A **package** is a set of proposals that are made by a government or organization. *...a Western economic aid package for Moscow.* [3] VERB When something **is packaged**, it is put into packets to be sold.

packaging /'pækɪdʒɪŋ/. N-U **Packaging** is the container or wrappings that something is sold in. *...layers of expensive, wasteful packaging.*

packet /'pækɪt/ **packets.** N-C A **packet** is a small box, bag, or envelope in which a quantity of something is sold. *The packet says the product contains cream... She was eating a packet of peanuts.*

pact /pækt/ **pacts.** N-C A **pact** is a formal agreement between two or more people, organizations, or governments. *He signed a new non-aggression pact with Germany.*

pad /pæd/ **pads.** [1] N-C A **pad** is a thick flat piece of a material such as cloth or foam rubber. Pads are used, for example, to clean things or for protection. *...a pad of cotton-wool.* [2] N-C A **pad** of paper is a number of pieces of paper which are fixed together along the top or the side, so that each piece can be torn off when it has been used. *Keep a pad handy to jot down queries as they occur.*

padded /'pædɪd/. ADJ Something that is **padded** has soft material on it or inside it which makes it less hard, protects it, or gives it a different shape. *...a man in a padded jacket.*

padding /'pædɪŋ/. N-U **Padding** is soft material on the outside or inside of something which makes it less hard, protects it, or gives it a different shape. *Players must wear padding to protect them from injury.*

paddle /'pædəl/ **paddles, paddling, paddled.** [1] N-C A **paddle** is a short pole with a wide flat part at one end or at both ends used to move a small boat through water. [2] VERB & N-C If you **paddle**, or if you go for a **paddle**, you walk or stand in shallow water, for example at the edge of the sea, for pleasure. *...a lovely little stream that you can paddle in.*

paddock /'pædək/ **paddocks.** [1] N-C A **paddock** is a small field where horses are kept. [2] N-C In horse racing, the **paddock** is the place where the horses walk about before a race.

paddy /'pædi/ **paddies.** N-C A **paddy** or a **paddy**

field is a flooded field that is used for growing rice.

padlock /'pædlɒk/ **padlocks, padlocking, padlocked.** N-C & VERB A **padlock** is a lock used for fastening two things or two parts of something together. When you **padlock** something, you lock it or fasten it using a padlock. *Eddie parked his cycle against a lamp post and padlocked it.*

paediatrician (AM **pediatrician**) /ˌpiːdiə'trɪʃən/ **paediatricians.** N-C A **paediatrician** is a doctor who specializes in treating sick children.

paediatrics (AM **pediatrics**) /ˌpiːdi'ætrɪks/ **paediatric.** The form **paediatric** is used as a modifier. N-U **Paediatrics** is the area of medicine that is concerned with the treatment of children's illnesses. *...a paediatric surgeon.*

pagan /'peɪgən/ **pagans.** ADJ **Pagan** beliefs and activities do not belong to any of the main religions of the world and take nature and a belief in many gods as a basis. They are older than other religions.

page /peɪdʒ/ **pages, paging, paged.** [1] N-C A **page** is a side of one of the pieces of paper in a book, magazine, or newspaper. *Turn to page 4.* [2] N-C The **pages** of a book, magazine, or newspaper are the pieces of paper it consists of. *He turned the pages of his notebook.*

pageant /'pædʒənt/ **pageants.** N-C A **pageant** is a colourful public parade, show, or ceremony, often organized to celebrate a historic event.

paid /peɪd/. [1] **Paid** is the past tense and past participle of **pay.** [2] ADJ **Paid** means to do with the money a worker receives from his or her employer. You can say, for example, that someone is **well paid** when they receive a lot of money for the work that they do. *...a legal right to paid holiday leave.*

pain /peɪn/ **pains, paining, pained.** [1] N-VAR If you feel **pain,** or if you are **in pain,** you feel great discomfort in a part of your body, because of illness or an injury. *...a bone disease that caused excruciating pain... I felt a sharp pain in my lower back.* [2] N-U **Pain** is the unhappiness that you feel when something very upsetting happens. *...grey eyes that seemed filled with pain.* [3] VERB If something **pains** you, it makes you feel upset or unhappy. *It pains me to think of you struggling all alone.* ♦**pained** ADJ *A pained expression came over her face.*

PHRASES ● If you say that something or someone is a **pain** or a **pain in the neck,** you mean they are very annoying or irritating; INFORMAL. *You can be a real pain in the neck sometimes.* ● If you **take pains** to do something, you try hard to do it successfully. *He took great pains to entertain me.*

painful /'peɪnful/. [1] ADJ If a part of your body is **painful,** it hurts. *Her glands were swollen and painful.* ♦**painfully** ADV *His tooth had started to throb painfully.* [2] ADJ If something such as an illness, injury, or operation is **painful,** it causes you a lot of physical pain. *...a painful back injury.* ♦**painfully** ADV *...cracking his head painfully against the cupboard.* [3] ADJ Situations, memories, or experiences that are **painful** are difficult and unpleasant to deal

with, and often make you feel sad and upset. *She finds it too painful to return there without him.*

painfully /'peɪnfuli/. ADV You use **painfully** to emphasize a quality or situation that is undesirable. *Things are moving painfully slowly... He was painfully aware of the gaps in his education.*

painkiller /'peɪnkɪlə/ **painkillers.** N-C A **painkiller** is a drug which reduces or stops physical pain.

painless /'peɪnləs/. [1] ADJ Something such as a treatment that is **painless** causes no physical pain. *The operation itself is a brief, painless procedure.* ♦**painlessly** ADV *She died peacefully and painlessly.* [2] ADJ If a process or activity is **painless,** you do not have to make a great effort or suffer in any way. *There are no easy or painless solutions to the nation's economic ills.* ♦**painlessly** ADV *...a game for children which painlessly teaches essential pre-reading skills.*

painstaking /'peɪnsteɪkɪŋ/. ADJ A **painstaking** search, examination, or investigation is done extremely carefully and thoroughly. ♦**painstakingly** ADV *Broken bones were painstakingly pieced together.*

paint /peɪnt/ **paints, painting, painted.** [1] N-VAR **Paint** is a coloured liquid that you put on a wall or other surface with a brush in order to protect the surface or to make it look nice, or that you use to produce a picture. *They saw some large letters in white paint... The paint was peeling on the window frames.* [2] VERB If you **paint** a wall or an object, you cover it with paint. *I painted the walls white.* [3] VERB If you **paint** something, or if you **paint** a picture of it, you produce a picture of it using paint. *He is painting a huge volcano.*

paintbrush /'peɪntbrʌʃ/ **paintbrushes.** N-C A **paintbrush** is a brush which you use for painting.

painter /'peɪntə/ **painters.** [1] N-C A **painter** is an artist who paints pictures. *...England's greatest modern painter.* [2] N-C A **painter** is someone who paints walls, doors, and some other parts of buildings as their job.

painting /'peɪntɪŋ/ **paintings.** [1] N-C A **painting** is a picture which someone has painted. [2] N-U **Painting** is the activity of painting pictures. *She really enjoyed painting and gardening.*

pair /peə/ **pairs.** [1] N-C A **pair** of things are two things of the same size and shape that are intended to be used together. *...a pair of socks. ...a pair of earrings.* [2] N-C Some objects that have two main parts of the same size and shape are referred to as a **pair.** *...a pair of faded jeans. ...a pair of binoculars.* [3] N-SING You can refer to two people as a **pair** when they are standing or walking together. *A pair of teenage boys were smoking cigarettes.* [4] See also **au pair.**

pajamas /pə'dʒɑːməz/. See **pyjamas.**

pal /pæl/. N-C Your **pals** are your friends; INFORMAL. *The two women became close pals.*

palace /'pælɪs/ **palaces.** N-C A **palace** is a very large splendid house, especially the home of a king, queen, or president.

palatable 442

palatable /'pælətəbəl/. [1] ADJ If you describe food or drink as **palatable**, you mean that it tastes pleasant; FORMAL. ...*some very palatable red wines*. [2] ADJ If you describe an idea or proposal as **palatable**, you mean that it is easy to accept. ...*direct payments to make the cuts more palatable to farmers*.

palate /'pælɪt/ **palates.** [1] N-C Your **palate** is the top part of the inside of your mouth. [2] N-C You can refer to someone's ability to judge good food and wine as their **palate**. ...*fresh pasta sauces to tempt more demanding palates*.

pale /peɪl/ **paler, palest.** [1] ADJ Something that is **pale** is not strong or bright in colour. ...*pale blue*. [2] ADJ If someone looks **pale**, their face is a lighter colour than usual, because they are ill, frightened, or shocked.

palette /'pælɪt/ **palettes.** N-C A **palette** is a flat piece of wood or plastic on which an artist mixes paints.

pall /pɔːl/ **palls, palling, palled.** [1] VERB If something **palls**, it becomes less interesting or less enjoyable. *The job was beginning to pall*. [2] N-C A **pall** of smoke is a thick cloud of it; LITERARY.

palm /pɑːm/ **palms.** [1] N-C A **palm** or **palm tree** is a tree that grows in hot countries. It has long leaves at the top and no branches. [2] N-C The **palm** of your hand is the flat surface which your fingers can bend towards.

palpable /'pælpəbəl/. ADJ Something that is **palpable** is very obvious. *The tension was palpable.* ♦**palpably** /'pælpəbli/ ADV *The policeman was palpably nervous.*

paltry /'pɔːltri/. ADJ A **paltry** amount of money or something else is very small. ...*a paltry 0.2% rise in manufacturing*.

pamper /'pæmpə/ **pampers, pampering, pampered.** VERB If you **pamper** someone, you do everything for them, and give them everything they want. ♦**pampered** ADJ *I was a very pampered child.*

pamphlet /'pæmflət/ **pamphlets.** N-C A **pamphlet** is a very thin book with a paper cover, which gives information about something.

pan /pæn/ **pans.** N-C A **pan** is a round metal container with a long handle, which is used for cooking things, usually on top of a cooker.

panacea /ˌpænə'siːə/ **panaceas.** N-C If you say that something is not a **panacea** for a particular set of problems, you mean that it will not solve all those problems. *Western aid may help but will not be a panacea.*

panache /pə'næʃ/. N-U If you do something with **panache**, you do it in a confident and stylish way. *The whole orchestra performed with great panache.*

pancake /'pænkeɪk/ **pancakes.** N-C A **pancake** is a thin, flat, circular piece of cooked batter that is usually eaten hot, often with a sweet or savoury filling.

panda /'pændə/ **pandas.** N-C A **panda** is a large animal with black and white fur which lives in China.

pander /'pændə/ **panders, pandering, pandered.** VERB If you **pander** to someone, you do everything they want, often to get some advantage for yourself; used showing disapproval. ...*politicians who pander to millionaires*.

pane /peɪn/ **panes.** N-C A **pane** of glass is a flat sheet of glass in a window or door.

panel /'pænəl/ **panels.** [1] N-C A **panel** is a small group of people who are chosen to do something, for example to discuss something in public or to make a decision. *The case will now go before a panel of judges.* [2] N-C A **panel** is a flat rectangular piece of wood or other material that forms part of a larger object such as a door. [3] N-C A control **panel** or instrument **panel** is a board containing switches and controls.

panelled (AM **paneled**) /'pænəld/. ADJ If something such as a room or door is **panelled**, its walls or surface are covered in decorative wooden panels. ...*panelled walls*.

pang /pæŋ/ **pangs.** N-C A **pang** is a sudden strong feeling, for example of sadness or pain. *Ruth felt a pang of guilt.*

panic /'pænɪk/ **panics, panicking, panicked.** [1] N-VAR **Panic** is a strong feeling of anxiety or fear that makes you act without thinking carefully. *He felt a sudden rush of panic at the thought... In a panic, I rushed to the kitchen.* [2] VERB If you **panic**, or if someone or something **panics** you, you become anxious or afraid, and act without thinking carefully. *Jason panicked when the spider fell onto his knee.*

panorama /ˌpænə'rɑːmə, -'ræmə/ **panoramas.** N-C A **panorama** is a view in which you can see a long way over a wide area of land. *You look out onto a breathtaking panorama of London.* ♦**panoramic** /ˌpænə'ræmɪk/ ADJ *We had a panoramic view of the beach.*

pant /pænt/ **pants, panting, panted.** VERB If you **pant**, you breathe quickly and loudly, because you have been doing something energetic. *She was panting for air.*

pantomime /'pæntəmaɪm/ **pantomimes.** N-VAR A **pantomime** is a funny musical play for children, usually performed at Christmas. *She regularly appeared in pantomime.*

pants /pænts/. [1] N-PL In British English, **pants** are a piece of underwear with two holes to put your legs through and elastic around the top. The usual American word is **underpants**. [2] N-PL In American English, **pants** are a piece of clothing that you wear over your body from the waist downwards, and that cover each leg separately. The usual British word is **trousers**.

papa /pə'pɑː, AM 'pɑːpə/ **papas.** N-C & N-VOC Some people refer to or address their father as **papa**; DATED.

papal /'peɪpəl/. ADJ BEFORE N **Papal** is used to describe things relating to the Pope. ...*a papal visit to Japan*.

paper /'peɪpə/ **papers, papering, papered.** [1] N-U **Paper** is a material that you write on or wrap things with. ...*a piece of paper. ...a paper bag.* [2] PHRASE If you put your thoughts down **on paper**, you write them down. [3] N-C A **paper** is a newspaper. ...*the daily papers.* [4] N-PL **Papers** are sheets of paper with information on them. ...*a briefcase carrying personal papers.* [5] N-PL Your **papers** are your official documents, for example your passport or identity card. *To his surprise the officer asked him in English for his papers.* [6] N-C A **paper** is a long essay on an academic subject. [7] N-C A **paper** prepared by a government or a committee is a report on a question they have been considering or a set of proposals for changes in the law. *...a new government paper on European policy.* [8] VERB If you **paper** a wall, you put wallpaper on it. *We papered all four bedrooms.*

paperback /ˈpeɪpəbæk/ **paperbacks.** N-VAR A **paperback** is a book with a paper cover. *...a cheap paperback... The book is now out in paperback.*

paperwork /ˈpeɪpəwɜːk/. N-U **Paperwork** consists of the letters, reports, and records which have to be dealt with as the routine part of a job. *He does his paperwork here.*

par /pɑː/.
PHRASES ● If you say that someone or something is **below par**, you mean that they are below the standard you expected. *Duffy's guitar playing is well below par.* ● If one thing is **on a par** with another, the two things are equally good or bad. *This match was on a par with the German Cup Final.*

parable /ˈpærəbəl/ **parables.** N-C A **parable** is a short story which makes a moral or religious point.

parachute /ˈpærəʃuːt/ **parachutes, parachuting, parachuted.** [1] N-C A **parachute** is a device which enables a person to jump from an aircraft and float safely to the ground. It consists of a large piece of thin cloth attached to your body by strings. [2] VERB If a person **parachutes**, or if someone **parachutes** them somewhere, they jump from an aircraft using a parachute. *They had been parachuted into the country at night.*

parade /pəˈreɪd/ **parades, parading, paraded.** [1] N-C A **parade** is a line of people or vehicles moving together through a public place in order to celebrate an important day or event. [2] VERB When people **parade**, they walk together in a formal group or in a line, usually in front of spectators. *Soldiers paraded down the Champs Elysee.* [3] VERB If someone **parades** something, they show it in public in order to impress people or to gain some advantage for themselves. *I paraded all the paintings in front of them... Five leading Communist fighters have been captured and paraded before the media.*

paradise /ˈpærədaɪs/ **paradises.** [1] N-PROPER According to some religions, **paradise** is a wonderful place where people go after they die, if they have led good lives. [2] N-VAR You can refer to a place or situation that seems perfect as **paradise** or a **paradise**.

paradox /ˈpærədɒks/ **paradoxes.** [1] N-C You describe a situation as a **paradox** when it involves two or more facts or qualities which seem to contradict each other. ♦ **paradoxical** ADJ *Some sedatives produce the paradoxical effect of making the person more anxious.* ♦ **paradoxically** ADV *Paradoxically, the less you have to do the more you may resent the work that does come your way.* [2] N-VAR A **paradox** is a statement in which it seems that if one part of it is true, the other part of it cannot be true.

paraffin /ˈpærəfɪn/. N-U **Paraffin** is a strong-smelling liquid which is used as a fuel in heaters, lamps, and engines. The usual American word is **kerosene**.

paragon /ˈpærəɡɒn/ **paragons.** N-C If you say that someone is a **paragon** of virtue, or some other good quality, you mean that they have a lot of that quality. *...a paragon of neatness, efficiency and reliability.*

paragraph /ˈpærəɡrɑːf, -ɡræf/ **paragraphs.** N-C A **paragraph** is a section of a piece of writing. A paragraph always begins on a new line and contains at least one sentence.

parallel /ˈpærəlel/ **parallels, parallelling, parallelled** (AM **paralleling, paralleled**). [1] N-C If something has a **parallel**, or if there are **parallels** between two or more things, they are similar to each other in some way. *It's an ecological disaster with no parallel anywhere else in the world... Detailed study of folk music from a variety of countries reveals many close parallels.* [2] VERB & ADJ If one thing **parallels** another, or if two things are **parallel**, they happen at the same time or are similar, and often seem to be connected. *His remarks paralleled those of the president. ...parallel talks between the two countries' Foreign Ministers.* [3] ADJ If two lines or two objects are **parallel**, they are the same distance apart along their whole length.

paralyse (AM **paralyze**) /ˈpærəlaɪz/ **paralyses, paralysing, paralysed.** [1] VERB If someone is **paralysed** by an accident or illness, they have no feeling in their body, or in part of their body, and are unable to move. ♦ **paralysed** ADJ *...a paralysed right arm.* [2] VERB If a person, place, or organization is **paralysed** by something, they are unable to act or function properly. *The government has been paralysed by indecision.*

paralysis /pəˈrælɪsɪs/. N-U **Paralysis** is the loss of feeling in all or part of your body and the inability to move. *...paralysis of the leg.*

parameter /pəˈræmɪtə/ **parameters.** N-C **Parameters** are factors or limits which affect the way that something can be done or made. *...the parameters of our loan agreement.*

paramilitary /ˌpærəˈmɪlɪtri, AM -teri/ **paramilitaries.** ADJ BEFORE N & N-C **Paramilitary** organizations are groups who are organized like an army but do not belong to any official army. **Paramilitaries** are members of a paramilitary organization.

paramount /ˈpærəmaʊnt/. ADJ Something that is **paramount** or of **paramount** importance is more important than anything else. *The child's welfare must be seen as paramount.*

paranoia /ˌpærəˈnɔɪə/. [1] N-U If you say that someone suffers from **paranoia**, you think that they are too suspicious and afraid of other people. *...the mounting paranoia with which he viewed the world.* [2] N-U If someone suffers from **paranoia**, they are suffering from a mental illness which makes them wrongly believe that other people are trying to harm them; TECHNICAL.

paranoid /ˈpærənɔɪd/. [1] ADJ If you say that someone is **paranoid**, you mean that they are extremely suspicious and afraid of other peo-

ple. *I'm not going to get paranoid about it.*
[2] ADJ Someone who is **paranoid** suffers from
the mental illness of paranoia; TECHNICAL. *...a
paranoid schizophrenic.*

paraphernalia /ˌpærəfə'neɪliə/. N-U You can refer to a large number of objects that someone
has with them or that are connected with a
particular activity as **paraphernalia**. *...ciga-
rettes and ashtrays and other paraphernalia associated with smoking.*

paraphrase /'pærəfreɪz/ **paraphrases, paraphrasing, paraphrased.** VERB & N-C If you
paraphrase someone, or if you **paraphrase**
something that they have said or written, you
express what they have said or written in a different way. A **paraphrase** is something that
has been paraphrased. *I'm paraphrasing but
this is honestly what he said... The writer here
has attempted a paraphrase of Mabry's words.*

parasite /'pærəsaɪt/ **parasites.** [1] N-C A **parasite** is a small animal or plant that lives on or
inside a larger animal or plant. ♦**parasitic**
/ˌpærə'sɪtɪk/ ADJ *...parasitic worms.* [2] N-C If you
call someone a **parasite**, you disapprove of
them because you think that they get money
or other things from people without doing
anything in return.

paratrooper /'pærətruːpə/ **paratroopers.** N-C
Paratroopers are soldiers who are trained to
be dropped by parachute into battle or into
enemy territory.

parcel /'pɑːsəl/ **parcels.** N-C A **parcel** is something wrapped in paper, usually so that it can
be sent to someone by post. The more usual
American word is **package.** ● **part and parcel:**
see **part.**

parched /pɑːtʃt/. [1] ADJ If the ground is
parched, it is very dry, because there has been
no rain. *...a hill of parched brown grass.* [2] ADJ
If your mouth, throat, or lips are **parched**, they
are unpleasantly dry. [3] ADJ AFTER LINK-V If you
say you are **parched**, you mean that you are
very thirsty.

pardon /'pɑːdən/ **pardons, pardoning, pardoned.** [1] CONVENTION You say '**Pardon?**', or '**I
beg your pardon?**' or, in American English,
'**Pardon me?**' when you want someone to repeat what they have just said, either because
you have not heard or understood it or because you are surprised by it. *'Will you let me
open it?'—'Pardon?'—'Can I open it?'*
[2] CONVENTION You say '**I beg your pardon**' or '**I
do beg your pardon**' as a way of apologizing
for accidentally doing something wrong, such
as disturbing someone or making a mistake. *I
was impolite and I do beg your pardon.* [3] VERB
& N-C If someone who has been found guilty of
a crime **is pardoned** or is given a **pardon**, they
are officially allowed to go free and are not
punished.

pare /peə/ **pares, paring, pared.** [1] VERB
When you **pare** something, or **pare** part of it
off or away, you cut off its skin or its outer layer. *He took out a slab of cheese and pared off a
slice.* [2] VERB If you **pare** something **down** or
back, or if you **pare** it up, you reduce it. *The number of Ministries has been pared down by a
third.*

parent /'peərənt/ **parents.** N-C Your **parents** are
your father and mother. ♦**parental** /pə'rentəl/
ADJ *Parental attitudes vary widely.*

parenthood /'peərənthʊd/. N-U **Parenthood** is
the state of being a parent.

parenting /'peərəntɪŋ/. N-U **Parenting** is the activity of bring up and looking after your child.

parish /'pærɪʃ/ **parishes.** [1] N-C A **parish** is a
village or part of a town which has its own
church and clergyman. [2] N-C A **parish** is a
small country area in England with its own
elected council.

parishioner /pə'rɪʃənə/ **parishioners.** N-C A
clergyman's **parishioners** are the people in his
parish.

parity /'pærɪti/. N-U If there is **parity** between
two things, they are equal; FORMAL. *Women
have yet to achieve wage or occupational parity.*

park /pɑːk/ **parks, parking, parked.** [1] N-C A
park is a public area of land with grass and
trees, usually in a town, where people go to relax and enjoy themselves. [2] N-VAR In Britain, a
private area of grass and trees around a large
country house is referred to as a **park**. [3] VERB
& ADJ When you **park** a vehicle, or when you
park somewhere, you drive the vehicle into a
position where it can stay for a period of time
and leave it. *Could you park over there? ...rows
of parked cars.* ♦**parking** N-U *...parking is allowed only on one side of the street.* ● See also
car park, national park.

> Note that you do not use the word **park-
> ing** to refer to a place where cars are
> parked. Instead, you refer to a **car park**
> in British English, and a **parking lot** in
> American English. **Parking** is used only
> to refer to the action of parking your car,
> or the state of being parked. *...a 'No
> Parking' sign.*

'parking lot, parking lots. N-C In American
English, a **parking lot** is an area of ground
where people can leave their cars. The British
term is **car park.**

parliament /'pɑːləmənt/ **parliaments.** N-VAR
The **parliament** of a country is the group of
people who make or change its laws. ● See
note at **government.** See also **Member of Parliament.**

parliamentary /ˌpɑːlə'mentəri/. ADJ BEFORE N
Parliamentary is used to describe things that
are connected with a parliament. *...a parliamentary candidate.*

parlour (AM **parlor**) /'pɑːlə/ **parlours.** N-C **Parlour** is used in the names of some types of
shops which provide a service. *...a pizza parlour.*

parochial /pə'rəʊkiəl/. ADJ If you describe
someone as **parochial**, you are critical of them
because they are too concerned with their own
local affairs and interests.

parody /'pærədi/ **parodies, parodying, paro-
died.** VERB & N-VAR When someone **parodies** a
particular work, thing, or person, they imitate
them in an amusing or exaggerated way. You
call an imitation like this a **parody.** *...parody-*

445

particularly

ing a number of television and film genres. ...a parody of his favourite comic book.

parole /pəˈrəʊl/ **paroles, paroling, paroled.**
[1] N-U & PASSIVE-VERB When prisoners are given **parole**, or when they **are paroled**, they are released before their sentence is due to end, on condition that they behave well. [2] PHRASE If someone is **on parole**, they will stay out of prison if they behave well.

parrot /ˈpærət/ **parrots, parroting, parroted.**
[1] N-C A **parrot** is a tropical bird with a curved beak and brightly-coloured or grey feathers. Parrots can be kept as pets. [2] VERB If you **parrot** what someone else has said, you repeat it without really understanding what it means. *Students all over the world have learnt to parrot the standard explanations.*

parsley /ˈpɑːsli, AM -zli/. N-U **Parsley** is a small plant with curly leaves used for flavouring or decorating savoury food.

parsnip /ˈpɑːsnɪp/ **parsnips.** N-C A **parsnip** is a root vegetable similar in shape to a carrot.

part 1 piece, section

part /pɑːt/ **parts.** [1] N-VAR If one thing is a **part** of another thing or **part** of it, the first thing is one of the pieces, sections, or elements that the second thing consists of. *I like that part of Cape Town... Respect is a very important part of any relationship... Switzerland is not part of the EC.* [2] N-C A **part** for a machine or vehicle is one of the smaller pieces that is used to make it. *...spare parts for military equipment.*

PHRASES ● The **best part** or the **better part of** a period of time or an amount means most of that time or that amount. *We spent the better part of an hour searching for her.* ● You use **in part** to indicate that something exists or happens to some extent but not completely. *The levels of blood glucose depend in part on what you eat.* ● For the **most part** means mostly or usually. *For the most part, the travellers lived as the locals did.* ● If you say that something is **part and parcel** of something else, you mean that it is involved or included in it. *Violence is part and parcel of everyday life round here.*

part 2 role

part /pɑːt/ **parts.** [1] N-C A **part** in a play or film is one of the roles in it. *I'd got a part in a romantic comedy.* [2] N-SING Your **part** in something that happens is your involvement in it. *If only he could conceal his part in the accident.*

PHRASES ● You can say, for example, that **for** your **part** you thought or did something, to introduce what you thought or did. *The soldiers, for their part, agreed not to disrupt the election campaign.* ● If someone **looks the part**, they dress or behave in the way that is characteristic of a particular kind of person. *If you go to an interview looking the part you can command a much higher salary.* ● If you talk about a feeling or action **on** someone's **part**, you are referring to something that they feel or do. *That was actually an error on my part.* ● You can say that someone or something **plays a part in** something to talk about the fact that they are involved in it and the effect they have on it. *Work plays an important part in a single woman's life.* ● If you **take part** in an ac-

tivity, you are involved in it with other people. *He did not take part in the meeting.*

part 3 separate

part /pɑːt/ **parts, parting, parted.** [1] VERB If things which are touching **part**, or if they **are parted**, they move away from each other. *Her lips parted and she smiled... Livy parted the curtains.* [2] VERB If your hair **is parted**, it is combed in two different directions so that there is a straight line from the front of your head to the back. [3] VERB When two people **part**, they leave each other or separate; FORMAL. *He is parting from his Swedish-born wife Eva.* ◆ **parting, partings** N-VAR *After her parting with Jackson she lived in Provence.*
▶ **part with.** PHR-VERB If you **part with** something that you would prefer to keep, you give it or sell it to someone else. *Think carefully before parting with money.*

partial /ˈpɑːʃəl/. [1] ADJ You use **partial** to refer to something that is true or exists to some extent, but is not complete or total. *The event was only a partial success.* ◆ **partially** ADV *I am partially deaf.* [2] ADJ AFTER LINK-V If you are **partial** to something, you like it. *Wasn't his uncle rather partial to asparagus?*

participant /pɑːˈtɪsɪpənt/ **participants.** N-C The **participants** in an activity are the people who take part in it.

participate /pɑːˈtɪsɪpeɪt/ **participates, participating, participated.** VERB If you **participate** in an activity, you are involved in it with other people. *All the warring parties agreed to participate in talks.* ◆ **participation** N-U *...participation in religious activities.*

participle /ˈpɑːtɪsɪpəl/ **participles.** N-C In grammar, a **participle** is a form of a verb that can be used in compound tenses of the verb. English verbs have a past participle, which usually ends in '-ed', and a present participle, which ends in '-ing'.

particle /ˈpɑːtɪkəl/ **particles.** N-C A **particle** of something is a very small piece or amount of it. *...food particles.*

particular /pəˈtɪkjʊlə/ **particulars.** [1] ADJ BEFORE N You use **particular** to emphasize that you are talking about one thing or one kind of thing rather than other similar ones. *One particular memory still haunts me.* [2] PHRASE You use **in particular** to indicate that what you are saying applies especially to one thing or person. *Why should he notice her car in particular?* [3] ADJ BEFORE N If a person or thing has a **particular** quality or possession, it belongs only to them. *I have a particular responsibility to ensure that I make the right decision.* [4] ADJ BEFORE N You can use **particular** to emphasize that something is greater or more intense than usual. *Particular emphasis will be placed on oral language training.* [5] ADJ Someone who is **particular** chooses or does things very carefully and is not easily satisfied. *Ted was very particular about the colors he used.*

particularly /pəˈtɪkjʊləli/. ADV You use **particularly** to indicate that what you are saying applies especially to one thing or situation. *Keep your office space looking good, particularly your desk... I particularly liked the wooden chests and chairs.*

particulars

446

particulars /pəˈtɪkjʊləz/. N-PL The **particulars** of something or someone are facts or details about them which are kept as a record. *The nurses at the admission desk asked her for particulars.*

partisan /ˌpɑːtɪˈzæn, AM -zən/ **partisans.** ① ADJ & N-C Someone who is **partisan** or a **partisan** strongly supports a particular person or cause, often without thinking carefully about what they represent. ② N-C **Partisans** are people who get together to fight enemy soldiers who are occupying their country.

partition /pɑːˈtɪʃən/ **partitions, partitioning, partitioned.** ① N-C A **partition** is a wall or screen separating one part of a room or vehicle from another. ② VERB If you **partition** a room, you separate one part of it from another by means of a partition. ③ VERB & N-U To **partition** a country means to divide it into two or more independent countries. The **partition** of a country is the act of dividing it like this.

partly /ˈpɑːtli/. ADV You use **partly** to indicate that something is true or exists to some extent, but not completely. *It's partly my fault... Margaret was always several steps behind her sister, partly because of her age.*

partner /ˈpɑːtnə/ **partners, partnering partnered.** ① N-C Your **partner** is the person you are married to or are having a long-term sexual relationship with. ② N-C Your **partner** in an activity such as a game or dance is the person you are playing or dancing with. ③ VERB If you **partner** someone, you are their partner in a game or in a dance. ④ N-C The **partners** in a firm or business are the people who share the ownership of it. *He's a partner in a Chicago law firm.* ⑤ N-C The **partner** of a country or organization is another country or organization with which they have an alliance or agreement. *...Britain's major trading partners in Europe.*

partnership /ˈpɑːtnəʃɪp/ **partnerships.** N-VAR A **partnership** is a relationship in which two or more people or organizations work together as partners. *Management must work in partnership with their employees and unions.*

part-'time. ADJ & ADV If someone is a **part-time** worker or has a **part-time** job, they work for only part of each day or week. You can also say they work **part-time**.

party /ˈpɑːti/ **parties, partying, partied.** ① N-C A **party** is a social event at which people enjoy themselves doing things such as eating, drinking, or dancing. *We threw a huge birthday party.* ② N-C A political **party** is an organization whose members have similar aims and beliefs, and that tries to get its members elected to government. *...the Labour party.* ③ N-C A **party** of people is a group of them doing something together, for example travelling. *...a party of sightseers.* ④ VERB If you **party**, you enjoy yourself doing things such as going drinking and dancing. *They drank and partied all night.* ⑤ N-C One of the people involved in a legal agreement or dispute can be referred to as a particular **party**; TECHNICAL. *It has to be proved that they are the guilty party.* ⑥ PHRASE If you **are party to** an action or agreement, or **are a party to** it, you are involved in it, and are

therefore partly responsible for it. *Crook had resigned his post rather than be party to such treachery.*

pass /pɑːs, pæs/ **passes, passing, passed.** ① VERB To **pass** someone or something means to go past them. *We passed the mountains of Torres Vedras... Jane stood aside to let her pass.* ② VERB To **pass** in a particular direction means to move or go in that direction. *He passed through the doorway into Ward B... The route passes through St-Paul-sur-Ubaye.* ③ VERB If you **pass** something through, over, or round something else, you move or push it through, over, or round that thing. *She passed the needle through the rough cloth... He has written a hand wearily over his eyes.* ④ VERB If you **pass** an object to someone, you pick it up and give it to them. If you **pass** a ball to someone, you hit, kick, or throw it to them. *Pass the salt, please.* ⑤ VERB & PHR-VERB If something **passes** from one person to another, or if it **is passed** or **passed on** to them, the second person is given it. *His mother's small estate had passed to him after her death... He has written a note asking me to pass on his thanks.* ⑥ VERB When a period of time **passes**, it happens and ends. *Several minutes passed before the girls were noticed.* ♦ **passing** N-SING *...the passing of time.* ⑦ VERB If you **pass** time in a particular way, you spend it in that way. *The children passed the time playing in the streets.* ⑧ VERB If an amount **passes** a particular total or level, it becomes greater than that total or level. *Today the population of the globe has passed five billion.* ⑨ VERB & N-C If someone or something **passes** a test or **is passed**, they are considered to be of an acceptable standard. To get a **pass** in a test means to pass it. *Kevin has just passed his driving test... The medical board would not pass him fit for General Service... It could mean the difference between a pass and a fail.* ● See note at **exam.** ⑩ N-C A **pass** is a document that allows you to do something. *Don't let any cars onto the land unless they've got a pass.* ⑪ VERB When people in authority **pass** a new law or a proposal, they formally agree to it or approve it. *Congress passed a law that regulates the disposal of waste.* ⑫ VERB If something **passes** without comment or **passes** unnoticed, nobody comments on it or notices it. *I cannot allow this nonsense to pass unchallenged.* ⑬ VERB To **pass for** or to **pass as** a particular thing means to be accepted as that thing, in spite of not having all the right qualities. *...a woman passing as a man.* ⑭ N-C A **pass** is a narrow way between two mountains. ⑮ See also **passing.** ● to **pass the buck**: see **buck.** ● to **pass sentence**: see **sentence.**

▶ **pass around** or **pass round.** PHR-VERB If a group of people **pass** something **around**, or **pass** it **round**, they each take it and then give it to the next person. *A bottle of whisky was passed around.*

▶ **pass away.** PHR-VERB You can say that someone **passed away** to mean that they died, if you want to avoid using the word 'die'.

▶ **pass off.** PHR-VERB If an event **passes off** without any trouble, it ends without any trouble;

BRITISH. *The main demonstration passed off peacefully.*

▶ **pass off as.** PHR-VERB If someone **passes** something **off** as another thing, they dishonestly convince people that it is that other thing. *She'd decided to pass herself off as a Canadian.*

▶ **pass on.** See **pass** 5.

▶ **pass out.** PHR-VERB If you **pass out**, you faint or collapse.

▶ **pass over.** PHR-VERB If someone **is passed over** for a job, they do not get the job and someone younger or less experienced is chosen instead. *She was repeatedly passed over for promotion.*

▶ **pass round.** See **pass around**.

▶ **pass up.** PHR-VERB If you **pass up** an opportunity, you do not take advantage of it. *We can't pass up a chance like this.*

passage /'pæsɪdʒ/ **passages.** [1] N-C A **passage** is a long, narrow space between walls or fences, connecting one room or place with another. [2] N-C A **passage** in a book, speech, or piece of music is a section of it. *He reads a passage from Milton.* [3] N-U The **passage** of someone or something is their movement or progress from one place or stage to another. *...the passage of food through the digestive tract... Relief convoys were to be guaranteed safe passage through rebel-held areas.* [4] N-SING The **passage** of time is the fact of it passing.

passageway /'pæsɪdʒweɪ/ **passageways.** N-C A **passageway** is a long, narrow space between walls or fences, connecting one room or place with another.

passenger /'pæsɪndʒə/ **passengers.** N-C A **passenger** in a bus, boat, or plane is a person who is travelling in it, but who is not driving it or working on it.

passing /'pɑːsɪŋ, 'pæs-/. [1] ADJ BEFORE N A **passing** feeling or action is brief and not very serious or important. *He had never taken more than a passing interest in the girl... It was just a passing comment.* [2] PHRASE If you mention something **in passing**, you mention it briefly while you are talking or writing about something else. [3] N-SING You can talk about the **passing** of a person or thing to mean the fact of their dying or coming to an end, especially when you are sad about it. *The business world is a duller place for his passing. We have mourned the passing of the old ways.* [4] See also **pass**.

passion /'pæʃən/ **passions.** [1] N-U **Passion** is a very strong feeling of sexual attraction for someone. *...my passion for a dark-haired, slender boy named James.* [2] N-U **Passion** is a very strong belief in something, to the point where you become excited or emotional about it. *He spoke with great passion.* [3] N-C If you have a **passion** for something, you like it very much. *...her childhood passion for collecting.*

passionate /'pæʃənət/. [1] ADJ A **passionate** person has very strong feelings about something. *I'm a passionate believer in public art. ...his passionate commitment to peace.* ◆**passionately** ADV *I am passionately opposed to the death penalty.* [2] ADJ A **passionate** person has strong romantic or sexual feelings and

expresses them in their behaviour. ◆**passionately** ADV *He was passionately in love with her.*

passive /'pæsɪv/ **passives.** [1] ADJ If you describe someone as **passive**, you mean they do not take action but instead let things happen to them; used showing disapproval. ◆**passively** ADV *...sitting passively in front of the TV.* [2] N-C In grammar, the **passive** is formed using 'be' and the past participle of a verb. The subject of a passive clause does not perform the action expressed by the verb but is affected by it. For example, in 'He's been murdered', the verb is in the **passive**. Compare **active**.

Passover /'pɑːsəʊvə, 'pæs-/. N-U **Passover** is a Jewish festival beginning in March or April and lasting for seven or eight days.

passport /'pɑːspɔːt, 'pæs-/ **passports.** [1] N-C Your **passport** is an official document which you need to show when you enter or leave a country. [2] N-C If you say that something is a **passport** to something such as success, you mean that it makes that thing possible. *It could be your passport to riches.*

password /'pɑːswɜːd, 'pæs-/ **passwords.** N-C A **password** is a secret word or phrase that enables you to enter a place or use a computer system. *No-one could use the computer unless they had a password.*

past /pɑːst, pæst/ **pasts.** [1] N-SING The **past** is the period of time before the present, and the things that happened in that period. *In the past they have been the target of racist abuse.* [2] ADJ BEFORE N **Past** events and things happened or existed before the present time. *...details of his past activities.* [3] N-C Your **past** consists of all the things that you have done or that have happened to you. *...revelations about his past. ...Germany's recent past.* [4] ADJ BEFORE N You use **past** to talk about a period of time that has just finished. *...the momentous events of the past few days... I have been homeless for the past year.* [5] ADJ BEFORE N The **past** tense of a verb is used to refer to things that happened or existed before the time when you are speaking or writing. For regular verbs, the past tense is the '-ed' form, for example 'They walked back to the car'. [6] PREP & ADV You use **past** when you are stating the time, when it is thirty minutes or less after a particular time. *It's ten past eleven... At a quarter past seven, we left the hotel... I have my lunch at half past.* [7] PREP & ADV If you go **past** someone or something, you go near them and keep moving, so that they are then behind you. *I dashed past him... An ambulance drove past.* [8] PREP If something is **past** a place, it is on the other side of it. *The farm was just past the next village.*

pasta /'pæstə, AM 'pɑːstə/. N-U **Pasta** is a type of food made from a mixture of flour, eggs, and water that is formed into different shapes. Spaghetti and macaroni are types of pasta.

paste /peɪst/ **pastes, pasting, pasted.** [1] N-VAR **Paste** is a soft, wet, sticky mixture of a substance, which can be spread easily. *...wallpaper paste. ...tomato paste.* [2] VERB If you **paste** something on a surface, you stick it to the surface with glue or adhesive paste. *The children were busy pasting gold stars on a chart.*

pastel /'pæstəl, AM pæ'stel/ **pastels.** ADJ & N-C Pastel colours are pale rather than dark or bright. *...delicate pastel shades... The lobby is decorated in pastels.*

pastime /'pɑːstaɪm, 'pæs-/ **pastimes.** N-C A **pastime** is something that you enjoy doing in your spare time. *His favourite pastime is golf.*

pastoral /'pɑːstərəl, 'pæst-/. [1] ADJ BEFORE N The **pastoral** activities of a religious leader relate to the general needs of people, rather than just their religious needs. *...the pastoral care of the sick.* [2] ADJ BEFORE N Pastoral means characteristic of peaceful country life. *...the pastoral beauty of a park.*

pastry /'peɪstri/ **pastries.** [1] N-U Pastry is a food made of flour, fat, and water that is used for making pies and flans. [2] N-C A **pastry** is a small cake made with pastry.

pasture /'pɑːstʃə, 'pæs-/ **pastures.** N-VAR Pasture is land that has grass growing on it and that is used for farm animals to graze on.

pat /pæt/ **pats, patting, patted.** VERB & N-C If you **pat** something or someone, or if you give them a **pat**, you tap them lightly with your hand held flat, usually as a sign of encouragement, affection, or friendship. *'Don't you worry about any of this,' she said patting me on the knee... He gave her an encouraging pat on the shoulder.*

patch /pætʃ/ **patches, patching, patched.** [1] N-C A **patch** on a surface is a part of it which is different in appearance from the area around it. *...the bald patch on the top of his head. ...two big damp patches on the carpet.* [2] N-C A **patch** of land is a small area of land, often one used for growing a particular crop. *...a vegetable patch.* [3] N-C A **patch** is a piece of material used to cover a hole in something. [4] VERB If you **patch** something that has a hole in it, you mend it by fixing something over the hole. *He and Walker patched the barn roof.* [5] PHRASE If you go through a **bad patch** or a **rough patch**, you have a lot of problems for a time.

▶ **patch up.** [1] PHR-VERB If you **patch up** a quarrel or relationship, you try to be friendly again and not to quarrel any more. *She has gone on holiday with her husband to try to patch up their marriage.* [2] PHR-VERB If you **patch up** something which is damaged, you mend it.

patchwork /'pætʃwɜːk/. ADJ BEFORE N **patchwork** quilt or dress has been made by sewing small pieces of material together.

patchy /'pætʃi/. [1] ADJ A **patchy** substance or colour is not spread evenly, but is scattered around in small quantities. *...thick patchy fog.* [2] ADJ If something is **patchy**, it is not completely reliable or satisfactory because it is not always good. *The evidence is patchy.*

pâté /'pæteɪ, AM pɑː'teɪ/ **pâtés.** N-VAR Pâté is a mixture of meat, fish, or vegetables with various flavourings, which is blended into a paste and eaten cold.

patent /'peɪtənt, AM 'pæt-/ **patents, patenting, patented.** The pronunciation /'pætənt/ is also used for meanings 1 and 2 in British English.

[1] N-C A **patent** is an official right to be the only person or company to make and sell a new product. *P&G applied for a patent on its cookies.* [2] VERB If you **patent** something, you obtain a patent for it. *The invention has been patented by the university.* [3] ADJ You use **patent** to emphasize that the nature or existence of something, especially something bad, is obvious. *This was patent nonsense.* ♦ **patently** ADV *He made his displeasure patently obvious.*

paternal /pə'tɜːnəl/. ADJ BEFORE N **Paternal** is used to describe feelings or actions which are typical of those of a father towards his child. *...paternal love for his children.*

path /pɑːθ, pæθ/ **paths.** [1] N-C A **path** is a strip of ground that people walk along. *...the garden path.* [2] N-C Your **path** is the space ahead of you as you move along. *A group of reporters blocked his path.* [3] N-C The **path** of something is the line which it moves along in a particular direction. *He stepped without looking into the path of a reversing car.* [4] N-C A **path** that you take is a particular course of action or way of doing something. *...a crucial step on the path of peace.*

pathetic /pə'θetɪk/. [1] ADJ If you describe a person or animal as **pathetic**, you mean that they are sad and weak or helpless, and they make you feel very sorry for them. *...a pathetic little dog with a curly tail.* ♦ **pathetically** ADV *She was pathetically thin.* [2] ADJ If you describe someone or something as **pathetic**, you mean that they make you feel impatient or angry, often because they are very bad or weak. *What pathetic excuses.* ♦ **pathetically** ADV *Five women in a group of 18 people is a pathetically small number.*

pathological /ˌpæθə'lɒdʒɪkəl/. [1] ADJ You describe a person as **pathological** when they behave in an extreme and unacceptable way, and have very powerful feelings which they cannot control. *He experiences chronic, almost pathological jealousy.* [2] ADJ Pathological means relating to pathology. *Students are trained in the use of pathological tests.*

pathology /pə'θɒlədʒi/. N-U Pathology is the study of the way diseases and illnesses develop, and examining dead bodies in order to find out the cause of death; TECHNICAL. ♦ **pathologist, pathologists** N-C *...the pathologist who conducted the autopsy.*

pathos /'peɪθɒs/. N-U Pathos is a quality in a situation that makes people feel sadness and pity. *...the pathos of man's isolation.*

pathway /'pɑːθweɪ, 'pæθ-/ **pathways.** N-C A **pathway** is the same as a **path**.

patience /'peɪʃəns/. N-U If you have **patience**, you are able to stay calm and not get annoyed, for example when something takes a long time. *He doesn't have the patience to wait.*

patient /'peɪʃənt/ **patients.** [1] N-C A **patient** is a person who is receiving treatment from a doctor or who is registered with a doctor. *The earlier the treatment is given, the better the patient's chances.* [2] ADJ If you are **patient**, you stay calm and do not get annoyed, for example when something takes a long time. *I've got to be patient and wait.* ♦ **patiently** ADV *She waited patiently for Frances to finish talking.*

patio /ˈpætiəʊ/ **patios.** N-C A **patio** is a paved area in a garden, where people can sit to eat or relax. *We had lunch on the patio.*

patriot /ˈpætriət, ˈpeɪt-/ **patriots.** N-C A **patriot** is someone who loves their country.

patriotic /ˌpætriˈɒtɪk, ˌpeɪt-/. ADJ Someone who is **patriotic** loves their country and feels very loyal towards it. ♦ **patriotism** /ˈpætriətɪzəm, ˈpeɪt-/ N-U ...*a country boy who had joined the army out of a sense of patriotism.*

patrol /pəˈtrəʊl/ **patrols, patrolling, patrolled.** [1] VERB & N-VAR When soldiers, police, or guards **patrol** an area or building, or when they do a **patrol** of it, they move around it in order to make sure that there is no trouble. *100 police were on patrol.* [2] N-C A **patrol** is a group of soldiers or vehicles that are patrolling an area. *A hand grenade was thrown at an army patrol.*

patron /ˈpeɪtrən/ **patrons.** [1] N-C A **patron** is a person who supports and gives money to artists, writers, or musicians. ...*a patron of modern art.* [2] N-C The **patron** of a charity, group, or campaign is an important person who allows his or her name to be connected with it for publicity. *The Princess is patron of the National AIDS Trust.* [3] N-C The **patrons** of a place such as a pub or a hotel are its customers. *Many of the bar's patrons are military.*

patronage /ˈpætrənɪdʒ, ˈpeɪt-/. N-U **Patronage** is the support and money given by someone to a person or a group such as a charity. ...*government patronage of the arts.*

patronize (BR also **patronise**) /ˈpætrənaɪz, AM ˈpeɪt-/ **patronizes, patronizing, patronized.** VERB If someone **patronizes** you, they speak or behave towards you in a way which seems friendly, but which shows that they think they are superior to you. *Don't you patronize me!* ♦ **patronizing** ADJ ...*his patronising attitude to the homeless.*

patter /ˈpætə/ **patters, pattering, pattered.** VERB & N-SING If something **patters** on a surface, it hits it quickly several times, making quiet tapping sounds. You can refer to these sounds as a **patter**. *Rain pattered gently outside.* ...*the patter of lots of little hands being clapped together.*

pattern /ˈpætən/ **patterns.** [1] N-C A **pattern** is a particular way in which something is usually or repeatedly done. *His sleeping pattern was bad.* [2] N-C A **pattern** is a design of lines or shapes repeated at regular intervals. ...*a three-dimensional pattern of colored dots.* [3] N-C A **pattern** is a diagram or shape that you can use as a guide when you are making something such as a model or a piece of clothing.

patterned /ˈpætənd/. ADJ Something that is **patterned** is covered with a pattern or design. ...*a patterned sweater.*

pause /pɔːz/ **pauses, pausing, paused.** [1] VERB If you **pause** while you are speaking or doing something, you stop for a short time and then continue. *The crowd paused for a minute, wondering what to do next.* [2] N-C A **pause** is a short period when something stops before it continues again. *There was a pause while the barmaid set down two plates.*

pave /peɪv/ **paves, paving, paved.** [1] VERB When an area of ground **has been paved**, it has been covered with blocks of stone or concrete. [2] PHRASE If one thing **paves the way** for another, it creates a situation in which the other thing is able to happen. *The invention of the first dynamo paved the way for the large scale generation of electric power.*

pavement /ˈpeɪvmənt/ **pavements.** [1] N-C In British English, a **pavement** is a path with a hard surface by the side of a road. The usual American word is **sidewalk**. [2] N-C The **pavement** is the hard surface of a road; AMERICAN. *The car spun on the slippery pavement.*

pavilion /pəˈvɪliən/ **pavilions.** [1] N-C A **pavilion** is a building on the edge of a sports field where players can change their clothes and wash; BRITISH. [2] N-C A **pavilion** is a large temporary structure such as a tent, which is used at outdoor public events.

paw /pɔː/ **paws, pawing, pawed.** [1] N-C The **paws** of an animal such as a cat, dog, or bear are its feet. [2] VERB If an animal **paws** something, it draws its paw or hoof over it.

pawn /pɔːn/ **pawns, pawning, pawned.** [1] VERB If you **pawn** something that you own, you leave it with a pawnbroker, who gives you money for it and who can sell it if you do not pay back the money before a certain time. [2] N-C In chess, a **pawn** is the smallest and least valuable playing piece. [3] N-C If you say that someone is using you as a **pawn**, you mean that they are using you for their own advantage. *They are the pawns in the power game played by their unseen captors.*

pawnbroker /ˈpɔːnbrəʊkə/ **pawnbrokers.** N-C A **pawnbroker** is a person who will lend you money if you give them something that you own. The pawnbroker can sell that thing if you do not pay back the money before a certain time.

pay /peɪ/ **pays, paying, paid.** [1] VERB When you **pay** an amount of money to someone, you give it to them because you are buying something from them or because you owe it to them. When you **pay** something such as a bill or a debt, you pay the amount that you owe. *The wealthier may have to pay a little more in taxes... All you pay for is breakfast and dinner... She paid £300,000 for the 34-room mansion... You can pay by credit card.* [2] VERB & N-U When you are **paid**, or when you receive your **pay**, you get your wages or salary from your employer. *I get paid monthly... They have not had a pay rise for two years.*

> When used as a noun, **pay** is a general word which you can use to refer to the money you get from your employer for doing your job. Professional people and office workers receive a **salary**, which is paid monthly. However, when talking about someone's salary, you usually give the annual figure. *I'm paid a salary of £15,000 a year.* Manual workers are paid **wages**, or **a wage**. The plural is more common than the singular, especially when you are talking about the actual cash that someone receives. *Every*

week he handed all his wages in cash to his wife. Wages are usually paid, and quoted, as a weekly sum. *Your starting wage will be eleven dollars a week.* Your **income** consists of all the money you receive from all sources, including your pay.

3 VERB If a course of action **pays**, it results in some advantage or benefit for you. *It pays to invest in protective clothing.* **4** VERB If you **pay** for something that you do or have, you suffer as a result. *She committed a terrible crime and will pay the penalty.* **5** VERB You use **pay** with some nouns, for example in the expressions **pay a visit** and **pay attention**, to indicate that something is given or done. *He felt a heavy bump, but paid no attention to it.* **6** PHRASE If you **pay** your **way**, you have or earn enough money to pay for what you need, without needing other people to give or lend you money. *I went to college anyway, as a part-time student, paying my own way.* **7** See also **paid**.

▶ **pay back.** PHR-VERB If you **pay back** money that you have borrowed from someone, you give them an equal amount at a later time.

▶ **pay off.** **1** PHR-VERB If you **pay off** a debt, you give someone all the money that you owe them. **2** PHR-VERB If an action **pays off**, it is successful. *Sandra was determined to become a doctor and her persistence paid off.* **3** See also **payoff**.

▶ **pay out.** PHR-VERB If you **pay out** money, usually a large amount, you spend it on something. *...football clubs who pay out millions of pounds for players.*

▶ **pay up.** PHR-VERB If you **pay up** you give someone the money that you owe them.

payable /ˈpeɪəbəl/. **1** ADJ If an amount of money is **payable**, it has to be paid or it can be paid. *Purchase tax was not payable on goods for export.* **2** ADJ If a cheque is made **payable** to you, it has your name written on it to indicate that you are the person who will receive the money.

payer /ˈpeɪə/ **payers.** N-C You can refer to someone as a **payer** if they pay a particular kind of bill or fee. For example, a tax **payer** is someone who pays taxes.

payment /ˈpeɪmənt/ **payments.** **1** N-U **Payment** is the act of paying money to someone or of being paid. *Players now expect payment for interviews.* **2** N-C A **payment** is an amount of money that is paid to someone. *...mortgage payments.*

payoff /ˈpeɪɒf/ **payoffs.** **1** N-C A **payoff** is a payment which is made to someone, often secretly or illegally, so that they will not cause trouble. **2** N-C A **payoff** is an advantage or benefit that results from an action.

payroll /ˈpeɪrəʊl/ **payrolls.** N-C The people on the **payroll** of a company or an organization are the people who work for it and are paid by it.

PC /ˌpiː ˈsiː/ **PCs.** **1** N-C & N-TITLE In Britain, a **PC** is a male police officer of the lowest rank. It is an abbreviation for 'police constable'. **2** N-C A **PC** is a computer that is used by one person in a small business, at school, or at home. It is an abbreviation for 'personal computer'.

pea /piː/ **peas.** N-C **Peas** are small, round, green seeds eaten as a vegetable.

peace /piːs/. **1** N-U **Peace** is a state of undisturbed quiet and calm. *One more question and I'll leave you in peace.* **2** N-U When a country is at **peace**, it is not involved in a war. *...a shared commitment to world peace.* **3** N-U & PHRASE If there is **peace** among a group of people, or if they live or work **in peace** with each other, they live or work together without fighting or quarrelling. *...a period of relative peace in the country's industrial relations.*

peaceful /ˈpiːsfʊl/. **1** ADJ A **peaceful** place or time is quiet, calm, and undisturbed. *Mornings are usually quiet and peaceful in Hueytown.* ♦ **peacefully** ADV *Except for nothing the night passed peacefully.* **2** ADJ Someone who feels or looks **peaceful** feels or looks calm and free from worry. ♦ **peacefully** ADV *Would she wake to find Gaston sleeping peacefully at her side?* **3** ADJ **Peaceful** means not involving violence or conflict. *...a peaceful demonstration.* ♦ **peacefully** ADV *Thousands have taken part in the protest which passed off peacefully.*

peach /piːtʃ/ **peaches.** **1** N-C A **peach** is a soft, round, juicy fruit with sweet yellow flesh and pinky-yellow skin. **2** ADJ & N-VAR Something that is **peach** is pale pinky-orange in colour. *...a peach silk blouse. ...a bedroom in peach and fern green.*

peak /piːk/ **peaks, peaking, peaked.** **1** N-C The **peak** of a process or activity is the point at which it is at its strongest, most successful, or most fully developed. *...the peak of the morning rush hour.* **2** ADJ BEFORE N The **peak** level or value of something is its highest level or value. *...a 10 per cent reduction in traffic at peak times.* **3** VERB When someone or something **peaks**, they reach their highest value or highest level of success. *Temperatures have peaked at over thirty degrees Celsius.* **4** N-C A **peak** is a mountain, or the top of a mountain. *...snow-covered peaks.* **5** N-C The **peak** of a cap is the part at the front that sticks out above your eyes.

peal /piːl/ **peals, pealing, pealed.** **1** VERB & N-C When bells **peal**, or when there is a **peal** of bells, they ring one after the other, making a musical sound. *Church bells pealed at the stroke of midnight.* **2** N-C A **peal** of laughter or thunder consists of a long loud series of sounds.

peanut /ˈpiːnʌt/ **peanuts.** N-C **Peanuts** are small nuts often eaten as a snack.

pear /peə/ **pears.** N-C A **pear** is a juicy fruit which is narrow at the top and wider at the bottom. It has white flesh and green or yellow skin.

pearl /pɜːl/ **pearls.** N-C A **pearl** is a hard, shiny, white ball-shaped object which grows inside the shell of an oyster. Pearls are used for making jewellery. *...a string of pearls. ...pearl earrings.*

peasant /ˈpezənt/ **peasants.** N-C People refer to the small farmers or farm labourers in a poor country as **peasants**.

peat /piːt/. N-U **Peat** is dark decaying plant material which is found in some cool wet regions.

pebble /'pebəl/ **pebbles**. N-C A **pebble** is a small stone.

peck /pek/ **pecks, pecking, pecked**. [1] VERB If a bird **pecks** something, it moves its beak forward quickly and bites at it. *A jay was pecking at a piece of bread someone had dropped... Chickens pecked in the dust.* [2] VERB & N-C If you **peck** someone **on** the cheek, or if you give them a **peck** on the cheek, you give them a quick light kiss.

peculiar /pɪˈkjuːliə/. [1] ADJ If you describe someone or something as **peculiar**, you think that they are strange or unusual, often in an unpleasant way. *Rachel thought it tasted peculiar.* ♦**peculiarly** ADV *His face had become peculiarly expressionless.* [2] ADJ AFTER LINK-V If something is **peculiar to** a particular thing, person, or situation, it belongs or relates only to that thing, person, or situation. *Punks, soldiers, hippies and Sumo wrestlers all have distinct hair styles, peculiar to their group.* ♦**peculiarly** ADV *Drinking too much at lunchtime is a peculiarly English habit.*

peculiarity /pɪˌkjuːliˈærɪti/ **peculiarities**. [1] N-C A **peculiarity** is a characteristic or quality which belongs or relates only to one person or thing. *I usually get out of my car very quickly – it's a peculiarity of mine. ...a peculiarity of the Soviet system.* [2] N-C A **peculiarity** that someone or something has is a strange or unusual characteristic or habit. *Joe's other peculiarity was that he was constantly munching hard candy.*

pedal /'pedəl/ **pedals, pedalling, pedalled** (AM **pedaling, pedaled**). [1] N-C The **pedals** on a bicycle are the two parts that you push with your feet in order to make the bicycle move. [2] VERB When you **pedal** a bicycle, you push the pedals around with your feet to make it move. *I pedalled to school.* [3] N-C A **pedal** in a car or on a machine is a lever that you press with your foot in order to control the car or machine. *...the brake pedal.*

peddle /'pedəl/ **peddles, peddling, peddled**. [1] VERB Someone who **peddles** things goes from place to place trying to sell them; DATED. [2] VERB Someone who **peddles** drugs sells them illegally. ♦**peddling** N-U *...the war against drug peddling.* [3] VERB If someone **peddles** an idea or piece of information, they try to get people to accept it; used showing disapproval. *Talk shows like these are a great place to peddle ideas to a large audience.*

pedestal /'pedɪstəl/ **pedestals**. N-C A **pedestal** is the base on which a statue or a column stands.

pedestrian /pɪˈdestriən/ **pedestrians**. [1] N-C A **pedestrian** is a person who is walking, especially in a town. *...streets crowded with pedestrians.* [2] ADJ If you describe something as **pedestrian**, you mean that it is ordinary and not at all interesting. *This book is depressingly pedestrian.*

pediatrician. See **paediatrician**.

pediatrics. See **paediatrics**.

pedigree /'pedɪgriː/ **pedigrees**. [1] N-C If a dog, cat, or other animal has a **pedigree**, its ances-

tors are known and recorded. [2] ADJ A **pedigree** animal is descended from animals which have all been of a particular breed, and is therefore considered to be of good quality. [3] N-C Someone's **pedigree** is their background or ancestry. *Jones has an impeccable pedigree.*

peek /piːk/ **peeks, peeking, peeked**. VERB & N-C If you **peek at** someone or something, or if you have a **peek** at them, you have a quick look at them, often secretly; INFORMAL. *On two occasions she had peeked at him through a crack in the wall.*

peel /piːl/ **peels, peeling, peeled**. [1] N-U The **peel** of a fruit such as a lemon or apple is its skin. In American English, you can also refer to a **peel**. *...grated lemon peel. ...a banana peel.* [2] VERB When you **peel** fruit or vegetables, you remove their skins. [3] VERB If you **peel** something off a surface, or if it **peels** off, it comes away from the surface. *It took me two days to peel off the labels... Paint was peeling off the walls... The acid makes skin peel slightly, revealing new skin beneath.*

peep /piːp/ **peeps, peeping, peeped**. [1] VERB & N-SING If you **peep** at something, or if you take a **peep** at it, you have a quick look at it, often secretly. *Now and then she peeped to see if he was noticing her.* [2] VERB If something **peeps** out from somewhere, a small part of it is visible. *Purple and yellow flowers peeped up between rocks.*

peer /pɪə/ **peers, peering, peered**. [1] VERB If you **peer** at something, you look at it very hard, usually because it is difficult to see clearly. *He watched the Customs official peer into the driver's window.* [2] N-C A **peer** is a member of the group of people in society who have titles and high social rank. [3] N-PL Your **peers** are people of the same age or status as you. *...children who are much cleverer than their peers.*

peerage /'pɪərɪdʒ/ **peerages**. [1] N-C If someone has a **peerage**, they have the rank of a peer. [2] N-SING The peers of a country are referred to as **the peerage**.

peg /peg/ **pegs, pegging, pegged**. [1] N-C A **peg** is a small hook or knob on a wall or door which is used for hanging things on. [2] N-C A **peg** is a small device which you use to fasten clothes to a washing line; BRITISH. [3] N-C A tent **peg** is a small piece of wood or metal that is hammered into the ground, keeping a section of the tent in place. [4] VERB If the price of something **is pegged** at a particular level, it is fixed at that level. You can also say that one country's currency **is pegged** to another country's when the value of the first currency is fixed in relation to the second; JOURNALISM. *A system was introduced, under which the peso is strictly pegged to the dollar.*

pellet /'pelɪt/ **pellets**. N-C A **pellet** is a small ball of paper, mud, lead, or other material.

pelt /pelt/ **pelts, pelting, pelted**. [1] N-C The **pelt** of an animal is its skin which can be used to make clothing or rugs. [2] VERB If you **pelt** someone **with** things, you throw things at them. *Crowds started to pelt police cars with stones.* [3] VERB If the rain is **pelting down**, it is raining very hard; INFORMAL. *The rain now was pelting down... We drove through pelting rain.*

pelvic /ˈpelvɪk/. ADJ BEFORE N **Pelvic** means near or relating to your pelvis.

pelvis /ˈpelvɪs/ **pelvises**. N-C Your **pelvis** is the wide curved group of bones at the level of your hips.

pen /pen/ **pens, penning, penned.** [1] N-C A **pen** is a writing instrument, which you use to write in ink. [2] VERB If someone **pens** a letter, article, or book, they write it. *She penned a short memo to his private secretary.* [3] N-C A **pen** is a small fenced area in which farm animals are kept for a short time. [4] VERB If people or animals **are penned** somewhere, they have to remain in a very small area. *I don't have to stay in my room penned up like a prisoner.*

penal /ˈpiːnəl/. ADJ BEFORE N **Penal** means relating to the punishment of criminals. *...a penal colony.*

penalize (BR also **penalise**) /ˈpiːnəlaɪz/ **penalizes, penalizing, penalized.** VERB If someone is **penalized** for something, they are made to suffer some disadvantage because of it. *Some of the players may, on occasion, break the rules and be penalized.*

penalty /ˈpenəlti/ **penalties.** [1] N-C A **penalty** is a punishment for doing something which is against a law or rule. *The death penalty for murder was abolished in Britain in 1969.* [2] N-C In sports such as football and hockey, a **penalty** is a free kick or hit at a goal, which is given to the attacking team if the defending team commit a foul near their own goal.

pence /pens/. See **penny**.

penchant /ˈpɒnʃɒn, ˈpentʃɑnt/. N-SING If someone has a **penchant for** something, they have a special liking for it or a tendency to do it; FORMAL. *...a stylish woman with a penchant for dark glasses.*

pencil /ˈpensəl/ **pencils, pencilling, pencilled.** [1] N-C A **pencil** is a thin wooden rod with graphite down the centre which is used for writing or drawing. [2] VERB If you **pencil** a letter or a note, you write it using a pencil. *He pencilled a note to Joseph Daniels.*

pendant /ˈpendənt/ **pendants.** N-C A **pendant** is an ornament on a chain worn round your neck.

pending /ˈpendɪŋ/. [1] ADJ If something such as a legal procedure is **pending**, it is waiting to be dealt with or settled; FORMAL. *As the court cases are pending we cannot say any more.* [2] PREP If something is done **pending** a future event, it is done until that event happens. *A judge has suspended a ban on the magazine pending a full inquiry.*

pendulum /ˈpendʒʊləm/ **pendulums.** [1] N-C The **pendulum** of a clock is a rod with a weight at the end which swings from side to side in order to make the clock keep regular time. [2] N-SING People use the word **pendulum** as a way of talking about regular changes in a situation or in people's opinions. *The pendulum has swung back and the American car companies have made dramatic advances in safety.*

penetrate /ˈpenɪtreɪt/ **penetrates, penetrating, penetrated.** [1] VERB If someone or something **penetrates** a physical object or an area, they succeed in getting into it or passing

through it. *His men had been ordered to shoot on sight anyone trying to penetrate the area.* ♦**penetration** N-U *The water has become clearer, permitting deeper penetration by the heat of the sun.* [2] VERB If someone **penetrates** an organization or a profession, they succeed in entering it although it is difficult to do so. *...the continuing failure of women to penetrate the higher levels of engineering.* [3] VERB If someone **penetrates** an enemy group, they succeed in joining it in order to get information or cause trouble. ♦**penetration** N-U *...the successful penetration by the KGB of the French intelligence service.*

penetrating /ˈpenɪtreɪtɪŋ/. [1] ADJ A **penetrating** sound is loud and clear. [2] ADJ If someone gives you a **penetrating** look, you feel that they know what you are thinking. [3] ADJ Someone who has a **penetrating** mind understands and recognizes things quickly and thoroughly. *He never stopped asking penetrating questions.*

penguin /ˈpeŋgwɪn/ **penguins.** N-C A **penguin** is a black and white sea bird found mainly in the South Pole. Penguins cannot fly.

peninsula /pəˈnɪnsjʊlə/ **peninsulas.** N-C A **peninsula** is a long narrow piece of land that is joined at one part to the mainland and is almost completely surrounded by water.

penis /ˈpiːnɪs/ **penises.** N-C A man's **penis** is the part of his body that he uses when urinating and when having sex.

penniless /ˈpenɪləs/. ADJ Someone who is **penniless** has not got any money.

penny /ˈpeni/ **pennies, pence.** The form **pence** is used for the plural of meaning 1. [1] N-C In Britain, a **penny** is a coin or an amount which is worth one hundredth of a pound. [2] N-C In America, a **penny** is a coin or an amount that is worth one cent; INFORMAL.

pension /ˈpenʃən/ **pensions.** N-C A **pension** is a sum of money which a retired, widowed, or disabled person regularly receives from the state or from a former employer.

pensioner /ˈpenʃənə/ **pensioners.** N-C A **pensioner** is a person who receives a pension.

penthouse /ˈpenthaʊs/ **penthouses.** N-C A **penthouse** is a luxurious flat or set of rooms at the top of a tall building.

pent-up /ˌpent ˈʌp/. ADJ **Pent-up** emotions have been held back and not expressed. *He still had a lot of pent-up anger to release.*

penultimate /peˈnʌltɪmət/. ADJ The **penultimate** thing in a series is the one before the last.

people /ˈpiːpəl/ **peoples; peopled.** [1] N-PL **People** are men, women, and children. **People** is normally used as the plural of **person**, instead of 'persons'. *Millions of people have lost their homes. ...the people of Angola.* [2] N-PL The **people** is sometimes used to refer to ordinary men and women, in contrast to the upper classes or the government. *...a tremendous rift between the people and their leadership.* [3] N-C A **people** consists of all the men, women, and children of a particular country or race. *...the native peoples of Central and South America.* [4] PASSIVE-VERB If a place **is peopled** by a particular group of people, those people live there.

pepper /ˈpepə/ peppers, peppering, pep-pered. [1] N-U **Pepper** is a hot-tasting spice which is used to flavour food. ...*freshly ground black pepper.* [2] N-C A **pepper** is a hollow green, red or yellow vegetable. [3] VERB If something **is peppered with** things, they hit it or are scattered over it. *The missile peppered the studio with jagged bits of metal. ...a retired bank manager who, like his son, peppers his conversation with jokes.*

peppermint /ˈpepəmɪnt/ peppermints. [1] N-U **Peppermint** is a strong fresh-tasting flavouring that is obtained from the peppermint plant or made artificially. [2] N-C A **peppermint** is a peppermint-flavoured sweet.

per /pɜː/ You use **per** to express rates and ratios. For example, if a vehicle is travelling at 40 miles per hour, it will travel 40 miles in an hour.

per annum /pər ˈænəm/. ADV A particular amount **per annum** means that amount each year. ...*a fee of £35 per annum.*

per capita /pə ˈkæpɪtə/. ADJ BEFORE N & ADV The **per capita** amount of something is the average amount of it for each person in a particular area or country; TECHNICAL. *They have the world's largest per capita income. ...the lowest oil consumption per capita in the world.*

perceive /pəˈsiːv/ perceives, perceiving, perceived. [1] VERB If you **perceive** something, especially something that is not obvious, you see, notice, or realize it. ...*to get pupils to perceive for themselves the relationship between success and effort.* [2] VERB If you **perceive** someone or something **as** doing or being a particular thing, it is your opinion that they do this thing or that they are that thing. *A woman cannot succeed if she is perceived as being too feminine.*

per cent (or **percent**) /pə ˈsent/; **per cent** is both the singular and the plural form. N-C & ADJ BEFORE N You use **per cent** to talk about amounts. For example, if an amount is 10 per cent (10%) of a larger amount, it is equal to 10 hundredths of the larger amount.

percentage /pəˈsentɪdʒ/ percentages. N-C A **percentage** is a fraction of an amount expressed as a particular number of hundredths.

perception /pəˈsepʃən/ perceptions. [1] N-C Your **perception** of something is the way that you think about it or the impression you have of it. *Our perceptions of death affect the way we live.* [2] N-U Someone who has **perception** realizes or notices things that are not obvious. [3] N-U **Perception** is the recognition of things by using your senses, especially the sense of sight.

perceptive /pəˈseptɪv/. ADJ A **perceptive** person realizes or notices things that are not obvious.

perch /pɜːtʃ/ perches, perching, perched. [1] VERB If you **perch** on something, you sit down lightly on the very edge of it. *I walked across the bridge, and perched on the narrow railing there.* [2] VERB If something **perches** on something, it is on the top or edge of something. ...*the vast slums that perch precariously on top of the hills.* [3] VERB If you **perch** one thing on another, you put it on the top or edge,

so that it looks as if it might fall off. *He picked up one of the baseball caps and perched it on his head.* [4] VERB When a bird **perches** on a branch or a wall, it lands on it and stays there.

percussion /pəˈkʌʃən/. N-U **Percussion** instruments are musical instruments that you hit, such as drums.

perennial /pəˈreniəl/. ADJ You use **perennial** to describe problems or situations that keep occurring or which seem to exist all the time. ...*the perennial urban problems of drugs and homelessness.*

perfect, perfects, perfecting, perfected. [1] ADJ /ˈpɜːfɪkt/ Something that is **perfect** is as good as it can possibly be. *He spoke perfect English... Hiring a nanny has turned out to be the perfect solution.* ♦**perfectly** ADV *The system worked perfectly.* [2] ADJ If you say that something is **perfect** for a particular person, thing, or activity, you are emphasizing that it is very suitable for them or for that activity. *Carpet tiles are perfect for kitchens because they're easy to take up and wash.* [3] ADJ BEFORE N You can use **perfect** to add emphasis. *What he had said to her made perfect sense.* ♦**perfectly** ADV *They made it perfectly clear that it was pointless to go on.* [4] ADJ BEFORE N The **perfect** tenses of a verb are the ones used to talk about things that happened or began before a particular time, as in 'He's already left' (present perfect) and 'They had always liked her' (past perfect). The present perfect tense is sometimes called the **perfect** tense. [5] VERB /pəˈfekt/ If you **perfect** something, you improve it so that it becomes as good as it can possibly be. *We perfected a hand-signal system.*

perfection /pəˈfekʃən/. N-U **Perfection** is the quality of being perfect. ...*fresh fish, cooked to perfection.*

perfectionist /pəˈfekʃənɪst/ perfectionists. N-C Someone who is a **perfectionist** refuses to do or accept anything that is not perfect.

perform /pəˈfɔːm/ performs, performing, performed. [1] VERB When you **perform** a task or action, you do it. ...*people of all ages who have performed outstanding acts of bravery.* [2] VERB The way that someone or something **performs** is how well they work or achieve good results. *The point of the tables is to get a picture of how schools are performing.* ♦**performer, performers** N-C *Until 1987, Canada's industry had been the star performer.* [3] VERB To **perform** a play, a piece of music, or a dance means to do it in front of an audience. *He began performing regularly in the early fifties.* ♦**performer** N-C ...*a solo performer.*

performance /pəˈfɔːməns/ performances. [1] N-C A **performance** involves entertaining an audience by singing, dancing, or acting. ...*a performance of Bizet's Carmen.* [2] N-VAR Someone's or something's **performance** is how well they do something. *That study looked at the performance of 18 surgeons.*

perfume /ˈpɜːfjuːm, pəˈfjuːm/ perfumes. [1] N-VAR **Perfume** is a pleasant-smelling liquid which women put on their necks and wrists to make themselves smell nice. [2] N-C A **perfume**

is a pleasant smell; LITERARY. ...*the perfume of roses.*

perhaps /pə'hæps, præps/. ADV You use **perhaps** to indicate that you are not sure whether something is true, possible, or likely. *In the end they love millions, perhaps billions... It was bulky, perhaps three feet long and almost as high... Perhaps, in time, the message will get through.*

peril /'perɪl/ **perils.** [1] N-VAR & PHRASE **Perils** are great dangers. If someone or something is in **peril**, they are in great danger; FORMAL. ...*the perils of the sea.* [2] N-PL The **perils** of a particular activity or course of action are the dangers or problems that can arise from doing it. ...*the perils of starring in a television commercial.*

perilous /'perɪləs/. ADJ Something that is **perilous** is very dangerous. ...*a perilous journey across the war-zone.* ♦**perilously** ADV *The track snaked perilously upwards.*

perimeter /pə'rɪmɪtə/ **perimeters.** N-C The **perimeter** of an area of land is the whole of its outer edge or boundary.

period /'pɪərɪəd/ **periods.** [1] N-C A particular **period** is a particular length of time. ...*a period of a few months. ...a period of economic good health and expansion. ...the Roman period.* [2] ADJ **Period** costumes, furniture and instruments were made at an earlier time in history, or look as if they were made then. [3] N-C When a woman has a **period**, she bleeds from her womb. This usually happens once a month, unless she is pregnant. [4] N-C In American English, a **period** is the punctuation mark (.) which you use at the end of a sentence when it is not a question or an exclamation. The British expression is **full stop.**

periodic /,pɪərɪ'ɒdɪk/. ADJ A **periodic** event or situation happens occasionally, at fairly regular intervals. ...*periodic bouts of illness.*

periodical /,pɪərɪ'ɒdɪkəl/ **periodicals.** [1] N-C A **periodical** is a magazine. [2] ADJ **Periodical** means the same as **periodic.** ♦**periodically** ADV *Meetings are held periodically to monitor the project's progress.*

peripheral /pə'rɪfərəl/. [1] ADJ A **peripheral** activity or issue is not very important compared with other activities or issues. [2] ADJ **Peripheral** areas of land are ones which are on the edge of larger ones. ...*peripheral regions beyond the reach of powerful rulers.*

periphery /pə'rɪfəri/ **peripheries.** [1] N-C If something is on the **periphery** of an area, place, or thing, it is on the edge of it; FORMAL. [2] N-C The **periphery** of a subject is the part of it that is not considered to be as central and important as the main part. *He brought the centre and the periphery of American politics together.*

perish /'perɪʃ/ **perishes, perishing, perished.** [1] VERB To **perish** means to die or be destroyed; WRITTEN. ...*the ferry disaster in which 193 passengers perished.* [2] VERB If a substance or material **perishes**, it starts to fall to pieces. *Their tyres are slowly perishing.*

perjury /'pɜːdʒəri/. N-U If someone who is giving evidence in a court of law commits **perjury**, they lie; TECHNICAL.

perk /pɜːk/ **perks perking perked.** N-C **Perks** are benefits that are given to people who have a particular job or belong to a particular group. *One of the perks of being a student is cheap travel.*

▶ **perk up.** PHR-VERB If something **perks** you **up**, or if you **perk up**, you become cheerful, after feeling tired, bored, or depressed. ...*suggestions to make you smile and perk you up.*

perm /pɜːm/ **perms, perming, permed.** VERB & N-C When a hair stylist **perms** someone's hair, or when they give someone a **perm**, they curl their hair and treat it with chemicals so that it stays curly for several months; BRITISH. *She had her hair permed.*

permanent /'pɜːmənənt/. ADJ **Permanent** means lasting for ever or occurring all the time. ...*permanent damage to the brain... The ban is intended to be permanent. ...a permanent state of tension.* ♦**permanently** ADV *She lived permanently in Australia with her family. ...the only way to lose weight permanently.* ♦**permanence** N-U *Anything which threatens the permanence of the treaty is a threat to peace.*

permeate /'pɜːmɪeɪt/ **permeates, permeating, permeated.** [1] VERB If an idea, feeling, or attitude **permeates** society or a system, it affects every part of it. *An obvious change of attitude at the top will permeate through the system.* [2] VERB If a liquid, smell, or flavour **permeates** something, it spreads through it. *Eventually, the water will permeate through the surrounding concrete.*

permissible /pə'mɪsəbəl/. ADJ Something that is **permissible** is allowed because it does not break any laws or rules. *Religious practices are permissible under the Constitution.*

permission /pə'mɪʃən/. N-U If you give someone **permission** to do something, you tell them that they can do it. *He asked permission to leave the room... They cannot leave the country without permission... He got permission from his commanding officer to join me.*

permissive /pə'mɪsɪv/. ADJ A **permissive** person allows or tolerates things which other people disapprove of. ♦**permissiveness** N-U ...*sexual permissiveness.*

permit, permits, permitting, permitted. [1] VERB /pə'mɪt/ If someone **permits** you to do something, they allow you to do it; FORMAL. *The guards permitted me to bring my camera.* [2] VERB If a situation **permits** something, it makes it possible for that thing to exist, happen, or be done; FORMAL. *This method of cooking also permits heat to penetrate evenly.* [3] N-C /'pɜːmɪt/ A **permit** is an official document allowing you to do something. ...*a work permit.*

pernicious /pə'nɪʃəs/. ADJ If you describe something as **pernicious**, you mean that it is very harmful. ...*the pernicious influence of secret societies.*

perpetrate /'pɜːpɪtreɪt/ **perpetrates, perpetrating, perpetrated.** VERB If someone **perpetrates** an immoral or harmful act, they commit it; FORMAL. *A high proportion of crime in any country is perpetrated by young males.* ♦**perpetrator, perpetrators** N-C ...*perpetrators of terrorist acts.*

perpetual /pə'petʃuəl/. ADJ A **perpetual** feeling, state, or quality never ends or changes; FORMAL. *...his perpetual enthusiasm.* ◆ **perpetually** ADV *They were all perpetually starving.*

perpetuate /pə'petʃueɪt/ **perpetuates, perpetuating, perpetuated.** VERB To **perpetuate** a situation, system, or belief, especially one that is bad or wrong, means to cause it to continue. *...adverts that perpetuate the worst stereotypes about the Irish.*

perplexed /pə'plekst/. ADJ If you are **perplexed**, you are puzzled or do not know what to do. *She is perplexed about what to do for her daughter.*

persecute /'pɜːsɪkjuːt/ **persecutes, persecuting, persecuted.** VERB If someone is **persecuted**, they are treated cruelly and unfairly, often because of their race or beliefs. *The Communists began by brutally persecuting the Catholic Church.* ◆ **persecution** N-U *...victims of political persecution.* ◆ **persecutor, persecutors** N-C *How could he forgive his persecutors?*

persevere /ˌpɜːsɪ'vɪə/ **perseveres, persevering, persevered.** VERB If you **persevere** with something difficult, you continue doing it and do not give up. *...a school with a reputation for persevering with difficult and disruptive children.* ◆ **perseverance** N-U *Adam's perseverance proved worthwhile.*

persist /pə'sɪst/ **persists, persisting, persisted.** [1] VERB If something undesirable **persists**, it continues to exist. *Contact your doctor if the cough persists.* [2] VERB If you **persist** in doing something, you continue to do it, even though other people oppose you or it is difficult. *She knows how much this upsets me but she persists in doing it... Their coach persisted with his own ideas.*

persistent /pə'sɪstənt/. [1] ADJ If something undesirable is **persistent**, it continues to exist or happen for a long time. *His cough grew more persistent.* ◆ **persistently** ADV *The allegations have been persistently denied.* ◆ **persistence** N-U *...concern at the persistence of inflation.* [2] ADJ **Persistent** people continue trying to do something, even though other people oppose them or it is difficult. *He phoned again this morning. He's very persistent.* ◆ **persistently** ADV *Rachel gently but persistently imposed her will upon Douglas.* ◆ **persistence** N-U *Chandra was determined to become a doctor and her persistence paid off.*

person /'pɜːsən/ **persons.** The usual plural of person is **people**. The form **persons** is used as the plural in formal language. [1] N-C A **person** is a man or a woman. *The amount of sleep we need varies from person to person... At least fifty four people have been killed.* [2] PHRASE If you do something **in person**, you do it yourself rather than letting someone else do it. *You must collect the mail in person.* [3] PHRASE If you meet, hear, or see someone **in person**, you are in the same place as them, rather than speaking to them on the telephone or writing to them. [4] N-C In grammar, the term **first person** is used when referring to 'I' and 'we', **second person** when referring to 'you', and **third person** when referring to 'he', 'she', 'it', 'they',

and all other noun groups. **Person** is also used like this when referring to the verb forms that go with these pronouns and noun groups.

persona /pə'səunə/ **personas** or **personae**. N-C Someone's **persona** is the aspect of their character or nature that they present to other people; FORMAL. *...the contradictions between her private life and the public persona.*

personal /'pɜːsənəl/. [1] ADJ BEFORE N A **personal** opinion, quality, or thing belongs or relates to a particular person. *That's my personal opinion. ...books, furniture, and other personal belongings.* [2] ADJ BEFORE N If you give something your **personal** attention, you deal with it yourself rather than letting someone else deal with it. *...a personal letter from the President's secretary.* [3] ADJ **Personal** matters relate to your feelings, relationships, and health. *He had resigned for personal reasons.* [4] ADJ **Personal** comments are critical of someone's appearance or character in an offensive way. *Newspapers resorted to personal abuse... It does concern me when it gets personal and people attack my family.*

personal com'puter, personal computers. N-C A **personal computer** is a computer which is used by one person, normally independently. The abbreviation 'PC' is also used.

personality /ˌpɜːsə'nælɪti/ **personalities.** [1] N-VAR Your **personality** is your whole character and nature. *...a friendly personality... Nobody in politics doubts his force of personality.* [2] N-C **Personality** can refer to a famous person, especially in entertainment, broadcasting, or sport, as a **personality**. *...television personalities.*

personalized (BR also **personalised**) /'pɜːsənəlaɪzd/ ADJ **Personalized** objects are marked with the name or initials of its owner. *...personalised stationery.*

personally /'pɜːsənəli/. [1] ADV You use **personally** to emphasize that you are giving your own opinion. *Personally I think it's a waste of time.* [2] ADV If you do something **personally**, you do it yourself rather than letting someone else do it. *The minister is returning to Paris to answer the allegations personally.* [3] ADV If you meet or know someone **personally**, you have met them or you know them, rather than knowing about them or knowing their work. *He did not know them personally, but he was familiar with their reputation.*

personal 'pronoun, personal pronouns. N-C A **personal pronoun** is a pronoun such as 'I', 'you', 'she', or 'they' which is used to refer to the speaker or the person listening to them, or to a person or thing whose identity is clear.

personify /pə'sɒnɪfaɪ/ **personifies, personifying, personified.** VERB If you say that someone **personifies** a particular thing or quality, you mean that they are perfect example of that thing, or they have a lot of that quality. *She seemed to personify goodness.* ◆ **personification** /pə,sɒnɪfɪ'keɪʃən/ N-SING *Joplin was the personification of the '60s female rock singer.*

personnel /ˌpɜːsə'nel/. N-PL The **personnel** of an organization are the people who work for it.

perspective /pə'spektɪv/ **perspectives.** [1] N-C A **perspective** is a particular way of thinking about something. *The death of his father 18 months ago has given him a new perspective on life.* [2] PHRASE If you get something **in perspective** or **into perspective**, you judge its real importance by considering it in relation to everything else. If you get something **out of perspective**, you fail to do this.

perspiration /ˌpɜːspɪˈreɪʃən/. N-U **Perspiration** is the moisture that appears on your skin when you are hot or frightened.

persuade /pəˈsweɪd/ **persuades, persuading, persuaded.** [1] VERB If you **persuade** someone to do a particular thing, you get them to do it, usually by convincing them that it is a good idea. *My husband persuaded me to come.* [2] VERB If you **persuade** someone that something is true, you say things that eventually make them believe that it is true. *I've managed to persuade Steve that it's for his own good.*

persuasion /pəˈsweɪʒən/ **persuasions.** [1] N-U **Persuasion** is the act of persuading someone to do something or to believe that something is true. *Britain had achieved a great deal by persuasion.* [2] N-C If you are of a particular political or religious **persuasion**, you have that political or religious belief; FORMAL.

persuasive /pəˈsweɪsɪv/. ADJ Someone or something that is **persuasive** is likely to persuade you to do or believe a particular thing. *This is hardly persuasive evidence.* ♦**persuasively** ADV *...a trained lawyer who can be relied on to present arguments persuasively.*

pertain /pəˈteɪn/ **pertains, pertaining, pertained.** VERB Something that **pertains** to something else belongs or relates to it; FORMAL. *...information pertaining to terrorist activities.*

pertinent /ˈpɜːtɪnənt/. ADJ Something that is **pertinent** is relevant to a particular subject; FORMAL. *She had asked some pertinent questions.*

pervade /pəˈveɪd/ **pervades, pervading, pervaded.** VERB Something that **pervades** a place or thing is present or noticed throughout it; FORMAL. *The smell of sawdust and glue pervaded the factory.*

pervasive /pəˈveɪsɪv/. ADJ Something that is **pervasive** is present or felt throughout a place or thing; FORMAL. *...the pervasive influence of the army in national life.*

perverse /pəˈvɜːs/. ADJ Someone who is **perverse** deliberately does things that are unreasonable. ♦**perversely** ADV *She was perversely pleased to be causing trouble.* ♦**perversity** N-U *It would be wrong to continue out of perversity.*

perversion /pəˈvɜːʃən, -ʒən/ **perversions.** [1] N-VAR A **perversion** is a sexual desire or action that is considered abnormal and unacceptable. [2] N-VAR The **perversion** of something is the changing of it so that it is no longer what it should be. *...cases involving the perversion of justice.*

pervert, perverts, perverting, perverted. [1] VERB /pəˈvɜːt/ If you **pervert** something, you interfere with it so that it is not what it used to be or should be; FORMAL. *Any reform will destroy and pervert our constitution.* [2] N-C /ˈpɜːvɜːt/ People with abnormal or unacceptable sexual desires are called **perverts**.

perverted /pəˈvɜːtɪd/. ADJ Someone who is **perverted** has abnormal behaviour or ideas, especially sexual ones.

pessimism /ˈpesɪmɪzəm/. N-U **Pessimism** is the belief that bad things are going to happen. ♦**pessimist, pessimists** N-C *I don't consider myself a pessimist.* ♦**pessimistic** /ˌpesɪˈmɪstɪk/ ADJ *People are becoming much more pessimistic about the future.*

pest /pest/ **pests.** [1] N-C A **pest** is an insect or small animal which damages crops or food supplies. [2] N-C You can describe someone, especially a child, as a **pest** if they keep bothering you; INFORMAL.

pester /ˈpestə/ **pesters, pestering, pestered.** VERB If you say that someone is **pestering** you, you mean that they keep asking you to do something, or keep talking to you, and you find this annoying. *He gets fed up with people pestering him for money.*

pesticide /ˈpestɪsaɪd/ **pesticides.** N-VAR **Pesticides** are chemicals which farmers put on their crops to kill harmful insects.

pet /pet/ **pets, petting, petted.** [1] N-C A **pet** is an animal that you keep in your home to give you company and pleasure. *...dogs and other pets.* [2] ADJ BEFORE N Someone's **pet** subject is one that they particularly like. Someone's **pet** hate is something that they particularly dislike. [3] VERB If you **pet** an animal, you pat or stroke it affectionately.

petal /ˈpetəl/ **petals.** N-C The **petals** of a flower are the thin coloured outer parts which together form the flower.

peter /ˈpiːtə/ **peters, petering, petered.**
▶ **peter out.** PHR-VERB If something **peters out**, it gradually comes to an end. *The six-month strike seemed to be petering out.*

petite /pəˈtiːt/. ADJ A **petite** woman is small and slim.

petition /pəˈtɪʃən/ **petitions, petitioning, petitioned.** [1] N-C A **petition** is a document signed by a lot of people which asks for some official action to be taken. *...a petition calling for a halt to nuclear tests.* [2] VERB If you **petition** someone in authority, you make a formal request to them. *Her followers petitioned the Vatican to make her a saint.*

petrified /ˈpetrɪfaɪd/. ADJ If you are **petrified**, you are extremely frightened. *I've always been petrified of being alone.*

petrol /ˈpetrəl/. N-U In British English, **petrol** is a liquid used as a fuel for motor vehicles. The usual American word is **gas** or **gasoline**.

petroleum /pəˈtrəʊliəm/. N-U **Petroleum** is oil which is found underground or under the sea bed. Petrol and other fuels are obtained from petroleum.

petty /ˈpeti/. [1] ADJ You can use **petty** to describe things such as rules, problems, or arguments which you think are trivial or unimportant. *...endless rules and petty regulations.* [2] ADJ If you describe someone's behaviour as **petty**, you disapprove of it because you think it shows that they care too much about small, unimportant things. ♦**pettiness** N-U *Never had she met such spite and pettiness.* [3] ADJ BEFORE N **Petty** is used to describe minor crimes or criminals. *...petty crime, such as handbag-snatching.*

petulant /'petjʊlənt/. ADJ You can describe someone's behaviour as **petulant** when he or she is angry for no good reason and upset in a childish way. ♦**petulance** N-U *His petulance made me impatient.*

pew /pjuː/ **pews.** N-C A **pew** is a long wooden seat for people in church.

pewter /'pjuːtə/. N-U **Pewter** is a grey metal made by mixing tin and lead.

phantom /'fæntəm/ **phantoms.** [1] N-C A **phantom** is a ghost. [2] ADJ BEFORE N You use **phantom** to describe something which does not really exist, but which someone believes or pretends does exist. *...a phantom pregnancy. ...phantom companies run by her relations.*

pharmaceutical /ˌfɑːməˈsuːtɪkəl/ **pharmaceuticals.** [1] ADJ BEFORE N **Pharmaceutical** means connected with the industrial production of medicine. *...pharmaceutical companies.* [2] N-PL **Pharmaceuticals** are medicines.

pharmacist /'fɑːməsɪst/ **pharmacists.** N-C A **pharmacist** is a person who is qualified to prepare and sell medicines.

pharmacy /'fɑːməsi/ **pharmacies.** [1] N-C A **pharmacy** is a place where medicines are sold or given out. [2] N-U **Pharmacy** is the job or the science of preparing medicines.

> In British English, **pharmacy** is not the usual way of referring to a shop where medicines are sold or given out. The usual term is **chemist** or **chemist's**. *She went into a chemist's and bought some aspirin.* In American English, the word **drugstore** is used, but this usually refers to a shop where you can buy drinks, snacks, and other small items, as well as medicines. *At the drugstore I bought a can of Coke and the local papers.*

phase /feɪz/ **phases, phasing, phased.** [1] N-C A **phase** is a particular stage in a process or in the development of something. *This first phase of economic reform was popular in Vietnam.* [2] VERB If an action or change **is phased** over a period of time, it is done in stages. *The redundancies will be phased over two years.*

▶ **phase in.** PHR-VERB If a new way of doing something **is phased in**, it is introduced gradually. *...the government's policy of phasing in Arabic as the official academic language.*

▶ **phase out.** PHR-VERB If something is **phased out**, people gradually stop using it or doing it. *16,000 jobs are being phased out.*

PhD /ˌpiː eɪtʃ 'diː/ **PhDs.** N-C A **PhD** is a degree awarded to people who have done advanced research. **PhD** is an abbreviation for 'Doctor of Philosophy'.

pheasant /'fezənt/; the plural is **pheasant** or **pheasants.** N-C A **pheasant** is a bird with a long tail, sometimes shot for sport and then eaten.

phenomenal /fɪˈnɒmɪnəl/. ADJ Something that is **phenomenal** is extraordinarily great or good. ♦**phenomenally** ADV *...her phenomenally successful singing career.*

phenomenon /fɪˈnɒmɪnən, AM -nɑːn/ **phenomena** /fɪˈnɒmɪnə/. N-C A **phenomenon** is something that is observed to happen or exist; FORMAL. *...natural phenomena such as lightning.*

philosopher /fɪˈlɒsəfə/ **philosophers.** N-C A **philosopher** is a person who studies or writes about philosophy.

philosophic /ˌfɪləˈsɒfɪk/. ADJ **Philosophic** means the same as **philosophical**.

philosophical /ˌfɪləˈsɒfɪkəl/. [1] ADJ **Philosophical** means concerned with or relating to philosophy. *...philosophical discussions.* [2] ADJ Someone who is **philosophical** does not get upset when disappointing or disturbing things happen. *He was philosophical about his defeat.* ♦**philosophically** ADV *She says philosophically: 'It could have been far worse'.*

philosophy /fɪˈlɒsəfi/ **philosophies.** [1] N-U **Philosophy** is the study or creation of theories about basic things such as the nature of existence or how people should live. *...traditional Chinese philosophy.* [2] N-C A **philosophy** is a particular set of theories or beliefs. *The Republicans and Democrats have different philosophies.*

phobia /'fəʊbiə/ **phobias.** N-C A **phobia** is an irrational fear or hatred of something. *He had a phobia about flying.*

phone /fəʊn/ **phones, phoning, phoned.** [1] N-U The **phone** is an electrical system used to talk to someone in another place by dialling a number on a piece of equipment and speaking into it. *We never discuss any matters over the phone... Do you have an address and phone number for him?* [2] N-C A **phone** is the piece of equipment that is used to talk to someone by phone. *Jamie answered the phone.* [3] VERB & PHR-VERB When you **phone** someone, or when you **phone** them **up**, you dial their phone number and speak to them by phone. *He phoned me to say he was visiting Manchester... I waited for her to phone... I'll phone up and ask them.*
PHRASES ● If you are **on the phone**, you are speaking to someone by telephone. *He's constantly on the phone to his girlfriend.* ● If someone is **on the phone**, they have a telephone in their house or office which is connected to the rest of the telephone system. *The Frosts were not on the phone.*

'phone booth, phone booths. N-C In American English, a **phone booth** is a small shelter in the street in which there is a public telephone. The British term is **telephone box**.

'phone-in, phone-ins. N-C A **phone-in** is a radio or television programme in which people telephone with questions or opinions and their calls are broadcast.

phoney (or **phony**) /'fəʊni/ **phoneys.** [1] ADJ If you describe something as **phoney**, you disapprove of it because it is not genuine; INFORMAL. *He'd telephoned with some phoney excuse.* [2] ADJ & N-C If you say that someone is **phoney**, or if you say they are a **phoney**, you disapprove of them because they are pretending to be someone that they are not.

phosphate /'fɒsfeɪt/ **phosphates.** N-VAR A

phosphate is a chemical compound that is used in fertilizers.

photo /ˈfəʊtəʊ/ **photos**. N-C A **photo** is the same as a photograph; INFORMAL.

photocopier /ˈfəʊtəʊkɒpiə/ **photocopiers**. N-C A **photocopier** is a machine which quickly copies documents by photographing them.

photocopy /ˈfəʊtəʊkɒpi/ **photocopies, photocopying, photocopied**. [1] VERB If you **photocopy** a document, you make a copy of it with a photocopier. [2] N-C A **photocopy** is a document made by a photocopier.

photograph /ˈfəʊtəgrɑːf, -græf/ **photographs, photographing, photographed**. [1] N-C A **photograph** is a picture that is made using a camera. *Her photograph appeared on the front page of The New York Times.* [2] VERB When you **photograph** someone or something, you use a camera to obtain a picture of them. *They were photographed kissing.*

photographer /fəˈtɒɡrəfə/ **photographers**. N-C A **photographer** is someone who takes photographs, especially as their job.

photographic /ˌfəʊtəˈgræfɪk/. ADJ **Photographic** means connected with photographs or photography. ...*photographic equipment.*

photography /fəˈtɒɡrəfi/. N-U **Photography** is the skill, job, or process of producing photographs. ...*fashion photography.*

phrasal verb /ˌfreɪzəl ˈvɜːb/ **phrasal verbs**. N-C A **phrasal verb** is a combination of a verb and an adverb or preposition, for example 'shut up' or 'look after', which together have a particular meaning.

phrase /freɪz/ **phrases, phrasing, phrased**. [1] N-C A **phrase** is a short group of words that are used as a unit and whose meaning is not always obvious from the words contained in it. [2] VERB If you **phrase** something in a particular way, you say or write it in that way. *I would have phrased it quite differently.* [3] PHRASE If someone has a particular **turn of phrase**, they have a particular way of saying or writing something. *Rose's stories weren't bad; she had a nice turn of phrase.*

physical /ˈfɪzɪkəl/. [1] ADJ **Physical** means connected with a person's body, rather than with their mind. *Physical activity promotes good health... The attraction between them is physical.* ◆**physically** ADV ...*those who are physically disabled.* [2] ADJ BEFORE N **Physical** things are real things that can be touched or seen. *Physical and ideological barriers had come down in Eastern Europe.* [3] ADJ BEFORE N **Physical** means connected with physics. ...*physical laws.*

physician /fɪˈzɪʃən/ **physicians**. N-C A **physician** is a doctor; AMERICAN.

physicist /ˈfɪzɪsɪst/ **physicists**. N-C A **physicist** is a person who studies physics.

physics /ˈfɪzɪks/. N-U **Physics** is the scientific study of forces such as heat, light, sound, pressure, gravity, and electricity.

physiology /ˌfɪzɪˈɒlədʒi/. [1] N-U **Physiology** is the scientific study of how people, animals, and plants grow and function. [2] N-SING The **physiology** of an animal or plant is the way that it functions. ...*the reproductive physiology*

of rodents. ◆**physiological** /ˌfɪzɪəˈlɒdʒɪkəl/ ADJ ...*the physiological effects of stress.*

physiotherapist /ˌfɪzɪəʊˈθerəpɪst/ **physiotherapists**. N-C A **physiotherapist** is a person whose job is using physiotherapy to treat people.

physiotherapy /ˌfɪzɪəʊˈθerəpi/. N-U **Physiotherapy** is medical treatment given to people who cannot move a part of their body and involves exercise, massage, or heat treatment.

physique /fɪˈziːk/ **physiques**. N-VAR Your **physique** is the shape and size of your body. *He was strikingly handsome with a powerful physique.*

piano /piˈænəʊ/ **pianos**. N-C A **piano** is a large musical instrument with a row of black and white keys, which you strike with your fingers. ◆**pianist** /ˈpiːənɪst, AM piˈæn-/ **pianists** N-C *Howard is a talented pianist.*

pick /pɪk/ **picks, picking, picked**. [1] VERB If you **pick** a particular person or thing, you choose that one. *I had deliberately picked a city with a tropical climate.* [2] N-SING You can refer to the best things or people in a particular group as **the pick** of that group. *The corporation gets the pick of Japan's best graduates.* [3] VERB When you **pick** flowers, fruit, or leaves, you break them off the plant and collect them. [4] VERB If you **pick** something from a place, you take it from that place, using your fingers. *He picked the telephone off the wall bracket.* [5] VERB If you **pick** an argument or a fight with someone, you deliberately cause one. [6] VERB If someone **picks** a lock, they open it without using a key, for example by using a piece of wire. [7] PHRASE If you **pick** your **way** across an area, you walk across it very carefully in order to avoid obstacles or dangerous objects. *Rescue workers were still picking their way through tons of rubble.*

▸ **pick at**. PHR-VERB If you **pick at** the food you are eating, you eat only very small amounts of it.

▸ **pick on**. PHR-VERB If someone **picks on** you, they repeatedly criticize or attack you unfairly. *Bullies pick on younger children.*

▸ **pick out**. PHR-VERB If you can **pick out** something or someone, you recognize them when it is difficult to see them. *Through my binoculars I pick out a group of figures a mile or so away.*

▸ **pick up**. [1] PHR-VERB If you **pick** something **up**, you lift it upwards from a surface using your fingers. *Ridley picked up a pencil and fiddled with it.* [2] PHR-VERB When you **pick up** something or someone, you collect them from somewhere, usually in a car. *We drove to the airport the next morning to pick up Susan.* [3] PHR-VERB If you **pick up** a skill or an idea, you acquire it without effort; INFORMAL. *Where did you pick up your English?* [4] PHR-VERB If a piece of equipment **picks up** a signal or sound, it receives it or detects it. *We can pick up Italian television.* [5] PHR-VERB If trade or the economy of a country **picks up**, it improves. [6] PHR-VERB If you **pick up** an illness, you get it from somewhere or something. *Passengers had picked up a food poisoning bug abroad.*

pickaxe (AM **pickax**) /ˈpɪkæks/ **pickaxes**. N-C
A **pickaxe** is a large tool consisting of a curved,
pointed piece of metal with a long handle
joined to the middle. Pickaxes are used for
breaking up rocks or the ground.

picket /ˈpɪkɪt/ **pickets, picketing, picketed**.
1 VERB If people who are demonstrating or on
strike **picket** a place, they stand outside it in
order to make a protest or to prevent people
from going in. *More than 150 protesters picketed the Australian Embassy.* **2** N-C A **picket** is a
group of people who are picketing a place. *...a
twenty four hour picket.*

pickle /ˈpɪkəl/ **pickles**. **1** N-PL **Pickles** are vegetables or fruit which have been kept in vin-
egar or salt water for a long time to give them a
strong sharp taste. **2** N-VAR **Pickle** is a cold,
spicy sauce that is made by boiling chopped
vegetables and fruit with spices.

pickled /ˈpɪkəld/. ADJ **Pickled** food has been
kept in vinegar and salt water so that it develops a strong sharp taste and does not go bad.
...pickled cabbage served with peppers.

picnic /ˈpɪknɪk/ **picnics, picnicking, picnicked**. N-C & VERB When people have a **picnic**,
or when they **picnic** somewhere, they eat a
meal in the open air. *I took the kids for a picnic... We picnicked on the riverbank.*

pictorial /pɪkˈtɔːriəl/. ADJ **Pictorial** means relating to or using pictures. *...a pictorial history of
the Special Air Service.*

picture /ˈpɪktʃə/ **pictures, picturing, pictured**. **1** N-C A **picture** consists of lines and
shapes which are drawn, painted, or printed
on a surface and show a person, thing, or scene. **2** N-C A **picture** is a photograph. *The Observer carries a big front-page picture of rioters.*
3 VERB If someone or something **is pictured** in
a newspaper or magazine, they appear in a
photograph in it. *The proud owners are pictured with one of their winning entries.* **4** N-C
You can refer to the image you see on a television screen as a **picture**. **5** N-C You can refer
to a film as a **picture**. *...a director of epic action pictures.* **6** N-PL In British English, if you
go to **the pictures**, you go to a cinema to see a
film. The American word is **movies**. **7** VERB &
N-C If you **picture** something, or if you have a
picture of something in your mind, you have a
clear idea or memory of it in your mind. *He
pictured her with long black braided hair... We
do have a picture of how we'd like things to be.*
8 N-C If you give a **picture** of what something
is like, you describe it. *Her book paints a bleak
picture of the problems women now face.*
9 N-SING When you refer to the **picture** in a
particular place, you are referring to the situation there. *It's a similar picture across the border in Ethiopia.*
PHRASES ● If you **get the picture**, you understand a particular situation, especially one
which someone is describing to you; INFORMAL.
● If you **put** someone **in the picture**, you tell
them about a situation which they need to
know about.

picturesque /ˌpɪktʃəˈresk/. ADJ A **picturesque**
place is attractive, interesting, and unspoiled.
...a picturesque village in the Cotswolds.

pie /paɪ/ **pies**. N-VAR A **pie** consists of meat, vegetables, or fruit, baked in pastry. *...a slice of apple pie.*

piece /piːs/ **pieces, piecing, pieced**. **1** N-C A
piece of something is a portion, part, or section of it that has been removed, broken off, or
cut off. *...a piece of paper... Cut the ham into
pieces... The vehicle was blown to pieces by the
explosion.* **2** N-C A **piece** of something of a particular kind is an individual thing of that kind.
For example, you can refer to a particular
thing that someone is advised to do as a **piece
of advice**. *...a highly complex piece of legislation. ...a sturdy piece of furniture.* **3** N-C A
piece is something that is written or created,
such as an article, work of art, or musical composition. *There was a piece about him on television... He replaced the stolen carvings with
less valuable pieces.*
PHRASES ● If someone or something is still **in
one piece** after a dangerous journey or experience, they are safe and not damaged or hurt.
● If you have to **pick up the pieces** after a disaster, you have to try to get the situation back
to normal again. ● If you **go to pieces**, you are
so upset or nervous that you lose control of
yourself and cannot do what you should do; IN-
FORMAL.

● **piece together**. **1** PHR-VERB If you **piece together** the truth about something, you gradually discover it. *Francis was able to piece together what had happened.* **2** PHR-VERB If you
piece something **together**, you gradually make
it complete by joining its parts together. *Doctors painstakingly pieced together the broken
bones.*

piecemeal /ˈpiːsmiːl/. ADJ & ADV A **piecemeal**
process happens gradually and in irregular or
unconnected stages. *The report is rightly critical of this piecemeal approach to welfare... It
was built piecemeal over some 130 years.*

pier /pɪə/ **piers**. N-C A **pier** is a large platform
which sticks out into the sea and which people
can walk along.

pierce /pɪəs/ **pierces, piercing, pierced**. VERB
If a sharp object **pierces** something, or if you
pierce something with a sharp object, the object goes into it and makes a hole in it. *Pierce
the skin of the potato with a fork... I'm having
my ears pierced.*

piercing /ˈpɪəsɪŋ/. **1** ADJ A **piercing** sound is
high-pitched and sharp in an unpleasant way.
Suddenly there was a piercing scream. **2** ADJ
Someone with **piercing** eyes has bright eyes
which seem to look at you very intensely.

pig /pɪg/ **pigs**. **1** N-C A **pig** is a farm animal with
a pink, white, or black skin. Pigs are kept for
their meat, which is called pork, ham, or bacon. **2** N-C If you call someone a **pig**, you are
insulting them, usually because you think that
they are greedy or unkind.

pigeon /ˈpɪdʒɪn/ **pigeons**. N-C A **pigeon** is a
grey bird which is often seen in towns.

pigment /ˈpɪgmənt/ **pigments**. N-VAR A **pigment** is a substance that gives something a
particular colour; FORMAL. *Melanin is the dark
pigment in our skin.*

pike /paɪk/; the plural is **pike** or **pikes**. N-VAR

Pike are a type of large river fish that eat other fish.

pile /paɪl/ **piles, piling, piled.** ⚊ N-C A **pile** of things is a quantity of them lying on top of one another. *The leaves had been swept into huge piles. ...a pile of boxes.*

A **pile** of things can be tidy or untidy. A **heap** is usually untidy, and often has the shape of a hill or mound. *Now, the house is a heap of rubble.* A **stack** is usually tidy, and often consists of flat objects placed directly on top of each other. *...a neat stack of dishes.*

⚋ VERB If you **pile** a quantity of things somewhere, you put them there so that they form a pile. You can also say a surface **is piled** with things. *He was piling clothes into the suitcase.* ⚌ QUANT A **pile** of something or **piles** of it is a large amount of it; INFORMAL. *He had piles of money.* ⚍ VERB If people **pile** into or out of a place, they all get into it or out of it in a disorganized way. *A fleet of police cars suddenly arrived. Dozens of officers piled out.* ⚎ N-U The **pile** of a carpet is its soft surface, which consists of lots of little threads standing on end.

▸ **pile up.** ⚊ PHR-VERB If you **pile up** a quantity of things, or if they **pile up**, they gradually form a pile. *Mail was still piling up at the office.* ⚋ PHR-VERB If problems or losses **pile up**, or if you **pile** them **up**, you get more and more of them. *Problems were piling up at work... He piled up huge debts.*

pilgrim /ˈpɪlɡrɪm/ **pilgrims.** N-C A **pilgrim** is a person who makes a journey to a holy place.

pilgrimage /ˈpɪlɡrɪmɪdʒ/ **pilgrimages.** N-VAR If someone makes a **pilgrimage** to a place, they make a journey there because the place is holy according to their religion, or very important to them personally. *...a private pilgrimage to family graves.*

pill /pɪl/ **pills.** ⚊ N-C **Pills** are small solid round masses of medicine or vitamins that you swallow. ⚋ N-SING If a woman is on **the pill**, she takes a special pill that prevents her from becoming pregnant.

pillar /ˈpɪlə/ **pillars.** ⚊ N-C A **pillar** is a tall solid structure which is usually used to support part of a building. ⚋ N-C If you describe someone as a **pillar of** the community, you approve of them because they play an important and active part in the community.

pillow /ˈpɪləʊ/ **pillows.** N-C A **pillow** is a rectangular cushion which you rest your head on when you are in bed.

pilot /ˈpaɪlət/ **pilots, piloting, piloted.** ⚊ N-C A **pilot** is a person who is trained to fly an aircraft. ⚋ VERB When someone **pilots** an aircraft, they act as its pilot. ⚌ ADJ A **pilot** scheme or project is one which is used to test an idea before deciding whether to introduce it on a larger scale. ⚍ VERB If an organization or government **pilots** a new scheme, they test it before deciding whether to introduce it on a larger scale. *The Government piloted a scheme under which noisy neighbours faced instant fines.*

pimp /pɪmp/ **pimps.** N-C A **pimp** is a man who finds clients for a prostitute and takes a large part of the prostitute's earnings.

pin /pɪn/ **pins, pinning, pinned.** ⚊ N-C **Pins** are very small thin pieces of metal with points at one end, which are used to fasten things together. ⚋ VERB If you **pin** something somewhere, you fasten it there with a pin. *They pinned a notice to the door... General Carl Vuono pinned on the medals.* ⚌ N-C You can refer to any long narrow piece of metal or wood with a blunt end, especially one that is used to fasten two things together, as a **pin**. *Surgeons will insert a 12-inch pin in his leg.* ⚍ VERB If someone **pins** you in a particular position, they press you firmly against something so that you cannot move. *I pinned him against the wall.* ⚎ VERB If someone tries to **pin** something bad **on** you, they say that you were responsible for it. *They couldn't pin the killing on anyone.* ⚏ VERB If you **pin** your hopes on something or someone, your future success or happiness depends on them. *Are we right to pin our hopes on our young people?*

▸ **pin down.** ⚊ PHR-VERB If you try to **pin** something **down**, you try to discover exactly what, where, or when it is. *It has taken until now to pin down its exact location.* ⚋ PHR-VERB If you **pin** someone **down**, you force them to make a definite statement. *She couldn't pin him down to a date.*

pincer /ˈpɪnsə/ **pincers.** ⚊ N-PL **Pincers** consist of two pieces of metal that are hinged in the middle. They are used as a tool for gripping things or for pulling things out. ⚋ N-C The **pincers** of an animal such as a crab or a lobster are its front claws.

pinch /pɪntʃ/ **pinches, pinching, pinched.** ⚊ VERB & N-C If you **pinch** someone, or if you give them a **pinch**, you squeeze a part of their body between your thumb and first finger. *She pinched his cheek.* ⚋ N-SING A **pinch** of an ingredient such as salt is the amount of it that you can hold between your thumb and your first finger. *...a pinch of cinnamon.* ⚌ VERB If someone **pinches** something, especially something of little value, they steal it; INFORMAL. ⚍ PHRASE If a person or company is **feeling the pinch**, they do not have as much money as they used to, and cannot buy the things that they want.

pine /paɪn/ **pines, pining, pined.** ⚊ N-VAR A **pine** or a **pine tree** is a tall tree with long thin leaves which it keeps all year round. **Pine** is the wood of this tree. ⚋ VERB If you **are pining** for something or someone, you feel sad because you cannot have them or cannot be with them. *Make sure your pet won't pine while you're away.*

pineapple /ˈpaɪnæpəl/ **pineapples.** N-VAR A **pineapple** is a large oval fruit with sweet, juicy, yellow flesh and thick, brown, skin.

pink /pɪŋk/ **pinker, pinkest; pinks.** ADJ & N-VAR **Pink** is the colour between red and white. *...a soft pink.*

pinnacle /ˈpɪnɪkəl/ **pinnacles.** ⚊ N-C A **pinnacle** is a tall pointed piece of a building or a rock. ⚋ N-C The **pinnacle** of something is the best or highest level of it. *Do you regard your* *selection as Captain as the pinnacle of your career?*

pinpoint /ˈpɪnpɔɪnt/ **pinpoints, pinpointing, pinpointed.** VERB If you **pinpoint** something, you discover or describe exactly what or where it is. *There is no possibility of pinpointing the exact time of death... The control room can always pinpoint the location of a car.*

pint /paɪnt/ **pints.** N-C A **pint** is a unit of measurement for liquids. In Britain, it is equal to 568 cubic centimetres or one eighth of an imperial gallon. In America, it is equal to 473 cubic centimetres or one eighth of an American gallon. *...a pint of milk. ...glasses which can hold a full pint.*

'pin-up, pin-ups. N-C A **pin-up** is a picture of an attractive woman or man who appears on posters, often wearing very few clothes. *She was already a famous model and pin-up.*

pioneer /ˌpaɪəˈnɪə/ **pioneers, pioneering, pioneered.** [1] VERB & N-C Someone who **pioneers** a new activity, invention, or process is one of the first people to do it. You can also refer to such a person as a **pioneer** of it. *...Professor Alec Jeffreys, who invented and pioneered DNA tests. ...one of the leading pioneers of British photo journalism.* ♦**pioneering** ADJ *The school has won awards for its pioneering work with the community.* [2] N-C **Pioneers** are people who leave their own country to go and settle in a part of another country that has not been settled in before.

pious /ˈpaɪəs/. ADJ Someone who is **pious** is very religious and moral. *He was brought up by pious female relatives.* ♦**piously** ADV *Conti kneeled and crossed himself piously.*

pip /pɪp/ **pips, pipping, pipped.** [1] N-C **Pips** are the small hard seeds in a fruit such as an apple or orange. [2] VERB In British English, if someone **is pipped** to something, such as a prize or an award, they are narrowly defeated. *Lewis was pipped for the gold medal by world record-holder Evans.*

pipe /paɪp/ **pipes, piping, piped.** [1] N-C A **pipe** is a long, round, hollow object through which a liquid or gas can flow. *...water pipes.* [2] VERB If liquid or gas **is piped** somewhere, it is transferred from one place to another through a pipe. *Clean water is piped into our own homes.* [3] N-C A **pipe** is an object which is used for smoking tobacco. [4] N-C Organ **pipes** are the long hollow tubes which produce musical notes from an organ.

pipeline /ˈpaɪplaɪn/ **pipelines.** [1] N-C A **pipeline** is a large pipe used for carrying oil or gas over a long distance. [2] PHRASE If something is **in the pipeline**, it has already been planned or begun. *There are still four movies in the pipeline.*

piping /ˈpaɪpɪŋ/. [1] N-U **Piping** is lengths of pipe or tube made from metal or plastic. *...rolls of bright yellow plastic piping.* [2] N-U **Piping** is cloth made into a narrow tube, used to decorate the edges of clothing.

piracy /ˈpaɪrəsi/. [1] N-U **Piracy** was robbery at sea carried out by pirates. [2] N-U You can refer to the illegal copying of things such as video tapes and computer programs as **piracy**.

pirate /ˈpaɪrət/ **pirates, pirating, pirated.** [1] N-C **Pirates** were sailors who attacked other ships and stole property from them. [2] VERB Someone who **pirates** tapes, books, or computer programs copies and sells them when they have no right to do so. *...a pirated edition of the book.*

piste /piːst/ **pistes.** N-C A **piste** is a track of firm snow for skiing on.

pistol /ˈpɪstəl/ **pistols.** N-C A **pistol** is a small hand gun.

piston /ˈpɪstən/ **pistons.** N-C A **piston** is a cylinder or metal disc that is part of an engine.

pit /pɪt/ **pits, pitting, pitted.** [1] N-C A **pit** is a coal mine. [2] N-C A **pit** is a large hole that is dug in the ground. [3] N-C In motor racing, the **pits** are the areas where drivers stop for fuel and repairs during races. [4] VERB If two opposing things or people **are pitted against** one another, they are in conflict. *These were two strong men pitting their skills against each other.* [5] See also **pitted**.

pitch /pɪtʃ/ **pitches, pitching, pitched.** [1] N-C In British English, a **pitch** is an area of ground that is marked out and used for playing a game such as football, cricket, or hockey. The more usual American word is **field**. *...cricket pitches.* [2] VERB If you **pitch** something somewhere, you throw it forcefully but aiming carefully. *Simon pitched the empty bottle into the lake.* [3] VERB If someone or something **pitches** somewhere, or if they **are pitched** somewhere, they fall forwards suddenly and with a lot of force. *I was pitched into the water and swam ashore.* [4] N-U The **pitch** of a sound is how high or low it is. *He raised his voice to an even higher pitch.* [5] VERB If something **is pitched** at a particular level, it is set at that level. *Prices at the budget hotel would be pitched at just over £40 a night.* [6] N-SING If something such as a feeling or a situation rises to a high **pitch**, it rises to a high level. *...the competitors who have all worked themselves up to a very high pitch.* [7] VERB To **pitch** a tent means to put it up in a place where you are going to stay.

▸ **pitch in.** PHR-VERB If you **pitch in**, you join in and help with an activity; INFORMAL. *The entire company pitched in to help.*

pitcher /ˈpɪtʃə/ **pitchers.** [1] N-C A **pitcher** is a jug. [2] N-C In baseball, the **pitcher** is the person who throws the ball to the person who is batting.

pitfall /ˈpɪtfɔːl/ **pitfalls.** N-C The **pitfalls** involved in a particular activity or situation are the things that may go wrong or may cause problems. *The pitfalls of working abroad are numerous.*

pitiful /ˈpɪtɪfʊl/. [1] ADJ Someone or something that is **pitiful** is so sad, weak, or small that you feel pity for them. *It was the most pitiful sight I had ever seen.* ♦**pitifully** ADV *His legs were pitifully thin.* [2] ADJ If you describe something as **pitiful**, you mean that it does not deserve respect or consideration. *This argument seems to show a pitiful lack of confidence in the capabilities of our juries.*

pitted /ˈpɪtɪd/. ADJ If the surface of something is **pitted**, it is covered with a lot of small shallow holes. *...the pitted surface of the moon.*

pity /ˈpɪti/ **pities, pitying, pitied.** 1 N-U & VERB
If you feel **pity** for someone, or if you **pity**
them, you feel very sorry for them. *He felt a
sudden tender pity for her... I don't know
whether to hate or pity him.* 2 PHRASE If you
take pity on someone, you feel sorry for them
and help them. *No woman had ever felt the
need to take pity on him.* 3 N-SING If you say
that it is **a pity** that something is the case, you
mean that you feel disappointment or regret
about it. *It is a great pity that all pupils in the
city cannot have the same chances.*

pivot /ˈpɪvət/ **pivots, pivoting, pivoted.**
1 N-C The **pivot** in a situation is the most important thing which everything else is based
on or arranged around. *It was Johnny, however, who was the pivot of her life.* 2 VERB If
something or someone **pivots**, they balance or
turn on a central point. *He pivoted around
sharply and punched Graham.* 3 N-C A **pivot** is
the pin or central point on which something
balances or turns.

pivotal /ˈpɪvətəl/. ADJ A **pivotal** role, point, or
figure in something is one that is very important and affects the success of that thing. *The
Court of Appeal has a pivotal role in the English legal system.*

pizza /ˈpiːtsə/ **pizzas.** N-VAR A **pizza** is a flat
piece of dough covered with tomatoes, cheese,
and other savoury food, which is baked in an
oven.

placard /ˈplækɑːd/ **placards.** N-C A **placard** is a
large notice that is carried in a march or demonstration.

placate /pləˈkeɪt, AM ˈpleɪkeɪt/ **placates, pla-
cating, placated.** VERB If you **placate** someone, you stop them feeling angry or resentful
by doing or saying things that will please them.
...a gesture intended to placate me.

place /pleɪs/ **places, placing, placed.** 1 N-C A
place is any point, building, area, town, or
country. *...Temple Mount, the place where the
Temple actually stood... The snow along the
roadside was five or six feet deep in places.*
2 N-SING **Place** can be used after 'any', 'no',
'some', or 'every' to mean 'anywhere', 'nowhere', 'somewhere', or 'everywhere'; AMERI-
CAN, INFORMAL. *The poor guy obviously didn't
have any place to go... Why not go out and see if
there's some place we can dance?* 3 N-C Your
place is the house or flat where you live; INFOR-
MAL. *Let's all go back to my place!* 4 N-C &
PHRASE You can refer to the position where
something belongs, or where it is supposed to
be, as its **place**. If something is **in place**, it is in
its correct or usual position. If it is **out of
place**, it is not in its correct or usual position.
He returned the album to its place on the shelf.
5 N-C A **place** is a seat or position that is available for someone to occupy. *I found a place to
park.* 6 N-C The **place** of someone or something in a society, system, or situation is their
position or role in relation to it. *They want to
see more women take their place higher up the
corporate or professional ladder.* 7 N-C & VERB
Your **place** in a race or competition is your position in relation to the other competitors. If,
for example, a competitor **is placed** first, second, or last, that is their position at the end of

a race or competition. 8 N-C If you get a **place**
in a team, on a committee, or on a course, you
are allowed to join the team, committee, or
course. *I eventually got a place at York University.* 9 VERB If you **place** something somewhere, you put it in a particular position.
*Brand folded it in his handkerchief and placed
it in the inside pocket of his jacket.* 10 VERB
You can use **place** instead of 'put' or 'lay' in
certain expressions where the meaning is carried by the associated noun. *His government is
placing its faith in international diplomacy.*
11 VERB If you **place** someone or something in
a particular class or group, you classify them in
that way. *The authorities have placed the drug
in Class A.* 12 VERB If you **place** an order for
some goods or for a meal, you ask a company
to send you the goods or a waiter to bring you
the meal. 13 VERB If you **place** an advertisement in a newspaper, you arrange for the advertisement to appear in the newspaper. *They
placed an advertisement in the local paper for a
secretary.* 14 VERB If you say that you cannot
place someone, you mean that you recognize
them but cannot remember exactly who they
are or where you have met them before. *He felt
he should know him, but could not quite place
him.*

You do not normally use **place** on its
own to refer to somewhere where someone can sit. The word you need is **seat**.
*There was only one seat free on the
train.* More generally, you can refer to a
space which someone or something can
occupy. *He was clearing a space for her
to lie down.*
You do not use **place** as an uncount
noun to refer to an open or empty area.
You should use **room** or **space** instead.
Room is more likely to be used when
you are talking about space inside an
enclosed area. *There's not enough room
in the bathroom for both of us... Leave
plenty of space between you and the car
in front.*

PHRASES ● If you have been trying to understand something puzzling and then everything
falls into place, you suddenly understand how
different pieces of information are connected
and everything becomes clearer. ● If things
fall into place, events happen naturally to
produce a situation you want. *Once the decision was finally made, things fell into place
rapidly.* ● If something such as a law, a policy,
or an administrative structure is **in place**, it is
working or able to be used. *Similar legislation
is already in place in Wales.* ● If one thing or
person is used or appears **in place of** another
or **in** another's **place**, they replace the other
thing or person. *Cooked kidney beans can be
used in place of French beans.* ● You say **in the
first place** when you are talking about the beginning of a situation or about the situation as
it was before a series of events. *What brought
you to Washington in the first place?.* ● If you
put someone **in** their **place**, you show them
that they are less important or clever than

they think they are. ● When something **takes place**, it happens, especially in a controlled or organized way. *The discussion took place in a famous villa.*

placement /'pleɪsmənt/ **placements.** [1] N-U The **placement** of something is the act of putting it in a particular place. *...the placement of the gun just beyond the victim's right hand.* [2] N-C If someone who is training gets a **placement**, they get a job for a period of time which is intended to give them experience in the work they are training for. [3] N-U The **placement** of someone in a job, home, or school is the act or process of finding them a job, home, or school. *...placement in a foster care home.*

placid /'plæsɪd/. ADJ If you describe a person or animal as **placid**, you mean they are calm and do not become excited, angry, or upset very easily.

plague /pleɪg/ **plagues, plaguing, plagued.** [1] N-C A **plague** is an infectious disease that spreads quickly and kills large numbers of people. *A cholera plague had been killing many prisoners of war.* [2] N-C A **plague of** unpleasant things is a large number of them that arrive or happen at the same time. *...a plague of rats.* [3] VERB If you **are plagued** by unpleasant things, they continually cause you a lot of trouble or suffering. *Fears about job security plague nearly half the workforce.* [4] VERB If someone **plagues** you, they keep bothering you or asking you for something. *I'm not going to plague you with a lot more questions.*

plaice /pleɪs/; **plaice** is both the singular and the plural form. N-VAR A **plaice** is a flat sea fish. **Plaice** is the flesh of this fish eaten as food.

plain /pleɪn/ **plains; plainer, plainest.** [1] ADJ A **plain** object, surface, or fabric is entirely in one colour and has no pattern, design, or writing on it. *A plain carpet makes a room look bigger.* [2] ADJ **Plain** things are very simple in style. *...plain food, freshly made from good quality ingredients.* ◆**plainly** ADV *...plainly dressed.* [3] ADJ If a fact, situation, or statement is **plain**, it is easy to recognize or understand. *It was plain to him that I was having a nervous breakdown.* [4] ADJ If you describe someone, especially a woman or girl, as **plain**, you think they look ordinary and are not at all beautiful. [5] N-C A **plain** is a large, flat area of land with very few trees on it.

plainly /'pleɪnli/. [1] ADV If something is **plainly** the case, it is obviously the case. *The judge's conclusion was plainly wrong.* [2] ADV You use **plainly** to indicate that something is easily seen, noticed, or recognized. *I could plainly see him turning his head.* [3] ADV If you say something **plainly**, it is easy to understand and cannot be mistaken. *'You're a coward,' Mark said very plainly.*

plaintiff /'pleɪntɪf/ **plaintiffs.** N-C A **plaintiff** is a person who brings a legal case against someone in a court of law.

plaintive /'pleɪntɪv/. ADJ A **plaintive** sound or voice is sad and high-pitched; LITERARY. *...the plaintive cry of the seagulls.*

plait /plæt, AM pleɪt/ **plaits, plaiting, plaited.** [1] VERB If you **plait** three or more lengths of hair or rope together, you twist them over and

under each other to make one thick length. [2] N-C In British English, a **plait** is a length of hair that has been plaited. The American word is **braid**.

plan /plæn/ **plans, planning, planned.** [1] N-C & PHRASE A **plan** is a method of achieving something that you have worked out carefully in advance. When things are going **according to plan**, they are working out in the way that you had planned. *...a peace plan... It seemed a trouble-free race, everything going to plan, until lap nineteen.* [2] VERB If you **plan** what you are going to do, you decide in detail what you are going to do. *He planned to leave Baghdad on Monday... Plan for the future. ...when we plan road construction.* [3] N-PL If you have **plans**, you are intending to do a particular thing. *'I'm sorry,' she said. 'I have plans for tonight.'* [4] N-C A **plan** of something that is going to be built or made is a detailed diagram or drawing of it. [5] See also **planning**.

▶ **plan on.** PHR-VERB If you **plan on** doing something, you intend to do it. *They were planning on getting married.*

plane /pleɪn/ **planes.** [1] N-C A **plane** is a vehicle with wings and engines which can fly. *He had plenty of time to catch his plane.* [2] N-C A **plane** is a flat level surface which may be sloping at a particular angle. *...a building with angled planes.* [3] N-C If you say that something is **on a higher plane**, you mean that it is more spiritual or less concerned with worldly things. *...a mind nostalgic for a higher plane.* [4] N-C A **plane** is a tool that has a flat bottom with a sharp blade in it, used for shaping wood. [5] VERB If you **plane** a piece of wood, you make it smaller or smoother by using a plane.

planet /'plænɪt/ **planets.** N-C A **planet** is a large, round object in space that moves around a star. The Earth is a planet. *...the nine planets in the solar system.*

planetary /'plænɪtri, AM -teri/. ADJ BEFORE N **Planetary** means relating to or belonging to planets. *...planetary systems.*

plank /plæŋk/ **planks.** N-C A **plank** is a long rectangular piece of wood.

planner /'plænə/ **planners.** N-C **Planners** are people whose job is to make decisions about what is going to be done in the future. *...James, a 29-year-old town planner.*

planning /'plænɪŋ/. [1] N-U **Planning** is the process of deciding in detail how to do something before you actually start to do it. *The trip needs careful planning.* [2] N-U **Planning** is control by the local government of the way that land is used and of what new buildings are built.

plant /plɑːnt, plænt/ **plants, planting, planted.** [1] N-C A **plant** is a living thing that grows in earth and has a stem, leaves, and roots. *Water each plant as often as required.* [2] VERB When you **plant** a seed, plant, or young tree, you put it into earth so that it will grow. ◆**planting** N-U *Flooding in the country has delayed planting.* [3] VERB When someone **plants** land, they put plants or seeds into the land to grow. *Much of their energy has gone into planting a large vegetable garden.* [4] N-C A **plant** is a factory, or a place where power is generated. *...car assembly plants.* [5] N-U **Plant** is large machinery used in industrial processes; TECHNICAL. **6** VERB If you **plant** something somewhere, you put it there firmly. *She planted her feet wide.* **7** VERB If someone **plants** a bomb somewhere, they hide it in the place where they want it to explode. **8** VERB If something such as a weapon or drugs **is planted** on someone, it is put amongst their belongings or in their house so that they will be wrongly accused of a crime.

plantation /plɑːnˈteɪʃən, plæn-/ **plantations.** **1** N-C A **plantation** is a large piece of land, where crops such as cotton, tea, or sugar are grown. **2** N-C A **plantation** is a large number of trees planted together.

plaque /plæk, plɑːk/ **plaques.** **1** N-C A **plaque** is a flat piece of metal or wood, which is fixed to a wall or monument in memory of a person or event. **2** N-U **Plaque** is a harmful substance that forms on the surface of your teeth.

plasma /ˈplæzmə/. N-U **Plasma** is the clear fluid part of blood which contains the red and white cells.

plaster /ˈplɑːstə, ˈplæs-/ **plasters, plastering, plastered.** **1** N-U **Plaster** is a smooth paste made of sand, lime, and water which dries and forms a hard layer. Plaster is used to cover walls and ceilings. **2** VERB If you **plaster** a wall or ceiling, you cover it with a layer of plaster. **3** N-C A **plaster** is a strip of sticky material with a small pad, used for covering small cuts or sores on your body; BRITISH. **4** PHRASE If a broken leg or arm is **in plaster**, it is covered in a hard case made from a special type of plaster to protect the broken bones.

plastered /ˈplɑːstəd, ˈplæs-/. **1** ADJ AFTER LINK-V If something is **plastered** to a surface, it is sticking to the surface. *His hair was plastered down to his scalp.* **2** ADJ AFTER LINK-V If a surface is **plastered** with something, it is covered with it. *My hands, boots and trousers were plastered with mud.*

plastic /ˈplæstɪk/ **plastics.** N-VAR **Plastic** is a light but strong material produced by a chemical process. *...a black plastic bag.*

plastic 'surgery. N-U **Plastic surgery** is the practice of performing operations to repair or replace skin which has been damaged, or to improve people's appearance.

plate /pleɪt/ **plates.** **1** N-C A **plate** is a round or oval flat dish used to hold food. A **plate** of food is the amount of food on the plate. *...a huge plate of bacon and eggs.* **2** N-C A **plate** is a flat piece of metal, for example on part of a machine. **3** N-U **Plate** is dishes, bowls, and cups that are made of precious metal. **4** N-C A **plate** in a book is a picture or photograph which takes up a whole page. **5** N-C A dental **plate** is a piece of shaped plastic which a set of false teeth is attached to. **6** See also **number plate**.

plateau /ˈplætəʊ, AM plæˈtəʊ/ **plateaus** or **plateaux.** **1** N-C A **plateau** is a large area of high fairly flat land. **2** N-C If an activity or process has reached a **plateau**, it is going through a stage where there is no change or development.

plated /ˈpleɪtɪd/. ADJ AFTER LINK-V If something made of metal is **plated with** a thin layer of another type of metal, it is covered with it. *...solid brass, plated with 24-carat gold.*

platform /ˈplætfɔːm/ **platforms.** **1** N-C A **platform** is a flat raised structure or area on which someone or something can stand. *He walked towards a platform to begin his speech. ...a rocky platform where they could pitch their tents.* **2** N-C A **platform** in a railway station is the area beside the rails where you wait for or get off a train. **3** N-C The **platform** of a political party is what they say they will do if they are elected. *...a landslide victory on a nationalist platform.*

platinum /ˈplætɪnəm/. N-U **Platinum** is a very valuable silvery-grey metal.

platitude /ˈplætɪtjuːd, AM -tuːd/ **platitudes.** N-C A **platitude** is a statement considered to be meaningless because it has been made many times before in similar situations. *I had told her the truth, while everyone else had been mouthing platitudes.*

platonic /pləˈtɒnɪk/. ADJ A **platonic** relationship is one of friendship and does not involve sexual attraction.

platter /ˈplætə/ **platters.** N-C A **platter** is a large flat plate used for serving food.

plausible /ˈplɔːzɪbəl/. ADJ A **plausible** explanation or statement seems likely to be true or valid. *Is it plausible that the President did not know what was going on?* ◆**plausibly** /ˈplɔːzɪbli/ ADV *He could plausibly have been in contact with all these people.* ◆**plausibility** N-U *...the plausibility of the theory.*

play /pleɪ/ **plays, playing, played.** **1** VERB & N-U When children or animals **play**, or when they spend time in **play**, they spend time doing enjoyable things, such as using toys and taking part in games. *Polly was playing with her teddy bear. ...a few hours of play until the baby-sitter takes them off to bed.* **2** VERB & N-U When you **play** a sport, game, or match, you take part in it. **Play** is the activity of playing sport or the time during which a game or match is played. *Alain was playing cards with his friends... I want to play for my country. ...the Continental style of play.* **3** VERB When one person or team **plays** another, or **plays** against them, they compete against them in a sport or game. *Northern Ireland will play Latvia.* **4** N-C A **play** is a piece of writing performed in a theatre, on the radio, or on television. *It's my favourite Shakespeare play.* **5** VERB If an actor **plays** a character in a play or film, he or she performs as that character. *His ambition is to play the part of Dracula.* **6** VERB If you **play** a musical instrument, or if you **play** a tune on it, you produce music from it. **7** VERB If you **play** a record, CD, or tape, you put it onto a record player or into a tape recorder and sound is produced. *There is classical music playing in the background.* **8** VERB If you **play** a joke or a trick on someone, you deceive them or give them a surprise in a way that you think is funny, but may cause them problems or annoy them. *Someone had played a trick on her, stretched a piece of string at the top of those steps.*

PHRASES ● If you ask **what** someone **is playing at**, you are angry because you think they are doing something stupid or wrong; INFORMAL. ● If something or someone **plays a part** or

plays a role in a situation, they are involved in it and have an effect on it. *The UN would play a major role in monitoring a ceasefire.*

▶ **play along.** PHR-VERB If you **play along** with a person, you appear to agree with them and do what they want, even though you are not sure whether they are right. *He turned and led the way to the lift. Fox played along, following him.*

▶ **play around.** [1] PHR-VERB If you **play around**, you behave in a silly way to amuse yourself or other people; INFORMAL. *Stop playing around and eat!* [2] PHR-VERB If you **play around** with a problem or an arrangement of objects, you try different ways of organizing it in order to find the best solution or arrangement; INFORMAL.

▶ **play at.** PHR-VERB If you say that someone is **playing at** an activity, you disapprove of the fact that they are doing it casually and not very seriously. *He had the afternoon off and spent it at her stall, playing at being a market trader.*

▶ **play back.** PHR-VERB When you **play back** a tape or film, you listen to the sounds or watch the pictures after recording them.

▶ **play down.** PHR-VERB If you **play down** something, you try to make people think that it is less important than it really is. *The team coach played down the rivalry between the sides.*

▶ **play off against.** PHR-VERB If you **play** people **off against** each other, you make them compete or argue, so that you gain some advantage. *Gregory would interview them, and would play one off against the other.*

▶ **play on.** PHR-VERB If you **play on** someone's fears, you deliberately use them in order to achieve what you want. *...an election campaign which plays on the population's fear of change.*

▶ **play up.** PHR-VERB If something such as a machine or a part of your body **is playing up**, or if it **is playing** you **up**, it is not working properly; INFORMAL, BRITISH. *The engine had been playing up... It was his back playing him up.*

player /'pleɪə/ **players.** [1] N-C A **player** in a sport or game is a person who takes part. [2] N-C You can use **player** to refer to a musician. *...a professional trumpet player.* [3] N-C A **player** is an actor. *Oscar nominations went to all five leading players.* [4] See also **record player.**

playful /'pleɪfʊl/. ADJ A **playful** gesture is friendly and cheerful. *...a playful kiss.* ♦ **playfully** ADV *She pushed him away playfully.* ♦ **playfulness** N-U *...the child's natural playfulness.*

playground /'pleɪgraʊnd/ **playgrounds.** N-C A **playground** is a piece of land where children can play.

playgroup /'pleɪgruːp/ **playgroups.** N-VAR A **playgroup** is an informal kind of school for very young children where they learn by playing.

'**playing card, playing cards.** N-C **Playing cards** are thin pieces of card with numbers and pictures on them, which are used to play games.

'**playing field, playing fields.** [1] N-C A **playing field** is a large area of grass where people play sports. [2] PHRASE You talk about a **level playing field** to mean a situation that is fair, because no competitor or opponent has an advantage over another.

'**play-off** (or **playoff**)**, playoffs.** N-C A **playoff** is an extra game played to decide the winner of a sports competition when two or more people have got the same score.

playwright /'pleɪraɪt/ **playwrights.** N-C A **playwright** is a person who writes plays.

plaza /'plɑːzə, AM 'plæzə/ **plazas.** N-C A **plaza** is an open square in a city.

plc (or **PLC**) /,piː el 'siː/ **plcs.** In Britain, **plc** is an abbreviation for 'public limited company'. It is used after the name of a company whose shares can be bought by the public. *...British Telecommunications plc.*

plea /pliː/ **pleas.** [1] N-C A **plea** is a request for something made in an intense or emotional way; JOURNALISM. *...his emotional plea for help in solving the killing.* [2] N-C In a court of law, a person's **plea** is the answer that they give when they have been charged with a crime. *...a plea of not guilty.*

plead /pliːd/ **pleads, pleading, pleaded.** [1] VERB If you **plead** with someone to do something, you ask them in an intense, emotional way to do it. *He was kneeling on the floor pleading for mercy... I pleaded to be allowed to go.* [2] VERB When someone charged with a crime **pleads guilty** or **not guilty** in a court of law, they officially state that they are guilty or not guilty of the crime. [3] VERB If someone **pleads the case** or **cause** of someone or something, they speak out in their support or defence. *He would plead the cause of Russian unity.* [4] VERB If you **plead** a particular thing as a reason for doing or not doing something, you give it as your excuse. *Mr Giles pleads ignorance as his excuse.*

pleading /'pliːdɪŋ/ **pleadings.** [1] ADJ A **pleading** expression or gesture shows that you want something very much. *...his pleading eyes.* [2] N-VAR **Pleading** is asking someone for something you want very much, in an intense or emotional way. *His mother simply ignored Sid's pleading.*

pleasant /'plezənt/ **pleasanter, pleasantest.** [1] ADJ Something that is **pleasant** is enjoyable or attractive. *It's always pleasant to do what you're good at doing.* ♦ **pleasantly** ADV *The room was pleasantly warm.* [2] ADJ Someone who is **pleasant** is friendly and likeable.

please /pliːz/ **pleases, pleasing, pleased.** [1] CONVENTION You say **please** when you are politely asking or inviting someone to do something, or when you are asking someone for something. *Can you help us please?... Please come in.* [2] CONVENTION You say **please** when you are accepting something politely. *'Tea?'—'Yes, please.'* [3] VERB If someone or something **pleases** you, they make you feel happy and satisfied. *I was tidying my bedroom to please mum... Nothing pleased him.* [4] PHRASE You use **please** in expressions such as **as she pleases, whatever you please,** and **anything he pleases** to indicate that someone can do or have whatever they want. *Women should be free to dress and act as they please.* [5] CONVENTION You say '**please yourself**' to indicate in a rather rude way that you do not mind or care whether the person you are talking to does a particular thing or not; INFORMAL.

pleased /pliːzd/. [1] ADJ AFTER LINK-V If you are **pleased**, you are happy about something or satisfied with it. *I think he's going to be pleased that we identified the real problems... I'm pleased with the way things have been going... They're pleased to be going home.* [2] CONVENTION You say **'Pleased to meet you'** as a polite way of greeting someone you are meeting for the first time.

pleasing /pliːzɪŋ/. ADJ Something that is **pleasing** gives you pleasure and satisfaction. *...a pleasing climate.* ♦ **pleasingly** ADV *The interior design is pleasingly simple.*

pleasurable /pleʒərəbəl/. ADJ **Pleasurable** experiences or sensations are pleasant and enjoyable. *He found sailing more pleasurable than skiing.*

pleasure /pleʒə/ **pleasures.** [1] N-U If something gives you **pleasure**, you get a feeling of happiness, satisfaction, or enjoyment from it. *Everybody takes pleasure in eating.* [2] N-U **Pleasure** is the activity of enjoying yourself rather than working. *He mixed business and pleasure.* [3] N-C A **pleasure** is an activity or experience that you find very enjoyable and satisfying. *Watching TV is our only pleasure.* [4] CONVENTION You can say **'It's a pleasure'** or **'My pleasure'** as a polite way of replying to someone who has just thanked you for doing something. *'Thanks very much anyhow.'—'It's a pleasure.'*

pleat /pliːt/ **pleats.** N-C A **pleat** in a piece of clothing is a permanent fold made in the cloth.

pleated /pliːtɪd/. ADJ A **pleated** piece of clothing has pleats in it.

pledge /pledʒ/ **pledges, pledging, pledged.** [1] VERB & N-C When someone **pledges** to do something, or when they make a **pledge** to do it, they promise solemnly that they will do it or provide it. *Britain pledged $36 million to the refugees... Both sides pledged that a nuclear war must never be fought.* [2] VERB If you **pledge** yourself to something, you promise to follow a particular course of action. *The President pledged himself to increase taxes for the rich.*

plentiful /plentɪfʊl/. ADJ Things that are **plentiful** exist in such large amounts or numbers that there is enough for people's wants or needs. *...a plentiful supply of vegetables.*

plenty /plenti/. QUANT If there is **plenty** of something, there is a large amount of it, often more than is needed. *There was still plenty of time to take Jill out for pizza... I don't believe in long interviews. Fifteen minutes is plenty.*

pliers /plaɪəz/. N-PL **Pliers** are a tool with two handles at one end and two hard, flat, metal parts at the other. **Pliers** are used to hold or pull out things such as nails, or to bend or cut wire.

plight /plaɪt/. N-SING If you talk about someone's **plight**, you mean the difficult or dangerous situation they are in; FORMAL. *...the worsening plight of Third World countries.*

plod /plɒd/ **plods, plodding, plodded.** [1] VERB If someone **plods** somewhere, they walk there slowly and heavily. *He plodded down the road at an unhurried pace.* [2] VERB If

you **plod** on with a job, you keep on doing it, without worrying about how fast you are progressing. *He is plodding on with negotiations... Aircraft production continued to plod along at an agonizingly slow pace.*

plot /plɒt/ **plots, plotting, plotted.** [1] N-C & VERB If there is a **plot** to do something illegal or wrong, or if people **plot** to do something like this, they plan secretly to do it. *...a plot to overthrow the government... By the time they were married, she was already plotting against him.* ♦ **plotter, plotters** N-C *Plotters tried to seize power in Moscow.* [2] N-VAR The **plot** of a film, novel, or play is the story and the way in which it develops. [3] N-C A **plot** is a small piece of land, especially one that is intended for a purpose such as building houses or growing vegetables. [4] VERB When people **plot** a strategy or a course of action, they carefully plan each step of it. [5] VERB When someone **plots** something on a graph, they mark certain points on it and then join the points up. [6] VERB To **plot** the position or progress of something means to follow its position or progress and show it on a map or diagram.

plough (AM **plow**) /plaʊ/ **ploughs, ploughing, ploughed.** [1] N-C A **plough** is a large farming tool with sharp blades, which is attached to a tractor or an animal and used to turn over the soil before planting. [2] VERB When a farmer **ploughs** an area of land, they turn over the soil using a plough.

▶ **plough into** [1] PHR-VERB If something, for example a car, **ploughs into** something else, it crashes violently into it. [2] PHR-VERB If you say that money **is ploughed into** something such as a business, you are emphasizing that a large amount of money is being invested in it. *...the need to plough even more money into education and training.*

▶ **plough on** PHR-VERB If you **plough on**, you continue moving or trying to complete something, even though it takes a lot of effort. *This will not deter the Government from ploughing on with the sale.*

▶ **plough through** [1] PHR-VERB If you **plough through** something such as a large meal or a long piece of work, you finally finish it, although it takes a lot of effort. [2] PHR-VERB If a person or vehicle **ploughs through** a place or substance, they move through it with great force or effort. *...the satisfying noise made by the boat as it ploughs through the water.*

plow /plaʊ/. See **plough.**

ploy /plɔɪ/ **ploys.** N-C If you describe something someone does as a **ploy**, you mean that they have planned it carefully and are doing it in order to gain an advantage for themselves. *That's only a ploy to get me to take Chris's place.*

pluck /plʌk/ **plucks, plucking, plucked.** [1] VERB If you **pluck** a fruit, flower, or leaf, you take it between your fingers and pull it from its stalk; WRITTEN. *I plucked a lemon from the tree.* [2] VERB If you **pluck** something from somewhere, you take it in your fingers or hands and pull it sharply from where it is. *He plucked the cigarette from his mouth and tossed it out into the street.* [3] VERB If you **pluck** the strings of a musical instrument such as a guitar, you pull them with your fingers and let them go, so that they make a sound. [4] VERB If you **pluck** a bird that has been killed to be eaten, you pull its feathers out to prepare it for cooking. [5] VERB If you **pluck** your eyebrows, you shape them by pulling out some of the hairs, using a device called a tweezers. [6] VERB If someone is rescued from a dangerous or bad situation, you can say that they **are plucked from** it or **are plucked to** safety; JOURNALISM. *They were plucked from the icy river when residents heard cries for help.* [7] PHRASE If you **pluck up the courage** to do something frightening, you make an effort to be brave enough to do it. *I slept in my car for two more days until I plucked up courage to go home.*

▸ **pluck at** PHR-VERB If you **pluck at** something, you take it between your fingertips and pull it sharply but gently. *The boy plucked at Adam's sleeve.*

plug /plʌg/ **plugs, plugging, plugged.** [1] N-C A **plug** on a piece of electrical equipment is a small plastic object with two or three metal pins which fit into the holes of an electric socket. [2] N-C A **plug** is a thick circular piece of rubber or plastic that you use to block the hole in a bath or sink. when it is filled with water. [3] VERB If you **plug** a hole, a gap, or a leak, you block it with something. *Chet tore off his shirt and used it to plug the hole in the canoe.* [4] VERB & N-C If someone **plugs** something such as a book or a film, or if they give it a **plug**, they talk about it in order to encourage people to buy it or see it; INFORMAL. *...another actor plugging his latest book.* [5] PHRASE If someone in a position of power **pulls the plug on** a project or on someone's activities, they use their power to stop them continuing.

▸ **plug in** or **plug into.** PHR-VERB If you **plug** a piece of electrical equipment **into** an electricity supply, or if you **plug it in**, you push its plug into an electric socket so that it can work. *I filled the kettle while she was talking and plugged it in.*

plum /plʌm/ **plums.** [1] N-C A **plum** is a small sweet fruit with a smooth red or yellow skin and a stone in the middle. [2] ADJ BEFORE N A **plum** job is a very good job that a lot of people would like.

plumber /'plʌmə/ **plumbers.** N-C A **plumber** is a person whose job is to connect and repair things such as water and drainage pipes, baths, and toilets.

plumbing /'plʌmɪŋ/ [1] N-U The **plumbing** in a building consists of the water and drainage pipes, baths, and toilets in it. [2] N-U **Plumbing** is the work of connecting and repairing water and drainage pipes, baths, and toilets.

plume /pluːm/ **plumes.** N-C A **plume** of smoke, dust, fire, or water is a large quantity of it that rises into the air in a column.

plummet /'plʌmɪt/ **plummets, plummeting, plummeted.** VERB If an amount, rate, or price **plummets**, it decreases quickly by a large amount; JOURNALISM. *In Tokyo share prices have plummeted.*

plump /plʌmp/ **plumper, plumpest; plumps, plumping, plumped.** ADJ A **plump** person is rather fat. • See note at **fat**.

▸ **plump for.** PHR-VERB If you **plump for** someone or something, you choose them after hesitating and thinking. *They may well plump for a candidate with a higher qualification.*

plunder /'plʌndə/ **plunders, plundering, plundered.** VERB & N-U If someone **plunders** a place, or if they are involved in the **plunder** of a place, they steal things from it; WRITTEN. *This has been done by plundering £4 billion from the Government reserves. ...a guerrilla group infamous for torture and plunder.*

plunge /plʌndʒ/ **plunges, plunging, plunged.** [1] VERB If something or someone **plunges** in a particular direction, especially into water, they fall, rush, or throw themselves in that direction. *At least 50 people died when a bus plunged into a river.* [2] VERB If you **plunge** an object into something, you push it quickly or violently into it. *She plunged the knife into his chest.* [3] VERB If something **plunges** someone or something **into** a particular state or situation, or if they **plunge into** it, they are suddenly in that state or situation. *8,000 homes were plunged into darkness as electricity cables crashed down... The economy is plunging into recession.* [4] VERB If you **plunge into** an activity or **are plunged into** it, you become very involved in it. *He plunged himself into work.* [5] VERB & N-C If an amount or rate **plunges**, or if there is a **plunge** in an amount or rate, it decreases quickly and suddenly. *His weight began to plunge.* [6] PHRASE If you **take the plunge**, you decide to do something that you consider difficult or risky. *Lesley took the plunge and invited him back.*

plural /'pluərəl/ **plurals.** N-C & ADJ BEFORE N The **plural** of a word or its **plural** form is the form that is used when referring to more than one person or thing. *What is the plural of 'person'? ...the plural pronoun 'we'.*

pluralism /'pluərəlɪzəm/. N-U If there is **pluralism** within a society, it has many different groups and political parties; FORMAL.

plus /plʌs/ **pluses** or **plusses.** [1] CONJ You use **plus** to show that one number or quantity is being added to another. *Two plus two equals four... Send a cheque for £18.99 plus £2 for postage and packing.* [2] ADJ **Plus** before a number or quantity means that the number or quantity is greater than zero. *The aircraft was subjected to temperatures of minus 65 degrees and plus 120 degrees.* [3] CONJ You can use **plus** when mentioning an additional item or fact. *There's easily enough room for two adults and three children, plus a dog in the boot.* [4] ADJ You use **plus** after a number or quantity to indicate that the actual number or quantity is greater than the one mentioned. *There are only 35 staff to serve 30,000-plus customers.* [5] N-C A **plus** is an advantage or benefit; INFORMAL. *Experience of any career in sales is a big plus.*

plush /plʌʃ/. ADJ If you describe something as **plush**, you mean that it is very smart, comfortable, or expensive. *...a plush, four-storey, Georgian house in Mayfair.*

plutonium /pluː'təʊniəm/. N-U **Plutonium** is a radioactive element used especially in nuclear weapons and as a fuel in nuclear power stations.

ply /plaɪ/ **plies, plying, plied.** [1] VERB If someone **plies** you with food or drink, they keep giving it to you in an insistent way. *There they ply you with drink until you are throwing your money at them in handfuls.* [2] VERB If a ship, aircraft, or vehicle **plies** a route, it makes regular journeys along that route.

plywood /ˈplaɪwʊd/. N-U **Plywood** is wood that consists of thin layers of wood stuck together.

p.m. /ˌpi: ˈem/. ADV **p.m.** is used after a number to show that you are referring to a particular time between noon and midnight. *The spa is open from 7:00 a.m. to 9:00 p.m. every day.*

PM /ˌpi: ˈem/ **PMs.** N-C The **PM** is an abbreviation for the **Prime Minister**; INFORMAL.

pneumonia /njuːˈməʊniə/. N-U **Pneumonia** is a serious disease which affects your lungs and makes breathing difficult.

poach /pəʊtʃ/ **poaches, poaching, poached.** [1] VERB If someone **poaches** animals, fish, or birds, they illegally catch them on someone else's property. ♦**poacher, poachers** N-C *Security cameras have been installed to guard against poachers.* ♦**poaching** N-U *...a man accused of salmon poaching.* [2] VERB If an organization **poaches** members or customers from another organization, they secretly or dishonestly persuade them to join them or become their customers. *...allegations that it had poached members from other unions.* ♦**poaching** N-U *Measures were introduced to conserve labour and prevent poaching.* [3] VERB If you **poach** food such as fish or eggs, you cook it gently in boiling water or milk. *...a poached egg.*

pocket /ˈpɒkɪt/ **pockets, pocketing, pocketed.** [1] N-C A **pocket** is a small bag or pouch that forms part of a piece of clothing. *...his jacket pocket.* [2] N-C You can use **pocket** in expressions that refer to money that people have, get, or spend. *Tax cuts will put money in taxpayers' pockets.* [3] ADJ BEFORE N You use **pocket** to describe something that is small enough to fit into a pocket. *...a pocket calculator.* [4] VERB If someone **pockets** something, usually something that does not belong to them, they keep it or steal it; INFORMAL. *O'Connor pocketed the money to reduce his bank overdraft.* [5] PHRASE If you are **out of pocket**, you have less money than you should have or than you intended. *You're going to be out of pocket because the interest is more than the income.*

pocket money. N-U **Pocket money** is a small amount of money given regularly to children by their parents.

pod /pɒd/ **pods.** N-C A **pod** is a seed container that grows on some plants such as peas.

podium /ˈpəʊdiəm/ **podiums.** N-C A **podium** is a small platform on which someone stands in order to give a lecture or conduct an orchestra.

poem /ˈpəʊɪm/ **poems.** N-C A **poem** is a piece of writing in which the words are chosen for their beauty and sound and are carefully arranged, often in short lines.

poet /ˈpəʊɪt/ **poets.** N-C A **poet** is a person who writes poems.

poetic /pəʊˈetɪk/. [1] ADJ Something that is po-etic is very beautiful, expressive, and sensitive. *...a witty and poetic portrait of contemporary Dublin.* [2] ADJ **Poetic** means relating to poetry. *There's a very rich poetic tradition in Gaelic.*

poetry /ˈpəʊɪtri/. N-U Poems, considered as a form of literature, are referred to as **poetry**. *Lawrence Durrell wrote a great deal of poetry. ...a poetry book.*

poignant /ˈpɔɪnjənt/. ADJ Something that is **poignant** makes you feel very sad or full of pity. *A poignant moment in the movie is the untimely death of one of the characters.*

point /pɔɪnt/ **points, pointing, pointed.** [1] N-C A **point** is an opinion or fact expressed by someone. *The research made some valid points... He illustrates his point with an anecdote.* [2] N-C If you say that someone has a **point**, or if you take their **point** or see their **point**, you mean that you accept that what they have said is worth considering. *'If he'd already killed once, surely he'd have killed Sarah?' She had a point there.* [3] N-SING The **point** of what you are saying or discussing is the most important part. If you say that something is **beside the point**, you mean it is not relevant to what you are saying or discussing. *My point is that I'm not going to change... He has completely missed the point of recent student protests... He came straight to the point. 'It's bad news,' he said.* [4] N-SING If you ask what the **point** of something is, or say that there is **no point** in it, you are indicating that a particular action has no purpose or would not be useful. *Many do not even turn up to classes. They cannot see the point.* [5] N-C A **point** is an aspect or quality of something or someone. *Science was never my strong point at school.* [6] N-C A **point** is a particular position or time. *The pain originated from a point in his right thigh... At this point Diana arrived.* [7] N-C The **point** of something such as a needle or knife is the thin, sharp end of it. [8] N-C In some sports and games, a **point** is one of the single marks that are added together to give the total score. *New Zealand have beaten Scotland by 21 points to 18.* [9] N-C You use **point** to refer to the dot or mark in a decimal number that separates the whole numbers from the fractions; SPOKEN. *...seven point eight per cent.* [10] N-C The **points** of a compass are the marks on it that show the directions, especially North, South, East, and West. [11] VERB If you **point** at a thing or person, you hold out your finger or an object such as a stick to show someone where the thing or person is. *He pointed to a chair, signalling for her to sit.* [12] VERB If you **point** something at someone, you aim the tip or end of it towards them. *A man pointed a gun at them.* [13] VERB If something **points** to a place or **points** in a particular direction, it shows where that place is or faces in that direction. *An arrow pointed to the toilets.* [14] VERB If something **points** to a particular situation, it suggests that the situation exists or is likely to occur. *Private polls and embassy reports pointed to a no vote.*

PHRASES ● If you **make a point of** doing something, you do it in a deliberate or obvious way. *He had made a point of never talking about the episode.* ● If you are **on the point of** doing something, you are about to do it. *He was on the point of saying something when the phone rang.* ● If you say that something is true **up to a point**, you mean that it is partly but not completely true. *It worked up to a point.* ● See also **pointed**. ● **in point of fact**: see **fact**. ● **to point the finger at** someone: see **finger**.

▶ **point out.** **1** PHR-VERB If you **point out** an object or place to someone, you direct their attention to it. *They kept standing up to take pictures and point things out to each other.* **2** PHR-VERB If you **point out** a fact or mistake, you tell someone about it. *Critics point out that the prince, on his income, should be paying tax.*

,point-'blank. **1** ADV & ADJ BEFORE N If you say something **point-blank**, you say it very directly, without explaining or apologizing. *I asked him point-blank why he was doing it. ...their point blank refusal.* **2** ADV & ADJ BEFORE N If someone or something is shot **point-blank** or at **point-blank** range, they are shot by a gun which is held extremely close to them.

pointed /'pɔɪntɪd/. **1** ADJ An object that is **pointed** has a narrow end or tip. *...pointed shoes. ...pointed roofs.* **2** ADJ **Pointed** comments or behaviour express criticism in a clear and direct way. *The senators asked Klein some rather pointed questions.* ◆ **pointedly** ADV *They were pointedly absent from the news conference.*

pointer /'pɔɪntə/ **pointers.** N-C A **pointer** is a piece of advice or information which helps you to understand a situation or solve a problem. *Here are a few pointers to help you make a choice.*

pointless /'pɔɪntləs/. ADJ Something that is **pointless** has no purpose. *Violence is always pointless.* ◆ **pointlessly** ADV *More than four years of my life had been ruined, quite pointlessly.*

,point of 'view, points of view. **1** N-C You can refer to the opinions that you have about something as your **point of view**. **2** PHRASE If you consider something **from a** particular **point of view**, you are using one aspect of a situation to judge it. *Do you think that, from the point of view of results, this exercise was worth the cost?*

poised /pɔɪzd/. **1** ADJ If a part of your body is **poised**, it is completely still but ready to move at any moment. *He studied the keyboard carefully, one finger poised.* **2** ADJ AFTER LINK-V If someone is **poised** to do something, they are ready to take action at any moment. *US forces are poised for a massive air, land and sea assault.* **3** ADJ If you are **poised**, you are calm, dignified, and in control of your emotions.

poison /'pɔɪzən/ **poisons, poisoning, poisoned.** **1** N-VAR **Poison** is a substance that harms or kills people or animals if they swallow or absorb it. *Mercury is a known poison.* **2** VERB To **poison** someone or something means to give poison to them or to add poison to them, causing them harm. *...the rumours that she had poisoned him... The land has been completely poisoned by chemicals.* ◆ **poisoning,**

poisonings N-VAR *She was sentenced to twenty years' imprisonment for poisoning.* **3** VERB Something that **poisons** a good situation or relationship spoils it or destroys it. *The letter poisoned her relationship with her family for ever.*

poisonous /'pɔɪzənəs/. **1** ADJ Something that is **poisonous** will kill you or harm you if you swallow or absorb it. *Ten workmen breathed in poisonous gas.* **2** ADJ A **poisonous** animal produces a poison that will kill you or make you ill if the animal bites you.

poke /pəʊk/ **pokes, poking, poked.** **1** VERB & N-C If you **poke** someone or something, or if you give them a **poke**, you quickly push them with your finger or a sharp object. You can also say that you **poke** your finger or an object into someone or something. *Her mother opened the oven door and poked a fork into the turkey skin... John smiled at them and gave Richard a playful poke.* **2** VERB If something **pokes** from behind or under something, or if someone **pokes** it there, you can see part of it appearing from behind or under that thing. *His tiny head poked from the covers... Julie tapped on my door and poked her head in.* **3** to **poke fun at**: see **fun**.

▶ **poke around.** PHR-VERB If you **poke around** for something, you search for it, usually by moving lots of objects around; INFORMAL. *We opened up the car bonnet and he started poking around in my engine.*

▶ **poke at.** PHR-VERB If you **poke at** something, you make lots of little pushing movements at it with a sharp object.

poker /'pəʊkə/. N-U **Poker** is a card game that people usually play in order to win money.

polar /'pəʊlə/. ADJ BEFORE N **Polar** refers to the area around the North and South Poles. *...the polar regions of the Soviet Union.*

polarize (BR also **polarise**) /'pəʊləraɪz/ **polarizes, polarizing, polarized.** VERB If something **polarizes** people, it causes them to become two separate groups with opposite opinions or positions. *The issue of free trade was polarizing the country.* ◆ **polarization** N-U *...polarization between the blacks and whites in the US.*

pole /pəʊl/ **poles.** **1** N-C A **pole** is a long, thin piece of wood or metal, used especially for supporting things. *...a telegraph pole.* **2** N-C The earth's **poles** are the two opposite ends of its axis.

polemic /pə'lemɪk/ **polemics.** N-VAR A **polemic** is a fierce written or spoken attack on, or defence of, a particular belief or opinion. *...Edmund Burke's polemic against the French Revolution.*

police /pə'liːs/ **polices, policing, policed.** **1** N-SING & N-PL The **police** are the official organization that is responsible for making sure that people obey the law. The **police** can take the singular or plural form of the verb. The men and women who belong to this organization are referred to as **police**. *Police say they have arrested twenty people... More than one hundred police have ringed the area.* **2** VERB To **police** a place, an event, or an activity means to preserve law and order within it or to ensure that what is done is fair and legal. *It is extreme-*

ly difficult to police the border effectively. ...the Securities and Exchange Commission, which polices the stockmarkets.

police force, police forces. N-C A **police force** is the police organization in a particular country or area.

policeman /pə'li:smən/ **policemen.** N-C A **policeman** is a man who is a member of the police force.

po'lice officer, police officers. N-C A **police officer** is a member of the police force.

po'lice station, police stations. N-C A **police station** is the local office of a police force in a particular area.

policewoman /pə'li:swʊmən/ **policewomen.** N-C A **policewoman** is a woman who is a member of the police force.

policy /'pɒlɪsi/ **policies.** [1] N-VAR A **policy** is a set of plans or principles that is used as a basis for making decisions, especially in politics, economics, or business. *What is their policy on nuclear testing?* [2] N-C An insurance **policy** is a document which shows the agreement that you have made with an insurance company.

polio /'pəʊliəʊ/. N-U **Polio** is a serious infectious disease which can cause paralysis.

polish /'pɒlɪʃ/ **polishes, polishing, polished.** [1] N-U **Polish** is a substance that you put on the surface of an object in order to clean it, protect it, and make it shine. ...*furniture polish.* [2] VERB If you **polish** something, you put polish on it or rub it with a cloth to make it shine. ♦**polished** ADJ ...*a highly polished floor.* [3] N-U If you say that a person, performance, or piece of work has **polish**, you mean that they show confidence and sophistication. ♦**polished** ADJ *He is polished, charming, articulate.* [4] VERB & PHR-VERB If you **polish** your technique, performance, or skill at doing something, or if you **polish** it **up**, you work on improving it. *Polish up your writing skills.*

▸ **polish off.** PHR-VERB If you **polish off** food or drink, you finish it; INFORMAL.

polite /pə'laɪt/ **politer, politest.** ADJ A **polite** person has good manners and is not rude to other people. ...*polite conversation.* ♦**politely** ADV *'Your home is beautiful,' I said politely.* ♦**politeness** N-U *She listened to him, but only out of politeness.*

political /pə'lɪtɪkəl/. [1] ADJ **Political** means relating to the way power is achieved and used in a country or society. *All other political parties there have been completely banned.* ♦**politically** ADV *The killings were politically motivated.* [2] ADJ If you are **political**, you are interested in politics and hold strong beliefs about it.

politician /,pɒlɪ'tɪʃən/ **politicians.** N-C A **politician** is a person whose job is in politics, especially a member of parliament.

politics /'pɒlɪtɪks/. [1] N-PL **Politics** are the actions or activities which people use to achieve power in a country or organization. **Politics** can take the singular or plural form of the verb. *Politics is by no means the only arena in which women are excelling.* [2] N-PL Your **politics** are your beliefs about how a country ought to be governed. *His politics began in the Communist Party.*

poll /pəʊl/ **polls.** [1] N-C A **poll** is a survey in which people are asked their opinions about something. ● See also **opinion poll.** [2] N-PL The **polls** means an election for a country's government, or the place where people go to vote in an election. *Voters are due to go to the polls on Sunday.*

pollen /'pɒlən/. N-U **Pollen** is a powder produced by flowers in order to fertilize other flowers.

polling /'pəʊlɪŋ/. N-U **Polling** is the act of voting in an election.

pollutant /pə'lu:tənt/ **pollutants.** N-VAR **Pollutants** are substances that pollute the environment, especially poisonous chemicals that are produced as waste by vehicles and by industry.

pollute /pə'lu:t/ **pollutes, polluting, polluted.** VERB To **pollute** water, air, or land means to make it dirty and dangerous to live in or to use, especially with poisonous chemicals or sewage. ♦**polluted** ADJ ...*foul polluted water.*

pollution /pə'lu:ʃən/. [1] N-U **Pollution** is poisonous substances that are polluting water, air, or land. *The level of pollution in the river was falling.* [2] N-U **Pollution** is the process of polluting the water, air, or land.

polo /'pəʊləʊ/. N-U **Polo** is a ball game played between two teams of players riding on horses.

polyester /,pɒli'estə, AM -es-/ **polyesters.** N-VAR **Polyester** is a type of synthetic cloth used especially to make clothes.

polythene /'pɒlɪθi:n/. N-U **Polythene** is a type of plastic made into thin sheets or bags.

pomp /pɒmp/. N-U **Pomp** is the use of a lot of fine clothes, and decorations, and formal words or actions. ...*the pomp and ceremony of the Pope's visit.*

pompous /'pɒmpəs/. ADJ If you describe someone as **pompous**, you mean that they behave or speak in a very serious way because they think they are more important than they really are; used showing disapproval. ♦**pomposity** /pɒm'pɒsɪti/ N-U ...*a scientist who hated pomposity.* ♦**pompously** ADV *'This is clearly a very important project,' I said pompously.*

pond /pɒnd/ **ponds.** N-C A **pond** is a small, usually man-made, area of water. ...*a garden pond.*

ponder /'pɒndə/ **ponders, pondering, pondered.** VERB If you **ponder** a question, you think about it carefully. *I'm continually pondering how to improve the team.*

ponderous /'pɒndərəs/. [1] ADJ **Ponderous** speech or writing is dull and serious. ♦**ponderously** ADV ...*the ponderously named Association of Residential Letting Agents.* [2] ADJ A movement or action that is **ponderous** is very slow or clumsy; WRITTEN. ♦**ponderously** ADV *Wilson shifted ponderously in his chair.*

pony /'pəʊni/ **ponies.** N-C A **pony** is a type of small horse.

ponytail /'pəʊniteɪl/ **ponytails.** N-C If someone has their hair in a **ponytail**, it is tied up at the back so that it hangs down like a tail.

poodle /'pu:dəl/ **poodles.** N-C A **poodle** is a type of dog with thick curly hair.

pool /pu:l/ **pools, pooling, pooled.** [1] N-C A **pool** is the same as a **swimming pool.** [2] N-C A

pool is a small area of still water. ...*beautiful gardens filled with pools.* **3** N-C A **pool** of liquid or light is a small area of it. *She was found lying in a pool of blood.* **4** N-C A **pool** of people, money, or things is a number or quantity of them that is available for use. ...*a reserve pool of cash.* **5** VERB If people **pool** their money, knowledge, or equipment, they share it or put it together so that it can be used for a particular purpose. *Philip and I pooled our savings to start up my business.* **6** N-U **Pool** is a game played on a special table. Players use a long stick called a cue to hit a white ball so that it knocks coloured balls into six holes around the edge of the table. **7** N-PL If you do the **pools**, you take part in a gambling competition in which people try to guess the results of football matches; BRITISH.

poor /pʊə, pɔː/ **poorer, poorest. 1** ADJ & N-PL Someone who is **poor** has very little money and few possessions. **The poor** are people who are poor. *He was one of thirteen children from a poor family... Even the poor have their pride.* **2** ADJ A **poor** country or area is inhabited by people who are poor. ...*children in a poor neighborhood.* **3** ADJ BEFORE N You use **poor** to express sympathy for someone. *Poor Gordon!* **4** ADJ If you describe something as **poor**, you mean that it is of a low quality or standard. *The flat was in a poor state of repair.* ◆**poorly** ADV ...*poorly built dormitories.* **5** ADJ If you describe an amount, rate, or number as **poor**, you mean that it is less than expected or less than is considered reasonable. ...*poor wages and working conditions.* ◆**poorly** ADV *The evening meetings were poorly attended.* **6** ADJ You use **poor** to describe someone who is not very skilful in a particular activity. *He was a poor actor.* ◆**poorly** ADV *Today I played as poorly as I ever have.* **7** ADJ AFTER LINK-V If something is **poor in** a particular quality or substance, it contains very little of the quality or substance. *Some foods are very rich in energy but poor in vitamins.*

poorly /ˈpʊəli, ˈpɔː-/. ADJ If someone is **poorly**, they are ill; INFORMAL, BRITISH. *Miss Cartwright looks very poorly.*

pop /pɒp/ **pops, popping, popped. 1** N-U **Pop** is modern music that usually has a strong rhythm and uses electronic equipment. ...*a life-size poster of a pop star.* **2** VERB & N-C If something **pops**, it makes a short sharp sound, called a **pop**. *The cork popped and shot to the ceiling... His back tyre just went pop on a motorway.* **3** VERB If your eyes **pop**, or if they **pop out**, you look very surprised or excited; INFORMAL. *My eyes popped at the sight of the rich variety of food on show.* **4** VERB If you **pop** something somewhere, you put it there; INFORMAL. *He popped some chewing-gum into his mouth.* **5** VERB If someone **pops** somewhere, they go there for a short time; INFORMAL. *He's just popped out to the shops. He won't be a minute.*

▶ **pop up.** PHR-VERB If someone or something **pops up**, they appear in a place or situation unexpectedly. *You solved one problem and another would immediately pop up.*

popcorn /ˈpɒpkɔːn/. N-U **Popcorn** is a snack which consists of grains of maize that have been heated until they have burst and become large and light.

Pope /pəʊp/ **Popes.** N-C & N-TITLE The **Pope** is the head of the Roman Catholic Church. ...*Pope John Paul II.*

poppy /ˈpɒpi/ **poppies.** N-C A **poppy** is a plant with large, delicate, red flowers.

populace /ˈpɒpjʊləs/. N-SING The **populace** of a country is its people; FORMAL. ...*a large section of Pakistan's populace.*

popular /ˈpɒpjʊlə/. **1** ADJ Someone or something that is **popular** is liked by a lot of people. ...*the most popular politician in France... These delicious pastries will be very popular.* ◆**popularity** /ˌpɒpjʊˈlærɪti/ N-U ...*his popularity with ordinary people... Golf increased in popularity during the 1980s.* **2** ADJ **Popular** ideas or attitudes are approved of or held by most people. *The military government has been unable to win popular support.* ◆**popularity** N-U *Watson's views gained in popularity.* **3** ADJ BEFORE N **Popular** newspapers, television programmes, or forms of art are aimed at ordinary people and not at experts or intellectuals. ...*one of the classics of modern popular music.* **4** ADJ BEFORE N **Popular** is used to describe political activities which involve the ordinary people of a country. *President Ferdinand Marcos was overthrown by a popular uprising.*

popularize (also BR **popularise**) /ˈpɒpjʊləraɪz/ **popularizes, popularizing, popularized.** VERB To **popularize** something means to make a lot of people interested in it and able to enjoy or understand it. ◆**popularization** N-U ...*the popularisation of sport through television.*

popularly /ˈpɒpjʊləli/. **1** ADV If something or someone is **popularly** known as something, most people call them that, although it is not their official name or title. ...*an infection popularly called mad cow disease.* **2** ADV If something is **popularly** believed or supposed to be the case, most people believe or suppose it to be the case, although it may not be true. *Schizophrenia is not a 'split mind' as is popularly believed.*

populate /ˈpɒpjʊleɪt/ **populates, populating, populated.** VERB If an area **is populated** by people or animals, those people or animals live there. *Before all this the island was populated by native American Arawaks.* ◆**populated** ADJ *The southeast is the most densely populated area.*

population /ˌpɒpjʊˈleɪʃən/ **populations. 1** N-VAR The **population** of a place is the people who live there, or the number of people living there. *Bangladesh now has a population of about 110 million.* ...*a massive increase in population.* **2** N-C If you refer to a particular type of **population** in a place, you are referring to all the people or animals of that type there; FORMAL. ...*75.6 per cent of the male population over sixteen.*

porcelain /ˈpɔːsəlɪn/. N-U **Porcelain** is a hard, shiny substance made by heating clay. It is used to make cups, plates, and ornaments.

porch /pɔːtʃ/ **porches.** [1] N-C A **porch** is a sheltered area at the entrance to a building. It has a roof and sometimes walls. [2] N-C In American English, a **porch** is a raised platform built along the outside wall of a house and often covered with a roof. The British word is **veranda**.

pore /pɔː/ **pores, poring, pored.** [1] N-C Your **pores** are the tiny holes in your skin. [2] N-C The **pores** of a plant are the tiny holes on its surface.

▶ **pore over.** PHR-VERB If you **pore over** or **through** information, you look at it, studying it very carefully. *We spent hours poring over travel brochures.*

pork /pɔːk/. N-U **Pork** is meat from a pig, usually fresh and not smoked or salted.

porn /pɔːn/. N-U **Porn** is the same as **pornography;** INFORMAL.

pornography /pɔːˈnɒɡrəfi/. N-U **Pornography** refers to books, magazines, and films that are designed to cause sexual excitement; used showing disapproval. ♦ **pornographic** /ˌpɔːnəˈɡræfɪk/ ADJ *...pornographic videos.*

porous /ˈpɔːrəs/. ADJ Something that is **porous** has many small holes in it, allowing water and air to pass through. *...a porous material like sand or charcoal.*

porridge /ˈpɒrɪdʒ, AM ˈpɔːr-/. N-U **Porridge** is a thick sticky food made from oats that are cooked in water or milk and eaten hot, especially for breakfast.

port /pɔːt/ **ports.** [1] N-C A **port** is a town or a harbour area with docks and warehouses, where ships load or unload goods or passengers. *...the Mediterranean port of Marseilles.* [2] ADJ & N-U The **port** side of a ship is the left side when you are on it and facing towards the front. *...turn to port.* [3] N-VAR **Port** is a type of strong, sweet red wine.

portable /ˈpɔːtəbəl/. ADJ & N-C A **portable** machine or device is designed to be easily carried or moved. The machine or device can be called a **portable**. *...portable computer... We bought a colour portable for the bedroom.*

porter /ˈpɔːtə/ **porters.** [1] N-C A **porter** is a person whose job is to be in charge of the entrance of a building such as a hotel; BRITISH. [2] N-C A **porter** is a person whose job is to carry things, for example people's luggage at a railway station.

portfolio /pɔːtˈfəʊliəʊ/ **portfolios.** N-C A **portfolio** is a set of pictures or photographs of someone's work, which they show to potential employers. *Edith showed them a portfolio of her own political cartoons.*

portion /ˈpɔːʃən/ **portions.** [1] N-C A **portion** of something is a part of it. *Damage was confined to a small portion of the castle... I have spent a fairly considerable portion of my life here.* [2] N-C A **portion** is the amount of food that is given to one person at a meal. *Desserts can be substituted by a portion of fresh fruit.*

portrait /ˈpɔːtreɪt/ **portraits.** N-C A **portrait** is a painting, drawing, or photograph of a person. *...a portrait of the Queen.*

portray /pɔːˈtreɪ/ **portrays, portraying, portrayed.** [1] VERB When an actor or actress portrays someone, he or she plays that person in a play or film. *He portrayed the king in a Los Angeles revival of 'Camelot'.* [2] VERB To **portray** someone or something in a particular way means to represent them in that way, for example in a book or film. *...this northern novelist, who accurately portrays provincial domestic life.*

portrayal /pɔːˈtreɪəl/ **portrayals.** N-C A **portrayal** of someone or something is a representation of them in a book, film, or play. *...a sensitive and often funny portrayal of a friendship between two 11-year-old boys.*

pose /pəʊz/ **poses, posing, posed.** [1] VERB If something **poses** a problem or danger, it is the cause of that problem or danger. *His ill health poses serious problems for the future.* [2] VERB If you **pose** a question, you ask it; FORMAL. [3] VERB If you **pose as** someone, you pretend to be that person in order to deceive people. *The team posed as drug dealers to trap the ringleaders.* [4] VERB & N-C If you **pose for** a photograph or painting, you stay in a particular position so that someone can photograph or paint you. This position is called a **pose**. *How did you get him to pose for this picture?*

posh /pɒʃ/. [1] ADJ If you describe something as **posh** you mean that it is smart, fashionable, and expensive; INFORMAL. *...a posh hotel.* [2] ADJ If you describe a person as **posh**, you mean that they belong to or behave as if they belong to a high social class. *He sounded so posh on the phone.*

position /pəˈzɪʃən/ **positions, positioning, positioned.** [1] N-C The **position** of someone or something is the place where they are. *The ship's name and position were reported to the coastguard.* [2] N-C When someone or something is in a particular **position**, they are sitting, lying, or arranged in that way. *The upper back and neck are held in an erect position.* [3] VERB & PHRASE If you **position** someone or something somewhere, or if you place them **in position**, you put them exactly where you want them to be. *Position trailing plants near the edges... Some 28,000 US troops are moving into position.* [4] N-C Your **position** in society is the role and the importance that you have in it. *...adjustment to their changing role and position in society.* [5] N-C A **position** in a company or organization is a job; FORMAL. *He left a career in teaching to take up a position with the Council.* [6] N-C Your **position** in a race or competition is how well you did in relation to the other competitors or how well you are doing. *The car was running in eighth position.* [7] N-C You can describe your situation at a particular time by saying that you are in a particular **position**. *He's going to be in a very difficult position.* [8] PHRASE If you are **in a position** to do something, you are able to do it. *I am not in a position to comment.* [9] N-C Your **position** on a particular matter is your attitude towards it; FORMAL. *What's your position on abortion?*

positive /ˈpɒzɪtɪv/. [1] ADJ If you are **positive**, you are hopeful and confident, and think of the good aspects of a situation rather than the bad ones. *Be positive about your future.* ♦ **positively** ADV *Try thinking positively about* *yourself.* [2] ADJ A **positive** situation or experience is pleasant and helpful to you in some way. *Working abroad should be an exciting and positive experience.* [3] ADJ If you make a **positive** decision or take **positive** action, you do something definite in order to deal with a task or problem. *He was expected to make a very positive contribution to the 1996 Games organisation.* [4] ADJ A **positive** response shows agreement, approval, or encouragement. ♦**positively** ADV *Voters would respond positively to a good campaign argument.* [5] ADJ AFTER LINK-V If you are **positive** about something, you are completely sure about it. *I'm as positive as I can be about it.* [6] ADJ BEFORE N **Positive** evidence gives definite proof of something. *We have positive proof that he was a blackmailer.* ♦**positively** ADV *He has positively identified the body.* [7] ADJ AFTER LINK-V If a medical or scientific test is **positive**, it shows that something has happened or is present. *If the test is positive, a course of antibiotics may be prescribed.*

positively /'pɒzɪtɪvli/. ADV You use **positively** to emphasize that something is the case. *This is positively the worst thing that I can imagine.*

possess /pə'zes/ **possesses, possessing, possessed.** [1] VERB If you **possess** something, you have it or own it. *He is said to possess a fortune.* [2] VERB To **possess** a quality, ability, or feature means to have it. *...the practical skills that some people possess.*

possession /pə'zeʃən/ **possessions.** [1] N-U If you are in **possession** of something, you have it, because you have obtained it or because it belongs to you; FORMAL. *Those documents are now in the possession of the Guardian. ...illegal possession of firearms.* [2] N-C Your **possessions** are the things that you own or have with you at a particular time. *People had lost their homes and all their possessions.*

possessive /pə'zesɪv/ **possessives.** [1] ADJ If someone is **possessive**, they want all their partner's love and attention. *She became increasingly possessive and jealous.* ♦**possessiveness** N-U *I've ruined every relationship with my possessiveness.* [2] N-C In grammar, the **possessive** is the form of a noun or pronoun used to indicate possession, for example 'George's' and 'his'.

possibility /ˌpɒsɪ'bɪlɪti/ **possibilities.** [1] N-C If you say there is a **possibility** that something is the case or that something will happen, you mean that it might be the case or it might happen. *Tax on food has become a very real possibility.* [2] N-C A **possibility** is one of several things that could be done. *There were several possibilities open to each manufacturer.*

> Note that you do not use **possibility** in sentences like 'I had the possibility to do it'. The words you need are **opportunity** or **chance**. *Later Donald had the opportunity of driving the car... The people of Northern Ireland would have the chance to shape their own future.*

possible /'pɒsɪbəl/. [1] ADJ If it is **possible** to do something, it can be done. *If it is possible to find out where your brother is, we shall... I need to see you, right away if possible.* [2] ADJ If you do something **as soon as possible**, you do it as soon as you can. If you get **as much as possible** of something, you get as much of it as you can. *Mrs. Pollard decided to learn as much as possible about the People's Republic of China.* [3] ADJ A **possible** event is one that might happen. *Her family is discussing a possible move to America.* [4] ADJ If you say that it is **possible** that something is true or correct, you mean that you do not know whether it is true or correct, but you accept that it might be. *It is possible that there's an explanation for all this.* [5] ADJ You use **possible** with superlative adjectives to emphasize that something has more of a quality than anything else of its kind. *They have joined the job market at the worst possible time... He is doing the best job possible.* [6] N-SING The **possible** is everything that can be done in a situation. *He is a democrat with the skill, nerve, and ingenuity to push the limits of the possible.*

possibly /'pɒsɪbli/. [1] ADV You use **possibly** to indicate that you are not sure whether something is true or will happen. *This camera was rare and possibly a collector's item.* [2] ADV You use **possibly** to emphasize that you are surprised or puzzled. *How could they possibly eat that stuff?... What could this possibly mean?* [3] ADV You use **possibly** with a negative modal to emphasize that something cannot happen or cannot be done. *No I really can't possibly answer that!... There's nothing more they can possibly do.*

post 1 letters, parcels, and information

post /pəʊst/ **posts, posting, posted.** [1] N-SING In British English, the **post** is the public service by which letters and parcels are collected and delivered. The American word is **mail**. *The winner will be notified by post... The cheque is in the post.* ♦**postal** ADJ BEFORE N *...the American postal service.* [2] N-U In British English, you can use **post** to refer to letters and parcels that are delivered to you. The American word is **mail**. *He flipped through the post without opening any of it.* [3] VERB In British English, if you **post** a letter or parcel, you send it to someone by putting it in a letterbox or taking it to a post office. The American word is **mail**. *I'm posting you a cheque tonight.*

post 2 jobs and places

post /pəʊst/ **posts, posting, posted.** [1] N-C A **post** in a company or organization is a job or official position in it; FORMAL. *She had earlier resigned her post as President Menem's assistant.* [2] VERB If you **are posted** somewhere, you are sent there by your employers to work. *Eric was posted to the South Seas for a year.* [3] See also **posting**.

post 3 poles

post /pəʊst/ **posts.** N-C A **post** is an upright pole fixed into the ground. *The device is fixed to a post.*

postage /'pəʊstɪdʒ/. N-U **Postage** is the money that you pay for sending letters and parcels by post. *Send a cheque for £18.99 plus £2 for postage and packing.*

postcard /'pəʊstkɑːd/ **postcards.** N-C A **post-card** is a piece of card, often with a picture on one side, which you can write on and post to someone without using an envelope.

postcode /'pəʊstkəʊd/ **postcodes.** N-C In British English, your **postcode** is a short sequence of numbers and letters at the end of your address. The American term is **zip code**.

poster /'pəʊstə/ **posters.** N-C A **poster** is a large notice, advertisement, or picture that you stick on a wall.

posterity /pɒ'sterɪti/. N-U You can refer to everyone who will be alive in the future as **posterity**; FORMAL. *A photographer recorded the scene on video for posterity.*

postgraduate /ˌpəʊst'grædʒʊət/ **postgraduates.** N-C A **postgraduate** is a student with a first degree from a university who is studying or doing research at a more advanced level; BRITISH.

posting /'pəʊstɪŋ/ **postings.** N-C A **posting** is a job which involves going to a different town or country. *Relevant work experience is required for overseas postings.* ◆ See also **post**.

postman /'pəʊstmən/ **postmen.** N-C In British English, a **postman** is a man whose job is to collect and deliver letters and parcels that are sent by post. The usual American word is **mailman**.

post-mortem /ˌpəʊst 'mɔːtəm/ **post-mortems.** [1] N-C A **post-mortem** is a medical examination of a dead person's body to find out how they died. [2] N-C A **post-mortem** is an examination of something that has recently happened, especially something that has failed or gone wrong. *...the election post-mortem.*

'post office, post offices. N-C A **post office** is a building where you can buy stamps, post letters and parcels, and use other services provided by the national postal service.

postpone /pəʊs'pəʊn/ **postpones, postponing, postponed.** VERB If you **postpone** an event, you arrange for it to take place at a later time than was originally planned. *The visit has now been postponed indefinitely.* ◆**postponement, postponements** N-VAR *There were several postponements of the flight.*

postulate /'pɒstjʊleɪt/ **postulates, postulating, postulated.** VERB If you **postulate** something, you suggest it as the basis for a theory, argument, or calculation; FORMAL. *Freud postulated that we all have a death instinct.*

posture /'pɒstʃə/ **postures.** [1] N-VAR Your **posture** is the position or manner in which you stand or sit. *You can make your stomach look flatter instantly by improving your posture.* [2] N-C A **posture** is an attitude that you have towards something; FORMAL. *None of the banks changed their posture on the deal.*

,post-'war (or **postwar**). ADJ **Post-war** is used to describe things that happened, existed, or were made in the period immediately after a war, especially the Second World War (1939-45). *...postwar architecture.*

pot /pɒt/ **pots, potting, potted.** [1] N-C A **pot** is a deep round container for cooking food. *...metal cooking pots.* [2] N-C A **pot** is a teapot or coffee pot. *There's tea in the pot.* [3] VERB If you

pot a plant, you put it into a flowerpot filled with soil.

potato /pə'teɪtəʊ/ **potatoes.** N-VAR **Potatoes** are vegetables with brown or red skins and white insides.

potent /'pəʊtənt/. ADJ Something that is **potent** is effective and powerful. *The drug is extremely potent, but causes unpleasant side effects.* ◆**potency** /'pəʊtənsi/ N-U *Sunscreen can lose its potency if left over winter in the bathroom cabinet.*

potential /pə'tenʃəl/. [1] ADJ BEFORE N You use **potential** to say that someone or something is capable of developing into a particular kind of person or thing. *The firm has identified 60 potential customers.* ◆**potentially** ADV *This is a potentially dangerous situation.* [2] N-U If something has **potential**, it is capable of being useful or successful in the future. *The boy has great potential.* [3] N-U If you say that someone or something has **potential** for doing something, you mean that it is possible that they may do it. If there is **the potential** for something, it may happen. *John seemed as horrified as I about his potential for violence.*

potion /'pəʊʃən/ **potions.** N-C A **potion** is a drink that contains medicine, poison, or something that is supposed to have magic powers. *...a magic potion to get him better.*

potter /'pɒtə/ **potters, pottering, pottered.** N-C A **potter** is someone who makes pottery.
▶ **potter about** or **potter around.** PHR-VERB If you **potter about** or **potter around**, you spend your time slowly doing a few pleasant or unimportant tasks.

pottery /'pɒtəri/. [1] N-U **Pottery** is objects made from clay. [2] N-U **Pottery** is the craft or activity of making objects out of clay. *...pottery classes.*

potty /'pɒti/ **potties.** [1] N-C A **potty** is a deep bowl which a small child uses as a toilet. [2] ADJ If you say that someone is **potty**, you think that they are crazy or foolish; BRITISH, INFORMAL. *I have to get out of here. I'll go potty if I stay.*

pouch /paʊtʃ/ **pouches.** [1] N-C A **pouch** is a flexible container like a small bag. *On my belt in its little leather pouch was my Swiss penknife.* [2] N-C The **pouch** of an animal such as a kangaroo is the pocket of skin on its stomach in which its baby grows.

poultry /'pəʊltri/. N-PL You can refer to chickens, ducks, and other birds that are kept for their eggs and meat as **poultry**. Meat from these birds is also referred to as **poultry**. *...intensive methods of rearing poultry... The menu features roast meats and poultry.*

pounce /paʊns/ **pounces, pouncing, pounced.** [1] VERB If a person or animal **pounces** on another person or animal, they leap towards them and try to take hold of them or attack them. *He pounced on the photographer, beat him up and smashed his camera... Before I could let the pigeon the cat pounced.* [2] VERB If someone **pounces** on something such as a mistake, they draw attention to it, usually in order to gain some sort of advantage for themselves. *The Democrats were ready to pounce on any Republican failings.*

pound /paʊnd/ **pounds, pounding, pounded.** [1] N-C The **pound** is the unit of money

which is used in Britain. It is represented by the symbol £. Some other countries, for example Egypt, also have a unit of money called a **pound**. *Beer cost three pounds a bottle.* [2] N-C A **pound** is a unit of weight used mainly in Britain, America, and other countries where English is spoken. One pound is equal to 0.454 kilograms. *Her weight was under ninety pounds. ...a pound of cheese.* ● See note at **weight**. [3] VERB If you **pound** something, or if you **pound** on it, you hit it loudly and repeatedly with your fists. *He pounded the table with his fist... Somebody began pounding on the front door.* [4] VERB If your heart **is pounding**, it is beating with a strong fast rhythm, usually because you are afraid or excited. *I'm sweating, my heart is pounding. I can't breathe.*
♦**pounding** N-U *...the fast pounding of her heart.*

pour /pɔ:/ **pours, pouring, poured.** [1] VERB If you **pour** a liquid, you make it flow steadily out of a container by holding the container at an angle. *She poured some water into a plastic bowl.* [2] VERB If you **pour** someone a drink, you fill a cup or glass with it so that they can drink it. *He poured himself a Scotch.* [3] VERB When a liquid or other substance **pours** somewhere, it flows there quickly and in large quantities. *There was dense smoke pouring from all four engines... Tears poured down both our faces.* [4] VERB When it rains very heavily, you can say that **it is pouring**. *The rain was pouring down.* ♦**pouring** ADJ *They left the school in pouring rain.* [5] VERB If people **pour** into or out of a place, they go there quickly and in large numbers. *At six p.m. large groups poured from the numerous offices.* [6] VERB If something **pours** into a place, a lot of it is obtained or given. *Letters and cards of support have been pouring in.*

▶ **pour out.** PHR-VERB If you **pour out** a drink, you fill a cup or glass with it. *Carefully and slowly he poured the beer out.*

pout /paʊt/ **pouts, pouting, pouted.** VERB If you **pout**, you stick out your lips, especially as a way of showing that you are annoyed. *He whined and pouted when he did not get what he wanted.*

poverty /ˈpɒvəti/. N-U **Poverty** is the state of being very poor. *...people living in poverty.*

powder /ˈpaʊdə/ **powders, powdering, powdered.** N-VAR **Powder** consists of many tiny particles of a solid substance. *Her face was covered with white powder.*

powdered /ˈpaʊdəd/. ADJ A **powdered** substance is one which is in the form of a powder. *...powdered milk.*

power /ˈpaʊə/ **powers, powering, powered.** [1] N-U If someone has **power**, they have a lot of control over people and activities. *...women who have reached positions of great power and influence.* [2] N-U Your **power** to do something is your ability to do it. *He was so drunk that he had lost the power of speech.* [3] N-U If it is in your **power** to do something, you are able to do it or you have the resources to deal with it. *We must do everything in our power to ensure the success of the conference.* [4] N-VAR If someone in authority has the **power** to do some-

thing, they have the legal right to do it. *...the legal powers of British Customs officers.* [5] N-U If people take **power** or come to **power**, they take charge of a country's affairs. People who are **in power** are in charge of a country's affairs. [6] N-U The **power** of something is its physical strength or other capability. *The Roadrunner had better power, better tyres, and better brakes. ...massive computing power.* [7] N-U **Power** is energy, especially electricity, that is obtained in large quantities from a fuel source. *Power has been restored to most parts that were hit last night by high winds.* [8] VERB The device or fuel that **powers** a machine provides the energy that makes the machine work.

powerful /ˈpaʊəfʊl/. [1] ADJ A **powerful** person or organization is able to control or influence people and events. *...Russia and India, two large, powerful countries.* [2] ADJ You say that someone's body is **powerful** when it is physically strong. *...his powerful muscles.* ♦**powerfully** ADV *...a strong, powerfully-built man.* [3] ADJ A **powerful** machine or substance is effective because it is very strong. *...powerful computer systems.* ♦**powerfully** ADV *...this powerfully alcoholic wine.* [4] ADJ A **powerful** smell is very strong. [5] ADJ A **powerful** voice is loud and can be heard from a long way away. [6] ADJ You describe a piece of writing, speech, or work of art as **powerful** when it has a strong effect on people's feelings or beliefs. ♦**powerfully** ADV *...a powerfully acted play.*

powerless /ˈpaʊələs/. [1] ADJ Someone who is **powerless** is unable to control or influence events. ♦**powerlessness** N-U *...childhood feelings of powerlessness.* [2] ADJ AFTER LINK-V If you are **powerless** to do something, you are unable to do it. *He was sympathetic, but powerless to help.*

'**power line, power lines.** N-C A **power line** is a cable, especially above ground, along which electricity passes to an area or building.

'**power plant, power plants.** N-C A **power plant** is a place where electricity is generated.

'**power station, power stations.** N-C A **power station** is a place where electricity is generated.

pp. pp. is the plural of 'p' and means 'pages'. *See chapter 6, pp. 137-41.*

practicable /ˈpræktɪkəbəl/. ADJ If a task or plan is **practicable**, people are able to do it or carry it out. *Teachers can only be expected to do what is reasonable and practicable.*

practical /ˈpræktɪkəl/ **practicals.** [1] ADJ **Practical** means involving real situations, rather than ideas and theories. *They offer practical suggestions for healthy eating.* [2] ADJ You describe people as **practical** when they make sensible decisions and deal effectively with problems. *We are practical people who judge ideas and policies by results.* [3] ADJ **Practical** ideas and methods are likely to be effective or successful in a real situation. *Our system is the most practical way of preventing crime.* [4] ADJ You can describe clothes and things in your house as **practical** when they are useful rather than just being fashionable or attractive. *Our clothes are lightweight, fashionable, practical for holidays.* [5] N-C A **practical** is an examination or lesson in which you make things or do experiments rather than simply write answers to questions.

practicality /ˌpræktɪˈkælɪti/ **practicalities.** N-PL The **practicalities** of a situation are the aspects of it which are concerned with real events rather than with ideas or theories. ...the practicalities of financing your schemes.

practically /ˈpræktɪkəli/ **[1]** ADV **Practically** means almost. He'd known the old man practically all his life. **[2]** ADV You use **practically** to describe something which involves real actions or events rather than ideas or theories. The course is essentially more practically based than the Masters degree.

practice /ˈpræktɪs/ **practices.** **[1]** N-C You can refer to something that people do regularly as a **practice**. ...the modern practice of using chemicals to colour the hair. **[2]** N-VAR **Practice** means doing something regularly in order to do it better. A **practice** is a session of this. ...basketball practice... He recorded the fastest time in a final practice today. **[3]** N-U The work done by doctors and lawyers is referred to as the **practice** of medicine and law. People's religious activities are referred to as the **practice** of a religion. I had to change my attitude toward medical practice. ...freedom of conscience and religious practice. **[4]** N-C A doctor's or lawyer's **practice** is his or her business, often shared with other doctors or lawyers.

PHRASES • What happens **in practice** is what actually happens, in contrast to what is supposed to happen. This theoretical freedom of choice is not in practice available to the majority of the population. • If you are **out of practice** at doing something, you have not had much experience of it recently, although you used to do it a lot or be quite good at it. • If you **put** an idea or method **into practice**, you make use of it. The prime minister has another chance to put his new ideas into practice.

practise (AM **practice**) /ˈpræktɪs/ **practises, practising, practised.** **[1]** VERB If you **practise** something, you keep doing it regularly in order to do it better. Lauren practises the piano every day. **[2]** VERB When people **practise** something such as a custom, craft, or religion, they take part in the activities associated with it. ...a family which practised traditional Judaism... Acupuncture was practised in China as long ago as the third millennium BC. ◆ **practising** ADJ BEFORE N All employees must be practising Christians. **[3]** VERB Someone who **practises** medicine or law works as a doctor or lawyer. He practised as a lawyer until his retirement last year. ...a practising architect.

practised (AM **practiced**) /ˈpræktɪst/. ADJ Someone who is **practised** at something is good at it because they have had a lot of experience of it. ...a practised and experienced surgeon.

practitioner /prækˈtɪʃənə/ **practitioners.** N-C Doctors are sometimes referred to as **practitioners**; FORMAL.

pragmatic /prægˈmætɪk/. ADJ A **pragmatic** way of dealing with something is based on practical considerations, rather than theoretical ones. A **pragmatic** person deals with things in a practical way. ◆ **pragmatically** ADV These firms respond pragmatically to local conditions.

pragmatism /ˈprægmətɪzəm/. N-U **Pragmatism** means thinking or dealing with problems in a practical way, rather than by using theory or abstract principles; FORMAL. ◆ **pragmatist, pragmatists** N-U He is a political pragmatist, not an idealist.

prairie /ˈpreəri/ **prairies.** N-VAR A **prairie** is a large area of flat grassy land in North America.

praise /preɪz/ **praises, praising, praised.** **[1]** VERB & N-U If you **praise** someone or something, or if you express your **praise** for them, you express approval for their achievements or qualities. He praised the fans for their continued support... She is full of praise for the range of excellent services available. **[2]** VERB & N-U If you **praise** God, or if you offer him your **praise**, you express your respect, honour, and thanks to God. Hindus were singing hymns in praise of the god Rama. **[3]** PHRASE If you **sing** someone's **praises**, you praise them in an enthusiastic way.

pram /præm/ **prams.** N-C A **pram** is like a baby's cot on wheels, which you can push along when you want to take the baby somewhere.

prank /præŋk/ **pranks.** N-C A **prank** is a childish trick; DATED.

prawn /prɔːn/ **prawns.** N-C A **prawn** is a small edible shellfish, similar to a shrimp. The usual American word is **shrimp**.

pray /preɪ/ **prays, praying, prayed.** VERB When people **pray**, they speak to God in order to give thanks or to ask for help. Kelly prayed that God would judge her with mercy.

prayer /preə/ **prayers.** **[1]** N-U **Prayer** is the activity of speaking to God. The night was spent in prayer. **[2]** N-C A **prayer** is the words that someone says when they speak to God. **[3]** N-C You can refer to a strong hope that you have as your **prayer**. This drug could be the answer to our prayers. **[4]** N-PL A short religious service at which people gather to pray can be referred to as **prayers**. ...Muslims attending prayers.

preach /priːtʃ/ **preaches, preaching, preached.** **[1]** VERB When someone, especially a member of the clergy, **preaches**, he or she gives a talk on a religious or moral subject as part of a church service. The bishop preached to a crowd of several hundred local people. ◆ **preacher, preachers.** N-C ...acceptance of women preachers. **[2]** VERB When people **preach** a belief or a course of action, they try to persuade other people to accept the belief or take the course of action. For many years I have preached against war.

precarious /prɪˈkeəriəs/. **[1]** ADJ If your situation is **precarious**, you are not in complete control of events and might fail in what you are doing at any moment. ◆ **precariously** ADV This left him clinging precariously to his job. **[2]** ADJ Something that is **precarious**, is not securely held in place and is likely to fall at any moment. ...a very precarious ladder. ◆ **precariously** ADV One of my grocery bags was still precariously perched on the car bumper.

precaution /prɪˈkɔːʃən/ **precautions.** N-C A **precaution** is an action that is intended to prevent something dangerous or unpleasant from happening. *They took the precaution of seeking legal advice. ...safety precautions.*

precede /prɪ'siːd/ **precedes, preceding, preceded.** VERB If one event or period of time **precedes** another, it happens before it; FORMAL. *The earthquake was preceded by several smaller tremors. ...friends I had already met during the preceding months.*

precedence /'presɪdəns/. PHRASE If one thing **takes precedence** over another, the first thing is regarded as more important than the second one. *He took precedence over everyone else.*

precedent /'presɪdənt/ **precedents.** N-VAR If there is a **precedent** for an action or event, it has happened before, and this can be regarded as an argument for doing it again; FORMAL. *There are plenty of precedents in Hollywood for letting people out of contracts.*

precept /'priːsept/ **precepts.** N-C A **precept** is a general rule that helps you to decide how you should behave in particular circumstances; FORMAL. *...the moral precepts that govern civilised society.*

precinct /'priːsɪŋkt/ **precincts.** [1] N-C A shopping **precinct** is an area in the centre of a town in which cars are not allowed; BRITISH. [2] N-C In the United States, a **precinct** is a part of a city which has its own police force and fire service. [3] N-PL The **precincts** of an institution are its buildings and land; FORMAL.

precious /'preʃəs/. [1] ADJ If you say that something such as a resource is **precious**, you mean that it is valuable and should not be wasted or used badly. *A family break allows you to spend precious time together.* [2] ADJ **Precious** objects and materials are worth a lot of money because they are rare. [3] ADJ If something is **precious** to you, you regard it as important and do not want to lose it. *Her family's support is particularly precious to Josie.* [4] PHRASE If you say that there is **precious little** of something, you are emphasizing that there is very little of it, and that it would be better if there were more. *Precious few home-buyers will notice any reduction in their monthly repayments.*

precipitate, precipitates, precipitating, precipitated. [1] VERB /prɪ'sɪpəteɪt/ If something **precipitates** an event or situation, usually a bad one, it causes it to happen suddenly or sooner than normal; FORMAL. *A slight mistake could precipitate a disaster.* [2] ADJ /prɪ'sɪpɪtət/ A **precipitate** action or decision happens or is made more quickly or suddenly than most people think is sensible; FORMAL. ◆**precipitately** ADV *I fled precipitately in the opposite direction.*

precise /prɪ'saɪs/. [1] ADJ You use **precise** to emphasize that you are referring to an exact thing, rather than something vague. *...the precise location of the wreck.* [2] ADJ Something that is **precise** is exact and accurate in all its details. *They speak very precise English.*

precisely /prɪ'saɪsli/. [1] ADV **Precisely** means accurately and exactly. *The meeting began at precisely 4.00 p.m.* [2] ADV You use **precisely** to emphasize that a reason or fact is the only important one there is, or that it is obvious. *That is precisely the result the system is designed to produce.*

precision /prɪ'sɪʒən/. N-U If you do something with **precision**, you do it exactly as it should be done. *The choir sang with precision.*

preclude /prɪ'kluːd/ **precludes, precluding, precluded.** VERB If something **precludes** you **from** doing something or going somewhere, it prevents you from doing it or going there. *Poor English precluded them from ever finding a job.*

precocious /prɪ'kəʊʃəs/. ADJ **Precocious** children do or say things that seem very advanced for their age.

preconception /ˌpriːkən'sepʃən/ **preconceptions.** N-C Your **preconceptions** about something are the beliefs you form about it before you have enough information or experience. *...preconceptions about the sort of people who did computing.*

precondition /ˌpriːkən'dɪʃən/ **preconditions.** N-C If one thing is a **precondition** for another, it must happen or be done before the second thing can happen or exist; FORMAL. *Some basic preconditions are necessary for unions to work well.*

precursor /priː'kɜːsə/ **precursors.** N-C A **precursor** of something is a similar thing that happened or existed before it. *...the European Monetary Institute, the precursor of a European central bank.*

predator /'predətə/ **predators.** N-C A **predator** is an animal that kills and eats other animals.

predatory /'predətri, AM -tɔːri/. ADJ **Predatory** animals or birds kill and eat other animals. *...predatory birds like the eagle.*

predecessor /'priːdɪsesə, AM 'pred-/ **predecessors.** [1] N-C Your **predecessor** is the person who had your job before you. *He learned everything he knew from his predecessor.* [2] N-C The **predecessor** of an object or machine is the object or machine that came before it in a sequence or process of development. *The car is some 40mm shorter than its predecessor.*

predicament /prɪ'dɪkəmənt/ **predicaments.** N-C If you are in a **predicament**, you are in a difficult situation. *The decision will leave her in a peculiar predicament.*

predict /prɪ'dɪkt/ **predicts, predicting, predicted.** VERB If you **predict** an event, you say that it will happen. *He predicted that my hair would grow back 'in no time'.*

predictable /prɪ'dɪktəbəl/. ADJ Something that is **predictable** is obvious in advance and will happen. *The result was entirely predictable.* ◆**predictably** ADV *His article is, predictably, a scathing attack on capitalism.* ◆**predictability** N-U *...the predictability of climate in the North Atlantic.*

prediction /prɪ'dɪkʃən/ **predictions.** N-VAR If you make a **prediction**, you say what you think will happen. *...their prediction that he would change her life drastically.*

predispose /ˌpriːdɪ'spəʊz/ **predisposes, predisposing, predisposed.** [1] VERB If something **predisposes** you to think or behave in a particular way, it makes it likely that you will think or behave in that way; FORMAL. *His wife's suicide predisposed him to pessimism.* ◆**predisposed** ADJ AFTER LINK-V *Franklin was predisposed to believe him.* [2] VERB If something **predisposes** you **to** a disease or condition, it makes it likely that you will suffer from that disease or condition. ◆**predisposed** ADJ AFTER LINK-V *Some people are genetically predisposed to diabetes.*

predisposition /ˌpriːdɪspəˈzɪʃən/ **predispositions.** N-C If you have a **predisposition** to a particular disease, condition, or way of behaving, something in your nature makes it likely that you will suffer from that disease or condition, or that you will behave in that way. *...a predisposition to alcoholism. ...a woman's predisposition to use the right side of her brain.*

predominant /prɪˈdɒmɪnənt/. ADJ If something is **predominant**, it is more important or noticeable than anything else in a set of people or things. *Amanda's predominant emotion was that of confusion.* ◆**predominantly** ADV *Business is conducted predominantly by phone.* ◆**predominance** N-U *...the predominance of men in entertainment TV.*

predominate /prɪˈdɒmɪneɪt/ **predominates, predominating, predominated.** VERB If one type of person or thing **predominates** in a group, there are more of that type than any other; FORMAL. *In older age groups women predominate because men tend to die younger.*

pre-eminent. ADJ The **pre-eminent** person in a group is the most important or powerful one; FORMAL. *...the pre-eminent political figure in the country.* ◆**pre-eminence** N-U *...the pre-eminence of post-war US literature.*

pre-empt /priː ˈempt/ **pre-empts, pre-empting, pre-empted.** VERB If you **pre-empt** an action, you prevent it from happening by doing something before it can happen. *You can pre-empt pain by taking a painkiller at the first warning sign.*

pre-emptive /priː ˈemptɪv/. ADJ A **pre-emptive** attack or strike is intended to weaken or damage an enemy or opponent, for example by destroying their weapons before they can do any harm.

preface /ˈprefɪs/ **prefaces, prefacing, prefaced.** [1] N-C A **preface** is an introduction at the beginning of a book. [2] VERB If you **preface** an action or speech with something else, you do or say this other thing first. *She prefaced everything with, 'The trouble with doing that is...'*

prefer /prɪˈfɜː/ **prefers, preferring, preferred.** VERB If you **prefer** someone or something, you like that person or thing better than another. *Does he prefer a particular sort of music?... I preferred books and people to politics.*

> Note that **prefer** can often sound rather formal in ordinary conversation. Verbal expressions such as **like...better** and **would rather** are used more frequently. For example, instead of saying '**I prefer football to tennis**', you can say '**I like football better than tennis**', instead of '**I'd prefer an apple**', you can say '**I'd rather have an apple**', and instead of '**I'd prefer to walk**', you can say '**I'd rather walk**'.

preferable /ˈprefrəbəl/. ADJ If one thing is **preferable** to another, it is more desirable or suitable. *It is preferable to use only vegetable oil for cooking.* ◆**preferably** ADV *Take exercise, preferably in the fresh air.*

preference /ˈprefərəns/ **preferences.** [1] N-VAR If you have a **preference** for something, you would like to have or do that thing rather than something else. *His designs show a preference for using natural materials.* [2] N-U If you **give preference** to someone, you choose them rather than someone else. *The company gave preference to local workers.*

preferential /ˌprefəˈrenʃəl/. ADJ If you get **preferential** treatment, you are treated better than other people.

prefix /ˈpriːfɪks/ **prefixes.** N-C A **prefix** is a letter or group of letters which is added to the beginning of a word in order to form a different word. For example, the prefix 'un-' is added to 'happy' to form 'unhappy'.

pregnant /ˈpregnənt/. ADJ If a woman or female animal is **pregnant**, she has a baby or babies developing in her body. *Lena got pregnant... Tina was pregnant with their first daughter.* ◆**pregnancy** /ˈpregnənsi/ *It would be wiser to cut out all alcohol during pregnancy.*

preheat /ˌpriːˈhiːt/ **preheats, preheating, preheated.** VERB If you **preheat** an oven, you switch it on and allow it to reach a certain temperature before you put food inside it.

prehistoric /ˌpriːhɪˈstɒrɪk, AM -ˈtɔːr-/. ADJ **Prehistoric** people and things existed at a time before information was written down. *...the famous prehistoric cave paintings of Lascaux.*

prejudice /ˈpredʒʊdɪs/ **prejudices, prejudicing, prejudiced.** [1] N-VAR **Prejudice** is an unreasonable dislike of someone or something, or an unreasonable preference for one group over another. *...a deep-rooted racial prejudice... There is widespread prejudice against workers over 45.* [2] VERB To **prejudice** someone or something means to influence them in such a way that they are no longer fair and objective. *I think your South American youth has prejudiced you.* [3] VERB If someone **prejudices** another person's situation, they do something which makes it worse than it should be. *The council has prejudiced their health by failing to deal with the asbestos.*

prejudiced /ˈpredʒʊdɪst/. ADJ If someone is **prejudiced** against a particular group, they have an unreasonable dislike of them. *Some landlords and landladies are racially prejudiced.*

preliminary /prɪˈlɪmɪnri, AM -neri/ **preliminaries.** N-C & ADJ **Preliminaries**, or **preliminary** activities or discussions, take place in preparation for an event before it starts. *...alternative treatment as a preliminary to surgery. ...preliminary tests.*

prelude /ˈpreljuːd, AM ˈpreɪluːd/ **preludes.** N-C You describe an event as a **prelude** to a more important event when it happens before it and acts as an introduction to it. *For some, retirement can be a boring prelude to senility and death.*

premature /ˌpreməˈtʃʊə, AM ˌpriː-/. [1] ADJ Something that is **premature** happens too early or earlier than expected. *His career was brought to a premature end.* ♦**prematurely** ADV *The years in the harsh mountains had prematurely aged him.* [2] ADJ A **premature** baby is born before the date when it was due to be born.

premier /'premiə, AM prɪ'mɪr/ **premiers.** [1] N-C The leader of a government can be referred to as the **premier.** *...Australian premier Paul Keating.* [2] ADJ BEFORE N **Premier** is used to describe something that is considered to be the best or most important thing of its kind. *...the country's premier opera company.*

premiere /'premiɛə, AM prɪ'mjer/ **premieres.** N-C The **premiere** of a new play or film is the first public performance of it.

premiership /'premiəʃɪp, AM prɪ'mɪr-/. N-SING **Premiership** is the position of being the leader of a government. *...the final years of Margaret Thatcher's premiership.*

premise /'premɪs/ **premises; premiss** is also used in British English for sense 2. [1] N-PL The **premises** of a business are all the buildings and land that it occupies. *There is a kitchen on the premises... The business moved to premises in Brompton Road.* [2] N-C A **premise** is something that you suppose is true and that you use as a basis for developing an idea; FORMAL. *...the premise that men and women are on equal terms.*

premium /'pri:miəm/ **premiums.** [1] N-C A **premium** is money that you pay regularly to an insurance company for an insurance policy. [2] N-C A **premium** is a sum of money that you have to pay for something in addition to the normal cost. *Callers are charged a premium rate of 48p a minute.* [3] PHRASE If something is **at a premium,** it is wanted or needed, but is difficult to get or achieve. *If space is at a premium, choose adaptable furniture.*

premonition /,premə'nɪʃən, AM ,pri:-/ **premonitions.** N-C If you have a **premonition,** you have a feeling that something is going to happen, often something unpleasant. *She had a premonition of disaster before the flight.*

prenatal /,pri:'neɪtəl/. ADJ **Prenatal** things relate to the medical care of pregnant women.

preoccupy /pri'ɒkjupaɪ/ **preoccupies, preoccupying, preoccupied.** VERB If something is **preoccupying** you, you are thinking about it a lot. *...matters which were also increasingly preoccupying me.* ♦**preoccupied** ADJ *He's become preoccupied with insurance policies.* ♦**preoccupied, preoccupations** N-VAR *In his preoccupation with Robyn, Crook had neglected everything.*

preparation /,prepə'reɪʃən/ **preparations.** [1] N-U **Preparation** is the process of getting something ready for use or for a particular purpose. *Behind any successful event lay months of preparation. ...food preparation.* [2] N-PL **Preparations** are the arrangements that are made for a future event. *...preparations for the wedding.*

preparatory /prɪ'pærətri, AM -tɔːri/. ADJ **Preparatory** actions are done as a preparation for something else; FORMAL. *At least a year's preparatory work will be necessary before building can start.*

prepare /prɪ'peə/ **prepares, preparing, prepared.** [1] VERB If you **prepare** something, you make it ready for something that is going to happen. *Two technicians were preparing a videotape recording of last week's programme.* [2] VERB If you **prepare** for an event or action that will happen soon, you get yourself ready for it or make the necessary arrangements. *He had to go back to his hotel and prepare to catch a train.* [3] VERB When you **prepare** food, you get it ready to be eaten.

prepared /prɪ'peəd/. [1] ADJ AFTER LINK-V If you are **prepared** to do something, you are willing to do it. *I'm prepared to take any advice.* [2] ADJ AFTER LINK-V If you are **prepared for** something that you think is going to happen, you are ready for it. *Be prepared for both warm and cool weather.* ♦**preparedness** N-U *...the city's preparedness for war.* [3] ADJ Something that is **prepared** has been done or made beforehand, so that it is ready when it is needed. *He ended his prepared statement by thanking the police.*

preposition /,prepə'zɪʃən/ **prepositions.** N-C A **preposition** is a word such as 'by', 'for', 'into', or 'with', which usually has a noun group as its object.

preposterous /prɪ'pɒstərəs/. ADJ If you describe something as **preposterous,** you mean that it is extremely unreasonable and foolish. ♦**preposterously** ADV *Some prices are preposterously high.*

prerequisite /,pri:'rekwɪzɪt/ **prerequisites.** N-C If one thing is a **prerequisite** for another, it must happen or exist before the second thing is possible. *Good self-esteem is a prerequisite for a happy life.*

prerogative /prɪ'rɒgətɪv/ **prerogatives.** N-C Something that is the **prerogative** of a particular person or group is a privilege or a power that only they have; FORMAL. *Constitutional changes are exclusively the prerogative of the parliament.*

prescribe /prɪ'skraɪb/ **prescribes, prescribing, prescribed.** [1] VERB If a doctor **prescribes** treatment, he or she states what medicine or treatment a patient should have. [2] VERB If a person or set of laws or rules **prescribes** an action or duty, they state that it must be carried out; FORMAL. *...article II of the constitution, which prescribes the method of electing a president.*

prescription /prɪ'skrɪpʃən/ **prescriptions.** [1] N-C A **prescription** is a medicine which a doctor has told you to take, or the form on which the doctor has written the details of that medicine. [2] PHRASE If a medicine is available **on prescription,** you can get it from a chemist if a doctor gives you a prescription for it.

presence /'prezəns/. [1] N-SING Someone's **presence** in a place is the fact that they are there. *His presence in the village could only stir up trouble.* [2] N-U If you say that someone has **presence,** you mean that they impress people by their appearance and manner. *They do not seem to have the vast, authoritative presence of those great men.*

PHRASES ● If someone or something **makes** their **presence felt,** they do something which forces people to pay attention to them. • If you are **in** someone's **presence,** you are in the same place as they are, and are close enough to them to be seen or heard.

present 1 existing or happening now

present /'prezənt/. **1** ADJ BEFORE N You use **present** to describe people and things that exist now, rather than in the past or the future. *...the government's present economic difficulties... No statement can be made at the present time.* **2** N-SING **The present** is the period of time that we are in now and the things that are happening now. *...his struggle to reconcile the past with the present.* **3** ADJ BEFORE N The **present** tenses of a verb are the ones used to talk about things that happen regularly or situations that exist at this time.

PHRASES • A situation that exists **at present** exists now, although it may change. • **The present day** is the period of history that we are in now. *...Western European art from the period of Giotto to the present day.*

present 2 being somewhere

present /'prezənt/. **1** ADJ If someone is **present** at an event, they are there. *The whole family was present.* **2** ADJ If something, especially a substance or disease, is **present in** something else, it exists in that thing. *This special form of vitamin D is naturally present in breast milk.*

present 3 gift

present, /'prezənt/ **presents.** N-C A **present** is something that you give to someone, for example for their birthday or for Christmas. *This book would make a great Christmas present.*

present 4 verb uses

present, /prɪ'zent/ **presents, presenting, presented.** **1** VERB If you **present** someone with a prize or with information, or if you **present** it to them, you formally give it to them. *Prince Michael of Kent presented the prizes... We presented three options to the unions for discussion.* ◆**presentation,** /,prezən'teɪʃən, AM ,priːzən-/ **presentations** N-VAR *Then came the presentation of the awards.* **2** VERB Something that **presents** a difficulty or a challenge causes or provides it. *Public policy on the family presents liberals with a dilemma.* **3** VERB If you **present** someone or something in a particular way, you describe them in that way. *The British like to present themselves as a nation of dog-lovers.* **4** VERB If someone **presents** a programme on television or radio, they introduce each item in it. ◆**presenter, presenters** N-C *...the presenter of the BBC radio programme Law in Action.*

presentation /,prezən'teɪʃən, AM ,priːzən-/ **presentations.** **1** N-U **Presentation** is the appearance of something, which someone has worked to create. *...traditional French food cooked in a lighter way, keeping the presentation simple.* **2** N-C A **presentation** is a formal event at which someone is given a prize or award. **3** N-C When someone gives a **presentation,** they give a formal talk. *...a slide and video presentation.* **4** N-C A **presentation** is something that is performed before an audience. *...Blackpool Opera House's presentation of*

Buddy, the musical.

present-'day (or present day). ADJ BEFORE N **Present-day** things, situations, and people exist at the time in history we are now in. *Even by present-day standards these were large aircraft.*

presently /'prezəntli/. **1** ADV If you say that something is **presently** happening, you mean that it is happening now. *She is presently developing a number of projects... The island is presently uninhabited.* **2** ADV You use **presently** to indicate that something happened quite a short time after something you have just mentioned; WRITTEN. *He was shown to a small office. Presently, a young woman in a white coat came in.* **3** ADV If you say that something will happen **presently,** you mean that it will happen quite soon. *'Who's Agnes?'—'You'll be meeting her presently.'*

preservative /prɪ'zɜːvətɪv/ **preservatives.** N-VAR A **preservative** is a chemical that is added to substances to prevent them from decaying. *Nitrates are commonly used as preservatives in food manufacture.*

preserve /prɪ'zɜːv/ **preserves, preserving, preserved.** **1** VERB If you **preserve** a situation or condition, you make sure that it stays as it is, and does not change or end. *We will do everything to preserve peace.* ◆**preservation** /,prezə'veɪʃən/ N-U *...the preservation of the status quo.* **2** VERB If you **preserve** something, you take action to save it or protect it. *We need to preserve the forest.* ◆**preservation** N-U *...the preservation of historic houses.* **3** VERB If you **preserve** food, you treat it in order to prevent it from decaying.

preside /prɪ'zaɪd/ **presides, presiding, presided.** VERB If you **preside over** a meeting or event, you are in charge or act as the chairperson.

presidency /'prezɪdənsi/. **presidencies.** N-C The **presidency** of a country or organization is the position of being the president or the period of time during which someone is president. *Poverty had declined during his presidency.*

president /'prezɪdənt/ **presidents.** **1** N-C & N-TITLE The **president** of a country that has no king or queen is the person who has the highest political position and is the leader of the country. *...President Mubarak.* • See note at **government.** **2** N-C The **president** of an organization is the person with the highest position in it. *...the president of the medical commission.*

presidential /,prezɪ'denʃəl/. ADJ BEFORE N **Presidential** activities or things relate or belong to a president. *...campaigning for Peru's presidential election.*

press /pres/ **presses, pressing, pressed.** **1** VERB If you **press** something somewhere, you push it firmly against something else. *He pressed his back against the door... They pressed the silver knife into the cake.* **2** VERB If you **press** a button or switch, or if you give it a **press,** you push it with your finger in order to make a machine or device work. *Drago pressed a button and the door closed. ...a TV which rises from a table at the press of a button.* **3** VERB If you **press** on something, or if you **press down**

on it, you push against it with your hand or foot. *The engine stalled. He pressed the accelerator hard... She leaned forward with her hands pressing down on the desk.* [4] VERB If you **press** clothes, you iron them. [5] VERB If you **press for** something, you try hard to persuade someone to give it to you or agree to it. *Police might now press for changes in the law.* [6] VERB If you **press** someone, you try hard to persuade them to do or say something. *Trade unions are pressing him to stand firm... Mr King seems certain to be pressed for further details.* [7] VERB If you **press charges** against someone, you make an official accusation which has to be decided in a court of law. *Police have announced they will not be pressing charges.* [8] N-SING The **press** refers to newspapers and the journalists who write them. **The press** can take the singular or plural form of the verb. *A meeting was promised, but the Press was not admitted.* [9] N-C A **press** or a **printing press** is a machine used for printing books, newspapers, and leaflets. [10] See also **pressing**.

▸ **press on** or **press ahead**. PHR-VERB If you **press on**, you continue doing something in a determined way, and do not allow difficulties to delay you. *Poland pressed on with economic reform.*

'**press conference, press conferences.** N-C A **press conference** is a meeting held by a famous or important person in which they answer journalists' questions.

pressing /'presɪŋ/. ADJ A **pressing** problem, need, or issue has to be dealt with immediately.

'**press release, press releases.** N-C A **press release** is a written statement about a matter of public interest which is given to the press by an organization involved in the matter. *The government had put out a press release naming the men.*

pressure /'preʃə/ **pressures, pressuring, pressured.** [1] N-U **Pressure** is the force produced when you press hard on something. *The best way to treat such bleeding is to apply firm pressure.* [2] N-U The **pressure** in a place or container is the force produced by the quantity of gas or liquid in that place or container. *...another high pressure area over the North Sea.* ● See also **blood pressure**. [3] N-U If there is **pressure** on someone to do something, someone is trying to persuade or force them to do it. *He may have put pressure on her to agree... Its government is under pressure from the European Commission.* [4] N-VAR If you **feel pressure**, you feel that you have too much to do and not enough time to do it, or that people expect a lot from you. *Can you work under pressure?... The pressures of modern life are great.* [5] VERB If you **pressure** someone to do something, you try forcefully to persuade them to do it. *He will never pressure you to get married... Don't pressure me.* ◆ **pressured** ADJ *You're likely to feel anxious and pressured.*

'**pressure group, pressure groups.** N-C A **pressure group** is an organization that campaigns to try to persuade a government to do something. *...the environmental pressure group Greenpeace.*

pressurize (BR also **pressurise**) /'preʃəraɪz/ **pressurizes, pressurizing, pressurized.** VERB If you are **pressurized into** doing something, you are forcefully persuaded to do it. *He thought she was trying to pressurize him.*

pressurized (BR also **pressurised**) /'preʃəraɪzd/. ADJ In a **pressurized** container or area, the pressure inside is different from the pressure outside. *Supplementary oxygen is rarely needed in pressurized aircraft.*

prestige /pre'stiːʒ/. N-U If a person, a country, or an organization has **prestige**, they are admired and respected because they are important or successful. *...efforts to build up the prestige of the United Nations. ...high prestige jobs.*

prestigious /pre'stɪdʒəs/. ADJ A **prestigious** institution or activity is respected and admired by people. *...the largest and most prestigious businesses in America.*

presumably /prɪ'zjuːməbli, AM -'zuːm-/. ADV If you say that something is **presumably** the case, you mean that you think it is the case, although you are not certain. *Presumably the front door was locked?... He had gone to the reception desk, presumably to check out.*

presume /prɪ'zjuːm, AM -'zuːm/ **presumes, presuming, presumed.** [1] VERB If you **presume** that something is the case, you think that it is the case, although you are not certain. *I presume you're here on business... The missing person is presumed dead.* [2] VERB If you say that someone **presumes** to do something, you mean that they do it even though they have no right to do it; FORMAL. *I wouldn't presume to question your judgement.*

presumption /prɪ'zʌmpʃən/ **presumptions.** N-C A **presumption** is something that is accepted as true but is not certain to be true. *...the presumption that a defendant is innocent until proved guilty.*

presumptuous /prɪ'zʌmptʃʊəs/. ADJ If you describe someone as **presumptuous**, you disapprove of them because they do things that they have no right to do. *It would be presumptuous to judge what the outcome will be.*

pretence (AM **pretense**) /prɪ'tens, AM 'priːtens/ **pretences.** [1] N-VAR A **pretence** is way of behaving that is intended to make people believe something that is not true. *Welland made a pretence of writing a note in his pad.* [2] PHRASE If you do something under **false pretences**, you do it when people do not know the truth about you and your intentions. *Conrad had been imprisoned for a year for gaining money by false pretences.*

pretend /prɪ'tend/ **pretends, pretending, pretended.** [1] VERB If you **pretend** that something is the case, you try to make people believe that it is the case, although it is not. *Sometimes the boy pretended to be asleep.* [2] VERB If you **pretend** that you are doing something, you imagine that you are doing it, for example as part of a game. *She can sunbathe and pretend she's in Spain.*

pretension /prɪ'tenʃən/ **pretensions.** N-VAR Someone with **pretensions** pretends that they are more important than they really are. *We like him for his honesty, his lack of pretension.*

pretentious /prɪˈtenʃəs/. ADJ Someone or something that is **pretentious** tries to appear more important or significant than they really are. *The film was too boring and pretentious for me.*

pretext /ˈpriːtekst/ **pretexts.** N-C A **pretext** is a reason which you pretend has caused you to do something. *I darted into the bedroom on the pretext of looking for a book.*

pretty /ˈprɪti/ **prettier, prettiest.** [1] ADJ If you describe someone, especially a girl, as **pretty**, you mean that they look nice and are attractive in a delicate way. *...a shy, delicately pretty girl with enormous blue eyes.* ● See note at **beautiful.** [2] ADJ A place or a thing that is **pretty** is attractive and pleasant. *...a pretty flowered cotton dress.* ◆**prettily** ADV *The living-room was prettily decorated.* [3] ADV You can use **pretty** before an adjective or adverb to mean 'quite' or 'rather'; INFORMAL. *I'm a pretty good judge of character.* ● See note at **rather.** [4] PHRASE **Pretty much** or **pretty well** means 'almost'; INFORMAL. *I travel pretty well every week.*

prevail /prɪˈveɪl/ **prevails, prevailing, prevailed.** [1] VERB If a proposal, principle, or opinion **prevails**, it gains influence or is accepted. *Political and personal ambitions are starting to prevail over economic interests.* [2] VERB If a situation or attitude **prevails** in a particular place at a particular time, it is normal or most common at that place and time. *...the confusion which had prevailed at the time of the revolution.* [3] VERB If you **prevail upon** someone to do something, you succeed in persuading them to do it. *He was prevailed upon to sign copies of his book.*

prevalent /ˈprevələnt/. ADJ A condition or belief that is **prevalent** is very common. *Smoking is becoming increasingly prevalent among younger women.* ◆**prevalence** N-U *...the prevalence of behaviour problems in 3-year-old children.*

prevent /prɪˈvent/ **prevents, preventing, prevented.** VERB If you **prevent** something, you stop it happening or being done. *...measures to prevent the wastage of water. ...to prevent wild animals in Britain from suffering terrible cruelty.* ◆**prevention** N-U *...crime prevention.*

preventative /prɪˈventətɪv/. ADJ BEFORE N **Preventative** means the same as **preventive.**

preventive /prɪˈventɪv/. ADJ BEFORE N **Preventive** actions are intended to help prevent things such as disease or crime. *...preventive medicine.*

preview /ˈpriːvjuː/ **previews.** N-C A **preview** is an opportunity to see something such as a film or invention before it is open or available to the public.

previous /ˈpriːviəs/. ADJ BEFORE N A **previous** event or thing is one that occurred before the one you are talking about. *She has a teenage daughter from a previous marriage.*

previously /ˈpriːviəsli/. [1] ADV **Previously** means at some time before the period that you are talking about. *Previously she had very little time to work.* [2] ADV You can use **previously** to say how much earlier one event was than another. *She had rented the flat from the council some fourteen months previously.*

pre-'war. ADJ **Pre-war** things happened, existed, or were made before a war, especially the 1939-45 war in Europe. *It was 1950 before he returned to his pre-war job at the British Museum.*

prey /preɪ/ **preys, preying, preyed.** [1] N-U A creature's **prey** are the creatures that it hunts and eats in order to live. [2] VERB A creature that **preys on** other creatures lives by catching and eating them. *...mountain lions and bears that prey on sheep.* [3] N-U If someone or something is **prey to** something bad, they have a tendency to let themselves be affected by it. *He was prey to a growing despair.* [4] PHRASE To **fall prey to** something bad means to be affected by it. *Children in evacuation centres are falling prey to disease.*

price /praɪs/ **prices, pricing, priced.** [1] N-VAR The **price** of something is the amount of money that you must pay to buy it. *They expected house prices to rise... They haven't come down in price.*

> The **price** of goods is the amount of money that the seller is asking people to pay in order to buy them. *The price marked on the box was five pounds.* When you are referring to services, or to things that you pay to use, you usually talk about a **charge** or a **fee**, rather than a **price**. *There is a 50p handling charge for postal bookings. ...£400 in unpaid parking fees.* The **cost** of something is the amount of money that you actually pay, or would pay, for it. *The total cost of modernising the room came to just £800.* The **cost** of goods is usually the same as their **price**.

[2] VERB If something **is priced** at a particular amount, the price is set at that amount. *The book is priced at £8.99.* ◆**pricing** N-U *It's hard to maintain competitive pricing.* [3] N-SING The **price** that you pay for something is an unpleasant thing you have to do in order to get it. *Slovenia will have to pay a high price for independence.* [4] PHRASE If you want something **at any price**, you are determined to get it, even if unpleasant things happen as a result.

priceless /ˈpraɪsləs/. [1] ADJ Something that is **priceless** is worth a very large amount of money. *...his priceless collection of Chinese art.* [2] ADJ If you say that something is **priceless**, you mean that it is extremely useful. *Gillian is passing on some of her priceless skill and experience.*

pricey /ˈpraɪsi/ **pricier, priciest.** ADJ If something is **pricey**, it is expensive; INFORMAL.

prick /prɪk/ **pricks, pricking, pricked.** [1] VERB If you **prick** something, you make small holes in it with a sharp object such as a pin. *Prick the potatoes and rub the skins with salt.* [2] VERB & N-C If something sharp **pricks** you, or if you feel a **prick**, something sticks into you and causes you pain. *She had just pricked her finger with the needle... She felt a prick on her neck.*

prickly /ˈprɪkli/. [1] ADJ Something that is **prickly** feels rough and uncomfortable, as if it has a lot of sharp points. [2] ADJ Someone who is **prickly** loses their temper or gets upset very easily. *You know how prickly she can be sometimes.*

pride /praɪd/ **prides, priding, prided.** [1] N-U **Pride** is a feeling of satisfaction which you have because you or people close to you have done something good or possess something good. *...the sense of pride in a job well done... Take pride in your health and your figure.* [2] VERB If you **pride** yourself **on** a quality or skill that you have, you are very proud of it. *Smith prides himself on being able to organise his own life.* [3] N-U **Pride** is a sense of dignity and self-respect. *His own pride forbids him to ask Arthur's help.* [4] N-U Someone's **pride** is the feeling that they have that they are better or more important than other people; used showing disapproval. *His pride may still be his downfall.*
PHRASES ● Someone or something that is your **pride and joy** is very important to you and makes you feel very happy. *The bike soon became his pride and joy.* ● If something takes **pride of place**, it is treated as the most important thing in a group of things.

priest /priːst/ **priests.** [1] N-C A **priest** is a member of the Christian clergy in the Catholic, Anglican, or Orthodox church. [2] N-C In many non-Christian religions a **priest** is a man who has particular duties and responsibilities in a place where people worship.

priestess /ˈpriːstes/ **priestesses.** N-C A **priestess** is a woman in a non-Christian religion who has particular duties and responsibilities in a place where people worship.

priesthood /ˈpriːsthʊd/ [1] N-U **Priesthood** is the position of being a priest or the period of time during which someone is a priest. *He spent the first twenty-five years of his priesthood as an academic.* [2] N-SING **The priesthood** consists of all the members of the Christian clergy.

prim /prɪm/ ADJ If you describe someone as **prim**, you mean that they behave too correctly and are too easily shocked by anything rude or improper. ♦ **primly** ADV *We sat primly at either end of a long settee.*

primal /ˈpraɪməl/ ADJ **Primal** is used to describe something that relates to the origins of things or that is very basic; FORMAL. *Jealousy is a primal emotion.*

primarily /ˈpraɪmərɪli, AM praɪˈmeərɪli/ ADV You use **primarily** to say what is mainly true in a particular situation. *The body is made up primarily of bone, muscle, and fat.*

primary /ˈpraɪməri, AM -meri/ [1] ADJ BEFORE N You use **primary** to describe something that is extremely important or most important for someone or something; FORMAL. *The primary source of water in the region is the river.* [2] ADJ BEFORE N In Britain, **primary** education is given to pupils between the ages of 5 and 11. The American equivalent is **elementary** education.

primate /ˈpraɪmət/ **primates.** N-C A **primate** is a member of the group of mammals which includes humans, monkeys, and apes.

prime /praɪm/ **primes, priming, primed.** [1] ADJ BEFORE N You use **prime** to describe something that is most important in a situation. *The police will see me as the prime suspect... Its prime audience lies in the 17 to 24 age group.* [2] ADJ BEFORE N You use **prime** to describe something that is of the best possible quality. *...keeping a car in prime condition.* [3] ADJ BEFORE N A **prime** example of something is a very typical example of it. *New York is a prime example of a city where crime strangles small-business development.* [4] N-SING Your **prime** is the stage in your life when you are most active or most successful. *She was in her intellectual prime.* [5] VERB If you **prime** someone to do something, you prepare them to do it, for example by giving them information about it beforehand. *I'm pretty much primed to believe anything bad about her.*

Prime 'Minister, Prime Ministers. N-C The leader of the government in some countries is called **the Prime Minister**.

primitive /ˈprɪmɪtɪv/ [1] ADJ **Primitive** means belonging to a society in which people live in a very simple way, usually without industries or a writing system. *...primitive tribes.* [2] ADJ **Primitive** means belonging to a very early period in the development of an animal or plant. *It is a primitive instinct to flee a place of danger.* [3] ADJ If you describe something as **primitive**, you mean that it is very simple in style or that it is very old-fashioned. *It's using some rather primitive technology.*

primrose /ˈprɪmrəʊz/ **primroses.** N-C A **primrose** is a wild plant with pale yellow flowers.

prince /prɪns/ **princes.** N-C & N-TITLE A **prince** is a male member of a royal family, especially the son of a king or queen.

princess /ˌprɪnˈses, AM -ˈsəs/ **princesses.** N-C & N-TITLE A **princess** is a female member of a royal family, especially the daughter of a king or queen or the wife of a prince.

principal /ˈprɪnsɪpəl/ **principals.** [1] ADJ BEFORE N **Principal** means first in order of importance. *Salt is the principal source of sodium in our diets.* [2] N-C The **principal** of a school or college is the person in charge of it.

principally /ˈprɪnsɪpəli/ ADV **Principally** means more than anything else. *A sport such as cycling is principally about athletic achievement.*

principle /ˈprɪnsɪpəl/ **principles.** [1] N-VAR A **principle** is a belief that you have about the way you should behave. *...moral principles. ...a man of principle.* [2] N-C The **principles** of a particular theory or philosophy are its basic rules or laws. *...the principles of Buddhism.*
PHRASES ● If you refuse to do something **on principle**, you refuse to do it because of your beliefs. *He would vote against it on principle.* ● If you agree with something **in principle**, you agree in general terms to the idea of it, although you do not know the details or know if it will be possible. *The conference approved in principle a new policy-making process.*

principled /ˈprɪnsɪpəld/ ADJ If you describe someone as **principled**, you approve of them because they have strong moral principles.

print /prɪnt/ **prints, printing, printed.** [1] VERB If someone **prints** a book, newspaper, or leaflet, they produce it in large quantities by a mechanical process. ♦ **printing** N-U *...a printing* *and publishing company.* [2] VERB If a newspaper or magazine **prints** a piece of writing, it includes it or publishes it. [3] VERB If numbers or letters **are printed** on an object, they appear on it. *The company has for some time printed its phone number on its products.* [4] VERB If a text or a picture **is printed**, a copy of it is produced by means of a computer printer or some other type of equipment. *...machines that can print on both sides of a page.* [5] VERB If you **print**, you write in letters that are not joined together. [6] N-U **Print** is used to refer to letters and numbers as they appear on the pages of a printed document. *...columns of tiny print.*

PHRASES ● If you or your words appear **in print**, or get **into print**, what you say or write is published in a book or newspaper. ● If a book is **in print**, it is available from a publisher. If it is **out of print**, it is no longer available.

▸ **print out.** PHR-VERB If you **print out** a document or some information, you produce a copy of it on paper using a computer. You can also say that a computer **prints** something **out**. *Print it out and compare it to the old version of your file.* ● See also **printout**.

printer /ˈprɪntə/ **printers.** [1] N-C A **printer** is a machine that can be connected to a computer in order to make copies on paper of information held by the computer. [2] N-C A **printer** is a person or firm whose job is printing books, leaflets, or similar material.

printout (or **print-out**) /ˈprɪntaʊt/ **printouts.** N-VAR A **printout** is a piece of paper on which information from a computer has been printed.

prior /praɪə/. [1] ADJ BEFORE N You use **prior** to indicate that something has already happened, or must happen, before another event takes place; FORMAL. *These courses require prior knowledge of computing.* [2] PREP If something happens **prior to** a particular time or event, it happens before it; FORMAL. *...a man seen hanging around the area prior to the shooting.*

priority /praɪˈɒrɪti, AM -ˈɔːr-/ **priorities.** N-C If something is a **priority**, it is the most important thing you have to achieve or deal with before everything else. *Quality is our number one priority... Her first priority was to knock down the wall between the kitchen and dining area.*

PHRASES ● If you **give priority** to something or someone, you treat them as more important than anything or anyone else. *The school will give priority to science and maths.* ● If something **takes priority** or **has priority** over other things, it is regarded as being more important than them and is dealt with first. *Academic work takes priority over politics or social life for most students.*

priory /ˈpraɪəri/ **priories.** N-C A **priory** is a place where a small number of monks live and work together.

prise (AM **prize**) /praɪz/ **prises, prising, prised.** [1] VERB If you **prise** something open, or if you **prise** it away from a surface, you force it to open or force it to come away from the surface. *She prised open the window... We were unable to prise the lids off.* [2] VERB If you **prise** information **out of** someone, you persuade

them to tell you although they may be very unwilling to.

prison /ˈprɪzən/ **prisons.** N-VAR A **prison** is a building where criminals are kept.

prisoner /ˈprɪzənə/ **prisoners.** [1] N-C A **prisoner** is a person who is kept in a prison as a punishment or because they have been captured by an enemy. [2] PHRASE If someone is **taken prisoner**, they are captured. If someone **is held prisoner**, they are guarded so that they cannot escape.

pristine /ˈprɪstiːn/. ADJ **Pristine** things are extremely clean or new. *The house is in pristine condition.*

privacy /ˈprɪvəsi, AM ˈpraɪ-/. N-U **Privacy** is the fact of being alone so that you can do things without being seen or disturbed. *...exercises you can do in the privacy of your own home... I've always enjoyed my privacy.*

private /ˈpraɪvɪt/ **privates.** [1] ADJ **Private** industries and services are owned and controlled by an individual person or group, rather than by the state. *...private education.* ♦**privately** ADV *...privately owned businesses.* [2] ADJ If something is **private**, it is for the use of one person or group, rather than for the general public. *...his father's private plane. ... a private golf club.* [3] ADJ **Private** activities involve only a small number of people, and very little information about them is given to other people. ♦**privately** ADV *I had not talked to Winnette privately for weeks.* [4] PHRASE If you do something **in private**, you do it without other people being present, often because it is something that you want to keep secret. [5] ADJ Your **private** life is that part of your life that is concerned with your personal relationships and activities, rather than with your work or business. [6] ADJ Your **private** thoughts or feelings are ones that you do not talk about to other people. *We felt as if we were intruding on his private grief.* ♦**privately** ADV *Privately, she worries about whether she's really good enough.* [7] ADJ If you describe a place as **private**, you mean that it is a quiet place and you can be alone there without being disturbed. *Can't we go somewhere private to discuss this?* [8] N-C & N-TITLE A **private** is a soldier of the lowest rank.

,**private 'school, private schools.** N-C A **private school** is a school which is not supported financially by the government and which parents have to pay for their children to go to.

privatize (BR also **privatise**) /ˈpraɪvətaɪz/ **privatizes, privatizing, privatized.** VERB If an organization owned by the state **is privatized**, the government sells it to one or more private companies. ♦**privatization, privatizations** N-VAR *...the privatisation of British Rail.*

privilege /ˈprɪvɪlɪdʒ/ **privileges.** [1] N-C A **privilege** is a special right or advantage that only one person or group has. *...special privileges for government officials.* [2] N-U **Privilege** is the power and advantages that belong to a small group of people, usually because of their wealth or their high social class. *...a life of privilege.*

privileged /ˈprɪvɪlɪdʒd/. ADJ Someone who is **privileged** has an advantage or opportunity that most other people do not have, often because of their wealth or high social class. *...a very wealthy, privileged elite.*

prize /praɪz/ **prizes, prizing, prized.** ⓵ N-C A **prize** is something valuable, such as money or a trophy, that is given to the winner of a game or competition. *He won first prize... The winner won about £300 in prize money.* ⓶ ADJ BEFORE N You use **prize** to describe things that are of such good quality that they win prizes or deserve to win prizes. *...a prize bull.* ⓷ VERB Something that **is prized** is wanted and admired because it is considered to be very valuable or very good quality. *These shells were highly prized by the Indians.* ⓸ See also **prise**.

pro /prəʊ/ **pros.** ⓵ N-C A **pro** is a professional, especially a professional sportsman or sportswoman. ⓶ PHRASE The **pros and cons** of something are its advantages and disadvantages.

probability /ˌprɒbəˈbɪlɪti/ **probabilities.** ⓵ N-VAR The **probability** of something happening is how likely it is to happen, sometimes expressed as a fraction or a percentage. *Without a transfusion, the victim's probability of dying was 100%.* ⓶ N-VAR You say that there is a **probability** that something will happen when it is likely to happen. *The probability is that he will return to Gloucestershire.* ⓷ PHRASE You use **in all probability** when you are confident that something is true or correct, or is likely to happen. *In all probability, we shall never know.*

probable /ˈprɒbəbəl/. ADJ Something that is **probable** is likely to be true or likely to happen. *It is probable that the volcano will erupt again.*

probably /ˈprɒbəbli/. ADV If you say that something is **probably** the case, you think that it is likely to be the case, although you are not sure. *You probably won't understand this word... Van Gogh is probably the best-known painter in the world.*

probation /prəˈbeɪʃən, AM prəʊ-/. N-U **Probation** is a period of time during which a person who has committed a crime is supervised to ensure that they do not break the law again, rather than being in prison. *The young woman admitted three theft charges and was put on probation for two years.*

pro'bation officer, probation officers. N-C A **probation officer** is a person whose job is to supervise and help people who have been put on probation.

probe /prəʊb/ **probes, probing, probed.** ⓵ VERB & N-C If you **probe** into something, you ask questions or make enquiries in order to discover facts about it. This questioning or enquiring is called a **probe**. *The Office of Fair Trading has been probing banking practices. ...a new probe into burglary in Queensland.* ⓶ VERB If you **probe** a place, you search in it in order to find someone or something that you looking for. *I probed around for some time in the bushes.*

problem /ˈprɒbləm/ **problems.** ⓵ N-C A **problem** is an unsatisfactory situation that causes difficulties for people. *He left home at the age of 16 because of family problems... The main problem was that I had very little experience.* ⓶ N-C A **problem** is a puzzle that requires logical thought or mathematics to solve it.

problematic /ˌprɒbləˈmætɪk/. ADJ Something that is **problematic** involves problems and difficulties. *Some places are more problematic than others for women traveling alone.*

procedural /prəˈsiːdʒərəl/. ADJ **Procedural** means involving a formal procedure; FORMAL. *The discussions will probably focus on procedural matters.*

procedure /prəˈsiːdʒə/ **procedures.** N-VAR A **procedure** is a way of doing something, especially the usual or correct way. *The procedure is lengthy, complicated and quite secretive. ...safety procedures.*

proceed /prəˈsiːd/ **proceeds, proceeding, proceeded.** ⓵ VERB If you **proceed** to do something, you do it after doing something else. *He then proceeded to tell us everything.* ⓶ VERB To **proceed** means to continue as planned; FORMAL. *I do not believe that such a sensible way to proceed.* ⓷ VERB If you **proceed** in a particular direction, you go in that direction; FORMAL. *He proceeded down the spiral stairway.* ⓸ N-PL /ˈprəʊsiːdz/ The **proceeds** of an event or activity are the money that has been obtained from it. *The proceeds from the concert will go towards famine relief.*

proceedings /prəˈsiːdɪŋz/. ⓵ N-PL Legal **proceedings** are legal action taken against someone; FORMAL. *...a man facing criminal proceedings for kidnapping his daughter.* ⓶ N-PL You can refer to an organized series of events that happen in a place as the **proceedings**; FORMAL. *...the proceedings of the enquiry.*

process /ˈprəʊses, AM ˈprɑːses/ **processes, processing, processed.** ⓵ N-C A **process** is a series of actions or events which have a particular result. *...the 12-week training process. ...factors that accelerate the ageing process.* ⓶ VERB When raw materials or foods **are processed**, they are treated by a chemical or industrial process before they are used or sold. *...diets high in refined and processed foods.* ♦**processing** N-U *...nuclear fuel processing plant.* ⓷ VERB When a person or computer **processes** information, they deal with the information by putting it through a system or into a computer. ♦**processing** N-U *...data processing.* ⓸ See also **word processing**.

| PHRASES | ● If you **are in the process of** doing something, you have started to do it and are still doing it. ● If you are doing something and you do something else **in the process**, you do the second thing as a result of doing the first thing. *You have to let us struggle for ourselves, even if we must die in the process.*

procession /prəˈseʃən/ **processions.** N-C A **procession** is a group of people who are walking, riding, or driving in a line as part of a public event. *A funeral procession was coming up the hill.*

processor /ˈprəʊsesə, AM ˈprɑːs-/ **processors.** N-C A **processor** is the part of a computer that interprets commands and performs the processes the user has requested; TECHNICAL.

proclaim /prəˈkleɪm/ **proclaims, proclaiming, proclaimed.** VERB If people **proclaim** something, they formally announce it or make it known. *He still proclaims himself a believer in the Revolution.*

proclamation /ˌprɒkləˈmeɪʃən/ **proclamations.** N-C A **proclamation** is a public announcement about something important.

procure /prəˈkjʊə/ **procures, procuring, procured.** VERB If you **procure** something, especially something that is difficult to get, you obtain it; FORMAL. *It remained very difficult to procure food.* ♦**procurement** N-U *...procurement of new weapons.*

prod /prɒd/ **prods, prodding, prodded.** [1] VERB & N-C If you **prod** someone or something, or if you give them a **prod**, you give them a quick push with your finger or with a pointed object. *He prodded Murray with the shotgun.* [2] VERB If you **prod** someone into doing something, you remind them or persuade them to do it. *This question is designed to prod students into examining the idea.* ♦**prodding** N-U *She did her chores without prodding.*

prodigious /prəˈdɪdʒəs/. ADJ Something that is **prodigious** is very large or impressive; LITERARY. *...prodigious amounts of work.* ♦**prodigiously** ADV *She ate prodigiously.*

produce, produces, producing, produced. [1] VERB /prəˈdjuːs, AM -ˈduːs/ To **produce** something means to cause it to happen. *The drug is known to produce side-effects.* [2] VERB If you **produce** something, you make or create it. *We try to produce items that are the basics of a stylish wardrobe.* ♦**producer, producers** N-C *...the world's leading oil producer.* [3] VERB If you **produce** evidence or an argument, you show it or explain it to people. *They challenged him to produce evidence to support his allegations.* [4] VERB. If you **produce** an object from somewhere, you show it or bring it out so that it can be seen. *To hire a car you must produce a passport.* [5] VERB If someone **produces** a play, film, programme, or record, they organize it and decide how it should be made. ♦**producer** N-C *...a freelance film producer.* [6] N-U /ˈprɒdjuːs, AM -duːs/ **Produce** is food such as fruit and vegetables that are grown in large quantities to be sold.

product /ˈprɒdʌkt/ **products.** [1] N-C A **product** is something that is produced and sold in large quantities. [2] N-C If you say that someone or something is a **product** of a particular situation or process, you mean that the situation or process made that person or thing what they are. *The bank is the product of a 1971 merger of two Japanese banks.*

production /prəˈdʌkʃən/ **productions.** [1] N-U **Production** is the process of manufacturing or growing something in large quantities, or the amount of goods manufactured or grown. *That model won't go into production before late 1990... We needed to increase the volume of production.* [2] N-U The **production** of something is its creation as the result of a natural process. *These proteins stimulate the production of blood cells.* [3] N-U **Production** is the process of organizing and preparing a play, film, programme, or record. [4] N-C A **production** is a play, opera, or other show that is performed in a theatre. *...a new production of The Rocky Horror Show.*

pro'duction line, production lines. N-C A **production line** is an arrangement of machines in a factory where the products pass from one machine to another until they are finished.

productive /prəˈdʌktɪv/. [1] ADJ Something or someone that is **productive** is very efficient at producing something. *Training makes workers highly productive.* [2] ADJ If you say that a relationship is **productive**, you mean that good or useful things happen as a result of it. *Our discussions were amicable and productive.*

productivity /ˌprɒdʌkˈtɪvɪti/. N-U **Productivity** is the rate at which goods are produced. *...continued improvements in productivity.*

Prof. /prɒf/. N-TITLE **Prof.** is a written abbreviation for 'professor'. *...Prof. Richard Joyner.*

profess /prəˈfes/ **professes, professing, professed.** [1] VERB If you **profess** to do or have something, you claim that you do it or have it, often when you do not; FORMAL. *Why do organisations profess that they care?* [2] VERB If you **profess** a feeling, opinion, or belief, you express it; FORMAL. *He professed to be content... Bacher professed himself pleased with the Indian tour.*

profession /prəˈfeʃən/ **professions.** [1] N-C A **profession** is a type of job that requires advanced education or training. [2] N-C You use **profession** to refer to all the people who have the same profession. *...the medical profession.*

professional /prəˈfeʃənəl/ **professionals.** [1] ADJ BEFORE N **Professional** means relating to a person's work, especially work that requires special training. *His professional career started at Liverpool University.* ♦**professionally** ADV *...a professionally-qualified architect.* [2] N-C & ADJ BEFORE N A **professional**, or a **professional** person, has a job that requires advanced education or training. *My father wanted me to become a professional and have more stability.* [3] ADJ BEFORE N & N-C You use **professional** to describe people who do a particular thing to earn money rather than as a hobby. You call these people **professionals.** *...a professional footballer... He had been a professional since March 1985.* ♦**professionally** ADV *By age 16 he was playing professionally with bands.* [4] ADJ If you say that something that someone does or produces is **professional**, you approve of it because you think it shows skill and high standards. *...a truly professional but personal touch.* ♦**professionalism** N-U *American companies pride themselves on their professionalism.* ♦**professionally** ADV *These tickets have been produced very professionally.*

professor /prəˈfesə/ **professors.** [1] N-C & N-TITLE A **professor** in a British university is the most senior teacher in a department. *In 1979, only 2% of British professors were female.* [2] N-C & N-TITLE A **professor** in an American or Canadian university or college is a teacher there.

proffer /ˈprɒfə/ **proffers, proffering, proffered.** VERB If you **proffer** something to someone, you offer it to them; FORMAL. *The army has not yet proffered an explanation.*

proficient /prəˈfɪʃənt/. ADJ If you are **proficient** in something, you can do it well. *A great number of Egyptians are proficient in foreign lan-*

guages. ♦**proficiency** N-U ...*basic proficiency in English.*

profile /ˈprəʊfaɪl/ **profiles, profiling, profiled.** N-C Your **profile** is the outline of your face seen from the side.

PHRASES • If someone has a **high profile**, people notice them and what they do. *Football is a high profile business.* • If you keep a **low profile**, you avoid doing things that will make people notice you.

profit /ˈprɒfɪt/ **profits, profiting, profited.** [1] N-VAR A **profit** is an amount of money that you gain when you are paid more for something than it cost you. *The bank made pre-tax profits of £3.5 million.* [2] VERB If you **profit** from something, you earn a profit from it or gain some advantage or benefit from it. *The dealers profited shamefully at the expense of my family.*

profitable /ˈprɒfɪtəbəl/ [1] ADJ A **profitable** activity or organization makes a profit. *It was profitable for them to produce large amounts of food.* ♦**profitably** ADV *The 28 French stores are trading profitably.* ♦**profitability** N-U ...*an effort to increase profitability.* [2] ADJ Something that is **profitable** results in some benefit for you. ...*a profitable exchange of personnel and ideas.* ♦**profitably** ADV *He could scarcely have spent his time more profitably.*

profound /prəˈfaʊnd/ [1] ADJ You use **profound** to emphasize that something is very great or intense. ...*discoveries which had a profound effect on many areas of medicine.* ♦**profoundly** ADV *This has profoundly affected my life.* [2] ADJ A **profound** idea or work shows great intellectual depth and understanding. ...*one of the country's most profound minds.*

profuse /prəˈfjuːs/ ADJ **Profuse** means doing something or happening a lot. *He gave profuse thanks to Jimmy.* ♦**profusely** ADV *He was bleeding profusely.*

profusion /prəˈfjuːʒən/ N-SING & N-U If there is a **profusion** of something or if it occurs in **profusion**, there is a very large quantity or variety of it; FORMAL. *Wild flowers grew in profusion.*

prognosis /prɒgˈnəʊsɪs/ **prognoses** /prɒgˈnəʊsiːz/. N-C A **prognosis** is an estimate about the future of someone or something; FORMAL. *His wife had a brain tumour and the prognosis was poor.*

program /ˈprəʊgræm/ **programs, programming, programmed.** VERB & N-C When you **program** a computer, you give it a set of instructions called a **program**, to make it able to perform a particular task. ♦**programming** N-U ...*programming skills.* ♦**programmer, programmers** N-C ...*a computer programmer.*

programme (AM **program**) /ˈprəʊgræm/ **programmes, programming, programmed.** [1] N-C A **programme** of actions or events is a series of actions or events that are planned to be done. *The nuclear programme should still continue.* [2] N-C A television or radio **programme** is something that is broadcast on television or radio. ...*local news programmes.* [3] N-C A theatre or concert **programme** is a booklet giving information about the play or concert. [4] VERB When you **programme** a machine or system, you set its controls so that it

will work in a particular way. *Parents can programme the machine not to turn on at certain times.*

progress, progresses, progressing, progressed. [1] N-U /ˈprəʊgres, AM ˈprɑː-/ **Progress** is the process of gradually improving or getting nearer to achieving or completing something. *His teacher sees signs of progress in his reading.* [2] N-SING The **progress** of a situation or action is the way in which it develops. *He had retained a keen interest in the progress of the work.* [3] PHRASE If something is in **progress**, it has started and is still continuing. [4] VERB /prəˈgres/ To **progress** means to improve or to become more advanced or higher in rank. *He started only five years ago, sketching first and then progressing to painting.* [5] VERB If events **progress**, they continue to happen gradually over a period of time. *As her career progressed she made three other short films.*

progression /prəˈgreʃən/ **progressions.** N-C A **progression** is a gradual development from one state to another. *Both drugs slow the progression of AIDS.*

progressive /prəˈgresɪv/ **progressives.** [1] ADJ & N-C Someone who is **progressive** has modern ideas about how things should be done, rather than traditional ones. You can call someone like this a **progressive**. ...*one of the country's most progressive young theatre companies... The Republicans are deeply split between progressives and conservatives.* [2] ADJ A **progressive** change happens gradually over a period of time. ...*progressive loss of memory.* ♦**progressively** ADV *Her symptoms became progressively worse.*

prohibit /prəˈhɪbɪt, AM prəʊ-/ **prohibits, prohibiting, prohibited.** VERB If someone **prohibits** something, they forbid it or make it illegal; FORMAL. ...*a law that prohibits tobacco advertising.* ♦**prohibition** N-U *The review recommended prohibition of cannabis.*

prohibitive /prəˈhɪbɪtɪv, AM prəʊ-/. ADJ If something's cost is **prohibitive**, it is so high that many people cannot afford it. ...*the prohibitive prices charged for seats at the opera.* ♦**prohibitively** ADV *Meat and butter were prohibitively expensive.*

project, projects, projecting, projected. [1] N-C /ˈprɒdʒekt/ A **project** is a carefully planned task that requires a lot of time and effort. ...*local development projects such as hospitals and schools.* [2] N-C A **project** is a detailed study of a subject by a pupil or a student. [3] VERB /prəˈdʒekt/ If something is **projected**, it is planned or expected. *The industry is projecting a small increase in exports.* [4] VERB If you **project** a film or picture onto a screen or wall, you make it appear there. ...*a high-tech production projected onto a giant Cinemascope screen.* [5] VERB If you **project** a particular feeling or quality, you show it in your behaviour. If you **project** someone or something in a particular way, you try to make people see them in that way. *He just hasn't been able to project himself as the strong leader... His first job will be to project Glasgow as a friendly city.* [6] VERB If something **projects**, it sticks out beyond a particular surface or edge; FORMAL. ...*brown-*

*coloured boulders projecting above the oily sur-
face.*

projection /prə'dʒekʃən/ **projections.** 1 N-C A
projection is an estimate of a future amount.
...sales projections. 2 N-U The **projection** of a
film or picture is the act of projecting it onto a
screen or wall. *...the most up to date projection
facilities in the world.*

projector /prə'dʒektə/ **projectors.** N-C A **projector** is a machine that projects films or slides
onto a screen or wall.

proliferate /prə'lɪfəreɪt/ **proliferates, proliferating, proliferated.** VERB If things **proliferate,** they increase in number very quickly; FOR-
MAL. *Computerized data bases are proliferating
fast.* ◆**proliferation** N-U *...the proliferation of
nuclear weapons.*

prolific /prə'lɪfɪk/. ADJ A **prolific** writer, artist, or
composer produces a large number of works.

prologue /'prəʊlɒg, AM -lɔːg/ **prologues.** N-C A
prologue is a speech or section of text that
introduces a play or book.

prolong /prə'lɒŋ, AM -lɔːŋ/ **prolongs, prolonging, prolonged.** VERB To **prolong** something means to make it last longer. *Foreign
military aid was prolonging the war.*

prolonged /prə'lɒŋd, AM -lɔːŋd/. ADJ A **prolonged** event or situation continues for a long
time. *...a prolonged period of low interest rates.*

prominent /'prɒmɪnənt/. 1 ADJ Someone or
something that is **prominent** is well-known
and important or respected. *...the children of
very prominent or successful parents.
...Romania's most prominent independent
newspaper.* ◆**prominence** N-U *Crime prevention had to be given more prominence.* 2 ADJ
Something that is **prominent** is very noticeable. *...his prominent nose.* ◆**prominently** ADV
*Entries will be prominently displayed in the ex-
hibition hall.*

promiscuous /prə'mɪskjʊəs/. ADJ Someone
who is **promiscuous** has sex with many different people; used showing disapproval.
◆**promiscuity** /ˌprɒmɪ'skjuːɪti/ N-U *...an attempt
to limit promiscuity.*

promise /'prɒmɪs/ **promises, promising,
promised.** 1 VERB & N-C If you **promise** that
you will do something, or if you make a **promise** that you will do it, you say that you will
definitely do it. *He promised to wait... Promise
me you will not waste your time.* 2 VERB & N-C If
you **promise** someone something, or if you
make them a **promise** about it, you tell them
that you will definitely give it to them or make
sure that they have it. *We promise you an exciting and exhilarating trip.* 3 VERB If a situation
or event **promises** to have a particular quality,
it shows signs that it will have that quality. *The
seminar also promises to be most instructive.*
4 N-U If someone or something shows **promise,** they seem likely to be very good or successful.

promising /'prɒmɪsɪŋ/. ADJ Someone or something that is **promising** seems likely to be very
good or successful. *...one of the most promising
poets of his generation.*

promote /prə'məʊt/ **promotes, promoting,
promoted.** 1 VERB If people **promote** something, they help to make it happen, increase,

or become more popular. *In many ways, our
society actively promotes alcoholism... The island could be promoted as a tourist destination.* ◆**promotion, promotions** N-VAR *...TV
commercials and other promotions.* 2 VERB If
someone **is promoted,** they are given a more
important job in the organization they work
for. *I was promoted to editor.* ◆**promotion**
N-VAR *Consider changing jobs or trying for promotion.*

promoter /prə'məʊtə/ **promoters.** 1 N-C A
promoter is a person who helps organize and
finance an event, especially a sports event.
2 N-C The **promoter of** a cause or idea tries to
make it become popular. *...the most energetic
promoter of American music.*

promotional /prə'məʊʃənəl/. ADJ **Promotional**
material, events, or ideas are designed to advertise a product or service and increase its
sales.

prompt /prɒmpt/ **prompts, prompting,
prompted.** 1 VERB If something **prompts**
someone to do something, it makes them decide to do it. *Japan's recession has prompted
consumers to cut back on buying cars.* 2 VERB If
you **prompt** someone, you encourage or remind them to do something or to continue doing something. *'Well, Daniels?' Wilson prompted.* ◆**prompting, promptings** N-VAR *She telephoned Wychwood House at your prompting.*
3 ADJ A **prompt** action is done without any
delay. *It is not too late, but prompt action is
needed.*

promptly /'prɒmptli/. 1 ADV If you do something **promptly,** you do it immediately. *I set
my watch alarm for seven-thirty and promptly
fell asleep.* 2 ADV If you do something **promptly** at a particular time, you do it at exactly that
time. *Promptly at a quarter past seven, we left
the hotel and made our way to the car.*

prone /prəʊn/. ADJ AFTER LINK-V If someone or
something is **prone to** something, usually
something bad, they have a tendency to be affected by it or to do it. *We know males are
more prone to violence.* ◆**-prone** *...the most
injury-prone rider on the circuit.*

pronoun /'prəʊnaʊn/ **pronouns.** N-C A **pronoun** is a word which is used instead of a
noun group to refer to someone or something.
'He', 'she', 'them', and 'something' are pronouns.

pronounce /prə'naʊns/ **pronounces, pro-
nouncing, pronounced.** 1 VERB To **pronounce** a word means to say it. *He pronounced
it Per-sha, the way the English do.* 2 VERB If
you **pronounce** something, you state it formally or publicly; FORMAL. *The authorities took
time to pronounce their verdicts.*

pronounced /prə'naʊnst/. ADJ Something that
is **pronounced** is very noticeable. *Most of the
art exhibitions have a pronounced Scottish
theme.*

pronouncement /prə'naʊnsmənt/ **pronouncements.** N-C **Pronouncements** are
public or official statements on an important
subject. *...the President's pronouncements.*

pronunciation /prəˌnʌnsi'eɪʃən/ **pronunciations.** N-VAR The **pronunciation** of words is

the way they are pronounced. *You're going to have to forgive my pronunciation.*

proof /pruːf/ **proofs.** N-VAR **Proof** is a fact or a piece of evidence which shows that something is true or exists. *This is not necessarily proof that he is wrong.*

-proof /-pruːf/ **-proofs, -proofing, -proofed.** [1] **-proof** combines with nouns and verbs to form adjectives which indicate that something cannot be damaged or badly affected by a particular thing or person. *...a large microwave-proof dish.* [2] **-proof** combines with nouns to form verbs which refer to protecting something against being damaged or badly affected by the thing mentioned. *...the cost of draught-proofing your home.*

prop /prɒp/ **props, propping, propped.** [1] VERB & PHR-VERB If you prop an object **on** or **against** something, or if you prop it **up**, you support it by putting something underneath it or by resting it against something. *He propped his feet on the desk... Prop up your back against a wall.* [2] N-C A **prop** is a stick or other object used to support something. [3] N-C The **props** in a play or film are the objects and furniture used in it.

▶ **prop up.** [1] PHR-VERB To **prop up** something means to support it or help it to survive. *Investments in the U.S. money market have propped up the American dollar.* [2] See **prop** 1.

propaganda /ˌprɒpəˈɡændə/. N-U **Propaganda** is information, often inaccurate information, which an organization publishes or broadcasts in order to influence people; *used showing disapproval.* *...anti-abortion propaganda.*

propagate /ˈprɒpəɡeɪt/ **propagates, propagating, propagated.** VERB If people **propagate** an idea or a piece of information, they spread it and try to make people believe it or support it; FORMAL. ♦**propagation** N-U *...the propagation of true Buddhism.*

propel /prəˈpel/ **propels, propelling, propelled.** [1] VERB To **propel** something in a certain direction means to cause it to move in that direction. *Rebecca took Steve's elbow and propelled him towards the staircase.* [2] VERB If something **propels** you into a particular activity, it causes you to be involved in it. *University fees was the issue which propelled her into politics.*

propeller /prəˈpelə/ **propellers.** N-C A **propeller** on a boat or aircraft is a device with blades which is turned by the engine, causing the boat or aircraft to move.

propensity /prəˈpensɪti/ **propensities.** N-C If someone has a **propensity** to do something or a **propensity for** something, they tend to behave in a particular way; FORMAL. *Mr Bint has a propensity to put off decisions.*

proper /ˈprɒpə/. [1] ADJ BEFORE N You use **proper** to describe things that you consider to be real or satisfactory. *Two out of five people lack a proper job.* ♦**properly** ADV *You're too thin. You're not eating properly.* [2] ADJ BEFORE N The **proper** thing is the one that is correct or most suitable. *The proper procedures have been followed.* [3] ADJ If you say that a way of behaving is **proper**, you mean that it is considered socially acceptable and right. *It was not thought*

entirely proper for a woman to be on the stage. ♦**properly** ADV *It's about time he learnt to behave properly.*

'proper ˌnoun, proper nouns. N-C In grammar, a **proper noun** is a noun which refers to a particular person, place, or institution. Proper nouns begin with a capital letter.

property /ˈprɒpəti/ **properties.** [1] N-U Someone's **property** consists of all the things that belong to them, or something that belongs to them; FORMAL. *...stolen property.* [2] N-C A **property** is a building and the land belonging to it; FORMAL. [3] N-C The **properties** of a substance or object are the ways in which it behaves in particular conditions; TECHNICAL. *A radio signal has both electrical and magnetic properties.*

prophecy /ˈprɒfɪsi/ **prophecies.** N-VAR A **prophecy** is a statement in which someone says they strongly believe that something will happen.

prophesy /ˈprɒfɪsaɪ/ **prophesies, prophesying, prophesied.** VERB If you **prophesy** something, you say that you strongly believe that it will happen. *She prophesied a bad ending for the expedition.*

prophet /ˈprɒfɪt/ **prophets.** N-C A **prophet** is a person believed to be chosen by God to say the things that God wants to tell people.

prophetic /prəˈfetɪk/. ADJ If something was **prophetic**, it described or suggested something that did actually happen later. *This ominous warning soon proved prophetic.*

proponent /prəˈpəʊnənt/ **proponents.** N-C A **proponent** of a particular idea or course of action actively supports it; FORMAL. *He's a hard-line proponent of law and order.*

proportion /prəˈpɔːʃən/ **proportions.** [1] N-C A **proportion** of an amount or group is a part of it; FORMAL. *A large proportion of the dolphins in that area will eventually die.* [2] N-C The **proportion of** one kind of person or thing in a group is the number of people or things of that kind compared to the total number in the group. *The proportion of women in the profession had risen to 17.3%.* [3] N-PL If you refer to the **proportions** of something, you are referring to its size, usually when this is extremely large; WRITTEN. *In the tropics plants grow to huge proportions.*

PHRASES ● If one thing increases or decreases **in proportion to** another thing, it increases or decreases to the same degree as that thing. *The pressure in the cylinders would go up in proportion to the boiler pressure.* ● If something is small or large **in proportion to** something else, it is small or large when you compare it with that thing. *Children tend to have relatively larger heads than adults in proportion to the rest of their body.* ● If you get something **out of proportion**, you think it is more important or worrying than it really is. If you keep something **in proportion**, you have a realistic view of how important it is.

proportional /prəˈpɔːʃənəl/. ADJ If one amount is **proportional to** another, the two amounts increase and decrease at the same rate so there is always the same relationship between them.

Loss of weight is directly proportional to the rate at which the disease is progressing.

proportionate /prə'pɔ:ʃənət/. ADJ **Proportionate** means the same as **proportional**. ♦ **proportionately** ADV *Proportionately more Americans get married nowadays than before.*

proposal /prə'pəʊzəl/ **proposals.** [1] N-C A **proposal** is a suggestion or plan, often a formal or written one. *...the government's proposals to abolish free health care.* [2] N-C A **proposal** is the act of asking someone to marry you.

propose /prə'pəʊz/ **proposes, proposing, proposed.** [1] VERB If you **propose** a plan or idea, you suggest it. *Britain was about to propose changes to European Community institutions.* [2] VERB If you **propose** to do something, you intend to do it. *It's still far from clear what action the government proposes to take... And where do you propose building such a huge thing?* [3] VERB If you **propose** to someone, you ask them to marry you.

proposition /,prɒpə'zɪʃən/ **propositions.** [1] N-C If you describe something such as a task or an activity as, for example, a difficult **proposition** or an attractive **proposition**, you mean that it is difficult or pleasant to do. *Making easy money has always been an attractive proposition.* [2] N-C A **proposition** is a statement or an idea which people can consider or discuss to decide whether it is true; FORMAL. [3] N-C A **proposition** is an offer or suggestion. *You came to see me at my office the other day with a business proposition.*

proprietary /prə'praɪətri, AM -teri/. ADJ BEFORE N **Proprietary** substances are ones sold under a trade name; FORMAL. *...some proprietary brands of dog food.*

proprietor /prə'praɪətə/ **proprietors.** N-C The **proprietor** of a hotel, shop, newspaper, or other business is the person who owns it.

prosaic /prəʊ'zeɪk/. ADJ Something that is **prosaic** is dull and lacks interest. *The truth is more prosaic.*

prose /prəʊz/. N-U **Prose** is ordinary written language, in contrast to poetry. *He writes in prose.*

prosecute /'prɒsɪkju:t/ **prosecutes, prosecuting, prosecuted.** VERB If someone **is prosecuted**, they are charged with a crime and put on trial. *The police have decided not to prosecute.* ♦ **prosecution, prosecutions** N-VAR *The head of government called for the prosecution of those responsible.*

prosecution /,prɒsɪ'kju:ʃən/. N-SING The lawyers who try to prove that a person on trial is guilty are called **the prosecution**. *Colonel Pugh, for the prosecution, said that the offences occurred over a six-year period.*

prosecutor /'prɒsɪkju:tə/ **prosecutors.** N-C In some countries, a **prosecutor** is a lawyer or official who brings charges against alleged criminals or tries to prove in a trial that they are guilty.

prospect, prospects, prospecting, prospected. [1] N-VAR /'prɒspekt/ A **prospect** is a possibility or a possible event. *There is little prospect of seeing these big questions answered... They now face the prospect of having to wear a cycling helmet by law.* [2] N-PL Someone's **prospects** are their chances of be-

ing successful. *I chose to work abroad to improve my career prospects.* [3] VERB /prə'spekt, AM 'prɑ:spekt/ To **prospect** for a substance such as oil or gold means to look for it in the ground or under the sea. *The oil companies are already prospecting not far from here.*

prospective /prə'spektɪv, AM prɑ:-/. ADJ BEFORE N You use **prospective** to describe a person who wants to be the thing mentioned or is likely to be the thing mentioned. *The story should act as a warning to other prospective buyers.*

prospectus /prə'spektəs, AM prɑ:-/ **prospectuses.** N-C A **prospectus** is a document produced by a college, school, or company which gives details about it.

prosper /'prɒspə/ **prospers, prospering, prospered.** VERB If people or businesses **prosper**, they are financially successful.

prosperity /prɒ'sperɪti/. N-U **Prosperity** is a condition in which a person or community is being financially successful. *...a new era of peace and prosperity.*

prosperous /'prɒspərəs/. ADJ **Prosperous** people or places are rich and successful.

prostitute /'prɒstɪtju:t, AM -tu:t/ **prostitutes.** N-C A **prostitute** is a person, usually a woman, who has sex with men in exchange for money.

prostitution /,prɒstɪ'tju:ʃən, AM -'tu:-/. N-U **Prostitution** involves having sex in exchange for money.

protagonist /prə'tægənɪst, AM prəʊ-/ **protagonists.** [1] N-C A **protagonist** in a play, novel, or real event is one of the main people in it; FORMAL. *...the leading protagonists in the Gulf crisis.* [2] N-C A **protagonist of** an idea or movement is a supporter of it.

protect /prə'tekt/ **protects, protecting, protected.** VERB To **protect** someone or something means to prevent them from being harmed or damaged. *What can women do to protect themselves from heart disease?... The government is committed to protecting the interests of tenants.* ♦ **protector, protectors** N-C *The best protector of women in childbirth is a trained midwife.*

protection /prə'tekʃən/. N-U If something gives **protection** against something unpleasant, it prevents people or things from being harmed or damaged by it. *Such a diet is widely believed to offer protection against a number of cancers.*

protective /prə'tektɪv/. [1] ADJ **Protective** means designed or intended to protect something or someone from harm. *She had to wear protective gloves.* [2] ADJ If someone is **protective** towards you, they show a strong desire to keep you safe. *Glynis was beside her, putting a protective arm around her shoulders.*

protégé /'prɒtɪʒeɪ, AM 'prəʊt-/ **protégés;** also spelled **protégée** when referring to a woman. N-C The **protégé** of an older and more experienced person is a young person who is helped and guided by them over a period of time.

protein /'prəʊti:n/ **proteins.** N-VAR **Protein** is a substance which the body needs and which is found in meat, eggs, and milk. *...a high protein diet.*

protest, protests, protesting, protested.
[1] VERB /prə'test/ To **protest** means to say or show publicly that you object to something. In British English, you **protest about** something or **against** something. In American English, you **protest** something. *Groups of women took to the streets to protest against the arrests... They were protesting soaring prices.*
♦ **protester, protesters** N-C *...anti-abortion protesters.* [2] VERB If you **protest** that something is the case, you insist that it is the case, when other people think that it may not be. *She protested that she was a patriot, not a collaborator... 'I never said any of that to her,' he protested... He has always protested his innocence.*
[3] N-VAR /'prəʊtest/ A **protest** is the act of saying or showing publicly that you do not approve of something. *...a protest against the company's tests on live animals... Councillors walked out of the meeting in protest.*

Protestant /'prɒtɪstənt/ **Protestants.** N-C A **Protestant** is someone who belongs to the branch of the Christian church which separated from the Catholic church in the sixteenth century.

protocol /'prəʊtəkɒl, AM -kɔːl/ **protocols.** N-VAR **Protocol** is a system of rules or agreements about the correct way to act in formal situations. *...minor breaches of protocol.*

prototype /'prəʊtətaɪp/ **prototypes.** N-C A **prototype** is the first model or example of a new type of thing. *Dave set about obtaining a patent for his invention and building a prototype.*

protracted /prə'træktɪd, AM prəʊ-/. ADJ Something that is **protracted** lasts longer than usual or longer than you had hoped. *After protracted negotiations Ogden got the deal he wanted.*

protrude /prə'truːd, AM prəʊ-/ **protrudes, protruding, protruded.** VERB If something **protrudes** from somewhere, it sticks out; FORMAL. *...a huge round mass of smooth rock protruding from the water.*

proud /praʊd/ **prouder, proudest.** [1] ADJ If you feel **proud**, you feel pleasure and satisfaction at something that you own, have done, or are connected with. *I felt proud of his efforts... They are proud 'hat she is doing well at school. ...the proud father of a 5-month-old baby son.*
♦ **proudly** ADV *'That's the first part finished,' he said proudly.* [2] ADJ Someone who is **proud** has a lot of dignity and self-respect. *He was too proud to ask his family for help.* [3] ADJ Someone who is **proud** feels that they are better or more important than other people.

prove /pruːv/ **proves, proving, proved** or **proven.** [1] LINK-VERB If something **proves** to be true or to have a particular quality, it becomes clear after a period of time that it is true or has that quality. *Our reports proved to be true... This process of transition has often proven difficult. ...an experiment which was to prove a source of inspiration.* [2] VERB If you **prove** that something is true, you show by means of argument or evidence that it is definitely true. *Professor Cantor set out to prove his theory. ...trying to prove how groups of animals have evolved... That made me determined to prove him wrong.* [3] VERB If you **prove** yourself,

you show by your actions that you have a certain good quality. *I have to prove myself as a respectable, balanced person.*

proverbial /prə'vɜːbiəl/. ADJ BEFORE N You use **proverbial** to show that you know the way you are describing something is one that is often used or is part of a popular saying. *My audience certainly isn't the proverbial man in the street.*

provide /prə'vaɪd/ **provides, providing, provided.** [1] VERB If you **provide** something that someone needs or wants, you give it to them or make it available to them. *They would not provide any details... The government was not in a position to provide them with food.* [2] VERB If a law or agreement **provides** that something will happen, it states that it will happen; FORMAL. *The treaty provides that, by the end of the century, the United States must have removed its bases.*

▶ **provide for.** [1] PHR-VERB If you **provide for** someone, you support them financially and make sure that they have the things that they need. *Elaine wouldn't let him provide for her... Her father always ensured she was well provided for.* [2] PHR-VERB If you **provide for** something that might happen or that might need to be done, you make arrangements to deal with it; FORMAL. *James had provided for just such an emergency.*

provided /prə'vaɪdɪd/. CONJ If something will happen **provided** or **providing** that something else happens, the first thing will happen only if the second thing also happens. *Provided they are fit I see no reason why they shouldn't go on playing.*

providence /'prɒvɪdəns/. N-U **Providence** is God, or a force which is believed to arrange the things that happen to us; LITERARY.

providing /prə'vaɪdɪŋ/. See **provided.**

province /'prɒvɪns/ **provinces.** [1] N-C A **province** is a large section of a country which has its own administration. [2] N-PL **The provinces** are all the parts of a country except the part where the capital is situated. *The government plans to transfer some 30,000 government jobs from Paris to the provinces.*

provincial /prə'vɪnʃəl/. [1] ADJ BEFORE N **Provincial** means connected with the parts of a country outside the capital. *...provincial towns.* [2] ADJ If you describe someone or something as **provincial**, you disapprove of them because you think that they are not sophisticated. *The audience was dull and very provincial.*

provision /prə'vɪʒən/ **provisions.** [1] N-U The **provision** of something is the act of giving it or making it available to people who need or want it. *The department is responsible for the provision of residential care services.* [2] N-U If you make **provision** for a future need, you make arrangements to ensure that it is dealt with. *Mr King asked if it had ever occurred to her to make provision for her own pension.* [3] N-C A **provision** in an agreement or law is an arrangement included in it. [4] N-PL **Provisions** are supplies of food.

provisional /prə'vɪʒənəl/. ADJ You use **provisional** to describe something that has been arranged or appointed for the present, but may be changed soon. ...*a provisional coalition government.* ♦**provisionally** ADV *The European Community has provisionally agreed.*

provocation /ˌprɒvəˈkeɪʃən/ **provocations.** N-VAR **Provocation** is a deliberate attempt to make someone react angrily. *The soldiers fired without provocation.*

provocative /prəˈvɒkətɪv/ 1 ADJ Something that is **provocative** is intended to make people react angrily. ...*outspoken and sometimes provocative speeches.* 2 ADJ **Provocative** behaviour or dress is intended to make someone feel sexual desire.

provoke /prəˈvəʊk/ **provokes, provoking, provoked.** 1 VERB If you **provoke** someone, you deliberately annoy them and try to make them behave aggressively. *I provoked him into doing something really stupid.* 2 VERB If something **provokes** a violent or unpleasant reaction, it causes it. *The destruction of the mosque has provoked anger throughout the Muslim world.*

prowess /ˈpraʊɪs/. N-U Someone's **prowess** is their great ability at doing a particular thing; FORMAL. ...*his prowess as a cricketer.*

prowl /praʊl/ **prowls, prowling, prowled.** VERB When animals or people **prowl** around, they move around quietly, for example when they are hunting. *He prowled around the room, not sure what he was looking for.*

proximity /prɒkˈsɪmɪti/. N-U **Proximity** to a place or person is the fact of being near to them; FORMAL. *Families are no longer in close proximity to each other.*

proxy /ˈprɒksi/ **proxies.** N-VAR A **proxy** is a person or thing that is acting or being used in the place of someone or something else. If you do something **by proxy**, you arrange for someone else to do it for you. *Those not attending the meeting may vote by proxy.*

prude /pruːd/ **prudes.** N-C If you call someone a **prude**, you disapprove of them because you think that they are too easily shocked and embarrassed by nudity or sex.

prudent /ˈpruːdənt/. ADJ Someone who is **prudent** is sensible and careful. *It is always prudent to start any exercise programme gradually.* ♦**prudently** ADV *Prudently, Joanna spoke none of this aloud.* ♦**prudence** N-U *A lack of prudence may lead to financial problems.*

prune /pruːn/ **prunes, pruning, pruned.** 1 N-C A **prune** is a dried plum. 2 VERB When you **prune** a tree or bush, you cut off some of the branches so that it will grow better the next year.

pry /praɪ/ **pries, prying, pried.** 1 VERB If you say that someone is **prying**, you disapprove of them because they are trying to find out about someone else's private affairs. *We do not want people prying into our affairs.* 2 VERB If you **pry** something **open** or **pry** it away from a surface, you force it open or away from a surface. *She pried open his jaws... I pried the top off a can of chilli.*

PS /ˌpiː ˈes/. You write **PS** before a comment you add at the end of a letter, after you have signed it. *PS. Please show your friends this letter.*

pseudonym /ˈsjuːdənɪm, AM ˈsuː-/ **pseudonyms.** N-C A **pseudonym** is a name which someone, usually a writer, uses instead of his or her real name.

psyche /ˈsaɪki/ **psyches.** N-C Your **psyche** is your mind and your deepest feelings and attitudes. ...*disturbing elements of the human psyche.*

psychedelic /ˌsaɪkəˈdelɪk/. ADJ **Psychedelic** art has bright colours and strange patterns.

psychiatry /saɪˈkaɪətri, AM sɪ-/. N-U **Psychiatry** is the branch of medicine concerned with the treatment of mental illness. ♦**psychiatric** /ˌsaɪkiˈætrɪk/ ADJ ...*chronic psychiatric illnesses.* ♦**psychiatrist** /saɪˈkaɪətrɪst, AM sɪ-/ **psychiatrists** N-C *A colleague urged him to see a psychiatrist.*

psychic /ˈsaɪkɪk/. 1 N-C & ADJ If you believe that someone is a **psychic**, or is **psychic**, you believe that they have strange mental powers, such as being able to read the minds of other people or to see into the future. 2 ADJ **Psychic** means relating to the mind rather than the body; FORMAL. ...*psychic powers.*

psychoanalysis /ˌsaɪkəʊəˈnælɪsɪs/. N-U **Psychoanalysis** is the treatment of someone who has mental problems by asking them about their feelings and their past in order to discover what may be causing their condition. ♦**psychoanalyst** /ˌsaɪkəʊˈænəlɪst/ **psychoanalysts** N-C *Jane is seeing a psychoanalyst.*

psychological /ˌsaɪkəˈlɒdʒɪkəl/. ADJ **Psychological** means concerned with a person's mind and thoughts. *Robyn's loss of memory is a psychological problem.* ♦**psychologically** ADV *It was very important psychologically for us to succeed.*

psychology /saɪˈkɒlədʒi/. 1 N-U **Psychology** is the scientific study of the human mind and the reasons for people's behaviour. ♦**psychological** /ˌsaɪkəˈlɒdʒɪkəl/ ADJ ...*psychological testing.* ♦**psychologist, psychologists** N-C *She was referred to a psychologist.* 2 N-U The **psychology** of a person is the kind of mind that they have, which makes them think or behave in the way that they do. ...*the psychology of murderers.*

psychopath /ˈsaɪkəʊpæθ/ **psychopaths.** N-C A **psychopath** is someone who has serious mental problems and who may act in a violent way without feeling sorry for what they have done.

psychosis /saɪˈkəʊsɪs/ **psychoses.** N-VAR **Psychosis** is severe mental illness which can make people lose contact with reality; MEDICAL.

psychotherapy /ˌsaɪkəʊˈθerəpi/. N-U **Psychotherapy** is the use of psychological methods to treat people who are mentally ill. ♦**psychotherapist, psychotherapists** N-C *He arranged for him to see a psychotherapist.*

psychotic /saɪˈkɒtɪk/. N-C & ADJ A **psychotic** or someone who is **psychotic** has a severe mental illness which has made them lose contact with reality; MEDICAL.

pub /pʌb/ **pubs.** N-C In Britain, a **pub** is a building where people can buy and drink alcoholic drinks. ● See note at **café**.

puberty /ˈpjuːbəti/. N-U **Puberty** is the stage in someone's life when their body starts to become physically mature.

public /ˈpʌblɪk/. [1] N-SING You can refer to people in general as **the public**. **Public** can take the singular or plural form of the verb. *The public is certainly getting tired of hearing about it... The public have flocked to the show.* [2] ADJ BEFORE N **Public** means relating to all the people in a country or community. *The Turkish government is under pressure from public opinion.* [3] ADJ BEFORE N **Public** statements, actions, and events are made or done in such a way that everyone can see them or be aware of them. *...the ministry's first detailed public statement on the subject... Marilyn made her last public appearance at Madison Square Garden.* ♦ **publicly** ADV *He never spoke publicly about the affair.* [4] ADJ BEFORE N A **public** figure or a person in **public** life is known about by many people because they serve the public in their job. *Mr Mandela is by far the most popular public figure in South Africa.* [5] ADJ AFTER LINK-V If a fact is **made public** or **becomes public**, it becomes known to everyone rather than being kept secret. [6] ADJ BEFORE N **Public** means relating to the government or state, or things that are done by the state for the people. *The social services account for a substantial part of public spending.* [7] ADJ BEFORE N **Public** things and places are provided for everyone to use, or are open to anyone. *...the New York Public Library. ...public transport. ...public areas of international airports.*

PHRASES ● If someone is in **the public eye**, many people know who they are, because they are famous or because they are often mentioned on television or in the newspapers. *He has kept his wife and daughter out of the public eye.* ● If you say or do something in **public**, you say or do it when a group of other people are present. *By-laws are to make it illegal to smoke in public.*

publication /ˌpʌblɪˈkeɪʃən/. **publications**. [1] N-U The **publication** of a book or magazine is the act of printing it and making it available. *The final volume is due for publication in October.* [2] N-C A **publication** is a book, magazine, or article that has been published.

publicist /ˈpʌblɪsɪst/. **publicists**. N-C A **publicist** is a person who publicizes things, especially as part of a job in advertising or journalism.

publicity /pʌˈblɪsɪti/. [1] N-U **Publicity** is advertising, information, or actions intended to attract the public's attention to someone or something. *The publicity blitz uses stickers with bright red lettering.* [2] N-U When newspapers and television pay a lot of attention to something, you can say that it is receiving **publicity**. *Football now seems to be getting massive publicity.*

publicize (BR also **publicise**) /ˈpʌblɪsaɪz/. **publicizes, publicizing, publicized**. VERB If you **publicize** a fact or event, you make it widely known to the public. *The author appeared on television to publicize her latest book.*

,public re'lations. [1] N-U **Public relations** is the part of an organization's work that is concerned with obtaining the public's approval for what it does. The abbreviation 'PR' is also used. *The chairman's statement is merely a public relations exercise.* [2] N-PL **Public relations** are the state of the relationship between an organization and the public. *His behaviour was not good for public relations.*

,public 'school, public schools. [1] N-VAR In Britain, a **public school** is a private school that provides secondary education which parents have to pay for. [2] N-VAR In the USA, Australia, and some other countries, a **public school** is a school that is supported financially by the government and usually provides free education.

,public 'sector. N-SING The **public sector** is the part of a country's economy which is controlled or supported financially by the government.

publish /ˈpʌblɪʃ/. **publishes, publishing, published**. [1] VERB When a company **publishes** a book or magazine, it prints copies of it, which are sent to shops and sold. [2] VERB When the people in charge of a newspaper or magazine **publish** a piece of writing or a photograph, they print it in their newspaper or magazine. *The magazine published an article satirising the government.* [3] VERB If someone **publishes** a book or an article that they have written, they arrange to have it published. *He has published two collections of poetry.*

publisher /ˈpʌblɪʃə/. **publishers**. N-C A **publisher** is a person or company that publishes books, newspapers, or magazines.

publishing /ˈpʌblɪʃɪŋ/. N-U **Publishing** is the business of publishing books.

'publishing house, publishing houses. N-C A **publishing house** is a company which publishes books.

pudding /ˈpʊdɪŋ/. **puddings**. [1] N-VAR A **pudding** is a cooked sweet food made with flour, fat, and eggs, and usually served hot. [2] N-U Some people refer to the sweet course of a meal as the **pudding**; BRITISH. *What's for pudding?*

puddle /ˈpʌdəl/. **puddles**. N-C A **puddle** is a small shallow pool of rain or other liquid on the ground.

puff /pʌf/. **puffs, puffing, puffed**. [1] VERB & N-C If someone **puffs** at a cigarette, cigar, or pipe, or if they take a **puff** of it, they smoke it. *He nodded and puffed on a stubby pipe as he listened... She was taking quick puffs at her cigarette.* [2] VERB If you **are puffing**, you are breathing loudly and quickly with your mouth open because you are out of breath after a lot of physical effort. [3] N-C A **puff** of air or smoke is a small amount of it that is blown out from somewhere.

pull /pʊl/. **pulls, pulling, pulled**. [1] VERB & N-C When you **pull** something, you hold it firmly and move it towards you or away from its previous position. A **pull** is an instance of pulling. *I helped pull him out of the water... Pull as hard as you can... The feather must be removed with a straight, firm pull.* [2] VERB When a vehicle, animal, or person **pulls** a cart or piece of machinery, they are attached to it or hold it, so that it moves along behind them when they move forward. *...a freight train pulling wagons.*

3 VERB If you **pull** a part of your body in a particular direction, you move it with effort or force in that direction. *He pulled his arms out of the sleeves... She tried to pull her hand free.* **4** VERB If you **pull** a muscle, you injure it by straining it. **5** N-C A **pull** is a strong physical force which causes things to move in a particular direction. *...the pull of gravity.*

▶ **pull away.** **1** PHR-VERB When a vehicle or driver **pulls away**, the vehicle starts moving forward. **2** PHR-VERB If you **pull away** from someone that you have had close links with, you deliberately become less close to them. *The Soviet Union began pulling away from Cuba.*

▶ **pull back.** PHR-VERB If someone **pulls back** from an action, they decide not to continue or persist with it, because it could have bad consequences. *...unsold homes causing builders to pull back on new construction.*

▶ **pull down.** PHR-VERB To **pull down** a building or statue means to deliberately destroy it.

▶ **pull in.** PHR-VERB When a vehicle or driver **pulls in** somewhere, the vehicle stops there. *He pulled in at the side of the road.*

▶ **pull into.** PHR-VERB When a vehicle or driver **pulls into** a road or driveway, the vehicle makes a turn into the road or driveway and stops there.

▶ **pull off.** PHR-VERB If you **pull off** something very difficult, you manage to achieve it successfully. *It will be a very, very fine piece of mountaineering if they pull it off.*

▶ **pull out.** **1** PHR-VERB When a vehicle or driver **pulls out**, the vehicle moves out into the road or nearer the centre of the road. *She pulled out into the street.* **2** PHR-VERB If you **pull out of** an agreement, a contest, or an organization, you withdraw from it. **3** PHR-VERB If troops **pull out** of a place, they leave it.

▶ **pull over.** PHR-VERB When a vehicle or driver **pulls over**, the vehicle moves closer to the side of the road and stops there.

▶ **pull through.** PHR-VERB If someone with a serious illness or in a very difficult situation **pulls through**, they recover.

▶ **pull together.** **1** PHR-VERB If people **pull together**, they co-operate with each other. *The nation was urged to pull together to avoid a slide into complete chaos.* **2** PHR-VERB If you are upset or depressed and someone tells you to **pull** yourself **together**, they are telling you in a rather unsympathetic way to control your feelings and behave calmly.

▶ **pull up.** PHR-VERB When a vehicle or driver **pulls up**, the vehicle slows down and stops.

pullover /ˈpʊləʊvə/ **pullovers.** N-C A **pullover** is a woollen piece of clothing that covers the upper part of your body and your arms; BRITISH.

pulp /pʌlp/. **1** N-SING If an object is pressed into a **pulp**, it is crushed or beaten until it is soft, smooth, and wet. **2** N-SING In fruit and vegetables, **the pulp** is the soft inner part.

pulpit /ˈpʊlpɪt/ **pulpits.** N-C A **pulpit** is a small raised platform in a church with a rail around it, where a member of the clergy stands to preach.

pulsate /pʌlˈseɪt, AM ˈpʌlseɪt/ **pulsates, pulsating, pulsated.** VERB If something **pulsates**,

it moves in and out or shakes with strong regular movements. *...a pulsating blood vessel.*

pulse /pʌls/ **pulses, pulsing, pulsed.** **1** N-C Your **pulse** is the regular beating of blood through your body, which you can feel, for example, at your wrist or neck. *Mahoney's pulse was racing, and he felt confused.* **2** PHRASE When someone **takes** your **pulse** or **feels** your **pulse**, they find out the speed of your heartbeat by feeling the pulse in your wrist. **3** N-C A **pulse** of electrical current, light, or sound is a sharp temporary increase in its level. **4** N-PL Some large dried seeds which can be cooked and eaten are called **pulses**, for example the seeds of peas, beans, and lentils.

pump /pʌmp/ **pumps, pumping, pumped.** **1** N-C A **pump** is a machine that is used to force a liquid or gas to flow in strong regular movements in a particular direction. *...a petrol pump.* **2** VERB To **pump** a liquid or gas in a certain direction means to force it to flow in that direction, using a pump. *Pumping out the air is a laborious process.* **3** N-C A **pump** is a device for bringing water to the surface from below the ground. **4** VERB To **pump** water, oil, or gas means to get a supply of it from below the surface of the ground, using a pump. *The Russians have pumped huge amounts of oil... The water will be pumped up from chalk pits.* **5** N-C A **pump** is a device that you use to force air into something, for example a tyre. *...a bicycle pump.* **6** VERB If someone has their stomach **pumped**, doctors use a special pump to empty the contents of their stomach. **7** VERB If you **pump** money **into** a project or an industry, you invest a lot of money in it; INFORMAL. **8** N-C **Pumps** are canvas shoes with flat rubber soles which people wear for sports and leisure. *There was a pair of pumps by the bed.*

▶ **pump out.** PHR-VERB To **pump out** something means to produce or supply it continually and in large amounts. *Japanese companies have been pumping out plenty of innovative products.*

▶ **pump up.** PHR-VERB If you **pump up** something such as a tyre, you fill it with air, using a pump.

pumpkin /ˈpʌmpkɪn/ **pumpkins.** N-VAR A **pumpkin** is a large, round, orange-coloured vegetable with a thick skin.

pun /pʌn/ **puns.** N-C A **pun** is a clever and amusing use of a word with more than one meaning, or a word that sounds like another word, so that what you say has two different meanings.

punch /pʌntʃ/ **punches, punching, punched.** **1** VERB & N-C If you **punch** someone or something, or if you throw a **punch** at them, you hit them hard with your fist. *If anyone tried to stop me I'd punch him on the nose.* **2** VERB If you **punch** something such as the buttons on a keyboard, you touch them in order to store information on a machine such as a computer or to give the machine a command to do something. **3** VERB If you **punch holes** in something, you make holes in it by pushing or pressing it with something sharp. **4** N-C A **punch** is a tool used for making holes in something. **5** PHRASE If you say that someone does not **pull** their **punches** when they are criticizing someone or something, you mean that they say exactly what they think and do not moderate their criticism. [6] N-VAR **Punch** is a drink usually made from wine or spirits mixed with sugar, fruit, and spices.

▶ **punch in.** PHR-VERB If you **punch in** a number on a machine or **punch** numbers **into** it, you push the machine's numerical keys in order to give it a command to do something. *All you need to do is punch in a short code.*

punctual /'pʌŋktʃuəl/. ADJ Someone who is **punctual** arrives somewhere at the expected time at the right time and is not late. *He's always very punctual.* ♦ **punctually** ADV *My guest arrived punctually.*

punctuate /'pʌŋktʃueɪt/ **punctuates, punctuating, punctuated.** VERB If an activity or situation **is punctuated** by particular things, it is interrupted by them at intervals; FORMAL. *The silence of the night was punctuated by the distant rumble of traffic.*

punctuation /ˌpʌŋktʃu'eɪʃən/. N-U **Punctuation** is the system of signs such as full stops, commas, and question marks that you use in writing to divide words into sentences and clauses.

ˌpunctu'ation mark, punctuation marks. N-C A **punctuation mark** is a sign such as a full stop, comma, or question mark.

puncture /'pʌŋktʃə/ **punctures, puncturing, punctured.** [1] N-C A **puncture** is a small hole in a car or bicycle tyre that has been made by a sharp object. [2] VERB If a sharp object **punctures** something, it makes a hole in it. *A bullet punctured one of the front tyres.*

pundit /'pʌndɪt/ **pundits.** N-C A **pundit** is a person who knows a lot about a subject and is often asked to give information or their opinion about it to the public.

pungent /'pʌndʒənt/. ADJ Something that is **pungent** has a strong bitter smell or taste. *...the pungent smell of smoked fish.*

punish /'pʌnɪʃ/ **punishes, punishing, punished.** [1] VERB To **punish** someone means to make them suffer in some way because they have done something wrong. *I don't believe that George ever had to punish the children.* [2] VERB To **punish** a crime means to punish anyone who commits that crime. *Such behaviour is unacceptable and will be punished.*

punishing /'pʌnɪʃɪŋ/. ADJ A **punishing** schedule, activity, or experience requires a lot of physical effort and makes you very tired or weak.

punishment /'pʌnɪʃmənt/ **punishments.** [1] N-U **Punishment** is the act of punishing someone or being punished. *The man is guilty and he deserves punishment.* [2] N-VAR A **punishment** is a particular way of punishing someone. *The usual punishment is a fine.* [3] See also **capital punishment, corporal punishment.**

punitive /'pju:nɪtɪv/. ADJ **Punitive** actions are intended to punish people; FORMAL. *...punitive measures such as curfews and fines.*

punk /pʌŋk/ **punks.** [1] N-U **Punk** or punk rock is rock music that is played in a fast, loud, and aggressive way. Punk rock was particularly popular in the late 1970s. [2] N-C A **punk** or a

punk rocker is a person who likes punk music and dresses in a very noticeable and unconventional way. [3] N-C A **punk** is a young person who behaves in an unruly, aggressive, or antisocial manner; AMERICAN, INFORMAL.

punter /'pʌntə/ **punters.** [1] N-C A **punter** is a person who bets money; BRITISH, INFORMAL. [2] N-C People sometimes refer to their customers or clients as **punters**; BRITISH, INFORMAL.

pup /pʌp/ **pups.** N-C A **pup** is a young dog. The young of some other animals, for example seals, are called **pups.**

pupil /'pju:pɪl/ **pupils.** [1] N-C The **pupils** of a school are the children who go to it. [2] N-C A **pupil** of a painter, musician, or other expert is someone who studies with that expert, learning his or her skills. [3] N-C The **pupils** of your eyes are the small, round, black holes in the centre of them.

puppet /'pʌpɪt/ **puppets.** [1] N-C A **puppet** is a doll that you can move, either by pulling strings which are attached to it, or by putting your hand inside its body and moving your fingers. [2] N-C You can refer to a person or country as a **puppet** when you mean their actions are controlled by a more powerful person or government, even though they may appear to be independent. *...a puppet government.*

puppy /'pʌpi/ **puppies.** N-C A **puppy** is a young dog.

purchase /'pɜ:tʃɪs/ **purchases, purchasing, purchased.** [1] VERB When you **purchase** something, you buy it; FORMAL. ♦ **purchaser** N-C *The group is the second largest purchaser of fresh fruit in the US.* [2] N-U The **purchase** of something is the act of buying it; FORMAL. *This week he is to visit China to discuss the purchase of military supplies.* [3] N-C A **purchase** is something that you buy; FORMAL. *She opened the box and looked at her purchase.*

pure /pjʊə/ **purer, purest.** [1] ADJ **Pure** means not mixed with anything else. *This dress is pure silk... His hair was pure white.* ♦ **purity** /'pjʊərɪti/ N-U *...their obsession with ideological purity.* [2] ADJ Something that is **pure** is clean and does not contain any harmful substances. *...demands for purer and cleaner river water.* ♦ **purity** N-U *They worried about the purity of tap water.* [3] ADJ If you describe someone as **pure**, you mean that they are free from things that are considered to be sinful or bad, especially sex; LITERARY. ♦ **purity** N-U *...sexual purity.* [4] ADJ BEFORE N **Pure** science or **pure** research is concerned only with theory and not with how this theory can be used in practical ways. *...pure maths.* [5] ADJ BEFORE N **Pure** means complete and total. *This was pure coincidence. ...a look of pure surprise.*

puree /'pjʊəreɪ, AM pjuˈreɪ/ **purees.** N-VAR **Puree** is food which has been mashed, sieved, or blended so that it forms a thick, smooth sauce. *...a can of tomato puree.*

purely /'pjʊəli/. ADV You use **purely** to emphasize that the thing you are mentioning is the most important feature or that it is the only thing which should be considered. *It is a racing machine, designed purely for speed.*

purge /pɜːdʒ/ **purges, purging, purged.**
[1] VERB & N-C To **purge** an organization of its
unacceptable members, or to make a **purge** of
an organization, means to remove its unacceptable members from it. You can also talk about
purging people from an organization. *He recently purged the armed forces, sending hundreds of officers into retirement... Purges began
soon after the election.* [2] VERB If you **purge**
something of undesirable things, you get rid of
them. *He closed his eyes and lay still, trying to
purge his mind of anxiety.*

purify /ˈpjʊərɪfaɪ/ **purifies, purifying, puri-
fied.** VERB To **purify** a substance means to
make it pure by removing any harmful, dirty,
or inferior substances from it. ◆**purification**
N-U *...a water purification plant.*

purist /ˈpjʊərɪst/ **purists.** N-C A **purist** is someone who believes in absolute correctness, especially concerning a particular subject which
they know a lot about.

puritan /ˈpjʊərɪtən/ **puritans.** N-C & ADJ You describe someone as a **puritan**, or you describe
their behaviour as **puritan**, when they live according to very strict moral or religious principles, especially by avoiding physical pleasures;
used showing disapproval.

puritanical /ˌpjʊərɪˈtænɪkəl/. ADJ If you describe someone as **puritanical**, you mean that
they disapprove of pleasure, for example because they are strictly religious; used showing
disapproval. *...a puritanical attitude towards
sex.*

purple /ˈpɜːpəl/. ADJ Something that is **purple** is
of a reddish-blue colour.

purport /pəˈpɔːt/ **purports, purporting, pur-
ported.** VERB If someone or something **purports** to do or be a particular thing, they claim
to do or be that thing; FORMAL. *...a book that
purports to tell the whole truth.*

purpose /ˈpɜːpəs/ **purposes.** [1] N-C The **purpose** of something is the reason for which it is
made or done. *What is the purpose of your visit? ...the use of nuclear energy for military purposes.* [2] N-C Your **purpose** is the thing that
you want to achieve. *I don't know exactly what
their purpose is.* [3] N-U **Purpose** is the feeling of
having a definite aim and of being determined
to achieve it. *The teachers are enthusiastic and
have a sense of purpose.*
PHRASES ● You use **for all practical purposes**
or **to all intents and purposes** to suggest that a
situation is not exactly as you describe it, but
the effect is the same as if it were. *To all intents
and purposes he was my father.* ● If you do
something **on purpose**, you do it deliberately.
*Was it an accident or did David really do it on
purpose?*

purpose-'built. ADJ A **purpose-built** building
has been specially designed and built for a
particular use.

purposeful /ˈpɜːpəsfʊl/. ADJ If someone is **purposeful**, they show that they have a definite
aim and a strong desire to achieve it. *She had a
purposeful air.* ◆**purposefully** ADV *He strode
purposefully towards the barn.*

purr /pɜː/ **purrs, purring, purred.** [1] VERB
When a cat **purrs**, it makes a low vibrating
sound with its throat. [2] VERB & N-C When an

engine or machine **purrs**, it makes a quiet,
continuous, vibrating sound, called a **purr**.
*Both boats purred out of the cave mouth and
into open water.*

purse /pɜːs/ **purses, pursing, pursed.** [1] N-C
In British English, a **purse** is a very small bag
that people, especially women, keep their
money in. The usual American term is **change
purse.** [2] N-C In American English, a **purse** is a
small bag that women carry. The usual British
word is **handbag.** [3] VERB If you **purse your
lips**, you move them into a small rounded
shape.

pursue /pəˈsjuː, -ˈsuː/ **pursues, pursuing,
pursued.** [1] VERB If you **pursue** a particular
aim or result, you make efforts to achieve it or
to progress in it; FORMAL. *She had come to England to pursue an acting career.* [2] VERB If you
pursue a particular topic, you try to find out
more about it by asking questions; FORMAL. *If
your original request is denied, don't be afraid
to pursue the matter.* [3] VERB If you **pursue** a
person, vehicle, or animal, you follow them,
usually in order to catch them; FORMAL.
◆**pursuer, pursuers** N-C *He could hear the pursuers getting closer.*

pursuit /pəˈsjuːt, AM -ˈsuːt/ **pursuits.** [1] N-U
Your **pursuit** of something that you want consists of your attempts at achieving it. *...the pursuit of happiness... They frequently move
around the country in pursuit of a medical career.* [2] N-U If you are **in pursuit of** a person,
vehicle, or animal, you are chasing them; FOR-
MAL. [3] N-C Your **pursuits** are your activities,
usually activities that you enjoy when you are
not working. *They both love outdoor pursuits.*

purveyor /pəˈveɪər/ **purveyors.** N-C The **purveyors** of information, goods, or services are
the people who provide them; FORMAL. *...the
leading purveyors of traditional Irish music.*

push /pʊʃ/ **pushes, pushing, pushed.**
[1] VERB When you **push** something, you use
force to make it move away from you or away
from its previous position. You can also say
that you give it a **push**. *The woman pushed
back her chair and stood up... He pushed the
door open... He gave me a sharp push.* [2] VERB
If you **push** through things that are blocking
your way or **push** your way through them, you
use force in order to move past them. *Dix
pushed forward carrying a glass... He pushed
his way towards her, laughing.* [3] VERB To **push**
a value or amount up or down means to cause
it to increase or decrease. *Interest had pushed
the loan up to $27,000.* [4] VERB & N-C If you **push**
someone to do something or **push** them **into**
doing it, you urge, encourage, or force them to
do it. A **push** is the action of pushing someone
to do something. *James did not push her into
stealing the money... We need a push to take
the first step.* [5] VERB & N-C If you **push** for
something, or if you make a **push** for it, you try
very hard to achieve it. *Keep pushing for everything that you want. ...a final push to arrive at
an agreement.* [6] VERB If someone **pushes** an
idea, a point, or a product, they try in a forceful way to convince people to accept it or buy
it. *...taking bribes from big business in return
for pushing new projects.* [7] VERB When some-

one **pushes** drugs, they sell them illegally; IN-FORMAL. ♦**pusher, pushers** N-C ...*drug pushers.*

▸ **push ahead** or **push forward**. PHR-VERB If you **push ahead** or **push forward** with something, you make progress with it. *The governor has vowed to push ahead with the airport.*

▸ **push around**. PHR-VERB If someone **pushes** you **around**, they give you orders in a rude and insulting way.

▸ **push aside**. PHR-VERB If you **push** something **aside**, you ignore it or refuse to think about it. *...pushing aside unpleasant thoughts.*

▸ **push forward**. See **push ahead**.

▸ **push in**. PHR-VERB When someone **pushes in**, they come into a queue in front of other people; used showing disapproval.

▸ **push on**. PHR-VERB When you **push on**, you continue with a journey or task. *Although the journey was a long and lonely one, Tumalo pushed on.*

▸ **push over**. PHR-VERB If you **push** someone or something **over**, you push them so that they fall onto the ground. *...people damaging hedges, uprooting trees and pushing over walls.*

▸ **push through**. PHR-VERB If someone **pushes through** a law, reform, or policy, they succeed in getting it accepted, often despite opposition. *Lord Wyatt tried to push the amendment through Parliament.*

pushchair /ˈpʊʃtʃeə/ **pushchairs**. N-C In British English, a **pushchair** is a small chair on wheels, in which a small child can sit and be wheeled around. The usual American word is **stroller**.

put /pʊt/ **puts, putting, put**. 1 VERB When you **put** something in a particular place or position, you move it into that place or position. *Leaphorn put the photograph on the desk... Mishka put down a heavy shopping bag.* 2 VERB If you **put** someone somewhere, you cause them to go there and to stay there. *I'd put the children to bed.* 3 VERB To **put** someone or something in a particular state or situation means to cause them to be in that state or situation. *This is going to put them out of business... He was putting himself at risk.* 4 VERB If you **put** your trust, faith, or confidence **in** someone or something, you trust them or have faith or confidence in them. *Are we right to put our confidence in computers?* 5 VERB If you **put** time, strength, or energy **into** an activity, you use it in doing that activity. *Eleanor did not put much energy into the discussion.* 6 VERB When you **put** an idea or remark in a particular way, you express it in that way. *The security forces might have made some mistakes, as he put it... You can't put that sort of fear into words.* 7 VERB When you **put** a question to someone, you ask them the question. *Some workers may be afraid to put questions publicly.* 8 VERB If you **put** something **at** a particular value or **in** a particular category, or **put** a particular value or category label **on** it, you estimate it to have that value or to be in that category. *I would put her age at about 50... All the more technically advanced countries put a high value on science.* 9 VERB If you **put** written information some-

where, you write, type, or print it there. *They put an announcement in the local paper.*

▸ **put across** or **put over**. PHR-VERB When you **put** something **across** or **put** it **over**, you succeed in describing or explaining it to someone. *Andrew really enjoys putting across a technical argument.*

▸ **put aside**. PHR-VERB If you **put** something **aside**, you keep it to be dealt with or used at a later time. *She took up a slice of bread, broke it nervously, then put it aside.*

▸ **put away**. 1 PHR-VERB If you **put** something **away**, you put it into the place where it is normally kept when it is not being used. *She finished putting the milk away.* 2 PHR-VERB If someone **is put away**, they are sent to prison or to a mental hospital for a long time; INFORMAL.

▸ **put back**. PHR-VERB To **put** something **back** means to delay it or postpone it. *The trip has been put back to Easter.*

▸ **put by**. PHR-VERB If you **put** money **by**, you save it so that you can use it at a later time. *There was enough put by for her fare.*

▸ **put down**. 1 PHR-VERB If you **put** something **down** somewhere, you write or type it there. *I had prepared for the meeting by putting down what I wanted from them.* 2 PHR-VERB If you **put down** some money, you pay part of the price of something as a deposit. *He bought an investment property for $100,000 and put down $20,000.* 3 PHR-VERB If soldiers, police, or the government **put down** a riot or rebellion, they stop it by using force. 4 PHR-VERB If someone **puts** you **down**, they treat you in an unpleasant way by criticizing you in front of other people or making you appear foolish; INFORMAL. 5 PHR-VERB When an animal **is put down**, it is killed because it is dangerous or very ill.

▸ **put down to**. PHR-VERB If you **put** something **down to** a particular thing, you believe that it is caused by that thing. *Sales remain constantly high. I put it down to having good staff.*

▸ **put forward**. PHR-VERB If you **put forward** a plan, proposal, or name, you suggest that it should be considered for a particular purpose or job. *Mr Ryzhkov put his name forward for the presidency.*

▸ **put in**. 1 PHR-VERB If you **put in** an amount of time or effort doing something, you spend that time or effort doing it. *We had to put in three hours work a night.* 2 PHR-VERB If you **put in** a request or **put in** for something, you make a formal request or application. *I decided to put in for a job as deputy secretary.*

▸ **put off**. 1 PHR-VERB If you **put** something **off**, you delay doing it. *...women who put off having a baby.* 2 PHR-VERB If you **put** someone **off**, you make them wait for something that they want. *I got the impression she'd like a word or two with you, sir, and I didn't put her off.* 3 PHR-VERB If someone or something **puts** you **off**, they distract you from what you are trying to do and make it more difficult for you to do it; BRITISH. *It put her off revising for her exams.*

▸ **put on**. 1 PHR-VERB When you **put on** clothing or make-up, you place it on your body in order

to wear it. *I haven't even put any lipstick on.*
● See note at **wear.** [2] PHR-VERB If you **put on** a
way of behaving, you behave in a way that is
not natural to you or that does not express
your real feelings. *It was hard to believe she
was ill, she was putting it on.* [3] PHR-VERB When
people **put on** a show, exhibition, or service,
they perform it or organize it. *We put it on and
everybody said 'Oh it's a brilliant production'.*
[4] PHR-VERB If someone **puts on** weight, they
become heavier. *Luther's on three stone.*
[5] PHR-VERB If you **put on** a piece of equipment
or a device, you make it start working. *I put the
radio on.* [6] PHR-VERB If you **put on** a record,
tape, or CD, you place it on a record, tape, or
CD player and listen to it. [7] PHR-VERB If you
put something **on,** you begin to cook or heat
it. *Put on a large pan of water to simmer.*

▶ **put out.** [1] PHR-VERB If you **put out** an announcement or story, you make it known to a
lot of people. *The French news agency put out a
statement from the Trade Minister.* [2] PHR-VERB
If you **put out** a fire, candle, or cigarette, you
make it stop burning. *He lit a half-cigarette
and almost immediately put it out again.*
[3] PHR-VERB If you **put out** an electric light, you
make it stop shining by pressing a switch.
[4] PHR-VERB If you **put out** things that will be
needed, you place them somewhere ready to
be used. *I slowly unpacked the teapot and put
it out on the table.* [5] PHR-VERB If you **put out**
your hand, you move it forward, away from
your body. *She put her hand out and tried to
touch her mother's arm.* [6] PHR-VERB If you **put**
someone **out,** you cause them trouble or inconvenience because they have to do something for you. *I've always put myself out for
others.* ● See also **put out.**

▶ **put over.** See **put across.**

▶ **put through.** [1] PHR-VERB When someone
puts through a telephone call or a caller, they
make the connection that allows the caller to
speak to the person they are phoning. *The operator will put you through.* [2] PHR-VERB If
someone **puts** you **through** an unpleasant experience, they make you experience it. *She
wouldn't want to put them through the ordeal
of a huge ceremony.*

▶ **put together.** [1] PHR-VERB If you **put** something **together,** you join its different parts to
each other so that it can be used. *He took it all
to pieces, cleaned it inside and out and put it
together again.* [2] PHR-VERB If you **put together**
a group of people or things, you form them
into a team or collection. *He is trying to put a
team together for next season.* [3] PHR-VERB If

you **put together** an agreement, plan, or product, you design and create it. *We got to work
on putting the book together.*

▶ **put up.** [1] PHR-VERB If people **put up** a wall,
building, tent, or other structure, they construct it. *They put up their tents and settled
down for the night.* [2] PHR-VERB If you **put up** a
poster or notice, you fix it to a wall or board.
They're putting up new street signs up. [3] PHR-VERB
To **put up** resistance to something means to
resist it. *He was old and very frail. He couldn't
have put up a fight.* [4] PHR-VERB If you **put up**
money for something, you provide the money
that is needed to pay for it. *The merchant
banks raise capital for industry. They don't actually put it up themselves.* [5] PHR-VERB To **put**
up the price of something means to cause it to
increase. *They know he would put their taxes
up.* [6] PHR-VERB If a person or hotel **puts** you
up, you stay at the person's home or at the hotel for one or more nights. *He put up for the
night at a small hotel.*

▶ **put up with.** PHR-VERB If you **put up with**
something, you tolerate or accept it, even
though you find it unpleasant or unsatisfactory. *You're late, Shelly; and I'll tell you, I won't
put up with it.*

putt /pʌt/ **putts, putting, putted.** VERB In golf,
when you **putt** the ball, you hit it a short distance on the green.

puzzle /ˈpʌzəl/ **puzzles, puzzling, puzzled.**
[1] VERB If something or someone **puzzles** you,
you do not understand them and find them
confusing. *...a question which has puzzled me
for years... My sister puzzles me.* ◆ **puzzled** ADJ
A puzzled look came across his face. ◆ **puzzling**
ADJ *Some of this book is rather puzzling.*
[2] VERB If you **puzzle over** something, you try
hard to think of the answer or the explanation
for it. *She puzzled over his behavior for a moment.* [3] N-C A **puzzle** is a question, game, or
toy which you have to think about carefully in
order to answer it correctly or put it together
properly. [4] N-SING You can describe a person
or thing that is hard to understand as a **puzzle.**
'Women are a puzzle,' he said.

pyjamas (AM **pajamas**) /pɪˈdʒɑːməz/; N-PL A
pair of **pyjamas** consists of loose trousers and
a loose jacket that are worn in bed.

pyramid /ˈpɪrəmɪd/ **pyramids.** N-C A **pyramid**
is a three-dimensional shape with a flat base and
flat triangular sides which slope upwards to a
point.

python /ˈpaɪθən/ **pythons.** N-C A **python** is a
type of large snake.

Q q

quadruple /ˌkwɒˈdruːpəl/ **quadruples, quad-
rupling, quadrupled.** [1] VERB If someone
quadruples an amount, or if it **quadruples,** it
becomes four times bigger. *The price has
quadrupled in the last few years.* [2] PREDET If
one amount is **quadruple** another amount, it
is four times bigger. [3] ADJ You use **quadruple**
to indicate that something happens four times
or has four parts. *...a quadruple gold medalist.*

quail /kweɪl/ **quails.** N-C A **quail** is a small bird
which is often shot and eaten. The plural is
quails or **quail.**

quaint /kweɪnt/ **quainter, quaintest.** ADJ
Something that is **quaint** is attractive because
it is unusual and rather old-fashioned. *...a
quaint little cottage.*

quake /kweɪk/ **quakes, quaking, quaked.**
[1] N-C A **quake** is the same as an **earthquake**; INFORMAL. [2] VERB If you **quake**, you tremble or shake, usually because you are afraid. *I just stood there quaking with fear.*

qualification /ˌkwɒlɪfɪˈkeɪʃən/ **qualifications.**
[1] N-C Your **qualifications** are the examinations that you have passed. *...people with good academic qualifications.* [2] N-C The **qualifications** needed for a particular activity or task are the qualities and skills that you need in order to do it. *Responsibility and reliability are necessary qualifications.* [3] N-VAR A **qualification** is something that you add to a statement to make it less strong or less generalized. *This statement requires qualification and clarification.* [4] See also **qualify**.

qualified /ˈkwɒlɪfaɪd/. ADJ BEFORE N If you give someone or something **qualified** support or approval, you give support or approval that is not total and suggests that you have some doubts. *Wade answers both questions with a qualified yes.*

qualifier /ˈkwɒlɪfaɪə/ **qualifiers.** N-C A **qualifier** is an early game or round in a competition. *Wales lost 5 to 1 to Romania in a World Cup qualifier last night.*

qualify /ˈkwɒlɪfaɪ/ **qualifies, qualifying, qualified.**
[1] VERB When someone **qualifies**, they pass the examinations that they need to pass in order to work in a particular profession. *I qualified as a doctor. ...qualified teachers.* ◆ **qualification** /ˌkwɒlɪfɪˈkeɪʃən/ N-U *Following qualification, he worked as a social worker.* [2] VERB If someone **qualifies** for something, or if something **qualifies** them for it, they have the right to do it or to have it. *A few useful skills – English-teaching, for example – qualified foreigners for work visas.* [3] VERB If you **qualify** in a competition, you are successful in one part of it and go on to the next stage. *Nottingham Forest qualified for the final by beating Tranmere.* ◆ **qualifier, qualifiers** N-C *Kenya's Robert Kibe was the fastest qualifier for the 800 metres final.* [4] VERB If you **qualify** a statement, you add a detail or explanation to it to make it less strong or less generalized. *I would qualify that by putting it into context.* [5] See also **qualification**.

qualitative /ˈkwɒlɪtətɪv, AM -teɪt-/. ADJ **Qualitative** means relating to the quality of something; FORMAL. *...qualitative research in psychology.*

quality /ˈkwɒlɪti/ **qualities.** [1] N-U The **quality** of something is how good or bad it is. *...high quality paper.* [2] N-U Something of **quality** is of a high standard. *...a college of quality... We are offering a quality service.* [3] N-C Someone's **qualities** are their good characteristics. *...mature people with leadership qualities.* [4] N-C You can describe a particular characteristic of a person or thing as a **quality**. *Thyme tea can be used by adults for its antiseptic qualities.*

qualm /kwɑːm/ **qualms.** N-C If you have no **qualms** about what you are doing, you are not worried that it may be wrong. *I have no qualms about recommending the same approach to other doctors.*

quantifier /ˈkwɒntɪfaɪə/ **quantifiers.** N-C In grammar, a **quantifier** is a word or phrase like 'plenty' or 'a lot', which allows you to refer to the quantity of something without being absolutely precise. It is often followed by 'of', as in 'a lot of money'.

quantitative /ˈkwɒntɪtətɪv, AM -teɪt-/. ADJ **Quantitative** means relating to the different sizes or amounts of things. *...the quantitative analysis of migration.*

quantity /ˈkwɒntɪti/ **quantities.** [1] N-VAR A **quantity** is an amount that you can measure or count. *...a small quantity of water... Cheap goods are available, but not in sufficient quantities.* [2] N-U Things that are produced or available **in quantity** are produced or available in large amounts. *They can afford to import basic food stuffs and raw materials in quantity.* [3] PHRASE If you say that someone or something is an **unknown quantity**, you mean that not much is known about what they are like or how they will behave.

quantum /ˈkwɒntəm/. [1] ADJ BEFORE N In physics, **quantum** theory and **quantum** mechanics are concerned with the behaviour of atomic particles. [2] ADJ BEFORE N You can use **quantum** in the expressions **quantum leap** and **quantum jump**, which mean a very great and sudden increase in size, amount, or quality. *A vaccine which can halt this suffering represents a quantum leap in healthcare.*

quarantine /ˈkwɒrəntiːn, AM ˈkwɔːr-/. N-U If a person or animal is in **quarantine**, they are kept separate from other people or animals in case they have an infectious disease.

quarrel /ˈkwɒrəl, AM ˈkwɔːr-/ **quarrels, quarrelling, quarrelled** (AM **quarreling, quarreled**). [1] N-C & VERB If you have a **quarrel** with a friend or family member, or if you **quarrel** with them, you have an angry argument with them. *I had a terrible quarrel with my other brothers... My brother quarrelled with my father.* [2] N-SING If you say that you have no **quarrel** with someone, you mean that you do not disagree with them.

quarry /ˈkwɒri, AM ˈkwɔːri/ **quarries, quarrying, quarried.** [1] N-C A **quarry** is an area that is dug out from a piece of land or mountainside in order to extract stone, slate, or minerals. [2] VERB When stone or minerals **are quarried**, or when an area is **quarried** for them, they are removed from the area by digging, drilling, or using explosives.

quart /kwɔːt/ **quarts.** N-C A **quart** is a unit of volume that is equal to two pints.

quarter /ˈkwɔːtə/ **quarters.** [1] N-C & PREDET & ADJ BEFORE N A **quarter** is one of four equal parts of something. *Cut the peppers into quarters. ...an asteroid about a quarter the size of the moon. ...the past quarter century.* [2] N-C A **quarter** is a fixed period of three months. *We update that once a quarter.* [3] N-U When you are telling the time, you use **quarter** to talk about the fifteen minutes before or after the hour. For example, 8.15 is **quarter past** eight, and 8.45 is **quarter to** nine. In American English you can also say that 8.15 is a **quarter after** eight and 8.45 is a **quarter of** nine. [4] N-C

You can refer to the area in a town where a particular group of people live or work as a particular **quarter**. *...the Chinese quarter.* **5** N-C If you talk about feelings or reactions from a certain **quarter**, you mean the feelings or reactions of a group of people, but you do not want to mention the names of the people. *The threat of violence from this quarter has increased sharply.* **6** N-PL You can refer to the room or rooms provided for a person such as a soldier to live in as that person's **quarters**. *...the officers' quarters.* **7** PHRASE If you do something **at close quarters**, you do it from a place that is very near to someone or something. *You can watch aircraft take off or land at close quarters.*

,quarter-'final (or **quarterfinal**) **quarter-finals.** N-C A **quarter-final** is one of the four matches in a competition which decides which four players or four teams will compete in the semi-final.

quarterly /'kwɔ:təli/. ADJ & ADV A **quarterly** event happens four times a year, at intervals of three months. *...the latest Bank of Japan quarterly survey... Dividends are paid quarterly or annually.*

quartet /kwɔ:'tet/ **quartets.** **1** N-C A **quartet** is a group of four people who play musical instruments or sing together. **2** N-C A **quartet** is a piece of music for four instruments or four singers.

quartz /kwɔ:ts/. N-U **Quartz** is a kind of hard shiny crystal, used in making electronic equipment and very accurate watches and clocks.

quash /kwɒʃ/ **quashes, quashing, quashed.** VERB If someone in authority **quashes** a decision or judgment, they officially reject it and it becomes no longer legally valid. *The Appeal Court has quashed the convictions of all eleven people.*

quay /ki:/ **quays.** N-C A **quay** is a long platform beside the sea or a river where boats can be tied.

queen /kwi:n/ **queens.** **1** N-C & N-TITLE A **queen** is a woman who rules a country as its monarch, or a woman who is married to a king. *...Queen Victoria... The king and queen had fled.* **2** N-C In chess, the **queen** is the most powerful piece, which can be moved in any direction. **3** N-C A **queen** is a playing card with a picture of a queen on it. *...the queen of spades.*

queer /kwɪə/ **queerer, queerest.** ADJ **Queer** means strange; DATED. *There's something a bit queer going on.*

quell /kwel/ **quells, quelling, quelled.** **1** VERB To **quell** opposition or violence means to stop it by using persuasion or force. *Troops eventually quelled the unrest.* **2** VERB If you **quell** unpleasant feelings, you stop yourself or other people from having these feelings. *The Information Minister is trying to quell fears of a looming oil crisis.*

query /'kwɪəri/ **queries, querying, queried.** **1** N-VAR A **query** is a question about a particular point. *He is unable to answer queries personally.* **2** VERB If you **query** something, you check it by asking about it because you are not sure if it is correct. *No one queried my decision.*

3 VERB To **query** means to ask a question. *People queried whether any harm had been done.*

quest /kwest/ **quests.** N-C A **quest** is a long and difficult search for something. *My quest for a better bank continues.*

question /'kwestʃən/ **questions, questioning, questioned.** **1** N-C A **question** is something which you say or write in order to ask about a particular matter. *He refused to answer further questions.* **2** VERB If you **question** someone, you ask them questions about something. *I had questioned him on his Western adventures.* ◆**questioner, questioners** N-C *He told the questioner: 'I don't know about their activities.'* ◆**questioning** N-U *The police have detained thirty-two people for questioning.* **3** VERB If you **question** something, you express doubts about it. *It never occurs to them to question the doctor's decisions.* **4** N-U If there is some **question** about something, there is doubt about it. If something is **in question** or has been called **into question**, doubt has been expressed about it. *Why Marlowe was killed may be open to question.* **5** N-C A **question** is a problem or point which needs to be discussed. *The whole question of aid is a tricky political one.* **6** N-C The **questions** in an examination are the problems or topics which are set in order to test your knowledge or ability.

PHRASES ● The time, place, person, or thing **in question** is the one you have just been talking about. *The player in question is Mark Williams.* ● If something is **out of the question**, it is impossible. *For the homeless, private medical care is simply out of the question.* ● If you say **there is no question** of something happening, you are emphasizing that it is not going to happen. *There was no question of betraying his own comrades.* ● If you do something **without question**, you do it without arguing or asking why it is necessary.

questionable /'kwestʃənəbəl/. ADJ If you say that something is **questionable**, you do not consider it to be completely honest or reasonable. *...questionable business practices.*

'question mark, question marks. N-C A **question mark** is the punctuation mark (?) which is used in writing at the end of a question.

questionnaire /,kwestʃə'neə, ,kes-/ **questionnaires.** N-C A **questionnaire** is a written list of questions which are answered by a number of people in order to provide information for a report or survey. *Please fill in the questionnaire.*

queue /kju:/ **queues, queueing** (or **queuing**), **queued.** **1** N-C In British English, a **queue** is a line of people or vehicles that are waiting for something. The American word is **line**. *He got a tray and joined the queue.* **2** VERB In British English, when people **queue**, or when they **queue up**, they stand in a line waiting for something. The American term is **line up**.

quibble /'kwɪbəl/ **quibbles, quibbling, quibbled.** **1** VERB When people **quibble**, they argue about a small matter which is not important. *It seems silly to quibble over such trivial* *details.* [2] N-C A **quibble** is a minor objection to something.

quick /kwɪk/ **quicker, quickest.** [1] ADJ Someone or something that is **quick** moves or does things with great speed. *You'll have to be quick... He was a very quick learner.* ♦**quickly** ADV *Stop me if I'm speaking too quickly.* ♦**quickness** N-U ...*the natural quickness of his mind.* [2] ADJ Something that is **quick** takes or lasts only a short time. *He took one last quick look about the room.* ♦**quickly** ADV *You can become fitter than you are quickly.* [3] ADJ **Quick** means happening with very little delay. *They were quick to dismiss rumours of an off-screen romance. ...a quick end to the war.* ♦**quickly** ADV *We need to get it back as quickly as possible.*

quicken /'kwɪkən/ **quickens, quickening, quickened.** VERB If something **quickens**, or if you **quicken** it, it becomes faster or moves at a greater speed. *He quickened his pace a little.*

quid /kwɪd/ N-C A **quid** is a pound in money. **Quid** is the singular and plural form. BRITISH, INFORMAL. *It cost him five hundred quid.*

quiet /'kwaɪət/ **quieter, quietest.** [1] ADJ Something or someone that is **quiet** makes only a small amount of noise. *Tania kept the children reasonably quiet and content... The street was unnaturally quiet.* ♦**quietly** ADV *Two students whisper quietly to each other.* ♦**quietness** N-U *I was impressed by the smoothness and quietness of the flight.* [2] ADJ If a place, situation, or time is **quiet**, there is no excitement, activity, or trouble. *She wanted a quiet life.* ♦**quietly** ADV *He lives quietly in the country.* ♦**quietness** N-U *I do very much appreciate the quietness and privacy here.* [3] ADJ AFTER LINK-V & N-U If you are **quiet**, you are not saying anything. You say there is **quiet** when no one is talking. *I told them to be quiet and go to sleep... He called for quiet.* ♦**quietly** ADV *Amy stood quietly in the doorway watching him.* [4] PHRASE If you **keep quiet about** something, or if you **keep** something **quiet**, you do not say anything about it. *He denied the department had tried to keep the plan quiet.*

quieten /'kwaɪətən/ **quietens, quietening, quietened.** VERB If you **quieten** someone or something, or if they **quieten**, they become less noisy or less active. *A man shouted and the dogs suddenly quietened.*

quilt /kwɪlt/ **quilts.** [1] N-C A **quilt** is a bed-cover filled with warm soft material, which is often decorated with lines of stitching. [2] N-C A **quilt** is the same as a **duvet**; BRITISH.

quip /kwɪp/ **quips, quipping, quipped.** VERB & N-C To **quip** or to make a **quip** means to say something that is intended to be amusing or clever; WRITTEN. *'He'll have to go on a diet,' Ballard quipped.*

quirk /kwɜːk/ **quirks.** [1] N-C A **quirk** is a habit or aspect of a person's character which is odd or unusual. [2] N-C A **quirk** is a strange occurrence that is difficult to explain.

quirky /'kwɜːki/ **quirkier, quirkiest.** ADJ Someone or something that is **quirky** is rather odd or unpredictable in their appearance, character, or behaviour. ...*her quirky and original style.* ♦**quirkiness** N-U *You will probably notice an element of quirkiness in his behaviour.*

quit /kwɪt/ **quits, quitting, quit.** [1] VERB If you **quit** something, you leave it or you stop doing it. *He refused to quit the building... Nicotine patches are now widely used to help smokers quit the habit.* [2] PHRASE If you say you are going to **call it quits**, you mean that you have decided to stop doing something or being involved in something.

quite /kwaɪt/ [1] ADV You use **quite** to indicate that something is the case to a fairly great extent. **Quite** is less emphatic than 'very' and 'extremely'. *I felt quite bitter about it at the time... I was quite a long way away... I quite enjoy living here.* [2] ADV You use **quite** to indicate certainty or to emphasize that something is definitely the case. *It is quite clear that we were firing in self defence... I quite agree with you.* [3] ADV You use **quite** after a negative to weaken the force of your statement. *Something here is not quite right... I didn't quite understand what all this was about.* [4] PREDET You use **quite** in front of a noun group to emphasize that a person or thing is very impressive or unusual. *He's quite a character.* [5] ADV You can say '**quite**' to express your agreement with someone; SPOKEN. *'And if you buy the record it's your choice isn't it.'—'Quite.*

> You can use **quite** in front of **a** or **an** followed by an adjective followed by a noun. For example, as well as '**The car is quite old**', you can say '**It's quite an old car**' and as well as '**It was quite warm**', you can say '**It was quite a warm day**'. Note that, in sentences like these, **quite** comes in front of the indefinite article. You cannot say, for example, 'It's a quite old car'.
> See also the note at **rather**.

quiver /'kwɪvə/ **quivers, quivering, quivered.** [1] VERB If something **quivers**, it shakes with very small movements. *Her bottom lip quivered.* [2] VERB & N-C If you say that someone **is quivering with** an emotion such as rage or happiness, or if they feel a **quiver** of emotion, you mean that their appearance or voice clearly shows this emotion. *I recognized it instantly and felt a quiver of panic.*

quiz /kwɪz/ **quizzes, quizzing, quizzed.** [1] N-C A **quiz** is a game or competition in which someone tests your knowledge by asking you questions. [2] VERB If you **are quizzed** by someone about something, they ask you questions because they want to get information from you. *Four men were being quizzed by police.*

quota /'kwəʊtə/ **quotas.** [1] N-C A **quota** is the limited number or quantity which is officially allowed. ...*the quota of four tickets per person.* [2] N-C Someone's **quota** of something is their expected or deserved share of it. *They have the usual quota of human weaknesses.*

quotation /kwəʊ'teɪʃən/ **quotations.** [1] N-C A **quotation** is a sentence or phrase taken from a book, poem, or play. [2] N-C When someone gives you a **quotation**, they tell you how much they will charge you to do a particular piece of work; BRITISH: *Get several written quotations and check them.*

quo'tation mark, quotation marks. N-C Quotation marks are punctuation marks used in writing to show where speech or a quotation begins and ends. They are usually written or printed as (' ') and (" ").

quote /kwəʊt/ **quotes, quoting, quoted.** [1] VERB If you **quote** someone as saying something, you repeat what they have written or said. *She quoted a great line from a book by* Romain Gary. [2] VERB If you **quote** something such as a law or a fact, you state it because it supports what you are saying. *She quoted statistics to show how well Britain is doing.* [3] N-C A **quote** from a book, poem, or play is a sentence or phrase from it. [4] VERB & N-C If someone **quotes** you a price for doing something, or if they give you a **quote** for doing it, they say how much money they would charge you to do it. *British Telecom quoted him £50 to put in a telephone.* [5] N-PL **Quotes** are the same as **quotation marks.**

R r

rabbi /'ræbaɪ/ **rabbis.** N-C & N-TITLE A **rabbi** is a Jewish religious leader.

rabbit /'ræbɪt/ **rabbits.** [1] N-C A **rabbit** is a small furry animal with long ears. Rabbits live in holes in the ground. [2] N-U **Rabbit** is the flesh of this animal eaten as food.

rabble /'ræbəl/. N-SING A **rabble** is a crowd of noisy disorganized people; used showing disapproval.

rabies /'reɪbiːz/. N-U **Rabies** is a serious infectious disease which humans can get from the bite of an animal such as a dog which has the disease.

race /reɪs/ **races, racing, raced.** [1] N-C A **race** is a competition to see who is the fastest, for example in running or driving. [2] VERB If you **race**, you take part in a race. *Morris is the only other horse in the land who could race him... I haven't raced against a lot of my rivals this year.* [3] N-C A **race** is a situation in which people or organizations compete with each other for power or control. *The race for the White House begins in earnest today.* [4] VERB If you **race** somewhere, you go there as quickly as possible. *He raced across town to the State House building.* [5] VERB If something **races**, it moves at a very fast rate. *Her heart raced... Already her mind was racing ahead to the hundred and one things she had to do.* [6] N-VAR A **race** is one of the major groups which human beings can be divided into according to their physical features, such as their skin colour. *Discrimination by employers on the grounds of race and nationality was illegal.* [7] PHRASE You describe a situation as a **race against time** when you have to work very fast in order to do something before a particular time. ● See also **human race.**

racecourse (or **race course**) /'reɪskɔːs/ **racecourses.** N-C In British English, a **racecourse** is a track on which horses race. The American word is **racetrack.**

racehorse (or **race horse**) /'reɪshɔːs/ **racehorses.** N-C A **racehorse** is a horse that is trained to run in races.

racer /'reɪsə/ **racers.** [1] N-C A **racer** is a person or animal that takes part in races. *...a former champion powerboat racer.* [2] N-C A **racer** is a vehicle such as a car or bicycle that is designed to be used in races and therefore travels fast.

race re'lations. N-PL **Race relations** are the ways in which people of different races living together in the same community behave towards each other.

racetrack (or **race track**) /'reɪstræk/ **racetracks.** N-C A **racetrack** is a track for races.

racial /'reɪʃəl/. ADJ **Racial** describes things relating to people's race. *...racial discrimination.* ◆**racially** ADV *...racially mixed marriages.*

racing /'reɪsɪŋ/. N-U **Racing** refers to races between animals, especially horses, or between vehicles.

racist /'reɪsɪst/ **racists.** N-C & ADJ A **racist**, or a person with **racist** views, believes that people of some races are inferior to others. *...a gang of white racists. ...dealing with a racist society.* ◆**racism** /'reɪsɪzəm/ N-U *...the fight against racism.*

rack /ræk/ **racks, racking, racked.** The verb is also spelled **wrack** in American English. [1] N-C A **rack** is a piece of equipment used for holding things or for hanging things on. *...a luggage rack. ...racks of clothes.* [2] VERB If someone **is racked** by something, it causes them great suffering or pain. *...a teenager racked with guilt.*

racket /'rækɪt/ **rackets;** also spelled **racquet** in meaning 3. [1] N-SING A **racket** is a loud unpleasant noise. *He makes such a racket.* [2] N-C You can refer to an illegal activity used to make money as a **racket;** INFORMAL. *...a drugs racket.* [3] N-C A **racket** is an oval-shaped bat with strings across it which is used in games such as tennis.

racy /'reɪsi/ **racier, raciest.** ADJ **Racy** writing or behaviour is lively and slightly shocking.

radar /'reɪdɑː/. N-U **Radar** is a way of discovering the position or speed of objects such as aircraft or ships by using radio signals.

radiant /'reɪdiənt/. [1] ADJ Someone who is **radiant** is so happy that their joy shows in their face. *The bride looked truly radiant.* ◆**radiance** N-U *A sort of radiance envelops her.* [2] ADJ Something that is **radiant** glows brightly. *Out on the bay the morning is radiant.* ◆**radiance** N-U *...the radiance of early morning.*

radiate /'reɪdieɪt/ **radiates, radiating, radiated.** [1] VERB If things **radiate** from a place, they form a pattern that spreads out like lines drawn from the centre of a circle to its edge. *...paths radiating from a central circular paved area.* [2] VERB If you **radiate** an emotion or quality or if it **radiates** from you, people can see it very clearly in your face and in your behaviour. *She radiates happiness.*

radiation /ˌreɪdi'eɪʃən/. [1] N-U **Radiation** is very small particles of a radioactive substance. Large amounts of radiation can cause illness and death. [2] N-U **Radiation** is energy, often in waves of heat or light, that comes from a particular source.

radiator /'reɪdieɪtə/ **radiators**. [1] N-C A **radiator** is a hollow metal device which is connected to a central heating system and used to heat a room. [2] N-C A car **radiator** is the part of the engine which is used to cool the engine.

radical /'rædɪkəl/ **radicals**. [1] ADJ **Radical** changes and differences are very important and great in degree. *...radical economic reforms.* ♦**radically** ADV *...radically different beliefs.* [2] N-C & ADJ A **radical** or a person who has **radical** views believes that there should be great changes in society and tries to bring about these changes. *...tension between radical and conservative politicians.*

radii /'reɪdiaɪ/. **Radii** is the plural of **radius**.

radio /'reɪdiəʊ/ **radios, radioing, radioed.** [1] N-U **Radio** is the broadcasting of programmes for the public to listen to. You can refer to the programmes broadcast in this way as the **radio**. *The last 12 months have been difficult ones for local radio... He's been on the radio a lot recently.* [2] N-C A **radio** is the piece of equipment used to listen to radio programmes. [3] N-U **Radio** is a system of sending sound over a distance using electrical signals. *They are in twice daily radio contact with the rebel leader.* [4] N-C A **radio** is a piece of equipment that is used for sending and receiving messages. [5] VERB If you **radio** someone, you send a message to them by radio. *The officer radioed for advice.*

radioactive /ˌreɪdiəʊ'æktɪv/. ADJ Something that is **radioactive** contains a substance that produces energy in the form of powerful rays which are harmful in large doses. *...radioactive waste.* ♦**radioactivity** /ˌreɪdiəʊæk'tɪvɪti/ N-U *...waste which is contaminated with low levels of radioactivity.*

radius /'reɪdiəs/ **radii** /'reɪdiaɪ/. [1] N-SING The **radius** around a point is the distance from it in any direction. *Nigel has searched for work in a ten-mile radius around his home.* [2] N-C The **radius** of a circle is the distance from its centre to its outside edge.

RAF /ˌɑːr eɪ 'ef, ræf/. N-PROPER The **RAF** is the air force of the United Kingdom. **RAF** is an abbreviation for 'Royal Air Force'.

raffle /'ræfəl/ **raffles**. N-C A **raffle** is a competition in which you buy numbered tickets. If your ticket is chosen, you win a prize.

raft /rɑːft, ræft/ **rafts**. [1] N-C A **raft** is a floating platform made from large pieces of wood tied together. [2] N-C A **raft** is a small inflatable rubber or plastic boat. [3] N-C A **raft of** people or things is a lot of them. *He has surrounded himself with a raft of advisers.*

rafter /'rɑːftə, 'ræf-/ **rafters**. N-C **Rafters** are the sloping pieces of wood that support a roof.

rag /ræg/ **rags**. [1] N-VAR A **rag** is a piece of old cloth which you can use to clean or wipe things. *...dry it on some rag.* [2] N-PL **Rags** are

old torn clothes. *...small children, some dressed in rags.* [3] N-C People refer to a newspaper as a **rag** when they have a low opinion of it; INFORMAL. *I've read all about it in the local rag.*

rage /reɪdʒ/ **rages, raging, raged.** [1] N-VAR **Rage** is strong, uncontrollable anger. *I flew into a rage. ...a fit of rage.* [2] VERB You say that something powerful or unpleasant **rages** when it continues with great force or violence. *The fire raged for more than four hours.* ♦**raging** ADJ BEFORE N *...kayaking on a raging river.* [3] VERB If you **rage** about something, you speak or think very angrily about it. *He began to rage against his bad luck.* [4] N-SING When something is popular and fashionable, you can say that it is **the rage**; INFORMAL. *Chinese cooking is all the rage.*

ragged /'rægɪd/. [1] ADJ **Ragged** clothes are old and torn. If someone is **ragged**, they are wearing old torn clothing. *...ragged children played among the pot-holed streets.* [2] ADJ You can say that something is **ragged** when it is uneven or untidy. *O'Brien formed the men into a ragged line.*

raid /reɪd/ **raids, raiding, raided.** [1] VERB & N-C When soldiers or the police **raid** a place, they enter it by force to attack it, or to look for someone or something. This action is called a **raid**. *...a raid on a house by thirty armed police.* ♦**raider, raiders** N-C *The raiders continued on their mission – to seek out and destroy American air and sea forces.* [2] VERB & N-C If someone **raids** a building or place, they enter it by force in order to steal something. This action is called a **raid**. BRITISH. *A 19-year-old man has been found guilty of raiding a bank.* ♦**raider** N-C *The raiders escaped with cash and jewellery.*

rail /reɪl/ **rails**. [1] N-C A **rail** is a horizontal bar which is fixed to something and used as a fence or a support, or to hang things on. *She gripped the hand rail in the lift... This pair of curtains will fit a rail up to 7ft 6in wide.* [2] N-C **Rails** are the steel bars which trains run on. [3] N-U If you travel or send something by **rail**, you travel or send it on a train. *...the electric rail link between Manchester and Sheffield.*

railing /'reɪlɪŋ/ **railings**. N-C A fence made from metal bars is called a **railing** or **railings**.

railroad /'reɪlrəʊd/ **railroads**. N-C In American English, a **railroad** is the same as a **railway**.

railway /'reɪlweɪ/ **railways**. [1] N-C A **railway** is a route between two places along which trains travel on steel rails; BRITISH. [2] N-C A **railway** is a company or organization that operates railway routes; BRITISH. *...the state-owned French railway. ...the privatisation of the railways.*

rain /reɪn/ **rains, raining, rained.** [1] N-U **Rain** is water that falls from the clouds in small drops. *I hope you didn't get soaked standing out in the rain.* [2] VERB When rain falls, you can say that it **is raining**. *It rained the whole weekend.* [3] VERB If things **rain** on a person or place, or if they **rain down**, they fall on that person or place in large quantities. *The masked attacker rained blows on him... Guerrillas rained down mortar machine-gun fire.*

▶ **rain off.** PHR-VERB If a sports match **is rained off**, it cannot take place because of the rain.

rainbow /ˈreɪnbəʊ/ **rainbows.** N-C A **rainbow** is the arch of different colours that you sometimes see in the sky when it is raining.

raincoat /ˈreɪnkəʊt/ **raincoats.** N-C A **raincoat** is a waterproof coat.

raindrop /ˈreɪndrɒp/ **raindrops.** N-C A **raindrop** is a single drop of rain.

rainfall /ˈreɪnfɔːl/ **rainfalls.** N-VAR **Rainfall** is the amount of rain that falls in a place during a particular period of time. *...below average rainfall.*

rainforest /ˈreɪnfɒrɪst, AM -fɔːr-/ **rainforests.** N-VAR A **rainforest** is a thick forest of tall trees found in tropical areas where there is a lot of rain.

rainy /ˈreɪni/. ADJ If it is **rainy**, it is raining a lot. *...one rainy night in Seattle.*

raise /reɪz/ **raises, raising, raised.** [1] VERB If you **raise** something, you move it to a higher position. *She went to the window and raised the blinds... He raised his hand. ...a small raised platform.* [2] VERB If you **raise** the rate or level of something, you increase it. *The Republic of Ireland is expected to raise interest rates.* [3] VERB To **raise** the standard of something means to improve it. *...courses to raise the standard of coaching.* [4] VERB If you **raise** your voice, you speak more loudly. [5] VERB If an event raises a particular emotion or question, it makes people feel the emotion or consider the question. *The agreement has raised hopes that the war may end soon.* [6] VERB If you **raise** a subject, objection, or question, you mention it or bring it to someone's attention. *At no time did he raise the matter with me.* [7] N-C In American English, a **raise** is an increase in your wages or salary. The British word is **rise.** [8] VERB To **raise** money for a particular cause means to get people to donate money towards it. [9] VERB To **raise** a child means to look after it until it is grown up. [10] VERB To **raise** a particular type of animal or crop means to breed the animal or grow the crop. *They raise sheep for meat, skins, and wool.*

raisin /ˈreɪzən/ **raisins.** N-C **Raisins** are dried grapes.

rake /reɪk/ **rakes, raking, raked.** [1] N-C A **rake** is a garden tool consisting of a row of metal teeth attached to a long handle. [2] VERB To **rake** leaves or soil means to use a rake to gather the leaves or to make the soil smooth.

▶ **rake in.** PHR-VERB If someone **is raking in** money, they are earning a lot of it fairly easily; INFORMAL. *He raked in £33,000 profit from his shares.*

rally /ˈræli/ **rallies, rallying, rallied.** [1] N-C A **rally** is a large public meeting held in support of something such as a political party. *...a pre-election rally.* [2] N-C A **rally** is a competition in which vehicles are driven over public roads. *...an accomplished rally driver.* [3] VERB When people **rally** to something or when something **rallies** them, they unite to support it. *He attempted to rally his supporters.* [4] VERB When someone or something **rallies**, they begin to recover or improve after having been weak. *Stock markets began to rally worldwide.*

▶ **rally around** or **rally round.** PHR-VERB When people **rally around** or **rally round**, they work as a group in order to support someone at a difficult time. *Connie's friends rallied round her.*

ram /ræm/ **rams, ramming, rammed.** [1] VERB If one vehicle **rams** another, it crashes into it with a lot of force. [2] VERB If you **ram** something somewhere, you push it there with great force. *He rammed the key into the lock.* [3] N-C A **ram** is an adult male sheep.

ramble /ˈræmbəl/ **rambles, rambling, rambled.** [1] VERB & N-C If you **ramble**, or if you go on a **ramble**, you go on a long walk in the countryside. *...an hour's ramble through the woods.* ♦ **rambler, ramblers** N-C *...a popular route for ramblers.* [2] VERB If someone **rambles**, or if they **ramble on**, they talk for a long time in a confused way. *She began rambling on about her childhood.*

ramification /ˌræmɪfɪˈkeɪʃən/ **ramifications.** N-C The **ramifications** of a decision or event, are all its consequences and effects, especially ones which were not obvious at first. *...the political ramifications of the riots.*

ramp /ræmp/ **ramps.** N-C A **ramp** is a sloping surface between two places that are at different levels. *I pushed her wheelchair up the ramp.*

rampage, rampages, rampaging, rampaged; verb /ræmˈpeɪdʒ/; phrase /ˈræmpeɪdʒ/. VERB & PHRASE If people or animals **rampage** through a place, or if they **go on the rampage** through a place, they rush about in a wild or violent way, causing damage or destruction. *Hundreds of fans went on the rampage after the match.*

rampant /ˈræmpənt/. ADJ If something such as crime or a disease is **rampant**, it is growing or spreading in an uncontrolled way. *...rampant corruption.*

ramshackle /ˈræmʃækəl/. ADJ A **ramshackle** building is badly made or in a very bad condition.

ran /ræn/. **Ran** is the past tense of **run.**

ranch /rɑːntʃ, ræntʃ/ **ranches.** N-C A **ranch** is a large farm used for raising animals.

random /ˈrændəm/. ADJ & PHRASE Something that is done or chosen in a **random** way, or at **random**, is done or chosen without a definite plan or pattern. *...a random sample of 930 women... Names were selected at random by computer.* ♦ **randomly** ADV *...magazines left scattered randomly around.*

rang /ræŋ/. **Rang** is the past tense of some meanings of **ring.**

range /reɪndʒ/ **ranges, ranging, ranged.** [1] N-C A **range** of things is a number of different things of the same general kind. *...a wide range of furniture including dining chairs and tables. ...growing public concerns over a range of environmental issues.* [2] N-C A **range** is the complete group that is included between two points on a scale of measurement or scale. *The age range is from eighteen to forty. ...properties available in the price range they are looking for.* [3] N-C The **range** of something is the maximum area within which it can reach things or detect things. *...a missile with a range of 2,000 kilometres... A newborn baby's range* *of vision is about a foot or so.* **[4]** VERB If things **range between** two points or **range from** one point **to** another, they vary within these points on a scale of measurement or quality. *They range in price from $3 to $15.* **[5]** VERB If people or things **are ranged** somewhere, they are arranged in a row or in lines; FORMAL. *Wooden chairs were ranged against one wall.* **[6]** N-C A **range** of mountains or hills is a line of them. **[7]** N-C A rifle **range** or a firing **range** is a place where people can shoot at targets.

PHRASES ● If something is **in range** or **within range**, it is near enough to be reached or detected. If it is **out of range**, it is too far away to be reached or detected. ...*within range of their aircraft... The fish stayed 50 yards offshore, well out of range.* ● If you see or hit something at **close range**, or **from close range**, you are very close to it when you see it or hit it. ...*photographing wild animals from close range.*

ranger /ˈreɪndʒə/ **rangers.** N-C A **ranger** is a person whose job is to look after a forest or park.

rank /ræŋk/ **ranks, ranking, ranked.** **[1]** N-VAR Someone's **rank** is their position in an organization, or in society. ...*the rank of captain.* ...*a person of high rank.* **[2]** VERB When someone or something **is ranked** a particular position, they are at that position on a scale. *The British player, Michael Adams, already ranks 20th in the world.* ...*a remarkable scientist whose work ranked with that of Einstein.* **[3]** N-PL The **ranks** are the ordinary members of an organization, especially of the armed forces. ...*a former Lieutenant-Colonel who had risen from the ranks.* **[4]** N-PL When you become a member of a large group of people, you can say that you are joining its **ranks.** *He soon joined the ranks of the unemployed.* **[5]** ADJ You can describe something as **rank** when it has a strong and unpleasant smell; LITERARY. ...*the rank smell of unwashed skin.* **[6]** N-C A taxi **rank** is a place where taxis park and wait to be hired.

PHRASES ● If a member of a group or organization **breaks ranks**, they disobey the instructions of their group or organization. ● If the members of a group **close ranks**, they support each other in a united way to oppose any attack or criticism.

‚rank and 'file. N-SING The **rank and file** of an organization, are the ordinary members of an organization, rather than the leaders. *The rank and file of the party hadn't been consulted.*

ransack /ˈrænsæk/ **ransacks, ransacking, ransacked.** VERB If you **ransack** a building or a room, you disturb everything in it and leave it in a mess, often because they are looking for something. *The thieves ransacked the house.*

ransom /ˈrænsəm/ **ransoms.** **[1]** N-VAR A **ransom** is money that is demanded as payment for the return of someone who has been kidnapped. *The kidnappers are demanding a ransom of five million dollars.* **[2]** PHRASE If a kidnapper **holds** someone **to ransom**, they keep that person prisoner until they are given what they want.

rant /rænt/ **rants, ranting, ranted.** VERB & N-C If someone **rants**, or if they have a **rant**, they talk

in a loud, excited, and angry way. ...*a rant against the meat industry.* ♦**ranting, rantings** N-VAR *He had been listening to Goldstone's rantings all night.*

rap /ræp/ **raps, rapping, rapped.** **[1]** N-VAR & VERB **Rap** is a type of music in which the words are not sung but are spoken in a rapid, rhythmic way. Someone who **raps** performs rap. ♦**rapper, rappers** N-C ...*the French rapper MC Solaar.* **[2]** VERB & N-C If you **rap** on something, you hit it with a series of quick blows. A **rap** is a quick hit or knock on something. *Mike rapped the table... There was a rap on the door.*

rape /reɪp/ **rapes, raping, raped.** VERB & N-VAR If someone **is raped**, they are forced to have sex against their will. **Rape** is the crime of forcing someone to have sex. *She despised the men who had raped her.* ♦**rapist, rapists** N-C *The judge sentenced the two rapists to five years in prison.*

rapid /ˈræpɪd/. ADJ If something is **rapid**, it happens or moves very quickly. *His heart rate seemed abnormally rapid to him.* ♦**rapidly** ADV ...*Queensland's rapidly increasing population.* ♦**rapidity** /rəˈpɪdɪti/ N-U ...*the rapidity with which the weather can change.*

rapids /ˈræpɪdz/. N-PL **Rapids** are parts of a river where the water moves very fast.

rapport /ræˈpɔː/. N-U **Rapport** is a feeling of understanding and sympathy between two or more people. ...*the extraordinary rapport between the two leaders.*

rapture /ˈræptʃə/ **raptures.** N-VAR **Rapture** is a feeling of extreme joy or pleasure; LITERARY. *They will be in raptures over the French countryside.*

rapturous /ˈræptʃərəs/. ADJ A **rapturous** feeling or reaction is one of great happiness or enthusiasm. ♦**rapturously** ADV *The performance was greeted rapturously by the audience.*

rare /reə/ **rarer, rarest.** **[1]** ADJ If something is **rare**, it is not common, and is therefore interesting, valuable, or unusual. ...*rare breeds of cattle.* ...*those rare occasions when he did eat alone.* **[2]** ADJ Meat that is **rare** is cooked very lightly so that the inside is still red.

rarely /ˈreəli/. ADV **Rarely** means not very often. *I very rarely wear a raincoat.*

rarity /ˈreərɪti/ **rarities.** **[1]** N-C If someone or something is a **rarity**, they are interesting or valuable because they are so unusual. *Signatures on 18th century Irish furniture are a rarity.* **[2]** N-U The **rarity** of something is the fact that it is very uncommon. *It was a real prize due to its rarity and good condition.*

rash /ræʃ/ **rashes.** **[1]** ADJ If someone is **rash** or does **rash** things, they act without thinking carefully first. *I don't want to make any rash promises.* ♦**rashly** ADV *I made quite a lot of money, but I rashly gave most of it away.* **[2]** N-C A **rash** is an area of red spots on your skin which appear when you are ill or have an allergy. **[3]** N-SING A **rash** of events or things is a large number of them that all happen or appear within a short period of time. ...*a rash of scandals.*

rasp /rɑːsp, ræsp/ **rasps, rasping, rasped.** **[1]** VERB & N-SING If someone **rasps**, their voice or breathing is harsh and unpleasant to listen to.

A **rasp** is this sound. ...*the rasp of Rennie's voice.* [2] VERB & N-SING If something **rasps**, it makes a harsh, unpleasant sound as it rubs against something hard or rough. A **rasp** is this sound. ...*the rasp of something being drawn across the sand.*

raspberry /'rɑːzbri, AM 'ræzberi/ **raspberries.** N-C **Raspberries** are small, soft, red fruit that grow on bushes.

rat /ræt/ **rats.** N-C A **rat** is an animal which has a long tail and looks like a large mouse.

rate /reɪt/ **rates, rating, rated.** [1] N-C The **rate** at which something happens is the speed or frequency with which it happens. ...*the rate at which hair grows... New diet books appear at a rate of nearly one a week.* [2] N-C A **rate** is the amount of money that is charged for goods or services. ...*specially reduced rates for travellers using Gatwick Airport.* [3] N-C The **rate** of taxation or interest is its level, expressed as a percentage. *The richest Americans pay taxes at a rate of 28%.* [4] VERB If you **rate** someone or something as good or bad, you consider them to be good or bad. *The film was rated excellent.* [5] See also **rating.**

PHRASES ● You use **at any rate** to indicate that the important thing is what you are going to say now, and not what was said before. *Well, at any rate, let me thank you for all you did.* ● If you say that **at this rate** something bad or extreme will happen, you mean that it will happen if things continue to develop as they have been doing. *At this rate they'd be lucky to get home before eight.*

rather /'rɑːðə, 'ræð-/. [1] PREP & CONJ You use **rather than** when you are contrasting two things or situations. **Rather than** introduces the thing or situation that is not the case or that you do not want or approve of. *I use the bike if I can rather than the car... She made students think for themselves, rather than telling them what to think.* [2] ADV You use **rather** to introduce a correction or contrast to what you have just said. *Twenty million years ago, Idaho was not the arid place it is now. Rather, it was warm and damp.* [3] PHRASE If you **would rather** do something, you would prefer to do it. *Kids would rather play than study.* ● See note at **prefer.** [4] ADV You use **rather** to indicate that something is true to a fairly great extent. ...*rather unusual circumstances.*

Rather, pretty, quite, and **fairly** can all be used to modify adjectives and adverbs, but are all less strong than **very.** **Rather** and **pretty** are the strongest of the these words and are the closest to **very. Pretty,** in this sense, is informal. Therefore, if you said to someone, 'Your work is rather good' or 'Your work is pretty good', they would be more likely to be pleased than if you said 'Your work is quite good' or 'Your work is fairly good'. However, **rather** is commonly used with words indicating negative qualities. *I was feeling rather sad.* It is the only one of these words than can be used with comparatives, and with **too.** *Global warming could be made far worse than we think it*

will be... *He was becoming rather too friendly with my ex-boyfriend.* **Quite** is slightly stronger than **fairly,** and may suggest that something has more of a quality than expected. *Nobody here's ever heard of it but it is actually quite common.*

---

[5] ADV You use **rather** before verbs that introduce your thoughts and feelings, in order to express your opinion politely, especially when a different opinion has been expressed; BRITISH. *I rather think he was telling the truth.*

ratify /'rætɪfaɪ/ **ratifies, ratifying, ratified.** VERB When national leaders or organizations **ratify** a treaty or written agreement, they make it official by giving their formal approval to it, usually by signing it or voting for it. ◆**ratification** /ˌrætɪfɪ'keɪʃən/ **ratifications** N-C ...*the ratification of the Maastricht Treaty.*

rating /'reɪtɪŋ/ **ratings.** N-C A **rating** of something is a score or assessment of how good or popular it is. *A student with 95 percent in a final examination scored a rating of five.*

ratio /'reɪʃiəʊ, AM -ʃəʊ/ **ratios.** N-C The **ratio** of something is the relationship between two things expressed in numbers or amounts, to show how much greater one is than the other. *The adult to child ratio is 1 to 6.*

ration /'ræʃən/ **rations, rationing, rationed.** [1] N-C When there is a shortage of something, your **ration** of it is the amount that you are allowed to have. *Families get a ration of tea, oil, sugar and rice.* [2] VERB When something **is rationed**, you are only allowed to have a limited amount of it. *Motorists will be rationed to thirty litres of petrol a month.* ◆**rationing** N-U *Tea rationing ended in Britain in 1952.* [3] N-PL **Rations** are the food which is given to people with food shortages.

rational /'ræʃənəl/. [1] ADJ **Rational** decisions and thoughts are based on reason rather than on emotion. *Look at both sides of the case and come to a rational decision.* ◆**rationally** ADV *We discussed it rationally.* ◆**rationality** /ˌræʃə'nælɪti/ N-U *We live in an era of rationality.* [2] ADJ A **rational** person is someone who thinks clearly and is not emotionally or mentally unbalanced. *Rachel looked calmer and more rational now.*

rationale /ˌræʃə'nɑːl, -'næl/. N-C The **rationale** for a course of action or a belief is the set of reasons on which it is based. *The rationale behind the project was that 'where learning is fun, it is done better'.*

rationalist /'ræʃənəlɪst/ **rationalists.** N-C & ADJ A **rationalist,** or a person with **rationalist** views, believes that their life should be based on reason and logic, rather than emotions or religious beliefs. ◆**rationalism** /'ræʃənəlɪzəm/ N-U ...*the rationalism of Western culture.*

rationalize (BR also **rationalise**) /'ræʃənəlaɪz/ **rationalizes, rationalizing, rationalized.** [1] VERB If you try to **rationalize** attitudes or actions that are difficult to accept, you think of reasons to justify or explain them. ...*an attempt to rationalize my feelings.* ◆**rationalization** /ˌræʃənəlaɪ'zeɪʃən/ **rationalizations** N-VAR ...*the rationalization of middle-*

class values. [2] VERB When a company, system, or industry **is rationalized**, it is made more efficient, usually by getting rid of staff and equipment. ♦**rationalization** N-U ...*the recent rationalization of the textile industry.*

rationing /'ræʃənɪŋ/. See **ration**.

rattle /'rætəl/ **rattles, rattling, rattled.** [1] VERB & N-C When something **rattles**, or when you **rattle** it, it makes short sharp knocking sounds because it is being shaken or it keeps hitting against something hard. A **rattle** is this noise. ...*a train rattled by... There was a rattle of rifle-fire.* [2] N-C A **rattle** is a baby's toy with loose bits inside which make a noise when the baby shakes it. [3] VERB If something or someone **rattles** you, they make you nervous. *The question didn't rattle her.* ♦**rattled** ADJ *His supporters seem a bit rattled.*

▸ **rattle off.** PHR-VERB If you **rattle off** something, you say it or do it very quickly and without much effort. *He rattled off the names.*

raucous /'rɔːkəs/. ADJ A **raucous** sound is loud, harsh, and rather unpleasant. ...*the raucous cries of the sea-birds.* ♦**raucously** ADV *They laughed together raucously.*

ravage /'rævɪdʒ/ **ravages, ravaging, ravaged.** VERB A town, country, or economy that **has been ravaged** has been damaged so much that it is almost completely destroyed. *The country has been ravaged by civil war.*

ravages /'rævɪdʒɪz/. N-PL The **ravages** of time, war, or the weather are the damaging effects that they have. ...*the ravages of winter.*

rave /reɪv/ **raves, raving, raved.** [1] VERB If someone **raves**, they talk in an excited and uncontrolled way. *'What is wrong with you, acting like that,' she raved.* [2] VERB If you **rave** about something, you speak or write about it with great enthusiasm. *Rachel raved about the new foods she ate.* [3] N-C A **rave** review is a very enthusiastic one. *'Only the Truth Is Funny', has drawn raves from the critics.* [4] N-C A **rave** is a large musical event in a club or in the open air which attracts people who like dancing to modern, electronic, dance music. [5] See also **raving**.

raven /'reɪvən/ **ravens.** [1] N-C A **raven** is a large bird with shiny black feathers and a deep harsh call. [2] ADJ **Raven** hair is shiny, black, and smooth; WRITTEN.

ravine /rə'viːn/ **ravines.** N-C A **ravine** is a very deep narrow valley with steep sides.

raving /'reɪvɪŋ/. ADJ & ADV You use **raving** to describe someone who you think is completely mad; INFORMAL. *Malcolm looked at her as if she were a raving lunatic... Jean-Paul has gone raving mad.*

raw /rɔː/. [1] ADJ A **raw** substance is in its natural state before being processed. ...*two ships carrying raw sugar from Cuba.* [2] ADJ **Raw** food has not been cooked, or has not been cooked enough. ...*a popular dish made of raw fish.* [3] ADJ If a part of your body is **raw**, it is red and painful because the skin has been damaged. [4] ADJ If you describe someone in a new job as **raw**, or as a **raw** recruit, you mean that they lack experience in that job. *Davies is still raw but his potential shows.* [5] PHRASE If you say

that you are getting a **raw deal**, you mean that you are being treated unfairly; INFORMAL.

ray /reɪ/ **rays.** [1] N-C **Rays** of light are narrow beams of light. [2] N-SING A **ray** of hope, comfort, or other positive quality is a small amount that makes a bad situation seem less bad. *The drug is a ray of hope for the 500,000 victims of Alzheimer's in Britain today.*

razor /'reɪzə/ **razors.** N-C A **razor** is a tool that people use for shaving.

Rd. Rd is a written abbreviation for 'road'. *St Pancras Library, 100 Euston Rd, London, NW1.*

-'re. -'re is a shortened form of 'are' that is used in spoken English and in informal written English. *We're not, are we?... What're you going to do?... People're working on that now.*

reach /riːtʃ/ **reaches, reaching, reached.** [1] VERB When someone or something **reaches** a place, they arrive there. *He did not stop until he reached the door.* [2] VERB If you **reach** somewhere, you move your arm and hand to take or touch something. *Judy reached into her handbag.* [3] VERB If you can **reach** something, you are able to touch it by stretching out your arm or leg. *Can you reach your toes with your fingertips?* [4] VERB If you try to **reach** someone, you try to contact them, usually by telephone. *Has the doctor told you how to reach him or her in emergencies?* [5] VERB If someone or something has **reached** a certain stage or amount, they are at that stage or amount. *We're told the figure could reach 100,000 next year.* [6] VERB If something **reaches** a place or level, it extends as far as that place or level. ...*a nightshirt which reached to his knees.* [7] VERB When people **reach** an agreement or compromise, they succeed in achieving it. *They are meeting in Lusaka in an attempt to reach a compromise.*

react /ri'ækt/ **reacts, reacting, reacted.** [1] VERB When you **react** to something that has happened to you, you behave in a particular way because of it. *It's natural to react with disbelief if your child is accused of bullying.* [2] VERB If you **react against** someone's way of behaving, you deliberately behave in a different way. *My father never saved and perhaps I reacted against that.* [3] VERB If you **react** to a treatment or substance, you are affected unpleasantly or made ill by it. *He reacted very badly to the radiation therapy.* [4] VERB When one chemical substance **reacts** with another, they combine chemically to form another substance. *These two gases react readily to produce carbon dioxide and water.*

reaction /ri'ækʃən/ **reactions.** [1] N-VAR Your **reaction** to something that has happened or something that you have experienced is what you feel, say, or do because of it. *He was surprised that his answer should have caused such a strong reaction.* [2] N-C A **reaction** against something is a way of behaving or doing something that is deliberately different from what has been done before. *All new fashion starts out as a reaction against existing convention.* ...*a strong reaction against socialism.* [3] N-C If you have a **reaction** against a treatment or substance, you are affected unpleasantly or made ill by it. ...*life-threatening reactions to* anaesthetics. **4** N-PL Your **reactions** are your ability to move quickly in response to something. *The sport requires very fast reactions.* **5** N-C The **reaction** between two chemical substances is what happens when they combine to form another substance. *Ozone is produced by the reaction between oxygen and ultra-violet light.*

reactionary /ri'ækʃənri, AM -neri/ **reactionaries.** N-C & ADJ A **reactionary** or a **reactionary** person or group tries to prevent changes in the political or social system of their country; used showing disapproval. *...reactionary forces trying to spread fear, confusion and discontent.*

reactor /ri'æktə/ **reactors.** N-C A **reactor** is a device which produces nuclear energy.

read, reads, reading, read. When it is the present tense, **read** is pronounced /ri:d/; **read** is also the past tense and past participle, when it is pronounced /red/. **1** VERB & N-C When you **read** something such as a book or article, you look at and understand or say aloud the words that are written there. You can also say you have a **read.** *He read through the pages slowly... I read them a story before tucking them in... I settled down to have a good read.* **2** VERB If you can **read** music, you have the ability to look at and understand the written symbols that are used to represent musical sounds. **3** VERB You can use **read** when saying what is written somewhere. For example, if a notice **reads** 'Exit', the word 'Exit' is written on it. **4** VERB If you refer to how a piece of writing **reads**, you are referring to its style. *It reads very awkwardly.* **5** N-C If you say that a book is a good **read**, you mean that it is very enjoyable to read. **6** VERB If you **read** someone's mind or their mood, you know what they are thinking or feeling without them telling you. **7** VERB When you **read** a measuring device, you look at it to see what the measurement on it is. *It is essential that you are able to read a thermometer.* **8** See also **reading.** ● to **read between the lines:** see **line.**

▸ **read into.** PHR-VERB If you **read** a meaning **into** something, you think it is there although it may not be. *It would be wrong to try to read too much into such a light-hearted production.*

▸ **read out.** PHR-VERB If you **read** something **out,** you say the words aloud, especially in a loud, clear voice. *The evidence was read out to the court.*

▸ **read up on.** PHR-VERB If you **read up on** a subject, you read a lot about it so that you become informed on it.

readable /'ri:dəbəl/. ADJ If a book or article is **readable,** it is enjoyable and easy to read.

reader /'ri:də/ **readers.** N-C The **readers** of a book, newspaper, or magazine are the people who read it.

readership /'ri:dəʃip/. N-SING The **readership** of a book, newspaper, or magazine is the number or type of people who read it. *...a college-age readership.*

readily /'redɪli/. **1** ADV If you do something **readily,** you do it willingly. *When I was invited to the party, I readily accepted.* **2** ADV You use **readily** to say that something can be done or

obtained quickly and easily. *I don't readily make friends.*

reading /'ri:dɪŋ/ **readings.** **1** N-U **Reading** is the activity of reading books. *I have always loved reading.* **2** N-C A **reading** is an event at which extracts from books are read to an audience. **3** N-C The **reading** on a measuring device is the measurement that it shows.

readjust /,ri:ə'dʒʌst/ **readjusts, readjusting, readjusted.** **1** VERB When you **readjust** to a new situation, you adapt to it. *They are forced to take time to readjust after a holiday.* ◆ **readjustment, readjustments** N-VAR *...a period of readjustment.* **2** VERB If you **readjust** something, you change it so that it is more effective or appropriate. *The rebel army has readjusted its strategy.* ◆ **readjustment** N-VAR *...readjustment of state borders.*

ready /'redi/ **readies, readying, readied.** **1** ADJ AFTER LINK-V If someone or something is **ready,** they have reached the required stage for something or they are properly prepared for action or use. *It took her a long time to get ready for church... Your breakfast's ready.* ◆ **readiness** N-U *The newsletter was printed towards the end of June in readiness for ...* **2** ADJ AFTER LINK-V If you are **ready** to do something, you are willing to do it. *She was always ready to give interviews.* ◆ **readiness** N-U *...his readiness to accept criticism.* **3** ADJ AFTER LINK-V If someone or something is **ready** to do something, they are about to do it or likely to do it. *It's like a volcano ready to erupt.* **4** ADJ AFTER LINK-V If you are **ready** for something, you need it or want it. *After five days in the heat of Bangkok, we were ready for the beach.* **5** ADJ BEFORE N You use **ready** to describe things that are able to be used quickly and easily. *...a ready supply of well-trained workers.* **6** VERB When you **ready** something, you prepare it for a particular purpose; FORMAL. *Soldiers were readying themselves for the final assault.* **7** **Ready** combines with past participles to indicate that something has already been done, and that therefore you do not have to do it yourself. *...ready-printed forms.* **8** PHRASE If you have something **at the ready,** you have it in a position where it can be quickly and easily used. *...soldiers with guns at the ready.*

,ready-'made. **1** ADJ If something that you buy is **ready-made,** you can use it immediately. *...ready-made bedcovers.* **2** ADJ **Ready-made** means extremely convenient or useful for a particular purpose. *...a ready-made topic of conversation.*

reaffirm /,ri:ə'fɜ:m/ **reaffirms, reaffirming, reaffirmed.** If you **reaffirm** something, you state it again clearly and firmly; FORMAL. *The government has reaffirmed that it will take any steps necessary to maintain law and order.*

real /ri:l/. **1** ADJ Something that is **real** actually exists and is not imagined or theoretical. *No, it wasn't a dream. It was real.* **2** ADJ A material or object that is **real** is genuine and not artificial or an imitation. *...real leather... Who's to know if they're real guns or not?* **3** ADJ BEFORE N You can use **real** to say that someone or something has all the characteristics or qualities that such a person or thing typically has. *...his first real* girlfriend. [4] ADJ BEFORE N You can use **real** to describe something that is the true or original thing of its kind. *Her real name had been Miriam Pinckus.* [5] ADV You can use **real** to emphasize an adjective or adverb; INFORMAL, AMERICAN. *He is finding prison life 'real tough'.*

PHRASES ● If someone does something **for real**, they actually do it and do not just pretend to do it. *He thought it was all a big joke, he had no idea it was for real.* ● You use **in real terms** to refer to the actual value or cost of something. For example, if your pocket money rises by 5% but prices rise by 10%, in real terms you get less pocket money. ● If you say that a thing or event is **the real thing**, you mean that it is the actual thing or event, and not an imitation or rehearsal. *The counterfeits sell for about $20 less than the real thing.*

'**real estate.** N-U Real estate is property in the form of buildings and land; AMERICAN.

realise /ˈriːəlaɪz/. See **realize**.

realism /ˈriːəlɪzəm/. [1] N-U When people show **realism** in their behaviour, they recognize and accept the true nature of a situation and try to deal with it in a practical way. ♦**realist, realists** N-C *I see myself not as a cynic but as a realist.* [2] N-U If things and people are presented with **realism** in painting, novels, or films, they are presented in a way that is like real life; used showing approval. ♦**realist** ADJ BEFORE N *...the foremost realist painter of our times.*

realistic /ˌriːəˈlɪstɪk/. [1] ADJ If you are **realistic** about a situation, you recognize and accept its true nature and try to deal with it practically. *It's only realistic to acknowledge that something, some time, will go wrong.* ♦**realistically** ADV *As an adult, you can assess the situation realistically.* [2] ADJ You say that a painting, story, or film is **realistic** when the people and things in it are like people and things in real life. ♦**realistically** ADV *The film starts off realistically and then develops into a ridiculous fantasy.*

reality /riˈælɪti/ **realities.** [1] N-U You use **reality** to refer to real things or the real nature of things rather than imagined, invented, or theoretical ideas. *Fiction and reality were increasingly blurred.* [2] N-C The **reality** of a situation is the truth about it, especially when it is unpleasant. *...the harsh reality of top international competition.* [3] N-VAR If something becomes a **reality**, it actually exists or is actually happening. *The reality is that they are poor.* [4] PHRASE You can use **in reality** to introduce a statement about the real nature of something, when it contrasts with something incorrect that has just been described. *He came across as streetwise, but in reality he was not.*

realize (BR also **realise**) /ˈriːəlaɪz/ **realizes, realizing, realized.** [1] VERB If you **realize** that something is true, you become aware of that fact or understand it. *People don't realize how serious this recession has actually been.* ♦**realization, realizations** N-C *There is now a growing realisation that things cannot go on like this.* [2] VERB When someone **realizes** a design or an idea, they make or organize something based on that design or idea; FORMAL. *The characters in 'Terminator II' have been cleverly realised.* [3] VERB If your hopes, desires,

or fears **are realized**, the things that you hope for, desire, or fear actually happen; FORMAL. ♦**realization** N-U *...the realization of his worst fears.*

really /ˈriːəli/. [1] ADV You can use **really** to emphasize a statement; SPOKEN. *I'm very sorry. I really am... I really do feel that some people are being unfair.* [2] ADV You use **really** when you are discussing the real facts about something, in contrast to the ones someone wants you to believe. *My father didn't really love her... What was really going on?* [3] ADV People sometimes use the word **really** to slightly reduce the force of a negative statement. *I'm not really surprised... 'Did they hurt you?'—'Not really'.* [4] CONVENTION You can say '**Really?**' to express surprise or disbelief. *'We saw a very bright shooting star.'—'Did you really?'*

> When **really** is used in a negative sentence, its position in relation to the verb affects the meaning. For instance, if you say **I really don't like Richard**, with **really** in front of the verb, you are emphasizing how much you dislike Richard. However, if you say **I don't really like Richard**, with **really** coming after the negative, you are still saying that you dislike Richard, but the feeling is not particularly strong.

realm /relm/ **realms.** N-C You can use the word **realm** to refer to any area of activity, interest, or thought; FORMAL. *...the realm of politics.*

,**real 'world.** N-SING If you talk about **the real world**, you are referring to the world and life in general, in contrast to a particular person's own life, experience, and ideas. *When they eventually leave the school they will be totally ill-equipped to deal with the real world.*

reap /riːp/ **reaps, reaping, reaped.** VERB If you **reap** the benefits or the rewards of something, you enjoy the good things that happen as a result of it.

reappear /ˌriːəˈpɪə/ **reappears, reappearing, reappeared.** VERB When people or things **reappear**, they return after they have been away or out of sight for some time. ♦**reappearance, reappearances** N-C *...the reappearance of Cossack culture in Russia.*

rear /rɪə/. **rears, rearing, reared.** [1] N-SING The **rear** of something is the back part of it. *...the rear of the building... Manufacturers have been obliged to fit rear seat belts in all new cars.* [2] VERB If you **rear** children or young animals, you look after them until they are old enough to look after themselves. *I was reared in east Texas.* [3] VERB If a horse **rears** or **rears up**, it moves the front part of its body upwards, so that its front legs are high in the air and it is standing on its back legs.

rearrange /ˌriːəˈreɪndʒ/ **rearranges, rearranging, rearranged.** VERB If you **rearrange** things, you change the way they are organized or ordered. *She rearranged the furniture.* ♦**rearrangement, rearrangements** N-VAR *...a rearrangement of our parliamentary institutions.*

reason /ˈriːzən/ **reasons, reasoning, reasoned.** [1] N-C The **reason** for something is a fact or situation which explains why it happens. *Who would have a reason to want to kill her? ...the reason why Italian tomatoes have so much flavour... For some reason Herman decided not to play the piece.* [2] N-U If you say that you have **reason** to believe something or to have a particular emotion, you mean that you have evidence for your belief or there is a definite cause of your feeling. *He had every reason to be upset.* [3] N-U The ability that people have to think and to make sensible judgments can be referred to as **reason**. *...a conflict between emotion and reason.* [4] VERB If you **reason** that something is true, you decide that it is true after thinking carefully about all the facts. *I reasoned that if he could do it, so could I... 'Motherhood would be a full-time job,' she reasoned.* [5] PHRASE If one thing happens **by reason of** another, it happens because of it; FORMAL. [6] See also **reasoned, reasoning.**

▶ **reason with.** PHR-VERB If you try to **reason with** someone, you try to persuade them to do something or to accept something by using sensible arguments.

reasonable /ˈriːzənəbəl/. [1] ADJ If you think that someone is fair and sensible you can say they are **reasonable**. *...this moderate and reasonable man. ...a perfectly reasonable decision.* ♦ **reasonably** ADV *'I'm sorry, Andrew,' she said reasonably.* ♦ **reasonableness** N-U *Bertha spoke with calm reasonableness.* [2] ADJ If you say that an expectation or explanation is **reasonable**, you mean that there are good reasons why it may be correct. *It seems reasonable to expect rapid urban growth.* ♦ **reasonably** ADV *Today's young adults can reasonably expect to live well into their 70s.* [3] ADJ If you say that the price of something is **reasonable**, you mean that it is fair and not too high. ♦ **reasonably** ADV *...reasonably priced accommodation.* [4] ADJ You can use the word **reasonable** to describe something that is fairly good, but not very good. ♦ **reasonably** ADV *I can dance reasonably well.* [5] ADJ A **reasonable** amount of something is a fairly large amount of it. *There are a reasonable number of people here.* ♦ **reasonably** ADV *The repairs were made reasonably quickly.*

reasoned /ˈriːzənd/. ADJ A **reasoned** discussion or argument is based on sensible reasons, rather than on feelings.

reasoning /ˈriːzənɪŋ/. N-U **Reasoning** is the process by which you reach a conclusion after considering all the facts. *...the reasoning behind the decision.*

reassert /ˌriːəˈsɜːt/ **reasserts, reasserting, reasserted.** [1] VERB If you **reassert** your control or authority, you make it clear that you are still in a position of power, or you strengthen the power that you had. [2] VERB If something such as an idea or habit **reasserts** itself, it becomes noticeable again.

reassess /ˌriːəˈses/ **reassesses, reassessing, reassessed.** VERB If you **reassess** a situation, you think about it and decide whether you need to change your opinion about it. ♦ **reassessment, reassessments** N-VAR *We need an urgent reassessment of the entire programme.*

reassure /ˌriːəˈʃʊə/ **reassures, reassuring, reassured.** VERB If you **reassure** someone, you say or do things to make them stop worrying about something. ♦ **reassurance, reassurances** N-VAR *She needed reassurance that she belonged somewhere.*

reassured /ˌriːəˈʃʊəd/. ADJ If you feel **reassured**, you feel less worried about something. *We both felt reassured after a talk with the surgeon.*

reassuring /ˌriːəˈʃʊərɪŋ/. ADJ If you find someone's words or actions **reassuring**, they make you feel less worried. ♦ **reassuringly** ADV *'It's okay now,' he said reassuringly.*

rebate /ˈriːbeɪt/ **rebates.** N-C A **rebate** is an amount of money which is paid to you when you have paid more tax, rent, or rates than you needed to.

rebel, rebels, rebelling, rebelled; verb /rɪˈbel/, noun /ˈrebəl/. [1] N-C **Rebels** are people who are fighting against their own country's army in order to change the political system there. [2] VERB If politicians **rebel** against one of their own party's policies, they show that they oppose it. [3] N-C Politicians who show that they oppose their own party's policies are sometimes referred to as **rebels.** [4] VERB When someone **rebels**, they start to behave differently from other people and reject the values of society or of their parents. [5] N-C If you say that someone is a **rebel**, you mean that they behave differently from other people and reject the values of society or of their parents.

rebellion /rɪˈbeljən/ **rebellions.** [1] N-VAR A **rebellion** is a violent organized action by a large group of people who are trying to change their country's political system. [2] N-VAR A **rebellion** is a situation in which politicians show their opposition to their own party's policies.

rebellious /rɪˈbeljəs/. ADJ A **rebellious** person behaves in an unacceptable way and does not do what they are told. ♦ **rebelliousness** N-U *With adolescence his rebelliousness only increased.*

rebirth /ˌriːˈbɜːθ/. N-SING You can refer to a change that leads to a new period of growth and improvement in something as its **rebirth**. *...the rebirth of democracy in Latin America.*

rebound /rɪˈbaʊnd/ **rebounds, rebounding, rebounded.** [1] VERB If something **rebounds** from a solid surface, it bounces or springs back from it. *The ball rebounded off the wall.* [2] VERB If an action or situation **rebounds** on you, it has an unpleasant effect on you, especially when this effect was intended for someone else. *Mia realised her trick had rebounded on her.*

rebuff /rɪˈbʌf/ **rebuffs, rebuffing, rebuffed.** VERB & N-VAR If someone **rebuffs** your suggestion or advice, or if they treat it with a **rebuff**, they respond in an unfriendly way and refuse to accept it.

rebuild /ˌriːˈbɪld/ **rebuilds, rebuilding, rebuilt.** [1] VERB When people **rebuild** something such as a building, they build it again after it has been damaged or destroyed. [2] VERB When people **rebuild** something such as an institution, a system, or an aspect of their lives, they take action to restore it to its previous state.

rebuke /rɪˈbjuːk/ **rebukes, rebuking, rebuked.** VERB & N-VAR If you **rebuke** someone, or if you give them a **rebuke**, you speak severely to them because they have said or done something that you do not approve of; FORMAL.

recall /rɪˈkɔːl/ **recalls, recalling, recalled.** [1] VERB When you **recall** something, you remember it. *I recalled all that Ray had told me... She could not recall ever seeing him drunk.* [2] VERB When you **recall** something, you remember it and tell others about it. *Henderson recalled the he first met Pollard during a business trip... 'That evening, I felt he was friendly,' she recalled.* [3] VERB If you are **recalled** to your home, country, or the place where you work, you are ordered to return there. *Spain has recalled its Ambassador after a row over refugees.*

recapture /ˌriːˈkæptʃə/ **recaptures, recapturing, recaptured.** [1] VERB & N-SING When soldiers **recapture** a place, they win control of it again from an opposing army who had taken it from them. You can also refer to the **recapture** of a place. [2] VERB & N-SING To **recapture** a person or animal which has escaped from somewhere means to catch them again. You can also refer to the **recapture** of a person or animal. [3] VERB When you **recapture** something such as an experience, emotion, or a quality you had in the past, or when something **recaptures** it for you, you experience it again. *This macho behaviour is the way they try and recapture their youth.*

recede /rɪˈsiːd/ **recedes, receding, receded.** [1] VERB If something **recedes** from you, it moves away into the distance. *Luke's footsteps receded into the night.* [2] VERB When something such as a quality, problem, or illness **recedes**, it becomes weaker, smaller, or less intense. [3] VERB If a man's hair starts to **recede**, it no longer grows on the front of his head.

receipt /rɪˈsiːt/ **receipts.** [1] N-C A **receipt** is a piece of paper that you get from someone as confirmation that they have received money or goods from you. *I wrote her a receipt for the money.* [2] N-PL **Receipts** are the amount of money received during a particular period, for example by a shop or theatre. *On Saturdays Amos takes the week's receipts to the bank.* [3] N-U The **receipt** of something is the act of receiving it; FORMAL. *We cannot acknowledge receipt of letters.*

receive /rɪˈsiːv/ **receives, receiving, received.** [1] VERB When you **receive** something, you get it after someone gives it to you or sends it to you. *They will receive their awards at a ceremony in Stockholm.* [2] VERB You can use **receive** to say that certain kinds of thing happen to someone. For example if they are injured, you can say that they **received** an injury. *He received more of the blame than anyone.* [3] VERB If you say that something **is received** in a particular way, you mean that people react to it in that way. *The book's been well received.*

receiver /rɪˈsiːvə/ **receivers.** [1] N-C A telephone **receiver** is the part that you hold near to your ear and speak into. [2] N-C A **receiver** is the part of a radio or television that picks up incoming signals and converts them into sound or pictures. [3] N-C A **receiver** is someone who is officially appointed to manage the affairs of a business, usually when it has gone into bankruptcy.

recent /ˈriːsənt/. ADJ A **recent** event or period of time happened only a short while ago. *...her recent trip to Argentina... The situation has improved in recent years.*

recently /ˈriːsəntli/. ADV If you have done something **recently** or if something happened **recently**, it happened only a short time ago. *Mr Stevens recently celebrated his eightieth birthday... Until recently she was renting a house.*

reception /rɪˈsepʃən/ **receptions.** [1] N-U In a hotel, office, or hospital, **reception** is the place where people are received and their reservations, appointments, and inquiries are dealt with. *'For you,' the young lady at reception said. ...the hotel reception desk.* [2] N-C A **reception** is a formal party which is given to celebrate a special event or to welcome someone. *The wedding and the reception will be held on Saturday.* [3] N-C If something or someone has a particular kind of **reception**, that is the way people react to them. *He received a cool reception to his speech.* [4] N-U If you get good **reception** from your radio or television, the sound or picture is clear because the signal is strong.

receptionist /rɪˈsepʃənɪst/ **receptionists.** N-C In a hotel, office, or hospital, the **receptionist** is the person whose job is to answer the telephone, arrange reservations or appointments, and deal with people when they first arrive.

receptive /rɪˈseptɪv/. ADJ Someone who is **receptive** to new ideas or suggestions is prepared to consider them or accept them.

recess /rɪˈses, ˈriːses/ **recesses, recessing, recessed.** [1] N-VAR A **recess** is a break between the sessions of work of an official body such as a committee, a court of law, or a government. *The conference broke for a recess.* [2] VERB When formal proceedings **recess**, they stop temporarily. *The hearings have now recessed for dinner.* [3] N-C In a room, a **recess** is part of a wall which is built further back than the rest of the wall. [4] N-C The **recesses** of something are its deep or hidden parts. *He emerged from the dark recesses of the garage.*

recession /rɪˈseʃən/ **recessions.** N-VAR A **recession** is a period when the economy of a country is not very successful. *The oil price increases sent Europe into deep recession.*

recipe /ˈresɪpi/ **recipes.** [1] N-C A **recipe** is a list of ingredients and a set of instructions that tell you how to cook something. [2] N-SING If you say that something is **a recipe for** a particular situation, you mean that it is likely to result in that situation. *When two ladies are involved in the same kitchen, it is often a recipe for disaster.*

recipient /rɪˈsɪpɪənt/ **recipients.** N-C The **recipient** of something is the person who receives it; FORMAL. *...recipients of government grants.*

reciprocal /rɪˈsɪprəkəl/. ADJ A **reciprocal** action or agreement involves two people or groups who do the same thing to each other or agree to help each other in a similar way; FORMAL.

...the old reciprocal relationship that exists between workers and employers.

reciprocate /rɪˈsɪprəkeɪt/ **reciprocates, reciprocating, reciprocated.** VERB If your feelings or actions towards someone **are reciprocated**, the other person feels or behaves in the same way towards you as you have felt or behaved towards them. *I hope they reciprocate by coming to support us.*

recital /rɪˈsaɪtəl/ **recitals.** N-C A **recital** is a performance of music or poetry, usually given by one person.

recite /rɪˈsaɪt/ **recites, reciting, recited.** [1] VERB When someone **recites** a poem or other piece of writing, they say it aloud after they have learned it. [2] VERB If you **recite** something such as a list, you say it aloud. *All he could do was recite a list of Government failings.*

reckless /ˈrekləs/. ADJ A **reckless** person shows a lack of care about danger or about the results of their actions. *She was reckless and utterly without fear. ...reckless driving.* ◆ **recklessly** ADV *She spent money recklessly.* ◆ **recklessness** N-U *...the headstrong recklessness of youth.*

reckon /ˈrekən/ **reckons, reckoning, reckoned.** [1] VERB If you **reckon** that something is true, you think that it is true; INFORMAL. *Toni reckoned that it must be about three o'clock.* [2] VERB If something **is reckoned** to be a particular figure, it is calculated to be roughly that amount. *The amount being poured into East Germany was reckoned at 140 billion marks.*

▶ **reckon with.** [1] PHR-VERB If you had not **reckoned with** something, you had not expected it and so were not ready for it. *Giles had not reckoned with the strength of Sally's feelings for him.* [2] PHRASE If you refer to a person or force as someone or something **to be reckoned with**, you mean they will be difficult to deal with because they are quite powerful or skilful. *Women have become a force to be reckoned with.*

reckoning /ˈrekənɪŋ/ **reckonings.** N-VAR Someone's **reckoning** is a calculation they make about something. *By my reckoning 50% of the people in our team will be available.*

reclaim /rɪˈkleɪm/ **reclaims, reclaiming, reclaimed.** [1] VERB If you **reclaim** something that you have lost or had taken away from you, you succeed in getting it back. *We can reclaim the income tax which you have already paid on this money.* [2] VERB When people **reclaim** land, they make it suitable for use by draining or irrigating it. *...1,100 acres of reclaimed land in Tokyo Bay.*

recline /rɪˈklaɪn/ **reclines, reclining, reclined.** [1] VERB If you **recline** on something, you sit or lie on it with the upper part of your body supported at an angle. *Some guests recline in lounge chairs.* [2] VERB If a seat **reclines**, you can lower the back so that it is more comfortable to sit in. *First-class seats recline almost like beds.*

recluse /rɪˈkluːs, AM ˈrekluːs/ **recluses.** N-C A **recluse** is a person who lives alone and deliberately avoids other people.

reclusive /rɪˈkluːsɪv/. ADJ If someone is **reclusive**, they prefer to live on their own and deliberately avoid other people.

recognition /ˌrekəgˈnɪʃən/. [1] N-U **Recognition** is the act of recognizing someone or identifying something when you see it. *He searched for a sign of recognition on her face.* [2] N-U **Recognition** of something is an understanding and acceptance of it. *...their recognition of the workers' right to strike.* [3] N-U When a person receives **recognition** for the things that they have done, people acknowledge the value or skill of their work. *Her father's work has received popular recognition.* [4] PHRASE If something is done **in recognition of** someone's achievements, it is done as a way of showing official appreciation of them. *He was presented with a bottle of champagne in recognition of his services to Australian soccer.*

recognizable (BR also **recognisable**) /ˌrekəgˈnaɪzəbəl/. ADJ Something that is **recognizable** is easy to recognize or identify. *This tree is always recognizable by its extremely beautiful silvery bark.*

recognize (BR also **recognise**) /ˈrekəgnaɪz/ **recognizes, recognizing, recognized.** [1] VERB If you **recognize** someone or something, you know who or what they are, because you have seen or heard them before or because they have been described to you. *The receptionist recognized him at once. ...a man I easily recognized as Luke's father.* [2] VERB You say that you **recognize** something when you realize or accept that it exists or that it is true. *Of course I recognize that evil exists... They have been slow to recognize AIDS as a problem.* [3] VERB If people or organizations **recognize** something as valid, they officially accept it or approve of it. *Russia has recognized Ukraine independence.* [4] VERB When people **recognize** the work someone has done, they show their appreciation of it, often by giving that person an award.

recoil /rɪˈkɔɪl/ **recoils, recoiling, recoiled.** [1] VERB If something makes you **recoil**, you move your body quickly away from it because it frightens, offends, or hurts you. *I thought he was going to kiss me. I recoiled in horror.* [2] VERB If you say that someone **recoils** from doing something or **recoils** at the idea of something, you mean that they are reluctant to do it because they dislike it so much. *People used to recoil from the idea of getting into debt.*

recollection /ˌrekəˈlekʃən/ **recollections.** N-VAR If you have a **recollection** of something, you remember it. *Pat has vivid recollections of the trip... He had no recollection of the crash.*

recommend /ˌrekəˈmend/ **recommends, recommending, recommended.** [1] VERB If someone **recommends** something or someone to you, they suggest that you would find them good or useful. *I have just spent a holiday there and would recommend it to anyone... I'll recommend you for a promotion.* ◆ **recommended** ADJ *This book is highly recommended.* ◆ **recommendation, recommendations** N-C *Most people choose a product often on the recommendation of others.* [2] VERB If you **recommend** that something is done, you advise that it should be done. *It is recommended that you should consult your doctor.* ◆ **recommendation** N-C *The committee's recom-*

mendations are unlikely to be made public.
[3] VERB If something has a particular quality to **recommend** it, that quality makes it attractive or gives it an advantage over similar things. *La Noblesse restaurant has much to recommend it to diners.*

reconcile /'rekənsaɪl/ **reconciles, reconciling, reconciled.** [1] VERB If you **reconcile** two beliefs, facts, or demands that seem to be opposed or completely different, you find a way in which they can both be true or both be fulfilled. *It's difficult to reconcile the demands of my job and the desire to be a good father.* ♦**reconciliation** /ˌrekənsɪli'eɪʃən/ N-SING ...*a reconciliation of the values of equality and liberty.* [2] VERB If you **are reconciled** with someone, you become friendly with them again after a disagreement. *He never believed he and Susan would be reconciled. ...my attempt to reconcile him with Toby.* ♦**reconciliation, reconciliations** N-U *The couple have separated but he wants a reconciliation.* [3] VERB If you **reconcile** yourself to an unpleasant situation, you accept it. *She had reconciled herself to never seeing him again.* ♦**reconciled** ADJ AFTER LINK-V *He seemed reconciled to defeat.*

reconnaissance /rɪ'kɒnɪsəns/. N-U **Reconnaissance** is the process of obtaining military information about a place using soldiers, planes, or satellites.

reconsider /ˌriːkən'sɪdə/ **reconsiders, reconsidering, reconsidered.** VERB If you **reconsider** a decision or method, you think about it and try to decide whether it should be changed. *This has forced the United States to seriously reconsider its position.*

reconstruct /ˌriːkən'strʌkt/ **reconstructs, reconstructing, reconstructed.** [1] VERB If you **reconstruct** something that has been destroyed or badly damaged, you build it and make it work again. *He had plastic surgery to help reconstruct his badly damaged face.* ♦**reconstruction** N-U ...*the post-war reconstruction of Germany.* [2] VERB To **reconstruct** something such as a system means to change its construction so that it works in a different way. *She actually wanted to reconstruct the state and transform society.* [3] VERB If you **reconstruct** a past event, you obtain a complete description of it by combining a lot of small pieces of information. ♦**reconstruction** N-C *Mrs Kerr was too upset to take part in a reconstruction of her ordeal.*

record, records, recording, recorded; noun /'rekɔːd, AM -kərd/, verb /rɪ'kɔːd/. [1] N-C If you keep a **record** of something, or if you keep something **on record**, you keep an account of it in writing, photographs, or on a computer so that it can be referred to later. *The result will go on your medical records... A photograph of each customer will be kept on record.* [2] N-C Someone's **record** is the facts that are known about their achievements or character. *Professor Blainey has a distinguished record as a historical researcher.* [3] VERB If you **record** a piece of information or an event, you write it down, photograph it, or put it into a computer so that in the future people can refer to it. *Her letters record the domestic and social details of diplo-*

matic life. [4] VERB When music or speech **is recorded**, it is put onto a tape or a record, so that it can be heard again later. [5] N-C A **record** is a round flat piece of black plastic on which music is stored. You listen to the sound by playing the record on a record player. [6] N-C A **record** is the best result that has ever been achieved in a particular sport or activity, for example the fastest time or the furthest distance. ...*the 800 metres, where she is the world record holder.* [7] See also **recording, track record.**

PHRASES ● If you say something **off the record**, you do not intend what you say to be taken as official, or published with your name attached to it. ● If you **set the record straight** or **put the record straight**, you show that something which has been regarded as true is in fact not true.

recorder /rɪ'kɔːdə/ **recorders.** N-C A **recorder** is a hollow musical instrument that you play by blowing down one end and covering a series of holes with your fingers.

recording /rɪ'kɔːdɪŋ/ **recordings.** [1] N-C A **recording** of something is a record, tape, CD, or video of it. [2] N-U **Recording** is the process of making records, tapes, or videos. ...*the recording industry.*

'record player, record players. N-C A **record player** is a machine on which you play records.

recount, recounts, recounting, recounted. [1] VERB /rɪ'kaʊnt/ If you **recount** a story or event, you tell or describe it to people; FORMAL. *He recounted how Williams had visited him.* [2] N-C /'riːkaʊnt/ A **recount** is a second count of votes in an election when the result is very close.

recoup /rɪ'kuːp/ **recoups, recouping, recouped.** VERB If you **recoup** a sum of money that you have spent or lost, you get it back. *Insurance companies are trying to recoup their losses.*

recourse /rɪ'kɔːs/. N-U If you have **recourse** to something, you use it to help you in a difficult situation. *It enabled its members to settle their differences without recourse to war.*

recover /rɪ'kʌvə/ **recovers, recovering, recovered.** [1] VERB When you **recover** from an illness or an injury, you become well again. *A policeman was recovering in hospital last night after being stabbed.*

> **Recover** is a fairly formal word. In conversation, you usually say that someone **gets better.** *Qualified nurses help patients get better more quickly.*

[2] VERB If you **recover** from an unhappy or unpleasant experience, you stop being upset by it. *Her plane broke down and it was 18 hours before she got there. It took her three days to recover.* [3] VERB If you **recover** something that has been lost or stolen, you find it or get it back. *Police raided five houses in south-east London and recovered stolen goods.* [4] VERB If you **recover** your former mental or physical state, it comes back again. *She never recovered consciousness.*

recovery /rɪ'kʌvəri/ **recoveries.** [1] N-VAR If a sick person makes a **recovery**, he or she becomes well again. *He had been given less than a one in 500 chance of recovery.* [2] N-VAR When there is a **recovery** in a country's economy, it improves. [3] N-U You talk about the **recovery** of something when you get it back after it has been lost or stolen. *A substantial reward is being offered for the recovery of a painting by Turner.* [4] N-U You talk about the **recovery** of someone's physical or mental state when they return to this state. *...the abrupt loss and recovery of consciousness.*

recreate /ˌriːkri'eɪt/ **recreates, recreating, recreated.** VERB If you **recreate** something, you succeed in making it happen or exist again. *I am trying to recreate family life far from home.* ♦**recreation, recreations** N-C *...a faithful recreation of the original Elizabethan theatre.*

recreation /ˌrekri'eɪʃən/ **recreations.** N-VAR **Recreation** consists of things that you do in your spare time to relax. *All the family members need to have their own interests and recreations.* ♦**recreational** ADJ *...parks and other recreational facilities.*

recrimination /rɪˌkrɪmɪ'neɪʃən/ **recriminations.** N-VAR **Recriminations** are accusations that two people or groups make about each other. *The war sweeps up everyone in hatred and recrimination.*

recruit /rɪ'kruːt/ **recruits, recruiting, recruited.** [1] VERB If you **recruit** people for an organization, you get them to join it or work for it. *The police are trying to recruit more black and Asian officers.* ♦**recruiting** N-U *...an army recruiting office.* ♦**recruitment** N-U *...a crisis in teacher recruitment.* [2] N-C A **recruit** is a person who has recently joined an organization or army.

rectangle /'rektæŋɡəl/ **rectangles.** N-C A **rectangle** is a shape with four sides whose angles are all right angles. Each side of a rectangle is the same length as the one opposite to it.

rectangular /rek'tæŋɡjʊlə/. ADJ Something that is **rectangular** is shaped like a rectangle. *...a rectangular table.*

rectify /'rektɪfaɪ/ **rectifies, rectifying, rectified.** VERB If you **rectify** something that is wrong, you change it so that it becomes correct or satisfactory. *Only an act of Congress could rectify the situation.*

recuperate /rɪ'kuːpəreɪt/ **recuperates, recuperating, recuperated.** VERB When you **recuperate**, you recover your health or strength after you have been ill or injured. *He is recuperating from a serious back injury.* ♦**recuperation** N-U *Sleep is necessary for recuperation.*

recur /rɪ'kɜː/ **recurs, recurring, recurred.** VERB If something **recurs**, it happens more than once. *...a recurring nightmare she has had since childhood.* ♦**recurrence**, /rɪ'kʌrəns, AM -'kɜːr-/ **recurrences** N-VAR *Police are out in force to prevent a recurrence of the violence.*

recurrent /rɪ'kʌrənt, AM -'kɜːr-/. ADJ A **recurrent** event or feeling happens or is experienced more than once. *...buildings in which staff suffer recurrent illness.*

recycle /ˌriː'saɪkəl/ **recycles, recycling, recycled.** VERB If you **recycle** things that have already been used, such as bottles or sheets of paper, you process them so that they can be used again.

red /red/ **redder, reddest; reds.** [1] ADJ & N-VAR Something that is **red** is the colour of blood or of a ripe tomato. [2] ADJ You describe someone's hair as **red** when it is between red and brown in colour.
PHRASES ● If a person or company is **in the red** or if their bank account is **in the red**, they have spent more money than they have in their account and therefore they owe money to the bank. ● If you **see red**, you become very angry.

reddish /'redɪʃ/. ADJ **Reddish** means slightly red in colour.

redeem /rɪ'diːm/ **redeems, redeeming, redeemed.** [1] VERB If you **redeem** yourself, you do something that gives people a good opinion of you again after you have behaved or performed badly. *He had realized the mistake he had made and wanted to redeem himself.* [2] VERB When something **redeems** an unpleasant thing or situation, it prevents it from being completely bad. *Work is the way that people seek to redeem their lives from futility.* [3] VERB If you **redeem** a debt or an obligation, you pay money that you owe or that you promised to pay.

redemption /rɪ'dempʃən/. N-U **Redemption** is the act of redeeming something or of being redeemed by something. *He craves redemption for his sins. ...redemption of the loan.*

redevelopment /ˌriːdɪ'veləpmənt/. N-U When **redevelopment** takes place, old buildings in a part of a town are knocked down and new ones are built in their place.

red-'hot. ADJ Something that is **red-hot** is extremely hot.

redirect /ˌriːdɪ'rekt, -daɪ-/ **redirects, redirecting, redirected.** [1] VERB If you **redirect** your energy, resources, or ability, you begin doing something different or trying to achieve something different. *...the ability to redirect attention quickly.* [2] VERB If you **redirect** someone or something, you change their course. *She redirected them to the men's department.*

redistribute /ˌriːdɪ'strɪbjuːt/ **redistributes, redistributing, redistributed.** VERB If money or goods **are redistributed**, they are shared among people or organizations in a different way from the way that they were previously shared. *Taxes could be used to redistribute income.* ♦**redistribution** N-U *...a redistribution of wealth.*

redress /rɪ'dres/ **redresses, redressing, redressed.** [1] VERB If you **redress** something such as a wrong or a grievance, you do something to correct it or to improve things for the person who has been badly treated; FORMAL. *...laws designed to redress racial inequality.* [2] VERB If you **redress** the balance or the imbalance between two things that have become unequal, you make them equal again. *...to redress the economic imbalance between the developed countries and the developing countries.* [3] N-U **Redress** is compensation for something wrong that has been done; FORMAL. ...*their legal battle to seek some kind of a redress from the government.*

,red 'tape. N-U You refer to official rules and procedures as **red tape** when they seem unnecessary and cause delay.

reduce /rɪ'djuːs, AM -'duːs/ reduces, reducing, reduced. [1] VERB If you **reduce** something, you make it smaller. *It reduces the risks of heart disease.* [2] VERB If someone **is reduced** to a weaker or inferior state, they become weaker or inferior as a result of something that happens to them. *They were reduced to extreme poverty.* [3] VERB If something is changed to a different or less complicated form, you can say that it **is reduced** to that form. *All the buildings in the town have been reduced to rubble.* [4] VERB If you say that someone **is reduced** to doing something, you mean that they have to do it, although it is unpleasant or humiliating. *He was reduced to begging for a living.*

reduction /rɪ'dʌkʃən/ reductions. N-VAR When there is a **reduction** in something, it is made smaller. *Many companies have announced dramatic reductions in staff.*

redundancy /rɪ'dʌndənsi/ redundancies. N-VAR If there are **redundancies** within an organization, some of its employees are dismissed because their jobs are no longer necessary or because the organization can no longer afford to pay them; BRITISH. *Thousands of bank employees are facing redundancy.*

redundant /rɪ'dʌndənt/ [1] ADJ If you are made **redundant**, you lose your job because it is no longer necessary or because your employer cannot afford to keep paying you; BRITISH. ...*a redundant miner.* [2] ADJ Something that is **redundant** is no longer needed because it has been replaced by something else. *Changes in technology may mean that once-valued skills are now redundant.*

reed /riːd/ reeds. N-VAR Reeds are tall plants that grow in shallow water or wet ground.

reef /riːf/ reefs. N-C A **reef** is a long line of rocks or sand, the top of which is just above or just below the surface of the sea.

reek /riːk/ reeks, reeking, reeked. [1] VERB & N-SING If something **reeks** of something else, usually something unpleasant, it smells very strongly of it. You can also talk about the **reek** of something. *The entire house reeked... He smelt the reek of whisky.* [2] VERB If you say that something **reeks** of unpleasant ideas, feelings, or practices, you disapprove of it because it gives a firm impression that it involves those ideas, feelings, or practices. *The whole thing reeks of hypocrisy.*

reel /riːl/ reels, reeling, reeled. [1] N-C A **reel** is a cylinder-shaped object around which you wrap something such as thread or cinema film. [2] VERB When someone **reels**, they move about unsteadily as if they were going to fall. *He lost his balance and reeled back.* [3] VERB If you are **reeling** from a shock, you are feeling extremely surprised or upset because of it. *It left us reeling with disbelief.* [4] VERB If you say that your brain or your mind **is reeling**, you mean that

you are very confused because you have too much to think about.

▶ reel off. PHR-VERB If you **reel off** information, you repeat it from memory quickly and easily. *She reeled off the titles of a dozen or so of the novels.*

,re-e'lect, re-elects, re-electing, re-elected. VERB When someone such as a politician **is re-elected**, they win a new election and are therefore able to continue in their position as, for example, a member of parliament. *Juan Peron was re-elected president of Argentina in 1973.* ♦re-election N-U *I would like to see him stand for re-election.*

,re-ex'amine, re-examines, re-examining, re-examined. VERB If a person or group of people **re-examine** their ideas or beliefs, they think about them carefully because they are no longer sure if they are correct. *The European Community re-examined its policy towards South Africa.* ♦re-examination, re-examinations N-VAR *It was time for a re-examination of the situation.*

refer /rɪ'fɜː/ refers, referring, referred. [1] VERB If you **refer to** a particular subject or person, you mention them. *In his speech, he referred to a recent trip to Canada.* ♦reference /'refərəns/ references N-VAR *There was no reference to any agreement.* [2] VERB If you **refer to** someone or something by a particular name, you call them this name. *He always referred to his friend as Mr Lowry.* [3] VERB If a word or expression **refers to** something, it is used as a name for it. *The word 'banquet' refers to a feast.* [4] VERB If you **refer to** a book or other source of information, you look at it in order to find something out. *He had to keep referring to the manual.* ♦reference N-U *Keep this sheet for future reference.* [5] VERB If a person or problem **is referred** to another person or to an organization, that person or organization is asked to deal with them. *I was referred to an ear specialist... He referred the matter to the Police Complaints Authority.*

referee /,refə'riː/ referees, refereeing, refereed. [1] N-C The **referee** is the official who controls a sports match. [2] VERB If you **referee** a sports match, you act as referee.

reference /'refərəns/ references. [1] N-C A **reference** is something such as a number or a name that tells you where you can obtain information. ...*a map reference.* [2] ADJ BEFORE N **Reference** books are ones you look at when you need specific information about a subject. [3] PHRASE You use **with reference to** or **in reference to** to indicate who or what you are referring to. *I am writing with reference to your article on salaries.* [4] N-C A **reference** is a letter written by someone who knows you which describes your character and abilities. [5] See also **refer**.

referendum /,refə'rendəm/ referendums or referenda /,refə'rendə/. N-C A **referendum** is a vote in which all the people in a country are asked whether they agree or disagree with a particular policy. *Estonia said it too planned to hold a referendum on independence.*

referral /rɪ'fɜːrəl/ referrals. N-VAR Referral is the act of officially sending someone to a person or authority that is authorized or better qualified to deal with them. A **referral** is an instance of this. *...a 300% increase in referrals to his psychiatry practice.*

refill, refills, refilling, refilled; verb /ˌriːˈfɪl/, noun /ˈriːfɪl/. VERB & N-C If you **refill** something, or if you give it a **refill**, you fill it again after it has been emptied. *Max held out his cup for a refill.*

refine /rɪˈfaɪn/ **refines, refining, refined.**
[1] VERB When a substance **is refined**, it is made pure by the removal of other substances from it. *...refined sugar.* ◆ **refining** N-U *...oil refining.*
[2] VERB If something such as a process, a theory, or a machine **is refined**, it is improved by being changed in small ways. *Surgical techniques are constantly being refined.* ◆ **refinement, refinements** N-VAR *Further refinements are needed.*

refined /rɪˈfaɪnd/. ADJ **Refined** people are polite and well-mannered.

refinery /rɪˈfaɪnəri/ **refineries.** N-C A **refinery** is a factory which refines a substance such as oil or sugar.

refit, refits, refitting, refitted; verb /ˌriːˈfɪt/, noun /ˈriːfɪt/. VERB & N-C When a ship **is refitted**, or when it is given a **refit**, it is repaired or is given new parts, equipment, or furniture.

reflect /rɪˈflekt/ **reflects, reflecting, reflected.**
[1] VERB If something **reflects** an attitude or situation, it shows that the attitude or situation exists. *Concern at the economic situation was reflected in the government's budget.* [2] VERB When light or heat **is reflected** off a surface, it is sent back from the surface rather than passing through it. *The light reflects off the window. ...a layer of aluminium to reflect heat.* [3] VERB When something **is reflected** in a mirror or in water, you can see its image there. [4] VERB When you **reflect** on something, you think deeply about it. *I reflected on the child's future.* [5] VERB If an action or situation **reflects** in a particular way on someone or something, it gives people a good or bad impression of them. *The affair hardly reflected well on the British.*

reflection /rɪˈflekʃən/ **reflections.** [1] N-C A **reflection** is an image that you can see in a mirror or in water. [2] N-C A **reflection** of a person's attitude or a situation indicates that the attitude or situation exists. *Crumb's drawings turn out to be a reflection of his own self-loathing.* [3] N-SING If you say that something is a **reflection** on someone or a **sad reflection** on someone, you mean that it gives a bad impression of them. *It's no reflection on your ability as a mother.* [4] N-U **Reflection** is careful thought about a particular topic. *A moment's reflection reveals the weakness of such a defence... On reflection, he says, he very much regrets the comments.* [5] N-PL Your **reflections** are your thoughts about a particular topic. *...his reflections on the church.*

reflective /rɪˈflektɪv/. [1] ADJ If you are **reflective**, you think deeply about things; WRITTEN. ◆ **reflectively** ADV *He sipped his brandy reflectively.* [2] ADJ AFTER LINK-V If something is **reflective** of a particular situation or attitude, it shows that situation or attitude exists. *...a su-*

perb achievement reflective of rugby's booming popularity. [3] ADJ A **reflective** surface or material sends back light or heat; FORMAL. *...new reflective coatings.*

reflex /ˈriːfleks/ **reflexes.** [1] N-C A **reflex** or a **reflex action** is a normal uncontrollable reaction of your body to something that you feel, see, or experience. *Blushing is a reflex action linked to the nervous system.* [2] N-PL Your **reflexes** refer to your ability to react quickly when your body does something when something unexpected happens. *...the reflexes of an athlete.*

reflexive pronoun /rɪˈfleksɪv ˈprəʊnaʊn/ **reflexive pronouns.** N-C A **reflexive pronoun** is a pronoun such as 'myself' which refers back to the subject of a sentence or clause.

reflexive verb /rɪˈfleksɪv vɜːb/ **reflexive verbs.** N-C A **reflexive verb** is a transitive verb whose subject and object always refer to the same person or thing, so the object is always a reflexive pronoun. An example is 'to enjoy yourself'.

reform /rɪˈfɔːm/ **reforms, reforming, reformed.** [1] N-VAR **Reform** consists of changes and improvements to a law, social system, or institution. These changes can be called **reforms**. *He has urged reform of the welfare system.* [2] VERB To **reform** something such as a law, a social system, or an institution means to improve it by making changes. *...his proposals for reforming the legal system.* ◆ **reformer, reformers** N-C *...prison reformers.* [3] VERB When someone **reforms**, they stop doing something that society does not approve of. ◆ **reformed** ADJ *...a reformed alcoholic.*

refrain /rɪˈfreɪn/ **refrains, refraining, refrained.** [1] VERB If you **refrain** from doing something, you deliberately do not do it. *He appealed to all factions to refrain from violence.* [2] N-C A **refrain** is a short simple part of a song which you repeat several times.

refresh /rɪˈfreʃ/ **refreshes, refreshing, refreshed.** [1] VERB If something **refreshes** you when you are hot, tired, or thirsty, it makes you feel cooler or more energetic. ◆ **refreshed** ADJ *He awoke feeling completely refreshed.* ◆ **refreshing** ADJ *...refreshing drinks.* [2] PHRASE If someone **refreshes** your **memory**, they tell you something you have forgotten.

refreshing /rɪˈfreʃɪŋ/. ADJ If something is **refreshing**, it is pleasantly different from what you are used to. *It's refreshing to hear somebody speaking common sense.* ◆ **refreshingly** ADV *He was refreshingly honest.*

refreshment /rɪˈfreʃmənt/ **refreshments.** [1] N-PL **Refreshments** are drinks and small amounts of food that are provided, for example, during a meeting or journey. [2] N-U You can refer to food and drink as **refreshment**; FORMAL. *May I offer you some refreshment?*

refrigerate /rɪˈfrɪdʒəreɪt/ **refrigerates, refrigerating, refrigerated.** VERB If you **refrigerate** food, you make it cold, for example by putting it in a refrigerator. ◆ **refrigeration** N-U *Refrigeration slows down the growth of bacteria.*

refrigerator /rɪˈfrɪdʒəreɪtə/ **refrigerators.** N-C A **refrigerator** is a large container which is kept cool inside, usually by electricity, so that the food and drink in it stays fresh.

refuel /ˌriːˈfjuːəl/ **refuels, refuelling, refuelled** (AM **refueling, refueled**). VERB When an aircraft or other vehicle **refuels**, or when someone **refuels** it, it is filled with more fuel so that it can continue its journey. ♦**refuelling** N-U *It will make two refuelling stops.*

refuge /ˈrefjuːdʒ/ **refuges**. ① N-C If you take **refuge** somewhere, you try to protect yourself from physical harm by going there. *Many Cubans took refuge in the United States.* ② N-C A **refuge** is a place where you go for safety and protection. *...a refuge for battered women.*

refugee /ˌrefjuˈdʒiː/ **refugees**. N-C **Refugees** are people who have been forced to leave their country because there is a war there or because of their political or religious beliefs.

refund, refunds, refunding, refunded. ① N-C /ˈriːfʌnd/ A **refund** is a sum of money which is returned to you, for example because you have returned goods to a shop. *Dissatisfied customers can return the product for a full refund.* ② VERB /rɪˈfʌnd/ If someone **refunds** your money, they return it to you.

refurbish /riːˈfɜːbɪʃ/ **refurbishes, refurbishing, refurbished.** VERB To **refurbish** a building or room means to clean and decorate it, and make it more attractive or better equipped. ♦**refurbishment, refurbishments** N-VAR *The gallery is now closed for refurbishment.*

refusal /rɪˈfjuːzəl/ **refusals.** N-VAR A **refusal** is the fact of firmly saying or showing that you will not do, allow, or accept something. *...the Prince's repeated refusals to attend peace negotiations.*

refuse, refuses, refusing, refused. ① VERB /rɪˈfjuːz/ If you **refuse** to do something, you deliberately do not do it, or say firmly that you will not do it. *He expects me to stay on here and I can hardly refuse.* ② VERB If someone **refuses** you something, they do not allow you to have it. *The town council had refused permission for the march.* ③ VERB If you **refuse** something that is offered to you, you do not accept it. *The patient has the right to refuse treatment.* ④ N-U /ˈrefjuːs/ **Refuse** consists of the rubbish and unwanted things in a house, shop, or factory that are regularly thrown away; FORMAL.

refute /rɪˈfjuːt/ **refutes, refuting, refuted.** ① VERB If you **refute** something such as a theory or argument, you prove that it is wrong; FORMAL. *It was the kind of rumour that it is impossible to refute.* ② VERB If you **refute** an allegation or accusation, you deny that it is true; FORMAL. *He angrily refutes the charge.*

regain /rɪˈɡeɪn/ **regains, regaining, regained.** VERB If you **regain** something that you have lost, you get it back again. *Troops have regained control of the city.*

regal /ˈriːɡəl/. ADJ If you describe something as **regal**, you mean that it is suitable for a king or queen, because it is very splendid or dignified. *...his regal manner.*

regard /rɪˈɡɑːd/ **regards, regarding, regarded.** ① VERB If you **regard** someone or something in a particular way, you think of them in that way, or have that opinion of them. *He regarded drug dealers with loathing... He was regarded as the most successful Chancellor of*

modern times. ② N-U If you have a high **regard** for someone, you have a lot of respect for them. *She was pleased by Hugh's regard for her parents.* ③ N-PL **Regards** is used in expressions like 'best regards' and 'with warm regards' as a way of expressing friendly feelings towards someone. *Give my regards to your husband.*

PHRASES ● You can use **as regards**, with **regard to**, or **in regard to** to indicate what you are referring to. *As regards the war, Haig believed in victory at any price.* ● You can use **in this regard** or **in that regard** to refer back to something you have just said. *In this regard nothing has changed.*

regarding /rɪˈɡɑːdɪŋ/. PREP You can use **regarding** to indicate what you are referring to. *He refused to divulge any information regarding the man's whereabouts.*

regardless /rɪˈɡɑːdləs/. ① PHRASE If something happens **regardless of** something else, it is not affected or influenced at all by that other thing. *Regardless of whether he is right or wrong, we have to abide by his decisions.* ② ADV If you say someone did something **regardless**, you mean they did it even though there were problems that could have stopped them. *Britain's partners are pressing on regardless.*

regatta /rɪˈɡætə/ **regattas.** N-C A **regatta** is a sports event consisting of races between yachts or rowing boats.

regenerate /rɪˈdʒenəreɪt/ **regenerates, regenerating, regenerated.** VERB To **regenerate** something that has been declining means to develop and improve it to make it more active or successful. *The government will continue to try to regenerate inner city areas.* ♦**regeneration** N-U *...plans for the regeneration of the area.*

reggae /ˈreɡeɪ/. N-U **Reggae** is a kind of West Indian popular music with a very strong beat.

regime /reɪˈʒiːm/ **regimes.** N-C If you refer to a government as a **regime**, you are critical of it because you think it is not democratic and uses unacceptable methods. *...a military regime.*

regiment /ˈredʒɪmənt/ **regiments.** N-C A **regiment** is a large group of soldiers commanded by a colonel. ♦**regimental** /ˌredʒɪˈmentəl/ ADJ BEFORE N *...the regimental headquarters.*

region /ˈriːdʒən/ **regions.** ① N-C A **region** is an area of a country or of the world. *...a remote mountainous region of Afghanistan.* ♦**regional** ADJ *...regional conflicts.* ② PHRASE You say **in the region of** to indicate that you are mentioning an approximate amount. *The scheme will cost in the region of six million pounds.*

register /ˈredʒɪstə/ **registers, registering, registered.** ① N-C A **register** is an official list or record. *...the register of voters.* ② VERB If you **register** for something, you put your name on an official list. *He registered for a class in design.* ③ VERB If you **register** something, you have it recorded on an official list. *The boy's mother never registered his birth.* ④ VERB When something **registers** on a scale or measuring instrument, it shows a particular value. *The earthquake registered 5.3 points on the Richter* scale. **5** VERB If you **register** a feeling or opinion that you have, you make it clear to other people. *Her face registered her dismay... Workers stopped work to register their protest.*

registrar /ˌredʒɪ'strɑː, AM -'strɑːr/ **registrars.** **1** N-C A **registrar** is a person whose job is to keep official records, especially of births, marriages, and deaths. **2** N-C A **registrar** is a senior administrative official in a college or university.

registration /ˌredʒɪ'streɪʃən/. N-U The **registration** of something is the recording of it in an official list.

registry /'redʒɪstri/ **registries.** N-C A **registry** is a place where official records are kept.

regress /rɪ'gres/ **regresses, regressing, regressed.** VERB When people or things **regress**, they return to an earlier and less advanced stage of development; FORMAL. *...if your child regresses to babyish behaviour.* ◆**regression** /rɪ'greʃən/ N-U *...regression in a pupil's learning process.*

regret /rɪ'gret/ **regrets, regretting, regretted.** **1** VERB If you **regret** something that you have done, you wish that you had not done it. *I simply gave in to him, and I've regretted it ever since.* **2** N-VAR **Regret** is a feeling of sadness or disappointment. *He feels deep regret about his friend's death.* **3** N-U & VERB If someone expresses **regret** about something, or if they **regret** something, they are saying in a polite way that they are sorry about it; FORMAL. *She has accepted his resignation with regret... I regret to say that Mr Brand has been taken ill.*

regrettable /rɪ'gretəbəl/. ADJ You describe something as **regrettable** when you think that it is bad and that it should not happen or have happened. *Obviously, it is regrettable that we made the mistake.* ◆**regrettably** ADV *Regrettably we could find no sign of the man.*

regroup /ˌriː'gruːp/ **regroups, regrouping, regrouped.** VERB If a group of people who work as a team **regroup**, they reorganize themselves because their previous attempt to do something has failed.

regular /'regjʊlə/ **regulars.** **1** ADJ **Regular** things happen at equal intervals, or involve things happening at equal intervals. *Keep your eyes closed and let your breathing become regular. ...a regular pattern of sleeping and waking.* ◆**regularly** ADV *He also writes regularly for 'International Management' magazine.* ◆**regularity** /ˌregjʊ'lærɪti/ N-U *...the regularity of the beat.* **2** ADJ **Regular** events happen often. *They'd agreed to meet on a regular basis.* ◆**regularly** ADV *...if you regularly take snacks instead of eating properly.* ◆**regularity** N-U *Job losses are again being announced with monotonous regularity.* **3** N-C & ADJ BEFORE N If you are a **regular** at a place, or a **regular** visitor there, you go there often. *...regulars at his local pub. ...regular churchgoers.* **4** ADJ BEFORE N **Regular** means 'normal'. *The product looks and burns like a regular cigarette.* **5** ADJ If something has a **regular** shape, both halves are the same and it has straight edges or a smooth outline. *...a man of moderate height with regular features.* **6** ADJ A **regular** verb, noun, or adjective in-

flects in the same way as most other verbs, nouns, or adjectives in the same language.

regulate /'regjʊleɪt/ **regulates, regulating, regulated.** VERB To **regulate** an activity or process means to control it, especially by means of rules. *...proposals to regulate and limit animal testing.* ◆**regulation** N-U *...the regulation of nurseries.*

regulation /ˌregjʊ'leɪʃən/ **regulations.** N-C **Regulations** are rules made by a government or other authority in order to control the way something is done or the way people behave. *...the new safety regulations.*

regulator /'regjʊleɪtə/ **regulators.** N-C A **regulator** is a person or organization appointed by a government to regulate the activities of private companies who provide a service to the public. ◆**regulatory** /ˌregjʊ'leɪtəri/ ADJ BEFORE N *...the UK's financial regulatory system.*

rehabilitate /ˌriːhə'bɪlɪteɪt/ **rehabilitates, rehabilitating, rehabilitated.** VERB To **rehabilitate** someone who has been ill or in prison means to help them to live a normal life again. ◆**rehabilitation** N-U *...an alcohol and drug rehabilitation centre.*

rehearsal /rɪ'hɜːsəl/ **rehearsals.** N-VAR A **rehearsal** of a play, dance, or piece of music is the time when those taking part practice it. *...rehearsals for a concert tour.*

rehearse /rɪ'hɜːs/ **rehearses, rehearsing, rehearsed.** VERB When people **rehearse** a play, dance, or piece of music, they practise it. *Tens of thousands of people have been rehearsing for the opening ceremony.*

reign /reɪn/ **reigns, reigning, reigned.** **1** VERB If you say, for example, that silence **reigns** in a place, you mean that the place is silent. *A relative calm reigned over the city.* **2** VERB & N-C When a king or queen **reigns**, he or she is the leader of the country. The **reign** of a king or queen is the period when they reign. PHRASES ● Someone or something that **reigns supreme** is the most important or powerful element in a situation or period of time. *The bicycle reigned supreme as Britain's most popular mode of transport.* ● A **reign of terror** is a period during which there is a lot of violence and killing, especially by people who are in a position of power.

reimburse /ˌriːɪm'bɜːs/ **reimburses, reimbursing, reimbursed.** VERB If you **reimburse** someone for something, you pay them back the money they have spent or lost because of it; FORMAL. *I'll be happy to reimburse you for any expenses you might have incurred.* ◆**reimbursement, reimbursements** N-VAR *She is demanding reimbursement for medical and other expenses.*

rein /reɪn/ **reins, reining, reined.** N-PL **Reins** are the leather straps attached to a horse's bridle which are used to control the horse. PHRASES ● If you **give free rein** to someone, you give them a lot of freedom to do what they want. ► **rein in.** PHR-VERB To **rein in** something means to control it. *He has had to rein in his enthusiasm.*

reincarnation /ˌriːɪŋkɑː'neɪʃən/ **reincarnations.** **1** N-U If you believe in **reincarnation**, you believe that people are born again as other people or animals after they die. [2] N-C A **reincarnation** is a person or animal who is believed to contain the spirit of a dead person.

reindeer /'reɪndɪə/; **reindeer** is the singular and plural form. N-C A **reindeer** is a type of deer that lives in northern areas of Europe, Asia, and America.

reinforce /ˌriːɪn'fɔːs/ **reinforces, reinforcing, reinforced.** [1] VERB If something **reinforces** something such as a feeling, process, or belief, it makes it stronger. *They are determined to reinforce the message that they will not tolerate drug abuse.* ◆**reinforcement, reinforcements** N-VAR *...the role of science in the reinforcement of cruel but popular myths about race.* [2] VERB To **reinforce** an object means to make it stronger or harder. *They had to reinforce the walls with exterior beams. ...reinforced glass.*

reinforcements /ˌriːɪn'fɔːsmənts/. N-PL **Reinforcements** are soldiers who are sent to join an army in order to make it stronger.

reinstate /ˌriːɪn'steɪt/ **reinstates, reinstating, reinstated.** VERB If you **reinstate** someone, you give them back a job which had been taken from them. *They had not reinstated him as manager.* ◆**reinstatement** N-U *Parents campaigned in vain for her reinstatement.*

reiterate /riː'ɪtəreɪt/ **reiterates, reiterating, reiterated.** VERB If you **reiterate** something, you say it again or emphasize it; FORMAL. *Let me reiterate that I knew this about him.*

reject, rejects, rejecting, rejected. [1] VERB /rɪ'dʒekt/ If you **reject** something such as a proposal or request, you do not accept it or agree to it. *I think the president was correct to reject the offer.* ◆**rejection** N-VAR *...his rejection of our values.* [2] VERB If someone **is rejected** for a job or course of study, it is not offered to them. ◆**rejection** N-C *Be prepared for lots of rejections before you land a job.* [3] VERB If you **reject** someone who feels affection for you, you show them that you do not feel affection for them. ◆**rejection** N-VAR *...feelings of rejection and hurt.* [4] N-C /'riːdʒekt/ A **reject** is a product that has not been accepted for use or sale, because there is something wrong with it.

rejoice /rɪ'dʒɔɪs/ **rejoices, rejoicing, rejoiced.** VERB If you **rejoice**, you are very pleased about something and you show it in your behaviour; LITERARY. ◆**rejoicing** N-U *There was general rejoicing at the news.*

rejuvenate /rɪ'dʒuːvəneɪt/ **rejuvenates, rejuvenating, rejuvenated.** VERB If something **rejuvenates** you, it makes you feel or look young again. *The Italian climate would rejuvenate him.* ◆**rejuvenating** ADJ *...rejuvenating face-cream.*

rekindle /ˌriː'kɪndl/ **rekindles, rekindling, rekindled.** VERB If something **rekindles** an interest, feeling, or thought that you used to have, it makes you think about it or feel it again. *The tragedy rekindled memories.*

relapse, relapses, relapsing, relapsed; verb /rɪ'læps/, noun /rɪ'læps/ or /'riːlæps/. [1] VERB & N-C If someone **relapses into** a way of behaving, or if they have a **relapse**, they start to behave in that way again. *With this the Superintendent relapsed into silence. ...relapses*

into old habits. [2] VERB & N-C If a sick person **relapses**, or if they have a **relapse**, their health suddenly gets worse after it had been improving.

relate /rɪ'leɪt/ **relates, relating, related.** [1] VERB If something **relates to** a particular subject, it concerns that subject. *The word crafts relates to the production of the work.* ◆**-related** *...smoking-related diseases.* [2] VERB The way that two things **relate** is the connection between them. *...a shift in thinking about how the two sciences relate.* ◆**related** ADJ *Crime and poverty are closely related. ...diving and related activities.* [3] VERB The way that people **relate** is the way that they communicate with each other and behave towards each other. *They didn't know how to relate to my sister.* [4] VERB If you **relate** a story, you tell it; FORMAL.

related /rɪ'leɪtɪd/. [1] ADJ AFTER LINK-V People who are **related** belong to the same family. *There are two families of Elwoods in Galway, and we're not related.* [2] See also **relate**.

relation /rɪ'leɪʃən/ **relations.** [1] N-PL **Relations** between people, groups, or countries are contacts between them and the way they behave towards each other. *Greece has established full diplomatic relations with Israel.* [2] N-U The **relation** of one thing to another is the connection between them. *...the relation of artists to politics.* [3] PHRASE You can talk about something **in relation to** something else when you want to compare the size, condition, or position of the two things. *The money he'd been ordered to pay was minimal in relation to his salary.* [4] N-C Your **relations** are the members of your family.

relationship /rɪ'leɪʃənʃɪp/ **relationships.** [1] N-C The **relationship** between two people or groups is the way they feel and behave towards each other. *...close family relationships.* [2] N-C A **relationship** is a close friendship between two people, especially one involving romantic or sexual feelings. *Both of us felt the relationship wasn't really going anywhere.* [3] N-C The **relationship** between two things is the way in which they are connected. *...a relationship between diet and cancer.*

relative /'relətɪv/ **relatives.** [1] N-C Your **relatives** are the members of your family. *Get a relative to look after the children.* [2] ADJ You use **relative** when you are comparing two or more things, particularly their size or quality. *The fighting resumed after a period of relative calm. ...the relative merits of London and Paris as places to live... If you do 50mph on a motorway, it's very slow. It's all relative.* ◆**relatively** ADV *The sums needed are relatively small.* [3] PHRASE **Relative to** something means with reference to it or in comparison with it. *Japanese interest rates rose relative to America's.*

relative 'clause, relative clauses. N-C A **relative clause** is a subordinate clause which specifies or gives information about a person or thing. Relative clauses come after a noun or pronoun and, in English, often begin with a relative pronoun such as 'who', 'which', or 'that'.

,relative 'pronoun, relative pronouns. N-C
A **relative pronoun** is a word such as 'who',
'that', or 'which' that is used to introduce a
relative clause.

relax /rɪˈlæks/ **relaxes, relaxing, relaxed.**
[1] VERB If you **relax**, or if something **relaxes**
you, you feel calmer and less worried or tense.
*I ought to relax and stop worrying about it... Do
something that you know relaxes you.*
♦**relaxation** N-U *...relaxation techniques.*
♦**relaxed** ADJ *The atmosphere at lunch was relaxed.* ♦**relaxing** ADJ *...a quiet, relaxing holiday.* [2] VERB When your body or a part of it **relaxes**, it becomes less stiff, firm, or tense. *Massage is used to relax muscles.* [3] VERB If you **re-
lax** your grip on something, you hold it less
tightly than before. [4] VERB If you **relax** a rule,
you make it less strict. *Rules governing student
conduct have relaxed somewhat in recent years.*

relay, relays, relaying, relayed. [1] N-C/ˈriːleɪ/
A **relay** or a **relay race** is a race between two or
more teams in which each member of the
team runs or swims one section of the race.
[2] VERB /rɪˈleɪ/ To **relay** television or radio signals means to send them on or broadcast
them.

release /rɪˈliːs/ **releases, releasing, released.** [1] VERB & N-C If a prisoner or animal **is
released**, they are set free. You can also talk
about someone's **release**. *He called for the release of all political prisoners.* [2] VERB & N-C To
release someone from an obligation, task, or
feeling, or to give them **release** from it means
to free them from it; FORMAL. *Many look on life
at college as a release from the obligation to
work.* [3] VERB & N-U If someone in authority **releases** information, they make it available. You
can also talk about the **release** of information.
[4] VERB If you **release** someone or something,
you stop holding them; FORMAL. *He stopped
and faced her, releasing her wrist.* [5] VERB & N-C
When a form of energy or a substance such as
a gas **is released** from something, it escapes
from it. You can also talk about the **release** of
energy or a substance. *...the release of radioactive materials into the environment.* [6] VERB &
N-C When a new CD, record, video, or film **is
released**, it becomes available so that people
can buy it or see it. You refer to this new CD,
record, video or film as a new **release**. [7] See
also **press release**.

relegate /ˈrelɪɡeɪt/ **relegates, relegating, relegated.** [1] VERB If a team that competes in a
league **is relegated**, it is moved to a lower division because it finished at or near the bottom
of its division at the end of a season.
♦**relegation** N-U *Relegation to the Third Division would prove catastrophic.* [2] VERB If someone or something **is relegated to** a less important position or role, they are moved to that
position or role.

relent /rɪˈlent/ **relents, relenting, relented.**
VERB If you **relent**, you allow someone to do
something that you had previously refused to
allow them to do. *Finally his mother relented
and gave permission for her son to marry.*

relentless /rɪˈlentləs/. ADJ If something is **relentless**, it never stops or becomes less intense. *The pressure now was relentless... She*
moves with relentless energy from one project to
another. ♦**relentlessly** ADV *The sun is beating
down relentlessly.*

relevant /ˈreləvənt/. ADJ If something is **relevant** to a situation or person, it is important
or significant in that situation or to that person. *I can think of nothing less relevant to Australians of the 1990s than a celebration of
Queen Victoria's birthday... Dr Venter said the
relevant authorities would be consulted.*
♦**relevance** /ˈreləvəns/ N-U *Many of the experiments performed on animals had little relevance to humans.*

reliable /rɪˈlaɪəbəl/. [1] ADJ **Reliable** people or
things can be trusted to work well or to behave
in the way that you want them to. ♦**reliably**
ADV *It's been working reliably for years.*
♦**reliability** N-U *He's worried about his car's reliability.* [2] ADJ **Reliable** information is very
likely to be correct, because it comes from a
trustworthy or accurate source. ♦**reliably** ADV
*Sonia, we are reliably informed, loves her fami-
ly very much.* ♦**reliability** N-U *Both questioned
the reliability of recent opinion polls.*

reliant /rɪˈlaɪənt/. ADJ AFTER LINK-V A person or
thing that is **reliant** on something needs it and
often cannot live or work without it. ♦**reliance**
N-U *...the country's increasing reliance on foreign aid.*

relic /ˈrelɪk/ **relics.** [1] N-C If you describe something or someone as a **relic** of an earlier period, you dislike them and think that they
should not have survived into the present.
*Their radio communication system is a relic
from the 1950s which keeps on breaking down.*
[2] N-C A **relic** is something which was made or
used a long time ago and which is kept for its
historical significance. *...a museum of war relics.*

relief /rɪˈliːf/. [1] N-U If you feel a sense of **relief**,
you feel glad because something unpleasant
has not happened or is no longer happening. *I
breathed a sigh of relief... It's a great relief to be
back.* [2] N-U If something provides **relief** from
pain or distress, it stops the pain or distress, or
it makes it less intense. [3] N-U **Relief** is money,
food, or clothing that is provided for people
who are very poor or hungry, or who have
been affected by war or a natural disaster.

relieve /rɪˈliːv/ **relieves, relieving, relieved.**
[1] VERB To **relieve** an unpleasant feeling or
situation means to make it less unpleasant or
cause it to disappear completely. *Drugs can relieve much of the pain.* [2] VERB If someone **relieves** you **of** something, they take it away
from you. *A porter relieved her of the three
large cases she had been pushing on a trolley.*
[3] VERB If you **relieve** someone, you take their
place and do the job or task being done previously by that person.

relieved /rɪˈliːvd/. ADJ If you are **relieved**, you
feel glad because something unpleasant has
not happened or is no longer happening.

religion /rɪˈlɪdʒən/ **religions.** [1] N-U **Religion** is
belief in a god or gods. *...Indian philosophy
and religion.* [2] N-C A **religion** is a particular
set of beliefs in a god or gods and the activities
connected with these beliefs. *...the Christian
religion.*

religious /rɪˈlɪdʒəs/. [1] ADJ BEFORE N **Religious** means connected with religion or with one particular religion. ...*different religious beliefs.* [2] ADJ A **religious** person has a strong belief in a god or gods.

relinquish /rɪˈlɪŋkwɪʃ/ **relinquishes, relinquishing, relinquished.** VERB If you **relinquish** something such as power or control, you give it up; FORMAL.

relish /ˈrelɪʃ/ **relishes, relishing, relished.** VERB & N-U If you **relish** something, or if you do something with **relish**, you get a lot of enjoyment from it. *I relish the challenge of doing jobs that others turn down.*

relive /ˌriːˈlɪv/ **relives, reliving, relived.** VERB If you **relive** something that has happened to you in the past, you remember it and imagine that you are experiencing it again.

relocate /ˌriːˈləʊˈkeɪt, AM -ˈləʊkeɪt/ **relocates, relocating, relocated.** VERB If people or businesses **relocate**, or if they **are relocated**, they move to a different place. *The firm plans to relocate its headquarters from Saint Louis to San Antonio.* ◆**relocation** N-U ... *the railroad station's relocation out of the center of town.*

reluctant /rɪˈlʌktənt/. ADJ If you are **reluctant** to do something, you do not really want to do it. *We have reluctantly agreed to let him go.* ◆**reluctantly** ADV *Frank boarded his train with great reluctance.* ◆**reluctance** N-U

rely /rɪˈlaɪ/ **relies, relying, relied.** [1] VERB If you **rely** on someone or something, you need them in order to live or work properly. *The Association relies on member subscriptions for most of its income.* [2] VERB If you can **rely** on someone to work well or behave as you want them to, you can trust them to do this.

remain /rɪˈmeɪn/ **remains, remaining, remained.** [1] LINK-VERB To **remain** in a particular state means to stay in that state and not change. *The three men remained silent... He remained a formidable opponent.* [2] VERB If you **remain** in a place, you do not move away from it. *She remained at home, waiting for the phone to ring.* [3] VERB You can say that something **remains** when it still exists. *Other dangers still remain.* [4] LINK-VERB If something **remains** to be done, it still needs to be done. [5] N-PL The **remains** of something are the parts of it that are left after most of it has been taken away or destroyed. *...the charred remains of a tank.* [6] N-PL The **remains** of a person or animal are the parts of their body that are left after they have died. *...human remains.* [7] N-PL **Remains** are objects and parts of buildings from an earlier period of history. *...valuable Roman remains.* [8] See also **remaining**.

remainder /rɪˈmeɪndə/. N-SING The **remainder** of something is the part of it that remains after the other parts have gone or been dealt with. *He gulped down the remainder of his coffee.*

remaining /rɪˈmeɪnɪŋ/. [1] ADJ BEFORE N The **remaining** things or people out of a group are the things or people that still exist, are still present, or have not yet been dealt with. *Stir in the remaining ingredients.* [2] See also **remain**.

remake, remakes, remaking, remade; verb /ˌriːˈmeɪk/, noun /ˈriːmeɪk/. VERB & N-C If a film **is remade**, or if there is a **remake** of it, a new film

is made that has the same story, and often the same title, as the original film.

remand /rɪˈmɑːnd, -ˈmænd/ **remands, remanding, remanded.** VERB & N-U If a person who is accused of a crime **is remanded** in custody, or if they are on **remand**, they are kept in prison until their trial. If they **are remanded** on bail, they are released and told to return to the court at a later date, when their trial will take place. *She has already served a year on remand.*

remark /rɪˈmɑːk/ **remarks, remarking, remarked.** [1] VERB If you **remark** that something is the case, you say that it is the case. *'Some people have more money than sense,' Winston had remarked... On several occasions she had remarked on the boy's improvement.* [2] N-C If you make a **remark** about something, you say something about it.

remarkable /rɪˈmɑːkəbəl/. ADJ Someone or something that is **remarkable** is very impressive or unusual. ◆**remarkably** ADV *The book is remarkably accurate.*

remedial /rɪˈmiːdiəl/. ADJ **Remedial** activities are intended to improve something; FORMAL. *How bad does all this have to get before remedial action is taken?*

remedy /ˈremədi/ **remedies, remedying, remedied.** [1] VERB & N-C If you **remedy** something that is wrong or harmful, or if you find a **remedy** for it, you correct or improve it. *They took drastic action to remedy the situation. ... a remedy for unemployment.* [2] N-C A **remedy** is something that is intended to stop illness or pain. *...Chinese herbal remedies.*

remember /rɪˈmembə/ **remembers, remembering, remembered.** [1] VERB If you **remember** people or events from the past, you still have an idea of them in your mind and you are able to think about them. *I remember her perfectly... I don't remember talking to you at all... I remember that it used to snow quite a lot.* [2] VERB If you **remember** that something is the case, you suddenly become aware of it again after a time when you did not think about it. *She remembered that she was going to the social club that evening... Then I remembered the cheque, which cheered me up.* [3] VERB If you **remember** to do something, you do it when you intend to. *Please remember to enclose a stamped addressed envelope when writing.*

remembrance /rɪˈmembrəns/. N-U If you do something in **remembrance** of a dead person, you do it as a way of showing that you remember them and respect them; FORMAL.

remind /rɪˈmaɪnd/ **reminds, reminding, reminded.** [1] VERB If someone **reminds** you of a fact or event that you already know about, they say something which makes you think about it. *His father has constantly reminded him of the virtues of patience.* [2] VERB If someone **reminds** you to do something, they say something that makes you remember to do it. *Tutors always have to remind them to bring in their notes.* [3] VERB If someone or something **reminds** you **of** another person or thing, they are similar to the other person or thing and they make you think about them. *The presi-*

dent reminds me of some managers I've known in business.

reminder /rɪˈmaɪndə/ **reminders.** **1** N-C If one thing is a **reminder** of another, the first thing makes you think about the second. *His death is a reminder that they too are nearing the end of life's road.* **2** N-C A **reminder** is a letter that is sent to tell you that you have not done something such as pay a bill.

reminisce /ˌremɪˈnɪs/ **reminisces, reminiscing, reminisced.** VERB If you **reminisce** about something from your past, you write or talk about it with pleasure; FORMAL.

reminiscence /ˌremɪˈnɪsəns/ **reminiscences.** N-C Someone's **reminiscences** are things which they remember from the past, and which they talk or write about; FORMAL.

reminiscent /ˌremɪˈnɪsənt/. ADJ AFTER LINK-V If one thing is **reminiscent** of another, the first thing reminds you of the second; FORMAL. *...flat-roofed houses reminiscent of those found in the Atlas Mountains.*

remission /rɪˈmɪʃən/ **remissions.** **1** N-VAR If someone who has had a serious disease is in **remission** or if the disease is in **remission**, the disease has been controlled so that they are not as ill as they were. **2** N-U If someone in prison gets **remission**, their prison sentence is reduced, usually because they have behaved well; BRITISH.

remit /ˈriːmɪt/ **remits.** N-C Someone's **remit** is the area of activity which they are expected to deal with, or which they have authority to deal with. *The centre has a remit to advise Asian businesses.*

remnant /ˈremnənt/ **remnants.** N-C A **remnant** of something is a small part of it that is left when the main part has disappeared or been destroyed. *Remnants of an older building are incorporated into its walls.*

remorse /rɪˈmɔːs/. N-U **Remorse** is a strong feeling of guilt and regret about something wrong that you have done; FORMAL.

remote /rɪˈməʊt/ **remoter, remotest.** **1** ADJ **Remote** areas are far away from places where most people live. ◆**remoteness** N-U *...the remoteness of the island.* **2** ADJ If something is **remote** from what people want or need, it is not relevant to it because it is so different from it or has no connection with it. *...teenagers forced to study subjects that seem remote from their daily lives.* **3** ADJ If you describe someone as **remote**, you mean that they are not friendly and do not get closely involved with other people. **4** ADJ If there is a **remote** possibility that something will happen, there is only a very small possibility that it will happen.

re͵mote con'trol, remote controls. **1** N-U **Remote control** is a system of controlling a machine or vehicle from a distance by using radio or electronic signals. **2** N-C The **remote control** for a television, video recorder, or music system is the device that you use to control it from a distance.

remotely /rɪˈməʊtli/. ADV You use **remotely** to emphasize a negative statement. *Nobody was remotely interested.*

removal /rɪˈmuːvəl/ **removals.** **1** N-U The **re-moval** of something is the act of removing it.

...surgical removal of a tumor. **2** N-VAR **Re-moval** is the process of transporting furniture from one building to another; BRITISH. *He has bought 30 lorries to move into house removals. ...a removal van.*

remove /rɪˈmuːv/ **removes, removing, re-moved.** **1** VERB If you **remove** something from a place, you take it away. *He went to the refrigerator and removed a bottle of wine.* **2** VERB When you **remove** clothing, you take it off. **3** VERB If you **remove** an obstacle or a problem, you get rid of it. *Most of her fears had been removed.*

removed /rɪˈmuːvd/. ADJ If an idea or situation is far **removed from** something, it is very different from it. *Her teen fantasy may not be all that far removed from reality.*

renaissance /rɪˈneɪsɒns, AM ˌrenɪˈsɑːns/. N-SING If something experiences a **renaissance**, it becomes popular or successful again after a time when people were not interested in it.

render /ˈrendə/ **renders, rendering, ren-dered.** **1** VERB You can use **render** to say that something is changed into a different state. *It contained so many errors as to render it worthless.* **2** VERB If you **render** someone help or assistance, you help them; FORMAL. *He had a chance to render some service to his country.* **3** VERB To **render** something in a particular language or in a particular way means to express it in that language or in that way. *All the signs and announcements were rendered in English and Spanish.* ◆**rendering, renderings** N-C *...a rendering of Verdi's Requiem by the BBC Symphony Orchestra.*

rendezvous /ˈrɒndeɪvuː/ **rendezvousing, rendezvoused.** The form **rendezvous** is pronounced /ˈrɒndeɪvuːz/ when it is the plural of the noun or the third person singular of the verb. VERB & N-C If you **rendezvous** with someone or if the two of you **rendezvous**, you meet at a particular time and place, often secretly. Your meeting is called a **rendezvous**. *I rendezvoused with him at 1400 hours.*

renegade /ˈrenɪgeɪd/ **renegades.** N-C & ADJ BE-FORE N A **renegade** is a person who abandons their former group and joins an opposing or different group. You use **renegade** to describe a person who does this. *Three men were shot dead by a renegade policeman.*

renew /rɪˈnjuː, AM -ˈnuː/ **renews, renewing, renewed.** **1** VERB If you **renew** an activity or relationship, you begin it again. *When the two men met again after the war they renewed their friendship. ...renewed fighting.* **2** VERB When you **renew** something such as a licence or a contract, you extend the period of time for which it is valid. *Larry's landlord threatened not to renew his lease.* **3** VERB You can say that something **is renewed** when it grows or succeeds again after a time when it was destroyed, lost, or failing. *...a renewed interest in public transport systems.*

renewable /rɪˈnjuːəbəl, AM -ˈnuː-/. **1** ADJ **Re-newable** resources are ones such as wind, water, and sunlight, which are constantly replacing themselves and therefore do not become used up. **2** ADJ If a contract or agreement is

renewable, it can be extended when it reaches the end of a fixed period of time.

renewal /rɪ'njuːəl, -'nuː-/ **renewals**. [1] N-U If there is a **renewal** of an activity or situation, it starts again. [2] N-VAR The **renewal** of a document such as a licence or a contract is an official extension of the time for which it remains valid. *His contract came up for renewal.*

renounce /rɪ'naʊns/ **renounces, renouncing, renounced**. VERB If you **renounce** something, you reject it or give it up. *After a period of imprisonment she renounced terrorism... He renounced his claim to the French throne.*

renovate /'renəveɪt/ **renovates, renovating, renovated**. VERB If someone **renovates** an old building or machine, they repair it and get it back into good condition. ♦**renovation, renovations** N-VAR ...*a property which will need extensive renovation.*

renowned /rɪ'naʊn/ ADJ A person or place that is **renowned** for something, usually something good, is well known because of it. *The hotel is renowned for its friendliness to all visitors.*

rent /rent/ **rents, renting, rented**. [1] VERB If you **rent** something, you regularly pay its owner in order to have it and use it yourself. ...*a rented car.* [2] VERB & PHR-VERB If you **rent** something to someone, or if you **rent** it **out** to them, you let them have it and use it in exchange for a sum of money which they pay you regularly. *She rented rooms to university students.* [3] N-VAR **Rent** is the amount of money that you pay regularly for the use of a house, flat, or piece of land. *They recently put my rent up.*

rental /'rentəl/ **rentals**. [1] N-VAR The **rental** of something such as a car or television is the fact of paying an amount of money in order to have and use it. ...*Scotland's largest video rental company.* [2] N-C The **rental** is the amount of money that you have to pay to use something such as a television, telephone, car, or property; BRITISH. [3] ADJ BEFORE N You use **rental** to describe things that are connected with the renting out of goods, properties, and services. *She picked up a rental car.*

reorganize (BR also **reorganise**) /riː'ɔːɡənaɪz/ **reorganizes, reorganizing, reorganized**. VERB To **reorganize** something means to change the way in which it is organized or done. ♦**reorganization, reorganizations** N-VAR ...*the reorganization of the legal system.*

rep /rep/ **reps**. [1] N-C A **rep** is a person who travels round selling their company's products or services to other companies. [2] N-C A **rep** is a person who acts as a representative for a group of people. ...*the health and safety rep at your union.* [3] N-U In the theatre, **rep** is the same as **repertory**.

repaid /rɪ'peɪd/. **Repaid** is the past tense and past participle of **repay**.

repair /rɪ'peə/ **repairs, repairing, repaired**. [1] VERB If you **repair** something that has been damaged or is not working properly, you mend it. *A woman drove her car to the garage to have it repaired.* ♦**repairer, repairers** N-C ...*builders, plumbers and TV repairers.* [2] N-C A **repair** is something that you do to mend something that has been damaged. *Many women know how to carry out repairs on their cars... Her marriage is beyond repair.* [3] PHRASE If something such as a building is in **good repair**, it is in good condition. If it is in **bad repair**, it is in bad condition.

repatriate /ˌriː'pætrieɪt, AM -'peɪt-/ **repatriates, repatriating, repatriated**. VERB If a country **repatriates** someone, it sends them back to their home country. ♦**repatriation, repatriations** N-VAR ...*the forced repatriation of Vietnamese boat people.*

repay /rɪ'peɪ/ **repays, repaying, repaid**. [1] VERB If you **repay** a debt, you pay back the money you owe to somebody. [2] VERB If you **repay** a favour that someone did for you, you do something or give them something in return. *It was very kind. I don't know how I can ever repay you.*

repayment /rɪ'peɪmənt/ **repayments**. [1] N-C A **repayment** is an amount of money paid at regular intervals in order to repay a debt. [2] N-U The **repayment** of money is the act or process of paying it back to the person you borrowed it from.

repeal /rɪ'piːl/ **repeals, repealing, repealed**. VERB & N-C If the government **repeals** a law, it officially ends it so that it is no longer valid. You call this the **repeal** of a law.

repeat /rɪ'piːt/ **repeats, repeating, repeated**. [1] VERB If you **repeat** something, you say or write it again. *He repeated that he had been misquoted.* [2] VERB If you **repeat** something that someone else has said or written, you say or write the same thing. *She had an irritating habit of repeating everything I said to her.* [3] VERB If you **repeat** an action, you do it again. [4] VERB & N-C If an event or series of events **repeats** itself, or if there is a **repeat** of an event, it happens again. *The UN will have to work hard to stop history repeating itself.* [5] N-C A **repeat** is a television or radio programme that has been broadcast before.

repeated /rɪ'piːtɪd/. ADJ BEFORE N **Repeated** actions or events are ones which happen many times. ♦**repeatedly** ADV *Both men have repeatedly denied the allegations.*

repel /rɪ'pel/ **repels, repelling, repelled**. [1] VERB When an army **repels** an attack or an invasion, they successfully fight and drive back soldiers from another army; FORMAL. [2] VERB If something **repels** you, you find it horrible and disgusting. ♦**repelled** ADJ *She was very striking but in some way I felt repelled.*

repellent /rɪ'pelənt/ **repellents**; also spelled **repellant** for meaning 2. [1] ADJ If you think that something is horrible and disgusting, you can say it is **repellent**; FORMAL. ...*a very large, very repellent toad.* [2] N-VAR Insect **repellents** are chemical substances that you use to keep insects away.

repent /rɪ'pent/ **repents, repenting, repented**. VERB If you **repent**, you say or show you feel sorry for something wrong you have done. ♦**repentance** /rɪ'pentəns/ N-U *They showed no repentance during their trial.* ♦**repentant** ADJ ...*a repentant criminal.*

repercussions /ˌriːpə'kʌʃənz/. N-C If an action or event has **repercussions**, it causes unpleasant things to happen some time after the original action or event. ...*the political repercussions of voting for a big tax increase.*

repertoire /ˈrepətwɑː/. N-SING A performer's **repertoire** is all the pieces of music or parts in plays he or she has learned and can perform. ...*a wide repertoire of songs.*

repertory /ˈrepətri, AM -tɔːri/. [1] N-U A **repertory** company is a group of actors and actresses who perform plays for just a few weeks at a time. [2] N-SING **Repertory** means the same as **repertoire.**

repetition /ˌrepɪˈtɪʃən/ **repetitions.** N-VAR If there is a **repetition** of an event, it happens again. ...*a repetition of last month's violence.*

repetitive /rɪˈpetɪtɪv/. ADJ **Repetitive** actions are repeated many times and are therefore boring. ...*factory workers who do repetitive jobs.*

replace /rɪˈpleɪs/ **replaces, replacing, replaced.** [1] VERB To **replace** a person or thing means to put another person or thing in their place. ...*the city lawyer who replaced Bob as chairman... I clean out all the grease and replace it with oil.* ♦**replacement** N-U ...*a gradual replacement of staff with less experienced contractors.* [2] VERB If you **replace** something that is damaged or lost, you get a new one. ♦**replacement** N-U ...*the replacement of damaged or lost books.* [3] VERB If you **replace** something, you put it back where it was before. *Replace the caps on all the bottles.*

replacement /rɪˈpleɪsmənt/ **replacements.** N-C One thing or person that replaces another can be referred to as their **replacement.** *Taylor has nominated Adams as his replacement.*

replay, replays, replaying, replayed; verb /ˌriːˈpleɪ/, noun /ˈriːpleɪ/. [1] VERB & N-C In sport, if a match is **replayed**, it is played again, usually because there is no winner from the first match. The second match is called a **replay.** [2] N-C A **replay** of something which has been recorded on a video tape is another showing of it. ...*a slow-motion videotape replay.*

replenish /rɪˈplenɪʃ/ **replenishes, replenishing, replenished.** VERB If you **replenish** something, you make it full or complete again; FORMAL. *Three hundred thousand tons of cereals are needed to replenish stocks.* ♦**replenishment** N-U ...*the replenishment of its fuel supplies.*

replica /ˈreplɪkə/ **replicas.** N-C A **replica** of something such as a statue, machine, or weapon is an accurate copy of it.

reply /rɪˈplaɪ/ **replies, replying, replied.** [1] VERB & N-C When you **reply** to something that someone has said or written to you, you say or write something, called a **reply**, as an answer. *I've not replied to Lee's letter yet... David has had 12 replies to his ad.* [2] VERB If you **reply** to something such as an attack, you do something in response. *Farmers threw eggs and empty bottles at police, who replied with tear gas.*

report /rɪˈpɔːt/ **reports, reporting, reported.** [1] VERB If you **report** something that has happened, you tell people about it. *I reported the theft to the police. Estate agents report that*

business is reasonable... The foreign secretary is reported as saying that force will have to be used... She reported him missing the next day. [2] VERB & N-C If you **report** on an event or subject, or if you give someone a **report** on it, you tell people about it, because it is your job or duty to do so. *From now on I'll report to you every night. ...a progress report on how the project is going.* [3] N-C A **report** is a news article or broadcast which gives information about something that has happened. [4] N-C A school **report** is a written account of a pupil's work and behaviour for the previous term or year. [5] VERB If someone **reports** you to a person in authority, they tell the person about something wrong that you have done. *The Princess was reported for speeding.* [6] VERB If you **report** to a person or place, you go to them and say that you are ready to start work. *None of the men had reported for duty.*

reportedly /rɪˈpɔːtɪdli/. ADV If you say that something is **reportedly** the case, you mean that someone has said that it is the case, but you have no evidence of it; FORMAL. *More than two hundred people have reportedly been killed.*

reˌported ˈspeech. N-U **Reported speech** gives an account of something that someone has said, but without quoting their actual words. Reported speech is usually introduced by a verb such as 'say' or 'tell' followed by 'that', as in 'He said that he was tired'.

reporter /rɪˈpɔːtə/ **reporters.** N-C A **reporter** is someone who writes news articles or broadcasts news reports. ...*a TV reporter.*

reporting /rɪˈpɔːtɪŋ/. N-U **Reporting** is the presenting of news in newspapers, on radio, and on television. ...*impartial political reporting.*

repository /rɪˈpɒzɪtri, AM -tɔːri/ **repositories.** [1] N-C A **repository** is a place where something is kept safely; FORMAL. *A church in Moscow became a repository for police files.* [2] N-C A **repository** of information is someone who knows a lot of information about a particular subject; LITERARY. *The repository of all important knowledge in a small town was the chief barman of the local pub.*

repossess /ˌriːpəˈzes/ **repossesses, repossessing, repossessed.** VERB If a person's house or car **is repossessed**, it is taken from them because the loan payments have not been paid.

repossession /ˌriːpəˈzeʃən/ **repossessions.** [1] N-VAR The **repossession** of someone's house is the act of repossessing it. [2] N-C You can refer to a house or car that has been repossessed as a **repossession.** *Many of the cars you will see at auction are repossessions.*

represent /ˌreprɪˈzent/ **represents, representing, represented.** [1] VERB If someone **represents** you, they act on your behalf. ...*the politicians we elect to represent us.* [2] VERB If you say that something **represents** a change, achievement, or victory, you mean that it is a change, achievement, or victory. *These developments represented a major change in the established order.* [3] VERB If a sign or symbol **represents** something, it is accepted as meaning that thing. ...*a black dot in the middle of the* *circle is supposed to represent the source of the radiation.* **4** VERB If you **represent** a person or thing as a particular thing, you describe them as being that thing. *She represented him as the best husband a woman could have.*

representation /ˌreprɪzɛnˈteɪʃən/ **representations.** **1** N-U If a group or person has **representation** in a parliament or on a committee, someone in parliament or on the committee will vote or make decisions on their behalf. *Puerto Ricans are U.S. citizens but they have no representation in Congress.* **2** N-C You can describe a picture or statue of someone as a **representation** of them; FORMAL. *...a lifelike representation of Christ.*

representative /ˌreprɪˈzentətɪv/ **representatives.** **1** N-C A **representative** is a person who acts on behalf of another person or group of people. *...trade union representatives.* **2** ADJ BEFORE N A **representative** group acts on behalf of a larger group. **3** ADJ If something is **representative** of a group, it is typical of that group. *He was in no way representative of dog-trainers in general.*

repress /rɪˈpres/ **represses, repressing, repressed.** **1** VERB If you **repress** a feeling, you make a deliberate effort not to show it or to have this feeling; used showing disapproval. *People who repress their emotions risk having nightmares.* ♦ **repression** N-U *...the repression of his feelings about men.* **2** VERB If a section of society **is repressed**, their freedom is restricted by the people who have authority over them; used showing disapproval. *...a UN resolution banning him from repressing his people.* ♦ **repression, repressions** N-VAR *...a society conditioned by violence and repression.*

repressed /rɪˈprest/. ADJ **Repressed** people try to stop themselves having natural feelings and desires, especially sexual ones; used showing disapproval.

repressive /rɪˈpresɪv/. ADJ A **repressive** government is one which uses force to control people and to restrict their freedom.

reprieve /rɪˈpriːv/ **reprieves, reprieving, reprieved.** **1** VERB If someone who has been sentenced in court **is reprieved**, their punishment is officially postponed or cancelled. **2** N-C A **reprieve** is a delay before a very unpleasant or difficult situation which may or may not take place. *Homebuyers may have won a reprieve from higher interest rates.*

reprimand /ˈreprɪmɑːnd, -ˈmænd/ **reprimands, reprimanding, reprimanded.** VERB & N-C If someone in authority **reprimands** you, or if they give you a **reprimand**, they speak to you angrily or seriously for doing something wrong. *He was reprimanded by a teacher for talking in the corridor... He has been fined five thousand pounds and given a severe reprimand.*

reprint, reprints, reprinting, reprinted. **1** VERB If a book **is reprinted**, further copies of it are printed after all the other ones have been sold. **2** N-C /ˈriːprɪnt/ A **reprint** is a new copy of a book or article, printed because all the other ones have been sold or because minor changes have been made to the original.

reprisal /rɪˈpraɪzəl/ **reprisals.** N-VAR If you do something to someone in **reprisal**, you do something violent or unpleasant to them because they have done something similar to you. *Witnesses are unwilling to testify through fear of reprisals.*

reproach /rɪˈprəʊtʃ/ **reproaches, reproaching, reproached.** **1** VERB If you **reproach** someone, you say or show that you are disappointed, upset, or angry because they have done something wrong. *She had not even reproached him for breaking his promise.* **2** N-VAR If you look at or speak to someone with **reproach**, you indicate to them that you are sad and disappointed or angry because they have done something wrong. *Women in public life must be beyond reproach.*

reproduce /ˌriːprəˈdjuːs, AM -ˈduːs/ **reproduces, reproducing, reproduced.** **1** VERB If you **reproduce** something, you copy it. *I shall not try to reproduce the policemen's English.* **2** VERB When people, animals, or plants **reproduce**, they produce more of their own species. *...the mechanism by which human cells reproduce themselves.*

reproduction /ˌriːprəˈdʌkʃən/ **reproductions.** **1** N-C A **reproduction** is a copy of something such as an antique or a painting. **2** N-U **Reproduction** is the process by which living things produce more of their own species.

reproductive /ˌriːprəˈdʌktɪv/. ADJ **Reproductive** processes and organs are concerned with the reproduction of living things.

reptile /ˈreptaɪl, AM -tɪl/ **reptiles.** N-C **Reptiles** are a group of animals which have scales on their skin and lay eggs. Snakes and crocodiles are reptiles.

republic /rɪˈpʌblɪk/ **republics.** N-C A **republic** is a country that has a president or whose system of government is based on the idea that every citizen has equal status. *In 1918 Austria became a republic. ...the Republic of Ireland.*

republican /rɪˈpʌblɪkən/ **republicans.** **1** ADJ & N-C A **republican** government has a president or is based on the idea that every citizen has equal status. You can also talk about someone who has **republican** views, or who is a **republican**. *Some families have been republican for generations.* **2** N-C & ADJ In Northern Ireland, if someone is a **Republican** or if they have **republican** views, they believe that Northern Ireland should not be ruled by Britain but should become part of the Republic of Ireland.

repudiate /rɪˈpjuːdieɪt/ **repudiates, repudiating, repudiated.** VERB If you **repudiate** something or someone, you show that you strongly disagree with them and do not want to be connected with them. *Leaders urged people to turn out in large numbers to repudiate the violence.* ♦ **repudiation** N-U *...his public repudiation of the conference decision.*

repulsive /rɪˈpʌlsɪv/. ADJ **Repulsive** means horrible and disgusting. *...repulsive fat white slugs.*

reputable /ˈrepjʊtəbəl/. ADJ A **reputable** company or person is reliable and trustworthy.

reputation /ˌrepjʊˈteɪʃən/ **reputations.** **1** N-C To have a **reputation** for something means to be known or remembered for it. *...his reputation for honesty.* **2** N-C Your **reputation** is the opinion that people have of you. *The stories ruined his reputation.*

reputed /rɪ'pjuːtɪd/. ADJ If something is **reputed** to be true or to exist, some people say that it is true or that it exists. *He is reputed to earn ten million pounds a year.* ♦ **reputedly** ADV *The beaches of the east coast are reputedly beautiful.*

request /rɪ'kwest/ **requests, requesting, requested.** [1] VERB If you **request** something, you ask for it politely or formally. *She had requested that the door to her room be left open.* [2] N-C If you make a **request**, you politely ask for something or ask someone to do something. *Vietnam made an official request that the meeting be postponed.*
PHRASES ● If something is done **on request**, it is given or done when you ask for it. *Leaflets giving details are available on request.* ● If you do something **at** someone's **request**, you do it because they ask you to.

require /rɪ'kwaɪə/ **requires, requiring, required.** [1] VERB To **require** something means to need it. *...the kind of crisis that requires us to drop everything else.* [2] VERB If a law or rule **requires** you to do something, you have to do it; FORMAL. *...a law requiring prompt reporting of such malfunctions... Then he'll know exactly what's required of him.*

requirement /rɪ'kwaɪəmənt/ **requirements.** [1] N-C A **requirement** is a quality or qualification that you must have in order to be allowed to do something or to be suitable for something. *Its products met all legal requirements.* [2] N-C Your **requirements** are the things that you need. *Variations of this programme can be arranged to suit your requirements.*

requisite /'rekwɪzɪt/. ADJ **Requisite** means necessary for a particular purpose; FORMAL. *She filled in the requisite paperwork.*

rescue /'reskjuː/ **rescues, rescuing, rescued.** [1] VERB & N-VAR If you **rescue** someone, you get them out of a dangerous or unpleasant situation. A **rescue** is an attempt to save someone from a situation like this. *He had rescued her from a horrible life. ...a major air-sea rescue... Lights clipped onto life jackets improve the chances of rescue.* ♦ **rescuer, rescuers** N-C *It took rescuers 90 minutes to reach the trapped men.* [2] PHRASE If you **go to** someone's **rescue** or **come to** their **rescue**, you help them when they are in danger or difficulty.

research /rɪ'sɜːtʃ/ **researches, researching, researched.** VERB & N-VAR If you **research** something or if you do **research** into it, you try to discover facts about it. *She spent two years in South Florida researching and filming her documentary. ...cancer research.* ♦ **researcher, researchers** N-C *...a market researcher.*

resemblance /rɪ'zembləns/ **resemblances.** N-VAR If there is a **resemblance** between two people or things, they are similar to each other. *There was a remarkable resemblance between him and Pete.*

resemble /rɪ'zembəl/ **resembles, resembling, resembled.** VERB If one thing or person **resembles** another, they are similar to each other. *She so resembles her mother.*

resent /rɪ'zent/ **resents, resenting, resented.** VERB If you **resent** someone or something, you feel bitter and angry about them. *She resents her mother for being so tough on her.*

resentful /rɪ'zentfʊl/. ADJ If you are **resentful**, you feel resentment. *I felt very resentful and angry about losing my job.*

resentment /rɪ'zentmənt/ **resentments.** N-VAR **Resentment** is a feeling of bitterness and anger. *Inflation and unemployment still cause a lot of resentment.*

reservation /ˌrezə'veɪʃən/ **reservations.** [1] N-VAR If you have **reservations** about something, you are not sure that it is entirely good or right. [2] N-C If you make a **reservation**, you arrange for something such as a table in a restaurant to be kept for you. *Can I use your telephone to make a reservation?*

reserve /rɪ'zɜːv/ **reserves, reserving, reserved.** [1] VERB If something **is reserved** for a particular person or purpose, it is kept specially for that person or purpose. *A double room had been reserved for him... They reserved two seats on a Malaysian Airlines flight.* [2] N-C A **reserve** is a supply of something that is available for use when needed. *...the world's oil reserves.* [3] PHRASE If you have something **in reserve**, you have it available for use when it is needed. *...the bottle of whisky that he kept in reserve.* [4] N-C In sport, a **reserve** is someone who is available to play in a team if one of the members cannot play; BRITISH. [5] N-C A nature **reserve** is an area of land where animals, birds, and plants are officially protected. [6] N-U If someone shows **reserve**, they keep their feelings hidden. *I do hope that you'll overcome your reserve and let me know.*

reserved /rɪ'zɜːvd/. ADJ Someone who is **reserved** keeps their feelings hidden. *Even though I'm quite a reserved person, I like meeting people.*

reservoir /'rezəvwɑː/ **reservoirs.** [1] N-C A **reservoir** is a lake used for storing water before it is supplied to people. [2] N-C A **reservoir** of something is a large quantity of it that is available for use when needed. *...the body's short-term reservoir of energy.*

reside /rɪ'zaɪd/ **resides, residing, resided.** VERB If someone **resides** somewhere, they live there or are staying there; FORMAL. *Margaret resides with her invalid mother.*

residence /'rezɪdəns/ **residences.** [1] N-C A **residence** is a house where people live; FORMAL. *...Mr Kohl's private residence.* [2] N-U Your place of **residence** is the place where you live; FORMAL.
PHRASES ● If someone is **in residence** in a place, they are living there. ● If you **take up residence** somewhere, you start living there.

resident /'rezɪdənt/ **residents.** [1] N-C The **residents** of a house or area are the people who live there. [2] ADJ AFTER LINK-V Someone who is **resident** in a country or town lives there. *He had been resident in Brussels since 1967.*

residential /ˌrezɪ'denʃəl/. [1] ADJ A **residential** area contains houses rather than offices or factories. [2] ADJ A **residential** institution is one where you can live while you are studying there or being cared for there. *...a residential home for children with disabilities.*

residual /rɪˈzɪdʒʊəl/. ADJ **Residual** is used to describe what remains of something when most of it has gone. *Allow the residual heat to keep the mixture simmering.*

residue /ˈrezɪdjuː, AM -duː/ **residues.** N-C A **residue** of something is a small amount that remains after most of it has gone. *Always using the same shampoo means that a residue can build up on the hair.*

resign /rɪˈzaɪn/ **resigns, resigning, resigned.** [1] VERB If you **resign** from a job or position, you formally announce that you are leaving it. *He resigned as chairman of the Electricity Council.* [2] VERB If you **resign** yourself to an unpleasant situation or fact, you accept it because you cannot change it. *He seemed to resign himself to leaving me.* [3] See also **resigned.**

resignation /ˌrezɪgˈneɪʃən/ **resignations.** [1] N-VAR Your **resignation** is a formal statement of your intention to leave a job or position. *I'm not prepared to carry on and here's my resignation.* [2] N-U **Resignation** is the acceptance of an unpleasant situation or fact because you cannot change it. *He sighed with profound resignation.*

resigned /rɪˈzaɪnd/. ADJ If you are **resigned** to an unpleasant situation or fact, you accept it because you cannot change it. *He is resigned to the noise, the mess, the constant upheaval.*

resilient /rɪˈzɪliənt/. ADJ **Resilient** people are able to recover easily and quickly from unpleasant or damaging events. ◆**resilience** N-U *His friend's resilience had helped them through the difficult times.*

resin /ˈrezɪn/ **resins.** [1] N-VAR **Resin** is a sticky substance produced by some trees. [2] N-VAR **Resin** is a chemically produced substance used to make plastics.

resist /rɪˈzɪst/ **resists, resisting, resisted.** [1] VERB If you **resist** a change, you refuse to accept it and try to prevent it. *Both governments continue to resist the introduction of political freedom.* [2] VERB To **resist** someone or something means to fight back. *The man was shot outside his house as he tried to resist arrest.* [3] VERB If you **resist** the temptation to do something, you stop yourself from doing it although you would like to do it. *She cannot resist giving him advice.* [4] VERB If someone or something **resists** damage of some kind, they are not harmed or damaged by it. *...bodies trained and toughened to resist the cold.*

resistance /rɪˈzɪstəns/. [1] N-U **Resistance** to a change or a new idea is a refusal to accept it. *...his stubborn resistance to anything new.* [2] N-U When there is **resistance** to an attack, people fight back. *...the troops are encountering stiff resistance.* [3] N-U The **resistance** of your body to germs or diseases is its power to remain unharmed or unaffected by them.

resistant /rɪˈzɪstənt/. [1] ADJ People who are **resistant** to something are opposed to it and want to prevent it. *Some people are very resistant to the idea of exercise.* [2] ADJ If something is **resistant** to something else, it is not harmed

by it. *...how to improve plants to make them more resistant to disease.*

resolute /ˈrezəluːt/. ADJ Someone who is **resolute** refuses to change their mind or to give up a course of action; FORMAL. ◆**resolutely** ADV *He resolutely refused to speak English.*

resolution /ˌrezəˈluːʃən/ **resolutions.** [1] N-C A **resolution** is a formal decision taken at a meeting by means of a vote. *...a resolution declaring the republic fully independent.* [2] N-C If you make a **resolution**, you decide to try very hard to do something. *She made a resolution to get fit.* [3] N-U **Resolution** is determination to do something. *She acted with resolution, courage, and intelligence.* [4] N-U The **resolution** of a problem or difficulty is the solving of it; FORMAL. *...a peaceful resolution to the crisis.*

resolve /rɪˈzɒlv/ **resolves, resolving, resolved.** [1] VERB To **resolve** a problem or argument, means to find a solution to it; FORMAL. *We must find a way to resolve these problems.* [2] VERB If you **resolve** to do something, you make a firm decision to do it; FORMAL. *She resolved that, if Mimi forgot this promise, she would remind her.* [3] N-U **Resolve** is determination to do something; FORMAL. *...the American public's resolve to go to war if necessary.*

resolved /rɪˈzɒlvd/. ADJ If you are **resolved** to do something, you are determined to do it; FORMAL. *He was resolved to marry Mrs Simpson.*

resonant /ˈrezənənt/ ADJ If a sound is **resonant**, it is deep, clear, and echoing. ◆**resonance** N-U *His voice had lost its resonance; it was tense and strained.*

resonate /ˈrezəneɪt/ **resonates, resonating, resonated.** VERB If something **resonates**, it vibrates and produces a deep strong sound. *The bass guitar began to thump so loudly that it resonated in my head.*

resort /rɪˈzɔːt/ **resorts, resorting, resorted.** [1] VERB If you **resort** to a course of action that you disapprove of, you adopt it because you cannot see any other way of achieving what you want. *His punishing work schedule had made him resort to drugs.* [2] PHRASE If you do something **as a last resort**, you do it because you can find no other way of getting out of a difficult situation or solving a problem. *Nuclear weapons should be used only as a last resort.* [3] N-C A holiday **resort** is a place where people can spend their holidays.

resounding /rɪˈzaʊndɪŋ/. [1] ADJ **Resounding** means very successful. *The FIS won a resounding victory in local elections.* [2] ADJ A **resounding** sound is loud and echoing. *...a resounding slap on the face.*

resource /rɪˈzɔːs, AM ˈriːsɔːrs/ **resources.** N-C The **resources** of a country, organization, or person are the materials, money, and other things they have and can use. *...scarce water resources... Some families don't have the resources to feed themselves properly.*

resourceful /rɪˈzɔːsfʊl/. ADJ Someone who is **resourceful** is good at finding ways of dealing with problems. ◆**resourcefulness** N-U *I envy Theo his stamina and resourcefulness.*

respect /rɪˈspekt/ **respects, respecting, respected.** [1] VERB & N-U If you **respect** someone, or if you have **respect** for them, you have a good opinion of their character or ideas. *I want him to respect me as a career woman.* [2] VERB & N-U If you **respect** someone's wishes, rights, or customs, or if you show **respect** for them, you avoid doing things that they would dislike or regard as wrong. *Finally, trying to respect her wishes, I said I'd leave.*

PHRASES ● You use expressions like **in this respect** and **in many respects** to indicate that what you are saying applies to the feature you have just mentioned or to many features of something. *In many respects Asian women see themselves as equal to their men.* ● You use **with respect to**, or in British English **in respect of**, to say what something relates to; FORMAL. *Parents often have little choice with respect to the way their child is medically treated.* ● If you **pay** your **respects** to someone, you go to see them or speak to them in order to be polite; FORMAL. *Carl had asked him to visit the hospital and to pay his respects to Francis.*

respectable /rɪ'spektəbəl/. [1] ADJ Someone or something that is **respectable** is approved of by society and considered to be morally correct. *...a teacher and a respectable member of the community.* ♦ **respectability** N-U *If she divorced Tony, she would lose the respectability she had.* [2] ADJ **Respectable** means adequate or acceptable. *At last I have something respectable to wear!*

respected /rɪ'spektɪd/. ADJ Someone or something that is **respected** is admired and considered important by many people. *She is a well respected member of the international community.*

respectful /rɪ'spektfʊl/. ADJ If you are **respectful**, you show respect for someone. *The children in our family are always respectful.* ♦ **respectfully** ADV *'You are an artist,' she said respectfully.*

respective /rɪ'spektɪv/. ADJ BEFORE N **Respective** means relating separately to the people you have just mentioned. *They went into their respective bedrooms to pack.*

respectively /rɪ'spektɪvli/. ADV **Respectively** means in the same order as the items you have just mentioned. *Their sons, Ben and Jonathan, were three and six respectively.*

respiratory /'respərətri, AM -tɔːri/. ADJ **Respiratory** means relating to breathing; MEDICAL. *...respiratory disease.*

respite /'respaɪt, -pɪt/. N-SING A **respite** is a short period of rest from something unpleasant; FORMAL. *The heat can be unbearable, the only respite comes with cooler evenings.*

respond /rɪ'spɒnd/ **responds, responding, responded.** VERB When you **respond** to something that is done or said, you react by doing or saying something. *They are likely to respond positively to the President's request for aid... The army responded with gunfire and tear gas.*

response /rɪ'spɒns/ **responses.** N-C Your **response** to an event or to something that is said is your reply or reaction to it. *In response to my question he lifted his head and thought for a moment.*

responsibility /rɪ,spɒnsɪ'bɪlɪti/ **responsibilities.** [1] N-U If you have **responsibility** for something or someone, it is your job or duty to deal with them. *He has responsibility for five employees.* [2] N-PL Your **responsibilities** are the duties that you have because of your job or position. *...work and family responsibilities.* [3] N-SING If you think that you have a **responsibility** to do something, you feel that you ought to do it because it is morally right or your duty to do it. *As a doctor Francesca had a responsibility to her fellow creatures.* [4] N-U If you accept **responsibility** for something that has happened, you agree that you were to blame for it. *British Rail has now admitted responsibility for the accident.*

responsible /rɪ'spɒnsɪbəl/. [1] ADJ AFTER LINK-V If you are **responsible** for something bad that has happened, it is your fault. *He still felt responsible for her death.* [2] ADJ AFTER LINK-V If you are **responsible** for something, it is your job or duty to deal with it. *...the minister responsible for the environment.* [3] ADJ AFTER LINK-V If you are **responsible to** a person or group, you are controlled by them and have to report to them about what you have done. *I'm responsible to my board of directors.* [4] ADJ **Responsible** people behave properly, without needing to be supervised. ♦ **responsibly** ADV *He urged everyone to act responsibly.*

responsive /rɪ'spɒnsɪv/. ADJ A **responsive** person is quick to react to people or events and to show emotions such as pleasure and affection. *Harriet was an easy, responsive little girl.* ♦ **responsiveness** N-U *Its success is based on its responsiveness to consumer demand.*

rest 1 quantifier uses

rest /rest/. [1] QUANT The **rest** of something is all that remains of it. *He was unable to travel to Barcelona with the rest of the team... Only 55 per cent of the raw material is canned. The rest is thrown away.* [2] PHRASE You can add **and the rest** or **all the rest of it** to the end of a statement or list when you want to refer vaguely to other things associated with the ones you have already mentioned. *And what about racism and all the rest of it?*

rest 2 verb and noun uses

rest /rest/ **rests, resting, rested.** [1] VERB & N-VAR If you **rest**, or if you have a **rest**, you do not do anything active for a period of time. *Rest the injured limb as much as possible... I've worked for 47 years so I think I'm due for a rest by now.* ♦ **rested** ADJ AFTER LINK-V *He looked tanned and well rested after his vacation.* [2] VERB If something such as an idea **rests on** a particular thing, it depends on that thing; FORMAL. *Such a view rests on a number of incorrect assumptions.* [3] VERB If something **rests** somewhere, or if you **rest** it there, its weight is supported there. *His head was resting on my shoulder... He rested his arms on the back of the chair... He rested on his pickaxe for a while.*

PHRASES ● When an object that has been moving **comes to rest**, it stops.

restate /,riː'steɪt/ **restates, restating, restated.** VERB If you **restate** something, you say or write it again, expressing the same message in a slightly different way; FORMAL.

restaurant /'restərɒnt, AM -rənt/ **restaurants.**
N-C A **restaurant** is a place where you can buy and eat a meal. ● See note at **café**.

restless /'restləs/ [1] ADJ If you are **restless**, you are bored or dissatisfied, and want to do something else. ◆**restlessness** N-U *Many fears and anxieties cause a feeling of restlessness.* [2] ADJ You say that someone is **restless** when they keep moving around, because they find it difficult to stay still. ◆**restlessly** ADV *He paced up and down restlessly.*

restore /rɪ'stɔː/ **restores, restoring, restored.** [1] VERB To **restore** something means to cause it to exist again. *The army has recently been brought in to restore order.* ◆**restoration** /ˌrestə'reɪʃən/ N-U ...*the restoration of diplomatic relations.* [2] VERB To **restore** someone or something to a previous state or condition means to cause them to be in that state or condition again. *His country desperately needs Western aid to restore its ailing economy.* [3] VERB To **restore** an old building, painting, or piece of furniture means to repair and clean it, so that it looks like it did when it was new. ◆**restoration** N-U ...*the restoration of fire-damaged Windsor Castle.*

restrain /rɪ'streɪn/ **restrains, restraining, restrained.** [1] VERB If someone **restrains** you, they stop you from doing what you intended or wanted to do, usually by using physical strength. [2] VERB If you **restrain** an emotion or an impulsive action, you prevent yourself from showing that emotion or performing that impulsive action. *Nancy restrained herself from bringing up the subject.* ◆**restrained** ADJ *In the circumstances he felt he'd been very restrained.* [3] VERB To **restrain** something that is growing or increasing means to prevent it from getting too large. ...*efforts to restrain inflation.*

restraint /rɪ'streɪnt/ **restraints.** [1] N-VAR **restraints** are rules or conditions that limit or restrict someone or something. *The Prime Minister is calling for new restraints on trade unions.* [2] N-U **Restraint** is calm, controlled, and unemotional behaviour. *They behaved with more restraint than I'd expected.*

restrict /rɪ'strɪkt/ **restricts, restricting, restricted.** [1] VERB If you **restrict** something, you put a limit on it to stop it becoming too large. ...*passing laws to restrict foreign imports.* ◆**restricted** ADJ *Plants, like animals, often have restricted habitats.* ◆**restriction, restrictions** N-VAR ...*restrictions on official spending.* [2] VERB To **restrict** the movement or actions of someone or something means to prevent them from moving or acting freely. *These dams have restricted the flow of the river downstream.* ◆**restricted** ADJ *They warned that he was in restricted airspace.* ◆**restriction** N-VAR ...*the relaxation of travel restrictions.* [3] VERB If you **restrict** someone's activities **to** one thing, they can only do or deal with that thing. *He was, however, allowed to stay on at the temple as long as he restricted himself to his studies.* [4] VERB If something **is restricted to** a particular group, only that group can have it or do it. *Membership is restricted to men.*

restrictive /rɪ'strɪktɪv/. ADJ **Restrictive** things

make it difficult for you to do what you want to. ...*increasingly restrictive immigration laws.*

restructure /ˌriː'strʌktʃə/ **restructures, restructuring, restructured.** VERB To **restructure** an organization or system means to change the way it is organized, usually in order to make it work more effectively. ...*his plans to restructure Russia's local government.* ◆**restructuring, restructurings** N-VAR *The company's property losses will mean more financial restructuring.*

result /rɪ'zʌlt/ **results, resulting, resulted.** [1] N-C A **result** is something that happens or exists because of something else that has happened. ...*people who have developed asthma as a direct result of their work... It's worth spending more to get better results.* [2] VERB If something **results in** a particular situation or event, it causes that situation or event to happen. *Fifty per cent of road accidents result in head injuries.* [3] VERB If something **results** from a particular event or action, it is caused by that event or action. *Ignore the early warnings and illness could result.* [4] N-C A **result** is the situation that exists at the end of a contest. ...*election results.* [5] N-C A **result** is the number that you get when you do a calculation. *The laboratory, which calculated the results, had made an error.* [6] N-C Your **results** are the marks or grades that you get for examinations. *Kate's exam results were excellent.*

resultant /rɪ'zʌltənt/. ADJ BEFORE N **Resultant** means caused by the event just mentioned; FORMAL. *At least a quarter of a million people have died in the fighting and the resultant famines.*

resume /rɪ'zjuːm, AM -'zuːm/ **resumes, resuming, resumed.** VERB If you **resume** an activity, or if it **resumes**, it begins again; FORMAL. *The search is expected to resume early today.*

résumé (or **resumé**) /'rezjuːmeɪ, AM -zuːm-/ **résumés.** [1] N-C A **résumé** is a short account of something that has happened or that someone has said or written. *I will leave with you a résumé of his most recent speech.* [2] N-C In American English, your **résumé** is a brief account of your personal details, your education, and the jobs you have had. The usual British word is **CV.**

resumption /rɪ'zʌmpʃən/. N-U When there is a **resumption** in an activity, it begins again. ...*the dispute over the resumption of nuclear testing.*

resurgence /rɪ'sɜːdʒəns/. N-U If there is a **resurgence** of an attitude or activity, it reappears and grows; FORMAL. ...*the resurgence of nationalism in Europe.*

resurrect /ˌrezə'rekt/ **resurrects, resurrecting, resurrected.** VERB When you **resurrect** something that has ended, you cause it to exist again. *Attempts to resurrect the ceasefire have already failed once.*

resurrection /ˌrezə'rekʃən/. N-U The **resurrection** of something that had ended is the act of making it exist again. ...*a resourceful resurrection of wartime spirit.*

resuscitate /rɪ'sʌsɪteɪt/ **resuscitates, resuscitating, resuscitated.** VERB If you **resuscitate** someone who has stopped breathing, you

cause them to start breathing again; FORMAL.
♦**resuscitation** N-U *Despite attempts at resuscitation, Mr Hunt died.*

retail /'riːteɪl/ **retails, retailing, retailed.**
[1] N-U **Retail** is the activity of selling goods direct to the public. *Retail sales grew just 3.8 percent last year.* [2] VERB If an item in a shop **retails at** or **for** a particular price, it is for sale at that price.

retailer /'riːteɪlə/ **retailers.** N-C A **retailer** is a person or business that sells goods to the public.

retailing /'riːteɪlɪŋ/. N-U **Retailing** is the activity of selling goods direct to the public.

retain /rɪ'teɪn/ **retains, retaining, retained.** VERB To **retain** something means to continue to have that thing; FORMAL. *This rice will retain its heat for a good hour.*

retaliate /rɪ'tælieɪt/ **retaliates, retaliating, retaliated.** VERB If you **retaliate** when someone harms you, you harm them in return. *The militia responded by saying it would retaliate against any attacks.* ♦**retaliation** N-U *The attack was in retaliation for the death of the drug trafficker.*

retarded /rɪ'tɑːdɪd/. ADJ **Retarded** people are less advanced mentally than most people of their age. *Doctors said he would probably be mentally retarded.*

retention /rɪ'tenʃən/. N-U The **retention** of something is the keeping of it; FORMAL. *...the retention of sanctions.*

rethink /ˌriː'θɪŋk/ **rethinks, rethinking, rethought.** VERB & N-SING If you **rethink** something such as a plan, or if you have a **rethink** about it, you think about it again and change it. *I think all of us need to rethink our attitudes toward health and sickness. ...calls for a rethink of Britain's military aid policy to Bogota.*

reticent /'retɪsənt/. ADJ If you are **reticent** about something, you do not talk about it. *He is very reticent to say anything about himself.* ♦**reticence** N-U *Pearl didn't mind his reticence; in fact she liked it.*

retina /'retɪnə/ **retinas.** N-C Your **retina** is the part of your eye at the back of your eyeball.

retire /rɪ'taɪə/ **retires, retiring, retired.** [1] VERB When older people **retire**, they leave their job and stop working. *Why aren't MPs made to retire at 65? ...his decision to retire from grand prix racing at the end of the season.* ♦**retired** ADJ *...a retired policeman.* [2] VERB If you **retire to** another room or place, you go there; FORMAL.

retirement /rɪ'taɪəmənt/. [1] N-U **Retirement** is the time when a worker retires. *The Governor is going to take early retirement.* [2] N-U A person's **retirement** is the period in their life after they have retired. *...financial support during retirement.*

retort /rɪ'tɔːt/ **retorts, retorting, retorted.** VERB & N-C To **retort**, or to answer with a **retort**, means to reply angrily. *Was he afraid, he was asked. 'Afraid of what?' he retorted... Others retort that strong central power is a dangerous thing.*

retrace /rɪ'treɪs/ **retraces, retracing, retraced.** VERB If you **retrace** your steps, you re-

turn to where you started from using the same route. *He retraced his steps to the spot where he'd left the case.*

retract /rɪ'trækt/ **retracts, retracting, retracted.** VERB If you **retract** something that you have said or written, you say publicly that you did not mean it; FORMAL. *He later retracted the statement, claiming he made it when drunk.* ♦**retraction, retractions** N-C *Miss Pearce said she expected an unqualified retraction of his comments.*

retreat /rɪ'triːt/ **retreats, retreating, retreated.** [1] VERB If you **retreat** from someone or something, you move away from them. *He retreated to the kitchen to consider their quarrel.* [2] VERB & N-VAR If an army **retreats**, or if it is in **retreat**, it moves away from an enemy in order to avoid fighting. *The French, suddenly outnumbered, were forced to retreat. ...Napoleon's retreat from Moscow.* [3] N-C A **retreat** is a quiet secluded place where you go to rest or to do something in private.

retribution /ˌretrɪ'bjuːʃən/. N-U **Retribution** is punishment for a crime; FORMAL. *They did not want their names used for fear of retribution.*

retrieval /rɪ'triːvəl/. N-U The **retrieval** of something is the process of getting it back. *Data is now usually stored in a computer as the sorting and retrieval can be done very easily.*

retrieve /rɪ'triːv/ **retrieves, retrieving, retrieved.** VERB If you **retrieve** something, you get it back from the place where you left it. *He reached over and retrieved his jacket from the back seat.*

retro /'retrəʊ/. ADJ **Retro** clothes, music, and objects are based on the styles of the past. *...50s retro ballgowns.*

retrospect /'retrəspekt/. PHRASE The way that things seem **in retrospect** is the way they seem after an event, when you are able to consider them from a more experienced point of view. *In retrospect, I wish I hadn't done it.*

retrospective /ˌretrə'spektɪv/. [1] N-C A **retrospective** is an exhibition or showing of work done by an artist over many years, rather than his or her most recent work. [2] ADJ **Retrospective** laws or legal actions take effect from a date before the date when they are officially approved. ♦**retrospectively** ADV *...governments that impose taxes retrospectively.*

return /rɪ'tɜːn/ **returns, returning, returned.** [1] VERB & N-SING When you **return** to a place, you go back there. Your **return** is your arrival back at a place. *Three days after returning to Britain he was arrested... She returned home to Birmingham... Asthma had hardly bothered him since his return from Berlin.* [2] VERB & N-SING If you **return** something that you have borrowed or taken, you give it back or put it back. The **return** of something is the act of giving or putting it back. *He returned her passport. ...Japan's demand for the return of the islands.* [3] VERB If you **return** someone's action, you do the same thing to them as they have just done to you. If you **return** someone's feeling, you feel the same way towards them as they feel towards you. *I returned his smile... Why couldn't she return his affection and like him just a little?* [4] VERB & N-SING If you **return**

to a subject or an activity, you start talking about that subject or doing that activity again. A **return** to an activity is the starting of it again. *He called for an end to strikes and a return to work.* **5** VERB & N-SING If you **return** to a state you were in before, you go back to that state again. You can refer to a change back to a former state as a **return** to that state. *Life has not yet returned to normal. ...the conditions that would allow a lasting peace and a return to normality.* **6** VERB When a judge or jury **returns** a verdict, they announce whether a person is guilty or not. **7** N-C A **return** or a **return ticket** is a ticket that allows you to travel to a place and then back again. **8** N-VAR The **return** on an investment is the profit you get from it. *Investors require higher returns on riskier investments.*

PHRASES ● If you do something **in return** for what someone has done for you, you do it because of what they did. *There's little I can do for him in return.* ● You say **'many happy returns'** to wish someone a happy birthday.

reunification /ˌriːjuːnɪfɪˈkeɪʃən/. N-U The **reunification** of a country or city that has been divided into two or more parts for some time is the joining of it together again.

reunion /riːˈjuːniən/ **reunions.** N-VAR A **reunion** is a party or occasion when people who have not seen each other for a long time meet again. *...a family reunion... It was a very emotional reunion.*

reunite /ˌriːjuːˈnaɪt/ **reunites, reuniting, reunited.** **1** VERB If you **are reunited** with your family or friends, you meet them again after being separated from them. *For Mary it would mean the chance to be reunited with her sister.* **2** VERB To **reunite** a divided organization or country means to cause it to be united again. *His first job will be to reunite the army.*

rev /rev/ **revs, revving, revved.** **1** VERB & PHR-VERB To **rev** the engine of a vehicle, or **rev up** the engine of a vehicle, means to increase the engine speed by pressing the accelerator. *The old bus was revving its engine... The friend revved up his motorbike.* **2** N-PL An engine's **revs** is its speed, which is measured in revolutions per minute.

revamp /riːˈvæmp/ **revamps, revamping, revamped.** VERB & N-C If someone **revamps** something, they change things about it in order to try and improve it. **Revamps** are changes to something. *It is time to revamp the system. ...major organizational revamps.*

reveal /rɪˈviːl/ **reveals, revealing, revealed.** **1** VERB To **reveal** something means to make people aware of it. *Research revealed that neither the sex nor the age of the student makes a difference.* **2** VERB If you **reveal** something that has been out of sight, you uncover it so that people can see it. *A grey carpet was removed to reveal the original pine floor.*

revealing /rɪˈviːlɪŋ/. **1** ADJ A **revealing** action or statement tells you something that you were not aware of. *...a revealing comment.* **2** ADJ **Revealing** clothes show a lot of your body.

revel /ˈrevəl/ **revels, revelling, revelled** (AM **reveling revelled**). VERB If you **revel** in a

situation or experience, you enjoy it very much. *He revelled in his triumph.*

revelation /ˌrevəˈleɪʃən/ **revelations.** **1** N-VAR The **revelation** of something is the act of making it known. A **revelation** is an interesting fact that is made known to people. *...the revelation of his affair with a former secretary. ...revelations about his private life.* **2** N-SING If something is a **revelation** to you, it makes you aware of something that you did not know before. *The expression on his father's face was a revelation to him.*

revenge /rɪˈvendʒ/. N-U **Revenge** involves hurting someone who has hurt you. *...acts of revenge... The attackers were said to be taking revenge on the 14-year-old, claiming he was a school bully... The killings were said to have been in revenge for the murder of her lover.*

revenue /ˈrevənjuː/ **revenues.** N-U & N-PL **Revenue** is the money that a government or organization receives from people. *...a boom year at the cinema, with record advertising revenue. ...a 40% increase in revenues.*

reverberate /rɪˈvɜːbəreɪt/ **reverberates, reverberating, reverberated.** VERB When a loud sound **reverberates**, it echoes through a place. *The noise reverberated through the house.*

revere /rɪˈvɪə/ **reveres, revering, revered.** VERB If you **revere** someone, you respect and admire them greatly; FORMAL. *He revered his father.* ♦**revered** ADJ *...some of the country's most revered institutions.* ♦**reverence** /ˈrevərəns/ N-U *They shared a reverence for women.*

Reverend /ˈrevərənd/. N-TITLE **Reverend** is a title used before the name of a member of the clergy. *...the Reverend Jim Simons.*

reversal /rɪˈvɜːsəl/ **reversals.** N-C When there is a **reversal** of a process or policy, it is changed to the opposite process or policy. *The move represents a complete reversal of previous US policy.*

reverse /rɪˈvɜːs/ **reverses, reversing, reversed.** **1** VERB To **reverse** a process, decision, or policy means to change it to its opposite. *Complaints are already rising, reversing the trend of recent years.* **2** VERB If you **reverse** the order of a set of things, you arrange them in the opposite order, so that the first thing comes last. **3** VERB & N-U When a car **is being reversed**, or when it is being driven in reverse, it is being driven backwards. **4** ADJ & N-SING **Reverse** or the **reverse** means opposite to what has just been described or mentioned. *Instead of bringing about peace the meeting may well have the reverse effect... It's not difficult, quite the reverse.* **5** PHRASE If something happens **in reverse** or goes **into reverse**, it happens in the opposite way to usual or to what has been happening. *The process also works in reverse.*

revert /rɪˈvɜːt/ **reverts, reverting, reverted.** VERB When people or things **revert** to a former state, system, or type of behaviour, they go back to it. *She reverted to her old ways.*

review /rɪˈvjuː/ **reviews, reviewing, reviewed.** **1** VERB & N-C When someone **reviews** something such as a new book or play, they write a report or give a talk on television or radio in which they express their opinion of it.

This report is called a **review**. ♦ **reviewer, reviewers** N-C ...*a film reviewer.* [2] VERB & N-VAR If you **review** a situation or system, you examine it in order to decide whether changes are needed. This process is called a **review**. *He said the Government would review the situation in June... That policy was due for review this year.* [3] PHRASE If something is **under review**, it is being examined in order to decide whether changes are needed.

revise /rɪˈvaɪz/ **revises, revising, revised.** [1] VERB If you **revise** something, you alter it in order to make it better or more accurate. *I found myself revising my opinion of him... Experts are starting to revise their estimates of how big the oil spill may be.* ♦ **revision** /rɪˈvɪʒən/ **revisions** N-VAR *It is badly in need of revision.* [2] VERB When you **revise** for an examination, you read things again in order to learn them thoroughly; BRITISH. *She got up early to revise.* ♦ **revision** N-U ...*exam revision.*

revisit /ˌriːˈvɪzɪt/ **revisits, revisiting, revisited.** VERB If you **revisit** a place, you return there for a visit after you have been away for a long time.

revitalize (BR also **revitalise**) /ˌriːˈvaɪtəlaɪz/ **revitalizes, revitalizing, revitalized.** VERB To **revitalize** something means to make it more active or lively. ...*Government plans for revitalising the economy of South Wales .*

revival /rɪˈvaɪvəl/ **revivals.** [1] N-VAR When there is a **revival** of something, it becomes active or popular again. ...*recent signs of economic revival.* ...*the revival in classical music.* [2] N-C A **revival** is a new production of a play, an opera, or a ballet. ...*John Clement's revival of Chekhov's 'The Seagull'.*

revive /rɪˈvaɪv/ **revives, reviving, revived.** [1] VERB When something such as a feeling or a practice **revives** or **is revived**, it becomes active or successful again. ...*an attempt to revive the British economy.* [2] VERB When someone **revives** a play, opera, or ballet, they present a new production of it. [3] VERB If you **revive** someone who has fainted, or if they **revive**, they become conscious again. *She could not be revived.*

revoke /rɪˈvəʊk/ **revokes, revoking, revoked.** VERB When someone in authority **revokes** something such as an order, they cancel it; FORMAL. *The council revoked its decision and the library remained open.*

revolt /rɪˈvəʊlt/ **revolts, revolting, revolted.** [1] N-VAR A **revolt** is a violent attempt by a group of people to change their country's political system. [2] VERB When people **revolt**, they use violence to try to change a country's political system. *In 1848 the Hungarians revolted against Austrian rule.* [3] N-VAR A **revolt** by a person or group against someone or something is a rejection of the authority of that person or thing. *The Prime Minister is facing a revolt by some of his MPs.* [4] VERB When people **revolt**, they reject the authority of someone or something. *Caroline revolted against her ballet training at sixteen.*

revolting /rɪˈvəʊltɪŋ/ . ADJ **Revolting** means horrible and disgusting. *The smell was revolting.*

revolution /ˌrevəˈluːʃən/ **revolutions.** [1] N-VAR A **revolution** is a successful attempt by a large group of people to change their country's political system, using force. *The period since the revolution has been one of political turmoil... There was talk of revolution.* [2] N-C A **revolution** is an important change in a particular area of human activity. ...*the industrial revolution.*

revolutionary /ˌrevəˈluːʃənri, AM -neri/ **revolutionaries.** [1] ADJ **Revolutionary** activities, organizations, or people have the aim of causing a political revolution. ...*the Cuban revolutionary leader, Jose Marti.* [2] N-C A **revolutionary** is a person who tries to cause a revolution or who takes part in one. [3] ADJ **Revolutionary** ideas and developments involve great changes in the way something is done or made. ...*a revolutionary concept in aviation.*

revolutionize (BR also **revolutionise**) /ˌrevəˈluːʃənaɪz/ **revolutionizes, revolutionizing, revolutionized.** VERB When something **revolutionizes** an activity, it causes great changes in the way it is done. ...*ideas that will revolutionize the way people use computers.*

revolve /rɪˈvɒlv/ **revolves, revolving, revolved.** [1] VERB If one thing **revolves** around another thing, the second thing is the main feature or focus of the first thing. *Since childhood, her life has revolved around tennis... The conversation revolved around the terrible condition of the road.* [2] VERB When something **revolves**, it moves or turns in a circle around a central point or line. *The satellite revolves around the Earth once every hundred minutes.*

revolver /rɪˈvɒlvə/ **revolvers.** N-C A **revolver** is a kind of hand gun.

revue /rɪˈvjuː/ **revues.** N-C A **revue** is a light theatrical entertainment consisting of songs, dances, and jokes about recent events.

revulsion /rɪˈvʌlʃən/ . N-U **Revulsion** is a strong feeling of disgust or disapproval. *They expressed their shock and revulsion at his violent death.*

reward /rɪˈwɔːd/ **rewards, rewarding, rewarded.** [1] N-C A **reward** is something that you are given because you have behaved well, worked hard, or provided a service to the community. *As a reward for good behaviour, treat your child to a new toy.* [2] N-C A **reward** is a sum of money offered to anyone who can give information about lost or stolen property or about someone who is wanted by the police. [3] VERB If you do something and **are rewarded** with a particular benefit, you receive that benefit as a result of doing it. *Impress the buyer and you will be rewarded with a quicker sale.*

rewarding /rɪˈwɔːdɪŋ/ . ADJ Something that is **rewarding** gives you satisfaction or brings you benefits. ...*a rewarding and full career.*

rewrite /ˌriːˈraɪt/ **rewrites, rewriting, rewritten.** VERB If someone **rewrites** a piece of writing such as a book, a script, or a law, they write it in a different way in order to improve it. *Students rewrite their papers and submit them for final evaluation.*

rhetoric /ˈretərɪk/ . N-U **Rhetoric** is speech or writing that is meant to convince and impress people but may lack sincerity or honesty. *My speech contained facts, not empty rhetoric.*

rhetorical /rɪˈtɒrɪkəl, AM -ˈtɔːr-/. [1] ADJ A **rhetorical** question is used in order to make a statement rather than to get an answer. ◆**rhetorically** ADV *'Do these kids know how lucky they are?' Jackson asked rhetorically.* [2] ADJ **Rhetorical** language is intended to be grand and impressive; FORMAL.

rhino /ˈraɪnəʊ/ **rhinos.** N-C A **rhino** is the same as a **rhinoceros.**

rhinoceros /raɪˈnɒsərəs/ **rhinoceroses.** N-C A **rhinoceros** is a large African or Asian animal with thick grey skin and one or two horns on its nose.

rhyme /raɪm/ **rhymes, rhyming, rhymed.** [1] VERB If one word **rhymes** with another, they have a very similar sound. *York rhymes with pork. ...names that rhyme: Donnie, Ronnie, Connie.* [2] N-C A **rhyme** is a short poem with rhyming words at the ends of its lines. ● See also **nursery rhyme.** [3] N-U **Rhyme** is the use of rhyming words as a technique in poetry.

rhythm /ˈrɪðəm/ **rhythms.** N-VAR A **rhythm** is a regular series of sounds, movements, or actions. *His body twists and sways to the rhythm... Dozing in the day spoils the normal bodily rhythm.*

rhythmic /ˈrɪðmɪk/ or **rhythmical** /ˈrɪðmɪkəl/. ADJ A **rhythmic** movement or sound is repeated at regular intervals. *...the rhythmic beat of the surf.* ◆**rhythmically** ADV *She stood, swaying her hips, moving rhythmically.*

rib /rɪb/ **ribs.** N-C Your **ribs** are the curved bones that go from your backbone around your chest.

ribbon /ˈrɪbən/ **ribbons.** N-VAR A **ribbon** is a long narrow piece of cloth used as a fastening or decoration.

rice /raɪs/. N-U **Rice** consists of white or brown grains taken from a cereal plant.

rich /rɪtʃ/ **richer, richest; riches.** [1] ADJ & N-PL A **rich** person has a lot of money or valuable possessions. **The rich** are rich people. *Their one aim in life is to get rich. ...the rich and famous.* [2] N-PL **Riches** are valuable possessions or large amounts of money. *Some people want fame or riches.* [3] ADJ If something is **rich in** a useful or valuable substance, it has a lot of that substance. *Bananas are rich in vitamin A. ...Angola's northern oil-rich coastline.* [4] ADJ A **rich** life is one that is interesting because it is full of different events and activities. *...the rich history of the island.* ◆**richness** N-U *...the richness of human life.* [5] ADJ **Rich** food contains a lot of fat or oil.

richly /ˈrɪtʃli/. [1] ADV If something is **richly** coloured, flavoured, or scented, it has a pleasantly strong colour, flavour, or scent. *...richly coloured fabrics.* [2] ADV You use **richly** to say that a place or thing has a large amount of elaborate or valuable things. *...the richly decorated silver pot.* [3] ADV If you say that someone **richly** deserves an award, success, or victory, you feel very strongly that they deserve it. *He achieved the success he so richly deserved.*

rickety /ˈrɪkɪti/. ADJ A **rickety** building or piece of furniture seems likely to collapse or break. *Mona climbed the rickety wooden stairway.*

rid /rɪd/ **rids, ridding, rid.** [1] PHRASE When you **get rid of** something that you do not want or like, you take action so that you no longer have it. *The owner needs to get rid of the car for financial reasons.* [2] PHRASE If you **get rid of** someone who is causing problems for you, you make them leave. *...a senior manager who wanted to get rid of him.* [3] VERB If you **rid** a place or person of something undesirable or unwanted, you succeed in removing it completely. *Why couldn't he ever rid himself of those thoughts?* [4] ADJ AFTER LINK-V If you **are rid of** someone or something unpleasant or annoying, they are no longer with you or causing problems for you. *The family had sought a way to be rid of her.*

ridden /ˈrɪdən/. **Ridden** is the past participle of **ride.**

riddle /ˈrɪdəl/ **riddles.** [1] N-C A **riddle** is a puzzle in which you ask a question that seems to be nonsense but which has a clever or amusing answer. [2] N-C You can describe something that is puzzling as a **riddle.** *Do they know the answer to the riddle of why it was never finished?*

riddled /ˈrɪdəld/. [1] ADJ AFTER LINK-V If something **is riddled with** bullets or bullet holes, it is full of them. [2] ADJ If something **is riddled with** undesirable qualities or features, it is full of them. *The report was riddled with errors. ...a dangerous, crime-riddled, filthy city.*

ride /raɪd/ **rides, riding, rode, ridden.** [1] VERB If you **ride** a horse, you sit on it and control its movements. *Can you ride?... He mounted his horse and rode away.* [2] VERB If you **ride** a bicycle or a motorcycle you sit on it, control it, and travel along on it. *He rode to work on a bicycle.* [3] VERB When you **ride** in a vehicle such as a car, you travel in it. [4] N-C A **ride** is a journey on a horse or bicycle, or in a vehicle.

> When you want to mention that someone is controlling a horse, bicycle, or motorbike, you can use **ride** as a transitive verb, with the object coming immediately after it. *Whether you ride a motorbike, scooter or moped, get yourself properly trained.* However, if you want to mention that someone is a passenger in a vehicle, **ride** must be followed by a preposition. *I was riding on the back of a friend's bicycle... We are still letting our children ride in the front seat of our cars.* If **ride** is used without an object, a preposition, or any other phrase that specifies the context, it usually refers to the activity of riding a horse. *'Do you ride?'—'No, I've never been on a horse.'*

PHRASES ● If you say that someone or something **is riding high,** you mean that they are popular or successful at the present time. ● If you say that someone faces **a rough ride,** you think that things are going to be difficult for them; INFORMAL. ● See also **riding.**

rider /ˈraɪdə/ **riders.** N-C A **rider** is someone who rides a horse, bicycle, or motorcycle.

ridge /rɪdʒ/ **ridges.** [1] N-C A **ridge** is a long narrow piece of raised land. *...a narrow mountain* *ridge.* [2] N-C A **ridge** is a raised line on a flat surface. *...the bony ridge of the eye socket.*

ridicule /ˈrɪdɪkjuːl/ **ridicules, ridiculing, ridiculed.** VERB & N-U If you **ridicule** someone or something, or if you make them an object of **ridicule**, you make fun of them in an unkind way. *Mr Goss ridiculed that suggestion... The press has held the royals up to ridicule.*

ridiculous /rɪˈdɪkjʊləs/. ADJ If you say that something or someone is **ridiculous**, you mean that they are very foolish. *It is ridiculous to suggest that we are having a romance.*

ridiculously /rɪˈdɪkjʊləsli/. ADV You use **ridiculously** to emphasize the fact that you think something is unreasonable or very surprising. *She looked ridiculously young to be a mother.*

riding /ˈraɪdɪŋ/. N-U **Riding** is the activity or sport of riding horses. *I went riding.*

rife /raɪf/. ADJ AFTER LINK-V If something bad or unpleasant is **rife**, it is very common. *Bribery and corruption are rife in the industry.*

rifle /ˈraɪfəl/ **rifles, rifling, rifled.** [1] N-C A **rifle** is a gun with a long barrel. [2] VERB If you **rifle** through things, or if you **rifle** them, you make a quick search among them in order to find something or steal something. *The thief rifled through her handbag.*

rift /rɪft/ **rifts.** [1] N-C A **rift** between people is a serious quarrel that stops them having a co-operative relationship. *The serious rifts within the country could lead to civil war.* [2] N-C A **rift** is a large split that appears in the ground.

rig /rɪg/ **rigs, rigging, rigged.** [1] VERB If someone **rigs** a contest, they dishonestly arrange it to get the result they want or to give someone an unfair advantage. *She accused her opponents of rigging the vote.* ♦**rigging** N-U *There were reports of election rigging.* [2] N-C A **rig** is a large structure that is used for extracting oil or gas from the ground or the sea bed. *...gas rigs in the North Sea.*

▶ **rig up.** PHR-VERB If you **rig up** a device or structure, you make it or fix it in place using any materials that are available. *I'll rig up a curtain.*

right 1 correctness and morality

right /raɪt/ **rights, righting, righted.** [1] ADJ & ADV If something is **right**, it is correct according to the facts or plans. If someone is **right** about something, they are correct about it. *Clocks never told the right time. ...delivery of the right pizza to the right place... Am I right in thinking you've got something arranged?... You guessed right about some things.* [2] ADJ & N-U **Right** is used to refer to activities or actions that are considered to be morally or legally good and acceptable. If someone has behaved in a way which is right, you can say that they are **in the right**. *It was right and proper not to show the film... I was right to issue that order... At least he knew right from wrong... Legally, the local tax office is in the right.* ♦**rightness** N-U *Many people have very strong opinions about the rightness or wrongness of abortion.* [3] N-C If you have a **right** to do or to have something, you are morally or legally entitled to do it or to have it. Your **rights** are the things you are entitled to do or have. *People have the right to read any kind of material they wish. ...voting rights.*

[4] ADJ If something such as an action or decision is the **right** one, it is the best or most suitable one. *They decided the time was right for their escape... She's the right person for the job.* [5] ADJ AFTER LINK-V If a situation or thing is **right**, it is satisfactory and as you would like it to be. If something is not **right** about a situation or thing, there is something unsatisfactory or odd about it. *I was pleased with my performance on Saturday – everything went right... The name Sue Anne never seemed quite right.* [6] ADJ If you say that someone is seen in all the **right** places or knows all the **right** people, you mean that they go to places which are socially acceptable or know people who are socially acceptable. [7] VERB If you **right** a wrong, you do something to make up for a mistake or something bad you did in the past. [8] VERB If you **right** something that has fallen or rolled over, it returns to its normal upright position. *The boat righted itself.* [9] ADJ BEFORE N The **right** side of a material is the side that is intended to be seen.

PHRASES ● If something is not the case but you think that it should be, you can say that **by rights**, it should be the case. *She did work which by rights should be done by someone else.* ● If someone is a successful or respected person **in** their **own right**, they are successful or respected because of their own efforts and talents rather than those of the people they are connected with. ● **it serves** you **right**: see **serve.** ● **on the right side of** someone: see **side.**

right 2 direction and political groups

right /raɪt/; also written **Right** for meaning 2. [1] N-SING & ADV & ADJ BEFORE N The **right** is one of two opposite directions, sides, or positions. If you are facing north and you turn to the right, you will be facing east. **Right** is used to describe things which are on the right side of your body. *Parking is on the right... To her right was an orange grove... Turn right into the street... Her right arm was broken.* [2] N-SING You can refer to political ideas based on capitalist or conservative ideas, or to the people who support these ideas, as **the right**. *The Tory Right despise him.*

right 3 used for emphasis or in speech

right /raɪt/. [1] ADV You can use the word **right** to emphasize the exact position or time of something. *The back of a car appeared right in front of him... I had to decide right then.* [2] ADJ You can use the word **right** to emphasize a noun, usually referring to something bad; IN-FORMAL, BRITISH. *He made a right mess.* [3] PHRASE If you do something **right away** or **right off**, you do it immediately; SPOKEN. *Right off I want to confess that I was wrong.* [4] ADV You use **right** in order to attract someone's attention or to indicate that you have dealt with one thing so you can go on to another. *Right, let's go to our next caller.* [5] See also **all right.**

'right angle, right angles. [1] N-C A **right angle** is an angle of 90°. [2] PHRASE If two things are **at right angles**, they form an angle of 90° where they touch each other. You can also say that one thing is **at right angles** to another.

righteous /ˈraɪtʃəs/. ADJ Someone who is **righteous** is morally good, especially according to the rules of a religion. *He was full of righteous indignation.* ● See also **self-righteous**. ♦**righteousness** N-U *...God's message of righteousness.*

rightful /ˈraɪtfʊl/. ADJ BEFORE N If you say that someone or something has returned to their **rightful** place or position, you mean they have returned to the place or position that you think they should have. *The car must be returned to its rightful owner.* ♦**rightfully** ADV *She's inherited the money which is rightfully hers.*

right-hand. ADJ BEFORE N If something is on the **right-hand** side of something, it is positioned on the right of it. *...the upper right-hand corner of the picture.*

right-'handed. ADJ & ADV Someone who is **right-handed**, or who does things **right-handed**, uses their right hand rather than their left hand for activities such as writing or picking things up.

right-'wing; also **right wing** for meaning 2. ① ADJ A **right-wing** person or group has conservative or capitalist views. ♦**right-winger**, **right-wingers** N-C *Right-wingers demanded tax cuts.* ② N-SING The **right wing** of a political party consists of the members of it who have the most conservative or the most capitalist views.

rigid /ˈrɪdʒɪd/. ① ADJ If you describe laws, systems, or attitudes as **rigid**, you disapprove of them because they cannot be changed or because someone refuses to change them. *Hospital routines for nurses are very rigid.* ♦**rigidity** /rɪˈdʒɪdɪti/ N-U *...the rigidity of government policy.* ♦**rigidly** ADV *Our rule is rigidly enforced.* ② ADJ A **rigid** substance or object is stiff and does not bend or stretch easily. ♦**rigidity** N-U *...the strength and rigidity of glass.*

rigorous /ˈrɪgərəs/. ADJ If you describe something as **rigorous**, you approve of the fact that it is done thoroughly and strictly. *...rigorous military training.* ♦**rigorously** ADV *...rigorously conducted research.*

rigour (AM **rigor**) /ˈrɪgə/ **rigours**. ① N-PL If you refer to the **rigours** of an activity or job, you mean the difficult or unpleasant things that are associated with it. *...the rigours of childbirth.* ② N-U If something is done with **rigour**, it is done in a strict, thorough way.

rim /rɪm/ **rims**. N-C The **rim** of a container or a circular object is the edge which goes all the way round the top or round the outside. *...a round mirror with a white metal rim.*

rind /raɪnd/ **rinds**. ① N-VAR The **rind** of a fruit such as a lemon is its thick outer skin. ② N-VAR The **rind** of cheese or bacon is the hard outer edge which you do not usually eat.

ring 1 telephoning or making a sound

ring /rɪŋ/ **rings, ringing, rang, rung**. ① VERB & PHR-VERB & N-C In British English, if you **ring** someone, or if you **ring** them **up**, or if you give them a **ring**, you phone them. The usual American word is **call**. *She has rung home just once... Could someone ring for a taxi?* ② VERB & N-C When a telephone **rings**, it makes a sound called a **ring**, to let you know that someone is phoning you. ③ VERB & N-C When you **ring** a

bell or when a bell **rings**, it makes a metallic sound called a **ring**. *He heard the school bell ring.* ♦**ringing** N-U *...the ringing of church bells.* ④ N-SING You can use the word **ring** to describe a quality that something such as a statement or argument seems to have. For example, if an argument **has a plausible ring**, it seems quite plausible. ⑤ PHRASE If a statement **rings true**, it seems to be true or genuine. If it **rings hollow**, it does not seem to be true or genuine.

▶ **ring back**. PHR-VERB In British English, if you **ring** someone **back**, you phone them, either because they phoned you earlier and you were out or because you did not finish an earlier conversation. The American term is **call back**.

▶ **ring off**. PHR-VERB In British English, when you **ring off** you put down the receiver at the end of a telephone call. The American term is **hang up**.

ring 2 shapes and groups

ring /rɪŋ/ **rings, ringing, ringed**. ① N-C A **ring** is a small circle of metal that you wear on your finger. ② N-C An object or substance that is in the shape of a circle can be described as a **ring**. *...a ring of blue smoke.* ③ N-C At a boxing match or circus, the **ring** is the place where the contest or performance takes place. ④ PASSIVE-VERB If a place **is ringed** with something, it is surrounded by that thing. *The city is ringed by mountains.* ⑤ N-C You can refer to an organized group of people who are involved in an illegal activity as a **ring**. *...an international spy ring.*

ringing /ˈrɪŋɪŋ/. ADJ BEFORE N A **ringing** sound can be heard very clearly. *He hit the metal steps with a ringing crash.*

rink /rɪŋk/ **rinks**. N-C A **rink** is a large area where people go to skate.

rinse /rɪns/ **rinses, rinsing, rinsed**. ① VERB & N-C When you **rinse** something, or when you give it a **rinse**, you wash it in clean water in order to remove dirt or soap from it. *Shampoo and rinse your hair.* ② N-C A hair **rinse** is a hair dye which is not permanent but gradually fades over time.

riot /ˈraɪət/ **riots, rioting, rioted**. ① VERB & N-C When people **riot**, or when there is a **riot**, a crowd of people behave violently in a public place. *They rioted in protest against the Government.* ♦**rioter**, **rioters** N-C *The militia dispersed the rioters.* ♦**rioting** N-U *...three days of rioting.* ② PHRASE If people **run riot**, they behave in a wild and uncontrolled manner. *Parents use discipline to stop their child running riot.*

rip /rɪp/ **rips, ripping, ripped**. ① VERB If you **rip** something, you tear it forcefully with your hands or with a tool such as a knife. If something **rips**, it is torn forcefully. *I tried not to rip the paper as I unwrapped it.* ② N-C A **rip** is a long cut or split in something made of cloth or paper. ③ VERB If you **rip** something away, you remove it quickly and forcefully. *Her earring had been ripped off.*

▶ **rip off**. PHR-VERB If someone **rips** you **off**, they cheat you by charging too much for goods or services; INFORMAL. *People are buying them and getting ripped off.*

▸ **rip up.** PHR-VERB If you **rip** something **up**, you tear it into small pieces.

ripe /raɪp/ **riper, ripest.** [1] ADJ **Ripe** fruit or grain is fully grown and ready to be harvested or eaten. [2] ADJ AFTER LINK-V If something is **ripe for** a change, that change is likely to happen soon. *The nation was ripe for revolution.* [3] PHRASE If you say **the time is ripe** for something, you mean that a suitable time has arrived for doing it. *The time is ripe to send our first female ambassador to the region.*

ripen /ˈraɪpən/ **ripens, ripening, ripened.** VERB When crops **ripen**, they become ripe. *You can ripen the tomatoes on a sunny windowsill.*

ripple /ˈrɪpəl/ **ripples, rippling, rippled.** [1] N-C & VERB **Ripples** are little waves on the surface of water caused by the wind or by something moving. When water **ripples**, a number of little waves appear on its surface. [2] VERB If something such as a feeling **ripples** through a person or group, it gradually spreads across them. *A faint smile rippled across the landlady's face.*

rise /raɪz/ **rises, rising, rose, risen** /ˈrɪzən/. [1] VERB If something **rises** or **rises up**, it moves upwards. *Wilson watched the smoke rise from his cigarette.* [2] VERB When you **rise**, you stand up; FORMAL. *Luther rose slowly from the chair.* [3] VERB When you **rise**, you get out of bed; WRITTEN. *Tony had risen early.* [4] VERB When the sun or moon **rises**, it appears from below the horizon. [5] VERB If land **rises**, it slopes upwards. *He looked up the slope of land that rose from the house.* [6] VERB & N-C If an amount **rises**, or if there is a **rise** in an amount, the amount increases. *Profits rose from £842,000 to £1.82m... He will get a pay rise of nearly £4,000.* [7] VERB & N-SING If someone **rises** to a higher position or status, they become more powerful or successful. You can also talk about someone's **rise**. *He has risen rapidly through the ranks of government... The rise of the Nazis forced the family to move to London.* [8] VERB If a sound **rises**, it becomes louder or higher. *His voice rose almost to a scream.* [9] PHRASE If something **gives rise to** an event or situation, it causes that event or situation to happen. [10] to **rise to the challenge**: see **challenge**.

▸ **rise above.** PHR-VERB If you **rise above** a problem, you do not allow it to affect you. *We have to resolve to rise above our circumstances.*

▸ **rise up.** PHR-VERB When the people in a country **rise up**, they rebel against the people in authority and start fighting them. *People have risen up against their rulers.*

risk /rɪsk/ **risks, risking, risked.** [1] N-VAR If there is a **risk** of something unpleasant, there is a possibility that it will happen. *There is a small risk that his party might lose... There's no risk of them being sued.* [2] N-C If you say that something or someone is a **risk**, you mean they are likely to cause harm. *Salmon cannot be regarded as a health risk... He is a risk to national security.* [3] N-C If something that you do is a **risk**, it might have unpleasant or undesirable results. *You're taking a big risk showing this to Kravis.* [4] VERB If you **risk** something unpleasant, you do something knowing that the unpleasant thing might happen as a result. *He's willing to risk making a fool of himself.* [5] VERB If you **risk** doing something, you do it, even though you know that it might have undesirable consequences. *I risked a glance back.* [6] VERB If you **risk** your life or something that is worth having, you do something which might result in it being lost or harmed. *You shouldn't have risked your job for me.*

PHRASES • If someone or something is **at risk**, they are in a situation where something unpleasant might happen to them. *People are at risk of starvation.* • If you tell someone that they are doing something **at** their **own risk**, you are warning them that, if they are harmed, it will be their own responsibility. • If you **run** the **risk** of doing or experiencing something undesirable, you do something knowing that the undesirable thing might happen as a result. *The officers had run the risk of being dismissed.*

risky /ˈrɪski/ **riskier, riskiest.** ADJ If an activity or action is **risky**, it is dangerous or could fail. *Investing is risky.*

rite /raɪt/ **rites.** N-C A **rite** is a traditional ceremony that is carried out in a particular group or society. *...a fertility rite.*

ritual /ˈrɪtʃʊəl/ **rituals.** [1] N-VAR & ADJ BEFORE N A **ritual** is a religious service or other ceremony which involves a series of actions performed in a fixed order. **Ritual** activities happen as part of a ritual. *...ritual dances.* [2] N-C A **ritual** is a way of behaving or a series of actions which people regularly carry out in a particular situation. *Cocktails at the Plaza was a nightly ritual of their sophisticated world.*

rival /ˈraɪvəl/ **rivals, rivalling, rivalled.** (AM **rivaling, rivaled**). [1] N-C & ADJ If people or groups are **rivals**, they are competing against each other. You can also talk about **rival** groups. *He is well ahead of his nearest rival. ...a dispute between rival teenage gangs.* [2] VERB If you say that one thing **rivals** another, you mean that they are both of the same standard or quality. *In my opinion, French cooking is rivalled only by the cuisine of China.*

rivalry /ˈraɪvəlri/ **rivalries.** N-VAR **Rivalry** is competition or conflict between people or groups. *What causes rivalry between brothers?*

river /ˈrɪvə/ **rivers.** N-C A **river** is a large amount of fresh water flowing continuously in a long line across land.

riverside /ˈrɪvəsaɪd/. N-SING The **riverside** is the area of land by the banks of a river. *...a riverside path.*

rivet /ˈrɪvɪt/ **rivets, riveting, riveted.** [1] VERB If you **are riveted** by something, it fascinates you and holds your interest completely. ♦**riveting** ADJ *...the most riveting TV interview of the year.* [2] N-C A **rivet** is a type of bolt used for fastening pieces of metal together.

road /rəʊd/ **roads.** N-C A **road** is a long piece of hard ground built between two places so that people can drive or ride easily from one to the other. *There was very little traffic on the roads... They will travel by road to Jordan.*

roadside /ˈrəʊdsaɪd/ **roadsides.** N-C The **roadside** is the area at the edge of a road. *...roadside restaurants.*

roadworks /'rəʊdwɜːks/. N-PL **Roadworks** are repairs or other work being done on a road.

roam /rəʊm/ **roams, roaming, roamed.** VERB If you **roam** an area or **roam** around it, you wander around it without having a particular purpose. *Barefoot children roamed the streets.*

roar /rɔː/ **roars, roaring, roared.** ① VERB & N-C If something **roars**, it makes a very loud noise. This noise is called a **roar**. *Her heart was pounding and the blood roared in her ears... A police car roared past. ...the roar of traffic.* ② VERB If someone **roars**, they shout very loudly. If they **roar** with laughter, they laugh very loudly. *'Tell us your name!' he roared.* ③ VERB & N-C When a lion **roars**, or when it gives a **roar**, it makes the loud sound typical of a lion.

roaring /'rɔːrɪŋ/. ① ADJ BEFORE N A **roaring** fire has large flames and is sending out a lot of heat. ② ADJ BEFORE N If something is a **roaring** success, it is very successful indeed.

roast /rəʊst/ **roasts, roasting, roasted.** ① VERB When you **roast** meat or other food, you cook it by dry heat in an oven or over a fire. ● See note at **cook**. ② ADJ BEFORE N **Roast** meat has been roasted. *I love roast chicken.*

rob /rɒb/ **robs, robbing, robbed.** ① VERB If a person or place is **robbed**, money or property is stolen from them, often using force. *He attempted to rob a bank.* ◆ **robber, robbers** N-C *Armed robbers broke into a jeweller's.* ② VERB If someone **is robbed of** something that they should have, it is taken away from them. *Bad luck robbed him of victory.*

robbery /'rɒbəri/ **robberies.** N-VAR **Robbery** is the crime of stealing money or property, often using force. *The gang members committed dozens of armed robberies.*

robe /rəʊb/ **robes.** ① N-C A **robe** is a long, loose piece of clothing, usually worn in religious or official ceremonies. ② N-C A bath **robe** is a piece of clothing, similar to a coat, which people wear at home when they are not dressed.

robin /'rɒbɪn/ **robins.** N-C A **robin** is a small brown bird with a red breast.

robot /'rəʊbɒt, AM -bət/ **robots.** N-C A **robot** is a machine which moves and performs certain tasks automatically. *...a robot arm.*

robust /rəʊ'bʌst, 'rəʊbʌst/. ADJ Someone or something that is **robust** is very strong or healthy.

rock /rɒk/ **rocks, rocking, rocked.** ① N-U **Rock** is the hard substance which the Earth is made of. *The hills above the valley are bare rock.* ② N-C A **rock** is a large piece of rock that sticks up out of the ground or the sea, or that has broken away from a mountain or a cliff. ③ N-C A **rock** is a piece of rock that is small enough for you to pick up. ④ VERB When something **rocks**, or when you **rock** it, it moves slowly and regularly backwards and forwards or from side to side. *His body rocked from side to side with the train... She sat on the porch and rocked the baby.* ⑤ VERB If an event or a piece of news **rocks** people, it shocks and horrifies them; JOURNALISM. *...the scandals that have rocked the country.* ⑥ N-U **Rock** or **rock music** is loud music with a strong beat that is played using instruments including electric guitars and drums.

PHRASES ● If you say that something such as a marriage or a business is **on the rocks**, you mean that it is having severe difficulties and looks likely to end soon. ● If you say that something has reached or hit **rock bottom**, you mean that it is at such a low level that it cannot go any lower. *Morale in the armed forces was at rock bottom.* ● **rock the boat**: see **boat**.

rock and roll. N-U **Rock and roll** is a kind of pop music developed in the 1950s which has a strong beat for dancing.

rocket /'rɒkɪt/ **rockets, rocketing, rocketed.** ① N-C A **rocket** is a space vehicle shaped like a long tube. ② N-C A **rocket** is a missile containing explosive and powered by gas. *...an anti-tank rocket.* ③ VERB If prices or profits **rocket**, they suddenly increase very quickly; JOURNALISM. *The crisis has sent oil prices rocketing.*

rocky /'rɒki/. ADJ A **rocky** place is covered with rocks or consists of large areas of bare rock. *We made our way down the rocky path.*

rod /rɒd/ **rods.** N-C A **rod** is a long thin bar made of metal or wood.

rode /rəʊd/. **Rode** is the past tense of **ride**.

rodent /'rəʊdənt/ **rodents.** N-C **Rodents** are small mammals, for example rats and squirrels, with sharp front teeth.

rodeo /'rəʊdiəʊ, rəʊ'deɪəʊ/ **rodeos.** N-C In the United States, a **rodeo** is a public entertainment in which cowboys show skills such as riding wild horses.

rogue /rəʊg/ **rogues.** N-C A **rogue** is a man who behaves in a dishonest way; DATED.

role /rəʊl/ **roles.** ① N-C The **role** of someone or something in a situation is their function or position in it. *Parents need to be clear about their role in raising their children... Films have long played a major role in his life.* ② N-C A **role** is one of the characters that an actor or singer plays in a film, play, or opera. *He gave her a leading role in his film.*

role model, role models. N-C A **role model** is someone you admire and try to imitate.

roll /rəʊl/ **rolls, rolling, rolled.** ① VERB If something **rolls** or if you **roll** it, it moves along a surface, turning over many times. *The ball rolled into the net... Roll the meat in coarsely ground black pepper.* ② VERB When vehicles **roll** somewhere, they move there slowly. *Tanks rolled into eastern Croatia.* ③ VERB If drops of liquid **roll** down a surface, they move quickly down it. *Tears rolled down her cheeks.* ④ VERB & PHR-VERB If you **roll** something flexible into a cylinder or a ball, or if you **roll** it **up**, you form it into a cylinder or a ball by wrapping it around itself or by shaping it between your hands. *Stein rolled up the paper bag with the money inside.* ⑤ N-C A **roll** of paper, cloth, or plastic is a cylinder of it that has been wrapped around itself or around a tube. *...a dozen rolls of film.* ⑥ N-C A **roll** is a very small circular loaf of bread. ⑦ N-C A **roll** is an official list of people's names. *A new electoral roll should be drawn up.* ⑧ See also **rolling**.

PHRASES ● If someone is **on a roll**, they are having great success which seems likely to continue; INFORMAL. ● If something is several things **rolled into one**, it combines the main features or qualities of those things. *This is our kitchen, sitting and dining room all rolled into one.* ● to **start the ball rolling**: see **ball**.

▸ **roll in.** PHR-VERB If money or profits **are rolling in**, they are being received in large quantities; INFORMAL.

▸ **roll up.** [1] PHR-VERB If you **roll up** your sleeves or trouser legs, you fold the ends back several times, making them shorter. [2] See also **roll 4**.

roller /'rəʊlə/ **rollers.** N-C A **roller** is a cylinder that turns round in a machine or device.

'roller-coaster (or **roller coaster**), **roller-coasters.** [1] N-C A **roller-coaster** is a ride at a fairground consisting of a small railway that goes up and down steep slopes fast. [2] N-C If you say that someone or something is on a **roller-coaster**, you mean that they go through many dramatic changes in a short time; JOURNALISM. *I've been on an emotional roller coaster since I've been here.*

roller-skate /'rəʊləskeɪt/ **roller-skates.** N-C **Roller-skates** are shoes with four small wheels on the bottom.

rolling /'rəʊlɪŋ/. ADJ BEFORE N **Rolling** hills have gentle slopes that extend into the distance.

ROM /rɒm/. N-U **ROM** is the permanent part of a computer's memory. The information stored there can be used but not changed. **ROM** is an abbreviation for 'read-only memory'. ● See also **CD ROM**.

,Roman 'Catholic, Roman Catholics. N-C & ADJ **Roman Catholic** means the same as **Catholic**.

romance /rə'mæns, 'rəʊmæns/ **romances.** [1] N-C A **romance** is a relationship between two people who are in love with each other. *...a whirlwind romance.* [2] N-U **Romance** refers to the actions and feelings of people who are in love. *He still finds time for romance by cooking candlelit dinners for his girlfriend.* [3] N-U You can refer to the pleasure and excitement of doing something as **romance**. *...the romance of travel.* [4] N-C A **romance** is a novel about a love affair.

romantic /rəʊ'mæntɪk/ **romantics.** [1] ADJ Someone who is **romantic** or does **romantic** things says and does things that make their partner feel special and loved. *...a romantic dinner for two.* [2] ADJ BEFORE N **Romantic** means connected with love. *He was not interested in a romantic relationship with Ingrid.* ◆**romantically** ADV *We are not romantically involved.* [3] ADJ BEFORE N A **romantic** play, film, or story describes or represents a love affair. [4] ADJ & N-C If you say that someone has a **romantic** view or idea of things, or that they are a **romantic**, you are criticizing them because their view of things is unrealistic. *He has a romantic view of rural society.*

romp /rɒmp/ **romps, romping, romped.** VERB When children **romp**, they play and move around in a noisy happy way. *Dogs and little children romped happily in the garden.*

roof /ru:f/ **roofs.** The plural can be pronounced /ru:fs/ or /ru:vz/. [1] N-C The **roof** of a building or car is the covering on top of it. *...a white cottage with a red slate roof.* [2] N-C The **roof** of your mouth is the top part of the inside of it.

[3] N-C The **roof** of an underground space such as a cave or mine is the highest part of it.
[PHRASES] ● If the level or price of something **goes through the roof**, it increases very suddenly and rapidly; INFORMAL. *Prices for Korean art have gone through the roof.* ● If someone **hits the roof** or **goes through the roof**, they are very angry indeed; INFORMAL.

rooftop (or **roof-top**) /'ru:ftɒp/ **rooftops.** N-C A **rooftop** is the outside part of the roof of a building. *...an attic with views over the rooftops.*

rookie /'rʊki/ **rookies.** N-C A **rookie** is a person who does not have much experience because they are new to a job; AMERICAN, INFORMAL.

room /ru:m, rʊm/ **rooms.** [1] N-C & N-SING A **room** is one of the separate sections in a building. You can refer to all the people in a room as **the room**. *The largest conference room could seat 5,000 people... The whole room roared with laughter.* [2] N-C If you talk about your **room**, you are referring to a room that you alone use, especially your bedroom or your office. *Go to my room and bring down my sweater, please.* [3] N-U If there is **room** for something, there is enough space for it. *The shoe should have enough room for the toes to move.* ● See note at **place**. [4] N-U If there is **room** for a particular kind of behaviour, people are able to behave in that way. *Mr Hedge left no room for doubt that he was in charge.*

roommate (or **room-mate**) /'ru:mmeɪt, 'rʊm-/ **roommates.** [1] N-C Your **roommate** is the person you share an apartment or house with; AMERICAN. [2] N-C Your **roommate** is the person you share a rented room with; BRITISH.

roomy /'ru:mi/ **roomier, roomiest.** ADJ Something that is **roomy** has plenty of space. *...a roomy kitchen.*

roost /ru:st/ **roosts, roosting, roosted.** [1] N-C A **roost** is a place where birds or bats rest. [2] VERB When birds or bats **roost** somewhere, they rest there.

root /ru:t/ **roots, rooting, rooted.** [1] N-C The **roots** of a plant are the parts that grow underground. [2] N-C The **root** of a hair or tooth is the part beneath the skin. [3] N-PL You can refer to the place or culture that a person or their family comes from as their **roots**. *I am proud of my Brazilian roots.* [4] N-C You can refer to the cause of a problem or an unpleasant situation as the **root** of it or the **roots** of it. *They were treating symptoms and not the root cause.* [5] VERB If you **root** through things, you search through them thoroughly. *Dogs root in the debris at the roadside.* [6] PHRASE If an idea, belief, or custom **takes root**, it becomes established among a group of people. *Time would be needed for democracy to take root.* [7] See also **grass roots**.

▸ **root out.** [1] PHR-VERB If you **root out** a person, you find them and force them from the place they are in, usually in order to punish them. *It shouldn't take too long to root him out.* [2] PHR-VERB If you **root out** a problem or an unpleasant situation, you find out the cause of it and put an end to it. *...a major drive to root out corruption.*

rooted /'ru:tɪd/. **1** ADJ AFTER LINK-V If one thing is **rooted** in another, it is strongly influenced by it or has developed from it. *The crisis is rooted in deep rivalries between the two groups.* **2** ADJ A deeply **rooted** opinion is a firm one that is unlikely to change. *Racism is a deeply rooted prejudice.*

rope /rəʊp/ **ropes, roping, roped.** **1** N-VAR A **rope** is a very thick cord, made by twisting together several thinner cords. *He tied the rope around his waist.* **2** VERB If you **rope** one thing to another, you tie them together with a rope. *The climbers were roped together for safety.*

▶ **rope in.** PHR-VERB If you say that you **were roped** in to a particular task, you mean that someone persuaded you to help them do that task; INFORMAL.

rose /rəʊz/ **roses.** **1** N-C A **rose** is a flower which has a pleasant smell and grows on a bush with thorns. **2** **Rose** is the past tense of **rise**.

rosé /'rəʊzeɪ, AM rəʊ'zeɪ/. N-U **Rosé** is wine which is pink in colour.

rosette /rəʊ'zet/ **rosettes.** N-C A **rosette** is a large circular badge made from coloured ribbons which is worn as a prize or to show support for a sports team or political party.

roster /'rɒstə/ **rosters.** N-C A **roster** is a list of people, especially one giving details about who is employed to do a particular job, or the order in which people do their job.

rosy /'rəʊzi/. **1** ADJ **Rosy** means pink in colour. *She had bright, rosy cheeks.* **2** ADJ If you say that a situation looks **rosy**, you mean that it is likely to be good or successful.

rot /rɒt/ **rots, rotting, rotted.** **1** VERB When food, wood, or other substances **rot**, or when something **rots** them, they decay and fall apart. *...rotting vegetation... Sugary canned drinks rot your teeth.* **2** N-U If there is **rot** in something made of wood, parts of it have decayed and fallen apart. *...extensive rot in the main beams.* **3** N-SING You can use **the rot** to refer to a gradual worsening of something. *He made mistakes during the campaign but the rot had set in well before that.*

▶ **rot away.** PHR-VERB When something **rots away**, it decays. *The pillars rotted away and were replaced.*

rota /'rəʊtə/ **rotas.** N-C A **rota** is a list which gives details of the order in which different people have to do a particular job; BRITISH. *...a careful rota which will make it clear who tidies the room on which day.*

rotary /'rəʊtəri/. ADJ BEFORE N **Rotary** means turning or able to turn in a circular movement round a fixed point.

rotate /rəʊ'teɪt, AM 'rəʊteɪt/ **rotates, rotating, rotated.** **1** VERB When something **rotates**, or when you **rotate** it, it turns with a circular movement. *Gently rotate your hips.* ♦ **rotation, rotations** N-VAR *...the daily rotation of the earth.* **2** VERB If people or things **rotate**, or if someone **rotates** them, they take it in turns to do something. ♦ **rotation** N-VAR *...crop rotation.*

rotten /'rɒtən/. **1** ADJ If food, wood, or another substance is **rotten**, it has decayed and can no longer be used. *The front bay window is rotten.* **2** ADJ If you say that something is **rotten**, you think it is bad, unpleasant, or unfair; INFORMAL. *It's a rotten idea.*

rough /rʌf/ **rougher, roughest; roughs, roughing, roughed.** **1** ADJ If a surface is **rough**, it is uneven and not smooth. *His hands were rough and calloused.* ♦ **roughness** N-U *...the roughness of his jacket.* **2** ADJ You say that people are **rough** when they use too much force. ♦ **roughly** ADV *A hand roughly pushed him aside.* **3** ADJ A **rough** place is unpleasant and dangerous because there is a lot of violence or crime there. *...a rough part of our town.* **4** ADJ A **rough** calculation or guess is approximate rather than exact or detailed. ♦ **roughly** ADV *Gambling and tourism pay roughly half the entire state budget.* **5** ADJ If someone is having a **rough** time, they are experiencing something difficult or unpleasant. *Tomorrow, he knew, would be a rough day.* **6** ADV You say that someone is **sleeping rough** or **living rough** when they have nowhere to live.

roulette /ru:'let/. N-U **Roulette** is a gambling game in which a ball is dropped onto a revolving wheel with numbered holes in it. The players bet on which hole the ball will end up in.

round /raʊnd/. **1** PREP & ADV To be positioned **round** a place or object means to surround it or be on all sides of it. *They were sitting round the kitchen table... Visibility was good all round.* **2** PREP If you move **round** a corner or obstacle, you move to the other side of it. If you look **round** a corner or obstacle, you look to see what is on the other side. *Suddenly a car came round a corner... One of his men tapped and looked round the door.* **3** PREP & ADV You use **round** to say that something happens in or is near different parts of a place or area. *He happens to own half the land round here... Shirley found someone to show them round.* **4** ADV If you move things **round**, you move them so they are in different places. *He will be glad to refurnish where possible, change things round.* **5** ADV & PREP If you go **round** to someone's house, you visit them. *He came round with a bottle of champagne... I went round my wife's house.* **6** PREP If you get **round** a problem or difficulty, you find a way of dealing with it. **7** See note at **around**. • **round the corner**: see **corner**. • **all year round**: see **year**.

round /raʊnd/ **rounds.** **1** N-C A **round** of events is a series of related events, especially one which comes after or before a similar series of events. *Another round of preliminary talks would be held.* **2** N-C In a sporting competition, a **round** is a series of games in which the winner goes on to play in the next round. **3** N-C In a boxing or wrestling match, a **round** is one of the periods during which the participants fight. **4** N-C A **round** of golf is one game, usually including 18 holes. **5** N-C A doctor's **rounds** are a series of visits they make as part of their job. **6** N-C If you buy a **round** of drinks, you buy a drink for each member of the group of people that you are with. **7** N-C A **round** of ammunition is a bullet.

round 3 adjective use

round /raʊnd/ rounder, roundest. ADJ If something has a **round** shape, it has a curved shape, like a circle or ball. *She had small feet and hands and a flat, round face.*

round 4 verb uses

round /raʊnd/ rounds, rounding, rounded. [1] VERB If you **round** a place or obstacle, you move in a curve past the edge or corner of it. *The house disappeared from sight as we rounded a corner.* [2] VERB If you **round** an amount up or down, or if you **round** it off, you change it to the nearest whole number or nearest multiple of a number.

▶ **round on.** PHR-VERB In British English, if someone **rounds on** you, they criticize you fiercely. The usual American expression is **turn on**. *The Conservative Party rounded angrily on him for damaging the Government.*

▶ **round up.** PHR-VERB If people or animals **are rounded up**, someone gathers them together.

roundabout /'raʊndəbaʊt/ roundabouts. [1] N-C A **roundabout** is a circle at a place where several roads meet. [2] N-C In a fair or playground, a **roundabout** is a large circular platform with seats which goes round and round; BRITISH. [3] ADJ If you do something in a **roundabout** way, you deliberately avoid doing or saying it in a simple, clear, and direct way.

rounded /'raʊndɪd/. ADJ Something that is **rounded** is curved rather than pointed or sharp.

round 'trip, round trips. N-C If you make a **round trip**, you travel to a place and then back again.

rouse /raʊz/ rouses, rousing, roused. [1] VERB If someone **rouses** you when you are sleeping, or if you **rouse**, you wake up; FORMAL. *When I put my hand on his, he stirs but doesn't quite rouse.* [2] VERB If you **rouse** yourself to do something, you make yourself get up and do it. *He roused himself to work only when he felt like earning some money.* [3] VERB If something **rouses** you, it makes you very emotional or excited. *...a man not quickly roused to anger.*
♦ **rousing** ADJ *...a rousing speech.*

rout /raʊt/ routs, routing, routed. VERB & N-C If an army or a sports team **routs** its opponents, it defeats them completely and easily. You can refer to a defeat like this as a **rout**. *The retreat turned into a rout.*

route /ruːt, AM raʊt/ routes, routing, routed. [1] N-C A **route** is a way from one place to another. *...the most direct route to the town centre.* [2] VERB If vehicles, goods, or passengers **are routed** in a particular direction, they are made to travel in that direction. [3] PHRASE **En route** to a place means on the way to it. *The ship in question is en route from Spain to the Molucca Islands. ...holiday makers en route for the US.* [4] N-C You can refer to a way of achieving something as a **route**. *Researchers are trying to get at the same information through an indirect route.*

routine /ruː'tiːn/ routines. [1] ADJ **Routine** activities are done regularly as a normal part of a job or process. *...a series of routine medical tests.* ♦ **routinely** ADV *Banks routinely send new debit cards through the post.* [2] N-VAR A **routine**

is the usual series of things that you do at a particular time in a particular order. *...their daily routine... He checked up on you as a matter of routine.*

roving /rəʊvɪŋ/. ADJ BEFORE N You use **roving** to describe a person who travels around, rather than staying in a fixed place. *...a roving reporter.*

row, rows, rowing, rowed. [1] N-C /rəʊ/ A **row** of things or people is a number of them arranged in a line. *...a row of pretty little cottages.* [2] PHRASE If something happens several times **in a row**, it happens that number of times without a break. *They have won five championships in a row.* [3] VERB When you **row** a boat, you make it move through the water by using oars. *The boatman refused to row him back.* ♦ **rowing** N-U *...competitions in rowing, swimming and water skiing.* [4] N-C /raʊ/ A **row** is a serious disagreement between people or organizations, often one involving a noisy argument. *They risked what could be a major diplomatic row with France... Maxine and I had a terrible row about how I spent my money.* [5] VERB If two people **row**, or if one person **rows with** another, they have a noisy argument. *They rowed all the time... He had earlier rowed with his girlfriend.* [6] N-C If you say that someone is making a **row**, you mean that they are making a loud unpleasant noise; BRITISH, INFORMAL. *Our little van made an unholy row.* [7] See also **death row**.

rowdy /'raʊdi/ rowdier, rowdiest. ADJ If people are **rowdy**, they are noisy, rough, and likely to cause trouble. *He has complained to the police about rowdy neighbours.*

royal /'rɔɪəl/. ADJ **Royal** means related or belonging to a king, queen, or emperor, or to a member of their family. *...the Japanese royal couple.*

royalist /'rɔɪəlɪst/ royalists. N-C A **royalist** is someone who thinks it is right that their country should have a royal family.

royalty /'rɔɪəlti/ royalties. [1] N-U The members of a royal family can be referred to as **royalty**. *...a ceremony attended by royalty.* [2] N-PL **Royalties** are payments made to authors and musicians when their work is sold or performed.

rub /rʌb/ rubs, rubbing, rubbed. [1] VERB If you **rub** something, you move your hand or a cloth backwards and forwards over it while pressing firmly. *She took off her glasses and rubbed them hard.* [2] VERB If you **rub** a part of your body against a surface, you move it backwards and forwards while pressing it against the surface. *A cat was rubbing against my leg... She rubbed her finger up and down the shiny bonnet.* [3] VERB If you **rub** a substance onto a surface, you spread it over the surface using your hand. *He rubbed oil into my back.* [4] VERB If two things **rub together**, or if you **rub** them **together**, they move backwards and forwards, pressing against each other. *He rubbed his hands together.* [5] to **rub shoulders**: see **shoulder**.

▶ **rub off on.** PHR-VERB If someone's habits or characteristics **rub off on** you, you start developing the same habits or characteristics after spending time with them; INFORMAL. *He was a* *tremendously enthusiastic teacher and that rubbed off on all the children he taught.*

▶ **rub out.** PHR-VERB If you **rub out** something written on paper or on a blackboard, you remove it by rubbing it with a rubber or a cloth.

rubber /'rʌbə/ **rubbers.** ① N-U **Rubber** is a strong, waterproof, elastic substance used for making tyres, boots, and other products. ② N-C A **rubber** is a small piece of rubber used to rub out mistakes that you have made while writing or drawing; BRITISH.

,rubber 'stamp (or rubber-stamp) **rubber stamps, rubber stamping, rubber stamped.** VERB When someone in authority **rubber stamps** a decision, plan, or law, they agree to it. *A meeting of union leaders rubber stamped the deal.*

rubbish /'rʌbɪʃ/ **rubbishes, rubbishing, rubbished.** ① N-U **Rubbish** consists of unwanted things or waste material such as old food. ② N-U If you think that something is foolish or of very poor quality you can say that it is **rubbish**; INFORMAL. *These reports are total and utter rubbish... He described her book as absolute rubbish.*

> In British English, **rubbish** is the word most commonly used to refer to waste material that is thrown away. In American English, the words **garbage** and **trash** are more usual. *...the smell of rotting garbage... She threw the bottle into the trash.* **Garbage** and **trash** are sometimes used in British English, but only informally and metaphorically. *I don't have to listen to this garbage... The book was trash.*

③ VERB If you **rubbish** a person, their ideas, or their work, you say they are of little value. *Five whole pages of script were devoted to rubbishing her political opponents.*

rubble /'rʌbəl/. N-U **Rubble** consists of the pieces of brick, stone, or other materials that remain when a building is destroyed.

ruby /'ruːbi/ **rubies.** N-C A **ruby** is a dark red precious stone.

rucksack /'rʌksæk/ **rucksacks.** N-C A **rucksack** is a bag, often on a frame, used for carrying things on your back.

rudder /'rʌdə/ **rudders.** N-C A **rudder** is a device for steering a boat or aeroplane.

ruddy /'rʌdi/ **ruddier, ruddiest.** ADJ If someone has a **ruddy** complexion, their face is a reddish colour. *He had a ruddy face and sticking-out ears.*

rude /ruːd/ **ruder, rudest.** ① ADJ If someone is **rude**, they behave in a way that is not polite. *He's rude to her friends.* ◆**rudely** ADV *...why she felt compelled to behave so rudely to a friend.* ◆**rudeness** N-U *Midge ignored Mary's rudeness.* ② ADJ **Rude** words and behaviour are likely to embarrass or offend people, because they relate to sex or other bodily functions. *...a rude joke.* ③ ADJ BEFORE N **Rude** is used to describe events that are unexpected and unpleasant. *It will come as a rude shock when their salary cannot be cashed.* ◆**rudely** ADV *People were awakened rudely by a siren.*

rudimentary /,ruːdɪ'mentri/. ADJ **Rudimentary** means very basic or not developed to a satisfactory degree. *He had nothing more than a rudimentary knowledge of banking. ...the country's rudimentary legal system.*

rueful /'ruːfʊl/. ADJ If someone is **rueful**, they feel or express regret or sorrow in a quiet and gentle way; LITERARY. *He shook his head and gave me a rueful smile.* ◆**ruefully** ADV *He was left to reflect ruefully on how his side have failed to win a single game.*

ruffle /'rʌfəl/ **ruffles, ruffling, ruffled.** ① VERB If you **ruffle** someone's hair, you move your hand backwards and forwards through it as a way of showing your affection towards them. ② VERB If a bird **ruffles** its feathers, or if its feathers **ruffle**, they stand out on its body, for example when it is cleaning itself. ③ N-C **Ruffles** are folds of cloth at the neck or cuffs of a piece of clothing.

ruffled /'rʌfəld/. ① ADJ Something that is **ruffled** is no longer smooth or neat. *Her short hair was oddly ruffled.* ② ADJ BEFORE N **Ruffled** clothes are decorated with small folds of material.

rug /rʌg/ **rugs.** ① N-C A **rug** is a piece of thick material that you put on the floor and use like a carpet. *...a Persian rug.* ② N-C A **rug** is a small blanket which you use to cover your shoulders or your knees.

rugby /'rʌgbi/. N-U **Rugby** is a game played by two teams, who try to get an oval ball past a line at their opponents' end of the pitch.

rugged /'rʌgɪd/. ① ADJ A **rugged** area of land is rocky and uneven; LITERARY. *...a rugged mountainous terrain.* ② ADJ If you describe a man as **rugged**, you mean that he has strong masculine features; used showing approval. ③ ADJ A **rugged** piece of equipment is made of strong long-lasting material. *Due to the rugged construction of the 600 Series, no maintenance should be required.*

ruin /'ruːɪn/ **ruins, ruining, ruined.** ① VERB To **ruin** something means to severely harm, damage, or spoil it. *My wife was ruining her health through worry.* ② PHRASE If something is **in ruins**, it has gone completely wrong, and there is no chance of putting it right. *His travel plans lay in ruins.* ③ N-C & PHRASE A **ruin** is a building that has been partly destroyed. You can say that a building like this is **in ruins**. *It looked as though part of the roof had fallen in. Commonwood was a ruin... The ancient medieval town was in ruins.* ④ N-PL The **ruins** of something are the parts of it that remain after it has been severely damaged or weakened. *The new Turkish republic he helped to build emerged from the ruins of a great empire.* ⑤ VERB & N-U If someone or something **ruins** you, or if you face financial **ruin**, someone or something causes you to no longer have any money.

ruined /'ruːɪnd/. ADJ BEFORE N A **ruined** building has been badly damaged or has fallen apart. *...a ruined church.*

rule /ruːl/ **rules, ruling, ruled.** ① N-C **Rules** are specific, often written, instructions telling you what you can and cannot do. *...a thirty-two-page pamphlet explaining the rules of basket-*

ball... This was against the rules. **2** N-C The **rules** of something such as a language or a science are statements that describe the way that things usually happen in a particular situation. *...the rules of quantum theory.* **3** N-SING If something is **the rule**, it is the normal state of affairs. *For most people, seven hours sleep a night is the rule.* **4** VERB The person or group that **rules** a country controls its affairs. *For four centuries, he says, foreigners have ruled Angola.* **5** VERB When someone in authority **rules** on a particular matter, they give an official decision about it; FORMAL. *The Israeli court has not yet ruled on the case.* **6** See also **ruling**; **ground rule**.

PHRASES ● If you say that something happens **as a rule**, you mean that it usually happens. *As a rule she eats dinner with us.* ● If someone in authority **bends the rules**, they allow you to do something, even though it is against the rules.

▶ **rule out. 1** PHR-VERB If you **rule out** an idea or course of action, you reject it because it is impossible or unsuitable. **2** PHR-VERB If something **rules out** a situation, it prevents it from happening or from being possible. *Agassi's chest injury ruled him out of the Davis Cup final.*

ruler /ˈruːlə/ **rulers. 1** N-C A **ruler** is a person who rules a country. *He was a weak-willed and indecisive ruler.* **2** N-C A **ruler** is a long flat object with straight edges used for measuring things or drawing straight lines.

ruling /ˈruːlɪŋ/ **rulings. 1** ADJ BEFORE N The **ruling** group of people in an organization or country is the group that controls its affairs. *...voters' growing dissatisfaction with the ruling party.* **2** N-C A **ruling** is an official decision made by a judge or court. *Goodwin tried to have the court ruling overturned.*

rum /rʌm/ N-U **Rum** is an alcoholic drink made from sugar cane juice.

rumble /ˈrʌmbəl/ **rumbles, rumbling, rumbled.** VERB & N-C If something **rumbles**, or if it makes a **rumble**, it makes a low continuous noise, often while moving slowly. *...the distant rumble of traffic.*

rumbling /ˈrʌmblɪŋ/ **rumblings. 1** N-C A **rumbling** is a low continuous noise. *...the rumbling of an empty stomach.* **2** N-C **Rumblings** are signs that a bad situation is developing or that people are becoming dissatisfied. *There were rumblings of discontent within the ranks.*

rummage /ˈrʌmɪdʒ/ **rummages, rummaging, rummaged.** VERB & N-C If you **rummage** through something, or if you have a **rummage** through it, you search for something you want by moving things around in a careless or hurried way. *I like going down to the markets and rummaging around... Your sons have had a good rummage in the cupboard.*

rumour (AM **rumor**) /ˈruːmə/ **rumours.** N-C A **rumour** is a piece of information that may or may not be true, but that people are talking about.

rumoured (AM **rumored**) /ˈruːməd/ PASSIVE-VERB If something **is rumoured** to be the case, people are suggesting that it is the case, but they do not know for certain. *Her parents are rumoured to be on the verge of splitting up.*

rump /rʌmp/ **rumps.** N-C An animal's **rump** is its rear end.

run /rʌn/ **runs, running, ran, run. 1** VERB & N-C When you **run**, or when you have a **run**, you move quickly, leaving the ground during each stride. *I excused myself and ran back to the telephone... Antonia ran to meet them... After a six-mile run, Jackie returns home.* ◆ **running** N-U *...cross-country running. ...running shoes.* **2** VERB You say that something long, such as a road, **runs** in a particular direction when you are describing its course or position. *...the sun-dappled trail which ran through the beech woods... The hallway ran the length of the villa.* **3** VERB If you **run** an object or your hand over or through something, you move the object or your hand over it or through it. *He ran his hand over his ribs... Fumbling, he ran her card through the machine.* **4** VERB In American English, if someone **runs** in an election, they take part as a candidate. The usual British word is **stand**. *He announced he would run for president.* **5** VERB If you **run** an organization or an activity, you are in charge of it or you organize it. *Is this any way to run a country? ...a well-run, profitable organisation.* ◆ **running** N-SING *...the day-to-day running of the clinic.* **6** VERB If you talk about how a system, an organization, or someone's life **is running**, you are saying how well it is operating or progressing. *...the staff who have kept the bank running.* **7** VERB If you **run** an experiment, computer program, or other process, you start it and let it continue. *He ran a lot of tests... The program runs on a standard personal computer.* **8** VERB When a machine **is running**, or when you **are running** it, it is switched on and operating. *She ran the tape and found a message from Charles.* **9** VERB A machine that **runs** on or off a particular source of energy functions using that source of energy. *Black cabs run on diesel.* **10** VERB If a train or bus **runs** somewhere, it travels on a regular route at set times. *A shuttle bus runs frequently between the Inn and the Country Club.* **11** VERB If you **run** somewhere in a car, you drive there; INFORMAL. *Could you run me up to Baltimore?* **12** VERB If a liquid **runs** in a particular direction, it flows in that direction. *Tears were running down her cheeks.* **13** VERB If you **run** water, you cause it to flow from a tap. *They heard him running the kitchen tap... I ran a warm bath.* ◆ **running** ADJ BEFORE N *...cold running water.* **14** VERB If the dye in some cloth or the ink on some paper **runs**, it comes off or spreads when the cloth or paper gets wet. **15** VERB If a play, event, or legal contract **runs** for a particular period of time, it lasts for that period of time. *It pleased critics but ran for only three years in the West End... The contract was to run from 1992 to 2020.* **16** N-C In the theatre, a **run** is the period of time during which performances of a play are given. **17** VERB **Run** is used in combination with other words and phrases, where the meaning of the combination depends mostly on the other word or phrase. *Time is running* *short... I'm running late again... Today's RPI figure shows inflation running at 10.9 per cent.* [18] See also **running.**

[PHRASES] ● If you talk about what will happen **in the long run**, you are saying what you think will happen over a long period of time in the future. If you talk about what will happen **in the short run**, you are saying what you think will happen in the near future. ● If someone is **on the run**, they are trying to escape or hide from someone such as the police or an enemy.

▶ **run across.** PHR-VERB If you **run across** someone or something, you meet them or find them unexpectedly. *We ran across some old friends.*

▶ **run away.** PHR-VERB If you **run away** from a place, you secretly leave it. *I ran away from home when I was sixteen.*

▶ **run away with.** PHR-VERB If you let your emotions **run away with** you, you fail to control them.

▶ **run down.** [1] PHR-VERB If you **run down** people or things, you criticize them strongly. *...the British 'genius for running ourselves down'.* [2] PHR-VERB If a vehicle or its driver **runs** someone **down**, the vehicle hits them and injures them. [3] See also **run-down.**

▶ **run into.** [1] PHR-VERB If you **run into** problems or difficulties, you unexpectedly begin to experience them. *...companies that have run into trouble.* [2] PHR-VERB If you **run into** someone, you meet them unexpectedly. *He ran into Krettner in the corridor.* [3] PHR-VERB If a vehicle **runs into** something, it accidentally hits it. [4] PHR-VERB You use **run into** when indicating that the cost or amount of something is very great. *...tuition fees which could run into thousands of pounds.*

▶ **run off.** [1] PHR-VERB If you **run off** with someone, you secretly go away with them in order to live with them or marry them. *We could run off together.* [2] PHR-VERB If you **run off** copies of a piece of writing, you produce them using a machine.

▶ **run out.** [1] PHR-VERB If you **run out** of something, or if it **runs out**, you have no more of it left. *We had lots before but now we've run out... Time is running out.* [2] PHR-VERB When a legal document **runs out**, it stops being valid. [3] to **run out of steam**: see **steam.**

▶ **run over.** PHR-VERB If a vehicle **runs over** someone or something, it knocks them down. *He ran over a six-year-old child as he was driving back from a party.*

▶ **run through.** [1] PHR-VERB If you **run through** a performance or a series of actions, you rehearse it or practise it. [2] PHR-VERB If you **run through** a list of items, you read or mention all the items quickly. *I ran through the options with him.*

▶ **run up.** [1] PHR-VERB If someone **runs up** bills or debts, they acquire them by buying a lot of things or borrowing money. *He ran up a £1,400 bill at the Britannia Adelphi Hotel.* [2] See also **run-up.**

▶ **run up against.** PHR-VERB If you **run up against** problems, you suddenly begin to experience them.

runaway /ˈrʌnəweɪ/. [1] ADJ You use **runaway** to describe a situation in which something in-

creases or develops very quickly and cannot be controlled. *Our Grand Sale in June was a runaway success.* [2] N-C A **runaway** is someone, especially a child, who leaves home without telling anyone or without permission. [3] ADJ A **runaway** vehicle and its driver has lost control of it. *The runaway car careered into a bench.*

run-down. [1] ADJ /ˌrʌn ˈdaʊn/ If someone is **run-down**, they are tired or slightly ill; INFORMAL. [2] ADJ A **run-down** building or organization is in very poor condition. *...a run-down block of flats.* [3] N-SING /ˈrʌn daʊn/ If you give someone a **run-down** of a group of things or a **run-down** on something, you give them details of it; INFORMAL. *Here's a rundown of the options.*

rung /rʌŋ/ **rungs.** [1] **Rung** is the past participle of **ring.** [2] N-C The **rungs** of a ladder are the wooden or metal bars that form the steps. [3] N-C If you reach a particular **rung** in an organization or in a process, you reach that level in it. *...the first rung of the property ladder.*

'run-in, run-ins. N-C If you have a **run-in** with someone, you have an argument or quarrel with them; INFORMAL.

runner /ˈrʌnə/ **runners.** [1] N-C A **runner** is a person who runs, especially for sport or pleasure. *...a marathon runner... I am a very keen runner.* [2] N-C A drugs **runner** or gun **runner** is someone who illegally takes drugs or guns into a country. [3] N-C **Runners** are thin strips of wood or metal underneath something which help it to move smoothly. *...plastic drawer runners.*

'runner bean, runner beans. N-C **Runner beans** are long green beans that are eaten as a vegetable.

,runner-'up, runners-up. N-C A **runner-up** is someone who finishes in second place in a race or competition.

running /ˈrʌnɪŋ/. [1] ADJ BEFORE N You use **running** to describe things that continue or keep occurring over a period of time. *The song turned into a running joke.* [2] ADJ BEFORE N You use **running** to describe something that keeps being changed or added to as something progresses. *John gave the police control room a running commentary on the driver's antics.* [3] ADJ You can use **running** when indicating that something keeps happening. *She'll wear the same thing two days running... Spain won the Cup for the third year running.*

[PHRASES] ● If someone is **in the running** for something, they have a good chance of winning or obtaining it. If they are **out of the running**, they have no chance of winning or obtaining it.

'running mate, running mates. N-C In an American election campaign, a candidate's **running mate** is the person that they have chosen to be their deputy if they win.

runny /ˈrʌni/. [1] ADJ Something that is **runny** is more liquid than usual or than was intended. *Warm the honey until it becomes runny.* [2] ADJ If someone's nose or eyes are **runny**, liquid is flowing from them.

'run-up. N-SING The **run-up** to an event is the

period of time just before it. *...the run-up to the elections.*

runway /'rʌnweɪ/ **runways.** N-C At an airport, the **runway** is the long strip of ground with a hard surface which an aeroplane takes off from or lands on.

rupture /'rʌptʃə/ **ruptures, rupturing, ruptured.** [1] VERB & N-C If you **rupture** a part of your body, or if you have a **rupture**, a part of your body tears or bursts open. *His stomach might rupture from all the acid. ...a ruptured appendix.* [2] VERB & N-C If someone or something **ruptures** relations between people, or if there is a **rupture** in relations, they damage them, causing them to become worse or to end. *...a rupture of the family unit.*

rural /'rʊərəl/. ADJ **Rural** means relating to country areas as opposed to large towns. *...the closure of rural schools... He spoke with a heavy rural accent.*

ruse /ruːz, AM ruːs/ **ruses.** N-C A **ruse** is an action or plan which is intended to deceive someone; FORMAL. *The whole thing may be a ruse to up the price.*

rush /rʌʃ/ **rushes, rushing, rushed.** [1] VERB If you **rush** somewhere, you go there quickly. *I've got to rush. Got a meeting in a few minutes... Shop staff rushed to get help.* [2] VERB If people **rush** to do something, they do it as soon as they can, because they are very eager to do it. *Russian banks rushed to buy as many dollars as they could.* [3] N-SING A **rush** is a situation in which you need to go somewhere or do something very quickly. *The men left in a rush. ...the mad rush not to be late for school.* [4] N-SING If there is a **rush** for something, many people suddenly try to get it or do it. *...the rush for tickets.* [5] VERB If you **rush** something, you do it in a hurry. *Chew your food well and do not rush meals.* ◆**rushed** ADJ *...a rushed job.* [6] VERB If you **rush** someone or something to a place, you take them there quickly. *We got an ambulance and rushed her to hospital.* [7] VERB If you **rush** into something, or if you **are rushed** into it, you do it without thinking about it for long enough. *He will not rush into any decisions... Don't be rushed into committing yourself.* ◆**rushed** ADJ *At no time did I feel rushed or under pressure.* [8] N-SING If you ex-

perience a **rush** of a feeling, you suddenly experience it very strongly. *A rush of pure affection swept over him.* [9] N-C **Rushes** are plants with long thin stems that grow near water.

'rush hour. N-C The **rush hour** is one of the periods of the day when most people are travelling to or from work. *Try to avoid rush-hour traffic.*

rust /rʌst/ **rusts, rusting, rusted.** [1] N-U **Rust** is a brown substance that forms on iron or steel when it comes into contact with water. [2] VERB When a metal object **rusts**, it becomes covered in rust.

rustic /'rʌstɪk/. ADJ You can use **rustic** to describe things or people that are simple or unsophisticated in a way that is typical of the countryside; used showing approval. *...the rustic charm of a country lifestyle.*

rustle /'rʌsəl/ **rustles, rustling, rustled.** VERB & N-C When something thin and dry **rustles**, it makes soft sounds as it moves, called **rustles**. *The leaves rustled in the wind... She rustled her papers impatiently. ...a rustle of her frilled petticoats.* ◆**rustling, rustlings** N-VAR *There was a rustling of paper.*

rusty /'rʌsti/. [1] ADJ A **rusty** metal object has a lot of rust on it. *...a rusty old van.* [2] ADJ If a skill that you have or your knowledge of something is **rusty**, it is not as good as it used to be, because you have not used it for a long time. *Ginny tried to sharpen up some rusty typing skills.*

rut /rʌt/ **ruts.** [1] N-C If someone is in a **rut**, they have become fixed in their way of thinking and doing things, and find it difficult to change. *I don't like being in a rut - I like to keep moving on.* [2] N-C A **rut** is a deep narrow mark made in the ground by the wheels of a vehicle.

ruthless /'ruːθləs/. ADJ Someone who is **ruthless** is very harsh or determined, and will do anything that is necessary to achieve their aim. *...his ruthless treatment of employees.* ◆**ruthlessly** ADV *...the ruthlessly efficient woman her father wanted her to be.* ◆**ruthlessness** N-U *...a mixture of ambition and ruthlessness.*

rye /raɪ/. N-U **Rye** is a cereal grown in cold countries. Its grains can be used to make flour, bread, or other foods.

S s

Sabbath /'sæbəθ/. N-PROPER The **Sabbath** is the day of worship and rest for the members of some religious groups, especially Jews and Christians. For Jews, it is Saturday; for Christians, it is Sunday.

sabotage /'sæbətɑːʒ/ **sabotages, sabotaging, sabotaged.** [1] VERB & N-U If a machine, railway line, or bridge **is sabotaged**, it is deliberately damaged or destroyed, for example in a war. **Sabotage** is the act of sabotaging something. *The bombing was a spectacular act of sabotage.* [2] VERB If someone **sabotages** a plan or a meeting, they deliberately prevent it from being successful. *...her attempt to sabotage his relationship with Sarah.*

sack /sæk/ **sacks, sacking, sacked.** [1] N-C A **sack** is a large bag made of rough woven material. [2] VERB & N-SING If your employers **sack** you from your job, or if they give you the **sack**, they tell you that you can no longer work for them. *One girl got the sack for telling lies.* ◆**sacking, sackings** N-C *...the sacking of twenty-three-thousand miners.*

sacred /'seɪkrɪd/. [1] ADJ Something that is **sacred** is believed to be holy. ◆**sacredness** N-U *...the sacredness of the site.* [2] ADJ BEFORE N Something connected with religion or used in religious ceremonies is described as **sacred**. *...sacred songs or music.* [3] ADJ You can describe something as **sacred** when you regard it as too important to be changed or interfered with. ♦**sacredness** N-U ...*the sacredness of life.*

sacrifice /ˈsækrɪfaɪs/ **sacrifices, sacrificing, sacrificed.** [1] VERB & N-C To **sacrifice** an animal, or to offer it as a **sacrifice**, means to kill it in a special religious ceremony. ♦**sacrificial** /ˌsækrɪˈfɪʃəl/ ADJ BEFORE N ...*the sacrificial altar.* [2] VERB & N-VAR If you **sacrifice** something valuable or important, you give it up, usually to obtain something else. You call the thing you give up a **sacrifice**. *He was willing to make any sacrifice for peace.*

sad /sæd/ **sadder, saddest.** [1] ADJ If you are **sad**, you feel unhappy. **Sad** stories, situations, or events make you feel unhappy. *I'm sad that Julie's marriage is on the verge of splitting up. ...a sad story of how a naive girl was seduced by money and glamour.* ♦**sadly** ADV *He will be sadly missed by all who knew him.* ♦**sadness** N-U *It is with great sadness we have to face this difficult decision.* [2] ADJ **Sad** means unfortunate or undesirable. ♦**sadly** ADV *Sadly, bamboo plants die after flowering.*

sadden /ˈsædən/ **saddens, saddening, saddened.** VERB If something **saddens** you, it makes you feel sad. ♦**saddened** ADJ AFTER LINK-V *He is saddened that they did not win anything.*

saddle /ˈsædəl/ **saddles, saddling, saddled.** [1] N-C A **saddle** is a leather seat that you put on the back of an animal so that you can ride the animal. [2] N-C A **saddle** is a seat on a bicycle or motorcycle. [3] VERB & PHR-VERB If you **saddle** an animal, or if you **saddle** it **up**, you put a saddle on it. [4] VERB If you **saddle** someone with a problem or with a responsibility, you put them in a position where they have to deal with it. *An extravagant lifestyle left him saddled with debts of almost 5 million dollars.*
▸ **saddle up** See **saddle** 3.

sadism /ˈseɪdɪzəm/. N-U **Sadism** is behaviour in which a person gets pleasure from hurting other people. ♦**sadist** /ˈseɪdɪst/ **sadists** N-C ...*a sadist who tortured animals and people.* ♦**sadistic** ADJ ...*sadistic guards who would punch the hostages.*

sae (also **SAE** or **s.a.e.**) /ˌes eɪ ˈiː/ **saes.** N-C An **sae** is an envelope on which you put your name and address, and a stamp. You send it to someone in order to save them the cost of posting you something. **sae** is an abbreviation for 'stamped addressed envelope'.

safari /səˈfɑːri/ **safaris.** N-C A **safari** is an expedition for hunting or observing wild animals, especially in East Africa.

safe /seɪf/ **safer, safest; safes.** [1] ADJ Something that is **safe** does not cause physical harm or danger. *The only place it is truly safe to swim in is on a patrolled beach... The doll is safe for children.* ♦**safely** ADV *The dog was safely locked up... Learn to drive safely.* [2] ADJ AFTER LINK-V If someone or something is **safe**, they are not in danger of being harmed or damaged. *Crime Prevention Officers can visit your home and suggest ways to make it safer... Where is Sophy? Is she safe?* ♦**safely** ADV *Guests were brought out of the building safely by firemen.* [3] ADJ BEFORE N If people or things have a **safe** journey, they reach their destination without being harmed. ...*the safe delivery of food and other*

supplies. ♦**safely** ADV *Once Mrs Armsby was safely home, she called the police.* [4] ADJ A **safe** place is one where it is unlikely that any harm will happen to the people or things that are there. ♦**safely** ADV *Guns cannot be safely stored in homes.* [5] ADJ If it is **safe** to say or assume something, you can say it with little risk of being wrong. ♦**safely** ADV *If I go to a grocer I know and trust, I can safely assume the eggs will be fresh.* [6] N-C A **safe** is a strong metal cupboard with special locks, in which you keep money, jewellery, or other valuable things.

PHRASES ● If you say that someone or something is **in safe hands**, you mean that they are being looked after by a reliable person and will not be harmed or damaged. ● If you say you are doing something **to be on the safe side**, you mean that you are doing it as a precaution, in case something unexpected or unpleasant happens.

safeguard /ˈseɪfgɑːd/ **safeguards, safeguarding, safeguarded.** [1] VERB To **safeguard** something or someone means to protect them from being harmed or lost; FORMAL. ...*precautionary measures to safeguard their forces from the effects of chemical weapons.* [2] N-C A **safeguard** is a law or rule that is intended to prevent someone or something from being harmed. ...*civil rights legislation that offers safeguards against discrimination in the workplace.*

ˌ**safe** ˈ**sex** (or **safer sex**). N-U **Safe sex** is sexual activity in which people protect themselves against the risk of AIDS and other sexually transmitted diseases, usually by using condoms.

safety /ˈseɪfti/. [1] N-U **Safety** is the state of being safe from harm or danger. ...*a number of recommendations to improve safety on aircraft. ...the safety of one's own home.* [2] N-SING If you are concerned about the **safety** of something, you are concerned that it might be harmful or dangerous. If you are concerned for someone's **safety**, you are concerned that they might be in danger. ...*public fears about the safety of nuclear power... There is grave concern for the safety of witnesses.* [3] ADJ BEFORE N **Safety** features or measures are intended to make something less dangerous. *Inbuilt safety devices halted the train... It's wise to wear safety goggles.*

ˈ**safety belt, safety belts.** N-C A **safety belt** is a strap that you fasten across your body for safety when travelling in a car or aeroplane.

ˈ**safety net, safety nets.** N-C A **safety net** is something that you can rely on to help you if you get into a difficult situation. *Welfare is the only real safety net for low-income workers.*

sag /sæg/ **sags, sagging, sagged.** [1] VERB When something **sags**, it hangs down loosely or sinks downwards in the middle. ...*the sagging armchair.* [2] VERB To **sag** means to become weaker. *Her energy seemed to sag. ...their sagging popularity.*

saga /ˈsɑːgə/ **sagas.** N-C A **saga** is a long story, account, or sequence of events.

sage /seɪdʒ/ **sages.** [1] ADJ & N-C **Sage** means wise and knowledgeable. A **sage** is a person who is regarded as being very wise. ♦**sagely**

ADV *We all nodded sagely and pretended we understood.* 2 N-U **Sage** is a herb.

said /sed/. **Said** is the past tense and past participle of **say**.

sail /seɪl/ **sails, sailing, sailed.** 1 N-C **Sails** are large pieces of material attached to the mast of a boat. 2 VERB If you **sail** a boat, or if a boat **sails**, it moves across water using its sails. *I shall get myself a little boat and sail her around the world.* 3 VERB You say a ship **sails** when it moves over the sea. *The trawler had sailed from the port of Zeebrugge.* 4 PHRASE When a ship **sets sail**, it leaves a port. 5 VERB If someone or something **sails** somewhere, they move there steadily and fairly quickly. *We got into the lift and sailed to the top floor.*

▶ **sail through.** PHR-VERB If someone or something **sails through** a difficult situation or experience, they deal with it easily and successfully. *She sailed through her maths exams.*

sailing /ˈseɪlɪŋ/ **sailings.** 1 N-C A **sailing** is a voyage made by a ship carrying passengers. *We'll get the next sailing.* 2 N-U **Sailing** is the activity or sport of sailing boats. 3 PHRASE In British English, if you say that a task was not all **plain sailing**, you mean that it was not very easy. The American term is **clear sailing**. *Pregnancy wasn't all plain sailing and once again there were problems.*

sailor /ˈseɪlə/ **sailors.** N-C A **sailor** is a person who works on a ship as a member of its crew.

saint /seɪnt/ **saints.** 1 N-C & N-TITLE A **saint** is a dead person who is officially recognized and honoured by the Christian church because his or her life was a perfect example of the way Christians should live. 2 N-C If you refer to a living person as a **saint**, you mean that they are extremely kind and patient. ♦**saintly** ADJ *...his saintly wife.*

sake /seɪk/ **sakes.**

PHRASES ● If you do something **for the sake of** a particular thing, you do it for that purpose or in order to achieve that result. *For the sake of argument, let's assume that you're right.* ● If you do something **for its own sake**, you do it because you enjoy it, and not for any other reason. *...the pursuit of power for its own sake.* ● When you do something **for** someone's **sake**, you do it in order to help them or make them happy. *Linda knew that for both their sakes she must take drastic action.*

salad /ˈsæləd/ **salads.** N-VAR A **salad** is a mixture of uncooked vegetables, eaten as part of a meal.

salary /ˈsæləri/ **salaries.** N-VAR Your **salary** is the money that you are paid each month by your employer. ● See note at **pay**.

sale /seɪl/ **sales.** 1 N-SING The **sale** of goods is the selling of them for money. *Efforts were made to limit the sale of alcohol.* 2 N-PL The **sales** of a product are the quantity that is sold. *The newspaper has sales of 1.72 million.* 3 N-PL You refer to the part of a company that deals with selling as **sales**. *Sonia and Sue also work in sales. ...the sales department.* 4 N-C A **sale** is an occasion when a shop sells things at less than their normal price. *...a pair of jeans bought half-price in a sale.*

PHRASES ● If something is **for sale** or **up for**

sale, it is available to buy. *The company is up for sale.* ● Products that are **on sale** can be bought in shops. *Tickets go on sale this Friday.*

'sales clerk, sales clerks. N-C In American English, a **sales clerk** is a person who works in a shop, selling things to customers. The British word is **shop assistant**.

salesman /ˈseɪlzmən/ **salesmen.** N-C A **salesman** is a man whose job is selling things to people.

salesperson /ˈseɪlzpɜːsən/ **salespeople** or **salespersons.** N-C A **salesperson** is a person whose job is selling things to people.

saliva /səˈlaɪvə/. N-U **Saliva** is the watery liquid that forms in your mouth.

salmon /ˈsæmən/ **salmon** is both the singular and plural form. N-VAR A **salmon** is a large edible silver-coloured fish with pink flesh. **Salmon** is the flesh of this fish eaten as food.

salon /ˈsælɒn, AM səˈlɑːn/ **salons.** N-C A **salon** is a place where people such as hairdressers work. *...a new hair salon.*

saloon /səˈluːn/ **saloons.** 1 N-C In British English, a **saloon** or a **saloon car** is a car with seats for four or more people, a fixed roof, and a boot that is separated from the rear seats. 2 N-C A **saloon** is a place where alcoholic drinks are sold and drunk; AMERICAN.

salt /sɔːlt/ **salts, salting, salted.** 1 N-U **Salt** is a substance in the form of white powder or crystals, used to improve the flavour of food or to preserve it. 2 VERB When you **salt** food, you add salt to it. ♦**salted** ADJ *...lightly salted butter.*

salty /ˈsɔːlti/ **saltier, saltiest.** ADJ **Salty** things contain salt or taste of salt. *...salty water.*

salute /səˈluːt/ **salutes, saluting, saluted.** 1 VERB & N-C If you **salute** someone, you greet them or show your respect with a formal sign. Soldiers salute officers by raising their right hand so that their fingers touch their forehead. A **salute** is a formal sign of greeting or respect. *I stood to attention and saluted... The soldier gave the clenched-fist salute... He raised his arm in salute.* 2 VERB & N-C To **salute** a person or an achievement means to publicly show or state your admiration for them. A public show of admiration for someone or something is called a **salute**. *The students' performance will be a salute to Australian music.*

salvage /ˈsælvɪdʒ/ **salvages, salvaging, salvaged.** 1 VERB & N-U If something **is salvaged**, someone manages to save it, for example from a ship that has sunk or a building that has been destroyed. **Salvage** is the act of salvaging things from somewhere. *...components salvaged from a crashed aircraft. ...a huge salvage operation.* 2 N-U The **salvage** from wrecked ships or destroyed buildings consists of the things that are saved from them. *...the value of the salvage.* 3 VERB If you **salvage** something from a difficult situation, you manage to get something useful from it so that it is not a complete failure. *Diplomats are still hoping to salvage something from the meeting.*

salvation /sælˈveɪʃən/. 1 N-U In Christianity, **salvation** is being saved from sin. 2 N-U The **salvation** of someone or something is the act of saving them from harm. *...those whose marriages are beyond salvation.*

same /seɪm/. **[1]** ADJ If two or more things, actions, or qualities are the **same**, or if one is the **same** as another, the two are very similar or exactly like each other in some way. *The houses were all the same... Driving a boat is not the same as driving a car... Try to find potatoes that are all the same size.* **[2]** ADJ You use **same** to indicate that you are referring to only one place, time, or thing, and not to different ones. *Your birthday is on the same day as mine.* **[3]** ADJ Something that is still the **same** has not changed in any way. *Only 17% said the economy would improve, but 25% believed it would stay the same.* **[4]** ADJ & PRON You use **same** to refer to something that has already been mentioned. *I had the same experience when I became a teacher myself... We made the decision which was right for us. Other parents must do the same.* **[5]** **at the same time:** see **time**.

PHRASES ● You say **all the same** or **just the same** to indicate that a situation or your opinion has not changed, in spite of what has happened or been said. *I had a lot of support along the way today, but it was hard all the same.* ● If you say that two or more people or things which are thought to be different are **one and the same**, you mean that they are in fact the same person or thing, or they are very similar and should be considered as one thing. *Luckily, Nancy's father and her attorney were one and the same person.*

sample /ˈsɑːmpəl, ˈsæm-/ **samples, sampling, sampled.** **[1]** N-C A **sample** of a substance or product is a small quantity of it, showing you what it is like. *We're giving away 2000 free samples.* **[2]** N-C A **sample** of a substance is a small amount of it that is examined and analyzed scientifically. *They took samples of my blood.* **[3]** N-C A **sample** of people or things is a number of them chosen from a larger group and then used in tests or used to provide information about the whole group. *...a random sample of more than 200 males.* **[4]** VERB If you **sample** food or drink, you taste a small amount of it in order to find out if you like it. **[5]** VERB If you **sample** a place or situation, you experience it for a short time in order to find out about it. *...the chance to sample a different way of life.*

sanction /ˈsæŋkʃən/ **sanctions, sanctioning, sanctioned.** **[1]** VERB & N-U If someone in authority **sanctions** an action or practice, they officially approve of it and allow it to be done. The **sanction** of someone in authority is their official approval. *He may now be ready to sanction the use of force... The king could not enact laws without the sanction of Parliament.* **[2]** N-PL **Sanctions** are measures taken by countries to restrict trade and official contact with a country that has broken international law. *He expressed his opposition to the lifting of sanctions.* **[3]** N-C A **sanction** is a severe course of action which is intended to make people obey the law. *The ultimate sanction is expulsion from the League.*

sanctity /ˈsæŋktɪti/. N-U If you talk about the **sanctity** of something, you mean that it is very important and should be treated with respect. *...the sanctity of marriage.*

sanctuary /ˈsæŋktʃʊəri, AM -tʃʊeri/ **sanctuaries.** **[1]** N-VAR A **sanctuary** is a place of safety for people who are being persecuted. *His church became a sanctuary for thousands of people... They sought sanctuary in the French embassy.* **[2]** N-C A wildlife **sanctuary** is a place where birds or animals are protected and allowed to live freely.

sand /sænd/ **sands, sanding, sanded.** **[1]** N-U **Sand** is a powder that consists of extremely small pieces of stone. *They walked barefoot across the damp sand to the water's edge. ...grains of sand.* **[2]** N-PL **Sands** are a large area of sand, for example a beach. *...miles of golden sands.* **[3]** VERB If you **sand** an object, you rub it with an abrasive paper called sandpaper in order to make it smooth or to get rid of paint or rust. *Sand the surface softly and carefully.*

sandal /ˈsændəl/ **sandals.** N-C **Sandals** are light shoes that have straps instead of a solid part over the top of your foot.

sandstone /ˈsændstəʊn/. N-U **Sandstone** is a type of rock which contains a lot of sand. *...sandstone cliffs.*

sandwich /ˈsænwɪdʒ, -wɪtʃ/ **sandwiches, sandwiched.** **[1]** N-C A **sandwich** consists of two slices of bread with a layer of food between them. *...a ham sandwich.* **[2]** PASSIVE-VERB When something **is sandwiched** between two other things, it is in a narrow space between them. *...a small shop sandwiched between a bar and a laundrette.*

sandy /ˈsændi/. ADJ A **sandy** area is covered with sand. *...sandy beaches.*

sane /seɪn/ **saner, sanest.** **[1]** ADJ Someone who is **sane** is able to think and behave normally and reasonably, and is not mentally ill. *He appears to be quite sane.* **[2]** ADJ If you describe an action or idea as **sane**, you mean that it is reasonable and sensible. *...extremely sane advice.*

sang /sæŋ/. **Sang** is the past tense of **sing**.

sanitary /ˈsænɪtri, AM -teri/. ADJ **Sanitary** means concerned with keeping things clean and hygienic. *Sanitary conditions are appalling.*

sanitation /ˌsænɪˈteɪʃən/. N-U **Sanitation** is the process of keeping places clean and hygienic, especially by providing a sewage system and a clean water supply. *...the hazards of contaminated water and poor sanitation.*

sanity /ˈsænɪti/. **[1]** N-U A person's **sanity** is their ability to think and behave normally and reasonably. *It was enough to make us question our sanity.* **[2]** N-U If there is **sanity** in a situation or activity, there is a purpose and a regular pattern, rather than confusion and worry. *She should do what she can to restore sanity to the situation.*

sank /sæŋk/. **Sank** is the past tense of **sink**.

sap /sæp/ **saps, sapping, sapped.** **[1]** VERB If something **saps** your strength or confidence, it gradually weakens or destroys it. *The illness sapped his strength.* **[2]** N-U **Sap** is the watery liquid in plants and trees.

sarcasm /ˈsɑːkæzəm/. N-U **Sarcasm** refers to speech or writing which actually means the opposite of what it seems to say. Sarcasm is usually intended to mock or insult someone. *'Congratulations. I'm pleased.' Alan spoke with a bitter sarcasm.*

sarcastic /sɑːˈkæstɪk/. ADJ Someone who is **sarcastic** says the opposite of what they really mean in order to mock or insult someone. *...sarcastic remarks.* ♦ **sarcastically** ADV *'What a surprise!' Caroline murmured sarcastically.*

sardine /sɑːˈdiːn/ **sardines**. N-C **Sardines** are a kind of small sea fish, often eaten as food.

sardonic /sɑːˈdɒnɪk/. ADJ If you describe someone as **sardonic**, you mean that they are mocking or scornful, often in a rather calm, quiet way. *...a sardonic sense of humour.* ♦ **sardonically** ADV *He grinned sardonically.*

sat /sæt/. **Sat** is the past tense and past participle of **sit**.

Satan /ˈseɪtən/. N-PROPER **Satan** is a name sometimes given to the Devil. ♦ **satanic** ADJ *...satanic rituals.*

satellite /ˈsætəlaɪt/ **satellites**. 1 N-C A **satellite** is an object which has been sent into space in order to collect information or to be part of a communications system. *President Bush spoke by satellite last night to 34 campaign rallies across the country.* 2 N-C A **satellite** is a natural object in space that moves round a planet or star.

'satellite dish, satellite dishes. N-C A **satellite dish** is a piece of equipment which receives satellite television signals.

satin /ˈsætɪn/, AM -tən/. N-U **Satin** is a smooth and shiny type of cloth.

satire /ˈsætaɪə/ **satires.** 1 N-U **Satire** is the use of humour to mock or criticize political ideas or the way that people behave. *The commercial side of the Christmas season is an easy target for satire.* 2 N-C A **satire** is a play or piece of writing that uses satire. *...a sharp satire on the American political process.*

satirical /səˈtɪrɪkəl/. ADJ A **satirical** drawing, piece of writing, or comedy show uses satire to criticize something. *...a satirical novel about London life.*

satisfaction /ˌsætɪsˈfækʃən/. 1 N-U **Satisfaction** is the pleasure you feel when you do something you wanted or needed to do. *Both sides expressed satisfaction with the progress so far. ...job satisfaction.* 2 N-U If you get **satisfaction** from someone, you get money or an apology from them because of some harm or injustice which has been done to you. *If you can't get any satisfaction, complain to the park owner.*

satisfactory /ˌsætɪsˈfæktəri/. ADJ If something is **satisfactory**, it is acceptable to you or fulfils a particular need or purpose. *I never got a satisfactory answer.* ♦ **satisfactorily** /ˌsætɪsˈfæktərɪli/ ADV *Their motives have never been satisfactorily explained.*

satisfied /ˈsætɪsfaɪd/. ADJ If you are **satisfied** with something, you are pleased because you have got what you wanted. *...satisfied customers.*

satisfy /ˈsætɪsfaɪ/ **satisfies, satisfying, satisfied.** 1 VERB If someone or something **satisfies** you, they give you enough of what you want to make you pleased or contented. *The*

pace of change has not been quick enough to satisfy everyone. 2 VERB If someone **satisfies** you **that** something is true or has been done properly, they convince you by giving you more information or by showing you what has been done. *Satisfy yourself that it's safe.* 3 VERB If you **satisfy** the requirements for something, you are good enough or suitable to fulfil these requirements. *Candidates must satisfy the general conditions for admission.*

satisfying /ˈsætɪsfaɪɪŋ/. ADJ Something that is **satisfying** gives you a feeling of pleasure and fulfilment. *...intellectually satisfying work.*

saturate /ˈsætʃʊreɪt/ **saturates, saturating, saturated.** 1 VERB If people or things **saturate** a place or object, they fill it completely so that no more can be added. *No one wants to saturate the city with car parking.* ♦ **saturation** N-U *...the saturation of the market with various kinds of goods.* 2 VERB If someone or something **is saturated**, they become extremely wet. *His work clothes, having become saturated with oil, had to be cleaned.*

Saturday /ˈsætədeɪ, -di/ **Saturdays.** N-VAR **Saturday** is the day after Friday and before Sunday.

sauce /sɔːs/ **sauces.** N-VAR A **sauce** is a thick liquid which is served with other food. *...a sauce of garlic, tomatoes, and cheese.*

saucepan /ˈsɔːspən, AM -pæn/ **saucepans.** N-C A **saucepan** is a deep metal cooking pot, usually with a long handle and a lid.

saucer /ˈsɔːsə/ **saucers.** N-C A **saucer** is a small curved plate on which you stand a cup.

saucy /ˈsɔːsi/. ADJ Someone or something that is **saucy** refers to sex in a light-hearted amusing way. *...a saucy joke.*

sauna /ˈsɔːnə/ **saunas.** 1 N-C A **sauna** is a hot steam bath. 2 N-C A **sauna** is a room or building where you can have a sauna.

saunter /ˈsɔːntə/ **saunters, sauntering, sauntered.** VERB If you **saunter** somewhere, you walk there in a slow casual way. *He sauntered along the river.*

sausage /ˈsɒsɪdʒ, AM ˈsɔːs-/ **sausages.** N-VAR A **sausage** consists of minced meat, mixed with other ingredients, inside a long thin skin.

sauté /ˈsəʊteɪ, AM sɔːˈteɪ/ **sautés, sautéing, sautéed.** VERB When you **sauté** food, you fry it quickly in hot oil or butter.

savage /ˈsævɪdʒ/ **savages, savaging, savaged.** 1 ADJ If someone or something is **savage**, they are extremely cruel, violent, and uncontrolled. *...a savage attack on a defenceless young girl.* ♦ **savagely** ADV *He was savagely beaten.* 2 N-C If you refer to people as **savages**, you dislike them because you think that they are cruel, violent, or uncivilized. 3 VERB If someone **is savaged** by a dog or other animal, the animal attacks them violently. 4 VERB If someone or something that they have done **is savaged** by another person, that person criticizes them severely. *The show had already been savaged by critics.*

savagery /ˈsævɪdʒri/. N-U **Savagery** is extremely cruel and violent behaviour. *...the sheer savagery of war.*

save /seɪv/ **saves, saving, saved.** ① VERB If you **save** someone or something, you help them to avoid harm or to escape from a dangerous or unpleasant situation. *To save his life, doctors amputated his legs. ...a final attempt to save 40,000 jobs.* ② VERB & N-C If a goalkeeper **saves** a shot, or if they make a **save**, they prevent the ball from going into the goal. ③ VERB If you **save** something, you keep it because it will be needed later. *Drain the beans thoroughly and save the stock for soup.* ④ VERB & PHR-VERB If you **save**, or if you **save up**, you gradually collect money by spending less than you get, usually in order to buy something that you want. *Tim and Barbara are now saving for a house... Put money aside in order to save up enough to make one major expenditure.* ♦**saver, savers** N-C *Low interest rates are bad news for savers.* ⑤ VERB If you **save** something such as time or money, you prevent the loss or waste of it. *It saves time in the kitchen to have things you use a lot within reach. ...money-saving special offers.* ⑥ VERB If you **save** someone an unpleasant task or experience, you do something which helps or enables them to avoid it. *He arranges to collect the payment from the customer, thus saving the client the paperwork.* ⑦ PREP You can use **save** or **save for** to introduce the only things, people, or ideas that your main statement does not apply to; FORMAL. *The parking lot was virtually empty save for a few cars.*
▶ **save up.** See save 4.

savings /ˈseɪvɪŋz/. N-PL Your **savings** are the money that you have saved, especially in a bank or a building society. *Her savings were in the Post Office Savings Bank.*

saviour (AM **savior**) /ˈseɪvjə/ **saviours.** ① N-C A **saviour** is a person who saves someone or something from danger, ruin, or defeat. *...the saviour of English football... She regarded him as her saviour.* ② N-PROPER In the Christian religion, **the Saviour** is Jesus Christ.

savour (AM **savor**) /ˈseɪvə/ **savours, savouring, savoured.** VERB If you **savour** something pleasant, you enjoy it as much as you can or for as long as possible. *Savour the flavour of each mouthful... There's something about the Loire Valley that makes you want to savour every moment.*

savoury (AM **savory**) /ˈseɪvəri/ **savouries.** ① ADJ **Savoury** food has a salty or spicy flavour rather than a sweet one. *...savoury dishes.* ② N-C **Savouries** are small portions of savoury food, usually eaten as a snack; BRITISH.

saw /sɔː/ **saws, sawing, sawed, sawn.** ① **Saw** is the past tense of see. ② N-C A **saw** is a tool for cutting wood, which has a blade with sharp teeth along one edge. ③ VERB If you **saw** something, you cut it with a saw.

sawdust /ˈsɔːdʌst/. N-U **Sawdust** is the very fine fragments of wood which are produced when you saw wood.

sawn /sɔːn/. **Sawn** is the past participle of saw.

sax /sæks/ **saxes.** N-C A **sax** is the same as a **saxophone**; INFORMAL.

saxophone /ˈsæksəfəʊn/ **saxophones.** N-C A **saxophone** is a musical wind instrument in the shape of a curved metal tube with keys and a curved mouthpiece. ♦**saxophonist** /sækˈsɒfənɪst, AM ˈsæksəfənn-/ **saxophonists** N-C *...the great jazz saxophonist Sonny Rollins.*

say /seɪ/ **says** /sez/ **saying, said.** ① VERB When you **say** something, you speak words. You can also use **say** to signal that you are stating a fact or your opinion. *'I'm sorry,' he said... I packed and said goodbye to Charlie... Did he say where he was going?... I would say that Susan will learn a lot from what she did.* ② VERB You can mention the contents of a piece of writing by mentioning what it **says** or what someone **says** in it. *Auntie Winnie wrote back saying Mam wasn't well.* ③ VERB If you **say** something **to** yourself, you think it. *Perhaps I'm still dreaming, I said to myself.* ④ VERB You indicate the information given by something such as a clock, dial, or map by mentioning what it **says**. *The clock said four minutes past eleven.* ⑤ VERB If something **says** something **about** a person, situation, or thing, it reveals something about them. *The building says something about the importance of the project.* ⑥ CONVENTION You can use **say** when you mention something as an example or when you mention an approximate amount or time. *Someone with, say, between 300 and 500 acres could be losing thousands of pounds a year.* ⑦ N-SING If you have a **say** in something, you have the right to give your opinion and influence decisions. When you have your **say**, you use this right or give your opinion. *It's time the people of Glasgow had a say in the future of Europe.*

Note that, with the verb **say**, if you want to mention the person who is being addressed, you should use the preposition **to**. 'What did she say you?' is wrong. **'What did she say to you?'** is correct. The verb **tell**, however, is usually followed by a direct object indicating the person who is being addressed. *He told Alison he was suffering from leukaemia... What did she tell you?* 'What did she tell to you?' is wrong.

Say is the most general verb for reporting the words that someone speaks. **Tell** is used to report information that is given to someone. *The manufacturer told me that the product did not contain corn.* **Tell** can also be used with a 'to'-infinitive to report an order or instruction. *My mother told me to shut up and eat my dinner.*

PHRASES ● You can use **'You can say that again'** to express strong agreement with what someone has just said; INFORMAL. *'Must have been a fiddly job.'—'You can say that again.'* ● If something **goes without saying**, it is obvious or definitely true. *It goes without saying that if someone has lung problems they should not smoke.* ● If you say that something **says it all**, you mean that it shows you very clearly the truth about a situation or someone's feelings. *This is my third visit in a week, which says it all.* ● You use **to say nothing of** when you add something which gives even more strength to the point you are making. *Unemployment leads to a sense of uselessness, to say nothing of financial problems.* ● You use **that is to say** to indicate that you are about to express the same idea more clearly; FORMAL. *Good writers are those who keep the language efficient. That is to say, keep it accurate, keep it clear.* ● If you say there is a lot **to be said for** something, you think it has a lot of good qualities or aspects. *There's a lot to be said for being based in the country.*

saying /ˈseɪɪŋ/ **sayings.** N-C A **saying** is a traditional sentence that people often say and that gives advice or information about life. *We also realize the truth of that old saying: Charity begins at home.*

scaffolding /ˈskæfəldɪŋ/. N-U **Scaffolding** is a temporary framework of poles and boards that is used by workmen to stand on while they are working on the outside structure of a building.

scald /skɔːld/ **scalds, scalding, scalded.** ① VERB If you **scald** yourself, you burn yourself with very hot liquid or steam. *A patient jumped into a bath being prepared by a member of staff and scalded herself. ...scalding hot water.* ② N-C A **scald** is a burn caused by very hot liquid or steam.

scale /skeɪl/ **scales, scaling, scaled.** ① N-SING If you refer to the **scale** of something, you are referring to its size or extent, especially when it is very big. *...killing on a massive scale... The British aid programme is small in scale.* ② N-C A **scale** is a set of levels or numbers which are used in a particular system of measuring things or comparing things. *...an earthquake measuring five-point-five on the Richter scale. ...those on the high end of the pay scale.* ③ N-C In music, a **scale** is a fixed sequence of musical notes, each one higher than the next, which begins at a particular note. *...the scale of C major.* ④ N-VAR The **scale** of a map, plan, or model is the relationship between the size of something in the map, plan, or model and its size in the real world. *...the map, on a scale of 1:10,000.* ⑤ ADJ A **scale** model of something is smaller than the original, but the sizes of all the parts are in the same, exact relation to each other. *...an intricately detailed scale model of the house.* ⑥ PHRASE If the different parts of a map, drawing, or model are **to scale**, they are the right size in relation to each other. ⑦ N-PL **Scales** are a piece of equipment for weighing things or people. *...kitchen scales... I step on the scales practically every morning.* ⑧ N-C The **scales** of a fish or reptile are the small flat pieces of hard skin that cover its body. ⑨ VERB If you **scale** something such as a mountain or a wall, you climb up it or over it. *...the first British woman to scale Everest.*

▸ **scale down.** PHR-VERB If you **scale down** something, you make it smaller in size, amount, or extent than it used to be. *One Peking factory has had to scale down its workforce from six hundred to six.*

scalp /skælp/ **scalps.** N-C Your **scalp** is the skin under the hair on your head.

scamper /ˈskæmpə/ **scampers, scampering, scampered.** VERB When people or small animals **scamper** somewhere, they move there quickly with small light steps. *The child scampered off without waiting for his friend.*

scan /skæn/ **scans, scanning, scanned.** ① VERB When you **scan** an area, a group of things, or a piece of writing, you look at it carefully, usually because you are looking for something in particular. *Joss scanned the crowd for the child's mother... She scanned the advertisement pages of the newspapers.* ② VERB If a machine **scans** luggage or other items, it examines it quickly, for example by moving a beam of light or X-rays over it. ③ N-C A **scan** is a medical test in which a machine sends a beam of X-rays over a part of your body in order to check whether your organs are healthy. *...a brain scan.* ④ N-C If a pregnant woman has a **scan**, a machine using sound waves produces an image of her womb on a screen so that a doctor can see if her baby is developing normally.

scandal /ˈskændəl/ **scandals.** ① N-C A **scandal** is a situation, event, or someone's behaviour that shocks a lot of people because they think it is immoral. *...a financial scandal.* ② N-SING If you say that something is a **scandal**, you are angry about it and think that the people responsible for it should be ashamed. *It is a scandal that a person can be stopped for no reason by the police.*

scandalous /ˈskændələs/. ① ADJ You can describe something as **scandalous** if it makes you very angry and you think the people responsible for it should be ashamed. *...a scandalous waste of money.* ◆ **scandalously** ADV *Many workers were being paid scandalously low wages.* ② ADJ **Scandalous** behaviour or activity is considered immoral and shocking.

scanner /ˈskænə/ **scanners.** N-C A **scanner** is a machine which is used to examine, identify, or record things, for example by moving a beam of light, sound, or X-rays over them.

scant /skænt/. ADJ You use **scant** to indicate that there is very little of something or not as much of something as there should be. *She began to criticise the police for paying scant attention to the theft.*

scapegoat /ˈskeɪpɡəʊt/ **scapegoats.** N-C If someone is made a **scapegoat** for something bad that has happened, people blame them or punish them for it, although it may not be their fault. *I don't think I deserve to be messed about and made the scapegoat for a couple of bad results.*

scar /skɑː/ **scars, scarring, scarred.** ① N-C A **scar** is a mark on the skin which is left after a wound has healed. ② VERB If your skin **is scarred**, it is badly marked as a result of a wound. *He was scarred for life during a pub fight.* ③ VERB If a surface **is scarred**, it is damaged and there are ugly marks on it. *The arena was scarred by deep muddy ruts.* ④ N-C & VERB If an unpleasant physical or emotional experience leaves a **scar** on someone, or if it **scars** them, it has a permanent effect on their mind. *The emotional scars that he bears will never disappear.*

scarce /skeəs/ **scarcer, scarcest.** ADJ If something is **scarce**, there is not enough of it. *Jobs are becoming increasingly scarce.*

scarcely /'skeəsli/. **1** ADV You use **scarcely** to emphasize that something is only just true or only just the case. *He could scarcely breathe... Scarcely a week goes by without the news providing fresh examples of racism.* **2** ADV You can use **scarcely** to say that something is certainly not true or is certainly not the case. *It was scarcely in their interest to let too many people know.* **3** ADV If you say **scarcely** had one thing happened when something else happened, you mean that the first event was followed immediately by the second. *Bruce had scarcely shaken our hands when the phone rang.*

scarcity /'skeəsɪti/ **scarcities.** N-VAR If there is a **scarcity** of something, there is not enough of it; FORMAL. *Successive bad harvests have created a severe food scarcity.*

scare /skeə/ **scares, scaring, scared.** **1** VERB & N-C If someone or something **scares** you, or if they give you a **scare**, they frighten you. *I didn't mean to scare you... It scared him to realise how close he had come to losing everything... Don't you realize what a scare you've given us all?* **2** N-C A **scare** is a situation in which many people are afraid or worried because they think something dangerous is happening which will affect them all. *...an Aids scare.* **3** N-C A bomb **scare** or a security **scare** is a situation in which there is believed to be a bomb in a place.

▶ **scare off** or **scare away**. PHR-VERB If you **scare off** or **scare away** a person or animal, or if you **scare** them **away**, you frighten them so that they go away. *...an alarm to scare off an attacker.*

scared /skeəd/. **1** ADJ If you are **scared** of someone or something, you are frightened of them. *I was too scared to move.* **2** ADJ If you are **scared** that something unpleasant might happen, you are nervous and worried because you think that it might happen. *I was scared that I might be sick... He was scared of letting us down.*

scarf /skɑːf/ **scarfs** or **scarves** /skɑːvz/. N-C A **scarf** is a piece of cloth that you wear round your neck or head, usually to keep yourself warm.

scarlet /'skɑːlət/. ADJ & N-U Something that is **scarlet** is bright red.

scary /'skeəri/ **scarier, scariest.** ADJ Something that is **scary** is rather frightening; INFORMAL. *There's something very scary about him. ...scary movies.*

scathing /'skeɪðɪŋ/. ADJ If you say that someone is being **scathing** about something, you mean that they are being very critical and scornful of it. *He made some particularly scathing comments about the design.* ♦ **scathingly** ADV *'Oh, they want to be excused,' the other girl said scathingly.*

scatter /'skætə/ **scatters, scattering, scattered.** **1** VERB If you **scatter** things over an area, you throw or drop them so you that they spread all over the area. *She scattered the petals over the grave.* **2** VERB If a group of people **scatter**, they suddenly separate and move in different directions. *They stared for a second,* *then scattered in panic.*

scattered /'skætəd/. **1** ADJ **Scattered** things are spread over an area in an untidy or irregular way. *He picked up the scattered toys... Food was scattered across the floor.* **2** ADJ AFTER LINK-V If something is **scattered** with a lot of small things, they are spread all over it. *Every surface is scattered with photographs.*

scattering /'skætərɪŋ/. N-SING A **scattering of** things is a small number of them spread over an area. *...a road with an inn, a few shops and a scattering of houses.*

scavenge /'skævɪndʒ/ **scavenges, scavenging, scavenged.** VERB If people or animals **scavenge** for food or other things, they collect them by searching among waste or unwanted objects. *Children had to scavenge to survive.* ♦ **scavenger, scavengers** N-C *...scavengers such as rats.*

scenario /sɪ'nɑːriəʊ, AM -'ner-/ **scenarios.** N-C If you talk about a likely or possible **scenario**, you are talking about the way in which a situation may develop. *In the worst-case scenario, you could become a homeless person.*

scene /siːn/ **scenes.** **1** N-C A **scene** in a play, film, or book is part of it in which a series of events happen in the same place. *...the opening scene of 'A Christmas Carol'.* **2** N-C You refer to a place as a **scene** when you are describing its appearance and indicating what impression it makes on you. *It's a scene of complete devastation.* **3** N-C The **scene** of an event is the place where it happened. *The area has been the scene of fierce fighting.* **4** N-SING You can refer to an area of activity as a particular type of **scene**. *...the alternative music scene.* **5** N-C If you make a **scene**, you embarrass people by publicly showing your anger about something.

PHRASES ● If something is done **behind the scenes**, it is done secretly rather than in public. *But behind the scenes Mr Cain will be working quietly to try to get a deal done.* ● Something that **sets the scene for** a particular event creates the conditions in which the event is likely to happen. *Mr Yeltsin's declaration set the scene for a further confrontation.*

scenery /'siːnəri/. **1** N-U The **scenery** in a country area is the land, water, or plants that you can see around you. *...the island's spectacular scenery.* ● See note at **landscape**. **2** N-U In a theatre, the **scenery** is the painted cloth and boards at the back of the stage which represent where the action is taking place.

scenic /'siːnɪk/. ADJ **Scenic** places have attractive scenery. *...a well-known scenic spot.*

scent /sent/ **scents, scenting, scented.** **1** N-C The **scent** of something is the pleasant smell that it has. *...shiny-leaved bushes with white flowers and a wonderful scent.* **2** N-VAR **Scent** is a pleasant-smelling liquid which women put on their necks and wrists to make themselves smell nice. **3** N-VAR The **scent** of a person or animal is the smell that they give off. *It wouldn't take long for the dogs to pick up our scent.* **4** VERB When an animal **scents** something, it becomes aware of it by smelling it. *The horse acted as if she had scented a wild cat.*

scented /'sentɪd/. ADJ **Scented** things have a pleasant smell, either naturally or because perfume has been added to them. *...scented soap.*

sceptic (AM **skeptic**) /'skeptɪk/ **sceptics.** N-C A **sceptic** is a person who has doubts and asks questions about things that other people believe. *He now has to convince sceptics that he has a serious plan.*

sceptical (AM **skeptical**) /'skeptɪkəl/. ADJ If you are **sceptical** about something, you have doubts about it. *...his sceptical view of all ideologies.*

scepticism (AM **skepticism**) /'skeptɪsɪzəm/. N-U **Scepticism** is great doubt about whether something is true or useful. *The report has inevitably been greeted with scepticism.*

schedule /'ʃedjuːl, AM 'skedʒuːl/ **schedules, scheduling, scheduled.** [1] N-C A **schedule** is a plan that gives a list of events or tasks and the times at which each one should happen or be done. *He has been forced to adjust his schedule.* [2] N-U You can use the word **schedule** to refer to the time or way something is planned to be done. For example, if something is completed **on schedule**, it is completed at the time planned. *The jet arrived in Johannesburg two minutes ahead of schedule.* [3] VERB If something **is scheduled** to happen at a particular time, arrangements are made for it to happen at that time. *The meeting with Mr Bush is scheduled for tomorrow morning.* [4] N-C A **schedule** is a written list of things, for example a list of prices, details, or conditions.

scheme /skiːm/ **schemes, scheming, schemed.** [1] N-C A **scheme** is a plan or arrangement, especially one produced by a government or other organization. *...schemes to help combat unemployment. ...a private pension scheme.* [2] VERB If you say that people **are scheming**, you mean that they are making secret plans in order to gain something for themselves; used showing disapproval. *The bride's family were scheming to prevent a wedding. ...a scheming career woman.* [3] PHRASE The **scheme of things** is the way that everything in the world or in a particular situation seems to be organized. *He spends rather too much time examining his own role in the scheme of things.*

schizophrenia /,skɪtsə'friːniə/. N-U **Schizophrenia** is a serious mental illness that prevents people from relating their thoughts and feelings to what is happening around them.

schizophrenic /,skɪtsə'frenɪk/ **schizophrenics.** ADJ & N-C Someone who is **schizophrenic** or who is a **schizophrenic** is suffering from schizophrenia. *...a psychopath with schizophrenic tendencies.*

scholar /'skɒlə/ **scholars.** N-C A **scholar** is a person who studies an academic subject and knows a lot about it. *...a leading biblical scholar.*

scholarly /'skɒləli/. [1] ADJ A **scholarly** person spends a lot of time studying and knows a lot about academic subjects. [2] ADJ A **scholarly** book or article contains a lot of academic information and is intended for academic readers.

scholarship /'skɒləʃɪp/ **scholarships.** [1] N-C If you get a **scholarship** to a school or university, your studies are paid for by the school or university, or by some other organization. [2] N-U **Scholarship** is serious academic study and the knowledge that is obtained from it. *A new era of scholarship is now beginning.*

school /skuːl/ **schools.** [1] N-VAR A **school** is a place where children are educated. You usually refer to this place as **school** when you are talking about the time that children spend there. *...a school built in the Sixties. ...two boys wearing school uniform. ...a boy who was in my class at school.* [2] N-C A **school** is the pupils or staff at a school. **School** can take the singular or plural form of the verb. *The whole school's going to hate you.* [3] N-C A place where a particular skill or subject is taught can be referred to as a **school.** *...a riding school.* [4] N-VAR A university, college, or university department specializing in a particular type of subject can be referred to as a **school.** *...the school of veterinary medicine at the University of Pennsylvania.* [5] N-VAR **School** is used to refer to university or college; AMERICAN, INFORMAL. *Bill Clinton's an Oxford man – he went to school in England.* [6] PHRASE A **school of thought** is a theory or opinion shared by a group of people. *There are three main schools of thought on how the money would best be spent.* [7] N-C A **school** of fish or dolphins is a large group of them.

schoolboy /'skuːlbɔɪ/ **schoolboys.** N-C A **schoolboy** is a boy who goes to school.

schoolchild /'skuːltʃaɪld/ **schoolchildren.** N-C **Schoolchildren** are children who go to school.

schooldays (or **school days**) /'skuːldeɪz/. N-PL Your **schooldays** are the period of your life when you are at school. *...a girl he had known since his schooldays.*

schoolgirl /'skuːlgɜːl/ **schoolgirls.** N-C A **schoolgirl** is a girl who goes to school.

schooling /'skuːlɪŋ/. N-U **Schooling** is education that children receive at school. *...children whose schooling has been disrupted by illness.*

schoolteacher /'skuːltiːtʃə/ **schoolteachers.** N-C A **schoolteacher** is a teacher in a school.

science /'saɪəns/ **sciences.** [1] N-U **Science** is the study of the nature and behaviour of natural things and the knowledge that we obtain about them. *Technically advanced countries put a high value on science.* [2] N-C A **science** is a particular branch of science, for example physics or biology. [3] N-C A **science** is the study of some aspect of human behaviour, for example sociology or anthropology. [4] See also **social science**.

science 'fiction. N-U **Science fiction** consists of stories and films about events that take place in the future or in other parts of the universe.

scientific /,saɪən'tɪfɪk/. [1] ADJ **Scientific** is used to describe things that relate to science or to a particular science. *...scientific research.* ♦**scientifically** ADV *...scientifically advanced countries.* [2] ADJ If you do something in a **scientific** way, you do it carefully and thoroughly, using experiments or tests. *It's not a scientific way to test their opinions.* ♦**scientifically** ADV *Efforts are being made to research it scientifically.*

scientist /'saɪəntɪst/ **scientists.** N-C A **scientist** is someone who has studied science and whose job is to teach or do research in science.

sci-fi /'saɪ faɪ/. N-U **Sci-fi** is science fiction. ...low-budget sci-fi films.

scissors /'sɪzəz/. N-PL **Scissors** are a small tool with two sharp blades which are screwed together. You use scissors for cutting things such as paper and cloth. She picked up a pair of scissors.

scoff /skɒf/ **scoffs, scoffing, scoffed.** VERB If you **scoff**, you speak in a scornful, mocking way about something. Some people may scoff at the idea that animals communicate.

scold /skəʊld/ **scolds, scolding, scolded.** VERB If you **scold** someone, you speak angrily to them because they have done something wrong; FORMAL. 'You should be at school,' he scolded.

scoop /skuːp/ **scoops, scooping, scooped.** **1** VERB If you **scoop** someone or something somewhere, you put your hands or arms under or round them and quickly move them there. Michael knelt next to her and scooped her into his arms. **2** VERB To **scoop** something from a container means to remove it with something such as a spoon. She scooped the chicken bones back into the stewpot. **3** N-C A **scoop** is an object like a spoon which is used for picking up a quantity of a food such as ice cream or flour. She gave him an extra scoop of clotted cream. **4** N-C A **scoop** is an exciting news story which is reported in one newspaper before it appears anywhere else.

▸ **scoop out.** PHR-VERB If you **scoop out** part of something, you remove it using a spoon or other tool. Cut a marrow in half and scoop out the seeds.

▸ **scoop up.** PHR-VERB If you **scoop** something **up**, you put your hands or arms under it and lift it in a quick movement. Use both hands to scoop up the leaves.

scooter /'skuːtə/ **scooters.** **1** N-C A **scooter** is a small lightweight motorcycle. **2** N-C A **scooter** is a child's toy which has two wheels joined by a board and a handle on a long pole attached to the front wheel.

scope /skəʊp/. **1** N-U If there is **scope** for a particular kind of behaviour, you have the opportunity to act in this way. Banks have increased scope to develop new financial products. **2** N-U The **scope** of an activity, topic, or piece of work is the area which it deals with or includes. ...a job she is confident will grow in scope.

scorch /skɔːtʃ/ **scorches, scorching, scorched.** VERB To **scorch** something means to burn it slightly or damage it with heat. The bomb scorched the side of the building. ♦**scorched** ADJ ...scorched black earth.

scorching /'skɔːtʃɪŋ/. ADJ **Scorching** or **scorching hot** weather or temperatures are very hot indeed. It was a scorching hot day.

score /skɔː/ **scores, scoring, scored.** **1** VERB In a sport or game, if a player **scores** a goal or a point, they gain a goal or point. Gascoigne almost scored in the opening minute. ♦**scorer, scorers** N-C Who was the club's leading scorer? **2** N-C The **score** in a game is the number of goals, runs, or points obtained by the teams or players. 4-1 was the final score. **3** VERB If you **score** a success, a victory, or a hit, you are successful in what you are doing. A multiple rocket launcher scored a direct hit on the steeple of a church. **4** N-C The **score** of a piece of music is the written version of it. **5** QUANT **Scores** of things or people means a large number of them. Two people were killed and scores were injured. **6** VERB If you **score** a surface with something sharp, you cut or scratch a line in it.

PHRASES ● You can use **on that score** or **on this score** to refer to something that has just been mentioned, especially an area of difficulty or concern. I became pregnant easily. At least I've had no problems on that score. ● If you **settle a score** or **settle an old score** with someone, you take revenge on them for something they have done in the past.

scorn /skɔːn/ **scorns, scorning, scorned.** **1** N-U If you treat someone or something with **scorn**, you show contempt for them. He became the object of ridicule and scorn. **2** VERB If you **scorn** someone or something, you feel or show contempt for them. People scorn me as a single parent. **3** VERB If you **scorn** something, you refuse to accept it because you think it is not good enough or suitable for you. ...people who scorned traditional methods.

scornful /'skɔːnfəl/. ADJ If you are **scornful** of someone or something, you show contempt for them. He is deeply scornful of politicians. ♦**scornfully** ADV They laughed scornfully.

Scotch /skɒtʃ/ **Scotches.** N-VAR **Scotch** or **Scotch whisky** is whisky made in Scotland. ...a bottle of Scotch... She expected him to ask for a scotch.

scour /skaʊə/ **scours, scouring, scoured.** **1** VERB If you **scour** a place for someone or something, you make a thorough search there for them. They scoured antiques shops for honey-coloured furniture. **2** VERB If you **scour** something such as a sink, floor, or pan, you clean its surface by rubbing it hard with something rough.

scourge /skɜːdʒ/ **scourges.** N-C A **scourge** is something that causes a lot of trouble to a group of people. ...the scourge of terrorism.

scout /skaʊt/ **scouts, scouting, scouted.** **1** N-C A **scout** is someone who is sent to an area of countryside to find out the position of an enemy army. **2** VERB If you **scout** somewhere for something, you go through that area searching for it. They scouted around for more fuel.

scowl /skaʊl/ **scowls, scowling, scowled.** VERB & N-C When someone **scowls**, they frown to show that they are angry. A **scowl** is the expression on someone's face when they scowl. She scowled at the two men... Chris met the remark with a scowl.

scramble /'skræmbəl/ **scrambles, scrambling, scrambled.** **1** VERB If you **scramble** over rough or difficult ground, you move quickly over it using your hands to help you. She scrambled down rocks to reach him. **2** VERB To **scramble** means to move somewhere in a hurried and awkward way. She

managed to scramble out of the vehicle as it burst into flames. ③ VERB & N-C If a number of people **scramble** for something, or if there is a **scramble** for it, they compete with each other for it, in a rough way. *Business is booming and foreigners are scrambling to invest. ...the scramble for jobs.* ④ VERB If you **scramble** eggs, you mix the whites and yolks of the eggs, then cook the mixture by stirring and heating it in a pan.
♦ **scrambled** ADJ *...scrambled eggs and bacon.*

scrap /skræp/ **scraps, scrapping, scrapped.** ① N-C A **scrap** of something is a very small piece or amount of it. *...a fire fueled by scraps of wood... They need every scrap of information they can get.* ② VERB If you **scrap** something, you get rid of it or cancel it. *...the decision to scrap smoking compartments on Kent trains.* ③ N-U **Scrap** is metal from old or damaged machinery or cars. *...a lorry piled with scrap metal.* ④ N-C You can refer to a fight or a quarrel as a **scrap**; INFORMAL.

scrape /skreɪp/ **scrapes, scraping, scraped.** ① VERB If you **scrape** something from a surface, you remove it, especially by pulling a sharp object over the surface. *She went round the car scraping the frost off the windows.* ② VERB & N-SING If something **scrapes** against something else, it rubs against it, making a noise, called a **scrape**. *The cab driver struggled with her luggage, scraping a bag against the door. ...the scrape of a guard's boot.* ♦ **scraping** N-SING *...the scraping of a chair across the floor.* ③ VERB If you **scrape** a part of your body, you accidentally rub it against something hard and rough, and damage it slightly.

▶ **scrape through.** PHR-VERB If you **scrape through** an examination, you succeed in passing it but with a score that is so low that you almost failed. *...the minimum amount of work necessary to scrape through.*

▶ **scrape together.** PHR-VERB If you **scrape together** an amount of money or a number of things, you succeed in obtaining it with difficulty. *They only just managed to scrape the money together.*

scratch /skrætʃ/ **scratches, scratching, scratched.** ① VERB If you **scratch** yourself, you rub your fingernails against your skin because it is itching. *The old man lifted his cardigan to scratch his side.* ② VERB If a sharp object **scratches** something or someone, it makes small shallow cuts on their surface or skin. *Knives will scratch the worktop.* ③ N-C **Scratches** on someone or something are small shallow cuts.
PHRASES ● If you do something **from scratch**, you do it without making use of anything that has been done before. *...building a home from scratch.* ● If something is not **up to scratch**, it is not good enough. *...keeping his health up to scratch.*

scrawl /skrɔːl/ **scrawls, scrawling, scrawled.** ① VERB If you **scrawl** something, you write it in a careless and untidy way. *He scrawled a hasty note to his wife.* ② N-VAR You can refer to writing that looks careless and untidy as **scrawl**.

scream /skriːm/ **screams, screaming, screamed.** ① VERB & N-C When someone

screams, they make a loud high-pitched cry, called a **scream**, usually because they are in pain or frightened. *He staggered around the playground, screaming in agony. ...screams of terror.* ② VERB If you **scream** something, you shout it in a loud high-pitched voice. *I was screaming at them to get out of my house.*

screech /skriːtʃ/ **screeches, screeching, screeched.** ① VERB If a vehicle **screeches**, its tyres make an unpleasant high-pitched noise, called a **screech**, on the road. *A black Mercedes screeched to a halt beside the helicopter... He slowed the car with a screech of tyres.* ② VERB & N-C If you **screech** something, or if you give a **screech**, you shout something in a loud, unpleasant, high-pitched voice. *'Get me some water, Jeremy!' I screeched. ...her voice rising to a screech.*

screen /skriːn/ **screens, screening, screened.** ① N-C A **screen** is the flat vertical surface on which pictures or words are shown on a television, on a computer, or in a cinema. ② VERB When a film or a television programme **is screened**, it is shown in the cinema or broadcast on television. *Channel Nine has again refused to screen the West Indies cricket tour.* ♦ **screening, screenings** N-VAR *The filmmakers will be present at the screenings.* ③ N-C A **screen** is a vertical panel that is used to separate different parts of a room. *They put a screen in front of me so I couldn't see what was going on.* ④ VERB If something **is screened** by another thing, it is behind it and hidden by it. *Most of the road behind the hotel was screened by a block of flats.* ⑤ VERB To **screen** people for a disease means to examine them to make sure that they do not have it. *...a quick saliva test that would screen for people at risk of tooth decay.* ♦ **screening** N-VAR *...breast screening for cancer.*

screenplay /ˈskriːnpleɪ/ **screenplays.** N-C A **screenplay** is a script for a film including instructions for the cameras.

screenwriter /ˈskriːnraɪtə/ **screenwriters.** N-C A **screenwriter** is a person who writes screenplays.

screw /skruː/ **screws, screwing, screwed.** ① N-C A **screw** is a small metal device for fixing things together. It has a wide top, a pointed end, and a raised spiral groove along its length. ② VERB If you **screw** something somewhere, you fix it there by means of a screw or screws. *I had screwed the shelf on the wall... Screw down any loose floorboards.* ③ VERB To **screw** something somewhere means to fasten or fix it in place by twisting it round and round. *He screwed the cap back on and laid the bottle on the table.* ④ VERB If you **screw** your face or your eyes **into** an expression of pain or discomfort, you tighten the muscles of your face showing that you are in pain or uncomfortable. *He screwed his face into a horrible grimace.* ⑤ VERB If someone **screws** something, especially money, **out of** you, they get it from you by putting strong pressure on you; INFORMAL. *He's now screwing cheaper prices out of his own raw material suppliers.*

▶ **screw up.** PHR-VERB If someone **screws** something **up**, or if they **screw up**, they cause something to fail or be spoiled; INFORMAL. *You can't open the window because it screws up the air conditioning.*

screwdriver /ˈskruːdraɪvə/ **screwdrivers.** N-C A **screwdriver** is a tool for fixing screws into place.

scribble /ˈskrɪbəl/ **scribbles, scribbling, scribbled.** [1] VERB If you **scribble** something, you write it quickly and untidily. *Boxhall scribbled his calculation on a scrap of paper... As I scribbled in my diary, the light went out.* [2] VERB To **scribble** means to make meaningless marks or rough drawings using a pencil or pen. *When Caroline was five she scribbled on a wall.* [3] N-VAR **Scribble** is something that has been written or drawn quickly and roughly.

script /skrɪpt/ **scripts.** [1] N-C The **script** of a play, film, or television programme is the written version of it. [2] N-VAR A **script** is a particular system of writing. *...written in Arabic script.*

scripture /ˈskrɪptʃə/ **scriptures.** N-VAR **Scripture** or **the scriptures** refers to writings that are regarded as sacred in a particular religion, for example the Bible in Christianity.

scroll /skrəʊl/ **scrolls.** N-C A **scroll** is a long roll of paper or other material with writing on it. *...ancient scrolls.*

scrub /skrʌb/ **scrubs, scrubbing, scrubbed.** [1] VERB & N-SING If you **scrub** something, or if you give it a **scrub**, you rub it hard in order to clean it, using a stiff brush and water. *The corridors are scrubbed clean... I started to scrub the dirt... That floor needs a jolly good scrub.* [2] N-U **Scrub** is land consisting of low trees and bushes in an area which gets very little rain.

scruffy /ˈskrʌfi/ **scruffier, scruffiest.** ADJ **Scruffy** things or people are dirty and untidy. *...a scruffy basement flat.*

scrupulous /ˈskruːpjʊləs/. [1] ADJ A **scrupulous** person or organization takes great care to do what is fair, honest, or morally right. *The case is pursued with scrupulous fairness according to the rules.* ♦**scrupulously** ADV *He is scrupulously fair.* [2] ADJ **Scrupulous** means thorough, exact, and careful about details. *Observe scrupulous hygiene when preparing and cooking food.* ♦**scrupulously** ADV *The streets and parks were scrupulously clean.*

scrutinize (BR also **scrutinise**) /ˈskruːtɪnaɪz/ **scrutinizes, scrutinizing, scrutinized.** VERB If you **scrutinize** something, you examine it very carefully. *The insurance industry will continue to be closely scrutinized by Congress.*

scrutiny /ˈskruːtɪni/. N-U If something is under **scrutiny**, it is being studied or observed very carefully. *The holders of public office must always be subject to public scrutiny.*

scuffle /ˈskʌfəl/ **scuffles, scuffling, scuffled.** VERB & N-C If people **are scuffling**, or if they are involved in a **scuffle**, they are fighting for a short time in a disorganized way. *Police scuffled with some of the protesters... Violent scuffles broke out between rival groups.*

sculpt /skʌlpt/ **sculpts, sculpting, sculpted.** VERB When an artist **sculpts** something, they carve it or shape it out of a hard material such as stone. *...figures sculpted in stone.* ♦**sculptor, sculptors** N-C *...a sculptor who takes inspiration from all kinds of natural things.*

sculpture /ˈskʌlptʃə/ **sculptures.** [1] N-VAR A **sculpture** is a work of art that is produced by carving or shaping materials such as stone or clay. [2] N-U **Sculpture** is the art and craft of making sculptures.

scum /skʌm/. N-U **Scum** is a layer of a substance on the surface of a liquid which looks unpleasant. *...areas where the water is especially hard and prone to form scum.*

scupper /ˈskʌpə/ **scuppers, scuppering, scuppered.** VERB To **scupper** a plan or attempt means to spoil it completely; BRITISH. *...a deliberate attempt to scupper the peace talks.*

scurry /ˈskʌri, AM ˈskɜːri/ **scurries, scurrying, scurried.** [1] VERB When people or small animals **scurry** somewhere, they move quickly and hurriedly, especially because they are frightened. *The attack began, sending residents scurrying for cover.* [2] VERB If people **scurry** to do something, they do it as quickly as they can. *Reporters scurried to find telephones.*

scuttle /ˈskʌtəl/ **scuttles, scuttling, scuttled.** VERB When people or small animals **scuttle** somewhere, they run there with short quick steps. *Two very small children scuttled away in front of them.*

sea /siː/ **seas.** [1] N-SING The **sea** is the salty water that covers much of the earth's surface. *Most of the kids have never seen the sea.* [2] N-C A **sea** is a large area of salty water that is part of an ocean or is surrounded by land. You use **seas** when you are describing the sea at a particular time or in a particular area. *...the North Sea... The seas are warm further south.* [3] N-SING A **sea** of people or things is a very large number of them. *...the sea of bottles and glasses on the table.*

PHRASES ● **At sea** means on or under the sea, far away from land. *The boats remain at sea for an average of ten days.* ● If someone is all **at sea**, they are in a state of confusion.

seafood /ˈsiːfuːd/. N-U **Seafood** refers to shellfish and other sea creatures that you can eat.

seagull /ˈsiːgʌl/ **seagulls.** N-C A **seagull** is a type of bird that lives near the sea.

seal /siːl/ **seals, sealing, sealed.** [1] N-C A **seal** is an animal which eats fish and lives partly on land and partly in the sea. It has short fur and uses short limbs, called flippers, to enable it to swim. [2] VERB When you **seal** an envelope, you close it by sticking down the flap. *Write your letter and seal it in a blank envelope.* [3] VERB & N-C If you **seal** a container or an opening, or if you form a **seal**, you cover it with something in order to prevent air, liquid, or other material getting in or out. *...a lid to seal in heat and keep food moist... Wet the edges where the two crusts join, to form a seal.* [4] N-C A **seal** is a device, used for example in a machine, which closes an opening tightly so that air, liquid, or other substances cannot get in or out. *Checks seals on fridges and freezers regularly.* [5] N-C A **seal** is an official mark on a document which shows that it is genuine. [6] VERB & PHR-VERB If someone in authority **seals** an area, or if they **seal** it **off**, they stop people entering or passing through it, for example by placing barriers in the way. *The army has stepped up patrols in an* effort to seal the border... Police and troops sealed off the area.

'sea level N-U If you are at **sea level**, you are at the same level as the surface of the sea. *The stadium was 2275 metres above sea level.*

seam /siːm/ **seams.** [1] N-C A **seam** is a line of stitches joining two pieces of cloth together. [2] N-C A **seam** of coal is a long narrow layer of it beneath the ground. [3] PHRASE If a place is very full, you can say that it is **bursting at the seams.**

seaman /ˈsiːmən/ **seamen.** N-C A **seaman** is a sailor.

seamless /ˈsiːmləs/. ADJ You use **seamless** to describe something that has no breaks or gaps in it or which continues smoothly, without stopping. *It was a seamless procession of wonderful electronic music.* ♦ **seamlessly** ADV ...*allowing law and order to blend seamlessly.*

search /sɜːtʃ/ **searches, searching, searched.** [1] VERB If you **search for** something or someone, you look carefully for them. If you **search** a place, you look carefully for something there. *The Turkish security forces have started searching for the missing men... She searched her desk for the necessary information.* [2] N-C A **search** is an attempt to find something by looking for it carefully. *Following an hour-long search, police seized several items.* [3] VERB If the police **search** you, they examine your clothing for hidden objects. [4] PHRASE If you go **in search of** something, you try to find them. ...*people in search of better economic opportunities.*

searching /ˈsɜːtʃɪŋ/. ADJ A **searching** question is intended to discover the truth about something.

searing /ˈsɪərɪŋ/. [1] ADJ BEFORE N **Searing** is used to indicate that something such as pain or heat is very intense. ...*the searing heat of the Saudi Arabian desert.* [2] ADJ BEFORE N A **searing** speech or piece of writing is very critical. ...*a searing indictment of corruption at the top.*

seaside /ˈsiːsaɪd/. N-SING You can refer to an area that is close to the sea, especially where people go for their holidays, as **the seaside**; BRITISH.

season /ˈsiːzən/ **seasons, seasoning, seasoned.** [1] N-C The **seasons** are the periods into which a year is divided and which each have their own typical weather conditions. *Autumn's my favourite season.* ...*the rainy season.* [2] N-C A **season** is the period during each year when something usually happens. ...*the start of the football season.* [3] VERB If you **season** food, you add salt, pepper, or spices to it. *Season the meat with salt and pepper.*
| PHRASES | ● If fruit or vegetables are **in season**, it is the time of year when they are ready for eating and are widely available. ● If a female animal is **in season**, she is in a state where she is ready for mating.

seasonal /ˈsiːzənəl/. ADJ **Seasonal** means happening during one particular time of the year. ...*seasonal variations in temperature.* ♦ **seasonally** ADV ...*the seasonally adjusted unemployment figures.*

seasoned /ˈsiːzənd/. ADJ **Seasoned** is used to

describe people who have a lot of experience of something. ...*seasoned travellers.*

seasoning /ˈsiːzənɪŋ/. N-U **Seasoning** is salt, pepper, or spices that are added to food to improve its flavour.

'season ticket, season tickets. N-C A **season ticket** is a ticket that you can use repeatedly over a certain period without having to pay each time.

seat /siːt/ **seats, seating, seated.** [1] N-C A **seat** is an object that you can sit on, for example a chair. ...*the back seat of their car... All seats for the Variety performance will be priced at £12.00.* ● See note at **place.** [2] N-C The **seat** of a chair is the part that you sit on. [3] VERB If you **seat** yourself somewhere, you sit down. *I seated myself at the bar... The room was empty apart from one man seated beside the fire.* [4] VERB A building or vehicle that **seats** a particular number of people has enough seats for that number. *The Theatre seats 570.* [5] N-C When someone is elected to parliament, you can say that they or their party have won a **seat.** [6] N-C If someone has a **seat** on the board of a company or on a committee, they are a member of it.
| PHRASES | ● If you **take a back seat**, you allow other people to have all the power and to make all the decisions. ● If you say that someone is **in the driving seat** or **in the driver's seat**, you mean that they are in control in a situation. ...*a more accountable system that would put voters back in the driving seat.* ● If you **take a seat**, you sit down. *Take a seat. What can I do for you?*

'seat-belt (or **seatbelt**), **seat-belts.** N-C A **seat-belt** is a strap that you fasten across your body for safety when travelling in a car or aeroplane.

seating /ˈsiːtɪŋ/. N-U The **seating** in a place consists of the seats there. ...*the pleasant cafeteria, with seating for up to 200.*

seaweed /ˈsiːwiːd/ **seaweeds.** N-VAR **Seaweed** is a plant that grows in the sea.

secluded /sɪˈkluːdɪd/. ADJ A **secluded** place is quiet, private, and undisturbed.

seclusion /sɪˈkluːʒən/. N-U If you are in **seclusion**, you are in a quiet place away from other people. *They love the seclusion of their garden.*

second, /ˈsekənd/ **seconds.** N-C A **second** is one of the sixty parts that a minute is divided into. People often say **'a second'** or **'seconds'** when they simply mean a very short length of time. *It only takes forty seconds... Seconds later, firemen reached his door.*

second, /ˈsekənd/ **seconds, seconding, seconded.** [1] ORD The **second** item in a series is the one that you count as number two. *It is the second time I have heard the name.* ...*Cambodia's second biggest city... First, interest rates may take longer to fall than is hoped. Second, in real terms, lending may fall.* [2] PHRASE If you say that something is **second to none**, you are emphasizing that it is very good indeed or very large indeed exists.

3 PHRASE If you say that something is **second only to** something else, you mean that it is the best or biggest that exists, except for that thing. *As a major health risk hepatitis is second only to tobacco.* **4** N-C **Seconds** are goods that are sold cheaply because they are slightly faulty. **5** VERB If you **second** a proposal in a meeting or debate, you formally agree with it so that it can then be discussed or voted on. *...the members who proposed and seconded his nomination.* **6** VERB If you **second** what someone has said, you say that you agree with them or say the same thing yourself. *His concern was seconded by spokesmen from the National Association of Homebuilders.* **7 second nature**: see **nature**.

second 3 sending someone to do a job

second /sɪˈkɒnd/ **seconds, seconding, seconded.** VERB If you **are seconded** somewhere, you are moved there temporarily by the organization you work for in order to do special duties. *Several hundred soldiers have been seconded to help farmers.*

secondary /ˈsekəndri, AM -deri/. **1** ADJ If you describe something as **secondary**, you mean that it is less important than something else. *Money is considered to be of secondary importance in this scheme of things.* **2** ADJ In Britain, **secondary** education is for pupils between the ages of 11 and 18.

,second 'best. ADJ & N-SING Something that is **second best** or a **second best** is not as good as the best thing of its kind but is better than all the other things. *...his second best suit...* *He refused to settle for anything that was second best.*

,second-'class. ADJ BEFORE N **Second-class** things are regarded as less valuable or less important than others of the same kind. *He was not prepared to see Uzbekistan become a second class republic.*

,second-'hand. **1** ADJ & ADV **Second-hand** things are not new and have been owned by someone else. *Far more boats are bought second-hand than are bought brand new.* **2** ADJ BEFORE N A **second-hand** shop sells second-hand goods. **3** ADJ & ADV **Second-hand** information or opinions are those you learn about from other people rather than directly or from your own experience. *I heard stories second-hand that they were having a fantastic time.*

secondly /ˈsekəndli/. ADV You say **secondly** when you want to make a second point or give a second reason for something. *Firstly, I didn't know exactly when I was going to America; secondly, who was going to look after Doran?*

,second-'rate. ADJ If you describe something as **second-rate**, you mean that you think it is of poor quality.

,second 'thoughts. **1** N-PL If you have **second thoughts** about a decision, you have doubts and begin to wonder if it was wise. **2** PHRASE In British English, you can say **on second thoughts** when you suddenly change your mind about something that you are saying or something that you have decided to do. In American English, you say **on second thought**. *'On second thoughts,' he said, 'I guess I'll come with you.'*

secrecy /ˈsiːkrəsi/. N-U **Secrecy** is the act of keeping something secret, or the state of being kept secret. *He had signed a pledge of secrecy.*

secret /ˈsiːkrɪt/ **secrets.** **1** ADJ If something is **secret**, it is known about by only a small number of people, and is not told or shown to anyone else. *The police have been trying to keep the documents secret.* ♦ **secretly** ADV *The meeting had been secretly recorded.* **2** N-C A **secret** is a fact that is known by only a small number of people, and is not told to anyone else. *He enjoyed keeping our love a secret.* **3** N-SING If a way of behaving is the **secret** of achieving something, it is the best way or the only way to achieve it. *The secret of success is honesty.* **4** PHRASE If you do something **in secret**, you do it without anyone else knowing. *The plans were drawn up in secret.*

secretarial /ˌsekrəˈteəriəl/. ADJ **Secretarial** work or training involves the work of a secretary.

secretariat /ˌsekrəˈteəriæt/ **secretariats.** N-C A **secretariat** is a department responsible for the administration of an international political organization.

secretary /ˈsekrətri, AM -teri/ **secretaries.** **1** N-C A **secretary** is a person who is employed to do office work, such as typing letters or answering phone calls. **2** N-C The **secretary** of an organization such as a trade union or a club is its official manager. **3** N-C The **secretary** of a company is the person who has the legal duty of keeping the company's records. **4** N-C **Secretary** is used in the titles of ministers and officials who are in charge of main government departments. *...the British Foreign Secretary.*

,Secretary of 'State, Secretaries of State. **1** N-C In the United States, the **Secretary of State** is the head of the government department which deals with foreign affairs. **2** N-C In Britain, the **Secretary of State** for a particular government department is the head of that department.

secrete /sɪˈkriːt/ **secretes, secreting, secreted.** VERB If part of a plant or animal **secretes** a liquid, it produces it. ♦ **secretion** N-U *...insulin secretion.*

secretion /sɪˈkriːʃən/ **secretions.** N-C A **secretion** is a liquid that is produced by a plant or animal.

secretive /ˈsiːkrətɪv, sɪˈkriːt-/. ADJ If you are **secretive**, you like to keep your knowledge, feelings, or intentions hidden.

,secret po'lice. N-U The **secret police** is a police force, especially in a non-democratic country, that works secretly and is concerned with political crimes.

,secret 'service, secret services. N-C A country's **secret service** is a government department whose job is to find out enemy secrets and to prevent its own government's secrets from being discovered.

sect /sekt/ **sects.** N-C A **sect** is a group of people that has separated from a larger group and has a particular set of religious or political beliefs.

sectarian /sekˈteəriən/. ADJ **Sectarian** means resulting from the differences between different religious sects. *The murder was sectarian.*

section /ˈsekʃən/ **sections**. N-C A **section** of something is one of the parts that it is divided into. *A section of the Bay Bridge had collapsed... This paragraph is the longest section of the will.* ● See also **cross-section**.

sector /ˈsektə/ **sectors**. N-C A **sector** of something, especially a country's economy, is a particular part of it. *...the nation's manufacturing sector. ...the poorest parts of Pakistani society.*

secular /ˈsekjʊlə/. ADJ You use **secular** to describe things that have no connection with religion. *...a secular state.*

secure /sɪˈkjʊə/ **secures, securing, secured**. [1] ADJ If something such as a job or institution is **secure**, it is safe and reliable, and unlikely to be lost or to fail. *The industry has a strong and secure future.* [2] ADJ A **secure** place is tightly locked or well protected, so that people cannot enter it or leave it. ♦**securely** ADV *Drugs were always securely locked away.* [3] VERB If you **secure** a place, you make it safe from harm or attack; FORMAL. *Troops had secured the airport.* [4] ADJ If an object is **secure**, it is fixed firmly in position. ♦**securely** ADV *They tied the ends of the bags securely.* [5] VERB If you **secure** an object, you fasten it firmly to another object. *Rugs are secured to the floor with tacks.* [6] ADJ If you feel **secure**, you feel safe and happy and are not worried about your life. [7] VERB If you **secure** something, you get it after a lot of effort; FORMAL. *He failed to secure enough votes for outright victory.*

security /sɪˈkjʊərɪti/ **securities**. [1] N-U **Security** refers to all the precautions that are taken to protect a place. *Airport security was tightened... ...security guards.* [2] N-U A feeling of **security** is a feeling of being safe and free from worry. *He loves the security of a happy home life.* [3] N-U The **security** of something such as a job is the fact that it is safe or reliable, and unlikely to be lost or to fail. *Fears about job security plague nearly half the workforce.* [4] N-U If you pledge something as **security** for a loan, you promise to give it to the person who lends you money, if you fail to pay all the money back. [5] See also **social security**.

sedate /sɪˈdeɪt/ **sedates, sedating, sedated**. [1] ADJ If you describe someone as **sedate**, you mean that they are quiet and calm, though perhaps rather dull. [2] VERB If someone is **sedated**, they are given a drug to calm them or to make them sleep.

sedation /sɪˈdeɪʃən/. N-U If someone is under **sedation**, they have been given medicine or drugs in order to calm them or make them sleep.

sedative /ˈsedətɪv/ **sedatives**. N-C A **sedative** is a drug that calms you or makes you sleep. *Her doctor prescribed a sedative.*

sedentary /ˈsedəntəri, AM -teri/. ADJ Someone who has a **sedentary** lifestyle or job sits down a lot of the time and does not take much exercise.

sediment /ˈsedɪmənt/ **sediments**. N-VAR **Sediment** is solid material that settles at the bottom of a liquid.

seduce /sɪˈdjuːs, AM -ˈduːs/ **seduces, seducing, seduced**. [1] VERB If something **seduces** you, it is so attractive that it tempts you to do something that you would not normally approve of. *We are seduced into buying all these brilliantly packaged items.* ♦**seduction** /sɪˈdʌkʃən/ **seductions** N-VAR *The country had resisted the seductions of mass tourism.* [2] VERB If someone **seduces** another person, they use their charm to persuade that person to have sex with them. ♦**seduction** N-VAR *Her methods of seduction are subtle.*

seductive /sɪˈdʌktɪv/. [1] ADJ Something that is **seductive** is very attractive or tempting. *It's a seductive argument.* [2] ADJ A **seductive** person is sexually attractive. ♦**seductively** ADV *Her mouth is seductively large and full.*

see /siː/ **sees, seeing, saw, seen**. [1] VERB When you **see** something, you notice it using your eyes. *Did you see that policeman?... I saw a man making his way towards me... I saw her get out of the car... It's dark and I can't see.*

> You use **see** to talk about things that you are aware of because a visual impression reaches your eyes. You often use **can** in this case. *I can see the fax here on the desk.* If you want to say that someone is paying attention to something they can see, you say that they **are looking at** it or **watching** it. In general, you **look at** something that is not moving, while you **watch** something that is moving or changing. *I asked him to look at the picture above his bed... He watched Blake run down the stairs.* **Look** is never followed directly by an object. You must always use **at** or some other preposition. *I looked towards the plane.*

[2] VERB If you go to **see** someone, you visit them or meet them. *You need to see a doctor.* [3] VERB If you go to **see** an entertainment such as a film or sports game, you go to watch it. *It was one of the most amazing films I've ever seen.* [4] VERB If you **see** what something is or what it means, you realize or understand what it is or what it means. *Amy saw that he was challenging her... I really don't see any reason for changing it... 'He came home in my car.'—'I see.'* [5] VERB If you **see** someone or something as a certain thing or **see** a particular quality in them, you have the opinion that they are that thing or have that quality. *He saw her as a rival... I don't see it as my duty to take sides.* [6] VERB If you **see** something happening in the future, you imagine it, or predict that it will happen. *I can see them doing really well.* [7] VERB If you say that a period of time or a person **sees** a particular change or event, you mean that the change or event takes place during that period of time or while that person is alive. *Yesterday saw the resignation of the acting Interior Minister... He had worked with the General for three years and was sorry to see him go.* [8] VERB If you say that you will **see** what is happening, you mean that you will try to find out what is happening. If you say that

you will **see** if you can do something, you mean that you will try to do it. *Let me just see what the next song is... We'll see what we can do, miss.* [9] VERB If you **see** that something is done, or if you **see** to it that it is done, you make sure that it is done. *See that you take care of him... Catherine saw to it that the information went directly to Walter.* [10] VERB If you **see** someone to a particular place, you accompany them to make sure that they get there safely, or to show politeness. *'Goodnight.'—'I'll see you out.'* [11] VERB **See** is used in books to indicate to readers where they should look for more information. *See Chapter 7 below for further comments on the textile industry.*

PHRASES • People say '**let me see**' or '**let's see**' when they are trying to remember or calculate something, or are trying to find something. *Let's see, they're six – no, make that five hours ahead of us.* • People say '**I'll see**' or '**We'll see**' to indicate that they do not intend to make a decision immediately, and will decide later. • You can use **seeing that** or **seeing as** to introduce a reason for what you are saying or a reason why you think something is the case. *Seeing as I pay half the rent, I should be allowed to smoke.* • '**See you**', '**be seeing you**', and '**see you later**' are ways of saying goodbye to someone whom you expect to meet them again soon.

▸ **see about.** PHR-VERB When you **see about** something, you arrange for it to be done or provided. *I really must see about selling the house.*

▸ **see off.** [1] PHR-VERB If you **see off** an opponent, you defeat them. *He saw off a strong challenge from two other candidates.* [2] PHR-VERB When you **see** someone **off**, you go with them to the place that they are leaving from, and say goodbye to them there.

▸ **see through.** PHR-VERB If you **see through** someone or their behaviour, you realize what their intentions are, even though they are trying to hide them. *I saw through your little ruse from the start.* • See also **see-through**.

▸ **see to.** PHR-VERB If you **see to** something that needs attention, you deal with it. *Franklin saw to the luggage.*

seed /siːd/ **seeds.** [1] N-VAR A **seed** is one of the small hard parts of a plant from which a new plant grows. [2] N-PL You can refer to the beginning of a feeling or process that gradually develops as the **seeds** of that feeling or process. *...questions meant to plant seeds of doubts in the minds of jurors.*

seedling /ˈsiːdlɪŋ/ **seedlings.** N-C A **seedling** is a young plant grown from a seed.

seedy /ˈsiːdi/. ADJ If you describe a person or place as **seedy**, you disapprove of them because they look dirty and not respectable. *...a seedy hotel.*

seek /siːk/ **seeks, seeking, sought.** [1] VERB If you **seek** something, you try to find or obtain it; FORMAL. *Pat decided she would seek work.* ◆**seeker, seekers** N-C *The beaches draw sunseekers from all over Europe.* [2] VERB If you **seek** to do something, you try to do it. *We have never sought to impose our views.*

▸ **seek out.** PHR-VERB If you **seek out** someone or something, you keep looking for them until you find them. *The press began to seek him out.*

seem /siːm/ **seems, seeming, seemed.** [1] LINK-VERB You use **seem** to say that someone or something gives the impression of having a particular quality, or that something gives the impression of happening in the way you describe. *Everyone seems busy... They seemed an ideal couple... Audiences seem to love it... It seemed as if she'd been gone forever.* [2] VERB You use **seem** when you are describing your own feelings or thoughts, in order to make your statement less forceful. *I seem to have lost all my self-confidence... I seem to remember giving you very precise instructions.* [3] VERB If you say that you **cannot seem** or **could not seem** to do something, you mean that you have tried to do it and were unable to. *Kim's mother couldn't seem to stop crying.*

seeming /ˈsiːmɪŋ/. ADJ BEFORE N **Seeming** means appearing to be the case, but not necessarily the case; FORMAL. *...the company's seeming inability to control costs.* ◆**seemingly** ADV *He has moved to Spain, seemingly to enjoy a slower style of life.*

seen /siːn/. **Seen** is the past participle of **see**.

seep /siːp/ **seeps, seeping, seeped.** VERB If liquid or gas **seeps** into a place, it slowly leaks into it. *The gas is seeping out of the rocks.*

seethe /siːð/ **seethes, seething, seethed.** [1] VERB If you **are seething**, you are very angry about something but do not express your feelings about it. *I seethed with rage.* [2] VERB If you say that a place **is seething**, you are emphasizing that it is very full of people or things and that they are all moving about. *The bars and restaurants were seething with customers.* ◆**seething** ADJ *...a seething mass of soldiers.*

'see-through. ADJ **See-through** clothes are made of thin cloth, so that you can see a person's body or underwear through them. *...a see-through dress.*

segment /ˈsegmənt/ **segments.** N-C A **segment** of something is one part of it. *...the poorer segments of society.*

segregate /ˈsegrɪgeɪt/ **segregates, segregating, segregated.** VERB To **segregate** two groups or types of people or things means to keep them apart. *They segregate you from the rest of the community.* ◆**segregated** ADJ *...racially segregated schools.* ◆**segregation** N-U *...the sex segregation of work.*

seize /siːz/ **seizes, seizing, seized.** [1] VERB If you **seize** something, you take hold of it quickly and firmly. *He seized my arm.* [2] VERB When a group of people **seize** a place or **seize** control of it, they take control of it quickly and suddenly, using force. *Troops have seized the airport.* [3] VERB When someone **is seized**, they are arrested or captured. *Men carrying submachine guns seize the five soldiers.* [4] VERB If you **seize** an opportunity, you take advantage of it and do something that you want to do. *I seized the chance to interview Chris.*

▸ **seize on.** PHR-VERB If you **seize on** something, or if you **seize upon** it, you show great interest in it, often because it is useful to you. *Opposi-*

tion parties were quick to seize on the jobs figures.

▶ **seize up.** PHR-VERB If an engine or part of your body **seizes up**, it stops working.

seizure /ˈsiːʒə/ **seizures.** ⊡ N-C If someone has a **seizure**, they have a heart attack or an epileptic fit. *...a mild cardiac seizure.* ⊡ N-C If there is a **seizure** of power in a place, a group of people suddenly take control of it, using force. *...the seizure of territory through force.*

seldom /ˈseldəm/. ADV If something **seldom** happens, it does not happen often. *They seldom speak... We were seldom at home.*

select /sɪˈlekt/ **selects, selecting, selected.** ⊡ VERB If you **select** something, you choose it from a number of things of the same kind. *A panel of judges is now selecting the finalists.* ◆ **selection** N-U *The selection of jurors had to be at random.* ⊡ ADJ You use **select** to describe things that are considered to be among the best of their kind. *...a meeting of a very select club.*

selection /sɪˈlekʃən/ **selections.** ⊡ N-C A **selection** of people or things is a set of them chosen from a larger group. *...this selection of popular songs.* ⊡ N-SING The **selection** of goods in a shop is the range of goods available. *There is also a wide selection of silk ties at £10.* ⊡ See also **select**.

selective /sɪˈlektɪv/. ⊡ ADJ BEFORE N A **selective** process applies only to a few things or people. *...selective education.* ◆ **selectively** ADV *They apply the rules selectively and in their own favour.* ⊡ ADJ When someone is **selective**, they choose things carefully, for example the things that they buy or do. *Sales still happen, but buyers are more selective.* ◆ **selectively** ADV *...people on small incomes who wanted to shop selectively.*

self /self/ **selves.** N-C Your **self** is your basic personality or nature. *You're looking more like your usual self.*

self-ˈconfident. ADJ Someone who is **self-confident** behaves confidently because they feel sure of their abilities or value. ◆ **self-confidence** N-U *I've developed a lot of self-confidence.*

self-ˈconscious. ADJ Someone who is **self-conscious** is easily embarrassed and nervous about the way they look or appear. *I felt a bit self-conscious in my swimming costume.*

self-conˈtained. ⊡ ADJ You can describe someone as **self-contained** when they do not need help or resources from other people. *She's very self-contained.* ⊡ ADJ A **self-contained** flat has all its own facilities including a kitchen and bathroom.

self-conˈtrol. N-U Your **self-control** is your ability to control your feelings and appear calm. *I began to wish I'd shown more self-control.*

self-deˈfence. N-U **Self-defence** is the use of force to protect yourself against someone who is attacking you. *He acted in self-defence.*

self-determiˈnation. N-U **Self-determination** is the right of a country to be independent, instead of being controlled by a foreign country, and to choose its own form of government.

self-emˈployed. ADJ & N-PL **Self-employed** people or **the self-employed** are people who organize their own work and taxes and are paid by people for a service they provide, rather than being paid a regular salary by a company. *...a self-employed builder.*

self-esˈteem. N-U Your **self-esteem** is how you feel about yourself and whether you have a good opinion of yourself. *It was so humiliating, a terrible blow to my self-esteem.*

self-ˈevident. ADJ A fact or situation that is **self-evident** is so obvious that there is no need for proof or explanation. *It's self-evident that this man's not worth marrying.*

self-ˈhelp. N-U **Self-help** consists of people providing support and help for each other in an informal way, rather than relying on official organizations. *...a self-help group for parents with over-weight children.*

self-ˈimage. N-C Your **self-image** is your opinion of yourself. *You must strive constantly to improve your self-image.*

self-imˈposed. ADJ A **self-imposed** situation, restriction, or task is one that you have created or accepted for yourself. *All my problems were self-imposed. ...eleven years of self-imposed exile.*

self-inˈdulgent. ADJ If you are **self-indulgent**, you allow yourself to have things that you enjoy but do not need. *To buy flowers for myself seems wildly self-indulgent.* ◆ **self-indulgence, self-indulgences** N-VAR *Those days of carefree self-indulgence are over.*

self-ˈinterest. N-U If you accuse someone of **self-interest**, you disapprove of them because they always want to do what is best for themselves rather than for anyone else. *Their current protests are motivated purely by self-interest.*

selfish /ˈselfɪʃ/. ADJ If you say that someone is **selfish**, you disapprove of them because they care only about themselves, and not about other people. *...the selfish interests of a few people.* ◆ **selfishly** ADV *39% of women complain that their partners act selfishly.* ◆ **selfishness** N-U *...a world where everyone leads lives of utter selfishness.*

selfless /ˈselfləs/. ADJ If you say that someone is **selfless**, you approve of them because they care about other people more than themselves. *Her generosity to me was entirely selfless.*

self-ˈpity. N-U **Self-pity** is a feeling of unhappiness and depression that you have about your problems, especially when this is unnecessary or greatly exaggerated. *I was unable to shake off my self-pity.*

self-reˈspect. N-U **Self-respect** is a feeling of confidence and pride in your own ability and worth. *I'd lost all my self-respect.*

self-ˈrighteous. ADJ If you describe someone as **self-righteous**, you disapprove of them because they are convinced that they are morally right and that other people are wrong. *...self-righteous reformers.* ◆ **self-righteousness** N-U *...Heather's voice, resonant with self-righteousness.*

self-'styled. ADJ BEFORE N If you describe someone as a **self-styled** leader or expert, you disapprove of them because they claim to be a leader or expert but they do not have the right to call themselves this. *Two of these arrested are said to be self-styled area commanders.*

self-suf'ficient. ADJ If a country or group is **self-sufficient**, it is able to produce or make everything that it needs. *Rural areas tend to be more self-sufficient.* ♦**self-sufficiency** N-U ...*Japan's self-sufficiency in rice.*

sell /sel/ **sells, selling, sold.** [1] VERB If you **sell** something that you own, you let someone have it in return for money. *The directors sold the business for £14.8 million.* [2] VERB If a shop **sells** a product, people can buy it from that shop. *We sell cosmetics.* [3] VERB If something **sells** for a particular price, or if it **sells** at that price, that is what it costs. [4] VERB If something **sells**, it is bought in fairly large quantities. *The products will sell well in the run-up to Christmas.*

▶ **sell out.** [1] PHR-VERB If a shop **sells out** of something, it sells all its stocks of it. [2] PHR-VERB If a performance of a play, film, or other entertainment **is sold out**, all the tickets have been sold. [3] PHR-VERB If you accuse someone of **selling out**, you disapprove of the fact that they do something which used to be against their principles; INFORMAL. *They felt I had sold out to the liberals.*

seller /'selə/ **sellers.** [1] N-C A **seller** is a person or business that sells something. ...*Kraft, the largest seller of cheese in the United States.* [2] N-C If you describe a product as, for example, a big **seller**, you mean that large numbers of it are being sold. ● See also **best-seller.**

'**sell-off, sell-offs.** N-C The **sell-off** of something, for example an industry that is owned by the state, is the act of selling it.

'**sell-out, sell-outs.** [1] N-C If a play, sports event, or other entertainment is a **sell-out**, all the tickets for it are sold. [2] N-C If you describe someone's behaviour as a **sell-out**, you disapprove of them doing something which used to be against their principles. *He denounced the summit agreement as a sell-out.*

selves /selvz/. **Selves** is the plural of **self.**

semblance /'sembləns/. N-SING If there is a **semblance** of a particular condition or quality, it appears to exist, though in fact it may not; FORMAL. *A semblance of normality has been restored.*

semen /'si:men/. N-U **Semen** is the liquid containing sperm that is produced by the male sex organs.

,**semi-'colon, semi-colons.** N-C A **semi-colon** is the punctuation mark (;).

,**semi-de'tached.** ADJ A **semi-detached** house is a house that is joined to another house on one side by a shared wall.

'**semi-final, semi-finals.** N-C A **semi-final** is one of the two matches or races in a competition that are held to decide who will compete in the final.

seminal /'semɪnl/. ADJ **Seminal** is used to describe things such as books or events that have a great influence in a particular field. *He wrote a seminal book on the subject.*

seminar /'semɪnɑː/ **seminars.** N-C A **seminar** is a class at a university in which the teacher and a small group of students discuss a topic. ...*a weekly seminar.*

semitic /sɪ'mɪtɪk/. [1] ADJ **Semitic** is sometimes used to mean Jewish. [2] ADJ **Semitic** is used to describe a group of languages that includes Arabic and Hebrew, or the people who speak these languages.

Senate /'senɪt/. N-PROPER The **Senate** is the smaller and more important of the two councils in the government of some countries, such as the United States of America. **Senate** can take the singular or plural form of the verb. ● See note at **government.**

senator /'senɪtə/ **senators.** N-C A **senator** is a member of a law-making Senate. ● See note at **government.**

send /send/ **sends, sending, sent.** [1] VERB When you **send** someone something, you arrange for them to receive it, for example by post. *Myra sent me a note thanking me for dinner... I sent a copy to the minister for transport... He could work and send money back to his mother.* ♦**sender, senders** N-C *£200 will go to the sender of the first correct answer.* [2] VERB If you **send** someone somewhere, you arrange for them to go there or stay there. *Tom came up to see her, but she sent him away... The government sent troops to the region... I was sent for blood tests.* [3] VERB If you **send** a signal or message, you cause it to go to a place by means of radio waves. *The space probe Voyager sent back pictures of Neptune.* [4] VERB If something **sends** things or people in a particular direction, it causes them to move in that direction. *The explosion sent shrapnel flying through the sides of cars.* [5] VERB If something **sends** someone or something into a particular state, it causes them to be in that state. *Famine sent the country plunging into anarchy.*

▶ **send for.** [1] PHR-VERB If you **send for** someone, you send them a message asking them to come and see you. *I've sent for the doctor.* [2] PHR-VERB If you **send for** something, or if you **send off for** it, you write and ask for it to be sent to you.

▶ **send off.** [1] PHR-VERB If you **send off** a letter or parcel, you send it somewhere by post. [2] PHR-VERB If a footballer **is sent off**, the referee makes him or her leave the field during a game, as a punishment for seriously breaking the rules.

▶ **send off for.** See **send for** 2.

▶ **send out.** [1] PHR-VERB If you **send out** things such as leaflets or bills, you send them to a large number of people at the same time. *She had sent out well over four hundred invitations.* [2] PHR-VERB To **send out** a signal, sound, light, or heat means to produce it.

▶ **send out for.** PHR-VERB If you **send out for** food, you phone and ask for it to be delivered to you. *Let's send out for a pizza.*

senile /'si:naɪl/. ADJ If old people become **senile**, they become confused and are unable to look after themselves. ♦**senility** /sɪ'nɪlɪti/ N-U *Alzheimer's disease causes premature senility.*

senior /'si:njə/ **seniors.** [1] ADJ BEFORE N The **senior** people in an organization have the highest and most important jobs in it. ...*senior officials in the Israeli government.* [2] ADJ & N-C If someone is **senior** to you, or if they are your **senior**, they have a more important job or position than you. [3] N-SING **Senior** is used when indicating how much older one person is than another. *She became involved with a married man many years her senior.*

senior 'citizen /'si:njə 'sɪtɪzən/ **senior citizens.** N-C A **senior citizen** is a person who is old enough to receive an old-age pension.

sensation /sen'seɪʃən/ **sensations.** [1] N-VAR **Sensation** is the ability to feel things physically. A **sensation** is a particular physical feeling. *She had lost all sensation in her left leg. ...a tingling sensation.* [2] N-C A **sensation** is the general feeling caused by a particular experience. *It's a funny sensation to know someone's talking about you.* [3] N-C If a person or event is a **sensation**, they cause great excitement and interest. ...*the film that turned her into an overnight sensation.*

sensational /sen'seɪʃənəl/ [1] ADJ A **sensational** event or situation is so remarkable that it causes great excitement and interest. *The world champions suffered a sensational defeat.* ♦**sensationally** ADV *He sensationally announced that he is to quit.* [2] ADJ You can describe something as **sensational** when you think that it is extremely good. ♦**sensationally** ADV ...*sensationally good food.*

sense /sens/ **senses, sensing, sensed.** [1] N-C Your **senses** are the physical abilities of sight, smell, hearing, touch, and taste. ...*a keen sense of smell.* [2] VERB If you **sense** something, you become aware of it, although it is not very obvious. *She probably sensed that I wasn't telling her the whole story.* [3] N-SING If you have a **sense** of guilt or shame, for example, you feel guilty or ashamed. ...*the crushing sense of failure that redundancy often brings.* [4] N-U **Sense** is the ability to make good judgements and to behave sensibly. *They sometimes have the sense to seek help.* [5] N-C A **sense** of a word or expression is one of its possible meanings. [6] See also **common sense, sense of humour.**
PHRASES ● If something **makes sense**, or if you **make sense of** it, you understand it or find it sensible. *From an early age we try to make sense of the world... It makes sense to look after yourself.* ● If you say that someone **has come to** their **senses** or **has been brought to** their **senses**, you mean that they have stopped being foolish and are being sensible again.

senseless /'sensləs/ [1] ADJ A **senseless** action seems to have no meaning or purpose. ...*senseless violence.* [2] ADJ AFTER LINK-V If someone is **senseless**, they are unconscious. *I was beaten senseless.*

sense of 'humour. N-U Someone's **sense of humour** is the fact that they find certain things amusing. *We share the same sense of humour... He's got no sense of humour.*

sensibility /ˌsensɪ'bɪlɪti/ **sensibilities.** N-VAR Someone's **sensibility** is their ability to experience deep feelings; FORMAL.

sensible /'sensɪbəl/ ADJ A **sensible** person is able to make good decisions and judgements based on reason. *It might be sensible to get a solicitor.* ♦**sensibly** ADV *They have very sensibly adjusted their diet.*

> You do not use **sensible** to describe someone whose feelings or emotions are strongly affected by their experiences. The word you need is **sensitive**. ...*a highly sensitive artist.*

sensitive /'sensɪtɪv/ [1] ADJ If you are **sensitive** to other people's problems and feelings, you understand and are aware of them. *He was always so sensitive and caring.* ♦**sensitively** ADV *The abuse of women needs to be treated seriously and sensitively.* ♦**sensitivity** /ˌsensɪ'tɪvɪti/ N-U ...*sensitivity for each other's feelings.* [2] ADJ If you are **sensitive** about something, it worries or upsets you. *Young people are very sensitive about their appearance.* ♦**sensitivity, sensitivities** N-VAR *Do not offend the sensitivities of religious groups.* [3] ADJ A **sensitive** subject or issue needs to be dealt with carefully because it is likely to cause disagreement or make people upset. *Employment is a very sensitive issue.* [4] ADJ Something that is **sensitive** to a physical force or substance can be affected by it. ...*a chemical which is sensitive to light.* ♦**sensitivity** N-U ...*skin lacking all sensitivity to touch.* [5] ADJ A **sensitive** piece of scientific equipment is capable of measuring or recording very small changes. ...*an extremely sensitive microscope.*

sensor /'sensə/ **sensors.** N-C A **sensor** is an instrument which reacts to certain physical conditions such as heat or light.

sensory /'sensəri/ ADJ BEFORE N **Sensory** means relating to the physical senses. ...*sensory awareness.*

sensual /'sensjuəl/ [1] ADJ A **sensual** person has a great liking for physical pleasures, especially sexual pleasures. ♦**sensuality** /ˌsensju'ælɪti/ N-U *Her blonde curls gave her sensuality and youth.* [2] ADJ Something that is **sensual** gives pleasure to your physical senses rather than to your mind. ...*sensual dance rhythms.* ♦**sensuality** N-U *These perfumes have warmth and sensuality.*

sensuous /'sensjuəs/ [1] ADJ **Sensuous** things give pleasure to the mind or body through the senses. ...*sensuous, atmospheric camerawork.* ♦**sensuously** ADV ...*sensuously shaped opaque glass vases.* [2] ADJ **Sensuous** means showing or suggesting a great liking for sexual pleasure. ♦**sensuously** ADV ...*a woman with a sensuously curved torso.*

sent /sent/ **Sent** is the past tense and past participle of **send.**

sentence /'sentəns/ **sentences, sentencing, sentenced.** [1] N-C A **sentence** is a group of words which, when they are written down, begin with a capital letter and end with a full stop, question mark, or exclamation mark. Most sentences contain a subject and a verb. [2] N-VAR In a law court, a **sentence** is the punishment that a person receives after they have been found guilty of a crime. *He had served a* *prison sentence for bank robbery.* [3] VERB & PHRASE When judges **sentence** someone, or when they **pass sentence** on someone, they state in court what the person's punishment will be. *A military court sentenced him to death.*

sentiment /'sentɪmənt/ **sentiments.** [1] N-VAR A **sentiment** is an attitude, feeling, or opinion. *...nationalist sentiments.* [2] N-U **Sentiment** is an emotion such as tenderness, romance, or sadness, which influences a person's behaviour. *Laura kept the letter out of sentiment.*

sentimental /ˌsentɪ'mentəl/. [1] ADJ A **sentimental** person or thing feels or makes you feel emotions such as tenderness, romance, or sadness, sometimes in a way that is exaggerated or foolish. *...sentimental love songs... I'm trying not to be sentimental about the past.* ◆**sentimentality** N-U *In this book there is no sentimentality.* ◆**sentimentally** ADV *We look back sentimentally to a 'golden era'.* [2] ADJ **Sentimental** means relating to a person's emotions. *...objects of sentimental value.*

sentry /'sentri/ **sentries.** N-C A **sentry** is a soldier who guards a camp or a building.

separate, separates, separating, separated. [1] ADJ /'sepərət/ If one thing is **separate** from another, the two things are apart and are not connected. *I've always kept my private and professional life separate... The word 'quarter' has two completely separate meanings.* ◆**separately** ADV *Each case is dealt with separately.* [2] PHRASE When two or more people who have been together for some time **go their separate ways,** they go to different places or end their relationship. [3] VERB /'sepəreɪt/ If you **separate** people or things that are together, or if they **separate,** they move apart. *Fluff the rice with a fork to separate the grains... They separated. Stephen returned to the square.* ◆**separation, separations** N-VAR *Mrs Holland is trying to cope with separation from her family.* [4] VERB & PHR-VERB If you **separate** one idea or fact from another, or if you **separate** it **out,** you consider them individually and see or show that they are distinct and different things. *It is difficult to separate the two aims... It is virtually impossible to separate out biological from early social influences.* ◆**separation** N-VAR *...the separation of church and state.* [5] VERB A quality or factor that **separates** one thing from another is the reason why the two things are different from each other. *What separates man from machine is the ability to think.* [6] VERB If an object, distance, or period of time **separates** two people or things, it exists between them. *...the white-railed fence that separated the yard from the paddock... Just four miles separate the two communities.* [7] VERB & PHR-VERB If you **separate** a group of people or things, or if you **separate** them **out,** you divide them into smaller groups or elements. *The police had separated the men into three groups... If prepared many hours ahead, the mixture may separate out.* ◆**separation** N-VAR *...the Northern League, which advocates the separation of Italy into three republics.* [8] VERB If a couple who are married or living together **separate,** they decide to live apart.

◆**separated** ADJ AFTER LINK-V *Her parents are separated.* ◆**separation** N-VAR *They agreed to a trial separation.* [9] N-PL /'sepərəts/ **Separates** are clothes such as skirts, trousers, and shirts which cover just the top or bottom half of your body.

▶ **separate out.** See **separate** 4, 7.

separatist /'sepərətɪst/ **separatists.** N-C Separatists are people of an ethnic or cultural group within a country who want to establish their own separate government. ◆**separatism** N-U *...the issue of Sikh separatism.*

September /sep'tembə/. N-U **September** is the ninth month of the year.

sequel /'siːkwəl/ **sequels.** [1] N-C The **sequel** to a book or film is another book or film which continues the story. [2] N-C The **sequel** to an event is something that happened after it or because of it. *The clash was a sequel to yesterday's nationwide strike.*

sequence /'siːkwəns/ **sequences.** [1] N-C A **sequence** of things is a number of them that come one after another in a particular order. *...the sequence of events which led to the murder.* [2] N-C A particular **sequence** is a particular order in which things happen or are arranged. *...the colour sequence yellow, orange, purple, blue, green.* [3] N-C A film **sequence** is a short part of a film. *...the film's opening sequence.*

sequin /'siːkwɪn/ **sequins.** N-C **Sequins** are small, shiny discs that are sewn on clothes to decorate them.

serene /sɪ'riːn/. ADJ **Serene** means calm and quiet. ◆**serenely** ADV *She carried on serenely sipping her gin and tonic.* ◆**serenity** /sɪ'renti/ N-U *...the serenity of the mountains.*

sergeant /'sɑːdʒənt/ **sergeants.** [1] N-VOC & N-TITLE A **sergeant** is an officer of middle rank in the army or air force. [2] N-VOC & N-TITLE A **sergeant** is an officer in the police force.

'sergeant major, sergeant majors. N-VOC & N-TITLE A **sergeant major** is an army officer of high rank.

serial /'sɪəriəl/ **serials.** [1] N-C A **serial** is a story which is broadcast or published in a number of parts over a period of time. *...a popular radio serial.* [2] ADJ BEFORE N **Serial** killings or attacks are a series of killings or attacks committed by the same person. This person is known as a **serial** killer or attacker. *...a serial rapist.*

series /'sɪəriz/. [1] N-C A **series** is both the singular and plural form of the word. [1] N-C A **series** of things or events is a number of them that come one after the other. *...a series of explosions.* [2] N-C A radio or television **series** is a set of related programmes with the same title. *...a new drama series called Under The Hammer.*

serious /'sɪəriəs/. [1] ADJ **Serious** problems or situations are very bad and cause people to be worried or afraid. *Crime is an increasingly serious problem in Russian society. ...a serious accident.* ◆**seriously** ADV *His wife was seriously injured in the attack.* ◆**seriousness** N-U *...the seriousness of the crisis.* [2] ADJ **Serious** matters are important and deserve careful thought. *This latest incident has raised serious questions about the security precautions taken for such* *events... It was a question which deserved serious consideration.* ♦**seriously** ADV *The management will have to think seriously about their positions.* [3] ADJ If you are **serious** about something, you are sincere about it, and not joking. *You really are serious about this, aren't you?* ♦**seriously** ADV *I seriously hope it will never come to that.* ♦**seriousness** N-U *In all seriousness, there is nothing else I can do.* [4] ADJ **Serious** people are thoughtful, quiet, and do not laugh very often. ♦**seriously** ADV *They spoke to me very seriously but politely.*

seriously /ˈsɪəriəsli/. [1] ADV You say **seriously** to indicate that you really mean what you say, or to ask someone else if they really mean what they have said. *Seriously, I shall miss you... 'OK, eat it.'—'Seriously?'* [2] PHRASE If you **take** someone or something **seriously**, you believe that they are important and deserve attention. *The phrase was not meant to be taken seriously.*

sermon /ˈsɜːmən/ **sermons.** N-C A **sermon** is a talk on a religious or moral subject given during a church service.

serpent /ˈsɜːpənt/ **serpents.** N-C A **serpent** is a snake; LITERARY.

serum /ˈsɪərəm/ **serums.** N-VAR A **serum** is a liquid that is injected into someone's blood to protect them against a poison or disease.

servant /ˈsɜːvənt/ **servants.** N-C A **servant** is someone who is employed to work in another person's house, for example to cook or clean.
● See also **civil servant.**

serve /sɜːv/ **serves, serving, served.** [1] VERB If you **serve** your country, an organization, or a person, you do useful work for them. *They served the US government loyally for 30 years.* [2] VERB If something **serves** as a particular thing or **serves** a particular purpose, that is its use or function. *The small building served as a school... This serves to make attackers think twice before attacking... I really do not think that an inquiry would serve any useful purpose.* [3] VERB If something **serves** people or an area, it provides them with something that they need. *A typical NHS hospital serves about 250,000 people. ...small businesses which serve the community.* [4] VERB If you **serve** people or if you **serve** food and drink, you give people food and drink. *Our waiter served us quickly... We used to serve dinner to the airmen.* [5] VERB Someone who **serves** customers in a shop or a bar helps them and provides them with what they want to buy. *They wouldn't serve me in any pubs because I looked too young.* [6] VERB If you **serve** a prison sentence, you spend a period of time in jail. *He is serving a five-year sentence for robbery.* [7] VERB & N-C When you **serve** in a game like tennis, you start play by hitting the ball. A **serve** is the act of doing this. *He threw the ball up to serve... His second serve clipped the net.* [8] PHRASE If you say it **serves** someone **right** when something unpleasant happens to them, you mean that it is their own fault and you have no sympathy for them. *Serves her right for being so stubborn.* [9] See also **serving.**

▶ **serve up.** PHR-VERB If you **serve up** food, you give it to people. *When the dish was finally finished, he served it up on delicate white plates.*

server /ˈsɜːvə/ **servers.** N-C A **server** is part of a computer network which does a particular task, for example storing or processing information, for all or part of the network.

service /ˈsɜːvɪs/ **services, servicing, serviced.** [1] N-C A **service** is an organization or system that provides something for the public. *...the social services. ...the postal service. ...service industries, such as banks and airlines.* [2] N-C A **service** is a job that an organization or business can do for you. *...a one hour dry-cleaning service.* [3] N-C The **services** are the army, navy, and air force. [4] N-U **Service** is the state or activity of working for a particular person or organization. *Pat is leaving the company after 12 years service.* [5] N-U The level or standard of **service** provided by an organization or company is the amount or quality of the work it can do for you. *How do you think we could improve customer service?.* [6] N-U When you receive **service** in a restaurant, hotel, or shop, an employee asks you what you want or gives you what you have ordered. *Restaurants usually charge between 10 and 12.5 per cent for service.* [7] PHRASE If a machine or vehicle is **in service**, it is being used or is able to be used. If it is **out of service**, it cannot be used. [8] VERB & N-C If you **service** a machine or vehicle, or if it has a **service**, it is examined, adjusted, and cleaned so that it will keep working efficiently and safely. *Make sure that all gas fires are serviced annually... The car is due for a service.* [9] N-C A **service** is a religious ceremony. *...the chapel where the wedding service was to have been held.* [10] N-C **services** is a place on a motorway where there is a petrol station, restaurant, shop, and toilets. The plural is also **services**; BRITISH. *...a motorway services.* [11] See also **Civil Service.**

serviceman /ˈsɜːvɪsmən/ **servicemen.** N-C A **serviceman** is a man who is in the army, navy, or air force.

serving /ˈsɜːvɪŋ/ **servings.** N-C A **serving** is an amount of food given to one person at a meal. *Each serving contains 240 calories.*

session /ˈseʃən/ **sessions.** [1] N-C A **session** is a meeting or series of meetings of a court, parliament, or other official group. *...an emergency session of the UN Security Council. ...the start of the next parliamentary session in November.* [2] N-C A **session** of a particular activity is a period of that activity. *...a photo session.*

set 1 noun uses

set /set/ **sets.** [1] N-C A **set** of things is a number of things that are thought of as a group. *They had the spare set of keys. ...a chess set.* [2] N-C In tennis, a **set** is one of the groups of six or more games that form part of a match. [3] N-C The **set** for a play or film scene is the scenery and furniture that is used on the stage or in the studio. *...stars who behave badly on set.* [4] N-C A **television set** is a television.

set 2 verb and adjective uses

set /set/ **sets, setting, set.** [1] VERB If you **set** something somewhere, you put it there, especially in a careful or deliberate way. *He set the glass on the counter.* [2] ADJ AFTER LINK-V If something is **set** in a particular place or position, it is in that place or position. *The castle is set in 25 acres of beautiful grounds.* [3] ADJ AFTER LINK-V If something is **set** into a surface, it is fixed there and does not stick out. *...a gate set in a high wall.* [4] VERB You can use **set** to say that a person or thing causes something to be in a particular condition or situation. For example, if something **sets** someone free, it causes them to be free. *A phrase from the conference floor set my mind wandering... Dozens of people have been injured and many vehicles on fire.* [5] VERB When you **set** a clock or control, you adjust it to a particular point or level. *Set the volume as high as possible.* [6] VERB If you **set** a date, price, goal, or level, you decide what it will be. *He has not yet set a date for the wedding.* [7] VERB To **set** an examination or a question paper means to decide what questions will be asked in it. [8] VERB If you **set** something such as a record, an example, or a precedent, you create it for people to copy or to try to achieve. *If you are smoking in front of the children then you are setting them a bad example.* [9] VERB If someone **sets** you a task or a target, you have to do that task or achieve that target. *The secret to happiness is to keep setting yourself new challenges.* [10] ADJ AFTER LINK-V If a play, film, or story is **set** in a particular place or period of time, the events in it take place in that place or period. [11] PHRASE Something that **sets the scene for** a particular event or **sets the stage for** a particular event, creates the conditions in which the event is likely to happen. *That assassination set the stage for the 1986 revolution.* [12] ADJ You use **set** to describe something which is fixed and cannot be changed. *...a set price. ...a set menu.* [13] ADJ AFTER LINK-V If you are **set** to do something, you are ready to do it or are likely to do it. If something is **set** to happen, it is about to happen or likely to happen. *Roberto Baggio is set to become one of the greatest players of all-time.* [14] ADJ AFTER LINK-V If you are **set on** something, you are strongly determined to do or have it. *She was set on going to an all-girls school.* [15] VERB When something such as jelly, glue, or cement **sets**, it becomes firm or hard. [16] VERB When the sun **sets**, it goes below the horizon. [17] See also **setting**. ● to **set eyes on** something: see **eye**. ● to **set fire to** something: see **fire**. ● to **set foot** somewhere: see **foot**. ● to **set sail**: see **sail**.

▶ **set apart.** PHR-VERB If a characteristic **sets** you **apart** from other people, it makes you different from them in a noticeable way. *Even at that stage his natural ability set him apart.*

▶ **set aside.** [1] PHR-VERB If you **set** something **aside** for a special use or purpose, you keep it available for that use or purpose. *Try to set aside time each day to relax.* [2] PHR-VERB If you **set aside** a belief, principle, or feeling, you decide that you will not be influenced by it. *He urged the participants to set aside minor differences.*

▶ **set back.** [1] PHR-VERB If something **sets** you **back** or **sets back** a project or scheme, it causes a delay. [2] PHR-VERB If something **sets** you **back** a certain amount of money, it costs you that much money. [3] See also **setback**.

▶ **set down.** PHR-VERB If a committee or organization **sets down** rules or guidelines for doing something, they decide what they should be and officially record them. *...rules set down by the Personal Investment Authority.*

▶ **set in.** PHR-VERB If something unpleasant **sets in**, it begins and seems likely to continue or develop. *Panic was setting in.*

▶ **set off.** [1] PHR-VERB When you **set off**, you start a journey. *He set off for the station.* [2] PHR-VERB If something **sets off** something such as an alarm or a bomb, it activates it so that the alarm rings or the bomb explodes.

▶ **set out.** [1] PHR-VERB When you **set out**, you start a journey. *I set out for the cottage.* [2] PHR-VERB If you **set out** to do something, you start trying to do it. *We set out to find the truth behind the mystery.* [3] PHR-VERB If you **set** things **out**, you arrange or display them. *She set out the cups and saucers.* [4] PHR-VERB If you **set out** facts or opinions, you explain them in writing or speech in a clear, organized way. *The agreement sets out how the two countries will co-operate.*

▶ **set up.** [1] PHR-VERB If you **set** something **up**, you make the preparations that are necessary for it to start. *She wants to set up children's ski schools.* ◆**setting up** N-U *The government announced the setting up of a special fund.* [2] PHR-VERB If you **set up** a temporary structure, you place it or build it somewhere. *Brian set up a large, white tent on the lawn.* [3] PHR-VERB If you **set up** somewhere or **set** yourself **up** somewhere, you establish yourself in a new business or area. *The Hong Kong-based bank is thinking of setting up in Canada.* [4] See also **set-up.**

setback /'setbæk/ **setbacks.** N-C A **setback** is an event that delays your progress or reverses some of the progress that you have made. *He has suffered a serious setback in his political career.*

settee /se'tiː/ **settees.** N-C A **settee** is a long comfortable seat with a back and arms, for two or three people.

setting /'setɪŋ/ **settings.** [1] N-C The **setting** for something is the particular place or the type of surroundings in which it is located or where it happens. *The house is in a lovely setting in the Malvern hills.* [2] N-C A **setting** is one of the positions to which the controls of a device such as a cooker or heater can be adjusted. *You can boil the fish fillets on a high setting.*

settle /'setəl/ **settles, settling, settled.** [1] VERB If two people **settle** an argument or problem, or if someone or something **settles** it, they solve it by making a decision about who is right or about what to do. *Both sides are looking for ways to settle their differences.* [2] VERB If you **settle** a bill or debt, you pay the amount that you owe. [3] VERB If something **is settled**, it has all been decided and arranged. *That's settled then. We'll exchange addresses tonight.* [4] VERB When people **settle** in a place, they start living there permanently. *He visited Paris and eventually settled there.* [5] VERB If you **settle** yourself somewhere or **settle** somewhere, you sit down or make yourself comfortable. *He settled into a chair.* [6] VERB If something **set-**

tles, it sinks slowly and becomes still. *A black dust settled on the walls.* [7] **when the dust settles**: see **dust**. • **to settle a score**: see **score**.

▶ **settle down.** [1] PHR-VERB When someone **settles down**, they start living a quiet life in one place, especially when they get married or buy a house. [2] PHR-VERB If a situation or a person that has been going through a lot of problems or changes **settles down**, they become calm. *We saw the therapist four times, and the children have now settled down.* [3] PHR-VERB If you **settle down** to do something, or if you **settle down** to something, you prepare to do it and concentrate on it. *Daniel settled down to work.*

▶ **settle for.** PHR-VERB If you **settle for** something, you choose or accept it, especially when it is not what you really want but there is nothing else available. *England will have to settle for third or fourth place.*

▶ **settle into.** PHR-VERB If you **settle into** a new place, job, or routine, or **settle in**, you become used to it. *I'm sure they will settle in very well.*

▶ **settle on.** PHR-VERB If you **settle on** a particular thing, you choose it after considering other possible choices.

▶ **settle up.** PHR-VERB When you **settle up**, you pay a bill or a debt.

settled /'setəld/. [1] ADJ A **settled** situation or system stays the same all the time. *...a period of settled weather.* [2] ADJ AFTER LINK-V If you feel **settled**, you have been living or working in a place long enough to feel comfortable.

settlement /'setəlmənt/ **settlements.** [1] N-C A **settlement** is an official agreement between two sides who were involved in a conflict. *...a peace settlement. ...pay settlements.* [2] N-C A **settlement** is a place where people have come to live and have built homes. *...the oldest settlement in New Brunswick.*

settler /'setələ/ **settlers.** N-C **Settlers** are people who go to live in a new country. *...the early settlers in North America.*

'set-up, set-ups. N-C A particular **set-up** is a particular system or way of organizing something; INFORMAL. *It was a bit of a weird family set-up.*

seven /'sevən/ **sevens.** NUM **Seven** is the number 7.

seventeen /,sevən'ti:n/. NUM **Seventeen** is the number 17.

seventeenth /,sevən'ti:nθ/. ORD The **seventeenth** item in a series is the one that you count as number seventeen.

seventh /'sevənθ/ **sevenths.** [1] ORD The **seventh** item in a series is the one that you count as number seven. [2] N-C A **seventh** is one of seven equal parts of something.

seventieth /'sevəntiəθ/. ORD The **seventieth** item in a series is the one that you count as number seventy.

seventy /'sevənti/ **seventies.** NUM **Seventy** is the number 70. For examples of how numbers such as seventy and eighty are used see **eighty**.

sever /'sevə/ **severs, severing, severed.** [1] VERB To **sever** something means to cut right through it or cut it off. *He was hit by a train and his left arm was almost severed. ...a severed fuel line.* [2] VERB If you **sever** a relationship or connection with someone, you end it suddenly

and completely. *She severed her ties with England.*

several /'sevrəl/. QUANT **Several** is used to refer to a number of people or things that is not large but is greater than two. *Several hundred students gathered on campus... Several of my friends are doctors.*

severe /sɪ'vɪə/ **severer, severest.** [1] ADJ You use **severe** to emphasize how bad or serious something is. *This bomb would have caused severe damage. ...a severe shortage of drinking water.* ♦ **severely** ADV *He was severely injured in a fire.* ♦ **severity** /sɪ'verɪti/ N-U *Several drugs are used to lessen the severity of the symptoms.* [2] ADJ **Severe** punishments or actions are very extreme. *My mother launched into a severe reprimand.* ♦ **severely** ADV *...a campaign to try to change the law to punish dangerous drivers more severely.* ♦ **severity** N-U *The Bishop said he was sickened by the severity of the sentence.*

sew /səʊ/ **sews, sewing, sewed, sewn.** VERB When you **sew**, you use a needle and thread to make or mend something such as clothes. *Anyone can sew on a button... She taught her daughter to sew.* ♦ **sewing** N-U *I was very good at sewing.*

sewage /'su:ɪdʒ/. N-U **Sewage** is waste matter such as faeces or dirty water from homes and factories, which flows away through sewers.

sewer /'su:ə/ **sewers.** N-C A **sewer** is a large underground channel that carries waste matter and rain water away.

sewing /'səʊɪŋ/. N-U **Sewing** is clothes or other things that are being sewn. *She took out her sewing.*

sewn /səʊn/. **Sewn** is the past participle of **sew**.

sex /seks/ **sexes.** [1] N-C The **sexes** are the two groups, male and female, into which people and animals are divided. [2] N-C The **sex** of a person or animal is their characteristic of being either male or female. *We don't plan to find out the sex of the child before its birth. ...victims of sex discrimination.* [3] N-U **Sex** is the physical activity by which people can produce children. If two people **have sex**, they perform the physical act of sex.

sexist /'seksɪst/ **sexists.** ADJ & N-C If you describe someone as **sexist** or as a **sexist**, you mean that they show prejudice and discrimination against the members of one sex, usually women. *Old-fashioned sexist attitudes are still common.* ♦ **sexism** N-U *...their battle against sexism.*

sexual /'sekʃʊəl/. [1] ADJ **Sexual** feelings or activities are connected with the act of sex or with desire for sex. *This was the first sexual relationship I had.* ♦ **sexually** ADV *...sexually transmitted diseases.* [2] ADJ **Sexual** means relating to the differences between men and women. *...sexual discrimination.* [3] ADJ **Sexual** means relating to the biological process by which people and animals produce young. *...sexual maturity.* ♦ **sexually** ADV *...organisms which reproduce sexually.*

,sexual 'intercourse. N-U **Sexual intercourse** is the physical act of sex between two people; FORMAL.

sexuality /,sekʃʊ'ælɪti/. [1] N-U A person's **sexuality** is their sexual feelings. *...the growing dis-*

cussion of women's sexuality. [2] N-U You can refer to a person's **sexuality** when you are talking about whether they are heterosexual, homosexual, or bisexual.

sexy /ˈseksi/ **sexier, sexiest.** ADJ You can describe people and things as **sexy** if you think they are sexually exciting or sexually attractive.

sh /ʃ/. CONVENTION You can say **'Sh!'** to tell someone to be quiet. *Sh! I have only a moment to talk, and you must listen closely!*

shabby /ˈʃæbi/ **shabbier, shabbiest.** [1] ADJ **Shabby** things or places look old and in bad condition. [2] ADJ A **shabby** person is wearing old, worn clothes.

shack /ʃæk/ **shacks.** N-C A **shack** is a small hut built from bits of wood or metal.

shade /ʃeɪd/ **shades, shading, shaded.** [1] N-U **Shade** is a cool area of darkness where the sun does not reach. *These plants need some shade, humidity and fresh air.* [2] VERB If a place **is shaded** by something, that thing prevents light from falling on it. *Most plants prefer to be lightly shaded from direct sunlight. ...a shaded spot.* [3] N-U **Shade** is darkness or shadows as they are shown in a picture. *...Rembrandt's skilful use of light and shade.* [4] N-C The **shades** of a particular colour are its different forms. *The flowers were a lovely shade of pink.* [5] N-C The **shades** of something abstract are its many, slightly different forms. *...newspapers of every shade of opinion.* [6] N-C A **shade** is a decorative covering that is fitted round or over an electric light bulb. [7] N-C A **shade** is a piece of stiff cloth or heavy paper that you can pull down over a window in order to prevent sunlight from coming in.

shadow /ˈʃædəʊ/ **shadows, shadowing, shadowed.** [1] N-C A **shadow** is a dark shape on a surface that is made when something stands between a light and the surface. *An oak tree cast its shadow over a tiny round pool.* [2] N-U **Shadow** is darkness caused by light not reaching a place. *Most of the lake was in shadow.* [3] VERB If someone **shadows** you, they follow you very closely wherever you go. *I noticed a police car shadowing us.* [4] ADJ BEFORE N In Britain, the **Shadow** Cabinet consists of the leaders of the main opposition party.

shadowy /ˈʃædəʊi/. [1] ADJ A **shadowy** place is dark and full of shadows. [2] ADJ **Shadowy** activities or people are mysterious and secretive. *...the shadowy world of spies.*

shady /ˈʃeɪdi/. [1] ADJ A **shady** place is pleasant because it is sheltered from bright sunlight. [2] ADJ **Shady** activities or people seem to be dishonest or illegal. *John was a bit of a shady character.*

shaft /ʃɑːft, ʃæft/ **shafts.** [1] N-C A **shaft** is a long narrow passage made so that people or things can travel up and down it. *...a disused mine shaft.* [2] N-C A **shaft** in a machine is a rod that turns round and round to transfer movement in the machine. *...the drive shaft.* [3] N-C A **shaft** of light is a beam of light.

shaggy /ˈʃægi/. ADJ **Shaggy** hair or fur is long and untidy. *...a dark shaggy beard.*

shake /ʃeɪk/ **shakes, shaking, shook, shaken** /ˈʃeɪkən/. [1] VERB & N-C If you **shake** someone or something, or if you give them a **shake**, you move them quickly backwards and forwards or up and down. *Shake the rugs well... As soon as he got inside, the dog shook himself... She gave me a little shake.* [2] VERB If something **shakes**, or if a force **shakes** it, it moves from side to side or up and down with quick small movements. *...an explosion that shook buildings several kilometers away.* [3] VERB If an event or a piece of news **shakes** you, it makes you feel shocked or upset. *Well it shook me quite a bit, but I was feeling emotional.*

PHRASES • If you **shake** someone's **hand**, you hold their right hand in your own when you are meeting them, saying goodbye, congratulating them, or showing friendship. • If you **shake** your **head**, you move it from side to side in order to say 'no'.

▶ **shake off.** PHR-VERB If you **shake off** someone or something that you do not want, you manage to get away from them or get rid of them.

'shake-up (or **shakeup**) **shake-ups.** N-C A **shake-up** is a major set of changes in an organization or system. *...a radical shake-up of the welfare state.*

shaky /ˈʃeɪki/ **shakier, shakiest.** [1] ADJ If your body or your voice is **shaky**, you cannot control it properly and it trembles, for example because you are ill or nervous. *Even small operations can leave you feeling a bit shaky.* ◆**shakily** ADV *'I'm okay,' she said shakily.* [2] ADJ If you describe a situation as **shaky**, you mean that it is weak or unstable, and seems unlikely to end soon. *The Prime Minister's political position is becoming increasingly shaky.*

shall /ʃəl, STRONG ʃæl/. **Shall** is a modal verb. It is used with the base form of a verb. [1] MODAL You use **shall** with 'I' and 'we' in questions in order to make offers or suggestions, or to ask for advice. *Shall I get the keys?... Let's have a nice little stroll, shall we?... What shall I do?* [2] MODAL You use **shall**, usually with 'I' and 'we', when you are referring to something that you intend to do, or when you are referring to something that you are sure will happen to you in the future. *We shall be landing in Paris in sixteen minutes... I shall miss him terribly.* [3] MODAL If you say that something **shall** happen, you are saying that it must happen, usually because of a rule or law; FORMAL. *The president shall hold office for five years.*

shallow /ˈʃæləʊ/ **shallower, shallowest,.** [1] ADJ A **shallow** hole, container, or layer of water measures only a short distance from the top to the bottom. *The water is quite shallow.* [2] ADJ If you describe a person, piece of work, or idea as **shallow**, you disapprove of them because they lack any serious or careful thought. [3] ADJ If your breathing is **shallow**, you take only a small amount of air into your lungs at each breath.

shallows /ˈʃæləʊz/. N-PL The **shallows** are the shallow part of an area of water.

sham /ʃæm/ **shams.** N-C If you describe something as a **sham**, you disapprove of it because it is not what it seems to be. *The government's promises were exposed as a hollow sham.*

shambles /ˈʃæmbəlz/. N-SING If a place, event, or situation is a **shambles**, everything is in disorder. *The ship's interior was an utter shambles.*

shame /ʃeɪm/ **shames, shaming, shamed.**
1 N-U **Shame** is an uncomfortable feeling that you have when you know that you have done something wrong or embarrassing, or when someone close to you has. *She felt a deep sense of shame... I was, to my shame, a coward.* **2** N-U If someone brings **shame** on you, they make other people lose their respect for you. *I don't want to bring shame on the family name.* **3** VERB If something **shames** you, it causes you to feel shame. *Her son's affair had humiliated and shamed her.* **4** VERB If you **shame** someone into doing something, you force them to do it by making them feel ashamed not to. *They shamed him into giving some money.* **5** N-SING If you say that something is **a shame**, you are expressing your regret about it and indicating that you wish it had happened differently. *What a shame the weather was so poor... It would seem a shame to waste this opportunity.*

shameful /ˈʃeɪmfʊl/. ADJ You can describe someone's actions or attitude as **shameful** when they act or think in a way that you find unacceptable, and for which you think they should feel ashamed. *...the most shameful episode in US naval history.* ◆**shamefully** ADV *They have been shamefully neglected.*

shameless /ˈʃeɪmləs/. ADJ If you describe someone or their behaviour as **shameless**, you mean that their behaviour is extremely bad and they ought to be ashamed of it. *...a shameless attempt to get votes under false pretenses.* ◆**shamelessly** ADV *He admitted to lying to women and manipulating them shamelessly.*

shampoo /ʃæmˈpuː/ **shampoos, shampooing, shampooed.** **1** N-VAR **Shampoo** is a liquid that you use for washing your hair. **2** VERB When you **shampoo** your hair, you wash it using shampoo.

shan't /ʃɑːnt, ʃænt/. **Shan't** is the usual spoken form of 'shall not'.

shape /ʃeɪp/ **shapes, shaping, shaped.**
1 N-VAR The **shape** of an object, a person, or an area is the form or pattern of its outline. *...a keyring in the shape of a fish... The room was square in shape.* **2** N-C A **shape** is something which has a definite form, for example a circle or triangle. *...a kidney shape.* **3** VERB If you **shape** an object, you cause it to have a particular shape. *Cut the dough in half and shape each half into a loaf.* **4** N-SING The **shape** of something such as a plan or organization is its structure and size. *...the future shape of Western Europe.* **5** VERB To **shape** a situation or an activity means to strongly influence the way it develops. *Like it or not, our families shape our lives and make us what we are.* **6** PHRASE If someone or something is **in good shape**, they are healthy and fit. If they are **out of shape**, they are unhealthy and unfit.
▸ **shape up.** PHR-VERB The way that someone or something **is shaping up** is the way that they are developing. *This is shaping up to be the closest governor's race in recent memory.*

shaped /ʃeɪpt/. ADJ AFTER LINK-V Something that is **shaped** in a particular way has the shape indicated. *...a helmet shaped like a wedge of cheese. ...large, heart-shaped leaves.*

share /ʃeə/ **shares, sharing, shared.** **1** VERB If you **share** something with another person, you both have it, use it, do it, or experience it. *The village tribe is friendly and they share their water supply with you... We share similar opinions about music. ...the huge house that he shared with his sisters... Two Americans will share this year's Nobel Prize for Medicine... Yes, I want to share my life with you.* **2** N-C If you have or do your **share** of something, you have or do the amount that is reasonable or fair. *Women must receive their fair share of training.* **3** N-C The **shares** of a company are the equal parts into which its ownership is divided. *People can buy shares in a company as an investment.*
▸ **share out.** PHR-VERB If you **share** something **out,** you give each person in a group an equal or fair part of it. *...a formula for sharing out power among the various clans.*

shareholder /ˈʃeəhəʊldə/ **shareholders.** N-C In British English, a **shareholder** is a person who owns shares in a company. The usual American word is **stockholder.**

shark /ʃɑːk/ **sharks.** N-C **Sharks** are very large fish with sharp teeth.

sharp /ʃɑːp/ **sharper, sharpest.** **1** ADJ A **sharp** point or edge is very small or thin and can cut through things very easily. *The other end of the twig is sharpened into a sharp point.* **2** ADJ & ADV A **sharp** bend or turn is one that changes direction suddenly. *...a fairly sharp bend that swept downhill to the left... Do not cross the bridge but turn sharp left.* ◆**sharply** ADV *Downstream the canyon bend sharply to the north.* **3** ADJ If you describe someone as **sharp**, you are praising them because they are quick to notice or understand things or to react to them. *He is very sharp, a quick thinker.* ◆**sharpness** N-U *I liked their enthusiasm and sharpness of mind.* **4** ADJ If someone says something in a **sharp** way, they say it suddenly and rather firmly or angrily. *His sharp reply clearly made an impact.* ◆**sharply** ADV *Environmentalists were sharply critical of the policy.* ◆**sharpness** N-U *Malone was surprised at the sharpness in his voice.* **5** ADJ A **sharp** change, movement, or feeling occurs suddenly, and is great in amount, force, or degree. *There's been a sharp rise in the rate of inflation. ...a sharp pain.* ◆**sharply** ADV *Theft from farms has risen sharply this year.* **6** ADJ A **sharp** difference, image, or sound is very easy to see, hear, or distinguish. *All the footmarks are quite sharp and clear.* ◆**sharply** ADV *Opinions on this are sharply divided.* ◆**sharpness** N-U *They were amazed at the sharpness of the first picture.* **7** ADJ A **sharp** taste or smell is rather strong or bitter, but is often also clear and fresh. ◆**sharpness** N-U *The pesto vinaigrette added a stimulating sharpness.* **8** ADV **Sharp** is used after stating a particular time to show that something happens at exactly that time. *She planned to unlock the store at 8.00 sharp.* **9** ADJ **Sharp** is used after a letter representing a musical note to show that the note should be played or sung half a tone higher than the note which otherwise corresponds to that letter. **Sharp** is often represented by the symbol ♯.

sharpen /'ʃɑːpən/ **sharpens, sharpening, sharpened.** [1] VERB If you **sharpen** an object, you make its edge very thin or you make its end pointed. [2] VERB If something **sharpens** your skills, senses, or understanding, it makes you better at noticing things, thinking, or doing something. *You can sharpen your skills with rehearsal.*

▶ **sharpen up.** PHR-VERB If you **sharpen** something **up**, or if it **sharpens up**, it becomes smarter or better than it was; INFORMAL. *The fashion designers have sharpened up their act in the last few years.*

shatter /'ʃætə/ **shatters, shattering, shattered.** [1] VERB If something **shatters**, or if someone or something **shatters** it, it breaks into a lot of small pieces. *The force of the explosion shattered the windows.* ◆**shattering** N-U *...the shattering of glass.* [2] VERB If something **shatters** your beliefs or hopes, it destroys them. [3] VERB If someone **is shattered** by an event, it shocks and upsets them. *...the tragedy which had shattered his life.* ◆**shattering** ADJ *Yesterday's decision was another shattering blow.*

shattered /'ʃætəd/. [1] ADJ If you are **shattered**, you are shocked and upset. *His death was so sudden. I am shattered.* [2] ADJ If you say that you are **shattered**, you mean you are extremely tired and have no energy left; BRITISH. *He was shattered and too tired to concentrate on schoolwork.*

shave /ʃeɪv/ **shaves, shaving, shaved.** [1] VERB & N-C To **shave**, or have a **shave**, means to cut hair from your face or body using a razor or shaver. *Many women shave their legs.* ◆**shaving** N-U *...a range of shaving products.* [2] VERB If you **shave off** part of a piece of wood or other material, you cut very thin pieces from it. *She was shaving thin slices off a courgette.*

shaver /'ʃeɪvə/ **shavers.** N-C A **shaver** is an electric device used for shaving hair from the face and body.

shaving /'ʃeɪvɪŋ/ **shavings.** N-C **Shavings** are small, very thin pieces or wood or other material which have been cut from a larger piece. *...metal shavings.*

shawl /ʃɔːl/ **shawls.** N-C A **shawl** is a large piece of woollen cloth worn over a woman's shoulders or head, or wrapped around a baby to keep it warm.

she /ʃi, STRONG ʃiː/. PRON You use **she** to refer to a woman, girl, or female animal. **She** is used as the subject of a verb. *She was seventeen.*

shear /ʃɪə/ **shears, shearing, sheared, shorn.** The past participle can be **sheared** or **shorn**. [1] VERB To **shear** a sheep means to clip all its wool off. ◆**shearing** N-U *...a display of sheep shearing.* [2] N-PL A pair of **shears** is a garden tool like a large pair of scissors.

sheath /ʃiːθ/ **sheaths.** N-C A **sheath** is a covering for the blade of a knife.

shed /ʃed/ **sheds, shedding, shed.** [1] N-C A **shed** is a small building used for storing things such as garden tools. [2] VERB When a tree **sheds** its leaves, its leaves fall off, usually in the

autumn. When an animal **sheds** hair or skin, some of its hair or skin drops off. [3] VERB To **shed** something means to get rid of it; JOURNALISM. *The firm is to shed 700 jobs.* [4] VERB If you **shed** tears, you cry. *They will shed a few tears at their daughter's wedding.* [5] VERB To **shed** blood means to kill people in a violent way. *Gunmen in Ulster shed the first blood of the new year.* [6] to **shed light on** something: see **light**.

she'd /ʃiːd, ʃɪd/. **She'd** is the usual spoken form of 'she had', especially when 'had' is an auxiliary verb. **She'd** is also a spoken form of 'she would'. *She'd found a job... She'd do anything for a bit of money.*

sheen /ʃiːn/. N-SING If something has a **sheen**, it has a smooth and gentle brightness.

sheep /ʃiːp/. N-C A **sheep** is a farm animal with a thick woolly coat. **Sheep** is both the singular and plural form.

sheepish /'ʃiːpɪʃ/. ADJ If you look **sheepish**, you look slightly embarrassed because you feel foolish. ◆**sheepishly** ADV *He grinned sheepishly.*

sheer /ʃɪə/. [1] ADJ BEFORE N You can use **sheer** to emphasize that a state or situation is complete and does not involve anything else. *...acts of sheer desperation.* [2] ADJ BEFORE N A **sheer** cliff or drop is extremely steep or completely vertical. [3] ADJ BEFORE N **Sheer** material is very thin, light, and delicate. *...sheer black tights.*

sheet /ʃiːt/ **sheets.** [1] N-C A **sheet** is a large rectangular piece of cloth that you sleep on or cover yourself with in a bed. [2] N-C A **sheet** of paper is a rectangular piece of paper. [3] N-C A **sheet** of glass, metal, or wood is a large, flat, thin piece of it.

sheikh (also **sheik**) /ʃeɪk, AM ʃiːk/ **sheikhs.** N-C A **sheikh** is a male Arab chief or ruler.

shelf /ʃelf/ **shelves.** N-C A **shelf** is a flat piece of wood, metal, or glass which is attached to a wall or to the sides of a cupboard. *He took a book from the shelf.*

shell /ʃel/ **shells, shelling, shelled.** [1] N-VAR The **shell** of an egg or nut is the hard covering which surrounds it. The substance that a shell is made of is called **shell**. *...beads made from ostrich egg shell.* [2] N-C The **shell** of a tortoise, snail, or crab is the hard protective covering on its back. [3] N-C **Shells** are the coverings which surround, or used to surround, small sea creatures. *The sand was pure white, scattered with sea shells.* [4] VERB If you **shell** nuts, peas, prawns, or other food, you remove their natural outer covering. [5] N-C A **shell** is a weapon consisting of a metal container filled with explosives that can be fired from a large gun over long distances. [6] VERB To **shell** a place means to fire explosive shells at it. ◆**shelling, shellings** N-VAR *Out on the streets, the shelling continued.*

▶ **shell out.** PHR-VERB If you **shell out** for something, you spend a lot of money on it. *...an insurance premium which saves you from having to shell out for repairs.*

she'll /ʃiːl, ʃɪl/. **She'll** is the usual spoken form of 'she will'.

shellfish /'ʃelfɪʃ/. N-C A **shellfish** is a small creature with a shell that lives in the sea.

shelter /ˈʃeltə/ **shelters, sheltering, sheltered.** [1] N-C A **shelter** is a small building or covered place which is made to protect people from bad weather or danger. [2] N-U If a place provides **shelter**, it provides protection from bad weather and danger. *The number of families seeking shelter rose by 17 percent.* [3] VERB If you **shelter** in a place, you stay there and are protected from bad weather or danger. *...a man sheltering in a doorway.* [4] VERB If a place or thing **is sheltered** by something, it is protected by it from wind and rain. [5] VERB If a person **shelters** someone, usually someone who is being hunted by police or other people, they provide them with a place to stay or live. *A neighbor sheltered the boy for seven days.*

sheltered /ˈʃeltəd/ [1] ADJ A **sheltered** place is protected from wind and rain. *...a shallow-sloping beach next to a sheltered bay.* [2] ADJ If you say someone has had a **sheltered** life, you mean that they have not experienced things that most people of their age have experienced, and that as a result they are rather naive.

shelve /ʃelv/ **shelves, shelving, shelved.** [1] VERB If someone **shelves** a plan, they decide not to continue with it at that time. *The project has now been shelved.* [2] **Shelves** is the plural of **shelf.**

shepherd /ˈʃepəd/ **shepherds, shepherding, shepherded.** [1] N-C A **shepherd** is a person whose job is to look after sheep. [2] VERB If you **are shepherded** somewhere, someone takes you there to make sure you arrive at the right place safely. *Supporters will then be shepherded on to a special fleet of buses.*

sheriff /ˈʃerɪf/ **sheriffs.** N-C & N-TITLE In the United States, a **sheriff** is a person who is elected to make sure that the law is obeyed in a particular county.

sherry /ˈʃeri/ **sherries.** N-VAR **Sherry** is a type of strong wine that is made in south-western Spain.

she's /ʃiːz, ʃɪz/. **She's** is the usual spoken form of 'she is' or 'she has', especially when 'has' is an auxiliary verb. *She's having a baby... She's been married for seven years.*

shield /ʃiːld/ **shields, shielding, shielded.** [1] VERB If something or someone **shields** you **from** a danger or risk, they protect you from it. *He shielded his head from the sun with an old sack.* [2] N-C A **shield** is a large piece of metal or leather which soldiers used to carry to protect their bodies while they were fighting.

shift /ʃɪft/ **shifts, shifting, shifted.** [1] VERB If you **shift** something, or if it **shifts**, it moves slightly. *He shifted from foot to foot.* [2] VERB & N-C If someone's opinion, a situation, or a policy **shifts**, or if it **is shifted**, it changes slightly. You call a change like this a **shift**. *The emphasis should be shifted more towards Parliament.* [3] N-C A **shift** is a set period of work in a place like a factory or hospital. *His father worked shifts in a steel mill. ...the afternoon shift.*

shimmer /ˈʃɪmə/ **shimmers, shimmering, shimmered.** VERB & N-C If something **shimmers**, it shines with a faint unsteady light called a **shimmer**. *The lights shimmered on the water.*

shin /ʃɪn/ **shins.** N-C Your **shin** is the front part of your leg between your knee and ankle.

shine /ʃaɪn/ **shines, shining, shined, shone.** The past tense and past participle of the verb is **shone**, except for meaning 4 when it is **shined**. [1] VERB When the sun or a light **shines**, it gives out bright light. [2] VERB If you **shine** a torch or lamp somewhere, you point its light there. *One of the men shone a torch in his face.* [3] VERB & N-SING Something that **shines**, or that has a **shine**, is very bright because it is reflecting light. *This gel gives a beautiful shine to the hair.* [4] VERB Someone who **shines** at a skill or activity does it very well. *He failed to shine academically.*

shingle /ˈʃɪŋɡəl/. N-U **Shingle** is a mass of small stones on the shore of a sea or river.

shining /ˈʃaɪnɪŋ/. ADJ A **shining** achievement or quality is a very good one which should be admired. *She is a shining example to us all.*

shiny /ˈʃaɪni/ **shinier, shiniest.** ADJ **Shiny** things are bright and reflect light. *...a shiny new sports car.*

ship /ʃɪp/ **ships, shipping, shipped.** [1] N-C A **ship** is a large boat which carries passengers or cargo. *He will then go by ship to England.* [2] VERB If people or things **are shipped** somewhere, they are sent there by ship. ♦**shipment** N-U *The furniture was ready for shipment.*

shipment /ˈʃɪpmənt/ **shipments.** N-C A **shipment** is an amount of a particular kind of cargo that is sent to another country on a ship.

shipping /ˈʃɪpɪŋ/. N-U **Shipping** is the transport of cargo as a business, especially on ships.

shipwreck /ˈʃɪprek/ **shipwrecks, shipwrecked.** [1] N-VAR When there is a **shipwreck**, a ship is destroyed in an accident at sea. *...the perils of storm and shipwreck.* [2] N-C A **shipwreck** is a ship which has been destroyed in an accident at sea. [3] PASSIVE-VERB If someone **is shipwrecked**, their ship is destroyed in an accident at sea but they survive and reach land.

shipyard /ˈʃɪpjɑːd/ **shipyards.** N-C A **shipyard** is a place where ships are built and repaired.

shirt /ʃɜːt/ **shirts.** N-C A **shirt** is a piece of clothing worn on the upper part of your body with a collar, sleeves, and buttons down the front.

shiver /ˈʃɪvə/ **shivers, shivering, shivered.** VERB & N-C When you **shiver**, or when you feel a **shiver**, your body shakes slightly because you are cold or frightened. *The emptiness here sent shivers down my spine.*

shoal /ʃəʊl/ **shoals.** N-C A **shoal** of fish is a large group of them swimming together.

shock /ʃɒk/ **shocks, shocking, shocked.** [1] N-C If you have a **shock**, you suddenly have an unpleasant or surprising experience. *It took me a very long time to get over the shock of her death.* [2] N-U **Shock** is a person's emotional and physical condition when something frightening or upsetting has happened to them. *She's still in a state of shock.* [3] N-U If someone is **in shock**, they are suffering from a serious physical condition in which their blood cannot circulate properly, for example because they have had a bad injury. [4] VERB If something **shocks** you, it makes you feel very upset. *Her behaviour at her husband's funeral shocked her* friends. ◆**shocked** ADJ *This was a nasty attack and the woman is still very shocked.* [5] VERB If someone or something **shocks** you, it upsets or offends you because you think it is rude or morally wrong. *Pictures of emaciated prisoners shocked the world.* ◆**shocked** ADJ *I am very sad and very shocked by this terrible crime.* [6] N-VAR A **shock** is a slight movement in something when it is hit by something else. *Steel barriers can bend and absorb the shock.* [7] N-C If you get a **shock** or an **electric shock**, you get a sudden painful feeling when you touch something which is connected to a supply of electricity.

shocking /'ʃɒkɪŋ/ ADJ You can say that something is **shocking** if you think that it is very bad; INFORMAL. ◆**shockingly** ADV *His memory was becoming shockingly bad.*

'**shock wave, shock waves.** [1] N-C A **shock wave** is an area of intense pressure moving through the air caused by an explosion or an earthquake, or by an object travelling faster than the speed of sound. [2] N-C If the effect of something unpleasant or surprising sends **shock waves** through a place, more and more people are offended, shocked, or surprised as they find out about it. *The crime sent shock waves throughout the country.*

shod /ʃɒd/ [1] ADJ You can use **shod** when you are describing the kind of shoes that a person is wearing; FORMAL. *...her stoutly shod feet.* [2] **Shod** is the past tense and past participle of **shoe**.

shoddy /'ʃɒdi/ ADJ If you describe a product or someone's work as **shoddy**, you think that it has been made or done carelessly or badly. ◆**shoddily** ADV *...shoddily-built cars.*

shoe /ʃuː/ **shoes, shoeing, shod.** [1] N-C **Shoes** are objects worn on your feet. Shoes cover most of your foot but not your ankle. *I'll need a new pair of shoes.* [2] PHRASE If you talk about being **in** someone's **shoes**, you talk about what you would do or how you would feel if you were in their situation. *I wouldn't want to be in his shoes.* [3] VERB To **shoe** a horse means to fix horseshoes onto its hooves.

shone /ʃɒn, AM ʃəʊn/ **Shone** is the past tense and past participle of **shine**.

shook /ʃʊk/ **Shook** is the past tense of **shake**.

shoot /ʃuːt/ **shoots, shooting, shot.** [1] VERB To **shoot** a person or animal means to kill or injure them by firing a gun at them. *Her father shot himself in the head.* ◆**shooting, shootings** N-C *Two more bodies were found nearby after the shooting.* [2] VERB To **shoot** means to fire a bullet from a weapon such as a gun. *They started shooting at us.* [3] VERB If someone or something **shoots** in a particular direction, they move in that direction quickly and suddenly. *Another car shot out of a junction and smashed into the back of them.* [4] VERB & N-SING When people **shoot** a film or **shoot** photographs, they make a film or take photographs using a camera. A **shoot** is an instance of shooting a film or photograph. *...a barn presently being used for a video shoot.* [5] VERB In sports such as football or basketball, when someone **shoots**, they try to score by kicking, throwing, or hitting the ball towards the goal. [6] N-C **Shoots** are plants that are beginning to

grow, or new parts growing from a plant or tree. [7] See also **shot**.

▸ **shoot down.** [1] PHR-VERB If someone **shoots down** an aeroplane or helicopter, they make it fall to the ground by hitting it with a bullet or missile. [2] PHR-VERB If you **shoot** someone **down** or **shoot down** their ideas, you ridicule that person or their ideas.

▸ **shoot up.** PHR-VERB If something **shoots up**, it grows or increases very quickly. *Sales shot up by 9%.*

shop /ʃɒp/ **shops, shopping, shopped.** [1] N-C In British English, a **shop** is a building or part of a building where things are sold. The usual American word is **store**. *She had run her own antiques shop.* [2] VERB When you **shop**, you go to shops and buy things. *He always shopped at the Co-op.* ◆**shopper, shoppers** N-C *...crowds of Christmas shoppers.* [3] See also **shopping, coffee shop.**

> When you want to refer to a particular type of shop, you can often simply use the word for the person who owns or manages the shop. *Down the road there is another greengrocer... Bring me back a paper from the newsagent.* Alternatively, you can use the possessive form with **'s**, without a following noun. *...items which can be purchased at the greengrocer's... She also cleans offices and serves in a local newsagent's.* You can also use the same pattern with other words that refer to a person or business that provides a service, such as **hairdresser** or **dentist**. *Three or four times a week they'll go to the hairdresser... It's worse than being at the dentist's.*

▸ **shop around.** PHR-VERB If you **shop around**, you go to different shops or companies and compare prices and quality before buying something.

'**shop assistant, shop assistants.** N-C In British English, a **shop assistant** is a person who works in a shop selling things to customers. The usual American word is **sales clerk**.

,**shop 'floor.** N-SING The **shop floor** refers to all the workers in a factory or the area where they work, especially in contrast to the management. *Cost must be controlled, not just on the shop floor but in the boardroom too.*

shopkeeper /'ʃɒpkiːpə/ **shopkeepers.** N-C A **shopkeeper** is a person who owns a small shop; BRITISH.

shoplift /'ʃɒplɪft/ **shoplifts, shoplifting, shoplifted.** VERB If someone **shoplifts**, they steal goods from a shop during the time that the shop is open. ◆**shoplifter, shoplifters** N-C *...when staff confronted shoplifters.* ◆**shoplifting** N-U *The grocer accused her of shoplifting.*

shopping /'ʃɒpɪŋ/ [1] N-U When you do the **shopping**, you go to shops and buy things. [2] N-U Your **shopping** consists of things that you have just bought from shops, especially food.

'**shopping centre, shopping centres.** N-C A

shopping centre is an area in a town where a lot of shops have been built close together.

'shopping mall, shopping malls. N-C A **shopping mall** is a covered area where many shops have been built and where cars are not allowed.

shore /ʃɔː/ **shores, shoring, shored.** N-C & PHRASE The **shore** of a sea, lake, or wide river is the land along the edge of it. Someone who is **on shore** is on the land rather than on a ship.

▶ **shore up.** PHR-VERB If you **shore up** something which is becoming weak, you do something in order to strengthen it. *The Secretary of State for Education must act to shore up the system.*

shoreline /'ʃɔːlaɪn/ **shorelines.** N-C The **shoreline** is the edge of a sea, lake, or wide river.

shorn /ʃɔːn/ [1] ADJ If hair is **shorn**, it has been cut very short; LITERARY. [2] **Shorn** is the past participle of **shear**.

short 1 adjective and adverb uses

short /ʃɔːt/ **shorter, shortest.** [1] ADJ If something is **short** or lasts for a **short** time, it is not very long or does not last very long. *The announcement was made a short time ago... Mr Mandela took a short break before resuming his schedule.* [2] ADV If something is cut **short** or stops **short**, it is stopped before people expect it to or before it has finished. *Jackson cut short his trip to Africa.* [3] ADJ Someone who is **short** is not as tall as most people are. [4] ADJ Something that is **short** measures only a small amount from one end to the other. *The city centre and shops are only a short distance away.* [5] ADJ AFTER LINK-V If a name or abbreviation is **short for** another name, it is the short version of that name. *...her friend Kes (short for Kesewa).* [6] ADJ AFTER LINK-V If you are **short of** something or if it is **short**, you do not have enough of it. *Her father's illness left the family short of money.* [7] ADJ If you have a **short** temper, you get angry easily.

PHRASES ● If something is **short of** a place or amount, it has not quite reached it. *They were still 51 short of their target.* ● If someone **stops short** of doing something, they nearly do it but do not actually do it. *He stopped short of explicitly criticizing the government.* ● You use the expression **in short** when you have been giving a lot of details and you want to give a conclusion or summary. *Try tennis, badminton or windsurfing. In short, anything challenging.*

short 2 noun uses

short /ʃɔːt/ **shorts.** [1] N-PL **Shorts** are trousers with short legs. *I decided to put on a pair of shorts.* [2] N-PL **Shorts** are men's underpants that usually reach halfway down their thighs. [3] N-C A **short** is a small, strong alcoholic drink of a spirit such as whisky or gin; BRITISH.

shortage /'ʃɔːtɪdʒ/ **shortages.** N-VAR If there is a **shortage** of something, there is not enough of it. *Vietnam is suffering from food shortage.*

shortcoming /'ʃɔːtkʌmɪŋ/ **shortcomings.** N-C The **shortcomings** of a person or thing are their faults or weaknesses. *I recognize all of my own shortcomings.*

,short 'cut, short cuts. [1] N-C A **short cut** is a quicker route than the one that you usually take. *I tried to take a short cut and got lost.*

[2] N-C A **short cut** is a method of achieving something more quickly or more easily than if you use the usual methods. *Fame can be a shortcut to love and money.*

shorten /'ʃɔːtən/ **shortens, shortening, shortened.** [1] VERB If you **shorten** an event or the length of time that something lasts, or if it **shortens**, it does not last as long as it would otherwise do or as it used to do. *Smoking can shorten your life. ...when the days shorten in winter.* [2] VERB If you **shorten** an object, or if it **shortens**, it becomes smaller in length. *...an operation to shorten her nose.*

shortfall /'ʃɔːtfɔːl/ **shortfalls.** N-C If there is a **shortfall** in something, there is not enough of it. *The government has refused to make up a £30,000 shortfall in funding.*

shorthand /'ʃɔːthænd/. N-U **Shorthand** is a quick way of writing which uses signs to represent words or syllables.

shortlist /'ʃɔːtlɪst/ **shortlists, shortlisting, shortlisted.** [1] N-C A **shortlist** is a list of people or things which have been chosen from a larger group, for example for a job or a prize. The successful person or thing is then chosen from the small group; BRITISH. *...the six books on the shortlist for the Booker prize.* [2] VERB If someone or something **is shortlisted**, they are put on a shortlist; BRITISH.

,short-'lived. ADJ Something that is **short-lived** does not last very long. *Her sense of triumph was short-lived.*

shortly /'ʃɔːtli/. [1] ADV If something happens **shortly** after or before something else, it happens a short amount of time after or before it. *The telephone call came shortly before dinnertime.* [2] ADV If something is going to happen **shortly**, it is going to happen soon. *Their trial will shortly begin.*

,short-'sighted. [1] ADJ If you are **short-sighted**, you cannot see things properly when they are far away, because there is something wrong with your eyes. [2] ADJ If you say that someone's actions or decisions are **short-sighted**, you mean they fail to take account of things that will probably happen in the future. *This is a short-sighted approach to the problem of global warming.*

'short-term. ADJ **Short-term** is used to describe things that will last for a short time, or things that will have an effect soon rather than in the distant future. *They had a short-term vacancy for a person on the foreign desk... The short-term outlook for employment remains gloomy.*

shot /ʃɒt/ **shots.** [1] **Shot** is the past tense and past participle of **shoot**. [2] N-C If you fire a **shot**, you fire a gun once. *My first two shots missed the target.* [3] N-C Someone who is a **good shot** can shoot well. Someone who is a **bad shot** cannot shoot well. [4] N-C In sport, a **shot** is the act of kicking or hitting a ball, especially in an attempt to score. *He had only one shot at goal.* [5] N-C A **shot** is a photograph or a particular sequence of pictures in a film. *A video crew was taking shots of the lane.* [6] PHRASES If you **have a shot at** something, or if you **give it a shot**, you attempt to do it. [7] N-C A **shot** of a drug is an injection of it. *The doctor* *administered a shot of Nembutal.*

PHRASES ● If you **give** something your **best shot**, you do it as well as you possibly can; IN-FORMAL. ● The person who **calls the shots** is in a position to tell others what to do. *There is no mistaking who calls the shots.* ● If you describe something as a **long shot**, you mean that it is unlikely to succeed, but is worth trying. *The deal was a long shot, but Bagley had little to lose.* ● **a shot in the arm**: see **arm**.

shotgun /ˈʃɒtgʌn/ **shotguns.** N-C A **shotgun** is a gun which fires a lot of small metal balls at one time.

should /ʃəd, STRONG ʃʊd/. **Should** is a modal verb. It is used with the base form of a verb. **1** MODAL You use **should** when you are giving advice or recommendations or when you are mentioning things that are not the case but that you think ought to be. *I should exercise more... Should our children be taught to swim at school?* **2** MODAL You use **should** to tell someone what to do or to report a rule or law which tells someone what to do. *A High Court judge has ruled that the two men should stand trial.* **3** MODAL You use **should** in questions when you are asking someone for advice, permission, or information. *Should I or shouldn't I go to university?* **4** MODAL If you say that something **should have** happened, you mean that it did not happen, but that you wish it had happened or that you expected it to happen. *I should have gone this morning but I was feeling a bit ill... I shouldn't have said what I did.* **5** MODAL You use **should** when you are saying that something is probably the case or will probably happen in the way you are describing. If you say that something **should have** happened by a particular time, you mean that it will probably have happened by that time. *You should have no problem with reading this language... We should have finished by a quarter past two.* **6** MODAL You use **should** in 'that' clauses after some verbs and adjectives when you are talking about a future event or situation. *He raised his glass and indicated that I should do the same.* **7** MODAL You use **should** in expressions such as **I should imagine** to indicate that you think something is true but you are not sure. *I should think it's going to rain soon.*

shoulder /ˈʃəʊldə/ **shoulders, shouldering, shouldered.** **1** N-C Your **shoulders** are the parts of your body between your neck and the tops of your arms. *He glanced over his shoulder.* **2** VERB If you **shoulder** something heavy, you put it across one of your shoulders so that you can carry it more easily. *He shouldered his bike and walked across the finish line.* **3** N-PL When you talk about someone's problems or responsibilities, you can say that they carry them on their **shoulders**. *He recognizes and understands the burden that's on his shoulders.* **4** VERB If you **shoulder** the responsibility or blame for something, you accept it. *He has had to shoulder the responsibility of his father's mistakes.* **5** PHRASE If you **rub shoulders with** famous people, you meet them and talk to them. ● **a chip on** someone's **shoulder**: see **chip**.

shouldn't /ˈʃʊdənt/. **Shouldn't** is the usual spoken form of 'should not'.

should've /ˈʃʊdəv/. **Should've** is the usual spoken form of 'should have', especially when 'have' is an auxiliary verb.

shout /ʃaʊt/ **shouts, shouting, shouted.** **1** VERB & PHR-VERB If you **shout**, or **shout** something **out**, you say it very loudly. *'She's alive!' he shouted triumphantly... Andrew rushed out of the house, shouting for help... You will have to shout out your name to the auctioneer.* ◆**shouting** N-U *My grandchildren heard the shouting first.* **2** N-C A **shout** is the noise made when someone speaks very loudly. *I heard a distant shout.*

▶ **shout down.** PHR-VERB If people **shout down** someone who is trying to speak, they prevent them from being heard by shouting at them. *Hecklers began to shout down the speakers.*

▶ **shout out.** See **shout** 1.

shove /ʃʌv/ **shoves, shoving, shoved.** VERB & N-C If you **shove** someone or something, or if you give them a **shove**, you give them a hard push. *He shoved her out of the way... She gave Gracie a shove towards the house.*

shovel /ˈʃʌvəl/ **shovels, shovelling, shovelled** (AM **shoveling, shoveled**). **1** N-C A **shovel** is a tool like a spade, used for lifting and moving earth, coal, or snow. **2** VERB If you **shovel** earth, coal, or snow, you lift and move it with a shovel. *He has to get out and shovel snow.* **3** VERB If you **shovel** something somewhere, you push a lot of it there quickly. *...Randall, who was obliviously shoveling food into his mouth.*

show /ʃəʊ/ **shows, showing, showed, shown.** **1** VERB If something **shows** that a state of affairs exists, it gives information that proves it or makes it clear to people. *New research shows that an excess of meat and salt can contract muscles... These figures show an increase of over one million in unemployment. ...blood tests to show whether you have been infected.* **2** VERB If a picture, chart, film, or piece of writing **shows** something, it represents it or gives information about it. *Figure 4.1 shows the respiratory system.* **3** VERB If you **show** someone something, you give it to them, take them to it, or point to it, so that they can see it or know what you are referring to. *Cut out this article and show it to your bank manager... I showed them where the gun was.* **4** VERB If you **show** someone to a room or seat, you lead them to it. *Your office is ready for you. I'll show you the way.* **5** VERB If you **show** someone how to do something, you do it yourself so that they can watch and learn how to do it. *Claire showed us how to make a chocolate roulade... Dr. Reichert has shown us a new way to look at those behavior problems.* **6** VERB If something **shows**, or if you **show** it, it is visible or noticeable. *Faint glimmers of daylight were showing through the treetops... Ferguson was unhappy and it showed... He showed his teeth.* **7** VERB If something **shows** a quality or characteristic, or if that quality or characteristic **shows** itself, the quality or characteristic can be noticed or observed. *Peace talks in Washington showed signs of progress.* **8** N-C A **show** of a feeling or quality is an attempt by someone to make it clear that they have that feeling or quality. *Miners gathered in the centre of Bucharest in a show of support for the government.* [9] PHRASE If you **have** something **to show for** your efforts, you have achieved something as a result of what you have done. *It's about time I had something to show for my time in my job.* [10] N-C A television or radio **show** is a programme on television or radio. [11] N-C A **show** in a theatre is an entertainment or concert, especially one that includes different items such as music, dancing, and comedy. [12] VERB When a film or television programme **is shown**, it appears in a cinema or is broadcast on television. *American films are showing at Moscow's cinemas.* [13] N-C A **show** is a public exhibition. *...the Chelsea Flower Show.*

PHRASES ● If you say that something is **for show**, you mean that it has no real purpose and is done just to give a good impression. *Animals are not put on this earth just for show.* ● If something is **on show**, it has been put in a place where it can be seen by the public. *...the most valuable crops on show.*

▶ **show around.** PHR-VERB If you **show** someone **around** a place, you go round it with them, pointing out its interesting features. *She showed him around the flat.*

▶ **show off.** PHR-VERB If you say that someone **is showing off**, you are criticizing them for trying to impress people by showing in a very obvious way what they can do or what they own. *All right, there's no need to show off.* [2] PHR-VERB If you **show off** something that you have or own, you show it to a lot of people because you are proud of it. *Body builders shave their chests to show off their muscles.* ● See also **show-off.**

'show business. N-U **Show business** is the entertainment industry. *He started his career in show business by playing the saxophone.*

showdown /ˈʃəʊdaʊn/ **showdowns.** N-C A **showdown** is a big argument or conflict which is intended to settle a dispute. *They may be pushing the Prime Minister towards a final showdown with his party.*

shower /ʃaʊə/ **showers, showering, showered.** [1] N-C A **shower** is a device which sprays you with water so that you can wash yourself. *She heard him turn on the shower.* [2] N-C & VERB If you have a **shower**, or if you **shower**, you wash yourself by standing under a shower. *She took two showers a day... There wasn't time to shower.* [3] N-C A **shower** is a short period of light rain. *The weather forecast was for scattered showers.* [4] N-C You can refer to a lot of things that are falling as a **shower** of them. *Showers of sparks flew in all directions.* [5] VERB If you **are showered** with a lot of small objects or pieces, they are scattered over you. *They were showered with rice in the traditional manner.* [6] VERB If you **shower** someone **with** presents or kisses, you give them a lot of them.

shown /ʃəʊn/. **Shown** is the past participle of **show.**

'show-off, show-offs. N-C If you say that someone is a **show-off**, you are criticizing them for trying to impress people by showing

in a very obvious way what they can do or what they own; INFORMAL. *I was an awful show-off as a child.*

showpiece /ˈʃəʊpiːs/ **showpieces.** N-C A **showpiece** is something that is admired as a fine example of its type, especially something which is intended to make people admire its owner or creator. *The factory was to be a showpiece of Western investment in the East.*

showroom /ˈʃəʊruːm/ **showrooms.** N-C A **showroom** is a shop in which goods such as cars, furniture, or electrical appliances are displayed for sale.

shrank /ʃræŋk/. **Shrank** is the past tense of **shrink.**

shrapnel /ˈʃræpnəl/. N-U **Shrapnel** consists of small pieces of metal scattered from exploding bombs and shells.

shred /ʃred/ **shreds, shredding, shredded.** VERB & N-C If you **shred** something such as food or paper, or if you cut it into **shreds**, you cut or tear it into very small pieces. *Finely shred the carrots.*

shrewd /ʃruːd/ **shrewder, shrewdest.** ADJ A **shrewd** person is able to understand and judge situations quickly and to use this understanding to their own advantage. ◆**shrewdly** ADV *She looked at him shrewdly.* ◆**shrewdness** N-U *His natural shrewdness tells him what is needed to succeed.*

shriek /ʃriːk/ **shrieks, shrieking, shrieked.** VERB & N-C If you **shriek**, you give a sudden loud scream, called a **shriek**. *She shrieked and leapt from the bed... 'Stop it! Stop it!' shrieked Jane... Sue let out a terrific shriek.*

shrill /ʃrɪl/ **shriller, shrillest.** ADJ A **shrill** sound is high-pitched, piercing, and unpleasant to listen to. *...the shrill whistle of the engine.*

shrimp /ʃrɪmp/ **shrimps.** N-C **Shrimps** are small shellfish with long tails and many legs. The plural is **shrimps** or **shrimp.**

shrine /ʃraɪn/ **shrines.** N-C A **shrine** is a holy place associated with a sacred person or object. *...the holy shrine of Mecca.*

shrink /ʃrɪŋk/ **shrinks, shrinking, shrank, shrunk.** [1] VERB If something **shrinks**, it becomes smaller. *The vast forests of West Africa have shrunk.* [2] VERB If you **shrink** away from someone or something, you move away because you are frightened or horrified by them. *He reached for Benjy, who shrank back in fear... They didn't shrink from danger.* [3] N-C A **shrink** is a psychiatrist; INFORMAL.

shrivel /ˈʃrɪvəl/ **shrivels, shrivelling, shrivelled** (AM **shriveling, shriveled**). VERB When something **shrivels** or **shrivels** up, it becomes dry and wrinkled. *...dry weather that shrivelled this summer's crops... The leaves started to shrivel up.* ◆**shrivelled** ADJ *It looked old and shrivelled.*

shroud /ʃraʊd/ **shrouds, shrouding, shrouded.** N-C A **shroud** is a cloth used for wrapping a dead body. [2] PHRASE If something has been **shrouded in mystery** or **shrouded in secrecy**, very little information about it has been made available. *The origin of AIDS, like that of most diseases is shrouded in mystery.*

[3] VERB If darkness, fog, or smoke **shrouds** an area, it covers it so that it is difficult to see. *The area is shrouded in smoke.*

shrub /ʃrʌb/ **shrubs.** N-C **Shrubs** are low plants like small trees with several stems instead of a trunk.

shrug /ʃrʌg/ **shrugs, shrugging, shrugged.** VERB & N-C If you **shrug**, you raise your shoulders to show that you are not interested in something or that you do not know or care about something. This movement is called a **shrug.** *Anne shrugged, as if she didn't know... 'I suppose so,' said Anna with a shrug.*
▸ **shrug off.** PHR-VERB If you **shrug** something **off**, you treat it as not important or serious. *He shrugged off the criticism.*

shrunk /ʃrʌŋk/. **Shrunk** is the past participle of **shrink.**

shudder /ˈʃʌdə/ **shudders, shuddering, shuddered.** [1] VERB & N-C If you **shudder**, you tremble with fear or disgust. This movement is called a **shudder.** *She had shuddered at the thought... She gave a violent shudder.* [2] VERB If something such as a machine **shudders**, it shakes suddenly and violently. *The whole ship shuddered and trembled.*

shuffle /ˈʃʌfəl/ **shuffles, shuffling, shuffled.** [1] VERB & N-SING If you **shuffle**, or if you walk with a **shuffle**, you walk without lifting your feet properly. *An old man shuffled out of a doorway... She is quite frail and can only walk with a shuffle.* [2] VERB If you **shuffle** when you are sitting or standing, you move your bottom or your feet about, because you feel uncomfortable or embarrassed. *He grinned and shuffled his feet.* [3] VERB If you **shuffle** things such as pieces of paper, you move them around so that they are in a different order.

shun /ʃʌn/ **shuns, shunning, shunned.** VERB If you **shun** someone or something, you deliberately avoid them. *Everybody shunned him.*

shunt /ʃʌnt/ **shunts, shunting, shunted.** VERB If someone or something **is shunted** somewhere, they are moved or sent there, usually because someone finds them inconvenient. *He spent eight years being shunted between prisons.*

shut /ʃʌt/ **shuts, shutting, shut.** [1] VERB & ADJ AFTER LINK-V If you **shut** something such as a door, you move it so that it covers a hole or a space. If it is **shut**, it covers a hole or space. *The screen door shut gently... The windows were fastened tight shut.* [2] VERB & ADJ AFTER LINK-V If you **shut** your eyes or your mouth, or if they are **shut**, your eyelids are closed or your lips are placed together. [3] VERB & ADJ AFTER LINK-V When a shop or pub **shuts**, or if it is **shut**, it is closed and you cannot go into it until it opens again. *What time do the pubs shut?... The local shop may be shut.*
▸ **shut away.** PHR-VERB If you **shut** yourself **away**, you avoid going out and seeing other people. *She was desperately upset and shut herself away for the whole day.*
▸ **shut down.** PHR-VERB If a factory or business **is shut down**, it is closed permanently. *Smaller contractors had been forced to shut down.* ● See also **shutdown.**

▸ **shut in.** PHR-VERB If you **shut** someone or something **in** a room, you close the door so that they cannot leave it.
▸ **shut off.** PHR-VERB If you **shut off** something such as an engine or a power supply, you turn it off to stop it working. *The water was shut off.*
▸ **shut out.** [1] PHR-VERB If you **shut** someone or something **out**, you prevent them from getting into a place. *'I shut him out of the bedroom,' says Maureen.* [2] PHR-VERB If you **shut out** a thought or a feeling, you stop yourself thinking about it or feeling it. *I shut out the memory.*
▸ **shut up.** PHR-VERB If you **shut up**, you stop talking. If you say **'shut up'** to someone, you are rudely telling them to stop talking. *...the only way he knew of shutting her up.*

shutdown /ˈʃʌtdaʊn/ **shutdowns.** N-C A **shutdown** is the closing of a factory or other business.

shutter /ˈʃʌtə/ **shutters.** [1] N-C The **shutter** in a camera is the part which opens to allow light through the lens when a photograph is taken. [2] N-C **Shutters** are wooden or metal covers fitted to a window.

shuttle /ˈʃʌtəl/ **shuttles, shuttling, shuttled.** [1] N-C A **shuttle** is the same as a **space shuttle.** [2] ADJ A **shuttle** is a plane, bus, or train which makes frequent journeys between two places. [3] VERB If someone or something **is shuttled** from one place to another, they are frequently sent from one place to the other. *Refugees can be shuttled from one country to another.*

shy /ʃaɪ/ **shyer, shyest; shies, shying, shied.** [1] ADJ A **shy** person is nervous and uncomfortable in the company of other people. *He is painfully shy of women.* ◆**shyly** ADV *The children smiled shyly.* ◆**shyness** N-U *He overcame his shyness.* [2] ADJ & VERB If you are **shy of** doing something, or if you **shy away from** doing it, you are unwilling to do it, often because you are afraid or not confident enough. *You should not be shy of having your say in the running of the school... We frequently shy away from making decisions.* [3] VERB When a horse **shies**, it moves away suddenly because something has frightened it.

sibling /ˈsɪblɪŋ/ **siblings.** N-C Your **siblings** are your brothers and sisters; FORMAL. ● See note at **brother.**

sick /sɪk/ **sicker, sickest.** [1] ADJ & N-PL If you are **sick**, you are ill. **The sick** are people who are sick. *He's very sick. He needs medication... There were no doctors to treat the sick.* [2] ADJ AFTER LINK-V If you are being **sick**, the food that you have eaten comes up from your stomach and out of your mouth. If you feel **sick**, you feel as if you are going to be sick. *She got up and was sick in the handbasin.* [3] N-U **Sick** is vomit; BRITISH. [4] ADJ If you are **sick of** something, you are annoyed or bored by it and want it to stop. *I am sick and tired of hearing all these people moaning.* [5] ADJ If you describe something such as a joke or story as **sick**, you mean that it deals with death or suffering in an unpleasantly frivolous way. [6] PHRASE If someone or something **makes** you **sick**, they make you feel angry or disgusted. *The pictures made me sick.* [7] See note at **ill.**

sicken /'sɪkən/ sickens, sickening, sickened. VERB If something **sickens** you, it makes you feel disgusted. ♦ **sickening** ADJ ...*a sickening attack on a pregnant and defenceless woman.*

sickly /'sɪkli/ sicklier, sickliest. 1 ADJ A **sickly** person is weak and unhealthy. *He had been a sickly child.* 2 ADJ A **sickly** smell or taste is unpleasant and makes you feel slightly sick. ...*the sickly smell of burnt human flesh.*

sickness /'sɪknəs/ sicknesses. 1 N-U **Sickness** is the state of being ill or unhealthy. *In fifty-two years of working he had one week of sickness.* 2 N-U **Sickness** is the uncomfortable feeling that you are going to vomit. 3 N-C A **sickness** is a particular illness. ...*radiation sickness.*

side /saɪd/ sides, siding, sided. 1 N-C The **side** of something is a position to the left or right of it, rather than in front of it, behind it, or on it. ...*the nations on either side of the Pacific.* ...*both sides of the border... Park on the side of the road.* 2 N-C The **sides** of an object are the outside surfaces that are not the top or the bottom. *We put a notice on the side of the box... A carton of milk lay on its side.* 3 N-C The **sides** of a hollow or a container are its inside vertical surfaces. ...*narrow valleys with steep sides.* 4 N-C The two **sides** of an area, surface, or object are its two halves or surfaces. ...*the right side of your face... The new copiers only copy onto one side of the paper.* 5 N-C Your **sides** are the parts of your body from your armpits down to your hips. 6 ADJ BEFORE N **Side** is used to describe things that are not the main or most important ones of their kind. ...*a side street.* 7 N-C You can call the two groups of people involved in an argument, war, or game the two **sides** of that argument, war, or game. 8 N-C The two **sides** of an argument are the opposing points of view. ...*sharp reactions from people on both sides of the issue.* 9 VERB If you **side with** someone, you support them in an argument. 10 N-C A particular **side** of something is one aspect of it. *Anxiety has a mental and a physical side.*

PHRASES ● If someone stays **at your side** or **by your side**, they stay near you and support or comfort you. *He was constantly at his wife's side.* ● If two people or things are **side by side**, they are next to each other. *We sat side by side.* ● If something moves **from side to side**, it moves repeatedly to the left and to the right. *She was shaking her head from side to side.* ● If you are **on** someone's **side**, you are supporting them in an argument or a war. ● If you do something **on the side**, you do it in addition to your main work. ...*ways of making a little bit of money on the side.* ● If you **put** something **to one side**, you temporarily ignore it in order to concentrate on something else. *Health and safety regulations are often put to one side.* ● If you get **on the wrong side of** someone, you do something to annoy them and make them dislike you. If you stay **on the right side of** someone, you try to please them and avoid annoying them. ● to **err on the side of** something: see **err**. ● to **be on the safe side**: see **safe**.

'side-effect, **side-effects**. N-C The **side-effects** of a drug are the effects it has on you in addition to its function of curing illness or pain. ...*unpleasant side-effects, such as nausea, vomiting and sweating.*

sideline /'saɪdlaɪn/ sidelines. 1 N-C A **sideline** is something that you do in addition to your main job in order to earn extra money. *Mr. Means sold computer disks as a sideline.* 2 N-C The **sidelines** of a playing area such as a tennis court or football pitch are the lines marking the long sides. 3 N-PL If you are on the **sidelines** in a situation, you are not involved in it. *France no longer wants to be left on the sidelines when critical decisions are taken.*

sidestep (or **side-step**) /'saɪdstep/ sidesteps, sidestepping, sidestepped. VERB If you **sidestep** a problem, you avoid dealing with it. *Rarely, if ever, does he sidestep a question.*

sidewalk /'saɪdwɔːk/ sidewalks. N-C In American English, a **sidewalk** is a path with a hard surface by the side of a road. The British word is **pavement**.

sideways /'saɪdweɪz/. ADV & ADJ BEFORE N **Sideways** means from or to the side of something or someone. *I took a step sideways.* ...*a sideways glance.*

siege /siːdʒ/ sieges. N-VAR A **siege** is a military operation in which an army or police force surrounds a place in order to force the people to surrender and come out. *We must do everything possible to lift the siege.* ...*sending supplies to the city which has been under siege.*

sieve /sɪv/ sieves, sieving, sieved. 1 N-C A **sieve** is a tool consisting of a metal or plastic ring with a fine wire net attached. It is used for separating liquids from solids or larger pieces of something from smaller pieces. See picture at **kitchen**. 2 VERB When you **sieve** a liquid or a powder, you put it through a sieve. *Sieve the flour into a mixing bowl.*

sift /sɪft/ sifts, sifting, sifted. 1 VERB If you **sift** a substance such as flour or sand, you put it through a sieve to remove large lumps. 2 VERB If you **sift** through something such as evidence, you examine it thoroughly. *Experts spent all day sifting through the wreckage.*

sigh /saɪ/ sighs, sighing, sighed. VERB & N-C When you **sigh**, or when you let out a **sigh**, you let out a deep breath. *She sighed deeply... She kicked off her shoes with a sigh.*

sight /saɪt/ sights, sighting, sighted. 1 N-U Your **sight** is your ability to see. *My sight is failing, and I can't see to read any more.* 2 VERB If someone is **sighted** somewhere, they are seen there briefly or suddenly. *A woman looking like her was sighted near Enmore.* 3 N-SING The **sight** of something is the act of seeing it or an occasion on which you see it. *I faint at the sight of blood.* 4 N-PL The **sights** are interesting places often visited by tourists. *We'd toured the sights of Paris.* 5 N-PL The **sights** of a weapon such as a rifle are the part which help you aim it.

PHRASES ● If one thing is **a sight** better or **a sight** worse than a similar thing, it is very much better or very much worse; INFORMAL. *She's looking a damn sight better than I am.*

• If you **know** someone **by sight**, you can recognize them when you see them, but you have never spoken to them. • If you **catch sight of** someone, you see them suddenly or briefly. *Then he caught sight of her small black velvet hat in the crowd.* • If something is **in sight**, you can see it. If it is **out of sight**, you cannot see it. • If a result or a decision is **in sight** or **within sight**, it is likely to happen within a short time. *An agreement on many aspects of trade policy was in sight.* • If you **lose sight of** an important feature or detail, you no longer pay attention to it because you are worrying about less important things. • If members of a police force or an army have been ordered to arrest or shoot someone **on sight**, they have been told to arrest or shoot someone as soon as they see them. *Troops shot anyone suspicious on sight.* • If you **set** your **sights on** something, you are determined to have it. *They have set their sights on the world record.*

sighting /ˈsaɪtɪŋ/ **sightings.** N-C A **sighting** of something is an occasion on which it is seen. *...the sighting of a rare sea bird at Lundy island.*

sightseeing /ˈsaɪtsiːɪŋ/. N-U **Sightseeing** is the activity of visiting the interesting places that tourists usually visit.

sign 1 indicators

sign /saɪn/ **signs.** [1] N-C A **sign** is a mark or shape with a particular meaning, for example in mathematics or music. *...an equals sign.* [2] N-C A **sign** is a movement of your arms, hands, or head which is intended to have a particular meaning. *Lech Walesa is pictured giving the V-for-victory sign.* [3] N-C A **sign** is a piece of wood, metal, or plastic with words or pictures on it, giving information or instructions. *Follow the road signs on to the D111.* [4] N-C If there is a **sign** of something, there is evidence that it exists. *They are prepared to hand back a hundred prisoners of war a day as a sign of good will... The sky is clear and there's no sign of rain or snow.* [5] N-C In astrology, a zodiac **sign** is one of the twelve areas into which the heavens are divided.

sign 2 writing your name

sign /saɪn/ **signs, signing, signed.** [1] VERB When you **sign** a document, you put your signature on it. *Before an operation the patient will be asked to sign a consent form.* ♦ **signing** N-U *Spain's top priority is the signing of an EMU treaty.* [2] VERB If an organization **signs** someone, or if someone **signs** for an organization, they sign a contract agreeing to work for that organization for a specified period of time. *He has signed to play rugby league with the London Broncos.*

▶ **sign away.** PHR-VERB If you **sign** something **away**, you sign official documents to say that you no longer have a right to it. *The Duke signed away his inheritance.*

▶ **sign for.** PHR-VERB If you **sign for** something, you officially state that you have received it, by signing a form or book.

▶ **sign in.** PHR-VERB If you **sign in**, you officially indicate that you have arrived at a hotel or club by signing a book or form.

▶ **sign on.** [1] PHR-VERB When an unemployed person **signs on**, they officially inform the authorities that they are unemployed, so that they can receive money from the government in order to live; BRITISH. [2] PHR-VERB If you **sign on for** something, or if you **sign up** for it, you officially agree to work for an organization or do a course of study by signing a contract or form. *He had signed on for a driving course.*

▶ **sign out.** PHR-VERB If you **sign out**, you indicate that you have left a hotel or club by signing a book or form.

▶ **sign up.** See **sign on** 2.

signal /ˈsɪɡnəl/ **signals, signalling, signalled.** (AM **signaling, signaled**). [1] N-C A **signal** is a sound or action which is intended to send a particular message. *They fired three distress signals... You mustn't fire without my signal.* [2] VERB If you **signal** something, or if you **signal** to someone, you make a gesture or sound in order to give someone a particular message. *She signalled a passing taxi.* [3] VERB & N-C If something **signals** a situation, or if it is a **signal** of it, it suggests that the situation is happening or likely to happen. *The lifting of American sanctions signalled the end of an era... Rebel leaders saw the visit as an important signal of support.* [4] N-C A **signal** is a piece of equipment beside a railway, which tells train drivers when to stop. [5] N-C A **signal** is a series of sound or light waves which carry information. *...high-frequency radio signals.*

signatory /ˈsɪɡnətri, AM -tɔːri/ **signatories.** N-C The **signatories** to an official document are the people who sign it. *Australia was a signatory to the International Convention on Civil and Political Rights.*

signature /ˈsɪɡnətʃə/ **signatures.** N-C Your **signature** is your name, written in your own characteristic way.

significance /sɪɡˈnɪfɪkəns/. N-U The **significance** of something is its importance. *The President's visit to this country is loaded with symbolic significance.*

significant /sɪɡˈnɪfɪkənt/. [1] ADJ A **significant** amount something is large enough to be important or noticeable. ♦ **significantly** ADV *Cars can be made significantly more fuel-efficient.* [2] ADJ A **significant** action or gesture is intended to have a special meaning. *Mrs Bycraft gave Rose a significant glance.*

signify /ˈsɪɡnɪfaɪ/ **signifies, signifying, signified.** VERB An event or a sign or gesture that **signifies** something has a particular meaning. *Becoming a father signified that he was now an adult.*

Sikh /siːk/ **Sikhs.** N-C A **Sikh** is a member of an Indian religion which separated from Hinduism in the sixteenth century and which teaches that there is only one God.

silence /ˈsaɪləns/ **silences, silencing, silenced.** [1] N-VAR If there is **silence**, it is completely quiet. *They stood in silence.* [2] N-U Someone's **silence** about something is their refusal to tell people anything about it. *He broke his silence for the first time yesterday about his lovechild.* [3] VERB To **silence** someone or something means to stop them speaking or making a noise. *A ringing phone silenced her.* [4] VERB If someone **silences** you, they stop you expressing opinions that they do not agree with. *He tried to silence anyone who spoke out against him.*

silent /'saɪlənt/. **1** ADJ AFTER LINK-V Someone or something that is **silent** is making no sound. *The heavy guns have again fallen silent.* ◆**silently** ADV *She and Ned sat silently for a moment.* **2** ADJ BEFORE N If you describe someone as a **silent** person, you mean that they do not talk to people very much, sometimes giving the impression of being unfriendly. *He was the silent type who sat in a corner, painfully shy.* **3** ADJ AFTER LINK-V If you are **silent** about something, you do not tell people about it. *The government have told the scientists to remain silent about their work.*

silhouette /ˌsɪluː'et/ **silhouettes.** N-C A **silhouette** is the outline of a dark shape against a bright light or pale background. *The dark silhouette of the castle ruins stood out boldly against the fading light.*

silicon /'sɪlɪkən/. N-U **Silicon** is a non-metallic element that is found combined with oxygen in sand and in minerals such as quartz and granite. Silicon is used to make parts of computers and other electronic equipment.

silicone /'sɪlɪkəʊn/. N-U **Silicone** is a substance made from silicon, which is used to make things such as oils and polishes.

silk /sɪlk/ **silks.** N-VAR **Silk** is a very smooth, fine cloth made from a substance produced by a kind of moth. *Pauline wore a silk dress with a strand of pearls.*

silky /'sɪlki/. ADJ Something that is **silky** is smooth and soft. *...silky fabrics.*

sill /sɪl/ **sills.** N-C A **sill** is a ledge at the bottom of a window.

silly /'sɪli/ **sillier, silliest.** ADJ Someone who is being **silly** is behaving in a foolish or childish way. ◆**silliness** N-U *Let's not have any more of this silliness.*

silt /sɪlt/. N-U **Silt** is fine sand, soil, or mud which is carried along by a river.

silver /'sɪlvə/. **1** N-U **Silver** is a valuable greyish-white metal used for making jewellery and ornaments. *...a hand-crafted brooch made from silver.* **2** N-U **Silver** consists of coins that look like silver. *...£150,000 in silver.* **3** N-U You can use **silver** to refer to all the things in a house that are made of silver, especially the cutlery and dishes. *He beat the rugs and polished the silver.* **4** ADJ & N-U **Silver** is used to describe things that are shiny greyish-white in colour. *He had thick silver hair.*

silver 'medal, silver medals. N-C A **silver medal** is a medal made of silver which is awarded as second prize in a contest.

silvery /'sɪlvəri/. ADJ **Silvery** things look like silver or are the colour of silver. *...silvery hair.*

similar /'sɪmɪlə/. ADJ If one thing is **similar** to another, or if a number of things are **similar**, they have features that are the same. *The accident was similar to one that happened in 1973. ...a group of similar pictures.*

similarity /ˌsɪmɪ'lærɪti/ **similarities.** N-VAR If there is a **similarity** between two or more things, they share some features that are the same. *She is also 25 and a native of Birmingham, but the similarity ends there.*

similarly /'sɪmɪləli/. **1** ADV You use **similarly** to say that something is similar to something else. *...a self-help network for themselves and other similarly affected families.* **2** ADV You use **similarly** to say that there is a correspondence or similarity between the way two things happen or are done. *He learned his English mainly from comic books. Similarly, I owe most of my oral French to Tintin and Asterix.*

simmer /'sɪmə/ **simmers, simmering, simmered.** VERB When you **simmer** food, or when it **simmers**, you cook it gently at just below boiling point. *Turn the heat down so the sauce simmers gently.*

simple /'sɪmpəl/ **simpler, simplest.** **1** ADJ If something is **simple**, it is not complicated, and is therefore easy to understand or do. *...simple pictures and diagrams. ...simple maths.* ◆**simply** ADV *State simply and clearly the reasons why you need an extension.* **2** ADJ **Simple** means containing all the basic or necessary things, but nothing extra. *...a simple dinner of rice and beans.* ◆**simply** ADV *He dressed simply and led a quiet family life.* **3** ADJ BEFORE N You use **simple** to emphasize that the thing you are referring to is the only important or relevant reason for something. *His refusal to talk was simple stubbornness.* **4** ADJ In English grammar, **simple** tenses are ones which are not formed using the auxiliary verb 'be', as in 'I dressed and went for a walk' and 'These wines taste awful'. Compare **continuous**. ● See also **simply**.

simplicity /sɪm'plɪsɪti/. **1** N-U The **simplicity** of something is the fact that it is uncomplicated and can be understood or done easily. *Because of its simplicity, this test could be carried out easily by a family doctor.* **2** N-U When you talk about something's **simplicity**, you approve of it because it is natural and simple rather than elaborate or ornate. *...the classical simplicity of the design.*

simplify /'sɪmplɪfaɪ/ **simplifies, simplifying, simplified.** VERB If you **simplify** something, you make it easier to understand. *The aim of the scheme is to simplify the complex social security system.* ◆**simplified** ADJ *...a shorter, simplified version of his speech.* ◆**simplification** /ˌsɪmplɪfɪ'keɪʃən/ **simplifications** N-VAR *...the simplification of court procedures.*

simplistic /sɪm'plɪstɪk/. ADJ A **simplistic** view or interpretation of something makes it seem much simpler than it really is. *He has a simplistic view of the treatment of eczema.*

simply /'sɪmpli/. **1** ADV You use **simply** to emphasize that something consists of only one thing, happens for only one reason, or is done in only one way. *Most of the damage that's occurred was simply because of fallen trees.* **2** ADV You use **simply** to emphasize what you are saying. *...nine out of ten thought it was simply marvellous.* ● See also **simple** .

simulate /'sɪmjʊleɪt/ **simulates, simulating, simulated.** VERB To **simulate** something means to pretend to do it or to produce something like it. *We used this trick in the Army to simulate illness... The wood had been painted to simulate stone.* ◆**simulation, simulations**

N-VAR *Training includes realistic simulation of typical casualty procedures.*

simultaneous /ˌsɪməlˈteɪniəs, AM ˌsaɪm-/. ADJ Things which are **simultaneous** happen or exist at the same time. *...the simultaneous release of the book and the album.* ◆**simultaneously** ADV *The two guns fired almost simultaneously.*

sin /sɪn/ **sins, sinning, sinned.** N-VAR & VERB If someone commits a **sin**, or if they **sin**, they do something which is believed to break the laws of God. *The Spanish Inquisition charged him with sinning against God and man.* ◆**sinner, sinners** N-C *I do not mean to imply that you are sinners.*

since /sɪns/. [1] PREP & ADV & CONJ You use **since** when you are mentioning a time or event in the past and indicating that a situation has continued from then until now. *This research has been in progress since 1961... I simply gave in to him, and I've regretted it ever since... I've been bored to death since I left the army.* [2] ADV & CONJ You use **since** to mention a time or event in the past when you are describing an event or situation that has happened after that time. *I haven't seen powdered eggs since the war... So much has changed in the sport since I was a teenager.* [3] ADV When you are talking about an event or situation in the past, you use **since** to indicate that another event happened at some point later in time. *Six thousand people were arrested, several hundred of whom have since been released.* [4] PHRASE If you say that something has **long since** happened, you mean that it happened a long time ago. *Her parents have long since died.* [5] CONJ You use **since** to introduce a reason. *I'm forever on a diet, since I put on weight easily.*

sincere /sɪnˈsɪə/. ADJ If you say that someone is **sincere**, you approve of them because they really mean the things they say. ◆**sincerity** /sɪnˈserɪti/ N-U *I was greatly impressed with his deep sincerity.*

sincerely /sɪnˈsɪəli/. [1] ADV If you say or feel something **sincerely**, you really mean it or feel it. *...sincerely held religious beliefs.* [2] CONVENTION In British English, people write **Yours sincerely** before their signature at the end of a formal letter when they have addressed it to someone by name. The usual American expression is **Sincerely yours**.

sinful /ˈsɪnfʊl/. ADJ If you describe something or someone as **sinful**, you think that they are wicked or immoral. *...sinful thoughts about women.*

sing /sɪŋ/ **sings, singing, sang, sung.** [1] VERB If you **sing**, you make musical sounds with your voice, usually producing words that fit a tune. *Ms Turner sang the theme tune from Goldeneye... Sing us a song!* ◆**singing** N-U *The dancing and singing ended at midnight.* [2] VERB When birds or insects **sing**, they make pleasant high-pitched sounds. *The bird was singing a beautiful song.* ◆**singing** N-U *The singing of birds is drowned out by motorway traffic.* [3] to **sing** someone's **praises**: see **praise**.

▶ **sing along.** PHR-VERB If you **sing along** with a piece of music, you sing it while you are listening to someone else perform it. *...fifteen hundred people all singing along.*

singer /ˈsɪŋə/ **singers.** N-C A **singer** is a person who sings, especially as a job.

single /ˈsɪŋgəl/ **singles, singling, singled.** [1] ADJ BEFORE N You use **single** to emphasize that you are referring to one thing, and no more than one thing. *She hadn't uttered a single word.* [2] ADJ BEFORE N You use **single** to indicate that you are considering something on its own and separately from other things like it. *Every single house in town had been damaged. ...the world's single most important source of oil.* [3] ADJ Someone who is **single** is not married. *When I was single I never worried about money.* [4] ADJ A **single** bed or room is intended for one person. [5] ADJ & N-C In British English, a **single ticket** or a **single** is a ticket for a journey from one place to another but not back again. The usual American term is **one-way** ticket. *...a Club Class single to Los Angeles.* [6] N-C A **single** is a record which has one short song on each side. *...the band's British and American hit singles.* [7] N-U **Singles** is a game of tennis or badminton in which one player plays another.

▶ **single out.** PHR-VERB If you **single** someone **out**, you choose them and give them special attention or treatment. *His immediate superior has singled him out for a special mention.*

single-. Single- is used to form words which describe something that has one part or feature, rather than having two or more of them. *...a single-sex school. ...a single-track road.*

single-ˈhanded. ADV If you do something **single-handed**, you do it without help from anyone else. *I brought up my seven children single-handed.* ◆**single-handedly** ADV *Olga Korbut single-handedly turned gymnastics into a major event.*

single-ˈminded. ADJ A **single-minded** person has only one aim and is determined to achieve it. *...a single-minded determination to win.* ◆**single-mindedness** N-U *...the single-mindedness of the athletes as they train.*

single ˈparent, single-parents. N-C A **single-parent** is someone who is bringing up a child on their own, because the other parent is not living with them.

singular /ˈsɪŋgjʊlə/. [1] ADJ BEFORE N & N-SING The **singular** form of a word or **the singular** is the form that is used when referring to one person or thing. *The word 'you' can be singular or plural... The inhabitants of the Arctic are known as the Inuit. The singular is Inuk.* [2] ADJ **Singular** means very great and remarkable; FORMAL. ◆**singularly** ADV *...a former sales executive singularly unsuited for the job.*

sinister /ˈsɪnɪstə/. ADJ Someone or something that is **sinister** seems evil or harmful. *There was something sinister about him that Elizabeth found disturbing.*

sink /sɪŋk/ **sinks, sinking, sank, sunk.** [1] N-C A **sink** is a basin with taps that supply water. *There were dirty dishes in the sink.* [2] VERB If a boat **sinks**, or if something **sinks** it, it disappears below the surface of a mass of water. *In a naval battle your aim is to sink the enemy's ship.* [3] VERB If something **sinks**, it disappears below the surface of a mass of water. *A fresh* *egg will sink and an old egg will float.* [4] VERB If you **sink**, you move into a lower position, for example by sinking down in a chair or kneeling; WRITTEN. *She sank into an armchair and crossed her legs.* [5] VERB If something **sinks** to a lower level or standard, it falls to that level or standard. *Pay increases have sunk to around seven per cent.* [6] VERB If your voice **sinks**, it becomes quieter; WRITTEN. *She heard their voices sink into a confidential whisper.* [7] VERB To **sink** into an unpleasant or undesirable situation or state means to pass gradually into it. *Bulgaria's economy has sunk into chaos.* [8] VERB If your **heart sinks**, you become depressed. *My heart sank because I thought he was going to dump me for another girl.* [9] VERB If something sharp **sinks** or **is sunk** into something solid, it goes deeply into it. *He sinks the needle into my arm.* ● See also **sunken**.

▸ **sink in.** PHR-VERB When a statement or fact **sinks in**, you finally understand or realize it fully. *The implication took a while to sink in.*

sip /sɪp/ **sips, sipping, sipped.** VERB & N-C If you **sip** a drink, or if you drink it in **sips**, you drink a small amount at a time. *She sipped from her coffee mug.*

siphon (or **syphon**) /ˈsaɪfən/ **siphons, siphoning, siphoned.** [1] VERB If you **siphon** liquid, you draw it from somewhere through a tube by using atmospheric pressure. *The town wasn't able to siphon any water out of the river.* [2] N-C A **siphon** is a tube which is used for siphoning liquid.

sir /sɜː/. [1] N-VOC People sometimes say **sir** as a polite way of addressing a man whose name they do not know or a man of superior rank. 'Dear Sir' is used at the beginning of official letters addressed to men. *Good afternoon, sir, and welcome to The New World Diner.* [2] N-TITLE **Sir** is the title used in front of the name of a knight or baronet. *...Sir Geoffrey Howe.*

siren /ˈsaɪərən/ **sirens.** N-C A **siren** is a warning device which makes a long, loud, wailing noise. Most fire engines, ambulances, and police cars have sirens.

sister /ˈsɪstə/ **sisters.** [1] N-C Your **sister** is a girl or woman who has the same parents as you. ● See note at **brother**. [2] N-C & N-TITLE **Sister** is a title given to a woman who belongs to a religious community such as a convent. *I'm Sister Agnes.* [3] N-C & N-TITLE In Britain, a **sister** is a senior female nurse who supervises a hospital ward. *Sister Middleton followed the coffee trolley.* [4] N-C You might use **sister** to describe a woman who belongs to the same race, religion, country, or organization as you, or who has ideas that are similar to yours. *...our Jewish brothers and sisters in New York.*

'sister-in-law, sisters-in-law. N-C Your **sister-in-law** is the sister of your husband or wife, or the woman who is married to your brother.

sit /sɪt/ **sits, sitting, sat.** [1] VERB If you are **sitting** somewhere, for example in a chair, your weight is supported by your buttocks rather than your feet. *He was unable to sit still.* [2] VERB When you **sit** somewhere, you lower your body until you are sitting on something.

He set the cases against a wall and sat on them. [3] VERB If you **sit** someone somewhere, you tell them to sit there or put them in a sitting position. *He used to sit me on his lap.* [4] VERB If you **sit** on a committee, you are a member of it. [5] VERB In British English, if you **sit** an examination, you do it. In American English, you **take** an examination. ● See also at **exam**. [6] VERB When a parliament, law court, or other official body is **sitting**, it is officially carrying out its work; FORMAL. [7] PHRASE If you **sit tight**, you remain where you are and do not take any action. *Sit tight. I'll be right back.* ● to **sit on the fence**: see **fence**.

▸ **sit around**; the form **sit about** is also used in British English. PHR-VERB If you **sit around** or **sit about**, you spend time doing nothing useful; INFORMAL. *Eve isn't the type to sit around doing nothing.*

▸ **sit back.** PHR-VERB If you **sit back** while something is happening, you relax and do not become involved in it. *Get everyone talking and then sit back and enjoy the conversation.*

▸ **sit in on.** PHR-VERB If you **sit in on** a meeting or lesson, you are present while it is taking place but do not take part in it. *Will they permit you to sit in on a few classes?*

▸ **sit on.** PHR-VERB If you say that someone **is sitting on** something, you mean that they are deliberately not dealing with it or not revealing it to others. *He had been sitting on the document for at least two months.*

▸ **sit out.** PHR-VERB If you **sit** something **out**, you wait for it to finish, without taking any action. *He can afford to sit out the property slump.*

▸ **sit through.** PHR-VERB If you **sit through** something such as a film or lecture, you stay until it is finished, although you are not enjoying it. *I sat through a long interview with the minister for tourism.*

▸ **sit up.** [1] PHR-VERB If you **sit up**, you move into a sitting position when you have been leaning back or lying down. [2] PHR-VERB If you **sit up**, you do not go to bed although it is very late. *We sat up drinking and talking.*

site /saɪt/ **sites, siting, sited.** [1] N-C A **site** is a piece of ground that is used for a particular purpose or where a particular thing happens or is situated. *...a building site. ...the site of the worst ecological disaster on earth. ...the site of Moses' tomb.* [2] VERB If something **is sited** in a particular place or position, it is placed there. *He said chemical weapons had never been sited in Germany.* ◆**siting** N-SING *...controls on the siting of gas storage vessels.*

'sitting-room, sitting-rooms. N-C A **sitting-room** is a room in a house where people sit and relax; BRITISH.

situated /ˈsɪtjʊeɪtɪd/. ADJ If something is **situated** somewhere, it is in a particular place or position. *His hotel is situated in one of the loveliest places on the Loire.*

situation /ˌsɪtjʊˈeɪʃən/ **situations.** [1] N-C You use the word **situation** to refer generally to what is happening at a particular place and time, or to refer to what is happening to you. *Army officers said the situation was under control... Men are not used to coping with women as equals in a work situation... I must do what* *any person would do in my situation.* [2] N-C The **situation** of a building or town is its surroundings; FORMAL. *A minor disadvantage is the hotel's situation on an island.*

six /sɪks/ **sixes.** NUM Six is the number 6.

sixteen /ˌsɪks'tiːn/ **sixteens.** NUM Sixteen is the number 16.

sixteenth /ˌsɪks'tiːnθ/ **sixteenths.** [1] ORD The **sixteenth** item in a series is the one that you count as number sixteen. [2] N-C A **sixteenth** is one of sixteen equal parts of something.

sixth /sɪksθ/ **sixths.** [1] ORD The **sixth** item in a series is the one that you count as number six. [2] N-C A **sixth** is one of six equal parts of something.

'sixth form, sixth forms. N-C The **sixth form** in a British school consists of the classes that pupils go into at the age of sixteen to study for 'A' Levels.

sixtieth /'sɪkstiəθ/. ORD The **sixtieth** item in a series is the one that you count as number sixty.

sixty /'sɪksti/ **sixties.** NUM Sixty is the number 60.

sizable /'saɪzəbl/. See **sizeable**.

size /saɪz/ **sizes, sizing, sized.** [1] N-U The **size** of something is how big or small it is. *The company had more than doubled in size. ...an area five times the size of Britain... Cut the chicken into bite-size pieces.* ♦ **-sized** *...a medium-sized college.* [2] N-U The **size** of something is the fact that it is very large. *Jack walked around the hotel and was mesmerized by its sheer size.* [3] N-C A **size** is one of a series of graded measurements, especially for things such as clothes or shoes. *My sister is the same height but only a size 12.*

▸ **size up.** PHR-VERB If you **size up** a person or situation, you carefully look at the person or think about the situation, so that you can decide how to act; INFORMAL. *He spent the evening sizing me up intellectually.*

sizeable (or **sizable**) /'saɪzəbl/. ADJ **Sizeable** means fairly large. *...a sizeable chunk of land.*

sizzle /'sɪzl/ **sizzles, sizzling, sizzled.** VERB If something **sizzles**, it makes a hissing sound like the sound made by frying food. *The sausages and burgers sizzled.*

skate /skeɪt/ **skates, skating, skated.** [1] N-C **Skates** are ice-skates or roller-skates. [2] VERB If you **skate**, you move about wearing ice-skates or roller-skates. *Dan skated up to him.* ♦ **skater, skaters** N-C *His dream was to become a professional skater.* ♦ **skating** N-U *They all went skating together.*

skeletal /'skelɪtəl/. ADJ BEFORE N **Skeletal** means relating to skeletons. *...the skeletal remains of seven adults.*

skeleton /'skelɪtən/ **skeletons.** [1] N-C Your **skeleton** is the framework of bones in your body. [2] ADJ BEFORE N A **skeleton** staff is the smallest number of staff necessary to run an organization.

skeptic /'skeptɪk/. See **sceptic**.

skeptical /'skeptɪkəl/. See **sceptical**.

sketch /sketʃ/ **sketches, sketching, sketched.** [1] N-C A **sketch** is a drawing that is done quickly without a lot of details. *Make a rough sketch showing where the vehicles were.* [2] VERB If you **sketch** something, you make a quick rough drawing of it. *He sketched a map on the back of a menu.* [3] N-C A **sketch** of an incident or person is a brief description of them without many details. *Leonard had given a brief sketch of his childhood.* [4] VERB & PHR-VERB If you **sketch** or **sketch out** a plan or incident, you briefly describe or state its main points. *I had visited him in Johannesburg and sketched what I was trying to do.* [5] N-C A **sketch** is a short humorous piece of acting, usually forming part of a comedy show.

sketchy /'sketʃi/ **sketchier, sketchiest.** ADJ Something that is **sketchy** is incomplete and does not have many details. *Details are sketchy, but first reports say at least eight people were hit.*

skewer /'skjuːə/ **skewers, skewering, skewered.** [1] N-C A **skewer** is a long metal pin which is used to hold pieces of food together during cooking. [2] VERB If you **skewer** something, you push a long, thin, pointed object through it. *He skewered one of the sausages.*

ski /skiː/ **skis, skiing, skied.** [1] N-C **Skis** are long, flat, narrow pieces of wood, metal, or plastic that are fastened to boots so that you can move easily over snow. [2] VERB When people **ski**, they move over snow on skis. [3] N-C **ski, skiers** N-C *He is an enthusiastic skier.* ♦ **skiing** N-U *...a skiing holiday.* [3] ADJ BEFORE N **Ski** is used to refer to things that are concerned with skiing. *...a Swiss ski resort. ...ski boots.*

skid /skɪd/ **skids, skidding, skidded.** VERB & N-C If a vehicle **skids**, or if it goes into a **skid**, it slides sideways or forwards in an uncontrolled way. *There was heavy snow and the plane skidded on landing.*

skilful (AM **skillful**) /'skɪlfʊl/. ADJ Someone who is **skilful** at something does it very well. *He is a particularly skilful writer.* ♦ **skilfully** ADV *He dealt skilfully with a series of demanding clients.*

skill /skɪl/ **skills.** [1] N-C A **skill** is a type of activity or work which requires special training or knowledge. *We need to focus on the basic skills of literacy and numeracy.* [2] N-U **Skill** is the knowledge and ability that enables you to do something well. *I tried fishing but had no skill and no luck.*

skilled /skɪld/. [1] ADJ Someone who is **skilled** has the knowledge and ability to do something well. *A train driver is a highly skilled professional.* [2] ADJ **Skilled** work can only be done by people who have had some training.

skillful /'skɪlfʊl/. See **skilful**.

skim /skɪm/ **skims, skimming, skimmed.** [1] VERB If you **skim** something from the surface of a liquid, you remove it. *Skim the fat off the gravy.* [2] VERB If something **skims** a surface or **skims** over it, it moves quickly along just above it. *We'll watch the flying fishes skimming across the water.* [3] VERB If you **skim** through a piece or writing, you read through it quickly. *He skimmed the pages quickly, then read them again more carefully.*

skimpy /'skɪmpi/ **skimpier, skimpiest.** ADJ **Skimpy** means too small in size or quantity.

Skimpy clothes reveal a lot of someone's body. *...skimpy underwear.*

skin /skɪn/ **skins, skinning, skinned.** [1] N-VAR Your **skin** is the natural covering of your body. *His skin is clear and smooth.* [2] N-VAR An animal **skin** is skin which has been removed from a dead animal. *...a leopard skin coat.* [3] N-VAR The **skin** of a fruit or vegetable is its outer layer or covering. *...banana skins.* [4] N-VAR If a **skin** forms on the surface of a liquid, a thin solid layer forms on it. *Stir the custard occasionally to prevent a skin forming.* [5] VERB If you **skin** a dead animal, you remove its skin.

skinny /'skɪni/ **skinnier, skinniest.** ADJ If you say that someone is **skinny**, you mean that they are very thin in a way you find unattractive; INFORMAL. *She had stringy hair and skinny legs.*

skip /skɪp/ **skips, skipping, skipped.** [1] VERB & N-C If you **skip** along, you move along with a series of little jumps from one foot to the other, called **skips.** *They skipped down the street... Anna gave a little skip of joy.* [2] VERB When someone **skips**, they jump up and down over a rope which they or other people are holding at each end and turning round and round. ◆**skipping** N-U *I enjoy skipping, walking, singing and playing games.* [3] VERB If you **skip** something that you usually do or that most people do, you decide not to do it. *It is important not to skip meals.* [4] VERB If you **skip** a part of something you are reading or a story you are telling, you miss it out or pass over it quickly. *She reinvented her own life story, skipping over the war years.* [5] N-C A **skip** is a large, open, metal container used to hold and take away rubbish; BRITISH.

skipper /'skɪpə/ **skippers.** N-C The **skipper** of a boat or of a sports team is its captain; INFORMAL.

skirmish /'skɜːmɪʃ/ **skirmishes.** N-C A **skirmish** is a short battle which is not part of a planned war strategy. *One Federal soldier was killed in the skirmish that ensued.*

skirt /skɜːt/ **skirts, skirting, skirted.** [1] N-C A **skirt** is a piece of clothing worn by women and girls. It fastens at the waist and hangs down around the legs. [2] VERB Something that **skirts** an area is situated around the edge of it. *...the gravel path that skirted the main lawn.* [3] VERB If you **skirt** something, you go around the edge of it. *She skirted round the edge of the room to the door.* [4] VERB If you **skirt** a problem or question, you avoid dealing with it. *He skirted round his main differences with her.*

skull /skʌl/ **skulls.** N-C Your **skull** is the bony part of your head which encloses your brain. *He was left with a broken arm and a fractured skull.*

sky /skaɪ/ **skies.** N-VAR The **sky** is the space around the earth which you can see when you stand outside and look upwards. *...warm sunshine and clear blue skies.*

skyline /'skaɪlaɪn/ **skylines.** N-C The **skyline** is the line or shape that is formed where the sky meets buildings or the land. *The village church dominates the skyline.*

skyscraper /'skaɪskreɪpə/ **skyscrapers.** N-C A **skyscraper** is a very tall building in a city.

slab /slæb/ **slabs.** N-C A **slab** of something is a thick flat piece of it. *...enormous slabs of meat. ...huge concrete paving slabs.*

slack /slæk/ **slacker, slackest.** [1] ADJ Something that is **slack** is loose and not firmly stretched or tightly in position. *...her rather dull, slack skin.* [2] ADJ A **slack** period is one in which there is not much activity. *Business has been a bit slack.* [3] ADJ If someone is **slack** in their work, they do not do it properly.

slacken /'slækən/ **slackens, slackening, slackened.** [1] VERB If something **slackens**, or if you **slacken** it, it becomes slower, less active, or less intense. *The wind slackened... He slackened his pace for me.* [2] VERB If your grip or a part of your body **slackens**, or if you **slacken** it, it becomes looser or more relaxed. *Muscles stretch, slacken and relax during child-birth.*
▶ **slacken off.** PHR-VERB If something **slackens off**, it becomes slower, less active, or less intense. *At about five o'clock, business slackened off.*

slacks /slæks/. N-PL **Slacks** are casual trousers; DATED. *She was wearing black slacks.*

slain /sleɪn/. **Slain** is the past participle of **slay.**

slam /slæm/ **slams, slamming, slammed.** [1] VERB If you **slam** a door or window, or if it **slams**, it shuts noisily and with great force. *He slammed the gate shut behind him.* [2] VERB If you **slam** something down, you put it there quickly and with great force. *She was outraged and slammed down the phone.* [3] VERB If one thing **slams** into another, or if it **slams against** another, it crashes into it with great force. *He was killed when his car slammed into a truck... He slammed his fist against the wall.*

slander /'slɑːndə, 'slæn-/ **slanders, slandering, slandered.** [1] N-VAR **Slander** is an untrue spoken statement about someone which is intended to damage their reputation. *He is suing his former wife for slander. ...lies, rumours and slanders.* [2] VERB If someone **slanders** you, they make untrue spoken statements about you in order to damage your reputation.

slang /slæŋ/. N-U **Slang** is words, expressions, and meanings that are informal and are used by people who know each other very well or who have the same interests. *... US Army slang.*

slant /slɑːnt, slænt/ **slants, slanting, slanted.** [1] VERB Something that **slants** is sloping, rather than horizontal or vertical. *The morning sun slanted through the glass roof.* [2] N-SING If something is on a **slant**, it is in a sloping position. [3] VERB If information or a system **is slanted**, it is made to favour towards a particular group or opinion. *The programme was deliberately slanted to make the home team look good.* [4] N-SING A particular **slant** on a subject is a particular way of thinking about it, especially one that is unfair or biased. *They give a slant to every single news item that's put on the air.*

slap /slæp/ **slaps, slapping, slapped.** [1] VERB & N-C If you **slap** someone, or if you give them a **slap**, you hit them with the palm of your hand. *I slapped him hard across the face.* [2] PHRASE If you describe something that someone does as **a slap in the face**, you mean that it shocks or upsets you because it shows that they do not support you or respect you. **3** VERB If you **slap** someone **on** the back, you hit them in a friendly manner on their back. **4** VERB If you **slap** something onto a surface, you put it there quickly and carelessly, often with a lot of force. *I slapped the sweets down on the table... I'll show you how to slap a bit of paint on the wall.*

slash /slæʃ/ **slashes, slashing, slashed.** **1** VERB If you **slash** something, you make a long deep cut in it. *Four cars had their tyres slashed.* **2** VERB If you **slash at** something, you quickly hit at it with something. *She slashed at me with an unpleasantly large carving-knife.* **3** VERB To **slash** something such as costs or jobs means to reduce them by a large amount; INFORMAL.

slate /sleɪt/ **slates.** **1** N-U **Slate** is a dark grey rock that can be easily split into thin layers. **2** N-C A **slate** is one of the small flat pieces of slate that are used for covering roofs.

slaughter /ˈslɔːtə/ **slaughters, slaughtering, slaughtered.** **1** VERB & N-U If large numbers of people or animals **are slaughtered**, they are killed in a way that is cruel, unjust, or unnecessary. **Slaughter** is the cruel, unjust, or unnecessary killing of large numbers of people or animals. *...the imperial army's slaughter of Chinese civilians.* **2** VERB & N-U To **slaughter** animals such as cows and sheep means to kill them for their meat. **Slaughter** is the killing of animals for their meat. *Commercial pigs are ready for slaughter at four to six months.* **3** See note at **kill**.

slave /sleɪv/ **slaves.** **1** N-C A **slave** is a person who is owned by another person and has to work for that person without pay. **2** N-C If you say that someone is a **slave** to something, you mean that they are very strongly influenced or controlled by it. *Anthony was never a slave to possessions.*

slavery /ˈsleɪvəri/. N-U **Slavery** is the system by which people are owned by other people as slaves. *...a fervent campaigner for the abolition of slavery.*

slay /sleɪ/ **slays, slaying, slew, slain.** VERB To **slay** a person or animal means to kill them; LITERARY. *...the field where Saint George is reputed to have slain the dragon.*

sleazy /ˈsliːzi/ **sleazier, sleaziest.** **1** ADJ If you describe a place as **sleazy**, you dislike it because it looks dirty and not respectable; INFORMAL. *...sleazy bars.* **2** ADJ If you describe something or someone as **sleazy**, you disapprove of them because you think they are not respectable and are rather sordid; INFORMAL. *...sex shops and sleazy magazines.*

sled /sled/ **sleds.** N-C A **sled** is the same as a **sledge**; AMERICAN.

sledge /sledʒ/ **sledges.** N-C & VERB A **sledge** is a vehicle for travelling over snow. It consists of a framework which slides on two strips of wood or metal. BRITISH.

sleek /sliːk/ **sleeker, sleekest.** **1** ADJ **Sleek** hair or fur is smooth and shiny and looks healthy. **2** ADJ A **sleek** person looks rich and stylish. **3** ADJ **Sleek** vehicles, furniture, or other objects look smooth, shiny, and expensive.

sleep /sliːp/ **sleeps, sleeping, slept.** **1** N-U **Sleep** is the natural state of rest in which your eyes are closed, your body is inactive, and your mind does not think. *Try and get some sleep... Be quiet and go to sleep.* **2** VERB & N-C When you **sleep**, you rest with your eyes closed and your mind and body inactive. A **sleep** is a period of sleeping. *She slept till noon. ...a pool surrounded by sleeping sunbathers... I think he may be ready for a sleep soon.* **3** VERB If one person **sleeps with** another, or if two people **sleep together**, they have sex. **4** VERB If a building or room **sleeps** a particular number of people, it has beds for that number of people. *The villa sleeps 10.*

There are three verbal expressions in English which refer to the moment when you start to sleep. When you go to bed at night, you normally **go to sleep** or **fall asleep**. When you **go to sleep**, it is usually a deliberate action. *He didn't want to go to sleep.* You can **fall asleep** by accident, or at a time when you should be awake. *I've seen doctors fall asleep in the operating theatre.* If you have difficulty sleeping, you can say that you cannot **get to sleep**. *Sometimes the fever prevents the child from getting to sleep.*

PHRASES ● If you say that you did not **lose** any **sleep** over something, you mean that you did not worry about it at all. ● If a sick or injured animal **is put to sleep**, it is painlessly killed by a vet. ● to **sleep rough**: see **rough**.

▶ **sleep around.** PHR-VERB If you say that someone **sleeps around**, you disapprove of them because they have sex with a lot of different people; INFORMAL.

▶ **sleep off.** PHR-VERB If you **sleep off** the effects of too much drink, food, or travelling, you recover from it by sleeping. *It's a good idea to spend the first night of your holiday sleeping off the jet lag.*

▶ **sleep through.** PHR-VERB If you **sleep through** a noise, it does not wake you up. *They had slept right through the alarm.*

sleeper /ˈsliːpə/ **sleepers.** **1** N-C You can use the word **sleeper** to indicate how well someone sleeps. For example, if someone is a light **sleeper**, they are easily woken up. *I'm a very heavy sleeper.* **2** N-C A **sleeper** is a train with beds for passengers on overnight journeys. You can also refer to the beds themselves as **sleepers**. BRITISH. *The train is air-conditioned and has first and second class sleepers.* **3** N-C Railway **sleepers** are large heavy beams that support the rails of a railway track; BRITISH.

sleeping bag, sleeping bags. N-C A **sleeping bag** is a large warm bag for sleeping in, especially when you are camping.

sleepless /ˈsliːpləs/. **1** ADJ A **sleepless** night is one during which you do not sleep. **2** ADJ Someone who is **sleepless** is unable to sleep. *She was still sitting there, grim and sleepless, when Frank arrived.* ◆ **sleeplessness** N-U *He continued to suffer from sleeplessness.*

sleepy /ˈsliːpi/ **sleepier, sleepiest.** **1** ADJ If you feel **sleepy**, you feel tired and ready to go to sleep. *'Are we here, love?' she said in a* *hoarse, sleepy voice.* ◆**sleepily** ADV *Joanna sat up, blinking sleepily.* [2] ADJ A **sleepy** place is very quiet and does not have much activity or excitement. *...a sleepy fishing village.*

sleet /sli:t/. N-U **Sleet** is rain that is partly frozen.

sleeve /sli:v/ **sleeves.** [1] N-C The **sleeves** of a coat, shirt, or other item of clothing are the parts that cover your arms. *...a shirt with long sleeves.* [2] PHRASE If you have something **up** your **sleeve**, you have an idea or plan which you have not told anyone about. *I still have a few tricks up my sleeve.* [3] N-C A record **sleeve** is the stiff envelope in which a record is kept.

sleigh /sleɪ/ **sleighs.** N-C A **sleigh** is a vehicle like a sledge which can slide over snow. Sleighs are usually pulled by horses.

slender /ˈslendə/. [1] ADJ A **slender** person is thin and graceful in an attractive way; WRITTEN. *...a tall slender woman. ...her long slender legs.* [2] ADJ You can use **slender** to describe a situation which exists but only to a very small degree; WRITTEN. *...the slender majority won by his government.*

slept /slept/. **Slept** is the past tense and past participle of **sleep**.

slew /slu:/. [1] **Slew** is the past tense of **slay**. [2] N-SING A **slew** of things or people is a large number of them; AMERICAN. *They'd evidently had a slew of customers.*

slice /slaɪs/ **slices, slicing, sliced.** [1] N-C A **slice** of bread, meat, fruit, or other food is a thin piece that has been cut from a larger piece. *Cut the onion halves into slices.* [2] VERB If you **slice** food, you cut it into thin pieces. *Slice the steak into long thin slices... I usually buy sliced bread.* [3] VERB If something **slices through** a substance, it moves through it quickly, like a knife; LITERARY. *The ship sliced through the water.* [4] N-C If you talk about someone getting a **slice** of something, you mean that they get a part of it. *Other ports are determined to challenge Hong Kong for a larger slice of the region's trade.*

slick /slɪk/ **slicker, slickest; slicks.** [1] ADJ A **slick** performance, production, or advertisement is presented in an attractive and professional way. [2] ADJ A **slick** action is done quickly and smoothly, and without any obvious effort. [3] ADJ If you describe someone as **slick**, you dislike them because they speak easily and persuasively but are not sincere. *...slick politicians.* [4] N-C A **slick** is the same as an **oil slick**.

slide /slaɪd/ **slides, sliding, slid** /slɪd/. [1] VERB When something **slides** somewhere, or when you **slide** it somewhere, it moves smoothly over or against something else. *Tears were sliding down his cheeks... She slid the door open.* [2] VERB If you **slide** somewhere, you move there smoothly and quietly. *He slid into the driver's seat.* [3] N-C A **slide** in a playground is a structure that has a steep slope for children to slide down. [4] VERB To **slide into** a particular mood, attitude, or situation means to gradually start to have that mood, attitude, or situation, often without intending to. *She had slid into a depression.* [5] N-C A **slide** is a small piece of photographic film which you project onto a screen so that you can see the picture.

slight /slaɪt/ **slighter, slightest; slights, slighting, slighted.** [1] ADJ Something that is **slight** is very small in degree or quantity. *Doctors say he has made a slight improvement... He's not the slightest bit worried.* [2] PHRASE You use **in the slightest** to emphasize a negative statement. *That doesn't interest me in the slightest.* [3] ADJ A **slight** person has a slim and delicate body. [4] VERB & N-C If you **are slighted**, someone does or says something that insults you by treating you as if your views or feelings are not important. You refer to what that person does or says as a **slight**. *They felt slighted by not being adequately consulted.*

slightly /ˈslaɪtli/. ADV **Slightly** means to some degree but not to a very large degree. *His family then moved to a slightly larger house... You can adjust it slightly.*

slim /slɪm/ **slimmer, slimmest; slims, slimming, slimmed.** [1] ADJ A **slim** person has a thin nicely shaped body. [2] VERB If you **are slimming**, you are trying to make yourself thinner and lighter by eating less food. ◆**slimmer, slimmers** N-C *...meals for slimmers.* ◆**slimming** N-U *We live in a society which is obsessed with slimming.* [3] ADJ A **slim** book, wallet, or other object is thinner than usual. [4] ADJ A **slim** chance or possibility is a very small one. *The chances of a new author getting published are very slim.*

▶ **slim down.** PHR-VERB If a company or other organization **slims down**, or if it **is slimmed down**, it employs fewer people, in order to save money or become more efficient.

slime /slaɪm/. N-U **Slime** is a thick slippery substance, for example the substance which comes from a slug.

sling /slɪŋ/ **slings, slinging, slung.** [1] VERB If you **sling** something somewhere, you throw it there carelessly. *I saw him take off his anorak and sling it into the back seat.* [2] VERB If you **sling** something over your shoulder or over something such as a chair, you hang it there loosely. *He had a small green rucksack slung over one shoulder.* [3] VERB If a rope, blanket, or other object **is slung** between two points, it is hung loosely between them. *...a hammock slung between the trees.* [4] N-C A **sling** is an object made of ropes, straps, or cloth that is used for carrying things. *In many parts of Kenya, babies are carried in slings all day.* [5] N-C A **sling** is a piece of cloth used to support an injured arm. It goes under someone's lower arm and is tied around their neck. *Next day she was back at work with her arm in a sling.*

slip /slɪp/ **slips, slipping, slipped.** [1] VERB If you **slip**, you accidentally slide and lose your balance. *I guess I must have slipped on some ice.* [2] VERB If something **slips**, it slides out of place or out of your hand. *His glasses slipped down his nose... The hammer slipped out of her grasp.* [3] VERB If you **slip** somewhere, you go there quickly and quietly. *Amy slipped downstairs and out of the house... I slipped out of bed.* [4] VERB If you **slip** something somewhere, you put it there quickly in a way that does not attract attention. *He found a coin in his pocket and slipped it into her collecting tin.* [5] VERB If you **slip** something **to** someone, or if you **slip**

someone something, you give it to them secretly. *Robert had slipped her a note in school.* ⑥ VERB To **slip into** a particular state or situation means to pass gradually into it, in a way that is hardly noticed. *Don't slip into the habit of sleeping late.* ⑦ VERB If you **slip** into or **slip** out of clothes or shoes, you put them on or take them off quickly and easily. *Laila stood up and slipped on her coat before he could assist her... I slipped off my woollen gloves.* ⑧ N-C A **slip** is a small or unimportant mistake. ⑨ N-C A **slip** of paper is a small piece of paper.

▸ **slip up.** PHR-VERB If you **slip up**, you make a small or unimportant mistake.

slipper /'slɪpə/ **slippers.** N-C Slippers are loose soft shoes that you wear in the house.

slippery /'slɪpəri/. ① ADJ Something that is **slippery** is smooth, wet, or greasy, making it difficult to walk on or to hold. *Motorists were warned to beware of slippery conditions.* ② PHRASE If you say that someone is on a **slippery slope** to something bad, you mean that their behaviour or actions will inevitably lead to that condition in the near future. *It is the slippery slope to anarchy when one part of society is above the law.*

slit /slɪt/ **slits, slitting, slit.** ① VERB If you **slit** something, you make a long narrow cut in it. *He slit open the bag with a penknife... My girlfriend was threatening to slit her wrists.* ② N-C A **slit** is a long narrow cut or opening in something. *Make a slit in the stem about half an inch long... She watched them through a slit in the curtains.*

slither /'slɪðə/ **slithers, slithering, slithered.** VERB If you **slither** somewhere, you slide along, often in an uncontrolled way. *Robert lost his footing and slithered down the bank.*

sliver /'slɪvə/ **slivers.** N-C A **sliver** of something is a small thin piece or amount of it. *...slivers of glass.*

slog /slɒg/ **slogs, slogging, slogged.** ① VERB If you **slog** through something, you work hard and steadily through it; INFORMAL. *She has slogged her way through ballet classes since the age of six.* ② N-SING If you describe a task as a **slog**, you mean that it is tiring and requires a lot of effort; INFORMAL. ③ VERB & N-SING If you **slog** somewhere, you make a long and tiring journey there, which you can refer to as a **slog**; INFORMAL. *...a slog through heather and bracken to the top of a hill.*

slogan /'sləʊgən/ **slogans.** N-C A **slogan** is a short phrase that is easy to remember and is used in advertisements and by political parties.

slop /slɒp/ **slops, slopping, slopped.** VERB If you **slop** liquid, or if it **slops**, it spills over the edge of a container in a messy way. *She slopped some tea into the saucer.*

slope /sləʊp/ **slopes, sloping, sloped.** ① N-C A **slope** is a surface that is at an angle, so that one end is higher than the other. *The street must have been on a slope.* ② VERB If a surface **slopes**, it is at an angle, so that one end is higher than the other. *The bank sloped down sharply to the river.* ◆ **sloping** ADJ *...the gently sloping beach.* ③ VERB If something **slopes**, it leans to the right or to the left rather than be-

ing upright. *The writing sloped backwards.* ④ N-SING The **slope** of something is the angle at which it slopes. *...a slope of ten degrees.*

sloppy /'slɒpi/. ADJ Something that is **sloppy** is messy and careless; INFORMAL. *He has little patience for sloppy work.* ◆ **sloppiness** N-U *...the sloppiness of the young.*

slot /slɒt/ **slots, slotting, slotted.** ① N-C A **slot** is a narrow opening in a machine or container, for example a hole that you put coins in to make a machine work. ② VERB When something **slots** into something else, or when you **slot** it in, you put it into a space where it fits. *The car seat belt slotted into place easily.* ③ N-C A **slot** in a schedule or scheme is a place in it where an activity can take place. *...her daily slot on the TV programme Hot Chefs.*

slouch /slaʊtʃ/ **slouches, slouching, slouched.** VERB & N-SING If you **slouch**, or if your body is in a **slouch**, you sit, stand, or walk with your shoulders and head drooping down. *Try not to slouch when you are sitting down... He sat slouched over his coffee... He walked with a slouch.*

slow /sləʊ/ **slower, slowest; slows, slowing, slowed.** ① ADJ Something that is **slow** moves, happens, or is done without much speed. *The traffic is heavy and slow. ...slow, regular breathing... The distribution of passports has been a slow process.* ◆ **slowly** ADV *Christian backed slowly away... My resentment of her slowly began to fade.* ◆ **slowness** N-U *She lowered the glass with calculated slowness.* ② VERB If something **slows**, or if you **slow** it, it starts to move or happen more slowly. *She slowed the car and began driving up a narrow road.* ③ ADJ AFTER LINK-V If someone is **slow** to do something, they do it after a delay. *I've been a bit slow in making up my mind.* ④ ADJ If you describe a situation, place, or activity as **slow**, you mean that it is not very exciting. *The island is too slow for her liking.* ⑤ ADJ If a clock or watch is **slow**, it shows a time that is earlier than the correct time. ⑥ ADJ Someone who is **slow** is not very clever and takes a long time to understand things.

▸ **slow down.** ① PHR-VERB If something **slows down**, or if you **slow** it **down**, it starts to move or happen more slowly. *The car slowed down... We want to slow down the process of eating.* ② PHR-VERB If someone **slows down**, they become less active. *He was still taking some medication which slowed him down.* ● See also **slowdown.**

▸ **slow up.** PHR-VERB **Slow up** means the same as **slow down 1.** *...a new code of criminal procedure has also slowed up the system.*

slowdown /'sləʊdaʊn/ **slowdowns.** N-C A **slowdown** is a reduction in speed or activity. *There has been a sharp slowdown in economic growth.*

slow 'motion. N-U When film or television pictures are shown in **slow motion**, they are shown much more slowly than normal.

sludge /slʌdʒ/. N-U **Sludge** is thick mud.

slug /slʌg/ **slugs.** ① N-C A **slug** is a small slow-moving creature, with a long slippery body, like a snail without a shell. ② N-C A **slug** is a bullet; AMERICAN, INFORMAL.

sluggish /'slʌgɪʃ/. ADJ Something that is **sluggish** moves or works much more slowly than normal. *He felt old and sluggish.*

slum /slʌm/ **slums, slumming, slummed.** [1] N-C A **slum** is an area of a city where living conditions are very bad. [2] VERB If you say that someone **is slumming it** or **is slumming**, you mean they are spending time in a place or in conditions that are at a much lower social level than they are used to.

slumber /'slʌmbə/ **slumbers, slumbering, slumbered.** [1] N-VAR **Slumber** is sleep; LITERARY. *He roused his brother Charles from his slumbers.* [2] VERB Someone who **is slumbering** is sleeping; LITERARY.

slump /slʌmp/ **slumps, slumping, slumped.** [1] N-C & VERB If there is a **slump** in something such as the value of something, or if it **slumps**, it falls suddenly and by a large amount. *...a slump in property prices... Net profits slumped by 41%.* [2] N-C A **slump** is a time when there is a lot of unemployment and poverty. [3] VERB If you **slump** somewhere, you fall or sit down there heavily. *She slumped into a chair.*

slung /slʌŋ/. **Slung** is the past tense and past participle of **sling**.

slur /slɜ:/ **slurs, slurring, slurred.** [1] N-C A **slur** is an insulting remark which could damage someone's reputation. *This is yet another slur on the integrity of the Metropolitan Police.* [2] VERB If someone **slurs** their speech, they do not pronounce each word clearly, because they are drunk or sleepy. *The newscaster's speech began to slur.* ♦**slurred** ADJ *Her words were slurred, as though she were slightly drunk.*

sly /slaɪ/. [1] ADJ A **sly** look, expression, or remark shows that you know something that other people do not know. *He gave me a sly, meaningful look.* ♦**slyly** ADV *Anna grinned slyly.* [2] ADJ If you describe someone as **sly**, you mean that they are clever at deceiving people.

smack /smæk/ **smacks, smacking, smacked.** [1] VERB & N-C If you **smack** someone, or if you give them a **smack**, you hit them with your hand. *She smacked me on the side of the head. ...a smack across the face.* [2] VERB If you **smack** something somewhere, you put it or throw it there so that it makes a loud sharp noise. *He took the letter out of his jacket and smacked it down on the desk.* [3] VERB If something **smacks** of something that you consider bad, it reminds you of it or is like it. *Their use of trickery smacked of deceit.*

small /smɔ:l/ **smaller, smallest.** [1] ADJ Someone or something that is **small** is not large in physical size. *She is small for her age... The window was far too small for him to get through.* [2] ADJ A **small** group or quantity consists of only a few people or things. *Fairly small numbers of young people commit suicide. ...a small amount of money.* [3] ADJ A **small** child is a very young child. *What were you like when you were small?* [4] ADJ You use **small** to describe something that is not significant or great in degree. *No detail was too small to escape her attention. ...a relatively small problem.* [5] ADJ AFTER LINK-V If someone makes you look or feel **small**, they make you look or feel stupid, so that you are ashamed or humiliated. *When your children misbehave, tell them without making them feel small.* [6] N-SING **The small of** your back is the bottom part of your back that curves inwards slightly. [7] **small wonder**: see **wonder**.

> You can also use the adjective **little** to talk about things that are small, but it is not normally used to emphasize or draw attention to the fact that something is small. For instance, you cannot say 'The town is little' or 'I have a very little car'. **Little** is a less precise word than **small**, and may be used to suggest the speaker's feelings or attitude towards the person or thing being described. For that reason, **little** is often used after another adjective. *What a nice little house you've got here!... Shut up, you horrible little boy!* Do not confuse this meaning of **little** with its use before uncount nouns, when it refers to a small amount of something. *We had no money, but we did have a little food.*
> See also the note at **little**.

,small 'print. N-U The **small print** of a contract or agreement is the part of it that is written in very small print.

,small-'scale. ADJ A **small-scale** activity or organization is limited in extent. *...the small-scale production of farmhouse cheeses.*

smart /smɑ:t/ **smarter, smartest; smarts, smarting, smarted.** [1] ADJ **Smart** people and things are pleasantly neat and clean in appearance. *I wore a black dress and looked very smart. ...smart new offices.* ♦**smartly** ADV *He dressed very smartly which was important in those days.* ● See also **smartly**. [2] ADJ A **smart** place or event is connected with wealthy and fashionable people. *...smart London dinner parties.* [3] ADJ You can describe someone who is clever as **smart**. *He's a smart kid.* [4] VERB If a part of your body or a wound **smarts**, you feel a sharp stinging pain in it. *Her eyes were smarting from the smoke.* [5] VERB If you **are smarting** from something such as criticism or failure, you feel upset about it. *I'm still smarting over my missed opportunity.*

smartly /'smɑ:tli/. ADV If someone moves or does something **smartly**, they do it quickly and neatly; WRITTEN. *The housekeeper moved smartly to the Vicar's desk.* ● See also **smart**.

smash /smæʃ/ **smashes, smashing, smashed.** [1] VERB If something **smashes**, or if you **smash** it, it breaks into many pieces, for example when it is hit or dropped. *Two or three glasses fell off and smashed into pieces... Someone smashed a bottle.* [2] VERB If you **smash** through a wall, gate, or door, you get through it by hitting and breaking it. *Soldiers smashed their way into his office.* [3] VERB If something **smashes** or **is smashed** against something solid, it moves with great force against it. *He smashed his fist into Anthony's face.* [4] N-C You can refer to a car crash as a **smash**; INFORMAL. [5] VERB To **smash** a political group or system means to deliberately destroy it; INFORMAL. *The President said he would smash the communists.*

▶ **smash up.** PHR-VERB If you **smash** something **up**, you completely destroy it by hitting it and breaking it into many pieces. *She took revenge on her ex-boyfriend by smashing up his home.*

smashing /'smæʃɪŋ/. ADJ If you describe something or someone as **smashing**, you mean that you like them very much; BRITISH, DATED. *They are smashing people.*

smear /smɪə/ **smears, smearing, smeared.** [1] VERB If you **smear** a surface with a substance, or if you **smear** the substance onto the surface, you spread a layer of the substance over the surface. *My sister smeared herself with suntan oil... Smear a little olive oil over the inside of the salad bowl.* ♦ **smeared** ADJ *The other child's face was smeared with dirt.* [2] N-C A **smear** is a dirty or greasy mark. [3] VERB & N-C To **smear** someone means to spread unpleasant and untrue rumours or accusations about them in order to damage their reputation. A **smear** is an unpleasant and untrue rumour or accusation. *...a smear campaign by his political opponents.*

smell /smel/ **smells, smelling, smelled** or **smelt.** [1] N-C The **smell** of something is a quality it has which you become aware of through your nose. *...the smell of freshly baked bread.* [2] N-U Your sense of **smell** is the ability that your nose has to detect things. [3] VERB If something **smells** of a particular thing, it has a particular quality which you become aware of through your nose. *The room smelled of lemons... It smells delicious. ...a foul-smelling cloud of smoke.* [4] VERB If you say that something **smells**, you mean that it smells unpleasant. *Do my feet smell?* [5] VERB If you **smell** something, you become aware of it through your nose. *As soon as we opened the front door we could smell the gas.* [6] VERB If you **smell** something, you put your nose near it and breathe in, so that you can discover its smell. *I took a fresh rose out of the vase on our table, and smelled it.* [7] VERB If you **smell** something, you feel instinctively that it is likely to happen or be true. *He knew virtually nothing about music but he could smell a hit*

smelly /'smeli/ **smellier, smelliest.** ADJ Something that is **smelly** has an unpleasant smell. *He had extremely smelly feet.*

smelt /smelt/ **smelts, smelting, smelted.** [1] **Smelt** is a past tense and past participle of **smell.** [2] VERB To **smelt** a substance containing metal means to process it by heating it until it melts, so that the metal is extracted and changed chemically.

smile /smaɪl/ **smiles, smiling, smiled.** [1] VERB When you **smile**, the corners of your mouth curve outwards, usually because you are pleased or amused. *He loved to make people smile... Both of them smiled at the picture.* [2] N-C A **smile** is the expression that you have on your face when you smile. *She had a big smile on her face.* [3] VERB If you **smile** something, you express or say it with a smile. *'Aren't we daft?' she smiled.*

smirk /smɜːk/ **smirks, smirking, smirked.** VERB & N-C If you **smirk**, or if you give a **smirk**, you smile in an unpleasant way. *Charlene smirked at Mona's outfit... 'Yeah, right,' he said with a smirk.*

smog /smɒg/. N-U **Smog** is a mixture of fog and smoke which occurs in some industrial cities.

smoke /sməʊk/ **smokes, smoking, smoked.** [1] N-U **Smoke** consists of gas and small bits of solid material that are sent into the air when something burns. *...cigarette smoke.* [2] VERB If something **is smoking**, smoke is coming from it. *...a pile of smoking rubble.* [3] VERB When someone **smokes** a cigarette, cigar, or pipe, they suck smoke from it into their mouth and blow it out again. If you **smoke**, you regularly smoke cigarettes, cigars, or a pipe. *He sat and smoked quietly.* ♦ **smoker, smokers** N-C *He was not a heavy smoker.* ♦ **smoking** N-U *Smoking will not be allowed. ...a no-smoking area.* [4] VERB If fish or meat **is smoked**, it is hung over burning wood so that the smoke preserves it and gives it a special flavour. *...smoked salmon.*

smoky /'sməʊki/. [1] ADJ A **smoky** place has a lot of smoke in the air. [2] ADJ You can use **smoky** to describe something that looks or tastes like smoke. *The tea has a distinctive smoky flavour. ...the smoky blue of early dawn.*

smolder /'sməʊldə/. See **smoulder.**

smooth /smuːð/. **smoother, smoothest; smooths, smoothing, smoothed.** [1] ADJ A **smooth** surface has no roughness or holes. *Use a sheet of glass, perspex, or any smooth surface.* ♦ **smoothness** N-U *...the smoothness of her skin.* [2] ADJ A **smooth** liquid or mixture has been mixed well so that it has no lumps in it. *Blend the sauce to a smooth puree.* [3] ADJ A **smooth** movement or process happens or is done evenly and steadily with no sudden changes or breaks. *He turned her round in a smooth movement... Research shows the economy in a smooth curve.* ♦ **smoothly** ADV *Make sure that you execute all movements smoothly.* [4] ADJ **Smooth** means successful and without problems. *...the Czech Republic's smooth transition from communism to capitalism.* ♦ **smoothly** ADV *So far, talks at GM have gone smoothly.* [5] ADJ If you describe a drink such as wine, whisky, or coffee as **smooth**, you mean that it is not bitter and is pleasant to drink. [6] ADJ If you describe a man as **smooth**, you mean that he is extremely smart, confident, and polite, often in a way that you find rather unpleasant. [7] VERB If you **smooth** something, or if you **smooth** it **out** or **smooth** it **down**, you move your hands over its surface to make it smooth and flat. *She stood up and smoothed down her frock... Carefully Nick smoothed a sheet of newspaper across the front of the grate.* [8] PHRASE If you **smooth the path** or **smooth the way** towards something, you make it easier or more likely to happen. *Their talks were aimed at smoothing the path towards a treaty.*

▶ **smooth out** or **smooth over.** PHR-VERB If you **smooth out** or **smooth over** a problem or difficulty, you make it less serious and easier to deal with, especially by talking to the people concerned. *Baker was smoothing out differences with European allies.*

smother /ˈsmʌðə/ **smothers, smothering, smothered.** [1] VERB If you **smother** a fire, you cover it with something in order to put it out. [2] VERB To **smother** someone means to kill them by covering their face with something so that they cannot breathe. [3] VERB To **smother** something with things is to cover it completely with them. *He leapt up and smothered her with kisses. ...scones smothered in cream and jam.* [4] VERB To **smother** someone means to give them too much love and protection. *He smothered his youngest daughter in love.*

smoulder (AM **smolder**) /ˈsmoʊldə/ **smoulders, smouldering, smouldered.** [1] VERB If something **smoulders**, it burns slowly, producing smoke but not flames. *The remains of a fire smouldered in the log basket.* [2] VERB If a feeling **smoulders** inside you, you feel it intensely but rarely show it. *Anger still smoulders about the allegations.*

smudge /smʌdʒ/ **smudges, smudging, smudged.** [1] N-C A **smudge** is a dirty, blurred mark. [2] VERB If you **smudge** something, you make it dirty or messy by touching it. *They had to swim without smudging their make-up.*

smug /smʌɡ/. ADJ If you say that someone is **smug**, you are criticizing the fact they seem very pleased with how good, clever, or fortunate they are. ◆**smugly** ADV *The Major smiled smugly and sat down.*

smuggle /ˈsmʌɡl/ **smuggles, smuggling, smuggled.** VERB If someone **smuggles** things or people into a place or out of it, they take them there illegally or secretly. *He smuggled papers out each day and photocopied them... If you try to smuggle drugs you are stupid.* ◆**smuggler** smugglers N-C *...drug smugglers.* ◆**smuggling** N-U *...diamond smuggling.*

snack /snæk/ **snacks.** N-C A **snack** is a small, quick meal, or something eaten between meals.

snag /snæɡ/ **snags, snagging, snagged.** [1] N-C A **snag** is a small problem or disadvantage. *The boy was looking for work. The only snag was that he had no transportation.* [2] VERB If you **snag** part of your clothing on a sharp or rough object, it gets caught or torn on it. *An American submarine snagged the nets of a trawler... The tip of my shoe snagged on something.*

snail /sneɪl/ **snails.** N-C A **snail** is a small animal that has a spiral shell. It moves slowly, leaving behind a trail of slime.

snake /sneɪk/ **snakes, snaking, snaked.** [1] N-C A **snake** is a long, thin reptile with no legs. [2] VERB Something that **snakes** in a particular direction goes in that direction in a line with a lot of bends; LITERARY. *The road snaked through forested mountains.*

snap /snæp/ **snaps, snapping, snapped.** [1] VERB & N-SING If something **snaps**, or if you **snap** it, it breaks suddenly, usually with a sharp cracking noise called a **snap**. *The rope snapped... The brake pedal had just snapped off... The joint broke with a snap.* [2] VERB & N-SING If something **snaps** into a particular position, or if you **snap** it, it moves quickly into that position with a sharp sound called a **snap**. *The bag snapped open... He snapped the cap off*

a beer... He shut the book with a snap. [3] VERB If someone **snaps** at you, they speak to you in a sharp, unfriendly way. *'Of course I don't know her,' Roger snapped.* [4] VERB If an animal **snaps** at you, it opens and shuts its jaws quickly near you. [5] ADJ BEFORE N A **snap** decision or action is taken suddenly, without careful thought. *It's important not to make snap judgments.* [6] VERB & N-C If you **snap** someone or something, or if you take a **snap** of them, you take a photograph of them; INFORMAL. *...holiday snaps.*

▶ **snap up.** PHR-VERB If you **snap** something **up**, you buy it quickly because it is a bargain or because it is just what you want. *A chunk of Britain's rail network was snapped up by Japanese bankers.*

snapshot /ˈsnæpʃɒt/ **snapshots.** N-C A **snapshot** is a photograph that is taken quickly and casually.

snare /sneə/ **snares, snaring, snared.** [1] N-C A **snare** is a trap for catching birds or small animals. [2] VERB To **snare** a bird or animal means to catch it using a snare. [3] VERB If someone **snares** something, they get it by using cleverness and cunning. *Most of all I want to snare a husband.*

snarl /snɑːl/ **snarls, snarling, snarled.** [1] VERB & N-C When an animal **snarls**, or when it gives a **snarl**, it makes a fierce, rough sound while showing its teeth. *The dogs snarled at the intruders... With a snarl, the second dog made a dive for his heel.* [2] VERB If you **snarl** something, you say it in a fierce, angry way. *'Let go of me,' he snarled.*

snatch /snætʃ/ **snatches, snatching, snatched.** [1] VERB If you **snatch** something, or if you **snatch** at it, you take or pull it away quickly. *Mick snatched the cards from Archie's hand.* [2] VERB If you **snatch** an opportunity, you quickly make use of it. *I snatched a glance at the mirror.* [3] N-C A **snatch** of a conversation or a song is a very small piece of it.

sneak /sniːk/ **sneaks, sneaking, sneaked** (AM also **snuck**). [1] VERB If you **sneak** somewhere, you go there quietly on foot, trying to avoid being seen or heard. *He would sneak out of his house late at night to be with me.* [2] VERB If you **sneak** something somewhere, you take it there secretly. *...kids who want to sneak drinks into dance halls.* [3] VERB If you **sneak** a look at someone or something, you secretly have a quick look at them.

sneaker /ˈsniːkə/ **sneakers.** N-C In American English, **sneakers** are casual shoes with rubber soles used for sports. The usual British word is **trainers**.

sneer /snɪə/ **sneers, sneering, sneered.** VERB & N-C If you **sneer** at someone or something, or if you give them a **sneer**, you express your contempt for them by what you say or by the expression on your face. *It is becoming fashionable again to sneer at scientists. ...a contemptuous sneer.*

sneeze /sniːz/ **sneezes, sneezing, sneezed.** VERB & N-C When you **sneeze**, you suddenly take in your breath and then blow it down your nose noisily, because you have a cold or because something has irritated your nose. This action is called a **sneeze**.

sniff /snɪf/ **sniffs, sniffing, sniffed.** [1] VERB & N-C When you **sniff**, or when you give a **sniff**, you breathe in air noisily through your nose, for example when you are trying not to cry, or in order to show disapproval. *She wiped her face and sniffed loudly... 'Tourists!' she sniffed.* [2] VERB & N-C If you **sniff** something, or if you take a **sniff** of it, you smell it by sniffing. *He sniffed the perfume she wore... She sniffed at it suspiciously.*

snigger /snɪɡə/ **sniggers, sniggering, sniggered.** VERB & N-C If someone **sniggers**, or if they give a **snigger**, they laugh quietly in a way which shows lack of respect. *The tourists snigger at the locals' outdated ways.*

snip /snɪp/ **snips, snipping, snipped.** VERB If you **snip** something or if you **snip** at it, you cut part of it off with scissors or shears in a single quick action. *Jeremy snipped a length of new bandage.*

snipe /snaɪp/ **snipes, sniping, sniped.** [1] VERB If someone **snipes at** you, they criticize you, often in an unfair or unkind way. *She could not resist the temptation to snipe at her successor.* ♦**sniping** N-U *Despite the sniping of critics, we still managed to double our audience.* [2] VERB To **snipe at** someone means to shoot at them from a hidden position. ♦**sniper, snipers** N-C *...a sniper's bullet.* ♦**sniping** N-U *10,069 people have been killed in the shelling and sniping.*

snippet /snɪpɪt/ **snippets.** N-C A **snippet** of information or news is a small piece of it. *...intriguing snippets of evidence.*

snob /snɒb/ **snobs.** N-C If you call someone a **snob**, you disapprove of them because they admire upper class people and dislike lower class people.

snobbery /snɒbəri/ N-U **Snobbery** is the attitude of a snob. *There was very little snobbery or class-consciousness in the wartime navy.*

snooker /snuːkə, AM snʊk-/. N-U **Snooker** is a game involving balls on a large table. The players use long sticks called cues to hit a white ball, and score points by knocking coloured balls into the pockets at the sides of the table.

snoop /snuːp/ **snoops, snooping, snooped.** VERB & N-C If someone **snoops** around a place, or if they have a **snoop** around it, they secretly look around it in order to find out things. *He was the one she'd seen snooping around Kim's hotel room.* ♦**snooper, snoopers** N-C *They raised the wall to 10m, to thwart photographers and snoopers.*

snore /snɔː/ **snores, snoring, snored.** VERB & N-C When someone who is asleep **snores**, they make a loud noise, called a **snore**, each time they breathe. *His echoing snores keep me awake at night.*

snorkel /snɔːkəl/ **snorkels, snorkelling, snorkelled** (AM **snorkeling, snorkeled**). [1] N-C A **snorkel** is a tube through which a person swimming just under the surface of the sea can breathe. [2] VERB When someone **snorkels**, they swim under water using a snorkel.

snort /snɔːt/ **snorts, snorting, snorted.** VERB & N-C If people or animals **snort**, or if they give

a **snort**, they breathe air noisily out through their noses. People sometimes snort in order to express disapproval or amusement. *Harry snorted with laughter... He gave an exasperated snort.*

snow /snəʊ/ **snows, snowing, snowed.** [1] N-U **Snow** is the soft white bits of frozen water that fall from the sky in cold weather. *The ground was covered in snow.* [2] VERB When it **snows**, snow falls from the sky.

snowball /snəʊbɔːl/ **snowballs, snowballing, snowballed.** [1] N-C A **snowball** is a ball of snow. [2] VERB If something such as a campaign **snowballs**, it rapidly increases and grows. *From those early days the business has snowballed.*

snowy /snəʊi/. ADJ A **snowy** place is covered in snow. A **snowy** day is a day when a lot of snow has fallen.

snub /snʌb/ **snubs, snubbing, snubbed.** VERB & N-C If someone **snubs** you, or if they give you a **snub**, they insult you by ignoring you or by behaving rudely towards you. *He snubbed her in public and made her feel an idiot... This was not intended in any way as a snub to Robbie.*

snuck /snʌk/. **Snuck** is a past tense and past participle of **sneak**; AMERICAN .

snuff /snʌf/ **snuffs, snuffing, snuffed.** N-U **Snuff** is powdered tobacco which people take by sniffing it up their nose.
▶ **snuff out.** PHR-VERB If someone or something **snuffs out** something such as a rebellion or disagreement, they stop it, usually in a forceful or sudden way. *Every time a new flicker of resistance appeared, the government snuffed it out.*

snug /snʌɡ/. [1] ADJ If you feel **snug** or if you are in a **snug** place, you are very warm and comfortable. [2] ADJ If something is a **snug** fit, it fits tightly. ♦**snugly** ADV *The shoes fitted snugly.*

snuggle /snʌɡəl/ **snuggles, snuggling, snuggled.** VERB If you **snuggle** somewhere, you settle yourself into a warm, comfortable position, especially by moving closer to another person. *Jane snuggled up against his shoulder.*

so /səʊ/. [1] ADV You use **so** to refer back to something that has just been mentioned. *'Do you think that made much of a difference to the family?'—'I think so'... Almost all young women who turn to prostitution do so as a means of survival.* [2] ADV You use **so** when you are saying that something which has just been said about one person or thing is also true of another one. *They had a wonderful time and so did I.* [3] CONJ You use the structures **as...so** and **just as...so** to indicate that two events or situations are similar in a particular way. *Just as society has rules, so do schools.* [4] CONJ You use **so** and **so that** to introduce the result of the situation you have just mentioned. *I was an only child, and so had no experience of large families... There was snow everywhere, so that the shape of things was difficult to identify.* [5] CONJ You use **so**, **so that**, and **so as** to introduce the reason for doing the thing you have just mentioned. *Come over here so I can see you... I was beginning to feel alarm, but kept it*

to myself so as not to worry our two friends.
6 ADV You can use **so** in a conversation or an account when you are checking something, summarizing something, or moving on to a new stage. *So you're a footballer?... So that's how I knew.* **7** ADV You can use **so** to emphasize the degree or extent of something. *He was so tired that he slept for 15 hours... Her hands were so wet they kept slipping off the wheel.* **8** ADV You can use **so** to intensify the meaning of an adjective, adverb, or word such as 'much' or 'many'. *John makes me so angry... So many children cannot read or write.* ● See note at **very**. **9** ADV You can use **so** before words such as 'much' and 'many' to indicate that there is a limit to something. *There is only so much time in the day for answering letters... Even the greatest city can support only so many lawyers.* **10** CONVENTION You say **'So?'** and **'So what?'** to indicate that you think that what someone has said is unimportant. INFORMAL. *'My name's Bruno.'—'So?'... 'You take a chance on the weather if you holiday in the UK.'—'So what?'.* **11** **ever so**: see **ever**. ● **so far**: see **far**. ● **so long as**: see **long**. ● **so much for**: see **much**. ● **every so often**: see **often**.

PHRASES ● You use **and so on** or **and so forth** at the end of a list to indicate that there are other items that you could also mention. *...health, education, tax and so on.* ● You use **or so** when you are giving an approximate amount. *They'll be here within the next fortnight or so.* ● You use the structures **not so much** and **not so much...as** to say that something is one kind of thing rather than another kind. *This is not so much a political battle as an economic one.*

soak /səʊk/ **soaks, soaking, soaked.** **1** VERB When you **soak** something, or when you leave it to **soak**, you put it into a liquid and leave it there. *Soak the noodles in warm water for 20 minutes... He turned off the water and left the dishes to soak.* **2** VERB When a liquid **soaks** something, it makes it very wet. *Heavy rain had soaked the road surface.* ♦ **soaked** ADJ *Her dress was soaked.* ♦ **soaking** ADJ *She was soaking wet.* **3** VERB When a liquid **soaks** through something, it passes through it. *Dark patches of sweat had soaked through the fabric.* **4** VERB & N-C If someone **soaks**, or if they have a **soak**, they spend a long time in a hot bath, because they enjoy it. *I had a long soak in the bath.*
▶ **soak up.** PHR-VERB When a soft or dry substance **soaks up** a liquid, the liquid goes into the substance. *Stir until the wheat has soaked up all the water.*

,so-and-'so. N-U You use **so-and-so** instead of a word, expression, or name when talking generally rather than giving a specific example. *Civil servants may tell ministers that so-and-so is departmental policy.*

soap /səʊp/ **soaps, soaping, soaped.** **1** N-VAR **Soap** is a substance that you use with water for washing yourself or sometimes for washing clothes. *...a bar of lavender soap. ...a large packet of soap powder.* **2** N-C A **soap** is the same as a **soap opera**.

'soap opera, soap operas. N-C A **soap opera**

is a television drama serial about the daily lives of a group of people.

soar /sɔː/ **soars, soaring, soared.** **1** VERB If the amount or level of something **soars**, it quickly increases by a great deal; JOURNALISM. *The price of timber has soared.* **2** VERB If something **soars** into the air, it goes quickly up into the air; LITERARY. *...listening to the seabirds and watching them soar and dive.*

sob /sɒb/ **sobs, sobbing, sobbed.** VERB & N-C If you **sob**, you cry in a noisy way. A **sob** is one of the noises that you make when you are crying. *I want to go home, she said, between sobs.* ♦ **sobbing** N-U *The room was silent except for her sobbing.*

sober /'səʊbə/ **sobers, sobering, sobered.** **1** ADJ When you are **sober**, you are not drunk. **2** ADJ A **sober** person is serious and thoughtful. ♦ **soberly** ADV *'There's a new development,' he said soberly.* **3** ADJ **Sober** colours and clothes are plain and dull. ♦ **soberly** ADV *...a group of soberly dressed men.*
▶ **sober up.** PHR-VERB When someone **sobers up**, they become sober after being drunk.

sobering /'səʊbərɪŋ/. ADJ You say that something is a **sobering** thought or has a **sobering** effect when a situation seems serious and makes you become serious and thoughtful. *It was a sobering experience.*

,so-'called. **1** ADJ BEFORE N You use **so-called** in front of a word to indicate that you think that the word is incorrect or misleading. *...so-called environmentally-friendly products.* **2** ADJ BEFORE N You use **so-called** to indicate that something is generally referred to by a particular name. *She was one of the so-called Gang of Four.*

soccer /'sɒkə/. N-U In American English, **soccer** is a game played by two teams of eleven players who kick a ball around a field in an attempt to score goals. The British word is **football**.

sociable /'səʊʃəbəl/. ADJ **Sociable** people enjoy meeting and talking to other people.

social /'səʊʃəl/. **1** ADJ BEFORE N **Social** means relating to society. *...unemployment, low pay and other social problems.* ♦ **socially** ADV *It is more socially acceptable for a man to be fat.* **2** ADJ BEFORE N **Social** activities are leisure activities that involve meeting other people, as opposed to activities related to work. *We ought to organize more social events.* ♦ **socially** ADV *We have known each other socially for a long time.*

socialist /'səʊʃəlɪst/ **socialists.** N-C & ADJ A **socialist** or a person with **socialist** beliefs believes that the state should own industries on behalf of the people and that everyone should be equal. *...members of the ruling Socialist party.* ♦ **socialism** N-U *...the contest between capitalism and socialism.*

socialize (BR also **socialise**) /'səʊʃəlaɪz/ **socializes, socializing, socialized.** VERB If you **socialize**, you meet other people socially. *It would give people a place to socialize with each other.*

'social life, social lives. N-C Your **social life** consists of ways in which you spend time with your friends and acquaintances. *Their social life revolves around the theatre.*

,**social 'science, social sciences.** N-VAR **Social science** is the scientific study of society. *...sociology and the other social sciences.*

,**social se'curity.** N-U In Britain, **social security** is money that is paid by the government to people who are unemployed, poor, or ill. The American term is **welfare**.

'**social work.** N-U **Social work** is a job which involves giving help and advice to people with serious financial problems or family problems.

society /sə'saɪɪti/ **societies.** [1] N-VAR **Society** consists of all the people in a country or region, considered as a group. *...Western society... We live in a capitalist society.* [2] N-C A **society** is an organization for people who have the same interest or aim. *...the North of England Horticultural Society.* [3] N-U You can use the word **society** to refer to the rich, fashionable people in a particular place who meet on social occasions. *They are well-known in society circles.*

sociology /,səusi'ɒlədʒi/. N-U **Sociology** is the study of society or of the way society is organized. ◆**sociological** /,səusiə'lɒdʒikəl/ ADJ *...sociological research.* ◆**sociologist, sociologists** N-C *...her career as a sociologist.*

sock /sɒk/ **socks.** N-C **Socks** are pieces of clothing which cover your foot and ankle and are worn inside shoes.

socket /'sɒkɪt/ **sockets.** [1] N-C A **socket** is a device on a piece of electrical equipment into which you can put a plug or bulb. [2] N-C In British English, a **socket** is a device or point in a wall where you can connect electrical equipment to the power supply. The American word is **outlet**. [3] N-C You can refer to any hollow part or opening in a structure which another part fits into as a **socket**. *Her eyes were sunk deep into their sockets.*

soda /'səudə/ **sodas.** [1] N-U **Soda** or **soda water** is fizzy water used for mixing with alcoholic drinks or fruit juice. [2] N-VAR **Soda** is a fizzy drink. A **soda** is a bottle or glass of soda. AMERICAN.

sodden /'sɒdən/. ADJ Something that is **sodden** is extremely wet.

sofa /'səufə/ **sofas.** N-C A **sofa** is a long, comfortable seat with a back and arms, which two or three people can sit on.

soft /sɒft, AM sɔːft/ **softer, softest.** [1] ADJ Something that is **soft** is pleasant to touch, and not rough or hard. *...warm, soft, white towels.* ◆**softness** N-U *The sea air robbed her hair of its softness.* [2] ADJ Something that is **soft** changes shape or bends easily when you press it. *She lay down on the soft, comfortable bed. ...soft cheese.* [3] ADJ Something that is **soft** is very gentle and has no force. For example, a **soft** sound is quiet and not harsh. A **soft** colour is pleasant to look at because it is not bright. *A soft spring rain had fallen all day.* ◆**softly** ADV *She kissed him softly.* [4] ADJ If you are **soft** on someone, you do not treat them as severely as you should do; used showing disapproval. [5] ADJ BEFORE N **Soft** drugs are illegal drugs which many people do not consider to be strong, harmful, or addictive. [6] PHRASE If you **have a soft spot for** someone, you are especially fond of them.

,**soft 'drink, soft drinks.** N-C A **soft drink** is a cold non-alcoholic drink such as lemonade.

soften /'sɒfən, AM 'sɔːf-/ **softens, softening, softened.** [1] VERB If something **is softened**, it becomes less hard or firm. *Fry for about 4 minutes, until the onion has softened.* [2] VERB If one thing **softens** the impact or the damaging effect of another thing, it makes it seem less severe. [3] VERB If you **soften** your position, you become more sympathetic and less hostile or critical. *His party's policy has softened a lot in recent years.*

▶ **soften up.** PHR-VERB If you **soften** someone **up**, you put them into a good mood before asking them to do something; INFORMAL. *If they'd treated you well it was just to soften you up.*

software /'sɒftweə, AM 'sɔːf-/. N-U Computer programs are referred to as **software**.

soggy /'sɒgi/ **soggier, soggiest.** ADJ Something that is **soggy** is unpleasantly wet.

soil /sɔɪl/ **soils, soiling, soiled.** [1] N-U **Soil** is the substance on the surface of the earth in which plants grow. [2] N-U You can use **soil** to refer to a country's territory. *The issue of foreign troops on Turkish soil is a sensitive one.* [3] VERB If you **soil** something, you make it dirty; FORMAL. ◆**soiled** ADJ *...a soiled white apron.*

solace /'sɒlɪs/. [1] N-U **Solace** is a feeling of comfort that makes you feel less sad; FORMAL. *Henry was inclined to seek solace in drink.* [2] N-SING If something is a **solace** to you, it makes you feel less sad; FORMAL.

solar /'səulə/. [1] ADJ **Solar** is used to describe things relating to the sun. *...a total solar eclipse.* [2] ADJ **Solar** power is obtained from the sun's light and heat.

'**solar system.** N-PROPER The **solar system** is the sun and all the planets that go round it.

sold /səuld/. **Sold** is the past tense and past participle of **sell**.

soldier /'səuldʒə/ **soldiers.** N-C A **soldier** is a person who works in an army.

sole /səul/ **soles.** [1] ADJ BEFORE N The **sole** thing or person of a particular type is the only one of that type. *Their sole aim is to destabilize the government.* ◆**solely** ADV *Too often we make decisions based solely upon what we see in the magazines.* [2] ADJ BEFORE N If you have **sole** charge or ownership of something, you are the only person in charge of it or who owns it. *Many women are left as the sole providers in families.* [3] N-C The **sole** of your foot or of a shoe or sock is the underneath surface of it. [4] N-VAR A **sole** is a kind of flat fish. The form 'sole' is also used as the plural.

solemn /'sɒləm/. [1] ADJ Someone or something that is **solemn** is very serious rather than cheerful or humorous. ◆**solemnly** ADV *Her listeners nodded solemnly.* ◆**solemnity** /sə'lemnɪti/ N-U *...the solemnity attached to death.* [2] ADJ A **solemn** promise or agreement is formal and sincere. *The Government seems to have made solemn commitments.* ◆**solemnly** ADV *He solemnly swore an oath of allegiance.*

solicit /sə'lɪsɪt/ **solicits, soliciting, solicited.** [1] VERB If you **solicit** money, help, or an opin-

ion from someone, you ask them for it; FORMAL.
♦ **solicitation, solicitations** N-C ...*the solicitation of money from a foreign government.* [2] VERB When prostitutes **solicit**, they offer to have sex with people in return for money. ♦ **soliciting** N-U ...*soliciting or loitering in the central London area.*

solicitor /sə'lɪsɪtə/ **solicitors.** N-C In Britain, a **solicitor** is a lawyer who gives legal advice, prepares legal documents and cases, and represents clients in the lower courts of law.

solid /'sɒlɪd/ **solids.** [1] N-C & ADJ A **solid**, or a **solid** substance or object, stays the same shape whether it is in a container or not. *Solids turn to liquids at certain temperatures.* [2] ADJ A **solid** object or mass does not have a space inside it, or holes or gaps in it. ...*50ft of solid rock... The car park was absolutely packed solid with people.* [3] ADJ A **solid** structure is strong and is not likely to collapse or fall over. ♦ **solidly** ADV *Their house, which was solidly built, resisted the main shock.* ♦ **solidity** /sə'lɪdɪti/ N-U ...*the solidity of walls and floors.* [4] ADJ If you describe someone as **solid**, you mean they are very reliable and respectable. ♦ **solidly** ADV *Graham is so solidly consistent.* ♦ **solidity** N-U *He had the proverbial solidity of the English.* [5] ADJ **Solid** evidence or information is reliable because it is based on facts. *Solid advice or work is useful and reliable. All I am looking for is a good solid performance.* ♦ **solidly** ADV *She's played solidly throughout the spring.* [6] ADJ If you do something for a **solid** period of time, you do it without any pause or interruption throughout that time. *We had worked together for two solid years.* ♦ **solidly** ADV *For the next two hours they worked solidly on his new song.*

solidarity /ˌsɒlɪ'dærɪti/ N-U If a group of people show **solidarity**, they show complete unity and support for each other, especially in political or international affairs.

solidify /sə'lɪdɪfaɪ/ **solidifies, solidifying, solidified.** VERB When a liquid **solidifies**, it changes into a solid.

solitary /'sɒlɪtri, AM -teri/. [1] ADJ BEFORE N A **solitary** activity is one that you do alone. *His evenings were spent in solitary drinking.* [2] ADJ A person or animal that is **solitary** spends a lot of time alone. [3] ADJ BEFORE N A **solitary** person or object is alone and has no others nearby.

solitude /'sɒlɪtjuːd, AM -tuːd/. N-U **Solitude** is the state of being alone, especially when this is peaceful and pleasant. *Imagine long golden beaches where you can wander in solitude.*

solo /'səʊləʊ/ **solos.** N-C & ADJ & ADV A **solo**, or a **solo** performance, especially of a piece of music, is a performance done by one person. You can also say that someone does something **solo** when they do it on their own. *He had just completed his final solo album.*

soloist /'səʊləʊɪst/ **soloists.** N-C A **soloist** is a person who performs a solo, usually a piece of music.

soluble /'sɒljʊbəl/. ADJ A substance that is **soluble** will dissolve in a liquid.

solution /sə'luːʃən/ **solutions.** [1] N-C A **solution** to a problem is a way of dealing with it so that the difficulty is removed. ...*a peaceful so-*

lution to the conflict. [2] N-C The **solution** to a riddle or a puzzle is the answer to it. [3] N-C A **solution** is a liquid in which a solid substance has been dissolved.

solve /sɒlv/ **solves, solving, solved.** VERB If you **solve** a problem or a question, you find a solution or an answer to it. *Their domestic reforms did precisely nothing to solve the problem of unemployment.*

solvent /'sɒlvənt/ **solvents.** [1] ADJ If a person or a company is **solvent**, they have enough money to pay all their debts. [2] N-VAR A **solvent** is a liquid that can dissolve other substances.

sombre (AM **somber**) /'sɒmbə/. [1] ADJ If someone is **sombre**, they are serious, sad, or pessimistic. ♦ **sombrely** ADV *'All the same, I wish he'd come back,' Martha said sombrely.* [2] ADJ **Sombre** colours and places are dark and dull.

some /səm, STRONG sʌm/. [1] DET & PRON You use **some** to refer to a quantity of something or to a number of people or things, when you are not stating the quantity or number precisely. *He went to fetch some books... This year all the apples are all red. My niece and nephew are going to pick some.* [2] DET You can use **some** to emphasize that an amount or number is fairly large. For example, if an activity takes **some** time, it takes quite a lot of time. [3] QUANT If you refer to **some** of the people or things in a group, you mean a few of them but not all of them. If you refer to **some of** a particular thing, you mean a part of it but not all of it. *Spoon some of the sauce into a bowl... When the chicken is cooked I'll freeze some.* [4] DET If you refer to **some** person or thing, you are referring to that person or thing vaguely, without stating precisely which one you mean. *If you are worried about some aspect of your child's health, call us.* [5] ADV You can use **some** in front of a number to indicate that it is approximate. *I have kept birds for some 30 years.*

somebody /'sʌmbədi, AM -baːdi/. **Somebody** means the same as **someone**.

somehow /'sʌmhaʊ/. ADV You use **somehow** to say that you do not know or cannot say how something was done or will be done. *Somehow I knew he would tell me the truth.*

someone /'sʌmwʌn/ (or **somebody** /'sʌmbədi, AM -baːdi/). [1] PRON You use **someone** or **somebody** to refer to a person without saying exactly who you mean. *I need someone to help me.* [2] PRON If you say that a person is **someone** or **somebody** in a particular kind of work or in a particular place, you mean that they are considered to be important in that kind of work or in that place. *He was somebody in the law division.*

someplace /'sʌmpleɪs/. ADV **Someplace** means the same as **somewhere**; AMERICAN, INFORMAL. *The Simpsons lived over around Coyote Canyon someplace.*

something /'sʌmθɪŋ/. [1] PRON You use **something** to refer to a thing, situation, event, or idea, without saying exactly what it is. *He realized right away that there was something wrong... People are always out in their cars, watching television or busy doing something else.* [2] PRON You can use **something** in expressions like **'that's something'** when you think that a situation is not very good but is better that it might have been. *Well, at least he was in town. That was something.* **3** PRON If you say that a thing is **something of** a disappointment, you mean that it is quite disappointing. If you say that a person is **something of** an artist, you mean that they are quite good at art. *She received something of a surprise when Robert said that he was coming to New York.* **4** PRON If you say that there is **something** in an idea or suggestion, you mean that it is quite good and should be considered seriously. *Could there be something in what he said?* ● **something like**: see **like**.

sometime /'sʌmtaɪm/. ADV You use **sometime** to refer to a time in the future or the past that is unknown or that has not yet been decided. *Why don't you come and see me sometime.*

sometimes /'sʌmtaɪmz/. ADV You use **sometimes** to say that something happens on some occasions. *You must have noticed how tired he sometimes looks.*

somewhat /'sʌmwɒt/. ADV You use **somewhat** to indicate that something is the case to a limited extent or degree. *Conditions in the village had improved somewhat since January.*

somewhere /'sʌmweə/. **1** ADV You use **somewhere** to refer to a place without saying exactly where you mean. *I needed somewhere to live in London.* **2** ADV You use **somewhere** when giving an approximate amount, number, or time. *Caray is somewhere between 73 and 80 years of age.* **3** PHRASE If you say that you **are getting somewhere**, you mean that you are making progress towards achieving something. *At last they were agreeing, at last they were getting somewhere.*

son /sʌn/ **sons**. N-C A person's **son** is their male child.

sonata /sə'nɑːtə/ **sonatas**. N-C A **sonata** is a piece of classical music written for a single instrument, or for one instrument and a piano.

song /sɒŋ, AM sɔːŋ/ **songs**. **1** N-C A **song** is a piece of music which consists of words and music sung together. *...a love song.* **2** N-U **Song** is the art of singing. *...dance, music, mime and song.* **3** N-VAR A bird's **song** is the pleasant musical sounds that it makes.

sonic /'sɒnɪk/. ADJ BEFORE N **Sonic** is used to describe things related to sound. *...the sonic boom from a supersonic aeroplane.*

¹son-in-law, sons-in-law. N-C A person's **son-in-law** is the husband of their daughter.

sonnet /'sɒnɪt/ **sonnets**. N-C A **sonnet** is a poem with 14 lines. Each line has 14 syllables, and the poem has a fixed pattern of rhymes.

soon /suːn/ **sooner, soonest**. **1** ADV If something is going to happen **soon**, it will happen after a short time. *This chance has come sooner than I expected... The kidnapper is a man we must catch and the sooner the better.* **2** ADV If something happened **soon** after a particular time or event, it happened a short time after it. *Soon afterwards he separated from his wife.*

PHRASES ● If you say that something happens **as soon as** something else happens, you mean that it happens immediately after the other

thing. *You'll never guess what happened as soon as I left my room.* ● If you say that something will happen **sooner or later**, you mean that it will happen, though it might take a long time. ● If you say that **no sooner** has one thing happened **than** another thing happens, you mean that the second thing happens immediately after the first thing. *No sooner had he arrived in Rome than he was kidnapped.* ● If you say that you **would sooner** do something, you mean that you would prefer to do it. *I'd sooner not talk about it.*

soot /sʊt/. N-U **Soot** is black powder which rises in the smoke from a fire and collects on the inside of chimneys.

soothe /suːð/ **soothes, soothing, soothed.** **1** VERB If you **soothe** someone who is angry or upset, you make them calmer. *He would take her in his arms and soothe her.* ◆**soothing** ADJ *...some gentle, soothing music.* **2** VERB Something that **soothes** pain makes it less severe. ◆**soothing** ADJ *Cold tea is very soothing for burns.*

sophisticated /sə'fɪstɪkeɪtɪd/. **1** ADJ A **sophisticated** person is at ease in social situations and knows about culture, fashion, and other matters that are considered socially important. **2** ADJ A **sophisticated** machine or method of doing something contains more advanced features than other things of the same type. *...a large and sophisticated new British telescope.*

sophistication /sə,fɪstɪ'keɪʃən/. N-U **Sophistication** is the quality of being sophisticated.

soprano /sə'prɑːnəʊ, -'præn-/ **sopranos**. N-C A **soprano** is a woman, girl, or boy with a high singing voice.

sordid /'sɔːdɪd/. **1** ADJ If you describe someone's behaviour as **sordid**, you mean that it is immoral or dishonest. *I don't want to hear the sordid details of your relationship.* **2** ADJ If you describe a place as **sordid**, you mean that it is dirty, unpleasant, or depressing. *...the attic windows of their sordid little rooms.*

sore /sɔː/ **sores**. **1** ADJ If part of your body is **sore**, it causes you pain and discomfort. *...a sore throat.* **2** N-C A **sore** is a painful spot on your body where the skin is infected.

sorely /'sɔːli/. ADV **Sorely** is used to emphasize that a feeling such as disappointment or need is very strong. *He will be sorely missed.*

sorrow /'sɒrəʊ/. N-U **Sorrow** is a feeling of deep sadness or regret. *It was a time of great sorrow.*

sorrows /'sɒrəʊz/. N-PL **Sorrows** are events or situations that cause deep sadness. *...the joys and sorrows of everyday living.*

sorry /'sɒri/ **sorrier, sorriest.** **1** CONVENTION You say **'Sorry'** or **'I'm sorry'** as a way of expressing your disappointment or sadness that something you have done or have told someone has caused them hurt or trouble. *Sorry I took so long... I'm really sorry if I said anything wrong... I'm sorry to have to tell you that your son is dead... She was very sorry about all the trouble she'd caused.* **2** ADJ AFTER LINK-V If you feel **sorry for** someone who is unhappy or in an unpleasant situation, you feel sympathy and sadness for them. *I am very sorry for the family.* **3** ADJ BEFORE N If someone or something is in a **sorry** condition, they are in a bad condition, mentally or physically. *She is a sorry* sight. [4] CONVENTION You say **sorry** when you have not heard what someone has said and you want them to repeat it.

sort /sɔ:t/ **sorts, sorting, sorted.** [1] N-C A particular **sort** of something is one of its different kinds or types. *What sort of school did you go to?* [2] N-SING You describe someone as a particular **sort** when you are describing their character. *He seemed to be just the right sort for the job.* [3] VERB If you **sort** things, you arrange them into different groups or places. *The students are sorted into three ability groups... He unlatched the box and sorted through the papers.*

PHRASES ● You use **sort of** when you want to say that your description of something is not very precise. *In the end, she sort of pushed it.* ● If you describe something as a particular thing **of sorts**, you are suggesting that its quality or standard is poor. *He made a living of sorts selling pancakes from a van.*

▶ **sort out.** [1] PHR-VERB If you **sort out** a group of things, you organize or tidy them. *...trying to sort out fact from fiction.* [2] PHR-VERB If you **sort out** a problem, you solve it. *When we reported a fault, it was sorted out within 3 hours.*

sortie /'sɔ:ti/ **sorties.** [1] N-C A **sortie** is a brief trip away from your home base, especially a trip to an unfamiliar place; FORMAL. *From here we plan several sorties into the countryside.* [2] N-C You refer to a brief raid by a military force into their enemy's territory as a **sortie**.

soufflé (or **souffle**) /'su:fleɪ, AM su:'fleɪ/ **soufflés.** N-VAR A **soufflé** is a light food made from a mixture of beaten egg whites and other ingredients that is baked in the oven.

sought /sɔ:t/. **Sought** is the past tense and past participle of **seek**.

'sought-after. ADJ Something that is **sought-after** is in great demand, usually because it is rare or of very good quality. *...the most sought-after prize in world sport.*

soul /səʊl/ **souls.** [1] N-C A person's **soul** is the spiritual part of them which some people believe continues existing after their body is dead. *...mourning the souls of the people killed in the blast.* [2] N-C You can refer to your mind, character, thoughts, and feelings as your **soul**. *I will put my heart and soul into the job.* [3] N-SING You use **soul** in negative statements to mean nobody at all. *I've never harmed a soul.* [4] N-U **Soul** or **soul music** is a type of pop music performed mainly by black American musicians.

sound /saʊnd/ **sounds, sounding, sounded; sounder, soundest.** [1] N-C A **sound** is something that you hear. *Liza was so frightened she couldn't make a sound. ...the sounds of children playing.* [2] N-U **Sound** is what you hear when vibrations travel through air or water. *...twice the speed of sound.* [3] VERB If something such as a bell **sounds**, or if you **sound** it, it makes a noise. *He sounded his horn in frustration.* [4] LINK-VERB When you are describing a noise, you can talk about the way it **sounds**. *They heard what sounded like a huge explosion.* [5] LINK-VERB When you talk about the way someone **sounds**, you are describing the impression you have of them when they speak.

She sounded a bit worried. [6] LINK-VERB & N-SING You can give your opinion about something you have just read or heard by talking about the way it **sounds**, or talking about the **sound** of it. *It sounds like a wonderful idea.* [7] ADJ You can describe a building or part of someone's mind or body as **sound** when it is in good condition. *His body was still sound.* [8] ADJ If something such as advice is **sound**, it is reliable and sensible. [9] PHRASE If you are **sound asleep**, you are sleeping deeply.

▶ **sound out.** PHR-VERB If you **sound** someone **out**, you question them to find out their opinion. *We told the company management to sound out the views of the employees.*

soundly /'saʊndli/. [1] ADV If someone is **soundly** defeated, they are defeated thoroughly. [2] ADV If a decision, opinion, or statement is **soundly** based, there are sensible or reliable reasons behind it. [3] ADV If you sleep **soundly**, you sleep deeply.

soundtrack /'saʊndtræk/ **soundtracks.** N-C The **soundtrack** of a film is its sound, speech, and especially the music.

soup /su:p/ **soups.** N-VAR **Soup** is liquid food made by cooking meat, fish, or vegetables in water.

sour /saʊə/ **sours, souring, soured.** [1] ADJ Something that is **sour** has a sharp taste like the taste of a lemon. *The stewed apple was sour.* [2] ADJ **Sour** milk has an unpleasant taste because it is no longer fresh. [3] ADJ If you say that someone is **sour**, you think they are bad-tempered and unfriendly. *He gave Lane a sour look.* ◆**sourly** ADV *Digby smiled sourly. 'Politics isn't pleasant to explain.'* [4] ADJ If a situation or relationship goes **sour**, it stops being enjoyable or satisfactory. *Palestine's dream of new democracy has quickly turned sour.* [5] VERB If a friendship or attitude **sours**, or if something **sours** it, it becomes less friendly or hopeful. *Her mood soured a little.*

source /sɔ:s/ **sources.** [1] N-C The **source** of something is the person, place, or thing which you get it from, or where it comes from. *...renewable sources of energy. ...tourism, which is a major source of income for the city.* [2] N-C A **source** is a person or book that provides information for a news story or for a piece of research. *Military sources say the boat was heading south.* [3] N-SING The **source** of a river or stream is the place where it begins.

south /saʊθ/. [1] N-SING The **south** is the direction on your right when you are looking towards the place where the sun rises. *...warm breezes from the south.* [2] N-SING & ADJ The **south** of a place, or the **south** part of a place, is the part which is towards the south. *...holidays in the south of France. ...the south side of the gorge.* [3] ADV **South** means towards the south, or positioned to the south of a place or thing. *Troops had moved south... The hurricane hit Florida just south of Miami.* [4] ADJ A **south** wind blows from the south.

,south-'east. [1] N-SING The **south-east** is the direction halfway between south and east. *Look roughly to the south east.* [2] N-SING & ADJ The **south-east** of a place, or the **south-east** part of a place, is the part which is towards the south-east. ...*a suburb seven miles south-east of Havana.* ...*south-east London.* **3** ADV **South-east** means towards the south-east, or positioned to the south-east of a place or thing. *The monsoon should move south-east by late tomorrow.* **4** ADJ A **south-east** wind blows from the south.

south-'eastern. ADJ **South-eastern** means in or from the south-east of a region or country. ...*the south-eastern edge of the United States.*

southerly /'sʌðəli/. **1** ADJ A **southerly** point, area, or direction is to the south or towards the south. ...*the most southerly areas of Zimbabwe.* ...*a southerly direction.* **2** ADJ A **southerly** wind blows from the south.

southern /'sʌðən/. ADJ **Southern** means in or from the south of a region or country. *He comes not from Southern China, but from northern Thailand.*

southerner /'sʌðənə/ **southerners.** N-C A **southerner** is a person who was born in or who lives in the southern part of a place or country. *Bob Wilson is a southerner, from Texas.*

southward /'saʊθwəd/ or **southwards** /'saʊθwədz/. ADV & ADJ **Southward** or **southwards** means towards the south. *They drove southward.* ...*the southward drift of the oil slick.*

south-'west. **1** N-SING The **south-west** is the direction halfway between south and west. *Turn to the south-west to see the expanse of Lucy Bay.* **2** N-SING & ADJ The **south-west** of a place, or the **south-west** part of a place, is the part which is towards the south-west. ...*the mountains in the south west of the USA.* ...*the South-west tip of Grenada.* **3** ADV **South-west** means towards the south-west, or positioned to the south-west of a place or thing. *Go south-west until you reach the cliff.* **4** ADJ A **south-west** wind blows from the south-west.

south-'western. ADJ **South-western** means in or from the south-west of a region or country. ...*south western France.*

souvenir /ˌsuːvə'nɪə, AM 'suːvənɪr/ **souvenirs.** N-C A **souvenir** is something which you buy or keep to remind you of a holiday, place, or event. ...*a souvenir of the summer of 1992.*

sovereign /'sɒvrɪn/ **sovereigns.** **1** ADJ A **sovereign** state or country is independent and not under the authority of any other country. **2** ADJ **Sovereign** is used to describe the person or institution that has the highest power in a country. ...*the Armed Forces Ruling Council, Nigeria's sovereign body.* **3** N-C A **sovereign** is a king, queen, or other royal ruler.

sovereignty /'sɒvrɪnti/. N-U **Sovereignty** is the power that a country has to govern itself or to govern other countries. ...*the reversion of Hong Kong to Chinese sovereignty.*

sow, sows, sowing, sowed, sown. **1** VERB /səʊ/ If you sow seeds, you plant them in the ground. **2** VERB If someone **sows** an undesirable feeling or situation, they cause it to begin and develop. *He cleverly sowed doubts into the minds of his rivals.* **3** N-C /saʊ/. A **sow** is an adult female pig.

spa /spɑː/ **spas.** N-C A **spa** is a place where water with minerals in it bubbles out of the ground.

space /speɪs/ **spaces, spacing, spaced.** **1** N-VAR You use **space** to refer to an area of any size that is empty or available. ...*cutting down yet more trees to make space for houses...* List in the spaces below the specific changes you have made. ● See note at **place.** **2** N-SING A **space** of time is a period of time. *I have known dramatic changes occur in the space of a few minutes.* **3** VERB & PHR-VERB If you **space** a series of things, or if you **space** them **out**, you arrange them so that they have gaps between them. *Women once again are having fewer children and spacing them further apart...* *He talks slowly and spaces his words out.* **4** N-U **Space** is the vast area that lies beyond the Earth's atmosphere and surrounds the stars and planets. ...*launching satellites into space.* ● See also **spacing.**

spacecraft /'speɪskrɑːft, -kræft/. N-C A **spacecraft** is a rocket or other vehicle that can travel in space. **Spacecraft** is both the singular and the plural form.

spaceship /'speɪsʃɪp/ **spaceships.** N-C A **spaceship** is the same as a **spacecraft.**

'space station, space stations. N-C A **space station** is an object which is sent into space and then goes around the earth, and is used as a base by astronauts.

spacing /'speɪsɪŋ/. N-U **Spacing** refers to the way that typing or printing is arranged on a page. *Write clearly in double spacing.* ● See also **space.**

spacious /'speɪʃəs/. ADJ A **spacious** room or other place is large, so that you can move around freely in it. ...*spacious air-conditioned offices.*

spade /speɪd/ **spades.** **1** N-C A **spade** is a tool used for digging, with a flat metal blade and a long handle. **2** N-U **Spades** is one of the four suits in a pack of playing cards. Each card in the suit is called a **spade** and is marked with one or more black symbols: ♠.

spaghetti /spə'geti/. N-U **Spaghetti** is a type of pasta which looks like long pieces of string.

span /spæn/ **spans, spanning, spanned.** **1** N-C A **span** is a period of time between two dates or events during which something exists, functions, or happens. *The batteries had a life span of six hours.* **2** N-C Your **concentration span** or your **attention span** is the length of time you are able to concentrate on something or be interested in it. **3** VERB If something **spans** a long period of time, it lasts throughout that period of time or relates to the whole of it. *His professional career spanned 16 years.* **4** N-C The **span** of something that extends or is spread out sideways is its width. *It is a very pretty butterfly, with a 2 inch wing span.* **5** VERB A bridge or other structure that **spans** something such as a river stretches right across it.

spank /spæŋk/ **spanks, spanking, spanked.** VERB If someone **spanks** a child, they punish them by hitting them on the bottom several times.

spanner /'spænə/ **spanners.** N-C In British English, a **spanner** is a metal tool used for tightening a nut. The American word is **wrench**.

spar /spɑː/ **spars, sparring, sparred.** ☐ VERB When boxers **spar**, they box using fairly gentle blows instead of hitting their opponent hard, for example in training. *He could not get anyone to spar with Tyson.* ☐ VERB If you **spar** with someone, you argue with them but not in an aggressive or serious way. *He sparred with his friend Jesse Jackson over political tactics.*

spare /speə/ **spares, sparing, spared.** ☐ ADJ & N-C Spare things or spares are the same as things that you are already using that you are keeping ready in case others are needed. *Don't forget to take a few spare batteries. ...two discs, with one as a spare.* ☐ ADJ You use **spare** to describe something that is not being used by anyone, and is therefore available for someone to use. *They don't have a lot of spare cash. ...the spare bedroom.* ☐ PHRASE If you have something such as time, money, or space **to spare**, you have some extra that you have not used or which you do not need. *You got here with ninety seconds to spare.* ☐ VERB If you **spare** time or another resource for a particular purpose, you make it available for that purpose. *Miss Jackson could only spare 35 minutes for our meeting.* ☐ VERB To **spare** someone an unpleasant experience means to prevent them from having it. *Spare them the pain of discovering the real facts... Northern Somalia was largely spared from the famine.*

spare 'part, spare parts. N-C Spare parts are parts that you can buy separately to replace old or broken parts in a piece of equipment.

spare 'time. N-U Your spare time is the time during which you do not have to work when you can do whatever you like. *In her spare time she read books.*

sparing /'speərɪŋ/. ADJ If you are **sparing** with something, you use it or give it in very small quantities. ◆**sparingly** ADV *Medication is used sparingly.*

spark /spɑːk/ **sparks, sparking, sparked.** ☐ N-C A spark is a tiny bright piece of burning material that flies up from something that is burning. ☐ N-C A spark is a flash of light caused by electricity. ☐ N-C A spark of a quality or feeling, especially a desirable one, is a small but noticeable amount of it. *His music lacked that vital spark of imagination.* ☐ VERB & PHR-VERB If one thing **sparks** another, or if one thing **sparks off** another, the first thing causes the second thing to start happening. *...a political crisis sparked off by religious violence.*

sparkle /'spɑːkəl/ **sparkles, sparkling, sparkled.** VERB & N-U If something **sparkles**, or if it has **sparkle**, it is clear and bright and shines with a lot of very small points of light. *In the marina yachts sparkle in the sunshine. ...the sparkle of coloured glass.*

sparkling /'spɑːklɪŋ/. ADJ Sparkling drinks are slightly fizzy. *...a glass of sparkling wine.*

sparrow /'spærəʊ/ **sparrows.** N-C A sparrow is a small brown bird that is common in Britain.

sparse /spɑːs/. ADJ Something that is sparse is small in number or amount and spread out over an area. *...rock fields with sparse vegetation... Traffic was sparse on the highway.*

◆**sparsely** ADV *...the sparsely populated interior region.*

spartan /'spɑːtən/. ADJ A spartan place or way of life is very simple or strict, with no luxuries. *Felicity's bedroom was spartan but functional.*

spasm /'spæzəm/ **spasms.** N-VAR A spasm is a sudden tightening of your muscles, which you cannot control. *A lack of magnesium causes muscles to go into spasm.*

spat /spæt/. Spat is the past tense and past participle of **spit.**

spate /speɪt/. N-C A spate of things, especially unpleasant things, is a large number of them that happen or appear within a short period of time. *...the recent spate of attacks on horses.*

spatial /'speɪʃəl/. ADJ BEFORE N Spatial is used to describe things relating to size, area, or position. *...the intensity and spatial distribution of rainfall.* ◆**spatially** ADV *...jobs that are more spatially dispersed throughout the country.*

spatter /'spætə/ **spatters, spattering, spattered.** VERB If a liquid **spatters** a surface, or if it **is spattered**, drops of it fall on the surface. *Turn the fish, being careful not to spatter any hot butter on yourself.* ◆**-spattered** *...the blood-spattered body.*

speak /spiːk/ **speaks, speaking, spoke, spoken.** ☐ VERB When you **speak**, you use your voice in order to say something. *He tried to speak, but she interrupted him. ...as I spoke these idiotic words.* ◆**speaker, speakers** N-C *...responses made after the speaker has stopped talking.* ☐ VERB If you **speak for** a group of people, you make their views and demands known, or represent them. *It was the job of the Church to speak for the underprivileged.* ☐ VERB If you **speak** a foreign language, you know it and can use it. *He doesn't speak English.* ◆**speaker** N-C *...a fifth of the population are Russian speakers.* ☐ VERB If two people are not **speaking**, they no longer talk to each other because they have quarrelled. *He is not speaking to his mother because of her friendship with his ex-wife.* ☐ VERB If you **speak well of** someone or **speak highly of** someone, you say good things about them. If you **speak ill of** someone, you criticize them. ☐ VERB You use **speaking** in expressions such as **generally speaking** and **technically speaking** to indicate the way in which your statement is true or relevant. *Politically speaking, do you think that these moves have been effective?*

PHRASES ● You can say '**speaking as** a parent' or '**speaking as** a teacher', for example, to indicate that the opinion you are giving is based on your experience as a parent or as a teacher. ● If something **speaks for** itself, its meaning or qualities are obvious and do not need to be explained or pointed out. ● You can say **speaking of** something that has just been mentioned as a way of introducing a new topic which has some connection with that thing. *Drop hints for Christmas presents! And speaking of presents, we have 100 exclusive fragrance collections to give away.* ● Nothing **to speak of** means hardly anything or only unimportant things. *They have no weaponry to speak of.* ● You say **so to speak** to indicate that what you are saying is not literally true. *The five coun-*

tries have now all passed, so to speak, their entry test.

▶ **speak out.** PHR-VERB If you **speak out** in favour of something or against something, you say publicly that you think it is good or bad. *She continued to speak out at rallies around the country.*

▶ **speak up.** PHR-VERB If you ask someone to **speak up**, you are asking them to speak more loudly.

> There are some differences in the way the verbs **speak** and **talk** are used. When you **speak**, you could, for example, be addressing someone or making a speech. **Talk** is more likely to be used when you are referring to a conversation or discussion. *I talked about it with my family at dinner... Sometimes we'd talk all night.* **Talk** can also be used to emphasize the activity of saying things, rather than the words that are spoken. *She thought I talked too much.*

-speak /-spiːk/. **-speak** is used to form nouns which refer to the kind of language used by a particular person or by people involved in a particular activity. *...a classic example of management-speak.*

speaker /'spiːkə/ **speakers.** [1] N-C A **speaker** is a person who makes a speech. *Bruce Wyatt will be the guest speaker at next month's meeting.* [2] N-C A **speaker** is a piece of equipment, for example part of a radio or hi-fi system, through which sound comes out. [3] See also **speak**.

spear /spɪə/ **spears, spearing, speared.** [1] N-C A **spear** is a weapon consisting of a long pole with a sharp point. [2] VERB If you **spear** something, you push or throw a pointed object into it.

spearhead /'spɪəhed/ **spearheads, spearheading, spearheaded.** VERB & N-C If someone **spearheads** a campaign, or if they are involved in the **spearhead** of it, they lead it; JOURNALISM. *...spearheading a national campaign against bullying.*

specs /speks/. N-PL A pair of **specs** is a pair of glasses; INFORMAL.

special /'speʃəl/. [1] ADJ Someone or something that is **special** is different from normal, often in a way that makes it better or more important than other things. *You're very special to me, darling. ...a special variety of strawberry.* [2] ADJ BEFORE N **Special** means relating to one particular person, group, or place. *Every anxious person will have his or her own special problems.*

special ef'fect, special effects. N-C In film, **special effects** are unusual pictures or sounds that are created by using special techniques.

specialise. See **specialize.**

specialist /'speʃəlɪst/ **specialists.** N-C A **specialist** is a person who has a particular skill or knows a lot about a particular subject. *...health specialist Professor John Brimley Evans.*

speciality /speʃi'ælɪti/ **specialities.** [1] N-C Someone's **speciality** is the kind of work they do best or the subject they know most about.

His speciality was the history of Germany. [2] N-C A **speciality** of a place is a special food or product that is always very good there. *These potato dumplings are a speciality of northern Italy.*

specialize (BR also **specialise**) /'speʃəlaɪz/ **specializes, specializing, specialized.** VERB If you **specialize** in an area of study or a type of work, you know a lot about it and spend a lot of your time and attention on it. ◆**specialization** N-U *...specialization in particular products.*

specialized (BR also **specialised**) /'speʃəlaɪzd/. ADJ Someone or something that is **specialized** is trained or developed for a particular purpose. *...specialized training in teaching reading.*

specially /'speʃəli/. [1] ADV If something has been done **specially** for a particular person or purpose, it has been done only for that person or purpose. *...a soap specially designed for sensitive skins.* [2] ADV **Specially** is used to mean more than usually or more than other things; INFORMAL. *What was specially enjoyable about that job?*

specialty /'speʃəlti/ **specialties.** N-C A **specialty** is the same as a **speciality**; AMERICAN.

species /'spiːʃiz/. N-C A **species** is a class of plants or animals whose members have the same characteristics and are able to breed with each other. **Species** is the singular and plural.

specific /spɪ'sɪfɪk/. [1] ADJ BEFORE N You use **specific** to emphasize that you are talking about a particular thing or subject. *Massage may help to increase blood flow to specific areas of the body.* [2] ADJ If someone is **specific**, they give a description that is precise and exact. You can also use **specific** to describe their description. [3] ADJ Something that is **specific** to a particular thing is connected with that thing only. *...financial problems specific to students.* ◆**-specific** *Most studies of trade have been country-specific.*

specifically /spɪ'sɪfɪkli/. [1] ADV You use **specifically** to emphasize that a subject is being considered separately from other subjects. *...the first nursing home designed specifically for people with AIDS.* [2] ADV You use **specifically** to add something more precise or exact to what you have already said. *Death frightens me, specifically my own death.* [3] ADV You use **specifically** to indicate that you are stating or describing something precisely. *I asked her to repeat specifically the words that Patti had used.*

specification /spesɪfɪ'keɪʃən/ **specifications.** N-C A **specification** is a requirement which is clearly stated, for example about the necessary features in the design of something. *Handmade jewellery can be produced to your specifications.*

specifics /spɪ'sɪfɪks/. N-PL The **specifics** of a subject are the details of it that need to be considered. *I don't know the specifics of your problem.*

specify /'spesɪfaɪ/ **specifies, specifying, specified.** VERB If you **specify** something, you state it precisely. *One rule specifies that learner drivers must be supervised by adults.*

specimen /'spesɪmɪn/ **specimens.** N-C A **specimen** of something is an example or small amount of it which gives an idea of the whole. *Applicants have to submit a specimen of handwriting.*

speck /spek/ **specks.** N-C A **speck** is a very small stain or mark, or a very small piece of something. *He brushed a speck of dust off his shoes.*

spectacle /'spektəkəl/ **spectacles.** [1] N-PL Someone's **spectacles** are their glasses; FORMAL. *...a pair of spectacles.* [2] N-C A **spectacle** is an interesting or impressive sight or event. *Mahoney stared in astonishment at the spectacle before him.*

spectacular /spek'tækjʊlə/ **spectaculars.** [1] ADJ Something that is **spectacular** is very impressive or dramatic. ♦**spectacularly** ADV *Many of her movies had been spectacularly successful.* [2] N-C A **spectacular** is a grand and impressive show or performance. *...one of the world's great sporting spectaculars.*

spectator /spek'teɪtə, AM 'spekteɪtər/ **spectators.** N-C A **spectator** is someone who watches something, especially a sporting event.

spectre (AM **specter**) /'spektə/ **spectres.** N-C You talk about the **spectre** of something unpleasant when you are frightened that it might occur. *This has raised the spectre of a full-scale war.*

spectrum /'spektrəm/ **spectra** or **spectrums.** [1] N-SING The **spectrum** is the range of different colours produced when light passes through an object called a prism or through a drop of water. [2] N-C A **spectrum** is a range of a particular type of thing. *The term 'special needs' covers a wide spectrum of problems.*

speculate /'spekjʊleɪt/ **speculates, speculating, speculated.** [1] VERB If you **speculate** about something, you guess about its nature or identity, or about what might happen. *The reader can speculate what will happen next.* ♦**speculation, speculations** N-VAR *...speculation over the future of the economy.* [2] VERB When people **speculate** financially, they buy property or shares in the hope of being able to sell them at a profit. ♦**speculator, speculators** N-C *...a Florida real-estate speculator.*

speculative /'spekjʊlətɪv, AM -leɪt-/. ADJ A **speculative** statement or opinion is based on guesses rather than knowledge. *...speculative stories about the mysterious disappearance.*

sped /sped/. **Sped** is a past tense and past participle of **speed**.

speech /spiːtʃ/ **speeches.** [1] N-U **Speech** is the ability to speak or the act of speaking. *...the development of speech in children.* [2] N-SING Your **speech** is the way in which you speak. *His speech became increasingly thick and nasal.* [3] N-U **Speech** is spoken language. *...the way common letter clusters are usually pronounced in speech.* [4] N-C A **speech** is a formal talk given to an audience.

speechless /'spiːtʃləs/. ADJ If you are **speechless**, you are temporarily unable to speak, usually because something has shocked you. *Alex was almost speechless with rage.*

speed /spiːd/ **speeds, speeding, sped.** For the phrasal verb, the past tense and past participle is **speeded.** [1] N-VAR The **speed** of something is the rate at which it moves, happens, or is done. *He drove off at high speed... Each learner can proceed at his own speed.* [2] N-U **Speed** is very fast movement. *Speed is the essential ingredient of all athletics.* [3] VERB To **speed** somewhere means to move or travel there quickly. *Trains will speed through the Channel Tunnel at 186mph.* [4] VERB A motorist who **is speeding** is driving a vehicle faster than the legal speed limit. ♦**speeding** N-U *He was fined for speeding.*
▸ **speed up.** PHR-VERB When something **speeds up**, it moves, happens, or is done more quickly. *I had already taken steps to speed up a solution to the problem.*

'speed limit, speed limits. N-C The **speed limit** on a road is the maximum speed at which you are legally allowed to drive.

speedy /'spiːdi/. ADJ A **speedy** process, event, or action happens or is done very quickly. *We wish Bill a speedy recovery.* ♦**speedily** ADV *Deal speedily and efficiently with everyday cleaning tasks.*

spell /spel/ **spells, spelling, spelled** (BR also **spelt**). [1] VERB & PHR-VERB When you **spell** a word, or when you **spell** it **out**, you write or speak each letter in the word in the correct order. *How do you spell 'potato'?... If I don't know a word, I ask them to spell it out for me.* [2] VERB If something **spells** a particular result, it suggests that this will be the result. *...situations which are likely to spell disaster.* [3] N-C A **spell** of an activity or type of weather is a short period of it. *...a brief spell teaching religious education.* [4] N-C A **spell** is a situation in which events are controlled by a magical power. *They say she died after a witch cast a spell on her.*
▸ **spell out.** [1] PHR-VERB If you **spell** something **out**, you explain it in detail. *Be assertive and spell out exactly how you feel.* [2] See **spell** 1.

spelling /'spelɪŋ/ **spellings.** [1] N-C The **spelling** of a word is the correct sequence of letters in it. [2] N-U **Spelling** is the ability to spell words in the correct way. It is also an attempt to spell a word in the correct way. *His spelling is very bad.*

spelt /spelt/. **Spelt** is a past tense and past participle of **spell**; BRITISH.

spend /spend/ **spends, spending, spent.** [1] VERB When you **spend** money, you pay money for things that you want. *Every three months I spend a hundred pounds on clothes.* [2] VERB If you **spend** time or energy doing something, you use your time or effort doing it. If you **spend** a time in a place, you stay there for a period of time. *She had spent 29 years as a nurse... We spent the night in a hotel.*

spent /spent/. [1] **Spent** is the past tense and past participle of **spend**. [2] ADJ **Spent** substances or containers have been used and cannot be used again. *Radioactive waste is simply spent fuel.*

sperm /spɜːm/ **sperms.** [1] N-C A **sperm** is a cell produced in the sex organs of a male animal which can enter a female animal's egg and fertilize it. The plural is **sperm** or **sperms**. [2] N-U **Sperm** is the liquid that contains sperm when it is produced.

spew /spjuː/ **spews, spewing, spewed.** VERB
When things **spew** from a place, they come out
in large quantities. *Leaking oil spewed from the
tanker.*

sphere /sfɪə/ **spheres.** [1] N-C A **sphere** is an
object that is perfectly round in shape like a
ball. [2] N-C A **sphere** of activity or interest is a
particular area of activity or interest. *...nurses
working in all spheres of the health service.*

spice /spaɪs/ **spices, spicing, spiced.** N-VAR A
spice is a part of a plant, or a powder made
from that part, which you put in food to give it
flavour.

spiced /spaɪst/. ADJ When food is **spiced**, it has
had spices or other strong-tasting foods added
to it.

spicy /'spaɪsi/. ADJ **Spicy** food is strongly flavoured with spices.

spider /'spaɪdə/ **spiders.** N-C A **spider** is a small
creature with eight legs.

spike /spaɪk/ **spikes.** [1] N-C A **spike** is a long
piece of metal with a sharp point. *...a 15-foot
wall topped with iron spikes.* [2] N-C Some long
pointed objects can be referred to as **spikes**.
Her hair stood out in spikes.

spiked /spaɪkt/. ADJ **Spiked** things have spikes
or a spike on them. *...huge iron spiked gates.*

spiky /'spaɪki/. ADJ Something that is **spiky** has
sharp points. *...tall, spiky evergreen trees.*

spill /spɪl/ **spills, spilling, spilled** (BR also
spilt /spɪlt/). [1] VERB If you **spill** a liquid, it accidentally flows over the edge of its container.
*I almost spilled my drink... Don't spill water on
your suit.* [2] VERB If people or things **spill** out
of a place, they come out in large numbers.
The crowd spilled out into the street.

spin /spɪn/ **spins, spinning, spun.** [1] VERB If
something or someone **spins**, or if you **spin**
them, they turn quickly around a central point.
*He spun around, looking guilty... Ella spun the
wheel and turned on to Main Street.* [2] VERB
When someone **spins**, they make thread by
twisting together pieces of a fibre. *...machinery
for spinning cotton.* [3] VERB If someone **spins** a
story, they give you an account of something
that is untrue or only partly true.
▶ **spin out.** PHR-VERB If you **spin** something **out**,
you make it last longer than it normally would.
He deliberately spun out his speech.

spinach /'spɪnɪdʒ, -ɪtʃ/. N-U **Spinach** is a vegetable with large green leaves.

spinal /'spaɪnəl/. ADJ BEFORE N **Spinal** means relating to your spine. *...spinal injuries.*

spine /spaɪn/ **spines.** N-C Your **spine** is the row
of bones down your back.

'**spin-off, spin-offs.** [1] N-C A **spin-off** is something useful that unexpectedly happens as a
result of trying to achieve something else.
...commercial spin-offs from its research. [2] N-C
A **spin-off** is a book, film, or television series
that is derived from something similar that is
already successful.

spiral /'spaɪərəl/ **spirals, spiralling, spiralled**
(AM **spiraling spiraled**). [1] N-C & ADJ BEFORE
N A **spiral** is a shape which winds round and
round, with each curve above or outside the
previous one. **Spiral** things are in the shape of
a spiral. *...the spiral staircase.* [2] VERB If some-

thing **spirals** somewhere, it grows or moves in
a spiral curve. *Dense smoke spiralled upwards
from the ground.* [3] VERB If an amount or level
spirals upwards or downwards, it rises or falls
quickly and at an increasing rate. You can refer
this kind of change in a level or amount as a
particular kind of **spiral**. *Her drug habit was
spiralling out of control. ...oil's upward price
spiral.*

spire /spaɪə/ **spires.** N-C The **spire** of a church is
a tall cone-shaped structure on top of a tower.

spirit /'spɪrɪt/ **spirits, spiriting, spirited.**
[1] N-SING Your **spirit** is the part of you that is
not physical and that is connected with your
deepest thoughts and feelings. *Marian retains
a restless, youthful spirit.* [2] N-C A person's **spirit** is a part of them that is not physical and that
is believed to remain alive after their death.
[3] N-C A **spirit** is a ghost or supernatural being.
[4] N-U **Spirit** is courage, determination, and energy that someone shows during difficult
times. *Everyone who knew her admired her
spirit.* [5] N-PL You can refer to your **spirits**
when saying how happy or unhappy you are.
For example, if your spirits are high, you are
happy. *A bit of exercise will help lift his spirits.*
[6] N-SING The **spirit** in which you do something
is the attitude you have when you are doing it.
*They approached the talks in a conciliatory
spirit.* [7] N-SING The **spirit of** something such as
a law or an agreement is the way that it was intended to be interpreted or applied. *The requirement for work permits violates the spirit
of the 1950 treaty.* [8] VERB If someone or something **is spirited** away, they are taken from a
place quickly and secretly without anyone noticing. [9] N-PL In British English, **spirits** are
strong alcoholic drinks such as whisky and gin.
The American word is **liquor**.

spirited /'spɪrɪtɪd/. ADJ **Spirited** means showing
great energy, confidence, or courage. *Dr
Lawrence gave a spirited defence of his position.*

spiritual /'spɪrɪtʃʊəl/. [1] ADJ **Spiritual** means
relating to people's deepest thoughts and beliefs, rather than to their bodies and physical
surroundings. ◆ **spiritually** ADV *We were physically and spiritually exhausted.* ◆ **spirituality**
/ˌspɪrɪtʃʊˈælɪti/ N-U *...the peaceful spirituality of
Japanese culture.* [2] ADJ **Spiritual** means relating to people's religious beliefs. *...the spiritual
leader of Ireland's Catholics.*

spit /spɪt/ **spits, spitting, spat** (AM also **spit**).
[1] N-U **Spit** is the watery liquid produced in
your mouth. [2] VERB If someone **spits**, they
force an amount of spit out of their mouth. If
you **spit** liquid or food somewhere, you force a
small amount of it out of your mouth. *They
spat at me and taunted me... Spit out that gum.*

spite /spaɪt/. [1] PREP You use **in spite of** to
introduce a fact which makes the rest of the
statement you are making seem surprising. *He
hired her in spite of the fact that she had never
sung on stage.* [2] PREP If you do something **in
spite of** yourself, you do it although you did
not really intend to or expect to. *'What's Tony's
reaction to all this?' Amy asked, laughing in
spite of herself.* [3] VERB & N-U If you do something to **spite** someone, or if you do it out of

spite, you do it because you want to hurt or upset them. *Just to spite Loren again, Shannon kissed Pitt.*

splash /splæʃ/ **splashes, splashing, splashed.** [1] VERB & N-SING If you **splash** around in water, you hit or disturb the water in a noisy way. A **splash** is the sound made when something hits or falls into water. *Players spent most of their time splashing through puddles... It hit the water with a huge splash.* [2] VERB & N-C If you **splash** a liquid somewhere or if it **splashes**, it hits someone or something and scatters in a lot of small drops. A **splash** of liquid is a quantity of it that hits something in this way. *Tears splashed into her hands.* [3] PHRASE If you **make a splash**, you become noticed or become popular because of something that you have done; INFORMAL.

▶ **splash out.** PHR-VERB If you **splash out** on something, especially on a luxury, you buy it even though it costs a lot of money; BRITISH, INFORMAL. *Can you afford to splash out a little?*

splatter /ˈsplætə/ **splatters, splattering, splattered.** VERB If a liquid **splatters** on something or **is splattered** on it, it drops or is thrown over it. *The men were splattered with beer.*

splendid /ˈsplendɪd/. [1] ADJ If you say that something is **splendid**, you mean that it is very good; DATED. *What a splendid idea!* ◆ **splendidly** ADV *We get along splendidly.* [2] ADJ If you describe a building or work of art as **splendid**, you mean that it is beautiful and impressive. *...a splendid Victorian mansion.* ◆ **splendidly** ADV *Nigel's book is splendidly illustrated.*

splendour (AM **splendor**) /ˈsplendə/ **splendours.** N-VAR The **splendour** of something is its beautiful and impressive appearance or features. *...the splendour of the palace of Versailles.*

splinter /ˈsplɪntə/ **splinters, splintering, splintered.** [1] N-C A **splinter** is a very thin sharp piece of wood or glass which has broken off from a larger piece. [2] VERB If something **splinters** or **is splintered**, it breaks into splinters. *The stone rocketed into the glass, splintering it.*

split /splɪt/ **splits, splitting, split.** [1] VERB If something **splits**, or if you **split** it, it is divided into two or more parts. *In a severe gale the ship split in two. ...families split by the Korean war.* [2] VERB If an organization **splits**, or if it **is split**, one group of members disagree strongly with the other members, and may form a group of their own. You also refer to a disagreement of this kind as a **split**. *Women priests are accused of splitting the church.* [3] VERB If something such as wood or a piece of clothing **splits**, or if it **is split**, a long crack or tear appears in it. *I'd split the trousers I had on.* [4] VERB If two or more people **split** something, they share it between them. *I was happy to split the profits with them.*

▶ **split up.** [1] PHR-VERB If two people **split up**, they end their relationship or marriage. *I split up with my boyfriend last year.* [2] PHR-VERB If a group of people **split up**, they go away in dif-

ferent directions. *We had decided to split up in an attempt to get more done.* [3] PHR-VERB If you **split** something **up**, you divide it into a number of separate sections. *He split up the company.*

split 'second. N-SING A **split second** is a very short period of time. *I had to make a split-second decision.*

splutter /ˈsplʌtə/ **splutters, spluttering, spluttered.** [1] VERB If someone **splutters**, they make spitting sounds and have difficulty speaking clearly, often because they are embarrassed or angry. *'I don't understand,' spluttered Jack.* [2] VERB If something **splutters**, it makes a series of short sharp sounds. *The flame spluttered and went out.*

spoil /spɔɪl/ **spoils, spoiling, spoiled** (BR also **spoilt** /spɔɪlt/). [1] VERB If you **spoil** something, you prevent it from being successful or satisfactory. *It's important not to let mistakes spoil your life.* [2] VERB If you say that someone **spoils** their children, you mean that they give their children everything they want and that this has a bad effect on their character. ◆ **spoilt, spoiled** ADJ *A spoilt child is rarely popular with other children.* [3] VERB If you **spoil** yourself, or if you **spoil** someone you love, you give yourself or them something nice as a treat, or you do something special for them. [4] N-PL The **spoils** of something are things that people get as a result of winning a battle or of doing something successfully. *...the spoils of war.*

spoke /spəʊk/ **spokes.** [1] **Spoke** is the past tense of **speak.** [2] N-C The **spokes** of a wheel are the bars that join the outer ring to the centre.

spoken /ˈspəʊkən/. **Spoken** is the past participle of **speak.**

spokesman /ˈspəʊksmən/ **spokesmen.** N-C A **spokesman** is a male spokesperson.

spokesperson /ˈspəʊkspɜːsən/ **spokespersons.** N-C A **spokesperson** is a person who speaks as the representative of a group or organization.

spokeswoman /ˈspəʊkswʊmən/ **spokeswomen.** N-C A **spokeswoman** is a female spokesperson.

sponge /spʌndʒ/ **sponges, sponging, sponged.** [1] N-U **Sponge** is a very light absorbent substance with lots of little holes in it. Sponge can be either man-made or natural and is capable of absorbing a lot of water or of acting as an insulating material. [2] N-C A **sponge** is a piece of sponge that you use for washing yourself or for cleaning things. [3] VERB If you **sponge** something, you wipe it with a wet sponge. *Gently sponge your face.* [4] N-VAR A **sponge** is a light cake or pudding made from flour, eggs, sugar, and sometimes fat. *...chocolate sponge cake.*

▶ **sponge off** or **sponge on.** PHR-VERB If you say that someone **sponges off** other people or **sponges on** them, you disapprove of them because they get money from others, rather than trying to support themselves; INFORMAL.

sponsor /ˈspɒnsə/ **sponsors, sponsoring, sponsored.** [1] VERB If an organization **sponsors** something such as an event, it pays some or all of the expenses connected with it, often in order to get publicity for itself. [2] VERB In Britain, if you **sponsor** someone who is doing something to raise money for charity, you give them a sum of money for the charity if they succeed in doing it. [3] VERB If you **sponsor** a proposal, you officially put it forward and support it. *The resolution was sponsored by 13 nations.* [4] N-C A **sponsor** is a person or organization that sponsors something or someone.

sponsorship /ˈspɒnsəʃɪp/. N-U **Sponsorship** is financial support given by a sponsor. ...*skiers in need of sponsorship.*

spontaneity /ˌspɒntəˈneɪɪti/. N-U **Spontaneity** is spontaneous, natural behaviour. *He had the spontaneity of a child.*

spontaneous /spɒnˈteɪniəs/. [1] ADJ **Spontaneous** acts are not planned or arranged, but are done because someone suddenly wants to do them. *I joined in the spontaneous applause.* ♦**spontaneously** ADV *He was never spontaneously warm or friendly towards us.* [2] ADJ A **spontaneous** event happens because of processes within something, rather than being caused by things outside it. ...*a spontaneous explosion.* ♦**spontaneously** ADV *These images surface spontaneously in dreams.*

spooky /ˈspuːki/ **spookier, spookiest.** ADJ If something is **spooky**, it has a frightening and unnatural atmosphere; INFORMAL. *It's really spooky out here.*

spool /spuːl/ **spools.** N-C A **spool** is a round object in a machine such as a sewing machine or film projector onto which thread, tape, or film is wound.

spoon /spuːn/ **spoons, spooning, spooned.** [1] N-C A **spoon** is an implement used for eating, stirring, and serving food. It is shaped like a small shallow bowl with a long handle. [2] VERB If you **spoon** food somewhere, you put it there using a spoon. *Spoon the sauce over the meat.*

sporadic /spəˈrædɪk/. ADJ **Sporadic** events happen at irregular intervals. ♦**sporadically** ADV *Fighting has occurred sporadically since 1988.*

spore /spɔː/ **spores.** N-C **Spores** are cells produced by fungi such as mushrooms, which can develop into new fungi; TECHNICAL.

sport /spɔːt/ **sports, sporting, sported.** [1] N-VAR **Sports** are games and other competitive activities which need physical effort and skill. *She excels at sport.* [2] VERB If you say that someone **is sporting** something such as a distinctive item of clothing, you mean that they are wearing it. *He sported a collarless jacket with pleated black panels.*

sporting /ˈspɔːtɪŋ/. ADJ BEFORE N **Sporting** means relating to sport or used for sport. ...*sporting events.*

sportsman /ˈspɔːtsmən/ **sportsmen.** N-C A **sportsman** is a man who takes part in sports.

sportswoman /ˈspɔːtswʊmən/ **sportswomen.** N-C A **sportswoman** is a woman who takes part in sports.

sporty /ˈspɔːti/ **sportier, sportiest.** ADJ A **sporty** person enjoys playing sport.

spot /spɒt/ **spots, spotting, spotted.** [1] N-C **Spots** are small, round, coloured areas on a surface. *The swimsuit comes in navy with white spots.* [2] N-C **Spots** on a person's skin are small lumps or marks. [3] N-C A **spot of** a substance is a small amount of it. *Spots of rain had begun to fall.* [4] N-C You can refer to a particular place as a **spot**. ...*the island's top tourist spots.* [5] VERB If you **spot** something or someone, you notice them. *Smoke was spotted coming up the stairs.*

PHRASES ● If you are **on the spot**, you are at the actual place where something is happening. *Troops are on the spot and protecting civilians.* ● If you do something **on the spot**, you do it immediately. *He was sacked on the spot.* ● If you **put** someone **on the spot**, you force them to make a difficult decision or answer a difficult question. ● **have a soft spot for** someone: see **soft**.

spotlight /ˈspɒtlaɪt/ **spotlights, spotlighting, spotlighted.** [1] N-C A **spotlight** is a powerful light, used for example in a theatre, which can be directed so that it lights up a small area. [2] VERB To **spotlight** a particular problem or situation means to make people notice it and think about it. *The budget crisis also spotlighted a weakening American economy.*

spouse /spaʊs/ **spouses.** N-C Someone's **spouse** is the person they are married to; FORMAL.

spout /spaʊt/ **spouts, spouting, spouted.** [1] VERB If something **spouts** liquid or fire, or if liquid or fire **spouts** out of something, it comes out very quickly with a lot of force. ...*a fountain that spouts water 40 feet into the air.* [2] VERB If you say that someone **spouts** something, you disapprove of them because they say something which you think is wrong or insincere. *He accused Mr Brown of spouting nonsense.* [3] N-C The **spout** of a kettle or teapot is the tube that the liquid comes out of.

sprain /spreɪn/ **sprains, spraining, sprained.** [1] VERB If you **sprain** your ankle or wrist, you accidentally damage it by twisting it, for example when you fall. ...*a badly sprained ankle.* [2] N-C A **sprain** is the injury caused by spraining a joint.

sprang /spræŋ/. **Sprang** is the past tense of **spring**.

sprawl /sprɔːl/ **sprawls, sprawling, sprawled.** [1] VERB If you **sprawl** somewhere, you sit or lie down with your legs and arms spread out in a careless way. *I tripped the guy so he sprawled on the ground.* [2] VERB & N-U If a place **sprawls** over a large area of land, it completely covers that area. You can refer to this area as a **sprawl**. ...*Dublin's urban sprawl.*

spray /spreɪ/ **sprays, spraying, sprayed.** [1] N-U **Spray** consists of a lot of small drops of water which are being splashed or forced into the air. ...*the spray from the waterfall.* [2] VERB If you **spray** drops of a liquid or small pieces of something somewhere, or if they **spray** somewhere, they cover a place or shower someone. *He sprayed aftershave on his cheeks... The bullet slammed into the ceiling, spraying them with bits of plaster.* [3] N-VAR A **spray** is a liquid kept under pressure in a container, which you can force out in very small drops. ...*a can of insect spray.*

spread /spred/ **spreads, spreading.** 1 VERB If you **spread** something somewhere, you open it out or arrange it over a place or surface, so that all of it can be seen or used easily. *She spread a towel on the sand and lay on it.* 2 VERB If you **spread** your hands, arms, or legs, you move them far apart. *Sitting on the floor, spread your legs as far as they will go.* 3 VERB If you **spread** a substance on a surface, you put a thin layer of the substance over the surface. *Spread the bread with the cheese.* 4 N-VAR A **spread** is a soft food which is put on bread. *...a salad roll with low fat spread.* 5 VERB If something **spreads**, or if it **is spread** by people, it gradually reaches or affects a larger and larger area or more and more people. *Cholera is not spreading as quickly as it did in the past.* 6 N-SING The **spread** of something is its increasing presence or occurrence. *...the spread of modern technology.* 7 VERB If something **is spread over** a period of time, it is organized so that it takes place at regular intervals over that period. *The course is spread over a five week period.* 8 N-SING A **spread** of ideas, interests, or activities is a wide variety of them. *We have an enormous spread of industries.*

▸ **spread out.** 1 PHR-VERB If people, animals, or vehicles **spread out**, they move apart from each other. 2 PHR-VERB If you **spread** something **out**, you arrange it over a surface, so that all of it can be seen or used easily. *Tom was spreading out a map of Scandinavia on the bed.* 3 PHR-VERB If you **spread out**, you relax by sitting or lying with your legs and arms stretched far apart.

spree /spri:/ **sprees.** N-C If you go on something such as a spending **spree**, you do something such as spend money in an excessive way. *...an all-day drinking spree.*

sprig /sprɪɡ/ **sprigs.** N-C A **sprig** is a small twig or stem with leaves on it which has been picked from a bush or plant.

spring /sprɪŋ/ **springs, springing, sprang, sprung.** 1 N-VAR **Spring** is the season between winter and summer. In the spring the weather gets warmer and plants begin to grow. 2 N-C A **spring** is a coil of wire which returns to its original shape after it is pressed or pulled. 3 N-C A **spring** is a place where water comes up through the ground. *...the hot springs of Banyas de Sant Loan.* 4 VERB When a person or animal **springs**, they move suddenly upwards or forwards. *He sprang to his feet.* 5 VERB If something **springs** in a particular direction, it moves there suddenly and quickly. *The lid of the boot sprang open.* 6 VERB If one thing **springs from** another, the first thing is the result of the second. *His anger sprang from his suffering at the loss of work.* 7 VERB If you **spring** some news or an event on someone, you tell them something that they did not expect to hear, without warning them. *The Congress Party sprang a surprise yesterday by strongly opposing the bill.* 8 PHRASE If a boat or container **springs a leak**, liquid starts coming in or out through a hole or crack. *A tanker carrying propane gas sprang a leak.*

▸ **spring up.** PHR-VERB If something **springs up**, it suddenly appears or comes into existence. *Arts centres sprang up all over the country.*

sprinkle /ˈsprɪŋkəl/ **sprinkles, sprinkling, sprinkled.** VERB If you **sprinkle** a thing with a substance, you scatter the substance over it. *He sprinkled sand on the fire.*

sprint /sprɪnt/ **sprints, sprinting, sprinted.** 1 N-C A **sprint** is a short fast race. *...the 100-metres sprint.* 2 VERB & N-SING If you **sprint** somewhere, or if you break into a **sprint**, you run as fast as you can over a short distance. *Sergeant Horne sprinted to the car.* ◆ **sprinter, sprinters** N-C *...Europe's top sprinter.*

sprout /spraʊt/ **sprouts, sprouting, sprouted.** 1 VERB When plants, vegetables, or seeds **sprout**, they produce new shoots or leaves. *It only takes a few days for beans to sprout.* 2 VERB When leaves, shoots, or plants **sprout** somewhere, they grow there. *Leaf-shoots were beginning to sprout on the hawthorn.* 3 N-C **Sprouts** are the same as **Brussels sprouts.**

spruce /spru:s/ **spruces, sprucing, spruced.** **Spruce** can also be used as the plural form. N-VAR A **spruce** is a kind of evergreen tree. **Spruce** is the wood of this tree.

▸ **spruce up.** PHR-VERB If something **is spruced up**, its appearance is improved. *We spruced ourselves up a bit and went out for dinner.*

sprung /sprʌŋ/. **Sprung** is the past participle of **spring.**

spun /spʌn/. **Spun** is the past tense and past participle of **spin.**

spur /spɜː/ **spurs, spurring, spurred.** 1 VERB & PHR-VERB If something **spurs** you to do something, or if something **spurs** you **on** to do it, it encourages you to do it. *I know people want me to lose but that only spurs me on.* 2 N-SING Something that acts as a **spur** encourages someone to do something or makes something happen faster or sooner. *...a belief in competition as a spur to efficiency.* 3 PHRASE If you do something **on the spur of the moment**, you do it suddenly, without planning it. *They admitted they had stolen a vehicle on the spur of the moment.* 4 N-C **Spurs** are sharp metal points attached to the heels of a rider's boots and used to make the horse go faster.

spurious /ˈspjʊəriəs/. ADJ A **spurious** claim or argument seems to be correct or genuine, but is really false or dishonest; used showing disapproval. *He was arrested in 1979 on spurious corruption charges.*

spurn /spɜːn/ **spurns, spurning, spurned.** VERB If you **spurn** something, you refuse to accept it; FORMAL. *He spurned the advice of management consultants. ...a spurned lover.*

spurt /spɜːt/ **spurts, spurting, spurted.** 1 VERB & N-C If something **spurts** liquid or fire, or if liquid or fire **spurts** from somewhere or something, it comes out quickly in a thin powerful stream called a **spurt**. *I saw flames spurt from the roof... A spurt of diesel came from one valve.* 2 N-C A **spurt** of activity or emotion is a sudden brief period of it. *A spurt of anger flashed through me.* 3 VERB & N-C If someone or something **spurts** somewhere, or if they move there with a **spurt**, they suddenly increase their speed for a short while in order to get there. *The back wheels spun and the van spurted up the last few feet. ...at the end when the athlete puts on a spurt.*

spy /spaɪ/ **spies, spying, spied.** [1] N-C A **spy** is a person whose job is to find out secret information about another country or organization. [2] VERB Someone who **spies** for a country or organization tries to find out secret information for them about other countries or organizations. *Russian intelligence is still spying on Western countries.* ♦**spying** N-U *...a ten-year sentence for spying.* [3] VERB If you **spy on** someone, you watch them secretly. *He spied on her while pretending to work on the shrubs.* [4] VERB If you **spy** someone or something, you notice them; LITERARY. *He spied an old friend.*

sq. sq is used as a written abbreviation for 'square' when you are giving the measurement of an area. *...25,500 sq ft.*

squabble /'skwɒbəl/ **squabbles, squabbling, squabbled.** VERB & N-C When people **squabble**, or when they have a **squabble**, they quarrel about something unimportant. *The children were squabbling over the remote-control.*

squad /skwɒd/ **squads.** [1] N-C A **squad** is a section of a police force that is responsible for dealing with a particular type of crime. *...the fraud squad.* [2] N-C A **squad** is a group of players from which a sports team will be chosen. [3] N-C A **squad** of soldiers is a small group of them.

squadron /'skwɒdrən/ **squadrons.** N-C A **squadron** is a section of one of the armed forces, especially the air force.

squalid /'skwɒlɪd/. [1] ADJ A **squalid** place is dirty, untidy, and in bad condition. *...living in squalid conditions.* [2] ADJ If you describe an activity as **squalid**, you think that it is unpleasant and perhaps dishonest. *...the squalid pursuit of profit.*

squalor /'skwɒlə/. N-U You can refer to squalid conditions or surroundings as **squalor**. *He was out of work and living in squalor.*

squander /'skwɒndə/ **squanders, squandering, squandered.** VERB If you **squander** money, resources, or opportunities, you waste them. *They squander money on lottery tickets.*

square /skweə/ **squares, squaring, squared.** [1] N-C A **square** is a shape with four sides of the same length and four corners that are all right angles. [2] ADJ If something is **square**, it has a shape similar to a square. *...a square table.* [3] N-C In a town or city, a **square** is a flat open place, often in the shape of a square. [4] ADJ BEFORE N **Square** is used before units of length when mentioning the area of something. For example, if a rectangle is three metres long and two metres wide, its area is six square metres. [5] VERB To **square** a number means to multiply it by itself. [6] N-C The **square** of a number is the number produced when you multiply that number by itself. [7] VERB If two different situations or ideas **square with** each other, they can be accepted together or they seem compatible. *That explanation squares with the facts.*

squarely /'skweəli/. [1] ADV **Squarely** means directly and in the middle, rather than indirectly or at an angle. *I kept the gun aimed squarely at his eyes.* [2] ADV If you face something **squarely**, you face it directly, without trying to avoid it.

squash /skwɒʃ/ **squashes, squashing, squashed.** [1] VERB If someone or something **is squashed**, they are pressed or crushed with such force that they become injured or lose their shape. *She made clay models and squashed them flat again.* [2] ADJ AFTER LINK-V If people or things are **squashed into** a place, they are put into a place where there is not enough room for them to be. *There were 2000 people squashed into her recent show.* [3] N-U **Squash** is a game in which two players hit a small rubber ball against the walls of a court using rackets.

squat /skwɒt/ **squats, squatting, squatted.** [1] VERB If you **squat**, or if you **squat down**, you lower yourself towards the ground, balancing on your feet with your legs bent. *He came over and squatted on his heels, looking up at the boys.* [2] ADJ If you describe someone or something as **squat**, you mean they are short and thick, usually in an unattractive way. *...squat stone houses.* [3] VERB People who **squat** occupy an unused building or unused land illegally. [4] N-C A **squat** is an empty building that people are living in illegally.

squatter /'skwɒtə/ **squatters.** N-C A **squatter** is someone who occupies an unused building or unused land illegally; BRITISH.

squeak /skwiːk/ **squeaks, squeaking, squeaked.** VERB & N-C If something or someone **squeaks**, they make a short, high-pitched sound called a **squeak**. *The door squeaked open.*

squeal /skwiːl/ **squeals, squealing, squealed.** VERB & N-C If someone or something **squeals**, they make a long high-pitched sound called a **squeal**. *...a squeal of brakes.*

squeeze /skwiːz/ **squeezes, squeezing, squeezed.** [1] VERB & N-C If you **squeeze** something soft or flexible, or if you give it a **squeeze**, you press it firmly from two sides. *Dip the bread briefly in water, then squeeze it dry.* [2] VERB If you **squeeze** a liquid or a soft substance out of an object, you get the liquid or substance out by pressing the object. *Joe squeezed some detergent over the dishes.* [3] VERB If you **squeeze** someone or something somewhere, or if they **squeeze** there, they manage to get through or into a small space. *...youngsters who can squeeze through tiny windows.*

squid /skwɪd/ **squids.** Squid can also be used as the plural form. N-VAR A **squid** is a sea creature with a long soft body and many tentacles. **Squid** is pieces of this creature eaten as food.

squint /skwɪnt/ **squints, squinting, squinted.** [1] VERB If you **squint** at something, you look at it with your eyes partly closed. *He squinted his eyes and looked at the floor.* [2] N-C If someone has a **squint**, their eyes look in different directions from each other.

squirm /skwɜːm/ **squirms, squirming, squirmed.** VERB If you **squirm**, you wriggle, for example because you are nervous or uncomfortable. *We'll make him squirm.*

squirrel /ˈskwɪrəl, AM ˈskwɜːrəl/ **squirrels.** N-C
A **squirrel** is a small furry wild animal with a long bushy tail.

squirt /skwɜːt/ **squirts, squirting, squirted.**
VERB & N-C If you **squirt** liquid somewhere, or if the liquid **squirts** somewhere, it is forced through a narrow opening so that it comes out in a thin fast stream called a **squirt**. *It just needs a little squirt of oil.*

St. The plural for meaning 2 is **SS**. [1] **St** is a written abbreviation for 'Street'. *...116 Princess St.* [2] **St** is a written abbreviation for 'Saint'. *...St Thomas.*

stab /stæb/ **stabs, stabbing, stabbed.**
[1] VERB If someone **stabs** another person, they push a knife into their body. *Stephen was stabbed to death.* [2] VERB If you **stab** something or if you **stab at** it, you push at it with your finger or with something pointed. *He stabbed at Frank with his finger.* [3] N-C If you have a **stab at** something, you try to do it; INFORMAL. *I thought I'd take a stab at snowboarding.* [4] N-SING You can refer to a sudden, usually unpleasant feeling as a **stab of** that feeling; LITERARY. *She felt a stab of pity for him.*

stabbing /ˈstæbɪŋ/ **stabbings.** [1] N-C A **stabbing** is an incident in which someone stabs someone else with a knife. [2] ADJ BEFORE N A **stabbing** pain is a sudden sharp pain.

stabilize (BR also **stabilise**) /ˈsteɪbɪlaɪz/ **stabilizes, stabilizing, stabilized.** VERB If something **stabilizes**, or if someone or something **stabilizes** it, it becomes stable. *Although her illness is serious, her condition is beginning to stabilize.* ♦**stabilization** N-U *...the stabilisation of property prices.*

stable /ˈsteɪbəl/ **stabler, stablest; stables, stabling, stabled.** [1] ADJ If something is **stable**, it is not likely to change or come to an end suddenly. ♦**stability** /stəˈbɪlɪti/ N-U *...a time of political stability.* [2] ADJ If an object is **stable**, it is firmly fixed in position and is not likely to move or fall. [3] N-C A **stable** or **stables** is a building in which horses are kept. [4] VERB When horses are **stabled** they are put into a stable.

stack /stæk/ **stacks, stacking, stacked.**
[1] N-C A **stack** of things is a neat pile of them. *There were stacks of books on the bedside table.* ● See note at **pile.** [2] VERB & PHR-VERB If you **stack** a number of things, or if you **stack** them **up**, you arrange them in neat piles. *He ordered them to stack up pillows behind his back.* [3] N-PL **Stacks** of something means a lot of it; INFORMAL. *You'll have stacks of money.* [4] PHRASE When **the odds are stacked against** someone, they are unlikely to succeed because the conditions are not favourable. *The odds are stacked against civilians getting a fair trial.*

stadium /ˈsteɪdiəm/ **stadiums** (or **stadia**). N-C
A **stadium** is a large sports ground with rows of seats all round it.

staff /stɑːf, stæf/ **staffs, staffed.** [1] N-C The **staff** of an organization are the people who work for it. **Staff** can take the singular or plural form of the verb. *The staff were very good.* [2] PASSIVE-VERB If an organization **is staffed** by

particular people, they are the people who work for it. *They are staffed by volunteers.* ♦**staffed** ADJ *...poorly staffed hotels.*

staffing /ˈstɑːfɪŋ, ˈstæf-/. N-U **Staffing** refers to the number of workers employed to work in a particular organization or building. *Staffing levels in prisons are too low.*

stag /stæg/ **stags.** N-C A **stag** is an adult male deer.

stage /steɪdʒ/ **stages, staging, staged.** [1] N-C A **stage** of an activity, process, or period is one part of it. *...the final stage of a world tour.* [2] N-C In a theatre, the **stage** is an area where actors or entertainers perform. *I went on stage and did my show.* [3] N-SING You can refer to performing and the production of plays in a theatre as **the stage**. *He was the first comedian I ever saw on the stage.* [4] VERB If someone **stages** a play or other show, they organize and present a performance of it. [5] VERB To **stage** an event or ceremony means to organize it. *The conference is staging a debate on constitutional reform.* [6] **set the stage:** see **set.**

stagger /ˈstægə/ **staggers, staggering, staggered.** [1] VERB If you **stagger**, you walk very unsteadily, for example because you are ill or drunk. *She staggered back to the hospital.* [2] VERB If something **staggers** you, it surprises you very much. ♦**staggered** ADJ AFTER LINK-V *I'm absolutely staggered at the verdict.* [3] VERB To **stagger** things means to arrange them so that they do not all happen at the same time.

staggering /ˈstægərɪŋ/. ADJ Something that is **staggering** is very surprising. *...a staggering £25,000-a-week.* ♦**staggeringly** ADV *The South Pole expedition proved to be staggeringly successful.*

stagnant /ˈstægnənt/. [1] ADJ If something such as a business or society is **stagnant**, there is little activity or change; used showing disapproval. *He is seeking advice on how to revive the stagnant economy.* [2] ADJ **Stagnant** water is not flowing, and is therefore often dirty and unhealthy.

stagnate /stægˈneɪt, AM ˈstægneɪt/ **stagnates, stagnating, stagnated.** VERB If something such as a business or society **stagnates**, it becomes inactive or does not change; used showing disapproval. ♦**stagnation** N-U *...the stagnation of the steel industry.*

staid /steɪd/. ADJ If you say that someone or something is **staid**, you mean that they are serious, dull, and rather old-fashioned. *...the traditionally staid image of golf.*

stain /steɪn/ **stains, staining, stained.** [1] N-C A **stain** is a mark on something that is difficult to remove. *...grass stains.* [2] VERB If a liquid **stains** something, the thing becomes coloured or marked by the liquid. ♦**stained** ADJ *His clothing was stained with mud.* ♦**-stained** *...ink-stained fingers.*

stained 'glass. N-U **Stained glass** consists of pieces of glass of different colours used to make decorative windows or other objects.

stainless steel /ˌsteɪnləs ˈstiːl/. N-U **Stainless steel** is a metal which does not rust, made from steel and chromium.

stair /steə/ **stairs.** [1] N-PL **Stairs** are a set of steps inside a building which go from one floor

to another. *We walked up a flight of stairs.*
2 N-C A **stair** is one of the steps in a flight of
stairs. *Terry was sitting on the bottom stair.*

staircase /ˈsteəkeɪs/ **staircases.** N-C A **staircase** is a set of stairs inside a house.

stairway /ˈsteəweɪ/ **stairways.** N-C A **stairway**
is a flight of steps, inside or outside a building.

stake /steɪk/ **stakes, staking, staked.**
1 PHRASE If something is **at stake**, it is being
risked and might be lost or damaged if you are
not successful. *The tension was naturally high
for a game with so much at stake.* **2** N-PL The
stakes involved in a risky action or a contest
are the things that can be gained or lost. *The
players knew exactly how high the stakes were.*
3 VERB If you **stake** something such as your
money or your reputation on the result of
something, you risk your money or reputation
on it. *He again staked his reputation on getting
the treaty through.* **4** N-C If you have a **stake in**
something, its success matters to you, for example because you own part of it. *...investors
who want a more direct stake in overseas companies.* **5** N-C A **stake** is a pointed wooden
post in the ground. • to **stake** your **claim**: see
claim.

stale /steɪl/ **1** ADJ **Stale** food or air is no longer
fresh. **2** ADJ AFTER LINK-V If you feel **stale**, you
have no new ideas or enthusiasm for what you
are doing.

stalemate /ˈsteɪlmeɪt/ **stalemates.** N-VAR **Stalemate** is a situation in which neither side in an
argument or contest can make progress. *The
war had reached a stalemate.*

stalk /stɔːk/ **stalks, stalking, stalked.** **1** N-C
The **stalk** of a flower, leaf, or fruit is the thin
part that joins it to the plant or tree. **2** VERB If
you **stalk** a person or a wild animal, you follow
them quietly and secretly in order to catch
them or observe them. *The hunters stalked
their prey.* **3** VERB If you **stalk** somewhere, you
walk there in a stiff, proud, or angry way. *He
got up and stalked up and down the flat.*

stall /stɔːl/ **stalls, stalling, stalled.** **1** VERB If
a process **stalls**, or if someone or something
stalls it, the process stops but may continue at
a later time. *Continental's managers had a
good reason to stall the negotiations.* **2** VERB If
you **stall** someone, you deliberately prevent
them from doing something until later, for example by talking to them. *Brian talked to the
man until the police arrived.* **3** VERB If you
stall, you try to avoid doing something until
later. *Thomas had spent all week stalling over
his decision.* **4** VERB If a vehicle **stalls**, or if you
accidentally **stall** it, the engine stops suddenly.
5 N-C A **stall** is a large table on which you put
goods that you want to sell, or information
that you want to give people. *...market stalls
selling local fruits.* **6** N-PL The **stalls** in a theatre or concert hall are the seats on the ground
floor in front of the stage; BRITISH.

stallion /ˈstæliən/ **stallions.** N-C A **stallion** is a
male horse.

stalwart /ˈstɔːlwət/ **stalwarts.** N-C & ADJ A **stalwart**, or someone who is **stalwart**, is a loyal
and hard-working employee or supporter.
...my stalwart bodyguard.

stamina /ˈstæmɪnə/. N-U **Stamina** is the physical
or mental energy needed to do a tiring activity
for a long time. *You have to have a lot of stamina to be a top-class dancer.*

stammer /ˈstæmə/ **stammers, stammering,
stammered.** VERB & N-C If someone **stammers**,
or if they have a **stammer**, they speak with difficulty, hesitating and repeating words or
sounds. *He turned white and began to stammer.* ◆**stammering** N-U *...a speech therapist
specialising in stammering.*

stamp /stæmp/ **stamps, stamping,
stamped.** **1** N-C A **stamp** or a **postage stamp**
is a small piece of paper which you stick on an
envelope or parcel, to show that you have paid
the cost of posting it. **2** N-C A **stamp** is a small
block of wood or metal with words or a design
on it. You press it onto an ink pad and then
onto a document in order to produce a mark
on the document. The mark is also called a
stamp. **3** VERB If you **stamp** a mark or word
on an object, you press the mark or word onto
the object, using a stamp. *He examined her
passport and stamped it.* **4** VERB If you **stamp**,
or if you **stamp** your foot, you put your foot
down very hard on the ground, for example
because you are angry. *His foot stamped down
on the accelerator.* **5** See also **rubber stamp.**
▸ **stamp out.** PHR-VERB If you **stamp** something
out, you put an end to it. *...new laws to stamp
out sexual discrimination at work.*

stamped addressed 'envelope. See **sae.**

stampede /stæmˈpiːd/ **stampedes, stam-
peding, stampeded.** VERB & N-C If a group of
people or animals **stampede**, or if there is a
stampede, they run in a wild, uncontrolled
way. *There was a stampede for the exit.*

stance /stæns/ **stances.** **1** N-C Your **stance** on
a particular matter is your attitude to it. *...the
Catholic Church's stance on contraception.*
2 N-C Your **stance** is the way that you are
standing; FORMAL. *Take a comfortably wide
stance and flex your knees a little.*

stand /stænd/ **stands, standing, stood.**
1 VERB When you **are standing**, your body is
upright, your legs are straight, and your weight
is supported by your feet. *They told me to
stand still. ...a shop assistant who has to stand
up all day.* **2** VERB When someone who is sitting **stands**, they change their position so that
they are upright and on their feet. *When I
walked in, they all stood up.* **3** VERB If you
stand back, you move a short distance sideways or backwards, so that you are standing in
a different place. *I stood aside to let her pass.*
4 VERB If something such as a building **stands**
somewhere, it is upright in that position; WRIT-
TEN. *The house stands alone on top of a small
hill.* **5** VERB If you **stand** something somewhere, you put it there in an upright position.
*Stand the plant in the open in a sunny, shel-
tered place.* **6** N-C If you **make a stand**, or if
you **take a stand**, you do something or say
something in order to make it clear what your
attitude to a particular thing is. *He felt the need
to make a stand against racism.* **7** VERB If you
ask someone where they **stand** on an issue,
you want to know their attitude or view on it.
Where do you stand on feminism? **8** VERB If a

law, decision, or offer **stands**, it still exists and has not been changed or cancelled. *Although exceptions can be made, the rule still stands.* [9] VERB If something that can be measured **stands** at a particular level, it is at that level. *The inflation rate now stands at 3.6 per cent.* [10] VERB If something can **stand** a situation or a test, it is good enough or strong enough to cope with it. *The economy would not stand another rise in interest rates.* [11] VERB If you cannot **stand** someone or something, you hate them. *He cannot stand his boss... You eat like a pig. I can't stand looking at you.* [12] VERB If you **stand** to gain something, you are likely to gain it. *His shops stand to lose millions of pounds.* [13] VERB In British English, if you **stand** in an election, you are a candidate in it. The American word is **run**. *She is to stand as a Member of the European Parliament.* [14] N-C A **stand** is a small shop or stall, outdoors or in a large public building. *...a newspaper stand.* [15] N-C A **stand** is an object or piece of furniture that is designed for supporting or holding a particular kind of thing. *...a hat stand. ...a music stand.* PHRASES ● You can describe someone's final attempt to defend themselves before they are defeated as their **last stand**. *So is this really the last stand of the private investor?* ● See also **standing**. ● to **stand a chance**: see **chance**. ● to **stand firm**: see **firm**. ● to **stand on your own two feet**: see **foot**. ● to **stand trial**: see **trial**. ● to **stand your ground**: see **ground**. ● to **stand someone in good stead**: see **stead**.

▶ **stand aside.** See **stand down**.
▶ **stand by.** [1] PHR-VERB If you **are standing by**, you are ready and waiting to provide help or to take action. *Warships are standing by to evacuate their citizens if necessary.* [2] PHR-VERB If you **stand by** and let something bad happen, you do not do anything to stop it; used showing disapproval. *We cannot stand by and watch people starve.* ● See also **standby**.
▶ **stand down.** PHR-VERB If someone **stands down**, or if someone **stands aside**, they resign from an important job. *He stood down as chairman last January.*
▶ **stand for.** [1] PHR-VERB If letters **stand for** particular words, they are an abbreviation for those words. *AIDS stands for Acquired Immune Deficiency Syndrome.* [2] PHR-VERB The ideas or attitudes that someone or something **stands for** are the ones that they support or represent. *He hates us and everything we stand for.* [3] PHR-VERB If you will not **stand for** something, you will not allow it to happen or continue. *It's outrageous, and we won't stand for it any more.*
▶ **stand in.** PHR-VERB If you **stand in** for someone, you take their place or do their job, because they are ill or away. *He will stand in for Mr Goh when he is abroad.* ● See also **stand-in**.
▶ **stand out.** PHR-VERB If something **stands out**, it can be clearly noticed or is clearly better or more important than other similar things. *The dark silhouette of the castle ruins stood out boldly against the fading light... He played the violin, and he stood out from all the other musicians.*
▶ **stand up.** PHR-VERB If something such as a claim or a piece of evidence **stands up**, it is ac-

cepted as true or satisfactory after being carefully examined. *How well does this thesis stand up to close examination?*
▶ **stand up for.** PHR-VERB If you **stand up for** someone or something, you defend them openly; used showing approval. *Don't be afraid to stand up for yourself.*
▶ **stand up to.** [1] PHR-VERB If something **stands up to** rough treatment, it remains almost undamaged. *Is this building going to stand up to the strongest gales?* [2] PHR-VERB If you **stand up to** someone more powerful than you are, you defend yourself against their attacks or demands.

standard /ˈstændəd/ **standards.** [1] N-C A **standard** is a level of quality or achievement, especially a level that is thought to be acceptable. *...new national standards for hospital cleanliness.* [2] N-PL **Standards** are moral principles which affect people's attitudes and behaviour. *...the decline of moral standards.* [3] ADJ **Standard** means usual and normal. *Everyone wore suits, which is standard practice.*

standardize (BR also **standardise**) /ˈstændədaɪz/ **standardizes, standardizing, standardized.** VERB To **standardize** things means to change them so that they all have the same features. ◆ **standardization** N-U *...the need for standardisation of working hours in Community councils.*

,**standard of ˈliving, standards of living.** N-C Your **standard of living** is the level of comfort and wealth which you have.

standby /ˈstændbaɪ/ **standbys.** [1] N-C A **standby** is someone or something that is always ready to be used if they are needed. *We simply selected a standby from our second team.* [2] PHRASE If someone or something is **on standby**, they are ready to be used if needed. [3] ADJ BEFORE N A **standby** ticket for something such as the theatre or a plane journey is a cheap ticket that you buy just before the performance starts or the plane takes off, if there are still some seats left. *...standby flights from New York.*

'**stand-in, stand-ins.** N-C A **stand-in** is a person who takes someone else's place because the other person is ill or away.

standing /ˈstændɪŋ/ [1] N-U Someone's **standing** is their status or reputation. *...an artist of international standing.* [2] ADJ BEFORE N You use **standing** to describe something which is permanently in existence. *Elizabeth had a standing invitation to stay with her.* ● See also **stand; long-standing**.

'**stand-off, stand-offs.** N-C A **stand-off** is a situation in which neither of two opposing groups will make a move until the other one does something, so nothing can happen until one of them gives way.

standpoint /ˈstændpɔɪnt/ **standpoints.** N-C If you look at an event, situation, or idea from a particular **standpoint**, you look at it in a particular way. *From a military standpoint, the situation is under control.*

standstill /ˈstændstɪl/ N-SING If movement or an activity comes to a **standstill**, it stops completely. *The country was brought to a standstill by public sector strikes.*

stank /stæŋk/. **Stank** is the past tense of **stink**.

staple /'steɪpəl/ **staples, stapling, stapled.** 1 ADJ BEFORE A N A **staple** food, product, or activity is one that is basic and important in people's everyday lives. *Rice is the staple food of more than half the world's population.* 2 N-C **Staples** are small pieces of wire, used for holding sheets of paper together firmly. 3 VERB If you **staple** something, you fasten it to something else using staples.

star /stɑː/ **stars, starring, starred.** 1 N-C A **star** is a large ball of burning gas in space. Stars appear to us as small points of light in the sky on clear nights. 2 N-C You can refer to a shape or an object as a **star** when it has four or more points sticking out of it in a regular pattern. 3 N-C Famous actors, musicians, and sports players are often referred to as **stars**. 4 VERB If an actor or actress **stars** in a play or film, he or she has one of the most important parts in it. You can also say that a play or film **stars** a famous actor or actress. *He's starred in dozens of films.* 5 N-PL Your horoscope is sometimes referred to as your **stars**: INFORMAL. *My stars said I would find love.*

starboard /'stɑːbəd/. ADJ The **starboard** side of a ship is the right side when you are facing the front.

starch /stɑːtʃ/ **starches.** 1 N-VAR **Starch** is a carbohydrate found in foods such as bread, potatoes, and rice. 2 N-U **Starch** is a substance used for stiffening cloth.

stardom /'stɑːdəm/. N-U **Stardom** is the state of being very famous, usually as an actor, musician, or sports player. *She shot to stardom on Broadway.*

stare /steə/ **stares, staring, stared.** VERB & N-U If you **stare** at someone or something, or if you give someone or something a **stare**, you look at them for a long time. *Hlasek gave him a long, cold stare.* ● See note at **gaze**.

stark /stɑːk/ **starker, starkest.** 1 ADJ **Stark** choices or statements are harsh and unpleasant. *He issued a stark warning to Washington.* ◆ **starkly** ADV *The point is a starkly simple one.* 2 ADJ If two things are in **stark contrast** to one another, they are very different from each other.

start /stɑːt/ **starts, starting, started.** 1 VERB & N-C If you **start** to do something, or if you make a **start** on it, you do something you were not doing before. *The boy started crying... After several starts, she read the report properly.* 2 VERB & N-SING When something **starts**, or when someone **starts** it, it takes place or begins to exist from a particular time. You can also refer to the **start** of something. *The meeting starts at 10.30... We have started a campaign for better nursery services... She demanded to know why she had not been told from the start.* 3 VERB If someone **started** or **started off** as a particular thing, their first job was as that thing. *Mr. Dambar had started off as an assistant.* 4 VERB & PHR-VERB If you **start** an engine or car, or if you **start** it **up**, it begins to work. *The engine of the seaplane started up... The car won't start.* 5 N-C A **start** is a sudden jerky movement your body makes because you are surprised or frightened. *Sylvia woke with a start.*

PHRASES ● You use **for a start** or **to start with** to introduce the first of a number of things or reasons that you want to mention or could mention. *For a start, the beach is dreadful.* ● If you **get off to a good start**, you are successful in the early stages of doing something. If you **get off to a bad start**, you are not successful in the early stages of doing something. *Rescue efforts got off to a slow start.* ● See also **head start**. ● **get off to a flying start**: see **fly**.

▶ **start off.** PHR-VERB If you **start off** by doing something, you do it as the first part of an activity. *I started off by setting out the facts.*

▶ **start on.** PHR-VERB If you **start on** something that needs to be done, you begin doing it. *No need for you to start on the washing-up yet.*

▶ **start out.** 1 PHR-VERB If someone or something **starts out as** a particular thing, they are that thing at the beginning although they change later. *What started out as fun quickly became hard work.* 2 PHR-VERB If you **start out** by doing something, you do it at the beginning of an activity or process. *I started out by bringing up my children quite strictly.*

▶ **start over.** PHR-VERB If you **start over**, or if you **start** something **over**, you begin something again from the beginning; AMERICAN. *Okay, let's start over.*

▶ **start up.** 1 PHR-VERB If you **start up** something such as a new business, you create it or cause it to start. *You could start up your own newspaper.* 2 See **start** 4.

starter /'stɑːtə/ **starters.** 1 N-C A **starter** is a small quantity of food served as the first course of a meal. 2 N-C The **starter** of a car is a device that starts the engine. 3 PHRASE You use **for starters** when you mention something to indicate that it is the first item or point in a series. *What do Diana Ross and Judi Dench have in common? For starters, they both sing.*

'starting point, starting points. N-C Something that is a **starting point** for a discussion or process can be used to begin it or act as a basis for it. *These proposals represent a realistic starting point for negotiation.*

startle /'stɑːtəl/ **startles, startling, startled.** VERB If something sudden and unexpected **startles** you, it surprises you and frightens you slightly. *The sound of his voice startled her.* ◆ **startled** ADJ *Martha gave her a startled look.*

startling /'stɑːtəlɪŋ/. ADJ Something that is **startling** is so unexpected or remarkable that people are surprised by it. *There were some startling successes.*

starve /stɑːv/ **starves, starving, starved.** 1 VERB If people **starve**, they suffer greatly from lack of food which sometimes leads to their death. ◆ **starvation** /stɑː'veɪʃən/ N-U *Up to four million people face starvation.* 2 VERB To **starve** someone means to not give them any food. *Judy decided I was starving myself.* 3 VERB If someone or something **is starved of** something they need, they are suffering because they are not getting enough of it. *...a childhood which was starved of affection.*

starving /'stɑːvɪŋ/. ADJ AFTER LINK-V If you say you are **starving**, you mean you are very hungry; INFORMAL.

stash /stæʃ/ **stashes, stashing, stashed.**
[1] VERB If you **stash** something valuable in a
secret place, you store it there to keep it safe.
...the bottle of whiskey that we had stashed be-
hind the bookcase. [2] N-C You can refer to
something you have stashed as a **stash** of
something; INFORMAL. *A large stash of drugs*
had been found aboard the yacht.

state /steɪt/ **states, stating, stated.** [1] N-C
You can refer to countries as **states**, particularly when you are discussing politics. *...Albania,*
Europe's only remaining communist state.
● See note at **country**. [2] ADJ BEFORE N A **state**
occasion is a formal one involving the head of
a country. *...a state visit to India.* [3] N-C Some
large countries such as the USA are divided
into smaller areas called **states**. [4] N-PROPER
The USA is sometimes referred to as **the**
States; INFORMAL. [5] N-SING You can refer to the
government of a country as **the state**. *...the*
state social-security system. [6] VERB If you **state**
something, you say or write it in a formal or
definite way. *Please state your name.* [7] N-C
When you talk about the **state** of someone or
something, you are referring to the condition
they are in or what they are like at a particular
time. *I was then in a state of clinical depres-*
sion.

stately /ˈsteɪtli/. ADJ Something or someone
that is **stately** is impressive because they look
very graceful and dignified.

statement /ˈsteɪtmənt/ **statements.** [1] N-C A
statement is something that you say or write
which gives information in a formal or definite
way. *Her husband made a formal statement to*
the police... The statement by the military de-
nied any involvement. [2] N-C A **statement** is a
printed document showing all the money paid
into and taken out of a bank or building society account.

state of af'fairs. N-SING If you refer to a particular **state of affairs**, you mean the general
situation and circumstances connected with
someone or something. *...a more democratic,*
and modern, state of affairs.

'state of mind, states of mind. N-C Your
state of mind is your mood or mental state at
a particular time. *He's thought to be in a dis-*
turbed state of mind.

state-of-the-'art. If you describe something as **state-of-the-art**, you mean that it is
the best available because it has been made
using the most modern techniques and technology. *...state-of-the-art technology.*

statesman /ˈsteɪtsmən/ **statesmen.** N-C A
statesman is an important and experienced
politician, especially one who is widely known
and respected.

static /ˈstætɪk/. [1] ADJ Something that is **static**
does not move or change. *Property prices re-*
mained static between February and April.
[2] N-U **Static** or **static electricity** is electricity
which is caused by friction and which collects
in things such as your body or metal objects.
[3] N-U If there is **static** on the radio or television, you hear loud crackling noises.

station /ˈsteɪʃən/ **stations, stationing, sta-**
tioned. [1] N-C A **station** is a building by a railway line where a train stops. [2] N-C A **bus sta-**

tion or **coach station** is a place where buses or
coaches start a journey. ● See also **police sta-**
tion. [3] N-C If you talk about a particular radio
or television **station**, you are referring to the
programmes broadcast by a particular radio or
television company. *...an independent local ra-*
dio station. [4] VERB If soldiers or officials **are**
stationed somewhere, they are sent there to
do a job or to work for a period of time. *...Unit-*
ed States military personnel stationed in the
Philippines.

stationary /ˈsteɪʃənri, AM -neri/. ADJ Something
that is **stationary** is not moving.

stationery /ˈsteɪʃənri, AM -neri/. N-U **Stationery**
is paper, envelopes, and writing equipment.

statistic /stəˈtɪstɪk/ **statistics.** [1] N-C **Statistics**
are facts obtained from analyzing information
that is expressed in numbers. *Official statistics*
show real wages declining by 24%. ◆**statistical**
ADJ *...statistical proof.* ◆**statistically** ADV *The*
results are not statistically significant. [2] N-U
Statistics is a branch of mathematics concerned with the study of information that is
expressed in numbers.

statue /ˈstætʃuː/ **statues.** N-C A **statue** is a large
sculpture of a person or an animal, made of
stone, bronze, or some other hard material.

stature /ˈstætʃə/. [1] N-U Someone's **stature** is
their height. *She was a little short in stature.*
[2] N-U Someone's **stature** is their importance
and reputation. *It's good to see an actor of the*
stature of Tom Courtney on an Edinburgh
stage.

status /ˈsteɪtəs/. [1] N-U Your **status** is your social or professional position. *The status of chil-*
dren in society has long been underestimated.
[2] N-U **Status** is the prestige and importance
that someone or something has in the eyes of
other people. *He has risen to gain the status of*
a national hero... Men's work was given more
status. [3] N-U **Status** is an official classification
which gives a person, organization, or country
certain rights or advantages. *The personal al-*
lowance depends on your age and marital sta-
tus.

status quo /ˌsteɪtəs ˈkwəʊ/. N-SING The **status**
quo is the situation that exists at a particular
time; FORMAL. *The federation voted to maintain*
the status quo.

statute /ˈstætʃuːt/ **statutes.** N-C A **statute** is a
rule or law which has been formally written
down.

statutory /ˈstætʃutəri, AM -tɔːri/. ADJ **Statutory**
means relating to rules or laws which have
been formally written down; FORMAL. *We had a*
statutory duty to report to Parliament.

staunch /stɔːntʃ/ **stauncher, staunchest.** ADJ
A **staunch** supporter of someone or something
supports them very strongly and loyally.
◆**staunchly** ADV *She was staunchly anti-*
communist.

stave /steɪv/ **staves, staving, staved.**
PHR-VERB If you **stave off** something bad, you
succeed in stopping it happening for a while.
...a last-minute bid to stave off defeat.

stay /steɪ/ **stays, staying, stayed.** [1] VERB If
you **stay** in a place or position, you continue to
be there and do not leave. *She stayed at home*
to raise her children... Stay away from the

rocks. **2** VERB If you **stay** in a town or hotel, or at someone's house, you live there for a short time. *We stayed the night in a little hotel.* **3** N-C The time you spend in a place is referred to as your **stay** there. *He had a short stay in hospital.* **4** LINK-VERB If someone or something **stays** in a particular condition or situation, they continue to be in it. *The company was struggling to stay ahead of its rivals... Nothing stays the same for long.* **5** VERB If you **stay** out of something or **stay** away from it, you do not get involved in it. *He warned young people to stay away from drugs.*

PHRASES ● If you say that something is **here to stay**, you mean that people have accepted it and it has become a part of everyday life. *Satellite TV is here to stay.* ● If you **stay put**, you remain somewhere. *He is very happy to stay put in Lyon.*

▸ **stay in.** PHR-VERB If you **stay in**, you remain at home during the evening and do not go out.

▸ **stay on.** PHR-VERB If you **stay on** somewhere, you remain there after other people have left or after the time when you were going to leave. *He had managed to arrange to stay on in Adelaide.*

▸ **stay out.** PHR-VERB If you **stay out**, you remain away from home at night. *I met some friends and stayed out until eleven or twelve.*

▸ **stay up.** PHR-VERB If you **stay up**, you remain out of bed at a later time than normal. *I used to stay up late with my mom and watch movies.*

stead /sted/. PHRASE If something will **stand you in good stead**, it will be useful to you in the future. *My years of teaching stood me in good stead.*

steadfast /'stedfɑːst, -fæst/. ADJ If you are **steadfast** in your beliefs or opinions, you are convinced that they are right and you refuse to change them; used showing approval. *He remained steadfast in his belief that he had done the right thing.* ♦**steadfastly** ADV *She steadfastly refused to look his way.*

steady /'stedi/ **steadier, steadiest; steadies, steadying, steadied. 1** ADJ Something that is **steady** continues or develops gradually without any interruptions and is unlikely to change suddenly. *They were forecasting a steady rise in sales... I want to find a steady job.* ♦**steadily** ADV *Relax as much as possible and keep breathing steadily.* **2** ADJ If an object is **steady**, it is firm and does not move about. *Hold the camera steady.* **3** ADJ A **steady** look or voice is calm and controlled. ♦**steadily** ADV *He moved back a little and stared steadily at Elaine.* **4** VERB If you **steady** something, or if it **steadies**, it stops shaking or moving about. *She placed her hands on the controls again and steadied the plane.* **5** VERB If you **steady** yourself, you control your voice or expression, so that people will think that you are calm. *Somehow she steadied herself.*

steak /steɪk/ **steaks. 1** N-VAR **Steak** is beef without much fat on it. **2** N-C A fish **steak** is a large flat piece of fish.

steal /stiːl/ **steals, stealing, stole, stolen. 1** VERB If you **steal** something from someone, you take it away from them without their permission and without intending to return it. *He*

was accused of stealing a small boy's bicycle... We have now found the stolen car.* ♦**stealing** N-U *She has since been jailed for six months for stealing.* **2** VERB If you **steal** somewhere, you move there quietly and cautiously. *They can steal away at night and join us.*

stealth /stelθ/. N-U If you do something with **stealth**, you do it in a slow, quiet, and secretive way. *Reform has proceeded by stealth.*

steam /stiːm/ **steams, steaming, steamed. 1** N-U **Steam** is the hot mist that forms when water boils. **Steam** vehicles and machines are powered by steam. *...steam trains.* **2** VERB If something **steams**, it gives off steam. *The kettle began to steam.* **3** VERB If you **steam** food, you cook it in steam. *Boil or steam the rice.* ● See note at **cook. 4** PHRASE If you **run out of steam**, you stop doing something because you have no more energy or enthusiasm left; INFORMAL.

steamer /'stiːmə/ **steamers. 1** N-C A **steamer** is a ship that is powered by steam. **2** N-C A **steamer** is a special saucepan used for steaming food such as vegetables and fish.

steamy /'stiːmi/ **steamier, steamiest. 1** ADJ A **steamy** place is very hot and humid, usually because it is full of steam. *...a steamy kitchen.* **2** ADJ **Steamy** means erotic or passionate; INFORMAL. *...steamy sex scenes.*

steel /stiːl/ **steels, steeling, steeled. 1** N-U **Steel** is a very strong metal made mainly from iron. ● See also **stainless steel. 2** VERB If you **steel** yourself, you prepare to deal with something unpleasant. *I had been steeling myself for something like this.*

steely /'stiːli/. **1** ADJ You use **steely** to describe something that has a hard, greyish colour. *...the steely grey light.* **2** ADJ **Steely** is used to describe someone who is hard, strong, and determined. *Their indecision has been replaced by confidence and steely determination.*

steep /stiːp/ **steeper, steepest. 1** ADJ A **steep** slope rises at a very sharp angle and is difficult to go up. ♦**steeply** ADV *The ground rose steeply.* **2** ADJ A **steep** increase is very big. ♦**steeply** ADV *Unemployment is rising steeply.*

steeped /stiːpt/. PHRASE AFTER LINK-V If a place or person is **steeped** in a quality or characteristic, they are surrounded by it or deeply influenced by it. *The castle is steeped in history.*

steer /stɪə/ **steers, steering, steered. 1** VERB When you **steer** a car, boat, or plane, you control it so that it goes in the direction you want. *She would often let me steer the car along our driveway.* **2** VERB If you **steer** someone in a particular direction, you guide them there. *I steered him towards the door.* **3** PHRASE If you **steer clear** of someone or something, you deliberately avoid them. *The rabbis try to steer clear of political questions.*

'steering wheel, steering wheels. N-C The **steering wheel** in a vehicle is the wheel which the driver holds to steer the vehicle.

stem /stem/ **stems, stemming, stemmed. 1** N-C The **stem** of a plant is the thin upright part on which the flowers and leaves grow. **2** N-C The **stem** of a glass or vase is the long thin part which connects the bowl to the base. **3** VERB If you **stem** something that is spreading from one place to another, you stop it spreading; FORMAL. *The authorities seem powerless to stem the rising tide of violence.* 4 VERB If a condition or problem **stems** from something, that is what originally caused it. *Most of her problems stemmed from her childhood.*

stench /stentʃ/ **stenches.** N-C A **stench** is a strong, unpleasant smell. *...the stench of decaying fish.*

stencil /'stensəl/ **stencils, stencilling, stencilled** (AM **stenciling, stenciled**). 1 N-C A **stencil** is a piece of paper, plastic, or metal with a design cut out of it. You place the stencil on a surface and create a design by putting ink or paint over the cut area. 2 VERB If you **stencil** letters or designs, you print them using a stencil.

step /step/ **steps, stepping, stepped.** 1 N-C A **step** is the movement made by lifting your foot and putting it down in a different place. *I took another step back... He heard steps in the corridor.* 2 VERB If you **step** on something or **step** in a particular direction, you put your foot on the thing or move your foot in that direction. *He stepped on glass and cut his foot... Doug stepped sideways.* 3 N-C A **step** is one of a series of actions that you take in order to achieve something. *He greeted the agreement as the first step towards peace.* 4 N-C A **step** is a raised flat surface, often one of a series, on which you put your feet in order to walk up or down to a different level. *He sat down on the bottom step of the stairs.* PHRASES • If you stay **one step ahead** of someone or something, you manage to achieve more than they do or avoid competition or danger from them. *The Opposition, using last-minute knowledge, has managed to keep one step ahead.* • If people are **in step** with each other, their ideas or opinions are the same. If they are **out of step** with each other, their ideas or opinions are different. *Britain is out of step with the rest of Europe on this matter.* • If you do something **step by step**, you do it by progressing gradually from one stage to the next. *The king took the boy, step by step, through everything that had happened.*

▶ **step aside.** See **step down.**

▶ **step back.** PHR-VERB If you **step back** from a situation, you think about it in a fresh and detached way. *It was necessary to step back from the project and look at it as a whole.*

▶ **step down.** PHR-VERB If you **step down** or **step aside**, you resign from an important job or position. *Mr Orlando was forced to step down as mayor.*

▶ **step in.** PHR-VERB If you **step in**, you get involved in a difficult situation, in order to help. *President Bush had to step in to settle the dispute.*

▶ **step up.** PHR-VERB If you **step up** something, you increase it. *The Japanese then stepped up their campaign against the guerrillas.*

stepfather (or **step-father**) /'stepfɑːðə/ **stepfathers.** N-C Your **stepfather** is the man who has married your mother after the death or divorce of your father.

stepmother (or **step-mother**) /'stepmʌðə/ **stepmothers.** N-C Your **stepmother** is the

woman who has married your father after the death or divorce of your mother.

'stepping stone, stepping stones. 1 N-C A **stepping stone** is a job or event that helps you to make progress, especially in your career. *Many students now see university as a stepping stone to a good job.* 2 N-C **Stepping stones** are a line of stones which you can walk on in order to cross a shallow stream or river.

stereo /'steriəʊ/ **stereos.** 1 ADJ **Stereo** is used to describe a recording or a system of playing music in which the sound is directed through two speakers. *...a stereo cassette player.* 2 N-C A **stereo** is a record player with two speakers.

stereotype /'steriətaɪp/ **stereotypes, stereotyping, stereotyped.** 1 N-C A **stereotype** is a fixed general image or set of characteristics that a lot of people believe represent a particular type of person or thing. *...the stereotype of the polite, industrious Japanese.* 2 VERB If someone **is stereotyped** as something, people form a fixed general image of them, so that it is assumed that they will behave in a particular way. *...the way women are stereotyped in a lot of films.*

sterile /'steraɪl, AM -rəl/. 1 ADJ Something that is **sterile** is completely clean and free of germs. *...a sterile needle.* ♦ **sterility** /stə'rɪlɪti/ N-U *...the antiseptic sterility of the hospital.* 2 ADJ A person or animal that is **sterile** is unable to have or produce babies. ♦ **sterility** N-U *This disease causes sterility.* 3 ADJ A **sterile** situation is lacking in energy and new ideas. *Too much time has been wasted in sterile debate.* ♦ **sterility** N-U *They are quitting in disgust at the sterility of politics.*

sterilize (BR also **sterilise**) /'sterɪlaɪz/ **sterilizes, sterilizing, sterilized.** 1 VERB If you **sterilize** a thing or place, you make it completely clean and free from germs. *Sterilize a large needle by boiling it.* 2 VERB If a person or an animal **is sterilized**, they have an operation that makes it impossible for them to have or produce babies. ♦ **sterilization, sterilizations** N-VAR *...the decision to have a sterilization.*

sterling /'stɜːlɪŋ/. 1 N-U **Sterling** is the money system of Great Britain. 2 ADJ If you describe someone's work or character as **sterling**, you mean it is excellent; FORMAL. *Those are sterling qualities to be admired in anyone.*

stern /stɜːn/ **sterner, sternest; sterns.** 1 ADJ Someone or something that is **stern** is very serious and strict. *...a stern warning.* ♦ **sternly** ADV *'We will take the necessary steps,' she said sternly.* 2 N-C The **stern** of a boat is the back part of it.

steroid /'steroɪd, AM 'stɪr-/ **steroids.** N-C A **steroid** is a type of chemical substance which occurs naturally in the body, and can also be made artificially.

stew /stjuː, AM stuː/ **stews, stewing, stewed.** 1 N-VAR A **stew** is a meal made by cooking meat and vegetables in liquid at a low temperature. *...beef stew.* 2 VERB If you **stew** meat, vegetables, or fruit, you cook them slowly in liquid.

steward /'stjuːəd, AM 'stuː-/ **stewards.** 1 N-C A **steward** is a man whose job is to look after passengers on a ship, plane, or train. 2 N-C A

steward is someone who helps to organize a race, march, or other public event.

stewardess /ˌstjuːəˈdes, ˌstuː-/ **stewardesses.** N-C A **stewardess** is a woman whose job is to look after passengers on a ship, plane, or train.

stick 1 noun uses

stick /stɪk/ **sticks.** ① N-C A **stick** is a thin branch which has fallen off a tree. ...*bundles of dried sticks.* ② N-C A **stick** is a long thin piece of wood which is used for a particular purpose. ...*a walking stick.* ...*a hockey stick.* ③ N-C A **stick** of something is a long thin piece of it. ...*a stick of celery.* ...*a stick of dynamite.*

stick 2 verb uses

stick /stɪk/ **sticks, sticking, stuck.** ① VERB If you **stick** something somewhere, you put it there in a rather casual way; INFORMAL. *He folded the papers and stuck them in his desk drawer.* ② VERB If you **stick** a pointed object in something, you push it in. *The doctor stuck the needle in Joe's arm.* ③ VERB If you **stick** one thing to another, you attach it using glue, sticky tape, or another sticky substance. *I was going to stick a notice on the window saying 'Tickets For The Court'.* ④ VERB If something **sticks** somewhere, it becomes attached or fixed in one position and cannot be moved. *It stops the rice sticking to the pan.* ⑤ PHRASE If someone in an unpleasant or difficult situation **sticks it out**, they do not leave or give up. *I really didn't like New York, but I wanted to stick it out a little bit longer.* ⑥ See also **stuck**.

▶ **stick around.** PHR-VERB If you **stick around**, you stay where you are; INFORMAL. *I didn't stick around long enough to find out.*

▶ **stick by.** PHR-VERB If you **stick by** someone, you continue to help or support them. ...*friends who stuck by me during the difficult times.*

▶ **stick out.** PHR-VERB If something **sticks out**, or if you **stick** it **out**, it extends beyond something else. ...*a nozzle sticking out of the front grill... Eve stuck her head out the window.*

▶ **stick to.** ① PHR-VERB If you **stick to** something, you stay close to it or with it and do not change to something else. *Stick to the main road... I think he had better stick to acting.* ② PHR-VERB If you **stick to** a promise or agreement, you do what you said you would do.

▶ **stick together.** PHR-VERB If people **stick together**, they stay with each other and support each other. *If we all stick together, we ought to be okay.*

▶ **stick up.** ① PHR-VERB If you **stick up** a picture or a notice, you fix it to a wall. ② PHR-VERB If something **sticks up**, it points upwards. *His hair stuck up.*

▶ **stick up for.** PHR-VERB If you **stick up for** someone or something, you support or defend them forcefully. *Why do you always stick up for her?*

▶ **stick with.** PHR-VERB If you **stick with** someone or something, you stay with them and do not change to something else. *If you're in a job that keeps you busy, stick with it.*

sticker /ˈstɪkə/ **stickers.** N-C A **sticker** is a small piece of paper or plastic with writing or a picture on it, that you can stick onto a surface.

'stick insect, stick insects. N-C A **stick insect** is an insect with a long thin body and legs.

sticky /ˈstɪki/. ① ADJ A **sticky** substance can stick to other things. **Sticky** things are covered with a sticky substance. ...*sticky paper.* ② ADJ **Sticky** weather is unpleasantly hot and damp. ...*an uncomfortably sticky day.* ③ ADJ A **sticky** situation is difficult or embarrassing; INFORMAL. *Her research was going through a sticky patch.*

stiff /stɪf/ **stiffer, stiffest.** ① ADJ Something that is **stiff** is firm and does not bend easily. *His gaberdine trousers were brand new and stiff.* ◆ **stiffly** ADV *Moira sat stiffly upright in her straight-backed chair.* ② ADJ Something such as a drawer or door that is **stiff** does not move as easily as it should. *The gears were too stiff.* ③ ADJ If you are **stiff**, your muscles or joints ache when you move. ◆ **stiffly** ADV *He climbed stiffly from the car.* ◆ **stiffness** N-U ...*pain and stiffness in the neck.* ④ ADJ **Stiff** behaviour is rather formal and not relaxed. *She looked at him with a stiff smile.* ◆ **stiffly** ADV ...*a stiffly worded letter.* ⑤ ADJ **Stiff** means difficult or severe. ...*stiff anti-drugs laws.* ⑥ ADJ BEFORE N A **stiff** drink is a large amount of a strong alcoholic drink. ...*a stiff whisky.* ⑦ ADJ A **stiff** wind blows quite strongly. ⑧ ADV If you are bored **stiff**, worried **stiff**, or scared **stiff**, you are extremely bored, worried, or scared; INFORMAL. ⑨ **stiff upper lip**: see **lip**.

stiffen /ˈstɪfən/ **stiffens, stiffening, stiffened.** ① VERB If you **stiffen**, you stop moving and become very tense, for example because you are afraid or angry. *His father's face stiffened with dismay.* ② VERB & PHR-VERB If your muscles or joints **stiffen**, or if they **stiffen up**, they become difficult to bend or move. *My elbow was starting to stiffen up where I'd landed on it.* ③ VERB If attitudes or behaviour **stiffen**, they become stronger or more severe, and less likely to be changed. *Canada has recently stiffened its immigration rules.* ④ VERB When something such as cloth **is stiffened**, it is made firm. ...*paper that had been stiffened with a kind of paste.*

stifle /ˈstaɪfəl/ **stifles, stifling, stifled.** VERB To **stifle** something means to stop it happening or continuing. *Ed stifled a yawn and looked at his watch... Regulations on children stifled all their creativity.*

stifling /ˈstaɪfəlɪŋ/. ① ADJ **Stifling** heat is so intense that it makes you feel uncomfortable. ② ADJ If a situation is **stifling**, it makes you feel uncomfortable because you cannot do what you want. *Life at home with her parents and two sisters was stifling.*

stigma /ˈstɪɡmə/ **stigmas.** N-VAR If you say that something has a **stigma** attached to it, you mean that people consider it to be unacceptable or a disgrace, and you think this is unfair. ...*the stigma attached to mental illness.*

stigmatize (BR also **stigmatise**) /ˈstɪɡmətaɪz/ **stigmatizes, stigmatizing, stigmatized.** VERB If someone or something **is stigmatized**, they are unfairly regarded by many people as unacceptable or disgraceful.

stiletto /stɪˈletəʊ/ **stilettos.** N-C **Stilettos** are women's shoes that have high, very narrow heels.

still 1 adverb uses

still /stɪl/. **1** ADV If a situation that used to exist **still** exists, it has continued and exists now. *I still dream of home... Brian's toe is still badly swollen.* **2** ADV If something that has not yet happened could **still** happen, it is possible that it will happen. *We could still make it, but we won't get there till three.* **3** ADV You use **still** to emphasize that something remains the case or is true. *Despite the ruling, Boreham was still found guilty.* **4** ADV You use **still** before saying something that shows that you think what has just been said or mentioned is not important or is not worth worrying about. *'Any idea who is going to be here this weekend?'—'No. Still, who cares?'* **5** ADV You use **still** in expressions such as **still further**, **still another**, and **still more** to show that you find the number or quantity of things you are referring to surprising or excessive. *There are clouds forecast for tomorrow and they could delay the flight still further.* **6** ADV You use **still** with words such as 'better' or 'more' to indicate that something has even more of a quality than something else. *Pizza may be good for you, but spaghetti sauce is better still.*

still 2 not moving

still /stɪl/ **stiller, stillest**. **1** ADJ If you stay **still**, you stay in the same position without moving. *He played the tape through once, then sat very still for several minutes.* **2** ADJ If something is **still**, there is no movement or activity there. *The night air was very still.* ♦**stillness** N-U *...the beauty and stillness of the forest.*

still 'life, still lifes. N-VAR A **still life** is a painting or drawing of an arrangement of objects such as flowers or fruit. **Still life** is this type of painting or drawing.

stimulant /ˈstɪmjʊlənt/ **stimulants**. N-C A **stimulant** is a drug that increases your heart rate and makes you less likely to sleep.

stimulate /ˈstɪmjʊleɪt/ **stimulates, stimulating, stimulated**. **1** VERB To **stimulate** something means to encourage it to begin or develop further. *These businesses stimulate the creation of local jobs.* **2** VERB If you are **stimulated** by something, it makes you feel full of ideas and enthusiasm. ♦**stimulating** ADJ *It is complex yet stimulating book.* ♦**stimulation** N-U *...the mental stimulation of a challenging job.* **3** VERB If something **stimulates** a part of a person's body, it causes it to move or function automatically. ♦**stimulation** N-U *...electrical stimulation of the brain.*

stimulus /ˈstɪmjʊləs/ **stimuli** /ˈstɪmjʊlaɪ/. N-VAR A **stimulus** is something that encourages activity in people or things. *Headaches can be triggered by a vast range of stimuli.*

sting /stɪŋ/ **stings, stinging, stung**. **1** VERB If an insect or plant **stings** you, it pricks your skin, usually with poison, so that you feel a sharp pain. • See note at **bite**. **2** N-C The **sting** of an insect is the part that stings you. **3** VERB & N-SING If a part of your body **stings**, or if you feel a **sting**, you feel a sharp pain there. *His cheeks were stinging from the icy wind.* **4** VERB If someone's remarks **sting** you, they upset and annoy you. *Some of the criticism has stung him.* ♦**stinging** ADJ *...a stinging attack on the government.*

stink /stɪŋk/ **stinks, stinking, stank, stunk**. **1** VERB & N-SING If something **stinks**, it smells extremely unpleasant. A **stink** is a very unpleasant smell. *The place stinks of fried onions.* **2** VERB If you say that something **stinks**, you mean that it involves ideas, feelings, or practices that you do not like; INFORMAL. *They have done something very bad. It's illegal, it stinks.*

stint /stɪnt/ **stints**. N-C A **stint** is a period of time spent doing a particular job or activity. *...a five-year stint in Hong Kong.*

stipulate /ˈstɪpjʊleɪt/ **stipulates, stipulating, stipulated**. VERB If you **stipulate** that something must be done, you say clearly that it must be done. *The company's rules stipulate that board members must retire at 75.* ♦**stipulation, stipulations** N-C *Clifford's only stipulation is that his clients obey his advice.*

stir /stɜː/ **stirs, stirring, stirred**. **1** VERB When you **stir** a liquid, you mix it inside a container using something such as a spoon. *There was Mrs Bellingham, stirring sugar into her tea.* **2** VERB If you **stir**, you move slightly, for example because you are uncomfortable or beginning to wake up; WRITTEN. *Eileen shook him, and he started to stir.* **3** VERB If something **stirs** you or **stirs** an emotion in you, it makes you react with a strong emotion; WRITTEN. *Amy remembered the anger he had stirred in her.* **4** N-SING If an event causes a **stir**, it causes great excitement and interest, or anger. *His film has caused a stir in America.* **5** See also **stirring**.

▶ **stir up**. **1** PHR-VERB If something **stirs up** dust or mud, it causes it to move around. *They saw first a cloud of dust and then the car that was stirring it up.* **2** PHR-VERB If you **stir up** a particular mood or situation, usually a bad one, you cause it. *As usual, Harriet is trying to stir up trouble.*

stirring /ˈstɜːrɪŋ/ **stirrings**. **1** ADJ A **stirring** event, performance, or account of something makes people very excited or enthusiastic. *The Prime Minister made a stirring speech.* **2** N-C When there is a **stirring** of emotion, people begin to feel it. *...the first stirrings of a sense of guilt.*

stitch /stɪtʃ/ **stitches, stitching, stitched**. **1** VERB If you **stitch** cloth, you use a needle and thread to join two pieces together or to make a decoration. *Fold the fabric and stitch the two layers together.* **2** N-C **Stitches** are the short pieces of thread that have been sewn in a piece of cloth. **3** N-C A **stitch** is a loop made by one turn of wool around a knitting needle. **4** VERB & PHR-VERB When doctors **stitch** a wound, or when they **stitch** it **up**, they use a special needle and thread to sew the skin together. *Dr Armonson stitched up her wrist wounds.* **5** N-C A **stitch** is a piece of thread that has been used to stitch a wound. *He had six stitches in a head wound.* **6** N-SING A **stitch** is a sharp pain in your side, usually caused by running or laughing a lot.

stock /stɒk/ **stocks, stocking, stocked**. **1** N-VAR **Stocks** are shares in the ownership of a company. A company's **stock** consists of all the shares that people have bought in it. *...the* *buying and selling of stocks.* ② VERB A shop that **stocks** particular goods keeps a supply of them to sell. *The inn gift shop stocks quality Indian crafts.* ③ N-U A shop's **stock** is the total amount of goods which it has available to sell. ④ N-C A **stock** of things is a supply of them. *...stocks of paper and printing ink.* ⑤ N-VAR **Stock** is a liquid made by boiling meat, bones, or vegetables in water.

PHRASES ● If goods are **in stock**, a shop has them available to sell. If they are **out of stock**, it does not. ● If you **take stock**, you pause and think about a situation before deciding what to do next. *It was time to take stock of the situation.*

▸ **stock up**. PHR-VERB If you **stock up** with something, you buy a lot of it, in case you cannot get it later. *The authorities have urged people to stock up on fuel.*

stockbroker /'stɒkbrəʊkə/ **stockbrokers**. N-C A **stockbroker** is someone whose profession is buying and selling stocks and shares for clients.

stockbroking /'stɒkbrəʊkɪŋ/. N-U **Stockbroking** is the professional activity of buying and selling stocks and shares for clients.

'**stock exchange, stock exchanges**. N-C A **stock exchange** is a place where people buy and sell stocks and shares.

stockholder /'stɒkhəʊldə/ **stockholders**. N-C In American English, a **stockholder** is a person who owns shares in a company. The usual British word is **shareholder**.

stocking /'stɒkɪŋ/ **stockings**. N-C **Stockings** are items of women's clothing which fit closely over their feet and legs. Stockings are usually made of nylon or silk and are held in place by suspenders. *...a pair of silk stockings.*

stockist /'stɒkɪst/ **stockists**. N-C A **stockist** of a particular brand or type of goods is a person or shop that sells it; BRITISH. *Take it to your nearest Kodak Photo CD stockist.*

'**stock market, stock markets**. N-C The **stock market** consists of the activity of buying stocks and shares, and the people and institutions that organize it.

stockpile /'stɒkpaɪl/ **stockpiles, stockpiling, stockpiled**. ① VERB If people **stockpile** things, they store large quantities of them for future use. *People are stockpiling food for the coming winter.* ② N-C A **stockpile** is a large store of something. *...stockpiles of chemical weapons.*

stocky /'stɒki/. ADJ A **stocky** person has a body that is broad, solid, and short.

stoke /stəʊk/ **stokes, stoking, stoked**. ① VERB & PHR-VERB If you **stoke** a fire, or if you **stoke** it **up**, you put more fuel onto it. *He stoked up the fire in the hearth.* ② VERB & PHR-VERB If you **stoke** something such as a feeling, or if you **stoke** it **up**, you cause it to be felt more strongly. *These demands are helping to stoke fears of civil war.*

stole /stəʊl/. **Stole** is the past tense of **steal**.

stolen /'stəʊlən/. **Stolen** is the past participle of **steal**.

stomach /'stʌmək/ **stomachs, stomaching, stomached**. ① N-C Your **stomach** is the organ

inside your body where food is digested. *My stomach is completely full.* ② N-C You can refer to the front part of your body below your waist as your **stomach**. *The children lay down on their stomachs.* ③ VERB If you cannot **stomach** something, you strongly dislike it and cannot accept it. *He could not stomach violence.*

stomp /stɒmp/ **stomps, stomping, stomped**. VERB If you **stomp** somewhere, you walk there with heavy steps, often because you are angry. *He stomped out of the room.*

stone /stəʊn/ **stones, stoning, stoned**. ① N-VAR **Stone** is a hard solid substance found in the ground and often used for building. *He could not tell whether the floor was wood or stone.* ② N-C A **stone** is a small piece of rock. *He removed a stone from his shoe.* ③ VERB If people **stone** someone or something, they throw stones at them. *Youths burned cars and stoned police.* ④ N-C In British English, the **stone** in a fruit such as a peach or plum is the large seed in the middle of it. ⑤ N-C A **stone** is a measurement of a person's weight, equal to 14 pounds or 6.35 kilograms. The plural is **stone**. BRITISH. *I weighed around 16 stone.* ● See note at **weight**. ⑥ N-C You can refer to a jewel as a **stone**. *...a diamond ring with three stones.* ⑦ PHRASE If you say that one place is **a stone's throw** from another, you mean that the places are close to each other.

'**Stone Age**. N-PROPER The **Stone Age** is a very early period of human history, when people used tools and weapons made of stone, not metal.

stony /'stəʊni/. ① ADJ **Stony** ground is rough and contains a lot of stones. ② ADJ If someone's expression or behaviour is **stony**, they show no friendliness or sympathy. *He drove us home in stony silence.*

stood /stʊd/. **Stood** is the past tense and past participle of **stand**.

stool /stuːl/ **stools**. N-C A **stool** is a seat with legs but no support for your back or arms.

stoop /stuːp/ **stoops, stooping, stooped**. ① VERB & N-SING If you **stoop**, or if you have a **stoop**, you stand or walk with your shoulders bent forwards. *He was a tall, thin fellow with a slight stoop.* ② VERB If you **stoop**, **stoop down**, or **stoop over**, you bend your body forwards and downwards. *Stooping down, he picked up a big stone.* ③ VERB If you say that someone **stoops** to doing something, you are criticizing them because they do something wrong or immoral that they would not normally do. *How could anyone stoop so low?*

stop /stɒp/ **stops, stopping, stopped**. ① VERB If you **stop** doing something that you have been doing, you no longer do it. *He can't stop thinking about it... Does either of the parties want to stop the fighting?... I stopped to read the notices on the bulletin board.* ② VERB & PHRASE If you **stop** something, or if you **put a stop to** it, you prevent it from happening or continuing. *He tried to stop the show before it could open... She really would have liked to stop us seeing each other... Motherhood isn't stop me from pursuing my acting career... His daughter should have stood up and put a stop to all these rumours.* ③ VERB If an activity or process **stops**, it comes to an end. *The rain had stopped... The system overheated and filming had to stop.* [4] VERB If something such as a machine **stops**, it is no longer working or working. *The clock had stopped at 2.12 a.m... Arnold stopped the engine and got out of the car.* [5] VERB & N-SING When a moving person or vehicle **stops**, or when they come to a **stop**, they no longer move. *The car failed to stop at an army checkpoint... The event literally stopped the traffic... She slowed the car almost to a stop.* [6] VERB If you **stop** or **stop off** somewhere on a journey, you stay there for a short while before continuing. *The president stopped off in Poland on his way to Munich.* [7] N-C A **stop** is a place where buses or trains regularly stop so that people can get on and off. [8] to **stop dead**: see **dead**. ● to **stop short of**: see **short**.

> When an action comes to an end or stops, you say that someone **stops doing** it. *She stopped reading and closed the book.* However, if you say that someone **stops to do** something, you mean that they interrupt their movement or another activity in order to do that thing. The 'to'-infinitive indicates purpose. *I stopped to read the notices on the bulletin board.*

▸ **stop by.** PHR-VERB If you **stop by** somewhere, you make a short visit to a person or place; IN-FORMAL. *Perhaps I'll stop by the hospital.*

stoppage /'stɒpɪdʒ/ **stoppages.** N-C When there is a **stoppage**, people stop working because of a disagreement with their employers.

storage /'stɔːrɪdʒ/. N-U **Storage** is the process of keeping something in a particular place until it is needed. *Some of the space will at first be used for storage.*

store /stɔː/ **stores, storing, stored.** [1] N-C A **store** is a shop. In British English, **store** is used mainly to refer to a large shop selling a variety of goods, but in American English, a **store** can be any shop. [2] VERB & PHR-VERB To **store** something or to **store** it **away** means to keep it in a place until it is needed. *The information can be stored in a computer... He simply stored the tapes away.* [3] N-C A **store** of something is a supply of it kept in a place until it is needed. *I have a store of food and water here.* [4] N-VAR A **store** is a place where things are kept while they are not being used. *...a grain store.* [5] PHRASE If something is **in store** for you, it is going to happen at some time in the future. *Off we went into the night, not knowing what lay in store.* [6] See also **department store**.

▸ **store away.** See **store** 2.

▸ **store up.** PHR-VERB If you **store** something **up**, you keep it until you think that the time is right to use it. *Investors were storing up a lot of cash in anticipation of disaster.*

storey (AM **story**) /'stɔːri/ **storeys.** N-C The **storeys** of a building are its different floors or levels. *...a modern three-storey building.*

storm /stɔːm/ **storms, storming, stormed.** [1] N-C A **storm** is very bad weather, with heavy rain, strong winds, and often thunder and lightning. [2] N-C If something causes a **storm**, it

causes an angry or excited reaction from a large number of people. *The announcement provoked an immediate storm of protest.* [3] VERB If you **storm** into or out of a place, you enter or leave it quickly and noisily, because you are angry. *After a bit of an argument, he stormed out.* [4] VERB If a place that is being defended **is stormed**, a group of people attack it, usually in order to get inside it. *The refugees decided to storm the embassy.* ◆**storming** N-U *...the storming of the Bastille.* [5] PHRASE If someone or something **takes** a place **by storm**, they are extremely successful there. *Kenya's long distance runners have taken the athletics world by storm.*

stormy /'stɔːmi/ **stormier, stormiest.** [1] ADJ If there is **stormy** weather, there is a strong wind and heavy rain. [2] ADJ A **stormy** situation involves a lot of angry argument or criticism. *Their working relationship was stormy at times.*

story /'stɔːri/ **stories.** [1] N-C A **story** is a description of imaginary people and events, which is written or told in order to entertain. *I shall tell you a story about four little rabbits.* [2] N-C A **story** is a description or account of things that have happened. *...the story of the women's movement in Ireland.* [3] N-C A news **story** is a piece of news in a newspaper or in a news broadcast. [4] See also **storey**.

PHRASES ● You use **a different story** to refer to a situation, usually a bad one, which exists in one set of circumstances when you have mentioned that it does not exist in another set of circumstances. *Where Marcella lives, the rents are fairly cheap, but a little further north it's a different story.* ● If you say it's **the same old story** or **the old story**, you mean that something unpleasant or undesirable seems to happen again and again. *It's the same old story. They want one person to do three people's jobs.* ● If you say that something is **only part of the story** or is **not the whole story**, you mean that the explanation or information given is not enough for a situation to be fully understood. *This may be true but it is only part of the story.* ● If someone tells you **their side of the story**, they tell you why they behaved in a particular way and why they think they were right, when other people think that person behaved wrongly. *He had already made up his mind before even hearing her side of the story.*

stout /staʊt/ **stouter, stoutest.** [1] ADJ A **stout** person is rather fat. [2] ADJ **Stout** shoes, branches, or other objects are thick and strong. [3] ADJ If you use **stout** to describe someone's actions, attitudes, or beliefs, you approve of them because they are strong and determined. ◆**stoutly** ADV *She stoutly defended her husband.*

stove /staʊv/ **stoves.** N-C A **stove** is a piece of equipment for heating a room or cooking. *She put the kettle on the gas stove.*

stow /staʊ/ **stows, stowing, stowed.** VERB & PHR-VERB If you **stow** something somewhere, or if you **stow** it **away**, you put it carefully somewhere until it is needed. *I helped her stow her bags in the boot of the car.*

straddle /ˈstrædəl/ **straddles, straddling, straddled.** 1 VERB If you **straddle** something, you put or have one leg on either side of it. *He sat down, straddling the chair.* 2 VERB If something such as a bridge or town **straddles** a river, road, or border, it stretches across it or exists on both sides of it. *...the Rumaila oilfield, which straddles the border between Kuwait and Iraq.* 3 VERB Someone or something that **straddles** different periods, groups, or fields of activity exists in, belongs to, or takes elements from them all. *He straddles two cultures, having been brought up in Britain and later converted to Islam.*

straight /streɪt/ **straighter, straightest.** 1 ADJ & ADV If something is **straight**, it continues in one direction or line and does not bend or curve. *Keep the boat in a straight line... She looked straight at me... He couldn't walk straight.* 2 ADV If you go **straight** to a place, you go there immediately. *We went straight to the experts for advice... We'll go to a meeting in Birmingham and come straight back.* 3 ADJ BEFORE N A **straight** choice or a **straight** fight involves only two people or things. *It's a straight choice between low-paid jobs and no jobs.* 4 ADJ & ADV If you are **straight** with someone, you speak to them honestly and frankly. *Can't you give me a straight answer?... I wish if they were to tell you straight that they have used an illegal drug?* 5 PHRASE If you **get** something **straight**, you make sure that you understand it properly or that someone else does. *You need to get your facts straight... Let's get things straight. I didn't lunch with her.* 6 **a straight face:** see **face.** • **set the record straight:** see **record.**

straight a´way (or **straightaway**). ADV If you do something **straight away**, you do it immediately. *I knew straight away he was different.*

straighten /ˈstreɪtən/ **straightens, straightening, straightened.** 1 VERB & PHR-VERB If you **straighten** something, or if you **straighten** it **out**, it becomes straight rather than having bends or curls in it, or being in the wrong position. *She sipped her coffee and straightened a picture on the wall... I had my Afro hair straightened... The road twisted its way up the mountain then straightened out.* 2 VERB If you are bending and you then **straighten** or **straighten up**, you make your body straight and upright. *I straightened until rock bumped my head... He straightened up and looked around.*

▶ **straighten out.** 1 PHR-VERB If you **straighten out** a confused situation, you succeed in dealing with it or getting it properly organized. *...an appointment with him to straighten out a couple of things.* 2 See **straighten** 1.

straightforward /ˌstreɪtˈfɔːwəd/. 1 ADJ If something is **straightforward**, it is not complicated to do or understand. *Disposable nappies are fairly straightforward to put on... The question seemed straightforward enough.* ◆**straightforwardly** ADV *Acid rain is not straightforwardly attributable to the burning of coal.* 2 ADJ If you describe a person or their behaviour as **straightforward**, you approve of

them because they are honest and direct, and do not try to hide their feelings. ◆**straightforwardly** ADV *His daughter says straightforwardly that he was not good enough.*

strain /streɪn/ **strains, straining, strained.** 1 N-VAR If **strain** is put on a person or organization, they have to do more than they are really able to do. *The prison service is already under considerable strain... the stresses and strains of a busy and demanding career.* 2 N-U **Strain** is an injury to a muscle in your body, caused by using it too much or twisting it awkwardly. *Avoid muscle strain by warming up.* 3 VERB To **strain** something means to make it do more than it is really able to do. *The volume of scheduled flights is straining the air traffic control system.* 4 VERB If you **strain** a muscle, you injure it by using it suddenly or too much. 5 VERB If you **strain** to do something, you make a great effort to do it. *Several thousand supporters strained to catch a glimpse of the new president.* 6 VERB When you **strain** food, you separate the liquid part of it from the solid parts by sieving it.

strained /streɪnd/. 1 ADJ If someone's appearance, voice, or behaviour is **strained**, they seem worried and nervous. *His laughter seemed a little strained.* 2 ADJ If relations between people are **strained**, their relationship has become difficult because they no longer like or trust each other.

strait /streɪt/ **straits.** 1 N-C You can refer to a narrow strip of sea which joins two large areas of sea as a **strait** or the **straits**. 2 N-PL If someone is in **dire straits** or in **desperate straits**, they are in a very difficult situation. *The company's closure has left many small businessmen in desperate financial straits.*

strand /strænd/ **strands, stranding, stranded.** 1 N-C A **strand** of thread, wire, or hair is a thin piece of it. 2 N-C A **strand** of a plan, theory, or story is one aspect of it. *He's trying to bring together various strands of radical philosophic thought.* 3 VERB If you **are stranded**, you are prevented from leaving a place, for example because of bad weather. *Hundreds of motorists are preparing to spend a second night stranded in their cars.*

strange /streɪndʒ/ **stranger, strangest.** 1 ADJ **Strange** means unusual or unexpected. *I had a strange dream... There was something strange about the flickering blue light.* ◆**strangely** ADV *The hut suddenly seemed strangely silent... Strangely, the race didn't start until 8.15pm.* ◆**strangeness** N-U *There was a strangeness in her manner.* 2 ADJ BEFORE N A **strange** person or place is one that you do not know. *I ended up alone in a strange city.*

stranger /ˈstreɪndʒə/ **strangers.** 1 N-C A **stranger** is someone you have not met before or do not know at all. If two people are **strangers**, they have never met or do not know each other at all. *Telling a complete stranger about your life is difficult.* 2 N-C If you are a **stranger** in a place, you do not know the place at all. If you are a **stranger** to something, you have had no experience of it or do not understand it. *I'm a stranger here... He is no stranger to controversy.*

You do not use **stranger** to talk about someone who comes from a country which is not your own. You can refer to him or her as a **foreigner**, but this word can sound rather rude. It is better to talk about **someone from abroad** or **a person from overseas**.

strangle /ˈstræŋgəl/ **strangles, strangling, strangled.** [1] VERB To **strangle** someone means to kill them by tightly squeezing their throat. [2] VERB To **strangle** something means to prevent it from developing or succeeding. *The country's economic plight is strangling its scientific institutions.*

stranglehold /ˈstræŋgəlhəʊld/ **strangleholds.** N-C To have a **stranglehold** on something means to have control over it and prevent it being free or developing. *It took the country over 40 years to break the stranglehold of Communism.*

strap /stræp/ **straps, strapping, strapped.** [1] N-C A **strap** is a narrow piece of leather, cloth, or other material. Straps are used to carry things or hold them in place. *...the strap of her beach bag... I undid my watch strap.* [2] VERB If you **strap** something somewhere, you fasten it there with a strap.

strata /ˈstrɑːtə, AM ˈstreɪtə/. **Strata** is the plural of **stratum**.

strategic /strəˈtiːdʒɪk/. [1] ADJ **Strategic** means relating to the most important, general aspects of something such as a military operation or political policy. *...a strategic plan for reducing infant mortality.* ♦**strategically** ADV *...strategically important roads.* [2] ADJ **Strategic** weapons are very powerful, long-range weapons, and the decision to use them can be made only by a political leader. [3] ADJ If you put something in a **strategic** position, you place it cleverly in a position where it will be most useful or have the most effect. ♦**strategically** ADV *...a strategically placed chair.*

strategist /ˈstrætədʒɪst/ **strategists.** N-C A **strategist** is someone who is skilled in planning the best way to achieve something, especially in war.

strategy /ˈstrætədʒi/ **strategies.** [1] N-VAR A **strategy** is a general plan or set of plans intended to achieve something, especially over a long period. [2] N-U **Strategy** is the art of planning the best way to achieve something, especially in war. *...the basic rules of military strategy.*

stratum /ˈstrɑːtəm, AM ˈstreɪtəm/ **strata.** N-C A **stratum** of society is a group of people in it who are similar in their social class; FORMAL. *...the lower strata of American society.*

straw /strɔː/ **straws.** [1] N-U **Straw** is the dried yellowish stalks from crops such as wheat or barley. [2] N-C A **straw** is a thin tube of paper or plastic, which you use to suck a drink into your mouth. [3] PHRASE If you say that an event is **the last straw**, you mean that it is the latest in a series of unpleasant events, and makes you feel that you cannot tolerate a situation any longer.

strawberry /ˈstrɔːbri, AM -beri/ **strawberries.** N-C A **strawberry** is a small red fruit with tiny seeds in its skin.

stray /streɪ/ **strays, straying, strayed.** [1] VERB If someone **strays** somewhere, they wander away from where they should be. *Tourists often get lost and stray into dangerous areas.* [2] ADJ BEFORE N & N-C A **stray** dog or cat has wandered away from its owner's home. A **stray** is a stray dog or cat. [3] VERB If your mind or your eyes **stray**, you do not concentrate on or look at one particular subject, but start thinking about or looking at other things. *She could not keep her eyes from straying towards him.* [4] ADJ BEFORE N **Stray** things have become separated from other similar things. *She shrugged a stray lock of hair out of her eyes.*

streak /striːk/ **streaks, streaking, streaked.** [1] N-C A **streak** is a long narrow stripe or mark on something. *A streak of orange smoke shot up into the sky.* [2] VERB If something **streaks** a surface, it makes streaks on it. *His face was pale and streaked with dirt.* [3] N-C If someone has a **streak** of a particular type of behaviour, they sometimes behave in that way. *There is a streak of madness in us both.* [4] VERB To **streak** somewhere means to move there very quickly. *A meteorite streaked across the sky.*

stream /striːm/ **streams, streaming, streamed.** [1] N-C A **stream** is a small narrow river. [2] N-C A **stream** of things is a large number of them occurring one after another. *...a never-ending stream of jokes... We had a constant stream of visitors.* [3] VERB If a mass of people, liquid, or light **streams** somewhere, it enters or moves there in large amounts. *Refugees have been streaming into Travnik for months... Tears streamed down their faces.*

streamline /ˈstriːmlaɪn/ **streamlines, streamlining, streamlined.** VERB To **streamline** an organization or process means to make it more efficient by removing unnecessary parts of it. *Things should be better now that they have streamlined application procedures.* ♦**streamlined** ADJ *...the streamlined organisations of the future.*

streamlined /ˈstriːmlaɪnd/. ADJ A **streamlined** object or animal has a shape that allows it to move quickly or efficiently through air or water.

street /striːt/ **streets.** [1] N-C A **street** is a road in a town or village, usually with houses along it. *He walked briskly down the street. ...activities to keep young people off the streets.* [2] N-C You can use **the street** or **the streets** when talking about activities that happen out of doors in a town rather than in a building. *Changing money on the street is illegal. ...street theatre.* [3] PHRASE If you talk about **the man in the street**, you mean ordinary people in general. *What does all this mean for the man in the street?*

streetcar /ˈstriːtkɑː/ **streetcars.** N-C In American English, a **streetcar** is an electric vehicle for carrying people which travels on rails in the streets of a town. The British word is **tram**.

strength /streŋθ/ **strengths.** [1] N-U Your **strength** is the physical energy that you have, which gives you the ability to do things such as lift heavy objects. *He threw it forward with all his strength... You don't need strength to take part in this sport.* [2] N-U Someone's **strength** in a difficult situation is their courage and determination. *Something gave me the strength to overcome the difficulty... She had often displayed great strength of character.* [3] N-VAR Someone's **strengths** are the qualities and abilities that they have which are an advantage to them, or which make them successful. *Take into account your own strengths and weaknesses... The novel's greatest strength is its portrayal of daily life.* [4] N-U The **strength** of an object or material is its ability to be treated roughly or to support heavy weights. *He checked the strength of the cables.* [5] N-U The **strength** of a person, organization, or country is the power and influence that they have because they are successful. [6] N-U If you refer to the **strength** of a feeling, opinion, or belief, you are talking about how deeply it is felt or believed by people, or how much they are influenced by it. *He was surprised at the strength of his own feeling.* [7] N-U The **strength** of a group of people is the total number of people in it. *...elite forces, comprising about one-tenth of the strength of the army.*

[PHRASES] ● If a person or organization **goes from strength to strength**, they become more and more successful or confident. ● If one thing is done **on the strength of** another, it is done because of the influence of that other thing. *On the strength on those grades, he won a scholarship to Syracuse University.*

strengthen /ˈstreŋθən/ **strengthens, strengthening, strengthened.** VERB To **strengthen** something means to make it stronger. *Cycling strengthens all the muscles of the body.*

strenuous /ˈstrenjʊəs/. ADJ A **strenuous** action or activity involves a lot of effort or energy. *Avoid strenuous exercise in the evening... She made strenuous efforts to pay off her debts.* ◆**strenuously** ADV *The former ambassador has strenuously denied the allegations.*

stress /stres/ **stresses, stressing, stressed.** [1] VERB & N-U If you **stress** a point, or if you lay **stress on** it, you emphasize it because you think it is important. *Sir Colin was keen to stress that the technology division was doing particularly well. ...the military's stress on tradition and continuity.* [2] N-VAR If you feel under **stress**, you feel worried and tense because of difficulties in your life. *She was suffering from stress. ...the stresses of modern living.* [3] N-VAR **Stresses** are strong physical pressures applied to an object. *Earthquakes happen when stresses in rock are suddenly released as the rocks fracture.* [4] VERB & N-VAR If you **stress** a word or part of a word when you say it, you put emphasis called **stress** on it, so that it sounds slightly louder. *The stress falls on the last syllable.*

stressed /strest/. ADJ If you feel **stressed**, you feel tension and anxiety because of difficulties in your life.

stressful /ˈstresfʊl/. ADJ A **stressful** situation or experience causes someone to feel stress.

stretch /stretʃ/ **stretches, stretching, stretched.** [1] VERB Something that **stretches** over an area or distance covers or exists in the whole of that area or distance. *Vast forests stretched the length of the valley... The procession stretched for several miles.* [2] N-C A **stretch** of land or water is a length or area of it. [3] VERB When you stretch, or when you **stretch** your arms or legs, you put your arms or legs out straight and tighten your muscles. *He yawned and stretched.* [4] N-C A **stretch** of time is a period of time. *...an 18-month stretch in the army.* [5] VERB When something soft or elastic **stretches**, or when it **is stretched**, it becomes longer or bigger as well as thinner, usually because it is pulled. *The cables are designed not to stretch.* [6] VERB If something **stretches** your money or resources, it uses them up so you have hardly enough for your needs. ◆**stretched** ADJ *...the company's stretched finances.*

▸ **stretch out.** [1] PHR-VERB If you **stretch out**, or if you **stretch** yourself **out**, you lie with your legs and body in a straight line. *I stretched out in the bottom of the boat and closed my eyes.* [2] PHR-VERB If you **stretch out** a part of your body, you hold it out straight. *He was about to stretch out his hand to grab me.*

stretcher /ˈstretʃə/ **stretchers.** N-C A **stretcher** is a long piece of canvas with a pole along each side, which is used to carry an injured person.

strewn /struːn/. ADJ If a place is **strewn with** things, they are scattered everywhere in it. *...the rock-strewn hillside.*

stricken /ˈstrɪkən/. ADJ If a person or place is **stricken** by something such as an unpleasant feeling, illness, or natural disaster, they are severely affected by it. *...the drought-stricken region of Tigray.*

strict /strɪkt/ **stricter, strictest.** [1] ADJ A **strict** rule or order is very precise or severe and must be obeyed absolutely. *She gave me strict instructions not to say anything.* ◆**strictly** ADV *The acceptance of new members is strictly controlled.* [2] ADJ A **strict** person does not tolerate behaviour which is not polite or obedient, especially from children. *My parents were very strict.* ◆**strictly** ADV *My own mother was brought up very strictly.* [3] ADJ BEFORE N The **strict** meaning of something is its precise meaning. *It's not quite peace in the strictest sense of the word, rather the absence of war.* ◆**strictly** ADV *Actually, that is not strictly true... Strictly speaking, it is not one house at all, but three houses joined together.* [4] ADJ BEFORE N You use **strict** to describe someone who never does things that are against their beliefs. For example, a **strict** vegetarian never eats meat.

strictly /ˈstrɪktli/. ADV You use **strictly** to emphasize that something is of one particular type, or intended for one particular thing or person, rather than any other. *He seemed fond of her in a strictly professional way... Early horse racing in Virginia was strictly for aristocrats.*

stride /straɪd/ **strides, striding, strode.** [1] VERB If you **stride** somewhere, you walk there with quick long steps. *He turned abruptly and strode off down the corridor.* [2] N-C A **stride**

is a long step which you take when you are walking or running. **3** N-C If you make **strides** in something that you are doing, you make rapid progress in it. *The country has made enormous strides politically.* **4** PHRASE In British English, if you **take** a difficult situation in your **stride**, you deal with it calmly and easily. The American expression is **take** something **in stride**. *She has learned to take criticism in her stride.*

strident /ˈstraɪdənt/. **1** ADJ If you use **strident** to describe someone or the way they express themselves, you disapprove of the noticeable or persistent way that they make their feelings or opinions known. *...the unnecessarily strident tone of the President's remarks.* ♦ **stridently** ADV. **2** ADJ A **strident** voice or sound is loud and unpleasant.

strife /straɪf/. N-U **Strife** is strong disagreement or fighting. *Money is a major cause of strife in many marriages.*

strike /straɪk/ strikes, striking, struck. **1** N-C & VERB When workers go on **strike**, or when they **strike**, they stop working for a period of time, usually to try to get better pay or conditions. *Staff at the hospital went on strike in protest at the incidents... They shouldn't be striking for more money.* ♦ **striker, strikers** N-C *The strikers want higher wages.* **2** VERB If you **strike** someone or something, you deliberately hit them; FORMAL. *She took two quick steps forward and struck him across the mouth.* **3** VERB If something that is falling or moving **strikes** something, it hits it; FORMAL. *His head struck the bottom when he dived into the 6ft end of the pool.* **4** VERB To **strike** someone or something means to attack them or to affect them, quickly and violently. *The killer says he will strike again... A powerful earthquake struck the Italian island of Sicily.* **5** N-C A military **strike** is a military attack. **6** VERB If an idea or thought **strikes** you, it suddenly comes into your mind. *It suddenly struck me that I was wasting my time.* **7** VERB If something **strikes** you as being a particular thing, it gives you the impression of being that thing. *He struck me as a very serious but friendly person.* **8** PASSIVE-VERB If you **are struck** by something, you think it is very impressive, noticeable, or interesting. *She was struck by his energy.* **9** VERB You can use **strike** to indicate that you arrive at an agreement, decision, or situation. *You have to strike a balance between sleep and homework... I was struck dumb by this and had to think it over for a moment.* **10** VERB If something **strikes** fear or terror into people, it makes them very frightened or anxious. **11** VERB When a clock **strikes**, its bells make a sound to indicate what the time is. *The clock struck nine.* **12** VERB If you **strike** a match, you make it produce a flame by moving it quickly against something rough. **13** VERB To **strike** oil or gold means to discover it in the ground as a result of mining or drilling.

▶ **strike down.** PHR-VERB If someone **is struck down**, especially by an illness, they are killed or severely harmed; WRITTEN. *Frank had been struck down by a massive heart attack.*

▶ **strike off.** PHR-VERB If a doctor or lawyer **is struck off**, their name is removed from the official register and they are not allowed to practise their profession.

▶ **strike out.** **1** PHR-VERB If you **strike out** in a particular direction, you start travelling in that direction. *They left the car and struck out along the muddy track.* **2** PHR-VERB If you **strike out**, you begin to do something different, often because you want to become more independent. *She wanted me to strike out on my own.*

▶ **strike up.** PHR-VERB When you **strike up** a conversation or friendship, you begin it.

striking /ˈstraɪkɪŋ/. **1** ADJ Something that is **striking** is very noticeable or unusual. *He bears a striking resemblance to Lenin.* ♦ **strikingly** ADV *The men really were strikingly similar.* **2** ADJ A **striking** person is very attractive. *...the striking blond actor.* ♦ **strikingly** ADV *...a strikingly handsome man.*

string /strɪŋ/ strings, stringing, strung. **1** N-VAR **String** is thin rope made of twisted threads, used for tying things together or tying up parcels. **2** N-C A **string** of things is a number of them on a piece of string, thread, or wire. *She wore a string of pearls.* **3** N-C A **string** of places or objects is a number of them that form a line. *...a string of villages.* **4** N-C The **strings** on a musical instrument such as a violin or guitar are thin pieces of tightly-stretched wire or nylon. **5** N-PL The **strings** are the section of an orchestra which consists of instruments played with a bow. **6** VERB If you **string** something somewhere, you hang it up between two or more objects. *He had strung a banner across the wall.* **7** PHRASE If something is offered to you with **no strings attached**, it is offered without any special conditions. *Aid should be given to developing countries with no strings attached.*

▶ **string along.** PHR-VERB If you **string** someone **along**, you deceive them by letting them believe that you have the same desires, beliefs, or hopes as them; INFORMAL. *She took advantage of him, stringing him along for years even after they were divorced.*

▶ **string together.** PHR-VERB If you **string** things **together**, you make them into one thing by adding them to each other, one at a time. *The speaker strung together a series of jokes.*

stringent /ˈstrɪndʒənt/. ADJ **Stringent** laws, rules, or conditions are severe or are strictly controlled; FORMAL. *...stringent controls on the possession of weapons.*

strip /strɪp/ strips, stripping, stripped. **1** N-C A **strip** of something is a long narrow piece of it. *The simplest rag-rugs are made with strips of fabric.* **2** N-C A **strip** of land or water is a long narrow area of it. **3** VERB If you **strip**, or if someone **strips** you, your clothes are removed from your body. *Women residents stripped naked in protest.* **4** VERB If someone **is stripped**, their clothes are taken off by another person, for example in order to search for hidden or illegal things. **5** VERB To **strip** someone of their property, rights, or titles means to take those things away from them. *The soldiers have stripped the civilians of their passports.* **6** VERB To **strip** something means to remove everything that covers it. *I stripped the beds and vacuumed the carpets.* **7** N-C In a newspaper or magazine, a comic **strip** is a series of drawings which tell a story.

▶ **strip away.** PHR-VERB To **strip away** something misleading or unnecessary means to remove it completely, so that people can see what is important or true. *Strip away the disputes about terminology, and most theories about these diseases look very similar.*

▶ **strip off.** PHR-VERB If you **strip off**, or if you **strip** your clothes **off**, you take off your clothes. *He stripped off his wet clothes and stepped into the shower.*

stripe /straɪp/ **stripes.** N-C A **stripe** is a long line which is a different colour from the areas next to it. *The walls in the front bedroom are painted with broad, pale blue and white stripes.*

striped /straɪpt/. ADJ Something that is **striped** has stripes on it. *...striped wallpaper.*

stripper /ˈstrɪpə/ **strippers.** N-C A **stripper** is a person who earns money by taking off their clothes slowly and in a sexy way to music. *...a male stripper.*

strive /straɪv/ **strives, striving, strove** (or **strived**) **striven** (or **strived**). VERB If you **strive** for something or **strive** to do something, you make a great effort to get or do it. *The school strives to treat pupils as individuals.*

strode /strəʊd/. **Strode** is the past tense of **stride**.

stroke /strəʊk/ **strokes, stroking, stroked.** 1 VERB If you **stroke** someone or something, you move your hand slowly and gently over them. *He held her quietly, his hand stroking her hair.* 2 N-C If someone has a **stroke**, a blood vessel in their brain bursts or gets blocked, which may kill them or cause one side of their body to be paralysed. 3 N-C The **strokes** of a pen or brush are the movements or marks you make with it when you are writing or painting. *...short, upward strokes of the pencil.* 4 N-C When you are swimming or rowing, your **strokes** are the repeated movements you make with your arms or the oars. *I turned and swam a few strokes further out to sea.* 5 N-C A swimming **stroke** is a particular style or method of swimming. 6 N-C In sports such as tennis, cricket, and golf, a **stroke** is the action of hitting the ball. 7 N-C The **strokes** of a clock are the sounds that indicate each hour. *On the stroke of 12, fireworks suddenly exploded.* 8 N-SING A **stroke** of luck is something lucky that suddenly happens. *It didn't rain, which turned out to be a stroke of luck.* PHRASES • If something happens **at a stroke** or **in one stroke**, it happens suddenly and completely because of one single action. *How can Britain reduce its prison population in one stroke?*

stroll /strəʊl/ **strolls, strolling, strolled.** VERB & N-C If you **stroll** somewhere, or if you go for a **stroll**, you walk in a slow relaxed way. *After dinner, I took a stroll round the city.*

stroller /ˈstrəʊlə/ **strollers.** N-C In American English, a **stroller** is a small chair on wheels, in which a baby or small child can sit and be wheeled around. The British word is **pushchair.**

strong /strɒŋ, AM strɔːŋ/ **stronger, strongest.** 1 ADJ A **strong** person is healthy with good muscles. *I'm not strong enough to carry him... His strong hand eased the bag from her.* 2 ADJ **Strong** objects or materials are not easily broken. *The vacuum flask has a strong casing, which won't crack or chip.* ♦**strongly** ADV *The fence was very strongly built.* 3 ADJ Someone who is **strong** is confident and determined. *She had a strong and supportive sister.* 4 ADJ If you have **strong** opinions on something or express them using **strong** words, you have extreme or very definite opinions which you are willing to express or defend. *...a strong supporter of President Mandela's reforms.* ♦**strongly** ADV *I would strongly advise against it.* 5 ADJ **Strong** action is firm and severe. *The government has said it will take strong action against any further strikes.* 6 ADJ **Strong** means great in degree or intensity. *He was surprised that his answer should have caused such a strong reaction.* ♦**strongly** ADV *He is strongly influenced by Spanish painters.* 7 ADJ **Strong** is used to describe people or things that have all the qualities that make them likely to be successful. *She was a strong contender for Britain's Olympic team... He would have a strong case for arguing that he was unlikely to receive a fair trial.* 8 ADJ BEFORE N Your **strong** points are the things you are good at. *Discretion is not Jeremy's strong point.* 9 ADJ You use **strong** to say how many people there are in a group. For example, a group that is twenty **strong** has twenty people in it. 10 ADJ **Strong** drinks, chemicals, or drugs contain a lot of a particular substance. *...strong liquor.* 11 ADJ A **strong** colour, flavour, smell, sound, or light is intense and easily noticed. *The wine goes with strong and mild cheese alike.* ♦**strongly** ADV *He leaned over her, smelling strongly of sweat.* 12 PHRASE If someone or something is still **going strong**, they are still alive, in good condition, or popular after a long time.

stronghold /ˈstrɒŋhəʊld, AM ˈstrɔːŋ-/ **strongholds.** N-C If a place is a **stronghold** of an attitude or belief, many people there hold this attitude or belief. *...Europe's last stronghold of male dominance.*

strove /strəʊv/. **Strove** is a past tense of **strive**.

struck /strʌk/. **Struck** is the past tense and past participle of **strike**.

structural /ˈstrʌktʃərəl/. ADJ **Structural** means relating to or affecting the structure of something. *...structural alterations made to the house.* ♦**structurally** ADV *When we bought the house, it was structurally sound.*

structure /ˈstrʌktʃə/ **structures, structuring, structured.** 1 N-VAR The **structure** of something is the way in which it is made, built, or organized. *...the structure of French education.* 2 N-C A **structure** is something that is built from or consists of parts connected together in an ordered way. *The house was a handsome four-story brick structure.* 3 VERB If you **structure** something, you arrange it in an organized pattern or system. *By structuring the course this way, we're forced to produce something the companies think is valuable.* ♦**structured** ADJ *...a much more structured training programme.*

struggle /ˈstrʌgəl/ **struggles, struggling, struggled.** 1 VERB If you **struggle** to do something difficult, you try hard to do it. *Those who have lost their jobs struggle to pay their supermarket bills.* ② N-VAR A **struggle** is an attempt to obtain something or to defeat someone who is denying you something. *Life became a struggle for survival. ...a power struggle.* ③ VERB If you **struggle** when you are being held, you twist and turn your body in order to try to get free. *I struggled, but he was a tall man.* ④ VERB & N-C If two people **struggle** with each other, or if they are in a **struggle**, they fight. *He died in a struggle with prison officers.* ⑤ VERB If you **struggle** to move yourself or to move a heavy object, you manage to do it with great difficulty. *I struggled with my bags.* ⑥ N-SING An action or activity that is a **struggle** is very difficult for you to do. *Losing weight was a terrible struggle.*

strum /strʌm/ **strums, strumming, strummed.** VERB If you **strum** a guitar, you play it by moving your fingers up and down across the strings.

strung /strʌŋ/. **Strung** is the past tense and past participle of **string**.

strut /strʌt/ **struts, strutting, strutted.** ① VERB Someone who **struts** walks in a proud way, with their head high and their chest out; used showing disapproval. *He struts around town like he owns the place.* ② N-C A **strut** is a piece of wood or metal which strengthens or supports a building or structure.

stub /stʌb/ **stubs, stubbing, stubbed.** ① N-C The **stub** of a cigarette or a pencil is the short piece which remains when the rest has been used. *...an ashtray of cigarette stubs.* ② N-C The **stub** of a cheque or ticket is the small part that you keep. ③ VERB If you **stub** your **toe**, you hurt it by accidentally kicking something.

▶ **stub out.** PHR-VERB When someone **stubs out** a cigarette, they put it out by pressing it against something hard.

stubble /'stʌbəl/. ① N-U **Stubble** consists of the short stalks which are left in fields after corn or wheat has been harvested. ② N-U The very short hairs on a man's face when he has not shaved recently are referred to as **stubble**. *He scratched at the stubble on his jaw.*

stubborn /'stʌbən/. ① ADJ A **stubborn** person is determined to do what they want and refuses to change their mind. *...his stubborn resistance to anything new.* ◆ **stubbornly** ADV *He stubbornly refused to tell her how he had come to be in such a state.* ◆ **stubbornness** N-U *His refusal to talk was simple stubbornness.* ② ADJ A **stubborn** stain is difficult to remove. *This treatment removes the most stubborn stains.*

stuck /stʌk/. ① **Stuck** is the past tense and past participle of **stick**. ② ADJ AFTER LINK-V If something is **stuck** in a particular position, it is fixed there and cannot move. *The tanker is stuck fast on the rocks.* ③ ADJ AFTER LINK-V If you are **stuck** in a place or in an unpleasant situation, you want to get away from it, but are unable to. *He was stuck in a line of slow-moving traffic.* ④ ADJ AFTER LINK-V If you get **stuck** when you are trying to do something, you are unable to continue doing it because it is too difficult. *They will be there to help if you get stuck.*

stud /stʌd/ **studs.** ① N-C **Studs** are small pieces of metal which are attached to a surface for decoration. *...a canary yellow jacket with gold studs.* ② N-C **Studs** are small round earrings attached to a bar which goes through your ear. ③ N-U Horses or other animals that are kept for **stud** are kept to be used for breeding.

studded /'stʌdɪd/. ADJ Something that is **studded** is decorated with studs. *...a beautiful gold bracelet studded with diamonds.*

student /'stjuːdənt, 'stuː-/ **students.** N-C A **student** is a person who is studying at a university, college, or school. *...art students.*

studio /'stjuːdiəʊ, 'stuː-/ **studios.** ① N-C A **studio** is a room where a designer, painter, or photographer works. *...Giorgio Armani at work in his studio.* ② N-C A **studio** is a room where radio or television programmes, records, or films are made. *...a recording studio.*

study /'stʌdi/ **studies, studying, studied.** ① VERB & N-VAR If you study, or if you do a course of **study**, you spend time learning about a particular subject or subjects. *Kids would rather play than study... He studied History and Economics... It enabled students to devote more time to their studies.* ② N-C A **study** of a subject is a piece of research on it. *...the first study of English children's attitudes.* ③ N-PL **Studies** are educational subjects. *...a business studies course.* ④ VERB If you **study** something, you look at it or consider it carefully. *He studied her face for a moment.* ⑤ N-C A **study** in a house is a room used for reading, writing, and studying. ● See also **case study**.

stuff /stʌf/ **stuffs, stuffing, stuffed.** ① N-U You can use **stuff** to refer to things in a general way, without mentioning the things themselves by name. *Don't tell me you still believe in all that stuff? ...a place to buy computer stuff... He pointed to a duffle bag. 'That's my stuff.'* ② VERB If you **stuff** something somewhere, you push it there quickly and roughly. *I stuffed my hands in my pockets.* ③ VERB If you **stuff** a container or space with something, you fill it with something or with a quantity of things until it is full. *...wallets stuffed with dollars.* ④ VERB If you **stuff** a bird such as a chicken, or a vegetable such as a pepper, you put a mixture of food inside it before cooking it. ⑤ VERB If a dead animal is **stuffed**, it is filled with a substance so that it can be preserved and displayed.

stuffing /'stʌfɪŋ/ **stuffings.** ① N-VAR **Stuffing** is a mixture of food that is put inside a bird such as a chicken before it is cooked. ② N-U **Stuffing** is material that is put inside cushions or soft toys to fill them and make them firm.

stuffy /'stʌfi/. ① ADJ If you describe a person or institution as **stuffy**, you are criticizing them for being formal and old-fashioned; INFORMAL. *Why were grown-ups always so stuffy and slow to recognize good ideas?* ② ADJ If a place is **stuffy**, it is unpleasantly warm and there is not enough fresh air. *...that stuffy, overheated apartment.*

stumble /'stʌmbəl/ **stumbles, stumbling, stumbled.** ① VERB If you **stumble**, you nearly fall while walking or running. *I stumbled sideways before landing flat on my back.* ② VERB If you **stumble** while speaking, you make a mistake, and have to pause before saying the words properly. *She stumbled slightly over her words sometimes.*

▶ **stumble across** or **stumble on.** PHR-VERB If you **stumble across** something, or if you **stumble on** something, you discover it unexpectedly. *You may be fortunate enough to stumble across a village fiesta.*

'**stumbling block, stumbling blocks.** N-C A **stumbling block** is a problem which stops you from achieving something. *This issue has turned out to be the main stumbling block to convening the peace conference.*

stump /stʌmp/ **stumps, stumping, stumped.** ⃞1 N-C A **stump** is a small part of something that remains when the rest of it has been removed or broken off. *...a tree stump.* ⃞2 VERB If a question or problem **stumps** you, you cannot think of any solution or answer to it.

▶ **stump up.** PHR-VERB If you **stump up** a sum of money, you pay the money that is required for something, often reluctantly; BRITISH, INFORMAL. *Customers do not have to stump up any cash for at least four weeks.*

stun /stʌn/ **stuns, stunning, stunned.** ⃞1 VERB If you **are stunned** by something, you are shocked or astonished by it and are therefore unable to speak or do anything. *Many cinema-goers were stunned by the film's violent and tragic end.* ◆**stunned** ADJ *When they told me she had gone missing I was totally stunned.* ⃞2 VERB If a blow on the head **stuns** you, it makes you unconscious or confused and unsteady. ● See also **stunning.**

stung /stʌŋ/. **Stung** is the past tense and past participle of **sting.**

stunk /stʌŋk/. **Stunk** is the past participle of **stink.**

stunning /ˈstʌnɪŋ/. ADJ A **stunning** person or thing is extremely beautiful or impressive. *...how the top supermodels manage to look stunning. ...a stunning display of fireworks.* ◆**stunningly** ADV *...stunningly beautiful countryside.*

stunt /stʌnt/ **stunts, stunting, stunted.** ⃞1 N-C A **stunt** is something interesting that someone does to get attention or publicity. *...turning her wedding into a publicity stunt.* ⃞2 N-C A **stunt** is a dangerous and exciting piece of action in a film. *The team will perform daily stunts including ramp-to-ramp jumps.* ⃞3 VERB If something **stunts** the growth or development of a person or thing, it prevents them from growing or developing normally. *...a bone disease that stunted her growth.* ◆**stunted** ADJ *The blackthorns were so stunted they looked like plants rather than bushes.*

stupid /ˈstjuːpɪd, AM ˈstuː-/ **stupider, stupidest.** ⃞1 ADJ If you say that someone or something is **stupid**, you mean that they show a lack of good judgement or intelligence and they are not at all sensible. *How could I have been so stupid?... I made a stupid mistake.* ◆**stupidly** ADV *We had stupidly been looking at the wrong column of figures.* ◆**stupidity** /stjuːˈpɪdɪti, AM stuː-/ **stupidities** N-VAR *I stared at him, astonished by his stupidity.* ⃞2 ADJ You

say that something is **stupid** to indicate that you do not like it or that it annoys you; INFORMAL. *Friendship is much more important to me than a stupid old ring!*

sturdy /ˈstɜːdi/ **sturdier, sturdiest.** ADJ Someone or something that is **sturdy** looks strong and is unlikely to be easily injured or damaged. *She was a short, sturdy woman.* ◆**sturdily** ADV *...a tall, sturdily-built man.*

stutter /ˈstʌtə/ **stutters, stuttering, stuttered.** VERB & N-C If someone **stutters**, or if they have a **stutter**, they have difficulty speaking because they keep repeating the first sound of a word. *He spoke with a pronounced stutter.* ◆**stuttering** N-U *Gerard had suffered in school with his stuttering and stammering.*

style /staɪl/ **styles, styling, styled.** ⃞1 N-C The **style** of something is the general way it is done or presented. *Kenny's writing style is clear and straightforward. ...American-style management.* ⃞2 N-U If places or people have **style**, they are smart and elegant. *Bournemouth, you have to admit, has style.* ⃞3 N-VAR The **style** of a product is its design. *Several styles of hat were available... Each design is very different in style... Guests have been asked to dress 1920s-style.* ⃞4 VERB If something such as a car or someone's hair **is styled** in a particular way, it is designed or shaped in that way. *His thick blond hair had just been styled before his trip. ...classically styled clothes.*

stylish /ˈstaɪlɪʃ/. ADJ Someone or something that is **stylish** is smart, elegant, and fashionable. *...the stylish shops of Buchanan Street.* ◆**stylishly** ADV *...stylishly dressed middle-aged women.*

stylistic /staɪˈlɪstɪk/. ADJ **Stylistic** describes things relating to the methods and techniques used in creating a piece of writing, music, or art. ◆**stylistically** ADV *Stylistically, this book is a very different one from Remains of The Day.*

stylized (or **stylised**) /ˈstaɪlaɪzd/. ADJ Something that is **stylized** uses various artistic conventions in order to create an effect. *...highly stylised furniture designs.*

suave /swɑːv/ **suaver, suavest.** ADJ If you describe a men as **suave**, you think he is charming, polite, and elegant, but not sincere.

subcommittee (or **sub-committee**) /ˈsʌbkəmɪti/ **subcommittees.** N-C A **subcommittee** is a small committee made up of members of a larger committee.

subconscious /ˌsʌbˈkɒnʃəs/. ⃞1 N-SING Your **subconscious** is the part of your mind that can influence you even though you are not aware of it. *The memory of it all was locked deep in my subconscious.* ⃞2 ADJ A **subconscious** feeling or action exists in or is influenced by your subconscious. *...a subconscious cry for affection.* ◆**subconsciously** ADV *Subconsciously I had known that I would not be in personal danger.*

subculture /ˈsʌbkʌltʃə/ **subcultures.** N-C A **subculture** consists of the ideas, art, and way of life of a particular group within a society, which are different from those of the rest of the society. *...the violent subculture of London youth gangs.*

subdivision /ˌsʌbdɪ'vɪʒən/ **subdivisions.** N-C
A **subdivision** is an area or section which is a
part of a larger area or section. *Months are a
conventional subdivision of the year.*

subdue /səb'djuː, AM -'duː/ **subdues, subdu-
ing, subdued.** VERB If soldiers or the police
subdue a group of people, they defeat them or
bring them under control by using force. *They
have not been able to subdue the rebels.*

subdued /səb'djuːd, AM -'duːd/ [1] ADJ Someone who is **subdued** is quiet, often because
they are sad. *The audience are strangely subdued, clapping politely after each song.* [2] ADJ
Subdued lights, feelings, sounds, or colours
are not very noticeable. *...a night-club atmosphere with subdued lighting.*

subject, subjects, subjecting, subjected.
[1] N-C /'sʌbdʒɪkt/ The **subject** of a conversation,
letter, or book is the person or thing that is being discussed or written about. *We got on to
the subject of relationships... Their epic fight is
the subject of a new film... He's now the subject
of an official inquiry.* [2] N-C A **subject** is an area
of knowledge that is studied at school, college,
or university. *Mathematics was voted their favourite subject.* [3] N-C In grammar, the **subject**
of a clause is the noun group which refers to
the person or thing that does the action expressed by the verb. For example, in 'My cat
keeps catching birds', 'my cat' is the subject.
[4] ADJ AFTER LINK-V If someone or something is
subject to something, they are affected, or
likely to be affected, by it. *Prices may be subject
to alteration.* [5] PREP If an event will take place
subject to a condition, it will take place only if
that condition exists. *Tickets for both offers,
subject to availability, can be collected from the
information desk.* [6] N-C The people who live in
or belong to a particular country, usually one
ruled by a monarch, are the **subjects** of that
monarch or country. *...British subjects.* [7] VERB
/səb'dʒekt/ If you **subject** someone **to** something unpleasant, you make them experience
it. *...the man who had subjected her to four
years of beatings.*

subjective /səb'dʒektɪv/. ADJ Something that is
subjective is based on personal opinions and
feelings. *Taste in art is a subjective matter.*
♦**subjectively** ADV *She subjectively rated herself
a winner.* ♦**subjectivity** N-U *...the film-maker's
subjectivity.*

'subject matter. N-U The **subject matter** of a
conversation, book, or film is the thing, person, or idea that is being discussed, written
about, or shown. *Artists were given greater freedom in their choice of subject matter.*

subjunctive /səb'dʒʌŋktɪv/. N-SING In English,
a clause expressing a wish or suggestion can
be put in the **subjunctive**, or in the **subjunctive** mood, by using the base form of a verb or
'were'. An example is 'He asked that they all be
removed'.

sublime /sə'blaɪm/. ADJ & N-SING If you describe
something as **sublime**, or as **the sublime**, you
mean that it has a wonderful quality that affects you deeply; LITERARY. *She elevated every
rare small success to the sublime.*

submarine /ˌsʌbmə'riːn/ **submarines.** N-C A

submarine is a ship that can travel below the
surface of the sea.

submerge /səb'mɜːdʒ/ **submerges, submerging, submerged.** [1] VERB If something
submerges, it goes below the surface of the
water. *The river burst its banks, submerging an
entire village.* [2] VERB If you **submerge** yourself
in an activity, you give all your attention to it.
Vicky tried to submerge herself in her work.

submission /səb'mɪʃən/. [1] N-U **Submission** is
a state in which people accept that they are
under the control of someone else. *Singapore
island was being bombed, shelled, and starved
into submission.* [2] N-U The **submission** of a
proposal or application is the act of sending it
to someone, so they can decide whether to accept it or not; FORMAL.

submissive /səb'mɪsɪv/. ADJ If you are **submissive**, you behave in a quiet obedient way.
♦**submissively** ADV *The troops submissively lay
down their weapons.*

submit /səb'mɪt/ **submits, submitting, submitted.** [1] VERB If you **submit** to something,
you accept it reluctantly, for example because
you are not powerful enough to resist it. *Mrs.
Jones submitted to an operation on her right
knee.* [2] VERB If you **submit** a proposal or application to someone, you send it to them so
they can decide whether to accept it or not.
*Head teachers yesterday submitted a claim for a
9 per cent pay rise.*

**subordinate, subordinates, subordinat-
ing, subordinated.** [1] N-C /sə'bɔːdɪnət/ Your
subordinate is someone who is in less important position than you in the organization that
you both work for. [2] ADJ Something or someone who is **subordinate** to something or
someone else is considered to be less important than the other thing or person. *Science became subordinate to technology... Women were
regarded as subordinate to free men.* [3] VERB
/sə'bɔːdɪneɪt/ If you **subordinate** one thing to
another, you treat it as less important than the
other thing. *...subordinating Spain to wider
American defence needs.* ♦**subordination**
N-U *...governmental subordination to the president.*

**sub,ordinate 'clause, subordinate
clauses.** N-C A **subordinate clause** is a clause
in a sentence which adds to the information
given in the main clause. It cannot usually
stand alone as a sentence.

subscribe /səb'skraɪb/ **subscribes, sub-
scribing, subscribed.** [1] VERB If you **subscribe to** an opinion or belief, you are one of a
number of people who have this opinion or
belief. *Most scientists subscribe to the idea that
salt increases water retention.* [2] VERB If you
subscribe to a service, magazine, or organization, you pay money regularly to receive the
service or magazine, or to belong to or support
the organization. *...computer-users who subscribe to the Internet.* ♦**subscriber, subscrib-
ers** N-C *I have been a subscriber to Railway
Magazine for many years.*

subscription /səb'skrɪpʃən/ **subscriptions.**
N-C A **subscription** is an amount of money that
you pay regularly to receive a service or maga-

zine, or to belong to or support an organization.

subsequent /'sʌbsɪkwənt/. ADJ BEFORE N **Subsequent** means existing or happening after the time or event that has just been referred to. *The book was banned in the US, as were two subsequent books.* ◆**subsequently** ADV *He was born in Hong Kong where he subsequently practised as a lawyer.*

subservient /səb'sɜːviənt/. [1] ADJ If you are **subservient**, you do whatever someone wants you to do. *Verbal abuse was used to keep the women subservient.* ◆**subservience** N-U *...obedience and subservience to authority.* [2] ADJ AFTER LINK-V If you treat one thing as **subservient** to another, you treat it as less important than the other thing. *...the philosophy that the weak should be subservient to the strong.*

subside /səb'saɪd/ **subsides, subsiding, subsided.** [1] VERB If a feeling or sound **subsides**, it becomes less strong or loud. *Catherine's sobs finally subsided.* [2] VERB If the ground or a building **is subsiding**, it is sinking to a lower level.

subsidiary /səb'sɪdiəri, AM -dieri/ **subsidiaries.** [1] N-C A **subsidiary** is a company which is part of a larger and more important company. *...British Asia Airways, a subsidiary of British Airways.* [2] ADJ If something is **subsidiary**, it is less important than something else with which it is connected. *All the undergraduates take two subjects for their honours degree, and two subsidiary subjects.*

subsidize (BR also **subsidise**) /'sʌbsɪdaɪz/ **subsidizes, subsidizing, subsidized.** VERB If an authority **subsidizes** something, they pay part of the cost of it. *Governments have subsidized the housing of middle and low-income groups.* ◆**subsidized** ADJ *...Scotland's subsidised theatre.*

subsidy /'sʌbsɪdi/ **subsidies.** N-VAR A **subsidy** is money paid by an authority in order to help an industry or business, or to pay for a public service. *...farming subsidies.*

subsistence /səb'sɪstəns/. N-U **Subsistence** is the condition of only having just enough food or money to stay alive.

substance /'sʌbstəns/ **substances.** [1] N-C A **substance** is a solid, powder, liquid, or gas. *...a crumbly black substance that smells like fresh soil.* [2] N-U **Substance** is the quality of being important or significant; FORMAL. *Why do we chatter so wittily but say nothing of any substance?* [3] N-SING **The substance of** what someone says or writes is the main thing that they are trying to say. [4] N-U If you say that something has no **substance**, you mean that it is not true; FORMAL. *There is no substance in any of these allegations.*

substantial /səb'stænʃəl/. [1] ADJ **Substantial** means large in amount or degree. *That is a very substantial improvement.* ◆**substantially** ADV *Firms still expect to cut jobs substantially in the months ahead.* [2] ADJ A **substantial** building is large and strongly built. *...a substantial late Victorian house.*

substantially /səb'stænʃəli/. [1] ADV If something is **substantially** correct, it is generally correct; FORMAL. *He checked the details given*

and found them substantially correct. [2] See also **substantial**.

substantiate /səb'stænʃieɪt/ **substantiates, substantiating, substantiated.** VERB To **substantiate** a statement or a story means to supply evidence proving that it is true; FORMAL. *There is little scientific evidence to substantiate the claims.*

substantive /səb'stæntɪv/. ADJ **Substantive** issues, questions, or talks are meaningful and important; FORMAL. *They are prepared to discuss substantive issues tomorrow.*

substitute /'sʌbstɪtjuːt, AM -tuːt/ **substitutes, substituting, substituted.** [1] VERB If you **substitute** one thing for another, you use it instead of the other thing. *Would phone conversations substitute for cosy chats over lunch?* ◆**substitution, substitutions** N-VAR *...a straight substitution of carob for chocolate.* [2] N-C A **substitute** is something or someone that you use instead of something or someone else. *Reduced-calorie cheese is a great substitute for cream cheese.*

subterranean /ˌsʌbtə'reɪniən/. ADJ A **subterranean** river or tunnel is underground; FORMAL.

subtle /'sʌtəl/ **subtler, subtlest.** [1] ADJ Something **subtle** is not immediately obvious or noticeable. *...the slow and subtle changes that take place in all living things.* ◆**subtly** ADV *The truth is subtly different.* [2] ADJ **Subtle** smells, tastes, sounds, or colours are pleasantly complex and delicate. ◆**subtly** ADV *...subtly coloured rugs.*

subtlety /'sʌtəlti/ **subtleties.** [1] N-C **Subtleties** are very small details or differences which are not obvious. *...the subtleties of human behaviour.* [2] N-U **Subtlety** is the quality of not being immediately obvious or noticeable. *African dance is vigorous, but full of subtlety.* [3] N-U **Subtlety** is the ability to use indirect methods to achieve something. *They had obviously been hoping to approach the topic with more subtlety.*

subtract /səb'trækt/ **subtracts, subtracting, subtracted.** VERB If you **subtract** one number from another, you take the first number away from the second. ◆**subtraction, subtractions** N-VAR *She's ready to learn simple addition and subtraction.*

suburb /'sʌbɜːb/ **suburbs.** N-C The **suburbs** of a city are the areas on the edge of it where people live.

suburban /sə'bɜːbən/. [1] ADJ BEFORE N **Suburban** means relating to a suburb. *...a suburban shopping centre in Sydney.* [2] ADJ If you describe something as **suburban**, you mean that it is dull and conventional. *His clothes were conservative and suburban.*

suburbia /sə'bɜːbiə/. N-U **Suburbia** is sometimes used to refer to the suburbs of cities and large towns considered as a whole. *...bright summer mornings in leafy suburbia.*

subversion /səb'vɜːʃən, AM -ʒən/. N-U **Subversion** is the attempt to weaken or destroy a political system or a government. *He was arrested in parliament on charges of subversion.*

subversive /səb'vɜːsɪv/ **subversives.** [1] ADJ Something that is **subversive** is intended to weaken or destroy a political system or government. *The play was promptly banned as subversive.* **2** N-C **Subversives** are people who attempt to weaken or to destroy a political system or government.

subvert /səb'vɜ:t/ **subverts, subverting, subverted.** **1** VERB To **subvert** something means to destroy its power and influence; FORMAL. *...an alleged plot to subvert the state.*

subway /'sʌbweɪ/ **subways.** **1** N-C In British English, a **subway** is a passage for pedestrians underneath a busy road. **2** N-C In American English, a **subway** is an underground railway. The British word is **underground.**

succeed /sək'si:d/ **succeeds, succeeding, succeeded.** **1** VERB To **succeed** means to achieve the result that you wanted or to perform in a satisfactory way. *We have succeeded in persuading cinemas to show the video. ...the skills and qualities needed to succeed.* **2** VERB If you **succeed** another person, you take over their job or position when they leave. *Prince Rainier III succeeded to the throne on 9 May 1949.*

success /sək'ses/ **successes.** N-U **Success** is the achievement of something you have wanted to achieve. *Work was the key to success... Most of the cast was amazed by the play's success.*

successful /sək'sesfʊl/ ADJ Someone or something that is **successful** achieves a desired result or performs in a satisfactory way. *How successful will this new treatment be?... She is a successful lawyer.* ♦ **successfully** ADV *The doctors have successfully concluded preliminary tests.*

succession /sək'seʃən/ **successions.** **1** N-C A **succession** of things of the same kind is a number of them that exist or happen one after the other. *Adams took a succession of jobs. ...scoring three goals in quick succession.* **2** N-U **Succession** is the act or right of being the next person to have a particular job or position. *She is now seventh in line of succession to the throne.*

successive /sək'sesɪv/ ADJ **Successive** means happening or existing one after another without a break. *Jackson was the winner for a second successive year.*

successor /sək'sesə/ **successors.** N-C Someone's **successor** is the person who takes their job after they have left.

suc'cess story, success stories. N-C Someone or something that is a **success story** is very successful, often unexpectedly or in spite of unfavourable conditions.

succinct /sək'sɪŋkt/. ADJ Something that is **succinct** expresses facts or ideas clearly and in few words; used showing approval. ♦ **succinctly** ADV *Readers are told succinctly what they need to know.*

succulent /'sʌkjʊlənt/. ADJ **Succulent** food is juicy and delicious. *...succulent vegetables and well-fried chips.*

succumb /sə'kʌm/ **succumbs, succumbing, succumbed.** VERB If you **succumb to** persuasion or desire, you are unable to resist it. *Don't succumb to the temptation to have just one cigarette.*

such /sʌtʃ/. **1** PREDET & DET & PRON You use **such** to refer to the person or thing you have just mentioned or to something similar. *How can we make sense of such a story as this?... There have been previous attempts at coups. We regard such methods as entirely unacceptable... We are scared because we are being watched – such is the atmosphere in Pristina.*

> You do not use **such** when you are talking about something that is present, or about the place where you are. You need to use the phrases **like that** or **like this**. For example, if you are admiring someone's watch, you do not say 'I'd like such a watch'. You say **'I'd like a watch like that'.** Similarly, you do not say about the town where you are living 'There's not much to do in such a town'. You say **'There's not much to do in a town like this'.**

2 PREDET & DET You use **such** to emphasize the degree or extent of something. *It was such a pleasant surprise... One will never be able to understand why these political issues can acquire such force.*

PHRASES ● You use **such as** or **such...as** to introduce one or more examples of something. *...serious offences, such as assault. ...such careers as teaching, nursing, hairdressing and catering.* ● You use **such...that** when saying that the result or consequence of something is. *He was in such a hurry that he almost pushed me over on the stairs... He could put an idea in such a way that Alan would believe it was his own.* ● You use **such as it is** to indicate that something is not very good, important, or useful. *...the British Women's Movement, such as it is these days.* ● You use **as such** with a negative to indicate that a word or expression is not a very accurate description of the actual situation. *I am not a learner as such – I used to ride a bike years ago.* ● You use **as such** after a noun to indicate that you are considering that thing on its own, separately from other things or factors. *Mr Simon said he was not against taxes as such.* ● You use **such and such** to refer to something without being specific. *I said, 'Well what time'll I get to Leeds?' and he said such and such a time.*

suck /sʌk/ **sucks, sucking, sucked.** **1** VERB If you **suck** something, you hold it in your mouth and pull at it with the muscles in your cheeks and tongue, for example in order to get liquid out of it. *You may prefer to give her a dummy to suck instead... He sucked on his cigarette.* **2** VERB If something **sucks** a liquid, gas, or object in a particular direction, it draws it there with a powerful force. *...a simple air pump that continuously sucks in the air.*

sucker /'sʌkə/ **suckers.** **1** N-C If you call someone a **sucker**, you mean that it is easy to cheat or fool them; INFORMAL. **2** N-C If you describe someone as a **sucker for** something, you mean that they find it very difficult to resist it; INFORMAL. *I'm such a sucker for romance.* **3** N-C On a plant, a **sucker** is a new growth that is sent out from the base of the plant or from its root.

sudden /'sʌdən/. [1] ADJ Something that is **sudden** happens quickly and unexpectedly. ...*the sudden death of her father.* ♦**suddenly** ADV ...*David's account of why he had suddenly left London.* ♦**suddenness** N-U *The enemy seemed stunned by the suddenness of the attack.* [2] PHRASE If something happens **all of a sudden**, it happens quickly and unexpectedly. *All of a sudden she fell silent.*

sue /suː/ **sues, suing, sued.** VERB If you **sue** someone, you start a legal action against them to claim money from them because they have harmed you in some way. *She threatened to sue him for unfair dismissal... If I were her, I'd sue.*

suede /sweɪd/. N-U **Suede** is thin soft leather with a slightly rough surface.

suffer /'sʌfə/ **suffers, suffering, suffered.** [1] VERB If you **suffer** pain or an illness, or if you **suffer from** a pain or illness, you are badly affected by it. *She began to suffer stomach cramps... Many team members suffered from diarrhoea.* ♦**sufferer, sufferers** N-C ...*arthritis sufferers.* [2] VERB If you **suffer** something bad, you are in a situation in which something painful, harmful, or very unpleasant happens to you. ...*the possibility that they could suffer complete defeat.* [3] VERB If you **suffer**, you are badly affected by an unfavourable event or situation. *It is the poor who have suffered most from food shortages.* [4] VERB If something **suffers**, it becomes worse in quality or condition as a result of neglect or an unfavourable situation. *I'm not surprised that your studies are suffering.*

suffering /'sʌfərɪŋ/ **sufferings.** N-VAR **Suffering** is serious pain which someone feels in their body or their mind. *He wanted to die in order to put an end to his suffering.*

suffice /sə'faɪs/ **suffices, sufficing, sufficed.** VERB If something will **suffice**, it will be enough to achieve a purpose or to fulfil a need; FORMAL. *You don't even have to do it in person; a polite letter will suffice.*

sufficient /sə'fɪʃənt/. [1] ADJ If something is **sufficient** for a particular purpose, there is as much of it as is necessary. *His savings were not sufficient to cover the cost.* ♦**sufficiently** ADV *It was many months before I had sufficiently recovered to move about.* [2] ADJ BEFORE N If something is a **sufficient** cause or condition for something to happen, it can happen; FORMAL. *Discipline is a necessary, but certainly not a sufficient condition for learning to take place.*

suffix /'sʌfɪks/ **suffixes.** N-C A **suffix** is a letter or group of letters added to the end of a word in order to form a different word, often of a different word class.

suffocate /'sʌfəkeɪt/ **suffocates, suffocating, suffocated.** VERB If someone **suffocates**, or is **suffocated**, they die because there is no air for them to breathe. ♦**suffocation** N-U *Many of the victims died of suffocation.*

sugar /'ʃʊgə/ **sugars.** [1] N-U **Sugar** is a sweet substance, often in the form of white or brown crystals, used to sweeten food and drink. [2] N-C If someone takes **sugar** in their tea or coffee,

they have one or more small spoon of sugar in it. *How many sugars do you take?*

suggest /sə'dʒest, AM səg'dʒ-/ **suggests, suggesting, suggested.** [1] VERB If you **suggest** something, you put forward a plan or idea for someone to consider. *I suggested we walk to the park... I suggested that we should charter a boat... I suggested to Mike that we go out for a meal.*

> Note that **suggest** cannot usually be followed directly by a noun or pronoun referring to a person. You do not 'suggest someone something', you '**suggest something to someone**'. *John Caskey first suggested this idea to me.* Nor do you 'suggest someone to do something'. You '**suggest that someone does something**'. A subjunctive is sometimes used in the 'that'-clause. *Beatrice suggested that he spend the summer at their place.*

[2] VERB If you **suggest** that something is the case, you say something which you believe is the case. *I'm not suggesting that is what is happening.* [3] VERB If one thing **suggests** another, it implies it or makes you think that it is the case. *Earlier reports suggested that a meeting would take place on Sunday.*

suggestion /sə'dʒestʃən, AM səg'dʒ-/ **suggestions.** [1] N-C If you make a **suggestion**, you put forward an idea or plan for someone to think about. *John made some suggestions for improvements.* [2] N-C A **suggestion** is something that someone says which implies that something is the case. *There are suggestions that jealousy drove her to murder.* [3] N-SING If there is a **suggestion** of something, there is a slight sign of it. ...*that fashionably faint suggestion of a tan.* [4] N-U **Suggestion** means giving people a particular idea by associating it with other ideas. ...*the power of suggestion.*

suggestive /sə'dʒestɪv, AM səg'dʒ-/. [1] ADJ AFTER LINK-V If one thing is **suggestive of** another, it gives a hint of it or reminds you of it. ...*long, curving nails suggestive of animal claws.* [2] ADJ **Suggestive** remarks cause people to think about sex, often in a way that makes them feel uncomfortable. ♦**suggestively** ADV *She winked at him suggestively.*

suicidal /ˌsuːɪ'saɪdəl/. [1] ADJ People who are **suicidal** want to kill themselves. [2] ADJ If you describe an action or behaviour as **suicidal**, you mean that it is very dangerous. *It would have been suicidal to attempt the descent in the dark.*

suicide /'suːɪsaɪd/ **suicides.** [1] N-VAR People who commit **suicide** deliberately kill themselves. ...*a growing number of suicides in the community.* [2] ADJ BEFORE N The people involved in a **suicide** attack, mission, or bombing do not expect to survive. ...*a suicide bomber.*

suit /suːt/ **suits, suiting, suited.** [1] N-C A **suit** is a matching jacket and trousers, or a matching jacket and skirt. [2] N-C A **suit** can be a piece of clothing worn for a particular activity. ...*bathing suits.* [3] VERB If a piece of clothing or a particular style or colour **suits** you, it makes you look attractive. [4] VERB If you say that something **suits** you, you mean that it is convenient, acceptable, or appropriate for you. *Would nine o'clock suit you?* [5] N-C In a court of law, a **suit** is a legal action taken by one person against another. [6] N-C A **suit** is one of the four types of card in a set of playing cards. These are hearts, diamonds, clubs, and spades. [7] PHRASE If people **follow suit**, they do what someone else has just done. *Efforts to persuade the remainder to follow suit have continued.*

> You do not use the verb **suit** if clothes are simply not the right size for you. The verb you need is **fit**. *Even the smallest size doesn't fit him... The gloves didn't fit.* You can say that something **suits** a person or place if it looks attractive on that person or in that place. However, you cannot usually say that one colour, pattern, or object **suits** another. The verb you need is **match**. *She wears a straw hat with a yellow ribbon to match her yellow cheesecloth dress... His clothes don't quite match.*

suitable /ˈsuːtəbəl/ ADJ Someone or something that is **suitable** for a particular purpose or occasion is right or acceptable for it. *She had no other dress suitable for the occasion. ...a suitable venue.* ◆**suitability** N-U *...information on the suitability of a product for use in the home.* ◆**suitably** ADV *...suitably qualified staff.*

suitcase /ˈsuːtkeɪs/ **suitcases.** N-C A **suitcase** is a case for carrying your clothes when you are travelling.

suite /swiːt/ **suites.** [1] N-C A **suite** is a set of rooms in a hotel or other building. *...a new suite of offices.* [2] N-C A **suite** is a set of matching furniture. [3] N-C A bathroom **suite** is a matching bath, basin, and toilet.

suited /ˈsuːtɪd/ ADJ AFTER LINK-V If something or someone is **suited** to a particular purpose or person, they are right or appropriate for that purpose or person. *Satellites are uniquely suited to provide this information... As a couple they seemed ideally suited.*

suitor /ˈsuːtə/ **suitors.** N-C A woman's **suitor** is a man who wants to marry her; DATED.

sulfur (AM **sulfur**) /ˈsʌlfə/. See **sulphur**.

sulk /sʌlk/ **sulks, sulking, sulked.** VERB & N-C If you **sulk**, or if you go into a **sulk**, you are silent and bad-tempered for a while because you are annoyed. *If I ever beat him at anything, he'd go off and have a sulk.*

sullen /ˈsʌlən/. ADJ A **sullen** person is bad-tempered and does not speak much. ◆**sullenly** ADV *'I've never seen it before,' Harry said sullenly.*

sulphur (AM **sulfur**) /ˈsʌlfə/. N-U **Sulphur** is a yellow chemical which has a strong unpleasant smell.

sultan /ˈsʌltən/ **sultans.** N-C A **sultan** is a ruler in some Muslim countries.

sultry /ˈsʌltri/. [1] ADJ **Sultry** weather is hot and humid. [2] ADJ A **sultry** woman is attractive in a way that suggests hidden passion; WRITTEN.

sum /sʌm/ **sums, summing, summed.** [1] N-C A **sum** of money is an amount of it. *...the relatively modest sum of £50,000.* ● See also **lump sum.** [2] N-C A **sum** is a simple calculation in arithmetic. *I can't do my sums.* [3] N-SING In mathematics, the **sum** of two numbers is the number that is obtained when they are added together. *The sum of all the angles of a triangle is 180 degrees.* [4] PHRASE You use **in sum** to introduce a statement that briefly describes a situation; FORMAL. *In sum, all is proceeding as expected.*

▶ **sum up.** [1] PHR-VERB If you **sum up** or **sum** something **up**, you briefly describe the main features of something. *Well, to sum up, what is the message that you are trying to get across?... The atmosphere is best summed up as being peaceful.* [2] See also **summing up.**

summarize (BR also **summarise**) /ˈsʌməraɪz/ **summarizes, summarizing, summarized.** VERB If you **summarize** something, you give a brief description of its main points. *The article can be summarized in three sentences... To summarise, this is a clever approach to a common problem.*

summary /ˈsʌməri/ **summaries.** [1] N-C A **summary** is a short account of something giving the main points but not the details. *...a summary of the report.* [2] ADJ BEFORE N **Summary** actions are done without delay and without careful consideration; FORMAL. *...reports of summary executions.* ◆**summarily** ADV *Several detainees had been summarily executed.*

summer /ˈsʌmə/ **summers.** N-VAR **Summer** is the season between spring and autumn. In summer the weather is usually warm or hot. *...the summer of 1987.*

summertime (or **summer time**) /ˈsʌmətaɪm/. N-U **Summertime** is the period of time during which summer lasts. *It's a very beautiful place in the summertime.*

summing 'up, summings up. N-C In a court of law, the **summing up** is a summary of all the evidence that has been presented in the trial.

summit /ˈsʌmɪt/ **summits.** [1] N-C A **summit** is a meeting between the leaders of two or more countries to discuss important matters. *...last month's Arab summit in Baghdad.* [2] N-C The **summit** of a mountain is the top of it.

summon /ˈsʌmən/ **summons, summoning, summoned.** [1] VERB If you **summon** someone, you order them to come to you. *The Chief summoned me downstairs.* [2] VERB & PHR-VERB If you **summon** the courage, energy, or strength to do something, or if you **summon** it **up**, you make a great effort to do it. *It took her a full month to summon the courage to tell her mother.*

summons /ˈsʌmənz/ **summonses, summonsing, summonsed.** [1] N-C A **summons** is an order to come and see someone. *I received a summons to the Palace.* [2] N-C & VERB If someone receives a **summons**, or if they are **summonsed**, they are officially ordered to appear in court. *She was summonsed to appear before the magistrates.*

sumptuous /ˈsʌmptʃʊəs/. ADJ Something that is **sumptuous** is magnificent and obviously expensive. ...a variety of sumptuous fabrics.

sun /sʌn/ **suns**. 1 N-SING **The sun** is the ball of fire in the sky that the Earth goes round, and that gives us heat and light. The sun was low in the sky. 2 N-U You refer to the light and heat that reach us from the sun as **the sun**. How pleasant it would be to sit in the sun. ...environmental hazards such as wind and sun.

sunbathe /ˈsʌnbeɪθ/ **sunbathes, sunbathing, sunbathed**. VERB When people **sunbathe**, they sit or lie in a place where the sun shines on them, in order to get a suntan; FORMAL. ♦**sunbathing** N-U ...a huge deck-space for sunbathing.

sunburn /ˈsʌnbɜːn/. N-U If someone has **sunburn**, their skin is red and sore because they have spent too much time in the sun.

Sunday /ˈsʌndeɪ, -di/ **Sundays**. N-VAR **Sunday** is the day after Saturday and before Monday.

sundry /ˈsʌndri/. 1 ADJ If you refer to **sundry** people or things, you mean several people or things of various sorts; FORMAL. ...scientists, business people, and sundry others. 2 PHRASE **All and sundry** means everyone. I made tea for all and sundry at the office.

sunflower /ˈsʌnflaʊə/ **sunflowers**. N-C A **sunflower** is a tall plant with large yellow flowers.

sung /sʌŋ/. **Sung** is the past participle of **sing**.

sunglasses /ˈsʌnɡlɑːsɪz, -ɡlæs-/. N-PL **Sunglasses** are spectacles with dark lenses to protect your eyes from bright sunlight. A pair of designer sunglasses.

sunk /sʌŋk/. **Sunk** is the past participle of **sink**.

sunken /ˈsʌŋkən/. 1 ADJ BEFORE N **Sunken** ships have sunk to the bottom of a sea, ocean, or lake. ...the sunken sailing-boat. 2 ADJ BEFORE N **Sunken** gardens, roads, or other features are below the level of their surrounding area. The room was dominated by a sunken bath. 3 ADJ **Sunken** eyes or cheeks curve inwards and make you look thin and unwell. Her eyes were sunken and black-ringed.

sunlight /ˈsʌnlaɪt/. N-U **Sunlight** is the light that comes from the sun. The calm sea glistened in the sunlight. ...a ray of sunlight.

sunny /ˈsʌni/ **sunnier, sunniest**. 1 ADJ When it is **sunny**, the sun is shining brightly. ...a warm, sunny day. 2 ADJ **Sunny** places are brightly lit by the sun. ...a sunny windowsill.

sunrise /ˈsʌnraɪz/ **sunrises**. 1 N-U **Sunrise** is the time in the morning when the sun first appears. The rain began before sunrise. 2 N-C A **sunrise** is the colours and light that you see in the sky when the sun first appears. There was a spectacular sunrise yesterday.

sunscreen /ˈsʌnskriːn/ **sunscreens**. N-VAR A **sunscreen** is a cream that protects your skin from the sun's rays in hot weather.

sunset /ˈsʌnset/ **sunsets**. 1 N-U **Sunset** is the time in the evening when the sun disappears from the sky. The fast is broken at sunset. 2 N-C A **sunset** is the colours and light that you see in the sky when the sun disappears in the evening. There was a red sunset over Paris.

sunshine /ˈsʌnʃaɪn/. N-U **Sunshine** is the light

and heat that comes from the sun. The bay glittered in the sunshine.

suntan /ˈsʌntæn/ **suntans**. 1 N-C If you have a **suntan**, the sun has turned your skin an attractive brown colour. 2 ADJ BEFORE N **Suntan** lotion, oil, or cream protects your skin from the sun.

super /ˈsuːpə/. ADJ **Super** means very nice or good; BRITISH, INFORMAL. We had a super time.

superb /suːˈpɜːb/. ADJ If something is **superb**, it is very good indeed. ...a superb staircase made from oak. ♦**superbly** ADV The orchestra played superbly.

superficial /ˌsuːpəˈfɪʃəl/. 1 ADJ If you describe someone as **superficial**, you disapprove of them because they do not think deeply, and have little understanding of anything serious or important. ...someone boring, superficial and overly macho. ♦**superficiality** /ˌsuːpəfɪʃiˈælɪti/ N-U ...the superficiality of the music industry. 2 ADJ If you describe something such as an action, feeling, or relationship as **superficial**, you mean that it includes only the simplest and most obvious aspects of that thing. ...a superficial knowledge of music. ♦**superficiality** N-U ...the superficiality of the judgements we make when we first meet people. ♦**superficially** ADV The film touches on these difficult questions, but only superficially. 3 ADJ **Superficial** injuries are not very serious, and affect only the surface of the body. You can also describe damage to an object as **superficial**. ...four superficial wounds to his chest... The explosion caused superficial damage.

superfluous /suːˈpɜːfluəs/. ADJ Something that is **superfluous** is unnecessary or is no longer needed. Further comment was superfluous.

superimpose /ˌsuːpərɪmˈpəʊz/ **superimposes, superimposing, superimposed**. VERB If one image **is superimposed** on another, it is put on top of it so that you can see the second image through it. The features of different faces were superimposed over one another.

superintendent /ˌsuːpərɪnˈtendənt/ **superintendents**. N-C & N-TITLE In British English, a **superintendent** is a senior police officer of the rank above an inspector. In the United States, a **superintendent** is the head of a police department. ...Superintendent Appleby.

superior /suːˈpɪəriə/ **superiors**. 1 ADJ You use **superior** to describe someone or something that is better than other similar people or things. ...a woman greatly superior to her husband in education and sensitivity. ...superior quality coffee. ♦**superiority** /suːˌpɪəriˈɒrɪti, AM -ˈɔːrɪti/ N-U ...the technical superiority of laser discs over tape. 2 ADJ A **superior** person or thing has more authority or importance than another person or thing in the same organization or system. ...negotiations between the mutineers and their superior officers. 3 N-C Your **superior** in an organization that you work for is a person who has a higher rank than you. 4 ADJ If you describe someone as **superior**, you disapprove of them because they behave as if they are better or more important than other people. Finch gave a superior smile.

superlative /suːˈpɜːlətɪv/ **superlatives.** N-C & ADJ In grammar, the **superlative** or the **superlative** form of an adjective or adverb is the form that indicates that something has more of a quality than anything else. For example, 'biggest' is the superlative form of 'big'. Compare **comparative**.

supermarket /ˈsuːpəmɑːkɪt/ **supermarkets.** N-C A **supermarket** is a large shop which sells all kinds of food and some household goods.

supermodel /ˈsuːpəmɒdəl/ **supermodels.** N-C A **supermodel** is a fashion model who is famous all over the world.

supernatural /ˌsuːpəˈnætʃrəl/. ADJ & N-SING **Supernatural** creatures, forces, and events are believed by some people to exist or happen, although they are impossible according to scientific laws. You can refer to these things generally as **the supernatural**. ...*evil spirits who looked like humans and possessed supernatural powers.*

superpower /ˈsuːpəpaʊə/ **superpowers.** N-C A **superpower** is a very powerful and influential country, usually one that has nuclear weapons and is economically successful.

supersede /ˌsuːpəˈsiːd/ **supersedes, superseding, superseded.** VERB If something is **superseded** by something newer, it is replaced because it has become old-fashioned or unacceptable. *Hand tools are relics of the past that have now been superseded by the machine.*

supersonic /ˌsuːpəˈsɒnɪk/. ADJ BEFORE N **Supersonic** aircraft travel faster than the speed of sound.

superstar /ˈsuːpəstɑː/ **superstars.** N-C A **superstar** is a very famous entertainer or sports player; INFORMAL. ...*a Hollywood superstar.*

superstition /ˌsuːpəˈstɪʃən/ **superstitions.** N-VAR **Superstition** is belief in things that are not real or possible, for example magic. *Westerners, too, have their superstitions about numbers.*

superstitious /ˌsuːpəˈstɪʃəs/. ADJ People who are **superstitious** believe in things that are not real or possible, for example magic. *Jean was extremely superstitious and believed the colour green brought bad luck.*

supervise /ˈsuːpəvaɪz/ **supervises, supervising, supervised.** VERB If you **supervise** an activity or a person, you make sure that the activity is done correctly or that the person is behaving correctly. *I supervise the packing of all mail orders.* ♦**supervision** /ˌsuːpəˈvɪʒən/ N-U A toddler requires close supervision. ♦**supervisor, supervisors** N-C ...*a supervisor at a factory.*

supervisory /ˌsuːpəˈvaɪzəri/. ADJ BEFORE N **Supervisory** means concerned with the supervision of people or activities. ...*supervisory staff.*

supper /ˈsʌpə/ **suppers.** [1] N-VAR Some people refer to the main meal eaten in the early part of the evening as **supper**. *He invited me to supper.* [2] N-VAR **Supper** is a simple meal eaten just before you go to bed at night; BRITISH. [3] See note at **meal**.

supplant /səˈplɑːnt, -ˈplænt/ **supplants, supplanting, supplanted.** VERB If one thing **supplants** another, it takes its place; FORMAL. *By the 1930s the wristwatch had almost completely supplanted the pocket watch.*

supple /ˈsʌpəl/. [1] ADJ A **supple** object or material bends or changes shape easily without cracking or breaking. ...*supple leather driving gloves.* [2] ADJ A **supple** person can move and bend their body very easily.

supplement /ˈsʌplɪmənt/ **supplements, supplementing, supplemented.** [1] VERB If you **supplement** something, you add something to it in order to improve it. *I suggest supplementing your diet with vitamins E and A.* [2] N-C A **supplement** is something which is added to another thing in order to improve it. ...*a supplement to their basic pension.*

supplementary /ˌsʌplɪˈmentri, AM -teri/. ADJ **Supplementary** things are added to something in order to improve it. ...*whether or not we need to take supplementary vitamins.*

supplier /səˈplaɪə/ **suppliers.** N-C A **supplier** is a person or company that provides you with goods or equipment. ...*one of the UK's biggest food suppliers.*

supply /səˈplaɪ/ **supplies, supplying, supplied.** [1] VERB If you **supply** someone with something, you provide them with it. ...*an agreement not to produce or supply chemical weapons.* [2] N-PL You can use **supplies** to refer to food, equipment, and other essential things that people need, especially when these are provided in large quantities. ...*food and gasoline supplies.* [3] N-VAR A **supply** of something is an amount of it which is available for use. If something is **in short supply**, there is very little of it available. *The brain requires a constant supply of oxygen.* [4] N-U **Supply** is the quantity of goods and services that can be made available for people to buy. *Prices change according to supply and demand.*

support /səˈpɔːt/ **supports, supporting, supported.** [1] VERB & N-U If you **support** someone or their aims, or if you give them your **support**, you agree with them, and perhaps try to help them because you want them to succeed. *He thanked everyone who had supported the strike.* ... *Only 60 clubs pledged their support for the scheme.* ♦**supporter, supporters** N-C ...*supporters of the former President.* [2] N-U If you give **support** to someone during a difficult time, you are kind to them and help them. ...*mentally ill people in need of support.* [3] VERB & N-U If you **support** someone, or if you give them financial **support**, you provide them with money or the things that they need. *He has a wife and two young children to support.* [4] VERB & N-U If a fact **supports** a statement or a theory, or if it provides **support** for it, it helps to show that it is true or correct. *History offers some support for this view.* [5] VERB If you **support** a sports team, you want them to win and perhaps go regularly to their games. ♦**supporter** N-C *I'm a Liverpool supporter.* [6] VERB If something **supports** an object, it is underneath the object and holding it up. ...*the thick wooden posts that supported the ceiling.* [7] N-C A **support** is a bar or other object that supports something. [8] VERB & N-U If something **supports** you, or if it provides you with **support**, it prevents you from falling because you are holding onto it or leaning on it. *Alice was leaning against him as if for support.*

If you dislike something very much or get very annoyed by it, you do not say 'I can't support it'. You do not say 'I **can't bear it**' or 'I **can't stand it**'. *She can't bear the new Labour government... I cannot stand going shopping.*

---

supportive /səˈpɔːtɪv/ ADJ If you are **supportive**, you are kind and helpful to someone at a difficult time in their life.

suppose /səˈpəʊz/ **supposes, supposing, supposed.** [1] VERB You use **suppose** or **supposing** when you are considering a possible situation or action and trying to think what effects it would have. *Suppose someone gave you an egg and asked you to describe exactly what was inside... Supposing it wasn't the wind that had thrown the door open?* [2] VERB If you **suppose** that something is true, you believe that it is probably true. *I supposed you would have a meal somewhere with Rachel.* • See note at **think**. [3] PHRASE You can say **I suppose** before stating something that you believe to be true, or something that you think you should do, when you want to express slight uncertainty or reluctance about it; SPOKEN. *'What would you tell them?'—'The truth, I suppose.'... I suppose I'd better do some homework... 'Is that the right way up?'—'Yeah. I suppose so.'.*

supposed. [1] ADJ /səˈpəʊzd, səˈpəʊst/ If you say that something is **supposed** to happen, you mean that it is planned or expected. Sometimes this use suggests that the thing does not really happen in this way. *Public spending is supposed to fall, not rise, in the next few years... The first debate was supposed to have been held on Tuesday.* [2] ADJ If you say that something is **supposed** to be true, you mean that people say it is true but you do not know for certain that it is true. *'The Whipping Block' has never been published, but it's supposed to be a really good poem.* [3] ADJ BEFORE N /səˈpəʊzɪd/ You use **supposed** when you want to suggest that the following word or description is misleading, or when it is not definitely known to be true. *She had long suspected him and her supposed friend Michelle of being lovers.* ♦**supposedly** ADV *Thirty eight women have died while taking these supposedly safer pills.*

suppress /səˈpres/ **suppresses, suppressing, suppressed.** [1] VERB If someone in authority **suppresses** an activity, they prevent it from continuing, by using force or making it illegal. *The movement was suppressed by army troops.* ♦**suppression** /səˈpreʃən/ N-U *...the suppression of human rights.* [2] VERB If a natural function or reaction of your body **is suppressed**, it is stopped, for example by drugs or illness. [3] VERB If you **suppress** your feelings or reactions, you do not express them, even though you might want to. *I had a lot of suppressed anger.* ♦**suppression** N-U *A mother's*

suppression of her own feelings can cause problems.* [4] VERB If someone **suppresses** a piece of information, they prevent other people from learning it. ♦**suppression** N-U *...the deliberate suppression of information.*

supremacy /suːˈpreməsi/ N-U If one group of people has **supremacy** over another group, they are more powerful. *The president has been able to assert his ultimate supremacy over the prime minister.*

supreme /suːˈpriːm/ [1] ADJ BEFORE N **Supreme** is used in a title to indicate that a person or group is at the highest level of an organization or system. *...NATO's Supreme Commander in Europe. ...the Supreme Court.* [2] ADJ You use **supreme** to emphasize the greatness of a quality or thing. *Her approval was of supreme importance.* ♦**supremely** ADV *Mr Kohl is now in a supremely confident position.*

sure /ʃʊə/ **surer, surest.** [1] ADJ AFTER LINK-V If you are **sure** that something is true, you are certain that it is true. If you are not **sure** about something, you do not know for certain what the true situation is. *He was not even sure that he should have been teaching... It is impossible to be sure about the value of land.* [2] ADJ AFTER LINK-V If someone is **sure of** getting something, they will certainly get it. *Neither can be sure of success.* [3] ADJ AFTER LINK-V If you say that something is **sure** to happen, you are emphasizing your belief that it will happen. *Kids are sure to love crawling through the tunnel.* [4] ADJ **Sure** is used to emphasize that something such as a sign or ability is reliable or accurate. *Sharpe's leg and shoulder began to ache, a sure sign of rain... She has a sure grasp of social issues.* [5] CONVENTION **Sure** is a way of saying 'yes' or 'all right'; INFORMAL. *'He rang you?'—'Sure. Last night.'.*

PHRASES • You say **sure enough**, especially when telling a story, to confirm that something you thought was true or would happen was really true or actually happened. *I called the hotel and asked them to check the room. Sure enough, they had found the ticket in the blankets.* • If you say that something is **for sure**, or that you know it **for sure**, you mean that it is definitely true. *One thing is for sure: they will not be calling him James.* • If you **make sure** that something is done, you take action so that it is done. *Make sure that you follow the instructions carefully.* • If you **make sure** that something is the way that you want or expect it to be, you check that it is that way. *He looked in the bathroom to make sure that he was alone.* • If you are **sure of yourself**, you are very confident about your own abilities or opinions.

surely /ˈʃʊəli/ [1] ADV You use **surely** to emphasize that you think something should be true, and you would be surprised if it was not true. *You surely haven't forgotten Dr Walters?* [2] PHRASE If you say that something is happening **slowly but surely**, you mean that it is happening gradually but it is definitely happening.

surf /sɜːf/ **surfs, surfing, surfed.** [1] N-U **Surf** is the mass of white foam formed by waves as they fall on the shore. [2] VERB If you **surf**, you ride on big waves on a special board. ♦**surfer**,

surfers N-C ...*fanatical surfers who travel the world looking for the perfect wave.* ♦ **surfing** N-U *The best time for surfing in Waikiki is in January.* [3] VERB If you **surf** the net, you move from place to place on the Internet. ♦ **surfer** N-C ...*programs and games for net surfers to download.*

surface /'sɜːfɪs/ **surfaces, surfacing, surfaced.** [1] N-C The **surface** of something is the top part of it or the outside of it. ...*tiny little waves on the surface of the water... Its total surface area was seven thousand square feet.* [2] VERB If someone or something under water **surfaces**, they come up to the surface of the water. *He surfaced, gasping for air.* [3] N-SING **The surface** of a situation is what can be seen easily rather than what is not immediately obvious. *Back in Britain, things appear, on the surface, simpler... It's brought to the surface a much wider controversy.*

surge /sɜːdʒ/ **surges, surging, surged.** [1] N-C & VERB If there is a **surge** in the level or rate of something, or if the level or rate of something **surges**, there is a sudden large increase in it. *The shares surged from 43p to 163p earlier this year.* [2] N-C If you feel a **surge** of a particular emotion or feeling, you experience it suddenly and powerfully. *McKee felt a sudden surge of hope.* [3] N-C & VERB If there is a **surge** of a physical force such as water or electricity, or if it **surges**, there is a sudden powerful movement of it. *Thousands of volts surged through his car.* [4] VERB If people **surge** forward, they move forward suddenly and powerfully, usually in a crowd. *The crowd surged into the station.*

surgeon /'sɜːdʒən/ **surgeons.** N-C A **surgeon** is a doctor who performs surgery.

surgery /'sɜːdʒəri/ **surgeries.** [1] N-U **Surgery** is medical treatment which involves cutting open a person's body in order to repair or remove a diseased or damaged part. *Robson had had emergency surgery to remove a cancerous growth.* [2] N-C A **surgery** is the room or house where a doctor or dentist works; BRITISH. [3] N-VAR A doctor's or dentist's **surgery** is the period of time each day when he or she sees patients at his or her surgery; BRITISH. *Bring him along to the morning surgery.* [4] See also **plastic surgery.**

surgical /'sɜːdʒɪkəl/. ADJ BEFORE N **Surgical** means relating to surgery. ...*surgical instruments.* ...*a surgical operation.* ♦ **surgically** ADV *Some cysts do need to be surgically removed.*

surmise /sə'maɪz/ **surmises, surmising, surmised.** VERB If you **surmise** that something is true, you guess from the information available that it is true, but you do not know for certain; FORMAL. *There's so little to go on, we can only surmise what happened.*

surname /'sɜːneɪm/ **surnames.** N-C Your **surname** is the name that you share with other members of your family.

surpass /sə'pɑːs, -'pæs/ **surpasses, surpassing, surpassed.** VERB If one person or thing **surpasses** another, the first is better than, or has more of a particular quality than, the second; FORMAL. *He was determined to surpass the achievements of his older brothers.*

surplus /'sɜːpləs/ **surpluses.** [1] N-VAR & ADJ If there is a **surplus** of something, there is more than is needed. **Surplus** things are not needed because there are already enough of them. *Germany suffers from a surplus of teachers... Few people have large sums of surplus cash.* [2] N-C A **surplus** refers to a situation in which a person or organization receives more than it spends. For example, if a country has a trade **surplus**, it exports more than it imports.

surprise /sə'praɪz/ **surprises, surprising, surprised.** [1] N-C & ADJ BEFORE N A **surprise** or a **surprise** event or fact is an unexpected event or fact. *His success came as a surprise to many people... I have a surprise for you: We are moving to Switzerland!... Baxter arrived here this afternoon, on a surprise visit.* [2] N-U **Surprise** is the feeling that you have when something unexpected happens. *They looked at her in surprise... To my surprise, I found I liked it.* [3] VERB If something **surprises** you, it gives you a feeling of surprise. *It surprised me that a driver of Alain's experience should make those mistakes.*

surprised /sə'praɪzd/. ADJ If you are **surprised** at something, you have a feeling of surprise, because it is unexpected or unusual. *Chang seemed surprised to find the big living-room empty.*

surprising /sə'praɪzɪŋ/. ADJ Something that is **surprising** is unexpected or unusual and makes you feel surprised. *It is not surprising that children learn to read at different rates.* ♦ **surprisingly** ADV *Her voice was surprisingly good.*

surreal /sə'riːəl/. ADJ If you describe something as **surreal**, you mean that it is very strange and like a dream. *There is a surreal quality to this part of the rainforest.*

surrender /sə'rendə/ **surrenders, surrendering, surrendered.** [1] VERB & N-VAR If you **surrender**, you stop fighting or resisting someone or something and agree that you have been beaten. **Surrender** is the act of surrendering. *He surrendered to American troops. ...after the Japanese surrender in 1945.* [2] VERB & N-U If you **surrender** something you would rather keep, you give it up or let someone else have it, often after a struggle. **Surrender** is the act of surrendering something. *Nadja had to fill out forms surrendering all rights to her property. ...the deadline for the surrender of weapons.*

surrogate /'sʌrəgeɪt, AM 'sɜːr-/ **surrogates.** ADJ BEFORE N & N-C You use **surrogate** to describe a person or thing that acts as a substitute for someone or something else. *He had been a wonderful friend to all of us; a surrogate father... Arms control should not be made into a surrogate for peace.*

surround /sə'raʊnd/ **surrounds, surrounding, surrounded.** [1] VERB If something or someone **is surrounded** by something, that thing is situated all around them. ...*the fluid that surrounds the brain. ...in the surrounding hills.* [2] VERB If you **are surrounded** by people such as soldiers or police, they spread out so that they are in positions all the way around you. *He tried to run away but gave up when he found himself surrounded.* [3] VERB The circumstances, feelings, or ideas which **surround**

something are those that are closely associated with it. *Controversy surrounds the cause of his death.* [4] VERB If you **surround** yourself **with** certain people or things, you make sure that you have a lot of them near you all the time. *They love being surrounded by familiar possessions.*

surroundings /səˈraʊndɪŋz/. N-PL The place where someone or something is can be referred to as their **surroundings**. *...a peaceful holiday home in beautiful surroundings.*

surveillance /səˈveɪləns/. N-U **Surveillance** is the careful watching of someone, especially by the police or army. *The police kept Golding under surveillance.*

survey, surveys, surveying, surveyed; verb /səˈveɪ/, noun /ˈsɜːveɪ/. [1] VERB & N-C To **survey** people or organizations, or to make a **survey** of them, means to try to find out information about their opinions or behaviour by asking them questions. *A survey showed people were confused about what they should eat.* [2] VERB If you **survey** something, you look at or consider the whole of it carefully. *He pushed himself to his feet and surveyed the room.* [3] VERB & N-C To **survey** a building or area of land, or to do a **survey** of it, means to examine it and measure it, usually in order to make a map of it. *...the geological survey of India.* ♦**surveyor, surveyors** N-C *...the surveyor's maps.* [4] VERB & N-C If someone **surveys** a house, or if they do a **survey** of it, they examine it carefully and report on its structure. *...a structural survey undertaken by a qualified surveyor.* ♦**surveyor** N-C *Our surveyor warned us that the house needed totally rebuilding.*

survival /səˈvaɪvəl/ **survivals.** N-U **Survival** is the fact of continuing to live or exist in spite of great danger or difficulty. *An animal's sense of smell is still crucial to its survival. ...companies which have been struggling for survival.*

survive /səˈvaɪv/ **survives, surviving, survived.** [1] VERB If someone **survives** in a dangerous situation, they do not die. *Drugs that dissolve blood clots can help people survive heart attacks.* ♦**survivor, survivors** N-C *There were no survivors of the plane crash.* [2] VERB If you **survive** in difficult circumstances, you manage to continue in spite of them. *Jim Hogg survives on £65 pounds a fortnight... When the market economy is introduced, many factories will not survive.* ♦**survivor** N-C *...female survivors of domestic violence.* [3] VERB If you **survive** someone, you continue to live after they have died. *Most women will survive their spouses.*

susceptible /səˈseptɪbəl/. [1] ADJ AFTER LINK-V If you are **susceptible** to something or someone, you are likely to be influenced by them. *Young people are the most susceptible to advertisements.* [2] ADJ AFTER LINK-V If you are **susceptible to** a disease or injury, you are likely to be affected by it. [3] ADJ BEFORE N A **susceptible** person is very easily influenced emotionally.

suspect, suspects, suspecting, suspected. [1] VERB /səˈspekt/ If you **suspect** that something is true, you mean that you believe it is probably true, but you want to make it sound less strong or direct. *I suspect*

they were right... Do women really share such stupid jokes? We suspect not. [2] VERB If you **suspect** that something dishonest or unpleasant has been done, you believe that it has probably been done. *He suspected that the woman staying in the flat above was using heroin.* [3] N-C /ˈsʌspekt/ A **suspect** is a person who the police think may be guilty of a crime. [4] ADJ If something is **suspect**, it cannot be trusted or regarded as genuine. *The whole affair has been highly suspect.*

suspend /səˈspend/ **suspends, suspending, suspended.** [1] VERB If you **suspend** something, you delay or stop it for a while. *The union suspended strike action this week.* [2] VERB If someone **is suspended** from their job, they are prevented from doing it for a fixed period of time, usually as a punishment. *Julie was suspended from her job shortly after the incident.* [3] VERB If something **is suspended** from a high place, it is hung from that place. *...a map of Europe suspended from the ceiling.*

suspenders /səˈspendəz/. N-PL In American English, **suspenders** are a pair of straps that go over someone's shoulders and are fastened to their trousers at the front and at the back to prevent the trousers from falling down. The British word is **braces**.

suspense /səˈspens/. N-U **Suspense** is a state of excitement or anxiety about something that is going to happen very soon. *There was genuine suspense before Green was named the winner.*

suspension /səˈspenʃən/ **suspensions.** [1] N-U The **suspension** of something is the act of delaying or stopping it for a while. *...the suspension of flights between London and Manchester.* [2] N-VAR Someone's **suspension** is their removal from a job for a period of time, usually as a punishment. *...a two-year suspension following a positive drug test.* [3] N-U A vehicle's **suspension** consists of the springs and other devices, which give a smooth ride over bumps in the road.

suspicion /səˈspɪʃən/ **suspicions.** [1] N-VAR **Suspicion** is a belief or feeling that someone has committed a crime or done something wrong. *He was arrested on suspicion of drunk driving.* [2] N-VAR If there is **suspicion** of someone or something, people do not trust them or consider them to be reliable. *I was always regarded in the Army with a certain amount of suspicion.* [3] N-C A **suspicion** is a feeling that something is probably true or is likely to happen. *I had a sneaking suspicion she was enjoying herself.*

suspicious /səˈspɪʃəs/. [1] ADJ If you are **suspicious** of someone or something, you do not trust them. *He was suspicious of all journalists.* ♦**suspiciously** ADV *'What's the matter with you?' Jake asked suspiciously.* [2] ADJ If you describe someone or something as **suspicious**, you mean that there is some aspect of them which makes you think that they are involved in a crime or a dishonest activity. *Police last night found a suspicious package.* ♦**suspiciously** ADV *...suspiciously large sums of money.*

sustain /səˈsteɪn/ **sustains, sustaining, sustained.** [1] VERB If you **sustain** something, you continue it or maintain it for a period of time. *...how to get enough food to sustain life.* [2] VERB If you **sustain** something such as a defeat, loss, or injury, it happens to you; FORMAL. *He had sustained a cut on his left eyebrow.* [3] VERB If something **sustains** you, it supports you by giving you help, strength, or encouragement; FORMAL. *He'll have lots of great memories to sustain him when he's away.*

sustainable /sə'steɪnəbəl/. ADJ A **sustainable** plan, method, or system can be continued at the same pace or level of activity without harming its efficiency and the people affected by it. *...an efficient and sustainable transport system.*

swab /swɒb/ **swabs.** N-C A **swab** is a small piece of cotton wool used for cleaning a wound.

swagger /'swægə/ **swaggers, swaggering, swaggered.** VERB & N-SING If you **swagger**, or if you walk with a **swagger**, you walk in a proud way, holding your body upright and swinging your hips. *He swaggered confidently up to the bar.*

swallow /'swɒləʊ/ **swallows, swallowing, swallowed.** [1] VERB & N-C When you **swallow** something, or when you take a **swallow**, you cause something to go from your mouth down into your stomach. *You are asked to swallow a capsule containing vitamin B... Jan lifted her glass and took a quick swallow.* [2] VERB If someone **swallows** a story or a statement, they believe it completely. *I too found this story a little hard to swallow.* [3] VERB If you **swallow** your feelings, you do not express them, although you want to very much. *Gordon has swallowed the anger he felt.* [4] N-C A **swallow** is a small bird with pointed wings and a forked tail.

swam /swæm/. **Swam** is the past tense of **swim**.

swamp /swɒmp/ **swamps, swamping, swamped.** [1] N-VAR A **swamp** is an area of wet land with wild plants growing in it. [2] VERB If something **swamps** a place or object, it fills it with water. *The Ventura river burst its banks, swamping a mobile home park.* [3] VERB If you **are swamped** by things or people, you have more of them than you can deal with. *The railway station was swamped with thousands of families.*

swan /swɒn/ **swans.** N-C A **swan** is a large white bird with a long neck that lives on rivers and lakes.

swap (or **swop**) /swɒp/ **swaps, swapping, swapped.** [1] VERB & N-C If you **swap** something with someone, or if you do a **swap**, you give it to them and receive something else in exchange. *Next week they will swap places. ...if she ever fancies a job swap.* [2] VERB If you **swap** one thing for another, you remove the first thing and replace it with the second. *He'd swapped his overalls for a suit and tie.* [3] VERB When you **swap** stories or opinions with someone, you tell each other stories or give each other your opinions. *They all sat together at table, laughing and swapping stories.*

swarm /swɔːm/ **swarms, swarming, swarmed.** [1] N-C A **swarm** of bees or other insects is a large group of them flying together. [2] VERB When bees or other insects **swarm**, they move or fly in a large group. [3] VERB When people **swarm** somewhere, they move there quickly in a large group. *People swarmed to the shops, buying up everything in sight.* [4] VERB If a place **is swarming** with people, it is full of people moving about in a busy way. *Within minutes the area was swarming with officers.* [5] N-C A **swarm** of people is a large group of them moving about quickly.

swat /swɒt/ **swats, swatting, swatted.** VERB If you **swat** an insect, you hit it with a quick, swinging movement.

swathe (or **swath**) /sweɪð, AM swɑːθ/ **swathes, swathing, swathed.** [1] N-C A **swathe** of land is a long strip of land. *The army took over another swathe of territory.* [2] VERB To **swathe** someone or something **in** cloth means to wrap them in it completely. *She swathed her enormous body in thin black fabrics.*

sway /sweɪ/ **sways, swaying, swayed.** [1] VERB When people or things **sway**, they lean or swing slowly from one side to the other. *The people swayed back and forth.* [2] VERB If you **are swayed** by someone or something, you are influenced by them. *Don't ever be swayed by fashion.*
PHRASES ● If someone or something **holds sway**, they have great power or influence over a particular place or activity. *...ideas that held sway for centuries.*

swear /sweə/ **swears, swearing, swore, sworn.** [1] VERB If someone **swears**, they use language that is considered to be rude or offensive. *They swore at them and ran off.* [2] VERB If you **swear** to do something, you solemnly promise that you will do it. *Alan swore that he would do everything in his power to help us... He swore allegiance to the U.S. government.* [3] VERB If you **swear** that something is true, or if you say that you can **swear** to it, you say very firmly that it is true. *I swear I've told you all I know.* [4] VERB If someone **is sworn** to secrecy or silence, they promise another person that they will not reveal a secret. *She was bursting to announce the news but was sworn to secrecy.* [5] See also **sworn**.
▸ **swear by.** PHR-VERB If you **swear by** something, you believe that it can be relied on to have a particular effect. *Many people swear by vitamin C's ability to ward off colds.*
▸ **swear in.** PHR-VERB When someone **is sworn in**, they solemnly promise to fulfil the duties of a new job or appointment.

sweat /swet/ **sweats, sweating, sweated.** [1] N-U **Sweat** is the salty colourless liquid which comes through your skin when you are hot, ill, or afraid. *He wiped the sweat off his face.* [2] VERB When you **sweat**, sweat comes through your skin. ◆**sweating** N-U *...symptoms such as sweating, irritability, anxiety and depression.* [3] PHRASE If someone is **in a sweat** or **in a cold sweat**, they are sweating a lot, especially because they are afraid or ill. *The very thought brought me out in a cold sweat.*

sweater /'swetə/ **sweaters.** N-C A **sweater** is a warm knitted piece of clothing which covers the upper part of your body and your arms.

sweatshirt /'swetʃɜːt/ **sweatshirts.** N-C A **sweatshirt** is a loose warm piece of casual clothing, usually made of thick cotton, which covers the upper part of your body and your arms.

sweaty /'sweti/. ADJ If your clothing or body is **sweaty**, it is soaked or covered with sweat.

sweep /swiːp/ **sweeps, sweeping, swept.**
1 VERB If you **sweep** an area of ground, you push dirt or rubbish off it with a broom. *She was in the kitchen sweeping crumbs into a dust pan.* **2** VERB If you **sweep** things off something, you push them off with a quick smooth movement of your arm. *She swept the cards from the table.* **3** VERB If a strong force **sweeps** you along, it moves you quickly along. *...landslides that buried homes and swept cars into the sea.* **4** VERB If events or ideas **sweep** through a place, they spread quickly through it. *A flu epidemic is sweeping through Moscow. ...the wave of patriotism sweeping the country.* **5** VERB To **sweep** something away or aside means to remove it quickly and completely. *In times of war, governments often sweep human rights aside.* **6** VERB If your gaze or a light **sweeps** an area, it moves over it. *Helicopters with searchlights swept the park.* **7** PHRASE If someone **sweeps** something bad or wrong **under the carpet**, they try to prevent people from hearing about it.
▶ **sweep up.** PHR-VERB If you **sweep up** dirt or rubbish, you put it together with a brush and then remove it. *Get a broom and sweep up that glass.*

sweeping /'swiːpɪŋ/. **1** ADJ If someone makes a **sweeping** statement or generalization, they make a firm definite statement although they have not considered the relevant facts or details carefully; used showing disapproval. *You can't make sweeping generalizations about youngsters of today.* **2** ADJ **Sweeping** changes or reforms are large in scale and have very important or significant results.

sweet /swiːt/ **sweeter, sweetest; sweets.**
1 ADJ **Sweet** food or drink contains a lot of sugar. *...a mug of sweet tea.* ◆**sweetness** N-U *Florida oranges have a natural sweetness.* **2** N-C In British English, **sweets** are sweet things such as toffees, chocolates, or mints. In American English sweets are referred to as **candy.** **3** N-C A **sweet** is something sweet, such as fruit or a pudding, that you eat at the end of a meal; BRITISH. **4** ADJ A **sweet** smell is pleasant and fragrant. *...the sweet smell of her shampoo.* **5** ADJ A **sweet** sound is pleasant, smooth, and gentle. *...the sweet sounds of Mozart.* ◆**sweetly** ADV *He sang much more sweetly than he has before.* **6** ADJ If you describe something as **sweet**, you mean that it gives you great pleasure and satisfaction; WRITTEN. *There are few things quite as sweet as revenge.* **7** ADJ If you describe someone as **sweet**, you mean that they are pleasant, kind, and gentle towards other people. *How sweet of you to think of me!* ◆**sweetly** ADV *I just smiled sweetly.* **8** ADJ If you describe a small person or thing as **sweet**, you mean that they are attractive in a child-like way; INFORMAL. *...a sweet little baby girl.*

sweetcorn /'swiːtkɔːn/. N-U **Sweet corn** consists of the yellow seeds of the maize plant, which are eaten as a vegetable.

sweeten /'swiːtən/ **sweetens, sweetening, sweetened.** VERB If you **sweeten** food or drink, you add sugar, honey, or another sweet substance to it.

sweetener /'swiːtənə/ **sweeteners.** N-VAR A **sweetener** is an artificial substance that can be used instead of sugar.

sweetheart /'swiːthɑːt/ **sweethearts.**
1 N-VOC You call someone **sweetheart** if you are very fond of them. *Happy birthday, sweetheart.* **2** N-C Your **sweetheart** is your boyfriend or girlfriend; DATED.

swell /swel/ **swells, swelling, swelled, swollen.** The forms **swelled** and **swollen** are both used as the past participle. **1** VERB If the amount or size of something **swells**, it becomes larger than it was before. *His bank balance has swelled by £222,000... Women continue to swell the ranks of teachers.* **2** VERB If something such as a part of your body **swells**, or if it **swells up**, it becomes larger and rounder than normal. *The limbs swell to an enormous size... The glands in the neck swell up.* **3** VERB If you **swell with** a feeling, you are suddenly full of that feeling; LITERARY. *She could see her two sons swell with pride.* **4** See also **swollen.**

swelling /'swelɪŋ/ **swellings.** N-VAR A **swelling** is a raised curved shape on the surface of your body which appears as a result of an injury or an illness. *...painful swellings of the big toe joint... The cyst was causing swelling.*

sweltering /'sweltərɪŋ/. ADJ If the weather is **sweltering**, it is very hot. *In LA it's sweltering – 98 degrees in the shade. ...a day of sweltering heat.*

swept /swept/. **Swept** is the past tense and past participle of **sweep.**

swerve /swɜːv/ **swerves, swerving, swerved.** VERB & N-C If a vehicle or other moving thing **swerves**, it suddenly changes direction, often in order to avoid colliding with something else. This movement is called a **swerve.** *Her car swerved off the road... Ned swerved the truck... He swung the car to the left and that swerve saved Malone's life.*

swift /swɪft/ **swifter, swiftest. 1** ADJ A **swift** event or process happens very quickly or without delay. *The police were swift to act... We wish him a swift recovery.* ◆**swiftly** ADV *...the police failed to act swiftly enough.* ◆**swiftness** N-U *...the secrecy and swiftness of the invasion.* **2** ADJ Something that is **swift** moves very quickly. *With a swift movement, she reached into the cot.*

swim /swɪm/ **swims, swimming, swam, swum.** **1** VERB & N-SING When you **swim**, or when you go for a **swim**, you move through water by making movements with your arms and legs. *I swim a mile a day... When can we go for a swim?* ◆**swimmer, swimmers** N-C *I'm a good swimmer.* **2** VERB If objects **swim**, they seem to be moving backwards and forwards, usually because you are ill. *He felt too hot, he couldn't breathe, the room swam.* **3** VERB If your head **is swimming**, you feel dizzy.

swimming /'swɪmɪŋ/. N-U **Swimming** is the activity of swimming, especially as a sport or for pleasure. *It was too chilly for swimming... I now go swimming five times a week.*

'**swimming pool, swimming pools.** N-C A **swimming pool** is a place that has been built for people to swim in. It consists of a large hole that has been tiled and filled with water.

swimsuit /'swɪmsuːt/ **swimsuits.** N-C A **swimsuit** is a piece of clothing that is worn for swimming, especially by women and girls.

swindle /'swɪndəl/ **swindles, swindling, swindled.** VERB & N-C If someone **swindles** a person or an organization, or if someone is involved in a **swindle**, they deceive the person or organization in order to get money from them. *A City businessman swindled investors out of millions of pounds. ...a tax swindle.* ◆**swindler, swindlers** N-C *...an insurance swindler.*

swing /swɪŋ/ **swings, swinging, swung.** [1] VERB & N-C If something **swings**, or if you **swing** it, it moves backwards and forwards or from side to side from a fixed point, once or several times. You can refer to this movement as a **swing**. *The pendulum slowly started to swing... She was swinging a bottle of wine by its neck... Roy swung his legs carefully off the couch. ...walking with a slight swing to her hips.* [2] VERB If a vehicle **swings** in a particular direction, or if a driver **swings** his or her vehicle in a particular direction, he or she turns it suddenly in that direction. *He got into Margie's car and swung out onto the road... He swung the car off the road.* [3] VERB & N-C If you **swing at** someone or something, or if you take a **swing at** someone, you try to hit them. *I picked up his baseball bat and swung at the man's head... I often want to take a swing at someone.* [4] N-C A **swing** is a seat hanging by two ropes or chains from a metal frame or tree. You can sit on the seat and move backwards and forwards through the air. [5] VERB & N-C If people's opinions, attitudes, or feelings **swing**, or if there is a **swing** in them, they change significantly. *The mood amongst Tory MPs seems to be swinging away from the Prime Minister. ...violent mood swings.* [6] PHRASE If something is **in full swing**, it is operating fully and is no longer in its early stages. *The international rugby season is in full swing.*

swipe /swaɪp/ **swipes, swiping, swiped.** VERB & N-C If you **swipe at** a person or thing, or if you take a **swipe at** them, you try to hit them, making a swinging movement with your arm. *She swiped at Rusty as though he was a fly... She took a casual swipe at the nettles.*

swirl /swɜːl/ **swirls, swirling, swirled.** [1] VERB If you **swirl** something liquid or flowing, or if it **swirls**, it moves round and round quickly. *She swirled the ice-cold liquid around her mouth... The black water swirled around his legs.* [2] N-C A **swirl** is a pattern made by moving something round and round quickly. *...small swirls of chocolate cream.*

swish /swɪʃ/ **swishes, swishing, swished.** VERB & N-C If something **swishes**, it moves quickly through the air, making a soft sound. This action is called a **swish**. *A car swished by... She turned with a swish of her skirt.*

switch /swɪtʃ/ **switches, switching, switched.** [1] N-C A **switch** is a small control for an electrical device which you use to turn the device on or off. *...a light switch.* [2] VERB & N-C If you **switch** to something different, for example to a different system, task, or subject of conversation, or if there is a **switch** to it, you change to it from what you were doing or saying before. *The law would encourage companies to switch from coal to cleaner fuels... A friend spurred Chris into switching jobs... New technology made a switch to oil possible.* [3] VERB If you **switch** two things, you replace one with the other. *The ballot boxes have been switched.*

▶ **switch off.** [1] PHR-VERB If you **switch off** an electrical device, you stop it working by operating a switch. *The driver dipped the headlights and then switched them off.* [2] PHR-VERB If you **switch off**, you stop paying attention to something; INFORMAL. *You've got so many things to think about that it's difficult to switch off.*

▶ **switch on.** PHR-VERB If you **switch on** an electrical device, you make it start working by operating a switch. *He pointed the light at his feet and tried to switch it on.*

switchboard /'swɪtʃbɔːd/ **switchboards.** N-C A **switchboard** is a place in a large office or business where all the telephone calls are connected. *He asked to be connected to the central switchboard.*

swivel /'swɪvəl/ **swivels, swivelling, swivelled** (AM **swiveling, swiveled**). VERB If someone or something **swivels**, or if you **swivel** them, they turn around a central point so that they are facing in a different direction. *He swivelled round to face Sarah... She swivelled her chair round.*

swollen /'swəʊlən/. [1] **Swollen** is the past participle of **swell**. [2] ADJ If a part of your body is **swollen**, it is larger and rounder than normal, usually as a result of injury or illness. *Her glands were swollen and painful.*

swoon /swuːn/ **swoons, swooning, swooned.** VERB If you **swoon**, you are strongly affected by your feelings for someone you love or admire very much. *Virtually every woman in the '20s swooned over Valentino.*

swoop /swuːp/ **swoops, swooping, swooped.** [1] VERB & N-C If police or soldiers **swoop** on a place, or if they carry out a **swoop** on a place, they go there suddenly and quickly, usually in order to arrest someone or to attack the place. *The drugs squad swooped and discovered 240 kilograms of cannabis. ...a swoop on a German lorry.* [2] VERB When a bird or aeroplane **swoops**, it suddenly moves downwards through the air in a smooth curving movement. *More than 20 helicopters began swooping in low.*

swop /swɒp/. See **swap**.

sword /sɔːd/ **swords.** N-C A **sword** is a weapon with a handle and a long blade.

swore /swɔː/. **Swore** is the past tense of **swear**.

sworn /swɔːn/. [1] **Sworn** is the past participle of **swear**. [2] ADJ BEFORE N If you make a **sworn** statement or declaration, you swear that everything that you have said in it is true. ...*sworn legal statements.*

swum /swʌm/. **Swum** is the past participle of swim.

swung /swʌŋ/. **Swung** is the past tense and past participle of swing.

syllable /'sɪləbəl/ **syllables.** N-C A **syllable** is a part of a word that contains a single vowel-sound and that is pronounced as a unit. For example, 'book' has one syllable, and 'reading' has two syllables.

syllabus /'sɪləbəs/ **syllabuses.** N-C You can refer to the subjects that are studied in a particular course as the **syllabus**. ...*the GCSE history syllabus.*

symbol /'sɪmbəl/ **symbols.** ⚊1⚊ N-C Something that is a **symbol** of a society or aspect of life seems to represent it because it is typical of it. *To them, the monarchy is the special symbol of nationhood.* ⚊2⚊ N-C A **symbol** of something such as an idea is a shape or design that is used to represent it. *I frequently use sunflowers as symbols of strength.* ⚊3⚊ N-C A **symbol** for an item in a calculation or formula is a number, letter, or shape that represents the item. *What's the chemical symbol for mercury?*

symbolic /sɪm'bɒlɪk/. ⚊1⚊ ADJ If you describe an event, action, or procedure as **symbolic**, you mean that it represents an important change, although it has little practical effect. *The President's visit is loaded with symbolic significance.* ◆**symbolically** ADV *It was a simple enough gesture, but symbolically important.* ⚊2⚊ ADJ **Symbolic** is used to describe things involving or relating to symbols. ...*symbolic representations of landscape.* ◆**symbolism** /'sɪmbəlɪzəm/ N-U ...*a film much praised for its visual symbolism.*

symbolize (BR also **symbolise**) /'sɪmbəlaɪz/ **symbolizes, symbolizing, symbolized.** VERB If one thing **symbolizes** another, it is used or regarded as a symbol of it. *The fall of the Berlin Wall symbolised the end of the Cold War.*

symmetrical /sɪ'metrɪkəl/. ADJ If something is **symmetrical**, it has two halves which are exactly the same, except that one half is the mirror image of the other. ...*rows of perfectly symmetrical windows.* ◆**symmetrically** ADV *The hors d'oeuvres were arranged symmetrically on two plates.*

symmetry /'sɪmɪtri/ **symmetries.** N-VAR Something that has **symmetry** is symmetrical in shape, design, or structure. ...*the incredible beauty and symmetry of a snowflake.*

sympathetic /ˌsɪmpə'θetɪk/. ⚊1⚊ ADJ If you are **sympathetic** to someone who has had a misfortune, you are kind to them and show that you understand how they are feeling. *She was very sympathetic to the problems of adult students.* ...*a sympathetic friend.* ◆**sympathetically** ADV *She nodded sympathetically.* ⚊2⚊ ADJ If you are **sympathetic** to a proposal or action, you approve of it and are willing to support it. *The London galleries are sympathetic to new ideas.*

sympathize (BR also **sympathise**) /'sɪmpəθaɪz/ **sympathizes, sympathizing, sympathized.** ⚊1⚊ VERB If you **sympathize** with someone who has had a misfortune, you show that you are sorry for them. *Anyone who has*

been in a troubled relationship will sympathise with Sue... He would sympathize but he wouldn't understand. ⚊2⚊ VERB If you **sympathize** with someone's feelings, you understand them and are not critical of them. *He liked Max, and sympathized with his ambitions.* ⚊3⚊ VERB If you **sympathize** with a person or group, you approve of their actions or proposals. *Most of the people living there sympathized with the guerrillas.* ◆**sympathizer, sympathizers** N-C ...*a large group of Nazi sympathisers.*

sympathy /'sɪmpəθi/ **sympathies.** ⚊1⚊ N-U If you have **sympathy** for someone who has had a misfortune, you are sorry for them, and show this in the way you behave towards them. *I have had very little help from doctors and no sympathy whatsoever.* ⚊2⚊ N-VAR If you have **sympathy** with someone's ideas or opinions, you agree with them. *I have some sympathy with this point of view.* ⚊3⚊ N-U If you take some action **in sympathy** with someone else, you do it in order to show that you support them. *A few players grumbled in sympathy with each other.*

symphony /'sɪmfəni/ **symphonies.** N-C A **symphony** is a piece of music written to be played for an orchestra, usually in four parts.

'symphony orchestra, symphony orchestras. N-C A **symphony orchestra** is a large orchestra that plays classical music.

symposium /sɪm'pəʊziəm/ **symposiums.** N-C A **symposium** is a conference in which experts or scholars discuss a particular subject.

symptom /'sɪmptəm/ **symptoms.** ⚊1⚊ N-C A **symptom** of an illness is something wrong with your body that is a sign of the illness. ...*patients with flu symptoms.* ⚊2⚊ N-C A **symptom** of a bad situation is something that happens which is considered to be a sign of this situation. *Your problem with keeping boyfriends is just a symptom of a larger problem.*

symptomatic /ˌsɪmptə'mætɪk/. ADJ AFTER LINK-V If something is **symptomatic** of something else, especially something bad, it is a sign of it; FORMAL. *The city's problems are symptomatic of the crisis that is spreading throughout the country.*

synagogue /'sɪnəgɒg/ **synagogues.** N-C A **synagogue** is a building where Jewish people worship.

synchronize (BR also **synchronise**) /'sɪŋkrənaɪz/ **synchronizes, synchronizing, synchronized.** VERB If you **synchronize** two activities, processes, or movements, you cause them to happen at the same time and speed as each other. *It was virtually impossible to synchronise our lives so as to take holidays and weekends together.*

syndicate /'sɪndɪkət/ **syndicates.** N-C A **syndicate** is an association of people or organizations that is formed for business purposes or to carry out a project. ...*a major crime syndicate.*

syndrome /'sɪndrəʊm/ **syndromes.** ⚊1⚊ N-C A **syndrome** is a medical condition that is characterized by a particular group of symptoms. ...*sudden infant death syndrome.* ⚊2⚊ N-C You can refer to an undesirable condition that is characterized by a particular type of activity or behaviour as a **syndrome**. *Scientists call this the 'it won't affect me' syndrome.*

synonym /'sɪnənɪm/ **synonyms.** N-C A synonym is a word or expression which means the same as another one.

synonymous /sɪ'nɒnɪməs/. [1] ADJ Synonymous words or expressions have the same meaning as each other. [2] ADJ If you say that one thing is **synonymous** with another, you mean that the two things are very closely associated with each other. *In politics, power and popularity are not synonymous.*

synthesis /'sɪnθɪsɪs/ **syntheses** /'sɪnθɪsiːz/. N-C A synthesis of different ideas or styles is a mixture or combination of them; FORMAL. *...her synthesis of feminism and socialism.*

synthesize (BR also **synthesise**) /'sɪnθɪsaɪz/ **synthesizes, synthesizing, synthesized.** VERB If you **synthesize** different ideas, facts, or experiences, you combine them to develop a single idea or impression; FORMAL. *The movement synthesised elements of modern art that hadn't been brought together before.*

synthetic /sɪn'θetɪk/. ADJ Synthetic products are made from chemicals or artificial substances rather than from natural ones. *...synthetic rubber.*

syphon /'saɪfən/ **syphons.** See **siphon**.

syringe /sɪ'rɪndʒ/ **syringes.** N-C A syringe is a small tube with a fine hollow needle, used for injecting drugs or for taking blood from someone's body.

syrup /'sɪrəp/ **syrups.** N-VAR Syrup is a sweet liquid made by cooking sugar with water or fruit juice.

system /'sɪstəm/ **systems.** [1] N-C A system is a way of working, organizing, or doing something which follows a fixed plan or set of rules. *...the present system of funding for higher education.* [2] N-C You use **system** to refer to a set of equipment, parts, or devices. *...powerful computer systems.. ...a central heating system. ...the body's digestive system.* [3] N-C You use **system** to refer to a whole institution or aspect of society that is organized in a particular way. *...the British legal system. ...Australia's road and rail system.* [4] N-C A system is a set of rules, especially in mathematics or science, which is used to count or measure things. *...the decimal system of metric weights.* [5] N-SING People sometimes refer to the government or administration of a country as **the system**. *These feelings are likely to make people attempt to overthrow the system.* [6] See also **immune system**, **nervous system**, **solar system**.

systematic /ˌsɪstə'mætɪk/. ADJ Something that is done in a **systematic** way is done according to a fixed plan, in a thorough and efficient way. *They commenced a systematic search.* ♦**systematically** ADV *The army has systematically violated human rights.*

systemic /sɪ'stiːmɪk/. ADJ Systemic means affecting the whole of a system or organism. *The economy is locked in a systemic crisis.*

T t

tab /tæb/ **tabs.** N-C A tab is a small piece of cloth or paper that is attached to something, usually with information about that thing written on it.

PHRASES ● If someone **keeps tabs on** you, they make sure that they always know where you are and what you are doing, often in order to control you; INFORMAL. ● If you **pick up the tab**, you pay a bill on behalf of a group of people or provide the money that is needed for something.

table /'teɪbəl/ **tables, tabling, tabled.** [1] N-C A table is a piece of furniture with a flat top that you put things on or sit at. *...the kitchen table.* [2] N-C A table is a set of facts or figures arranged in columns and rows. [3] PHRASE If you **turn the tables on** someone who is causing you problems, you change the situation completely so that you cause problems for them instead. [4] VERB If someone **tables** a proposal, they say formally that they want it to be discussed at a meeting; BRITISH. *They've tabled a motion criticising the Government.*

tablecloth /'teɪbəlklɒθ, AM -klɔːθ/ **tablecloths.** N-C A tablecloth is a cloth used to cover a table.

tablespoon /'teɪbəlspuːn/ **tablespoons.** N-C A tablespoon is a fairly large spoon used for serving food and in cookery.

tablet /'tæblət/ **tablets.** N-C A tablet is a small, solid, round mass of medicine which you swallow. *I take herbal sleeping tablets.*

tabloid /'tæblɔɪd/ **tabloids.** N-C A tabloid is a newspaper with small pages, short articles, and lots of photographs.

taboo /tæ'buː/ **taboos.** N-C & ADJ If there is a **taboo** on a subject or activity, or if it is **taboo**, it is a social custom to avoid doing that activity or talking about that subject, because people find it embarrassing or offensive. *The topic of addiction remains something of a taboo... Cancer is a taboo subject.*

tacit /'tæsɪt/. ADJ If someone gives their **tacit** agreement or approval, they agree to something or approve it without actually saying so. *He gave tacit support to terrorists.* ♦**tacitly** ADV *He tacitly admitted that the government had breached regulations.*

tack /tæk/ **tacks, tacking, tacked.** [1] N-C A tack is a short nail with a broad flat head. [2] VERB If you **tack** something to a surface, you pin it there with tacks. *He had tacked this note to her door.* [3] N-U If you change **tack** or try a different **tack**, you try a different method for dealing with a situation. *This report takes a different tack from the 20 that have come before.*

▶ **tack on.** PHR-VERB If you say that something is **tacked on** to something else, you think that it is added in a hurried and unsatisfactory way. *The child-care bill is to be tacked on to the budget plan.*

tackle /'tækəl/ **tackles, tackling, tackled.** [1] VERB If you **tackle** a difficult task, you start dealing with it in a determined way. *Drastic measures are needed to tackle the crisis.* [2] VERB & N-C If you **tackle** someone in a game such as football, you try to take the ball away from them. This action is called a **tackle**. [3] VERB If you **tackle** someone about a difficult matter, you speak to them frankly about it, usually in order to get something changed or done. *I tackled him about how anyone could live amidst so much poverty.* [4] N-U **Tackle** is the equipment that you need for an activity, especially fishing.

tacky /ˈtæki/ **tackier, tackiest.** ADJ If you describe something as **tacky**, you dislike it because it is cheap and badly made or vulgar; IN-FORMAL. *...tacky red sunglasses.*

tact /tækt/. N-U **Tact** is the ability to avoid upsetting or offending people by being careful not to say or do things that would hurt their feelings. *He has handled the affair with great tact.*

tactful /ˈtæktfʊl/. ADJ If you describe someone as **tactful**, you approve of them because they are careful not to say or do anything that would offend or upset other people. *Sorry, that wasn't a very tactful question, was it?* ♦ **tactfully** ADV *Alex tactfully refrained from further comment.*

tactic /ˈtæktɪk/ **tactics.** N-C **Tactics** are the methods that you choose in order to achieve what you want. *...delaying tactics.*

tactical /ˈtæktɪkəl/. [1] ADJ A **tactical** action or plan is intended to help someone achieve what they want in the future, rather than immediately. *The security forces had made a tactical withdrawal from the area.* ♦ **tactically** ADV *Many will vote tactically for the party they think has the best possibility of beating the government.* [2] ADJ **Tactical** means relating to tactics. *He's made a tactical error.*

tag /tæg/ **tags, tagging, tagged.** [1] N-C A **tag** is a small piece of card or cloth which is attached to an object and has information about that object on it. *...baggage tags.* [2] VERB If you **tag** something, you attach something to it or mark it so that it can be identified later. *...ways of tagging chemical molecules.*

▶ **tag along.** PHR-VERB If you **tag along** with someone, you go with them, especially because you are interested in what they are doing. *He said we could tag along, just to find out what detective work was all about.*

tail /teɪl/ **tails, tailing, tailed.** [1] N-C The **tail** of an animal is the part extending beyond the end of its body. [2] N-C You can use **tail** to refer to the end or back of something, especially something long and thin. *...the tail of the plane.* [3] VERB To **tail** someone means to follow close behind them and watch what they do; INFORMAL. *He trusted her so little that he had her tailed.*

▶ **tail off.** PHR-VERB If something **tails off**, it gradually becomes less, and perhaps ends completely. *Last year, economic growth tailed off to below four percent.*

tailor /ˈteɪlə/ **tailors, tailoring, tailored.** [1] N-C A **tailor** is a person who makes clothes, especially for men. [2] VERB If you **tailor** something such as a plan or system to someone's needs

or purposes, you make it suitable for them by changing the details of it. *...scripts tailored to American comedy audiences.*

tailor-ˈmade. ADJ Something that is **tailor-made** for a person or purpose is very suitable or was specially designed for them. *These questions were tailor-made for Professor Posner.*

taint /teɪnt/ **taints, tainting, tainted.** [1] VERB If you say that something or someone **is tainted** by something undesirable or corrupt, you mean that their status or reputation is harmed by it. *...a series of political scandals that has tainted the political stars of a generation.* ♦ **tainted** ADJ *...tainted evidence.* [2] N-SING A **taint** is an undesirable quality in something which spoils it. *Her government never really shook off the taint of corruption.*

take /teɪk/ **takes, taking, took, taken.** [1] VERB You can use **take** to say that someone does something. For example, you can say **'he took a look'** instead of 'he looked'. *She was too tired to take a shower... Betty took a photograph of us.* [2] VERB You can use **take** with nouns instead of using a more specific and often more formal verb. For example, you can say **'he took control'** instead of 'he assumed control'. *President Collor de Mello took power in March... I felt it was important for her to take a leading role.*

take /teɪk/ **takes, taking, took, taken.** [1] VERB If you **take** something, you reach for it and hold it. *Let me take your coat... Opening a drawer, she took out a letter.* [2] VERB If you **take** something with you when you go somewhere, you carry it with you. *I'll take these papers home and read them.* [3] VERB If you **take** something from its owner, you steal it. [4] VERB If a person, vehicle, or path **takes** someone somewhere, they transport or lead them there. *She took me to a Mexican restaurant.* [5] VERB To **take** something or someone means to win or capture them from an enemy or opponent. *Marines went in, taking 15 prisoners.* [6] VERB If you **take** something that is offered to you, you accept it. *When I took the job I thought I could change the system.* [7] VERB If you **take** a road or route, you choose to travel along it. *Take the Chester Road to the outskirts of town.* [8] VERB If you **take** a car, train, bus, or plane, you use it to go from one place to another. *She took the train to New York.* [9] VERB If you **take** a particular size in shoes or clothes, that size fits you. *47 per cent of women in the UK take a size 16 or above.* [10] VERB If someone **takes** a drug or medicine, they swallow it. [11] VERB If you **take** an event or piece of news well or badly, you react to it well or badly. *No one took my messages seriously.* [12] VERB If something **takes** a certain amount of time, you need that amount of time in order to do it. *The sauce takes 25 minutes to prepare.* [13] VERB If something **takes** a particular quality or thing, it requires it. *Walking across the room took all her strength.* [14] VERB If you cannot **take** something unpleasant, you cannot bear it. *Don't ever ask me to look after those kids again. I just can't take it!* [15] VERB If you **take** a subject or course at school or university, you choose to study it. *Students are allowed to take European history and American history.* **16** VERB If you **take** an exam, you do it or take part in it. ● See note at **exam**. **17** VERB The teacher who **takes** a class for a subject teaches the class that subject; BRITISH. **18** See note at **bring**.

take 3 phrases

take /teɪk/ **takes, taking, took, taken.**

PHRASES ● You can say '**I take it**' to someone in order to confirm that you have understood their meaning or understood a situation. *I take it that neither of you reads 'The Times'.* ● If you say to someone '**take it or leave it**', you are telling them that they can accept something or not accept it, but that you are not prepared to discuss any other alternatives.

take 4 phrasal verbs

take /teɪk/ **takes, taking, took, taken.**

▶ **take after.** PHR-VERB If you **take after** a member of your family, you look or behave like them. *He takes after his dad.*
▶ **take apart.** PHR-VERB If you **take** something **apart**, you separate it into its different parts.
▶ **take away.** **1** PHR-VERB If you **take** something **away** from someone, you remove it from them. *'Give me the knife,' he said softly, 'or I'll take it away from you.'* **2** See also **takeaway**.
▶ **take back.** **1** PHR-VERB If you **take** something **back**, you return it. *I once took back a pair of shoes that fell apart after a week.* **2** PHR-VERB If you **take back** something that you said, you admit that it was wrong. *Take back what you said about Jeremy!*
▶ **take down.** **1** PHR-VERB When people **take down** a structure, they separate it into pieces and remove it. *The Canadian army took down the barricades.* **2** PHR-VERB If you **take down** information, you write it down. *I took down his comments in shorthand.*
▶ **take in.** **1** PHR-VERB If you **take** someone **in**, you allow them to stay in your house or country, especially when they are homeless or in trouble. *The monastery has taken in 26 refugees.* **2** PHR-VERB If you **are taken in** by someone or something, you are deceived or fooled by them. *He is a real charmer who totally took me in.* **3** PHR-VERB If you **take** something **in**, you pay attention to it and understand it when you hear or read it. *Robert took it all in without needing second explanations.*
▶ **take off.** **1** PHR-VERB When an aircraft **takes off**, it leaves the ground and starts flying. ● See also **takeoff**. **2** PHR-VERB If you **take off** something that you are wearing, you move it off your body. *She took off her spectacles.* ● See note at **wear**. **3** PHR-VERB If you **take** time **off**, you do not go to work. *She took two days off work.*
▶ **take on.** **1** PHR-VERB If you **take on** a job or responsibility, you accept it. *Don't take on more responsibilities than you can handle.* **2** PHR-VERB If you **take on** someone more powerful than you, you fight them or compete against them. **3** PHR-VERB If you **take** someone **on**, you give them a job. *The party has been taking on staff.* **4** PHR-VERB If something **takes on** a new appearance or quality, it develops that appearance or quality. *His writing took on a feverish intensity.*

▶ **take out.** **1** PHR-VERB If you **take out** something such as a loan or insurance policy, a company agrees to let you have it. **2** PHR-VERB If you **take** someone **out**, you take them to an enjoyable place, and you pay for both of you. *Rachel took me out to lunch.* **3** PHR-VERB If you **take** your unhappiness or anger **out on** someone, you behave in an unpleasant way towards them, even though it is not their fault that you feel upset. *Just because you've had a bad day at work, there's no need to take it out on us.*
▶ **take over.** **1** PHR-VERB To **take over** something such as a company or country means to gain control of it. *A British newspaper says British Airways plan to take over Trans World Airways.* ● See also **takeover**. **2** PHR-VERB If you **take over** a job, or if you **take over**, you start doing the job after someone else has stopped doing it. *In 1966, Pastor Albertz took over from him as governing mayor.*
▶ **take to.** **1** PHR-VERB If you **take to** someone or something, you like them immediately. *My wife Caroline and I immediately took to Alan.* **2** PHR-VERB If you **take to** doing something, you begin to do it regularly. *They had taken to wandering through the streets.*
▶ **take up.** **1** PHR-VERB If you **take up** an activity or job, you start doing it. *He left a job in the City to take up farming.* **2** PHR-VERB If you **take** someone **up on** an offer that they have made, you accept their offer. *Since she'd offered to babysit, I took her up on it.* **3** PHR-VERB If you **take up** a matter, you start to deal with it or discuss how you are going to deal with it. *Dr Mahathir intends to take up the proposal with the prime minister.*
▶ **take upon.** PHR-VERB If you **take** it **upon** yourself to do something, you do it even though it is not your duty. *He took upon himself the responsibility for protecting her.*

takeaway /ˈteɪkəweɪ/ **takeaways.** N-C In British English, a **takeaway** is a shop or restaurant which sells hot food to be eaten elsewhere. A meal that you buy there is also called a **takeaway**. The American word is **takeout**.

taken /ˈteɪkən/ **1** **Taken** is the past participle of **take**. **2** ADJ AFTER LINK-V If you are **taken with** something or someone, you find them attractive and interesting. *She seems very taken with the idea.*

takeoff /ˈteɪkɒf, AM -ɔːf/ **takeoffs.** N-VAR **Takeoff** is the beginning of a flight, when an aircraft leaves the ground. *The commuter plane was waiting for takeoff.*

takeout /ˈteɪkaʊt/ **takeouts.** See **takeaway**.

takeover /ˈteɪkəʊvə/ **takeovers.** **1** N-VAR A **takeover** is the act of gaining control of a company by buying a majority of its shares. *...the proposed £3.4 billion takeover of Midland Bank.* **2** N-C A **takeover** is the act of taking control of a country, political party, or movement by force. *There's been a military takeover of some kind.*

taker /ˈteɪkə/ **takers.** N-C If there are no **takers** or few **takers** for an offer or challenge, hardly anyone is willing to accept it.

takings /ˈteɪkɪŋz/ N-PL The **takings** of a business such as a shop or cinema consist of the amount of money it gets from selling its goods or tickets during a certain period; BRITISH.

tale /teɪl/ **tales.** [1] N-C A **tale** is a story, especially one involving adventure or magic. [2] N-C You can refer to an interesting, exciting, or dramatic account of a real event as a **tale**. *...tales of horror and loss resulting from Monday's earthquake.* [3] See also **fairy tale**.

talent /'tælənt/ **talents.** N-VAR **Talent** is the natural ability to do something well. *Both her children have a talent for music... It is important to use people's talents to the full.*

talented /'tæləntɪd/. ADJ Someone who is **talented** has a natural ability to do something well. *Howard is a talented pianist.*

talisman /'tælɪzmən/ **talismans.** N-C A **talisman** is an object which you believe has magic powers to protect you or bring you luck.

talk /tɔːk/ **talks, talking, talked.** [1] VERB & N-VAR When you **talk**, you say things to someone. **Talk** is the things you say. *They were talking about American food... A teacher reprimanded a girl for talking in class... We had a long talk about her father.* [2] VERB & N-C If you **talk**, or if you give a **talk** on or about something, you make an informal speech about it. *He intends to talk to young people about the dangers of AIDS.* [3] VERB & N-PL When different sides in a dispute or negotiation **talk**, or when they have **talks**, they have formal discussions. *Croats and Serbs still aren't prepared to talk to each other. ...peace talks.* [4] VERB If someone **talks** when they are being held by police or soldiers, they reveal important or secret information, usually unwillingly. [5] VERB If you **talk** politics or sport, for example, you discuss it. *...middle-aged men talking business.* [6] See notes at **discuss** and **speak**.

▸ **talk down.** PHR-VERB If someone **talks** something **down**, they reduce its value or importance by saying bad things about it. *Businessmen are tired of politicians talking the economy down.*

▸ **talk into.** PHR-VERB If you **talk** someone **into** doing something, you persuade them to do it.

▸ **talk out of.** PHR-VERB If you **talk** someone **out** of doing something, you persuade them not to do it.

▸ **talk over.** PHR-VERB If you **talk** something **over**, you discuss it thoroughly and honestly. *He always talked things over with his friends.*

▸ **talk through.** PHR-VERB To **talk through** a problem is the same as to **talk** it **over**. *That's how we cope, by talking things through.*

▸ **talk up.** PHR-VERB If someone **talks up** a particular thing, they increase its value, success, or importance by saying exaggerated things about it. *Politicians accuse the media of talking up the possibility of a riot.*

tall /tɔːl/ **taller, tallest.** [1] ADJ Someone or something that is **tall** is above average height. *He was very tall.* [2] ADJ You use **tall** to ask or talk about the height of someone or something. *How tall are you?... I'm only 5ft tall.* [3] PHRASE If something is **a tall order**, it is very difficult. *Financing your studies may seem like a tall order.* [4] See note at **high**.

tally /'tæli/ **tallies, tallying, tallied.** [1] N-C A **tally** is a record of amounts or numbers which you keep changing and adding to as the activity which affects it progresses. *The final tally was 817 votes for her and 731 for Mr Lee.* [2] VERB If two numbers or statements **tally**, they agree with each other or are exactly the same. *This description didn't seem to tally with what we saw.*

tame /teɪm/ **tamer, tamest; tames, taming, tamed.** [1] ADJ A **tame** animal or bird is not afraid of humans. [2] ADJ If you say that something or someone is **tame**, you are criticizing them for being weak and boring. *Some of today's political demonstrations look rather tame.* ♦**tamely** ADV *He tamely did what someone else told him.* [3] VERB If someone **tames** a wild animal or a wild bird, they train it not to be afraid of humans.

tamper /'tæmpə/ **tampers, tampering, tampered.** VERB If someone **tampers with** something, they interfere with it or try to change it when they have no right to do so. *He found his computer had been tampered with.* ♦**tampering** N-U *The phone lines also have a security code to prevent tampering.*

tampon /'tæmpɒn/ **tampons.** N-C A **tampon** is a firm piece of cotton wool that a woman puts inside her vagina when she has a period, in order to absorb the blood.

tan /tæn/ **tans, tanning, tanned.** [1] N-C If you have a **tan**, your skin has become darker than usual because you have been in the sun. [2] VERB If a part of your body **tans**, your skin becomes darker than usual because you spend time in the sun. ♦**tanned** ADJ *He is very tanned.*

tandem /'tændəm/ **tandems.** [1] N-C A **tandem** is a bicycle designed for two riders. [2] PHRASE If two things happen or are done **in tandem**, they happen or are done together.

tangible /'tændʒɪbl/. ADJ If something is **tangible**, it is clear enough to be easily seen, felt, or noticed. *...tangible evidence that the economy is starting to recover.*

tangle /'tæŋgl/ **tangles, tangling, tangled.** [1] N-C A **tangle** of something is a mass of it twisted together in a confusing manner. *...a tangle of wires.* [2] VERB If something **is tangled**, or if it **is tangled up**, it becomes twisted into a confusing mass that is difficult to separate into its original form. *Animals get tangled in fishing nets and drown.*

tank /tæŋk/ **tanks.** [1] N-C A **tank** is a large container for holding liquid or gas. *...a tank full of goldfish.* [2] N-C A **tank** is a military vehicle covered with armour and equipped with guns or rockets.

tanker /'tæŋkə/ **tankers.** N-C A **tanker** is a ship or truck used for transporting large quantities of gas or liquid, especially oil.

tanned /tænd/. See **tan.**

tantalize (BR also **tantalise**) /'tæntəlaɪz/ **tantalizes, tantalizing, tantalized.** VERB If something or someone **tantalizes** you, they make you feel hopeful and excited about something, usually before disappointing you. *...the dreams of democracy that have so tantalized them.* ♦**tantalizing** ADJ *...a tantalising aroma of roast beef.*

tantamount /'tæntəmaʊnt/. ADJ AFTER LINK-V If you say that one thing is **tantamount to** a second, more serious thing, you are emphasizing how bad or unfortunate the first thing is by saying it is almost the same as the second; FORMAL. *Slowing down can seem tantamount to admitting you're weak.*

tantrum /ˈtæntrəm/ **tantrums.** N-C If a child has a **tantrum**, it suddenly loses its temper in a noisy and uncontrolled way.

tap /tæp/ **taps, tapping, tapped.** [1] N-C A **tap** is a device that controls the flow of a liquid or gas from a pipe or container. *She turned on the tap and splashed her face with cold water.* [2] VERB & N-C If you **tap** something, or if you **tap** on it, you hit it with a quick light blow or a series of quick light blows. This kind of blow is called a **tap**. *O'Leary tapped the pavement with his foot... A tap on the door interrupted him.* [3] VERB If you **tap** a resource, you make use of it. *Hydro-electric power taps the energy of river water.* [4] VERB & N-C If someone **taps** your telephone, they attach a special device called a **tap** to the line so that they can secretly listen to your conversations.

tape /teɪp/ **tapes, taping, taped.** [1] N-U **Tape** is a narrow plastic strip covered with a magnetic substance. It is used to record sounds, pictures, and computer information. *Many students declined to be interviewed on tape.* [2] N-C A **tape** is a cassette with magnetic tape wound round it. [3] VERB If you **tape** music, sounds, or television pictures, you record them using a tape recorder or a video recorder. ♦ **taping, tapings** N-VAR *...an unauthorized taping.* [4] N-VAR A **tape** is a strip of cloth used to tie things together or to identify who a piece of clothing belongs to. *...name tapes.* [5] N-U **Tape** is a sticky strip of plastic used for sticking things together. *...adhesive tape.* [6] VERB If you **tape** one thing to another, you attach it using sticky tape. *The envelope was taped shut.* ● See also **red tape**.

▶ **tape up** PHR-VERB If you **tape** something **up**, you fasten tape around it firmly, in order to protect it or hold it in a fixed position.

'tape measure, tape measures. N-C A **tape measure** is a strip of metal, plastic, or cloth with marks on it, used for measuring.

taper /ˈteɪpə/ **tapers, tapering, tapered.** VERB If something **tapers**, or if you **taper** it, it gradually becomes thinner at one end. *...a beard that tapered to a sharp point.* ♦ **tapered** ADJ *...the elegantly tapered legs of the dressing-table.*

▶ **taper off** PHR-VERB If something **tapers off**, it gradually reduces in amount, number, or size. *The storm is expected to taper off today.*

'tape recorder, tape recorders. N-C A **tape recorder** is a machine used for recording and playing music, speech, or other sounds.

tapestry /ˈtæpɪstri/ **tapestries.** N-VAR A **tapestry** is a piece of heavy, good quality cloth with a picture or pattern sewn on it.

tar /tɑː/. N-U **Tar** is a thick, black, sticky substance used in making roads.

target /ˈtɑːgɪt/ **targets, targeting, targeted.** [1] N-C A **target** is something that someone is trying to hit with a weapon or other object. *Both his kicks missed the target... The mine could be a prime target for guerilla attack.* [2] VERB If someone **targets** someone or some-

thing, they decide to attack or criticize them. *Ms Garner also targeted feminists who criticised her.* [3] N-C The **target** of an attack or a criticism is the person or thing being attacked or criticized. *They have been the target of racist abuse.* [4] N-C A **target** is a result that you are trying to achieve. *...the park's annual target of 11 million visitors.* [5] PHRASE If someone or something is **on target**, they are making good progress and are likely to achieve the result that is wanted. [6] VERB If you **target** a particular group of people, you try to appeal to those people or affect them. *The union was particularly keen to target young people.*

tariff /ˈtærɪf/ **tariffs.** [1] N-C A **tariff** is a tax on goods coming into a country. [2] N-C A **tariff** is the rate at which you are charged for something; BRITISH.

tarmac /ˈtɑːmæk/. N-U **Tarmac** is a material used for making road surfaces, consisting of crushed stones mixed with tar; BRITISH. **Tarmac** is a trademark.

tarnish /ˈtɑːnɪʃ/ **tarnishes, tarnishing, tarnished.** [1] VERB If something **tarnishes** a person's reputation, it damages it and causes people to lose respect for that person. ♦ **tarnished** ADJ *He wants to improve the overall image of his country.* [2] VERB If metal **tarnishes**, or if something **tarnishes** it, it becomes stained and loses its brightness. ♦ **tarnished** ADJ *...brown surfaces of tarnished brass.*

tart /tɑːt/ **tarts.** [1] N-VAR A **tart** is a shallow pastry case with a filling of sweet food or fruit. *...jam tarts.* [2] ADJ If something such as fruit is **tart**, it has a sharp slightly bitter taste.

tartan /ˈtɑːtən/. ADJ **Tartan** cloth, which traditionally comes from Scotland, has different coloured stripes crossing each other.

task /tɑːsk, tæsk/ **tasks.** N-C A **task** is an activity or piece of work which you have to do. *Walker had the unenviable task of breaking the bad news to Hill... ...administrative tasks.*

taste /teɪst/ **tastes, tasting, tasted.** [1] N-U Your sense of **taste** is your ability to recognize the flavour of things with your tongue. [2] N-C The **taste** of something is the flavour that it has, for example whether it is sweet or salty. *I like the taste of wine.* [3] VERB If food or drink **tastes** of something, it has that particular flavour. *I drank a cup of tea that tasted of diesel... The pizza tastes delicious.* [4] VERB & N-SING If you **taste** some food or drink, or if you have a **taste** of it, you try a small amount of it in order to see what its flavour and texture is like. [5] VERB If you can **taste** something that you are eating or drinking, you are aware of its flavour. *You can taste the chilli in the dish.* [6] VERB & N-SING If you **taste** something such as a way of life or a pleasure, or if you have a **taste** of it, you experience it for a short period of time. [7] N-SING If you have a **taste for** something, you enjoy it. *That gave me a taste for reading.* [8] N-U & N-PL A person's **taste** is their choice in the things that they like or buy, for example their clothes, possessions, or favourite music. *There was music for all ages and all tastes.* [9] PHRASE If you say that something that is said or done is **in bad taste** or **in poor taste**, you mean that it is offensive, often because it concerns death or sex and is inappropriate for the situation.

tasteful /ˈteɪstfʊl/. ADJ If you describe something as **tasteful**, you mean that it is attractive and elegant. ...*a tasteful linen suit.* ♦**tastefully** ADV ...*a large and tastefully decorated home.*

tasteless /ˈteɪstləs/. [1] ADJ If you describe something as **tasteless**, you mean that it is vulgar and unattractive. [2] ADJ If you describe something such as a remark or joke as **tasteless**, you mean that it is offensive. [3] ADJ If you describe food or drink as **tasteless**, you mean that it has very little or no flavour.

tasty /ˈteɪsti/ **tastier, tastiest.** ADJ If you say that food, especially savoury food, is **tasty**, you mean that it has a pleasant and fairly strong flavour which makes it good to eat.

tattered /ˈtætəd/. ADJ If something such as clothing is **tattered**, it is torn or crumpled, especially because it is old and has been used a lot.

tatters /ˈtætəz/. [1] N-PL Clothes that are in **tatters** are badly torn in several places. [2] N-PL If you say that something such as a plan or relationship is in **tatters**, you are emphasizing that it is weak and has suffered a lot of damage.

tattoo /tæˈtuː/ **tattoos, tattooing, tattooed.** [1] N-C A **tattoo** is a design on someone's skin, made by pricking little holes and filling them with coloured dye. [2] VERB If someone **tattoos** you, they draw a design on your skin by pricking little holes and filling them with coloured dye. *He had the words 'Angie loves Ian' tattooed on his left shin.*

taught /tɔːt/. **Taught** is the past tense and past participle of **teach**.

taunt /tɔːnt/ **taunts, taunting, taunted.** [1] VERB If someone **taunts** you, they try to upset or annoy you by saying unkind or insulting things to you, especially about your weaknesses or failures. [2] N-C A **taunt** is an unkind or insulting comment that is intended to upset or annoy you. ...*racist taunts.*

taut /tɔːt/ **tauter, tautest.** ADJ Something that is **taut** is stretched very tight.

tax /tæks/ **taxes, taxing, taxed.** [1] N-VAR **Tax** is an amount of money that you have to pay to the government so that it can pay for public services. ...*the basic rate of income tax.* [2] VERB When a person or company **is taxed**, they have to pay a part of their income or profits to the government. When goods **are taxed**, a percentage of their price has to be paid to the government. *Biscuits and ice cream are taxed at 11 percent.* [3] VERB If something **taxes** your strength, your patience, or your resources, it uses nearly all of them, so that you have great difficulty in carrying out what you are trying to do. [4] See also **taxing**.

taxable /ˈtæksəbl/. ADJ **Taxable** income is income on which you have to pay tax.

taxation /tækˈseɪʃən/. [1] N-U **Taxation** is the system by which a government takes money from people so that it can use it to pay for public services. [2] N-U **Taxation** is the amount of money that people have to pay in taxes. *The result will be higher taxation.*

,tax-'free. ADJ **Tax-free** is used to describe income on which you do not have to pay tax. ...*a tax-free savings plan.*

taxi /ˈtæksi/ **taxis, taxiing, taxied.** [1] N-C A **taxi** is a car driven by a person whose job is to take people where they want to go in return for money. [2] VERB When an aircraft **taxis** along the ground, it moves slowly along it before taking off or after landing.

taxing /ˈtæksɪŋ/. ADJ A **taxing** task or problem requires a lot of mental or physical effort.

taxpayer /ˈtækspeɪə/ **taxpayers.** N-C **Taxpayers** are people who pay a percentage of their income to the government as tax.

TB /ˌtiː ˈbiː/. **TB** is a very serious infectious disease that affects someone's lungs and other parts of their body. **TB** is an abbreviation for **tuberculosis**.

tea /tiː/ **teas.** [1] N-VAR **Tea** is a drink made by pouring boiling water on the chopped dried leaves of a plant called the tea bush. A cup of tea can be referred to as a **tea**. *Would you like a cup of tea?* [2] N-VAR **Tea** is the chopped dried leaves that you use to make tea. ...*a packet of tea.* [3] N-VAR Drinks such as mint **tea** are made by pouring boiling water on the dried leaves of the particular plant or flower. ...*herbal teas.* [4] N-VAR **Tea** is a meal some people eat in the late afternoon, especially in Britain. It consists of food such as sandwiches and cakes, with tea to drink. [5] N-VAR Some people refer to the main meal that they eat in the early part of the evening as **tea**; BRITISH. [6] See also **meal**.

teach /tiːtʃ/ **teaches, teaching, taught.** [1] VERB If you **teach** someone something, you give them instructions so that they know about it or know how to do it. *George had taught him how to ride a horse... She taught Julie to read.* [2] VERB To **teach** someone something means to show them how to think, feel, or act in a new or different way. *We have to teach drivers to respect pedestrians and cyclists.* [3] VERB If you **teach**, your job is to help students to learn about a subject by explaining it or showing them how to do it. *Ingrid is currently teaching Mathematics at Shimla Public School.* ♦**teacher, teachers** N-C ...*her chemistry teacher.* ♦**teaching** N-U ...*the teaching of English in schools.* [4] to **teach someone a lesson**: see **lesson**.

teaching /ˈtiːtʃɪŋ/ **teachings.** N-C The **teachings** of a particular person, school of thought, or religion are all the ideas and principles that they teach.

teak /tiːk/. N-U **Teak** is a very hard wood.

team /tiːm/ **teams, teaming, teamed.** [1] N-C A **team** is a group of people who play together against another group in a sport or game. **Team** can take the singular or plural form of the verb. *The team is close to bottom of the League.* [2] N-C You can refer to any group of people who work together as a **team**. **Team** can take the singular or plural form of the verb. ...*a team of doctors.*

▶ **team up** PHR-VERB If you **team up** with someone, you join them in order to work together for a particular purpose. *A friend suggested that we team up for a working holiday in Europe.*

'**team-mate, team-mates.** N-C In a game or sport, your **team-mates** are the other members of your team.

teamwork /'ti:mwɜːk/. N-U **Teamwork** is the ability a group of people have to work well together.

teapot /'ti:pɒt/ **teapots.** N-C A **teapot** is a container with a lid, a handle, and a spout, used for making and serving tea.

tear 1 crying

tear /tɪə/ **tears.** ① N-C **Tears** are the drops of liquid that come out of your eyes when you are crying. ② N-PL You can use **tears** in expressions such as **in tears**, **burst into tears**, and **close to tears** to indicate that someone is crying or is almost crying. *He was in floods of tears.*

tear 2 damaging or moving

tear /teə/ **tears, tearing, tore, torn.** ① VERB & N-C If you **tear** something such as paper or cloth, you pull it into two pieces or you pull it so that a hole appears in it. A **tear** in something is a hole that has been made in it. *Mary Ann tore the edge off her napkin... He took a small notebook from his jacket pocket and tore out a page... Nancy quickly tore open the envelope... I peered through a tear in the van's curtains.* ② VERB To **tear** something from somewhere means to remove it violently. *She tore the windscreen wipers from his car.* ③ VERB If you **tear** somewhere, you move there very quickly, often in an uncontrolled or dangerous way. *The door flew open and Miranda tore into the room.* ④ See also **wear and tear**.

▶ **tear apart.** PHR-VERB If something **tears** people **apart**, it causes them to quarrel or to leave each other. *The quarrel tore the party apart.*

▶ **tear away.** PHR-VERB If you **tear** someone **away** from a place or activity, you force them to leave the place or stop doing the activity, even though they want to remain there or carry on. *She couldn't tear herself away from the radio.*

▶ **tear down.** PHR-VERB If you **tear** something **down**, you destroy it or remove it completely. *They tore the school down some years later.*

▶ **tear off.** PHR-VERB If you **tear off** your clothes, you take them off quickly in a rough way.

▶ **tear up.** PHR-VERB If you **tear up** a piece of paper, you tear it into a lot of small pieces. *Don't you dare tear up her ticket. ...a torn up old photograph.*

tearful /'tɪəfʊl/. ADJ If someone is **tearful**, their face or voice shows signs that they have been crying or that they want to cry.

tear gas /'tɪə gæs/. N-U **Tear gas** is a gas that causes your eyes to sting and fill with tears. It is used by the police to control violent crowds.

tease /tiːz/ **teases, teasing, teased.** VERB To **tease** someone means to laugh at them or make jokes about them in order to embarrass, annoy, or upset them. *'You must be expecting a young man,' she teased.*

teaspoon /'tiːspuːn/ **teaspoons.** ① N-C A **teaspoon** is a small spoon that you use to put sugar into tea or coffee. *He wants three teaspoons of sugar in his coffee.* ② N-C A **teaspoon** of food or liquid is the amount that a teaspoon will hold.

technical /'teknɪkəl/. ① ADJ **Technical** means involving the sorts of machines, processes, and materials used in industry, transport, and communications. *A number of technical problems will have to be solved. ...jobs that require technical knowledge.* ② ADJ You use **technical** to describe the practical skills and methods used to do an activity such as an art, a craft, or a sport. *Their technical ability is exceptional.* ♦ **technically** ADV *While Sade's voice isn't technically brilliant it has a quality which is unmistakable.* ③ ADJ **Technical** language involves using special words to describe the details of a specialized activity. *...a technical term.*

technicality /ˌteknɪ'kælɪti/ **technicalities.** ① N-PL The **technicalities** of a process or activity are the detailed methods used to do it. *...the technicalities of classroom teaching.* ② N-C A **technicality** is a point based on a strict interpretation of a law or a set of rules. *The earlier verdict was overturned on a legal technicality.*

technically /'teknɪkli/. ADV If something is **technically** true or possible, it is true or possible according to a strict interpretation of the facts, laws, or rules, but may not be important or relevant in a particular situation. *Technically, the two sides have been in a state of war ever since 1949.*

technician /tek'nɪʃən/ **technicians.** N-C A **technician** is someone whose job involves skilled practical work with scientific equipment, for example in a laboratory.

technique /tek'niːk/ **techniques.** ① N-C A **technique** is a particular method of doing an activity, usually a method that involves practical skills. *...the techniques of modern agriculture.* ② N-U **Technique** is skill and ability in an artistic, sporting, or other practical activity that is developed through training and practice. *...the band's lack of technique.*

technology /tek'nɒlədʒi/ **technologies.** N-VAR **Technology** refers to things which are the result of scientific knowledge being used for practical purposes. *...the rapid development of technology. ...the moral issues posed by new technologies.* ♦ **technological** /ˌteknə'lɒdʒɪkəl/ ADJ BEFORE N *...an era of very rapid technological change.* ♦ **technologically** /ˌteknə'lɒdʒɪkli/ ADV *...technologically advanced aircraft.*

teddy /'tedi/ **teddies.** N-C A **teddy** or a **teddy bear** is a soft toy that looks like a bear.

tedious /'tiːdiəs/. ADJ If you describe something such as a job or a situation as **tedious**, you mean it is boring and frustrating. ♦ **tediously** ADV *These introductory chapters are tediously repetitive.*

teem /tiːm/ **teems, teeming, teemed.** VERB If a place **is teeming** with people, there are a lot of people moving around in it. *The area is teeming with tourists. ...the teeming streets of Calcutta.*

teen /tiːn/ **teens.** ① N-PL If you are in your **teens**, you are between thirteen and nineteen years old. *I first met John in my late teens.* ② ADJ BEFORE N **Teen** is used to describe films, magazines, music, or activities that are aimed at or done by teenagers. *...a teen movie.*

teenage /'tiːneɪdʒ/. ADJ BEFORE N **Teenage** children are aged between thirteen and nineteen years old. *Almost one in four teenage girls now smoke. ...'Smash Hits', a teenage magazine.*

teenager /ˈtiːneɪdʒə/ **teenagers.** N-C A **teenager** is someone between thirteen and nineteen years of age.

teeter /ˈtiːtə/ **teeters, teetering, teetered.** [1] VERB **Teeter** is used in expressions such as **teeter on the brink** to emphasize that something seems to be in a very unstable situation or position. *His voice teetered on the edge of hysteria.* [2] VERB If someone or something **teeters**, they shake in an unsteady way, and seem to be about to lose their balance and fall over. *He watched the cup teeter on the edge before it fell.*

teeth /tiːθ/. **Teeth** is the plural of **tooth**.

TEFL /ˈtefəl/. N-U **TEFL** is the teaching of English to people whose first language is not English, especially people from a country where English is not spoken. **TEFL** is an abbreviation for 'teaching English as a foreign language'.

telecommunications /ˌtelɪkəmjuːnɪˈkeɪʃənz/. N-U **Telecommunications** is the technology of sending signals and messages over long distances using electronic equipment, for example by radio and telephone.

telepathy /tɪˈlepəθi/. N-U **Telepathy** is the direct communication of thoughts and feelings between people's minds, without the need to use speech or writing. ◆**telepathic** /ˌtelɪˈpæθɪk/ ADJ *They had a telepathic understanding.*

telephone /ˈtelɪfəʊn/ **telephones, telephoning, telephoned.** [1] N-U The **telephone** is an electrical system used to talk to someone in another place by dialling a number on a piece of equipment and speaking into it. *He made a telephone call to his wife.* [2] N-C A **telephone** is the piece of equipment used to talk to someone by telephone. *He got up and answered the telephone.* [3] VERB If you **telephone** someone, you dial their telephone number and speak to them by telephone. *They usually telephone first to see if she is at home.*

PHRASES ● If you are **on the telephone**, you are speaking to someone by telephone. *Linda remained on the telephone to the police for three hours.* ● If someone is **on the telephone**, they have a telephone in their house or office which is connected to the rest of the telephone system. *He's not on the telephone.*

'telephone box, telephone boxes. N-C In British English, a **telephone box** is a small shelter in the street in which there is a public telephone. The American term is **phone booth**.

telescope /ˈtelɪskəʊp/ **telescopes.** N-C A **telescope** is an instrument shaped like a tube. It has lenses inside it that make distant things seem larger and nearer when you look through it.

televise /ˈtelɪvaɪz/ **televises, televising, televised.** VERB If an event **is televised**, it is filmed and shown on television.

television /ˈtelɪvɪʒən, -ˈvɪʒ-/ **televisions.** [1] N-C A **television** or a **television set** is a piece of electrical equipment consisting of a box with a glass screen on which you can watch programmes with pictures and sounds. [2] N-U **Television** is the system of sending pictures and sounds by electrical signals over a distance so that people can receive them on a television set. *Toy manufacturers began promoting some of their products on television.*

tell /tel/ **tells, telling, told.** [1] VERB If you **tell** someone something, you give them information. *They told us the dreadful news... John just told me that your birthday is on the same day as mine... I had told people what he had been doing.* [2] VERB If you **tell** someone to do something, you order, instruct, or advise them to do it. *A passer-by told the driver to move his car.* [3] VERB If facts or events **tell** you something, they reveal certain information to you through ways other than speech. *The facts tell us that this is not true... The photographs tell a different story.* [4] VERB If you can **tell** what is happening or what is true, you are able to judge correctly what is happening or what is true. *You never can tell what life is going to bring you... You can tell he's joking.* [5] VERB If an unpleasant or tiring experience begins to **tell**, it begins to have a serious effect. *The strains of office are beginning to tell on the prime minister.* [6] See note at **say**.

▶ **tell apart.** PHR-VERB If you cannot **tell** people or things **apart**, you are not able to recognize the differences between them and cannot therefore identify them individually. *I can still only tell Mark and Dave apart by the colour of their shoes!*

▶ **tell off.** PHR-VERB If you **tell** someone **off**, you speak to them angrily or seriously because they have done something wrong. *I'm always being told off for being so awkward.*

telling /ˈtelɪŋ/. [1] ADJ If something is **telling**, it shows the true nature of a person or situation. *How a man shaves may be a telling clue to his age.* ◆**tellingly** ADV *Tellingly, fewer than 1.1 percent of people living there have university qualifications.* [2] PHRASE You use **there's no telling** to introduce a statement when you want to say that it is impossible to know what will happen in a situation. *There's no telling how long the talks could drag on.*

telly /ˈteli/ **tellies.** N-VAR **Telly** means the same as television; INFORMAL, BRITISH. *I've seen him on the telly.*

temper /ˈtempə/ **tempers, tempering, tempered.** [1] N-VAR If you say that someone has a **temper**, you mean that they become angry very easily. *I hope he can control his temper.* [2] PHRASE If you **lose your temper**, you become very angry. [3] N-VAR If someone is **in** a particular type of **temper**, that is the way they are feeling. *Lee stormed off the field in a furious temper.* [4] VERB To **temper** something means to make it less extreme; FORMAL. *He had to learn to temper his enthusiasm.*

temperament /ˈtemprəmənt/ **temperaments.** N-VAR Your **temperament** is your basic nature, especially as it is shown in the way that you react to situations or to people. *His impulsive temperament regularly got him into difficulties.*

temperamental /ˌtemprəˈmentəl/. [1] ADJ If you say that someone is **temperamental**, you are criticizing them for having moods that change often and suddenly. *...a man given to temperamental outbursts.* [2] ADJ If you describe something such as a machine or car as **temperamental**, you mean that it often does not work properly. *Old cars can be temperamental.*

temperate /'temprət/. ADJ A **temperate** climate or place is one that is never extremely hot or extremely cold.

temperature /'temprətʃə/ **temperatures.** [1] N-VAR The **temperature** of something is how hot or cold it is. *Winter closes in and the temperature drops below freezing.* [2] N-C Your **temperature** is the temperature of your body. *His temperature continued to rise.*

PHRASES ● If someone **takes** your **temperature**, they use a thermometer to measure your temperature. ● If you **have a temperature**, your temperature is higher than it usually is and you feel ill.

In Britain, two different scales are commonly used for measuring temperature. On the **Celsius** (formerly **Centigrade**) scale, water freezes at zero degrees and boils at 100 degrees. On the **Fahrenheit** scale, water freezes at 32 degrees and boils at 212 degrees. Celsius is the scale which is officially used for talking about the weather. Fahrenheit is considered more old-fashioned, but is still widely used. If you want to emphasize how cold it is, you are more likely to use Celsius, as the numbers are lower. Conversely, if you want to emphasize how warm it is, you are more likely to use Fahrenheit. The first of the following examples shows a temperature in Celsius and the second shows a temperature in Fahrenheit. *The temperature has been down to minus seven... With temperatures in the 70s, sun lovers have been flocking to resorts.* In the United States, the Fahrenheit scale is almost always used.

---

template /'templeɪt, AM -plɪt/ **templates.** N-C A **template** is a thin piece of metal or plastic which is cut into a particular shape. It is used to help you cut wood, paper, metal, or other materials accurately, or to reproduce the same shape many times.

temple /'tempəl/ **temples.** [1] N-C A **temple** is a building used for the worship of a god or gods, especially in the Buddhist and Hindu religions. [2] N-C Your **temples** are the flat parts on each side of the front part of your head, near your forehead.

tempo /'tempəʊ/ **tempos.** [1] N-SING The **tempo** of an event is the speed at which it happens. *He was dissatisfied with the tempo of political change.* [2] N-VAR The **tempo** of a piece of music is the speed at which it is played.

temporal /'tempərəl/. ADJ BEFORE N **Temporal** powers or matters relate to ordinary institutions and activities rather than to religious or spiritual ones; FORMAL. *...the spiritual and temporal leader of the Tibetan people.*

temporary /'tempərəri, AM -reri/. ADJ Something that is **temporary** lasts for only a limited time. *His job here is only temporary. ...a temporary loss of memory.* ♦**temporarily** ADV *Check-*

---

points between the two zones were temporarily closed.

tempt /tempt/ **tempts, tempting, tempted.** VERB Something that **tempts** you attracts you and makes you want it, even though it may be wrong or harmful. *Children not attending schools may be tempted into crime... Don't let credit tempt you to buy something you can't afford.* ♦**tempting** ADJ *...Raoul's tempting offer of the Palm Beach trip.*

temptation /temp'teɪʃən/ **temptations.** N-VAR **Temptation** is the state you are in when you want to do or have something, although you know it might be wrong or harmful. *Will they be able to resist the temptation to buy?*

tempted /'temptɪd/. ADJ AFTER LINK-V If you say that you are **tempted** to do something, you mean that you would like to do it. *I'm very tempted to sell my house.*

ten /ten/ **tens.** NUM **Ten** is the number 10.

tenacious /tɪ'neɪʃəs/. ADJ A **tenacious** person is very determined and does not give up easily. *...a tenacious and persistent interviewer.* ♦**tenaciously** ADV *In spite of his illness, he clung tenaciously to his job.*

tenacity /tɪ'næsɪti/. N-U If you have **tenacity**, you are very determined and do not give up easily. *Hard work and sheer tenacity are all crucial to career success.*

tenancy /'tenənsi/ **tenancies.** N-VAR **Tenancy** is the use that you have of land or property belonging to someone else, for which you pay rent. *His father took over the tenancy of the farm.*

tenant /'tenənt/ **tenants.** N-C A **tenant** is someone who pays rent for the place they live in, or for land or buildings that they use.

tend /tend/ **tends, tending, tended.** [1] VERB If something **tends** to happen, it usually happens or it happens often. *I tend to forget things.* [2] VERB If someone or something **tends** towards a particular characteristic, they often display that characteristic. *...the local cuisine which tends towards boiled meat dishes.* [3] VERB If you **tend** someone or something, or **tend to** them, you do what is necessary to keep them in a good condition; FORMAL. *He tends the flower beds and evergreens.*

tendency /'tendənsi/ **tendencies.** N-C A **tendency** is a worrying or unpleasant habit or action that keeps occurring. *Her suicidal tendencies continued... Shetland jumpers have a tendency to be annoyingly itchy.*

tender /'tendə/ **tenders, tendering, tendered.** [1] ADJ A **tender** person expresses gentle and caring feelings. ♦**tenderly** ADV *Mr. White tenderly embraced his wife.* ♦**tenderness** N-U *She smiled, politely rather than with tenderness.* [2] ADJ BEFORE N If someone is at a **tender** age, they are young and inexperienced. [3] ADJ Meat or other food that is **tender** is easy to cut or chew. [4] ADJ If a part of your body is **tender**, it is sensitive and painful when it is touched. [5] VERB & N-VAR If a company **tenders for** something, or if they put in a **tender** for it, it makes a formal offer to supply goods or do a job for a particular price. [6] VERB If you **tender** something such as a suggestion or money, you formally offer or present it; FORMAL. *She quickly tendered her resignation.*

tendon /ˈtendən/ **tendons.** N-C A **tendon** is a strong cord of tissue in your body joining a muscle to a bone.

tenement /ˈtenəmənt/ **tenements.** N-C A **tenement** is a large old terraced building divided into a lot of flats, also called **tenements.**

tenet /ˈtenɪt/ **tenets.** N-C The **tenets** of a theory or belief are the principles on which it is based; FORMAL. *Non-violence and patience are the central tenets of their faith.*

tennis /ˈtenɪs/. N-U **Tennis** is a game played by two or four players on a rectangular court with a net across the middle. The players use rackets to hit a ball over the net.

tenor /ˈtenə/ **tenors.** [1] N-C A **tenor** is a male singer with a fairly high voice. [2] ADJ A **tenor** musical instrument has a range of notes of fairly low pitch. [3] N-SING The **tenor** of something is the general meaning or mood that it expresses; FORMAL. *The whole tenor of discussions has changed.*

tense /tens/ **tenses, tensing, tensed.** [1] ADJ If you are **tense**, you are worried and nervous, and cannot relax. *Never had she seen him so tense.* [2] ADJ If your body is **tense**, your muscles are tight and not relaxed. [3] VERB & PHR-VERB If your muscles **tense**, or if they **tense up**, your muscles become tight and stiff, often because you are anxious or frightened. *Jane tensed her muscles to stop them from shaking.* [4] N-VAR The **tense** of a verb is the form which shows whether you are referring to past, present, or future time.

tension /ˈtenʃən/ **tensions.** [1] N-VAR **Tension** is a feeling of fear or nervousness produced before a difficult, dangerous, or important event. *The tension between the two countries is likely to remain.* [2] N-U **Tension** is a feeling of worry and nervousness which makes it difficult for you to relax. *Laughing has actually been shown to relieve tension.* [3] N-U The **tension** in a rope or wire is how tightly it is stretched.

tent /tent/ **tents.** N-C A **tent** is a shelter made of canvas or nylon and held up by poles and ropes, used mainly by people who are camping.

tentacle /ˈtentəkəl/ **tentacles.** N-C The **tentacles** of an animal such as an octopus are the long thin parts used for feeling, holding things, and moving.

tentative /ˈtentətɪv/. [1] ADJ **Tentative** agreements or plans are not definite or certain, but have been made as a first step. *...a tentative agreement to hold a preparatory conference.* [2] ADJ If someone is **tentative**, they are cautious and not very confident because they are uncertain or afraid. *She did not return his tentative smile.* ♦ **tentatively** ADV *I tentatively suggested an alternative route.*

tenth /tenθ/. ORD The **tenth** item in a series is the one that you count as number ten.

tenuous /ˈtenjʊəs/. ADJ If you describe something such as a connection, a reason, or someone's position as **tenuous**, you mean that it is very uncertain or weak. *This decision puts the President in a somewhat tenuous position.*

tenure /ˈtenjə/. [1] N-U **Tenure** is the legal right to live in a place or to use land or buildings for a period of time. [2] N-U **Tenure** is the period of time during which someone holds an important job. *...during his tenure as foreign minister.*

tepid /ˈtepɪd/. [1] ADJ A **tepid** liquid is slightly warm. [2] ADJ If you describe a feeling or reaction as **tepid**, you mean that it lacks enthusiasm or liveliness. *...their tepid applause.*

term /tɜːm/ **terms, terming, termed.** [1] PHRASE If you talk about something **in** particular **terms**, or **in terms of** a particular thing, you are specifying which aspect of it you are discussing. *The video explains in simple terms how the new tax works... Our goods compete in terms of product quality.* [2] N-C A **term** is a word or expression with a specific meaning. *Myocardial infarction is the medical term for a heart attack.* [3] VERB If you say that something **is termed** a particular thing, you mean that that is what people call it or that is their opinion of it. *He termed the war a humanitarian nightmare.* [4] N-VAR A **term** is one of the periods of time that a school, college, or university year is divided into. *...the last day of term.* [5] N-C A **term** is a period of time that someone spends doing a particular job or in a particular place. *Felipe Gonzalez won a fourth term of office. ...a seven-year prison term.* [6] N-PL The **terms** of an agreement or arrangement are the conditions that have been accepted by the people involved in it.

PHRASES ● If you **come to terms with** something difficult or unpleasant, you learn to accept it. *It was hard to come to terms with her death.* ● If two people are treated **on equal terms** or **on the same terms**, neither of them has an advantage over the other. ● If two people are **on good terms** or **on friendly terms**, they are friendly with each other. ● You use the expressions **in the long term**, **in the short term**, and **in the medium term** to talk about what will happen over that period of time. *In the long term the company hopes to open in Moscow.* ● If you say you are **thinking in terms of** doing something or **talking in terms of** doing it, you mean that you are considering it. *United should be thinking in terms of winning the European Cup.* ● **a contradiction in terms:** see **contradiction.** ● **in real terms:** see **real.** ● **in no uncertain terms:** see **uncertain.**

terminal /ˈtɜːmɪnəl/ **terminals.** [1] ADJ A **terminal** illness or disease cannot be cured and eventually causes death. ♦ **terminally** ADV *The patient is terminally ill.* [2] N-C A **terminal** is a place where vehicles, passengers, or goods begin or end a journey. [3] N-C A computer **terminal** is a piece of equipment consisting of a keyboard and a screen connected to a computer.

terminate /ˈtɜːmɪneɪt/ **terminates, terminating, terminated.** [1] VERB When something **terminates**, or when you **terminate** it, it ends completely; FORMAL. *His contract terminates at the season's end.* ♦ **termination** N-U *...the abrupt termination of trade.* [2] VERB When a train or bus **terminates** somewhere, it ends its journey there.

terminology /ˌtɜːmɪˈnɒlədʒi/ **terminologies.**
N-VAR The **terminology** of a subject is the set of
special words and expressions used in connection with it. ...*football terminology.*

termite /ˈtɜːmaɪt/ **termites.** N-C **Termites** are
small white insects that eat wood.

terrace /ˈterɪs/ **terraces.** [1] N-C A **terrace** is a
row of similar houses joined together by their
side walls; BRITISH. [2] N-C A **terrace** is a flat area
of stone or grass next to a building where people can sit. ...*a garden terrace.* [3] N-C **Terraces**
are a series of flat areas of ground built like
steps on a hillside so that crops can be grown
there.

,**terraced 'house, terraced houses.** ADJ A
terraced house or a **terrace house** is one of a
row of similar houses joined together by their
side walls; BRITISH.

terracotta /ˌterəˈkɒtə/. N-U **Terracotta** is a
brownish-red clay that has been baked but not
glazed and that is used for making things such
as flower pots and tiles.

terrain /təˈreɪn/. N-U The **terrain** in an area is
the type of land that is there. ...*a rugged mountainous terrain.*

terrible /ˈterɪbl/. [1] ADJ **Terrible** means extremely bad. *Her French is terrible.* ♦**terribly**
ADV *My son has suffered terribly.* [2] ADJ BEFORE N
You use **terrible** to emphasize the great extent
or degree of something. *Her death is a terrible
waste.* ♦**terribly** ADV *I'm terribly sorry to bother
you.*

terrific /təˈrɪfɪk/. [1] ADJ If you describe something or someone as **terrific**, you are very
pleased with them or very impressed by them;
INFORMAL. *You look terrific, Ann.* [2] ADJ BEFORE N
Terrific means very great in amount, degree,
or intensity. *There was a terrific bang.*

terrify /ˈterɪfaɪ/ **terrifies, terrifying, terrified.**
VERB If something **terrifies** you, it makes you
feel extremely frightened. *The idea of death
terrified me.* ♦**terrified** ADJ *He was terrified of
heights.*

terrifying /ˈterɪfaɪɪŋ/. ADJ If something is **terrifying**, it makes you very frightened. *Crime is
increasing at a terrifying rate.*

territorial /ˌterɪˈtɔːriəl/. ADJ **Territorial** means
concerned with the ownership of a particular
area of land or water. *Argentina feel very
strongly about their territorial claims to Antarctica.*

territory /ˈterɪtri, AM -tɔːri/ **territories.** [1] N-VAR
Territory is land which is controlled by a particular country or ruler. *The government denies
that any of its territory is under rebel control.*
[2] N-U You can use **territory** to refer to an area
of knowledge or experience. ...*on their own familiar territory of trade.* [3] N-U **Territory** is
land with a particular character. ...*mountainous territory.*

terror /ˈterə/ **terrors.** [1] N-VAR **Terror** is very
great fear. *I shook with terror... He had a real
terror of facing people.* [2] **reign of terror**: see
reign.

terrorist /ˈterərɪst/ **terrorists.** N-C A **terrorist** is
a person who uses violence in order to achieve
political aims. ...*terrorist attacks.* ♦**terrorism**
N-U ...*indiscriminate acts of terrorism.*

terrorize (BR also **terrorise**) /ˈterəraɪz/ **terrorizes, terrorizing, terrorized.** VERB If someone **terrorizes** you, they frighten you by making it seem likely that they will attack you.
...*pensioners terrorised by anonymous telephone calls.*

terse /tɜːs/. ADJ A **terse** comment or statement
is brief and unfriendly. ♦**tersely** ADV *'It's too
late,' he said tersely.*

tertiary /ˈtɜːʃəri, AM -ʃieri/. ADJ BEFORE N **Tertiary**
education is education at university or college
level.

test /test/ **tests, testing, tested.** [1] VERB & N-C
When you **test** something, or when you conduct a **test** on it, you try using it in order to
find out what it is, what condition it is in, or
how well it works. ...*travelling to Holland to
test a British-built boat.* ...*the banning of nuclear tests.* [2] VERB & N-C If you **test** someone, or
if you give them a **test**, you ask them questions
to find out how much they know about something. ...*an arithmetic test.* [3] N-C If an event or
situation is a **test** of a person or thing, it reveals their qualities or effectiveness. *The test of
any civilised society is how it treats its minorities.* [4] VERB If you **are tested** for a particular
disease or medical condition, you are examined in order to find out whether you have that
disease or condition. *My doctor wants me to be
tested for diabetes.* [5] N-C A medical **test** is an
examination of your body in order to check
that you are healthy. [6] PHRASE If you **put**
something **to the test**, you find out how useful
or effective it is by using it. *Ramsay's comic
skills were first put to the test on the big screen.*

testament /ˈtestəmənt/ **testaments.** N-VAR If
one thing is a **testament** to another thing, it
shows that the other thing exists or is true; FOR-
MAL. *That he has recovered so swiftly is a testament to his will power.*

,**test 'case, test cases.** N-C A **test case** is a legal case which becomes an example for deciding other similar cases.

testicle /ˈtestɪkl/ **testicles.** N-C A man's **testicles** are the two sex glands that produce
sperm.

testify /ˈtestɪfaɪ/ **testifies, testifying, testi-
fied.** [1] VERB When someone **testifies** in a
court of law, they give a statement of what
they saw someone do or what they know of a
situation, after having promised to tell the
truth. [2] VERB If one thing **testifies** to another,
it supports the belief that the second thing is
true; FORMAL. *Crumbling mansions and cathedrals testify to every stage of the city's long
history.*

testimonial /ˌtestɪˈməʊniəl/ **testimonials.** N-C
A **testimonial** is a written statement about a
person's character and abilities, often written
by their employer.

testimony /ˈtestɪməni, AM -məʊni/ **testimo-
nies.** [1] N-VAR In a court of law, someone's **testimony** is a formal statement that they make
about what they saw someone do or what they
know of a situation, after having promised to
tell the truth. [2] N-U If one thing is **testimony**
to another, it shows that the second thing has
a particular quality. *The environmental move-*

ment is testimony to the widespread feelings of support for nature.

testosterone /tɛˈstɒstərəʊn/. N-U **Testosterone** is a hormone found in higher levels in men than in women.

tether /ˈtɛðə/ **tethers, tethering, tethered.** 1 PHRASE If you are **at the end of** your **tether**, you are so worried or tired because of your problems that you feel you cannot cope. 2 VERB If you **tether** an animal or object to something, you attach it there with a rope or chain.

text /tɛkst/ **texts.** 1 N-VAR **Text** is any written material. *A CD-ROM can store more than 250,000 pages of typed text.* 2 N-C A **text** is a book or other piece of writing, especially one connected with science or education. *His early plays are set texts in universities.*

textbook /ˈtɛkstbʊk/ **textbooks.** N-C A **text-book** is a book about a particular subject that is intended for students.

textile /ˈtɛkstaɪl/ **textiles.** 1 N-C **Textiles** are types of woven cloth. 2 N-PL **Textiles** are the industries concerned with making cloth. *75,000 jobs will be lost in textiles and clothing.*

texture /ˈtɛkstʃə/ **textures.** N-VAR The **texture** of something is the way that it feels when you touch it. *Her skin is pale, the texture of fine wax.*

than /ðən, STRONG ðæn/. PREP & CONJ You use **than** to link two parts of a comparison or contrast. *...a package smaller than a cigarette box... It contains less than 1 per cent fat... He could have helped her more than he did... The arrangement was more a formality than a genuine partnership.* • **less than:** see **less.** • **more than:** see **more.** • **more often than not:** see **often.** • **other than:** see **other.** • **rather than:** see **rather.**

thank /θæŋk/ **thanks, thanking, thanked.** 1 CONVENTION You say **thank you** or, more informally, **thanks** to express your gratitude or acknowledgement when someone does something for you or gives you something. *Thank you very much for your call... Thanks for the information... 'Would you like a cigarette?'—'No thank you.'* 2 VERB & N-PL When you **thank** someone, or when you give them your **thanks,** you express your gratitude to them for something. *I thanked them for their kind and loyal service... They accepted their certificates with words of thanks.* 3 CONVENTION You can use **thank you** to say firmly that you do not want someone's help or to tell them that you do not like the way they are behaving towards you. *I can stir my own tea, thank you.*

PHRASES • You say **'Thank God'**, **'Thank Goodness'**, or **'Thank heavens'** when you are very relieved about something. *Thank heavens we have you here.* • If something happens **thanks to** someone or something, they are responsible for it or caused it to happen. *Thanks to recent research, effective treatments are available.*

thankful /ˈθæŋkfʊl/. ADJ When you are **thankful,** you feel happy and relieved that something has happened. *I'm just thankful that I've got a job.* ◆**thankfully** ADV *Simon thankfully*

slipped off his uniform and relaxed.

thankfully /ˈθæŋkfʊli/. ADV You use **thankfully** to express approval and relief about a statement that you are making. *Thankfully, he had not been injured.*

Thanksgiving /ˌθæŋksˈɡɪvɪŋ/. N-U In the United States, **Thanksgiving** or **Thanksgiving Day** is a public holiday on the fourth Thursday in November.

that 1 demonstrative uses

that /ðæt/. 1 PRON & DET You use **that** to refer back to an idea, situation, or period of time that you have referred to previously. *You particularly wanted to talk to me. Why was that?... 'I've never been to Paris.'—'That's a pity.'... She returned to work later that week.* 2 DET & PRON You use **that** when you are referring to someone or something which is a distance away from you, especially when you indicate or point to them. *You see that man over there?... What's that you're writing?... That looks heavy.* 3 DET If something is not **that** bad, funny, or expensive, for example, it is not as bad, funny, or expensive as it might be or as has been suggested. *Do I look that stupid?*

PHRASES • You use **that is** or **that is to** say to indicate that you are about to explain something more clearly, more specifically, or in more detail. *...random genetic change – that is, mutations.* • You use **that's that** or **that's it** to indicate that there is nothing more to be done or said, or that the end has been reached. *I'm staying here, and that's that... When he left the office, that was it, the workday was over.* • See also **those.** • **this and that:** see **this.**

that 2 conjunction and relative pronoun uses

that /ðət, STRONG ðæt/. 1 CONJ You use **that** after many verbs, nouns, and adjectives to introduce a clause. *He said that he did not want to be seen. ...breaking the news that your marriage is over... It's obvious that you need more time.* 2 PRON You use **that** immediately after a noun to introduce a clause which gives more information about the noun. *...a car that won't start. ...a man that Maddock has known for nearly 20 years.* 3 CONJ You use **that** after expressions with 'so' and 'such' in order to introduce the result or effect of something. *She came towards me so quickly that she knocked a chair over.*

thatched /θætʃt/. ADJ A **thatched** house has a roof made of straw or reeds.

that's /ðæts/. **That's** is a spoken form of 'that is'.

thaw /θɔː/ **thaws, thawing, thawed.** 1 VERB When something frozen **thaws,** or when you **thaw** it, it melts. *It's so cold the snow doesn't get a chance to thaw... Always thaw frozen pastry thoroughly.* 2 N-C A **thaw** is a period of warmer weather when the snow and ice melt. 3 VERB & N-SING If something **thaws** relations between people, or if there is a **thaw** in relations, people become friendly again after a period of tension. *It took up to Christmas for political relations to thaw.*

the; usually pronounced /ðə/ before a consonant and /ði/ before a vowel, but pronounced /ðiː/ when you are emphasizing it. 1 DET **The** is the definite article. You use **the** at the beginning of noun groups to refer to someone or something when they are generally known about or when it is clear which particular person or thing you are referring to. *Amy sat outside in the sun... Who was that on the phone?... I patted him on the head.* **2** DET You can use **the** in front of a singular noun to refer to all people or things of that type. *The computer has made considerable strides in recent years.* **3** DET You use **the** in front of an adjective when you are referring to a particular thing that is described by that adjective. *He's wishing for the impossible.* **4** DET You can use **the** in front of adjectives and plural nouns to refer to all people of a particular type or nationality, or to a couple or family with a particular name. *...care for the elderly... The Germans and the French both have identity-card systems.* **5** DET You use **the** in front of numbers that refer to days and dates. *The meeting should take place on the fifth of May. ...how bad things were in the thirties.* **6** DET You use **the** in front of superlative adjectives and adverbs. *Brisk daily walks are still the best exercise.* **7** DET You use **the** in front of two comparative adjectives or adverbs to describe how one amount or quality changes in relation to another. *The more confidence you build up in yourself, the greater are your chances of success.* **8** DET The is used in rates, prices, and measurements to refer to a single unit, which is related or compared to a number of units of a different kind. *The exchange rate would soon be $2 to the pound.*

theatre (AM **theater**) /ˈθiːətə/ **theatres.** **1** N-C A **theatre** is a building with a stage on which plays and other entertainments are performed. *We went to the theatre.* **2** N-U **Theatre** is entertainment involving the performance of plays. *...theatre for children.* **3** N-C In American English, a **theater** or a **movie theater** is a place where people go to watch films. The British word is **cinema.** **4** N-C In a hospital, a **theatre** is a room where surgeons carry out operations.

theatrical /θiˈætrɪkəl/ **1** ADJ BEFORE N **Theatrical** means relating to the theatre. *...outstanding British theatrical performances.* **2** ADJ **Theatrical** behaviour is deliberately exaggerated and unnatural. *...her big, theatrical gestures.* ♦**theatrically** /θiˈætrɪkli/ ADV *He looked theatrically at his watch.*

theft /θeft/ **thefts.** N-VAR **Theft** is the criminal act of stealing. *...the theft of classified documents from a car.*

their /ðeə/ **1** DET You use **their** to indicate that something belongs or relates to the group of people, animals, or things you are talking about. *Janis and Kurt have announced their engagement... The trees shed their leaves.* **2** DET You use **their** instead of 'his or her' to indicate that something belongs or relates to a person without saying whether that person is a man or a woman. Some people think this use is incorrect. *...anyone looking for an adequate income from their investments.*

theirs /ðeəz/ **1** PRON You use **theirs** to indicate that something belongs or relates to the group of people, animals, or things that you are talking about. *...at the table next to theirs... Theirs*

had been a happy and satisfactory marriage. **2** PRON You use **theirs** instead of 'his or hers' to indicate that something belongs or relates to a person without saying whether that person is a man or a woman. Some people think this use is incorrect. *I don't know whose handkerchief it is. Somebody must have left theirs.*

them /ðəm, STRONG ðem/. **1** PRON **Them** is used as the object of a verb or preposition. You use **them** to refer to a group of people, animals, or things. *The Beatles – I never get tired of listening to them... His dark socks, I could see, had a stripe on them.* **2** PRON You use **them** instead of 'him or her' to refer to a person without saying whether that person is a man or a woman. Some people think this use is incorrect. *It takes great courage to face your child and tell them the truth.*

theme /θiːm/ **themes.** N-C A **theme** in a piece of writing, a discussion, or a work of art is an important idea or subject that runs through it. *The book's central theme is power.*

themselves /ðəmˈselvz/. **1** PRON You use **themselves** to refer to people, animals, or things when the object of a verb or preposition refers to the same people or things as the subject of the verb. *They all seemed to be enjoying themselves... The men talked amongst themselves.* **2** PRON You use **themselves** to emphasize the people or things that you are referring to. **Themselves** is also sometimes used instead of 'them' as the object of a verb or preposition. *The islands themselves are largely uninhabitable. ...men and women who are in the same position as themselves.* **3** PRON You use **themselves** instead of 'himself or herself' to refer back to the person who is the subject of sentence without saying whether it is a man or a woman. Some people think this use is incorrect. *What can a patient with emphysema do to help themselves?*

then /ðen/. **1** ADV **Then** means at a particular time in the past or in the future. *Things were simpler, clearer then... Since then, Knowles has published around 50 titles... I'm coming up on Friday so I can drop it off then.* **2** ADV You use **then** to say that one thing happens after another, or is after another on a list. *He thought a bit and then answered... He'll speak first, then Robert's mother, then me.* **3** ADV You use **then** to introduce a summary or conclusion to what you have just said, or to end a conversation. *By 1931, then, France alone in Europe was a country of massive immigration... He stood up. 'That's settled then.'... Bye bye then.* **4** ADV You use **then** with words like 'now', 'well', and 'okay', to introduce a new topic or a new point of view. *Well then, I'll put the kettle on.* **5** ADV You use **then** to introduce the second part of a sentence which begins with 'if'. The first part of the sentence describes a possible situation, and **then** introduces the result of the situation. *If the answer is 'yes', then we must decide on an appropriate course of action.* **6** ADV You use **then** at the beginning of a sentence or after 'and' or 'but' to introduce a comment or an extra piece of information. *He sounded sincere, but then, he always did.* **7** now and then: see now. ● there and then: see there.

theologian /ˌθiːəˈləʊdʒən/ **theologians.** N-C A **theologian** is someone who studies religion and the nature of God.

theology /θiˈɒlədʒi/. N-U **Theology** is the study of religion and the nature of God. ♦ **theological** /ˌθiːəˈlɒdʒɪkəl/ ADJ ...a theological college.

theoretical /ˌθiːəˈretɪkəl/. ADJ **Theoretical** means based on or using the ideas and abstract principles of a subject, rather than the practical aspects of it. ...a lecturer in theoretical physics.

theoretically /ˌθiːəˈretɪkəli/. ADV You use **theoretically** to say that although something is supposed to be true or to exist in the way stated, it may not in fact be true or exist in that way. Theoretically, the price is supposed to be marked... No one believes it will happen. But it is theoretically possible.

theorize (BR also **theorise**) /ˈθiːəraɪz/ **theorizes, theorizing, theorized.** VERB If you **theorize** that something is true, or if you **theorize** about something, you develop a set of abstract ideas about it in order to explain it. By studying the way people behave, we can theorize about what is going on in their mind. ♦ **theorist, theorists** N-C ...the leading theorist of the French Communist Party.

theory /ˈθiːəri/ **theories.** [1] N-C A **theory** is a formal idea or set of ideas intended to explain something. ...Darwin's theory of evolution. [2] N-C If you have a **theory** about something, you have your own opinion about it which you cannot prove but which you think is true. My theory is that male fashion designers really don't like women. [3] N-U The **theory** of a practical subject or skill is the set of rules and principles that form the basis of it. ...the theory and practice of sustainable agriculture. [4] PHRASE You use **in theory** to say that although something is supposed to be true or to happen in the way stated, it may not in fact be true or happen in that way. In theory I'm on call day and night.

therapeutic /ˌθerəˈpjuːtɪk/. [1] ADJ If something is **therapeutic**, it helps you to feel happier and more relaxed. Day-dreaming is very therapeutic. [2] ADJ **Therapeutic** treatment is designed to treat a disease or to improve a person's health; TECHNICAL. ...therapeutic drugs.

therapist /ˈθerəpɪst/ **therapists.** N-C A **therapist** is a person skilled in a type of therapy.

therapy /ˈθerəpi/. N-U **Therapy** is the treatment of mental or physical illness without the use of drugs or operations. ...group therapy sessions for men who batter their wives.

there. Pronounced /ðə, STRONG ðeə/ for meanings 1 and 2, and /ðeə/ for all other meanings. [1] PRON You use **there** as the subject of the verb 'be' to say that something exists or does not exist, or to draw attention to it. There must be an option other than war... There's no way we can afford to buy a house... There are no cars on some of the islands.

> **There** is normally followed by a plural form of the verb **be** when it is used to introduce a count noun in the plural. There were policemen everywhere.

However, when it introduces a series of nouns in the singular, linked by **and**, a singular form of the verb **be** is normally used. There is a time and a place for everything... There was a street fair and an old-fashioned brass band.

[2] ADV If something is **there**, it exists or is available. The group of old buildings by the main road is still there today... The book is there for people to read. [3] ADV You use **there** to refer to a place that has already been mentioned. Durrell was born in India in 1912; the families of both his parents had lived there for generations. [4] ADV You say **there** to indicate a place that you are pointing to or looking at. The toilets are over there... Where did I put it? – Oh there it is. [5] ADV You use **there** when speaking on the telephone to ask if someone is available to speak to you. Hello, is Gordon there please? [6] ADV You use **there** to refer to a point that someone has made in a conversation. I think you're right there John. [7] ADV You use **there** to refer to a stage that has been reached in an activity or process. We are making further investigations and will take the matter from there. [8] ADV You can use **there** in expressions such as **there you go** or **there we are** when accepting that an unsatisfactory situation cannot be changed; SPOKEN. It's the wages that count. Not over-generous, but there you are. [9] ADV You can use **there** in expressions such as **there you go** and **there we are** when emphasizing that something proves that you were right; SPOKEN. 'There you are, you see!' she exclaimed. 'I knew you'd say that!'

PHRASES ● You use **there again** to introduce an extra piece of information which either contradicts what has been said or gives an alternative to it. You may strike lucky and find a sympathetic and helpful clerk, but, there again, you might not. ● If something happens **there and then** or **then and there**, it happens immediately. ● You say **'there you are'** or **'there you go'** when you are offering something to someone. There you are, Lennie, you take the nice biscuit.

thereafter /ðeərˈɑːftə, -ˈæftə/. ADV **Thereafter** means after the event or date mentioned; FORMAL. In 1954 he met, and shortly thereafter married, Simone Forti.

thereby /ˌðeəˈbaɪ/. ADV You use **thereby** to introduce a result or consequence of the event or action just mentioned; FORMAL. Our bodies can sweat, thereby losing heat by evaporation.

therefore /ˈðeəfɔː/. ADV You use **therefore** to introduce a logical result or conclusion. The process is said to be much quicker and therefore cheaper.

therein /ˌðeərˈɪn/. [1] ADV **Therein** means in the place just mentioned; FORMAL. ...the documents, or the information contained therein. [2] ADV When you say **therein** lies a situation or problem, you mean that an existing situation has caused that situation or problem; FORMAL, DATED. Santa Maria di Castellabate is barely mentioned in guidebooks; therein lies its charm.

thermal /'θɜːməl/. [1] ADJ BEFORE N **Thermal** means relating to heat or caused by heat. ...*thermal power stations*. [2] ADJ BEFORE N **Thermal** clothes are specially designed to keep you warm. ...*thermal underwear*.

thermometer /θə'mɒmɪtə/ **thermometers**. N-C A **thermometer** is an instrument for measuring the temperature of a room or of a person's body.

these /ðiːz/. [1] DET & PRON You use **these** to refer to people or things that have been mentioned. *Switch to an interest-paying current account. Most banks and larger building societies now offer these accounts... Please bring with you any drugs that you are taking. These must be handed to the sister.* [2] DET & PRON You use **these** to introduce people or things that you are going to talk about. *If you're converting your loft, these addresses will be useful... These are some of the things you can do.* [3] DET People use **these** to introduce people or things into a story; INFORMAL, SPOKEN. *I was on my own and these fellows came along.* [4] PRON You use **these** when you are identifying someone or asking about their identity. *These are my children.* [5] DET & PRON You use **these** to refer to people or things that are near you, especially when you touch them or point to them. *These scissors are awfully heavy... These are the only tapes we have.* [6] PHRASE If you say that **these days** something happens, you mean that at the present time it happens, in contrast to in the past. *Living in Bootham these days can be depressing.*

thesis /'θiːsɪs/ **theses** /'θiːsiːz/. [1] N-C A **thesis** is an idea or theory that is expressed as a statement and discussed in a logical way. [2] N-C A **thesis** is a long piece of writing based on your own ideas and research that you do as part of a university degree.

they /ðeɪ/. [1] PRON You use **they** to refer to a group of people, animals, or things. *The two men were far more alike than they would ever admit.* [2] PRON You use **they** instead of 'he' or 'she' to refer to a person without saying whether that person is a man or a woman. Some people think this is incorrect. *The teacher is not responsible for the student's success or failure. They are only there to help the student learn.* [3] PRON You use **they** in expressions such as 'they say' or 'they call it' when you want to refer vaguely to what people in general say, think, or do. *They say there's plenty of opportunities.*

they'd /ðeɪd/. **They'd** is the usual spoken form of 'they had', especially when 'had' is an auxiliary verb. **They'd** is also a spoken form of 'they would'. *They'd both lived in this road all their lives... He agreed that they'd visit her.*

they'll /ðeɪl/. **They'll** is the usual spoken form of 'they will'.

they're /ðeə, ðeɪə/. **They're** is the usual spoken form of 'they are'.

they've /ðeɪv/. **They've** is the usual spoken form of 'they have', especially when 'have' is an auxiliary verb. *They've gone out.*

thick /θɪk/ **thicker, thickest.** [1] ADJ Something that is **thick** has a large distance between its two opposite surfaces. ...*a thick stone wall.*

♦**thickly** ADV *Slice the meat thickly.* [2] ADJ You can use **thick** to talk or ask about how wide or deep something is. *The folder was two inches thick... How thick are these walls? ...a plant with a brown root as thick as a finger.* ♦**thickness, thicknesses** N-VAR *The size of the fish will determine the thickness of the steaks.* [3] ADJ If something that consists of several things is **thick**, it has a large number of them very close together. ...*our father's thick, wavy hair.* ♦**thickly** ADV *The trees grew thickly here by the river.* [4] ADJ **Thick** smoke, fog, or cloud is difficult to see through. [5] ADJ **Thick** liquids are fairly stiff and solid and do not flow easily. *They had to battle through thick mud.* [6] ADJ If you describe someone as **thick**, you think that they are stupid; INFORMAL, BRITISH.

PHRASES ● If things happen **thick and fast**, they happen very quickly and in large numbers. *The rumours have been coming thick and fast.* ● If you are **in the thick of** an activity or situation, you are very involved in it. *The AWPA ran into political trouble and Naomi was in the thick of it.*

thicken /'θɪkən/ **thickens, thickening, thickened.** VERB If something **thickens**, or if you **thicken** it, it becomes thicker. *The crowds around him began to thicken... Thicken the sauce by adding the cream.*

thief /θiːf/ **thieves.** N-C A **thief** is a person who steals something from another person.

thigh /θaɪ/ **thighs.** N-C Your **thighs** are the top parts of your legs, between your knees and your hips.

thin /θɪn/ **thinner, thinnest; thins, thinning, thinned.** [1] ADJ If something is **thin**, there is a small distance between its two opposite surfaces. ...*a thin cable... The material was too thin.* ♦**thinly** ADV *Peel and thinly slice the onion.* [2] ADJ A **thin** person or animal has no extra fat on their body. [3] ADJ **Thin** liquids are weak and watery. [4] VERB & PHR-VERB If something **thins** or **thins out**, it becomes less crowded because people or things have been removed from it. *By midnight the crowd had thinned... As soon as seedlings are large enough to handle, start thinning them out.*

PHRASES ● If you say that people or things are **thin on the ground**, you mean that there are not very many of them and so they are hard to find. *Good managers are often thin on the ground.*

thing /θɪŋ/ **things.** [1] N-C You use **thing** as a substitute for another word when you are unable to be more precise, or you do not need or want to be more precise. *What's that thing in the middle of the fountain?. ...iron and silicon and things like that... Getting drunk is a thing all young men do.* [2] N-SING The word **thing** is often used instead of the pronouns 'anything,' or 'everything' in order to emphasize what you are saying. *Don't you worry about a thing.* [3] N-C A **thing** is a physical object that is considered as having no life of its own. *It's not a thing, Beauchamp. It's a human being!.* [4] N-C You can call a person or an animal a particular **thing** when you are expressing your feelings towards them; INFORMAL. *Oh you lucky thing!* [5] N-PL Your **things** are your clothes or possessions. *Sara told him to take all his things and not to return.* **6** N-PL **Things** can refer to life in general and the way it affects you. *How are things going?*

PHRASES ● If you do something **first thing**, you do it at the beginning of the day, before you do anything else. If you do it **last thing**, you do it at the end of the day. *I always do it last thing on a Saturday.* ● If you **have a thing** about someone or something, you have very strong positive or negative feelings about them; INFORMAL. *He's got this thing about ties.* ● You say **for one thing** when you give only one reason for something, but want to indicate that there are other reasons. *She was unable to sell it, because for one thing its size was awkward.* ● If you **do** your **own thing**, you live or behave in the way you want to, without paying attention to convention or depending on other people. ● You can say **'The thing is'** to introduce an explanation or opinion relating to something that has just been said. *I'm getting a grant for a speech therapy course. But the thing is, I don't know whether I want to do it any more.*

think /θɪŋk/ **thinks, thinking, thought.** **1** VERB If you **think** that something is the case, you have the opinion that it is the case. *I certainly think there should be a ban on tobacco advertising... What do you think of my theory?* ◆**thinking** N-U *...his thinking on welfare provisions.* **2** VERB If you say that you **think** that something is true or will happen, you mean that you have the impression that it is true or will happen, although you are not certain of the facts. *Nora thought he was seventeen years old... The storm is thought to be responsible for as many as four deaths.*

Note that when you are using the verb **think** with a that-clause in order to state a negative opinion or belief, you normally make **think** negative, rather than the verb in the that-clause. For instance, it is more usual to say **'I don't think he saw me'** than 'I think he didn't see me'. The same pattern applies to other verbs with a similar meaning, such as **believe**, **consider**, and **suppose**. *He didn't believe she could do it... I don't consider that you kept your promise... I don't suppose he ever saw it.*

3 VERB If you **think** a lot of someone or something, you admire them. *People at the club think very highly of him.* **4** VERB & N-SING When you **think** about ideas or problems, or when you have a **think** about them, you make a mental effort to consider them or solve them. *She closed her eyes for a moment, trying to think... I'll have a think about that.* ◆**thinking** N-U *...quick thinking.* **5** VERB When you **think** of something, you remember it or it comes into your mind. *Nobody could think of anything to say... I was trying to think what else we had to do.* **6** VERB When you **are thinking** something, you have words or ideas in your mind without saying them out loud. *I remember thinking how lovely he looked.* **7** VERB If

you **are thinking of** doing something, you are considering doing it. *Martin was thinking of taking legal action against Zuckerman.* **8** See also **thought.**

PHRASES ● You can use **'I think'** as a way of being polite when you are explaining or suggesting something, giving your opinion, or responding to an offer. *I think he means 'at' rather than 'to'... 'Would you like to do that another time.'—'Yes I think so.'* ● If you say that someone would **think nothing of** doing something difficult or strange, you mean that they would do it and not think that it was difficult or strange at all. *I thought nothing of betting £1,000 on a horse.*

▶ **think back.** PHR-VERB If you **think back**, you remember things that happened in the past. *I thought back to the time in 1975 when my son was desperately ill.*

▶ **think over.** PHR-VERB If you **think** something **over**, you consider it carefully before making a decision.

▶ **think through.** PHR-VERB If you **think** a problem or situation **through**, you consider it thoroughly. *I didn't think through the consequences of promotion.*

▶ **think up.** PHR-VERB If you **think** something **up**, for example an idea or plan, you invent it using mental effort. *Julian has been thinking up new ways of raising money.*

thinker /ˈθɪŋkə/ **thinkers.** N-C A **thinker** is a person who spends a lot of time thinking deeply about important things, especially a philosopher who is famous for thinking of new ideas.

thinking /ˈθɪŋkɪŋ/. **1** See **think.** **2** See also **wishful thinking.**

third /θɜːd/ **thirds.** **1** ORD The **third** item in a series is the one that you count as number three. **2** N-C A **third** is one of three equal parts of something.

thirdly /ˈθɜːdli/. ADV You use **thirdly** when you are about to mention the third thing in a series of items. *First of all, there are not many of them, and secondly, they have little money and, thirdly, they have few big businesses.*

third 'party, third parties. N-C A **third party** is someone who is not one of the two main people or groups involved in a business or legal matter, but who becomes involved in a minor way.

Third 'World. N PROPER The countries of Africa, Asia, and South America are sometimes referred to as **the Third World.**

thirst /θɜːst/ **thirsts.** **1** N-VAR **Thirst** is the feeling that you need to drink something. *Drink water to quench your thirst.* **2** N-U **Thirst** is the condition of not having enough to drink. *They died of thirst.* **3** N-SING A **thirst** for something is a very strong desire for it. *Children show a real thirst for learning.*

thirsty /ˈθɜːsti/. ADJ If you are **thirsty**, you feel a need to drink something.

thirteen /ˌθɜːˈtiːn/. NUM **Thirteen** is the number 13.

thirteenth /ˌθɜːˈtiːnθ/. ORD The **thirteenth** item in a series is the one that you count as number thirteen.

thirtieth /ˈθɜːtiəθ/. ORD The **thirtieth** item in a series is the one that you count as number thirty.

thirty /ˈθɜːti/ **thirties.** NUM **Thirty** is the number 30. For examples of how numbers such as thirty and eighty are used see **eighty**.

this /ðɪs/. **1** DET & PRON You use **this** to refer to a person or thing that has been mentioned. *President Clinton had long prepared for this challenge... I had been on many film sets, but never one like this.* **2** PRON & DET You use **this** to introduce someone or something that you are going to talk about. *This is what I will do. I will telephone Anna and explain... This report is from our Jerusalem correspondent, Gerald Butt.* **3** PRON & DET You use **this** to refer to a person or thing that is near you now, or to the present time. When there are two or more people or things near you, **this** refers to the nearest one. *Is this what you were looking for?... This is my colleague, Mr Arnold Landon... This place is run like a hotel.* **4** PRON You use **this** when you refer to a situation which is happening or has just happened and which you feel involved in. *Tim, this is awful... Is this what you want to do with the rest of your life?* **5** DET You use **this** to refer to the next occurrence of a particular day, month, season, or festival. *...this Sunday's 7.45 performance... We're getting married this June.* **6** PRON You use **this** in order to say who you are when you are speaking on the telephone, radio, or television. *'Hello, is this Mr Brown?'—'Yeah, who's this?'.* **7** PHRASE You can refer to a variety of things that you are doing or talking about as **this and that** or **this, that and the other**. *'And what are you doing now?'—'Oh, you know, this and that.'*

thorn /θɔːn/ **thorns.** N-C **Thorns** are the sharp points on some plants and trees.

thorny /ˈθɔːni/. **1** ADJ A **thorny** plant or tree is covered with thorns. **2** ADJ A **thorny** problem or question is difficult to deal with.

thorough /ˈθʌrə, AM ˈθɜːrəʊ/. **1** ADJ A **thorough** action is done very carefully and methodically. *We are making a thorough investigation.* ♦**thoroughly** ADV *Food that is being offered hot must be reheated thoroughly.* ♦**thoroughness** N-U *...the fairness and thoroughness of the disciplinary process.* **2** ADJ Someone who is **thorough** does things in a careful and methodical way. ♦**thoroughness** N-U *His thoroughness and attention to detail is legendary.* **3** ADJ You can use **thorough** for emphasis. *The management has got itself into a thorough mess.* ♦**thoroughly** ADV *I thoroughly enjoy your programme.*

those /ðəʊz/. **1** DET & PRON You use **those** to refer to people, things, or situations which have already been mentioned. *Most of those crimes are committed by boys... Waterfalls never fail to attract and those at the Falls of Clyde are no exception.* **2** DET & PRON You use **those** when you are referring to people or things that are a distance away from you in position or time, often when you indicate or point to them. *What are those buildings?... Those are nice shoes.* **3** PRON You use **those** to mean 'people'. *He caused much anguish to those around him.*

though /ðəʊ/. **1** CONJ & ADV You use **though** to introduce a fact or comment which contrasts with something else that is being said, or makes it seem surprising. *Gaelic has been a dying language for many years, though children are nowadays taught it in school... I like him. Though he makes me angry sometimes.* **2** **as though:** see **as**.

thought /θɔːt/ **thoughts.** **1** **Thought** is the past tense and past participle of **think**. **2** N-C A **thought** is an idea or opinion. *The thought of someone suffering through a mistake of mine makes me shiver... ...his thoughts on love and fatherhood.* **3** N-U **Thought** is the activity of thinking, especially deeply, logically, or with concentration. *After much thought I decided to end my marriage.* **4** N-U **Thought** is the group of ideas and beliefs or way of thinking which belongs, for example, to a particular religion or political party. *This school of thought argues that depression is best treated by drugs.* **5** See also **second thoughts.**

thoughtful /ˈθɔːtfʊl/. **1** ADJ If you are **thoughtful**, you are quiet and serious because you are thinking about something. ♦**thoughtfully** ADV *Daniel nodded thoughtfully.* **2** ADJ If you describe someone as **thoughtful**, you approve of them because they remember what other people want, need, or feel, and try not to upset them. ♦**thoughtfully** ADV *...the bottle of wine he had thoughtfully purchased for the celebrations.*

thoughtless /ˈθɔːtləs/. ADJ If you describe someone as **thoughtless**, you are critical of them because they forget or ignore other people's wants, needs, or feelings. ♦**thoughtlessly** ADV *They thoughtlessly planned a picnic without him.*

thousand /ˈθaʊzənd/ **thousands.** **1** NUM A **thousand** or one **thousand** is the number 1,000. **2** N-PL & PRON If you refer to **thousands of** things or people, you are emphasizing that there are very many of them. **Thousands** means very many. *I must have driven past that place thousands of times.*

thousandth /ˈθaʊzənθ/. ORD The **thousandth** item in a series is the one you count as number one thousand.

thrash /θræʃ/ **thrashes, thrashing, thrashed.** **1** VERB If one player or team **thrashes** another in a game or contest, they defeat them easily; INFORMAL. ♦**thrashing,** **thrashings** N-C *...his team's 5-0 thrashing of the home team.* **2** VERB If someone **thrashes** you, they hit you several times as a punishment. ♦**thrashing** N-C *If Sarah caught her, she would get a thrashing.* **3** VERB If someone **thrashes** about, they move in a wild or violent way, often hitting against something. *Jimmy collapsed on the floor, thrashing his legs about.*

▶ **thrash out.** PHR-VERB If people **thrash out** something such as a problem or a plan, they discuss it in detail until a solution is reached. *...a sincere effort by two people to thrash out differences.*

thread /θred/ **threads, threading, threaded.** **1** N-VAR & VERB **Thread** or a **thread** is a long, thin piece of cotton, silk, nylon, or wool. When you **thread** a needle, you put a piece of thread

through the hole in the top of the needle.
2 VERB If you **thread** small objects such as beads onto a string, you join them together by pushing the string through them. **3** N-C The **thread** on a screw, or on something such as a lid, is the raised spiral line of metal or plastic around it which allows it to be fixed in place by twisting. **4** N-C The **thread** of a story or a situation is an aspect of it that connects all the different parts together. *He lost the thread of Wan Da's narrative.* **5** VERB If you **thread** your way through a group of people or things, you move through it carefully. *Anna threaded her way through the crowded room.*

threat /θret/ **threats.** **1** N-VAR A **threat** to someone or something is a danger that something unpleasant might happen to them. *A* **threat** is also the cause of this danger. *Some couples see single women as a threat to their relationships. ...small projects under threat from spending cuts.* **2** N-SING A **threat** is a statement by someone that they will do something unpleasant, especially if you do not do what they want. *He may be forced to carry out his threat to resign.*

threaten /ˈθretən/ **threatens, threatening, threatened.** **1** VERB If someone **threatens** to do something unpleasant to you, or if they **threaten** you, they say or imply that they will do something unpleasant to you, especially if you do not do what they want. ◆**threatening** ADJ *...a threatening phone call.* **2** VERB If something **threatens** people or things, it is likely to harm them. *30 percent of reptiles, birds, and fish are currently threatened with extinction.* **3** VERB If something unpleasant **threatens** to happen, it seems likely to happen. *The fighting is threatening to turn into full-scale war.*

three /θriː/ **threes.** NUM **Three** is the number 3.

three-di'mensional. ADJ A **three-dimensional** object is solid rather than flat, because it can be measured in three dimensions, usually the height, depth, and width.

three-'quarters. QUANT **Three-quarters** is an amount that is three out of four equal parts of something. *Three-quarters of the country's workers took part in the strike... Road deaths have increased by three-quarters.*

threshold /ˈθreʃhəʊld/ **thresholds.** **1** N-C The **threshold** of a building or room is the floor in the doorway, or the doorway itself. **2** N-C A **threshold** is an amount, level, or limit on a scale. *She has a low threshold of boredom.* **3** PHRASE If you are **on the threshold of** something exciting or new, you are about to experience it. *We are on the threshold of a new era in astronomy.*

threw /θruː/. **Threw** is the past tense of **throw**.

thrill /θrɪl/ **thrills, thrilling, thrilled.** VERB & N-C If something **thrills** you, or if something gives you a **thrill**, it gives you a feeling of great pleasure or excitement. *I can still remember the thrill of not knowing what I would get on Christmas morning.*

thrilled /θrɪld/. ADJ AFTER LINK-V If you are **thrilled** about something, you are pleased and excited about it. *I was so thrilled to get a good report.*

thriller /ˈθrɪlə/ **thrillers.** N-C A **thriller** is a book, film, or play that tells an exciting story about something such as criminal activities or spying.

thrilling /ˈθrɪlɪŋ/. ADJ Something that is **thrilling** is very exciting and enjoyable. *...a thrilling adventure movie.*

thrive /θraɪv/ **thrives, thriving, thrived.** VERB If someone or something **thrives**, they do well and are successful, healthy, or strong. *...a thriving business... He thrived on such adversity.*

throat /θrəʊt/ **throats.** **1** N-C Your **throat** is the back of your mouth and the top part of the tubes that go down into your stomach and your lungs. **2** N-C Your **throat** is the front part of your neck.

PHRASES ● If you **clear** your **throat**, you cough once in order to make it easier to speak or to attract people's attention.

throb /θrɒb/ **throbs, throbbing, throbbed.** **1** VERB & N-SING If a part of your body **throbs**, you feel a series of strong and usually painful beats there. You can refer to this feeling as a **throb**. *...the throbbing pain in her ankle.* **2** VERB & N-SING If something **throbs**, it vibrates and makes a rhythmic noise, called a **throb**; LITERARY. *The music throbbed hypnotically.*

throne /θrəʊn/ **thrones.** **1** N-C A **throne** is an ornate chair used by a king, queen, or emperor on important occasions. **2** N-SING You can talk about **the throne** as a way of referring to the position of being king, queen, or emperor. *...the heir to the throne.*

throng /θrɒŋ, AM θrɔːŋ/ **throngs, thronging, thronged.** **1** N-C A **throng** is a large crowd of people. **2** VERB When people **throng** somewhere, they go there in great numbers. ◆**thronged** ADJ AFTER LINK-V *The streets are thronged with people.*

throttle /ˈθrɒtəl/ **throttles, throttling, throttled.** **1** VERB To **throttle** someone means to kill or injure them by holding them tightly by the throat so that they cannot breathe. **2** N-C The **throttle** of a motor vehicle or aircraft is a device that controls the quantity of fuel entering the engine and is used to control the vehicle's speed.

through /θruː/. **1** PREP & ADV To move, cut, or travel **through** something, means to move, cut, or travel from one side or end to the other. *Go straight through that door under the EXIT sign... He went straight through to the kitchen... The exhaust pipe had been cut through.* **2** PREP If you can see, hear, or feel something **through** a particular thing, that thing is between you and the thing you can see, hear, or feel. *They could hear music pulsing through the walls of the house.* **3** PREP & ADV If something happens **through** a period of time, it happens from the beginning until the end. *...hard work right through to the summer.* **4** PREP If you go **through** a particular experience or event, you experience it. *We have been going through a bad time.* **5** ADJ AFTER LINK-V If you are **through** with something or if it is **through**, you have finished doing it and will never do it again. If you are **through** with someone, you do not want to have anything to do with them again.

I'm through with women. **6** PREP If something happens because of something else, you can say that it happens **through** it. *Geoff had to retire early through ill health.* **7** PREP & ADV If someone gets **through** an examination or a round of a competition, they succeed or win. **8** PREP If you go **through** or look **through** a lot of things, you deal with them one after another. *Try working through the opening exercises in this chapter.*

throughout /θruː'aʊt/. **1** PREP & ADV If something happens **throughout** a particular period of time, it happens during the whole of that period. *The school runs cookery and sewing courses throughout the year... It was an absorbing contest throughout.* **2** PREP & ADV If something happens or exists **throughout** a place, it happens or exists in all parts of it. *The route is well sign-posted throughout.*

throw /θrəʊ/ **throws, throwing, threw, thrown.** **1** VERB If you **throw** an object that you are holding, you move your hand quickly and let go of the object, so that it moves through the air. *He spent hours throwing a tennis ball against a wall... He threw Brian a rope.* **2** VERB To **throw** something into a place or position means to cause it to fall there. *Fox threw his coat on the nearest chair... He threw me to the ground.* **3** VERB If you **throw** a part of your body somewhere, you move it there suddenly and with a lot of force. *She threw her hands into the air... He threw himself on his bed.* **4** VERB If a horse **throws** its rider, it makes the rider fall off. **5** VERB If a person or thing **is thrown** into an unpleasant situation or state, something causes them to be in it. *Abidjan was thrown into turmoil because of a protest by taxi drivers.* **6** VERB If you **throw** yourself, your energy, or your money into a particular job or activity, you become involved in it very enthusiastically. **7** VERB If someone **throws** a fit or tantrum, they are suddenly very angry and start to behave in an uncontrolled way. **8** VERB When someone **throws** a party, they organize one; INFORMAL. **9** VERB If something such as a remark or an experience **throws** you, it confuses you because it is unexpected. *That reporter really threw me.*

▸ **throw away.** **1** PHR-VERB If you **throw away** or **throw out** something you do not want, you get rid of it. *I never throw anything away.* **2** PHR-VERB If you **throw away** something good that you have, you waste it. *Failing to tackle the deficit would be throwing away an opportunity.*

▸ **throw in.** PHR-VERB If someone who is selling or offering something **throws in** something else, they add it to what they are selling or offering for no extra charge. *...a weekend break in Paris—with free beer thrown in.*

▸ **throw off.** PHR-VERB If you **throw off** something that is restricting you or making you unhappy, you get rid of it. *Resorts need to throw off their outdated image.*

▸ **throw out.** **1** See **throw away** 1. **2** PHR-VERB If you **throw** someone **out**, you force them to leave. *I wanted to kill him, but instead I just threw him out of the house.* **3** PHR-VERB If a

court or committee **throws out** a case, proposal, or request, they reject it.

▸ **throw up.** PHR-VERB To **throw up** means to vomit; INFORMAL.

thrown /θrəʊn/. **Thrown** is the past participle of **throw**.

thrush /θrʌʃ/ **thrushes.** N-C A **thrush** is a small brown bird with small marks on its chest.

thrust /θrʌst/ **thrusts, thrusting, thrust.** **1** VERB & N-C If you **thrust** something somewhere, or if you make a **thrust** with it, you push or move it there quickly with a lot of force. *They thrust him into the back of a jeep. ...knife thrusts.* **2** N-SING The **thrust** of an activity or idea is the main or essential things it involves. *The main thrust of the research will be the study of the early Universe.*

thud /θʌd/ **thuds, thudding, thudded.** N-C & VERB A **thud** is a dull sound, usually made by a solid, heavy object hitting something soft. If something **thuds** somewhere, it makes this sound as it hits it. *She tripped and fell with a sickening thud... She ran up the stairs, her bare feet thudding on the wood.*

thug /θʌg/ **thugs.** N-C If you refer to someone as a **thug**, you disapprove of them and think they are violent or a criminal.

thumb /θʌm/ **thumbs, thumbing, thumbed.** N-C Your **thumb** is the short, thick digit on the side of your hand next to your first finger.

▸ **thumb through.** PHR-VERB If you **thumb through** a book or magazine, you glance at each page quickly rather than reading them carefully.

thump /θʌmp/ **thumps, thumping, thumped.** **1** VERB & N-C If you **thump** someone or something, or if you give them a **thump**, you hit them hard with your fist. *I'll thump you... I heard you thumping on the door... He felt a thump on his shoulder.* **2** VERB & N-C If you **thump** something somewhere, or if it **thumps** there, it hits something else with a loud, dull sound called a **thump**. *He thumped the can down on the table.* **3** VERB When your heart **thumps**, it beats strongly and quickly, usually because you are afraid or excited.

thunder /'θʌndə/ **thunders, thundering, thundered.** **1** N-U & VERB **Thunder** is the loud noise that you hear from the sky after a flash of lightning. When it **thunders**, you hear thunder. **2** N-U & VERB The **thunder** of something such as traffic is the loud, deep, continuous noise it makes. If something **thunders**, it makes this noise. *...the thunder of the sea on the rocks.*

thunderous /'θʌndərəs/. ADJ A **thunderous** noise is very loud and deep. *They greeted him with thunderous applause.*

thunderstorm /'θʌndəstɔːm/ **thunderstorms.** N-C A **thunderstorm** is a storm in which there is thunder, lightning, and heavy rain.

Thursday /'θɜːzdeɪ, -di/ **Thursdays.** N-VAR **Thursday** is the day after Wednesday and before Friday.

thus /ðʌs/. **1** ADV You use **thus** to introduce the consequence or conclusion of something that you have just mentioned; FORMAL. *Neither of them thought of turning on the lunch-time* news. *Thus Caroline didn't hear of John's death until Peter telephoned... Some people will be more capable and thus better paid than others.* [2] ADV *If you say that something is **thus** or happens **thus** you mean that it is, or happens, as you describe;* FORMAL. *Joanna was pouring the drink. While she was thus engaged, Charles sat on one of the bar-stools.*

thwart /θwɔːt/ **thwarts, thwarting, thwarted.** VERB *If you **thwart** someone or **thwart** their plans, you prevent them from doing or getting what they want. The security forces were doing all they could to thwart terrorists.*

thyme /taɪm/. N-U *Thyme is a type of herb.*

tick /tɪk/ **ticks, ticking, ticked.** [1] N-C *In British English, a **tick** is a written mark like a V with the right side extended. You use it to show that something is correct or has been dealt with. The usual American word is **check**. Place a tick in the appropriate box.* [2] VERB *If you **tick** something that is written on a piece of paper, you put a tick next to it. Please tick this box if you do not wish to receive such mailings.* [3] VERB & N-C *When a clock or watch **ticks**, it makes a regular series of short sounds as it works. The **tick** of a clock is this series of short sounds.* ♦**ticking** N-U *...the endless ticking of clocks.* [4] VERB *If you talk about what makes someone **tick**, you are talking about the reasons for their character and behaviour;* INFORMAL. *Their parents simply don't understand what makes them tick.*

▶ **tick away** or **tick by.** PHR-VERB *If you say that the clock or time is **ticking away** or **ticking by**, you mean that time is passing, especially when there is something urgent that needs to be done or when someone is waiting for something to happen.*

▶ **tick off.** [1] PHR-VERB *If you **tick off** an item on a list, you put a tick by it to show that it has been dealt with.* [2] PHR-VERB *If you **tick** someone **off**, you speak to them angrily because they have done something wrong;* INFORMAL. *Harry will be ticked off for being careless.* ♦**ticking off, tickings off** N-C *They got a ticking off from the police.*

▶ **tick over.** PHR-VERB *Something that **is ticking over** is working or operating steadily, but not producing very much or making much progress. Zambia will be able to afford enough imports to keep the economy ticking over.*

ticket /ˈtɪkɪt/ **tickets.** [1] N-C *A **ticket** is an official piece of paper or card which shows that you have paid for a journey or have paid to enter a place of entertainment.* ● *See also **season ticket**.* [2] N-C *If you get a **ticket**, you are given a piece of paper which orders you to pay a fine or to appear in court because you have committed a driving or parking offence. ...the money she owed on an unpaid parking ticket.*

tickle /ˈtɪkəl/ **tickles, tickling, tickled.** [1] VERB *When you **tickle** someone, you move your fingers lightly over their body, often in order to make them laugh.* [2] VERB *If something **tickles**, it causes an irritating feeling by lightly touching a part of your body. A beard doesn't scratch, it just tickles.*

tidal /ˈtaɪdəl/. ADJ *Tidal means relating to or produced by tides. ...tidal energy.*

'tidal wave, tidal waves. [1] N-C *A **tidal wave** is a very large wave, often caused by an earthquake.* [2] N-C *A **tidal wave** of emotions, things, or people is a very large number of them all occurring at the same time. A tidal wave of refugees was sweeping across Bosnia.*

tide /taɪd/ **tides, tiding, tided.** [1] N-C *The **tide** is the regular change in the level of the sea on the shore. The tide was going out.* [2] N-C *The **tide** of opinion or fashion is what the majority of people think or do at a particular time. The tide of opinion seems overwhelmingly in his favour.*

▶ **tide over.** PHR-VERB *If someone or something **tides** you **over**, they help you to get through a period when you are having difficulties, especially by providing you with money. He can fall back on odd jobs to tide him over.*

tidy /ˈtaɪdi/ **tidier, tidiest; tidies, tidying, tidied.** [1] ADJ *Something that is **tidy** is neat and arranged in an orderly way. ...a tidy desk.* ♦**tidily** ADV *...books and magazines stacked tidily on shelves.* ♦**tidiness** N-U *...the tidiness of his Swiss apartment.* [2] ADJ *Tidy people keep their things tidy. She's obsessively tidy.* ♦**tidiness** N-U *I'm very impressed by your tidiness.* [3] VERB *When you **tidy** a place, you make it neat by putting things in their proper places. He tidied his garage.* [4] ADJ BEFORE N *A **tidy** amount of money is a large amount;* INFORMAL. *He has made a tidy profit.*

▶ **tidy away.** PHR-VERB *When you **tidy** something **away**, you put it in a cupboard or drawer so that it is not in the way. McMinn tidied away the glasses and tea-cups.*

▶ **tidy up.** PHR-VERB *When you **tidy up** or **tidy** a place **up**, you put things back in their proper places so that everything is neat. Kelly spent an hour tidying things up around the shop.*

tie /taɪ/ **ties, tying, tied.** [1] VERB & PHR-VERB *If you **tie** two things together, or if you **tie** them **up**, you fasten them together with a knot. They tied the ends of the bags securely... He tied up the bag and took it outside.* [2] VERB & PHR-VERB *If you **tie** someone or something in a place or position, or if you **tie** them **up**, you put them in that place or position and fasten them using rope or string. He tied her hands behind her back... He had tied the dog to one of the trees.* [3] VERB *If you **tie** a piece of string or cloth around something, you put a piece of string or cloth around it and fasten the ends together in a knot or bow. Roll the meat and tie it with string.* [4] VERB *If you **tie** something in a knot or bow, you fasten the ends together in a knot or bow. She tied a knot in a cherry stem.* [5] N-C *A **tie** is a long narrow piece of cloth that is worn round the neck under a shirt collar and tied in a knot at the front.* [6] VERB *If one thing is **tied** to another, the two things have a close connection or link. ...their bonuses, which are tied to the company's profits.* [7] N-C *Ties are the connections you have with people or a place. ...France's close ties with the Arab world.* [8] VERB & N-C *If two people **tie** in a competition or game, or if there is a **tie** between them, they have the same number of points or the same* degree of success. *Ronan Rafferty had tied with Frank Nobilo... The first game ended in a tie.*

▶ **tie up.** See **tie** 1 and 2.

tier /tɪə/ **tiers.** N-C A **tier** is a row or layer of something that has other layers above or below it. *...the auditorium with the tiers of seats around and above it.*

tiger /ˈtaɪɡə/ **tigers.** N-C A **tiger** is a large fierce animal belonging to the cat family. Tigers are orange with black stripes.

tight /taɪt/ **tighter, tightest; tights.** [1] ADJ **Tight** clothes or shoes fit very closely. *...her tight black jeans.* ◆**tightly** ADV *He buttoned his collar tightly round his thick neck.* [2] ADV & ADJ If you hold someone or something **tight**, you hold them firmly. *Hold on tight!... He kept a tight hold of her arm.* ◆**tightly** ADV *She climbed back into bed and wrapped her arms tightly round her body.* [3] ADJ **Tight** controls or rules are very strict. ◆**tightly** ADV *Germany's armed forces are tightly controlled by government.* [4] ADJ Skin, cloth, or string that is **tight** is stretched or pulled so that it is smooth or straight. ◆**tightly** ADV *Her sallow skin was drawn tightly across the bones of her face.* [5] ADJ **Tight** is used to describe an amount of something or a group of things that is closely packed together. *She curled up in a tight ball.* ◆**tightly** ADV *Many animals travel in tightly packed lorries.* [6] ADJ A **tight** schedule or budget allows very little time or money for unexpected events or expenses. *Financially, things are a bit tight.* ● to **sit tight**: see **sit**.

tighten /ˈtaɪtən/ **tightens, tightening, tightened.** [1] VERB If you **tighten** your grip on something, or if your grip on something **tightens**, you hold it more firmly or securely. *I could feel him tighten his hold on the stick.* [2] VERB If you **tighten** a rope or chain, or if a rope or chain **tightens**, it stretches until it is straight. [3] VERB & PHR-VERB When you **tighten** a screw, nut, or other device, or when you **tighten** it **up**, you turn it or move it so that it is more firmly in place or holds something more firmly. *I used my thumbnail to tighten the screw... It's important to tighten up the wheels properly.* [4] VERB To **tighten** rules or controls means to make them stricter. *...an attempt by anti-abortionists to tighten the rules. ...his plans to tighten his grip on the machinery of central government.* [5] to **tighten** your **belt**: see **belt**.

tights /taɪts/. N-PL **Tights** are a piece of clothing made of thin material such as nylon that covers your hips and each of your legs and feet separately. *...a new pair of tights.*

tile /taɪl/ **tiles.** N-VAR **Tiles** are flat square pieces of baked clay, carpet, cork, or other substance, which are fixed as a covering onto a floor, wall, or roof. *The cabins had linoleum tile floors.*

tiled /taɪld/. ADJ A **tiled** surface is covered with tiles. *...the hard tiled floor.*

till /tɪl/ **tills.** [1] PREP & CONJ **Till** is often used instead of **until**. *They had to wait till Monday... They slept till the alarm bleeper woke them.* [2] N-C In a shop or other place of business, a **till** is a counter or cash register where money is kept, and where customers pay for what they

have bought. *...long queues at tills... There was money in the till.*

tilt /tɪlt/ **tilts, tilting, tilted.** VERB If you **tilt** an object, or if it **tilts**, you change its position so that one end or side is higher than the other. *Leonard tilted his chair back on two legs and stretched his long body.*

timber /ˈtɪmbə/. N-U In British English, **timber** is wood used for building houses and making furniture. The American word is **lumber**. *...a single-storey timber building.*

time /taɪm/ **times, timing, timed.** [1] N-U **Time** is what we measure in minutes, hours, days, and years. *...a two-week period of time... Time passed, and still Ma did not appear... Religion has changed over time.* [2] N-SING You use **time** to ask or talk about a specific point in the day, which can be stated in hours and minutes and is shown on clocks. *'What time is it?'—'Eight o'clock.'... He asked me the time.* [3] N-C The **time** when something happens is the point in the day when it happens or is supposed to happen. *Departure times are 0815 from St Quay, and 1815 from St Helier.* [4] N-U & PHRASE You use **time** to refer to the period that someone spends doing something or when something has been happening. If something happens **all the time**, it happens continually. *Adam spent a lot of time in his grandfather's office... I haven't got much time... We can't be together all the time.* [5] N-SING If you say that something happens for **a time**, you mean that it happens for a fairly long period of time. *He stayed for quite a time.* [6] N-C You use **time** or **times** to talk about a period of time. *We were in the same college, which was male-only at that time... During the time I was married I tried to be the perfect wife... Homes are more affordable than at any time in the past five years. ...one of the most severe recessions in modern times.* [7] N-C When you describe the **time** that you had on a particular occasion or during a particular part of your life, you are describing the sort of experience that you had then. *I had a great time while the kids were away.* [8] N-U If you say it is **time** for something, you mean that this thing ought to happen or be done now. *It was time for him to go to work... This was no time to make a speech.* [9] N-C When you talk about a **time** when something happens, you are referring to a specific occasion when it happens. *The last time I saw her was about sixteen years ago.* [10] N-C You use **time** after numbers to say how often something happens. *It was her job to make tea three times a day... How many times has your mother told you?* [11] N-PL You use **times** after numbers when comparing one thing to another and saying, for example, how much bigger, smaller, better, or worse it is. *...an area five times the size of Britain.* [12] VERB You use **times** in arithmetic to link numbers or amounts that are multiplied together. *Four times six is 24.* [13] VERB If you **time** something, you plan or decide to do it or cause it to happen at a particular time. *We had timed our visit for March 7... He had timed his intervention well.* [14] VERB If you **time** an action or activity, you measure how long it lasts. *He timed each performance with a stop-*

watch. [15] See also **timing**.

PHRASES • If you say it is **about time** that something was done, or that it is **high time** that something was done, you are emphasizing that it should be done now, and really should have happened or been done sooner. *It's about time he learnt to behave properly.* • If someone is **ahead of** their **time** or **before** their **time**, they have new ideas a long time before other people start to think in the same way. • If you say that someone or something is, for example, the best writer **of all time**, or the most successful film **of all time**, you mean that they are the best or most successful that there has ever been. • If something is the case **for the time being**, it is the case, but only until something else becomes possible or happens. *The situation is calm for the time being.* • If you are **in time** for a particular event, or if you are **on time**, you are not late. *I arrived just in time for my flight... Their planes usually arrive on time.* • If something will happen **in time**, it will happen eventually. *He would sort out his own problems, in time.* • If you say that something will happen, for example, **in a week's time**, you mean that it will happen a week from now. • **Once upon a time** is used at the beginning of children's stories to indicate that something happened or existed a long time ago or in an imaginary world. *'Once upon a time,' he began, 'there was a man who had everything.'.* • If you say that something was the case **at one time**, you mean that it was the case during a particular period in the past. *At one time 400 men, women and children lived in the village.* • You use **at the same time** to introduce a statement that contrasts with the previous statement. *I was afraid of her, but at the same time I really liked her.* • If you **take** your **time** doing something, you do it slowly and do not hurry. • If you say that something will **take time**, you mean that it will take a long time. *Change will come, but it will take time.* • If you do something **from time to time**, you do it occasionally. • See also **timing**. • **time and again**: see **again**.

'**time-honoured.** ADJ BEFORE N A **time-honoured** tradition or way of doing something is one that has been used and appreciated for a very long time. *The beer is brewed in the time-honoured way.*

timeless /ˈtaɪmləs/. ADJ If you describe something as **timeless**, you mean that it is so good or beautiful that it cannot be affected by changes in society or fashion. *There is a timeless quality to his best work.*

timely /ˈtaɪmli/. ADJ If you describe an event as **timely**, you mean that it happens at exactly the right moment. *Disaster was only averted by the timely arrival of the maintenance man.*

timetable /ˈtaɪmteɪbəl/ **timetables.** [1] N-C A **timetable** is a plan of the times when particular events are to take place. *Don't you realize we're working to a timetable?* [2] N-C A **timetable** is a list of the times when trains, boats, buses, or aeroplanes arrive at or depart from a place.

timid /ˈtɪmɪd/. ADJ **Timid** people are shy, nervous, and have no courage or self-confidence.

♦**timidly** ADV *The little boy stepped forward timidly.* ♦**timidity** /tɪˈmɪdɪti/ N-U *She doesn't ridicule my timidity.*

timing /ˈtaɪmɪŋ/. [1] N-U **Timing** is the skill or action of judging the right moment in a situation or activity at which to do something. *His photo is a wonderful happy moment caught with perfect timing.* [2] N-U You can refer to the time at which something happens or is planned to happen as its **timing**. *The timing of the announcement from the Iraqi leader is seen as significant.* • See also **time**.

tin /tɪn/ **tins.** [1] N-U **Tin** is a soft silvery-white metal. [2] N-C In British English, a **tin** is a sealed metal container filled with food. The usual American word is **can**. *...a tin of tomatoes.* [3] N-C A **tin** is a metal container with a lid. *Store the cookies in an airtight tin.* [4] N-C A baking **tin** is a metal container used for baking things such as cakes and bread in an oven.

tinge /tɪndʒ/ **tinges.** N-C A **tinge** of a colour, feeling, or quality is a small amount of it. *His skin had an unhealthy greyish tinge. ...a tinge of guilt.*

tinged /tɪndʒd/. ADJ If something is **tinged** with a colour, feeling, or quality, it has a small amount of that colour, feeling, or quality in it. *Her homecoming was tinged with sadness.* ♦**-tinged** *...pink-tinged flowers.*

tingle /ˈtɪŋgəl/ **tingles, tingling, tingled.** [1] VERB When a part of your body **tingles**, you feel a slight prickly sensation there. ♦**tingling** N-U *A sensation of burning or tingling may be experienced in the hands.* [2] VERB & N-C If you **tingle** with a feeling such as excitement, or if you feel a **tingle** of that feeling, you feel it very strongly. *When I look over and see Terry I tingle all over. ...a sudden tingle of excitement.*

tinker /ˈtɪŋkə/ **tinkers, tinkering, tinkered.** VERB If you **tinker with** something, you make some small alterations to it in order to repair or improve it. *They tinkered with the engine.*

tinned /tɪnd/. ADJ In British English, **tinned** food has been preserved by being sealed in a tin. The usual American word is **canned**. *...tinned fish.*

tint /tɪnt/ **tints, tinted, tinting.** [1] N-C A **tint** is a small amount of a colour. *...the unusual green tint of these glass bottles.* [2] VERB If something **is tinted**, it has a small amount of a particular colour or dye in it. *Eyebrows can be tinted with the same dye.* ♦**-tinted** *The General wore green-tinted glasses.*

tiny /ˈtaɪni/ **tinier, tiniest.** ADJ Someone or something that is **tiny** is extremely small. *Though she was tiny, she had a very loud voice.*

tip /tɪp/ **tips, tipping, tipped.** [1] N-C The **tip** of something long and narrow is the end of it. *...the tips of his fingers. ...the southern tip of Florida.* [2] PHRASE If you say that a problem is **the tip of the iceberg**, you mean that it is one small part of a much larger problem. *The above complaints are, I suspect, just the tip of the iceberg.* [3] VERB If an object or part of your body **tips**, or if you **tip** it, it moves into a sloping position with one end or side higher than the other. *She had to tip her head back to see him.* [4] VERB If you **tip** something somewhere, you pour it there. *Tip the vegetables into a* *bowl... Tip away the salt and wipe the pan.* **5** N-C A **tip** is a place where rubbish is left; BRITISH. **6** N-C & VERB If you give someone such as a waiter a **tip**, or if you **tip** them, you give them some money for their services. *She tipped the barmen 10 dollars.* **7** N-C A **tip** is a useful piece of advice. *A good tip is to buy the most expensive lens you can afford.* **8** VERB If a person **is tipped to** do something or **is tipped for** success at something, experts or journalists believe that they will do that thing or achieve that success. *He is tipped to be the country's next foreign minister.*

▶ **tip off.** PHR-VERB If someone **tips** you **off**, they give you information about something that has happened or is going to happen. ◆ **tip-off, tip-offs** N-C *The man was arrested at his home after a tip-off to police.*

▶ **tip over.** PHR-VERB If something **tips over**, it falls over or turns over.

tiptoe /'tɪptəʊ/ **tiptoes, tiptoeing, tiptoed.** VERB & PHRASE If you **tiptoe** somewhere, or if you walk somewhere **on tiptoe**, you walk there very quietly without putting your heels on the floor. *She slipped out of bed and tiptoed to the window.*

tirade /taɪ'reɪd/ **tirades.** N-C A **tirade** is a long angry speech criticizing someone or something.

tire /taɪə/ **tires, tiring, tired.** **1** VERB & PHR-VERB If something **tires** you, or if it **tires** you **out**, it uses a lot of your energy, leaving you very tired and needing to rest. *The oppressive afternoon heat had quite tired him out.* **2** VERB If you **tire of** something, you become bored with it. *He would never tire of international cricket.* **3** See also **tyre.**

tired /taɪəd/ **1** ADJ If you are **tired**, you feel that you want to rest or sleep. *She was too tired to take a shower.* ◆ **tiredness** N-U *He felt half dead with tiredness.* **2** ADJ AFTER LINK-V If you are **tired** of something, you do not want it to continue because you are bored with it. *I was tired of being a bookkeeper.*

tireless /'taɪələs/. ADJ If you describe someone or their efforts as **tireless**, you approve of the fact that they put a lot of hard work into something, and refuse to give up. ◆ **tirelessly** ADV *He worked tirelessly for the cause of health and safety.*

tiresome /'taɪəsəm/. ADJ If you describe someone or something as **tiresome**, you mean that you find them irritating or boring. *...the tiresome old lady next door.*

tiring /'taɪərɪŋ/. ADJ If you describe something as **tiring**, you mean that it makes you tired so that you want to rest or sleep. *Travelling is tiring. ...a long and tiring day.*

tissue /'tɪʃuː, 'tɪsjuː/ **tissues.** **1** N-VAR In animals and plants, **tissue** consists of cells that are similar in appearance and function. *...muscle tissue.* **2** N-U **Tissue** or **tissue paper** is thin paper used for wrapping things that are easily damaged. **3** N-C A **tissue** is a piece of thin soft paper that you use as a handkerchief. *...a box of tissues.*

titillate /'tɪtɪleɪt/ **titillates, titillating, titillated.** VERB If something **titillates** someone, it pleases and excites them, especially in a sexual

way. ◆ **titillating** ADJ *...titillating gossip.* ◆ **titillation** N-U *People buy sex manuals for titillation they don't buy them for ideas.*

title /'taɪtl/ **titles.** **1** N-C The **title** of a book, play, film, or piece of music is its name. **2** N-C Someone's **title** is a word such as 'Lord' or 'Mrs' that is used before their name to show their status or profession. *She has been awarded the title Professor.* **3** N-C A **title** in a sports competition is the position of champion. *He has retained his title as world chess champion.*

to 1 preposition and adverb uses

to. Usually pronounced /tə/ before a consonant and /tʊ/ before a vowel, but pronounced /tuː/ when you are emphasizing it. **1** PREP You use **to** when indicating the place that someone or something visits, moves towards, or points at. *Ramsay made a second visit to Italy... She went to the window and looked out... He pointed to a chair.* **2** PREP If you go to an event, you go where it is taking place. *We went to a party at the leisure centre.* **3** PHRASE If someone moves **to and fro**, they move repeatedly from one place to another and back again. *She stood up and began to pace to and fro.* **4** PREP If something is attached **to** something larger or fixed **to** it, the two things are joined together. *There was a piece of cloth tied to the dog's collar.* **5** PREP You use **to** when indicating the position of something. For example, if something is **to** your left, it is nearer your left side than your right. *Atlanta was only an hour's drive to the north.* **6** PREP When you give something **to** someone, they receive it. **7** PREP You use **to** to indicate who or what an action or a feeling is directed towards. *...troops loyal to the government. ...repairs to the house.* **8** PREP You use **to** when indicating someone's reaction to something. *To his surprise, the bedroom door was locked.* **9** PREP You use **to** when indicating the person whose opinion you are stating. *It was clear to me that he respected his boss.* **10** PREP You use **to** when indicating the state that someone or something gradually starts to be in. *...an old ranch house that has been converted to a nature centre. ...a return to active politics.* **11** PREP You use **to** when indicating the last thing in a range of things. *I read everything from fiction to history and science.* **12** PREP You use **to** when you are stating a time. For example, 'five to eight' means five minutes before eight o'clock. **13** PREP You use **to** in ratios and rates. *...a mixture of one part milk to two parts water.* **14** ADV If you push a door **to**, you close it but do not shut it completely. *He slipped out, pulling the door to.*

to 2 used before the base form of a verb

to. Pronounced /tə/ before a consonant and /tʊ/ before a vowel. **1** You use **to** with an infinitive when indicating the purpose of an action. *...programs set up to save animals.* **2** You use **to** with an infinitive when commenting on your attitude or intention in making a statement. *I'm disappointed, to be honest.* **3** You use **to** with an infinitive in various other constructions when talking about an action or state. *The management wanted to know... Nuclear plants are expensive to build. ...advice *about how to do her job... The Foreign Minister is to visit China.*

toad /təʊd/ **toads.** N-C A **toad** is an animal like a frog, but with a drier skin.

toast /təʊst/ **toasts, toasting, toasted.** [1] N-U **Toast** is slices of bread heated until they are brown and crisp. *...a piece of toast.* [2] VERB When you **toast** bread, you heat it so that it becomes brown and crisp. ● See note at **cook**. [3] N-C & VERB When you drink a **toast** to someone, or when you **toast** them, you wish them success or good health, and then drink some alcoholic drink.

toaster /'təʊstə/ **toasters.** N-C A **toaster** is a piece of electric equipment used to toast bread.

tobacco /tə'bækəʊ/ **tobaccos.** N-VAR **Tobacco** is the dried leaves of a plant which people smoke in pipes, cigars, and cigarettes.

today /tə'deɪ/ [1] ADV & N-U **Today** means the day on which you are speaking or writing. *How are you feeling today?... Today is Friday.* [2] ADV & N-U You can refer to the present period of history as **today**. *The United States is in a serious recession today. ...the Africa of today.*

toddler /'tɒdlə/ **toddlers.** N-C A **toddler** is a young child who has only just learnt to walk.

toe /təʊ/ **toes, toeing, toed.** [1] N-C Your **toes** are the five movable parts at the end of each foot. [2] N-C The **toe** of a shoe or sock is the part that covers the end of your foot. [3] PHRASE If you **toe the line**, you behave in the way that people in authority expect you to. *...politicians that wouldn't toe the party line.*

toenail /'təʊneɪl/ **toenails.** N-C Your **toenails** are the thin hard areas at the end of your toes.

toffee /'tɒfi, AM 'tɔːfi/ **toffees.** N-VAR A **toffee** is a sweet made by boiling sugar and butter together with water.

together /tə'geðə/. [1] ADV If people do something **together**, they do it with each other. *We went on long bicycle rides together... They all live together in a three-bedroom house... Together they swam to the ship.* [2] ADV If two things happen **together**, they happen at the same time. *Three horses crossed the finish line together.* [3] ADV If things are joined **together**, they are joined to each other so that they touch or form one whole. *Mix the ingredients together thoroughly... She clasped her hands together on her lap.* [4] ADV If things or people are situated **together**, they are in the same place and very near to each other. *The trees grew close together... We gathered our things together.* [5] ADV You use **together** when you are adding two or more amounts or things to each other in order to consider a total amount or effect. *The two main opposition parties together won 29.8 per cent.* [6] PREP **Together with** something means as well as that thing. *Return the completed questionnaire, together with your cheque for £60.*

toil /tɔɪl/ **toils, toiling, toiled.** VERB & N-U If you say that people **toil**, or if you describe their work as **toil**, you mean that they work hard doing unpleasant or tiring tasks; LITERARY. *Workers toiled long hours... Hours of toil paid off in the end.*

toilet /'tɔɪlət/ **toilets.** [1] N-C A **toilet** is a large bowl connected to the drains which you use when you want to get rid of urine or faeces from your body. *She flushed the toilet and went back in the bedroom.* [2] N-C In British English, a **toilet** is a small room containing a toilet. The American word is **bathroom**.

'toilet paper. N-U **Toilet paper** is paper that you use to clean yourself after getting rid of urine or faeces from your body.

toiletries /'tɔɪlətriz/. N-PL **Toiletries** are things that you use when cleaning or taking care of your body, such as soap and toothpaste.

token /'təʊkən/ **tokens.** [1] N-C A **token** is a piece of paper, plastic, or metal which can be used instead of money. *...£10 book tokens. ...subway tokens.* [2] N-C If you give something to someone as a **token** of your feelings for them, you give it as a way of expressing those feelings. *The ring was given as a token of love.* [3] ADJ BEFORE N You use **token** to describe things or actions which show your intentions or feelings but are small or unimportant. *...token gestures of force.* [4] PHRASE You use **by the same token** to introduce a statement that you think is true for the same reasons that were given for a previous statement. *If you give up exercise, your muscles shrink and fat increases. By the same token, if you expend more energy you will lose fat.*

told /təʊld/. [1] **Told** is the past tense and past participle of **tell**. [2] PHRASE You can use **all told** to indicate a summary, generalization, or total. *All told, he went to 14 different schools.*

tolerable /'tɒlərəbəl/. ADJ If something is **tolerable**, it is acceptable or bearable, but not pleasant or good. *The pain was tolerable.*
♦ **tolerably** ADV *Their captors treated them tolerably well.*

tolerant /'tɒlərənt/. ADJ If you are **tolerant**, you let other people say and do what they like, even if you do not agree with it or approve of it. *People are becoming more tolerant of homosexuals.* ♦ **tolerance** N-U *...religious tolerance.*

tolerate /'tɒləreɪt/ **tolerates, tolerating, tolerated.** [1] VERB If you **tolerate** things that you do not agree with or approve of, you allow them to exist or happen. *We will not tolerate such behaviour.* [2] VERB If you can **tolerate** something unpleasant or painful, you are able to bear it. *Women tolerate pain better than men.*

toll /təʊl/ **tolls, tolling, tolled.** [1] VERB When a bell **tolls**, it rings slowly and repeatedly, often as a sign that someone has died. [2] N-C A **toll** is a sum of money that you have to pay in order to use a particular bridge or road. [3] PHRASE If something **takes a toll** or **takes its toll**, it has a bad effect on someone or something, or causes a lot of suffering. *Winter takes its toll on your health.* [4] See also **death toll**.

tomato /tə'mɑːtəʊ, AM -'meɪ-/ **tomatoes.** N-VAR A **tomato** is a small, soft, red vegetable that is used in cooking or eaten raw.

tomb /tuːm/ **tombs.** N-C A **tomb** is a stone structure containing the body of a dead person.

tombstone /'tuːmstəʊn/ **tombstones.** N-C A **tombstone** is a large flat piece of stone on someone's grave, with their name written on it.

tomorrow /tə'mɒrəʊ, AM -'mɔːr-/. **1** ADV & N-U **Tomorrow** refers to the day after today. *The results will be announced tomorrow... Tomorrow is her thirteenth birthday.* **2** ADV & N-U You can refer to the future as **tomorrow**. *What is education going to look like tomorrow? ...tomorrow's computer industry.*

ton /tʌn/ **tons**. **1** N-C A non-metric **ton** is a unit of weight equal to 2,240 pounds in Britain and 2,000 pounds in the United States. **2** N-C A metric **ton** is a unit of weight equal to 100 kilograms.

tone /təʊn/ **tones, toning, toned**. **1** N-C The **tone** of a sound is its particular quality. *They began speaking in low tones. ...the clear tone of the bell.* **2** N-C Someone's **tone** is a quality in their voice which shows what they are feeling or thinking. *I still didn't like his tone of voice... Her tone implied that her patience was limited.* **3** N-U The **tone** of a speech or piece of writing is its style and the feelings expressed in it. *The tone of the letter was very friendly... His comments to reporters were conciliatory in tone.* **4** VERB & PHR-VERB Something that **tones** or **tones up** your body makes it firm and strong. *The massage tones up the child's muscles.*

▶ **tone down**. PHR-VERB If you **tone down** something that you have written or said, you make it less forceful, severe, or offensive. *It would help if you toned down your language.*

tongue /tʌŋ/ **tongues**. **1** N-C Your **tongue** is the soft movable part inside your mouth that you use for tasting, licking, and speaking. **2** N-C A **tongue** is a language; LITERARY. *English is not her native tongue.* **3** PHRASE A **tongue-in-cheek** remark is made as a joke, and is not serious or sincere. **4** To **bite your tongue**: see **bite**.

tonic /'tɒnɪk/ **tonics**. **1** N-VAR **Tonic** or **tonic water** is a colourless, fizzy drink that has a slightly bitter flavour. *...a gin and tonic.* **2** N-C You can refer to anything that makes you feel stronger or more cheerful as a **tonic**. *Seeing Marcus at that moment was a great tonic.*

tonight /tə'naɪt/. ADV & N-U **Tonight** refers to the evening or night that will come at the end of today. *What are you doing tonight?... Tonight is the opening night of the opera.*

tonne /tʌn/ **tonnes**. N-C A **tonne** is a unit of weight equal to 1,000 kilograms.

too /tuː/. **1** ADV You use **too** after mentioning another person, thing, or aspect that a previous statement applies to or includes. *'Nice to talk to you.'—'Nice to talk to you too.'... I've got a great feeling about it.'—'Me too.'... Depression may be expressed physically too... He doesn't want to meet me. I, too, have been afraid to talk to him.* **2** ADV You use **too** after adding a piece of information or a comment to a statement, in order to emphasize it. *We did learn to read, and quickly too... 'That money's mine.'—'Of course it is, and quite right too.'* **3** ADV You use **too** to indicate that there is more of a thing or quality than is desirable or acceptable. *Eggs shouldn't be kept in the fridge, it's too cold... She was drinking too much... We have too much to do today.* ● See note at **very**. **4** ADV

You can use **too** to make a negative opinion politer or more cautious. *Americans are never too keen to leave their beloved country... I wasn't too happy with what I'd written so far.* **5** **too bad**: see **bad**. ● **none too**: see **none**.

PHRASES ● You use **all too** or **only too** to emphasize that something happens to a greater degree than is pleasant or desirable. *She remembered it all too well... The letter spoke only too clearly of his anxiety for her.*

> **Too** is not generally used to modify an adjective inside a noun group. For instance, you cannot say 'the too heavy boxes' or 'too expensive jewellery'. There is one exception to this rule, which is when the noun group begins with **a** or **an**. Notice the word order in the following examples. *...if the products have been stored at too high a temperature... He found it too good an opportunity to miss... It was too long a drive for one day.* See also the note at **very**.

took /tʊk/. **Took** is the past tense of **take**.

tool /tuːl/ **tools**. **1** N-C A **tool** is any instrument or simple piece of equipment, for example a hammer or a knife, that you hold in your hands and use to do a particular kind of work. **2** N-C You can refer to anything that you use for a particular purpose as a particular type of **tool**. *The video has become an invaluable teaching tool.*

tooth /tuːθ/ **teeth**. **1** N-C Your **teeth** are the hard, white objects in your mouth that you use for biting and chewing. **2** N-PL The **teeth** of a comb, saw, or zip are the parts that stick out in a row. **3** To **grit your teeth**: see **grit**.

toothbrush /'tuːθbrʌʃ/ **toothbrushes**. N-C A **toothbrush** is a small brush used for cleaning your teeth.

toothpaste /'tuːθpeɪst/ **toothpastes**. N-VAR **Toothpaste** is a thick substance which you use to clean your teeth.

top /tɒp/ **tops, topping, topped**. **1** N-C The **top** of something is its highest point or part. *I waited at the top of the stairs... Don't fill it up to the top.* **2** ADJ BEFORE N The **top** thing or layer in a series of things or layers is the highest one. *Our new flat was on the top floor.* **3** PHRASE If one thing is **on top** of another, it is on its highest part. *...hot chocolate with whipped cream on top.* **4** N-C The **top** of a bottle, jar, or tube is its cap or lid. **5** ADJ BEFORE N You can use **top** to describe the highest level of a scale or measurement. *The vehicles have a top speed of 80 kilometres per hour.* **6** ADJ & N-SING If someone is **top** of a table or league, or if they are at **the top** of it, their performance is better than that of all the other people involved. *She came top in French and second in maths.* **7** N-SING & ADJ BEFORE N If someone is at **the top** of an organization or career, they are among the most senior, important, or successful people in it. You can also refer to the **top** people in an organization or career. *He has got to the top on natural talent. ...a top model.* **8** See also **topped**.

PHRASES ● **On top of** other things means in

addition to them. *An extra 700 jobs are being cut on top of the 2,000 that were lost last year.*
● If you are **on top of** a task, you are dealing with it successfully. ● If you say that something is **over the top**, you mean that it is unacceptable because it is too extreme; BRITISH, INFORMAL. *Her paintings are over the top.*

▸ **top up.** PHR-VERB If you **top up** a container, you fill it again when it has been partly emptied. *He topped her glass up.*

,**top 'class.** ADJ **Top class** means amongst the finest of its kind. *You have to have a lot of stamina to be a top-class dancer.*

topic /'tɒpɪk/ **topics.** N-C A **topic** is a particular subject that you write about or discuss. *The weather is a constant topic of conversation in Britain.*

topical /'tɒpɪkəl/. ADJ **Topical** means relating to events that are happening at the time when you are speaking or writing. *The magazine's aim is to discuss topical issues.*

topless /'tɒpləs/. ADJ If a woman goes **topless**, she does not wear anything to cover her breasts. *...a topless dancer.*

topped /tɒpt/. ADJ If something is **topped** by or with another thing, the other thing is on top of it. *...hot scones topped with fresh cream.*

topple /'tɒpəl/ **topples, toppling, toppled.** 1 VERB If someone or something **topples** somewhere, or if they **topple over**, they become unsteady and fall over. *His foot slipped and he toppled into the boat head first.* 2 VERB To **topple** a government or leader means to cause them to lose power; JOURNALISM. *...the revolution which toppled the communist regime.*

,**top 'secret.** ADJ **Top secret** information or activity is intended to be kept completely secret. *...a top-secret military mission.*

torch /tɔːtʃ/ **torches.** 1 N-C In British English, a **torch** is a small, battery-powered electric light which you carry in your hand. The American word is **flashlight**. 2 N-C A **torch** is a long stick with burning material at one end, used to provide light or to set things on fire.

tore /tɔː/. **Tore** is the past tense of **tear**.

torment, torments, tormenting, tormented. 1 N-VAR /'tɔːment/ **Torment** is extreme suffering, usually mental suffering. *He spent years in torment going from psychiatrist to psychiatrist. ...the torments of being a writer.* 2 VERB /tɔː'ment/ If something **torments** you, it causes you extreme mental suffering. *He had lain awake all night, tormented by jealousy.* 3 VERB To **torment** a person or animal means to annoy them in a playful, rather cruel way, for your own amusement.

torn /tɔːn/. **Torn** is the past participle of **tear**.

tornado /tɔː'neɪdəʊ/ **tornadoes** or **tornados.** N-C A **tornado** is a violent storm with strong circular winds.

torpedo /tɔː'piːdəʊ/ **torpedoes, torpedoing, torpedoed.** 1 N-C A **torpedo** is a bomb shaped like a tube that travels underwater. 2 VERB If a ship is **torpedoed**, it is hit and, usually sunk, by a torpedo.

torrent /'tɒrənt/, AM 'tɔːr-/ **torrents.** 1 N-C A **torrent** is a lot of water falling or flowing rap-

idly or violently. *Torrents of water gushed into the reservoir... The rain came down in torrents.* 2 N-C A **torrent** of abuse or questions is a lot of insults or questions directed continuously at someone.

torrential /təˈrenʃəl/, AM tɔːr-/. ADJ **Torrential** rain falls very fast and very heavily.

torso /'tɔːsəʊ/ **torsos.** N-C Your **torso** is the main part of your body, excluding your head, arms, and legs; FORMAL.

tortoise /'tɔːtəs/ **tortoises.** N-C A **tortoise** is a slow-moving animal with a shell into which it can pull its head and legs for protection.

tortuous /'tɔːtʃuəs/. 1 ADJ A **tortuous** road is full of bends and twists; FORMAL. 2 ADJ A **tortuous** process is long and complicated; FORMAL.

torture /'tɔːtʃə/ **tortures, torturing, tortured.** VERB & N-VAR If someone **is tortured**, or if they are subjected to **torture**, another person deliberately causes them great pain, in order to punish them or make them reveal information. *Many died under torture, others committed suicide. ...a medieval torture.*

toss /tɒs, AM tɔːs/ **tosses, tossing, tossed.** 1 VERB If you **toss** something somewhere, you throw it there lightly and carelessly. *She tossed her suitcase onto one of the beds... He tossed Malone a can of beer.* 2 VERB If you **toss** your head, you move it backwards quickly and suddenly, often as a way of expressing anger or contempt. 3 VERB & N-C In sports and informal situations, if you decide something by **tossing** a coin, or by the **toss** of a coin, you spin a coin into the air and guess which side of the coin will face upwards when it lands. 4 VERB If something such as the wind or sea **tosses** an object, it causes it to move from side to side or up and down. *The seas grew turbulent, tossing the small boat like a cork.*

total /'təʊtəl/ **totals, totalling, totalled** (AM **totaling, totaled**). 1 N-C & ADV BEFORE N A **total** is the number that you get when you add several numbers together or when you count how many things there are in a group. *The companies have a total of 1,776 employees... The total cost of the project would be more than $240 million.* 2 PHRASE If there are a number of things **in total**, there are that number of them when you count or add them all together. *I was with my husband for eight years in total.* 3 VERB If several numbers **total** a certain figure, that is the figure you get when all the numbers are added together. *They will compete for prizes totalling nearly £300.* 4 ADJ **Total** means complete. *I have total confidence that things will change.* ◆**totally** ADV *...something totally different... The fire totally destroyed the top floor.*

totalitarian /ˌtəʊtælɪˈteəriən/. ADJ A **totalitarian** political system is one in which one political party controls everything and does not allow any other parties to exist.

totter /'tɒtə/ **totters, tottering, tottered.** VERB When someone **totters** somewhere, they walk there in an unsteady way.

touch /tʌtʃ/ **touches, touching, touched.** 1 VERB & N-SING If you **touch** something, or if you give it a **touch**, you put your fingers or hand on it. *Kate leaned forward and touched* *his hand reassuringly... Don't touch that dial. ...a gentle touch on the hand.* [2] VERB When two things **touch**, or when one thing **touches** another, their surfaces come into contact with each other. *Their knees were touching... Annie lowered her legs, until her feet touched the floor.* [3] N-U Your sense of **touch** is your ability to tell what something is like when you feel it with your hands. *The wine should feel decidedly cold to the touch.* [4] VERB If you **touch on** a particular subject, you mention it briefly. [5] VERB If something that someone says or does **touches** you, it affects you emotionally, often because that person is suffering or is being very kind. ♦**touched** ADJ AFTER LINK-V *He was touched that we came.* ♦**touching** ADJ *...a touching tale of love and romance.* [6] N-C A **touch** is a detail which is added to something to improve it. *They called the event 'a tribute to heroes', which was a nice touch.* [7] QUANT A **touch of** something is a very small amount of it. *She just had a touch of flu.* [8] N-U If you are in **touch** with someone, you write, phone, or visit each other regularly. *We have to keep in touch by phone... We lost touch for many years.*

PHRASES ● If you say that something is **touch and go**, you mean that it is uncertain whether it will happen or succeed. *It was touch and go whether we'd go bankrupt.* ● If you are **in touch** with a subject or situation, you know the latest information about it. If you are **out of touch** with it, your knowledge of it is out of date.

▶ **touch down.** PHR-VERB When an aircraft **touches down**, it lands.

touchy /'tʌtʃi/ **touchier, touchiest.** [1] ADJ **Touchy** people are easily upset or irritated. [2] ADJ A **touchy** subject is one that needs to be dealt with carefully, because it might upset or offend people.

tough /tʌf/ **tougher, toughest.** [1] ADJ A **tough** person has a strong character and can tolerate difficulty or hardship. ♦**toughness** N-U *Mrs Potter has won a reputation for toughness and determination.* [2] ADJ A **tough** substance is strong, and difficult to break or cut. *...dark brown beans with a rather tough outer skin.* [3] ADJ A **tough** task or way of life is difficult or full of hardship. *She had a pretty tough childhood.*

toughen /'tʌfən/ **toughens, toughening, toughened.** [1] VERB If you **toughen** something, or if it **toughens**, you make it stronger so that it will not break easily. *...toughened glass.* [2] VERB & PHR-VERB If an experience **toughens** you, or if it **toughens up**, it makes you stronger in character. *He thinks boxing is good for kids, that it toughens them up.*

tour /tʊə/ **tours, touring, toured.** [1] VERB & N-VAR When people such as musicians, politicians, or theatre companies **tour**, or when they go on **tour**, they go to several different places, stopping to meet people or perform. *He toured for nearly two years... Their British tour was a virtual sell-out.* [2] N-C A **tour** is a trip or journey to an interesting place or around several interesting places. [3] VERB If you **tour** a place, you go on a journey or trip round it.

tourism /'tʊərɪzəm/. N-U **Tourism** is the business of providing services for people on holiday.

tourist /'tʊərɪst/ **tourists.** N-C A **tourist** is a person who is visiting a place for pleasure, especially when they are on holiday.

tournament /'tʊənəmənt/ **tournaments.** N-C A **tournament** is a sports competition in which players who win a match continue to play further matches until just one person or team is left.

tout /taʊt/ **touts, touting, touted.** [1] VERB If someone **touts** something, they try to sell it or convince people that it is good; used showing disapproval. *The product is touted as being completely natural.* [2] VERB If someone **touts** for business or custom, they try to obtain it; BRITISH. [3] N-C A **tout** is someone who unofficially sells tickets outside a sports ground or theatre, often for more than their original value; BRITISH.

tow /təʊ/ **tows, towing, towed.** [1] VERB If one vehicle **tows** another, the first vehicle pulls the second along behind it. *They threatened to tow away my car.* [2] PHRASE If you have someone in **tow**, they are following you closely because you are looking after them or you are leading them somewhere; INFORMAL. *There she was on my doorstep with child in tow.*

towards /tə'wɔːdz, AM tɔːrdz/. The form **toward** is also used and is the more usual form in American English. [1] PREP If you move or look **towards** something or someone, you move or look in their direction. *Caroline leant across the table towards him.* [2] PREP If people move **towards** a particular situation, that situation becomes nearer in time or more likely to happen. *She also began moving toward a different life-style.* [3] PREP If you have a particular attitude **towards** something or someone, you feel like that about them. *Not everyone in the world will be kind and caring towards you.* [4] PREP If something happens **towards** a particular time, it happens just before that time. *The Channel tunnel was due to open towards the end of 1993.* [5] PREP If something is **towards** part of a place or thing, it is near that part. *The home of the Morgan family was up Gloucester Road, towards the top of the hill.* [6] PREP If you give money **towards** something, you give it to help pay for that thing. *He gave them £20,000 towards a house.*

towel /taʊəl/ **towels, towelling, towelled;** (AM **toweling, toweled).** [1] N-C A **towel** is a piece of thick, soft cloth that you use to dry yourself with. [2] VERB If you **towel** something, you dry it with a towel. *I towelled myself dry.* [3] PHRASE If you **throw in the towel**, you stop trying to do something because you realize that you cannot succeed.

tower /taʊə/ **towers, towering, towered.** [1] N-C A **tower** is a tall narrow structure, that is often part of a church or castle. [2] VERB Someone or something that **towers** over surrounding people or things is a lot taller than they are.

towering /'taʊərɪŋ/. ADJ BEFORE N If you describe something such as a mountain or cliff as **towering**, you mean that it is very high and therefore impressive; LITERARY.

town /taʊn/ **towns.** ① N-C A **town** is a place with many streets and buildings where people live and work. ② N-U You use **town** in order to refer to the town where you live. *She left town.*

town 'hall (also **Town Hall**), **town halls.** N-C The **town hall** in a town is a large building owned and used by the town council, often as its headquarters.

township /'taʊnʃɪp/ **townships.** N-C In South Africa, a **township** was a town where only black people lived.

toxic /'tɒksɪk/ ADJ A **toxic** substance is poisonous. ♦**toxicity** /tɒk'sɪsɪti/ **toxicities** N-VAR ...*data on the toxicity of chemicals.*

toy /tɔɪ/ **toys, toying, toyed.** N-C A **toy** is an object that children play with, for example a doll or a model car.
▶ **toy with.** ① PHR-VERB If you **toy with** an idea, you consider it casually, without making any decisions about it. ② PHR-VERB If you **toy with** an object or with your food, you keep moving it around but do not eat it properly or eat it, especially because you are thinking about something else.

trace /treɪs/ **traces, tracing, traced.** ① VERB If you **trace** someone or something, you find them after looking for them. *They traced the van to a New Jersey car rental agency.* ② VERB & PHR-VERB If you **trace** the origin or development of something, or if you **trace** it **back**, you find out or describe how it started or developed. *He can trace his jealousy back to when he was age two.* ③ VERB If you **trace** a picture, you copy it by covering it with a piece of transparent paper and drawing over the lines underneath. ④ N-C A **trace** is a sign which shows that someone or something has been in a place. ...*traces of chemicals in food and water.*

track /træk/ **tracks, tracking, tracked.** ① N-C A **track** is a narrow road or path. ② N-C A **track** is a piece of ground that is used for races. ③ N-C Railway **tracks** are the rails that a train travels along. ④ N-PL Animal **tracks** are the footprints that animals make. ⑤ VERB If you **track** animals or people, you try to find them by following their footprints or other signs.

PHRASES ● If a place is **off the beaten track**, it is in a quiet and isolated area. ● If you **keep track of** a situation or a person, you have accurate information about them all the time. If you **lose track of** them, you no longer know where they are or what is happening. *It's so easy to lose track of who's playing who and when.* ● If you are **on the right track**, you are acting or progressing in a way that is likely to result in success.
▶ **track down.** PHR-VERB If you **track down** someone or something, you find them after a long and difficult search. *It took two years to track him down.*

track 'record, track records. N-C If you talk about the **track record** of a person, company, or product, you are referring to their past achievements or actions.

tracksuit /'træksuːt/ **tracksuits.** N-C A **tracksuit** is a loose, warm suit consisting of trousers and a sweatshirt, worn mainly when exercising.

tractor /'træktə/ **tractors.** N-C A **tractor** is a farm vehicle that is used for pulling farm machinery.

trade /treɪd/ **trades, trading, traded.** VERB & N-U When people or countries **trade**, they buy, sell, or exchange goods or services. This activity is called **trade**. *Texas has a long history of trade with Mexico.* ♦**trading** N-U ...*trading on the stock exchange.*

trademark /'treɪdmɑːk/ **trademarks.** N-C A **trademark** is a name or symbol that a company uses on its products and that cannot legally be used by another company.

trader /'treɪdə/ **traders.** N-C A **trader** is a person whose job is to trade in goods or stocks.

trade 'union (or **trades union**) **trade unions.** N-C A **trade union** is an organization formed by workers in order to represent their rights and interests to their employers.

trade 'unionist, (or **trades unionist**) **trade unionists.** N-C A **trade unionist** is an active member of a trade union.

tradition /trə'dɪʃən/ **traditions.** N-VAR A **tradition** is a custom or belief that has existed for a long time. ...*the rich traditions of Afro-Cuban music.* ♦**traditional** ADJ ...*traditional teaching methods.* ♦**traditionally** ADV *Married women have traditionally been treated as dependent on their husbands.*

traffic /'træfɪk/ **traffics, trafficking, trafficked.** ① N-U **Traffic** refers to all the vehicles that are moving along the roads in an area. *Traffic was unusually light for that time of day.* ② N-U **Traffic** refers to the movement of ships, trains, or aircraft between one place and another. *Air traffic had returned to normal.* ③ VERB & N-U If someone **traffics** in illegal or stolen goods, or if they are involved in the **traffic** of such goods, they buy and sell them illegally. *Traffic in illicit drugs was now worth some $500 thousand million a year.* ♦**trafficking** N-U ...*charges of drug trafficking.* ♦**trafficker, traffickers** N-C *Mexican police have arrested a powerful drug trafficker.*

'traffic jam, traffic jams. N-C A **traffic jam** is a long line of vehicles that cannot move because there is too much traffic, or because the road is blocked.

'traffic light, traffic lights. N-C **Traffic lights** are the coloured lights at road junctions which control the flow of traffic.

tragedy /'trædʒɪdi/ **tragedies.** ① N-VAR A **tragedy** is an extremely sad event or situation. *They have suffered an enormous personal tragedy.* ② N-VAR **Tragedy** is a type of serious drama, usually ending in the death of the main character.

tragic /'trædʒɪk/. ① ADJ Something that is **tragic** is extremely sad, usually because it involves death or suffering. *It was just a tragic accident.* ♦**tragically** /'trædʒɪkli/ ADV *He died tragically young.* ② ADJ BEFORE N **Tragic** is used to refer to literary tragedy. ...*Shakespearian tragic heroes.*

trail /treɪl/ **trails, trailing, trailed.** ① N-C A **trail** is a rough path across open country or through forests. ② N-C A **trail** is a series of marks or other signs left by someone or something as they move along. *He left a trail of clues at the scenes of his crimes.* ③ PHRASE If you are **on the trail**

of a person or thing, you are trying to find them. ...*on the trail of the world's most ruthless terrorist.* [4] VERB If you **trail** someone or something, you follow them secretly. *I trailed her to a shop in Kensington.* [5] VERB If you **trail** something, it hangs down loosely behind you as you move along. *He let his fingers trail in the water.* [6] VERB If someone **trails** somewhere, they move there slowly and without enthusiasm. *He trailed through the wet Manhattan streets.* [7] VERB In a contest, if someone **is trailing**, they are behind their opponents. *They trailed by nine points to six at half-time.*

▶ **trail away** or **trail off.** PHR-VERB If a speaker's voice **trails off** or **trails away**, their voice becomes quieter and they hesitate until they stop speaking completely.

trailer /ˈtreɪlə/ **trailers.** [1] N-C A **trailer** is a vehicle without an engine which is pulled by a car or lorry. [2] N-C A **trailer** for a film or television programme is a set of short extracts which are shown to advertise it.

train /treɪn/ **trains, training, trained.** [1] N-C A **train** is a number of carriages or trucks pulled by a railway engine. *He arrived in Shenyang by train.* [2] N-C A **train** of thought or a **train** of events is a connected series of thoughts or events. *He lost his train of thought for a moment.* [3] VERB If you **train** to do something, or if someone **trains** you to do it, they teach you the skills that you need in order to do it. *Stavros was training to be a priest... They train teachers in counselling skills... I'm a trained nurse.* ♦**-trained** ...*an American-trained lawyer.* ♦**trainer, trainers** N-C ...*teacher trainers.* ♦**training** N-U *Kennedy had no formal training as a decorator.* [4] VERB If you **train** for an activity such as a race, or if someone **trains** you for it, you prepare for it by doing particular physical exercises. ♦**trainer** N-C *She went to the gym with her trainer.* ♦**training** N-U *He will soon be back in training for next year's National.* [5] VERB If you **train** something such as a gun, a camera, or a light **on** someone or something, you keep it pointing steadily towards them. *She trained her binoculars on the distant horizon.*

trainee /treɪˈniː/ **trainees.** N-C A **trainee** is a junior employee who is being taught how to do a job.

trainer /ˈtreɪnə/ **trainers.** N-C In British English, **trainers** are shoes with rubber soles used for sports. The usual American word is **sneakers.**

trait /treɪt, treɪ/ **traits.** N-C A **trait** is a characteristic, quality, or tendency that someone or something has. *Creativity is a human trait.*

traitor /ˈtreɪtə/ **traitors.** N-C A **traitor** is someone who betrays their country or a group of which they are a member by helping their enemies.

tram /træm/ **trams.** N-C In British English, a **tram** is a public transport vehicle, usually powered by electricity, which travels along rails laid in the surface of a street. The usual American word is **streetcar.**

tramp /træmp/ **tramps, tramping, tramped.** [1] N-C A **tramp** is a person with no home or job who travels around and gets money by doing occasional work or by begging. [2] VERB If you

tramp somewhere, you walk with slow heavy footsteps, for a long time. *She spent all day yesterday tramping the streets.*

trample /ˈtræmpəl/ **tramples, trampling, trampled.** [1] VERB To **trample** on someone's rights or values means to deliberately ignore or disregard them. *Diplomats denounced the leaders for trampling their citizens' civil rights.* [2] VERB If someone **is trampled**, they are injured or killed by being trodden on by animals or people. [3] VERB If you **trample** on something, you tread heavily on it and damage it. *They don't want people trampling the grass.*

trance /trɑːns, træns/ **trances.** N-C If someone is in a **trance**, they seem to be asleep, but they can see and hear things and respond to commands.

tranquil /ˈtræŋkwɪl/ ADJ **Tranquil** means calm and peaceful. ♦**tranquillity** N-U *He enjoyed the tranquillity of village life.*

tranquillize (BR also **tranquillise**, AM also **tranquilize**) /ˈtræŋkwɪlaɪz/ **tranquillizes, tranquillizing, tranquillized.** VERB To **tranquillize** a person or an animal means to make them become calm, sleepy, or unconscious by means of a drug.

tranquillizer (BR also **tranquilliser**, AM also **tranquilizer**) /ˈtræŋkwɪlaɪzə/ **tranquillizers.** N-C A **tranquillizer** is a drug that is used to tranquillize people or animals.

transaction /trænˈzækʃən/ **transactions.** N-C A **transaction** is a business deal.

transatlantic /ˌtrænzətˈlæntɪk/. [1] ADJ BEFORE N **Transatlantic** flights or signals go across the Atlantic Ocean, usually between the United States and Britain. *Many transatlantic flights land there.* [2] ADJ BEFORE N **Transatlantic** is used to refer to something that happens, exists, or originates in the United States; BRITISH. ...*transatlantic fashions.*

transcend /trænˈsend/ **transcends, transcending, transcended.** VERB Something that **transcends** normal limits or boundaries goes beyond them, because it is more significant than them. *Human rights transcend age, class and race.*

transcribe /trænˈskraɪb/ **transcribes, transcribing, transcribed.** VERB If you **transcribe** something that is spoken or written, you write it down, copy it, or change it into a different form of writing.

transcript /ˈtrænskrɪpt/ **transcripts.** N-C A **transcript** of something that is spoken is a written copy of it.

transfer, transfers, transferring, transferred; verb /trænsˈfɜː/, noun /ˈtrænsfɜː/. [1] VERB & N-VAR If you **transfer** something or someone from one place to another, they go from the first place to the second. The **transfer** of something or someone is the act of transferring them. *He wants to transfer some money to her account... Arrange for the transfer of medical records to your new doctor.* [2] VERB & N-VAR If you **are transferred** to a different place or job, or if you get a **transfer**, you move to a different place or job within the same organization. *Two senior members of staff had been transferred.*

transform /trænsˈfɔːm/ **transforms, transforming, transformed.** VERB To **transform**

someone or something means to change them completely. ...*transforming them from a guerrilla force into a regular army.* ♦**transformation** /ˌtrænsfəˈmeɪʃən/ **transformations** N-VAR ...*the transformation of an attic into a study.*

transfusion /trænsˈfjuːʒən/ **transfusions.** N-C A blood **transfusion** is a process in which blood is injected into the body of a person who is badly injured or ill.

transient /ˈtrænziənt, AM -nʃənt/ **transients.** [1] ADJ Something that is **transient** does not last very long or is constantly changing; FORMAL. *In most cases, pain is transient.* ♦**transience** /ˈtrænziəns AM -nʃəns/ N-U *There is a sense of transience about her.* [2] N-C **Transients** are people who stay in a place for only a short time and do not have a fixed home; FORMAL.

transistor /trænˈzɪstə/ **transistors.** [1] N-C A **transistor** is a small electronic component in something such as a television or radio, which is used to amplify or control electronic signals. [2] N-C A **transistor** or a **transistor radio** is a small portable radio; DATED.

transit /ˈtrænzɪt/. [1] N-U & PHRASE **Transit** is the carrying of goods or people by vehicle from one place to another. People or things that are **in transit** are travelling or being taken from one place to another. ...*goods lost in transit.* [2] ADJ BEFORE N A **transit** area or building is a place where people wait or where goods are kept between different stages of a journey. ...*a transit lounge at Moscow airport.* [3] N-U In American English, a **transit** system is a system for moving people or goods from one place to another, for use on buses or trains. The usual British word is **transport**. ...*the Chicago Transit Authority.*

transition /trænˈzɪʃən/ **transitions.** N-VAR **Transition** is the process in which something changes from one state to another. ♦**transitional** ADJ ...*the transitional stage between the old and new methods.*

transitive /ˈtrænzɪtɪv/. ADJ A **transitive** verb has an object.

translate /trænzˈleɪt/ **translates, translating, translated.** [1] VERB If something that someone has said or written **is translated**, it is said or written again in a different language. *Martin Luther translated the Bible into German.* ♦**translation** N-U *The papers have been sent to Saudi Arabia for translation.* ♦**translator, translators** N-C *To work as a translator, you need fluency in at least one foreign language.* [2] VERB To **translate** one thing into another means to convert it into something else. *Your decision must be translated into specific, concrete actions.*

translation /trænzˈleɪʃən/ **translations.** N-C A **translation** is a piece of writing or speech that has been translated from a different language.

translucent /trænzˈluːsənt/. ADJ If a material is **translucent**, some light can pass through it. ...*translucent plastic sheeting.*

transmission /trænzˈmɪʃən/ **transmissions.** [1] N-U The **transmission** of something involves passing or sending it to a different place or person. ...*the fax machine and other forms of*

electronic data transmission. [2] N-U The **transmission** of television or radio programmes is the broadcasting of them. [3] N-C A **transmission** is a television or radio broadcast. [4] N-VAR A vehicle's **transmission**, is the system of gears by which the power from the engine reaches and turns the wheels.

transmit /trænzˈmɪt/ **transmits, transmitting, transmitted.** [1] VERB When a message or electronic signal **is transmitted**, it is sent by wires, radio waves, or satellite. *This is currently the most efficient way to transmit certain types of data like electronic mail.* [2] VERB To **transmit** something to a different place or person means to pass or send it to the place or person; FORMAL. ...*transmitting the infection through operations.*

transmitter /trænzˈmɪtə/ **transmitters.** N-C A **transmitter** is a piece of equipment used for broadcasting television or radio programmes.

transparency /trænsˈpærənsi, AM -ˈper-/ **transparencies.** [1] N-C A **transparency** is a small piece of photographic film in a frame which can be projected onto a screen. [2] N-U **Transparency** is the quality that an object or substance has if you can see through it.

transparent /trænsˈpærənt, AM -ˈper-/. [1] ADJ If an object or substance is **transparent**, you can see through it. ...*a sheet of transparent plastic.* [2] ADJ If a situation, system, or activity is **transparent**, it is easily understood or recognized. ♦**transparently** ADV *He had been transparently honest with her.*

transpire /trænˈspaɪə/ **transpires, transpiring, transpired.** [1] VERB When it **transpires** that something is the case, people discover that it is the case; FORMAL. *It transpired that there was something wrong with the roof.* [2] VERB When something **transpires**, it happens; FORMAL.

transplant, transplants, transplanting, transplanted. [1] N-VAR /ˈtrænsplɑːnt, -plænt/ A **transplant** is a surgical operation in which a part of a person's body is replaced because it is diseased. ...*a heart transplant.* [2] VERB /trænsˈplɑːnt, -ˈplænt/ To **transplant** someone or something means to move them to a different place. *Marriage had transplanted Rebecca from London to Manchester.*

transport, transports, transporting, transported. [1] N-U /ˈtrænspɔːt/ **Transport** refers to any type of vehicle that you can travel in. *Have you got your own transport?* ...*public transport.* [2] N-U **Transport** is the moving of goods or people from one place to another. *The transport of soldiers and equipment is now complete.* [3] VERB /trænsˈpɔːt/ When goods or people are **transported** from one place to another, they are moved there.

transportation /ˌtrænspɔːˈteɪʃən/. N-U **Transportation** is the same as **transport**; AMERICAN.

trap /træp/ **traps, trapping, trapped.** [1] N-C & VERB A **trap** is a device for catching animals. If you **trap** animals, you catch them using a trap. [2] VERB & N-C If someone **traps** you, they trick you so that you do or say something which you did not want to. A **trap** is a trick that is intended to catch or deceive someone. *Were you trying to trap her into making some admission?*.

3 VERB If you **are trapped** somewhere, something falls onto you or blocks your way, preventing you from moving. *His car pushed another vehicle forward, temporarily trapping a young boy.*

trapped /træpt/. ADJ If you feel **trapped**, you are in an unpleasant situation in which you lack freedom, and you feel you cannot escape from it. *Gordon found himself trapped in a dead-end job.*

trappings /'træpɪŋz/. N-PL The **trappings** of power or wealth are the extra things, such as decorations and luxury items, that go with it; used showing disapproval.

trash /træʃ/. N-U In American English, **trash** consists of unwanted things or waste material such as old food. The British word is **rubbish**.
● See note at **rubbish**.

trauma /'trɔːmə, AM 'traumə/ **traumas**. N-VAR **Trauma** is a very severe shock or very upsetting experience, which may cause psychological damage. *...the trauma of divorce.*

traumatic /trɔː'mætɪk, AM trau-/. ADJ A **traumatic** experience is very shocking or upsetting, and may cause psychological damage.

travel /'trævəl/ **travels, travelling, travelled** (AM **traveling, traveled**). **1** VERB If you **travel**, you go from one place to another, often to a place that is far away. *Students often travel hundreds of miles to get here.* **2** N-U **Travel** is the act of travelling. *Information on travel in New Zealand is available at the hotel.* **3** N-PL Someone's **travels** are the journeys they make to places a long way from their home. *He also collects things for the house on his travels abroad.* **4** VERB When light, sound, or news from one place reaches another, you say that it **travels** to the other place. *When sound travels through water, strange things can happen.*

The noun **travel** is used to talk about the general activity of travelling. It is either uncount or plural. You cannot say 'a travel'. If you want to talk about a particular instance of someone going somewhere, you should refer to it as a **trip** or a **journey**. *He suggested I cancel my trip to China. ...a journey by train from Berlin.* **Voyage** is a more literary word, and is used only when you are talking about travelling by ship or spacecraft.

'travel agent, travel agents. **1** N-C A **travel agent** or **travel agent's** is a shop where you can arrange a holiday or journey. **2** N-C A **travel agent** is a person or business that arranges holidays and journeys.

traveller (AM **traveler**) /'trævələ/ **travellers**. N-C A **traveller** is a person who is making a journey or who travels a lot.

'traveller's cheque (AM **traveler's check**), **traveller's cheques**. N-C **Traveller's cheques** are special cheques that you can exchange for local currency when you are abroad.

traverse /'trævɜːs, trə'vɜːs/ **traverses, traversing, traversed**. VERB If someone or something **traverses** an area of land or water, they go across it; FORMAL. *...the muddy path that traversed the meadow.*

travesty /'trævəsti/ **travesties**. N-C If you describe something as a **travesty** of something else, you mean that it is a very bad representation of the other thing. *They issued a statement calling the judgment a 'travesty of justice'.*

trawler /'trɔːlə/ **trawlers**. N-C A **trawler** is a fishing boat with large nets that are dragged along the bottom of the sea.

tray /treɪ/ **trays**. N-C A **tray** is a flat piece of wood, plastic, or metal that has raised edges and that is used for carrying food or drinks.

treacherous /'tretʃərəs/. **1** ADJ If you describe someone as **treacherous**, you think they are likely to betray you; FORMAL. **2** ADJ If you say that something is **treacherous**, you mean that it is dangerous and unpredictable. *Blizzards had made the roads treacherous.*

treachery /'tretʃəri/. N-U **Treachery** is behaviour in which someone betrays their country or betrays a person who trusts them; FORMAL.

tread /tred/ **treads, treading, trod, trodden**. **1** VERB If you **tread on** something, you put your foot on it when you are walking or standing. *Oh, sorry, I didn't mean to tread on your foot.* **2** VERB If you **tread** in a particular way, you walk that way; LITERARY. *He trod softly up the stairs.* **3** N-SING Someone's **tread** is the sound made by their feet as they walk; WRITTEN. *She had heard the creak of his heavy tread.* **4** VERB If you **tread** carefully, you behave with caution. **5** N-C The **tread** of a tyre is the pattern of grooves on it.

treadmill /'tredmɪl/ **treadmills**. N-C You can refer to a task or a job as a **treadmill** when you have to keep doing it although it is unpleasant.

treason /'triːzən/. N-U **Treason** is the crime of betraying your country.

treasure /'treʒə/ **treasures, treasuring, treasured**. **1** N-U In children's stories, **treasure** is a collection of valuable old objects, such as gold coins and jewels. **2** N-C **Treasures** are valuable objects, especially works of art and items of historical value. *...stolen art treasures.* **3** VERB If you **treasure** something that you have, you keep it carefully because it gives you great pleasure and you think it is very special. *She treasures her memories of those joyous days.* ◆ **treasured** ADJ BEFORE N *...my most treasured possessions.*

treasurer /'treʒərə/ **treasurers**. N-C The **treasurer** of a society or organization is the person in charge of its finances.

treat /triːt/ **treats, treating, treated**. **1** VERB If you **treat** someone or something in a particular way, you behave towards them in that way. *Stop treating me like a child... All faiths should be treated with respect.* **2** VERB When a doctor **treats** a patient or an illness, he or she tries to make the patient well again. *The boy was treated for a minor head wound.* **3** VERB If something **is treated** with a particular substance, the substance is put onto or into it, for example in order to clean it. *If you use timber it is vital to have it treated with preservative.* **4** N-C & VERB If you give someone a **treat**, or if you **treat** them, you buy or arrange something special for them which they will enjoy. *Sometimes as a special treat my grandfather took me to the docks... Go on, treat yourself to a new dress.*

treatment /'tri:tmənt/ **treatments.** [1] N-VAR **Treatment** is medical attention given to a sick or injured person or animal. *There are two standard treatments for this disease.* [2] N-U Your **treatment** of someone is the way you behave towards them. *We don't want any special treatment.*

treaty /'tri:ti/ **treaties.** N-C A **treaty** is a written agreement between countries.

treble /'trebəl/ **trebles, trebling, trebled.** VERB If something **trebles**, or if you **treble** it, it becomes three times greater in number or amount. *The number of claims has almost trebled this year.*

tree /tri:/ **trees.** N-C A **tree** is a tall plant with a hard trunk, branches, and leaves.

trek /trek/ **treks, trekking, trekked.** VERB & N-C If you **trek** somewhere, or if you go on a **trek**, you go on a long journey across difficult terrain, usually on foot. *...trekking through the jungles.*

tremble /'trembəl/ **trembles, trembling, trembled.** [1] VERB If you **tremble**, you shake slightly, usually because you are frightened or cold. *I was trembling with fear.* [2] VERB If something **trembles**, it shakes slightly; LITERARY. *He felt the earth tremble under him.*

tremendous /trɪ'mendəs/. [1] ADJ You use **tremendous** to emphasize how strong a feeling or quality is, or how large an amount is. *I felt a tremendous pressure on my chest. ...a tremendous amount of information.* ♦**tremendously** ADV *I enjoyed it tremendously.* [2] ADJ You can describe someone or something as **tremendous** when you think they are very impressive.

tremor /'tremə/ **tremors.** [1] N-C A **tremor** is a small earthquake. [2] N-C A **tremor** is a shaking of your body or voice that you cannot control. *Winslow felt a little tremor of excitement.*

trench /trentʃ/ **trenches.** N-C A **trench** is a long narrow channel dug in the ground.

trend /trend/ **trends.** N-C A **trend** is a change towards something different. *...the growing trend towards overseas investment.*

trendy /'trendi/ **trendier, trendiest.** ADJ If you say that something or someone is **trendy**, you mean that they are very fashionable and modern; INFORMAL. *...a trendy London restaurant.*

trepidation /,trepɪ'deɪʃən/. N-U **Trepidation** is fear or anxiety about something that you are going to do or experience; FORMAL. *They will await the outcome with some trepidation.*

trespass /'trespəs/ **trespasses, trespassing, trespassed.** VERB If you **trespass** on someone's land, you go onto it without their permission.

trial /traɪəl/ **trials.** [1] N-VAR & PHRASE A **trial** is the legal process in which a judge and jury listen to evidence and decide whether a person is guilty of a crime. You say that the person being judged is **on trial** or that they **stand trial**. *New evidence showed the police lied at the trial.* [2] N-VAR & PHRASE A **trial** is an act of testing something or someone to see how well they perform a task. You say that the thing or person being tested is **on trial**. *The vaccine is about to go on trial in the US.* [3] PHRASE If you

do something by **trial and error**, you try different ways of doing it until you find the best one.

triangle /'traɪæŋgəl/ **triangles.** N-C A **triangle** is a shape with three straight sides. ♦**triangular** /traɪ'æŋgjʊlə/ ADJ *...the triangular frame.*

tribe /traɪb/ **tribes.** N-C **Tribe** is sometimes used to refer to a group of people of the same race, language, and customs, especially in a developing country. Some people disapprove of this use. **Tribe** can take the singular or plural form of the verb. *...the Xhosa tribe.* ♦**tribal** /'traɪbəl/ ADJ *...tribal lands.*

tribulation /,trɪbjʊ'leɪʃən/ **tribulations.** N-VAR You can refer to the suffering or difficulty that you experience in a particular situation as **tribulations**; FORMAL. *...the trials and tribulations of everyday life.*

tribunal /traɪ'bju:nəl/ **tribunals.** N-C A **tribunal** is a special court or committee that is appointed to deal with particular problems. **Tribunal** can take the singular or plural form of the verb. *...an industrial tribunal.*

tribute /'trɪbju:t/ **tributes.** [1] N-VAR A **tribute** is something that you say or do to show your admiration and respect for someone. *He paid tribute to the organising committee.* [2] N-SING If one thing is a **tribute** to another, it is the result of the other thing and shows how good it is. *Their success is a tribute to their discipline.*

trick /trɪk/ **tricks, tricking, tricked.** [1] VERB & N-C If someone **tricks** you, or if they play a **trick** on you, they deceive you, often in order to make you do something. *His family tricked him into going to Pakistan.* [2] N-C A **trick** is a clever or skilful action that someone does in order to entertain people. *...card tricks.* [3] N-C A **trick** is a special way of doing something. *There is a trick to installing it properly.* [4] PHRASE If something **does the trick**, it achieves what you wanted; INFORMAL. *Sometimes a few choice words will do the trick.*

trickle /'trɪkəl/ **trickles, trickling, trickled.** [1] VERB & N-C If a liquid **trickles** somewhere, or if there is a **trickle** of it, it flows slowly in a thin stream. *A tear trickled down the old man's cheek. ...a trickle of water.* [2] VERB & N-C If people or things **trickle** somewhere, or if there is a **trickle** of them to that place, they move there slowly in small amounts. *The flood of cars has now slowed to a trickle.*

tricky /'trɪki/ **trickier, trickiest.** ADJ A **tricky** task or problem is difficult to deal with.

tried /traɪd/. **Tried** is the past tense and past participle of **try**.

trifle /'traɪfəl/ **trifles, trifling, trifled.** [1] PHRASE You can use **a trifle** to mean slightly. *He seemed a trifle annoyed.* [2] N-C **Trifles** are things that are not considered important. *He didn't waste himself over trifles.* [3] N-VAR **Trifle** is a cold dessert made of layers of sponge cake, fruit, jelly, and custard.

trigger /'trɪgə/ **triggers, triggering, triggered.** [1] N-C The **trigger** of a gun is the small lever which you pull to fire it. [2] VERB To **trigger** a bomb or system means to cause it to work. *The thieves must have deliberately triggered the alarm.* [3] VERB & PHR-VERB If something **triggers** an event, or if it **triggers off** an event, it causes the event to happen. *It is still* *not clear what events triggered off the demonstrations.* [4] N-C If something acts as a **trigger** for another thing, the first thing causes the second thing to begin. *Stress may act as a trigger for these illnesses.*

trillion /ˈtrɪljən/. NUM A **trillion** is a million million.

trilogy /ˈtrɪlədʒi/ **trilogies**. N-C A **trilogy** is a series of three books, plays, or films with the same characters or subject.

trim /trɪm/ **trimmer, trimmest; trims, trimming, trimmed.** [1] ADJ Something that is **trim** is neat and attractive. *The neighbours' gardens were trim and neat.* [2] ADJ If someone has a **trim** figure, they are slim. *...a trim woman in her forties.* [3] VERB & N-C If you **trim** something, or if you give it a **trim**, you cut off small amounts of it to make it look neater. *His hair needed a trim.* [4] VERB If something such as a piece of clothing **is trimmed** with a type of material or design, it is decorated with it, usually along its edges. *...an ivory dress trimmed with blue bows.* [5] N-VAR The **trim** on something such as a piece of clothing is a decoration along its edges in a different colour or material. *...black leather boots with fur trim.*

▸ **trim off.** PHR-VERB If you **trim off** parts of something, you cut them off, because they are not needed. *Trim the fat off the ham.*

trimming /ˈtrɪmɪŋ/ **trimmings.** [1] N-VAR The **trimming** on something such as a piece of clothing is the decoration along its edges in a different colour or material. *...the lace trimming on her satin nightgown.* [2] N-PL **Trimmings** are extra things that can be added to something or included in something. *...roast turkey with all the trimmings.*

trio /ˈtriːəʊ/ **trios.** N-C A **trio** is a group of three people, especially musicians or singers.

trip /trɪp/ **trips, tripping, tripped.** [1] N-C A **trip** is a journey that you make to a place and back again. ● *We went out on a day trip. ...a business trip.* ● See also **round trip.** [2] N-C A **trip** is an imaginary experience caused by taking drugs; INFORMAL. [3] VERB If you **trip** when you are walking, or if you **trip up**, you knock your foot against something and fall over. *He was just coming down the ramp when he tripped up.* [4] VERB & PHR-VERB If you **trip** someone who is walking, or if you **trip them up**, you put your foot or something else in front of them so that they knock their own foot against it and fall.

triple /ˈtrɪpəl/ **triples, tripling, tripled.** [1] ADJ BEFORE N **Triple** means consisting of three things or parts. *...a triple somersault.* [2] VERB If something **triples**, or if you **triple** it, it becomes three times greater in size or number. *The Exhibition has tripled in size from last year.*

triplet /ˈtrɪplət/ **triplets.** N-C **Triplets** are three children born at the same time to the same mother.

tripod /ˈtraɪpɒd/ **tripods.** N-C A **tripod** is a stand with three legs, used to support something such as a camera.

triumph /ˈtraɪʌmf/ **triumphs, triumphing, triumphed.** [1] N-VAR A **triumph** is a great success or achievement. *The building is a triumph of modern design.* [2] N-U **Triumph** is a feeling

of great satisfaction when you win or achieve something. *Any feeling of triumph will be short-lived.* [3] VERB If you **triumph**, you win a victory or succeed in overcoming something. *The film is about good triumphing over evil.*

triumphant /traɪˈʌmfənt/. ADJ If you are **triumphant**, you feel very happy because you have won a victory or achieved something. ◆ **triumphantly** ADV *They marched triumphantly into the capital.*

trivia /ˈtrɪviə/. N-U **Trivia** consists of unimportant facts or details. *The two men chatted about such trivia as their favourite kinds of fast food.*

trivial /ˈtrɪviəl/. ADJ If you describe something as **trivial**, you think that it is unimportant and not serious. *...trivial details.*

triviality /ˌtrɪviˈælɪti/ **trivialities.** N-VAR If you refer to something as a **triviality**, you think it is unimportant.

trod /trɒd/. **Trod** is the past tense of **tread.**

trodden /ˈtrɒdən/. **Trodden** is the past participle of **tread.**

trolley /ˈtrɒli/ **trolleys.** [1] N-C A **trolley** is a small cart on wheels that you use to carry things such as shopping or luggage; BRITISH. *...supermarket trolleys.* [2] N-C A **trolley** is a small table on wheels on which food and drinks can be carried; BRITISH. [3] N-C In American English, a **trolley** is an electric vehicle which travels on rails along a street. The British word is **tram.**

trombone /trɒmˈbəʊn/ **trombones.** N-C A **trombone** is a brass musical instrument which you play by blowing into it and sliding part of it backwards and forwards.

troop /truːp/ **troops, trooping, trooped.** [1] N-PL **Troops** are soldiers. *...more than 35,000 troops from a dozen countries.* [2] N-C A **troop** is a group of soldiers within a cavalry or armoured regiment. [3] VERB If people **troop** somewhere, they walk there in a group. *They all trooped back to the house.*

trooper /ˈtruːpə/ **troopers.** [1] N-C A **trooper** is a soldier of low rank in the cavalry or in an armoured regiment in the army. [2] N-C In the United States, a **trooper** is a police officer in a state police force.

trophy /ˈtrəʊfi/ **trophies.** N-C A **trophy** is a prize such as a cup, given to the winner of a competition.

tropical /ˈtrɒpɪkəl/. ADJ **Tropical** means belonging to or typical of the tropics. *...tropical diseases. ...tropical weather.*

tropics /ˈtrɒpɪks/. N-PL The **tropics** are the hottest parts of the world, near the equator.

trot /trɒt/ **trots, trotting, trotted.** [1] VERB & N-SING When an animal such as a horse **trots**, or when it breaks into a **trot**, it moves fairly fast, taking quick small steps. *Pete got on his horse and started trotting across the field.* [2] VERB If you **trot** somewhere, you move fairly fast, taking quick small steps. *I trotted down the steps.* [3] PHRASE If several things happen **on the trot**, they happen one after the other, without a break; INFORMAL. *She lost five games on the trot.*

▶ **trot out.** PHR-VERB If you say that someone **is trotting out** old ideas or information, you mean that they are repeating them in a boring way.

trouble /'trʌbəl/ troubles, troubling, troubled. [1] N-VAR You can refer to problems or difficulties as **trouble**. *I had trouble parking. ...financial troubles.* [2] N-SING If you say that one aspect of a situation is **the trouble**, you mean that it is the aspect which is causing problems. *The trouble is that these restrictions have remained.* [3] VERB If something **troubles** you, it makes you feel worried. *He was troubled by the lifestyle of his son.* ◆**troubling** ADJ *...troubling chest pains.* [4] N-U If you have back **trouble**, for example, there is something wrong with your back. [5] N-U If there is **trouble**, people are quarrelling or fighting. *...fans who make trouble during the World Cup.* PHRASES ● If someone is **in trouble**, they have broken a rule or law and are likely to be punished by someone in authority. *He was in trouble with his teachers.* ● If you **take the trouble** to do something, you do it although it requires some time or effort. *Alexander rolled up his trouser legs.*

troubled /'trʌbəld/. ADJ **Troubled** means worried or full of problems. *Rose sounded deeply troubled. ...this troubled country.*

troublemaker /'trʌbəlmeɪkə/ troublemakers. N-C A **troublemaker** is someone who causes trouble.

troublesome /'trʌbəlsəm/. ADJ Someone or something that is **troublesome** causes problems or difficulties. *...a troublesome back injury.*

trough /trɒf, AM trɔːf/ troughs. [1] N-C A **trough** is a long container from which farm animals drink or eat. [2] N-C A **trough** is a low point in a pattern that has regular high and low points. *American bank shares have risen by 60% since their trough last October.*

troupe /truːp/ troupes. N-C A **troupe** is a group of actors, singers, or dancers who work together.

trousers /'traʊzəz/; the form **trouser** is used as a modifier. N-PL In British English, **trousers** are a piece of clothing that you wear over your body from the waist downwards, and that cover each leg separately. You can also say a **pair of trousers**. The usual American word is **pants**.

trout /traʊt/ trouts. N-VAR A **trout** is a kind of fish that lives in rivers and streams. **Trout** is the flesh of this fish eaten as food.

truant /'truːənt/ truants. [1] N-C A **truant** is a child who stays away from school without permission. [2] PHRASE If children **play truant**, they stay away from school without permission.

truce /truːs/ truces. N-C A **truce** is an agreement between two people or groups to stop fighting or quarrelling for a short time.

truck /trʌk/ trucks. [1] N-C In American English a **truck** is a large vehicle that is used to transport goods by road. The usual British word is **lorry**. [2] N-C A **truck** is an open vehicle used for carrying goods on a railway; BRITISH.

trudge /trʌdʒ/ trudges, trudging, trudged. VERB & N-SING If you **trudge** somewhere, you walk there with slow heavy steps. This way of walking is called a **trudge**. *...the long trudge home.*

true /truː/ truer, truest. [1] ADJ If something is **true**, it is based on facts and is not invented or imagined. *He said it was true that a collision had happened... The film is based on a true story.* [2] ADJ BEFORE N **True** means real, genuine, or typical. *This country professes to be a true democracy... The true cost often differs from that.* PHRASES ● If a dream, wish, or prediction **comes true**, it actually happens. ● If a general statement **holds true** in particular circumstances, or if your previous statement **holds true** in different circumstances, it is true or valid in those circumstances. *The nearer the cinema, the worse the restaurant. This rule holds true across most of London.*

truly /'truːli/. [1] ADV **Truly** means completely and genuinely. *Not all doctors truly understand the reproductive cycle... Believe me, Susan, I am truly sorry.* [2] ADV You can use **truly** in order to emphasize your description of something. *They were truly appalling.* [3] ADV You can use **truly** to emphasize that what you are saying is true. *I do not expect a war between my country and yours. Truly I do not.* [4] CONVENTION You can write **Yours truly** before your signature at the end of a letter to someone you do not know very well. [5] **well and truly**: see **well.**

trump /trʌmp/ trumps. [1] N-U In a game of cards, **trumps** is the suit which is chosen to have the highest value in a particular game. [2] PHRASE Your **trump card** is the most powerful thing that you can use or do to gain an advantage. *Mr Amato's trump card is his colleagues' fear of an early election.*

trumpet /'trʌmpɪt/ trumpets. N-C A **trumpet** is a brass wind instrument.

trumpeter /'trʌmpɪtə/ trumpeters. N-C A **trumpeter** is someone who plays a trumpet.

trundle /'trʌndəl/ trundles, trundling, trundled. [1] VERB If a vehicle **trundles** somewhere, it moves there slowly. *The train eventually trundled in at 7.54.* [2] VERB If you **trundle** something somewhere, especially an object with wheels, you move or roll it along slowly. *The old man lifted the barrow and trundled it away.*

trunk /trʌŋk/ trunks. [1] N-C The **trunk** of a tree is the large main stem from which the branches grow. [2] N-C A **trunk** is a large strong case or box used for storing things or for taking on a journey. [3] N-C An elephant's **trunk** is its long nose. [4] N-C In American English, the **trunk** of a car is a covered space at the back or front that is used for luggage. The usual British word is **boot.**

trust /trʌst/ trusts, trusting, trusted. [1] VERB & N-U If you **trust** someone, or if you have **trust** in them, you believe that they are honest and will not deliberately do anything to harm you. *The president can't be trusted... You've betrayed their trust.* [2] VERB If you **trust** someone to do something, you believe that they will do it. *I knew I could trust him to meet a tight deadline.* [3] VERB If you **trust** someone **with** something, you allow them to look after it or deal with it. *I'd trust him with my life.* [4] N-U **Trust** is responsibility that you are given to deal with important, valuable, or secret things. ...*a position of trust which was generously paid.* **5** VERB If you do not **trust** something, you feel that it is not safe or reliable. *He didn't trust his legs to hold him up.* **6** VERB If you **trust** someone's judgement or advice, you believe that it is good or right. **7** N-C A **trust** is a financial arrangement in which an organization keeps and invests money for someone. *They've set up a trust fund for their daughter... The money will be put in trust until she is 18.*

trustee /trʌ'stiː/ **trustees.** N-C A **trustee** is someone with legal control of money or property that is kept or invested for another person.

trusting /'trʌstɪŋ/ ADJ A **trusting** person believes that people are honest and sincere and do not intend to harm him or her.

trustworthy /'trʌstwɜːði/. ADJ A **trustworthy** person is reliable, responsible, and can be trusted completely.

truth /truːθ/ **truths.** **1** N-U The **truth** about something is all the facts about it, rather than things that are imagined or invented. *In the town very few know the whole truth... I want you to tell me the truth.* **2** N-U If you say that there is some **truth** in a statement or story, you mean that it is true, or partly true. *The criticisms have at least an element of truth.* **3** N-C A **truth** is something that is generally accepted to be true. ...*universal truths.*

truthful /'truːθfʊl/. ADJ If a person or their comments are **truthful**, they are honest and do not tell any lies. ♦ **truthfully** ADV *I answered all their questions truthfully.* ♦ **truthfulness** N-U ...*qualities such as honesty and truthfulness.*

try /traɪ/ **tries, trying, tried.** **1** VERB & N-C If you **try** to do something, or if you have a **try** at doing something, you make an effort to do it. *I tried hard to persuade him to stay... I must try and see him... I tried calling him when I got here but he wasn't at home... After a few tries Patrick had given up.* **2** VERB & N-C If you **try** something new or different, or if you give it a **try**, you use it or do it in order to find out how useful, effective, or enjoyable it is. *You could try a little cheese melted on the top.* **3** VERB If you **try** a particular place or person, you go to that place or person because you think they may be able to provide you with what you want. *Have you tried the local music shops?* **4** VERB When a person is **tried**, they appear in court and are found innocent or guilty after the judge and jury have heard the evidence. **5** N-C In the game of rugby, a **try** is the action of scoring by putting the ball down behind the goal line of the opposing team. **6** to **try** your **hand**: see **hand**. ● to **try** your **luck**: see **luck**.

▸ **try on.** PHR-VERB If you **try on** a piece of clothing, you put it on to see if it fits you or if it looks nice.

▸ **try out.** PHR-VERB If you **try** something **out**, you test it in order to find out how useful or effective it is. *London Transport hopes to try out the system in September.*

trying /'traɪɪŋ/. ADJ Someone or something that is **trying** is difficult to deal with and makes you feel impatient or annoyed. *The whole business has been very trying.*

'T-shirt (or tee-shirt) T-shirts. N-C A **T-shirt** is a cotton shirt with short sleeves and no collar or buttons.

tub /tʌb/ **tubs.** **1** N-C A **tub** is a deep container of any size. ...*four tubs of ice cream.* **2** N-C In American English, a **tub** is a container which you fill with water and sit in while you wash your body. The British word is **bath**.

tube /tjuːb, AM tuːb/ **tubes.** **1** N-C A **tube** is a long hollow cylinder. *He is fed by a tube that enters his nose.* **2** N-C A **tube** of paste is a long thin container which you squeeze in order to force the paste out. ...*a tube of toothpaste.* **3** N-SING The **Tube** is the underground railway system in London; BRITISH. *He travelled by tube.*

tuberculosis /tjuːˌbɜːkjʊ'ləʊsɪs, AM tuː-/. N-U **Tuberculosis**, or 'TB', is a serious infectious disease that affects the lungs.

tubing /'tjuːbɪŋ, AM tuː-/. N-U **Tubing** is plastic, rubber, or other material made in the shape of a tube.

tuck /tʌk/ **tucks, tucking, tucked.** VERB If you **tuck** something somewhere, you put it there so that it is safe, comfortable, or neat. *He tried to tuck his flapping shirt inside his trousers.*

▸ **tuck away.** **1** PHR-VERB If you **tuck away** something such as money, you store it in a safe place. *I tucked the box away in the linen drawer.* **2** PHR-VERB If someone or something **is tucked away**, they are well hidden in a quiet place where very few people go. *His home in Bexley is tucked away in a miniature forest.*

▸ **tuck in.** **1** PHR-VERB If you **tuck in** a piece of material, you secure it in position by placing the edge of it behind or under something else. *Tuck the sheets in firmly... Straighten your cap and tuck your shirt in.* **2** PHR-VERB If you **tuck** a child **in** bed, or if you **tuck** them **in**, you make them comfortable by straightening the sheets and blankets and pushing the loose ends under the mattress.

▸ **tuck into or tuck in** PHR-VERB If someone **tucks into** a meal, or if they **tuck in**, they start eating enthusiastically or hungrily; BRITISH, INFORMAL. *Tuck in while it's hot.*

Tuesday /'tjuːzdeɪ, -di, AM 'tuːz-/ **Tuesdays.** N-VAR **Tuesday** is the day after Monday and before Wednesday.

tug /tʌɡ/ **tugs, tugging, tugged.** **1** VERB & N-C If you **tug** something, if you **tug** at it, or if you give it a **tug**, you give it a quick pull. *Anna tugged at Martha's arm. 'Look,' she said.* **2** N-C A **tug** is a small powerful boat which pulls large ships, usually when they come into a port.

tuition /tjʊ'ɪʃən, AM tuː-/. N-U If you are given **tuition** in a particular subject, you are taught about that subject, especially on your own or in a small group. *I've seriously been considering having private tuition.*

tulip /'tjuːlɪp, AM 'tuː-/ **tulips.** N-C **Tulips** are garden flowers that grow in the spring.

tumble /'tʌmbəl/ **tumbles, tumbling, tumbled.** VERB & N-C If someone or something **tumbles**, or if they take a **tumble**, they fall with a rolling or bouncing movement. ...*the gun tum-*

bled out of his hand... He injured his ribs in a tumble from his horse.

tummy /ˈtʌmi/ **tummies.** N-C Your **tummy** is your stomach; INFORMAL.

tumour (AM **tumor**) /ˈtjuːmə, AM ˈtuː-/ **tumours.** N-C A **tumour** is a mass of diseased or abnormal cells that has grown in someone's body.

tumultuous /tjuːˈmʌltʃuəs, AM tuː-/. **1** ADJ **Tumultuous** feelings or events are very exciting or confusing. *...the tumultuous changes taking place in Eastern Europe.* **2** ADJ A **tumultuous** reaction to something is very noisy, because the people involved are very happy or excited. *...tumultuous applause.*

tuna /ˈtjuːnə, AM ˈtuːnə/; the plural is **tuna** or **tunas.** N-VAR A **tuna** or a **tuna fish** is a large fish that lives in warm seas. **Tuna** or **tuna fish** is the flesh of this fish eaten as food.

tune /tjuːn, AM tuːn/ **tunes, tuning, tuned.** **1** N-C A **tune** is a series of musical notes that is pleasant to listen to. *...a merry little tune.* **2** VERB When someone **tunes** or **tunes up** a musical instrument, they adjust it so that it produces the right notes. **3** VERB If your radio or television **is tuned** to a particular broadcasting station, you are listening to or watching the programmes being broadcast on that station. PHRASES ● A person or musical instrument that is **in tune** produces exactly the right notes. ● If you say that someone **has changed** their **tune**, you are criticizing them because they have changed their opinion or way of doing things. ● **To the tune of** a particular amount means to the extent of that amount. *The family suddenly found itself in debt to the tune of some $5,000.*
▸ **tune in.** PHR-VERB If you **tune in** to a particular television or radio station or programme, you watch or listen to it.

tunic /ˈtjuːnɪk, AM ˈtuː-/ **tunics.** N-C A **tunic** is a loose garment that is worn on the top part of your body.

tunnel /ˈtʌnəl/ **tunnels, tunnelling, tunnelled** (AM **tunneling, tunneled**). **1** N-C A **tunnel** is a long passage which has been made under the ground, usually through a hill or under the sea. **2** VERB To **tunnel** somewhere means to make a tunnel there. *The rebels tunnelled out of a maximum security jail.*

turbine /ˈtɜːbaɪn, AM -bɪn/ **turbines.** N-C A **turbine** is a machine or engine which uses a stream of air, gas, water, or steam to turn a wheel and produce power.

turbulent /ˈtɜːbjʊlənt/. **1** ADJ A **turbulent** time, place, or relationship is one in which there is a lot of change and confusion. *...six turbulent years of rows and reconciliations.* ◆**turbulence** /ˈtɜːbjʊləns/ N-U *...a region often beset by political turbulence.* **2** ADJ **Turbulent** water or air contains strong currents which change direction suddenly. ◆**turbulence** N-U *His plane encountered severe turbulence.*

turf /tɜːf/ **turfs, turfing, turfed.** N-U **Turf** is short, thick, even grass.
▸ **turf out.** PHR-VERB If someone **is turfed out** of a place or position, they are forced to leave;

BRITISH, INFORMAL. *She should have been turfed out of her job years ago.*

turkey /ˈtɜːki/ **turkeys.** **1** N-C A **turkey** is a large bird that is kept on a farm for its meat. **2** N-U **Turkey** is the meat of a turkey eaten as food.

turmoil /ˈtɜːmɔɪl/. N-U **Turmoil** is a state of confusion or great anxiety. *...the political turmoil of 1989... Her marriage was in turmoil.*

turn 1 to change in direction or nature

turn /tɜːn/ **turns, turning, turned.** **1** VERB To **turn** means to move in a different direction or to move into a different position. **Turn around** or **turn round** means the same as **turn**. *He turned his head left and right... She had turned the bedside chair to face the door.* **2** VERB & N-C When you **turn** in a particular direction, you change the direction in which you are moving or travelling. A **turn** is a change of direction. *Now turn right to follow West Ferry Road... You can't do a right-hand turn here.* ● See also **turning**. **3** VERB If you **turn to** a particular page in a book, you open it at that page. **4** VERB If you **turn** your attention or thoughts **to** a particular person or thing, you start thinking about them or discussing them. *We turn now to the British news.* **5** VERB If you **turn to** someone, you ask for their help or advice. *There was no one to turn to.* **6** VERB When something **turns** into something else, or when you **turn** it into something else, it becomes something different. *...the government's plans to turn the country into a one-party-state.* **7** N-C If a situation or trend takes a particular kind of **turn**, it changes so that it starts developing in a different or opposite way. *...the latest turn in the fighting.* **8** **to turn your back**: see **back**. ● **to turn the tables**: see **table**.

turn 2 your time or occasion to do something

turn /tɜːn/ **turns.** N-C If it is your **turn** to do something, you now have the right or duty to do it, when other people have done it before you or will do it after you. *Tonight it's my turn to cook.* PHRASES ● You use **in turn** to refer to actions or events that are in a sequence one after the other, for example because one causes the other. *Cuba buys rice from China which in turn purchases sugar from the island.* ● If two or more people **take turns** to do something or **take it in turns** to do it, they do it one after the other several times, rather than doing it together.

turn 3 phrasal verbs

turn /tɜːn/ **turns, turning, turned.**
▸ **turn against.** PHR-VERB If you **turn against** someone or something, or if something **turns** you **against** them, you stop supporting them, trusting them, or liking them. *Working with the police has turned me against the use of violent scenes as entertainment.*
▸ **turn around** or **turn round.** **1** See **turn 1**. **2** PHR-VERB If you **turn** something **around**, or if it **turns around**, it is moved so that it faces the opposite direction. *I turned the car around and headed south.*
▸ **turn away.** PHR-VERB If you **turn** someone **away**, you reject them or send them away.

Hard times are forcing many community colleges to turn away students.

▶ **turn back.** PHR-VERB If you **turn back**, or if someone **turns** you **back** when you are going somewhere, you change direction and go towards where you started from. *Police attempted to turn back protesters.*

▶ **turn down.** [1] PHR-VERB If you **turn down** a person or their request or offer, you refuse their request or offer. *After careful consideration I turned the invitation down.* [2] PHR-VERB When you **turn down** a radio, heater, or other piece of equipment, you reduce the amount of sound or heat being produced, by adjusting the controls. *He kept turning the central heating down.*

▶ **turn off.** [1] PHR-VERB If you **turn off** the road or path you are going along, you start going along a different road or path which leads away from it. *Turn off at the sign to Walton.* [2] PHR-VERB When you **turn off** a piece of equipment or a supply of something, you stop heat, sound, or water being produced by adjusting the controls. *The light's a bit too harsh. You can turn it off.*

▶ **turn on.** [1] PHR-VERB When you **turn on** a piece of equipment or a supply of something, you cause heat, sound, or water to be produced by adjusting the controls. *She asked them why they hadn't turned the lights on.* [2] PHR-VERB If someone **turns on** you, they attack you or speak angrily to you.

▶ **turn out.** [1] PHR-VERB If something **turns out** a particular way, it happens in that way or has the result or degree of success indicated. *I was positive things were going to turn out fine.* [2] PHR-VERB If something **turns out** to be a particular thing, it is discovered to be that thing. *It turned out that I knew the person who got shot.* [3] PHR-VERB When you **turn out** something such as a light or gas, you move the device that controls it so that it stops giving out light or heat. *Turn the lights out.* [4] PHR-VERB If people **turn out** for a particular event or activity, they go and take part in it or watch it. [5] See also **turnout**.

▶ **turn over.** [1] PHR-VERB If you **turn** something **over**, or if it **turns over**, it is moved so that the top part is now facing downwards. *I don't suppose you thought to turn over the tape, did you?.* [2] PHR-VERB If you **turn** something **over** in your mind, you think carefully about it. [3] PHR-VERB If you **turn** something **over** to someone, you give it to them when they ask for it, because they have a right to it. *The lawyer turned over the release papers.* [4] See also **turnover**.

▶ **turn round.** See **turn around**.

▶ **turn up.** [1] PHR-VERB If you say that someone or something **turns up**, you mean that they arrive, often unexpectedly or after you have been waiting a long time. *This is similar to waiting for a bus that never turns up.* [2] PHR-VERB When you **turn up** a radio, heater, or other piece of equipment, you increase the amount of sound, heat, or power being produced. *I turned the volume up.*

turning /'tɜːnɪŋ/ **turnings.** N-C If you take a particular **turning**, you go along a road which

leads away from the side of another road. *Take the next turning on the right.* ● See also **turn**.

'**turning point, turning points.** N-C A **turning point** is a time at which an important change takes place which affects the future of a person or thing. *Hungary's opening of the border was a turning point for the refugees.*

turnip /'tɜːnɪp/ **turnips.** N-VAR A **turnip** is a round vegetable with a green and white skin.

turnout (or **turn-out**) /'tɜːnaʊt/ **turnouts.** N-C The **turnout** at an event is the number of people who go to it. *It was a marvellous afternoon with a huge turnout of people.*

turnover /'tɜːnəʊvə/. [1] N-U The **turnover** of a company is the value of goods or services sold during a particular period of time. *The zoo has an annual turnover of £7 million.* [2] N-U The **turnover** of people in an organization is the rate at which people leave and are replaced. *Short-term contracts increase staff turnover.*

turquoise /'tɜːkwɔɪz/ **turquoises.** ADJ & N-VAR Something that is **turquoise** is of a greenish-blue colour. *I glanced out at the turquoise sea.*

turtle /'tɜːtəl/ **turtles.** N-C A **turtle** is a large reptile with a thick shell which lives in the sea.

tusk /tʌsk/ **tusks.** N-C The **tusks** of an elephant or wild boar are its two very long pointed teeth.

tussle /'tʌsəl/ **tussles, tussling, tussled.** VERB & N-C If one person **tussles** with another, or if they **tussle**, they grab hold of and struggle with each other. A **tussle** is a struggle in which people grab hold of each other.

tutor /'tjuːtə, AM 'tuːt-/ **tutors, tutoring, tutored.** [1] N-C A **tutor** is a teacher at a British university or college. [2] N-C A **tutor** is someone who gives private lessons to a pupil or a small group of pupils. [3] VERB If someone **tutors** a person or subject, they teach that person or subject. *She was tutored at home by her parents... He still tutors medical students in anatomy.*

tutorial /tjuː'tɔːriəl, AM 'tuːt-/ **tutorials.** N-C In a university or college, a **tutorial** is a regular meeting between a tutor and one or several students, for discussion of a subject that is being studied.

tuxedo /tʌk'siːdəʊ/ **tuxedos.** N-C A **tuxedo** is a black or white jacket worn by men for formal social events.

TV /ˌtiː 'viː/ **TVs.** N-VAR **TV** means the same as **television**. *I prefer going to the cinema to watching TV. ...a brand-new TV.*

tweed /twiːd/ **tweeds.** N-VAR **Tweed** is a thick woollen cloth, often woven from different coloured threads.

twelfth /twelfθ/ **twelfths.** [1] ORD The **twelfth** item in a series is the one that you count as number twelve. [2] N-C A **twelfth** is one of twelve equal parts of something.

twelve /twelv/ **twelves.** NUM **Twelve** is the number 12.

twentieth /'twentiəθ/. ORD The **twentieth** item in a series is the one that you count as number twenty.

twenty /'twenti/ **twenties.** NUM **Twenty** is the number 20. For examples of how numbers such as twenty and eighty are used see **eighty**.

twice /twaɪs/. **1** ADV If something happens **twice**, it happens two times. *I've visited Africa twice... Try to do this exercise at least twice a day.* **2** ADV If one thing is, for example, **twice as** big or old as another thing, or if it is **twice the** size or age of another thing, it is two times as big or old as the other thing. *It took us nearly twice as long to return to the station as it had to come from it... Unemployment in Northern Ireland is twice the national average.*

twig /twɪg/ **twigs.** N-C A **twig** is a very small thin branch of a tree or bush.

twilight /ˈtwaɪlaɪt/. **1** N-U **Twilight** is the time after sunset when it is just getting dark. *They returned at twilight.* **2** N-U **Twilight** is the dim light that there is outside just after sunset. *...the deepening autumn twilight.*

twin /twɪn/ **twins.** **1** N-C If two people are **twins**, they have the same mother and were born on the same day. *...her twin sister.* **2** ADJ BEFORE N **Twin** is used to describe a pair of things that look the same and are close together. *...the twin towers of a new office development. ...the world's largest twin-engined aircraft.*

twinkle /ˈtwɪŋkəl/ **twinkles, twinkling, twinkled.** **1** VERB If a star or a light **twinkles**, it shines with an unsteady light which rapidly and constantly changes from bright to faint. **2** VERB & N-SING If you say that someone's eyes **twinkle**, or that there is a **twinkle** in their eye, you mean that their face expresses good humour, amusement, or mischief.

twirl /twɜːl/ **twirls, twirling, twirled.** **1** VERB If you **twirl** something, or if it **twirls**, it turns round and round with a smooth fairly fast movement. *Bonnie twirled her empty glass in her fingers.* **2** VERB If you **twirl**, you move round and round rapidly, for example when you are dancing. *She bounded out of bed, startling Boris, and twirled around the room on her toes.*

twist /twɪst/ **twists, twisting, twisted.** **1** VERB If you **twist** something, you turn it to make a spiral shape, for example by turning the two ends of it in opposite directions. *Her hands began to twist the handles of the bag... She twisted her hair into a bun.* **2** VERB If you **twist** something, especially a part of your body, or if it **twists**, it moves into a strange, uncomfortable, or distorted shape or position. *He twisted her arms behind her back. ...the twisted wreckage of a train.* **3** VERB If you **twist** part of your body such as your head or your shoulders, you turn that part while keeping the rest of your body still. *She twisted her head sideways... Susan twisted round in her seat.* **4** VERB If you **twist** a part of your body such as your ankle or your wrist, you injure it by turning it too sharply or in an unusual direction. *I twisted my knee last year playing tennis.* **5** VERB If you **twist** something, you turn it so that it moves around in a circular direction. *He takes out a jar and twists the lid off.* **6** VERB If someone **twists** what you say, they repeat it in a way that changes its meaning, in order to harm you or benefit themselves. *You're twisting my words around.* **7** N-C A **twist** in something is an

unexpected and significant development. *The long-running battle took a new twist last night.*

twisted /ˈtwɪstɪd/. ADJ If you describe a person as **twisted**, you dislike them because you think they are strange in an unpleasant way.

twitch /twɪtʃ/ **twitches, twitching, twitched.** VERB & N-C If a part of your body **twitches**, it makes a little jerking movement, called a **twitch**. *He saw the corners of Alex's mouth twitch... He developed a nervous twitch.*

two /tuː/ **twos.** NUM **Two** is the number 2.

two-'thirds (or **two thirds**). QUANT **Two-thirds** is an amount that is two out of three equal parts of something. *Two-thirds of families in Britain already own their homes. ...a treaty to cut their nuclear arsenals by two-thirds.*

two-'way. ADJ **Two-way** means moving or working in two opposite directions. *The bridge is now open to two-way traffic... We all carry two-way radios.*

tycoon /taɪˈkuːn/ **tycoons.** N-C A **tycoon** is a person who is successful in business and so has become rich and powerful.

type 1 sort or kind

type /taɪp/ **types.** **1** N-C A **type** of something is a group of those things that have particular features in common. *...several types of lettuce... In 1990, 25% of households use of this type.* **2** N-C If you refer to a particular thing or person as a **type** of something more general, you are considering that thing or person as an example of that more general group. *Have you done this type of work before?... I am a very determined type of person.* **3** N-C If you refer to a person as a particular **type**, you mean that they have that particular appearance, character, or type of behaviour. *I was rather an outdoor type... She was certainly not the type to murder her husband.*

type 2 writing and printing

type /taɪp/ **types, typing, typed.** VERB If you **type** something, you use a typewriter or word processor to write it. *I had never really learnt to type properly.* ♦**typing** N-U *He learnt shorthand and typing.*

▸ **type in** or **type into.** PHR-VERB If you **type** information **into** a computer or **type** it **in**, you press keys on the keyboard so that the computer stores or processes the information.

▸ **type up.** PHR-VERB If you **type up** a handwritten text, you produce a typed copy of it.

typewriter /ˈtaɪpraɪtə/ **typewriters.** N-C A **typewriter** is a machine with keys which are pressed in order to print letters, numbers, or other characters onto paper.

typhoon /taɪˈfuːn/ **typhoons.** N-C A **typhoon** is a very violent tropical storm.

typical /ˈtɪpɪkəl/. **1** ADJ You use **typical** to describe someone or something that shows the most usual characteristics of a particular type of person or thing, and is therefore a good example of that type. *Aaron was brought up as a typical American child... A typical day begins at 8.30.* **2** ADJ If a particular action or feature is **typical** of someone or something, it shows their usual qualities or characteristics. *This is* *not typical of Chinese, but is a feature of the Thai language.*

typically /'tɪpɪkəli/. **1** ADV You use **typically** to say that something usually happens in the way that you are describing it. *The day typically begins with exercises and swimming.* **2** ADV You use **typically** to say that something shows all the most usual characteristics of a particular type of person or thing. *Ashley's pretty bedroom looks typically English.* **3** ADV You use **typically** to indicate that someone has behaved in the way that they normally do. *Typically, he took the setback in good humour.*

typify /'tɪpɪfaɪ/ **typifies, typifying, typified.** VERB To **typify** something means to be a typical example of it. *The design typifies Ercol's furniture: elegant and substantial.*

tyranny /'tɪrəni/. N-U **Tyranny** is cruel and unjust rule by a person or small group of people.

tyrant /'taɪərənt/ **tyrants.** N-C A **tyrant** is someone who treats the people they have authority over in a cruel and unfair way.

tyre (AM **tire**) /taɪə/ **tyres.** N-C A **tyre** is a thick ring of rubber filled with air and fitted round the wheel of a vehicle.

U u

ubiquitous /juː'bɪkwɪtəs/. ADJ If you describe something as **ubiquitous**, you mean that it seems to be everywhere at the same time. *The video camcorder has become ubiquitous.*

ugly /'ʌgli/ **uglier, ugliest.** **1** ADJ If you say that someone or something is **ugly**, you mean that they are unattractive and unpleasant to look at. ♦**ugliness** N-U *...the raw ugliness of his native city.* **2** ADJ If you refer to a situation as **ugly**, you mean that it is very unpleasant, usually because it involves violence. *There have been some ugly scenes.*

ulcer /'ʌlsə/ **ulcers.** N-C An **ulcer** is a sore area on or inside a part of your body which is very painful and may bleed.

ultimate /'ʌltɪmət/. **1** ADJ BEFORE N You use **ultimate** to describe the final result or the original cause of a long series of events. *It is still not possible to predict the ultimate outcome.* **2** ADJ BEFORE N You use **ultimate** to describe the most important or extreme thing of a particular kind. *The ultimate authority remained the presidency... The death penalty would be the ultimate abuse of human rights.* **3** PHRASE **The ultimate in** something is the best or most advanced thing of its kind. *This hotel is the ultimate in luxury.*

ultimately /'ʌltɪmətli/. **1** ADV **Ultimately** means finally, after a long series of events. *That struggle will ultimately succeed.* **2** ADV You use **ultimately** to emphasize that what you are saying is the most important point in a discussion. *Ultimately, the problem lies with employers.*

ultimatum /ˌʌltɪ'meɪtəm/ **ultimatums.** N-C An **ultimatum** is a warning that unless someone acts in a particular way within a particular time limit, action will be taken against them. *Workers have issued an ultimatum to the government.*

ultrasound /'ʌltrəsaʊnd/ **ultrasounds.** **1** N-U **Ultrasound** refers to sound waves which travel at such a high frequency that they cannot be heard by humans. **2** N-C An **ultrasound** or an **ultrasound scan** is a medical test in which ultrasound waves are used to form a picture of the inside of someone's body.

ultraviolet /ˌʌltrə'vaɪələt/. ADJ **Ultraviolet** light or radiation causes your skin to darken after you have been in sunlight.

umbrella /ʌm'brelə/ **umbrellas.** **1** N-C An **umbrella** is an object which you use to protect yourself from the rain or hot sun. It consists of a long stick with a folding frame covered in cloth. **2** N-SING **Umbrella** refers to a single idea or group that includes a lot of different ideas or groups. *Does coincidence come under the umbrella of the paranormal? ...an umbrella group of several human rights organisations.*

umpire /'ʌmpaɪə/ **umpires, umpiring, umpired.** **1** N-C An **umpire** is a person whose job is to make sure that a sports match or contest is played fairly and that the rules are not broken. **2** VERB If you **umpire** a game, you are its umpire.

unable /ʌn'eɪbəl/. ADJ If you are **unable to** do something, it is impossible for you to do it. *I was unable to accept the invitation... Mary felt herself blushing and unable to meet his eyes.*

unacceptable /ˌʌnək'septəbəl/. ADJ If you describe something as **unacceptable**, you strongly disapprove of it or object to it and feel that it should not be allowed to happen or continue. *It is totally unacceptable for children to swear.*

unaffected /ˌʌnə'fektɪd/. **1** ADJ AFTER LINK-V If someone or something is **unaffected** by an event, they are not changed by it in any way. *She seemed totally unaffected by what she'd drunk.* **2** ADJ If you describe someone as **unaffected**, you approve of them because they are natural and genuine in their behaviour.

unanimity /ˌjuːnə'nɪmɪti/. N-U When there is **unanimity** among a group of people, they all agree about something.

unanimous /juː'nænɪməs/. ADJ When a group of people or their opinion is **unanimous**, they all agree about something. ♦**unanimously** ADV *Its executive committee voted unanimously to reject the proposals.*

unannounced /ˌʌnə'naʊnst/. ADJ If someone arrives or does something **unannounced**, they do it unexpectedly and without anyone having being told about it beforehand. *He had just arrived unannounced from South America.*

unanswered /ˌʌn'ɑːnsəd, -'æns-/. ADJ Something such as a question or letter that is **unanswered** has not been answered. *Some of the most important questions remain unanswered.*

unarmed /ˌʌn'ɑːmd/. ADJ If a person or vehicle is **unarmed**, they are not carrying any weapons.

unashamed /ˌʌnəˈʃeɪmd/. ADJ If you describe someone's behaviour or attitude as **unashamed**, you mean that they are open and honest about things that other people might find embarrassing or shocking. ♦**unashamedly** ADV ...an unashamedly traditional view.

unattractive /ˌʌnəˈtræktɪv/. [1] ADJ **Unattractive** people and things are unpleasant in their appearance. [2] ADJ If you describe something as **unattractive**, you mean that people do not like it and do not want to be involved with it. The market is still unattractive to many insurers.

unauthorized (BR also **unauthorised**) /ˌʌnˈɔːθəraɪzd/. ADJ If something is **unauthorized**, it has been produced or is happening without official permission. ...a new unauthorized biography of the Russian President.

unavailable /ˌʌnəˈveɪləbəl/. ADJ When things or people are **unavailable**, you cannot obtain them, meet them, or talk to them. Mr Icke is out of the country and so unavailable for comment.

unavoidable /ˌʌnəˈvɔɪdəbəl/. ADJ If something bad is **unavoidable**, it cannot be avoided or prevented. The job losses were unavoidable.

unaware /ˌʌnəˈweə/. ADJ AFTER LINK-V If you are **unaware** of something, you do not know about it. She was unaware that she was being filmed.

unbalanced /ˌʌnˈbælənst/. [1] ADJ If you describe someone as **unbalanced**, you mean that they appear to be very disturbed and upset, and perhaps slightly mad. He was shown to be mentally unbalanced. [2] ADJ If you describe something such as a report or argument as **unbalanced**, you think that it is unfair or inaccurate because it emphasizes some things and ignores others.

unbearable /ˌʌnˈbeərəbəl/. ADJ If you describe something as **unbearable**, you mean that it is so unpleasant, painful, or upsetting that you feel unable to accept it or deal with it. War has made life almost unbearable for the civilians. ♦**unbearably** ADV It had become unbearably hot.

unbeatable /ˌʌnˈbiːtəbəl/. ADJ If you describe something as **unbeatable**, you mean that it is the best thing of its kind. These resorts, like Magaluf and Arenal, remain unbeatable in terms of price.

unbeaten /ˌʌnˈbiːtən/. ADJ In sport, if a person or their performance is **unbeaten**, nobody has ever beaten them. He's unbeaten in 20 fights.

unbelievable /ˌʌnbɪˈliːvəbəl/. [1] ADJ If you say that something is **unbelievable**, you are emphasizing that it is very extreme, impressive, or shocking. The pressure they put us under there was unbelievable... It was an unbelievable moment when Chris won... I find it unbelievable that people can accept this sort of behaviour. ♦**unbelievably** ADV What you did was unbelievably stupid. [2] ADJ If an idea or theory is **unbelievable**, it is so unlikely or so illogical that you cannot believe it. I know it sounds unbelievable but I never wanted to cheat. ♦**unbelievably** ADV Lainey was, unbelievably, pregnant again.

unborn /ˌʌnˈbɔːn/. ADJ & N-PL An **unborn** child is still inside its mother's womb or is going to be born in the future. **The unborn** are children who are not born yet. They will affect generations of Britons still unborn.

unbroken /ˌʌnˈbrəʊkən/. ADJ If something is **unbroken**, it is continuous or complete. ...an unbroken run of 38 match wins... We've had ten days of almost unbroken sunshine.

uncanny /ʌnˈkæni/. ADJ If something is **uncanny**, it is strange and difficult to explain. I had this uncanny feeling that I was seeing the future. ♦**uncannily** ADV The night was uncannily still.

uncertain /ʌnˈsɜːtən/. [1] ADJ If you are **uncertain** about something, you do not know what to do. They were baffled and uncertain how to proceed. ♦**uncertainly** ADV He entered the hallway and stood uncertainly. [2] ADJ If something is **uncertain**, it is not known or not definite. It's uncertain whether they will accept the plan. [3] PHRASE If you say that someone tells a person something **in no uncertain terms**, you are emphasizing that they say it firmly and clearly so that there is no doubt about what they mean.

uncertainty /ʌnˈsɜːtənti/ **uncertainties.** N-VAR **Uncertainty** is a state of doubt about the future or about what is the right thing to do. ...the uncertainties concerning the future funding of the company.

unchallenged /ˌʌnˈtʃælɪndʒd/. ADJ When something is **unchallenged**, people accept it without questioning whether it is right or wrong. This new research has not gone unchallenged.

unchanged /ˌʌnˈtʃeɪndʒd/. ADJ Something that is **unchanged** has stayed the same during a period of time. Prices have remained virtually unchanged.

uncharacteristic /ˌʌnkærɪktəˈrɪstɪk/. ADJ If an action or mood is **uncharacteristic** of someone, it is not their usual type of behaviour. She made an uncharacteristic error of judgement. ♦**uncharacteristically** ADV Owen has been uncharacteristically silent.

unchecked /ˌʌnˈtʃekt/. ADJ If something undesirable is left **unchecked**, it keeps growing without anyone trying to stop it. ...the corruption which flourished unchecked.

uncle /ˈʌŋkəl/ **uncles.** N-C Your **uncle** is the brother of your mother or father, or the husband of your aunt.

unclear /ˌʌnˈklɪə/. [1] ADJ If something is **unclear**, it is not known or not certain. It is unclear how much support they have. [2] ADJ AFTER LINK-V If you are **unclear** about something, you do not understand it properly or are not sure about it. He is still unclear about his own future.

uncomfortable /ˌʌnˈkʌmfətəbəl/. [1] ADJ If you are **uncomfortable**, you are not physically relaxed, and feel slight pain or discomfort. ♦**uncomfortably** ADV He awoke to find himself lying uncomfortably on a pile of firewood. [2] ADJ If you are **uncomfortable**, you are slightly worried or embarrassed, and not relaxed and confident. ♦**uncomfortably** ADV Dr Wilding pulled uncomfortably at his tie. [3] ADJ

Something that is **uncomfortable** makes you feel slight pain or physical discomfort when you experience it or use it. ...*an uncomfortable chair.*

uncomplicated /ˌʌnˈkɒmplɪkeɪtɪd/. ADJ **Uncomplicated** things are simple and straightforward. ...*his uncomplicated sense of humour.*

uncompromising /ˌʌnˈkɒmprəmaɪzɪŋ/. ADJ If you describe someone as **uncompromising**, you mean that they are determined not to change their opinions or aims in any way. ...*a tough and uncompromising politician.*

unconcerned /ˌʌnkənˈsɜːnd/. ADJ If someone is **unconcerned** about something, they are not interested in it or not worried about it. *Sue is unconcerned about her health.*

unconditional /ˌʌnkənˈdɪʃənəl/. ADJ Something that is **unconditional** is done or given to someone freely, without anything being required in return. *Children need unconditional love.* ♦**unconditionally** ADV *The hostages were released unconditionally.*

unconfirmed /ˌʌnkənˈfɜːmd/. ADJ If a report or rumour is **unconfirmed**, there is not yet any definite proof that it is true.

unconnected /ˌʌnkəˈnektɪd/. ADJ If two things are **unconnected** with each other, they are not related to each other in any way. *I can't believe that those two murders are unconnected.*

unconscious /ʌnˈkɒnʃəs/. [1] ADJ Someone who is **unconscious** is in a state similar to sleep, as a result of a shock, accident, or injury. *He was dragged from his van and beaten unconscious.* ♦**unconsciousness** N-U *He slipped into unconsciousness.* [2] ADJ If you are **unconscious** of something, you are unaware of it. Similarly, if feelings or attitudes are **unconscious**, you are unaware of them. *Mr Battersby was apparently quite unconscious of their presence.* ...*an unconscious hatred for men.* ♦**unconsciously** ADV *Bob stared at it, unconsciously holding his breath.* [3] N-SING In psychology, the **unconscious** is the part of your mind which contains feelings and ideas that you do not know about or cannot control.

unconstitutional /ˌʌnkɒnstɪˈtjuːʃənəl, AM -ˈtuː-/. ADJ Something that is **unconstitutional** is against the rules of an organization or political system. *The Moldavian parliament has declared the elections unconstitutional.*

uncontrollable /ˌʌnkənˈtrəʊləbəl/. ADJ If something such as an emotion is **uncontrollable**, you can do nothing to prevent it or control it. *He burst into uncontrollable laughter.* ♦**uncontrollably** ADV *I started shaking uncontrollably.*

uncontrolled /ˌʌnkənˈtrəʊld/. ADJ If something such as a feeling or activity is **uncontrolled**, no attempt is made to stop or restrain it. ...*the dangers of uncontrolled economic growth.*

unconventional /ˌʌnkənˈvenʃənəl/. ADJ If someone is **unconventional**, they do not behave in the same way as most other people in their society. *He had rather unconventional work habits, preferring to work through the night.*

unconvincing /ˌʌnkənˈvɪnsɪŋ/. ADJ If you describe a statement, argument, or explanation as **unconvincing**, you do not believe it is true

or valid. *The reasons given were unconvincing.* ♦**unconvincingly** ADV *'It is doing me no harm,'* he said, unconvincingly.

uncount noun /ˌʌnkaʊnt ˈnaʊn/ **uncount nouns.** N-C An **uncount noun** is a noun such as 'gold' or 'information' which has only one form and can be used without a determiner.

uncover /ʌnˈkʌvə/ **uncovers, uncovering, uncovered.** [1] VERB If you **uncover** something secret, you find out about it. *Auditors said they had uncovered evidence of widespread fraud.* [2] VERB To **uncover** something means to remove a cover from it.

undaunted /ʌnˈdɔːntɪd/. ADJ If you are **undaunted**, you are confident about dealing with something that would frighten or worry most people. *He seems undaunted by such setbacks.*

undecided /ˌʌndɪˈsaɪdɪd/. ADJ If you are **undecided** about something, you have not yet made a decision about it. *She was still undecided as to what career she wanted to pursue.*

undemocratic /ˌʌndeməˈkrætɪk/. ADJ In an **undemocratic** system, decisions are made by a small number of powerful people without consulting all the people who are affected; used showing disapproval.

undeniable /ˌʌndɪˈnaɪəbəl/. ADJ If something is **undeniable**, it is definitely true or definitely exists. *Her charm is undeniable.* ♦**undeniably** ADV *Bringing up a baby is undeniably hard work.*

under /ˈʌndə/. [1] PREP If something is **under** something else, it is directly below or beneath it. ...*a labyrinth of tunnels under the ground... He'd been held under the water and drowned... I had my head under the blanket... A river boat passed under the bridge.* [2] PREP & ADV If something or someone is **under** a particular age or amount, they are less than that age or amount. *Expenditure this year should be just under 15 billion pounds. ...a film for very young viewers – aged, say, six and under.* [3] PREP If something happens **under** particular circumstances or conditions, it happens when those circumstances or conditions exist. *Under normal circumstances, these three men would probably never have met... They had to be able to work under pressure... Under current laws, charges must be laid by the alleged victim.* [4] PREP If people live or work **under** a particular person, that person is their ruler, boss, or teacher. ...*the Baltic Republics, forcibly incorporated into the Soviet Union under Stalin... I am the new manager and you will be working under me. ...the artists who had studied under Beuys.* [5] PREP If you do something **under** a particular name, you use that name instead of your real name. *Mrs Coke is a novelist, writing under the name Claire Hunter... The patient was registered under a false name.* [6] PREP You use **under** to say which section of a list, book, or system something is classified in. *This study is described under 'General Diseases of the Eye'... 'Where would it be?'—'Filed under C, second drawer down.'*

underclass /ˈʌndəklɑːs, -klæs/ **underclasses.** N-C The **underclass** consists of people who are poor, and who have little chance of improving their situation.

undercover /ˌʌndəˈkʌvə/. ADJ **Undercover** work involves secretly obtaining information for the government or the police. ...*an undercover operation designed to catch drug smugglers.*

undercurrent /ˈʌndəkʌrənt, -kɜːr-/ **undercurrents.** N-C If there is an **undercurrent** of a feeling, the feeling exists in a weak form, and may become powerful later. ...*a growing undercurrent of fear.*

undercut /ˌʌndəˈkʌt/ **undercuts, undercutting, undercut.** VERB If a business **undercuts** its competitors or their prices, it sells a product more cheaply than its competitors.

underdeveloped /ˌʌndədɪˈveləpt/. ADJ An **underdeveloped** country does not have modern industries and usually has a low standard of living. Some people dislike this term and prefer to use **developing**.

underdog /ˈʌndədɒg, AM -dɔːg/ **underdogs.** N-C The **underdog** in a contest is the person who seems least likely to succeed or win.

underestimate /ˌʌndərˈestɪmeɪt/ **underestimates, underestimating, underestimated.** [1] VERB If you **underestimate** something, you do not realize how large it is or will be. *They had underestimated how much tax would be demanded.* [2] VERB If you **underestimate** someone, you do not realize what they are capable of doing. *Opponents make the mistake of underestimating him.*

undergo /ˌʌndəˈɡəʊ/ **undergoes, undergoing, underwent, undergone.** VERB If you **undergo** something necessary or unpleasant, it happens to you. *New recruits have been undergoing training... He recently underwent brain surgery.*

undergraduate /ˌʌndəˈɡrædʒuət/ **undergraduates.** N-C An **undergraduate** is a student at a university or college who is studying for his or her first degree. ...*a 21-year-old history undergraduate.*

underground; adverb /ˌʌndəˈɡraʊnd/; noun and adjective /ˈʌndəɡraʊnd/. [1] ADJ & ADJ BEFORE N Something that is **underground** is below the surface of the ground. *The plane hit so hard that one engine was buried 16 feet underground.* ...*an underground car park.* [2] N-SING In British English, the **underground** in a city is the railway system in which electric trains travel below the ground in tunnels. The American word is **subway.** [3] ADJ BEFORE N **Underground** political activities take place secretly, and are directed against the government. ...*the underground Kashmir Liberation Front.*

undergrowth /ˈʌndəɡrəʊθ/. N-U **Undergrowth** consists of bushes and plants growing closely together under trees; BRITISH. *He pushed his way through the undergrowth.*

underlie /ˌʌndəˈlaɪ/ **underlies, underlying, underlay, underlain.** VERB If something **underlies** a feeling or situation, it is the cause or basis of it. *Try to figure out what feeling underlies your anger.*

underline /ˌʌndəˈlaɪn/ **underlines, underlining, underlined.** [1] VERB In British English, if a person or event **underlines** something, they draw attention to it and emphasize its importance. The American word is **underscore.** *The*

Second World War underlined the importance of science and technology. [2] VERB In British English, if you **underline** a word or sentence, you draw a line underneath it. The American word is **underscore.**

underlying /ˌʌndəˈlaɪɪŋ/. ADJ BEFORE N The **underlying** aspects of an event or situation are the aspects that are not obvious but that have great significance or effect. *To stop a problem you have to understand its underlying causes.*

undermine /ˌʌndəˈmaɪn/ **undermines, undermining, undermined.** VERB To **undermine** a feeling or a system means to make it less certain or less secure. *The conversations were designed to undermine her authority.*

underneath /ˌʌndəˈniːθ/. [1] PREP & ADV If one thing is **underneath** another, it is directly below or beneath it. *We all dived underneath the tables... Pull back a bit of this carpet to see what's underneath.* [2] ADV & N-SING The part of something which is **underneath** is the part which normally touches the ground or faces towards the ground. **The underneath** of something is the part which is underneath. *Check the actual construction of the chair by looking underneath... I know what the underneath of a car looks like.* [3] ADV & PREP You use **underneath** when you are talking about feelings and emotions that people do not show in their behaviour. *Underneath, Sofia was deeply committed to her husband.*

underpants /ˈʌndəpænts/. N-PL **Underpants** are a piece of underwear with two holes for your legs and elastic around the waist. In British English, **underpants** refers only to men's underwear. In American English it refers to both men's and women's.

underrate /ˌʌndəˈreɪt/ **underrates, underrating, underrated.** VERB If you **underrate** someone, you do not realize how clever, able, or important they are. ♦**underrated** ADJ *He is a very underrated poet.*

underscore /ˌʌndəˈskɔː/ **underscores, underscoring, underscored.** [1] VERB In American English, if a person or an event **underscores** something, they draw attention to it and emphasize its importance. The British word is **underline.** *The recent violence in Los Angeles underscores how real the problems are.* [2] VERB In American English, if you **underscore** a word or a sentence, you draw a line underneath it. The British word is **underline.**

underside /ˈʌndəsaɪd/ **undersides.** N-C The **underside** of something is the part of it which normally faces towards the ground.

understand /ˌʌndəˈstænd/ **understands, understanding, understood.** [1] VERB If you **understand** someone, or if you **understand** what they are saying, you know what they mean. *I don't understand what you are talking about... She could barely understand a word of English.* [2] VERB To **understand** someone means to know how they feel and why they behave in the way that they do. *My husband and I understand each other very well.* [3] VERB You say that you **understand** something when you know why or how it happens. *They are too young to understand what is going on.* [4] VERB If you say that you **understand** that something is the case, you mean that you think it is the case because you have heard or read that it is; FORMAL. *I understand that he's just taken early retirement... He was understood to be reluctant to take over.*

understandable /ˌʌndəˈstændəbəl/. ADJ If you describe someone's behaviour or feelings as **understandable**, you mean that they have reacted to a situation in a natural way or in the way you would expect. *It is understandable that Mr Khan should want something to be done.* ♦**understandably** ADV *Most organizations are, quite understandably, suspicious of new ideas.*

understanding /ˌʌndəˈstændɪŋ/ **understandings.** [1] N-SING & N-U If you have an **understanding** of something, you know how it works or what it means. *They have to have a basic understanding of computers... Mr Smith seems to have little understanding of the procedures.* [2] ADJ If you are **understanding** towards someone, you are kind and forgiving. *Fortunately for John, he had an understanding wife.* [3] N-U If there is **understanding** between people, they are friendly towards each other and trust each other. *...a foundation which works to promote understanding between Muslims, Christians and Jews.* [4] N-C An **understanding** is an informal agreement about something. *We had an understanding that we'd talk in the summer... He left half the shares to Grandma on the understanding that she'd leave hers to Mum.*

understate /ˌʌndəˈsteɪt/ **understates, understating, understated.** VERB If you **understate** something, you describe it in a way that suggests that it is less important or serious than it really is. *The figures probably understate the extent of the epidemic.*

understated /ˌʌndəˈsteɪtɪd/. ADJ BEFORE N If you describe a style, colour, or effect as **understated**, you like it because it is not obvious. *...understated elegance.*

understatement /ˈʌndəsteɪtmənt/ **understatements.** N-VAR An **understatement** is a statement which does not fully express the extent to which something is true. *To say I'm disappointed is an understatement.*

understood /ˌʌndəˈstʊd/. **Understood** is the past tense and past participle of **understand**.

undertake /ˌʌndəˈteɪk/ **undertakes, undertaking, undertook, undertaken.** [1] VERB When you **undertake** a task or job, you start doing it and accept responsibility for it; FORMAL. *She undertook a major reorganization of the legal department.* ♦**undertaking, undertakings** N-C *Organizing the show has been a massive undertaking.* [2] VERB If you **undertake** to do something, you promise that you will do it; FORMAL. *He undertook to edit the text himself.* ♦**undertaking** N-C *Frank would have to give an undertaking to be a responsible parent.*

undertaker /ˈʌndəteɪkə/ **undertakers.** N-C In British English, an **undertaker** is a person whose job is to deal with the bodies of people who have died and to arrange funerals. The American word is **mortician**.

undertook /ˌʌndəˈtʊk/. **Undertook** is the past tense of **undertake**.

undervalue /ˌʌndəˈvæljuː/ **undervalues, undervaluing, undervalued.** VERB If you **undervalue** something, you fail to recognize how valuable or important it is. *We must never undervalue freedom.*

underwater /ˌʌndəˈwɔːtə/. ADV & ADJ BEFORE N Something that exists or happens **underwater** exists or happens below the surface of the sea, a river, or a lake. *Some stretches of beach are completely underwater. ...underwater photography.*

underway /ˌʌndəˈweɪ/. ADJ AFTER LINK-V If an activity gets **underway**, it starts. If an activity is **underway**, it has already started. *An investigation is underway.*

underwear /ˈʌndəweə/. N-U **Underwear** is clothing which you wear next to your skin under your other clothes.

underwent /ˌʌndəˈwent/. **Underwent** is the past tense of **undergo**.

underworld /ˈʌndəwɜːld/. N-SING The **underworld** consists of organized crime and the people involved in it. *...a wealthy businessman with underworld connections.*

underwrite /ˌʌndəˈraɪt/ **underwrites, underwriting, underwrote, underwritten.** VERB When an insurance company or other organization **underwrites** an activity or **underwrites** the cost of it, they agree to provide any money that is needed to cover losses or buy special equipment, often for an agreed fee; TECHNICAL.

undesirable /ˌʌndɪˈzaɪərəbəl/. ADJ If you describe something or someone as **undesirable**, you think they will have harmful effects. *There can be undesirable side-effects... It is clearly undesirable that people should be exposed to this.*

undid /ˌʌnˈdɪd/. **Undid** is the past tense of **undo**.

undisclosed /ˌʌndɪsˈkləʊzd/. ADJ **Undisclosed** information has not been revealed to the public. *She was paid an undisclosed sum in damages.*

undisputed /ˌʌndɪˈspjuːtɪd/. ADJ If you describe something as **undisputed**, you mean that everyone accepts that it exists or is true. *Japan is now the undisputed champion of consumer electronics.*

undisturbed /ˌʌndɪˈstɜːbd/. [1] ADJ Something that remains **undisturbed** has not been touched, moved, or changed. *The desk looked undisturbed.* [2] ADJ If you are **undisturbed** in something that you are doing, you are able to continue doing it and are not affected by something that is happening. *He was able to work undisturbed.*

undo /ʌnˈduː/ **undoes, undoing, undid, undone.** [1] VERB If you **undo** something, you unfasten, loosen, or untie it. *She undid the buttons of her jacket... Her hair had come undone.* [2] VERB To **undo** something that has been done means to reverse its effect. *It would be difficult to undo the damage.*

undoing /ʌnˈduːɪŋ/. N-SING If you say that something is someone's **undoing**, you mean that it is the cause of their failure. *His lack of experience may prove to be his undoing.*

undoubted /ʌnˈdaʊtɪd/. ADJ You can use **undoubted** to emphasize that something exists or is true. *The event was an undoubted success.* ◆ **undoubtedly** ADV *He is undoubtedly a highly talented player.*

undress /ˌʌnˈdres/ **undresses, undressing, undressed.** VERB When you undress, you take off your clothes. If you undress someone, you take off their clothes. ◆ **undressed** ADJ *He got undressed in the bathroom.* ● See note at **wear**.

undue /ˌʌnˈdjuː, AM -ˈduː/. ADJ BEFORE N If you describe something bad as undue, you mean that it is greater or more extreme than you think is reasonable. *This would help the families to survive the drought without undue suffering.* ◆ **unduly** ADV *He appealed to firms not to increase their prices unduly.*

undulating /ˈʌndʒʊleɪtɪŋ/. ADJ Undulating means having gentle curves or slopes, or moving gently and slowly up and down or from side to side; LITERARY. *...gently undulating hills.*

unearth /ˌʌnˈɜːθ/ **unearths, unearthing, unearthed.** VERB If someone unearths something hidden or secret, they discover it. *Investigators have unearthed evidence of systematic fraud.*

unease /ˌʌnˈiːz/. N-U If you have a feeling of unease, you feel that something is wrong and you are anxious or uncomfortable about it. *The atmosphere on the streets was one of unease.*

uneasy /ˌʌnˈiːzi/. **1** ADJ If you are uneasy, you feel that something is wrong and you are anxious or uncomfortable about it. *Richard was uneasy about how best to approach his elderly mother.* ◆ **uneasily** ADV *Meg shifted uneasily on her chair.* ◆ **uneasiness** N-U *I felt a great uneasiness about meeting her again.* **2** ADJ If you describe a situation or relationship as uneasy, you mean that it is not settled and may not last. *An uneasy calm has settled over Los Angeles.* ◆ **uneasily** ADV *...a country whose component parts fit uneasily together.*

unemployed /ˌʌnɪmˈplɔɪd/. ADJ & N-PL Someone who is unemployed does not have a job although they want one. **The unemployed** are people who are unemployed.

unemployment /ˌʌnɪmˈplɔɪmənt/. N-U Unemployment is the fact that people who want jobs cannot get them. *...the highest unemployment rate in western Europe.*

unequivocal /ˌʌnɪˈkwɪvəkəl/. ADJ If you describe someone's attitude as unequivocal, you mean that it is very clear and firm; FORMAL. *The message to him was unequivocal: 'Get out'.* ◆ **unequivocally** ADV *He stated unequivocally that the French forces were ready to go to war.*

unethical /ʌnˈeθɪkəl/. ADJ If you describe someone's behaviour as unethical, you think it is morally wrong; FORMAL. *It is unethical to sell properties at clearly inflated prices.*

uneven /ʌnˈiːvən/. **1** ADJ An uneven surface is not level or smooth. *...the uneven surface of the car park.* **2** ADJ Something that is uneven is not regular or consistent. *Her breathing was uneven.*

unexpected /ˌʌnɪkˈspektɪd/. ADJ Something that is unexpected surprises you because you did not think it was likely to happen. *His death was totally unexpected.* ◆ **unexpectedly** ADV *Mr Kirk had unexpectedly strong support.*

unexplained /ˌʌnɪkˈspleɪnd/. ADJ If something is unexplained, the reason for it or cause of it is unclear or is not known. *...the unexplained death of an opposition leader.*

unfair /ʌnˈfeə/. ADJ Something that is unfair is not right or not just. *It was unfair that he should suffer so much.* ◆ **unfairly** ADV *She claims she was unfairly dismissed.* ◆ **unfairness** N-U *He raged at the unfairness of life.*

unfaithful /ʌnˈfeɪθfʊl/. ADJ If someone is unfaithful to their lover or to the person they are married to, they have a sexual relationship with someone else. *...her unfaithful husband.*

unfamiliar /ˌʌnfəˈmɪliə/. ADJ If something is unfamiliar to you, or if you are unfamiliar with it, you know very little about it and have not seen or experienced it before. *She speaks no Japanese and is unfamiliar with Japanese culture.*

unfashionable /ʌnˈfæʃənəbəl/. ADJ If something is unfashionable, it is not approved of or done by most people. *Wearing fur has become deeply unfashionable.*

unfavourable (AM **unfavorable**) /ʌnˈfeɪvərəbəl/. **1** ADJ Unfavourable conditions or circumstances cause problems and reduce the chance of success. *...unfavourable conditions for the development of British industry.* **2** ADJ If you have an unfavourable reaction to something, you do not like it. ◆ **unfavourably** ADV *I was forever being compared to her unfavourably.*

unfettered /ʌnˈfetəd/. ADJ Unfettered activities are not restricted in any way; FORMAL. *Unfettered free trade is an ideal, never achieved.*

unfinished /ʌnˈfɪnɪʃt/. ADJ If something is unfinished, it has not been completed. *...Jane Austen's unfinished novel.*

unfit /ʌnˈfɪt/. **1** ADJ If you are unfit, your body is not in good condition because you have not been taking regular exercise. **2** ADJ If someone or something is unfit for a particular purpose, they are not suitable or not of a good enough quality. *He declared her mentally unfit for duty... The wine was unfit for human consumption.*

unfold /ʌnˈfəʊld/ **unfolds, unfolding, unfolded.** **1** VERB When a situation or story unfolds, it develops and becomes known or understood. *The facts started to unfold before them.* **2** VERB If someone unfolds something which has been folded or if it unfolds, it is opened out and becomes flat. *He quickly unfolded the blankets.*

unforeseen /ˌʌnfəˈsiːn/. ADJ An unforeseen event happens unexpectedly. *Her office was shut due to unforeseen circumstances.*

unforgettable /ˌʌnfəˈgetəbəl/. ADJ If something is unforgettable, it is so impressive that you are likely to remember it for a long time. *A visit to the Museum is an unforgettable experience.*

unfortunate /ʌnˈfɔːtʃənət/. **1** ADJ If you say that someone is unfortunate, you mean that something unpleasant or unlucky has happened to them. *He was one of those unfortunate people who put on weight very easily.* **2** ADJ If you say that something that has happened is unfortunate, you mean that it is a pity that it happened. *He described the alleged plot as a 'very unfortunate incident'.*

unfortunately /ʌnˈfɔːtʃunətli/. ADV You can use **unfortunately** to express regret about what you are saying. *Unfortunately, my time is limited... Unfortunately for us, he is panicking.*

unfounded /ʌnˈfaʊndɪd/. ADJ If you say that a belief is **unfounded** you mean that it is wrong, and is not based on facts or evidence. *There were unfounded rumours of alcohol abuse.*

unfriendly /ʌnˈfrendli/. ADJ If you describe someone as **unfriendly**, you mean that they behave in an unkind or hostile way. *His manner was unfriendly.*

unfulfilled /ˌʌnfʊlˈfɪld/. 1 ADJ You say that a hope is **unfulfilled** when the thing that you hoped for has not happened. *Do you have any unfulfilled ambitions?* 2 ADJ If someone feels **unfulfilled**, they feel dissatisfied with life or with their achievements.

unfurl /ʌnˈfɜːl/ **unfurls, unfurling, unfurled.** VERB If you **unfurl** something such as a flag or umbrella, or if it **unfurls**, you unroll or unfold it so that it is flat or open and can be used. *Anti-nuclear protesters unfurled a banner.*

unhappy /ʌnˈhæpi/ **unhappier, unhappiest.** 1 ADJ If you are **unhappy**, you are sad and depressed. ♦**unhappily** ADV *...an unhappily married woman.* ♦**unhappiness** N-U *There was a lot of unhappiness in my adolescence.* 2 ADJ AFTER LINK-V If you are **unhappy** about something, you are not pleased about it or not satisfied with it. *Republicans are unhappy that the government isn't doing more.* ♦**unhappiness** N-U *...his unhappiness with the government's decision.* 3 ADJ BEFORE N An **unhappy** situation is not satisfactory or desirable. *This event is a symptom of the unhappy state of British politics.*

unharmed /ʌnˈhɑːmd/. ADJ If someone or something is **unharmed** after an accident or violent incident, they are not hurt or damaged in any way. *His eleven year old daughter was unharmed in the attack.*

unhealthy /ʌnˈhelθi/. 1 ADJ Something that is **unhealthy** is likely to cause illness or poor health. *...unhealthy foods such as hamburger and chips.* 2 ADJ If you are **unhealthy**, you are not very fit or well.

unheard of /ʌnˈhɜːd ɒv/. ADJ You can say that an event or situation is **unheard of** when it never happens, or has never happened before. *My mother was a career woman, which was unheard of in those days.*

unhelpful /ʌnˈhelpfʊl/. ADJ If you say that someone or something is **unhelpful**, you mean that they do not help you or improve a situation, and may even make things worse. *The criticism is both unfair and unhelpful.*

unhurt /ʌnˈhɜːt/. ADJ If someone who has been attacked, or involved in an accident, is **unhurt**, they are not injured. *The lorry driver escaped unhurt, but a pedestrian was injured.*

unidentified /ˌʌnaɪˈdentɪfaɪd/. ADJ If you describe someone or something as **unidentified**, you mean that nobody knows who or what they are. *He was shot this morning by unidentified intruders.*

unification /ˌjuːnɪfɪˈkeɪʃən/. N-U **Unification** is the process by which two or more countries join together and become one country.

uniform /ˈjuːnɪfɔːm/ **uniforms.** 1 N-VAR A **uniform** is a special set of clothes which some people wear to work in, and which some children wear at school. *Philippe was in uniform.* 2 ADJ If something is **uniform**, it does not vary, but is even and regular throughout. *Chips should be cut into uniform size.* ♦**uniformity** /ˌjuːnɪˈfɔːmɪti/ *...uniformity of color.* ♦**uniformly** ADV *Microwaves heat water uniformly.* 3 ADJ If you describe a number of things as **uniform**, you mean that they are all the same. *Along each wall stretched uniform green metal filing cabinets.* ♦**uniformity** N-U *...the dull uniformity of the houses.* ♦**uniformly** ADV *The natives uniformly agreed.*

uniformed /ˈjuːnɪfɔːmd/. ADJ **Uniformed** people such as police officers are wearing a uniform while doing their job. *You have to pass uniformed staff at the bottom of the stairs.*

unify /ˈjuːnɪfaɪ/ **unifies, unifying, unified.** VERB If something **unifies** different things or parts, they are brought together to form one thing. *He had unified the party.* ♦**unified** ADJ *...a unified system of taxation.*

unilateral /ˌjuːnɪˈlætərəl/. ADJ A **unilateral** decision or action is taken by only one of the groups or countries involved in a particular situation, without the agreement of the others. *...unilateral nuclear disarmament.*

unimaginable /ˌʌnɪˈmædʒɪnəbəl/. ADJ If you describe something as **unimaginable**, you are emphasizing that it is difficult to imagine or understand properly, because it is not part of people's normal experience. *The children here have lived through unimaginable horrors.* ♦**unimaginably** /ˌʌnɪˈmædʒɪnəbli/ ADV *Conditions in prisons out there are unimaginably bad.*

unimportant /ˌʌnɪmˈpɔːtənt/. ADJ If you describe something or someone as **unimportant**, you mean that they do not have much effect or value, and are therefore not worth considering.

unimpressed /ˌʌnɪmˈprest/. ADJ AFTER LINK-V If you are **unimpressed** by something or someone, you do not think they are particularly good or important.

uninhibited /ˌʌnɪnˈhɪbɪtɪd/. ADJ If you describe a person as **uninhibited**, you mean that they express their opinions and feelings openly, and behave as they want to, without worrying what other people think.

unintentional /ˌʌnɪnˈtenʃənəl/. ADJ Something that is **unintentional** is not done deliberately, but happens by accident. ♦**unintentionally** ADV *...an unintentionally funny adaptation of 'Dracula'.*

uninterrupted /ˌʌnɪntəˈrʌptɪd/. ADJ If something is **uninterrupted**, it continues without any breaks or interruptions. *This enables the healing process to continue uninterrupted.*

union /ˈjuːnjən/ **unions.** 1 N-C A **union** is the same as a **trade union.** 2 N-U When the **union** of two or more things occurs, they are joined together and become one thing. *Britain should move towards closer union with our partners.*

unionist /'juːnjənɪst/ **unionists.** N-C A **unionist** is someone who believes in the set of political principles based on the idea that two or more political or national units should be joined or remain together.

unique /juːˈniːk/. **1** ADJ Something that is **unique**, is the only one of its kind. *Each person's signature is unique.* ♦**uniquely** ADV *The Antarctic is a uniquely fragile environment.* ♦**uniqueness** N-U *...the uniqueness of China's own experience.* **2** ADJ AFTER LINK-V If something is **unique** to one thing or person, it concerns or belongs only to that thing or person. *This creature is unique to Borneo.* ♦**uniquely** ADV *The problem isn't uniquely American.* **3** ADJ Some people use **unique** to mean very unusual and special. *Kauffman was a woman of unique talent.* ♦**uniquely** ADV *...this uniquely beautiful city.*

unison /'juːnɪsən, -zən/. PHRASE If a group of people do something **in unison**, they all do it together at the same time.

unit /'juːnɪt/ **units.** **1** N-C If you consider something as a **unit**, you consider it as a single complete thing. *...the basic family unit.* **2** N-C A **unit** is a group of people who work together at a specific job, often in a particular place. *...the health services research unit.* **3** N-C A **unit** is a small machine which has a particular function, often part of a larger machine. *The unit plugs into any TV set.* **4** N-C A **unit** of measurement is a fixed, standard length, quantity, or weight. *The litre, the centimetre, and the ounce are all units.*

unite /juːˈnaɪt/ **unites, uniting, united.** VERB If a group of people or things **unite**, they join together and act as a group. *Only the president can unite the people.*

united /juːˈnaɪtɪd/. **1** ADJ When people are **united** about something, they agree about it and act together. *Every party is united on the need for parliamentary democracy.* **2** ADJ **United** is used to describe a country which has been formed from two or more countries or states. *...a united Germany.*

unity /'juːnɪti/. **1** N-U **Unity** is the state of different areas or groups being joined together to form a single country or organization. *...European economic unity.* **2** N-U When there is **unity**, people are in agreement and act together for a particular purpose. *The choice was meant to create an impression of party unity.*

universal /ˌjuːnɪˈvɜːsəl/. ADJ Something that is **universal** relates to everyone in the world or to everyone in a particular group or society. *...universal health care.* ♦**universally** ADV *...a universally accepted point of view.*

universe /'juːnɪvɜːs/. N-C The **universe** is the whole of space, and all the stars, planets, and other forms of matter and energy in it.

university /ˌjuːnɪˈvɜːsɪti/ **universities.** N-VAR A **university** is an institution where students study for degrees and where academic research is done. *They want their daughter to go to university.*

unjust /ˌʌnˈdʒʌst/. ADJ If you describe an action, system, or law as **unjust**, you think that it treats a person or group badly in a way that they do not deserve. ♦**unjustly** ADV *She was unjustly accused of stealing money.*

unjustified /ˌʌnˈdʒʌstɪfaɪd/. ADJ If you describe a belief or action as **unjustified**, you think that there is no good reason for having it or doing it. *...totally unjustified allegations.*

unkind /ʌnˈkaɪnd/ **unkinder, unkindest.** ADJ If someone is **unkind**, they behave in an unpleasant, unfriendly, or slightly cruel way. *I think it's very unkind of you to make up stories about him... No one has an unkind word to say about him.* ♦**unkindly** ADV *Several viewers commented unkindly on her costume.* ♦**unkindness** N-U *He realized the unkindness of the remark.*

unknown /ˌʌnˈnəʊn/ **unknowns.** **1** ADJ & N-C If something or someone is **unknown** to you, you do not know what or who they are. An **unknown** is something that is unknown. *An unknown number of demonstrators were arrested... The length of the war is one of the biggest unknowns.* **2** ADJ & N-C An **unknown** person is not famous or publicly recognized. You can refer to a person like this as an **unknown**. *A group of complete unknowns had established a wholly original form of humour.* **3** N-SING The **unknown** refers generally to things or places that people do not know about or understand. *Fear of the unknown is what brings out prejudice.*

unlawful /ˌʌnˈlɔːfʊl/. ADJ If something is **unlawful**, the law does not allow you to do it; FORMAL. *...employees who believe their dismissal was unlawful.* ♦**unlawfully** ADV *The government acted unlawfully in imposing the restrictions.*

unleaded /ˌʌnˈledɪd/. ADJ & N-U **Unleaded** fuels contain a reduced amount of lead in order to reduce the pollution caused when they are burned. You can refer to such fuels as **unleaded**. *All its V8 engines will run happily on unleaded.*

unleash /ˌʌnˈliːʃ/ **unleashes, unleashing, unleashed.** VERB If you say that someone or something **unleashes** a powerful movement or feeling, you mean that it starts suddenly and has an immediate strong effect. *Food rationing will unleash a new stream of refugees.*

unless /ʌnˈles/. CONJ You use **unless** to introduce the only circumstances in which an event you are mentioning will not take place or in which a statement you are making is not true. *I'm not happy unless I ride or drive every day.*

unlike /ˌʌnˈlaɪk/. **1** PREP If one thing is **unlike** another thing, the two things have different features from each other. *This was a foreign country, so unlike San Jose.* **2** PREP You can use **unlike** to contrast two people or things and show how they are different. *Unlike aerobics, walking entails no expensive fees for classes or clubs.* **3** PREP If you describe something that someone has done as **unlike** them, you mean that it is not typical of their normal behaviour. *It was so unlike him to say something like that.*

unlikely /ʌnˈlaɪkli/ **unlikeliest.** **1** ADJ If you say that something is **unlikely** to happen or **unlikely** to be true, you believe that it will not happen or that it is not true, although you are not completely sure. *In the unlikely event of* *anybody phoning, could you just scribble a message down?* **2** ADJ BEFORE N If you describe someone or something as **unlikely**, you mean it is surprising that they have a particular role or have done a particular thing. *Bespectacled Potter, a yoga fanatic, looks an unlikely drugs dealer.*

unlimited /ʌnˈlɪmɪtɪd/. ADJ If there is an **unlimited** quantity of something, you can have as much of it as you want. *You'll also have unlimited access to the swimming pool.*

unload /ˌʌnˈləʊd/ **unloads, unloading, unloaded.** VERB If you **unload** goods from a vehicle, or if you **unload** a vehicle, you remove the goods from the vehicle. *...a petrol tanker which was unloading at a power station.*

unlock /ˌʌnˈlɒk/ **unlocks, unlocking, unlocked.** VERB If you **unlock** something such as a door, a room, or a container, you open it using a key. *He unlocked the car and threw the coat on to the back seat... Who left this door unlocked?*

unlucky /ʌnˈlʌki/. **1** ADJ If you are **unlucky**, you have bad luck. *They were unlucky not to reach the World Cup Final.* **2** ADJ **Unlucky** is used to describe something that is thought to cause bad luck. *Sixteen is her unlucky number.*

unmarked /ˌʌnˈmɑːkt/. **1** ADJ Something that is **unmarked** has no marks of damage or injury on it. *Her shoes are still white and unmarked.* **2** ADJ Something that is **unmarked** has no signs on it which identify what it is or whose it is. *...an unmarked police car.*

unmistakable (or **unmistakeable**) /ˌʌnmɪsˈteɪkəbəl/. ADJ If you describe something as **unmistakable**, you mean that it is so obvious that it cannot be mistaken for anything else. *He didn't give his name, but the voice was unmistakable.* ◆**unmistakably** ADV *The name was unmistakably French.*

unmoved /ˌʌnˈmuːvd/. ADJ AFTER LINK-V If you are **unmoved** by something, you are not emotionally affected by it.

unnamed /ˌʌnˈneɪmd/. ADJ **Unnamed** people or things are talked about but their names are not mentioned. *The cash comes from an unnamed source.*

unnatural /ʌnˈnætʃərəl/. **1** ADJ If you describe something as **unnatural**, you mean that it is strange and often frightening, because it is different from what you normally expect. *The aircraft rose with unnatural speed.* ◆**unnaturally** ADV *The house was unnaturally silent.* **2** ADJ If you describe someone's behaviour as **unnatural**, you mean that it does not seem normal or spontaneous. *She gave him a bright, determined smile which seemed unnatural.* ◆**unnaturally** ADV *Try to avoid shouting or speaking unnaturally.*

unnecessary /ʌnˈnesəsri, AM -seri/. ADJ If you describe something as **unnecessary**, you mean that it is not needed or does not have to be done. *He accused Diana of making an unnecessary fuss.* ◆**unnecessarily** ADV *I didn't want to upset my husband or my daughter unnecessarily.*

unnerve /ˌʌnˈnɜːv/ **unnerves, unnerving, unnerved.** VERB If something **unnerves** you, it frightens, worries, or startles you. *The news*

about Dermot had unnerved me. ◆**unnerving** /ˌʌnˈnɜːvɪŋ/ ADJ *He has always found flying to be an unnerving experience.*

unnoticed /ˌʌnˈnəʊtɪst/. ADJ If something happens or passes **unnoticed**, it is not seen or noticed by anyone. *I tried to slip up the stairs unnoticed.*

unobtrusive /ˌʌnəbˈtruːsɪv/. ADJ If you describe something or someone as **unobtrusive**, you mean that they are not easily noticed or do not draw attention to themselves; FORMAL. *He managed the factory with unobtrusive efficiency.* ◆**unobtrusively** ADV *They slipped away unobtrusively.*

unofficial /ˌʌnəˈfɪʃəl/. ADJ An **unofficial** action is not authorized, approved, or organized by a person in authority. *...an unofficial strike.* ◆**unofficially** ADV *The replica is unofficially valued at nearly £500.*

unorthodox /ʌnˈɔːθədɒks/. ADJ If you describe someone's behaviour, beliefs, or customs as **unorthodox**, you mean that they are different from what is generally accepted. *...his unorthodox management style.*

unpack /ˌʌnˈpæk/ **unpacks, unpacking, unpacked.** VERB When you **unpack** a suitcase, box, or bag, or when you **unpack** the things inside it, you take the things out of it. *When I'd unpacked I went and tapped on his door.*

unpaid /ˌʌnˈpeɪd/. **1** ADJ BEFORE N If you do **unpaid** work, you do a job without receiving any money for it. **2** ADJ **Unpaid** taxes or bills have not been paid yet.

unpalatable /ʌnˈpælɪtəbəl/. ADJ If you describe an idea as **unpalatable**, you mean that you find it unpleasant and difficult to accept; FORMAL. *I began to learn the unpalatable truth about John.*

unparalleled /ʌnˈpærəleld/. ADJ If you describe something as **unparalleled**, you are emphasizing that it is, for example, bigger, better, or worse than anything else of its kind. *The country is facing a crisis unparalleled since the Second World War.*

unpleasant /ʌnˈplezənt/. **1** ADJ If something is **unpleasant**, it gives you bad feelings, for example by making you feel upset or uncomfortable. *The symptoms can be uncomfortable, unpleasant and serious.* ◆**unpleasantly** ADV *The smell was unpleasantly strong.* **2** ADJ An **unpleasant** person is unfriendly and rude. ◆**unpleasantly** ADV *Melissa laughed unpleasantly.*

unplug /ˌʌnˈplʌg/ **unplugs, unplugging, unplugged.** VERB If you **unplug** a piece of electrical equipment, you take its plug out of the socket.

unpopular /ˌʌnˈpɒpjʊlə/. ADJ If something or someone is **unpopular**, most people do not like them. *He had been unpopular at school.* ◆**unpopularity** N-U *...the unpopularity of the new tax.*

unprecedented /ʌnˈpresɪdentɪd/. **1** ADJ If something is **unprecedented**, it has never happened before. *Such policies would require unprecedented cooperation between nations.* **2** ADJ If you describe something as **unprecedented**, you are emphasizing that it is very great in quality, amount, or scale. ...*an unprecedented success.*

unpredictable /ˌʌnprɪˈdɪktəbəl/. ADJ If someone or something is **unpredictable**, you cannot tell what they are going to do or how they are going to behave. *Britain's notoriously unpredictable weather.* ♦**unpredictability** N-U *...his unpredictability and his tendency to make scandalous remarks.*

unprepared /ˌʌnprɪˈpeəd/. **1** ADJ If you are **unprepared** for something, you are not ready for it, and are therefore surprised or at a disadvantage when it happens. *She was totally unprepared for the shattering news.* **2** ADJ If you are **unprepared** to do something, you are not willing to do it. *He was unprepared to co-operate.*

unproductive /ˌʌnprəˈdʌktɪv/. ADJ Something that is **unproductive** does not produce anything useful. ...*unproductive land.* ...*a busy but unproductive night.*

unprofitable /ˌʌnˈprɒfɪtəbəl/. ADJ An industry, company, or product that is **unprofitable** does not make enough profit.

unprotected /ˌʌnprəˈtektɪd/. **1** ADJ An **unprotected** person or place is not looked after or defended, and so they may be harmed or attacked. *Two-dozen soldiers raced down the hillside toward the unprotected camp.* **2** ADJ If something is **unprotected**, it is not covered or treated with anything, and so it may easily be damaged. *If we are unprotected from the sun for long enough, our skin will burn.*

unpublished /ˌʌnˈpʌblɪʃt/. ADJ An **unpublished** book, letter, or report has never been published.

unqualified /ˌʌnˈkwɒlɪfaɪd/. **1** ADJ If you are **unqualified**, you do not have any qualifications, or do not have the right qualifications for a particular job. **2** ADJ **Unqualified** means total, unlimited, and complete. *The event was an unqualified success.*

unquestionable /ˌʌnˈkwestʃənəbəl/. ADJ If you describe something as **unquestionable**, you are emphasizing that it is so obviously true or real that nobody can doubt it. *His loyalty and devotion to the King were unquestionable.* ♦**unquestionably** ADV *The next two years were unquestionably the happiest of his life.*

unravel /ʌnˈrævəl/ **unravels, unravelling, unravelled** (AM **unraveling, unraveled**). VERB If you **unravel** a mystery or puzzle, or if it **unravels**, it gradually becomes clearer and you can work out the answer to it. *Carter was still trying to unravel the truth of the woman's story.*

unreal /ˌʌnˈriːl/. ADJ AFTER LINK-V If you say that a situation is **unreal**, you mean that it is so strange that you find it difficult to believe it is happening. ♦**unreality** /ˌʌnriˈælɪti/ N-U *The rest of the weekend had a strange air of unreality.*

unrealistic /ˌʌnriəˈlɪstɪk/. ADJ If you say that someone is being **unrealistic**, you mean that they do not recognize the truth about a situation, especially about the difficulties involved. ...*their unrealistic expectations of parenthood.*

unreasonable /ˌʌnˈriːzənəbəl/. **1** ADJ If you say that someone is being **unreasonable**, you mean that they are behaving in a way that is not fair or sensible. ♦**unreasonably** ADV *We unreasonably expect near perfect behaviour from our children.* **2** ADJ An **unreasonable** decision, action, price, or amount seems unfair and difficult to justify. ♦**unreasonably** ADV *The banks' charges are unreasonably high.*

unrelated /ˌʌnrɪˈleɪtɪd/. ADJ If one thing is **unrelated** to another, there is no connection between them. *Two of them died from apparently unrelated causes.*

unrelenting /ˌʌnrɪˈlentɪŋ/. **1** ADJ If you describe someone's behaviour as **unrelenting**, you mean that they are continuing to do something in a very determined way. *She established her authority with unrelenting thoroughness.* **2** ADJ If you describe something unpleasant as **unrelenting**, you mean that it is continuing without stopping. ...*the unrelenting pressures of his job.*

unreliable /ˌʌnrɪˈlaɪəbəl/. ADJ If you describe a person, machine, or method as **unreliable**, you mean that you cannot trust them to do or provide what you want. *The car was horribly slow and unreliable.*

unremarkable /ˌʌnrɪˈmɑːkəbəl/. ADJ If you describe someone or something as **unremarkable**, you mean that they do not have many exciting, original, or attractive qualities. ...*a tall, lean man, with an unremarkable face.*

unrepentant /ˌʌnrɪˈpentənt/. ADJ If you are **unrepentant**, you are not ashamed of your beliefs or actions. *Pamela was unrepentant about her strong language.*

unresolved /ˌʌnrɪˈzɒlvd/. ADJ If a problem or difficulty is **unresolved**, no satisfactory solution has been found to it; FORMAL.

unrest /ˌʌnˈrest/. N-U If there is **unrest** in a particular place or society, people are expressing anger and dissatisfaction, often by demonstrating or rioting; JOURNALISM. *There is growing unrest among students in several major cities.*

unrestricted /ˌʌnrɪˈstrɪktɪd/. ADJ If an activity is **unrestricted**, you are free to do it in the way that you want, without being limited by any rules.

unrivalled (AM **unrivaled**) /ʌnˈraɪvəld/. ADJ If you describe something as **unrivalled**, you are emphasizing that it is better than anything else of the same kind. ...*an unrivalled knowledge of south Arabian society.*

unruly /ʌnˈruːli/. **1** ADJ If you describe people as **unruly**, you mean that they behave badly and are difficult to control. **2** ADJ **Unruly** hair is difficult to keep tidy.

unsafe /ˌʌnˈseɪf/. **1** ADJ If a building, machine, activity, or area is **unsafe**, it is dangerous. *Critics claim the trucks are unsafe.* **2** ADJ AFTER LINK-V If you are **unsafe**, you are in danger of being harmed. *I felt very unsafe.*

unsatisfactory /ˌʌnsætɪsˈfæktəri/. ADJ If you describe something as **unsatisfactory**, you mean that it is not as good as it should be, and cannot be considered acceptable. ...*questions to which he received unsatisfactory answers.*

unsavoury (AM **unsavory**) /ʌnˈseɪvəri/. ADJ If you describe someone or something as **unsavoury**, you mean that you find them unpleasant or morally unacceptable. *Mr King had written a string of unsavoury reports.*

unscathed /ʌnˈskeɪðd/. ADJ If you are **unscathed** after a dangerous experience, you have not been injured or harmed by it.

unscrupulous /ʌnˈskruːpjʊləs/. ADJ If you describe a person as **unscrupulous**, you are critical of the fact that they are prepared to act in a dishonest or immoral way in order to get what they want.

unseeded /ˌʌnˈsiːdɪd/. ADJ In sports competitions such as tennis or badminton, an **unseeded** player is someone who has not been ranked amongst the top 16 players by the tournament's organizers.

unseen /ˌʌnˈsiːn/. ADJ You use **unseen** to describe things that you cannot see or have not seen. *There was barely time for the two boys to escape unseen. ...a spectacular ballroom, unseen by the public for over 30 years.*

unsettled /ʌnˈsetəld/. [1] ADJ In an **unsettled** situation, there is a lot of uncertainty about what will happen. *...Britain's unsettled political scene.* [2] ADJ AFTER LINK-V If you are **unsettled**, you cannot concentrate on anything, because you are worried. *To tell the truth, I'm a bit unsettled tonight.*

unsettling /ʌnˈsetəlɪŋ/. ADJ If you describe something as **unsettling**, you mean that it causes you to feel restless or rather worried. *His sense of humour was really unsettling.*

unsightly /ʌnˈsaɪtlɪ/. ADJ If you describe something as **unsightly**, you mean that it is unattractive to look at. *...an unsightly hole in the garden.*

unskilled /ʌnˈskɪld/. [1] ADJ People who are **unskilled** do not have any special training for a job. *...work as an unskilled labourer.* [2] ADJ **Unskilled** work does not require any special training. *...low-paid, unskilled jobs.*

unsolicited /ˌʌnsəˈlɪsɪtɪd/. ADJ Something that is **unsolicited** is given without being asked for and may not have been wanted. *...unsolicited advice.*

unsolved /ˌʌnˈsɒlvd/. ADJ An **unsolved** problem or mystery has never been solved.

unspeakable /ʌnˈspiːkəbəl/. ADJ If you describe something as **unspeakable**, you are emphasizing that it is extremely unpleasant. *...the unspeakable horrors of chemical weapons.* ◆**unspeakably** /ʌnˈspiːkəblɪ/ ADV *The novel was unspeakably boring.*

unspecified /ˌʌnˈspesɪfaɪd/. ADJ You say that something is **unspecified** when you are not told exactly what it is. *He was arrested on unspecified charges.*

unspoiled /ˌʌnˈspɔɪld/ (BR also **unspoilt** /ˌʌnˈspɔɪlt/). ADJ If you describe a place as **unspoiled**, you think it is beautiful because it has not been changed or built on for a long time. *...the unspoiled island of Cozumel.*

unspoken /ˌʌnˈspəʊkən/. ADJ If your thoughts or feelings are **unspoken**, you do not speak about them.

unstable /ʌnˈsteɪbəl/. [1] ADJ You can describe something as **unstable** if it is likely to change suddenly, especially if this creates difficulty. *The situation is unstable and potentially dan-*

gerous. [2] ADJ **Unstable** objects are likely to move or fall. *...unstable rock formations.* [3] ADJ If people are **unstable**, their emotions and behaviour keep changing because their minds are disturbed. *He was emotionally unstable.*

unsteady /ʌnˈstedɪ/. [1] ADJ If you are **unsteady**, you have difficulty doing something because you cannot completely control your body. *The boy was very unsteady and had staggered around when he got up.* ◆**unsteadily** ADV *She pulled herself unsteadily from the bed.* [2] ADJ If you describe something as **unsteady**, you mean that it is not regular or stable. *His voice was unsteady and only just audible.* [3] ADJ **Unsteady** objects are not held, fixed, or balanced securely. *...a slightly unsteady item of furniture.*

unsubstantiated /ˌʌnsəbˈstænʃieɪtɪd/. ADJ An **unsubstantiated** statement or story has not been proved true.

unsuccessful /ˌʌnsəkˈsesfʊl/. [1] ADJ Something that is **unsuccessful** does not achieve what it was intended to achieve. *...a second unsuccessful operation on his knee.* ◆**unsuccessfully** ADV *He has been trying unsuccessfully to sell the business.* [2] ADJ Someone who is **unsuccessful** does not achieve what they intended to achieve. *He and his friend Boris were unsuccessful in getting a job.*

unsuitable /ʌnˈsuːtəbəl/. ADJ Someone or something that is **unsuitable** for a particular purpose or situation does not have the right qualities for it. *Amy's shoes were unsuitable for walking.*

unsure /ˌʌnˈʃʊə/. [1] ADJ If you are **unsure** of yourself, you lack confidence. *He made her feel hot, and awkward, and unsure of herself.* [2] ADJ AFTER LINK-V If you are **unsure** about something, you feel uncertain about it. *Fifty-two per cent were unsure about the idea.*

unsuspecting /ˌʌnsəˈspektɪŋ/. ADJ You can use **unsuspecting** to describe someone who is not aware of something that is happening or going to happen. *...his unsuspecting victim.*

unsympathetic /ˌʌnsɪmpəˈθetɪk/. [1] ADJ If someone is **unsympathetic**, they are not kind or helpful to a person in difficulties. *Her husband was unsympathetic and she felt she had no one to turn to.* [2] ADJ An **unsympathetic** person is unpleasant and difficult to like. *...a very unsympathetic main character.*

untenable /ʌnˈtenəbəl/. ADJ An argument or position that is **untenable** cannot be defended successfully against criticism or attack. *He claimed the charges against him were untenable.*

unthinkable /ʌnˈθɪŋkəbəl/. [1] ADJ & N-SING If you say that something is **unthinkable**, you mean that it cannot possibly be accepted or imagined as a possibility. The **unthinkable** is something that is unthinkable. *Any thought of splitting up the company was unthinkable... The unthinkable had happened – a power failure.* [2] ADJ You can use **unthinkable** to describe a situation or event which is extremely unpleasant to imagine or remember. *This place is going to be unthinkable without you.*

untidy /ʌnˈtaɪdɪ/ **untidier, untidiest.** [1] ADJ Something that is **untidy** is messy, and not neatly arranged. *Clothes were thrown in the luggage in an untidy heap.* ♦ **untidily** ADV *Her long hair tumbles untidily around her shoulders.* **2** ADJ If you describe a person as **untidy**, you mean that they do not care about whether things are neat and well arranged. *I'm untidy in most ways.*

untie /ˌʌn'taɪ/ **unties, untying, untied. 1** VERB If you **untie** something that is tied to another thing, or if you **untie** two things that are tied together, you remove the string or rope that holds them. *Just untie my hands.* **2** VERB If you **untie** something such as string or rope, you undo the knot in it.

until /ʌn'tɪl/. **1** PREP & CONJ If something happens **until** a particular time, it happens during the period before that time and stops at that time. *...consumers who have waited until after the Christmas holiday to do that holiday shopping... I waited until it got dark.* **2** PREP & CONJ If something does not happen **until** a particular time, it does not happen before that time and only happens after it. *The traffic laws don't take effect until the end of the year.*

> Note that you only use **until** or **till** when you are talking about time. You do not use these words to talk about place or position. Instead, you should use **as far as** or **up to**. *Then you'll be riding with us as far as the village?... We walked up to where his bicycle was.*

untold /ˌʌn'təʊld/. **1** ADJ BEFORE N You can use **untold** to emphasize how unpleasant something is. *This might do untold damage to her health.* **2** ADJ BEFORE N You can use **untold** to emphasize that an amount or quantity is very large, especially when you are not sure how large it is. *An Olympic gold medal can lead to untold riches for an athlete.*

untouched /ˌʌn'tʌtʃt/. **1** ADJ Something that is **untouched** has not been changed or damaged in any way. *The western part of the island is still untouched by tourism... There was one building that remained untouched.* **2** ADJ If food or drink is **untouched**, none of it has been eaten or drunk. *The coffee was untouched.*

untrained /ˌʌn'treɪnd/. **1** ADJ Someone who is **untrained** has not been taught the skills that they need for a particular job. **2** ADJ You use **untrained** with words like 'eye' and 'ear' to describe how something seems to someone who is not an expert. *They don't look very different to the untrained eye.*

untreated /ˌʌn'triːtɪd/. **1** ADJ If an injury or illness is left **untreated**, it is not being used at medical treatment. **2** ADJ **Untreated** materials, water, or chemicals are harmful and have not been made safe.

untrue /ˌʌn'truː/. ADJ Something that is **untrue** is not true. *Such remarks are both offensive and untrue.*

unused. 1 ADJ /ˌʌn'juːzd/ Something that is **unused** has not been used or is not being used at the moment. *Any unused land should return to farm land.* **2** ADJ AFTER LINK-V /ʌn'juːst/ If you are **unused** to something, you have not often

done it or experienced it. *He was unused to having his speeches interrupted.*

unusual /ʌn'juːʒʊəl/. ADJ If something is **unusual**, it does not happen very often or you do not see it or hear it very often. *It's very unusual for him to make a mistake. ...rare and unusual plants.* ♦ **unusually** ADV *...an unusually harsh winter.*

unveil /ˌʌn'veɪl/ **unveils, unveiling, unveiled. 1** VERB If someone **unveils** something such as a new statue or painting, they draw back the curtain which is covering it, in a special ceremony. **2** VERB If you **unveil** something that has been kept secret, you make it known to the public. *The company unveiled plans to open 100 new stores.*

unwanted /ˌʌn'wɒntɪd/. ADJ You say that something is **unwanted** when someone does not want it. *...unwanted pregnancies... Every year thousands of unwanted animals are abandoned.*

unwarranted /ˌʌn'wɒrəntɪd, AM -'wɔːr-/. ADJ Something that is **unwarranted** is not justified or deserved; FORMAL. *He accused the police of using unwarranted brutality.*

unwelcome /ʌn'welkəm/. **1** ADJ An **unwelcome** experience is one that you do not like and did not want. *The media has brought more unwelcome attention to the Royal Family.* **2** ADJ If a visitor is **unwelcome**, you did not want them to come. *She was, quite deliberately, making him feel unwelcome.*

unwell /ˌʌn'wel/. ADJ AFTER LINK-V If you are **unwell**, you are ill. *Mrs Potter was too unwell to go with him.*

unwieldy /ʌn'wiːldi/. **1** ADJ An **unwieldy** object is difficult to move or carry because it is big or heavy. **2** ADJ An **unwieldy** system does not work well because it is too large or is badly organized. *...France's unwieldy welfare system.*

unwilling /ˌʌn'wɪlɪŋ/. ADJ If you are **unwilling** to do something, you do not want to do it. *He was unwilling to discuss the matter.* ♦ **unwillingly** ADV *Unwillingly, she moved aside.* ♦ **unwillingness** N-U *...the unwillingness of banks to grant loans.*

unwind /ˌʌn'waɪnd/ **unwinds, unwinding, unwound. 1** VERB When you **unwind** after working hard, you relax. *It is the perfect place to unwind.* **2** VERB If you **unwind** something that is wrapped round something else, you undo it or straighten it out.

unwise /ˌʌn'waɪz/. ADJ Something that is **unwise** is foolish. *It would be unwise to expect too much.* ♦ **unwisely** ADV *She had acted unwisely.*

unwitting /ʌn'wɪtɪŋ/. ADJ If you describe a person or their actions as **unwitting**, you mean that the person does something or is involved in something without realizing it. *It had been an unwitting blunder on Blair's part.* ♦ **unwittingly** ADV *...a woman who had unwittingly bought a stolen car.*

unworkable /ˌʌn'wɜːkəbəl/. ADJ If an idea or plan is **unworkable**, it cannot succeed. *This proposal would be unworkable.*

unworthy /ʌn'wɜːði/. **1** ADJ If someone is **unworthy** of something, they do not deserve it; LITERARY. *She felt unworthy of any respect.*

2 ADJ If you say that an action is **unworthy** of someone, you mean that it is not a nice thing to do and someone with their reputation or position should not do it. *His accusations are unworthy of a prime minister.*

unwound /ˌʌnˈwaʊnd/. **Unwound** is the past tense and past participle of **unwind.**

unwrap /ˌʌnˈræp/ **unwraps, unwrapping, unwrapped.** VERB When you **unwrap** something, you take off the paper or covering that is around it.

unwritten /ˌʌnˈrɪtən/. ADJ **Unwritten** things have not been printed or written down. *The book he had meant to write remained unwritten.*

<hr>

up 1 preposition, adverb, and adjective uses

up /ʌp/ **ups.** **1** PREP & ADV **Up** means towards a higher place, or in a higher place. *I ran up the stairs... The Newton Hotel is halfway up a steep hill... He put his hand up.* **2** ADV If someone stands **up**, they move so that they are standing. *He got up and went out into the foyer.* **3** ADV **Up** means in the north or towards the north. *Mark was travelling up to London by train.* **4** PREP If you go **up** something such as a road or river, you go along it. *Several tanks came up the road.* **5** ADV If you go **up** to something or someone, you move to the place where they are and stop there. *The girl ran up to the car... A boy of about ten came up on roller skates.* **6** ADJ AFTER LINK-V If you are **up**, you are not in bed. *He was up at 6am.* **7** ADV If an amount goes **up**, it increases. If an amount of something is **up**, it is at a higher level than it was. *They recently put my rent up.* **8** ADJ AFTER LINK-V If a period of time is **up**, it has come to an end. *When the six weeks were up, everybody was sad that she had to leave.*

PHRASES • If you move **up and down**, you move repeatedly in one direction and then in the opposite direction. *Her son started to jump up and down... I strolled up and down thoughtfully before calling a taxi.* • If you have **ups and downs**, you experience a mixture of good things and bad things. *Every relationship has a lot of ups and downs.* • If you are **up against** something, you have a difficult situation or problem to deal with. *They were up against a good team but did very well.* • If someone or something is **up for** discussion, election, or review, they are about to be considered or judged. *The whole question of school curriculum is up for discussion.* • You use **up to** to say how large something can be or what level it has reached. *Up to twenty thousand students paid between five and six thousand dollars... It could be up to two years before the process is complete.* • If you do not feel **up to** doing something, you do not feel well enough to do it. • If you say that it is **up to** someone to do a particular thing, you mean that it is their responsibility to do it. *It is up to you to tell them.* • If something happens **up to** or **up until** a particular time, it happens until that time. *Please feel free to call me any time up until half past nine.*

up 2 verb uses

up /ʌp/ **ups, upping, upped.** VERB If you **up** something such as the amount of money you

are offering for something, you increase it. *We are talking about upping everybody's pay.*

up-and-'coming. ADJ BEFORE N **Up-and-coming** people are likely to be successful in the future.

upbeat /ˈʌpbiːt/. ADJ If you describe someone as **upbeat**, you mean they are cheerful and optimistic about a situation; INFORMAL. *Ann was in an upbeat mood.*

upbringing /ˈʌpbrɪŋɪŋ/. N-U Your **upbringing** is the way your parents treat you and the things that they teach you. *Her son had a good upbringing.*

upcoming /ˈʌpkʌmɪŋ/. ADJ BEFORE N **Upcoming** events will happen in the near future.

update, updates, updating, updated. **1** VERB /ʌpˈdeɪt/ If you **update** something, you make it more modern, usually by adding newer parts to it. *...an updated edition of the book.* **2** N-C /ˈʌpdeɪt/ An **update** is a news item which has been rewritten so that it includes the latest developments in a situation.

up 'front (or **upfront**). **1** ADV If a payment is made **up front**, it is made in advance , so that the person being paid can be sure that they will be paid. *Some companies charge a fee up front.* **2** ADJ If you are **up front** about something, you act openly or publicly so that people know what you are doing or what you believe. *I'm very upfront about being happily married.*

upgrade /ˌʌpˈgreɪd/ **upgrades, upgrading, upgraded.** VERB & N-C To **upgrade** something, or to give it an **upgrade**, means to change it so that it is more important or better. *...upgraded catering facilities. ...an upgrade of the sports facilities.*

upheaval /ʌpˈhiːvəl/ **upheavals.** N-VAR An **upheaval** is a big change which causes a lot of trouble and confusion. *Algeria has been going through political upheaval for the past two months.*

upheld /ʌpˈheld/. **Upheld** is the past tense and past participle of **uphold.**

uphill /ʌpˈhɪl/. **1** ADV & ADJ If you go **uphill**, you go up a slope. *We walked uphill in single file. ...a long, uphill journey.* **2** ADJ BEFORE N If you refer to something as an **uphill** struggle, you mean that it requires a great deal of effort and determination.

uphold /ʌpˈhəʊld/ **upholds, upholding, upheld.** VERB If you **uphold** a law, principle, or decision, you support and maintain it. *...upholding the artist's right to creative freedom.*

upholstery /ʌpˈhəʊlstəri/. N-U **Upholstery** is the soft covering on chairs and sofas that makes them comfortable.

upkeep /ˈʌpkiːp/. **1** N-U The **upkeep** of a building or place is the continual process of keeping it in good condition. *The maintenance department is responsible for the general upkeep of the park.* **2** N-U The **upkeep** of a group of people or services is the process of providing them with the things that they need. *He offered to pay £100 a month towards his son's upkeep.*

uplifting /ʌpˈlɪftɪŋ/. ADJ If something is **uplifting**, it makes you feel cheerful and happy. *...a very uplifting experience.*

upmarket /ˌʌpˈmɑːkɪt/. ADJ **Upmarket** places or products are intended to appeal to people with sophisticated and expensive tastes; BRITISH. *...an upmarket hotel.*

upon /əˈpɒn/. **1** PREP If one thing is **upon** another, it is on it; FORMAL. *He set the tray upon the table... I imagined the eyes of the others in the room upon me.* **2** PREP You use **upon** when mentioning an event that is followed immediately by another. *Upon leaving the club, he collapsed. ...row upon row of women.* **3** PREP You use **upon** between two occurrences of the same noun in order to say that there are large numbers of the thing mentioned. *...row upon row of women.* **4** PREP If an event is **upon** you, it is just about to happen. *The football season is upon us.*

upper /ˈʌpə/. **1** ADJ You use **upper** to describe something that is above something else. *...a smart restaurant on the upper floor.* **2** ADJ The **upper** part of something is the higher part. *...the upper rungs of the ladder.* **3** PHRASE If you have **the upper hand** in a situation, you have more power than the other people involved and can make decisions about what happens.

upper ˈclass, upper classes. N-C & ADJ The **upper class** or the **upper classes** are the group of people in a society who own the most property and have the highest social status. You say people like this are **upper class**. *...wealthy, upper class families.*

upright /ˈʌpraɪt/. **1** ADJ If you are sitting or standing **upright**, you have your back straight and are not bending or lying down. *The wind was so strong I couldn't stand upright.* **2** ADJ You can describe people as **upright** when they are careful to follow acceptable rules of behaviour and behave in a moral way. *...an upright citizen.*

uprising /ˈʌpraɪzɪŋ/ **uprisings.** N-C When there is an **uprising**, a group of people start fighting against the people who are in power in their country.

uproar /ˈʌprɔː/. **1** N-U & N-SING An **uproar** is a lot of shouting and noise because people are very angry or upset about something. **2** N-U & N-SING An **uproar** is a lot of public criticism and debate about something that has made people angry. *...last year's uproar over school spending cuts.*

uproot /ʌpˈruːt/ **uproots, uprooting, uprooted.** **1** VERB If you **uproot** yourself, or if you **are uprooted**, you leave or are made to leave a place where you have lived for a long time. *He was not prepared to uproot his family from the Midlands.* **2** VERB If someone **uproots** a tree or plant, or if the wind **uproots** it, it is pulled out of the ground.

upset, upsets, upsetting, upset; verb and adjective /ʌpˈset/, noun /ˈʌpset/. **1** ADJ If you are **upset**, you are unhappy or disappointed because something unpleasant has happened. *They are terribly upset by the break-up of their parents' marriage.* **2** VERB If something **upsets** you, it makes you feel worried or unhappy. *I'm sorry if I've upset you.* ♦ **upsetting** ADJ *The whole incident was very upsetting.* **3** VERB If events **upset** something such as a procedure or a state of affairs, they cause it to go wrong. *Po-

litical problems could upset agreements between Moscow and Kabul.* **4** N-C & ADJ BEFORE N If you have a stomach **upset**, or if you have an **upset** stomach, you have a slight illness in your stomach caused by an infection or by something that you have eaten.

upside down (or **upside-down**) /ˌʌpsaɪd ˈdaʊn/. **1** ADV & ADJ If something has been put **upside down**, it has been turned round so that the part that is usually lowest is above the part that is usually highest. *The painting was hung upside down. ...an upside-down map of Britain.* **2** PHRASE If you **turn** a place **upside down**, you move everything around and make it untidy, because you are looking for something.

upstage /ˌʌpˈsteɪdʒ/ **upstages, upstaging, upstaged.** VERB To **upstage** someone is to draw attention away from them by being more attractive or interesting.

upstairs /ˌʌpˈsteəz/. **1** ADV If you go **upstairs** in a building, you go up a staircase towards a higher floor. *Maureen ran upstairs to her bedroom.* **2** ADV & ADJ If something or someone is **upstairs** in a building, they are on a floor that is higher than the ground floor. *There is another bar upstairs. ...the upstairs apartment.* **3** N-SING **The upstairs** of a building is the floor or floors that are higher than the ground floor.

upstart /ˈʌpstɑːt/ **upstarts.** N-C You can refer to someone as an **upstart** when they behave as if they are important, but you think that they are too new in a place or job to be treated as important.

upstream /ˌʌpˈstriːm/. ADV Something that is moving **upstream** is moving along a river towards the source of the river. Something that is **upstream** is towards the source of a river. *He lives about 60 miles upstream from Oahe.*

upsurge /ˈʌpsɜːdʒ/. N-SING If there is an **upsurge** in something, there is a sudden large increase in it; FORMAL. *...the upsurge in oil prices.*

uptight /ˌʌpˈtaɪt/. ADJ If someone is **uptight**, they are very tense, because they are worried or annoyed about something; INFORMAL.

ˌup-to-ˈdate (or **up to date**). **1** ADJ If something is **up-to-date**, it is the newest thing of its kind. *...Germany's most up to date electric power station.* **2** ADJ If you are **up-to-date** with something, you have the latest information about it.

uptown /ˌʌpˈtaʊn/. ADV & ADJ BEFORE N If you go **uptown**, or go to a place **uptown**, you go away from the centre of a town or city towards one of its suburbs; AMERICAN. *Susan continued to live uptown. ...uptown New Orleans.*

upturn /ˈʌptɜːn/ **upturns.** N-C If there is an **upturn** in the economy or in a company or industry, it becomes more successful.

upwards /ˈʌpwədz/. In British English, **upwards** is an adverb and **upward** is an adjective. In informal British English and American English, **upward** is both an adjective and an adverb. **1** ADV & ADJ BEFORE N If you move or look **upwards**, you move or look up towards a higher place. *They climbed upward along the steep cliffs surrounding the village... Lie face upwards with a cushion under your head... She

started once again on the steep upward climb.
2 ADV If an amount or rate moves **upwards**, it increases. *The share price is likely to leap upwards.* **3** PREP A quantity that is **upwards of** a particular number is more than that number. *...projects worth upwards of 200 million pounds.*

uranium /jʊˈreɪniəm/. N-U **Uranium** is a radioactive metal that is used to produce nuclear energy and weapons.

urban /ˈɜːbən/. ADJ **Urban** means belonging to, or relating to, a town or city. *...densely populated urban areas.*

urge /ɜːdʒ/ **urges, urging, urged.** **1** VERB If you **urge** someone to do something, you try hard to persuade them to do it. *He had urged her to come to Ireland... 'Now read,' I urged.* **2** N-C If you have an **urge** to do or have something, you have a strong wish to do or have it. *The urge to have children was beginning to take over her life. ...his urge for revenge.*

▸ **urge on** PHR-VERB If you **urge** someone **on**, you encourage them to do something. *Urged on by his strong-willed mother, he set out to become a doctor.*

urgent /ˈɜːdʒənt/. **1** ADJ If something is **urgent**, it needs to be dealt with as soon as possible. *...an urgent need for food and water... He had urgent business in New York.* ♦ **urgency** N-U *It is a matter of utmost urgency.* ♦ **urgently** ADV *An alternative road is urgently needed.* **2** ADJ If you speak in an **urgent** way, you show that you are anxious for people to notice something or do something. ♦ **urgency** N-U *She was surprised at the urgency in his voice.* ♦ **urgently** ADV *'Are you still there?' Jerrold asked urgently.*

urinate /ˈjʊərɪneɪt/ **urinates, urinating, urinated.** VERB When you **urinate**, you get rid of urine from your body.

urine /ˈjʊərɪn/. N-U **Urine** is the liquid that you get rid of from your body when you go to the toilet.

urn /ɜːn/ **urns.** **1** N-C An **urn** is a container like a large vase, especially one in which the ashes of a cremated person are kept. **2** N-C An **urn** is a metal container used for making a large quantity of tea or coffee and keeping it hot.

us /əs, STRONG ʌs/. PRON A speaker or writer uses **us** to refer to a group of people which includes himself or herself. *Neither of us forgot about it... He told us we had to leave Delhi by 7am.*

usable /ˈjuːzəbəl/. ADJ If something is **usable**, it is in a good enough state or condition to be used. *There is very little usable land left.*

usage /ˈjuːsɪdʒ/ **usages.** **1** N-U **Usage** is the way in which words are actually used in particular contexts, especially with regard to their meanings. *...an Australian Guide to Modern English Usage.* **2** N-U **Usage** is the degree to which something is used or the way in which it is used. *The motor wore out because of constant usage.*

use 1 verb uses

use /juːz/ **uses, using, used.** **1** VERB If you **use** a particular thing, you do something with it in order to do a job or to achieve something. *May I use your phone?... Use a very sharp knife to cut the beef... He had never used violence.*

2 VERB & PHR-VERB If you **use** a supply of something, or if you **use** it **up**, you finish it so that none of it is left. *It isn't them who use up the world's resources.* **3** VERB If you **use** a particular word or expression, you say or write it. **4** VERB If you say that someone **uses** people, you disapprove of them because they are only interested in other people when they can benefit from them.

use 2 noun uses

use /juːs/ **uses.** **1** N-U Your **use** of something is the action or fact of your using it. *...the use of any artificial drugs. ...microcomputers and their use in classrooms.* **2** N-VAR If something has a particular **use**, it is intended for a particular purpose. *Infrared detectors have many uses... They both loved the fabric, but couldn't find a use for it in TV.* **3** N-U If you have the **use** of something, you have the permission or ability to use it. *They had regular use of a car... Crippled by polio in 1921, he had lost the use of his legs.* **4** N-C A **use** of a word is a particular meaning that it has or a particular way in which it can be used.

PHRASES ● If something such as a technique, building, or machine is **in use**, it is used regularly. If it has gone **out of use**, it is no longer used regularly. ● If you **make use of** something, you do something with it in order to do a job or achieve something. *I shall make use of this time to see to the washing.* ● You use expressions such as **it's no use**, **there's no use** and **what's the use** to indicate that an action will not achieve anything. *It's no use arguing with a drunk.*

used 1 modal uses and phrases

used /juːst/. **1** MODAL If something **used to** be done or **used to** be the case, it was done regularly in the past or was the case in the past. *People used to come and visit him every day... The gallery in north London used to be a warehouse.* **2** PHRASE If you **are used to** something, you are familiar with it because you have done it or experienced it many times before. If you **get used to** something, you become familiar with it. *I'm used to having my sleep interrupted.*

used 2 adjective uses

used /juːzd/. **1** ADJ A **used** handkerchief, glass, or other object is dirty or spoiled because it has been used. **2** ADJ A **used** car has already had one or more owners.

useful /ˈjuːsfʊl/. **1** ADJ If something is **useful**, you can use it to do something or to help you. *...useful information.* ♦ **usefully** ADV *...the problems to which computers could be usefully applied.* ♦ **usefulness** N-U *...the usefulness of his work.* **2** PHRASE If an object or skill **comes in useful**, it can help you achieve something in a particular situation.

useless /ˈjuːsləs/. **1** ADJ If something is **useless**, you cannot use it. *Their money was useless in this country.* **2** ADJ If a course of action is **useless**, it does not achieve anything. *She knew it was useless to protest.* **3** ADJ If you say that someone or something is **useless**, you mean that they are no good at all; INFORMAL. *He was useless at any game with a ball.*

user /'ju:zə/ **users.** N-C The **users** of a product, machine, service, or place are the people who use it. *Beach users have complained that the bikes are noisy.*

user-'friendly. ADJ If you describe something such as a machine or system as **user-friendly**, you mean that it is well designed and easy to use.

usher /'ʌʃə/ **ushers, ushering, ushered.** 1 VERB If you **usher** someone somewhere, you show them where they should go, often by going with them. *I ushered him into the office.* 2 N-C An **usher** is a person who shows people where they are going to sit, for example at a wedding or concert.
▶ **usher in.** PHR-VERB If a person or event **ushers in** an important change, they help make it happen; JOURNALISM. *...a unique opportunity to usher in a new era of stability in Europe.*

usual /'ju:ʒʊəl/. ADJ **Usual** is used to describe what happens or what is done most often in a particular situation. *An officer was asking the usual questions... The winter has been colder than usual... It is usual to tip waiters.*
PHRASES ● You use **as usual** to indicate that you are describing something that normally happens or that is usually the case. *As usual when he was nervous, his stomach began to rumble.* ● If something happens **as usual**, it happens in the way that it normally does. *When somebody died everything went on as usual.*

usually /'ju:ʒʊəli/. ADV If something **usually** happens, it is the thing that most often happens in a particular situation. *We usually eat in here.*

usurp /ju:'zɜ:p/ **usurps, usurping, usurped.** VERB If you say that someone **usurps** a job, role, title, or position, you mean that they take it from someone when they have no right to do this; FORMAL.

utensil /ju:'tensəl/ **utensils.** N-C **Utensils** are tools or other objects that you use when you are cooking or doing other tasks in your home. *...aluminium cooking utensils.*

uterus /'ju:tərəs/ **uteruses.** N-C A woman's **uterus** is her womb; TECHNICAL.

utilise /'ju:tlaɪz/. See **utilize.**

utilitarian /,ju:tɪlɪ'teəriən/. ADJ **Utilitarian** objects and buildings are designed to be useful rather than beautiful.

utility /ju:'tɪlɪti/ **utilities.** 1 N-C A **utility** is an important service such as water, electricity, or gas that is provided for everyone, and that everyone pays for. 2 N-U The **utility** of something is its usefulness; FORMAL. *He inwardly questioned the utility of his work.*

utilize (BR also **utilise**) /'ju:tɪlaɪz/ **utilizes, utilizing, utilized.** VERB If you **utilize** something, you use it; FORMAL. *...ways in which their skill and experience could be utilized.*
♦ **utilization** N-U *...the utilisation of human resources.*

utmost /'ʌtməʊst/. 1 ADJ BEFORE N You can use **utmost** to emphasize the importance or seriousness of something or to emphasize the way that it is done; FORMAL. *I have a matter of the utmost urgency to discuss with you... Utmost care must be taken not to spill any of the contents.* 2 N-SING If you say that you are doing your **utmost** to do something, you are emphasizing that you are trying as hard as you can to do it. *He will try his utmost to help them.*

Utopia /ju:'təʊpiə/ **Utopias.** N-VAR If you refer to an imaginary situation as a **utopia**, you mean that it is one in which society is perfect and everyone is happy, but which you feel is not possible.

utopian /ju:'təʊpiən/. ADJ If you describe a plan or idea as **utopian**, you are criticizing it because it is unrealistic and shows a belief that things can be improved much more than is possible.

utter /'ʌtə/ **utters, uttering, uttered.** 1 VERB If someone **utters** sounds or words, they say them; LITERARY. *They departed without uttering a word.* 2 ADJ BEFORE N You use **utter** to emphasize the great degree or amount of something bad. *This, of course, is utter nonsense. ...this utter lack of responsibility.*

utterance /'ʌtərəns/ **utterances.** N-C Someone's **utterances** are the things that they say; FORMAL. *...the Queen's public utterances.*

utterly /'ʌtəli/. ADV You use **utterly** to emphasize the great degree or amount of something bad. *The new laws coming in are utterly ridiculous.*

'U-turn, U-turns. 1 N-C If you make a **U-turn** when you are driving or cycling, you turn in a half circle in one movement, so that you are then going in the opposite direction. 2 N-C When a government does a **U-turn**, it abandons a policy and does something completely different.

V v

V, v /vi:/ **V's, v's.** V or v is an abbreviation of 'versus'. It is used to indicate that two teams are competing against each other. *...Newcastle United v Leicester City.*

vacancy /'veɪkənsi/ **vacancies.** 1 N-C A **vacancy** is a job or position that has not been filled. *We have a vacancy for an editorial assistant.* 2 N-C If there are **vacancies** at a hotel, there are rooms still available for people to stay in.

vacant /'veɪkənt/. 1 ADJ If something is **vacant**, it is not being used by anyone. *...a vacant seat.* 2 ADJ If a job or position is **vacant**, it has not yet been filled, and people can apply for it. *The post has been vacant since June.* 3 ADJ A **vacant** look suggests that someone does not understand or that they are not concentrating. ♦ **vacantly** ADV *He looked vacantly out of the window.*

vacate /'veɪ'keɪt/, AM **'veɪkeɪt/ vacates, vacating, vacated.** VERB If you **vacate** a place or a job, you leave it and make it available for other people; FORMAL. *He vacated the flat and went to stay with an uncle.*

vacation /vəˈkeɪʃən, AM veɪ-/ **vacations.**
[1] N-VAR In American English, a **vacation** is a period of time when you are not working and are away from home for relaxation. The British word is **holiday**. *We went on vacation to Puerto Rico.* [2] N-C A **vacation** is a period of the year when universities or colleges are officially closed. *During his summer vacation he visited Russia.*

vaccinate /ˈvæksɪneɪt/ **vaccinates, vaccinating, vaccinated.** VERB If a person or animal is **vaccinated**, they are given a vaccine, usually by injection, to prevent them from getting a disease. *Have you had your child vaccinated against whooping cough?* ♦**vaccination, vaccinations** N-VAR *Consider getting a vaccination.*

vaccine /ˈvæksiːn, AM vækˈsiːn/ **vaccines.** N-VAR A **vaccine** is a substance containing the germs that cause a disease. It is given to people to prevent them getting the disease.

vacuum /ˈvækjuːm, -juːəm/ **vacuums, vacuuming, vacuumed.** [1] N-C If someone or something creates a **vacuum**, they leave a place or position which then needs to be filled by someone or something else. *The collapse of the army left a vacuum in the area.* [2] N-C A **vacuum** is a space that contains no air or other gas. [3] VERB If you **vacuum** something, you clean it using a vacuum cleaner.

'vacuum cleaner, vacuum cleaners. N-C A **vacuum cleaner** or a **vacuum** is an electric machine which sucks up dust and dirt from floors and carpets.

vagary /ˈveɪɡəri/ **vagaries.** N-C The **vagaries** of something are the unexpected and unpredictable changes in it; FORMAL. *...the vagaries of the weather.*

vagina /vəˈdʒaɪnə/ **vaginas.** N-C A woman's **vagina** is the passage connecting her outer sex organs to her womb. ♦**vaginal** ADJ BEFORE N *...vaginal infections.*

vague /veɪɡ/ **vaguer, vaguest.** [1] ADJ If something is **vague**, it is not clear, distinct, or definite. You can also say that someone is **vague** about something. *The description was pretty vague... They have only a vague idea of the amount of water available.* ♦**vaguely** ADV *Judith could vaguely remember her mother lying on the sofa.* [2] ADJ If you describe someone as **vague**, you mean that they do not seem to be thinking clearly. ♦**vaguely** ADV *He looked vaguely around the room.* [3] ADJ A **vague** shape or outline is not clear or easy to see.

vaguely /ˈveɪɡli/. ADV **Vaguely** means to a small degree. *The voice on the line was vaguely familiar to me.*

vain /veɪn/ **vainer, vainest.** [1] ADJ BEFORE N & PHRASE A **vain** attempt to do something does not succeed. If you do something **in vain**, what you do has no effect. *He searched everywhere in the vain hope that he had simply mislaid it... It became obvious that all my complaints were in vain.* ♦**vainly** ADV *He hunted vainly through his pockets for a piece of paper.* [2] ADJ If you describe someone as **vain**, you disapprove of them because they are too proud of their appearance.

valiant /ˈvæliənt/. ADJ **Valiant** means very

brave. ♦**valiantly** ADV *They have fought valiantly to defend her freedom.*

valid /ˈvælɪd/. [1] ADJ A **valid** reason or argument is logical and reasonable, and therefore worth taking seriously. *He recognized the valid points that both sides were making.* ♦**validity** /vəˈlɪdɪti/ N-U *This argument has lost much of its validity.* [2] ADJ If a ticket or document is **valid**, it can be used and will be accepted by people in authority. *You will need a valid passport.*

validate /ˈvælɪdeɪt/ **validates, validating, validated.** VERB To **validate** a statement or claim means to prove that it is true or correct. *This discovery seems to validate the claims of popular astrology.* ♦**validation, validations** N-VAR *There had been no recent assessment or validation of the allegations.*

valley /ˈvæli/ **valleys.** N-C A **valley** is a low area of land between hills, often with a river flowing through it.

valuable /ˈvæljʊəbəl/. [1] ADJ Something that is **valuable** is very useful. *...the valuable contribution of ambulancemen to patient care.* [2] ADJ **Valuable** objects are worth a lot of money. *...valuable books.*

valuables /ˈvæljʊəbəlz/. N-PL **Valuables** are things that you own that are worth a lot of money, especially small objects such as jewellery.

valuation /ˌvæljʊˈeɪʃən/ **valuations.** N-VAR A **valuation** is a judgement about how much money something is worth. *...an independent valuation of the company.*

value /ˈvæljuː/ **values, valuing, valued.** [1] N-U The **value** of something such as a quality or a method is its importance or usefulness. *The value of this work experience should not be underestimated.* [2] VERB If you **value** someone or something, you think that they are important and you appreciate them. *She genuinely values his opinion.* [3] N-VAR The **value** of something is the amount of money it is worth. *The company's market value rose to $5.5 billion... Italy's currency went down in value by 3.5 per cent. ...land of little value.* [4] VERB When experts **value** something, they decide how much money it is worth. *...cocaine valued at around $53 million.* [5] N-U A thing's **value** is its worth in relation to the money that it costs. *Scottish salmon is excellent value for money.* [6] N-PL The **values** of a person or group are their moral principles and beliefs. *...traditional family values.* [7] See also **face value.**

valve /vælv/ **valves.** N-C A **valve** is a device which controls the flow of a gas or liquid, for example in a pipe or tube.

vampire /ˈvæmpaɪə/ **vampires.** N-C In horror stories, **vampires** are creature who come out of their graves at night and suck the blood of living people.

van /væn/ **vans.** N-C A **van** is a medium-sized road vehicle that is used for carrying goods.

vandal /ˈvændəl/ **vandals.** N-C A **vandal** is someone who deliberately damages things, especially public property.

vandalism /ˈvændəlɪzəm/. N-U **Vandalism** is the deliberate damaging of things, especially public property.

vandalize (BR also **vandalise**) /'vændəlaɪz/ **vandalizes, vandalizing, vandalized.** VERB If something **is vandalized** by someone, they deliberately damage it. *The walls had been horribly vandalized with spray paint.*

vanguard /'vænɡɑːd/. N-SING If someone is **in the vanguard of** something such as a revolution or an area of research, they are involved in the most advanced part of it.

vanilla /və'nɪlə/. N-U **Vanilla** is a flavouring used in ice cream and other sweet food.

vanish /'vænɪʃ/ **vanishes, vanishing, vanished.** VERB If someone or something **vanishes**, they disappear suddenly or cease to exist altogether. *Anne vanished from outside her home last Wednesday. ...endangered animals and those species which have vanished.*

vanity /'vænɪti/. N-U If you refer to someone's **vanity**, you disapprove of them because they are too interested in their own appearance, or in other good qualities they believe they possess. *With my usual vanity, I thought he might be falling in love with me.*

vantage point /'vɑːntɪdʒ pɔɪnt, 'vænt-/ **vantage points.** N-C A **vantage point** is a place from which you can see a lot of things. *From a concealed vantage point, he saw a car arrive.*

vapour (AM **vapor**) /'veɪpə/ **vapours.** N-VAR **Vapour** consists of tiny drops of water or other liquids in the air, which appear as mist.

variable /'veəriəbəl/ **variables.** [1] ADJ Something that is **variable** is likely to change at any time. *The potassium content of foodstuffs is very variable.* ♦**variability** N-U *...the variability in the climate.* [2] N-C A **variable** is a factor in a situation that can change. *The major economic variables are not under control.*

variance /'veəriəns/. PHRASE If one thing is **at variance** with another, the two things seem to contradict each other; FORMAL. *Many of his statements were at variance with the facts.*

variant /'veəriənt/ **variants.** N-C A **variant** of something has a different form from the usual one. *Many words have variant spellings.*

variation /ˌveəri'eɪʃən/ **variations.** [1] N-C A **variation on** something is the same thing presented in a different form. *...this delicious variation on an omelette.* [2] N-VAR A **variation** is a difference in a level, amount, or quantity. *...a wide variation in the prices charged for canteen food.*

varied /'veərid/. ADJ Something that is **varied** consists of things of different types, sizes, or qualities. *It is essential that your diet is varied and balanced.* ● See also **vary.**

variety /və'raɪəti/ **varieties.** [1] N-U If something has **variety**, it consists of things which are different from each other. *Susan's idea of freedom was to have variety in her life style.* [2] N-SING A **variety** of things is a number of different kinds or examples of the same thing. *Hampstead has a variety of good shops and supermarkets.* [3] N-C A **variety** of something is a type of it. *She has 12 varieties of old-fashioned roses.*

various /'veəriəs/. ADJ If you say that there are **various** things, you mean there are several different things of the type mentioned. *Various*

countries will be putting forward ideas... *The joys of gardening are many and various.*

variously /'veəriəsli/. ADV You can use **variously** to introduce a number of different ways in which something is described. *He is variously described as a designer, stylist, and a photographer.*

varnish /'vɑːnɪʃ/ **varnishes, varnishing, varnished.** [1] N-VAR **Varnish** is an oily liquid which is painted onto wood to give it a hard, clear, shiny surface. [2] VERB If you **varnish** something, you paint it with varnish.

vary /'veəri/ **varies, varying, varied.** [1] VERB If things **vary**, they are different in size, amount, or degree. *As they're handmade, each one varies slightly... The amount of sleep we need varies from person to person.* [2] VERB If something **varies**, or if you **vary** it, it becomes different or it changes. *The cost of the alcohol duty varies according to the amount of wine in the bottle.* [3] See also **varied.**

vase /vɑːz, AM veɪs/ **vases.** N-C A **vase** is a jar used for holding cut flowers or as an ornament.

vast /vɑːst, væst/. ADJ Something that is **vast** is extremely large. *...vast stretches of land.*

vastly /'vɑːstli, 'væst-/. ADV **Vastly** means to an extremely great degree or extent. *...two vastly different accounts of what happened.*

vault /vɔːlt/ **vaults, vaulting, vaulted.** [1] N-C A **vault** is a secure room where money and other valuable things can be kept safely. *...bank vaults.* [2] N-C A **vault** is a room underneath a church or in a cemetery where people are buried. [3] N-C A **vault** is an arched roof or ceiling. [4] VERB If you **vault** something or **vault** over it, you jump over it, putting one or both of your hands on it. *He could easily vault the wall.*

VCR /ˌviː siː 'ɑː/ **VCRs.** N-C A **VCR** is a machine that can be used to record television programmes or films onto video tapes. **VCR** is an abbreviation for 'video cassette recorder'.

VDU /ˌviː diː 'juː/ **VDUs.** N-C A **VDU** is a machine with a screen which is used to display information from a computer. **VDU** is an abbreviation for 'visual display unit'.

veal /viːl/. N-U **Veal** is meat from a calf.

veer /vɪə/ **veers, veering, veered.** VERB If something **veers** in a particular direction, it suddenly moves in that direction. *The plane veered off the runway.*

vegetable /'vedʒtəbəl/ **vegetables.** N-C **Vegetables** are edible plants such as cabbages, potatoes, and onions.

vegetarian /ˌvedʒɪ'teəriən/ **vegetarians.** [1] N-C & ADJ A **vegetarian** is someone who does not eat meat or fish. *...a strict vegetarian diet.*

vegetation /ˌvedʒɪ'teɪʃən/. N-U **Vegetation** is plants, trees and flowers; FORMAL.

vehement /'viːəmənt/. ADJ **Vehement** feeling and opinions are strongly held and forcefully expressed. ♦**vehemence** N-U *He spoke with more vehemence than he had intended.* ♦**vehemently** ADV *Krabbe has always vehemently denied using drugs.*

vehicle /'viːɪkəl/ **vehicles.** [1] N-C A **vehicle** is a machine with an engine, for example a car, that carries people or things from place to place. [2] N-C You can use **vehicle** to refer to something that you use in order to achieve a particular purpose. *Her art became a vehicle for her political beliefs.*

veil /veɪl/ **veils.** [1] N-C A **veil** is a piece of thin soft cloth that women sometimes wear over their heads and which can also cover their face. [2] N-C You can refer to something that hides a situation or activity as a **veil**. *...the chilling facts behind this veil of silence.*

veiled /veɪld/. [1] ADJ BEFORE N A **veiled** comment is expressed in a disguised form rather than directly and openly. *This last clause is a thinly-veiled threat.* [2] ADJ A **veiled** person is wearing a veil.

vein /veɪn/ **veins.** [1] N-C Your **veins** are the tubes in your body through which your blood flows towards your heart. [2] N-C The **veins** on a leaf are the thin lines on it. [3] N-U Something that is written or spoken in a particular **vein** is written or spoken in that style or mood. *The girl now replies in similar vein.*

velocity /vɪ'lɒsɪti/ **velocities.** N-VAR **Velocity** is the speed at which something moves; TECHNICAL.

velvet /'velvɪt/. N-U **Velvet** is a soft fabric with a thick layer of short cut threads on one side. *...a velvet collar.*

vendetta /ven'detə/ **vendettas.** N-VAR If one person has a **vendetta** against another, the first person wants revenge for something the second person did to them in the past. *The cartoonist has a personal vendetta against him.*

vendor /'vendə/ **vendors.** N-C A **vendor** is someone who sells things such as newspapers or hamburgers from a small stall or cart. *...ice-cream vendors.*

veneer /vɪ'nɪə/. N-SING If you refer to the pleasant way that someone behaves or that something appears as a **veneer**, you are critical of them because you believe that their true nature is unpleasant, and this is being hidden. *He was able to fool the world with his veneer of education.*

venerable /'venərəbəl/. [1] ADJ **Venerable** people deserve respect because they are old and wise. [2] ADJ **Venerable** things are impressive because they are old and historically important. *...venerable institutions like the Theatre National de l'Odeon.*

vengeance /'vendʒəns/. [1] N-U **Vengeance** is the act of harming someone because they have harmed you. *He swore vengeance on everyone involved in the murder.* [2] PHRASE If you say that something happens **with a vengeance**, you are emphasizing that it happens to a great extent. *It began to rain again with a vengeance.*

venison /'venɪzən/. N-U **Venison** is the meat of a deer eaten as food.

venom /'venəm/. [1] N-U **Venom** is a feeling of great bitterness or anger towards someone. *There was no mistaking the venom in his voice.* [2] N-U The **venom** of certain snakes, spiders, or other creatures is the poison that they inject into animals, insects, or people when they bite or sting them.

vent /vent/ **vents, venting, vented.** [1] N-C A **vent** is a hole in something which allows air to come in and smoke, gas, or smells to go out. *There was a small air vent in the ceiling.* [2] VERB If you **vent** your feelings, you express them forcefully. *The rioters were prevented from venting their anger on the police.*

ventilate /'ventɪleɪt/ **ventilates, ventilating, ventilated.** VERB If you **ventilate** a room or building, you allow fresh air to get into it. *...badly ventilated rooms.* ♦ **ventilation** N-U *The only ventilation comes from tiny sliding windows.*

venture /'ventʃə/ **ventures, venturing, ventured.** [1] N-C A **venture** is a new project or activity which is exciting and difficult because it involves the risk of failure. *...his latest writing venture.* [2] VERB If you **venture into** an activity, you do something that involves the risk of failure because it is new and different. *He enjoyed little success when he ventured into business.* [3] VERB If you **venture** somewhere, you go there, although it might be dangerous. *People are afraid to venture out for fear of sniper attacks.*

venue /'venjuː/ **venues.** N-C The **venue** for an event or activity is the place where it will happen. *The Embassy was the venue for a New Year's Eve party.*

veranda (or **verandah**) /və'rændə/ **verandas.** N-C A **veranda** is a platform with a roof along the outside wall of a house.

verb /vɜːb/ **verbs.** N-C A **verb** is a word such as 'sing' or 'feel' which is used to say what someone or something does or what happens to them, or to give information about them.

verbal /'vɜːbəl/. [1] ADJ You use **verbal** to indicate that something is expressed in speech rather than in writing or action. *We have a verbal agreement with her.* ♦ **verbally** ADV *Twins often have difficulty expressing themselves verbally.* [2] ADJ You use **verbal** to indicate that something is connected with words and the use of words. *Wayne has great verbal dexterity.*

verdict /'vɜːdɪkt/ **verdicts.** [1] N-C In a law court, a **verdict** is the decision that is given by the jury or judge at the end of a trial. *The jury returned a unanimous guilty verdict.* [2] N-C Someone's **verdict** on something is their opinion of it, after thinking about it or investigating it. *The doctor's verdict was that he was entirely healthy.*

verge /vɜːdʒ/ **verges, verging, verged.** [1] PHRASE If you are **on the verge of** something, you are about to do it or it is about to happen. *Carole was on the verge of tears.* [2] N-C The **verge** of a road is the narrow strip of grassy ground at the side; BRITISH.

▸ **verge on.** PHR-VERB If someone or something **verges on** a particular state or quality, they are almost the same as that state or quality. *...a fury that verged on madness.*

verify /'verɪfaɪ/ **verifies, verifying, verified.** VERB If you **verify** something, you check or confirm that it is true. *A clerk simply verifies that the payment and invoice amounts match.* ♦ **verification** /ˌverɪfɪ'keɪʃən/ N-U *...the agency's verification procedures.*

veritable /'verɪtəbəl/. ADJ You can use **veritable**

to emphasize the size or nature of something. *...a veritable feast of pre-match entertainment.*

vernacular /vəˈnækjʊlə/ **vernaculars.** N-C The **vernacular** is the language or dialect that is most widely spoken by ordinary people in a region or country. *...books or plays written in the vernacular.*

versatile /ˈvɜːsətaɪl, AM -təl/. [1] ADJ If you say that a person is **versatile**, you approve of them because they have many different skills. *...one of the game's most versatile athletes.* ◆**versatility** /ˌvɜːsəˈtɪlɪti/ N-U *...her incredible versatility as an actress.* [2] ADJ A **versatile** activity, material, or machine can be used for many different purposes. *Never before has computing been so versatile.* ◆**versatility** N-U *Velvet is not known for its versatility.*

verse /vɜːs/ **verses.** [1] N-U **Verse** is writing arranged in lines which have rhythm and which often rhyme at the end. *I have been moved to write a few lines of verse.* [2] N-C A **verse** is one of the parts into which a poem, a song, or a chapter of the Bible or Koran is divided.

version /ˈvɜːʃən, -ʒən/ **versions.** [1] N-C A **version** of something is a form of it in which some details are different from earlier or later forms. *...an updated version of his book.* [2] N-C Someone's **version** of an event is their personal account of it.

versus /ˈvɜːsəs/. [1] PREP You use **versus** to say that two ideas or things are opposed. *...the debate about bottle-feeding versus breastfeeding.* [2] PREP **Versus** is used to indicate that two people or teams are competing against each other in a sporting event. *...the Lennox Lewis versus Frank Bruno boxing confrontation.*

vertebra /ˈvɜːtɪbrə/ **vertebrae** /ˈvɜːtɪbreɪ/. N-C **Vertebrae** are the small circular bones that form your backbone.

vertical /ˈvɜːtɪkəl/. ADJ Something that is **vertical** stands or points straight upwards. *...a vertical wall of rock.* ◆**vertically** ADV *Cut each bulb in half vertically.*

very /ˈveri/. [1] ADV **Very** is used to give emphasis to an adjective or adverb. *The problem and the answer are very simple... Thank you very much.* [2] ADJ BEFORE N You use **very** with certain nouns in order to specify an extreme position or extreme point in time. *I turned to the very end of the book, to read the final words... He was wrong from the very beginning.* [3] ADJ BEFORE N You use **very** with nouns to emphasize that something is exactly the right one or exactly the same one. *She died in this very house.* [4] CONVENTION **Very well** is used to say that you agree to do something or you accept someone's answer, even though you might not be completely satisfied with it. *'I know that as well as you do.'—'Very well, we won't argue about it.'* [5] PHRASE The expression **very much so** is an emphatic way of answering 'yes' or something or saying that it is true or correct. *'Are you enjoying your holiday?'—'Very much so.'.*

> **Very**, **so**, and **too** can all be used to intensify the meaning of an adjective, an adverb, or a word like **much** or **many**. However, they are not used in the same way. **Very** is the simplest intensifier. It has no other meaning beyond that. **So** can suggest an emotional reaction on the part of the speaker, such as pleasure, surprise, or disappointment. *John makes me so angry!... Oh thank you so much!* **So** can also refer forward to a result clause introduced by **that**. *The procession was forced to move so slowly that he arrived three hours late.* **Too** suggests an excessive or undesirable amount, often so much that a particular result does not or cannot happen. *She does wear too much make-up at times... He was too late to save her.*

vessel /ˈvesəl/ **vessels.** [1] N-C A **vessel** is a ship or a large boat; FORMAL. *...a New Zealand navy vessel.* [2] N-C A **vessel** is a bowl or other container in which liquid is kept; FORMAL. *...storage vessels.* [3] See also **blood vessel**.

vest /vest/ **vests, vesting, vested.** [1] N-C A **vest** is a piece of underwear which is worn to keep the top part of your body warm; BRITISH. [2] N-C In American English, a **vest** is a sleeveless piece of clothing with buttons which people usually wear over a shirt. The British word is **waistcoat**. [3] VERB If something **is vested** in you, or if you **are vested** with it, it is given to you as a right or responsibility; FORMAL. *The mass media have been vested with significant power.*

vested 'interest, vested interests. N-C If you have a **vested interest** in something, you have a very strong reason for acting in a particular way, for example to protect your money or reputation. *The administration has no vested interest in proving public schools good or bad.*

vestige /ˈvestɪdʒ/ **vestiges.** N-C The **vestiges** of something are the small parts that still remain after most of it has gone. *...the last vestige of a UN force that once numbered more than 30,000.*

vet /vet/ **vets, vetting, vetted.** [1] N-C A **vet** is someone who is qualified to treat sick or injured animals. [2] VERB If someone or something **is vetted**, that person or thing is checked carefully to make sure that they reach certain standards, particularly standards of morality or trust; BRITISH. *He had not been allowed to read any book until his mother had vetted it.* ◆**vetting** N-U *...the procedure for carrying out security vetting.*

veteran /ˈvetərən/ **veterans.** [1] N-C A **veteran** is someone who has served in the armed forces of their country, especially during a war. [2] N-C A **veteran** is someone who has been involved in a particular activity for a long time. *...the veteran television campaigner Mary Whitehouse.*

veterinary /ˈvetərənəri, AM -neri/. ADJ BEFORE N **Veterinary** is used to describe the work of a person whose job is to treat sick or injured animals, or to describe the medical treatment of animals. *...a veterinary examination.*

veto /ˈviːtəʊ/ **vetoes, vetoing, vetoed.** [1] VERB & N-C If someone in authority **vetoes** something, or if they put a **veto** on it, they forbid it, or stop it being put into action. *The President vetoed the economic package passed by Congress. ...the veto was a calculated political risk.* [2] N-U **Veto** is the right that someone in authority has to forbid something. *...the President's power of veto.*

vex /veks/ **vexes, vexing, vexed.** VERB If someone or something **vexes** you, they make you feel annoyed. *Everything about her vexed him.* ♦**vexed** ADJ *Farmers and industrialists alike are vexed and blame the government.* ♦**vexing** ADJ *There remains, however, another and more vexing problem.*

via /vaɪə, viːə/. [1] PREP If you go somewhere **via** a particular place, you go through that place on the way to your destination. *Mr Baker will return home via Britain and France.* [2] PREP If you do something **via** a particular means or person, you do it by making use of that means or person. *...the technology to allow relief workers to contact the outside world via satellite.*

viable /vaɪəbəl/. ADJ Something that is **viable** is capable of doing what it is intended to do. *Cash alone will not make Eastern Europe's banks viable.* ♦**viability** N-U *...the shaky financial viability of the nuclear industry.*

vibrant /vaɪbrənt/. [1] ADJ Something or someone that is **vibrant** is full of energy and enthusiasm. *...her vibrant personality.* ♦**vibrancy** N-U *She was a woman with extraordinary vibrancy.* [2] ADJ **Vibrant** colours are very bright and clear. *The grass was a vibrant green.* ♦**vibrantly** ADV *...vibrantly coloured rugs.*

vibrate /vaɪˈbreɪt, AM ˈvaɪbreɪt/ **vibrates, vibrating, vibrated.** VERB If something **vibrates**, or if you **vibrate** it, it shakes with repeated small quick movements. *The noise vibrated the table.* ♦**vibration, vibrations** N-VAR *The vibrations of the vehicles rattled the shop windows.*

vicar /vɪkə/ **vicars.** N-C A **vicar** is a priest in the Church of England.

vice /vaɪs/ **vices;** spelled **vise** in American English for meaning 3. [1] N-C A **vice** is a habit which is regarded as a weakness in someone's character, but not usually as a serious fault. *I spend too much on clothes, that's my only vice.* [2] N-U **Vice** refers to criminal activities connected with pornography or prostitution. [3] N-C A **vice** or **vise** is a tool with a pair of jaws that hold an object tightly while you do work on it.

vice versa /vaɪsə ˈvɜːsə/. PHRASE **Vice versa** is used to indicate that the reverse of what you have said is also true. For example, 'Women may bring their husbands with them, and vice versa' means that men may also bring their wives with them.

vicinity /vɪˈsɪnɪti/. N-SING If something is in the **vicinity** of a place, it is in the nearby area. *No enemy aircraft was seen in the vicinity.*

vicious /vɪʃəs/. [1] ADJ A **vicious** person is violent and cruel. ♦**viciously** ADV *She had been viciously attacked with a hammer.* ♦**viciousness** N-U *...the intensity and viciousness of these attacks.* [2] ADJ A **vicious** remark is cruel and intended to upset someone. ♦**viciously** ADV *'He deserved to die,' said Penelope viciously.*

vicious 'circle. N-SING A **vicious circle** is a problem or difficult situation that has the effect of creating new problems which then cause the original problem or situation to occur again.

victim /vɪktɪm/ **victims.** N-C A **victim** is someone who has been hurt or killed by someone or something. *...the victims of violent crime.*

victimize (BR **victimise**) /vɪktɪmaɪz/ **victimizes, victimizing, victimized.** VERB If someone **is victimized**, they are deliberately treated unfairly. *The students had been victimized because they'd voiced opposition to the government.* ♦**victimization** N-U *...society's cruel victimization of women.*

victor /vɪktə/ **victors.** N-C The **victor** in a contest or battle is the person who wins; LITERARY.

Victorian /vɪkˈtɔːriən/ **Victorians.** [1] ADJ **Victorian** means belonging to, connected with, or typical of Britain in the middle and last parts of the 19th century, when Victoria was Queen. *...a lovely old Victorian house.* [2] ADJ You can use **Victorian** to describe people who have old-fashioned qualities, especially in relation to discipline and morals. *Victorian values are much misunderstood.* [3] N-C The **Victorians** were the people who lived in the reign of Queen Victoria.

victorious /vɪkˈtɔːriəs/. ADJ You use **victorious** to describe someone who has won a victory in a struggle, war, or competition. *...a member of the victorious British team.*

victory /vɪktəri/ **victories.** N-VAR A **victory** is a success in a war or a competition. *The New Democracy party has claimed victory.*

video /vɪdiəʊ/ **videos, videoing, videoed.** [1] N-C A **video** is a film or television programme recorded on videotape. [2] N-U **Video** is the recording and showing of films and events, using a video recorder, videotapes, and a television set. *She has watched the race on video.* [3] N-C A **video** is the same as a **VCR.** [4] VERB If you **video** something, you record it on magnetic tape, either by using a video recorder or camera.

'video recorder, video recorders. N-C A **video recorder** or a **video cassette recorder** is the same as a **VCR.**

videotape, /vɪdiəʊteɪp/ **videotapes.** N-VAR **Videotape** is magnetic tape that is used to record pictures and sounds which can be shown on television.

vie /vaɪ/ **vies, vying, vied.** VERB If one person **vies** with another to do something, or if they **vie** to do it, they both try hard to do it sooner or better than the other person; FORMAL. *He will vie with Mr Bush for the votes of the young.*

view 1 opinions

view /vjuː/ **views, viewing, viewed.** [1] N-C Your **views** on something are the opinions or beliefs that you have about it. *I take the view that she should be stopped as soon as possible... In my view things won't change.* [2] N-SING Your **view** of a particular subject is the way that you understand and think about it. *...a Christian-centred view of religion.* • See also **point of view.** [3] VERB If you **view** something in a particular way, you think of it in that way. *We would view favourably any sensible suggestion.* [4] PREP You use **in view of** when you are taking into consideration facts that have just been mentioned or are just about to be mentioned. *She has to be extra careful in view of her past medical history.* [5] PHRASE If you do something **with a view to** a particular result, you do it to achieve that result. *He has called a meeting of all parties tomorrow, with a view to forming a national reconciliation government.*

view 2 being able to see things

view /vjuː/ **views, viewing, viewed.** [1] N-C The **view** from a particular place is everything you can see from that place, especially when it is considered to be beautiful. [2] N-SING If you have a **view** of something, you can see it. *He stopped in the doorway, blocking her view.* [3] N-U You use **view** in expressions to do with being able to see something. For example, if something is **in view**, you can see it. If something is **in full view of everyone**, everyone can see it. *A group of riders came into view.* [4] VERB If you **view** something, you inspect it or look at it for a particular purpose; FORMAL. *Check out the motor museum and view the classic cars.* [5] PHRASE If something such as a work or art is **on view**, it is being exhibited in public.

viewer /'vjuːə/ **viewers.** N-C Viewers are people who watch television.

viewpoint /'vjuːpɔɪnt/ **viewpoints.** N-C Someone's **viewpoint** is the way they think about things in general or about a particular thing. *The novel is shown entirely from the girl's viewpoint.*

vigil /'vɪdʒɪl/ **vigils.** N-C A **vigil** is a period of time when people remain quietly in a place, especially at night, for example because they are praying or are making a political protest. *Protesters are holding a twenty-four hour vigil.*

vigilant /'vɪdʒɪlənt/. ADJ Someone who is **vigilant** gives careful attention to a particular problem or situation and concentrates on noticing any danger or trouble that there might be. *Inspector Murphy warned the public to be vigilant and report anything suspicious.* ♦**vigilance** /'vɪdʒɪləns/ N-U *Drugs are a problem that requires constant vigilance.*

vigilante /ˌvɪdʒɪˈlænti/ **vigilantes.** N-C Vigilantes are people who organize themselves into an unofficial group to protect their community and to catch and punish criminals.

vigorous /'vɪɡərəs/. ADJ **Vigorous** actions involve using a lot of energy and enthusiasm. *...the benefits of vigorous exercise.* ♦**vigorously** ADV *He shook his head vigorously... The police vigorously denied that excessive force had been used.*

vigour (AM **vigor**) /'vɪɡə/. N-U **Vigour** is physical or mental energy and enthusiasm. *The election was fought with vigour.*

vile /vaɪl/ **viler, vilest.** ADJ If you say that someone or something is **vile**, you mean that they are extremely unpleasant.

villa /'vɪlə/ **villas.** N-C A **villa** is a fairly large house, especially one that is used for holidays in Mediterranean countries.

village /'vɪlɪdʒ/ **villages.** N-C A **village** consists of a group of houses, together with other buildings such as a church and school, in a country area.

villager /'vɪlɪdʒə/ **villagers.** N-C You refer to the people who live in a village as the **villagers**.

villain /'vɪlən/ **villains.** N-C A **villain** is someone who deliberately harms other people or breaks the law in order to get what he or she wants.

vindicate /'vɪndɪkeɪt/ **vindicates, vindicating, vindicated.** VERB If a person **is vindicated**, they are proved to be correct, after people have said that they were wrong; FORMAL. *The director said he had been vindicated by the experts' report.* ♦**vindication, vindications** N-VAR *He called the success of his party's free-market economic policy.*

vindictive /vɪn'dɪktɪv/. ADJ Someone who is **vindictive** deliberately tries to upset or cause trouble for people who they think have done them harm. ♦**vindictiveness** N-U *He is letting vindictiveness get in the way of his judgment.*

vine /vaɪn/ **vines.** N-C A **vine** is a climbing or trailing plant, especially one which produces grapes.

vinegar /'vɪnɪɡə/. N-U **Vinegar** is a sharp-tasting liquid, usually made from sour wine or malt, which is used to make things such as salad dressing.

vineyard /'vɪnjəd/ **vineyards.** N-C A **vineyard** is an area of land where grape vines are grown in order to produce wine.

vintage /'vɪntɪdʒ/. [1] N-C The **vintage** of a good quality wine is the year and place that it was made. [2] ADJ BEFORE N **Vintage** wine is good quality wine that has been stored for several years in order to improve its quality. [3] ADJ BEFORE N **Vintage** cars or aeroplanes are old but are admired because they are considered to be the best of their kind.

vinyl /'vaɪnɪl/. N-U **Vinyl** is a strong plastic used for making things such as floor coverings and furniture.

viola /viˈəʊlə/ **violas.** N-C A **viola** is a musical instrument which looks like a violin but is slightly larger.

violate /'vaɪəleɪt/ **violates, violating, violated.** [1] VERB If someone **violates** an agreement, law, or promise, they break it. *They violated the ceasefire agreement.* ♦**violation, violations** N-VAR *To deprive the boy of his education is a violation of state law.* [2] VERB If you **violate** someone's privacy or peace, you disturb it; FORMAL. [3] VERB If someone **violates** a special place, for example a tomb, they damage it or treat it without respect. ♦**violation** N-VAR *...the violation of the graves.*

violence /'vaɪələns/. [1] N-U **Violence** is behaviour which is intended to hurt or kill people. *Twenty people were killed in the violence.* [2] N-U If you do or say something with **violence**, you use a lot of force and energy in doing or saying it, often because you are angry; LITERARY. *The violence in her tone gave Alistair a shock.*

violent /'vaɪələnt/. [1] ADJ If someone is **violent**, or if they do something which is **violent**, they use physical force or weapons to hurt or kill other people. *A quarter of current inmates have* committed *violent crimes.* ◆**violently** ADV *Some opposition activists have been violently attacked.* [2] ADJ A **violent** event happens suddenly and with great force. *A violent impact hurtled her forward.* ◆**violently** ADV *A nearby volcano erupted violently.* [3] ADJ If you describe something as **violent**, you mean that it is said, done, or felt with great force and energy. *He had violent stomach pains.* ◆**violently** ADV *Other experts violently disagree.*

violet /'vaɪəlɪt/ **violets.** [1] N-C A **violet** is a small purple or white flower that blooms in the spring. [2] ADJ & N-U Something that is **violet** in colour is bluish-purple.

violin /ˌvaɪə'lɪn/ **violins.** N-C A **violin** is a musical instrument with four strings stretched over a shaped hollow box. You hold a violin under your chin and play it with a bow. ◆**violinist** /ˌvaɪə'lɪnɪst/ **violinists** N-C *...the famous jazz violinist.*

VIP /ˌviː aɪ 'piː/ **VIPs.** N-C A **VIP** is someone who is given better treatment than ordinary people because he or she is famous or important. **VIP** is an abbreviation for 'very important person'.

virgin /'vɜːdʒɪn/ **virgins.** [1] N-C A **virgin** is someone who has never had sex. ◆**virginity** /və'dʒɪnɪti/ N-U *She lost her virginity when she was 20.* [2] ADJ You use **virgin** to describe something such as land that has never been used or spoiled. *...a sloping field of virgin snow.*

virile /'vɪraɪl, AM -rəl/. ADJ If you describe a man as **virile**, you mean he has the qualities that a man is traditionally expected to have, such as strength and sexuality. ◆**virility** /vɪ'rɪlɪti/ N-U *Children are also considered to be proof of a man's virility.*

virtual /'vɜːtʃuəl/. ADJ BEFORE N You can use **virtual** to indicate that something is so nearly true that for most purposes it can be regarded as being true. *...the virtual banning of religion.* ◆**virtually** ADV *Virtually all cooking was done over coal-fired ranges.*

virtual re'ality. N-U **Virtual reality** is an environment which is produced by a computer and seems very like reality to the person experiencing it.

virtue /'vɜːtʃuː/ **virtues.** [1] N-U **Virtue** is thinking and doing what is right, and avoiding what is wrong. [2] N-C A **virtue** is a good quality or way of behaving. *His virtue is patience.* [3] N-VAR The **virtue** of something is an advantage or benefit that it has, especially in comparison with something else. *Its other great virtue, of course, is its hard-wearing quality.* [4] PREP You use **by virtue of** to explain why something happens or is true; FORMAL. *Mr Olaechea has British residency by virtue of his marriage.*

virtuoso /ˌvɜːtʃu'əʊzəʊ/ **virtuosos** or **virtuosi** /ˌvɜːtʃu'əʊzi/. [1] N-C A **virtuoso** is someone who is exceptionally good at playing a musical instrument. [2] ADJ A **virtuoso** performance or display shows exceptional skill.

virtuous /'vɜːtʃuəs/. [1] ADJ A **virtuous** person behaves in a moral and correct way. *...virtuous people who obey the rules and are nice to others.* [2] ADJ If you describe someone as **virtuous**, you mean that they feel very pleased with their own good behaviour; often used showing disapproval. *I cleaned the flat, which left me*

feeling *virtuous.* ◆**virtuously** ADV *'I've already done that,' said Ronnie virtuously.*

virulent /'vɪrjʊlənt/. [1] ADJ **Virulent** feelings or actions are extremely bitter and hostile. *Now he faces virulent attacks from the Italian media.* ◆**virulently** ADV *The talk was virulently hostile.* ◆**virulence** N-U *The virulence of the café owner's anger had appalled her.* [2] ADJ A **virulent** disease or poison is extremely powerful and dangerous. ◆**virulence** N-U *...the virulence of the epidemic.*

virus /'vaɪərəs/ **viruses.** [1] N-C A **virus** is a kind of germ that can cause disease. [2] N-C In computer technology, a **virus** is a program that introduces itself into a system, altering or destroying the information stored there.

visa /'viːzə/ **visas.** N-C A **visa** is an official document or a stamp put in your passport which allows you to enter or leave a particular country.

vise /vaɪs/. See **vice.**

visibility /ˌvɪzɪ'bɪlɪti/. N-U **Visibility** is how far or how clearly you can see in particular weather conditions. *Visibility was poor.*

visible /'vɪzɪbəl/. [1] ADJ If an object is **visible**, it can be seen. *The mainland is clearly visible from their island.* [2] ADJ You use **visible** to describe something or someone that people notice or recognize. *He was making a visible effort to control himself.* ◆**visibly** ADV *They emerged visibly distressed.*

vision /'vɪʒən/ **visions.** [1] N-C Your **vision** of a future situation or society is what you imagine or hope it would be like, if things were very different from the way they are now. *I have a vision of a society that is free of exploitation and injustice.* [2] N-U Your **vision** is your ability to see clearly with your eyes. *It causes blindness or serious loss of vision.*

visionary /'vɪʒənri, AM -neri/ **visionaries.** [1] N-C A **visionary** is someone who has strong original ideas about how things might be different in the future, especially about how things might be improved. [2] ADJ You use **visionary** to describe the strong original ideas of a visionary. *...the visionary architecture of Etienne Boullée.*

visit /'vɪzɪt/ **visits, visiting, visited.** [1] VERB & N-C If you **visit** someone, or if you pay them a **visit**, you go to see them and spend time with them. *Bill would visit on weekends.* [2] VERB & N-C If you **visit** a place, or if you make a **visit** to a place, you go to see it. *...the Pope's visit to Canada.*

▶ **visit with.** PHR-VERB If you **visit with** someone, you go to see them and spend time with them; AMERICAN. *I visited with him in San Francisco.*

visitor /'vɪzɪtə/ **visitors.** N-C A **visitor** is someone who is visiting a person or place.

vista /'vɪstə/ **vistas.** [1] N-C A **vista** is view, especially a beautiful view from a high place. *I looked out on a crowded scene of hills and rooftops.* [2] N-C A **vista** is a vision of a situation or of a range of possibilities. *...a vista of a future without hope.*

visual /'vɪʒuəl/. ADJ **Visual** means relating to sight, or to things that you can see. *Watching TV requires the processing of visual images.*

...*careers in the visual arts.* ♦**visually** ADV ...*visually handicapped boys and girls.*

visualize (BR also **visualise**) /ˈvɪʒʊəlaɪz/ **visualizes, visualizing, visualized.** VERB If you **visualize** something, you imagine what it is like by forming a mental picture of it. *He could not visualize her as old... It was hard to visualize how it could have been done.*

vital /ˈvaɪtəl/. [1] ADJ If something is **vital**, it is necessary or very important. *It is vital that action is taken quickly. ...vital information.* ♦**vitally** ADV *Lesley's career in the church is vitally important to her.* [2] ADJ **Vital** people, organizations, or activities are very energetic and full of life. *He was a vital and witty man.*

vitality /vaɪˈtælɪti/. N-U If someone or something has **vitality**, they have great energy and liveliness. *He had enormous vitality. ...the financial vitality of the corporation.*

vitamin /ˈvɪtəmɪn, AM ˈvaɪt-/ **vitamins.** N-C Vitamins are organic substances in food which you need in order to remain healthy. *...vitamin D. ...vitamin supplements.*

vivid /ˈvɪvɪd/. [1] ADJ **Vivid** memories and descriptions are very clear and detailed. *...a very vivid dream.* ♦**vividly** ADV *I remember the phone call vividly.* [2] ADJ Something that is **vivid** is very bright in colour. *...a vivid blue sky.* ♦**vividly** ADV *...vividly coloured birds.*

vocabulary /vəʊˈkæbjʊləri, AM -leri/ **vocabularies.** [1] N-VAR Your **vocabulary** is the total number of words you know in a particular language. *...people with a limited vocabulary.* [2] N-SING The **vocabulary** of a language is all the words in it. *...a new word in the German vocabulary.*

vocal /ˈvəʊkəl/. [1] ADJ You say that people are **vocal** when they speak forcefully and with feeling about something. *She continued to be very vocal in opposing his business.* [2] ADJ BEFORE N **Vocal** means involving the use of the human voice, especially in singing.

vocalist /ˈvəʊkəlɪst/ **vocalists.** N-C A **vocalist** is a singer who sings with a pop group. *...the band's lead vocalist.*

vocals /ˈvəʊkəlz/. N-PL In a pop song, the **vocals** are the singing, in contrast to the playing of instruments.

vocation /vəʊˈkeɪʃən/ **vocations.** N-VAR If you have a **vocation**, you have a strong feeling that you are especially suited to a particular job or role in life. You can also call your job a **vocation** if you feel like this about it. *He found his vocation early: poetry and classical scholarship.*

vocational /vəʊˈkeɪʃənəl/. ADJ **Vocational** training and skills are the training and skills needed for a particular job or profession. *...newer universities offering more vocational courses.*

vociferous /vəˈsɪfərəs, AM vəʊs-/. ADJ If you describe someone as **vociferous**, you mean that they speak with great energy and determination, because they want their views to be heard; FORMAL. *He was a vociferous opponent of communism.* ♦**vociferously** ADV *The Prime Minister has campaigned vociferously for this result.*

vodka /ˈvɒdkə/ **vodkas.** N-VAR **Vodka** is a strong clear alcoholic drink.

vogue /vəʊg/. [1] N-SING If there is a **vogue** for something, it is very popular and fashionable. *...the vogue for so-called health teas.* [2] PHRASE If something is **in vogue**, it is very popular and fashionable. If it comes **into vogue**, it becomes very popular and fashionable.

voice /vɔɪs/ **voices, voicing, voiced.** [1] N-C When someone speaks or sings, you hear their **voice**. *'The police are here,' she said in a low voice.* [2] N-C You can use **voice** to refer to someone's opinion on a particular topic. *There were no dissenting voices.* [3] N-SING If you have a **voice** in something, you have the right to express an opinion on it. *But your partners will have no voice in how you operate your company.* [4] VERB If you **voice** an opinion or an emotion, you say what you think or feel. *Some scientists have voiced concern that the disease could be passed on to humans.* [5] N-SING In grammar, if a verb is in the **active voice**, the person who performs the action is the subject of the verb. If a verb is in the **passive voice**, the thing or person affected by the action is the subject of the verb.

void /vɔɪd/ **voids.** [1] N-C If you describe a situation or a feeling as a **void**, you mean that it seems empty because there is nothing interesting or worthwhile about it. *His sudden death left a very deep void in my life.* [2] N-C You can describe a large or frightening space as a **void**. *The ship moved silently through the black void.* [3] ADJ AFTER LINK-V Something that is **void** is officially considered to have no value or authority. *The vote was declared void.*

volatile /ˈvɒlətaɪl, AM -təl/. [1] ADJ A **volatile** situation is likely to change suddenly and unexpectedly. *Armed soldiers guard the streets in this volatile atmosphere.* [2] ADJ A **volatile** person is someone whose moods or attitudes change quickly and frequently.

volcanic /vɒlˈkænɪk/. ADJ **Volcanic** means coming from or created by volcanoes. *St Vincent is a lush, volcanic island.*

volcano /vɒlˈkeɪnəʊ/ **volcanoes.** N-C A **volcano** is a mountain from which hot melted rock, gas, steam and ash sometimes burst. *The volcano erupted last year killing about 600 people.*

volley /ˈvɒli/ **volleys, volleying, volleyed.** [1] N-C A **volley** of gunfire is a lot of bullets that are fired at the same time. *A volley of shots rang out.* [2] VERB & N-C In sports such as tennis and football, if someone **volleys**, they hit or kick the ball before it touches the ground. A **volley** is a shot like this. *He volleyed the ball spectacularly into the far corner of the net.*

volleyball /ˈvɒlibɔːl/. N-U **Volleyball** is a sport in which two teams use their hands to hit a large ball over a high net.

volt /vəʊlt/ **volts.** N-C A **volt** is a unit used to measure the force of an electric current.

voltage /ˈvəʊltɪdʒ/ **voltages.** N-VAR The **voltage** of an electrical current is its force measured in volts. *...high-voltage power lines.*

volume /ˈvɒljuːm/ **volumes.** [1] N-C The **volume** of something is the amount of it that there is. *The volume of sales has increased slightly. ...the sheer volume of traffic.* [2] N-C The **volume** of an object is the amount of space that it contains or occupies. *When egg* *whites are beaten they can rise to seven or eight times their original volume.* **3** N-C A **volume** is one book in a series of books. *...the first volume of his autobiography.* **4** N-U The **volume** of a radio, TV, or sound system is how loud it is. *He turned down the volume.*

voluntary /'vɒləntri, AM -teri/. **1** ADJ **Voluntary** is used to describe actions and activities that you do because you choose them, rather than because you have to do them. *...classes where attendance is voluntary.* ◆**voluntarily** ADV *He asked people to surrender their firearms voluntarily.* **2** ADJ **Voluntary** work is work which people do not get paid for, but which they do to help an organization such as a charity. **3** ADJ BEFORE N A **voluntary** organization, for example a charity, is controlled by the people who have chosen to work for it, often without being paid.

volunteer /ˌvɒlən'tɪə/ **volunteers, volunteering, volunteered.** **1** N-C A **volunteer** is someone who does work without being paid for it, especially for an organization such as a charity. *She now helps in a local school as a volunteer.* **2** N-C A **volunteer** is someone who offers to do a particular task without being forced to do it. *What I want now is two volunteers to come down to the front.* **3** N-C A **volunteer** is someone who chooses to join the armed forces, especially in wartime, as opposed to someone who is forced to join by law. **4** VERB If you **volunteer** to do something, you offer to do it without being forced to do it. *Mary volunteered to clean up the kitchen... He volunteered for overseas service.* **5** VERB If you **volunteer** information, you tell someone something without being asked; FORMAL. *No one volunteered any further information... 'They were both great supporters of Franco,' Ryle volunteered.*

vomit /'vɒmɪt/ **vomits, vomiting, vomited.** **1** VERB If you **vomit**, food and drink comes back up from your stomach and out through your mouth. **2** N-U **Vomit** is partly digested food and drink that comes out of someone's mouth when they vomit.

voracious /və'reɪʃəs, AM vɔːr-/. ADJ If you describe a person, or their appetite for something, as **voracious**, you mean that they want a lot of it; LITERARY. *She was a voracious reader.*

vote /vəʊt/ **votes, voting, voted.** **1** N-C A **vote** is a choice made by a particular person or group in a meeting or an election. *He walked to the local polling centre to cast his vote... Mr Reynolds was re-elected by 102 votes to 60... They took a vote and decided not to do it.* **2** N-SING The **vote** is the total number of votes or voters in an election, or the number of votes received or cast by a particular group. *The vote was overwhelmingly in favour of the Democratic Party. ...a huge majority of the white male vote.* **3** N-SING If you have the **vote** in an election, or have a **vote** in a meeting, you have the legal right to indicate your choice. *In Italy women did not get the vote until 1945.* **4** VERB

When you **vote**, you indicate your choice officially at a meeting or in an election, for example by raising your hand or writing on a piece of paper. *Who are you going to vote for?... Recently the parliament voted to allow greater political and religious freedoms.* ◆**voting** N-U *Voting began about two hours ago.* ◆**voter, voters** N-C *Nearly a third of the voters were either still undecided or said they would abstain.*

voucher /'vaʊtʃə/ **vouchers.** N-C A **voucher** is a piece of paper that can be used instead of money to pay for something. *...a voucher for a pair of cinema tickets.*

vow /vaʊ/ **vows, vowing, vowed.** **1** VERB If you **vow** to do something, you make a solemn promise or decision that you will do it. *I solemnly vowed that some day I would return to live in Europe... 'I'll kill him,' she vowed.* **2** N-C A **vow** is a solemn promise. *I made a silent vow to be more careful in the future... I took my marriage vows and kept them.*

vowel /'vaʊəl/ **vowels.** N-C A **vowel** is a sound such as the ones represented in writing by the letters 'a', 'e' 'i', 'o' and 'u', which you pronounce with your mouth open, allowing the air to flow through it.

voyage /'vɔɪɪdʒ/ **voyages.** N-C A **voyage** is a long journey on a ship or in a spacecraft. *...Columbus's voyage to the West Indies.* ● See note at **travel**.

vs. vs. is an written abbreviation for 'versus'. *What happened in the Broncos vs Canberra game?*

vulgar /'vʌlgə/. **1** ADJ If you describe something as **vulgar**, you think it is in bad taste or of poor artistic quality. *I think it's a very vulgar house. ...vulgar consumerism.* ◆**vulgarity** N-U *I hate the vulgarity of this room.* **2** ADJ If you describe someone or something as **vulgar**, you dislike them because they use bad language, or because they refer to sex or the body in an unpleasant way. *'Don't be vulgar,' she reprimanded. ...vulgar jokes.* ◆**vulgarity** N-U *It's his vulgarity that I can't take.*

vulnerable /'vʌlnərəbəl/. **1** ADJ If someone or something is **vulnerable** to something, they have some weakness or disadvantage which makes them more likely to be harmed or affected by that thing. *People with high blood pressure are especially vulnerable to diabetes. ...attacks on vulnerable targets.* ◆**vulnerability** N-U *...anxieties about the country's vulnerability to invasion.* **2** ADJ A **vulnerable** person is weak and without protection, with the result that they are easily hurt physically or emotionally. *Old people are particularly vulnerable members of our society.* ◆**vulnerability** /ˌvʌlnərə'bɪlɪtɪ/ N-U *...the special emotional vulnerability of childhood.*

vulture /'vʌltʃə/ **vultures.** N-C A **vulture** is a large bird which lives in hot countries and eats the flesh of dead animals.

vying /'vaɪɪŋ/. **Vying** is the present participle of **vie**.

W w

wacky (or **whacky**) /'wæki/ **wackier, wacki-est.** ADJ If you describe something or someone as **wacky**, you mean that they are eccentric, unusual, and often funny; INFORMAL. *...a wacky new television comedy series.*

wad /wɒd/ **wads.** N-C A **wad** of something such as paper or banknotes is a thick, tightly packed bundle of it.

wade /weɪd/ **wades, wading, waded.** VERB If you **wade** through mud or water, you walk through it with difficulty.

▸ **wade through.** PHR-VERB If you **wade through** a difficult book or document, you spend a lot of time and effort reading it. *Managers have no time to wade through the reports.*

▸ **wade in** or **wade into.** PHR-VERB If someone **wades in**, or if they **wade into** something, they intervene in something in a very determined and forceful way, often without thinking about the consequences. *They don't just listen sympathetically. They wade in with remarks like, 'If I were you...'*

wafer /'weɪfə/ **wafers.** N-C A **wafer** is a thin crisp biscuit, often eaten with ice cream.

waffle /'wɒfəl/ **waffles, waffling, waffled.** [1] VERB & N-U If someone **waffles**, they talk or write a lot without saying anything clear or important. You can call what they say or write **waffle**. *We had 15 seconds of comment and 15 minutes of waffle.* [2] N-C A **waffle** is a type of thick pancake.

waft /wɒft, wæft/ **wafts, wafting, wafted.** [1] VERB If sounds or scents **waft** through the air, or if something **wafts** them, they move gently through the air. *A slight breeze rose, wafting the heavy scent of flowers past her.* [2] N-C You can call a sound or scent which has been carried on the air a **waft**. *A waft of perfume drifted into Ingrid's nostrils.*

wag /wæg/ **wags, wagging, wagged.** [1] VERB When a dog **wags** its tail, or when its tail **wags**, its tail moves repeatedly from side to side. [2] VERB If you **wag** your finger, you shake it repeatedly and quickly from side to side, usually because you are telling someone off.

wage /weɪdʒ/ **wages, waging, waged.** [1] N-C Someone's **wages** are the amount of money that is regularly paid to them for the work that they do. *His wages have gone up.* ● See note at **pay.** [2] VERB To **wage** a campaign or war means to start it and carry it on over a period of time. *Peter waged a 17-month legal battle to fight the move.*

wager /'weɪdʒə/ **wagers, wagering, wagered.** VERB & N-C If you **wager** on the result of a horse race, football match, or other event, or if you have a **wager** on it, you bet money on the result.

wagon (BR also **waggon**) /'wægən/ **wagons.** N-C A **wagon** is a strong vehicle with four wheels which is used for carrying heavy loads, and which is usually pulled by a horse or tractor.

wail /weɪl/ **wails, wailing, wailed.** [1] VERB & N-C If you **wail**, or if you let out a **wail**, you cry loudly. *'Now look what you've done!' Shirley wailed... Alice let out a wail of terror.* [2] VERB & N-C If something such as a siren **wails**, or if it makes a wail, it makes long, high-pitched, piercing sounds. *...the wail of sirens.*

waist /weɪst/ **waists.** [1] N-C Your **waist** is the middle part of your body, above your hips. [2] N-C The **waist** of a garment such as a dress or pair of trousers is the part of it which covers the middle part of your body.

waistcoat /'weɪstkəʊt, 'weskət/ **waistcoats.** N-C In British English, a **waistcoat** is a sleeveless piece of clothing with buttons, usually worn over a shirt. The American word is **vest**.

wait /weɪt/ **waits, waiting, waited.** [1] VERB If you **wait**, you spend some time, usually doing very little, before something happens. *Stop waiting for things to happen. Make them happen... I waited to see how she responded... We will have to wait a week or so before we know whether the operation is a success.* ♦**waiting** ADJ *She headed toward the waiting car.* [2] N-C A **wait** is a period of time in which you do very little, before something happens. *...the four-hour wait for the organizers to declare the result.* [3] VERB If something **is waiting** for you, it is ready for you to use, have, or do. *When we came home we had a meal waiting for us.* [4] VERB If you say that something can **wait**, you mean that it can be dealt with later. *I want to talk to you, but it can wait.* [5] VERB **Wait** is used in expressions such as **wait a minute** and **wait a moment** to interrupt someone when they are speaking, for example because you object to what they are saying or because you want them to repeat something. [6] PHRASE If you **can't wait** to do something, or **can hardly wait** to do it, you are very excited about it and eager to do it; SPOKEN.

▸ **wait around** or **wait about.** PHR-VERB If you **wait around**, or if you **wait about**, you stay in the same place, usually doing very little, because you cannot act before something happens or before someone arrives. *The attacker may have been waiting around for an opportunity to strike.*

waiter /'weɪtə/ **waiters.** N-C A **waiter** is a man who serves food and drink in a restaurant.

'waiting list, waiting lists. N-C A **waiting list** is a list of people who have asked for something which cannot be given to them immediately, for example medical treatment or housing, and who must therefore wait until it is available. *There were 20,000 people on the waiting list for a new home.*

'waiting-room, waiting-rooms. N-C A **waiting-room** is a room in a place such as a railway station or a doctor's surgery, where people can sit and wait.

waitress /'weɪtrəs/ **waitresses.** N-C A **waitress** is a woman whose job is to serve food and drink in a restaurant.

waive /weɪv/ **waives, waiving, waived.**
[1] VERB If you **waive** your right to something, for example legal representation, or if someone else **waives** it, you no longer have the right to receive it. [2] VERB If someone **waives** a rule, they decide not to enforce it. *The art gallery waives admission charges on Sundays.*

waiver /'weɪvə/ **waivers.** N-C A **waiver** is an agreement by a person, government, or organization to give up a right or claim or to not enforce a particular rule or law. *Non-members do not qualify for the tax waiver.*

wake /weɪk/ **wakes, waking, woke, woken.** The form **waked** is used in American English for the past tense. [1] VERB & PHR-VERB When you **wake**, or when you **wake up**, you become conscious again after being asleep. *She woke to find her dark room lit by flashing lights... At dawn I woke him up and said we were leaving.* [2] N-C A **wake** is a gathering of people who have collected together to mourn someone's death. [3] N-C The **wake** of a boat is the track of waves that it makes behind it as it moves through the water.
[PHRASES] ● If one thing follows **in the wake of** another, it happens after the other thing is over, often as a result of it. *The governor has enjoyed a huge surge in the polls in the wake of last week's convention.* ● If you leave something **in your wake**, you leave it behind you as you go. *Adam stumbles on, leaving a trail of devastation in his wake.*

▸ **wake up.** [1] See **wake** 1. [2] PHR-VERB If you **wake up** to something, you become aware of it. *People should wake up to the fact that people with disabilities have got a vote as well.*

walk /wɔːk/ **walks, walking, walked.** [1] VERB & N-SING When you **walk**, or when you move at a **walk**, you move along by putting one foot in front of the other on the ground. *They would stop the car and walk a few steps... When I was your age I walked five miles to school... She slowed to a steady walk.* [2] N-C A **walk** is an outing made by walking. *He often took long walks in the hills.* [3] N-SING A **walk** of a particular distance is the distance which a person has to walk to get somewhere. *The hotel is a short walk from the Empire State Building.* [4] VERB If you **walk** someone somewhere, you walk there with them. *I walked her to the car.* [5] VERB If you **walk** your dog, you take it for a walk in order to keep it healthy.

▸ **walk off with.** [1] PHR-VERB If someone **walks off with** something that does not belong to them, they take it without permission; INFORMAL. [2] PHR-VERB If you **walk off with** something such as a prize, you win it very easily; JOURNALISM.

▸ **walk out.** [1] PHR-VERB If you **walk out of** a meeting, performance, or unpleasant situation, you leave it suddenly, usually to show that you are angry or bored. *Mr. Mason walked out during the performance.* ◆**walkout** /'wɔːkaʊt/ **walkouts** N-C *This protest included a staged walkout by the U.S. representative.* [2] PHR-VERB If someone **walks out** on their family or their partner, they leave them suddenly. [3] PHR-VERB If workers **walk out**, they go

on strike. ◆**walkout** N-C *County public works employees staged a one-day walkout today.*

walker /'wɔːkə/ **walkers.** N-C A **walker** is a person who walks, especially in the countryside for pleasure.

walking /'wɔːkɪŋ/ N-U **Walking** is the activity of going for walks in the country. *I've started to do a lot of walking and cycling.*

walk of 'life, walks of life. N-C The **walk of life** that you come from is the position that you have in society and the kind of job you have. *...people from all walks of life.*

walkway /'wɔːkweɪ/ **walkways.** N-C A **walkway** is a path or passage for pedestrians, especially one which is raised above the ground.

wall /wɔːl/ **walls.** [1] N-C A **wall** is one of the vertical sides of a building or room. *...the bedroom walls.* [2] N-C A **wall** is a long narrow vertical structure made of stone or brick that surrounds or divides an area of land. *He climbed over a garden wall to steal apples.* [3] N-C The **wall** of something hollow is its side. *...the stomach wall.*

walled /wɔːld/. ADJ A **walled** area of land is surrounded by a wall. *...a walled rose garden.*

wallet /'wɒlɪt/ **wallets.** N-C A **wallet** is a small flat folded case where you can keep banknotes and credit cards.

wallow /'wɒləʊ/ **wallows, wallowing, wallowed.** [1] VERB If you say that someone **is wallowing in** an unpleasant situation or feeling, you are criticizing them for being deliberately unhappy. *He was drunk, wallowing in self-pity.* [2] VERB When an animal **wallows** in mud or water, it lies or rolls about in it slowly.

wallpaper /'wɔːlpeɪpə/ **wallpapers, wallpapering, wallpapered.** [1] N-VAR **Wallpaper** is thick coloured or patterned paper that is used to decorate the walls of rooms. [2] VERB If someone **wallpapers** a room, they cover the walls with wallpaper.

walnut /'wɔːlnʌt/ **walnuts.** N-C **Walnuts** are light brown edible nuts which have a wrinkled shape and a very hard round shell.

waltz /wɔːlts/ **waltzes, waltzing, waltzed.** [1] N-C A **waltz** is a piece of music with a rhythm of three beats in each bar, which people can dance to. [2] N-C & VERB When two people do a **waltz**, or when they **waltz**, they dance a waltz together. *Couples are waltzing round the wooden floor.* [3] VERB If you **waltz** into a place, you enter in a quick confident way that makes other people notice you; INFORMAL. *Suddenly this guy waltzed in, and asked for my autograph.*

wander /'wɒndə/ **wanders, wandering, wandered.** [1] VERB & N-SING If you **wander** around a place, or if you take a **wander** round it, you walk around in a casual way. *I was perfectly happy simply to wander the streets every now and then... A wander around any market will reveal stalls piled high with vegetables.* [2] VERB If a person or animal **wanders** from a place where they are supposed to stay, they move away from the place without going in a particular direction. *He has wandered off somewhere.* [3] VERB If your mind **wanders** or your thoughts **wander**, you stop concentrating on something and start thinking about other things.

wane /weɪn/ **wanes, waning, waned.** [1] VERB If a condition, attitude, or emotion **wanes**, it becomes weaker, often so that it eventually disappears. *His interest in these sports began to wane.* ◆**waning** ADJ *...her mother's waning strength.* [2] PHRASE If a condition, attitude, or emotion is **on the wane**, it is becoming weaker. *The influence of the leadership was clearly on the wane.*

want /wɒnt/ **wants, wanting, wanted.** [1] VERB If you **want** something, you feel a desire or a need for it. *I want a drink... People wanted to know who this talented designer was... He wanted his power recognised... Do you want another cup of coffee?* [2] VERB If you say that something **wants** doing, you think that it needs to be done; INFORMAL. *The windows wanted cleaning.* [3] VERB If you tell someone that they **want** to do a particular thing, you are advising them to do it; INFORMAL. *You want to be careful what you say.* [4] VERB If someone is **wanted** by the police, the police are searching for them. ◆**wanted** ADJ BEFORE N *He is one of the most wanted criminals in Europe.* [5] N-SING A **want** of something is a lack of it; FORMAL. *The men were daily becoming weaker from want of rest.*

PHRASES ● You say **if you want** when you are making or agreeing to an offer or suggestion in a casual way. *Mary says you're welcome to stay the night if you want.* ● If you do something **for want of** something else, you do it because the other thing is not available or not possible. *Many of them had gone into teaching for want of anything better to do.*

wanting /wɒntɪŋ/ ADJ If you find something **wanting**, or if it proves **wanting**, it is not as good as you think it should be. *He analysed his game and found it wanting.*

war /wɔː/ **wars.** [1] N-VAR A **war** is a period of fighting between countries. *They've been at war for the last fifteen years.* [2] N-VAR **War** is intense economic competition between countries or organizations. *...a trade war.* [3] See also civil war. [4] PHRASE If two people, countries, or organizations have a **war of words**, they criticize each other because they strongly disagree about something; JOURNALISM.

ward /wɔːd/ **wards, warding, warded.** [1] N-C A **ward** is a room in a hospital which has beds for many people, often people who need similar treatment. [2] N-C A **ward** is a district which forms part of a political constituency or local council. [3] N-C Someone's **ward** is a child who they are responsible for as their appointed guardian.

▶ **ward off.** PHR-VERB To **ward off** a danger or illness means to do something to prevent it from affecting you or harming you. *...urgent measures to ward off the threat of starvation.*

warden /wɔːdən/ **wardens.** [1] N-C A **warden** is an official who is responsible for a particular place or thing, and for making sure that certain laws are obeyed. *...a safari park warden.* [2] N-C In British English, a **warden** is someone who works in a prison supervising the prisoners. The American word is **guard**.

warder /wɔːdə/ **warders.** N-C A **warder** is the same as a prison **warden**; BRITISH.

wardrobe /wɔːdrəʊb/ **wardrobes.** [1] N-C A **wardrobe** is a tall cupboard in which you hang your clothes. [2] N-C Someone's **wardrobe** is the total collection of clothes that they own. *She asked her friend for advice on building up her wardrobe.*

ware /weə/ **wares.** [1] **Ware** is used to form nouns that refer to objects that are made of a particular material, or that are used for a particular purpose. *...porcelain cooking ware.* [2] N-PL Someone's **wares** are the things that they sell, usually in the street or in a market; DATED.

warehouse /weəhaʊs/ **warehouses.** N-C A **warehouse** is a large building where raw materials or manufactured goods are stored.

warfare /wɔːfeə/. N-U **Warfare** is the activity of fighting a war. *...the threat of chemical warfare.*

warhead /wɔːhed/ **warheads.** N-C A **warhead** is the front end of a bomb or missile, where the explosives are carried.

warm /wɔːm/ **warmer, warmest; warms, warming, warmed.** [1] ADJ Something that is **warm** has some heat but not enough to be hot. *Because it was warm, David wore only a white cotton shirt. ...warm water.* ● See note at **hot**. [2] ADJ **Warm** clothes and blankets are made of a material such as wool which protects you from the cold. ◆**warmly** ADV *Remember to wrap up warmly on cold days.* [3] ADJ A **warm** person is friendly and affectionate. ◆**warmly** ADV *He greeted me warmly.* [4] VERB If you **warm** a part of your body, or if something hot **warms** it, it stops feeling cold and starts to feel hotter. *She went to warm her hands by the log fire.* [5] VERB If you **warm to** a person or an idea, you become fonder of the person or more interested in the idea. *Those who got to know him better warmed to his openness and honesty.*

▶ **warm up.** [1] PHR-VERB If you **warm** something **up**, or if it **warms up**, it gets hotter. *Have you warmed the potato up, Mum?... The weather had warmed up.* [2] PHR-VERB If you **warm up** for an event such as a race, you prepare yourself for it by doing exercises or by practising just before it starts. ◆**warm-up, warm-ups.** N-C *The exercises can be fun and a good warm-up for the latter part of the programme.* [3] PHR-VERB When an engine **warms up**, it becomes ready for use a little while after being switched on or started. *We spent a frustrating five minutes while the pilot warmed up the engines.*

warmth /wɔːmθ/. [1] N-U The **warmth** of something is the heat that it has or produces. *...the warmth of the fire.* [2] N-U The **warmth** of something such as a garment or blanket is the protection that it gives you against the cold. [3] N-U Someone who has **warmth** is friendly and enthusiastic in their behaviour towards others.

warn /wɔːn/ **warns, warning, warned.** [1] VERB If you **warn** someone about a possible danger or problem, you tell them about it so that they are aware of it. *United Nations officials warn of epidemics and famine... When I* *had my first baby friends warned me that children were expensive.* **2** VERB If you **warn** someone not to do something, you advise them not to do it in order to avoid possible danger or punishment. *'Don't do anything yet,' he warned... Officials warned people against eating or picking mushrooms.*

warning /ˈwɔːnɪŋ/ **warnings.** N-VAR A **warning** is something which is said or written to tell people of a possible danger, problem, or other unpleasant thing that might happen. *The police have issued a warning to parents that he could be anywhere in Britain by now... The soldiers opened fire without warning.*

warp /wɔːp/ **warps, warping, warped.** **1** VERB If something **warps** or **is warped**, it becomes damaged by bending or curving, often because of the effect of heat or water. *The wood had started to warp.* ♦**warped** ADJ *The door was warped.* **2** VERB If something **warps** someone's character or mind, it damages them or influences them in a bad way. ♦**warped** ADJ *...the sort of appalling deed which is committed by the warped mind.*

warrant /ˈwɒrənt, AM ˈwɔːr-/ **warrants, warranting, warranted.** **1** VERB If something **warrants** a particular action, it makes the action seem necessary or appropriate. *The allegations are serious enough to warrant an investigation.* **2** N-C A **warrant** is an official document signed by a judge or magistrate, which gives the police special permission to do something such as arrest someone or search their house.

warranty /ˈwɒrənti, AM ˈwɔːr-/ **warranties.** N-C A **warranty** is a written guarantee which enables you to get a product repaired or replaced free of charge within a certain period of time. *The equipment is still under warranty.*

warrior /ˈwɒriə, AM ˈwɔːr-/ **warriors.** N-C A **warrior** is a fighter or soldier, especially one in former times who was very brave and experienced in fighting.

warship /ˈwɔːʃɪp/ **warships.** N-C A **warship** is a ship with guns that is used for fighting in wars.

wart /wɔːt/ **warts.** N-C A **wart** is a small lump which grows on your skin and which is usually caused by a virus.

wartime /ˈwɔːtaɪm/. N-U **Wartime** is a period of time when there is a war. *...his wartime experiences in France.*

wary /ˈweəri/. ADJ If you are **wary** of someone or something, you are cautious because you do not know much about them and you believe they may be dangerous or cause problems. *They were very wary about giving him a contract.* ♦**warily** ADV *She studied me warily.*

was /wəz, STRONG wɒz, AM wʌz/. **Was** is the first and third person singular of the past tense of **be.**

wash /wɒʃ/ **washes, washing, washed.** **1** VERB & N-C If you **wash** something, or if you give it a **wash**, you clean it using water and soap or detergent. *It took a long time to wash the mud out of his hair... Rub down the door and wash off the dust... That coat could do with a wash.* **2** VERB & N-C If you **wash**, or if you have a **wash**, you clean part of your body using soap and water. *She washed her face with cold wa-*

ter... You are going to have your dinner, get washed, and go to bed... She had a wash and changed her clothes. **3** N-SING **The wash** is all the clothes, sheets and other things that are washed together at one time. *His grey socks were in the wash.* **4** VERB If a sea or river or something carried by a sea or river **washes** somewhere or **is washed** there, it flows there gently. *The force of the water washed him back into the cave.* **5** to **wash** your **hands** of something: see **hand.** ● See also **washing.**

▶ **wash away.** PHR-VERB If rain or floods **wash away** something, they destroy it and carry it away. *Flood waters washed away one of the main bridges.*

▶ **wash down.** PHR-VERB If you **wash** something **down** with a drink, you swallow it and then drink the drink, for example to make it easier to swallow or digest. *...a massive beef sandwich washed down by a bottle of beer.*

▶ **wash up.** **1** PHR-VERB If you **wash up**, you wash the pans, plates, cups, and cutlery which have been used in cooking and eating a meal; BRITISH. *I bet you make breakfast and wash up their plates, too.* **2** PHR-VERB If something **is washed up** on a piece of land, it is carried there by a river or the sea and left there. **3** See also **washing-up.**

washable /ˈwɒʃəbəl/. ADJ **Washable** clothes or materials can be washed without being damaged. *...washable vinyl.*

washbasin (or **wash basin**) /ˈwɒʃbeɪsən/ **washbasins.** N-C A **washbasin** is a large bowl for washing your hands and face. It is usually fixed to a wall, with taps for hot and cold water.

washer /ˈwɒʃə/ **washers.** **1** N-C A **washer** is a thin flat ring made of metal or plastic, which is placed over a bolt before the nut is screwed on. **2** N-C A **washer** is the same as a **washing machine**; INFORMAL.

washing /ˈwɒʃɪŋ/. N-U **Washing** is clothes, sheets, and other things that need to be washed, are being washed, or have just been washed. *They were anxious to bring the washing in before it rained.*

ˈwashing machine, washing machines. N-C A **washing machine** is a machine that you use to wash clothes in.

ˌwashing-ˈup. N-U To **do the washing-up** means to wash the pans, plates, cups, and cutlery which have been used in cooking and eating a meal; BRITISH.

wasn't /ˈwɒzənt, AM ˈwʌz-/. In informal English, **was not** is usually said or written as **wasn't.**

wasp /wɒsp/ **wasps.** N-C A **wasp** is a small insect with a painful sting. It has yellow and black stripes across its body.

waste /weɪst/ **wastes, wasting, wasted.** **1** VERB & N-SING If you **waste** something such as time, money, or energy, you use too much of it doing something that is not important or necessary, or is unlikely to succeed. You can say that doing this is a **waste** of time, money, or energy. *The last thing she wanted to do was waste time looking at old cars... I resolved not to waste money on a hotel... It was just a waste of government money... I thought it was a waste* of time moaning about it. [2] VERB If you **waste** an opportunity, you do not take advantage of it when it is available. [3] N-U & N-PL **Waste** or **wastes** is material which has been used and is no longer wanted, for example because the valuable or useful part has been removed. ...*industrial waste.* [4] ADJ **Waste** land is land which is not used or looked after by anyone. [5] N-PL **Wastes** are a large area of land, for example a desert, in which there are very few people, plants, or animals. ...*the barren wastes of the Sahara.*

▶ **waste away.** PHR-VERB If someone **wastes away**, they become extremely thin and weak because they are ill or are not eating properly.

wasteful /ˈweɪstfʊl/. ADJ Action that is **wasteful** uses too much of something valuable such as time, money, or energy. *This kind of training is ineffective, and wasteful of scarce resources.*

wasteland /ˈweɪstlænd/ **wastelands.** N-VAR A **wasteland** is an area of land which cannot be used, for example because it is infertile or because it has been misused by people.

watch 1 looking and paying attention

watch /wɒtʃ/ **watches, watching, watched.** [1] VERB If you **watch** someone or something, you look at them, usually for a period of time. *Two girls stood chewing slowly, watching the ambulance... They had been sitting watching television.* [2] VERB If you **watch** a situation, you pay attention to it or you are aware of it, but are not participating in it. *Human rights groups have been closely watching the case.* [3] VERB If you tell someone to **watch** a particular person or thing, you are warning them to be careful that the person or thing does not get out of control or do something unpleasant. *You really ought to watch these quiet types.* [4] See note at **see.**
| PHRASES | • You say '**watch it**' in order to warn someone to be careful; INFORMAL. • If someone **keeps watch**, they look around all the time, usually when other people are asleep, so that they can warn the others of danger or an attack. • If you **keep watch** on events or a situation, you pay attention to what is happening, so that you can take action at the right moment.

▶ **watch for** or **watch out for.** PHR-VERB If you **watch for** something, or if you **watch out for** it, you pay attention so that you notice it, either because you do not want to miss it or because you want to avoid it. *We'll be watching for any developments... Watch out for hidden sugar in food by reading the nutrition label carefully.*

▶ **watch out.** PHR-VERB If you tell someone to **watch out**, you are warning them to be careful, because something unpleasant might happen to them or they might get into difficulties. *You have to watch out because there are land mines all over the place.*

▶ **watch out for.** See **watch for.**

watch 2 instrument that tells the time

watch /wɒtʃ/ **watches.** N-C A **watch** is a small clock which you wear on a strap on your wrist or on a chain.

watchdog /ˈwɒtʃdɒg, AM -dɔːg/ **watchdogs.** N-C A **watchdog** is a person or committee

whose job is to make sure that companies do not act illegally or irresponsibly. ...*the head of Britain's gas industry watchdog.*

watchful /ˈwɒtʃfʊl/. ADJ Someone who is **watchful** is careful to notice everything that is happening. *They had been alert and watchful, but had seen nothing suspicious.*

water /ˈwɔːtə/ **waters, watering, watered.** [1] N-U **Water** is a clear thin liquid that has no colour or taste when it is pure. It falls from clouds as rain. *Get me a glass of water.* [2] N-U & N-PL When people are talking about a large area of water, for example a lake or sea, they sometimes call it the **water** or the **waters.** *Monique ran down to the water's edge. ...the calm waters of Cowes Harbour.* [3] N-PL A country's **waters** consist of the area of sea which is near it and which is regarded as belonging to it. ...*ferries operating in British waters.* [4] VERB If you **water** plants, you pour water into the soil to help them to grow. [5] VERB If your eyes **are watering**, you have tears in them because they are sore or because you are upset. [6] VERB If you say that your mouth **is watering**, you mean that you can smell or see some appetizing food.

▶ **water down.** PHR-VERB If something, especially a proposal, speech, or statement **is watered down**, it is made much weaker and less forceful or less controversial.

watercolour (AM **watercolor**) /ˈwɔːtəkʌlə/ **watercolours.** [1] N-PL **Watercolours** are coloured paints, used for painting pictures, which you apply with a wet brush or dissolve in water first. [2] N-C A **watercolour** is a picture which has been painted using watercolours.

waterfall /ˈwɔːtəfɔːl/ **waterfalls.** N-C A **waterfall** is a place where water flows over the edge of a steep cliff and falls into a pool below.

waterfront /ˈwɔːtəfrʌnt/ **waterfronts.** N-C A **waterfront** is a street or piece of land which is next to an area of water, for example a harbour or the sea. ...*a two-bedroom apartment on the waterfront.*

waterproof /ˈwɔːtəpruːf/. ADJ Something that is **waterproof** does not let water pass through it. ...*waterproof clothing.*

watershed /ˈwɔːtəʃed/ **watersheds.** N-C If something such as an event is a **watershed** in the history or development of something, it is very important because it represents the beginning of a new stage in it. *Many observers expected this election to be a watershed in Malaysia's political history.*

watertight /ˈwɔːtətaɪt/. [1] ADJ Something that is **watertight** does not allow water to pass through it, for example because it is tightly sealed. *The batteries are safely enclosed in a watertight compartment.* [2] ADJ A **watertight** case or agreement is one that nobody can disapprove or find fault with. *The police had a watertight case.*

waterway /ˈwɔːtəweɪ/ **waterways.** N-C A **waterway** is a canal, river, or narrow channel of sea which ships or boats can sail along.

watery /ˈwɔːtəri/. [1] ADJ Something that is **watery** is weak or pale. *A watery light began to show through the branches.* [2] ADJ **Watery** food or drink contains too much water or is thin and tasteless like water. ...*a plateful of watery soup.* [3] ADJ Something that is **watery** contains, resembles, or consists of water. *Diana's eyes went red and watery.*

watt /wɒt/ **watts.** N-C A **watt** is a unit of measurement of electrical power. *...a 100-watt light-bulb.*

wave /weɪv/ **waves, waving, waved.** [1] VERB & N-C If you **wave** or **wave** your hand, or if you give a **wave**, you move your hand from side to side in the air, usually in order to say hello or goodbye to someone. *He smiled and waved to journalists... Paddy spotted Mary Ann and gave her a cheery wave.* [2] VERB If you **wave** someone somewhere, you make a movement with your hand to indicate that they should move in a particular direction. *Leshka waved him away with a show of irritation.* [3] VERB If you **wave** something, you hold it up and move it rapidly from side to side. *More than 4000 people waved flags and sang nationalist songs.* [4] N-C A **wave** is a raised mass of water on the sea or a lake, caused by the wind or the tide. [5] N-C A **wave** is a sudden increase in a particular feeling, activity, or type of behaviour, especially an undesirable or unpleasant one. *...the current wave of violence... The loneliness and grief comes in waves.* [6] N-C **Wave** is used to refer to the way in which things such as sound, light, and radio signals travel. *Radio waves have a certain frequency.* [7] See also **new wave, shock wave, tidal wave**.

wavelength /ˈweɪvleŋθ/ **wavelengths.** [1] N-C A **wavelength** is the distance between the same point on consecutive cycles of a wave of energy such as light or sound. *Blue light has a shorter wavelength than red.* [2] N-C A **wavelength** is the size of radio wave which a particular radio station uses to broadcast its programmes. [3] PHRASE If two people are **on the same wavelength**, they find it easy to understand each other and they tend to agree, because they share similar interests or opinions.

waver /ˈweɪvə/ **wavers, wavering, wavered.** [1] VERB If you **waver**, you are uncertain or indecisive about something. *Some military commanders wavered over whether to support the coup.* [2] VERB If something **wavers**, it shakes with very slight movements or changes. *The shadows of the dancers wavered continually.*

wavy /ˈweɪvi/ **wavier, waviest.** ADJ **Wavy** hair is not straight or curly, but curves slightly.

wax /wæks/. N-U **Wax** is a solid, slightly shiny substance made of fat or oil which is used to make candles and polish.

way /weɪ/ **ways.** [1] N-C If you refer to a **way** of doing something, you are referring to how you can do it, for example the method you can use to achieve it. *Another way of making new friends is to go to an evening class... I can't think of a worse way to spend my time.* [2] N-C You can refer to the **way** that an action is done to indicate the quality that it has. *She smiled in a friendly way.* [3] N-PL The **ways** of a particular person or group of people are their customs or their usual behaviour. *I won't alter my ways because I'm under pressure.* [4] N-C If a general statement or description is true in a particular **way**, that is a particular manner or form that it

takes in a specific case. *She was afraid in a way that was quite new to her... In some ways, the official opening is a formality.* [5] N-SING The **way** you feel about something is your attitude to it or your opinion about it. *I'm terribly sorry, I had no idea you felt that way.* [6] N-C The **way** to a particular place is the route that you must take in order to get there. *Does anybody know the way to the bathroom?... We'll go out the back way... This is the way in.* [7] N-SING You use **way** to indicate the direction or position of something. *As he strode into the kitchen, he passed Pop coming the other way... Turn the cake the right way up.* [8] N-SING If someone or something is in the **way**, they prevent you from moving freely or from seeing clearly. *Get out of my way!* [9] N-SING You use **way** in expressions such as **push your way** and **make your way** to indicate movement or progression, especially when this is difficult or slow. *He elbowed his way to the bar... Fergus sat at the desk working his way through a mass of papers.* [10] N-SING You use **way** in expressions such as **a long way** and **a little way** to say how far away something is. *We've a fair way to go yet.* [11] N-SING You use **way** in expressions such as **all the way, most of the way,** and **half the way** to refer to the extent to which an action has been completed. *When was the last time you listened to an album all the way through?* [12] ADV You can use **way** to emphasize, for example, that something is a great distance away or is very much below or above a particular level or amount. *Way down in the valley to the west is the town of Freiburg... I have to decide my plan way in advance.*

PHRASES ● If an object that is supporting something **gives way**, it breaks or collapses. *He fell when a ledge gave way beneath him.* ● If you **give way** to someone or something that you have been resisting, you stop resisting and allow yourself to be persuaded or controlled by them. *The President has given way to pressure from the hardliners.* ● If a moving person or a vehicle or its driver **gives way**, they slow down or stop in order to allow other people or vehicles to pass in front of them; BRITISH. ● If you **lose your way**, you become lost when you are trying to go somewhere. ● If one person or thing **makes way** for another, the first is replaced by the second. *The building will be demolished in January to make way for new offices.* ● If you **go out of** your **way** to do something, you make a special effort to do it. *She went out of her way to make him feel at home.* ● If you **keep out of** someone's **way**, you avoid them. ● When something is **out of the way**, it is over or you have dealt with it. *The plan has to remain confidential at least until the local elections are out of the way.* ● If an activity or plan is **under way**, it has begun and is now taking place. *Peace talks are under way.* ● If someone **gets** their **way** or **has** their **way**, nobody stops them doing what they want to do. You can also say that someone **gets** their **own way** or **has** their **own way**. *As long as she got her own way, she could be a delightful child.* ● If someone says that you **can't have it both ways**, they mean that you have to choose between two things and cannot do or have them both. ● If you say that someone or something **has a way** of doing a particular thing, you mean they often do it. *Bosses have a way of always finding out about such things.* ● You say **by the way** when you add something, especially something that you have just thought of; SPOKEN. *By the way, how is your back?* ● You use **in a way** to indicate that your statement is true to some extent or in one respect. *In a way, I suppose I'm frightened of failing.*

,way of 'life, ways of life. N-C Someone's **way of life** consists of their habits and their daily activities.

wayward /'weɪwəd/. ADJ A **wayward** person is likely to change suddenly, and is therefore difficult to control.

we /wɪ, STRONG wiː/. PRON **We** is used as the subject of a verb. A speaker or writer uses **we** to refer to a group of people which includes himself or herself. *We ordered another bottle of champagne... We students outnumbered our teachers.*

weak /wiːk/ **weaker, weakest.** [1] ADJ If someone is **weak**, they do not have very much strength or energy. ♦**weakly** ADV *Sharon shook her head weakly.* ♦**weakness** N-U *Symptoms of infection include weakness, nausea and vomiting.* [2] ADJ Something that is **weak** is not strong or good, and is likely to break or fail. *Ron has weak eyesight... She had a weak heart.* [3] ADJ If you describe someone as **weak**, you mean that they are not very confident or determined, so that they are often frightened or worried, or easily influenced by other people. ♦**weakness** N-U *Many people felt that admitting to stress was a sign of weakness.* [4] ADJ If something such as an argument or case is **weak**, it is not convincing or there is little evidence to support it. *The evidence against him was weak.* [5] ADJ A **weak** drink, chemical, or drug contains very little of a particular substance, for example because it has been diluted with a lot of water. *...a cup of weak tea.*

weaken /'wiːkən/ **weakens, weakening, weakened.** [1] VERB To **weaken** something means to make it less strong or less powerful. *The recession has weakened so many firms that many can no longer survive... Family structures are weakening and breaking up.* [2] VERB If someone **weakens**, they become less certain about a decision they have made. *Jennie weakened, and finally relented... The verdict hasn't weakened his resolve to fight the charges against him.*

weakness /'wiːknəs/ **weaknesses.** N-C If you have a **weakness** for something, you like it very much. *Stephen had a weakness for cats.*

wealth /welθ/. [1] N-U **Wealth** is a large amount of money or property owned by someone, or the possession of it. *His own wealth grew.* [2] N-SING A **wealth** of something means a very large amount of it; LITERARY. *The city boasts a wealth of beautiful churches.*

wealthy /'welθi/ **wealthier, wealthiest.** ADJ & N-PL **Wealthy** people have a large amount of money or property. You can call people like this **the wealthy**.

wean /wiːn/ **weans, weaning, weaned.** [1] VERB When a mother **weans** her baby, she stops feeding it with milk from her breast and starts giving it other food. [2] VERB If you **wean** someone off a bad habit, you gradually make them stop doing it or liking it. *...a programme to wean addicts off drugs.*

weapon /'wepən/ **weapons.** N-C A **weapon** is an object such as a gun, knife, or missile.

weaponry /'wepənri/. N-U **Weaponry** is all the weapons that a group or country has or that are available to it.

wear /weə/ **wears, wearing, wore, worn.** [1] VERB When you **wear** clothes, shoes, or jewellery, you have them on your body. *He was wearing a brown uniform.* [2] VERB If you **wear** your hair in a particular way, it is cut or styled in that way. *She wore her hair in a long braid.* [3] N-U You can use **wear** to refer to clothes that are suitable for a particular time or occasion. *...an extensive range of beach wear.* [4] N-U **Wear** is the amount or type of use that something has over a period of time. *You'll get more wear out of a hat if you choose one in a neutral colour.* [5] VERB & N-U If something **wears**, or if it shows signs of **wear**, it becomes thinner or weaker from constant use. *Your horse needs new shoes if the shoe has worn thin or smooth. ...a large, well-upholstered armchair which showed signs of wear.* [6] See also **worn**.

After you get up in the morning, you **get dressed**, or you **dress**, by **putting on** your clothes. *He put on his shoes and socks.* Small children and sick people may be unable to **dress themselves**, so someone else has to **dress** them.

When you **are dressed**, you **are wearing** your clothes, or you **have** them **wearing**. *Edith had her hat on... They ought to stop walking round the house with nothing on.*

During the day you might want to **get changed**, or to **change**, or to **change** your clothes. *She returned having changed from trousers and a pullover into a short-sleeved blouse and a skirt... Adams changed his shirt a couple of times a day.*

Before you go to bed, you **get undressed**, or you **undress**, by **taking off** your clothes. *He won't take his clothes off in front of me.*

See also the note at **clothes**.

▸ **wear away.** PHR-VERB If you **wear** something **away**, it becomes thin and eventually disappears because it is used a lot or rubbed a lot. *The softer rock wears away.*

▸ **wear down.** [1] PHR-VERB If you **wear** something **down**, it becomes flatter or smoother as a result of constantly rubbing against something else. [2] PHR-VERB If someone **wears** you **down**, they weaken you by continually attacking or criticizing you, or trying to persuade you to do something. *They hoped the waiting and the uncertainty would wear down my resistance.*

▸ **wear off.** PHR-VERB If a feeling or sensation **wears off**, it slowly disappears. *Now that the* *initial shock was wearing off, he was in considerable pain.*

▶ **wear out.** ① PHR-VERB When something **wears out**, it is used so much that it becomes thin or weak and cannot be used any more. *He wore out his shoes wandering around Mexico City.* • See also **worn-out.** ② PHR-VERB If something **wears** you **out**, it makes you feel extremely tired; INFORMAL.

weary /'wɪəri/ **wearier, weariest; wearies, wearying, wearied.** ① ADJ If you are **weary**, you are very tired. ♦**wearily** ADV *I sighed wearily.* ♦**weariness** N-U *Despite his weariness, Brand mustered a wan smile.* ② VERB & ADJ AFTER LINK-V If you **weary** of something, or if you are **weary** of it, you become tired of it. *He had wearied of teaching in state universities... She was weary of being alone.*

weather /'weðə/ **weathers, weathering, weathered.** ① N-U The **weather** is the condition of the atmosphere in an area at a particular time, for example, whether it is raining, hot, or windy. *The weather was bad. ...cold weather.* ② VERB If something such as rock or wood **weathers**, it changes colour or shape as a result of the effects of wind, sun, rain, or frost. ③ VERB If you **weather** a difficult time, you survive it. *The company has weathered the recession.*

weave /wiːv/ **weaves, weaving, wove, woven.** The form **weaved** is used for the past tense and past participle for meaning 3. ① VERB If you **weave** cloth, you make it by crossing threads over and under each other using a machine called a loom. ♦**weaver, weavers** N-C *...a linen weaver from Ireland.* ♦**weaving** N-U *I studied weaving.* ② N-C The **weave** of a cloth is the way in which the threads are arranged. *Fabrics with a close weave.* ③ VERB If you **weave** your way somewhere, you move between and around things as you go there. *He weaves his way through a crowd.*

web /web/ **webs.** ① N-C A spider's **web** is the thin net which it makes from the sticky substance it produces in its body. ② N-C A **web** is a complicated pattern of connections or relationships, often considered as an obstacle or a danger. *They accused him of weaving a web of lies and deceit.*

wed /wed/ **weds, wedded.** The form **wed** is used in the present tense and is the past tense. The past participle can be either **wed** or **wedded.** VERB If one person **weds** another or if two people **wed**, they get married; JOURNALISM.

we'd /wɪd, wiːd/. **We'd** is the usual spoken form of 'we would' or 'we had', especially when 'had' is an auxiliary verb. *I don't know how we'd have managed without her!*

wedding /'wedɪŋ/ **weddings.** N-C A **wedding** is a marriage ceremony and the celebration that often takes place afterwards.

wedge /wedʒ/ **wedges, wedging, wedged.** ① N-C A **wedge** is an object with one pointed edge and one thick edge, which you put under a door to keep it firmly in position. ② VERB If you **wedge** something such as a door or window, you keep it firmly in position by pushing a wedge or a similar object between it and the

surface next to it. *We slammed the gate after them, wedging it shut with planks.* ③ VERB If you **wedge** something somewhere, you fit it there tightly. *Wedge the plug into the hole.* ④ PHRASE If someone **drives a wedge** between two people who are close, they cause ill feelings between them in order to weaken their relationship.

Wednesday /'wenzdeɪ, -di/ **Wednesdays.** N-VAR **Wednesday** is the day after Tuesday and before Thursday.

wee /wiː/. ADJ **Wee** means small or little; used especially in Scotland. *...a wee child.*

weed /wiːd/ **weeds, weeding, weeded.** ① N-C A **weed** is a wild plant growing where it is not wanted, for example in a garden. ② VERB If you **weed** an area, you remove the weeds from it. *The Hodges are busy weeding and planting.*

▶ **weed out.** PHR-VERB If you **weed out** things or people that are not wanted in a group, you find them and get rid of them. *He is keen to weed out the many applicants he believes may be frauds.*

week /wiːk/ **weeks.** ① N-VAR A **week** is a period of seven days, which is often considered to start on Monday and end on Sunday. *I had a letter from my mother last week... Her mother stayed for another two weeks.* ② N-C Your working **week** is the hours that you spend at work during a week. *...workers on a three-day week because of the slump.* ③ N-SING The **week** is the part of the week that does not include Saturday and Sunday. *...looking after the children during the week.*

weekday /'wiːkdeɪ/ **weekdays.** N-C A **weekday** is any day of the week except Saturday and Sunday.

weekend /ˌwiːk'end/ **weekends.** N-C A **weekend** is Saturday and Sunday. *I'll phone you at the weekend.*

weekly /'wiːkli/ **weeklies.** ① ADJ BEFORE N & ADV **Weekly** is used to describe something that happens or appears once a week. *...a weekly newspaper... The group meets weekly.* ② N-C A **weekly** is a newspaper or magazine that is published once a week.

weep /wiːp/ **weeps, weeping, wept.** VERB & N-SING If someone **weeps** or if they have a **weep**, they cry. *She wept tears of joy... There are times when I sit down and have a good weep.*

weigh /weɪ/ **weighs, weighing, weighed.** ① VERB If someone or something **weighs** a particular amount, that is how heavy they are. *He weighs 19 stone.* ② VERB If you **weigh** someone or something, you measure how heavy they are. ③ VERB & PHR-VERB If you **weigh** the facts about a situation, or if you **weigh** them **up**, you consider them very carefully before you decide or say anything. *She weighed her options... 'I've been weighing up all the alternatives.'* ④ VERB If a problem **weighs** on you, it makes you worried or unhappy. *The separation weighed on both of them.*

▶ **weigh down.** ① PHR-VERB If something that you are wearing or carrying **weighs** you **down**, it stops you moving easily because it is heavy. *...soldiers weighed down by their heavy packs.*

2 PHR-VERB If you **are weighed down** by something, it is makes you very worried or causes you great problems. *...countries that are weighed down by the burden of overseas debt.*

weight /weɪt/ **weights, weighting, weighted.** **1** N-VAR The **weight** of a person or thing is how heavy they are, measured in units such as kilos or pounds. *What is your height and weight?... This reduced the weight of the load.*

> In British English, a person's weight is normally measured in **stones** and **pounds**. A **stone** is equivalent to 14 pounds, or 6.35 kilograms. When you are mentioning someone's weight, you often omit the word **pounds** and **stone** usually has a singular form although its meaning is plural. *Jodie confessed she now weighed 9 stone 12.*
> In American English, only **pounds** are used. *I weigh 110 pounds.*

2 N-C **Weights** are metal objects which weigh a known amount. *I was in the gym lifting weights.* **3** N-C You can refer to a heavy object as a **weight**. *Straining to lift heavy weights can lead to a rise in blood pressure.* **4** N-SING If you feel a **weight** on you, you have a worrying problem or responsibility. *A great weight lifted from me... I feel a much greater weight of responsibility in my current job.*

PHRASES ● If someone is not **pulling** their **weight**, they are not working as hard as everyone else who is involved in the same task. ● If you **throw** your **weight behind** a person or a plan, you use all your influence and do everything you can to support them.

▸ **weight down.** PHR-VERB If you **weight** something **down**, you put something heavy on it or in it, often so that it cannot move easily.

weighted /'weɪtɪd/ ADJ A system that is **weighted** in favour of a person or group is organized so that this person or group has an advantage. *The peace process is so heavily weighted against them that it will never achieve results.*

weighty /'weɪti/ **weightier, weightiest.** ADJ **Weighty** issues seem serious or important; FORMAL. *Surely such weighty matters merit a higher level of debate?*

weir /wɪə/ **weirs,** N-C A **weir** is a low dam built across a river to control the flow of water.

weird /wɪəd/ **weirder, weirdest.** ADJ **Weird** means strange and peculiar. *It must be really weird to be rich.* ◆ **weirdly** ADV *...men who dressed weirdly.*

welcome /'welkəm/ **welcomes, welcoming, welcomed.** **1** VERB & N-C If you **welcome** someone or if you give them a **welcome**, you greet them in a friendly way when they arrive. *She was there to welcome him home from war... There would be a fantastic welcome awaiting him.* **2** CONVENTION You can say '**Welcome**' to someone who has just arrived. *Welcome to Washington... Welcome back, Deborah – It's good to have you here.* **3** ADJ If you say that someone is **welcome** in a particular place, you are encouraging them to go there by assuring them that they will be accepted. *New members are always welcome.* **4** PHRASE If you

make someone **welcome** or **make** them **feel welcome**, you make them feel happy and accepted in a new place. **5** VERB & ADJ If you **welcome** an action or decision, or if you say it is **welcome**, you approve of it and support it. *The leadership issued a statement welcoming the coup... This was certainly a welcome change of fortune.* **6** ADJ AFTER LINK-V If you tell someone that they are **welcome** to do something, you are encouraging them to do it. *...a conservatory which guests are welcome to use.* **7** CONVENTION You can acknowledge someone's thanks by saying '**You're welcome**'. *'Thank you for the information.'—'You're welcome.'*

weld /weld/ **welds, welding, welded.** **1** VERB If you **weld** one piece of metal to another, you join them by heating their edges and putting them together so that they cool and harden into one piece. **2** N-C A **weld** is a join where two pieces of metal have been welded together.

welfare /'welfeə/ **1** N-U The **welfare** of a person or group is their health, comfort, and prosperity. *I do not think he is considering Emma's welfare.* **2** ADJ **Welfare** services are provided to help with people's living conditions and financial problems. *He has urged complete reform of the welfare system.* **3** N-U In American English, **welfare** is money that is paid by the government to people who are unemployed, poor, or ill. The British term is **social security**.

welfare 'state. N-SING In Britain and some other countries, the **welfare state** is a system in which the government uses money collected from taxes to provides social services such as health and education and gives money to people when they are unable to work.

well 1 *discourse uses*

well /wel/. **Well** is used mainly in spoken English. **1** ADV You say **well** to indicate that you are about to say something else, especially when you are hesitating, when you are trying to make your statement less strong, when you are about to correct a statement, or when you are changing the topic. *Well, I thought she was a bit unfair about me... There was a note. Well, not really a note.* **2** CONVENTION You say **oh well** to indicate that you accept a situation or that someone else should accept it, even though you or they are not very happy about it. *Oh well, it could be worse.* ● **very well**: see **very**.

well 2 *adverb uses*

well /wel/ **better, best.** **1** ADV If you do something **well**, you do it to a high standard or to a great extent. *All the Indian batsmen played well... He speaks English better than I do... People live longer nowadays, and they are better educated... I don't really know her very well.* **2** ADV If you do something **well**, you do it thoroughly and completely. *Mix all the ingredients well.* **3** ADV You use **well** to ask or talk about the extent or standard of something. *How well do you remember your mother, Franzi?... He wasn't dressed any better than me.* **4** ADV You use **well** in front of prepositions and a few adjectives in order to emphasize them. For example, if you say that one thing happened **well before** another, you mean that it happened a long time before it. *Franklin did not turn up* *until well after midnight... The show is well worth a visit.* **5** ADV You use **well** after verbs such as 'may' and 'could' when you are saying what you think is likely to happen. *The murderer may well come from the estate.*

well 3 phrases

well /wel/.

PHRASES ● If one thing is involved and another thing is involved **as well**, the second thing is also involved. *It is most often diagnosed in women in their thirties and forties, although I've seen it in many younger women, as well.* ● If one thing is involved **as well as** another, the first thing is involved in addition to the second. *Jim Morrison was a poet as well as a singer.* ● If you say that something that has happened **is just as well**, you mean that it is fortunate that it happened in the way it did. *Judging from everything you've said, it was just as well she wasn't there.* ● If you say that you **might as well** do something, or that you **may as well** do it, you mean that you will do it although you do not have a strong desire to do it and may even feel slightly reluctant about it. *Anyway, you're here; you might as well stay.* ● If you say that something is **well and truly** over, you are emphasizing that it is completely finished or gone. *The war is well and truly over.*

well 4 adjective use

well /wel/. ADJ If you are **well**, you are healthy and not ill. *I'm not very well today.*

well 5 noun uses

well /wel/ **wells**. **1** N-C A **well** is a hole in the ground from which a supply of water is extracted. **2** N-C A **well** is an oil well.

well 6 verb use

well /wel/ **wells, welling, welled.** VERB & PHR-VERB If tears **well** in your eyes, or if they **well up** in your eyes, they come to the surface. *Tears well up in her eyes when she recalls the tragic loss.*

we'll /wil, STRONG wiːl/. **We'll** is the usual spoken form of 'we shall' or 'we will'. *Whatever you want to chat about, we'll do it tonight.*

,well-'balanced. **1** ADJ Someone who is **well-balanced** is sensible and does not have many emotional problems. **2** ADJ If you describe something that is made up of several parts as **well-balanced**, you mean that the way that there is a good mixture of each part. *...a well-balanced diet.*

'well-being (or **wellbeing**). N-U Someone's **well-being** is their health and happiness. *Singing can create a sense of wellbeing.*

,well 'done. **1** CONVENTION You say **'Well done'** to indicate that you are pleased that someone has got something right or done something good. **2** ADJ If meat is **well done**, it has been cooked thoroughly.

,well-'dressed. ADJ Someone who is **well-dressed** is wearing smart or elegant clothes.

,well-es'tablished. ADJ If something is **well-established**, it has existed for quite a long time and is successful. *...well-established companies.*

,well-in'formed. ADJ Someone who is **well-informed** knows a lot about many different subjects or about one particular subject.

,well-in'tentioned. ADJ **Well-intentioned** means the same as **well-meaning**.

,well-'known. ADJ Something or someone that is **well-known** is famous or familiar. *She was a very well-known author.* ● See note at **famous**.

,well-'meaning. ADJ Someone who is **well-meaning** tries to be helpful, but is usually unsuccessful or causes unfortunate results.

,well-'off. ADJ Someone who is **well-off** is rich enough to be able to do and buy most of the things that they want.

,well-'paid. ADJ If you say that a person or their job is **well-paid**, you mean that they receive a lot of money for the work that they do.

,well-to-'do. ADJ **Well-to-do** means the same as **well-off**.

went /went/. **Went** is the past tense of **go**.

wept /wept/. **Wept** is the past tense and past participle of **weep**.

were /wə, STRONG wɜː/. **1** **Were** is the plural and the second person singular of the past tense of **be**. **2** **Were** is sometimes used instead of 'was' in certain structures, for example in conditional clauses or after the verb 'wish'; FORMAL. *If she were to marry, her husband would have to live at Park Villa... Jerry wished he were back in Washington.*

we're /wɪə/. **We're** is the usual spoken form of 'we are'. *I'm married, but we're not separated.*

weren't /wɜːnt/. **Weren't** is the usual spoken form of 'were not'. *We weren't totally happy with the way things sounded.*

west /west/. **1** N-SING The **west** is the direction in which you look to see the sun set. **2** N-SING & ADJ The **west** of a place, or the **west** part of a place, is the part which is towards the west. *...a house in the west of the city... He's from the west coast of Africa.* **3** ADV **West** means towards the west, or positioned to the west of a place or thing. *We'll drive west to Kanchanaburi... The plan is to build a huge new film studio just west of London.* **4** ADJ A **west** wind blows from the west. **5** N-SING The **West** is used to refer to the United States, Canada, and the countries of Western, Northern, and Southern Europe.

westerly /ˈwestəli/. **1** ADJ A **westerly** point, area, or direction is to the west or towards the west. *They set out in a westerly direction along the riverbank.* **2** ADJ A **westerly** wind blows from the west.

western /ˈwestən/ **westerns**. **1** ADJ **Western** means in or from the west of a region or country. **2** ADJ **Western** means coming from or associated with the societies of the United States, Canada, and the countries of Western, Northern, and Southern Europe. **3** N-C A **western** is a film or book about the life of cowboys.

westerner /ˈwestənə/ **westerners**. N-C A **westerner** is a person who was born in or who lives in the United States, Canada, or Western, Northern, or Southern Europe.

westward /ˈwestwəd/ (or **westwards**) /ˈwestwədz/. ADV & ADJ **Westward** or **westwards** means towards the west. *...the settlers who moved westwards in the 19th century. ...the one-hour westward flight over the Andes to Lima.*

wet /wet/ **wetter, wettest; wets, wetting, wetted.** The forms **wet** and **wetted** are both used as the past tense and past participle of the verb. **1** ADJ If something is **wet**, it is covered in water or another liquid. *My gloves were soaking wet.* **2** VERB To **wet** something means to cause it to have water or another liquid on it. *For the best results wet the hair and work the shampoo well into the scalp.* **3** ADJ When the weather is **wet**, it is raining. *It was very wet and windy the day I drove over to Milland.* **4** ADJ If something such as paint or cement is **wet**, it is not yet dry. **5** VERB If someone **wets** their beds or clothes, or if they **wet** themselves, they urinate in their beds or clothes because they cannot control their bladder. *To put it plainly, they wet themselves.*

wetland /'wetlænd/ **wetlands.** N-VAR A **wetland** is an area of very wet muddy land with wild plants growing in it. You can also refer to a wetland as **wetlands.** *...a scheme that aims to protect the wilderness of the wetlands.*

we've /wɪv, STRONG wiːv/. **We've** is the usual spoken form of 'we have', especially when 'have' is an auxiliary verb. *'Hello, I don't think we've met,' Robert introduced himself.*

whack /wæk/ **whacks, whacking, whacked.** VERB If you **whack** someone or something, you hit them hard; INFORMAL. *Someone whacked him on the head.*

whacky See **wacky.**

whale /weɪl/ **whales.** N-C A **whale** is a very large sea mammal.

whaling /'weɪlɪŋ/. N-U **Whaling** is the activity of hunting and killing whales. *...commercial whaling in Antarctica.*

wharf /wɔːf/ **wharves.** N-C A **wharf** is a platform by a river or the sea where ships can be tied up.

what /wɒt/. **1** PRON & DET You use **what** in questions when you are asking for information. *What do you want?... 'Has something happened?'—'Indeed it has.'—'What?'... Hey! What are you doing? ...What kind of poetry does he like?* **2** CONJ & DET You use **what** after certain words, especially verbs and adjectives, when you are referring to a situation that is unknown or has not been specified. *I want to know what happened to Norman... She turned scarlet from embarrassment, once she realized what she had done.* **3** CONJ You use **what** at the beginning of a clause in structures where you are changing the order of the information to give special emphasis to something. *What she does possess is the ability to get straight to the core of a problem.* **4** CONJ & DET You use **what** to indicate that you are talking about the whole of an amount. *He drinks what is left in his glass as if it were water... They had had to use what money they had.* **5** PREDET & DET You use **what** to express your opinion of something, for example when you are surprised by it. *What a horrible thing to do... What ugly things; throw them away.* **6** CONVENTION You say **'What?'** when you want someone to repeat something because you did not hear it properly. 'What' is not as polite as 'pardon' or 'sorry'. *'They could paint this place,' she said. 'What?' he asked.* **7** CONVENTION You can say **'What'** to express surprise or disbelief. *'We've got the car that killed Myra Moss.'—'What!'*

PHRASES • You use **what about** when you are making a suggestion or offer. *What about a cup of tea?* • You use **what if** at the beginning of a question about the consequences of something, especially something undesirable. *What if this doesn't work out?* • If you know **what's what**, you know the important things that need to be known about a situation. • You say **what with** to introduce the reasons for a situation, especially an undesirable one. *Maybe they are tired, what with all the sleep they're losing.* • **what's more**: see **more.**

whatever /wɒt'evə/. **1** CONJ & DET You use **whatever** to refer to anything or everything of a particular type. *Franklin was free to do pretty much whatever he pleased... Whatever doubts he might have had about Ingrid were all over now.* **2** CONJ You use **whatever** when you are indicating that you do not know the precise identity, meaning, or value of the thing just mentioned. *'I love you,' he said.—'Whatever that means,' she said.* **3** CONJ You use **whatever** to say that something is the case in all circumstances. *We shall love you whatever happens, Diana... People will judge you whatever you do.* **4** ADV You use **whatever** after a noun group to emphasize a negative statement. *I have nothing whatever to say.* **5** ADV You use **whatever** to ask in an emphatic way about something which you are very surprised about. *Whatever is the matter with you both?*

what's /wɒts/. **What's** is the usual spoken form of 'what is' or 'what has', especially when 'has' is an auxiliary verb.

whatsoever /ˌwɒtsəʊ'evə/. ADV You use **whatsoever** after a noun group in order to emphasize a negative statement. *My school did nothing whatsoever in the way of athletics.*

wheat /wiːt/. N-U **Wheat** is a cereal crop grown for its grain, which is ground into flour to make bread.

wheel /wiːl/ **wheels, wheeling, wheeled.** **1** N-C A **wheel** is a circular object which turns round on a rod attached to its centre. Wheels are fixed underneath vehicles so that they can move along. *The car wheels spun and slipped on some oil.* **2** N-C A **wheel** is the same as a **steering wheel.** **3** VERB If you **wheel** an object that has wheels somewhere, you push it along. *He wheeled his bike into the alley.* **4** VERB If you **wheel** round, you turn round suddenly. *He wheeled around to face her.*

wheelchair /'wiːltʃeə/ **wheelchairs.** N-C A **wheelchair** is a chair with wheels that sick or disabled people use in order to move about.

wheeze /wiːz/ **wheezes, wheezing, wheezed.** VERB If you **wheeze**, you breathe with difficulty, making a hissing or whistling sound.

when /wen/. **1** ADV You use **when** to ask questions about the time at which things happen. *When did you get married?... 'I'll be there this afternoon.'—'When?'* **2** CONJ You use **when** to introduce a clause where you refer to the time at which something happens. *I asked him when he'd be back to pick me up... I don't know* when the decision was made... When I met the Gills, I had been gardening for nearly ten years... She remembered clearly that day when she'd gone exploring the rockpools. [3] CONJ You use **when** to introduce the reason for an opinion or question. How can you understand, when you don't have kids? [4] CONJ You use **when** in order to introduce a fact or comment which makes the other part of the sentence rather surprising or unlikely. The temperature sensor is making the computer think the engine is cold when, in fact, it's hot.

whenever /wen'evə/. CONJ You use **whenever** to refer to any time or every time that something happens or is true. She always called at the vicarage whenever she was in the area... Avoid processed foods whenever possible.

where /weə/. [1] ADV You use **where** to ask questions about the place something is in, or is coming from or going to. Where did you meet him?... 'You'll never believe where Julie and I are going.'—'Where?' [2] CONJ & PRON You use **where** to specify or refer to the place in which something is situated or happens. People began looking across to see where the noise was coming from... He knew where Henry Carter had gone... Conditions which apply to your flight are available at the travel agency where you book your holiday. [3] CONJ & PRON & ADV You use **where** when you are referring to or asking about a situation, a stage in something, or an aspect of something. It's not hard to see where she got her feelings about herself... The government is at a stage where it is willing to talk... Where will it all end? [4] CONJ **Where** is used to introduce a clause which contrasts with what is said in the main clause. Sometimes a teacher will be listened to, where a parent might not.

whereabouts. [1] N-SING /'weərəbauts/ The **whereabouts** of a person or thing is the place where they are. ...a map showing the whereabouts of local castles. [2] ADV /,weərə'bauts/ You use **whereabouts** in questions when you are asking precisely where something is. Whereabouts in Liverpool are you from?

whereas /weər'æz/. CONJ You use **whereas** to introduce a comment which contrasts with what is said in the main clause. She shows her feelings, whereas I don't.

whereby /weə'bai/. PRON A system or action **whereby** something happens is one that makes that thing happen; FORMAL. ...a deal whereby the union will receive nearly a million pounds.

wherein /weər'in/. [1] PRON **Wherein** means in which place; FORMAL. ...a little room wherein are five cubicles. [2] ADV & CONJ **Wherein** means in which part or respect; FORMAL. Wherein lies the truth?... It is difficult to know wherein Mr Ritchie hoped to find salvation for his country.

whereupon /,weərə'ppn/. CONJ You use **whereupon** to say that one thing happens immediately after another thing and usually as a result of it; FORMAL. 'Well, get on with it then,' said Dobson, whereupon Davies started to explain.

wherever /weər'evə/. [1] CONJ You use **wherever** to say that something happens or is true in any place or situation. Some people enjoy themselves wherever they are. [2] CONJ You use

wherever to indicate that you do not know where a place or person is. 'Till we meet again, wherever that is,' said the chairman.

whether /'weðə/. [1] CONJ You use **whether** to talk about a choice or doubt between two or more alternatives. They now have two weeks to decide whether or not to buy. [2] CONJ You use **whether** to say that something is true in any of the circumstances you mention. We're in this together, whether we like it or not.

which /witʃ/. [1] PRON & DET You use **which** to ask questions when there are two or more possible answers or alternatives. Which is your cabin ?... Which woman or man do you most admire? [2] DET & PRON You use **which** to refer to a choice between two or more possible answers or alternatives. I wanted to know which school it was you went to... There are so many diets on the market, how do you know which to choose? [3] PRON You use **which** at the beginning of a relative clause that specifies the thing you are talking about or that gives more information about it. Soldiers opened fire on a car which failed to stop at an army checkpoint. [4] PRON & DET You use **which** to refer back to what has just been said. They ran out of drink. Which actually didn't bother me because I wasn't drinking... It could be a sign she has an infection, in which case she needs to see a doctor.

whichever /witʃ'evə/. [1] DET & CONJ You use **whichever** to indicate that it does not matter which of the possible alternatives happens or is chosen. Whichever way you look at it, nuclear power is the energy of the future... We will gladly exchange your goods, or refund your money, whichever you prefer. [2] DET & CONJ You use **whichever** to specify which of a number of possibilities is the right one or the one you mean. ...learning to relax by whichever method suits you best... Fishing is from 6 am to dusk or 10.30pm, whichever is sooner.

whiff /wif/ **whiffs**. [1] N-C If there is a **whiff** of something, there is a faint smell of it. He caught a whiff of her perfume. [2] N-C A **whiff** of something bad or harmful is a slight sign of it. Just a whiff of a scandal would destroy us.

while /wail/ **whiles, whiling, whiled**. [1] CONJ If one thing happens **while** another thing is happening, the two things happen at the same time. I sat on the settee to unwrap the package while he stood by... Her parents could help with child care while she works. [2] CONJ You use **while** to introduce a clause which contrasts with the other part of the sentence. The first two services are free, while the third costs £35.00. [3] CONJ You use **while** in a clause to say that although something is the case, it does not affect the truth of the other part of the sentence. While the war, so far, has been good, there may be days ahead when it is bad. [4] N-SING A **while** is a period of time. They walked on in silence for a while... He was married a little while ago. ● to be **worth** your **while**: see **worth**.

PHRASES ● You use **all the while** in order to say that something happens continually or that it happens throughout the time when something else is happening. *All the while the people at the next table watched me eat.* • If something happens **once in a while**, it happens occasionally.

▶ **while away.** PHR-VERB If you **while away** the time in a particular way, you spend time in that way because you are waiting for something or because you have nothing else to do. *They whiled away the hours telling stories.*

whilst /waɪlst/. CONJ **Whilst** means the same as **while** when it is used as a conjunction; BRITISH. *The girls met four years ago whilst singing backing vocals for local Birmingham bands.*

whim /wɪm/ **whims.** N-VAR A **whim** is a sudden desire to do or have something without any particular reason. *We decided, more or less on a whim, to sail to Morocco.*

whimper /ˈwɪmpə/ **whimpers, whimpering, whimpered.** VERB & N-VAR If someone **whimpers**, they make quiet unhappy or frightened sounds called **whimpers**, as if they are about to start crying. *She lay at the bottom of the stairs, whimpering in pain... David's crying subsided to a whimper.*

whimsical /ˈwɪmzɪkəl/. ADJ Something that is **whimsical** is unusual and slightly playful, and is not trying to make a serious point. *...his gentle and whimsical humour.*

whine /waɪn/ **whines, whining, whined.** [1] VERB & N-C If something or someone **whines**, they make a long, high-pitched noise called a **whine**, which often sounds sad or unpleasant. *The dog started to whine with impatience. ...the whine of air-raid sirens.* [2] VERB If someone **whines** about something, they complain about it in an annoying way.

whinge /wɪndʒ/ **whinges, whingeing, whinged.** VERB & N-C If you say that someone **is whingeing** or having a **whinge**, you mean that they are complaining in an annoying way about something unimportant; BRITISH, INFORMAL. *...listening to everybody's whinges.*

whip /wɪp/ **whips, whipping, whipped.** [1] N-C A **whip** is a long thin piece of leather or rope fastened to a handle. It is used for hitting animals or people. [2] VERB If someone **whips** an animal or person, they hit them with a whip. ◆**whipping, whippings** N-C *He threatened to give her a whipping.* [3] VERB If you **whip** something out or **whip** something off, you take it out or take it off very quickly and suddenly. *Bob whipped out his notebook... She whipped off her skis and charged up the hill.* [4] VERB If you **whip** cream or eggs, you stir them very quickly to make them thick or stiff. *Serve warm or cold with whipped cream.*

▶ **whip up.** PHR-VERB If someone **whips up** an emotion such as hatred, they deliberately cause and encourage people to feel that emotion. *He accused politicians of whipping up anti-foreign sentiments.*

whir /wɜː/. See **whirr.**

whirl /wɜːl/ **whirls, whirling, whirled.** [1] VERB If something or someone **whirls** round, or if you **whirl** them round, they move round or turn round very quickly. *He whirled around and began to run back down the alley. ...whirling snow.* [2] N-C You can refer to a lot of intense activity as a **whirl** of activity.

whirlwind /ˈwɜːlwɪnd/ **whirlwinds.** N-C A **whirlwind** is a tall column of air which spins round and round very fast and moves across the land or sea.

whirr (or **whir**) /wɜː/ **whirrs, whirring, whirred.** VERB & N-C If something such as a machine **whirrs**, it makes a series of low sounds so quickly that they seem like one continuous sound. This sound is called a **whirr**. *...the constant whirr of his electric fan.*

whisk /wɪsk/ **whisks, whisking, whisked.** [1] VERB If you **whisk** someone or something somewhere, you take them there quickly. *I was whisked away in a police car.* [2] VERB If you **whisk** eggs or cream, you stir air into them very fast. [3] N-C A **whisk** is a kitchen tool used for whisking eggs or cream.

whisker /ˈwɪskə/ **whiskers.** [1] N-C The **whiskers** of an animal such as a cat or mouse are the long stiff hairs that grow near its mouth. [2] N-PL People sometimes refer to the hair on a man's face as his **whiskers**.

whiskey /ˈwɪski/ **whiskeys.** N-VAR **Whiskey** is whisky made in Ireland or the United States.

whisky /ˈwɪski/ **whiskies.** N-VAR **Whisky** is a strong alcoholic drink made, especially in Scotland, from grain such as barley or rye.

whisper /ˈwɪspə/ **whispers, whispering, whispered.** VERB & N-C If you **whisper** something, or if you say it in a **whisper**, you say it very quietly, using only your breath and not your voice. *'Keep your voice down,' I whispered... He whispered the message to David... They spoke in whispers.*

whistle /ˈwɪsəl/ **whistles, whistling, whistled.** [1] VERB When you **whistle**, you make sounds by forcing your breath out between your lips or teeth. *He whistled a tune... He whistled, surprised but not shocked.* [2] VERB If something such as a train or a kettle **whistles**, it makes a loud, high sound. *Somewhere a train whistled.* [3] VERB If something such as the wind or a bullet **whistles** somewhere, it moves there, making a loud high sound. *As I stood up a bullet whistled past my back.* [4] N-C A **whistle** is a small metal tube which you blow in order to produce a loud sound and attract someone's attention.

white /waɪt/ **whiter, whitest; whites.** [1] ADJ & N-VAR Something that is **white** is the colour of snow or milk. [2] ADJ & N-C A **white** person has a pale skin and belongs to a race of European origin. **Whites** are white people. *He was white, with brown shoulder-length hair. ...a law that has kept blacks and whites apart.* [3] ADJ **White** wine is wine of a pale yellowish colour. [4] ADJ **White** coffee contains milk or cream; BRITISH. [5] N-VAR The **white** of an egg is the transparent liquid surrounding the yolk. [6] N-C The **white** of your eye is the white part of your eyeball.

white-'collar. ADJ BEFORE N **White-collar** workers work in offices rather than doing manual work in industry.

whitewash /ˈwaɪtwɒʃ/. [1] N-U **Whitewash** is a mixture of lime or chalk and water used for painting walls white. [2] N-SING A **whitewash** is an attempt to hide the unpleasant facts about something from the public in order to make a situation look less serious than it really is. *He has described the investigation as a white-wash.*

whittle /ˈwɪtəl/ **whittles, whittling, whittled.**
► **whittle away** or
► **whittle down.** PHR-VERB To **whittle** something **away** or to **whittle** it **down** means to make it smaller or less effective. *He had whittled eight interviewees down to two.*

whizz /wɪz/ **whizzes, whizzing, whizzed.**
VERB If something **whizzes** somewhere, it moves there very fast; INFORMAL. *Stewart felt a bottle whizz past his head.*

who /huː/. [1] PRON You use **who** when asking questions about the name or identity of a person or group of people. *Who's there?... Who did you ask?... Who do you work for?... 'You reminded me of somebody.'—'Who?'* [2] CONJ You use **who** to introduce a clause where you talk about the identity of a person or a group of people. *I was suddenly curious and asked who she was... They haven't found out who did it.* [3] PRON You use **who** at the beginning of a relative clause when specifying the person or group of people you are talking about or when giving more information about them. *The woman, who needs constant attention, is cared for by relatives... The hijacker gave himself up to police, who are now questioning him.*

who'd /huːd/. **Who'd** is the usual spoken form of 'who had', especially when 'had' is an auxiliary verb. **Who'd** is also a spoken form of 'who would'.

whoever /huːˈevə/. [1] PRON You use **whoever** to refer to someone when their identity is not yet known. *Whoever was responsible for this crime is a very dangerous man... Whoever wins this year is going to be famous for life.* [2] CONJ You use **whoever** to indicate that the actual identity of the person who does something will not affect a situation. *You can have whoever you like to visit you... Everybody who goes into this region, whoever they are, is at risk of being taken hostage.*

whole /həʊl/. [1] QUANT If you refer to the **whole** of something, you mean all of it. *I was cold throughout the whole of my body... We spent the whole summer in Italy.* [2] N-SING A **whole** is a single thing which contains several different parts. *The group's various businesses do not yet form a coherent whole.* [3] ADJ AFTER LINK-V If something is **whole**, it is in one piece and is not broken or damaged. *Much of the temple was ruined, but the front was whole... He plucked an ice cube from the glass and swallowed it whole.* [4] ADJ BEFORE N You use **whole** to emphasize what you are saying; INFORMAL. *...a whole new way of doing business... There's a whole group of friends who doesn't want you to meet.*
PHRASES • If you refer to something **as a whole**, you are referring to it generally and as a single unit. *In rural India as a whole, 80% of women are illiterate.* • You say **on the whole** to indicate that what you are saying is only true in general and may not be true in every case. *The wines they make are, on the whole, of a high standard.*

Whole is often used to mean the same as **all**, but when used in front of plurals **whole** and **all** have different meanings. For example, if you say '**Whole buildings have been destroyed**', you mean that some buildings have been destroyed completely. If you say '**All the buildings have been destroyed**', you mean that every building has been destroyed.

---

wholehearted /ˌhəʊlˈhɑːtɪd/. ADJ If you support something or agree to something in a **wholehearted** way, you support or agree to it enthusiastically and completely. *He has my wholehearted support.* ◆**wholeheartedly** ADV *I agree wholeheartedly with you.*

wholesale /ˈhəʊlseɪl/. [1] ADJ & ADV **Wholesale** goods or goods that are bought **wholesale** are bought cheaply in large quantities and then sold again to shops. *...the decline in wholesale prices over the past three months... Each tablet is sold wholesale for just 2p or 3p.* [2] ADJ BEFORE N & ADV You use **wholesale** to describe something undesirable or unpleasant that is done to an excessive extent. *...a campaign to stop the wholesale destruction of villages.*

wholesaler /ˈhəʊlseɪlə/ **wholesalers.** N-C A **wholesaler** is a person whose business is buying large quantities of goods and selling them in smaller amounts to shops.

wholesome /ˈhəʊlsəm/. [1] ADJ If you describe something as **wholesome**, you approve of it because you think it will have a positive influence on people, especially because it does not involve anything sexually immoral. *...good, wholesome fun.* [2] ADJ If you describe food as **wholesome**, you approve of it because you think it is good for your health.

who'll /huːl/. **Who'll** is a spoken form of 'who will' or 'who shall'.

wholly /ˈhəʊlli/. ADV **Wholly** means completely. *This is a wholly new approach.*

whom /huːm/. **Whom** is used in formal or written English instead of 'who' when it is the object of a verb or preposition. [1] PRON You use **whom** in questions when you ask about the name or identity of a person or group of people. *'I want to send a telegram.' 'Fine, to whom?'... Whom did he expect to answer his phone?* [2] CONJ You use **whom** to introduce a clause where you talk about the name or identity of a person or a group of people. *He asked whom I'd told about his having been away... They have a free hand to appoint whom they like.* [3] PRON You use **whom** at the beginning of a relative clause when specifying the person or people you are talking about, or when giving more information about them. *One writer in whom I had taken an interest was Immanuel Velikovsky... The Homewood residents whom I knew had little money and little free time.*

whoop /wuːp, AM huːp/ **whoops, whooping, whooped.** VERB & N-C If you **whoop**, or if you let out a **whoop**, you shout loudly in a very happy or excited way; WRITTEN. *Harry whooped with delight. ...loud whoops and yells.*

whore /hɔː/ **whores.** N-C A **whore** is the same as a **prostitute**.

who're /ˈhuːə/. **Who're** is a spoken form of 'who are'.

who's /huːz/. **Who's** is the usual spoken form of 'who is' or 'who has', especially when 'has' is an auxiliary verb.

whose /huːz/. [1] PRON You use **whose** at the beginning of a relative clause to indicate that something belongs to or is associated with the person or thing mentioned in the previous clause. *I saw a man shouting at a driver whose car was blocking the street.* [2] PRON & DET You use **whose** in questions to ask about the person or thing that something belongs to or is associated with. *Whose was the better performance?... Whose is this?... Whose daughter is she?* [3] DET & CONJ You use **whose** to introduce a clause where you talk about the person or thing that something belongs to or is associated with. *I can't remember whose idea it was for us to meet again... It doesn't matter whose it is.*

who've /huːv/. **Who've** is the usual spoken form of 'who have', especially when 'have' is an auxiliary verb.

why /waɪ/. [1] ADV You use **why** when asking questions about the reason for something. *Why hasn't he brought the whisky?... 'I just want to see him.'—'Why?'... Why should I leave?* [2] CONJ & ADV You use **why** at the beginning of a clause in which you talk about the reason for something. *Experts wonder why the US government is not taking similarly strong actions... I don't know why... Here's why.* [3] ADV You use **why** with 'not' to introduce a suggestion in the form of a question. *Why not give Claire a call?... Why don't we talk it through?* [4] CONVENTION You say **why not** in order to agree with what someone has suggested. *'Want to spend the afternoon with me?'—'Why not?'*

wicked /ˈwɪkɪd/. [1] ADJ You use **wicked** to describe someone or something that is very bad in a way that is deliberately harmful to people. *She described the shooting as a wicked attack.* ◆**wickedness** N-U *...the wickedness of nuclear weapons.* [2] ADJ If you describe someone or something as **wicked**, you mean that they are mischievous in a way that you find enjoyable. *She had a wicked sense of humour.* ◆**wickedly** ADV *...a wickedly funny parody.*

wicker /ˈwɪkə/. N-U **Wicker** is material made by weaving canes or twigs together, which is used to make baskets and furniture.

wide /waɪd/ **wider, widest.** [1] ADJ Something that is **wide** measures a large distance from one side to the other. *...a wide-brimmed sun-hat... Wreckage was scattered over a wide area.* [2] ADV If you open or spread something **wide**, you open or spread it to its fullest extent. *Open your mouth wide... 'It was huge,' he announced, spreading his arms wide.* [3] ADJ You use **wide** to talk or ask about how much something measures from one side or edge to the other. *The road is only one track wide. ...a desk that was almost as wide as the room.* [4] ADJ You use **wide** to describe something that includes a large number of different things or people. *...a wide choice of hotels. ...a wide*

range of topics... The case has attracted wide publicity. ◆**widely** ADV *He published widely in scientific journals.* [5] ADJ BEFORE N **Wider** is used to describe something relating to the most important or general parts of a situation rather than the details. *He emphasised the wider issue of superpower cooperation.* [6] ADJ A **wide** shot or punch does not hit its target. *Nearly half the missiles landed wide.* [7] **far and wide**: see **far**. ● **wide of the mark**: see **mark**.

'wide-eyed. [1] ADJ If you describe someone as **wide-eyed**, you mean that they seem inexperienced, and perhaps lack common sense. *...a wide-eyed boy ready to explore.* [2] ADJ & ADV If someone is **wide-eyed**, their eyes are more open than usual, especially because they are surprised or frightened. *...an expression of wide-eyed amazement... Trevor was staring wide-eyed at me.*

widen /ˈwaɪdən/ **widens, widening, widened.** [1] VERB If you **widen** something, or if it **widens**, it becomes bigger from one side or edge to the other. *The river widens considerably as it begins to turn east.* [2] VERB If something **widens**, or if you **widen** it, it becomes greater in range, size, or variety or affects a larger number of people or things. *The search for my brother widened... Newspapers enjoyed a widening circle of readers.*

‚wide-'ranging. ADJ If something is **wide-ranging**, it affects or deals with a great variety of different things. *...a wide-ranging debate about the party's goals.*

widespread /ˈwaɪdspred/. ADJ Something that is **widespread** exists or happens over a large area or to a very great extent. *Food shortages are widespread.*

widow /ˈwɪdəʊ/ **widows.** N-C A **widow** is a woman whose husband has died.

widowed /ˈwɪdəʊd/. ADJ If someone is **widowed**, their husband or wife has died.

widower /ˈwɪdəʊə/ **widowers.** N-C A **widower** is a man whose wife has died.

width /wɪdθ/ **widths.** N-VAR The **width** of something is the distance that it measures from one side to the other. *Measure the full width of the window... The road was reduced to 18ft in width.*

wield /wiːld/ **wields, wielding, wielded.** [1] VERB If you **wield** a weapon or tool, you carry it and use it. *...a gang member wielding a knife.* [2] VERB If someone **wields** power, they have it and are able to use it. *He remains chairman, but wields little power at the company.*

wife /waɪf/ **wives.** N-C A man's **wife** is the woman he is married to.

wig /wɪg/ **wigs.** N-C A **wig** is a mass of false hair which is worn on your head.

wiggle /ˈwɪgəl/ **wiggles, wiggling, wiggled.** VERB & N-C If you **wiggle** something, or if it **wiggles**, it moves around with small, quick movements, called **wiggles**. *Your baby will try to shuffle or wiggle along the floor. ...a wiggle of the hips.*

wild /waɪld/ **wilder, wildest; wilds.** [1] ADJ **Wild** animals and plants live or grow in natural surroundings and are not looked after by people. [2] ADJ Wild land is natural and not cultivated. ...forests and other wild areas. [3] N-PL The wilds are remote areas, far away from towns. [4] ADJ Wild behaviour is uncontrolled, excited, or energetic. As George himself came on stage they went wild. ◆wildly ADV The crowd clapped wildly. [5] ADJ BEFORE N A wild idea or guess is unusual and made without much thought. ◆wildly ADV 'Thirteen?' he guessed wildly. [6] PHRASE If something or someone runs wild, they behave in a natural, free or uncontrolled way. Molly has let that girl run wild.

wilderness /'wɪldənəs/ **wildernesses.** N-C A **wilderness** is an area of natural land which is not cultivated. ...one of the largest wilderness areas in North America.

wildlife /'waɪldlaɪf/. N-U You can use **wildlife** to refer to animals and other living things that live in the wild. Pets or wildlife could be affected by the pesticides.

wildly /'waɪldli/. ADV You use **wildly** to emphasize the degree, amount, or intensity of something. The community and police have wildly different stories of what happened... The island's hotels vary wildly. ● See also **wild**.

wilful (AM **willful**) /'wɪlfʊl/. [1] ADJ BEFORE N **Wilful** actions or attitudes are done or expressed deliberately, especially with the intention of hurting someone. Wilful neglect of our manufacturing industry has caused this problem. ◆wilfully ADV ...claims that the Front has wilfully perverted democracy. [2] ADJ A **wilful** person is obstinate and determined to get what they want. He is a wilful and indeed rather spiteful young man.

will 1 modal verb uses

will /wɪl/. The usual spoken form of **will not** is **won't.** [1] MODAL You use **will** to indicate that you hope, think, or have evidence that something is going to happen in the future. 70 per cent of airports in the Far East will have to be upgraded... Will you ever feel at home here? [2] MODAL You use **will** to talk about someone's intention to do something. 'Dinner's ready.'— 'Thanks, Carrie, but we'll have a drink first.'... What will you do next?... Will you be remaining in the city? [3] MODAL You use **will** to say that someone or something is able to do something in the future. How will I recognize you? [4] MODAL You use **will** when making offers, invitations, or requests. Will you stay for supper?... Won't you sit down? [5] MODAL You use **will** to say that someone is willing to do something. You use **will not** or **won't** to indicate that someone refuses to do something. All right, I'll forgive you... I'll answer the phone... If you won't let me pay for a taxi, then at least allow me to lend you something.

will 2 wanting something to happen

will /wɪl/ **wills, willing, willed.** [1] N-VAR **Will** is the determination to do something. He was said to have lost his will to live... It's a constant battle of wills with your children. ● See also **free will.** [2] N-SING If something is the **will** of a person or group of people with authority, they want it to happen. He has submitted himself to the will of God... Democracy responds and adjusts to the will of the people. [3] VERB If you **will** something to happen, you try to make it hap

pen using mental rather than physical effort. I looked at the telephone, willing it to ring. [4] N-C A **will** is a legal document stating what you want to happen to your money and property when you die. [5] PHRASE If you can do something **at will**, you can do it whenever you want. ...scientists who can adjust their experiments at will.

willing /'wɪlɪŋ/. [1] ADJ If someone is **willing** to do something, they do not mind doing it or have no objection to doing it. ◆willingly ADV I am glad you have come here so willingly. ◆willingness N-U I had to prove my willingness to work hard. [2] ADJ If you describe someone as **willing**, you mean that they are eager and enthusiastic. He was a natural and willing pupil.

willow /'wɪləʊ/ **willows.** N-C A **willow** is a tree with long narrow leaves and branches that hang down.

willpower (also **will-power** or **will power**) /'wɪlpaʊə/. N-U **Willpower** is a very strong determination to do something. His attempts to stop smoking by willpower alone failed.

wilt /wɪlt/ **wilts, wilting, wilted.** VERB If a plant **wilts**, it gradually bends downwards and becomes weak, because it needs more water or is dying.

wily /'waɪli/ **wilier, wiliest.** ADJ **Wily** people are clever and cunning. ...the wily old general.

wimp /wɪmp/ **wimps.** N-C If you call someone a **wimp**, you disapprove of them because they lack confidence or determination, or because they are often afraid of things; INFORMAL.

win /wɪn/ **wins, winning, won.** [1] VERB & N-C If you **win** a fight, game, or argument, you defeat your opponent, or you do better than everyone else involved. You can also talk about a **win**. I don't think they'll win the election... Sanchez Vicario won 2-6, 6-4, 6-3. ...eight games without a win. [2] VERB If you **win** a prize or medal, you get it because you have defeated everyone else in a competition, or you have been very successful at something. The first correct entry wins the prize... He won a silver medal at the 1994 World Championships. [3] VERB If you **win** something that you want or need, you succeed in getting it. British Aerospace has won an order worth $340 million. [4] See also **winning**.

▶ **win over** or **win round.** PHR-VERB If you **win** someone **over** or **win** them **round**, you persuade them to support you or agree with you. Not all my staff agree but I am winning them over.

wince /wɪns/ **winces, wincing, winced.** VERB & N-C If you **wince**, or if you give a **wince**, the muscles of your face tighten suddenly because you are in pain or have experienced something unpleasant. Just reading about it makes you wince.

winch /wɪntʃ/ **winches, winching, winched.** [1] N-C A **winch** is a machine for lifting heavy objects. It consists of a cylinder around which a rope or chain is wound. [2] VERB If you **winch** an object or person somewhere, you lift or lower them using a winch.

wind 1 air

wind /wɪnd/ **winds, winding, winded.** [1] N-VAR A **wind** is a current of air moving across the earth's surface. *There was a strong wind blowing... A gust of wind had blown the pot over.* [2] VERB If you **are winded** by something such as a blow, you have difficulty breathing for a short time. *The cow stamped on his side, winding him.* [3] N-U **Wind** is the air that you sometimes swallow with food or drink, or gas that is produced in your intestines, which causes an uncomfortable feeling.

wind 2 turning or wrapping

wind /waɪnd/ **winds, winding, wound.**
[1] VERB If a road, river, or line of people **winds** in a particular direction, it goes in that direction with a lot of bends or twists in it. *The convoy wound its way through the West Bank.* [2] VERB When you **wind** something round something else, you wrap it round it several times. *She wound the bandage around his knee.* [3] VERB When you **wind** a mechanical device, for example a watch, you turn a key or handle on it round and round in order to make it operate.

▸ **wind down.** PHR-VERB If someone **winds down** a business or activity, they gradually reduce the amount of work that is done or the number of people that are involved. *Aid workers have already begun winding down their operation.*

▸ **wind up.** PHR-VERB If someone **winds up** a business or activity, they close it down or finish it. *Could we wind up this meeting as quickly as possible?*

windfall /ˈwɪndfɔːl/ **windfalls.** N-C A **windfall** is a sum of money that you receive unexpectedly.

windmill /ˈwɪndmɪl/ **windmills.** N-C A **windmill** is a tall building with sails which turn as the wind blows. Windmills are used to grind grain or pump water.

window /ˈwɪndəʊ/ **windows.** [1] N-C A **window** is a space in the wall of a building or in the side of a vehicle, which has glass in it so that light can pass through and people can see in or out. *He looked out of the window. It was a lovely day.* [2] N-C On a computer screen, a **window** is one of the work areas into which the screen can be divided into.

windscreen /ˈwɪndskriːn/ **windscreens.** N-C In British English, the **windscreen** of a car or other vehicle is the glass window at the front through which the driver looks. The usual American word is **windshield.**

windshield /ˈwɪndʃiːld/ **windshields.** See **windscreen.**

windy /ˈwɪndi/ **windier, windiest.** ADJ If it is **windy,** the wind is blowing a lot.

wine /waɪn/ **wines.** N-VAR **Wine** is an alcoholic drink, usually made from grapes.

'wine bar, wine bars. N-C A **wine bar** is a place where people can buy and drink wine, and sometimes eat food as well.

wing /wɪŋ/ **wings.** [1] N-C The **wings** of a bird or insect are the parts of its body that it uses for flying. [2] N-C The **wings** of an aeroplane are the long flat parts at each side which support it while it is flying. [3] N-C A **wing** of a building is a part of it which sticks out from the main part. *...the east wing of the palace.* [4] N-C A **wing** of

an organization is a group within it which has a particular function or has particular beliefs. *...the military wing of the African National Congress.* ● See also **left-wing, right-wing.**
[5] N-C The **wings** of a car are the parts around the wheels; BRITISH. [6] N-PL In a theatre, **the wings** are the sides of the stage which are hidden from the audience by curtains or scenery.

winged /wɪŋd/. ADJ A **winged** insect or other creature has wings.

wink /wɪŋk/ **winks, winking, winked.** VERB & N-C If you **wink** at someone, or if you give them a **wink,** you look towards them and close one eye very briefly, usually as a signal that something is a joke or a secret.

winner /ˈwɪnə/ **winners.** N-C The **winner** of a prize, race, or competition is the person, animal, or thing that wins it.

winning /ˈwɪnɪŋ/ **winnings.** [1] ADJ BEFORE N You can use **winning** to describe a person or thing that wins something such as a competition, game, or election. *Donovan scored the winning goal.* [2] ADJ BEFORE N **Winning** is used to describe actions or qualities that please people and make them feel friendly towards you. *...his winning personality.*

winnings /ˈwɪnɪŋz/. N-PL You can refer to the money that someone wins in a competition or by gambling as their **winnings**.

winter /ˈwɪntə/ **winters.** N-VAR **Winter** is the season between autumn and spring. In winter the weather is usually cold.

wipe /waɪp/ **wipes, wiping, wiped.** [1] VERB & N-C If you **wipe** something, or if you give it a **wipe,** you rub its surface to remove dirt or liquid from it. *He began to wipe the basin clean... Lainey wiped her hands on the towel... I'm going to give the toys a good wipe.* [2] VERB If you **wipe** dirt or liquid from something, you remove it, for example by using a cloth or your hand. *Nancy wiped the sweat from her face.*

▸ **wipe out.** PHR-VERB To **wipe out** a place or a group of people or animals means to destroy it completely. *...the epidemic that wiped out thousands of seals in Europe.*

wire /waɪə/ **wires, wiring, wired.** [1] N-VAR A **wire** is a long thin piece of metal that is used to fasten things or to carry electric current. *...fine copper wire.* [2] See also **barbed wire.**

▸ **wire up.** PHR-VERB If you **wire up** something such as a building or piece of equipment, you install or connect wires inside it so that electricity or signals can pass into or through it. *I even wired up the alarm system.*

wireless /ˈwaɪələs/ **wirelesses.** N-C A **wireless** is a radio; DATED.

wiring /ˈwaɪərɪŋ/. N-U The **wiring** in a building or machine is the system of wires that supply electricity to the different parts of it.

wiry /ˈwaɪəri/ [1] ADJ Someone who is **wiry** is rather thin but is also strong. [2] ADJ Something such as hair or grass that is **wiry** is stiff and rough to touch.

wisdom /ˈwɪzdəm/. [1] N-U **Wisdom** is the ability to use your experience and knowledge to make sensible decisions and judgments. *...the patience and wisdom that comes from old age.*
[2] N-SING If you talk about the **wisdom** of an ac-

tion or decision, you are talking about how sensible it is. *I have grave doubts about the wisdom of resuming nuclear tests.*

wise /waɪz/ **wiser, wisest.** ADJ A **wise** person is able to use their experience and knowledge to make sensible decisions and judgments. *He has made a wise choice of publisher.* ♦ **wisely** ADV *They've invested their money wisely.*

wish /wɪʃ/ **wishes, wishing, wished.** ☐ N-C A **wish** is a desire for something. *Her wish is to be in films.* ☐ VERB If you **wish** to do something, you want to do it; FORMAL. *I wish to leave a message.* ☐ VERB If you **wish** that something were the case, you would like it to be the case, even though it is impossible or unlikely. *I wish I could paint like that.* ☐ VERB & N-C If you **wish for** something, or if you make a **wish**, you express the desire for something silently to yourself. In fairy stories, when someone wishes for something, it often happens by magic. *What did you wish for?* ☐ VERB If you **wish** someone something such as luck or happiness, you express the hope that they will be lucky or happy. *I wish you both a very good journey.* ☐ N-PL If you express your good **wishes** towards someone, you are politely expressing your friendly feelings towards them and your hope that they will be successful or happy. *Please give him my best wishes.*

wishful 'thinking. N-U If a hope or wish is **wishful thinking,** it is unlikely to come true. *It is wishful thinking to expect deeper change under his leadership.*

wistful /ˈwɪstful/. ADJ If someone is **wistful,** they are sad because they want something and know they cannot have it. *He looked a little wistful.* ♦ **wistfully** ADV *'I wish I had a little brother,' said Daphne wistfully.*

wit /wɪt/ **wits.** ☐ N-U **Wit** is the ability to use words or ideas in an amusing and clever way. *He writes beautifully and with great wit.* ☐ N-PL You can refer to someone's ability to think quickly in a difficult situation as their **wits.** *She'd better learn to keep her wits about her.*

witch /wɪtʃ/ **witches.** N-C A **witch** is a woman who is believed to have magic powers, especially evil ones.

witchcraft /ˈwɪtʃkrɑːft, -kræft/. N-U **Witchcraft** is the use of magic powers, especially evil ones.

'witch-hunt, witch-hunts. N-C A **witch-hunt** is an attempt to find and punish a particular group of people who are being blamed for something, often simply because of their opinions and not because they have actually done anything wrong; used showing disapproval. *He accused the police of conducting a witch hunt against the former party members.*

with /wɪð, wɪθ/. ☐ PREP If one thing or person is **with** another, they are together in one place. *She is currently staying with her father... She walked with her to the front door.* ☐ PREP If you discuss something **with** someone, or if you fight or argue **with** someone, you are both involved in a discussion, fight, or argument. *We didn't even discuss it with each other... I must have been arguing with him for fifteen minutes... The war with Spain was over.* ☐ PREP If you do something **with** a particular tool, ob-

ject, or substance, you do it using that tool or object. *Wipe the mushrooms with a damp cloth... She had never been allowed to eat with her fingers.* ☐ PREP If someone stands or goes somewhere **with** something, they are carrying it. *A man came round with a tray of chocolates.* ☐ PREP Someone or something **with** a particular feature or possession has that feature or possession. *She was six feet tall with red hair. ...a single-storey house with a flat roof.* ☐ PREP If something is filled or covered **with** a substance or **with** things, it has that substance or those things in it or on it. *His legs were caked with dried mud.* ☐ PREP You use **with** to indicate what a state, quality, or action relates to, involves, or affects. *He still has a serious problem with money... Depression lowers the human ability to cope with disease.* ☐ PREP You use **with** when indicating the way something is done or the feeling that someone has when they do something. *He listened with great care... He agreed, but with reluctance.* ☐ PREP You use **with** when indicating a sound, gesture, or facial expression that is made at the same time as an action. *'Broken again,' Jane said with a sigh... The front door closed with a crash.* ☐ PREP You use **with** to indicate the feeling that makes someone behave in a particular way. *Gil was white and trembling with anger.* ☐ PREP You use **with** when mentioning the position or appearance of someone or something at the time that they do something, or what someone else is doing at that time. *Joanne stood with her hands on the sink, staring out the window... She walked back to the bus stop, with him following.* ☐ PREP You use **with** to introduce a current situation that is a factor affecting another situation. *With all the night school courses available, there is no excuse for not getting some sort of training.*

withdraw /wɪðˈdrɔː/ **withdraws, withdrawing, withdrew, withdrawn.** ☐ VERB If you **withdraw** something from a place, you remove it or take it away; FORMAL. *He reached into his pocket and withdrew a sheet of notepaper.* ☐ VERB When troops **withdraw,** or when someone **withdraws** them, they leave the place where they are fighting or where they are based and return nearer home. ☐ VERB If you **withdraw** money from a bank account, you take it out of that account. *He withdrew £750 from his account.* ☐ VERB If you **withdraw** from an activity or organization, you stop taking part in it. *The African National Congress threatened to withdraw from the talks.* ☐ VERB If you **withdraw** a remark or statement you have made, you say that you want people to ignore it; FORMAL. *I demand that the Prime Minister withdraw that totally offensive remark.*

withdrawal /wɪðˈdrɔːəl/ **withdrawals.** ☐ N-VAR The **withdrawal** of something is the act or process of removing it or ending it; FORMAL. *...the withdrawal of American troops from South Vietnam.* ☐ N-U Someone's **withdrawal** from an activity or an organization is their decision to stop taking part in it. *...his withdrawal from government in 1946.* ☐ N-C If you make a **withdrawal** from your bank account, you take money out of it. ☐ N-U **Withdrawal** is the period during which someone feels ill after they have stopped taking a drug which they were addicted to. *...vitamins to help addicts overcome the first stages of withdrawal.* 5 N-U **Withdrawal** is behaviour in which someone prefers to be alone and does not want to talk to other people. *Her periods of withdrawal and mental illness increased.*

withdrawn /wɪð'drɔːn/. 1 **Withdrawn** is the past participle of **withdraw**. 2 ADJ AFTER LINK-V Someone who is **withdrawn** is quiet and shy.

withdrew /wɪð'druː/. **Withdrew** is the past tense of **withdraw**.

wither /'wɪðə/ **withers, withering, withered.** 1 VERB If something **withers** away, it becomes weaker until it no longer exists or is no longer effective. *The Party still predicts that ultimately religion will wither away.* 2 VERB If a plant **withers**, or if something **withers** it, it shrinks, dries up, and dies.

withered /'wɪðəd/. ADJ If a person or a part of their body is **withered**, their skin is very wrinkled and dry, and looks old. *...a withered old man.*

withhold /wɪð'həʊld/ **withholds, withholding, withheld.** VERB If you **withhold** something that someone wants, you do not let them have it; FORMAL. *The Council gave no reason for withholding these particular documents.*

within /wɪ'ðɪn/. 1 PREP & ADV If something is **within** a place, area, or object, it is inside it or surrounded by it; FORMAL. *...one of the quiet villages within the Forest of Dean... A small voice called from within. 'Yes, just coming.'* 2 PREP & ADV Something that happens or exists **within** a society, organization, or system, happens or exists inside it or to something that is part of it. *...the motives that attract people to work within a social service... Why not join the enemy and destroy it from within?* 3 PREP & ADV If you have a feeling, you can say that it is **within** you; LITERARY. *She could almost feel fresh life and hope rising within her. ...a profound sense of loneliness deep within.* 4 PREP If something is **within** a particular limit, it does not go beyond that limit. *The film will be finished within its budget.* 5 PREP If you are **within** a particular distance of a place, you are less than that distance from it. *The man was within a few feet of him... It was within easy walking distance of the hotel.* 6 PREP **Within** a particular length of time means before that length of time has passed. *And within twenty-four hours I'd got the money.* 7 PREP If something is **within sight**, **within earshot**, or **within reach**, you can see it, hear it, or reach it.

without /wɪ'ðaʊt/. 1 PREP You use **without** to indicate that someone or something does not have or use the thing mentioned. *I don't like myself without a beard. ...a meal without barbecue sauce.* 2 PREP If one thing happens **without** another thing, or if you do something **without** doing something else, the second thing does not happen or occur. *They worked without a break until about eight in the evening... Alex had done this without consulting her.* 3 PREP If you do something **without** a particular feeling, you do not have that feeling when you do it. *'Hello, Swanson,' he said without surprise.* 4 PREP If you do something **without** someone else, they are not with you when you do it. *We would never go anywhere without you.*

withstand /wɪð'stænd/ **withstands, withstanding, withstood** /wɪð'stʊd/. VERB To **withstand** a force or action means to survive it or not to give in to it; FORMAL. *The buildings should withstand the severest earthquake.*

witness /'wɪtnəs/ **witnesses, witnessing, witnessed.** 1 N-C A **witness** to an event such as an accident or crime is a person who saw it. 2 VERB & PHRASE If you **witness** something, or if you **are witness to** it, you see it happen. *Anyone who witnessed the attack should call the police.* 3 N-C A **witness** is someone who appears in a court of law to say what they know about a crime or other event. *Eleven witnesses will be called to testify.* 4 N-C A **witness** is someone who writes their name on a document that you have signed, to confirm that it really is your signature. 5 VERB If someone **witnesses** your signature, they write their name after it, to confirm that it really is your signature. 6 PHRASE If something or someone **bears witness** to something else, they show or say that it exists or happened; FORMAL. *Many of these poems bear witness to his years spent in India.*

witty /'wɪti/ **wittier, wittiest.** ADJ Someone or something that is **witty** is amusing in a clever way. *His plays were very good, very witty.*

wives /waɪvz/. **Wives** is the plural of **wife**.

wizard /'wɪzəd/ **wizards.** 1 N-C In legends and fairy stories, a **wizard** is a man who has magic powers. 2 N-C If you say that someone is a **wizard** at a particular kind of activity, you mean that they are very good at it. *...a financial wizard.*

wobble /'wɒbəl/ **wobbles, wobbling, wobbled.** VERB If someone or something **wobbles**, they make small movements from side to side, for example because they are unsteady. *...a cyclist who wobbled into my path.*

wobbly /'wɒbli/. 1 ADJ If something is **wobbly**, it moves unsteadily from side to side. *I was sitting on a wobbly plastic chair.* 2 ADJ If you feel **wobbly**, or if your legs feel **wobbly**, you feel weak and have difficulty standing up, especially because you are afraid, ill, or exhausted.

woe /wəʊ/ **woes.** 1 N-U **Woe** is very great sadness; LITERARY. *He turned to my tale of woe.* 2 N-PL You can refer to someone's problems or misfortunes as their **woes**; WRITTEN.

woeful /'wəʊfʊl/. ADJ You can use **woeful** to emphasize that something is very bad or undesirable. *...the woeful state of the economy.* ♦ **woefully** ADV *Public expenditure on the arts is woefully inadequate.*

woke /wəʊk/. **Woke** is the past tense of **wake**.

woken /'wəʊkən/. **Woken** is the past participle of **wake**.

wolf /wʊlf/ **wolves, wolfs, wolfing, wolfed.** 1 N-C A **wolf** is a wild animal that looks like a large dog. 2 VERB & PHR-VERB If someone **wolfs** their food, or if they **wolf** it **down**, they eat it all very quickly and greedily; INFORMAL. *Pitt wolfed down a peanut butter sandwich.*

woman /'wʊmən/ **women.** N-C A **woman** is an adult female human being.

womanhood /'wʊmənhʊd/. N-U **Womanhood** is the state of being a woman rather than a girl, or the period of a woman's adult life. ...*young girls approaching womanhood.*

womb /wuːm/ **wombs.** N-C A woman's **womb** is the part inside her body where a baby grows before it is born.

women /'wɪmɪn/. **Women** is the plural of **woman.**

won /wʌn/. **Won** is the past tense and past participle of **win.**

wonder /'wʌndə/ **wonders, wondering, wondered.** ① VERB If you **wonder** about something, you think about it and try to guess or understand more about it. *I wondered what that noise was... 'Why does she want to get in there?' Pete wondered.* ② VERB If you **wonder** at something, you are surprised and amazed about it. *He liked to sit and wonder at all that had happened.* ③ N-SING If you say that it is a **wonder** that something happened, you mean it is very surprising that it happened. *It's a wonder that it took almost ten years.* ④ N-U **Wonder** is a feeling of surprise and amazement. *'That's right!' Bobby exclaimed in wonder.* ⑤ N-C A **wonder** is something remarkable that people admire. ...*the wonders of space and space exploration.*

PHRASES ● If you say **'no wonder', 'little wonder'**, or **'small wonder'**, you mean that you are not surprised by something that has happened. *No wonder my brother wasn't feeling well.* ● If you say that something or someone **works wonders** or **does wonders**, you mean that they have a very good effect on something. *A few moments of relaxation can work wonders.*

wonderful /'wʌndəfʊl/. ADJ If you describe something or someone as **wonderful**, you think they are extremely good. *The cold, misty air felt wonderful on his face... It's wonderful to see you.* ◆**wonderfully** ADV *It's a system that works wonderfully well.*

won't /wəʊnt/. **Won't** is the usual spoken form of 'will not'.

woo /wuː/ **woos, wooing, wooed.** ① VERB If you **woo** people, you try to get them to help or support you. *They wooed customers by offering low interest rates.* ② VERB If a man **woos** a woman, he spends time with her and tries to persuade her to marry him; DATED.

wood /wʊd/ **woods.** ① N-VAR **Wood** is the material which forms the trunks and branches of trees. *Their dishes were made of wood.* ② N-C A **wood** is a large area of trees growing near each other. You can refer to one or several of these areas as **woods.** ...*a walk in the woods.*

wooded /'wʊdɪd/. ADJ A **wooded** area is covered in trees. ...*a wooded valley.*

wooden /'wʊdən/. ADJ A **wooden** object is made of wood. ...*faded wooden floorboards.*

woodland /'wʊdlənd/ **woodlands.** N-VAR **Woodland** is land covered with trees.

woodwork /'wʊdwɜːk/. ① N-U You can refer to the doors and other wooden parts of a house as the **woodwork.** ...*fresh paint on the wood-*

work. ② N-U **Woodwork** is the activity or skill of making things out of wood.

wool /wʊl/ **wools.** ① N-U **Wool** is the hair that grows on sheep and on some other animals. ② N-VAR **Wool** is a material made from animal's wool. It is used for making clothes, blankets, and carpets. ③ See also **cotton wool.**

woollen (AM **woolen**) /'wʊlən/. ADJ **Woollen** clothes are made from wool. ...*woollen socks.*

woolly (AM **wooly**) /'wʊli/ **woollier, woolliest.** ① ADJ Something that is **woolly** is made of wool or looks like wool. *He wore a light blue woolly hat.* ② ADJ If you describe people or their ideas as **woolly**, you are criticizing them for being inconsistent or confused. *He abhors woolly thinking.*

word /wɜːd/ **words, wording, worded.** ① N-C A **word** is a single unit of language in writing or speech. In English, a word has a space on either side of it when it is written. *The words stood out clearly on the page.* ② N-C If you have a **word** with someone, you have a short conversation with them, usually in private; SPOKEN. *James, could I have a quiet word?* ③ N-C If you offer someone a **word** of warning, advice, or praise, you warn, advise, or praise them. *May I also say a word of thanks to all the people who sent letters.* ④ N-SING If you say that someone does not hear, understand, or say a **word**, you are emphasizing that they hear, understand, or say nothing at all. *Not a word was spoken.* ⑤ N-U If there is **word** of something, people receive news or information about it. *There is no word from the authorities on the reported attack.* ⑥ N-SING If you give your **word**, you promise to do something. ...*an adult who gave his word the boy would be supervised.* ⑦ VERB To **word** something in a particular way means to choose to use particular words to express it. *If I had written the letter, I might have worded it differently.* ◆**-worded** ...*a carefully-worded speech.*

PHRASES ● If one person **has words with** another, they have a serious discussion or argument, especially because one has complained about the other's behaviour. *We had words and she stormed out.* ● You say **in a word** to indicate that you are summarizing what you have just been saying. *Victor, in a word, got increasingly fed up.* ● If you have **the last word** in an argument, you make the comment that finishes it and defeats the other person. ● You say **in other words** when introducing a simpler or clearer explanation of something that has just been said. *The mobile library services have been reorganised – in other words, they visit fewer places.* ● If you say that someone has said something, but not **in so many words**, you mean that they said it or expressed it, but in an indirect way. *'And has she agreed to go with you?'—'Not in so many words. But I read her thoughts.'* ● If you repeat something **word for word**, you repeat it exactly as it was originally said or written. *I don't try to memorize speeches word for word.*

wording /'wɜːdɪŋ/. N-U The **wording** of a piece of writing or a speech is the words that are used in it, especially when these are chosen to have a particular effect. *The wording is so* *vague that no one actually knows what it means.*

,word 'processing. N-U Word processing is the work or skill of producing printed material using a word processor.

,word 'processor, word processors. N-C A **word processor** is a computer which is used to produce printed material such as letters and books.

wore /wɔː/. Wore is the past tense of **wear**.

work /wɜːk/ works, working, worked. **1** VERB People who **work** have a job, usually one which they are paid to do. *Weiner works for the US Department of Transport... He worked as a bricklayer's mate.* ● See note at **live**. **2** N-U People who have **work**, or who are in **work**, have a job, usually one which they are paid to do. *I was out of work at the time... What kind of work do you do?* **3** VERB When you **work**, you do tasks which your job involves, or a task that needs to be done. *We work really hard and we get the lowest pay. ...people like me who were working 24 hours a day to survive.* **4** N-U Work consists of the tasks which your job involves, or any tasks which need to be done. *I've got work to do... There have been days when I have finished work at 2pm.* **5** N-U Work is the place where you do your job. *Many people travel to work by car.* **6** N-C A **work** is something such as a painting, book, or piece of music. *The church has several valuable works of art.* **7** VERB If a machine or piece of equipment **works**, it operates and performs its function. *The pump doesn't work and we have no running water.* **8** VERB If an idea, method, or system **works**, it is successful. *95 per cent of these diets do not work... A methodical approach works best.* **9** VERB If you **work** a machine or piece of equipment, you operate it. *Many adults still depend on their children to work the video.* **10** See also **working**, **social work**.

PHRASES ● If you **work** your **way** somewhere, you move or progress there slowly, and with a lot of effort or work. *Many personnel managers started as secretaries or personnel assistants and worked their way up.* ● If you say that you will **have your work cut out** to do something, you mean that it will be a very difficult task. *He will have his work cut out to get into the team.*

▶ **work into.** PHR-VERB If you **work** one substance **into** another, you add it to the other substance and mix the two together thoroughly. *Gradually pour the liquid into the flour, working it in carefully with a wooden spoon.*

▶ **work off.** PHR-VERB If you **work off** energy or anger, you get rid of it by doing something that requires a lot of physical effort. *If I've had a bad day I'll work it off by cooking.*

▶ **work out.** **1** PHR-VERB If you **work out** a solution to a problem or mystery, you find the answer by thinking or talking about it. *Negotiators are due to meet later today to work out a compromise.* **2** PHR-VERB If something **works out** at a particular amount, it is calculated to be that amount. *It will probably work out cheaper to hire a van and move your own things.* **3** PHR-VERB If a situation **works out**, it happens or progresses in a satisfactory way.

The deal just isn't working out the way we were promised. **4** PHR-VERB If you **work out**, you go through a physical exercise routine. ● See also **workout**.

▶ **work up.** **1** PHR-VERB If you **work** yourself **up**, you make yourself very upset or angry about something. *She worked herself up into a bit of a state.* ♦**worked up** ADJ AFTER LINK-V *Steve shouted at her. He was really worked up now.* **2** PHR-VERB If you **work up** the enthusiasm or courage to do something, you gradually make yourself feel it. *She had never worked up the nerve to tell anyone.*

workable /'wɜːkəbəl/. ADJ A **workable** idea or system is realistic and practical, and likely to be effective.

worker /'wɜːkə/ workers. **1** N-C Workers are people who are employed in industry or business and who are not managers. **2** N-C You can use **worker** to say how well or badly someone works. *He is a hard worker.*

workforce /'wɜːkfɔːs/ workforces. **1** N-C The **workforce** is the total number of people in a country or region who are physically able to do a job and are available for work. **2** N-C The **workforce** is the total number of people who are employed by a particular company.

working /'wɜːkɪŋ/ workings. **1** ADJ BEFORE N Working people have jobs which they are paid to do. *Like working women anywhere, Asian women are buying convenience foods.* **2** ADJ BEFORE N A **working** day or week is the number of hours that you work during a day or a week. *...a shorter, more flexible working week.* **3** ADJ BEFORE N If you have a **working** knowledge of a subject, you have a useful but not very thorough knowledge of it. **4** N-PL The **workings** of a piece of equipment, an organization, or a system are the ways in which it operates. ● **in working order**: see **order**. **5** See also **work**.

,working 'class, working classes. N-C & ADJ The **working class** or **working classes** are the people in a society who do not own much property, who have low social status, and whose work involves physical skills rather than intellectual skills. You can also say that someone is from a **working class** background.

workload /'wɜːkləʊd/ workloads. N-C Your **workload** is the amount of work that you have to do. *Wilson has had a heavy workload this season.*

workman /'wɜːkmən/ workmen. N-C A **workman** is a man who works with his hands, for example a builder or plumber.

,work of 'art, works of art. **1** N-C A **work of art** is a painting or piece of sculpture of high quality. **2** N-C You can refer to something that has been skilfully produced as a **work of art**. *The chocolate-and-brandy fig cake was a real work of art.*

workout /'wɜːkaʊt/ workouts. N-C A **workout** is a period of physical exercise or training. *...a 35-minute aerobic workout.*

workplace /'wɜːkpleɪs/ workplaces. N-C Your **workplace** is the place where you work. *...the difficulties facing women in the workplace.*

workshop /'wɜːkʃɒp/ workshops. **1** N-C A **workshop** is a room or building containing tools or machinery for making or repairing things. **2** N-C A **workshop** is a period of discussion or practical work on a particular subject in which a group of people share their knowledge or experience. *...a writers' workshop.*

workstation /'wɜːksteɪʃən/ **workstations.** N-C A **workstation** is a computer.

world /wɜːld/ **worlds.** **1** N-SING The **world** is the planet that we live on. *It's a beautiful part of the world... More than anything, I'd like to drive around the world.* **2** N-C A **world** is a planet. *...the possibility of life on other worlds.* **3** ADJ BEFORE N You can use **world** to describe someone or something that is one of the most important or significant of its kind on earth. *Like Japan, China has emerged as a world power. ...a world authority on heart-diseases.* **4** N-C Someone's **world** is the life they lead, the people they have contact with, and the things they experience. *I lost my job and it was like my world collapsed.* **5** N-SING You can use **world** to refer to a particular field of activity, and the people involved in it. *...the latest news from the world of finance.* **6** N-SING You can use **world** to refer to a particular group of living things, for example **the animal world**, **the plant world,** and **the insect world**. PHRASES ● **The world over** means throughout the world. *Some problems are the same the world over.* ● If you say that someone has **the best of both worlds,** you mean that they have the benefits of two things and none of the disadvantages. *Her living room provides the best of both worlds, with an office at one end and comfortable sofas at the other.* ● You can use **the outside world** to refer to all the people who do not live in a particular place or who are not involved in a particular situation. *For many, the post office is the only link with the outside world.*

world-'class. ADJ A **world-class** competitor in a sporting event is one of the best in the world at what they do; JOURNALISM.

world-'famous. ADJ Someone or something that is **world-famous** is known about by people all over the world. *...the world-famous Oxford Street.*

worldly /'wɜːldli/. **1** ADJ **Worldly** is used to talk about the ordinary things of life, especially things like possessions, rather than spiritual things; LITERARY. *Neither parent had left much in the way of worldly goods behind them.* **2** ADJ Someone who is **worldly** is experienced, practical, and knowledgeable about life.

world 'view, world views. N-C A person's **world view** is the way they see and understand the world, especially regarding issues such as politics, philosophy, and religion.

world 'war, world wars. N-VAR-VAR A **world war** is a war involving countries from all over the world.

worldwide /ˌwɜːld'waɪd/. ADJ & ADV **Worldwide** means happening throughout the world. *Today, doctors are fearing a worldwide epidemic... His books have sold more than 20 million copies worldwide.*

World-Wide 'Web. N-PROPER The **World-Wide Web** is a system which links documents and pictures into an information database that is stored in computers in many different parts of the world and which can be accessed with a single program. **The World-Wide Web** is often abbreviated to 'the Web'.

worm /wɜːm/ **worms, worming, wormed.** **1** N-C A **worm** is a small thin animal without bones or legs which lives in the soil. **2** N-PL If animals or people have **worms,** worms are living as parasites in their intestines. **3** VERB If you **worm** an animal, you give it medicine in order to kill the worms that are living in its intestines. **4** VERB If you **worm** your way somewhere, you move there slowly and with difficulty.

worn /wɔːn/. **1** **Worn** is the past participle of **wear**. **2** ADJ **Worn** things are damaged or thin because they are old and have been used a lot. *...a worn blue carpet.* **3** ADJ AFTER LINK-V If someone looks **worn,** they look old and tired.

worn-'out. **1** ADJ **Worn-out** things are too old, damaged, or thin from use to be used any more. *...his worn-out shoes.* **2** ADJ If you are **worn-out,** you are extremely tired.

worry /'wʌri, AM 'wɜːri/ **worries, worrying, worried.** **1** VERB If you **worry,** you keep thinking about a problem or about something unpleasant that might happen. *Don't worry, your luggage will come on afterwards by taxi... I worry about her constantly.* ◆**worried** ADJ *I'm worried about what is going to happen if we get in the same situation again.* **2** VERB If someone or something **worries** you, they cause you to worry. *'Why didn't you tell us?'—'I didn't want to worry you.'* **3** N-U **Worry** is the state or feeling of anxiety and unhappiness caused by the problems that you have or by thinking about unpleasant things that might happen. *His last years were overshadowed by financial worry.* **4** N-C A **worry** is a problem that you keep thinking about and that makes you unhappy. *My main worry was that Madeleine Johnson would still be there.*

worrying /'wʌriɪŋ, AM 'wɜːriɪŋ/. ADJ If something is **worrying,** it causes people to worry. *This is a very worrying incident.*

worse /wɜːs/. **Worse** is the comparative of **bad** and **badly**. PHRASES ● If a situation **goes from bad to worse,** it becomes even more unpleasant or unsatisfactory. ● If a situation changes **for the worse,** it becomes more unpleasant or more difficult. ● If you tell someone that they **could do worse** than do a particular thing, you are advising them that it would be quite a good thing to do. *Scientists in search of a challenging career could do worse than consider forensic science.*

worsen /'wɜːsən/ **worsens, worsening, worsened.** VERB If a situation **worsens,** or if something **worsens** it, it becomes more difficult, unpleasant, or unacceptable. *The security forces had to intervene to prevent the situation worsening... These options would actually worsen the economy.*

worship /'wɜːʃɪp/ **worships, worshipping, worshipped** (AM **worshiping, worshiped**). **1** VERB & N-U To **worship** God or a god means to show your respect to God or a god, for example by saying prayers. The act of showing respect in this way is called **worship**. *...Jews* *worshipping at the Wailing Wall. ...places of worship.* ♦**worshipper, worshippers** N-C *The mosque will hold 1,000 worshippers.* **2** VERB If you **worship** someone or something, you love them or admire them very much. *He worships his father.*

worst /wɜːst/. **1** **Worst** is the superlative of **bad** and **badly**. **2** N-SING **The worst** is the most unpleasant or unfavourable thing that could happen or does happen. *The country had come through the worst of the recession.*

[PHRASES] • You use **at worst** when considering a situation in the most unfavourable or most pessimistic way. *At best Nella would be an invalid; at worst she would die.* • If someone is **at their worst**, they are behaving as unpleasantly or doing something as unsuccessfully as it is possible for them to do. *This was their mother at her worst.*

worth /wɜːθ/. **1** PREP If something is **worth** an amount of money, it can be sold for that amount or has that value. *These books might be worth £50 or £60 or more to a collector.* **2** **Worth** combines with amounts of money, so that when you talk about a particular amount of money's **worth** of something, you mean the quantity of it that you can buy for that amount of money. *I went and bought about six dollars' worth of potato chips.* **3** N-U Someone's **worth** is their value, usefulness, or importance. *...highly skilled people who had already proven their worth to their companies.* **4** PREP You use **worth** to say that something is so enjoyable or useful that it is a good thing to do or have. *This restaurant is well worth a visit... He's decided to get a look at the house and see if it might be worth buying.* **5** PHRASE If an action or activity is **worth** your **while**, it is helpful or useful to you. *It might be worth your while to go to court and ask for the agreement to be changed.*

worthless /ˈwɜːθləs/. ADJ Something that is **worthless** is of no real use or value. *...a worthless piece of old junk.*

worthwhile /ˌwɜːθˈwaɪl/. ADJ If something is **worthwhile**, it is enjoyable or useful, and worth the time, money, or effort spent on it. *...a worthwhile movie that was compelling enough to watch again... It might be worthwhile to consider your attitude to an insurance policy.*

worthy /ˈwɜːði/. **worthier**, **worthiest**. ADJ If someone or something is **worthy** of something, they deserve it because they have the qualities or abilities required; FORMAL. *The bank might think you're worthy of a loan... Agassi was a worthy winner.*

would /wəd STRONG wʊd/ In spoken English, **would** is often abbreviated to **'d**. **1** MODAL You use **would** when you are saying what someone believed, hoped, or expected to happen or be the case. *Would he always be like this?... A report yesterday that said British unemployment would continue to rise.* **2** MODAL You use **would** when you are referring to the result or effect of a possible situation. *It would be fun to be taken to fabulous restaurants.* **3** MODAL You use **would** to say that someone was willing to do something. You use **would not** to indicate that

someone refused to do something. *She indicated that she would help her husband... He wouldn't say where he had picked up the information.* **4** MODAL You use **would**, especially with verbs such as 'like', 'love', and 'wish' when saying that someone wants to do or have something or wants something to happen. *She asked me what I would like to do... Ideally, she would love to become pregnant again... Anne wouldn't mind going to Italy or France to live.* **5** MODAL You use **would** in polite questions and requests. *Would you like a drink?... Do you think it would be all right if I smoked?* **6** MODAL You say that someone **would** do something when it is or was typical of them. *I was amazed, during a 'Women In Rock' debate, to be told, 'Well, you would say that: you're a man.'... Sunday mornings my mother would bake. I'd stand by the fridge and help.* **7** MODAL You use **would** or **would have** to express your opinion about something that you think is true. *I think you'd agree he's a very respected columnist... I would have thought it a proper job for the Army to fight rebellion.* **8** MODAL If you talk about what **would have** happened if a possible event had occurred, you are talking about the result or effect of that event. *My daughter would have been 17 this week if she had lived.* **9** MODAL If you say that someone **would have** liked or preferred something, you mean that they wanted to do it or have it but were unable to. *I would have liked a bit more time.*

'would-be. ADJ BEFORE N You use **would-be** to describe what someone wants to do or become. For example, if someone is a **would-be** writer, they want to become a writer. *...would-be singers.*

wouldn't /ˈwʊdənt/. **Wouldn't** is the usual spoken form of 'would not'.

would've /ˈwʊdəv/. **Would've** is a spoken form of 'would have', especially when 'have' is an auxiliary verb.

wound, wounds, wounding, wounded. **1** /waʊnd/. **Wound** is the past tense and past participle of **wind 2**. **2** N-C /wuːnd/ A **wound** is an injury to your body, especially a cut or hole caused by a gun, knife, or similar weapon. **3** VERB If a weapon or something sharp **wounds** you, it injures your body. *A bomb exploded in a hotel, killing six people and wounding another five. ...two wounded men.* **4** VERB If you **are wounded** by what someone says or does, they make you feel hurt and upset. *He was deeply wounded by the treachery of close aides.*

> Note that when someone is hurt accidentally, for example, in a car crash or when they are playing sport, you do not say that they **are wounded** or that they receive a **wound**. You say that **are injured** or that they receive an **injury**. In more formal English, **injury** can also be an uncount noun. *A man and his baby were injured in the explosion... Many of the deaths that occur in cycling are due to head injuries... Two teenagers escaped serious injury when their car*

rolled down an embankment. **Wound** is normally restricted to soldiers who are injured in battle, or to deliberate acts of violence against a particular person.

wound 'up. ADJ If someone is **wound up**, they are very tense and nervous or angry; INFORMAL.

wove /wəʊv/. **Wove** is the past tense of **weave**.

woven /ˈwəʊvən/. **Woven** is the past participle of **weave**.

wow /waʊ/. EXCLAM You can say **'wow'** when you are very impressed, surprised, or pleased; IN-FORMAL. *Wow, this is so exciting.*

wrangle /ˈræŋɡəl/ **wrangles, wrangling, wrangled.** VERB & N-C If two people **are wrangling** over something, or if they are involved in a **wrangle** over it, they are arguing angrily for a long time about it. *There have been diplomatic wrangles over how to mark the occasion.* ♦**wrangling, wranglings** N-VAR *Their decision follows months of wrangling.*

wrap /ræp/ **wraps, wrapping, wrapped.** ① VERB & PHR-VERB If you **wrap** something, or if you **wrap** it **up**, you fold paper or cloth tightly round it to cover it. *Diana is taking the opportunity to wrap up the family presents.* ② VERB If you **wrap** something such as a piece of paper or cloth round another thing, you put it around it. *She wrapped a handkerchief around her bleeding palm.* ③ VERB If you **wrap** your arms, fingers, or legs around something, you put them tightly around it. *He wrapped his arms around her and held her for half a minute.* ④ See also **wrapping**.
▸ **wrap up.** ① PHR-VERB If you **wrap up**, you put warm clothes on. *It can be breezy, so wrap up well.* ② PHR-VERB If you **wrap up** something such as a job or an agreement, you complete it in a satisfactory way. *The deal was wrapped up in just 24 hours.* ③ See also **wrap** 1.

,wrapped 'up. ADJ AFTER LINK-V If someone is **wrapped up** in something or someone, they spend nearly all their time thinking about them, so that they forget about other things which may be important. *They were totally wrapped up in their own problems.*

wrapper /ˈræpə/ **wrappers.** N-C A **wrapper** is a piece of paper, plastic, or foil which covers and protects something that you buy, especially food.

wrapping /ˈræpɪŋ/ **wrappings.** N-VAR **Wrapping** is something such as paper or plastic which is used to cover and protect something. *I tore off the wrapping and opened the box.*

wrath /rɒθ, AM ræθ/. N-U **Wrath** means anger; LITERARY.

wreak /riːk/ **wreaks, wreaking, wreaked** or **wrought**. ① VERB Something or someone that **wreaks** havoc or destruction causes a great amount of disorder or damage; JOURNALISM. *Torrential rain wreaked havoc on the Gold Coast yesterday.* ② VERB If you **wreak** revenge or vengeance on someone, you do something to harm them, because they have harmed you; LITERARY. ③ See also **wrought**.

wreath /riːθ/ **wreaths.** N-C A **wreath** is a ring of flowers and leaves which is put onto a grave as a sign of remembrance for the dead person.

wreck /rek/ **wrecks, wrecking, wrecked.** ① VERB To **wreck** something means to completely destroy or ruin it. *Twenty-one people were killed and 50 houses wrecked. ...the injuries which nearly wrecked his career.* ② N-C A **wreck** is something such as ship, car, plane, or building which has been destroyed, usually in an accident.

wreckage /ˈrekɪdʒ/. N-U When a plane, car, or building has been destroyed, you can refer to what remains as the **wreckage**.

wren /ren/ **wrens.** N-C A **wren** is a very small brown bird.

wrench /rentʃ/ **wrenches, wrenching, wrenched.** ① VERB If you **wrench** something, usually something that is in a fixed position, you pull or twist it violently. *He felt two men wrench the suitcase from his hand... She wrenched herself from his grasp.* ② VERB If you **wrench** a limb or one of your joints, you twist it and injure it. ③ N-SING If you say that leaving someone or something is a **wrench**, you feel very sad about it. ④ N-C A **wrench** is an adjustable metal tool used for tightening or loosening nuts and bolts.

wrestle /ˈresəl/ **wrestles, wrestling, wrestled.** ① VERB If you **wrestle** with a difficult problem or situation, you try to solve it. ② VERB If you **wrestle** with someone, you fight them by forcing them into painful positions or throwing them to the ground, rather than by hitting them. Some people wrestle as a sport.

wrestler /ˈreslə/ **wrestlers.** N-C A **wrestler** is someone who wrestles as a sport.

wrestling /ˈreslɪŋ/. N-U **Wrestling** is a sport in which two people wrestle and try to throw each other to the ground.

wretched /ˈretʃɪd/. ① ADJ You describe someone as **wretched** when you feel sorry for them because they are in an unpleasant situation or have suffered unpleasant experiences; FORMAL. *...wretched people who had to sell or starve.* ② ADJ If you describe something or someone as **wretched**, you think that they are very bad; SPOKEN. *The pay has always been wretched... Wretched woman, he thought, why the hell can't she wait?*

wriggle /ˈrɪɡəl/ **wriggles, wriggling, wriggled.** VERB If you **wriggle**, or if you **wriggle** a part of your body, you twist and turn your body with quick movements. *Janey wriggled out of her father's arms... She pulled off her shoes and stockings and wriggled her toes.*
▸ **wriggle out of.** PHR-VERB If you **wriggle out of** doing something that you do not want to do, you manage to avoid doing it; INFORMAL. *I had wriggled out of the washing up.*

wring /rɪŋ/ **wrings, wringing, wrung.** VERB If you **wring** something out of someone, you manage to make them give it to you even though they do not want to.
▸ **wring out.** PHR-VERB When you **wring out** a wet cloth or a wet piece of clothing, you squeeze the water out of it by twisting it strongly.

wrinkle /ˈrɪŋkəl/ **wrinkles, wrinkling, wrinkled.** ① N-C **Wrinkles** are lines which form on someone's face as they grow old. ② VERB When you **wrinkle** your nose or forehead, or when it

wrinkles, you tighten the muscles in your face so that the skin folds. *Jack wrinkled his nose at that distasteful thought.*

wrinkled /'rɪŋkəld/. **1** ADJ Someone who has **wrinkled** skin has a lot of wrinkles. *...the old man's wrinkled face.* **2** ADJ **Wrinkled** clothes have lots of small untidy folds or lines in them. *His white uniform was dirty and wrinkled.*

wrist /rɪst/ **wrists**. N-C Your **wrist** is the part of your body between your hand and arm which bends when you move your hand.

writ /rɪt/ **writs**. N-C A **writ** is a legal document that orders a person to do a particular thing.

write /raɪt/ **writes, writing, wrote, written**. **1** VERB When you **write** something on a surface, you use something such as a pen or pencil to produce words, letters, or numbers on it. *They were still trying to teach her to read and write... She took a card out and wrote an address on it.* **2** VERB If you **write** something such as a book, a poem, or a piece of music, you create it and record it on paper or perhaps on a computer. *She writes for many papers, including the Sunday Times.* **3** VERB When you **write** to someone, or when you **write** them a letter, you give them information, ask them something, or express your feelings in a letter. In American English, you can also **write** someone. *She had written him a note a couple of weeks earlier... The next day I wrote a letter to the manager.* **4** VERB & PHR-VERB When someone **writes** something such as a cheque, receipt, or prescription, or when they **write** it **out**, they put the necessary information on it and usually sign it. *I'll write you a cheque in a moment... Get my wife to write you out a receipt before you leave.* **5** See also **writing, written**.

▶ **write down**. PHR-VERB When you **write** something **down**, you record it on a piece of paper using a pen or pencil. *I did write down what I thought was good about the course.*

▶ **write in**. PHR-VERB If you **write in** to an organization, you send them a letter. *What's the point in writing in when you only print half the letter anyway?*

▶ **write into**. PHR-VERB If a rule or detail **is written into** a law or agreement, it is included in it when the law or agreement is made.

▶ **write off**. **1** PHR-VERB If you **write off** to a company or organization, you send them a letter asking for something. *He wrote off to the New Zealand Government for these pamphlets.* **2** PHR-VERB If you **write off** an amount of money you have lost, you accept that you will never get it back. *He had long since written off the money.* **3** PHR-VERB If you **write** someone or something **off**, you decide that they are unimportant or useless and that they are not worth further serious attention. *He is fed up with people writing him off because of his age.* **4** PHR-VERB If someone **writes off** a vehicle, they have a crash in it and it is so badly damaged that it is not worth repairing. *One of Pete's friends wrote his car off there.*

▶ **write out**. See write 4.

▶ **write up**. PHR-VERB If you **write up** something that has been done or said, you record it on paper in a neat and complete form, usually using notes that you have made. *Mr Sadler conducted interviews, and his girlfriend wrote them up.*

'write-off, write-offs. N-C If a vehicle is a **write-off**, it is so badly damaged in an accident that it is not worth repairing.

writer /raɪtə/ **writers**. **1** N-C A **writer** is a person whose job is writing books, stories, or articles. **2** N-C The **writer** of a story or other piece of writing is the person who wrote it.

writhe /raɪð/ **writhes, writhing, writhed**. VERB If you **writhe**, you twist and turn your body violently backwards and forwards, usually because you are in great pain.

writing /'raɪtɪŋ/ **writings**. **1** N-U **Writing** is something that has been written or printed. *Joe tried to read the writing on the opposite page... If you have a complaint about your holiday, please inform us in writing.* **2** N-U You can refer to any piece of written work as **writing**, especially when you are considering the style of language used in it. *It was such a brilliant piece of writing.* **3** N-U **Writing** is the activity of writing, especially of writing books for money. **4** N-U Your **writing** is the way the words that you write down look when you see them on paper. *It was a little difficult to read your writing.*

written /'rɪtən/. **1** **Written** is the past participle of **write**. **2** ADJ A **written** test or piece of work is one which involves writing rather than doing something practical or giving spoken answers. **3** ADJ BEFORE N A **written** agreement or law has been officially written down. *We're waiting for written confirmation from the Americans.*

wrong /rɒŋ, AM rɔːŋ/ **wrongs, wronging, wronged**. **1** ADJ AFTER LINK-V If you say that there is something **wrong**, you mean that there is something unsatisfactory about the situation, person, or thing you are talking about. *Pain is the body's way of telling us that something is wrong. ...a relationship that felt wrong from the start... What's wrong with him?* **2** ADJ BEFORE N & ADV **Wrong** means not correct or not suitable. *The wrong man had been punished... I really made the wrong decision there... You've done it wrong.* ◆**wrongly** ADV *She was wrongly blamed for breaking a vase.* **3** ADJ AFTER LINK-V If you are **wrong** about something, what you say or think about it is not correct. *I was wrong about it being a casual meeting.* ◆**wrongly** ADV *People believed (wrongly) that the disease could be transmitted in saliva.* **4** ADJ AFTER LINK-V If you say that something someone does is **wrong**, you mean that it is bad or immoral. *She was wrong to leave her child alone... We don't consider we did anything wrong.* **5** N-U **Wrong** is used to refer to actions that are bad or immoral. *Johnson didn't seem to be able to tell the difference between right and wrong.* **6** N-C A **wrong** is an unjust action or situation. *We too should be compensated financially for the terrible wrongs done to us.* **7** VERB If someone **wrongs** you, they treat you in an unfair way; LITERARY.

PHRASES ● If something **goes wrong**, it stops working or is no longer successful. *Something went wrong with the lift. ...when my marriage started to go wrong.* ● If someone who is involved in an argument or dispute is **in the wrong**, they have behaved in a way which is morally or legally wrong.

wrongdoing /ˈrɒŋduːɪŋ, AM ˈrɔːŋ-/ **wrongdoings**. N-VAR **Wrongdoing** is behaviour that is illegal or immoral. *The bank has denied any wrongdoing.*

wrote /rəʊt/. **Wrote** is the past tense of **write**.

wrought /rɔːt/. **[1]** VERB If something **has wrought** a change, it has caused it; LITERARY. *Events in Paris wrought a change in British*

opinion towards France. **[2] Wrought** is a past tense and past participle of **wreak**.

wrung /rʌŋ/. **Wrung** is the past tense and past participle of **wring**.

wry /raɪ/. ADJ If someone responds to a bad or difficult situation with a **wry** remark or facial expression, it shows that they find a bad or difficult situation slightly amusing or ironic. *There is a wry sense of humour in his work.* ♦**wryly** ADV *She turned and smiled wryly.*

Xx Yy Zz

xenophobia /ˌzenəˈfəʊbiə/. N-U **Xenophobia** is fear or strong dislike of people from other countries. ♦**xenophobic** ADJ *Stalin was obsessively xenophobic.*

Xerox /ˈzɪərɒks/ **Xeroxes, Xeroxing, Xeroxed**. **[1]** N-C A **Xerox** is a machine that can make copies of pieces of paper which have writing or other marks on them. **Xerox** is a trademark. **[2]** VERB & N-C If you **Xerox** a document, or if you make a **Xerox** of it, you make a copy of it using a Xerox machine.

'X-ray, X-rays, X-raying, X-rayed. **[1]** N-C An **X-ray** is a type of radiation that can pass through most solid materials. X-rays are used by doctors to examine the bones or organs inside your body, and at airports to see inside people's luggage. **[2]** N-C An **X-ray** is a picture made by sending X-rays through something. **[3]** VERB If someone or something **is X-rayed**, an x-ray picture is taken of them.

yacht /jɒt/ **yachts**. N-C A **yacht** is a large boat with sails or a motor, used for racing or for pleasure trips.

yachting /ˈjɒtɪŋ/. N-U **Yachting** is the sport or activity of sailing a yacht.

yank /jæŋk/ **yanks, yanking, yanked**. VERB & N-C If you **yank** something somewhere, or if you give it a **yank**, you pull it suddenly with a lot of force. *She yanked open the drawer... Grabbing his ponytail, Shirley gave it a yank.*

yard /jɑːd/ **yards**. **[1]** N-C A **yard** is a unit of length equal to 36 inches or approximately 91.4 centimetres. **[2]** N-C A **yard** is a flat area of concrete or stone that is next to a building and often has a wall around it. **[3]** N-C You can refer to a large open area where a particular type of work is done as a **yard**. *...a ship repair yard.* **[4]** N-C In American English, a **yard** is an area of land next to a house, with plants, trees, and grass. The usual British word is **garden**.

yardstick /ˈjɑːdstɪk/ **yardsticks**. N-C If you use someone or something as a **yardstick**, you use them as a standard for comparison when you are judging other people or things. *The best yardstick was to measure traffic against the 1990 figures.*

yarn /jɑːn/ **yarns**. **[1]** N-VAR **Yarn** is thread that is used for knitting or making cloth. **[2]** N-C A **yarn** is a story that someone tells, often with invented details which make it more interesting.

yawn /jɔːn/ **yawns, yawning, yawned**.

[1] VERB & N-C When you **yawn**, you open your mouth wide and breathe in more air than usual, often when you are tired. A **yawn** is an act of yawning. *Rosanna stifled a huge yawn.* **[2]** VERB A gap or opening that **yawns** is large and wide, and often frightening; LITERARY. *Liddie's doorway yawned blackly open.*

yd, yds. N-C **yd** is a written abbreviation for 'yard'. *...200 yds further on.*

yeah /jeə/. CONVENTION **Yeah** is used in written English to represent the way **yes** is pronounced in informal speech. *'Bring us something to drink.'—'Yeah, yeah.'*

year /jɪə/ **years**. **[1]** N-C A **year** is a period of twelve months, beginning on the first of January and ending on the thirty-first of December. **[2]** N-C A **year** is any period of twelve months. *The museums attract more than two and a half million visitors a year.* **[3]** N-C A period of the year which is connected with schools or business can be called a school **year** or a business **year**. **[4]** N-PL You can use **years** to emphasize that you are referring to a very long time. *I haven't laughed so much in years.* **[5]** PHRASE If you something happens **all year round**, it happens continually throughout the year. **[6]** See also **New Year**.

yearly /ˈjɪəli/. **[1]** ADJ BEFORE N & ADV A **yearly** event happens once a year or every year. *...their yearly meeting in London... Clients normally pay fees in advance, monthly, quarterly, or yearly.* **[2]** ADJ BEFORE N & ADV You use **yearly** to describe something such as an amount that relates to a period of one year. *...a yearly budget for health care... Novello says college students will spend $4.2 billion yearly on alcoholic beverages.*

yearn /jɜːn/ **yearns, yearning, yearned**. VERB If someone **yearns** for something, they want it very much. *I yearned to be a movie actor.* ♦**yearning, yearnings** N-VAR *...a yearning for a child of my own.*

-year-old, -year-olds. **-year-old** combines with numbers to form adjectives and nouns that indicate the age of people or things. *She has a six-year-old daughter called Ceri. ...a ski school for 3- to 6-year-olds.*

yeast /jiːst/ **yeasts**. N-VAR **Yeast** is a kind of fungus which is used to make bread rise, and in making alcoholic drinks such as beer.

yell /jel/ **yells, yelling, yelled**. VERB & N-C If you **yell** or **yell out**, or if you give a **yell**, you shout loudly, usually because you are excited, angry, or in pain. *I'm sorry I yelled at you last night... He let out a yell.*

yellow /'jeləʊ/ **yellows, yellowing, yellowed.** [1] ADJ & N-VAR Something that is **yellow** is the colour of lemons or egg yolks. *...the soft yellows of the desert sands.* [2] VERB If something **yellows**, it becomes yellow in colour, often because it is old.

yes /jes/. [1] CONVENTION You use **yes** to give a positive response to a question, or when you are saying that something is true, accepting an offer or request, or giving permission. *'Are you a friend of Nick's?'—'Yes.'... 'That's a type of whitefly, is it?'—'Yes, it is a whitefly.'... 'Can I ask you something?'—'Yes, of course.'* [2] CONVENTION You can use **yes** when contradicting something that someone says. *'I don't know what you're talking about.'—'Yes, you do.'*

yesterday /'jestədeɪ, -di/. ADV & N-U You use **yesterday** to refer to the day before today. *She left yesterday. ...yesterday's meeting.*

yet /jet/. [1] ADV You use **yet** in negative statements to indicate that something has not happened up to the present time, although it probably will happen. You also use **yet** in questions to ask if something has happened up to the present time. *No decision has yet been made... He had asked around and learned that Billy was not yet here... Have you got satellite TV yet?*

> In British English, **yet** and **already** are usually used with the present perfect tense. *Have they said sorry or not yet?... I have already started knitting baby clothes.* In American English, a past tense is commonly used. *I didn't get any sleep yet... She already told the neighbors not to come.* This usage is becoming more common in British English.

[2] ADV If you say that something should not or cannot be done **yet**, you mean that it should not or cannot be done now, although it will have to be done at a later time. *Don't give up yet.* [3] ADV You use **yet** to say that there is still a possibility that something will happen. *A negotiated settlement might yet be possible.* [4] ADV You use **yet** after an expression referring to a period of time, when you want to say how much longer a situation will continue. *Unemployment will go on rising for some time yet.* [5] ADV If you say that you have **yet** to do something, you mean that you have never done it. *He has been nominated three times for the Oscar but has yet to win.* [6] CONJ You can use **yet** to introduce a fact which seems rather surprising after the previous fact you have just mentioned. *I don't eat much, yet I am a size 16.* [7] ADV You can use **yet** to emphasize a word, especially when you are saying that something is surprising because it is more extreme than previous things of its kind, or a further case of them. *I saw yet another doctor.*

yield /jiːld/ **yields, yielding, yielded.** [1] VERB If you **yield** to someone or something, you stop resisting them. *Gessler was the first to*

yield, announcing his resignation in January. [2] VERB If you **yield** something that you have control of or responsibility for, you allow someone else to have control or responsibility. *The President is now under pressure to yield power to the republics.* [3] VERB If something **yields**, it breaks or moves position because pressure has been put on it. *He reached the massive door of the barn and pushed. It yielded.* [4] VERB & N-C When something **yields** an amount of something such as food or money, it produces that amount. The amount produced is called a **yield**. *The vineyard yields 200 tonnes of grapes annually... A yield of more than 7 per cent is expected from the shares.*

yoga /'jəʊgə/. N-U **Yoga** is a type of exercise in which you move your body into various positions in order to become more fit or flexible, to improve your breathing, and to relax your mind.

yogurt (or **yoghurt**) /'jɒgət, AM 'jəʊ-/ **yogurts.** N-VAR **Yoghurt** is a slightly sour thick liquid made by adding bacteria to milk. A **yogurt** is a small pot of yogurt.

yoke /jəʊk/ **yokes, yoking, yoked.** [1] N-SING If you say that people are under the **yoke** of something or someone bad, you mean they are forced to live in a difficult or unhappy state because of that thing or person; LITERARY. *People are still suffering under the yoke of slavery.* [2] VERB If two or more people or things **are yoked** together, they are forced to be closely linked with each other. *The pact signed in 1965 yoked Ontario into the United States economy.*

yolk /jəʊk/ **yolks.** N-VAR The **yolk** of an egg is the yellow part in the middle.

you /juː/. [1] PRON A speaker or writer uses **you** to refer to the person or people that he or she is speaking to. *When I saw you across the room I knew I'd met you before.* [2] PRON A speaker or writer sometimes uses **you** to refer to people in general. *In those days you did what you were told.'*

you'd /juːd/. **You'd** is the usual spoken form of 'you had', especially when 'had' is an auxiliary verb. **You'd** is also a spoken form of 'you would'. *I think you'd better tell us why you're asking these questions.*

you'll /juːl/. **You'll** is the usual spoken form of 'you will'.

young /jʌŋ/ **younger** /'jʌŋgə/ **youngest** /'jʌŋgəst/. [1] ADJ & N-PL A **young** person, animal, or plant has not lived or existed for long and is not yet mature. You can refer to people who are young as **the young**. *...his younger brother.* [2] N-PL The **young** of an animal are its babies.

youngster /'jʌŋstə/ **youngsters.** N-C Young people, especially children, are sometimes referred to as **youngsters**.

your /jɔː, jʊə/. [1] DET A speaker or writer uses **your** to indicate that something belongs or relates to the person or people that he or she is talking or writing to. *Emma, I trust your opinion a great deal... I left all of your messages on your desk.* [2] DET A speaker or writer sometimes uses **your** to indicate that something belongs or relates to people in general. *Pain-*

killers are very useful in small amounts to bring your temperature down.

you're /jɔː, jʊə/. **You're** is the usual spoken form of 'you are'.

yours /jɔːz, jʊəz/. **1** PRON A speaker or writer uses **yours** to refer to something that belongs or relates to the person or people that he or she is talking or writing to. *I'll take my coat upstairs. Shall I take yours, Roberta?... I believe Paul was a friend of yours.* **2** CONVENTION People write **Yours**, **Yours sincerely**, or **Yours faithfully** at the end of a letter before they sign their name. *With best regards, Yours, George... Yours faithfully, Michael Moore, London Business School.*

yourself /jɔːˈself, jʊə-/ **yourselves.** **1** PRON A speaker or writer uses **yourself** to refer to the person that he or she is talking or writing to. **Yourself** is used when the object of a verb or preposition refers to the same person as the subject of the verb. *Treat yourselves to a glass of wine to help you relax.* **2** PRON You use **yourself** to emphasize the person that you are referring to. *They mean to share the business between them, after you yourself are gone.*

youth /juːθ/ **youths** /juːðz/. **1** N-UNCOUNT Someone's **youth** is the period of their life when they are a child, before they are a fully mature adult. *In my youth my ambition had been to be an inventor.* **2** N-UNCOUNT **Youth** is the quality or state of being young and perhaps immature or inexperienced. *The team is now a good mixture of experience and youth.* **3** N-COUNT Journalists often refer to young men as **youths**. *...gangs of youths who broke windows and looted shops.* **4** N-PLURAL The **youth** are young people considered as a group. *He represents the opinions of the youth of today.*

youthful /ˈjuːθfʊl/. ADJ Someone who is **youthful** behaves as if they are young or younger than they really are. *I'm a very youthful 50.*

you've /juːv/. **You've** is the usual spoken form of 'you have', especially when 'have' is an auxiliary verb.

yr, yrs. N-COUNT **Yr** is a written abbreviation for 'year'.

yuppie /ˈjʌpi/ **yuppies.** N-COUNT A **yuppie** is a young middle-class person with a well-paid job, who likes to have an expensive lifestyle; used showing disapproval.

zap /zæp/ **zaps, zapping, zapped.** VERB To **zap** someone or something means to kill, destroy, or hit them, usually using a gun, spray, or laser; INFORMAL. *A guard zapped him with the stun gun.*

zeal /ziːl/. N-UNCOUNT **Zeal** is great enthusiasm, especially in connection with work, religion, or politics. *Mr Lopez approached his task with a religious zeal.*

zealous /ˈzeləs/. ADJ Someone who is **zealous** spends a lot of time or energy supporting something that they believe in very strongly, especially a political or religious ideal. ♦**zealously** ADV *Details of the group's past activities were zealously guarded.*

zebra /ˈzebrə, ˈziː-/ **zebras**; the plural can be **zebra** or **zebras**. N-COUNT A **zebra** is an African wild horse which has black and white stripes.

zero /ˈzɪərəʊ/ **zeros (or zeroes), zeroing, ze-**

roed. **1** NUM **Zero** is the number 0. **2** N-UNCOUNT **Zero** is freezing point on the Centigrade scale. It is often written as 0° C. *...thirty degrees below zero.* **3** ADJ You can use **zero** to say that there is none at all of the thing mentioned. *His chances are zero.*

zest /zest/. **1** N-UNCOUNT **Zest** is a feeling of pleasure and enthusiasm. *...a lovable girl with a zest for life.* **2** N-UNCOUNT **Zest** is a quality in an activity or situation which you find exciting. *Live interviews add zest and a touch of the unexpected to any piece of research.*

zigzag (or **zig-zag**) /ˈzɪɡzæɡ/ **zigzags, zigzagging, zigzagged.** **1** N-COUNT A **zigzag** is a line with a series of angles in it, like a continuous series of 'W's. **2** VERB If you **zigzag**, you move forward by going at an angle first to one side then to the other. *He zigzagged his way across the field.*

zinc /zɪŋk/. N-UNCOUNT **Zinc** is a bluish-white metal which is used to make other metals such as brass or to cover other metals such as iron to stop them rusting.

zip /zɪp/ **zips, zipping, zipped.** **1** N-COUNT In British English, a **zip** is a device used to open and close parts of clothes and bags. It consists of two rows of metal or plastic teeth which separate or fasten together as you pull a small tag along them. The usual American word is **zipper**. **2** VERB When you **zip** something, or when you **zip up** something, you close it using a zip. *He zipped up his jeans.*

zipper /ˈzɪpə/ **zippers.** N-COUNT A **zipper** is the same as a **zip**; AMERICAN.

zodiac /ˈzəʊdiæk/. N-SING The **zodiac** is a diagram used by astrologers to represent the positions of the planets and stars. It is divided into twelve sections, each with a special name and symbol.

zone /zəʊn/ **zones, zoning, zoned.** **1** N-COUNT A **zone** is an area that has particular features or characteristics. *The area has been declared a disaster zone.* **2** VERB If an area of land is **zoned**, it is formally set aside for a particular purpose. *The land was not zoned for commercial purposes.* ♦**zoning** N-UNCOUNT *...the use of zoning to preserve agricultural land.*

zoo /zuː/ **zoos.** N-COUNT A **zoo** is a park where live animals are kept so that people can look at them.

zoology /zuːˈɒlədʒi, zəʊ-/. N-UNCOUNT **Zoology** is the scientific study of animals. *...the Cambridge Museum of Zoology.* ♦**zoological** ADJ BEFORE N *...zoological specimens.* ♦**zoologist, zoologists** N-COUNT *...a renowned zoologist and writer.*

zoom /zuːm/ **zooms, zooming, zoomed.** VERB If you **zoom** somewhere, you go there very quickly. *We zoomed through the gallery.*

▶ **zoom in.** PHR-VERB If a camera **zooms in** on something that is being filmed or photographed, it gives a close-up picture of it. *...a tracking system which can follow a burglar round a building and zoom in on his face.*

zucchini /zuːˈkiːni/ **zucchinis.** The plural can be either **zucchini** or **zucchinis**. N-VAR In American English, **zucchini** are long thin green vegetables of the marrow family; the British word is **courgette**.